# WELCOME TO WALTHERS 2008 HO REFERENCE BOOK

Dear Model Railroading Friends,

As this is written in the summer of 2007, Wm. K. Walthers, Inc. is celebrating its 75th anniversary. It's fun to look back at the people and events that helped make the business what it is today. But our happiness is tempered somewhat by the loss of my father, Bruce, this past January.

I know he was looking forward to this milestone year. Even as his health failed, he was still working on several projects, grateful for the extra time God granted him. One of the last projects he helped complete was the "Along the Route" history timeline, which appears in this edition. Working from Bill Walthers' original letters and notes, a never-published book manuscript, and his own lifetime of experiences, Bruce shared a lot of stories through e-mails and interviews that made this feature possible.

Bruce's 60-plus years of service to the company began in the mid-1930s, helping his dad over school holidays and summer vacations for 20¢ an hour. In 1937, he began studying accounting and business at the University of Wisconsin in Madison. Shortly after graduation, World War II put a temporary hold on his future plans. Bruce served three years active duty in the Navy as a meteorologist on Kwajelein Atoll. Returning home in 1946, he went to work for his dad full-time.

The next 10 years were some of the toughest the hobby and the company would ever face. Smaller homes drastically reduced demand for O Scale models, then the mainstay of the Walthers line. Television took many people away from the workbench. A flood of new hobby products created more problems, as wholesalers would only distribute bestselling items. At this point, Walthers began selling it's own products directly to hobby shops, laying the groundwork for our wholesale operations. Bill was ready to call it quits when help arrived in [illegible] form of undecorated Athearn models. Demand for Walthers decals took off, leading to more sales of paint, parts and other supplies. This influx of cash saved the company, allowing Bill to retire and turn over operations to Bruce in 1959.

But problems were far from over. Many distributors all but stopped carrying model trains as slot cars raced to the front of hobby sales. Under Bruce's leadership in1960, the company became the first full-line wholesaler dedicated to model railroad products. This would set the pace for the next 20 years, firmly establishing Walthers leadership role in the industry.

In the early 1980s, an import program to offer a wider selection of models from around the world was introduced, starting with Marklin and eventually including Kibri, Faller, Vollmer and more.

Bruce turned the throttle over to me in 1984, but stayed active as Chairman of the Board. Always willing to offer help, ideas and suggestions, he was involved in our transition into the electronic age, our continued growth as a manufacturer and distributor, and most recently, with our acquisition of Life-Like Products in 2005.

Though not an active model railroader, Bruce's real hobby was finding new ways to use his many skills helping others achieve success. He was a life-long volunteer, serving many organizations within the hobby industry, his church and other groups.

With that in mind, we gratefully dedicate the 2008 HO Reference Book to his memory. You can read more about Bruce's life in the tribute that introduces the "Along the Route" feature.

And we're still building on that legacy in 2008, showcasing our many new items, and listings from over 300 different manufacturers.

It's always a pleasure to present our "Magic of Model Railroading" photo contest to inspire your modeling! A Magic photo introduces each section of the Book, with more photos in the Magic Section.

Helpful Information Station articles bring you fun facts, tips, history and modeling ideas.

Our F[illegible]res [illegible]al [illegible] promote the new Hiawatha on your railroad. The sheet can easily be removed without damaging your Book.

You can update your Book at walthers.com, every business day with new product announcements photos, news and more. The site is your best on-line resource for finding must-have products, as well as nearby hobby shops, where you can see items in person, ask questions and place special orders. You can check our entire inventory to see what's in stock and our Product Locator™ can put you in touch with dealers that ordered scarce items from us in the past and may have them available for immediate delivery.

Your comments and suggestions for improvements are always welcome, as they help us build towards a better future.

Happy Modeling

Phil Walthers

Phil Walthers

**WALTHERS**
P.O. Box 3039
Milwaukee, WI 53201-3039
(414) 527-0770
www.walthers.com

**ISBN**
**0-941952-78-9**

Printed in the USA

ISBN 0941952789
9 780941 952781

# In Memoriam – Bruce J. Walthers, 1919-2007

Bruce J. Walthers was born in Plymouth, Wisconsin, on September 9, 1919 and left this world at his home in Solana Beach, California, on January 28, 2007, after a valiant battle with multiple cancers.

Bruce was actively involved in many different industry, civic and church groups, often serving as their diligent and hard-working president. A graduate of South Division High School, Milwaukee, and the University of Wisconsin-Madison, Bruce served in the Navy during WWII as a meteorologist on Kwajalein Atoll in the South Pacific. After active duty, he continued to serve in the Navy Reserves at the Glenview Air Station, achieving the rank of Commander.

Bruce's civilian career spanned 60 years at Wm. K. Walthers, Inc. He became President in 1958 and under his leadership the company became the largest distributor of model railroad products in the world. He successfully transferred the family business to the third generation in 1984, remaining active as Chairman of the Board of Wm. K. Walthers, Inc. He was a Board member and served as President of both the Model Railroad Industry Association and the Hobby Industry Association of America (HIAA). The HIAA awarded him their highest honors, the Meritorious Award of Honor and Lifetime Membership in recognition of his many years of service and significant contributions to the industry.

Bruce was a lifelong learner and mentor to others. Early in his business life he overcame a fear of public speaking by completing the Dale Carnegie training course. He used his new skills to help others do the same, both as a Dale Carnegie volunteer leader and later as an alumnus of the program. As a member of the HIAA Board, Bruce was often designated at the national meetings to interact on behalf of the association with the celebrity performing that year. He had fond memories of sparring on stage with Joan Rivers, Mel Torme, Bill Cosby, George Burns, Joel Grey, Alan King, Julie Budd, Vic Damone and Billy Crystal. As the President of the Milwaukee chapter of the Council of Independent Managers and Organizer and President of the National Council of Independent Managers, he helped to strengthen the expertise of countless small business owners. A community leader, he served as a Board member of Cardinal Stritch University and Board member and President of St. Anthony's Hospital.

In retirement, Bruce was a frequent traveler, and participated in numerous Elderhostel programs. He stayed active by bicycling, researching family genealogy and serving as Board member and President of condominium associations in Whitefish Bay, Wisconsin, and Solana Beach, California. He was a founding member of Holy Family Parish in Whitefish Bay, served as President of the Holy Name Society and was a Parish and Regional Chair of the Catholic Family Movement. Bruce had a home in Solana Beach and was actively involved in the community there, especially at St. James Catholic Church, at the time of his death.

# Along the Route

New Year's Eve 1899 was a pivotal time in seven year-old Kearney Walthers life. (William Kearney Walthers was called by his middle name – a family tradition – until he was married and his wife insisted he be called Bill). Kearney had just received his first wind-up toy train as a Christmas present. He was fascinated by the new toy—so much so that he wound it up so many times he got blisters on his thumb! This great gift was the catalyst for his lifelong interest in trains of all kinds. Since little Kearney received that train on the dawn of the 20th Century, model and real railroading have both experienced enormous changes.

Leaps in technology have spurred improvements and refinements to railroads large and small. The introduction of small electric motors to model railroading revolutionized the industry; electric trains replaced wind-up toy trains. Over time, detailed plastic models have taken the place of stamped metal and wood models. Prototype railroads have seen the progression from steam to diesel, wooden cars to steel, and the loss of most passenger traffic to the automobile, but they have never been more important for moving the nation's freight. Many non-modelers think trains are dead because they don't ride them, but, in truth, trains are more important than ever for moving goods to market in the global economy.

Walthers, as a model railroad company, has undergone tremendous change over the years. Bill Walthers was a railroad hobbyist. He started Walthers as a manufacturing business to share his modeling ideas and inventions with others. It was the Depression and his main business, the Findex Company, was in bankruptcy, so he used his time to share his ideas and fulfill a thirty-year ambition. If he could feed his family in the process, so much the better. $500 for the first year's sales was a lot back then!

When Bill's son, Bruce, took the reins of the company, his goal was to make sure that every hobbyist would have a chance to buy the products he needed and wanted. Because model railroad items were typically sold in low volumes, toy distributors were reluctant to carry the product line. That's why Bruce turned Walthers into a successful specialty hobby distributor, a wholesaler that would carry each manufacturer's full line and promote it in a catalog — a revolutionary idea at the time.

Phil Walthers took the throttle of a progressive model railroad distributor and manufacturer in 1984. Under his leadership, the Walthers product line has undergone many changes. Cornerstone Series® kits, Trainline® train sets and Walthers HO rolling stock have proven popular with hobbyists.

As with real railroad companies, mergers and takeovers in the model railroad industry have changed the business. Since its founding in 1932, Walthers has acquired a number of companies including Ulrich, Magnuson, Train Miniature and HO West to name a few.

Most recently, the acquisition of Life-Like, has positioned the company for growth in the HO and N Scale arenas. Through Life-Like products, Walthers now offers train sets and road race sets to beginners through mass market outlets where many potential modelers have their first exposure to the hobby. Trainline® sets and accessories appeal to intermediate railroaders looking for hobby quality items. Walthers and PROTO™ series models appeal to serious model railroaders concerned with detail and authenticity.

Of course, as the real railroad industry has changed, Walthers has kept up the pace by offering models of new prototype trains along with those from the early days.

So, as Walthers celebrates its 75th anniversary, let's take a look at events along the way that have shaped model railroading since Bill received his first train in 1899.

**1899**

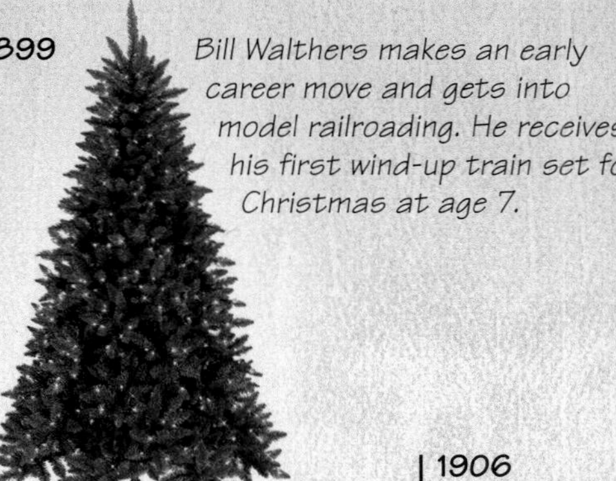

*Bill Walthers makes an early career move and gets into model railroading. He receives his first wind-up train set for Christmas at age 7.*

**1902**

*NYC 20th Century Limited makes first run.*

**1906**

*American Flyer predecessor Edmonds-Metzel Hardware Company founded. AF name introduced in 1910.*

**1903**

*Wright Brothers first flight at Kitty Hawk, NC. While many ups and downs were to come, airliners would eventually eclipse rail passenger traffic. But, don't forget — steel rails, not the friendly skies, built this country!*

**1900**

*Lionel® founded in New York.*

*NP North Coast Limited makes inaugural run.*

**1912**
PRR Broadway Limited makes first run. Luxury travel from New York to Chicago was now even better.

**1913**

The Dan Patch line in Minnesota tries something new — a GE oil-electric boxcab — the first commercially successful internal-combustion loco in the U.S. While not a diesel, it proved that internal combustion had a place in railroading.
Photo by Dennis Pehoski

**1915**
Canadian Government to the rescue: Canadian Government Railways formed to control the Intercolonial and National Transcontinental railways.

**1917**

U.S. enters World War I.

United States Railway Administration (USRA) takes charge of U.S. railroad network. Its mission is standardization to keep railroads running reliably during the War.

GE builds first diesel-electric loco. The 225-horsepower experiment never made it past the gate; it lived at the company's Erie Works laboratory, but was a test bed for the propulsion systems that led to modern locos.

**1918**
First United States Railway Administration design locomotive constructed, becomes B&O #4500.

**1919**
Marx Trains founded.

Canadian Government Railways becomes Canadian National Railway.

**1922**
Smaller is better! OO Gauge trains introduced in England by Bing.

**1923**
GE/Ingersoll Rand build first standardized 60-ton boxcab diesel-electric.

H.L. Hamilton's Electro-Motive Engineering Corporation begins building gas-electric "Doodlebug" self-propelled railcars in Cleveland.
Collection of Bob Gallegos

**1925**
Small switcher success! Alco/GE/Ingersoll Rand diesel-electric unit delivered to CNJ; operates on Bronx line until 1957.

**1928**
The Canadians were first! Diesel-electric passenger loco built by Canadian Locomotive Company, Baldwin and Commonwealth Steel speeds passengers at up to 63m.p.h.

**1929**
GN "Empire Builder," named for GN founder James J. Hill, makes first run. The Builder makes it easy to "See America First!". The Great Northern Railroad built Glacier Park to provide a vacation destination.

**1930**
Electro-Motive Corporation purchased by General Motors.

B&O gives passengers a cool ride — introduces first successful air conditioned car, a diner named Martha Washington.

## 1932

IMPROVE YOUR TOY RAILROAD

Why not make your toy railroad into a *Model System?* Send 15 cents in stamps for 24 page catalog on signal and control equipment, rails, ties and track; real automatic switches; reversing mechanisms, automatic couplers and uncouplers, supplies, parts, drawings, etc. Also SIGNAL AND CONTROL MANUAL — 250 pages and drawings — $3.00.

W. K. WALTHERS

1566 W. Pierce Street Milwaukee, Wis.

Bill Walthers starts his business. His first ad in the May, 1932 issue of Model Maker magazine offers signaling and electrical products so modelers could improve their "toy" railroads. His first catalog was 24 pages and sold for 15¢. $500 sales in first year. Bill also offered his first book, the Signal & Control Manual; it sold for $3.00.

Catalog and Price List

W. K. Walthers

Walthers first catalog is published in 1932.

## 1934

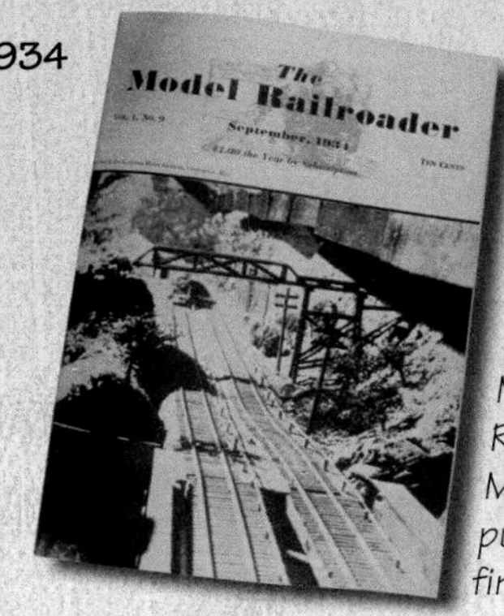
The Model Railroader

September, 1934

TEN CENTS

Model Railroader Magazine publishes first issue.

First diesel-electric streamliner in the U.S., CB&Q's Pioneer Zephyr dedicated. Screams across the prairies from Denver to Chicago on a record-breaking, nonstop run in May. Collection of Bob Gallegos

UP M-10000, first U.S. distillate-powered streamliner dedicated. Barnstorms the U.S. with 12,625-mile exhibition trip. 1.2 million see it.

Milwaukee Road constructs first practical, light-weight, streamlined standard passenger car.

Electro-Motive Division of General Motors opens first plant in LaGrange, IL.

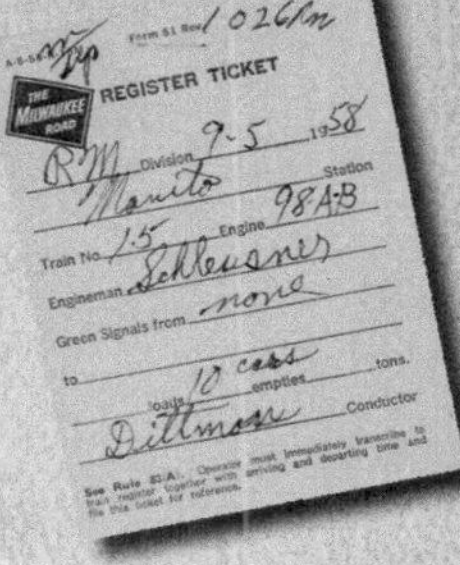
REGISTER TICKET

Pennsy begins construction of first streamlined electric locomotive—the legendary GG1.

## 1933

THE MODEL CRAFTSMAN

Building and Equipping Model Railroads

By EDWIN P. ALEXANDER

Railroad Model Craftsman magazine publishes first issue.

WORLD'S FAIR

CHICAGO

1833 · A CENTURY OF PROGRESS · 1933

Look at the little trains! Century of Progress Exposition at the Chicago World's Fair puts model railroading before the public eye.

## 1935

B&M/MEC Flying Yankee enters service.

National Model Railroad Association founded in Milwaukee.

Bill Walthers, Al Kalmbach and soon-to-be Milwaukee Mayor Frank Zeidler are key founding members.

First streamlined "Hiawatha" passenger trains operated by the Milwaukee Road.

EMC constructs #511 & 512, first self-contained diesel passenger locomotives in the U.S.

Collection of Bob Gallegos

Bill Walthers is given a wild project! Popular Science Magazine commissioned him to design, build, photograph and prepare an article on how to build a model of UP's M-10001 streamliner—in only five days! It's done on time.

**1937**

Walthers moves to bigger quarters — 241 E. Erie St., Milwaukee. This was the "Terminal Building" from which Terminal Hobby Shop took its name. The business is incorporated as Wm. K. Walthers, Inc.

ATSF "Super Chief" hits the high iron between Chicago and L.A.

SP "Daylight" zips up the California coast for the first time. Photo by Bob Gallegos

**1939**

New York World's Fair "Railroads on Parade." By this time a well-respected busnessman in the model railroad field, Bill Walthers is asked to produce cars for the huge O Scale layout display. They become the basis for the streamlined passenger car line.

Somewhere in between HO and O: S Scale trains introduced by A.C. Gilbert/American Flyer.

Beginning of the end for steam locomotives: EMD Builds FT Demo Set — the first mass-produced diesel-electric road freight locomotive.

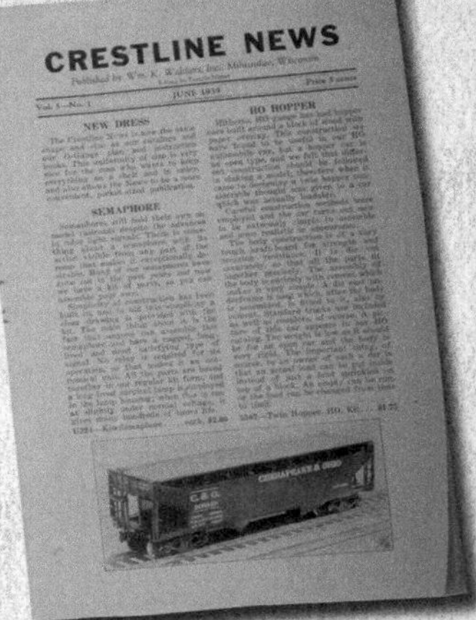


Walthers Crestline News kept modelers informed of new releases in O and HO.

**1936**

CN steam-powered streamliner makes 112.5mph run.

UP/CNW/SP City of San Francisco inaugurated.

N&W receives first Class A 2-6-6-4.

**Mid-1930s**

The company that eventually became Life-Like founded by Sol and Lou Kramer.

**1938**

AC Gilbert purchases American Flyer, introduces line of HO Scale.

Walthers starts HO Scale line. Wartime restrictions delay further development until after the war.

Walthers Crestline O and HO cars feature metal sides, a wood core and cast-metal details.

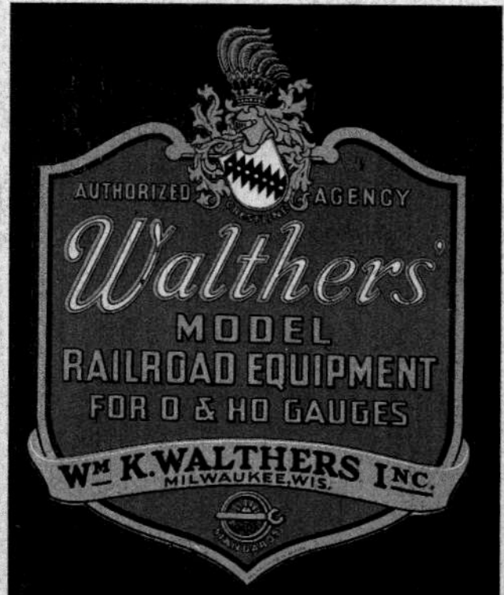


Dealers who carried Walthers kits and parts displayed these window stickers beginning in the 40s.

1940

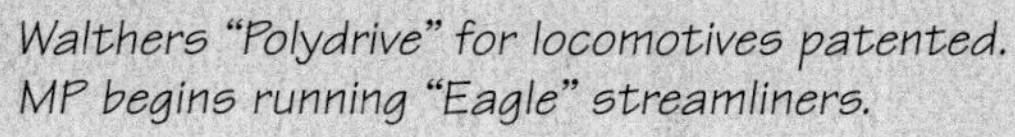

Walthers "Polydrive" for locomotives patented. MP begins running "Eagle" streamliners.

Biggest of the big steam locos delivered: UP receives Alco "Big Boy" 4-8-8-4s.

Baldwin M-3 "Yellowstone" 2-8-8-4 delivered to Duluth, Missabe & Iron Range.

"Willie" first appeared at Walthers in the early 40s.

First Lima "Allegheny" 2-6-6-6 delivered to C&O. Photo courtesy of Railfan & Railroad Magazine

1945

Last Shay locomotive built - WM #6

1946

Bruce Walthers joins his father's company. He had spent the last three years in the U.S. Navy and knew relatively little about what was happening in the postwar model railroad market.

Life-Like started producing paper maché train tunnels.

1950s

Life-Like produces first foam model railroad tunnels and grass mats.

1951

Booming business: GN re-equips "Empire Builder" with state-of-the-art streamlined cars.

1953

ATSF re-equips Super Chief with new cars.

Southern Railway is the first major railroad to completely dieselize.

1941

Last Heisler geared steam locomotive constructed.

U.S. Enters World War II - Walthers scraped the bottom of the barrel for materials because of wartime restrictions. Most companies switched to war production work. Walthers was one of a few that continued to make model kits. Bill sought war work, but his equipment was not suitable for volume production. It was tough. Materials were rationed, prices controlled and all of the experienced employees either enlisted or left for war production work, but Bill had rent to pay and a family to feed, so he kept at it. His wartime ads helped build morale and sustained interest in the hobby during what would otherwise have been a bleak period. Both of Bill's sons and one of two daughters served in the armed forces and returned safely.

1944

Fairbanks-Morse of Beloit, Wisconsin, begins locomotive production. Collection of Bob Gallegos

NKP receives S-2 Class 2-8-4 "Berkshire" locos from Lima. Collection of Bob Gallegos

1947

Postwar passenger premier: GN inaugurates streamlined "Empire Builder".

First American Freedom Train tours U.S. behind new Alco PA loco. Cars loaded with historical displays make patriotic journey.

Bill Walthers had hoped to continue with his prewar plans to expand O Scale, but the market moved off in a different direction with the development of plastics, HO Scale and ever easier-to-build kits. Old-time modelers kidded, "all you have to do is shake the box", but it wasn't much of a joke. Walthers barely survived, until a competitor unknowingly came to the rescue.

1949

California Zephyr makes first run Chicago-Oakland.

**1957**

WALTHERS
25th ANNIVERSARY EDITION
REFERENCE MANUAL AND CATALOG
for HO MODEL RAILROADERS

Walthers celebrates 25th Anniversary.

Walthers, producing HO but still emphasizing O gauge is struggling in the post-war market. The turning point came when Athearn produced unlettered HO cars and locos. Walthers decals became the second hottest thing on the market. Profits earned selling decals for these cars and locos provided the capital for Walthers expansion into the wholesale business.

**1960**

Walthers becomes a full-line model railroad distributor. Toy distributors weren't interested in low-volume hobby products, so Bruce decided to make the company a distributor of specialty hobby products, to make sure every modeler could buy the things he wants and needs. Profits from sale of decals for Athearn's unlettered plastic cars and locomotives make this possible.

ARNOLD

Models get even smaller: N Scale introduced in Germany by Arnold.

So long steam! GTW operates last scheduled steam-powered passenger train from Durand to Detroit, MI. In the U.S. a few mainline roads were still running steam in freight service, but not on a regular basis. Shortlines, a few Canadian lines and the National Railways of Mexico still boasted regular operations, but these were on the way out.

GE introduces U25B – first of its "Universal" series of mainline diesel-electric locos. Photo by Bob Gallegos

**1963**

FM delivers its final H16-44 roadswitchers to Mexico.

**1966**

Toy Train Operating Society organized.

**1967**

The beginning of the end: U.S. Post Office pulls most railroad mail contracts, railroads begin discontinuing passenger trains en masse.

Model Railroad Industry Association founded.

**1968**

Set up for failure: NYC and PRR merge to form Penn Central. Overbuilt, under-trafficked and subject to company infighting, the road declares bankruptcy by 1970.

**1954**

Walthers purchases Hobsco (the Hobby Supply Co. - manufacturer of a power truck).

Train Collectors Association formed.

**1955**

GN Empire Builder at its zenith: luxury train receives dome coaches and dome lounge. This is the prototype for the train introduced by Walthers in 2006.

Montreal-Vancouver passenger trains get a streamlined look: CP's "Canadian" and CN's "Super Continental" hit the rails.

**1956**

Baldwin exits locomotive business; last models built were S-12 and RS-12 roadswitchers.

**1958**

Bill Walthers retires, hands throttle to Bruce Walthers.

Walthers moves into its own building: 1245-47 N. Water Street, Milwaukee.

**1961**

Chihuahua al Pacifico completes last Mexican mainline between Chihuahua and the port of Topolombampo. Originally, the line was to connect with Kansas City.

**1962**

B&O merged into C&O. This merger signals the beginning of a trend in the railroad industry that leads to many favorite lines becoming "fallen flags."

N Scale introduced in U.S.

**1969**

Walthers moves to 4050 N. 34th St. Milwaukee, doubles its space, expands the wholesale business.

Bigger and better: UP purchases DDA40X "Centennial," the largest, most powerful diesel ever built on a single frame. Named for Golden Spike 100th anniversary.
Photo by Bob Gallegos

**1970s**

**INSTANT HORIZONS™**

Walthers purchases HO West, renamed Instant Horizons™.

**1970**

The largest merger to date: Burlington Northern gobbles up GN, NP, CB&Q, SP&S and Pacific Coast RR.

Congress passes Rail Passenger Service Act creating the National Rail Passenger Corporation—Amtrak®.

Walthers purchases Ulrich, manufacturer of metal freight cars and vehicles.

**1973**

Walthers HO Catalog reaches 200 pages.

Walthers offers its first N Scale decals.

**1975**

American Freedom Train begins two-year tour for U.S. Bicentennial celebration.

**1976**

Walthers moves to 5601 W. Florist Ave. With nearly two and a half acres under roof, the wholesale business is greatly expanded. What had started out as a Walthers Catalog is rapidly becoming a Reference Book for the industry.

Trains get even smaller: Walthers publishes first full N&Z Scale Catalog.

U.S. government-created Conrail (Consolidated Rail Corporation) rises from the ashes of bankrupt PC, EL, RDG, LV, L&HR, CNJ and other northeastern roads.

**1980s**

Walthers purchases Train-Miniature.

**1980**

Congress passes Staggers Act deregulating rail rates and allowing railroads to act as businesses.

Rock Island liquidated.

**1982**

Walthers celebrates 50 years in business.

Walthers Catalog reaches 576 pages.

Purchases Magnuson Models.

**1988**

CP opens 9.1-mile Mount MacDonald Tunnel in British Columbia - longest in the Americas.

GE introduces Dash 8-40B.

**1971**

Amtrak takes over U.S. intercity passenger service on May 1st.

**1972**

Phil Walthers joins his family's business.

More flags fall: Previously merged C&O/B&O system (now including WM) is officially renamed Chessie System.

Marklin introduces Z Scale. At 1/220 Scale, these are the smallest commercially available model trains.

EMD introduces GP38-2 roadswitcher.

**1977**

Via Rail Canada incorporated to assume operation of Canadian intercity passenger service. Photo by Bob Gallegos

Milwaukee Road bankrupt.

**1979**

Montreal Locomotive Works (MLW) acquired by Bombardier.

**märklin®**

Marklin, the premier European manufacturer selects Walthers as its U.S. marketing partner. Other European firms follow and the Walthers catalog is expanded with many new imported lines.

**1983**

UP merges MP, WP into system.

**1984**

Bruce hands throttle to Phil Walthers.

**1985**

Walthers HO Code 83 track system introduced

Cabooseless operation takes hold in U.S.

1989

Walthers introduces its popular "Great Circus Train" series. With these detailed kits, modelers could build a complete circus train based on actual equipment at the Circus World Museum in Baraboo, Wisconsin.

Life-Like produces its first HO racing sets.

Walthers introduces its revolutionary, easy-to-build Cornerstone Series® injection-molded plastic structures.

Bombardier acquired by GE.

Life-Like introduces first PROTO 2000 HO locomotive, the EMD BL2.

First cabooseless trains run in Canada.

1998

Rails meet water: Cornerstone Series® "Waterfront" rail-marine series introduced.

1999

Gold Ribbon Series™ multi-colored kits introduced. Detailed models offer snap-together main pieces; siding and trim colors are molded into a single part.

Cornerstone Series® "America's Driving Force" brings the auto industry to HO.

2005

Walthers acquires Life-Like Products. The acquisition of Life-Like complements Walthers product offerings. PROTO series locos and cars appeal to serious model railroaders, Life-Like train sets (and other products) place Walthers products in mass market stores where beginners get their first taste of the hobby. Life-Like also places Walthers solidly in the N Scale market. Outside of model railroading, Walthers reaches kids of all ages through Life-Like Racing™, Darda™ Toys and Bolz™ Tops.

1992

Life-Like starts making NASCAR® licensed racing sets.

1993

TRAINLINE®

First Walthers Trainline® train sets introduced.

Mexico begins privatizing railroad system.

1995

Merger mania: BN/ATSF merger forms Burlington Northern & Santa Fe Railway Company.

UP takes over C&NW.

1996

Big steel on a small scale: Cornerstone Series "The Works" steel works series debuts.

UP gets even bigger; purchases SP/DRGW.

1997

Modern logging and paper mills: Cornerstone Series "Trees & Trains" forest products series offered.

2001

Ultimate detail: Life-Like introduces first HO PROTO 2000 Heritage Steam collection loco, the 2-8-8-2.

2002

More detail in N: first N Scale PROTO 2000 Heritage Steam collection loco, the 2-8-8-2, hits the rails.

2003

Walthers introduces complete ATSF "Super Chief" train in HO Scale. Photo by V. S. Roseman

2004

The best gets even better: Life-Like releases PROTO 2000 Heritage 2-8-8-2 with factory-installed Quantum® sound and DCC.

Amtrak celebrates the Empire Builder's 75th anniversary.

Dedicated to serving all your model railroading needs, Walthers has 150 full-time team members at our offices in Milwaukee and Baltimore.

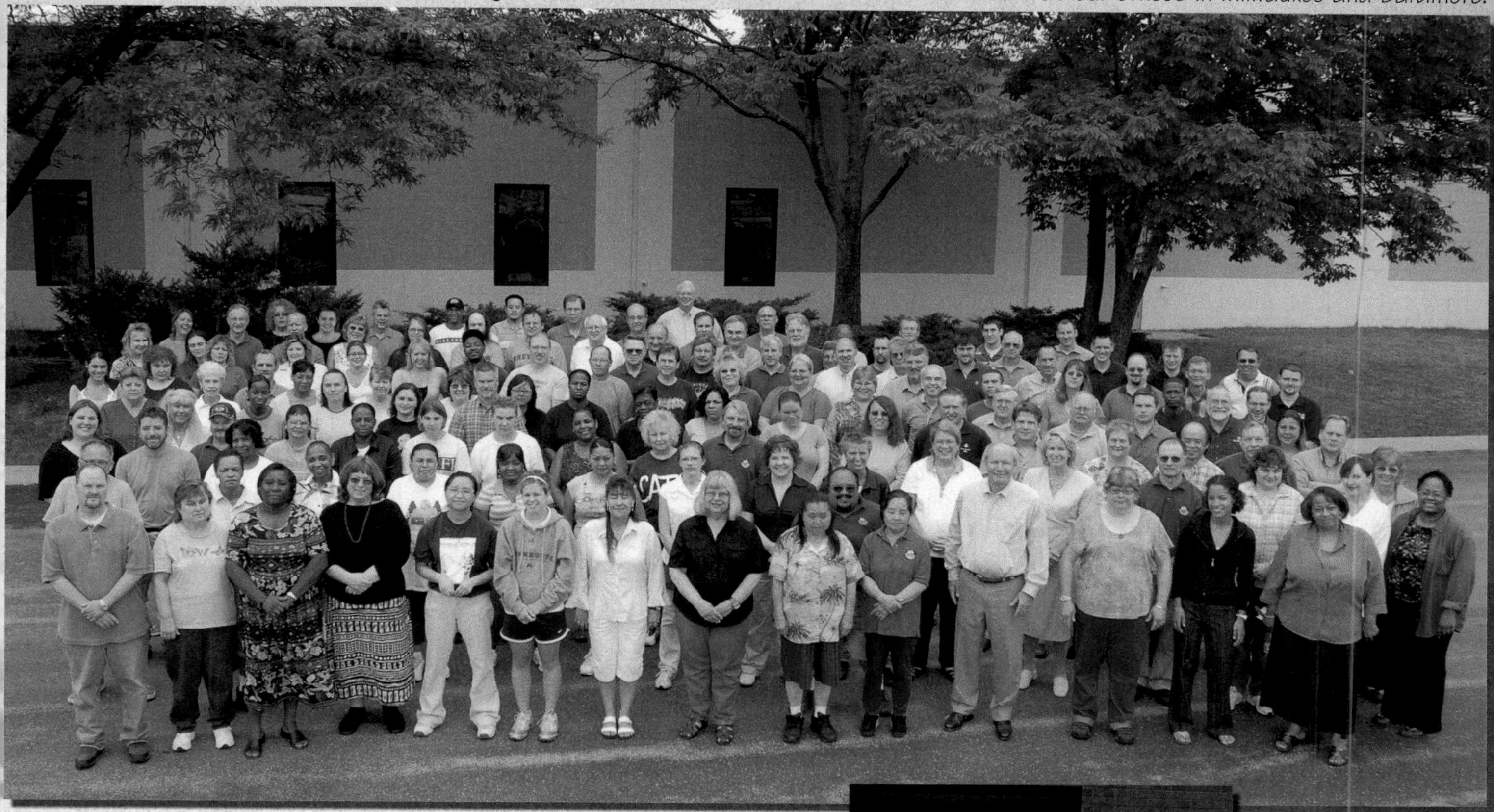

The Milwaukee Crew

The Baltimore Crew

2007

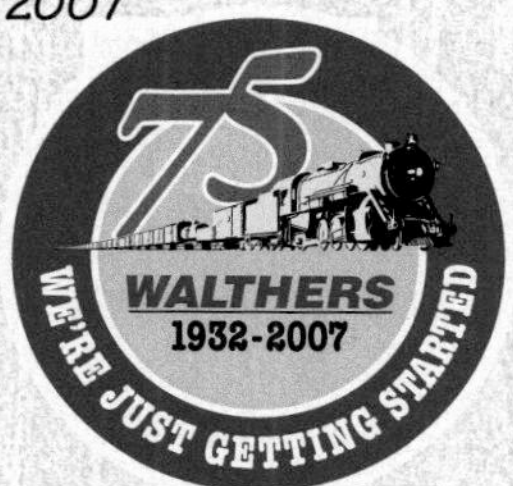


Walthers 75th Anniversary Celebration officially began on Founder's Day, May 10th (Bill Walthers birthday).

Produced especially for Walthers 75th Anniversary, HO Hiawatha train and structures are unveiled to the public for the first time at NMRA convention in Detroit.

# Walthers.com is the most comprehensive source of model railroading product information on the Internet.

**Only at walthers.com will you find the kind of information you want:**

- **Current stock information on over 100,000 items in a searchable online catalog**
- **Daily updates to your Walthers Model Railroad Reference Books**
- **Online ordering from your favorite participating dealer**
- **Product Locator™ for hard-to-find products**
- **Nearly 40,000 product photos**
- **Breaking news on new product releases**
- **Current retail prices**

**Find Out More About Walthers**

Everything from company history to the most frequently asked questions about Walthers can be found on the Web site.

**Product Pix And Write-ups!**

Walthers Web site offers more color product photos than we could possibly print in the Reference Book. Along with more product information and up-to-date availability and pricing, walthers.com is a great tool for keeping your Model Railroad Reference Books current all year long!

**Product Locator™ Service**

Find it even if it's already sold out!

The Web site can show you where to look for limited-run and hard-to-find products. The search page checks to see which participating dealers purchased the item from Walthers and lists them for you to contact.

**Online Hobby Shops**

Walthers.com includes an online gathering of Walthers dealers from which you can order through our Web site. Each participating dealer has a storefront, and all you have to do is select which dealer you want to order from. Your shopping cart order goes directly to the dealer.

**Contests**

Get all the info about the annual Walthers "Magic of Model Railroading" photo contest. Prize-winning photos are published each year in the "Magic of Model Railroading" section of each Reference Book. Check out the entry rules, deadlines and a few fantastic photos on the site.

**Keep Your Model Railroad Reference Book Current**

The Walthers Web site is the best way to update the information in your Model Railroad Reference Books. With the click of your mouse you can keep track of constantly changing availability and pricing. You'll also be in the know about new products introduced between Reference Books. With all the information updated on the site each day, you'll want to keep walthers.com bookmarked and check it often!

**Hobby Shop Locator**

Find the top Walthers dealers from around the world with our Dealer Locator. Use this service to find a nearby store or to find stores along your travel and vacation routes!

**Who Makes What?**

Our Manufacturer List is a great way to learn a little more about your favorite manufacturers. Selected manufacturer listings tell about the history of the vendor and the products they produce.

**We're Taking Suggestions**

Have an idea for a new product you would like us to produce? Please take a few minutes to fill out a customer suggestion form. It'll be mailed directly to our marketing department. We read 'em all, so your suggestions and ideas for new products really count!

**Online Customer Service**

Have a question about a Walthers product? Contact our customer service department with a click of your mouse.

**Get The Latest Scoop!**

Get the most current information on what's hot and what's new. The site is updated daily, so you'll always know what's in stock. Just try the search page — it covers every item we have on hand and more. Check availability on the Web site, along with your Reference Book, when putting together your shopping list before visiting your favorite hobby shop! You might just find some products you didn't know existed!

**Walthers.com is your greatest resource for finding the products you need!**

**walthers.com**

# FREQUENTLY ASKED QUESTIONS

### WHAT DOES WALTHERS DO?

We're a manufacturer of passenger cars, freight cars, locomotives, Trainline® Models, Cornerstone Series® buildings, Life-Like products and other kits.

We're also a wholesaler, distributing products from over 300 manufacturers to hobby shops worldwide.

And we're an importer, bringing you products from around the world.

Combined as one operation, we're the world's largest distributor of model railroad products, offering over 100,000 items so you and your dealer have the best possible selection.

### DOES WALTHERS HAVE A WORLD WIDE WEB SITE?

Yes, **www.walthers.com** is the quickest and easiest way to contact Walthers.

### HOW DOES THIS REFERENCE BOOK HELP ME AND MY DEALER?

This is a comprehensive listing of merchandise that's available or will be delivered shortly.

All manufacturers have reviewed and updated their listings. Based on this, Walthers lists items we believe will be available during the life of this book.

### HOW DO I PURCHASE ITEMS SHOWN IN THIS REFERENCE BOOK?

Walthers is a wholesaler and sells to approved hobby shops who are committed to helping you enjoy the hobby and supplying products from this book. Please support your local shop by purchasing materials and supplies there.

If your dealer has Walthers EXPRES™ III, he or she can find out almost instantly if we have the product you want in stock and the current price. We can usually ship it the next day.

### THE PRODUCT I WANT IS LISTED IN THE REFERENCE BOOK AND ON THE WEB SITE, BUT WALTHERS DOESN'T HAVE IT IN STOCK. HOW CAN I GET IT?

With the Product Locator™ service on our Web site, we can help you find any item that's out of stock or has been discontinued. This search page draws upon the purchase history of dealers to see who ordered the item from us in the past. Even though Walthers may no longer have the item, the Product Locator™ will be able to lead you to dealers that may still have it in stock.

### HOW DO I FIND A HOBBY SHOP IN MY AREA?

Simply send Walthers a SASE and we will send you a list of dealers in your area. Please send to:

Walthers—DEALER LIST
5601 W. Florist Ave.
P.O. Box 3039
Milwaukee, WI 53201-3039

Walthers.com also has a dealer locator that lists quality hobby shops around the world.

### WHAT IF MY DEALER DOESN'T HAVE THE ITEM I WANT?

There are more products than your dealer can possibly have in stock. If you don't find what you want, ask to place a special order.

### THE ITEM IS OUT OF STOCK - WHAT DOES THAT MEAN?

We try to stock these products at all times, but some manufacturers' products run out and are temporarily unavailable. Ask your dealer to place it on backorder.

### I RECEIVED THE ITEM, BUT I'M NOT HAPPY - WHO CAN HELP?

We try to describe each item in this Reference Book accurately. If it's not what you expected, your dealer can return it. If the kit is too difficult, it can be returned BEFORE starting construction. We cannot accept returns of items that have been worked on or are partially assembled.

### I STILL DON'T HAVE MY ORDER - WHY NOT?

Most manufacturers make every effort to ship products on schedule, but many are small businesses with limited resources. They may rely on outside suppliers for parts, packaging, use of a molding machine, etc., which they can't always get. This means items may be temporarily out of stock, or in extreme cases, may never go into production.

Some manufacturers use "batch production," making just enough product to satisfy current demand. Orders are then allowed to accumulate to a specific level before another batch is made. With slow-moving items, there can be long delays (sometimes several years) until enough orders are received.

### WHY ARE SOME LISTINGS PRINTED IN BLUE INK?

This is Walthers way of letting you know we haven't received these products for quite some time, and they may not be in stock. They haven't been discontinued, but you may not be able to get them right away. We expect delivery sometime this year and suggest you backorder them with your dealer.

### HOW CAN I KEEP THIS REFERENCE BOOK UPDATED?

Visit www.walthers.com. You'll find new product and new arrival information updated daily. Or, if you don't have on-line access, ask your dealer about the latest arrivals and product announcements.

### WHO SHOULD I CONTACT WITH A QUESTION ABOUT A PRODUCT?

We do our best to describe each item in this Reference Book accurately. We are happy to answer all questions sent to us with a SASE or on-line.

For questions about techniques or materials, see your dealer. There are many "how-to" books and videos available that may have the answers you need. Your dealer probably knows several experienced modelers who visit the shop and can answer your questions.

There may also be a club in your area where you can visit their layout. You can ask questions, watch trains and see how things are done.

A membership in the National Model Railroad Association (NMRA) will put you in touch with thousands of modelers worldwide. A monthly magazine, "Scale Rails," provides listings of clubs, special interest groups and helpful articles.

(An application for membership is printed in this Reference Book; please see the index listing under NMRA for the page.)

If you are looking for information on an actual car, locomotive or rail line, consider joining a railroad historical society. These addresses are listed in some hobby magazines. Members are dedicated to studying and preserving the history and equipment of their favorite lines. Most issue a newsletter or magazine and can answer in-depth questions.

# WALTHERS REFERENCE BOOK POLICY/ WARRANTY INFORMATION

### WALTHERS REFERENCE BOOK POLICY

We realize there are more products listed in this book than the average hobby shop can stock at one time. Therefore, we try to describe every item accurately so you can special order them with confidence. However, if the item is not as you expected, your dealer can return it to us. If it is clearly our mistake, we will pay return transportation; otherwise your dealer must pay the return transportation, plus restock fees.

### PRICES

All prices are subject to change without notice. All items are invoiced at the prices in effect at the time of shipment.

### IMPORTANT NOTE

There are certain things beyond Walthers control, therefore: 1) All items offered are subject to availability at the time of shipment. 2) We reserve the right to correct errors, change prices and modify designs without notice and without obligation to previous purchasers. If you do not like the change or correction, the item may be returned by your dealer.

### ABOUT WARRANTIES

As a prospective buyer of materials offered in this book, you benefit from three separate warranties:

1) The warranty offered by the manufacturer
2) The warranty we extend to our dealers
3) The warranty offered by the dealer to you, the purchaser

Some warranties are better than others; we suggest you ask before you buy.

### WALTHERS LIMITED WARRANTY

We will replace any part of a Walthers kit that's defective at the time of purchase. We reserve the right to ask you to send the damaged or defective part back to Walthers; however, DO NOT send it back until we ask for it, as we will not be responsible for this shipping cost. If the part was defective, we'll pay the transportation costs to send you a new one. If you are asking for a replacement because the part was lost or damaged during assembly, please include $5.00 service fee payment (in U.S. funds), payable to Wm. K. Walthers, Inc. This warranty applies to the original purchaser only, with a time limit of 90 days.

Walthers reserves the right to request proof of purchase. To save time, write to Walthers directly regarding replacement or repair and DO NOT RETURN THE MERCHANDISE UNLESS REQUESTED. Since Walthers designs are subject to change, Walthers reserves the right to make reasonable substitution if the item requested is no longer available. Remember, Walthers warranties apply ONLY to merchandise purchased through authorized retail establishments.

### OTHER MANUFACTURERS' WARRANTIES

Manufacturers establish their own policies. Detailed information may be included with the product, or may be obtained by contacting the company. Most require that parts be returned to them with proof of purchase. Under Federal regulations, this is defined as a limited warranty.

Your rights on warranty repairs vary depending on which state you live in. If you have problems with another manufacturer's warranty, Walthers will try to help, but again, DON'T SEND MERCHANDISE UNLESS WALTHERS ASKS FOR IT.

### DEALER WARRANTIES AND POLICIES

Dealers set their own policies for returns, refunds, credits or exchanges. Ask before you buy, as some are unable or unwilling to return merchandise. Walthers can't accept responsibility or issue refunds for merchandise sent without authorization.

### KITS VS ASSEMBLY

Unless stated otherwise, the merchandise offered is in kit form, for assembly by you. If you feel that you are unable to put it together, this is a reason for return under Walthers policy, but please do this BEFORE starting construction. Walthers normally will not accept the return of items that have been worked on or are otherwise in unsellable condition. Please note that Walthers does not have an assembly service.

# PUT "SAFETY FIRST" ON YOUR RAILROAD

Working on a real railroad can be dangerous. The "Safety First" message on equipment reminds employees to work carefully, think about what they're doing and follow proper procedures.

"Safety First" is a good message for model railroaders, too. Properly used, hobby products provide hours of enjoyment. But you must understand and appreciate the tools and materials. That's especially important if younger members of the family are going to help.

The items in this Reference Book are NOT toys, and should only be used by children with adult supervision. You can set a good example by working carefully and taking the time to read and follow directions.

The use of hazardous substances in hobby products is declining, but you can be exposed to TOXIC, MECHANICAL (including heat) and ELECTRICAL hazards.

### SAFETY IS HABIT FORMING

By paying attention, reading instructions and using common sense, you can safely use a variety of materials. Model railroading is fun, and by making safety a habit, you can keep it that way!

# LEGEND & TRADEMARK INFORMATION

## NORTH AMERICAN ROADNAME ABBREVIATION KEY

**AA** Ann Arbor

**A&WP** Atlanta & West Point

**ACL** Atlantic Coast Line

**ACY** Akron, Canton & Youngstown

**ART** American Refrigerator Transit

**ATSF** Santa Fe (Actual = Atchison, Topeka & Santa Fe)

**B&M** Boston & Maine

**B&O** Baltimore & Ohio

**BCOL** British Columbia Railway

**BCIT** BC Rail

**BN** Burlington Northern

**BNSF** Burlington Northern Santa Fe (1996 Merger)

**BS** Birmingham Southern

**C&G** Columbus & Greenville

**C&O** Chesapeake & Ohio

**C&S** Colorado & Southern (CB&Q Subsidiary)

**CB&Q** Chicago, Burlington & Quincy

**CG** Central of Georgia

**CN** Canadian National

**CNJ** Central Railroad of New Jersey/Jersey Central

**CNW** Chicago & North Western

**CP** Canadian Pacific

**CR** Conrail

**CRR** Clinchfield (Actual = Carolina, Clinchfield & Ohio)

**CSX** CSX Transportation

**D&H** Delaware & Hudson

**DL&W** Delaware, Lackawanna & Western (a.k.a. Lackawanna)

**DT&I** Detroit, Toledo & Ironton

**DMIR** Duluth, Missabe & Iron Range (a.k.a. Missabe Road)

**DRGW** Rio Grande (Actual = Denver & Rio Grande Western)

**EL** Erie-Lackawanna

**FEC** Florida East Coast

**FGE** Fruit Growers Express

**FNM** Ferrocarriles Nacionales de Mexico (Actual = Mexican National Railways)

**GF** Georgia & Florida

**GM&O** Gulf, Mobile & Ohio

**GN** Great Northern

**GTW** Grand Trunk Western

**IC** Illinois Central

**KCS** Kansas City Southern

**KCSM** Kansas City Southern de Mexico

**L&N** Louisville & Nashville

**LS&I** Lake Superior & Ishpeming

**LV** Lehigh Valley

**MEC** Maine Central

**MILW** Milwaukee Road (Actual = Chicago, Milwaukee, St. Paul & Pacific)

**MKT** Katy (Actual = Missouri-Kansas-Texas)

**MN&S** Minneapolis, Northfield & Southern

**MON** Monon (Actual = Chicago, Indianapolis & Louisville)

**MOW** Maintenance-Of-Way

**MP** Missouri Pacific

**NdeM** National Railways of Mexico

**NH** New Haven (Actual = New York, New Haven & Hartford)

**NKP** Nickel Plate Road (Actual = New York, Chicago & St. Louis)

**NP** Northern Pacific

**NS** Norfolk Southern

**N&W** Norfolk & Western

**NYC** New York Central

**PC** Penn Central

**PFE** Pacific Fruit Express

**PRR** Pennsylvania Railroad (Also "Pennsy")

**RDG** Reading

**RI** Rock Island (Actual = Chicago, Rock Island & Pacific)

**RUT** Rutland

**SAL** Seaboard Air Line (a.k.a. "Seaboard")

**SCL** Seaboard Coast Line

**SLSF** St. Louis-San Francisco "Frisco"

**SOO** Soo Line (Actual = Minneapolis, St. Paul & Sault Ste. Marie)

**SOU** Southern Railway

**SP** Southern Pacific

**SP&S** Spokane, Portland & Seattle

**SSW** Cotton Belt (Actual = St. Louis-Southwestern)

**UP** Union Pacific

**TFM** Transportacion Ferroviaria Mexicano

**TTX** TTX Corporation

**W of A** Western Railway of Alabama

**WC** Wisconsin Central Limited

**WM** Western Maryland

**WP** Western Pacific

## SYMBOLS

**NEW** - Identifies a brand new item appearing for the first time in this book.

Items listed below are available by Special Order (see Legend Page). These items are currently available, but are not stocked in the Walthers warehouse. Walthers orders them directly from the manufacturer and ships them to you as soon as received.

**NEW SUPPLIER** - Identifies an all-new line of products making their first appearance in this book.

Blue Line Items

When an item is listed in blue, it's because the manufacturer has not been able to deliver them regularly. The item was out of stock when the catalog was printed and delivery was not known. All "blue line" items CAN still be placed on backorder. Ask your dealer or check our Web site at www.walthers.com for current delivery information.

**Limited Quantity Available**

When a product appears under this heading, it means we are running out of the item and are unable to order more. The item may have been discontinued by the manufacturer, or is produced on an irregular schedule and will not be available again for quite some time.

**PACKAGE QUANTITY** - pkg(#) - Indicates the number of items included in the package. Some items used in pairs (trucks, diaphragms) are listed as 1 Pair, 2 Pair, etc.

**RETIRED MODEL** - Indicates a Walthers product which has been taken out of production. Supplies are limited to the remaining inventory at your dealer or in our warehouse. A future production run may be scheduled.

## TRADEMARK INFORMATION

Wm. K. Walthers, Inc. is an authorized Amtrak supplier. Amtrak is a registered service mark of the National Railroad Passenger Association.

CSX proprietary marks used by permission of CSX Transportation, Inc.

Products bearing American Refrigerator Transit Company, ART, Chicago & North Western Railway, Chicago & North Western System, Chicago & North Western, CNW, C&NW, Denver & Rio Grande Western, DRGW, D&RG, D&RGW, Rio Grande, Katy Railroad, The Katy, Missouri-Kansas-Texas, MKT, M-K-T, Missouri Pacific Lines, Missouri Pacific, Mo-Pac, MP, Pacific Fruit Express Company, Pacific Fruit Express, PFE, Southern Pacific Rail Corporation, Southern Pacific Lines, Southern Pacific, SP, St. Louis Southwestern, SSW, Cotton Belt, Cotton Belt Route, Texas & Pacific, T&P, TP, Union Pacific Railroad Company, Union Pacific Railroad, Union Pacific, UP, Union Pacific Fruit Express, UPFE, Western Pacific & WP marks are made under trademark license from Union Pacific Railroad Company.

## LICENSING INFORMATION

© 2007 Good Humor-Breyers Ice Cream. All Rights Reserved. Trademark used under license. Licensed by Broad Street Licensing Group, LLC

© 1923,1925,1935,1938 SEPS: Licensed by Curtis Publishing, Indianapolis IN. All Rights Reserved.

The yellow/black color scheme is a trademark for DEWALT® Power Tools and Accessories. The DEWALT® trademarks, Roush Racing trademarks and Matt Kenseth's name and/or likeness used by authority of Roush Racing, Livonia, MI.

®Unless otherwise indicated, all trademarks are owned by Newell Rubbermaid, Inc. or its subsidiaries, and are used by permission. All rights reserved. The Roush Racing trademarks and Jamie McMurray's name and/or likeness used by authority of Roush Racing, Livonia, MI.

The name Office Depot and the Office Depot logo are registered trademarks of Office Depot. The Roush Racing trademarks and Carl Edwards name and/or likeness used by authority of Roush Racing, Livonia, MI.

The Roush Racing trademarks and Greg Biffle's name and/or likeness used by authority of Roush Racing, Livonia, MI. ©2007 Ameriquest Mortgage Company. Trade/servicemarks are the property of Ameriquest Mortgage Company and/or its subsidiaries. All rights reserved.

© 2007 Evernham Motorsports, LLC. The stylized E with checkered flag® and 9® are registered trademarks and service marks of Evernham Motorsports, LLC, used under license. Kasey Kahne™ likeness and signature are trademarks of Kasey Kahne Inc. licensed by Evernham Motorsports, LLC. Dodge is a trademark of DaimlerChrysler Corporation.

© 2007 Evernham Motorsports, LLC. The stylized E with checkered flag® and 19® are registered trademarks and service marks of Evernham Motorsports, LLC, used under license. Elliott Sadler™ likeness and signature are trademarks of Elliott Sadler Enterprises, Inc. licensed by Evernham Motorsports, LLC. Dodge is a trademark of DaimlerChrysler Corporation.

© 2007 Valvoline Evernham Racing, LLC. The VER logo and stylized No. 10 are trademarks and service marks of Valvoline Evernham Racing, LLC and Evernham Motorsports, LLC respectively. Scott Riggs likeness and signature are trademarks of Scott Riggs Enterprises licensed by Valvoline Evernham Racing, LLC. V® and Valvoline, used under License and are registered trademarks of Ashland. Stanley and Stanley in a notched rectangle design are registered trademarks of Stanley Logistics, Inc., or its affiliates.

General Motors trademarks used under license to Wm. K. Walthers, Inc.

Dodge is a trademark of the DaimlerChrysler Corporation.

'Ford' and 'Fusion' trademarks used under the license from Ford Motor Company.

Honda Official Licensed Products are for sale only in the U.S., U.S. territories, Canada and Mexico. Designed, manufactured and distributed by Wm. K. Walthers, Inc. Honda trademarks are distinctive design elements of Honda Products are intellectual property of Honda Motor Co., Inc., used under license. All rights reserved.

Goodyear is a trademark of The Goodyear Tire & Rubber Company used under license by Wm. K. Walthers, Inc.

NASCAR® is a registered trademark of The National Association for Stock Car Auto Racing, Inc.

© 2007 HGL, LLC The name, likeness and signature of Jeff Gordon and the signature of Jeff Gordon the likeness of the #24 DuPont Chevrolet are used under license granted by HGL, LLC

© HGL, LLC The name, likeness and signature of Jimmie Johnson and the likeness of the #48 Lowe's Chevrolet are used under license granted by HGL, LLC.

© 2007 HGL, LLC. The name, likeness and signature of Kyle Busch and the likeness of the #5 HMS Chevrolet are used under license granted by HGL, LLC. © 2007 Kellogg NA Company.

"J.J. Yeley®", "#18®" and "Interstate® Batteries" licensed under authority of Joe Gibbs Racing, Huntersville, NC.

"Tony Stewart®", "#20®", and "The Home Depot®" licensed under authority of Joe Gibbs Racing, Huntersville, NC.

"Denny Hamlin™", "#11™" and "FedEx®" licensed under authority of Joe Gibbs Racing, Huntersville, NC.

# INDEX

"THE GREAT LITTLE KIT..."
Bar Mills
SCALE MODEL WORKS
"FROM THE GREAT STATE OF MAINE"

Blair Line LLC
PRODUCTS FOR MODEL RAILROADERS





BLMA MODELS

BRAWA
LIEBE ZUM DETAIL

BUSCH

Circuitron
Electronic Hobby Products

CLASSIC
METAL
WORKS
PRECISION CAST REPLICA

CMK

WALTHERS
CORNERSTONE®
SERIES

# INDEX

# INDEX

2008
HO
Model Railroad
Reference Book

# LOCOMOTIVES

Model and Photo by Neil Schofield

Old Man Winter visited all of his fury on the Newport area over the past 24 hours. Schools were closed. Moms and dads gave up trying to go to work. Airliners sat lonely and snow-covered at the terminals. Semis stood on the sidelines at truck stops, as state and county highway crews couldn't keep ahead of the storm. Through it all, the railroads kept moving. Sure, it was a fight, and RS-2 #8400 still carries plenty of snow on the walkways to mark its pre-dawn passage through the drifts. Just as things were looking up on arrival at the yards, the crew finds one of the switch leads jammed with snow and ice. All of it will have to be shoveled out by hand, a job which the brakeman has been assigned by the more senior members of the engine crew, who at least offered to share their coffee - when he gets back!

With the cab heaters running flat out, you just know it's a bitterly cold Vermont morning on Neil Schofield's layout in Seekonk, Massachusetts. The loco is a heavily modified Kato model, which sees regular service along the line, which is set in the early 80s and serves northeast Vermont. Last night's "storm" was actually a mix of Woodland Scenics and Noch snow, which was sprinkled over the layout for a staged Christmas card scene. Once the shots were made, the snow was removed with a vacuum cleaner.

Locomotives are the defining features of any railroad. Whether it's a tiny 4-4-0 or a giant AC4400 moving the tonnage, nothing sets the time and place of your railroad quite like its motive power. Inside this section, you'll find a wide range of engines, from early steam to contemporary diesels, ready to take on the challenges of moving freight and passengers on your pike.

From Walthers

From Walthers

# You're not Just Modeling History – You're Making it

The EMD BL-2 changed the face of railroading — prototype and model — forever. When EMD launched its BL-2 in the late 40s, it represented an entirely new concept in locomotive design. So too did the HO replica from Life-Like that appeared in 1989.

Here's where it all began, with the EMD BL-2, introduced in 1989

### *Building on Success*

From that initial launch, Life-Like broke new ground, releasing many models that had only been dreamed of, with new features to improve realism and performance.

### *New Trains of Thought*

If engines could look and run this well, why not freight cars? The first PROTO 2000 first kits appeared a few years later, complete with separate grab irons, brake gear, knuckle couplers, metal wheels and more.

EMD E8A from 2003

### *Revisiting Railroading's Glorious Heritage*

Designers next took on the challenge of making a PROTO 2000-quality steam loco. Over two years and 14,000 work-hours passed before the roll out of the PROTO 2000 Heritage Series 2-8-8-2 in 1999. Complete in every detail, only the soot and cinders were missing!

The newest member of the PROTO 2000 Heritage Series, these new 2-10-2's are now available.

### *Continuing the Traditions*

Today, PROTO 2000 still delivers the quality and realism that first defined the line. New locos feature 14:1 gearing, helical gears for quiet operation, more prototype-specific details and come in your choice of Quantum Sound & DCC equipped, or standard DC powered versions.

The following pages showcase the newest PROTO 2000 (and PROTO 1000) locos, which will be arriving through May of 2008. Be sure to check out the Freight Cars section for more new releases!

New RSC-2 diesels are expected shortly

From Walthers

EMD SD50 from 2004

## *Taking the Right Track to Success*

Chances are, your life-long involvement with model railroading began with a basic train set. But once you discovered better models, the set was abandoned.

But what if you could have started with advanced, affordably priced models?

That was the goal for Life-Like engineers when they unveiled the PROTO 1000 series in 1999.

EMD GP38-2 from second series, released in 2004

## *The Best of Both Worlds*

The first PROTO 1000 EMD F3s appeared to rave reviews. By molding smaller details on the body, the engines were tough enough for younger modelers. Sharing drive components and other features of PROTO 2000 engines, ensured top-notch performance. And less assembly meant more affordable prices.

And it wasn't long before the F3A was pulling PROTO 1000 freight cars, also built to offer superb detail at an affordable price.

EMD SD45, first released in 2003

## *Unique Ideas Brought to Life*

It wasn't just newcomers who took notice — experienced modelers were soon running PROTO 1000 equipment too! And the line kept growing, with R17 subway cars, Rail Diesel Cars (RDC), RS-2 diesels, unique box cars and other freight equipment, offered for the first time as affordable plastic models.

## *Meet Each New Challenge*

Whether you're just getting started or your railroad is growing, you'll find PROTO 1000 models to meet each new challenge. Check out the listings here and in the Freight Cars Section for more exciting releases!

Thrall All-Door Box Car from 1998

From Walthers

# EMD F7

Mainline freight service was the last stronghold for steam power in America. By the late 1930s, diesels had proven themselves as switchers and as power for the new streamlined trains, but there were doubts that they could ever be practical in freight service.

That all changed in late 1939 when EMD rolled out its brand-new FT locomotive. Borrowing some basic design elements from E series passenger power, but in a shorter, more powerful package, the demonstrator set out on a 35-state tour that covered nearly 90,000 miles. Railroads were amazed at what this single A-B-B-A lash-up with its incredible 5400 horsepower could do, and orders came quickly. With its proven track record, EMD was the only builder allowed to construct road diesel power during the material shortages of World War II.

Starting in 1945, the basic design underwent a number of changes, resulting in the F2, F3 and F5. But with the arrival of the F7 in 1949, EMD had exactly what the railroads needed to begin dieselizing with a vengeance. The F7 retained the 1500 horsepower 567B prime mover of the F3, but with better electrical equipment, it had a tonnage rating some 30% greater than the earlier model. The units could be geared for freight or passenger service, and were equally at home in either assignment. Over the next four years EMD built over 2200 A and 1400 B units, which were delivered in a rainbow of schemes to nearly every railroad in America. Tough and durable, many soldiered on into the early 70s and several have been preserved.

**Order Now! Limited Availability**

Please Note: All Proto Series manufacturer numbers have changed from 433 to 920.

EMD F7 A-B Set C&O 920-40581

## EMD F7

### Fall 2007 Delivery (Unless Noted)

- All-New Drive
  - * 14:1 Gear Ratio for Easy Multiple-Unit Operations
  - * Helical Gears for Ultra-Quiet & Smooth Running
  - * Five-Pole, Skew-Wound, High Torque, High Efficiency Can Motor
  - * Heavily Weighted for Maximum Traction
  - * Both A&B Units Powered
- Painted Metal Grab Irons, Ladder Stand-Offs, Handrails & Lift Rings
- Correct Coupling Distance Between A & B Units
- Most Authentic "Bulldog" Nose Ever Done
- Correct Windshield Slope
- Roof Panel Weld Lines
- Correctly Sized Bolt Heads
- Complete Scale Fuel Tank w/Hangers, Battery Box, Air Tank & Underframe Detail
- Working Headlight w/Bezel & Recessed Lens
- Working Mars Light as Appropriate - Works on DC or DCC
- With or Without Dynamic Brakes to Match Prototypes
- Correct Style Lighted Numberboards
- Bright "Sunny White" LED Lighting
- Separate, Clear Class Lights
- Full Cab Interior w/Crew Figures
- New Insulated Diecast Magnetic Knuckle Couplers
- Full or Partial Fuel Tank Skirts to Match Prototypes
- Correct Grab Iron Style & Placement for Each Roadname
- Freight, Passenger or Snowplow Pilot
- All-New Sideframes w/Road Specific Journals & With or Without Speed Recorder
- Nose Lift Rings as Appropriate
- Operating Diaphragms as Appropriate
- Etched Metal Farr or Horizontal Grilles
- Visible Details Behind Grilles & Under Fan Covers
- Available with Dual Mode QSI Sound & DCC** or Standard DC Models

**Sound and DCC-equipped models can be operated on either DC or DCC layouts, and feature authentic EMD 567 prime mover recordings that include exhaust, road-specific horn tone to match prototype, improved throttle notching and transition sounds for change in traction motor electrical connection during acceleration, bell, squealing brakes, doppler effect, air let off and much more.

### A-B Sets

**369.98 w/Sound & DCC**

**269.98 Standard DC**

**Santa Fe**

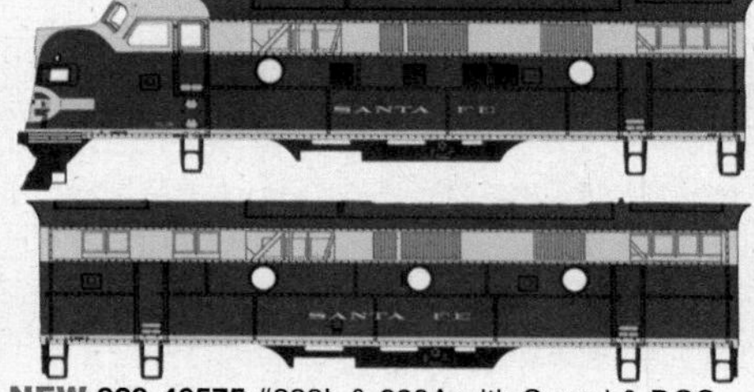

**NEW 920-40575** #233L & 233A with Sound & DCC

**NEW 920-40576** #251L & 251A with Sound & DCC

**NEW 920-40577** #238C & 238B Standard DC

**NEW 920-40578** #258L & 258A Standard DC

**Chesapeake & Ohio**

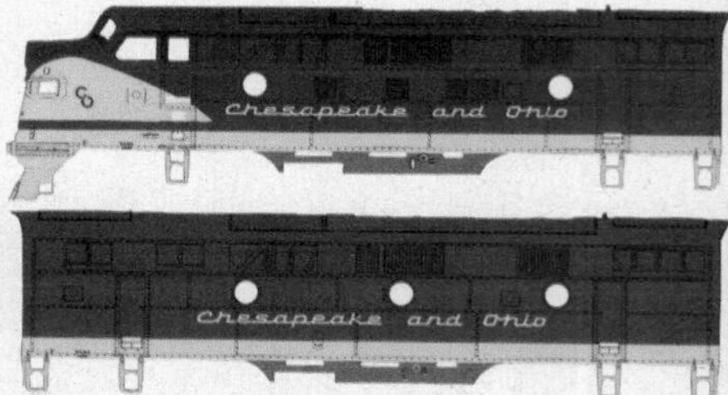


**NEW 920-40579** #7000 & 7500 with Sound & DCC

**NEW 920-40621** #7004 & 7502 with Sound & DCC

**NEW 920-40581** #7016 & 7508 Standard DC

**NEW 920-47621** #7028 & 7514 Standard DC

*complete listings continue p.36*

## Prototype-Specific Details Include:

### Chesapeake & Ohio
- Wind Deflectors
- Whip Radio Antenna Base w/Conduit
- 5-Chime Forward-Facing Nathan M5 Airhorn
- 2 Vertical Wire Grab Irons on Nose
- Roller Bearing Journal Boxes
- Freight Pilot
- Full Side Skirts
- Nondynamic Roof Detail

### Santa Fe (not pictured)
- Leslie Typhon A-200 Single-Chime Airhorns
- Front Numberplate
- Nose Lift Rings
- Wind Deflectors
- Full Nose Grab Irons
- Roller Bearing Journal Boxes
- Freight Pilot
- Partial Side Skirts
- Dynamic Brakes

### Chicago, Burlington & Quincy
- Leslie Typhon A-200 Single-Chime Airhorns
- Front-Mounted Wagonwheel Radio Antenna
- Conduit Between Windshields
- Mars Light
- Partial Side Skirts
- Dynamic Brake
- Square Journal Boxes
- Passenger Pilot

### Great Northern
- 3-Chime Leslie S-3L Air Horns
- Winterization Hatch
- Roof-Mounted Cooling Coil
- Correct Steam Generator Air Intake
- Straight Radio Antenna
- Partial Side Skirts
- Roller Bearing Journal Boxes
- Snowplow Pilot
- Matches Walthers Empire Builder Cars

†Union Pacific licensed product.

### New York Central
- Leslie Typhon A-200 Single-Chime Airhorns
- Sinclair Radio Antenna
- Wind Deflectors
- Partial Side Skirts
- Dynamic Brake
- Roller Bearing Journal Boxes
- Passenger Pilot

### Soo Line
- Leslie Typhon A-200 Single-Chime Airhorns
- Firecracker Radio Antenna
- Full Nose Grab Irons
- Winterization Hatch
- Mars Light
- Partial Side Skirts
- Nondynamic Roof Detail
- ACI Labels
- Roller Bearing Journal Boxes
- Freight Pilot

### Southern Pacific†
- Leslie Typhon A-200 Single-Chime Airhorns
- Whip Radio Antenna
- Wind Deflectors
- Conduit Between Windshields
- Mars Light
- Partial Side Skirts
- Dynamic Brake
- Roller Bearing Journal Boxes
- Snowplow Pilot

### Milwaukee Road
- Leslie Typhon A-200 Single-Chime Airhorns
- Straight Radio Antenna
- Wind Deflectors
- Conduit Between Windshields
- Winterization Hatch
- Mars Light
- Dynamic Brake
- Roller Bearing Journal Boxes
- Passenger Pilot

Preproduction models shown. Some details may vary.

From Walthers

## A-B Sets (Unless Noted)

**369.98 w/Sound & DCC**
**269.98 Standard DC**

### Chicago, Burlington & Quincy

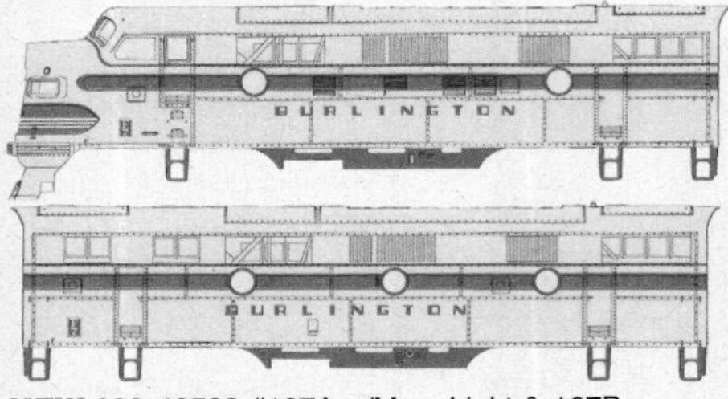


**NEW 920-40583** #167A w/Mars Light & 167B with Sound & DCC

**NEW 920-40608** #168A w/Mars Light & 168B with Sound & DCC

**NEW 920-40585** #167A w/Mars Light & 167B Standard DC

**NEW 920-40610** #169A & 169-B Standard DC

### Great Northern

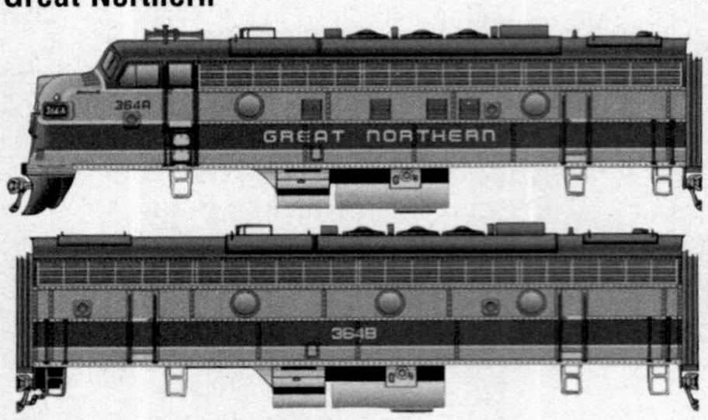


**NEW 920-40587** #363A w/Mars Light & 363B with Sound & DCC

**NEW 920-40607** #270A w/Mars Light & 270B with Sound & DCC

**NEW 920-40589** #269A w/Mars Light & 269B Standard DC

**NEW 920-40619** #365A w/Mars Light & 365B Standard DC

### Milwaukee Road

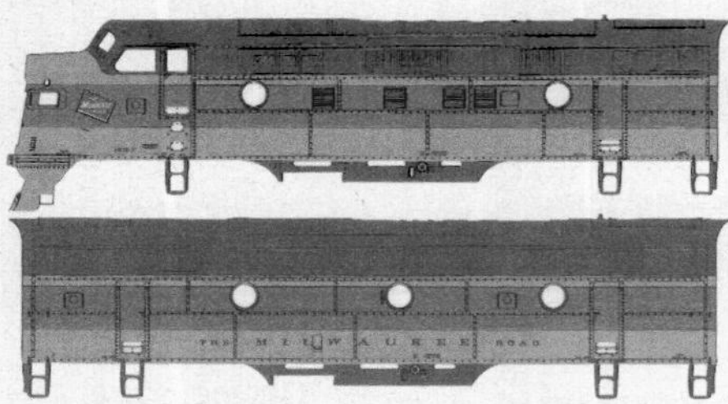

**NEW 920-40591** #70A w/Mars Light & 70B with Sound & DCC

**NEW 920-40623** #69A w/Mars Light & 69B with Sound & DCC

**NEW 920-40593** #72A w/Mars Light & 72B Standard DC

**NEW 920-47623** #71A w/Mars Light & 71B Standard DC

## Order Now! Limited Availability

Please Note: All Proto Series manufacturer numbers have changed from 433 to 920.

### New York Central

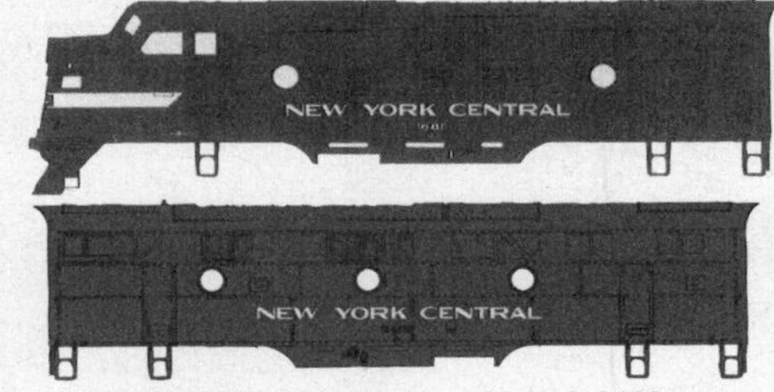


**NEW 920-40595** #1681 w/Mars Light & 2438 with Sound & DCC

**NEW 920-40597** #1684 w/Mars Light & 2440 Standard DC

### Soo Line

**NEW 920-40599** #2225A w/Mars Light & 502C with Sound & DCC

**NEW 920-40627** #2226A w/Mars Light & 503C with Sound & DCC

**NEW 920-40601** #2226A w/Mars Light & #503C Standard DC

**NEW 920-47627** #2225A & 502C Standard DC

### Southern Pacific†

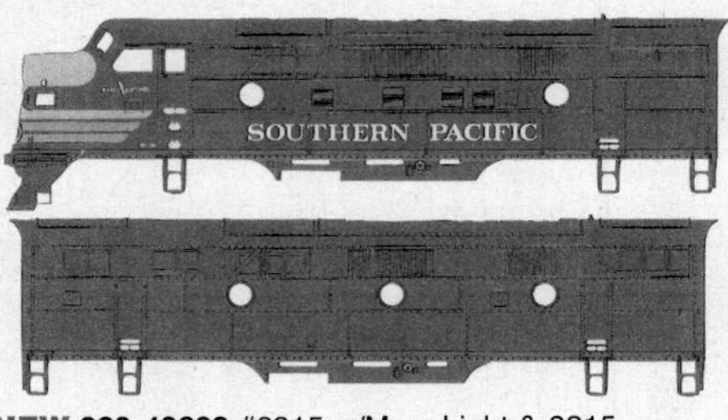


**NEW 920-40603** #6315 w/Mars Light & 8215 with Sound & DCC

**NEW 920-40604** #6320 w/Mars Light & 8220 with Sound & DCC

**NEW 920-40605** #6323 w/Mars Light & 8223 Standard DC

**NEW 920-40603** #6325 w/Mars Light & 8225 Standard DC

### Undecorated

**NEW 920-40615** With Sound & DCC

**NEW 920-40617** Standard DC

### Winter 2007-08 Delivery

### Union Pacific†

**NEW 920-40631** #1 with Sound & DCC

**NEW 920-40632** #2 with Sound & DCC

**NEW 920-47631** #3 Standard DC

**NEW 920-47632** #4 Standard DC

### Pennsylvania

**NEW 920-40635** #1 with Sound & DCC

**NEW 920-40636** #2 with Sound & DCC

**NEW 920-47635** #3 Standard DC

**NEW 920-47636** #4 Standard DC

### Baltimore & Ohio

**NEW 920-40639** #1 with Sound & DCC

**NEW 920-40640** #2 with Sound & DCC

**NEW 920-47639** #3 Standard DC

**NEW 920-47640** #4 Standard DC

### Wabash (A-A Sets)

**NEW 920-40643** #1 with Sound & DCC

**NEW 920-40644** #2 with Sound & DCC

**NEW 920-47643** #3 Standard DC

**NEW 920-47644** #4 Standard DC

### Chicago & North Western†

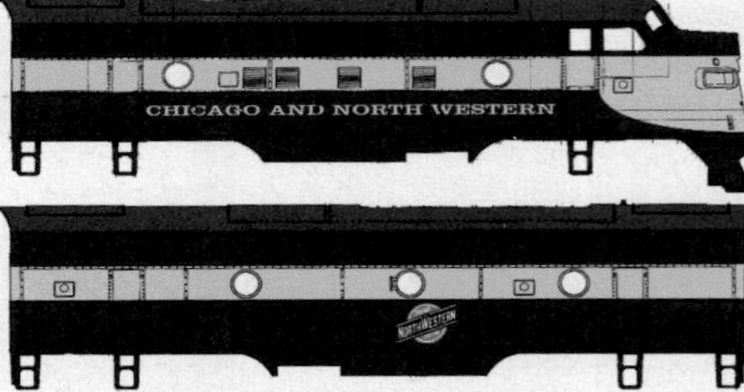


**NEW 920-40647** #1 with Sound & DCC

**NEW 920-40648** #2 with Sound & DCC

**NEW 920-47647** #3 Standard DC

**NEW 920-47648** #4 Standard DC

### Rock Island

**NEW 920-40649** #1 with Sound & DCC

**NEW 920-40650** #2 with Sound & DCC

**NEW 920-47649** #3 Standard DC

**NEW 920-47650** #4 Standard DC

### Denver & Rio Grande Western†

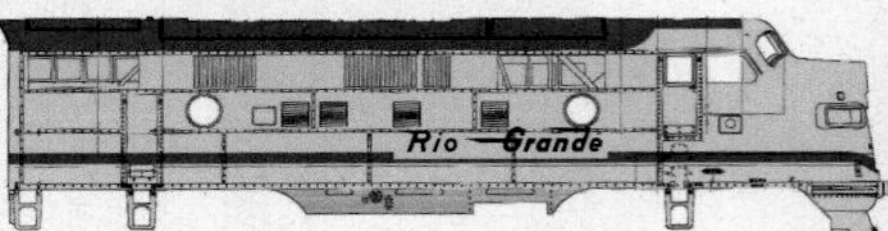


**NEW 920-40653** #1 with Sound & DCC

**NEW 920-40654** #2 with Sound & DCC

**NEW 920-47653** #3 Standard DC

**NEW 920-47654** #4 Standard DC

From Walthers

### Canadian National

**NEW 920-40657** #1 with Sound & DCC
**NEW 920-40658** #2 with Sound & DCC
**NEW 920-47657** #3 Standard DC
**NEW 920-47658** #4 Standard DC

### Great Northern - Big Sky Blue

**NEW 920-40659** #1 with Sound & DCC
**NEW 920-40660** #2 with Sound & DCC
**NEW 920-47659** #3 Standard DC
**NEW 920-47660** #4 Standard DC

## A Unit Only

**189.98 w/Sound & DCC**
**139.98 Standard DC**

### Chesapeake & Ohio

**NEW 920-40580** #7001 with Sound & DCC
**NEW 920-40622** #7005 with Sound & DCC
**NEW 920-40582** #7017 Standard DC
**NEW 920-47622** #7029 Standard DC

### Chicago, Burlington & Quincy

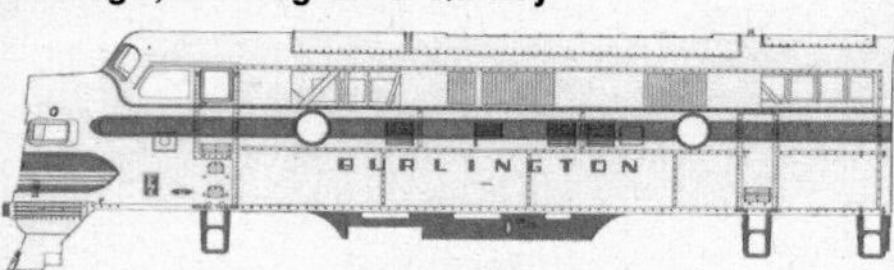


**NEW 920-40584** #167C w/Mars Light with Sound & DCC
**NEW 920-40609** #168C w/Mars Light with Sound & DCC
**NEW 920-40586** #167C w/Mars Light Standard DC
**NEW 920-40611** #169C w/Mars Light Standard DC

### Great Northern - Empire Builder

**NEW 920-40588** #363C w/Mars Light with Sound & DCC
**NEW 920-40612** #268A w/Mars Light with Sound & DCC
**NEW 920-40590** #268A w/Mars Light Standard DC
**NEW 920-40620** #365C w/Mars Light Standard DC

## Order Now! Limited Availability

Please Note: All Proto Series manufacturer numbers have changed from 433 to 920.

### Milwaukee Road

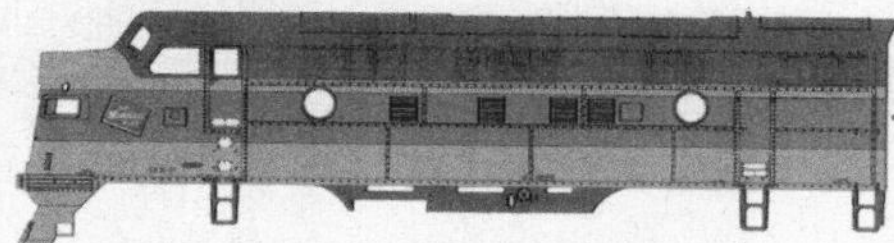

**NEW 920-40592** #70C w/Mars Light with Sound & DCC
**NEW 920-40624** #69C w/Mars Light with Sound & DCC
**NEW 920-40594** #72C w/Mars Light Standard DC
**NEW 920-47624** #71C w/Mars Light Standard DC

### New York Central

**NEW 920-40596** #1693 w/Mars Light with Sound & DCC
**NEW 920-40598** #1701 w/Mars Light Standard DC

### Soo Line

**NEW 920-40600** #2225B w/Mars Light with Sound & DCC
**NEW 920-40628** #2226B w/Mars Light with Sound & DCC
**NEW 920-40602** #2226B w/Mars Light Standard DC
**NEW 920-47628** #2225B w/Mars Light Standard DC

### Undecorated

**NEW 920-40616** With Sound & DCC
**NEW 920-40618** Standard DC

### Winter 2007-08 Delivery

### Pennsylvania

**NEW 920-40637** #1 with Sound & DCC
**NEW 920-40638** #2 with Sound & DCC
**NEW 920-47637** #3 Standard DC
**NEW 920-47638** #4 Standard DC

### Baltimore & Ohio

**NEW 920-40641** #1 with Sound & DCC
**NEW 920-40642** #2 with Sound & DCC
**NEW 920-47641** #3 Standard DC
**NEW 920-47642** #4 Standard DC

†Union Pacific licensed product.

### Wabash

**NEW 920-40645** #1 with Sound & DCC
**NEW 920-40646** #2 with Sound & DCC
**NEW 920-47645** #3 Standard DC
**NEW 920-47646** #4 Standard DC

### Rock Island

**NEW 920-40651** #1 with Sound & DCC
**NEW 920-40652** #2 with Sound & DCC
**NEW 920-47651** #3 Standard DC
**NEW 920-47652** #4 Standard DC

## B Unit Only

**189.98 w/Sound & DCC**
**139.98 Standard DC**

### Great Northern - Empire Builder

**NEW 920-40613** #362B with Sound & DCC
**NEW 920-40629** #268B with Sound & DCC
**NEW 920-40614** #359B Standard DC
**NEW 920-40630** #360B Standard DC

### Winter 2007-08 Delivery

### Union Pacific†

**NEW 920-40633** #1 with Sound & DCC
**NEW 920-40634** #2 with Sound & DCC
**NEW 920-47633** #3 Standard DC
**NEW 920-47634** #4 Standard DC

### Denver & Rio Grande Western†

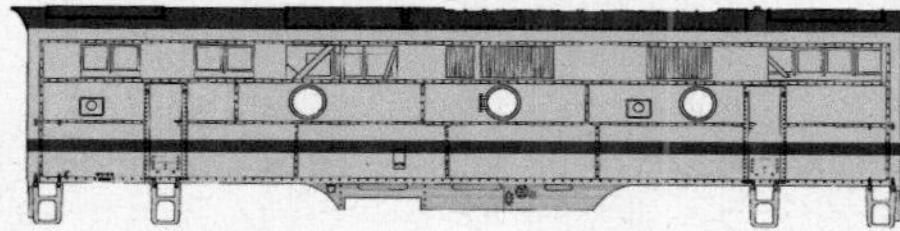

**NEW 920-40655** #1 with Sound & DCC
**NEW 920-40656** #2 with Sound & DCC
**NEW 920-47655** #3 Standard DC
**NEW 920-47656** #4 Standard DC

Get Your Daily Dose of Product News at
**www.walthers.com**

From Walthers

# GP7/9

While the road switcher concept had appeared as early as 1940, EMD preferred to concentrate on its F series cab unit diesels for freight service. But with no footboards and no rearward visibility, F units were not well liked by crews on locals and similar runs where there was a lot of switching or reverse running. EMD entered the road switcher market tentatively in 1948 with its BL1 and BL2, which mounted a semi-streamlined body on the same frame and machinery as the F3. This was a start, but in 1949, EMD found exactly what the railroads wanted in its new General Purpose series. Simple and rugged, the squared-off lines of the new GP7 weren't necessarily handsome, but this didn't matter to the new owners. In short order, buyers were using GP7s for everything from road freights to commuter service. Production continued with minor changes along the way (these spotting features are referred to as "phases" by railfans to differentiate variations among the otherwise similar locos) through 1954 when the more powerful GP9 was introduced. Reliable and versatile, many have lead long lives and are still working for shortlines and industrial operators.

## Order Now! Limited Availability

Please Note: All Proto Series manufacturer numbers have changed from 433 to 920.

920-40451
Model Shown for Illustration Only

### GP7/9

**Winter 2007-08 Delivery**

**224.98 with Sound & DCC**

**124.98 Standard DC**

- Prototype-Specific Detailing
- Magnetic Knuckle Couplers
- All-Wheel Drive & Electrical Pick-Up
- Machined Brass Flywheels
- Constant & Directional Headlights
- RP-25 Wheels
- Heavy Diecast Chassis
- Five-Pole Skew-Wound Motor
- Available With or Without Factory-Installed Sound & DCC

Sound can be operated with standard DC power pack or DCC controllers. Sound features include: Diesel Engine, Horn, Bell, Squealing Brakes, Doppler Effect, Air Let Off (in neutral), Headlight, and Trailer which mutes whistle and bell for double heading.

**Iowa Interstate**

**NEW 920-40850** GP9 Phase II #309 with Sound & DCC

**NEW 920-40851** GP7 Phase II #325 with Sound & DCC

**NEW 920-47850** GP9 Phase II #309 Standard DC

**NEW 920-47851** GP7 Phase II #325 Standard DC

**Algoma Central**

**NEW 920-40852** GP7 Phase I #158 with Sound & DCC

**NEW 920-40853** GP7 Phase I #161 with Sound & DCC

**NEW 920-47852** GP7 Phase I #152 Standard DC

**NEW 920-47853** GP7 Phase I #153 Standard DC

**Chicago & North Western†**

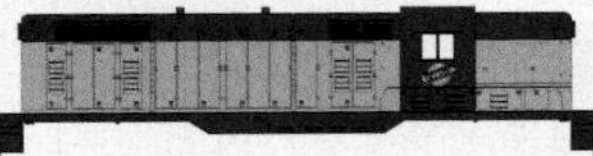

**NEW 920-40854** GP9 Phase III #1748 with Sound & DCC

**NEW 920-40855** GP9 Phase III #1756 with Sound & DCC

**NEW 920-47854** GP7 Phase II #1568 Standard DC

**NEW 920-47855** GP7 Phase II #1569 Standard DC

**Soo Line**

**NEW 920-40856** GP9 Phase I #2551 with Sound & DCC

**NEW 920-40857** GP9 Phase I #2554 with Sound & DCC

**NEW 920-47856** GP9 Phase I #2407 Standard DC

**NEW 920-47857** GP9 Phase I #2409 Standard DC

**Toledo, Peoria & Western**

**NEW 920-40858** GP7 Phase I #102 with Sound & DCC

**NEW 920-40859** GP7 Phase I #103 with Sound & DCC

**NEW 920-47858** GP7 Phase I #102 Standard DC

**NEW 920-47859** GP7 Phase I #103 Standard DC

**Ohio Central**

**NEW 920-40860** GP9 Phase II #91 with Sound & DCC

**NEW 920-40861** GP7 Phase I #1501 with Sound & DCC

**NEW 920-47860** GP9 Phase II #91 Standard DC

**NEW 920-47861** GP7 Phase I #1501 Standard DC

**North Central Texas**

**NEW 920-40862** GP7 Phase II #612 with Sound & DCC

**NEW 920-47862** GP7 Phase II #613 Standard DC

**NEW 920-47863** GP7 Phase II #614 Standard DC

**Dakota, Minnesota & Eastern**

**NEW 920-40864** GP9 Phase III #1463 with Sound & DCC

**NEW 920-40865** GP9 Phase III #1471 with Sound & DCC

**NEW 920-47864** GP9 Phase III #1483 Standard DC

**NEW 920-47865** GP9 Phase III #1484 Standard DC

**Cedar Rapids & Iowa City**

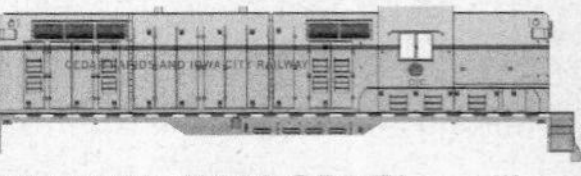

**NEW 920-40866** GP9 Phase III #101 with Sound & DCC

**NEW 920-47866** GP9 Phase III #101 Standard DC

**Undecorated**

**GP7**

**NEW 920-40870** Phase I with Sound & DCC

**NEW 920-47870** Phase I Standard DC

**GP9**

**NEW 920-40871** Phase II with Sound & DCC

**NEW 920-47871** Phase II Standard DC

†Union Pacific licensed product.

From Walthers

# Fairbanks-Morse H10-44

In the early 1930s, Fairbanks-Morse expanded its line of prime movers with the Model 38, which used opposed pistons for the combustion chamber. Although mechanically complex, it was smooth-running and quiet. This caught the eye of the US Navy, who ordered several for submarines. As WWII began winding down, F-M was given the OK to build a loco to test civilian applications for the Model 38. On August 21, 1944, F-M rolled out its first H10-44; "H" for a hood-type body, "10" for 1000 horsepower and "44" for a B-B (four axles and four traction motors) wheel arrangement. The loco went to work for the Milwaukee Road, who ordered 10 in 1945. Some 197 were built through May of 1950 when a 1200-horsepower version (H12-44) was introduced. Some H10s soldiered on into the 1980s, often working for shortline and industrial users. The first H10 was restored by the Illinois Railway Museum.

## Fairbanks-Morse H10-44

**Winter 2007-08 Delivery**

**204.98 w/Sound & DCC**

**104.98 Standard DC**

- Completely New Model
- Prototype-Specific Detailing
- Magnetic Knuckle Couplers
- All-Wheel Drive & Electrical Pick-Up
- Machined Brass Flywheels
- Constant & Directional Headlights
- RP-25 Wheels
- Heavy Diecast Chassis
- Five-Pole Skew-Wound Motor
- Available With or Without Factory-Installed Sound & DCC

Sound can be operated with standard DC power pack or DCC controllers. Sound features include: Diesel Engine, Horn, Bell, Squealing Brakes, Doppler Effect, Air Let Off (in neutral), Headlight, and Trailer which mutes whistle and bell for double heading.

**Order Now! Limited Availability**

Please Note: All Proto Series manufacturer numbers have changed from 433 to 920.

### Santa Fe

**NEW 920-40775** #1 with Sound & DCC

**NEW 920-40776** #2 with Sound & DCC

**NEW 920-47775** #3 Standard DC

**NEW 920-47776** #4 Standard DC

### Baltimore & Ohio

**NEW 920-40777** #1 with Sound & DCC

**NEW 920-40778** #2 with Sound & DCC

**NEW 920-47777** #3 Standard DC

**NEW 920-47778** #4 Standard DC

### Chicago & North Western†

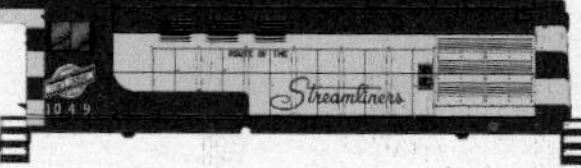


**NEW 920-40779** #1 with Sound & DCC

**NEW 920-40780** #2 with Sound & DCC

**NEW 920-47779** #3 Standard DC

**NEW 920-47780** #4 Standard DC

### Central of New Jersey

**NEW 920-40781** #1 with Sound & DCC

**NEW 920-40782** #2 with Sound & DCC

**NEW 920-47781** #3 Standard DC

**NEW 920-47782** #4 Standard DC

### Milwaukee Road

**NEW 920-40783** #1 with Sound & DCC

**NEW 920-40784** #2 with Sound & DCC

**NEW 920-47783** #3 Standard DC

**NEW 920-47784** #4 Standard DC

### Nickel Plate Road

**NEW 920-40785** #1 with Sound & DCC

**NEW 920-40786** #2 with Sound & DCC

**NEW 920-47785** #3 Standard DC

**NEW 920-47786** #4 Standard DC

### New York Central

**NEW 920-40787** #1 with Sound & DCC

**NEW 920-40788** #2 with Sound & DCC

**NEW 920-47787** #3 Standard DC

**NEW 920-47788** #4 Standard DC

### Pennsylvania

**NEW 920-40789** #1 with Sound & DCC

**NEW 920-40790** #2 with Sound & DCC

**NEW 920-47789** #3 Standard DC

**NEW 920-47790** #4 Standard DC

### Undecorated

**NEW 920-40793** With Sound & DCC

**NEW 920-47793** Standard DC

For Up-To-Date Information and News Bookmark Walthers Web site at

**www.walthers.com**

# EMD SD7

Originally intended for use on branch lines, EMD launched its "Special Duty" series in 1952 with the SD7. This loco also introduced the three-axle Flexi-Coil truck with its powered center axle. This was a major departure from earlier three-axle designs where an unpowered center axle was used to spread the engine's weight over more wheels, reducing the strain on the lighter rail and lower capacity bridges found on branches. EMD's design not only spread the weight but the extra traction motors provided a bit more power to get trains started. The SD's longer trucks required a longer frame, and buyers could also specify a heavier frame for engines working transfers and other low speed service. Somewhat underpowered with only 1500 horsepower (same as a four-axle GP7), only 188 SD7s were built from February of 1952 through November of 1953; the more powerful SD9 was introduced the following January.

**Order Now! Limited Availability**

Please Note: All Proto Series manufacturer numbers have changed from 433 to 920.

EMD SD7 PRR 920-40733

## EMD SD7

- Prototype-Specific Detailing
- Magnetic Knuckle Couplers
- All Wheel Drive & Electrical Pick-Up
- Dual Machined Brass Flywheels
- Constant & Directional Headlights
- RP-25 Wheels
- Heavy Diecast Chassis
- Five-Pole Skew-Wound Motor
- Available With or Without Factory-Installed Sound & DCC

Sound can be operated with standard DC power pack or DCC controllers. Sound features include: Diesel Engine, Horn, Bell, Squealing Brakes, Doppler Effect, Air Let Off (in neutral), Headlight, and Trailer which mutes whistle and bell for double heading.

**Quantum® Sound & DCC Equipped, 224.98 Each**

**Standard DC, 124.98 Each**

### Bessemer & Lake Erie

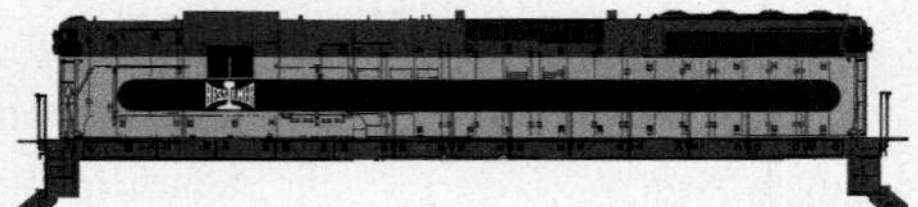

**NEW 920-40725** #452 With Sound & DCC
**NEW 920-40726** #453 With Sound & DCC
**NEW 920-47725** #451 Standard DC
**NEW 920-47726** #454 Standard DC

### EMD Demonstrator

**NEW 920-40727** #990 With Sound & DCC
**NEW 920-40728** #991 With Sound & DCC
**NEW 920-40777** #990 With Sound & DCC
**NEW 920-40778** #991 With Sound & DCC

†Union Pacific licensed product.

### Chicago & North Western†

**NEW 920-40729** #1661 With Sound & DCC
**NEW 920-40730** #1663 With Sound & DCC
**NEW 920-47729** #1660 Standard DC
**NEW 920-47730** #1662 Standard DC

### Great Northern

**NEW 920-40731** #561 With Sound & DCC
**NEW 920-40732** #562 With Sound & DCC
**NEW 920-47731** #569 Standard DC
**NEW 920-47732** #570 Standard DC

### Pennsylvania

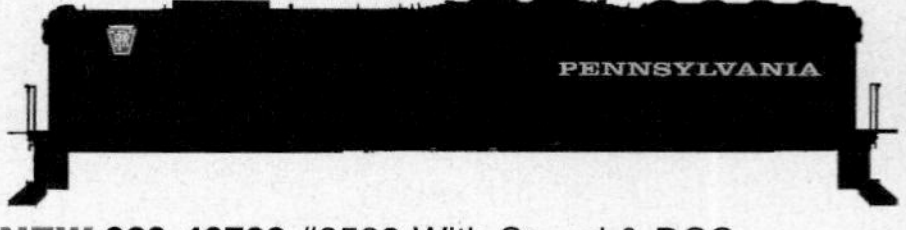


**NEW 920-40733** #8588 With Sound & DCC
**NEW 920-40734** #8589 With Sound & DCC
**NEW 920-47733** #8588 Standard DC
**NEW 920-47734** #8589 Standard DC

### Chessie

**NEW 920-40735** #1827 With Sound & DCC
**NEW 920-40736** #1830 With Sound & DCC
**NEW 920-47735** #1826 Standard DC
**NEW 920-47736** #1829 Standard DC

### Undecorated

**NEW 920-40737** With Sound & DCC
**NEW 920-47737** Standard DC

PROTO 1000 SERIES™
From Walthers

# RS-2

The RS-2 was Alco's first roadswitcher to incorporate its new 244-Series prime mover. The 1,500-horsepower units were designed for versatility - they were equally at home working road freights or switch runs. If equipped with a steam generator, they were adept at working commuter and secondary passenger runs. Production began in 1946 with just over 350 units constructed for U.S. and Canadian roads before the unit was succeeded by the 1,600-horsepower RS-3 in 1950 (although a few late RS-2s were rated at 1,600 horsepower).

RS-2s have worked for Class I, shortline and industrial lines across the continent. The engines have been long lived, with one survivor still holding down daily freight duties in 2007. A few others still see service at museum and tourist lines.

**Order Now! Limited Availability**

Please Note: All Proto Series manufacturer numbers have changed from 433 to 920.

ALCO RS-2 GB&W 920-35100

## RS-2

**99.98 ea**

- Magnetic Knuckle Couplers
- All Wheel Drive & Electrical Pick-Up
- Dual Machined Brass Flywheels
- Constant & Directional Headlights
- RP-25 Contour Blackened Wheels
- Heavy Diecast Chassis
- Five-Pole Skew-Wound Motor

### Green Bay & Western

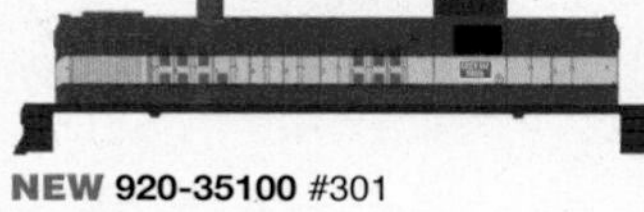

**NEW** 920-35100 #301
**NEW** 920-35101 #303

### Chesapeake & Ohio

**NEW** 920-35102 #5500
**NEW** 920-35103 #5501

### Maine Central

**NEW** 920-35104 #551
**NEW** 920-35105 #554

### Delaware & Hudson

**NEW** 920-35106 #4005
**NEW** 920-35107 #4023

### Louisville & Nashville

**NEW** 920-35108 #260
**NEW** 920-35109 #266

### Spokane, Portland & Seattle

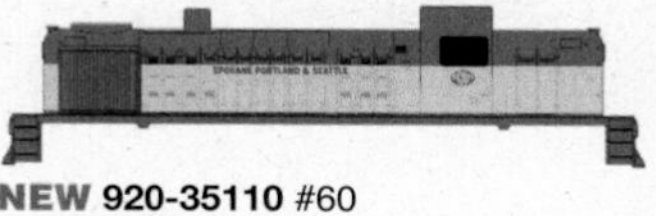

**NEW** 920-35110 #60
**NEW** 920-35111 #61

### Undecorated

**NEW** 920-35112

### Winter 2007-08 Delivery

### Chicago & North Western†

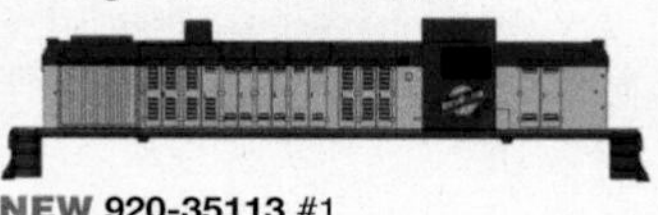

**NEW** 920-35113 #1
**NEW** 920-35114 #2

### Canadian Pacific

**NEW** 920-35115 #1
**NEW** 920-35116 #2

### Elgin, Joliet & Eastern

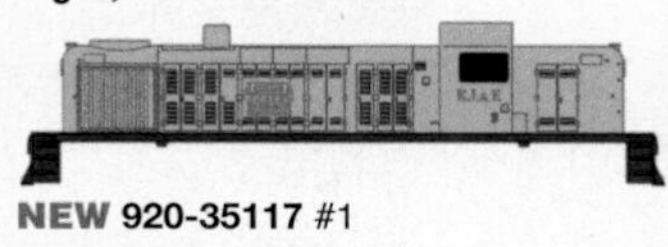


**NEW** 920-35117 #1
**NEW** 920-35118 #2

### Chicago Great Western

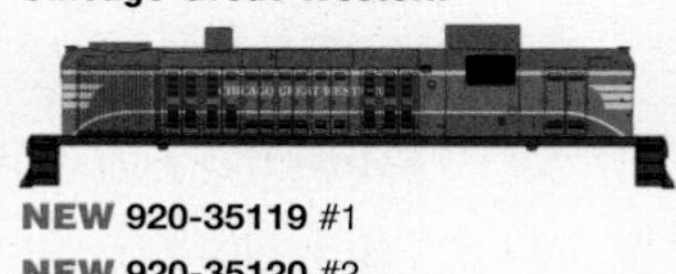

**NEW** 920-35119 #1
**NEW** 920-35120 #2

### Toledo, Peoria & Western

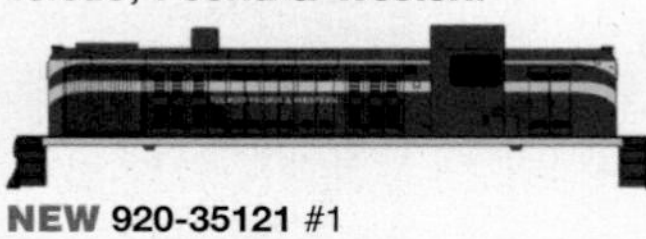

**NEW** 920-35121 #1
**NEW** 920-35122 #2

### Union Pacific†

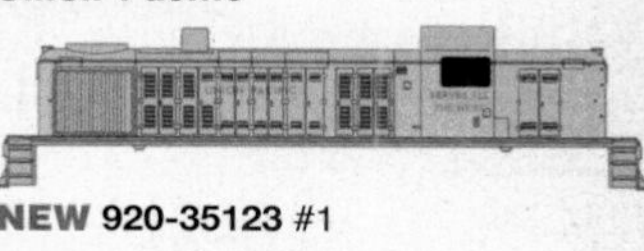

**NEW** 920-35123 #1
**NEW** 920-35124 #2

## RSC-2

**94.98 ea**

### Winter 2007-08 Delivery

### Milwaukee Road

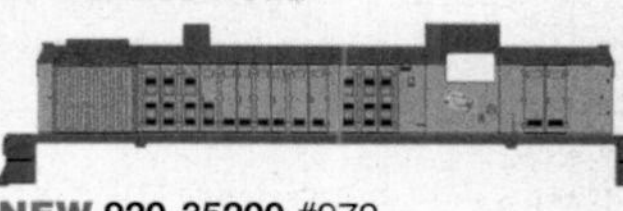

**NEW** 920-35200 #979
**NEW** 920-35201 #982

### Seaboard Coast Line

**NEW** 920-35202 #1101
**NEW** 920-35203 #1105

### Soo Line

**NEW** 920-35204 #369
**NEW** 920-35205 #371

### Union Pacific†

**NEW** 920-35206 #1283
**NEW** 920-35207 #1289

See What's Available at
**www.walthers.com**

PROTO 2000™

HERITAGE

STEAM COLLECTION

From Walthers

# USRA Heavy 2-10-2

The 1900s was an era of larger and more powerful locomotive design. The adoption of the wide firebox carried on a trailing truck, stokers, larger cylinders, feedwater heaters and other devices led to the development of the 4-6-2 and 2-8-2. In turn, the idea of a better 2-8-2 created the first modern 2-10-2s just before World War I. Roads that needed to move maximum tonnage found Santa Fe types (the first 2-10-2 was built for the Santa Fe in 1903) had pulling power that was only dreamed of a few years earlier.

Once the US entered the war, the United States Railway Administration (USRA) designed both light and heavy 2-10-2s to meet weight restrictions on various railroads. In addition to larger boilers and drivers, the heavy 2-10-2s were designed with, and many were constructed with Southern valve gear. A total of 175 USRA heavy 2-10-2s were built and allocated to the Bessemer & Lake Erie (5), the Burlington (10), Erie (25), Fort Worth & Denver City (Colorado & Southern; 5) and the Pennsylvania (130).

After the war, the original USRA heavy 2-10-2s found their niche moving coal, ore and similar traffic where tonnage was more important than speed. Several roads that needed big power ordered copies. While newer and more powerful engines quickly overtook the design after 1930, the heavy 2-10-2s continued to give a good account of themselves well into the late 1950s.

**Order Now! Limited Availability**

Please Note: All Proto Series manufacturer numbers have changed from 433 to 920.

## PROTO 2000 HERITAGE STEAM COLLECTION FROM WALTHERS

- Available With or Without Sound
- Fully Assembled
- Hand-Applied Details
- Authentic Paint & Lettering
- Weighted for Maximum Traction
- RP-25 Wheels
- Driver & Tender Electrical Pick-Up
- 5-Pole Motor with Skew-Wound Balanced Armature
- Precisely Meshed Gears
- Magnetic Knuckle Couplers
- History Booklet & Certificate of Quality

USRA Heavy 2-10-2 C&S 920-60011

## USRA HEAVY 2-10-2

**425.00 w/Sound & DCC**

**325.00 Standard DC**

- All-New - 1st Time in Plastic!
- Available With or Without Sound & DCC
- Sound operates with standard DC or DCC controllers. Features Steam Sounds, Whistle, Bell, Squealing Brakes, Doppler Effect, Generator Whine and Trailer mode to mute whistle and bell for double-heading.
- Separate Driver Set w/Traction Tires
- Southern or Baker Valve Gear
- History Booklet & Certificate of Quality

### 1st Release

- Southern Valve Gear

**PRR**

**920-60000** #7190 w/Sound & DCC
**920-60001** #7326 w/Sound & DCC
**920-60002** #8263 Standard DC
**920-60003** #8360 Standard DC

**Erie**

**920-60004** #4212 w/Sound & DCC
**920-60005** #4217 w/Sound & DCC
**920-60006** #4214 Standard DC
**920-60007** #4224 Standard DC

**Colorado & Southern**

**920-60008** #905 w/Sound & DCC
**920-60009** #906 w/Sound & DCC
**920-60010** #908 Standard DC
**920-60011** #909 Standard DC

Sharp paint and lettering accents the many fine details.

**Painted, Unlettered**

**920-60012** w/Sound & DCC
**920-60013** Standard DC

### 2nd Release

**CB&Q**

- Southern Valve Gear

**920-60014** #1 w/Sound & DCC
**920-60015** #2 w/Sound & DCC
**920-60016** #3 Standard DC
**920-60017** #4 Standard DC

**IC**

- Baker Valve Gear

**920-60018** #1 w/Sound & DCC
**920-60019** #2 w/Sound & DCC
**920-60020** #3 Standard DC
**920-60021** #4 Standard DC

**Bessemer & Lake Erie**

- Southern Valve Gear

**920-60022** #1 w/Sound & DCC
**920-60023** #2 w/Sound & DCC
**920-60024** #3 Standard DC
**920-60025** #4 Standard DC

**Painted, Unlettered**

- Baker Valve Gear

**920-60026** w/Sound & DCC
**920-60027** Standard DC

Working headlight, working front knuckle coupler, brass bell with with wire "rope" and more all included.

From Walthers

With superb rivet detail, fine wire grabs and railings, plus dozens of separately applied parts, the new USRA Heavy 2-10-2 looks great from any angle.

Climb in the cab for a close-up look at the many fine details inside, including firebox doors, stokers, seats, positionable side windows, gauges and much, much more.

Ready for service, the USRA Heavy 2-10-2 includes a working knuckle coupler at front and rear.

Loaded with fine detail from coal load to reversing headlight, the models include an authentic USRA 12,000-Gallon Tender.

Models feature Southern or Baker valve gear; drivers and unique brake shoe details have plenty of side-to-side movement built in to handle layout curves.

Perfect power for coal, ore and similar traffic, the USRA Heavy 2-10-2 will be a great addition to your steam-era railroad.

PROTO 2000 HERITAGE™ STEAM COLLECTION

From Walthers

# USRA 0-6-0

As the US entered World War I, many roads soon found their switchers weren't up to the job. Once the United States Railway Administration (USRA) assumed control, construction of a new 0-6-0 design began in 1918.

Larger and more powerful than many 0-6-0s, the USRA locos could handle all types of switching and some transfer work.

Production ended in 1919 with 255 engines built and in service on 28 railroads. Following the end of USRA control in 1920, some roads ordered copies of these engines, while others used the design as a starting point for improved 0-6-0s. Owners of original engines also began modifying them to match their own standards; many rebuilt tender coal bunkers to improve rearward visibility, and/or replaced headlights, bells and other appliances. Many remained in use until the end of steam.

**Order Now! Limited Availability**

Please Note: All Proto Series manufacturer numbers have changed from 433 to 920.

USRA 0-6-0 CNJ 920-31775

## USRA 0-6-0

**325.00 w/Sound & DCC**

**225.00 Standard DC**

- Now Available With or Without Factory-Installed Sound & DCC
- Sound operates on standard DC or DCC systems. Features Steam Engine Sounds, Whistle, Bell, Squealing Brakes, Doppler Effect, Generator Whine and Trailer mode to mute whistle and bell.
- Separate Driver Set w/Traction Tires
- Slow Speed Under 3 Scale Miles Per Hour - 59 Scale Miles Per Hour Fast Speed
- Over 120 Hand-Applied Details
- Operating Cab Windows & Meticulously Detailed Cab Interior
- Tender Coal Bunker Style Appropriate to Road
- Constant, Directional Lights
- Cast Metal Rods & Valve Gear
- Handles 18" Radius Curves & #4 Turnouts

**ACL**

**920-31764** #1139 w/Sound & DCC
**920-31765** #1143 w/Sound & DCC
**920-31766** #1145 Standard DC

**CNW†**

**920-31767** #2608 w/Sound & DCC
**920-31768** #2614 w/Sound & DCC
**920-31769** #2618 Standard DC

**Gulf, Mobile & Ohio**

**920-31770** #43 w/Sound & DCC
**920-31771** #56 w/Sound & DCC
**920-31772** #62 Standard DC

**CNJ**

**920-31773** #104 w/Sound & DCC
**920-31774** #106 w/Sound & DCC
**920-31775** #108 Standard DC

**PRR**

**920-31776** #7030 w/Sound & DCC
**920-31777** #7258 w/Sound & DCC
**920-31778** #9212 Standard DC

**Rock Island**

**920-31779** #281 w/Sound & DCC
**920-31780** #284 w/Sound & DCC
**920-31781** #282 Standard DC

**Unlettered**

**920-31783** Standard DC

†Union Pacific licensed product.

USRA 0-6-0 PRR 920-31778

**From Walthers**

Each model includes an 8,000-gallon clear vision tender complete with separate ladder, handrail, cut lever and working reverse lamp.

Packing big detail in a small package, the USRA 0-6-0 includes working valve gear, yellow LED lights at front and rear and is offered in a sound-equipped version for maximum realism.

Factory-applied parts like the wire bell and whistle ropes, sand lines, piping, generator, air compressor and more transform each model into a superdetailed replica.

Working knuckle couplers at front and rear make the USRA 0-6-0 the perfect power for yard or industrial swithcing; optional driver set with traction tires can be installed for more pulling power if desired.

Authentic cab interior includes full backhead detail, deckplate, seats, positionable side windows and much, much more.

From Walthers

# USRA 0-8-0

By 1917, the arrival of larger and much heavier freight cars had pushed most 0-6-0 designs to their limits. Realizing that railroads needed bigger and more powerful switchers to handle these modern cars, the United States Railway Administration developed plans for an all-new 0-8-0.

Up-to-date in all respects, these big switchers were the equals in power of many road freight locomotives from just a few years earlier! Unlike some USRA designs, the 0-8-0 was well liked by the railroads that received it; 175 were completed before government control ended in 1920.

But the 0-8-0's ultimate success came in the years that followed as the USRA design was eventually copied by 35 different roads. In fact, the last new steam locos built in the US were a series of 0-8-0s, constructed by the N&W in 1951-53 that followed the general outline of the decades-old USRA design!

**Order Now! Limited Availability**

Please Note: All Proto Series manufacturer numbers have changed from 433 to 920.

USRA 0-8-0
CB&Q 920-60102

## USRA 0-8-0

**349.98 w/Sound & DCC**

**249.98 Standard DC**

- Available With or Without Factory-Installed Sound & DCC
- Now with Loco & Tender Electrical Pick-Up
- Improved Tractive Effort - Now With Traction Tires
- Weighted for Maximum Tractive Effort - Pulls 60 or More Cars
- Nickel-Silver Plated RP-25 Wheels
- Operating Cab Windows and Meticulously Detailed Cab Interior
- Tender Coal Bunker Style as Appropriate to Road
- Slow Speed Less than 3 Scale Miles Per Hour and up to 59 Scale Miles Per Hour Fast Speed
- 10-Page History Booklet & Certificate of Quality
- New Roadnames & Numbers
- Limited Availability

Sound can be operated with standard DC power pack as well as DCC controllers. Sound features include: Dual Steam Engine Sounds, Whistle, Bell, Squealing Brakes, Doppler Effect, Air Let Off (in neutral), Headlight, and Trailer which mutes whistle and bell for doubleheading. Includes QSI Sound Reference Manual.

**Boston & Maine**

**NEW 920-60100** #612 with Sound & DCC

**NEW 920-60101** #618 with Sound & DCC

**NEW 920-67100** #630 Standard DC

**Chicago, Burlington & Quincy**

**NEW 920-60102** #540 with Sound & DCC

**NEW 920-60103** #544 with Sound & DCC

**NEW 920-67102** #547 Standard DC

**Nickel Plate Road**

**NEW 920-60104** #206 with Sound & DCC

**NEW 920-60105** #207 with Sound & DCC

**NEW 920-67104** #205 Standard DC

**Northern Pacific**

**NEW 920-60106** #1170 with Sound & DCC

**NEW 920-60107** #1171 with Sound & DCC

**NEW 920-67106** #1172 Standard DC

**Pere Marquette**

**NEW 920-60108** #1401 with Sound & DCC

**NEW 920-60109** #1406 with Sound & DCC

**NEW 920-67108** #1410 Standard DC

**Painted, Unlettered**

**NEW 920-60110** with Sound & DCC

**NEW 920-67110** Standard DC

920-31579
Roadname Shown Not Available

Looking like she just rolled out of the shop, this powerful steam switcher packs true-to-life details, applied metal handrails, laser-sharp lettering and crisp paint.

Although packed with detail like authentic valve gear, separately applied piping, readable data on the air reservoir and more, you can still see-through the space under boiler - just like on the prototypes!

Give your engineer and fireman some fresh air on hot days—simply open the the sliding cab windows! Other features include a painted cab interior and full backhead detail.

Separate metal grab irons and handrails, a realistic coal load and more add to this model's good looks.

The clear-vision tender matches later modifications done by many roads. Separately applied footboards, realistic poling pockets and more add realism; metal wheelsets with electrical pickups and magnetic knuckle couplers ensure reliable performance.

**Order Now! Limited Availability**

Please Note: All Proto Series manufacturer numbers have changed from 433 to 920.

PROTO 2000 HERITAGE™ STEAM COLLECTION

**From Walthers**

# Y-3 2-8-8-2

First built for the Southern Pacific in 1909 to tame its tough western grades, the 2-8-8-2 articulated Mallet soon caught the attention of roads facing similar problems. In 1910, Norfolk and Western ordered five 2-8-8-2s (Class Y-1) similar to the SP models from Baldwin. By 1918, lessons learned from the first group led to an improved version, the Y-2; with minor changes to the cylinders, these became Class Y-2a, which served as the basis for the United States Railway Administration (USRA) 2-8-8-2.

Although delivered too late for the war effort, the N&W received 50 of the USRA engines in 1919, which it classified as Y-3. In 1923 another 30 were ordered with larger tenders (Y-3a), followed by 10 more in 1927 fitted with feedwater heaters.

During World War II, several Y-3s were sold to various western railroads that were desperate to ease motive power shortages. Although well suited to coal-hauling duties in the Appalachians, the big articulateds proved too slow for most of their new owners and they were retired or sold following the war. At home, Y-3s remained in service until 1958.

Tender is complete with working reverse lamp; includes optional "dog house" for head brakeman that can be added if desired.

Authentic pilot details include working knuckle coupler and headlight.

Detailed to match their prototypes, each 2-8-8-2 includes a feedwater heater, separate piping, low water alarm, and more.

Complete cab interior features positionable side windows.

From Walthers

## Y-3 2-8-8-2

**495.00 w/Sound & DCC**

**395.00 Standard DC**

- Now Available With or Without Sound & DCC
- Sound operates on standard DC or DCC systems. Features Dual Steam Engine Sounds, Whistle, Bell, Squealing Brakes, Doppler Effect, Generator Whine and Trailer mode to mute whistle and bell for double-heading.
- Separate Driver Set w/Traction Tires
- 200 Hand-Applied Details
- Detailed Cab Interior w/Operating Windows
- Constant & Directional Lights
- Handles 18" Radius Curves & #4 Turnouts!
- Slow Speed Under 3 Scale MPH; Fast speed to 65 Scale MPH
- 16-Wheel Drive and 24-Wheel Electrical Pick-Up
- Dual Flywheels

### ATSF

**920-32000** #1792 w/Sound & DCC
**920-32001** #1794 w/Sound & DCC
**920-32002** #1797 Standard DC

### N&W

**920-32003** #2012 w/Sound & DCC
**920-32004** #2037 w/Sound & DCC
**920-32005** #2040 Standard DC

### PRR

**920-32006** #374 w/Sound & DCC
**920-32007** #375 w/Sound & DCC
**920-32008** #377 Standard DC

### UP†

**920-32009** #3670 w/Sound & DCC
**920-32010** #3672 w/Sound & DCC
**920-32011** #3674 Standard DC

### Virginian

**920-32012** #738 w/Sound & DCC
**920-32013** #741 w/Sound & DCC
**920-32014** #740 Standard DC

### Painted, Unlettered

**920-32015** w/Sound & DCC
**920-32016** Standard DC

†Union Pacific licensed product.

Latest New Product News Daily! Visit Walthers Web site at

**www.walthers.com**

**Order Now! Limited Availability**

Please Note: All Proto Series manufacturer numbers have changed from 433 to 920.

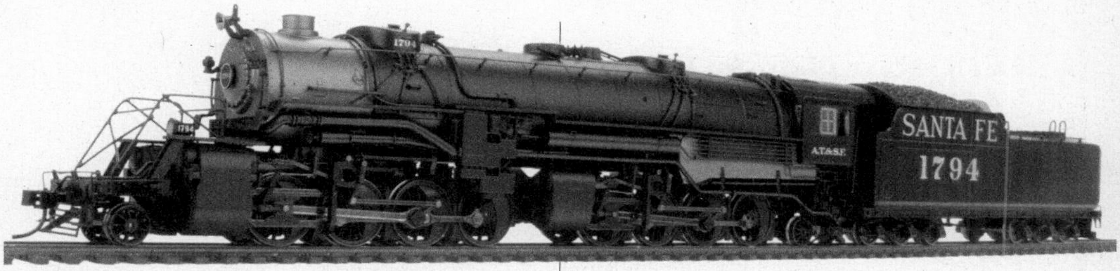

920-32001

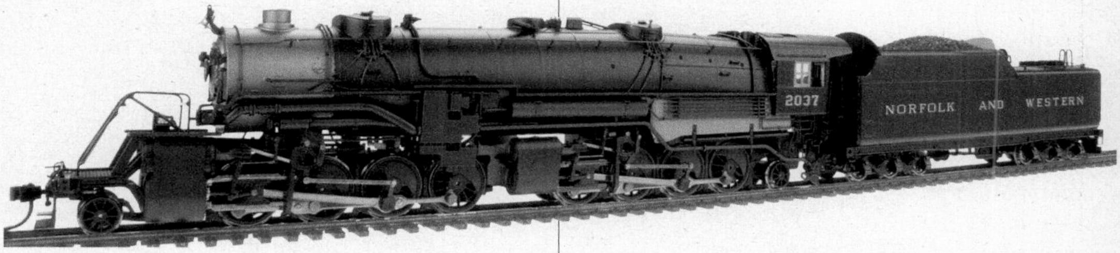

920-32004

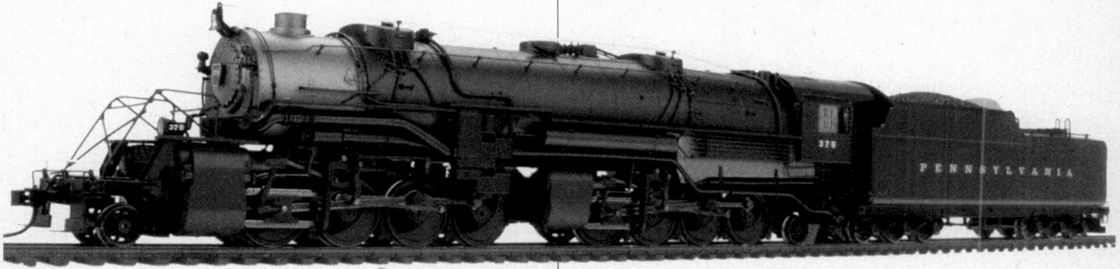

920-32007

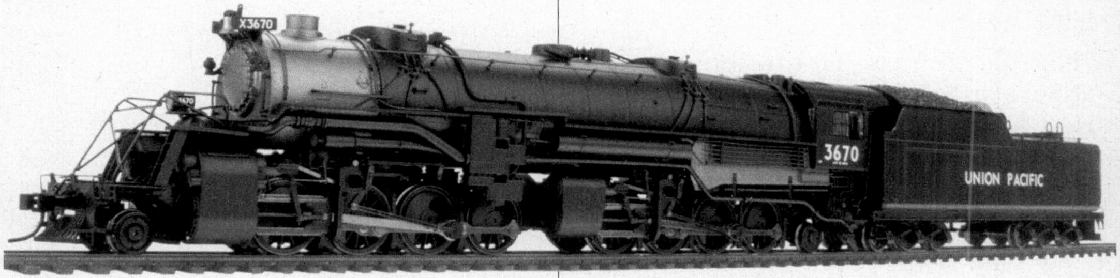

920-32009

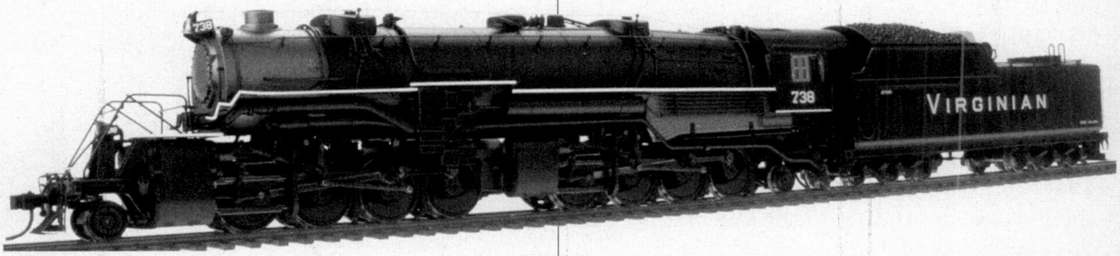

920-32012

PROTO 2000 HERITAGE STEAM COLLECTION™

From Walthers

# 2-8-4 "Berkshire"

Introduced in 1924, the 2-8-4 ushered in the super-power era. Its larger firebox and other improvements produced a combination of speed and power that was ideal for many railroads.

Among these were C&O, Nickel Plate and Pere Marquette, which were controlled by the Van Sweringen brothers. In 1929, management pooled the talents of the road's engineering departments to create the "Advisory Mechanical Committee" that would oversee future locomotive developments, including new 2-8-4s.

The Committee's first 2-8-4s were delivered to the Nickel Plate in 1934 and these speed demons worked fast freights between Bellevue, Ohio, and Buffalo, as well as Bellevue and Frankfort, Indiana. Building on this success, a new series was designed for Pere Marquette in 1937, followed by additional classes delivered in 1941 and 1944. During the war years when production was limited to existing designs, C&O ordered 40 2-8-4s based on these earlier locos, but with numerous mechanical improvements and other changes to match C&O practices. Between 1945 and 1947, 50 more were ordered by the C&O; the PM was absorbed in to the C&O in 1947 and some of its 2-8-4s remained in use there until 1953. Five near-copies of the C&O locos were delivered to the Virginian (though it was never a Van Sweringen-controlled road) in 1946.

Several Van Sweringen Berkshires were operation.

**Order Now! Limited Availability**

Please Note: All Proto Series manufacturer numbers have changed from 433 to 920.

Van Sweringen Berkshire 2-8-4 PM 920-31680

## VAN SWERINGEN BERKSHIRE 2-8-4

**410.00 w/Sound & DCC**

**310.00 Standard DC**

- Specific Prototype Details:
  - *Three Different Tenders*
  - *Three Different Cabs*
  - *Three Different Boilers*
  - *Friction or Roller Bearing Front & Rear Trucks*
- Outstanding Laser-Sharp Printing
- Authentic Painting & Lettering
- Improved Driver Appearance
- Over 120 Hand-Applied Detail Parts
- Metal Handrails & Cut Levers
- Brass Bell
- 12-Page History Booklet & Certificate of Quality
- Operates on Code 83 Track, 18" Radius Curves & #4 Turnouts
- Available with Factory Installed Sound & DCC or Without

Sound can be operated with standard DC power pack as well as DCC controllers. Sound features include: Dual Steam Engine Sounds, Whistle, Bell, Squealing Brakes, Doppler Effect, Air Let Off (in neutral), Headlight, and Trailer which mutes whistle and bell for doubleheading.

- Limited Availability

**Chesapeake & Ohio**

**920-31672** #2744 with Sound & DCC

**920-31673** #2759 with Sound & DCC

**920-31674** #2746 - Standard DC

**Nickel Plate**

**920-31675** #772 w/Mars Light; with Sound & DCC

**920-31676** #776 w/Mars Light; with Sound & DCC

**920-31677** #774 w/Mars Light - Standard DC

**Pere Marquette**

**920-31678** #1235 with Sound & DCC

**920-31679** #1239 with Sound & DCC

**920-31680** #1236 - Standard DC

**Unlettered**

**920-31681** Black with Sound & DCC

**920-31682** Black - Standard DC

From Walthers

# EMD GP20

By the mid 50s, increasing pressure from long-haul trucks, declining passenger revenues and mounting costs forced western railroads to find new ways to improve service. Faced with expensive overhauls of early cab and hood unit diesels, many began looking at new equipment as well as ways to improve existing motive power. In 1955 Union Pacific equipped several GP9s with turbochargers as an experiment. Their success inspired EMD to create its own turbocharger for the 567 prime mover, leading to the introduction of the six-axle SD24 in 1958. Further experiments in 1959 created a four-axle version, dubbed the GP20. The first GP20s, which were built for GN and WP, were delivered with high, short hoods, and were the only units so equipped as later buyers favored the improved visibility of the short nose. Early in their careers, GP20s were typically assigned priority freights that demanded higher speeds. With the arrival of newer power, they were gradually bumped into secondary runs, and eventually spent their last years in local and yard service. Following their retirement, a few went to work for shortline operators.

**Order Now! Limited Availability**

Please Note: All Proto Series manufacturer numbers have changed from 433 to 920.

EMD High-Hood GP20
GN 920-31906

## EMD HIGH-HOOD GP20

**225.00 w/Sound & DCC**

**125.00 Standard DC**

- Factory-Installed Sound & DCC
- Operates with DC power pack or DCC controllers. Sound features include: Diesel Engine Sounds, Horn, Bell, Squealing Brakes, Doppler Effect, Air Let Off (in neutral), Headlight, and Trailer mode which mutes whistle and bell for double-heading.
- New High Short Hood Version
- Prototype Specific Details
- Over 135 Factory-Applied Parts
- Consumer-Applied Parts Pack Included

**BN - Green & Black**

**920-31897** #2002 w/Sound & DCC
**920-31898** #2014 w/Sound &DCC
**920-31899** #2009 Standard DC
**920-31900** #2017 Standard DC

**BN - Big Sky Blue**

**920-31901** #2004 w/Sound & DCC
**920-31902** #2006 w/Sound & DCC
**920-31903** #2003 Standard DC
**920-31904** #2015 Standard DC

**GN - Green & Orange**

**920-31905** #2010 w/Sound & DCC
**920-31906** #2013 w/Sound & DCC
**920-31907** #2007 Standard DC
**920-31908** #2016 Standard DC

**GN - Big Sky Blue**

**920-31909** #2000 w/Sound & DCC
**920-31910** #2005 w/Sound & DCC
**920-31911** #2004 Standard DC
**920-31912** #2012 Standard DC

**UP†**

**920-31913** #488 w/Sound & DCC
**920-31914** #488 Standard DC

**WP† - Silver & Orange**

**920-31915** #2001 w/Sound & DCC
**920-31916** #2008 w/Sound & DCC
**920-31917** #2003 Standard DC
**920-31918** #2010 Standard DC

**WP† - Green Stripes**

**920-31919** #2002 w/Sound & DCC
**920-31920** #2005 w/Sound & DCC
**920-31921** #2004 Standard DC
**920-31922** #2007 Standard DC

**Undecorated**
**920-31923** w/Sound & DC
**920-31924** Standard DC

†Union Pacific licensed product.

# EMD GP30

Introduced in 1961, the GP30 was possibly the most distinctive diesel ever built in large numbers. Although longer and wider than previous EMD designs, a slight bulge was needed in the long hood just behind the cab to accommodate air handling and electrical equipment. Influenced by GM's auto styling staff, the bulge was covered with a rounded metal fairing that extended back to the middle of the long hood and to the front edge of the cab roof. The appearance of the new locos could also be changed by customer specifications. Some roads traded in older power and their new GP30s rode on AAR trucks, usually from retired ALCO units. As the extra length of these older trucks required a slightly shorter fuel tank, three sizes were made available. Some roads operated under union rules that required an engineer, fireman and head brakeman on the engine, so the fireman's side of the cab was extended by 12" to provide room for a third seat. Both the Southern and the Norfolk & Western ordered GP30s with high, short hoods, designating the long end as the front. This improved crew safety in the event of a collision; the area under the high short hood housed a toilet. Although replaced by the new 35 Line in 1963, GP30s led long, productive lives in mainline service, and a few remain in revenue service on shortlines today.

**Order Now! Limited Availability**

Please Note: All Proto Series manufacturer numbers have changed from 433 to 920.

EMD Low-Hood GP30
GM&O 920-31882

## EMD LOW-HOOD GP30

**225.00 w/Sound & DCC**

**125.00 Standard DC**

- Available in Two Versions: With or Without Factory-Installed Sound & DCC

Sound can be operated with standard DC power pack or DCC controllers. Sound features include: Diesel Engine, Horn, Bell, Squealing Brakes, Doppler Effect, Air Let Off (in neutral). Trailer mode is also available to mute the whistle and bell for double heading.

- LED Headlights
- Super-Detailing Kit - now with all-weather windows & wind deflectors
- Prototype-Specific Details:
  *With or without low hood headlights*
  *With or without drop steps*
  *With or without dynamic brakes*
  *Blomberg (EMD) or AAR (ALCO) trucks*
  *Three sizes of fuel tanks*
  *Standard or extended cab*
- Subtle Weathering
- Magnetic Knuckle Couplers
- Heavy Diecast Chassis
- 5-Pole Skew Wound Armature Motor
- Precisely Meshed Worm Gear & Spur Teeth for Silent Running

**ATSF**

**920-31861** #2764 with Sound & DCC
**920-31862** #2778 with Sound & DCC
**920-31863** #2759 - Standard DC
**920-31864** #2784 - Standard DC

**B&O**

**920-31865** #6904 with Sound & DCC
**920-31866** #6955 with Sound & DCC
**920-31867** #6905 - Standard DC
**920-31868** #6957 - Standard DC

**BNSF**

**920-31869** #2436 with Sound & DCC
**920-31870** #2470 with Sound & DCC
**920-31871** #2452 - Standard DC
**920-31872** #2463 - Standard DC

**C&O**

**920-31873** #3024 with Sound & DCC
**920-31874** #3030 with Sound & DCC
**920-31875** #3026 - Standard DC
**920-31876** #3034 - Standard DC

From Walthers

**CNW†**

**920-31877** #804 with Sound & DCC
**920-31878** #818 with Sound & DCC
**920-31879** #806 - Standard DC
**920-31880** #823 - Standard DC

**Gulf, Mobile & Ohio**

**920-31881** #500 with Sound & DCC
**920-31882** #521 with Sound & DCC
**920-31883** #509 - Standard DC
**920-31884** #530 - Standard DC

**Southern Pacific Santa Fe**

**920-31885** #2750 with Sound & DCC
**920-31886** #2752 with Sound & DCC
**920-31887** #2759 - Standard DC
**920-31888** #2772 - Standard DC

**UP†**

**920-31889** #701 with Sound & DCC
**920-31890** #834 with Sound & DCC
**920-31891** #726 - Standard DC
**920-31892** #874 - Standard DC

**Undecorated**
**920-31893** With Sound & DCC
**920-31894** Standard DC

## Order Now! Limited Availability

Please Note: All Proto Series manufacturer numbers have changed from 433 to 920.

EMD High-Hood GP30
Indiana & Ohio Railroad
920-40162

# EMD HIGH-HOOD GP30

**225.00 w/Sound & DCC**
**125.00 Standard DC**

- Factory-Installed Sound & DCC
- Operates with DC power pack or DCC controllers. Sound features include: Diesel Engine Sounds, Horn, Bell, Squealing Brakes, Doppler Effect, Air Let Off (in neutral), Headlight, and Trailer mode which mutes whistle and bell for double-heading.
- New High Short Hood Version
- Prototype Specific Details
- Consumer-Applied Parts Pack Included

**N&W - Gothic Herald (Phase 1)**

**920-40150** #525 w/Sound & DCC
**920-40151** #558 w/Sound & DCC
**920-40152** #539 Standard DC
**920-40153** #542 Standard DC

**N&W - "Hamburger" Herald (Phase 1)**

**920-40154** #522 w/Sound & DCC
**920-40155** #555 w/Sound & DCC
**920-40156** #533 Standard DC
**920-40157** #556 Standard DC

**N&W - Block NW Lettering (Phase 1)**

**920-40158** #541 w/Sound & DCC
**920-40159** #549 w/Sound & DCC
**920-40160** #534 Standard DC
**920-40161** #563 Standard DC

**Indiana & Ohio Railroad (Phase 2)**

**920-40162** #81 w/Sound & DCC
**920-40163** #82 w/Sound & DCC
**920-40164** #81 Standard DC
**920-40165** #82 Standard DC

**NS (Phase 2)**

**920-40166** #2598 w/Sound & DCC
**920-40167** #2612 w/Sound & DCC
**920-40168** #2600 Standard DC
**920-40169** #2595 Standard DC

**SOU (Phase 2)**

**920-40170** #2590 w/Sound & DCC
**920-40171** #2607 w/Sound & DCC
**920-40172** #2593 Standard DC
**920-40173** #2623 Standard DC

**Undecorated**
**920-40174** Phase 1 w/Sound & DCC
**920-40175** Phase 1 Standard DC
**920-40176** Phase 2 w/Sound & DCC
**920-40177** Phase 2 Standard DC

†Union Pacific licensed product.

From Walthers

# EMD E7

When EMD was given the green light to build new passenger diesels in early 1945, it unveiled an improved version of the successful E6, designated the E7. A pair of 567A prime movers, rated at 2000 total horsepower, now supplied power. Most of the notable changes were seen on the body and included a new and much smaller "bulldog" nose, as well as a large, vertical louver directly behind the cab doors.

Introduced just as American railroads began upgrading and rebuilding passenger service, the E7 was the most successful passenger diesel ever built, with 428 A units and 82 cabless B units produced through April of 1949 when the E8 was unveiled.

## EMD E7

- Factory-Installed Sound & DCC
- Operates with DC power pack or DCC controllers. Sound features include: Diesel Engine Sounds, Horn, Bell, Squealing Brakes, Doppler Effect, Air Let Off (in neutral), Headlight, and Trailer mode which mutes whistle and bell for double-heading.
- Working Diaphragms
- See-Through Steps
- Visible Interior Bracing
- Side Frames With Floating Journal Covers
- Laser-Quality Paint Schemes & Lettering
- Freight & Passenger Pilots
- A Units feature Cab Interior w/Crew & Molded-On Windshield Wipers
- 12-Wheel Electrical Pickup
- Correct "Bulldog Nose"
- Dual Machined Brass Flywheels
- Prototype Specific Details:
  *Mars Light on Select Models*
  *Dual Air Intake Grills*
  *Straight or Angled Number Boards*
  *Standard or Extended Range Fuel & Water Tanks*

EMD E7 A-B Set
CB&Q 920-40533

### A Units Only

**225.00 w/Sound & DCC**
**125.00 Standard DC**

**B&O**

**920-40525** #1424 w/Sound & DCC
**920-40526** #1428 w/Sound & DCC
**920-40527** #1425 Standard DC
**920-40528** #1432 Standard DC

**CNW† w/Mars Light**

**920-40529** #5011-A w/Sound & DCC
**920-40530** #5011-B w/Sound & DCC
**920-40531** #5018-A Standard DC
**920-40532** #5018-B Standard DC

**CB&Q w/Mars Light**

**920-40533** #9917-B w/Sound & DCC
**920-40534** #9922-A w/Sound & DCC
**920-40535** #9919-B Standard DC
**920-40536** #9923-A Standard DC

### A-A Sets

**GN Empire Builder w/Mars Light**

**920-40537** #502A & 502B w/Sound & DCC **315.00**
Powered A, Dummy A
**920-40538** #503A & 503B Standard DC **205.00**
Both units powered.

†Union Pacific licensed product.

### A-B Sets

**315.00 w/Sound & DCC (Powered A, Dummy B)**
**205.00 Standard DC (Both Units Powered)**

**NYC**

**920-40539** #4000 & 4100 w/Sound & DCC
**920-40540** #4005 & 4103 w/Sound & DCC
**920-40541** #4004 & 4104 Standard DC
**920-40542** #4007 & 4106 Standard DC

**PRR**

**920-40543** #5852A & 5258B w/Sound & DCC
**920-40544** #5853A & 5854B w/Sound & DCC
**920-40545** #5858A & 5858B Standard DC
**920-40546** #5859A & 5854B Standard DC

**UP† w/Mars Light**

**920-40547** #990 & 996B w/Sound & DCC
**920-40548** #998 & 998B w/Sound & DCC
**920-40549** #988 & 988B Standard DC
**920-40550** #999 & 994B Standard DC

**Undecorated w/Mars Light**

**920-40551** A Unit Only w/Sound & DCC
**920-40552** A Unit Only Standard DC
**920-40553** A-B Set w/Sound & DCC
**920-40554** A-B Set Standard DC

# EMD GP7

While the road switcher concept had appeared as early as 1940, EMD preferred to concentrate on its F series cab unit diesels for freight service. But with no footboards and no rearward visibility, F units were not well liked by crews on locals and similar runs where there was a lot of switching or reverse running. EMD entered the road switcher market tentatively in 1948 with its BL1 and BL2, which mounted a semi-streamlined body on the same frame and machinery as the F3. This was a start, but in 1949, EMD found exactly what the railroads wanted in its new General Purpose series. Simple and rugged, the squared-off lines of the new GP7 weren't necessarily handsome, but this didn't matter to the new owners. In short order, buyers were using GP7s for everything from road freights to commuter service. Production continued with minor changes along the way (these spotting features are referred to as "phases" by railfans to differentiate variations among the otherwise similar locos) through 1954 when the more powerful GP9 was introduced.

## EMD GP7 - PHASE II

**225.00 w/Sound & DCC**
**125.00 Standard DC**

- Factory-Installed Sound & DCC
- Operates with DC power pack or DCC controllers. Sound features include: Diesel Engine Sounds, Horn, Bell, Squealing Brakes, Doppler Effect, Air Let Off (in neutral), Headlight, and Trailer mode which mutes whistle and bell for double heading.
- Prototype Specific Details
- Consumer-Applied Parts Pack Included

EMD GP7 WP 920-40479

**ATSF**

**920-40450** #2837 w/Sound & DCC
**920-40451** #2849 w/Sound & DCC
**920-40452** #2831 Standard DC
**920-40453** #2860 Standard DC

**Chessie B&O**

**920-40454** #5608 w/Sound & DCC
**920-40455** #5611 w/Sound & DCC
**920-40456** #5618 Standard DC
**920-40457** #5624 Standard DC

**C&O**

**920-40458** #5751 w/Sound & DCC
**920-40459** #5772 w/Sound & DCC
**920-40460** #5767 Standard DC
**920-40461** #5771 Standard DC

**Kansas City Southern**

**920-40462** #157 w/Sound & DCC
**920-40463** #159 w/Sound & DCC
**920-40464** #156 Standard DC
**920-40465** #161 Standard DC

**PRR**

**920-40466** #8569 w/Sound & DCC
**920-40467** #8577 w/Sound & DCC
**920-40468** #8579 Standard DC
**920-40469** #8580 Standard DC

**Rock Island - Maroon, White Stripes**

**920-40470** #1269 w/Sound & DCC
**920-40471** #1277 w/Sound & DCC
**920-40472** #1272 Standard DC
**920-40473** #1275 Standard DC

**UP†**

**920-40474** #105 w/Sound & DCC
**920-40475** #107 w/Sound & DCC
**920-40476** #104 Standard DC
**920-40477** #109 Standard DC

**WP† - Green w/Orange Lettering**

**920-40478** #702 w/Sound & DCC
**920-40479** #704 w/Sound & DCC
**920-40480** #703 Standard DC
**920-40481** #706 Standard DC

**Undecorated**
**920-40482** w/Sound & DCC
**920-40483** Standard DC

**Order Now! Limited Availability**

Please Note: All Proto Series manufacturer numbers have changed from 433 to 920.

ALCO PA-PB Set
PRR 920-40108

# ALCO PA

As World War II drew to a close, American railroads began planning, promoting and ordering equipment for all-new streamlined trains. In addition to new cars, these much-publicized "trains of tomorrow" demanded equally stylish motive power, and in 1946, many buyers found exactly what they wanted in the American Locomotive Company's (ALCo.) PA diesel.

With its long nose and sleek, square body, the PA projected strength and power whether flying along the mainline or waiting for departure. Under the hood was a turbocharged 16-cylinder 244 prime mover that generated an amazing 2000 horsepower. For buyers who needed additional pulling power, a cabless B unit was also available. Finished in a rainbow of color schemes, PAs could soon be found at the head of many flagship trains. Production of the first series, designated PA-1, continued until 1950 when the more powerful but outwardly identical PA-2 was introduced. With the decline of passenger traffic in the 50s and 60s, some PAs were bumped into freight service. Most reached the end of the line in the late 60s. Today, a handful of survivors remain, including one being restored to operating condition.

## ALCO PA-PB

- DCC Ready
- Powered B Units
- With or Without Mars Light
- With or Without Dynamic Brakes
- Flat or Angled Number Boards
- 2 Styles of Add-on Pilot Doors
- Add-on Rooftop Numberboard
- Close Coupling with Working Diaphragms
- Photo-Etched Radiator Screens
- Air or Water Cooled Exhaust Stacks
- Heavy Diecast Underframe
- All-Wheel Electrical Pick-Up

### PA-PB Sets 179.95

**ATSF**

**920-40100** #59B w/Mars Light & #58A

**920-40101** #62B w/Mars Light & #60A

**DRGW**†

**920-40104** #6001 w/Mars Light & #6002

**920-40105** #6013 w/Mars Light & #6012

†Union Pacific licensed product.

**PRR**

**920-40108** #5756A & #5756B

**920-40109** #5759A & #5752B

**UP**†

**920-40110** #605 w/Mars Light & #600B

**920-40111** #606 w/Mars Light & #606B

**ALCO Demonstrator**

**920-40112** #8375 & 8375B

### PAs Only 89.98

**D&H**

**920-40102** #17 w/Mars Light

**920-40103** #19 w/Mars Light

**NH**

**920-40106** #0762

**920-40107** #0769

# EMD E8/9

As America's railroads rebuilt their passenger service following World War II, premiere trains received new equipment from engine to observation car. And once production resumed in 1945, many were led by brand-new E7 diesels from EMD. By 1948, the 567B prime mover was ready and the more powerful E8 entered production. These units were built through 1954, when the virtually identical E9 with its 567C prime movers was introduced. Speedy, powerful and economical, E8s and their kin proved to be an excellent choice for long-distance name trains. Despite the many changes in passenger service over the years, E8s were among the first diesels to serve Amtrak® when operations began in 1971; others ended their days in commuter service a few years later.

## PROTO 2000 DIESELS

## EMD E8/9

- Heavy Diecast Chassis
- DC Motor with 5-Pole Skew-Wound Armature
- Precisely Meshed Worm Gear & Spur Teeth for Silent Running
- Operating Mars Light as Appropriate
- LED Directional Headlights
- Magnetic Knuckle Couplers
- Available With or Without Factory-Installed Sound & DCC

Sound can be operated with a standard DC power pack as well as DCC controllers. Sound features in the A unit include: Dual Diesel Engine Sounds, Horn, Bell, Squealing Brakes, Doppler Effect, Air Let Off (in neutral), Headlight, and Trailer which mutes whistle and bell for doubleheading.

- Limited Availability

EMD E8/9 A-B Set
B&O 920-31731

### E8/9 A

**225.00 w/Sound & DCC**
**125.00 Standard DC**

**Atlantic Coast Line**

**920-31701** #547 w/Mars Light Sound & DCC
**920-31702** #548 w/Mars Light, Sound & DCC
**920-31703** #545 w/Mars Light - Standard DC
**920-31704** #546 w/Mars Light - Standard DC

**Erie**

**920-31705** #827 with Sound & DCC
**920-31706** #830 with Sound & DCC
**920-31707** #821 - Standard DC
**920-31708** #822 - Standard DC

**New York Central**

**920-31709** #4066 with Sound & DCC
**920-31710** #4068 with Sound & DCC
**920-31711** #4088 - Standard DC
**920-31712** #4089 - Standard DC

**Pennsylvania**

**920-31713** #5701 with Mars Light, Sound & DCC
**920-31714** #5768 with Sound & DCC
**920-31715** #5700 w/Mars Light - Standard DC
**920-31716** #5765 - Standard DC

**Rock Island**

**920-31717** #650 w/Mars Light, Sound & DCC
**920-31718** #655 w/Mars Light, Sound & DCC
**920-31719** #644 w/Mars Light - Standard DC
**920-31720** #645 w/Mars Light - Standard DC

**Seaboard Air Line**

**920-31721** #3057 w/Mars Light, Sound & DCC
**920-31722** #3058 w/Mars Light, Sound & DCC
**920-31723** #3053 w/Mars Light - Standard DC
**920-31724** #3054 w/Mars Light - Standard DC

**Southern Pacific†**

**920-31725** #6046 w/Mars Light, Sound & DCC
**920-31726** #6047 w/Mars Light, Sound & DCC
**920-31727** #6018 w/Mars Light - Standard DC
**920-31728** #6050 w/Mars Light - Standard DC

### EMD E8/9 Powered A, Dummy B Sets

**295.00 w/Sound & DCC**
**195.00 Standard DC**

**Baltimore & Ohio**

**920-31731** #1437 & #2417 with Sound & DCC
**920-31732** #1436 & #2418 with Sound & DCC
**920-31733** #1433 & #2414 - Standard DC
**920-31734** #1435 & #2415 - Standard DC

**Illinois Central**

**920-31735** #4035 & #2100 w/Mars Light, Sound & DCC
**920-31736** #4039 & #4105 w/Mars Light, Sound & DCC
**920-31737** #4020 w/Mars Light & #4107 - Standard DC
**920-31738** #4027 w/Mars Light & #4108 - Standard DC

**Union Pacific†**

**920-31739** #925 & #925B w/Mars Light, Sound & DCC
**920-31740** #939 & #939B w/Mars Light, Sound & DCC
**920-31741** #900 w/Mars Light & #900B - Standard DC
**920-31742** #930 w/Mars Light & #930B - Standard DC

**Undecorated**

**920-31729** A w/Mars Light -B Set with Sound & DCC
**920-31730** A w/Mars Light -B Set - Standard DC

From Walthers

# EMD GP20

By the mid 50s, increasing pressure from long-haul trucks, declining passenger revenues and mounting costs forced western railroads to find new ways to improve service. Faced with expensive overhauls of early cab and hood unit diesels, many began looking at new equipment as well as ways to improve existing motive power. In 1955 Union Pacific equipped several GP9s with turbochargers as an experiment. Their success inspired EMD to create its own turbocharger for the 567 prime mover, leading to the introduction of the six-axle SD24 in 1958. Further experiments in 1959 created a four-axle version, dubbed the GP20. The first GP20s, which were built for GN and WP, were delivered with high, short hoods, and were the only units so equipped as later buyers favored the improved visibility of the short nose. Early in their careers, GP20s were typically assigned priority freights that demanded higher speeds. With the arrival of newer power, they were gradually bumped into secondary runs, and eventually spent their last years in local and yard service. Following their retirement, a few went to work for shortline operators.

EMD GP20 BN 920-31478

## EMD GP20

### 165.00 Standard DC

- Retooled Handrails & Other Parts for More Accurate Detail
- Over 135 Factory-Applied Parts
- Consumer-Applied Parts Pack Included
- Heavy Diecast Chassis
- 5-Pole Motor with Skew-Wound Armature
- Precisely Meshed Worm Gear & Spur Teeth for Silent Running
- LED Directional Headlights
- Magnetic Knuckle Couplers
- Limited Availability

**Burlington Northern**

**920-31478** #2042 - Standard DC

**920-31479** #2064 - Standard DC

**New York Central**

**920-31482** #2109 - Standard DC

**920-31483** #2112 - Standard DC

**Penn Central**

**920-31484** #2102 - Standard DC

**Limited Quantity Available**

**920-31485** #2105 - Standard DC

EMD GP20 NYC 920-31482

From Walthers

# ALCO RS-27

As the horsepower race between major locomotive builders began heating up, ALCO rolled out its new RS-27 in late 1959. While the design used the running gear of the RS-11, the new model was powered by a larger 16-cylinder prime mover that generated 2400 horsepower. To accommodate its extra length, the cab was moved forward, and the front hood shortened, giving the RS-27s a very distinctive appearance. Under relentless pressure from GE and EMD, ALCO was able to sell just 35 RS-27s before production ended in 1962.

## ALCO RS-27

**225.00 w/Sound & DCC**

**125.00 Standard DC**

- Heavy Diecast Chassis
- DC Motor with 5-Pole Skew-Wound Armature
- Precisely Meshed Worm Gear & Spur Teeth for Silent Running
- Magnetic Knuckle Couplers
- Prototype Specific Details Including:
  *With or Without Dynamic Brakes*
  *With or Without Drop Steps*
  *Two Styles of Class Lights*
  *Standard or Large Fuel Tank*
- Available With or Without Factory-Installed Sound & DCC

Sound can be operated with a standard DC power pack as well as DCC controllers. Sound features include: Diesel Engine, Horn, Bell, Squealing Brakes, Doppler Effect, Air Let Off (in neutral), Headlight, and Trailer which mutes whistle and bell for doubleheading.

- Limited Availability

**Order Now! Limited Availability**

Please Note: All Proto Series manufacturer numbers have changed from 433 to 920.

ALCO RS-2 CR 920-31364

### Chicago & North Western[†]

**920-31333** #902 with Sound & DCC
**920-31334** #903 with Sound & DCC
**920-31331** #900 - Standard DC
**920-31332** #901 - Standard DC

### Demonstrator

**920-31337** #640-3 with Sound & DCC
**920-31338** #640-4 with Sound & DCC
**920-31335** #640-1 - Standard DC
**920-31336** #640-2 - Standard DC

### Green Bay & Western

**920-31341** #316 with Sound & DCC
**920-31342** #317 with Sound & DCC

### Pennsylvania

**920-31345** #2408 with Sound & DCC
**920-31346** #2410 with Sound & DCC
**920-31343** #2400 - Standard DC
**920-31344** #2405 - Standard DC

[†]Union Pacific licensed product.

### SOO

**920-31349** #415 with Sound & DCC
**920-31350** #416 with Sound & DCC
**920-31347** #415 - Standard DC
**920-31348** #416 - Standard DC

### Union Pacific[†]

**920-31353** #677 with Sound & DCC
**920-31354** #678 with Sound & DCC
**920-31351** #675 - Standard DC
**920-31352** #676 - Standard DC

### Penn Central

**920-31359** #2407 with Sound & DCC
**920-31360** #2414 with Sound & DCC
**920-31357** #2402 - Standard DC
**920-31358** #2413 - Standard DC

### Conrail

**920-31363** #2411 with Sound & DCC
**920-31364** #2414 with Sound & DCC
**920-31361** #2402 - Standard DC
**920-31362** #2412 - Standard DC

### Undecorated

**920-31356** With Sound & DCC
**920-31355** Standard DC

# EMD GP38-2

EMD changed the face of railroading in 1972 with the introduction of its Dash 2 series, which was based on existing designs, but equipped with new electrical systems and other improvements. Of these, the GP38-2 became the standard medium-sized diesel in the line and one of the most successful EMD designs ever built, with over 2200 constructed through 1987.

These reliable, non-turbocharged 2,000-horsepower units proved ideal for all kinds of road and switching chores. Hundreds are still in use by railroads of all sizes including all Class I lines down to shortlines and industrial lines. As with most EMD production, there were numerous owner-specified changes resulting in some variations including high, short hood models for Southern and N&W as well as steam-boiler passenger units for the National Railways of Mexico. Federal requirements to make engine cabs safer led to the introduction of a slightly larger 88" nose (81" had been standard) in 1977.

**Order Now! Limited Availability**

Please Note: All Proto Series manufacturer numbers have changed from 433 to 920.

EMD GP38-2 CSX 920-31049

## EMD GP38-2 W/88" NOSE

**125.00 ea**

- Dynamic Brake Option (Applied As Appropriate)
- Magnetic Knuckle Couplers
- Dual Machined Brass Flywheels
- Limited Availability

**Burlington Northern Santa Fe**

**920-31020** #2371 - Standard DC
**920-31021** #2373 - Standard DC

**Clinchfield**

**920-31022** #6001 - Standard DC
**920-31023** #6003 - Standard DC

**Lousiville & Nashville**

**920-31024** #6022 - Standard DC
**920-31025** #6043 - Standard DC

**Norfolk Southern**

**920-31026** #5334 - Standard DC
**920-31027** #5385 - Standard DC

**Pittsburgh & Lake Erie**

**920-31028** #2051 - Standard DC
**920-31029** #2053 - Standard DC

**Rock Island**

**920-31030** #4374 - Standard DC
**920-31031** #4379 - Standard DC

**Seaboard System**

**920-31032** #2680 - Standard DC
**920-31033** #2690 - Standard DC

**Santa Fe**

**920-31040** #3563 - Standard DC
**920-31041** #3570 - Standard DC

**Burlington Northern**

**920-31042** #2151 - Standard DC
**920-31043** #2154 - Standard DC

## Order Now! Limited Availability

Please Note: All Proto Series manufacturer numbers have changed from 433 to 920.

From Walthers

### Chicago & North Western†

**920-31044** #4629 - Standard DC
**920-31045** #4632 - Standard DC

### Conrail

**920-31046** #8206 - Standard DC
**920-31047** #8227 - Standard DC

### CSX

**920-31048** #2764 - Standard DC
**920-31049** #2771 - Standard DC

### Missouri Pacific†

**920-31052** #2138 - Standard DC
**920-31053** #2164 - Standard DC

### Southern Pacific†

**920-31054** #4810 - Standard DC
**920-31055** #4827 - Standard DC

### Union Pacific†

**920-31056** #2139 - Standard DC
**920-31057** #2142 - Standard DC

### Undecorated

**920-31036** - Standard DC

## EMD GP38-2

**125.00 ea**

- Dynamic Brake Option (As Appropriate)
- Magnetic Knuckle Couplers
- Dual Machined Brass Flywheels
- Limited Availability

### Illinois Central Gulf

**920-30760** #9561 - Standard DC
**920-30761** #9569 - Standard DC

### Norfolk Southern

**920-30765** #5324 - Standard DC

### Seaboard Coast Line

**920-30766** #500 - Standard DC
**920-30767** #509 - Standard DC

### CSX

**920-30770** #2738 - Standard DC
**920-30771** #2749 - Standard DC

### Boston & Maine

**920-30776** #204 - Standard DC
**920-30777** #212 - Standard DC

### Burlington Northern

**920-30778** #2084 - Standard DC
**920-30779** #2336 - Standard DC

### Conrail

**920-30780** #7966 - Standard DC
**920-30781** #7993 - Standard DC

### Gulf, Mobile & Ohio

**920-30782** #742 - Standard DC
**920-30783** #748 - Standard DC

### Louisville & Nashville

**920-30784** #4055 - Standard DC
**920-30785** #4060 - Standard DC

### Missouri Pacific†

**920-30786** #2026 - Standard DC
**920-30787** #2038 - Standard DC

### Delaware & Hudson

**920-30788** #7309 - Standard DC
**920-30789** #7312 - Standard DC

### Union Pacific†

**920-30790** #2027 - Standard DC
**920-30791** #2040 - Standard DC

†Union Pacific licensed product.

From Walthers

# EMD SW8/9/600

Switchers had been an important part of EMD production from the early 1930s on. The SC (cast frames) and SW (welded frames) models were first introduced in 1936 and paved the way for many future models. The later development of improved power plants and other equipment led to a succession of higher horsepower units.

Introduced by EMD in 1950, the SW8 offered railroads and industry a rugged and reliable unit for switching chores, replacing the last of steam or earlier diesel switchers still in service. Powered by the famed 567B, the engines delivered 800 horsepower. In 1954, industry demand for a more powerful switcher led EMD to introduce the SW900, producing 100 additional horsepower from the 567C prime mover. Outwardly, these units (and the SW600 of which only 15 were built) were virtually identical. Production ended in late 1965 with a combined total of 743 engines. Well into the 1980s, these early switchers served railroads large and small and some remain in industrial service today.

**Order Now! Limited Availability**

Please Note: All Proto Series manufacturer numbers have changed from 433 to 920.

EMD SW8/9/600 Rock Island
920-31436

## EMD SW8/9/600

**205.00 w/Sound & DCC**

**105.00 Standard DC**

- Heavy Diecast Chassis and DC Motor with 5-Pole Skew-Wound Armature
- Precisely Meshed Worm Gear & Spur Teeth for Silent Running
- More Than 135 Factory Applied Detail Parts
- Modeler-Applied Parts Package
- Retooled Handrails & Other Parts for More Accurate Detail
- LED Directional Headlights
- Magnetic Knuckle Couplers
- Available With or Without Factory-Installed Sound & DCC

Sound can be operated with a standard DC power pack as well as DCC controllers. Sound features include: Diesel Engine, Horn, Bell, Squealing Brakes, Doppler Effect, Air Let Off (in neutral), Headlight, and Trailer which mutes whistle and bell for doubleheading.

**Conrail**

**920-31456** #8604 with Sound & DCC
**920-31457** #8615 with Sound & DCC
**920-31426** #8606 - Standard DC
**920-31427** #8620 - Standard DC

**Delaware, Lackawanna & Western**

**920-31458** #501 with Sound & DCC
**920-31459** #506 with Sound & DCC
**920-31428** #504 - Standard DC
**920-31429** #509 - Standard DC

**Santa Fe**

**920-31461** #651 with Sound & DCC
**920-31430** #652 - Standard DC
**920-31431** #653 - Standard DC

**Norfolk & Western**

**920-31462** #2111 with Sound & DCC
**920-31463** #3124 with Sound & DCC
**920-31432** #2108 - Standard DC
**920-31433** #3122 - Standard DC

**Nickel Plate Road**

**920-31464** #107 with Sound & DCC
**920-31465** #110 with Sound & DCC
**920-31434** #109 - Standard DC
**920-31435** #112 - Standard DC

**Rock Island**

**920-31466** #811 with Sound & DCC
**920-31467** #833 with Sound & DCC
**920-31436** #820 - Standard DC
**920-31437** #837 - Standard DC

**Southern Pacific†**

**920-31469** #1112 with Sound & DCC
**920-31438** #1110 - Standard DC
**920-31439** #1116 - Standard DC

**Wabash**

**920-31470** #120 with Sound & DCC
**920-31471** #127 with Sound & DCC
**920-31440** #123 - Standard DC
**920-31441** #130 - Standard DC

**Undecorated**

**920-31472** With Sound & DCC

# GE U28B & U30B

By the 1950s, railroads were shopping for more powerful units to replace earlier diesels, and a horsepower race between EMD, ALCO and General Electric began in earnest. GE took a bold step forward, unveiling its brutish new Universal series in 1959. Production began with a 2500-horsepower, four-axle unit, known as the U25B in 1960 – and railfans quickly nicknamed them "U-boats." The success of the new series soon pushed GE into the number two spot in locomotive sales.

In 1966 a 2800-horsepower prime mover was added to create the U28B. Only 148 units were built that year. Late production units (which are the prototypes for these models) had a shorter nose and some differences in the radiator intakes, which were carried over into early U30B production.

Late in 1966, GE introduced a 3000 horsepower prime mover in the U30B. Many features were carried over into the new body, however later production units (the prototypes for these models) had revised air intakes. Total production ended at 296 units in 1975.

**Order Now! Limited Availability**

Please Note: All Proto Series manufacturer numbers have changed from 433 to 920.

## GENERAL ELECTRIC U28B

**225.00 w/Sound & DCC**

**125.00 Standard DC**

- Available With or Without Factory-Installed Sound & DCC

Sound can be operated with a standard DC power pack as well as DCC controllers. Sound features include: Diesel Engine, Horn, Bell, Squealing Brakes, Doppler Effect, Air Let Off (in neutral), Headlight, and Trailer which mutes whistle and bell for doubleheading.

### Chicago, Burlington & Quincy

**920-31383** #107 with Sound & DCC
**920-31384** #112 with Sound & DCC
**920-31075** #109 - Standard DC
**920-31076** #114 - Standard DC

### New York Central

**920-31385** #2822 with Sound & DCC
**920-31386** #2823 with Sound & DCC
**920-31077** #2822 - Standard DC
**920-31078** #2823 - Standard DC

### Louisville & Nashville

**920-31387** #2500 with Sound & DCC
**920-31388** #2502 with Sound & DCC
**920-31079** #2501 - Standard DC
**920-31080** #2504 - Standard DC

### Great Northern

**920-31389** #2524 with Sound & DCC
**920-31390** #2526 with Sound & DCC
**920-31081** #2525 - Standard DC
**920-31082** #2529 - Standard DC

### Rock Island

**920-31391** #258 with Sound & DCC
**920-31392** #260 with Sound & DCC
**920-31083** #259 - Standard DC
**920-31084** #261 - Standard DC

### Union Pacific†

**920-31393** #506 with Sound & DCC
**920-31394** #507 with Sound & DCC
**920-31085** #510 - Standard DC
**920-31086** #517 - Standard DC

## GENERAL ELECTRIC U30B

**225.00 w/Sound & DCC**

**125.00 Standard DC**

- EMD or GE Trucks as Appropriate

### Atlantic Coast Line

**920-31401** #975 with Sound & DCC
**920-31402** #976 with Sound & DCC
**920-31110** #977 - Standard DC
**920-31111** #978 - Standard DC

### GE Demonstrator

**920-31403** #301 with Sound & DCC
**920-31404** #302 with Sound & DCC
**920-31112** #303 - Standard DC
**920-31113** #304 - Standard DC

### Illinois Central

**920-31405** #5001 with Sound & DCC
**920-31406** #5003 with Sound & DCC
**920-31114** #5002 - Standard DC
**920-31115** #5005 - Standard DC

### Louisville & Nashville

**920-31407** #2505 with Sound & DCC
**920-31408** #2507 with Sound & DCC
**920-31108** #2506 - Standard DC
**920-31109** #2509 - Standard DC

### Seaboard Air Line

**920-31409** #803 with Sound & DCC
**920-31410** #806 with Sound & DCC
**920-31116** #804 - Standard DC
**920-31117** #809 - Standard DC

### Western Pacific†

**920-31411** #751 with Sound & DCC
**920-31412** #754 with Sound & DCC
**920-31118** #752 - Standard DC
**920-31119** #755 - Standard DC

### CB&Q

**920-31473** #142 with Sound & DCC
**920-31474** #149 with Sound & DCC
**920-31106** #141 - Standard DC
**920-31107** #144 - Standard DC

### Undecorated

**920-31413** with Sound & DCC
**920-31120** Standard DC

†Union Pacific licensed product.

# EMD E6

920-31211
Roadname Shown Not Available

In the early 30s, lightweight, oil-electric streamliners like the "Zephyr" and M-10000 ushered in a new era in passenger train travel. At this same time, diesel-electric switchers were proving the technology had merit, leading some major roads to experiment with new diesels for their premiere passenger trains.

Many buyers turned to EMD for these early diesels, which were custom-built in very small numbers, using parts from various suppliers. Sensing a market for an off-the-shelf passenger diesel, EMD introduced its new E6 in November of 1939. This standardized model was built entirely with EMD-manufactured components including a pair of 5676C prime movers generating 2000 total horsepower. Geared for speed this proved an ideal combination and the E6 soon found a home at the front of some of the finest new trains. Its sleek body, accented by a pronounced sloping nose, gave it a distinctive appearance that complimented streamlined cars. Over 100 were built until production was halted for the war effort in 1942.

**Order Now! Limited Availability**

Please Note: All Proto Series manufacturer numbers have changed from 433 to 920.

## EMD E6

### A Units Only

- Parts for Open or Closed Pilot
- Perfectly Contoured Nose
- Authentic Period Paint & Lettering
- Magnetic Knuckle Couplers
- Available With or Without Factory-Installed Sound & DCC
- All-Wheel Drive & Electrical Pickup
- Heavy Diecast Chassis
- 5-Pole Motor with Skew-Wound Armature
- Precisely Meshed Worm Gear & Spur Teeth for Silent Running
- Limited Availability

Sound can be operated with a standard DC power pack as well as DCC controllers. Sound features in the A unit include: Dual Diesel Engine Sounds, Horn, Bell, Squealing Brakes, Doppler Effect, Air Let Off (in neutral), Headlight, and Trailer which mutes whistle and bell for doubleheading.

**Louisville & Nashville**

**920-31198** #776 - Standard DC **125.00**

**Undecorated**

**920-31216** With Sound & DCC **225.00**

†Union Pacific licensed product.

### A (Powered) & B (Dummy) Sets

- Parts for Open or Closed Pilot
- Perfectly Contoured A Unit Nose
- Authentic Period Paint & Lettering
- Magnetic Knuckle Couplers
- Available With or Without Factory-Installed Sound & DCC
- All-Wheel Drive & Electrical Pick-Up
- Heavy Diecast Chassis
- 5-Pole Motor with Skew-Wound Armature
- Precisely Meshed Worm Gear & Spur Teeth for Silent Running
- Limited Availability

Sound can be operated with a standard DC power pack as well as DCC controllers. Sound features in the A unit include: Dual Diesel Engine Sounds, Horn, Bell, Squealing Brakes, Doppler Effect, Air Let Off (in neutral), Headlight, and Trailer which mutes whistle and bell for double heading.

**Union Pacific†**

**920-31214** UP #957A & 926B - Standard DC **195.00**

**Undecorated**

**920-31217** Standard DC **195.00**

## QUANTUM ENGINEER

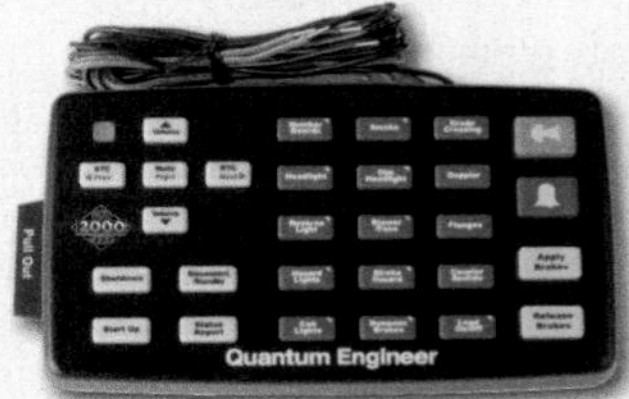


**920-5990 54.98**

- Enjoy Full Sound Control on DC Layouts
- Pushbutton Operation & Programming
- Operates all Sound, Lights & Automatic Features
- Use with any Loco with Quantum Sound
- Works with any Power Pack
- Easy to Hook-Up & Operate

From Walthers

**Order Now! Limited Availability**
Please Note: All Proto Series manufacturer numbers have changed from 433 to 920.

- Magnetic Knuckle Couplers
- Constant & Directional LED Lighting
- Dual Machined Brass Flywheels
- Balanced 5-Pole Skew-Wound Armature
- Separately Applied Pantograph Gates
- Heavy Diecast Chassis

DL-109 CNW 920-31953

## DL-109

**75.00 ea**

- LED Headlight
- 8-Pin NMRA DCC Plug
- Advanced Coupler Design allows Operation on 18" Radius Curves
- All-Wheel Drive & Electrical Pickup

**CNW**†
**920-31953** #5007A

**Gulf, Mobile & Ohio**

**920-31954** #270

**920-31955** #271

**MILW**

**920-31956** #14A

**920-31957** #14B

**Rock Island**

**920-31960** #622

**920-31961** #623

**SOU**

**920-31962** #6400

**920-31963** #6401

## EMD F3S

**A-B Sets 145.00**

**A Units Only 79.98**

- New Paint Schemes
- Both Units Powered
- Different Numbers - Mix & Match for A-B-B-A
- NMRA DCC eight-pin plug
- All-Wheel Drive & Electrical Pickup
- Directional LED Headlight on A Unit

**CGW**
**920-35000** #104A & 104B
**920-35001** #107A & 107B

**Delaware, Lackawanna & Western**
**920-35002** #660A & 660B
**920-35003** #660D & 660C

**MP**†
**920-35004** #702 & 792B
**920-35005** #705 & 795B

**NP**
**920-35006** #6004A & 6004B
**920-35007** #6004D & 6004C

**Seaboard Air Line - A Unit Only**
**920-35008** #4026
**920-35009** #4028

**SP**†
**920-35010** #6100A & 6100B
**920-35011** #6100D & 6100C

EMD F3 A-B Set NP 920-35006

From Walthers

## R17 NYC SUBWAY CARS

**185.00 ea**

- 5-Pole Skew-Wound Motor with Dual Flywheels
- Close Coupled
- Directional Lighting
- Interior Lighting
- Magnetic Knuckle Couplers

**920-31015** R-17 Bright Red
This set is finished in the same bright red as earlier releases to model a longer train. Includes powered unit #6604, and three unpowered units: #6513, 6529 and 6619.

New York City "Red Bird" R17 Subway Cars, limited availability

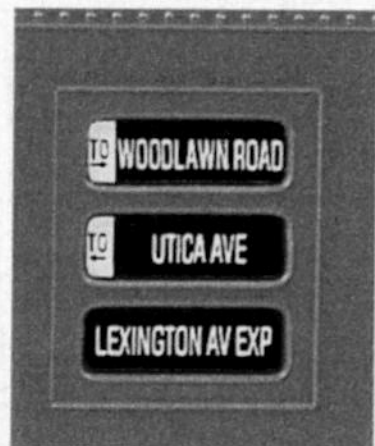


**Order Now! Limited Availability**
Please Note: All Proto Series manufacturer numbers have changed from 433 to 920.

R21-22 NYC Subway Cars 920-31016

## R21-22 NEW YORK CITY SUBWAY CARS

- All-New Model

**920-31016** 4-Car Set **185.00**

R17 NYC Subway Cars 920-31015

**Order Now! Limited Availability**

Please Note: All Proto Series manufacturer numbers have changed from 433 to 920.

EMD F3 A-B Set WP 920-31424

# EMD F3 A-B SETS

**145.00 ea**

- All-Wheel Drive & Electrical Pickup
- Dual Machined Brass Flywheels
- Directional LED Headlight
- NMRA 8-Pin DCC Plug
- Blackened-Metal Wheels
- Magnetic Knuckle Couplers

### Bangor & Aroostook

**920-31414** #500A & #600B
**920-31415** #507A & #602B

### Baltimore & Ohio

**920-31416** #82A & #82AX
**920-31417** #84A & #84AX

### Monon

**920-31418** #62A & #62C
**920-31419** #64A & #64C

### Central of New Jersey

**920-31420** #50 & #1A
**920-31421** #51 & #2B

### Erie

**920-31422** #714A & #714B
**920-31423** #714D & #714C

### Western Pacific†

**920-31424** #801A & #801B
**920-31425** #801D & #801C

EMD F3 A-B Set B&O
920-31416

†Union Pacific licensed product.

From Walthers

**Order Now! Limited Availability**

Please Note: All Proto Series manufacturer numbers have changed from 433 to 920.

F-M C-Liner NYC 920-31594

## FAIRBANKS-MORSE C-LINER

- Magnetic Knuckle Couplers
- Constant & Directional LED Lighting
- Dual Machined Brass Flywheels
- Balanced 5-Pole Skew-Wound Armature
- Heavy Diecast Chassis
- RP25 Contour Blackened Wheels
- 8-Wheel Drive & Electrical Pickup

### A-B Sets 150.00 ea

**Milwaukee Road**

**920-31590** #24A & #24B
**920-31592** #28A & #28B

**New York Central**

**920-31594** #6601 & #6900
**920-31596** #5006 & #6902

**Pennsylvania**

**920-31598** #9450 & #9450B
**920-31600** #9448 & #9448B

### A Unit Only 75.00 ea

**Milwaukee Road**
**920-31591** #24C
**920-31593** #28C

**New York Central**
**920-31595** #6603
**920-31597** #6604

**Pennsylvania**
**920-31599** #9451
**920-31601** #9497

**920-31696** PRR #9466A & #9466B
**920-31698** UP† #651 & #654B

### A Unit Only 75.00 ea

**920-31689** ATSF #90A

**920-31690** CNW† #60002A
**920-31691** CNW† #60002B
**920-31693** MILW #12B

**920-31695** NYC #4401
**920-31697** PRR #9467A

**920-31699** UP† #652

## FAIRBANKS-MORSE ERIE-BUILT

- Magnetic Knuckle Couplers
- Dual Machined Brass Flywheels
- Balanced 5-Pole Skew-Wound Armature
- Heavy Diecast Chassis
- RP25 Contour Blackened Wheels
- 8-Wheel Drive, 12-Wheel Electrical Pickup

### A-B Sets 150.00 ea

**920-31688** ATSF #90 & #90B

**920-31692** MILW #9A & #9B
**920-31694** NYC #4400 & #5100

†Union Pacific licensed product.

From Walthers

## ALCO RSC-2

**95.00 ea**

- Powerful Motor with Skew-Wound Armature & Dual Flywheels
- 12-Wheel Drive & 12-Wheel Electrical Pickup
- Directional Lighting
- Magnetic Knuckle Couplers
- RP25 Contour Blackened Wheels

### Milwaukee Road

**920-31291** #988 **920-31292** #992

### Seaboard Air Line

**920-31293** #1520 **920-31294** #1523

### SOO Line

**920-31295** #368 **920-31296** #370

### Union Pacific†

**920-31297** #1282 **920-31298** #1286

### Undecorated

**920-31299**

ALCO RS-2 NH 920-31279

**Order Now! Limited Availability**

Please Note: All Proto Series manufacturer numbers have changed from 433 to 920.

ALCO RSC-2 SOO 920-31296

## ALCO RS-2

- Magnetic Knuckle Couplers
- All-Wheel Drive & Electrical Pickup
- Dual Machined Brass Flywheels
- Constant & Directional Headlights
- RP25 Contour Blackened Wheels
- Heavy Diecast Chassis
- 5-Pole Skew-Wound Motor

### Delaware & Hudson

**920-31274** #4018

### New Haven

**920-31279** #0509

**920-31280** #0513

### Erie-Lackawanna

**920-31281** #909

**920-31282** #911

### Rock Island

**920-31283** #450

**920-31284** #452

### Western Maryland

**920-31285** #182

**920-31286** #183

### Undecorated

**920-31287**

Get the Scoop!
Get the Skinny!
Get the Score!
Check Out Walthers
Web site at

**www.walthers.com**

From Walthers

**Order Now! Limited Availability**

Please Note: All Proto Series manufacturer numbers have changed from 433 to 920.

Budd RDC-1 SP 920-31250

# BUDD RAIL DIESEL CARS

**85.00 ea**

- 3 Popular Body Styles
- Magnetic Knuckle Couplers
- 4-Wheel Drive & 8-Wheel Electrical Pickup
- 5-Pole Skew-Wound Motor
- Flywheel Equipped

## RDC-1; Coach

**920-31239** CNJ #553

**920-31240** CNJ #559

**920-31242** LV #40

**920-31249** Pennsylvania-Reading Seashore Line #M413

**920-31250** SP† #SP-10

**920-31254** Susquehanna #M-1

**920-31255** Susquehanna #M-2

**920-31251** Undecorated

## RDC-2; Coach-Baggage

**920-31236** CNW† #9935

**920-31238** C&O #9935

**920-31243** LV #41

**920-31247** NYC #M-480

**920-31252** Undecorated

## RDC-3; Coach-Baggage-Railway Post Office

**920-31241** GN #2350

**920-31244** MKT† #20

**920-31245** Northern Pacific #B40

**920-31246** Northern Pacific #B42

**920-31253** Undecorated

Authentically contoured radiator with realistic fan details.

Cab ends feature windshield wiper details and single-chime airhorns.

Realistic trap door, step details and authentic baggage doors on RDC-2 & RDC-3 models.

†Union Pacific licensed product.

# TRAINLINE®
## by WALTHERS

TRAINLINE® DIESELS
- Ready to Run
- Working Headlight
- Knuckle Couplers
- Diecast Metal Frames
- 5-Pole Motor w/Skew-Wound Armature
- Flywheels

## EMD F40PH

**54.98 ea**
- New Motor
- Dual Flywheels
- Add-on Pilot Plow Included
- Directional Headlight
- Looks Great with Walthers Passenger Cars

**931-330** Amtrak® - Phase III Scheme

**931-331** Metra

**931-332** VIA Rail

**931-333** Regional Transportation Authority (RTA) – Chicago

**931-334** CSX

**931-335** Amtrak - Phase IV Scheme

For Up-To-Date Information and News Bookmark Walthers Web site at

**www.walthers.com**

## EMD GP9M DIESEL

**39.98 ea**
- New Motor
- Dual Flywheels
- Perfect Choice for Freight Service

**931-101** BN (white front)

**931-102** UP†

**931-103** ATSF - Freight

**931-104** CN ("North America")

**931-105** CSX

**931-106** CR

**931-108** NS

**931-109** PRR

**931-111** MILW

**931-113** ATSF (Superfleet®)

**931-114** CP

EMD F40PH Diesel Amtrak - Phase IV Scheme 931-335

EMD F40PH Diesel VIA Rail 931-332

EMD GP9M Diesel DRGW 931-129

EMD GP9M Diesel Genessee & Wyoming 931-132

**931-118** WC

**931-120** BNSF ("Pumpkin")

**931-123** Amtrak

**931-128** SOO (Candy Apple Red, white)

**931-129** DRGW†

**931-130** PRR (Tuscan Red)

†Union Pacific licensed product.

**931-131** Amtrak - Switcher Scheme

**931-132** Genessee & Wyoming

**931-133** IC (orange, white)

# TRAINLINE®
## by WALTHERS

## GP9M LOCO & CABOOSE SETS

**39.98 ea**

- Fully Assembled
- Matching Caboose
- Different Numbers from Individual Locos & Cars

**931-700** Alaska Railroad Loco has correct ALCO Type B trucks.

**931-701** US Army

**931-707** BNSF

**931-708** ATSF ("Warbonnet")

## ALCO FA-1 & FB-1

**39.98 ea**

- Period Paint & Lettering
- Matching B Units per Prototype

### GN

**931-201** FA-1 #310A

**931-261** FB-1 #310B

**931-235** FA-1 #279A

**931-275** FB-1 #279B

### UP†

**931-203** FA-1 #1500A

**931-262** FB-1 #1524B

### PRR

**931-205** FA-1 #9600

**931-263** FB-1 #9601B

### ATSF

**931-207** FA-1 #202A

**931-264** FB-1 #202B

### SOU

**931-209** FA-1 #2853A

**931-265** FB-1 #2853B

### NYC

**931-211** FA-1 #1000A

**931-266** FB-1 #2304B

### NH

**931-223** FA-1 #0400

**931-271** FB-1 #0464

**931-236** FA-1 #0419

**931-276** FB-1 #0453

### Lehigh Valley

**931-227** FA-1 #538

**931-274** FB-1 #531

### Soo Line

**931-229** FA-1 #207A

### Spokane, Portland & Seattle

**931-237** FA-1

**931-277** FB-1

### Long Island Railroad

**931-238** FA-1

### Undecorated

**931-200** FA-1 #310A

**931-260** FB-1 #310B

Alaska Railroad 931-700

US Army 931-701

BNSF 931-707

Santa Fe 931-708

ATSF 931-708

Alco FA-1 & FB-1 Diesel NYC 931-211/931-266

Alco FA-1 & FB-1 Diesel Lehigh Valley 931-227/931-274

†Union Pacific licensed product.

Daily New Product Announcements! Visit Walthers Web site at **www.walthers.com**

## STEAM

### Union Pacific 4-8-8-4 "Big Boy"

635-HR2005 #4003 **299.98**

To eliminate helpers over the rugged grades of the Wasatch Mountains, Union Pacific designers created an entirely new class of articulated power in the early 1940s. The massive size and weight required eight axles per engine, while four-wheel pilot and trailing trucks were added front and rear. During construction at ALCO, an unknown worker chalked the name "Big Boy" on one of the new 4-8-8-4s and a legend was born. Delivered in the fall of 1941, locos #4000-4019 were soon handling an incredible volume of wartime traffic. To keep pace, five more (#4020-4024) were delivered in 1944. Big Boys remained in regular freight service into the late 1950s, and as some of the last big steam in service, caught the attention of railfans worldwide. Officially retired in 1962, several were preserved by museums to inspire a new generation of fans.

The model comes fully assembled and finished in black and graphite paint and features blackened, fine-flanged wheels for operation on Code 70, 83 and 100 track, razor-sharp graphics, realistic matte finish and formed metal handrails.

### Chesapeake & Ohio 2-6-6-6 "Allegheny"

**NEW** 635-2051 #1603
w/Sound & DCC **459.95**

Steep grades and heavy coal trains were the rule on Chesapeake & Ohio's Allegheny Subdivision. By 1940, the road's aging 2-8-8-2s were getting expensive to maintain. When C&O began looking for a replacement, Lima proposed an all-new 2-6-6-6 articulated. C&O ordered 10, classified H-8 and named "Allegheny" to honor the mountain range where they would soon be working. Running 80 miles between Hinton, West Virginia, and Clifton Forge, Virginia, a pair of 2-6-6-6s regularly lifted 140 loaded hoppers westbound over the steep grades. In 1944, 25 more were delivered. In 1948, C&O purchased 15 more Alleghenies and began running the class on the line from Russell, Kentucky, to Walbridge, Ohio. On this flatter stretch of railroad, the Alleghenies easily rolled heavy time freights and coal at speed. But the onslaught of diesels and a drop in demand for coal led to retirement in July of 1956. Two were saved; #1601 is displayed at the Henry Ford Museum in Dearborn, Michigan, and #1604 at the B&O Railroad Museum in Baltimore, Maryland.

A superb replica of the prototype, this model comes ready for service with an incredible level of detailing. The loco operates on 18" radius (22" or larger radius is recommended) curves and Code 70, 83 or 100 rail.

### New York Central 4-6-4 "Hudson"

635-HR2007 #5442 **229.98**

With 10 years of practical experience using 4-6-4s on premiere passenger trains, The New York Central introduced its class J3a in 1937. Some 50 engines were built (the last 10 were streamlined), and were assigned to the road's finest trains, including the flagship 20th Century Limited. While they were bumped from their elite status by the late 40s, Hudsons continued to handle important passenger runs until the end of steam.

Fast and powerful, these six-coupled speedsters feature a smooth-running mechanism, fine detailing and great-looking paint , making them the perfect choice for fast passenger trains on your HO mainline.

Atlas engines feature prepainted and lettered plastic bodies with plenty of applied details. All locomotives are powered unless noted. A heavy diecast frame supports a mechanism which features a can motor and dual flywheels for smooth operation. All-wheel drive provides plenty of pulling power and all-wheel electrical pickup ensures smooth operation. Other features include directional lighting and factory-installed AccuMate® knuckle couplers. Sound and DCC equipped models feature the QSI® Quantum Sound® system with dual speaker system, diesel engine sounds, squealing brakes, doppler effect and muting options for the bell and whistle. Atlas announces new products on a monthly basis. Visit Walthers Web site at www.walthers.com for the latest additions to the Atlas line.

**Limited Quantity Available On All Items**

## NEW PRODUCTS

### Diesel Locomotives

### Atlas Master Silver™ GE U30C

Built by General Electric between 1966 and 1976, the six-axle, 3000hp U30C locomotive was primarily used in heavy-haul road freight and unit train service. The Phase II carbody style first appeared in December 1967 with the delivery of 6 units to Delaware & Hudson. This style was produced through 1969 when production of phase III units began. Details include separately installed scale windshield wipers, metal grab irons and fine scale handrails, directional lighting, crew members and separately applied drop steps and marker light lenses. Nose headlights, snowplows, accurate Adirondack floating-bolster trucks with or without bearing caps, non-operating cab rooftop beacon and antenna details are included as appropriate for each roadname. Units are equipped with an 8-pin DCC decoder socket (decoder sold separately).

**Phase II 124.95 ea (Unless Noted)**

**NEW 150-7364** D&H #709 ("Lightning Stripe" blue, gray)

**NEW 150-7365** D&H #711 ("Lightning Stripe" blue, gray)

**NEW 150-7366** D&H #712 ("Lightning Stripe" blue, gray)

**NEW 150-7367** SOO #801 (white, red w/"Parllelogram" logo)

**NEW 150-7368** SOO #803 (white, red w/"Parllelogram" logo)

**NEW 150-7369** SOO #809 (white, red w/"Parllelogram" logo)

**NEW 150-7302** Undecorated **109.95**

**NEW 150-7303** Undecorated w/Nose Headlight **109.95**

**Phase III 124.95 ea (Unless Noted)**

**NEW 150-7370** BN #5341 (Cascade Green)

**NEW 150-7371** BN #5348 (Cascade Green)

**NEW 150-7372** BN #5352 (Cascade Green)

**NEW 150-7373** CSX #7207 (gray, blue)

**NEW 150-7374** CSX #7222 (gray, blue)

**NEW 150-7375** CSX #7259 (gray, black)

**NEW 150-7376** MP #2974 (blue, white)

**NEW 150-7377** MP #2980 (blue, white)

**NEW 150-7378** MP #2984 (blue, white)

**NEW 150-7379** SBD #7203 (gray, red, yellow)

**NEW 150-7380** SBD #7205 (gray, red, yellow)

**NEW 150-7381** SBD #7250 (gray, red, yellow)

**NEW 150-7382** SP #7930 (1970s Repaint gray, scarlet)

**NEW 150-7383** SP #7383 (1970s Repaint gray, scarlet)

**NEW 150-7384** SP #7935 (1970s Repaint gray, scarlet)

**NEW 150-7385** BN #1776 (red, white, blue) **139.95**

**NEW 150-7386** US Department of Transportation #001 (red, white, blue) **139.95**

## DIESEL LOCOMOTIVES

### Master Line® EMD SD24

Produced by EMD between July 1958 and March 1963, the SD-24 locomotive generated a total of 2,400hp with its turbocharged 567D-3 prime mover and C-C wheel arrangement. These models come in four variations with appropriate roadname-specific bodies and detailing.

**Atlas Master Gold w/Sound & DCC 244.95 ea (Unless Noted)**

**High Nose**

**NEW 150-7587** EMD Demonstrator #5579 (maroon, red, yellow) **254.95**

**NEW 150-7591** CB&Q #507 (red, gray, white)

**NEW 150-7592** CB&Q #510 (red, gray, white)

**NEW 150-7593** SOU #2511 (black, Imitation Aluminum, gold)

**NEW 150-7594** SOU #2520 (black, Imitation Aluminum, gold)

**NEW 150-7597** UP #448 ("Dependable Transportation" Slogan)

**150-7550** Undecorated - CB&Q Style

**150-7552** Undecorated - SOU Style

**Low Nose**

**NEW 150-7588** Kennecott Copper #904 (green, yellow)

**NEW 150-7589** ATSF #4508 (blue, yellow "Warbonnet")

**NEW 150-7590** ATSF #4525 (blue, yellow "Warbonnet")

**NEW 150-7595** UP #402 ("Dependable Transportation" Slogan)

**NEW 150-7596** UP #421 ("Dependable Transportation" Slogan)

**150-7551** Undecorated - ATSF Style

**150-7553** Undecorated - UP Style

**Atlas Master Silver Standard DC 124.95 ea (Unless Noted)**

**High Nose**

**NEW 150-7537** EMD Demonstrator #5579 (maroon, red, yellow) **134.95**

**NEW 150-7541** CB&Q #500 (red, gray, white)

**NEW 150-7542** CB&Q #512 (red, gray, white)

**NEW 150-7543** SOU #2506 (black, Imitation Aluminum, gold)

**NEW 150-7544** SOU #2517 (black, Imitation Aluminum, gold)

**NEW 150-7547** UP #448 ("Dependable Transportation" Slogan)

**150-7500** Undecorated - CB&Q Style

**150-7502** Undecorated - SOU Style

**Low Nose**

**NEW 150-7538** Kennecott Copper #904 (green, yellow)

**NEW 150-7539** ATSF #4502 (blue, yellow "Warbonnet")

**NEW 150-7540** ATSF #4526 (blue, yellow "Warbonnet")

**NEW 150-7545** UP #415 ("Dependable Transport ation" Slogan)

**NEW 150-7546** UP #429 ("Dependable Transportation" Slogan)

**150-7501** Undecorated - ATSF Style

**150-7503** Undecorated - UP Style

### Master Line® FM H24-66 Trainmaster

Advertised by Fairbanks-Morse as "the most useful locomotive ever built," the H24-66 Train Master was first introduced in 1953. In its era, this versatile 2,400hp locomotive was the most powerful single-engine unit in production. Ordered by several roads, it easily handled heavy freights, passenger and commuter trains.

**Atlas Master Gold w/Sound & DCC 259.95 ea**

**Phase 1A**

**NEW 150-7750** Fairbanks-Morse Demonstrator #TM-3 (orange, yellow, black)

**NEW 150-7751** Fairbanks-Morse Demonstrator #TM-4 (orange, yellow, black)

**NEW 150-7753** DL&W #852 (gray, maroon, yellow)

**NEW 150-7754** DL&W #857 (gray, maroon, yellow)

**150-7700** Undecorated, Single Headlight, Small Number Boards

**Phase 1B**

**NEW 150-7755** RDG #201 (green, yellow)

**NEW 150-7756** RDG #801 (green, yellow)

**NEW 150-7757** SP #3030 (post-1971; gray, scarlet)

**NEW 150-7758** SP #3035 (post-1971; gray, scarlet)

**150-7703** Undecorated, Dual Headlights, Small Number Boards

**Phase 2**

**NEW 150-7759** N&W #173 (NW repaint black, white)

**NEW 150-7760** RDG #265 (green, yellow)

**NEW 150-7761** RDG #867 (green, yellow)

**NEW 150-7762** Virginian #69 (black, yellow)

**NEW 150-7763** Virginian #71 (black, yellow)

**150-7702** Undecorated, Single Headlight, Large Number Boards

**Atlas Master Silver Standard DC 149.95 ea**

**Phase 1A**

**NEW 150-7856** Fairbanks-Morse Demonstrator #TM-1 (orange, yellow, black)

**NEW 150-7857** Fairbanks-Morse Demonstrator #TM-2 (orange, yellow, black)

**NEW 150-7858** DL&W #851 (gray, maroon, yellow)

**NEW 150-7859** DL&W #856 (gray, maroon, yellow)

**150-7800** Undecorated, Single Headlight, Small Number Boards

**Phase 1B**

**NEW 150-7860** RDG #201 (green, yellow)

**NEW 150-7861** RDG #801 (green, yellow)

**NEW 150-7862** SP #3026 (post-1971 gray, scarlet)

**NEW 150-7863** SP #3033 (post-1971 gray, scarlet)

**150-7803** Undecorated, Dual Headlights, Small Number Boards

**Phase 2**

**NEW 150-7864** N&W #173 (NW repaint, black, white)

**NEW 150-7865** RDG #265 (green, yellow)

**NEW 150-7866** RDG #867 (green, yellow)

**NEW 150-7867** Virginian #70 (black, yellow)

**NEW 150-7868** Virginian #72 (black, yellow)

**150-7802** Undecorated, Single Headlight, Large Number Boards

### Master Line® GE B23-7/30-7

General Electric's "Dash 7" locomotive line replaced the "Universal Series" of the 60s and early 70s. The B23-7 was a direct replacement for the 2,250hp U23B model, while the B30-7 replaced the 3,000hp U30B; production lasted to 1984 and 1981 respectively. These models feature roadname-specific details such as truck sideframes, anticlimbers, front headlights, bell and cab windows.

**Atlas Master Gold B23-7 w/Sound & DCC 259.95 ea**

**NEW 150-8162** CR "Keep It Moving" #1980 (blue, white)

**NEW 150-8163** CR #1967 (blue, white)

**NEW 150-8164** CR #1984 (blue, white)

**NEW 150-8165** Minnesota Commercial #1971 (red, white, black)

**NEW 150-8166** Minnesota Commercial #1978 (red, white, black)

**NEW 150-8167** Minnesota Commercial #1983 (red, white, black)

**NEW 150-8168** MP #4659 (blue, white)

**NEW 150-8169** MP #4665 (blue, white)

**NEW 150-8170** SP #5105 (gray, scarlet)

**NEW 150-8171** SP #5108 (gray, scarlet)

**NEW 150-8172** SP #5113 (gray, scarlet)

**NEW 150-8173** UP #144 (yellow, gray, red)

**NEW 150-8174** UP #152 (yellow, gray, red)

**NEW 150-8105** Undecorated, Phase 2, No Nose Headlight

### Atlas Master Gold B30-7 w/Sound & DCC 259.95 ea

**NEW 150-8175** CSX "Transportation" #5508 (Early Scheme, gray, blue)

**NEW 150-8176** CSX "Transportation" #5511 (Early Scheme, gray, blue)

**NEW 150-8177** SBD #5502 (gray, red, yellow)

**NEW 150-8178** SBD #5509 (gray, red, yellow)

**NEW 150-8179** SBD #5515 (gray, red, yellow)

**NEW 150-8108** Undecorated Phase 2, Nose Headlight

### Atlas Master Silver B23-7 Standard DC 149.95 ea

**NEW 150-8062** CR "Keep It Moving" #1980

**NEW 150-8063** CR #1971 (blue, white)

**NEW 150-8064** CR #1987 (blue, white)

**NEW 150-8065** Minnesota Commercial #1971 (red, white, black)

**NEW 150-8066** Minnesota Commercial #1978 (red, white, black)

**NEW 150-8067** Minnesota Commercial #1983 (red, white, black)

**NEW 150-8068** MP #4643 (blue, white)

**NEW 150-8069** MP #4661 (blue, white)

**NEW 150-8070** SP #5103 (gray, scarlet)

**NEW 150-8071** SP #5110 (gray, scarlet)

**NEW 150-8072** SP #5112 (gray, scarlet)

**NEW 150-8073** UP #158 (yellow, gray, red)

**NEW 150-8074** UP #166 (yellow, gray, red)

**NEW 150-8005** Undecorated, Phase 2, No Nose Headlight

### Atlas Master Silver B23-7 Standard DC 149.95 ea

**NEW 150-8075** CSX "Transportation" #5508 (Early Scheme, gray, blue)

**NEW 150-8076** CSX "Transportation" #5511 (Early Scheme, gray, blue)

**NEW 150-8077** SBD #5500 (gray, red, yellow)

**NEW 150-8079** SBD #5516 (gray, red, yellow)

**NEW 150-8008** Undecorated Phase II, Low Nose w/Nose Headlight

### Alco S-Series Switchers

Alco S-series switchers are just the thing for yards, shortlines and industrial operations. The 600hp S1 and 1000hp S-2 were produced from 1940 to 1950 and both rode on Blunt trucks. The 1000hp S-4 was introduced in 1950 and rides on AAR trucks.

### S-1 Standard DC 94.95 ea

**NEW 150-10000029** Alco Demonstrator #5 (dark green, yellow, black)

**NEW 150-10000030** Bath & Hammondsport #4 (red, black, yellow)

**NEW 150-10000031** Bath & Hammondsport #5 (red, black, yellow)

**NEW 150-10000032** RDG #50 (dark green, gold)

**NEW 150-10000033** RDG #53 (dark green, gold)

**150-8850** Undecorated

### S-2 Standard DC 94.95 ea

**NEW 150-10000034** LV #157 (red, gray, yellow)

**NEW 150-10000035** LV #163 (red, gray, yellow)

**NEW 150-10000036** NYC/P&LE #8452 (dark green, black, white)

**NEW 150-10000037** NYC/P&LE #8548 (dark green, black, white)

**NEW 150-10000038** San Francisco Belt #23 (black, yellow)

**NEW 150-10000039** San Francisco Belt #25 (black,yellow)

**NEW 150-10000040** SP (T&NO) #51 (black, orange)

**NEW 150-10000041** SP (T&NO) #69 (black, orange)

**NEW 150-10000042** WP #551 (black, white)

**NEW 150-10000043** WP #555 (black, white)

**NEW 150-10000044** SOU #2228 (green, yellow, black)

**NEW 150-10000045** SOU #2229 (green, yellow, black)

**150-8700** Undecorated

### S-4 Standard DC 94.95 ea

**NEW 150-10000046** B&M #1268 (blue, white)

**NEW 150-10000047** B&M #1269 (blue, white)

**NEW 150-10000048** B&M #1274 (blue, black, white)

**NEW 150-10000049** Morristown & Erie #14 (red, blue, yellow)

**150-8750** Undecorated

See What's Available at

**www.walthers.com**

### Alco RS-1 104.95 ea

The RS-1 was introduced by Alco in March of 1941. Revolutionary for the time, it combined a switcher's accessibility with the higher-speed tracking of a road unit. These detailed models feature separately applied wire grab irons and coupler cut levers, improved radiator detail and revised roof detail.

**NEW 150-7141** Chattahoochee Industrial #38 (white, red, blue)

**NEW 150-7142** Chattahoochee Industrial #97 (white, red, blue)

**NEW 150-7143** Duluth South Shore & Atlantic #101 (green, yellow, red)

**NEW 150-7144** Duluth South Shore & Atlantic #105 (green, yellow, red)

**NEW 150-7145** SLSF #101 (black, yellow)

**NEW 150-7146** SLSF #111 (black, yellow)

**NEW 150-7147** Genesee & Wyoming #30 (orange, black)

**NEW 150-7148** Genesee & Wyoming #43 (orange, black)

**NEW 150-7149** Illinois Terminal #750 (black, white)

**NEW 150-7150** Illinois Terminal #752 (black, white)

**NEW 150-7151** Minneapolis & St. Louis #546 (blue, gray, yellow)

**NEW 150-7152** Minneapolis & St. Louis #244 (blue, gray, yellow)

**NEW 150-7153** NYC #9909 (black, white)

**NEW 150-7154** NYC #9910 (black, white)

**NEW 150-7155** PRR #8857 (green, yellow)

**NEW 150-7156** PRR #8858 (green yellow)

**150-7100** Undecorated

### EMD MP15DC 134.95 ea

The first MP15DCs were built for MP in 1974 and a total of 246 units were produced through the end of production in November 1980. The MPD15DC is a versatile locomotive that is employed by both large and small railroads across North America in road freight and switching duties. It was also used for plant switching service. Model features 3 different hood styles: standard air filter, square air filter box, angled air filter box.

GE U23B ATSF #6346 150-8299

Fairbanks-Morse H16-44
Roadname Shown Not Available

### Atlas Master™ Gold Series w/DCC Decoder & Sound 244.95 ea (Unless Noted)

**150-9410** Undecorated - Standard Hood **249.95**

**Limited Quantity Available**

**150-9440** Frisco No Number

**150-9442** L&N #5038

**150-9443** L&N No Number

### Atlas Master™ Silver Series No DCC Decoder, No Sound 134.95 ea (Unless Noted)

**Limited Quantity Available**

**150-9928** Frisco #362

**150-9929** Frisco #364

**150-9930** Frisco No Number

**150-9931** L&N #5031

**150-9932** L&N #5037

**150-9933** L&N No Number

**150-9934** MP #1539

**150-9935** MP #1541

**150-9900** Undecorated - Standard Hood **139.95**

**150-9901** Undecorated - Square Air Filter Box **139.95**

### Alco RS-3 104.95 ea (Unless Noted)

Produced by the American Locomotive Company during the 1950s, the RS-3 was used in freight and commuter passenger service throughout North America. The new Atlas RS-3 features thinner handrails and stanchions including separate drop step detail.

**150-8450** Undecorated

### Alco RSD-4/5 104.95 ea

Contemporaries of the RS-3, these units spread their weight over six axles, making them ideal for light-railed branch lines.

**150-8490** Undecorated

### GE U23B 109.95 ea

These popular four-axle units were GE's mid-horsepower roadswitcher offering. Hundreds were built beginning in 1968, making them GE's second best-selling "Universal Series" locos. these detailed models feature a PC board with directional headlights and an eight-pin DCC plug, applied grab irons, smooth-running mechanism and roadname-specific trucks and cab versions.

**Limited Quantity Available**

**150-8261** CSX #3278

**150-8262** CSX #3289

**150-8291** MP #4512

**150-8293** MP #4530

**150-8298** ATSF #6330

**150-8299** ATSF #6346

**150-8650** Undecorated (AAR Trucks)

**150-8651** Undecorated (FB-2/Blomberg Trucks)

### Alco C-424/C-425 99.95 ea

Built in the early 1960s, Alco Century locomotives could be found in service on many railroads across the country. Some are still running on shortlines today.

### C-424 Phase 3

**150-9400** Undecorated

### C-425 Phase 1

**150-9360** Undecorated

### Fairbanks-Morse H16-44 w/Early "Loewy" Body & Cab, Sill-Mounted Handrails

As Atlas Master locomotives, these new units come factory-equipped with an Atlas 4-Function, Dual-Mode DCC decoder installed. Dual-mode decoders allow operation on either DCC or conventional DC layouts with no difference in performance.

**150-9518** Undecorated **149.95**

## Dash 8 Locomotives

Feature crew figures; separately installed scale windshield wipers, metal grab irons and fine-scale handrails; highly detailed coupler cut bars, MU hoses, snowplow, shock absorbers and piping on trucks; diecast underframe; five-pole skewed armature motor with dual flywheels for optimum performance at all speeds; directional lighting; simulated ditch lights; and factory-equipped with AccuMate® couplers. Units also come equipped with the HO Dual-Mode™ Decoder pre-installed.

### Dash 8-40BW 149.95 ea

**150-9050** Undecorated, Standard Cab Roof

**150-9051** Undecorated Gull Wing Cab

### Dash 8-32BHW

**150-9070** Undecorated **149.95**

### Dash 8-40C

**Atlas Master™ Gold Series w/DCC Decoder & Sound 259.95 ea**

**Limited Quantity Available**

**150-9656** CR #6031

**150-9657** CR #6049

**150-9658** CSX "YN3" #7497

**150-9659** CSX "YN3" #7591

**150-9695** Undecorated (Phase I)

**150-9696** Undecorated (Phase II)

**Atlas Master™ Silver Series No DCC Decoder, No Sound 149.95 ea (Unless Noted)**

**150-7600** Undecorated (Phase I)

**150-7601** Undecorated (Phase II)

**Limited Quantity Available**

**150-7666** CR #6026 (blue, white)

**150-7669** CSX "YN3" #7599 (dark blue, yellow)

**150-7673** UP #9209 (yellow sill stripe)

Dash 8-40C CR
Different Roadnumber Shown

### Dash 8-40CW

Produced by General Electrical between 1989 and 1993, this was the follow-up engine to the Dash 8-40C.

**Atlas Master™ Gold Series w/DCC Decoder & Sound 259.95 ea**

**NEW 150-9675** CR #6190 ("Quality" blue, white)

**NEW 150-9676** CR #6225 ("Quality" blue, white)

**NEW 150-9677** CSX #7681 (gray, blue, yellow)

**NEW 150-9678** CSX #7741 (gray, blue, yellow)

**NEW 150-9679** ATSF #841 ("Warbonnet" silver, red)

**NEW 150-9680** ATSF #880 ("Warbonnet" silver, red)

**NEW 150-9681** ATSF #891 ("Warbonnet" silver, red)

**NEW 150-9682** CSX #7812 ("Spirit of America" gray, blue, yellow)

**NEW 150-9683** UP #9390 (yellow, gray w/"Wings")

**NEW 150-9684** UP #9425 (yellow, gray w/"Wings")

**NEW 150-9685** UP #9527 (yellow, gray w/"Wings")

**150-9697** Undecorated - CSX/UP Style

**150-9698** Undecorated - ATSF Style

**150-9699** Undecorated - CR Style

**Atlas Master™ Silver Series No DCC Decoder, No Sound 149.95 ea**

**NEW 150-7686** CR #6187 ("Quality" blue, white)

**NEW 150-7687** CR #6213 ("Quality" blue, white)

**NEW 150-7688** CSX #7677 (gray, blue, yellow)

**NEW 150-7689** CSX #7799 (gray, blue, yellow)

**NEW 150-7690** ATSF #838 ("Warbonnet" silver, red)

**NEW 150-7691** ATSF #876 ("Warbonnet" silver, red)

**NEW 150-7692** ATSF #881 ("Warbonnet" silver, red)

**NEW 150-7693** CSX #7812 ("Spirit of America" gray, blue, yellow)

**NEW 150-7694** UP #9370 (yellow, gray w/"Wings")

**NEW 150-7695** UP #9387 (yellow, gray w/"Wings")

**NEW 150-7696** UP #9523 (yellow, gray w/"Wings")

**150-7602** Undecorated - CSX/UP Style

**150-7603** Undecorated - ATSF Style

**150-7604** Undecorated - CR Style

**Limited Quantity Available**

**150-7682** LMS - Locomotive Management Services #715

## DIESEL SHELL ASSEMBLIES

Bodies are molded in gray plastic and are complete with window "glass," add-on details and full sets of handrails, which are molded in black engineering plastic.

### Undecorated

**Limited Quantity Available**

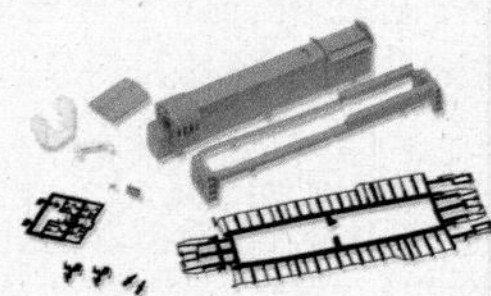

**150-805210** C424 Phase II **12.50**

**150-805225** C424 Phase I **12.75**

## LOCOMOTIVE MAINTENANCE

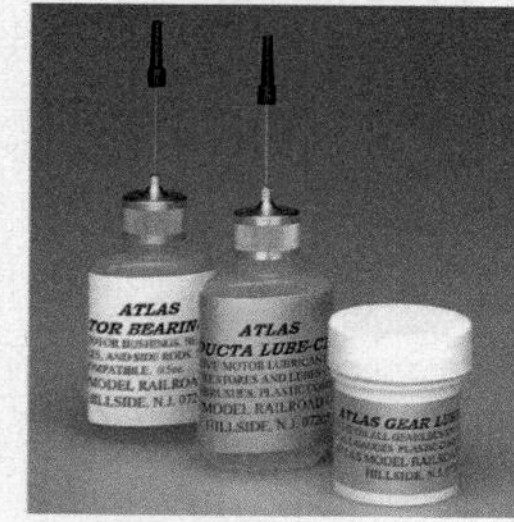


**150-193** Loco & Track Maintenance 3-Pack **27.50**



## DIAPHRAGMS

### For Stewart Hobbies F Units

147-9900

Designed for Kadee® #450 close couplers. Includes diaphragms and an alignment spacer.

**147-9900** Gray, 1 Pair **4.75**

**147-9903** Gray, 3 Pair **12.95**

**147-9910** Black, 1 Pair **4.75**

**147-9913** Black, 3 Pair **12.95**

### Stewart FT A-B Sets 4.95 ea

Includes new diaphragm for connection of A-B set.

**147-9700** Gray

**147-9710** Black

### For Athearn F Units

Draft gear boxes fit Kadee #5 couplers.

**147-9800** 1 Pair **4.95**
One pair of diaphragms and draft gear boxes for two A units or one B unit.

**147-6100** 2 Pair **2.75**
Draft gear box for A-B-A set (4 locomotive ends).

**147-9803** 3 Pair **13.95**
Diaphragms and draft gear for A-B-B-A sets (six locomotive ends).

**147-9810** Black **4.95**

**147-9813** Black, 3 Pair **13.95**

**147-9850** Athearn Genesis A-B Set, Gray, 1 Pair **4.95**

**147-9860** Athearn Genesis A-B Set, Black, 1 Pair **4.95**

## AMERICAN PLASTICS

### Train Display Cases

Showcase your favorite models in any setting with these handsome cases, ideal for home, office, layout room or shows. Each features a durable base with rubber "feet" so they're safe to place on any surface, and a crystal-clear cover to protect your work from dust and curious hands! Track and train not included.

### Plastic

**146-AD50** 18" 45.7cm **25.95**

**146-AD51** 24" 60.9cm **32.95**

**146-AD72** 30" 76.2cm **42.95**

### Wood Base

**146-H2024** Two-Tier 24" 60.9cm **115.00**

HO Scale locomotives are ready to run and feature prepainted and lettered plastic bodies, operating headlights and E-Z Mate® couplers. Engines feature an all-metal chassis with additional weight, worm gear and flywheel drive, five-pole motor and idler gear box.

## NEW PRODUCTS

### Loco Test/Display Rollers

### E-Z Riders™

Make sure your fleet is running smoothly with these handy ball-bearing rollers. E-Z Riders allow you to run your loco in place on your workbench or in a display case. Simply place them on a powered piece of track and place one under each of your loco's powered axles. Non-rolling (fixed) versions are also available to support unpowered axles. E-Z Riders work for HO and On30 locos.

**NEW 160-42901** Rolling pkg(4) **50.00**

**NEW 160-42902** Non-Rolling (Fixed) pkg(4) **25.00**

## STEAM LOCOMOTIVES

### USRA 0-6-0 65.00 ea

#### Vanderbilt Tender w/Smoke

**160-50701** UP Greyhound

**160-50711** GN

**160-50735** Erie

**NEW 160-50746** SAL (black, silver)

#### Short Haul Tender

**160-50440** Smokey Mountain Express

#### Slope Tender w/Smoke

**NEW 160-50601** UP #4432 (silver, black)

**160-50602** ATSF

**160-50612** B&O

**160-50614** PRR

**160-50620** NYC

**160-50649** Painted, Unlettered

### 2-6-0 Mogul 87.00 ea

**NEW 160-56501** DRGW (Flying Rio Grande Lettering)

**160-56508** Rock Island

**160-56513** CN

**160-56514** PRR

**160-56520** NYC

**160-56549** Painted, Unlettered

### 2-6-2 Prairie w/Smoke 87.00 ea

**160-51501** UP

**NEW 160-51504** SOU (green)

**160-51511** B&O

**NEW 160-51517** DRGW (Flying Rio Grande Lettering)

**160-51520** NYC

**160-51525** WP

**160-51549** Painted, Unlettered

### 4-4-0 American & Tender 85.00 ea

**160-51101** UP #119

**160-51112** B&O

**160-51114** PRR

**160-51116** CB&Q

**160-51124** Central Pacific "Jupiter"

**NEW 160-51144** B&O 1890's Version (Royal Blue)

## DIESEL LOCOMOTIVES

### MDT Plymouth Switchers 38.00 ea

**160-60002** ATSF (black, yellow)

**160-60016** CB&Q

**160-60039** Industrial (yellow w/red stripes)

### B23/B30-7 46.00 ea

Features flywheel and eight-wheel drive.

**160-11103** UP

**160-11105** ATSF (blue, yellow)

**160-11107** CR

**160-11112** BN

**160-11114** MP

**160-11116** CSX (blue, gray, yellow)

### GP50 Powered 40.00 ea

**160-61241** NS

**160-61242** N&W

### FT A Units 40.00 ea

Locomotives feature eight-wheel drive and E-Z Mate couplers.

**160-11702** ATSF (red & silver Warbonnet)

**160-11703** DRGW (yellow w/black)

**160-11704** CB&Q (white & red)

**160-11705** SAL (green, orange, yellow)

**160-11706** B&O (blue & gray)

**160-11707** NYC (Lightning Stripe)

**160-11708** Erie (yellow & black)

**NEW 160-11709** ATSF (blue, yellow)

USRA 0-6-0 Vanderbilt Tender w/Smoke UP Greyhound 160-50701

USRA 0-6-0 Short Haul Tender Smokey Mountain Express 160-50440

2-6-0 Mogul CN 160-56513

2-6-2 Prairie w/Smoke UP 160-51501

American 4-4-0 & Tender UP #119 160-51101

B23/B30-7 MP 160-11114

FT A Unit SAL 160-11705

## EMD FT B Unit - Powered 40.00 ea

Features eight-wheel drive.

**160-11802** ATSF (red & silver warbonnet)
**160-11803** DRGW (yellow, black)
**160-11804** CB&Q (white, red)
**160-11805** SAL (green, orange, yellow)
**160-11806** B&O (blue, gray)
**160-11807** NYC (lightning stripe)
**160-11808** Erie (yellow, black)
**NEW 160-11809** ATSF (blue, yellow)

## EMD GP38-2 Powered 49.00 ea

**160-61701** ATSF ("Warbonnet" blue, yellow)
**160-61702** NS
**160-61703** CSX ("Bright Future")
**160-61704** D&H (blue, gray)
**160-61705** Chessie System (blue, yellow, vermillion)
**160-61706** CP Rail (Action Red w/Multimark)

## EMD GP40 Powered 40.00 ea

Locomotives feature eight-wheel drive and E-Z Mate® couplers.

**160-63501** UP
**160-63502** ATSF
**160-63506** CR

**160-63509** C&O
**160-63537** WM (red, white & black)
**160-63548** Alaska

## Fairbanks-Morse H16-44 Powered 55.00 ea

Features flywheels and an eight-wheel drive.

**160-64102** ATSF ("Zebra Stripes" black, silver)
**160-64112** B&O (Cobalt Blue)
**160-64129** Canadian Pacific (gray, maroon w/script lettering)
**160-64130** Virginian (yellow, black)
**160-64131** NH (black, orange)
**160-64142** N&W (black, yellow)

## EMD SD40-2 Powered 49.00 ea

**160-67003** ATSF ("Warbonnet" blue, yellow)
**160-67004** NS
**160-67005** CSX ("Bright Future")
**160-67006** UP
**160-67007** BN (Cascade Green)
**160-67008** CP Rail (Action Red w/Multimark)

# TROLLEYS

These models are ready to run and feature prepainted and lettered plastic bodies, operating headlights and horn-hook couplers.

## Brill Trolley Car 32.00 ea

**160-61040** Christmas

**160-61047** Mainstreet
**NEW 160-61043** Green
**160-61048** Yellow #36

## PCC Trolley 35.00 ea

**160-62945** Philadelphia Transportation Company (dark green, tan)
**NEW 160-62947** BTC Powered (yellow, cream)

## Cable Cars 38.00 ea

**160-60530** Municipal Rail (red)

**160-60531** Municipal Rail (green)

**160-60532** Blue

# MAINTENANCE OF WAY VEHICLES

## Self-Propelled High Rail Vehicles 43.00 ea (Unless Noted)

**160-46201** Pick Up Truck

**160-46204** Rail Detector Step Van

**160-46207** 1950s 4x4

**NEW 160-46211** Bus

## Operating Gandy Dancer

**160-46210** Christmas **32.00**

# SMOKE FLUID

**160-99993** 2-1/4 fl. oz. **6.50**

# DCC EQUIPPED LOCOMOTIVES

## Steam Locomotives

## SP GS4 4-8-4 Powered w/DCC Decoder 159.00 ea

**160-50201** SP #4449 ("Railfan Daylight" red, orange, black)
**160-50202** SP #4446 ("Daylight" red, orange, black)
**160-50203** SP #4459 (Post-War Scheme black, silver)
**160-50204** SP #4464 (Post-War Scheme black)
**NEW 160-50205** 1976 American Freedom Train #4449

## NYC 4-8-4 "Niagara" Post-War Powered w/DCC Decoder 159.00 ea

**160-50301** NYC #6009
**160-50302** NYC #6014

**160-50303** NYC #6016
**160-50304** NYC #6020

NYC 4-8-4 "Niagara" Post-War Powered w/DCC Decoder 160-50302

EMD FT B Unit Powered ATSF 160-11802

EMD GP38-2 Powered D&H 160-61704

EMD GP40 Powered Alaska 160-63548

Fairbanks-Morse H16-44 Powered Virginian 160-64130

EMD SD40-2 Powered NS 160-67004

SP GS4 4-8-4 Powered w/DCC Decoder SP #4449 160-50201

### ATSF 4-8-4 Powered w/DCC Decoder 159.00 ea

Locos wear the 40s-50s scheme, black with silver lettering and trim.

**160-50801** ATSF #3777
**160-50802** ATSF #3781
**160-50803** ATSF #3783
**160-50804** ATSF #3784

## Diesel Locomotives

### EMD SD40-2 Powered w/DCC Decoder 65.00 ea

**160-60901** ATSF ("Warbonnet" blue, yellow)
**160-60902** NS

**160-60903** CSX ("Bright Future")

**160-60904** UP
**160-60905** BN (Cascade Green)
**160-60906** CP (Action Red w/ Multimark)

### EMD GP38-2 Powered w/DCC Decoder 65.00 ea

**160-61101** ATSF ("Warbonnet" blue, yellow)
**160-61102** NS
**160-61103** CSX ("Bright Future")
**160-61104** D&H (blue, gray)
**160-61105** Chessie System (blue, yellow, vermillion)
**160-61106** CP (Action Red w/ Multimark)
**NEW 160-61107** UP

### GE 70-Tonner Powered w/DCC Decoder 60.00 ea

Perfect for switching and branch line runs, the 70-Tonner was owned by many railroads and industries to handle switching and operations over light-railed branches.

**160-60601** SP #5101
**160-60602** SP #5106

**160-60603** L&N #98
**160-60604** L&N #99
**160-60605** Bethlehem Steel #56
**160-60606** Bethlehem Steel #58

**160-60607** Painted, Unlettered (yellow w/black stripes)
**160-60608** Painted, Unlettered (green)
**160-60609** Painted, Unlettered (red)

### EMD GP35 Powered w/DCC Decoder 60.00 ea

This 60s-era road unit is perfect for powering fast freights on your railroad.

**160-60701** CR #2273
**160-60702** CR #2269
**160-60703** CSX #4402
**160-60704** CSX #4406

**160-60705** CP #8205
**160-60706** CP #8210
**160-60707** WM #3576
**160-60708** WM #3579

**160-60709** CP Rail (Multimark) #5003
**160-60710** CP Rail (Multimark) #5009
**160-60711** Undecorated
**NEW 160-60712** DRGW (Flying Rio Grande Lettering) 60.00

### EMD GP30 Powered w/DCC Decoder 60.00 ea

This early 60s road unit was the GP35's predecessor; its distinctive styling will add variety to your loco fleet.

**160-60801** RDG #5516
**160-60802** RDG #5518
**160-60803** GN #3007
**160-60804** GN #3009

**160-60805** B&O #6918
**160-60806** B&O #6936
**160-60807** PRR #2205
**160-60808** PRR #2208

**160-60809** NKP #903
**160-60810** NKP #905
**160-60812** ATSF #3230 ("Warbonnet" blue, yellow)

**160-60813** ATSF #3232 ("Warbonnet" blue, yellow)
**160-60811** Undecorated

### E-Z Command® EMD FT Locomotives w/DCC Decoder Powered

Each includes a DCC decoder. See the Bachmann listing in the Command Control section of this Reference Book for more details on the E-Z Command control system.

**EMD FT-A 60.00 ea**

**160-60102** ATSF (silver, red)
**160-60112** B&O

**160-60116** CB&Q
**160-60117** DRGW

**160-60120** NYC
**160-60135** Erie

**NEW 160-60139** ATSF (blue, yellow)
**160-60147** SAL

**FT-B Powered 60.00 ea**

Cabless boosters are have all the features of their companion FT-As and are decorated to match.

**160-60202** ATSF (silver, red)

**160-60212** B&O

**160-60216** CB&Q
**160-60217** DRGW

ATSF 4-8-4 Powered w/DCC Decoder ATSF #3781 160-50802

EMD SD40-2 BN 160-60905

GE 70-Tonner SP #5106 160-60602

EMD GP35 WM #3576 160-60707

EMD GP30 GN #3007 160-60803

EMD FT-A DRGW 160-60117

EMD FT-B DRGW 160-60217

**160-60220** NYC

**160-60235** Erie

**NEW 160-60239** ATSF (blue, yellow)

**160-60247** Seaboard

### EMD GP40 w/DCC Decoder 60.00 ea

**160-60301** UP

**160-60302** ATSF (blue, yellow)

**160-60306** CR

**160-60309** Chessie

**160-60337** WM

**160-60348** Alaska Railroad

### EMD GP50 w/DCC Decoder 60.00 ea

**160-60404** SOU

**160-60441** NS

**160-60442** N&W

EMD FT-B ATSF 160-60239

EMD GP40 WM 160-60337

EMD GP50 NS 160-60441

Spectrum®

Spectrum locomotives take detailing to a higher level. Locos feature five-pole, skew-wound motors, flywheels, detailed bodies loaded with hand-applied details and accurate painting and printing. All locos are DCC-ready and those so noted come with factory-installed DCC decoders.

USRA Light 2-10-2 w/Long Tender Duluth, Missabe & Iron Range #506 160-83803

N&W Class J 4-8-4 (Passenger Version) N&W #611 160-83904

4-8-2 Heavy Mountain w/Long Tender C&O J2 #544 160-84202

4-8-2 Heavy Mountain w/Long Tender SP #4361 160-84204

2-10-0 Russian Decapod ATSF #2552 160-84302

PRR K4 4-6-2 Pacific PRR #5404 160-84402

Baldwin 2-8-0 Consolidation w/Medium Tender SOU #721 160-84503

## NEW PRODUCTS

### Steam Locomotives

### Sound & DCC Decoder Equipped

Bachmann sound-equipped locomotives feature Soundtraxx™ Tsunami® sound and DCC decoder that allows operation on any DCC- or standard DC-controlled layout with no modifications. Other DCC features include short, extended, and advanced consisting addressing modes, paged, register, direct, and operations-mode programming and an extensive range of CVs. In addition to sound and DCC decoders, these locos also have all the detail features of other Spectrum locos.

### USRA Light 2-10-2 w/Long Tender 345.00 ea

**NEW 160-83802** SOU #5216

**NEW 160-83803** Duluth, Missabe & Iron Range #506

**NEW 160-83804** SAL #2489

**NEW 160-83801** Painted, Unlettered

### N&W Class J 4-8-4 (Passenger Version) 325.00 ea

**NEW 160-83902** N&W #606 (1950s scheme)

**NEW 160-83903** N&W #612 (1950s scheme)

**NEW 160-83904** N&W #611 (1981-1993 excursion scheme)

### 4-8-2 Heavy Mountain w/Long Tender 310.00 ea

**NEW 160-84202** C&O J2 #544 (w/Flying Pumps & Vanderbilt Tender)

**NEW 160-84203** N&W #118

**NEW 160-84204** SP #4361

### 2-10-0 Russian Decapod 290.00 ea

**NEW 160-84302** ATSF #2552

**NEW 160-84303** WM #1107

### PRR K4 4-6-2 Pacific 270.00 ea

**NEW 160-84402** PRR #5404; 1920s Multi-Stripe Scheme (Brunsiwck Green, gold)

**NEW 160-84403** PRR #1361; Post-War w/Modern Pilot

**NEW 160-84404** PRR #5442; Pre-War w/Slat Pilot

### Baldwin 2-8-0 Consolidation w/Medium Tender 275.00 ea

**NEW 160-84502** B&O #2788

**NEW 160-84503** SOU #721

**NEW 160-84504** WM #744

**NEW 160-84505** ATSF #2528

**NEW 160-84501** Painted Black, Unlettered

## DCC Decoder Equipped

### Chinese Class SY 2-8-2 Mikado 335.00 ea

Class SY 2-8-2s were constructed in China until the 1990s, and some were still in use in 2007 hauling coal. Susquehanna #142 was built for excursion service in 1989. These detailed, smooth-running models come equipped with a DCC decoder and E-Z Mate® couplers.

**NEW 160-83212** Susquehanna #142

**NEW 160-83211** Painted, Unlettered

## Gas-Electric Railcars

### EMC Gas Electric Doodlebug w/Coach Trailer & DCC Decoder 180.00 ea

Based on cars built by the Electro-Motive Corporation in the 20s and 30s, these models come equipped with a factory-installed DCC decoder. In service, the prototypes often towed a trailer coach to boost passenger capacity on busy days. These sets include the Doodlebug and a 72' trailer; both feature lighted interiors with seat details.

**NEW 160-81422** B&O (Pullman Green)

**NEW 160-81423** B&M (maroon)

**NEW 160-81424** Maryland & Pennsylvania #81

**NEW 160-81425** SAL

**NEW 160-81426** NYC

**NEW 160-81421** Unlettered (Pullman Green)

## SPECTRUM STEAM LOCOMOTIVES

### Norfolk & Western Class J 4-8-4 w/DCC Decoder 235.00 ea

#### Passenger Version

Designed for optimum speeds at the head of the road's crack passenger trains, the J was tested at speeds of 115mph, but the engineer closed the throttle out of concern for safety. These well-liked locos lasted in service into the late 1950s. One notable surviving J, #611, was the star on excursion trains into the early 1990s.

**160-82121** #610

**160-82122** #611

#### Freight Version

The same locomotive that was a star performer on varnish was also adept at handling long drag freights. In service, these engines carried an auxilliary water tender which extended its operating range. This model includes a tender with doghouse and water tender.

**160-82104** #603

**160-82105** #608

### USRA Light 2-10-2 w/DCC Decoder 225.00 ea

Designed for heavy drag freight service, the USRA Light was used by a variety of railroads. This detailed model is patterned after these locos as they looked in the middle to late-steam era. Features include diecast boiler, frame and cylinders, and railroad-specific details such Southern or Walschaert valve gear and appropriate tenders for each roadname.

**160-83302** Chicago & Illinois Midland #600

**160-83303** Chicago & Illinois Midland #603

**160-83304** SOU #5212

**160-83305** SOU #5224

**160-83306** Duluth, Missabe & Iron Range #508

**160-83307** Duluth, Missabe & Iron Range #511

**160-83308** CN #4202

**160-83309** CN #4209

**160-83310** Seaboard Air Line #2485

**160-83311** Seaboard Air Line #2491

**160-83312** Kansas City Southern #220

**160-83313** Kansas City Southern #223

**160-83301** Painted, Unlettered (black)

### 2-8-0 Consolidation w/DCC Decoder 171.00 ea

Loaded with plenty of applied details and featuring a smooth-running mechanism, these 2-8-0s are perfect for any freight your steam-era railroad needs to run.

**160-83602** B&O #2781

**160-83603** SOU #722 (green)

**160-83604** WM #761 ("Fireball" Scheme)

**160-83605** ATSF #2526

**160-83606** Rock Island #2119

**160-83607** UP #618 w/Medium Vanderbilt Coal Tender

**160-83601** Painted, Unlettered (black)

N&W J Class 4-8-4 Powered w/Tender Freight Version #608 160-82105

## SPECTRUM DIESEL LOCOMOTIVES

### SD45 w/DCC Decoder 115.00 ea

In the 60s when the 3600-horsepower SD45 was the last word in heavy road units. Owned by railroads across the U.S., many of these units are still in service today. this model features many applied details, a smooth-running, flywheel-equipped mechanism, factory installed DCC decoder and E-Z Mate knuckle couplers.

**160-82712** EL #3614

**160-82713** NP #3605

**160-82714** GN #407

**160-82715** RDG #7604

**160-82716** PRR #6122

**160-82717** CR #6144

**160-82718** UP #17

**160-82719** ATSF #5418

**160-82711** Undecorated

### GE Dash 8-40CW w/DCC Decoder 160.00 ea

Packing 4000 horsepower, this powerful locomotive is at home hauling any modern-era freight. In service since the 1990s, the loco features a wide nose for added crew comfort and protection. The spectrum replical includes a detailed body, many applied details, a smooth-running, flywheel-equipped mechanism, factory installed DCC decoder and E-Z Mate knuckle couplers.

**160-83502** UP #9374

**160-83503** ATSF #808

**160-83504** CR #6087

**160-83505** CSX #7661

**160-83506** BNSF #812

**160-83501** Undecorated

Chinese Class SY 2-8-2 Mikado Susquehanna #142 160-83212

EMC Gas Electric Doodlebug w/Coach Trailer & DCC Decoder Unlettered 160-81421

USRA Light 2-10-2 w/DCC Decoder Chicago & Illinois Midland #600 160-83302

USRA Light 2-10-2 w/DCC Decoder CN #4202 160-83308

2-8-0 Consolidation SOU #722 160-83603

2-8-0 Consolidation UP #618 160-83607

GE Dash 8-40CW w/DCC Decoder BNSF #812 160-83506

## STEAM LOCOMOTIVES

### Baldwin 4-6-0 175.00 ea

These DCC-ready locomotive include all-metal valve gear, operating headlight, detailed backhead, RP25 metal wheels and body-mounted E-Z Mate® Mark II couplers.

**With Low Boiler**

**160-82302** Maryland & Pennsylvania

**160-82301** Painted, Unlettered (black)

**With High Boiler**

**160-82307** Painted, Unlettered (black)

### USRA Heavy Mountain 4-8-2 210.00 ea

The DCC-ready locomotives feature a glowing firebox, diecast detail parts, cab window glazing, detailed cab interior, realistic tender load and body-mounted E-Z Mate Mark II couplers.

**With Flying Pumps & Vandy Tender**

**160-82503** C&O J2

**With Large Coal Tender**

**160-82505** Richmond, Fredericksburg & Potomac

**160-82506** IC

**160-82501** Painted, Unlettered

### 2-8-0 Consolidation

**Limited Quantity Available**

**160-11417** Baldwin Loco Works (Demo) 140.00

### K4 4-6-2 Pacific Powered w/Tender 155.00 ea

**Pre-War w/Slat Pilot**

Engines are DCC ready.

**160-84113** PRR #5448

**160-84114** PRR #5475

**Post-War w/Modern Pilot**

**160-84013** PRR #3750

**160-84014** PRR #1361

### 2-10-0 Russian Decapod Powered 170.00 ea

Engines are DCC ready.

**160-81702** WM ("Fireball" Scheme)

**160-81703** Atlantic Coast Line

**160-81706** Seaboard Air Line

**160-81707** Susquehanna

**160-81708** Nashville, Chattanooga & St. Louis

**160-81701** Painted, Unlettered

### 55-Ton Class B Two-Truck Climax - Powered 275.00 ea

These DCC-ready engines feature diecast construction, a five-pole skew-wound motor, all-wheel electrical pickup, three-gearbox power train, scale-speed gearing, detailed cab interior, amber LED headlight and backup light, and various separately applied details.

**160-82802** Moore Keppel Lumber Company #3

**160-82803** West Virginia Pulp & Paper #6

**160-82805** W. M. Ritter Lumber Co.

**160-82806** Clear Lake Lumber Co.

### Shay 80-Ton Three-Truck Powered 275.00 ea

Engines are DCC ready.

**160-81903** Greenbrier & Elk River, Wood Cab

**160-81904** Ely Thomas Lumber Co., Wood Cab

**160-81905** Weyerhauser Timber, Steel Cab

**160-81908** W.M. Ritter Lumber Company w/Wood Cab

**160-81909** West Virginia Pulp &Paper w/Wood Cab

**160-81901** Painted, Unlettered, Wood Cab

**160-81902** Painted, Unlettered, Steel Cab

**160-81907** Painted, Unlettered w/Oil Burner & Steel Cab

## Tenders

### Auxiliary Water Tenders 35.00 ea

**160-89922** N&W (maroon)

**160-89923** N&W (black w/yellow)

**160-89924** B&O

**160-89921** Painted, Unlettered (black)

### Vanderbilt Tenders

**Medium Length 43.00 ea**

These four-wheel tenders are DCC ready.

**160-89902** UP

**160-89903** SP

**160-89904** B&O

**160-89901** Painted, Unlettered w/Coal Load

**160-89905** Painted, Unlettered w/Oil Bunker

**Long 43.00 ea**

**160-89841** C&O; Painted & Lettered, No Engine Number

**160-89842** Painted, Unlettered

**Hicken Style 43.00 ea**

**160-89912** SP

**160-89911** Painted, Unlettered

### Baldwin Small Stock Tender

**160-89821** Painted, Unlettered 43.00

### USRA Coal Tenders 43.00 ea

**Medium**

**160-89731** Painted, Unlettered

**Long (12,000-Gallon)**

**160-89832** C&O

**160-89831** Painted, Unlettered

55-Ton Class B Two-Truck Climax West Virginia Pulp & Paper #6 160-82803

Baldwin 4-6-0 w/Low Boiler Maryland & Pennsylvania 160-82302

USRA Heavy Mountain w/Large Coal Tender Richmond, Fredericksburg & Potomac 160-82505

K4 4-6-2 Pacific Pre-War w/Slat Pilot PRR 160-84114

K4 4-6-2 Pacific Post-War w/Modern Pilot PRR 160-84014

2-10-0 Russian Decapod WM 160-81702

Shay 80-Ton Three-Truck Powered WVP&P 160-81909

Auxiliary Water Tender N&W 160-89922

## DIESEL LOCOMOTIVES

### GE 44-Tonner Powered Switchers 85.00 ea

These DCC-ready switchers feature a directional headlight, a five-pole skew-wound motor, diecast chassis, blackened RP25 wheels, and E-Z Mate® Mark II couplers. Each locomotive features such separately applied details as grab irons, windshield wipers and handrails.

**160-80038** PRR

**160-80039** NH

**160-80041** ATSF

**160-80043** WM

**160-80044** B&O

**160-80035** Unlettered, Yellow w/Safety Stripes

## ELECTRIC LOCOMOTIVES

### Amtrak® Acela℠ Dual Locomotive Set

**160-81949 180.00**
Includes one powered and one dummy electric loco with directional headlights, ditch lights and markers. May be run from track or overhead power. DCC ready.

### Amtrak Acela HHP Powered 158.00 ea

These DCC-ready locomotives feature an interior selector switch for choice between rail or pantograph operation, diecast gear towers and chassis, a five-pole skew-wound motor, operating doors and directional headlights, ditchlights and markers.

**160-83003** #655
**160-83004** #656
**160-83005** #664

### GE E-33 130.00 ea

These DCC-ready engines are perfect for any electrified operation on your HO Scale layout! Locomotives feature a diecast frame, operating pantograph, working headlight, 12-wheel drive and body-mounted E-Z Mate Mark IIcouplers. Available in two roadnumbers, unless noted.

**160-82402** Virginian
**160-82403** N&W
Available with or without roadnumbers.
**160-82405** PC

**160-82406** CR

**160-82407** NH #304

Amtrak Acela Dual Locomotive Set 160-81949

Blackstone Models™

DIVISION OF SOUNDTRAXX™

## NEW PRODUCTS

## K-27 PARTS

**NEW 678-370101** Snowplow **24.95**

**NEW 678-370102** Doghouse **8.95**

**NEW 678-826501** Tsumani Sound System **119.00**
This high-performance digital decoder integrates a full-featured sound system with 22 steam sound effects, lighting, a motor controller and a DCC decoder into a single, integrated package. Compatible with the NMRA DCC standards and Recommended Practices, can also be used on DC layouts and controlled with a conventional power pack. The Tsunami is designed specifically for plug-and-play installation in the Blackstone Models K-27 locomotive series.

## DENVER & RIO GRANDE WESTERN K-27 2-8-2 STEAM LOCOS

One of the best-known narrow gauge steam locos, the K-27 (originally Class 125) "Mudhens" were first delivered to the Denver & Rio Grande in 1903. With a tractive effort of over 27,000 pounds, these were some of the biggest and most powerful locos on the narrow gauge at that time. All 15 (#450-464) were delivered with Vauclain compound cylinders, which were later replaced with single expansion cylinders and slide valves due to high maintenance costs. In later years, 11 engines were refitted with modern piston valve cylinders, which are the prototype for this model.

Denver & Rio Grande Western K-27 2-8-2 #453 w/Outboard Piston Valves 678-310102S

Denver & Rio Grande Western K-27 2-8-2 #456 w/Inboard Piston Valves 678-310122S

Affordably priced, these authentic HOn3 replicas feature period paint schemes and prototype-specific details. Engines are available with a SoundTraxx™ Tsunami™ digital sound decoder, which provides authentic sound for DCC or DC operations; standard DC-powered locos without sound are also available.

### With Outboard Piston Valves

#### With Tsunami Sound Decoder 419.00 ea (Unless Noted)

**678-310102S** #453 w/Doghouse, Switcher Pilot/Tender Steps, Backup Light, Square-Corner Tender

**678-310106S** #463 w/Road Pilot & Backup Light

**678-310107S** #464 w/Snowplow, Backup Light & Square Corner Tender

**Pre-1936 "Royal Gorge" Herald**
**678-310103S** #455 w/Green Boiler

**Late 30s "Moffat Tunnel" Herald**
**678-310104S** #459 w/Road Pilot, Backup Light

**Rio Grande Southern w/"Sunrise" Herald**
**678-310131S** #455 w/Plow; Post Wreck Details & Tender **449.00**

**Painted, Unlettered**
**678-310100S** w/Road Pilot, Backup Light

#### No Sound 339.00 ea (Unless Noted)

**678-310102** #453 w/Doghouse, Switcher Pilot/Tender Steps, Backup Light, Square-Corner Tender

**678-310106** #463 w/Road Pilot & Backup Light

**678-310107** #464 w/Snowplow, Backup Light & Square Corner Tender

**Pre-1936 "Royal Gorge" Herald**
**678-310103** #455 w/Green Boiler

**Late 30s "Moffat Tunnel" Herald**
**678-310104** #459 w/Road Pilot, Backup Light

**Rio Grande Southern w/"Sunrise" Herald**
**678-310131** #455 w/Plow; Post Wreck Details & Tender **369.00**

**Painted, Unlettered**
**678-310100** w/Road Pilot, Backup Light

### With Inboard Piston Valves

#### With Tsunami Sound Decoder 419.00 ea

**"Flying" Rio Grande**
**678-310121S** #454 Switcher Pilot/Tender Steps, Backup Light

**678-310124S** #461 w/Road Pilot

**Late 30s "Moffat Tunnel" Herald**
**678-310122S** #456 w/Switcher Pilot/Tender Steps, Backup Light

**Rio Grande Southern w/"Sunrise" Herald**
**678-310125S** #461 w/Road Pilot

#### No Sound 339.00 ea

**"Flying" Rio Grande**
**678-310121** #454 Switcher Pilot/Tender Steps, Backup Light

**678-310124** #461 w/Road Pilot

**Late 30s "Moffat Tunnel" Herald**
**678-310122** #456 w/Switcher Pilot/Tender Steps, Backup Light

**Rio Grande Southern w/"Sunrise" Herald**
**678-310125** #461 w/Road Pilot

NEW NH I-5 4-6-4 187-1284

**HO BlueLine Series**

BlueLine locomotives are designed for operation on standard DC layouts, but are DCC ready. Each includes a factory-installed sound system, smooth-running mechanism with five-pole motor and dual flywheels and Precision Motor Control, magnetic knuckle couplers and plenty of applied details. They will operate on Code 70, 83 and 100 rail and can be operated on minimum 18" radius curves. For easy plug-and-play to DCC locos come equipped with and eight-pin DCC socket so you can add the decoder of your choice (sold separately).

**HO Paragon Series Brass-Hybrid**

Brass-hybrids are accurately detailed models made of brass and other materials. All brass-hybrid models include factory-installed sound and are equipped for DC or DCC operation. Other features include nickel silver rods and valve gear, full cab detail, Kadee® operating scale couplers, builder's plate, prototypical light operation with golden white LED headlight and premium caliber painting.

**HO Broadway Brass Museum Series**

Broadway Brass Museum Series locos feature a all-brass locomotive and tender with full underbody detail, all the performance features of brass-hybrid locos plus window glazing, sprung drivers, operating power reverse, trust plate on tender and premium caliber painting. A state-of-the-art display case with roller bearings and power inputs is included for in-place display operation.

NEW C&O T-1 2-10-4 C&O #3007 187-5017

Different Roadnumber Shown

NEW PRR M1a 4-8-2 187-5033

# NEW PRODUCTS

## Steam

### NH I-5 4-6-4

The ten 4-6-4 Baldwin-built locomotives New Haven bought in 1937 were its last steam locos. These streamlined, stainless-steel striped engines remained in service until the early 50s.

**Brass-Hybrid 450.00 ea**

**NEW 187-1280** NH #1401 (Original Block Lettering)

**NEW 187-1281** NH #1402 (Small Script)

**NEW 187-1282** NH #1406 (Large Script)

**NEW 187-1283** NH #1407 (Large Script)

**NEW 187-1820** NH #1403 (Original Block Lettering)

**NEW 187-1821** NH #1400 (Small Shoreline Service Script)

**NEW 187-1822** NH #1405 (Small Shoreline Service Script)

**NEW 187-1284** Unnumbered, Includes Decals

**Broadway Brass Museum Series 1695.00 ea**

**NEW 187-1087** NH #1403 (Original Block Lettering)

**NEW 187-1088** NH #1400 (Small Shoreline Service Script)

**NEW 187-1089** NH #1409 (Small Shoreline Service Script)

**NEW 187-1817** NH #1401 (Original Block Lettering)

**NEW 187-1818** NH #1402 (Small Shoreline Service Script)

**NEW 187-1819** NH #1407 (Small Shoreline Service Script)

**NEW 187-1816** Unpainted

NEW N&W Class A 2-6-6-4 N&W #1218 187-5078

### NYC L-4 Mohawk 4-8-2

Because their route was flat, New York Central called their 4-8-2s "Mohawks" after the Mohawk River instead of the more familiar "Mountains." NYC had four different classes of Mohawks, L-1 through L-4 used for both freight and passenger service. The fifty L-4s produced by Lima Locomotive Works in 1943 had huge coal tenders riding on two six-wheel trucks. Smoke deflectors were added to many units in later years.

**Brass-Hybrid 450.00 ea**

**NEW 187-1285** L-4a Boxpok Drivers, Louvered Pump Shield NYC #3101

**NEW 187-1286** L-4a Scullin Drivers, Screen Pump Shield NYC #3124

**NEW 187-1287** L-4b Scullin Drivers, Louvered Pump Shield NYC #3149

**NEW 187-1288** L-4b Boxpok Drivers, Screen Pump Shield NYC #3144

**NEW 187-1335** L-4b Boxpok Drivers, Screen Pump Shield Undecorated

**Broadway Brass Museum Series 1795.00 ea**

**NEW 187-1289** L-4a Boxpok Drivers, Louvered Pump Shield NYC #3110

**NEW 187-1290** L-4a Scullin Drivers, Screen Pump Shield NYC #3122

**NEW 187-1291** L-4b Scullin Drivers, Louvered Pump Shield NYC #3136

**NEW 187-1292** L-4b Boxpok Drivers, Screen Pump Shield NYC #3143

**NEW 187-1336** L-4b Boxpok Drivers, Screen Pump Shield Undecorated

### UP Class TTT-6 2-10-2

Union Pacific labeled their 2-10-2s with "TTT" to designate the wheel configuration. These powerful locomotives were ideal for hauling heavy tonnage. UP's TTT-6 and 7 were the last and the largest of the class. The TTTs received many modifications through their careers and served until the mid 50s. These detailed models are replicas of modernized engines equipped with Young valve gear, Worthington 4BL feedwater heater and 13,500-gallon oil or coal tender as indicated. All are decorated in black and graphite with aluminum lettering unless noted.

**Brass-Hybrid 450.00 ea**

**NEW 187-1293** Coal UP #5044

**NEW 187-1294** Coal UP #5053

**NEW 187-1295** Oil UP #5507

**NEW 187-1296** Oil UP #5509

**NEW 187-1337** Oil Undecorated

**Broadway Brass Museum Series 1795.00 ea**

**NEW 187-1297** Coal UP #5043

**NEW 187-1298** Coal UP #5057

**NEW 187-1299** Oil UP #5516

**NEW 187-1300** Oil UP #5518

**NEW 187-1338** Oil Unpainted

### C&O T-1 2-10-4 w/Sound

**Blue Line Series 299.99 ea**

**NEW 187-5017** C&O #3007

**NEW 187-5018** C&O #3023

**NEW 187-5019** Undecorated

For Up-To-Date Information and News Bookmark Walthers Web site at

**www.walthers.com**

## PRR M1a 4-8-2 w/Sound

**BlueLine Series 269.99 ea**

**NEW 187-5033** PRR #6778 Post 1946 Version

**NEW 187-5034** PRR #6791 Post 1946 Version

**NEW 187-5035** Unlettered, Unnumbered

## PRR M1b 4-8-2 w/Sound

**BlueLine Series 269.99 ea**

**NEW 187-5036** PRR #6755 Standard Version

**NEW 187-5037** PRR #6794 Standard Version

**NEW 187-5038** Unlettered, Unnumbered

## N&W Class A 2-6-6-4 w/Sound

**BlueLine Series 399.99 ea**

**NEW 187-5077** N&W #1214

**NEW 187-5078** N&W #1218

**NEW 187-5079** Unnumbered, Unlettered

## UP Big Boy 4-8-8-4 w/Sound

**BlueLine Series 427.99 ea**

**NEW 187-5080** UP #4004 (1941, After Cooler)

**NEW 187-5081** UP #4017 (1941, After Cooler)

**NEW 187-5082** UP #4020 (1944)

**NEW 187-5083** UP #4023 (1944)

## PRR J1 2-10-4 w/Sound

**BlueLine Series 299.99 ea**

**NEW 187-5085** PRR #6165

**NEW 187-5086** PRR #6432

**NEW 187-5087** Unnumbered, Unlettered

## BlueLine Diesels w/Sound

## EMD F7 w/Sound

**Powered A/Unpowered B Sets 269.99 ea**

**NEW 187-5101** ATSF #38L/38A (Warbonnet, silver, red)

**NEW 187-5102** MILW #84A/84B (orange, maroon As-Delivered)

**NEW 187-5103** NYC #1638/2426 (Lightning Stripe)

**NEW 187-5104** PRR #9648A/9648B (Brunswick Green, Single Stripe)

**NEW 187-5105** UP #1467/1467B

**Powered A Unit 169.99 ea**

**NEW 187-5106** ATSF #38C (Warbonnet, silver, red)

**NEW 187-5108** MILW #84D (orange, maroon As-Delivered)

**NEW 187-5110** NYC #1646 (Lightning Stripe)

**NEW 187-5112** PRR #9650A (Brunswick Green, Single Stripe)

**NEW 187-5114** UP #1469

**NEW 187-5116** Undecorated

**Powered B Unit 159.99 ea**

**NEW 187-5107** ATSF #38B (Warbonnet, silver, red)

**NEW 187-5109** MILW #84C (orange, maroon As-Delivered)

**NEW 187-5111** NYC #2429 (Lightning Stripe)

**NEW 187-5113** PRR #9650B (Brunswick Green, Single Stripe)

**NEW 187-5115** UP #1474C

**NEW 187-5117** Undecorated

**NEW** PRR M1a 4-8-2 Unlettered, Unnumbered 187-5035

**NEW** PRR M1b 4-8-2 PRR #6755 187-5036

**NEW** PRR J1 2-10-4 PRR #6165 187-5085

**NEW** UP Big Boy 4-8-8-4 UP #4023 187-5083

## EMD SD40-2 w/Sound
**169.99 ea**

**NEW 187-5000** ATSF #5032

**NEW 187-5001** ATSF #5042

**NEW 187-5002** Chessie/B&O #7600

**NEW 187-5003** Chessie/B&O #7606

**NEW 187-5004** BNSF #6701

**NEW 187-5005** BNSF #6705

**NEW 187-5006** CN (GTW) #5931

**NEW 187-5007** CN (GTW) #5932

**NEW 187-5008** FEC #701

**NEW 187-5009** FEC #703

**NEW 187-5010** MILW #133

**NEW 187-5011** MILW #136

**NEW 187-5012** NS #1643

**NEW 187-5013** NS #1649

**NEW 187-5014** UP #3055

**NEW 187-5015** UP #3162

**NEW 187-5016** Undecorated

## EMD SD9 w/Sound
**169.99 ea**

**NEW 187-5020** MILW #508

**NEW 187-5021** MILW #533

**NEW 187-5022** PC #6913

**NEW 187-5023** PC #6915

**NEW 187-5024** PRR #7600

**NEW 187-5025** PRR #7611

**NEW 187-5026** CNW #1701

**NEW 187-5027** CNW #1702

Different Roadnumber Shown

**NEW 187-5028** BN #6128

**NEW 187-5029** BN #6131

**NEW 187-5030** SOU #202

**NEW 187-5031** SOU #203

**NEW 187-5032** Undecorated

## GE C30-7 w/Sound
**169.99 ea**

**NEW 187-5040** ATSF #8022 (Warbonnet, blue, yellow)

**NEW 187-5041** ATSF #8023 (Warbonnet, blue, yellow)

**NEW 187-5042** ATSF #8018 (Merger Scheme, red, yellow)

**NEW 187-5043** ATSF #8051 (Merger Scheme, red, yellow)

**NEW 187-5044** Family Lines/L&N #7051

**NEW 187-5045** Family Lines/ L&N #7050

**NEW 187-5046** Lake Superior & Ishpeming #3073 (BN Patch)

**NEW 187-5047** Lake Superior & Ishpeming #3074 (BN Patch)

**NEW 187-5048** NS #8004 (black)

Different Roadnumber Shown

**NEW 187-5049** NS #8005 (black)

Different Roadnumber Shown

**NEW 187-5050** UP #2477 (We Will Deliver Slogan)

**NEW 187-5051** UP #2451 (We Will Deliver Slogan)

**NEW 187-5052** Undecorated

**NEW** EMD SD40-2 ATSF #5032 187-5000

**NEW** EMD SD40-2 Chessie/B&O #7600 187-5002

**NEW** EMD SD40-2 BNSF #6701 187-5004

**NEW** EMD SD40-2 MILW #133 187-5010

## GE AC6000CW w/Sound 169.99 ea

**NEW 187-5055** UP #7510 (Low Ditch Lights)

**NEW 187-5056** UP #7549 (Low Ditch Lights)

**NEW 187-5057** CSX #5000 (Diversity Scheme; High Ditch Lights)

**NEW 187-5058** CSX #5001 (Diversity Scheme; High Ditch Lights)

**NEW 187-5059** BHP Iron Ore #6071 (Blue Scheme; Low Ditch Lights)

**NEW 187-5060** BHP Iron Ore #6076 (Bubbles Scheme; Low Ditch Lights)

**NEW 187-5061** SP #601 (Speed Lettering; Low Ditch Lights)

**NEW 187-5062** SP #602 (Speed Lettering; Low Ditch Lights)

**NEW 187-5063** CP #9800 (Golden Beaver Scheme; High Ditch Light)

**NEW 187-5064** CP #9801 (Golden Beaver Scheme; High Ditch Light)

**NEW 187-5065** Unpainted w/UP Details & Low Ditch Lights

**NEW 187-5066** Unpainted w/CSX Details & High Ditch Lights

## EMD SD7 w/Sound 169.99 ea

Different Roadnumber Shown

**NEW 187-5067** B&O #762 (blue, gray)

**NEW 187-5068** B&O #763 (blue, gray)

Different Roadnumber Shown

**NEW 187-5069** BN #6011 (Cascade Green, black)

**NEW 187-5070** BN #6015 (Cascade Green, black)

Different Roadnumber Shown

**NEW 187-5071** PRR #8588 (Brunswick Green)

**NEW 187-5072** PRR #8589 (Brunswick Green)

**NEW 187-5073** UP #776 (Dependable Transportation Slogan)

**NEW 187-5074** UP #778 (Dependable Transportation Slogan)

**NEW 187-5075** Undecorated

## Alco RSD-15 w/Sound

### Low Hood 169.99 ea

**NEW 187-5090** ATSF #9821 (blue, yellow)

**NEW 187-5091** ATSF #9822 (blue, yellow)

**NEW 187-5092** ATSF #808 (Zebra Stripe)

**NEW 187-5093** ATSF #815 (Zebra Stripe)

**NEW 187-5097** SP #250 (dark gray, scarlet)

**NEW 187-5098** SP #251 (dark gray, scarlet)

**NEW 187-5099** Undecorated

### High Hood 169.99 ea

**NEW 187-5089** CN #1754

**NEW 187-5094** DM&IR #50 (maroon)

**NEW 187-5095** PRR #8614 (Brunswick Green)

**NEW 187-5096** PRR #8616 (Brunswick Green)

**NEW 187-5100** Undecorated

## Alco FA/FB w/Sound

### Powered A/Unpowered B Sets 269.99

**NEW 187-5120** CP #4000/4400 (gray, maroon)

**NEW 187-5121** NYC #1002/2302 (Lightning Stripe)

**NEW 187-5122** PRR #9607/9607B (Brunswick Green, Single Stripe)

**NEW 187-5123** UP #1628A/1626C

### Powered A Unit 169.99 ea

**NEW 187-5124** CN #9400 (olive green, yellow)

**NEW 187-5125** CN #9401 (olive green, yellow)

**NEW 187-5126** CP #4003 (gray, maroon)

**NEW 187-5128** Long Island #615 (blue-gray, white, black)

**NEW 187-5129** Long Island #616 (blue-gray, white, black)

**NEW 187-5130** NYC #1003 (Lightning Stripe)

**NEW 187-5132** PRR #9605 (Brunswick Green, Single Stripe)

**NEW 187-5134** UP #1629A

**NEW 187-5136** Undecorated

### Powered B Unit 159.99 ea

**NEW 187-5127** CP #4403 (gray, maroon)

**NEW 187-5131** NYC #2303 (Lightning Stripe)

**NEW 187-5133** PRR #9605B (Brunswick Green, Single Stripe)

**NEW 187-5135** UP #1624C

**NEW 187-5137** Undecorated

**NEW** GE AC6000CW UP #7510 187-5056

**NEW** GE AC6000CW CSX #5000 187-5057

**NEW** GE AC6000CW BHP Iron Ore #6071 187-5059

**NEW** GE AC6000CW BHP Iron Ore #6076 187-5060

**NEW** GE AC6000CW SP #602 187-5062

**NEW** GE AC6000CW CP #9801 187-5064

**NEW** PRR #8614 187-5095

## CLEAR CASE

Protect your investment in your favorite models. These handmade cases are constructed of rich-grain solid oak or walnut with a mitered edge to ensure a dust-free enclosure and felt pad feet to protect your furniture. The cover is crystal clear optical grade acrylic to make your model look like a museum masterpiece.

**Limited Quantity Available On All Items**

### Display Cases

**248-1005** 3-3/4 x 3-3/4 x 5" **22.99**

**248-1011** Light Oak 14 x 12 x 6" **81.99**

**248-1013** Light Oak 18 x 12 x 8" **111.99**

**248-1103** Light Oak 6 x 6 x 3-3/4" **34.99**

**248-1248** 12 x 6 x 4" **56.99**

**248-8710** Light Oak 10-5/8 x 2-3/4 x 3-1/4" **37.99**

**248-12453** Medium Oak 10 x 3-3/4 x 5-1/2" **44.99**

### Sports Display Medium Oak

**248-1615** Football Case **75.99**

**248-1620** Football Helmet **114.99**

### Multi-Shelf Display Units

Eight shelves per case.

**248-1836** Light Oak 38-1/2 x 27-1/2 x 5" **375.99**

**248-8706** Wall Shelf w/8 Shelves & Mirror Back 27 x 9" **81.99**

**248-18221** Dark Oak 38-1/2 x 27-1/2 x 5" **251.99**

### Anti-Static Cleaner

**248-500** Spray Cleaner 4oz **6.59**
For plastic and acrylics. Polishes, repels dust and resists fingerprints.

Daily New Product Announcements! Visit Walthers Web site at **www.walthers.com**

# PIERCE ARROW "GALLOPING GOOSE"

The Pierce Arrow "Galloping Goose" was built in 1931 using the chassis and drive train from a 1926 Pierce Arrow limousine. Con-Cor's original Galloping Goose was modeled after the Goose in the early 1950s when they remodeled the original "PA" Goose using a bus body to accommodate more passengers. Now Con-Cor is backdating that model to the 1931 freight version. Delivery is scheduled for 2008.

**Pierce Arrow Galloping Goose**
**Freight Version TBA**
**NEW 223-4111** Rio Grande Southern #5
**NEW 223-4112** DRGW
**NEW 223-4113** ATSF
**NEW 223-4114** PRR
**NEW 223-4115** GN
**NEW 223-4116** UP
**NEW 223-4117** SP
**NEW 223-4118** NYC
**NEW 223-4119** MOW
**NEW 223-4110** Undecorated (silver, no lettering)

**HOn3 TBA ea**
**223-4126** Rio Grande Southern #5
**223-4127** DRGW
**223-4125** Undecorated (silver, no lettering)

# HO SCALE ELECTROLINER

America's first "All Electric Luxury Trains" proclaimed the ads announcing the first run of the "Electroliners" on Feb. 9, 1941. The design of these unique trains was influenced by the competition on the Chicago to Milwaukee run of C&NW's 400 trains and Milwaukee Road's Hiawatha trains. Also influencing the design was the fact that the Electroliners had to circumnavigate Chicago's EL tracks above the Loop and run down the middle of city streets in Milwaukee.

In later years Electroliners were sold to the City of Philadelphia and known as "Liberty Liners". One of the Electroliner train sets is alive and well today and totally restored at the Illinois Train Museum in Union, Illinois.

Con-Cor's Electroliners feature the turquoise and salmon color scheme and an undecorated version is also available for customizing.

**4-Car Set $419.98 ea**
**223-8718** #801-802
**223-8719** #803-804
**223-8717** Undecorated

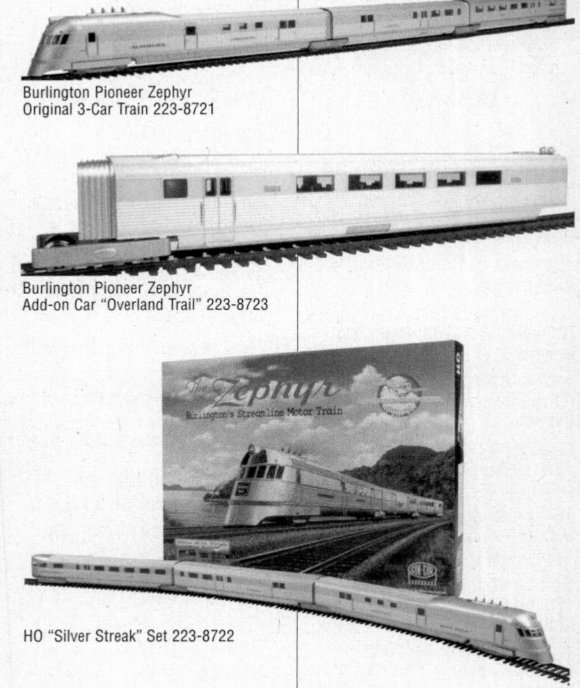

Burlington Pioneer Zephyr
Original 3-Car Train 223-8721

Burlington Pioneer Zephyr
Add-on Car "Overland Trail" 223-8723

HO "Silver Streak" Set 223-8722

## NEW PRODUCTS

### M-10,000 Original 3-Car Passenger Train Set

Based on the original 1934 three-car train, this detailed model is DCC ready and features a full interior with lighting plus reversing headlights and tail lights.

**NEW 223-8781** UP (brown, yellow) **429.98**

**NEW 223-8780** Undecorated (silver, no lettering) **429.98**

**NEW 223-8782** Pullman Add-on Car UP (brown, yellow) **129.98**

## BURLINGTON PIONEER ZEPHYR

### Original 3-Car Train

This model is fully ready to run and comes with a factory-installed, standard 8-pin DCC-ready board plus two extra pins for speaker mounting meeting NMRA standards so it will be easy to install the DCC decoder of your choice.

**223-8721** Pioneer Zephyr Lettering **398.98**

**223-8720** Undecorated (silver, no lettering) **398.98**

**223-8723** Add-on Car "Overland Trail" **139.98**



### "Silver Streak" Set 429.98 ea

This limited run version of the three-car Pioneer Zephyr is lettered as it appeared in the 1934 movie "The Sliver Streak". A special DVD with a copy of the original movie and other railroad movie clips is included.

**223-8722** HO Scale

## DIESEL LOCOMOTIVES

### EMD MP15 99.98 ea

Model is equipped with factory-installed "Dual-Mode" printed circuit board so it will run on DC and DCC layouts. Additional features include factory-mounted Kadee™ couplers, dual flywheels and highly detailed paint schemes.

**NEW 223-1165101** BN #1000
**NEW 223-1165102** BN #1003
**NEW 223-1165201** SP #2695 (speed lettering)
**NEW 223-1165202** SP #2698 (speed lettering)
**NEW 223-1165301** UP #1004 (yellow, red)
**NEW 223-1165302** UP #1107 (yellow, red)
**NEW 223-1165401** Chessie System #5311
**NEW 223-1165402** Chessie System #5316
**NEW 223-1165501** ATSF #912 (blue)
**NEW 223-1165502** ATSF #924 (blue)
**NEW 223-1165601** CR #9627
**NEW 223-1165602** CR #9630
**NEW 223-1165701** NS #2380
**NEW 223-1165702** NS #2384

Galloping Goose Railbus - Freight Version
NYC 223-4108

Galloping Goose Railbus -
Tourist Version 223-4131

**NEW 223-1165801** WC #1559
**NEW 223-1165802** WC #1565
**NEW 223-1166001** ATSF #1212 (silver)
**NEW 223-1160002** ATSF #1215 (silver)
**NEW 223-1166101** CB&Q #580
**NEW 223-1166102** CB&Q #576
**NEW 223-1166201** MP #1379 (black, white, red)
**NEW 223-1166202** MP #1382 (black, white, red)
**NEW 223-1166301** IC #1356 (black, white)
**NEW 223-1166302** IC #1359 (black, white)
**NEW 223-1166401** Amtrak #531
**NEW 223-1166402** Amtrak #536
**NEW 223-1166501** SP #2690 (gray, red)
**NEW 223-1166502** SP #2700 (gray, red)
**NEW 223-1165000** Undecorated

## RAILBUSES

### Galloping Goose - Freight Version 189.98 ea

These ready-to-run rail cars come with a factory-installed PC board designed to NMRA standards. They can easily be outfitted with a DCC decoder (sold separately) and are available for operation on standard HO or Narrow Gauge track.

#### HO Standard Gauge

**223-4101** Rio Grande Southern #5
**223-4102** DRGW
**223-4103** ATSF
**223-4104** PRR
**223-4105** GN
**223-4106** UP
**223-4107** SP
**223-4108** NYC
**223-4109** MOW
**223-4100** Undecorated (silver, no lettering)

#### HOn3 Narrow Gauge

**223-4121** Rio Grande Southern #5
**223-4122** DRGW
**223-4120** Undecorated (silver, no lettering)

### Galloping Goose - Tourist Version 189.98 ea

Similar in construction to the Freight Version (see the information above), the Tourist Version of the Galloping Goose comes with an alternate snow plow.

#### HO Standard Gauge

**223-4131** Rio Grande Southern #5 (As In Dolores, Colorado)
**223-4132** DRGW
**223-4140** Rio Grande Southern #4 (As In Telluride, Colorado)
**223-4130** Undecorated (silver, no lettering)

#### HOn3 Narrow Gauge

**223-4151** Rio Grande Southern #5 (As In Dolores, Colorado)
**223-4152** DRGW
**223-4153** Rio Grande Southern #4 (As In Telluride, Colorado)
**223-4150** Undecorated (silver, no lettering)

## Aerotrain

"This Train will save an Industry" declared a New York Central advertisement in 1956. With passenger traffic declining in the mid-1950s due to the rapid expansion of the Interstate Highway system, railroads were looking for ways to attract more ridership. Many, including the Pennsy, NYC, UP and others hoped the AeroTrain would do just that. Featuring a wraparound windshield, multiple headlights, a low center of gravity and new air suspension, EMD's stylish AeroTrain debuted in 1955 at the GM Powerama. Modelers can easily recreate the original 10-car consist by combining our four-car introductory set with two add-on three-car sets.

**Introductory Four Car Set**
**$429.98 ea**
Includes engine, two coaches and observation car.
223-8741 GM Demonstrator
223-8742 PRR
223-8743 NYC
223-8744 UP
223-8746 RI
223-8740 Undecorated

**Add-on Three Car Coach Set**
**$219.98 ea**
223-8751 GM Demonstrator
223-8752 PRR
223-8753 NYC
223-8754 UP
223-8756 RI
223-8750 Undecorated

## UNION PACIFIC M-10000

Union Pacific won the race to place a modern streamlined high-speed train into service. Their M-10000 streamliner hit the rails in February 1934, two months before the rival Pioneer Zephyr. Although the Zephyr received far more publicity, UP's M-10000 was exhibited across the U.S. on a coast-to-coast tour. Over one million people climbed aboard for a look at the beautiful interior and each received a souvenir coin made of the same aluminum material as the M-10000 body.

These models are based on the original three-car train as delivered in 1934. Each three-car set includes a replica souvenir coin. A Pullman built for the M-10001 was tested for several months on the M-10000. This Pullman fourth car will be available separately as an add-on car.

**HO M-10000 3-Car Train Set**
**$429.98 ea (Unless Noted)**
**223-8781** UP (brown & yellow paint scheme)
**223-8780** Undecorated (silver, no lettering)
**223-8782** Pullman 4th Car "Overland Trail" **$139.98**
**223-8793** Pullman Add-On Car "Oregon Trail" **$139.98**

**N M-10000 3-Car Train Set**
**$429.98 ea (Unless Noted)**
**223-8791** UP (brown & yellow paint scheme)
**223-8790** Undecorated (silver, no lettering)
**223-8792** Pullman 4th Car "Overland Trail **$139.98**
**223-8793** Pullman Add-On Car "Oregon Trail" **$139.98**

# EXAMPLES OF THE FINE ART OF GERMAN LOCOMOTIVE CONSTRUCTION

## FROM FLEISCHMANN Die Modellbahn der Profis

German locomotive builders have shaped railroad history for generations. And great engines are still rolling out of Siemens, Krupp, Krauss-Maffei and Bombardier for service in Germany, across Europe and around the world.

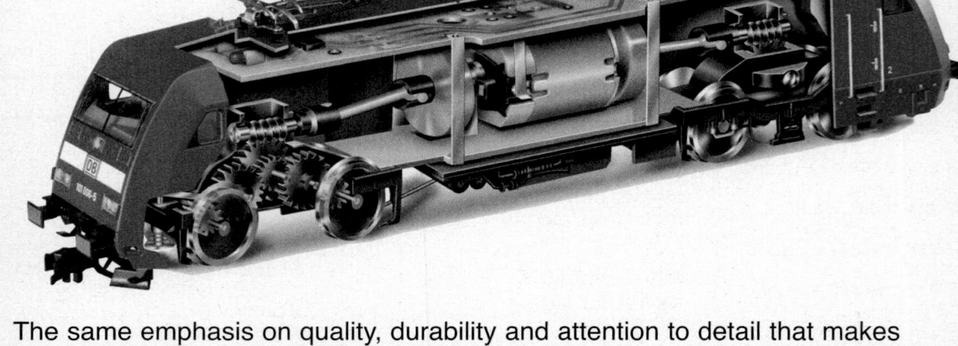


The same emphasis on quality, durability and attention to detail that makes these prototype engine manufacturers so successful is also used by Germany's famous engine builder — FLEISCHMANN. The company, which is still owned and run by the current third and fourth generations of the family, is now celebrating its 120$^{th}$ birthday.

No model locomotives or cars leave their works halls at Nüremberg until it successfully passes the most demanding tests!

*Whether steam, diesel or electric, you're always "on the right track" when you choose Fleischmann locos for your railroad.*

**FLEISCHMANN**

*FLEISCHMANN Model Railways... Quality down to the finest detail!*

# FLEISCHMANN

IMPORTED FROM GERMANY BY WALTHERS

Capture the power and excitement of European railroading for your layout or collection with these superb replicas. Fully assembled and ready for service, each features authentic detail and lettering to match the prototype during a specific time in its career.

## DIESEL

### German Federal Railways - DB

**277-4224** Class 361 Switcher - Powered w/Standard NEM Socket **TBA**

**277-4228** Class 211, Era IV - Powered **TBA**

**277-4235** Class 221, Era IV - Powered w/Standard NEM Socket **TBA**

### Class VT 95 Rail Car Era III

**NEW 277-4405** Standard DC **TBA**

**NEW 277-74405** DCC & Sound Equipped **TBA**

### Class VB 142 Era III Trailer

**NEW 277-4406** Non-Powered **TBA**
Use with VT95 rail cars, sold separately.

### German Railway Union - DB-AG

**277-4236** Class 218.3, Era V DCC-Ready w/NEM Socket **TBA**

**Limited Quantity Available**

**277-4233** Class 218.4, Era V DCC-Ready w/NEM Socket **269.99**

## ELECTRIC

### German Federal Railways - DB

**277-4380** Class 151, Era IV **TBA**

### Class 103.1 Era IV

**277-4376** Standard DC **TBA**

**NEW 277-74376** DCC & Sound Equipped **TBA**



### Class E19.1, Era III

**NEW 277-4318** Green - DCC-Ready w/NEM Socket **TBA**

**277-4319** Blue - DCC-Ready w/NEM Socket **TBA**

### German Railway Union - DB-AG (DB Cargo)

**277-4320** Class 145, Era V DCC-Ready w/NEM Socket **TBA**

**NEW 277-4324** Class 146, Era V DCC-Ready w/NEM Socket **TBA**

**277-4355** Class 101, Era V DCC-Ready w/NEM Socket **TBA**

### SBB Cargo Swiss Federal Railway

**277-4323** Class 481, Era V DCC-Ready w/NEM Socket **TBA**

# FLEISCHMANN

IMPORTED FROM GERMANY BY WALTHERS

## STEAM

### German State Railways - DRG

**277-4103** Class 03 4-6-2 Express Era III **TBA**

**277-4132** Class 41 2-8-2 "Oxen" Era II DCC-Ready w/NEM Socket **TBA**

**277-4171** Class 03 Streamlined 4-6-2 Era II DCC-Ready w/NEM Socket **TBA**

### Class 17 4-6-0 Express Engine Era II

**NEW 277-4117** DCC-Ready w/NEM Socket **TBA**

**NEW 277-74117** DCC & Sound Equipped **TBA**

### German Federal Railways - DB

### Class 18 4-6-2 "Bavarian Diva" Era III

**277-4118** DCC-Ready w/NEM Socket **TBA**

## GRAND CENTRAL GEMS

## LOCOMOTIVE STORAGE BOXES

Organize, store and protect your valuable motive power and rolling stock in these rugged boxes. Each is made of sturdy cardboard and includes an end label. Plastic storage bags are provided to wrap engines, while the interior is fitted with a custom cellular foam liner for added protection; an additional foam strip is provided that can be cut to fit the openings as needed to hold smaller equipment securely.

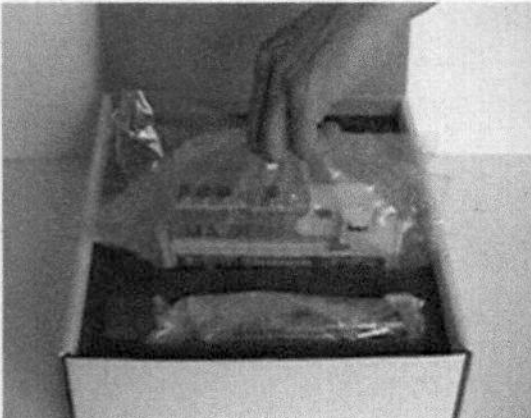

**295-B1** Standard pkg(4) **15.00**
Holds engines up to a Dash 9-40CW.

**295-B2** Extra-Large pkg(4) **20.00**
Ideal for big steam and similar large engines.

Designed, Manufactured & Assembled entirely in the U.S.A.

### Loco Driver Cleaner

**380-236** Speedi-Driver Cleaner **11.95**
Cleans corrosion from loco driver treads to improve electrical conductivity. No special wiring is needed to operate. HOn3 to O Scale.

## GRANDT LINE

These HO Scale kits contain injection-molded, black plastic parts and nonmagnetic wheelsets. They will accept Kadee® couplers. Powered kits include Mabuchi Motor and Grandt Line gears with 80:1 reduction.

## INDUSTRIAL LOCOMOTIVES

### GE 25-Ton Locomotives 50.00 ea

300-7090

Small switchers like these are owned and operated by many types of heavy industries including steel mills, cement plants, grain elevators and more. This powered model accepts Kadee® No. 714 (narrow gauge) or No. 711 (standard gauge) couplers.

**300-7091** HO

**300-7090** HOn3

### 23-Ton Box Cab Diesel Locomotives 50.00 ea

300-7088

Early box cab diesels were found in many large cities, where smoke from steam locos and tight clearances created problems. In later years, they were often sold to on-line industries for use as plant switchers.

**300-7089** Standard Gauge

**300-7088** Narrow Gauge

For Up-To-Date Information and News Bookmark Walthers Web site at

**www.walthers.com**

## Information STATION

### Loco Care & Maintenance

It is important to remember that your model railroad equipment is not a toy and should not be exposed to rough handling, especially locomotives. Yes, it is true that they will stand up to considerable abuse, but, as with all things, they will last longer and work better if they are treated well.

Dirt is responsible for most problems affecting performance. Dirty wheels and track will reduce electrical pick-up and cause an engine to slow or stutter. Wheels and track should be inspected for dirt and cleaned regularly. Liquid cleaners made especially for model railroad products provide fast results, but there are others, such as rubber abrasive cleaning blocks and electronic cleaners. When using liquids, avoid cloth or paper products that shed lint.

Proper lubrication is also necessary to avoid performance dilemmas. Read your locomotive manuals carefully and follow their advice. Oil should be applied sparingly as a tiny drop is all that's needed. Always use compatible lubricants made especially for model railroad products as most household lubricants and oils are not safe for plastics. Most engines can be disassembled easily for service with basic tools, but don't be afraid to ask your local hobby dealer for help if you're not familiar with the procedure.

When treated properly, your locomotives, and all railroad equipment, should last a lifetime.

# JAM CREATIONS/SOLUTIONS

## "STEALTH" TRACK CLEANING LOCOS

These track cleaners, disguised as locomotives, are made to run up front and remove grime before powered units run over it. Four independent, spring-loaded cleaning feet are built into the fuel tank and can be fitted with any combination of abrasive or felt discs, which ride the rail to remove oxidation, grime and dirt. Cleaning feet are set slightly inward of the rail center to force some rotation as the cleaner encounters curves, so the whole disk is used, rather than simply wearing down the same point . No liquids are used and the Stealth System can be used any time you run trains.

### STEWART F UNITS

#### Chassis Only

Fits F3, F7 and F9 body.

**343-1069** **89.00**
Modified with cleaning feet and live trucks; use with your own body shell will handle 18" minimum radius curves. Includes assortment pack of 16 cleaning disks.

#### A Units Only 149.00 ea

**F3**
**NEW 343-1079** NYC
**NEW 343-1085** CB&Q

**F7**
**NEW 343-1088** PRR
**343-1089** CN
**NEW 343-1090** Amtrak
**NEW 343-1091** B&O

**NEW 343-1096** Rock Island
**NEW 343-1098** L&N

**F9**
**343-1110** ATSF
**NEW 343-1112** MILW
**343-1113** UP

#### A-B Sets - Powered B 229.00 ea

A unit track cleaner and matching powered B unit. Models are fully detailed and DCC-ready.

**F7**
**NEW 343-1212** PRR
**NEW 343-1214** Rock Island

**NEW 343-1215** SP
**NEW 343-1228** Amtrak
**NEW 343-1229** B&O
**NEW 343-1233** L&N

**F9**
**NEW 343-1216** ATSF (Cigar)
**NEW 343-1223** DRGW
**NEW 343-1373** UP

### ATHEARN GP UNITS

Units are free-rolling and include power trucks and drive shafts.

#### GP40-2 179.00 ea

**343-1129** DRGW
**NEW 343-1135** Chessie/C&O

**NEW 343-1140** UP
**NEW 343-1141** CSX YN2
**NEW 343-1153** SP
**NEW 343-1161** BN

#### GP38-2 179.00 ea

**343-1127** NS (Horse)
**343-1162** CP
**343-1164** SP
**NEW 343-1166** BN
**NEW 343-1172** CR Operation Life Saver
**NEW 343-1176** CR "Q"
**NEW 343-1180** CSX YN2

#### Chassis Only

**343-1070** **89.00**
Modified with cleaning feet and live trucks; use with your own body shell (accepts GP38-2, 40-2, 50, or 60 body), and will handle 20" minimum radius curves.

### CLEANING DISKS

#### Abrasive pkg(20) 2.99 ea

**343-1187** 120 Grit
**343-1188** 180 Grit
**343-1189** 220 Grit

#### Soft pkg(20) 2.99 ea

**343-1190** Felt on Foam
**343-1191** Felt on Fabric

#### Assortment

**343-1192** Felt & Abrasive pkg(20) **2.99**

## NEW PRODUCTS

### EMD Mid-Production SD40-2

#### 179.00 ea

One of the best-selling EMD locos ever built, over 3,000 SD40-2s were sold in the US and Canada. During production, some prototype features were changed, and these new ready-to-run models are based on mid-production units. Like the prototype, the Kato SD40-2 incorporates a number of exciting features, including functioning ditch lights which can be switched between alternating (flashing) and steady lighting modes on the fly in DC (for DCC operation, ditch lights can be synchronized with horn or bell functions by installing an 8-pin sound decoder, sold separately). The models also come with all details and handrails installed, Golden White LED headlights and illuminated, printed numberboards. And for modelers who wish to add sound, the units feature DCC friendly construction, with a 1.1" (28mm) speaker housing in the fuel tank.

**NEW 381-376601** BN #6770 (White Face)

**NEW 381-376601A** BN #6992 (White Face)

**NEW 381-376603** CN #6253 (IC Cab Sublettering)

**NEW 381-376603A** CN #6256 (IC Cab Sublettering)

**NEW 381-376600** Undecorated

## DIESELS

Add the color and variety of contemporary railroading to your roster with these models. Each is powered and includes Kato knuckle couplers and directional LED headlight.

### EMD SD38-2 145.00 ea (Unless Noted)

Accurate replicas of the heavy-duty locos used by the steel industry and some major railroads. Models feature 8-pin DCC socket. Units are sound-friendly and accept a 1-1/10" 28 mm diameter speaker; sound unit & speaker sold separately.

**381-376482** Elgin, Joliet & Eastern #660 **140.00**

**381-376491** US Steel #1 (Two-Tone Blue) **140.00**

**381-376501** UP #2801 (Traditional Scheme)

**381-376502** UP #2804 (Traditional Scheme)

**381-376511** UP #Y833 (Mini-Winged Shield & Lightning Bolt)

**381-376512** UP #Y835 (Mini-Winged Shield & Lightning Bolt)

**381-376522** CNW #6656 (Traditional Yellow & green)

**381-376532** DM&IR #212 (Arrowhead Scheme) **140.00**

### F40PH

Widely used, the F40PH served Amtrak for over 20 years, as well as many commuter lines. Units are sound friendly and accept a 1.1" (28mm) diameter speaker; sound unit and speaker both sold separately. Shock absorber construction provides stable running performance. All units come prepainted to provide the best color match for Kato bi-level cab and coach cars, listed in the Passenger Cars section.

**381-376551** Amtrak® Phase III #375 **125.00**

**381-376552** Amtrak Phase III #391 **125.00**

**381-376553** Amtrak Phase III #400 **125.00**

**381-376561** Chicago RTA #135 **130.00**

**381-376562** Chicago RTA #157 **130.00**

### EMD SD70MAC

Introduced in 1993, more than 900 are now in service. Models feature lighted ditch lights and numberboards along with a factory-installed DCC socket.

#### With Cab Headlight 150.00 ea (Unless Noted)

**381-376381** BN #9580

**381-376382** BN #9615

**381-376408** CSX #734 **149.98**

#### With Nose Headlight 149.98 ea

**381-376451** BNSF #8802

**381-376452** BNSF #9959

**381-376455** Grupo Transportacion Ferroviaria Mexicana - TFM #1602

**381-376456** Grupo Transportacion Ferroviaria Mexicana - TFM #1634

### EMD SD80MAC 149.98 ea

Models are equipped with 8-pin DCC socket and include detail parts such as windshield wipers and MU hoses.

**381-376347** NS #7213

### EMD SD90/43MAC 149.98 ea

**381-376360** CEFX #118 w/CIT Logo

**381-376361** CEFX - No CIT Logo #123

**381-376362** UP #8242

### EMD SD45 134.98 ea

**381-371741** CNW #6544

**381-371742** PRR #6200

**381-371744** WC #6677

#### ATSF

These models come with all details parts installed.

**NEW 381-371745A** #5592

**NEW 381-371746A** #5596

### GE AC4400CW 150.00 ea (Unless Noted)

GE first delivered the AC4400CW in 1994. Models feature 8-pin DCC socket, lighted ditch lights and numberboards and are sound-friendly. accepts 1-1/10" 28 mm diameter speaker; sound unit & speaker sold separately.

**381-376431** CEFX Leasing #1006

**381-376432** CEFX Leasing #1021

**381-376441** BNSF #5608 (Heritage II)

**381-376442** BNSF #5615 (Heritage II)

# HIGHLINERS

## F UNIT BODY SHELL KITS

Body shell kits can build any version of the F Unit. Use with Athearn Genesis, or Stewart F Unit drives.

B Unit kits include molded plastic detail parts: four versions of the dynamic brake hatch, tall and short roof fans, five sets of side panel inserts, steam generator parts, two styles of sand filler hatches, flush-mounted porthole "glass," photo-etched stainless steel fan grilles, door handles, lift rings and other detail parts.

A Unit kits include all the details found in the B Unit kits plus true-to-scale headlights, three styles of number boards, two styles of pilots, two styles of cab doors, three nose doors (with and without lights), horns, five types of side porthole arrangement inserts, "winterization hatch" and coupler door cover, photo-etched stainless steel windshield wipers, windshield and porthole "gaskets," cab side-window "wind wings," cab door "kick plates," pilot corner steps and winterization hatch screen.

**328-1001** A Unit, Complete Kit **49.95**

**328-1002** B Unit, Complete Kit **36.95**

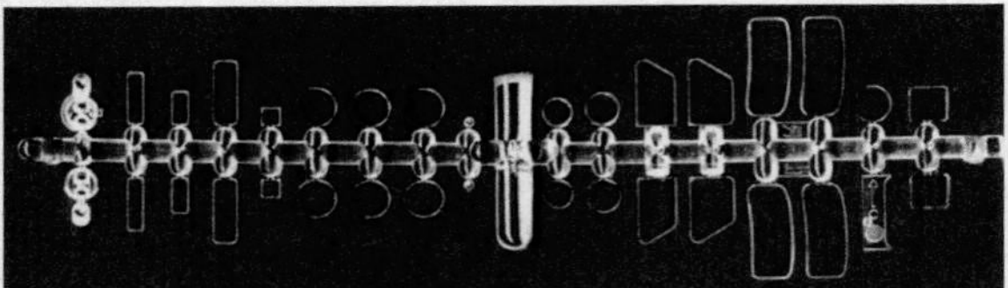

**328-4001** A/B "Glass" Unit **12.95**
Includes two end windows, numberboard alignment tool, two pairs of windshields, two pairs of cab-side windows, five headlight covers, two classification light lenses, six side porthole glasses, two cab door windows, three pairs of numberboard covers and two types of dual-sealed beam headlights.

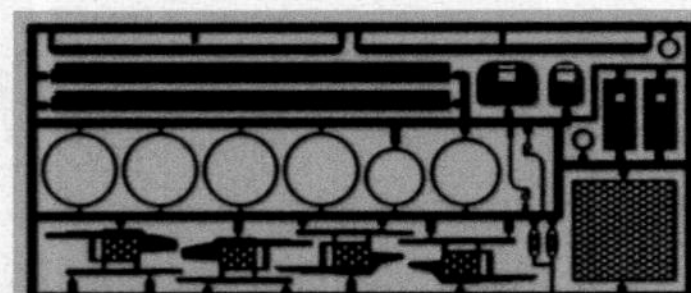

**328-2004** Preblackened Stainless Steel **8.95**
Includes winterization hatch screen, four pilot corner steps, two cab steps, two class light bezel rings, four F9 porthole gaskets, two F9 headlight gaskets, two pilot cut-bar links, two pilot cut-bar handles, MU doors, two F9 nose access panels and two door frames.

**328-2003** Etched Stainless Steel **6.95**
Includes four pairs of side kick plates, two windshield wipers, two early water filler hatches, and two each standard and tall "wind wings."

328-2001

**328-1005** A Unit, Shell Only **19.95**

**328-1006** B Unit, Shell Only **19.95**

## DETAIL PARTS SETS

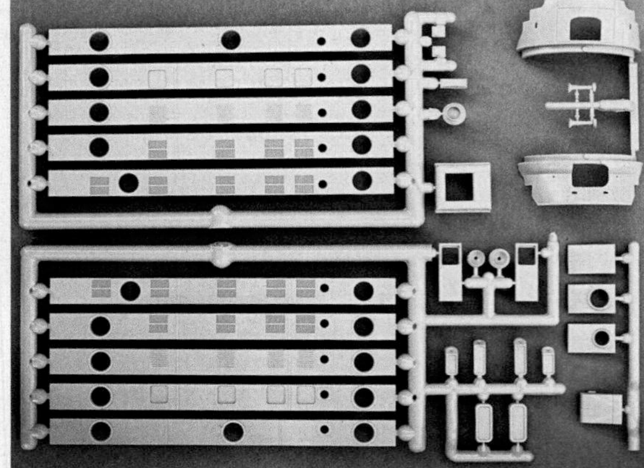

**328-3001** A Unit **19.95**
Includes two pilots, "snap-on/off" passenger pilot coupler door cover, two horns, three nose doors, three sets of numberboards, two reversible cab doors, two headlight reflectors, two water fill hatches, bumper, roof vent, winterization hatch, and five pairs of side panels.

## FAN & DETAIL PARTS SETS

Includes five 36" low fans, four 34" tall fans, one 48" fan, eight sand filler hatches, four exhaust stacks, steam generator vents etc. Used for E/F units, GP7, GP9, GP18, GP20 and SD units.

**328-2001** #1 **14.95**

**328-2002** #2 Photo-Etched Fan Grilles and Detail Parts **5.95**

**328-5001** FP7/9 Conversion Parts Set **19.95**

## WIRE SCREENING

These "see-through," photo-etched, preblackened, .003" thick stainless-steel screens simulate the "chicken wire" applied over air intakes on prototype F3s.

**328-10010** A Unit **14.95**

**328-10013** A Unit, Extra Fine **16.95**

**328-10020** B Unit **14.95**

**328-10023** B Unit, Extra Fine **16.95**

328-10010

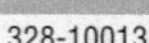
328-10013

328-10017

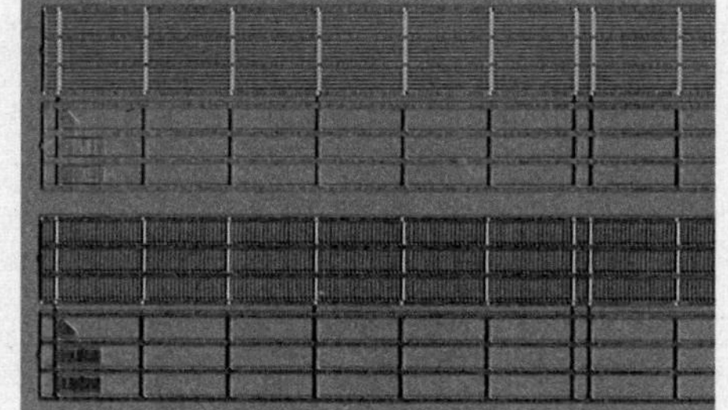

328-10019

## STAINLESS STEEL "FARR" AIR GRILLES

**328-10017** A Unit F7 pkg(2) **16.95**

**328-10019** A Unit F9 pkg(2) **16.95**

**328-10027** B Unit F7 pkg(2) **18.95**

**328-10029** B Unit F9 pkg(2) **18.95**

HO Scale locomotives are ready-to-run with plastic and diecast bodies that are prepainted and lettered. Steam locos feature working valve gear. All locos have working headlights and Magic Mate couplers.

Items listed in blue ink may not be available at all times (see Legend Page).

## NEW PRODUCTS

### Command XXV Premier Gold Series Steam Locomotives

These impressive models feature applied handrails and coupler lift bars, operating headlight and tender backup light, working knuckle couplers and blackened-metal RP-25 contour wheels for operation on Code 70 and larger rail. Models come equipped with an 8-pin DCC socket for easy addition of a DCC decoder (sold separately).

#### 4-6-2 Pacific 139.98 ea

**NEW 348-25005** Alton
**NEW 348-25016** MILW
**NEW 348-25021** PRR
**NEW 348-25025** SP (Daylight)
**NEW 348-25028** UP
**NEW 348-25030** CNJ (Blue Comet)
**NEW 348-25063** ACL (FDR Special)
**NEW 348-25066** DRGW

#### Semi-Streamlined 4-6-2 Pacific 139.98 ea

**NEW 348-26007** DL&W
**NEW 348-26022** Reading (Crusader)

#### 2-8-2 Mikado 139.98 ea

**NEW 348-27000** ATSF
**NEW 348-27001** SOU
**NEW 348-27003** C&O
**NEW 348-27005** GN
**NEW 348-27021** B&O
**NEW 348-27024** CB&Q
**NEW 348-27025** CP
**NEW 348-27040** B&M
**NEW 348-27050** KCS



## PREMIER SERIES STEAM LOCOMOTIVES

These authentically reproduced models feature additional body details, extra pick-ups in the tenders and metal handrails.

### 2-10-2 "Santa Fe" Powered 129.98 ea (Unless Noted)

These impressive models feature applied body details, extra pick-ups in the tenders, working knuckle couplers and metal handrails. Models come equipped with an 8-pin DCC socket for easy addition of a DCC decoder (sold separately).

**348-23400** ATSF #3803
**348-23401** CB&Q #6000

**348-23402** B&O #6185 **149.98**
**NEW 348-23403** Erie **149.98**
**NEW 348-23404** GN **149.98**
**348-23408** IC
**348-23409** PRR #4882 **149.98**
**348-23411** SOU #5200 **149.98**
**NEW 348-23412** UP **149.98**
**348-23414** DMIR

**348-23415** B&M #3006
**NEW 348-23416** SP **149.98**
**348-23417** WM **149.98**
**348-23418** Wabash #2507
**348-23419** C&O
**348-23420** LV
**348-23421** RI
**348-23422** ACL
**348-23423** NH
**348-23424** KCS
**NEW 348-23425** CP **149.98**
**NEW 348-23426** MILW
**NEW 348-23427** DL&W
**NEW 348-23429** NKP
**NEW 348-23430** MEC
**NEW 348-23431** Toronto, Hamilton & Buffalo
**NEW 348-23432** SLSF
**NEW 348-23433** FEC
**NEW 348-23434** NYC
**NEW 348-23435** DRGW **149.98**
**348-23413** Undecorated

#### With Vanderbilt Tender

**348-23404** GN #2100 **149.98**
**348-23412** UP #5009 **149.98**
**348-23416** SP #3711 **149.98**

### 0-8-0 Shifter Powered 69.98 ea

#### With USRA Tender

**348-23700** Atlantic Coast Line
**348-23701** B&O
**348-23707** CB&Q
**348-23709** Erie
**348-23710** Grand Trunk Western
**348-23714** Lehigh & New England
**348-23715** LV
**348-23716** Long Island Railroad
**348-23717** L&N
**348-23720** MP
**348-23722** NYC
**348-23725** NP
**348-23727** PRR
**348-23730** ATSF
**348-23731** SOU
**348-23732** SP
**348-23733** UP
**348-23734** U.S. Army

#### With Extended Bunker Tender

**348-23702** Boston & Maine
**348-23703** Belt Railway of Chicago
**348-23704** CP
**348-23705** CV
**348-23706** C&O
**348-23711** GN
**348-23712** IC
**348-23713** Delaware, Lackawanna & Western
**348-23719** MKT
**348-23721** NH
**348-23723** NKP
**348-23724** N&W
**348-23728** Rock Island
**348-23735** Wabash
**348-23736** Undecorated

### 2-8-2 Mikado 88.98 ea

**348-9800** ATSF
**348-9801** SOU
**348-9802** SP
**348-9803** C&O
**348-9804** C&O Chessie
**348-9805** GN
**348-9806** PRR
**348-9807** Atlantic Coast Line
**348-9808** L&N
**348-9809** CN
**348-9810** CNW
**348-9811** UP
**348-9813** WM
**348-9814** RDG
**348-9815** SP
**348-9816** NYC
**348-9817** NKP
**348-9818** Frisco
**348-9819** MILW
**348-9820** Erie
**348-9821** B&O

2-10-2 Santa Fe Powered ATSF #3803 348-23400

2-10-2 Santa Fe Powered with Vanderbilt Tender GN #2100 348-23404

0-8-0 Shifter Powered w/USRA Tender B&O 348-23701

2-8-2 Mikado Western Maryland 348-9813

4-8-2 Mountain with Tender CB&Q 348-903

**348-9822** NH
**348-9823** Lackawanna
**348-9824** CB&Q
**348-9825** CP
**348-9826** LV
**348-9827** DRGW
**348-9828** NP
**348-9829** Texas & Pacific
**348-9830** NdeM (National of Mexico)
**348-9831** Maine Central
**348-9812** Undecorated

### 4-8-2 Mountain 104.98 ea

For more realism, each engine includes the correct style of tender used by the prototype. The rectangular type, matching the style used by most roads, is highly detailed and features a working back-up light. Roads that used Vanderbilt tenders include that style.

#### With Tender

**348-902** Boston & Maine
**348-903** CB&Q
**348-984** SP
**348-986** Texas & Pacific

#### With Square Tender

**348-910** Florida East Coast
**348-931** Seaboard
**348-940** Western Pacific
**348-966** LV
**348-976** PRR

#### With Vanderbilt Tender

**348-955** C&O
**348-971** NH
**348-977** RDG
**348-982** SOU

#### With Deck-Mounted Air Pumps

**348-903** Bangor & Aroostook
**348-906** Rock Island
**348-911** Frisco

#### Type "C" Powered

**348-980** N&W
**348-988** UP #7000 (Rectangular Tender)
**348-993** NKP #844 (Rectangular Tender)
**348-994** SP "Daylight" (Rectangular Tender)
**348-995** UP "Overland" #700 (Rectangular Tender) (gray)

International Hobby Corp.

### Steam 4-6-4 Hudson Powered 99.98 ea
**348-23000** ATSF #3456
**348-23001** B&O #5047
**348-23003** CN #5700
**348-23005** C&O #301
**348-23006** CB&Q #3011
**348-23007** MILW #6400
**348-23008** CNW #4001
**348-23009** Delaware, Lackawanna & Western (Lackawanna) #1151
**348-23010** IC #2499
**348-23011** Maine Central #702
**348-23014** NKP
**348-23015** NH #1400
**348-23016** Frisco
**348-23017** Toronto, Hamilton & Buffalo
**348-23018** Wabash #703
**348-23019** PRR #2003 (Rectangular Tender)
**348-23020** UP #2003 (Vanderbilt Tender)
**348-23021** GN #2003 (Vanderbilt Tender)

### 2-6-0 "Camelback" - "Mother Hubbard" 91.98 ea (Unless Noted)
Finely detailed and ready for service on your railroad, each comes equipped with Magic Mate couplers, which can be used with horn-hook or knuckle type couplers.
**348-23150** Atlantic City Railroad
**348-23151** Atlantic Coast Line
**348-23152** ATSF
**348-23153** B&O
**348-23154** Boston & Maine
**348-23155** CN **76.98**
**348-23156** CP
**348-23157** CNJ **66.98**
**348-23158** C&O
**348-23159** Chicago, Milwaukee, St. Paul & Pacific
**348-23161** D&H
**348-23162** DRGW
**348-23163** Lackawanna
**348-23164** Erie
**348-23166** GN
**348-23169** Lehigh Coal & Navigation
**348-23170** LV
**348-23174** NYC & Hudson
**348-23175** New Haven
**348-23176** N&W
**348-23177** Pennsylvania Lines **66.98**
**348-23178** RDG
**348-23180** SOU **66.98**
**348-23181** SP
**348-23182** UP
**348-23207** New York, Ontario & Western River **66.98**
**348-23202** Undecorated

### 2-6-0 Mogul 70.98 ea
#### With Oil Tender
**348-510** ATSF
**348-511** PRR
**348-512** SP
**348-513** SOU (green)
**348-514** Central Vermont
**348-515** B&O
**348-516** CNW
**348-517** Green Bay & Western
**348-518** NYC
**348-519** Central of Georgia
**348-520** NH
**348-521** Texas & Pacific
**348-522** IC
**348-523** CN
**348-526** Boston & Maine
**348-527** New York, Ontario & Western
**348-524** Undecorated

#### With Coal Tender
**348-528** ATSF
**348-529** PRR
**348-530** SP
**348-531** SOU
**348-532** Central Vermont
**348-533** B&O
**348-534** CNW
**348-535** Green Bay & Western
**348-536** NYC
**348-537** Central of Georgia
**348-538** NH
**348-539** Texas & Pacific
**348-540** IC
**348-541** CN
**348-543** Boston & Maine
**348-544** RDG
**348-545** C&O
**348-546** L&N
**348-547** Richmond, Fredericksburg & Potomac
**348-548** LV
**348-549** Florida East Coast
**348-550** GN
**348-551** NP
**348-552** CNJ
**348-553** Atlantic Coast Line
**348-554** MP
**348-555** Kansas City Southern
**348-556** WM
**348-557** UP
**348-558** D&H
**348-542** Undecorated

### 4-6-2 Pacific 79.98 ea
Includes can motor with flywheel, metal handrails mounted on boiler, retooled drivers for smoother operation, real brass bell, metal coupler lift bar on tender body, reversing headlight on tender and additional weight in cab and smokebox. Pacifics are equipped with Magic Mate couplers, compatible with horn-hook and knuckle type couplers.
**348-9888** Florida East Coast
**348-9889** N&W
**348-9890** Pere Marquette
**348-9891** Atlantic Coast Line (FDR Special)
**348-9892** Rock Island
**348-9893** LV
**348-9894** DRGW
**348-9895** Boston & Maine
**348-9896** B&O (Royal Blue)
**348-9897** NP
**348-9898** Texas & Pacific
**348-9899** Toronto, Hamilton & Buffalo
**348-9900** Atlantic Coast Line
**348-9901** ATSF
**348-9902** B&O President Washington
**348-9903** B&O President Fillmore
**348-9904** CB&Q
**348-9905** Chicago & Alton
**348-9906** CNW
**348-9907** C&O
**348-9908** C&O Chessie
**348-9909** CN
**348-9910** CP
**348-9911** Erie
**348-9912** Frisco
**348-9913** GN
**348-9914** L&N
**348-9915** Delaware, Lackawanna & Western
**348-9916** MILW
**348-9917** MILW Chippewa
**348-9918** NH
**348-9919** NKP
**348-9920** NYC
**348-9921** PRR
**348-9922** RDG
**348-9923** SOU
**348-9924** Southern Crescent
**348-9925** SP
**348-9926** SP Line
**348-9928** UP
**348-9929** WM
**348-9930** CNJ
**348-9931** B&O
**348-9932** B&O President Lincoln
**348-9933** B&O President Polk
**348-9934** B&O President Jefferson
**348-9927** Undecorated

### 2-8-0 Consolidation 65.98 ea (Unless Noted)
**348-9500** ATSF
**348-9501** Atlantic Coast Line
**348-9502** B&O
**348-9503** Bessmer & Lake Erie
**348-9504** Boston & Maine
**348-9505** CN
**348-9506** CP
**348-9507** Central Vermont
**348-9508** C&O
**348-9509** CB&Q
**348-9510** CNW
**348-9511** D&H
**348-9513** DRGW
**348-9514** Erie
**348-9515** Frisco

Steam 4-6-4 Hudson Powered ATSF #3456 348-23000

2-6-0 "Camelback" "Mother Hubbard" Erie 348-23164

2-6-0 Mogul SP 348-512

4-6-2 Pacific RDG 348-9922

2-8-0 Consolidation WM 348-9541

**348-9516** GN
**348-9517** IC
**348-9518** Kansas City Southern
**348-9519** Lehigh & New England
**348-9520** LV **59.98**
**348-9521** L&N
**348-9522** Maine Central
**348-9523** MILW
**348-9524** MKT
**348-9525** MP
**348-9526** MON
**348-9527** NH
**348-9528** NYC
**348-9529** New York, Ontario & Western
**348-9530** NKP **59.98**
**348-9531** N&W
**348-9532** NP
**348-9533** Pennsylvania Lines
**348-9534** Philadelphia & Reading
**348-9535** Rock Island
**348-9536** Seaboard
**348-9537** Southern
**348-9538** SP
**348-9539** UP
**348-9540** Wabash
**348-9541** WM
**348-9542** Western Pacific
**348-9543** Duluth, Missabe & Iron Range
**348-9544** Lake Superior & Ishpeming
**348-9545** Buffalo Creek & Gauley
**348-9546** Grand Trunk Western
**348-9547** Lehigh & Hudson River
**348-9548** Florida East Coast
**348-9549** Spokane, Portland & Seattle
**348-9551** Virginian
**348-9552** Long Island
**348-9553** Duluth, Winnipeg & Pacific

International Hobby Corp.

348-9554 Chicago Great Western
348-9555 Wheeling & Lake Erie
348-9556 SOO
348-9557 Bangor & Aroostook
348-9558 Chicago & Illinois Midland
348-9559 NdeM (National of Mexico)
348-9560 Susquehanna & New York
348-9562 Pere Marquette
348-9550 Undecorated

## Semi-Streamlined Pacifics 89.98 ea

These spectacular models feature Mabuchi motors with precision flywheels, metal handrails and lift bars, and directional lighting.

348-9850 ATSF #1369 (Valley Flyer)
348-9851 B&O #5304 (The Royal Blue)
348-9852 D&H #3607 (Loree)
348-9853 LV #2022 (Asa Packer)
348-9855 NYC #6515 (The Mercury)
348-9856 Boston & Maine #3710
348-9857 Lackawanna #1124
348-9858 Frisco
348-9859 Wabash (Blue Bird)
348-9860 PRR #5399
348-9861 RDG #210

348-9862 SP #4365 (Sunbeam)
348-9863 UP #2906
348-9864 MILW #6160 (Hiawatha)
348-9865 CNW (Route of the 400)
348-9866 L&N (South Wind)
348-9867 CP
348-9868 SOU (Tennessean)

## 4-4-0 American 74.98 ea

These historic models come fully assembled and are equipped with Magic Mate Couplers, which can be used with horn-hook or knuckle type couplers.

348-13800 ATSF
348-13801 PRR
348-13802 SP
348-13803 SOU
348-13804 B&O
348-13805 CNW
348-13806 NYC
348-13809 IC
348-13811 Green Bay & Western
348-13812 NH
348-13813 CN
348-13815 Boston & Maine
348-13817 L&N
348-13818 GN
348-13821 UP
348-13822 Virginia & Truckee
348-13814 Undecorated

Items listed below are available by Special Order (see Legend Page).

348-13807 Central of Georgia
348-13808 RDG
348-13810 Central Vermont
348-13816 New York, Ontario & Western
348-13819 LV
348-13820 Delaware, Lackawanna & Western

## 4-4-0 Old Timer 44.98 ea

Roadname Shown Not Available

348-34017 GN

# DIESEL LOCOMOTIVES

## EMD SD24 34.98 ea

348-3800 ATSF #960
348-3801 Amtrak®
348-3802 Atlantic Coast Line
348-3803 B&O
348-3805 CB&Q #505
348-3807 Canadian Pacific
348-3808 C&O Chessie
348-3809 CNW
348-3811 DRGW
348-3816 GN
348-3820 Long Island Railroad
348-3824 MP
348-3825 NH
348-3826 NYC
348-3830 PRR #7105
348-3834 Royal American Shows
348-3835 SOU
348-3839 UP #429
348-3842 Presidential

## ALCO C-415 Powered 29.98 ea

These prototype-accurate locomotives feature a high cab design, smooth running gearing, operating headlight, Magic-Mate coupler and a precision can motor.

348-24000 Amtrak® (Platinum Mist, black)
348-24001 ATSF ("Zebra Stripes")
348-24002 B&O (blue, yellow)
348-24003 BN (green, black, white)
348-24004 CNW (green, yellow)
348-24005 CNJ ("Red Baron")
348-24006 DRGW (black, orange)

4-4-0 American Virginia & Truckee 348-13822

348-24007 EL (gray, maroon, yellow)
348-24008 LV ("Yellow Bird")
348-24010 NYC (black, white)
348-24011 PRR (black, yellow)
348-24012 RDG (green, yellow)
348-24013 Rock Island (yellow, red, white)
348-24015 SOU (green, white)
348-24016 UP (Armour Yellow, gray, red)
348-24017 Undecorated (Weyerhauser Green, yellow)

## ALCO C-628 Powered 24.98 ea

348-23250 ATSF #1814 (blue & yellow)
348-23251 CP #4503 (Tuscan, gray, black & gold)
348-23252 D&H #602 (blue, gray & yellow)
348-23253 L&N #1413
348-23254 L&N #1405
348-23255 LV #628 (Cornell Red)
348-23256 LV #629 (Cornell Red)
348-23257 LV #630 Snowbird
348-23258 LV #631 Snowbird
348-23259 MON #404 (black & gold)
348-23260 PRR #6311 (black)
348-23261 PRR #6310 (black)
348-23262 SP #3125 "Black Widow"
348-23263 SP #4850 "Black Widow"
348-23264 UP #3222 (yellow & red)
348-23265 LV #625 (gray)
348-23266 LV #627 (gray)
348-23267 NH #800 ("McGinnis" Scheme)
348-23268 NH #802 ("McGinnis" Scheme)
348-23269 EL #3616
348-23270 EL #3617
348-23271 ATSF "War Bonnet" #400
348-23272 ATSF "War Bonnet" #403
348-23273 Susquehanna #3008
348-23274 Susquehanna #3002
348-23275 RDG #5301 (yellow)
348-23276 RDG #5308 (yellow)

Semi-Streamlined Pacific B&O #5304 348-9851

EMD SD24 ATSF #960 348-3800

EMD SD24 MP 348-3824

ALCO C-415 Powered RDG 348-24012

Alco C-628 Powered UP #3222 348-23264

Alco C-628 Powered NH #800 ("McGinnis" Scheme) 348-23267

Brill Trolley Downtown 348-9384

GG-1 PRR #4899 348-9661

**348-23277** Penn Central #6306

**348-23278** Penn Central #6301

**348-23279** Western Pacific #800

**348-23280** Western Pacific #803

**348-23281** N&W #1110

**348-23282** N&W #1113

**348-23283** Seaboard Coast Line #2211

**348-23284** Seaboard Coast Line #2213

**348-23285** CB&Q #576

**348-23286** CB&Q #579

**348-23287** NP #2802

**348-23288** NP #2811

**348-23289** Atlantic Coast Line #2000

**348-23290** Atlantic Coast Line #2003

**348-23291** CNW #6711

**348-23292** CNW #6713

### SD35 34.98 ea

**348-13700** CR

**348-13702** Atlantic Coast Line

**348-13703** B&O

**348-13704** CP

**348-13705** CSX

**348-13706** CNJ

**348-13707** Family Lines System L&N

**348-13708** Gulf, Mobile & Ohio

**348-13709** L&N

**348-13711** PRR

**348-13712** Seaboard System

**348-13713** SP

**348-13714** UP

**348-13715** WM

**348-13716** CN

## ELECTRICS

### Brill Trolley 34.98 ea

These four-wheel cars were common on big city streetcar lines. Set features a powered unit pulling a trailer.

**348-9382** Connecticut Company

**348-9383** United Transit Lines

**348-9384** Downtown

### GG-1 79.98 ea

**348-9650** PRR #4828 (Tuscan)

**348-9651** PRR #4828 (Brunswick Green)

**348-9652** PRR #4880 (silver)

**348-9654** PRR #4907 (Single Stripe Tuscan)

**348-9655** PRR #4907 (Single Stripe Brunswick Green)

**348-9656** PRR #4856 (5-Stripe Tuscan)

**348-9658** PRR #4824 5-Stripe "Futura"

**348-9659** CR #4800 (blue)

**348-9660** Amtrak #902 (black)

**348-9661** PRR #4899 Pre-Loewy

**348-9662** Amtrak® #902 "Bloody Nose"

**348-9664** Amtrak #921 "Savings Bond"

**348-9665** Penn Central, JFK Funeral

**348-9666** PRR Spirit of '76 (white)

**348-9667** CR Spirit of '76 (red, white & blue)

**348-9668** PRR #4829 (Dark Green Stripe)

**348-9670** Milwaukee Premier

**348-9671** NH Premier

**348-9672** VGN Premier

348-9673 GN Premier

**348-9674** NYC Lightning Premier

## JORDAN HIGHWAY MINIATURES

### 15-Ton Mack Switcher Locomotive

**360-302 10.95**
Kit is based on the Mack gas-electric switcher locomotive that was in use from 1930 to 1980. Unpowered model molded of styrene plastic.

## KEYSTONE LOCOMOTIVE WORKS

Craft train kits contain unpainted metal parts.

### Cab Interiors
**9.98 ea**

**395-3304** EMD 1st Generation GP/SD
Fits the following models: GP7 9, 18, 20, and SD7, 9, 18, and 24.

**395-3305** EMD 2nd Generation GP/SD
Fits the following models: 40-2, 38-2, 35, 40 and 50. Can also be modified to fit Bachmann GP30.

**395-3309** E Unit

### Steam Locomotives

**Shay 49.95 ea**

**395-105** 20-Ton Class A, HO

**395-1053** 20-Ton Class A, HOn3

## ON-TRAK MODEL PRODUCTS

HO Scale, cast-metal Craft Train kits.

### Shay Conversion Boiler

**786-5019 16.95**
Cast-alloy boiler will backdate the Roundhouse Shay prior to 1915. Boiler is straight version with a fluted steam and sand dome.

### Loco Kits Unpowered

**786-5203** Mack BR Special Switcher **24.95**

**786-5205** Westminster Kerosene **18.95**
HO/HOn3.

## MANTUA

## STEAM LOCOMOTIVES

All steam locomotives are DCC ready.

### Metal 4-6-2 "Pacific"

**With Vanderbilt Tender 137.99 ea**

**455-340001** UP Grey Goose

**455-340002** B&O (blue)

**455-340003** SP

**455-340004** Undecorated

**With Long Haul Tender 129.99 ea**

**455-349001** ATSF

**455-349002** PRR

**455-349003** NP

**455-349005** CN

**455-349006** CP

**455-349004** Undecorated

### 4-6-2 "Pacific" Camelback Type w/Tender 99.99 ea

**455-323001** UP

**455-323002** LV

**455-323003** SOU

**455-323005** New Jersey Central

**455-323004** Undecorated

### 0-6-0 "Goat" Camelback Type Switcher w/Tender B7-B8A 79.99 ea (Unless Noted)

**455-389001** RDG

**455-389002** ATSF

**455-389003** SOU

**455-389005** DRGW **82.99**

**455-389004** Undecorated

For Daily Product Updates Point Your Browser to

**www.walthers.com**

### 2-6-6-2 Articulated Logger Powered w/Flywheel Drive

**With Tender 153.99 ea**

**455-345001** GN

**455-345002** WM

**455-345003** N&W

**455-345005** SP

**455-345004** Undecorated

**Tank Engine - No Tender 142.99 ea**

**455-351600** Weyerhaeuser (green)

**455-351601** CP

**455-351602** Uintah Railway

**455-351603** Undecorated

### 0-6-0 Switchers – Tank Engine Type, No Tender 54.99 ea

Roadname Shown Not Available

**455-393001** ATSF

**455-393002** B&O

**455-393003** PRR

**455-393005** UP

**455-393006** Bethlehem Steel

**455-393007** CP

**455-393004** Undecorated

## TOMAR INDUSTRIES

### Traction Drumheads

Drumheads were used for many years on the last car of interurbans, making it easy for passengers to find their train in a terminal. The lighted sign was also useful for advertising, especially after dark. These kits are complete with cast and machined drum housing, 1.5V micro-miniature lamp, full color sign, light diffuser, diodes, hookup wire and complete instructions. For a complete listing of drumheads, visit Walthers Web site at www.walthers.com.

All locomotives come with magnetic couplers installed or included in the box. All models are ready to run.

# DIESEL LOCOMOTIVES

## METALTRAIN™ F7A Metal 65.98 ea

These lighted diesel locomotives feature a metal body, flywheel drive, magnetic knuckle couplers and standard couplers. DCC ready.

**490-2160** ATSF
**490-2161** Amtrak®
**490-2162** UP
**490-2163** PRR
**490-2164** CN
**490-2165** CP
**490-2166** Alaska

## ALCO Dual Drive Lighted 44.98 ea

### RS-2

490-6842

**490-6841** CN (black)
**490-6842** CP
**490-6843** ATSF
**490-6844** BN
**490-6845** CR
**490-6846** SOU

### C-430

**490-6773** CR

## EMD Dual Drive Lighted

### F3A

Eight-wheel pick-up with metal chassis. Painted in ATSF scheme.

### F2A 38.98 ea (Unless Noted)

490-6801

**490-6800** ATSF
**490-6801** PRR
**490-6802** Chessie
**490-6803** UP
**490-6804** SP
**490-6805** BN
**490-6806** Amtrak
**490-6807** CR
**490-6808** SOU
**490-6809** CN
**490-6810** CP
**490-6811** PRR - Raymond Loewy **42.98**
**490-6812** SP "Daylight"
**490-6813** United States Army
**490-6814** US Air Force
**490-6870** ATSF Dummy **16.50**

### GP9 42.98 ea

Roadname Shown Not Available

**490-6751** SOU
**490-6752** CR
**490-6754** CN
**490-6755** BN
**490-6756** BNSF

## Baldwin "Shark Nose" Collector Series

### A Unit Dummy 18.98 ea

**490-730** ATSF
**490-731** PRR
**490-733** CN

**Limited Quantity Available**
**490-729** Undecorated

### B Unit Dummy 16.98 ea

**490-750** ATSF
**490-754** NYC

### Lighted, A Unit Dummy, B Unit Dummy

**490-7307** ATSF **24.98**

## FB-2 Lighted A-B-A Set 89.98 ea

**490-8608** ATSF
**490-8610** PRR
**490-8638** UP

## ALCO Collector Series

**Limited Quantity Available**

### FB2 87.99 ea

**490-840** ATSF
**490-842** PRR
**490-844** UP
**490-845** BN

### FA2 Dummy Lighted 18.99 ea

**490-850** ATSF
**490-852** CP

### FB2 Dummy

Roadname Shown Not Available

**490-864** BN **17.99**

## Porter Hustler Lighted 32.98 ea

Directional lighting.

**490-6705** ATSF
**490-6706** BN
**490-6707** SOU
**490-6708** SP
**490-6709** PRR
**490-6710** Chessie
**490-6711** Amtrak
**490-6712** CN

## DDT Plymouth Industrial Diesel 32.98 ea (Unless Noted)

490-6674

**490-6669** BN
**490-6670** ATSF
**490-6673** CN
**490-6674** CP
**490-6676** Amtrak
**490-6678** Chessie
**490-6679** CR
**490-6680** DRGW **34.98**

# STEAM LOCOMOTIVES

## 2-6-0 Lighted w/Tender 43.98 ea

**490-6720** ATSF
**490-6721** PRR
**490-6722** GN
**490-6723** SOU

## Old Time Shifter w/Tender 43.98 ea

**490-6780** ATSF
**490-6781** PRR
**490-6782** SOU
**490-6783** CP
**490-6784** DRGW
**490-6785** Pennzoil

## 0-4-0 Lighted 33.98 ea (Unless Noted)

490-6501

**490-6500** ATSF
**490-6501** PRR
**490-6502** CN
**490-6503** Number Only **32.98**
**490-6504** SOU
**490-6505** B&O
**490-6507** CP
**490-6508** RDG
**490-6509** C&O
**490-6510** UP

## 0-4-0 w/Tender 43.98 ea

490-6635

**490-6632** CN
**490-6633** CP
**490-6634** ATSF
**490-6635** PRR
**490-6636** SOU

## *Information* STATION

### Headlights

Faced with heavy traffic, in 1832 the South Carolina Railroad became the first to run at night.

But how was the engineer supposed to see? The first effort to light the tracks put two flat cars ahead of the engine. The first was covered with sand, and a fire was started. A sheet of iron was used as a reflector on the second car.

The idea continued to evolve, with oil-burning lamps becoming common by 1860.

Battery-operated electric lamps appeared in 1874. The first electric headlights appeared in 1883 when a French railroad company tried using a steam turbine to generate electricity. Electric headlights made their way to the Americas in the 1890s. By 1915, federal law required electric headlights on all locomotives.

As train speeds increased, new types of warning lights appeared on engines. This included high-power searchlights, as well as motorized warning lights that swept a beam of lamp across the tracks.

High-powered, sealed beam lamps became standard equipment on later diesel locomotives.

Today, three lights are required on the front of each locomotive, one headlight and two pilot-mounted "ditch lights."

RAPIDO®
TRAINS INC.
QUALITY. STYLE. SPIRIT.™
www.rapidotrains.com
Pre-production model shown.

Preproduction Model Shown

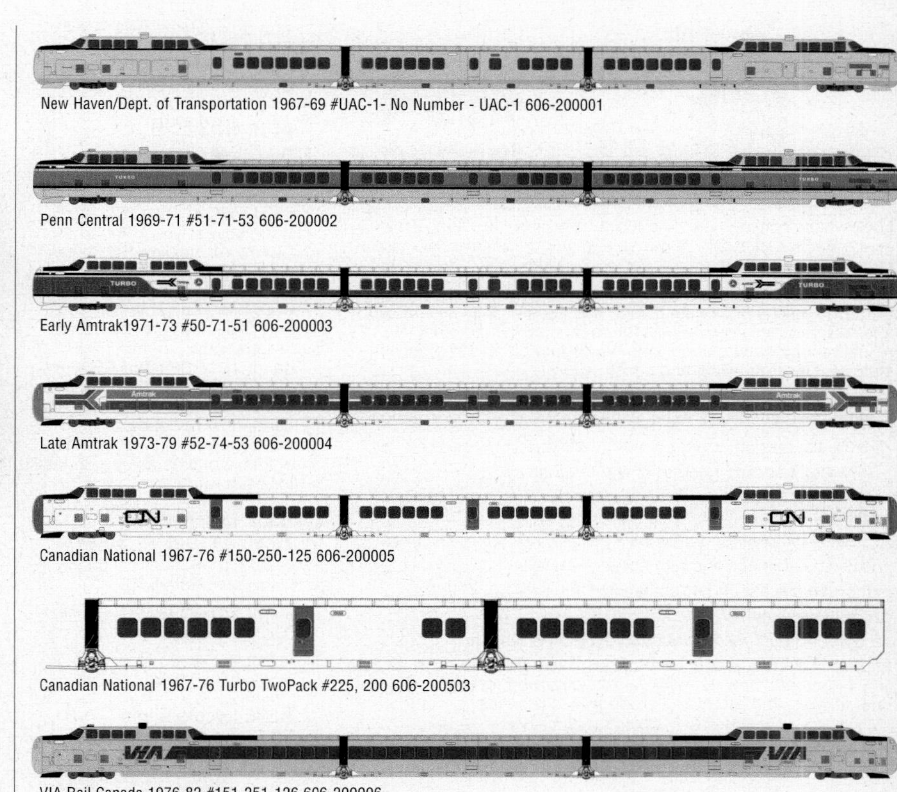

New Haven/Dept. of Transportation 1967-69 #UAC-1- No Number - UAC-1 606-200001

Penn Central 1969-71 #51-71-53 606-200002

Early Amtrak1971-73 #50-71-51 606-200003

Late Amtrak 1973-79 #52-74-53 606-200004

Canadian National 1967-76 #150-250-125 606-200005

Canadian National 1967-76 Turbo TwoPack #225, 200 606-200503

VIA Rail Canada 1976-82 #151-251-126 606-200006

VIA Rail Canada 1976-82 Turbo TwoPack #226, 201 606-200603

**TurboTrain**
NORTH AMERICA'S FASTEST TRAIN

On December 20, 1967, the United Aircraft TurboTrain reached a record-shattering 170.8 MPH on the Pennsylvania Railroad in New Jersey. To this day, this is still the fastest speed ever achieved by a production train in North America.

Rapido Trains Inc. is proud to present the first ever accurate model of this unique train in any scale. Each train features one Intermediate Car and two Power Dome Car locomotives. For speed and reliability, both engines are powered, and both engines have sound decoders and speakers. More Intermediate Cars are available to make a longer train. Several different Coach, Cafe and Club cars are available, depending on the choice of paint scheme. The TurboTrain operates with or without sound on both DC and DCC.

The TurboTrain comes with numerous factory-applied detail parts; working full-width diaphragms; full interior lighting; constant directional headlights and operating Gyralites; a decal sheet with additional logos and car numbers; TurboTrain: A Journey, a full-color book on the history of the TurboTrain featuring dozens of never-before-published photographs; and a hand-held controller for operating the train sounds in DC.

The TurboTrain features interior detail that has rarely been attempted in HO scale, including "padded" armrests, faucets in the bathroom sinks, gauges in the engineman's cab, and a microwave behind the counter in the cafe car. The models are fully prototype-specific, with three different Power Dome Car designs represented and five different Intermediate Car styles available. Minimum radius is 18" without diaphragms, 24" with diaphragms.

# UNITED AIRCRAFT TURBOTRAIN

## New Haven/Dept. of Transportation 1967-69

**606-200001** #UAC-1- No Number -UAC-1 **499.95**

**606-200101** TurboCoach Intermediate Car - No Number **39.95**

## Penn Central 1969-71

**606-200002** #52-71-53 **499.95**

**606-200201** TurboCoach Intermediate Car #70 **39.95**

**606-200202** TurboCoach Intermediate Car #72 **39.95**

## Early Amtrak 1971-73

In 1972, the Department of Transportation increased Amtrak's TurboTrains to 5 cars each. Products 606-200003, 200301 and 200302 together have the correct car numbers for Amtrak Turbo 1

**606-200003** #50-71-51 **499.95**

### TurboCoach Intermediate Car 39.95 ea

Correct window arrangements and interiors for cars added in 1972; models are different from the Turbo Cafe-Coach included with #200003.

**606-200301** #70

**606-200302** #72

See What's New and Exciting at
**www.walthers.com**

## Late Amtrak 1973-79

Amtrak ran its TurboTrains in this paint scheme in 4- and 5-car configurations. Products 606-200004, 200401 and 200402 together have the correct car numbers for Amtrak Turbo 2.

**606-200004** #52-74-53 **499.95**

### TurboCoach Intermediate Car 39.95 ea

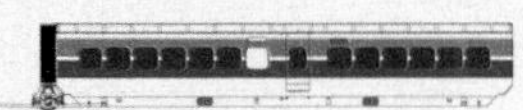

**606-200401** #73

**606-200402** #75

## Canadian National 1967-76

Canadian National converted its Turbos to 9-car trains. Products 606-200005, 606-200501, 606-200502, 200503 and 200504 together have the correct car numbers for CN Turbo 1.

Preproduction Model Shown

**606-200005** #150-250-125 **499.95**

Like the prototypes, the Power Cars of this set differ; #150 (PDC-27) is a TurboCoach, while #125 (PDC-26) is equipped as a TurboClub.

### TurboCoach Intermediate Car 39.95 ea

**606-200501** #255

**606-200502** #260

### Turbo TwoPack 69.95 ea

These sets include a TurboCafe and Turbo Club Intermediate cars, which differ from the standard TurboCoach, and feature unique window and interior arrangements.

**606-200503** #225 & 200

**606-200504** #227 & 202

## VIA Rail Canada 1976-82

VIA Rail Canada (and VIA-CN before it became an independent crown corporation) only ran its Turbos in 9-car trains. Products 606-200006, 200601, 200602, 200603 and 200604 together have the correct car numbers for VIA Turbo 2.

**606-200006** #151-251-126 **499.95**

Decals are provided for the red CN logos used on the nose until 1978 and the Montreal 1976 Olympics logo used in 1976. Like the prototypes, the Power Cars of this set differ; #151 (PDC-27) is a TurboCoach, while #126 (PDC-26) is equipped as a TurboClub.

### TurboCoach Intermediate Car 39.95 ea

**606-200601** #256

**606-200602** #261

### Turbo TwoPack 69.95 ea

These sets include a TurboCafe and TurboClub Intermediate cars, which differ from the standard TurboCoach, and feature unique window and interior arrangements.

**606-200603** #226, 201

**606-200604** #228, 203

Look what's coming down the "right track" from the Atlas Trainamn™ — a collection of quality, affordable, high performance HO model railroad locos and cars!

Meticulously engineered by Atlas, and designed for compatibility with any existing HO Scale layout, each comes fully assembled and ready to run. They're built for dependability and smooth, reliable performance; combining handsome paint schemes with state-of-the-art detailing and construction.

Trainman HO Scale locos come fully assembled and feature:

- Same drive as basic Master Series™ in an affordable locomotive
- Five-pole skewed armature motor with dual flywheels
- Separately applied hand rails and end railings
- Matching cabooses available separately (See the Freight Car Section)
- Locating dimples for grab irons
- True scale dimensions with accurate details
- Realistic diecast underframes
- AccuMate® Couplers
- 2,600 or 3,600 gallon fuel tank to match prototype

And, all Trainman products will be available year 'round at all times, so you can add new items to your layouts whenever you choose. With this exciting line of HO products, we promise…

***HO SCALE FUN FOR EVERYONE!™***

EMD GP38-2 BN 751-901

EMD GP38-2 CR 751-903

EMD GP38-2 UP "Baby Wings" 751-907

EMD GP38-2 CP 751-958

## NEW PRODUCTS

### Diesel Locomotives

### Alco RS32/36

Designated as a DL721 by ALCo, the 2,000hp RS32 was intended to compete with EMD's GP20 and GE's U25B locomotives. The 1,800hp DL701, also called RS36 was produced concurrently. Only 35 RS32 and 40 RS36 units were produced between 1961 and 1963. Despite their very low production numbers, a handful of RS32 and RS36 locomotives are still in service in 2007 on a few US shortline and tourist railroads. These models come with or without dynamic brakes as appropriate for each roadname.

**RS32 Locomotives**
**79.95 ea (Unless Noted)**

**NEW 751-8392** NYC (black, "Simplified Scheme")

**NEW 751-8393** NYC (black, "Simplified Scheme")

**NEW 751-8380** Undecorated No Dynamic Brakes **69.95**

**RS36 Locomotives**
**79.95 ea (Unless Noted)**

**NEW 751-8384** D&H (blue, gray, "Lightning Stripe")

**NEW 751-8385** D&H (blue, gray, "Lightning Stripe")

**NEW 751-8394** L&N (gray, yellow, "Late Scheme")

**NEW 751-8395** L&N (gray, yellow, "Late Scheme")

**NEW 751-8396** N&W (blue, yellow)

**NEW 751-8397** N&W (blue, yellow)

**NEW 751-8398** Tennessee Central (black, white)

**NEW 751-8399** Tennessee Central (black, white)

**NEW 751-8381** Undecorated w/Dynamic Brakes **69.95**

**NEW 751-8391** Undecorated No Dynamic Brakes **69.95**

Get the Scoop!
Get the Skinny!
Get the Score!
Check Out Walthers
Web site at
**www.walthers.com**

## DIESEL LOCOMOTIVES

### EMD GP38-2 "Late Production" 79.95 ea (Unless Noted)

The Dash 2 series, unveiled by EMD in 1972, featured significant internal upgrades, such as a solid-state, modular electrical control system and improved engine components designed to increase traction and reduce exhaust emissions. A reliable workhorse, the GP38-2 remains one of the most successful diesels ever built and most are still in service today.

**751-901** BN

**751-902** BN

**751-903** CR

**751-904** CR

**751-905** CSX "YN2"

**751-906** CSX "YN2"

**751-907** UP "Baby Wings"

**751-908** UP "Baby Wings"

**751-958** CP (Action Red w/Multimark)

**751-959** CP (Action Red w/Multimark)

**751-960** NS (black)

**751-961** NS (black)

**751-962** ATSF ("Warbonnet" blue, yellow)

**751-963** ATSF ("Warbonnet" blue, yellow)

**751-964** SP (gray, scarlet)

**751-965** SP (gray, scarlet)

**NEW 751-10000021** BNSF (green, orange)

**NEW 751-10000022** BNSF (green, orange)

**NEW 751-10000023** CNW (yellow, green, Operation Lifesaver Logo)

**NEW 751-10000024** CNW (yellow, green, Operation Lifesaver Logo)

**NEW 751-10000025** CSX ("YN3" blue, yellow)

**NEW 751-10000026** CSX ("YN3" blue, yellow)

**NEW 751-10000027** SOO (white, red)

**NEW 751-10000028** SOO (white, red)

**751-900** Undecorated **69.95**

## *Information* STATION

### The A Team, or The B Team?

Diesels changed the way railroads assigned locos to trains. In the steam era, one engine powered each train, except on grades, or with heavy trains, where a second loco and crew was added for more power.

Later diesels were modular; additional locos could be added or removed as needed. While each was independent, electrical or air cables from the lead engine allowed simultaneous control.

This concept became popular in the 1940s with the introduction of the EMD F unit. Lead or A units with cabs were coupled to cabless booster or B units, and run as one high-horsepower engine by a single crew.

In operation, locomotives were assigned to trains depending on tonnage, grades and weather conditions. A short train might have an A-B set of engines while a long train headed for heavy grades could have an A-B-B-B-A or A-B-B-B-B consist.

As with steam locos, A units had to be turned, a time-consuming process. To avoid this, many roads operated with opposite-facing A units at each end.

These diesel locomotive models feature plastic bodies and diecast frames, trucks, Buehler motor with flywheels and drive train with NMRA DCC plug. All locomotives include horn-hook, Northwest Shortline wheels and Accumater couplers.

# NEW PRODUCTS

## Sound Chassis w/LokSound

Replacement chassis for F units makes it easy to add sound and DCC to new or older units. Each includes a high quality digital decoder with motor control and a digital sound module on one circuit board. The sound is adjusted to the running mode: when the loco starts moving, you hear the primemover rev up and when it stops, you hear the engine slow down and braking sounds. All units come with a preprogrammed #72428 LokSound V.3.5, featuring the 16-cylinder_ EMD 567 prime mover, dynamic brakes, and a single chime air horn._ Can be used on DC layouts with a Precision Craft DCMaster #1001 Analog Control Module (sold separately) for pushbutton sound activation of bell and horn, volume control and programming. Sound units start at a slightly high voltage when operated on DC systems.

### EMD F3, 7 & 9

**A Unit w/Black Sideframes**
**NEW 691-1201** Unpowered **149.95**

**NEW 691-1203** Powered **199.95**

**B Unit w/Black Sideframes**
**NEW 691-1202** Unpowered **149.95**

**NEW 691-1204** Powered **199.95**

**A Unit w/Silver Sideframes**

**NEW 691-1205** Unpowered **149.95**

**NEW 691-1207** Powered **199.95**

**B Unit w/Silver Sideframes**
**NEW 691-1206** Unpowered **149.95**

**NEW 691-1208** Powered **199.95**

### EMC FT

**A Unit w/Black Sideframes**
**NEW 691-1209** Unpowered **149.95**

**NEW 691-1210** Powered **199.95**

**B Unit w/Black Sideframes**

**NEW 691-1213** Unpowered **149.95**

**NEW 691-1214** Powered **199.95**

**A Unit w/Silver Sideframes**

**NEW 691-1211** Unpowered **149.95**

**NEW 691-1212** Powered **199.95**

**B Unit w/Silver Sideframes**

**NEW 691-1215** Unpowered **149.95**

**NEW 691-1216** Powered **199.95**

## Tradition Line Diesels

### Baldwin VO-1000 Powered 120.00 ea

**NEW 691-4757** PRR #4757 (tuscan)

**NEW 691-4758** Elgin, Joliet, & Eastern #484

**NEW 691-4759** Elgin, Joliet, & Eastern #476

**NEW 691-4760** LV #137 (Tuscan w/orange handrails)

### Baldwin S-12 Powered 120.00 ea

**NEW 691-4941** LV #240 (tuscan)

**NEW 691-4942** LV #235 (tuscan)

### EMD F3

**Phase II Late A Unit Powered**
**NEW 691-5320** Bangor & Aroostook #45 (blue, yellow) **120.00**

**Phase II Late A (Powered) & B (Non-Powered) Set**
**NEW 691-5321** Maine Central #672A & 672B (green, Dulux) **160.00**

### EMD F7

**Phase I Early A (Powered) & B (Non-Powered) Set**

**NEW 691-5647** Soo Line #2202A & #2202C (maroon & Dulux Gold) **160.00**

**NEW 691-5649** CR #1652 & #3869 (black; Ex-PC "Patch" Paint) **170.00**

**Phase I Early A Unit Powered**
**NEW 691-5648** CR #1648 (blue) **135.00**

**Phase I Late A (Powered) & B (Non-Powered) Set**
**NEW 691-5716** Penn Central #1865, #3439 (white P) **170.00**

**Phase II A (Powered) & B (Non-Powered) Set**
**NEW 691-5821** Penn Central #1707, #712 (red P) **170.00**

## Executive Line Diesels

### GE U25B

**Powered 159.95 ea**
**NEW 691-23112** GN #2503 Phase 2

**NEW 691-23113** GN #2506 Phase 2

**NEW 691-23116** EL #2520 (late scheme) Phase 4

**NEW 691-23117** EL #2527 (late scheme) Phase 4

**NEW 691-23120** ATSF #6605 Phase 2

**NEW 691-23121** ATSF #6612 Phase 2

**NEW 691-23128** N&W #3516 Phase 2

**NEW 691-23129** N&W #3524 Phase 2

**NEW 691-23132** NH #2519 Phase 4

**NEW 691-23133** NH #2521 Phase 4

**NEW 691-23136** CB&Q #101 Phase 2

**NEW 691-23137** CB&Q #105 Phase 2

**Powered w/DCC & Loksound 259.95 ea**
**NEW 691-23114** GN #2500 Phase 2

**NEW 691-23115** GN #2504 Phase 2

**NEW 691-23118** EL #2517 (late scheme) Phase 4

**NEW 691-23119** EL #2524 (late scheme) Phase 4

**NEW 691-23122** ATSF #6601 Phase 2

**NEW 691-23123** ATSF #6608 Phase 2

**NEW 691-23130** N&W #3522 Phase 2

**NEW 691-23131** N&W #3529 Phase 2

**NEW 691-23134** NH #2514 Phase 4

**NEW 691-23135** NH #2525 Phase 4

**NEW 691-23138** CB&Q #102 Phase 2

**NEW 691-23139** CB&Q #104 Phase 2

### Early U28B

**Powered 159.95**
**NEW 691-23124** SP #7026

**NEW 691-23125** SP #7028

**Powered w/DCC & Loksound 259.95 ea**
**NEW 691-23126** SP #7025

**NEW 691-23127** SP #7027

# EXECUTIVE LINE DIESELS

Executive Line diesels come fully assembled and ready to run. Each has appropriate details including brass MU hoses, air hoses and windshield wipers. Wire grab irons and coupler lift bars are also included. Other features include an operating headlight, window glazing, installed handrails, a Buehler can motor, brass flywheels, nickel silver wheels with RP-25 flanges and knuckle couplers. Units are DCC ready.

## Baldwin

**DS-6-6-1500 159.95 ea**
**691-23201** EL #1150

**691-23202** EL #1152

**691-23203** Elgin, Joliet & Eastern #500

**691-23204** Elgin, Joliet & Eastern #501

**AS-16 Powered 159.95 ea**
**691-23301** B&O "Sunburst" #6203

**691-23302** B&O "Sunburst" #6205

**AS-616 Powered 159.95 ea**
**691-23205** SOO #393

**691-23206** SOO #395

**691-23207** Bessemer & Lake Erie #409

**691-23208** Bessemer & Lake Erie #404

## GE

### U25B

**Phase II w/ Brass Train Phone Antenna 159.95 ea**
**691-23107** PRR #2506

**691-23108** PRR #2502 w/Brass Train Phone Antenna

**Phase IV Powered 149.95 ea (Unless Noted)**
**691-23109** Guilford/Maine Central #225

**691-23110** Guilford/Maine Central #226

**691-23111** SP "Bicentennial" **169.95**

**With Snow Plows 159.95 ea**
**691-23103** MILW #5007

**691-23104** MILW #5058

**Early Version Cab Powered 149.95 ea**
**691-23105** Pittsburgh & Lake Erie #2818

**691-23106** Pittsburgh & Lake Erie #2808

# BALDWIN

## AS-16 Powered 115.00 ea

**691-4201** WM #175 (Speed Lettering)

**691-4202** WM #176 (Speed Lettering)

**691-4203** RDG #531

**691-4204** RDG #561

**691-4207** B&O #2234

**691-4208** B&O #2236

**691-4209** WM "Fireball" #173

**691-4210** WM "Fireball" #174

**691-4211** WM "Fireball" #175

**691-4212** WM "Fireball" #176

**691-4200** Undecorated

## AS-616 Powered 115.00 ea

**691-6601** PRR #8966

**691-6605** SP "Black Widow" #2

**691-6606** SP "Black Widow" #2

## Baldwin VO-660 120.00 ea

**691-4623** Chicago & Eastern Illinois #110 – Phase II

**691-4625** CNW #1246 – Phase III

**691-4626** CNW – Painted, No Unit Number - Phase III

**691-4627** DRGW #66 – Phase I

**691-4629** DRGW #73 – Phase I

**691-4630** DRGW – Painted, No Unit Number – Phase I

**691-4632** Elgin, Joliet & Eastern #272 – Phase I

**691-4633** CNJ #1040 – Phase II

**691-4634** CNJ #1041 – Phase II

**691-4635** CNJ #1042 – Phase II

**691-4636** CNJ #1043 – Phase II

**691-4637** KCS #1150 – Phase III

**691-4638** L&N #20 – Phase II

**691-4639** L&N #21 – Phase II

**691-4640** L&N #22 – Phase II

**691-4641** L&N #23 – Phase II

**691-4643** MP #9012 – Phase I

**691-4645** NP #129 – Phase II

**691-4647** NYC #501 – Phase I

**691-4648** NYC #754 – Phase II

**691-4649** NYC – Painted, No Unit Number – Phase II

**691-4650** NYC #761 – Phase III

**691-4651** NYC – Painted, No Unit Number – Phase III

**691-4655** PRR #5941 – Phase III

**691-4658** RDG #66 – Phase I

**691-4659** RDG – Painted, No Unit Number – Phase I

**691-4660** RDG #68 – Phase II

**691-4661** RDG – Painted, No Unit Number – Phase II

**691-4662** SLSF #600 – Phase II

**691-4663** SLSF #601 – Phase II

**691-4667** Terminal Railroad Association of St. Louis #533 – Phase II

**691-4668** Terminal Railroad Association of St. Louis #534 – Phase II

**691-4671** WM #103 – Phase II

**691-4672** WM #104 – Phase II

**691-4620** Undecorated – Phase I

**691-4621** Undecorated – Phase II

**691-4622** Undecorated – Phase III

## VO-1000 Powered 115.00 ea

**691-4712** B&O No Unit Number

**691-4721** UP No Unit Number

**691-4722** SAL #1402

**691-4723** SAL #1416

**691-4725** SLSF #213

**691-4726** SLSF #224

**691-4735** MP #9119

**691-4742** St. SLSF #214 ("Frisco" black, yellow)

## DS-4-4-1000 Powered 115.00 ea (Unless Noted)

**691-4808** SP #1401 "Tiger Stripes"

**691-4811** Chicago Great Western #36 (maroon)

**691-4812** Chicago Great Western #38 (maroon)

**691-4813** LV #140 (As Delivered Scheme)

**691-4814** LV #148 (As Delivered Scheme)

**691-4815** SOO #311 (black, yellow)

**691-4816** SOO #312 (black, yellow)

**691-4817** RDG #714

**691-4818** RDG #716

**691-4819** SLSF #238 ("Frisco" black, yellow)

**691-4820** St. Louis - San Francisco #241 ("Frisco" black, yellow)

**691-4821** Ironton #750

**691-4822** Ironton #751

**691-4823** B&O Mid 1960s #1

**691-4824** B&O Mid 1960s #2

**691-4827** MP #1 (black)

**691-4828** MP #2 (black)

**691-4829** EL #1 (black, yellow)

**691-4830** EL #2 (black, yellow)

**691-4833** Terminal Railroad Association of St. Louis (red)

**691-4834** PRR #9122

**691-4835** PRR #9252

**691-4837** ATSF #2273 (blue & yellow)

**691-4838** PC #7955

**691-4839** PC #7956

**691-4840** PRR #9071 **120.00**

**691-4841** PRR #9274 **120.00**

**691-4842** ATSF #2266 (Zebra Stripes) **120.00**

**691-4843** ATSF #2288 (Zebra Stripes) **120.00**

**691-4800** Undecorated

## S-8 Powered 115.00 ea

**691-4881** Rock Island (black)

**691-4882** Pennsylvania-Reading Seashore Lines

**691-4883** PRR #8996

**691-4884** PRR #8998

**691-4885** Rock Island #805 (red)

**691-4880** Undecorated

## S-12 Powered 115.00 ea (Unless Noted)

**691-4901** PRR #1

**691-4902** PRR #2

**691-4903** B&O As Delivered #1

**691-4904** B&O As Delivered #2

**691-4905** SP "Tiger Stripes" #1

**691-4906** SP "Tiger Stripes" #2

**691-4907** SOO (black, yellow) #1

**691-4908** SOO (black, yellow) #2

**691-4909** CNJ #1072

**691-4910** CNJ #1073

**691-4911** Erie #620

**691-4912** Erie #623

**691-4913** LV #234

**691-4914** LV #242

**691-4915** MKT #1211

**691-4916** MKT #1212

**691-4917** MP (black) #9226

**691-4918** MP (black) #9228

**691-4919** NYC (Cigar Band) #8100

**691-4920** NYC (Cigar Band) #8112

**691-4921** SAL #1462

**691-4922** Seaboard #1465

**691-4923** SOU (green) #2292

**691-4924** SOU (green) #2299

**691-4925** Wabash #305

**691-4926** Wabash #306

**691-4927** MKT w/Safety Stencil #306

**691-4928** Rock Island #759 (red)

**691-4930** SMS Rail Service #300

**691-4931** PC #8117

**691-4932** PC #8193

**691-4933** SMS Rail Service #301 "Old Blue"

**691-4934** EL #619 (gray & maroon) **120.00**

**691-4935** EL #621 (gray & maroon) **120.00**

**691-4936** EL #623 (gray & maroon) **120.00**

**691-4937** EL #626 (gray & maroon) **120.00**

**691-4938** EL #627 (gray & maroon) **120.00**

**691-4939** PRR #8753 **120.00**

**691-4940** PRR #8790 **120.00**

## RS-12 Powered 115.00 ea

**691-4602** NYC #6226

**691-4603** NYC #6228

**691-4604** CNJ #1206

**691-4605** PC #8300

**691-4600** Undecorated

# GE

## U25B

### Phase II Powered 115.00 ea (Unless Noted)

**691-7207** PRR #2501

**691-7208** PC #2501

**691-7211** NH #2505

**691-7224** GN #2503 (Big Sky Blue, white) **120.00**

**691-7225** GN #2503 (Big Sky Blue, white) **120.00**

**691-7201** Undecorated

### Phase IV Powered

**691-7401** Undecorated **115.00**

# ALCO

## Century C-630 Powered 135.00 ea (Unless Noted)

**691-6310** PRR

**691-6311** SP

**691-6312** PC

**691-6313** L&N

**691-6314** CR (Ex-PC/PRR Unit)

**691-6315** CR (Ex-RDG Unit)

**691-6316** ACL

**691-6319** SCL

**691-6323** N de M #8315 **140.00**

**691-6324** N de M #8326 **140.00**

**691-6325** L&N #1425 **140.00**

**691-6326** PRR #6320 **140.00**

**691-6327** SP #6327 **140.00**

**691-6300** Undecorated Single Sand Filler - CR, L&N, PC, PRR, SP & UP

**691-6301** Undecorated Dual Sand Filler - Atlantic Coast Line, Seaboard Coast Line

## Century C-630 High Hood Powered 135.00 ea

**691-6351** N&W #1 As Delivered (blue)

**691-6352** N&W #2 As Delivered (blue)

**691-6353** N&W #3 As Delivered (blue)

**691-6354** N&W #1130 (black w/white "NW" logo)

**691-6355** N&W #1133 (black w/white "NW" logo)

**691-6356** N&W #1134 (black w/white "NW" logo)

**691-6357** N&W #1131 (black w/white "NORFOLK AND WESTERN" lettering)

**691-6350** Undecorated

## Century C-628 Powered 135.00 ea (Unless Noted)

**691-6210** PRR

**691-6212** PC

**691-6213** Alco Demonstrator #628-1

**691-6214** Alco Demonstrator #628-2

**691-6215** L&N

**691-6216** CR (Ex-PC/PRR)

**691-6218** ACL

**691-6219** MON

**691-6221** D&H Small Herald

**691-6222** CR (Ex-LV)

**691-6223** SCL

**691-6227** N de M #8327 **140.00**

**691-6228** N de M #8331 **140.00**

**691-6229** D&H #602 **140.00**

**691-6230** PRR #6303 **140.00**

**691-6231** LV #627 (Tuscan) **140.00**

**691-6232** LV #630 (Tuscan) **140.00**

**691-6233** CR #6748 **140.00**

**691-6234** PC #6302 **140.00**

**691-6328** PC #6318 **140.00**

**691-6200** Undecorated Single Sand Filler

**691-6201** Undecorated Double Sand Filler

## Century C-628 High Hood Powered 135.00 ea

**691-6251** N&W #1 As-Delivered (black)

**691-6252** N&W #2 As-Delivered (black)

**691-6253** N&W #3 As-Delivered (black)

**691-6257** N&W As-Delivered Scheme #1113 (blue)

**691-6258** N&W As-Delivered Scheme #1114 (blue)

**691-6259** N&W As-Delivered Scheme #1117 (blue)

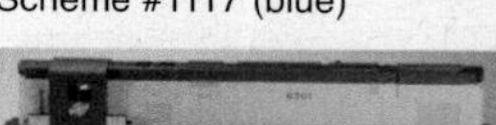

**691-6260** CNW w/Green Cab #6701

**691-6261** CNW w/Green Cab #6718

**691-6262** CNW w/Green Cab #6723
**691-6250** Undecorated

# EMD

## FT A-B Set 185.00 ea
Includes powered A unit & dummy B unit.
**691-5018** DRGW
**691-5019** DRGW (5 Port Holes in B Unit)
**691-5020** LV (Cornell Red)
**691-5021** SOU (green)
**691-5022** GN
**691-5023** GN (Light Side Panel)
**691-5027** SSW "Black Widow"
**691-5029** ATSF Passenger
**691-5030** B&M
**691-5031** CB&Q
**691-5032** WP
**691-5033** Erie
**691-5034** B&O
**691-5036** ATSF "Catwhisker" (Nose Stripe)
**691-5037** ATSF "Catwhisker" (No Stripe)
**691-5040** Rock Island
**691-5041** RDG #1
**691-5042** RDG #2
**691-5043** NP #1
**691-5044** NP #2
**691-5045** York, Ontario & Western #1
**691-5046** New York, Ontario & Western #2
**691-5047** MILW (As Delivered) #1
**691-5048** MILW (As Delivered) #2
**691-5049** ACL #1 (black & yellow)
**691-5050** ACL #2 (black & yellow)
**691-5051** MP #1
**691-5052** MP #2
**691-5064** SOU #4102-4302 (green)
**691-5067** SSW #923-922 (Black Widow)

**691-5068** ATSF #163 (Passenger Warbonnet)
**691-5069** B&M #4211 (Minute Man Scheme – No Wings)
**691-5074** ATSF #167 (Passenger Warbonnet)
**691-5075** Erie #701 (black w/yellow stripes)

## FTA Single Headlight 185.00 ea (Unless Noted)

**691-5014** NYC **130.00**
**691-5053** WP #911A-B
**691-5054** WP #911C-D
**691-5055** ATSF #118 (Cigar Band)
**691-5056** ATSF #140 (Cigar Band)
**691-5057** ATSF #TBA (blue)
**691-5000** Undecorated w/Light Side Panel **130.00**
**691-5001** Undecorated w/Large Side Panels **130.00**

**Limited Quantity Available**
**691-5058** MP #510A-B

## FTA Double Headlight 130.00 ea
**691-5002** Undecorated
**691-5003** Undecorated w/Large Side Panels

## FTB Dummy 55.00 ea
**691-5015** NYC
**691-5004** Undecorated
**691-5005** Undecorated, 5 Port Holes

# EMD F UNIT A-B SETS
Includes powered A unit and unpowered B unit unless noted.

## F3 150.00 ea (Unless Noted)

### Phase I Powered
Includes chicken wire, three-porthole A units and high fans.
**691-5122** DL&W #656 "Gray Ghost" **115.00**
**691-5100** Undecorated Single Headlight
**691-5101** Undecorated Double Headlight

### Phase II Early
**691-5210** Chicago Great Western B Unit Only **45.00**
**691-5211** NYC (gray, "3/4 Lightning Stripe")
**691-5212** NYC (black, "3/4 Lightning Stripe")
**691-5214** CB&Q Passenger
**691-5215** CB&Q Passenger A Unit Only **115.00**

**691-5218** WM "Fireball" A Unit Only **115.00**
**691-5220** NYC #1611-2409 (black, 3/4 Lightning Stripe) **160.00**
**691-5221** NYC #3503-3601 (gray, 3/4 Lightning Stripe) **160.00**
**691-5222** CB&Q #9962A, 9962B **160.00**
**691-5223** CB&Q Passenger #9962C A Unit Only **120.00**
**691-5200** Undecorated Single Headlight
**691-5201** Undecorated Double Headlight

### Phase II Late

**691-5310** Bangor & Aroostook A Unit Only (blue & yellow) **115.00**
**691-5312** Maine Central (green & yellow)
**691-5315** Chicago & Eastern Illinois (Simplified) Nondynamic
**691-5316** Chicago & Eastern Illinois (Simplified) Nondynamic A Unit Only **115.00**
**691-5318** Bangor & Aroostook A Unit Only (blue, gray) **115.00**
**691-5300** Undecorated Single Headlight
**691-5301** Undecorated Double Headlight

### Phase III
Includes chicken wire, horizontal louvers and low fans.
**691-5400** Undecorated Single Headlight
**691-5401** Undecorated Double Headlight

### Phase IV
**691-5510** CB&Q Double Headlight
**691-5511** MILW (As Delivered) Double Headlight
**691-5512** Maine Central A Unit Only (green & yellow) **115.00**
**691-5515** SOO Double Headlight As Delivered (maroon)
**691-5517** SOO #2200A/2200C **160.00**
**691-5500** Undecorated Single Headlight
**691-5501** Undecorated Double Headlight

## F7 150.00 ea (Unless Noted)
Includes powered A unit and unpowered B unit unless noted

### Phase I Early
**691-5610** PRR Single Headlight
**691-5611** CN "Wet Noodle"
**691-5612** SP "Black Widow" Double Headlight
**691-5613** Amtrak® Double Headlight
**691-5614** B&O Mid-1960s Scheme Single Headlight
**691-5615** Minneapolis & St. Louis Single Headlight A Unit Only (red & white) **115.00**
**691-5616** LV (As Delivered) Scheme Single Headlight
**691-5617** RDG Single Headlight
**691-5619** CNW (Freight, Simplified) Double Headlight
**691-5621** WP (Freight 1955-1965) Single Headlight
**691-5622** Rock Island Single Headlight (red & black)
**691-5623** MP Single Headlight
**691-5625** L&N Double Headlight (Freight Scheme)
**691-5626** Rock Island A Unit Only (red & black) **115.00**
**691-5627** N&W Nondynamic A Unit Only **115.00**
**691-5628** CNJ A Unit Only (blue, Ex-B&O) **115.00**
**691-5633** WM "Fireball"
**691-5634** WM "Fireball" A Unit Only **115.00**
**691-5635** SOU #4260 - 4403 ("Black Tuxedo") **160.00**
**691-5636** SOU #4267 - 4423 ("Black Tuxedo") **160.00**
**691-5637** SOU – Painted ("Black Tuxedo"), No Unit Numbers **160.00**
**691-5638** PRR #1470 - 3518 **160.00**
**691-5639** RDG #272 **160.00**
**691-5640** Amtrak #102/150 **160.00**
**691-5641** Amtrak #101/154 **160.00**
**691-5642** B&O (Mid-60s Scheme) #4528/5475 **160.00**
**691-5643** B&O (Mid-60s Scheme) #4539/5507 **160.00**
**691-5644** RI #121A/121B **160.00**
**691-5645** RI #118 A Unit Only **120.00**
**691-5646** L&N #846/706 **160.00**
**691-5600** Undecorated Single Headlight
**691-5601** Undecorated Double Headlight

### Phase I Late

**691-5711** SP (red & gray)
**691-5712** SSW (red & gray)
**691-5700** Undecorated Single Headlight
**691-5701** Undecorated Double Headlight

### Phase II
48" dynamic fan, low fans and vertical grille and louvers.
**691-5812** WM "Speed Lettering" Scheme Single Headlight **160.00**

**691-5819** A Unit Only; Wellsville, Addison & Galeton #2200 **120.00**
**691-5820** WM #242/406 (Speed Lettering) **160.00**
**691-5800** Undecorated Single Nose Headlight
**691-5801** Undecorated Double Nose Headlight

## F9 150.00 ea
48" dynamic fan, extra louvers, low fans and vertical grille and louvers.
**691-5910** ATSF Freight Scheme Single Headlight
**691-5911** BN Double Headlight
**691-5912** DRGW Double Headlight (yellow w/single black stripe)
**691-5913** NP Passenger Scheme Double Headlight
**691-5914** MILW Double Headlight (orange, black)

**691-5916** UP Single Headlight
**691-5923** DRGW #5771/5762 (Single Stripe) **160.00**
**691-5924** BN #788/773 **160.00**
**691-5925** BN #770/807 **160.00**
**691-5900** Undecorated Single Headlight
**691-5901** Undecorated Double Headlight

### A Units 120.00 ea
**691-5917** N de M #TBA
**691-5918** N de M #TBA

# POWER CHASSIS

## Power Chassis Only 95.00 ea (Unless Noted)
Includes frame, motor and trucks, no body shell.
**691-4299** Baldwin AS-16
**691-4699** Alco RS-12 - Stewart Drive
**691-5198** F3A/F7A/F9A
**691-5199** F3B/F7B/F9B
**691-5999** FTB **85.00**
**691-6299** C628
**691-6399** C630
**691-6699** AS-616

# UNDECORATED BODY SHELLS

## ALCO RS-3 11.00 ea
**691-1075** Phase 1B
**691-2075** Phase 2A
**691-3075** Phase 3

# UNSURPASSED DETAIL

## The Classic Big Boy Roars To Life!

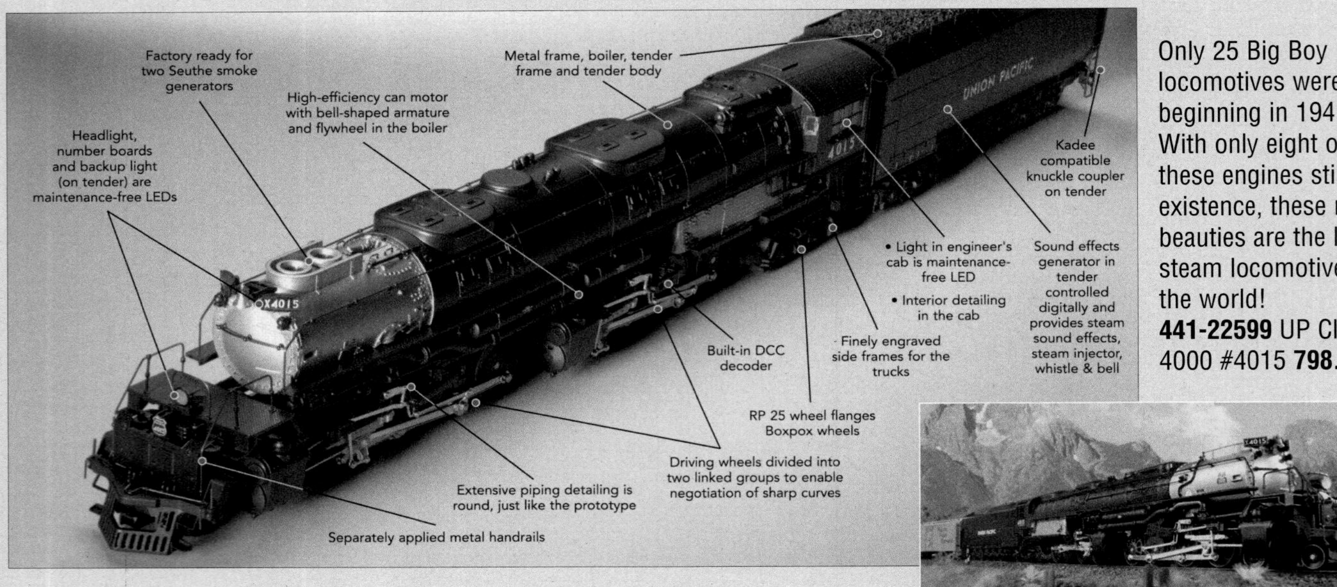


Only 25 Big Boy locomotives were built beginning in 1941. With only eight of these engines still in existence, these rare beauties are the largest steam locomotives in the world!
**441-22599** UP Class 4000 #4015 **798.00**

TRIX

TRIX

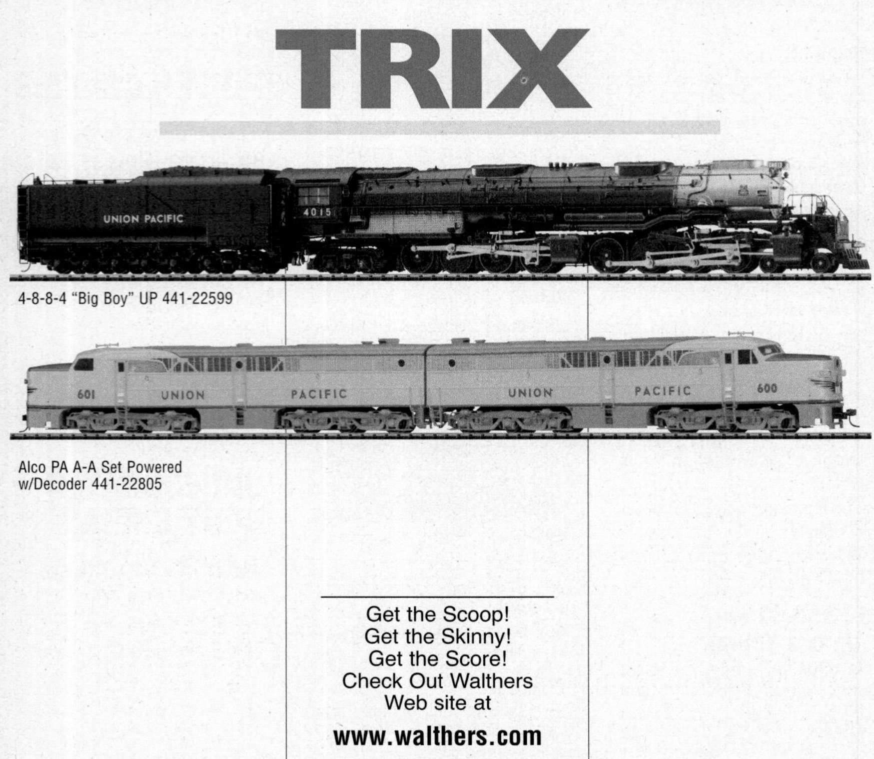

4-8-8-4 "Big Boy" UP 441-22599

Alco PA A-A Set Powered w/Decoder 441-22805

Get the Scoop!
Get the Skinny!
Get the Score!
Check Out Walthers Web site at
**www.walthers.com**

## STEAM LOCOMOTIVES

### 4-8-8-4 "Big Boy"

**441-22599** UP **798.00**
Designed for two-rail DC model railroading, this impressive engine features all-metal construction (with a metal frame, boiler, tender body and tender frame), a built-in DCC decoder (for steam sound effects and control of whistle, bell, lights, braking and speed), high-efficiency motor, RP-25 wheel flanges, Kadee-compatible coupler, and synchronized and asynchronized sound.

## DIESEL LOCOMOTIVES

### Alco PA-1 A-A Set Powered w/Decoder

**441-22805** UP **339.00**
This dynamic diesel set features diecast metal frame and bodies, two five-pole high-efficiency motors, built-in DCC-Selectrix decoder, RP-25 wheels, Kadee-compatible couplers, and a Mars light.

### Locomotive Wheel Cleaning Brush

**441-66602 28.49**
This easy-to-use brush cleans wheels for improved conductivity and prevention of radio/television interference. Two-rail DC.

Relive the glory days of railroading with this line of detailed locos. Models are offered in DCC versions with LokSound for use with DCC systems or DC layouts (requires separate controller to activate sounds) or without sound for DC only.

All engines feature a powerful five-pole can motor with flywheel/s, plus exceptional weight for pulling power; an optional traction tire-equipped driver is also included. Models are detailed, painted and lettered to match specific prototypes, and feature working headlight and back-up light, where applicable. Operating Kadee® couplers are standard.

Engines equipped with LokSound combine silent running decoders with a super high output amplifier, and adjustable volume for synchronized chuff, whistle, bell, squealing brakes, flange squeal, Doppler effect and air let off (in neutral). The system also features load dependent sound, 8Mbit of memory to handle complex sounds, and four-channel sound. New 20-function mapping lets you create custom sound and function operations, and units are compatible with LokSound Programmer for PC control, upgrades or adding custom sounds. Load compensation, switcher mode and Dynamic Drive Control features are also included.

Baldwin Sharknose BF-16 PRR 588-120

PRR Class I1sa 2-10-0 588-88

# NEW PRODUCTS

## Diesel

### Baldwin Sharknose BF-16

**Powered A-B Set w/LokSound 389.99 ea (Unless Noted)**

**NEW 588-120** PRR #2004A/2004B (5-Stripe w/Train Phone Antenna) **399.99**

**NEW 588-121** PRR #2007A/2007B (5-Stripe w/Train Phone Antenna) **399.99**

**NEW 588-124** B&O #851-A/851X (blue, gray, gold)

**NEW 588-125** B&O #853-A/853X (blue, gray, gold)

**NEW 588-128** NYC #1212/3706 (Cigar Band)

**NEW 588-129** NYC #1217/3704 (Cigar Band)

**Powered A Unit w/LokSound**

**NEW 588-122** PRR #2007A (5-Stripe w/Train Phone Antenna) **259.99**

**NEW 588-126** B&O #853-A (blue, gray, gold) **249.99**

**NEW 588-130** NYC #1217 (Cigar Band) **249.99**

**NEW 588-132** Unpainted, PRR Type w/Tall Nose Door & Train Phone Antenna **249.99**

**NEW 588-133** Unpainted, B&O Type w/Short Nose Door **239.99**

**NEW 588-134** NYC Type w/Tall Nose Door **239.99**

**Dummy B Unit 149.99 ea (Unless Noted)**

**NEW 588-123** PRR #2012B (5-Stripe)

**NEW 588-127** B&O #853X (blue, gray, gold)

**NEW 588-131** NYC #3704 (Cigar Band)

**NEW 588-135** Unpainted **139.99**

**DC Powered A-B Set 279.99 (Unless Noted)**

**NEW 588-162** PRR #2004A/2004B (5-Stripe w/Train Phone Antenna) **289.99**

**NEW 588-163** PRR #2007A/2012B (5-Stripe w/Train Phone Antenna) **289.99**

**NEW 588-166** B&O #851-A/851X (blue, gray, gold)

**NEW 588-167** B&O #853-A/853X (blue, gray, gold)

**NEW 588-170** NYC #1212/3706 (Cigar Band)

**NEW 588-171** NYC #1217/3704 (Cigar Band)

**DC Powered**

**NEW 588-164** PRR #2007A (5-Stripe w/Train Phone Antenna) **159.99**

**NEW 588-168** B&O #853-A (blue, gray, gold) **149.99**

**NEW 588-172** NYC #1212 (Cigar Band) **149.99**

**NEW 588-174** Unpainted PRR Type w/Tall Nose Door & Train Phone Antenna **149.99**

**NEW 588-175** Unpainted B&O Type w/Short Nose Door **139.99**

**NEW 588-176** Unpainted NYC Type w/Tall Nose Door **139.99**

**DC Powered B Unit 13.99 ea (Unless Noted)**

**NEW 588-165** PRR #2012B (5-Stripe)

**NEW 588-169** B&O #853X (blue, gray, gold)

**NEW 588-173** NYC #2706 (Cigar Band)

**NEW 588-177** Unpainted **129.99**

### Sharknose B Unit Chassis Upgrade

**NEW 588-395** w/LokSound **149.99**

## STEAM

### PRR Class I1sa 2-10-0

**Powered w/LokSound 399.99 ea**

**588-88** #4471 High Headlight

**588-89** #4268 High Headlight

**588-91** #4440 Low Headlight

**588-92** #4538 Low Headlight

**NEW 588-880** #4324 Modern Headlight

**NEW 588-881** #4595 Modern Headlight

**588-90** Unlettered High Headlight

**588-93** Unlettered Low Headlight

**NEW 588-882** Unlettered Modern Headlight

**DC Powered 299.99 ea**

**588-94** #4383 High Headlight

**588-95** #4637 High Headlight

**588-97** #4447 Low Headlight

**588-98** #4304 Low Headlight

**NEW 588-883** #4324 Modern Headlight

**NEW 588-884** #4595 Modern Headlight

**588-96** Unlettered High Headlight

**588-99** Unlettered Low Headlight

**NEW 588-885** Unlettered Modern Headlight Position

2008
HO
Model Railroad
Reference Book

# TRAIN SETS

Models and Photo by Ken Nelson

A brilliant summer sunrise welcomes the start of another busy workday on the Poco Valley Railroad. Early morning commuters fold their newspapers and gulp the last of their coffee from paper cups as a pair of rail diesel cars arrive to begin the morning rush.

Built by Ken Nelson of Scotia, New York, this impressive layout is served by a pair of repainted Life-Like RDCs, easing to a stop in front of an Atlas station.

If you're just getting started, or looking to share the fun of model railroading with family or friends, you'll find a great assortment of sets for every interest in the Train Sets Section which follows.

# TRAINLINE®
## by WALTHERS

Baggage Car Not Shown

931-840

## NEW PRODUCTS

### Trainline® Wayfreight HO Train Set

**Fall 2007 Delivery**
- Complete Starter Set
- PROTO 1000 F3 Diesel with Working Headlight
- Metal Wheels & Knuckle Couplers on All Cars
- Flat Car with Removable Grader
- Log Car with Removable Logs
- Bay Window Caboose Matches Loco
- Solid State MRC™ Power Pack
- 3 SceneMaster™ Vehicles
- 36 x 54" 91.4 x 137.1cm Oval of Nickel Silver Track
- Compatible with Thousands of HO Scale Products

### With Atlas® Track 119.98 ea

**NEW 931-850** Santa Fe

**NEW 931-851** Chicago & North Western

**NEW 931-852** Pennsylvania

**NEW 931-853** Union Pacific†

**NEW 931-854** Baltimore & Ohio

**NEW 931-855** Canadian National

### With Bachmann® EZ-Track® 119.98 ea

**NEW 931-840** Santa Fe

**NEW 931-841** Chicago & North Western

**NEW 931-842** Pennsylvania

**NEW 931-843** Union Pacific

**NEW 931-844** Baltimore & Ohio

**NEW 931-845** Canadian National

## CITY EXPRESS
### 149.98 ea

- Free Video & Booklet
- Ready to Run
- Powered FA-1 Diesel w/Working Headlight
- 60' Heavyweight Baggage, Coach & Combine
- Cars feature Interiors & Metal RP-25 Wheels
- Knuckle Couplers
- Snap-Together Station Kit
- MRC™ Power Pack
- 44 x 71" 110 x 177.5cm Oval of Atlas Snap-Track

**Limited Quantity Available**

**931-46** GN

**931-48** PRR

**931-50** UP

For Up-To-Date Information and News Bookmark Walthers Web site at

**www.walthers.com**

Ready-to-run electric train sets include lighted locomotives, steel track, power packs with hook-up wire and instructions. Locomotives feature all-wheel drive.

## NEW PRODUCTS

### Metal Train Metalset™

These ready-to-run train sets feature all-metal locomotives and all-metal cars. Sets come complete with 45 x 36" roadbed track oval and deluxe UL-Listed power pack.

### The Explorer 2

**NEW 490-801 TBA**
Includes F7 freight locomotive, three cars and six hand-painted figures.

### Metalforce

**NEW 490-830 TBA**
All-metal US Army F7 locomotive pulls US Army tank car, box car, search light car and caboose. Set includes 72 US Army figures and authentic detailed tank.

### Holiday Spirit

**NEW 490-835 TBA**
This delightful set features an F7 locomotive followed by the Three Elves Egg Nog Tank, North Pole Tree Service Hopper with three Christmas trees, Mister Frosty's Reefer and Season's Greetings Caboose. Includes special edition Santa's Gift Delivery Van.

### Trains, Trucks & Automobiles 190.99 ea

Ready-to run all-metal set includes two lighted F7 locomotives, four cars, three diecast autos, tractor-trailer auto carrier, loading dock, 45 x 36" oval track and deluxe UL pack w/DC and AC terminals.

**490-820** UP

**490-821** PRR

**490-822** CP

## TRAIN SETS

### Iron Duke

**490-1035 115.00**
Lighted steam locomotive with all-wheel pickup, four heavy weight cars w/knuckle couplers, deluxe transformer, 45 x 36" oval roadbed track and 22-piece accessory kit. Sets up in minutes.

### Bumble Bee

**490-1026 69.00**
Includes a DRGW locomotive, hopper, box car, crane and caboose.

### Evening Star

**490-1027 69.00**
Features a dual lighted 0-4-0 steam locomotive, flat car with logs, reefer and wood caboose.

### The Classic

**490-1028 74.00**
Set comes with one each hobby-quality F-2 locomotive with eight-wheel drive, tank car, box car and caboose.

### The Canadian Classic

**490-1029 74.00**
Includes one each hobby-quality F-2 locomotive with eight-wheel drive, tank car, box car and caboose, all decorated in Canadian paint schemes.

**Limited Quantity Available**

### Thunder Jet

**490-1040 132.00**
Features a 2-6-0 steam locomotive with tender, five pieces of rolling stock, a station with figures and accessories, telephone poles, signals, targets, and a 200-piece 54 x 36" track oval.

### High-Speed Train Sets 132.00 ea

These state-of-the-art train sets include three high-speed units, power pack and a 45 x 36" oval of track.

**490-2500** Amtrak

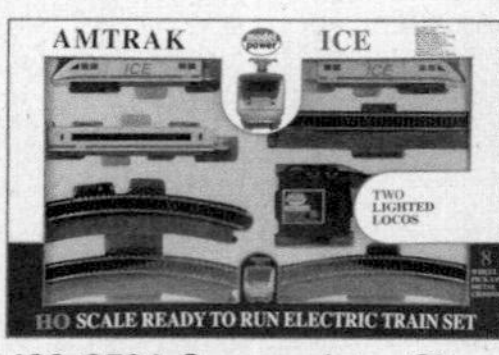


**490-2501** German Inter City Express (ICE)

**Limited Quantity Available**

### Double Diesel

**490-1061 142.00**
Powered and dummy diesel locomotives, four freight cars, caboose, bridge and trestle set, 40-piece building set, 22 telephone poles and signs, figures, tunnel and 54 x 36" oval of track.

### Midnight Express

**490-1065 96.00**
0-4-0 steam locomotive, three freight cars, caboose and 36" circle of track.

**Limited Quantity Available**

### Christmas Train Set

**490-1093 129.00**
A lighted gear-driven locomotive pulls four dynamic freight cars: a Holiday Express hopper, a Season's Greetings box car, a flat car pulling Santa Claus riding in a sleigh, and a white-and-gold caboose.

Division of
Wm. K. Walthers, Inc.

# TRAIN SETS W/POWER-LOC™ TRACK

These sets include Life-Like's Power-Loc track, the unique side-locking track system that clicks together instantly and locks track securely in place. There's no need for rail joiners, so set-up is quick and easy. Solid roadbed base offers durability and support on any surface (even carpet), eliminating the need for boards, nails, screws or tools. Sets also include a UL-listed power pack with forward and reverse, and a terminal rerailer.

## NEW PRODUCTS

### Warbonnet Charger

**NEW 433-8992 59.99**
Now with Bilingual instructions and packaging in English and Spanish. Keep freight moving on schedule with this exciting set! Includes hi-nose GP38-2 diesel with working headlight in Santa Fe red and silver, matching caboose, plus gondola, tank car and box car, 38" 0.9m circle of Power-Loc track with terminal rerailer, UL-listed power pack with forward and reverse, plug-in wires, extra couplers and complete instructions.

### Freight Runner

**NEW 433-9100 109.99**
Now with Bilingual instructions and packaging in English and Spanish. Loaded with model railroading fun, this big set delivers plenty of railroad action. A rugged GP38-2 diesel with working headlight leads a Sliding Door Box Car, Two-Bay Hopper, Tank Car, Thrall Door Box Car, Stock car and a Matching Caboose down the line. The set includes a Stock Yard complete with pigs, cows and people, along with a simple snap-together Passenger and Freight Station building. There's a working Crossing Gate with Dual Arms that raise and lower as the train passes. Three trees, two automobiles, a truck and over 100 signs are also included. Setting up the giant 89 x 38" 2.26 x 0.9m figure 8 of Power-Loc track will be easy, thanks to the new 90° Degree Crossing Track that eliminates separate bridges and piers.

### Nostalgic Heartland Express

**NEW 433-8993 89.99**
Ring in the holidays for years to come with this wonderful starter set! Featuring officially licensed reproductions of Saturday Evening Post covers, the four freight cars, matching caboose and powered 0-4-0 steam loco with tender will brighten any layout under the tree or a Christmas village. For more fun, there are five glitter-decorated Christmas trees and a snap-together station in cheery holiday colors. The complete set also comes with a 56 x 38" 1.4 x 0.9m oval of Power-Loc track with terminal rerailer, UL-listed power pack, plug-in wires, extra couplers and complete instructions.



### Super City Elevated Rails

**NEW 433-8994 199.99**
Twice the fun in one complete set! With both freight and passenger trains running on two levels, this set is packed with big-time railroading action. The freight train includes a GP38-2 diesel with working light, Wooden Box Car, Tank Car and Sliding Door Box Car, while the passenger train features a powered F7 diesel with headlight pulling a Coach and Observation cars, which also have interior lights. The action takes place on two complete loops of track: a 65 x 38" 1.6 x 0.9m oval for the lower, plus a 47 x 38" 1.1 x 0.9m oval with snap-in elevation piers for the upper level. Each level also has its own UL-listed power pack for independent control. For more big city fun, the set comes with a snap-together railroad station, plus Fire House and Police Station building kits, 24 signs, telephone poles, automobiles, street lights and much, much more.

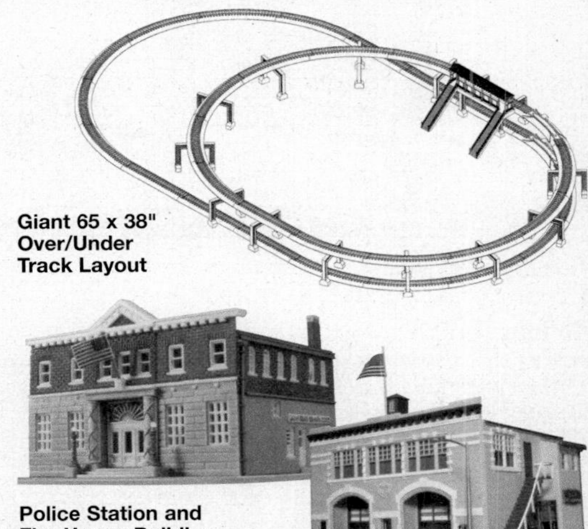

Giant 65 x 38" Over/Under Track Layout

Police Station and Fire House Building Kits Included

13 Snap-In Piers for Elevated Fun

Division of
Wm. K. Walthers, Inc.

All sets are complete with UL-Listed power pack, plug-in terminal wires, extra couplers and complete instructions.

Freightline USA 433-8644

Diesel Thunder 433-8951

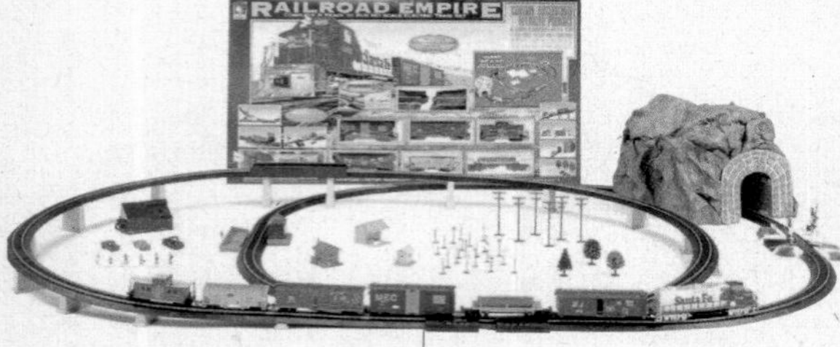

Railroad Empire 433-8646

## Holiday Rails

**433-8198 84.99**
Powered F7 Diesel with working headlight leads a tank car, a gondola with glittering Christmas trees, a flat car carrying packages and a caboose. For the finishing touch, there's a snap-together station decorated for the holidays. Includes 56 x 38" 140 x 95cm oval of Power-Loc track with terminal rerailer.

## Rail Runner

**433-8635 89.99**
GP38-2 ATSF low nose diesel with headlight, five cars, 65 x 38" track oval with terminal rerailer, operating dual crossing gate, three trackside shanty kits, seven vehicles, 10-piece bridge and pier set, 91 railroad, street and road signs and 12 utility poles.

## Santa Fe Flyer

**433-8660 84.99**
Includes F7 diesel with working headlight, five cars, 56 x 38" track oval, station, two cars, one truck, three trees, 86 signs, 12 utility poles and log dump station.

## Freight Hauler

**433-8630 89.99**
GP38-2 hi-nose diesel with working headlight, six cars, 65 x 33" elevated track oval, 10-piece bridge-and-pier set, signal bridge with trackside accessories, 110 signs and 12 utility poles.

## Iron Horse

**433-8619 84.99**
Includes 0-4-0 steam loco and tender, four freight cars, 47 x 38" oval track, 10-piece bridge and pier set, 62 signs, 12 utility poles and more.

## Freightline USA

**433-8644 159.99**
GP38-2 diesel, six cars, 49 x 76" double loop track, two manual switches, 18-piece bridge-and-pier set, coal tipple, gravel dump station, operating crossing gate, three shanty kits, three vehicles, six figures, three trees, tunnel, signal bridge, 24 authentic street signs, six utility signs and more.

## Diesel Thunder

**433-8951 94.99**
GP38-2 diesel loco with working headlight, GP38-2 unpowered loco, five cars, 74 x 38" track oval, bridge-and-pier set, three trackside shanty kits, livestock pen, six cows, six pigs, six farmers, four automobiles, three pick up trucks, three trees, one signal bridge, 91 authentic railroad, street and road signs and 12 utility poles.

## Railroad Empire

**433-8646 139.99**
GP38-2 diesel with working headlight, five cars, 65 x 47" elevated double-oval track, 18-piece bridge-and-pier set, three shanty kits, livestock pen, six cows, six pigs, six people, two automobiles, one pick-up truck, three trees, 19 authentic railroad signs, six utility poles and tunnel.

## Branch Line

**433-8607 54.99**
F7 diesel with working headlight, five cars and 38" track circle.

## Rail Master

**433-8608 59.99**
Includes F40PH diesel, three cars, 47 x 38" oval track, 62 signs, six utility poles and more.

# TRAIN SET W/ CONVENTIONAL TRACK

## Golden Flyer

**433-8803 55.00**
Includes F40PH diesel with working headlight, three cars and Track-Loc™ track circle.



## ATLAS TRAINMAN®

# NEW PRODUCT

## Train Set

### Trainman Diesel Freight Set 175.00 ea

Get started right with this hobby-quality train set. Heading up the train is a reliable, realistic EMD GP38-2 locomotive with true-scale dimensions and accurate details, a smooth-running five-pole motor with dual flywheels, working headlight and a heavy diecast underframe. It pulls a box car, gondola, covered hopper and matching caboose, all with true scale dimensions, weighted and detailed underframes and free-rolling metal wheels. Cars and loco are equipped with Accumate® knuckle couplers. Also included are a 4 x 3' oval of Atlas True-Track® roadbed-style track, a power pack, instructions, warranty card, Atlas CD catalog and a Blueprints for Ten True-Track Layouts book.

**NEW 751-30** ATSF
**NEW 751-31** CP
**NEW 751-32** NS

### True-Track Add-On Pack

**NEW 751-29 24.95**
Pack includes all the necessary pieces to turn the 4 x 3' oval in the Diesel Freight Set into a figure 8. Includes two 9" straights, six 18" radius curves, four 6" straights and 90° crossing.

Bachmann train sets feature ready-to-run locos and cars, Bachmann E-Z Track® roadbed-style track suitable for set-up on any flat surface, power pack and speed controller and an illustrated instruction manual. Locos and cars feature body-mounted E-Z Mate® knuckle couplers.

# NEW PRODUCTS

## E-Z Command® DCC Train Sets

Enjoy the benefits of command control with these sets. Command control allows you to control each locomotive individually — just like the real thing! Each includes a "DCC On Board" DCC decoder-equipped locomotive, E-Z Command control center w/wall pack and simple plug-in wiring, rolling stock, E-Z Track and accessories. Locos and cars come equipped with E-Z Mate knuckle couplers. Locos are compatible with other DCC compliant command control systems and other decoder-equipped engines can be controlled with E-Z Command, making these sets ideal for expansion. Conventional DC locomotives and power packs cannot be used with these sets.

### Digital Commander Diesel Train Set

**NEW 160-501** ATSF **250.00**
This action-packed includes two powered DCC-equipped locomotives for two-loco operation. Included are DCC decoder-equipped EMD GP40, and EMD FT-A locomotives with operating headlights, plug-door box car, open quad hopper, extended-vision caboose, 56 x 38" oval of E-Z Track with one manual turnout and track for a siding with bumper, under-track magnetic uncoupler with brakeman figure, complete E-Z Command instruction video DVD and an illustrated instruction manual.

### Digital Commander Steam Train Set

**NEW 160-502** UP **225.00**
Old meets new with this digitally controlled steam train set. This set includes a DCC decoder-equipped 0-6-0 steam loco with operating headlights, box car, gondola, extended-vision caboose, 56 x 38" oval of E-Z Track with one manual turnout and track for a siding with bumper, under-track magnetic uncoupler with brakeman figure, complete E-Z Command instruction video DVD and an illustrated instruction manual.

## Standard DC Train Sets

### Hershey's™ Express

**NEW 160-672 120.00**
Got a sweet tooth? Satisfy it with this collector's-style train set. Includes milk chocolate EMD GP40, Reese's Pieces open quad hopper, Bubble Yum plug-door box car, Twizzlers caboose, 47 x 38" oval of E-Z Track, wall power pack, speed controller and illustrated instruction manual.

### Walt Disney's Carolwood Pacific Railroad

**NEW 160-675 200.00**
Walt Disney, a well-known train lover, built the Carolwood Pacific Railroad in the backyard of his Holmby Hills, California, home. This HO Scale set is inspired by his one-eighth scale outdoor railroad and its equipment that was hand crafted by Walt and his team of talented precision machinists at Disney Studios. The set includes 4-4-0 American steam locomotive and tender with operating headlight, old-time box car, two old-time gondolas, old-time bobber caboose, 47 x 38" oval of E-Z Track, wall power pack, speed controller and illustrated instruction manual.

### Shrek's Holiday Special

**NEW 160-676 99.00**
Shrek puts his unique spin on the holidays with this festive train set. The set includes an EMD FT-A diesel loco with working headlight, flat car, plug-door box car, and offset-cupola caboose, all dressed in a special Shrek paint scheme. Also includes a 36" circle of E-Z Track, wall power pack, speed controller and illustrated instruction manual.

## STANDARD DC TRAIN SETS

### Thunderbolt

**160-612 92.00**
A distant roar and the trembling earth can mean only one thing: the Thunderbolt is on its way! With a flash of silver and red, a mighty locomotive bolts past, transporting freight to far-off destinations. The Thunderbolt train set includes an EMD GP40 loco with operating headlight pulls a plug-door box car, single-dome tank car, off-center cupola caboose and 36" diameter oval of snap-together E-Z Track. Also includes a power pack, speed controller and illustrated instruction manual.

### Casey Jones

**160-617 140.00**
Behind schedule and trying to make up time, engineer John Luther Jones raced his way into railroading history when his need for speed cost him his life near the town of Vaughan, Mississippi. Ever after known by his nickname, John Luther lives on as the railroad folk hero "Casey Jones." This ready-to-run train set includes an 0-6-0 steam locomotive and tender with operating headlight, plug-door box car, single-dome tank car, open quad hopper, off-center cupola caboose, all equipped with body-mounted E-Z Mate couplers. Also included are plenty of items to begin your railroading adventure: 47 x 38" oval of snap-fit E-Z Track, suburban station, signal bridge, 48 figures, 36 telephone poles, 48 railroad and street signs, power pack and speed controller and an illustrated instruction manual.

### Silver Streak

**160-627 160.00**
With their crimson and silver "Warbonnet" paint scheme, twin locomotives move with seemingly unstoppable force as they haul freight up and over towering mountain passes you create with this set's 14-piece graduated pier set. This big set includes one powered (with headlight) and one unpowered EMD GP40 locomotive, a single-dome tank car, steel gondola, wood stock car and off-center cupola caboose, all equipped with body-mounted E-Z Mate couplers. The Silver Streak also includes a 56 x 38" oval of snap-fit E-Z Track, 14-piece graduated pier set, signal bridge, 12 figures, 12 telephone poles, 24 railroad and street signs, crossing signals and gates (12 pieces), power pack and speed controller and an illustrated instruction manual.

### The Grinch's Whoville Special

**160-658 83.00**
Inspired by the story that has warmed the hearts of generations, the Grinch's Whoville Special train set delivers good cheer to children of all ages. This whimsical, ready-to-run set includes an EMD FT diesel with working headlight, open quad hopper, plug-door box car, off-center cupola caboose and 36" circle of E-Z Track.

### Yuletide

**160-664 160.00**
Festively decorated for a very Merry Christmas, this colorful set is perfect for under-the-tree enjoyment. The Yuletide Special features a 47 x 38" oval of Bachmann E-Z Track. Also included is a USRA 0-6-0 steam locomotive and tender with operating headlight, gondola, box car, old-time combine, power pack, speed controller illustrated instruction manual. the loco and rolling stock are equipped with E-Z Mate knuckle couplers.

### Santa Fe Flyer

**160-647 83.00**
The set is pulled by a mighty Santa Fe diesel locomotive with a diecast chassis, operating headlight and eight-wheel drive, painted in the distinctive "Warbonnet" color scheme. Also included is an open quad hopper, gondola and wide-vision caboose. (All cars are outfitted with E-Z Mate couplers.) Set runs on a 36" circle of E-Z Track, including 11 curved track sections and one curved plug-in terminal rerailer. Also included are a UL-listed power pack and an illustrated instruction manual.

### Reversing Trolley Car Sets 150.00 ea

Featuring electronic auto-reversing E-Z Track, this set is the perfect solution for point-to-point passenger transit on your layout. A stop time of five to seven seconds allows plenty of time for HO scale shoppers and travelers to board, and a variable speed controller lets you determine the rate of travel. Sets include trolley car, four 18"-radius curved and three 9" straight sections of E-Z Track, one piece of straight E-Z Track with attached trolley depot, Hayes bumper, power pack and instructions.

**160-401** Main Street

**160-402** Christmas

### Rail King

**160-657 120.00**
This 130-piece set has everything you need to start a model railroad. Includes an EMD GP40 locomotive with headlight, gondola, open quad hopper, reefer, off-center cupola caboose, 47 x 38" oval of E-Z Track, signal bridge, 36 figures, 24 telephone poles, 48 railroad and street signs, power pack and speed controller and complete instructions.

## McKinley Explorer

**160-624 130.00**
The set includes an EMD GP40 diesel locomotive with operating headlight, four full-dome passenger cars named after the Alaskan Rivers *Talkeetna, Kenai, Knik* and *Deshka*, a 56 x 38" oval of E-Z Track® (including 16 pieces of 22" radius curved track, three sections of straight track and one plug-in terminal rerailer), a UL-listed power pack, and illustrated instruction manual.

## Overland Limited

**160-614 225.00**
Union Pacific 4-8-4 steam loco with tender and operating smoke and headlight, three-dome tank car, grain car, flat car with logs, center flow hopper, open quad offset hopper, two plug door box cars, wood stock car, wide vision caboose, 65 x 38" oval of E-Z Track, power pack and instructions.

# BACHMANN COLLECTOR SERIES TRAIN SETS

## The Lafayette

**160-628 115.00**
Set includes a Norris 4-2-0 B&O Lafayette locomotive with skew-wound motor with hardened carbon brushes, a hand-tooled coal load in tender, three historical B&O passenger cars, metal detail parts, nickel-silver wheels, a 47 x 38" oval of nickel-silver E-Z Track, a UL-listed power pack and an illustrated instructional manual.

## The John Bull

**160-640 115.00**
The set includes a John Bull locomotive with skew-wound motor featuring hardened carbon brushes and a hand-tooled coal load in tender, finely detailed parts, a 47 x 38" oval of nickel-silver E-Z Track (including 12 pieces of curved track, one straight track section and one plug-in terminal rerailer), a UL-listed power pack, and illustrated instruction manual.

## The DeWitt Clinton Historic Set

**160-641 99.00**
Set includes the DeWitt Clinton locomotive and tender (featuring skew-wound motor with hardened carbon brushes, diecast wood load and water barrels) and three DeWitt Clinton coaches. Also features nickel-silver wheels, a 47 x 38" oval of nickel-silver E-Z Track, a UL-listed power pack and an illustrated instruction manual.

## SPECTRUM® SILVER SERIES® TRAIN SETS

Premium quality sets featuring an oval of nickel-silver E-Z Track, a Spectrum Series locomotive with operating headlight, upgraded rolling stock (with detailed under-frames, brass nonmagnetic axles and body-mounted couplers) and a Spectrum power pack.

### The Frontiersman 295.00 ea

DCC ON BOARD Sets feature a Baldwin 2-8-0 locomotive with DCC on Board for authentic speed, direction and headlight control, open quad hopper, plug door box car and extended vision caboose. Also included are a 56 x 38" oval of E-Z Track and a DVD video with complete instructions.

**160-1301** UP

**160-1302** WM

**160-1303** SOU

### The Explorer 345.00 ea

DCC ON BOARD Sets feature a Baldwin 2-8-0 locomotive with DCC on Board for authentic speed, direction and headlight control. This detailed machine totes a train of three heavyweight cars: a combine, a coach and and observation, all equipped with interior lighting. Also included are a 63 x 45" oval of E-Z Track, power pack and controller, and a DVD video with complete instructions.

**160-1306** UP

**160-1307** NYC

**160-1308** ATSF

### The Cavalier

**160-1311 365.00**

DCC ON BOARD While the Norfolk & Western was known for its extensive coal hauling operations, its passenger trains were known for their class. An example was the Cavalier, which swept passengers between Norfolk and Cleveland in comfort. This detailed set includes a replica of one of N&W's Class J 4-8-4s complete with a DCC decoder for realistic speed and headlight control and heavyweight combine, coach and observation cars with interior lights. It travels on a 63 x 45" oval of E-Z Track and includes a power pack, speed controller and DVD video with complete instructions.

### The Continental

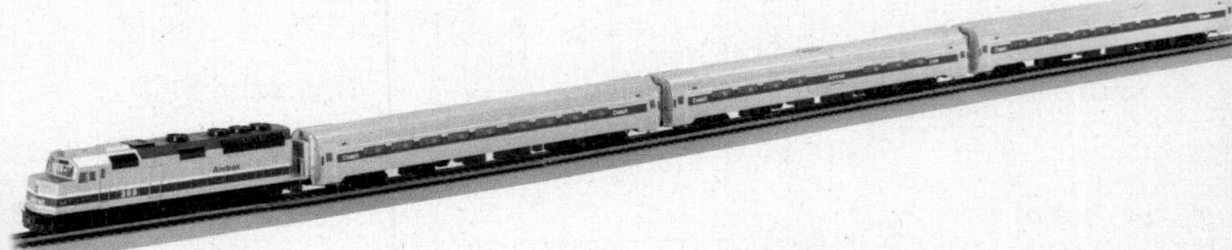

**160-1312 310.00**

DCC ON BOARD Patterned after Amtrak® trains that operate from coast to coast, the Continental carries leisure and business travelers in style. Set includes an F40PH locomotive with strobe lights and DCC on Board for excellent speed and headlight control, two Amfleet® Coaches and a Café Car dressed in the Phase IV scheme, a 63 x 45" oval of E-Z Track, power pack, speed controller and a DVD video with complete instructions.

### Amtrak® Acela℠ Express Train Set

**160-1202 370.00**

Ready for service, complete set includes: Powered and Dummy Acela Electric Locos (with directional headlights, ditch lights and markers), First Class Coach, Café Acela and Business-Class Cars with full interiors and working lights (additional cars also available separately), 63 x 45" 157.5 x 112.5cm oval of nickel silver EZ-Track with 22" 55cm radius curves and a Spectrum power pack. Set is DCC ready.

# THOMAS THE TANK ENGINE®

All Thomas & Friends railroad equipment comes equipped with international-style hook-and-loop couplers.

## Thomas & Friends® Locomotives

**NEW 160-58746** Edward w/Moving Eyes **64.00**

**NEW 160-58801** Mavis w/Moving Eyes **43.00**

## Thomas & Friends Freight Cars 17.00 ea (Unless Noted)

**NEW 160-77029** Coal Wagon w/Load

**NEW 160-77030** Cattle Wagon

**NEW 160-77031** Well Wagon **20.00**

**NEW 160-77032** Cream Tank Car

**NEW 160-77033** Raspberry Syrup Tank Car

**NEW 160-77034** Salt Wagon

**NEW 160-77035** RF Container Wagon

**NEW 160-77036** 6-Ton Wagon

## Thomas & Friends Structures

**NEW 160-45231** Sodor Junction Station **25.00**

**NEW 160-45232** Water Tower **25.00**

**NEW 160-45233** Coaling Station **30.00**

**NEW 160-45234** Pedestrian Bridge **25.00**

**NEW 160-45235** Signal Gantry pkg(2) **35.00**

## Thomas & Friends Accessories

**NEW 160-78979** Spare Hook-and-Loop Couplers pkg(6) **6.50**

## Thomas The Tank Engine & Accessories

### Locomotives

Each engine features eyes that move from side to side as the locomotive heads down the tracks.

**160-58741** Thomas the Tank Engine **37.50**

**160-58742** Percy the Small Engine **37.50**

**160-58743** James the Red Engine **48.00**

**160-58744** Gordon the Big Express Engine **64.00**

**160-58745** Henry the Green Engine **64.00**

**160-58747** Toby the Tram Engine **43.00**

**160-58748** Emily **59.00**

**160-58749** Spencer **75.00**

### Freight Cars 15.00 ea (Unless Noted)

**160-77037** Open Wagon

**160-77038** Oil Tank

**160-77039** Sodor Fuel Tank

**160-77041** S.C. Ruffey

**160-77042** Open Wagon

**160-77043** Cargo Car

**160-77045** Brake Van

**160-77046** Troublesome Truck #1 **12.00**

**160-77047** Troublesome Truck #2 **12.00**

Sodor Junction Station 160-45231

Pedestrian Bridge 160-45234

James the Red Engine 160-58743

Gordon the Big Express Engine 160-58744

Henry the Green Engine 160-58745

Emily 160-58748

Spencer 160-58749

160-77048 Tidmouth Milk Tank

160-77049 Tar Tank

### Coaches

160-76042 Emily's Coach 13.00

160-76043 Emily's Brake Coach 13.00

160-76044 Annie 13.00

160-76045 Clarabel 13.00

160-76046 Brake Coach 32.00

160-76047 Composite Coach 32.00

160-76048 Gordon's Express Brake Coach 32.00

160-76049 Gordon's Composite Coach 32.00

## Thomas w/Annie & Clarabel

**160-642 94.00**
Traveling across the faraway island of Sodor is this deluxe train set commemorating the animated adventures of the classic train. Thomas the Tank Engine travels around a 36" circle of snap-fit E-Z Track®, pulling along Annie and Clarabel coaches with international-style hook-and-loop couplers. Thomas is equipped with eyes that look from side to side as he moves across the tracks. Includes a power pack and illustrated instruction manual.

## Deluxe Thomas w/Annie & Clarabel

**160-644 130.00**
This set comes with a Thomas the Tank Engine with moving eyes, Annie and Clarabel coaches with international-style hook-and-loop couplers, Bertie the Bus, Harold the Helicopter, Sir Topham Hatt figure, a 56 x 38" oval of E-Z Track, power pack and illustrated instruction manual.

### Vehicles 13.00 ea

160-42441 Harold the Helicopter

160-42442 Bertie the Bus

### Figures

160-42443 Sir Topham Hatt 7.00

### Crane

160-42444 Cranky the Crane w/Working Crane Action 27.00

## Gordon's Express Set

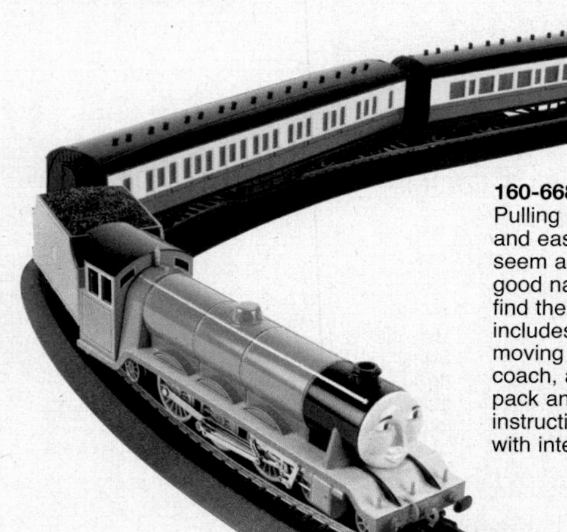

**160-668 160.00**
Pulling heavy passenger coaches with the pride and ease of a natural leader may make Gordon seem a bit bossy at times, but his kind heart and good nature always save the day when his friends find themselves in trouble. This fun train set includes Gordon the Big Express Engine with moving eyes, a composite coach, an express brake coach, a 63 x 45" oval of snap-fit E-Z Track, power pack and speed controller and an illustrated instruction manual. Loco and cars come equipped with international-style hook-and-loop couplers.

## James the Red Engine Freight Set

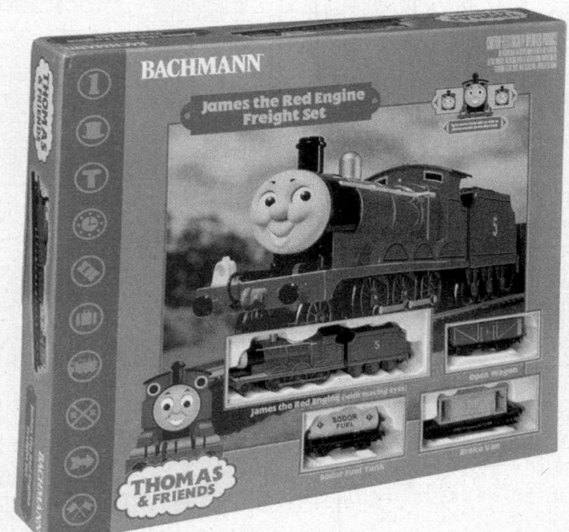


**160-656 120.00**
With a scarlet coat and brass dome, James fancies himself to be a really splendid engine. His high opinion of himself can lead to trouble when it comes to getting work done on the Island of Sodor. This set includes James the Red Engine with moving eyes, Sodor fuel tank, open wagon and brake van with international-style hook and loop couplers, a 56" x 38" oval of snap-fit E-Z Track power pack, speed controller and an illustrated instruction manual.

SOU Mogul Train Set 348-313

PRR Steam Passenger 4-6-2 Streamlined Train Set 348-19592

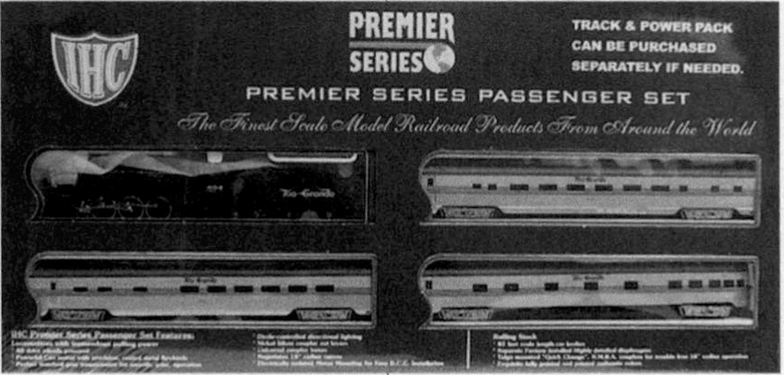

DRGW Steam Passenger 4-6-2 Pacific Train Set 348-20676

Strates Carnival Show Train Set 348-318

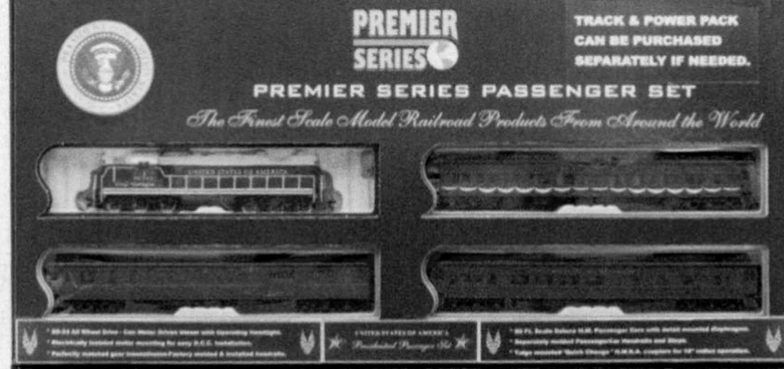

The Presidential Train Set 348-320

# STEAM TRAIN SETS

## Premier Series Mogul Train Sets

Sets include a 2-6-0 steam engine and tender, five freight cars, an oval of track and a deluxe UL-listed power pack with automatic resetting circuit breaker.

**348-313** SOU **79.98**

## Steam Passenger 4-6-2 Streamlined Train Sets

Items listed below are available by Special Order (see Legend Page).

### With Track & Power Pack 134.98 ea

**348-19574** Delaware, Lackawanna & Western "Lackawanna" w/3 Smoothside Cars

**348-19580** Frisco w/3 Frisco Corrugated Side Cars

**348-19586** Wabash w/3 Corrugated Side Cars

**348-19592** PRR "Fleet Of Modernism" w/3 Corrugated Cars

**348-19593** PRR "Congressional" w/3 Corrugated Side Cars

**348-19594** PRR w/3 Corrugated Side Cars (Aluminum/Tuscan)

**348-19595** PRR w/3 Corrugated Side Cars (Tuscan)

**348-19596** PRR "Fleet Of Modernism" w/3 Smoothside Cars

**348-19598** RDG w/3 Aluminum Corrugated Side Cars

**348-19604** SP "Sunbeam" w/3 Corrugated Side Cars

**348-19605** SP "Sunbeam" w/3 Smoothside Cars

**348-19628** L&N w/3 Corrugated Side Cars (aluminum)

### With No Track or Power Pack 110.98 ea

**348-20568** Boston & Maine "Peter Cooper" w/3 Corrugated Side Cars

**348-20574** Lackawanna w/3 Smoothside Cars

**348-20580** Frisco w/3 Corrugated Side Cars

**348-20586** Wabash w/3 Corrugated Side Cars

**348-20592** PRR "Fleet Of Modernism" w/3 Corrugated Cars

**348-20593** PRR "Congressional" w/3 Corrugated Side Cars

**348-20594** PRR w/3 Corrugated Side Cars (aluminum, Tuscan)

**348-20595** PRR w/3 Corrugated Side Cars (Tuscan)

**348-20596** PRR "Fleet Of Modernism" w/3 Smoothside Cars

**348-20598** RDG w/3 Corrugated Side Cars (aluminum)

GG-1 Passenger Train Set 348-19449

**348-20599** RDG w/3 Smoothside Cars (aluminum)

**348-20604** SP "Sunbeam" w/3 Corrugated Side Cars

**348-20605** SP "Sunbeam" w/3 Smoothside Cars

## Steam Passenger 4-6-2 Pacific Train Sets

Items listed below are available by Special Order (see Legend Page).

### With Track & Power Pack 129.98 ea

**348-19640** Florida East Coast w/3 Corrugated Side Cars (aluminum)

**348-19646** N&W w/3 Smoothside Cars (maroon)

**348-19658** Atlantic Coast Line w/3 Corrugated Side Cars (aluminum)

**348-19664** Rock Island w/3 Corrugated Side Cars (red)

**348-19665** Rock Island w/3 Smoothside Cars (red, yellow)

**348-19676** DRGW w/3 Smoothside Cars

**348-19682** Boston & Maine w/3 Corrugated Side Cars (aluminum)

**348-19694** NP w/3 Smoothside Cars (Two-Tone Green)

**348-19736** Chicago & Alton w/3 Smoothside Cars (red, maroon)

**348-19790** Lackawanna w/3 Smoothside Cars

**348-19832** SOU w/3 Corrugated Side Cars

### With No Track or Power Pack 110.98 ea (Unless Noted)

**348-20640** Florida East Coast w/3 Corrugated Side Cars (aluminum)

**348-20646** N&W w/3 Smoothside Cars (maroon)

**348-20658** Atlantic Coast Line w/3 Corrugated Side Cars (aluminum, purple)

**348-20664** Rock Island w/3 Corrugated Side Cars (aluminum, red)

**348-20665** Rock Island w/3 Smoothside Cars (red, yellow)

**348-20676** DRGW w/3 Smoothside Cars

**348-20682** Boston & Maine w/3 Corrugated Side Cars (aluminum) **108.98**

**348-20694** NP w/3 Smoothside Cars (Two-Tone Green)

**348-20736** Chicago & Alton w/3 Smoothside Cars (red, maroon)

**348-20790** Lackawanna w/3 Smoothside Cars

**348-20832** SOU w/3 Corrugated Side Cars

# DIESEL TRAIN SETS

Each set is led by a SD-24 diesel locomotive.

## Strates Carnival Show Train Sets

Along for the ride are four heavyweight passenger cars: baggage car, sleeper, coach and observation car.

**348-318** With No Track Or Power Pack **49.98**

## The Presidential Train Set

Accompanying heavyweight passenger cars include a combine/communications car, a Secret Service 8-1-2 sleeper, and a Ferdinand Magellan observation car.

**348-319** With Track & Power Pack **61.98**

**348-320** With No Track Or Power Pack **41.98**

# ELECTRIC TRAIN SETS

## GG-1 Passenger Train Sets

### With Track & Power Pack 104.98 ea (Unless Noted)

**348-19401** PRR #4228 (Tuscan 5-Stripe) w/3 Aluminum Corrugated Side Cars **118.98**

**348-19402** PRR #4228 (Tuscan 5-Stripe) w/3 Corrugated Side Cars

**348-19404** PRR #4228 (Tuscan 5-Stripe) w/3 Smoothside Cars

**348-19412** PRR #4228 (silver) w/3 Corrugated Side Cars

**348-19448** Amtrak® #902 (black) w/3 PRR Aluminum Corrugated Side Cars

**348-19449** Amtrak #902 (black) w/3 PRR Aluminum Smoothside Cars **118.98**

Items listed below are available by Special Order (see Legend Page).

**348-19400** PRR (Tuscan 5-Stripe) w/3 Smoothside Cars (Tuscan) **118.98**

**348-19403** PRR #4228 (Tuscan 5-Stripe) w/3 Corrugated Side Cars

**348-19430** PRR #4856 (Tuscan 5-Stripe) w/3 Smoothside Cars

**348-19431** PRR #4856 (Tuscan 5-Stripe) w/3 Aluminum Corrugated Side Cars

**348-19432** PRR #4856 (Tuscan 5-Stripe) w/3 Corrugated Side Cars

**348-19433** PRR #4856 (Tuscan 5-Stripe) w/3 Corrugated Side Cars (Tuscan)

**348-19434** PRR #4856 (Tuscan 5-Stripe) w/3 Smoothside Cars (silver)

**348-19460** Amtrak #921 ("Savings Bond") w/3 PRR Corrugated Side Cars

**348-19461** Amtrak #921 ("Savings Bond") w/3 PRR Smoothside Cars

**348-19466** Penn Central #4901 (black) w/3 PRR Corrugated Cars

### With No Track or Power Pack 83.98 ea (Unless Noted)

**348-20400** PRR #4228 (Tuscan 5-Stripe) w/3 Smoothside Cars (Tuscan)

**348-20401** PRR #4228 (Tuscan 5-Stripe) w/3 Aluminum Corrugated Side Cars **108.98**

**348-20404** PRR #4228 (Tuscan 5-Stripe) w/3 Smoothside Cars

**348-20412** PRR #4880 (silver) w/3 Corrugated Side Cars (aluminum) **108.98**

**348-20431** PRR #4856 w/3 Aluminum Corrugated Side Cars

**348-20433** PRR #4856 (Tuscan 5-Stripe) w/3 Corrugated Side Cars (Tuscan) **108.98**

**348-20448** Amtrak #902 (black) w/3 PRR Corrugated Side Cars (aluminum)

**348-20449** Amtrak #902 (black) w/3 PRR Smoothside Cars (aluminum)

Items listed below are available by Special Order (see Legend Page).

**348-20402** PRR #4228 (Tuscan 5-Stripe) w/3 Corrugated Side Cars

**348-20403** PRR #4228 (Tuscan 5-Stripe) w/3 PRR Tuscan Corrugated Side Cars **108.98**

**348-20430** PRR #4856 (Tuscan 5-Stripe) w/3 Smoothside Cars

**348-20432** PRR #4856 (Tuscan 5-Stripe) w/3 Corrugated Side Cars

**348-20434** PRR #4856 (Tuscan 5-Stripe) w/3 Smoothside Cars (aluminum)

**348-20454** New Jersey Transit #4876 ("Ugly Duckling") w/3 PRR Smoothside Cars (aluminum) **108.98**

**348-20460** Amtrak #921 ("Savings Bond") w/3 PRR Corrugated Cars (aluminum)

**348-20461** Amtrak #921 ("Savings Bond") w/3 PRR Smoothside Cars (aluminum)

**348-20466** Penn Central #4901 (black) w/3 PRR Corrugated Cars (aluminum

**MANTUA**

## TRAIN SETS

### Classic Six Train Set 110.00 ea

Each ready-to-run set features one twin lighted 0-6-0 tank loco, four old-time cars, six steam-era figures, 45 x 36" track oval and power pack. DCC ready.

**455-30000** ATSF

**455-30001** B&O

**455-30002** CP

märklin®

NYC ALCO PA-1 American Freight Starter Set 441-29571

Fire Department Digital Starter Set 441-29755

## DIGITAL STARTER SETS

### Fire Department Digital Starter Set

**441-29755 301.75**

This German-style freight set is perfect for getting started with Marklin model trains. The set features a DCC decoder-equipped Class 212 diesel with working headlights and three cars decorated as a German fire department relief train. Also included is a 73 x 34" 184 x 84cm oval of Marklin C Track with two curved turnouts and track to create a siding, Mobile Station digital controller, 18VA transformer, necessary hardware and complete instructions.

### Fire Train Accessories

#### Type X05 Flat Car w/Fire Department Volkswagen Beetle Load

**NEW 441-46063** German Federal Railroad (DB) **43.50** VW Beetle in FD Version w/blue light.

#### "Relief Train" Add-On Car Set

**NEW 441-78050 69.98**

Includes a tank car, low-side car, track and emergency vehicles.

### NYC ALCO PA-1 American Freight Starter Set

Mobile Station Included with NYC ALCO PA-1 American Freight Starter Set

**441-29571 595.75**

Includes a diesel locomotive, box car, reefer, gondola, center-cupola caboose, large "C" track layout, transformer and Mobile Station.

"Relief Train" Add-On Car Set 441-78050

EXTERMINATION
FUMIGATION
MOTH PROOFING

Models by Dan Darnell and Photo by Jason Shron and Dan Garcia, Toronto, Ontario

Escaping steam heat and patches of dirty snow tell us that it's a cold March morning in Toronto's Spadina yard. A hostler has just fitted the kerosene markers onto the rear car of the morning train to Windsor and the Montreal Locomotive Works S13 switcher on the next track will soon drag it to Union Station to collect its passengers. On the far track, last night's Cavalier has just arrived from Montreal and will be cleaned, turned and prepared for tonight's journey back east.

Locomotive 6525, a General Motors FP9A pulls forward from under the large concrete and brick coaling tower, an obsolete remnant from the not-too-distant past when this yard was filled with the hiss and chuff of steam engines.

The passenger cars are Super Continental Line™ models from Rapido Trains Inc. The S13 and FP9A are brass models owned by Dan Darnell from Van Hobbies and Overland, respectively. The background is a photo taken by Bill Morisson near this spot in the real Spadina Yard before it was demolished to make way for the Rogers Centre, home of the Toronto Blue Jays.

Spend some time looking through the Passenger Car Section and you'll discover a wide variety of cars, from sleepers to observation lounges to baggage cars and more, to create a great passenger consist on your layout.

# Hiawatha

## FIRST OF THE SPEEDLINERS

### From Teakettles to Tearing Up the High Iron

From its humble beginnings to a time when it was the pinnacle of technology and style, the Milwaukee Road's passenger service was long-lived and fascinating.

Roll back the clock to 1850. For the first time, teakettle

Milwaukee ad 4-4-2 Atlantic #1 "Hiawatha" is being inspected for the run west to the Twin Ci The Everett St. Station clock tower looms large in the background. Photo Walth archives

steamer "Number 1"
hauled tw s packed with
VIPs west f Milwaukee
over five mi f newly
completed M ukee &
Mississippi R ck at the
breakneck spe 25 miles
per hour, maki e
Milwaukee Road decessor
the first and fas ilroad
in Wisconsin.

After a long perio
expansion and im
the Milwaukee Roa ent,
known leader in pa
service. But in 1933,
experiment in the ro
passenger car shop w
soon become a standa
against which all mode
intercity passenger trai
would be judged.

Early in 1934, UP and CB&Q debuted streamlined trains amid much fanfare. On February 12, UP's M-10000, a lightweight, aluminum-bodied, distillate-powered, three-car limited hit the high iron. As things played out, its limited, fixed passenger capacity and limited reliability led to its early retirement by 1940. The CB&Q's diesel-powered "Zephyr" was successful from the start. Its nonstop dawn-to-dusk run between Denver and Chicago on May 26th broke records for the longest nonstop run and highest average speed – 77.5mph. Though a success, its limited capacity landed it on midwestern short-haul routes where it ran until 1960; today, it's a star attraction at the Chicago Museum of Science and Industry. Both trains were sleek, fast and lightweight and instilled hope for a better tomorrow in an America deep in the throes f the Great Depression.

In the shadows of all the hoopla over the streamliners, Milwaukee Road car designers had already cooked up their answer to the new trains in the road's backshops. On February 3rd, only a few days before M-10000 debuted, lightweight coach #4400 and rebuilt "streamstyled" heavyweight coach #4000 had been quietly unveiled at a public display at Chicago Union Station. Coach #4400 featured lightweight, welded construction, sleek, smooth sides, air conditioning and a luxury interior. But, in contrast to other streamliners, it was a single car, the first of 42, built for high-speed service.

Coach #4400 and its siblings were extremely significant developments in streamline car design because they offered something streamlined trains didn't—the flexibility to tailor train length to passenger demand and servicing needs. It was the pattern for most streamliners introduced from that point on.

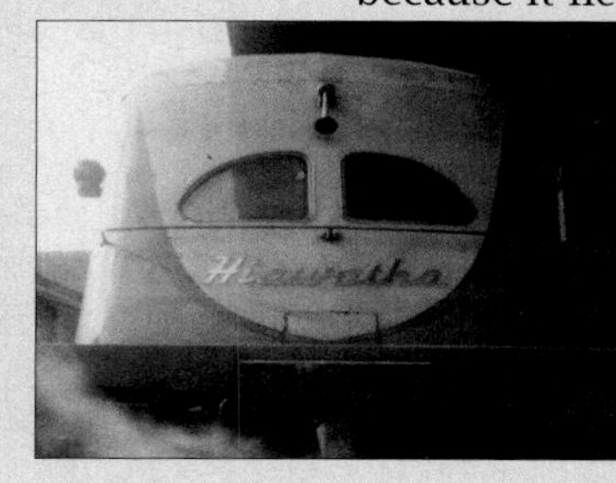


With their sloped ends and wedge windows, Beaver Tail lounges were unlike anything else on rails at the time. Photo Walthers archives

### The First of the Speedliners

By the end of 1934 the Milwaukee was running more streamlined cars (over 75) but still had no "streamliner." Ever pragmatic and looking to save a dime, the railroad decided to use tried-and-true technology to power its streamliners—steam. Internal-combustion power was in its infancy, the railroad was already equipped to handle steam and with money being tight (the Great Depression was in full swing), steam locos were cheaper to construct.

While a third lighter than standard cars, two-truck lightweight cars were still heavier than the one-truck cars on articulated streamliners. The Milwaukee placed an order with Alco for streamlined 4-4-2 Atlantics because it needed the most modern steam locos possible for speed, pulling power and reliability. Sporting a shovel-nosed shroud and spectacularly adorned in gray, orange

Workers in the Milwaukee Road's shops add the finishing touches to a rubber-tired loco for use in parades. Photo Walthers archives

Hiawatha pride even extended to home-built box cars that received stylish ribbed sides and passenger train ad slogans. Photo Walthers archives

and maroon with stainless steel nose wings and chrome trim, they were, without a doubt, the fastest-looking steam locos in America.

Back in the Milwaukee's shops two coaches were turned into wildly unique lounges. Each was given a sloped end and rear windows—they looked like they were speeding away even when they were standing still! The railroad dubbed them "Beaver Tail" lounges and they were to be the finishing touch for the new trains.

On May 29th, 1935 America's first steam-powered streamliner was launched. "Hiawatha, First of the Speedliners" proclaimed newspaper ads (some in color!) in 70 cities. Hiawatha, the fleet-footed figure in the popular Henry Wadsworth Longfellow poem, denoted speed and Native American imagery. Hiawatha was allowed to run free on the highly competitive route between Chicago and the Twin Cities, a market already enjoying the CB&Q's "Twin Zephyr" streamliners, just over a month old, and the Chicago & North Western's "400," a fast train cobbled together from rebuilt heavyweight cars, introduced in January.

The Hiawatha thrust the Milwaukee into the forefront of modern steam-powered streamliners. It broke speed records and was proclaimed by some to be the fastest steam-hauled train in the world. With its flashy, high-drivered locomotive capable of over 120 miles per hour, the train was pure excitement for the throngs of people who lined the tracks along its route to see it speed by.

The speedster was the start of a fleet of premier Hiawatha trains beginning with the connecting "Hiawatha—North Woods Service" in 1936 from New Lisbon, Wisconsin, north to resort areas near Star Lake. By 1950, Hiawatha service extended north into Michigan's upper peninsula and west to Sioux Falls, South Dakota, and Seattle/Tacoma, Washington.

### On Time & Ahead of Their Time

A success from the start, the Hiawatha turned a profit in an era when automobile travel was growing. Through March 1937 the trains averaged over 750 passengers daily and had a sterling on-time record. Second sections hauled by fast 4-6-2 "Pacifics" were often necessary. Even with an extra car (which made schedule keeping difficult), passenger demand outstripped capacity, so a bigger, better Hiawatha was planned.

Hiawatha consists were re-equipped for the second time in 1937 with the first ribbed-side cars, but more improvements were in the offing. In October 1938 the "Hiawatha of 1939" featured all-new ribbed-side cars and more powerful F-7 4-6-4 "Hudsons" styled by noted industrial designer Otto Kuhler. The new higher-capacity nine-car trains weighed slightly less and offered passengers the Tip Top Tap, a full-service diner, or conversation areas in the lounges. The Beaver Tail received a new look replete with Art Deco fins. Building on their success, train frequency doubled in 1939 and the trains were renamed "Morning Hiawatha" and "Afternoon Hiawatha."

The stylish Hiawatha logo appeared on cars, promotional items, timetables and on the railroad's final paint scheme in the early 1980s. Photo by Bob Gallegos

Mechanically, the new cars incorporated an innovative new truck designed by Milwaukee Road mechanical engineer Karl Nystrom. Unlike anything else to date, it incorporated lightweight steel alloy, swing bolster suspension, rubber components and hydraulic shock absorbers to provide the smoothest ride ever.

Older Hiawatha equipment cascaded to Hiawatha trains on other important routes. The road's passenger service soldiered on into World War II with only minor changes, but the fleet was stretched to the limit and Hiawatha locos and cars were frequently used for troop movements.

As with other railroads, the Milwaukee Road sought to expand its streamliner fleet in the postwar era. The Twin Cities Hiawathas were to be re-equipped for the fourth time and the new Olympian Hiawatha would begin service. Industrial designer Brooks Stevens gave the road's huge 1947 order for 127 new home-built cars, plus a few from Pullman, a new look. The cars were styled with smooth sides, rectangular windows in passenger-seating areas and oval or round porthole windows elsewhere.

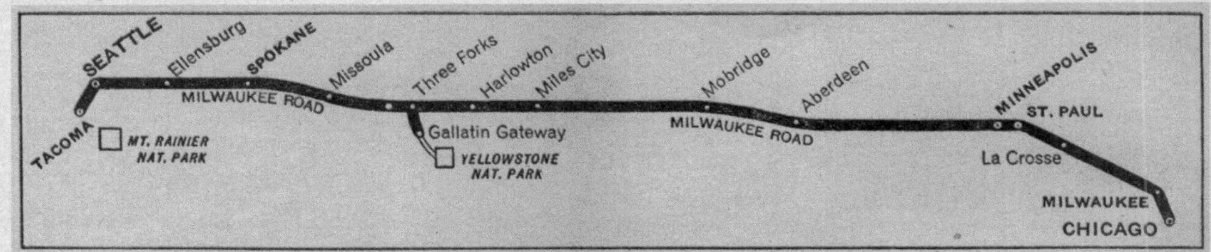


Hiawatha service reached as far as the Pacific into the 1960s. The Twin Cities Hiawathas traveled only as far west as Minneapolis.

Restored Skytop "Cedar Rapids" offers travelers a great Mississippi River view at the rear of an excursion north of Winona, Minnesota in July 2004. Photo by Bob Gallegos

The most exotic observation cars ever were included in the order.

"Skytop" observation cars, with their greenhouse-like rounded ends, gave passengers a spectacular 180° view on the road's most scenic routes. Pullman built six Skytops with bedrooms for the new transcontinental train and four home-built Skytop parlor cars went to the new Twin Cities trains. Again ahead of their time, the cars featured smooth-riding trucks, electropneumatic braking and corrosion-resistant Cor-Ten® steel alloy construction.

This time, diesels were the power of choice. The Olympian Hiawatha was assigned Fairbanks-Morse "Erie Builts," adorned with flashy stainless steel trim, which headed the train on non-electrified lines. EMD E7s initially powered the Twin Cities trains, although as newer E, F and FP-series units were acquired, they supplemented the E7s.

Super Domes, the country's first all-dome lounge cars, came to the Olympian and Twin Cities Hiawathas in 1952. The Olympian Hiawatha became the first train to offer dome service to the Pacific Northwest. Introduced at displays along the route during December 1952, the expensive $320,000 cars were a bargain in terms of the publicity they garnered.

### From Apex to Amtrak®

With the 1948 inauguration of the Olympian Hiawatha and the re-equipping of the Twin Cities Hiawatha and subsequent upgrade with Super Domes, Hiawatha service had reached its high point. The Chicago-Milwaukee-Green Bay-Ontanagon, Michigan "Chippewa Hiawatha" was the last introduced but it was short lived and made its last run as a Hiawatha in 1957.

In the wake of a few high-speed rail disasters in the mid 1940s, a general slowdown of American passenger trains began with an Interstate Commerce Commission ruling on maximum safe train speeds. Combined with competition from air and auto travel, passenger loadings on all Hiawathas, as well as other Milwaukee Road trains, dwindled. With the slowdown, the introduction of domes, Super Domes and other specialty cars marked a shift by railroads to appeal to vacation travelers. These passengers were looking for an experience, not necessarily a quick trip from A to B—for speed they could drive or fly—and unfortunately, many did.

In 1955 UP and the Milwaukee Road teamed up to operate UP's Overland Route trains between Chicago and Omaha, rerouting them off the deteriorating parallel C&NW line. UP's flagship "City of San Francisco" and other "City" streamliners connected to, and shared cars with Milwaukee Road's Chicago-Omaha trains. Service was better, but the catch was that UP insisted all equipment on its trains wear its colors. The route's Midwest Hiawatha was dropped; UP's "Challenger"

Skytop Lounges offered a great view of the scenery. Restored car "Cedar Rapids," owned by the Friends of the 261, rests at the Twin Cities. Photo by Bob Gallegos.

Super Domes offered passengers comfort and a great view. Restored Super Dome glides through Atalissa, Iowa in 2006. Photo by Bob Gallegos

Into the 1960s the Milwaukee Road heavily promoted its Super Domes. This full-page illustration in a 1959 timetable promoted Hiawatha dome service, as well as domes operated in conjunction with the UP. Walthers archives.

operated on a similar schedule. Instead of maintaining two fleets of differently painted cars, the Milwaukee dropped its orange and maroon colors, standardizing on UP's Armour Yellow and Harbor Mist Gray with Milwaukee Road lettering.

In response to low ridership, many trains were dropped or truncated. In the 60s, the Milwaukee offset Hiawatha and other passenger losses by adding mail storage cars and occasional Flexi-Van container flat cars, sometimes tacked on the rear behind the Skytop!

By Amtrak's first day on May 1, 1971, only the Morning Hiawatha retained its Hiawatha status. Amtrak's "Empire Builder" and the "North Coast Hiawatha" (discontinued in 1980) continued on the Hiawatha route from Chicago to the Twin Cities, and in 2007, Amtrak's Chicago-Milwaukee "Hiawatha Service" trains make seven daily trips in each direction. All trains on the route max out at only 79 m.p.h.—a far cry from the 110 m.p.h. and faster speeds in Milwaukee Road days.

## The Hiawatha in HO

For Walthers 75th anniversary, it's only fitting that we introduce a passenger train based on our hometown favorite. The Morning and Afternoon Hiawathas were longtime fixtures and offered the best service to the Twin Cities. Right up to the end, the trains were a pleasure to ride, and even in retirement the Super Dome and Skytop Lounge, both operated in excursion service by the Friends of the 261 group, are passenger favorites.

Our HO Scale Hiawatha is based on the train as it was running in 1955, just before all cars were repainted into UP colors. At the time, E7, E8, E9, FP7 and F7 locomotive consists could be seen, including consists that mixed the various loco models. Car consists varied during busy travel seasons with extra coaches and mail cars added as needed. The train was not normally switched along its route.

Setting the scene for your Hiawatha is easy thanks to new structures being introduced with the train. The limited-run Milwaukee-Style Station & Train Shed is inspired by the road's 1887-built Milwaukee depot and shed. The structure has been designed to capture the monumental look of the building in a layout-sized structure. If you're modeling the city of Milwaukee, you need this station.

The Train Shed is based on the structure used in Milwaukee, but a similar one was also used in Minneapolis and others were used by lines across the continent. Other structures based on Milwaukee Road prototypes that will look great along your line include the octagonal Gateman's Tower, Yard Office and the Freight House and Office, all sold separately.

Bumped from Twin Cities Hiawatha duties by new diesels, F-7 Hudson 4-6-4s hauled other passenger trains such as this mail train. Photo Walthers archives

# Bring the Legendary *Hiawatha* to Your Layout!

- 10 All-New & Authentic Milwaukee Road Cars
- Upgraded PROTO 2000 E7 Diesels
- Based on 1955 Twin Cities Hiawatha
- Correct 8' Wheelbase Nystrom Trucks
- GSC 6-Wheel Trucks on Superdome
- Diecast Knuckle Couplers
- Produced Especially for Walthers 75th Anniversary
- First Car Arrives November 2007

**PROTO 2000™ E7 A-A Diesels** August 2008

**Sound & DCC**

A-A Set $369.98 Each
920-40950 #1 920-40951 #2
Undecorated 920-40954

Matching A Units $189.98 Each
920-40952 #1 920-40953 #2
Undecorated 920-40955

**Standard DC**

A-A Set $269.98 Each
920-47950 #1 920-47951 #2
Undecorated 920-47954

Matching A Units $139.98 Each
920-47952 #1 920-47953 #2
Undecorated 920-47955

PROTO 2000 EMD E7 Diesel — August 2008

Choose A-A Sets or Single A Units — Complete list shown above

Railway Post Office #2152-2153 $44.98 March 2008
Painted — 932-9201; Undecorated — 932-9210

Express Car – Version 2 #1317-29 $44.98 April 2008
Painted — 932-9209; Undecorated — 932-9290

Express Car w/Conductor's Window #1330-36 $44.98 January 2008
Painted — 932-9202; Undecorated — 932-9220

52-Seat Coach #498 Series $44.98 November 2007
Painted — 932-9200; Undecorated — 932-9300

Coach #535 Series $44.98 February 2008
Painted — 932-9208; Undecorated — 932-9280

P-S Super Dome #50-59 $49.98 August 2008
Painted — 932-9207; Undecorated — 932-9270

26-Seat Tap Lounge #172-173 $44.98 June 2008
Painted — 932-9204; Undecorated — 932-9240

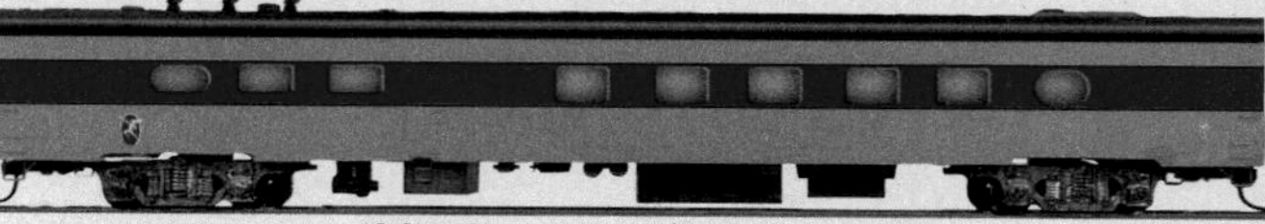
48-Seat Diner #121-26 $44.98 May 2008
Painted — 932-9203; Undecorated — 932-9230

30-Seat Parlor Car "...Valley" Series #190-197 $44.98 December 2007
Painted — 932-9205; Undecorated — 932-9250

Skytop Lounge "...Rapids" Series #186-189 $49.98 July 2008
Painted — 932-9206; Undecorated — 932-9260

Delivery dates shown were accurate at press time; for updated information, see walthers.com. Sketches are for illustration only; details of actual models may vary.

# All-New Structures to Complement your *Hiawatha* Collection

- **Designed Especially for the New Hiawatha**
- **Illustrated Instructions**
- **Detailed Plastic Parts**
- **Use on any Layout**
- **Easy to Build**

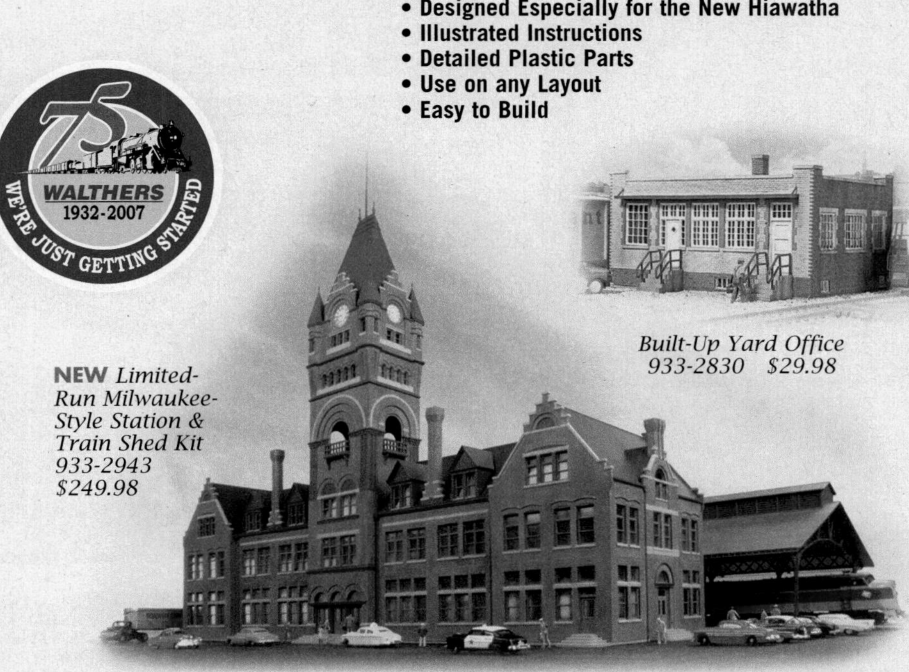


*Built-Up Yard Office*
*933-2830 $29.98*

**NEW** *Limited-Run Milwaukee-Style Station & Train Shed Kit*
*933-2943*
*$249.98*

**NEW** *Freight House Kit*
*933-2954 $29.98*

**NEW** *Freight House & Freight Office Combo Kit (Not pictured)*
*933-2950 $49.98*

**NEW** *Freight Office Kit*
*933-2953 $31.98*

**NEW** *Train Shed Only Kit*
*933-2949 $99.98*

**NEW** *Gateman's Tower Kit*
*933-2944 $32.98*

*Built-Up Walthers Water Street Building*
*933-2814 $39.98*

Photos show preproduction models, details and colors may vary.

Complete the scene on your layout with these Milwaukee structures alongside your new fleet of Hiawatha streamliners! Based on several historic railroad structures that served the Milwaukee Road in its namesake city, these HO Scale kits capture the look of the prototypes in a size that fits most layouts.

### *Limited-Run Milwaukee-Style Station & Train Shed Kit*

**933-2943 $249.98**
**November Delivery**

- Two Complete Kits
- Sized to Fit Most Layouts
- Used from 1887 to 1965
- Inspired by Milwaukee's Everett Street Station

### *Train Shed Only Kit*

**933-2949 $99.98**
**December Delivery**

- Classic American Design
- Used at Many Big City Stations
- Easily Combine Kits for Larger Facility

### *Freight Office Kit*

**933-2953 $31.98**
**March 2008 Delivery**

- Perfect Office for Large Industries
- Authentic Signs

### *Freight House Kit*

**933-2954 $29.98**
**March 2008 Delivery**

- Easily Expanded
- Similar Structures in Many Cities

### *Freight House & Freight Office Combo Kit*

**933-2950 $49.98**
**March 2008 Delivery**

- #2953 & 2954 in One Complete Kit

### *Gateman's Tower Kit*

**933-2944 $32.98**
**October Delivery**

- Includes Shed & Toolbox
- Authentic Eight-Sided Design
- Compact Size, Perfect for City Scenes
- Similar Buildings Used by Many Railroads

### *Built-Up Yard Office*

**933-2830 $29.98**
**In Stock**

- Milwaukee Prototype
- Great for any Layout
- Packed with Realistic Detail
- Perfect Location for Small Businesses

### *Built-Up Walthers Water Street Building*

**933-2814 $39.98**
**September Delivery**

- Walthers "Home" from 1958-69
- Authentic Details
- Fits any Business District
- Colorful Signs

**WALTHERS**

# Go Great! Go Great Northern!

932-9039

932-9039
932-9031
932-9034
932-9036
932-9032
932-9035
932-9037
932-9033
932-9040

## EMPIRE BUILDER CARS

### 44.98 ea (Unless Noted)

- 10 Authentic GN Prototypes
- Based on Equipment used from 1955 On
- CB&Q and SP&S Cars Available Separately for Larger Trains
- Power Your Train with Matching GN PROTO 2000 F7 Diesels

**932-9031** ACF 60-Seat Coach #1209-1214

**932-9032** ACF Baggage-Mail #37-42

**932-9033** P-S 7-4-3-1 Sleeper "...River" Series

**932-9034** ACF Ranch Coffee Shop Lounge #1240-1245 "... Lake" Series

**932-9035** ACF Baggage-Dormitory #1200-1205

**932-9036** P-S 6-5-2 Sleeper "... Pass" Series

**932-9037** ACF 36-Seat Diner "Lake..." Series

**932-9038** P-S 6-4-1 Observation "... Coulee" Series **49.98**

**932-9039** Budd 46-Seat Vista Dome Coach #1320-1335 **49.98**

**932-9040** Budd Great Dome Lounge "... River" Series **49.98**

920-40587

## GREAT NORTHERN EMPIRE BUILDER EMD F7 DIESELS

Equip your Empire Builder with the most authentic HO Scale F units available! Only PROTO 2000 models include authentic GN-style:

- Snowplow Pilot
- 3-Chime Air Horns
- Winterization Hatch
- Roof-Mounted Cooling Coil
- Steam Generator Air Intake
- Correct Style & Location of Grab Irons & Ladder Stand-Offs on Nose
- Radio Antenna
- Paint & Lettering to Match Walthers Empire Builder Cars

### Sound & DCC Equipped

**NEW 920-40587** A-B Set #363-A & 363-B **369.98**

**NEW 920-40607** A-B Set #270-A & 270-B **369.98**

**NEW 920-40588** Matching A Unit #363-C **189.98**

**NEW 920-40612** Matching A Unit #268-C **189.98**

**NEW 920-40613** Matching B Unit #362-B **189.98**

**NEW 920-40629** Matching B Unit #268-B **189.98**

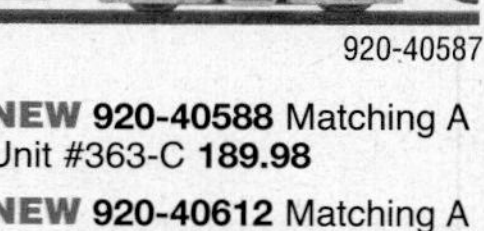

### Standard DC Power - No Sound

**NEW 920-40589** A-B Set #269-A & 269-B **269.98**

**NEW 920-40619** A-B Set #365-A & 365-B **269.98**

**NEW 920-40620** Matching A Unit #365-C **139.98**

**NEW 920-40590** Matching A Unit #268-A **139.98**

**NEW 920-40614** Matching B Unit #359-B **139.98**

**NEW 920-40630** Matching B Unit #360-B **139.98**

# WALTHERS

ACF 60-Seat Coach BN "Hockey Stick" 932-9044

ACF Ranch Coffee Shop Lounge GN 932-9062

Pullman-Standard 7-4-3-1 Sleeper Amtrak Phase I 932-9059

Budd Great Dome 932-6523

ACF Streamlined 36-Seat Diner Amtrak Phase I 932-9082

ACF Railway Post Office-Baggage Car GN 932-9048

ACF Baggage-Dormitory Car BN 932-9068

Pullman-Standard Streamlined 6-5-2 Sleeper GN 932-9072

ACF 6-4-1 Observation BN 932-9086

Budd 46-Seat Vista Dome Coach Amtrak Phase I 932-9097

Budd Great Dome GN 932-6521

## MATCHING EMPIRE BUILDER CARS WITH CB&Q/SP&S DECALS

### 44.98 ea (Unless Noted)

For a larger train, matching Empire Builder cars with decals to add sub-lettering for equipment owned by the Chicago, Burlington & Quincy or Spokane, Portland & Seattle are available:

**932-6523** Budd Great Dome 49.98

**932-9045** ACF 60-Seat Coach

**932-9057** P-S 7-4-3-1 Sleeper

**932-9065** ACF Ranch Coffee Shop Lounge

**932-9074** P-S 6-5-2 Sleeper

**932-9083** ACF 36-Seat Diner

**932-9087** 6-4-1 Observation 49.98

**932-9093** Budd 46-Seat Vista Dome Coach **49.98**

## FORMER EMPIRE BUILDER CARS

- Prototype Variations of Empire Builder Equipment
- Superbly Detailed Inside & Out
- Authentic Paint & Lettering
- Car Name & Number Decals

### ACF 60-Seat Coach 44.98 ea

**932-9043** GN - Big Sky Blue

**932-9044** BN "Hockey Stick"

**932-9042** Undecorated

### ACF Railway Post Office-Baggage Car 44.98 ea

**932-9048** GN - Big Sky Blue

**932-9049** BN "Hockey Stick"

**932-9047** Undecorated

### Pullman-Standard 7-4-3-1 Sleeper 44.98 ea

**932-9055** GN - Big Sky Blue

**932-9056** BN "Hockey Stick"

**NEW 932-9059** Amtrak® Phase I

**932-9054** Undecorated

### ACF Ranch Coffee Shop Lounge 44.98 ea

**932-9062** GN - Big Sky Blue

**932-9063** BN "Hockey Stick"

**NEW 932-9064** Amtrak® Phase I

**NEW 932-9275** GN (orange, green)

**932-9061** Undecorated

### ACF Baggage-Dormitory Car 44.98 ea

**932-9067** GN - Big Sky Blue

**932-9068** BN "Hockey Stick"

**NEW 932-9069** Amtrak® Phase I

**932-9066** Undecorated

See What's Available at **www.walthers.com**

### Pullman-Standard Streamlined 6-5-2 Sleeper 44.98 ea

**932-9072** GN - Big Sky Blue

**932-9073** BN "Hockey Stick"

**NEW 932-9077** National Railways of Mexico

**932-9071** Undecorated

### ACF Streamlined 36-Seat Diner 44.98 ea

**932-9080** GN - Big Sky Blue

**932-9081** BN "Hockey Stick"

**NEW 932-9082** Amtrak Phase I

**932-9079** Undecorated

### ACF 6-4-1 Observation 49.98 ea

**932-9085** GN - Big Sky Blue

**932-9086** BN "Hockey Stick"

**932-9084** Undecorated

### Budd 46-Seat Vista Dome Coach 49.98 ea

**932-9091** GN - Big Sky Blue

**932-9092** BN "Hockey Stick"

**NEW 932-9094** GN (Cascade Green, white)

**NEW 932-9095** NP

**NEW 932-9276** GN (orange, green)

**932-9090** Undecorated

### Budd Great Dome 49.98 ea

**NEW 932-6521** GN - Big Sky Blue

**NEW 932-6522** BN - "Hockey Stick"

**NEW 932-6520** Undecorated

# WALTHERS

## BRING THE LEGENDARY SUPER CHIEF TO YOUR LAYOUT!

- Fully assembled, ready to run
- Working diaphragms
- Flush-fitting windows
- Full interiors
- Removable roof with separate details
- Diecast GSC trucks and RP-25 metal wheels
- Working knuckle couplers (optional horn-hook couplers included)
- Swinging drawbars improve performance on curves
- Wire grab irons
- Molded drill starter points
- Razor-sharp painting & lettering
- Car name & number decals included
- Includes equipment from Budd and Pullman-Standard
- Cars can be illuminated with lighting kit #933-1049 (except Pleasure Dome #932-9006, which uses lighting kit #933-1083)

## SANTA FE "SUPER CHIEF" CARS

### Budd Cars 39.98 ea

**932-9001** "Pine" Series 10-6 Sleeper

**932-9002** 73' Baggage Car

**932-9007** 63' Railway Post Office

### Pullman-Standard Cars 39.98 ea (Unless Noted)

**932-9003** 36-Seat Diner

**932-9004** 29-Seat Dormitory-Lounge

**932-9005** "Hotevilla" Series 4-4-2 Sleeper

**932-9006** Pleasure Dome **49.98**

**932-9008** "Vista" Series Observation-Lounge **44.98**

932-9001

932-9002

932-9007

**Model your Super Chief with Walthers All-New HO Mission Style Depot with Freight House (for more details, see the Structures Section)**

**933-2924** Mission Style Combination Depot w/Freight House **54.98**

**933-2920** Mission Style Depot **39.98**

**933-2921** Mission Style Freight House **29.98**

932-9003

932-9006

932-9008

932-9004

## Just $44.98 each!

- Based on Pullman Plans
- Multi-Colored Interiors
- Perfect for 1930s to 60s
- Fit Popular Modeling Eras
- Authentic Prototypes
- Metal Wheelsets
- Knuckle Couplers
- Ready to Run
- Built-in Contacts for Walthers Lighting Kits (Sold Separately)
- Realistic Detail Inside & Out

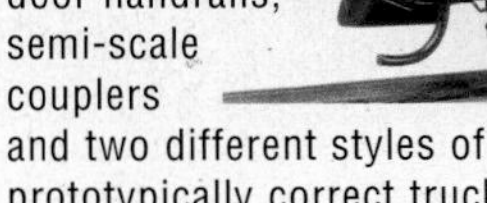

Prototype details include sprung diaphragms, factory-applied door handrails, semi-scale couplers and two different styles of prototypically correct trucks.

Seats, floors, walls and other interior parts are molded and painted in realistic colors, taking interior detailing to a new level of realism.

Preproduction models shown, some details may vary.

Got a Mouse? Click Walthers Web Site at **www.walthers.com**

## Perfect Companions for your Heavyweights

### Walthers Heavyweight 6-Wheel Trucks

**933-1085** Type 242A Fits Walthers 12-1 Sleeper, 14-Section Sleeper and 3-2 Observation **12.98**

**933-1086** Type 2411 Fits Walthers 8-1-2 Sleeper, Diner and Coach **12.98**

### Walthers Heavyweight Passenger Car Interior Lighting Kits

**933-1087** DC Version **10.98**

**933-1088** DCC Version **7.98**

Amazing underbody includes brake gear, air conditioning, water tanks, generators and more.

# WALTHERS

### Pullman Heavyweight Solarium-Observation 44.98 ea
• Enclosed Observation Area
**932-10451** Pullman
**932-10452** ATSF
**932-10453** CB&Q
**932-10454** PRR
**932-10455** UP† (gray)
**932-10456** CNW†
**932-10457** NYC
**932-10458** UP† (yellow)
**932-10459** SP†
**932-10460** B&O
**932-10461** DRGW†
**932-10462** MILW
**932-10463** GN
**932-10464** SOO
**932-10465** C&EI
**932-10466** IC
**932-10467** NH
**932-10450** Undecorated

### Pullman Heavyweight 28-1 Parlor Car 44.98 ea
**932-10301** Pullman
**932-10302** ATSF
**932-10303** CB&Q
**932-10304** PRR
**932-10305** UP† (gray)
**932-10306** CNW†
**932-10307** NYC
**932-10308** UP† (yellow)
**932-10309** SP†
**932-10310** B&O
**932-10311** DRGW†
**932-10312** MILW
**932-10313** GN
**932-10314** Long Island
**932-10315** NH
**932-10316** MP†
**932-10317** SOU
**932-10318** SAL
**932-10300** Undecorated

†Union Pacific licensed product.

### Pullman Heavyweight 6-3 Sleeper 44.98 ea
**932-10401** Pullman
**932-10402** ATSF
**932-10403** CB&Q
**932-10404** PRR
**932-10405** UP† (gray)
**932-10406** CNW†
**932-10407** NYC
**932-10408** UP† (yellow)
**932-10409** SP†
**932-10410** B&O
**932-10411** DRGW†
**932-10412** MILW
**932-10413** GN
**932-10414** ACL
**932-10415** Rock Island
**932-10416** Pullman (Two-Tone Gray)
**932-10400** Undecorated

### American Car & Foundry 70' Baggage Car 44.98 ea
**932-10502** ATSF
**932-10503** CB&Q
**932-10504** PRR
**932-10505** UP† (gray)
**932-10506** CNW†
**932-10507** NYC
**932-10508** UP† (yellow)
**932-10509** SP†
**932-10510** B&O
**932-10511** DRGW†
**932-10512** MILW
**932-10513** GN
**932-10514** MP†
**932-10515** Wabash
**932-10516** L&N
**932-10517** SOO
**932-10549** Express Car Painted, Unlettered
**932-10500** Undecorated - Mail Storage
**932-10548** Undecorated - Baggage-Express



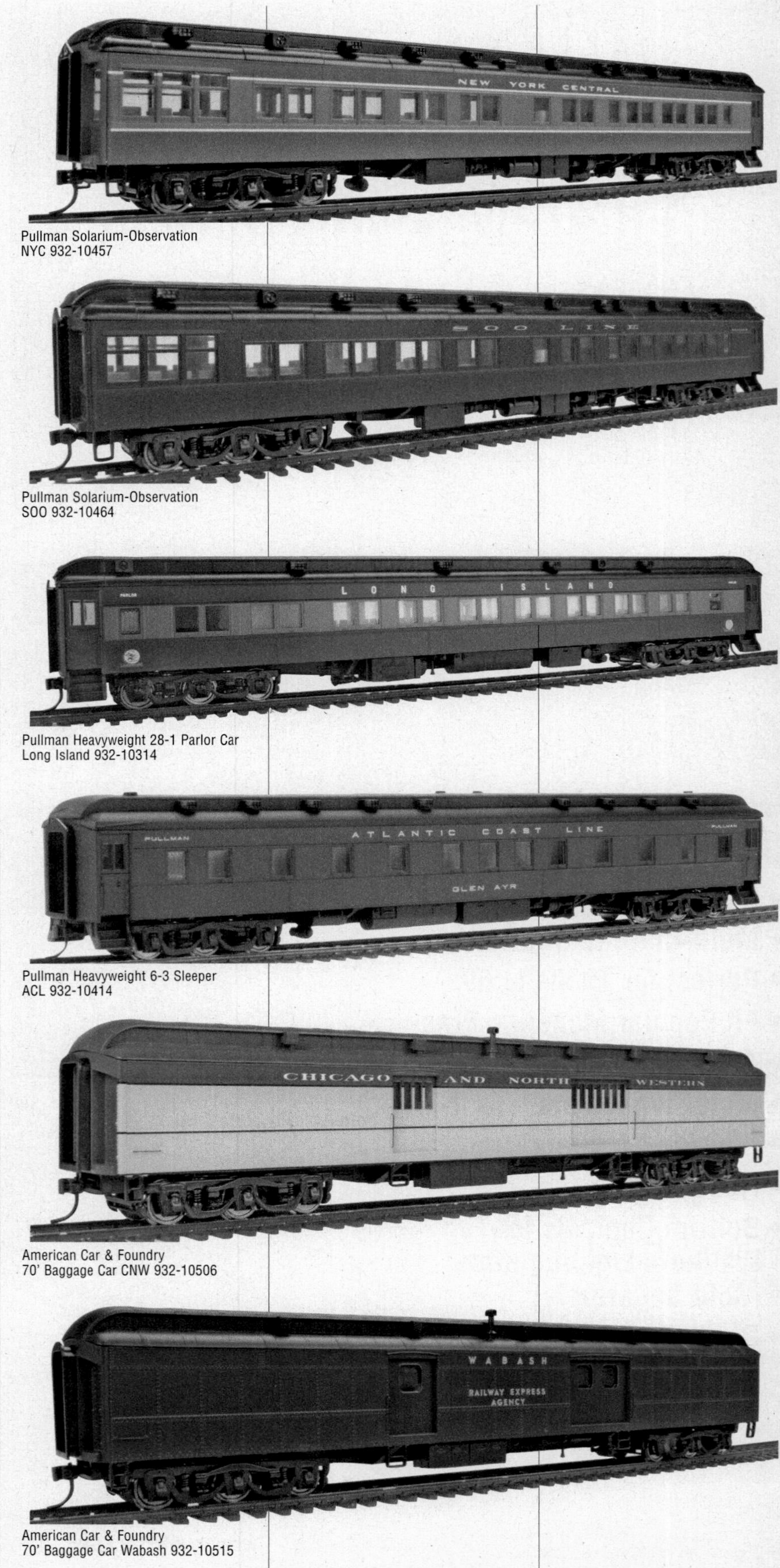


Pullman Solarium-Observation NYC 932-10457

Pullman Solarium-Observation SOO 932-10464

Pullman Heavyweight 28-1 Parlor Car Long Island 932-10314

Pullman Heavyweight 6-3 Sleeper ACL 932-10414

American Car & Foundry 70' Baggage Car CNW 932-10506

American Car & Foundry 70' Baggage Car Wabash 932-10515

# WALTHERS

### Pullman Heavyweight 10-1-2 Sleeper 44.98 ea

932-10551 Pullman
932-10552 ATSF
932-10553 CB&Q
932-10554 PRR
932-10555 UP† (gray)
932-10556 CNW†
932-10557 NYC
932-10558 UP† (yellow)
932-10559 SP†
932-10560 B&O
932-10561 DRGW†
932-10562 MILW
932-10563 GN
932-10564 SOO
932-10565 ACL
932-10566 L&N
932-10567 IC
932-10568 SOU
932-10569 LV
932-10550 Undecorated

### Pullman-Built Heavyweight 36-Seat Diner 44.98 ea

932-10152 ATSF
932-10153 CB&Q
932-10154 PRR
932-10155 UP† (gray)
932-10156 CNW†
932-10157 NYC
932-10158 UP† (yellow)
932-10159 SP†
932-10160 B&O
932-10161 DRGW†
932-10162 MILW
932-10163 GN
932-10164 SOU
932-10165 SAL
932-10166 SOO
932-10167 ACL
932-10168 C&O
932-10169 NKP
932-10199 Painted, Unlettered
932-10150 Undecorated

### Pullman 12-1 Sleeper 44.98 ea

932-10002 ATSF
932-10003 CB&Q
932-10004 PRR
932-10005 UP† (gray)
932-10006 CNW†
932-10007 NYC
932-10008 UP† (yellow)
932-10009 SP†
932-10010 B&O
932-10011 DRGW†
932-10012 MILW
932-10013 GN
932-10014 SOO
932-10015 Louisville & Nashville
932-10016 IC
932-10017 NH
932-10018 C&O
932-10019 SOU
932-10001 Pullman
932-10000 Undecorated

### Pullman 8-1-2 Sleeper 44.98 ea

932-10051 Pullman
932-10052 ATSF
932-10053 CB&Q
932-10054 PRR
932-10055 UP† (gray)
932-10056 CNW†
932-10057 NYC
932-10058 UP† (yellow)
932-10059 SP†
932-10060 B&O
932-10061 DRGW†
932-10062 MILW
932-10063 GN
932-10064 SOO
932-10065 ACL
932-10066 IC
932-10067 Louisville & Nashville
932-10068 C&O
932-10069 SOU
932-10050 Undecorated

### Roadname Color Key

- Solarium-Observations
- 28-1 Parlor Cars
- 6-3 Sleepers
- ACF 70' Baggage Cars
- 10-1-2 Sleepers
- 12-1 Sleepers
- 8-1-2 Sleepers
- 36-Seat Diners

Pullman

ATSF (Pullman Green w/Black Roof)

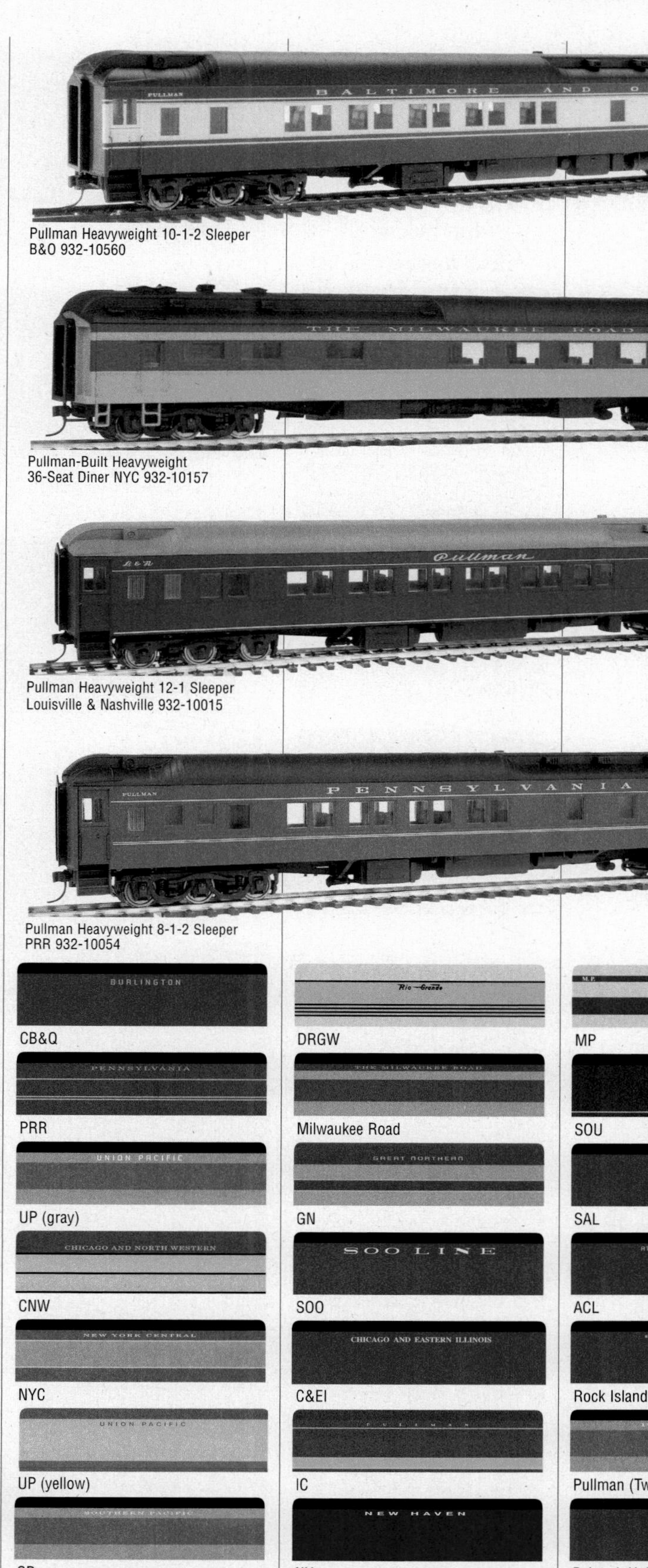

Pullman Heavyweight 10-1-2 Sleeper B&O 932-10560

Pullman-Built Heavyweight 36-Seat Diner NYC 932-10157

Pullman Heavyweight 12-1 Sleeper Louisville & Nashville 932-10015

Pullman Heavyweight 8-1-2 Sleeper PRR 932-10054

CB&Q
DRGW
MP
PRR
Milwaukee Road
SOU
UP (gray)
GN
SAL
CNW
SOO
ACL
NYC
C&EI
Rock Island
UP (yellow)
IC
Pullman (Two-Tone Gray)
SP
NH
Painted, Unlettered (Pullman Style)
B&O
Long Island
L&N

# WALTHERS

## Pullman 14-Section Sleeper 44.98 ea

**932-10201** Pullman
**932-10202** ATSF
**932-10203** CB&Q
**932-10204** PRR
**932-10205** UP† (gray)
**932-10206** CNW†
**932-10207** NYC
**932-10208** UP† (yellow)
**932-10209** SP†
**932-10210** B&O
**932-10211** DRGW†
**932-10212** MILW
**932-10213** GN
**932-10214** Boston & Maine
**932-10215** C&O
**932-10216** IC
**932-10217** Louisville & Nashville
**932-10218** NH
**932-10219** Wabash
**932-10200** Undecorated

## 3-Compartment, 2-Drawing Room Observation-Lounge 44.98 ea

**932-10251** Pullman
**932-10252** ATSF
**932-10253** CB&Q
**932-10254** PRR
**932-10255** UP† (gray)
**932-10256** CNW†
**932-10257** NYC
**932-10258** UP† (yellow)
**932-10259** SP†
**932-10260** B&O
**932-10261** DRGW†
**932-10262** MILW
**932-10263** GN
**932-10264** SOU
**932-10265** Louisville & Nashville
**932-10266** C&O
**932-10267** NH
**932-10268** IC
**932-10269** Wabash
**932-10250** Undecorated

## Pullman-Built Paired-Window Coach 44.98 ea

**932-10102** ATSF
**932-10103** CB&Q
**932-10104** PRR
**932-10105** UP† (gray)
**932-10106** CNW†
**932-10107** NYC
**932-10108** UP† (yellow)
**932-10109** SP†
**932-10110** B&O
**932-10111** DRGW†
**932-10112** MILW
**932-10113** GN
**932-10114** B&O (Modernized)
**932-10115** IC
**932-10116** Wabash
**932-10117** NH
**932-10118** N&W
**932-10119** C&O
**932-10149** Painted, Unlettered
**932-10100** Undecorated

## Roadname Color Key

- 14-Section Sleepers
- 3-2 Observations
- Paired-Window Coaches

Pullman

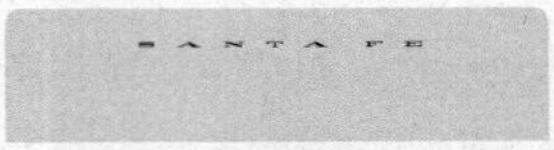

ATSF (Pullman Green w/Black Roof)

CB&Q

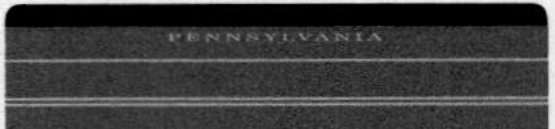

PRR

UP (gray)

CNW

NYC

UP (yellow)

SP

B&O

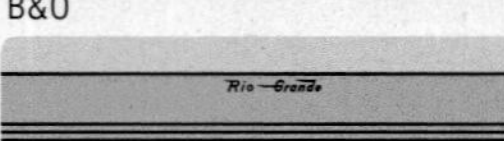

DRGW

Milwaukee Road

GN

SOO

†Union Pacific licensed product.

Pullman 14-Section Sleeper DRGW 932-10211

3-Compartment, 2-Drawing Room Observation-Lounge B&O 932-10260

Pullman-Built Paired-Window Coach N&W 932-10118

Heavyweight Santa Fe-Style Coach ATSF #2 932-10352

C&EI

IC

NH

Long Island

MP

SOU

SAL

ACL

Rock Island

Pullman (Two-Tone Gray)

Painted, Unlettered (Pullman Style)

L&N

## Heavyweight Santa Fe-Style Coach 44.98 ea

- Railroad-Specific Prototype
- Operated System-wide & on Connecting Railroads

**932-10351** ATSF (Pullman Green w/black roof)
**932-10352** ATSF (Pullman Green w/silver roof)
**932-10353** ATSF (Two-Tone Gray)
**932-10350** Undecorated

## Roadname Color Key

- Heavyweight Santa Fe-Style Coach

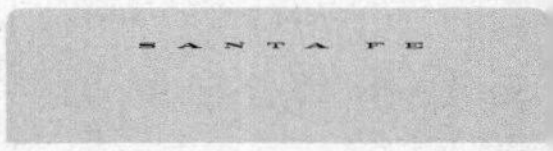

932-10351 ATSF #1

932-10352 ATSF #2

932-10353 ATSF #3

# WALTHERS

## CLASSIC CARS FROM THE FIRST DAYS OF AMTRAK®

- Fully assembled, ready to run
- Working diaphragms
- Full interiors
- Trucks with blackened metal wheelsets
- Wire handrails and grab irons
- Replicas of cars built for the legendary Santa Fe "Super Chief"
- Includes flush-fitting windows and metal truck sideframes
- Built-in electrical contacts for installing interior lights using Walthers Passenger Car Interior Lighting Kits #933-1049 (except Pleasure Dome #932-9021, which uses lighting kit #933-1083), sold separately

36-Seat Diner Amtrak Phase I 932-9017

### 36-Seat Diners 39.98 ea

**932-9017** Amtrak Phase I

**932-9016** Undecorated

Dormitory-Lounge Car Amtrak Phase I 932-9019

### Dormitory-Lounge Cars 39.98 ea

**932-9019** Amtrak Phase I

**932-9018** Undecorated

## CARRY COMMUTERS IN FASHIONABLE STYLE

- Purchased by SP in the 1950s
- Features extra windows found on SP cars
- Interior Details
- Working Diaphragms
- Electrical contacts for Interior Lighting Kit (sold separately)

### Pullman-Standard SP Commuter Cars 34.98 ea

**932-5971** SP† (Two-Tone Gray)

**932-5972** SP† (Gray)

**932-5970** Undecorated

Bring your Commuter Cars to life with this interior lighting conversion kit.

**933-1058 10.98**

Latest New Product News Daily! Visit Walthers Web site at

**www.walthers.com**

### Budd "Pine" Series 10-6 Sleepers 39.98 ea

**932-9011** Amtrak Phase I

**932-9012** Amtrak Phase II

**932-9013** Amtrak Phase III

**932-9014** Phase IV (narrow blue stripe & Dorm-Lounge lettering)

**932-9010** Undecorated

Amtrak Phase I 932-9011

Amtrak Phase II 932-9012

Amtrak Phase III 932-9013

Amtrak Phase IV 932-9014

Undecorated 932-9010

### Pleasure Dome Cars 49.98 ea

**932-9021** Amtrak Phase I

**932-9020** Undecorated

Pleasure Dome Car Amtrak Phase I 932-9021

Pullman-Standard SP Commuter Car SP 932-5972

# WALTHERS

## PULLMAN-STANDARD CARS ADD VARIETY AND COLOR TO YOUR PASSENGER CONSISTS!

- Walthers Pullman-Standard cars feature as many as four body styles—smooth or fluted sides, with or without skirting—as appropriate for each roadname
- All cars, unless noted, have built-in contacts for the Walthers Passenger Car Interior Lighting Kit 933-1049, $10.98 (sold separately)
- First time in plastic
- Fully assembled, ready to run
- Prototypical side skirting
- Fluted car sides as appropriate
- Full interiors
- Flush-fitting windows
- Wire grab irons
- Molded drill starter points
- Removable roof with separate details
- Working diaphragms
- Complete underbody detail
- Diecast GSC 41-HR trucks
- RP-25 blackened-metal wheels
- Swinging drawbars improve performance on curves
- Working knuckle couplers (optional horn-hook couplers also included)
- Factory-installed electrical pickups
- Car name & number decals included

### Pullman-Standard 10-6 Sleeper 34.98 ea

**932-6841** GN
**932-6842** ATSF
**932-6843** CNW†
**932-6844** Amtrak Phase I
**932-6845** SP†
**932-6846** NP
**932-6847** PRR
**932-6848** DRGW†
**932-6849** C&O
**932-6850** Rock Island
**932-6851** UP†
**932-6852** NYC
**932-6840** Undecorated

**COMING SOON!**

**Summer 2007 Delivery**
- New Roadnames

**NEW 932-6853** SOU
**NEW 932-6854** PRR
**NEW 932-6855** L&N
**NEW 932-6856** ACL
**NEW 932-6857** CN

### Pullman-Standard 48-Seat Diner 34.98 ea

- All-New Tooling

**932-6821** GN
**932-6822** ATSF
**932-6823** CNW†
**932-6824** Amtrak® Phase I
**932-6825** SP†
**932-6826** NP
**932-6827** PRR
**932-6828** DRGW†
**932-6829** C&O
**932-6830** Rock Island
**932-6831** UP†
**932-6832** NYC
**932-6833** IC
**932-6834** MP†
**932-6835** L&N
**932-6836** Wabash
**932-6820** Undecorated

### Pullman-Standard 64-Seat Coach 34.98 ea

- Based on Pullman Plan #7484
- Fluted & Smoothside Body Styles
- Skirted & Non-Skirted Versions

**932-6781** GN
**932-6782** ATSF
**932-6783** CNW†
**932-6784** Amtrak Phase I
**932-6785** SP†
**932-6786** NP
**932-6787** PRR
**932-6788** DRGW†
**932-6789** C&O
**932-6790** Rock Island
**932-6791** UP†
**932-6792** NYC
**932-16781** NYC (Smoothside)
**932-16782** IC (Smoothside)
**932-16783** L&N
**932-16784** N&W
**932-16785** NYC
**932-16786** PC
**932-16787** MP†
**932-6780** Undecorated
**932-6799** Undecorated (Smoothside w/o Skirts)

†Union Pacific licensed product.



Pullman-Standard 48-Seat Diner CNW 932-6823

Pullman-Standard 48-Seat Diner NP 932-6826

Pullman-Standard 10-6 Sleeper Amtrak Phase I 932-6824

Pullman-Standard 10-6 Sleeper SOU 932-6853

Pullman-Standard 64-Seat Coach C&O 932-6789

Pullman-Standard 64-Seat Coach NYC 932-16785

# WALTHERS

Troop Sleeper Pullman 932-4151

Troop Kitchen Car 932-4181

Troop Sleeper Baggage Car Conversion
Alaska 932-4163

Converted Kitchen Car CB&Q 932-4182

Converted Kitchen Car Monon 932-4183

Pullman-Standard 4-4-2 Sleeper
Rock Island 932-6710

Pullman-Standard 6-6-4 Sleeper
UP 932-6731

Pullman-Standard "Vista Series"
Observation Car Undecorated 932-9022

Pullman-Standard 10-5 Sleeper
B&O 932-16745

## Pullman-Standard 4-4-2 Sleepers 34.98 ea

**932-6701** GN "Empire Builder"

**932-6702** ATSF (fluted sides)

**932-6703** CNW† ("Cities" Scheme, Armour Yellow)

**932-6704** Amtrak® Phase I

**932-6705** SP† (silver, red stripe)

**932-6706** NP

**932-6707** PRR (Late Scheme)

**932-6708** DRGW† ("Four-Stripe" Scheme)

**932-6709** C&O

**932-6710** Rock Island

**932-6711** UP†

**932-6712** NYC (Two-Tone Gray w/single band)

**932-16701** Pullman Pool Scheme (Two-Tone Gray)

**932-16702** IC

**932-16703** CN

**932-16704** PRR "Fleet of Modernism" Scheme

**932-16705** ACL

**932-16706** National Railways of Mexico (NdeM)

**932-16707** NYC (1938 Scheme)

**932-16708** ATSF (No Skirting)

**932-6700** Undecorated

## Pullman-Standard 6-6-4 Sleepers 34.98 ea

**932-6721** GN "Empire Builder"

**932-6722** ATSF (gray, silver)

**932-6723** CNW† (Early Scheme, yellow, green)

**932-6724** Amtrak Phase I

**932-6725** SP† (silver, red stripe)

**932-6726** NP

**932-6727** PRR (Late Scheme)

**932-6728** DRGW† ("Four-Stripe" Scheme)

**932-6729** C&O

**932-6730** Rock Island

**932-6731** UP†

**932-6732** NYC (Two-Tone Gray w/single band)

**932-16721** Pullman Pool Scheme (Two-Tone Gray)

**932-16722** Erie

**932-16723** IC

**932-16724** MP†

**932-16725** National Railways of Mexico (NdeM)

**932-16726** ATSF (Two-Tone Gray)

**932-16727** CNW† (Late)

**932-16728** UP† (No Skirts)

**932-6720** Undecorated

## Pullman-Standard "Vista Series" Observation Car

- Based on a "Super Chief" design, similar to cars used by other roads

**932-9022** Undecorated (unpainted) **44.98**

## Pullman-Standard 10-5 Sleepers 34.98 ea

**932-6741** GN "Empire Builder"

**932-6742** ATSF (gray)

**932-6743** CNW† (Early Scheme)

**932-6744** Amtrak Phase I

**932-6745** SP† (silver, red stripe)

**932-6746** NP (Two-Tone Green)

**932-6747** PRR (Late Scheme)

**932-6748** DRGW† ("Four-Stripe" Scheme)

**932-6749** C&O

**932-6750** Rock Island

**932-6751** UP†

**932-6752** NYC (Two-Tone Gray w/single band)

**932-16741** NYC (1938 Scheme)

**932-16742** PRR ("Fleet of Modernism" Scheme)

**932-16743** IC

**932-16744** CP

**932-16745** B&O

**932-16746** ATSF

**932-6740** Undecorated

## Troop Sleepers 24.98 ea

**932-4151** Pullman

**932-4150** Undecorated

## Troop Kitchen Cars 24.98 ea

**932-4181** Troop Kitchen

**932-4180** Undecorated

## Troop Sleeper Baggage Car Conversions

### Single Cars 24.98 ea

**932-4161** NYC

**932-4162** EL

**932-4163** Alaska

**932-4164** Rock Island

**932-4160** Undecorated

### Limited-Run 2-Packs 44.98 ea

**932-24163** Alaska

**932-24164** Rock Island

## Converted Kitchen Cars 24.98 ea

**932-4182** CB&Q

**932-4183** Monon

**932-4199** Undecorated

# WALTHERS

Pullman-Standard 52 Seat Coach
SF 932-6762

Pullman-Standard 52 Seat Coach
CNW 932-6763

Pullman-Standard 52 Seat Coach
UYP 932-6771

Pullman-Standard Bilevel Commuter
Coach Rock Island 932-6254

Pullman-Standard Bilevel Cab Car/Coach
Amtrak® Phase III 932-6266

Pullman-Standard 52-Seat Coach
C&O 932-6769

Pullman-Standard 52-Seat Coach
C&O (Fluted, No Skirts) 932-16766

## Pullman-Standard 52-Seat Coach 34.98 ea

**932-6761** GN "Empire Builder"
**932-6762** ATSF
**932-6763** CNW†
**932-6764** Amtrak Phase I
**932-6765** SP†
**932-6766** NP (Two-Tone Green)
**932-6767** PRR (Late Scheme)
**932-6768** DRGW† ("Four-Stripe" Scheme)
**932-6769** C&O
**932-6770** Rock Island
**932-6771** UP†
**932-6772** NYC (Two-Tone Gray w/single band)
**932-16761** NKP
**932-16762** Delaware & Hudson
**932-16763** N&W
**932-16764** ACL
**932-16765** Seaboard Air Line
**932-16766** C&O; Fluted, No Skirts
**932-6760** Undecorated

Seated 590-1014009

Standing/Walking for Platform
590-1014008

# CLASSIC COMMUTER CARS

- Fully assembled, ready to run
- Full interiors
- Flush-fitting tinted windows
- Removable roof with separate details
- Working diaphragms
- Separate wire grab irons
- Number decals
- Authentic trucks
- RP-25 metal wheels
- Knuckle couplers (optional horn-hooks also provided)
- Swinging coupler pockets for better performance
- Factory-installed electrical pickups for use with the Bilevel Car Lighting Kit (#933-1058, sold separately)

## Pullman-Standard Bilevel Commuter Coach 32.98 ea

**932-6251** CNW† (green, yellow)
**932-6252** Metra (Chicago Area 1984+)
**932-6253** Regional Transportation Authority (RTA; Chicago 1974-84)
**932-6254** Rock Island
**932-6255** Virginia Railway Express
**932-6256** Amtrak Phase III
**932-6250** Undecorated

## Pullman-Standard Bilevel Cab Cars/Coach 32.98 ea

**932-6261** CNW† (green, yellow)
**932-6262** Metra (Chicago Area 1984+)
**932-6263** Regional Transportation Authority (RTA; Chicago 1974-84)
**932-6264** Rock Island
**932-6266** Amtrak Phase III
**932-6260** Undecorated

## Bilevel Car Lighting Kit

**933-1058** For 6250, 6260 & 5970 Series Cars **10.98**

- Fully assembled accessory
- Easy-to-install drop-in mounting

## Passenger Figure Sets 36.98 ea

- Use Standing/Walking Passengers outside Walthers City Station (#933-2904) or the Wood Station Shed & Platform (#933-3188), both sold separately
- Molded in plastic and hand-painted for more realism

**590-1014008** Standing/Walking for Platform pkg(36)
**590-1014009** Seated pkg(36)

†Union Pacific licensed product.

# WALTHERS

## THE BUDD-BUILT TRAINS OF TOMORROW ARE HERE TODAY!

- Fully assembled, ready to run
- As-Built & Amtrak® versions
- Full interiors
- Flush-fitting windows
- Prototypical side skirting
- Wire grab irons
- Molded drill starter points
- Removable roof with separate details
- Working diaphragms
- Complete underbody detail
- Diecast GSC Commonwealth trucks with RP-25 metal wheels
- Swinging drawbars improve performance on curves
- Working knuckle couplers (optional horn-hook couplers also included)
- Factory-installed electrical pickups
- Snap-in interior lighting kit available separately
- Car name & number decals included

Thanks Model Railroader readers for selecting Walthers Budd Cars for this great honor!

Budd Dome Coach
VIA (Modern Scheme) 932-16483

Budd Dome Coach
IC 932-16482

### Budd Dome Coach 39.98 ea

**932-6481** Amtrak Phase I
**932-6482** Amtrak Phase II*
**932-6483** Amtrak Phase III*
**932-6484** Amtrak Phase IV*
**932-6485** ATSF
**932-6486** PRR
**932-6487** CB&Q
**932-6488** NYC
**932-6489** CP
**932-6492** Rock Island
**932-6493** SP†
**932-6494** UP†
**932-6495** Penn Central
**932-16481** D&H
**932-16482** IC
**932-16483** VIA (Modern Scheme)
**932-6480** Undecorated

*Model Features Head-End Power Underframe

Add realism to your Budd Dome Coaches with the Walthers Dome Car Interior Lighting Kit.
**933-1065 12.98**

For Up-To-Date Information and News Bookmark Walthers Web site at
**www.walthers.com**

Budd Tavern-Observation Car
Amtrak Phase I 932-6501

Budd Tavern-Observation Car
NYC 932-6508

Budd Baggage/Dormitory Car
Seaboard Coast Line 932-16462

### Budd Tavern-Observation Cars 39.98 ea

- Comes with or without rear warning light
- Operating rear knuckle coupler

**932-6501** Amtrak Phase I
**932-6502** Amtrak Phase II
**932-6503** Amtrak Phase III
**932-6504** Amtrak Phase IV
**932-6505** ATSF
**932-6506** PRR
**932-6507** CB&Q
**932-6508** NYC
**932-6509** CP
**932-6512** Rock Island
**932-6513** SP†
**932-6514** UP†
**932-6515** Penn Central
**932-16501** VIA
**932-16502** Seaboard Coast Line
**932-16503** Seaboard Air Line
**932-6500** Undecorated

### Budd Baggage/ Dormitory Cars 34.98 ea

**932-6461** Amtrak Phase I
**932-6462** Amtrak Phase II*
**932-6463** Amtrak Phase III*
**932-6464** Amtrak Phase IV*
**932-6465** ATSF
**932-6466** PRR
**932-6467** CB&Q
**932-6468** NYC
**932-6469** CP
**932-6472** Rock Island
**932-6473** SP†
**932-6474** UP†
**932-6475** Penn Central
**932-16461** VIA
**932-16462** Seaboard Coast Line
**932-16463** Seaboard Air Line
**932-6460** Undecorated

*Model Features Head-End Power Underframe.

These Budd Cars can be made brighter with the Passenger Car Interior Lighting Conversion Kit.
**933-1049 10.98**

# WALTHERS

## Budd 63' Railway Post Office 34.98 ea

**932-6441** Amtrak® Phase I
**932-6442** Amtrak Phase II
**932-6443** Amtrak Phase III
**932-6444** Amtrak Phase IV
**932-6445** ATSF
**932-6446** PRR
**932-6447** CB&Q
**932-6448** NYC
**932-6449** CP
**932-6450** ACL
**932-6451** SOU
**932-6452** Rock Island
**932-6453** SP†
**932-6454** UP†
**932-16441** Seaboard Coast Line

**932-16442** ATSF (no side skirting)
**932-6440** Undecorated

## Passenger Train Crew

**590-10452** Transition-Era Passenger Train Crew pkg(6) **15.99**

- Set provides a complete crew for any size passenger train of the 1940s to the 1960s
- Includes a seated engineer, hardworking fireman, a uniformed conductor, trainman, porter and waiter/steward

## Budd 73' Baggage Car 32.98 ea

**932-6401** Amtrak Phase I
**932-6402** Amtrak Phase II*
**932-6403** Amtrak Phase III*
**932-6404** Amtrak Phase IV*
**932-6405** ATSF
**932-6406** PRR
**932-6409** CP
**932-6412** Rock Island
**932-6413** SP†
**932-6414** UP†
**932-6415** Penn Central
**932-16401** VIA
**932-16402** Seaboard Coast Line
**932-16403** ATSF (No Car Skirting)
**932-6400** Undecorated

## Budd Lounge Car (1 Drawing Room, 29 Seats) 34.98 ea

**932-6421** Amtrak® Phase I
**932-6422** Amtrak Phase II*

**932-6423** Amtrak Phase III*

**932-6424** Amtrak Phase IV*
**932-6425** ATSF

**932-6426** PRR

**932-6427** CB&Q

**932-6428** NYC
**932-6429** CP
**932-6430** ACL
**932-6431** SOU
**932-6432** Rock Island
**932-6433** SP†
**932-6434** UP†
**932-6435** Penn Central
**932-16422** Seaboard Coast Line
**932-6420** Undecorated

> These Budd Cars can be made brighter with the Passenger Car Interior Lighting Conversion Kit.
> **933-1049 10.98**

## Budd 52-Seat Coach 34.98 ea

**932-6381** Amtrak Phase I

**932-6382** Amtrak Phase II*

**932-6383** Amtrak Phase III*

**932-6384** Amtrak Phase IV*

**932-6385** ATSF

**932-6386** PRR

**932-6387** CB&Q
**932-6388** NYC
**932-6389** CP
**932-6392** Rock Island
**932-6393** SP†
**932-6394** UP†
**932-6395** Penn Central
**932-16381** Seaboard Coast Line
**932-16382** Seaboard Air Line
**932-6380** Undecorated

*Model Features Head-End Power Underframe.

†Union Pacific licensed product.

Budd Streamline 63' Railway Post Office Rock Island 932-6452

Budd Streamline 73' Baggage Car UP 932-6414

Budd 52-Seat Coach Seaboard Air Line 932-16382

Budd Lounge Car CP 932-6429

# WALTHERS

Budd 24-8 Slumber Coach
NP 932-16362

Budd 46-Seat Coach
Seaboard Coast Line 932-16302

Budd 10-6 Sleeper MILW 932-16344

Budd Diner NYC 932-16322

## Budd 24-8 Slumber Coach 34.98 ea

**932-6361** Amtrak Phase I
**932-9362** Amtrak Phase II*
**932-6363** Amtrak Phase III*
**932-6364** Amtrak Phase IV*
**932-6365** ATSF
**932-6366** PRR
**932-6367** CB&Q
**932-6368** NYC
**932-6372** Rock Island
**932-6373** SP†
**932-6374** UP†
**932-16361** NYC (black roof)
**932-16362** NP
**932-16363** MP†
**932-16364** B&O
**932-6360** Undecorated

## Budd 46-Seat Coach 34.98 ea

**932-6301** Amtrak Phase I
**932-6302** Amtrak Phase II*
**932-6303** Amtrak Phase III*
**932-6307** CB&Q
**932-6309** CP
**932-6310** ACL
**932-6311** SOU
**932-6312** Rock Island
**932-6313** SP†
**932-6314** UP†
**932-16301** VIA*
**932-16302** Seaboard Coast Line
**932-16303** ATSF (No Car Skirting)
**932-6300** Undecorated

## Budd 10-6 Sleeper 34.98 ea

**932-6342** Amtrak Phase II*
**932-6343** Amtrak Phase III*
**932-6344** Amtrak Phase IV*
**932-6347** CB&Q
**932-6350** ACL
**932-6351** SOU
**932-6352** Rock Island
**932-16341** VIA*
**932-16342** Seaboard Coast Line
**932-16343** UP† (Non-Pullman)
**932-16344** MILW
**932-16345** Amtrak Phase IV (Dormitory Car)*

*Model Features Head-End Power Underframe.

## Budd Diner 34.98 ea

**932-6322** Amtrak Phase II*
**932-6323** Amtrak Phase III*
**932-6324** Amtrak Phase IV*
**932-6329** CP
**932-6332** Rock Island
**932-6334** UP†
**932-6335** Penn Central
**932-16321** VIA*
**932-16322** NYC (black roof)

## Drop-In Interior Lighting Kit

**933-1049** For Budd Cars **10.98**

- Fully assembled and designed for easy snap-in mounting
- Includes step-by-step instructions for removing car roof and adding lighting unit
- Note: ***NOT*** for use with Pleasure Dome #932-9006, which uses lighting kit #933-1083

## Budd Passenger Car Underbody Details

**933-1057 9.98**

- Includes the main underbody detail parts found on Walthers Budd passenger cars.
- Use it to add realism to other manufacturers' passenger cars

# REVISED AMTRAK® SUPERLINER® I & II PASSENGER CARS

## 34.98 ea

- Totally Re-Tooled
- Full Interiors
- Built-In Electrical Contacts for Interior Lighting Kit
- Upgraded Trucks w/Metal Sideframes
- Amtrak Phase IVb Scheme
- Correct Details
- Wire Grab Irons
- Working Diaphragms
- Knuckle Couplers

**COMING SOON!**

**Fall 2007 Delivery**

### Superliner I

**NEW 932-6164** Coach
**NEW 932-6174** Sleeper

### Superliner II

**NEW 932-6102** Coach
**NEW 932-6112** Sleeper

See What's Available at
**www.walthers.com**

Superliner II Sleeper 932-6112
Image Courtesy of Bruce Jacobs

Superliner I Coach 932-6164

Superliner I Sleeper 932-6174

Superliner II Coach 932-6102
Images Courtesy of T.J. Van Haag

**COMING SOON!**

**Winter 2007-08 Delivery**

### Superliner I

**NEW 932-6184** Diner
**NEW 932-6194** Sightseer Lounge

### Superliner II

**NEW 932-6122** Sightseer Lounge
**NEW 932-6132** Diner

# SUPERLINER ACCESSORIES

**COMING SOON!**

**Fall 2007 Delivery**

### Interior Lighting Kit

**NEW 933-6004 10.98**

- Fits New Amtrak Superliner Cars
- Completely Assembled
- For DC or DCC Layouts

**COMING SOON!**

**Fall 2007 Delivery**

### GSC Trucks

**NEW 933-1321** For Superliner II 1 Pair **10.98**

- Revised Design
- Metal Sideframes
- RP-25 Metal Wheels

**COMING SOON!**

**Winter 2007-08 Delivery**

### Airbag Trucks

**NEW 933-1320** Superliner I As-Delivered 1 Pair **10.98**

- Revised Design
- Metal Sideframes
- RP-25 Metal Wheels

# WALTHERS

## SUPERLINER® I & II CARS

- Fully assembled, ready to run
- Authentic paint
- Decals for car markings & numbers
- Working knuckle couplers
- Correct trucks with metal wheels
- Tinted windows
- Complete underbody
- Swinging coupler pockets
- Preformed wire grab irons
- Movable diaphragms
- Complete instructions

### Superliner I 27.98 ea

**Limited Quantity Available**

**Coach/Baggage**

**932-6151** Phase III

**932-6152** Phase IV

**932-6153** Phase II

**932-6154** Coach-Smoker Phase IV

**932-6150** Undecorated

**Limited Quantity Available**

**Coach**

**932-6161** Phase II

**932-6162** Phase III

**932-6163** Phase IV

**932-6160** Undecorated

**Limited Quantity Available**

**Sleeper**

**932-6171** Phase II

**932-6172** Phase III

**932-6173** Phase IV

**932-6170** Undecorated

**Limited Quantity Available**

**Diner**

**932-6181** Phase II

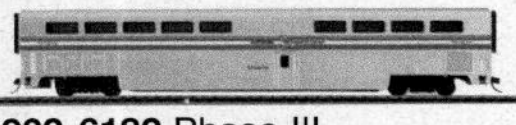

**932-6182** Phase III

**932-6183** Phase IV

**932-6180** Undecorated

**Limited Quantity Available**

**Lounge**

**932-6191** Phase II

**932-6192** Phase III

**932-6193** Phase IV

**932-6190** Undecorated

### Superliner II 27.98 ea

- Outwardly similar to Superliner I but with wider entryways and other modifications to comply with the Americans with Disabilities Act
- Prepainted in the Phase IV scheme

**Limited Quantity Available**

**Amtrak Phase IV**

**932-6101** Coach

**932-6111** Sleeper

**932-6121** Lounge

**932-6131** Diner

**932-6141** Transition Sleeper

**Limited Quantity Available**

**Undecorated**

**932-6100** Coach

**932-6110** Sleeper

**932-6120** Lounge

**932-6130** Diner

**932-6140** Transition Sleeper

Superliner I Coach/Baggage
Phase IV 932-6152

Superliner I Coach/Baggage
Phase II 932-6153

Superliner I Coach
Phase II 932-6161

Superliner I Sleeper
Phase IV 932-6173

Superliner II Transition Sleeper
Undecorated 932-6140

# WALTHERS

## AMFLEET℠ I CARS 24.98 ea

- Offered in all four paint schemes (called Phases) used on both coach and food service cars since they were first delivered
- Feature improved inside bearing trucks with electrical pickup

### Phase I

As-built scheme with wide red and blue stripes, separated by narrow white stripes, plus the original pointless arrow logo

**932-6002** Coach

**932-6012** Food Service

### Phase II

Wide red and blue stripes with white pinstripes between

**932-6001** Coach

**932-6011** Food Service

### Phase III

Equal width red, white and blue stripes, with Amtrak logo in black on white background

**932-6003** Coach

**932-6013** Food Service

### Phase IV

Large blue stripe with small red and white stripes.

**932-6004** Coach

**932-6014** Food Service

### Phase IV - "Northeast Direct"

**932-6005** Coach

**932-6015** Food Service

## AMFLEET II CARS 24.98 ea

- Suitable for period or contemporary trains
- Models feature the correct larger windows, a single vestibule, tinted windows, metal wheelsets and body-mounted knuckle couplers

### Coach

**932-6202** Phase III

**932-6203** Phase IV

**932-6200** Undecorated

### Food Service

**932-6212** Phase III

**932-6213** Phase IV

**932-6210** Undecorated

## HORIZON FLEET CARS 24.98 ea

- Authentic paint and lettering
- Decals for car markings and numbers
- Tinted windows
- Complete underbody with correct GSI trucks
- Swinging coupler pockets for improved performance on curves

### Coaches

**932-6051** Amtrak Phase III

**932-6052** Amtrak Phase IV

**932-6050** Undecorated

### Food Service

**932-6061** Amtrak Phase III

**932-6062** Amtrak Phase IV

**932-6060** Undecorated

## VIEWLINER SLEEPERS 27.98 ea

- Triangular shock supports mounted above trucks
- Tinted windows
- Authentic Amtrak® paint and lettering
- Separate wire grabs and stirrups
- Includes electrical conduit on the roof
- Free-rolling trucks and working knuckle couplers

**932-6091** Amtrak Phase IV

**932-6090** Undecorated

## DIAPHRAGMS 1 Pair 2.98 ea

- Easy to build and install
- Kits are offered in the bellows style for heavyweights or the black rubber style for modern streamlined cars
- Two complete diaphragms each, enough for one car

**933-429** Folded Bellows With vinyl striker plate, for heavyweight cars

**933-977** Black Rubber One-piece molding, for streamlined cars.

Amfleet I Food Service Car Phase I Scheme 932-6012

Amfleet II Food Service Phase III 932-6212

Amfleet II Food Service Phase IV 932-6213

## HORIZON COMMUTER SERVICE CARS 24.98 ea

- For commuter operations, a cab car for push-pull service was built
- Fully assembled, ready to run
- Features authentic paint schemes
- Includes decals for car markings and numbers, correct inside-bearing trucks, tinted windows, complete underbody details, swinging coupler pockets, working knuckle couplers with additional horn-hook couplers included

### Virginia Rail Express

**932-6077** Coach

**932-6087** Cab Car

### Boston (MBTA)

**932-6073** Coach

**932-6083** Cab Car

### New York (NY Metro MTA)

**932-6074** Coach

**932-6084** Cab Car

### Connecticut DOT

**932-6075** Coach

**932-6085** Cab Car

### New Jersey Transit

**932-6072** Coach

**932-6082** Cab Car

### Undecorated

(see Legend Page)

**932-6070** Coach

**932-6080** Cab Car

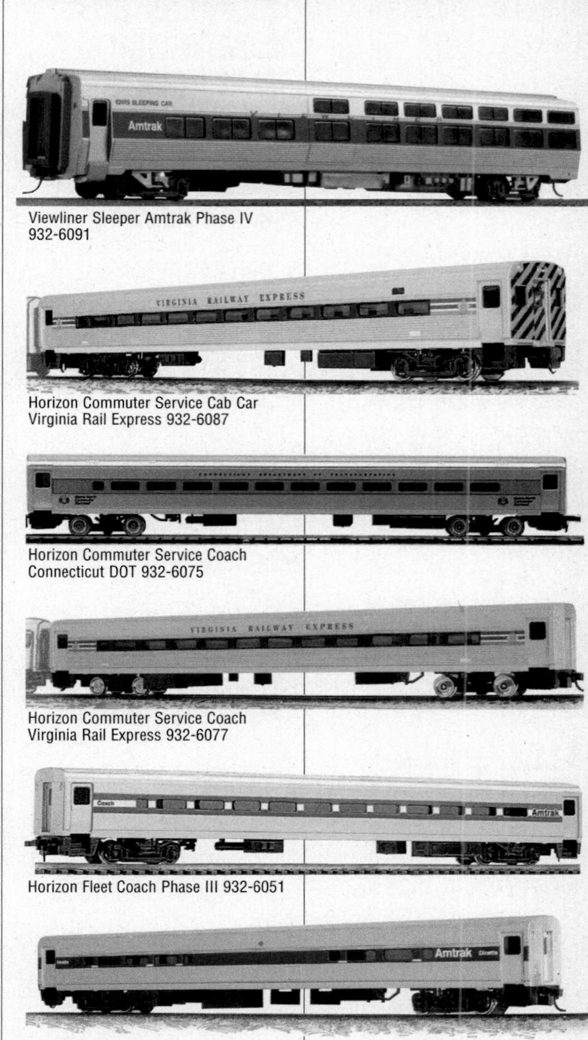

Viewliner Sleeper Amtrak Phase IV 932-6091

Horizon Commuter Service Cab Car Virginia Rail Express 932-6087

Horizon Commuter Service Coach Connecticut DOT 932-6075

Horizon Commuter Service Coach Virginia Rail Express 932-6077

Horizon Fleet Coach Phase III 932-6051

Horizon Fleet Food Service Car Phase IV 932-6062

# WALTHERS

## GOLD LINE™ FLEXI-VAN FLAT CAR W/TWO TRAILERS

COMING SOON!

Winter 2007-08 Delivery
- All-New Tooling
- Includes Two 40' Trailers
- Run in Freight or Passenger Service
- Three Car Numbers Available
- Mark III Cars
- More Trailers & Bogies Available Separately

### Single Cars 42.98 ea (Unless Noted)

**NEW 932-3921** NYC #1
**NEW 932-3922** MILW #1
**NEW 932-3923** IC **45.98**
**NEW 932-3925** NYC #2
**NEW 932-3926** MILW #2
**NEW 932-3927** Seaboard Air Line
**NEW 932-3928** SOU **45.98**
**NEW 932-3929** WP†
**NEW 932-3920** Undecorated

### Limited-Run 2-Packs 81.98 ea (Unless Noted)

**NEW 932-23921** NYC #1
**NEW 932-23922** MILW #1
**NEW 932-23923** IC **86.98**
**NEW 932-23925** NYC #2
**NEW 932-23926** MILW #2
**NEW 932-23927** SAL
**NEW 932-23928** SOU **86.98**
**NEW 932-23929** WP†

COMING SOON!

Winter 2007-08 Delivery

## FLEXI-VAN 40' TRAILERS

### 12.98 ea

- All-New Model
- Perfect for Flexi-Van Flats
- Use as Highway, Dock or Car Detail
- Includes Trailer Bogie

**NEW 933-1681** NYC
**NEW 933-1682** MILW
**NEW 933-1683** IC
**NEW 933-1685** CB&Q
**NEW 933-1686** SAL
**NEW 933-1687** SOU
**NEW 933-1688** WP†
**NEW 933-1689** L&N
**NEW 933-1690** Soo Line
**NEW 933-1680** Undecorated

COMING SOON!

Winter 2007-08 Delivery

## FLEXI-VAN TRAILER BOGIES

- Great Terminal Detail
- Use with 40' Flexi-Van Trailers

**NEW 933-1318 6.98**

## NYC-STYLE EXPRESS BOX CAR TROOP SLEEPER CONVERSION

COMING SOON!

Winter 2007-08 Delivery
- Great Addition to Post-War Passenger Trains
- Ready-to-Run
- New Paint & Lettering Schemes
- Knuckle Couplers
- Correct Trucks w/RP-25 Metal Wheels
- Add-On Wire Grab Irons

### Single Cars 24.98 ea

**NEW 932-4155** NYC 1947-48
**NEW 932-4156** NYC Leased (1960)
**NEW 932-4157** Rock Island (Pullman Green)
**NEW 932-4158** Erie
**NEW 932-4159** Lackawanna

### Limited-Run 2-Packs 49.98 ea

**NEW 932-24155** NYC 1947-48
**NEW 932-24156** NYC Leased (1960)
**NEW 932-24157** Rock Island (Pullman Green)
**NEW 932-24158** Erie
**NEW 932-24159** Lackawanna

### HO Allied Full-Cushion Express Truck

COMING SOON!

Winter 2007-08 Delivery
- Matches trucks used on Walthers Express Box Cars and Troop Cars

**NEW 933-1319** 1 Pair **9.98**

## C&O-STYLE EXPRESS BOX CAR TROOP SLEEPER CONVERSION

COMING SOON!

Fall 2007 Delivery
- Great Addition to Post-War Passenger Trains
- Ready-to-Run
- New Paint & Lettering Schemes
- Knuckle Couplers
- Correct Trucks w/RP-25 Metal Wheels
- Add-On Wire Grab Irons

### Single Cars 26.98 ea

**NEW 932-4166** C&O (Pullman Green)
**NEW 932-4167** C&O (blue, gray, yellow)
**NEW 932-4168** B&O (MOW Scheme)
**NEW 932-4169** B&O (Dark Blue, yellow )
**NEW 932-4170** B&M (Maroon, Dulux Gold)
**NEW 932-4165** Undecorated

### Limited-Run 2-Packs 49.98 ea

**NEW 932-24166** C&O (Pullman Green)
**NEW 932-24167** C&O (blue, gray, yellow)
**NEW 932-24168** B&O (MOW Scheme)
**NEW 932-24169** B&O (Dark Blue, yellow )
**NEW 932-24170** B&M (Maroon, Dulux Gold)

## AMTRAK 1700 SERIES BAGGAGE CARS

### 32.98 ea

- Prepainted in Phase IV and US Mail schemes
- Fully assembled
- Working diaphragms
- Swinging couplers
- Add-on wire grab irons
- Metal GSC Commonwealth trucks
- 36" metal wheels
- Authentic Amtrak-style ends
- Car number decals
- Interior bulkheads
- Knuckle couplers

**932-6231** Amtrak Phase IV
**932-6232** Amtrak Phase IV w/U.S. Postal Service Markings
**932-6230** Undecorated

Flexi-Van Flat Car w/Two Trailers
Image Courtesy of Bob's Photo

C&O-Style Express Box Car Troop Sleeper Conversion
C&O 932-4167

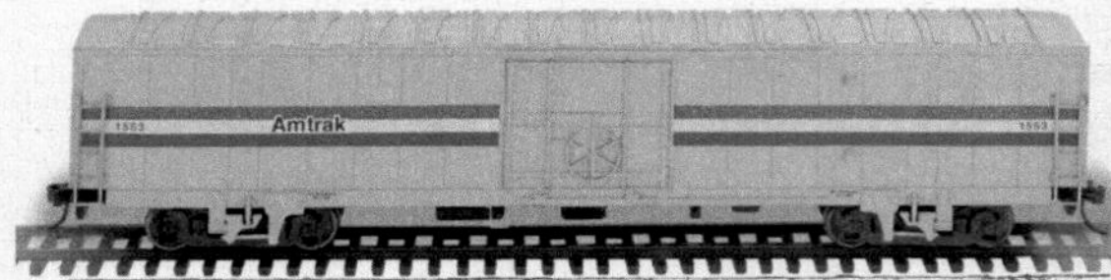

Amtrak Phase III
Material Handling Car 932-6021

60' Express Box Car
Amtrak Phase IV 932-6041

## AMTRAK MATERIAL HANDLING CARS

- Fully assembled
- Separate ladders
- GSC trucks
- Knuckle couplers

### Single Cars 21.98 ea

**932-6021** Phase III (Tri-Stripe)
**932-6022** Phase III w/US Mail Emblem
**932-6023** Phase IV
**932-6020** Undecorated

### Limited-Run 2-Packs

**932-26021** Phase III (Tri-Stripe) **43.98**

## 60' EXPRESS BOX CARS

### 21.98 ea

- Fully assembled
- Separate door latch bars & release wheels
- Separate ladders
- Knuckle couplers

**932-6041** Amtrak Phase IV
**932-6042** Amtrak Silver Scheme
**932-6043** NS
**932-6044** International Bridge & Terminal Co.
**932-6045** Amtrak Phase V (New Scheme)
**932-6040** Undecorated

# WALTHERS

## 75' AUTO CARRIERS

- Fully assembled
- Short or long ladders
- Optional roofwalks
- Separate door details
- Brake gear
- GSC trucks
- Knuckle couplers

### Auto Train Corporation

**932-6224** Short & Tall Ladders, Roofwalk **21.98**

**932-26224** Tall & Short Ladders, Roofwalk pkg(2) **43.98**

### Amtrak

**932-6221** Phase III (Short Ladders, Optional Roofwalk) **21.98**

**932-6222** Phase IV (Short Ladders, Optional Roofwalk) **21.98**

**932-26221** Phase III (Short Ladders, Optional Roofwalk) **43.98**

**932-26222** Phase IV (Short Ladders, Optional Roofwalk) pkg(2) **43.98**

### Canadian National

**932-6223** Tall Ladders & Roofwalk **21.98**

### Undecorated

**932-6220 21.98**

## 50' GACX WOOD EXPRESS REEFERS

- Used from the 1920s to the 60s
- Carried perishables, mail and packages
- Use with heavyweight or streamlined cars
- Fully assembled
- Add-on wire grab irons included

### With Pullman Trucks

### Single Cars 25.98 ea

**932-5471** REA

**932-5472** PFE†

**932-5473** American Refrigerator Transit†

**932-5474** Frisco

**932-5475** MP†

**932-5476** Wabash

**932-5477** NKP

**932-5485** REA #3

**932-5487** PFE† #2

**932-5492** REA - Dulux lettering, large herald

**932-5470** Undecorated

### Limited-Run 2-Packs 44.98 ea

**932-25473** American Refrigerator Transit†

**932-25474** Frisco

**932-25475** MP†

**932-25476** Wabash

**932-25485** REA #3

**932-25487** PFE† #2

**932-25492** REA - Dulux lettering, large herald (Pullman Truck)

### With GSC Trucks

### Single Cars 25.98 ea

**932-5478** Rock Island (GSC Trucks)

**932-5479** DRGW†

**932-5480** REA

**932-5481** Seaboard Air Line

**932-5482** SOO

**932-5483** Union Refrigerator Transit

**932-5484** WP†

**932-5486** Union Refrigerator Transit (orange)

**932-5488** Louisville & Nashville

**932-5489** KCS

**932-5490** MKT†

**932-5491** REA - white lettering, large herald

**932-5493** REA - gold lettering

**932-5494** PFE†

**932-5495** URTX

**932-5499** Undecorated

### Limited-Run 2-Packs 44.98 ea

**932-25478** Rock Island

**932-25479** DRGW†

**932-25480** REA

**932-25481** Seaboard Air Line

**932-25482** SOO

**932-25483** Union Refrigerator Transit

**932-25484** WP†

**932-25486** Union Refrigerator Transit

**932-25489** KCS

**932-25490** MKT†

**932-25491** REA - white lettering, large herald

**932-25493** REA - gold lettering

**932-25494** PFE†

**932-25495** URTX

See What's Available at

**www.walthers.com**

## RAILWAY EXPRESS AGENCY 50' RIVETED STEEL EXPRESS REEFERS

- Based on a series of cars first ordered in 1957
- Fully assembled, ready to run
- Highly-detailed one-piece body with ice hatches, ladders and roofwalks
- Separate wire grab irons
- Complete underbody details
- High-speed trucks with metal wheelsets
- Working knuckle couplers

### Single Cars 24.98 ea

**932-6241** Railway Express Agency (Hunter Green)

**932-6242** REA Express – Hunter Green

**932-6243** REA Express - Chromate Green

**932-6244** ATSF

**932-6245** GN

**932-6246** ACL

**932-6247** San Luis Central

**932-6248** SFRD Santa Fe Freight

**932-6249** Railway Express Agency (Striped Scheme)

**932-6240** Undecorated

### Limited-Run 2-Packs 49.98 ea

**932-26247** San Luis Central

**932-26248** SFRD Santa Fe Freight

**932-26249** Railway Express Agency (Striped Scheme)

## 53' GENERAL AMERICAN-PFAUDLER MILK CARS

- First Time in Plastic
- Five Authentic Schemes
- Used from 1920s to the 60s
- Perfect for Sterling Consolidated Dairy Complex (#933-3799) Sold Separately

### Single Cars 25.98 ea

**932-5461** H. P. Hood

**932-5462** Dairymen's League

**932-5463** Sheffield

**932-5464** United Farmers

**932-5465** White Brothers

**932-5460** Undecorated

†Union Pacific licensed product.

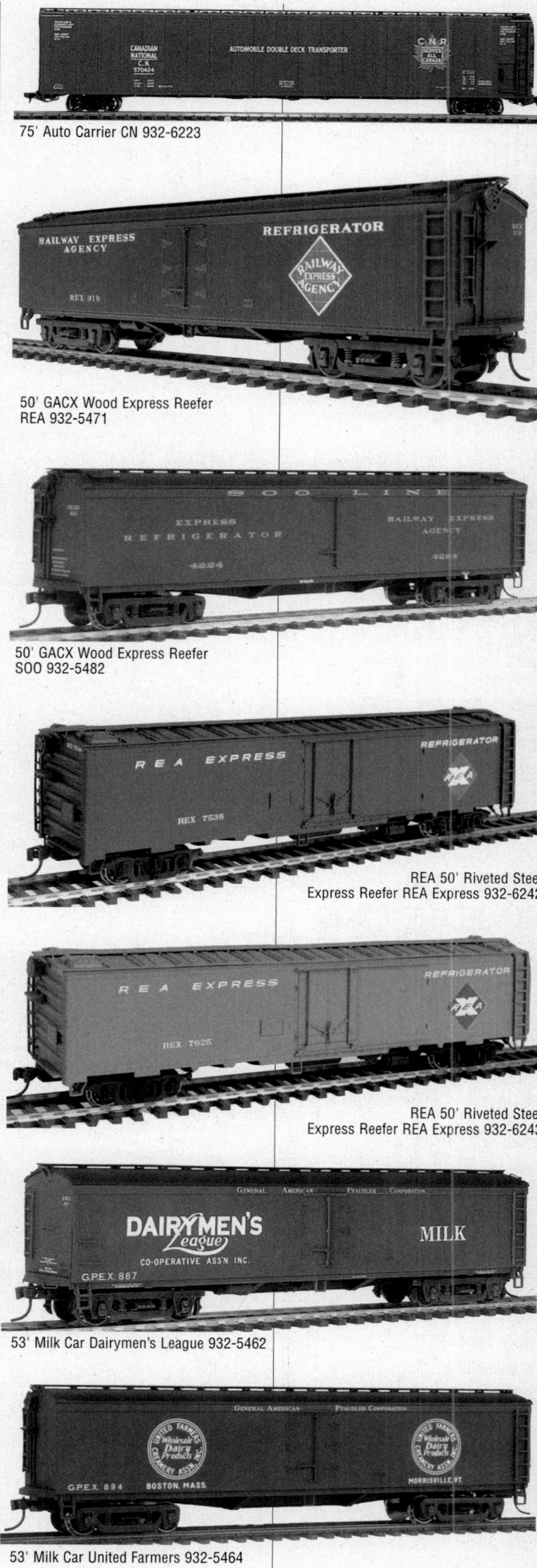


75' Auto Carrier CN 932-6223

50' GACX Wood Express Reefer REA 932-5471

50' GACX Wood Express Reefer SOO 932-5482

REA 50' Riveted Steel Express Reefer REA Express 932-6242

REA 50' Riveted Steel Express Reefer REA Express 932-6243

53' Milk Car Dairymen's League 932-5462

53' Milk Car United Farmers 932-5464

# WALTHERS

## PRR R50b EXPRESS REEFERS

**24.98 ea**

- Fully assembled, ready to run
- Equipped with 2D-P5 trucks and metal wheelsets
- Separate roofwalks and ladders
- Molded-in drill starter points for installing the supplied wire grab irons

**932-5881** PRR (Prewar Scheme)

**932-5882** PRR (Postwar Scheme)

**932-5883** PRR (Keystone Herald)

**932-5884** PRR (1939 Scheme)

**932-5885** PRR (Tuscan Red Scheme 1943-44)

**932-5886** PRR (Tuscan Red, No REA Logo 1954)

**932-5887** PRR 1936-38 Scheme (Tuscan, olive, brown, buff)

**932-5888** PRR Summer 1945 Scheme (Medium Tuscan, black, buff)

**932-5880** Undecorated

## PRR B60b BAGGAGE CARS

**34.98 ea**

- Fully Assembled
- Metal RP-25 Wheels
- Knuckle Couplers
- Razor-Sharp Paint and Lettering
- Modeler-Installed Grab Irons Included

**932-5871** PRR

**932-5872** PRR - Modern w/Keystone Heralds

**932-5873** Long Island Railroad

**932-5874** N&W

**932-5875** PC

**932-5876** PRR - Messenger Car

**932-5831** PRR

**932-5832** PRR

**932-5833** PRR

**932-5834** PC #2

**932-5870** Undecorated

PRR R50b Express Reefer 932-5887

PRR R50b Express Reefer 932-5888

PRR R50b Express Reefer 932-5883

PRR B60b Baggage Car PC 932-5875

PRR B60b Baggage Car 932-5876

Division of Wm.K.Walthers, Inc.

Ready-to-run cars are made of colored plastic, and include trucks plus horn-hook couplers.

## 60' STREAMLINED CARS W/LIGHTS

### Amtrak® 17.25 ea

**433-8077** Observation

**433-8078** Full Dome

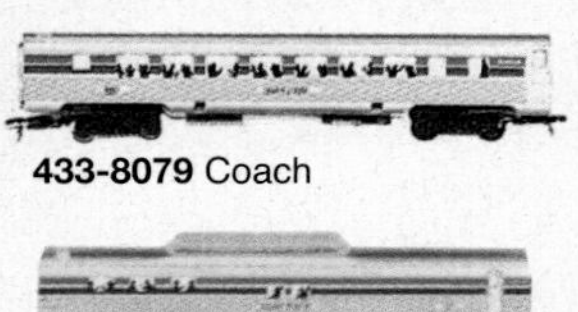

**433-8079** Coach

**433-8090** Diner

**433-8091** Vista Dome

Observation 433-8077

Vista Dome 433-8091

Vista Dome 433-8052

Full Dome 433-8059

Diner 433-8093

### ATSF 17.25 ea

**433-8052** Vista Dome

**433-8056** Diner

**433-8059** Full Dome

### B&O 17.25 ea

**433-8093** Diner

**433-8094** Vista Dome

### Car Assortments pkg(12)

Includes three each of Coach and Vista Dome, and two each of Observation, Full Dome and Diner.

**433-8076** Amtrak **207.00**

60' Coach Chicago & North Western 635-HR4037

60' Baggage Car Chicago & North Western 635-HR4038

60' Coach Pennsylvania 635-HR4040

60' Baggage Car Pennsylvania 635-HR4041

## NEW PRODUCTS

### 60' Passenger Cars

From branchline to mainline, these 60' Heavyweight cars are a great way to expand passenger service. Serving for decades on important trains, in commuter service, at the rear of rural mixed trains and as trailers behind gas electrics, the ready-to-run models will be at home on just about any layout. For more realism, these cars can be fitted with Walthers Interior Lighting Kits (#933-1075 for Coaches, #933-1076 for Baggage Cars) available separately.

### Chicago & North Western

**NEW 635-4036** Coach 3-Pack **89.99**

**NEW 635-4037** Single Coach **29.99**

**NEW 635-4038** Baggage Car **29.99**

### Pennsylvania

**NEW 635-4039** Coach 3-Pack **89.99**

**NEW 635-4040** Single Coach **29.99**

**NEW 635-4041** Baggage Car **29.99**

## 60' PASSENGER CAR LIGHTING KITS

### 17.98 ea

Fully assembled, easy to install (will also fit older Trainline and Rivarossi 60' cars).

**933-1075** For Cars w/4-Wheel Trucks

**933-1076** For Cars w/6-Wheel Trucks

## STREAMLINE CAR LIGHTING KITS

Add constant lighting to newer Rivarossi cars. Includes snap-in light bar, wiring components and replacement truck sideframes.

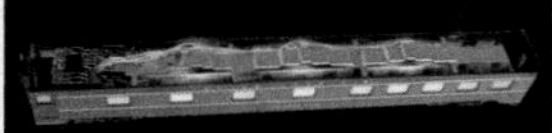

**933-1051** For Coach, 10-6 Sleeper & Diner **15.98**

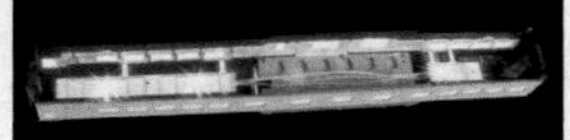

**933-1052** For Dome & Dome-Observation **17.98**

## 1930S ERA STREAMLINED CARS

### 26.98 ea

Fully assembled with RP-25 metal wheels, interior and superb paint and lettering.

**Limited Quantity Available on All Items**

### Denver & Rio Grande Western

**635-2893** Diner

### Missouri Pacific "The Colorado Eagle"

**635-2748** Roomette Sleeper

### Northern Pacific

**635-2817** Diner

## NEW PRODUCTS

### SP 1953 Coast Daylight Passenger Cars

These detailed models are based on the post-war version of the train with unskirted bodies and Southern Pacific lettering. Each ready-to-run car features an injection-molded body, lighted interior, operating diaphragms, appropriate trucks and more.

### Train #98 Series

**NEW 187-1570** Baggage - Chair Car #3302 **74.99**

**NEW 187-1571** Articulated Chair Car w/Antenna #W2462/M2461 **134.99**

**NEW 187-1572** Articulated Chair Car w/Antenna #W2474/M2473 **134.99**

**NEW 187-1573** Chair Car #2485 **69.99**

**NEW 187-1574** Parlor Car #3002 **69.99**

**NEW 187-1575** Parlor Observation w/Antenna #2954 **89.99**

**NEW 187-1576** Articulated Coffee Shop, Kitchen, Diner #10258/#10257/#10256 **189.99**

**NEW 187-1577** Tavern #10314 **74.99**

**NEW 187-1578** Articulated Chair Car #W2458/#M2457 **134.99**

**NEW 187-1579** Articulated Chair Car #W2460/#M2459 **134.99**

### Train #99 Series

**NEW 187-1580** Baggage-Chair Car w/Antenna #3303 **74.99**

**NEW 187-1581** Articulated Chair Car #W2470/#M2469 **134.99**

**NEW 187-1582** Articulated Chair Car #W2476/M2475 **134.99**

**NEW 187-1583** Chair Car #2486 **69.99**

**NEW 187-1584** Parlor #3003 **69.99**

**NEW 187-1585** Parlor Observation w/Antenna #2955 **89.99**

**NEW 187-1586** Articulated Coffee Shop, Kitchen, Diner #10261/#10260/#10259 **189.99**

**NEW 187-1587** Tavern w/Antenna #10315 **74.99**

**NEW 187-1588** Articulated Chair Car #W2466/#M2465 **134.99**

**NEW 187-1589** Articulated Chair Car #W2468/#M2467 **134.99**

The Coach Yard

## COUPLER POCKET

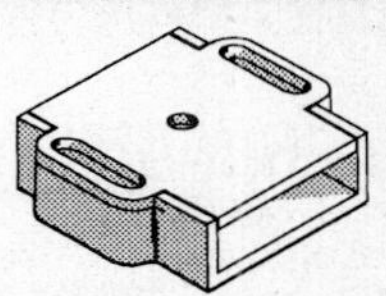

**224-8** Darwin Universal Coupler Pocket 6 Pair w/Screws (1.4mm) **4.95**
Allows for correct spacing between passenger cars. Fits most HO scale passenger cars. Accepts most couplers.

## WORKING FULL-WIDTH DIAPHRAGMS

Detail your streamliner fleet with working diaphragms, based on equipment designed to fit the 1937 AAR end profile, which was the standard for all lightweight passenger cars built in the U.S. Each diaphragm is fully assembled with a super flexible material between detailed metal ends.

### One Pair 17.95 ea

**224-6A** Gray

**224-6B** "Daylight" Red

**224-6C** Silver

**224-6D** "Empire Builder" Green

**224-6E** Tuscan Red

**224-6F** Armour Yellow

### 6 Pair 102.95 ea

**224-7A** Gray

**224-7B** "Daylight" Red

**224-7C** Silver

**224-7D** "Empire Builder" Green

**224-7E** Tuscan Red

**224-7F** Armour Yellow

## POWER TRUCKS

DCC-compatible power trucks are perfect for use under streetcars and motor cars. Use under a passenger car to provide a boost for your head-end power. Features 36" wheels, a can motor and provisions for mounting 8'-6" or 9' truck sideframes.

**224-9** 2-Axle 8'6" to 9' wheelbase **109.95**

**224-10** 3-Axle 11' wheelbase **119.95**

# DIAPHRAGMS

Easy-to-build kits feature injection-molded plastic parts, in black or gray plastic. Sprung to hold together on curves down to 24" radius, no minimum radius limitation. Will not interfere with operation of most couplers. All kits include complete instructions.

## Walthers Pullman Passenger Cars

Pullman-style striking plate and coupler adapters.

### Single (1 Pair) 4.95 ea

**147-9680** Gray

**147-9690** Black

### 6 Pair 23.95 ea

**147-9686** Gray

**147-9696** Black

## Walthers Budd Cars

Budd-style striker plate and new coupler adapters to provide correct coupling for the diaphragms.

**147-9600** 1 Pair **4.95**

**147-9606** 6 Pair **23.95**

## Streamline Cars-Gray

Can be modified to look like Pullman or Budd diaphragms. Fit on Athearn Streamliners.

**147-9000** 1 Pair **4.45**

**147-9006** 6 Pair **20.95**

## Streamline Cars-Black

**147-9010** 1 Pair **4.45**

**147-9016** 6 Pair **20.95**

## Full-Width for Streamline Cars

**147-9500** 1 Pair **5.25**

**147-9504** 4 Pair **18.95**

## Heavyweight Cars-Athearn-Black

**147-9100** 1 Pair **4.45**

**147-9106** 6 Pair **20.95**

## Heavyweight Cars-Branchline Pullman

Includes coupling adapters to close up the coupling distance.

**147-9160** 1 Pair **4.95**

**147-9166** 6 Pair **23.95**

## Heavyweight Cars-Rivarossi & Others

**147-9200** 1 Pair **4.45**

**147-9206** 6 Pair **20.95**

## MDC Harriman Cars

**147-9150** 1 Pair **4.45**

**147-9156** 6 Pair **20.95**

## Bachmann Spectrum Cars-Black

Complete set includes car end doors. Unit is designed for use with Kadee® #23 couplers.

**147-9300** 1 Pair **4.45**

**147-9306** 6 Pair **20.95**

## Con-Cor Superliners-Gray

Simplifies installation of knuckle-type couplers (sold separately) and provides prototypical close-coupling between cars. Kits include diaphragms molded in gray plastic, coupler and truck adapter in black plastic, plus mounting screws.

**147-9400** 1 Pair **4.75**

**147-9406** 6 Pair **23.95**

# F UNIT DIESEL DIAPHRAGMS

## FT 4.95 ea

Uses the loco's scale (short) drawbar and includes three complete diaphragm assemblies, enough for one A and one B unit.

**147-9700** Gray

**147-9710** Black

## Stewart F3/F7 A&B Units

### Single (1 Pair) 4.75 ea

Parts for two A or one B unit. Includes spacers and works with close-coupling adapter.

**147-9900** Gray

**147-9910** Black

### Set Of 6 (3 Pair) 12.95 ea

Three complete sets for A-B-B-A or other combinations.

**147-9903** Gray

**147-9913** Black

## Athearn F7 A&B Units

Draft gear boxes accept Kadee #5 couplers (sold separately) and sets the units at 32" between diaphragm mounts.

### Single (1 Pair) 4.95 ea

Enough parts to do two A or one B unit.

**147-9800** Gray

**147-9810** Black

**147-9850** Athearn Genesis, Gray

**147-9860** Athearn Genesis, Black

### Set Of 6 (3 Pair) 13.95 ea

Enough parts to do an A-B-B-A set, or other combinations.

**147-9803** Gray

**147-9813** Black

# EASTERN CAR WORKS INC.

Easy-to-build kits feature molded plastic parts and are undecorated. Cars are compatible with Kadee® draft gear (not included) and feature trucks with RP-25, 36" Delrin® wheel sets. Less couplers. Important Note: This listing includes items which are available by special order only. Please see the Legend Page for information, and visit www.walthers.com for a complete listing of in-stock and special order products.

## P-70 Series 80' Standard Heavyweights

### Car Core Kits

Kits include roof and floor to complete American Model Builders Limited car side conversions, sold separately.

**117-1200** Basic Core **10.00**

**117-1299** Pullman Standard Core **10.00**

## Pullman-Standard Lightweights

### Undecorated Stainless Steel 25.00 ea

**117-1310** Commuter Coach

**117-1311** Baggage/Lounge

# FUNARO & CAMERLENGO

Craft Train Kits consist of thin flexible styro-urethane castings with details molded in place, stripwood, wire and instructions. Cars are less trucks and couplers unless noted. Important Note: This listing includes items which are available by special order only. Please see the Legend Page for information, and visit www.walthers.com for a complete listing of in-stock and special order products.

## PRR MP-54 Coach 59.99 ea

Cars feature a detailed, one-piece, cast-resin body and each includes cast truck sideframes and decals. Less pantographs and wheelsets.

**279-6960** With 2CP2 Fabricated Trucks

**279-6961** With Hyatt Trucks

# Information STATION

## Passenger Car Ductwork

Ever think of airflow while riding on a passenger cars? Probably not. But it took engineering know-how to install the correct type of ductwork inside commuter traveling cars.

Air ducts are sheet metalwork atop roofed passenger cars. These ducts carry cool air from the air compressor unit to the clerestory openings. This allowed for the flow of air to be controlled from within the passenger cars. The ductwork was usually designed to fit the contours and needs of the individual car.

You'll find these air ducts placed above passenger-occupied areas (like observation areas, lounge seating, Pullman sections and compartment spaces) but not in passageways, kitchens, vestibules or restroom facilities. On heavyweight cars, these are the bulges running parallel to the clerestory. Passengers and train staff could then control the airflow from inside. This design also allowed efficient air routing to avoid exhausting unfresh air into lounges and rooms.

A variety of designs allowed the end of the ductwork to blend into the clerestory. Some featured a straight cut, while others favored an angled appearance. And there were some ducts that gradually tapered into the clerestory, creating a more streamlined appearance.

Ready-to-run passenger cars feature molded plastic bodies, which are prepainted and lettered. Complete with trucks and E-Z Mate® knuckle couplers.

## NEW PRODUCTS

### Passenger Cars

#### Open-Sided Excursion Cars w/Seats 30.00 ea

**NEW 160-17432** Durango & Silverton

**NEW 160-17445** Cass Scenic Railroad

**NEW 160-17447** Unlettered (silver, black)

**NEW 160-17448** Unlettered (silver, yellow)

**NEW 160-17449** Unlettered (red, green, gold)

## SILVER SERIES® PASSENGER CARS

All cars feature lighted interiors.

### 85' Amtrak® Amfleet Passenger Cars 34.00 ea

#### Coaches

**160-13106** Phase II

**160-13107** Phase III

**160-13108** Phase IV

**160-13109** Acela℠ Regional

**160-13114** Phase IVB

**160-13116** Phase V

#### Cafe

**160-13110** Phase II

**160-13111** Phase III

**160-13112** Phase IV

**160-13113** Acela Regional

**160-13115** Phase IVB

**160-13117** Phase V

### 85' Full-Dome Cars 30.00 ea

**160-13002** ATSF

**160-13005** Amtrak

**160-13032** Amtrak Phase II

**160-13037** McKinley Explorer

## SPECTRUM® HEAVYWEIGHTS

Plastic bodies are prepainted and lettered in period schemes. Details include working lights, separate metal grab irons, rubber diaphragms and full underbody with brake gear. Cars come with weights, trucks and swing coupler pockets with E-Z Mate knuckle couplers. Four-car sets listed below include coach, combine, diner and observation cars.

### Baltimore & Ohio

**160-89340** Set pkg(4) **128.00**

**160-89047** Pullman "Loch Ness" **32.00**

**160-89345** Coach #5490 **32.00**

### Great Northern

**160-89330** Set pkg(4) **128.00**

**160-89037** Pullman "Buccaneer" **32.00**

**160-89335** Coach #956 **32.00**

### New Haven

**160-89200** Set pkg(4) **128.00**

**160-89205** Coach **32.00**

**160-89207** Pullman **32.00**

### New York Central

**160-89400** Set pkg(4) **128.00**

**160-89405** Coach #965 **32.00**

### Norfolk & Western

**160-89410** Set pkg(4) **128.00**

**160-89415** Coach #1647 **32.00**

### Pennsylvania

#### Post-War Scheme

**160-89240** Set pkg(4) **128.00**

**160-89245** Coach #3816 **32.00**

**160-89117** Pullman "Edgar Allan Poe" **32.00**

#### Pre-War Scheme

**160-89300** Set pkg(4) **128.00**

**160-89305** Coach #1704 **32.00**

### Santa Fe

**160-89310** Set pkg(4) **128.00**

**160-89147** Pullman "Echo Lake" **32.00**

**160-89315** Coach #892 **32.00**

### Southern

**160-89440** Set pkg(4) **128.00**

**160-89445** Coach **32.00**

**160-89447** Pullman **32.00**

### Union Pacific

**160-89325** Coach #1125 **32.00**

### Undecorated

These unlettered cars are painted Pullman Green.

**160-89520** Set pkg(4) **128.00**

**160-89522** Coach **32.00**

**160-89527** Pullman **32.00**

## AMTRAK ACELA EXPRESS CARS

### 48.00 ea

Fully assembled with complete interior and working lights, flush windows and working tilt chassis; matches equipment in set #160-1202 sold separately.

**160-89941** Café

**160-89942** First Class Car

**160-89943** Business-Class Car

**160-89944** End-Business Class Car

85' Amtrak Amfleet Passenger Coach Acela℠ Regional 160-13109

85' Amtrak Amfleet Passenger Cafe Phase II 160-13110

85' Full-Dome Car ATSF 160-13002

Spectrum Heavyweight Baltimore & Ohio Pullman "Loch Ness" 160-89047

Amtrak Acela Express Café 160-89941

Amtrak Acela Express First Class Car 160-89942

Amtrak Acela Express Business-Class Car 160-89943

Amtrak Acela Express End-Business Class Car 160-89944

# BRANCHLINE TRAINS

**BLUEPRINT SERIES**

## NEW PRODUCTS

### 80' Paired Window Coach Kit

### Single Cars 39.95 ea

**NEW 181-5701** B&O (green)
**NEW 181-5702** B&O (blue)
**NEW 181-5703** Seaboard (green)
**NEW 181-5704** CN
**NEW 181-5705** CP
**NEW 181-5706** UP
**NEW 181-5707** FEC
**NEW 181-5708** C&O (green)
**NEW 181-5709** C&O (blue, gray, yellow)
**NEW 181-5711** IC (green)
**NEW 181-5712** CNW (green)
**NEW 181-5713** UP "Challenger" (green)
**NEW 181-5714** IC (orange, brown)
**NEW 181-5715** NP (Pine Tree)
**NEW 181-5716** MILW (orange, maroon)
**NEW 181-5700** Undecorated - Unpainted
**NEW 181-5799** Undecorated - Green

### 3-Pack 119.85 ea

**NEW 181-57033** Seaboard (green)
**NEW 181-57113** Illinois Central (green)
**NEW 181-57123** CNW (green)
**NEW 181-57133** UP "Challenger" (green)
**NEW 181-57143** IC (orange, brown)
**NEW 181-57153** NP (Pine Tree)
**NEW 181-57163** MILW (orange, maroon)

### Assembled Cars

### 8-1-2 Pullman Sleeper 54.98 ea

**NEW 181-15004** GN "General W.C. Brown"
**NEW 181-15005** GN "General Sully"
**NEW 181-15006** GN "General Sherman"
**NEW 181-15030** C&O "Potomac"
**NEW 181-15031** C&O "Mount Vernon"
**NEW 181-15032** C&O "First Citizen"
**NEW 181-15040** MILW "Hiawatha"
**NEW 181-15041** MILW "Okoboji"
**NEW 181-15042** MILW "Michigamme"

### Pullman 12-1 Sleeper 54.98 ea

**NEW 181-15304** Pullman Pool "Pecos" (Green, Dulux Gold)
**NEW 181-15305** Pullman Pool "Coronado" (Green, Dulux Gold)
**NEW 181-15320** PRR 1948-53 Scheme Alexandria
**NEW 181-15312** SP "Marblehead" (Pullman Green w/Dulux Gold lettering)
**NEW 181-15316** PRR 1947 Scheme "Samuel Adams" (Tuscan Red, gold stripes & Pullman lettering
**NEW 181-15324** PRR 1943-68 Scheme "Queensville" (Tuscan Red, Buff stripes & Pennsylvania lettering)
**NEW 181-15328** PRR 1941-47 Fleet of Modernism "Robert Morris" (Block Pullman lettering)
**NEW 181-15332** L&N "John Audubon"
**NEW 181-15333** L&N "Leetsdale"
**NEW 181-15334** L&N "Cassius Clay"
**NEW 181-15336** NH "Israel Putnam"
**NEW 181-15338** NH "John Winthrop"
**NEW 181-15358** NH "East Columbia"
**NEW 181-15359** NH "St. Leonards"

### Single Window Coach 54.98 ea

**NEW 181-251011** NYC (green, Roman) #1
**NEW 181-251012** NYC (green, Roman) #2
**NEW 181-251013** NYC (green, Roman) #3
**NEW 181-251031** NH (green) #1
**NEW 181-251032** NH (green) #2
**NEW 181-251033** NH (green) #3
**NEW 181-251101** MP (green) #1
**NEW 181-251102** MP (green) #2
**NEW 181-251103** MP (green) #3
**NEW 181-251161** L&N (green) #1
**NEW 181-251162** L&N (green) #2
**NEW 181-251163** L&N (green) #3
**NEW 181-251171** NH (McGinnis Scheme) #1
**NEW 181-251172** NH (McGinnis Scheme) #2
**NEW 181-251173** NH (McGinnis Scheme) #3
**NEW 181-251201** Erie #1
**NEW 181-251202** Erie #2
**NEW 181-251203** Erie #3
**NEW 181-251221** CB&Q green #1
**NEW 181-251222** CB&Q (green) #2
**NEW 181-251223** CB&Q (green) #3
**NEW 181-251301** Rutland #1
**NEW 181-251302** Rutland #2
**NEW 181-251303** Rutland #3

### 78' Single Window Coach 54.98 ea

**NEW 181-251091** Boston & Albany #475
**NEW 181-251092** Boston & Albany #468
**NEW 181-251093** Boston & Albany #482
**NEW 181-251281** L&N (blue, gray) #1842
**NEW 181-251282** L&N (blue, gray) #1853
**NEW 181-251283** L&N (blue, gray) #1845
**NEW 181-251291** DL&W #1
**NEW 181-251292** DL&W #2
**NEW 181-251293** DL&W #3

## PASSENGER CARS

### Blueprint Series Kits

Branchline Blueprint Series kits feature detailed plastic bodies, full underbody with brake rigging, working diaphragms, interior, metal wheels, air conditioner components, accurate six-wheel trucks and more as appropriate for each car style. They are designed to operate on a 22" radius making them great for layouts of any size. Individual cars are mixed road numbers; four packs include one each of four car numbers. Some schemes and/or car names may be subject to change.

### 80' Single-Window Coaches 39.95 ea

**181-5101** NYC (green w/Roman lettering)
**181-5102** SOU
**181-5103** NH (green)
**181-5104** Pere Marquette
**181-5105** C&O
**181-5106** CP
**181-5107** Boston & Maine
**181-5108** GN (green, Omaha Orange)
**181-5109** Boston & Albany
**181-5110** MP
**181-5112** Gulf, Mobile & Ohio
**181-5113** Pittsburgh & Lake Erie
**181-5114** NYC (CCC&St.L Big Four)
**181-5115** NYC (two-tone gray)
**181-5116** L&N (green)
**181-5117** NH (McGinnis black, red)
**181-5118** NKP
**181-5119** N&W
**181-5120** Erie
**181-5121** GN (green)
**181-5122** CB&Q (green)

80' Paired Window Coach B&O
181-5701

8-1-2 Pullman Sleeper GN
"General W.C. Brown" 181-15004

Single Window Coach NYC #3
181-251013

78' Single Window Coach L&N #1842
181-251281

**181-5123** Spokane, Portland & Seattle (green)
**181-5124** EL (gray, maroon)
**181-5125** Seaboard (green)
**181-5126** D&H
**181-5127** NYC (green w/Gothic lettering)
**181-5128** Lackawanna (green)
**181-5129** L&N (blue, gray)
**181-5130** Rutland (green)
**181-5100** Undecorated

### 80' Single-Window Coach 3-Packs 119.85

Items listed below are available by Special Order (see Legend Page).

**181-51013** NYC (green w/roman lettering)
**181-51023** SOU
**181-51033** NH (green)
**181-51043** Pere Marquette
**181-51053** C&O
**181-51063** CP
**181-51073** Boston & Maine
**181-51083** GN (green, Omaha Orange)
**181-51093** Boston & Albany
**181-51103** MP
**181-51123** Gulf, Mobile & Ohio
**181-51133** Pittsburgh & Lake Erie
**181-51143** NYC (CCC&St.L Big Four)
**181-51153** NYC (two-tone gray)
**181-51163** L&N (green)
**181-51173** NH (McGinnis black, red)
**181-51183** NKP
**181-51193** N&W
**181-51203** Erie
**181-51213** GN (green)
**181-51223** CB&Q
**181-51233** Spokane, Portland & Seattle
**181-51243** EL
**181-51253** Seaboard
**181-51263** D&H
**181-51273** NYC (green, Gothic lettering)
**181-51283** Lackawanna
**181-51293** L&N (blue)
**181-51303** Rutland

### 80' Paired-Window Coaches 39.95 ea

**181-5701** B&O (green)
**181-5702** B&O (blue)
**181-5704** CN
**181-5705** CP
**181-5706** UP
**181-5707** Florida East Coast
**181-5708** C&O (green)
**181-5709** C&O (blue, gray, yellow)
**181-5710** Monon
**181-5700** Undecorated

### 80' Paired-Window Coach 3-Packs 119.85

Items listed below are available by Special Order (see Legend Page).

**181-57013** B&O (green)
**181-57023** B&O (blue)
**181-57043** CN
**181-57053** CP
**181-57063** UP
**181-57073** Florida East Coast
**181-57083** C&O (green)
**181-57093** C&O (blue, gray, yellow)
**181-57103** Monon

## BRANCHLINE TRAINS

### BLUEPRINT SERIES

**Pullman 8-1-2 Sleepers 39.95 ea**

All cars are Pullman Green unless noted.

**181-5001** Pullman "Rock Harbor"

**181-5002** Pullman "Reas Pass"

**181-5003** Pullman "Centford"

**181-5004** GN "Empire Builder" "General W.C. Brown"

**181-5005** GN "Empire Builder" "General Sully"

**181-5006** GN "Empire Builder" "General Sherman"

**181-5007** NYC "Centdoya" (two-tone gray)

**181-5008** NYC "Fawcett Gap" (two-tone gray)

**181-5009** NYC "Ausable Pass" (two-tone gray)

**181-5010** Atlantic Coast Line "Cameron Pass"

**181-5011** Atlantic Coast Line "Algonquin Park"

**181-5012** Atlantic Coast Line "Rock Cliff"

**181-5014** ATSF "Centwell" (two-tone gray)

**181-5015** ATSF "Centash" (two-tone gray)

**181-5016** ATSF "Centoak" (two-tone gray)

**181-5017** SP "Rock Bay"

**181-5018** SP "De Wolf"

**181-5019** SP "Des Plaines"

**181-5020** PRR "Centfaun" (Postwar Scheme, Tuscan Red, buff lettering)

**181-5021** PRR "Centwood" (Postwar Scheme, Tuscan Red, buff lettering)

**181-5022** PRR "Centhill" (Postwar Scheme, Tuscan Red, buff lettering)

**181-5023** CN "Morning Glory" (green black)

**181-5025** CN "John Jacob Astor" (green black)

**181-5026** CN "Island Park" (green black)

**181-5027** L&N "Rock Haven" (silver & blue shadowlined)

**181-5028** L&N "Kings Crown" (silver & blue shadowlined)

**181-5029** L&N "Henry M. Rice" (silver & blue shadowlined)

**181-5030** C&O "Potomac" ("George Washington" Scheme)

**181-5031** C&O "Mount Vernon" ("George Washington" Scheme)

**181-5032** C&O "First Citizen" ("George Washington" Scheme)

**181-5033** Wabash "Riverdale Park" (blue)

**181-5034** Wabash "Rock Pass" (blue)

**181-5035** Wabash "Centstar" (blue)

**181-5036** SOO "Centeburne" (maroon)

**181-5037** SOO "Centsalva" (maroon)

**181-5038** B&O "Centabella" (blue, gray)

**181-5039** B&O "Centonia" (blue, gray)

**181-5040** MILW "Hiawatha" (orange, red)

**181-5041** MILW "Okoboji" (orange, red)

**181-5042** MILW "Michigamme" (orange, red)

**181-5043** IC "John McLoughlin" (orange, brown)

**181-5044** IC "Centessa" (orange, brown)

**181-5099** Painted, Unlettered

**181-5000** Undecorated

**10-1-2 Pullman Sleepers 39.95 ea**

All cars are Pullman Green unless noted.

**181-5201** Pullman "Lake Augusta"

**181-5202** Pullman "Lake Vineyard"

**181-5203** Pullman "Lake George"

**181-5204** SOU "Lake Williams"

**181-5205** SOU "Lake Harriet"

**181-5206** SOU "Lake Andrew"

**181-5207** PRR "Lake Merritt" (Postwar Scheme, Tuscan Red, buff lettering)

**181-5208** PRR "Lake Maitland" (Postwar Scheme, Tuscan Red, buff lettering)

**181-5209** PRR "Lake Stearns" (Postwar Scheme, Tuscan Red, buff lettering)

**181-5210** MP "Lake Fortuna" ("Eagle" Scheme, blue, gray)

**181-5211** MP "Lake Woodruf" ("Eagle" Scheme, blue, gray)

**181-5212** MP "Lake Okeechobee" ("Eagle" Scheme, blue, gray)

**181-5213** UP "Lake James" (yellow, gray)

**181-5214** UP "Lake Champlain" (yellow, gray)

**181-5216** B&O "Lake Erie" (blue, gray)

**181-5217** B&O "Lake Lapourde" (blue, gray)

**181-5218** B&O "Lake Vista" (blue, gray)

**181-5219** Atlantic Coast Line "Lake Elmo"

**181-5220** Atlantic Coast Line "Lake Winnebago"

**181-5221** Atlantic Coast Line "Lake Pelican"

**181-5222** LV "Lake Tracy" (red)

**181-5223** LV "Lake Long" (red)

**181-5224** LV "Lake Vale" (red)

**181-5225** CNW "Lake Forest" (yellow, green)

**181-5226** CNW "Lake Gardner" (yellow, green)

**181-5227** CNW "Lake Bluff" (yellow, green)

**181-5228** Pullman "Lake Ontario" (gray)

**181-5229** Pullman "Lake Calumet" (two-tone gray)

**181-5230** Pullman "Lake Drummond" (two-tone gray)

**181-5231** Lackawanna "Devils Lake"

**181-5232** Lackawanna "Bowman Lake"

**181-5233** Lackawanna "Medicine Lake"

**181-5234** IC "Lake Peigneu"

**181-5235** IC "Lake Ferguson"

**181-5236** SOO "Lake Ann" (maroon)

**181-5237** SOO "Lake View" (maroon)

**181-5238** Erie "Josephine Lake"

**181-5239** Erie "Lake Worth"

**181-5240** SP "Lake Hancock"

**181-5241** SP "Lake Ariana"

**181-5242** SP "Lake Sheridan"

**181-5243** Florida East Coast "Lake Goodwin"

**181-5244** Florida East Coast "Lake Michigan"

**181-5245** Seaboard "Lake Chicot"

**181-5246** DRGW "Harrison Lake" (yellow, silver)

**181-5247** DRGW "Gunsight Lake" (yellow, silver)

**181-5248** Atlanta & West Point "Lake Belanona" (blue)

**181-5299** Painted, Unlettered

**181-5200** Undecorated

**12-1 Pullman Sleepers 39.95 ea**

All cars are Pullman Green unless noted.

**181-5301** Pullman "St. Carvan"

**181-5302** Pullman "Orange County"

**181-5303** Pullman "McBridesville"

**181-5304** PRR "Hawkins" (Tuscan Red, buff lettering)

**181-5305** PRR "Francis Hopkinson" (Tuscan Red, buff lettering)

**181-5306** PRR "John Jay" (Tuscan Red, buff lettering)

**181-5307** SP "Goliad"

**181-5308** SP "Calafia"

**181-5309** SP "McVean"

**181-5310** CNW "Red Bridge" (yellow, green)

**181-5311** CNW "McClellan" (yellow, green)

**181-5312** CNW "Orange Cove" (yellow, green)

**181-5313** SOU "Walton"

**181-5314** SOU "McQuaid"

**181-5315** SOU "Litchfield"

**181-5316** NYC "Brockway" (two-tone gray)

**181-5317** NYC "McMada" (two-tone gray)

**181-5318** NYC "East Chester" (two-tone gray)

**181-5319** UP "Newburyport" (yellow, gray)

**181-5320** UP "Multnomah" (yellow, gray)

**181-5321** UP "Nolando" (yellow, gray)

**181-5322** L&N "John James Audubon" (blue, gray)

**181-5323** L&N "Leetsdale" (blue, gray)

**181-5324** L&N "Cassius M. Clay" (blue, gray)

**181-5325** CN "Red House" (green, black)

**181-5326** CN "Red Hook" (green, black)

**181-5327** CN "Red Line" (green, black)

**181-5328** B&O "East Chicago" (blue, gray)

**181-5329** B&O "Thendara" (blue, gray)

**181-5330** B&O "Midlothian" (blue, gray)

**181-5331** Wabash "Knollwood" (blue)

**181-5332** Wabash "Dorchester" (blue)

**181-5333** Wabash "Tuscaloosa" (blue)

**181-5334** N&W "Sunstar Rose" (Tuscan Red, buff lettering)

**181-5335** N&W "Vulcan" (Tuscan Red, buff lettering)

**181-5336** NH "Israel Putnam" (Tuscan Red, buff lettering)

**181-5338** NH "John Winthrop" (Tuscan Red, buff lettering)

**181-5339** Boston & Maine "McDade"

**181-5340** Gulf, Mobile & Ohio "Trinity" (maroon, red)

**181-5341** Gulf, Mobile & Ohio "Orange State" (maroon, red)

**181-5342** Fort Worth & Denver "Anaconda" (silver)

**181-5343** Fort Worth & Denver "Wadena" (silver)

**181-5344** Fort Worth & Denver "Maximilian" (silver)

**181-5345** NKP "East Charleroi"

**181-5346** SOU "Knickerbocker" (silver "Shadowline" scheme)

**181-5347** MP "McGlashens" ("Eagle" Scheme, blue, gray)

**181-5348** MP "Wentachee"

**181-5349** GN "Anacortes" ("Empire Builder" lettering)

**181-5350** GN "Bison" ("Empire Builder" lettering)

**181-5351** GN "Cashmere" ("Empire Builder" lettering)

**181-5352** C&O "Chancellor Livingston" ("George Washington" lettering)

**181-5353** C&O "Frederick Muhlenberg" ("George Washington" lettering)

**181-5354** C&O "Mary Washington" ("George Washington" lettering)

**181-5355** PRR "Daniel Webster" ("Fleet Of Modernism" scheme, two-tone red)

**181-5356** PRR "Nathaniel Greene" ("Fleet Of Modernism" scheme, two-tone red)

**181-5357** PRR "Henry Clay" ("Fleet Of Modernism" scheme, two-tone red)

**181-5358** NH "East Columbia"

**181-5359** NH "St. Leonards"

**181-5360** Pullman "Red Canon" (two-tone gray)

**181-5361** Pullman "Red Lion" (two-tone gray)

**181-5362** Pullman "Red Lodge" (two-tone gray)

**181-5399** Painted, Unlettered

**181-5300** Undecorated

**14-Section Pullman Sleepers 39.95 ea**

All cars are Pullman Green unless noted.

**181-5401** Pullman "Robert Fulton"

**181-5402** Pullman "Overcot"

**181-5403** Pullman "Samuel P. Langley"

**181-5404** NYC "Park Point"

**181-5405** NYC "Star Light"

**181-5406** NYC "Star Flower"

**181-5407** MILW "Avalon"

**181-5408** MILW "Le Seur"

**181-5409** MILW "Red Wing"

**181-5410** ATSF "Geo. Stephenson"

**181-5411** ATSF "John Stephens"

**181-5412** ATSF "Isaac Newton"

**181-5413** Gulf, Mobile & Ohio "New Marshfield"

**181-5414** Gulf, Mobile & Ohio "Port Lewis"

**181-5416** Gulf, Mobile & Ohio "Micheal Farday"

**181-5417** CN "Port Hope"

**181-5418** CN "Port Stanley"

**181-5419** CB&Q "American Legion"

**181-5420** CB&Q "New Omaha"

**181-5421** CB&Q "New Capitol"

**181-5422** IC "Luthur Burbank"

**181-5423** IC "New Grove"

**181-5424** CNW "Humbird"

**181-5425** CNW "Shorewood"

**181-5426** Wabash "New Columbia"

**181-5427** Wabash "New Prospect"

**181-5431** PRR "New Nicolette"

**181-5432** PRR "New Palmer"

**181-5433** PRR "Samuel Morse"

**181-5434** NH "New Franklin"

**181-5435** NKP "Park Summit"

**181-5436** NKP "Part Terrace"

**181-5437** B&M "New Hamburg"

**NEW 181-5438** Nashville, Chattanooga & St. Louis "Christopher Wren"

**181-5499** Painted, Unlettered

**181-5400** Undecorated

**10-1-1 Pullman Sleepers 39.95 ea**

All cars are Pullman Green unless noted.

**181-5501** Pullman "Chief Red Tomahawk

**181-5502** Pullman "Blue Bird Lake"

**181-5503** Pullman "Rice Lake"

**181-5504** Pullman "Chief Iron Tail" (two-tone gray)

**181-5505** Pullman "McCarron Lake" (two-tone gray)

## BRANCHLINE TRAINS

### BLUEPRINT SERIES

**181-5506** Pullman "Fleetnor" (two-tone gray)
**181-5507** Atlantic Coast Line "Island Home"
**181-5508** Atlantic Coast Line "La Boheme"
**181-5509** Atlantic Coast Line "La Gioconda"
**181-5510** CB&Q "Carter Lake"
**181-5511** CB&Q "Linoma Lake"
**181-5512** CB&Q "Gull Lake" (silver "Shadowline" scheme)
**181-5513** CB&Q "Lariet Range" (silver "Shadowline" scheme)
**181-5514** CB&Q "Lariet Crest" (silver "Shadowline" scheme)
**181-5515** CNW "Floyd River"
**181-5516** CNW "Fox River"
**181-5517** CNW "Mount Rushmore"
**181-5518** IC "Chief Goliah"
**181-5519** IC "Chief Pine Shooter"
**181-5520** IC "Chief Sitting Bull"
**181-5521** L&N "Chief Comcomly"
**181-5522** L&N "Chief Joseph"
**181-5523** MILW "Tomahawk"
**181-5524** MILW "Arrowhead"
**181-5525** N&W "Island Regal"
**181-5526** N&W "Island Rose"
**181-5527** NP "Chief Black Bear"
**181-5528** NP "Chief Many Horns"
**181-5529** NP "Chief Standing Buffalo"
**181-5530** PRR "Le Reine"
**181-5531** SP "Palouse Falls"
**181-5532** SP "Prior Lake"
**181-5533** UP "Balsam Fir"
**181-5534** UP "Columbia Gorge"
**181-5535** UP "Crown Point"
**181-5599** Painted, Unlettered
**181-5500** Undecorated

### 6-3 Pullman Sleepers 39.95 ea

All cars are Pullman Green unless noted.

**181-5601** Pullman "Michaelangelo"
**181-5602** Pullman "Brahms"
**181-5603** Pullman "Shakespeare"
**181-5604** Pullman "Glen Airlie"
**181-5605** Pullman "Glen Willow"
**181-5606** Pullman "Glen Manor"
**181-5607** Pullman "Glen Dee" (two-tone gray)
**181-5608** Pullman "Glen Springs" (two-tone gray)
**181-5609** Pullman "Glen Sannox" (two-tone gray)
**181-5610** Pullman "Schumann" (two-tone gray)
**181-5611** PRR "Monument Square"
**181-5612** PRR "Times Square"
**181-5613** PRR "Logan Square"
**181-5614** NYC "Glen Adelaide"
**181-5615** NYC "Glen Echo"
**181-5616** NYC "Glen Road"
**181-5617** Seaboard "Glen Crag"
**181-5618** Seaboard "Glen Dale"
**181-5619** Seaboard "Glen Eagles"
**181-5620** SOU "Bizet"
**181-5621** SOU "Corot"
**181-5622** SOU "Glen Summit"
**181-5623** SP "Glen Moriston"
**181-5624** SP "Glen Elleyn"
**181-5625** SP "Glen Aladale"
**181-5626** NH "Hogarth"
**181-5627** Alaska "Mt. Susitna"
**181-5628** Alaska "Mt. Illiamna"
**181-5699** Painted, Unlettered
**181-5600** Undecorated

### 50' Welded-Side Express Reefers 24.98 ea

Based on the popular 1947-era 50' welded-side express reefer, this kit offers all-new tooling with separate ladders and grabs, full underbody, correct trucks and more. Individual cars are mixed road numbers; four packs include one each of four car numbers.

**181-2501** Railway Express Agency (green, no herald)
**181-2502** Railway Express Agency (green, 1950s herald)
**181-2503** Railway Express Agency (green, 1960s herald)
**181-2504** Railway Express Agency As-Delivered Scheme (green, silver, yellow)
**181-2505** Atlantic Coast Line (green)
**181-2506** Atlantic Coast Line As-Delivered Scheme (silver, purple)
**181-2500** Undecorated

### 50' Welded-Side Express Reefers 4-Packs 99.92

**181-25024** Railway Express Agency (green, 1950s herald)
Items listed below are available by Special Order (see Legend Page).
**181-25014** Railway Express Agency (green, no herald)
**181-25034** Railway Express Agency (green, 1960s herald)
**181-25044** Railway Express Agency As-Delivered Scheme (green, silver, yellow)
**181-25054** Atlantic Coast Line (green)
**181-25064** Atlantic Coast Line As-Delivered Scheme (silver, purple)



# BRASS CAR SIDES

Photo-etched brass sides and kits for streamlined passenger cars. Window openings and grab iron holes are etched through, with additional etched details on front. These craft train kits can be used with either Basic (#173-101) or Deluxe (#173-102) Body Kits. Many side sets are also designed to be used as an overlay on ready-to-run plastic cars and core kits, without shortening the body. See Walthers Web site (manufacturer #173) for illustrations and overlay and core kit recommendations.

## CAR SIDES

### CN 31.75 ea

**173-38** "Elgin" Series 8-4-4 Sleeper CN 1110-1161
**173-39** CCF Coach CN 5437-5654

### C&O/DRGW/NKP 31.75 ea

PS Plan 7600 52-seat coach with smooth sides. Later used on D&H, SP, SAL, CNW and Amtrak.

**173-45** Original Skirts
**173-46** Partial Skirts

### CNW 31.75 ea

**173-1** "400" 56-Seat Coach CNW 3431-3476
Also used on GP, NP, CB&Q.
**173-6** P-S "Northern" Series 16-3-1 Sleeper

### L&N/C&EI/NC&STL

**173-35** "Pine" Series 6-4-6 PS 4183 Sleeper **31.75**

### PRR 31.75 ea

**173-32** P-85B 44-Seat Coach 4068-91, 4100-69
**173-33** "Rapids" P-S 10-6 4140 Sleeper N&W, L&N

### GN/CB&Q/SP&S Empire Builder 31.75 ea (Unless Noted)

**173-10** "Ranch" Coffee Shop GN 1240-1245
**173-11** "River" Series 7-4-3-1 Sleeper GN 1260-1274
**173-12** 48-Seat Coach GN 1215-1231, SP&S 350
**173-13** "Pass" Series 6-5-2 Sleeper GN 1370-1384
**173-14** 60-Seat Coach GN 1209-1214
**173-15** "Lake" Series Diner GN 1250-1255
**173-18** Baggage-Dorm GN 1200-1205
**173-20** Budd Dome Coach GN 1320-1331, SP&S 1332, CB&Q 1333-35
**173-25** "Glacier" Series P-S 16-4 Sleeper "Western Star" GN 1181-1188
**173-27** "View" Great Dome Lounge GN 1390-1395
**173-43** Mail-Baggage GN 37-44 **36.75**
Also UP & CNW.
**NEW 173-62** "Club" 8-2 Buffet Lounge Sleeper For Winnipeg Ltd. GN 1198-1199
**NEW 173-63** P-S Mail Baggage GN 1100-1104 **TBA**

### IC 31.75 ea

**173-41** "C" Series P-S 10-6 Sleeper B&O 7040-7049
**173-44** P-S 56-Seat Coach IC 2614-2640

### MILW 31.75 ea (Unless Noted)

**173-2** 52-Seat Coach 1948 Hiawatha MILW 480-497, 535-551, 600-Series
**173-3** "Valley" Series Parlor MILW 190-197
**173-7** "Raymond" Series P-S 16-4 Sleeper
**173-8** "River" Series P-S 8-6-4 Sleeper
**173-52** RPO Express w/Four Separate Doors MILW 1208-30 **36.75**
**173-53** "Tap Lounge" MILW 162-167, 172-173
**173-54** 75' Express w/Four Separate Doors MILW 1317-1329 **36.75**
**173-55** Dining Car For 1947-48 Olympian & Twin Cities Hiawatha MILW 115-126
**173-57** Baggage-Dorm w/Integral Doors 1309-1314 **32.75**
**173-58** "Touralux" P-S 14-Section Sleeper "Mountain"
**173-59** 60' Postal Car w/Four Doors #2152-2153 **36.75**
**173-60** "Grove" Cafe-Parlor #180-185

### NP/CB&Q/SP&S "North Coast Limited" 31.75 ea (Unless Noted)

**173-4** P-S 56-Seat Coach NP 588-597, CB&Q 598-599
**173-5** P-S 8-6-3-1 Sleeper NP 350-363, CB&Q 480-482
**173-19** "Travelers Rest" Lounge NP 494-499
**173-20** Budd Dome Coach NP 549-556, CB&Q 557-558
**173-24** Budd Dome Sleeper NP 307-314, CB&Q 304-305
**173-29** Budd Diner NP 459-463, CB&Q 498
**173-30** P-S 56-Seat Coach NP 500-517, SP&S 301-305
**173-50** Mail-Dorm w/Doors NP 425-429 **34.75**
**173-56** Water-Baggage w/Four Separate Doors NP 400-404, CB&Q 405 **36.75**
**NEW 173-61** P-S Diner NP 450-455

### Pullman Sleepers 31.75 ea

**173-9** "American" Series Plan 4099 6-6-4 UP, SP, CNW, ATSF, Erie, MP, IC, RI
**173-16** "Imperial" Series Plan 4069 4-4-2 NYC, PRR, UP, SP, CNW, RI, IC, CN
**173-17** "Cascade" Series Plan 4072 10-5 NYC, PRR, B&O, SP, ATSF, CP
**173-21** "County" Plan 4071 13-Bedroom NYC, PRR, SP
**173-23** "City" Plan 4068 18-Roomette NYC, PRR, NKP, CN
**173-28** Plan 4153 14-4 B&O, MP, Texas & Pacific, Kansas City Southern
**173-37** Plan 4122 22-Roomette NYC, CN, IC, SP
**173-51** Plan 4140C 10-6 SP 9030-9052, NP 364-365

### UP

**173-22** Dome Diner 8000-8009 Rivarossi Overlay **31.75**
**173-26** Dome Lounge One-Piece Rivarossi Overlay **37.25**
**173-31** "Challenger" 48-Seat Chair Car UP 5331-5365 **31.75**
**173-36** Dome Observation Lounge One-Piece Rivarossi Overlay UP 9000-9015 **37.25**
**173-40** ACF 44-Seat Chair Car UP 5450-5487, CNW 3477-3492 **31.75**
Also GN, GTW, SP.
**173-43** Mail-Baggage UP 5900-5902, CNW 8225-8226 **36.75**

## BODY KITS

Use with all non-dome brass side sets. Some cutting required for shorter cars. Instructions included. Less trucks and couplers.

**173-101** Basic Kit **11.75**
Pewter metal ends, scale-width milled basswood roof, floor and centersill for one car.
**173-102** Deluxe Kit **19.75**
Lost-wax brass ends, heavy copper-clad fiberglass pc board floor, milled basswood roof for one car.

## BAGGAGE-MAIL DOORS

### pkg(2) 5.75 ea

One-piece photo-etched brass.

**173-300** 3' Two-Window GN
**173-301** 5' Three-Window GN
**173-302** 3' One-Window MILW
**173-303** 8' Two-Window MILW
**173-304** 5' Three-Window NP
**173-305** 7' Three-Window NP

## CAR ENDS

**173-200** American Pewter (Included w/Basic Body Kit #173-101) 1 Pair **5.75**
Streamlined one-piece castings match ends used by P-S or ACF on lightweight non-dome cars.

Make your roster of passenger equipment more authentic with this selection of kits, based on a wide range of prototypes. For more accurate modeling, the kits are offered in various styles to better match the original wood or steel construction. All kits are less trucks and couplers.

## PLASTIC KITS

### 29.95 ea (Unless Noted)

**718-230** Class BAv Baggage Car - Reading

**718-240** Class BAa Baggage Express - Reading

**718-310** Class PBm Clerestory Roof Coach - Central of New Jersey/Reading **39.95**

**718-320** Class CVh Clerestory Roof Combine - Central of New Jersey/Reading **39.95**

**718-330** Class BE Baggage Car - Central of New Jersey

**718-440** Class M70b Railway Post Office - Pennsylvania

**718-530** Class BA Baggage Car - Western Maryland

**718-610** Class A-e Coach - Baltimore & Ohio **39.95**

### Class PBn Arch Roof Coach

**718-210** Reading/ Central of New Jersey

**718-211** Boston & Maine/Maine Central

**718-213** Seaboard Air Line

### Class CVI Arch Roof Combine

**718-220** Reading/ Central of New Jersey

**718-221** Boston & Maine

Class BAa Baggage Express - Reading 718-240

Class PBn Arch Roof Coach Seaboard Air Line 718-213

PRR B62 Baggage Express Car 718-432

Coach & Club Car - Reading "Wall Street" 718-2000

### Plastic Kits with Eastern Car Works Core Kit 39.95 ea

**718-733** ACF Baggage Car - Soo Line #1635-1636

**718-831** Modern Baggage Express Car - Erie

**718-832** Baggage Express Car - Erie Lackawanna

**718-833** Modern RPO/Baggage - Erie

**718-834** RPO/Baggage Car - Erie Lackawanna

**718-835** Modern Dormitory Mail Car - Erie

## KITS WITH BRASS CAR SIDES

### 59.95 ea (Unless Noted)

Kits include brass cars sides; some also include brass underframes.

**718-236** Class MBr Railway Post Office - Reading

**NEW 718-237** D&H RPO/ Baggage Car #701-708 **67.50**

**718-261** Cafe Car "Giacobini" - Central of New Jersey "Blue Comet" **75.00**

**NEW 718-431** PRR B70 Baggage Express Car #6000-6054

**NEW 718-432** PRR B62 Baggage Express Car

**NEW 718-433** PRR B60 Baggage Express Car

**NEW 718-434** PRR B60 Baggage Express Car (Original Doors)

**NEW 718-436** PRR Theatrical Scenery Express Car (Modern Doors)

**NEW 718-436A** PRR Theatrical Scenery Express Car (Original Doors)

**NEW 718-437** PRR Horse Car

**NEW 718-438** PRR B60a Baggage Car (Modern Doors)

**NEW 718-439** PRR B60a Baggage Car (Original Doors)

**NEW 718-811** Erie Modernized Coach #1000 **67.50**

**718-1187** Cafe Car - Reading #1187 **75.00**

**718-1230** Class G74 Baggage Car - New York Central

**718-1231** NYC Horse Express Car #5600-5614 **67.50**

**718-1240** Railway Post Office - New York Central

**718-1430** Class BEk Baggage Express Car - Norfolk & Western

**718-2000** Coach & Club Car - Reading "Wall Street"

## EXPRESS BOX CARS

### National Steel Car 40' Express Box Cars 19.95 ea

Based on one of Canada's most numerous box cars from the 1950s to the 1990s, some were rebuilt for high-speed passenger service. Each ready-to-run car features sliding doors, applied details, free-rolling trucks and working knuckle couplers.

**326-12016** CP (maroon, gold)

**326-12017** CP (silver, maroon)

**326-12018** CN (green, black)

**326-12019** CN (green, yellow)

**326-12020** CN (black, gray)

All Con-Cor passenger cars now come assembled and complete with operating knuckle couplers and metal screw and post-mounted trucks. Most streamlined cars are available in 72' (ideal for smaller layouts or tight radius curves) and full-length, 85' versions.

# ASSEMBLED 72' PASSENGER

## 18.69 ea (Unless Noted)

**Cars feature operating knuckle couplers and metal screw and post-mounted trucks. Include a factory-installed Passenger Car Upgrade Kit (#223-270).**

### Amtrak

**Phase II**

**223-906** Coach
**223-926** Railway Post Office
**223-946** Vista Dome
**223-966** Observation Car
**223-986** Sleeper
**223-11006** Diner
**223-11026** Baggage

**Phase IV 19.98 ea**
Include a factory installed Passenger Car Upgrade Kit (#223-1000270).

**223-10090023** Coach
**223-10092023** Railway Post Office

**223-10094023** Regular Vista Dome
**223-10096023** Tail End Observation
**223-10098023** Pullman Sleeper
**223-10100023** Diner
**223-10102023** Baggage Car

### Atchison, Topeka & Santa Fe

**"Valley Flyer"**
(silver, with red, black, yellow trim)
**223-910** Coach
**223-930** Railway Post Office
**223-950** Vista Dome
**223-970** Observation Car
**223-990** Sleeper
**223-11010** Diner
**223-11030** Baggage

**"Scout"**
(two-tone gray)
**223-10004** Diner
**223-10204** Baggage
**223-19004** Coach
**223-19204** Railway Post Office
**223-19404** Vista Dome
**223-19604** Observation Car
**223-19804** Sleeper

### Baltimore & Ohio

(blue, gray)
**223-10003** Diner
**223-10203** Baggage
**223-19003** Coach
**223-19203** Railway Post Office
**223-19403** Vista Dome
**223-19603** Observation Car
**223-19803** Sleeper

### Burlington Northern Executive

(green, gray)
**223-190013** Coach
**223-192013** Railway Post Office
**223-194013** Vista Dome
**223-196013** Observation Car
**223-198013** Sleeper
**223-1100013** Diner
**223-1102013** Baggage
**223-92031** 4-Pack (Coach, RPO, Dome, Observation) **74.49**

### Canadian National

(green, black)
**223-190011** Coach
**223-192011** Railway Post Office
**223-194011** Vista Dome
**223-196011** Observation Car
**223-198011** Sleeper
**223-1100011** Diner
**223-1102011** Baggage
**223-92029** 4-Pack (Coach, RPO, Dome & Observation Car) **74.49**

### Chesapeake & Ohio

(silver)
**223-919** Coach
**223-939** Railway Post Office
**223-959** Vista Dome
**223-979** Observation Car
**223-999** Sleeper
**223-11019** Diner
**223-11039** Baggage

### Chicago & North Western

(yellow, green)
**223-916** Coach
**223-936** Railway Post Office
**223-956** Vista Dome
**223-976** Observation Car
**223-996** Sleeper
**223-11016** Diner
**223-11036** Baggage

## HO SANTA FE EL CAPITAN BI-LEVEL CARS

The hi-level passenger car was developed jointly between the Budd Company and the Santa Fe Railroad. In 1956 Budd delivered an order of 47 assorted cars to the Santa Fe. They were an instant hit and more orders followed. In later years Amtrak based its first Superliner car designs on the railroad's experience with the El Capitan cars.

In order to "interchange" with the traditional passenger cars, one series of bi-level coach cars had a stairwell to the lower level at one end of the car. Another version of the coach cars had pass-through doors from car to car only at the upper deck level.

**There were 4 different body types:**

- Coaches with stairwell at one end (#s528-549)
- Coaches with pass-through doors at both ends, upper level only (#s700-736)
- Diners (#s650-655)
- Lounge Cafe (#s575-580)

Two baggage cars were converted to crew cars and had an aerodynamic end fitted on one end to match the height of the El Capitan cars.

### Delaware & Hudson

(silver, blue, yellow)
**223-190012** Coach
**223-192012** Railway Post Office
**223-194012** Vista Dome
**223-196012** Observation Car
**223-198012** Sleeper
**223-1100012** Diner
**223-1102012** Baggage
**223-92030** 4-Pack (Coach, RPO, Dome & Observation Car) **74.49**

### Erie

(green, cream)
**223-19008** Coach
**223-19208** Railway Post Office
**223-19408** Vista Dome
**223-19608** Observation Car
**223-19808** Sleeper
**223-110008** Diner
**223-110208** Baggage

### Erie-Lackawanna

(gray, yellow and maroon scheme)
**223-190010** Coach
**223-192010** Railway Post Office
**223-194010** Vista Dome
**223-196010** Observation Car
**223-198010** Sleeper
**223-1100010** Diner
**223-1102010** Baggage Car
**223-92028** 4-Pack (Coach, RPO, Dome & Observation Car) **74.49**

### Great Northern "Empire Builder"

(orange, green, yellow)
**223-903** Coach
**223-923** Railway Post Office
**223-943** Vista Dome
**223-963** Observation Car
**223-983** Sleeper
**223-11003** Diner
**223-11023** Baggage

### Illinois Central

(brown, orange scheme)
**223-19006** Coach
**223-19206** Railway Post Office

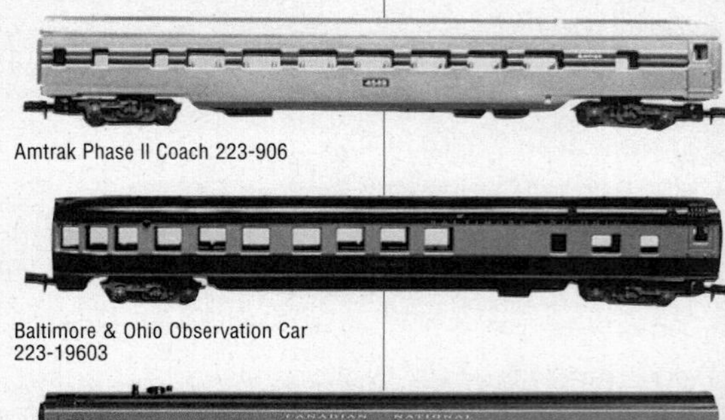

Amtrak Phase II Coach 223-906

Baltimore & Ohio Observation Car 223-19603

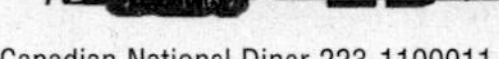

Canadian National Diner 223-1100011

Chesapeake & Ohio Sleeper 223-999

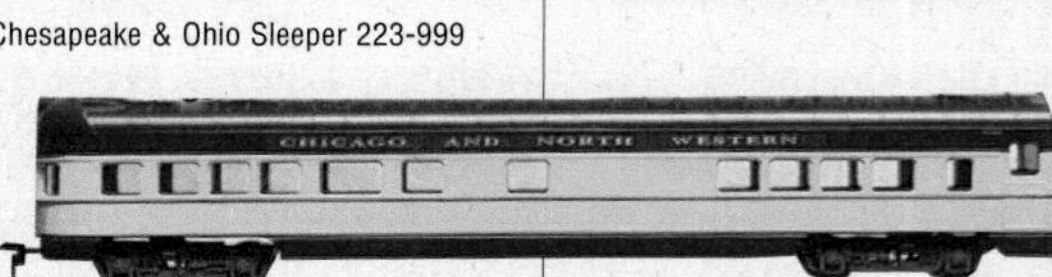

Chicago & North Western Observation Car 223-976

**223-19406** Vista Dome
**223-19606** Observation Car
**223-19806** Sleeper
**223-110006** Diner
**223-110206** Baggage Car
**223-92025** 4-Pack (Coach, RPO, Dome & Observation Car) **74.49**

### Kansas City Southern

(black, silver)
**223-19005** Coach
**223-19205** Railway Post Office
**223-19405** Vista Dome
**223-19605** Observation Car
**223-19805** Sleeper
**223-110005** Diner
**223-110205** Baggage

### Lackawanna

(gray, yellow and maroon scheme)
**223-19007** Coach

**223-19207** Railway Post Office
**223-19407** Vista Dome
**223-19607** Observation Car
**223-19807** Sleeper
**223-110007** Diner
**223-110207** Baggage Car
**223-92026** 4-Pack (Coach, RPO, Dome & Observation Car) **74.49**

## Louisville & Nashville
(L&N Blue, gold)
**223-190017** Coach
**223-192017** Railway Post Office
**223-194017** Vista Dome
**223-196017** Observation Car
**223-198017** Sleeper
**223-1100017** Diner
**223-1102017** Baggage
**223-92034** 4-Pack (Coach, RPO, Dome, Observation Car) **74.49**

## Milwaukee Road
(yellow, gray)
**223-909** Coach
**223-929** Railway Post Office
**223-949** Vista Dome
**223-969** Observation Car
**223-989** Sleeper
**223-11009** Diner
**223-11029** Baggage

## Missouri Pacific
(gray, blue, silver)
**223-190018** Coach
**223-192018** Railway Post Office
**223-194018** Vista Dome
**223-196018** Observation Car
**223-198018** Sleeper
**223-1100018** Diner
**223-1102018** Baggage
**223-92035** 4-Pack (Coach, RPO, Dome, Observation Car) **74.49**

## New York Central
(two-tone gray)
**223-913** Coach
**223-933** Railway Post Office
**223-953** Vista Dome
**223-973** Observation Car
**223-993** Sleeper
**223-11013** Diner
**223-11033** Baggage

### "20th Century" Scheme
(gray, blue, black)
**223-190016** Coach
**223-192016** Railway Post Office
**223-194016** Vista Dome
**223-196016** Observation Car
**223-198016** Sleeper
**223-1100016** Diner
**223-1102016** Baggage
**223-92033** 4-Pack (Coach, RPO, Dome, Observation Car) **74.49**

## Nickel Plate Road
(silver, blue)
**223-10002** Diner
**223-10202** Baggage
**223-19002** Coach
**223-19202** Railway Post Office
**223-19402** Vista Dome
**223-19602** Observation Car
**223-19802** Sleeper

## Norfolk Southern
(maroon, gold)
**223-911** Coach
**223-931** Railway Post Office
**223-951** Vista Dome
**223-971** Observation Car
**223-991** Sleeper
**223-11011** Diner
**223-11031** Baggage

## Norfolk & Western
(Tuscan with gold stripes)
**223-907** Coach
**223-927** Railway Post Office
**223-947** Vista Dome
**223-967** Observation Car
**223-987** Sleeper
**223-11007** Diner
**223-11027** Baggage

## Northern Pacific
(two-tone green)
**223-190019** Coach
**223-192019** Railway Post Office
**223-194019** Vista Dome
**223-196019** Observation Car
**223-198019** Sleeper
**223-1100019** Diner
**223-1102019** Baggage
**223-92036** 4-Pack (Coach, RPO, Dome, Observation Car) **74.49**

## Pennsylvania
(Tuscan Red w/Dulux Gold)
**223-905** Coach
**223-925** Railway Post Office
**223-945** Vista Dome
**223-965** Observation Car
**223-985** Sleeper
**223-11005** Diner
**223-11025** Baggage

### "Senator"
(silver, Tuscan letterboards, Dulux lettering)
**223-917** Coach
**223-937** Railway Post Office
**223-957** Vista Dome
**223-977** Observation Car
**223-997** Sleeper

**223-11017** Diner
**223-11037** Baggage

## Rio Grande "Ski Train"
(orange, silver)
**223-10001** Diner
**223-10201** Baggage
**223-19001** Coach
**223-19201** Railway Post Office
**223-19401** Vista Dome
**223-19601** Observation Car
**223-19801** Sleeper

See What's New and Exciting at
**www.walthers.com**

## Royal American Shows Carnival
(red, yellow)
**223-908** Coach
**223-928** Railway Post Office
**223-948** Vista Dome
**223-968** Observation Car
**223-988** Sleeper
**223-11008** Diner

**223-11028** Baggage

## Southern Pacific
### "Daylight"
(orange, red)
**223-902** Coach
**223-922** Railway Post Office
**223-942** Vista Dome
**223-962** Observation Car
**223-982** Sleeper
**223-11002** Diner
**223-11022** Baggage

### "San Joaquin"
(red, silver)
**223-918** Coach
**223-938** Railway Post Office
**223-958** Vista Dome
**223-978** Observation Car
**223-998** Sleeper
**223-11018** Diner
**223-11038** Baggage

### "Lark"
(gray, white)
**223-914** Coach
**223-934** Railway Post Office
**223-954** Vista Dome
**223-974** Observation Car
**223-994** Sleeper
**223-11014** Diner
**223-11034** Baggage

### "SP/RI (Rock Island) Golden State"
(silver, red)
**223-190020** Coach
**223-192020** Railway Post Office
**223-194020** Vista Dome
**223-196020** Observation Car

**223-198020** Sleeper
**223-1100020** Diner
**223-1102020** Baggage
**223-92037** 4-Pack (Coach, RPO, Dome, Observation Car) **74.49**

## Southern Railway "Crescent Limited"
(Two-Tone Green, Dulux lettering, black roof)
**223-904** Coach
**223-924** Railway Post Office
**223-944** Vista Dome
**223-964** Observation Car
**223-984** Sleeper
**223-11004** Diner
**223-11024** Baggage

NP Vista Dome 223-194019, MP Coach 223-190018, & NYC 20th Century Ltd. Sleeper 223-198016

NYC "20th Century" Baggage 223-1102016

Rio Grande "Ski Train" Vista Dome 223-19401

Southern Pacific "Daylight" RPO 223-922

Southern Railway "Crescent Limited" RPO 223-924

## Union Pacific
(yellow, gray)

**223-901** Coach
**223-921** Railway Post Office
**223-941** Vista Dome
**223-961** Observation Car
**223-981** Sleeper
**223-11001** Diner
**223-11021** Baggage

### "Overland"
(gray)
**223-915** Coach
**223-935** Railway Post Office
**223-955** Vista Dome
**223-975** Observation Car
**223-995** Sleeper
**223-11015** Diner
**223-11035** Baggage

## VIA
(blue, yellow stripes)
**223-912** Coach
**223-932** Railway Post Office
**223-952** Vista Dome
**223-972** Observation Car
**223-992** Sleeper
**223-11012** Diner

**223-11032** Baggage

## Wabash
Following prototype practice, the coach, Sleeper and Dome, which interchanged with UP, are painted in matching UP colors (but lettered for Wabash). The other cars are painted in the Wabash blue and gray scheme.
**223-190022** Coach
**223-192022** Railway Post Office
**223-194022** Vista Dome
**223-196022** Observation Car
**223-198022** Sleeper

223-1100022 Diner
223-1102022 Baggage
223-92038 4-Pack (Coach, Dome, RPO & Observation Car) **74.49**

**Undecorated**
223-900 Coach
223-920 Railway Post Office
223-940 Vista Dome
223-960 Observation Car
223-980 Sleeper
223-11000 Diner
223-11020 Baggage

## ASSEMBLED 85' STREAMLINED SUPERLINER COACH 19.98 ea

**Cars feature operating knuckle couplers and metal screw and post-mounted trucks. Include a factory-installed Passenger Car Upgrade Kit (#223-271).**

**Amtrak Phase II**

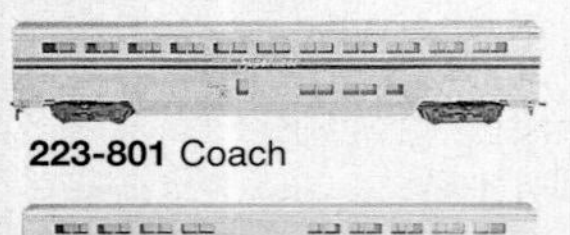

223-801 Coach
223-811 Diner
223-821 Coach/Baggage
223-831 Sleeper
223-841 Lounge/Cafe

**Amtrak Phase III**
223-802 Coach
223-812 Diner
223-822 Coach/Baggage
223-832 Sleeper
223-842 Lounge/Cafe

**Amtrak Phase IV**
223-803 Coach
223-813 Diner

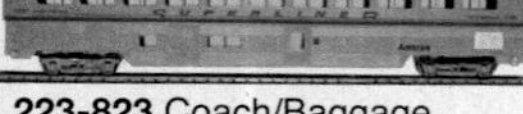

223-823 Coach/Baggage

223-833 Sleeper

223-843 Lounge/Cafe

**Undecorated**
223-800 Coach
223-810 Diner
223-820 Coach/Baggage
223-830 Sleeper
223-840 Lounge/Cafe

## ASSEMBLED 85' CORRUGATED PASSENGER

### 19.49 ea

**Cars are assembled and complete with operating knuckle couplers and metal screw and post-mounted trucks.**

**Amtrak®**
223-7105 Coach
223-7205 Dome
223-7305 Diner
223-7405 Observation Car
223-7505 70' Baggage
223-7605 Budd Slumbercoach
223-7805 Dome-Observation
223-7905 Budd-Dome

**Atlantic Coast Line**
(with purple letterboards)
223-70101 Coach
223-71101 Dome
223-72101 Diner
223-73101 Observation Car
223-74101 70' Baggage
223-75101 Slumbercoach
223-77101 Dome-Observation
223-78101 Budd-Dome
223-79101 10-6 Sleeper

**Atchison, Topeka & Santa Fe**
223-702 Coach
223-712 Dome
223-722 Diner
223-732 Observation Car
223-742 70' Baggage
223-752 Slumbercoach
223-772 Dome-Observation
223-782 Budd-Dome
223-792 10-6 Sleeper

**"California Zephyr"**
223-706 Coach
223-716 Dome
223-726 Diner
223-736 Observation Car
223-746 70' Baggage
223-756 Slumbercoach
223-776 Dome-Observation
223-786 Budd-Dome
223-796 10-6 Sleeper

**Canadian Pacific**
223-70109 Coach
223-71109 Dome
223-72109 Diner
223-73109 Observation Car
223-74109 70' Baggage
223-75109 Slumbercoach
223-77109 Dome-Observation
223-78109 Budd-Dome
223-79109 10-6 Sleeper



**Canadian Pacific w/"Beaver" Logo**
223-709 Coach
223-719 Dome
223-729 Diner
223-739 Observation Car
223-749 70' Baggage
223-759 Slumbercoach
223-779 Dome-Observation
223-789 Budd-Dome
223-799 10-6 Sleeper

**Chicago, Burlington & Quincy**
(silver)
223-70102 Coach
223-71102 Dome
223-72102 Diner
223-73102 Observation Car
223-74102 70' Baggage
223-75102 Slumbercoach
223-77102 Dome-Observation
223-78102 Budd-Dome
223-79102 10-6 Sleeper

**Frisco "Texas Special"**
(red, silver)
223-70104 Coach
223-71104 Dome
223-72104 Diner
223-73104 Observation Car
223-74104 70' Baggage
223-75104 Slumbercoach
223-77104 Dome-Observation
223-78104 Budd-Dome
223-79104 10-6 Sleeper

**New Haven**
(silver, red)
223-70103 Coach
223-71103 Dome
223-72103 Diner
223-73103 Observation Car
223-74103 70' Baggage
223-75103 Slumbercoach
223-77103 Dome-Observation
223-78103 Budd-Dome
223-79103 10-6 Sleeper

**New York Central**
223-705 Coach
223-715 Dome
223-725 Diner
223-735 Observation Car
223-745 70' Baggage
223-755 Slumbercoach
223-775 Dome-Observation
223-785 Budd-Dome
223-795 10-6 Pullman

**Pennsylvania**
223-703 Coach
223-713 Dome
223-723 Diner
223-733 Observation Car
223-743 70' Baggage
223-753 Slumbercoach
223-773 Dome-Observation
223-783 Budd-Dome
223-793 10-6 Sleeper

**Pennsylvania "Senator"**
223-708 Coach
223-718 Dome
223-728 Diner
223-738 Observation Car
223-748 70' Baggage
223-758 Slumbercoach
223-778 Dome-Observation
223-788 Budd-Dome
223-798 10-6 Sleeper

**Southern**
(black, silver)
223-17106 Coach
223-17206 Dome
223-17306 Diner
223-17406 Observation Car
223-17506 70' Baggage
223-17606 Slumbercoach
223-17806 Dome-Observation
223-17906 Budd-Dome
223-18006 10-6 Sleeper

**Undecorated**
223-701 Coach
223-711 Dome
223-721 Diner
223-731 Observation Car
223-741 70' Baggage
223-751 Slumbercoach
223-771 Dome-Observation
223-781 Budd-Dome
223-791 10-6 Sleeper

## ASSEMBLED 85' CORRUGATED PASSENGER CARS

### 19.98 ea

**Cars feature operating knuckle couplers and metal screw and post-mounted trucks. Include a factory-installed Passenger Car Upgrade Kit (#223-271).**

**Amtrak**
**Phase IV**
223-70110 Coach
223-71110 ACF Dome
223-72110 Diner
223-73110 Observation Car
223-74110 70' Baggage
223-75110 Slumbercoach
223-77110 Dome-Observation
223-78110 Budd-Dome
223-79110 10/6 Sleeper

**Southern "Crescent"**
(green)
223-70113 Coach
223-71113 ACF Dome
223-72113 Diner
223-73113 Observation Car
223-74113 70' Baggage
223-75113 Slumbercoach
223-77113 Dome-Observation
223-78113 Budd-Dome
223-79113 10/6 Sleeper

**Southern Pacific "Daylight"**
(orange, red)
223-70107 Coach
223-71107 ACF Dome
223-72107 Diner
223-73107 Observation Car
223-74107 70' Baggage
223-75107 Slumbercoach
223-77107 Dome-Observation
223-78107 Budd-Dome
223-79107 10/6 Sleeper

**Union Pacific**
(yellow, gray)
223-70112 Coach
223-71112 ACF Dome
223-72112 Diner
223-73112 Observation Car
223-74112 70' Baggage
223-75112 Slumbercoach
223-77112 Dome-Observation
223-78112 Budd-Dome
223-79112 10/6 Sleeper

**Via Rail**
(silver, blue)
223-70111 Coach
223-71111 ACF Dome
223-72111 Diner
223-73111 Observation Car
223-74111 70' Baggage
223-75111 Slumbercoach
223-77111 Dome-Observation
223-78111 Budd-Dome
223-79111 10/6 Sleeper

## PASSENGER CAR PARTS

223-73 Standard Roof pkg(2) **8.98**
223-74 Passenger Car Truck Pin pkg(8) **1.99**

**Budd Style Car Roofs pkg(2) 7.98 ea**
223-70 Regular
223-72 Dome

## PASSENGER CAR UPGRADE KITS

### 4.29 ea

Upgrade your Con-Cor passenger cars to accept an interior lighting kit! Kits include two brass posts, two shouldered truck screws and two McHenry knuckle couplers.

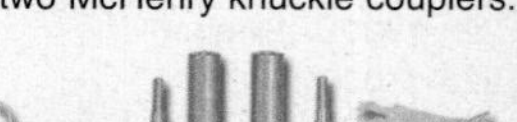

223-270 For Con-Cor 72' Cars
223-271 For Con-Cor 85' Cars

## HEAVYWEIGHTS

**9.98 ea (Unless Noted)**
Each car features separately molded grab irons, strap steps and roof vents.

### Atlantic Coast Line
**348-49000** Baggage
**348-49001** Coach
**348-49002** Combine
**348-49003** Diner
**348-49004** Observation
**348-49005** RPO
**348-49006** 8-1-2 Sleeper
**348-49007** 12-1 Sleeper
**348-49008** 8-Car Set **79.84**

### Atchison, Topeka & Santa Fe "Valley Flyer"
**348-49030** Baggage
**348-49031** Coach
**348-49032** Combine
**348-49033** Diner
**348-49034** Observation
**348-49035** RPO
**348-49036** 8-1-2 Sleeper
**348-49037** 12-1 Sleeper
**348-49038** 8-Car Set **79.84**

### Baltimore & Ohio
**348-49050** Baggage
**348-49051** Coach
**348-49052** Combine
**348-49053** Diner
**348-49054** Observation
**348-49055** RPO
**348-49056** 8-1-2 Sleeper
**348-49057** 12-1 Sleeper
**348-49058** 8-Car Set **79.84**

### Canadian National
**348-49100** Baggage
**348-49101** Coach
**348-49102** Combine
**348-49103** Diner
**348-49104** Observation
**348-49105** RPO
**348-49106** 8-1-2 Sleeper
**348-49107** 12-1 Sleeper
**348-49108** 8-Car Set **79.84**

### Canadian Pacific
**348-49110** Baggage
**348-49111** Coach
**348-49112** Combine
**348-49113** Diner
**348-49114** Observation
**348-49115** RPO
**348-49116** 8-1-2 Sleeper
**348-49117** 12-1 Sleeper
**348-49118** 8-Car Set **79.84**

### CNJ "Blue Comet"
**348-49120** Baggage
**348-49121** Coach
**348-49122** Combine
**348-49123** Diner
**348-49124** Observation
**348-49125** RPO
**348-49126** 8-1-2 Sleeper
**348-49127** 12-1 Sleeper
**348-49128** 8-Car Set **79.84**

### Chesapeake & Ohio
**348-49160** Baggage
**348-49161** Coach
**348-49162** Combine
**348-49163** Diner
**348-49164** Observation
**348-49165** RPO
**348-49166** 8-1-2 Sleeper
**348-49167** 12-1 Sleeper
**348-49168** 8-Car Set **79.84**

### Chicago & Alton "Alton Limited"
**348-49130** Baggage
**348-49131** Coach
**348-49132** Combine
**348-49133** Diner
**348-49134** Observation
**348-49135** RPO
**348-49136** 8-1-2 Sleeper
**348-49137** 12-1 Sleeper
**348-49138** 8-Car Set **79.84**

### Chicago & North Western "North Western Limited"
**348-49210** Baggage
**348-49211** Coach
**348-49212** Combine
**348-49213** Diner
**348-49214** Observation
**348-49215** RPO
**348-49216** 8-1-2 Sleeper
**348-49217** 12-1 Sleeper
**348-49218** 8-Car Set **79.84**

### Delaware & Hudson
**348-49220** Baggage
**348-49221** Coach
**348-49222** Combine
**348-49223** Diner
**348-49224** Observation
**348-49225** RPO
**348-49226** 8-1-2 Sleeper
**348-49227** 12-1 Sleeper
**348-49228** 8-Car Set **79.84**

### Delaware, Lackawanna & Western
**348-49340** Baggage
**348-49341** Coach
**348-49342** Combine
**348-49343** Diner
**348-49344** Observation
**348-49345** RPO
**348-49346** 8-1-2 Sleeper
**348-49347** 12-1 Sleeper
**348-49348** 8-Car Set **79.84**

### Denver & Rio Grande Western
**348-49230** Baggage
**348-49231** Coach
**348-49232** Combine
**348-49233** Diner
**348-49234** Observation
**348-49235** RPO
**348-49236** 8-1-2 Sleeper
**348-49237** 12-1 Sleeper
**348-49238** 8-Car Set **79.84**

### Erie
**348-49240** Baggage
**348-49241** Coach
**348-49242** Combine
**348-49243** Diner
**348-49244** Observation
**348-49245** RPO
**348-49246** 8-1-2 Sleeper
**348-49247** 12-1 Sleeper
**348-49248** 8-Car Set **79.84**

### Frisco "Firefly"
**348-49260** Baggage
**348-49261** Coach
**348-49262** Combine
**348-49263** Diner
**348-49264** Observation
**348-49265** RPO
**348-49266** 8-1-2 Sleeper
**348-49267** 12-1 Sleeper
**348-49268** 8-Car Set **79.84**

### Great Northern "Western Star"
**348-49280** Baggage
**348-49281** Coach
**348-49282** Combine
**348-49283** Diner
**348-49284** Observation
**348-49285** RPO
**348-49286** 8-1-2 Sleeper
**348-49287** 12-1 Sleeper
**348-49288** 8-Car Set **79.84**

### Gulf, Mobile & Ohio "The Rebel"
**348-49300** Baggage
**348-49301** Coach
**348-49302** Combine
**348-49303** Diner
**348-49304** Observation
**348-49305** RPO
**348-49306** 8-1-2 Sleeper
**348-49307** 12-1 Sleeper
**348-49308** 8-Car Set **79.84**

### Kansas City Southern
**348-49320** Baggage
**348-49321** Coach
**348-49322** Combine
**348-49323** Diner
**348-49324** Observation
**348-49325** RPO
**348-49326** 8-1-2 Sleeper
**348-49327** 12-1 Sleeper
**348-49328** 8-Car Set **79.84**

### Lehigh Valley "Asa Packer"
**348-49360** Baggage
**348-49361** Coach
**348-49362** Combine
**348-49363** Diner
**348-49364** Observation
**348-49365** RPO
**348-49366** 8-1-2 Sleeper
**348-49367** 12-1 Sleeper
**348-49368** 8-Car Set **79.84**

### Long Island Railroad
**348-49380** Baggage
**348-49381** Coach
**348-49382** Combine
**348-49383** Diner
**348-49384** Observation
**348-49385** RPO
**348-49386** 8-1-2 Sleeper
**348-49387** 12-1 Sleeper
**348-49388** 8-Car Set **79.84**

### Louisville & Nashville
**348-49390** Baggage
**348-49391** Coach
**348-49392** Combine
**348-49393** Diner
**348-49394** Observation
**348-49395** RPO
**348-49396** 8-1-2 Sleeper
**348-49397** 12-1 Sleeper
**348-49398** 8-Car Set **79.84**

### Milwaukee
**348-49400** Baggage
**348-49401** Coach
**348-49402** Combine
**348-49403** Diner
**348-49404** Observation
**348-49405** RPO
**348-49406** 8-1-2 Sleeper
**348-49407** 12-1 Sleeper
**348-49408** 8-Car Set **79.84**

### Monon "Thoroughbred"
**348-49440** Baggage
**348-49441** Coach
**348-49442** Combine
**348-49443** Diner
**348-49444** Observation
**348-49445** RPO
**348-49446** 8-1-2 Sleeper
**348-49447** 12-1 Sleeper
**348-49448** 8-Car Set **79.84**

### New Haven
**348-49470** Baggage
**348-49471** Coach
**348-49472** Combine
**348-49473** Diner
**348-49474** Observation
**348-49475** RPO
**348-49476** 8-1-2 Sleeper
**348-49477** 12-1 Sleeper
**348-49478** 8-Car Set **79.84**

### New York Central
**348-49490** Baggage
**348-49491** Coach
**348-49492** Combine
**348-49493** Diner
**348-49494** Observation
**348-49495** RPO
**348-49496** 8-1-2 Sleeper
**348-49497** 12-1 Sleeper
**348-49498** 8-Car Set **79.84**

### Norfolk & Western
**348-49510** Baggage
**348-49511** Coach
**348-49512** Combine
**348-49513** Diner
**348-49514** Observation
**348-49515** RPO
**348-49516** 8-1-2 Sleeper
**348-49517** 12-1 Sleeper
**348-49518** 8-Car Set **79.84**

### Northern Pacific
**348-49520** Baggage
**348-49521** Coach
**348-49522** Combine
**348-49523** Diner
**348-49524** Observation
**348-49525** RPO
**348-49526** 8-1-2 Sleeper
**348-49527** 12-1 Sleeper
**348-49528** 8-Car Set **79.84**

### Pennsylvania
**348-49540** Baggage
**348-49541** Coach
**348-49542** Combine
**348-49543** Diner
**348-49544** Observation
**348-49545** RPO
**348-49546** 8-1-2 Sleeper
**348-49547** 12-1 Sleeper
**348-49548** 8-Car Set **79.84**

### Reading
**348-49570** Baggage
**348-49571** Coach
**348-49572** Combine
**348-49573** Diner
**348-49574** Observation
**348-49575** RPO
**348-49576** 8-1-2 Sleeper
**348-49577** 12-1 Sleeper
**348-49578** 8-Car Set **79.84**

### Royal American Shows
**348-49590** Baggage
**348-49591** Coach
**348-49592** Combine
**348-49593** Diner
**348-49594** Observation
**348-49595** RPO
**348-49596** 8-1-2 Sleeper
**348-49597** 12-1 Sleeper
**348-49598** 8-Car Set **79.84**

### Seaboard Air Line "Orange Blossom Special"
**348-49600** Baggage
**348-49601** Coach
**348-49602** Combine
**348-49603** Diner
**348-49604** Observation
**348-49605** RPO
**348-49606** 8-1-2 Sleeper
**348-49607** 12-1 Sleeper
**348-49608** 8-Car Set **79.84**

### Southern "Crescent Limited"
**348-49630** Baggage
**348-49631** Coach
**348-49632** Combine
**348-49633** Diner
**348-49634** Observation
**348-49635** RPO
**348-49636** 8-1-2 Sleeper
**348-49637** 12-1 Sleeper
**348-49638** 8-Car Set **79.84**

### Southern Pacific "Lark"
**348-49660** Baggage
**348-49661** Coach
**348-49662** Combine
**348-49663** Diner
**348-49664** Observation
**348-49665** RPO
**348-49666** 8-1-2 Sleeper
**348-49667** 12-1 Sleeper
**348-49668** 8-Car Set **79.84**

### Union Pacific (yellow, gray)
**348-49690** Baggage
**348-49691** Coach
**348-49692** Combine
**348-49693** Diner
**348-49694** Observation
**348-49695** RPO
**348-49696** 8-1-2 Sleeper
**348-49697** 12-1 Sleeper
**348-49698** 8-Car Set **79.84**

### Union Pacific "Overland" (two-tone gray)
**348-49700** Baggage
**348-49701** Coach
**348-49702** Combine
**348-49703** Diner
**348-49704** Observation
**348-49705** RPO
**348-49706** 8-1-2 Sleeper
**348-49707** 12-1 Sleeper
**348-49708** 8-Car Set **79.84**

### Heavyweight Passenger Car Interiors 4.98 ea
**348-20170** Baggage
**348-20171** Coach
**348-20172** Combine
**348-20173** Diner
**348-20174** Observation
**348-20175** Railway Post Office
**348-20176** 8-1-2 Sleeper
**348-20177** 12-1 Sleeper

## PULLMAN-STANDARD CARS

### Streamlined With Corrugated Sides 9.98 ea (Unless Noted)

### Atlantic Coast Line
**348-47750** Baggage
**348-47751** Coach
**348-47752** Diner
**348-47753** Observation
**348-47755** RPO
**348-47756** Sleeper
**348-147754** Combine
**348-147757** Vista Dome
**348-147758** 8-Car Set **79.84**

### Algoma Central
**348-47760** Baggage
**348-47762** Diner
**348-47763** Observation
**348-47765** RPO
**348-47766** Sleeper
**348-147761** Coach
**348-147764** Combine
**348-147767** Vista Dome
**348-147768** 8-Car Set **79.84**

### Amtrak®
**348-47770** Baggage
**348-47773** Observation
**348-47777** Vista Dome
**348-147771** Coach
**348-147772** Diner
**348-147774** Combine
**348-147775** RPO
**348-147776** Sleeper
**348-47778** 8-Car Set **79.84**

### Atchison, Topeka & Santa Fe
**348-47781** Coach
**348-47782** Diner
**348-47783** Observation
**348-47784** Combine
**348-47786** Sleeper
**348-47787** Vista Dome
**348-147780** Baggage
**348-147785** RPO
**348-47788** 8-Car Set **79.84**

### Baltimore & Ohio
**348-47800** Baggage
**348-47801** Coach
**348-47802** Diner
**348-47803** Observation
**348-47804** Combine
**348-47805** RPO
**348-47806** Sleeper
**348-47807** Vista Dome
**348-47808** 8-Car Set **79.84**

### Boston & Maine
**348-47790** Baggage
**348-47791** Coach
**348-47792** Diner
**348-47793** Observation
**348-47794** Combine
**348-47795** RPO
**348-147796** Sleeper
**348-147797** Vista Dome
**348-147798** 8-Car Set **79.84**

### California Zephyr
**348-47830** Baggage
**348-47831** Coach
**348-47832** Diner
**348-47833** Observation
**348-47834** Combine
**348-47835** RPO
**348-47836** Sleeper
**348-47837** Vista Dome
**348-47838** 8-Car Set **79.84**

### Canadian Pacific
**348-47850** Baggage
**348-47851** Coach
**348-47852** Diner
**348-47853** Observation
**348-47854** Combine
**348-47855** RPO
**348-47856** Sleeper
**348-47857** Vista Dome
**348-47858** 8-Car Set **79.84**

### Chesapeake & Ohio
**348-47820** Baggage
**348-47821** Coach
**348-47822** Diner
**348-47823** Observation
**348-47824** Combine
**348-47825** RPO
**348-47826** Sleeper
**348-47827** Vista Dome
**348-47828** 8-Car Set **79.84**

### C&O "The Chessie"
**348-47310** Baggage
**348-47311** Coach
**348-47312** Diner
**348-47313** Observation
**348-47314** Combine
**348-47315** RPO
**348-47316** Sleeper
**348-47317** Vista Dome
**348-47318** 8-Car Set **79.84**

### Chicago, Burlington & Quincy
**348-47810** Baggage
**348-47811** Coach
**348-47812** Diner
**348-47813** Observation
**348-47814** Combine
**348-47815** RPO
**348-47816** Sleeper
**348-47817** Vista Dome
**348-47818** 8-Car Set **79.84**

### CB&Q "Texas Zephyr"
**348-47300** Baggage
**348-47301** Coach
**348-47302** Diner

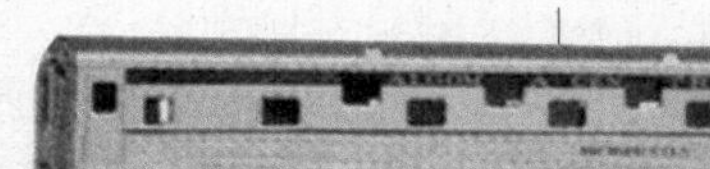
Algoma Central Sleeper Car 348-47766

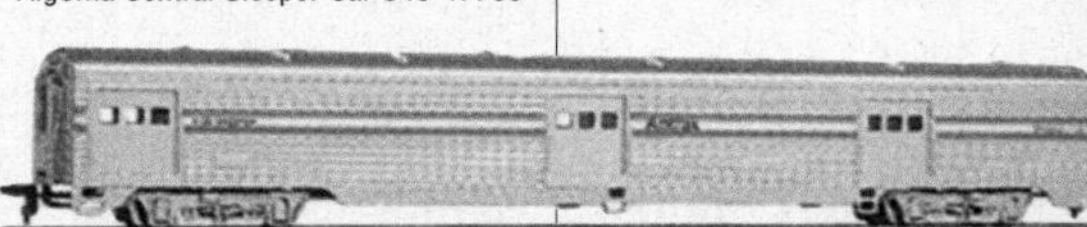
Amtrak Baggage Car 348-47770

**348-47303** Observation
**348-47304** Combine
**348-47305** RPO
**348-47306** Sleeper
**348-47307** Vista Dome
**348-47308** 8-Car Set **79.84**

### Delaware & Hudson
**348-47320** Baggage
**348-47321** Coach
**348-47322** Diner
**348-47323** Observation
**348-47324** Combine
**348-47325** RPO
**348-47326** Sleeper
**348-47327** Vista Dome
**348-47328** 8-Car Set **79.84**

### Denver, Rio Grande & Western
**348-47330** Baggage
**348-47331** Coach
**348-47332** Diner
**348-47333** Observation
**348-47334** Combine
**348-47335** RPO
**348-47336** Sleeper
**348-47337** Vista Dome
**348-47338** 8-Car Set **79.84**

### Florida East Coast
**348-47860** Baggage
**348-47861** Coach
**348-47862** Diner
**348-47863** Observation
**348-47864** Combine
**348-47865** RPO
**348-47866** Sleeper
**348-47867** Vista Dome
**348-47868** 8-Car Set **79.84**

### Frisco
**348-47870** Baggage
**348-47871** Coach
**348-47872** Diner
**348-47873** Observation
**348-47874** Combine
**348-47875** RPO
**348-47876** Sleeper
**348-47877** Vista Dome
**348-47878** 8-Car Set **79.84**

### Louisville & Nashville
**348-47880** Baggage
**348-47881** Coach
**348-47882** Diner
**348-47883** Observation
**348-47884** Combine
**348-47885** RPO
**348-47886** Sleeper
**348-47887** Vista Dome
**348-47888** 8-Car Set **79.84**

### Louisville & Nashville "The Hummingbird"
**348-47340** Baggage
**348-47341** Coach
**348-47342** Diner
**348-47343** Observation
**348-47344** Combine
**348-47345** RPO
**348-47346** Sleeper
**348-47347** Vista Dome
**348-47348** 8-Car Set **79.84**

### Missouri Pacific
**348-47350** Baggage
**348-47351** Coach
**348-47352** Diner
**348-47353** Observation
**348-47354** Combine
**348-47355** RPO
**348-47356** Sleeper
**348-47357** Vista Dome
**348-47358** 8-Car Set **79.84**

### New Haven "Patriot"
**348-47360** Baggage
**348-47361** Coach
**348-47362** Diner
**348-47363** Observation
**348-47364** Combine
**348-47365** RPO
**348-47366** Sleeper
**348-47367** Vista Dome
**348-47368** 8-Car Set **79.84**

### New York Central
**348-47890** Baggage
**348-47891** Coach
**348-47892** Diner
**348-47893** Observation
**348-47894** Combine
**348-47895** RPO
**348-47896** Sleeper
**348-47897** Vista Dome
**348-47898** 8-Car Set **79.84**

### New York Central "Empire State Express"
**348-47370** Baggage
**348-47371** Coach
**348-47372** Diner
**348-47373** Observation
**348-47374** Combine
**348-47375** RPO
**348-47376** Sleeper
**348-47377** Vista Dome
**348-47378** 8-Car Set **79.84**

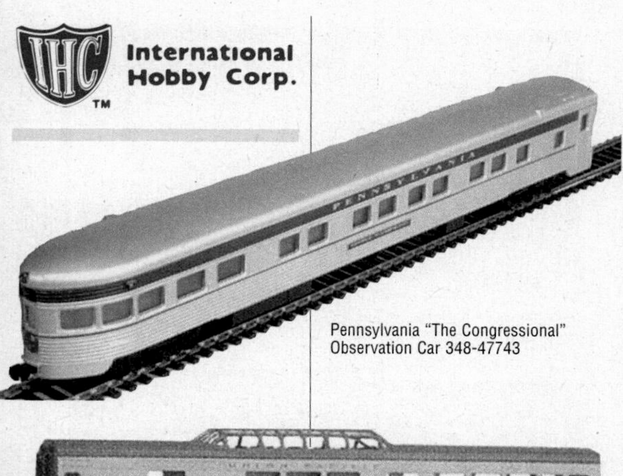


Pennsylvania "The Congressional" Observation Car 348-47743

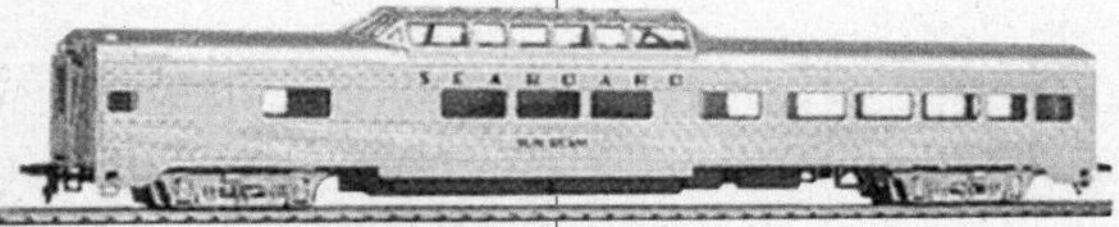

Union Pacific Vista Dome Car 348-47967

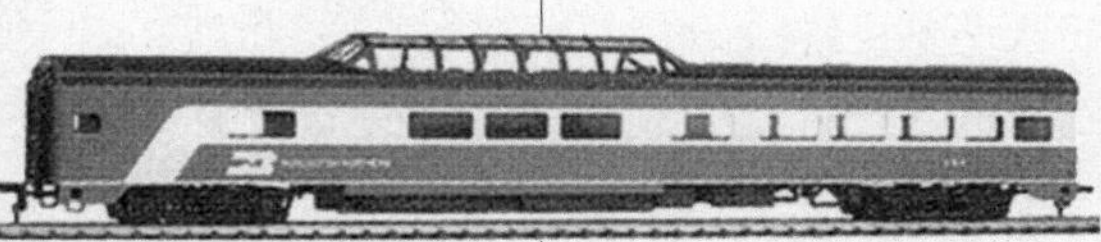

Seaboard Vista Dome Car 348-47937

Burlington Northern Vista Dome Car 348-48037

**Penn Central**
**348-47980** Baggage
**348-47981** Coach
**348-47982** Diner
**348-47983** Observation
**348-47984** Combine
**348-47985** RPO
**348-47986** Sleeper
**348-47987** Vista Dome
**348-47988** 8-Car Set **79.84**

**Pennsylvania**
**348-47900** Baggage
**348-47901** Coach
**348-47902** Diner
**348-47903** Observation
**348-47904** Combine
**348-47905** RPO
**348-47906** Sleeper
**348-47907** Vista Dome
**348-47908** 8-Car Set **79.84**

**Pennsylvania "The Congressional"**
**348-47740** Baggage
**348-47741** Coach
**348-47742** Diner
**348-47743** Observation
**348-47744** Combine
**348-47745** RPO
**348-47746** Sleeper
**348-47747** Vista Dome
**348-47748** 8-Car Set **79.84**

**Pennsylvania "The Fleet of Modernism"**
**348-47730** Baggage
**348-47731** Coach
**348-47732** Diner
**348-47733** Observation
**348-47734** Combine
**348-47735** RPO
**348-47736** Sleeper
**348-47737** Vista Dome
**348-47738** 8-Car Set **79.84**

**Reading**
**348-47910** Baggage
**348-47911** Coach
**348-47912** Diner
**348-47913** Observation
**348-47914** Combine
**348-47915** RPO
**348-47916** Sleeper
**348-47917** Vista Dome
**348-47918** 8-Car Set **79.84**

**Rock Island "Golden Rocket"**
**348-47920** Baggage
**348-47921** Coach
**348-47922** Diner
**348-47923** Observation
**348-47924** Combine
**348-47925** RPO
**348-47926** Sleeper
**348-47927** Vista Dome
**348-47928** 8-Car Set **79.84**

**Rock Island "Rocky Mountain Rocket"**
**348-47380** Baggage
**348-47381** Coach
**348-47382** Diner
**348-47383** Observation
**348-47384** Combine
**348-47385** RPO
**348-47386** Sleeper
**348-47387** Vista Dome
**348-47388** 8-Car Set **79.84**

**Seaboard**
**348-47930** Baggage
**348-47931** Coach
**348-47932** Diner
**348-47933** Observation
**348-47934** Combine
**348-47935** RPO
**348-47936** Sleeper
**348-47937** Vista Dome
**348-47938** 8-Car Set **79.84**

**Southern Pacific "Sunbeam"**
**348-47390** Baggage
**348-47391** Coach
**348-47392** Diner
**348-47393** Observation
**348-47394** Combine
**348-47395** RPO
**348-47396** Sleeper
**348-47397** Vista Dome
**348-47398** 8-Car Set **79.84**

**Southern Pacific "Sunset Limited"**
**348-47950** Baggage
**348-47951** Coach
**348-47952** Diner
**348-47953** Observation
**348-47954** Combine
**348-47955** RPO
**348-47956** Sleeper
**348-47957** Vista Dome
**348-47958** 8-Car Set **79.84**

**Southern Railway**
**348-47940** Baggage
**348-47941** Coach
**348-47942** Diner
**348-47943** Observation
**348-47944** Combine
**348-47945** RPO
**348-47946** Sleeper
**348-47947** Vista Dome
**348-47948** 8-Car Set **79.84**

**Texas Special**
**348-47720** Baggage
**348-47721** Coach
**348-47722** Diner
**348-47723** Observation
**348-47724** Combine
**348-47725** RPO
**348-47726** Sleeper
**348-47727** Vista Dome
**348-47728** 8-Car Set **79.84**

**Union Pacific**
**348-47960** Baggage
**348-47961** Coach
**348-47962** Diner
**348-47963** Observation
**348-47964** Combine
**348-47965** RPO
**348-47966** Sleeper
**348-47967** Vista Dome
**348-47968** 8-Car Set **79.84**



**Wabash**
**348-47970** Baggage
**348-47971** Coach
**348-47972** Diner
**348-47973** Observation
**348-47974** Combine
**348-47975** RPO
**348-47976** Sleeper
**348-47977** Vista Dome
**348-47978** 8-Car Set **79.84**

**Undecorated**
**348-47710** Baggage
**348-47711** Coach
**348-47712** Diner
**348-47713** Observation
**348-47714** Combine
**348-47715** RPO
**348-47716** Sleeper
**348-47717** Vista Dome
**348-47718** 8-Car Set **79.84**

## Streamlined With Smooth Sides 9.98 ea (Unless Noted)

**Amtrak®**
**348-48000** Baggage
**348-48001** Coach
**348-48002** Diner
**348-48003** Observation
**348-48004** Combine
**348-48005** RPO
**348-48006** Sleeper
**348-48007** Vista Dome
**348-48008** 8-Car Set **79.84**

**Atchison, Topeka & Santa Fe**
**348-48010** Baggage
**348-48011** Coach
**348-48012** Diner
**348-48013** Observation
**348-48014** Combine
**348-48015** RPO
**348-48016** Sleeper
**348-48017** Vista Dome
**348-48018** 8-Car Set **79.84**

**Baltimore & Ohio**
**348-48020** Baggage
**348-48021** Coach
**348-48022** Diner
**348-48023** Observation
**348-48024** Combine
**348-48025** RPO
**348-48026** Sleeper
**348-48027** Vista Dome
**348-48028** 8-Car Set **79.84**

**Burlington Northern**
**348-48030** Baggage
**348-48031** Coach
**348-48032** Diner
**348-48033** Observation
**348-48034** Combine
**348-48035** RPO
**348-48036** Sleeper
**348-48037** Vista Dome
**348-48038** 8-Car Set **79.84**

**Canadian National**
**348-48050** Baggage
**348-48051** Coach
**348-48052** Diner
**348-48053** Observation
**348-48054** Combine
**348-48055** RPO
**348-48056** Sleeper
**348-48057** Vista Dome
**348-48058** 8-Car Set **79.84**

**Chessie "Steam Special"**
**348-48350** Baggage
**348-48351** Coach
**348-48352** Diner
**348-48353** Observation
**348-48354** Combine
**348-48355** RPO
**348-48356** Sleeper
**348-48357** Vista Dome
**348-48358** 8-Car Set **79.84**

**Chicago & North Western**
**348-48040** Baggage
**348-48041** Coach
**348-48042** Diner
**348-48043** Observation
**348-48044** Combine
**348-48045** RPO
**348-48046** Sleeper
**348-48047** Vista Dome
**348-48048** 8-Car Set **79.84**

**Delaware, Lackawanna & Western**
**348-48140** Baggage
**348-48141** Coach
**348-48142** Diner
**348-48143** Observation
**348-48144** Combine
**348-48145** RPO
**348-48146** Sleeper
**348-48147** Vista Dome
**348-48148** 8-Car Set **79.84**

**Denver & Rio Grande Western**
**348-48060** Baggage
**348-48061** Coach
**348-48062** Diner
**348-48063** Observation
**348-48064** Combine
**348-48065** RPO
**348-48066** Sleeper
**348-48067** Vista Dome
**348-48068** 8-Car Set **79.84**

**Erie**
**348-48070** Baggage
**348-48071** Coach
**348-48072** Diner
**348-48073** Observation
**348-48074** Combine
**348-48075** RPO
**348-48076** Sleeper
**348-48077** Vista Dome
**348-48078** 8-Car Set **79.84**

# PASSENGER CARS

International Hobby Corp.

### Erie Lackawanna
**348-48300** Baggage
**348-48301** Coach
**348-48302** Diner
**348-48303** Observation
**348-48304** Combine
**348-48305** RPO
**348-48306** Sleeper
**348-48307** Vista Dome
**348-48308** 8-Car Set **79.84**

### Gulf, Mobile & Ohio
**348-48080** Baggage
**348-48081** Coach
**348-48082** Diner
**348-48083** Observation
**348-48084** Combine
**348-48085** RPO
**348-48086** Sleeper
**348-48087** Vista Dome
**348-48088** 8-Car Set **79.84**

### Great Northern
**348-48090** Baggage
**348-48091** Coach
**348-48092** Diner
**348-48093** Observation
**348-48094** Combine
**348-48095** RPO
**348-48096** Sleeper
**348-48097** Vista Dome
**348-48098** 8-Car Set **79.84**

### Illinois Central
**348-48110** Baggage
**348-48111** Coach
**348-48112** Diner
**348-48113** Observation
**348-48114** Combine
**348-48115** RPO
**348-48116** Sleeper
**348-48117** Vista Dome
**348-48118** 8-Car Set **79.84**

### Illinois Central "City of Miami"
**348-48330** Baggage
**348-48331** Coach
**348-48332** Diner
**348-48333** Observation
**348-48334** Combine
**348-48335** RPO
**348-48336** Sleeper
**348-48337** Vista Dome
**348-48338** 8-Car Set **79.84**

### Kansas City Southern
**348-48120** Baggage
**348-48121** Coach
**348-48122** Diner
**348-48123** Observation
**348-48124** Combine
**348-48125** RPO
**348-48126** Sleeper
**348-48127** Vista Dome
**348-48128** 8-Car Set **79.84**

### Lehigh Valley "John Wilkes"
**348-48150** Baggage
**348-48151** Coach
**348-48152** Diner
**348-48153** Observation
**348-48154** Combine
**348-48155** RPO
**348-48156** Sleeper
**348-48157** Vista Dome
**348-48158** 8-Car Set **79.84**

### Louisville & Nashville
**348-48130** Baggage
**348-48131** Coach
**348-48132** Diner
**348-48133** Observation
**348-48134** Combine
**348-48135** RPO
**348-48136** Sleeper
**348-48137** Vista Dome
**348-48138** 8-Car Set **79.84**

### Missouri Pacific
**348-48160** Baggage
**348-48161** Coach
**348-48162** Diner
**348-48163** Observation
**348-48164** Combine
**348-48165** RPO
**348-48166** Sleeper
**348-48167** Vista Dome
**348-48168** 8-Car Set **79.84**

### New Jersey Transit
**348-48180** Baggage
**348-48181** Coach
**348-48182** Diner
**348-48183** Observation
**348-48184** Combine
**348-48185** RPO
**348-48186** Sleeper
**348-48187** Vista Dome

Item listed below is available by Special Order (see Legend Page).
**348-48188** 8-Car Set **79.84**

### New York Central
**348-48200** Baggage
**348-48201** Coach
**348-48202** Diner
**348-48203** Observation
**348-48204** Combine
**348-48205** RPO
**348-48206** Sleeper
**348-48207** Vista Dome
**348-48208** 8-Car Set **79.84**

### New York Central "Mercury"
**348-48290** Baggage
**348-48291** Coach
**348-48292** Diner
**348-48293** Observation
**348-48294** Combine
**348-48295** RPO
**348-48296** Sleeper
**348-48297** Vista Dome
**348-48298** 8-Car Set **79.84**

### Norfolk & Western
**348-48170** Baggage
**348-48171** Coach
**348-48172** Diner
**348-48173** Observation
**348-48174** Combine
**348-48175** RPO
**348-48176** Sleeper
**348-48177** Vista Dome
**348-48178** 8-Car Set **79.84**

### Northern Pacific "North Coast Limited"
**348-48190** Baggage
**348-48191** Coach
**348-48192** Diner
**348-48193** Observation
**348-48194** Combine
**348-48195** RPO
**348-48196** Sleeper
**348-48197** Vista Dome
**348-48198** 8-Car Set **79.84**

### Pennsylvania
**348-48210** Baggage
**348-48211** Coach
**348-48212** Diner
**348-48213** Observation
**348-48214** Combine
**348-48215** RPO
**348-48216** Sleeper
**348-48217** Vista Dome
**348-48218** 8-Car Set **79.84**

### Pennsylvania "Eastwind"
**348-48320** Baggage
**348-48321** Coach
**348-48322** Diner
**348-48323** Observation
**348-48324** Combine
**348-48325** RPO
**348-48326** Sleeper
**348-48327** Vista Dome
**348-48328** 8-Car Set **79.84**

### Pennsylvania "The Fleet of Modernism"
**348-48310** Baggage
**348-48311** Coach
**348-48312** Diner
**348-48313** Observation
**348-48314** Combine
**348-48315** RPO
**348-48316** Sleeper
**348-48317** Vista Dome
**348-48318** 8-Car Set **79.84**

### Reading
**348-48220** Baggage
**348-48221** Coach
**348-48222** Diner
**348-48223** Observation
**348-48224** Combine
**348-48225** RPO
**348-48226** Sleeper
**348-48227** Vista Dome
**348-48228** 8-Car Set **79.84**

### Richmond, Fredericksburg & Potomac
**348-48230** Baggage
**348-48231** Coach
**348-48232** Diner
**348-48233** Observation

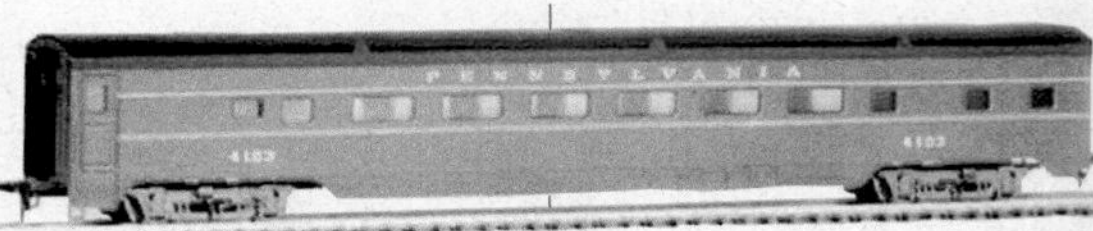


Pennsylvania Coach Car 348-48211

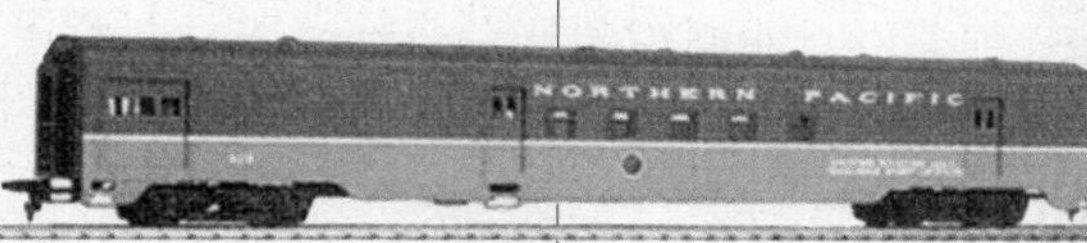


Northern Pacific "North Coast Lmited" RPO Car 348-48195

Vista Dome Interior 348-20157

**348-48234** Combine
**348-48235** RPO
**348-48236** Sleeper
**348-48237** Vista Dome
**348-48238** 8-Car Set **79.84**

### Rock Island
**348-48240** Baggage
**348-48241** Coach
**348-48242** Diner
**348-48243** Observation
**348-48244** Combine
**348-48245** RPO
**348-48246** Sleeper
**348-48247** Vista Dome
**348-48248** 8-Car Set **79.84**

### Southern Pacific "Daylight"
**348-48250** Baggage
**348-48251** Coach
**348-48252** Diner
**348-48253** Observation
**348-48254** Combine
**348-48255** RPO
**348-48256** Sleeper
**348-48257** Vista Dome
**348-48258** 8-Car Set **79.84**

### Southern Pacific "Golden State"
**348-48100** Baggage
**348-48101** Coach
**348-48102** Diner
**348-48103** Observation
**348-48104** Combine
**348-48105** RPO
**348-48106** Sleeper
**348-48107** Vista Dome
**348-48108** 8-Car Set **79.84**

### Spokane, Portland & Seattle
**348-48340** Baggage
**348-48341** Coach
**348-48342** Diner
**348-48343** Observation
**348-48344** Combine
**348-48345** RPO
**348-48346** Sleeper
**348-48347** Vista Dome
**348-48348** 8-Car Set **79.84**

### Union Pacific
**348-48270** Baggage
**348-48271** Coach
**348-48272** Diner
**348-48273** Observation
**348-48274** Combine
**348-48275** RPO
**348-48276** Sleeper
**348-48277** Vista Dome
**348-48278** 8-Car Set **79.84**

### VIA
**348-48280** Baggage
**348-48281** Coach
**348-48282** Diner
**348-48283** Observation
**348-48284** Combine
**348-48285** RPO
**348-48286** Sleeper
**348-48287** Vista Dome
**348-48288** 8-Car Set **79.84**

### Undecorated
**348-48260** Baggage
**348-48261** Coach
**348-48262** Diner
**348-48263** Observation
**348-48264** Combine
**348-48265** RPO
**348-48266** Sleeper
**348-48267** Vista Dome
**348-48268** 8-Car Set **79.84**

## INTERIORS

### 4.98 ea
For smoothside and corrugated-side passenger cars.
**348-20150** Baggage
**348-20151** Coach
**348-20152** Diner
**348-20153** Observation
**348-20154** Combine
**348-20155** RPO
**348-20156** Sleeper
**348-20157** Vista Dome

## DIAPHRAGMS

### 10.95 ea

Add realism *between* your passenger cars with Hi-Tech Details passenger car diaphragms. Available in seven different prototype styles, these easy-to-build parts feature real working springs and real stainless steel striker plates for reliable operation—they even flex as trains move through curves. Parts come molded in neutral gray or appropriate colors that match popular passenger car color schemes. Diaphragms are listed by style.

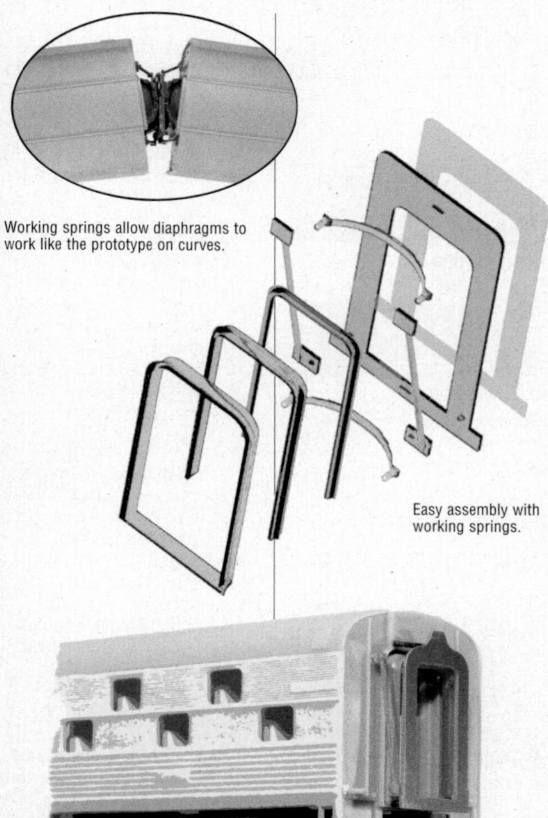

Working springs allow diaphragms to work like the prototype on curves.

Easy assembly with working springs.

331-9600 Installed on passenger car.

### Common Standard Pair

**331-9000** Neutral Gray
**331-9001** Black
**331-9002** Daylight Red
**331-9003** Tuscan Red
**331-9004** Harbor Mist Gray

### Fowler Pair

**331-9100** Neutral Gray
**331-9101** Black
**331-9103** Tuscan Red
**331-9104** Harbor Mist Gray

### Common Standard Tall Pair

**331-9200** Neutral Gray
**331-9201** Black
**331-9203** Tuscan Red
**331-9204** Harbor Mist Gray

### Western Tall Pair

**331-9300** Neutral Gray
**331-9302** Daylight Red
**331-9304** Harbor Mist Gray

### Opera Window Pair

**331-9400** Neutral Gray
**331-9402** Daylight Red
**331-9404** Harbor Mist Gray

### Bat Wing Tall Pair

**331-9500** Neutral Gray
**331-9501** Black
**331-9503** Tuscan Red
**331-9504** Harbor Mist Gray

### Western Short Pair

**331-9600** Neutral Gray
**331-9601** Black
**331-9603** Tuscan Red
**331-9604** Harbor Mist Gray

See What's Available at
**www.walthers.com**

OK ENGINES/STREAMLINERS METAL MODEL PRODUCTS

These easy-to-assemble passenger cars feature all-metal construction, weighted trucks and detailed castings.

Please visit Walthers Web site at www.walthers.com for a complete listing of all available items including parts.

## PULLMAN PASSENGER CARS

### Smoothside Cars

These cars are representative of the steel-sided, lightweight cars common on many railroads. All cars are undecorated.

#### Kits 27.00 ea (Unless Noted)

**543-11** Coach
**543-12** Domed Coach
**543-13** Observation Car **29.95**
**543-15** Baggage-Dorm
**543-16** Sleeper
**543-17** Diner
**543-18** RPO

Item listed below is available by Special Order (see Legend Page).
**543-14** Baggage Car

#### Assembled Models 35.00 ea (Unless Noted)

**543-11A** Coach
**543-12A** Domed Coach
**543-13A** Observation Car **39.95**
**543-14A** Baggage Car
**543-15A** Baggage-Dorm
**543-16A** Sleeper
**543-17A** Diner
**543-18A** RPO

### Streamliner Cars

These cars could be found on most railroads from the late steam-era of the 1930s to the first days of Amtrak® in the 1970s. All cars come undecorated.

#### Kits 27.00 ea (Unless Noted)

**543-21** 48-Seat Coach
**543-23** Observation Car **29.95**
**543-25** Baggage-Dorm
**543-222** Domed Coach
**543-224** Baggage
**543-226** Sleeper
**543-227** Diner
**543-228** RPO
**543-229** Domed Observation **29.95**

#### Assembled Models 35.00 ea (Unless Noted)

**543-21A** 48-Seat Coach
**543-23A** Observation Car **39.95**
**543-25A** Baggage-Dorm
**543-222A** Domed Coach
**543-224A** Baggage
**543-226A** Sleeper
**543-227A** Diner
**543-228A** RPO
**543-229A** Domed Observation **39.95**

### Budd-Style Streamliner Cars

A staple of postwar era passenger service.

#### Kits 27.00 ea (Unless Noted)

**543-44** Baggage
**543-46** Sleeper
**543-47** Diner
**543-48** RPO

Items listed below are available by Special Order (see Legend Page).
**543-41** 48-Seat Coach
**543-42** Domed Coach
**543-43** Observation Car **29.95**
**543-45** Baggage-Dorm
**543-49** Domed Observation **29.95**

#### Assembled Models 35.00 ea (Unless Noted)

**543-41A** 48-Seat Coach
**543-42A** Domed Coach
**543-43A** Observation Car **39.95**
**543-44A** Baggage
**543-45A** Baggage-Dorm
**543-46A** Sleeper
**543-47A** Diner
**543-48A** RPO
**543-49A** Domed Observation **39.95**

Smoothside Cars Baggage Car 543-14

Streamliner Cars Diner 543-227

Pullman Four-Window Cab Coach Amtrak Phase III 381-356021

Pullman Four-Window Cab Coach Chicago Regional Transit Authority #8713 381-356023

Pullman Four-Window Coach CNW 381-356032

Pullman Four-Window Coach Chicago Regional Transit Authority #7700 381-356033

Pullman Six-Window Coach Chicago RTA 381-356042

Business Car CP 381-356002

Business Car B&O 381-356008

Business Car NP 381-356010

## NEW PRODUCTS

### Material Handling Car

**NEW 381-356101** Amtrak Phase III **TBA**

## BI-LEVEL COMMUTER CARS

All cars come prepainted to provide the best color match for Kato F40PH diesels, listed in the Locomotives section.

### Pullman Four-Window Cab Coaches

**381-356021** Amtrak® Phase III **57.00**
**381-356022** CNW **65.00**
**NEW 381-356023** Chicago Regional Transit Authority (RTA) #8713 **67.00**
**NEW 381-356023A** Chicago Regional Transit Authority (RTA) #8716 **67.00**
**NEW 381-356024** Rock Island #CC115 **67.00**

### Pullman Four-Window Coach

**381-356031** Amtrak Phase III **50.00**
**381-356032** CNW **52.00**
**NEW 381-356033** Chicago Regional Transit Authority (RTA) #7700 **55.00**
**NEW 381-356033A** Chicago Regional Transit Authority (RTA) #7708 **55.00**
**NEW 381-356034** Rock Island #155 **67.00**

### Pullman Six-Window Coach 52.00 ea

**381-356041** CNW
**381-356042** Chicago RTA

## BUSINESS CARS

### 47.98 ea (Unless Noted)

Models feature finely scaled body corrugations and window gaskets, body interior, knuckle couplers and lighted tail lights/marker lights. Cars are designed to accept the Passenger Lighting Kits (#381-7501 with bulbs and #381-7502 with LED), sold separately.

**381-356001** Amtrak "Track Inspection Car 10000" (stainless steel silver with Phase III stripes)
**381-356002** CP "Algonquin"
**381-356003** CB&Q "Burlington" (stainless steel silver)

**381-356004** NYC "Gotham"

**381-356006** SP "SP150"
**381-356008** B&O "902"
**381-356010** NP "Yellowstone"
**381-356012** UP "Sunset" **50.00**

### Lighting Kits

**381-7502** w/LEDs **17.00**

## MANTUA

Ready-to-run models are prepainted plastic, and include trucks and knuckle couplers.

## OLD-TIME CARS – WOOD STYLE

### 10.99 ea

### 1860 Era

#### Combines

**455-717004** NP

**455-718520** PRR

#### Coaches

**455-717100** NYC & Hudson

**455-717520** PRR
**455-718004** NP

### 1890 Era

#### Combines

**455-717110** NYC & Hudson

**455-720008** DRGW

**455-720525** B&O

#### Coaches

**455-719008** DRGW

**455-719525** B&O

## Information STATION

### Who Owns That Passenger Car?

In the days of premier trains, many railroads offered through cars, or worked with connecting lines to offer long-distance service. Each road supplied equipment, often painted to match specific consists.

For example, the "Empire Builder" was GN's premier train between Chicago and Seattle/Portland. A joint effort between GN and its affiliates Spokane, Portland & Seattle and Chicago, Burlington & Quincy, it was painted in GN colors but letterboards read "Empire Builder." Very small lettering indicated who actually owned each car.

A few other trains that carried sublettered cars included IC's "City of Miami" with Central of Georgia and IC cars; UP's "City of San Francisco," which hauled cars from PRR, CNW, SP and Wabash (and later MILW and N&W); and the "California Zephyr," which carried cars from WP, DRGW & CB&Q plus a through sleeper from the Pennsy. And don't forget, many streamlined sleepers operated by Pullman carried that name on the letterboards until the cars were sold to the railroads. At that time Pullman became the sublettering on some road's cars.

Sublettering is easy to model on your passenger fleet. Cars often come with decals for car numbers and names, and many include sublettering too. Some decal manufacturers also include appropriate sublettering on some of their sets.

Ready-to-run cars feature plastic bodies and come prepainted and lettered. Budd cars and old-time cars feature brass wheels and axles, plus full interiors.

# PASSENGER CARS

## Amtrak

### Budd Cars 17.98 ea

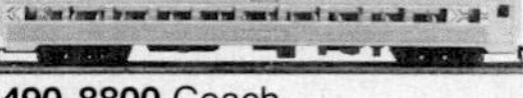

**490-8800** Coach

**490-8801** Baggage

**490-8803** Observation

**490-8804** Sleeper

## Baltimore & Ohio

### 67' Harriman Cars w/ Interior (blue) 18.98 ea

**490-9903** Coach

**490-9913** Observation Car

## Canadian National

### 67' Harriman Cars w/Interior (green) 18.98 ea

**490-9906** Coach (gray, black)

**490-9908** Coach

**490-9916** Observation Car (modern gray, black)

**490-9918** Observation Car

### Budd Cars 16.98 ea

**490-8840** Coach

**490-8841** Baggage

**490-8842** Dining

**490-8843** Observation

**490-8844** Sleeper

## Canadian Pacific

### 48' Old-Time Wood Cars 17.98 ea

**490-5508** Coach

**490-5518** Baggage

### 67' Harriman Cars w/Interior (silver, red) 18.98 ea

**490-9905** Coach

**490-9907** Coach (older Maroon scheme)

**490-9915** Observation Car

**490-9917** Observation Car (older Maroon scheme)

### Budd Cars 17.98 ea

**490-8850** Coach

**490-8851** Baggage

**490-8852** Dining

**490-8853** Observation

**490-8854** Sleeper

## Dickens Railroad 16.98 ea

These 48' old-time wooden cars are painted and lettered to match equipment in Christmas Village Sets.

**490-5504** Deluxe Coach

**490-5514** Baggage

## Pennsylvania

### 48' Old-Time Wood Cars

**490-5506** Coach **17.98**

### 67' Harriman Cars w/Interior 18.98 ea

**490-9909** Coach

**490-9919** Observation Car

## Rio Grande

### 48' Old-Time Wood Cars 18.98 ea

**490-5509** Coach

**490-5519** Baggage

## Santa Fe

### 48' Old-Time Wood Cars 17.98 ea

**490-5505** Coach

**490-5515** Baggage

### 67' Harriman Cars w/Interior (silver) 18.98 ea

**490-9904** Coach

**490-9914** Observation

### Budd Cars 16.98 ea

**490-8860** Coach

**490-8861** Baggage

**490-8862** Dining

**490-8863** Observation

**490-8864** Sleeper

## Southern

### 48' Old-Time Wood Cars 17.98 ea

**490-5507** Coach

**490-5517** Baggage

### 67' Harriman Cars w/Interior (green) 18.98 ea

**490-9902** Coach

**490-9912** Observation Car

## Southern Pacific

### 67' Harriman Cars w/Interior (red, orange) 19.98 ea

**490-9901** Coach

**490-9911** Observation Car

### Budd Cars 17.98 ea

**490-8820** Coach

**490-8821** Baggage

**490-8822** Dining

**490-8823** Observation

**490-8824** Sleeper

## Undecorated

### 67' Harriman Cars w/Interior 18.98 ea

**490-9899** Coach

**490-9900** Observation Car

Modernize and detail passenger car interiors quickly and easily with these injection molded parts. Easily painted and installed in ready-to-run cars, kits or scratchbuilt models, parts are typical of seating found in many types of cars.

# NEW PRODUCTS

## Parlor Car Chairs

**NEW 548-5002100** pkg(100) **22.50**

## Lounge Seats

**NEW 548-5004100** pkg(100) **21.50**

## Dining Car Parts

**NEW 548-5134** Serving Counter pkg(2) **3.95**

**NEW 548-5137** Locker 2 Each of 3 Sizes pkg(6) **4.95**

**NEW 548-5138** Refrigerators 3 Each of 2 Sizes pkg(6) **4.95**

**NEW 548-5139** Steward's Desk pkg(2) **2.95**

**NEW 548-500524** Café Booths pkg(24) **19.95**

**NEW 548-500748** Dining Chairs - Paired pkg(48) **27.50**

## Underbody Details

**NEW 548-4002** Propane Carrier Three cylinder style pkg(4) **4.95**

**NEW 548-4003** Four Tread Fixed Steps pkg(4) **4.95** For Rock Island rebuilt coaches.

## Battery Boxes

**NEW 548-4001** Four Strap-Hinge Style pkg(4) **4.95**

**NEW 548-4011** Two-Strap Hinge Style pkg(4) **4.95**

## Vestibule Bulkhead

**NEW 548-5114** Wood Style for MDC Palace Cars 1 Pair **4.25**

# PASSENGER CAR INTERIOR DETAILS

## Streamliner Coach Seats

**548-500136** pkg(36) **7.95**

**548-5001100** pkg(100) **18.95**

## Individual Seats

**548-500236** Parlor Car pkg(36) **9.50**

**548-500430** Lounge Car pkg(30) **7.50**

## Dining Car Parts

Includes cut styrene parts for tabletops.

**548-500510** Café Booths pkg(10) **8.95**

**548-500724** Dining Chairs - Paired pkg(24) **14.50**

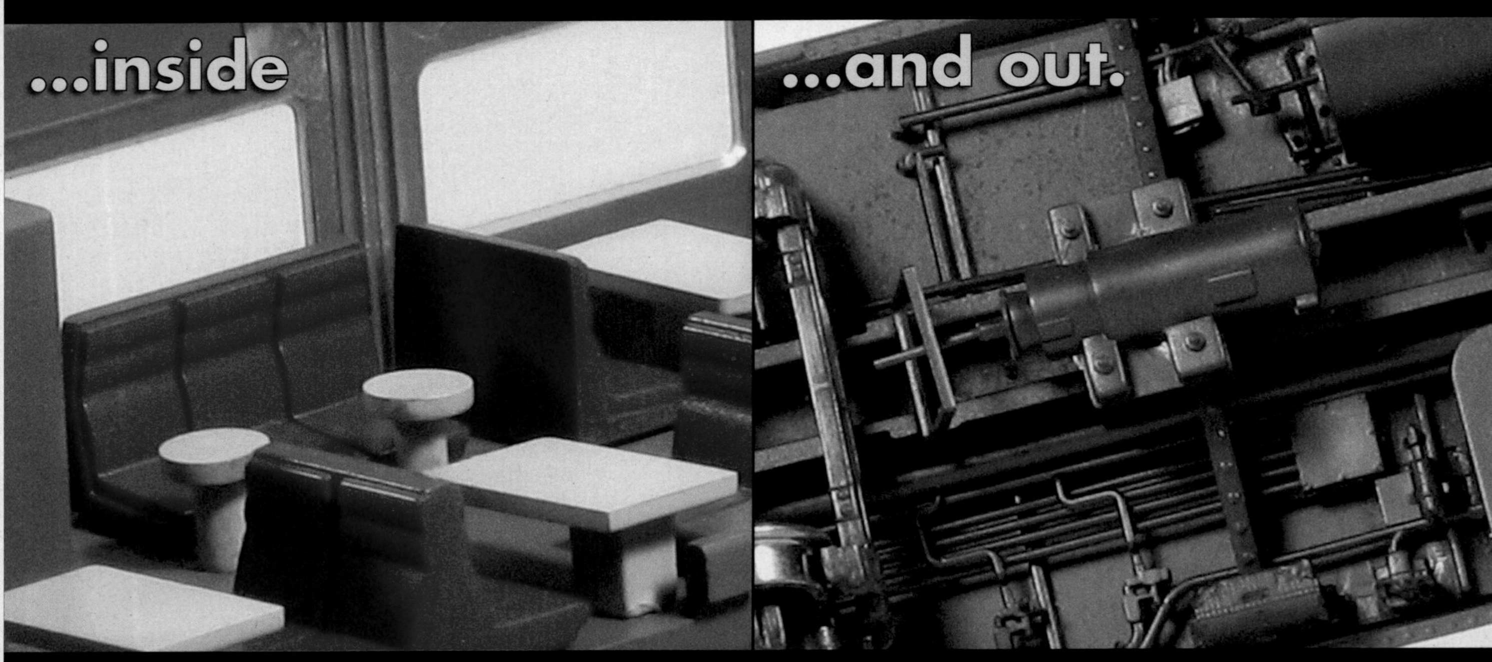

**Limited Quantity Available On All Items**

# SUPER CONTINENTAL LINE PASSENGER CARS

## 59.95 ea (Unless Noted)

The Super Continental Line from Rapido Trains Inc. has become synonymous with quality, detail and craftsmanship. These super-detailed, full-length passenger cars feature:

- Ready-to-run, injection-molded plastic models
- Fully decorated in many different paint scheme
- Detailed underbody with separate steam, air and electrical lines
- Flush-fitting windows with raised and painted window frames
- Factory-applied grab irons and uncoupling levers
- Fully detailed interior cast or painted in appropriate colors
- Battery-powered LED lighting operated by magnetic wand (included)
- Separate, removable marker lamps and end gates
- Scale-size knuckle couplers and operating diaphragms with support bars
- 18" minimum radius (24" or greater recommended)
- Multiple car names/numbers available for each railroad and type of car
- Detailed, illustrated, 12-page instruction booklet
- Limited manufacturer warranty for replacement or repair of defective products

The first two releases in the series were a lightweight coach and a 4 bedroom, 8 roomette, 4 section duplex sleeper. 2007 saw the delivery of a cafe-bar-lounge car and a 10 roomette, 5-bedroom sleeper. More cars are arriving in 2008. Cars come with partial skirts or fixed steps as appropriate. New releases are announced regularly. Visit walthers.com for the latest additions.

### Algoma Central

**Lightweight Coach "Route of the Black Bear"**
NEW 606-100185 #5441
NEW 606-100186 #5462
NEW 606-100187 #5474
NEW 606-100188 #5483
NEW 606-100189 #5494

### Amtrak (Phase 1)

**Lightweight Coach 49.95 ea**
606-100043 #5688
606-100045 #5691

Amtrak (Phase I) Lightweight Coach #5691 606-100045

**Duplex Sleeper 49.95 ea**
606-101041 #2400
606-101042 #2401
606-101043 #2402
606-101044 #2420
606-101045 #2460

**Café-Bar-Lounge**
NEW 606-103016 #8380
NEW 606-103017 #8381
NEW 606-103018 #8382

**10-5 Sleeper**
NEW 606-104019 #2800
NEW 606-104020 #2801
NEW 606-104021 #2802
NEW 606-104022 #2803
NEW 606-104023 #2805

### Amtrak (Phase 3)

Duplex Sleeper-Car Not Available

**Café-Bar-Lounge**
NEW 606-103019 #3100
NEW 606-103020 #3101
NEW 606-103021 #3105

**10-5 Sleeper**
NEW 606-104024 #2804
NEW 606-104025 #2863
NEW 606-104026 #2864
NEW 606-104027 #2865
NEW 606-104028 #2866

## Atchison, Topeka & Santa Fe

### 10-5 Sleeper
**NEW** 606-104029 "Cascade Mills"

**NEW** 606-104030 "Cascade Shoals"

## Baltimore & Ohio

Lightweight Coach-Car Shown Not Available

### Lightweight Coach 49.95 ea
606-100072 "Cumberland"

606-100074 "New Castle"

606-100075 "Youngstown"

### Café-Bar-Lounge
**NEW** 606-103022 #1083

**NEW** 606-103023 #1084

### 10-5 Sleeper
**NEW** 606-104031 "Cascade Bluff"

**NEW** 606-104032 "Cascade Boulders"

**NEW** 606-104033 "Cascade Gully"

**NEW** 606-104034 "Cascade Locks"

**NEW** 606-104035 "Cascade Music"

## Canadian National 1954 Scheme

### Lightweight Coach 49.95 ea
606-100011 #5437

606-100012 #5465

606-100013 #5470

606-100015 #5533

606-100016 #5541

606-100017 #5552

606-100018 #5564

### Duplex Sleeper 49.95 ea
606-101011 "Eastport"

606-101013 "Elmsdale"

606-101014 "Emperor"

606-101017 "Ernestown"

606-101018 "Estcourt"

606-101019 "Ethelbert"

606-101020 "Euclid"

### Café-Bar-Lounge
**NEW** 606-103006 #2500

**NEW** 606-103007 #2502

**NEW** 606-103008 #2508

**NEW** 606-103009 #2512

**NEW** 606-103010 #2514

### 10-5 Sleeper
**NEW** 606-104007 "Buckley Bay"

**NEW** 606-104008 "Hudson Bay"

**NEW** 606-104009 "Chaleur Bay"

**NEW** 606-104010 "Glace Bay"

**NEW** 606-104011 "Fortune Bay"

**NEW** 606-104012 "Thunder Bay"

## Canadian National 1961 Scheme

### Lightweight Coach 49.95 ea
606-100021 #5443

606-100022 #5455

606-100023 #5476

606-100025 #5500

606-100026 #5502

606-100027 #5549

606-100029 #5574

606-100030 #5588

### Duplex Sleeper 49.95 ea
606-101021 "Edson"

606-101022 "Ekhart"

606-101023 "Elgin"

606-101025 "Emerald"

606-101026 "Endako"

606-101027 "Entrance"

606-101028 "Escuminac"

606-101029 "Essex"

606-101030 "Extew"

### Café-Bar-Lounge
**NEW** 606-103011 #2503

**NEW** 606-103012 #2504

**NEW** 606-103013 #2506

**NEW** 606-103014 #2509

**NEW** 606-103015 #2511

### 10-5 Sleeper
**NEW** 606-104013 "Buckley Bay"

**NEW** 606-104015 "Chaleur Bay"

**NEW** 606-104016 "Glace Bay"

**NEW** 606-104017 "Fortune Bay"

**NEW** 606-104018 "Thunder Bay"

Canadian National 1961 Scheme
Duplex Sleeper "Emerald" 606-101025

## Canadian Pacific Railway

### 10-5 Sleeper
**NEW** 606-104036 "Armdale"

**NEW** 606-104037 "Brookdale"

**NEW** 606-104038 "Cloverdale"

**NEW** 606-104039 "Riverdale"

## Chesapeake & Ohio

### Lightweight Coach
**NEW** 606-100190 #1613

**NEW** 606-100191 #1621

**NEW** 606-100192 #1637

**NEW** 606-100193 #1641

**NEW** 606-100194 #1655

### Café-Bar-Lounge
**NEW** 606-103055 "Blue Ridge Club" #1923

**NEW** 606-103056 "Bluegrass Club" #1924

**NEW** 606-103057 "Allegheny Club" #1925

### 10-5 Sleeper
**NEW** 606-104089 "District of Columbia" #2602

**NEW** 606-104090 "City of Richmond" #2611

**NEW** 606-104091 "Virginia Hot Springs" 2614

**NEW** 606-104092 "City of Grand Rapids" #2636

**NEW** 606-104093 "City of Saginaw" #2640

## Chicago & North Western

Duplex Sleeper-Car Shown Not Available

### Café-Bar-Lounge
**NEW** 606-103024 #7900

**NEW** 606-103025 #7901

**NEW** 606-103026 #7902

### 10-5 Sleeper
**NEW** 606-104040 "Western Frontier"

**NEW** 606-104041 "Western Lake"

**NEW** 606-104042 "Western Peak"

## Delaware & Hudson

### Lightweight Coach
**NEW** 606-100195 "Ausable River" #31

**NEW** 606-100196 "Bulwagga Bay" #32

**NEW** 606-100197 "Schroon Lake" #33

**NEW** 606-100198 "Whiteface Mountain" #34

**NEW** 606-100199 "Lake Placid" #202

### Café-Bar-Lounge
**NEW** 606-103058 "Saratoga Inn" #41

**NEW** 606-103059 "Adirondack Lodge" #42

## Delaware, Lackawanna & Western

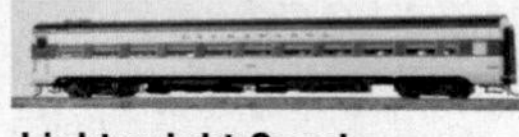

### Lightweight Coach
**NEW** 606-100200 #316

**NEW** 606-100201 #317

**NEW** 606-100202 #319

**NEW** 606-100203 #322

**NEW** 606-100204 #324

### 10-5 Sleeper
**NEW** 606-104094 "Kittatinny"

**NEW** 606-104095 "Lakawanna"

**NEW** 606-104096 "Tioughnioga"

**NEW** 606-104097 "Tobyhanna"

**NEW** 606-104098 "Tunkhannock"



## Erie

### Lightweight Coach
**NEW** 606-100180 #1002

**NEW** 606-100181 #1007

**NEW** 606-100182 #1010

**NEW** 606-100183 #1011

**NEW** 606-100184 #1014

### 10-5 Sleeper
**NEW** 606-104043 "Pride of Youngstown"

**NEW** 606-104044 "Spirit of Youngstown"

## Erie-Lackawanna

### Lightweight Coach
**NEW** 606-100205 #1304

**NEW** 606-100206 #1305

**NEW** 606-100207 #1310

**NEW** 606-100208 #1321

**NEW** 606-100209 #1325

### 10-5 Sleeper
**NEW** 606-104045 "Pride of Youngstown"

**NEW** 606-104046 "Spirit of Youngstown"

## Grand Trunk Western

### Lightweight Coach
**NEW** 606-100210 #4884

**NEW** 606-100211 #4885

**NEW** 606-100212 #4886

**NEW** 606-100213 #4887

**NEW** 606-100214 #4888

## Great Northern

### Lightweight Coach

### Duplex Sleeper
606-101032 "Triple Divide Pass"

### Café-Bar-Lounge
**NEW 606-103027** #1145

**NEW 606-103028** #1146

## Great Northern "Big Sky Blue"

### Lightweight Coach
**NEW 606-100215** #1076

**NEW 606-100216** #1079

**NEW 606-100217** #1080

**NEW 606-100218** #1081

**NEW 606-100219** #1083

### Duplex Sleeper
**NEW 606-101105** "Ptarmigan Pass" #1161

**NEW 606-101106** "Dawson Pass" #1162

**NEW 606-101107** "Piegan Pass" #1163

**NEW 606-101108** "Logan Pass" #1164

**NEW 606-101109** "Red Gap Pass" #1168

### Café-Bar-Lounge
**NEW 606-103060** "Waterton Lake" #1140

**NEW 606-103061** "St. Mary Lake" #1141

**NEW 606-103062** "Two Medicine Lake" #1142

## Illinois Central

Lightweight Coach-Car Shown Not Available

### Café-Bar-Lounge
**NEW 606-103029** #3341

**NEW 606-103030** #3344

**NEW 606-103031** #3345

### 10-5 Sleeper
**NEW 606-104047** "Decatur"

**NEW 606-104048** "Detrehan"

**NEW 606-104049** "Durant"

**NEW 606-104050** "Summit"

## Louisville & Nashville

### Café-Bar-Lounge
**NEW 606-103032** "Churchill Downs" #3000

**NEW 606-103033** "Carnival Club" #3001

**NEW 606-103034** "Belle Meade" #3002

### 10-5 Sleeper
**NEW 606-104051** "Alabama Pine"

**NEW 606-104052** "Curly Pine"

**NEW 606-104053** "Deep Woods Pine"

**NEW 606-104054** "Green Pine"

**NEW 606-104055** "Holiday Pine"

## Milwaukee Road 1950 Scheme

### Lightweight Coach
**NEW 606-100081** #543

**NEW 606-100082** #544

**NEW 606-100085** #547

### Duplex Sleeper
**NEW 606-101081** "Minnesota River"

**NEW 606-101082** "Zumbro River"

### Café-Bar-Lounge
**NEW 606-103035** #162

**NEW 606-103036** #165

## Milwaukee Road 1955 UP Scheme

### Duplex Sleeper
**NEW 606-101101** "Minnesota River"

**NEW 606-101102** "Zumbro River"

### Café-Bar-Lounge
**NEW 606-103037** #164

**NEW 606-103038** #167

Great Northern Lightweight Coach #1116 606-100032

Milwaukee Road 1950 Scheme Lightweight Coach #546 606-100084

## Missouri Pacific "Eagle" Scheme

### Lightweight Coach
**NEW 606-100220** #450 (T&P)

**NEW 606-100221** #451 (T&P)

**NEW 606-100222** #454 (T&P)

**NEW 606-100223** #459 (T&P)

**NEW 606-100224** #830 (MOPAC)

### Café-Bar-Lounge
**NEW 606-103063** #841 (MOPAC)

**NEW 606-103064** #842 (MOPAC)

**NEW 606-103065** #843 (MOPAC)

### 10-5 Sleeper
**NEW 606-104099** "Cascade Drive (B&O)"

**NEW 606-104100** "Cascade Sound (B&O)"

**NEW 606-104101** "Cascade Hollow (PRR)"

**NEW 606-104102** "Cascade Mantle (PRR)"

**NEW 606-104103** "Cascade Pinnacle (PRR)"

## Missouri Pacific "Jenks Blue"

### Café-Bar-Lounge
**NEW 606-103039** #571

**NEW 606-103040** #572

### 10-5 Sleeper
**NEW 606-104056** "Eagle Creek"

**NEW 606-104057** "Eagle Forest"

**NEW 606-104058** "Eagle Lake"

**NEW 606-104059** "Eagle Preserve"

**NEW 606-104060** "Eagle Valley"

## New York Central

### Café-Bar-Lounge
**NEW 606-103041** "Atlantic Shore"

**NEW 606-103042** "Lake Shore"

### 10-5 Sleeper
**NEW 606-104061** "Cascade Rainbow"

**NEW 606-104062** "Cascade Torrent"

**NEW 606-104063** "Cascade Crystals"

**NEW 606-104064** "Cascade Spray"

**NEW 606-104065** "Cascade Green"

## Norfolk & Western

### Lightweight Coach
**NEW 606-100225** #1720

**NEW 606-100226** #1721

**NEW 606-100227** #1728

**NEW 606-100228** #1731

**NEW 606-100229** #1732

### Café-Bar-Lounge
**NEW 606-103066** #1050

**NEW 606-103067** #1051

**NEW 606-103068** #1052

## Northern Pacific

### Lightweight Coach 49.95 ea
606-100037 #582

606-100040 #585

### Duplex Sleeper 49.95 ea
606-101036 #367

606-101037 #368

606-101038 #369

606-101039 #371

### Café-Bar-Lounge
**NEW 606-103043** "Holiday Lounge" #492

**NEW 606-103044** "Holiday Lounge" #493

### 10-5 Sleeper
**NEW 606-104066** #364

**NEW 606-104067** #365

## Pennsylvania Railroad

### Lightweight Coach
**NEW 606-100230** #3909

**NEW 606-100231** #3910

**NEW 606-100232** #3918

**NEW 606-100233** #3921

**NEW 606-100234** #3925

### Duplex Sleeper
**NEW 606-101111** "Center Creek"

**NEW 606-101112** "Chippewa Creek"

**NEW 606-101113** "College Creek"

**NEW 606-101114** "Country Creek"

**NEW 606-101115** "Crystal Creek"

### 10-5 Sleeper
**NEW 606-104070** "Cascade Ledge"

**NEW 606-104072** "Cascade Roar"

## Pullman Standard

### 10-5 Sleeper
**NEW 606-104073** "Cascade Banks"

**NEW 606-104074** "Cascade Basin"

**NEW 606-104075** "Cascade Mills"

**NEW 606-104076** "Cascade Shoals"

## Southern Pacific

Lightweight Coach-Car Shown Not Available

### Café-Bar-Lounge
**NEW 606-103048** #10316

**NEW 606-103049** #10317

### 10-5 Sleeper
**NEW 606-104077** #9202

**NEW 606-104078** #9203

**NEW 606-104079** #9205

**NEW 606-104080** #9209

**NEW 606-104081** #9210

VIA Rail Canada Duplex Sleeper "Exeter" 606-101010

## Union Pacific

Duplex Sleeper-Car Shown Not Available

### Café-Bar Lounge
**NEW 606-103050** #6201

**NEW 606-103051** #6204

**NEW 606-103052** #6205

### 10-5 Sleeper
**NEW 606-104082** "Imperial Cape"

**NEW 606-104083** "Imperial Flower"

**NEW 606-104086** "Imperial Palm"

**NEW 606-104087** "Imperial Sea"

**NEW 606-104088** "Imperial Star"

## VIA Rail Canada

### Lightweight Coach 49.95 ea
**606-100006** #5514

**606-100007** #5517

**606-100008** #5531

**606-100009** #5560

### Duplex Sleeper 49.95 ea
**606-101001** "Edgeley"

**606-101002** "Edmonton"

**606-101003** "Enfield"

**606-101004** "Enterprise"

**606-101005** "Erickson"

**606-101009** "Eldorado"

**606-101010** "Exeter"

### Café-Bar-Lounge
**NEW 606-103001** #2501

**NEW 606-103002** #2505

**NEW 606-103003** #2507

**NEW 606-103004** #2510

**NEW 606-103005** #2513

### 10-5 Sleeper
**NEW 606-104001** "Buckley Bay"

**NEW 606-104002** "Hudson Bay"

**NEW 606-104003** "Chaleur Bay"

**NEW 606-104004** "Glace Bay"

**NEW 606-104005** "Thunder Bay"

**NEW 606-104006** "Fortune Bay"

## Undecorated

### Lightweight Coach 49.95 ea
**606-100088** Fixed Steps

### Café-Bar-Lounge
**NEW 606-103053** Fixed Steps

**NEW 606-103054** Partial Skirts

### 10-5 Sleeper
**NEW 606-104084** Fixed Steps

**NEW 606-104085** Partial Skirts

## REPLACEMENT LIGHTING BATTERIES

**606-102000 11.95**

## SP MORNING "DAYLIGHT" STREAMLINED CARS

Patterned after cars from SP's flagship train between Los Angeles and San Francisco, the "Daylight" was called by some "The most beautiful train in the world." These replicas feature authentic design and accurate color schemes. ABS plastic bodies feature plenty of applied details including antennae and cars feature properly colored detailed interiors. Operating details include working exterior lighting where applicable, sprung diaphragms and working drumhead and markers on the observation car. Cars feature Kadee®-compatible knuckle couplers and will operate on Code 70 or larger rail and 22" radius or larger curves. Cars are an ideal match for PCM SP GS-4 and Alco PA/PB locomotives.

**588-680** Baggage-Chair #3302 w/Antenna **74.99**

**588-681** Articulated Chair W #2462 & Chair M #2461 w/Antenna **134.99**

**588-682** Articulated Chair W #2474 & Chair M #2473 w/Antenna **134.99**

**588-683** Chair #2485 **69.99**

**588-684** Parlor #3002 **69.99**

**588-685** Parlor-Observation #2954 w/Antenna **89.99**

**588-686** Articulated Coffee Shop #10258, Kitchen #10257 & Diner #10256 **189.99**

**588-687** Tavern #10314 w/Antenna **74.99**

**588-688** Articulated Chair W #2548 & Chair M #2457 **134.99**

**588-689** Articulated Chair W #2460 & Chair M #2459 **134.99**

**588-690** Baggage-Chair #3303 **74.99**

**588-691** Articulated Chair W #2470 & Chair M #2469 **134.99**

**588-692** Articulated Chair W #2476 & Chair M #2475 **134.99**

**588-693** Chair #2486 **69.99**

**588-694** Parlor #3003 **69.99**

**588-695** Parlor-Observation #2955 **89.99**

**588-696** Articulated Coffee Shop #10261, Kitchen #1026 & Diner #10259 **189.99**

**588-697** Tavern #10315 w/Antenna **74.99**

**588-698** Articulated Chair W #2466 & Chair M #2465 **134.99**

**588-699** Articulated Chair W #2468 & Chair M #2467 **134.99**

Chair #2485 588-683

Tavern #10315 w/Antenna 588-697

Transform your streamlined car fleet with these interior fittings based on actual equipment used by major car builders. All parts are highly detailed and molded in gray plastic for ease in painting. Kits include detailed assembly and painting instructions, a parts identification guide that also lists the correct time frame when the items were in use and prototype photos.

## COACH & CHAIR CAR SEATING

**630-111001** Coach & Car Equipment Co #829; Heywood Wakefield 981-129-ES pkg(24) **12.95**
Standard equipment for the New York Central and many other roads, these seats were used by Budd, Pullman-Standard and American Car & Foundry (ACF) on various new cars. Parts are correct for Eastern Car Works and Rivarossi Budd coaches, as well as all brass cars and feature adjustable back and footrests.

**630-112001** S. Karpen & Brothers #A4081-2 pkg(24) **12.95**
This style of seat was the standard for Santa Fe cars and was also used on cars assigned to Union Pacific's "Overland." Cars built by ACF, Budd, Pullman-Standard and St. Louis Car Company in the mid-1950s also used these seats. Designed for use with American Model Builders 5400-Series Union Pacific Coaches, Rivarossi 44-Seat Coaches and all brass models. Like the prototypes, these parts feature adjustable back, leg and footrests.

## PARLOR CHAIRS

Kits include complete instructions covering assembly and painting (including suggested paint numbers) plus prototype history and photos.

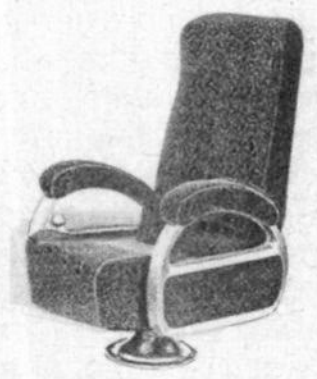

**630-131** Heywood Wakefield #981P pkg(24) **10.95**
Models can be rotated and include adjustable back and leg rests.

**630-133** pkg(24) **10.95**
Kits feature prototype style bases and can be rotated just like the real thing.

## LOUNGE CAR FURNISHINGS

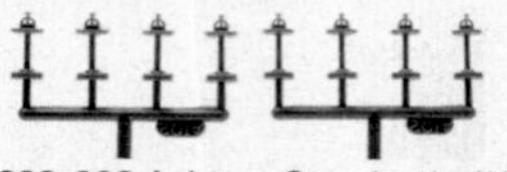

**630-308** Ashtray Stands pkg(8) **2.95**

**630-311** Heywood Wakefield #630P Chairs pkg(12) **5.95**
Installed on cars used on the SP "Daylight," CNW "400," UP "Overland" and "Cities" trains, as well as by the MP, GN, SP&S, IC and most other roads.

Coach Interior 630-100

**630-312** Heywood Wakefield #630P-2 Sofa pkg(6) **5.95**
Installed on cars used on the SP "Daylight," CNW "400," UP "Overland" and "Cities" trains, as well as by the MP, GN, SP&S, IC and most other roads.

**630-314** Heywood Wakefield #635P Seats pkg(6) **5.95**
This type of seat was installed on cars used with the SP "Daylight," CNW "400," UP "Overland" and "Cities" trains, as well as by the MP, IC C&O and others.

**630-317** S. Karpen & Brothers #R-234 Club Lounge Chair **5.95**
This style of Pullman lounge/club chair was used on various trains, including those of the Santa Fe, New York Central and others.

Coach Interior Detail 630-100

## HEYWOOD WAKEFIELD "SLEEPY HOLLOW" CAR SEAT KITS

### #803 48-Seat Coaches/ Chair Cars pkg(24) 12.95 ea

Used by most railroads from 1947 on, this set provides accurate seating for a 48-seat coach or chair car. Kits can be built to match the 830 or 830C style seat and include bulkhead footrests. Complete instructions cover assembly and painting (including suggested paint numbers) and include prototype history and photos.

These seats are scale models of the prototype. For a proper fit and more realistic appearance inside plastic models with molded-on roofs and windows, the windows will need to be removed and replaced with Evergreen .005" or .010" clear styrene (sold separately).

**630-1130001** Gray
**630-1130002** Tan
**630-1130003** Blue
**630-1130004** Dark Blue
**630-1130005** Brown
**630-1130006** Pea Green

# UNIVERSAL PARTITION KITS

Add authentic interior detail to lightweight cars with these kits. Modular design allows you to re-create most prototype variations built for each car type. Kits include highly detailed plastic parts engineered to match the originals, which assemble like a plastic airplane or ship model. Complete instructions and HO Scale floor plans for both ready-to-run and car core kits are provided, along with information on car histories, numbers and in-service interior variations.

**630-100** Coach **16.95**
Builds various cars from 1937 to the 1970s including all chair cars, combines, parlor cars, some lounges (without a bar) and most original single-deck commuter cars. Use this kit to build coaches constructed from 1937 on for the ATSF, NP, GN, SP&S, SP, UP, NYC and PRR.

**630-200** Dining Car **TBA**
Models all dining cars from 1937 to the 1970s with (non-kitchen) refrigerator configurations, lockers and cabinets as built by Pullman-Standard, AC&F and St. Louis Car Co. for most railroads.

# RESTROOM DETAILS

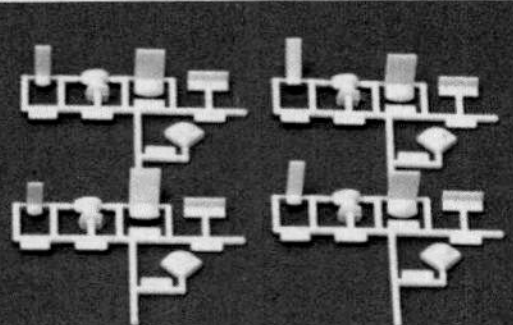

**630-123** Restroom Fixtures (16 Pieces) **3.95**
Includes four each straight sinks, corner sinks, dental bowl sinks and toilets.

**630-124** Complete Kit with Fixtures, Accessories & Mirrors **5.25**
Includes all fixtures found in Restroom Fixtures #630-123 (sold separately).

**630-125** Restroom w/Lounge **11.95**
Includes Karpen Bros. sofas, Mandrel Bros. women's lounge chairs, ashtray stands, and 12 various styles of mirrors.

**630-151** Restroom Sofas/ Modular Sofa pkg(3) **3.95**
Includes one restroom sofa for early stream or transition from heavyweights. Also includes modular sofas.

General Electric water cooler cup filling type, partition wall recessed trash and dixie cup No. 1970 dispenser.

**630-120** Free-Standing Water Coolers 1930s (Art Deco) to 60s pkg(7) **4.95**
Also used in stations and offices.

# VESTIBULE/ BLIND END DOORS

Designed to replace doors on ready to run plastic cars as well as those in car core kits. Doors are positionable and include different detail on both sides including kickplates, hardware and more. Each comes with laser-cut windows and no gluing is required.

## 060 Series Doors - Latch Lock w/Twist or Push-Pull Hardware 3.95 ea

### Square Oblong Window

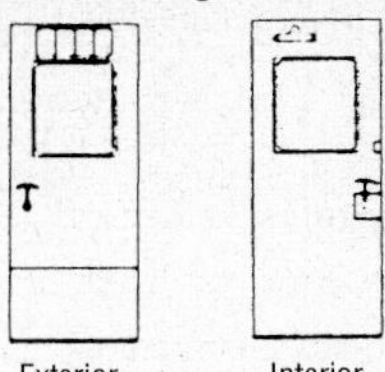


**630-6001** Large Numberboard pkg(2)
Used 1937-50 by Pullman-Standard (P-S), similar to early American Car & Foundry (ACF) and Budd Co. types.

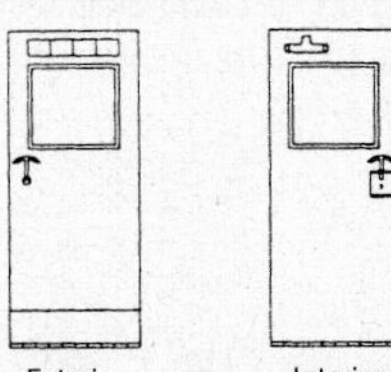


**630-6003** Small Numberboard pkg(2)
Used in the 1940s by P-S, similar to ACF type.

### Large Round Windows

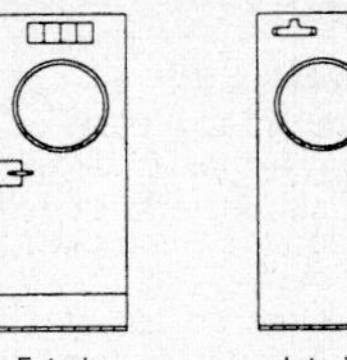


**630-6006** Milwaukee Road Shops pkg(2)
Features exterior twist handle with latch and interior twist handle with mounting plate, lock and pneumatic door closer.

### Small Round Windows

Used 1937-mid 40s by Pullman-Standard on UP, PRR, SP and other cars.

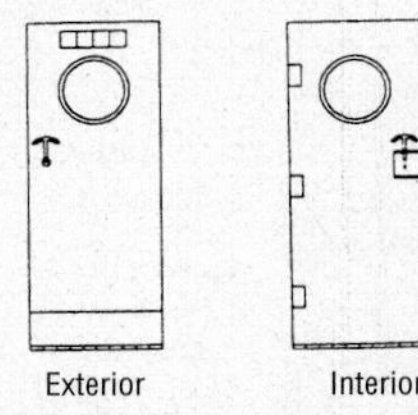


**630-6004** Sliding Door Lock pkg(2)

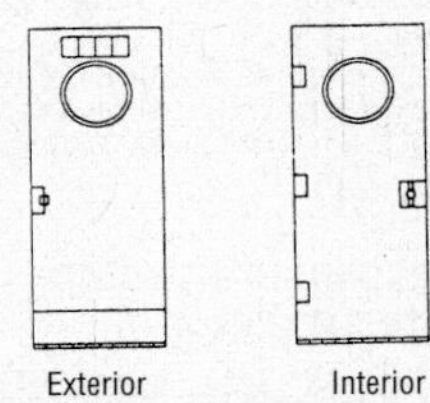


**630-6005** Door Lock & Latch pkg(2)

### No Windows

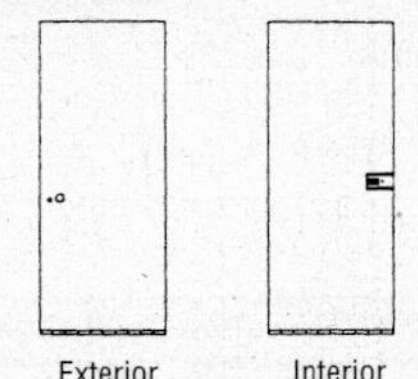


**630-6002** pkg(2)
For combine or baggage cars built from early 1930s to 1960s. Features simulated Adlake hardware.

## 061 Series Doors w/Pushbars 3.95 ea

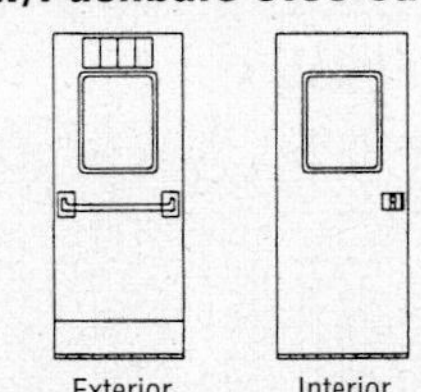


**630-6101** Oblong Windows pkg(2)
Typical style for P-S and AC&F cars with exterior pushbar and interior latch handle.

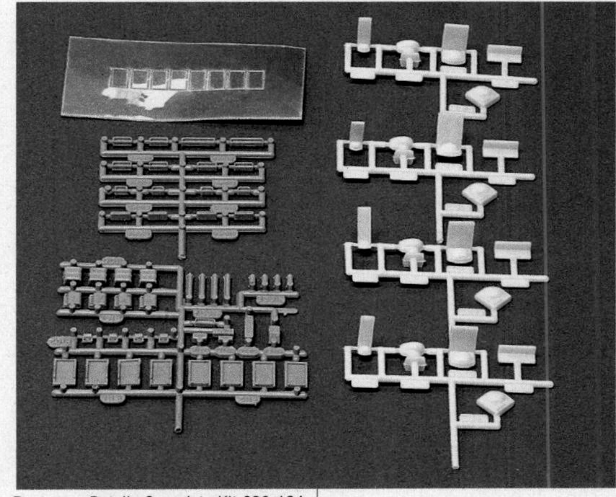

Restroom Details Complete Kit 630-124

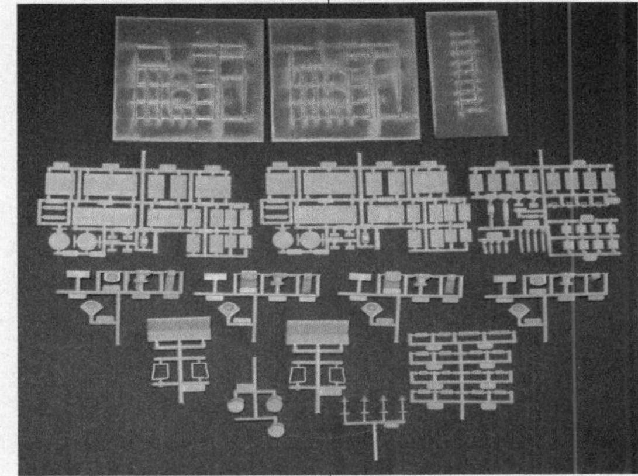

Restroom w/Lounge 630-125

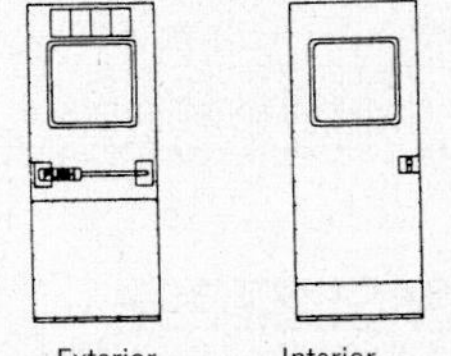


**630-6102** Oblong Thermo-pane Window pkg(2)
Used on Budd cars built from 1946 to the 50s with exterior "PUSH" tab on bar and turning handle on interior.

**630-6103** Oblong Windows pkg(2)
Used on P-S "American Flyer Cars" from 1948-50 with pneumatic exterior pushbar and interior latch pull handle.



## 62 Series Air-Activated Sliding Doors 3.95 ea

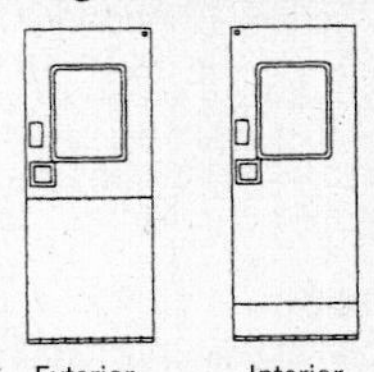


**630-6201** Oblong Thermopane Windows pkg(2)
Used on P-S and ACF cars in the 1950s.

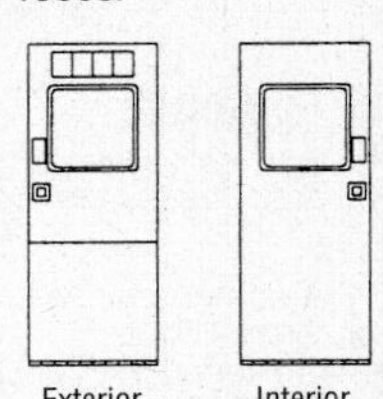


**630-6202** Square Thermo-pane Windows pkg(2)
Used on Budd cars in the 1950s.

All products made in the USA.

# NEW PRODUCTS

## Passenger Car Interiors

### UP Dome Diner

Interiors fit Dome Diner 932-871, sold separately.

**NEW 732-9666** Main Level Only (Not Dome Area) **33.95**

**NEW 732-9667** Dome Dining Area Only **21.95**

**NEW 732-9668** Main Level & Dome Dining Area Combo **49.95**

### Dome Car Upgrade Kit

**NEW 732-513** For Rivarossi/ AHM Dome Coach **18.95**
Includes truck sideframes, coupler drawbars, end door gates, interior bulkhead walls, underbody details and more. All parts are injection-molded plastic.

# BUDD HI-LEVEL PASSENGER CARS

Introduced on Santa Fe's "El Capitan" in 1956, these streamlined, hi-level cars were later acquired by Amtrak®. Easy-to-build kits feature plastic bodies and are available undecorated (correct for ATSF or Amtrak schemes) or as ATSF cars, painted silver with black lettering. Models are also offered with blackened brass wheelsets as noted.

### Coach

**732-820** Less Couplers & Wheels **25.95**

**732-822** ATSF w/Blackened Wheels **32.95**

**732-802** Undecorated Body **10.95**

### Step-Up Coach

These cars were used between conventional equipment and hi-level cars.

**732-434** Amtrak Hi-Level Coach-Dorm Window Inserts/Amfleet Style Window Frames **4.95**
Converts Train Station Products/Detail Associates High-Level, Step-Up Coach to a modern Amtrak Hi-Level Coach-Dorm.

**732-810** Less Couplers & Wheels **25.95**

**732-811** Painted Silver w/Blackened Wheels **29.95**

**732-812** ATSF w/Blackened Wheels **32.95**

**732-818** Unpainted Amtrak Remodeled Coach-Dorm **29.95**

**732-801** Undecorated Body **10.95**

### Diner

**732-830** Less Couplers & Wheels **25.95**

**732-831** Painted Silver w/Blackened Wheels **32.95**

**732-832** ATSF w/Blackened Wheels **35.95**

**732-803** Undecorated Body **10.95**

# THEATER INSPECTION CARS

**732-860** BN Theatre (Glacier View) **49.95**

**732-861** BNSF Theatre (Fluted Sides, Glacier View) **59.95**

# DOME DINER

**732-871** UP Dome **49.95**

# BAGGAGE CAR

**732-870** Amtrak® 50' Short Baggage **59.95**
Based on a United States Army kitchen car, this kit includes everything except couplers and superdetailing items.

# PASSENGER CAR PARTS

## Detail Kits

### Walthers Amtrak 1700 Series Baggage Car

**732-454 14.95**
Now with correct Budd ends. Includes 9' wheel base outside swing hanger trucks, tubular diaphragms and end gates.

### Passenger Car Parts

Includes air condition units, water tanks, wheel generators, battery and propane tank holders, among others.

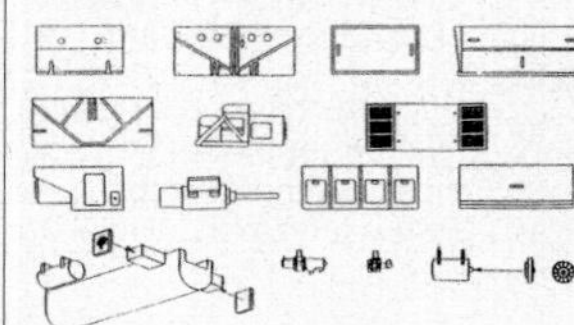

Not all parts in kit shown

**732-460 12.95**

**732-461** With 85' Frame/Floor **15.95**

## Material Handling Car Parts

### Conversion Kit

**732-440** MHC II **10.95**
Modernizes the Con-Cor Material Handling Car from the MHC I to the current MHC II (1500 series) cars now in Amtrak service. Includes side ladders, door locking wheels and the correct GSI trucks. All parts are also sold separately.

### Individual Parts

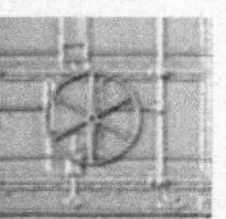

**732-441** Locking Wheels pkg(2) **3.95**
Now in use on MHC I (1400 series) and newer MHC II (1500 series) cars.

**732-442** Side Ladders pkg(4) **3.95**
Current style, now in use on most MHC I and MHC II cars.

**732-443** Ladder & Wheel Set **5.95**
Complete set of four ladders and two locking wheels, as used on MHC I and MHC II type cars.

## Passenger Car Core Kits 18.95 ea

**732-806** Budd Type Cars

**732-807** Pullman-Standard

**NEW 732-877** American Car & Foundry (ACF)

**732-492** Core Kit Sides Only .030" thick pkg(2) **8.95**
To be used with Train Station Products Core Kits #732-806 and 807. Also works with Athabasca, Brass Car Sides, Laser Horizons, Chicago Coach Works and NKP Car.

## Door Gates

**732-408** Passenger Car End pkg(4) **2.95**
Fits Con-Cor, AHM, Rivarossi, Walthers, Athearn, brass and other passenger cars. Two each of two basic styles of gates are included.

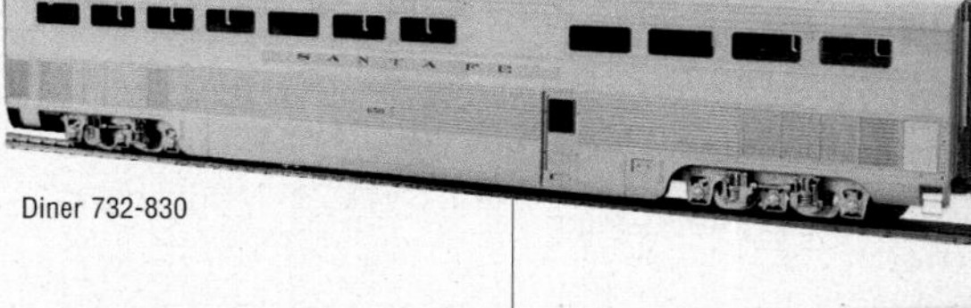

Step-Up Coach 732-812
Coach 732-822

Diner 732-830

Amtrak Coach Dorm 732-818

50' Amtrak Baggage Car 732-870; Prototype Photo Shown

## Diaphragms

Unpainted plastic parts, unless noted.

### Amfleet Style

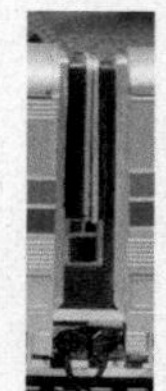

For Amfleet, Superliner I and II, Horizon, High-Level, Metroliner/Cab Control cars and some Heritage Fleet cars. Fits Train Station Products, Detail Associates, Con-Cor, Bachmann, Walthers and others.

**732-400** 1 Pair **3.95**

**732-401** 3 Pair **8.95**

### Hi-Level Style

A unique design, used on the Budd Hi-Level cars which operated on Santa Fe's "El Capitan," and were later acquired by Amtrak. Includes support bars and leaf springs.

**732-407** 1 Pair **2.95**

**732-452** Working 1 Pair **5.95**

### UP Style

For Con-Cor, AHM, Rivarossi, Athearn, brass and other models. Easily modified to make other styles. This diaphragm was installed on most of Union Pacific's modern passenger fleet and remained in use when the cars entered Amtrak service. Includes end gates, support bars and leaf springs.

**732-403** 1 Pair **3.95**

**732-404** 3 Pair **8.95**

**732-453** Working 1 Pair **5.95**

## Working Diaphragm Conversion Kit

**732-450** 1 Pair **4.95**
Converts Train Station Products diaphragms #732-403, 404, 406 and 407 into working or moveable diaphragms. Also works with Rivarossi or IHC diaphragms.

### Tubular Style

**732-405** 1 Pair **4.95**
For Con-Cor, AHM, Rivarossi, Athearn, brass and other models. This style of diaphragm is still in use on most privately owned cars and was found on many Amtrak Heritage Fleet cars.

### Standard Modern Style

Many railroads used this style of diaphragm, or a very similar style, on modern, streamlined cars. Subsequently, they could be found on much of Amtrak's Heritage Fleet. Includes support bars and leaf springs.

**732-406** 1 Pair **2.95**

**732-451** Working 1 Pair **5.95**

## Step Covers

**732-430** pkg(4) **2.95**
Fits Walthers Amtrak® Horizon Cars. Can be used on other passenger cars where a smooth step cover is needed.

## Air Conditioners

**732-468** Waukesha I.C.E **2.95**

**732-469** Frigidaire (ER3684/ER2810) **2.95**

**732-470** Frigidaire (ER7001/ER2914) **2.95**

**732-471** Safety Car Heating & Light **3.95**

**732-478** Belt Driven Passenger Car Air Conditioner w/etched see-thru belt guard pkg(4) **13.95**

**732-510** Roof Top pkg(4) **5.95**
For use with passenger cars, RVs & Passenger Engines

**NEW 732-511** ATSF-Style Steam Injection **8.95**

## Air Conditioner Compressors pkg(2) 3.95 ea

**732-472** Direct Drive - Safety Car Heating & Light

**732-473** Belt Driven

## Compressor Belt Guards

**732-479** pkg(4) **9.95**
See-through etched-metal parts are replicas of those used on belt-driven air conditioning compressors.

## Baggage Car Parts

### Doors

**732-505** Amtrak pkg(4) **6.95**
For Walthers 73' Budd Baggage Car

### End Doors

**732-507** pkg(2) **4.95**
For use with Train Station Products' Core Kits #732-806, 807 and 877.

### Upgrade Kit

**732-506** **18.95**
This kit enhances the realism and detail found in the Walthers Amtrak Budd 73' Baggage Car. The kit contains the detailed "Commonwealth" (41-N) trucks that run under these Budd cars along with the correct Budd ends with the proper gap in the roof, exterior brake wheel, end lights, and solid end doors. It also contains the correct tubular diaphragms found on these cars along with the 6'6" baggage doors that have a small single window as used by Amtrak when the baggage cars were refurbished. The correct paint scheme for these cars is Phase III or Phase IV.

## Battery Boxes 3.95 ea

**732-465** Budd Style pkg(5)

**732-476** Pullman-Standard/ American Car & Foundry pkg(6)

## Brake Equipment

**732-467** For 2 Passenger Cars **5.95**
Includes control relay, relay valve, combined and supply reservoirs.

## Engine Generators

**732-475** pkg(2) **2.95**

## Equipment/Control Box

**732-477** pkg(2) **3.95**

## Propane Fuel Carriers

**732-464** pkg(6) **3.95**
Four of one style, two of another.

## Water Tanks

**732-466** pkg(6) **4.95**
Includes two tanks with side fills and side fill plates and two water-raising reservoirs.

## Waukesha Enginators

**732-474** pkg(2) **5.95**

## Wheel Generator

**732-463** Belt-Driven Wheel Generator **2.95**
Includes generator, pulley and belt, and guard.

## Cable Ducts

**732-486** 170' (Fits 2 85' Cars) **2.95**
These rooftop cable ducts were used on streamline passenger cars run by Amtrak, Union Pacific and other railroads.

## Car Ends

**732-480** Budd pkg(2) **5.95**
Also comes with two end door face plates.

**732-482** Pullman-Standard/ American Car & Foundry pkg(2) **5.95**
End doors are not molded in.

**732-489** St. Louis pkg(2) **12.95**
End doors are not molded in.

**732-493** BN Theatre Car End **9.95**

**732-494** Theatre/Track Inspection Car End **8.95**

## End Doors

**732-491** For ACF Cars as used by the Union Pacific pkg(4) **5.95**
These doors are designed to be used with Train Station Products' Core Kits #732-806 and 807. Also works with Rivarossi, Walthers, and other manufacturers' passenger cars.

**732-508** For ACF Cars as used by the Union Pacific **4.95**
These are the same doors as found in Kit #491, but they are wider to fit Train Station Products diaphragm frame.

## End Roof Sections

### Boat-Tail Observation Car 10.95 ea

To be used with Train Station Products Budd or Pullman-Standard passenger car Core Kits or Eastern Car Works Core Kit.

**732-500** Plain - No End Light

**732-501** With Large End Light

**732-502** With Small End Light

**732-503** NYC w/Small Light & Roof Vent

### Blunt End Observation Car

**732-504** 4' Long **10.95**

## End Windows

**732-509** Large Picture Window **3.95**
For use with Theater/Track Passenger Cars Kits #492, 493, 860 and 861

## Grilles

**732-438** pkg(4) **3.95**
Can be used on Walthers and Three Brothers bi-level commuter car side vents, on passenger car skirts, or as a see-through roof vent. Two each of two different sizes.

## Interior Kits

**732-9611** Budd "El Capitan" Hi-Level Car Step-Up/Step-Down Passenger Chair Car **23.95**
Includes an upper level floor, two stairways with one water dispenser, and seats for the 68-seat chair car.

**732-9612** Budd "El Capitan" Hi-Level Car 72-Seat Passenger Chair Kit **19.95**
Includes an upper level floor, one stairway with a water dispenser, and seats for the 72-seat chair car.

**732-9663** Budd "El Capitan" Hi-Level Dining Car **29.00**

**732-9690** For Budd BN or BNSF Theater Passenger cars **38.95**

## Marker Lights

**732-488** End Mounted pkg(8) **3.95**
Non-working lights that are used on the ends of the modern (1930s to present) passenger cars. Two lights used on each end.

## Lift Rings

**732-496** pkg(12) **4.95**

## Roofs 5.95 ea

**732-481** 85' Budd Car

**732-483** Pullman-Standard

**732-484** American Car & Foundry/Pullman Standard

## Vestibule Partition & End Doors

**732-485** **5.95**
Includes four separate different style end doors (including a set of baggage car end doors).

## Exhaust Pipes

**732-431** pkg(4) **2.95**
Fits Train Station Products/ Detail Associates Budd "El Capitan" Hi-Level passenger cars.

## Hi-Level Transition Top

**732-805** **10.95**
For roof of baggage-dorm on Santa Fe "El Capitan" passenger train.

## Wheel Recorders

**732-432** Decelostats pkg(8) **3.95**
Fits journal covers of Train Station Products/Detail Associates Outside Swing Hanger Passenger Car Trucks. Used by UP, ATSF and others.

## Window Inserts

**732-433** Superliner II Sleeping Car **2.95**

## Roof Vents

**732-435** Rectangular Wire Screen pkg(12) **3.95**
Commonly used on most modern Budd passenger cars. Enough parts for two or three cars, depending on number of prototype vents.

**732-448** Pullman Standard/American Car Foundry pkg(12) **4.95**

**732-498** Pullman Standard pkg(6) **4.95**

## Stirrup Steps

**732-436** pkg(12) **2.95**
Same parts as used on Train Station High-Level cars. Same style is used on prototype Budd and other cars.

**732-487** 6' Stirrup Steps pkg(8) **3.95**
Used on the sides of some baggage cars. Can be cut into 2' or 4' steps for dining car or lounge car use.

### Truck Mounting Posts

**732-439** pkg(4) **3.95**
Fits Train Station Products, Rivarossi, Con-Cor and other trucks to the floor/frame of a car. Enough parts for two cars.

### Underframe/Floor

**732-800** 85' **5.95**
Same parts used in Train Station Products/Detail Associates High-Level Car kits. Suitable for scratchbuilding.

### Passenger Trucks

#### Superliner I 1 Pair 8.95 ea (Unless Noted)

Accepts Con-Cor, Kadee® or Jay-Bee 36" wheelsets.

**732-410** Con-Cor
Coupler pocket accepts most couplers.

**732-411** Original Style w/Pneumatic Air Springs, Without Wheelsets

**732-412** Original Style w/Pneumatic Air Springs. For Walthers Superliner Cars

**732-413** Current Style Fits Walthers Superliner I

#### Superliner II 1 Pair 8.95 ea

Accepts Con-Cor, Jay-Bee and Kadee 36" wheelsets.

**732-422** Con-Cor
Coupler pockets accept Intermountain, McHenry or Kadee #5 couplers.

**732-423** Fits Walthers Superliner Cars

#### Commonwealth

Fits Train Station Products, Athabasca, AMB Laser Kits, NKP Car, Rivarossi, Concord Junction, Con-Cor, Athearn, AHM, IHC and other passenger cars. Accepts Jay-Bee, Northwest Short Line, Intermountain, Kadee and other wheelsets.

**732-427** 41-N Without Wheelsets **9.95**

**732-428** 41-N w/Metal Wheelsets **16.95**

**732-429** 41-NV Without Wheelsets 10.95

#### Disc Brake 8'-6" 41-ND or 41-DN

Fits Train Station Products, Athabasca, AMB Laser Kits, Rivarossi, NKP Car, Concord Junction, Athearn, Con-Cor, AHM, IHC and others.

**732-455** No Wheelsets Pair **9.95**

**732-456** With Metal Wheelsets Pair **16.95**

#### PRR 41-NP Trucks

**732-457** No Wheelsets Pair **9.95**

#### Ex-Army Kitchen Car Trucks

**732-458** 6'-6" Wheelbase With Metal Wheelsets Pair **16.95**
Used under Army Kitchen Cars, these trucks feature clasp brake detail, exposed roller bearings and vertical struts as applied by Amtrak when the cars were converted into the "shorty" baggage cars in the 1970s.

#### GSI Roller Bearing

**732-420** 1 Pair **8.95**
For Amtrak Horizon Passenger Cars. Fits Walthers and other passenger cars.

#### Modern Six-Wheel Passenger Cars Without Wheelsets

Accepts Con-Cor, Jay-Bee and Kadee 36" wheelsets. Coupler pockets accept Intermountain, McHenry or Kadee #5 couplers.

**732-424** UP **10.95**

**732-425** UP (silver) **11.95**

**732-426** ATSF **10.95**

#### Outside Swing Hanger

**732-414** 41-CUDO 1 Pair **9.95**
Used by Amtrak, UP, ATSF and others. Fits Rivarossi, Con-Cor, AHM, Athearn and other cars. Accepts Kadee, Con-Cor and Jay-Bee 36" wheelsets. Coupler pocket accepts Intermountain or Kadee® No. 5 couplers.

**732-415** 41-CUDO With Blackened 36" Brass Wheelsets 1 Pair **16.95**

**732-418** 41-CUDO Fits Walthers Passenger Cars **10.95**

**732-419** 41-BNO w/Clasp Brake Shoes & External Cylinders 1 Pair **11.95**

### Truck Parts

**732-402** Mounting Screws pkg(12) **4.95**

**732-409** Truck Bolster w/Coupler Boxes pkg(4) **5.95**

**732-416** Bolster Anchors & Timkin Wheel Journal Covers **4.95**

**732-437** Passenger Car Brake Cylinders & Adjusters pkg(12) **4.95**

**732-490** Truck Bolsters pkg(4) **4.95**
Must use European NEM (0.970" long) axles.

**732-495** Bolster Mounting Plates pkg(4) **5.95**
Fits Train Station Products passenger car frame/floor so that shorter passenger cars can be built and modeler can decrease distance between the trucks. Mounting plates are notched to fit the center sill.

#### Brake Cylinders

**732-445** With Short Pistons **3.95**
For mounting on passenger car trucks.

#### Brake Cylinder/Slack Adjuster Units

**732-444** Two Each Right and Left; Enough For 1 Car **3.95**

#### Springs

Four each left and right for outside swing hanger trucks.

**732-446** With Bolster Anchor pkg(8) **4.95**

**732-447** pkg(8) **3.95**



## TOMAR INDUSTRIES

### LIGHTED DRUMHEAD KITS

Drumhead kits include illustrated instructions, cast and machined housing, 1.5V micro-miniature lamp, full-color sign, light diffuser and constant lighting components (four diodes, ballast lamp and hookup wire) which operate from track power. (Cars may require modification to provide electrical pick-up.) Kits can also be battery powered using #81-812, (sold separately). For a complete listing of both varieties of drumhead kits, visit Walthers web site at www.walthers.com.

### ACCESSORIES

#### Battery Power Hook-Up Kit

**81-812 3.60**
Use wherever 1.5V is needed. Ideal for drumheads, markers, etc. Fits inside most HO or larger cars. Includes AA battery holder (less battery), micro-switch and wire.

#### Pick-Up Shoes

Preformed metal shoes for better electrical pick-up.

**81-801** Constant Intensity Light **3.60**
Includes 14V ballast lamp, four diodes and hook-up wire. Powers up to four 1.5V lamps from track power.

**81-816** Ballast Bulb pkg(2) **1.60**
Replacement for Constant Intensity Light #81-801, sold separately.

**81-802** Micro Miniature Slide Switch pkg(2) **2.90**
Very small SPDT switch.

**81-804** Passenger Car pkg(4) **4.50**
Includes drawings, wire, instructions and screws.

**81-805** Loco pkg(4) **4.50**
Includes drawings, wire, instructions and screws.

#### Bulk Packs pkg(8) 3.60 ea

With shoes only. Less hardware and instructions.

**81-814** Passenger & Caboose

**81-815** Locomotive Only

#### Axialight Lamp

**81-820** 1.5V Clear pkg(2) **3.80**
Very small size, ideal for limited space.

#### End-Of-Train Device 13.95 ea

**81-806** Amber

**81-822** Red

**81-819** 1.5V Lamps pkg(2) **5.5**
Replacement bulbs for #81-806 or #81-822, each sol separately.

#### Adlake Marker Lights 14.60 ea

**81-807** Green & Red

**81-809** Yellow & Red

#### Replacement Lamps

**81-818** Adlake Replacement Lamps pkg(2) **5.50**
1.5V bulbs for #81-807 or #81 809, also fits all drumheads.

**81-813** Red Tail Light Kit **4.15**
Includes 1.5V red lamp and instructions.

### CATALOG

For a free copy of the latest catalog, please write Tomar at 9520 E. Napier Ave., Benton Harbor, MI 49022

# FREIGHT

Models and Photo by Alex Mantle

Looks like those guys on the F7 will be springing for lunch again! While they're good engines in every respect, trying to see out the cab when you're backing up is not as easy as it sounds. A quick call to the local café confirms today's specials are to everyone's liking. A little discussion about picking up the check and the switch crew will be happy to pull and spot empties for the through freight.

Before that happens however, there are a few additional cars that need to be spotted over at the Continental Foods warehouse along Alex Mantle's Chicago, Denver & Northern in Buffalo, Wyoming. All of the engines and rolling stock are detailed, painted and decaled Athearn equipment. The warehouse was kitbashed from a Pikestuff engine house kit, while the nearby billboard is a Bar Mills model. Woodland Scenics materials were used to complete the scene, with Walthers code 83 track on the mainline and Shinohara code 70 on the sidings.

Freight pays the bills on virtually every railroad from tiny narrow gauge shortline to contemporary class one. Finding the right cars to serve customers along your railroad is fast and fun - check out the many selections on the following pages!

# WALTHERS

## PLATINUM LINE™ CABOOSES

### Platinum Line features:

- Fully assembled, ready to run
- All grab irons installed; including handrails
- All detail parts added
- Detailed interiors
- Metal wheelsets
- Knuckle couplers
- Superb paint and lettering
- Singles and 2-packs offer three different roadnumbers

### Pennsylvania Center-Cupola N6B Wood Cabin Car

COMING SOON!

**Winter 2007-08 Delivery**

- New Centered-Cupola Version
- Authentic Pennsylvania Prototype
- Perfect for Steam- and Diesel-Era Layouts
- Sloped-Side Cupola
- Correct Trucks
- Use w/932-7640-Series w/Offset Cupola

**Single Cars 34.98 ea**

**NEW 932-7651** Roman Lettering & Bars

**NEW 932-7652** Keystone at Top

**NEW 932-7653** Keystone in Middle

**NEW 932-7650** Undecorated Kit - Some Assembly Required*

**Limited-Run 2-Packs 69.98 ea**

**NEW 932-27651** Roman Lettering & Bars

**NEW 932-27652** Keystone at Top

**NEW 932-27653** Keystone in Middle

932-7651 Roman Lettering & Bars

932-7652 Keystone at Top

932-7653 Keystone in Middle

### Milwaukee Road Rib-Side Caboose

COMING SOON!

**Winter 2007-08 Delivery**

- Authentic Milwaukee Road Prototype
- All-New Car – First Ever Ready-to-Run Version
- Used System-wide from 1939-80s
- Roof-Mounted Lantern Smokejack
- Side-Mounted Tool Box

**Single Cars 34.98 ea**

**NEW 932-7661** Lettered

**NEW 932-7662** Herald on Bay Window

**NEW 932-7663** 70s-Era Scheme

**NEW 932-7660** Undecorated Kit - Some Assembly Required*

**Limited-Run 2-Packs 69.98 ea**

**NEW 932-27661** Lettered

**NEW 932-27662** Herald on Bay Window

**NEW 932-27663** 70s-Era Scheme

932-7661 Full Name

932-7662 Early Herald

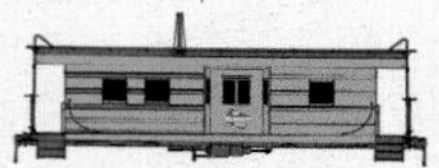
932-7663 1970s Herald

*PLEASE NOTE: For easier customizing, all undecorated versions include modeler-installed grab irons and details - some assembly is required.

### Milwaukee Road Caboose Rigid Truck

COMING SOON!

**Winter 2007-08 Delivery**

**NEW 933-1322** 1 Pair **9.98**

- Authentic MILW Design
- Matches 932-7660-Series Models

### Steel Bay Window Caboose

- Roadname-specific detailing
- Three different roof and bay window styles
- Three different ends

PRR Center-Cupola N6B Wood Cabin Car
Image courtesy of Robert Johnson

MILW Rib-Side Caboose 932-7661

Steel Bay Window Caboose
RI 932-7630

Steel Bay Window Caboose
P&LE 932-7631

**Single Cars 31.98 ea**

**932-7621** MILW

**932-7622** CR

**932-7623** CNW†

**932-7624** UP†

**932-7625** Green Bay & Western

**932-7626** ATSF

**932-7627** BN

**932-7628** B&O/Chessie

**932-7629** PC

**932-7630** RI

**932-7631** Pittsburgh & Lake Erie

**932-7632** MILW

**932-7633** SOO

**932-7620** Undecorated (CNW† Version) - Some Assembly Required*

**932-7638** Undecorated (MILW Version) - Some Assembly Required*

**932-7639** Undecorated (Penn Central Version) - Some Assembly Required*

**Limited Quantity Available**

**Limited-Run 2-Packs 54.98 ea**

**932-27626** ATSF

**932-27627** BN

**932-27628** B&O/Chessie

**932-27629** PC

**932-27630** RI

**932-27631** Pittsburgh & Lake Erie

†Union Pacific licensed product.

# WALTHERS

## PLATINUM LINE™ CABOOSES

### PRR N6B Wood Cabin Car 34.98 ea

- All-new tooling
- Authentic PRR prototype

**932-7641** PRR

**932-7642** PRR

**932-7643** PRR

**932-7640** Undecorated*

932-7641 PRR

932-7642 PRR

932-7643 PRR

### 30' 3-Window Wood Caboose w/Offset Cupola 29.98 ea

- Based on Grand Trunk Western prototype
- Classic offset cupola design
- Similar cars used by many roads

**932-7515** DRGW[†]

**932-7516** GN

**932-7517** GTW

**932-7518** CN

932-7515 DRGW

932-7516 GN

932-7517 Grand Trunk Western

932-7518 CN

*PLEASE NOTE: For easier customizing, all undecorated versions include modeler-installed grab irons and details - some assembly is required.

### SP[†] Class C-30-1 Wood Caboose 34.98 ea

- Used from 1917 through the 1960s
- Three authentic lettering schemes

**932-7608** Roman with Bars

**932-7609** Modern Gothic

**932-7610** Radio Equipped

**932-7611** Roman, No Bars

**932-7612** Roman w/Bars

**932-7613** Gothic

932-7611 Roman, No Bars

932-7612 Roman w/Bars

932-7613 Gothic

### 25' Wood Caboose – C&O Style 34.98 ea

- Introduced in 1924
- Correct 3-window cupola
- Choose steam- or diesel-era schemes

**932-7527** C&O (red)

**932-7528** C&O (red, "Progress")

**932-7529** C&O (yellow, "Progress")

**932-7530** B&O

932-7527 C&O

932-7528 C&O

932-7529 C&O

932-7530 B&O



### ATSF 1300-Series Wood Caboose 34.98 ea

- In service from 1923 to the 1960s
- Prototypical window arrangement
- Authentic lettering schemes from different eras

**932-7584** A.T.&S.F.

**932-7585** A.T.S.F.

**932-7586** ATSF

932-7585 A.T.S.F.

932-7586 ATSF

### Four-Window Wood Caboose 29.98 ea

- Served from 1900s to the 70s
- Similar cars used by CNW

**932-7569** CB&Q (Caboose Red)

**932-7570** CB&Q (Box Car Red)

**932-7571** BN

**932-7572** CNW[†]

932-7569 CB&Q

932-7570 CB&Q

932-7571 BN

932-7572 CNW

Platinum 30' Wood Caboose GN 932-7516

Platinum ATSF Wood Caboose A.T.&S.F. 932-7584

Platinum Four-Window Wood Caboose CNW 932-7572

Platinum 25' Wood Caboose B&O 932-7530

Platinum PRR N6B Wood Cabin PRR 932-7641

# WALTHERS

## GOLD LINE™ CABOOSES

A high-quality caboose designed for the modeler who enjoys superdetailing.

**Gold Line features:**

- Fully assembled, ready to run
- Includes modeler-applied wire grab irons
- Molded starter points simplify drilling
- Detailed interiors
- Separately applied "wood" roofwalks, window glazing and molded end ladders
- Metal wheelsets
- Knuckle couplers
- Superb paint and lettering
- Singles and 2-packs offer three different roadnumbers

### SP† Class C-30-1 Wood Caboose

**Single Cars 24.98 ea**

**932-7605** Northwestern Pacific

**932-7606** SP (no bars over roadname)

**932-7607** SP (w/"Radio-Equipped" Logo)

**Limited-Run 2-Packs 49.98 ea**

**932-27606** SP (no bars over roadname)

**932-27607** SP (w/"Radio-Equipped" Logo)

### ATSF 1300-Series Wood Caboose

**Single Cars 24.98 ea**

**932-7581** A.T.&S.F.

**932-7582** A.T.S.F.

**932-7583** ATSF

**932-7580** Undecorated

**Limited-Run 2-Packs 49.98 ea**

**932-27581** A.T.&S.F.

**932-27582** A.T.S.F.

**932-27583** ATSF

SP C-30-1 Wood Caboose NWP 932-7605

SP C-30-1 Wood Caboose 932-7606

ATSF 1300-Series Wood Caboose 932-7582

## GOLD LINE™ FREIGHT CARS

**Gold Line features:**

- Better operation
- Enhanced appearance
- Assembled, ready to run
- Includes modeler-applied wire grab irons on select models
- Molded starter points simplify drilling
- Metal wheelsets
- Knuckle couplers
- Superb paint and lettering

## BOX CARS

### Thrall 56' All-Door Box Car

- For post-60s lumber fleets

**Single Cars 21.98 ea**

**932-7026** Lignum

**932-7027** Netherlands Overseas

**932-7028** Canfor (red, white)

**932-7029** FURX

**932-7030** Thrall Demonstrator

**932-7031** Spokane Moulding

**932-7032** Chandler

**932-7033** St. Regis

**932-7034** McMillan-Bloedell

**Limited-Run 2-Packs 39.98 ea**

**932-27031** Spokane Moulding

**932-27032** Chandler

**932-27033** St. Regis

**932-27034** McMillan-Bloedell

### 50' Gunderson Hi-Cube Paper Service Box Car

- Separate door details
- End ladders & brake platform
- Detailed underframe

**Single Cars 19.98 ea**

**932-7101** BN

**932-7106** CN

**932-7117** McCloud River

**932-7118** WC #2

**932-7119** Arkansas-Oklahoma (AOK)

**932-7120** Northwestern Oklahoma (NOKL) #2

**932-7121** CN (CNA)

**Limited-Run 2-Packs 37.98 ea**

**932-27117** McCloud River

**932-27119** Arkansas-Oklahoma (AOK)

**932-27120** Northwestern Oklahoma (NOKL) #2

**932-27121** CN (CNA)

Thrall 56' All-Door Box Car Spokane Moulding 932-7031

Thrall 56' All-Door Box Car Chandler 932-7032

50' Gunderson Hi-Cube Paper Service Box Car NOKL 932-7120

50' Gunderson Hi-Cube Paper Service Box Car AOK 932-7119

# WALTHERS

## GOLD LINE™ FREIGHT CARS

### PRR X-29 Box Car 3-Pack

- Three authentic paint schemes
- A must for steam- or classic diesel-era fleets

**932-9023** PRR (Three schemes) **44.98**

### Pullman-Standard 60' Single-Door Auto Parts Box Car

- Revised Tooling
- Great for Post-60s Layouts

**Single Cars 21.98 ea**

**932-35511** UP†
**932-35512** ATSF
**932-35513** BNSF
**932-35514** CSX
**932-35515** NYC
**932-35516** CR
**932-35510** Undecorated

**Limited-Run 2-Packs 41.98 ea**

**932-235511** UP†
**932-235512** ATSF
**932-235513** BNSF
**932-235514** CSX
**932-235515** NYC
**932-235516** CR

932-35511 UP

932-35512 ATSF

932-35513 BNSF

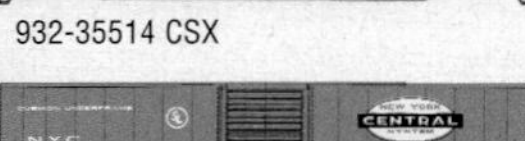
932-35514 CSX

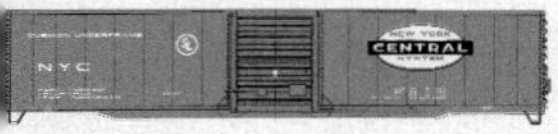

932-35515 NYC

932-35516 CR

†Union Pacific licensed product.

**COMING SOON!**

**Winter 2007-08 Delivery**
- New Roadnames

**Single Cars 24.98 ea**

**NEW 932-35517** CN
**NEW 932-35518** B&O
**NEW 932-35519** MILW
**NEW 932-35520** CP (Script Lettering)
**NEW 932-35521** Rock Island

**Limited-Run 2-Packs 49.98 ea**

**NEW 932-235517** CN
**NEW 932-235518** B&O
**NEW 932-235519** MILW
**NEW 932-235520** CP (Script Lettering)
**NEW 932-235521** Rock Island

932-35517 CN

932-35518 B&O

932-35519 MILW

932-35520 CP

932-35521 Rock Island

### Pullman-Standard 60' Double-Door Auto Parts Box Car

- Revised tooling
- A common variation of the Pullman-Standard 60' auto parts box cars
- Used to carry engine blocks, axles, transmissions or brake drums

**Single Cars 21.98 ea**

**932-35811** UP†
**932-35812** CB&Q
**932-35813** NYC
**932-35814** GTW
**932-35815** BN
**932-35816** ATSF
**932-35810** Undecorated

**Limited-Run 2-Packs 39.98 ea**

**932-235811** UP†
**932-235812** CB&Q
**932-235813** NYC
**932-235814** GTW
**932-235815** BN
**932-235816** ATSF

**COMING SOON!**

**Winter 2007-08 Delivery**
- New Roadnames

**Single Cars 21.98 ea**

**NEW 932-35817** MILW
**NEW 932-35818** CR
**NEW 932-35819** ATSF

**Limited-Run 2-Packs 41.98 ea**

**NEW 932-235817** MILW
**NEW 932-235818** CR
**NEW 932-235819** ATSF

932-35817 MILW

932-35818 CR

932-35819 ATSF

### Pullman-Standard 86' 8-Door Hi-Cube Auto Parts Box Car

- Revised Tooling
- Great for Post-60s Layouts

**Single Cars 24.98 ea**

**932-35311** SOU
**932-35312** UP†
**932-35313** MILW
**932-35314** PRR
**932-35315** GTW
**932-35310** Undecorated

**Limited-Run 2-Packs 49.98 ea**

**932-235311** SOU
**932-235312** UP†
**932-235313** MILW
**932-235314** PRR
**932-235315** GTW

932-35311 SOU

932-35312 UP

932-35313 MILW

932-35314 PRR

932-35315 GTW

See What's Available at **www.walthers.com**

Pullman-Standard 60' Single-Door Auto Parts Box Car B&O 932-35518

Pullman-Standard 60' Double-Door Auto Parts Box Car NYC 932-35813

Pullman-Standard 86' 8-Door Hi-Cube Auto Parts Box Car GTW 932-35315

PRR X-29 Box Car PRR 932-9023

**COMING SOON!**

**Winter 2007-08 Delivery**
- New Roadnames

**Single Cars 24.98 ea**

**NEW 932-35316** CR
**NEW 932-35317** B&O
**NEW 932-35318** NYC

**Limited-Run 2-Packs 49.98 ea**

**NEW 932-235316** CR
**NEW 932-235317** B&O
**NEW 932-235318** NYC

932-35316 CR

932-35317 B&O

932-35318 NYC

# WALTHERS

## GOLD LINE™ FREIGHT CARS

### Pullman-Standard 86' 4-Door Hi-Cube Box Car

- Revised tooling
- New roadnames & numbers
- Designed to move lightweight sheet metal parts
- Based on the common four-door design originally built for Ford and Chrysler plants
- Models feature correct ribbed ends and unique sidesills with visible interior posts

**Single Cars 24.98 ea**

**932-35011** CR/NYC

**932-35012** BN

**932-35013** CP (CPAA)

**932-35014** PRR

**932-35015** Cotton Belt†

**932-35016** MILW

**932-35010** Undecorated

**Limited Run 2-Packs 44.98 ea**

**932-235011** CR/NYC

**932-235012** BN

**932-235013** CP (CPAA)

**932-235014** PRR

**932-235015** Cotton Belt†

**932-235016** MILW

932-35011 CR

932-35012 BN

932-35013 CP (CPAA)

932-35014 PRR

932-35015 Cotton Belt

932-35016 MILW (Tuscan)

### COMING SOON!

**Fall 2007 Delivery**

- New Roadnames

**Single Cars 24.98 ea**

**NEW 932-35017** DT&I

**NEW 932-35018** CR

**NEW 932-35019** GTW

**NEW 932-35020** CSX/NYC

**NEW 932-35021** N&W

**Limited-Run 2-Packs 49.98 ea**

**NEW 932-235017** DT&I

**NEW 932-235018** CR

**NEW 932-235019** GTW

**NEW 932-235020** CSX/NYC

**NEW 932-235021** N&W

932-35017 DT&I

932-35018 CR

932-35019 GTW

932-35020 CSX/NYC

932-35021 N&W

## AUTO CARRIERS

### 89' Tri-Level Enclosed Auto Carrier 25.98 ea

- 28" wheels to reduce overall height

**932-4871** St. Louis - San Francisco

**932-4872** CP Rail

**932-4873** ATSF

**932-4874** BNSF (black & white logo)

**932-4875** CNW† (Box Car Red)

**932-4876** C&O (Chessie)

**932-4877** KCS

**932-4878** UP† (SSW or SP reporting marks)

**932-4879** Illinois Central Gulf

**932-4880** GTW

**932-4881** CSX

**932-4882** UP†

**932-4883** N&W

†Union Pacific licensed product.

Pullman-Standard 86' 4-Door Hi-Cube Box Car GTW 932-35019

Pullman-Standard 86' 4-Door Hi-Cube Box Car Cotton Belt 932-35015

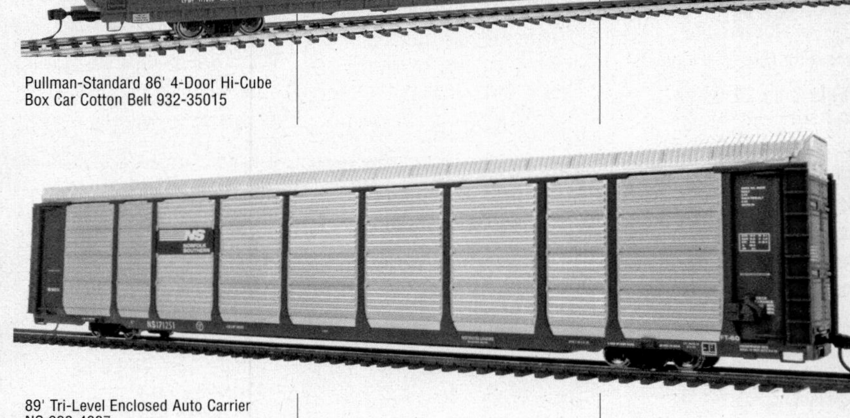

89' Tri-Level Enclosed Auto Carrier NS 932-4887

89' Tri-Level Enclosed Auto Carrier ATSF 932-4873

932-4879 Illinois Central Gulf

932-4880 Grand Trunk Western

932-4881 CSX

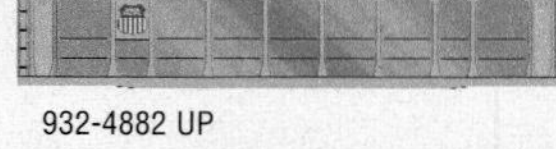
932-4882 UP

932-4883 N&W

### COMING SOON!

**Winter 2007-08 Delivery**

- New Paint Schemes
- New Roadnumbers
- Knuckle Couplers
- Metal RP-25 Wheels

**Single Cars 25.98 ea**

**NEW 932-4884** UP† ("Building America" Slogan)

**NEW 932-4885** BNSF (2005 "Power Bar" Logo)

**NEW 932-4886** GTW (blue)

**NEW 932-4887** NS

**NEW 932-4888** CR

**Limited-Run 2-Packs 49.98 ea**

**NEW 932-24884** UP† ("Building America" Slogan)

**NEW 932-24885** BNSF (2005 "Power Bar" Logo)

**NEW 932-24886** GTW (blue)

**NEW 932-24887** NS

**NEW 932-24888** CR

932-4884 UP

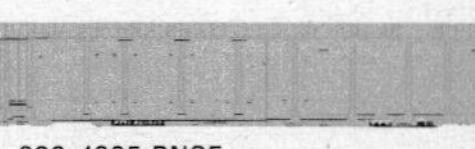
932-4885 BNSF

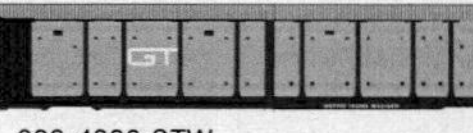

932-4886 GTW

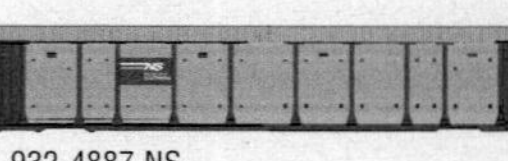
932-4887 NS

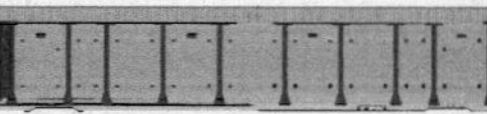
932-4888 CR

# WALTHERS

## GOLD LINE™ FREIGHT CARS

## AUTO CARRIERS

### Bi-Level Enclosed Auto Carriers

**COMING SOON!**

**Spring 2008 Delivery**
- All-New Tooling
- Knuckle Couplers
- Metal RP-25 Wheels

**Single Cars 29.98 ea**
**NEW 932-40101** UP†
**NEW 932-40102** SP†
**NEW 932-40103** BNSF
**NEW 932-40104** GTW
**NEW 932-40105** MILW
**NEW 932-40106** ATSF
**NEW 932-40107** CR
**NEW 932-40108** SCL
**NEW 932-40109** SOO (red)
**NEW 932-40100** Undecorated Kit - Some Assembly Required*

**Limited-Run 2-Packs 59.98 ea**
**NEW 932-240101** UP†
**NEW 932-240102** SP†
**NEW 932-240103** BNSF
**NEW 932-240104** GTW
**NEW 932-240105** MILW
**NEW 932-240106** ATSF
**NEW 932-240107** CR
**NEW 932-240108** SCL
**NEW 932-240109** SOO (red)

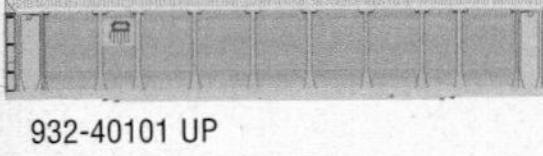
932-40101 UP

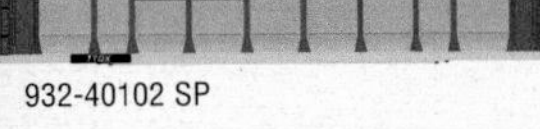
932-40102 SP

932-40103 BNSF

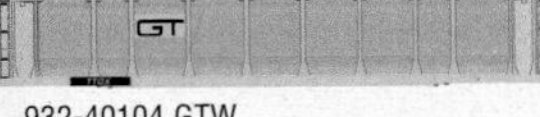

932-40104 GTW

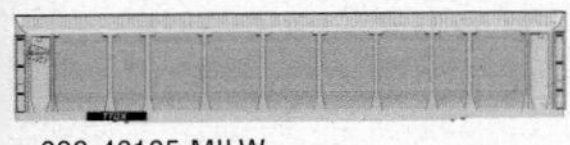
932-40105 MILW

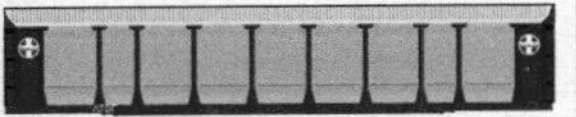
932-40106 ATSF

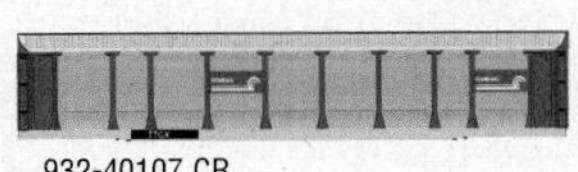
932-40107 CR

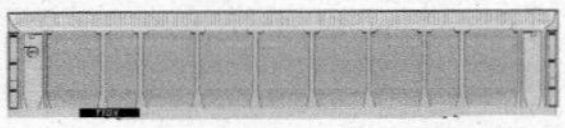

932-40108 SCL

932-40109 SOO

## REEFERS

### 40' General American Meat Reefer
- New Roadnames & Roadnumbers
- Perfect for Transition-Era Consists

**Single Cars 17.98 ea**
**932-2579** Dugdale Packing
**932-2580** Black Hills Packing Co.
**932-2581** American Refrigerator Transit† (MP/NW)
**932-2582** Liebmann Packing
**932-2583** Armour (PCX)
**NEW 932-2584** Bookey #65070
**NEW 932-2585** Schuyler - WCLX #2099
**NEW 932-2586** Central Packing #91499
**NEW 932-2587** Kansas Beef #91662
**NEW 932-2588** Greenlee #69101
**NEW 932-2589** Hormel - NADX #159
**NEW 932-2590** Spencer #60067

**Limited-Run 2-Packs 31.98 ea**
**932-22579** Dugdale Packing
**932-22580** Black Hills Packing Co.
**932-22581** American Refrigerator Transit† (MP/NW)
**932-22582** Liebmann Packing
**932-22583** Armour (PCX)
**NEW 932-22584** Bookey #65071, #65074
**NEW 932-22585** Schuyler - WCLX #2107, #2115
**NEW 932-22586** Central Packing #91495, #91497
**NEW 932-22587** Kansas Beef ##91663, #91665
**NEW 932-22588** Greenlee #69102)
**NEW 932-22589** Hormel - NADX #115, #186
**NEW 932-22590** Spencer #60064, #60069

Bi-Level Enclosed Auto Carrier
Image Courtesy of Darin Umlauft

40' General American Reefer American Refrigerator Transit (MP/NW) 932-2581

40' General American Reefer Bookey 932-2584

40' General American Reefer Schuyler (WCLX) 932-2585

932-2584 Bookey

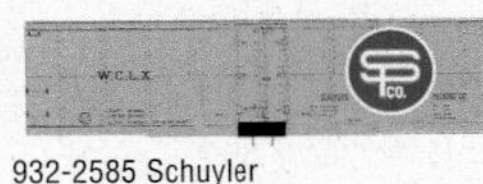
932-2585 Schuyler

932-2588 Greenlee

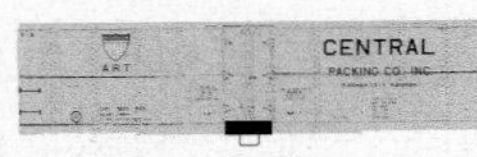

932-2586 Central Packing

932-2589 Hormel

932-2587 Kansas Beef

932-2590 Spencer

# WALTHERS

## GOLD LINE™ FREIGHT CARS

## HOPPERS

### 100-Ton 2-Bay Greenville Hopper

- New Roadnames & Roadnumbers
- Perfect for Quarry & Stone Service

**Single Cars 19.98 ea**

**932-7412** SP†

**932-7413** UP† (w/SP Reporting Marks)

**932-7414** Golden West/SP (Patch)

**932-7415** NS

**932-7416** Golden West

**Limited-Run 2-Packs 37.98 ea**

**932-27413** UP† (w/SP Reporting Marks)

**932-27415** NS

932-7412 SP

932-7413 UP (w/SP Reporting Marks)

932-7414 Golden West/SP (Patch)

932-7415 NS

932-7416 Golden West

### 40' Ortner 100-Ton Open Aggregate Hopper

- One of the most distinctive cars in service today
- Built for rough service and heavy hauling
- Includes simulated load

**Single Cars 14.98 ea**

**932-7051** CSX

**932-7052** CR

**932-7053** Florida East Coast

**932-7056** WC/Restenciled Algoma Central Car

**932-7060** Golden West Service

**932-7062** Algoma Central

**932-7063** SSAM/Wisconsin Central

**932-7065** Blue Circle Cement

**932-7050** Undecorated

**Limited-Run 3-Packs 39.98 ea**

**932-37070** Florida East Coast

**932-37071** Georgetown Railroad

**932-37072** CSX

**932-37073** WC

932-37070 Florida East Coast

932-37071 Georgetown Railroad

932-37072 CSX

932-37073 WC

### 50' Airslide® Covered Hopper

- Available individually and in limited-run two-packs for a total of three roadnumbers per roadname

**Single Cars 19.98 ea**

**932-3721** CNW† (gray)

**932-3722** ICG (orange)

**932-3723** CCLX

**932-3724** GACX (baby blue)

**932-3725** MILW (small logo)

**932-3726** NP

**Limited-Run 2-Packs 37.98 ea**

**932-23724** GACX (baby blue)

**932-23725** MILW (small logo)

932-3721 CNW (gray)

932-3722 ICG (orange)

932-3723 CCLX

932-3724 GACX (baby blue)

50' Airslide Covered Hopper CCLX 932-3723

932-3725 MILW (small logo)

932-3726 NP

### Trinity 2-Bay Cement Service Covered Hopper

- Detailed body
- Roof hatches
- A thin profile roofwalk

**Single Cars 19.98 ea**

**932-5379** BN (plain)

**932-5380** MKT†

**932-5381** Dakota, Minnesota & Eastern

**932-5382** Chicago Heights Terminal & Transfer (UP Subsidiary)

**932-5383** Blue Circle Cement

**932-5384** Green Bay & Western

**932-5385** GATX

**932-5386** N&W

**932-5387** Griffin

**932-5388** Calaveras Cement

**932-5389** SOU

932-5385 GATX

932-5386 N&W

932-5387 Griffin

932-5388 Calaveras Cement

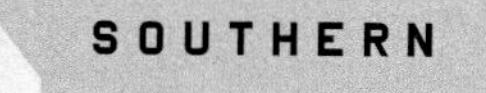

932-5389 SOU

†Union Pacific licensed product.

100-Ton 2-Bay Greenville Hopper Golden West 932-7416

Trinity 2-Bay Cement Service Hopper Griffin 932-5387

40' Ortner 100-Ton Open Aggregate Hopper FEC 932-37070

For Up-To-Date Information and News Bookmark Walthers Web site at **www.walthers.com**

# WALTHERS

## GOLD LINE™ FREIGHT CARS

### 41' Ballast Hopper 3-Packs 39.98 ea

- Expand your maintenance fleet in minutes with these sets
- Three roadnumbers per roadname
- Also available: undecorated single car

**932-34221** UP†
**932-34222** CSX
**932-34223** ATSF
**932-34224** CR
**932-34225** BNSF
**932-34226** CNW†
**932-34227** SP†
**932-34228** Amtrak
**932-34229** MILW
**932-34230** CN
**932-34231** SOO
**932-34232** CP
**932-34233** BN
**932-34234** NS
**932-34235** DRGW†
**932-34236** N&W
**932-34237** SOU
**932-4200** Undecorated Single Car **11.98**

932-34233 BN

932-34234 NS

932-34235 DRGW

932-34236 N&W

932-34237 SOU

### Trinity RD-4 Coal Hopper 6-Packs 89.98 ea

- Perfect for unit coal trains
- One-piece body, heavy diecast underframe, separately applied door mechanism, brake details and interior bracing
- Available in six different roadnumbers, so building a unit train is easy

**932-7818** BNSF #3
**932-7819** OMAX
**932-7820** Alaska Railroad
**932-7821** NS #3
**932-7822** BNSF #4
**932-7823** NS #4
**932-7824** OMAX #2
**932-7825** Flex Leasing Corp.
**932-7826** Virginia Power
**932-7827** NS
**932-7828** BNSF
**932-7829** CNW†
**932-7830** BNSF ("Wedge" Scheme)
**932-7831** UP† "Building America"/CMO

932-7826 Virginia Power

932-7827 NS

932-7828 BNSF

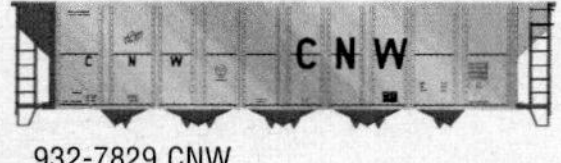

932-7829 CNW

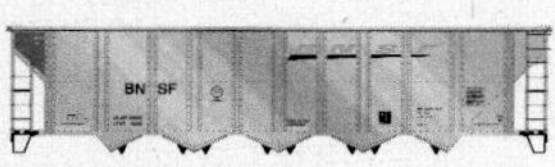

932-7830 BNSF ("Wedge" Scheme)

932-7831 UP "Building America"/CMO

**COMING SOON!**

**Winter 2007-08 Delivery**

- New Roadnumbers
- New Roadnames

**NEW 932-7832** BNSF - New Logo
**NEW 932-7833** NS
**NEW 932-7834** UP†
**NEW 932-7835** NVPX
**NEW 932-7836** COMX

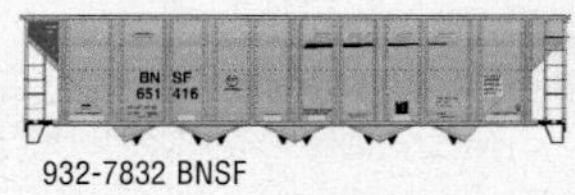

932-7832 BNSF

932-7833 NS

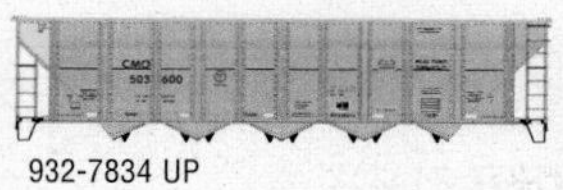

932-7834 UP

932-7835 NVPX

932-7835 COMX

### Bethlehem 4,000 Cubic-Foot Three-Bay Coal Hopper 6-Packs 79.98 ea (Unless Noted)

- All-new model
- New roadnumbers
- Easily expands unit trains
- One of America's most common coal cars
- Used from the 70s 'til now

**932-7851** BN
**932-7852** WP†
**932-7853** SOO
**932-7854** MILW
**932-7855** CNW†
**932-7856** AEPX
**932-7857** MRL
**932-7858** BN #2
**932-7859** CNW† #2
**932-7860** SOO #2
**932-7861** MRL #2
**932-7862** MILW #2
**932-7863** BNSF #2
**932-7864** MILW (Patched ex-PC&N)
**932-7865** WC (Patched ex-BN)
**932-7866** UMP
**932-7867** BN
**932-7868** SOO New Scheme
**932-7869** WP†
**932-7850** Undecorated Single **14.98**

932-7864 MILW (Patched ex-PC&N)

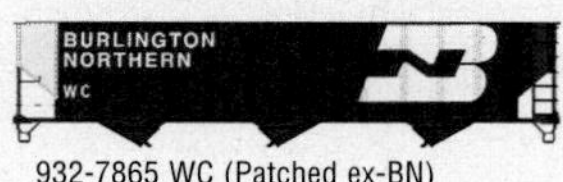

932-7865 WC (Patched ex-BN)

932-7866 UMP

932-7867 BN

932-7868 SOO New Scheme

41' Ballast Hoppers N&W
932-34236

Trinity RD-4 Hopper BNSF 932-7832

Bethlehem 4,000 Cubic-Foot Hopper
MILW (Patched ex-PC&N) 932-7864

932-7869 WP

**COMING SOON!**

**Winter 2007-08 Delivery**

- New Roadnumbers

**NEW 932-7870** MILW
**NEW 932-7871** SOO
**NEW 932-7872** WC
**NEW 932-7873** BN
**NEW 932-7874** MILW (ex-Point Comfort & Northern patch)
**NEW 932-7875** BNSF (Oxide Red)

932-7870 MILW

932-7871 SOO

932-7872 WC

932-7873 BN

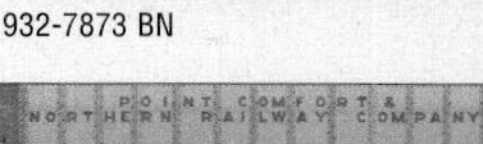

932-7874 MILW

932-7875 BNSF

# WALTHERS

## GOLD LINE™ FREIGHT CARS

### Pullman-Standard 2,893 Cubic-Foot Covered Hopper

- New roadnames
- Perfect for classic diesel- and modern-era layouts

**Single Cars 22.98 ea**

**932-7951** ATSF
**932-7952** CB&Q
**932-7953** GN
**932-7954** NYC
**932-7955** SP†
**932-7956** SOO/WC
**932-7957** MILW
**932-7958** SOU
**932-7959** WC
**932-7960** BN
**932-7961** CR
**932-7962** CNW†
**932-7963** PC
**932-7964** NP
**NEW 932-7965** ATSF
**NEW 932-7966** B&O
**NEW 932-7967** Central of Georgia
**NEW 932-7968** DRGW†
**NEW 932-7969** IC
**NEW 932-7970** MKT†
**NEW 932-7971** Reynolds NAHX
**NEW 932-7972** SOU
**932-7950** Undecorated

**Limited-Run 2-Packs 41.98 ea**

**NEW 932-27965** ATSF
**NEW 932-27966** B&O
**NEW 932-27967** Central of Georgia
**NEW 932-27968** DRGW†
**NEW 932-27969** IC
**NEW 932-27970** MKT†
**NEW 932-27971** Reynolds NAHX
**NEW 932-27972** SOU

932-7959 WC

932-7960 BN

932-7961 CR

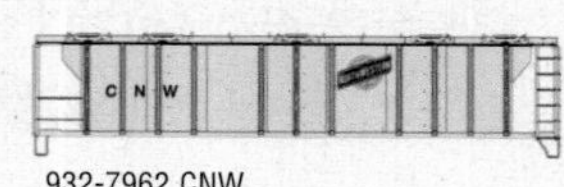
932-7962 CNW

932-7963 PC

932-7964 NP

932-7965 ATSF

932-7966 B&O

932-7967 Central of Georgia

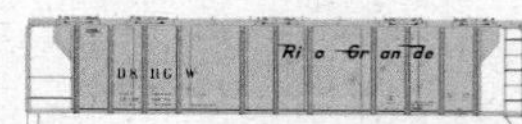
932-7968 DRGW

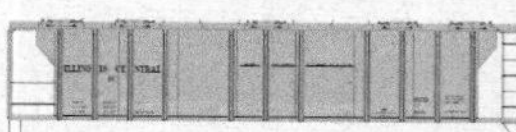
932-7969 IC

932-7970 MKT

932-7971 Reynolds NAHX

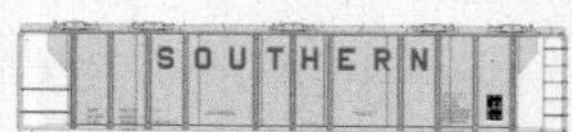

932-7972 SOU

## GONDOLAS

### Thrall 53' Gondola

- All-New Tooling
- Steel & Scrap Industry Favorites

**Single Cars 19.98 ea**

**932-40251** SOO
**932-40252** WC
**932-40253** MILW
**932-40254** Green Bay & Western
**932-40255** UP†
**932-40256** CR
**932-40250** Undecorated

†Union Pacific licensed product.

**Limited-Run 2-Packs 37.98 ea**

**932-240251** SOO
**932-240252** WC
**932-240253** MILW
**932-240254** Green Bay & Western
**932-240255** UP†
**932-240256** CR

**COMING SOON!**

**Winter 2007-08 Delivery**

**Single Cars 19.98 ea**

**NEW 932-40257** DT&I
**NEW 932-40258** Illinois Terminal
**NEW 932-40259** DRGW†
**NEW 932-40260** FEC
**NEW 932-40261** MKT†
**NEW 932-40262** WC

**Limited-Run 2-Packs 37.98 ea**

**NEW 932-240257** DT&I
**NEW 932-240258** Illinois Terminal
**NEW 932-240259** DRGW†
**NEW 932-240260** FEC
**NEW 932-240261** MKT†
**NEW 932-240262** WC

932-40251 SOO

932-40252 WC

932-40253 MILW

932-40254 Green Bay & Western

932-40255 UP

932-40256 CR

932-40257 DT&I

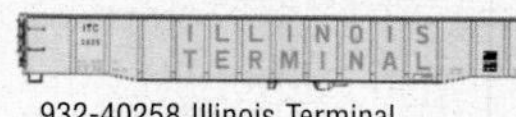

932-40258 Illinois Terminal

932-40259 DRGW

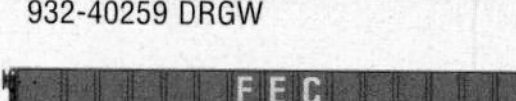

932-40260 FEC

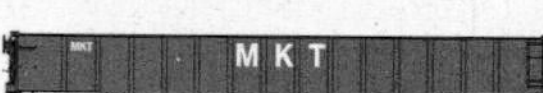

932-40261 MKT

932-40262 WC

P-S 2,893 Cubic-Foot Covered Hopper ATSF 932-7965

P-S 2,893 Cubic-Foot Covered Hopper BN 932-7960

P-S 2,893 Cubic-Foot Covered Hopper B&O 932-7966

P-S 2,893 Cubic-Foot Covered Hopper MKT 932-7970

Thrall 53' Gondola SOO 932-40251

Thrall 53' Gondola GB&W 932-40254

Thrall 53' Gondola WC 932-40252

# WALTHERS

## GOLD LINE™ FREIGHT CARS

### Bethgon Coalporter™ Gondola 6-Packs 89.98 ea

- Model a unit train in minutes with six-packs; each car features a different roadnumber
- New interior bracing
- Hidden weight for better operation

**932-5301** BN #1
**932-5302** CSXT #1
**932-5303** UP† #1
**932-5304** NS #1
**932-5336** BNSF #3
**932-5337** BN (black) #3
**932-5338** CSXT #3
**932-5339** NS #3
**932-5340** UP† #3
**932-5341** AEPX
**932-5342** BNSF New Scheme
**932-5343** Detroit Edison DEEX
**932-5344** Edgewater Generating Station EDGX
**932-5345** UP†
**932-5346** NS

### Bethgon Coalporter Single Car

**932-5300** Undecorated Kit **14.98**

932-5336 BNSF

932-5337 BN (black)

932-5338 CSXT

932-5339 NS

932-5340 UP

932-5341 AEPX

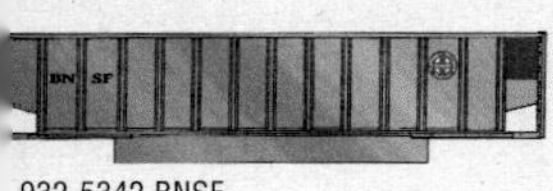
932-5342 BNSF

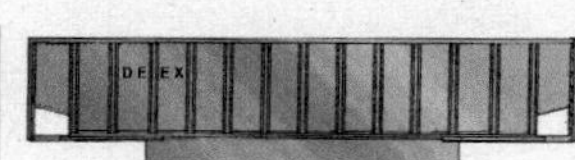
932-5343 DEEX

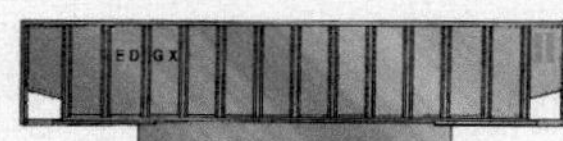
932-5344 EDGX

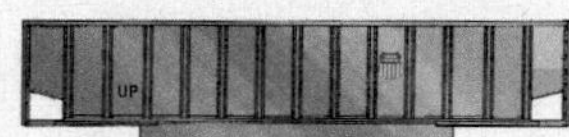
932-5345 UP

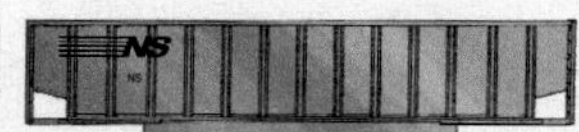

932-5346 NS

## COMING SOON!

### Winter 2007-08 Delivery

- New Roadnumbers

**NEW 932-40401** UP†
**NEW 932-40402** BNSF (green ends)
**NEW 932-40403** BNSF (Mineral Brown ends)
**NEW 932-40404** CSX
**NEW 932-40405** DEEX

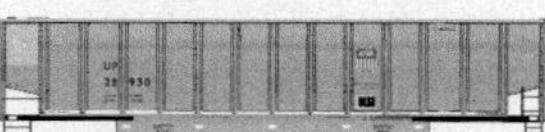
932-40401 UP

932-40402 BNSF (green ends)

932-40403 BNSF

932-40404 CSX

932-40405 DEEX

### Coal Loads

One-piece resin castings are designed especially for the cars listed and feature realistic texture. Drop-in mount.

#### Bethgon Coalporters

**933-1038** Two-Pack **7.98**
**933-1039** Six-Pack **17.98**

#### 100-Ton Quad Hoppers

**933-1037** 2-Pack **7.98**

See What's Available at **www.walthers.com**

Bethgon Coalporter Gondola BNSF 932-5342

Bethgon Coalporter Gondola UP 932-5340

Bethgon Coalporter Gondola AEPX 932-5341

USRA 46' Gondola B&O 932-7469

USRA 46' Gondola NYC 932-7468

### USRA 46' Steel Gondola

- New Roadnames & Schemes
- Great for Steam & Transition-Era Railroads

#### Single Cars 17.98 ea

**932-7466** PRR (Circle Keystone)
**932-7467** NKP #2
**932-7468** NYC
**932-7469** B&O
**932-7470** Pittsburgh & Lake Erie

#### Limited-Run 2-Packs 32.98 ea

**932-27466** PRR (Circle Keystone)
**932-27467** NKP #2
**932-27468** NYC
**932-27469** B&O
**932-27470** Pittsburgh & Lake Erie

932-7466 PRR (Circle Keystone)

932-7467 NKP #2

932-7468 NYC

932-7469 B&O

932-7470 Pittsburgh & Lake Erie

# WALTHERS

## GOLD LINE™ FREIGHT CARS

### Difco® Dump Car

- New roadnumbers
- Perfect for work trains

**Single Cars 24.98 ea**

**932-7901** UP†

**932-7902** Duluth, Missabe & Iron Range

**932-7903** ATSF

**932-7904** BNSF

**932-7905** CSX

**932-7906** Maintenance Of Way

**932-7907** SP†

**932-7908** NS

**932-7909** DRGW†

**932-7910** MILW

**932-7911** Amtrak

**932-7912** CP

**932-7900** Undecorated

**Limited Quantity Available**

**Limited Run 3-Packs 64.98 ea**

**932-37904** BNSF

**932-37905** CSX

**932-37908** NS

**932-37911** Amtrak

**COMING SOON!**

**Winter 2007-08 Delivery**

- New Roadnames & Numbers

**Single Cars 24.98 ea**

**NEW 932-7913** CP (black)

**NEW 932-7914** Alaska

**NEW 932-7915** BN

**NEW 932-7917** UP† (green)

**Limited Run 3-Packs 64.98 ea**

**NEW 932-37913** CP (black)

**NEW 932-37914** Alaska

**NEW 932-37915** BN

**NEW 932-37917** UP† (green)

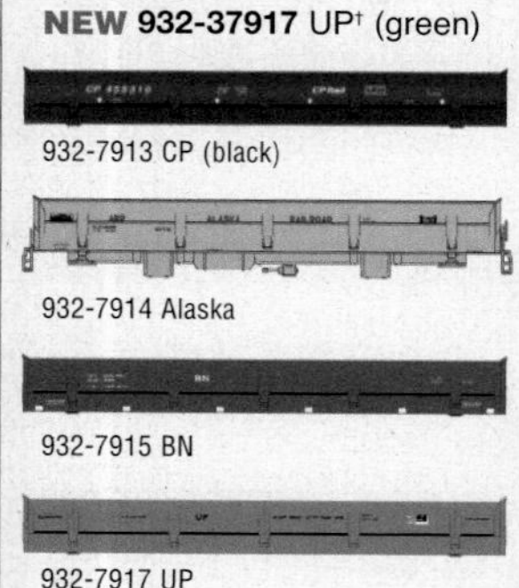

932-7913 CP (black)

932-7914 Alaska

932-7915 BN

932-7917 UP

## EVANS 100-TON 55' CUSHION COIL CARS

- Correct-length, heavy diecast frame for better tracking
- Drill starter points for installing the supplied wire grab irons
- Angled or round hoods as appropriate for each roadname

**Single Cars 21.98 ea**

**932-3822** CSX

**932-3823** CR

**932-3825** UP†

**932-3826** Grand Trunk Western

**932-3827** Indiana Harbor Belt

**932-3828** Elgin, Joliet & Eastern

**932-3832** Ohio Central

**932-3835** ICG

**932-3836** CP

**932-3837** NYC (Jade Green)

**932-3838** Detroit, Toledo & Ironton

**932-3839** C&O

**932-3840** B&O

**932-3841** Indiana Harbor Belt

**932-3842** IC

**932-3843** RDG

**932-3844** MP†

**932-3845** NS

**932-3846** MILW

**932-3820** Undecorated

(see Legend Page)

**932-3829** MKT†

**932-3830** South Shore

**932-3831** UP/CNW†

**932-3833** N&W

**932-3834** CSX (Angled Hoods)

**Limited-Run 2-Packs 36.98 ea**

**932-23841** Indiana Harbor Belt

**932-23842** IC

**932-23843** RDG

**932-23844** MP†

**932-23845** NS

**932-23846** MILW

932-3842 IC

932-3843 RDG

932-3844 MP

932-3845 NS

932-3846 MILW

### Steel Coil Load Kit

**933-1499** pkg(12) **5.98**
Injection molded parts capture the look of huge coils, but are easy to build. Parts for twelve coils in two sizes.

## FLAT CARS

### Canadian 50' Bulkhead Flat Car

- All-New Tooling
- Separate Applied Ladders
- Great for Post-70s Layouts
- Perfect for Lumber Service
- Prototypes Operate All Over North America

**Single Cars 19.98 ea**

**932-40051** CN

**932-40052** Duluth, Winnipeg & Pacific

**932-40053** BC Rail (BCOL)

**932-40054** Algoma Central

**932-40050** Undecorated

**COMING SOON!**

**Fall 2007 Delivery**

- New Roadnames

**Single Cars 19.98 ea**

**NEW 932-40055** British Columbia Railway

**NEW 932-40056** Ontario Northland

**NEW 932-40057** Algoma Central (green)

**NEW 932-40058** BC Rail (BCIT Reporting Marks)

**NEW 932-40059** NAFX(orange, black)

**NEW 932-40060** TPFX(orange, black)

**NEW 932-40061** Finley Forest Products

**NEW 932-40062** MRL (blue)

**Limited-Run 2-Packs 39.98 ea**

**NEW 932-240055** British Columbia Railway

**NEW 932-240056** Ontario Northland

**NEW 932-240057** Algoma Central (green)

**NEW 932-240058** BC Rail (BCIT Reporting Marks)

**NEW 932-240059** NAFX (orange, black)

**NEW 932-240060** TPFX (orange, black)

**NEW 932-240061** Finley Forest Products

**NEW 932-240062** MRL (blue)

Difco Dump Car CP 932-7913

Difco Dump Car CSX 932-7905

Difco Dump Car DRGW 932-7909

Evans 100-Ton 55' Cushion Coil Car IC 932-3842

Evans 100-Ton 55' Cushion Coil Car MILW 932-3846

Canadian 50' Bulkhead Flat Car BCOL 932-40055

932-40055 BCOL

932-40059 NAFX

932-40056 Ontario Northland

932-40060 TPFX

932-40057 Algoma Central

932-40061 Finley Forest Products

932-40058 BC Rail

932-40062 MRL

# WALTHERS

## GOLD LINE™ FREIGHT CARS

### 72' Centerbeam Flat Car

- Offered in either standard or distinctive opera window centerbeam with oval cutouts
- Appropriate type of center beam for each prototype
- Snap-in lumber loads that are available in a variety of schemes (sold separately)

**Single Cars 21.98 ea**

**932-4103** TTX (standard)
**932-4123** UP† (brown w/shield herald, opera)
**932-4124** CN (yellow, opera)
**932-4130** BC Rail - Opera
**932-4131** NOKL - Standard
**932-4132** CBRY - Opera
**932-4133** TSE - Standard
**932-4134** CP (green, standard)
**932-4135** TTX (brown, standard)
**932-4136** SOO (brown, standard)
**932-4137** CHTT (UP† Subsidiary, brown, standard)
**932-4100** Undecorated - Standard

932-4134 CP (green, standard)

932-4135 TTX (brown, standard)

932-4136 SOO (brown, standard)

932-4137 CHTT (UP subsidiary, brown, standard)

### 72' Centerbeam Flat Car Loads 8.98 ea

- Assembles in minutes, with no cutting or gluing
- One-piece plastic load (one for each side of the car)
- Prepainted and lettered

**933-1101** Georgia-Pacific
**933-1102** Slocan Group
**933-1103** Louisiana Pacific
**933-1104** Plum Creek
**933-1106** High Cascade Lumber
**933-1107** Mountain Lumber
**933-1112** Weyerhaeuser Lumber
**933-1113** Finlay Premium
**933-1114** Tolko
**933-1115** Potlach

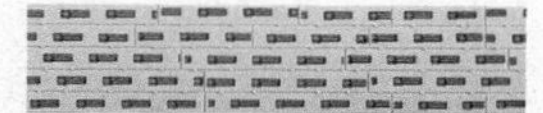

**933-1116** Williamette Industries
**933-1100** Undecorated

### Pulpwood Loads

- Designed to fit the trailer included with the Pulpwood Truck (#933-4014, sold separately)

**933-1036** Pulpwood Truck Load **6.98**

### Woodchip Loads

One-piece castings with realistic look (not molded in color) are designed for drop-in mounting on Walthers 61' Woodchip Hoppers and Truck.

**933-1034** 61' Woodchip Car Load 2-Pack **6.98**

**933-1035** Woodchip Truck Load **2.98**

### Log Loads

**933-1031** For Walthers 45' Logging Flats pkg(30) **9.98**
One-piece resin castings. Use as car loads, fresh-cut trees at the cutting site or floating logs in a mill pond.

## INTERMODAL EQUIPMENT

### Flexi-Van Flat Car w/Two Trailers

**COMING SOON!**

**Fall 2007 Delivery**

- All-New Tooling
- Includes Two 40' Trailers
- Run in Freight or Passenger Service
- Three Different Roadnumbers
- Mark III Cars
- More Trailers & Bogies Available Separately

**Single Cars 42.98 ea (Unless Noted)**

**NEW 932-3921** NYC #1
**NEW 932-3922** MILW #1
**NEW 932-3923** IC **45.98**
**NEW 932-3925** NYC #2
**NEW 932-3926** MILW #2
**NEW 932-3927** SAL
**NEW 932-3928** SOU **45.98**
**NEW 932-3929** WP†
**NEW 932-3920** Undecorated

72' Centerbeam Flat Car TSE 932-4133

72' Centerbeam Flat Car CHTT 932-4137

Flexi-Van Flat Car w/Two Trailers Prototype Photo Shown

**Limited-Run 2-Packs 81.98 ea (Unless Noted)**

**NEW 932-23921** NYC #1
**NEW 932-23922** MILW #1
**NEW 932-23923** IC **86.98**
**NEW 932-23925** NYC #2
**NEW 932-23926** MILW #2
**NEW 932-23927** SAL
**NEW 932-23928** SOU **86.98**
**NEW 932-23929** WP†

932-3921 NYC #1

932-3922 MILW #1

932-3923 IC

932-3925 NYC #2

932-3926 MILW #2

932-3927 SAL

932-3928 SOU

932-3929 WP

### Flexi-Van 40' Trailers 12.98 ea

- All-New Model
- Perfect for Flexi-Van Flats
- Use as Highway, Dock or Car Detail
- Includes Trailer Bogie

**NEW 933-1681** NYC
**NEW 933-1682** MILW
**NEW 933-1683** IC
**NEW 933-1686** Seaboard Air Line
**NEW 933-1687** SOU
**NEW 933-1688** WP†
**NEW 933-1689** L&N
**NEW 933-1690** Soo Line
**NEW 933-1680** Undecorated

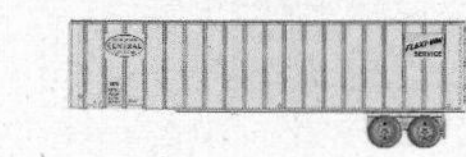

933-1681 NYC

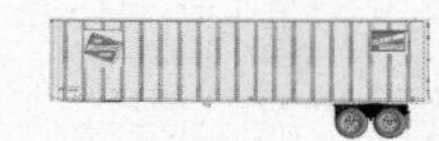

933-1682 MILW

See What's New and Exciting at **www.walthers.com**

933-1683 IC

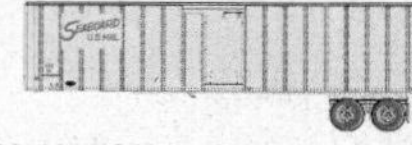

933-1686 SAL

933-1687 SOU

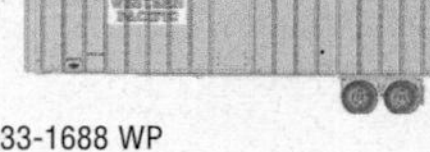

933-1688 WP

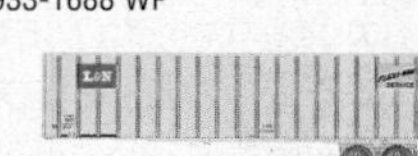

933-1689 L&N

933-1690 SOO

†Union Pacific licensed product.

# WALTHERS

## GOLD LINE™ FREIGHT CARS

### Bethlehem 89' Flush-Deck Flat Car

- All-New Tooling
- Underbody Detail
- Great for Intermodal Consists

**Single Cars 24.98 ea**

**932-40301** TTX

**932-40302** WTTX

**932-40303** ATSF

**932-40304** FEC

**932-40305** SOU

**932-40306** SP†

**932-40307** WC

**932-40300** Undecorated

932-40301 TTX

932-40302 TTWX

932-40303 ATSF

932-40304 FEC

932-40305 SOU

932-40306 SP

932-40307 WC

## COMING SOON!

**Fall 2007 Delivery**

- New Roadnames
- Three New Hitch Arrangements

**Single Cars 24.98 ea**

**NEW 932-40308** New Orleans Public Belt

**NEW 932-40309** ATSF

**RTTX Version**

**NEW 932-40316** RTTX (Trailer-Train yellow)

**NEW 932-40317** RTTX (TTX)

**NEW 932-40315** Undecorated

**KTTX Version (Collapsible Hitch Back-to-Back)**

**NEW 932-40321** KTTX (Trailer-Train yellow)

**NEW 932-40322** KTTX (TTX)

**NEW 932-40320** Undecorated

**KTTX Version (Rigid Hitch Back-to-Back)**

**NEW 932-40326** KTTX (Trailer-Train yellow)

**NEW 932-40327** KTTX (TTX)

**NEW 932-40325** Undecorated

**Limited-Run 2-Packs 47.98 ea**

**NEW 932-240308** New Orleans Public Belt

**NEW 932-240309** ATSF

**RTTX Version**

**NEW 932-240316** RTTX (Trailer-Train yellow)

**NEW 932-240317** RTTX (TTX)

**NEW 932-240315** Undecorated

**KTTX Version (Collapsible Hitch Back-to-Back)**

**NEW 932-240321** KTTX (Trailer-Train yellow)

**NEW 932-240322** KTTX (TTX)

**NEW 932-240320** Undecorated

**KTTX Version (Rigid Hitch Back-to-Back)**

**NEW 932-240326** KTTX (Trailer-Train yellow)

**NEW 932-240327** KTTX (TTX)

**NEW 932-240325** Undecorated

932-40308 NOPB

932-40309 ATSF

932-40316 RTTX (Trailer Train yellow)

932-40317 RTTX (TTX)

932-40321 KTTX (Trailer Train yellow)

932-40322 KTTX (TTX)

932-40326 KTTX (Trailer Train yellow)

932-40327 KTTX (TTX)

### Front Runner with Trailer 19.98 ea

- Includes assembled 45' or 48' Trailer
- Adds authenticity to HO Intermodal consists

**932-39811** Trailer-Train with 45' TransAmerica Trailer

**932-39812** Trailer-Train with 45' SP† Trailer

**932-39813** Trailer-Train with 45' Tote Trailer

**932-39814** TTX with 48' Schneider Trailer

**932-39815** TTX with 48' Xtra Trailer

**932-39816** TTX with 48' JB Hunt Trailer

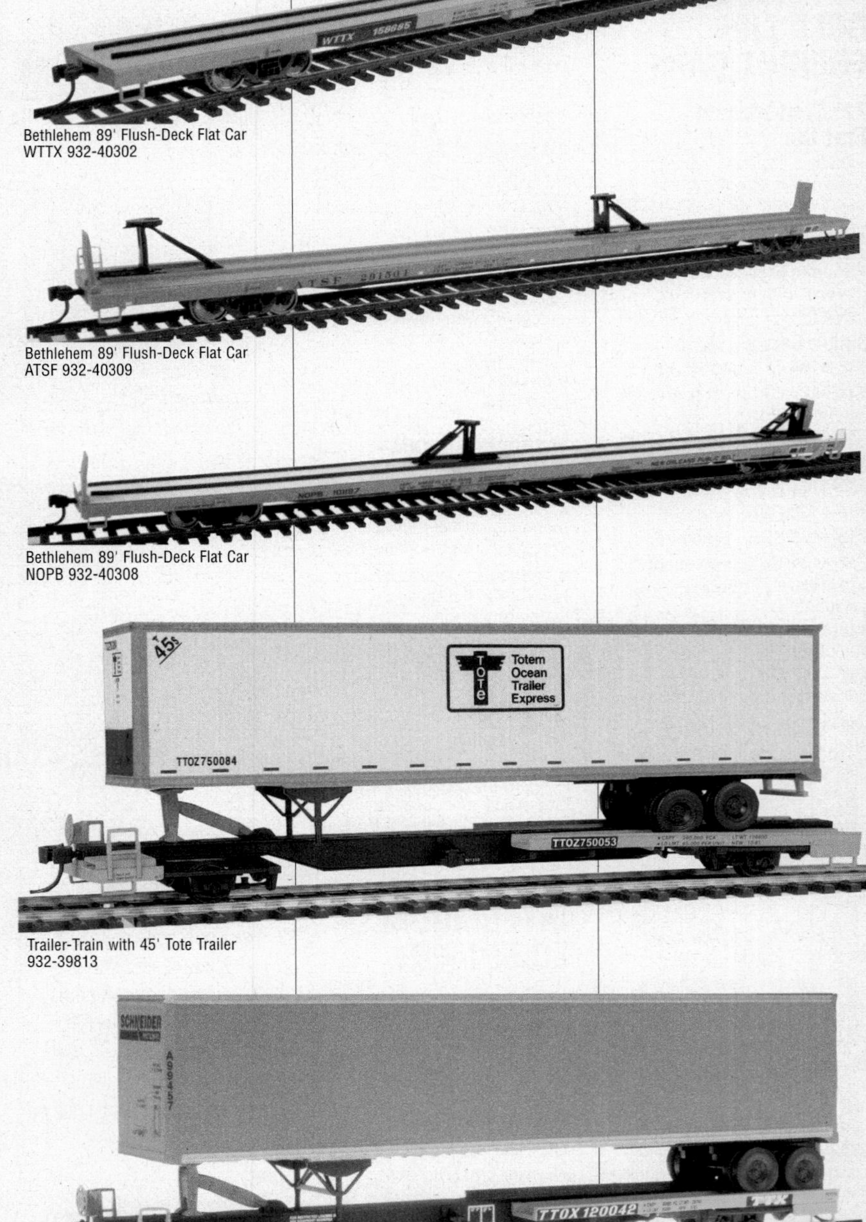


Bethlehem 89' Flush-Deck Flat Car WTTX 932-40302

Bethlehem 89' Flush-Deck Flat Car ATSF 932-40309

Bethlehem 89' Flush-Deck Flat Car NOPB 932-40308

Trailer-Train with 45' Tote Trailer 932-39813

TTX with 48' Schneider Trailer 932-39814

932-39811 Trailer-Train with 45' TransAmerica Trailer

932-39813 Trailer-Train with 45' Tote Trailer

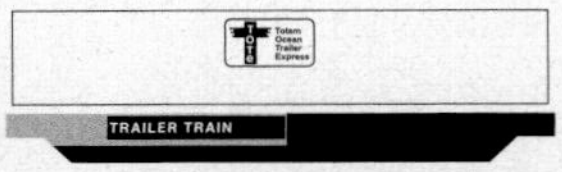

932-39815 TTX with 48' Xtra Trailer

932-39812 Trailer-Train with 45' SP Trailer

932-39814 TTX with 48' Schneider Trailer

932-39816 TTX with 48' JB Hunt Trailer

# WALTHERS

## GOLD LINE™ FREIGHT CARS

### 4-Axle, 90-Ton GSC Depressed-Center Flat Car 19.98 ea

- All-new tooling
- Diecast metal body for optimum performance
- Accurate replica of cars currently in service

**932-7881** TTX
**932-7882** Trailer-Train
**932-7883** Kasgro (KRL)
**932-7884** SOO
**932-7885** UP†
**932-7886** CR
**932-7887** NYC
**932-7888** MILW
**932-7889** CNW†
**932-7890** WC
**932-7891** SOU
**932-7892** Westinghouse
**932-7893** Pittsburgh & Lake Erie
**932-7894** SOO
**932-7880** Undecorated

932-7881 TTX

932-7882 Trailer-Train

932-7883 Kasgro (KRL)

932-7884 SOO

932-7885 UP

932-7886 CR

932-7887 NYC

932-7888 MILW

932-7889 CNW

932-7890 WC

932-7891 SOU

932-7892 Westinghouse

†Union Pacific licensed product.

932-7893 Pittsburgh & Lake Erie

932-7894 SOO

### 63' Pulpwood Flat Car

**COMING SOON!**

**Winter 2007-08 Delivery**
- New Roadnumbers
- Used to move pulpwood to paper mills
- Great for post-70s layouts

**Single Cars 17.98 ea**
**NEW 932-3157** CN
**NEW 932-3158** CP
**NEW 932-3159** WC
**NEW 932-3160** Georgia-Pacific
**NEW 932-3161** TTX
**NEW 932-3162** SOU

**Limited-Run 2-Packs 34.98 ea**
**NEW 932-23157** CN
**NEW 932-23158** CP
**NEW 932-23159** WC
**NEW 932-23160** Georgia-Pacific
**NEW 932-23161** TTX
**NEW 932-23162** SOU

932-3157 CN

932-3158 CP

932-3159 WC

932-3160 Georgia-Pacific

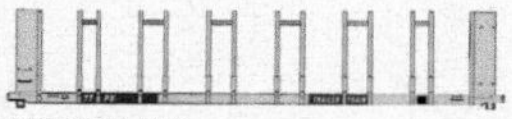

932-3161 TTX

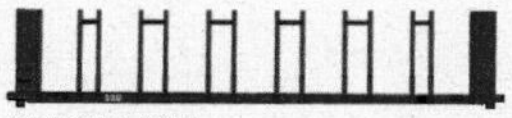

932-3162 SOU

### 81' 4-Truck Depressed Center Flat Cars 29.98 ea

- Diecast metal body for optimum performance

**932-5620** TTX
**932-5621** BN
**932-5622** Department of Defense
**932-5623** UP†
**932-5625** GECX
**932-5628** CR
**932-5629** Kasgro Rail
**932-5630** ATSF
**932-5631** NS
**932-5632** GE (yellow)
**932-5619** Undecorated

4-Axle, 90-Ton GSC Depressed-Center Flat Car UP 932-7885

4-Axle, 90-Ton GSC Depressed-Center Flat Car CR 932-7886

4-Axle, 90-Ton GSC Depressed-Center Flat Car CNW 932-7889

81' 4-Truck Depressed Center Flat Car TTX 932-5620

81' 4-Truck Depressed Center Flat Car GECX 932-5625

81' 4-Truck Depressed Center Flat Car Department of Defense 932-5622

63' Pulpwood Flat Car
Car Number Shown Not Available

# WALTHERS

## GOLD LINE™ FREIGHT CARS

### 66' Heavy-Duty 4-Truck Flat Cars 29.98 ea

- Diecast metal body for optimum performance
- Looks great carrying machinery, off-road vehicles and other big loads

**932-5641** TTX #1

**932-5645** UP†

**932-5646** SOO

**932-5647** CSX

**932-5648** SP†

**932-5640** Undecorated

## FUNNEL-FLOW® TANK CARS

- Correct sloped body
- Realistic hatches and fittings
- Wire handrails
- Sharp lettering
- 16,000- and 23,000-Gallon versions

### 40' 16,000-Gallon Funnel-Flow Tank Car 21.98 ea

**932-7223** ADM Corn Syrup (New Logo)

**932-7224** Procor White

**932-7226** Amaizo (UTLX)

**932-7227** Cerestar (UTLX)

**932-7228** Procor (SHLX) Optimiser

**932-7229** UCLX (black)

**932-7231** GATX (Caustic Soda)

**932-7232** Cargill (old logo)

**932-7233** Georgia Marble (HARX)

**932-7234** TILX (black w/white band)

**932-7235** ITDX (black)

**932-7236** PPTX

**932-7237** WAGX

**932-7238** UTLX (Potassium Chloride)

**932-7200** Undecorated

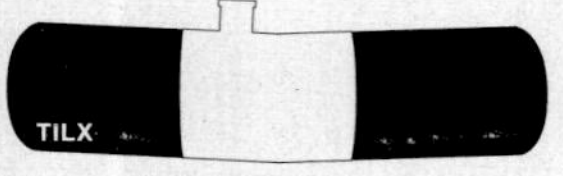


932-7234 TILX (black w/white band)

932-7235 ITDX (black)

932-7236 PPTX

932-7237 WAGX

932-7238 UTLX (Potassium Chloride)

### 54' 23,000-Gallon Funnel-Flow Tank Car 21.98 ea

932-7270 Terra

932-7271 United States Army

932-7272 Darling (UTLX)

932-7273 Shell Oil Company (SCMX)

932-7274 Celtran, Inc. (CELX)

932-7275 NGO-Chemical (UTLX)

932-7276 UTLX (Optimiser)

932-7277 Kerr-McGee (SHPX)

932-7278 UTLX (100th Anniversary)

932-7276 UTLX (Optimiser)

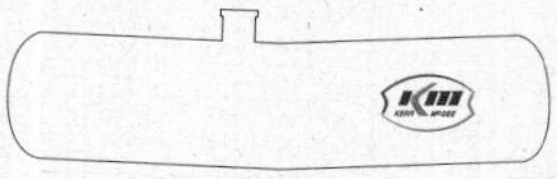

932-7277 Kerr-McGee (SHPX)

932-7278 UTLX (100th Anniversary)

40' 16,000-Gallon Funnel-Flow Tank Car
ADM 932-7223

54' 23,000-Gallon Funnel-Flow Tank Car
Darling 932-7272

54' 23,000-Gallon Funnel-Flow Tank Car
Celtran 932-7274

66' Heavy-Duty 4-Truck Flat Car
SP 932-5648

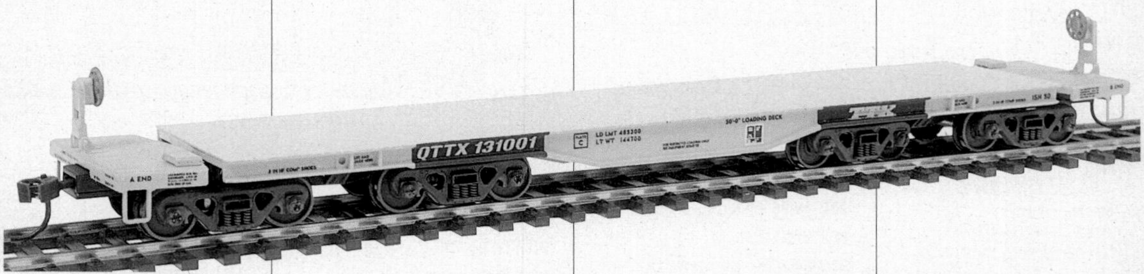

66' Heavy-Duty 4-Truck Flat Car
TTX 932-5641

# WALTHERS

## GOLD LINE™ FREIGHT CARS

## ORE CARS

- Authentic "Minnesota" cars
- Diecast underframe
- Detailed brake system
- Knuckle (or horn hook) couplers for end cars; dummy couplers for intermediate cars

### 4-Packs 29.98 ea

**932-4401** UP†
**932-4402** GN
**932-4403** CNW†
**932-4404** DM&IR
**932-4406** Bessemer & Lake Erie
**932-4407** SOO
**932-4408** Data Only (oxide)
**932-4400** Undecorated

### Taconite Ore Car 12-Packs 79.98 ea

- Side and End Extensions
- Diecast Underframe
- Detailed brake system
- Knuckle (or horn hook) couplers for end cars
- Dummy couplers or drawbars for intermediate cars to match prototype practice

**932-4557** BN #2
**932-4558** DMIR
**932-4559** GN #2
**932-4560** DM&IR (new scheme)
**932-4561** BN
**932-4562** GN
**932-4563** Lake Superior & Ishpeming

DMIR

932-4560 DM&IR (new scheme)

932-4561 BN

GREAT NORTHERN

932-4562 GN

932-4563 Lake Superior & Ishpeming

Daily New Product Announcements! Visit Walthers Web site at **www.walthers.com**

## WELL CARS

### 69' All-Purpose Husky-Stacks®

- Authentic paint schemes
- Diecast body
- Unique car numbers
- See-through floor

### Single Cars 16.98 ea

**932-4301** TTX
**932-4302** BN
**932-4303** NS
**932-4304** CRLE
**932-4305** TTX - Limited-Run
**932-4300** Undecorated

### National Steel Car 53' 3-Unit Well Cars

- Three drawbar-connected platforms
- Holds 53' containers
- Free-rolling trucks
- Knuckle couplers
- Detailed, diecast metal bodies with appropriate plastic details
- Modeler Installed Grab Irons
- Available in 3-Unit Sets or Stand Alone

### Stand-Alone Cars 16.98 ea

**932-3945** TTX #4
**932-3946** TTX #5
**932-3948** CP
**932-3949** TTX #6
**932-3944** Undecorated

### 3-Unit Sets 44.98 ea

**932-3941** TTX #1
**932-3942** TTX #2
**932-3943** TTX #3
**932-3944** CP #1
**932-3947** CP #2
**932-3950** TTX #4

932-3948 CP

932-3949 TTX

932-3947 CP

National Steel Car 53' 3-Unit Well Car 933-3941 Early sample shown; car will include metal wheels

†Union Pacific licensed product.

69' All-Purpose Husky-Stack TTX 932-4301

69' All-Purpose Husky-Stack NS 932-4303

National Steel 53' Well Car CP 932-3948

Ore Car GN 932-4402

Taconite Ore Car DMIR 932-4560

Taconite Ore Car LS&I 932-4563

Superbly detailed replicas of cars used by many American railroads in the steam, transition and diesel eras, PROTO 2000 cars feature scale size handrails & grab irons, correct weight for optimum operation, correct trucks with metal RP-25 wheels and magnetic knuckle couplers. Most are offered in your choice of assembled or kit versions with up to four different roadnumbers for each scheme.

## NEW PRODUCTS

### PS2CD 4427 3-Bay Covered Hopper

**October 2007 Delivery**

Valued for its large capacity, trough-style roof hatches, and center discharge gates, the PS-2 Center Discharge 4427 High-Side Covered Hopper was introduced in the 1960s and can still be found hauling grain and other medium-density loads today.

- Fully Assembled Single Cars & 2-Packs
- 13-Rib High-Side Body
- Full Underbody Detail
- Detailed Brake System
- Barber S-2 100-Ton Trucks w/36" Wheels
- New Roadnames & Numbers

#### Milwaukee Road

**NEW 920-54675** Single Car **29.98**

**NEW 920-254675** Limited-Run 2-Pack **59.98**

#### ADM®

**NEW 920-54676** Single Car **29.98**

**NEW 920-254676** Limited-Run 2-Pack **59.98**

#### Cooper Feeds

**NEW 920-54677** Single Car **29.98**

**NEW 920-254677** Limited-Run 2-Pack **59.98**

#### Chicago & North Western[†]

**NEW 920-54678** Single Car **29.98**

**NEW 920-254678** Limited-Run 2-Pack **59.98**

#### Cargill

**NEW 920-54679** Single Car **29.98**

**NEW 920-254679** Limited-Run 2-Pack **59.98**

#### Peavey

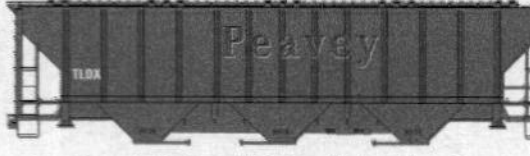

**NEW 920-54680** Single Car **29.98**

**NEW 920-254680** Limited-Run 2-Pack **59.98**

#### Missouri-Kansas-Texas

**NEW 920-54681** Single Car **29.98**

**NEW 920-254681** Limited-Run 2-Pack **59.98**

#### Undecorated

**NEW 920-21869** Single Car **29.98**



PS2CD 4427 3-Bay Covered Hopper
Roadname Shown Not Available

AAR 53'-6" 50-Ton Flat Car with Load - Ready to Run
Kansas City Southern w/Wagon Boxes & Frames 920-54533

### AAR 53'-6" 50-Ton Flat Car with Load

**October 2007 Delivery for Kits**

**January 2008 Delivery for Ready to Run Cars**

Based on the AAR standard design first submitted in 1941, cars of this type remained in revenue service into the 1980s and can still be found in maintenance service today. The models are highly detailed with a realistic deck, and an authentic load with appropriate blocking, strapping and tie downs. Each features a hidden metal weight for improved performance, plus authentic paint and lettering. Kits can be assembled in about an hour.

- New Roadnames & Roadnumbers
- Realistic Loads

#### Atlantic Coast Line w/Generators

**NEW 920-54475** Kit #77000 **17.00**

**NEW 920-54476** Kit #77042 **17.00**

**NEW 920-54525** Ready to Run #77105 **29.98**

**NEW 920-54526** Ready to Run #77146 **29.98**

#### Missouri-Kansas-Texas[†] w/Generators

**NEW 920-54477** Kit #13701 **17.00**

**NEW 920-54478** Kit #13719 **17.00**

**NEW 920-54527** Ready to Run #13711 **29.98**

**NEW 920-54528** Ready to Run #13725 **29.98**

#### Elgin, Joliet & Eastern w/Generators

**NEW 920-54479** Kit #6575 **17.00**

**NEW 920-54480** Kit #6701 **17.00**

**NEW 920-54529** Ready to Run #6673 **29.98**

**NEW 920-54530** Ready to Run #6759 **29.98**

#### Norfolk & Western w/Wagon Boxes & Frames

**NEW 920-54481** Kit #32807 **17.00**

**NEW 920-54482** Kit #32826 **17.00**

**NEW 920-54531** Ready to Run #32815 **29.98**

**NEW 920-54532** Ready to Run #32843 **29.98**

#### Kansas City Southern w/Wagon Boxes & Frames

**NEW 920-54483** Kit #1053 **17.00**

**NEW 920-54484** Kit #1109 **17.00**

**NEW 920-54533** Ready to Run #1099 **29.98**

**NEW 920-54434** Ready to Run #1167 **29.98**

#### Western Maryland w/Generators

**NEW 920-54485** Kit #2605 **17.00**

**NEW 920-54486** Kit #2629 **17.00**

**NEW 920-54535** Ready to Run #2614 **29.98**

**NEW 920-54536** Ready to Run #2640 **29.98**

#### Undecorated

**NEW 920-54487** Kit w/Generator **17.00**

**NEW 920-54487** Kit w/Grain Wagon Boxes & Chassis **17.00**

[†]Union Pacific licensed product.

From Walthers

## Mather Stock Cars

**November 2007 Delivery for Ready to Run Cars**

For nearly 100 years, railroads moved all kinds of livestock from western ranges to eastern markets. For most roads however, this traffic was limited to just a few weeks each year. And since stock cars didn't lend themselves to handling other loads, most railroads were reluctant to invest in such specialized cars that were needed only for short periods. From 1915 on, many roads found it easier to lease stock cars from the Mather Stock Car Company of Chicago on an as-needed basis. Built to it's own modular design (which was considered quite radical at the time), Mather cars were simple to repair or rebuild, and these cost-saving measures were reflected in lower lease rates to customers. Some of these venerable cars were still running in the 1960s, until changes in the meatpacking and processing industry all but eliminated the need for stock cars.

- New Roadnames & Roadnumbers
- Single or Double Deck as Appropriate

### Akron, Canton & Youngstown

**NEW 920-54575** Kit #286 Double Deck **17.00**

**NEW 920-54576** Kit #294 Double Deck **17.00**

**NEW 920-54675** Ready to Run #3 Double Deck **29.98**

**NEW 920-54676** Ready to Run #4 Double Deck **29.98**

### Baltimore & Ohio

**NEW 920-54577** Kit #110355 Double Deck **17.00**

**NEW 920-54578** Kit #111088 Double Deck **17.00**

**NEW 920-54594** Kit #112085 Single Deck **17.00**

**NEW 920-54595** Kit #112537 Single Deck **17.00**

**NEW 920-54677** Ready to Run #3 Double Deck **29.98**

**NEW 920-54678** Ready to Run #4 Single Deck **29.98**

### Great Northern

**NEW 920-54579** Kit #55063 Single Deck **17.00**

**NEW 920-54580** Kit #55149 Single Deck **17.00**

**NEW 920-54679** Ready to Run #3 Single Deck **29.98**

**NEW 920-54680** Ready to Run #4 Single Deck **29.98**

### Gotham Stock Express

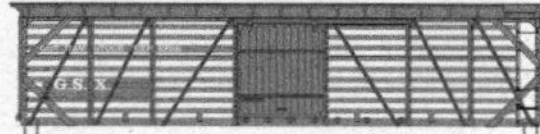

**NEW 920-54581** Kit #4004 Double Deck **17.00**

**NEW 920-54582** Kit #4135 Double Deck **17.00**

**NEW 920-54681** Ready to Run #3 Double Deck **29.98**

**NEW 920-54682** Ready to Run #4 Double Deck **29.98**

### Louisville & Nashville

**NEW 920-54583** Kit #88004 Single Deck **17.00**

**NEW 920-54584** Kit #88076 Single Deck **17.00**

**NEW 920-54683** Ready to Run #3 Single Deck **29.98**

**NEW 920-54684** Ready to Run #4 Single Deck **29.98**

### Mather Stock Car

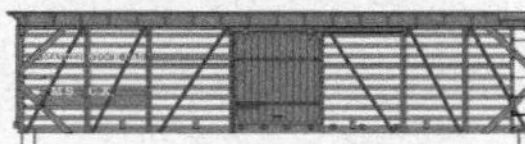

**NEW 920-54585** Kit #1793 Single Deck **17.00**

**NEW 920-54586** Kit #2100 Single Deck **17.00**

**NEW 920-54685** Ready to Run #3 Single Deck **29.98**

**NEW 920-54686** Ready to Run #4 Single Deck **29.98**

### Northern Pacific

**NEW 920-54587** Kit #80073 Double Deck **17.00**

**NEW 920-54588** Kit #80084 Double Deck **17.00**

**NEW 920-54596** Kit #80108 Single Deck **17.00**

**NEW 920-54597** Kit #80144 Single Deck **17.00**

**NEW 920-54687** Ready to Run #3 Single Deck **29.98**

**NEW 920-54688** Ready to Run #4 Double Deck **29.98**

### Undecorated

**NEW 920-54589** Kit **17.00**

## ICC Type-21 8,000-Gallon Tank Car - Early Version w/K Brakes

**September 2007 Delivery for Kits**

**December 2007 Delivery for Ready to Run Cars**

Demand for tank cars skyrocketed in the 1920s as automobiles and trucks became more common. Moving gasoline, lubricants and other petroleum products over long distances required larger and stronger tank cars. In 1921, American Car & Foundry rolled out the first of its new 10,000-gallon, riveted steel cars, which came to be known as the Type 21.

Tough and durable, the cars kept rolling into the 1960s, often hauling many other kinds of liquids in later years. This series of models is based on steam-era cars with the original K-type brake system and early lettering schemes.

- Authentic Steam-Era Schemes
- Detailed Underframe with K Brake

Mather Stock Car L&N 920-54583

ICC Type-21 8,000-Gallon Tank Car Chicago Tank Car Co. 920-54400

### Chicago Tank Car Co.

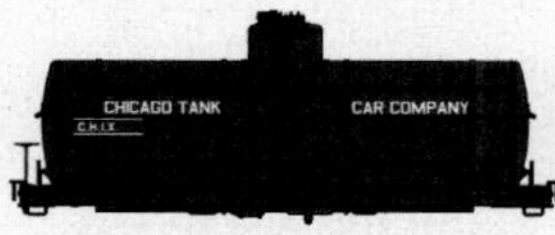

**NEW 920-54350** Kit #1163 **17.00**

**NEW 920-54351** Kit #1136 **17.00**

**NEW 920-54400** Ready to Run #1123 **30.00**

**NEW 920-54401** Ready to Run #1147 **30.00**

### Continental Oil Co.

**NEW 920-54352** Kit #8152 **17.00**

**NEW 920-54353** Kit #8029 **17.00**

**NEW 920-54402** Ready to Run #8034 **30.00**

**NEW 920-54403** Ready to Run #8015 **30.00**

### National Oil Co.

**NEW 920-54354** Kit #8046 **17.00**

**NEW 920-54355** Kit #8017 **17.00**

**NEW 920-54404** Ready to Run #8034 **30.00**

**NEW 920-54405** Ready to Run #8015 **30.00**

### Philadelphia Quartz Co.

**NEW 920-54356** Kit #806 **17.00**

**NEW 920-54357** Kit #809 **17.00**

**NEW 920-54406** Ready to Run #802 **30.00**

**NEW 920-54407** Ready to Run #805 **30.00**

### Roxana Petroleum - Shell

**NEW 920-54358** Kit #2412 **17.00**

**NEW 920-54359** Kit #2395 **17.00**

**NEW 920-54408** Ready to Run #2351 **30.00**

**NEW 920-54409** Ready to Run #2488 **30.00**

### Stauffer Chemical Co.

**NEW 920-54360** Kit #82 **17.00**

**NEW 920-54361** Kit #89 **17.00**

**NEW 920-54410** Ready to Run #81 **30.00**

**NEW 920-54411** Ready to Run #86 **30.00**

### Mid-Continent Petroleum

**NEW 920-54362** Kit #2954 **17.00**

**NEW 920-54363** Kit #2957 **17.00**

**NEW 920-54412** Ready to Run #2956 **30.00**

**NEW 920-54413** Ready to Run #2957 **30.00**

### Undecorated

**NEW 920-54364** Kit **17.00**

**NEW 920-54414** Ready to Run **30.00**

From Walthers

## 40' MATHER BOX CAR

- New Roadnumbers
- Perfect for Steam and Transition-Era
- Choose Time-Saver Kits® or Assembled Models
- 4 Different Numbers for Each Roadname
- Laser Quality Painting & Printing
- Scale Size Handrails & Grab Irons
- Correct Trucks
- Metal RP-25 Wheels
- Magnetic Knuckle Couplers
- Correct Weight for Optimum Operation

### Akron, Canton & Youngstown

**920-54175** Ready To Run #1125 **24.98**

**920-54176** Ready To Run #1184 **24.98**

**920-54150** Kit #1102 **16.98**

**920-54151** Kit #1136 **16.98**

### Chicago & Eastern Illinois

**920-54177** Ready To Run #422 **24.98**

**920-54178** Ready To Run #473 **24.98**

**920-54152** Kit #405 **16.98**

**920-54153** Kit #449 **16.98**

### Chicago & Illinois Midland

**920-54179** Ready To Run #8196 **24.98**

**920-54180** Ready To Run #8409 **24.98**

**920-54154** Kit #8062 **16.98**

**920-54155** Kit #8250 **16.98**

### Fort Dodge, Des Moines & Southern

**920-54181** Ready To Run #14004 **24.98**

**920-54182** Ready To Run #14007 **24.98**

**920-54156** Kit #14002 **16.98**

**920-54157** Kit #14005 **16.98**

### Illinois Northern

**920-54183** Ready To Run #2023 **24.98**

**920-54184** Ready To Run #2086 **24.98**

**920-54158** Kit #2009 **16.98**

**920-54159** Kit #2038 **16.98**

**920-30897** #2073 Ready To Run **30.00**

### Manufacturers Railway

**920-54185** Ready To Run #7532 **24.98**

**920-54186** Ready To Run #7584 **24.98**

**920-54160** Kit #7507 **16.98**

**920-54161** Kit #7557 **16.98**

### Muncie & Western

**920-54187** Ready To Run #1229 **24.98**

**920-54188** Ready To Run #1272 **24.98**

**920-54162** Kit #1204 **16.98**

**920-54163** Kit #1236 **16.98**

### Port Huron & Detroit

**920-54189** Ready To Run #1295 **24.98**

**920-54190** Ready To Run #1603 **24.98**

**920-54164** Kit #1030 **16.98**

**920-54165** Kit #1466 **16.98**

**920-30901** Ready To Run #1509 **30.00**

### Tennessee Central

**920-54191** Ready To Run #7736 **24.98**

**920-54192** Ready To Run #7783 **24.98**

**920-54166** Kit #7723 **16.98**

**920-54167** Kit #7752 **16.98**

### Undecorated

**920-54168** Kit **16.98**

Latest New Product News Daily! Visit Walthers Web site at **www.walthers.com**

50' Single Door Box Car
Cotton Belt #20064 920-54284

## 50' SINGLE DOOR BOX CAR

- Choose Kit or Assembled Versions
- New Car Numbers
- 4 Different Numbers for Each Roadname
- Great for any Layout
- Laser Quality Painting & Printing
- Scale Size Handrails & Grab Irons
- Correct Trucks
- Metal RP-25 Wheels
- Magnetic Knuckle Couplers
- Correct Weight for Optimum Operation
- Time-Saver Kits Coming Fall 06
- Ready to Run Coming Spring 07

### CB&Q

**920-54276** Ready to Run #21004 **24.98**

**920-54277** Ready to Run #21243 **24.98**

**920-54251** Kit #21058 **16.98**

**920-54252** Kit #21246 **16.98**

### Grand Trunk Western

**920-54278** Ready to Run #595372 **24.98**

**920-54279** Ready to Run #595456 **24.98**

**920-54253** Kit #595099 **16.98**

**920-54254** Kit #595268 **16.98**

### NYC

**920-54280** Ready to Run #176646 **24.98**

**920-54281** Ready to Run #176737 **24.98**

**920-54255** Kit #176422 **16.98**

**920-54256** Kit #176598 **16.98**

### Pittsburgh & Lake Erie

**920-54282** Ready to Run #35990 **24.98**

**920-54283** Ready to Run #35922 **24.98**

**920-54257** Kit #35933 **16.98**

**920-54258** Kit #35966 **16.98**

40' Mather Box Car Akron, Canton & Youngstown 920-54175

40' Mather Box Car Chicago & Illinois Midland 920-54179

50' Single Door Box Car
CB&Q 920-54276

50' Single Door Box Car
NYC 920-54281

### Cotton Belt†

**920-54284** Ready to Run #20064 **24.98**

**920-54285** Ready to Run #20168 **24.98**

**920-54259** Kit #20032 **16.98**

**920-54260** Kit #20130 **16.98**

†Union Pacific licensed product.

### SP†

**920-54286** Ready to Run #81768 **24.98**

**920-54287** Ready to Run #81936 **24.98**

**920-54261** Kit #81649 **16.98**

**920-54262** Kit #81865 **16.98**

### Undecorated

**920-54263** Kit **16.98**

From Walthers

# 52'6" DROP END MILL GONDOLA W/LOAD

- Now with Realistic Load
- New Roadnumbers
- Time-Saver Kit® Coming Summer 06
- Ready to Run Coming Winter 06-07

### CR (brown)

**920-54075** Ready To Run #510907 w/Duct Work **29.98**

**920-54076** Ready To Run #510992 w/Riveted Girder **29.98**

**920-31975** Kit #510862 w/Duct Work **24.98**

**920-31976** Kit #510934 w/Riveted Girder **24.98**

### Erie (As Delivered Scheme)

**920-54077** Ready To Run #10432 w/Large Gears **29.98**

**920-54078** Ready To Run #10524 w/Duct Work **29.98**

**920-31977** Kit #10355 w/Large Gears **24.98**

**920-31978** Kit #10376 w/Duct Work **24.98**

### NKP (As Delivered Scheme)

**920-54079** Ready To Run #66025 w/Riveted Girder **29.98**

**920-54080** Ready To Run #66040 w/Large Gears **29.98**

**920-31979** Kit #66015 w/Riveted Girder **24.98**

**920-31980** Kit #66036 w/Large Gears **24.98**

### NYC (As Delivered Scheme)

**920-54081** Ready To Run #712516 w/Duct Work **29.98**

**920-54082** Ready To Run #712593 w/Riveted Girder **29.98**

**920-31981** Kit #712540 w/Duct Work **24.98**

**920-31982** Kit #712689 w/Riveted Girder **24.98**

### Patapsco & Back Rivers (As Delivered Scheme)

**920-54083** Ready To Run #115 w/Large Gears **29.98**

**920-54084** Ready To Run #150 w/Duct Work **29.98**

**920-31983** Kit #140 w/Large Gears **24.98**

**920-31984** Kit #181 w/Duct Work **24.98**

### Pere Marquette (As Delivered Scheme)

**920-54085** Ready To Run #18858 w/Riveted Girder **29.98**

**920-54086** Ready To Run #18939 w/Large Gears **29.98**

**920-31985** Kit #18872 w/Riveted Girder **24.98**

**920-31986** Kit #18908 w/Large Gears **24.98**

### Undecorated

**920-31987** Kit w/Riveted Girder **24.98**

# WAR EMERGENCY STEEL-SIDE HOPPERS

- Non-Magnetic Blackened Metal Wheels
- Free-Rolling 50-Ton Spring Plankless Trucks
- AB Brake System
- Magnetic Knuckle Couplers
- 2 Styles of Handbrakes
- 2 Styles of Door Locks
- Fully Weighted for Trouble-Free Operation
- Partially Assembled Timesaver Kits – Build in Less Than One Hour
- Also Available Factory Assembled

### Atlantic Coast Line

**920-31513** #82331 (black, white) Timesaver Kit **17.00**

**920-31514** #82409 (black, white) Timesaver Kit **17.00**

**920-31611** #82007 (black, white) Assembled **30.00**

**920-31612** #82164 (black, white) Assembled **30.00**

### Santa Fe

**920-31613** #180706 (Mineral Red, white) Assembled **30.00**

**920-31614** #180637 (Mineral Red, white) Assembled **30.00**

### Baltimore & Ohio

**920-31518** #733183 (black, white) Timesaver Kit **17.00**

**920-31615** #733031 (black, white) Assembled **30.00**

**920-31616** #733169 (black, white) Assembled **30.00**

### Chesapeake & Ohio

**920-31519** #54443 (black, white) Timesaver Kit **17.00**

**920-31520** #55999 (black, white) Timesaver Kit **17.00**

**920-31617** #54284 (black, white) Assembled **30.00**

**920-31618** #55090 (black, white) Assembled **30.00**

### Norfolk & Western

**920-31521** #339156 (black, white) Timesaver Kit **17.00**

**920-31522** #339399 (black, white) Timesaver Kit **17.00**

**920-31619** #339032 (black, white) Assembled **30.00**

**920-31620** #339260 (black, white) Assembled **30.00**

### Seaboard Coast Line

**920-31523** #682130 (black, white) Timesaver Kit **17.00**

**920-31524** #682698 (black, white) Timesaver Kit **17.00**

**920-31621** #682090 (black, white) Assembled **30.00**

**920-31622** #682478 (black, white) Assembled **30.00**

### Southern

**920-31525** #104934 (black, white) Timesaver Kit **17.00**

**920-31526** #105949 (black, white) Timesaver Kit **17.00**

**920-31623** #104500 (black, white) Assembled **30.00**

**920-31624** #105187 (black, white) Assembled **30.00**

### Wabash

**920-31527** #39162 (black, white) Timesaver Kit **17.00**

**920-31528** #39394 (black, white) Timesaver Kit **17.00**

**920-31625** #39000 (black, white) Assembled **30.00**

**920-31626** #39253 (black, white) Assembled **30.00**

### Undecorated

**920-31529** Timesaver Kit **17.00**

# 4427 COVERED HOPPER

### Factory-Assembled 30.00 ea

- Exact Replica
- Full Underbody Detail
- Complete Brake System
- Accurately Scaled 13-Rib High-Side Body
- Extremely Free-Rolling Barber S-2 100 Ton Trucks with 36" Wheels
- Full Recommended NMRA Weight
- PROTO 2000 Magnetic Knuckle Couplers

### Northern Pacific

**920-31666** #76826 (gray, billboard "Northern Pacific")

**920-31667** #76933 (gray, billboard "Northern Pacific")

52'6" Drop End Mill Gondola w/Large Gears Patapsco & Back Rivers 920-31983

War Emergency Steel-Side Hopper Seaboard Coast Line #682478 920-31622

4427 Covered Hopper St. Louis-San Francisco #79061 920-31668

Northeastern Steel Center Cupola Caboose Chessie/WM Safety #901806 920-31258

### St. Louis-San Francisco

**920-31668** #79061 (gray, billboard "Frisco")

**920-31669** #79086 (gray, billboard "Frisco")

# 10,000 GALLON INSULATED TYPE 21 TANK CAR

### Time-Saver Kits 17.00 ea

- Authentic Placards
- Detailed Underframe with Brake Gear
- Prototypically Correct Laser Quality Painting & Printing
- Magnetic Knuckle Couplers
- Partially Assembled – Build in Less Than One Hour

### MPCX Magnolia

**920-31531** #1627 (white tank, black underframe)

# NORTHEASTERN STEEL CENTER CUPOLA CABOOSE

### Factory-Assembled 30.00 ea

- Authentic Replica of USRA Design
- Used by over 40 Railroads
- Over 75 Separate Parts
- Detailed Interior
- Flush Widows
- Complete Underbody Detail
- Bettendorf Swing Motion Caboose Trucks
- Magnetic Knuckle Couplers

### Chessie/WM Safety

**920-31257** #901803 (green w/large safety slogan)

**920-31258** #901806 (orange w/large safety slogan)

# WALTHERS

## BULK MATERIAL CONTAINERS

Designed for hauling smaller loads to on-line industries, these containers make great details for vintage terminal scenes and loads for the new USRA Steel Gondolas listed elsewhere in this section.

### Coke Containers pkg(3) 10.98 ea

Fully loaded USRA Gondola holds nine Coke Containers.

**933-2121** B&O

**933-2122** PRR
**933-2123** NYC
**933-2124** Erie
**933-2125** NKP
**933-2126** WM
**933-2127** MP†
**933-2128** LV
**933-2129** MILW
**933-2130** MON
**933-2131** EL
**933-2132** N&W
**933-2120** Undecorated

### Bulk Containers pkg(3) 10.98 ea

Fully loaded USRA Gondola holds 12 Bulk Containers.

**933-2101** B&O
**933-2102** PRR
**933-2103** NYC
**933-2104** Erie

**933-2105** NKP
**933-2106** WM
**933-2107** MP†
**933-2108** LV
**933-2109** ACL
**933-2110** DL&W
**933-2111** RDG
**933-2112** D&H
**933-2113** N&W
**933-2100** Undecorated

## CONTAINERS

Walthers containers, available in the four most common prototype lengths of 20, 28, 40 and 48', are great loads for any modern intermodal car and a must for realistic terminal scenes. Each package includes one pre-painted and assembled container.

### 20' Ribbed-Side Containers 4.49 ea

**933-1751** Maersk
**933-1752** K-Line
**933-1753** Hanjin

**933-1754** Evergreen
**933-1755** Genstar
**933-1756** OOCL
**933-1757** Mitsui OSK
**933-1758** Triton
**933-1759** Nedlloyd
**933-1761** CP Ships
**933-1762** CAST
**933-1763** American President Lines (APL)
**933-1764** Flexi-Van
**933-1765** NOL
**933-1766** NYK
**933-1767** Hamburg Sud
**933-1768** Xtra International
**933-1769** UASC
**933-1750** Undecorated

### 20' Tank Containers 4.98 ea

**933-1951** ATSF
**933-1952** UP
**933-1953** SEACO
**933-1954** TransAmerica
**933-1955** K&W Alaska
**933-1957** Tiphook
**933-1961** Bond
**933-1962** Vanhool
**933-1963** Hoyer
**933-1964** Stolt
**933-1966** Miller
**933-1950** Undecorated

†Union Pacific licensed product.

### 20' Hi-Cube Corrugated-Side Containers 4.98 ea

**933-2001** Maersk-Sealand
**933-2002** K-Line
**933-2003** Xtra
**933-2004** Genstar
**933-2005** OOCL
**933-2006** Gateway
**933-2007** Triton
**933-2008** Tiphook
**933-2009** P&O
**933-2010** SEACO
**933-2011** Tex
**933-2012** Yang Ming
**933-2013** Cosco

**933-2014** CMA
**933-2015** GE Seaco
**933-2016** Hapag-Lloyd
**933-2017** China Shipping

**933-2018** MSC
**933-2019** Hamburg Sud
**933-2020** Capital
**933-2021** CMA/CGM
**933-2022** MSC (Red)
**933-2023** Maersk
**933-2000** Undecorated

933-2019 Hamburg Sud

933-2020 Capital

933-2021 CMA/CGM

933-2023 Maersk

40' Reefer Container Maersk 933-1855

20' Tank Container SEACO 933-1953

20' Corrugated Side Container 933-2002

### 40' High-Cube Containers 4.49 ea

**933-1701** Maersk
**933-1702** APL
**933-1703** Evergreen
**933-1704** K-Line

**933-1705** Hapag-Lloyd
**933-1706** Matson
**933-1707** ITEL
**933-1708** CAST
**933-1709** CP Ship
**933-1710** OOCL
**933-1711** Hyundai
**933-1712** Hanjin
**933-1713** TransAmerica
**933-1714** Genstar
**933-1715** XTRA
**933-1716** Tropical
**933-1717** P&O
**933-1718** Nedlloyd
**933-1719** Yang Ming Line
**933-1720** Columbus Line
**933-1721** Crowley
**933-1700** Undecorated

### 40' Reefer Containers 4.98 ea

Equipped with a "picture frame" refrigeration unit that draws power from a separate generator, these containers are lighter and carry more than other containers of this type.

**933-1851** K-Line
**933-1852** Sea-Land
**933-1853** TransAmerica
**933-1854** Evergreen
**933-1855** Maersk
**933-1856** APL
**933-1857** Dole
**933-1859** MOL
**933-1861** NYK
**933-1862** P&O
**933-1863** Cosco
**933-1864** Trans Ocean
**933-1850** Undecorated

# WALTHERS

## CONTAINERS

### 40' Hi-Cube Corrugated-Side Containers 4.98 ea

**933-2051** APL
**933-2052** K-Line
**933-2053** Hyundai
**933-2054** Genstar
**933-2055** Seaco
**933-2056** Hapag-Lloyd
**933-2057** OOCL
**933-2058** PO Nedlloyd
**933-2059** Maersk-Sealand
**933-2060** Triton
**933-2061** Capitol
**933-2062** Uniglory

**933-2063** China Shipping

**933-2064** TEX

**933-2065** APL (No Eagle)

**933-2066** OOCL (Small, High Logo)

**933-2067** CMA/GMA (Earth)

**933-2068** Amficon
**933-2050** Undecorated

### 40' Corrugated-Side Containers 4.98 ea

- New Tooling
- Perfect for use with other double-stack cars

**933-1501** China Shipping

**933-1502** P&O/Nedlloyd

**933-1503** Genstar

**933-1504** K-Line

**933-1505** Yang Ming

**933-1506** Xtra Leasing

**933-1507** Cosco

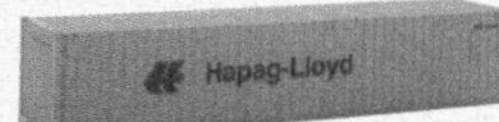


**933-1508** Hapag-Lloyd

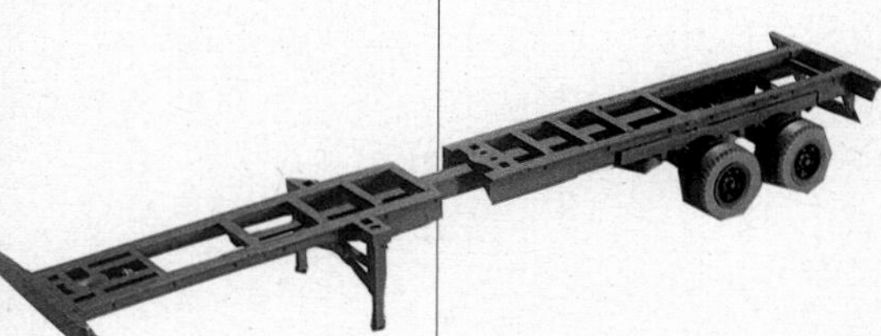

Extendable Container Chassis 933-3110

Mi-Jack Crane 933-3122

### 48' Stoughton Ribside Exterior-Post Containers 4.98 ea

**933-1805** NS
**933-1816** EMP
**933-1817** ATSF

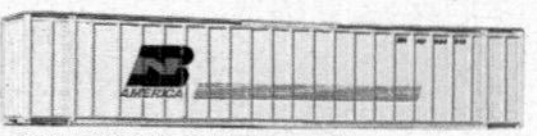

**933-1818** BN America
**933-1819** J.B. Hunt®
**933-1820** APL
**933-1821** NACS
**933-1823** UP†
**933-1849** Undecorated

### 48' Stoughton Smoothside Containers 4.98 ea

**933-1801** CP/US Service
**933-1802** CN Laser
**933-1803** BN America
**933-1804** Conrail Mercury
**933-1806** APL
**933-1807** Conquest
**933-1808** Genstar
**933-1809** CSX/SL
**933-1810** XTRA
**933-1811** ATSF
**933-1812** SP†
**933-1813** UP/Genstar
**933-1814** ITEL
**933-1815** J.B. Hunt
**933-1800** Undecorated

### Extendable Container Chassis

**933-3110** pkg(2) **8.98**
These special telescoping chassis are adjustable from 40 to 48'.

48' Stoughton Smoothside Container 933-1807

Kalmar Container Crane 933-3109

## CONTAINER CRANES

### Mi-Jack Translift Intermodal Crane

**933-3122 21.98**

- Used to lift trailers or containers; wide enough to straddle the intermodal car and two rows of trailers or containers parked side by side
- Many parts are adjustable to simulate a working crane
- Magnets hold containers securely without gluing
- Decals and complete instructions are included

### Kalmar Container Crane

**933-3109 19.98**

- Used for side loading or unloading and are well suited to smaller terminals
- Model is molded in safety yellow and includes decals and instructions

## MAINTENANCE-OF-WAY EQUIPMENT

### 25-Ton Crane Kit 14.98 ea

**932-5610** Vulcan Steel
**932-5611** Brownhoist
**932-5612** Electric Company
**932-5500** Undecorated

# WALTHERS

48' Stoughton Semi Trailer
XTRA Intermodal 933-1901

48' Stoughton Semi Trailer
J.B. Hunt 933-1904

48' Stoughton Semi Trailer
Schneider 933-1906

48' Stoughton Semi Trailer
Strick Lease 933-1907

26' Parcel Trailer w/Decals 933-1581

53' Stoughton Van Trailer
Swift 933-1453

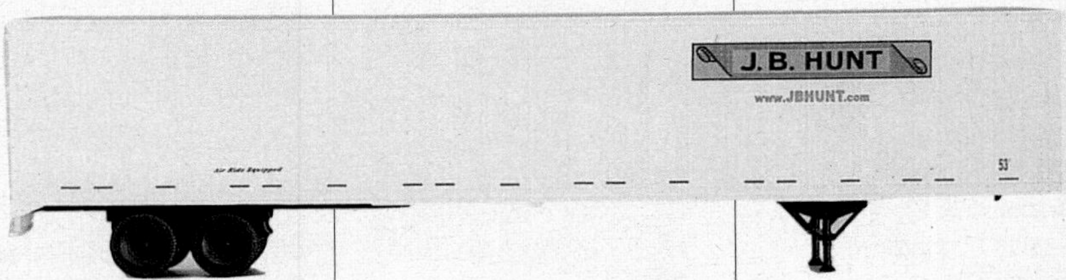

53' Stoughton Van Trailer
J.B. Hunt 933-1460

## TRUCKS & TRAILERS

### 48' Stoughton Semi Trailers 5.98 ea

Some of the most common trailers on the road or the rails are the 48' Stoughton Semi Trailers. These easy-to-build kits come decorated in a variety of popular roadnames, which are seen on intermodal trains throughout the US.

**933-1901** XTRA Intermodal (white)

**933-1904** J.B. Hunt (white)

**933-1906** Schneider (white)

**933-1907** Strick Lease (white)

**933-1908** Tip Lease (white)

**933-1909** Schneider (orange)

**933-1919** BNSF

**933-1925** Werner

**933-1900** Undecorated

### 53' Stoughton Van Trailers 6.98 ea

**933-1453** Swift

**933-1454** Bison

**933-1455** Yanke

**933-1459** Klyson

**933-1460** J.B. Hunt

**933-1461** Schneider

**933-1462** MS Carriers

**933-1450** Undecorated

## TRAILERS

### 26' Parcel Trailers 4.98 ea

**933-1581** Parcel Van w/Decals

**933-1580** Undecorated

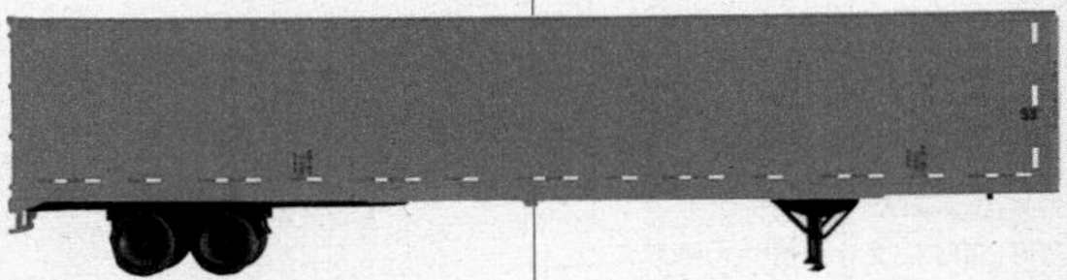

53' Stoughton Van Trailer
Schneider 933-1461

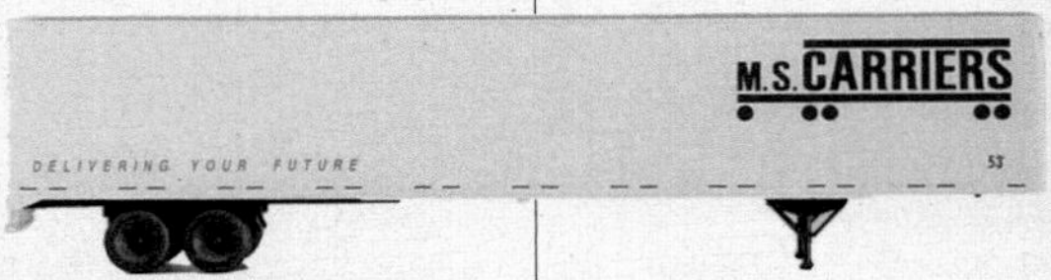

53' Stoughton Van Trailer
MS Carriers 933-1462

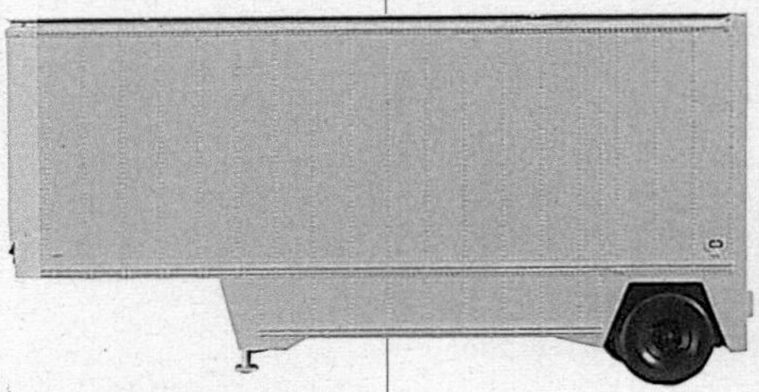

26' Parcel Trailer Undecorated 933-1580

# WALTHERS

## "THE WORKS"

These steel-service cars are ready to meet the vigorous demands of a blistering day at any steel works.

### Hot Metal Car Kit

- Easy-to-build, highly detailed cars feature a positionable ladle, six-wheel trucks, drive housing and working knuckle couplers

**932-3130** Hot Metal Car **16.98**

**932-3131** Hot Metal Car 3-Pack **49.98**

### Slag Car Kit

- Kit features separate ladle, simulated dump mechanism, trucks and working knuckle couplers

**932-3140** Slag Car **15.98**

**932-3141** Slag Car 3-Pack **44.98**

### Coke Car Kit

- Converted from older 36' two-bay hoppers and feature side and end extensions

**932-3091** Coke Car 3-Pack **24.98**

## FREIGHT CAR ACCESSORIES

Simulate end-of-car cushioning devices on modern freight cars with these kits.

### Cushion Car Couplers

- Molded in rust-colored styrene
- Assembly drawings and detailed instructions
- Parts to modify four cars
- Use with knuckle or horn-hook couplers

**933-1030** Cushion Car Coupler Pocket Kit 4 Pair **3.98**

### Horn-Hook Couplers

**933-995** X2F Horn-Hook Couplers pkg(12) **1.98**
Standard replacement fits all Walthers kits. Molded in Delrin® plastic.

### Athearn Coupler Pocket Conversion Kit

**933-997** 2 Pair **5.98**
Converts Athearn 85' Hi-Cube box cars and 85' flat cars to a body-mounted swinging coupler bar system as used on Walthers Enclosed Auto Carrier. Kit includes parts to convert two cars.

## REDISCOVER DO-IT-YOURSELF FUN WITH WALTHERS CLASSIC KITS!

### Classic Kit features:

- Easy to build
- Affordable fun
- Widely used prototypes
- Authentic color schemes
- Includes trucks and working knuckle couplers

### 49' Quad Hopper Kits 9.98 ea

- Perfect for 1970s-era and later coal trains

**932-4911** BN

**932-4912** GN

**932-4913** DRGW†

**932-4914** CNW†

**932-4915** CSX

**932-4916** WC

**932-4917** Clinchfield

**932-4918** CB&Q

932-4911 BN

932-4912 GN

932-4913 DRGW

932-4914 CNW

932-4915 CSX

932-4916 WC

932-4917 Clinchfield

932-4918 CB&Q

†Union Pacific licensed product.

### Coal Loads

One-piece resin castings are designed especially for the cars listed and feature realistic texture. Drop-in mount.

### 100-Ton Quad Hoppers

**933-1037** 2-Pack **7.98**

### GSC "Commonwealth" 54' Flat Car Kits 9.98 ea

- Build one of four ways: Standard Flat Car, Bulkhead, early Piggyback and Late Piggyback

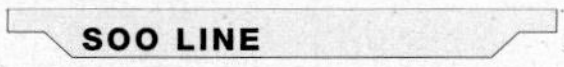

**932-3774** SOO

**932-3775** PRR

**932-3776** UP†

**932-3777** ATSF

**932-3778** BN

**932-3779** CR

**932-3780** SP†

**932-3781** NP

**932-3773** Undecorated

SOO LINE
932-3774 SOO

PENNSYLVANIA
932-3775 PRR

UP
932-3776 UP

ATSF
932-3777 ATSF

BN
932-3778 BN

CR
932-3779 CR

SP
932-3780 SP

NORTHERN PACIFIC
932-3781 NP

### Fruit Growers Express-Style 50' RBL Insulated Box Car Kits 9.98 ea

- Used from the early 1960s to the present

**932-4772** Fruit Growers Express

**932-4773** UP†

**932-4774** DRGW†

**932-4775** BN

**932-4776** CNW†

**932-4777** CSXT

**932-4778** CR

**932-4779** Golden West Service

**932-4771** Undecorated

For Daily Product Updates Point Your Browser to
**www.walthers.com**

Hot Metal Car Kit 932-3130

Slag Car Kit 932-3140

Coke Car Kit 932-3091

49' Quad Hopper Kit 932-4912

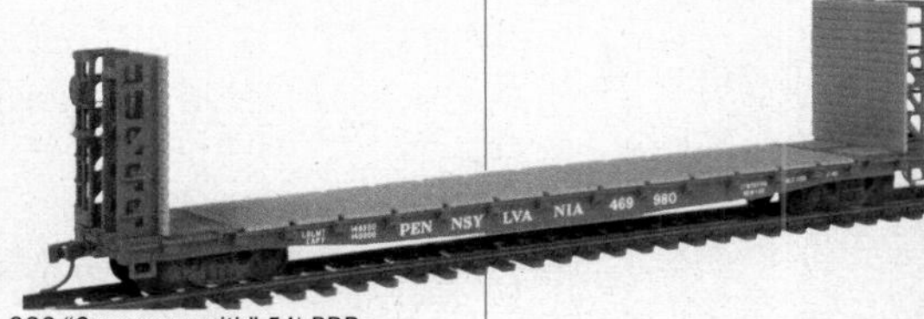

GSC "Commonwealth" 54' PRR Flat Car Kit 932-3775

Fruit Growers Express-Style 50' RBL Insulated Box Car Kit

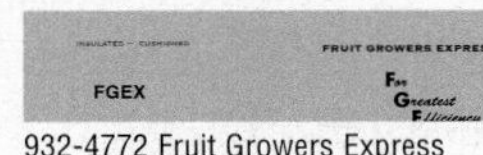

932-4772 Fruit Growers Express

CN W
932-4776 CNW

932-4773 UP

CSX
932-4777 CSXT

Rio Grande
D & R G W
932-4774 DRGW

CONRAIL
932-4778 CR

932-4775 BN

932-4779 Golden West Service

From Walthers

Ready to use on layouts of any size, PROTO 1000 freight cars make it easy - and affordable - to upgrade your steam- or diesel-era layout. With molded-on details, these cars are perfect for the demanding environment of operating layouts or displays. A wide range of realistic paint and lettering schemes are available, each with three different numbers. Each car comes complete with magnetic knuckle couplers, and blackened RP-25 metal wheelsets.

## NEW PRODUCTS

### 100-Ton Three-Bay Open Hopper

**September 2007 Delivery**

Developed by the N&W in the early 60s, cars of this design were also constructed by the PRR, RDG, C&O, B&O and Frisco as well as by Bethlehem Steel and ACF for several other roads. These cars were the unofficial standard coal hopper of the 60s, 70s and 80s and some are still in service in 2006.

- Great for 60s or Later Coal Trains

#### Pennsylvania

**NEW 920-37001** Single Car **9.98**

**NEW 920-237001** Limited-Run Two-Pack **19.98**

#### New York Central

**NEW 920-37002** Single Car **9.98**

**NEW 920-237002** Limited-Run Two-Pack **19.98**

#### Louisville & Nashville

**NEW 920-37003** Single Car **9.98**

**NEW 920-237003** Limited-Run Two-Pack **19.98**

#### Milwaukee Road

**NEW 920-37004** Single Car **9.98**

**NEW 920-237004** Limited-Run Two-Pack **19.98**

#### Soo Line

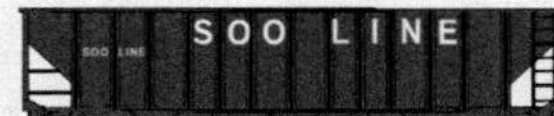


**NEW 920-37005** Single Car **9.98**

**NEW 920-237005** Limited-Run Two-Pack **19.98**

#### Illinois Central

**NEW 920-37006** Single Car **9.98**

**NEW 920-237006** Limited-Run Two-Pack **19.98**

#### Norfolk & Western

**NEW 920-37007** Single Car **9.98**

**NEW 920-237007** Limited-Run Two-Pack **19.98**

#### Chesapeake & Ohio

**NEW 920-37008** Single Car **9.98**

**NEW 920-237008** Limited-Run Two-Pack **19.98**

#### Baltimore & Ohio

**NEW 920-37009** Single Car **9.98**

**NEW 920-237009** Limited-Run Two-Pack **19.98**

#### Chessie/B&O

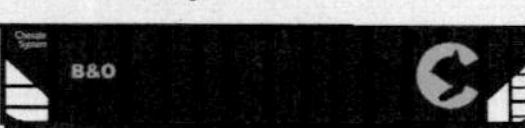

**NEW 920-37010** Single Car **9.98**

**NEW 920-237010** Limited-Run Two-Pack **19.98**

B&O 920-37009

N&W 920-37007

#### St. Louis-San Francisco

**NEW 920-37011** Single Car **9.98**

**NEW 920-237011** Limited-Run Two-Pack **19.98**

#### Reading

**NEW 920-37012** Single Car **9.98**

**NEW 920-237012** Limited-Run Two-Pack **19.98**

#### Conrail

**NEW 920-37013** Single Car **9.98**

**NEW 920-237013** Limited-Run Two-Pack **19.98**

#### Penn Central

**NEW 920-37014** Single Car **9.98**

**NEW 920-237014** Limited-Run Two-Pack **19.98**

#### Undecorated

**NEW 920-37000** Single Car **9.98**

Milwaukee Road 920-37004

Chessie/B&O 920-37010

St. Louis-San Francisco 920-37011

Penn Central 920-37014

From Walthers

## USRA 50-Ton Drop-Bottom Composite Gondola

**October 2007 Delivery**
In the early 20th century, many railroads preferred composite construction for freight cars exposed to rough service. Roads handling coal were partial to composite gondolas, as wooden sides and floors were better able to withstand exposure to wet coal, which produced sulfuric acid. Coal was critical for war production during World War I, and to keep it moving, the USRA designed a composite gondola with drop doors in the floor for fast unloading. The design proved very popular, and over 20,000 cars were eventually assigned to over 25 railroads.

- New Roadnames & Roadnumbers
- Fits Steam Era Layouts

### Milwaukee Road

**NEW 920-37051** Single Car **9.98**

**NEW 920-237051** Limited-Run Two-Pack **19.98**

### Chicago, Burlington & Quincy

**NEW 920-37052** Single Car **9.98**

**NEW 920-237052** Limited-Run Two-Pack **19.98**

### St. Louis-San Francisco

**NEW 920-37053** Single Car **9.98**

**NEW 920-237053** Limited-Run Two-Pack **19.98**

### Atlantic Coast Line

**NEW 920-37054** Single Car **9.98**

**NEW 920-237054** Limited-Run Two-Pack **19.98**

### Santa Fe

**NEW 920-37055** Single Car **9.98**

**NEW 920-237055** Limited-Run Two-Pack **19.98**

### Illinois Central

**NEW 920-37056** Single Car **9.98**

**NEW 920-237056** Limited-Run Two-Pack **19.98**

### Chicago & North Western†

**NEW 920-37057** Single Car **9.98**

**NEW 920-237057** Limited-Run Two-Pack **19.98**

### Great Northern

**NEW 920-37058** Single Car **9.98**

**NEW 920-237058** Limited-Run Two-Pack **19.98**

### New York Central

**NEW 920-37059** Single Car **9.98**

**NEW 920-237059** Limited-Run Two-Pack **19.98**

### Union Pacific†

**NEW 920-37060** Single Car **9.98**

**NEW 920-237060** Limited-Run Two-Pack **19.98**

### Rock Island

**NEW 920-37061** Single Car **9.98**

**NEW 920-237061** Limited-Run Two-Pack **19.98**

### Chesapeake & Ohio

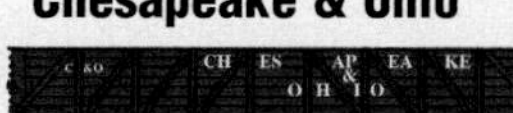

**NEW 920-37062** Single Car **9.98**

**NEW 920-237062** Limited-Run Two-Pack **19.98**

### Undecorated

**NEW 920-37050** Single Car **9.98**

†Union Pacific licensed product.

## Evans 50' High-Roof Box Car

**October 2007 Delivery**
Based on the 70-ton box cars constructed in 1972 by Evans Products subsidiary U.S. Railway Equipment, these cars feature 10' doors for easy loading by forklift, and the highest roof allowable to maximize cubic capacity under the "Plate C" clearance diagram. They're favorites for high-value shipments of manufactured goods and large paper rolls used by printers.

- New Roadnames & Roadnumbers
- Great for Post-70s Layouts

### Penn Central

**NEW 920-37101** Single Car **9.98**

**NEW 920-237101** Limited-Run Two-Pack **19.98**

### Conrail - Green

**NEW 920-37102** Single Car **9.98**

**NEW 920-237102** Limited-Run Two-Pack **19.98**

### Conrail - Brown

**NEW 920-37103** Single Car **9.98**

**NEW 920-237103** Limited-Run Two-Pack **19.98**

### Canadian National

**NEW 920-37104** Single Car **9.98**

**NEW 920-237104** Limited-Run Two-Pack **19.98**

### Western Pacific†

**NEW 920-37105** Single Car **9.98**

**NEW 920-237105** Limited-Run Two-Pack **19.98**

### Undecorated

**NEW 920-37150** Single Car **9.98**

See What's New and Exciting at **www.walthers.com**

USRA 50-Ton Drop-Bottom Composite Gondola C&O 920-37062

Evans 50' High-Roof Box Car Penn Central 920-37101

Evans 50' High-Roof Box Car WP 920-37105

Newsprint Car Canadian Pacific 920-31099

Newsprint Car Minnesota, Dakota & Western 920-31102

## NEWSPRINT CARS

**Ready to Run 20.00 ea**

- Prototypes used from the 1960s to the Present
- Built to Handle Newsprint Rolls
- Authentic Ends
- Correct Youngstown 9' Plug Doors
- Wire Grab Irons
- Non-Magnetic Blackened Metal Wheels
- Magnetic Knuckle Couplers

### Canadian Pacific - Green

**920-31098** #80969

**920-31099** #81135

### Minnesota, Dakota & Western

**920-31102** #7002 (Boise Cascade)

**920-31103** #7048 (Boise Cascade)

# TRAINLINE® by WALTHERS

## READY-TO-RUN FREIGHT CARS

- Fully assembled, ready to run
- Finished in authentic paint schemes
- Quality construction and features
- Free-rolling wheels and strong metal axles
- Body-mounted working knuckle couplers
- Some photos show preproduction models with horn-hook couplers

### 50' Plug-Door Box Cars 9.98 ea

**931-670** PRR

**931-671** SOO

**931-672** UP†

**931-673** CP (green w/pine tree)

**931-674** MKT†

**931-675** WP†

### 40' Offset-Side Quad Hoppers 9.98 ea

**931-650** UP†

**931-651** ATSF

**931-652** CB&Q

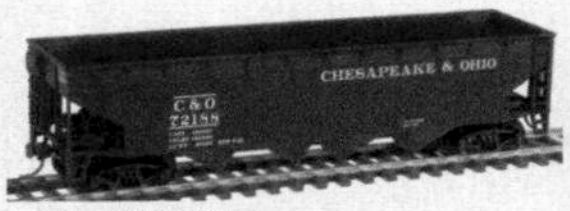

**931-653** C&O

**931-654** NYC

**931-655** N&W

### Pullman-Standard 34' PS-3 2-Bay Coal Hoppers 9.98 ea

**931-640** L&N

**931-641** Clinchfield

**931-642** IC

**931-643** UP†

**931-644** SP†

**931-645** RDG

†Union Pacific licensed product.

### 40' PS-3 Stock Cars 9.98 ea

**931-680** UP†

**931-681** ATSF

**931-682** GN

**931-683** DRGW†

**931-684** Swift

### 40' X-29 Box Cars 8.98 ea

**931-621** PRR

**931-622** Reading

**931-623** NKP

### 40' Tank Cars 8.98 ea

**931-611** Sinclair

**931-612** Gulf

**931-613** Standard

**931-614** Conoco

### 50' Flat Cars 8.98 ea

**931-601** BN

**931-602** CR

**931-603** UP†

**931-604** NS

50' Plug-Door Box Car SOO 931-671

40' Offset-Side Quad Hopper CB&Q 931-652

Pullman-Standard 34' PS-3 2-Bay Coal Hopper L&N 931-640

### 40' Plug-Door Box Car-Track Cleaning Cars 15.98 ea

- Cleans tracks for better performance while you run your trains
- Soft-abrasive pad mounted under car wipes away grime without scratching rail surfaces

**931-751** UP†

**931-752** CSX

### Logging Cars

**931-761** Log Dump Car & Crane Car Set **15.98**
Crane car features movable cab, boom and grapple. Log dump car will dump included logs when used with Trainline Sawmill #931-801.

**931-764** Log Dump Car w/Logs **9.98**
Same car as in set listed above, but with different road number.

**931-767** Firefighting Car **9.98**
Complete with pump details and movable water cannon!

### Wide Vision Cabooses 7.98 ea

**931-501** BN

**931-502** UP†

**931-503** ATSF

**931-504** CN

**931-505** CSX

**931-506** CR

**931-508** NS

**931-509** PRR

**931-510** CNW†

**931-511** MILW

**931-514** CP

**931-518** WC

**931-520** BNSF

**931-523** Amtrak

**931-524** C&O Chessie

**931-526** Alaska Railroad

Division of
Wm. K. Walthers, Inc.

## OPERATING COAL TIPPLE

**433-8306** With Hopper Car **22.75**

## 50' BI-LEVEL AUTO CARRIER

**433-8303** ATSF/Trailer Train w/6 Cars (red, yellow) **18.00**

## FREIGHT CAR ASSORTMENT

**Limited Quantity Available**
**433-8452** pkg(24) **198.00**
Includes four each: Seaboard 50' Hi-Roof Box Car, RDG 50' Hi-Roof Box Car, BN 100-Ton Hopper, CR 100-Ton Hopper, Weyerhaeuser 60' Thrall Door Box Car, and Illinois Terminal 60' Thrall Door Box Car.

## SCENEMASTER™ FLAT CAR LOADS

### 9.75 ea (Unless Noted)

**433-1513** Large Gears **8.49**

**433-1514** Duct Work **8.49**

**433-1515** Girder **8.49**

**433-1509** Metal Rail

**433-1510** Steel Pipe

**433-1511** Wrapped Machinery

**433-1512** Concrete Pipe

**433-1659** Power Generator

**433-1660** Grain Boxes (Wagon Parts)

**433-1661** Corn Head (For Combine)

**433-1662** Vertical Hoist

**433-1663** Industrial Machinery

**433-1664** Large Vertical Crates

**433-1665** Palletized Boxes

**433-1666** Milled Lumber

**433-1670** Counter Display Assortment pkg(24) **234.00**
Includes three each of flat car loads #1659 through 1666.

Latest New Product News Daily! Visit Walthers Web site at
**www.walthers.com**

## C M SHOPS, INC.

## HOPPER LOADS

### Coal pkg(2) 4.50 ea

**12-3101** Athearn Twin Hopper, Single "Hump" Contour
**12-3102** Athearn Twin Hopper, Double "Hump" Contour
**12-3103** Stewart Fishbelly Hopper
**12-3104** Athearn Quad Hopper
**12-3108** MDC Triple Hopper
**12-3110** MDC Thrall Gondola
**12-3112** Con-Cor Triple Hopper
**12-3114** MDC Bathtub
**12-3116** Walthers/TMI Twin Hopper or Gondola
**12-3118** MDC Ortner Hopper
**12-3121** Stewart AAR 14-Panel Hopper
**12-3123** Stewart H39 12-Panel Hopper
**12-3124** Stewart Offset-Side 9-Panel Hopper
**12-3125** Bowser H21 Hopper
**12-3126** Bowser 100-Ton Triple Hopper
**12-3127** Accurail USRA Two-Bay Hopper
**12-3128** Walthers BethGon Coalporter
**12-3129** Walthers Quad Hopper
**12-3130** Atlas Two-Bay Hopper

### Gravel pkg(2) 4.50 ea

**12-3106** Athearn Twin Hopper
**12-3107** Athearn Quad Hopper
**12-3109** MDC Triple Hopper
**12-3119** Walthers/TMI Twin Hopper

### Ore 4.50 ea

**12-3105** MDC 21' Ore Car pkg(2)
**12-3115** MDC Modern 26' Gondola pkg(2)

### Sand

**12-3113** Athearn 50' Gondola pkg(2) **4.50**

### Woodchip Hopper

**12-3117** Walthers/TMI 36' Hopper pkg(2) **4.50**

## SKELETON LOG CAR 2-PACKS

**39.98 ea**

No bones about it! You need reliable, rugged equipment in the woods and Rivarossi Skeleton Log Cars can handle the toughest jobs!

These superb HO Scale replicas are based on 38' skeleton cars that served logging operations as long as timber moved by train.

Fully assembled and ready for service, they feature diecast metal bodies, separate K type airbrakes, optional log loads and tie-down chains. Plus, they come prepainted and lettered so you can model a complete train in minutes.

**635-HR6016** Northern Pacific
**635-HR6017** McCloud River
**635-HR6020** Ohio Match
**635-HR6021** Coos Bay Lumber Co.
**635-HR6022** West Side Lumber Co.
**635-HR6024** St. Regis Paper Co.

**Limited Quantity Available**
**635-HR6018** Georgia Pacific
**635-HR6023** Weyerhaeuser Timber

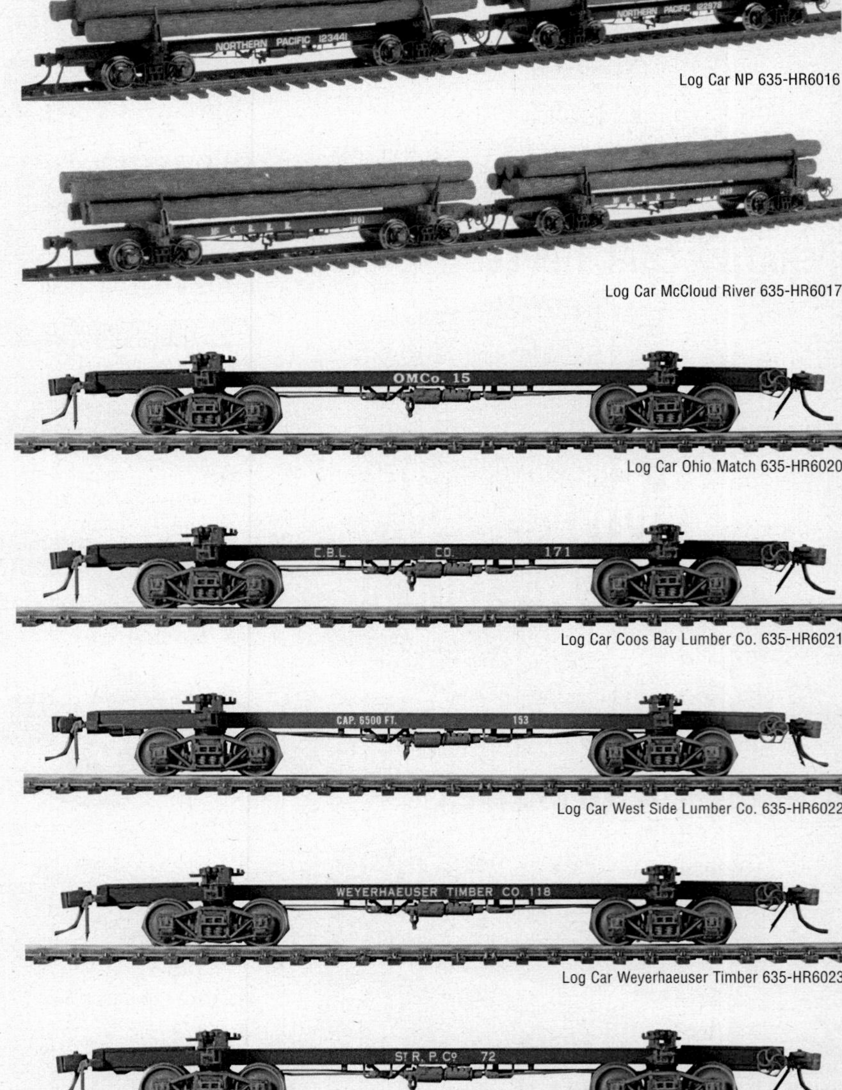

Log Car NP 635-HR6016

Log Car McCloud River 635-HR6017

Log Car Ohio Match 635-HR6020

Log Car Coos Bay Lumber Co. 635-HR6021

Log Car West Side Lumber Co. 635-HR6022

Log Car Weyerhaeuser Timber 635-HR6023

Log Car St. Regis Paper Co. 635-HR6024

Logging operations created clearings like this all across the continent to keep their engines supplied with water. A locomotive and its consist of fully loaded log cars pulls away from the tower while two Heislers wait patiently for their turn under the water tower.

# ACCURAIL®

These easy-to-build HO Scale plastic car kits feature a one-piece body with details molded in place. Decorated models feature authentic paint and lettering schemes with end reporting marks. Cars feature appropriate trucks and include body-mounted AccuMate® knuckle couplers. See walthers.com for a complete listing of all cars and current availability.

Items listed in blue ink may not be available at all times (see Legend Page).

50' Plug-Door AAR Boxcar
CB&Q RBBX #79468 112-82000

50' Combo-Door Box Car
UP #165458 112-82030

50' Double Plug-Door AAR Box Car
ATSF #18213 112-82050

50' Riveted AAR Steel Box Car
WP #3046 112-82071

40' Wood Outside-Braced Box Car
Western Pacific 112-4106

## NEW PRODUCTS

### 41' AAR Steel Gondola

**12.98 ea**

**Late 2007 Delivery**

**NEW 112-3701** DRGW (black)

**NEW 112-3702** CNW (oxide)

**NEW 112-3703** Pittsburgh & West Virginia (black)

**NEW 112-3704** Texas & Pacific (oxide)

**NEW 112-3705** D&H (black)

**NEW 112-3706** Gulf, Mobile & Ohio (black)

**NEW 112-3707** PRR (Oxide Red, Circle Keystone)

**NEW 112-3708** SP (Mineral Red)

**NEW 112-3709** Atlantic Coast Line (black)

**NEW 112-3710** C&O (black)

**NEW 112-3711** MP (Mineral Red)

**NEW 112-3712** GN (Mineral Red)

**NEW 112-3797** Data Only - Black

**NEW 112-3799** Data Only - Oxide

**NEW 112-3700** Undecorated

### Accuready™ Fully-Assembled Cars

**19.98 ea**

### 50' Plug-Door AAR Box Car

**NEW 112-82000** CB&Q RBBX #79468 (deep green, yellow stripe)

**NEW 112-82001** CB&Q RBBX #79473 (deep green, yellow stripe)

**NEW 112-82020** MILW #2563 (oxide w/large yellow stripe)

### 50' Combo-Door Box Car

**NEW 112-82030** UP #165458 Automated Railway

**NEW 112-82031** UP #165463 Automated Railway

**NEW 112-82032** UP #165479 Automated Railway

**NEW 112-82040** GN #36489 (Glacier Green w/Rocky logo)

**NEW 112-82041** GN #36372 (Glacier Green w/Rocky logo)

**NEW 112-82060** CP #201092 (Action Red w/Multi-Mark)

**NEW 112-82061** CP #201478 (Action Red w/Multi-Mark)

41' AAR Steel Gondola PRR 112-3707

### 50' Double Plug-Door AAR Box Car

**NEW 112-82050** ATSF #18213 (red, black roof & ends, large white logo)

**NEW 112-82051** ATSF #18227 (red, black roof & ends, large white logo)

**NEW 112-82052** ATSF #18236 (red, black roof & ends, large white logo)

### 50' Riveted AAR Steel Box Car

**NEW 112-82070** WP #3027 (orange w/large silver feather)

**NEW 112-82071** WP #3046 (orange w/large silver Feather)

**NEW 112-82080** Central of Georgia #1534 (black, gray "Blimp" scheme)

## BOX CARS

### USRA 40' Double-Sheathed Wood Box Cars 12.98 ea

Cars are finished in WWII and Post-War schemes.

**112-4601** ATSF

**112-4602** CNW

**112-4603** CB&Q

**112-4604** GN

**112-4606** NYC

**112-4610** NP

**112-4613** UP

**112-4620** NH

**112-4621** LV (Mineral Red)

**112-4624** Spokane, Portland & Seattle

**112-4625** L&N - Post-War Scheme

**112-4626** Duluth, Missabe & Iron Range - Post-War Scheme

**112-4627** Florida East Coast (Oxide)

**112-4628** Pere Marquette (Mineral Red)

**112-4629** Kansas City Southern (Oxide)

**112-4630** CCC&St.L (Big Four/NYC, Mineral Red)

**NEW 112-4631** DRGW

**112-4698** Data Only (Mineral Red)

**112-4699** Data Only (Oxide)

**112-4600** Undecorated

### 40' PS-1 Steel Cars 12.98 ea

**112-1603** Rock Island "100 Years" (Mineral Red, black & white lettering)

**112-3413** CN (dark red)

**112-3422** Atlanta & West Point

**112-3429** NH (Mineral Red)

**112-3430** Clinchfield (Oxide)

**112-3431** D&H (blue)

**112-3432** Gulf, Mobile & Ohio (orange)

**112-3433** Frisco (Oxide)

**112-3434** Richmond, Fredericksburg & Potomac (blue, white, silver)

**112-3435** Erie (Mineral Red)

**112-3436** Chicago Great Western (Mineral Red)

**112-3437** NP (Mineral Red)

**112-3438** SOO (Oxide)

**112-3496** Data Only (Bright Red)

**112-3498** Data Only (Mineral Red)

**112-3400** Undecorated

### 40' Wood Outside-Braced Box Cars 12.98 ea

#### With Wood Doors & Ends

**112-4101** CB&Q (Mineral Red)

**112-4102** CN (Oxide)

**112-4103** MILW

**112-4106** Western Pacific (Oxide)

**112-4107** Grand Trunk Western (Mineral Red)

**112-4108** Maine Central (Oxide)

**112-4111** Virginian (Mineral Red)

**112-4112** SP (Oxide)

**NEW 112-4113** MKT

**112-4100** Undecorated

#### With Wood Doors & Metal Ends

**112-4304** PRR (Oxide)

**112-4307** Lehigh & New England (Mineral Red)

**112-4308** CP (Mineral Red)

**112-4309** Erie Railroad (Mineral Red)

See What's New and Exciting at **www.walthers.com**

## ACCURAIL®

**112-4312** CB&Q (Oxide)

**112-4313** WM (Oxide)

**112-4314** N&W (Mineral Red)

**112-4315** Clinchfield (Oxide)

**112-4316** Ann Arbor

**112-4317** D&H

**112-4318** Frisco (Mineral Red)

**112-4319** Wabash (Oxide)

**112-4398** Data Only (Mineral Red)

**112-4399** Data Only (Oxide)

**112-4300** Undecorated

### With Metal Doors & Ends

**112-4504** MP (Oxide)

**112-4506** Duluth, Missabe & Iron Range (Mineral Red)

**112-4507** Wabash (Oxide)

**112-4500** Undecoratred

### 50' Exterior Post 12.98 ea

Different Roadname Shown

**112-5607** Frisco

**112-5617** BNSF (Mineral Red)

**112-5618** IC (light green)

**112-5621** Golden West (blue)

**112-5623** MILW (Mineral Red)

**112-5625** Kansas City Southern (Oxide)

**112-5626** LV (white)

**112-5627** CP Rail

**112-5628** NS

**112-5629** Chessie System

**112-5630** Green Bay & Western (blue)

**112-5631** MILW (yellow w/"America's Resourceful Railroad" slogan)

**NEW 112-5632** PRR

**NEW 112-5633** Richmond, Fredericksburg & Potomac

**NEW 112-5634** CR

**NEW 112-5635** Atlantic Coast Line (gray)

**112-5698** Data Only

**112-5699** Data Only (Oxide)

**112-5600** Undecorated

### 40' Wood 6-Panel Outside-Braced Box Cars 12.98 ea

#### With Wood Ends

**112-7002** Erie Railroad (Mineral Red)

**112-7003** Chicago & Illinois Midland (yellow)

**112-7006** Lehigh & New England (Oxide)

**112-7007** Green Bay & Western (Mineral Red)

**112-7008** DRGW (Oxide)

**112-7009** IC (Mineral Red)

**112-7010** Muncie & Western (yellow)

**112-7012** Chicago, St. Paul, Minneapolis & Omaha (Mineral Red)

**NEW 112-7013** CP

**NEW 112-7014** B&M

**112-7098** Data Only (Mineral Red)

**112-7099** Data Only (Oxide)

**112-7000** Undecorated

#### 3-Pack

**112-3380** Wood; CB&Q, Fort Worth & Denver, Colorado & Southern **35.98**

#### With Dreadnaught Ends

**112-7105** MP (Mineral Red)

**112-7107** GN (Mineral Red)

**112-7108** Frisco (Oxide)

**112-7110** Rock Island (Mineral Red)

**112-7111** Chicago & Eastern Illinois (Oxide)

**112-7198** Data Only (Mineral Red)

**112-7199** Data Only (Oxide)

**112-7100** Undecorated

### 40' AAR Box Cars 12.98 ea

#### Plug Doors

Cars feature high ladders and roofwalks.

**112-3103** Fruit Growers Express (yellow)

**112-3106** Frisco (Mineral Red)

**112-3109** GN (blue)

**112-3110** Grand Trunk Western

**112-3111** L&N (blue)

**112-3112** NH (Mineral Red)

**NEW 112-3113** C&O (yellow, black)

**112-3114** MILW (orange)

**112-3199** Data Only (Oxide)

**112-3100** Undecorated

#### Single-Door Steel

**112-3502** NP

**112-3507** SP (Mineral Red)

**112-3509** GN (red)

**112-3510** CB&Q (red)

**112-3511** B&O (Oxide)

**112-3512** SOO (Oxide)

**112-3513** CNW (Mineral Red)

**112-3514** C&O (Mineral Red)

**112-3515** BN (green)

**112-3516** Western Pacific (Oxide)

**112-3517** IC (Mineral Red)

**112-3518** Rock Island (Oxide)

**112-3519** NKP (Oxide)

**112-3520** MKT (Oxide)

**112-3521** Grand Trunk Western (Mineral Red)

**112-3522** NP (Mineral Red)

**112-3523** CP (Mineral Red w/"Spans the World" logo)

**112-3524** NYC (Jade Green)

**112-3525** Erie (Large Herald)

**112-3526** L&N (blue)

**112-3527** Lackawanna (Mineral Red w/Phoebe Snow slogan)

**112-3528** Gulf, Mobile & Ohio (red w/"Wings")

**112-3529** NP (Oxide)

**112-3530** NH (orange "McGinnis" scheme)

**112-3531** Minneapolis & St. Louis (red w/white stripes)

**112-3532** SOU (Oxide)

**112-3533** CN (Oxide w/"Noodle")

**112-3534** Atlantic Coast Line (silver)

**112-3535** EL (gray, maroon lettering)

**112-3536** LV (Jade Green)

**112-3537** Rock Island (blue)

**112-3598** Data Only (Mineral Red)

**112-3599** Data Only (Oxide)

**112-3500** Undecorated

#### 3-Pack

**112-3381** Steel; NP w/Large Tri-Colored Monad Herald **35.98**

#### Double-Door

**112-3603** NYC (Mineral Red)

**112-3605** UP (Oxide)

**112-3607** SP (Mineral Red)

40' AAR Plug Door Box Car
Roadmane Shown Not Available

40' AAR Double-Door Box Car
BN 112-3613

50' Steel Double-Door Box Car
Different Roadname Shown

**112-3608** Frisco (Oxide)

**112-3609** NP (green)

**112-3610** Seaboard Railroad (Oxide)

**112-3611** B&O (Oxide)

**112-3612** CNW (Mineral Red)

**112-3613** BN (green)

**112-3614** CB&Q (red)

**112-3615** CN (Mineral Red)

**112-3616** MILW (Mineral Red)

**112-3617** N&W (Mineral Red)

**112-3618** Cotton Belt (SSW, Oxide)

**112-3619** SOU (Oxide)

**112-3620** MP (Mineral Red)

**112-3621** GTW (Mineral Red)

**112-3622** Wabash (Mineral Red)

**112-3623** IC (Mineral Red)

**112-3624** Gulf, Mobile & Ohio (Oxide)

**112-3625** Wheeling & Lake Erie (Oxide)

**112-3698** Data Only (Mineral Red)

**112-3699** Data Only (Oxide)

**112-3600** Undecorated

### 50' Steel Cars-Riveted Sides 12.98 ea

#### Single Door

**112-5001** ATSF (Mineral Red)

**112-5006** PRR (Oxide)

**112-5007** B&O (Oxide)

**112-5008** CB&Q (Oxide)

**112-5013** Chessie System (blue)

**112-5015** Texas & Pacific (Oxide)

**112-5016** MKT (Mineral Red)

**112-5017** Cotton Belt (Oxide)

**112-5018** Wabash (Oxide)

**112-5019** Missouri Pacific (Mineral Red)

**112-5020** Atlantic Coast Line (black)

**112-5022** B&O (Oxide)

**112-5098** Data Only (Mineral Red)

**112-5099** Data Only (Oxide)

**112-5000** Undecorated

#### Double-Door

**112-5206** SP (Mineral Red)

**112-5208** MKT (yellow)

**112-5212** Texas & Pacific (Mineral Red)

**112-5213** Southern (Oxide)

**112-5214** Western Pacific (Oxide)

**112-5215** NKP (Oxide)

**112-5216** NH (orange)

**112-5217** Detroit, Toledo & Ironton (Mineral Red)

**112-5218** LV (Mineral Red)

**112-5219** N&W (black)

**112-5220** Detroit & Toledo Shore Line (blue)

**112-5221** MON (Mineral Red)

**112-5222** Spokane, Portland & Seattle (Mineral Red)

ACCURAIL®

50' AAR Plug Door Riveted Box Car Roadmane Shown Not Available

112-5223 SOU (Oxide)
112-5224 Rock Island (blue)
112-5225 N&W (Mineral Red)
112-5226 Grand Trunk Western (blue)
112-5276 Grand Trunk Western
112-5298 Data Only (Mineral Red)
112-5299 Data Only (Oxide)
112-5200 Undecorated

### 50' AAR Cars

**Plug Door Riveted 12.98 ea**
Cars feature high ladders and roofwalks.

112-5105 SP (Oxide)
112-5106 NKP (Mineral Red)
112-5107 WP (Mineral Red)
112-5109 Frisco (Oxide)
112-5110 CNW (yellow)
112-5111 N&W (black)
112-5112 Gulf, Mobile & Ohio (green)
112-5113 Wabash (Mineral Red)
112-5114 IC (Oxide)
112-5115 CP (green)
112-5116 Green Bay & Western (yellow)
112-5117 Maine Central (Harvest Gold, green lettering & door)
112-5118 L&N (blue)
NEW 112-5119 ATSF (red w/Shock Control logo)
NEW 112-5120 CB&Q - BREX (green, white)
NEW 112-5121 Chessie/C&O (blue, yellow)
112-5198 Data Only (Mineral Red)
112-5199 Data Only (Oxide)
112-5100 Undecorated



**Sliding Doors 12.98 ea**
Cars feature low ladders and no roofwalks.

112-5703 WM (Oxide)
112-5705 MKT
112-5706 Chessie System (blue)
112-5707 Gulf, Mobile & Ohio (green)
112-5708 WM (Oxide)
112-5709 Seaboard Coast Line/L&N (Mineral Red)
112-5711 SOU (Mineral Red)
112-5712 N&W (black)
112-5713 Richmond, Fredericksburg & Potomac (blue)
112-5714 Seaboard (Oxide)
112-5715 Boston & Maine (blue, black door)
112-5716 Western Pacific (Oxide)
112-5798 Data Only (Mineral Red)
112-5799 Data Only (Oxide)
112-5700 Undecorated

**Plug Door Welded 12.98 ea**
Cars feature low ladders and no roofwalks.

112-5801 ATSF (bright red)
112-5803 EL (Oxide)
112-5805 LV (white)
112-5806 MP (Oxide)
112-5807 Fruit Growers Express (yellow)
112-5808 Frisco (Oxide)
112-5809 WP (yellow)
112-5810 CP (green)
112-5811 DRGW (orange)
112-5812 CNW (yellow)
NEW 112-5813 Montana Rail Link
NEW 112-5814 UP "Chilled Express"
112-5898 Data Only (Mineral Red)
112-5899 Data Only (Oxide)
112-5800 Undecorated

AAR Offset-Side Three-Bay Hopper Prototype Photo Shown; Photo By G. Speir

**Double-Door 11.98 ea**
Cars feature low ladders and no roofwalks.

112-5901 ATSF (Mineral Red)
112-5905 N&W (Mineral Red)
112-5906 MKT (green)
112-5907 Bessemer & Lake Erie (Oxide)
112-5908 CNW (Oxide)
112-5910 GN (blue)

112-5911 SOO (Oxide)
112-5912 Texas & Pacific (Mineral Red)
112-5913 DRGW (Mineral Red)
112-5998 Data Only (Mineral Red)
112-5999 Data Only (Oxide)
112-5900 Undecorated

**50' Combo-Door Riveted Cars 12.98 ea**
Cars feature high ladders and roofwalks.

NEW 112-5307 MILW (Oxide Red)

112-5309 ACL (black)
112-5310 NS-Old (gray)
112-5311 EL (Oxide)
112-5312 CP (Mineral Red, Script Lettering)
112-5313 N&W (black)
112-5314 SP (Oxide)
112-5398 Data Only (Mineral Red)
112-5399 Data Only (Oxide)
112-5300 Undecorated

## STOCK CARS

**40' Wood Stock Cars 15.98 ea**

112-4701 ATSF (Box Car Red)
NEW 112-4702 Great Northern (red)
112-4708 Grand Trunk Western (brown)
112-4710 C&O (Mineral Red)
112-4712 IC (Mineral Red)
112-4714 DRGW (black)
112-4715 Rock Island (Oxide)
112-4716 Seaboard Railroad (Mineral Red)
112-4717 Boston & Maine
112-4718 Kansas City Southern
112-4719 SOU (Oxide)

NEW 112-4720 B&O

NEW 112-4721 UP
NEW 112-4722 PRR
NEW 112-4723 CB&Q
NEW 112-4724 Chicago Great Western
112-4799 Data Only (Oxide)
112-4700 Undecorated

**Three-Number Sets 35.98 ea**

112-4764 GN
112-4774 DRGW

**Limited-Run 3-Packs**

112-3378 DRGW (black, flying Rio Grande) 35.98

## HOPPERS

**AAR Offset-Side Hoppers 12.98 ea**

112-7501 ATSF (Mineral Red)
112-7502 B&O (black)
112-7503 CNW (black)
112-7504 SP (Oxide)
112-7505 Pittsburgh & Lake Erie (black)
112-7506 SOO (Mineral Red)
112-7507 MOPAC (Mineral Red)
112-7508 Nickel Plate Road (Oxide)
112-7509 CB&Q (red)
112-7510 NYC (black)
112-7511 Rock Island (black)
112-7512 CN (Oxide)
112-7513 Kansas City Southern (black)
112-7514 Seaboard Air Line (Oxide)
112-7515 Grand Trunk Western (black)
112-7516 CP (Mineral Red)
112-7517 IC (black)
112-7518 ACL (black)
NEW 112-7519 N&W (black)
112-7520 C&O
112-7521 NP
112-7522 SP&S
112-7523 UP
112-7524 Chessie System
NEW 112-7525 DRGW
NEW 112-7526 B&O (Capitol Dome, black)
NEW 112-7527 Lackawanna
NEW 112-7528 Pere Marquette
NEW 112-7529 Erie
NEW 112-7530 Toledo, Peoria & Western
NEW 112-7531 CN (Gothic Lettering)

**NEW 112-7532** MILW

**NEW 112-7533** Seaboard Coast Line

**NEW 112-7534** Central of Georgia

**112-7597** Data Only (black)

**112-7598** Data Only (Mineral Red)

**112-7599** Data Only (Oxide Red)

**112-7500** Undecorated

## Limited-Run 6-Pack

**NEW 112-7601** SP **65.98**

## Coal Loads

### For Accurail AAR Offset-Side Hoppers

**NEW 112-303** pkg(12) **11.98**

**NEW 112-353** pkg(48) **44.98**

## 47' ACF 3-Bay Center Flow Hoppers 13.98 ea

These cars carry 4600 cubic feet and were "Plate B" cars used on a large number of 2001 railroads.

**112-2001** ACFX (light gray)

**112-2002** ATSF (Mineral Red)

**112-2005** UP (light gray)

**112-2006** CNW

**112-2007** MILW

**112-2008** SP

**112-2011** WP

**112-2012** MP

**112-2013** CR (brown)

**112-2014** GTW (blue)

**112-2015** BN (green)

**112-2017** CB&Q

**112-2018** SOO (white)

**112-2019** Rock Island (blue)

**112-2021** SSW (light gray)

**112-2023** CSX

**112-2026** L&N (blue)

**112-2029** Erie Lackawanna (light gray)

**112-2030** CP-SOO (light gray)

**112-2034** DRGW (orange)

**112-2039** Reading

**112-2040** C&O (gray)

**112-2043** Montana Rail Link

**112-2046** CN (light gray)

**112-2049** BNSF (brown)

**112-2055** IC (gray)

**112-2063** Sterling Salt (light gray)

**112-2071** Gulf, Mobile & Ohio

**112-2073** ADM - New Logo (light gray)

**112-2074** ICG (orange)

**112-2075** B&O (gray)

**112-2076** SSW (gray)

**112-2077** KCS (green, yellow)

**112-2078** BNSF 2005 "Wedge" Scheme

**NEW 112-2079** CN/WC (Mineral Red)

**NEW 112-2080** GN Grain Loading (light gray)

**112-2096** Data Only (gray)

**112-2000** Undecorated

## Limited-Run 6-Packs

**NEW 112-22002** Eastern Road Fallen Flags **71.98**
One each B&O, C&O, SCL, L&N, EL & CR.

## 3-Bay Covered Hoppers

**112-1605** Chessie System (yellow w/blue, black & white lettering) **13.98**

## USRA 55-Ton Hoppers

### Original Builder's Lettering Schemes 3-Packs 30.98 ea

**112-2451** Cleveland, Cincinnati, Chicago & St. Louis - NYC (black, white)

**112-2452** C&O (black, white)

**112-2464** Colorado & Southern

### 6-Packs

Includes six cars painted in the same scheme, with different numbers.

**112-2602** N&W **59.98**

### Original Lettering 11.98 ea

Hoppers feature the original builders' lettering scheme and Andrews trucks.

**112-2401** Cleveland, Cincinnati, Chicago & St. Louis-Big Four (black)

**112-2402** C&O (black)

**112-2403** Clinchfield (black)

**112-2408** Cincinnati Northern

**112-2409** NYC (black)

**112-2410** IC (black)

**112-2411** BR&P (NYC, black)

**NEW 112-2412** GTW

### Later Schemes 11.98 ea

**112-2501** ATSF (Oxide)

**112-2502** N&W (black)

**112-2503** Lackawanna

**112-2504** NYC

**112-2505** B&O

**112-2506** PRR

**112-2508** C&O (black)

**112-2509** RDG

**112-2511** CN

**112-2514** SP

**112-2515** Wabash (black)

**112-2518** IC (black)

**112-2520** Virginian (black)

**112-2521** Akron, Canton & Youngstown (black)

**112-2524** Minneapolis & St. Louis (Oxide)

**112-2525** NH

**112-2531** L&N (black)

**112-2533** B&O (black w/large lettering)

**112-2535** Chicago & Eastern Illinois (black)

**112-2540** Gulf, Mobile & Ohio (black)

**112-2541** Seaboard (black)

**112-2542** Richmond, Fredericksburg & Potomac (black)

**112-2543** CNJ (black)

**112-2545** Ann Arbor (black)

**112-2546** Rock Island (black)

**112-2547** Duluth, Missabe & Northern (Mineral Red

**112-2548** New York, Ontario & Western (black)

**112-2549** RDG (early, black)

**NEW 112-2550** Green Bay & Western

**112-2551** Central Vermont

**112-2552** CB&Q (red)

**NEW 112-2553** Central of Georgia

**NEW 112-2554** Chicago & Illinois Midland

**112-2597** Data Only (black)

**112-2599** Data Only (Oxide)

**112-2500** Undecorated

### Three-Number Sets 27.98 ea

**112-2561** ATSF

**112-2562** N&W

**112-2563** NYC

**112-2569** RDG

**112-2862** C&O

### Six-Number Set

**NEW 112-2614** SP **62.98**

### Panel-Side Twin 11.98 ea

**112-2802** C&O (black)

**112-2806** Frisco (Oxide)

**112-2808** D&H (black)

**112-2809** Ann Arbor (black)

**112-2810** PRR

**112-2811** CN

**112-2812** Central Vermont

**NEW 112-2813** MP

**112-2897** Data Only (black)

**112-2899** Data Only (Oxide)

**112-2800** Undecorated

### Three-Number Set

**112-2861** NYC **30.98**

47' ACF 3-Bay Center Flow Hopper
112-2006

55-Ton USRA Hopper
Different Roadname Shown

### Wood-Side Twin 11.98 ea

**112-2701** ATSF (Mineral Red)

Prototype Photo Shown

**112-2702** PRR (Oxide)

**112-2703** Wabash (black)

**112-2704** C&O (black)

**112-2706** CB&Q (Oxide)

**112-2708** Clinchfield (black)

**112-2709** L&N (Oxide)

**112-2710** UP (Oxide)

**112-2711** Southern (Oxide)

**112-2712** LV (Oxide)

**112-2713** MON (black)

**112-2714** Ann Arbor

**112-2715** Alton (black)

**112-2797** Data Only (black)

**112-2799** Data Only (Oxide)

**112-2700** Undecorated

### Canton Car Co.-Built 2-Bay Hoppers 11.98 ea

### 55-Ton

**112-2301** GN (Oxide)

**112-2303** Virginian

**112-2300** Undecorated

## Coal Loads

### For Accurail Twin Hoppers

**112-301** pkg(12) **11.98**

**112-351** pkg(48) **44.98**

### For Athearn Twin Hoppers

**112-302** pkg(12) **11.98**

**112-352** pkg(48) **44.98**

### Load Removal Magnet

**112-300** **7.98**

# REEFERS

## 40' Wooden Reefers 13.98 ea (Unless Noted)

**112-4802** Fruit Growers Express

**112-4803** Western Fruit Express

**112-4807** CN

**112-4810** NYC

**112-4811** NKP

**112-4813** Erie

**112-4814** ATSF "Grand Canyon"

**112-4816** ATSF-Map- "Super Chief" (orange, black)

**112-4820** Swift (silver)

**112-4821** National Car Co. (Mineral Red, Railbox Yellow)

**112-4822** CP (Mineral Red)

**112-4824** New York Dispatch (Mineral Red, ATSF Orange)

**112-4826** North American Despatch (Mineral Red, orange)

**112-4827** Patrick Cudahy (Mineral Red, white)

## ACCURAIL®

112-4829 IC (Mineral Red, orange)

NEW 112-4831 DM&IR

112-4832 Grand Trunk Western (orange, Mineral Red, black, white)

112-4833 PFE w/UP & SP Heralds (orange, Tuscan Red)

NEW 112-4834 Pacific Great Eastern

NEW 112-4835 Pere Marquette

112-4895 Data Only (Yellow, Brown)

112-4800 Undecorated

### Limited-Run 3-Packs 38.98 ea

112-3377 ATSF; 1 Each El Capitan, Super Chief & Grand Canyon w/Map

112-3379 NYC/MDT w/Early Bird Logo (orange, tuscan, white & blue logo)

NEW 112-3383 Swift, WFE, West Indian Fruit & Steamship

NEW 112-3384 Erie, New York Central, Nickel Plate Road

## A.I.M. PRODUCTS

### Pulpwood Load

110-925 For Roundhouse 60' Bulkhead Car 8.95

## TANK CONTAINERS

Molded in color, easy to assemble, and are compatible with the Athearn 86' intermodal flat car, Walthers All-Purpose Spine Car, and all well cars, where they are often placed on the lower level. Kits also include full-color Microscale® decals.

### 20' Tank Container Trailers 8.95 ea (Unless Noted)

147-7710 UP (yellow)

147-7720 Blue

147-7800 BNSF 12.95

147-7810 UP 12.95

### Unframed Tank Containers 5.95 ea

Also called "beam" tanks, the prototype is designed for the U.S. domestic market.

147-7510 UP Bulktainer® With "New American Tank Truck" graphics.

147-7515 UP Bulktainer With newest graphics.

147-7520 Alaska West Express

### Framed Tank Containers 5.95 ea (Unless Noted)

These tanks are a European prototype commonly seen in the United States and around the world.

147-7610 Stolt

147-7620 Eurotainer

147-7630 TransAmerica Leasing

147-7640 ATSF QTC

147-7600 Undecorated 5.49

### Tank Container Decal Sets

For use with undecorated tank container #147-7600 or Walthers 20' Tank Container.

147-6210 Stolt pkg(2) 3.00

147-6220 Eurotainer pkg(2) 3.00

147-6200 Placards & Chemical Stencils 2.50

## BROADWAY LIMITED IMPORTS

## STOCK CARS

Different Roadnumber Shown

187-868 K-7 Class PRR pkg(4) 99.99

## NEW PRODUCTS

### Painted Steel Plate Loads 7.74 ea

Three sizes for Athearn and other 65' mill gondolas.

NEW 143-215 Mixed

NEW 143-7043 6 x 620"

### Built Up Steel Plate Loads 16.95 ea

Designed for flat cars or gondolas.

#### Triple Stack For 40' cars.

NEW 143-8200 6 x 10'

NEW 143-8201 6 x 12'

#### Double Stack

NEW 143-8202 6 x 16'6" Fits 40' Cars

NEW 143-8203 4 x 20' Fits 45' Cars

NEW 143-8204 5 x 20' Fits 45' Cars

NEW 143-8205 6 x 20' Fits 45' Cars

NEW 143-8206 6 x 24' Fits 52' Cars

#### Single Stack

NEW 143-8207 6 x 30' For 40' Cars

NEW 143-8208 6 x 40' For 45' Cars

### Built Up Single Stack Steel Slab Load 18.95 ea

For 48' flat cars or gondolas.

NEW 143-8250 5 x 45'

NEW 143-8251 6 x 45'
For 65' flat cars or gondolas.

NEW 143-8252 5 x 60'

NEW 143-8253 6 x 60'

## LOADS

### Steel Plate Loads

Neat way to add weight to gondolas, flat cars, or intermodal flatbed trailers! Each kit includes precut, nontoxic lead alloy pieces that match common sizes of steel plate, which are primed and ready for painting. To hold the load, three wooden spacers for each piece, and a spacing guide to simplify installation, are included.

#### 6 x 20'

143-7014 Heavy 5.14

143-7015 Light 3.84

#### 5 x 20'

143-7016 Heavy 5.14

143-7017 Light 3.84

#### 4 x 20'

143-7018 Heavy 5.72

143-7019 Light 4.42

#### Mixed Size Loads

143-7026 6 x 10' 5.14

143-7027 6 x 12' 5.14

143-7028 6 x 30' 5.72

### Painted Steel Slab Loads

Usually rust free. For gondolas only. Transfer loads from steel mill to remote rolling mill. Special lumber for slab use only.

#### Thick

143-7035 6 x 45' 5.14

143-7036 6 x 60' 5.72

#### Thin

143-7037 5 x 45' 5.14

143-7038 5 x 60' 5.72

## CENTRAL VALLEY

### Stock Car Kit

210-1001 Undecorated (Less Trucks & Couplers) 11.95
After the round-up, ship your livestock to market in this detailed car. Based on a NP prototype, it's typical of stock cars used by many Western roads from the 1930s into the early 1970s. Champ decal HC-112 provides the correct lettering for the NP car this model is based on. This easy-to-build HO Scale kit features highly detailed plastic parts with separate details and a detailed underframe.

## EVERGREEN HILL DESIGNS

## FLAT CARS

261-401 28' Carter Bros. 44.95
Kit features one-piece laser-cut frame, Rio Grande Models trucks and Northwest Short Line wheelsets. HOn3 Scale.

Laser-Cut Wood Caboose
152-863

Laser-Cut Wood Caboose
152-867

Laser-Cut Wood Caboose
152-870

## LASER-CUT WOOD CABOOSE KITS

### 46.95 ea

Cabooses feature tabbed-and-slotted sub wall construction, peel-and-stick windows and doors, and laser-scribed siding. Kits also include accurate caboose bodies based on prototype plans with cast-resin end platforms, steps, center sill, and brake details. Additional detail parts are required to complete models.

**152-850** Katy #751-795 Series

**152-851** NKP

**152-852** IC (Side-Door)

**152-853** C-30-1 SP Caboose

**152-854** Seaboard Air Line Class 5CC Wood Caboose

**152-855** CB&Q 4-Window Waycar

**152-856** Chicago Great Western 33' Extended-Vision Caboose

**152-857** Chicago Great Western 28' Extended-Vision Caboose

**152-858** CB&Q 30' Side-Door Waycar

**152-859** Atlantic Coast Line M3 Wood-Sheathed Caboose

**152-860** Seaboard Air Line Class 5CC Plywood-Sheathed Version

**152-861** GN 25' Caboose

**152-862** IC "Iowa Division" Wood Caboose

**152-863** Frisco Wood Caboose

**152-864** N&W CF Caboose

**152-865** ATSF Caboose

**152-866** CB&Q 28' 3-Window Waycar

**152-867** Minneapolis & St. Louis 25' Bay Window Caboose

**152-868** Rock Island Wood Caboose

**152-869** Atlantic Coast Line M3 Class Caboose, Plywood-Sheathed Version

**152-870** Illinois Terminal Bay Window Caboose

**152-871** NP 24' 1200-Series Caboose

**152-872** FEC (As-Built #700-800 Series w/Side Door)

**152-873** Nashville, Chattanooga & St. Louis/L&N (Post-1949 Rebuild)

## FREIGHT CAR LOADS

### Gondola Loads

**152-350** Auto Frame Rack
**19.95**
Use with Tichy War Emergency Gondola and J.J.M Railroad Enterprises Auto Frames (shown in photo; all sold separately). Includes laser-scribed wood car deck and cast resin and laser-cut wood rack assembly.

### Flat Car Loads
### 12.95 ea

Neat detail for any era car, loads are laser-cut from wood or acrylic and fit together easily. Includes laser-cut bracing to hold load in place.

**152-287** Wood Crate/Box Load-Plywood w/Wood Bracing

**152-288** Crankshaft-Acrylic w/Wood Bracing

**152-289** Stacked Lumber-All Wood

## GRAND CENTRAL GEMS

### Lumber Loads

**295-LL1 20.00**
Detail your modern bulkhead or centerbeam flat cars in minutes with these loads made of real wood. Lumber stacks come fully assembled with banding and printed logos, additional scale lumber strips are included to model dunnage and bracing as needed. Each package contains lumber to fill one HO 60' flat or bulkhead car.

These easy-to-build HO Scale kits are based on contemporary intermodal equipment used by many roads. They include unpainted injection-molded plastic parts, trucks, weights and step-by-step instructions. Kits are less couplers, but accept horn-hook or Kadee® styles.

# DOUBLE STACK CONTAINER CARS

## 40' & 45' Thrall

These five-unit cars are used by American President Lines/ APC and Trailer Train/TTX. The 40 and 45' units can carry two 20' or one 40 or 45' container on the bottom, and a 40, 45, 48 or 53' container on the top (depending on the kit).

**116-26103** 40' 5-Unit Set, Undecorated **49.95**

**116-26105** 40'/45' 5-Unit Set, Undecorated **51.95**
This kit includes two 40' end units and three 45' mid units.

**116-26900** Thrall Extra-Detail Kit **12.95**

## Gunderson

### Twin-Stack

These five-unit cars are used by Trailer Train, ATSF, SP, BN, CR, SOO, Sea Land (NYSW & CSX) and others. Units can carry two 20' or one 40' container on the bottom, and a 40, 45 or 48' container on top.

**116-27103** 5-Unit Set, Undecorated **53.95**

**116-27900** Twin Stack Extra-Detail Kit **9.95**
One package will detail five cars.

### Husky-Stack®

**116-27200** Undecorated **10.95**
This single-unit, 48' well car is used by Trailer Train/TTX, BN, Greenbrier Leasing, Coe Rail and others. The car can carry either two 20' or one 40, 45 or 48' container on the bottom, and a 40, 45, 48 or 53' container on top.

# FLAT CARS

## 85' Flat Car w/End Weight

**116-13202** Undecorated **14.95**
This flat car kit includes an undecorated Athearn body with trucks. The custom end weights improve performance of the car by lowering the car height and center of gravity. End weights simplify installing body-mounted couplers and come with springs to simulate cushioning effect. Center sill weights #116-13201 are also available for additional added weight. See A-Line listing in Super Detailing Parts section.

# CONTAINERS

## 20 & 40' Corrugated pkg(2) 7.95 ea (Unless Noted)

Used by NYK, Mitsui, OSK, YS Line, OOCL, Triton, Hyundai, Matson, IEA, CGM, Evergreen, Transamerica, Maersk and others. Each kit features the "beveled" style of corrugation, two-logo panel or all corrugated sides, smooth or corrugated doors, see-through forklift pockets, corrugated roofs and one-piece body with separate floor, stacking pins, vents and door bars.

**116-25500** 20' Undecorated 2-Logo Panel Sides/Smooth Doors

**116-25510** 20' Undecorated 2-Logo Panel Sides/ Corrugated Doors

**116-25520** 20' Undecorated Corrugated Sides/Smooth Doors

**116-25530** 20' Undecorated Corrugated Sides & Doors

## 48 & 53' Smooth Side

Used by APL/APC, BN, SP, CSX/CSL, ITEL, XTRA, CN, Genstar, Con-Way and CR, ATSF, Canadian Pacific and others. Based on a Monon prototype, these are the most common domestic containers in use today.

Each kit features a one-piece body with separate roof and stacking pins. The undecorated containers are molded in white styrene. Decorated containers are ready to run.

**116-25301** 48' ATSF pkg(2) **13.50**

**116-25300** 48' Undecorated pkg(2) **9.50**

**116-25400** 53' Undecorated pkg(2) **9.50**

Gunderson "Twin Stack" 116-27103
Sealand Decals 116-27705
45' Ribbed Container 116-25200
Maersk Decal 116-25803

20' Containers 116-25520 & 116-25530
Maersk Decal 116-25803
NOL Decal 116-25819

40' Ribbed Container 116-25100
45' Ribbed Container 116-25200
APL 40'/45' Decals 116-25800

Thrall Double-Stack 116-26103
APL/APC Decals 116-26700
40' Ribbed 116-25100
45' Ribbed Container 116-25200
APL 40' and 45' Decals 116-25800

Gunderson Husky-Stack 116-27200
BN Decals 116-27805
48' Smooth Containers 116-25300
48' BN American Decal 116-25804
48' BN American Special Decal 116-25814

Gunderson "Twin Stack" 116-27103
TTX Decals 116-27700
48' Smooth Container 116-25300
APC 48' Decal 116-25805

53' Smooth Container 116-25400
48' Smooth Container 116-25300
53' APC Decals 116-25806
48' APC Decals 116-25805

## 40 & 45' Ribbed Side

Used by APL, Maersk, Sea Land and others, these containers are seen around the world. These kits feature a one-piece body with separate floor and stacking pins. Undecorated containers are molded in silver styrene. Painted containers are ready for decals, which are available separately.

**116-25101** 40' Painted (silver) pkg(2) **9.95**

**116-25201** 45' Painted (silver) pkg(2) **9.95**

**116-25100** 40' Undecorated pkg(2) **9.50**

**116-25200** 45' Undecorated pkg(2) **9.50**

# DECALS

## Container 4.95 ea (Unless Noted)

Each set includes detailed lettering diagram of container.

**116-25800** APL 40'/45'

**116-25801** Maersk 20'/40' (Original)

**116-25802** Sea Land 40'

**116-25803** Maersk 40'/45'

**116-25804** BN America 48'

**116-25805** APC 48'

**116-25806** APC 53'

**116-25807** ITEL/BN/ITEL 48'

**116-25808** ATSF 45'/48'/53'

**116-25809** CSX/CSL 48'

**116-25810** XTRA 48'

**116-25811** SP 48'

**116-25812** CN Intermodal 48'

**116-25813** CP Intermodal 48'

**116-25814** BN America Special 48' **6.00**

**116-25815** CR Mercury 48'

**116-25816** CR Mercury 53'

**116-25817** Con-Quest 48'

**116-25819** NOL 20'/40'

## Locomotive

**116-25900** Maersk GP60M **4.95**

## Thrall Car 4.95 ea

Each set includes complete decals for one five-unit set and detailed lettering diagram.

**116-26700** APL/APC (blue or red car)

**116-26701** Trailer Train (yellow car)

## Twin-Stack Car 4.95 ea

Each set includes complete decals for one five-unit set and detailed lettering diagram.

**116-27700** TTX/SP (yellow car)

**116-27701** TTX/ATSF (yellow car)

**116-27702** TTX/BN (yellow car)

**116-27703** SP (red car)

**116-27704** ATSF (red car)

**116-27705** Sea Land (red car)

**116-27706** BN (Cascade Green car)

**116-27707** SOO (red car)

**116-27708** CR (Box Car Red)

**116-27711** Twin-Stack (red car)

**116-27712** Gunderson TTX/ Modern (yellow car)

## Husky-Stack® 4.95 ea

Each set includes detailed lettering diagram of car.

**116-27800** TTX
Enough to do four single cars.

**116-27805** BN
Enough to do two single and one three-stack units.

**116-27806** GBRX/BN

**116-27807** CRLE/GBRX

# HOBBY-TOTE SYSTEM™

## Hobby-Tote Storage Containers

Protect your valuable model railroad equipment with these versatile and economical storage containers. For club members or anyone who stores and/or transports model railroad equipment, Hobby-Tote storage containers are a must. They are also handy for storing modeling materials such as styrene, stripwood, wire, detail parts, etc. Hobby-Tote storage containers will last indefinitely with normal use. Designed to also fit into the Hobby-Tote nylon carrying case for easy transport.

Innovative storage container features:

- Tray lids insure dust-free storage and maximum protection during transport
- Removable chip board dividers with foam cushioning
- Made from heavy-duty 250lb test, double wall corrugated cardboard
- Easy assembly; instruction included
- Clean white exterior
- Approximate tray capacity: HO Scale – 16 40' box cars or 8 85' passenger cars; N Scale – approximate 72 40' box cars or 36 85' passenger cars
- Additional foam spacers available to provide additional cushioning for the ends of models.

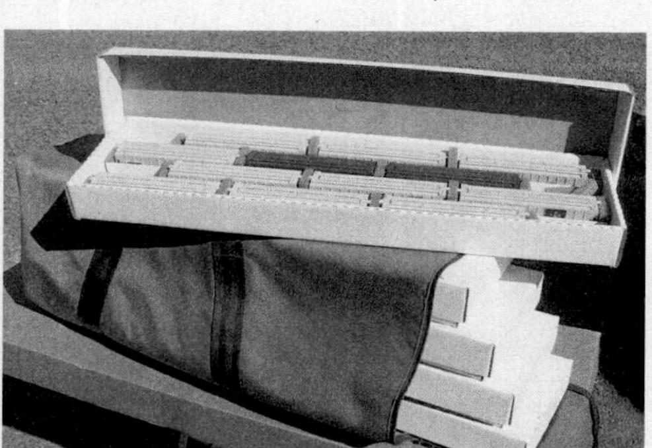

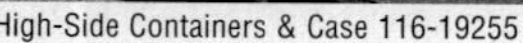
High-Side Containers & Case 116-19255

### High Sides

Inside dimensions of container: 27" long x 7" wide x 2-3/4" height; four containers fit into nylon case.

**116-19251** pkg(2) **39.00**

**116-19252** pkg(4) **58.00**

**116-19255** Case & 4 Containers, Plus Free Sample Package of Foam Spacers **107.00**

**116-19300** Foam Spacers pkg(24) **3.75**
Foam is placed between ends of cars to protect and separate equipment while in trays. One package will do one tray.

New low-sided containers (2-1/4") were designed to hold most locomotives and standard height HO Scale equipment, not auto racks or hi-cube cars. These low-side containers utilize space more efficiently for N Scale equipment and HO Scale vehicles. They are also excellent for unit trains, coal, grain, cement, etc. They also allow five containers to be carried in one nylon case.

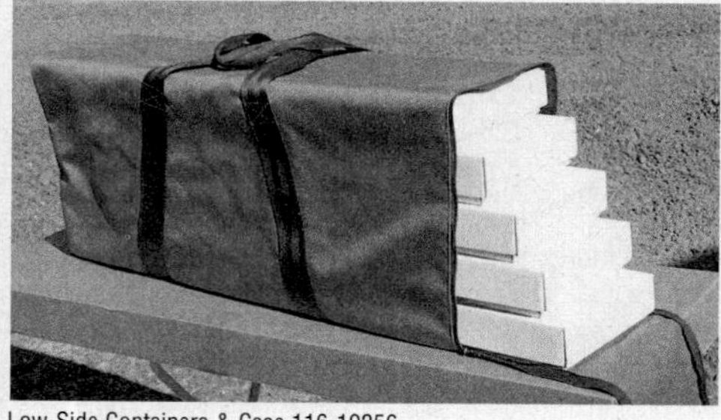
Low-Side Containers & Case 116-19256

### Low Sides

Inside dimensions of container: 27" long x 7" wide x 2-1/4" height; five containers fit into nylon case.

**116-19253** pkg(2) **39.00**

**116-19254** pkg(5) **68.00**

**116-19256** Case & 5 Containers, Plus Free Sample Package of Foam Spacers **120.00**

**116-19300** Foam Spacers pkg(24) **3.75**
Foam is placed between ends of cars to protect and separate equipment while in trays. One package will do one tray.

### Hobby-Tote Nylon Carrying Case

**116-19250 47.50**
Transport your model roster anywhere in confidence with this convenient and reliable nylon carrying case. Accommodates up to four hi-side or five low-side storage containers and can be used to transport virtually any scale models and/or supplies. Made from tough, heavy cordura fabric. Features a heavy-duty double zipper closure and strong, comfortable, integral carrying straps.

### Foam Liner Material

**116-19301 5.95**
2' Wide x 10' Long x 3/32" Thick

Use this strong, lightweight foam liner material to make a "cradle" to lift equipment in and out of the storage containers. This material provides for even less handling of models, extra protection from damage to painted finish and details, and no more bent locomotive handrails. Foam liner material is virtually crushproof, lint free, non-abrasive, and chemically inert.

IMPORTED FROM GERMANY BY WALTHERS

# FREIGHT CAR LOADS

**189-7600** Coal **8.99**

**189-7601** Sand **8.99**

**189-7603** Scrap Metal Load **8.99**

**189-7604** Tires **12.99**

**189-7607** Two Bundles of Wood **12.99**

**189-7611** Dirt/Top Soil **9.99**

**189-7617** Covered Machinery Load **8.99**
Measures 3-7/8 x 1-1/8" 9.6 x 3cm.

Items listed below are available by Special Order (see Legend Page).

**189-7606** Truck Cabs **19.99**

**189-7616** Covered Tour Bus **8.99**
Measures 3-7/8 x 1-1/8" 9.6 x 3cm.

## BLACKSTONE MODELS

DIVISION OF SOUNDTRAXX™

### DRGW Arch Bar Freight Trucks

### 1 Pair TBA ea

A faithful reproduction of the Rio Grande 3'7" design, used extensively on narrow gauge equipment.

**NEW 678-370103** Black

**NEW 678-370104** Brown

# NARROW GAUGE FREIGHT CARS

Fully assembled and finished in authentic schemes with different roadnumbers. Each features a diecast chassis with plastic parts, separate wire grab irons, brake rigging and underbody details, plus trucks and Kadee® couplers.

### 3000-Series 30' Box Cars 36.95 ea

**"Flying" Rio Grande**

**678-340100** DRGW #3000

**678-340101** DRGW #3028

**678-340102** DRGW #3044

**"Moffat Tunnel" Herald**

**678-340103** DRGW #3066

**678-340104** DRGW #3298

**678-340105** DRGW #3194

### 5500-Series 30' Stock Cars 36.95 ea

**"Flying" Rio Grande**

**678-340200** DRGW #5500

**678-340201** DRGW #5508

**678-340202** DRGW #5536

**678-340203** DRGW #5561

**678-340204** DRGW #5575

**678-340205** DRGW #5586

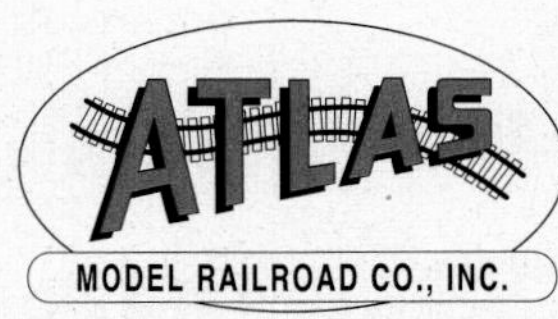


Atlas freight cars feature appropriate trucks with blackened-metal wheelsets and body-mounted Accumate® kncuckle couplers.

Master Line models feature accurate paint schemes, etched-metal, see-through roofwalks and walkways where appropriate, detailed brake gear and screw-attached coupler pockets with Accumate knuckle couplers.

Atlas announces new products on a monthly basis. Visit Walthers Web site at www.walthers.com for the latest additions to the Atlas line.

## NEW PRODUCTS

**Limited Quantity Available on all Items Except Undecorated Models**

### Master Line® Box Cars

#### Evans 53' Double-Plug Door Box Car 20.95 ea (Unless Noted)

Roadnumber Shown Not Available

Features 70-ton roller-bearing trucks, blackened metal wheels, a two-piece underframe, separate brake cylinder, air reservoir and end platforms.

**NEW 150-20000104** BC Rail #800502 (green)

**NEW 150-20000105** BC Rail #800520 (green)

**NEW 150-20000106** BC Rail #800539 (green)

**NEW 150-20000107** CHTT #50371 ("Green Repaint")

**NEW 150-20000108** CHTT #50434 ("Green Repaint")

**NEW 150-20000109** Keokuk Junction Railway #5254 (blue)

**NEW 150-20000110** Keokuk Junction Railway #5267 (blue)

**NEW 150-20000111** Louisville, New Albany & Corydon "Repaint" #5614 (brown)

**NEW 150-20000112** BNSF (SFLC) #11145 (brown w/Conspicuity Stripes)

**NEW 150-20000113** Santa Fe (SFLC) #11174 (brown "Berwind Repaint")

**NEW 150-20000114** Santa Fe (SFLC) #11283 (brown, "Repaint")

**NEW 150-20000115** Toledo, Peoria & Western #50581 (red, white, "Links East & West" Slogan)

**NEW 150-20000116** Toledo, Peoria & Western #50588 (red, white, "Links East & West" Slogan)

**NEW 150-20000117** Wisconsin & Southern #503019 (brown)

**NEW 150-20000118** Wisconsin & Southern #503032 (brown)

**NEW 150-20000119** Wisconsin & Southern #503141 (brown)

**150-1750** Undecorated **16.95**

#### ACF® 60' Auto-Parts Box Car

Cars feature 70-ton roller-bearing trucks, separate brake system details, cushion underframe details and roof overspray where appropriate.

**Single Door 20.95 ea (Unless Noted)**

**NEW 150-16641** Chessie System/B&O #491463 (blue, yellow)

**NEW 150-16642** Chessie System/B&O #491943 (blue, yellow)

**NEW 150-16651** GTW #306839 (brown, white)

**NEW 150-16652** GTW #306855 (brown, white)

**NEW 150-16661** MP #265109 (brown, white)

**NEW 150-16662** MP #265115 (brown, white)

**NEW 150-16671** NS #463002 (brown, white)

**NEW 150-16681** N&W #600859 (brown, white)

**NEW 150-16682** N&W #600883 (brown, white)

**150-1650** Undecorated **18.95**

**Double Door 20.95 ea (Unless Noted)**

**NEW 150-16821** MILW #4160 (brown, white)

**NEW 150-16822** MILW #4162 (brown, white)

**NEW 150-16831** MKT #8520 (red, white)

**NEW 150-16832** MKT #8528 (red, white)

**NEW 150-16841** WM #495996 (brown, white)

**NEW 150-16842** WM #495999 (brown, white)

**150-1670** Undecorated **18.95**

### Master Line® Reefers

#### 36' Wood Reefer 29.95 ea (Unless Noted)

**NEW 150-61331** Atlantic Seaboard Despatch #1925 (orange, red, brown)

**NEW 150-61332** Atlantic Seaboard Despatch #1938 (orange, red, brown)

**NEW 150-61341** Libby's #1464 (yellow, brown, red, blue)

**NEW 150-61342** Libby's #1465 (yellow, brown, red, blue)

**NEW 150-61351** New York, Ontario & Western #6401 (brown, white)

**NEW 150-61352** New York, Ontario & Western #6404 (brown, white)

**NEW 150-61361** Swift "Premium Bacon" #1860 (orange, brown, black)

**NEW 150-61362** Swift "Premium Ham" #1944 (orange, brown, black)

**NEW 150-61371** T.N. Fosse #3100 (orange, brown, black, red)

**NEW 150-61372** T.N. Fosse #3101 (orange, brown, black, red)

**NEW 150-61381** Wescott & Winks "Jersey Gold" #1055 (yellow, brown, black, red)

**NEW 150-61382** Wescott & Winks "Jersey Gold" #1056 (yellow, brown, black, red)

### Master Line® Covered Hoppers

#### ACF 4650 3-Bay Centerflow Covered Hopper

These models include etched-metal, see-through roofwalks, detailed brake gear and authentic 100-ton roller bearing trucks. Undecorated models come with optional parts for three different types of loading hatches and two styles of discharge outlets.

**Pre-1971 Body 26.95 ea**

**NEW 150-20000082** Golden West #77391 (blue)

**NEW 150-20000081** Golden West #77382 (blue)

**NEW 150-1400** Undecorated

**Post-1971 Body 26.95 ea**

**NEW 150-20000065** ADM #6505 (light gray, blue, white, black)

**NEW 150-20000066** ADM #65035 (light gray, blue, white, black)

**NEW 150-20000067** The Andersons #8498 (gray, black)

**NEW 150-20000068** The Andersons #8499 (gray, black)

**NEW 150-20000069** BN #458397 (green, 1990s Scheme)

**NEW 150-20000070** BN #458495 (green, 1990s Scheme)

**NEW 150-20000071** BNSF #402021 (brown)

**NEW 150-20000072** BNSF #403678 (brown)

**NEW 150-20000073** IMC #10207 (brown)

**NEW 150-20000074** IMC #10345 (brown)

**NEW 150-20000075** SSW #70433 (gray)

**NEW 150-20000076** SSW #70447 (gray)

**NEW 150-20000077** Texas Rail Car Leasing #74108 (gray)

**NEW 150-20000078** Texas Rail Car Leasing #74125 (gray)

**NEW 150-20000079** Farmland Industries #7417 (gray)

**NEW 150-20000080** Farmland Industries #7450 (gray)

**NEW 150-1450** Undecorated

#### ACF® 5701 Centerflow Plastics Hopper 29.95 ea

This 1970s-era and later car body features eight full-width panels with nine seams, ten 20" hatches, longitudinally mounted air reservoir and pneumatic outlets.

**NEW 150-20000001** DUPX #37234 (red)

**NEW 150-20000002** DUPX #37280 (red)

**NEW 150-20000003** ACFX #98087 (gray, red, black)

**NEW 150-20000004** ACFX #98525 (gray, red, black)

**NEW 150-20000005** Arco Polymers #496 (blue)

**NEW 150-20000006** Arco Polymers #574 (blue)

**NEW 150-20000007** American Hoechst Plastics Division (ACFX) #98319 (gray, blue, white)

**NEW 150-20000008** American Hoechst Plastics Division (ACFX) #98791 (gray, blue, white)

**NEW 150-20000009** ELTX #116 (gray)

**NEW 150-20000010** ELTX #149 (gray)

**NEW 150-20000011** Occidental Chemical (FPCX) #70050 (gray)

**NEW 150-20000012** Occidental Chemical (FPCX) #70054 (gray)

**NEW 150-20000000** Undecorated

### Master Line® Gondolas

#### Thrall 2743 Gondola

This 1990s-era and later car features a scale-height body with 14 side posts, etched-metal platform and end reinforcement plate, metal grabirons and brake rods, air hoses, corner pins and correct open notch and more. Includes optional coupler pockets for Kadee® No.5® or Accumate® scale couplers.

**NEW 150-4001** CP #346579 (black w/red & white Conspicuity Markings)

**NEW 150-4002** CP #346597 (black w/red & white Conspicuity Markings)

**NEW 150-4003** Environmental Rail Solutions #520196 (black, white, yellow, orange)

**NEW 150-4004** Environmental Rail Solutions #520201 (black, white, yellow, orange)

**NEW 150-4005** David J. Joseph Company #30109 (black, white, yellow, blue)

**NEW 150-4006** David J. Joseph Company #30152 (black, white, yellow, blue)

**NEW 150-4007** Gondola Connection #3096 (blue)

**NEW 150-4008** Gondola Connection #3121 (blue)

**NEW 150-4009** Joseph Transportation #98515 (black, white, yellow, green)

**NEW 150-4010** Joseph Transportation #98522 (black, white yellow, green)

**NEW 150-4011** NS #194221 (black, white)

**NEW 150-4012** NS #194267 (black, white)

**NEW 150-4000** Undecorated

Daily New Arrival Updates! Visit Walthers Web site at

**www.walthers.com**

## Master Line® Flat Cars

### ACF® 89'4" Flat Car

**Body Style A w/Mid & End Hitches 32.95 ea (Unless Noted)**

**NEW 150-20000017** Erie Western #250050 (white)

**NEW 150-20000018** Erie Western #250065 (white)

**NEW 150-20000019** Erie Western #250083 (white)

**NEW 150-20000020** Erie Western #250099 (white)

**NEW 150-20000021** Providence & Worcester

**NEW 150-20000022** Providence & Worcester

**NEW 150-20000023** Providence & Worcester

**NEW 150-20000024** Providence & Worcester

**NEW 150-20000025** FEC #2700 (brown, white)

**NEW 150-20000026** FEC #2764 (brown, white)

**NEW 150-20000027** FEC #2801 (brown, white)

**NEW 150-20000028** FEC #2949 (brown, white)

**NEW 150-20000029** Trailer Train #974325 (yellow)

**NEW 150-20000030** Trailer Train #974437 (yellow)

**NEW 150-20000031** Trailer Train #974730 (yellow)

**NEW 150-20000032** Trailer Train #974834 (yellow)

**NEW 150-20000013** Undecorated **27.95**

**Style R w/Triple Hitches 32.95 ea (Unless Noted)**

**NEW 150-20000033** TTX #603724 (yellow)

**NEW 150-20000034** TTX #604130 (yellow)

**NEW 150-20000035** TTX #604345 (yellow)

**NEW 150-20000036** TTX #604642 (yellow)

**NEW 150-20000014** Undecorated **27.95**

## Master Line® Tank Cars

### GATX 20,700-Gallon Tank Car

This general-purpose, non-pressire, non-insulated, 1960s and later tank car is afavorite for handling diesel fuel, oils, tallow, fertilizers and glycols. The body features five-secion construction, detailed top platform, see-through end walkways, bottom outlet, safety vent, manway, control housing, stuffing box and safety box details. Car comes equipped with McHenry double-shelf couplers. Two variations of saddles are available and two top platform variations are applied as appropriate.

**Type 10 Saddles 29.95 ea (Unless Noted)**

**NEW 150-20000085** GATX #52301 (black, white)

**NEW 150-20000086** Target GATX #98193 (black, white)

**NEW 150-20000087** GATX #98512 (black, white, yellow)

**NEW 150-20000088** Service Driven GATX #98934 (white, black, blue)

**NEW 150-20000089** Pennzoil GATX #99525 (black, white, yellow, red)

**NEW 150-20000083** Undecorated **24.95**

**Type 20 Saddles 29.95 ea (Unless Noted)**

**NEW 150-20000090** Relco Trank Line RTLX #2053 (black, white)

**NEW 150-20000091** Dow Chemical DOWX #4743 (black, white)

**NEW 150-20000092** Quality Liquid Feeds GATX #10148 (black, white, red)

**NEW 150-20000093** GATX #11774 (black, white)

**NEW 150-20000094** Monfort Packing GATX #35819 (white, black)

**NEW 150-20000084** Undecorated **24.95**

### American Car & Foundry 33,000-Gallon Tank Car 23.95 ea

This tank car is used to carry liquefied petroleum gas and anhydrous ammonia. Features 100-ton roller bearing trucks and improved coupler pockets with screw attached covers. Details include end ladders arched over the sides, air reservoir, walkway and end platforms.

**NEW 150-17217** ACFX #19906 (black)

**NEW 150-17218** ACFX #19907 (black)

**NEW 150-17297** Suburban Propane CNTX #1308 (tan)

**NEW 150-17298** Suburban Propane CNTX #1318 (tan)

**NEW 150-17353** ACFX #17213 (white)

**NEW 150-17354** ACFX #17716 (white)

**NEW 150-17371** Delta Gas SHPX #17040 (white, blue, black)

**NEW 150-17372** Delta Gas SHPX #17031 (white, blue, black)

**NEW 150-17381** CITX #30069 (black)

**NEW 150-17382** DCTX #30067 (black, white w/orange stripe)

**NEW 150-17391** Wanda Petroleum ACFX #17074 (white, blue, black)

**NEW 150-17392** Wanda Petroleum ACFX #17077 (white, blue, black)

## Master Line® Thrall Articulated Auto Carrier

### 59.95 ea

Built in 1997 by Thrall for TTX, these articulated auto carriers were designed to haul new trucks, vans or sport utility vehicles from assembly plants to distribution facilities. Models feature a diecast chassis for superb tracking, prototypical paint and lettering, end door details, articulated diaphragm, 70-ton roller bearing trucks, Accumate® couplers and require 22" or larger curves. All cars are yellow with appropriate markings.

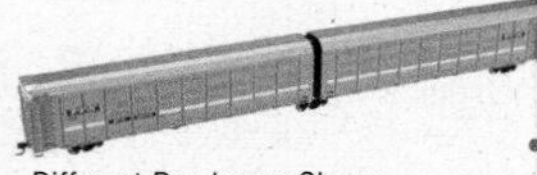

Different Roadname Shown

**NEW 150-20000053** NS Scheme 2 #110142

**NEW 150-20000054** NS Scheme 2 #110178

**NEW 150-20000055** NS Scheme 2 #110236

**NEW 150-20000056** NS Scheme 2 #110555

**NEW 150-20000057** TTX #880230

**NEW 150-20000058** TTX #880255

**NEW 150-20000059** UP #880059

**NEW 150-20000060** UP #880064

**NEW 150-20000061** FEC #110625

**NEW 150-20000062** FEC #110637

**NEW 150-20000063** FEC #110660

**NEW 150-20000064** FEC #110674

**150-6330** Undecorated

# BOX CARS

### ACF 60' Auto Single-Door Box Car

**Limited Quantity Available**

**150-16572** WM #495985 **19.95**

# FLAT CAR LOAD

### Girders

**150-790** Girder Load pkg(4) **3.65**
Molded in black styrene plastic.

# REEFERS

### 36' Wood Refrigerator Car 29.95 ea (Unless Noted)

Based on the reefers built by the General American Car Company for the Cudahy Packing Co. in 1925, these 36' reefers are similar to thousands of cars that transported meat, dairy, beer and food products well into the 1960s. The cars feature separately applied door hardware, grab irons, ladders and stirrups and opening doors and hatches. Truss rods and two styles of ice hatches are applied as appropriate for each roadname.

**150-6100** Undecorated, Standard Hatch, Grab Irons **19.95**

**150-6101** Undecorated, Standard Hatch, Ladders **19.95**

**Limited Quantity Available**

Different Roadnumber Shown

**150-61322** Meyer Kornblum #119

# GONDOLAS

### HO Coalveyor Bathtub Gondolas

Built in the 1980s by ACF®, Coalveyor Bathtub Gondolas can be found running in unit trains throughout the country. These detailed, ready-to-run cars feature a diecast chassis, interior bracing and a removable coal loads.

Roadname Shown Not Available

**Limited Quantity Available**

**150-1002** OSGX-Iowa Southern Utilities **22.95**

**150-1003** RTPX Wheelabrator Coal Services (black w/white end) **18.95**

**150-1004** UFIX Utility Fuels (black w/orange end) **22.95**

# FLAT CARS

### Pulpwood Flat Car 24.95 ea (Unless Noted)

These cars feature realistic detailing and a pulpwood load.

**150-1600** Undecorated - Open Ends **19.95**

**150-1601** Undecorated - Closed Ends **19.95**

**Limited Quantity Available**

**150-16112** BN #611301

**150-16123** D&H #8000

**150-16124** D&H #8059

**150-16075** WM #402

**150-16076** WM #406

**150-16171** St. Louis, Brownsville & Mexico #1050

**150-16172** St. Louis, Brownsville & Mexico #1052

# CABOOSES

### Standard-Cupola Caboose

Based on 60s-era prototypes, these cars feature thin-profile end railings, realistic window glazing, applied brake and stack details, roller bearing caboose trucks and roofwalks as appropriate.

**150-1300** Undecorated **18.95**

### Extended-Vision Caboose

Based on 60s-era prototypes, these cars feature a wider cupola for an extended view ahead. Model features include thin-profile end railings, realistic window glazing, applied brake and stack details, roller bearing caboose trucks and roofwalks as appropriate.

**150-1900** Undecorated No Roofwalk **18.95**

**150-1999** Undecorated With Roofwalk **18.95**

**Limited Quantity Available**

**150-62082** Family Lines/CRR #1091 (orange, black) **21.95**

# BRANCHLINE TRAINS

## NEW PRODUCTS

YARDMASTER SERIES

### 40' Steel Box Car Kits

**NEW 181-9019** Lancaster & Chester **9.98**

**NEW 181-9021** WP **14.98**

**NEW 181-9026** CMStP&O/CNW "Overland Route" **15.98**

**NEW 181-9027** UP/OSL "Be Specific" **10.98**

**NEW 181-9028** DRGW "Cookie Box" **12.98**

BLUEPRINT SERIES

### Assembled Cars

### 40' AAR Postwar Box Car w/6' Door 25.98 ea

**NEW 181-114041** CB&Q #1

**NEW 181-114042** CB&Q #2

**NEW 181-114043** CB&Q #3

**NEW 181-114044** CB&Q #4

**NEW 181-114251** NP #1

**NEW 181-114252** NP #2

**NEW 181-114253** NP #3

**NEW 181-114254** NP #4

**NEW 181-114381** ATSF Bx44 (Mineral Brown) #1

**NEW 181-114382** ATSF Bx44 (Mineral Brown) #2

**NEW 181-114383** ATSF Bx44 (Mineral Brown) #3

**NEW 181-114384** ATSF Bx44 (Mineral Brown) #4

**NEW 181-114501** NYC #1

**NEW 181-114502** NYC #2

**NEW 181-114503** NYC #3

**NEW 181-114504** NYC #4

**NEW 181-114121** Georgia #1

**NEW 181-114122** Georgia #2

**NEW 181-114123** Georgia #3

**NEW 181-114124** Georgia #4

**NEW 181-114191** L&N #1

**NEW 181-114192** L&N #2

**NEW 181-114193** L&N #3

**NEW 181-114194** L&N #4

**NEW 181-114221** NC&StL #1

**NEW 181-114222** NC&StL #2

**NEW 181-114223** NC&StL #3

**NEW 181-114224** NC&StL #4

**NEW 181-114361** WofA #1

**NEW 181-114362** WofA #2

**NEW 181-114363** WofA #3

**NEW 181-114364** WofA #4

**NEW 181-190051** BN #1

**NEW 181-190052** BN #2

**NEW 181-190053** BN #3

**NEW 181-190054** BN #4

**NEW 181-190131** SP&S #1

**NEW 181-190132** SP&S #2

**NEW 181-190133** SP&S #3

**NEW 181-190134** SP&S #4

**NEW 181-190261** CNW/Omaha #1

**NEW 181-190262** CNW/Omaha #2

**NEW 181-190263** CNW/Omaha #3

**NEW 181-190264** CNW/Omaha #4

### 40' AAR Postwar Box Car w/8' Door 25.98 ea

**NEW 181-115121** PRR (Circle Keystone) #1

**NEW 181-115122** PRR (Circle Keystone) #2

**NEW 181-115123** PRR (Circle Keystone) #3

**NEW 181-115124** PRR (Circle Keystone) #4

**NEW 181-115211** PRR (Shadow Keystone) #1

**NEW 181-115212** PRR (Shadow Keystone) #2

**NEW 181-115213** PRR (Shadow Keystone) #3

**NEW 181-115214** PRR (Shadow Keystone) #4

**NEW 181-115141** SOU #1

**NEW 181-115142** SOU #2

**NEW 181-115143** SOU #3

**NEW 181-115144** SOU #4

### 40' AAR Postwar Box Car w/7' Door 25.98 ea

**NEW 181-116011** Buffalo Creek #1

**NEW 181-116012** Buffalo Creek #2

**NEW 181-116013** Buffalo Creek #3

**NEW 181-116014** Buffalo Creek #4

**NEW 181-116031** Erie #1

**NEW 181-116032** Erie #2

**NEW 181-116033** Erie #3

**NEW 181-116034** Erie #4

**NEW 181-116071** NKP #1

**NEW 181-116072** NKP #2

**NEW 181-116073** NKP #3

**NEW 181-116074** NKP #4

**NEW 181-116081** PRR (Circle Keystone) #1

**NEW 181-116082** PRR (Circle Keystone) #2

**NEW 181-116083** PRR (Circle Keystone) #3

**NEW 181-116084** PRR (Circle Keystone) #4

**NEW 181-116121** WP #1

**NEW 181-116122** WP #2

**NEW 181-116123** WP #3

**NEW 181-116124** WP #4

### 50' Riveted Box Car w/8' Door 25.98 ea (Unless Noted)

**NEW 181-110011** ATSF #1

**NEW 181-110012** ATSF #2

**NEW 181-110013** ATSF #3

**NEW 181-110014** ATSF #4

**NEW 181-110051** NP #1

**NEW 181-110052** NP #2

**NEW 181-110053** NP #3

**NEW 181-110054** NP #4

**NEW 181-110061** T&P #71813

**NEW 181-110062** T&P #71815

**NEW 181-110063** T&P #71834

**NEW 181-110064** T&P #71837

**NEW 181-110071** MKT (As Delivered) #99206

**NEW 181-110072** MKT (As Delivered) #99201

**NEW 181-110073** MKT (As Delivered) #99209

**NEW 181-110074** MKT (As Delivered) #99207

**NEW 181-110081** IC #1 **26.98**

**NEW 181-110082** IC #2 **26.98**

**NEW 181-110083** IC #3 **26.98**

**NEW 181-110084** IC #4 **26.98**

**NEW 181-110111** PRR (Circle Keystone) #604083

**NEW 181-110112** PRR (Circle Keystone) #604392

**NEW 181-110113** PRR (Circle Keystone) #604158

**NEW 181-110114** PRR (Circle Keystone) #604241

**NEW 181-110131** B&O #1

**NEW 181-110132** B&O #2

**NEW 181-110133** B&O #3

**NEW 181-110134** B&O #4

**NEW 181-110201** General American - Evans #1 **26.98**

**NEW 181-110202** General American - Evans #2 **26.98**

**NEW 181-110203** General American - Evans #3 **26.98**

**NEW 181-110204** General American - Evans #4 **26.98**

**NEW 181-110091** NYC #1

**NEW 181-110092** NYC #2

**NEW 181-110093** NYC #3

**NEW 181-110094** NYC #4

### 50' Riveted Double-Door Box Car 25.98 ea (Unless Noted)

**NEW 181-111011** C&O #1

**NEW 181-111012** C&O #2

**NEW 181-111013** C&O #3

**NEW 181-111014** C&O #4

**NEW 181-111031** NKP #1

**NEW 181-111032** NKP #2

**NEW 181-111033** NKP #3

**NEW 181-111034** NKP #4

**NEW 181-111141** Erie #1

**NEW 181-111142** Erie #2

**NEW 181-111143** Erie #3

40' AAR Postwar Box Car w/6' Door
NC&SIL #3 181-114223

40' AAR Postwar Box Car w/8' Door
SOU #4 181-115144

50' Riveted Box Car w/8' Door
ATSF #2 181-110012

50' Riveted Double-Door Box Car
Erie #2 181-111142

50' Plug Door Box Car
KO&G #3 181-117043

**NEW 181-111144** Erie #4

**NEW 181-111161** NYC Early Bird #1

**NEW 181-111162** NYC Early Bird #2

**NEW 181-111163** NYC Early Bird #3

**NEW 181-111164** NYC Early Bird #4

**NEW 181-111201** Monon #1 **26.98**

**NEW 181-111202** Monon #2 **26.98**

**NEW 181-111203** Monon #3 **26.98**

**NEW 181-111204** Monon #4 **26.98**

### 50' Plug Door Box Car 25.98 ea

**NEW 181-117041** KO&G #1

**NEW 181-117042** KO&G #2

**NEW 181-117043** KO&G #3

**NEW 181-117044** KO&G #4

**NEW 181-117111** WFE #1

**NEW 181-117112** WFE #2

**NEW 181-117113** WFE #3

**NEW 181-117114** WFE #4

**NEW 181-117151** ART #1

**NEW 181-117152** ART #2

**NEW 181-117153** ART #3

**NEW 181-117154** ART #4

## BRANCHLINE TRAINS

### BLUEPRINT SERIES

### 50' GARX-Style Plug Door Box Car 25.98 ea

**NEW 181-118011** GARX #1
**NEW 181-118012** GARX #2
**NEW 181-118013** GARX #3
**NEW 181-118014** GARX #4
**NEW 181-118051** SP/GARX #1
**NEW 181-118052** SP/GARX #2
**NEW 181-118053** SP/GARX #3
**NEW 181-118054** SP/GARX #4
**NEW 181-118081** NKP/GARX #1
**NEW 181-118082** NKP/GARX #2
**NEW 181-118083** NKP/GARX #3
**NEW 181-118084** NKP/GARX #4
**NEW 181-118091** Quanah, Acme & Pacific/GARX #1
**NEW 181-118092** Quanah, Acme & Pacific/GARX #2
**NEW 181-118093** Quanah, Acme & Pacific/GARX #3
**NEW 181-118094** Quanah, Acme & Pacific/GARX #4
**NEW 181-118101** CNW/ GARX #1
**NEW 181-118102** CNW/ GARX #2
**NEW 181-118103** CNW/ GARX #3
**NEW 181-118104** CNW/ GARX #4
**NEW 181-118131** SSW/GARX #51736
**NEW 181-118132** SSW/GARX #51737
**NEW 181-118133** SSW/GARX #51738
**NEW 181-118134** SSW/GARX #51739

### 50' Welded Box Car w/9' Door 25.98 ea

**NEW 181-119031** BAR State of Maine #10108 27.98
**NEW 181-119032** BAR State of Maine #10125 27.98
**NEW 181-119033** BAR State of Maine #10134 27.98
**NEW 181-119034** BAR State of Maine #10162 27.98
**NEW 181-119035** BAR State of Maine #5
**NEW 181-119036** BAR State of Maine #6
**NEW 181-119037** BAR State of Maine #7
**NEW 181-119038** BAR State of Maine #8
**NEW 181-119091** SAL #1
**NEW 181-119092** SAL #2
**NEW 181-119093** SAL #3
**NEW 181-119094** SAL #4
**NEW 181-119101** ACL #1
**NEW 181-119102** ACL #2
**NEW 181-119103** ACL #3
**NEW 181-119104** ACL #4

### 50' Riveted Box Car w/9' Door 25.98 ea (Unless Noted)

**NEW 181-120011** ACL #1
**NEW 181-120012** ACL #2
**NEW 181-120013** ACL #3
**NEW 181-120014** ACL #4
**NEW 181-120031** GM&O #1 26.98
**NEW 181-120032** GM&O #2 26.98
**NEW 181-120033** GM&O #3 26.98
**NEW 181-120034** GM&O #4 26.98
**NEW 181-120041** LV #1
**NEW 181-120042** LV #2
**NEW 181-120043** LV #3
**NEW 181-120044** LV #4
**NEW 181-120061** MILW #1
**NEW 181-120062** MILW #2
**NEW 181-120063** MILW #3
**NEW 181-120064** MILW #4
**NEW 181-120111** C&O #1
**NEW 181-120112** C&O #2
**NEW 181-120113** C&O #3
**NEW 181-120114** C&O #4

### 40' Billboard Reefers 26.98 ea (Unless Noted)

**NEW 181-112091** Premier Pabst
**NEW 181-112231** Schlitz #92132
**NEW 181-112501** Prima Beer
**NEW 181-113221** Blatz Beer
**NEW 181-113351** Heilemans
**NEW 181-113481** Pabst-ett - Pabst Beer
**NEW 181-112011** CMSTP 1927 Scheme #87003
**NEW 181-112012** CMSTP 1927 Scheme #87019
**NEW 181-112013** CMSTP 1927 Scheme #87028
**NEW 181-112014** CMSTP 1927 Scheme #87029
**NEW 181-112081** Oscar Mayer (1957 Scheme) #1
**NEW 181-112082** Oscar Mayer (1957 Scheme) #2
**NEW 181-112083** Oscar Mayer (1957 Scheme) #3
**NEW 181-112084** Oscar Mayer (1957 Scheme) #4
**NEW 181-112131** MILW/URTX 1950S-60s #7066
**NEW 181-112132** MILW/URTX 1950S-60s #7044
**NEW 181-112133** MILW/URTX 1950S-60s #7572
**NEW 181-112134** MILW/URTX 1950S-60s #7728
**NEW 181-112141** NKP Late 40s #1567
**NEW 181-112142** NKP Late 40s #1568
**NEW 181-112143** NKP Late 40s #1561
**NEW 181-112144** NKP Late 40s #1565
**NEW 181-112151** NWX early gray 1920s-30s #1
**NEW 181-112152** NWX early gray 1920s-30s #2
**NEW 181-112153** NWX early gray 1920s-30s #3
**NEW 181-112154** NWX early gray 1920s-30s #4
**NEW 181-112161** NWX 1930s-53 #70269
**NEW 181-112162** NWX 1930s-53 #70352
**NEW 181-112163** NWX 1930s-53 #15103
**NEW 181-112164** NWX 1930s-53 #70320
**NEW 181-112171** NWX 1953-70s #2741
**NEW 181-112172** NWX 1953-70s #2785
**NEW 181-112173** NWX 1953-70s #5235
**NEW 181-112174** NWX 1953-70s #70153
**NEW 181-112181** MILW 1940s #87235
**NEW 181-112182** MILW 1940s #87287
**NEW 181-112183** MILW 1940s #87292
**NEW 181-112184** MILW 1940s #85348
**NEW 181-113571** Iowa State #12407 (1932 Scheme)
**NEW 181-112241** SOO 1940s #50292
**NEW 181-112242** SOO 1940s #50291
**NEW 181-112243** SOO 1940s #50083
**NEW 181-112244** SOO 1940s #50057
**NEW 181-113011** Kraft Cheese #1 27.98
**NEW 181-113012** Kraft Cheese #2 27.98
**NEW 181-113013** Kraft Cheese #3 27.98
**NEW 181-113014** Kraft Cheese #4 27.98
**NEW 181-113041** JH Neil Produce #1 27.98
**NEW 181-113042** JH Neil Produce #2 27.98
**NEW 181-113043** JH Neil Produce #3 27.98

50' GARX-Style Plug Door Box Car
Quanah, Acme & Pacific/GARX #3
181-118093

50' Welded Box Car w/9' Door
ACL #3 181-119103

50' Riveted Box Car w/9' Door
LV #1 181-120041

40' Billboard Reefers
Schlitz #92132 181-112231

40' AAR Box Car w/6' Door
Nashville, Chattanooga & St. Louis
181-1422

## FREIGHT CARS

### BLUEPRINT SERIES

### Blueprint Series Kits

Blueprint series kits feature detailed plastic bodies and include trucks with metal wheelsets, individual grab irons and ladders, correct ends, doors and roofs, accurate paint and lettering. Individual cars are mixed road numbers, multi-car packs include one each of either three or four road numbers.

### 40' AAR Box Cars w/6' Door 15.98 ea (Unless Noted)

All cars are Box Car Red with appropriate lettering unless noted.

**181-1401** Atlanta & West Point
**181-1404** CB&Q 17.98
**181-1406** CN
**181-1407** CNW 17.98
**181-1408** CP w/ "Spans The World" Slogan 17.98
**181-1409** D&H w/ "100 Years Of Anthracite" Herald
**181-1410** Erie (Small Diamond Logo)
**181-1412** Georgia RR
**181-1413** Gulf, Mobile & Ohio 17.98
**181-1416** IC 17.98
**181-1417** Illinois Terminal
**181-1419** L&N
**181-1420** M-K-T
**181-1421** MP
**181-1422** Nashville, Chattanooga & St Louis

## BRANCHLINE TRAINS

### BLUEPRINT SERIES

**181-1424** NKP

**181-1425** NP

**181-1427** NYC (Jade Green)

**181-1430** SOO **17.98**

**181-1431** Spokane, Portland & Seattle **17.98**

**181-1433** Texas & Pacific

**181-1434** UP As-Delivered Scheme **17.98**

**181-1435** Wabash

**181-1436** Western Of Alabama (silver)

**181-1438** ATSF Class Bx-44 (Mineral Red)

**181-1450** NYC **17.98**

**181-1400** Undecorated

### 40' AAR Box Cars w/6' Door 4-Packs 63.92 ea (Unless Noted)

Items listed below are available by Special Order (see Legend Page).

**181-14014** Atlanta & West Point

**181-14044** CB&Q **71.92**

**181-14064** CN

**181-14074** CNW **71.92**

**181-14084** CP **71.92**

**181-14094** D&H

**181-14104** Erie

**181-14124** Georgia

**181-14134** Gulf, Mobile & Ohio **71.92**

**181-14164** IC **71.92**

**181-14174** Illinois Terminal

**181-14194** L&N

**181-14204** M-K-T

**181-14214** MP

**181-14224** Nashville, Chattanooga & St Louis

**181-14244** NKP

**181-14254** NP

**181-14274** NYC

**181-14304** SOO **71.92**

**181-14314** Spokane, Portland & Seattle **71.92**

**181-14334** Texas & Pacific

**181-14344** UP **71.92**

**181-14354** Wabash

**181-14364** Western Railway of Alabama

**181-14384** ATSF

**181-14504** NYC **71.92**

### 40' AAR Box Cars w/7' Door 15.98 ea

All cars are Box Car Red with appropriate lettering unless noted.

**181-1601** Buffalo Creek w/Flour Sack Herald

**181-1602** D&TS

**181-1603** Erie w/Large Diamond Herald

**181-1604** Grand Trunk Western (blue)

**181-1605** Grand Trunk Western

**181-1606** LV

**181-1607** NKP

**181-1608** PRR w/Circle Keystone (Freight Car Red)

**181-1609** PRR w/Shadow Keystone (Freight Car Red)

**181-1610** Toledo, Peoria & Western

**181-1611** WM (Oxide Red, Speed Lettering)

**181-1612** Western Pacific

**181-1600** Undecorated

### 40' AAR Box Cars w/7' Door 4-Packs 63.92 ea

Items listed below are available by Special Order (see Legend Page).

**181-16014** Buffalo Creek w/Flour Sack Herald

**181-16024** D&TS

**181-16034** Erie

**181-16044** Grand Trunk Western (blue)

**181-16054** Grand Trunk Western (Box Car Red)

**181-16064** LV

**181-16074** NKP

**181-16084** PRR w/Circle Keystone

**181-16094** PRR w/Shadow Keystone

**181-16104** Toledo Peoria & Western

**181-16114** WM

**181-16124** Western Pacific

### 40' AAR Box Cars w/8' Door 15.98 ea

All cars are Box Car Red with appropriate lettering unless noted.

**181-1504** Detroit, Toledo & Ironton

**181-1505** Erie w/Large Diamond Herald

**181-1506** IC

**181-1507** Kansas City Southern

**181-1509** MP

**181-1511** Pittsburgh & West Virginia

**181-1512** PRR w/Circle Keystone (Freight Car Red)

**181-1513** RDG

**181-1514** SOU

**181-1517** Maine Central (yellow)

**181-1520** RDG (green)

**181-1521** PRR w/Shadow Keystone (Freight Car Red)

**181-1500** Undecorated

### 40' AAR Box Cars w/8' Door 4-Packs 63.92 ea

Items listed below are available by Special Order (see Legend Page).

**181-15044** Detroit, Toledo & Ironton

**181-15054** Erie

**181-15064** IC

**181-15074** Kansas City Southern

**181-15094** MP

**181-15114** Pittsburgh & West Virginia

**181-15124** PRR w/Circle Keystone

**181-15134** RDG (Box Car Red)

**181-15144** SOU

**181-15174** Maine Central

**181-15204** RDG (green)

**181-15214** PRR w/Shadow Keystone

### 50' AAR Single-Door Riveted-Side Box Cars w/8' Door 15.98 ea (Unless Noted)

All cars are Box Car Red w/appropriate graphics unless noted.

**181-1001** ATSF Class Bx-69 (Mineral Red)

**181-1002** Erie

**181-1005** NP (As-Delivered Scheme)

**181-1006** Texas & Pacific

**181-1007** IC "Mainline of Mid America"

**181-1008** M-K-T

**181-1009** NYC

**181-1010** CB&Q (Chinese Red)

**181-1011** PRR Class X44 (Red Circle Keystone)

**181-1012** Wabash w/Heart Herald

**181-1013** B&O (Oxide Red, w/"13 States" Herald)

**181-1016** Chicago & Eastern Illinois

**181-1017** EL

**181-1018** WM (Oxide Red w/Speed Lettering)

**181-1019** CB&Q w/"Way of the Zephyrs" Slogan

**181-1020** General American/Evans (GAEX) (green w/yellow stripe)

**181-1021** Rock Island w/"Route of the Rockets" Slogan

**181-1023** Grand Trunk Western

**181-1024** Peoria & Eastern/ NYC (Jade Green)

**181-1025** Monon

**181-1027** NP (green)

**181-1028** ATSF Class Bx-70 (Mineral Red)

**181-1029** Erie

**181-1030** Chessie (dark blue, yellow lettering)

**181-1000A** Undecorated w/Straight Sill **14.98**

**181-1000B** Undecorated w/Drop Sill **14.98**

**181-1000C** Undecorated w/Tabbed Sill **14.98**

40' AAR Box Car w/7' Door Western Pacific 181-1612

50' AAR Single-Door Riveted-Side Box Car w/8' Door Peoria & Eastern/NYC 181-1024

### 50' AAR Single-Door Riveted-Side Box Cars w/8' Door 3-Packs 47.94 ea

Items listed below are available by Special Order (see Legend Page).

**181-10283** ATSF Class Bx-70

**181-10293** Erie

**181-10303** Chessie

### HO 50' AAR Single-Door Riveted-Side Box Cars w/8' Door 4-Packs 63.92 ea

Items listed below are available by Special Order (see Legend Page).

**181-10014** ATSF Class Bx-69

**181-10024** Erie

**181-10054** NP

**181-10064** Texas & Pacific

**181-10074** IC

**181-10084** M-K-T

**181-10094** NYC

**181-10104** CB&Q (Chinese Red)

**181-10114** PRR

**181-10124** Wabash

**181-10134** B&O

**181-10144** Gulf, Mobile & Ohio

**181-10164** Chicago & Eastern Illinois

**181-10174** EL

**181-10184** WM

**181-10194** CB&Q (Mineral Red)

**181-10204** General American/ Evans

**181-10214** Rock Island

**181-10234** Grand Trunk Western

**181-10244** Peoria & Eastern/ NYC

**181-10254** Monon

**181-10274** NP



### 50' AAR Double-Door Box Cars 15.98 ea (Unless Noted)

All cars are Box Car Red w/appropriate graphics unless noted.

**181-1101** C&O **17.98**

**181-1102** Gulf, Mobile & Ohio

**181-1103** NKP

**181-1104** B&O

**181-1105** NYC

**181-1106** Spokane, Portland & Seattle

**181-1107** Detroit, Toledo & Ironton

**181-1108** IC

**181-1110** GN (bright red)

**181-1111** NJI&I (Wabash)

**181-1112** Texas & Pacific

**181-1113** Chicago Great Western (CNW)

**181-1114** Erie

**181-1115** CR

**181-1116** NYC "Early Bird"

**181-1117** Wabash

**181-1118** Detroit & Toledo Shore Line

**181-1119** ATSF (Mineral Red)

**181-1120** Monon

**181-1122** BN (Cascade Green)

**181-1123** Penn Central (Jade Green)

**181-1124** EL

**181-1125** Chessie/C&O (blue)

**181-1100** Undecorated

### 50' AAR Double-Door Box Car 3-Packs 47.94 ea (Unless Noted)

Items listed below are available by Special Order (see Legend Page).

**181-11023** Gulf, Mobile & Ohio

**181-11033** NKP

**181-11043** B&O

**181-11053** NYC (Standard)

**181-11073** Detroit, Toledo & Ironton

## BRANCHLINE TRAINS

### BLUEPRINT SERIES

**181-11083** IC

**181-11113** NJI&I (Wabash)

**181-11123** Texas & Pacific **44.94**

**181-11143** Erie

**181-11153** CR

**181-11163** NYC "Early Bird"

**181-11173** Wabash

**181-11183** Detroit & Toledo Shore Line

**181-11193** ATSF

### 50' AAR Double-Door Box Car 4-Packs 63.92 ea (Unless Noted)

Items listed below are available by Special Order (see Legend Page).

**181-11014** C&O **71.92**

**181-11064** Spokane, Portland & Seattle

**181-11104** GN

**181-11124** Texas & Pacific

**181-11134** Chicago Great Western (CNW)

**181-11164** NYC "Early Bird"

**181-11194** ATSF

**181-11204** Monon

**181-11224** BN

**181-11234** Penn Central

**181-11244** EL

**181-11254** Chessie/C&O

### 50' Standard-Style Plug-Door Box Cars 15.98 ea

**181-1701** C&O

**181-1702** Chicago Great Western

**181-1704** Kansas, Oklahoma & Gulf (blue)

**181-1705** Minneapolis & St Louis (Bright Red)

**181-1706** American Refrigerator Transit (MODX, yellow)

**181-1707** NKP (Box Car Red)

**181-1709** CB&Q (RBBX, green w/yellow stripe)

**181-1710** Fruit Growers Express (yellow)

**181-1711** Western Fruit Express (yellow)

**181-1713** Texas & Pacific (yellow)

**181-1714** UP (orange)

**181-1715** American Refrigerator Transit (WADX, yellow)

**181-1717** PRR (Red Shadow Keystone)

**181-1718** ATSF (Indian Red w/Large Herald)

**181-1700** Undecorated

### 50' Standard-Style Plug-Door Box Car 3-Packs 47.94 ea

Items listed below are available by Special Order (see Legend Page).

**181-17013** C&O

**181-17023** Chicago Great Western

**181-17043** Kansas, Oklahoma & Gulf

**181-17053** Minneapolis & St Louis

**181-17063** American Refrigerator Transit (MODX)

**181-17073** NKP

**181-17103** Fruit Growers Express

**181-17133** Texas & Pacific

**181-17143** UP

**181-17153** American Refrigerator Transit (WADX)

**181-17173** PRR

### 50' Standard-Style Plug-Door Box Car 4-Packs 63.92 ea (Unless Noted)

Items listed below are available by Special Order (see Legend Page).

**181-17024** Chicago Great Western **59.92**

**181-17094** CB&Q (RBBX)

**181-17114** Western Fruit Express

**181-17174** PRR

**181-17184** ATSF

### 50' GARX Plug-Door Box Cars 15.98 ea

Cars wear yellow with black lettering unless noted.

**181-1801** GARX

**181-1802** GARX/Frisco

**181-1803** UP

**181-1804** GARX/Texas & Pacific

**181-1805** GARX/SP

**181-1806** SP (Box Car Red)

**181-1807** GARX/N&W

**181-1808** GARX/NKP

**181-1809** GARX/Quanah, Acme & Pacific

**181-1810** GARX/CNW

**181-1811** GARX/M-K-T

**181-1812** GARX/Toledo Peoria & Western

**181-1813** GARX/Cotton Belt

**181-1814** GARX/Rock Island

**181-1815** DRGW

**181-1817** GARX/DRGW (yellow, silver, black lettering)

**181-1819** UP

**181-1800** Undecorated

### 50' GARX Plug-Door Box Car 3-Packs 47.94 ea (Unless Noted)

Items listed below are available by Special Order (see Legend Page).

**181-18013** GARX

**181-18023** GARX/Frisco

**181-18034** GARX/UP 4-Pack **63.92**

**181-18043** GARX/Texas & Pacific

**181-18053** GARX/SP (yellow)

**181-18063** SP (Box Car Red)

**181-18073** GARX/N&W

**181-18083** GARX/NKP

**181-18093** GARX/Quanah, Acme & Pacific

**181-18103** GARX/CNW

**181-18113** GARX/M-K-T

**181-18133** GARX/Cotton Belt

**181-18143** GARX/Rock Island

**181-18153** GARX/ DRGW

**181-18193** UP

### 50' Single-Door Welded-Side Box Cars w/9' Door 15.98 ea (Unless Noted)

All cars are Box Car Red with appropriate lettering unless noted.

**181-1901** N&W As-Delivered Scheme

**181-1902** Savannah & Atlanta

**181-1903** Bangor & Aroostook "State of Maine" Scheme

**181-1904** Bangor & Aroostook

**181-1905** L&N (blue, yellow)

**181-1906** Rock Island

**181-1908** N&W 1960s Scheme

**181-1909** Seaboard

**181-1910** Atlantic Coast Line

**181-1911** Kansas City Southern

**181-1912** Lackawanna w/"Phoebe Snow" Slogan

**181-1913** Seaboard Coast Line

**181-1914** EL

**181-1915** L&N/Family Lines (black, yellow)

**181-1900B** Undecorated w/Fishbelly Sill **14.98**

**181-1900C** Undecorated w/Tabbed Sill **14.98**

### 50' Single-Door Welded-Side Box Cars w/9' Door 4-Packs 63.92 ea

Items listed below are available by Special Order (see Legend Page).

**181-19014** N&W

**181-19024** Savannah & Atlanta

**181-19034** Bangor & Aroostook "State of Maine" Scheme

**181-19044** Bangor & Aroostook (Box Car Red)

**181-19054** L&N

**181-19074** Rock Island

**181-19084** N&W

**181-19094** Seaboard

**181-19104** Atlantic Coast Line

**181-19114** Kansas City Southern

**181-19124** Lackawanna

**181-19134** Seaboard Coast Line

**181-19144** EL

**181-19154** L&N/Family Lines

50' Standard-Style Plug-Door Box Car ATSF 181-1718

### 50' Single-Door Riveted-Side Box Cars w/9' Door 15.98 ea (Unless Noted)

All cars are Box Car Red with appropriate lettering unless noted.

**181-2001** Atlantic Coast Line

**181-2002** C&O (As-Delivered Scheme, black)

**181-2003** Gulf, Mobile & Ohio

**181-2004** LV

**181-2005** Maine Central (green)

**181-2006** MILW

**181-2007** Texas & Pacific

**181-2008** Seaboard Line

**181-2010** C&O (blue)

**181-2011** C&O (1960s Box Car Red Scheme)

**181-2000B** Undecorated Fishbelly Sill **14.98**

181-2000C Undecorated Tabbed Sill **14.98**

### 50' Single-Door Riveted-Side Box Cars w/9' Door 4-Packs 63.92 ea

Items listed below are available by Special Order (see Legend Page).

**181-20014** Atlantic Coast Line

**181-20024** C&O (black)

**181-20034** Gulf, Mobile & Ohio

**181-20044** LV

**181-20054** Maine Central

**181-20064** MILW

**181-20074** Texas &

**181-20084** Seaboard Coast Line

**181-20104** C&O

**181-20114** C&O (Box Car Red)

### 50' Berwick Box Cars 15.98 ea

**181-2101** Bangor & Aroostook (As-Delivered Scheme, red w/Herald)

**181-2102** Bangor & Aroostook (red w/reporting marks only)

**181-2103** BN (Cascade Green)

**181-2105** CP (CPAA Reporting Marks, red)

**181-2106** CP (Ex-Ma & Pa, CPAA Reporting Marks, black)

**181-2107** Chessie (blue)

**181-2108** Columbus & Greenville

**181-2109** CSX (blue)

**181-2110** D&H (red)

**181-2111** Detroit & Mackinac (red)

**181-2112** Genesee & Wyoming (orange)

**181-2113** Grand Trunk Western (blue)

**181-2115** Maine Central (yellow)

**181-2116** Middletown & New Jersey (NRUC Blue )

**181-2117** Maryland & Pennsylvania (black)

**181-2118** Nevada Northern (yellow)

**181-2119** New Hope & Ivyland (green)

**181-2120** Peninsula Terminal (NRUC Blue)

**181-2121** Pickens (NRUC Blue)

**181-2122** Railbox Original Scheme (bright yellow)

**181-2123** Railbox Repaint (pale yellow)

**181-2124** St. Lawrence Railroad (NRUC Blue)

**181-2125** Wisconsin Central (maroon)

**181-2127** CNW (red)

**181-2129** IC (gray)

**181-2131** Illinois Central Gulf (orange)

**181-2132** Detroit, Toledo & Ironton (Box Car Red)

**181-2100** Undecorated

### 50' Berwick Box Cars 3-Packs 47.94 ea

Items listed below are available by Special Order (see Legend Page).

**181-21013** Bangor & Aroostook Original Scheme

**181-21033** BN

**181-21083** Columbus & Greenville

**181-21093** CSX

**181-21103** D&H

**181-21113** Detroit & Mackinac

**181-21123** Genesee & Wyoming

**181-21133** Grand Trunk Western

**181-21163** Middletown & New Jersey

**181-21173** Maryland & Pennsylvania

**181-21183** Nevada Northern

**181-21193** Nevada Northern

**181-21203** Peninsula Terminal

**181-21213** Pickens

**181-21223** Railbox Original Scheme

BRANCHLINE TRAINS

BLUEPRINT SERIES

**181-21233** Railbox Repaint

**181-21243** St. Lawrence Railroad

**181-21273** CNW

**181-21293** IC

**181-21313** Illinois Central Gulf

**181-21323** Detroit, Toledo & Ironton

## 50' Berwick Box Cars 4-Packs 63.92 ea

Items listed below are available by Special Order (see Legend Page).

**181-21024** Bangor & Aroostook Repaint

**181-21054** CP (CPAA, red)

**181-21064** CP (CPAA, black)

**181-21074** Chessie

**181-21154** Maine Central

**181-21254** Wisconsin Central

**181-21324** Detroit Toledo & Ironton

## 40' ACF/URTX Wood Reefers

**181-1201** CM&St.P (MILW) **15.98**

**181-1202** Van Camp's **17.98**

**181-1204** Jerpe - NWX **17.98**

**181-1205** Wescott & Winks **17.98**

**181-1208** Oscar Mayer **17.98**

**181-1209** Pabst Premier Blue Ribbon **19.98**

**181-1210** Priebe Poultry - NWX **17.98**

**181-1211** Green Bay & Western **15.98**

**181-1212** Hershey's (Billboard) **17.98**

**181-1213** MILW (1940s Scheme) **15.98**

**181-1214** NKP **17.98**

**181-1215** NWX 1930s Gray Scheme **17.98**

**181-1216** NWX 1940s Gray Scheme **15.98**

**181-1217** NWX 1950s Yellow & Green Scheme **17.98**

**181-1218** URTX - MILW (1950s Scheme) **15.98**

**181-1220** Minneapolis & St Louis **15.98**

**181-1223** Schlitz **19.98**

**181-1224** SOO **15.98**

**181-1250** Prima Beer **19.98**

**181-1301** Kraft Cheese **17.98**

**181-1302** George Tracy - NWX **17.98**

**181-1303** J. Lynard - NWX **17.98**

**181-1304** J.H. Neil - NWX **17.98**

**181-1305** Land O' Lakes **17.98**

**181-1306** Nevada Poultry - NWX **17.98**

**181-1308** Priebe (PRLX) **15.98**

**181-1311** Jewell Produce - NWX **17.98**

**181-1314** Lakeshire Cheese **17.98**

**181-1316** Morrell Bacon **17.98**

**181-1317** Morrell Meat **17.98**

**181-1318** Morrell Ham **17.98**

**181-1319** Wisconsin Cheese **17.98**

**181-1322** Blatz Old Heidelberg Beer **19.98**

**181-1323** Borden's **19.98**

**181-1329** Edelweiss **19.98**

**181-1332** Gerber's Baby Food **19.98**

**181-1334** Hardings Cream **17.98**

**181-1335** Heileman's Beer **19.98**

**181-1336** IGA Foods **19.98**

**181-1343** Monarch Foods **19.98**

**181-1344** N. Dorman Co. **19.98**

**181-1346** Nucoa **19.98**

**181-1347** Our Mother's Cocoa **19.98**

**181-1348** Pabst Ett **19.98**

**181-1349** Pacific Central Egg **15.98**

**181-1353** Wilson's Milk **19.98**

**181-1356** Fairmont Creamery **17.98**

**181-1357** Iowa State Creamery **19.98**

**181-1200** Undecorated **15.98**

## 40' ACF/URTX Wood Reefer 3-Packs 53.94 ea (Unless Noted)

Items listed below are available by Special Order (see Legend Page).

**181-12023** Van Camp's

**181-12043** Jerpe - NWX

**181-12053** Wescott & Winks

**181-12083** Oscar Mayer **47.94**

**181-12103** Priebe Poultry - NWX

**181-12123** Hersheys **50.94**

**181-12143** NKP **47.94**

**181-12183** URTX - MILW **47.94**

**181-12203** Minneapolis & St. Louis **47.94**

**181-13013** Kraft Cheese **50.94**

**181-13023** George Tracy

**181-13033** J. Lynard

**181-13043** J. H. Neil

**181-13053** Land O' Lakes

**181-13063** Nevada Poultry

**181-13113** Jewell Produce

**181-13143** Lakeshire Cheese

**181-13163** Morrell

**181-13193** Wisconsin Cheese

**181-13343** Hardings Creamery

**181-13433** Monarch Fine Foods **59.94**

**181-13493** Pacific Central Egg **47.94**

**181-13563** Fairmont Creamery

## 40' ACF/URTX Wood Reefer 4-Packs

Items listed below are available by Special Order (see Legend Page).

**181-12014** MILW (CM&St.P) **63.92**

**181-12084** Oscar Mayer **71.92**

**181-12094** Pabst Premier Beer **79.92**

**181-12104** Priebe - NWX **71.92**

**181-12114** Green Bay & Western **62.92**

**181-12134** MILW Late Scheme **62.92**

**181-12144** NKP **71.92**

**181-12154** NWX (1930s Scheme) **71.92**

**181-12164** NWX (1940s Scheme) **62.92**

**181-12174** NWX (1950s Scheme) **71.92**

**181-12184** URTX - MILW **63.92**

**181-12244** SOO **63.92**

**181-13014** Kraft Cheese **71.92**

**181-13054** Land O' Lakes **71.92**

YARDMASTER SERIES

## Yardmaster Series Kits

Yardmaster series kits feature cast-on details for simple five-minute assembly, but with the same great painting and decorating found on Blueprint Series cars. Individual cars are mixed road numbers, four packs include one each of four car numbers.

## 40' 1937 AAR Box Cars 10.98 ea (Unless Noted)

All cars are Box Car Red with appropriate lettering unless noted.

**181-8001** Atlantic & East Carolina

**181-8002** Boston & Maine

**181-8003** C&O

**181-8004** CN w/Maple Leaf Herald

**181-8005** Lackawanna w/"Phoebe Snow" Slogan

**181-8006** Erie w/Large Diamond Logo

**181-8007** L&N

**181-8008** LV

**181-8009** Maine Central

**181-8010** NH w/Script Herald

**181-8011** NH McGinnis Scheme (black)

**181-8012** NKP

**181-8013** NP

**181-8014** Seaboard

**181-8015** Linde Tank Car

**181-8016** Frisco (Express, green w/yellow lettering)

**181-8017** SOU

40' 1937 AAR Box Car Lackawanna w/"Phoebe Snow" Slogan 181-8005

**181-8018** SP

**181-8019** UP

**181-8020** WM w/Circle Herald

**181-8021** NYC

**181-8022** Atlantic Coast Line

**181-8023** Minneapolis & St Louis (green w/yellow lettering)

**181-8024** CP

**181-8025** Atlanta & West Point

**181-8026** Florida East Coast w/"Speedway To Florida" Slogan

**181-8027** VGN

**181-8028** Gulf, Mobile & Ohio "Rebel Route" (red)

**181-8029** Central of Georgia

**181-8030** Nashville, Chattanooga & St Louis w/"To & From Dixieland" Slogan

**181-8031** Erie w/Small Diamond Herald

**181-8033** NH (McGinnis Orange)

**181-8034** Minneapolis & St Louis (bright red)

**181-8036** Georgia RR

**181-8037** Indiana Harbor Belt

**181-8039** Pittsburgh & Lake Erie

**181-8040** Pere Marquette

**181-8041** SOO

**181-8042** Texas & Pacific

**181-8043** Wabash

**181-8044** Western Pacific Merchandise Service **11.98**

**181-8045** ATSF

**NEW 181-8046** SLSF "Ship It On Frisco" **10.98**

**181-8000** Undecorated **9.98**

## 40' 1937 AAR Box Car 4-Packs 43.92 ea

Items listed below are available by Special Order (see Legend Page).

**181-80014** Atlantic & East Carolina

**181-80024** Boston & Maine

**181-80034** C&O

**181-80044** CN

**181-80054** Lackawanna

**181-80064** Erie

**181-80074** L&N

**181-80084** LV

**181-80094** Maine Central

**181-80104** NH w/Script

**181-80114** NH (black)

**181-80124** NKP

**181-80134** NP

**181-80144** Seaboard

**181-80154** Linde Tank Car

**181-80164** Frisco

**181-80174** SOU

**181-80184** SP

**181-80194** UP

**181-80204** WM

**181-80214** NYC

**181-80224** Atlantic Coast Line

**181-80234** Minneapolis & St Louis

**181-80244** CP

**181-80254** Atlanta & West Point

**181-80264** Florida East Coast

**181-80274** VGN

**181-80284** Gulf, Mobile & Ohio

**181-80294** Central of Georgia

**181-80304** Nashville, Chattanooga & St. Louis

**181-80314** Erie

**181-80334** NH (orange)

**181-80344** Minneapolis & St. Louis

**181-80364** Georgia RR

**181-80374** Indiana Harbor Belt

**181-80394** Pittsburgh & Lake Erie

**181-80404** Pere Marquette

**181-80414** SOO

**181-80424** Texas & Pacific

**181-80434** Wabash

**181-80444** Western Pacific

**181-80454** ATSF

**NEW 181-80464** SLSF "Ship It On Frisco"

See What's Available at

**www.walthers.com**

## NEW PRODUCTS

### Ready-To-Run Freight Cars 21.95 ea

These assembled cars include knuckle couplers and metal wheels.

#### X31 Round Roof Box Car

**NEW 6-40219** PRR #67405 (Circle Keystone)
**NEW 6-40220** PRR #67427 (Circle Keystone)
**NEW 6-40221** PRR #67412 (Circle Keystone)
**NEW 6-40222** N&W #46005
**NEW 6-40223** N&W #46124
**NEW 6-40224** N&W #46098

#### K-11 Stock Car

**NEW 6-40237** PRR #130554
**NEW 6-40238** PRR #130550
**NEW 6-40239** PRR #130547
**NEW 6-40240** PRR #130545
**NEW 6-40241** PRR #130532
**NEW 6-40242** PRR #130536

#### 100-Ton Triple Hopper

**NEW 6-40201** PRR #225027
**NEW 6-40202** PRR #225031
**NEW 6-40203** PRR #225045
**NEW 6-40204** NS #144711
**NEW 6-40205** NS #144725
**NEW 6-40206** NS #144753
**NEW 6-40207** CSX #810230
**NEW 6-40208** CSX #825880
**NEW 6-40209** CSX #830161
**NEW 6-40210** CR #478754
**NEW 6-40211** CR #478084
**NEW 6-40212** CR #479021
**NEW 6-40213** Reading & Northern #7265
**NEW 6-40214** Reading & Northern #7268
**NEW 6-40215** Reading & Northern #7209
**NEW 6-40216** UP #37168
**NEW 6-40217** UP #37165
**NEW 6-40218** UP #37160

#### 14-Panel Triple Hopper

**NEW 6-40225** ATSF #80098
**NEW 6-40226** ATSF #80075
**NEW 6-40227** ATSF #80067
**NEW 6-40228** Chessie/WM #80049
**NEW 6-40229** Chessie/WM #80037
**NEW 6-40230** Chessie/WM #80028
**NEW 6-40231** EL #32788
**NEW 6-40232** EL #32810
**NEW 6-40233** EL #32775
**NEW 6-40234** D&H #9319
**NEW 6-40235** D&H #9276
**NEW 6-40236** D&H #9316

## FREIGHT CARS

Bowser easy-to-build kits feature plastic molded bodies, underframes, brake platforms, brake wheels, coal loads (where appropriate), free-rolling trucks, nonmagnetic wheels, x2f couplers. Other features include authentic painting and printing, and coupler pockets that accept Kadee® #5 couplers.

### 70-Ton 2-Bay Open-Side Covered Hoppers 12.95 ea

**6-55601** N&W
**6-55602** C&O
**6-55603** UP
**6-55604** GN
**6-55605** Monon
**6-55606** DMIR
**6-55607** Edgar Clays
**6-55609** DL&W
**6-55611** Lehigh & New England
**6-55612** Central of Georgia

**6-55613** Rock Island (blue)
**6-55614** Atlantic Coast Line
**6-55615** DRGW
**6-55616** L&N (gray)
**6-55618** Gulf, Mobile & Ohio
**6-55619** McMillen Feeds
**6-55620** GE Mazda Lamps
**6-55621** Kosmos
**6-55622** Shippers Car Line
**6-55623** Colgate Palmolive
**6-55625** Clinchfield
**6-55626** ATSF
**6-55627** IC
**6-55628** SOO
**6-55629** Wabash
**6-55630** Kansas, Oklahoma & Gulf
**6-55631** NKP
**6-55632** NS
**6-55633** Pere Marquette
**6-55634** DT&I
**6-55635** GTW
**6-55636** MKT
**6-55637** Frisco
**6-55638** ACL **TBA**
**6-55639** SOU (black)
**6-55641** ACY
**6-55643** Clinchfield (black)
**6-55644** BN (gray)
**6-55645** DT&I
**6-55646** RDG
**6-55647** Elgin, Joliet & Eastern
**6-55649** NH
**6-55650** SOU (gray)
**6-55651** WM (Speed Lettering)
**6-55652** Chessie System
**6-55653** Rock Island
**6-55656** RDG
**6-55657** GE Lamps
**6-55659** ACL
**6-55660** C&O ("Progress")
**6-55661** Chicago & Illinois Western
**6-55662** Clinchfield
**6-55663** Genesee & Wyoming
**6-55664** Elgin, Joliet & Eastern
**6-55665** GM&O
**6-55666** ICG
**6-55668** N&W
**6-55669** SOO
**6-55670** Monon
**6-55671** WM
**6-55673** SCL
**6-55675** ACL (beige)
**6-55676** LaSalle
**6-55677** L&N ("Dixie Line")
**6-55678** Wabash
**6-55679** GN (Big Sky Blue)
**6-55680** GN (gray)
**6-55681** GN
**6-55682** GN
**6-55683** Alum Ore Co. (silver)
**6-55684** Edgar Clays
**6-55685** Alum Ore Co. (black)
**6-55686** Alum Ore Co. (gray)
**6-55688** GM&O - black
**6-55689** Akron, Canton & Youngstown
**6-55690** ACY
**6-55691** B&M ("Minute Man")
**6-55692** CG
**6-55693** KCS
**6-55694** L&N
**6-55695** MEC
**6-55697** Missouri-Illinois
**6-55698** Spokane International
**6-55699** St. Louis, Brownsville & Mexico
**6-55800** SP
**6-55801** SP
**6-55804** MILW
**6-55806** Electro Metallurgical Co.
**6-55807** Dewey Portland Cement
**6-55809** Missouri Portland
**6-55811** Monsanto Chemical Co
**6-55812** Libby Owens
**6-55814** Westvaco Chlorine
**6-55815** Sherwin Williams
**6-55817** Kimberly Clark
**6-55818** Philadelphia Quartz
**6-55819** Maine Central
**6-55821** Westvaco
**6-55822** Seaboard Air Line
**6-55824** Kimberly Clark Corp.
**6-55827** GE Lamps
**6-55828** Frisco
**6-55829** Minneapolis & St. Louis
**6-55836** Detroit & Toledo Shore Line
**6-55837** Cedar Heights Clay
**6-55838** SHPX
**6-55840** Seaboard System
**6-55842** Grand Truck Western (brown)
**6-55844** SCL **TBA**
**6-55845** D&H (silver)
**6-55846** D&H (gray)
**6-55847** Virginian
**6-55850** SAL
**6-55851** Ann Arbor
**6-55852** GTW (brown)
**6-55856** Shippers Car Line
**6-55858** SP - Texas & New Orleans
**6-55859** NP
**6-55861** SOU (gray, black)
**6-55863** Frisco
**6-55865** Nashville, Chattanooga & St. Louis w/"Dixie Line" Slogan
**6-55866** Nashville, Chattanooga & St. Louis
**6-55867** L&N
**6-55868** Central Soya McMillen Feed Division
**6-55870** DT&I
**6-55871** L&N
**6-55872** L&N
**6-55873** SCL
**6-55874** ACL (gray)
**6-55875** NH
**6-55876** EL
**6-55877** CSX #1
**6-55878** Wabash
**6-55879** N&W
**6-55880** B&M
**6-55881** CNJ
**6-55882** DT&I (gray)
**6-55887** CSX #2
**6-55600** Undecorated

### 70-Ton 2-Bay Closed-Side Covered Hoppers 12.95 ea

**6-56101** BN
**6-56102** CB&Q
**6-56103** EL
**6-56104** NYC
**6-56105** Northampton & Bath
**6-56107** GE Lamps
**6-56108** ATSF
**6-56109** SP
**6-56110** Cotton Belt
**6-56111** UP
**6-56112** CB&Q
**6-56113** C&O ("Progress")
**6-56114** DRGW

**6-56115** MILW
**6-56116** Detroit & Toledo Shore Line
**6-56118** EL
**6-56119** GE Lamps
**6-56120** West End Chemical
**6-56121** Napierville Junction
**6-56122** D&H
**6-56123** D&H (silver)
**6-56124** D&H
**6-56125** SP (T&NO)
**6-56126** CB&Q
**6-56127** CB&Q
**6-56128** CB&Q
**6-56129** Chicago & Eastern Illinois
**6-56131** MKT
**6-56132** UP (gray)
**6-56133** GE Lamps
**6-56134** ILDX
**6-56135** ILDX GE Lamps
**6-56136** SP
**6-56142** EL (gray)
**6-56144** Monon
**6-56145** CB&Q
**6-56146** LV
**6-56147** Northampton & Bath
**6-56148** Central of Georgia
**6-56149** NP
**6-56150** C&O
**6-56151** Pittsburgh & West Virginia
**6-56152** SSW
**6-56100** Undecorated

### Plate-Wall RoadRailer® 15.95 ea

**6-55501** Triple Crown w/Medium Logo
**6-55502** Schneider National
**6-55503** Triple Crown w/Large Logo
**6-55504** Triple Crown w/Small Logo
**6-55505** White w/Silver Trim
**6-55506** Swift
**6-55507** ATSF

**6-55508** Wabash Map
**6-55509** Amtrak®
**6-55510** Amtrak
**6-55511** Wabash Lease
**6-55512** Swift w/Wabash Logo
**6-55500** Undecorated

### Side-Door RoadRailer

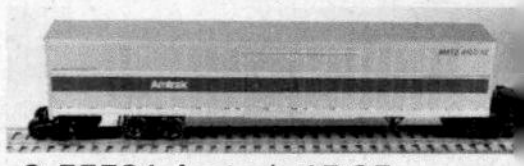

**6-55521** Amtrak **15.95**

### Smooth-Wall RoadRailers 15.95 ea

**6-55525** Ice Cold Express
**6-55527** ICEZ
**6-55528** TMM
**6-55530** Clipper
**6-55531** Amtrak "Express Tra

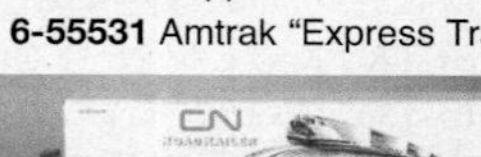


**6-55532** CN
**6-55533** Alliance ReeferRailer
**6-55534** Southwest ReeferRailer
**6-55539** CN
**6-55541** Clipper ReeferRailer
**6-55535** Undecorated

## Duraplate RoadRailer 15.95 ea

**6-55536** Triple Crown

**6-55538** Swift

## Smooth-Wall RoadRailers 15.95 ea

Based on "Super Wedge"-style trailers.

**6-55701** Amtrak US Mail
**6-55702** Swift
**6-55703** Super Wedge

**6-55704** Triple Crown
**6-55707** White w/Silver Rib
**6-55708** UP
**6-55709** Triple Crown (ex-UP)
**6-55700** Undecorated

## RoadRailer Accessories

**6-55498** CouplerMate **6.95**
Only one needed per train, this truck/coupler assembly is the interface between conventional locomotives or cars and RoadRailer consists.

**6-55499** Railing and Steps for CouplerMate **9.95**

## PRR 40' GS Gondolas 12.95 ea

**6-55901** PRR
**6-55902** Circle Keystone
**6-55903** Shadow Keystone
**6-55904** PRR Original Lettering
**6-55905** Vandalia
**6-55906** TWV&O PRR
**6-55907** E&PRR
**6-55908** Grand Rapids & Indiana
**6-55909** A.V.R. Pennsylvania
**6-55910** Penna Ontario Coal Line
**6-55911** Westmoreland Coal
**6-55900** Undecorated

## PRR X-31 Series 40' Round-Roof Single-Door Box Cars 12.95 ea

### Flush Roof

**6-55301** PRR Circle Keystone

**6-55304** SAL "Silver Meteor"
**6-55305** N&W
**6-55310** Undecorated

### X-31a Inset Roof

**6-55302** PRR Shadow Keystone
**6-55303** PRR Plain Keystone
**6-55306** PRR Company Service
**6-55300** Undecorated

## PRR X-31 Series 40' Round-Roof Double-Door Box Cars 12.95 ea

### Flush Roof

**6-55345** Seaboard Air Line
**6-55346** N&W
**6-55347** NP
**6-55348** DT&I
**6-55349** PRR Circle Keystone
**6-55351** PRR Circle Keystone "Automobiles"
**6-55352** PRR Shadow Keystone
**6-55353** SAL "Route of Courteous Service"
**6-55354** SAL "Orange Blossom Special"

**6-55355** Ashley, Drew & Northern
**6-55356** SCL
**6-55361** SAL "Robert E. Lee"
**6-55350** Undecorated

### X-31a Inset Roof

**6-55341** PRR Circle Keystone
**6-55342** PRR Circle Keystone "Autos"
**6-55343** PRR Circle Keystone "War Bonds"
**6-55344** PRR Shadow Keystone
**6-55340** Undecorated

## PRR 40' X-31F "Turtle Roof" Box Cars 12.95 ea

**6-55358** PRR Circle Keystone
**6-55359** PRR Shadow Keystone

**6-55360** PRR Modern Lettering
**6-55362** Ashley, Drew & Northern
**6-55363** Undecorated

## PRR 50' Single-Door Round-Roof Box Cars w/Flush Roof 12.95 ea

**6-55421** PRR Circle Keystone
**6-55422** PRR Shadow Keystone

**6-55423** Oregon, Pacific & Eastern
**6-55420** Undecorated

## PRR 50' Double-Door Round-Roof Box Cars w/Flush Roof 12.95 ea

**6-55401** PRR Circle Keystone
**6-55402** PRR Circle Keystone "Automobiles"
**6-55403** PRR Shadow Keystone
**6-55404** Norfolk & Western
**6-55405** DT&I
**6-55406** Wabash
**6-55407** NP
**6-55408** D&H

**6-55409** Tennessee, Alabama & Georgia
**6-55410** Virginian
**6-55411** Manufacturers Railway
**6-55412** Detroit & Mackinac
**6-55413** Texas-South Eastern RR
**6-55414** Oregon, Pacific & Eastern
**6-55400** Undecorated

## PRR X-33 Series End-Door 50' Box Cars 12.95 ea

**6-55461** PRR Circle Keystone
**6-55463** PRR Shadow Keystone

For Daily Product Updates Point Your Browser to
**www.walthers.com**

## PRR K-11 Series 40' Stock Cars 12.95 ea (Unless Noted)

**6-55451** PRR
**6-55452** PRR "Livestock" (silver roof) **19.95**
**6-55450** Undecorated

## PRR K-9 Series 50' Stock Cars 12.95 ea (Unless Noted)

**6-55466** PRR "Livestock"
**6-55467** PRR (Block Lettering)

**6-55468** PRR "Livestock" (silver roof) **19.95**
**6-55469** PRR w/Block Lettering (black roof) **19.95**
**6-55465** Undecorated

## 100-Ton 3-Bay Hopper Cars 12.95 ea (Unless Noted)

**6-55101** PRR Class H-43
**6-55102** C&O
**6-55103** N&W

**6-55104** UP
**6-55105** CR
**6-55106** Shawmut Line
**6-55107** RDG
**6-55108** D&H
**6-55109** RDG
**6-55110** Frisco
**6-55111** N&W
**6-55112** Chessie System/B&O
**6-55113** Chessie System/C&O
**6-55114** Chessie System/CSX
**6-55115** Chessie System/WM
**6-55116** Rock Island
**6-55117** Lake Erie, Franklin & Clarion
**6-55118** Seaboard Air Line
**6-55119** L&N
**6-55120** DRGW
**6-55121** MKT
**6-55122** Pittsburgh & Lake Erie
**6-55123** NS
**6-55124** NASA
**6-55125** D&H
**6-55126** CN (black)
**6-55127** Chessie System/ CSXT
**6-55128** Penn Central
**6-55129** WM
**6-55130** BN
**6-55131** Clinchfield
**6-55132** Bessemer & Lake Erie
**6-55133** RDG "Speed Lettering"
**6-55134** Upper Marion & Plymouth
**6-55135** Cambria & Indiana
**6-55136** EL
**6-55137** SOU
**6-55138** CSX/WM
**6-55140** D & H
**6-55141** CR "Quality"
**6-55142** Data Only (black)
**6-55143** Data Only (brown)
**6-55144** L&N (orange)
**6-55145** D&H
**6-55146** Lake Erie, Franklin & Clarion (Small Ball Logo)
**6-55147** BDMX
**6-55148** PLWX **19.95**
**6-55149** MKT (black)
**6-55150** N&W (Bold Lettering)
**6-55151** C&O
**6-55153** SOU (black)
**6-55154** Shawmut Line w/Diamond Logo
**6-55156** AEPX **19.95**
**6-55157** C&O/CSX
**6-55158** B&O/CSX
**6-55159** NP
**6-55160** BN "Stealth Lettering"
**6-55161** BN "New Image"
**6-55162** BNSF
**6-55163** ATSF
**6-55164** BN "Stealth" Logo
**6-55166** BN w/large logo & white end **19.95**
**6-55168** BN #1
**6-55169** BN #2 **19.95**
**6-55173** SOO
**6-55174** MILW
**6-55178** CN (brown)
**6-55179** CR w/NYC Reporting Marks
**6-55180** CSX w/NYC Reporting Marks
**6-55100** Undecorated

## PRR H-21a 4-Bay Hoppers 12.95 ea

**6-54051** PRR Circle Keystone
**6-54054** PRR Circle Keystone, No Car Number
**6-54052** PRR Shadow Keystone
**6-54055** PRR Shadow Keystone, No Car Number
**6-54053** PRR Modern Lettering
**6-54056** PRR Modern, No Car Number (black)
**6-54057** PRR Early Version
**6-54062** PRR Early Lettering, No Car Number
**6-54058** PRR Block Lettering
**6-54063** PRR Block Lettering, No Car Number
**6-54061** PRR Circle Keystone w/"Coal Goes To War"
**6-54064** PRR Circle Keystone "Coal Goes To War," No Car Number
**6-54059** PC (black)
**6-54065** PC (black), No Car Number

Bowser

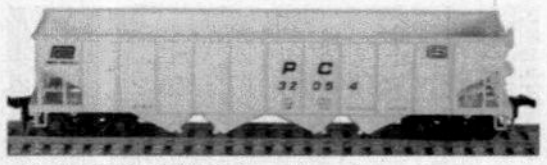

**6-54060** PC (yellow)
**6-54066** N&W
**6-54068** Virginian
**6-54069** PRR Ice Breaker Car **19.95**
**6-54050** Undecorated

## PRR H-21 Hopper w/Clamshell Hopper Doors 12.95 ea

**6-54101** PRR
**6-54102** PRR Circle Keystone

**6-54103** Bertha Coal Co.
**6-54104** Donora Southern
**6-54105** Erie
**6-54106** B&O
**6-54108** Bethlehem Mines
**6-54111** PRR Lines
**6-54112** Fairport, Painesville & Eastern
**6-54113** Rainey Wood Coke Co.
**6-54114** Alcoa Ore Co.
**6-54115** Republic Iron & Steel
**6-54116** Youngstown Sheet & Tube Co.
**6-54117** Davies Steel
**6-54100** Undecorated

## PRR H-22A 4-Bay Hopper 12.95 ea

**6-56001** PRR Early Lettering
**6-56003** PRR Early Lettering, No Car Numbers
**6-56004** PRR Circle Keystone, No Car Numbers
**6-56000** Undecorated

## H-22 Hoppers w/Clamshell Hopper Doors 12.95 ea

**6-56011** PRR
**6-56012** PRR Circle Keystone
**6-56013** PRR Lines
**6-56010** Undecorated

## PRR GLa 2-Bay Hopper Cars 13.95 ea

**6-56201** PRR Circle Keystone
**6-56202** PRR Shadow Keystone

**6-56203** PRR Plain Keystone
**6-56204** Berwind
**6-56205** PRR "Early"
**6-56206** PRR Lines
**6-56207** Westmoreland Coal Co.
**6-56208** Berwind, NR&PCC Co.
**6-56209** Berwind, NRBX
**6-56210** Penn Gas Coal Co.
**6-56211** National Mining
**6-56212** Jamison Coal & Coke
**6-56213** Keystone Coal & Coke
**6-56214** Panther Creek
**6-56215** H.C. Frick Coke
**6-56216** CN (brown)
**6-56217** AGS "Queen & Crescent Route"
**6-56218** Alton & Southern
**6-56219** Aluminum Company of America
**6-56220** B&O
**6-56221** NYC ("Big Four")
**6-56222** Chicago, New Orleans, Texas & Pacific ("Queen & Crescent Route")
**6-56223** LV
**6-56224** Milliken Brothers
**6-56225** NH
**6-56226** NYC - Pittsburgh & Lake Erie
**6-56227** NYC - Pittsburgh, McKeesport & Youghiogheny
**6-56228** Pennsylvania Salt & Manufacturing Co
**6-56229** TSP Co
**6-56230** Westmoreland Coal Co. (black)
**6-56231** CN (black)
**6-56232** Berwind BMCM Co. (black)
**6-56234** Buffalo, Rochester & Pittsburgh
**6-56235** C&O
**6-56236** Rutland
**6-56237** PSM Co.
**6-56238** CI&S
**6-56239** Lake Shore & Michigan Southern
**6-56240** The ALH & P Co
**6-56241** Thurlow Railway Co
**6-56242** Union Carbide Co of Canada Limited
**6-56243** WPT Ry Co
**6-56244** WM
**6-56200** Undecorated

## PRR 50' F-30a Flat Cars 12.95 ea

**6-55951** PRR

**6-55952** CR-MOW (gray)
**6-55953** CR-MOW (yellow)
**6-55954** PRR 1950s Lettering
**6-55955** PRR 1960s Lettering
**6-55956** Penn Central (green)
**6-55957** LV (Box Car Red)
**NEW 6-55958** PRR (yellow, black)

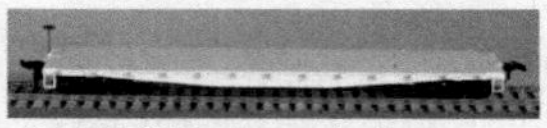

**6-55950** Undecorated

## PRR N-8 Cabooses 29.95 ea

**6-56301** PRR Circle Keystone Eastern Region
**6-56302** PRR Circle Keystone Central Region
**6-56303** PRR Circle Keystone Pittsburgh
**6-56304** PRR Shadow Keystone
**6-56305** PRR Shadow Keystone Buckeye Region
**6-56306** PRR Shadow Keystone Pittsburgh Region
**6-56307** PRR Shadow Keystone Chesapeake Region
**6-56308** PRR Shadow Keystone Susquehanna Division
**6-56309** PRR Plain Keystone (red w/black roof)
**6-56310** PRR Plain Keystone (red w/yellow cupola)
**6-56311** PRR Plain Keystone Buckeye Region (red w/yellow cupola)
**6-56312** PRR Plain Keystone (Focal Orange)
**6-56313** "PEN"

**6-56314** CR (blue)
**6-56315** CR (blue w/large logo)
**6-56316** CR (green)
**6-56317** Penn Central
**6-56318** Penn Central w/"P" logo
**6-56319** Penn Central
**6-56320** Illinois Central Gulf
**6-56300** Undecorated

## PRR N-5C Cabooses 14.95 ea (Unless Noted)

**6-54001** Old Style Eastern Region
**6-54002** Old Style New York Zone
**6-54003** Old Style Western Region
**6-54004** Old Style Central Region
**6-54023** Old Style Eastern Region
**6-54024** Old Style, No Car Number
**6-54005** Shadow Keystone Pittsburgh Region
**6-54006** Shadow Keystone East Region
**6-54007** Shadow Keystone Philadelphia Region
**6-54008** Shadow Keystone New York Region
**6-54009** Shadow Keystone Northern Region
**6-54012** Shadow Keystone Buckeye Region
**6-54013** Shadow Keystone Lake Region
**6-54014** Shadow Keystone Chesapeake Region
**6-54015** Shadow Keystone Pittsburgh Region
**6-54016** Shadow Keystone Philadelphia Region
**6-54025** Shadow Keystone, No Car Number
**6-54010** New Style (orange)
**6-54020** New Style (Caboose Red)
**6-54021** New Style (orange)
**6-54026** New Style, No Car Number (orange)
**6-54027** New Style, No Car Number (red)
**6-54011** CR
**6-54017** CR
**6-54028** CR, No Car Number (blue)
**6-54030** CR (brown) **15.95**
**6-54018** PC North Region Canada Division
**6-54029** PC (green), No Car Number
**6-54019** PC Central Region
**6-54032** PC **15.95**
**6-54000** Undecorated

## PRR N-5 Cabooses 15.95 ea

**6-55001** PRR Old Style Eastern Region
**6-55002** PRR Old Style Pittsburgh Division
**6-55003** PRR Old Style Buckeye Region
**6-55004** PRR Old Style Philadelphia Division

**6-55005** PRR Shadow Keystone Pittsburgh Region
**6-55006** PRR Shadow Keystone Eastern Region
**6-55007** PRR Shadow Keystone Philadelphia Region
**6-55008** PRR Shadow Keystone Buckeye Region
**6-55009** PRR New Style
**6-55010** CR
**6-55011** Penn Central
**6-55012** NH
**6-55013** Amtrak (orange)
**6-55014** Amtrak (orange)
**6-55015** Boston & Maine (blu
**6-55016** Cambria & Indiana
**6-55017** CR (gray)
**6-55018** Detroit & Mackinac
**6-55019** Long Island RR (orange)
**6-55020** Pennsy Cr. Seashore Line
**6-55021** PRR New Style Central Region
**6-55022** PRR New Style Southern Region
**6-55023** PRR New Style Western Region
**6-55024** NH
**6-55025** PRR New Style
**6-55026** Pennsylvania Readir Seashore Lines
**6-55027** Cambria & Indiana
**6-55028** Long Island RR
**6-55029** PRR New Style
**6-55030** PRR
**6-55031** PC
**6-55032** PRR New Style (red w/yellow cupola)
**6-55033** B&M w/Minute Man Logo
**6-55034** PRR Circle Keystone Over PRR
**6-55035** PRR Circle Keystone Under PRR
**6-55036** PRR Shadow Keystone "Assigned to Passenger Service Railway Express"
**6-55037** NH "American Railway Express"
**6-55038** PRR Shadow Keystone "American Express Agency"
**6-55039** PRR "Buy War Bond
**6-55000** Undecorated

## N-5, N-5c and N-8 Caboose Details

### Antenna Sets

**6-455** Brass **12.95**
**6-474** Plastic **4.85**

### Window Sets

**6-54033** N-5c **3.00**
**6-55040** N-5 **3.00**

Flat Car with Crated Load MEC 160-18902

Flat Car with Pipe Load SAL 160-18918

Flat Car with Steel Load WM 160-18929

# NEW PRODUCTS

## Silver Series® Freight Cars

### Flat Car w/Load 20.00 ea

These ready-to-run cars feature assembled loads for extra realism.

**With Container Load**

**NEW 160-18901** MEC
**NEW 160-18906** PRR
**NEW 160-18911** ATSF
**NEW 160-18916** SAL
**NEW 160-18921** UP
**NEW 160-18926** WM

**With Crated Load**

**NEW 160-18902** MEC
**NEW 160-18907** PRR
**NEW 160-18912** ATSF
**NEW 160-18917** SAL
**NEW 160-18922** UP
**NEW 160-18927** WM

**With Pipe Load**

**NEW 160-18903** MEC
**NEW 160-18908** PRR
**NEW 160-18913** ATSF
**NEW 160-18918** SAL
**NEW 160-18923** UP
**NEW 160-18928** WM

**With Steel Load**

**NEW 160-18904** MEC
**NEW 160-18909** PRR
**NEW 160-18914** ATSF
**NEW 160-18919** SAL
**NEW 160-18924** UP
**NEW 160-18929** WM

# BACHMANN SILVER SERIES®

HO deluxe freight cars with metal wheels, anti-magnetic axle and EZ-Mate magnetic couplers.

# BOX CARS

## 40' Box Cars 15.00 ea

**NEW 160-17004** SOU ("Look Ahead Look South" Slogan)
("Through the Heart of Dixie" Slogan)
**160-17012** B&O Timesaver
**160-17014** PRR Merchandise Service
**160-17020** NYC "Pacemaker"
**160-17025** C&IM
**160-17029** RUT
**160-17031** NH
**160-17032** Toledo, Peoria & Western
**160-17033** Lancaster & Chester
**160-17037** WM

**160-17038** Bangor & Aroostook
**160-17039** DRGW

**NEW 160-17040** Christmas
**NEW 160-17046** SAL

**160-17048** Boston & Maine

## Evans All-Door Box Cars 15.00 ea

**160-18104** SOU
**160-18107** SP

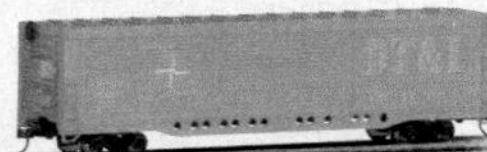

**160-18132** Detroit, Toledo & Ironton
**160-18133** Bennett Lumber

## 50' Plug-Door 13.00 ea

**160-18002** ATSF

**160-18008** Rock Island- The Rock

**160-18010** RDG
**160-18012** B&O
**160-18022** C&O (yellow, blue)

**160-18025** Frisco
**160-18029** D&H

**160-18037** WM (Speed Lettering)

**160-18045** Spokane, Portland & Seattle

40' Box Car PRR Merchandise Service 160-17014

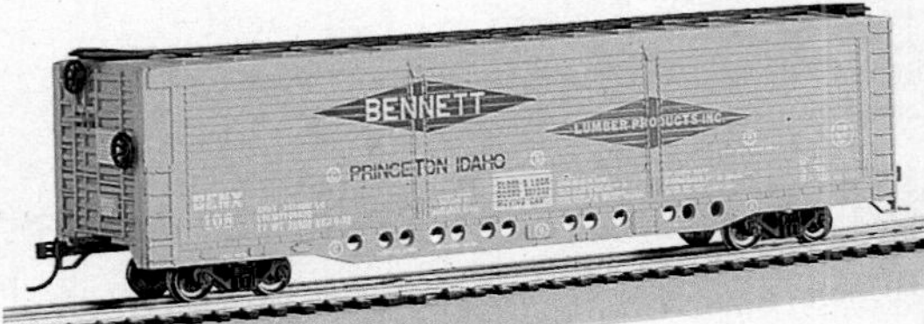


Evans All-Door Box Car Bennett Lumber 160-18133

50' Plug-Door Box Car B&O 160-18012

50' Steel Reefer Safeway 160-17944

40' Stock Car CP 160-18524

# REEFERS

## 50' Steel 13.00 ea

**160-17901** UP
**160-17902** ATSF
**NEW 160-17903** BN
**160-17913** CN
**160-17927** LV

**160-17936** Swift Premium
**160-17940** Fruit Growers Express
**160-17944** Safeway

**160-17947** Tropicana
**160-17948** Pacific Fruit Express

## 40' Stock Cars 14.00 ea

**160-18501** UP
**160-18502** ATSF
**160-18507** SP
**160-18511** GN
**160-18512** B&O
**160-18520** NYC
**160-18524** CP
**160-18535** NP

**160-18549** Humane Livestock Car

## HOPPERS

### 56' ACF Centerflow 14.00 ea

**160-17502** ATSF
**160-17512** B&O
**NEW 160-17518** CSX
**160-17513** CN
**160-17520** NYC (Jade Green)
**160-17523** NYC (gray)
**NEW 160-17528** EL
**NEW 160-17532** DT&I
**160-17534** Shell

**160-17537** ACF Cannonaide
**160-17545** Corning
**160-17547** Monsanto

### 40' Quad 13.00 ea

**160-17604** Southern
**160-17610** RDG
**160-17614** PRR
**160-17618** CSX
**160-17620** NYC
**160-17622** C&O
**160-17642** N&W
**160-17647** Seaboard

### 3-Bay 100-Ton Hoppers 18.00 ea

**160-18701** UP
**160-18702** UP

**160-18703** BN
**160-18704** BN

**160-18710** RDG
**160-18711** RDG
**160-18715** PRR "Yellow Ball" #180671
**160-18722** C&O
**160-18723** C&O #78951

40' Quad Hopper C&O 160-17622

56' ACF Centerflow Hopper ATSF 160-17502

40' 3-Dome Tank Car Pennsalt Chemical 160-17127

**160-18732** Clinchfield
**160-18733** CRR #56857
**160-18735** NP
**160-18738** WM #63787
**160-18741** NS
**160-18743** NS #144927

### Ore Cars 13.00 ea

**160-18601** UP
**160-18606** CR
**160-18614** PRR
**NEW 160-18629** Lake Superior & Ishpeming
**160-18642** N&W

**160-18643** Duluth, Missabe & Iron Range (yellow)
**160-18644** Duluth, Missabe & Iron Range (Mineral Red)

### Canadian Grain Hoppers 15.00 ea

**160-19102** ATSF

**160-19111** GN
**NEW 160-19113** CN
**160-19129** CP
**160-19131** Canada Grain
**160-19132** CN "Environmental Mode"
**160-19134** Government of Canada
**160-19139** Heritage Fund
**160-19140** Saskatchewan

## GONDOLAS

### 40' 13.00 ea

**160-17201** UP

**160-17204** Southern
**160-17213** CN
**160-17214** PRR
**160-17216** CB&Q
**160-17234** Wabash
**160-17235** NKP
**160-17242** N&W

## FLAT CARS

### 52' Depressed Center

**160-18344** Desert Military w/Missile **19.00**
**160-18345** Military w/Camouflaged Missile **19.00**
**160-18346** With Boiler **18.00**
**160-18347** With Missile Load **19.00**

**160-18348** With Transformer Load **16.00**

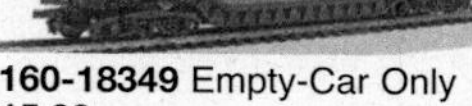

**160-18349** Empty-Car Only **15.00**

Ore Car PRR 160-18614

Canadian Grain Hoppers ATSF 160-19102

40' Gondola CN 160-17213

52' Depressed Center Flat Car Desert Military w/Missile 160-18344

52' Flat Car NP 160-17333

ACF 40' Log Cars w/Logs 1906-1935 160-18332

### 52' Flat Car 14.00 ea

**160-17302** ATSF
**160-17314** PRR
**160-17325** WP
**160-17333** NP
**160-17334** WM
**160-17335** Maine Central
**160-17346** SAL

### ACF 40' Log Cars w/Logs 36.00 ea

**160-18332** 1906-1935
**160-18849** 1935-1960

## TANK CARS

### 40' 3-Dome 14.00 ea

HO deluxe freight cars with metal wheels and EZ-Mate™ magnetic couplers.
**160-17127** Pennsalt Chemical (red)

**160-17130** Deep Rock
**160-17134** Shell
**160-17135** Cosden & Co.

**160-17137** Quaker State

**160-17139** Panhandle Refining Co.
**160-17140** Phillips 66

**160-17141** Northern California Wineries
**160-17142** Transcontinental Oil Company

### 40' Single-Dome 14.00 ea

**160-17825** Pennsalt (red)
**160-17831** Magnolia
**160-17832** Gramps

**160-17834** Shell
**160-17837** Quaker State
**160-17838** Exxon

**160-17840** Phillips 66
**160-17843** Tagolene
**160-17845** Owenwood Motor Oil

## CABOOSES

### Bobber Caboose 13.00 ea

**NEW 160-18439** Maryland & Pennsylvania

**160-18444** Weyerhaeuser Timber

36' Wide Vision Caboose RDG 160-17710

250-Ton Crane Cars & Boom Tender MOW 160-16138

Speeder With Work Crane & Cart 160-16946

40' Single-Dome Tank Car Magnolia 160-17831

**160-18445** Cass Scenic Railroad

**NEW 160-18447** Unlettered (yellow)

**160-18448** Boston & Maine
**160-18449** Painted, Unlettered

### 36' Wide Vision 13.00 ea

**160-17701** UP
**160-17702** ATSF

**160-17703** BN

**160-17709** Chessie
**160-17710** RDG

**160-17728** EL

## MISCELLANEOUS

### Gandy Dancer Hand Xmas Car

**160-46202** Powered (yellow, red, green) **32.00**

### 250-Ton Crane Cars & Boom Tenders 35.00 ea

**160-16110** RDG
**160-16114** PRR
**160-16138** MOW

**160-16149** Painted, Unlettered

## MAINTENANCE-OF-WAY VEHICLES

Each self-propelled MOW car includes finescale interior detail, a precision skew-wound motor, RP25 wheels and body-mounted E-Z Mate® Mark II couplers.

### Speeder

**160-16946** With Work Crane & Cart **64.00**

### Ballast Regulator

**160-16947** **64.00**

### Ballast Vehicle

**160-16948** With Crane **64.00**

## EASTERN CAR WORKS INC.

These undecorated HO Scale kits feature highly detailed plastic parts and include trucks. Couplers are not included, but Kadee® couplers can be easily installed.

Important Note: This listing includes items which are available by special order only. Please see the Legend Page for information, and visit www.walthers.com for a complete listing of in-stock and special order products.

## HOPPERS

### 70-Ton Enterprise Covered Hopper

Developed by the Enterprise Railway Equipment Company to compete with the ACF 70-ton covered hopper.

**117-2020** NYC Version **10.00**

### 40' Airslide® Covered Hopper

**117-2600** 2600 Cubic Feet **10.00**
Includes parts to model early or late version.

### 3500 Cubic Foot Dry Flo Car® Covered Hopper

**117-2640** Undecorated **20.00**

## GONDOLAS

### 65' Mill Gondola 10.00 ea

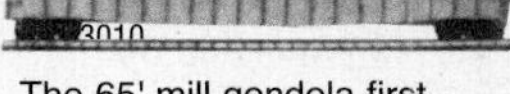

The 65' mill gondola first appeared in the 1930s. The two most common were Pennsy's G-26 and the AAR 70-ton.

**117-3000** PRR G-26
**117-3010** AAR 70-Ton

Get the Scoop!
Get the Skinny!
Get the Score!
Check Out Walthers Web site at
**www.walthers.com**

Model accurate freight trains of the 1940s to the 1960s with this line of easy-to-build, HO Scale kits. These colorful models capture the details found on their prototypes and come prepainted and lettered in period schemes. Additional styles and/or roadnames can be special ordered. Please visit www.walthers.com for a complete listing of in-stock and special order products.

Items listed in blue ink may not be available at all times (see Legend Page).

# REEFERS

## ATSF Steel Rebuilt Ice-Cooled Reefers

### Version A 13.88 ea (Unless Noted)

5' swing doors 3" eaves and recessed ends.

**193-7001** Orange Ends Without Map or Slogan

**193-7003** Big Circle Herald-1959

**193-7005** "El Capitan"/Ship & Travel Class Rr23

**193-7006** "Chief"/Ship and Travel, Class Rr23

**193-7012** "Chief", Pullman/ Ship & Travel, Class Rr25

**193-7014** "Super Chief"/Ship & Travel, Class Rr25

**193-7016** Big Circle Herald, Class Rr25

**193-7018** Black Ends Without Map or Slogan, Class Rr27

**193-7019** "Grand Canyon"/ Curved Line Map, Class Rr27

**193-7021** "Scout"/Curved Line Map, Class Rr27 1940

**193-7025** "Chief"/Straight Line Map, Class Rr28 1940

**193-7027** Grand Canyon Straight Line Map Class Rr28

**193-7028** "El Capitan"/Ship & Travel, Class Rr28 1947

**193-7034** Texas Chief Ship and Travel Class Rr28 1948

**193-7035** Big Circle Herald Class Rr28

**193-7037** "Super Chief"/ Straight Line Map Class Rr32

**193-7040** "Scout"/Straight Line Map, Class Rr32

**193-7042** "San Francisco Chief"/Ship & Travel, Class Rr32

**193-7000** Undecorated **11.88**

### Version B 13.88 ea (Unless Noted)

4/4 dreadnaught ends. 5' swing door and 3" eaves.

**193-7102** "Super Chief"/ Straight Line Map Class Rr34

**193-7103** "Grand Canyon"/ Straight Line Map Class Rr33

**193-7104** "El Capitan"/Straight Line Map Class Rr34

**193-7105** "Scout"/Straight Line Map Class Rr33

**193-7106** "Chief" w/Pullman/ Ship & Travel Class Rr34

**193-7107** "Chief"/Ship & Travel, Class Rr34

**193-7108** "Super Chief"/Ship & Travel Class Rr34

**193-7109** "Grand Canyon"/ Ship & Travel Class Rr34

**193-7110** "El Capitan"/Ship & Travel Class Rr33

**193-7111** "San Francisco Chief"/Ship & Travel Class Rr33

**193-7100** Undecorated **11.88**

### Version C

**193-7200** Undecorated **11.88**
5" swing door, 7" eave and 4/4 ends.

### Version D

**193-7300** Undecorated **11.88**
5" swing door, 7" eave and 3/3 ends.

# BOX CARS

## AAR 40' Box Cars 8.98 ea

Models feature 10 panel side, flat roof and 4-4 ends, unless noted.

### 6' Doors

**193-10101** Wabash

**193-10107** NH Script Herald

**193-10109** D&H, Round Herald "Bridge Route"

**193-10113** Illinois Terminal (Early)

**193-10114** CNW (Early)

**193-10115** IC "Mainline of Mid-America"

**193-10116** Monon "Hoosier Script"

**193-10117** N&W 1944 Railroad Roman

**193-10118** N&W 1954 Railroad Roman

**193-10119** N&W Half Moon Herald

**193-10100** Undecorated

### 6' Doors, Angle Roof

**193-12104** CP Script

**193-12105** CP Block Lettering

**193-12100** Undecorated

### 6' Doors, 4/3/1 Ends

**193-10901** MP "Route of the Eagles"

**193-10904** Texas & Pacific (Box Car Red)

### 6' Doors, 4/3/1 Ends

**193-13102** MKT "Serving The Southwest"

**193-13103** GM&O w/Bright Red Wings

**193-13107** D&H Later Oxide Red

**193-13108** CNW/Minneapolis & St. Louis "Employee Owned" (Box Car Red)

**193-13100** Undecorated

### 6' Doors, 4/3/1 Ends, 12-Panel Diagonal Roof

**193-13500** Undecorated

### 6' Doors, 12 Panel

**193-10502** ATSF "El Capitan"/ Straight Line Map

**193-10504** ATSF "Super Chief"/Straight Line Map

**193-10505** ATSF "Grand Canyon"/Straight Line Map

**193-10506** DRGW (Box Car Red)

**193-10507** Rock Island Rockets

**193-10508** Erie Large Diamond Herald

**193-10500** Undecorated

### 6' Doors, 12 Panel, 4/3/1 Ends

**193-11302** SP Early Ball Herald

**193-11303** SP Late Ball Herald

**193-11300** Undecorated

### ATSF 6' Doors, 12 Panel, Diagonal Roof

**193-12501** "Chief" Bx53

**193-12502** "El Capitan" Bx60

**193-12503** "Super Chief" Bx62

**193-12504** "Grand Canyon" Bx63

**193-10900** Undecorated

### 7' Doors

**193-10201** B&O "Timesaver" (Vermillion)

**193-10202** B&O "Sentinel" (Vermillion)

**193-10203** WM Round Herald

**193-10204** B&O M-55H Round Herald

**193-10205** PRR X-43 Tuscan Round Keystone)

**193-10207** NYC (Oxide Red oval herald)

**193-10208** WP (1940s)

**193-10211** NKP

**193-10200** Undecorated

### 7' Doors, 4/3/1 Ends

**193-11001** Genesee & Wyoming 1960s Scheme

### 7' Doors, 12-Panel, 4/3/1 Ends, Angle Roof

**193-13601** PRR X-43a, SK2a Modern Shadow Keystone

**193-13600** Undecorated

### 7' Doors, 4/3/1 Ends, Angle Roof

**193-13203** NYC Early Pacemaker

**193-13204** WM Speed Lettering

**193-13206** Bessemer & Lake Erie "Pittsburgh Bicentennial"

**193-13200** Undecorated

### 7' Doors, 12 Panel

**193-10601** PRR X-43a, Tuscan Red Keystone

**193-10600** Undecorated

### 7' Doors, 12 Panel, 4/3/1 Ends

**193-11401** West India Fruit & Steamship

**193-11400** Undecorated

### 8' Doors

**193-10305** RDG Large Diamond

**193-10306** RDG (Box Car Red w/orange "DF" on door)

### 8' Doors, 4/3/1 Ends

**193-13301** PRR X-43c, SK2a Shadow Keystone

**193-13302** PRR X-43c, SK2b Modern Shadow Keystone

**193-13303** Frisco, "Ship It" High Visability Scheme

**193-13304** BN (Cascade Green)

**193-13305** Seaboard Coast Line "Service Customers Like"

**193-11100** Undecorated

**193-13300** Undecorated

### 8' Doors, 4/3/1 Ends, Angle Roof

**193-13704** Atlantic Coast Line

**193-13700** Undecorated

### 14' Double-Doors, 4/3/1 Ends, Diagonal Roof

**193-13400** Undecorated

### Staggered 14' Double-Doors, 4/3/1 Ends

**193-11201** MP "Route of the Eagles"

**193-11200** Undecorated

### Staggered Double-Doors

**193-10401** ATSF "Scout"/ Straight Line Map

**193-10402** ATSF "El Capitan"/ Straight Line Map

**193-10403** ATSF "Chief"/ Straight Line Map

**193-10404** ATSF "Super Chief"/ Straight Line Map

**193-10405** ATSF "Grand Canyon"/Straight Line Map

**193-10406** Wabash w/Flag Herald

**193-10408** NYC Oxide Red Oval

**193-10410** DRGW Automobile Service (Box Car Red)

**193-10414** Seaboard Air Line "Route of Courteous Service"

**193-10415** Seaboard Air Line "Route of the Silver Meteor"

**193-10400** Undecorated

## GN Experimental Schemes 8.98 ea

### 14' Double-Doors, Taper Ends, Diagonal Panel Roof

**193-14401** #6 Gray #3345

**193-14402** #7 Box Car Red #3384

**193-14404** #9 Vermillion Red #3249

**193-14405** #10 Box Car Red #3486

### Angle Roof, Taper End & Staggered Double Door

**193-14400** Undecorated

### 6' Doors, Taper Ends, 12 Panel Diagonal Roof

**193-14500** Undecorated

# HOPPER

**193-990001** East Broad Top w/Trucks HOn3 **19.98**

# TRUCKS

## Freight Car

**193-990003** Vulcan HOn3 **6.9**

# DECALS

## ATSF 40' Reefer Decal Sets 2.50 ea

**193-90001** No Map, No Sloga for Cars w/Black or Orange En

**193-90005** "Chief" w/Straight Line Map

**193-90006** "Super Chief" w/Straight Line Map

**193-90007** "Grand Canyon" w/Straight Line Map

**193-90008** "El Capitan" w/Straight Line Map

**193-90009** "Scout" w/Straight Line Map

**193-90010** "Chief" w/"All Pullman" & "Ship & Travel" Slogans

**193-90013** "Grand Canyon" w/"Ship & Travel" Slogan

**193-90014** "El Capitan" w/"Ship & Travel" Slogan

**193-90016** "Texas Chief" w/"Ship & Travel Slogan 1947-58

Chooch loads are realistically hand painted and weathered resin castings. Most will fit in all open cars made by most manufacturers. You can cut them up with a metal cutting razor saw. Many new items can be used "off track" for scenery, truck vehicles or industrial details. Our new loads are all HO and come small, medium and large, also suitable for N and S and even O scale. Cars shown are sold separately.

# FREIGHT CAR LOADS

## Rock Crusher & Pulley Load 14.99 ea

**214-7277** 40 Ton
Main pulley is 2" long

**214-7278** 80 Ton
Main pulley is 2.75" long

**214-7279** 120 Ton
Main pulley is 3.75" long



## Steam Boiler Equipment

**214-7280** 40 Ton **13.99**
Boiler diameter is .75"

**214-7281** 80 Ton **17.99**
Boiler diameters are 1" and 1.25"

**214-7282** 120 Ton **16.99**
Boiler diameter is 1.75"

## Driveshaft & Pulley

**214-7283** 10 Ton **13.99**
Nautical drive shaft bearing is 2.5" long

Parts from kit #7277 for HO scale truck vehicles

**214-7284** 80 Ton **15.99**
Nautical drive shaft bearings are 3.75" and 4.25" long

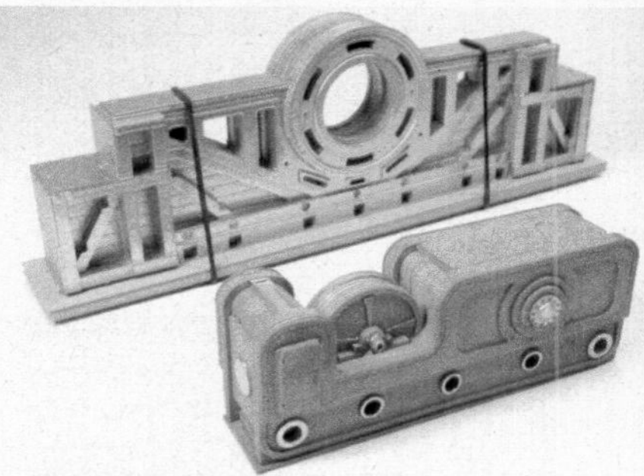

**214-7285** 120 Ton **16.99**
Nautical drive shaft bearing is 6.25" long

## Barium Oxide Bins

**214-7286** Small **8.99**
These "tote bins" are used to transport barium oxide and granulated products, usually for foundry work. Each bin is a large batch of material.

**214-7287** Large **14.99**
These "tote bins" are used to transport barium oxide and granulated products, usually for foundry work. Each bin is a large batch of material.

Parts from kit #7277 for HO scale truck vehicles

Although all the loads on this page are for HO, the larger loads can fit in S or even O scale. But all the larger sized loads will fit on the HO heavy and depressed flat cars made by Walthers and Athearn.

## GONDOLA & FLAT CAR LOADS

**214-7221** Coiled Wire **7.99**

**214-7222** Baled Scrap **7.99**

**214-7223** Random Baled Scrap **7.99**

**214-7229** Wire Coil **7.99**

**214-7230** Scrap Railroad Car Wheels **7.99**

**214-7231** New Railroad Car Wheels **7.99**

**214-7232** Heavy Equipment **9.99**

**214-7235** Coil Steel **9.99**

**214-7236** Heavy Equipment Tires **8.99**

**214-7238** Stamping Scrap **7.99**

**214-7244** Oil Pipe Connectors **8.99**

**214-7245** Light Cable Spools **8.99**

**214-7248** Wire Spool **7.99**

### Machinery

214-7220 214-7247

**214-7220** Wrapped Machinery pkg(6) **9.99**
**214-7247** Heavy Machines pkg(3) **13.99**

**214-7249** Crank Shaft w/Pallets pkg(3) **10.99**

**214-7250** Large Machines **9.99**

## Coils

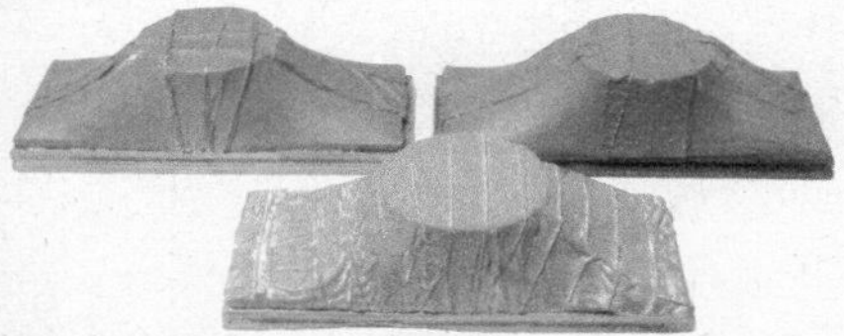

**214-7252** Intermodal 20' Covered Coils pkg(3) **10.99**

**214-7253** Intermodal 20' Coils pkg(2) **9.99**

**214-7254** Steel Coils Large & Small (9 Pieces) **13.99**

**214-7271** Single Palleted Small **13.99**
5/8" coil diameter
6 pieces

**214-7272** Single Palleted Medium **14.99**
1 & 13/16" coil diameter 4 pieces, 2 each

**214-7273** Single Palleted Large **14.99**
1-1/4 & 1-13/16" coil diameter 3 pieces, 1 each size

## Cable Reels & Spools

**214-7246** Heavy Cable Spool **8.99**

**214-7268** Steel Ribbed Small **13.99**
1/2" reel diameter 6 pieces, 2 each

**214-7269** Steel Ribbed Medium **10.99**
1" reel diameter 4 pieces, 2 each

**214-7270** Steel Ribbed Large **10.99**
1-1/2" reel diameter 2 pieces, 1 each

## Vehicles

**214-7255** Covered Trucks pkg(3) **12.99**

## Crates

**214-7243** Wood Sheathed Heavy pkg(5) **12.99**
Longest crate 3-1/2"

**214-7251** Open Crates pkg(6) **15.99**

**214-7265** Wood Sheathed Small 3-5/8 x 5/8" **13.99**
Longest crate 3-5/8" 4 pieces, 1 each size

**214-7266** Wood Sheathed Medium 4-3/4 x 1" **15.99**
Longest crate 4-3/4" 4 pieces, 1 each size

**214-7267** Wood Sheathed Large 6 x 1-1/4" **16.99**
Longest crate 6" 2 pieces, 1 each size

### Military

**214-7256** Covered Army Tanks pkg(3) **12.99**

**214-7257** Covered Artillery pkg(3) **11.99**

### Structural Beams

**214-7274** 20 Ton Small pkg(2) 3-1/2 x 3/4" **10.99**

**214-7275** 40 Ton Medium 5-3/4 x 3/4" **9.99**

**214-7276** 60 Ton Large 7-3/4 x 1-1/8" **12.99**

## GONDOLA & HOPPER LOADS

### Coal pkg(2) 7.99 ea

**214-7056** For Athearn 40' Quad Hopper 5-3/4 x 1-1/4"

**214-7057** For Athearn 34' Offset-Side Twin Hopper 4-1/2 x 1-1/4"

**214-7063** For MDC 3-Bay Hoppers

**214-7089** For Accurail USRA 55-Ton 2-Bay Open Hoppers

**214-7203** For Walthers Bethgon Coalporter

**214-7204** For Walthers 100-Ton Quad Hoppers

### Bulk Packs pkg(6) 17.99 ea

**214-70561** For Athearn 40' Quad Hopper 5-3/4 x 1-1/4"

**214-70571** For Athearn 34' Offset-Side Twin Hopper 4-1/2 x 1-1/4"

**214-70631** For MDC 3-Bay Hopper

**214-70891** For Accurail USRA 55-Ton 2-Bay Open Hoppers

### Iron Ore

**214-7212** For Walthers Ore Cars pkg(4) **8.99**

### Taconite

**214-7213** For Walthers Taconite/Ore Cars pkg(4) **8.99**

## PULPWOOD LOADS

**214-7259** Pulpwood For Walthers 52' Cars **10.99**

**214-7260** Pulpwood Load for Atlas Pulpwood Car **9.99**

## NEW PRODUCT

### 2007 Christmas Car

**NEW 223-1000078** Ten Lords-A-Leaping **17.98**

## HOPPERS

### Greenville 12-Panel Hopper 8.98 ea

**223-9300** Data (black)
**223-9301** Data (red)
**223-9302** Chessie
**223-9304** SOU
**223-9305** SP

**223-9306** BN
**223-9307** DRGW
**223-9308** ATSF
**223-9309** UP
**223-9310** N&W

**223-9311** CNW
**223-9313** Frisco
**223-9314** Illinois Central

**223-9315** PRR
**223-9316** Seaboard
**223-9317** Chattahoochee Industrial
**223-9318** SOO
**223-9319** WP
**223-9322** DRGW

**223-9324** CR
**223-9325** CNW
**223-9326** BN #2
**223-9328** UP (oxide)
**223-9329** UP (black)
**223-9331** NS 1990s
**223-9332** ATSF
**223-9320** Undecorated

### Greenville 15-Panel Hopper 8.98 ea

**223-9350** Data (black)
**223-9351** Data (red)
**223-9532** B&O
**223-9353** Detroit, Toledo & Ironton
**223-9354** Western Maryland
**223-9355** ATSF
**223-9356** L&N
**223-9357** N&W
**223-9359** L&N (Dixie)
**223-9360** EL
**223-9361** D&H
**223-9362** NP
**223-9363** CB&Q
**223-9364** NYC
**223-9365** ATSF
**223-9358** Undecorated

## GONDOLAS

### 54' Mill Gondola 8.98 ea

**223-9001** CNW
**223-9002** UP
**223-9005** ATSF
**223-9006** Wabash
**223-9007** CR
**223-9008** CSX
**223-9010** SP
**223-9011** BN
**223-9013** PL&E
**223-9014** C&O
**223-9015** L&N
**223-9016** MO PAC
**223-9019** Cotton Belt
**223-9022** SOU
**223-9023** MILW
**223-9024** D&H
**223-9025** Data (black)
**223-9026** Date (red)
**223-9028** Alaska
**223-9000** Undecorated

### 54' Mill Gondola w/Scrap Load 8.49 ea

**223-9029** WC
**223-9030** Montana Rail
**223-9031** CNJ
**223-9032** CR
**223-9033** UP
**223-9034** WC
**223-9035** NS

## FLAT CARS

### 54' Pulpwood Flat Car 8.98 ea

**223-9201** ATSF

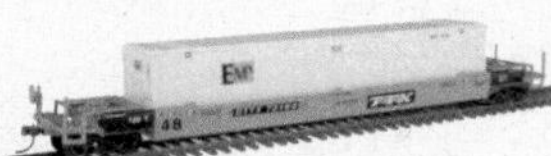

**223-9202** Trailer Train
**223-9203** SOO
**223-9204** BN
**223-9205** SOU
**223-9206** Ontario Northland
**223-9207** GN
**223-9208** N&W
**223-9209** CNW
**223-9200** Undecorated

### 54' Flat Car w/Removable Cable Reel 8.98 ea

**223-9251** SP

**223-9252** Trailer Train
**223-9253** BN
**223-9254** Illinois Central Gulf
**223-9255** N&W
**223-9256** UP
**223-9257** ATSF
**223-9258** Rio Grande (orange)
**223-9259** CR (Box Car Red)
**223-9260** CSX Transportation
**223-9262** Family Lines
**223-9250** Undecorated

### 54' Flat Car w/Trailer 10.98 ea

**223-9277** Rio Grande (black, gray)
**223-9282** N&W

### 54' Coil Car 13.98 ea

**223-9051** ATSF
**223-9052** NS
**223-9053** Chessie System
**223-9054** CR
**223-9055** PRR
**223-9057** NYC
**223-9058** GTW
**223-9060** WC
**223-9062** UP
**223-9063** N&W
**223-9064** CR

## INTERMODAL

### 125-Ton Gunderson Container Car w/48' Container 26.98 ea

Ready-to-run cars come with automatic couplers and one container.

**223-198701** Pacer Stack Train #BRAN 6348 w/Pacer #PATU 548115
**223-198702** Pacer Stack Train #BRAN 6351 w/Pacer #PATU 548122

**223-198801** Southwind #CRLE 5041 w/NS #TCZU 8506742
**223-198802** Southwind #CRLE 5023 w/NS #TCZU 8506759

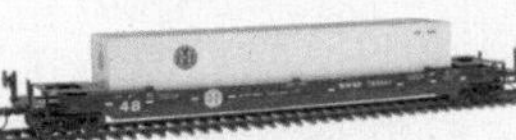

**223-198901** BNSF #153541 w/BNSF #SFCZ 420819
**223-198902** BNSF #153556 w/BNSF #SFCZ 420842

**223-199001** UP #410725 w/APL #APLU 480217
**223-199002** UP #410727 w/APL #APLU

**223-199101** Rail Bridge #RLBX 53602 w/K Line #KLFU 4339201
**223-199102** Rail Bridge #RLBX 53607 w/K Line #KLFU 4338161

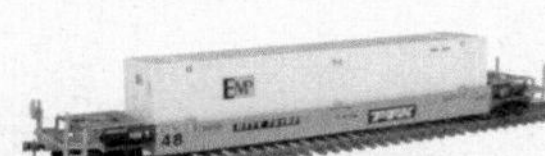

**223-199201** Trailer Train #DTTX 73192 w/EMP #EMPU 148121
**223-199202** Trailer Train #DTTX 73196 w/EMP #EMPU 148129



## CMX PRODUCTS

### Clean Machine Track Cleaning Car

**226-CMXHO** w/10 Cleaning Pads **124.95**
Clean tracks completely and quickly with this specially designed car. Unit applies and wipes solvents (sold separately) in one pass, or can be used as an abrasive type cleaner. Solid brass construction (except for trucks) resists all solvents. Unit weighs about one pound for maximum contact and deep-cleaning action. Special drag pads won't catch on trackwork and are easily changed when dirty. Unit comes assembled with body-mount Kadee couplers and complete instructions.

### Replacement Pads

**226-CMXHOPADS** pkg(20) **5.00**
Use with the Clean Machine Track Cleaning Car (sold separately).

## KEYSTONE LOCOMOTIVE WORKS

All items are HO Scale craft train kits.

For a complete listing of products, visit www.walthers.com

### Lumber Cars

#### Barnhart Log Loader

**395-104 39.95**

#### Climax Log Car

**395-107** pkg(2) **11.95**

#### Log Buggie

**395-100** pkg(2) **11.95**
Less trucks and couplers.

#### Logging Caboose

**395-106 18.95**
Includes trucks, less couplers.

#### Skeleton Log Car

**395-103** 29' pkg(2) **11.95**
Less trucks and couplers.

### Caboose Interior

#### Wide Vision

**395-3501 12.98**
Fits Athearn, Bachmann and AHM wide-vision cabooses without modification.

# Custom Finishing

These HO Scale Craft Train kits feature detailed brass and white-metal parts, and include rotating, insulated wheels. All kits include decals. For a complete listing of Custom Finishing products, visit www.walthers.com.

## TRACK MAINTENANCE EQUIPMENT

**247-7057** Burro Crane Model 30 **54.95**
This 7-1/2-ton crane can rotate or be secured by a pivot system. Over 55 detail parts, including a brass boom, windshield wipers, window glazing and a 39" magnet. Couplers not included.

**247-7282** Clamshell Bucket **16.95**
This 1/2-cubic-yard bucket includes brass castings and can be assembled to operate.

**247-7283** Crane Accessories **6.95**
This set of brass castings includes a 39" nonoperating magnet, hoistblock, hook and railtongs.

**247-7007** Swingmaster Speed Swing Model 181 **29.95**

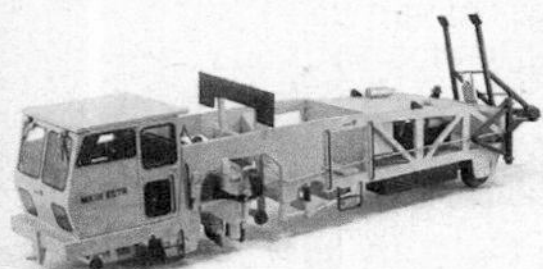

**247-7014** Tamper Track Alignment Machine w/Laser Alignment Buggy Model MK III **55.95**

**247-7027** Kershaw Ballast Regulator Model 26 **76.95**
This kit has many parts that are positionable. The side wing plows can be raised and lowered by cable and drum like the prototype. The front transfer plow blade swings, and can be raised and lowered, as can the sweeping machinery at the rear. The model includes a full cab interior, plus decals, window glazing and etched brass windshield wipers. The kit features over 100 metal parts and includes complete assembly instructions.

**247-7029** Kershaw 150-Ton Wrecking Crane **99.95**

### Fairmont Tamper

**247-7031** Mark IV Production Tamper w/Laser Alignment Buggy Kit **95.95**

**247-7034** Model TR-10 Tie Exchanger **58.95**

**247-7086** Jet Snow Melter **75.95**

**247-7042** Automatic Rail Lifter **17.95**

Truck Shown Sold Separately

**247-7047** 50' Equipment Transport Flatbed Trailer **25.95**
Heavy duty detachable gooseneck. Fits Herpa/Con-Cor and other tractors (not included).

**247-7048** 18-Ton Steel-Decked Equipment Trailer w/Pintel Hook **21.95**

**247-7248** Operating Pintel Hooks pkg(3) **4.95**

**247-7049** Kershaw RCT 130 Mobile Wrecking Crane Kit **84.95**
The stabilizers of this 130-ton wrecking crane are positionable. Over 150 detail parts, including windshield wipers and window glazing. Cabs feature full interior detail.

**247-7056** Fairmont A4 Series E Motor Car **26.95**
This double kit features over 30 detail parts, including windshield wipers and window glazing.

Truck Shown Sold Separately

**247-7060** National Telescoping Boom Truck Body **34.95**

**247-7061** Badger Cruz-Air Rubber Tire Excavator **64.95**

**247-7069** Kershaw Rail Carrier Buggies 1 Pair **11.95**
Features insulated wheels, pulling bar and spreader bar.

**247-7070** Tracked Crawler/ Dozer D-7 Similar **25.95**
Includes fully detailed motor, two styles of motor hoods and intake filters, front bumper and rear hitch.

**247-7271** Dozer Blade 10'-6" **9.95**
Fits Tracked Crawler/Dozer #247-7070, sold separately. Blade can be raised and lowered.

**247-7272** Heavy-Duty Rear Mounted Winch **8.95**
Fits Tracked Crawler/Dozer #247-7070, sold separately. Comes with windable cable drum, cable and weighted hook.

**247-7274** Side Boom Pipelayer **27.95**
Fits Tracked Crawler/Dozer #247-7070, sold separately. Boom, hook and block can be raised and lowered. Features de-mountable weight plates.

Truck Shown Sold Separately

**247-7072** Wreck Crane Supply Carrier Body **43.95**
Fits Atlas Ford LNT 9000 Tractor. Functional service crane swivels 360°, while hy-rail wheels raise and lower.

**247-7073** Kershaw Model 44 Rotary Tie Bed Scarifier **59.95**
The inserter can be positioned up or down via hydraulic cylinders. Can be modeled in an open or closed cab style. Includes window glazing, wipers and decals.

**247-7074** Nordco Tie Spacer **22.95**
Brass telescopic hydraulic cylinders on each side of the machine can position clamps. Over 32 parts. Includes decals and an unpainted operator figure.



## LOG STAKE CAR

**247-318** 62' 9" National Steel Car Company **19.95**
This log car is easily assembled and features an all pewter make-up. Kit includes all castings, preformed grabs, predrilled end platforms for truck installation (brass screws included) and illustrated instructions. Less trucks, couplers and decals.

## ACCESSORIES

### Hy-Rail Wheels

Trucks Not Included

**247-7009** Guide, For Light-Duty Vehicles **4.95**

**247-7276** Medium/Heavy Duty **14.95**

**247-7016** Flat Car Loading Ramp **9.95**
For Track Maintenance Equipment.

**247-7024** Compressor 160 psi, w/Hy-Rail Wheels **11.95**

**247-7036** Seated Figures pkg(6) **4.95**
Hard hat operators for maintenance equipment. Three each of two different positions.

**247-7059** Welders/Boxes pkg(8) **15.95**
Set includes two Miller Air-Pak welders and six on-site job tool boxes.

Truck Not Included

**247-7071** Snow Plow Attachment 1 Pair **9.95**
For Light Duty Trucks. Fits Trident four-wheel drive vehicles.

These HO and HOn3 craft train kits include various combinations of wood, plastic, cast-metal and cardstock parts. Special note: The Wheel Works line of freight cars has been acquired by Durango Press.

## GONDOLAS

All gondolas are HOn3 scale DRGW Prototype.

### High-Side Gondola

**254-112 18.95**

### Pipe Gondola

**254-114 18.95**

## FLAT CARS

### Westside Lumber Co.

Car bodies are one-piece metal castings, so no extra weight is needed. All add-on details are also cast metal. Trucks included.

**254-50** HOn3 **19.95**

**254-53** Aged Deck HOn3 **19.95**
Includes a weathered deck with rotten boards.

### Idler Flat Car

**254-116** DRGW HOn3 **16.95**

## INTERMODAL EQUIPMENT

Now in use on some major railroads, the RoadRailer® can be operated as a truck trailer or rail car using the retractable running gear. A special coupler is used so that RoadRailers are run as unit trains. Kits include unpainted plastic and metal parts.

### AdapterRailer®

**254-102 21.95**
This unit is used as an idler between the loco and other RoadRailer units. It has a standard coupler at the front, and the special RoadRailer coupler at the rear.

### RoadRailer

**254-101 17.95**
Kit is designed to run on rails, but can be modified for highway use with some scratchbuilding.

## CABOOSE

### Westside Lumber Co.

**254-55** HOn3 **22.95**
All-plastic kit with trucks.

## MAINTENANCE-OF-WAY

### Rotary Snow Plow Kits 109.95 ea

Meet winter head-on with this rugged rotary plow. The kit is based on Rotary OM, which was built by Cooke and delivered to the Rio Grande narrow gauge in 1889. The same design was also used by many standard-gauge roads.

**254-30** HOn3
Includes decals for Rio Grande Rotary OM.

**254-31** HO
Includes decals for SP, UP, CP, GN and SOO.

### Drag Flangers

**254-42** HOn3 Rio Grande Southern #02 Plow Flanger **64.95**

**254-51** RGS Drag Flanger #01 HOn3 **37.95**
Came to the RGS new in 1890 from the Denver & Rio Grande shops.

**254-126** Rio Grande Southern Decals **1.00**
Set includes numbers and data for use with #254-51 as shown above, printed in white.

### Hand Cars

Taken directly from Rio Grande plans, this kit consists of detailed metal castings, brass wire and scale lumber.

**254-12** HO **10.95**

**254-22** HOn3 **11.95**

**254-14** Hand Car Wheels pkg(4) **2.95**
These wheels are for use with kits #254-12 and 254-22, each sold separately.

### Track Maintenance Equipment

### Fairmont Speeders

**254-36** Early MT-14 **9.95**

**254-37 9.95**

**254-38** HOn3 **9.95**
Cast metal kit features an older version roof, front & rear support design. Used 1930s-1960s. Uses a narrow wood simulated main body to accommodate 3' gauge track.

Track "Crew" Work Train 254-90

Track Equipment Set 254-100

### Tie Carts & Tools

**254-88 12.95**

### "Crew" Cars

**254-89** pkg(2) **9.95**

### Track "Crew" Work Train

**254-90 41.95**
Includes three nonpowered speeders, two trailers and one trailer with small crane.

### Fairmont Spike Puller

**254-97 8.95**
The prototype of this unit is used to pull spikes from bad ties.

### Fairmont Tie Shear

**254-98 22.95**
The prototype of this machine cuts bad ties in half, for faster removal.

### Kershaw Tie Crane

**254-99 22.95**
This small crane is used to lift new ties and put them in place.

### Track Equipment Set

**254-100 59.95**
This set includes one each of the following kits: Fairmont Speeder (#254-37), Fairmont Tie Shear (#254-98), Fairmont Spike Puller (#254-97) and Kershaw Tie Crane (#254-99).

## LOG CAR

### New Mexico Lumber Co.

**254-58 13.95**
This car was used by the New Mexico Lumber Co. and other lumber companies along the Rio Grande line.

## MINING EQUIPMENT

**254-43** 18" Gauge Mine Car **4.95**

**254-47** 18" Gauge Timber Car **4.95**

### Deluxe Mining Detail Set

**254-44** 18" Gauge **14.95**
Includes mine car, timber car, tools, picks, helmets and more.

## FUNARO & CAMERLENGO

These kits consist of thin flexible styro-urethane castings, Tichy brake parts, preformed wire grab irons and instructions. Cars do not include couplers or trucks. Kits include decals where noted.

Important Note: Please see the Legend Page for information, and visit www.walthers.com for a complete listing of in-stock and special order products.

### NEW PRODUCTS

#### Box Cars

**FEC Rebuilt Insulated Box Car**

**NEW 279-6416** Palm Tree Herald Decals **39.99**
One-piece body.

**M15L/M Wagontop Automobile Car**

**NEW 279-7020** B&O **39.99**
One-piece body, resin kit.

**Central Vermont 40' Smoothside Cars 31.99 ea**

**NEW 279-7060** #40000 Series - Standard

**NEW 279-7061** #40000 Series - Flour Loading w/Hatches & Hoppers

#### Stock Cars

**Reading Class SMC**

**NEW 279-7040** K Brakes; w/Decals **31.99**

#### Hoppers

**B&O Wagontop Covered Hoppers 39.99 ea**

One-piece body, resin kits with decals.

**NEW 279-7050** Steam Era

**NEW 279-7051** Large B&O

#### Flat Cars

**PRR F22 Heavy-Duty Cars 34.99 ea**

Resin kits with decals.

**NEW 279-7010** K Brake

**NEW 279-7011** AB Brake

**PRR F23 30' Steel Deck Cars 34.99 ea**

Resin kits with decals.

**NEW 279-7070** K Brake

**NEW 279-7071** AB Brake

#### Tank Cars

**ACF AAR Type 2 39.99 ea**

One-piece tank with frame and decals.

**NEW 279-7030** National Oil Co.

**NEW 279-7031** Associated Oil Co.

#### Cabooses

**PRR Class ND 39.99 ea**

Resin kits with one-piece, roof, cupola and decals.

**NEW 279-514** K Brakes

**NEW 279-515** AB Brakes

**PRR Class NDA 39.99 ea**

Resin kits with one-piece, roof, cupola and decals.

**NEW 279-516** K Brakes

**NEW 279-517** AB Brakes

### BOX CARS

**PRR X-28A 39.99 ea**

One-piece body with decals.

**279-7000** Creco Door & K Brake

**279-7001** Creco Door & AB Brake

**279-7002** Youngstown Door & K Brake

**279-7003** Youngstown Door & AB Brake

**B&O M50 Wagontop 39.99 ea**

One-piece body with decals.
**279-6935** White Decals

**279-6936** Black Decals

**B&O M53 Wagontop 39.99 ea**

One-piece body with decals.

**279-6930** Plain Door

**279-6931** Creco Door

**279-6932** Youngstown Door

**279-6933** Express Version Plain Door

**279-6934** Express Version Creco Door

**40' Box Car**

**279-1008** NP 1918 **31.99**
8'9" inside height, truss rod steel center sill and underframe; includes decals.

**1890s Wooden Car**

**279-3801** DL&W 1890-1911 Details w/Decals **31.99**

### STOCK CARS

**Rutland 36' Single Deck 31.99 ea**

**279-6690** #1940-1999

**279-6691** #1970-1973

### HOPPERS

**Phosphate-Fertilizer Covered Hopper**

**279-6880** Shippers Car Line Corp. **34.99**

**PRR H30 Covered Hopper 31.99 ea**

**279-6840** White Circle Keystone

**279-6841** Black Circle Keystone

**279-6842** Shadow Keystone

**279-6843** Plain Keystone

**279-6844** White Penn Central

**279-6845** Black Penn Central

**PRR H32 Covered Hopper 31.99 ea (Unless Noted)**

**279-2091** White Circle Keystone

**279-2092** Shadow Keystone

**279-2094** Black Circle Keystone

**NEW 279-2095** Shadow Keystone, Vibrator Underframe **34.99**

### FLAT CARS

**F33 Well Hole Car**

**279-6940** PRR **39.99**
One-piece body with decals.

### TANK CARS

**PRR TM8 8000-Gallon Tank Car w/K Brake 39.99 ea**

**279-6990** White Lettering

**279-6991** Black Lettering

**20,000-Gallon Steel Coal Tar Tank Car**

**279-6970** Jones & Laughlin w/Decals **49.99**

**Borden's "Butterdish" Milk Tank Car 39.99 ea**

**279-1010** White

**279-1011** Yellow

## RIX PRODUCTS

**Ingot Buggies & Molds**

**628-601** pkg(3) **11.95**

**Ingot Molds w/Stools**

**628-602** pkg(2) **2.99**

## SHEEPSCOT SCALE PRODUCTS

**Pile Driver Conversion**

**668-75005** Industrial Brownhoist Type **25.00**
Convert any Walthers 25-Ton Crane (sold separately) into a pile driver with this kit.

## TOMAR INDUSTRIES

**Pick-Up Shoes pkg(4) 4.50 ea**

Shoes mount on the trucks of passenger cars, cabooses or locomotives. Kits include detailed installation drawings.

**81-804** For Passenger Cars & Cabooses

**81-805** For Locomotives
Comes with wires and screws.

## GRANDT LINE

Narrow gauge styrene craftsman car kits. Underbody details, brake gear, wire parts, dummy couplers, trucks and decals (where appropriate) are included. All kits are HOn3 unless noted.

## NARROW GAUGE CARS

### 30' Reefer

**300-5231** Colorado & Southern/ Rio Grande Southern **22.95**

### Steel Underframe Stock Car

**300-5253** Colorado & Southern/ Rio Grande Southern **22.95**
Over 60 parts; Murphy roof and positionable door.

### 30' Gondolas

**300-5188** Drop Bottom DRGW **33.95**
Includes over 200 parts.

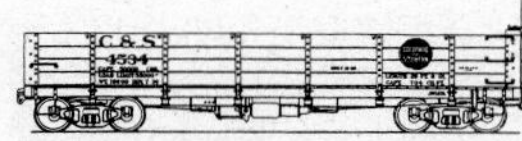

**300-5214** Steel Underframe Colorado & Southern **22.95**

### 30' Flat Car

**300-5186** DRGW **19.95**

### 30' Caboose

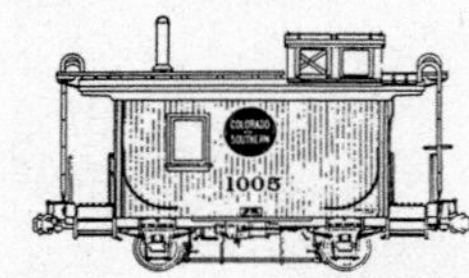

**300-5235** Colorado & Southern **21.95**

### 30' Wheel & Tie Car

**300-5187** DRGW **23.95**

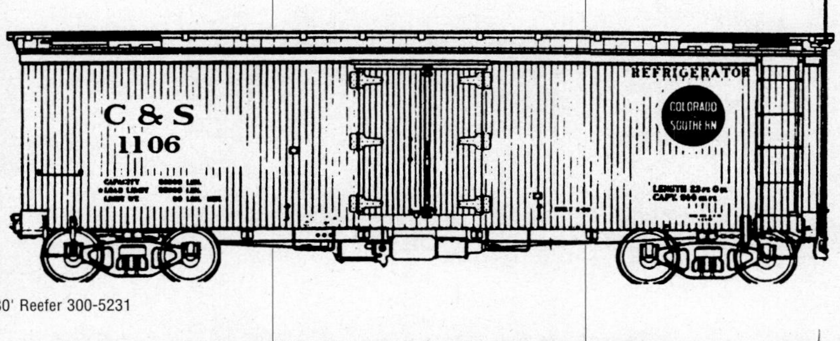


30' Reefer 300-5231

Steel Underfame Stock Car 300-5253

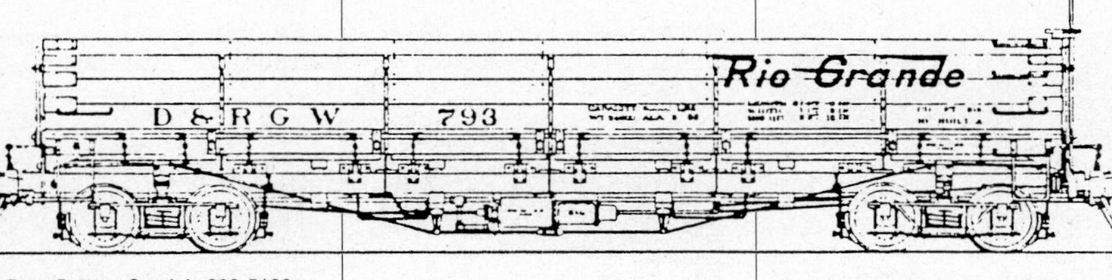


30' Drop Bottom Gondola 300-5188

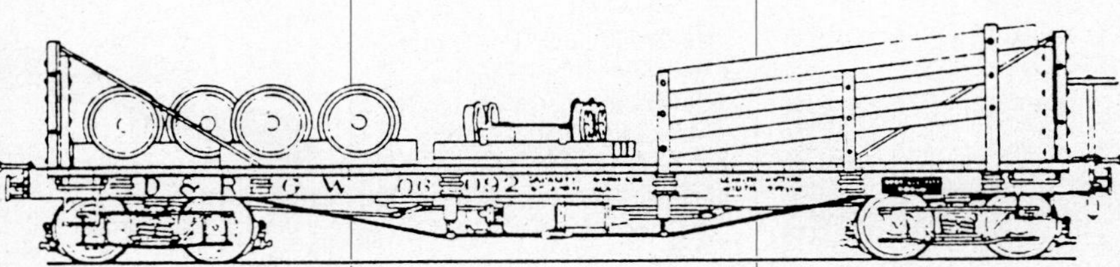


30' Wheel & Tie Car 300-5187

## Hi-Tech Details

331-7000

331-7105

## BOX CARS

### Pullman-Standard 40' Hi-Cube Box Car

**331-7000** Undecorated **13.95**
A highly detailed, injection-molded styrene kit. This type of car was most commonly used by the CB&Q, DRGW, MILW, IC, NP and BN railroads.

### PS-1 40' Hy-Cube Box Cars 19.95 ea

All cars feature CB&Q markings and are painted Chinese Red.

**331-7102** #19856

**331-7103** #19869

**331-7104** #19871

**331-7105** #19874

HEICO MODELL

IMPORTED FROM GERMANY BY WALTHERS

Transform empty cars into detailed models in seconds! Fully assembled, one-piece loads are complete with real wood bracing and are ideal for use with various flat cars and gondolas. Simply set in place for loads-in/empties out operation, or glue down for permanent detail. Can be used to model finished products stacked for loading or unloading alongside industries too. Short loads may be kitbashed for use with trucks. Dimension shown is overall length. Freight cars and tractor/trailers shown in pictures are not included.

## FREIGHT CAR LOADS

**335-87005** Heated Containers pkg(2) **25.99**

**335-87015** Machine Component 3-1/8" 8cm **24.99**

**335-87017** Turbine in Wood Case **46.99**

**335-87026** Rolled Steel Sheets 4" 10cm pkg(2) **27.99**

**335-87030** Banded Aluminum 2-3/8" 6cm pkg(2) **26.99**

**335-87032** Aluminum Slabs 2-3/8" 6cm pkg(2) **19.99**

**335-87041** Short Steel Pipe 5-1/2" 14cm **17.99**

**335-87043** Large Diameter Pipe "Mannesmann" 5-3/8" 13.5cm **17.99**

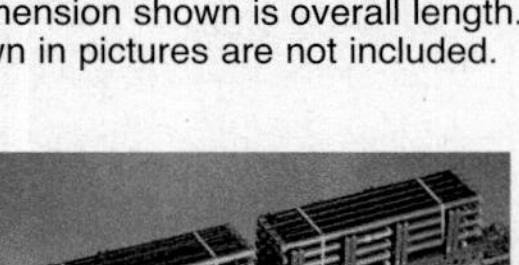

**335-87046** Steel Pipe 4" 10cm pkg(2) **24.99**

**335-87051** Banded Steel Pipe 5-3/8" 13.5cm **17.99**

**335-87100** Motor **29.99**

**335-87124** Iron Bars **21.99**

**335-87132** Radio Antenna 7-13/16" 19.5cm **24.99**

**335-87311** Concrete Water/Sewer Pipe 3-3/8" 8.5cm **21.99**

**335-87314** Reinforced Concrete "Betomax" 5" 12.5cm **29.99**

**335-87316** Finished Concrete Parts "Clement" **29.99**

**335-87406** Old Railroad Tie Stacks 5-5/16" 13.5cm **19.99**



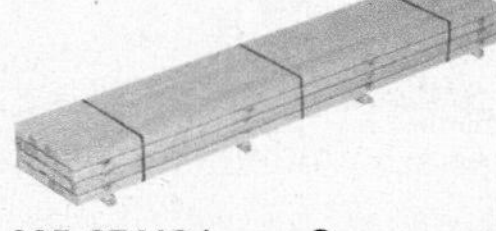

**335-87412** Large Square Wooden Beams 5-1/2" 14cm **18.99**

**335-87415** Banded Square Wooden Beams Small 2" 5cm pkg(2) **18.99**

**335-87431** Cut Board Lumber 3-1/2" 9cm **18.99**

**335-87473** Plastic-Wrapped Lumber Load "Trinkl" 2-3/8" 6cm pkg(3) **29.99**

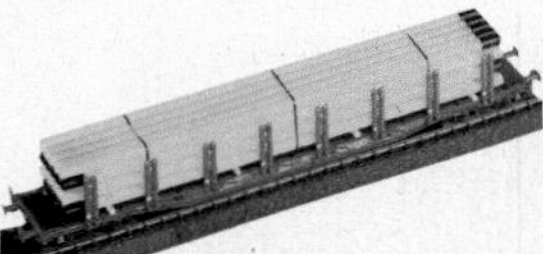

**335-87507** Banded Gas Pipes w/Fitting Flanges Large (yellow) 7-7/8" 20cm **21.99**

**335-87503** Coated Pipe Load (green) 2-3/8" 6cm pkg(2) **24.99**

**335-87510** Aluminum Tubes **19.99**

**335-87511** Aluminum Pipe "VAM Europipe AG" 5-3/8" 13.5cm **23.99**

**335-87513** Gas Pipes "Fuchs" **23.99**

**335-87813** Large Tank "Bitterfeld" 4-7/8" 12.5cm **21.99**

**335-87815** Powered Cement Silo 3-3/4" 9.5cm **21.99**

**335-87816** Dust Collector 3-3/4" 9.5cm **21.99**

**335-87827** Wheel Loader Parts **42.99**

**335-87834** Ship's Diesel Engine 2-3/4" 7cm **24.99**

**335-87835** Large Air Compressor 5-3/8" 13.5cm **24.99**

**335-87837** Diesel Engine "May Brook" Load pkg(2) **51.99**

**335-87838** Locomotive Engine w/Crate Load 5-5/8" 14cm **35.99**

**335-87855** Newsprint Paper Rolls 5-3/8" 13.5cm **21.99**

**335-87860** Locomotive Body Under Tarp 13/16 x 2-5/8" 2 x 6.5cm **26.99**

**335-87870** Air Conditioner w/Air Duct Piping 5-3/8" 13.5cm **19.99**

**335-87880** AEG Transformer Load 5-5/8" 14cm **25.99**

**335-87885** Machine Tools Under Tarp 13/16 x 2-5/8" 2 x 6.5cm **32.99**

**335-87934** Feed Crates "Henschel" 1-1/2" 4cm pkg(3) **29.99**

**335-87936** Overseas Crates "Hamburg Seehafen" 2-1/2" 6.5cm pkg(2) **24.99**

**335-87931** Crated Machinery 3-7/8" 10cm **16.99**

Items listed below are available by Special Order (see Legend Page).

**335-87001** Locomotive Shell Under Tarp **43.99**

**335-87122** Ingot Molds For Steel Works 4-7/8" 12.5cm **24.99**

**335-87123** Steel Coils w/Bracing 5" 12.5cm **24.99**

**335-87417** Pressure-Treated Lumber 7-7/8" 20cm **44.99**

## TRACTOR/ TRAILER LOADS

**335-77041** Steel Pipe 2" 5cm and 2-3/4" 7cm **21.99**

**335-77311** Concrete Sewer Pipe 5-7/8" 15cm **31.99**

**335-77321** Precast Concrete Culvert Sections 5-7/8" 15cm **17.99**

**335-77874** Oil Cooled Industrial Transformer 3-3/4" 9.5cm **24.99**

## NEW PRODUCTS

### Cylindrical Covered Hoppers

**24.95 ea**

Seen in grain service, these colorful covered hoppers can be found all over Canada and the US, The models come fully assembled and will handle 15" radius curves.

**NEW 326-12051** Alberta (Take an Alberta Break)

**NEW 326-12052** Government of Canada (Red)

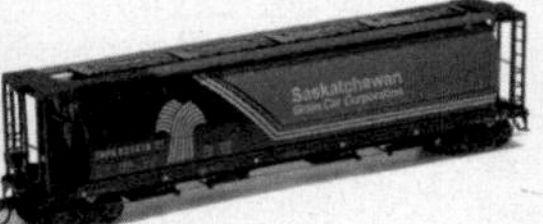

**NEW 326-12053** Saskatchewan Grain Car Corp.

**NEW 326-12054** CP Rail

**NEW 326-12055** Government of Canada (Tan)

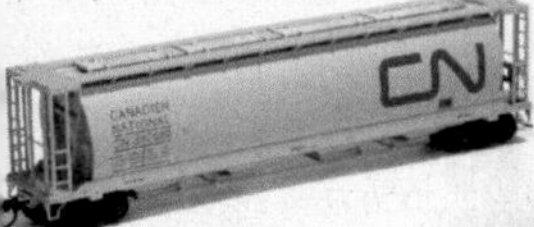

**NEW 326-12056** CN

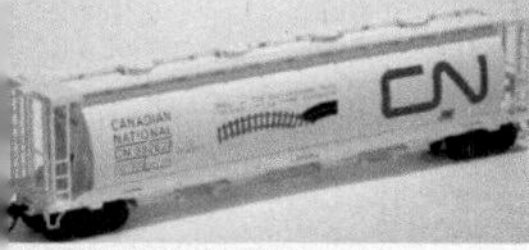

**NEW 326-12057** CN (Environment Mode)

**NEW 326-12058** Canadian Wheat Board

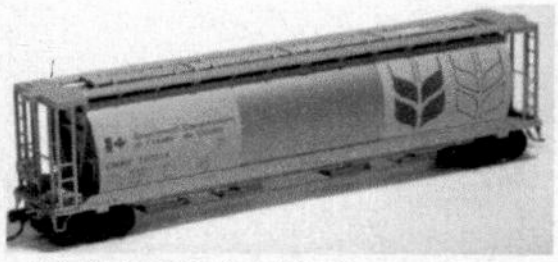

**NEW 326-12059** Government of Canada (Aluminum)

**NEW 326-12060** Toronto, Hamilton & Buffalo

### 40' Track Cleaning Box Cars

**24.95 ea**

Clean track while your run your trains. Fully assembled box cars are fitted with a spring-loaded abrasive pad that removes dirt and grime from rail surfaces.

**NEW 326-13109** CP (green, Multi-mark)

**NEW 326-13117** CP (silver)

**NEW 326-13119** CN (green)

**NEW 326-13120** CN (black & gray)

**NEW 326-13126** CN Manitoba

**NEW 326-13128** CN (Noodle w/wheat logo)

**NEW 326-13130** Esquimault & Nanaimo (red w/Multi-mark)

**NEW 326-13131** CP Rail (yellow door)

## NATIONAL STEEL CAR 40' BOX CARS

Based on one of Canada's most numerous box cars from the 1950s to the 1990s, these ready-to-run cars feature sliding doors, applied details, free-rolling trucks and working knuckle couplers.

### As-Built With Roofwalk & Long Ladders 19.95 ea

**326-12001** CP (Block Lettering)

**326-12003** CN (Maple Leaf "Serves All Canada" logo)

**326-12006** Pacific Great Eastern (w/Initials Logo)

**326-12021** CP (Box Car Red, Script Lettering)

**326-12023** CN (Maple Leaf "Serves All Canada" logo)

**326-12024** CN (Maple Leaf "Canada's Largest Railway" logo)

**326-12025** CP ("Newsprint Service" logo and block lettering)

**326-12032** CP (Block Lettering, red door)

Cylindrical Covered Hopper Alberta (Take an Alberta Break) 326-12051

**326-12997** Painted CN #11 Red, Unlettered

**326-12998** Painted CP Oxide Brow), Unlettered

**326-12999** Undecorated

### Rebuilt No Roofwalk, Short Ladders 19.95 ea

**326-12008** CP Rail

**326-12009** CP Rail

**326-12011** CN ("Noodle" logo)

**326-12012** CN ("Noodle" logo, yellow door)

**326-12013** Pacific Great Eastern (gray map herald)

**326-12022** CP Grain Service (Script Lettering)

**326-12026** CN Manitoba Grain

**326-12027** CP ("Newsprint Service" logo and script lettering)

**326-12028** CN Modern Grain Service ("Noodle" logo)

**326-12029** CN Grain Service ("Serves All Canada," straight rectangle Maple Leaf logo)

**326-12030** Esquimault & Nanaimo

**326-12031** CP Rail

**326-12033** CP (Block Lettering, "Movable Bulkheads" lettering)

**326-12034** Toronto, Hamilton & Buffalo Ti-Cat (yellow, black)

**326-12035** Toronto, Hamilton & Buffalo '67 Centennial (yellow, black)

**326-12994** Painted CN #11 Red, Unlettered

**326-12995** Painted Oxide Red, Unlettered

**326-12996** Undecorated

# Jaeger

Easy-to-build load kits include coated paper, wood blocks, banding material, spacers and instructions.

Protected Building Product Load 347-3900

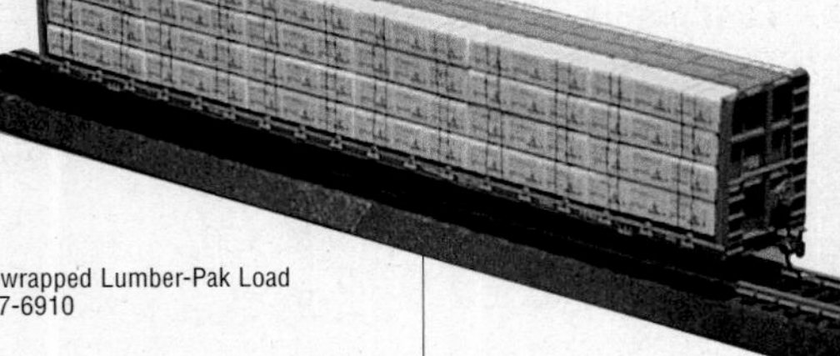

Unwrapped Lumber-Pak Load 347-6910

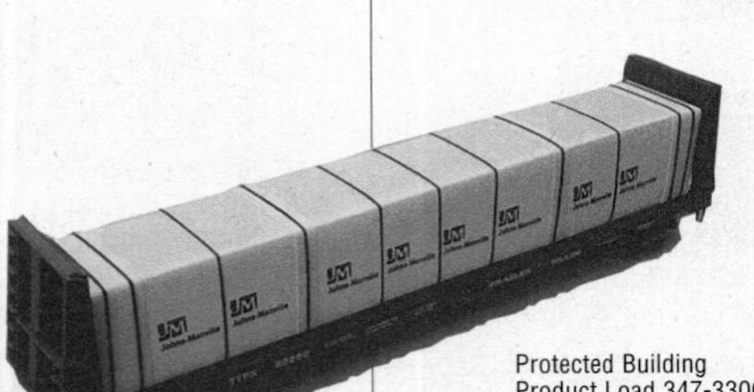

Protected Building Product Load 347-3300

Timber Load 347-2525

60' Flat Car Lumber Load 347-6000

## LOADS

### 40'/50' Flat Car Lumber Load Kits 10.00 ea

Fits standard or bulkhead car.

**347-100** Boise Cascade
**347-200** Bulkley Valley
**347-250** Canfor
**347-300** Edward Hines
**347-400** Georgia-Pacific
**347-450** Georgia-Pacific (blue)
**347-500** Pack River
**347-600** Weyerhaeuser Shed-Pak
**347-650** ATCO Lumber Ltd.
**347-700** Babine
**347-750** Croman Corp.
**347-800** Idapine Mills
**347-900** Louisiana-Pacific
**347-1000** Modoc
**347-1100** St. Regis
**347-1150** Tricon Timber, Inc.
**347-1200** West Fraser
**347-1300** Bennett Lumber
**347-1400** Collins Pine Co.
**347-1450** Crown Pacific
**347-1500** High Cascade
**347-1600** International Paper-IP Building Materials
**347-1700** Keystone
**347-1800** Potlatch
**347-1900** Weldwood

### Utility Pole Load Kits

Two complete loads for gondolas or bulkhead flats.

**347-2300** Natural **10.00**
**347-2350** Dark Brown **15.00**

### Pipe Load Kit

**347-2900** Aluminum **16.00**
Builds two complete loads, fits most 40 or 50' flats or gondolas.

### Timber Load Kits 18.00 ea

Four assembled, stained and banded bundles for Athearn 40 or 50' flat cars.

**347-2500** No Markings
**347-2525** Georgia-Pacific
**347-2550** Publishers Forest Products

### Ingot Load Kit

**347-2600** Aluminum **15.00**
Two loads for 50' gondolas or 60' bulkhead flats.

Get Your Daily Dose of Product News at **www.walthers.com**

### Protected Building Product Load Kits 12.00 ea

Assembled, fits Roundhouse 60' bulkhead flats.

**347-3100** Evans Products
**347-3200** Gold Bond Products
**347-3300** Johns-Manville Building Products
**347-3350** Ligmun
**347-3400** Masonite
**347-3500** Plum Creek Timber Co.
**347-3600** US Gypsum
**347-3700** Centex
**347-3800** Georgia-Pacific
**347-3850** Georgia-Pacific (blue)
**347-3900** Louisiana-Pacific
**347-3950** Louisiana-Pacific (Particle Board)
**347-3000** Undecorated (black)

### 60' Flat Car Lumber Load Kits 15.00 ea

Fits standard or bulkhead car.

**347-4000** ATCO Lumber Ltd.
**347-4100** Canfor
**347-4200** Carrier Western Lumber
**347-4300** Champion Lumber
**347-4400** Crown Zellerbach
**347-4500** Evans Products
**347-4600** Grande Prairie
**347-4700** Hines
**347-4800** Northwood
**347-4900** Pope & Talbot
**347-5000** Publishers Forest Products
**347-5100** Roseburg
**347-5200** Simpson Timber
**347-5300** Washington Idaho Forest Products
**347-5400** Weyerhaeuser Building Products
**347-5500** Clearwater Forest Industries
**347-5600** Great West Timber
**347-5700** Hanel Lumber Company
**347-5800** Sierra Pacific
**347-5900** Slocan
**347-6000** Weyerhaeuser Lumber/Kamloops

### Walthers GSC Flat Car Lumber Load Kits 13.00 ea

**347-6800** ATCO Lumber Ltd.
**347-6805** Bennett Lumber

**347-6810** Boise Cascade
**347-6815** Champion Lumber
**347-6820** Georgia-Pacific
**347-6825** Grande Prairie
**347-6830** High Cascade
**347-6835** Idaho Timber
**347-6840** Idapine Mills
**347-6845** International Paper
**347-6850** Louisiana-Pacific
**347-6855** MacMillan Bloedel
**347-6860** Northwood
**347-6865** Plum Creek Timber
**347-6870** Publishers Forest Products
**347-6875** Ranger
**347-6880** Rustad Brothers
**347-6885** St. Regis
**347-6890** Weldwood
**347-6895** Weyerhaeuser

### Lumber-Pak Kits For Walthers 73' Centerbeam Cars 18.00 ea

**347-6900** Boise Cascade
**347-6910** Clearwater/Idapine
**347-6920** Hampton Lumber
**347-6930** Lignum
**347-6940** Manfor Ltd.
**347-6950** Moose River Lumber Co.
**347-6960** Weyerhaeuser
**347-6970** Norwegian Termite
**347-6980** Simpson Timber

### Centerbeam Lumber Load Kits 15.00 ea

**347-7000** Boise Cascade
**347-7100** MacMillan Bloedel
**347-7200** Quandra Wood Products
**347-7300** Rustad Brothers
**347-7400** Snow Mountain Pine Co.
**347-7500** Weyerhaeuser
**347-7600** Jacobson Brothers
**347-7650** Jacobson Brothers (red, green)
**347-7700** Millar Western
**347-7800** Plum Creek Timber
**347-7900** Ranger
**347-8000** Georgia-Pacific
**347-8100** Idaho Timber
**347-8200** Potlatch
**347-8300** Simpson

## SIGNODE GRAIN DOORS

### pkg(24) 1.00 ea

**347-2000** Red Lettering pkg(24)
**347-2050** Grain Tainer, Green Lettering pkg(24)

## FREIGHT CAR PLACARDS

Assorted placards for gondolas, box and flat cars.

**347-2100** Set 1 pkg(400) **1.00**
**347-2150** Set 2 **2.00**
Includes modern "Home Shop For Repairs" on green paper.

## DETAILING KIT

**347-2275** Lumber Yard (144 Pieces) **50.00**

# Kadee® Cars

**Designed, Manufactured & Assembled entirely in the U.S.A.**

40' PS-1 Box Car

50' PS-1 Box Car

PS-2 Hopper

Kadee® prides itself in creating and manufacturing premium "RTR" rolling stock as close to scale and detail as possible. Model railroaders can expect only the best quality and craftsmanship with every Kadee quality product. Nothing stacks up to the accuracy, detail, quality & authenticity of Kadee® Cars over all other "RTR" cars on the market.

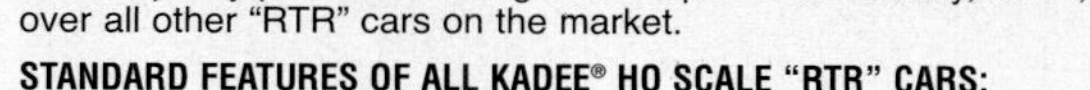

**STANDARD FEATURES OF ALL KADEE® HO SCALE "RTR" CARS:**

- Fully Assembled, Ready To Run
- Kadee® Magne-Matic® "Scale" Metal Couplers with delayed centering action for strong, accurate, reliable, trouble free coupling & uncoupling
- Kadee® smooth rolling, fully sprung, self-centering trucks with RP-25 non magnetic metal wheels
- Premium scale detailed grab irons, ladders, stirrups, handrails, see-through roofwalk & brake step
- Brake wheels & brake rigging when prototypical
- Accurate, legible, highly detailed prototypical heralds & lettering
- N.M.R.A. standard weight, low center of gravity for optimum operating performance
- Limited production, making them valuable to collectors
- Made & Assembled Entirely in the U.S.A.

Made & Assembled Entirely in the U.S.A.

End details include scale incredibly detailed hand brake and rigging.

See-through running board and brake step.

Highly detailed movable doors.

Sharp, prototypically accurate, legible lettering.

Details include scale ladders and grab irons.

Scale rivets, grabs, air lines, chains, & AB valve.

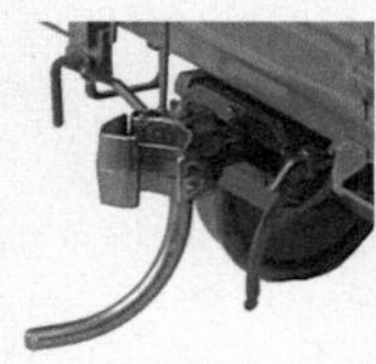
Kadee® Magne-Matic® "Scale" size coupler and molded on narrow draft gear box with patented delayed centering action.

Self-centering Bettendorf, A-3 Ride Control or Roller Bearing trucks.

CNW, DRGW, MKT, MP, SP, SSW, UP, & WP marks are made under trademark license from Union Pacific Railroad Company

**New Roads Released Monthly**

## 40' PS-1 BOX CARS

**380-4052** MILW #35016 **32.95**

**380-4067** L&BC #170961 **29.95**

**380-4069** ATSF #31627 **31.95**

**380-4512** MKT #977630 **30.95**

**380-4513** CCLX #400210 **31.95**

**380-4514** AA #334 **29.95**

**380-4816** BM #75161 **29.95**

**380-4817** MEC #21284 **30.95**

**380-5009** VGN #63162 **30.95**

**380-5010** SSW #33974 **31.95**

**380-5270** SA #202 **29.95**

**380-5271** BM #76428 **31.95**

**380-5275** USN #61-06463 **31.95**

**380-5276** C&G #3417 **29.95**

Designed, Manufactured & Assembled entirely in the U.S.A.

**380-6902** 2005 Anniversary Car **39.95**

**380-6904** 2006 60th Anniversary Car **36.95**

**380-6906** 61st Anniversary Car w/Dale Edwards Signature **41.95**

## 50' PS-1 BOX CARS

**380-6115** GF #442 **31.95**

**380-6118** MEC #9435 **31.95**

**380-6119** SOO #177518 **35.95**

**380-6207** WofA #17260 **29.95**

**380-6724** MKT #949 **31.95**

**380-6725** SSW #47500 **31.95**

**380-6726** NH #40503 **31.95**

**380-6727** DSS&A #15502 **31.95**

## AAR STANDARD 50-TON TWO-BAY OPEN HOPPERS

**380-7012** C&I #600 **42.95**

**380-7014** D&H #6116 **40.95**

**380-7015** CIL #4001 **40.95**

**380-7016** CIL #4048 **40.95**

**380-7018** CG #21823 **40.95**

**380-7020** NSR #9162 **40.95**

**380-7021** NSR #9129 **40.95**

**380-7023** NC&StL #48457 **40.95**

**380-7024** SB #116 **39.95**

**380-7511** GM&O #32523 **40.95**

**380-7512** Alton #61099 **40.95**

**380-7513** Alton #6116 **40.95**

## OPEN HOPPER COAL LOADS

**380-171** Lump/Egg Coal (small) pkg(6) **14.99**

**380-172** Large Lump Coal (medium) pkg(6) **14.99**

**380-173** Mine Run Coal (large) pkg(6) **14.99**

**380-174** Coal Load Weights pkg(3) **4.95**

## PS-2 TWO-BAY COVERED HOPPERS

**380-8012** SLSF #84084 **39.95**

**380-8021** SSW #77167 **41.95**

**380-8022** GN #71465 **41.95**

**380-8023** GN #71501 **41.95**

**380-8024** UP #11443 **41.95**

**380-8215** CNW #95330 **40.95**

**380-8216** CNW #95297 **40.95**

**380-8323** NAHX #31229 **40.95**

**380-8327** PRR #257213 **41.95**

**380-8615** MKT #34220 **41.95**

**380-8619** CNW #69475 **40.95**

**380-8620** D&H #12089 **41.95**

**380-8626** FEC #14093 **38.95**

**380-8632** P&WV #1955 **40.95**

**380-8633** D&H #12046 **41.95**

Designed, Manufactured & Assembled entirely in the U.S.A.

## UNDECORATED CARS

### PS-1 40' Box Cars 24.65 ea

Current production models are now available with multiple door styles.

**Assorted 6' Doors**

380-3997 Red Oxide

380-3998 Dark Tuscan

380-4297 Red Oxide

380-4298 Box Car Red

380-4497 Red Oxide

380-4498 Box Car Red

**Assorted 7' Doors**

380-4797 Red Oxide

380-4798 Box Car Red

380-4897 Red Oxide

380-4898 Box Car Red

**Assorted 8' Doors**

380-4997 Red Oxide

380-4998 Dark Tuscan

380-5097 Red Oxide

380-5098 Dark Tuscan

380-5197 Red Oxide

380-5198 Box Car Red

### 50' PS-1 Box Cars 24.65 ea

**Assorted 9' Doors**

380-5997 Red Oxide

380-5998 Box Car Red

380-6097 Red Oxide

380-6098 Box Car Red

380-6197 Red Oxide

380-6198 Box Car Red

**Assorted 15' Doors**

380-6697 Red Oxide

380-6698 Box Car Red

### AAR Standard 50-Ton Two-Bay Open Hoppers

Cars are black.

380-7001 Wine 36.95

### PS-2 Two-Bay Covered Hoppers 35.95 ea

Cars wear Alkali-Resisting Light Gray

380-8201 Hat End Rib*

380-8601 Channel End Rib*

*=Cars equipped with "Scale" coupler.

## FREIGHT CAR BOXES

380-3000 Plastic Box Only 3.35

380-3010 Plastic Box & 40' Box Car Nest 3.65

380-3011 Plastic Box & 50' Box Car Nest 3.65

380-3012 Plastic Box & Hopper Nest 3.80

## LOGGING EQUIPMENT KITS

These Master Craft kits feature metal and plastic parts, Kadee couplers and metal trucks.

### Log Cars w/Logs

Metal cars with three unpainted logs.

380-101 Disconnect Log Car 21.50

380-102 Skeleton Log Car 25.75

380-103 Truss Log Car 32.25

### Log Cars Without Logs

Arch bar-style trucks with couplers and footboards in kit form.

380-107 Disconnect Log Car 1 Pair 17.50

### Logging Caboose

380-104 Red 19.75

Kit features all-metal trucks and wheels, insulated couplers and plastic molded body with removable roof.



## JAM CREATIONS/SOLUTIONS

## "STEALTH" TRACK CLEANING CARS

Keep your railroad running at its best with these modified Bowser hoppers. Four independent, spring-loaded cleaning feet are built into the bottom that can be fitted with any combination of abrasive or felt discs, which ride the rail to remove oxidation, grime and dirt. Cleaning feet are slightly inward of the rail center to force some rotation of the foot as the cleaner encounters curves, so the whole disk is used, rather than simply wearing down the same point. No liquids are used and the Stealth System can be used any time you run trains.

## NEW PRODUCTS

### 100-Ton 45' Triple Hopper w/Coal Load

**Standard**

**Assembled 49.95 ea**

NEW 343-1303 PRR

NEW 343-1305 N&W

NEW 343-1306 UP

NEW 343-1307 CR "Q"

NEW 343-1311 ATSF

NEW 343-1314 Chessie/C&O

NEW 343-1318 CSXT

NEW 343-1321 L&N

NEW 343-1322 DRGW

NEW 343-1323 NS

NEW 343-1326 CN (black)

NEW 343-1331 BN w/White End

**Kits 39.95 ea**

NEW 343-1338 PRR

NEW 343-1339 N&W

NEW 343-1340 UP

NEW 343-1341 CR "Q"

NEW 343-1346 ATSF

NEW 343-1349 Chessie/C&O

NEW 343-1353 CSXT

NEW 343-1356 L&N

NEW 343-1357 DRGW

NEW 343-1358 NS

NEW 343-1361 CN (black)

NEW 343-1366 BN w/White End

**Deluxe with Kadee® Trucks & Couplers**

**Assembled 59.95 ea**

NEW 343-13031 PRR

NEW 343-13051 N&W

NEW 343-13061 UP

NEW 343-13071 CR "Q"

NEW 343-13111 ATSF

NEW 343-13141 Chessie/C&O

NEW 343-13181 CSXT

NEW 343-13211 L&N

NEW 343-13221 DRGW

NEW 343-13231 NS

NEW 343-13261 CN (black)

NEW 343-13311 BN w/White End

**Deluxe Kits 49.95 ea**

NEW 343-13381 PRR

NEW 343-13391 N&W

NEW 343-13401 UP

NEW 343-13411 CR "Q"

NEW 343-13461 ATSF

NEW 343-13491 Chessie/C&O

NEW 343-13531 CSXT

NEW 343-13561 L&N

NEW 343-13571 DRGW

NEW 343-13581 NS

NEW 343-13611 CN (black)

NEW 343-13661 BN w/White End

## 70-TON TWO-BAY COVERED HOPPERS

**Standard**

**Assembled 49.95 ea**

NEW 343-1034 ICG

NEW 343-1038 DRGW

NEW 343-1039 BN

NEW 343-1042 Detroit, Toledo & Ironton (gray)

NEW 343-1043 UP

NEW 343-1045 N&W

NEW 343-1049 Clinchfield

NEW 343-1050 ATSF

NEW 343-1057 SOO

NEW 343-1205 CRR

**Kit 39.95 ea**

NEW 343-1001 Detroit, Toledo & Ironton (gray)

NEW 343-1002 ICG

NEW 343-1006 DRGW

NEW 343-1007 BN

NEW 343-1012 UP

NEW 343-1013 N&W

NEW 343-1017 Clinchfield

NEW 343-1018 ATSF

NEW 343-1025 SOO

NEW 343-1204 C&O (black)

**Deluxe with Kadee® Trucks & Couplers**

**Assembled 59.95 ea**

NEW 343-10341 ICG

NEW 343-10381 DRGW

NEW 343-10391 BN

NEW 343-10421 Detroit, Toledo & Ironton (gray)

NEW 343-10431 UP

NEW 343-10451 N&W

NEW 343-10491 Clinchfield

NEW 343-10501 ATSF

NEW 343-10571 SOO

NEW 343-12051 Clinchfield

**Deluxe Kit 49.95 ea**

NEW 343-10011 Detroit, Toledo & Ironton (gray)

NEW 343-10021 ICG

NEW 343-10061 DRGW

NEW 343-10071 BN

NEW 343-10121 UP

NEW 343-10131 N&W

NEW 343-10171 Clinchfield

NEW 343-10181 ATSF

NEW 343-10251 SOO

NEW 343-12041 C&O (black)

## CLEANING DISKS

### Abrasive pkg(20) 2.99 ea

343-1187 120 Grit

343-1188 180 Grit

343-1189 220 Grit

### Soft pkg(20) 2.99 ea

343-1190 Felt on Foam

343-1191 Felt on Fabric

### Assortment

343-1192 Soft & Abrasive pkg(20) 2.99

kibri®

IMPORTED FROM GERMANY BY WALTHERS
These easy-to-build, nonpowered plastic kits feature parts molded in several realistic colors. Construction is fast and easy with numbered parts and exploded view instructions.

## NEW PRODUCTS

### Work Train Equipment

**NEW 405-16307** Unimog HyRail Flatbed w/Excavator **45.99**

**NEW 405-16308** Hyrail Flatbed w/Wheel Loader **47.99**

## FLAT CARS

### Depressed Center 12-Axle Heavy-Duty Flat Car

**405-16504** w/Transformer Load **71.99**

**405-16508** DB Cargo w/Generator Loads **144.99**

**405-16510** DB w/Large Shipping Crate Load (black, white) **71.99**

### 20-Axle Heavy-Duty Flat Car

Item listed below is available by Special Order (see Legend Page).

**405-16500** Heavy-Duty 20-Axle Transformer Carrier **155.99**

**405-16507** DB Class Uaai 687.9 w/Generator Load **151.99**

Item listed below is available by Special Order (see Legend Page).

**405-16506** DB Cargo Class Uaai 836 **107.99**

### 2-Axle Low Side Flat Cars

**Limited Quantity Available**

**405-16256** With Side Stakes & Log Load **43.99**

**405-16260** Flat Car w/Kaelble DB Highway Truck Load **61.99**

### With Low Drop Sides & Ends

Item listed below is available by Special Order (see Legend Page).

**405-16204** KBS 442 Era IV (Ocean Blue) **34.99**

**Limited Quantity Available**

**405-16259** With Side Stakes & Timber Load **41.99**

### KLS 442 Flat Cars

Items listed below are available by Special Order (see Legend Page).

**405-16200** Yellow **34.99**

**405-16202** Brown **34.99**

## WORK TRAIN EQUIPMENT

**405-16000** 100-Ton Crane w/Telescoping Boom "Swietelsky" (yellow) **132.99**

**405-16006** Liebherr 4-Axle Hy-Rail Truck Crane (yellow) **48.99**

Item listed below is available by Special Order (see Legend Page).

**405-16007** PIKO Railcar & Crane **263.99**

**405-16010** DEMAG w/Idler Flat Car Leonhard Weiss **158.99**

**405-16050** Plasser & Theurer Ballast Cleaner/ Tamper **154.99**

Prototype Photo Shown

**405-16060** Plasser & Theurer USP 2000 SWS Track & Ballast Maintenance Machine **181.99**

Items listed below are available by Special Order (see Legend Page).

**405-16062** Mercedes Hyrail Unimog w/Catenary Wire Repair Flat Car **84.99**

**405-16070** Plasser & Theurer DGS 62 N Open Version **163.99**

**405-16072** Plasser & Theurer DGS 62 N Ballast Tamper Closed Cab Version **160.99**

**405-16080** Plasser & Theurer MTW 100 Catenary Repair/ Inspection Unit w/Cherrypicker **189.99**

**405-16090** Plasser & Theurer Track Tamper **278.99**

Item listed below is available by Special Order (see Legend Page).

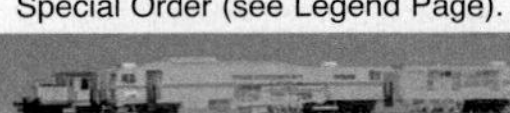

**405-16092** PIKO Stopfexpress **316.99**

Prototype Photo Shown

**405-16100** SKL "Bullok" Maintenance Vehicle w/Crane **105.99**

Item listed below is available by Special Order (see Legend Page).

**405-16102** "Bullok" Transporter w/Loading Crane **129.99**

**405-16104** Bullock Loco w/DGB Flat Car & Backhoe **70.99**

**405-16150** MFS 100 Ballast Cleaning/Collecting Conveyor Car **123.99**

**405-16302** Atlas 1604 Hyrail Excavator **45.99**

**405-16303** Unimog Euro II Hyrail Weed Sprayer Truck - DB **69.99**

**405-16306** Unimog Flatbed w/Snow Thrower & Plow Blade **53.99**

**405-16502** Heavy-Duty Generator Transport Car (No Load) **122.99**

**405-16600** Tunnel Inspection Train w/Bullok MOW Unit, 2 Flats, Scaffold & Accessories **167.99**

**405-16602** Contractor's Repair Train w/Bullok MOW Unit, 2 Flats & Accessories **154.99**

**Limited Quantity Available**

**405-16103** SKL Bullok MOW Car w/Flat Car & Backhoe **115.99**

Red Oak 357-1847

Red Oak 357-1740

## Wood Display Cases

Great for displaying HO Scale equipment, these cases feature a solid oak frame and shelves, white plastic back and plastic sliding doors. Mounting hardware and self-sticking door handles also included.

**18 x 47 x 2-1/2"**

**357-1847** Red Oak **196.95**
For HO Scale.

**17 x 47 x 2-1/2"**

**357-1740** Red Oak **199.95**
Sized for HO Narrow Gauge or TT scales. Identical construction as the HO case listed above.

## Plastic Polishing Kit

**357-1339** Plastic Polish/Anti-Static Cleaning Solution 2oz **6.95**
A handy kit containing a pump spray and polishing cloth. Use on display case doors or any other hard shiny surfaces. Cleaned surface resists dust and fingerprints. Kit comes in resealable polybag with hang hole for easy storage.

Hot New Products Announced Daily! Visit Walthers Web site at

**www.walthers.com**

KATO
PRECISION RAILROAD MODELS

NKP 381-380109

GN 381-380203

## HOPPERS

These easy-to-assemble three-car kits are crisply printed and precisely detailed. Kits include ASF "Ride Control" trucks, metal wheels, semi-automatic knuckle couplers and heavy brass weights. An open space between the two bays distinguishes the Open from the Closed Side units.

### AC&F 70-Ton Covered Hopper 3-Packs 45.00 ea

**Closed Side**

**381-380111** Seaboard Air Line 8100, 8165 & 8247

**381-380109** NKP 91034, 91067 & 91085

**Open Side**

**381-380201** Boston & Maine 5502, 5511 & 5516 (gray)

**381-380202** GE Lamps 313, 317 & 318 (black)

**381-380203** GN 71233, 71247 & 71283 (gray)

**381-380204** MON 4331, 4376 & 4382 (gray)

**381-380205** Wabash 30000, 30001 & 30004 (black)

**381-380206** WM 5102, 5124 & 5187 (gray)

## PLASTRUCT

### Hot Metal Cars

**570-1040** Undecorated pkg(2) **23.45**
Perfect for hauling hot metal from blast furnaces to converters, these Pollock 12-wheel cars are a must for any layout serving the steel industry. Includes plastic parts to build two cars, based on Dean Freytag's article in the November 1994 issue of *Railroad Model Craftsman*. A reprint of the article is provided for instructions. Kits are less trucks, hardware and couplers; some model building experience is helpful in constructing this scratch model kit.

## PRE-SIZE MODEL SPECIALTIES

### Loads

All loads are trim to fit.

**Ballast Loads 6.25 ea**

**483-455** Ballast For Walthers 4200 Series Ballast Hoppers

**483-456** Ballast For MDC 40' Hoppers 1-1/4 x 5-7/16"

**483-457** Ballast For Athearn 40' Quad Hoppers 1-1/4 x 5-7/16"

**Scrap Loads 6.75 ea**

483-454

**483-453** For Walthers 53' Thrall Gondola

**483-454** For MDC Roundhouse 1680 Series 50' Mill Gondola

## RIBBONRAIL

### Track Cleaning Car

**170-6** For Standard 2-Rail Track **34.95**
Ready-to-run model is equipped with rubber blocks impregnated with fine grain abrasives that clean the rails as the car rolls around the track. Features solid brass body and trucks. Comes without couplers.

MANTUA

All Mantua rolling stock are heavyweight cars with RP-25 wheels, metal axles and knuckle couplers.

1860s Era Wooden Water Car
B&O 455-723025

50' Plug-Door Box Car PRR 455-755020

36' Hopper with Coal
RDG (Diamond Herald) 455-729721

## 1860S ERA WOODEN FREIGHT CARS

### Box Cars 10.99 ea

**455-721011** SP

**455-721044** Western & Atlantic

**455-721050** UP

**455-721303** Maryland & Pennsylvania

**455-721322** G.H. Hammond Co.

### Horse Cars 10.99 ea

**455-722003** UP

**455-722050** PRR

### Water Cars 10.99 ea

**455-723003** UP

**455-723020** PRR

**455-723025** B&O

### Log Cars 10.99 ea

**455-724008** DRGW

**455-724020** PRR

**455-724021** Weyerhaeuser

### Long Caboose 10.99 ea

**455-725006** CP

**455-725008** DRGW

**455-725025** B&O

**455-725026** ATSF

**455-725027** CP

## BOX CARS

### 40' Flat Cars w/Crates 10.99 ea

**455-727001** ATSF

**455-727002** RDG

**455-727003** ICF

### 41' Box Cars w/Sliding Doors 10.99 ea

**455-734010** Lifesaver

**455-734011** Oreo

**455-734012** Frisco

**455-734186** RDG Freedom w/Flag

**455-734231** Railbox

**455-734549** PRR Merchandise Service

### 41' Wooden Cattle Cars w/Sliding Doors 10.99 ea

**455-735003** UP

**455-735064** CNW

**455-735077** MKT

**455-735420** PRR

### 50' Plug-Door Box Cars 10.99 ea

**455-755020** PRR

**455-755021** RDG

**455-755235** Rohm & Haas

## REEFERS

### 41' Steel Refrigerator Cars 10.99 ea

**455-733001** ATSF

**455-733080** CP

**455-733130** Bangor & Aroostook (red, white & blue)

**455-733306** Carnation

## HOPPERS

### 36' Hoppers 10.99 ea

**With Coal**

**455-729018** Peabody

**455-729620** PRR

**455-729721** RDG (Diamond Herald)

**No Coal**

**455-728001** Ritz

**455-728002** Milkbone

## GONDOLAS

### 40' Gondolas 10.99 ea

**With Coal**

**455-731062** CB&Q

**455-731224** Railgon

**No Coal**

**455-730001** Fig Newton

**455-730002** Planters Peanuts

## TANK CARS

### 40' Single-Dome Tank Cars 10.99 ea

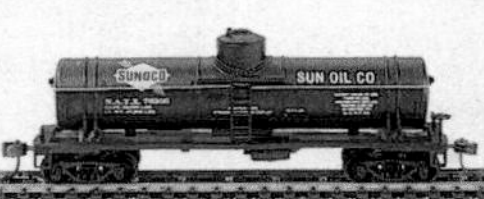
**455-732184** Sunoco

**455-732307** Union Carbide

**455-732308** Sherwin-Williams

**455-732520** PRR

**455-732694** Mobil w/Pegasus

## CABOOSES

### 36' Steel Cabooses 10.99 ea

**455-726002** ATSF

**455-726008** DRGW

**455-726020** PRR

**455-726503** UP Safety

**455-729018** Peabody

These HO Scale ready-to-run cars are prepainted and lettered. An asterisk (*) after a car name indicates that the model is a "Heavy Weight" series car, which features a heavier weight for improved performance, metal springs for coupler return and coupler height pockets. Includes easily installed knuckle couplers.

## METAL TRAINS CARS

This line of ready-to-run freight cars feature an all-metal body, along with state-of-the-art metal detailing in the chassis, wheels and axles. Each car also comes with magnetic knuckle and standard couplers.

### U-29 Steel Ore Cars

**Single Cars 15.98 ea**

**490-1900** DMIR #40108
**490-1901** SP #467526
**490-1902** UP #27186 (silver)
**490-1903** Bessemer & Lake Erie #20696
**490-1904** GN #95629 (green)
**490-1905** BN #96044
**490-1906** CN #344007
**490-1907** CP #377246 (black)
**490-1908** CNW #810253

**3-Packs**
**43.98 ea (Unless Noted)**

**490-3990** DMIR
**490-3991** SP **47.98**
**490-3992** UP (silver)
**490-3993** Bessemer & Lake Erie
**490-3994** GN (green)
**490-3995** BN
**490-3996** CN
**490-3997** CP (black)
**490-3998** CNW

### 40' Box Cars w/Sliding Doors 15.98 ea

490-2172

**490-2171** ATSF (red & black w/large "Ship & Travel" logo)
**490-2172** NYC (black & green w/large logo)
**490-2173** SOO
**490-2174** CP w/Pac-Man

### 40' Steel Box Car 15.98 ea

**490-2176** Union Carbide

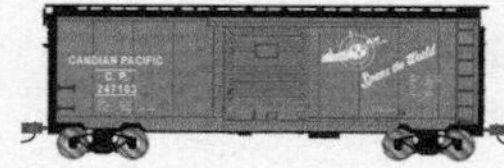

**490-2177** CP w/"Spans the World" Logo

### 41' Steel Reefer 15.98 ea

**490-2230** State of Maine "New Haven"

**490-2231** White Rock Water

### 41' Reefers 15.98 ea

490-2227

**490-2226** Bangor & Aroostock (red, white & blue)
**490-2227** Swift
**490-2228** Burlington Refrigerator
**490-2229** Armour

### 40' Ballast-Style Quad Hoppers 15.98 ea

490-2212

**490-2211** Alaska
**490-2212** BNSF
**490-2213** UP
**490-2214** PRR

Info, Images, Inspiration! Get It All at
**www.walthers.com**

### 57' Flat Cars 15.98 ea

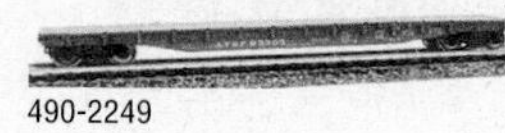
490-2249

**490-2246** TTX
**490-2247** PRR
**490-2248** CN
**490-2249** ATSF

**490-2250** C&O

### 40' Tank Cars 15.98 ea

490-2192

**490-2190** ATSF (black, orange, silver)
**490-2191** Mobil – Pegasus Horse
**490-2192** Shell – Shell Emblem
**490-2193** Hooker (orange w/black)

### 34' Cupola Cabooses 15.98 ea

**490-2270** ATSF
**490-2271** BNSF
**490-2272** PRR
**490-2273** CN
**490-2274** CP

**490-2275** Alaska
**490-2276** UP

## BOX CARS

### 40' 8.98 ea

**With Sliding Doors**

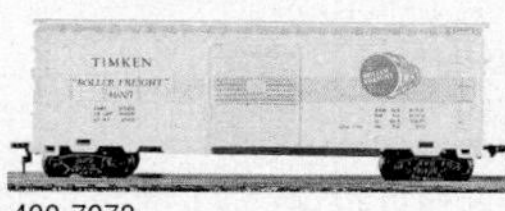

490-7973

**490-7970** B&O Sentinel* (silver, blue)
**490-97971** GN* (green w/orange stripe)
**490-7972** Central of Georgia* (purple, silver)
**490-7973** Timken* (yellow, silver)
**490-97974** SP* (brown)
**490-7976** Operation Lifesaver*
**490-7977** PRR "Don't Stand Me Still"

**Heavyweight Canadian**

**490-7950** Algoma Central*
**490-7951** BC Rail*
**490-7952** CP*
**490-7953** CN*
**490-7954** Grand Trunk Western*
**490-7955** Ontario Northland*
**490-7956** Pacific Great Eastern*
**490-7957** Toronto, Hamilton & Buffalo*
**490-7958** CN Manitoba*
**490-7960** Unlettered (white)*

### Sliding-Door Steel 8.98 ea (Unless Noted)

490-8002

**490-8001** CR
**490-8002** Baby Ruth (red)
**490-8003** Maine Central (bright orange)
**490-8004** CN
**490-8005** CP Rail
**490-8006** Domino
**490-8008** Napa Filters
**490-80052** Champion Plugs

### Plug-Door/Sliding-Door Combo

Roadname Shown Not Available

**490-9037** Frisco (yellow) **8.98**

**Limited Quantity Available**

**490-9031** WP (silver w/orange feather) **6.98**
**490-9034** Illinois Central Gulf (orange) **7.98**

## REEFERS

### 40' Generation 2-Steel

These heavyweight reefers offer smooth operation, metal wheels and body-mounted couplers.

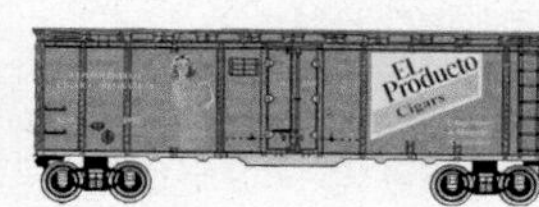

490-8256

**490-8255** Antonio y Cleopatra **12.98**
**490-8256** El Producto **12.98**
**490-8257** Dutch Masters **12.98**
**490-8258** Muriel **12.98**
**490-8259** State of Maine* **11.98**
**490-8260** ATSF w/Map* **11.98**
**490-8261** Wescott & Winks Jersey Gold* **11.98**
**490-8262** Illinois Central Gulf* **11.98**
**490-8263** GN* **11.98**
**490-8264** CN* **11.98**

## HOPPERS

### 36' 2-Bay 8.98 ea

**Covered**

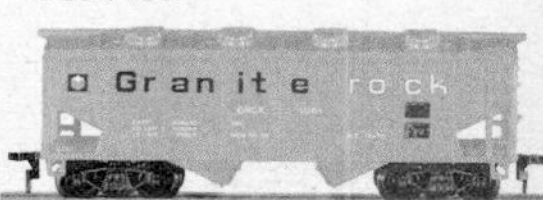

490-8084

**490-8080** N&W* (gray)
**490-8081** Portland Cement* (gray)
**490-8082** Ontario Northland* (blue)
**490-8083** Jack Frost Cane Sugar* (gray, blue)
**490-8084** Granite Rock* (orange)

**Open**

**490-98060** L&N-Dixie Line* (gray)
**490-98061** WM* (red)

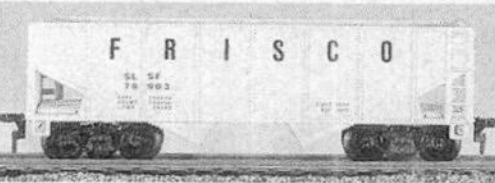


**490-8062** Frisco* (white)
**490-8063** PRR* (Tuscan)
**490-8064** SP* (red)
**490-8065** CN
**490-8066** C&O

**490-8067** NYC
**490-8069** DRGW

## GONDOLAS

### 40' 8.98 ea

490-8503

**490-8501** SP* (brown)
**490-8502** PRR* (tuscan)
**490-98503** SOU* (silver)
**490-8504** CN* (tuscan)
**490-8506** SOO* (white)
**490-8507** Recycled Steel* (white)
**490-8508** Recycled Steel* (black)
**490-8509** CSX-B&O

# FLAT CARS

## 40' Depressed Center

### With Searchlight

**490-8220** Safety First* (red) **10.98**
All-metal car features dual electrical pickup, constant lighting and two handpainted figures.

### With 2 Cables & Figures 10.98 ea

**490-8221** ATSF*
**490-8222** PRR*
**490-8223** CN*
**490-8224** Jet Copter (red)

## 40' w/Logs

**490-98210** CB&Q* (red) **10.98**

## 40' w/Twin Removable Tanks 10.98 ea

490-8161

**490-8160** Cities Service*
**490-8161** Gulf* (blue w/white tanks)
**490-8162** Sonoma Wine*
**490-8163** Water Car*

## 40' w/Guard Rails 8.98 ea

**490-8230** ATSF*
**490-8231** PRR*
**490-8232** CP*
**490-8233** SOU*

## 51' w/2 Containers 14.49 ea (Unless Noted)

490-8308

**490-8303** ATSF
**490-8304** PRR
**490-8305** Trailer Train
**490-8306** Southern
**490-8307** DRGW **15.49**
**490-8308** Maine Casket Co.

## 51' w/40' Trailer 15.99 ea (Unless Noted)

**490-8350** ATSF w/Union 76 Trailer
**490-8351** PRR
**490-8352** CR
**490-8353** SP
**490-8354** CP
**490-8355** SOU w/US Mail Trailer
**490-8356** CNW w/Fed Ex Trailer **16.98**
**490-8357** Schenker
**490-8358** Union 76
**490-8359** Phillips 66
**490-8360** Conoco

**490-8361** Marathon
**490-8362** ATSF Unlettered
**490-8363** TTX
**490-8364** ATSF w/Sunkist
**490-8365** Mason Dixon

### With Grader Load 17.99 ea

490-6972

**490-6970** ATSF
**490-6971** PRR
**490-6972** Southern
**490-9159** US Army



### With 50' Tractor & 32' Trailer 17.99 ea

**490-6950** ATSF

**490-6951** PRR
**490-6952** US Mail

**490-6953** US Army

# TANK CARS

## 40' 8.98 ea

490-8032

**490-6921** DuPont (yellow, Olive Green)
**490-98032** Cities Service Oils (green)
**490-8034** Hooker
**490-8035** Celanese
**490-8103** Shell

## Chemical Tank Car 8.98 ea

490-8125

**490-98101** Tank Train*
**490-98102** Kodak*
**490-8103** Shell

**490-8104** Hudson's Bay Oil & Gas* (yellow)
**490-98105** Exxon*
**490-98106** Texaco*
**490-8110** Champion Oil
**490-8111** Dominion Sugar Co. Ltd.
**490-8112** Imperial Oil Ltd.
**490-8119** Ashland Oil
**490-98120** Union 76

**490-8122** Phillips 66
**490-8123** Conoco
**490-98125** SP
**490-8126** MCP Corn

# CABOOSES

## 32' Wood 9.98 ea

Wooden cabooses were used well into the 1950s by many railroads, so this handsome model is right at home behind your favorite steam or early diesel power.

490-9143

**490-9141** PRR
**490-9142** B&O
**490-9143** ATSF
**490-9144** SP
**490-9145** SOU
**490-9146** DRGW
**490-9147** CP
**490-9148** CN
**490-9149** Transfer

## 36' Bay-Window 8.98 ea

**490-8240** Safety*
**490-8241** ATSF
**490-8242** CR*
**490-8243** PRR*
**490-8244** SOU*
**490-8245** BN*

**490-8246** CN*
**490-8247** SP*
**490-8248** CP Rail



**490-8249** BNSF

## 40' Work 10.98 ea (Unless Noted)

### With Tank

**490-8181** Amtrak*
**490-8182** Weed Control*
**490-8180** Undecorated* (white)

### With Crane

**490-8191** ATSF*
**490-98192** PRR
**490-98193** DRGW
**490-8194** C&O
**490-8190** Undecorated

### With Tool Boxes

**490-8200** Safety First* (red, silver) **11.98**

# MAINTENANCE OF WAY

## Railroad Crane w/Metal Wheels

Roadname Shown Not Available

**490-9175** ATSF **32.98**

# CONTAINERS

## With Opening Door

**490-7850** #1 pkg(4) **12.98**
Contains Fed Ex, Consolidated Freight, US Mail and US Army.

**490-7851** #2 pkg(4) **11.98**
Contains Evergreen, K-Line, Hanjin and Schenkers.

**490-7852** #3 pkg(4) **11.98**
Contains CR, PRR, ATSF and CP.

# CHRISTMAS CARS

**490-9700** 4-Car Set **34.98**
Special Christmas set includes a Season's Greetings caboose, Millie's Egg Nog tank car, Christmas Tree box car and Mother's Apple Cider flat car with two tanks.

**490-9701** 4-Car Set **34.98**
Includes Season's Greetings box car, Holiday Express hopper, flat car with sleigh and Santa, and a white and gold caboose.

Here's a quick and easy way to make almost any car look and run better! Highly detailed one-piece loads capture the appearance of various bulk cargoes, making passing freights more fun to watch. Plus, the added weight of the plaster castings improves car performance without a lot of extra work. Each is hand-cast from a very strong gypsum material that picks up fine details much like dental plaster. Loads are then handpainted to bring out the many details. While some loads will fit in almost any car, most are custom measured to fit specific models as shown. (All cars shown in photos are sold separately.)

Athearn Coal Load 506-230

Athearn Coal Load 506-240

## Coal Loads pkg(2) 5.94 ea

Keep coal revenues climbing on your railroad with these affordable loads, sculpted to capture the gleaming, faceted appearance of the real thing. Made for exact fit in the car shown, this is a quick and easy way to add the extra weight that hoppers and gondolas so often need to be good runners.

### Accurail®

**506-1920** 2-Bay USRA Hoppers

### Athearn

**506-230** 34' 2-Bay Hoppers

**506-240** Quad Hoppers

### Atlas

**506-1980** Offset Side 2-Bay Hopper

### Bowser

**506-1660** H-21 4-Bay Hoppers

**506-1900** H-22a 4-Bay Hopper

**506-1970** H-43 100-Ton, 3-Bay Hopper

### Con-Cor

**506-250** 100-Ton Hoppers Also fits McKean Cars.

### E&C Shops

**506-1960** Coal Porter Gondola

### PROTO™ 2000

**506-232** 50-Ton War Emergency Hopper

### Roundhouse

**506-260** 3-Bay Hopper

**506-280** Thrall Gondolas

**506-290** "Bathtub" Gondolas

**506-300** Roundhouse 5-Bay Rapid Discharge Hoppers

**506-2020** 40' Gondola

### Stewart Hobbies

**506-1260** 70-Ton Hoppers

**506-1280** 55-Ton Hoppers

**506-1630** 70-Ton Class H-39 Hoppers

**506-1950** Offset Side Hoppers

**506-1990** "U" Channel 2-Bay Hoppers

**506-2030** H37-B 70-Ton, 13-Panel Triple Hopper

### Tichy Train Group

**506-780** USRA 2-Bay Hoppers

### Varney

**506-220** 2-Bay Hopper

### Walthers Train Miniature

**506-270** 36' 2-Bay Hoppers Also fits Train Miniature cars.

**506-1620** 100-Ton Quad Hoppers

**506-2000** Bethgon Coalporter

## Lumber, Timber & Wood Loads

### Banded Heavy Timbers 7.55 ea

Fits most flat cars or gondolas.

**506-720** Untreated

**506-2050** Creosoted Bridge Timbers
Great detail at a bridge or trestle construction site!

### Banded Lumber Stacks pkg(2) 5.70 ea

Fits most flat cars; looks great inside lumber sheds or as a load for a flatbed truck.

**506-130** Red Ends

**506-140** Green Ends

**506-141** Plain Ends - No Color

**506-142** Blue Ends

**506-143** Orange Ends

### Stacked Lumber For Open-Door Box Car

**506-1670** Painted pkg(4) **5.94**
Fits virtually any length box car.

### Pulpwood For Athearn Bulkhead Flats 7.55 ea

**506-1930** 8' Wide Logs

**506-1940** 4' Wide Logs pkg(2)

### Woodchips

**506-310** Roundhouse 5-Bay Rapid Discharge Cars pkg(2) **5.94**

**506-1910** E&C Shops 62' FMC Cars pkg(2) **7.55**

## Ore & Stone Loads

### Cut Stone Blocks w/Drill Marks

**506-1680** Unpainted pkg(3) **5.94**

### Ballast/Stone Loads pkg(2) 7.02 ea

Each casting is topped with real stone.

**506-235** For Athearn 34' 2-Bay Hopper

**506-265** For Roundhouse 3-Bay Hopper

**506-275** For Walthers Train Miniature 36' 2-Bay Hopper

**506-1285** For Stewart 55-Ton Hopper

**506-1925** For Accurail 2-Bay USRA Hopper

**506-1985** For Atlas Offset-Side 2-Bay Hopper

**506-1995** For Stewart "U"-Channel 2-Bay Hopper

**506-2025** For Roundhouse 40' Gondola

### Ore Loads pkg(2) 5.94 ea

**506-320** Roundhouse 21' Cars

**506-330** Roundhouse 26' Cars

**506-790** Tichy Wooden Cars

**506-1290** Old Varney Cars

**506-1510** Roundhouse 3-Bay Hopper

**506-1520** Walthers Train Miniature 36' 2-Bay Hopper

**506-1530** Athearn 34' Hoppers

### Taconite Loads For Walthers Cars

**506-2040** pkg(2) **5.94**

## Steel & Scrap Loads

### Crushed Aluminum Bales pkg(2) 8.10 ea

**506-380** Athearn 50' Gondolas

**506-390** Roundhouse 50' Gondolas

**506-1190** Con-Cor 54' Mill Gondolas

### Rebar & Coiled Steel Rods pkg(2) 8.10 ea

**506-360** Athearn 50' Gondolas

**506-370** Roundhouse 50' Gondolas

**506-1210** Con-Cor 54' Mill Gondolas

### Stamping Plant Scraps pkg(2) 8.10 ea

**506-400** Athearn 50' Gondolas

**506-410** Roundhouse 50' Gondolas

**506-1200** Con-Cor 54' Mill Gondolas

### Junk Loads For Gondolas pkg(2) 8.10 ea

**506-340** Athearn 50' Cars

**506-350** Roundhouse 50' Cars

**506-420** Roundhouse 40' Cars

**506-770** Con-Cor 54' Mill Cars

**506-1180** Eastern Car Works 65' Mill Cars

### Tarp-Covered Loads pkg(2) 8.10 ea

**506-730** Roundhouse 40' Gondolas

**506-740** Athearn 50' Gondolas

**506-750** Roundhouse 50' Gondolas

**506-760** Con-Cor 54' Mill Gondolas

Junk Load for Gondola 506-420

Tarp-Covered Load 506-730

Internal Workings of MNP Track Cleaning Cars (517-7101 Interior Shown)

## MOTORIZED TRACK CLEANING CARS

### 50' High Cube Box Cars 109.98 ea

Keeping your track clean has never been easier! These fully assembled cars feature accurate paint schemes and lettering; high-torque dual-geared electric motors; pressure-sensitive, easily adjustable cleaning discs; and easy peel-and-stick pads.

**517-7101** BN

**NEW 517-7105** BNSF

**517-7106** CN

**NEW 517-7118** WC

### Cleaning Pads

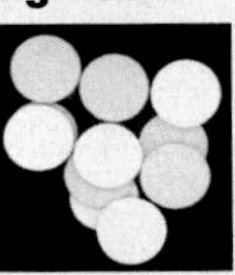

**517-CP1H001** 3/4" Diameter pkg(12) **3.50**
These pressure-sensitive pads gently keep track clean as rolling stock heads down the rails. For use with Motorized Track Cleaning Cars - 50' High-Cube Box Cars #517-7101, 7106 and 40' High-Cube Box Car #517-99149. No cleaning solution required.

### Motorized Track Cleaning Car for DCC

**517-99149** 40' Hi-Cube Box Car MOW **149.98**
Includes factory-installed DCC decoder; motors can be run faster or slower as needed, independent of engine speed.

Got a Mouse? Click Walthers Web Site at
**www.walthers.com**

## TICHY TRAIN GROUP

These easy-to-build HO Scale kits feature unpainted plastic parts, underbody details, separate ladders and grab irons (unless noted). Coupler pockets accept horn-hook or Kadee® couplers. Visit Walthers Web site at www.walthers.com for a compete listing of Tichy Train Group freight cars and accessories.

## BOX CARS

### 40' USRA Wood Box Cars Rebuilt w/Steel Sides Upgrade

Kits feature both ribbed and nonribbed extended ends, plus AB-type brake gear.

**293-4028** Single Car **14.50**

**293-40284** Single Car, w/Decals **16.50**
Lettering for NYC, Pittsburgh & Lake Erie and Pittsburgh, McKeesport & Youghiogheny.

### 40' USRA Single-Sheathed Box Car

**293-4026** Single Car **14.50**

## REEFER

### 40' PFE Wood Reefer

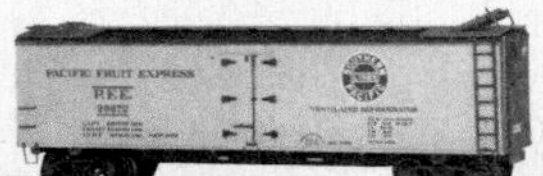

**293-4024** Single Car **14.50**
Kit is based on class R-40 PFE wood reefers as operated by the SP/UP and WP railroads.

## HOPPERS

### USRA 36' 2-Bay

**293-4027** Single Car **14.50**

## GONDOLAS

### War Emergency Composite Mill Gondolas

**293-1042** ATSF **17.95**

**293-61041** NYC pkg(6) **90.00**

**293-4041** Undecorated **14.95**

**293-40414** Undecorated w/Decals **16.95**
With decals for PRR, NYC, ATSF, N&W and Rock Island.

## FLAT CARS

### 40' Flat Cars

#### 50-Ton Steel

Features molded deck, straight side sills, detailed underframe and complete brake rigging.

**293-4021** Single Car **8.95**

**293-6021** 6-Pack **46.00**

### 40' Company Wheel Service

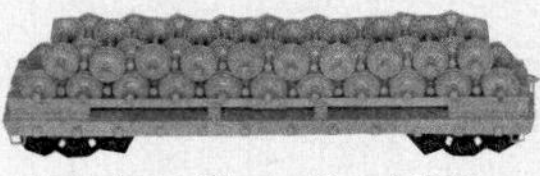

**293-4023** Single Car **14.50**
These cars were converted by the Milwaukee and other lines to transport wheelsets for company use. Kit includes 40 wheelsets.

**293-3010** Extra Wheelset pkg(96) **9.50**
Nonoperating wheelsets for use with kit #4023, sold separately.

### 53' GSC Commonwealth Flat Car

These prepainted and decorated kits include trucks and couplers.

**293-1004** UP **9.00**

**293-1000** Undecorated **8.00**

### Flat Car Load

**293-3056** Pipe Load pkg(2 Loads) **9.50**

### Atlantic Coast Line Style Flat Cars

These undecorated kits feature optional wood gondola sides.

**293-4040** Single Car **14.50**

**293-40404** Single Car, w/Decals **16.50**

## TANK CARS

### 36' USRA Tank Cars 14.50 ea

The 36' USRA 10,000 gallon tank car was used from the 1920s through the 1960s to haul crude oil and other products.

**293-4020** 54" Dome

**293-4025** 60" Dome

## MAINTENANCE-OF-WAY

### 120-Ton Brownhoist Crane

**293-4010** Undecorated **28.50**
The detailed model has over 200 parts and features a working boom plus heavy-duty trucks. Complete instructions are included.

### 40' Boom Car

**293-4022** Single Car **14.50**
This kit features a toolbox underframe, deck cabin and many accessories to customize the design.

## ORE CARS

### 22' Wood Ore Car

The heavy-duty "Great Lakes" ore car captures the look of Eastern and Western mining equipment.

**293-4012** 2-Car Set **14.50**

**293-6012** 12-Car Set **75.00**

## HAND CARS

**293-4011** Handcars/Trailers pkg(12) **9.50**
This kit contains six handcars with optional side benches and six trailers.

# RED CABOOSE

All freight car kits come with McHenry couplers.

Important Note: This listing includes items which are available by Special Order only. Please see the Legend Page for more information, and visit www.walthers.com for a complete listing of in-stock and special order products.

Items listed in blue ink may not be available at all times (see Legend Page).

X-29 Box Car
Roadname Shown Not Available

R-30-12-9
Roadname Shown Not Available

Drop-Bottom Gondola w/Composite Sides
Roadname Shown Not Available

Flat Car w/Wood Deck
Roadname Shown Not Available

Coil Car ATSF 629-32538

## NEW PRODUCTS

### Ready-to-Run Freight Cars

#### 42' 10" Flat Car 23.95 ea

Assembled car comes with metal wheels, couplers and weights installed.

**NEW 629-32301** ATSF

**NEW 629-32302** DRGW

**NEW 629-32303** NP

**NEW 629-32304** C&O

**NEW 629-32305** NYC

**NEW 629-32306** GN

#### S-40-5 Stock Car 39.95 ea

**NEW 629-39003** SP Post-1952 Scheme

**NEW 629-39010** North Western Pacific 1946/47 Scheme

#### F-70-7 Flat Car w/Piggyback TOFC Deck (plastic)

**NEW 629-32201** SP **39.95**

## FREIGHT CAR KITS

### Box Cars

#### 1937 AAR Single-Door 16.95 ea

**629-8001** Undecorated Square Corner

**629-8002** Undecorated "W" Corner

#### 40' Double-Door

**629-8500** Undecorated "W" Corner **16.95**

**629-8501** Undecorated Square Corner **16.95**

#### X-29

**629-70021** Undecorated 1924 Body w/Steel Plate Ends **16.95**

**629-7003** Undecorated AAR Body w/Steel Plate Ends **16.95**

#### ACF 4-3-1 10' 6"

**Riveted Sides**

**629-8600** Undecorated **16.95**

**Riveted Sides 8' Door**

**629-8700** Undecorated **16.95**

**Welded Sides 8' Door**

**629-8900** Undecorated **16.95**

### Reefers

#### R-30-12-9 "Reconditioned" Wood Reefers 26.95 ea (Unless Noted)

Reconditioned cars with wooden or steel ice hatches, Equipco brake gear, ladders, K type brakes or AB Brakes and Bettendorf trucks.

**629-4451** American Refrigerator Transport MP/Wabash Emblems

**629-4250** Undecorated w/Wood Hatches **16.95**

#### Wine R-30 Reefer

**629-4300** Undecorated **16.95**

#### 37' Mather Meat Reefer

**629-1000** Undecorated **16.95**

### Gondolas

#### Drop Bottom Gondolas

**With Steel Sides**

**629-50071** DRGW **24.95**

**629-50001** Undecorated - SP Style Ends **16.95**

**629-50201** Undecorated - UP Style Ends **16.95**

**With Composite Sides**

**629-5101** SP w/Black & White Herald **26.95**

**629-5100** Undecorated **16.95**

**With Composite Sides & Sugar Beet Extensions**

**629-5171** Undecorated w/Board Extensions-UP Style Ends **21.95**

**629-5172** Undecorated w/Plywood Extensions-UP Style Ends **21.95**

**629-5175** Undecorated w/Board Extensions-SP Style Ends **21.95**

**629-5176** Undecorated w/Plywood Extensions-SP Style Ends **21.95**

**With Steel Sides & Sugar Beet Extensions Undecorated 21.95 ea**

**629-5169** With Board Extensions-UP Style Ends

**629-5170** With Plywood Extensions-UP Style Ends

### Flat Cars

#### F-70-7 Flat Cars

**629-2101** Undecorated w/SP Decals & Wood Deck **29.95**

**629-2103** Undecorated w/Texas & New Orleans Decals & Wood Deck **29.95**

#### 42' Flat Cars 10.95 ea (Unless Noted)

**629-2206** UP (red)

**629-2207** C&O (black)

**629-2212** NP (black)

**629-2213** DRGW (black)

**629-2216** CP (black)

**629-2217** Western Pacific (red)

**629-2218** CN (red)

**629-2224** NYC (red)

**629-2227** Erie

**629-2233** L&N

**629-2248** Duluth, South Shore & Atlantic

**629-2250** Pacific Great Eastern

**629-2254** Wheeling & Lake Erie

**629-2262** Toledo, Peoria & Western

**629-2264** ATSF MOW Service

**629-2267** Clinchfield

**629-2268** Illinois Terminal

**629-2200** Undecorated (gray) **9.95**

### Tank Cars

Each kit features detailed plastic parts and comes prepainted and lettered.

#### 10,000-Gallon Tank Cars 20.95 ea (Unless Noted)

**629-3021** Roma Wine

**629-3022** Fruit Industries Limited Wine

**629-3026** Skelgas

**629-3027** Anchor

**629-3029** Humble

**629-3000** Undecorated **16.95**

## READY-TO-RUN FREIGHT CARS

### Flat Cars

#### With Wood Deck 37.95 ea

**629-32103** SP

**629-32105** Texas & New Orleans

### Coil Cars 35.95 ea (Unless Noted)

**629-32501** CSX **36.95**

**629-32502** Elgin, Joliet & Eastern **36.95**

**629-32503** CB&Q

**629-32505** SOU **36.95**

**629-32507** C&O

**629-32509** N&W **37.95**

**629-32510** NS **37.95**

**629-32511** BN **34.95**

**629-32513** IC (orange)

**629-32515** CR

**629-32517** Rock Island

**629-32518** CSS

**629-32528** Ohio Central

**629-32529** Iowa Interstate

**629-32530** Chessie System

**629-32532** GM&O

**629-32533** Illinois Central Gulf

**629-32535** NS "Protect II" **37.95**

**629-32536** Frisco

**629-32537** B&O

**629-32538** ATSF (red) **37.95**

**629-32539** IC Modern w/ICG Lettered Body **37.95**

**629-32540** CSX (blue & gray) **36.95**

**629-32541** Detroit & Toledo Shore Line w/GT & Chessie Hoods **36.95**

**629-32542** CNW

**629-32544** BNSF "New Image" w/Round Hoods **36.95**

**629-32550** Undecorated w/Angled Hoods **30.95**

**629-32551** Undecorated w/Round Hoods **30.95**

### Box Cars

#### X-29 w/Plate End

**629-37026** PRR "Merchandise Service" **29.95**

**629-37101** Seaboard Air Line "Orange Blossom Special" **28.85**

#### X-29 w/Body Patch 29.95 ea (Unless Noted)

**629-37201** PRR Circle Keystone

**629-37202** PRR Shadow Keystone

**629-37203** PRR/REA **30.95**

**NEW 629-37204** PRR "Merchandise Service" **31.95**

**629-37210** Chicago Great Western

**NEW 629-37211** PC **30.95**

## RED CABOOSE

1937 40' AAR Box Car
Seaboard "Cement" 629-38090

Drop-Bottom Gondolas
DRGW w/Steel Sides 629-35007

10,000-Gallon Welded Tank Car
Sunoco 629-33010

### AAR
**629-37157** B&O

### 1937 40' AAR
**629-38009** CP **39.95**

**629-38027** St. Louis - San Francisco "Frisco"

**629-38063** CRR

**629-38070** NH (black, orange)

**629-38085** ATSF "Grand Canyon"

**629-38088** SP

**629-38090** Seaboard "Cement"

**629-38091** ACL

**629-38092** Pittsburgh & Lake Erie w/Oval Herald

### Reefers
#### Wood Refrigerator Cars 29.95 ea (Unless Noted)
629-34151 PFE w/UP & SP Colored Heralds w/Wooden Hatches

629-34154 PFE w/UP/SP B&W Heralds

**NEW 629-34158** PFE **31.95**

**629-34231** PFE/Western Pacific w/Wooden Hatches

**629-34429** NP ("Yellowstone" Herald)

**629-34431** NP

**629-34435** NP – Post-1942

629-34440 MDT

629-34448 Western Fruit Express/GN (Reefer yellow, Freight Car Red)

**629-34451** ART MP/Wabash

**629-34461** BREX

### Gondolas
#### Drop-Bottom Gondolas 30.95 ea (Unless Noted)
Item listed below is available by special order (see Legend Page).
**629-35002** UP w/Steel Sides

**629-35004** NP w/Steel Sides

**629-35007** DRGW w/Steel Sides

**629-35010** GN w/Steel Sides

629-35019 SP 1955-57 Scheme w/Steel Sides

**629-35014** MILW w/Steel Sides **29.95**

**NEW 629-35107** DRGW

### Tank Cars
#### 10,000-Gallon Welded Tank Car 28.95 ea (Unless Noted)
**629-33001** UTLX (black) **29.95**

**629-33002** SHPX (black)

**629-33010** Sunoco **29.95**

**629-33020** Carter

**629-33022** Fruit Industries Limited Wine (silver)

**629-33025** Magnolia

**629-33026** Skelgas

**629-33027** Anchor (black)

**629-33044** ACL **29.95**

## RAIL LINE

30' Box Car 620-130

30' Idler Flat Car 620-131

30' Stock Car 620-132

## NARROW GAUGE CARS
These HOn3 kits are based on Rio Grande prototypes. They feature injection-molded styrene bodies, detailed underframes, separate wire grab irons and other details. They also include dummy couplers, but do not come with trucks or decals.

### 30' Box Car
**620-130** Rio Grande **15.95**
Haul in supplies to the high country aboard this authentic 30' box car, a replica of the Rio Grande's rebuilt 3000 series cars. Sliding side doors are great for showing off interior details.

### 30' Idler Flat Car
**620-131** Rio Grande **14.95**
These 6700 series flat cars were converted from 5500 series stock cars in 1955 for pipe train service.

### 30' Stock Car
**620-132** Rio Grande **15.95**
Based on 5500 series cars as rebuilt after 1940. The kit features sliding doors, positionable end door and molded details.

New Arrivals Updated Every Day! Visit Walthers Web site at
**www.walthers.com**

## STEWART PRODUCTS
These HO Scale craft train kits feature unpainted metal castings.

### Flat Car Loads 8.40 ea (Unless Noted)
**683-203** Air-Cooled Transformer

**683-204** Turbine Gear & Block

**683-205** Diesel Generator

**683-209** Ship Propellers pkg(4)

**683-210** Steel Coils pkg(6)

**683-216** Refinery Pressure Tank **10.50**

**683-217** Extra Sections for Tank No. 216 pkg(4) **7.30**

**683-220** High-Voltage Cells pkg(3)

## TAURUS PRODUCTS/ TROUT CREEK ENGINEERING
These kits feature scale lumber and plastic and metal detail parts. They do not include trucks or couplers. Custom decals are included with all kits except ore cars.

### HO 40' Wood Sheathed Reefers 23.00 ea
**707-2871** PFE
UP herald on one side and SP herald on the other.

**707-2872** Rock Island

### HOn3 Tank Cars
**707-3180** Conoco **44.00**

**707-3881** Standard Oil **45.00**

**707-3882** Zerolene Oil **44.00**

**707-3883** RPM Oil **44.00**

### HO Stock Car
**707-2870** Oregon Short Line **22.00**

### 20' Wood Ore Cars pkg(2) 26.00 ea
Typical of small wooden ore cars used by narrow- and standard-gauge railroads around the country.

**707-2860** HO Undecorated

**707-3860** HOn3 Undecorated
Comes with wire and screws.

These easy-to-build kits feature one-piece plastic bodies, which are prepainted and lettered. Models are complete with trucks and weights; coupler pockets accept Kadee® couplers, sold separately.

# HOPPERS

## 70-Ton Cars 12.95 ea

Kits include friction or roller bearing style trucks as noted.

### 14-Panel Triple

**691-10901** Data Only – Black (Friction Bearing)

**691-10902** Boston & Albany (Friction Bearing)

**691-10903** Clinchfield (Roller Bearing)

**691-10904** Chessie/C&O (Roller Bearing)

**691-10905** Chessie/WM (Roller Bearing)

**691-10906** CR (Friction Bearing)

**691-10907** Chicago & Eastern Illinois (Friction Bearing)

**691-10908** Detroit & Mackinack (Friction Bearing)

**691-10909** DRGW (Friction Bearing)

**691-10910** D&H (Friction Bearings)

**691-10911** DT&I (Friction Bearing)

**691-10912** EL (Roller Bearing)

**691-10913** FEC – Large Numbers (Roller Bearing)

**691-10914** FEC – Small Numbers (Roller Bearing)

**691-10915** GN (Friction Bearing)

**691-10916** Montour (Friction Bearing)

**691-10917** NYC (Friction Bearing)

**691-10918** Pittsburgh & Shawmut (Friction Bearing)

**691-10919** PC (Friction Bearing)

**691-10920** ATSF (Roller Bearing)

**691-10921** SAL (Friction Bearing)

**691-10922** SCL (Roller Bearing)

**691-10923** WM (Roller Bearings)

**691-10900** Undecorated – Friction Bearings

### 12-Panel Triple

Kits include friction or roller bearing style trucks as noted.

**691-10951** Data Only – Black (Friction Bearing)

**691-10952** CR (Roller Bearing)

**691-10953** CN (Friction Bearing)

**691-10954** CSX (Roller Bearing)

**691-10955** DRGW (Friction Bearing)

**691-10956** EL (Roller Bearing)

**691-10957** L&N (Roller Bearing)

**691-10958** MILW (Friction Bearing)

**691-10959** PC (Friction Bearing)

**691-10960** PRR (Friction Bearing)

**691-10961** Pittsburgh & Lake Erie

**691-10962** SOU (Roller Bearing)

**691-10963** WM (Roller Bearing)

**691-10964** PRR

**NEW 691-10965** CN Modernized (black w/white "Noodle")

**691-10950** Undecorated (Friction Bearing)

### 12-Panel Peaked End Triple w/Friction Bearing Trucks

**691-10976** PRR

**691-10977** C&O

**691-10978** N&W

**691-10975** Undecorated

### 13-Panel Triple w/Friction Bearing Trucks

**691-11071** Data Only

**691-11072** PRR As-Built Scheme

**691-11073** PRR Simplified Scheme

**691-11070** Undecorated

### Offset Triple

**691-11001** Data Only

**691-11002** ACL w/Stripes

**691-11003** ACL No Stripes

**691-11004** Bangor & Aroostook – Two Schemes

**691-11005** Bangor & Aroostook – Two Schemes

**691-11006** B&O – Round Herald

**691-11007** B&O – Billboard Scheme

**691-11008** B&O – W7 Class As-Delivered

**691-11009** B&O – Yellow Stripe

**691-11010** B&O – W9

**691-11011** B&M

**691-11012** CN #1

**691-11013** CN #2

**691-11014** CP #1

**691-11015** CP #2

**691-11016** CP #3

**691-11017** Carbon County

**691-11018** CB&Q (Chinese Red)

**691-11019** CB&Q (Chinese Red) w/C&S Reporting Marks

**691-11020** CB&Q (Mineral Red; As-Built)

**691-11021** Chicago Great Western

**691-11022** Chicago Great Western/Minneapolis & St. Louis – CGW Number

**691-11023** Chicago Great Western/Minneapolis & St. Louis – M&StL Number

**691-11024** CNW/Omaha – CNW Number

**691-11025** CNW/Omaha – CStPM&O Number

**691-11026** DT&I

**691-11027** Family Lines/SCL

**691-11028** Illinois Terminal #1

**691-11029** Illinois Terminal #2

**691-11030** KCS As-Built

**691-11031** MP – As-Built

**691-11032** MP – Missouri Illinois

**691-11033** Minneapolis & St. Louis

**691-11034** NYC – As-Built

**691-11035** NKP

**691-11036** Pittsburgh & Lake Erie (black)

**691-11037** Rock Island – As Built

**691-11038** SCL

**691-11039** ATSF Class GA-73

**691-11040** SAL – As-Built

**691-11041** SP/Texas & New Orleans – As-Built

**691-11042** SOU (black)

**691-11043** Toronto, Hamilton & Buffalo

**691-11044** Chessie/B&O

**691-11045** Canada Southern

**691-11046** CN

**691-11047** RI "The ROCK"

**691-11048** IC

**691-11049** SP

**691-11050** CP

**691-11000** Undecorated

## 55-Ton Cars 12.95 ea

### With Fishbelly Underframe

**691-10101** Data Only (black)

**691-10701** WM

**691-10702** RDG

**691-10703** RDG – Anthracite

**691-10704** RDG – Speed

**691-10705** CNJ

**691-10706** D&H #1

**691-10707** D&H #2

**691-10708** D&H #3

**691-10709** LV

**691-10710** ACL

**691-10711** B&O

**691-10712** C&O

**691-10713** Cambria & Indiana

**691-10714** CNJ Central Railroad of Pennsylvania

**691-10715** D&H #4

**NEW 691-10716** Norfolk Southern Railway (black, white)

**691-10100** Undecorated

### With Fishbelly Underframe & Peaked Ends

**691-10801** N&W

**691-10802** ACL #1

**691-10803** Atlantic Coast Line #2

### With U-Channel Underframe

**691-10751** Data Only

**691-10752** WM – Circular Herald

**691-10753** WM – Speed Lettering

**691-10754** Pittsburgh & West Virginia

**691-10755** B&M

**691-10756** Toronto, Hamilton & Buffalo

**691-10750** Undecorated

# ORE CARS

## G39 Series 70-Ton 15.98 ea

### G39a

**691-10672** Data Only – Black

**691-10673** Data Only – Red

**691-10674** PRR As-Delivered

**691-10675** PRR Re-Trucked

**691-10676** PC

**691-10677** CR (red)

**691-10670** Undecorated – Black

**691-10671** Undecorated – Red

### G39 with Crown Trucks

**691-10679** Data Only

**691-10680** PRR

**691-10681** PC

**691-10678** Undecorated

### G39b with Friction Bearing Trucks

**691-10683** Data Only

**691-10684** PRR #14034

**691-10685** PC #501021

**691-10686** CR #500999

**691-10687** PRR

**691-10682** Undecorated

Look what's coming down the "right track" from the Atlas Trainman™ — a collection of quality, affordable, high performance HO model railroad locos and cars!

Meticulously engineered by Atlas, and designed for compatibility with any existing HO Scale layout, each comes fully assembled and ready to run. They're built for dependability and smooth, reliable performance; combining handsome paint schemes with state-of-the-art detailing and construction.

All Cars feature:

- True scale dimensions with accurate details
- Weighted, detailed underframes
- Equipped with AccuMate® Knuckle Couplers
- Trucks equipped with free-rolling metal wheels
- Accurate painting and lettering

And, all Trainman products will be available year 'round at all times, so you can add new items to your layout whenever you choose. With this exciting line of HO products, we promise...

***HO SCALE FUN FOR EVERYONE!™***

## NEW PRODUCTS

### Covered Hopper

### Thrall 4750 Covered Hopper 12.95 ea (Unless Noted)

This covered hopper model is based on a late-1970s 263,000 lbs GRL (Gross Rail Loading) 4750 cubic-foot capacity designed by Thrall Car primarily for grain transport. These cars operate individually and in solid trains across the continent.

**NEW 751-20000120** BN (green, white)

**NEW 751-20000121** BN (green, white)

**NEW 751-20000122** Transportation Corporation of America (NOKL) (red, white diagonal "sash")

**NEW 751-20000123** Transportation Corporation of America (NOKL) (red, white diagonal "sash")

**NEW 751-20000124** DM&E (gray, black)

**NEW 751-20000125** DM&E (gray, black)

**NEW 751-20000126** Union Equity (TCAX) (yellow, black, white, green)

**NEW 751-20000127** Union Equity (TCAX) (yellow, black, white, green)

**NEW 751-20000128** Undecorated **9.95**

## BOX CARS

### American Car & Foundry 50'6" Cars 12.95 ea (Unless Noted)

In 1974, American Car & Foundry (ACF)® built the first box car for Railbox, a subsidiary of the Trailer Train Company. They went on to produce 5,400 50' cars over the next six years, receiving large orders from Class I railroads, shortlines and box car leasing companies.

**751-919** Atlanta & St. Andrews Bay

**751-920** Atlanta & St. Andrews Bay

**751-921** CSX

**751-922** CSX

**751-923** Railbox

**751-924** Railbox

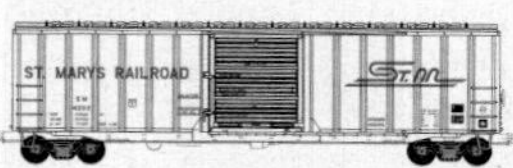


**751-925** St. Mary's Railroad

**751-926** St. Mary's Railroad

**NEW 751-1180** Atlantic & Western (red, black "Patch Job")

**NEW 751-1181** Atlantic & Western (red, black "Patch Job")

**NEW 751-1182** East Erie Commercial (brown, white)

**NEW 751-1183** East Erie Commercial (brown, white)

**NEW 751-1184** Family Lines (black, yellow)

**NEW 751-1185** Family Lines (black, yellow)

**NEW 751-1186** Minneapolis, Northfield & Southern (blue, red, white)

**NEW 751-1187** Minneapolis, Northfield & Southern (blue, red, white)

**751-918** Undecorated **9.95**

## HOPPERS

### AAR 70-Ton 3-Bay Open Hopper 12.95 ea (Unless Noted)

An industry standard since the 1930s, the 3-bay hopper was adopted as an AAR recommended design. Although offering greater carrying capacity than flat-sided cars, the joints were easily damaged by sulfuric acid (created by wet coal), and the cars fell out of favor by the mid-1950s as repair costs mounted.

**751-928** Minneapolis & St. Louis

**751-929** Minneapolis & St. Louis

**751-930** DRGW

**751-931** DRGW

**751-932** SOU

**751-933** SOU

**751-934** BN

**751-935** BN

**NEW 751-1188** BN #172532 (black, white, red)

**NEW 751-1189** BN #172731 (black, white, red)

**NEW 751-1190** Chessie/C&O #143754 (black, yellow)

**NEW 751-1191** Chessie/C&O #143603 (black, yellow)

**NEW 751-1192** NH #80333 (brown, white)

**NEW 751-1193** NH #80516 (brown, white)

**NEW 751-1194** RDG #60192 (black, white)

**NEW 751-1195** RDG #60455 (black, white)

**751-927** Undecorated, Standard Ends **9.95**

### ACF® 3560 Center Flow Covered Hopper 12.95 ea (Unless Noted)

The three-compartment American Car & Foundry (ACF)® 3560 Center Flow Covered Hopper was designed to transport high-density, dry, bulk loads including salt, fertilizer, starch, bauxite and clay. Over 2,000 were built from 1967-72. All cars are gray with appropriate graphics unless noted.

**751-937** C&O

**751-938** C&O

**751-939** Corn Products

**751-940** Corn Products

**751-941** DMIR

American Car & Foundry 50'6" Cars
Railbox 751-923

AAR 70-Ton 3-Bay Open Hopper
Minneapolis & St. Louis 751-929

ACF 3560 Center Flow Covered Hopper
Corn Products 751-939

**751-942** DMIR

**751-943** Stauffer Chemical

**751-944** Stauffer Chemical

**NEW 751-18917** Alaska Railroad

**NEW 751-18918** Alaska Railroad

**NEW 751-18919** ACFX

**NEW 751-18920** ACFX

**NEW 751-18921** Chessie/C&O (yellow, blue)

**NEW 751-18922** Chessie/C&O (yellow, blue)

**NEW 751-18923** Kerr-McGee

**NEW 751-18924** Kerr-McGee

**751-936** Undecorated **9.95**

### 2-Bay Offset-Side Hopper w/Flat Ends 12.95 ea (Unless Noted)

All cars black with white lettering unless noted.

Different Roadnumber Shown

**751-18871** B&O

**751-18872** B&O

**751-18873** IC (brown, white)

**751-18874** IC (brown, white)

**751-18875** MILW (oxide red, white)

**751-18876** MILW (oxide red, white)

**751-18877** NKP

**751-18878** NKP

**751-18881** EL

**751-18882** EL

**751-18883** GN (Mineral Red, white, black)

**751-18884** GN (Mineral Red, white, black)

**751-18885** CNJ

**751-18886** CNJ

**751-18887** ATSF (Mineral Red, white, black)

**751-18888** ATSF (Mineral Red, white, black)

**NEW 751-18901** BAR

**NEW 751-18902** BAR

**NEW 751-18903** Kewaunee, Green Bay & Western (Oxide Red)

**NEW 751-18904** Kewaunee, Green Bay & Western (Oxide Red)

**NEW 751-18905** N&W

**NEW 751-18906** N&W

**NEW 751-18907** P&LE

**NEW 751-18908** P&LE
**NEW 751-18909** SLSF
**NEW 751-18910** SLSF
**NEW 751-18911** RDG
**NEW 751-18912** RDG
**NEW 751-18913** South Buffalo (brown, yellow)
**NEW 751-18914** South Buffalo (brown, yellow)
**NEW 751-18915** Tennessee Central
**NEW 751-18916** Tennessee Central
**751-18870** Undecorated **9.95**

### PS-2 Covered Hopper 12.95 ea (Unless Noted)

All cars gray with black lettering unless noted or shown.

Different Roadnumber Shown

**751-17171** BN
**751-17172** BN
**751-17173** MP
**751-17174** MP
**751-17175** PC
**751-17176** PC
**751-17177** ATSF
**751-17178** ATSF

**751-17181** CNJ
**751-17182** CNJ
**751-17183** MILW
**751-17184** MILW
**751-17185** DRGW
**751-17186** DRGW
**751-17187** SOU
**751-17188** SOU
**NEW 751-17189** D&H
**NEW 751-17190** D&H
**NEW 751-17191** Olin Chemicals (NHIX)
**NEW 751-17192** Olin Chemicals (NHIX)
**NEW 751-17193** WM
**NEW 751-17194** WM
**NEW 751-17195** WP
**NEW 751-17196** WP
**NEW 751-17197** Clinchfield
**NEW 751-17198** Clinchfield
**NEW 751-17199** CR
**NEW 751-17200** CR
**NEW 751-17201** Elgin Joliet & Eastern
**NEW 751-17202** Elgin Joliet & Eastern
**NEW 751-17203** SP
**NEW 751-17204** SP
**751-17170** Undecorated **9.95**

## GONDOLAS

### Evans 52' Gondola 12.95 ea (Unless Noted)

Some of the hardest working cars in all of railroading, gondolas are called on to move all kinds of loads that don't require protection from the weather. A favorite of the steel industry, the open tops and low sides make it easy to load big, heavy items such as structural steel, or scrap metal.

**751-910** Atlantic & Western
**751-911** Atlantic & Western

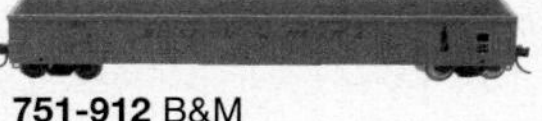

**751-912** B&M
**751-913** B&M
**751-914** CNW
**751-915** CNW
**751-916** GTW
**751-917** GTW
**NEW 751-20000096** Herzog #3902 (brown, white, yellow)
**NEW 751-20000097** Herzog #3906 (brown, white, yellow)
**NEW 751-20000098** Newburgh & South Shore #130346 (brown, white)
**NEW 751-20000099** Newburgh & South Shore #130349 (brown, white)
**NEW 751-20000100** Tuscola & Saginaw Bay Railway Company #5714 (black, white)
**NEW 751-20000101** Tuscola & Saginaw Bay Railway #5730 (black, white)
**NEW 751-20000102** Upper Merion & Plymouth #5501 (black, white)
**NEW 751-20000103** Upper Merion & Plymouth #5540 (black, white)
**751-909** Undecorated **9.95**

## CABOOSES

### C&O-Style Center Cupola Caboose 12.95 ea (Unless Noted)

Introduced in 1937 by the C&O, these rugged steel cabooses led long lives. Similar cars were also built for other railroads, and many remained in use until the 1980s. In addition to the standard features of other Trainman cars, these models also include clear window inserts and separately applied side railings.

**751-946** BN
**751-947** BN
**751-948** C&O
**751-949** C&O

Evans 52' Gondola
Grand Trunk Western 751-917

C&O-Style Center Cupola Caboose
D&H 751-1137

C&O-Style Center Cupola Caboose
C&O 751-948

C&O-Style Center Cupola Caboose
Chessie System 751-951

**751-950** Chessie System
**751-951** Chessie System
**751-952** CR
**751-953** CR
**751-954** UP
**751-955** UP
**751-956** Virginian
**751-957** Virginian
**751-1122** C&O (red, white, black)
**751-1123** C&O (red, white, black)
**751-1124** CP Rail (yellow, black, white)
**751-1125** CP Rail (yellow, black, white)
**751-1126** NS (red, white)
**751-1127** NS (red, white)
**751-1128** ATSF (red, yellow)
**751-1129** ATSF (red, yellow)
**751-1130** SP (brown, orange)
**751-1131** SP (brown, orange)
**751-1132** Pere Marquette (red, white)
**751-1133** Pere Marquette (red, white)
**NEW 751-1134** CNW (yellow, green)
**NEW 751-1135** CNW (yellow, green)
**NEW 751-1136** D&H (red, white)
**NEW 751-1137** D&H (red, white)
**NEW 751-1138** NYC (brown, white)
**NEW 751-1139** NYC (brown, white)
**NEW 751-1144** L&N (red, yellow)
**NEW 751-1145** L&N (red, yellow)
**NEW 751-1146** MP (red, white)
**NEW 751-1147** MP (red, white)
**NEW 751-1148** N&W (red, white)
**NEW 751-1149** N&W (red, white)
**NEW 751-1196** SOO (white, red, black)
**NEW 751-1197** SOO (white, red, black)
**NEW 751-1198** Tennessee Central (red, white, black)
**NEW 751-1199** Tennessee Central (red, white, black)
**751-945** Undecorated **9.95**

## *Information* STATION

### One Train, One Commodity

Unit trains are the most efficient way to ship many bulk commodities. Coal, potash, sulfur, fertilizer, aggregates and grain are the bread and butter of many railroads' business. Because many of these materials move in huge quantities from a single producer to a single destination, unit trains allow railroads to run a single train from supplier to end users or transloading terminals cheaply, and with as few delays for classification as possible.

For example, a unit grain train, on some railroads as few as 26 cars, on others sometimes over 100, loads at a single elevator. All the cars typically have the same capacity (usually 100 tons), and are often identical. The cars are kept together as a unit (hence the name), are treated as a single shipment, and often operate as a single train until they're unloaded at an export terminal or processing plant. They avoid classification yards and most other terminal delays.

N Scale lends itself well to modeling unit trains. Because of its size, long trains don't take up much space. Long mainline runs on home or modular layouts allow you to let your locomotives strut their stuff. Just imagine a 50-car unit grain train of matched PS2CD 4427 Covered Hoppers snaking across the countryside on your home or modular layout – an impressive sight indeed!

márklin®

Beer Car Warsteiner 441-4417

Beer Car Doppelbock Dunkel 441-4421

Beer Car Binding 441-44189

## NEW PRODUCTS

### 3-Rail AC Freight Cars

Ready-to-run cars come equipped with AC wheelsets and NEM hook-and-loop couplers.

### Beer Cars 18.40 ea (Unless Noted)

**NEW 441-4417** Warsteiner

**NEW 441-4421** Doppelbock Dunkel

**NEW 441-44184** Karlsberg

**NEW 441-44189** Binding

**NEW 441-44191** Erdinger

**NEW 441-44193** Schofferhofer

**NEW 441-44195** Kostritzer Schwarzbrauerei **19.55**

**NEW 441-45021** Lowenbrau **35.59**

**NEW 441-46202** Kulmbach **34.29**

TRIX

40' Steel Single-Door Box Car UP 441-24900

## MAINTENANCE OF WAY SET

**441-T24916** Railroad Maintenance 3-Car Set UP (Silver MOW Scheme, 2 40' Box Cars, 1 CA-3 Caboose) **89.00**

## BOX CARS

### 40' Steel Single-Door Box Cars

**441-24900** UP pkg(20) **535.00** This ready-to-run series of box cars features 20 Union Pacific cars with different slogans and car number. Each model features sliding doors, inside floor planking, diecast metal chassis and floor, RP-25 wheels and a Kadee®-compatible special coupler.

### Single-Door Box Cars

**441-T24912** Class XM 40' Box Car 3-Car Set PRR (2 Shadow Keystone, 1 "Merchandise Service") pkg(3) **69.00**

### 40' Steel Box Car Set

**441-T24907** NYC ("Pacemaker" gray, red, white) pkg(3) **69.00**

### Double-Door Box Cars

**441-T24913** Class XM 40' Box Car 3-Car Set ATSF (1 Each "Scout" & "Super Chief" Slogans & 1 w/Map Logo) pkg(3) **69.00**

## REFRIGERATOR CARS

### R-40-14 Steel Reefer Set

**441-T24906** PFE (black & white UP & SP heralds) pkg(3) **69.00**

## STOCK CARS

### UP S-40-12 Stock Cars

**441-T24905** 2 Yellow, 1 Oxide Red pkg(3) **69.00**

## TANK CARS

### ACF Type 105A Tank Cars

**441-T24908** Penn Salt, Electro Bleaching & Mathieson Chemical pkg(3) **49.50**

## FREIGHT CAR ASSORTMENT

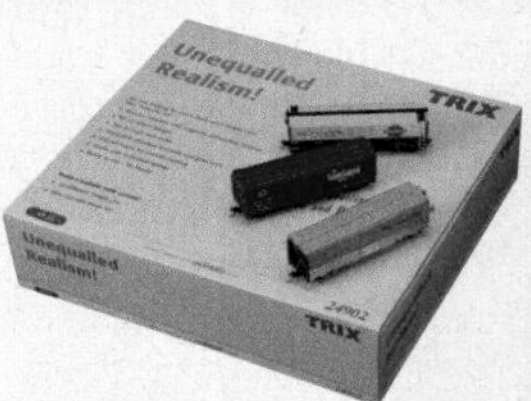

**441-24902** pkg(20) **295.00** An assortment of box cars, hoppers, reefers and automobile cars, all featuring different lettering! Each car is outfitted with RP-25 wheelsets, detailed trucks, close coupler mechanism, NEM coupler pockets, Kadee-compatible special couplers, and separately applied detail parts.

*State Tool & Die Co.*

## STEEL MILL CARS

All cars feature trucks and magnetic knuckle couplers.

### Kit Bash Series Mill Gondolas

**661-770** Single Car **10.50**

**661-7703** pkg(3) **27.90**

### Universal Steel Mill Car

**661-780 9.95**

**661-7803** w/Kadee couplers pkg(3) **26.90**

### Hot Metal Cars w/Kadee Couplers

**661-720** Pollock 75-Ton Kling **19.20**

**661-725** 3-in-1 Open Top w/Extended Ladle and "Add-on" Wings **21.75**

### Spacer Car w/Kadee Couplers

**661-740 12.95**

### Ingot Mold Car

**NEW 661-730** pkg(3) **38.95**

## FREIGHT CAR ACCESSORIES

### Caboose Conversion Kit

**661-900** C&O **4.25**

### Coil Car Hoods

**Corrugated**

**661-2012** Set of 2 **4.25**

**661-2016** Set of 6 **11.95**

**Round - Revised**

**661-1012** Set of 2 **3.79**

**661-1016** Set of 6 **9.95**

### Universal Coil Cradles

**661-151** Single Unit **2.95**

**661-1513** pkg(3) **7.50**

### GE 52 Coil Cradle

**NEW 661-161 2.95**

### Kling Ladle Kit

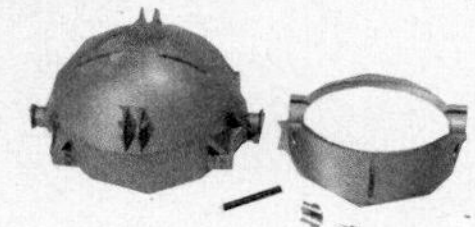

**661-760 6.95**

### Drawbars

**661-600** Multi-Purpose Drawbars pkg(10) **3.00**

### Steel Slabs pkg(10) 4.00 ea

**661-7853** Cold (silver or gray w/painting instructions)

**661-7858** Hot (orange-red w/painting instructions)

**661-78518** Rust (rust colored)

2008
HO
Model Railroad
Reference Book

# DECALS

Models and Photo by Edward Wall

Waiting patiently for a back up signal, a hard-working Diablo & Western switcher takes a quick break. In a sea of brown box cars and black hoppers, a cut of reefers really stands out from the crowd! Resplendent in bright colors and lavishly decorated, sign painters have transformed them into rolling billboards for the companies that lease them. While the "billboard" era ended in the 1930s, the blazing colors of yesterday live on in this scene by Edward Wall from Salem, Oregon. These reefers were scratchbuilt and proudly wear period lettering from Clover House.

Capturing the color of your favorite era is easy with decals, like those you'll find on the following ages.

## WALTHERS

### MODULAR DECAL SET

**934-1030 14.98**

- Adds that Final Touch of Realism
- Specially Designed for Cornerstone Modulars™ System
- Variety of Signs & Business Names Included
- Use with Most Buildings

### BLANK DECAL PAPER

Create custom decals for any kind of models with these blank sheets. The same high-quality paper used in Walthers decals and ready to use. Choose from larger 8-1/2 x 11" sheets in flat or gloss finishes, or the standard 6 x 9" sheets. For use with either an Alps printer or silkscreen printing.

**9 x 6" 22.5 x 15cm Sheets pkg(4) 3.98 ea**

**934-706820** Flat (Dull) Finish

**934-706823** Gloss (Shiny) Finish

**8-1/2 x 11" 21.2 x 27.5cm Sheets pkg(4) 7.98 ea**

**934-706821** Flat (Dull) Finish

**934-706822** Gloss (Shiny) Finish

## DECAL SETS

### 3.00 ea (Unless Noted)

**Alphabet**

**NEW 718-245** Railroad Roman 1/16" Letters (Bronze Gold)

**Baltimore & Ohio**

**NEW 718-203** Passenger Cars (Dulux Gold)

**NEW 718-206** Railway Post Office (Dulux Gold)

**Boston & Maine**

**718-227** Passenger Cars (Dulux Gold)

**NEW 718-228** Baggage Cars (Dulux Gold)

**Central of New Jersey**

**718-325** "Blue Comet" (Bronze Gold) **8.50**

**718-335** Baggage Car (Bronze Gold)

**Central of New Jersey/Reading**

**718-225** Passenger Cars (Bronze Gold)

**718-226** Passenger Cars (Dulux Gold)

**Colorado Midland**

**718-SP10** Various Equipment **10.00**

**Delaware, Lackawanna & Western**

**NEW 718-204** Passenger Cars (Dulux Gold)

**NEW 718-205** Passenger Cars (maroon)

**NEW 718-251** Passenger Cars (maroon)

**Erie**

**718-800** Passenger Cars (Dulux Gold)

**Erie-Lackawanna**

**NEW 718-252** Passenger Cars (maroon)

**Interstate**

**NEW 718-246** Caboose (white) **6.00**

**Lehigh & Hudson River**

**NEW 718-208** Caboose (white)

**NEW 718-209** Caboose Lehigh & Hudson River (yellow)

**NEW 718-209A** Caboose Lehigh & Hudson River (yellow w/ACI block)

**Lehigh Valley**

**718-701** Dulux Gold **6.00**

**Nashville, Chattanooga & St Louis**

**718-712A** Passenger Cars (Dulux Gold)

**New Haven**

**718-446A** Passenger Cars (white)

**New York Central**

**NEW 718-217** Postal Cars (Dulux Gold)

**NEW 718-218** Horse Car (Dulux Gold)

**Nickel Plate Road**

**NEW 718-202** Passenger Cars (Dulux Gold)

**NEW 718-253** Reefer (black)

**Norfolk & Western**

**NEW 718-229** Baggage Cars (Dulux Gold)

**Pennsylvania**

**718-401** Parlor Car (Bronze Gold) **6.00**

**718-442** Middle Division Railway Post Office **6.00**

**718-SP2** Steel Stock Car K9/K11 (white) **6.00**

**NEW 718-214** Baggage Cars (Bronze Gold)

**NEW 718-215** Baggage Car (Dulux Gold)

**NEW 718-436B** Theatrical Scenery Car (Bronze Gold) **6.00**

**NEW 718-437A** Horse Cars (Bronze Gold) **6.00**

**Pere Marquette**

**718-445A** Passenger Cars (Bronze Gold)

**Private Owner**

**NEW 718-255** Reefer ERDX (black)

**NEW 718-853** Reefer Merchant's Despatch Transportation (black) **4.00**

**Pullman**

**NEW 718-239** Pullman Sleepers (Dulux Gold)

**Raritan River**

**NEW 718-238** Caboose (black)

**Reading**

**NEW 718-219** Milk Car (Dulux Gold)

**NEW 718-207** Caboose (white)

**Rutland**

**NEW 718-852** Reefer (Dulux Gold, white)

**Seaboard Air Line**

**718-213A** Passenger Cars (Dulux Gold)

**Southern Pacific**

**NEW 718-SP** Passenger Cars (Dulux Gold)

**Western Maryland**

**NEW 718-216** Passenger Cars (Dulux Gold)

## EVAN DESIGNS

### INKJET DECAL PAPER

**266-P7** HobbyCal 8-1/2 x 11" Decal Paper (white) pkg(5) **15.00**

Create great decals with ANY inkjet printer. Ink is absorbed into the special coating on the decal paper. No oversprays required. Simply print, water slip and apply to any surface. Thin decals easily conform to smooth or irregular surfaces. Matte finish. Background dries white, can be made clear. Instructions included. Customize your layout!

## RAPIDO TRAINS

### NEW PRODUCTS

**Decals**

**NEW 606-1** VIA Rail HEP2 **7.95**

**NEW 606-2** VIA Rail LRC **7.95**

**NEW 606-8** CN Trackside Signs Kit **15.95**

Designed, Manufactured & Assembled entirely in the U.S.A.

### DECALS

**Blank Decal Paper**

**380-3099** Clear 8.5 x 11" Single Sheet **2.95**

**Boxcar Lettering**

**380-3101** B&M w/Large B&M Herald (black, white) **3.75**

**380-3104** B&M Minuteman Herald **3.25**

**380-3105** Erie Black & White Diamond Herald **3.75**

**380-3107** SLSF - Black & White Frisco Heralds, "Frisco Fast Freight" **3.75**

**380-3108** CG - Square White Herald, "The Right Way" Script Slogan **3.25**

**380-3112** DRGW - Flying Rio Grande, DF Logos **3.25**

**380-3129** WP - Silver & Black Herald, Large Silver Feather w/Orange DF Logo **4.75**

**Hopper Decals**

**380-3103** ATSF - Class Ga-105 **3.75**

**380-3106** MKT - Black **3.25**

**380-3109** FEC - Black **3.25**

**380-3110** PRR - Black w/Large Shadow Keystone Heralds **3.25**

**380-3121** CG - Black, "The Right Way" Script Slogan **3.25**

**380-3127** SP - Red **3.75**

**380-3128** SP - Black **3.75**

**380-3130** RDG - Red, Black & White Herald, White Lettering **4.75**

**380-3111** Pullman Builders Badge Decal **3.75**

**Building Decals**

**380-3113** Old West #1 - Assorted Period Business Names in White **3.85**

**Street Marking Decals 3.75 ea**

**380-3122** Dash - White Lines

**380-3123** Dash - Yellow Lines

**380-3124** Solid/Dash - Yellow Lines

**380-3125** Solid/Solid - White

**380-3126** Solid/Solid - Yellow

## BARN SIGN DECAL SETS

**5.00 ea**

Prototypical use was on barn and structure walls. Size varies, most are scale 17' wide, 3 signs per set.

**184-2250** #1, Eat More Possum, Redman, Dr. Pierce

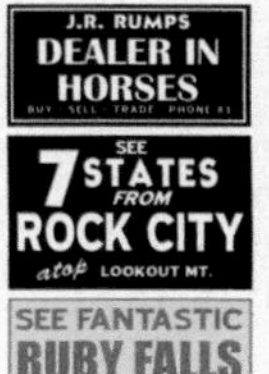


**184-2251** #2, Ruby Falls, Rock City, Horse Trader

**184-2252** #3, Meramec Caverns, Bank, Meet God

**184-2253** #4, Kentucky Club, Meramec Caverns, Repent

**184-2254** #5, Melo Crown, Mail Pouch, One Nation

**184-2255** #6 Mail Pouch, Bull Durham, United

## MODERN "TAGGER" GRAFFITI DECAL SETS 3.00 ea

All decals are reproductions of graffiti found on real railroad cars. Use on freight and passenger cars, buildings, walls, bridges and everywhere. Decals are not shown actual size.

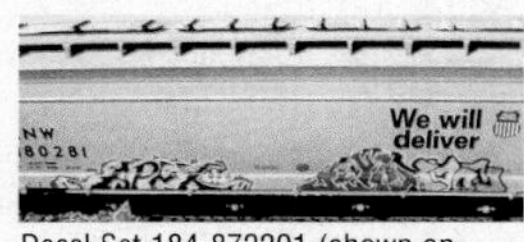


Decal Set 184-872201 (shown on rolling stock, not included)

**184-2221** PAYDIRT

**184-2222** ELVIS/SUSI

**184-2223** CHOOCHOO/FACE

**184-2224** KROS/SENIK

**184-2225** HETASEVER/RTZ

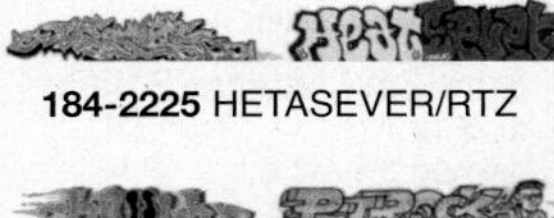

**184-2226** PETROCK/BOUS

**184-2227** DEBT/EMIR/OREC

**184-2228** DOS

**184-2229** HEAT/TCI

Decal Set 184-872210 (shown on rolling stock, not included)

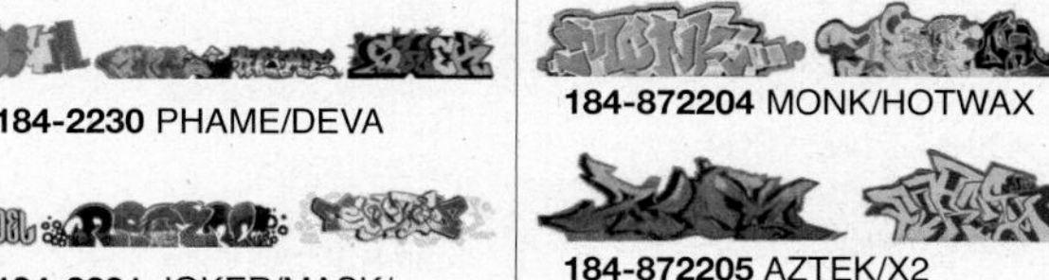

**184-2230** PHAME/DEVA

**184-2231** JOKER/MASK/NOEL

**184-2232** KING/RESA

**184-2233** ASIC/TAKO

**184-2234** FAME/RKRE

**184-2235** HALLOWEEN/BATUI

**184-2236** ISRAEL/NEXT

**184-2237** WONE/BULL/TVC

**184-2238** JASE/SKETCH

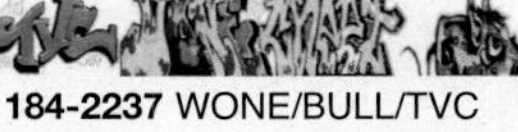

**184-2239** GISK/VEEGEE

**184-2240** TATOO/NOMADS

**184-2241** GODZILLA

**184-2242** MUSE

**184-872201** APEX/ZOOM

**184-872202** PEASER/QUISP

**184-872203** XYDE/QUASHE

**184-872204** MONK/HOTWAX

**184-872205** AZTEK/X2

**184-872206** HEK/JUNK

**184-872207** APART/TCI

**184-872208** FUSE/GLIOTW

**184-872209** ZOOM/PRAE

**184-872210** TNS

**184-872211** ANVL/JAIT

**184-872212** SMOG/MBER/NISE

**184-872213** WILD/BUG

**184-872214** DRANE/FROG

**184-872215** JESO/HM

**184-872216** DISKO/CROME

**184-872217** WEVER/AHUE

**184-872218** NEZ/HOAX

**184-872219** ONOROK/INCA

**184-872220** MONK/MUZE

## MODERN "TAGGER" GRAFFITI DECAL MEGA SETS

**5.00 ea**

**184-2244** #1 pkg(8)

**184-2245** #2 pkg(9)

**184-2246** #3 pkg(8)

**184-2247** #4 pkg(3)

**184-2248** #5 pkg(8)

**184-2249** #6 pkg(9)

MICROSCALE®

## DECAL ACCESSORIES

**460-50** Microscale System Pack **24.75**
Complete starter kit with one bottle each: Micro Set, Micro Sol, Micro Coat Flat, Satin and Gloss finishes, Micro Mask, Kristal Kleer, Micro Metal Foil Adhesive, Micro Weld Cement, Micro Liquitape and Micro Liquid Decal Film.

### Adhesives 1oz (30ml) 2.50 ea

**460-114** Kristal Kleer
Perfect for attaching window glass, aircraft canopies, headlights and other clear parts to models.

**460-115** Micro Liquitape
Make any part removable with this special formula.

**460-116** Micro Metal Foil Adhesive

### Liquid Decal Film

**460-117** 1oz (30ml) **2.50**

### Masking Liquid

**460-110** Micro Mask 1oz (30ml) **2.50**
For use with solvent-based paints. (Micro Mask is water soluble.)

### Decal Setting Solution 1oz (30ml) 2.50 ea

Setting solutions soften decal film, allowing it to stretch over details. Formulated especially for Micro Scale decals, can be used with most other brands.

**460-104** Micro Set

**460-105** Micro Sol
A stronger formula, for use on larger details or stubborn areas.

### Micro Coat Clear Finish 2.50 ea

**460-103** Flat
Dead-flat for dirty, weathered or camouflaged look.

**460-106** Satin
Semi-gloss, for a less shiny or slightly dirty look.

**460-108** Gloss
Provides a smooth surface for decaling and produces a high-gloss, "wet look" when dry.

## ACCESSORY DECAL SETS

### Trim Film 2.20 ea

Sheets measure 4-1/2 x 7"

**460-1** White
**460-2** Black
**460-3** Metallic Gold
**460-4** Metallic Silver
**460-5** Red
**460-6** Yellow
**460-7** Dark Blue
**460-8** Dulux Gold
**460-9** Dark Green
**460-10** SP "Daylight" Orange
**460-11** Guilford Gray
**460-12** UP/Amtrak® Blue
**460-13** Brown
**460-14** Bright Blue
**460-15** Gray Green
**460-16** B&M Gray
**460-17** Emerald Green
**460-18** Maroon
**460-19** Light Blue
**460-20** DRGW Orange
**460-21** NYC Gray
**460-22** Royal Blue
**460-23** CR Blue
**460-24** Box Car Red
**460-25** Caboose Red
**460-26** Pullman Green
**460-27** Stainless Steel
**460-29** Dayglow Orange
**460-38** Flat Black
**460-39** Dark Dulux Gold
**460-41** Jade
**460-100** Clear
**460-40** "Micro-Glo" Glow-In-The-Dark Material
Great for signs, signals, special effects and much more on your layout.

### 8-1/2 x 11" Sheets 2.50 ea

**460-200** Clear
**460-210** White

### Parallel Stripes 2.20 ea (Unless Noted)

Each sheet includes several stripes of the same width and color as shown.

#### Black

**460-212** 1/2"
**460-214** 1/4"
**460-218** 1/8"
**460-2116** 1/16"
**460-2132** 1/32"
**460-2164** 1/64"

#### Gold

**460-312** 1/2"
**460-314** 1/4"
**460-318** 1/8"
**460-3116** 1/16"
**460-3132** 1/32"
**460-3164** 1/64"

#### Silver

**460-412** 1/2"
**460-414** 1/4"
**460-418** 1/8"
**460-4132** 1/32" **3.60**
**460-4164** 1/64" **3.60**

#### Red

**460-512** 1/2"
**460-514** 1/4"
**460-518** 1/8"
**460-5116** 1/16"
**460-5132** 1/32"
**460-5164** 1/64"

#### Yellow

**460-612** 1/2"
**460-614** 1/4"
**460-618** 1/8"
**460-6116** 1/16"
**460-6132** 1/32"
**460-6164** 1/64"

#### White

**460-1112** 1/2"
**460-1114** 1/4"
**460-1116** 1/16"
**460-1118** 1/8"
**460-1132** 1/32"
**460-1164** 1/64"

#### Dark Blue

**460-712** 1/2"
**460-714** 1/4"
**460-718** 1/8"
**460-7116** 1/16"
**460-7132** 1/32"
**460-7164** 1/64"

#### Dulux Gold

**460-812** 1/2"
**460-814** 1/4"
**460-818** 1/8"
**460-8116** 1/16"
**460-8132** 1/32"
**460-8164** 1/64"

### HO Scale Width Stripes 6.00 ea

#### 1 & 2" Wide

**460-91111** White
**460-91112** Black
**460-91113** Gold
**460-91114** Silver
**460-91115** Red
**460-91116** Yellow
**460-91117** Blue
**460-91118** Dulux Gold
**460-91119** Dark Green
**460-91121** SP Gray

#### 3 & 4-3/4" Wide

**460-91101** White
**460-91102** Black
**460-91103** Gold
**460-91104** Silver
**460-91105** Red (Fits UP Diesels)
**460-91106** Yellow
**460-91108** Dulux
**460-91109** Dark Green

#### 4 & 6" Wide

**460-91131** White
**460-91132** Black
**460-91133** Gold
**460-91134** Silver
**460-91135** Red
**460-91136** Yellow
**460-91138** Dulux Gold
**460-91139** Green

### Barricade Stripes 6.00 ea

#### 6" Wide

**460-91141** White
**460-91142** Black
**460-91143** Gold
**460-91144** Silver
**460-91146** Yellow
**460-91147** Blue
**460-91148** Dulux Gold
**460-91149** Green

#### 45° Angle

**460-91151** White
**460-91152** Black
**460-91154** Silver
**460-91155** Red
**460-91156** Yellow
**460-91157** Dark Blue
**460-91158** Dulux Gold
**460-91159** Green

#### 8" Wide

**460-91171** White
**460-91172** Black
**460-91174** Silver
**460-91175** Red
**460-91179** Dark Green

### Alphabet & Number Sets 6.00 ea

#### Ornate Railroad

**460-90241** White w/Black Shadow

#### Art Deco-Condensed

**460-90141** White
**460-90142** Black

#### Extra Bold Modern Gothic 4, 6 & 12"

**460-90151** White
**460-90152** Black

#### Railroad Roman

**460-90001** White
**460-90002** Black
**460-90003** Gold
**460-90004** Silver
**460-90005** Red
**460-90006** Yellow
**460-90007** Dark Blue
**460-90008** Dulux Gold
**460-90009** Green

#### Railroad Gothic

**460-90101** White
**460-90102** Black
**460-90103** Gold
**460-90104** Silver
**460-90105** Red
**460-90106** Yellow
**460-90107** Blue
**460-90108** Dulux Gold
**460-90109** Green
**460-90120** Orange

#### Extended Roman-Passenger Cars

**460-90011** White
**460-90012** Black
**460-90013** Gold
**460-90014** Silver
**460-90015** Red
**460-90016** Yellow
**460-90017** Blue
**460-90018** Dulux Gold
**460-90019** Green

#### Condensed Gothic

**460-90021** White
**460-90022** Black
**460-90023** Gold
**460-90024** Silver
**460-90025** Red
**460-90026** Yellow
**460-90027** Blue
**460-90029** Green

#### Condensed Roman

**460-90031** White
**460-90032** Black
**460-90033** Gold
**460-90034** Silver
**460-90035** Red
**460-90036** Yellow
**460-90039** Green

#### Eurostyle

**460-90191** White
**460-90192** Black

#### Neon

**460-90182** Neon Lettering-Black Background

#### Roman Stencil

**460-90111** White
**460-90112** Black

#### Old West

**460-90041** White
**460-90042** Black
**460-90044** Silver
**460-90045** Red
**460-90046** Yellow
**460-90047** Blue
**460-90048** Dulux Gold
**460-90049** Green

#### Block Gothic

**460-90051** White
**460-90052** Black
**460-90053** Gold
**460-90054** Silver
**460-90055** Red
**460-90056** Yellow
**460-90057** Blue
**460-90058** Dulux Gold
**460-90059** Dark Green

# MICROSCALE®

### Extended Roman-Southern Pacific Style
**6 & 15"**
**460-90061** White
**460-90062** Black
**460-90063** Gold
**460-90064** Silver
**460-90065** Red
**460-90066** Yellow
**460-90067** Blue
**460-90068** Dulux Gold
**460-90069** Green

**3, 9 & 12"**
**460-90071** White
**460-90072** Black
**460-90073** Gold
**460-90074** Silver
**460-90075** Red
**460-90076** Yellow
**460-90077** Blue
**460-90078** Dulux Gold
**460-90079** Green

### Extended Gothic-New Haven Style
**460-90081** White
**460-90082** Black
**460-90083** Gold
**460-90084** Silver
**460-90085** Red
**460-90086** Yellow
**460-90087** Blue
**460-90088** Dulux Gold
**460-90089** Green

### Quentin
**460-90091** White
**460-90092** Black
**460-90093** Gold
**460-90094** Silver
**460-90095** Red
**460-90096** Yellow
**460-90097** Blue
**460-90098** Dulux Gold
**460-90099** Green

### 1920s Style Ultra-Modern
**460-90132** 4, 6 & 12" Black

### UP-Style Lettering
**With No Outline**
**460-90161** White
**460-90162** Black
**460-90163** Gold
**460-90164** Silver
**460-90165** Red
**460-90166** Yellow

**With Black Outline**
**460-90171** White
**460-90173** Gold
**460-90174** Silver
**460-90175** Red
**460-90176** Yellow

## Data Sets 6.00 ea (Unless Noted)

### Freight Cars
Ideal for use with custom decals.

**460-4280** Automatic Car Identification ACI Kartrack Computer ID Plates 1967-77 **3.60**

**460-4309** Builder's Plates & Logos **3.60**

**460-87236** Tank Cars-Yellow; GATX, UTLX, SHPX & More

**460-87840** Hazardous Material Placards US & Canada 1984+

### Diesels
**460-8748** Data & Builders Plates (black & white)

**460-87527** GE & EMD Late 1980s Data & Builders Plates

**460-87925** GE Dash-9 & AC-4400 Data 1995+

# RAILROAD SETS

## 6.00 ea (Unless Noted)

### American Car & Foundry ACFX
**460-4123** Pressure Aide Covered Hoppers 1994+ **3.60**

### American Freedom Train
**460-871065** Alco PA Diesel & Passenger Cars (red, blue, gold)

**460-871066** Additional Striping (matches 460-871065)

### Amtrak®
**460-4155** Material Handling Cars 1986+ **3.60**

**460-4170** Vermonter Baggage Cars 1995+ **3.60**

**460-4314** Pacific Parlor Lounge 1997+ **3.60**

**460-8799** Cars Phase II (white lettering)

**460-87100** E, F & F40 Diesels Phase I 1970

**460-87423** E8, F40PH & SDP40F Phase II 1970-80

**460-87424** F40PH Phase III 1980+

**460-87425** Superliners Phase II 1970-80

**460-87427** Superliner Phase II Scotchlite Striping (Use with #87425)

**460-87428** Heritage Fleet Phase III Striping (Use with #87426)

**460-87525** Amfleet Cars Phase III Paint

**460-87526** Amfleet Cars Stripes Phase III (Use with #87525)

**460-87675** Dash 8-32BWH Phase IV 1991+

**460-87950** Hi-Level Car Stripes Phase III 1980+

**460-87971** Amfleet Cars, Phase IV 1996+

**460-871021** P40/P42 Diesels 1996+

**460-871022** P-42 Northeast Direct Diesels 1997+

**460-871244** Station Signs 1971+

**NEW 460-871267** GE P40/42 Diesels (Late)

### Apache Railway
**460-4323** Woodchip Cars **3.60**

### Atlantic Coast Line
**460-87768** Diesels (yellow & black) 1957-66

**460-87773** E & F Units (purple & silver) 1939-57

**460-87907** ACL-Subsidiaries Late Switchers & GP7 1950-57

**460-87908** Diesel Stripes (purple & silver) 1949-57

**460-87976** Cabooses 1930-67

### Baltimore & Ohio
**460-4053** GP30 Sunburst Scheme **3.60**

**460-8783** Medium Steam Locos

**460-87396** E-Units 1950-60 (blue & gray scheme)

**460-87401** EMD & GE Diesels 1970

**460-87486** 2-Bay Covered Hoppers Class N-42 & N-43

**460-87797** Passenger Cars 1949-70

**460-87798** Passenger Car Stripes 1949-70

**460-871178** Steam Locomotives

**460-871179** Freight & Passenger Cars

**460-871224** "Timer Saver Service" Box Cars

### Boston & Maine
**460-4208** E7 Diesels As-Delivered 1945-48 **3.60**

**460-4397** Bicentennial GP38-2 #200 1975+ **3.60**

**460-87863** Passenger Cars; 1945-70

**460-87934** Late Blue Scheme 1978-85

**460-871193** Bicentennial Diesels 1976+

### Burlington - Chicago, Burlington & Quincy
**460-8715** Diesel Hood Units (red, black, gray) 1950-70

**460-8798** Passenger Diesels E5, E7, E8

**460-87108** California Zephyr Passenger Cars 1950-70

**460-87412** XM-32 40' Steel Box Cars

**460-871110** California Zephyr Lounges 1949-70

**460-871130** Steam Locos 1927-60

**460-871134** Denver/Texas Zephyr 1936+

**460-871140** Superpower Steam Locos

**460-871197** Waycars/Cabooses (Orange Scheme) 1954-70

**460-871198** Waycars/Cabooses (Chinese Red & Pre-BN Green) 1959-70

**460-871217** Cabooses & MOW Cars (Box Car Red) 1927-47

### Burlington Northern
**460-4106** BN/Western Fruit Express 57' Mechanical Reefers 1993+ **3.60**

**460-8725** Diesels (green & black)

**460-87190** Early BN, Late CB&Q Diesels (green, black, white lettering)

**460-87251** General Freight

**460-87364** GP30/35 Diesels w/Nose Stripes

**460-87484** SD40, GP50 & SD60 "Tiger Stripe Nose" 1985

**460-87492** Fuel Tenders & Locomotive Data

**460-87549** Diesels w/White Front 1989

**460-87621** Desert Storm SD60M 1991

**460-87649** Hoppers, Box Cars 1990 Scheme w/Herald

**460-87716** Diesel Data 1980s+

**460-87723** BN America 48' Container #2, 48' Chassis & Terminal Tractor 1990+

**460-87760** SD60M 1990+

**460-87780** Business Train Stripes 1989+

**460-87803** SD70MAC 1994+

**460-87826** Gunderson Maxi III Double-Stack Car 1990+

**460-87842** Cabooses 1970+

### Burlington Northern Santa Fe - BNSF
**460-4178** Aluminum Coalporter Gondolas 1996+ **3.60**

**460-4254** Patches for Renumbered Diesels (yellow & green) **3.60**
Use with #871035 and standard BN or ATSF sets.

**460-4258** 48' Trailers or Containers 1997+ **3.60**

**460-4380** ACF Center Flow Covered Hoppers **3.60**

**NEW 460-4383** Switchers & Slugs

**460-87943** SD75M Diesels-Super Fleet Colors 1996+

**460-87944** SD70MAC Diesels-BN Executive Colors 1996+

**460-87979** GE Dash-8 Diesels (red & silver) 1996+

**460-871023** Orange & Green Repainted Diesels 1996+

**460-871037** Centerflow Covered Hoppers 1996+

**460-871044** SD70MAC Premium Heritage Hood Unit Diesels w/Cigar-Band Nose Herald

**460-871076** GE Dash 9-44CW & AC4400CW Diesels w/Nose Logo w/Large Lettering: 4900, 4300 & 4400 Classes 1998+

**460-871211** Maersk-Painted NS SD40-2 & ATSF SDF40-2 Locomotives 2002



**460-871255** GE ES44DC Diesels 2005+

**460-871263** Standard Cab Hood Unit Repaints - 2005+

### B.C. HYDRO
**460-871256** SW9, MP15 & SD38-2 Diesels 1961-88

### Canadian National
**460-4227** Modern Cabooses, Noodle Scheme 1970+ **3.30**

**460-87234** General Freight & Cabooses 1970-80

**460-87374** F Unit Diesels 1940-50

**460-87568** Hood Unit Diesel Stripes 1990+

**460-87707** 4-Bay Cylindrical Covered Hoppers

**460-87746** CN North America Diesels 1992+

**460-87939** Diesels 1995+

**460-87947** Freight Diesels (green & yellow) 1953-60

**460-87948** GP7/9 & RS-10/18 (green & yellow) 1953-60

**460-871019** Steam Locos 1931-60

**460-871033** Wood Cabooses 1920-61

**460-871073** EMD SD70I & SD75 Diesels 1997+ (Designed to Fit Athearn Genesis Models, Sold Separately)

**460-871226** Expo '86 Diesels

### Canadian Pacific/CP Rail System
**460-4137** 3-Bay Centerflow Covered Hoppers 1994+ **3.60**

**460-4142** SD40-2 Diesels in UP Colors 1995+ **3.60**

**460-4339** Cabooses 1969+ **3.60**

**460-8792** Hood Unit Diesels

**460-87221** General Freight 1970-80

**460-87706** Cylindrical Covered Hoppers

**460-87733** Diesels 1969+

**460-87738** Diesel 8" Stripes Mid 1970s to Date

**460-87754** Dual Flag Scheme Diesels 1993+

**460-87844** Bathtub Gondolas 1985

**460-871052** Golden Beaver Modern Hood Unit Diesels

**460-871131** Diesel Nose Stripes 5"

**460-871152** Hood Unit Diesels 1998+

**460-871160** Passenger Car CB-01 1969-78

**460-871226** Expo '86 Diesels

### Central California Traction Company
**460-4334** SW1500 Diesels; 100th Anniversary 2005+ **3.60**

## MICROSCALE®

### ALL SETS $6.00 (UNLESS NOTED)

#### Central Of Georgia

**460-4062** Switchers 1952-69 **3.60**

**460-87382** Freight & Passenger Diesels F3A, E7A & E8A 1950-60

**460-87604** Hood Unit Diesels RS-3, GP9 & SD9 1950s

**460-871079** 40 & 50' Box Cars 1937-71

**460-871093** 2 & 3-Bay Covered Hoppers 1940-63

**460-871126** Streamlined Passenger Cars 1947-63

**460-871194** Steam Locomotives 1931-53

**460-871219** Cabooses

#### Chesapeake & Ohio

**460-4245** Piggyback Flat Cars 1959-70 **3.60**

**460-8795** C&O/Pere Marquette Berkshire Steam Locos

**460-87401** EMD & GE Hood Unit Diesels 1970

**460-87875** Diesel Road Units & Switchers 1950-60

**460-87881** Hood & Cab Unit Diesels 1957-1965

**460-871042** C&O or Pere Marquette E7A Cab Unit Diesels 1948-1955

**460-871045** Open Top Coal Hoppers w/Roman Lettering 1935-56+

#### Chessie System

**460-4257** Chessie/EMD 50th Anniversary Diesel **3.60**

**460-4325** 2,600 Cubic-Foot HC-44 Class Centerflow Covered Hopper

**460-87400** EMD & GE Diesels 1970-80

**460-87790** Chessie/WM Safety Cabooses

**460-871228** Covered Hoppers #1 - ACF & P-S Cars 1972-89

#### Chicago & North Western

**460-8751** Cab Diesels; E6 through E8 1950-60

**460-8789** Steam Locos 1930-50

**460-87290** Employee Owned & Falcon Service Slogan SD40-2 Diesels 1970-80

**460-87541** Late 1980s GE & EMD Diesels

**460-87560** F Unit Diesels 1949-75 (Use #87561 for Stripes)

**460-87561** E & F Unit Striping (Use w/#8751 or #87560) 1950s

**460-87735** Fowler 40' Wood Box Cars 1914-59

**460-87781** Operation Life Saver Diesels 1990+

**460-87845** Freight Cars w/Large Block CNW Letters 1992+

**460-87859** Lightweight Passenger Cars 1940+

**460-87928** GE AC4400CW & Dash-9 Diesels w/Operation Lifesaver Logos 1995+

**460-87962** Early Hood Unit Diesels & Switchers 1948-60

**460-87963** Early Hood Unit Diesel & Switcher Stripes 1948-60

**460-871006** 40' Slogan Box Cars 1937-58

**460-871167** Cabooses

#### Clinchfield

**460-87913** Diesels 1948-77

**460-87966** 40 & 50' Box Cars 1947-70

#### Connecticut Department of Transportation

**460-87930** Passenger Cars 1990+

**460-871196** P32AC-DM Diesels NH Scheme

#### Conrail

**460-4049** Desert Storm SD50 Diesel #6707 1991 **3.60**

**460-4255** Keep It Moving With Conrail B23-7 Diesel #1980 **3.60**

**460-87157** Hood Unit Diesels 1970-80

**460-87614** GE Painted Diesels & Labor-Management Project Nose Art 1976-92

**460-87627** EMD & CR Painted Diesels 1970-Present

**460-87628** Diesel Data & Stripes

**460-87742** 50' Coil Steel Cars 1 Each CR, CNW, IAIS, LRWN

**460-87856** Hoppers w/Quality Logos 1985+

**460-87987** Quality Diesels Repainted by CR 1995+

**460-87994** SD80MAC Diesels 1996+

**460-871034** United Way/ Savings Bonds Diesels

**460-871046** Assorted 50' Box Cars
Includes PRR and NYC reporting marks to show cars going to CSX or NS.

**460-871051** SD70MAC Hood Unit Diesels (blue, white matches SD80MACS)

#### CSX

**460-4075** Bay Window Cabooses 1991+ **3.60**

**460-4141** Maintenance of Way Locos & Cabooses 1995+ **3.60**

**460-4162** CSX Diesel Data 1990+ **3.60**

**460-4324** Diesel Names & "Spirit of..." Lettering **3.60**

**460-87497** CSX & CSX Transportation Diesels 1986

**460-87504** CSX Transportation Box Cars, Open & Covered Hoppers & Gondola 1986

**460-87575** Diesels (blue, gray & yellow) 1990

See What's Available at
**www.walthers.com**

**460-87915** GE Wide Cab Dash 8/9 & AC Units 1990+

**460-87988** Freight Car Data 1985+

**460-871180** Diesels (dark blue scheme) 2002+

**460-871181** Diesels

#### Delaware & Hudson - D&H

**460-4385** 40' Box Car **3.60**

#### Rio Grande - Denver & Rio Grande Western

**460-4083** GP60 Diesels 1991+ **3.60**

**460-4311** Mini-Cal 40' Hi-Cube Box Car 1967+ **3.60**

**460-4405** Mini-Cal Airslide Covered Hoppers 1960+ **3.60**

**460-8728** Diesels-Large & Small Lettering 1960-80

**460-8796** Early Hood Unit Diesels (black & yellow)

**460-87108** California Zephyr Passenger Cars 1950-70

**460-87199** Cabooses (orange) 1970-80

**460-87271** Stripes for EMD Hood Unit Diesels 1960-80

**460-871128** Hood Unit Diesels & Switcher 1962-84

**460-871213** Box Cars - 50' Wood Packer, 50' Hi-Cube, 51' PC&F RBL

#### Detroit, Toledo & Ironton

**460-4041** 70-Ton, 14-Panel Triple Bay Hopper **3.60**

**460-4268** 50' Outside-Post Railbox Box Car 1973+ **3.60**

**460-4303** Diesels (orange & black) w/Compass Herald 1962-77 **3.60**

**460-4304** Diesels 1977-80 **3.60**

**460-4305** Diesels 1980-83 **3.60**

**460-4329** Bicentennial GP38-2 1975-80 **3.60**

#### Duluth, Missabe & Iron Range - DMIR

**NEW 460-871269** Hood Diesels w/Gopher Style Lettering

#### Elgin, Joliet & Eastern - EJ&E

**460-871259** EMD SD38-2 #668 Bicentennial Scheme - 1976

**460-4326** BL-20-2 Demonstrator Unit **3.60**

#### Erie

**460-8791** Steam Locos 1930-50

**460-87360** F Unit Diesels 1940-60

**460-87876** Road Units & Switchers 1945-1960

#### Erie Lackawanna

**460-8716** Diesels (maroon & yellow lettering) 1960-70

**460-87573** Stripes for E, F & PA 1960-75

#### Family Lines

**460-87397** EMD & GE Diesels 1970s

**460-87399** F Units & Switchers 1970

#### Florida East Coast

**460-4244** Ortner Hopper Cars 1996+ **3.60**

**460-87556** Hood Unit Diesels 1980s

**460-871157** ex-UP SD40-2 Diesels 2002+

**460-871158** Diesels (blue) 2002+

#### Frisco - St. Louis San Francisco

**460-8785** Cab Unit Diesels & Cabooses 1960-70

**460-87115** Diesels 1970-80

**460-87137** Modern 50 to 86' Box Cars (yellow) 1970

**460-87149** 40-50' Box Cars (black & white) "Ship It On The Frisco!" 1970-80

**460-87455** EMD E Unit Diesels 1950-60

#### Fruit Growers Express

**460-4022** Real Cold 57' Mechanical Reefers 1986 **3.60**

**460-87238** Mechanical Reefers; For Greater Efficiency, N&W Herald

**460-87450** 50' Insulated Box Cars & 57' Mechanical Reefers Solid Cold/Gold & The Chiller Slogans

#### Gateway Western/ Gateway Eastern

**460-4008** Gateway Western Operation Lifesaver & Gateway Eastern Diesels 1993+ **3.30**

#### GATX-General American

**460-4058** Capital Corp. Ex-UP SD40-2 Diesels 1991 **3.60**

**460-4076** 63 & 66' Liquid Petroleum Gas Tank Cars 1990 **3.60**

**460-4146** Lamb Weston Cryogenic Box Cars, Arcticar, 1995+ **3.60**

**460-87413** Tank Train 50' Tank Cars (black w/white lettering) 1980

**460-87736** 50' Tank Cars 1970

**460-87770** Covered Hoppers; 50' Airslide®, 4-Bay ACF 1970+

#### General Electric

**460-4056** Builders Plates - US & Canadian **3.60**

**460-4129** Number Boards 1960+ **3.60**

**460-4237** GECX AC4400-CW Diesels 1997+ **3.60**

**460-87532** GECX Leasing Dash 8-40B 1987

#### Golden West Service

**460-87658** Freight Cars 1990

**460-87693** 62' Bulkhead Flat, Ballast Hopper, 89' Flat Car, 60' Woodchip Car 1992

**460-87694** 57' Mechanical & 60' Cryogenic Reefers 1992

#### Grand Trunk Western

**460-4350** Mini-Cal 50' Box Cars **3.60**

**460-87103** Cab & Hood Unit Diesels 1950-60

**460-87366** F3 Diesels 1940-50

**460-87650** Late Diesels (large GT Herald)

#### Great Northern

**460-4014** Passenger-Script Lettering for E7 Diesels 1950 **3.60**

**460-8786** Switchers 1940-60

**460-87153** "Empire Builder" Passenger Cars 1950-60

**460-87154** Passenger Car Gold & Silver Stripes 1950-60

**460-87185** 40' Single-Door Box Car 1950-60

**460-87284** Hood & Cab Unit Diesels (Big Sky Blue) 1970

**460-87285** SD45-Hustle Muscle, RCU Cars & Cabooses (Big Sky Blue) 1970

**460-87926** 40' Glacier Green Box Cars 1961-1967

**460-871261** Steam Locos - Silver & White Lettering

#### Gulf, Mobile & Ohio

**460-4359** Cabooses Red & White Scheme 1966-72 **3.60**

**460-8743** Hood & Cab Unit Diesels 1960-70

**460-87365** GP30 & GP35 Diesels 1960-70

#### Illinois Central

**460-4210** Operation Lifesaver Diesels 1993+ **3.60**

**460-8727** Diesels (white & orange) & Cabooses (black & orange) 1970

**460-87528** Diesels Black w/White Lettering & Deathstar Herald 1988

**460-87655** Diesel & Passenger Car Stripes 1980+

#### Illinois Central Gulf

**460-8742** Hood Unit Diesels & Cabooses (orange & white) 1970

**460-87402** Modern Hood Unit & Diesel Switchers (gray & orange) 1980

#### Intermodal Equipment

**460-4095** APC Thrall Double-Stack Cars (Use w/#87788) 1986+ **3.60**

**460-4096** APL Thrall Double-Stack Cars (Use w/#87788) 1986+ **3.60**

**460-4286** Strick Lease 48' Trailers & Railtrailer **3.60**

**460-4341** American President Lines 53' Containers **3.60**

**460-4405** Mini-Cal Wan Hai Lines Ltd. 40' Container **3.60**

**460-4410** North American Container Systems (NACS) 53' Containers **3.60**

**460-4411** North American Container Systems (NACS) Extra Container Logos **3.60**

**460-87487** American President Lines 40 & 45' Containers & Chassis

**460-871249** STAX 53' Domestic Containers

#### Kansas City Southern

**460-4364** Diesel Handrail Stripes **3.60**

**460-87138** E & F Unit Diesels 1950-60

**460-87148** Switchers 1950-60

# MICROSCALE®

## ALL SETS $6.00 (UNLESS NOTED)

**460-87430** SD40-2 & GP7 Diesels 1950-80

**460-87550** Diesels (gray) 1989

**460-87656** Freight Cars 1970s

**460-87942** Diesels with Cab Side Logo (gray) 1995+

**460-871100** GE AC4400CW Diesels 1999+

**460-871104** "NAFTA" EMD SD50 & GE AC4400CW Diesels; Enclosed Autoracks 1998+

### Lease Fleet Diesels

**460-4154** LMS (Lease Management Services) 8-40CW 1994+ **3.60**

**460-87520** GE Leasing LMX B39-8 1988

**460-87601** Capital Corporation (GATX) Diesels 1990

**460-871250** Loco Leasing Partners - LLPX Diesel Hoods & Switchers 2000+

### Lehigh Valley

**460-4098** Pre-War Switchers 1937-45 **3.60**

**460-87775** Diesels (Cornell Red & black stripe) 1940-60

**460-87776** Diesel Stripes (Cornell Red & black) 1940-60

**460-87855** Late Cornell Red GP38, GP38-2, U-23B Diesels 1970-76

**460-87880** Alco C-420 & C-628 Diesels As-Delivered 1964-76

**460-87922** Cabooses 1932-80

**460-87995** Diesels (Tuscan Red w/White Flag) 1966-72

### Logging Lines

**460-878** LK&L, Coos Bay, Long Bell, Pickering Lumber, Weyerhauser, St. Regis 1930-50

### Louisville & Nashville

**460-4105** Cabooses 1963-80 **3.60**

**460-4387** 40' Box Car **3.60**

**460-8761** E & F Unit Diesels (tan & orange stripes) 1950-60

**460-87824** Diesel Stripes (gray & yellow) 1963-70

**460-87917** Diesels, (solid blue or black) 1958-62

**460-4404** Diesel GP30 1962+ **3.60**

### Metrolink

**460-4089** Metrolink Diesels & Passenger Cars 1992+ **3.60**

### Metro-North

**460-4151** Metro North Commuter Railroad Diesels 1985+ **3.60**

**460-87929** Commuter Passenger Cars 1990+

**460-871195** Diesel P32AC-DM 1997+

### Milwaukee Road

**460-8753** E & F Unit Diesels 1953-60

**460-87441** Diesels New Hiawatha Scheme 1980

**460-87514** 50' Box Cars 1970s

**460-87789** Diesels (orange & black) 1960-87

**460-871113** Diesel SD40-2 Bicentennial

### Missouri Pacific

**460-4091** Cabooses 1979-90 **3.60**

**460-4377** Mini-Cal Bicentennial GP9/18 Diesels 1976+ **3.60**

**460-8774** Hood Unit Diesels (dark blue w/Eagle) 1960-70

**460-87113** EMD & GE Diesels w/Buzzsaw & Eagle Heralds 1970-80

**460-87442** Diesels UP North Little Rock Lettering 1980

**460-8711070** Steam Locomotives w/Silver Lettering 1930-50

**460-871222** Box Cars

### Missouri-Kansas-Texas Katy

**460-87180** Diesel Numbers & Letters (green & yellow) 1970-80

**460-87181** Diesel Stripes (green & yellow) 1970-80

**460-87277** Diesel Numbers & Letters (red & white) 1950-80

**460-87278** Diesel Heralds & Stripes (red & white) 1950-80

**460-87446** Freight Cars 1970-80

**460-87479** General Freight; 50' Box Car, 2-Bay Covered Hopper, 50' Flat Car 1960-70

**460-871124** Airslide Covered Hoppers

### Montana Rail Link

**NEW 460-4406** Remote Receiver Caboose **3.60**

**460-87544** Diesels 1988

**460-87600** ACF Centerflow & Pullman-Standard Hopper, 52' Gondola 1987

**460-87605** 50' Box Cars 1988+

**460-87606** Cabooses & Freight Cars #2 1988

**460-87954** Diesels w/New Image Lions Head Logo 1996+

### New Haven - New York, New Haven & Hartford

**460-8768** Diesels; McGinnis & Alpert Schemes 1954-68

**460-87207** Passenger Cars 1950-60

**460-87666** EF-4 Electrics

**460-87864** Steam Locos 1900-55

**460-87937** Cab Diesels 1954-68

**460-871001** Hood Unit Diesels (green & orange) 1947-55

**460-871062** Electric Locos w/Green & Yellow Scheme 1947-65

**460-871199** Caboose & MOW 1929-68

### National Railway Equipment - NREX

**460-871266** Lease Diesel Locos (Ex- BNSF, CP, SP, UP etc.)

### National Railways of Mexico NdeM

**460-4337** Box Cars **3.60**

### New York Central

**460-4004** Diesel Switchers Alco, Baldwin & EMD 1950 **3.60**

**460-4186** 50' Mather Stock Cars 1963-70 **3.60**

**460-8749** Cab Unit Diesels Red Herald, Gray Stripes 1950-60

**460-8758** 40 & 50' Jade Green Box Cars 1960-68

**460-8778** Steam Locos-Medium 1930-50

**460-8788** Single Stripe Cab Unit Diesels 1960

**460-87618** Lightning Stripes for Hood Unit Diesels 1950s

**460-871248** Flexi-Van Flats & Containers

### Norfolk & Western

**460-8722** Hood Unit Diesels (blue or black) 1950-70

**460-87106** Steam Locos 1930-80

**460-87554** Hood Unit Diesels & Switchers 1982

**460-87728** Auto Racks 1980+

### Norfolk Southern

**460-4147** Southern Railway 100th Anniversary GP59 Diesel #4610 1994+ **3.60**

**460-4392** GP59 #4611 w/Transcaer Logo 2000+ **3.60**

**460-87435** Thoroughbred for GE & EMD Diesels 1984

**460-87591** Covered Hoppers, Coil Steel Car 1988+

**460-87945** GE Dash-8/9 Diesels 1984+

**460-871182** Diesel Numbers & Patches for Ex-CR Locos

**460-871225** Diesels 2002+

### Northern Pacific

**460-8737** 40, 50 & 60' Box Cars, Large Billboard, NP & Monad 1958-70

**460-8746** Freight Cab Unit Diesels 1950-70

**460-87118** Steam Locos 1920-50

**460-87584** Stripes for Freight F Unit Diesels 1950

**460-87787** Stripes for Two-Tone Green Passenger Cars 1946-54

### New York, Susquehanna & Western

**460-4195** SD70M Diesels 1996+ **3.60**

**460-87531** Diesels 1988

### Pacific Electric

**460-87563** Trolleys 1911-47

**460-87564** Car Stripes 1911-47

**460-87589** Freight Motors 1903-65

### Penn Central

**460-8784** Cab & Hood Unit Diesels

**460-871094** Box Cars w/PRR-Style Car Numbers 1968-76

**460-871096** Box Cars w/PC-Style Lettering 1968-76

**NEW 460-871097** 86' Hi-Cube Box Cars **6.00**

**460-871098** Box Car Esoterica - TOC, P&E Lettering, Black & Multicolor PC Logos

### Pennsylvania

**460-8721** Hood Unit Diesels (Tuscan Red & Dulux Gold or white) 1960-70

**460-8739** 5-Stripe E, F, PA, PB Diesels & GG1 Electrics 1950-60

**460-8766** Steam Locos

**460-87677** 5-Stripe Gold Leaf Scheme Locos 1939-52

**460-87810** Single Stripe E Unit Diesels 1953-68

**460-87891** Tuscan Red Passenger Cars 1947-68

**460-87892** Stripes for Tuscan Red Passenger Cars 1947-68

**460-871141** Heavyweight Passenger Cars 1912-45

**460-871200** 40' Box Cars Classes X26A, X26C, X28A, X29, X29A, X29B 1954-60

**460-871210** Cabin Cars (Cabooses) 1927-68

**460-871262** Class F30 (F30a, D & E) Flat Cars

### Pittsburgh & Lake Erie

**460-871227** Diesels

### Private Owner Cars

**460-4124** Minnesota Corn Processors 40 & 50' Tank Cars 1994+ **3.60**

**460-4298** Mini-Cal New Orleans Public Belt 50' Outside Post Per Diem Box Car 1977+ **3.60**

**460-4310** Evergreen Freight Car Corp 50' Insulated Box Cars 1966-79 **3.60**

**460-4312** Minnesota Soybean Processors 5,461 Cubic Foot Covered Hoppers 2004+ **3.60**

**460-4313** Farmland 5,161 Cubic Foot Covered Hoppers 1996+ **3.60**

**460-4370** ADM Corporation Tank Cars (new logo) **3.60**

**460-87660** ACF Covered Hoppers; Private Owners (gray & aluminum) 1939-70

**460-87727** Corn Products; 40' Tank Car, 4-Bay ACF Hopper

### Pullman Company

**460-871220** Heavyweight Passenger Cars w/Dulux Lettering

**460-871221** Heavyweight Passenger Cars w/Gold Lettering

### Railbox

**460-4173** Repainted 50' Box Cars 1992+ **3.60**

**460-87160** 50' Outside-Braced Single-Door Box Cars

**460-87316** 50' Plug & Single Door Box Car, Rail Gon 52' Gondola 1970-80

### Reflective Conspicuity Markings 2005+ (Reflector Stripes) 3.60 ea

Now being applied to new and older equipment; mounted vertically on tank cars, horizontally or vertically on all other types of cars and locos.

**460-4389** Yellow

**460-4390** White

### Rock - Rock Island-Chicago, Rock Island & Pacific

**460-8718** Hood & Cab Unit Diesels 1960-70

**460-8719** Freight Cars-Block Lettering 1960-70

**460-8720** Freight Cars-Speed Lettering 1960-70

**460-87230** ROCK Hood Unit Diesels 1970

**460-87956** E & F Unit Diesels Rocket Scheme 1943-60

**460-87989** GP7 & RS-3 Diesels Rocket Scheme 1950-60

**460-871041** GP7/9 Diesels THE ROCK w/Names 1975-80

**460-871229** Cabooses Part I; Wood & Early Steel

**460-871230** Cabooses Part II; Late Steel & Transfer Cars

### Santa Fe - Atchison, Topeka & Santa Fe

**460-4346** Mini Cal ACF Centerflow Hoppers **3.60**

**460-4401** Cabooses 1910-71 **3.60**

**460-8729** Freight Diesels (blue & yellow) Warbonnet 1972

**460-8730** Freight Cars w/Large Round Herald (black & white lettering) 1972

**460-8764** Steam Locos-Silver Lettering 1930-50

**460-8772** Passenger Warbonnet E3, E6, PA-1 & PB-1 Diesels 1946-69

**460-8777** Early Freight F Units 1940-70

**460-87101** Warbonnet Passenger Diesels 1950-70

**460-87114** Super Chief Passenger Cars 1946-72

**460-87248** Zebra Stripes for Hood Unit Diesels (silver) 1950-60

**460-87383** Heavyweight Passenger Cars 1920-50

**460-87444** 4-Bay Cylindrical & 3-Bay Covered Hoppers 1970

**460-87483** Bicentennial SD45-2 Diesel 1976

**460-87506** 40 & 50' Damage Free Box Cars Texas Chief, Chief, Ship & Travel ATSF All the Way & Grand Canyon Line (white) 1947-59

**460-87516** 40' Box Cars w/Curved Line Map 1940

**460-87517** 40' Ice Reefers w/Curved Line Map 1930-40

**460-87663** Valley Flyer Steam Loco Stripes 1938-40s

**460-87699** F Unit Cat Whiskers Scheme 1940-52

## MICROSCALE®

**ALL SETS $6.00 (UNLESS NOTED)**

**460-87772** Thrall 5-Unit Articulated Double-Stack Cars 1989+

**460-87791** Quality Covered Hoppers 1990+

**460-87906** SD75M Diesels 1995+

**460-87914** Late Cabooses, Ce-1 to Ce-13 1979+

**460-91154** Zebra Stripes (Silver)

**460-871072** Early E3-E6 A&B Passenger Diesels 1939-68 (Fits Life-Like Proto 2000 Engines, Sold Separately)

**460-871161** Hood Unit Diesels & Switchers w/White Zebra Stripes, Black & Silver Logos 1934-60

**460-871164** Steam Locos 1930-50 (white lettering)

**460-871254** SK Class Stock Cars; Sk-Q, R, S, T, U, Z, 2, 3, 4, & 5

**460-871264** 100-Ton Ga-176, -189, -195 & -203 Class Coal Hoppers 1969-95

**460-871265** 40' Ice Reefer Car Numbers for Ends, Roof & Ice Hatches

### SPSF Proposed Merger

(Merger denied July, 1986 by the ICC.)

**460-4273** SPSF Cabooses 1986+ **3.60**

**460-87469** Premerger Experimental Scheme w/Large SP or ATSF Lettering 1985

**460-87475** Merger Warbonnet Yellow Outlines for ATSF Blue/ Yellow Diesels

**460-87476** Merger Warbonnet Red Outlines for SPSF Red/ Yellow Diesels

**460-87496** Premerger Diesels (red, yellow Kodachromes) w/Large SP or SF 1986

### Seaboard Air Line

**460-4013** Passenger EMD E7 Diesels 1950 **3.60**

**460-87151** Cabooses 1950-60

**460-87439** EMD E Unit Diesels 1950-60

**460-87565** Switchers & Diesel Freight Units 1950s

**460-87566** Freight Diesel Stripes 1950s

### Seaboard Coast Line

**460-8706** Freight Cars 1960-70

**460-87896** Diesels 1967-72

### Seaboard System

**460-87398** EMD & GE Diesels 1980

### Shortlines

**460-4287** Central California Traction Co. GP7, GP18 Diesel or Caboose 1976+ **3.60**

**460-4295** Arcata & Mad River 50' Double-Door Box Car 1978+ **3.60**

**460-87825** Arizona & California/California Northern Diesels 1992+

**460-871189** Durham & Southern - Diesel Hood Units

**460-MC4365** Chattahoochee Industrial Railway 50' Box Cars **3.60**

### Soo Line

**460-87117** Diesels (red, white) 1962-89

**460-87119** Diesel Switchers (black, Dulux Gold) 1954-61

**460-87553** Diesels (Candy Apple Red) 1989

**460-871116** 50' Box Car Colormark Variations 1974-86

**460-871136** Steam Locos 1920-55

**460-871215** Cabooses

### Southern Pacific

**460-4298** 89' Enclosed Autoracks w/Speed Lettering 1991-96 **3.60**

**460-4381** Overnight Box Car Number Set **3.60**

**460-4382** Speed Lettering for GP38-2 Diesels **3.60**

**460-4388** 40' Box Car **3.60**

**460-4400** Diesels w/ Sans-Serif Lettering 1958+ **3.60**

Add AT F – under Southern Pacific

**NEW 460-4407** "Research & Tests" Instrument Car **3.60**

**460-8733** Steam Locos-Daylight, Sunbeam & San Joaquin 1940-50

**460-8734** Passenger Cars Daylight, Sun Beam & San Joaquin SP Lines 1940-60

**460-8750** Daylight Diesels; PA, PB, E7, E8A & B & FP7 1950-60

**460-8765** Medium Steam Locos 1920-50

**460-8771** Tiger Stripe Switchers 1950-60

**460-8775** Heavy Steam Locos 1940-50

**460-87178** Letterboard Striping for Sunset Limited Passenger Cars 1960-80

**460-87201** Black Widow E, F, GP9, SD9 & Trainmaster Diesels 1950-60

**460-87227** Cabooses 1940-80

**460-87239** Covered Hoppers

**460-87262** Daylight Passenger Car Stripes

**460-87390** Two-Tone Gray Passenger Car Stripes 1940+

**460-87447** Diesels Red Wings Scheme (use with #87612) 1980

**460-87464** SD40 Diesel & 45' Trailers in Olympic Schemes 1980s

**460-87472** 4-Pack Intermodal Flat Cars 1980

**460-87529** 57' Mechanical Reefers w/8 Different Colored Heralds 1980s

**460-87611** Police Cabooses & Passenger Cars 1985

**460-87612** Diesel Road Names & Numbers (red, use with #87447) 1989

**460-87617** Red Wings for Atlas, Athearn, Con-Cor & Rail Power Model Diesels 1950s

**460-87620** Speed Lettering Merger Scheme-Rebuilt GP40s 1991

**460-87646** GP60 Diesels w/Speed Lettering 1991+

**460-87835** Bicentennial Diesels & Caboose 1975-80

**460-87857** Speed Lettering for SD70, Dash 9-44CW & Switchers 1994

**460-87911** Single-Sheathed Wood Box Cars Classes B-50-13, B-50-14, 1923-62

**460-871148** Bridges 1959+

**460-871165** Heavyweight Passenger Cars w/Dulux Gold Lettering 1920-50

**460-871212** 50' Box Cars SP/SSW 1968+

**460-871213** 100-Ton Open Hoppers

**460-871251** 86' Hi-Cube Auto Parts Box Cars; Classes B-100-19, 1968-96

**460-871252** 86' Hi-Cube Auto Parts Box Cars w/Gray Striping & Arrows 1968-96

**460-871253** ACF 4,650 Cubic-Foot Centerflow Covered Hoppers 1966-96

**460-871260** Diesel Hood Numbers (Lettering Gray)

### Southern Railway

**460-4084** Bay Window Cabooses 1960-90 **3.60**

**460-4196** Coil Steel Car 1974-85 **3.60**

**460-8714** Freight Cars; Green Light, White Lettering, DF Logos 1960-70

**460-8732** Hood Unit Diesels, Southern, Interstate, Savannah & Atlanta, Central of Georgia 1950-70

**460-87878** Early Hood Unit Diesels & Switchers, (green) 1940-60

**460-87879** Early Cab Units (green) 1940-60

### Southern Railway of British Columbia

**NEW 460-871257** EMD MP15 & SD38 Diesels

### Spokane, Portland & Seattle

**460-4016** EMD or Alco Cab Unit Diesels 1950 **3.60**

**460-4345** 40' Box Cars **3.60**

**460-87102** E, F & FA Diesels 1950-70

**460-87195** Hood Unit Diesels (yellow & green) 1960-70

**460-87196** Diesel Switchers (black) 1950-60

**460-871026** 40 & 50' Steel Box Cars 1946-68

### SRY Rail Link

**460-871258** Diesel Hood Units & Switchers

### Texas Mexican

**460-4373** Hood Diesels 1950-98 **3.60**

### Texas & Pacific

**460-4088** Diesel Switchers (orange & black) 1950-62 **3.60**

**460-87452** Cab Unit Diesels

**460-87764** Early Hood Unit Diesels 1950-62

### Toledo, Peoria & Western

**460-87129** Hood Unit Diesels 1950-70

**460-87648** Diesels 1991

**460-871064** Hood Diesels Orange & White Scheme 1969-83

### Trailer Train - TTX

**NEW 460-4386** NTTX Container Spine Cars **3.60**

**460-87552** 50, 60, 68, 85 & 89' Flat Cars (Box Car Red)

**460-87579** 89' & Long Runner Flat Cars (yellow)

**460-87670** Trailer Train/TTX Husky Stack Container Cars 1991+

**460-87747** TTX Long Runner Flat Cars (2 89' Cars) 1990+

**460-87788** Trailer Train/TTX Thrall 5-Unit Articulated Double-Stack Car 1989+

**460-87792** TTX Gunderson Maxi III 5-Unit Articulated Double-Stack Cars 1992+

**460-87822** Trailer Train/TTX 48 & 53' All-Purpose Spine Cars 1990+

**460-87839** TTX Twin Stack 5-Unit Articulated Double-Stack Cars 1993+

### Turtle Creek Central

**460-5001** Mini-Cal Freight Cars **3.60**

### Union Pacific

**460-4077** 57' Mechanical Reefers Late 1980s **3.60**

**460-4328** Patch Renumbered Diesels (Ex-CNW, DRGW, SP, SSW Units w/New Road Numbers on Paint Patches) 2000+ **3.60**

**460-4402** Reefer Chilled Express 2002+ **3.60**

**460-4403** 57' Reefer Building America Logo 2002+ **3.60**

**460-8735** Diesels & Turbine (gray & yellow) 1960-80

**460-8763** Steam Locos-White, Yellow or Silver Lettering 1930-80 **9.85**

**460-87109** Passenger E & F Unit Diesels 1950-80

**460-87265** 100-Ton Grain Hoppers 1960-80

**460-87354** Hood Unit Diesels 1970-80

**460-87522** Diesels w/North Little Rock Style Lettering 1987

**460-87616** Passenger Cars 1947-89 (Stripes in #871105)

**460-87851** United Way Campaign SD40-2 Diesel 1994

**460-87905** Early Cabooses CA-1 to -9 (red or yellow) 1941-77

**460-87997** SD90MAC Diesels 1996+

**460-871084** Head End Pasenger Cars w/Green Scheme 1939-47

**460-871085** Chair Cars & Coaches - Gold Lettering (1920-1938)

**460-871087** Diner, Lounge & Observation Cars - Gold Lettering 1920-38)

**460-871090** Pullman Assigned Sleepers #1 w/Dulux Lettering 1938+

**460-871092** Pullman Assigned Sleepers #2 w/Dulux Lettering 1938+

**460-871102** UPY Diesel Yard Switchers; SW1500, MP15, SD38-2 & GP15 2000+

**460-871125** Diesels w/Smaller Winged Shield 2001+

**460-871145** SD70M Building America 2001+

**460-871147** Dash 9-44CW/ AC4400CW 2000+

**460-871150** Building America Diesels 2002+

### VIA Rail Canada

**460-87667** Diesels 1979-92

**460-87672** Passenger Cars 1990+

**460-87673** Passenger Car Stripes 1990+

**460-871153** P42 Diesels 2002-

### Western Maryland

**460-87130** Hood Unit Diesels 1950-70

**460-87700** Cabooses 1936-80

**460-871005** Hood & Cab Unit Diesels Fireball Scheme 1947-54

### Western Pacific

**460-4266** 50' Single-Sheathed Automobile Service Box Cars-Original White Lettering **3.60**

**460-4274** Bicentennial GP40 Diesel **3.60**

**460-4349** 50' Box Cars w/Metric Data **3.60**

**460-8726** Silver & Orange Hood & Cab Unit Diesels (Sacramento Northern) 1950-70

**460-87187** Green Diesels (Sacramento Northern, Tidewater Southern) 1970

**460-87272** Freight Cars-New Image 1980

**460-87274** Hood Unit Diesels (Sacramento Northern)-New Image 1970-80

**460-87445** Merger Cabooses (UP red lettering) 1980

**460-871151** Heavyweight Passenger Cars 1910+

**460-871240** 89' Piggyback Flats (Includes DRGW and KCS Re-Stencil)

# MICROSCALE®

## ALL SETS $6.00 (UNLESS NOTED)

### Wisconsin Central
**460-4102** Model Railroader 60th Anniversary 50' Box Car 1993 **3.60**
**460-4409** 50' Berwick Forge Box Cars **3.60**
**460-87534** Diesel Stripes-30" Wide (yellow) 1988+
**460-87546** Box Cars 1989+
**460-87547** Hoppers & Gondolas 1989
**460-87712** GP40 Diesels 1991 New Paint Scheme
**460-87921** F45 Diesels 1995+

### Yreka Western
**460-4294** Mini-Cal 50' Box Cars **3.60**

## MULTIPLE FREIGHT CAR SETS

### 6.00 ea (Unless Noted)
Sets include lettering for various individual cars.

### Airslide® Hoppers
**40' Cars**
**460-87417** UP, NP, GN
**460-87419** Atlantic Coast Line, SOU, SP, Chicago Great Western
**460-87749** Domino Sugar, Bay State Milling, Golden Loaf Flour
**50' Cars**
**460-87515** BN, CNW, DRGW
**460-87503** ATSF, SP & SSW
**460-87507** UP, WP, MP

### Auto Racks
**460-87692** MILW, SOO, CNW
**460-87709** CR & Waterloo (WLO)

### Box Cars
**460-8738** SSW 50' Double-Door, PRR, L&N, CPR, D&H 40' Single Door
**460-87217** 50' Outside-Braced Rahway Valley, St. Lawrence, Western Erie, Railbox
**460-87303** Family Lines, Sandersville, V&S
**460-87321** 50' UP & Providence & Worchester

### 62' Bulkhead Centerbeam Flat Cars
**460-87339** Trailer Train, CP Rail, CR

### Covered Hoppers
**460-4296** Wonder Bread/ Hostess Special US Bicentennial Scheme ACF 4-Bay Covered Hopper 1974+ **3.60**

### Reefers
**460-87418** 57' Mechanical SOO, Bangor & Aroostook & 50' Maine Central

## SIGNS

### 6.00 ea (Unless Noted)

### American Flags
**460-4201** 48 Star 1912-59 **3.60**
**460-4202** 50 Star 1960+ **3.60**

### Canadian Flags
**460-4372** 1965+ 2.50 **3.60**

### Canadian Grain Elevators
**460-87866** Alberta 1980+
**460-87870** Saskatchewan 1985+
**460-87898** Manitoba 1980+

### City Building Signs
**460-87275** Streets & Buildings
**460-87848** Set #1 1960+
**460-87982** Diners #1 1950+
**460-87983** Diners #2 1950+
**460-871049** Commercial Buildings/Stores Late 1950s - Mid 1960s

### Farm Community
**460-87163** Small Towns
**460-87166** Rural Towns 1800-1920
**460-87795** #1 Grain Elevators, Feed Stores 1960
**460-87811** #2 Grain Elevators, Feed Stores 1960+

### Gas Stations
**460-87853** Detail Signs 1945+
**460-87902** Gulf 1936-63
**460-87938** Mobil 1940-66
**460-87959** Esso 1946-65
**460-87969** Sinclair 1935-60
**460-87993** Shell 1935-60
**460-871002** Ashland & Pepper 1924-60
**460-871017** Atlantic Refining Co. 1935-60

### Industrial Signs
**460-87165** Town & City Industry Signs
**460-87273** Set #1
**460-87289** Set #2
**460-87924** Industrial Safety and Warning Signs 1985+
**460-87941** Superior & Suburban Propane 1985+

### Packing House/Cold Storage
**460-87771** Sunkist Packing House 1955+
**460-87806** #1 1970+
**460-87807** #2 1970+
**NEW 460-871268** Sunkist, Pure Gold, Mutual Citrus (2 Sheet set)

### Railroad Signs
**460-87206** Right-Of-Way Crossing, Warnings, etc. (black) **6.00**
**460-871162** Right-of-Way, Black Lettering w/Clear Background; Yard Limit, No Clearance & More

### Western Town Signs
**460-87162** Cowtowns
**460-87164** Town Signs

### 20th-Century Signs
**460-87197** 1900-1930
**460-87198** Mid Century

### 1930s & 40s Signs
**460-87287** 1930s Window Signs
**460-87420** Commercial Signs
**460-87421** Commercial Signs
**460-87422** Commercial Signs

## TRUCK & VEHICLE SETS

### 6.00 ea (Unless Noted)

### Semi Trailers
**460-4331** Mini Cal 48' Or 53' Trailer & Tractor (1996+) **3.60**
**460-8705** 40' SCL, REA, DRGW, WM, Monon, EL, PC, L&N, MP
**460-87276** 40' IC, Family Lines, CNW
**460-87292** 40' Crab, Orchard & Egyptian, Texas Mexican, BN
**460-87308** 40' Chief, Chessie, NYC & SOU

### Trucking Companies
**460-4330** Roads West 53' Trailer & Tractor 1997+ **3.60**
**460-4051** J.B. Hunt 48' Trailers & Tractor **3.60**
**460-87769** J.B. Hunt 48 & 53' Containers & Chassis 1993+
**460-87873** Tractor Striping and May Trucking Tractors 1989+
**460-87508** 45' CSX, Seaboard System, US Mail & XTRA

### Vehicle Markings
**460-4122** Red & White Trailer Safety Striping 1993+ **3.60**
**460-87281** Custom Truck Tractor Schemes - Owner/ Operators **6.00**

## CUSTOM DECAL SYSTEM

**704-9198 9.25**
The Custom Decal System allows you to electronically download a series of custom art images and turn them into decals that can be printed on your own computer. Designed for use with any laser and/or inkjet printer, each set includes special water-soluble decaling film, spray decal bonder, a series of custom graphics, and complete instructions.

### Decal Bonder Refill Spray
**704-9200** 3oz **4.59**
Apply a few mist coats of Decal Bonder to seal any decal. Also works well for refreshing older decals that have begun showing signs of decay.

### Decal Paper pkg(6) 9.99 ea
Each sheet measures 5-1/2 x 8-1/2".

**704-9201** Clear
**704-9202** White
**704-9203** Assortment Includes three each clear and white.

# Information STATION

### Decals for Realism

While decals are great for lettering railroad equipment and vehicles, they have plenty of other uses that can add realism to your layout.

Because decals are printed on transparent film, they're great for dressing up windows on your structures. Several manufacturers make business sign decals or dry transfers. The dry transfers can be applied to decal film for easier application into tight spaces, especially where a burnishing tool won't fit. If there aren't any signs available that fit your scene, don't worry; signs, banners, and even simulated stained glass can be printed on blank decal film.

Decals are also great for use on vehicle windows to imply a detailed interior or for adding stickers and windshield wiper marks on the surface. On structures or scenery, you can use decals when you're trying to recreate a surface that's difficult to match. Just scan in a photo of the prototype on your computer, scale it to fit your model, print it onto decal film and apply it. This is especially good for one-time uses on structures such as numbers or logos engraved in stone or concrete, or unique plaques.

Railflyer Model Prototypes Inc.

## NEW PRODUCTS

Transform your collection of modern equipment with these decal sets based on North American prototypes. Each is carefully researched and accurately reproduced in an exact to scale format. All markings are contained within the decal set and many options are included for additional road numbers or paint scheme variations. All sets are printed for the highest quality possible using the waterslide and screen-printing technology.

### Railroad Decals

**11.49 ea (Unless Noted)**

#### New Brunswick Southern Railway

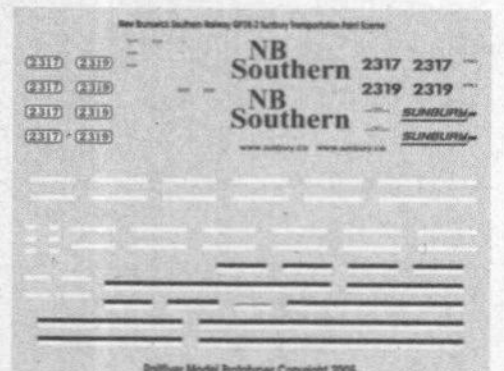


**NEW 631-11** GP38-2 #2317 or #2319 (2003) **8.99**
In 2003, the New Brunswick Southern Railway painted two units to inaugurate a new intermodal service offered by the NBSR and Sunbury Transportation. Both units can be found throughout southern New Brunswick and Northern Maine.

#### Chicago, Fort Wayne & Eastern

**NEW 631-21** GP38-2 Diesels 2004+ **8.99**
Began operations in 2004 as part of the Rail America network, with ten former CNW engines purchased from National Railway Equipment.

#### Algoma Central Railway

**NEW 631-22** 1st Generation Locos

**NEW 631-23** 2nd Generation Locos

#### British Columbia Railway

**NEW 631-24** SD40-2 Early Lightning Scheme

**NEW 631-25** SD40-2 Late

#### Canadian National Railway

**NEW 631-26** GP38-2/GP38-2W/GP40-2W

**NEW 631-27** SD38-2/SD40-2/SD40-2W

**NEW 631-28** SD50F/SD50AF/SD60F

**NEW 631-29** SD70I/SD75I/SD70M-2

**NEW 631-30** C40-8M/C44-9WL

#### Canadian Pacific Railway

**NEW 631-80** GP38-2

**NEW 631-81** GP38-2 Heritage

**NEW 631-82** SD40/SD40-2 Heritage

**NEW 631-83** SD40/SD40-2 Early

**NEW 631-84** SD40-2 Mid

**NEW 631-85** SD40-2 Dual Flags

**NEW 631-86** SD40-2 Late

#### Guilford (Pam Am Railways)

**NEW 631-90** 2nd Generation Locos

#### New Brunswick East Coast Railway

**NEW 631-91** Alco Locos

**NEW 631-92** SD40 Locos

#### Ontario Northland Railway

**NEW 631-93** 2nd Generation Locos Early

**NEW 631-94** 2nd Generation Locos Mid

**NEW 631-94** 2nd Generations Locos Late GP38-2/SD40-2

**NEW 631-95** 2nd Generation Locos SD75I

### Intermodal Decals

**11.49 ea**

#### Armour

**NEW 631-01** 53' Hyundai Containers

**NEW 631-02** 53' Trailers - Mond & Trailmobile

**NEW 631-03** 53' Trailers - Other

**NEW 631-04** 53' Extendable Container Chassis

#### Midland

**NEW 631-05** 53' Stoughton Containers

**NEW 631-06** 53' Trailers - Great Dane

**NEW 631-07** 53' Extendable Container Chassis

#### TransX

**NEW 631-08** 53' Containers

#### Maritime Ontario 53' Containers

**NEW 631-09** Stoughton

**NEW 631-10** Transtech

#### Canadian Tire 53' Containers

**NEW 631-12** CIMC

**NEW 631-13** Stoughton

#### Sunbury Transportation

A part of the Irving Oil Corporation, Sunbury Transportation equipment can be seen throughout the Maritime Provinces and New England. Two years of photographic research have provided some interesting variations in this attractive paint scheme, currently used on containers and equipment.

**NEW 631-41** 53' Hyundai & Stoughton Containers

**NEW 631-42** 53' Mond or Trailmobile Trailers

**NEW 631-43** 53' Extendable Container Chassis

#### CN Intermodal 53' Containers

Based on equipment now in service, all sets are complete with markings and warning labels.

**NEW 631-51** Stoughton Rib Side 8.99

**NEW 631-52** CIMC "Jindo" Containers 8.99

**NEW 631-53** Hyundai Containers w/Train Art

**NEW 631-54** CN World Wide Hyundai Containers 2005+

**NEW 631-55** Stoughton Containers w/Train Art; Carrier Heaters

**NEW 631-56** 53' Extended Container Chassis

**NEW 631-57** CIMC "We Deliver" Containers

**NEW 631-58** CN World Wide CIMC Containers

**NEW 631-59** CIMC "We Deliver" Heated Containers

Daily New Product Announcements! Visit Walthers Web site at **www.walthers.com**

Express your creativity while customizing your locomotives and rolling stock by creating your own decals. Vitachrome Graphics provides kits and individual products that allow modelers to design their own easy-to-apply decals. By using your existing inkjet printer (paper compatible with most printers), the options are limitless in creating unique and imaginative semi-permanent designs.

Decal Paper 768-5000

Clear Sealer Spray 786-5050

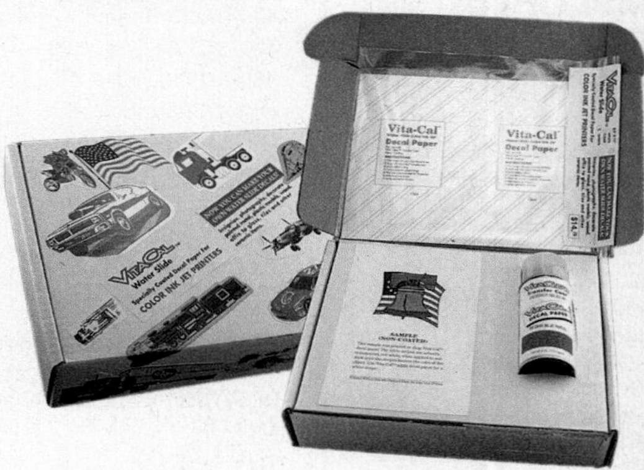


Inkjet Decal Starter Kit 768-5070

## DECAL PAPER

Create your own decals using VitaCal™ decal paper. Compatible with most inkjet printers, decal paper has a high-gloss finish. Paper is easy to apply and adheres to most hard, smooth surfaces. Sheets measure 8-1/2 x 11" 20 x 27.5cm. Color indicated reflects background color.

**768-5000** White pkg(5) **24.95**

**768-5020** Clear pkg(5) **24.95**

**768-5030** White pkg(100) **350.00**

**768-5040** Clear pkg(100) **350.00**

## CLEAR SEALER SPRAY

**768-5050** 4oz **10.95**
Sealer for use with decal paper. Childproof packaging.

## DECAL STARTER KIT

**768-5070 26.95**
Use your inkjet printer to create decals right away. Includes two sheets each of clear and white VitaCal decal paper, each sheet measuring 8-1/2 x 11" 20 x 27.5cm. Also includes one can of 4oz Clear Sealer spray.

Products bearing Union Pacific, Southern Pacific and Rio Grande marks are made under trademark license from Union Pacific Railroad Company.

# NEW PRODUCTS

## Model Graphics® Dry Transfer Alphabets & Numbers

**5.49 ea**

Designed for the critical hobbyist, these Dry Transfers are easy to use. Position as desired and rub into place with the Dry Transfer Burnisher (#785-600 sold separately). Intricate detailing is quicker, easier and more realistic than when attempted with water slide decals. Each set comes on a sheet measuring 5-1/2 x 8-1/4"; sets include lettering sizes 1/16, 3/32, 1/8, 3/16, 1/4 & 5/16" unless noted.

### Railroad Roman

#### Alphabets & Numbers

**NEW 785-701** Black
**NEW 785-702** White
**NEW 785-703** Gold
**NEW 785-704** Red
**NEW 785-705** Yellow
**NEW 785-706** Silver

#### Numbers Only

**NEW 785-707** Black
**NEW 785-708** White
**NEW 785-709** Gold
**NEW 785-710** Red
**NEW 785-711** Yellow
**NEW 785-712** Silver

#### 3/8 & 1/2" Alphabets & Numbers

**NEW 785-713** Black
**NEW 785-714** White

### Extended Railroad Roman

#### Alphabets & Numbers

**NEW 785-715** Black
**NEW 785-716** White
**NEW 785-717** Gold

### Condensed Railroad Roman

#### Alphabets & Numbers

**NEW 785-718** Black
**NEW 785-719** White

### Railroad Gothic

#### Alphabets & Numbers

**NEW 785-720** Black
**NEW 785-721** White
**NEW 785-722** Gold
**NEW 785-723** Red
**NEW 785-724** Yellow
**NEW 785-725** Silver

#### Numbers Only

**NEW 785-726** Black
**NEW 785-727** White
**NEW 785-728** Gold
**NEW 785-729** Red
**NEW 785-730** Yellow
**NEW 785-731** Silver

#### 3/8 & 1/2" Alphabets & Numbers

**NEW 785-732** Black
**NEW 785-733** White

### Extended Railroad Gothic

**NEW 785-734** Black
**NEW 785-735** White
**NEW 785-736** Gold

### Condensed Railroad Gothic

**NEW 785-737** Black
**NEW 785-738** White

### 45° USA Gothic

Standard lettering style for US military vehicles and aircraft.

#### Alphabets & Numbers

**NEW 785-739** Black
**NEW 785-740** White
**NEW 785-741** Red
**NEW 785-742** Yellow
**NEW 785-743** Silver

#### Numbers Only

**NEW 785-746** Black
**NEW 785-747** White
**NEW 785-748** Red
**NEW 785-749** Yellow
**NEW 785-750** Silver

#### 3/8 & 1/2" Alphabets & Numbers

**NEW 785-744** Black
**NEW 785-745** White

### Stencil & Block Roman

3/32, 1/8 & 1/4".

**NEW 785-751** Black
**NEW 785-752** White
**NEW 785-753** Red
**NEW 785-754** Yellow

### Script & Old English

3/16 & 5/16".

**NEW 785-755** Black
**NEW 785-756** White
**NEW 785-757** Gold
**NEW 785-758** Silver

### Stripes

.010, 1/64, .022, 1/32, 3/64".

**NEW 785-759** Black
**NEW 785-760** White
**NEW 785-761** Gold
**NEW 785-762** Red
**NEW 785-763** Yellow
**NEW 785-764** Silver

## Dry Transfer Alphabet & Number Sets

**4.49 ea**

A quick and easy way to add color to buildings, fences, signs and more. Position where desired, rub gently with the Woodland Scenics Dry Transfer Burnisher (#785-600 sold separately), and remove the carrier sheet. Each set comes on a sheet measuring 4 x 5"; sets include lettering sizes as shown.

### Tuscan & Playbill

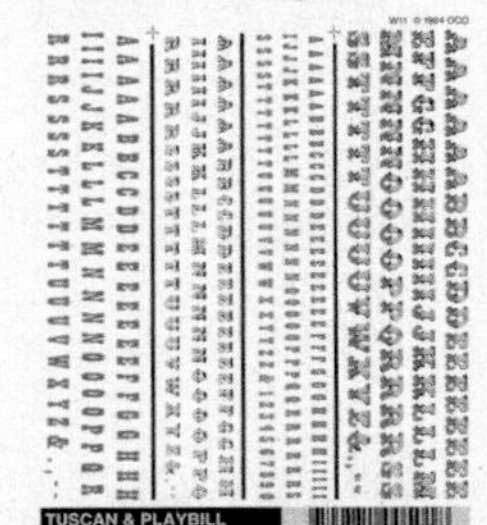


**NEW 785-501** 1/16, 3/32, 1/8 & 3/16"

### Benton & Windsor

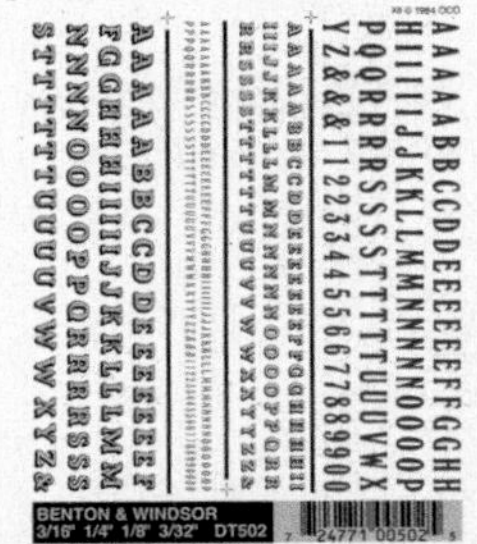


**NEW 785-502** 3/32, 1/8, 3/16 & 1/4"

### Gothic Outline & Sign Painter

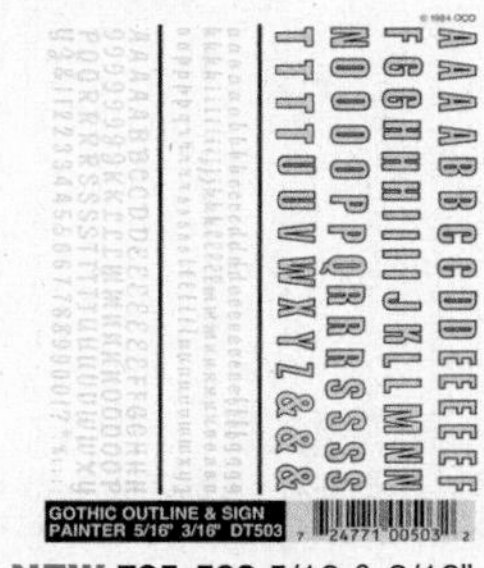


**NEW 785-503** 5/16 & 3/16"

### Railroad Roman

1/16, 3/32, 1/8 & 3/16"

#### Alphabets & Numbers

**NEW 785-504** Red & Gold
**NEW 785-505** Black
**NEW 785-506** White

#### Numbers Only

**NEW 785-509** Black
**NEW 785-510** White

### Railroad Gothic

1/16, 3/32, 1/8 & 3/16"

#### Alphabets & Numbers

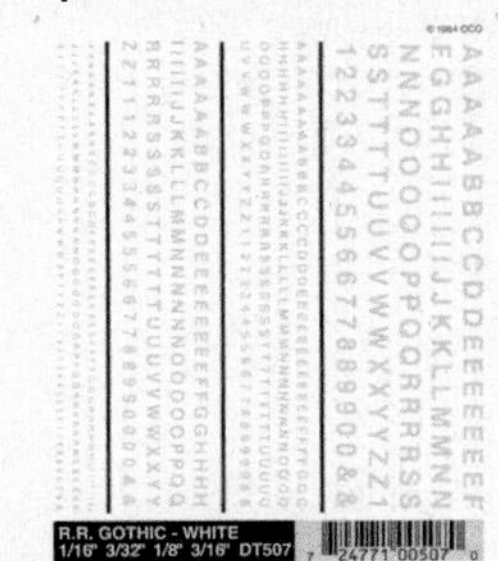


**NEW 785-507** White
**NEW 785-508** Black

#### Numbers Only

**NEW 785-511** Black
**NEW 785-512** White

### Stripes

1/64, 3/32, 1/8, 3/16"

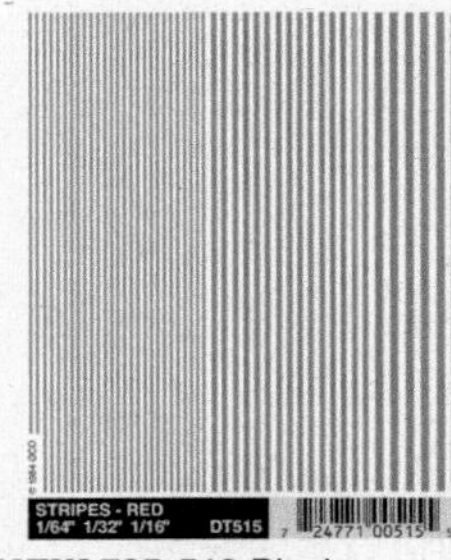


**NEW 785-513** Black
**NEW 785-514** White
**NEW 785-515** Red
**NEW 785-516** Yellow

# DRY TRANSFER SIGN SETS

## Dry Transfer Signs

**5.98 ea**

Full-color dry transfers can be applied to a smooth or textured surface such as wood, metal or plastic by positioning the sign in the desired area, rubbing gently on the back and peeling away the carrier sheet. One 4" x 5" sheet per package.

**785-245** Series One Signs

785-551 Tavern, Gas Station and Commercial Signs

785-552 Assorted Business Signs

785-553 Depot, REA and Advertising Signs

785-554 Product and Advertising Signs

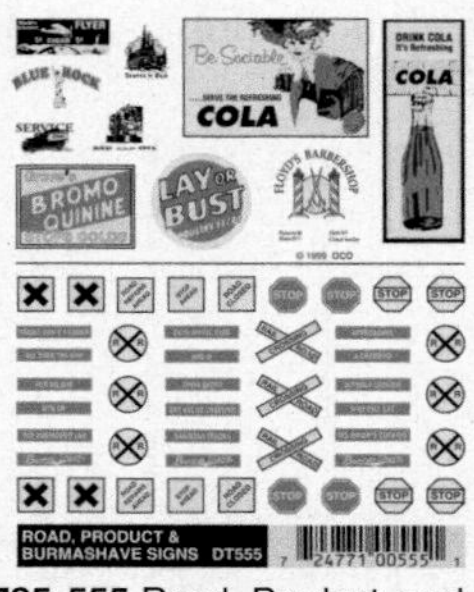

785-555 Road, Product, and Burma Shave Signs

785-556 Assorted Logos and Advertising Signs

785-557 Data/Warning Labels and Commercial Signs

785-558 Railroad Heralds

785-559 Business Signs

785-560 Crate Labels and Warning Signs

785-561 1960s Signs and Posters

785-562 1950s Signs and Posters

785-563 1940s Signs and Posters

## Mini-Series Dry Transfer Signs 5.98 ea (Unless Noted)

These N Scale transfers can be used as small signs for HO Scale.

785-570 Product Logos

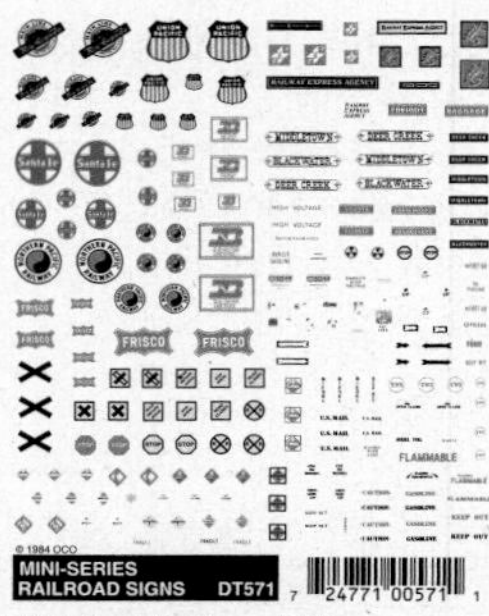

785-571 Railroad Signs

785-572 Business Signs

785-573 Signs and Posters

785-574 Service Station Signs

785-575 Mini-Lettering (black & white) 4.49



## DRY TRANSFER RAILROAD LETTERING SETS

### 4.49 ea

### Box Cars

785-603 UP "Automated Railway" & "Ship & Travel"

785-604 ATSF "El Capitan" & "Super Chief" w/Straight Line Map

785-605 ATSF "Super Shock Control","Ship & Travel" w/Large Herald

785-606 Rock Island w/Soft Touch & Damage Free (DF) Logos

785-607 BN & CB&Q "Way of the Zephyrs", "Everywhere West"

785-608 SLSF "Ship It" & "Fa Freight"

785-609 SP w/Hydra-Cushior & Damage-Free Logos

785-610 GN w/Modern Rocky Logos

### Freight Car Data (white, black)

785-601 Railroad Roman

785-602 Railroad Gothic

### Reefers

785-611 Armour, Miller & Hormel

## DRY TRANSFER BURNISHER

785-600 5.29

For applying dry transfers. Gently rub burnisher over dry transfer to apply.

# COUPLERS

Models and Photo by Greg Drewiske

Being gentle with something that weighs several tons and packs hundreds of horsepower can be a daunting task. But to prevent expensive damage to loads and equipment, it's a skill that every engineer has to master. With a resounding "CLLLLLUNKKK" metal meets metal as coupler knuckles slide past each other and close tightly. The head brakeman disappears between engine and car, re-connect the air line and signals all is ready. Air compressors throb to life as he climbs aboard, and this train is about to get underway once more.

About to get underway on Greg Drewiske's layout in Wisconsin Rapids, Wisconsin, we're just in time to watch the crew pickup a custom painted and decaled Athearn 40' box car. Doing the honors on today's C&NW freight is a Life-Like GP7. The right-of-way has also been detailed with products from Super Trees and Woodland Scenics.

Couplers are just as important to model railroads as they are in the real world! Here in the Trucks and Couplers Section, you'll find all types of couplers, along with freight, engine and passenger car trucks, wheelsets, special tools and other accessories that you can use to take your models to a new level of operation and appearance.

# WALTHERS

## NEW PRODUCTS

### Caboose Trucks

**COMING SOON**

**Winter 2007-08 Delivery**

### Milwaukee Road Caboose Rigid Truck

**NEW 933-1322** 1 Pair **9.98**

- Authentic MILW Design
- Matches 932-7660-Series Models

### Passenger Car Trucks

### Revised Superliner Trucks

**COMING SOON**

**Fall 2007 Delivery**

**GSC Style**

**NEW 933-1321** For Superliner II 1 Pair **10.98**

- Metal Sideframes
- RP-25 Metal Wheels

**Airbag Style**

**NEW 933-1320** Superliner I As-Delivered 1 Pair **10.98**

- Metal Sideframes
- RP-25 Metal Wheels

### Allied Full-Cushion Express Truck

**COMING SOON**

**Winter 2007-08 Delivery**

**933-1319** 1 Pair **9.98**

- Matches trucks used on Walthers Express Box Cars and Troop Cars

## COUPLERS

### Athearn Coupler Pocket Conversion Kit

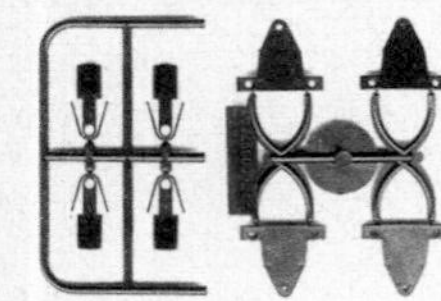

**933-997** 2 Pair **5.98**

- Fits Athearn 85' Hi-Cube Box & Flat Cars
- Body-Mounting Couplers
- Swinging Couplers Improve Curve Performance
- Parts to Convert 2 Cars

### Cushion Car Coupler Pocket

**933-1030** pkg(8) **3.98**

- Easy to Install
- Simulates End-of-Car Cushioning
- Used on Many Types of Cars
- Longer Draft Gear
- More Prototypical Appearance
- Accepts Kadee® or Horn-Hook Couplers
- Parts to Convert 4 Cars

### Dummy Couplers

**933-1045** 12 Pair **2.98**

### Horn-Hook Couplers

**933-995** pkg(12) **1.98**
Replacement coupler

- Fits All Walthers Cars
- Molded in Delrin®

## PASSENGER CAR TRUCKS

- Fully Assembled
- Diecast Sideframes
- RP-25 Blackened Metal Wheels

### Superliner Cars

**933-1046** Air Sprung Type 1 Pair **5.98**
Original style used on Superliner cars, prototypes were fitted with a large airbag in place of springs.

### GSC 41-NDO (CIB) Outside Swing Hanger Trucks 1 Pair 10.98 ea

Based on widely used trucks manufactured by General Steel Castings, these detailed replicas match those used on Walthers Budd passenger cars.

- Used on Walthers Budd Cars
- 36" Wheels

**933-1060** Black

**933-1061** Silver

### GSC 41-HR Passenger Trucks 1 Pair 10.98 ea

- Used on Walthers Pullman-Standard Cars
- 36" Wheels

**933-1067** Black

**933-1068** Silver

### GSC BX Express Trucks

**933-1062** 1 Pair **5.98**

- Used on Various Cars
- 33" Wheels

### GSC 41-N-11 (CIB) 1 Pair 10.98 ea

**933-1069** Black

**933-1070** Silver

### GSC 41-CNS-11 (CIB) 1 Pair 10.98 ea

**933-1071** Black

**933-1072** Silver

### Pennsylvania 2-DP-5 Trucks 1 Pair 10.98

- Authentic PRR Design Used on Many Cars

**933-1303** Olive Green

**933-1304** Tuscan

**933-1313** Black

### Lightweight Passenger Trucks

**GSC 41-N-11 w/Disc Brakes 1 Pair 10.98**

**933-1305** Black

**933-1311** Silver

**GSC 41-CNS-11 w/Disc Brakes 1 Pair 10.98**

**933-1306** Black

**933-1312** Silver

### Commonwealth Straight Equalized Truck

**Inside Stabilizing Bearing 1 Pair 12.98 ea**

**933-1307** Friction Bearings

**933-1308** Roller Bearings

**Outside Stabilizing Bearing 1 Pair 12.98 ea**

**933-1309** Friction Bearings

**933-1310** Roller Bearings

### Heavyweight Car Trucks

**4-Wheel Trucks**

**933-1077** 1 Pair **10.98**

**Pullman-Standard 6-Wheel Trucks 1 Pair 12.98 ea**

**933-1078** 106W Wood Beam w/Friction Bearings

**933-1079** 106W w/Roller Bearing

**933-1085** Type 242A

**933-1086** Type 2411

## FREIGHT TRUCKS

- For all Types of Freight Cars
- Black Delrin Sideframes
- RP-25 Metal Wheelsets w/Plastic Axles

### Rigid Plastic w/Plastic Wheels 1 Pair 2.98 ea

**933-1010** Arch Bar

**933-1011** "T" Section

**933-1012** Bettendorf

**933-1013** Roller Bearing

### Rigid Plastic w/Metal Wheels 1 Pair 3.98 ea

**933-1007** Roller Bearing

**933-1008** Bettendorf

**933-1009** "T" Section

**933-1018** Arch Bar 1 Pair

### Sprung Plastic w/Plastic Wheels 1 Pair 3.98 ea

- Easy to Assemble
- Sprung & Equalized

**933-1001** Bettendorf

**933-1002** Diamond Arch Bar

# WALTHERS

933-1003 "T" Section Bettendorf

933-1004 Andrews

933-1005 Roller Bearing

## WHEELSETS

With nonmagnetic brass axles.

### Blackened Brass Wheels pkg(4) 3.98 ea

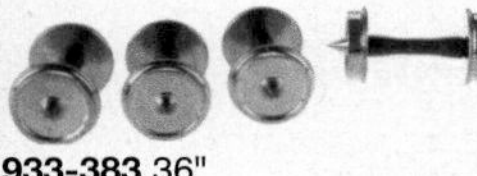
933-383 36"

933-870 33"
933-1048 28"

### Black Plastic Wheels

933-1006 33" pkg(12) 3.98

# LIFE-LIKE®

Div. of Wm. K. Walthers, Inc.

## COUPLERS

433-1410 Horn-Hook pkg(4) 4.75

## TRUCKS

433-1413 Bettendorf 1 Pair 4.75
Ready-to-run, with couplers.

From Walthers

### Proto 2000 Couplers

920-21095 1 Pair 2.00

920-21096 10 Pair 15.50

## TRUCKS

### Proto 2000 Trucks pkg(2) 5.50 ea

**Andrews**
920-23207 With 33" Flat Back Wheelsets

920-23399 With 33" Ribbed Back Wheelsets

### 50-Ton Spring Plankless w/33" WheelSets

920-21251 Ribbed Back

920-21253 Flat Back

### National B-1 w/33" WheelSets

920-21254 Ribbed Back

920-21255 Flat Back

### Barber S-2 100-Ton

920-21256 With 36" Wheelsets pkg(2)

## WHEELSETS

### Proto 2000 Wheelsets pkg(12) 9.00 ea

920-21257 36"

920-21258 33" Flat Back

920-21259 33" Ribbed Back

# ACCURAIL®

## NEW PRODUCT

### Coupler Height Gauge

NEW 112-1010 2.49

## COUPLERS

### Accumate Couplers

Easy-to-use coupler works well manually or magnetically, and can be dropped into the coupler box of most cars. With no tiny springs or small metal stampings to lose, it's great for beginners. Draftless knuckle profile allows operation of long, heavy trains without the effects of "coupler rideup."

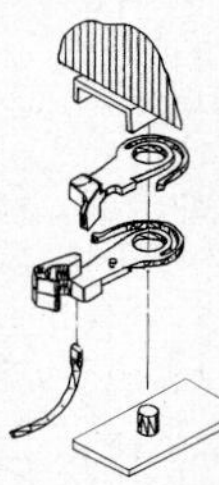
112-1011 2 Pair 1.59

112-1012 12 Pair 8.98

112-1020 Scale Knuckle & Draft Gear Box 2 Pair 2.98

112-1030 Scale-Size Knuckle Couplers w/Draft Gear Box 12 Pair 15.98

### Coupler Tools

112-1001 Accumate Switchman 1.99
Hand-held uncoupler works anywhere on your layout; simply insert between Accumate couplers and turn.

## TRUCKS

### 100-Series 1 Pair 3.49 ea

Trucks feature acetal plastic sideframes and wheelsets.

112-100 Bettendorf

112-102 Roller Bearing

112-103 Andrews

### 200-Series 1 Pair 5.98 ea

200-Series trucks feature acetal plastic sideframes and metal wheelsets.

112-200 Bettendorf

112-202 Roller Bearing

112-203 Andrews

## WHEELSETS

112-101 33" Acetal Plastic pkg(12) 3.49

# ALEXANDER SCALE MODELS

DIVISION OF TOMAR INDUSTRIES

## COUPLERS

120-6001 Horn-Hook Plastic 1 Pair 1.30

120-6002 Metal Link & Pin pkg(2) 4.20

### Coupler Pocket Mounts pkg(2)

120-6003 Screw Mounting 1.90

120-6004 Pin Mounting 1.60

# AMERICAN LIMITED MODELS

### Coupling Kit

147-6100 Close Coupling Adaptor Kit 2.75
For Athearn F7A/B diaphragms and draft gear box.



# ATLAS

### Freight Car Trucks 1 Pair 4.75 ea

Trucks feature Delrin® sideframes and metal wheelsets.

150-180000 70-Ton Roller-Bearing

150-185000 50-Ton Bettendorf Friction-Bearing

150-190000 Barber Bettendorf Roller-Bearing Caboose

150-195000 100-Ton Roller-Bearing

### Freight Car Wheelset Bulk Packs

150-180100 33" Metal Wheels For Atlas Freight Cars pkg(100) 76.95

150-190100 33" Metal Wheels For Atlas Cabooses pkg(100) 76.95

150-195100 36" Metal Wheels pkg(100) 82.50

# BRAWA

IMPORTED FROM GERMANY BY WALTHERS

### Rigid Coupling

186-2250 For Standard Coupling Shafts pkg(10) 10.99

## KITBITS TRUCKS

Detail your rolling stock in minutes with these authentic replicas of various freight and passenger car trucks. Each pair features unpainted metal sideframes and includes metal wheelsets.

### Passenger Car Trucks – 4-Wheel 1 Pair 11.95 ea (Unless Noted)

**718-92** Standard Motor Car Trucks

**718-95A** Commonwealth Bolted Journals

**718-98** Stillwell

**718-99** Top Equalized

**718-121** Roller Bearing

**718-127** Pennsylvania Type 2D-5P w/8' Wheelbase

**718-139** 9' Wheelbase

**NEW 718-151** PRR 2D-5P2 Passenger Car Trucks **11.95**

**718-231** B&O Express Car Trucks

**718-1250** Commonwealth; 8' Wheelbase

**718-1252** Standard Roller Bearing

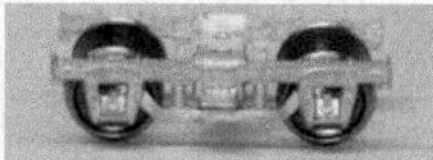

**718-1260** Old Style 7'3" Wheelbase

**718-1263** "Challenger" Style

**718-1265** 7' Wheelbase

### Passenger Car Trucks – 6-Wheel 1 Pair 16.95 ea (Unless Noted)

**718-97** Top Equalized

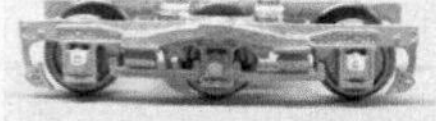

**718-123** Pennsylvania Type 3D-5P2 **19.95**

**718-1241** N&W Pilchner Patent

**718-1272** Pullman

### Caboose Trucks 1 Pair 9.95 ea (Unless Noted)

**718-124** 6' Wheelbase

**718-125** Wolfe 5-1/2'

**718-126** Symington - 5'6" Wheelbase

**718-128** Symington - 5'3" Wheelbase

**718-129** Express Box Car & Caboose Trucks – Erie **11.95**

### Tender Trucks 1 Pair 9.95 ea (Unless Noted)

**718-199** 4-Wheel; GSC 7' Wheelbase **11.95**

**718-1212** 4-Wheel; Symington-Gould

**718-1228** 4-Wheel; Andrews w/Leaf Spring 5'6" Wheelbase

### Freight Trucks 1 Pair 9.95 ea (Unless Noted)

**718-1203** Gould Heavy-Duty w/5'6" Wheelbase

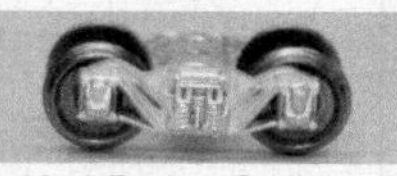

**718-1216** Barber Stabilized 5'6" Wheelbase

**718-1219** Symington-Gould Hi-Speed 5'6" Wheelbase

**718-1220** Vulcan 5'6" Wheelbase

**718-1223** Fox Pressed Steel 5'6" Wheelbase

**718-1224** Dalman Two-Level 5'6" Wheelbase

**718-1225** National Type B

**718-1227** Andrews w/Coil Springs

### Arch Bar 1 Pair 9.95 ea (Unless Noted)

**718-134** 4'9" Wheelbase

**718-135** PSC; 5'6" Wheelbase

**718-1209** With Leaf Springs Freight Trucks; 5'6" Wheelbase

**718-1215** Pilchner Trussed 5'6" Wheelbase

### Bettendorf 1 Pair 9.95 ea

**718-1202** Heavy-Duty; 5'6" Wheelbase

**718-1204** T-Section; 5'6" Wheelbase

### Taylor 1 Pair 9.95 ea

**718-1217** Coil Spring; 5'6" Wheelbase

**718-1218** Leaf Springs; 5'6" Wheelbase

## BOWSER

## TRUCKS

Trucks feature plastic sideframes, 33" wheels and nonmagnetic axles.

### 1 Pair 3.16 ea

**6-74013** N5 & N5c Caboose

**6-74091** Crown

**6-74190** Coil-Leaf

**6-74277** AAR 70-Ton

**6-74256** 100-Ton Roller Bearing

**6-74326** Arch Bar

**6-74225** 70-Ton Roller Bearing

## BRANCHLINE TRAINS

## TRUCKS

### 1 Pair 4.98 ea

All trucks are less wheelsets unless noted.

**181-100019** Barber S2a Freight. Includes 33" turned-metal wheelsets.

**181-150001** Pullman 2411 Bottom-Equalized

**181-150002** Pullman 242 A Top-Equalized

**181-150004** REA Express Reefer

## WHEELSETS

### Turned Metal pkg(12) 9.98 ea

**181-161001** 33" Standard Tread

**181-161002** 36" .088 Tread

**181-161003** 33" Standard Tread

**181-161004** 36" .088 Tread

### Turned Metal pkg(100) 74.98 ea

**181-161005** 33" Standard Tread

**181-161007** 33" .008 Tread

Items listed below are available by Special Order (see Legend Page).

**181-161006** 36" Standard Tread

**181-161008** 36" .088 Tread

# COUPLERS

## E-Z Mate® Magnetic Knuckle Couplers

E-Z Mate knuckle couplers have springs molded as an integral part of the knuckle coupler. They operate with a standard metal "glad hand" and under-track magnet. Completely compatible with all magnetically operated knuckle couplers currently on the market. Features a center - set shank.

**160-78005** Medium 12 Pair **12.00**

**160-78105** Medium 25 Pair **21.00**

## E-Z Mate Mark II 12 Pair 18.00 ea

Features metal coil springs.

### Over Shank

**160-78021** Long

**160-78022** Medium

**160-78023** Short

### Center Shank

**160-78024** Long

**160-78025** Medium

**160-78026** Short

### Under Shank

**160-78027** Long

**160-78028** Medium

**160-78029** Short

### Medium Center Shank

**160-78125** 25 Pair **29.00**

### NEM Coupler

**160-78035** Center Shank Medium 1 pair **1.50**
Fits into standard European coupler pocket for simple conversion to E-Z Mate operation.

# MAGNET

**160-78999** With Brakeman Figure **2.75**

# CAL-SCALE

HO Scale couplers and truck kits are cast in brass.

# COUPLERS

## Dummy Couplers

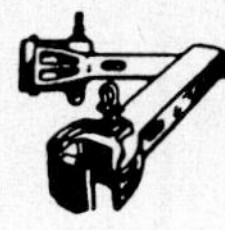
292

302

**190-292** Standard 1 Pair **3.60**

**190-302** Standard "E" 1 Pair **3.45**

### Brass Wheels pkg(4) 4.85 ea

**190-467** 30" 1/16 Diameter

**190-468** 36" Needle Point

**190-469** 33" Needle Point

**190-470** 30" Needle Point

**190-471** 36" Flush

**190-472** 33" Flush

**190-473** 30" Flush

### Non-Magnetic Nickel-Plated WheelSets 4.85 ea

**190-453** 36"

**190-454** 33"

# TRUCKS

## Tender Trucks 24.10 ea

**190-310** Andrews 1 Pair

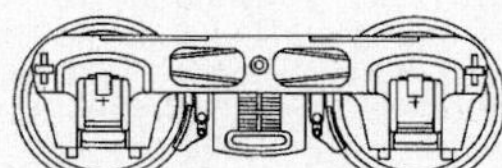

**190-311** 4-Wheel USRA 1 Pair

# CALUMET TRAINS

Vinyl traction tires increase pulling power and give a smoother ride with less bounce. These tires can only be used on wheels that had traction tires on them originally. Wheels must be grooved to accept tires.

## Super Traction Tire Assortments 6.95 ea

**192-505** Diesel Tires pkg(20)

**192-510** Small Steam pkg(18)
Fits AHM GG-1, 0-8-0 Switcher, 2-8-8-2 Mallet and others.

**192-511** Medium Steam pkg(18)
Fits AHM Mikado, Berkshire, Bowser, Challenger, Reno and others.

**192-512** Large Steam pkg(18)
Fits AHM Hudson, Heavy Pacific and others.

**192-513** Steam Assortment pkg(18)
Includes six each of Nos. 510, 511 and 512.

**192-515** Steam Tender Tires pkg(20)
Fits TYCO "Chattanooga" and 0-8-0 Tender Drives.

## Traction Tire Tool

**192-504 11.95**
For easy application and replacement of diesel traction tires. Includes ten tires.

# KEYSTONE LOCOMOTIVE WORKS

All-metal craft train kits, unless noted.

## Freight Trucks

**395-30** Grasse River Log Buggie 1 Pair **3.95**
Includes cast-metal bolsters and sideframes, plus RP25 wheels.

## Passenger Trucks

**395-9** PRR 6-Wheel 1 Pair **10.95**
Pre-assembled with NorthWest Short Line nickel-silver wheelsets.

# EASTERN CAR WORKS

Easy-to-build kits with plastic parts. Kits come without wheels, but wheelsets are available separately.

Important Note: This listing includes items which are available by special order only. Please see the Legend Page for information, and visit www.walthers.com for a complete listing of in-stock and special order products.

# TRUCKS

## 4-Wheel Freight Trucks 1 Pair 3.00 ea

**117-9051** Barber-Bettendorf Caboose

**117-9052** Taylor 70-Ton Caboose/Freight

**117-9053** Bettendorf Friction Bearing

**117-9055** Birdsboro/Andrews Caboose/Freight

**117-9056** Bettendorf Roller Bearing Conversion

**117-9057** Pyle-National B-1

**117-9058** Buckeye Roller Bearing 125-Ton

**117-9059** C-1 Friction Bearing

**117-9061** 2 Level Dalman

**117-9068** Vulcan

## 4-Wheel Passenger Trucks 1 Pair 5.00 ea

**117-9001** Pennsylvania 2D-P5

**117-9002** Commonwealth Leaf Spring

**117-9005** Pullman Standard

## 6-Wheel Freight Trucks 1 Pair 4.00 ea

**117-9081** Commonwealth Integral Pedestal

**117-9082** Buckeye Friction Bearing

**117-9083** Buckeye Roller Bearing

## 6-Wheel Passenger Trucks 1 Pair 5.00 ea

**117-9021** Pennsylvania 3D-P1, 3D-P7

**117-9022** Pennsylvania 3D5P2

**117-9023** Pullman-Standard 61-NO

**117-9024** Commonwealth

## Express Trucks 1 Pair 5.00 ea

**117-9040** Commonwealth, 8' Wheel Base

**117-9041** ACF Mechanical Ventilation Fans, 6' Wheel Base

# ERNST MANUFACTURING

## Gearing Kit

Self-lubricating gearing kits for Athearn locomotive trucks. Kits produce more realistic control and smoother operation, with lower low speeds, twice the power and brighter headlights. Keeps motor running cooler, increasing motor life. Triple reduction.

**259-2** Gearing Kit For Hustler **11.98**
Provides a 36:1 gear ratio with two 1/2" flywheels. Includes two flywheels, brass worms and gearboxes with all gears necessary.

**259-3** Gearing Kit For RDC **11.98**
Provides a 12:1 gear ratio with a large flywheel for smoother operation. Includes a gearbox, geared axle pieces, worm gears, 1" flywheel and added components.

**259-6** Super Gearing Kit For 6-Axle Trucks **7.98**
EMD SD9, F45, SDP40, SD45, U28C, U33C, Trainmaster, Alco PA-1 and PB-2 (Alco requires modeling skill).

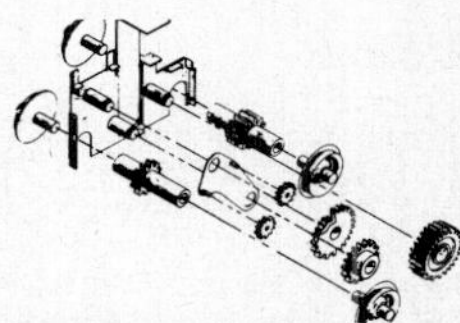

**259-44** Gearing Kit MKII For 4-Axle Trucks **7.98**
F7 A & B, GP9, GP35, U28B, S12, SW7 Cow and Calf.

**259-66** Gearing Kit For SD40-2 **7.98**
Converts 12:1 ratio of the stock SD40-2 to a 32:1 gear ratio. Greater pulling power, slower speed and less current draw.

See What's New and Exciting at
**www.walthers.com**

GRANDT LINE

Trucks are ready-to-run and molded in Delrin®.

Items listed in blue ink may not be available at all times (see Legend Page).

## TRUCKS

### Bettendorf

**300-5120** 54" Wheelbase, HOn3 Brown 1 Pair **6.25**
Used by Colorado & Southern, Rio Grande Southern and White Pass & Yukon.

### Andrews Hon3 1 Pair 6.25 ea

DRGW style for 5900 stock car, 150 reefer and 6400 flat. 4'-8" wheelbase.

**300-5144** Brown

**300-5145** Black

### Archbar

**300-5159** Brown 1 Pair **6.25**
DRGW style, 4'-8" wheelbase.

**300-5257** Sandy River & Rangeley Lakes/Northwest Shortline Wheels **9.00**

### Freight Car 1 Pair 6.25 ea

DRGW style, 3'-7" wheelbase.

**300-5110** Brown HOn3

**300-5111** Black HOn3

International Hobby Corp.

## COUPLERS

**348-19001** Magic Mate 4 Pair **4.98**

## TRUCKS

### Passenger Trucks

#### Commonwealth 4-Wheel

For use on IHC/Rivarossi passenger cars and other equipment. One side of the nickel-silver wheels is insulated to allow for interior lighting.

**348-4240** Black 1 Pair **20.98**

**348-4241** Silver 1 Pair **20.98**

**348-4242** IHC/Rivarossi Adapters **3.98**

### 6-Wheel 24.98 ea

**348-4256** Friction Bearing (black)

**348-4257** Friction Bearing (silver)

**348-4258** Roller Bearing (black)

**348-4259** Roller Bearing (silver)

## WHEELSETS

### 31" RP25 Metal

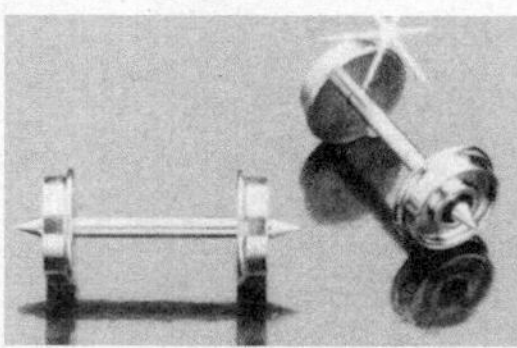

Nickel-silver plated wheelsets are insulated on one side and are nonmagnetic.

**348-4254** pkg(12) **13.98**

**348-4255** pkg(36) **38.98**

**348-5996** pkg(12) **13.98**

**348-5997** pkg(36) **38.98**

Item listed below is available by Special Order (see Legend Page).
**348-5994** pkg(100) **99.98**
For corrugated or smoothside Pullman-Standard passenger cars.

All wheelsets are brass with black nickel plating (unless noted) and are RP-25 contour, .110" tread.

Please visit Walthers Web site at www.walthers.com for a complete listing of all available items.

## METAL WHEELSETS & AXLES

### Athearn Diesel

**369-100** 36" Wheels w/Half Axle pkg(12) **9.00**

**369-101** 42" Wheels w/Half Axle pkg(8) **6.75**

**369-102** 40" Solid Nickel Silver Wheels w/1/2 Axle pkg(8) **10.80**
For use in newer Athearn diesels with molded plastic sideframes. Includes parts to convert one four-axle locomotive.

### Blunt End Axles pkg(4) 6.65 ea

**369-1011** 42"

**369-1061** 36"

**369-1081** 33"

**369-1091** 40"

### Euro-Type RP-25 w/110 Tread

**369-2009** 40" pkg(12) **14.00**

**369-2098** 38" pkg(12) **13.80**

**369-2106** 36" pkg(12) **13.50**

**369-2108** 33" pkg(12) **13.15**

**369-2109** 42" pkg(12) **14.25**

### For Athearn EMD SD60

**369-10242** 42" Solid Nickel Half Axle **16.30**

### Metal Wheel Replacements pkg(6) 8.75 ea

**369-1094** 40" Wheelset For Athearn Dummy

**369-1095** 42" Wheelset For Athearn Dummy

### Pointed-Axle Wheelsets - Bulk Packs

**369-106100** 36" pkg(100) **94.40**

**369-108100** 33" pkg(100) **91.40**

**369-108200** 33" pkg(200) **180.00**

Items listed below are available by Special Order (see Legend Page).

**369-106200** 36" pkg(200) **185.75**

**369-106500** 36" pkg(500) **445.00**

**369-108500** 33" pkg(500) **418.00**

### Pointed-End Axles

**369-98** 38" pkg(12) **15.40**

**369-106** 36" pkg(12) **14.50**

**369-107** 28" pkg(8) **8.75**

**369-108** 33" pkg(12) **14.15**

**369-109** 40" pkg(4) **6.15**

**369-988** 33" & 38" pkg(12) **14.60**
Includes four 33" and eight 38" pointed-end axles for Walthers Double Stack cars.

### Shoulder End Axles pkg(4) 6.65 ea

**369-1012** 42"

**369-1062** 36"

**369-1072** 28"

**369-1082** 33"

**369-1092** 40"

### With Pointed Axles & Built-In Resistors

**369-10605** 36" Wheels, 5.1k Ohm pkg(12) **24.00**

**369-10610** 36" Wheels, 10k Ohm pkg(12) **24.00**

**369-10620** 36" Wheels, 20k Ohm pkg(12) **24.00**

**369-10639** 36" Wheels, 38k Ohm pkg(12) **24.00**

**369-10805** 33" Wheels, 5.1k Ohm pkg(12) **22.90**

**369-10810** 33" Wheels, 10k Ohm pkg(12) **22.90**

**369-10820** 33" Wheels, 20k Ohm pkg(12) **22.90**

**369-10839** 33" Wheels, 39k Ohm pkg(12) **22.90**

## COUPLER MOUNT PADS

Improve the handling of long HO Scale passenger cars by replacing the Talgo couplers with these body-mounted coupler mounting pads. Use to mount Kadee® type couplers to Athearn, Bachmann, Con-Cor, Rivarossi and Roundhouse cars. When used with the proper size wheels, these pads provide correct coupler heights. Each mounting pad is adjustable, so cars can be spaced close together or apart when coupled. Parts to convert three cars are included in each pack.

### Athearn 3.75 ea

**369-113** Streamline

**369-114** Heavyweight

### Bachmann

**369-118** Spectrum Cars **3.75**

### Con-Cor 3.75 ea

**369-115** Budd 72 & 85' Cars

**369-116** Superliners

### Detail Associates

**369-120** ATSF "El Capitan" **3.75**

### Rail Power

#### SD90MAC & Athearn SD40-2

**369-10245** 45" Solid Nickel Half Axle **17.50**

### Rivarossi 3.75 ea

**369-110** 1920 Baggage Cars

**369-111** 1920 Cars Except Baggage

**369-112** 1930 Cars

**369-117** 1940 Cars

## TRUCKS WITH ELECTRICAL PICK-UPS

**147-1533** Athearn Freight **10.40**

HERPA/TRAINS CANADA

## WHEELSETS

Smooth-rolling plastic wheels on turned-brass nonmagnetic axles.

### 33" Wheels

**326-3000** pkg(12) **6.95**

**326-3001** pkg(24) **12.95**

**326-3003** pkg(100) **42.95**

### 36" Wheels

**326-3004** pkg(12) **7.95**

**326-3005** pkg(24) **14.95**

**326-3007** pkg(100) **46.95**

## COUPLERS

### Horn-Hook

**326-3010** pkg(12) **2.95**

**326-3011** pkg(24) **5.50**

**326-3013** pkg(100) **19.95**

## TRUCKS

**326-3050** Bettendorf Pair **3.50**
Builds either standard friction style or converted roller bearing style.

Designed, Manufactured & Assembled entirely in the U.S.A.

Kadee® Magne-Matic® Delayed Magnetic Action® couplers automatically uncouple when stopped over a magnetic uncoupler (see illustrations below). Kadee® makes both delayed action and nondelayed action uncouplers to fit different coupling and uncoupling requirements.

See the Coupler Conversion List on the following pages for aid in adapting and installing Kadee® couplers.

Made and assembled entirely in the USA

## Creators of the Magne-Matic® Coupling and Uncoupling System

# MAGNE-MATIC®

| Coupler | Description | Diagram |
|---|---|---|
| #21 #31 #41 | **Long** underset shank raises knuckle height | Long Underset Shank (.250" · .505" · .100" · .050" · .3906") |
| #26 #36 #46 #156 | **Long** centerset shank knuckle is centered | |
| #29 #39 #49 | **Long** overset shank lowers knuckle height | |
| #27 #37 #47 | **Medium** underset shank raises knuckle height | Medium Centerset Shank (.250" · .405" · .050" · .050" · .28125") |
| #3 #9 #5 #58 #118 #119 #148 & #158 | **Medium** metal centerset shank knuckle is centered **(#10, #11, & #12 pack)** | |
| #28 #38 | **Medium** plastic centerset shank **(same as #5)** | |
| #22 #32 #42 | **Medium** overset shank lowers knuckle height | |
| #24 #34 #44 | **Short** underset shank raises knuckle height | Short Overset Shank (.250" · .365" · .050" · .100" · .25") |
| #23 #33 #43 #153 | **Short** centerset shank knuckle is centered | |
| #25 #35 #45 | **Short** overset shank lowers knuckle height | |

Stopped over a magnetic upcoupler allowing slack to occur between the couplers. Knuckles have opened.

Withdraw slightly to disengage couplers. Magnetic force of the uncoupler draws couplers apart, uncoupling them.

Enter over uncoupler again, Couplers are in delayed position allowing pushing of car(s) without causing re-coupling.

Withdraw, leaving uncoupled car(s) on desired track. Couplers automatically return to normal coupling position.

### What is Delayed Uncoupling?

1. Uncouple Here
2. "Spot" Car Anywhere

## MAGNE-MATIC® COUPLERS

### No.5®

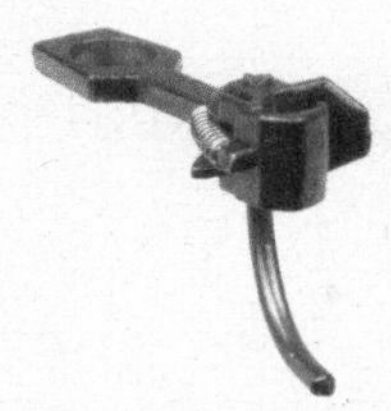

The most popular Kadee® coupler, fits most HO equipment. Metal coupler with insulated plastic gear box.

**380-3** Fully Assembled 2 Pair **5.80**

**380-5** Kit 2 Pair **3.50**

**380-9** Truck Mounting 2 Pair **3.85**
For metal Tyco truck mounting. Couplers have a small hole in the draft gear box.

380-10 380-11 380-12

**380-10** Less Draft Gear Box 10 Pair **14.65**

**380-11** Less Draft Gear Box 20 Pair **25.75**

**380-12** #58 "Scale" Couplers Less Draft Gear Boxes 20 Pair **29.95**

### Whisker® Couplers

These unique metal, drop-in, Self-Centering, Centerset Shank couplers fit many coupler pockets that are too shallow for a standard No.5® type centering spring. Whisker® couplers may be mounted with the supplied draft gear boxes, other Kadee® gear boxes or in manufacturers' cast-on coupler pockets. All Kadee® couplers are designed and tested for reliablility and durability, and feature Delayed Magnetic Uncoupling® with Delayed-Action.

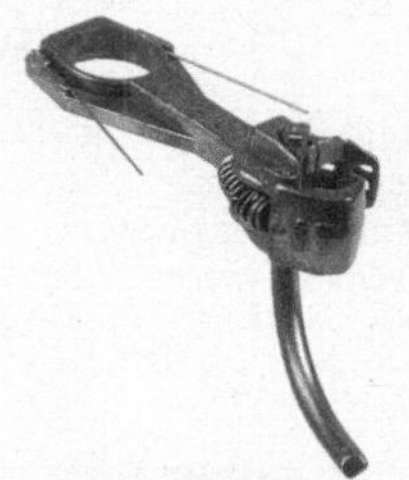

### "Scale" Metal Couplers 2 Pair 3.95

**NEW 380-153** Short (1/4") Centerset Shank 2 Pair

**NEW 380-156** Long (25/64") Centerset Shank

**NEW 380-158** Medium (9/32") Centerset Shank
Can be used in the place of #58 coupler.

### Standard Metal Couplers

**380-148** Medium (9/32") Centerset Shank 2 Pair **3.85**
Can be used in the place of No.5® coupler.

### Functional All-Metal Shelf Couplers 2 Pair

Centerset shank. Used on tank and pasenger cars.

**380-118** Type "SF" Shelf Couple. Medium (9/32") 2 Pair **3.95**

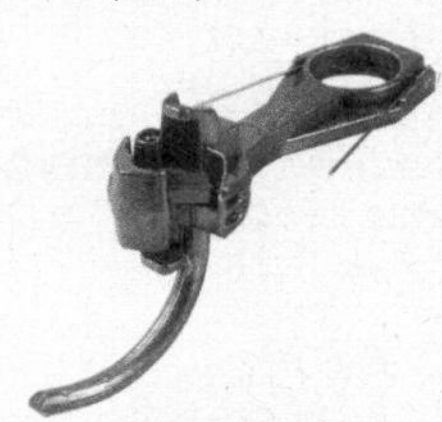

**NEW 380-119** Type "SE" Whisker® Shelf Coupler Medium (9/32") 2 Pair **3.95**

### #4 Couplers

**380-4** 4 Standard 2 Pair **3.50**
All-metal coupler. Especially for mounting on wooden floored car kits and trains that require additional drawbar slack action.

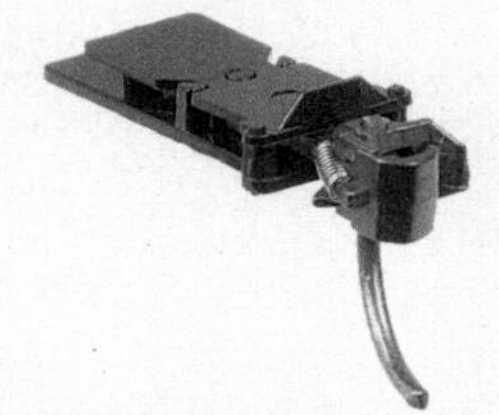

**380-15** Low Profile 2 Pair **3.75**
Metal coupler with plastic insulating draft gear box.

### 20 Series Couplers 2 Pair 4.25 ea

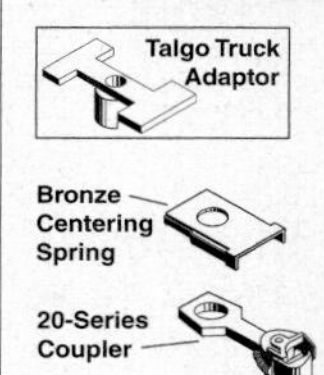

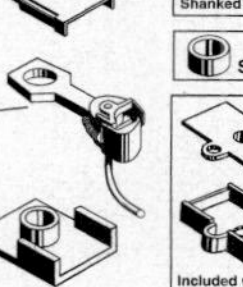

Multi-purpose insulated coupler kit for Talgo truck or body mounting on locomotives or rolling stock. Includes adaptors and No.5® draft gear box. 20 Series coupler may be replaced with the appropriate 40 Series metal coupler for added strength.

**380-21** Long (25/64") Underset Shank

**380-22** Medium (9/32") Overset Shank

**380-23** Short (1/4") Centerset Shank

**380-24** Short (1/4") Underset Shank

**380-25** Short (1/4") Overset Shank

**380-26** Long (25/64") Centerset Shank

**380-27** Medium (9/32") Underset Shank

**380-28** Medium (19/64") Centerset Shank

**380-29** Long (25/64") Overset Shank

### 30 Series Couplers 2 Pair 3.75 ea

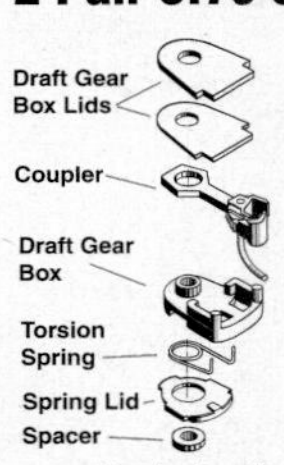

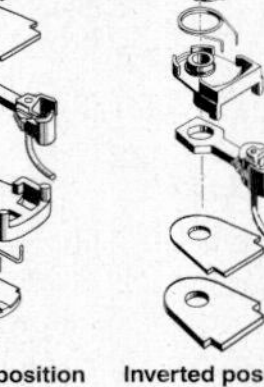


Multi-purpose insulated coupler kit has a small gear box for mounting in small openings. Coupler assembly may be mounted from the top or mounted from the bottom. Draft gear assembly may be inverted for additional variations in coupler mounting heights. 30 Series coupler may be replaced with the appropriate 40 Series coupler for added strength.

**380-31** Long (25/64") Underset Shank

**380-32** Medium (9/32") Overset Shank

**380-33** Short (1/4") Centerset Shank

**380-34** Short (1/4") Underset Shank

**380-35** Short (1/4") Overset Shank

**380-36** Long (25/64") Centerset Shank

**380-37** Medium (9/32") Underset Shank

**380-38** Medium (9/32") Centerset Shank

**380-39** Long (25/64") Overset Shank

## 40 Series Offset-Metal Couplers 2 Pair 3.50 ea

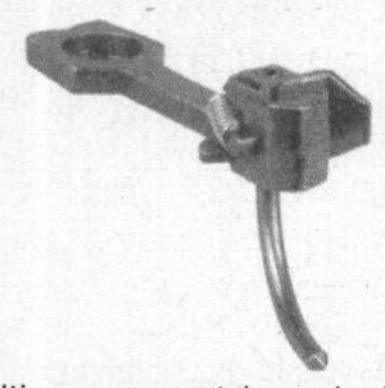

Multi-purpose metal coupler kit with insulated No. 5® gear box with strength you can count on for your long haul. Ideal for body mounting on locomotives and rolling stock.

**380-41** Long (25/64") Underset Shank

**380-42** Medium (9/32") Overset Shank

**380-43** Short (1/4") Centerset Shank

**380-44** Short (1/4") Underset Shank

**380-45** Short (1/4") Overset Shank

**380-46** Long (25/64") Centerset Shank

**380-47** Medium (9/32") Underset Shank

**380-49** Long (25/64") Overset Shank

## #58 "Scale" Metal Coupler

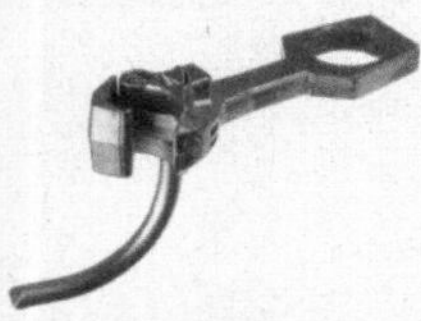

**380-58** Medium (9/32") Centerset Shank 2 Pair **3.75**
All-metal coupler with insulated draft gear box and bronze centering spring. Designed and tested for compatible operation with Kadee® HO Scale couplers. Can be used instead of No.5® coupler for most applications.

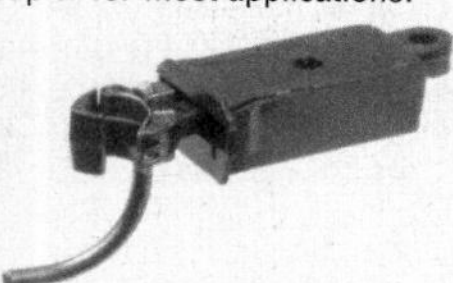

**380-78** Medium (9/32") 2 Pair **5.95**
Centerset shank, scale all-metal coupler with insulated scale draft gear box. Fully assembled.

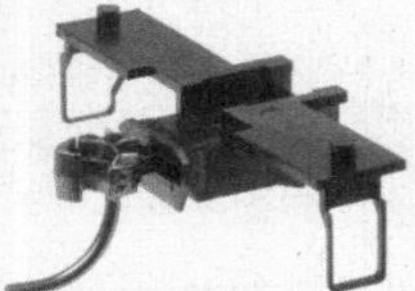

**380-2100** Scale All-Metal Coupler w/Kadee® PS-1 Gear Box 1 Pair **3.50**
Retrofit/replacement of scale coupler and gear box for Kadee® PS-1 box cars. Fully assembled.

## NEM (362) European Style Mount 2 Pair 4.50

**380-17** Short 7.11mm .280"

**380-18** Medium 8.63mm .340"
**380-19** Long 10.76mm .400"
**380-20** Extra Long 11.68mm .460"

## Old-Time Couplers 2 Pair

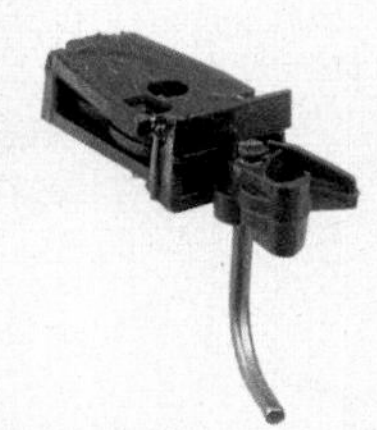

3/4-size couplers for old-time locomotives and cars.
**380-711** HO **3.35**
**380-714** HOn3 **3.40**

## Couplers For Limited-Space Mounting 2 Pair 3.75 ea

**380-6** 13/32" Long Shank
**380-7** 1/4" Long Underset Shank
**380-8** 5/16" Long Shank
**380-16** 1/4" Long Shank

## Coupler Sample Kits

Find out which couplers are right for your cars and locomotives with this sample set of HO couplers.

**380-13** Sampler Kit **27.50**
Includes couplers #4-9, 21-29, 31-39 & 711. Also includes Magne-Matic® Uncouplers #308 & 321.

**380-1030** HO Starter Kit **48.95**
Includes No.5®, 42, 43, 46, 47, 205, 208, 209, 211, 231, 237, 241, 256, 321 and 334.

## Talgo Truck Adaptors

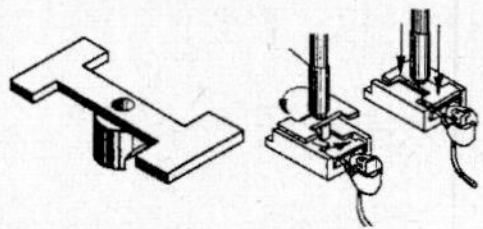

**380-212** pkg(24) **3.35**
Couplers Conversion Kits

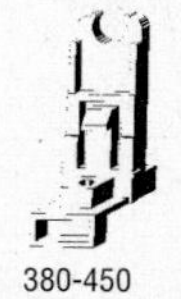
380-450

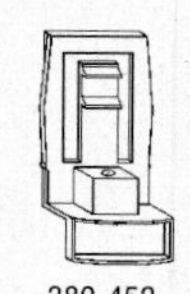
380-452

**380-450** Stewart F Units 1 Pair **5.65**
Coupler conversion for Stewart F3, F7, F9 and A & B units.

**380-452** Bachmann F7 A & B Units 1 Pair **6.75**

**380-453** Life Like PROTO™ 2000 E8/9 1 Set **12.95**

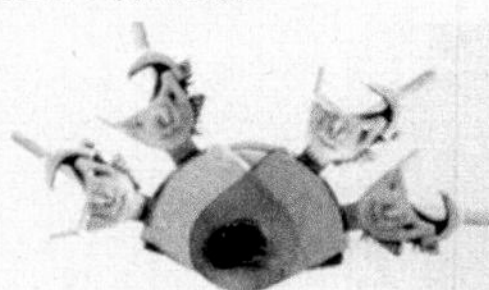

**380-454** Swing Bracket Adaptor Kit 1 Set **7.75**

**380-455** Life-Like PROTO™ 2000 E7A & B or PA & PB Set **9.95**

## Passenger Truck Conversion Bolsters w/Couplers 3.95 ea

Each package contains two conversion bolsters and one Pair of No.5® couplers.

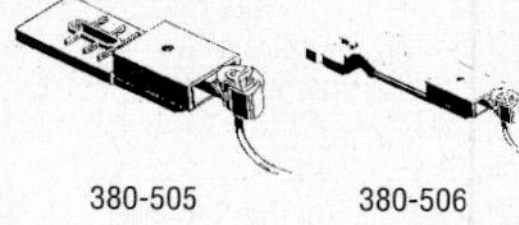
380-505 380-506

**380-505** For AHM, IHC, Rivarossi & Con-Cor six-wheel passenger trucks. Adjusts to different car lengths.

**380-506** For Central Valley 4-Wheel Passenger Trucks

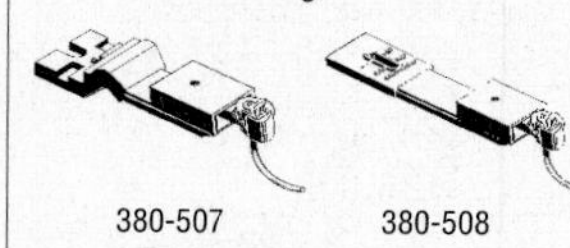
380-507 380-508

**380-507** For Central Valley 6-Wheel Passenger Trucks

**380-508** For AHM, IHC, Rivarossi & Con-Cor four-wheel passenger trucks. Adjusts to different car lengths.

## Coupler Draft Gear Boxes & Shims

380-211 380-232

Draft gear boxes with covers only.

**380-211** Draft Gear Shims pkg(40) **1.75**
For #4-9 couplers. Includes 20 each of .010" and .015" thick draft gear shims.

**380-213** Boxes & Sleeves for 20 Series pkg(24) **3.35**

**380-228** For #4 Couplers, Metal 10 Pair **2.90**

**380-232** For #3, No.5®, 20 Series, 40 Series, #58, #505-508,#148 and #118 Couplers, Plastic 10 Pair **2.85**

**380-233** For 30 Series Couplers 10 Pair **3.95**

**380-234** Boxes w/Lids for #23-25 & 43-45 Couplers 10 Pair **2.85**

**380-242** Universal Snap-Together Gear Box for No.5®, 20, 40-Series, #58, 118 & Whisker® Couplers **2.95**

## Minimum Space Adapter Plate

**380-204** pkg(20) **2.80**
Use with #4 coupler where space is limited. Takes place of #4 draft gear box and cover plate.

# UNCOUPLERS

## Magne-Matic® Uncouplers

For use with Kadee® couplers.

### Under Track

**380-308 4.50**
Extra strong magnet can be completely concealed under ties and ballasted over. For use from HOn3 to O Scale.

### Nondelayed

**380-312** pkg(2) **5.15**
Automatically uncouples cars when couplers are stopped over magnet. You can then pull away, leaving the cars.

### Delayed

When couplers are stopped over uncoupler, knuckles open and move off center to "delayed" position (see Magne-Matic® system diagram at beginning of listing). You can then push uncoupled cars to any location, beyond the uncoupler, without recoupling.

**380-321** pkg(2) **5.15**
**380-709** HOn3 pkg(2) **5.25**

## Uncoupler Gluing Jig

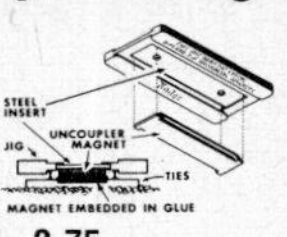


**380-334 2.75**
For installing #312 & 321 magnetic uncouplers in track.

## Magne-Electric Uncouplers

Delayed Magnetic Action® uncoupler effectively eliminates false uncoupling sometimes experienced with permanent magnetic uncouplers. Push-button switch (not included) activates magnet. Ideal for secondary and siding tracks. Mounts through the track.

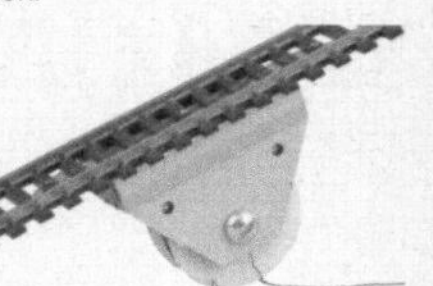

**380-309** HO **16.95**
**380-708** HOn3 **13.95**

# SPRINGS

## Centering Springs

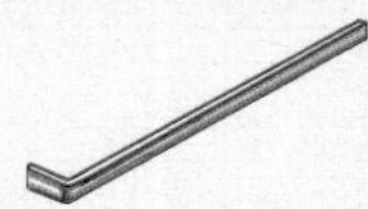

**380-620** For #17-20 Couplers pkg(20) **2.30**

**380-623** For #4 & #205 Height Gauge Couplers, w/Spacer Dowels pkg(12) **1.25**

380-634 380-635

**380-634** For#3, No.5®, 20 Series, 40 Series, #58 & #505-508 Couplers, Plastic pkg(12) **2.75**

**380-635** For #6, 7, 8 & 16 Couplers pkg(12) **1.15**

**380-636** For #711 & 714 Couplers pkg(12) **1.35**

## Knuckle Springs

**380-622** pkg(12) **1.15**
For use with all Kadee® HO Scale couplers (except #58, 78, 150 Series, 711 and 2100).

**380-625** pkg(12) **1.25**
For use with Kadee® #58, 78, 150 Series, 2100 "Scale" metal couplers.

## Torsion Springs

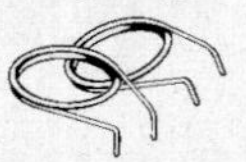

**380-621** For 30 Series Gear Boxes pkg(12) **1.85**

### Truck Springs

**380-624** HOn3 pkg(12) **1.25**

**380-637** HO pkg(18) **2.25**
**380-638** HO pkg(18) **2.50**
For #513 roller bearing trucks.

## SCREWS

### Coupler Mounting Screws pkg(24) 4.55 ea (Unless Noted)

Metal round head screws; 0-48 size.
**380-400** 1/8" Long
**380-401** 3/16" Long
**380-402** 1/4" Long **4.60**
**380-403** 3/8" Long **4.60**

### Plastic Screws

**380-256** 2-56 x 1/2" Long pkg(12) **1.80**
Insulated phillips head screws. Uses include mounting couplers, draft gear boxes and trucks. Can be easily trimmed to appropriate length.

## TRUCKS

Kadee® offers three styles of trucks, Standard, Self-Centering and Talgo (with couplers and coupler pockets mounted on truck). All trucks feature blackened nonmagnetic metal sideframes and RP-25 wheels with insulated axles. Cannot be used for car lighting unless wipers are used on wheels.

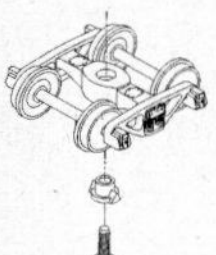

Self-Centering style trucks: when car is picked up the trucks self-align with the car

### Bettendorf Trucks

**380-500** Standard 1 Pair **6.50**
With 33" smooth-back wheels.
**380-550** Self-Centering 1 Pair **6.99**
With 33" smooth-back wheels.

**380-502** Talgo 1 Pair **8.95**
With 33" smooth-back wheels and ready-to-mount couplers.

**380-511** T-Section, Standard 1 Pair **6.50**
With 33" ribbed-back wheels.
**380-554** T Section, Self-Centering 1 Pair **6.99**
With 33" ribbed-back wheels.

**380-512** T-Section, Talgo 1 Pair **8.95**
With 33" ribbed-back wheels and ready-to-mount couplers.

### Arch Bar Trucks

With 33" ribbed-back wheels.

**380-501** Standard 1 Pair **6.50**
**380-551** Self-Centering 1 Pair **6.99**

**380-503** Talgo 1 Pair **8.95**
With ready-to-mount couplers.

### Andrews Trucks

With 33" ribbed-back wheels.

**380-509** Standard 1 Pair **6.50**
**380-553** Self-Centering 1 Pair **6.99**

**380-510** Talgo 1 Pair **8.95**
With ready-to-mount couplers.

### Roller Bearing Trucks

With 36" smooth-back wheels.

**380-513** Standard 1 Pair **8.50**
**380-555** Self-Centering 1 Pair **8.95**

### Barber S-2 70-Ton Roller Bearing Trucks

33" smooth-back wheels.

**380-518** Standard 1 Pair **7.65**
**380-558** Self-Centering 1 Pair **8.50**

### Vulcan Double-Truss Trucks

With 33" ribbed-back wheels.

**380-515** Standard 1 Pair **6.50**
**380-556** Self-Centering 1 Pair **6.99**

**380-516** Talgo 1 Pair **8.95**
With ready-to-mount couplers.

### ASF 50-Ton Ride Control Trucks

With 33" smooth-back wheels.

**380-504** Standard 1 Pair **6.50**
**380-552** Self-Centering 1 Pair **6.99**

### PRR Class 2DF8 50-Ton Trucks

**380-517** Standard 1 Pair **6.75**
With 33" smooth-back wheels.
**380-557** Self-Centering 1 Pair **7.25**
With 33" ribbed-back wheels.

### Disconnect Logging Trucks

**380-107** 1 Pair **17.50**
Two trucks to make a disconnect logging car. Ribbed-back wheels. Includes two pairs of couplers.

### HOn3 Trucks 1 Pair 8.99 ea

Kits include body and truck bolsters, sideframes, spring planks, wheelsets with ribbed-back wheels, truck bushings and springs.

**380-716** 3' 7" Wheel Centers

**380-717** 4' 6" Wheel Centers

## WHEELSETS

RP-25 contour, tapered axles and founding data on wheels.

### Freight Car Wheelsets pkg(12) 8.50 ea

380-520 380-523 380-524

**380-520** 33" Smooth-Back Wheels
**380-523** 33" Ribbed-Back Wheels
**380-524** 28" Smooth-Back Wheels
For modern freight cars such as TOFC and auto carriers.

### Passenger Car Wheelsets pkg(12) 10.50 ea

380-521 380-522

**380-521** 36" Ribbed-Back Wheels
**380-522** 36" Smooth-Back Wheels

### HOn3 Scale Wheelsets

**380-718** 26" Ribbed-Back pkg(8) **8.50**
Same as wheelsets used on trucks #380-716 and 380-717, each sold separately.

## WASHERS

### Fiber Washers pkg(48) 2.55 ea

Truck spacer washers for adjusting car height or coupler height.

380-208 380-209

**380-208** .015" Thick
**380-209** .010" Thick

## TOOLS

### Coupler Height Gauges

A critical tool that ensures top performance. Gauges coupler, trip pin, and magnet uncoupler height, includes built-in track gauge.
**380-205** HO w/Standard & Scale Couplers **4.50**
**380-704** HOn3 **6.50**

### Adapter Insertion Pic

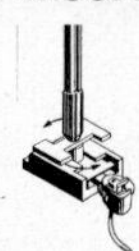

**380-230 2.65**
For use with the #212 and 20 Series Talgo truck mounting adaptors. Sets the adapter into the Talgo mount holding the spring and coupler.

### Grippers

**380-239** Five-Prong Gripper **5.95**

### Pin Vise

**380-240** Double-Headed Pin Vise **5.95**

### Uncoupler/Spring Pic

**380-241** Dual Tool Manual **1.95**
For manually uncoupling Scale, Standard and Shelf couplers. Blade end has a built-in spring pic.

### Tweezers

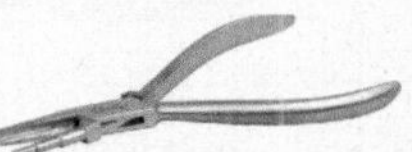

**380-1020** Coupler Tweezers **3.95**

### Trip Pin Pliers

**380-237 12.35**
Special pliers for adjusting the height of coupler trip pins. Jaws of pliers are curved to conform to the correct bend in the trip pin and prevent kinking.

### Coupler Assembly Fixtures 8.50 ea (Unless Noted)

Fixtures hold coupler parts in place for easier assembly.
**380-701** For #4, No.5®, 9, 43, 46 & 58 Couplers
**380-702** For #711 & 714 Couplers **8.95**
**380-703** For #6, 7 & 8 Couplers

### Tap & Drill Sets 5.95 ea

**380-246** 2-56 Tap, #43 & 50 Drills
For 2-56 screw mounting most HO couplers and trucks.
**380-780** 0-80 Tap, #52 & 55 Drills
For 0-80 and 0-48 screws used in the side lugs of the #4, No.5®, 9, 78, 234, 711 and 714 gear box.
**380-247** 1-72 Tap, #48 & 53 Drills
**380-1059** 00-90 Tap, #62 & #56 Drills **6.25**

## HOn3 TRUCK ASSEMBLY FIXTURE

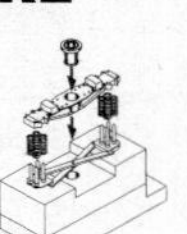

**380-715 4.50**
Fixture holds truck parts in place for easier assembly.

## LUBRICANT

### Greas-em Lubricant

**380-231** 1/4oz Tube **2.25**
A multi-purpose dry lubricant ideal for couplers, wheelsets and trucks, and many other applications.

# HO SCALE COUPLER CONVERSION LIST

Kadee®
Designed, Manufactured & Assembled entirely in the U.S.A.

Most of the listings below have converson instructions listed on the internet at www.kadee.com/conv/ho.htm

### ACCURAIL

All Rolling Stock . . . . . . . . . .MCS

### AHM (RIVAROSSI)

**STEAM**
0-4-0 Dockside (Early model) . . . . . . . . . . . . .34 Pilot, 31 Rear
0-4-0 Dockside (Late model) . . . . . . . . . . . . .34 Pilot, 34 Rear
0-4-0 Switcher w/Tender . . . . .37
0-8-0 Switcher .38 Pilot, 5 Tender
2-4-0 Bowker (Tender only) . . .34
2-8-4 Berkshire 34 Pilot, 26 Tender
2-10-2 Santa Fe Class, . . . . . . .38
2-8-8-2 USRA Mallet . . . . . . . . . . . . . . . . . . . . .33 Pilot, 27 Tender
4-4-0 Genoa or Reno (Tender only) . . . . . . . . . . . . . . . . . . . . . . . .34
4-6-0 Casey Jones (Tender only) . . . . . . . . . . . . . . . . . . . . . . . .37
4-6-2 Heavy Pacific . . . . . . . . . . . . . . . . . . . . .33 Pilot, 27 Tender
4-6-4 J3a Hudson Pilot . . . . .28
Tender . . . . . . . . . . . . . . . .MCS
4-6-6-4 Challenger . . . . . . . . . . .33 Pilot, 27 Tender
4-8-8-2 Cab Forward (Early model) . . . . . . . . . . . . . . . . . . .34
4-8-8-2 Cab Forward (Late model) . . . . .Pilot 33, Tender 27
4-8-8-4 Big Boy . . . . . . . . . . . . . . . . . . . . . . .33 Pilot, 27 Tender
Heisler (2&3 truck) BM 32 TM 21
**DIESEL**
Alco C424 . . . . . . . . . . . . . . .31
Alco RS-2 . . . . . . . . . . . . . .MCS
EMD BL-2 . . . . . . . . . . . . . .MCS
EMD E-8/9 . . . . .27 Pilot, 24 Rear
EMD GP-18 . . . . . . . . . . . . . .21
SD-40 . . . . . . . . . . . .153 or 148
Fairbanks Morse 'C' Liner . . . . . . . . . . . . . . . . . . . .31 Pilot, 37 Rear
GE 1000 . .Modified 20, NEM 362
GE U25C . . . . . . . . . . . . . . . .38
GG1 . . . . . . . . . . . . . . . . . . . .37
Krauss/Maffei . .5, 58, 148 or 28
Plymouth MDT Switcher . . . . . .27
Whitcomb Switcher . . . . . . . . .38
**ROLLING STOCK**
All Freight Cars-Talgo Trucks . . . . . . . . . . . . . . . . . . . . . . . .37 TM
All Freight Cars-Body Mount . . . . . . . . . . . . . . . . . . . . . . .MCS BM
Old Time Freight Cars . . . . . . . . . . . . . . . . . . . . . . . . . . . .MCS
Old Time 4-Wheel Pass. Truck . . . . . . . . . . . . . . . . . . . . . . . .508
4-Wheel Pass. Trucks . . . . . .508
6-Wheel Pass. Trucks . . . . . .505
Tavern Lounge or Observation, dummy coupler end . . . . . . . .38

**NOTE:**
**1. See "Rivarossi" for post 1993 models.**
**2. Most late model RTR European Locos and Rolling Stock come equipped with "NEM" style couplers. Kadee® offers HO-Scale NEM-362 Couplers in four different lengths** . . . . . . . . . . . . .17, 18, 19 & 20

### A-LINE (Proto Power West)

All Rolling Stock . . . . . . . . . .MCS

### AMERICAN MODEL BUILDERS

All Passenger Car Kits . . . . .MCS

### AMERICAN TRAIN & TRACK

**DIESEL**
Alco 415 . . . . . . . . . . . . .MCS TM
Plymouth MDT Switcher . . . . .27
**ROLLING STOCK**
All Freight Cars (Generic) .37 TM
Box Car & Reefers . . . . . . . . . . . . . . . . . . . . . . . . . . . . .MCS BM
Flat Car, 3 Container . . . . . . . . . . . . . . . . . . . . . . . . . . . .MCS BM
Coach, Old Time . . . . . . . . . . . .27

### ATHEARN

**STEAM (EARLY PRODUCTION)**
0-4-2T "Little Monster" .27 or 37
0-6-0 Switcher w/Tender . . . . . . . . . . . . . . . . . . . . . . . . . . . . .MCS
4-6-2 Pacific . . . . . . . . . . . . .MCS
**DIESEL**
Alco PA-1 & PB-1 . . . . .27 or 37
AMD-103 P40 and P42 . . . . . .27
Baldwin S-12 . . . . . . . . . . . . .27
Budd RDC . . .37 Metal Body, 21 Plastic Body
EMD DD40 . . . . . . . . . . . . . . . .38
EMD CF7 . . . . . . . . . . . . . . MCS
EMD F7A & B (Rubberband Drive) . . . . . . . . . . . . . . . . . . . . . . . 31
EMD F7A & B (Gear Drive) . . .37
EMD F45 . . . . . . . . . . . . . . . .38
EMD FP45 . . . . . . . . . . . . . . .38
EMD GP9 . . . . . . . . . . . . . . . .38
EMD GP30 . . . . . . . . . . . . . . .38
EMD GP35 . . . . . . . . . . . . . . .32
EMD GP38-2 . . . . . . . . . . . . . .37
EMD GP40-2 . . . . . . . . . . . . . .38
EMD GP50 . . . . . . . . . . . . . . .38
EMD GP50 Phase II . . . . . . . . .38
EMD GP60 . . . . . . . . . . . . . . .38
EMD SD9 . . . . . . . . . . . . . . . .38
EMD SD35 . . . . . . . . . . . . . . .37
EMD SDP40 . . . . . . . . . . . . . .37
EMD SD40-2 . . . . . . . . . . . . . .37
EMD SD40-2 Snoot Nose . . . . . . . . . . . . . . . . . . . . . . . . . . . .MCS
EMD SD40T-2 . . . . . . . . . . . . .37
EMD SD45 . . . . . . . . . . . . . . .37
EMD SW7 . . . . . . . . . . . . . .MCS
EMD SW7, Calf . . . . . . . . . . .MCS
EMD SW1000 (Late) 38 (Early) 37
EMD SW1500 (Late) 38 (Early) . . . . . . . . . . . . . . . . . . . . . . . .MCS
FM H 24-66 (Trainmaster) . . . .37
GE Dash 9-44CW . . . . . .27 or 28
GE U28B . . . . . . . . . . . . . . . .37
GE U28C . . . . . . . . . . . . . . . .38
GE U30B . . . . . . . . . . . . . . . .37
GE U30C . . . . . . . . . . . . . . . .38
GE U33C . . . . . . . . . . . . . . . .38
GE U33B . . . . . . . . . . . . . . . .37
GE AC 4400 . . . . . . . . . . . . . .28
Hustler . . . . . . . . . . . . . . . .MCS
**ROLLING STOCK**
Freight Cars-Generic (Metal/Wood) . . . . . . . . . . . . . . . . . . . . . . . .4
Box Car 86' Hi-Cube . . . . . . . .27
Caboose ATSF Type . . . . . . . .27
Caboose Bay Window . . . . . . .27
Caboose Extended Type . . . . . .27
Container Well Car . . . . . . . . .27
Flat Car 86' . . . . . . . . . . . . . .27
Husky Stack Gunderson GWF-10 . . . . . . . . . . . . . . . . . . . . . . . .27
ImpackEnd Car or Unit . . . . . . .22
Stock Car . . . . . . . . . . . . . . . .27
Tank Car, 62' . . . . . . . . . . . . .27
TOFC, 86' . . . . . . . . . . . . . . . .27
Other Rolling Stock . . . . . . .MCS

### ATHEARN CONT'D

Work Caboose on Flat . . . . . . .27
Passenger Car Heavyweight . . . . . . . . . . . . . . . . . . . . . . . . .MCS TM
Passenger Car Streamline . . . . . . . . . . . . . . . . .5, 58, 148 or 26 TM

### ATHEARN GENESIS

**STEAM**
USRA 2-8-2 Light Mikado (Both Pilots) . . . . . . . . . . . . . . . . . . . . . . . . . . . . .36 Pilot, MCS Tender
USRA 2-8-2 Light Mikado (Step Pilot) . . . . . . . . . . . . . . . . . . . . . . . . . . . . .34 Pilot, MCS Tender
4-6-2 Pacific 36 Pilot, MCS Tender
4-6-6-4 Challenger . . .153 or 148
48-8-4 Big Boy . . . . . .153 or 148
**DIESEL**
EMD F7 "A" . . . .36 Pilot 38 Rear
EMD F7 "B" . . . . . .38 Both Ends
EMD F3, F7 & F9 "A" . . . . . . . . . . . . . . . . . . . . . . . .36 Pilot, 38 Rear
EMD SD70, 70I, 70M, 75I, 75M . . . . . . .28 Use 26 w/snow Plow
**ROLLING STOCK**
Auto-Max . . . . . . . . . . . .42 or 22
5161 Cubic Foot Trinity Hopper . . . . . . . . . . . . . . . . . . . . . . . . . .78
Caboose, Extended Vision . . . .27
Other Rolling Stock . . . . . . .MCS

### ATHEARN "RTR"

**DIESEL**
EMD CF7 . . . . . . . . . . . . . .MCS
EMD F7 "A" & "B" . . . . . . . . . .33
EMD F-59 PHI . . . .38, 36 w/plow
EMD GP38-2 . . . . . .38 Both ends
EMD GP60M & GP60B . . . . . . . . . . . . . . . . . . . . .27 Both ends
EMD SD40-2 . . . . . . . . . . . .MCS
**ROLLING STOCK**
Bombadier Coach . . . . . . . .MCS
Caboose . . . . . . . . . . . . . .MCS

### ATLAS

**DIESEL**
AEM-7 . . . . . . . . . . . . . . . .MCS
ALP-44 . . . . . . . . . . . . . . . .MCS
Alco C-424/425 . . . . . . . . . .MCS
Alco RS-1 . . . . . . . . . . . . . .MCS
Alco RS-3 . . . . . . . . . . . . . .MCS
Alco RS-11 . . . . . . . . . . . . .MCS
Alco RSD-4/5 . . . . . . . . . . . . .38
Alco RSD-12 . . . . . . . . . . . .MCS
Alco S-1 . . . . . . . . . . . . . . . .28
Alco S-2 . . . . . . . . . . . . . . . .27
Alco S-3 . . . . . . . . . . . . . . . .28
Alco S-4 . . . . . . . . . . . . . . . .27
EMD F3 . . . . . . . . . . . . . . . . .37
EMD F7 . . . . . . . . . . . . . . . . .37
EMD FP7 Austria . . . . . . . . . .34
EMD FP7 . . . . . . . . . . . . . . . .38
EMD GP7 . . . . . . . . . . . . . . . .38
EMD GP7 New Production . . . . . . . . . . . . . . . . . . . . . . . . . . . .MCS
EMD GP38 . . . . . . . . . . . . . . .37
EMD GP-38 New Production . . . . . . . . . . . . . . . . . . . . . . . . . . .MCS
EMD GP40 . . . . . . . . . . . . . . .37
EMD GP40 New Production . . . . . . . . . . . . . . . . . . . . . . . . . . .MCS
EMD SD9 . . . . . . . . . . . . . . . .38
EMD SD24 . . . . . . . . . . . . . . .37
EMD SD-24 (New Production) . . . . . . . . . . . . . . . . . . . . . . . . . . .MCS
EMD SD35 . . . . . . . . . . . . . . .37
H15-44 H16-44 . . . . . . . . . . .MCS
GE C30-7 . . . . . . .33 or 454 Kit
GE U30C . . . . . . . . . . . . . . .MCS
GE Dash 8-40C . . . . . . . . . . .MCS
GEU23B . . . . . . . . . . . . . . .MCS
GE U33/36C . . . . . .38 or 454 Kit
GE Dash 8-40B . . . . . . . . . . .MCS

### BACHMANN

**STEAM**
0-6-0 Switcher (Late) . . . . . . . . . . . . . . . . . . . . .34 Pilot, 33 Tender
0-6-0 USRA Switcher . . . . . . . . . . . . . . . . . . . . . . . . . . . . . . .MCS
2-6-2 Prairie . . . . . . . . . . .MCS ?
2-8-0 Consolidation . . . . . . .MCS
2-8-2 Mikado . . . . . . . . . . .MCS ?
2-10-4 Texas . . . . . . . . . . .MCS ?
4-4-0 American & Jupiter (Older, Tender Only) . . . . . . . . . . . . .33
4-8-4 GS4 (Tender Only) . . . . .37
**DIESEL**
EMD F9 . . . . . . . . . . . . . . . . .37
EMD F45 . . . . . . . . . . . . . . . .37
EMD GP18 . . . . . . . . . . . . . . .28
EMD GP40 . . . . . . . . . . . . . . .37
EMD GP50 . . . . . . . . . . . . . . .37
EMD SD40-2 . . . . . . . . . . . . . .27
GE E60-CP Electric (Amtrak) . .38
GE U36-B . . . . . . . . . . . . . . . .37
Plymouth 35 Ton Switcher . . . .37
**ROLLING STOCK**
All Freight Cars (Generic) . . . . . . . . . . . . . .37 TM or MCS BM
Box Car, 56' All Door . . . . . . . .38
All Cabooses . . . . . . . . . . . . . .37
Crane Car (Lifting) . . . . . . . .27 ?
Budd 85' Coach . . .38 TM or 454
Passenger Cars 85' . . .37 or 454

### BACHMANN SILVER SERIES

**ROLLING STOCK**
Freight Cars . . . . . . . . . . . .MCS

### BACHMANN PLUS

**STEAM**
4-8-4 GS-4 (Tender Only) . . . .37
4-8-4 N&W J (Tender Only) . . .37
4-8-4 Niagara (Tender Only) . .37
4-8-4 Northern (Tender Only) .37
**DIESEL**
EMD F7 A & B . . . . . . . . . . . .452
EMD GP35 . . . . . . . . . . . . . . .27
EMD SD45 . . . . . . . . . . . . . . .38
GE B23-7 . . . . . . . . . . . . . . .MCS
GE B30-7 . . . . . . . . . . . . . . . .33

### BACHMANN SPECTRUM

**STEAM**
0-6-0 Tank Switcher . . . . . . .MCS
4-6-0 Ten Wheeler . . . . . . . . . .22 Pilot, 5, 58, 148 or 28 Tender
4-6-2 K4 Pacific 4 Pilot, 37 Tender
4-6-2 Pacific (new) . . . . . . . . . . . . . . . . . . . . .32 Pilot, MCS Tender
2-8-0 Consolidation . . . . . . . . . . . . . . . . . . . . .36 Pilot,38 Tender
4-8-2 Mountain . . . . . . . . . . . . . . . . . . . . . . . . .39 Pilot, 33 Tender
2-10-0 Russian Decapod . . . . . . . . . . . . . . . . . . . . . . . . . . . . .MCS
Shay 3-Truck . . . . . . . . . . . .MCS
**DIESEL**
EMC Gas Elec Doodlebug . . . . . . . . . . .Rear 5, 58, 148 or 38 .For Small Radius Track 454 w/31
EMD DD40AX . . . . . . . . . . . . .38
EMD F40PH . . . . . . . . . . . . . .27
EMD GP7 . . . . . . . . . . . . . . . .38
**ELECTRIC**
Acela Set . . . . . . . . . .#118 on Flexable arm or #454 with #118
EMD SD45 . . . . . . . . . . . . . . .33
FM H16-44 . . . . . . . . . . . . . . .34
GE 44-Tonner . . . . . . . . . . . . .33
GE 70-Tonner . . . . . . . . . . . . .21
GE 70-Ton Switcher . . . . . . . .22
GE Dash 8-40C 37, (31 Front w/Plow)
GE Dash 8-40CW Wide Cab 37, ( 31 Front w/Plow)

### BACHMANN SPECTRUM CONT'D

**ROLLING STOCK**
Observation Car Front 27, Rear 27+5 box
Passenger Cars (non obs.) . . .27
When running Bachmann Spectru Passenger Cars on tight radius track use . . . . . . . . . . . .454+36
1998 Production Passenger cars . . . . . . . . . . . . . . . . . . . . . . . .MCS

### BRANCHLINE

Passenger Cars (Con-Cor) . . .508
Other Rolling Stock . . . . . . .MCS

### BOWSER

**STEAM**
2-8-0 Consolidation . . . . . . .MCS
2-8-2 Mikado . . . . . . . . . . .MCS
2-10-0 Decapod . . . . . . . . .MCS
4-4-2 Atlantic . . . . . . . . . . .MCS
4-6-2 Pacific . . . . . . . . . . . .MCS
4-8-2 Mountain . . . . . . . . .MCS ?
4-6-6-4 Challenger . . . . . . . . . . . . . . . . . . . .36 Pilot, MCS Tender
Tenders (Penn Line) . . . . . . .MCS
T-7 Type Tender . . . . . . . . .MCS
**DIESEL**
FM H-16 -44 Diesel (Bowser Box) 28 (In a Kadee Box) . . . . . . MCS
Other Rolling Stock . . . . . . .MCS

### BRAWA (See LIFE-LIKE)

**NOTE: Most late model RTR European Locos and Rolling Stock come equipped with "NEM" style couplers. Kadee also offers HO-Scale NEM-362 Couplers in four different lengths** . . . . . . . . . . . . .17, 18, 19 & 20

### BROADWAY LIMITED

**STEAM**
4-6-4 Hudson . . . . . . . . . . . . . . . . . . . . . . . . . .78 Pilot, MCS Tender
SY 2-8-4 Mikado . . . . . . . . . . . . . . . . . . . . .MCS Pilot, 17 Tender
USRA 2-8-4 Heavy Mikado . . . . . . . . . . . . . . . .33 Pilot, 23 Tender

### CANADIAN RAILWAY MODEL

All Freight Cars . . . . . . . . . .MCS

### CASCADE MODELS

Wood Chip Car . . . . . . . . . .MCS

### C&BT

AAR 40' Box Car . . . . . . . . . .27

### C&M SHOPS

All Rolling Stock . . . . . . . . . .MCS

### CENTRAL VALLEY

All Freight Cars . . . . . . . . . .4 or 5
Passenger Cars 4 Wheel Truck 50 . . . . . . . . . . . .6 Wheel Truck 50

### CHALLENGER IMPORTS (Brass)

All Rolling Stock .5, 58, 38 or 148

### CON-COR

**STEAM**
4-6-4 Hudson . . . . . . . . . . . . . . . . . . . . . . .28 Pilot, MCS Tend
4-8-8-4 Big Boy 33 Pilot, 27 Tend
**DIESEL**
BUDD RDC (Plastic Body) . . .21
EMD E7A & B . .Pilot 31, Rear 33

KEY: MCS = No.5®, 28, 58, 118, 119, 148 or 158 Medium Centerset Shank Coupler BM = Mounting, CM = Clip Mounting, SM = Screw Mounting, TM = Truck Mounting, ?5 Or ? = Not Verified/Converted by Kadee®

# HO SCALE COUPLER CONVERSION LIST

Designed, Manufactured & Assembled entirely in the U.S.A.

## CON-COR CONT'D

EMD GP38 .37
EMD GP40 .37
EMD MP15 .22
EMD SD24 .37
EMD SD35 .37
EMD SD40 .38
EMD SW7 .37
**ROLLING STOCK**
All Freight Car Kits (Wood) .4, MCS
Box Cars 60' Greenville .27
Box Cars (Empire Builder Series) .MCS
Box Car PS-1 .27
Flat Car .MCS
Flat Car 54' .MCS
Mill Gondola 54" .MCS
Hopper Greenville .27 ?
Covered Hopper Airslide .27 ?
Covered Hopper PS-2 .38
Reefer .27
1890 Oldie Passenger Car .33
Gunderson 5 Unit Twin Stack MCS
Amtrak Mail Car (60' PD Box Car) .MCS
Amtrak Phase III Car. .508 & 22
Streamlined Passenger Car .MCS BM, 37 TM
Amtrak Superliner .27 in 5 box
New Passenger Cars .4 Wheel Trucks 508
.6 Wheel Trucks 505
72' Passenger Cars w/4 Wheel Trucks .505

## COOPER & OSHTEMO

All Rolling Stock .MCS

## CROWN (Brass)

See Manufacturers Instructions .MCS

## CUSTOM RAIL

89' TOFC .MCS

## DETAIL ASSOCIATES

Covered Hopper ACF 2970 .MCS
Gondola 40' GS .MCS

## DETAILS WEST

Box Car, Comb. Door 50' .MCS
Box Car, Plug Door 50' .MCS

## E&B VALLEY

Mill Gondola 65' .MCS
Covered Hopper .22

## EASTERN CAR WORKS

All Feright Cars .MCS
All Heavywt. Passenger Cars .MCS BM, 21 TM
All Streamlined Passenger Cars 22

## E&C SHOPS

**ROLLING STOCK**
Freight Cars .MCS

## ERM

Insulated Box (Beer) 62'Car .26

## ERTL

All Rolling Stock .MCS

## EURO-MODELS IMPORTERS LTD.

**DIESEL**
EMD FP7 .34
Baldwin Shark .34
**ROLLING STOCK**
Track Cleaning Car (Roco) .37 BM, 21 TM
**DIESEL**
0-C-0 Switcher (German) .37
**ROLLING STOCK**
Non-"NEM" .39

## FLEISCHMANN (Germany)

Most Fleischmann cars and locomotives that do not have "NEM" coupler pockets will use the #39 coupler mounted on the original pin or screw hole.
**NOTE: Most late model RTR European Locos and Rolling Stock come equipped with "NEM" style couplers. Kadee® also offers HO-Scale NEM-362 Couplers in four different lengths** .17, 18, 19, & 20

## FRATESCHI (E.R. MODELS)

**DIESEL**
FA-1 (Brazil) .37

## FUNARO AND CAMERLENGO

See Manufacturers Instructions .MCS

## GEM MODELS (Brass)

Promontory Pass Set .27 in 5 Box
All Rolling Stock .MCS

## GLOOR CRAFT MODELS

All Rolling Stock .MCS

## GOULD CO.

**ROLLING STOCK**
120-Ton Wrecking Crane .22
All Rolling Stock .MCS

## GRANDT LINE HOn3

All HOn3 Rolling Stock .714

## HALLMARK (Brass)

See Manufacturers Instructions .27 or 28

## HOBBYTOWN

**DIESEL**
ALCO 1600 HP RS/RSD .6
EMD GP9 and GP30 (Athearn) .8
Chassis GP20 (TYCO) .8
Chassis SDP40, SD45 .6
Chassis GE U-28C .6

## IHC (Mehano)

**STEAM**
0-4-0 Dockside .27
0-4-0 Switcher 34 Pilot, 34 Tender
0-8-0 Switcher .MCS
2-6-0 Mogul (Mehano) .38 Pilot, 27 Tender
2-6-0 Mogul .38 Pilot, 38 or .28 TM Tender
2-6-0 Camelback Mother Hubbard .Pilot 26
.Tender Talgo Type 28

## IHC (Mehano) CONT'D

2-8-0 Consolidation .39 Pilot, MCS Tender
2-8-2 Mikado .38 Pilot, 27 Tender
4-4-0 American29 Pilot, 28 Tender
4-6-2 Pacific (Mehano) .38 Pilot, 27 Tender
4-6-2 Pacific (IHC) .31 Pilot, MCS Tender
4-6-4 Hudson .36 Pilot, .5or 8 Tender
4-8-2 Mountain .36 Pilot, MCS Tender
**DIESEL**
Alco C-628 .29 TM
Alco C-415 .33
Center-Cab Switcher .27
EMD E8/9 A and B Units .26 Pilot, 27 Rear
EMD SD35 .23
EMD SD40 .22
GG-1 Electric .New 27 Old 37
MDT Switcher .31
**SETS**
Thunder Bolt Set (Mehano) .SD40 Loco 22
.Cars 28
**ROLLING STOCK**
Crane Car and Boom Tender .28 TM or 22 BM
Log Car (Buggy) .MCS
Freight Cars .27 TM or 28 TM
(New) Old Time Freight Cars .MCS
Heavyweight Pass Cars 6 wheel trucks .505
Streamlined Pass Cars 4 wheel trucks .508
Passenger Car Truck, 6 Wheel Die Cast Metal (After Market) 505
Tavern Lounge or Observation, dummy coupler .38

## IMWX

Box Cars .MCS

## INTERMOUNTAIN

**DIESEL**
EMD F-7 A .
26 or 46 Pilot, MCS Rear
EMD F-7 B .MCS Both Ends
**ROLLING STOCK**
All Freight Cars .MCS

## J-C MODELS

All Passenger Cars Kits . MCS

## KATO (Japan)

**DIESEL**
Alco RS-2 .33
Alco RSC-2 .33
EMD GP35 .MCS
EMD GP35 Phase 1A & 1C .MCS
EMD NW2 ... .27 in 5 Box
EMD SD40-2 .23 Rear, 28w/Plow
EMD SD40-2 "Snoot Nose" .23 Rear, 28 w/Plow
SD40 .MCS
SD45 .33
SD45 (New Production) .MCS
SD-70MAC .MCS
SD-80MAC .MCS
SD-90/43MAC .MCS
GE C44-9C (Dash 9) .38 or MCS
**FREIGHT CARS**
ACF 70 TON Covered Hopper .MCS
Business Car .38

## KEY (Brass)

See Manufacturers Instructions .MCS

## KEYSTONE LOCOMOTIVE

Log Buggy .MCS
Climax Log Car (HOn3) .711
(HO) .MCS

## LA BELLE

All Rolling Stock Kits .MCS

## LAMBERT ASSOCIATES

See Manufacturers Instructions .MCS

## LBF COMPANY

**ROLLING STOCK**
Freight Cars .MCS

## LIMA

**STEAM**
2-8-2 Mikado .37 Tender
**DIESEL**
Alco C-420 .38

## MANTUA

**STEAM**
0-4-0 Booster .37
0-4-0 Camelback .37
0-4-0 Switcher .37
0-6-0 Tank Switcher .37
0-6-0 Little Six Switcher .37
0-8-0 USRA Switcher .27 Pilot, 37 Tender
2-6-0 Mogul .37
2-6-2 Prairie .37
2-8-0 Consolidation .37
2-8-2 Mikado (Camelback) .37
2-8-2 Mikado (Old- Pwr. in Tender) .MCS
2-8-2 Mikado .38
2-8-4 Berkshire .37
2-6-6-2 Logger .22 Pilot, 28 Rear
2-6-6-2 Mallet .22 Pilot, 28 Rear
4-4-0 American 31 Pilot, 37 Tender
4-4-2 Atlantic .33
4-6-0 Ten Wheeler (Rogers) .31 Pilot, 37 Tender
4-6-2 Pacific .39 Pilot, 37 Tender
4-6-2 Pacific (Newer) 36 Pilot, 37 Tender
4-6-4 Hudson .31 Pilot, 38 Tender
**DIESEL**
EMD F7A & B .28 TM
EMD GP20 .28 TM
**ROLLING STOCK**
Freight Car Kits .38
Water Car (Old Time) .27
Streamlined Pass. Car (Metal) .28
Passenger Cars, Old Time 1860 .27

## MARKLIN

**Most Marklin Cars and locomotives that have Non-NEM coupler pockets can easily be adapted to use Kadee couplers (mostly 30 series). Contact Kadee with the type of car or locomotive and the Marklin product number.**
***NOTE*: Most late model RTR European Locos and Rolling Stock come equipped with "NEM" style couplers. Kadee also offers HO-Scale NEM-362 Couplers in four different lengths .17, 18, 19, & 20**
**DIESEL**
#83341 (3341) RC 2 SL Electric Loco (Amtrak) .20
**ROLLING STOCK**
#49950 "Goliath" Crane w/Boom & Counterweight Cars .19

## MARKLIN/TRIX

**STEAM**
2-8-2 USRA Mikado . 33,58,or78 .#17 or #18 NEM Tender
**ROLLING STOCK**
40' Box Cars .17
Caboose .17

## MDC-MODEL DIE CASTING CO. (ROUNDHOUSE)

**STEAM**
0-6-0 Yard Hog (Metal) .4
0-6-0 Switcher (Old) .26 Pilot, 4 Tender
0-6-0 Switcher (New) .26 Pilot, 28 Tender
2-6-0 Mogul (Old) .26 Pilot, 4 Tender
2-6-0 Mogul (New) .26 Pilot, 28 Tender
2-6-2 Prairie (Old) .26 Pilot, 4 Tender
2-6-2 Prairie (New) .26 Pilot, 28 Tender
2-8-0 Consolidation (Old) .26 Pilot, 4 Tender
2-8-0 Consolidation (New) .26 Pilot, 28 Tender
4-4-2 Atlantic (Old) .26 Pilot, 4 Tender
4-4-2 Atlantic (New) .26 Pilot, 28 Tender
4-6-0 Ten Wheeler (Old) .26 Pilot, 4 Tender
4-6-0 Ten Wheeler (New) .26 Pilot, 28 Tender
Climax .MCS
Shay .27
**DIESEL**
Alco RS-3 .MCS
Box Cab Diesel .MCS
EMD Model 40 "Critter" .38
Track Cleaner .MCS
**ROLLING STOCK**
All Rolling Stock .MCS
Hopper, Sand (Metal) 4 with 204
Ore Car (Older Metal) .37
All Old-Time Rolling Stock .28
Pullman Palace Cars .MCS
Old-Time 50'Passenger Car .MCS
Harriman Passenger Cars .MCS

## MEHANO (See IHC)

## MICRO-ENGINEERING

**ROLLING STOCK**
All HOn3 Rolling Stock .714
Adapte-Railer .5

## MODEL POWER

**STEAM**
0-4-0 Shifter w/Tender .19
0-4-0 Switcher .27
2-6-0 Switcher w/Tender .33 Pilot, 36 Tender
2-8-0 Consolidation .26 Pilot .MCS Tender
4-6-0 Casey Jones .26 Pilot .MCS Tender
4-6-2 Pacific .38 Pilot .27 Tender
**DIESEL**
Alco 1000 Diesel Switcher .19
ALCO C-430 .28
ALCO C-628 .25
ALCO FA-2 & FB-2 .Front 37 .Rear 27
ALCO RS-11 .33 BM, 29 TM
Baldwin Shark Nose A & B .Front 37, Rear 27
EMD E7 .Front 36, Rear 38
EMD E8/9 .Front 36, Rear 38

KEY: MCS = No.5®, 28, 58, 118, 119, 148 or 158 Medium Centerset Shank Coupler BM = Mounting, CM = Clip Mounting, SM = Screw Mounting, TM = Truck Mounting, ?5 Or ? = Not Verified/Converted by Kadee®

# HO SCALE COUPLER CONVERSION LIST

Designed, Manufactured & Assembled entirely in the U.S.A.

**MODEL POWER CONT'D**

EMD F-2 ................MCS
EMD F3 .................MCS
**Steam (Early Production)**
0-4-2T "Little Monster" ....MCS
0-6-0 Switcher w/Tender ........................MCS
4-6-2 Pacific ..............28
Porter Hustler ...........MCS
**ROLLING STOCK**
250-Ton Crane ..........36 BM
2-Pack Ore Cars .........27 TM
32' Wood Cabooses .........23
Depressed-Center Flat Car ....36
All Freight Cars (Generic) ...................MCS BM, 28 TM
Harriman Passenger/Observation Car ...................28 TM
Old-Time Passenger Car ..28 TM
Streamlined Pass. Cars (Tri-Ang)37
Streamlined Passenger Cars 27 TM

**MODEL EXPO (RIVAROSSI)**

All Rolling Stock see Rivarossi

**MRC**

EMD F7 ................MCS

**MTS IMPORTS (Brass)**

See Manufacturers Instructions .. ......................MCS

**NEW ENGLAND RAIL SERVICE**

All Rolling Stock ..........MCS

**NICKEL PLATE PRODUCTS**

See Manufacturers Instructions .. ......................MCS

**NORTHEASTERN**

All Rolling Stock ..........MCS

**NORTHWEST SHORTLINE**

All HO Rolling Stock .......MCS
All HOn3 Rolling Stock .....714

**OVERLAND MODELS (BRASS)**

See Manufacturers Instructions .. ......................MCS

**PECOS RIVER BRASS**

See Manufacturers Instructions .. ......................MCS

**PFM (Brass)**

See Manufacturers Instructions
HO ................... MCS
HOn3 .................. 714

**PMI (LIMA)**

**STEAM**
0-4-0 Switcher ...........27 ?
2-8-2 Mikado .38 Pilot, 27 Tender
**DIESEL**
ALCO C 420 ...........27 TM
EMD FP45 .....27 with MCS Lid
**ROLLING STOCK**
All Freight Cars ............38
Caboose ................MCS
All Passenger Cars .......27 TM
All Products in HO ........MCS
All Products in HOn3 ......714

**PROTO POWER WEST**

Thrall Container Car .......MCS

**QUALITY CRAFT MODELS**

All Rolling Stock ..........MCS

**RAIL POWER PRODUCTS**

**DIESEL**
EMD CF7 .................38
EMD GP60 (All Versions) ........................MCS
EMD SD38,SD40 ...........38
EMD SD45, SD45-2 .........38
EMD SD60 ................38
EMD SD7/9 ...............38
EMD SD90MAC ..........MCS
EMD SD60M SD75M ........27
GE DASH 9-44CW ..........38
GE DASH 9-40CW ..........38
GE DASH 8-40B ............27
**ROLLING STOCK**
Gunderson Well Car .......MCS
See Manufacturers Instructions for other Kadee coupler recommendations.

**RAILWORKS (Brass)**

See Manufacturers Instructions .. ......................MCS

**RAPIDO TRAINS**

HO Passenger Cars .......MCS

**RED CABOOSE**

All Rolling Stock ..........MCS

**RIVAROSSI (Post 1993)**

**STEAM**
0-8-0 Switcher ........38 Pilot, 38 Tender BM
2-8-4 Berkshire 34 Pilot, 26 Tender
2-8-4 Berkshire (new production) .........33 Pilot, MCS Tender
2-6-6-6 Allegheny ..........MCS
2-8-8-0 and 2-8-8-2 Mallet 33 Pilot
Vanderbilt Tender ...........38
Non-Vanderbilt Tender ....27BM
4-4-0 Amer, Inyo, Reno, Genoa .. ....................38 Tender
4-6-2 Pacific .........33 Pilot: Tender 5, 58 or 148 BM 31 TM
4-6-4 Hudson ..28 Pilot, 5 Tender
4-8-4 UP Northern ............33 Pilot, 27 Tender
4-6-6-4 Challenger ............33 Pilot, 27 Tender
4-8-8-2 Cab Forward ............33 Pilot, 27 Tender
4-8-8-4 Big Boy 33 Pilot, 27 Tender
Heisler Two and Three Truck (new production) ......32 BM, 31 TM
Heisler Two and Three Truck .... ................32 BM 21 TM
Heisler (Walthers) Two and Three Truck (Latest Production) ...... MCS
**DIESEL**
ALCO C-420 .............MCS
EMD E8/9 .....27 Pilot, 24 Rear
**ROLLING STOCK**
Snow Plow ..............38BM
Log Car ..................MCS
Log Car Buggy ..............33
Hvywt. Passenger Car, 6 Wheel 505
Streamlined Pass. Car,4 Wheel 508

**ROCO**

**LOCOMOTIVES**
4169B Locomotive ..........19
**ROLLING STOCK**
200-Ton Crane .............31
All Passenger Cars (NEM-362) 18
***NOTE:* Most late model RTR European Locos and Rolling Stock come equipped with "NEM" style couplers. Kadee® also offers HO-Scale NEM-362 Couplers in four different lengths** 17, 18, 19, & 20

**ROLLER BEARING MODELS**

All Rolling Stock ..........MCS

**ROUNDHOUSE (MDC)**

See MDC-Model Die Casting Co.

**SAMHONGSA (BRASS)**

**STEAM**
4-6-2 Pacific ..................4 Pilot, MCS Tender

**SPECTRUM (See Bachmann)**

**S. SOHO AND CO. (Brass)**

See Manufacturers Instructions .. ......................MCS

**STEWART HOBBIES**

**DIESEL**
ALCO RS-3 .............MCS
Baldwin AS-16 .............22
Baldwin VO-1000 ..........MCS
Alco C-628 "Century" ......26/46
Alco C-630 "Century" ......26/46
EMD FT A & B (Pilot and Rear of B) ........................MCS
(Between A & B) ........... 35
EMD F3 A & B ............450
EMD F7 A & B ............450
EMD F7 A&B ...........35 Pilot, 5/28 Rear, ...........Close Coupling 450
EMD F9 A & B Units ...........35 Pilot, 5/28 Rear, ...........Close Coupling 450
GE U25B ..............MCS
**ROLLING STOCK**
Freight Cars .............MCS

**SUNSET MODELS (Brass)**

See Manufacturers Instructions .. MCS

**SUNSHINE MODELS**

All Rolling Stock ..........MCS

**SYLVAN**

All Rolling Stock (w/Kadee #500 Trucks) .................MCS

**TENSHODO**

See Mfrs Instructions ..... MCS

**THREE BROTHERS (HOLGATE & REYNOLDS)**

Passenger Cars .......MCS BM

**TICHY TRAIN GROUP**

All Rolling Stock .........MCS

**TIGER VALLEY**

All Diesels ..............MCS

**TRAIN-MASTER**

All Rolling Stock .........MCS

**TRAIN MINIATURE**

**DIESEL**
Alco FA-1 ........6 Pilot, 8 Rear
Alco FB-1 .................8

**TRAIN STATION PRODUCTS**

Hi- Level Passenger Car ....MCS

**TRU-SCALE**

All Rolling Stock ..........MCS

**TYCO**

**STEAM**
0-4-0 Booster37 Pilot, MCS Tender
0-6-0 Little Six .........................37 Pilot, MCS Tender
0-6-0 Big Six .............37
0-8-0 Chattanooga .....................5 Pilot, 27 TM Tender
2-6-2 Prairie ...............37
2-8-2 Mikado ...............38
4-4-0 General (Tender Only) .... ........................MCS
4-6-2 Pacific 39 Pilot, 37 Tender
**DIESEL**
ALCO C-430 ...........27 TM
EMD F9 A & B..33 BM and 33 TM
EMD GP20 .................9
GG-1 Electric ..........26 TM
Plymouth Switcher ........MCS
**ROLLING STOCK**
New Rolling Stock .........28
Old Rolling Stock ...........9
Streamlined Passenger Cars ........................MCS
Old-Time Passenger Cars .....9

**U.S. HOBBIES, INC. (Brass)**

See Manufacturers Instructions ......................MCS

**VAN HOBBIES MODELS**

Canadian Models sold by PFM ......................MCS

**VARNEY**

F-3 ......................33
F-7 ......................33

**WALTHERS**

**ROLLING STOCK**
Freight Cars (Except as Noted) .. ......................MCS
M.O.W. Difco Dump Car (Metal Chassis) .................28
Jordan Spreader ..........Front 36, Rear MCS
**Passenger Cars**
Amfleet Passenger Car ......... ......................MCS
Budd Passenger Cars ...28 or 46
Horizon Commuter Pass. Car ............MCS or 454 w/36
Superliner Passenger Cars ....26
On small radius curves use 454 with 38
**DIESEL**
EMD SW-1 Switcher .......MCS
FM H10/12-44 ..........MCS
Sperry Rail Inspection Car ...... ..........MCS or 38 Rear Only

**WALTHERS LIFE-LIKE®**

**STEAM**
0-4-0 Old Time Tea Kettle ....28
0-4-0 Tank (Dockside) .......27
0-4-0 Switcher ............27
**DIESEL**
EMD F7A ............Pilot 37, ...........Rear 35 or 27 TM
EMD F7B .........35 or 27 TM
EMD F40PH ...........28TM
EMD GP38-2 ................New 33 BM, Old 28 TM
**ROLLING STOCK**
Truck-Mounted Freight Cars .... ..................27 or 28 TM
Body-Mounted Freight Cars ...................MCS BM

**WALTHERS LIFE-LIKE® PROTO 1000™ SERIES**

**DIESEL**
ALCO DL-109 ...........MCS
ALCO RS-2 .............MCS
C-Liner ................MCS
Erie-Built ..5 Pilot, 23 or 43 Rear
F3A .......23 Regular, 33 Close
R-17 Subway Car .........MCS
Budd RDC-1 .............MCS
**ROLLING STOCK**
Freight Cars ............MCS

**WALTHERS LIFE-LIKE PROTO 2000™ HERITAGE**

**STEAM**
USRA 0-6-0 Steam Loco ....... ......................MCS
USRA 0-8-0 Steam Loco ....... ......................MCS
2-8-4 Berkshire .........MCS
2-8-8-2 Mallet .......... MCS

**WALTHERS LIFE-LIKE PROTO 2000™ SERIES**

**DIESEL**
Alco FA-1 ..............MCS
Alco FB-1 ..............MCS
Alco FA-2 ......36 or 26 Front, ................38 or 28 Rear
Alco FB-2 ............38 or 28
Alco PA/PB 26 Pilot, 23 Ends, For
Alco S-1 ...............MCS
EMD BL-2 Diesel ......32 or 22
EMD E6 A&B 23, For Close Coupling ................455
EMD E8/9 A ..........33 or 453
EMD E7 A&B 26 Pilot 23 Ends, For Close-Coupling ........455
EMD E8/9A .........33 or 453
EMD GP9 ...............MCS
EMD GP18 ..........38 or 28
EMD GP18 (New Production) ... ......................MCS
EMD GP20 ..............MCS
EMD GP30 ..............MCS
EMD GP38-2 ............MCS
EMD GP60 ..............MCS
EMD SD7 .........33 or 23 CM
EMD SD9 .................33
EMD SD45 ..............MCS
EMD SD60, SD60M .......MCS
EMD SW 9/1200 .........MCS
EMD SW600, 8, 900 ......MCS
**ROLLING STOCK**
Box Car, 50' DD Auto ..................5, 58 or 1483
Caboose .................38
Other Freight Car Kits ......................MCS
Factory Assembled Cars (RTR) .. ......................MCS

**WALTHERS TRAINLINE®**

**DIESEL**
Alco FA-1 and FB-1 .......MCS
EMD F40PH ...............28
EMD GP9M ...............28
GE Dash 8-40B ..........MCS

**WALTHERS TRAINLINE SETS**

**DIESEL**
EMD GP9M ...............28
**ROLLING STOCK**
Box Car ..................29
Caboose, Extended Vision ....27
Flat Car ..................28
Gondola ..................28
Tank Car .................22

KEY: MCS = No.5®, 28, 58, 118, 119, 148 or 158 Medium Centerset Shank Coupler BM = Mounting, CM = Clip Mounting, SM = Screw Mounting, TM = Truck Mounting, ?5 Or ? = Not Verified/Converted by Kadee®

Designed, Manufactured & Assembled entirely in the U.S.A.

WESTERFIELD

All Rolling Stock Kits ...... MCS

WESTSIDE MODEL CO. (Brass)

See Manufacturers Instructions .. MCS

YANKEE CLIPPER MODELS

All Rolling Stock Kits ...... MCS

YE OLDE HUFF-N-PUFF

ROLLING STOCK
All HO Rolling Stock Kits ........................ MCS
All HOn3 Rolling Stock Kits ...... 714

ALL HOn3 MANUFACTURERS

You may choose HOn3 Kadee® #714 couplers. The "Old Time" 3/4-size Kadee® #711, 58 and 78 may be able to be modified. Be sure to always use the #704 coupler height gauge to check for proper trip pin clearance and coupler height.

COUPLER MOUNTING HELPFUL HINTS

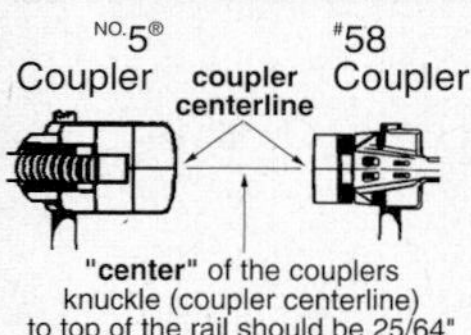


To attain peak coupler performance, all couplers need to be at the same height. The NMRA standard S-1 requires HO coupler height to be 25/64" above the rail, measured from the top of the rail to the center of the couplers.

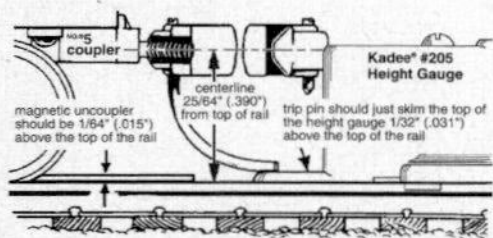


Also, for the most dependable operations, the trip pin height and uncoupler height needs to be at the above measurements.

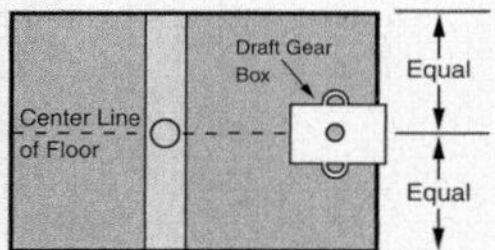


Always mount the couplers on the centerline of all rolling stock and locomotives.

NorthWest Short Line

A NorthWest Short Line 100 + page catalog (#53-1, **9.00**) is available for more detailed information on these products.

## DRIVE UNITS

### Flea II 59.95 ea (Unless Noted)

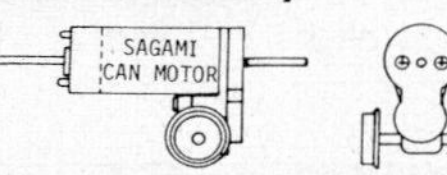


**53-2046** With Economy Motor & 33"/88 Tread Wheelset **49.95**

**53-2056** With NWSL 1020 Motor & 33"/88 Tread Wheelset

**53-2066** With NWSL 1025 Motor & 33"/88 Tread Wheelset

### Flea II Geared Wheelsets 7.95 ea

Geared wheelsets have a 3/32" shoulder style axle, except for #53-20196, which is flush.1/16" journal on shouldered style. Wheelsets fit Flea II #53-2056, #53-2066 or Auxiliary Gearbox #53-2076.

**53-20016** 33"/110 Wheels

**53-20026** 36"/110 Wheels

**53-20186** 26"/88 Wheels, HOn3

**53-20196** 26"/88 Wheels, Flush Axle

**53-20096** 33"/88 Wheels

**53-20106** 36"/88 Wheels

**53-20236** 3/32" Shaft (Axle) w/Gear

## WHEELSETS

Nonmagnetic wheelsets (insulated on one side). Solid nickel-silver wheels weathered in a rust color that can be removed with an eraser or allowed to wear off the tread with use. In general, 110 size tread is used in HO Gauge, 88 in HOn3 and HO semi-finescale.

### Athearn Outside (Metal Sideframe) Frame pkg(12) 9.95 ea

**53-371384** 36"/110 Wheels

**53-371394** 40"/110 Wheels

**53-371404** 42"/110 Wheels

**53-372394** 40"/88 Wheels

**53-372404** 42"/88 Wheels

### Athearn Inside (Plastic Sideframe) Frame, Some Life-Like pkg(12) 9.95 ea

**53-371414** 40"/110 Wheels

**53-371424** 42"/110 Wheels

**53-371434** 36"/110 Wheels

**53-371444** 45"/110 Wheels

**53-372414** 40"/88 Wheels

**53-372424** 42"/88 Wheels

**53-372444** 45"/88 Wheels

### 1.5mm Half-Axle Wheels Kato/Stewart/Atlas/Athearn Genesis/Some Life-Like pkg(12) 9.95 ea

**53-371914** 40"/110

**53-371924** 42"/110

**53-372914** 40"/88

**53-372924** 42"/88

### Blunt Axle Wheelsets 9.95 ea

**53-371094** 40"/110 Wheels Fits early Athearn dummy diesels.

**53-371104** 42"/110 Wheels pkg(6) Fit early Athearn dummy diesels.

**53-371294** 40"/110 Wheels Fit later Athearn dummy diesels.

**53-371304** 42"/110 Wheels Fit later Athearn dummy diesels.

### Flush Axle Wheelsets

**53-371234** 26"/110 Wheels pkg(4) **6.95**

**53-371254** 28"/110 Wheels pkg(4) **6.95**

**53-371274** 33"/110 Wheels pkg(4) **6.95**

**53-371284** 36"/110 Wheels pkg(6) **9.95**

**53-371294** 40"/110 Wheels pkg(6) **9.95**

**53-371304** 42"/110 Wheels pkg(6) **9.95**

**53-372234** 26"/88 Wheels pkg(4) **6.95**

**53-372254** 28"/88 Wheels pkg(4) **6.95**

**53-372274** 33"/88 Wheels pkg(4) **6.95**

### Pointed 1.015" Axle Wheelsets

Athearn, MDC, etc.

**53-371134** 26"/110 Wheels pkg(4) **6.95**

**53-371154** 28"/110 Wheels pkg(4) **6.95**

**53-371164** 30"/110 Wheels pkg(4) **6.95**

**53-371174** 33"/110 Wheels pkg(4) **6.95**

**53-371184** 36"/110 Wheels pkg(6) **9.95**

**53-371194** 40"/110 Wheels pkg(6) **9.95**

**53-371204** 42"/110 Wheels pkg(6) **9.95**

**53-372134** 26"/88 Wheels pkg(4) **6.95**

**53-372154** 28"/88 Wheels pkg(4) **6.95**

**53-372164** 30"/88 Wheels pkg(4) **6.95**

**53-372174** 33"/88 Wheels pkg(4) **6.95**

**53-372184** 36"/88 Wheels pkg(6) **9.95**

### Pointed .970" Axle Wheelsets

European wheelsets for Roco and Rivarossi products.

**53-371674** 33"/110 Wheels pkg(4) **6.95**

**53-371684** 36"/110 Wheels pkg(6) **9.95**

**53-372674** 33"/88 Wheels pkg(4) **6.95**

**53-372684** 36"/88 Wheels pkg(6) **9.95**

### Pointed .944" Axle Wheelsets

For use with Atlas items.

**53-371874** 33"/110 Wheels pkg(4) **6.95**

**53-371884** 36"/110 Wheels pkg(6) **9.95**

**53-372874** 33"/88 Wheels pkg(4) **6.95**

**53-372884** 36"/88 Wheels pkg(6) **9.95**

### Shouldered Axle Wheelsets

Wheelsets are non-magnetic weathered nickel-silver.

**53-371034** 26"/110 Wheels pkg(4) **6.95**

**53-371054** 28"/110 Wheels pkg(4) **6.95**

**53-371064** 30"/110 Wheels pkg(4) **6.95**

**53-371074** 33"/110 Wheels pkg(4) **6.95**

**53-371084** 36"/110 Wheels pkg(6) **9.95**

**53-371094** 45"/110 SD80/90 Wheels **9.95**

**53-372034** 26"/88 Wheels pkg(4) **6.95**

**53-372054** 28"/88 Wheels pkg(4) **6.95**

**53-372074** 33"/88 Wheels pkg(4) **6.95**

**53-372084** 36"/88 Wheels pkg(6) **9.95**

### Life-Like Proto 2000 E8, E9 Units pkg(12) 10.95 ea

Half axle with needle point, available in two tread sizes.

**53-371454** 36"/110

**53-372454** 36"/88

### Spoked Wheelsets pkg(2) 6.95 ea

Nine-spoke, double-insulated, nickel-plated tire.

**53-471074** HO 33"/110 Shoulder 3/32" Axle

**53-471084** HO 36"/110 Shoulder 3/32" Axle

**53-471174** HO 33"/110 Point 3/32" Axle

**53-471184** HO 36"/110 Point 3/32" Axle

**53-471274** HO 33"/110 Flush 3/32" Axle

**53-472034** HO 26"/88 Shoulder 2mm Axle

**53-472134** HO 26"/88 Point 2mm Axle

**53-472164** HO 30"/88 Point 1.5mm Axle

**53-472234** HO 26"/88 Flush 2mm Axle

**53-472264** HO 30"/88 Flush 1.5mm Axle

**53-472364** HO 38"/88 Point 1.5mm Axle

**53-473034** HOn3 26"/88 Shoulder 2mm Axle

**53-473134** HOn3 26"/88 Point 2mm Axle

**53-473164** HOn3 30"/88 Point 2mm Axle

**53-473234** HOn3 26"/88 Flush 2mm Axle

KATO

## TRUCKS

### ASF Ride Control Trucks

**381-31601** A-3 pkg(2) **5.98**
Based on American Steel Foundries A-3 freight car truck. Fully assembled, molded in black plastic with metal wheels. Designed to fit most freight cars.

### Barber S-2 Trucks

**381-31602** 70-Ton Roller Bearing pkg(2) **5.98**
Features a wheel bearing cap that spins as truck is rolling, simultaneously maintaining the car's smooth rolling ability.

## RAIL LINE

### Couplers

620-101

620-107

**620-101** Magnetic w/Draft Gear pkg(4) **2.50**

**620-106** Regular NMRA Style w/Draft Gear pkg(4) **2.00**

**620-107** Regular NMRA Style, Less Draft Gear pkg(4) **1.20**

**620-116** HOn3 "Sharon" pkg(6) **1.00**

### Uncouplers

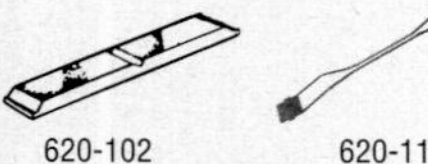
620-102 620-112

**620-102** Magnet for #620-101 pkg(2) **3.00**

**620-112** Uncoupling Ramp, Stationary pkg(2) **1.20**
One-piece, black nylon uncoupling ramp assures positive, automatic switching. Installs anywhere on your layout.

## RAPIDO TRAINS

### NEW PRODUCT

### Passenger Trucks

**NEW 606-102001** 41-BNO-11 Outside Swinghanger Passenger Truck 1 Pair **14.95**
These 41-BNO-11 4-wheel, outside-swinghanger trucks were originally built by General Steel Castings and Canadian Car & Foundry from 1947 until the 1960s. They were the most common passenger car trucks used on new and rebuilt cars during that time period, and most are still in use on VIA, Amtrak, business cars, private cars and tourist lines. The models feature:

- Fully ready-to-run
- Detailed on all four sides with 8 separately-applied parts per truck
- Serial number moulded on each truck
- Slippery Celcon plastic bearings
- Insulated blackened metal RP-25 wheelsets included

## RED CABOOSE

Items listed in blue ink may not be available at all times (see Legend Page).

### Freight Trucks

#### Barber

**629-5016** With Plastic Wheels **2.75**

**629-5018** Without Wheels **2.00**

#### T Section

**629-5004** With Plastic Wheels Black **2.75**

**629-5011** Bettendorf Truck Less Wheels 1 Pair, Black **2.00**

#### Andrews

**629-5007** With Plastic Wheels **2.75**

#### PRR 2DF8

**629-5009** With Plastic Wheels Black **2.75**

**629-5013** Less Wheels, Black **2.00**

### Weights

#### Gondola

**629-5022 1.85**

**629-5023** pkg(2) **2.95**

#### Flat Car

**629-200013 1.85**

**629-200014** pkg(2) **2.95**

## RIX PRODUCTS

### Uncoupling Tool

**628-14 3.49**
When inserted between two cars or engines with magnetically activated couplers, the tool will cause the couplers to release.

## SMOKEY VALLEY

These detailed plastic parts can be combined with other manufacturers' products to create customized or super-detailed cars and locomotives. Basic instructions for assembly and installation are included.

Please visit Walthers Web site at www.walthers.com for a complete listing of all available items.

### SIDEFRAMES

### 9.45 ea

All kits include one set of sideframes.

**676-24** Athearn AAR Switcher w/Roller Bearings
Fits switcher trucks.

#### GE

#### GSC Dash 8

**676-78** Fits Athearn "C" Three-Axle Power Trucks

**676-79** Fits Bachmann Dash 8-40C Power Trucks

#### EMD

**676-90** Blomberg "M" Phase 2
Fits Athearn "B" two-axle power trucks.

**676-120** SW Flex-i-Coil "B" Type Switcher
Fits Athearn switcher power trucks.

**676-145** HTCR II Radial
Fits Athearn three-axle Dash 2 power trucks.

**676-146** HTCR II Radial **9.95**
Fits Athearn three-axle Genesis power trucks.

### Truck Parts

**676-122** Truck Exposed Roller-Bearing Journals pkg(8) **4.45**

**676-300** Low-Mounted Brake Cylinders w/Brake Shoes pkg(8) **4.45**

**676-332** Vertical Struts/Shock Absorbers for EMD HTC & Other Trucks pkg(8) **3.45**

## TICHY TRAIN GROUP

Please visit Walthers Web site at www.walthers.com for a complete listing of all available items.

### FREIGHT TRUCKS

Heavy-duty trucks have a 5-1/2' wheel base and include wheelsets. Arch bar trucks are molded in paintable styrene with nylon bearings. All other trucks are molded black Delrin and self-lubricating.

#### Arch Bar Kits

**293-3002** 1 Pair **2.95**

**293-3035** 10 Pair **14.50**

#### Andrews 2.95 ea

**293-3012** Kit 1 Pair

**293-3026** Assembled 1 Pair

#### Bettendorf 2.95 ea

**293-3024** Assembled 1 Pair

**293-3049** Leaf/Coil 1 Pair

**293-3051** Caboose, Leaf Springs 1 Pair

# TRACK

Models by Christian Grenier and Pierre Dion, Photos by Pierre Dion

Clean ballast marks the completion of a curve realignment in the busy terminal at White River Junction, Vermont. The steady pounding of heavy freight and passenger trains moving back and forth from the US and Canada puts quite a load on these rails, and frequent inspections keep things moving smoothly. You can guarantee that the section foreman will be hearing from the agent about those weeds that have already crept in!

Serving trains of the Boston & Maine and Central Vermont, the joint station scene was built by Christian Grenier for his home layout. Today, the action includes the CP "Alouette" about to depart for Montreal via Wells River, followed by the "Seaview" in place of the usual "Cape." The weathered and detailed motive power is the work of Pierre Dion, who also took the photo.

One of the most important models on your layout, good track can easily make or break any railroad, model or prototype! On the pages the follow, you'll find everything you need to construct a solid right-of-way for operations on your line.

# WALTHERS

MADE EXCLUSIVELY FOR WALTHERS BY SHINOHARA

## NOW FEATURING DCC-FRIENDLY TURNOUTS

Track is one of the most important models on your layout. Walthers Code 83 Track System, makes building realistic yards, mainlines and industrial sidings is fast, easy and fun.

Now that more and more layouts are using Digital Command Control, we've revised our entire selection of turnouts to make them DCC-Friendly. These versions feature electrically isolated frogs and points to eliminate polarity problems that may cause short circuits when decoder-equipped locos or cars with metal wheels enter the turnout.

### DCC-Friendly Turnouts

- Isolated Frogs
- Isolated Points
- Eliminates Short Circuits Crossing Turnouts
- Completely Compatible with Original Walthers Code 83 Track
- Pre-wired jumper
- Isolated frog with built-in connection; an access point allows you to convert to a live frog if desired
- Improved point clearance gaps to prevent short circuits from metal wheelsets
- Insulated tie bar
- Tab reinforcement to hold points more securely
- Option to power frog through switch machines

### Outstanding Realism...

- Simulates 132-lb rail used on most lines
- Models look more massive and realistic
- Thin, dark brown ties with woodgrain
- Rail joiners with bolt detail
- Spike Mounting holes next to the rail
- Realistic spike head and fishplate details

### Easy To Use...

- Realism of hand-laid track without the work
- Complete system, wide selection

### Great Selection...

- DCC-Friendly Turnouts in 5 popular sizes
- Flex Track

### Superb Performance...

- Nickel-silver rail improves electrical conductivity

### Unique Items...

- Double-Slip turnouts
- Double Crossovers
- Code 83-100 & 70-83 Transition Tracks
- Bridge Track sections with guardrails
- DCC-Friendly Curved Turnouts in 4 sizes
- DCC-Friendly Wye Turnouts in 5 sizes

Models and Photo by Ken Patterson

Get the Scoop!
Get the Skinny!
Get the Score!
Check Out Walthers Web site at
**www.walthers.com**

# WALTHERS

MADE EXCLUSIVELY BY SHINOHARA FOR WALTHERS

Like a spider web of steel, a complex network of track keeps trains moving. Big city yards often shoehorned miles of track and turnouts into narrow spaces. The result was some mighty busy railroading with trains arriving, switching and departing around the clock. This diorama by Ken Patterson is based on the tracks at St. Louis Union Station. Ken used Walthers fully-assembled #6 Double Slip and #10 Turnouts to make construction quick and easy, then completed the work with sections of Flex Track cut to length and spiked in place. A few extras such as motor drives to simulate powered turnouts, switchstands, ballast and period equipment complete the scene.

## CODE 83 "DCC-FRIENDLY" TURNOUTS

With more layouts using Digital Command Control, our entire selection of turnouts is now DCC-Friendly with electrically isolated frogs and points to eliminate polarity problems that may cause short circuits when decoder-equipped locos, or cars with metal wheels enter the turnout.

### #4 18.98 ea

Total length: 8-15/16" 22.3cm.

Ideal for small layouts or modeling tighter trackage found in industrial areas. Perfect for new layouts too — #4s are among the most commonly specified turnouts in track plans.

**948-8801** Left

**948-8802** Right

### #5 18.98 ea

A: Total length: 10-3/8" 263.5mm

B: Points to Frog: 5-21/32" 143.7mm

C: Frog Angle: 11° 26'

**948-8891** Left

**948-8892** Right

### #6 18.98 ea

A: Total length: 11-5/16" 287.3mm

B: Points to Frog: 6-9/16" 166.7mm

C: Frog Angle: 9° 32'

**948-8803** Left

**948-8804** Right

### #8 19.98 ea

A: Total length: 13-7/8" 352.4mm

B: Points to Frog: 8-1/32" 204mm

C: Frog Angle: 7° 9'

**948-8805** Left

**948-8806** Right

### #10 28.98 ea

Total length: 16-1/8" 41.2cm

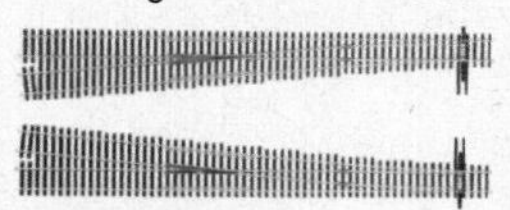

**948-8884** Left

**948-8885** Right

### Wye Turnouts 18.98 ea

**948-8887** #2 (Matches #4 Turnouts)

A: Total length: 6" 15cm

Well suited to any layout or era, this is a perfect choice for modelers working in limited space. Matches #4 turnouts #948-8801 and 8802 (both sold separately) for more planning possibilities.

**948-8890** #2-1/2 (Matches #5 Turnouts)

A: Total length: 7-3/16" 182.6mm

B: Points to Frog: 3-19/32" 91.3mm

C: Frog Angle: 22° 54'

**948-8893** #3

A: Total length: 7-7/8" 200mm

B: Points to Frog: 3-3/4" 95.2mm

C: Frog Angle: 19° 5'

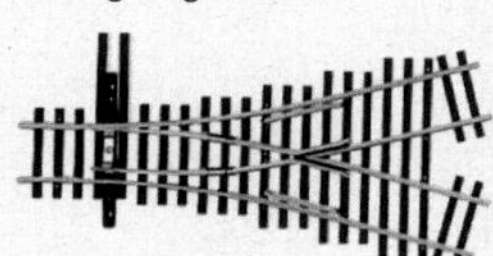

**948-8807** #4 (Matches #8 Turnouts)

A: Total length: 9-23/32" 247.8mm

B: Points to Frog: 4-5/16" 134.9mm

C: Frog Angle: 14° 15'

**948-8883** #5

A: Total length: 13-7/8" 352.4mm

B: Points to Frog: 8-1/32" 204mm

C: Frog Angle: 7° 9'

### Curved Turnouts 33.98 ea (Unless Noted)

#### #6-1/2

A: Total length: 12-25/32" 324.6mm

R1: Inside Radius 20" 508mm

R2: Outside Radius 24" 609.6mm

**948-8826** Left **31.98**

**948-8827** Right **31.98**

#### #7

A: Total length: 14-31/32" 380.2mm

R1: Inside Radius 24" 609.6mm

R2: Outside Radius 28" 711.2mm

**948-8894** Left

**948-8895** Right

#### #7-1/2

A: Total length: 17-7/32" 437.4mm

R1: Inside Radius 28" 711.2mm

R2: Outside Radius 32" 812.8mm

**948-8888** Left

**948-8889** Right

#### #8

A: Total length: 19" 482.6mm

R1: Inside Radius 32" 812.8mm

R2: Outside Radius 36" 914.4mm

**948-8828** Left

**948-8829** Right

### #6 Specialty Turnouts

#### Three-Way

**948-8808 39.98**

A: Total Length: 13-3/8" 339.7mm

B: Points to Frog: 5-1/8" 130.2mm

C: Width: 3-23/32" 94.4mm

#### Double Crossover

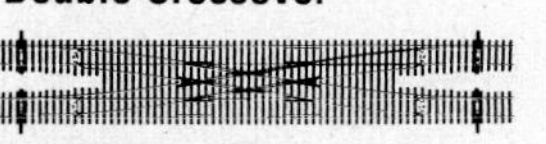

**948-8812 59.98**

A: Total Length: 19-5/32" 486.6mm

B: Points to Frog: 6-19/32" 167.5mm

C: Frog Angle: 9° 30'

### Double Slip Turnouts

**948-8814** #6 **54.98**

A: Total Length: 15-7/16" 392.1mm

B: Points to Frog: 7" 177.8mm

C: Frog Angle: 9° 30'

**948-8896** #8 **64.98**

A: Total Length: 20-1/4" 515mm

B: Points to Frog: 7-7/8" 200mm

C: Frog Angle: 7° 9'

Flex Track

Turnout

Wye Turnout

Curved Turnout

Three-Way Turnout

Crossing

Double Crossover

Dimensions shown with all listings indicate:

A: Overall length

B: Distance from points to frog

C: Frog angle in degrees and minutes

## CODE 83 TRACK

### Flex Track

**948-815** 39" Section **6.98**

Dealers MUST order in multiples of 10.

### Crossings 17.98 ea

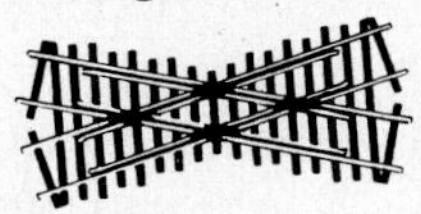

**948-830** 30°

A: Total Length: 6-11/32" 161.5mm

B: Angle: 30°

**948-831** 45°

A: Total Length: 5-9/16" 141.9mm

B: Angle: 45°

**948-832** 60°

A: Total Length: 4-13/16" 123mm

B: Angle: 60°

**948-833** 90°

A: Total Length: 3-7/32" 82mm

B: Angle: 90°

# WALTHERS

MADE EXCLUSIVELY BY SHINOHARA FOR WALTHERS

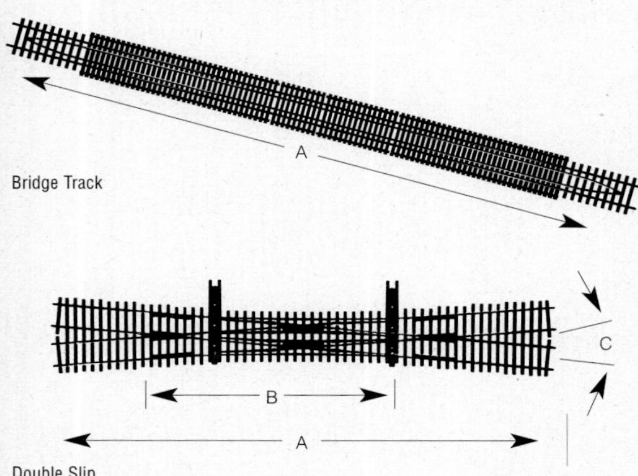


Dimensions shown with all listings indicate:

A: Overall length

B: Distance from points to frog

C: Frog angle in degrees and minutes

## Bridge Track

**948-886** Bridge Track w/Guard Rails & Separate Approach "V" Sections **18.98**

Total Length: About 18" 1/2 Meter

Designed as an add-on accessory for Walthers Cornerstone Series® bridge kits, easily used with other models and scratchbuilt projects. Features Code 83 outside rails and Code 70 inside guardrails, plus separate V-shaped end rails used on the approach and exit to the span.

**948-899** Truss Bridge Track **19.99**

A: Total Length: 19-11/16" 500mm

Designed especially for the Cornerstone Series® Double-Track Truss Bridge, (#933-3012 sold separately) this single track section features detailed bridge ties and inside guard rails with Code 70 rail. Two bridge tracks required for each bridge. Can also be used with most HO bridges.

## Bulk Rail

**948-870** 150' 45m pkg(50) **100.00**

Includes 50 rail sections, each 3' long.

## Transition Track 5.98 ea

These transition tracks can combine other rail sizes with Walthers Code 83 system to create realistic mainlines, yards and sidings. Each 6" section has a small section of Code 83, combined with Code 100 or 70 track.

**948-897** Code 83 to Code 100

**948-898** Code 83 to Code 70

## Rail Spikes

**948-360** .024 x 3/8" pkg(500*) **5.80**

For Code 83 or Code 70 track. *Package is sold by weight, number shown is approximate.

## Rail Joiners

**948-841** Code 83 pkg(50) **7.98**

Got a Mouse? Click Walthers Web Site at

**www.walthers.com**

## BRIGHT BOY TRACK CLEANER

Easy-to-use Bright Boy track cleaning block keeps rails and wheels clean and bright. Just run Bright Boy over rails for clean track with better conductivity.

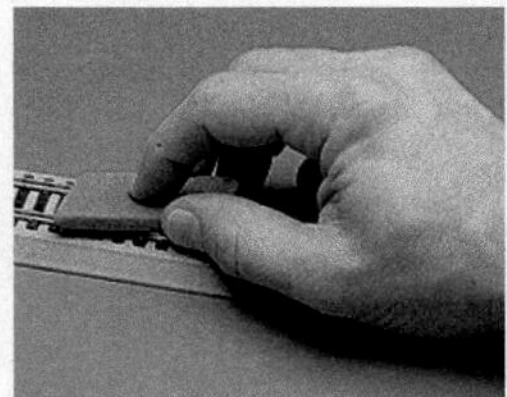

**949-521** Bright Boy 2 x 1 x 1/4" **5.98**

**NEW 949-522** Bright Boy Extra-Fine 3 x 1 x 1/4" **7.49**

# WALTHERS CODE 83 TRACK PLANNING TEMPLATE SCALE 3/4"=1'

## Use this Handy Template to Plan Code 83 Track Projects

Planning your next track improvement or layout rebuilding project is easy with this template. Simply photocopy or scan this page, then cut out and arrange the pieces as needed. All items are scaled at 3/4" = 1'. By placing them on appropriately sized graph paper, you can create scale drawings for larger projects or track profiles for your entire layout. Names and part numbers are included so you can make a bill of materials that will simplify ordering the exact Code 83 items you need.

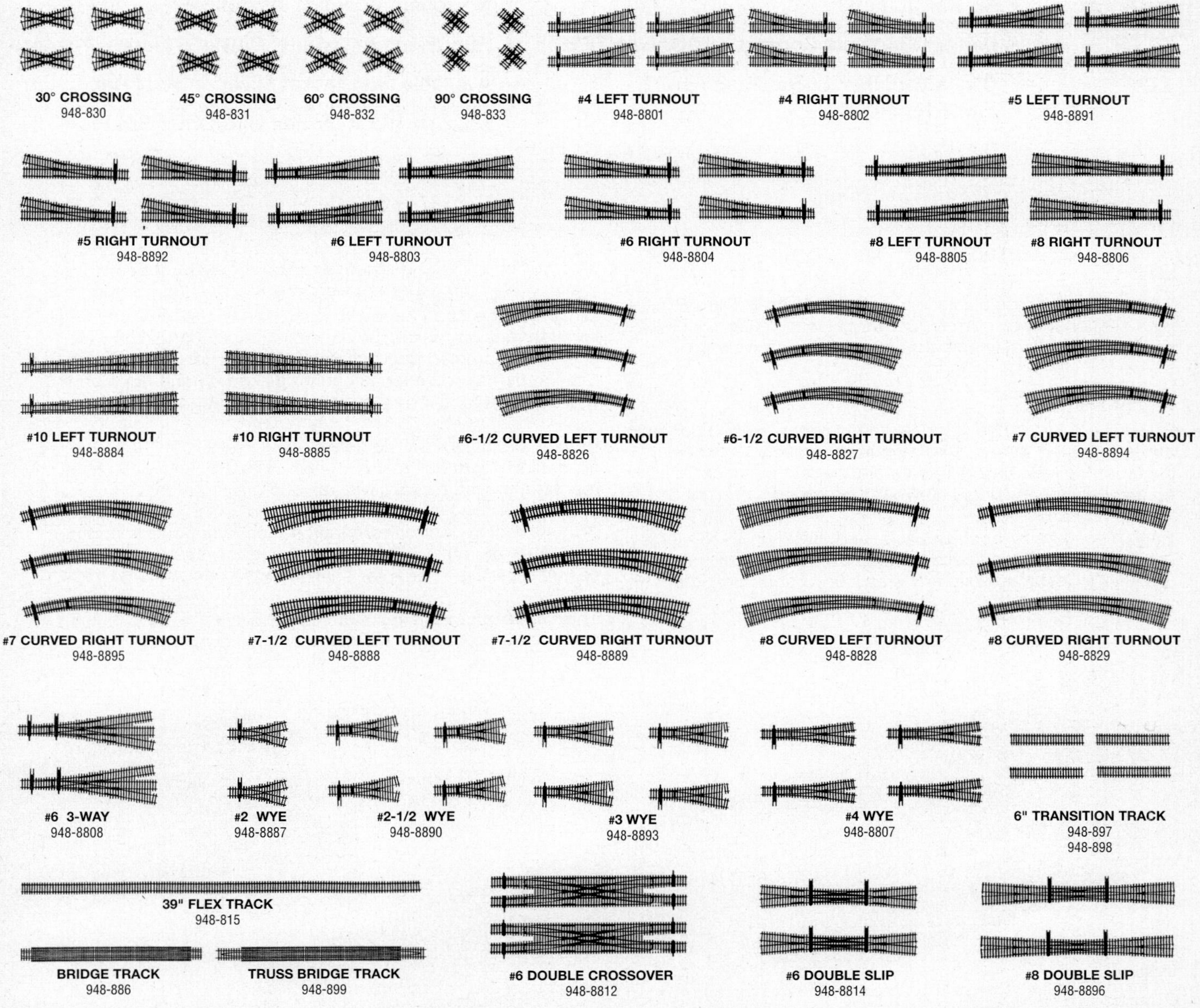

**30° CROSSING** 948-830

**45° CROSSING** 948-831

**60° CROSSING** 948-832

**90° CROSSING** 948-833

**#4 LEFT TURNOUT** 948-8801

**#4 RIGHT TURNOUT** 948-8802

**#5 LEFT TURNOUT** 948-8891

**#5 RIGHT TURNOUT** 948-8892

**#6 LEFT TURNOUT** 948-8803

**#6 RIGHT TURNOUT** 948-8804

**#8 LEFT TURNOUT** 948-8805

**#8 RIGHT TURNOUT** 948-8806

**#10 LEFT TURNOUT** 948-8884

**#10 RIGHT TURNOUT** 948-8885

**#6-1/2 CURVED LEFT TURNOUT** 948-8826

**#6-1/2 CURVED RIGHT TURNOUT** 948-8827

**#7 CURVED LEFT TURNOUT** 948-8894

**#7 CURVED RIGHT TURNOUT** 948-8895

**#7-1/2 CURVED LEFT TURNOUT** 948-8888

**#7-1/2 CURVED RIGHT TURNOUT** 948-8889

**#8 CURVED LEFT TURNOUT** 948-8828

**#8 CURVED RIGHT TURNOUT** 948-8829

**#6 3-WAY** 948-8808

**#2 WYE** 948-8887

**#2-1/2 WYE** 948-8890

**#3 WYE** 948-8893

**#4 WYE** 948-8807

**6" TRANSITION TRACK** 948-897, 948-898

**39" FLEX TRACK** 948-815

**BRIDGE TRACK** 948-886

**TRUSS BRIDGE TRACK** 948-899

**#6 DOUBLE CROSSOVER** 948-8812

**#6 DOUBLE SLIP** 948-8814

**#8 DOUBLE SLIP** 948-8896

Division of Wm.K.Walthers, Inc.

# Guess what we removed to

- No Rail Joiners!
- Perfect Electrical Contact — GUARANTEED
- Clicks Together, Locks Together, Stays Together!
- No Tools Needed to Assemble
- Run Trains Anywhere: Carpets, Floors or Tables
- Available with Nickel Silver or Steel Rail
- Adapter Track for use with Other Brands

## How can something as tiny as a rail joiner cause such big problems?

**Easy!**

Without all that careful aligning, tightening and fiddling around, your sectional track system just won't work, creating electrical problems and derailments that seriously spoil your fun.

**Not any more!**

Power-Loc® Track has NO pesky rail joiners! Built-in contacts and a patented side-locking mechanism give you perfect alignment for fewer derailments and perfect electrical connections every single time — guaranteed.

Each piece snaps together easily and quickly with NO tools needed. Simply place sections side-by-side and click them together to instantly build any size loop... or a complete, permanent layout.

And with its solid roadbed base, you can set up Power-Loc Track on rugs, floors or tables. On carpeting, the roadbed eliminates the need for layout boards, nails, screws and tools. Its offset design makes the strongest track connection ever and the assembled track won't bend. So when you're finished running trains, entire loops can be picked up and hung on the wall or stored as a complete assembly under a bed.

Best of all, there's a wide selection of Power-Loc track available in both HO and N Scales, with steel rail and black roadbed, or with nickel silver rail and gray roadbed.

And upgrading your current train set or layout built with other brands of track that use rail joiners is easy! Just connect the special Power-Loc adapter section to the conventional track.

Then raise your conventional track to the same height using a shim or cork roadbed and you're all set.

# make our track connect better?

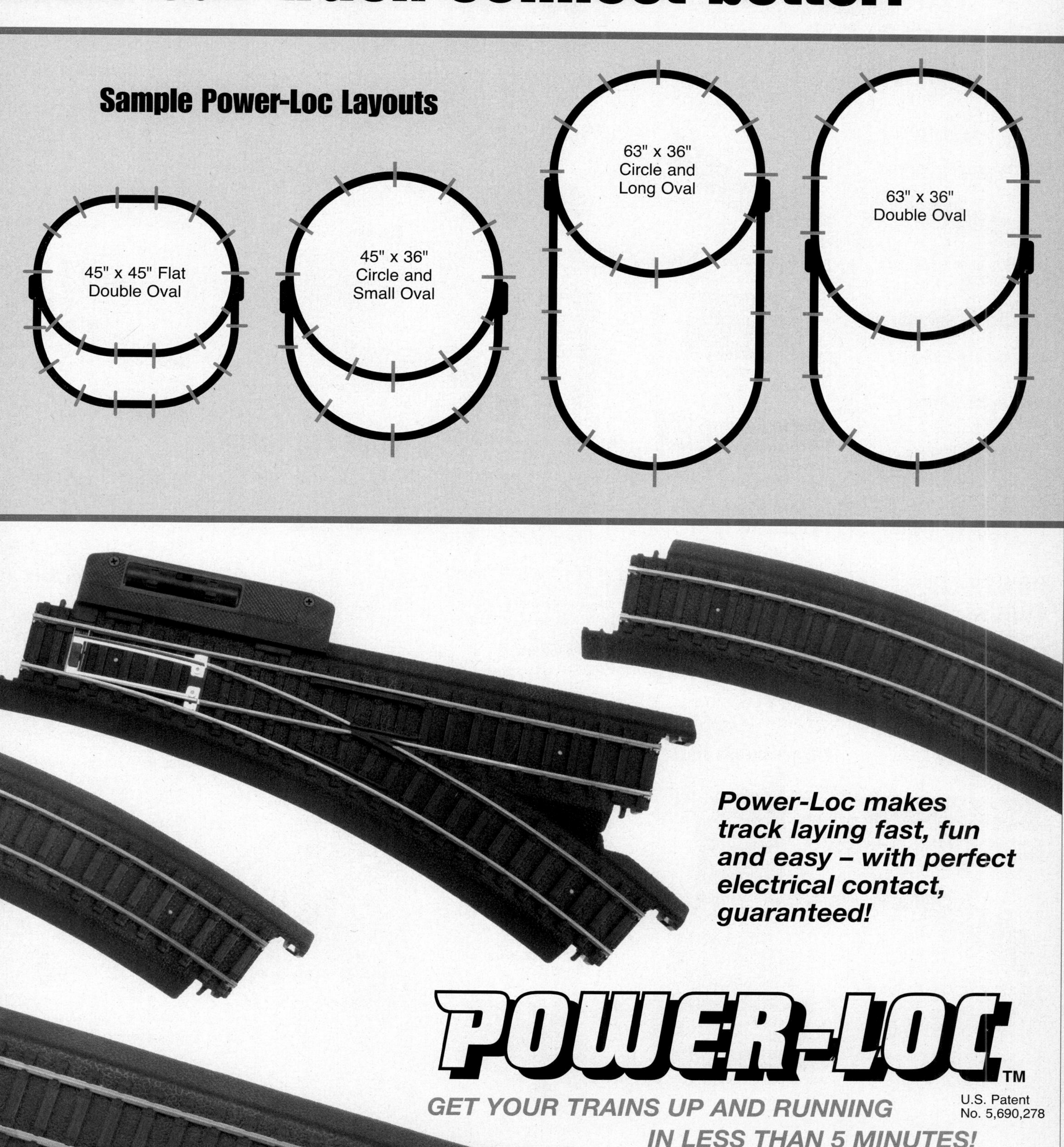


GET YOUR TRAINS UP AND RUNNING IN LESS THAN 5 MINUTES!

U.S. Patent No. 5,690,278

Division of
Wm. K. Walthers, Inc.

## NEW PRODUCTS

### 9" Straight 50-Packs

**NEW 433-8893** Nickel Silver Rail **105.00**

**NEW 433-21167** Steel Rail **72.50**

### 18" Radius Curves 50-Packs

**NEW 433-8894** Nickel Silver Rail **105.00**

**NEW 433-21177** Steel Rail **72.50**

## POWER-LOC TRACK

This side-locking track system and solid roadbed base offer durability and support on any surface (even carpet) eliminating the need for boards, nails, screws and other tools. Maximum strength without frustrating rail joiners. So simple, beginners can set up an entire layout in five minutes or less.

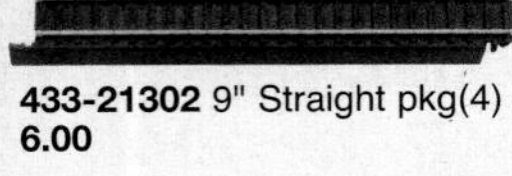

**433-21302** 9" Straight pkg(4) **6.00**

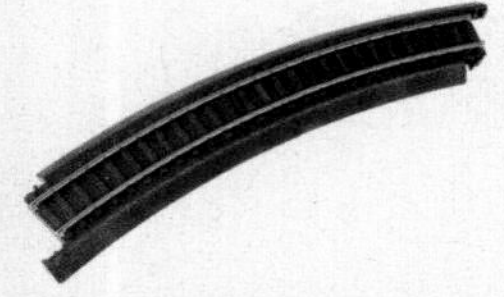

**433-21303** 18" Curved pkg(4) **6.00**

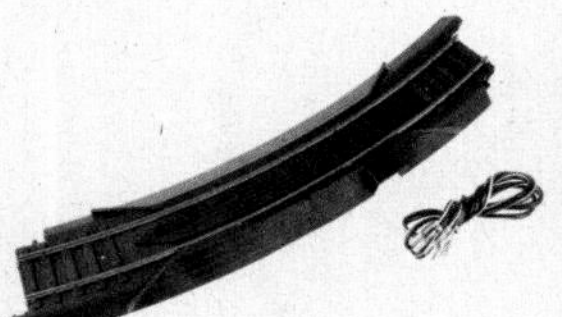

**433-21304** Curved Terminal Rerailer **6.00**

**433-21317** 3" Straight Track pkg(4) **6.00**

**433-21318** 22" Curved Track pkg(4) **8.00**

### Remote Control Turnouts 12.00 ea

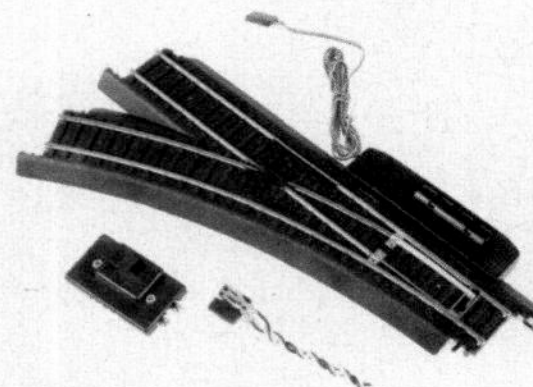

**433-21305** Right Hand

**433-21306** Left Hand

### Miscellaneous Track

**433-21308** Illuminated Bumpers pkg(2) **6.75**

**433-21314** Power Link Adapter Track **3.50**
Allows modeler to connect Power-Loc to existing layouts and all standard rail joiner track.

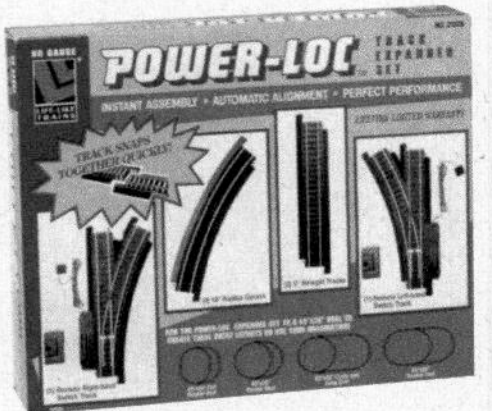


**433-21328** Double Oval Track Expander Set **34.98**

**433-21715** Steel 90-Degree Crossing **6.00**

**433-8794** Figure 8 Track Expander **34.98**

- Converts Set Oval to Figure 8
- Set-up Instructions Included
- Two 9" Steel Rail Straight Tracks
- Six 18" Radius Curve Steel Rail Tracks
- Eight 3" Steel Rail Straight Tracks
- 90-Degree Cross Track
- Use with 47 x 38" Oval

### Nickel-Silver Power-Loc

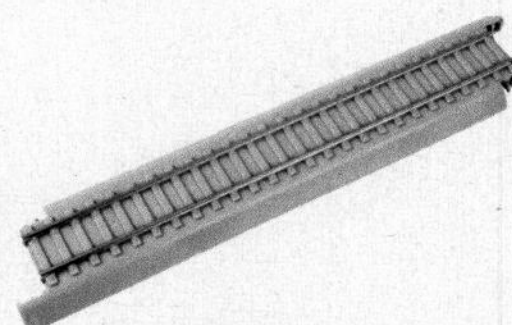

**433-21332** 9" Straight pkg(4) **8.75**

**433-21347** 3" Straight pkg(4) **6.75**

**433-21333** 18" Radius pkg(4) **8.75**

**433-21348** 22" Radius pkg(4) **11.50**

### Remote Control Turnouts 16.75 ea

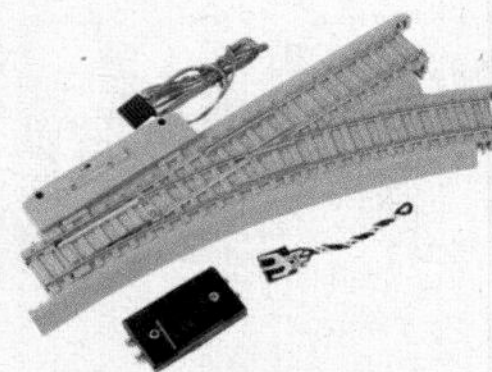

**433-21335** Right Hand

**433-21336** Left Hand

### Terminal/Rerailer

**433-21334** 18" Radius **8.75**

### Power Link Adaptor

**433-21344** **4.00**

### Bumpers

**433-21338** Illuminated pkg(2) **6.00**

## CODE 100 TRACK

Code 100 track and accessories. Track features steel rails, unless noted.

### Straight Track

**433-8609** 9" pkg(4) **3.50**

### Curved Track

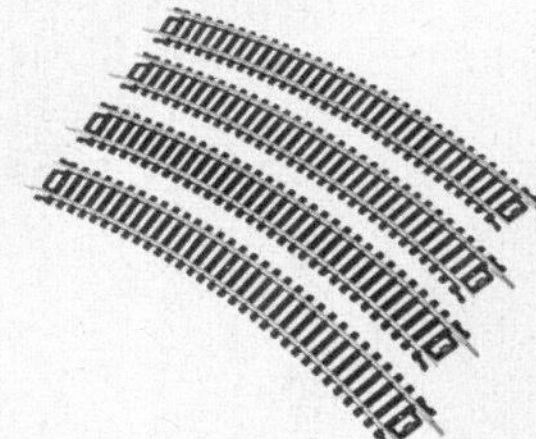

**433-8602** 18" Radius pkg(4) **3.50**
Two packages make a full circle.

See What's New and Exciting at
**www.walthers.com**

### Rail Joiners

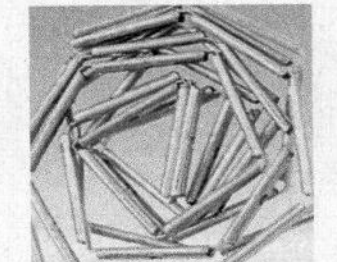

**433-1412** Steel pkg(24) **4.75**

### Nails/Screws/Spikes 4.75 ea

433-1402

433-1406

**433-1402** 1/2" Track Nails pkg(20g)

**433-1406** HO Spikes pkg(20g)

**433-1411** 3/4" Track Nails for Cork pkg(20g)

### Bumpers

**433-8628** Lighted pkg(2) **5.00**

### Track Expander Sets

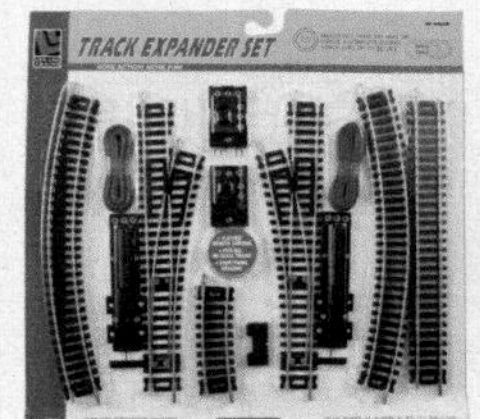


**433-8617** Double Oval **28.00**
Turns an oval into a double oval.

### Remote Control Turnouts 11.00 ea

**433-8610** Right Hand

**433-8611** Left Hand

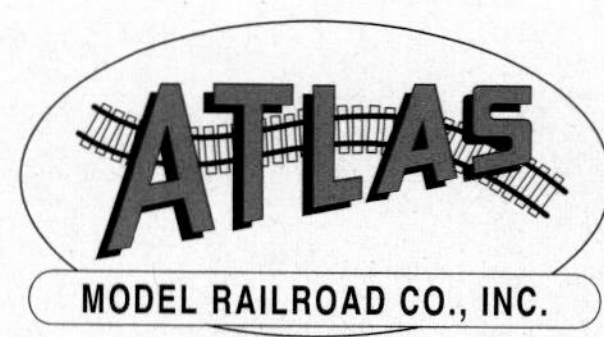


# TRACK PACKS

## World's Greatest Hobby Track Pack

**150-489 129.95**
This set contains the track you need to create the World's Greatest Hobby Layout. This 4 x 8' layout makes a great first layout for beginning model railroaders. This pack features realistic Atlas HO True-Track, a premium "all-in-one" roadbed track featuring Atlas Code 83 track. Also included is the official "Building your First Railroad" instructional video. Narrated by actor and model railroader Michael Gross, this 60-minute VHS video teaches you everything you need to know about building a model railroad layout, including easy methods for laying track, wiring techniques and more!

## River Pass Track Pack

**150-578 71.50**
This Atlas track pack gives you all the components required for the Woodland Scenics 4 x 8' River Pass Layout in one convenient pack. The track in this pack features realistic brown ties and scale-height Code 83 rail for realism, and matches the track described in the Woodland Scenics River Pass layout instructions (#785-1484, 1488 and 1487, each sold separately).

## Grand Valley Track Pack

**150-589 82.50**
Includes all the Code 83 track, switches, bridges and rail joiners needed to build a railroad on the 4 x 8' Grand Valley HO Scale Layout from Woodland Scenics (#785-1483, sold separately).

## Starter Set

**150-588** Starter Set **38.50**

# TRUE-TRACK®

Get your trains running right away with True-Track, designed for fast and easy set-up on virtually any surface. Ready to use, each piece features Code 83 nickel-silver rail on realistic brown ties, plus roadbed molded in gray and detailed to look like real ballast. Just connect the sections together, wire to your power pack, and your railroad is up and running!

Best of all, True-Track is adaptable to your changing needs. It can be nailed down for use on a permanent layout. Or remove and paint the roadbed sections for added realism. The sections can also be removed from the roadbed and used with cork roadbed, ballast and other Atlas Code 83 track products to build a traditional layout.

## Straight Sections

**150-450** 9" pkg(4) **6.25**
**150-451** 6" pkg(4) **6.25**
**150-452** 3" pkg(4) **4.25**
**150-453** 1-1/2" pkg(4) **4.25**
**150-454** 2" pkg(4) **4.25**
**150-476** 90° Crossing **10.75**

## Curved Sections pkg(4) 6.25 ea (Unless Noted)

**150-460** 18" Radius Curve
**150-463** 22" Radius Curve
**150-464** 1/3 22" Radius Curve **4.25**
**150-468** 24" Radius Curve

## Bulk Sections Case 67.50 ea

Items must be purchased in cases of 50.
**150-410** 9" Straight
**150-411** 18" Radius
**150-412** 22" Radius

## Track Accessories

**150-465** Terminal Joiners pkg(2) **2.35**
**150-470** Track Bumpers pkg(2) **2.50**
**150-471** Rerailers pkg(2) **5.90**

## Manual Snap-Switches 13.95 ea

**150-478** Left Hand
**150-479** Right Hand

## Manual Switch Machines 3.65 ea

**150-586** Left Hand
**150-587** Right Hand

## Remote Snap-Switches 18.95 ea

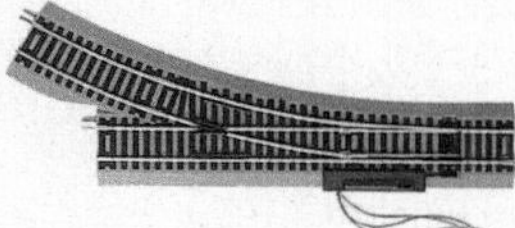

**150-480** Left Hand
**150-481** Right Hand

## Starter Kit

**150-488** True-Track Starter Set **54.95** Includes 18 sections of track, plus two manual switches and terminal rail joiners, enough track for a 38 x 56" layout.

## Remote Switch Machines 8.75 ea

**150-584** Left Hand
**150-585** Right Hand

## Terminal Track

**150-466** 9" Straight **5.75**

# CODE 100 TRACK

Code 100 comes with black ties and nickel-silver rail. For all skill levels, it can be used to build any one of the 36 HO layouts featured in the Atlas layout instruction books that appear in the Books, Videos & Railroadiana section of this Reference Book.

## HO Scale Snap-Track® Starter Set

**150-88** Nickel-Silver Rail, Black Ties **37.95**

## 36" Super-Flex Track

**150-168** Black Ties **3.85**
**150-178** Black Ties pkg(5) **19.95**

## Straight Snap-Track

**150-821** 9", Black Ties pkg(6) **5.50**
**150-822** 6", Black Ties pkg(4) **2.95**
**150-823** 3", Black Ties pkg(4) **2.95**
**150-825** 1-1/2", Black Ties pkg(4) **2.95**

## Curved Snap-Track

**150-831** 15" Radius, Black Ties pkg(6) **5.50**
**150-832** 1/2 - 15" Radius, Black Ties pkg(4) **2.95**

**150-833** 18" Radius, Black Ties pkg(6) **5.50**
**150-834** 1/2 - 18" Radius, Black Ties pkg(4) **2.95**
**150-835** 1/3 - 18" Radius, Black Ties pkg(4) **2.95**
**150-836** 22" Radius, Black Ties pkg(6) **5.50**

## Snap-Track Assortment

**150-847** Black Ties **3.85**

## Bulk Snap-Track

Items must be purchased in cases of 100.

## Nickel-Silver Rail - Black Ties Case 90.00 ea

**150-150** 9" Straight Track
**150-151** 15" Radius
**150-152** 18" Radius
**150-153** 22" Radius

## Snap Crossings

**150-839** 30°, Black Ties **7.75**

## Snap-Track Terminal Sections

**3.85 ea**
**150-840** 9" Straight, Black Ties

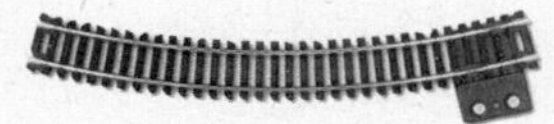

**150-845** 18" Radius Curved, Black Ties

## Snap-Switches®

**Remote Control 16.50 ea**

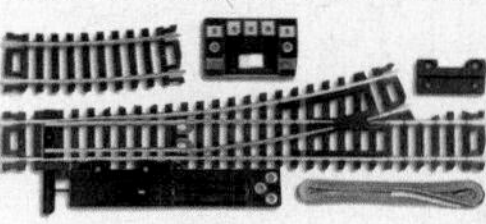

**150-850** Left Hand, Black Ties
**150-851** Right Hand, Black Ties

**Manual 10.75 ea**
**150-860** Left Hand, Black Ties

**150-861** Right Hand, Black Ties

## Rail Joiners

**150-55** Plastic Insulating pkg(24) **1.35**

**150-170** Nickel Silver pkg(48) **2.35**

## Switch Machines

**Remote Control 8.25 ea (Unless Noted)**
**150-52** Left Hand, Black Ties
**150-53** Right Hand, Black Ties
**150-65** Under-Table Right or Left
**150-66** Under-Table Deluxe w/Snap Relay Right or Left **15.50**

**Manual 2.50 ea**
**150-62** Left Hand, Black Ties
**150-63** Right Hand, Black Ties

## Bumper

**150-843** Black Ties pkg(2) **2.95**

## Rerailer

**150-155** Black Ties **1.75**
**150-844** Black Ties pkg(3) **6.25**

## Terminal Joiners

**150-842** 1 Pair **2.65**

## Custom-Line® Crossings

**7.75 ea (Unless Noted)**
**150-171** 19° - 6", Black Ties
**150-172** 25° - 4-1/2", Black Ties
**150-173** 30° - 4", Black Ties
**150-174** 45° - 3", Black Ties

**150-175** 60° - 3", Black Ties
**150-176** 90° - 6", Black Ties
**150-177** 12-1/2° - 9", Black Ties **8.25**

### Custom-Line Mark 3 Turnouts 12.50 ea

**150-280** Wye, Black Ties

**150-281** #4 Left, Black Ties
**150-282** #4 Right, Black Ties
**150-283** #6 Left, Black Ties
**150-284** #6 Right, Black Ties

## CODE 83 TRACK

Code 83 track features brown ties and nickel-silver rail. Perfect for modelers of all skill levels looking for high-quality, prototypical-looking track. Can be used to build any one of the 36 HO layouts featured in the Atlas layout instruction books that appear in the Books, Videos & Railroadiana section of this Reference Book.

### Switch Machines

For use with Code 83 Snap-Switches (#150-540 through #543, each sold separately).

**Remote 8.75 ea**
**150-584** Left Hand
**150-585** Right Hand

**Manual 3.65 ea**
**150-586** Left Hand
**150-587** Right Hand

### Snap-Track®

**Straight Sections**
**150-520** 9" pkg(6) **5.50**
**150-521** 6" pkg(4) **2.95**
**150-522** 3" pkg(4) **2.95**
**150-523** 1-1/2" pkg(4) **2.95**
**150-524** Assortment **3.85**
**150-525** 2" pkg(4) **2.95**

**Curved Sections**
**150-530** 15" Radius pkg(6) **5.50**
**150-531** 1/2 - 15" Radius pkg(4) **2.95**
**150-532** 18" Radius pkg(6) **5.50**
**150-533** 1/2 - 18" Radius pkg(4) **2.95**
**150-534** 1/3 - 18" Radius pkg(4) **2.95**
**150-535** 22" Radius pkg(6) **5.50**
**150-536** 24" Radius pkg(6) **5.50**
**150-537** 1/3 - 22" Radius pkg(4) **2.95**

### Bulk Case 90.00 ea

Items must be purchased in cases of 100.

**150-510** 9" Straight
**150-511** 15" Radius Curve
**150-512** 18" Radius Curve
**150-513** 22" Radius Curve

### Rail Joiners

**150-551** Transition (Code 83 to 100), Nickel Silver pkg(12) **2.60**
**150-552** Plastic Insulating pkg(24) **1.50**

### Bumper

**150-518** pkg(2) **3.65**

### Rerailer

**150-519** 9" pkg(3) **5.75**

### Terminal Joiners

**150-553** Nickel Silver (1 Pair) **2.75**

### 36" Super-Flex® Track 4.65 ea

**150-500** Brown Ties
**150-502** Concrete Ties

### Flex-Track End Ties pkg(6) 2.35 ea

Use these individual ties to fill gaps between track sections.
**150-598** Brown
**150-599** Concrete

### Crossings

Each crossing includes brown ties and nickel silver rail.
**150-571** 12-1/2° **8.25**
**150-572** 19° **7.75**
**150-573** 25° **7.75**
**150-574** 30° **8.75**
**150-575** 45° **7.75**
**150-576** 60° **7.75**
**150-577** 90° **7.75**

### Terminal Track w/Wire

**150-554** 9" Straight **4.25**

### Code 83 #6 Turnouts 14.95 ea

**150-505** Left Hand

**150-506** Right Hand

### Snap-Switches®

**Remote (18" Radius) 16.50 ea**

**150-540** Left Hand
**150-541** Right Hand

**Manual 10.75 ea**
**150-542** Left Hand
**150-543** Right Hand

### Custom-Line Turnouts 13.95 ea (Unless Noted)

**150-560** Wye
**150-561** #4 Left Hand
**150-562** #4 Right Hand
**150-563** #6 Left Hand
**150-564** #6 Right Hand
**150-565** #8 Left Hand **14.25**
**150-566** #8 Right Hand **14.25**

## ELECTRICAL CONTROLS

### Snap Relay

**150-200 10.25**
Feeds control panel lamps and allows selective power control (i.e., frogs and signals).

### Connector

**150-205 7.95**
Features three SPST on-off switches in parallel for controlling sidings, accessories, etc. Can be coupled together.

### Switch Control Box

**150-56 3.75**

### Selector

**150-215 7.95**
Four SPDT switches provide two-cab operation for four blocks. May be coupled together to control additional blocks without interswitch wiring. Can be used as area selectors for four-cab operation. Can be used with controller (#150-220, sold separately).

### Controller

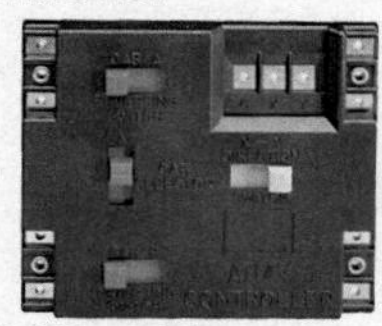

**150-220 8.25**
Simple way to wire and control reversing loops, wyes and turntables. Has reversing switches for two mainline cabs plus a switch, selectable for either cab, for directional control on reversing loops, etc. Can be used with selector (#150-215, sold separately).

### Twin

**150-210 7.95**
Two DPDT switches in parallel. Useful for reversing section and turntable control on single-cab layouts, etc.

## WIRE & ACCESSORIES

### 20 Gauge Hook-Up Wire 6.95 ea

Each role includes 50' of stranded, copper wire.

**150-315** Black
**150-316** Red
**150-317** Green
**150-318** Yellow
**150-319** Light Blue

### Spade Connectors

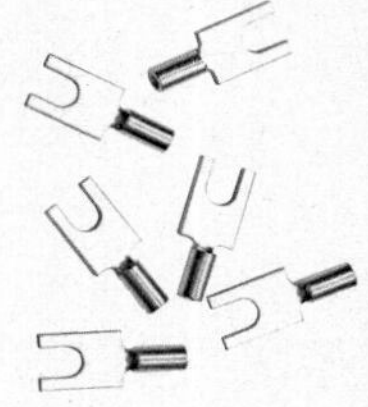

**150-201** #3 pkg(24) **4.25**

### 5-Conductor Ribbon Wire

**150-312 18.95**
Includes 50' of wire that matches what is included with all Atlas switches. Can be used for any scale.

### Turntable

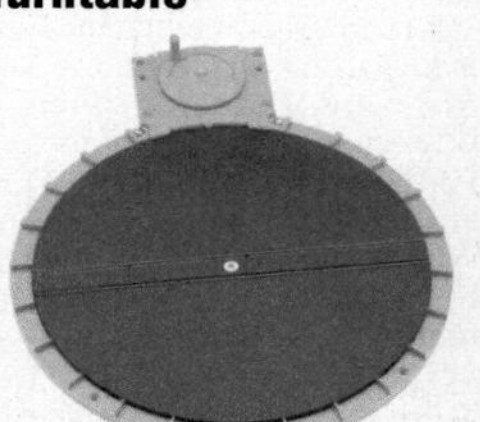

**150-305 25.75**
Fully assembled, 9" diameter turntable has the ability to stop at 21 positions, 15° apart. Geneva movement locks table in exact position every time. Simulated wood brown turntable deck and concrete pit ring. Surface mount; no cutting necessary. Manual crank operation; can be motorized for remote control operation with the Turntable Drive Unit(#304, sold separately).

**150-304** Turntable Drive Unit **25.75**

## ACCESSORIES

### Modeler's Super Saw

**150-400** Super Saw **3.25**

### Track Nails

**150-2540** Track Nails (2oz) **3.75**
Number 19, 1/2" long, round head, black oxidized steel.

### Track Planning Template Set

**150-361 4.75**
Exact paper replicas of all currently available Atlas track. Just cut out and position, like pieces of track, into the desired layout shape.

## ATLAS FANTASTIC LAYOUTS BOOKLET

**150-4** Revised Edition **1.00**
Whether you're contemplating your first layout or your 21st, you've got everything here that you need to make the right decision. This booklet is designed to make it easy for you to choose your fantastic layout! All 54 Classic Atlas HO & N scale layouts, plus twelve HO True-Track® layouts and five N Code 55 layouts are included in simple graphics, along with the vital information you need to decide which layout is right for you.

## CONTROLLERS

### Lighted Switch Controllers

Will operate all switches and switch motors including Lionel®, Atlas®, and others. Light remains on after corresponding button is pressed. Instructions, red and green light bulbs, mounting screws and self-stick number sheet are included.

Each #498 and #444 comes with a contact plate. Each #894 and #888 is equipped with electro-mechanical switching circuitry controls and switches red and green light automatically. No need for contact plates or relays; unit is completely self-contained. Bulbs use the AC current from the power supply.

#### Surface Mount

**105-444** Standard **12.40**

**105-888** Electro-Mechanical **19.80**

#### Insert Mount

**105-498 11.00**

**105-894 18.90**

**105-4994** GE Bulb 12-18V (red) pkg(2) **.80**

**105-4995** GE Bulb 12-18V (blue) pkg(2) **.80**

## PUSH-BUTTON UNITS

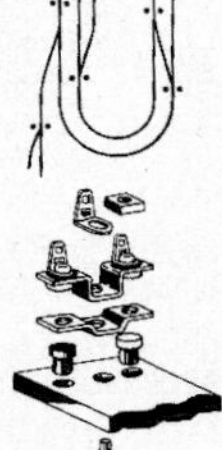

**105-439** Double **3.40**
Can be installed in any position. Dealers MUST order multiples of 12.

## PANELS

### Frame-Mounted

With polished aluminum mounting frame.

**105-401** Operates 1 Switch **6.45**

**105-402** Operates 2 Switches **8.75**

**105-403** Operates 3 Switches **11.00**

**105-404** Operates 4 Switches **13.35**

**105-405** Operates 5 Switches **14.75**

**105-406** Operates 6 Switches **17.20**

**105-407** Operates 7 Switches **19.25**

**105-408** Operates 8 Switches **22.05**

**105-916** Operates 16 Switches **41.35**

### Terminal Panels

**105-416** Less Switches **11.50**

**105-516** With Switches **13.95**

### Flush-Mounted

EXCLUSIVE FEATURE: All Acme switch controllers are equipped with crimp or solder terminals.

**105-301** Operates 1 Switch **5.20**

**105-302** Operates 2 Switches **7.25**

**105-303** Operates 3 Switches **9.30**

**105-304** Operates 4 Switches **11.75**

**105-305** Operates 5 Switches **13.35**

**105-306** Operates 6 Switches **15.55**

**105-307** Operates 7 Switches **17.00**

**105-308** Operates 8 Switches **19.95**

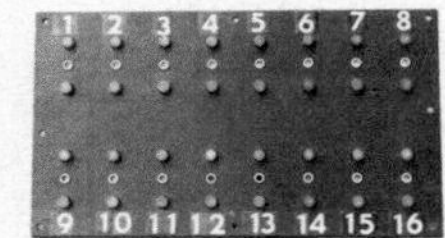

**105-816** Operates 16 Switches **36.75**

**BK Enterprises**
QUALITY TRACK PRODUCTS

Recommended for the advanced modeler, these turnouts feature accurately gauged nickel-silver rails, without ties (ties are available separately). PLEASE NOTE: All kits are made to order and are not available for immediate delivery. A backorder is required for all track items. Please visit Walthers Web site at www.walthers.com for complete listing of all available items.

## CODE 83

### HO Assembled Turnouts

**#4 23.60 ea**
**180-241** Right Hand
**180-242** Left Hand

**#6 21.40 ea**
**180-261** Right Hand
**180-262** Left Hand

**#8 22.20 ea**
**180-281** Right Hand
**180-282** Left Hand

**Wye**
**180-292** #4 **20.60**

### HO Curved Turnouts

**#6 28.00 ea**
**180-2261** Right Hand
**180-2262** Left Hand

### HO Double Slip Crossings

**180-238** #4 Frog **52.00**
**180-239** #6 Frog **54.00**

## CODE 100

### HO Turnouts

**#4 24.00 ea**
**180-141** Right Hand
**180-142** Left Hand

**#5 21.40 ea**
**180-151** Right Hand
**180-152** Left Hand

**#6 21.80 ea**
**180-161** Right Hand
**180-162** Left Hand

**#7 25.20 ea**
**180-171** Right Hand
**180-172** Left Hand

**#8 22.60 ea**
**180-181** Right Hand
**180-182** Left Hand

**#8-1/2 22.80 ea**
**180-1811** Right Hand
**180-1821** Left Hand

**#10 26.80 ea**
**180-111** Right Hand
**180-112** Left Hand

**#12 27.60 ea**
**180-1111** Right Hand
**180-1121** Left Hand

**#16 29.20 ea**
**180-101** Right Hand
**180-102** Left Hand

**Wye**
**180-191** #2-1/2 **21.00**
**180-192** #4 **21.00**
**180-1921** #5 **21.40**
**180-1922** #6 **21.80**
**180-1923** #8 **22.60**

## BUSCH

IMPORTED FROM GERMANY BY WALTHERS

## NEW PRODUCTS

### Ballast

#### Printed Ballast/ Crushed Stone Sheet

**NEW 189-7181** pkg(2) **5.99**
26-3/4 x 19-1/4" 68 x 49cm

Use this printed ballast sheet underneath turnouts and other movable track pieces. Its color matches Busch ballast #189-7127, sold separately.

Track ballast tape and cork roadbed for HO and HOn3 track.

#### Track Ballast Tape

**189-7119** Ballast Tape **11.99**
10' 3.3m long, 1-5/8" 41mm wide.

#### Cork Roadbed

3/16" 5mm thick.

**189-7501** 8' 3" 2.5m Long, 45° Beveled Edge **17.99**

**189-7502** Cork Sheet 12 x 8" 300 x 200mm **9.99**

## BRAWA

**186-99700** Track Cleaner Abrasive Pad **5.99**

## E-Z TRACK®

Each section combines track and roadbed into a single unit, with snap-fit assembly and plug-in wiring to provide instant railroad fun. A hidden locking feature holds sections securely together until you're ready to take them apart. Easy to set up on any surface, including floors and rugs: no special tools, nails or boards are needed. A great system for Christmas, displays or permanent layouts. Twelve sections of curved 18" radius track make a full circle; 16 sections of curved 22" radius track make a full circle.

### Nickel-Silver Track w/Gray Roadbed

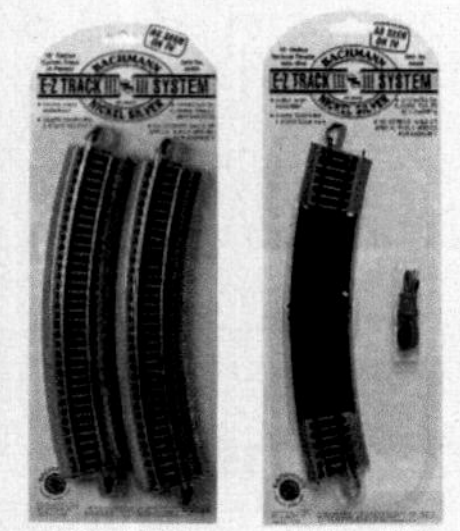

160-44501 160-44502

**160-44501** 18" Radius Curved pkg(4) **11.00**

**160-44502** 18" Radius Terminal/Rerailer **8.50**

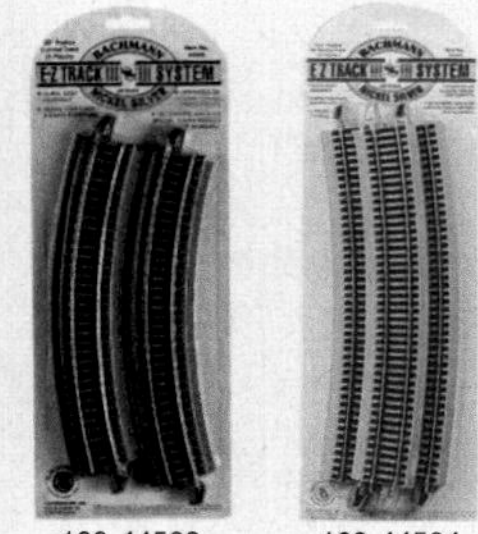

160-44503 160-44504

**160-44503** 22" Radius Curved pkg(4) **14.50**

**160-44504** 33-1/4" Radius, 18° Curve pkg(5) **18.00**

**160-44505** 15" Radius Curve Track pkg(4) **12.00**

**160-44506** 28" Radius Curve pkg(5) **15.50**

See What's Available at

**www.walthers.com**

160-44507 160-44508

**160-44507** 35-1/2" Radius, 18° Curve pkg(5) **18.00**

**160-44508** 33-1/4" Radius, 6° Curve pkg(4) **14.00**

160-44509 160-44510

**160-44509** 33-1/4" Radius, 12° Curve pkg(4) **14.00**

**160-44510** 9" Straight Terminal/Rerailer **8.50**

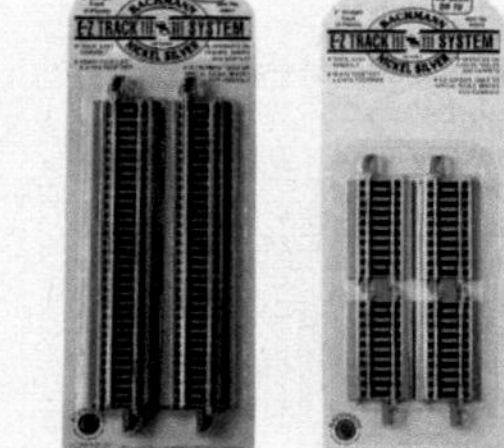

160-44511 160-44512

**160-44511** 9" Straight pkg(4) **11.50**

**160-44512** 3" Straight pkg(4) **7.50**

160-44513 160-44514 160-44528

**160-44513** 2-1/4" Straight pkg(4) **7.50**

**160-44514** 4-1/2" Straight pkg(4) **8.50**

**160-44519** 26" Radius Curve pkg(5) **15.50**

**160-44528** 9" Straight Rerailer pkg(2) **7.50**

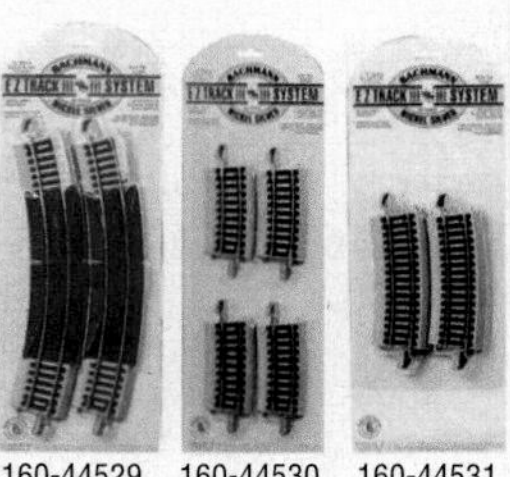

160-44529 160-44530 160-44531

**160-44529** 18" Radius Curved Rerailer pkg(2) **7.50**

**160-44530** 1/3 18" Radius Curve pkg(4) **7.50**

**160-44531** 1/2 18" Radius Curve pkg(4) **7.50**

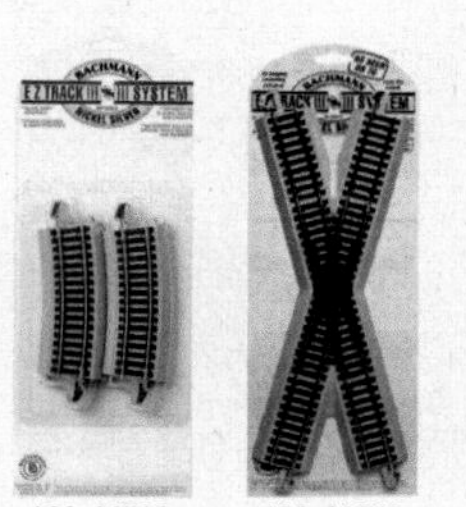

160-44532 160-44540

**160-44532** 1/2 22" Radius Curve pkg(4) **13.00**

**160-44540** 30° Crossing **12.00**

160-44541

160-44542

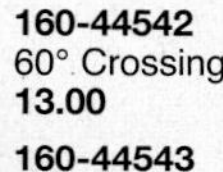

160-44543

**160-44541** 90° Crossing **15.00**

**160-44542** 60° Crossing **13.00**

**160-44543** 45-Degree Crossing **13.00**

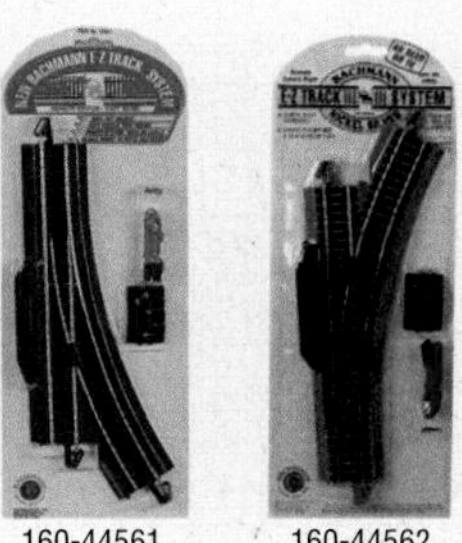

160-44561 160-44562

**160-44561** Remote Left Hand Switch **20.00**

**160-44562** Remote Right Hand Switch **20.00**

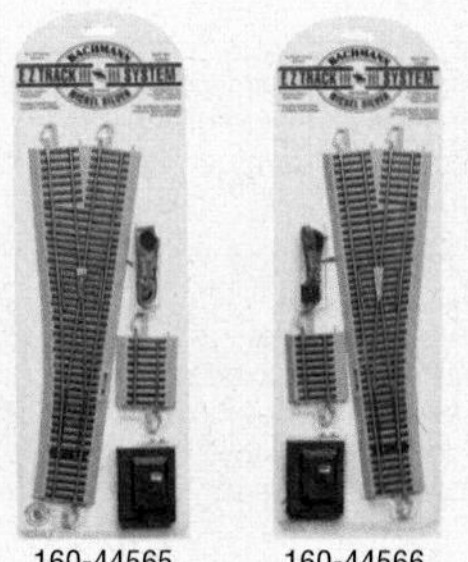

160-44565 160-44566

**160-44565** #5 Left Hand Remote Switch **30.00**

**160-44566** #5 Right Hand Remote Switch **30.00**

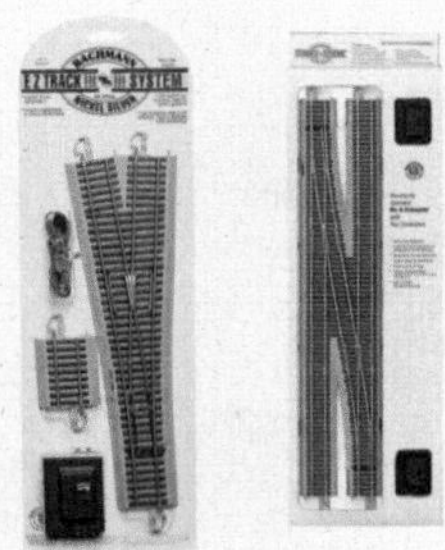

160-44569 160-44575

**160-44569** #5 Wye Switch **30.00**

**160-44575** #6 Left Hand Remote Crossover Turnout **55.00**

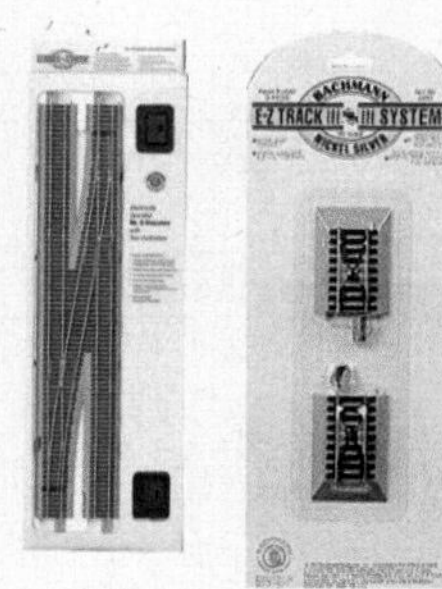

160-44576 160-44591

**160-44576** #6 Right Hand Remote Crossover Turnout **55.00**

**160-44591** Hayes Bumpers pkg(2) **11.00**

**160-44594** Layout Expander **72.00**

### "World's Greatest Hobby" Track Pack

This track set includes: nine 9" straight sections, a 9" terminal rerailer, a 9" rerailer, twenty 18" radius curve sections, two 3" straight sections, two left hand remote switches, two right hand remote switches, an E-Z Track terminal wire, four E-Z Track switch wires and an instructional DVD.

**160-44596** Nickel Silver **105.00**

**NEW 160-44497** Steel Alloy **65.00**

### Steel Track w/Black Roadbed

**160-44401** 18" Radius Curved pkg(4) **8.50**

**160-44402** 18" Radius Terminal/Rerailer **7.50**

**160-44403** 22" Radius Curved pkg(4) **10.00**

**160-44410** 9" Straight Terminal/Rerailer **7.50**

**160-44411** 9" Straight pkg(4) **8.50**

**160-44412** 3" Straight pkg(4) **6.00**

**160-44428** 9" Straight Rerailer pkg(2) **5.00**

**160-44429** 18" Radius Curved Rerailer pkg(2) **5.00**

**160-44440** 30° Crossing **6.50**

**160-44441** 90° Crossing **11.00**

**160-44461** Remote Left Hand Switch **14.50**

**160-44462** Remote Right Hand Switch **14.50**

**160-44491** Hayes Bumpers pkg(2) **11.00**

**160-44494** Expander Set **52.00**

Deluxe Dual Crossing Gate 160-44579

Tall 8-Piece E-Z Track Pier Set 160-44472

## E-Z Track® Accessory Set

**160-44493** Steel Rail on Black Roadbed **75.00**

## Bulk Track - Case Of 50

### Nickel Silver

**160-44580** 18" Radius Curved **107.00**

**160-44581** 9" Straight **107.00**

**160-44583** 22" Radius Curve **153.00**

**160-44584** 36" Straight Track pkg(25) **242.00**

### Steel

**160-44480** 18" Steel Radius Curved **72.00**

**160-44481** 9" Straight **72.00**

**160-44483** 22" Steel Radius Curved **103.00**

## Deluxe Dual Crossing Gate

**160-44579 29.00**

## Pier Sets

**160-44471** 14-Piece E-Z Track Pier Set **17.00**

**160-44472** Tall 8 Pieces **14.00**

## 18-Piece E-Z Track Graduated Pier Set

**160-44595 27.00**

# TRACK ACCESSORIES

## Extension Wire

10' long.

160-44498 160-44598

**160-44498** Terminal Connector/Hook-Up Wire **6.00**

**160-44598** Green Switch **6.50**

**NEW 160-44332** E-Z Track Rail Joiners pkg(48) **2.50**

CABOOSE INDUSTRIES

# OPERATING GROUND THROWS

Strong, self-lubricating, black Delrin® ground throws with external cam for strength and maximum throw. Molded on a pin for direct mounting. All 100 series (Rigid) stands require modelers to fabricate a spring connecting link between the stand and the turnout. All 200 series stands have internal springs so they can be connected directly to the turnout throwbar.

## .135" Travel (N)

**97-105** Rigid **3.03**

**97-206** Sprung **3.20**

## .190" Travel (HO)

**97-101** Rigid **2.93**

**97-202** Sprung **3.10**

**97-5202** Sprung 5-Pack **14.75**

## .280" Travel (O)

**97-107** Rigid **3.13**

**97-208** Sprung **3.30**

## .190" Travel w/Targets

**97-109** Rigid **4.08**

**97-210** Sprung **4.25**

## .165" Travel w/Selectable End Fittings (N or HO)

Operating ground throws including five different connectors: flat blade for Roco, small diameter pin for Micro Engineering, .083" hole for Peco, 90° slender shaft for Atlas, and large pin for most other turnouts. Also includes shim plate to raise the stand to tie height if needed.

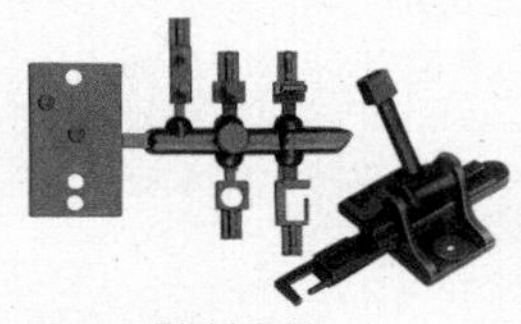

**97-117** Rigid **3.03**

**97-218** Sprung **3.20**

**97-5218** Sprung 5-Pack **15.25**

## .165" Travel w/SPDT Contacts

Includes parts to assemble one low current SPDT contact set.

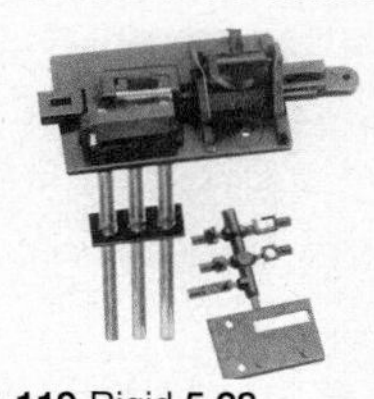

**97-119** Rigid **5.28**

**97-220** Sprung **5.50**

# HIGH LEVEL SWITCH STANDS

These operating models are typical of switch stands used by many railroads. Working parts are Delrin, but kit also includes six targets, nonworking lantern and a square diamond made of ABS plastic. Manual targets can be adapted to operate from an electric switch machine (sold separately) below the benchwork, .190" travel. Kits include a shim to raise the stand to tie level, along with five different fittings for use with most turnouts, including Atlas®, Roco, Peco, Micro Engineering and Shinohara.

**97-103** Rigid **6.68**

**97-204** Sprung **6.90**

## CAMPBELL SCALE MODELS

HO Scale track ties and accessories.

### Profile Ties 17.71 ea

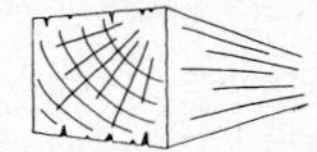

**200-796** Standard pkg(1000)

**200-797** Turnout & Crossover pkg(250)

**200-798** Bridge pkg(500)

**200-799** Narrow Gauge pkg(1000)

### TracTk Test Light

**200-550 9.20**
When set on track, test light shines if power is on. Works with any gauge. In green, red or amber.

## *Information* STATION

### Why Narrow Gauge?

Many narrow gauge railroads, those with a track gauge of less than standard gauge's four feet, eight and one-half inches, could once be found all across North America. Construction was generally cheaper because smaller trains, sharper curves and smaller clearances required less grading. Because they carried less than standard gauge lines, most were victims of automobile and truck competition. Here are a few notable narrow gauge lines.

New England, was home to a number of light duty two-foot gauge common carriers such as the Sandy River & Rangeley Lakes RR.

Three foot, six inch gauge was used through 1989 by Canadian National in Newfoundland and by many streetcar lines.

Three foot gauge, the most popular of the narrow gauges, was extensively used by logging and mining railroads. Notable narrow gauge common carriers included the Denver & Rio Grande, Colorado & Southern, East Broad Top, Southern Pacific, South Pacific Coast, White Pass & Yukon and the Oahu Railway. While a few lines remain as tourist operations, U.S. Gypsum's 26-mile mine railroad at Plaster City, California and a few small mine and in-plant industrial railroads still haul freight.

Model railroaders designate narrow track gauge by adding a suffix of "n3" or "n42" to the scale; for example, HOn3 is three foot-gauge HO Scale. HOn3 is the most popular modeling narrow gauge.

### The Tortoise Switch Machine

**800-6000 18.95**
Easy-to-mount slow-motion switch machine features:
• Prototypical slow-motion action - three seconds to complete throw
• Precision-engineered gear drive mechanism
• Simple mounting with linkage included - no additional brackets or linkage necessary
• Convenient auxilliary contacts- two sets SPDT provided
• Easy wiring - two-wire connection possible

### Tortoise Value Packs

(Dealers Note: items are not labeled for individual sale.)

**800-6006** pkg(6) **110.00**

**800-6012** pkg(12) **210.00**

### Switch Machine w/Internal DCC Decoder

**800-6200 39.95**
Same size and mounting as the TORTOISE™. Compatible with all DCC systems that provide accessory address control. Two wire connection to DCC bus with no external power necessary. Easy programming. May also be controlled with panel switches or detection circuits. Adjustable throw speed. Power up position user definable or will default to last used. Other specifications same as TORTOISE.

### SMAIL™ Value Packs

(Dealers Note: Items are not labeled for individual sale.)

**800-6206** pkg(6) **230.00**

**800-6212** pkg(12) **440.00**

### Terminal Blocks

Set of two screw-type terminal blocks that can be soldered to the SMAIL circuit board to allow easy under-layout connections.

**800-6301** Single **4.95**

**800-6306** pkg(6) **24.95**

**800-6312** pkg(12) **42.95**

### SMAIL w/Terminal Blocks

Includes factory installed screw-type terminal blocks for simple connections without soldering.

**800-6200TB 46.95**

(Dealers Note: Items below are not labeled for individual sale.)

**800-6206TB** pkg(6) **270.00**

**800-6212TB** pkg(12) **520.00**

### Remote Tortoise Mount

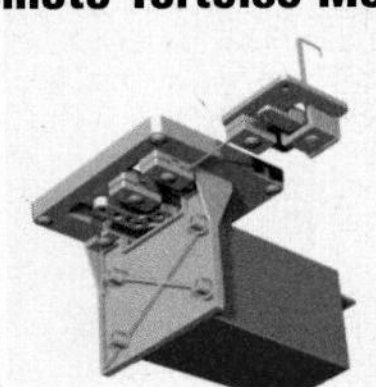

**800-6100 10.95**
Mounting bracket and special linkage allow you to mount the Tortoise above or below the benchwork and up to 18" from the turnout. Suitable for all scales and brands of turnouts.

**800-6101** For Crossovers & Double Slip Switches **5.95**
Extra cable and Actuator may be used with Remote Tortoise Mount (#800-6100, sold separately) to allow two sets of points to be thrown simultaneously by one Tortoise.

### Drilling Template

**800-6190 5.95**
Laser-cut template of thin acrylic allows precise location of TORTOISE or SMAIL mounting holes.

### AC Adapter

**800-7212 12.95**
110V AC wall plug adapter outputs filtered 12V DC at 500 mA, sufficient to power up to 30 Tortoise Switch Machines.

## CTT, Inc.

Designing and planning your next layout will be easy with CTT track-planning templates and layout design sheets. All items are calibrated to a 1" = 12" scale.

### Template

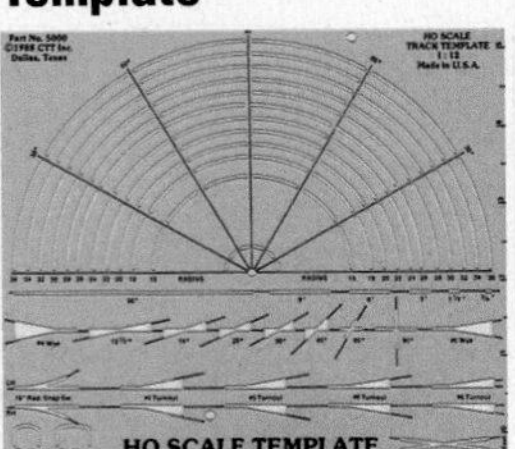


Template is molded in tough, see-through plastic with outlines for HO Scale curves, crossings, turnouts and other track.

**233-5000** Template Only **14.99**

**233-5003** Template & Layout Design Paper Kit **19.99**

### Layout Design Paper

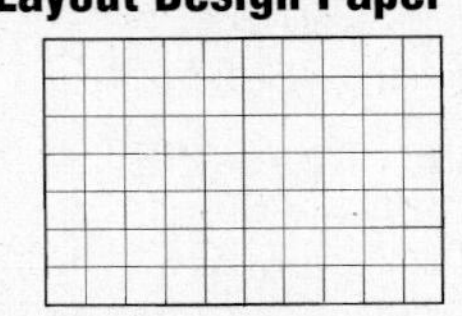

Design sheets feature a 1" square grid pattern, printed in light gray. Available for 7 x 10', 9 x 16', or 16 x 23' rooms. (Sheets can be overlapped for larger areas.)

**233-4001** 7 x 10' **.59**

**233-4002** 9 x 16' **1.59**

**233-4003** 16 x 23' **3.99**

**233-4000** Paper Kit **7.99**
Includes four layout design sheets #4001, two layout design sheets #4002 and one layout design sheet #4003.

### Scale Rulers 4.29 ea

12" clear plastic. Includes scale feet, inches, full-size inch, millimeter, decimal and metric conversion table.

**233-9020** 1:20.3 (G) Scale

**233-9022** 1:22.5 (G) Scale

**233-9024** 1:24 (G) Scale

**233-9025** 1:25 (G) Scale

**233-9029** 1:29 (G) Scale

**233-9032** 1:32 (G) Scale

**233-9035** 1:35 (G) Scale

**233-9048** 1:48 (O) Scale

**233-9064** 1:64 (S) Scale

**233-9072** 1:72 (S) Scale

**233-9087** 1:87 (HO) Scale

**233-9160** 1:160 (N) Scale

## CVMW
CENTRAL VALLEY MODEL WORKS

## CURVABLE TURNOUT KITS

These fantastic self-gauging switch kits allow for greater, free-flowing track options. Each kit includes one pair of detailed nickel-silver points, one insulated frog spacer, joint bars, rail braces, detailed guardrails, working switch stand and a complete set of instructions with diagrams and crossover dimensions.

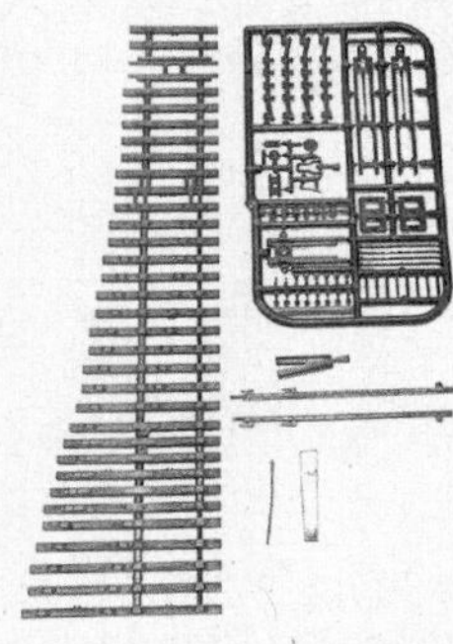

### Code 70 Turnout Kits

**#5**
**210-2571** Left **11.95**
**210-2572** Right **11.95**

**#6**
**210-2671** Left **11.95**
**210-2672** Right **11.95**

**#7**
**210-2771** Left **11.95**
**210-2772** Right **11.95**

**#8**
**210-2871** Left **12.95**
**210-2872** Right **12.95**

**#9**
**210-2971** Left **12.95**
**210-2972** Right **12.95**

### Code 83 Turnout Kits

**#5**
**210-2581** Left **11.95**
**210-2582** Right **11.95**

**#6**
**210-2681** Left **11.95**
**210-2682** Right **11.95**

**#7**
**210-2781** Left **11.95**
**210-2782** Right **11.95**

**#8**
**210-2881** Left **12.95**
**210-2882** Right **12.95**

**#9**
**210-2981** Left **12.95**
**210-2982** Right **12.95**

## CVT
CENTRAL VALLEY TIES

## TIES

These self-gauging tie strips allow trouble-free, museum-grade detail for almost any skill level of modeler. These CVT ties allow for Code 83, 70 and 55 rail with no need for a track gauge if using RP25 wheelsets gauged to NMRA standards.

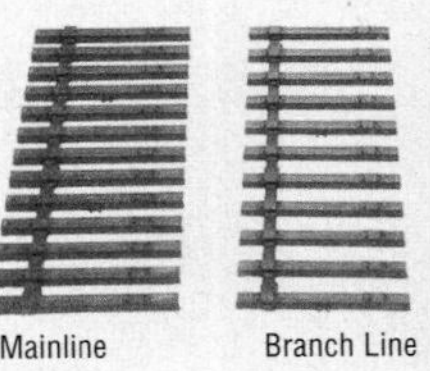


### Mainline Tie Strips

**210-20016** pkg(6) **5.98**

**210-2001** pkg(50) **41.98**

### Branch Line Tie Strips

**210-20026** pkg(6) **5.98**

**210-2002** pkg(50) **41.98**

### Curvable Switch Ties pkg(2) 8.95 ea

**#5**
**210-2501** Left
**210-2502** Right

**#6**
**210-2601** Left
**210-2602** Right

**#7**
**210-2701** Left
**210-2702** Right

**#8**
**210-2801** Left
**210-2802** Right

**#9**
**210-2901** Left
**210-2902** Right

## SWITCH DETAIL PARTS

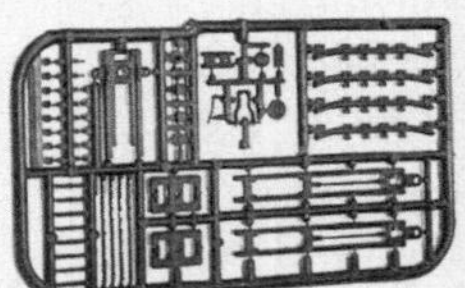

**210-1603 5.98**
Includes three switch stands, 24 fish plates, 42 rail braces, 12 frog bolt bars, six each of Code 70 and 83 guardrails, and more!

## HO ROADBED

One-piece cork roadbed turnout sections provide a smooth transition between turnouts and track. Each section is 3/16" 5mm thick with beveled edges. Color and profile match other popular brands of roadbed. Works with all HO Scale track.

### #4/#6 Turnouts 5.15 ea

**357-1500** Right Hand pkg(2)

**357-1501** Left Hand pkg(2)

### #8 Turnouts 6.05 ea

**357-1502** Right Hand pkg(2)

**357-1503** Left Hand pkg(2)

### Crossings & Wye

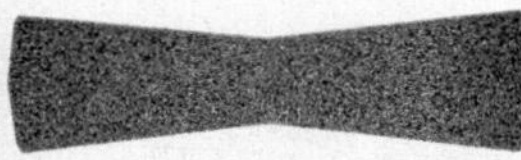

**357-1504** 12.5° Crossing **3.95**

**357-1505** 25/30° Crossing **3.80**

**357-1506** Wye **3.90**

### Multi-Track Yard Pads

**357-1518** 6 x 18" **5.25**
Yard pads are beveled along the 18" edges for easy transition with other roadbed pieces

Dealers MUST Order Multiples of 12.

## HOm & TT ROADBED

### 18" Single Track

**357-1400** pkg(5) **6.95**

**357-14001** pkg(24) **26.50**

### Curved Turnouts 2.65 ea

**357-1403** Right Hand

**357-1404** Left Hand

**357-1405** 15° Crossing

### Turnouts pkg(2) 3.80 ea

**357-1401** Right Hand

**357-1402** Left Hand

## GC LASER

## GRADE CROSSINGS

### 2-Pack 9.99 ea

Each kit Includes six laser-cut pieces, instructions with isometric drawings, laser-etched planks and bolt heads with shim stock. Easy to install; use with Code 100 or 83 rail.

**292-11271** Straight

**292-11274** 15" Radius Curve

**292-11275** 18" Radius Curve

**292-11277** 22" Radius Curve

New Arrivals Updated Every Day! Visit Walthers Web site at **www.walthers.com**

Designed, Manufactured & Assembled entirely in the U.S.A.

### "Quickie" Panel Switches pkg(3) 3.95 ea

Single pole, single throw, momentary push-button switches for uncouplers, turnout motors, etc. 16V AC or DC, 1 amp.

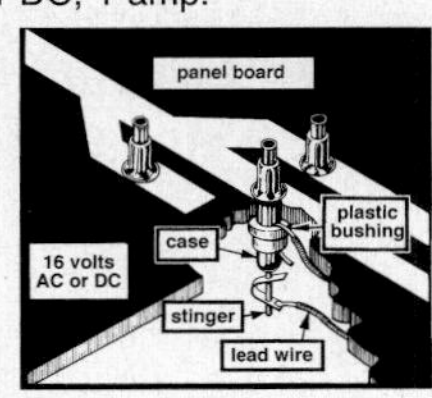


**380-160** Amber
**380-161** Green
**380-162** Red

### Track Gauges 3.50 ea

"Flip-over" multi-purpose gauge.

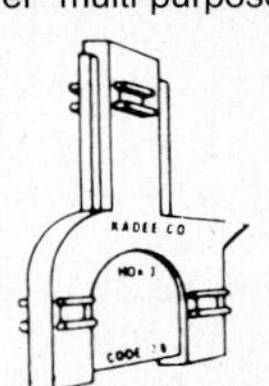

**380-341** Code 70 & 100
**380-342** Code 55, 66 & 70 HOn3

### Track Spikes For Kadee Rail Spiker pkg(4000) 11.99 ea

These spikes can only be used with the Kadee Rail Spiker.

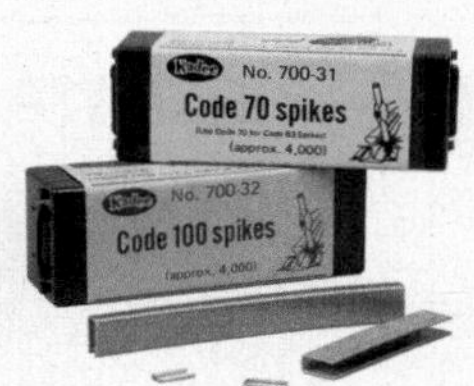


**380-372** Code 70 & 83
**380-392** Code 100

## EVERGREEN HILL DESIGNS

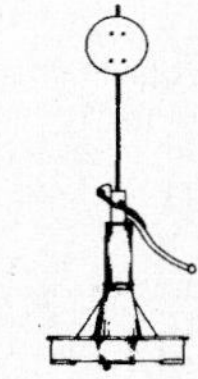

### Switch Stand

**261-620** Sierra Switch Stand **2.75**
Nonoperating, cast white-metal HO Scale kit.

Track tools for use with HO and HOn3 track.

## TRACK TOOLS

### Ballast Spreaders 10.05 ea

Easy to use. Adjustable for heavy or light flow.

**479-5008** HO Scale

**479-5010** HOn3 Scale

### Track Laying Tools 3.85 ea

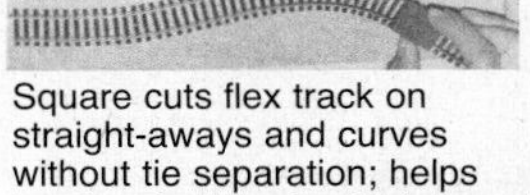

Square cuts flex track on straight-aways and curves without tie separation; helps locate misaligned rail joints and straightens used flex track in seconds.

**479-5001** HO

**479-5003** HO & HOn3

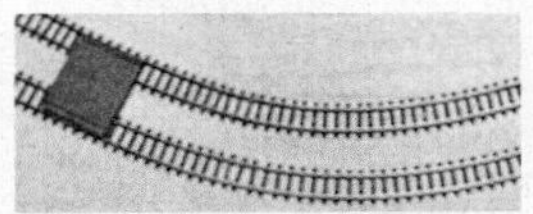

**479-5002** Parallel, HO & HOn3
Allows uniform spacing maintenance on straight-aways and curves while laying parallel tracks with HO or HOn3 track.

### Solder Tools 3.85 ea

Tool holds rail alignment for soldering rail joint.

**479-5005** HO

**479-5006** HOn3

### Radius Tool

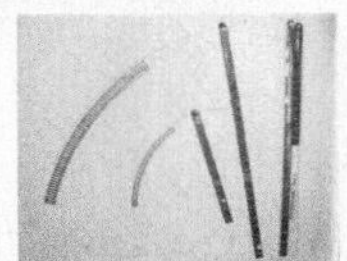

**479-5007 8.57**
Set contains two units – short unit will swing a radius from 7 to 11", long unit 11 to 23".

### Flex Track Alignment Tools 5.15 ea

8" section will keep rail straight during construction of hand-laid mainlines, sidings and yard tracks.

**479-5016** HO

**479-5017** HOn3

### Track Tool Sets

Sets contain track tool, parallel tool, soldering tool and ballast spreader.

**479-5012** HO **20.57**

**479-5013** HOn3 **20.57**

**479-5019** Deluxe HO **35.09**
Also includes radius tool and flex track alignment tool.

## KAPPLER MILL & LUMBER CO.

These HO and HOn3 Scale ties are made of unstained sugar pine. Dimensions are in prototype inches.

### Regular Ties

#### HOn3 pkg(1000) 12.95 ea

**385-51** 5" x 7" x 6'

**385-52** 5" x 7" x 6-1/2'

#### HO pkg(1000) 13.95 ea

**385-53** 7" x 9" x 8'

**385-54** 7" x 9" x 8-1/2'

### Switch Ties

**385-59** 5" x 7" x 12', HOn3 pkg(500) **12.95**

**385-60** 7" x 9" x 16', HO pkg(500) **13.95**

### Low-Profile Switch Ties

**385-84** 4" x 7" x 12', HOn3 pkg(500) **12.95**

**385-85** 4" x 9" x 16', HO pkg(500) **13.95**

### Bridge & Trestle Ties

**385-69** 8" x 8" x 10', HO/HOn3 pkg(500) **13.95**

### Low-Profile Cross Ties

Low-profile cross ties are about half the thickness of regular scale ties in order to use less ballast.

#### HOn3 pkg(1000) 12.95 ea

**385-72** 4" x 7" x 6'

**385-73** 4" x 7" x 6-1/2'

#### HO pkg(1000) 13.95 ea

**385-74** 4" x 9" x 8'

**385-75** 4" x 9" x 8-1/2'

## Analog DC & Manual Turnout

With this setting, you can run a train on the mainline and store additional trains on sidings on a DC layout.

### Set to Power Routing

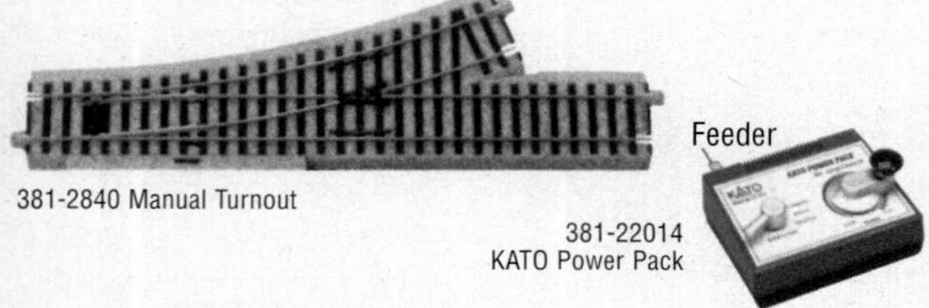


## DCC & Manual Turnout

This setting allows you to control multiple trains at the same time; the KATO Power Pack can be connected to the JUMP port on the Zephyr as the second control source.

### Set to Non-Power Routing

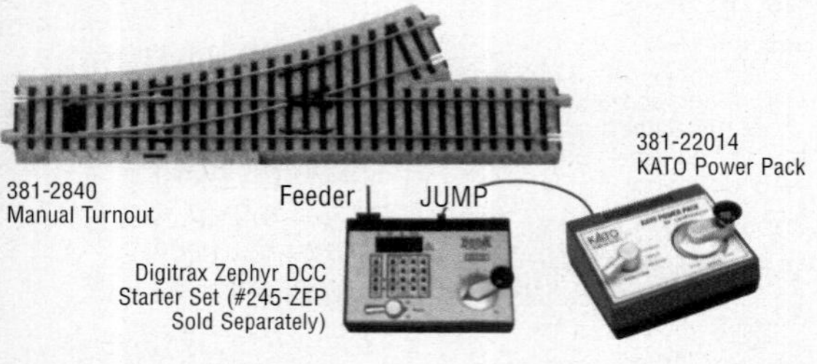


- **Power Routing** comes factory set on a KATO turnout to allow electricity to only go to the route the turnout is thrown and not to the other route. Using a Manual Turnout and a KATO Power Pack, you can run a train on the mainline and store additional trains on sidings.
- **Non-Power Routing** is ideal for multiple train operation on DCC-powered layouts. By selecting Non-Power Routing, electricity flows to both routes regardless of the turnout position.

# UNITRACK

- The Unijoiner reliably and securely connects track sections time after time - minimizes the potential of frustrating breaks in the rail and derailments.
- Code 83 Nickel Silver Rail is used for optimal model performance.
- UNITRACK turnouts meet your operation needs for both Analog DC and DCC (Digital Command Control) environments:

## Analog DC & Remote Turnout

This setting lets you control a switch like a railroad dispatcher on a DC layout. A Turnout Control Switch (381-24840) and a DC Turnout Machine (381-2503), both sold separately, are required.

### Set to Power Routing

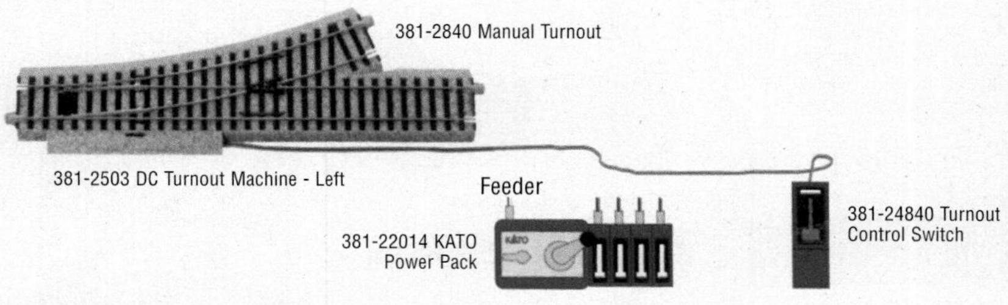


## DCC & Remote Turnout

### Set to Non-Power Routing

With a DC Turnout machine (#381-2503), this setting is ideal for two-train operation on the same track; controlling the switch from a switch controller lets you operate like a railroad dispatcher and engineer. The KATO Power Pack can be connected to the JUMP port on the Zephyr as the second control source.

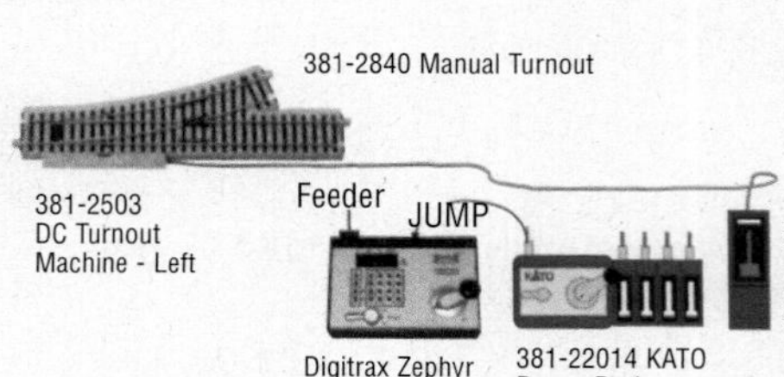


### Or Set to Non-Power Routing

With the Digitrax DCC Turnout Machine #245-DS61K1L (left) or #245-DS61K1R (right) you can run two trains on the same track with modern remote control of switches using the Zephyr. The KATO Power Pack can be connected to the JUMP port on the Zephyr as the second control source.

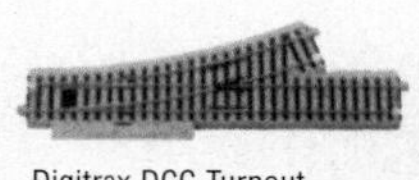


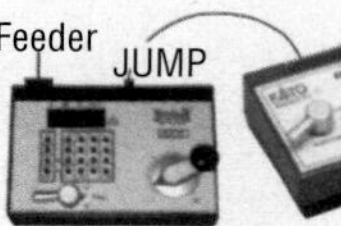

## KATO POWER PACK

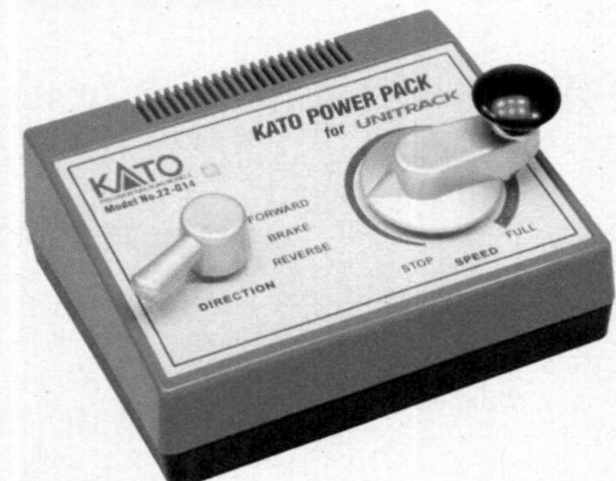


**381-22014 65.00**
Provides Analog DC power and simplified wiring connections to the "Feeder Track" using a unique keyed plug/socket system. Also provides simple connection to Turnout Control Switch (#381-24840 sold separately). Features direction and speed controls, plus circuit breaker with reset button. 12V DC, 1 Amp Output. Includes Adapter Cord to connect to other brands of track.

## HO BASIC UNITRAK SET

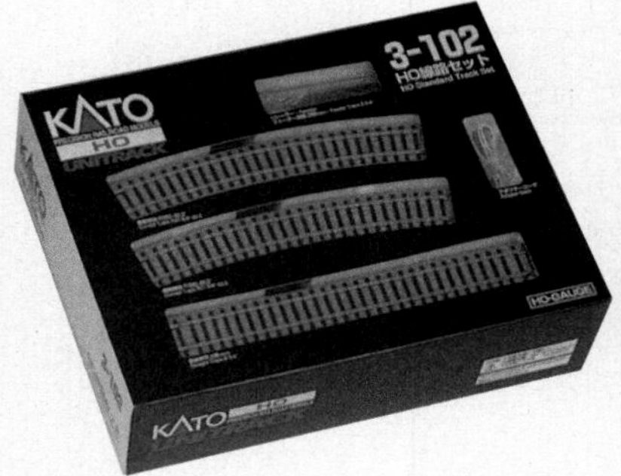


**381-3102 65.98**
This basic starter set builds an approximate 6'11" x 3'10" oval layout. Use the HO Track Set as packaged for simple operations, or combine it with additional Unitrack sections and turnouts to create a larger and more elaborate layout.

Includes: 9-3/4" Straight Track- 7 Pieces, 9-3/4" Feeder Track - 1 Piece, 21-5/8" Radius Curved Track - 16 Pieces, Rerailer, Power Pack Adapter Cord

## HO UNITRACK WORLD'S GREATEST HOBBY PLAN SET

**381-3103 198.00**
Includes all the track needed to build the 4x8' layout recommended in the World's Greatest Hobby video "Building Your First Layout." Turnouts are selectable for power routing for DC operations, or non-power routing for DCC operations.

Includes: Left-Hand Manual Turnouts - 2 Pieces, Right-Hand Manual Turnouts - 2 Pieces, 9-3/4" Straight Track- 4 Pieces, 9-3/4" Feeder Track - 1 Piece, 22.5° Curved Track (specially designed for this track pack) - 29 Pieces, 6-7/8" Straight Track - 4 Pieces, 4-7/8" Straight Track - 3 Pieces, Track Bumpers - 2 Pieces, Rerailer, Power Pack Adapter Cord

## STRAIGHT TRACK

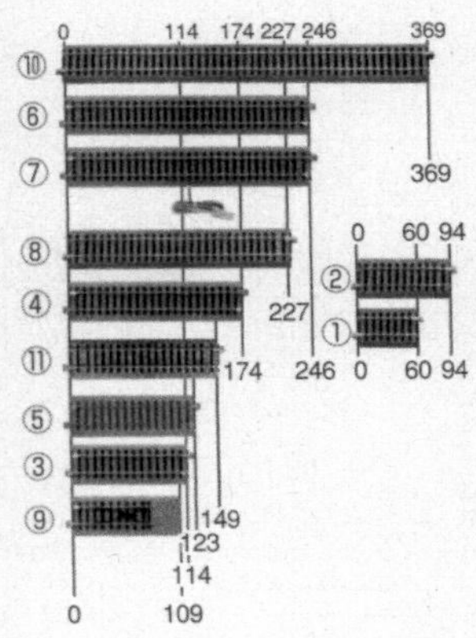

**#1 2-3/8" 60mm**
**381-2105** pkg(4) **10.00**

**#2 3-11/16" 94mm**
**381-2111** pkg(2) **5.00**

**#3 4-1/2" 114mm**
**381-2120** pkg(4) **10.00**

**#4 6-7/8" 174mm**
**381-2130** pkg(4) **10.50**

**#5 4-7/8" 123mm**
**381-2140** pkg(4) **10.00**

**#6 9-3/4" 246mm**
**381-2150** pkg(4) **11.00**

**#7 9-3/4" 246mm Feeder Track**
**381-2151 5.00**

**#8 8-15/16" 227mm**
**381-2160** pkg(2) **5.50**

**#9 4-1/4" 109mm Bumper Track**
**381-2170** pkg(2) **10.00**

**#10 14-1/2" 369mm**
**381-2180** pkg(4) **17.00**

**#11 5-7/8" 149mm**
**381-2193** pkg(2) **5.00**

**#12 2-3/8" 60mm 90° Crossing**
**381-2401 11.00**

## CURVED TRACK

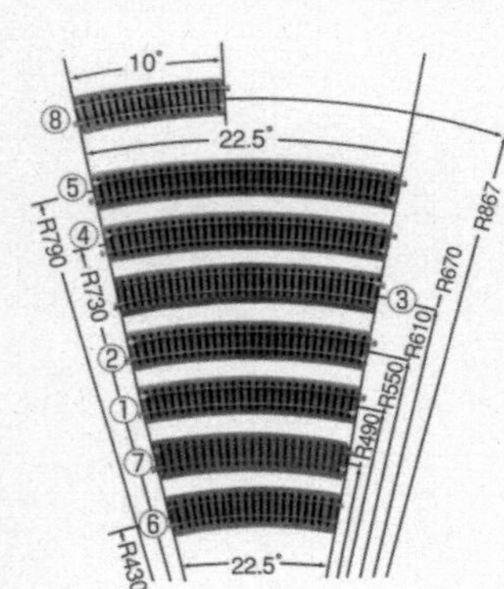

All items are 22.5° Radius unless noted.

**#1 21-5/8" 550mm**
**381-2210** pkg(4) **11.00**

**#2 24" 610mm**
**381-2220** pkg(4) **12.00**

**#3 26-3/8" 670mm**
**381-2230** pkg(4) **13.00**

**#4 28-3/4" 730mm**
**381-2240** pkg(4) **13.00**

**#5 31-1/8" 790mm**
**381-2250** pkg(4) **14.00**

**#6 16-7/8" 430mm**
**381-2260** pkg(4) **10.00**

**#7 19-1/4" 490mm**
**381-2270** pkg(4) **10.00**

**#8 34-1/8" 867mm**
**381-2290** 10° Radius pkg(2) **5.00**

## TURNOUTS & TURNOUT MACHINES

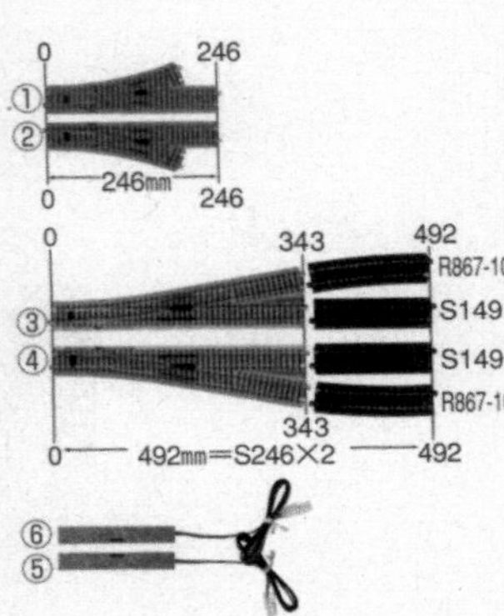

**#1 Left Manual - 19-3/4" 490mm Radius**
**381-2840 22.00**

**#2 Right Manual - 19-3/4" 490mm Radius**
**381-2841 22.00**

**#3 #6 Left Manual - 34-1/8" 867mm Radius**
**381-2862 22.00**

**#4 #6 Right Manual - 34-1/8" 867mm Radius**
**381-2863 22.00**

**#5 DC Turnout Machine - Left**
**381-2503** Fits #2840 & 2862 **10.00**

**#6 DC Turnout Machine - Right**
**381-2504** Fits #2841 & 2863 **10.00**

## ADDITIONAL COMPONENTS

### Rerailer

**381-2502 3.60**
Simply place on top of track to easily guide loco and car wheels on to the rails.

### Unitrak Ballast

**381-24039** 200 Grams **9.00**
Ballast mixed to match Unitrack; use between tracks, and to blend roadbed to surrounding scenery.

### Unijoiner - Track Connectors

**381-24815** pkg(20) **5.25**
Simple design provides reliable and secure connections between tracks.

### Insulated Unijoiner

**381-24816** pkg(20) **5.25**
Use to electrically separate sections of track into "blocks" on your layout.

### Terminal Unijoiner

**381-24818 4.25**
Prewired, use in place of a Feeder Track. Makes it easy to feed power to curves, between switches and to areas where you don not want to install a small piece of straight track.

### DC Extension Cord

**381-24825 3.25**
Use to extend the wire distance between Power Pack and track power feeds. Plugs into the power cord on the power pack and the plug on the track power cord.

### 3-Way Extension Cord

**381-24827 5.25**
Simplifies wiring, allows you to connect three items together to a power feed,

### Turnout Control Switch

**381-24840 7.75**
Use alongside the power pack to operate a remote turnout anywhere on your layout.

### Turnout Extension Cord

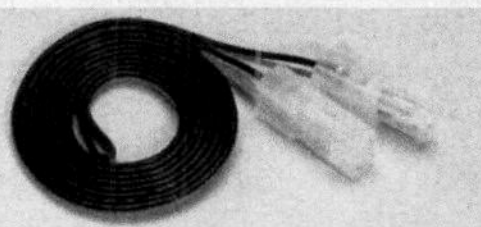

**381-24841 3.25**
Use to extend the wire distance between a Turnout and a Turnout Control Switch.

### DC Converter for Turnout Control Switches

**381-24842 6.50**
Connects to power supply's 18V AC output and converts the AC to DC for use by the Turnout Switch Control.

### Power Pack Adapter Cord

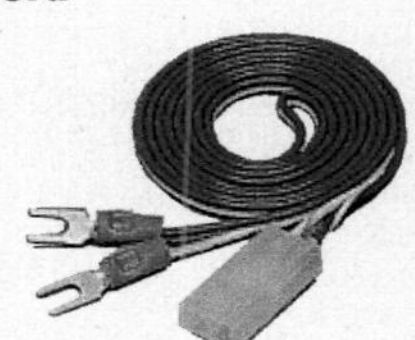

**381-24843 3.25**
Connects Kato plugs to any power pack screw terminals.

## LAYOUT SETS

Get a railroad running in no time with these complete track sets. Each includes a full assortment of Unitrack and Power Pack to create the layout plan as shown.

### Let's DCC

There's plenty of operating action in this 4 x 8' layout, with separate stations for Amtrak or regional commuter service and busy industrial sidings that can be worked by a local freight.

**NEW 381-30640** HO Unitrack & Power Pack Assortment **464.00**

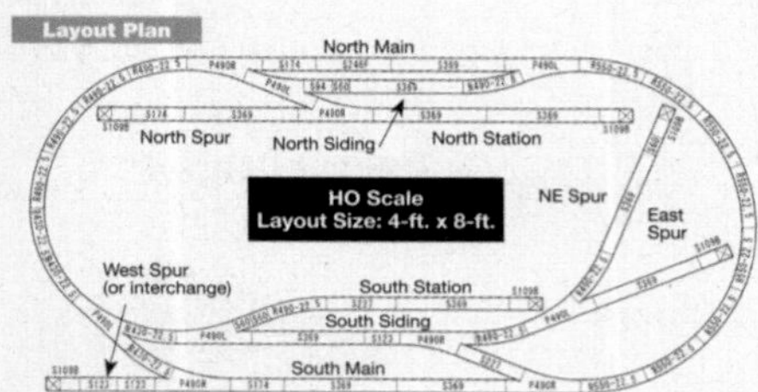


### Dispatchers Orders

This busy railroad may need a dispatcher to help keep trains moving on time. There's plenty of action built into this 4x8' layout with a busy double-track mainline and several sidings that need to be switched.

**381-30610** HO Unitrak & Power Pack Assortment **639.25**

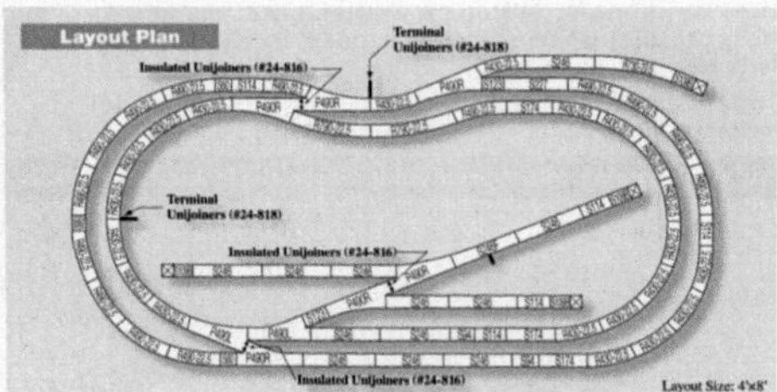


### Yard Job One

Sorting and blocking cars will keep a yard switcher busy on this layout, and once the train is made up, there's more work serving the industrial sidings along the main line. Enough track for a 4x8' area.

**381-30620** HO Unitrak & Power Pack Assortment **530.25**

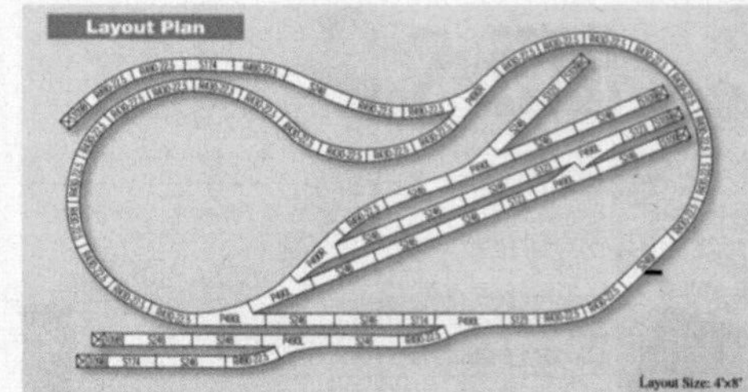

# FLEX-TRAK™

Flex-Trak features scale size ties, tie plates and spikes, irregular tie spacing, natural brown tie color and nickel-silver rail. 3' lengths. The weathered Flex-Trak also features pre-colored brown rails.

### HO Standard Gauge Non-Weathered Flex-Trak

**255-10102** Code 100 pkg(6) **33.40**

**255-10104** Code 83 pkg(6) **32.95**

**255-10105** Code 83 w/Concrete Ties, pkg(6) **32.95**

**255-10106** Code 70 pkg(6) **32.95**

**255-10108** Code 55 pkg(6) **31.45**

### HO Standard Gauge Weathered Flex-Trak

**255-12102** Code 100 pkg(6) **34.80**

**255-12104** Code 83 pkg(6) **34.55**

**255-12105** Code 83 w/Concrete Ties, pkg(6) **34.55**

**255-12106** Code 70 pkg(6) **34.55**

**255-12108** Code 55 pkg(6) **32.90**

### HO-HOn3 Dual Gauge Non-Weathered Flex-Trak

**255-10110** Code 70 pkg(6) **40.65**

**255-10112** Code 55 pkg(6) **38.70**

### HO-HOn3 Dual Gauge Weathered Flex-Trak

**255-12110** Code 70 pkg(6) **43.90**

**255-12112** Code 55 pkg(6) **41.85**

### HOn3 Narrow Gauge Non-Weathered Flex-Trak

**255-10114** Code 70 pkg(6) **32.95**

**255-10116** Code 55 pkg(6) **29.55**

**255-10118** Code 40 pkg(6) **29.55**

### HOn3 Narrow Gauge Weathered Flex-Trak

**255-12114** Code 70 pkg(6) **34.55**

**255-12116** Code 55 pkg(6) **30.80**

**255-12118** Code 40 pkg(6) **30.80**

### Bridge Flex-Trak

Flex-Trak with bridge tie dimensions. Ties are wider with closer spacing. The HO track includes guard rails, guard timbers and four barrel platforms with barrels. Non-weathered.

**255-11101** HO Code 83 pkg(1) **10.20**
36" length.

**255-11103** HO Code 70 pkg(1) **10.20**
36" length.

**255-11102** HOn3 Code 55 pkg(2) **6.10**
7" length.

### Flex-Trak Turnouts 18.95 ea

Flex-Trak turnouts are DCC and analog (standard DC) compatible right from the box with no modifications necessary. These turnouts feature scale-size, wood-grained plastic ties that match Micro Engineering Flex-Trak, American-style spike heads and tie plates, all-metal frog and guard rails, rail brace and slide plate details, snap-action sprung switch points, non-operating switch stand and a super detailing kit.

**255-14705** HO Code 83, #6 Left Hand

**255-14706** HO Code 83, #6 Right Hand

**255-14805** HO Code 70, #6 Left Hand

**255-14806** HO Code 70, #6 Right Hand

### Laser-Cut Tie Turnouts 22.95 ea

Feature laser-cut, stained wood ties.

**255-15205** HOn3 Code 55, #6 Left Hand

**255-15206** HOn3 Code 55, #6 Right Hand

### Turnout Parts

**255-80301** Switch Stand, Nonoperating pkg(2) **2.50**

### Turnout Kits 8.95 ea

Includes a cast frog with a rib along its bottom, a pair of guard rails and a switch assembly with a molded-on plastic throw bar.

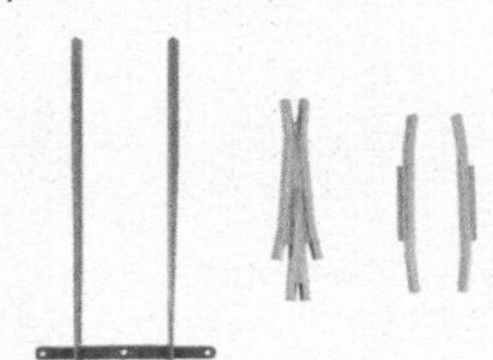

**255-80316** HO Code 83 #6

**255-80320** HO Code 70 #6

# NICKEL SILVER RAIL

3' lengths.

### Non-Weathered

**255-17040** Code 40 pkg(17) **25.65**

**255-17055** Code 55 pkg(33) **44.20**

**255-17070** Code 70 pkg(33) **55.95**

**255-17083** Code 83 pkg(33) **59.95**

**255-17100** Code 100 pkg(33) **64.25**

### Weathered

Pre-colored, dark brown rail.

**255-16040** Code 40 pkg(17) **27.80**

**255-16055** Code 55 pkg(33) **48.00**

**255-16070** Code 70 pkg(33) **60.10**

**255-16083** Code 83 pkg(33) **64.55**

**255-16100** Code 100 pkg(33) **68.95**

# ACCESSORIES

### Rail Joiners-Metal

Low profile, nickel silver, slip-on type joiners.

**255-26040** Code 40 pkg(20) **4.20**

**255-26055** Code 55 pkg(50) **8.05**

**255-26070** Code 70 pkg(50) **8.05**

**255-26083** Code 83 pkg(50) **8.05**

**255-26100** Code 100 pkg(48) **6.05**

### Rail Joiners-Plastic Insulated 3.85 ea

**255-26084** Code 83 pkg(12)

**255-26071** Code 70 pkg(12)

**255-26056** Code 55 pkg(12)

### Transition Rail Joiners-Plastic 4 Pair 3.85 ea

**255-26001** Code 100 to 83

**255-26002** Code 100 to 70

**255-26003** Code 83 to 70

**255-26005** Code 70 to 55

### Spikes

Blackened metal.

**255-30101** Large, 1/2" pkg(7500) **113.25**

**255-30102** Large, 1/2" pkg(500) **9.40**

**255-30103** Medium, 3/8" pkg(12,000) **136.25**

**255-30104** Medium 3/8" pkg(800) **10.85**

**255-30105** Small 1/4" Pointed Tip pkg(15,000) **110.55**

**255-30106** Small 1/4" Pointed Tip pkg(1000) **9.40**

**255-30110** Small 1/4" Chisel Tip pkg(1000) **9.40**

**255-30108** Micro 3/16" pkg(1000) **9.40**

### Non-Weathered Ties

Scale ties in natural wood.

#### Full Profile

**255-37101** HO Regular Length pkg(1000) **13.15**

**255-37102** HO Turnout Length pkg(250) **7.15**

**255-37103** HOn3 Regular Length pkg(1000) **11.50**

**255-37104** HOn3 Turnout Length pkg(250) **6.30**

#### Low Profile

**255-37107** HO Regular Length pkg(1000) **13.15**

**255-37108** HO Turnout Length pkg(250) **7.15**

### Weathered Ties

Scale ties, stained and weathered brown.

#### Full Profile

**255-36101** HO Regular Length pkg(1000) **14.50**

**255-36102** HO Turnout Length pkg(250) **7.90**

**255-36103** HOn3 Regular Length pkg(1000) **13.25**

**255-36104** HOn3 Turnout Length pkg(250) **7.20**

#### Low Profile

**255-36107** HO Regular Length pkg(1000) **14.50**

**255-36108** HO Turnout Length pkg(250) **7.90**

### Rail Weathering Solution

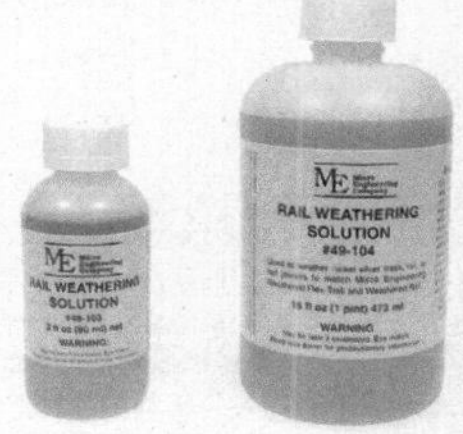


This is the same solution Micro Engineering uses for weathering its Flex-Trak™ and rail.

**255-49103** 4oz **9.85**

**255-49104** 16oz (1pt) **25.25**

# TOOLS

### Track Gauges 4.85 ea

Three-point, diecast metal track gauge keeps rails aligned when hand-laying track.

**255-42101** HO Code 100

**255-42102** HO Code 83

**255-42103** HO Code 70

**255-42104** HO Code 55

**255-42105** HOn3 Code 70

**255-42106** HOn3 Code 55

**255-42107** HOn3 Code 40

### Track Tools

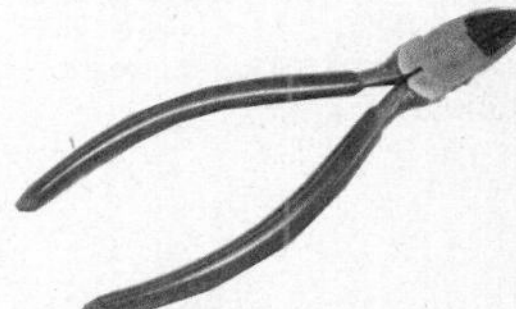

**255-48101** Rail Cutter, Heavy Duty **27.70**

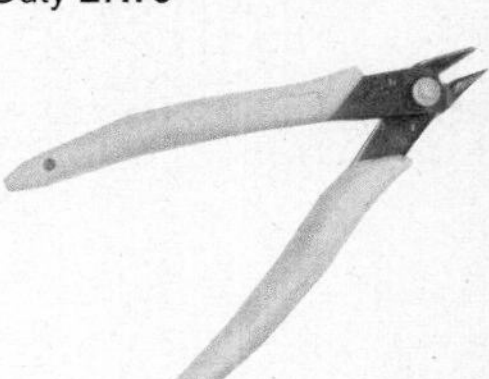

**255-48102** Rail Nipper, Light Duty **13.80**

HO Scale cork roadbed and sheet.

## CORK ROADBED

These lightweight pieces of cork roadbed are easy to use by any modeler: materials can be easily shaped and cut. Constructed with consistent thickness, each section is beveled for a realistic look. Features excellent sound absorption.

### 3' Sections

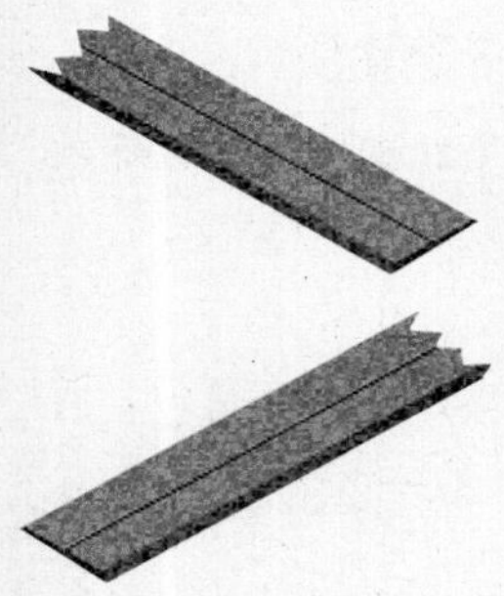

**472-3013 1.39**
Dealers MUST order multiples of 25.

**472-3015** pkg(5) **8.95**

### #4/6 Turnouts

Install roadbed under turnouts in seconds with these precut, easy-to-use cork sections. Simply position and nail in place. One-piece design eliminates difficult alignment of diverging route and cutting. Beveled edges, height and color match other cork roadbed and sheets. Can be used with most United States standard turnouts.

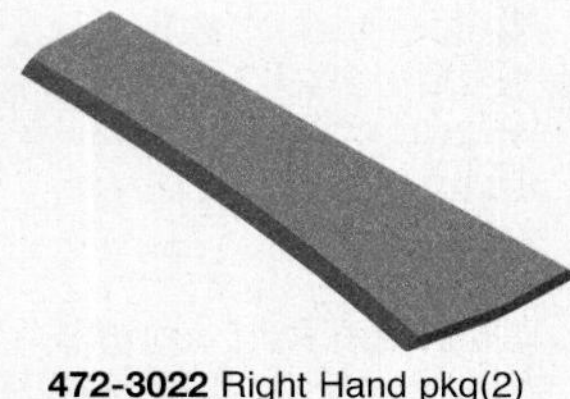

**472-3022** Right Hand pkg(2) **6.78**
3/16 x 2-15/16 x 8-5/8"

**472-3023** Left Hand pkg(2) **6.78**
3/16 x 2-15/16 x 8-5/8"

**472-3024** Wye **4.79**
3/16 x 3-1/8 x 8-23/32"

## CORKSHEET PACKS

**472-3014 3.79**
Sheet stock can be used on switches, sidings, yards and loading areas. Each sheet is 5mm x 5 x 36". Dealers MUST order multiples of 9.

**472-3030** Wide **7.99**
These cork sheets measure 11-3/4" wide – more than twice as wide as standard corksheet pack, making them perfect for siding and yards. Constructed from the same material as Midwest Products cork roadbed. Dealer MUST order in multiples of 5.

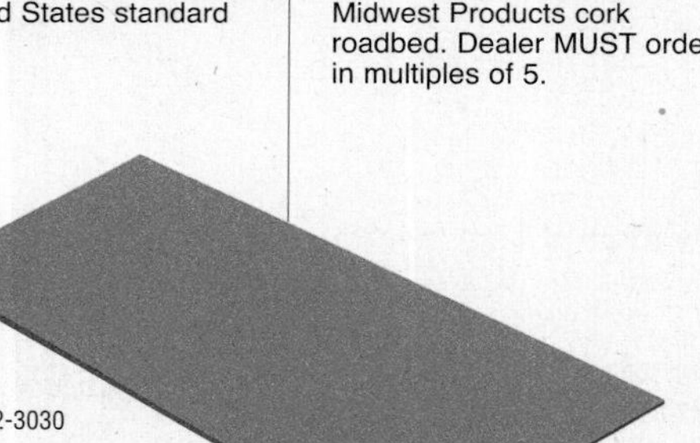

Corksheet 472-3030

Add a finishing touch of realism to trackside scenes with these detailed, one-piece castings. Each is hand-cast from a very strong gypsum material that picks up fine details much like dental plaster. Items are handpainted to bring out the many details, and are ready to install on your railroad.

### Track Bumpers 5.70 ea

**506-8** End-of-Track w/Heavy Timbers

**506-9** End-of-Track w/Light Timbers

**506-100** Pennsy Concrete Style pkg(4)

### Loading Ramps 6.99 ea

**506-170** Wooden End-of-Track Style

**506-180** Wood & Stone Trackside Style

### Tie Pile

**506-150** Stack of Wooden Railroad Ties pkg(2) **5.70**

Get the Scoop!
Get the Skinny!
Get the Score!
Check Out Walthers
Web site at
**www.walthers.com**

*Peerless Industries Inc.*

Peerless Industries offers easy-to-install electronic controls for directional reversing, delayed reversing and intermediate stops. The units come completely assembled with color-coded wires and easy-to-follow instructions.

### Automatic Reversing Unit

Automatically reverses train direction without the need for special switches, optical sensors, lights or magnets. Operates from a 12V DC power pack. Unit is less track. Can be used for:

- automatic single or multitrack point-to-point operation
- a wall or bookcase mini-layout or display track for your favorite locomotive
- a test or break-in track

**564-525** HO Scale **74.95**

**564-535** N Scale **74.95**

**564-542** G Scale **84.50**

**564-545** O Scale **79.50**

### Automatic Train Stop Control

**564-550 79.50**
For use with the #525, 535, 542 or 545. Provides automatic delayed stops at the end points of your reversing section. Delay is adjustable up to 30 seconds. Takes only a few minutes to install and operates from your power pack accessory terminals.

### Automatic Intermediate Train Stop

**564-555 79.50**
Train stops—delays up to 30 seconds—restarts automatically at preset locations such as at a train station, water tower, etc. Use with #525, 535, 542, 545 or alone in a continuous-loop layout. Operates from power pack accessory terminals.

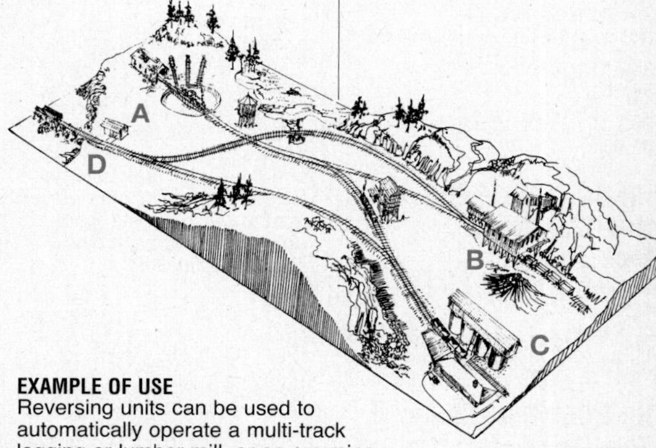


**EXAMPLE OF USE**
Reversing units can be used to automatically operate a multi-track logging or lumber mill, or an ore mine.

In this example, a train can start at point A, travel to point B, automatically stop and reverse to point D, then automatically stop and reverse to point C, before finally stopping and reversing automatically back to point A. Basic plans available from manufacturer.

# PECO STREAMLINE 83 LINE TRACK:

## HO Scale North American-Style Track for your Railroad

Flexi Track available with wooden ties!

Turnouts suitable for DC and DCC operating systems!

Crossing geometry complements turnouts!

If you're model railroading in the U.S or Canada, Peco's Streamline Code 83 track system will add realism along your right-of-way. Based on American Railway Engineering Association drawings for utmost authenticity, all components have been designed to meet NMRA standards. This line of track is a worthy addition to Peco's 50+ year history of providing dependable and durable track systems designed for years of reliable service.

It's the attention to detail that makes this track a standout! Turnout geometry makes it easy to combine turnouts and crossings to fit your track plan. All track and turnouts feature the correct prototypical tie spacing; once laid and ballasted, each piece looks at home on your North American-style layout. The wiring system also allows for any DC or DCC operating system to be used with the track!

- **Suitable for DC or DCC**
- **Choose Insulfrog or Electrofrog components**
- **Correct prototypical tie spacing**
- **Wood-grain plastic ties molded in creosote color**
- **Realistic North American-style tieplate and spike detail**
- **Over-center spring for positive throw**
- **Nickel silver rail**
- **#5, #6, #7 or #8 frog angles**

# PECO

IMPORTED FROM GREAT BRITAIN BY WALTHERS
Peco track features nickel-silver rail for excellent conductivity. Setrack is a sectional track system ideal for beginners. Streamline is a more advanced, flexible track system. Insulfrog turnouts feature an insulated plastic frog for easier wiring. Electrofrog turnouts provide continuous electrical current across the frog to help prevent stalling and hesitation. Turnouts are route selective.

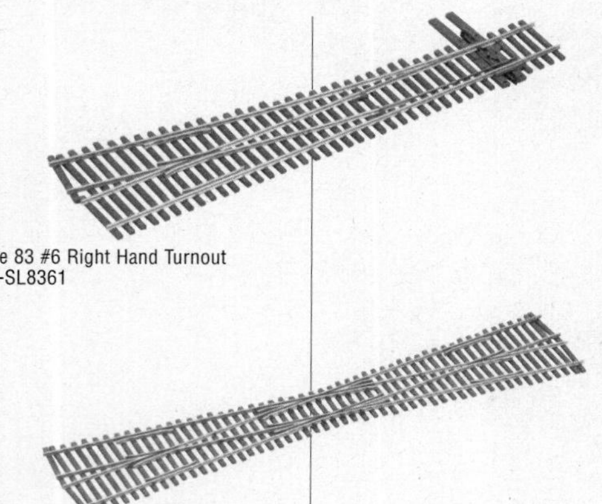

Code 83 #6 Right Hand Turnout 552-SL8361

Code 83 #6 Crossing 552-SL8364

## NEW PRODUCTS

### North American-Style Code 83 Track

#### Turnouts 42.99 ea

**NEW 552-SL8376** #7 Right Insulfrog

**NEW 552-SL8377** #7 Left Insulfrog

**NEW 552-SLE8376** #7 Right Electrofrog

**NEW 552-SLE8377** #7 Left Electrofrog

### Hayes Bumper

**NEW 552-SL8340 4.99**

### Code 100 Setrack

**NEW 552-ST247** Medium-Radius Wye Insulfrog **21.99**
6-11/16" 170mm Long, 33-27/32" 85.96cm Radius

### Turnout Motors

**NEW 552-PL11** Side-Mounting Turnout Motor **TBA**

**NEW 552-PL10WE** Low-Amp Motor w/Extended Pin **14.99**

### Bulk Bull-Head Rail

#### Code 124, 36" sections

**NEW 552-IL7BH** Nickel Silver pkg(6) **24.99**

**NEW 552-IL7SBH** Bright Coated Steel pkg(6) **15.99**

## STREAMLINE TRACK

### North American-Style Code 83 Track

Based on North American prototype track, Peco Streamline Code 83 track features nickel silver rail and creosote-colored plastic ties that look right at home on U.S. and Canadian-style layouts.

#### Flexi Track

**552-SL8300** 36" Length **7.60**
Dealers must order in multiples of 25.

#### Turnouts

**With Insulfrog**

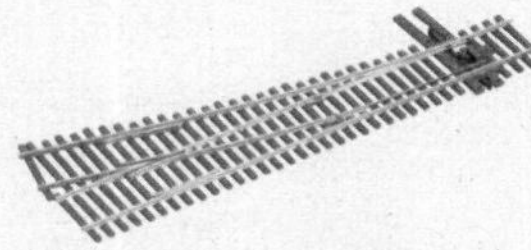

**552-SL8351** #5 Right Hand **36.99**

**552-SL8352** #5 Left Hand **36.99**

**552-SL8361** #6 Right Hand **36.99**

**552-SL8362** #6 Left Hand **36.99**

**552-SL8381** #8 Right Hand **42.99**

**552-SL8382** #8 Left Hand **42.99**

**With Electrofrog**

**552-SLE8351** #5 Right Hand **36.99**

**552-SLE8352** #5 Left Hand **36.99**

**552-SLE8361** #6 Right Hand **36.99**

**552-SLE8362** #6 Left Hand **36.99**

**552-SLE8381** #8 Right Hand **42.99**

**552-SLE8382** #8 Left Hand **42.99**

#### Crossings

**552-SL8364** Insulfrog **38.99**

**552-SLE8364** Electrofrog **39.99**

#### Track Inspection Pit

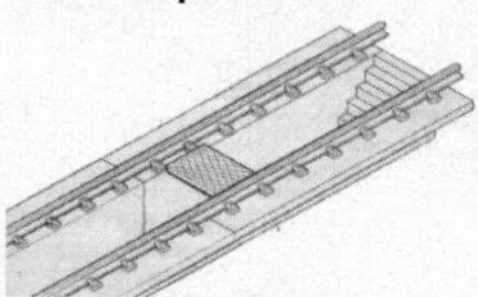

**552-SL8356 15.99**
Perfect for use in loco servicing scenes, roundhouses, engine houses and more. Includes pit, Code 83 rail and details.

#### Rail Joiners

Dealers must order in multiples of 12.

**552-SL8310** Metal **4.83**

**552-SL8311** Insulating **4.83**

#### Track Pins

**552-SL8314 2.67**
Dealers must order in multiples of 12.

### Code 75

#### Flex Track

**552-1163** Wooden Ties pkg(25) **189.99**
Each piece measures 36" long and features nickel-silver rail. Dealers must order in multiples of 25.

#### Crossings

**552-529** Short, Insulfrog **25.99**

**552-193** Short, Electrofrog **26.99**

**552-1194** Long, Insulfrog **24.99**

#### Double Slip

**552-190** Insulfrog **93.99**

#### Single Slip

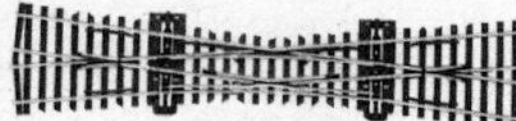

**552-1180** Insulfrog **86.99**

#### Wye Turnouts

Nominal Radius: 610mm 24", Angle: 24°, Length: 148mm 5-13/16".

**552-1197** Small Radius, Electrofrog **27.99**

**552-1198** Large Radius, Electrofrog **28.99**

#### Curved Double Radius Turnouts 31.99 ea

Nominal Radius Outside: 1524mm 60", Inside: 762mm 30", Length: 256mm 10-5/32".

**552-917** Right Hand, Electrofrog

**552-918** Left Hand, Electrofrog

#### Small Radius Turnouts 26.99 ea

Nominal Radius: 610mm 24", Angle: 12°, Length: 185mm 7-9/32".

**552-1916** Right Hand, Electrofrog

**552-1917** Left Hand, Electrofrog

#### Medium Radius Turnouts 27.99 ea

Nominal Radius: 914mm 36", Angle: 12°, Length: 219mm 8-5/8".

**552-1912** Right Hand, Electrofrog

**552-1913** Left Hand, Electrofrog

#### Large Radius Turnouts 31.99 ea

Nominal Radius: 1524mm 60", Angle: 12°, Length: 258mm 10-5/32".

**552-1914** Right Hand, Electrofrog

**552-1915** Left Hand, Electrofrog

#### 3-Way Turnout

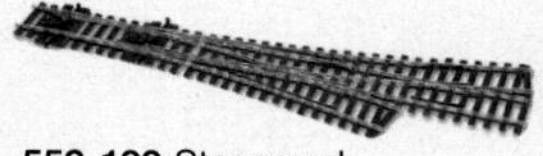

**552-199** Staggered w/Electrofrog **71.99**

### Code 100

#### Flex Track 7.12 ea

Each piece measures 36" long and features nickel-silver rail. Dealers must order in multiples of 25.

**552-1162** Concrete Ties
Simulates modern concrete ties used on some railroads.

**552-11603** Wooden Ties

#### Crossings

**552-1049** Short, Insulfrog, **21.99**
Approximate length: 5" 127mm, Angle: 24°.

**552-1050** Long, Insulfrog **25.99**
Approximate length: 10" 250mm, Angle: 12°.

#### 3-Way Turnouts

Nominal Radius: 914mm 36", Angle: 12°, Length: 220mm, 8-21/32".

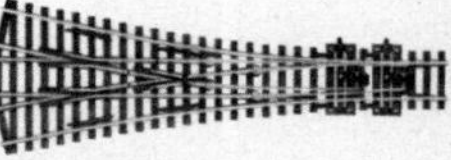

**552-1055** Medium Radius, Insulfrog **62.99**

**552-1907** Medium Radius Electrofrog **63.99**

#### Single Slip

**552-80** Insulfrog-New Design **74.99**

#### Double Slip

**552-90** Insulfrog-New Design **81.99**

#### Wye Turnouts

Nominal Radius: 610mm 24", Angle: 24°, Length: 148mm 5-13/16".

**552-1053** Small Radius, Insulfrog **23.99**

**552-1054** Large Radius, Insulfrog **27.99**

**552-1901** Small Radius, Electrofrog **24.99**

**552-1902** Large Radius, Electrofrog **27.99**

#### Curved Double-Radius Turnouts 29.99 ea

Nominal Radius Outside: 1524mm 60", Inside: 762mm 30", Length: 256mm 10-5/32".

**552-1042** Right Hand, Insulfrog

**552-1043** Left Hand, Insulfrog

**552-1910** Right Hand, Electrofrog

**552-1911** Left Hand, Electrofrog

IMPORTED FROM GREAT BRITAIN BY WALTHERS

### Small Radius Turnouts 23.99 ea

Nominal Radius: 610mm 24", Angle: 12°, Length: 185mm 7-9/32".

**552-1047** Right Hand, Insulfrog

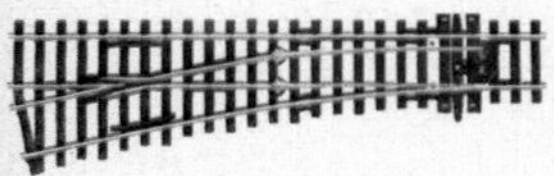

**552-1048** Left Hand, Insulfrog

**552-1903** Right Hand, Electrofrog

**552-1904** Left Hand, Electrofrog

### Medium Radius Turnouts 25.99 ea

Nominal Radius: 914mm 36", Angle: 12°, Length: 219mm 8-5/8".

**552-1051** Right Hand, Insulfrog

**552-1052** Left Hand, Insulfrog

**552-1905** Right Hand, Electrofrog

**552-1906** Left Hand, Electrofrog

### Large Radius Turnouts

Nominal Radius: 1524mm 60", Angle: 12°, Length: 258mm 10-5/32".

**552-1044** Right Hand, Insulfrog **28.99**

**552-1045** Left Hand, Insulfrog **28.99**

**552-1908** Right Hand, Electrofrog **29.99**

**552-1909** Left Hand, Electrofrog **29.99**

## SETRACK

### Curved Track

Items listed below are available by Special Order (see Legend Page).

**552-408** No. 3 Radius, Standard Curve pkg(36) **169.99**

**552-409** No. 3 Radius, Double Curve pkg(24) **147.99**

### Turnouts 21.99 ea

Radius: 17-1/4" 438mm, Length: 6-5/8" 168mm, Angle: 22-1/2°.

**552-1240** Right Hand, Insulfrog

**552-1241** Left Hand, Insulfrog

### Curved Double-Radius Turnouts 34.99 ea

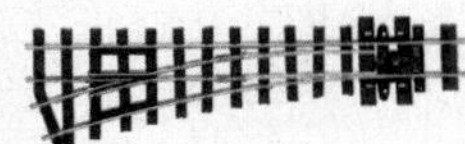

**552-244** Code 100, Right Hand

**552-245** Code 100, Left Hand

## STREAMLINE NARROW GAUGE TRACK

### Metre Gauge Track

Used throughout Switzerland. Metre gauge can also be found in parts of Europe, Asia and South America. In HO, it scales out to 3'-6" (HOn3-1/2), which is used in many parts of the world. Modelers working in OO can use this trackage for OOn3, matching the 3' gauge lines used in Ireland and on the Isle of Man. The selection includes flex track, turnouts and other accessories, which are fully assembled with simulated wood ties and Code 75 nickel-silver rail.

### Flex Track

Dealers MUST order in multiples of 25.

**552-1400 9.88**

### Crossings

**552-1493** Short Crossing 20° Angle w/Electrofrog **23.99**

### Medium Radius Turnouts w/Electrofrogs 31.99 ea

**552-1495** Right Hand

**552-1496** Left Hand

### Curved Turnouts 43.99 ea

**552-1486** Right Hand

**552-1487** Left Hand

### Accessories

**552-1440** Buffer Stop Rail Type pkg(6) **20.99**

### HOe (HOn2-1/2) Narrow Gauge Flex Track

**552-500** 36" **7.60**

Features Code 80 nickel-silver rail and randomly spaced-wooden ties.

Dealers MUST order in multiples of 25.



### HOe (HOn2-1/2) Narrow Gauge Turnouts 22.99 ea

Features Code 80 nickel-silver rail and randomly spaced wooden ties. Turnouts feature electrofrogs.

**552-491** Right Hand, 12" Radius

**552-492** Left Hand, 12" Radius

**552-497** Wye, 18" Radius

## ACCESSORIES

### Loco Lifter

**552-43** Loco-Lift & Storage 305mm 12" **29.99**

Pick up, move, and store your locos without touching them! Perfect way to handle your favorite motive power and equipment without damaging details or paint jobs. Can be used anywhere along your layout. Simply place on tracks and rails in the lifter are electrified so the whole train can run through. Stacking beams at both ends allow the units to be used for storage between operating sessions.

### Bulk Rail 36"

Simulate the wide variety of rail sizes found on mainlines and sidings with these packs of bulk rail. Rail is made of nickel-silver for realistic appearance and improved electrical conductivity.

**552-4000** Code 60 pkg(6) **13.99**

**552-4002** Code 75 pkg(6) **16.99**

**552-4003** Code 80 pkg(6) **16.99**

**552-4004** Code 100 pkg(6) **19.99**

### Rail Joiners

Dealers MUST order in multiples of 12.

552-1164

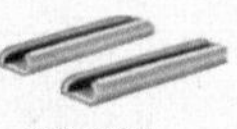

552-1165

### Code 75 4.83 ea

**552-1164** Nylon-Insulated

**552-1165** Nickel-Silver

### Code 100 4.58 ea

**552-10** Nickel-Silver

**552-11** Nylon-Insulated

### Third Rail Conductor Mounts

**552-4009** Code 60 Rail pkg(100) **9.99**

### Switch Machine & Accessories

Unit installs directly beneath the turnout and makes positive contact without linkage or other complex connections. Just cut a hole in your benchwork deep enough to clear the motor and install. An extension pin is included to mount the motor beneath the benchwork. Can be adapted to other brands of turnouts with extension pin (included) and motor adapter, available separately.

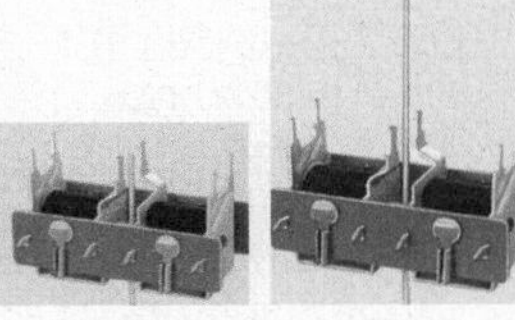

552-3010 552-105

**552-3010** Switch Machine **12.99**

**552-105** Switch Machine w/Extended Pin **12.99**

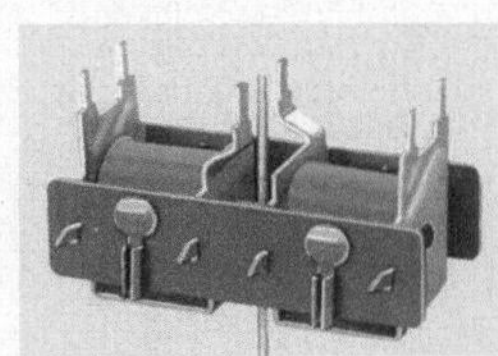

**552-1023** Switch Machine For Digital Applications **14.99**

Designed to consume less power than standard Switch Machine #552-3010.

### Push-On Terminal Connectors & Shrouds

**552-PL31 5.99**

Connectors slide-fit on contact pins on Peco turnout motors. Includes slide-on insulating shroud.

### Motor Adapter

**552-3003 3.99**

Allows mounting of the switch machine on the benchwork, alongside of the turnout. Can be adapted for use with various makes of turnouts.

### Accessory Switch

**552-3013 6.99**

Can be used with switch machine to control turnout polarity, operate signals or other trackside devices.

### Micro Switch

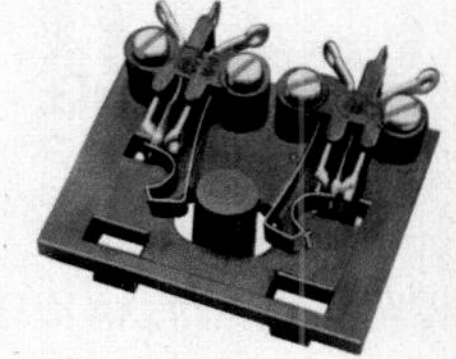

**552-15 16.99**

## STREAMLINE TRACK

### Code 83

### Mounting Plate

**552-9 5.99**

For switch machines #552-3010, 105 and 1023, each sold separately.

### Passing Contact Switches 12.99 ea

552-26 552-22

Lever-type switch for turnout control. Can be mounted on a panel or inside switch console #552-28, sold separately.

**552-26** Black

**552-30** White

**552-31** Yellow

**552-32** Red

**552-22** On/Off Switch Light Blue

**552-23** On/On Green

### Switch Accessories

**552-24** Switch Joining Bar **5.99**

**552-29** Mounting Plates For Contact Switches pkg(6) **4.99**

### Switch Console

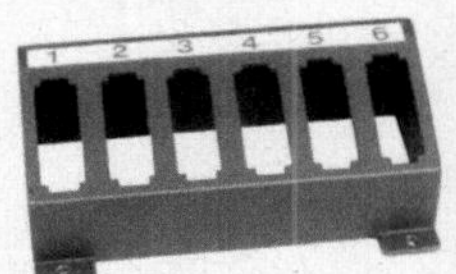


**552-28 8.99**

Create a neat-looking control panel in minutes. Plastic unit holds up to six Passing Contact Switches, #552-22, 23, 26 and 32, (switches sold separately). Small size can easily be hidden behind scenery or inside some structures if mounting space is limited.

PECO

IMPORTED FROM GREAT BRITAIN BY WALTHERS

### Subway Staircase Kit

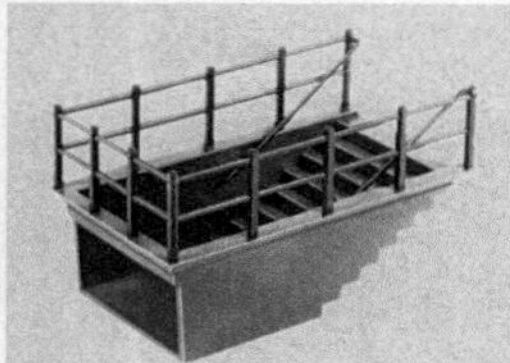

552-7 12.99

### Peco Catalog

552-1995 8.99
Features the complete line of Peco products, including track, locomotives and rolling stock, structures, scenery and more.

## NEW PRODUCTS

### Flex Link™

Simplify installation of control knobs for Blue Point™ Turnout Controllers (sold separately) with this complete and easy to use system. A clear acrylic knob mounted on the fascia is connected to a nylon push-pull tube, which then connects to the Controller. Tubes are 3' (91.4cm) long, and can be bent into tight curves, or cut to fit as needed.

### Flex Link Starter Kit

**NEW 501-40022 9.95**
Everything you need to install one Blue Point Controller (sold separately) including one pre-drilled acrylic knob, one 2-56 screw to attach the knob to the inner tube, one 3' flexible tube (contains both an inner and outer tube), two tube clamps with screws that anchor the outer tube at each end, one steel clamp to hold the outer tube at the Blue Point end, and one 2-56 threaded rod and clevis to attach inner tube to Blue Point.

### Flex Link Hardware Kit

**NEW 501-400235 34.95**
All of the hardware needed to hook-up five Blue Point Controllers; NOTE: Flex Link Tubing (#501-40024) is needed but not included with this set.

### Flex Link Tubing

**NEW 501-400245** 5-Pack **9.95**
Includes five nylon push-pull tubes, each 3' (91.4cm) long, which can be cut shorter as needed.

## BLUE POINT™ TURNOUT CONTROLLERS

This innovative electrical component makes it easy to power frogs and route power on manual turnouts. Under-the-benchwork, manually thrown turnout control includes two sets of 5A electrical contacts for turnout frog or accessories such as signals. Features include locking slider tension and throw adjustment, plus dual attach points for fascia control. Also includes .032 turnout throw wire and complete instructions.

**501-40018** Single **12.95**
**501-400185** pkg(5) **59.95**
**501-4001810** pkg(10) **99.95**

## TRACK ACCESSORIES

### Switch Stands 8.99 ea

All brass-jeweled, operating.

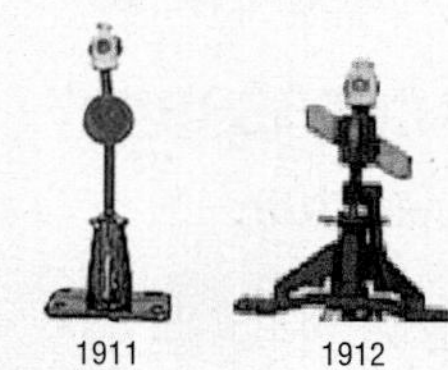


**525-1911** Star
**525-1912** Branch Line

**525-1913** Main Line
**525-1914** Low Ramapo
**525-1915** High Ramapo

### Assembled High-Star Type Operating Switch Stands 8.99 ea

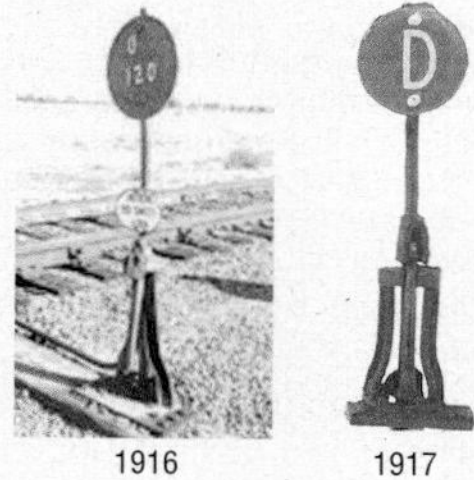


**525-1916** Standard Red Target
**525-1917** Derail Blue Target

### Switch Indicator 17.99 ea

All brass with LEDs.

**525-1300** Silver (1 Pair)
**525-1301** Black (1 Pair)

## TRACK ACCESSORIES

HO Scale switch machines and accessories.

### CTC Knob Kit

**628-61** pkg(2) **8.95**

### Mounting Brackets

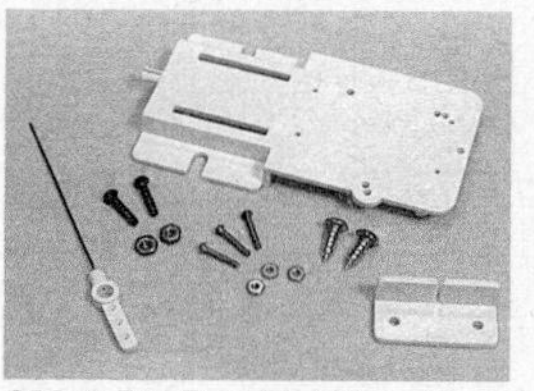

**628-5** Rix-Rax Flat Mounting Bracket Kit **3.49**
Under layout mounting bracket works with most any switch machine for flat mounting.

**628-21** Rix-Rax II **3.49**
Under layout mounting bracket complete with press-on linkage to motor shaft, adjustable limit stop blocks to limit the force on the switch points, mounting holes for most brands of adjustable limit switches and all hardware. Designed for use with the Hanscraft Display Motor. Works with all scales.

**628-1** Rix-Rax Mounting Bracket **3.49**
Under layout bracket, completely adjustable. Includes nuts, bolts, screws and throw rod. For use with most twin coil switch machines.

### Rail-It

**628-2 2.99**
Set on track and roll cars down ramp; automatically places wheels on track. Works with Code 70, 83 and 100 track.

### Rix Adjusto Pad

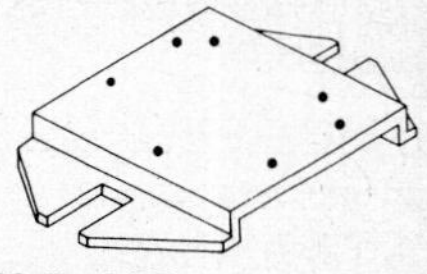

**628-7 2.75**
For mounting switch machine above or below layout. Includes wood and switch machine screws. Adjustable and interchangeable.

### Switch Machines

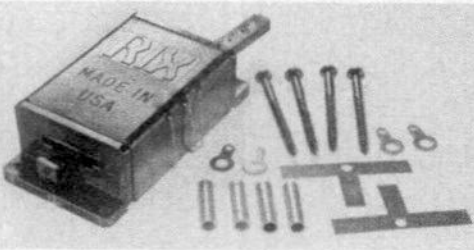

**628-4** T-C **10.99**
Controls turnouts from above or below the layout. Includes two SPDT add-on sets of contacts and needed hardware. Operates on 6-32V.

**628-15** Economy **10.25**
Same as #628-4 less contacts and mounting screws.

### Turnout Linkage

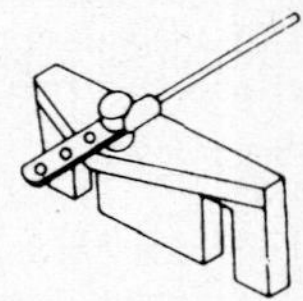

**628-6** Pivoting Turnout Linkage **2.75**
For controlling turnout from underneath layout.

### Switch Stand Kit

**628-13** Shorty Type, 2' **3.49**
Works directly off throw bar from any type turnout. 90° rotation. Includes switch ties, throw bar, target, linkage and housing.

## NOCH

IMPORTED FROM GERMANY BY WALTHERS

### Bumpers pkg(2) 11.99 ea

Based on rural and branchline installations, these layout-ready bumpers will keep cars from rolling off the ends of your spurs and industrial sidings.

**528-58640** Rural/Branchline, Wood-Reinforced Rock Pile

**528-58642** Rural/Branchline Rock Pile

### Snap-On Track Cleaners

**528-60157** pkg(5) **9.99**
This track cleaning pad is a sturdy brush that keeps the rails free of dust and dirt. Each pad has a molded-on clip that attaches to the inner axle of a freight or passenger wheelset. Run the car as normal, and watch the brush wipe your track clean! The axle clip works with a 5/64" 2mm diameter or smaller axle. When the brush gets dirty, simply replace it.

## SELLEY FINISHING TOUCHES

Assembled details are unpainted metal castings.

### Bumper

**675-89** End of Line **3.30**

### Hayes Wheel Stops

**675-677** pkg(6) **2.60**

## SHINOHARA

Build busy mainlines, sidings and yards all along your layout with this line of ready-to-use track and accessories. Available in two popular sizes, Code 100 simulates heavy (155+ pounds) mainline trackage, while Code 70 can be used for medium rail (100 pounds) found on branchlines and sidings. The two can be combined for a more realistic variety of rail sizes, or used with other brands of track. All items come fully assembled, ready to install with nickel-silver rail and dark brown plastic ties, unless noted.

## CODE 100

### #4 Turnouts 17.95 ea

**669-101** Left Hand

**669-102** Right Hand

### #6 Turnouts 17.95 ea

**669-103** Left Hand

**669-104** Right Hand

### #8 Turnouts 19.50 ea

Measures 12-3/4", frog angle 7° 9'.

**669-105** Left Hand

**669-106** Right Hand

### Wye Turnouts

**669-107** #4 **19.00**
Measures 9-5/8", frog angle 14° 15'.

**669-118** #6 **19.50**

### Three-Way Turnout

**669-108** #6 **38.00**
Measures 12-1/16".

### Crossovers

**669-109** #6 Single Left Hand **34.35**
Measures 9-3/8", frog angle 9° 30'.

**669-110** #6 Single Right Hand **34.35**
Measures 9-3/8", frog angle 9° 30'.

**669-111** #4 Double **57.25**
Measures 14-15/32", frog angle 14°.

**669-112** #6 Double **57.25**
Measures 19-1/8", frog angle 9° 30'.

### Double Slip Switches

**669-113** #4 **51.98**
Measures 9-3/4", frog angle 15°.

**669-114** #6 **51.98**
Measures 12-1/8" frog angle 9° 30'.

### Flex-Track

**669-115** pkg(10) **88.95**

**669-116** Single Guard Rail pkg(10) **95.00**
20" (50cm) long.

**669-117** Double Guard Rail pkg(10) **155.00**
39" (1m) long.

**669-119** For Branch Line pkg(10) **87.95**

### Curved Turnouts

#### #5 17.95 ea

**669-191** Left Hand

**669-192** Right Hand

#### #6 28.98 ea

Measures 12-31/32".

**669-126** Left Hand

**669-127** Right Hand

#### #8 31.75 ea

Measures 16-11/16".

**669-128** Left Hand

**669-129** Right Hand

### Turnout Accessories

**669-173** Throw Bar pkg(12) **1.25**

**669-178** Linkage **8.40**

### Crossings 18.25 ea (Unless Noted)

**669-130** 30°

**669-131** 45°
Measures 4-17/32".

**669-132** 60°
Measures 4-15/32".

**669-133** 90°
Measures 3-3/32".

**669-134** 9-1/2° Left Hand **24.95**

**669-135** 9-1/2° Right Hand **24.95**

### Straight Track

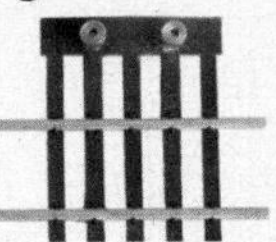

**669-144** 2" Terminal Section **3.35**

**669-145** 9" Straight Track pkg(10) **46.98**

**669-146** 9" Terminal Section **4.50**

### Curved Track pkg(12)

**669-147** 16" Radius **46.98**

**669-148** 18" Radius **46.98**

**669-149** 20" Radius **48.98**

**669-150** 22" Radius 30° **48.98**

**669-151** 24" Radius 30° **48.98**

**669-152** 26" Radius 30° **64.98**

**669-153** 28" Radius 30° **64.98**

**669-154** 30" Radius 30° **69.98**

**669-155** 32" Radius 30° **69.98**

**669-156** 34" Radius 30° **69.98**

**669-157** 36" Radius 30° **69.98**

### Track w/Concrete Ties

Some roads have experimented with concrete ties in place of wood. Track sections feature plastic ties molded in concrete gray, with prototypical mountings.

**669-185** Flex-Track 1m long **9.98**

### Code 100 Track Accessories

**669-141** Rail Joiners-Nickel Silver pkg(50) **8.40**

**669-160** Spikes .35 oz (10g) pkg **5.80**

### Spacer Ties pkg(24) 2.75 ea

Use to fill in "empty" spaces between track sections.

**669-175** Brown (Wood)

**669-179** Cement

### Uncoupler

**669-172** Uncoupling Base **1.50**

### Track Cleaner

**669-177** Rail Cleaner **2.98**

## CODE 70

### #4 Turnouts 17.25 ea

**669-301** Left Hand

**669-302** Right Hand

### #6 Turnouts 17.25 ea

Measures 10-7/8", frog angle 9° 30'.

**669-303** Left Hand

**669-304** Right Hand

### #8 Turnouts 18.85 ea

Measures 14-13/32", frog angle 7° 9'.

**669-305** Left Hand

**669-306** Right Hand

### Special Turnouts

**669-307** #4 Wye **17.25**

**669-308** #6 Three-Way **38.00**

**669-312** #6 Double Crossover **54.75**

**669-314** #6 Double Slip Switch **51.98**

### Flex Track

**669-315** pkg(10) **82.95**

**669-317** Double Guard Rails pkg(10) **155.00**
39" (1m) long.

### #6 Curved Turnouts 31.65 ea

**669-326** Left Hand

**669-327** Right Hand

### Curvable Turnouts 31.65 ea

**669-371** Left Hand

**669-372** Right Hand

### Crossings 18.25 ea

**669-330** 30°
Measures 5-13/32".

**669-331** 45°
Measures 4-23/32".

**669-332** 60°
Measures 4-3/32".

**669-333** 90°
Measures 4-3/32".

### Code 70 Track Accessories

**669-375** Space Tie pkg(24) **2.75**

**669-341** Rail Joiner-Nickel Silver pkg(50) **8.40**

**669-342** Insulated Rail Joiners pkg(12) **2.00**

## HOn3

### #3 Wye Turnout

**669-493 15.40**

### #4 Turnouts 15.40 ea

**669-401** Left Hand

**669-402** Right Hand

### #6 Turnouts 15.40 ea

**669-403** Left Hand

**669-404** Right Hand

### Flex Track

**669-415** pkg(10) **82.95**

**669-465** Dual Gauge pkg(10) **132.95**

### Crossings 16.90 ea

**669-430** 30°

**669-431** 45°

**669-432** 60°

**669-433** 90°

### Dual Gauge #6 Turnouts 39.95 ea

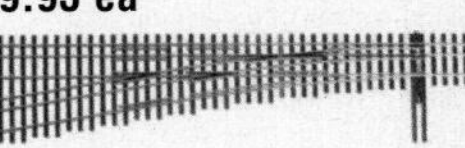

**669-450** Left Hand-1
Narrow gauge on left.

**669-451** Left Hand-2
Narrow gauge on right.

**669-452** Right Hand-1
Narrow gauge on right.

**669-453** Right Hand-2
Narrow gauge on left.

### Transition Track 12.00 ea

**669-470** Narrow Gauge-Left

**669-471** Narrow Gauge-Right

# märklin®

## NEW PRODUCT

### German Federal Railroad (DB) Class 701 Maintenance Car

**NEW 441-39970 613.45**
Based on a protoype used to check and repair overhead catenary, this powered, DCC-equipped model features sound and a moving work platform that raises as well as rotates and a double arm pantograph, which can also be raised and lowered. LED head and marker lights are standard. Fine details include cab interior, separately applied skylight antenna, horn, windshield wipers, and ladders. Length over buffers 16.0 cm/6-5/16".

## CATENARY

Add the excitement of electric railroading to your layout. This system is patterned after modern systems and will look great along heavy passenger, light rail or commuter lines. Contact and messenger wire components are made of welded steel where appropriate. Designed for use with Marklin track systems.

### Starter Set

**441-70000** Basic Catenary Assortment Set **230.90**
Contents: 9 sections of wire 14-3/16" for straight track.
18 section of wire 5-9/16" for standard curve. 6 sections of wire 6-5/8" for parallel curve.
31 regular masts and 1 feeder mast with outrigger arms, base, and clip for C Track.
1 mast positioning jig set.
1 installation jig for the catenary wire. Instructions and tips for setup.

### Contact Wire pkg(5)

16 pieces of catenary wire required for a circle, each piece with a 22.5° of curvature.

**441-70142** 5-9/16" Long **11.20**
For radii under 14-3/16" (C Track, K Track, M Track).

**441-70167** 6-5/8" Long **11.20**
For radii under 16-11/16" (K Track).

**441-70172** 6-13/16" Long **12.65**
For radii under 17-1/4" (C Track, M Track).

**441-70203** 8" Long **13.89**
For radii under 20-9/32" (C Track).

**441-70228** 8-15/16" Long **15.75**
For radii under 22-13/16" (C Track).

**441-70253** 9-15/16" Long **17.15**
For radii under 25-11/32" (C Track)

**441-70360** 14-3/16" Long **18.45**
Standard length. Designed for straight lengths of track.

### For Crossings

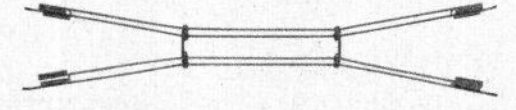

**441-70131** 5-1/2" Long pkg(1) **13.89**
Pre-finished for crossings and double slip switches with a crossing angle of 22.5° and 24.3°. 4 each 70231 adjustment sections required at ends.

### Transition Pieces

**441-70143** 5-9/16" Long pkg(3) **11.20**
For transition from old Marklin catenary to new catenary.

### Contact Wire Accessories

For electrical separation of the power circuit in the catenary. Install at any point by separating the contact wire and fixing in place in the insulation. Skids for a continuous voltage pick-up with variable holders. Set with 1 unit.

**441-70221** Wire Interrupter **3.25**

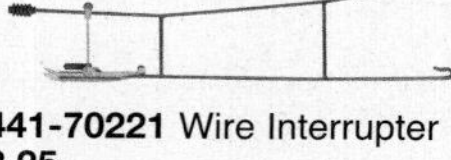

**441-70231** Wire Adjustment Section pkg(5) **22.39**

### Masts 3-15/16" pkg(5) 28.49 ea (Unless Noted)

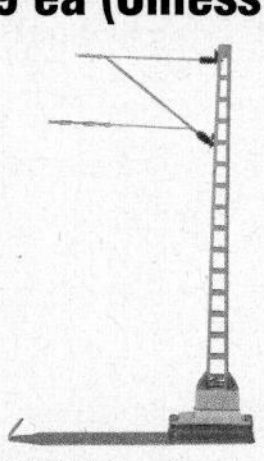

**441-74101** Standard
Metal lattice mast. Base with mounting screw and plug-in connection. Additional base mounting bracket for C Track.

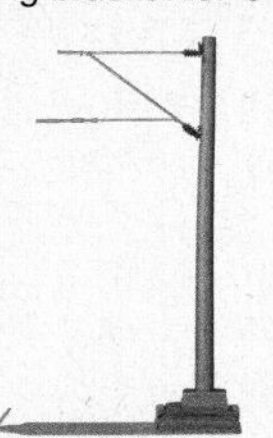

**441-74103** Concrete
Metal round mast. Base with mounting screw and plug-in connection. Additional base as a mounting bracket for C Track.

**441-74104** Bridge
Metal lattice mast. Base with plug-in connection plus additional mast bracket for Marklin-bridge system.

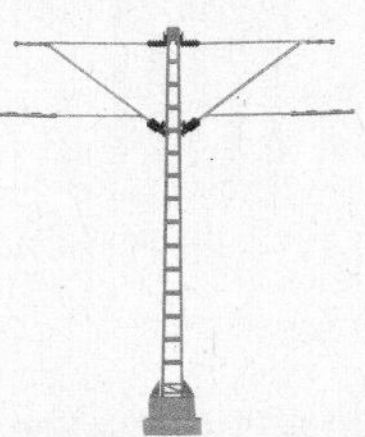

**441-74105** Center pkg(1) **6.55**
Lattice mast and two insulated hanger arms. Base includes mounting screw and plug, plus clip for C Track.

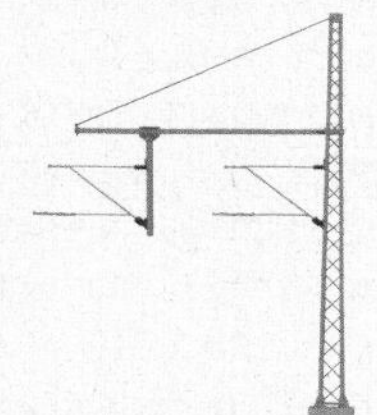

**441-74106** Tower Mast w/Tubular Outrigger Beam for Hanger Arm 5-7/8" pkg(1) **26.35**
Mast with additional beam and 2 insulated arms. Outer arm is adjustable to 4-5/8".

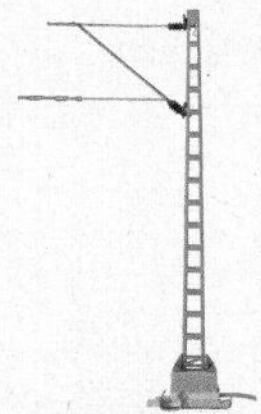

**441-74121** Feeder Mast **8.65**
For supplying power to catenary and for signal blocks. Includes base with plug in connection, feeder wire and additional base for C Track.

**441-74141** Lattice Tower Mast w/Light **22.39**
Mast height without light 6-11/16". Base with mounting screw and plug-in connection. Suitable for cross spans or individual outrigger arms. Can be used with all track systems. Lighting with a clear light bulb.

**441-74142** Lattice Tower Mast 6-11/16" **12.89**
Base with mounting screw and plug connection. Suitable for cross spans or outrigger arms. Mounting points on all four sides. Can be used for all track systems.

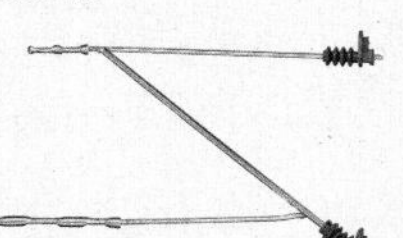

**441-74151** Single Outrigger Arm pkg(5) **13.89**
Includes hanger for contact and messenger wire. Can be installed on regular and tower masts.

### Mast Bases

**441-74109** Base for Catenary Masts pkg(20) **15.59**
Matches C Track. For replacing bases on M Track or K Track versions of the masts.

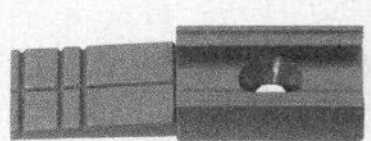

**441-74110** Replacement Bases for Standard Masts pkg(20) **11.20**
Can be shortened to fit all HO track systems with or without roadbed. Includes mounting screw.

### Cross Span Assembly

Assembled unit includes cross span adjusters, wires, and 3 adjustable catenary wire hangers. 2 metal tower masts on bases with mounting screws and plug-in connection. Steel cross span adjuster, elastic cross span wires. Masts and catenary wire hangers are electrically separated.

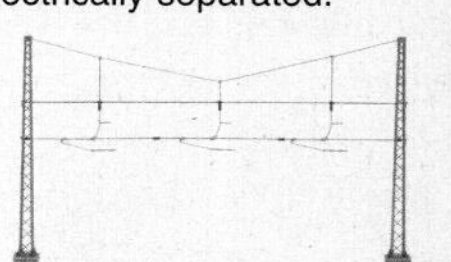

**441-74131** 3 Track 5-7/8" **40.95**
Mast spacing can be adjusted up to 9-1/4".

**441-74132** 4 Track 6-11/16" **47.45**
Mast spacing can be adjusted up to 12-5/16".

**441-74133** Catenary Cross Span Kit **13.89**
For a custom set-up. The kit consists of cross span tension wires, cross span wires, insulators and 5 catenary wire hangers. 2 tower masts are required at distance of up to 19-11/16". The cross span wires are made of steel; tension wires can be tensioned. Wire hangers are electrically insulated. This kit comes with set-up instructions.

### Jigs

**441-70011** Mast Positioning Jig Set **7.25**
Tool for determining the position of masts and wire on curves. Includes 2 positioning jigs, catenary branch-off jig, and 2 marking pens.

**441-70012** Catenary Installation Jig pkg(5) **17.15**
For determining the height and side position of the catenary wire. Can be adapted to all track systems.

## BOOKS

**441-3902** Catenary Handbook **43.49**
English text. An introduction into catenary in prototype and model railroading. Detailed description with tips to build and use HO catenary. 100 pages.

# TRIX

## TRIX C TRACK

Building a North American-style two-rail layout with Trix C track is a snap. This new two-rail track system features a detailed all-plastic roadbed with ballast detail and Code 90 nickel silver rail for reliable electrical pickup. For added realism, there is a realistic air space between the bottom of the rail and the top of the ballast, and its dark brown ties feature wood grain and tie plate details. Trix C track is easy to assemble, it clicks together. Under-the-ties electrical contacts welded to the rails ensure reliable, carefree electrical continuity. The design also allows you to add electrical features anywhere on the track pieces. Track system geometry ensures easy layout design. With its durable base, the track can be used on any surface including carpet for temporary layouts, or as part of a permanent layout.

### Straight Sections pkg(10)

**441-T62064** 2-9/16" **40.80**

**441-T62071** 2-13/16" **45.65**

**441-T62077** 3-1/16" **31.20**

**441-T62094** 3-3/4" **32.59**

**441-T62172** 6-3/4" **19.55**

**441-T62188** 7-13/32" **19.55**

**441-T62229** 9" **45.65**

**441-T62236** 9-5/16" **45.65**

### Curved Sections pkg(6)

Trix C Track offers a variety of curve radii. The smallest radii are ideal for smaller North American equipment like trolleys, 40' cars and small four-axle locos. Larger radii curves such as 20-1/4" are suitable for most manufacturer's North American locos and freight cars; full-length 85' cars may require larger curves. Degree measurements specify how much of a complete circle each track piece is, for example: twelve 30° sections make a complete circle.

**441-T62107** 14-3/16" Radius 7.5° **17.75**

**441-T62115** 14-3/16" Radius 15° **19.15**

**441-T62130** 14-3/16" Radius 30° **19.55**

**441-T62206** 17-1/4" Radius 5.7° **19.15**

**441-T62207** 17-1/4" Radius 7.5° **19.55**

**441-T62215** 17-1/4" Radius 15° **19.55**

**441-T62224** 17-1/4" Radius 24.3° **21.25**

**441-T62230** 17-1/4" Radius 30° **22.55**

**441-T62330** 20-1/4" Radius 30° **21.25**

**441-T62430** 22-3/16" Radius 30° **34.45**

**441-T62530** 25-5/16" Radius 30° **36.55**

**441-T62912** 43-7/8" Radius 12.1° **38.25**

### Turnouts

All turnouts are manual, but are easily motorized by adding the Electric Turnout Mechanism #441-74490, (sold separately).

**Standard 20.29 ea**

Radius: 7-13/32" Length: 7-13/32" Curve: 24.3°

**441-T62611** Left

**441-T62612** Right

**Wide Radius 30.49 ea**

Length: 9-5/16" Branch Track Radius: 43-7/8" Turnout Curve: 12.1° 10° Metal Frog, can be polarized.

**441-T62711** Left Hand

**441-T62712** Right Hand

**Curved 20.29 ea**

Radius: 14-3/16" Curve: 30° Outer curve 30° in the parallel curve spacing of 3-1/16".

**441-T62671** Left

**441-T62672** Right

See What's New and Exciting at **www.walthers.com**

**Double Slip**

**441-T62624 73.95**
Radius: 17-7/32" Length: 17-13/32" Curve: 24.3°

Manual hand lever, turnout mechanism, and lighted double slip switch can be installed to the right or the left. Clear setting for traversing through the curve or straight across. Electric turnout mechanism and lantern already installed.

### Track Accessories

**441-T62951** Code 83 Adapter Track 1-9/16" **6.50**

**441-T62977** Track Ends w/Bumpers 3-1/4" **8.39**
Attached frame with a buffer beam. The rails end in the roadbed.

**441-T62001** Roadbed End Pieces Length 5/8" pkg(10) **11.60**

### Uncoupler

**441-T62997** 3-3/4" **24.80**
With hand lever and built-in electric mechanism. Compatible with most common European coupler systems; will not work with horn-hook or knuckle couplers.

### Märklin Accessories for Trix C Track

**441-74030** Rail Joint Insulator pkg(5) **12.00**

**441-74040** Feeder Wire Set pkg(5) **21.95**

**441-74042** Supplemental Feeder Wire Set pkg(5) **24.79**

**441-74470** Turnout Lanterns **94.25**

**441-74490** Electric Turnout Mechanism pkg(5) **105.55**

**441-74990** Track Screws pkg(200) **8.65**

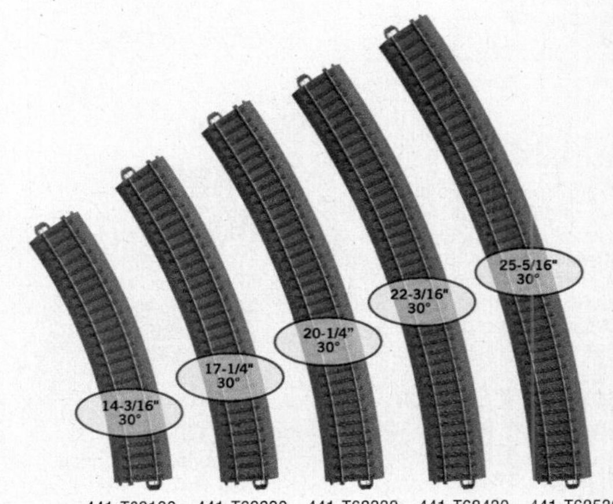


Assorted Curved Track Sections Showing Parallel Radii

Straight Section 9-5/16" 441-T62236

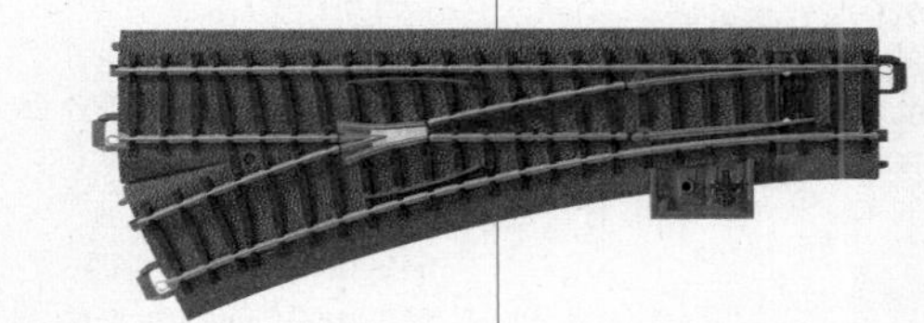

Standard Left Turnout 441-T62611

Wide-Radius Left Turnout 441-T62711

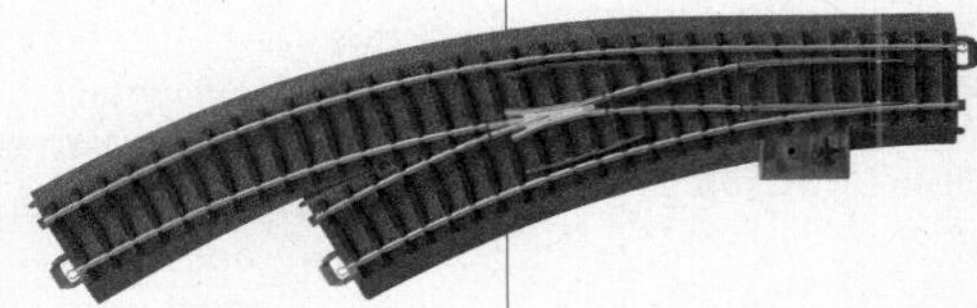

Curved Left Turnout 441-T62671

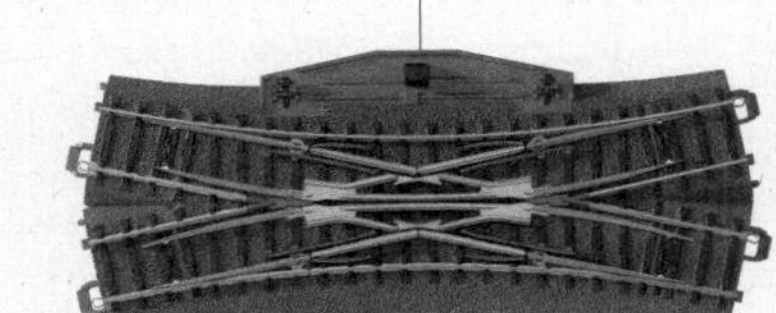

Double-Slip Turnout 441-T62624

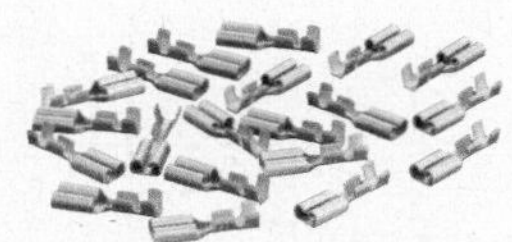

**441-74995** Spade Connectors pkg(20) **4.95**

**441-74997** Light Mast for Uncoupler Track **13.89**

**441-7555** Switch Contact **12.65**

## RIBBONRAIL

### ROADBED

Precut Upson board pieces feature beveled edges. Available in 1" radius increments from 15 to 48", and #4, 6 and 8 turnout blocks. Visit www.walthers.com for a complete listing of Ribbonrail track products.

#### Flex Track Section

**170-9020** 24" pkg(4) **8.00**

#### Straight Section

**170-9010** 24" pkg(4) **5.50**

#### Curved Sections 6.75 ea (Unless Noted)

**8 Pieces (Complete Circle)**

**170-9180** 18" pkg(4) **5.75**

**170-9220** 22" pkg(4) **5.75**

**170-9240** 24" pkg(4)

**170-9260** 26" pkg(4)

**170-9280** 28" pkg(4)

**12 Pieces (Complete Circle)**

**170-9300** 30" pkg(4)

**170-9320** 32" pkg(4)

**170-9340** 34" pkg(4)

**170-9360** 36" pkg(4)

### TRACK ALIGNMENT GAUGES (HO)

These alignment gauges help take the kinks and headaches out of laying flex track or hand-laying rail. Simply match the gauge to the desired radius, slip the gauge between the rails, and secure the track when the gauge slides easily.

#### Straight Gauges

**170-5** 5" **3.95**

**170-10** 10" **4.15**

#### Radius Gauges 3.95 ea

**170-15** 15"
**170-16** 16"
**170-17** 17"
**170-18** 18"
**170-19** 19"
**170-20** 20"
**170-21** 21"
**170-22** 22"
**170-23** 23"
**170-24** 24"
**170-25** 25"
**170-26** 26"
**170-27** 27"
**170-28** 28"
**170-29** 29"
**170-30** 30"
**170-31** 31"
**170-32** 32"
**170-33** 33"
**170-34** 34"
**170-35** 35"
**170-36** 36"
**170-37** 37"
**170-38** 38"
**170-39** 39"
**170-40** 40"
**170-41** 41"
**170-42** 42"
**170-43** 43"
**170-44** 44"
**170-45** 45"
**170-46** 46"
**170-47** 47"
**170-48** 48"

## SCALE SHOPS

### TURNOUT MOTORS

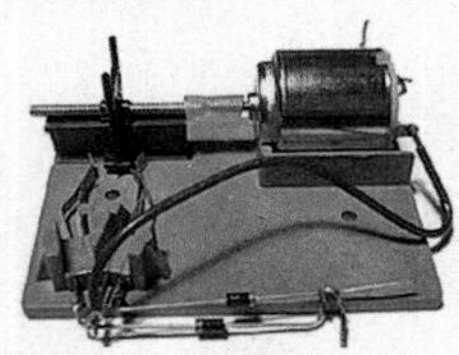

Slow motion, motorized, threaded-shaft type switch machine. Available fully assembled and in kit form. Each kit includes one pair of contacts and turnout linkage. Easy-to-build kits assemble in six steps. Includes cut-out contacts, diodes and complete assembly, wiring and installation instructions.

#### 3-Volt

**Assembled**

**649-1040** Single Unit **17.98**

**Kits**

**649-1006** pkg(6) **56.98**

**649-1012** pkg(12) **98.98**

**649-1030** Single Unit **10.98**

#### 12-Volt

These machines have the same features as the 3-Volt versions, but allow for easier use with wall transformers and DCC stationary decoders.

**Assembled**

**NEW 649-1240** Single Unit **17.98**

**Kits**

**NEW 649-1206** pkg(6) **56.98**

**NEW 649-1212** pkg(12) **98.98**

**NEW 649-1230** Single Unit **10.98**

#### Turnout Motor Contacts

**649-4080** pkg(2) **.98**

**649-4082** pkg(12) **4.98**

**649-4085** pkg(50) **16.98**



## TOMAR INDUSTRIES

#### Hayes Wheel Stop

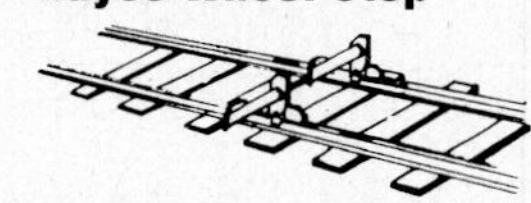

**81-803** Type SF pkg(4) **2.05**
Cast white-metal "stops" protect your spur ends. They won't come off when bumped by a car. Used on heavy or lightweight service.

#### Bumping Posts

**81-808** Hayes **4.35**
Assembled post mounted on track with insulated rail joiners.

**81-80870** For Code 70 Track **4.75**

**81-80883** For Code 83 Track **4.75**

## TRAIN AMERICA STUDIOS

#### Torquemaster Switch Motors

Offers quiet, reliable operation ideal for N, HO, S, O and G Scales (working great for both standard and narrow gauges alike). Unit is powered by a 12V DC supply (provisions are made for higher voltages). A resistor is added to one lead of the input power, drawing approximately 20 milliamps. One unit has enough power to control signal aspects and panel lights. Each Torquemaster kit includes all mounting hardware required to successfully install one motor. A DPDT toggle switch is required for operation (sold separately).

**703-4052** Single Unit **15.95**

**703-4062** pkg(6) **89.95**

Item listed below is available by Special Order (see Legend Page).
**703-4054** Bulk Pack (25 Units) **358.95**

#### Panel Mount Kit

**703-4060 5.75**
For use with Torquemaster Switch Motors, listed above. Includes bi-polar LEDs, DPDT toggle switch and mounting hardware.

## VOLLMER

IMPORTED FROM GERMANY BY WALTHERS

Complete HO Scale catenary system is designed to provide overhead power or can be used for nonoperating catenary with standard track power. Based on German Railways prototypes, equipment can be adapted for any model railroad.

All wiring is made from chrome-nickel steel for improved conductivity. Masts are molded in break-resistant plastic to prevent short circuits. Each is approximately 3-7/8" tall (9.7cm) and provides a wire height of about 3" (7.6cm).

### CATENARY

#### Masts

770-1300 770-1301

**770-1300** Mast w/Short Arm pkg(10) **62.99**

**770-1301** Mast w/Long Arm pkg(10) **62.99**

770-1304 770-1308

**770-1304** Terminal/Feeder pkg(5) **52.99**

**770-1308** Tower Mast pkg(10) **83.99**

**770-1311** Registration For Tower Mast pkg(5) **21.99**
For use with masts #1300 and #1301, each sold separately.

Item listed below is available by Special Order (see Legend Page).
**770-1314** Mast Bracket pkg(10) **29.99**

#### Wire

**770-1310** Cross Span w/Accessories 31cm Long **16.99**

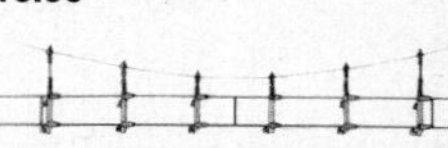

**770-1315** Bridging Section pkg(5) **21.99**
Used between two bridges.

**770-1316** Bridging Section pkg(5) **17.99**

**770-1320** Insulating Unit 1" pkg(5) **23.99**

**770-1331** 3.9" pkg(10) **37.99**
For radii under 10" 28cm.

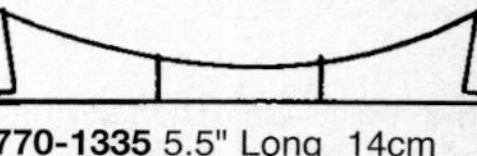

**770-1335** 5.5" Long 14cm pkg(10) **42.99**
For radii over 10" 28cm.

**770-1339** 1.95 x 7.4" 19cm pkg(10) **44.99**
For radii over 17.5" 43.7cm.

**770-1343** Contact Wire 15.8" pkg(10) **49.99**

**770-1345** For Loco Shed #5750 pkg(2) **11.99**

**770-1347** For Loco Shed #5752 pkg(2) **14.99**

Wire listed below is available by Special Order (see Legend Page).
**770-1349** For Loco Shed #5760 pkg(2) **14.99**

**770-1351** For Bridge #2506 pkg(2) **14.99**

#### Set

770-1390 Overhead Set 199.99
This set includes nine #1300, ten #1301, one #1304, 18 #1335 and two contact wires 15.6" long.

## TRACK-BED

Track-Bed provides smooth, quiet train operation and absorbs irregularities in your layout. A high-quality, economical alternative to other roadbed materials, Track-Bed remains flexible, won't dry out, become brittle, or crack. It aligns well with cork on any layout and comes in strips, sheets and rolls for an almost seamless application.

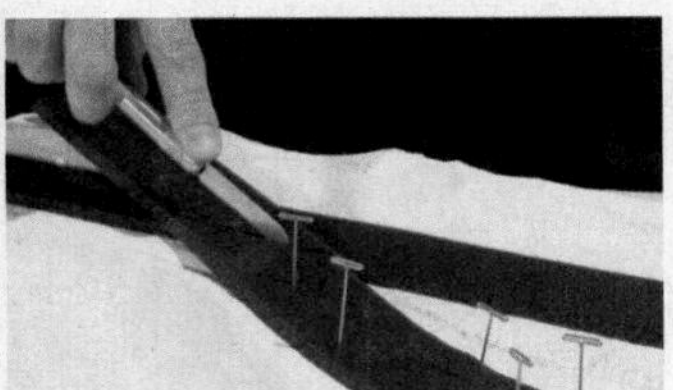

### Track-Bed Strips

Each piece is 2' (60cm) long.

**785-1461** Bulk Pack pkg(36) **28.47**

**785-1471** Standard Pack pkg(12) **9.49**

### Track-Bed Roll

**785-1474** 24' (720cm) Long **9.49**
Same great material in a continuous 24' roll for almost seamless installation.

### Track-Bed Sheets

**785-1470** 5 x 24" (12.5 x 60cm) pkg(6) **13.49**
All sheets are 5mm thick; use in yards, stations or other areas.

### Super Sheets

**785-1477** 12 x 24" (30 x 60cm) **4.29**

Dealers must order in multiples of 6.

### HO Scale Track-Bed

**Conforms To Applicable NMRA Standards**

- **Quieter Operation** (Sound Deadening Material)
- **Smoother Operation** (Cushions Vibrations)
- **Easier to Use** (Tack or Glue Down, Flexible, No Soaking, Compatible with Cork, Won't Dry Out or Crumble)
- **Better Value** (Higher Quality...Lower Cost)

2008
HO
Model Railroad
Reference Book

# SIGNALS

Models and Photo by George Dutka

For decades, trains approaching the busy station trackage at White River have arrived and departed safely under the watchful eye of the signalman and the venerable old ball signal that still guards the right-of-way. Steam power may be just a memory, but these signals can still be seen in daily service at some important points. George Dutka, of London, Ontario, brings us this station scene from his layout, where an S2 (Atlas) and GP9 (Life-Like) wait in the clear as a B&M E7 (Broadway Limited) moves through. Both the station and historic signal were scratchbuilt.

Dating from the earliest days of railroading, and commonly used in New England, a large red ball on a staff was lowered to indicate that trains should stop or raised if it was safe to proceed. Crews seeing the "high ball" displayed could keep right on going, eventually giving us the slang expression "highball." At stations like this, various combinations of balls were raised and lowered to control train movements on different routes.

Signals are a fun accessory that adds a lot of realism to any scene. For more realism, working models can be installed to control trains much like the prototype. You'll find plenty of ideas for adding this great detail to your railroad on the pages inside the Signals Section.

# WALTHERS

**Built-ups**

## NEW PRODUCTS

### Working Street Lamps

- New North American Prototypes
- Interchangeable with Other Cornerstone Series Street Lamps
- Easily Added to New or Existing Scenes

### "Tear Drop" Style

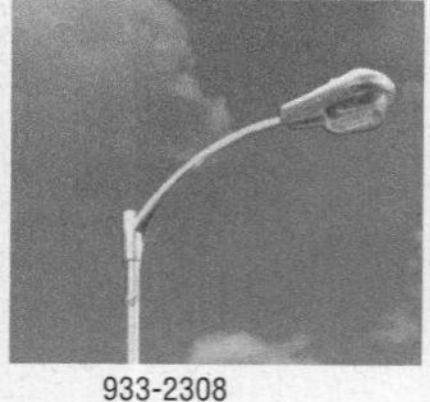
933-2308

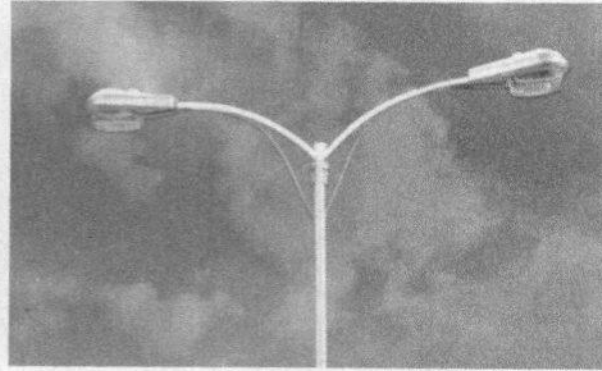
933-2309

**NEW 933-2308** Single-Arm **12.98**
**NEW 933-2309** Double-Arm **15.98**

### Modern "Arm" Style

933-2310

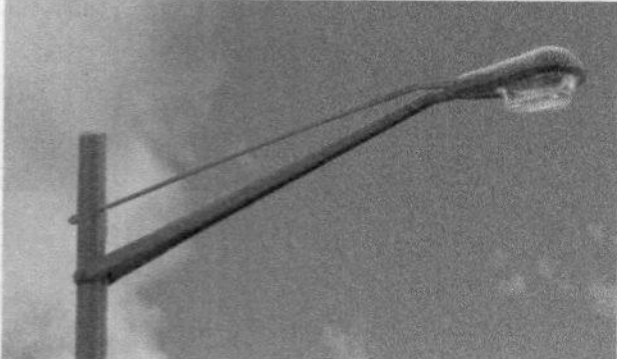
933-2310

**NEW 933-2310** Short - Wall Mount **12.98**
**NEW 933-2311** Long **15.98**

### "Acorn" Style

933-2313

933-2315

**NEW 933-2313** Single Arm **14.98**
**NEW 933-2315** Double Arm Style **17.98**

### "Pneumatic" Crossing Gates

**NEW 933-2312** Crossing Gates pkg(2) **24.98**

- Classic Steam-Era Design
- North American Prototype
- Moving Parts - Use w/Any Drive System
- Two Complete Gates
- Great Alongside Crossing Shanties & Towers

## ROADSIDE BILLBOARDS

**933-3133** Plain Billboards Without Signs pkg(2) **4.98**

### Post-60s Cantilever Crossing Signals

**NEW 933-2314 24.98**

**Winter 2007-08 Delivery**
- Authentic American Style
- Perfect for Post-60s Layouts
- Use with Crossing Signal Controller #933-2307 (sold separately)
- Easy Installation

## TRAFFIC LIGHTS

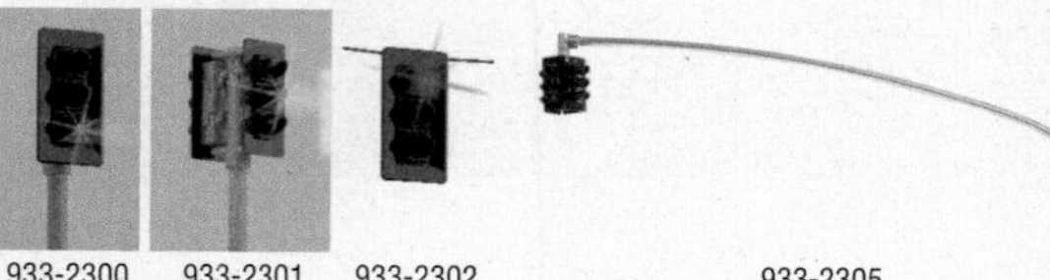
933-2300 933-2301 933-2302 933-2305

**933-2300** Single-Sided **10.98**
**933-2301** Double-Sided **14.98**
**933-2302** Single-Head Hanging **9.98**
**933-2305** Four-Way Hanging **24.98**
- Fully Assembled
- Plugs Into Controller - Sold Separately
- Three Styles to Fit any Intersection
- Great City Detail

## TRAFFIC LIGHT CONTROLLER

**933-2306 34.98**
- Use with New Traffic Lights (Each Sold Separately)
- Fully Assembled
- Plug-in Wiring
- Two Circuits

## CANTILEVER CROSSING SIGNALS

933-2304 933-2303

**933-2304** Modern Single Lane **24.98**
**933-2303** Modern Two Lane **34.98**
- Fully Assembled
- Easy to Connect to Existing Wiring
- Detail Modern Highway Scenes
- Detector & Flasher Control

## CANTILEVER SIGNAL CONTROLLER

**933-2307 34.98**
- Use with New Cantilver Signals (Each Sold Separately)
- Fully Assembled
- Screw Terminals for Easy Wiring
- Detector & Flasher Control

## WORKING STREET LAMPS

**9.98 ea (Unless Noted)**
- Fully-Assembled
- Durable Plastic & Metal Construction
- Fits Popular Modeling Eras
- Plug-In Installation for Most Models

933-1080

933-1081

**933-1080** Double-Arm Style Boulevard Type

**933-1081** Single-Arm Style

933-1082

933-1090

**933-1082** Small Street Lamps pkg(2) **10.98**
**933-1090** Bishop's Crook

933-1082

933-1092

**933-1082** Cast Iron Column pkg(2) **10.98**
**933-1092** Concrete Column pkg(2)

See What's New and Exciting at
**www.walthers.com**

## WALTHERS

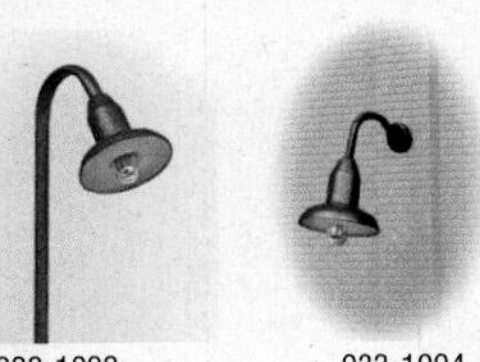
933-1093 933-1094

933-1095

**933-1093** Station Platform*
**933-1094** Wall-Mounted Lamps* pkg(3)
**933-1095** Double Arm Lamp

933-1096 933-1097

933-1098

**933-1096** Modern Street Lamp
**933-1097** Single Arm Lamp
**933-1098** Ornate Wall-Mounted Lamps* pkg(3)

*Designed for permanent mounting, will not include plug-in sockets.

## OLD TIME STREET LAMPS

933-1022 933-1023

Operating lamps can be used in scenes from the 1920s to the present for lighting streets, boulevards or station platforms. Lamps are fully assembled, unpainted brass with plastic globes.

**933-1023** Double-Arm, 3-1/2" Tall (18V bulb) **9.98**

**Limited Quantity Available**

**933-1022** Single-Arm, 3-1/2" Tall (18V bulb) **7.98**

Division of Wm. K. Walthers, Inc.

## SCENEMASTER™ SIGNALS

**433-1253** Railroad Signal **9.75**

## LIGHT-UPS

Detailed, lighted accessories molded in appropriately colored plastic.

### Spotlights

**433-1628** pkg(2) **10.00**
Lights swivel up and down and turn 360°.

### Lights pkg(3) 10.00 ea

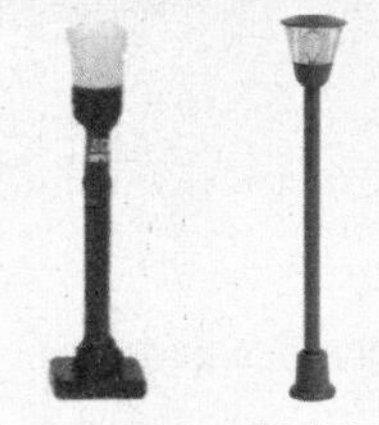
433-1254 433-1257

**433-1254** Street
**433-1257** Gas

### Expressway Lights

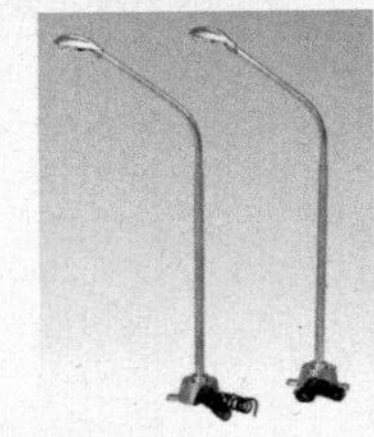

**433-1629** pkg(2) **10.00**
Suitable for use with HO or S Scale.

## ACCESSORIES

Appropriately colored, molded plastic accessories.

### Utility Poles

**433-1621** pkg(12) **9.75**

### City Sidewalks

**433-1622 9.75**
Includes street signs, streetlights, telephone booth, benches and fire hydrants.

### Signs

**433-1602** Street & Highway pkg(24) **9.75**

## OPERATING ACCESSORIES

9" brass straight track included.

### Switchman

**433-8203** With Lighted Building **24.00**
Switchman emerges automatically from lighted shack as train nears, goes inside after last car passes.

### Crossing Gate

**433-8314 16.25**
Gate lowers automatically as train nears, raises after last car crosses.

### Power-Loc™ Operating Accessories

For use with Power-Loc track.

### Dual Crossing Gate

**433-8309 21.75**
Safety gates lower to warn oncoming traffic as train approaches and remain down until the last car passes.

### Switchman

**433-8310 24.00**
As train approaches grade crossing, switchman emerges from the lighted shack; goes back inside after the last car passes.

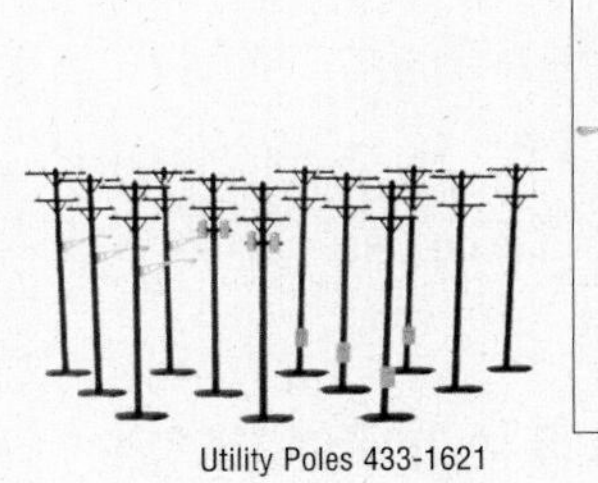
Utility Poles 433-1621

Close-up images show pole details

Street & Highway Signs 433-1602

Close-up image shows sign details

City Sidewalks 433-1622

Close-up image shows accessory details

Switchman With Lighted Building 433-8203

Dual Crossing Gate 433-8309

## SIGNALS SYSTEM & ACCESSORIES

The Atlas Model RR Signal System features true scale dimensions and details, and includes circuitry for North American prototype operation. These signals can be used as a stand-alone accessory, or connected to one another for complete dynamic integration. Features include easy setup, scale signal structures that have true scale dimensions and details, prototypical operation circuitry, expandable with your railroad, modular design with telephone-style cord connections (for use with multiple signals, sold separately). Visit atlasrr.com for complete information and downloadable wiring diagrams and instructions.

### Type G Signals

All signals include one jumper wire (signal plug to RJ-11 jack) and signal bungalow per signal.

150-235

150-238

150-239

**150-235** Single Target **29.95**

**150-236** Single Target w/Signal Control PCB and 2-Rail (Analog) Block Detector **49.95**

**150-237** Single Target pkg(4) **99.95**

**150-238** Double Target **39.95**

**150-239** Bi-Directional Single Target **39.95**

### Signal System Accessories

**150-233** Analog Block Detector **12.95**

**150-234** Signal Control Board **19.95**

### Signal Cable

**150-230** 7' **3.95**

**150-231** 15' **7.25**

**150-232** 25' **10.95**

American Limited MODELS

## OPERATING WIGWAG CROSSING SIGNALS KIT

Designed for easy construction, the signals are powered by an under-table drive system. Rayon thread is used to make the signals swing almost invisibly at a prototypical speed. When shut off, the signals stop straight down, just like the prototypes.

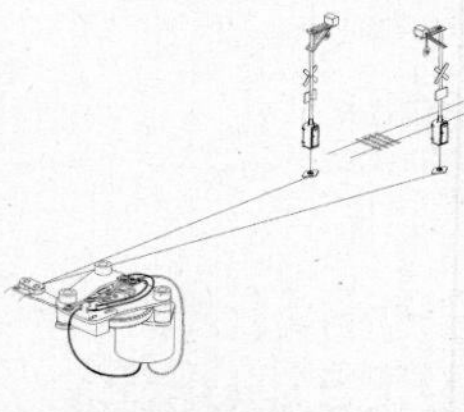

**147-5400** Without Detector **35.95**

**147-5410** With Detector **43.95** Includes a crossing detector and activation switches that operate in either direction. Detector requires 12V DC power; two "D" batteries (sold separately) will provide 30+ hours of power to the signal drive.

## OPERATING WIGWAG CROSSING SIGNALS ACCESSORIES

### Grade Crossing Detector & Switches

**147-5420** **11.95**

### Track Switches

**147-5430** pkg(4) **3.95**

Precolored plastic signals, lights and signs.

## SIGNALS

**160-42101** Block Signals pkg(4) **6.50**

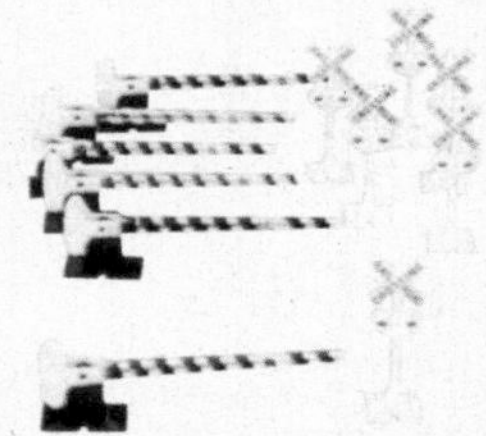

**160-42200** Crossing Signals & Gates (6 each) pkg(12) **6.50**

### Signal Bridge

**160-45134** **10.00**

### Grade Crossing

**160-42208** Nonoperating **6.50**

## SIGNS

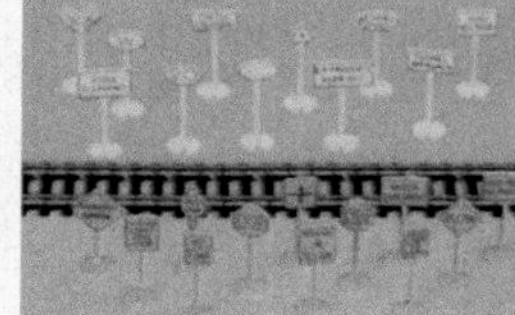

**160-42204** Rail & Street Signs pkg(24) **6.50**

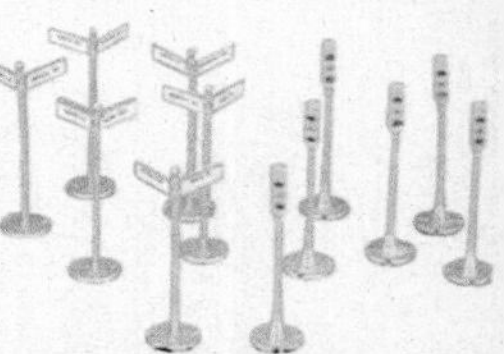

**160-42207** Traffic Lights & Signs pkg(12) **6.50**

**ACCURATE DESIGNS**

## CIRCUS BANNERS

"Step right up! Step right up! Come and see the world's most amazing freaks at the circus sideshow! If that isn't enough to totally amaze you, let the sight of revolting reptiles put a chill down your spine." Printed in color on 100% polyester.

**145-971** Sideshows pkg(6) **26.49**

**145-972** Reptiles pkg(4) **15.95**

**Blair Line LLC**™
PRODUCTS FOR MODEL RAILROADERS

# LASER-CUT BILLBOARD FRAME KITS WITH SIGNS

## 9.95 ea (Unless Noted)

Accurate reproductions of period billboard frames fit cities, small towns or any roadside. Kits include one laser-cut frame, several era-appropriate signs and lampshades.

**184-2429** Deco — 1930s-60s

**184-2430** City Beautiful — 1920s-50s

**184-2431** Lattice —1900s-60s

**184-2432** Grill —1940s-60s

**184-2433** Pole — 1950s-Present

**184-2434** Pylon — 1960s-Present

**184-2435** Wall — 1930s-Present

# LASER-CUT BILLBOARD SIGNS

These laser-cut billboard signs are great for rooftops, or as stand-alone roadside attention-getters. Small versions of signs are designed for HO, Z and N Scale use, while large signs are meant for HO, S and O Scales.

### Western Auto

**184-1501** Small (2-1/2 x 2") **7.95**

**184-2501** Large (3-3/4 x 3") **9.95**

### Freight Station

Includes 30 railroad heralds.

**184-1503** Small (2-1/2 x 1-3/8") **9.95**

**184-2503** Large (3-1/2 x 2") **11.95**

### Jesus Saves

**184-1507** Small (2-1/4 x 1-5/8") **9.95**

**184-2507** Large (3-1/2 x 2-1/2") **10.95**

### Union Pacific

**184-1509** Small (1-1/2 x 2") **9.95**

**184-2509** Large (2-1/2 x 3-3/8") **11.95**

### Esso

**184-1510** Small (2-1/8 x 1-7/8") **9.95**

**184-2510** Large (3-3/8 x 3") **11.95**

### Santa Fe

**184-1511** Small (3-3/4 x 1-1/5") **9.95**

**184-2511** Large (6 x 2") **11.95**

### TV Broadcast Tower

**184-2516** Large (1 x 8") **15.95**
Personalize the tower with your own station number included.

### Hotel

**184-1517** Small (2-1/5 x 1-1/4") **9.95**

**184-2517** Large (3-1/2 x 2-1/8") **11.95**

### Red Cross

**184-1519** Small (1-4/5 x 1-4/5") **9.95**

**184-2519** Large (3 x 3") **11.95**

### Patriotic U.S. Flag

Includes the following slogans: In God We Trust, Buy War Bonds, United We Stand, and Support Our Troops.

**184-1520** Small (1-4/5 x 1-4/5") **9.95**

**184-2520** Large (3 x 3") **11.95**

### Hollywood

**184-1526** Small (4-1/2 x 4/5") **9.95**

**184-2526** Large (7-1/2 x 1-3/10") **11.95**

### Missouri Pacific Lines

**184-1530** Small (2-1/4 x 1-1/2") **9.95**

**184-2530** Large (4-1/8 x 2-1/4") **11.95**

### Ship Texas & Pacific

**184-1531** Small (1-5/8 x 1-5/8") **9.95**

**184-2531** Large (3 x 3") **11.95**

### Do-It-Yourself Custom Billboard

Includes laser-cut framing and letters to make custom signs for roof or wall mounting.

**184-1550** Small (2-5/8 x 1-1/8") **11.95**

**184-2550** Large (4-3/4 x 2") **13.95**

### Eat & Business District

Includes two different signs; "EAT" for rooftop and roadside sign for the business district.

**184-1532** Small (2-5/32 x 1-5/16") **9.95**

**184-2532** Large (3-5/8 x 2-1/8") **11.95**

### Welcome To Your Town

**184-2528** **13.95** (3-1/2 x 2-1/10")

Includes custom letters to make your own town name and organization shields, such as VFW, Kiwanis, Masons, Lions Club, etc.

# SIGNS

## Storefront, Industrial & Business Sign Sets 5.00 ea

Signs printed in color on thin plastic for easy application to your commercial or scratchbuilt structure. Designed to duplicate porcelain and tin signs. Use for any era. Use as wall advertising and small roadside signs, too. Adds realistic detail to any layout. Many signs may be assembled back-to-back.

**184-150** Modern Storefront Signs

**184-151** "Main St." Storefront Signs I

**184-154** "Main St." Storefront Signs II

**184-158** "Main St." Storefront Signs III

**184-152** Safety, Warning & Miscellaneous Signs

**184-153** Service Station Signs

**184-155** Signs for Industries

**184-156** Railroad Stations & Depot Signs

**184-157** Feed & Seed Store Signs

**184-159** Tavern & Liquor Store Signs

## Highway & Railroad Signs 5.00 ea (Unless Noted)

Scale signs, printed in color on thin plastic for easy assembly. Each set of signs includes scale posts. CAD designed to Federal Specifications for accuracy and authenticity. Great roadside, streetside and trackside details.

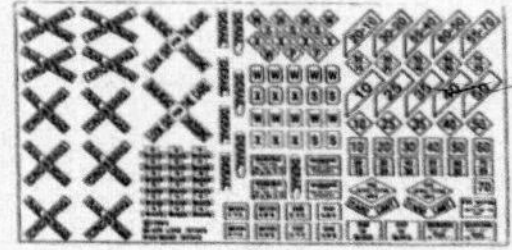

**184-101** Railroad Right-Of-Way Signs (1900s-Present)

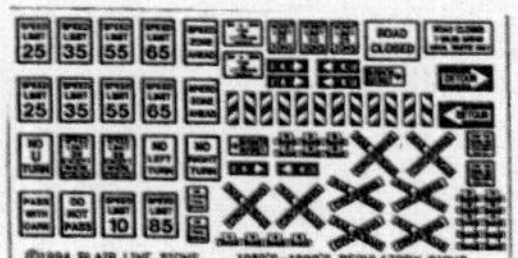

**184-102** Regulatory Signs #1 (1948-Present)

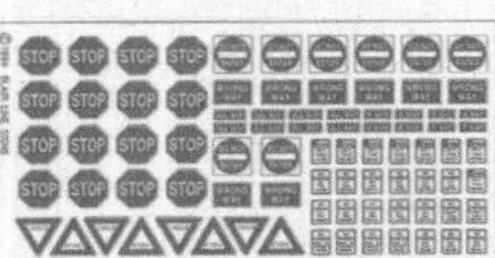

**184-103** Regulatory Signs #2 (1930s-Present)

**184-104** Construction Warning Signs (1950s-Present)

**184-105** Warning & Symbol Signs #1 (1971-Present)

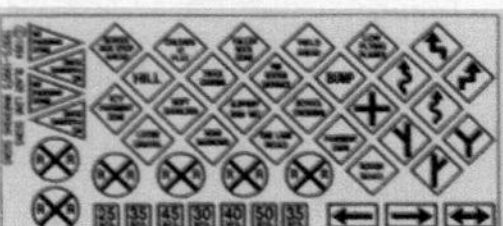

**184-106** Warning Signs #2 (1948-Present)

**184-107** Warning Signs #3 (1948-Present)

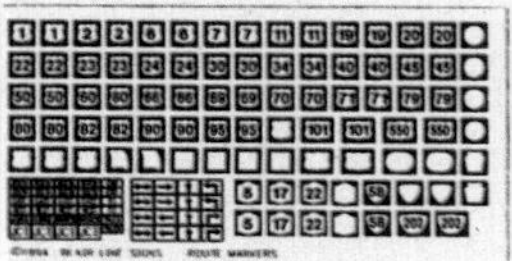

**184-108** US Highway Route Markers (1950s-Present)

**184-109** Street Signs, Any Era pkg(109)

**184-110** Warning Signs #4 (1948-Present)

**184-142** Vintage Regulatory Signs (1930s-1950s)

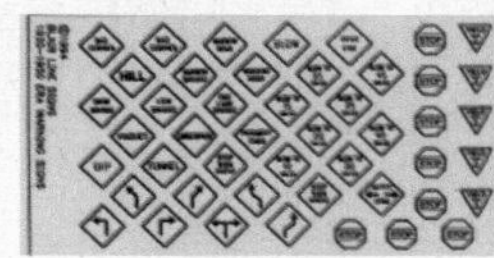

**184-143** Vintage Warning/ Stop Signs (1930s-1950s)

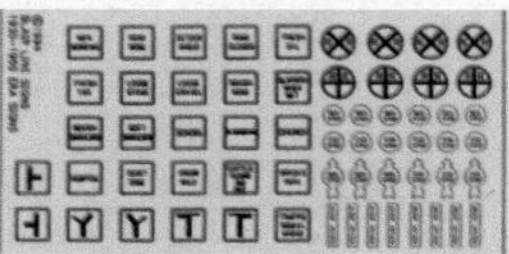

**184-144** Vintage Caution Signs (1930s-1950s)

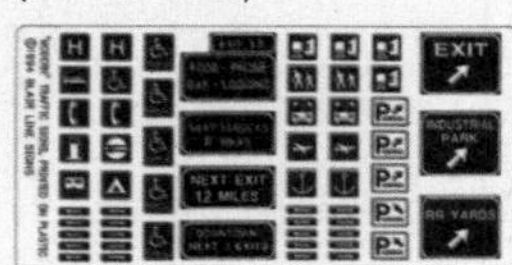

**184-146** Freeway & Symbol Signs (1971-Present)

**184-147** Modern Traffic & Symbol Signs

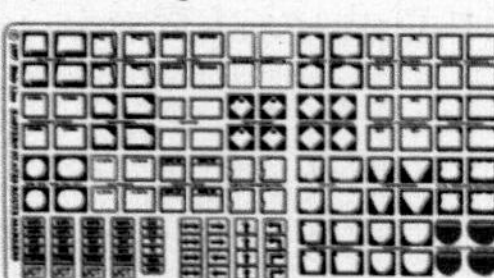

**184-148** State Highway Route Signs (Eastern USA) Includes number decals.

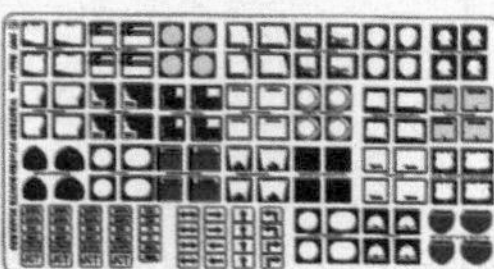

**184-149** State Highway Route Signs (Western USA) Includes number decals.

**184-198** Square Wood Posts for Signs pkg(20) **2.00**

**184-199** Round Plastic Posts for Signs pkg(20) **2.00**

## NEW PRODUCT

### Signals

#### Modern Cantilever Signal Bridge

**NEW 176-4030 89.95**
Based on modern tubular signal bridges used by several major Class I lines and modern commuter railroads, this layout-ready signal bridge is ideal for double-track lines. Each model includes four prewired, micro-LED signal heads with three aspects per head (red, yellow, green). The accurately scaled model features durable plastic parts and etched-metal walkways. Each supporting leg houses four wires, (one common and one for each LED). It's ready for hookup to your choice of detection circuitry, sold separately. Specifications: LEDs require 2 to 2.2VDC @ 25 - 30mA. Bridge is wired in the common anode configuration.

#### Signal Head

**176-4000** Target-Style pkg(3) **9.95**
These non-operating metal signal head kits are the perfect complement to BLMA all-metal signal bridges #176-4010 and 176-4020 (sold separately). Features cast metal body, etched metal components and metal mount. Easy to modify with hollow centers for installation of LEDs (not included).



### Signal Bridges

**176-4010** ATSF Style Double-Track **79.95**
Santa Fe style "A" Frame bridges built in the 1930s and 40s were a common sight along the mainline for well over half a century. Like the prototype, this model is entirely metal (steel and brass) with etched stainless steel handrails. Kit includes two non-operating signal heads, four concrete footings and non-operating electrical box. Easily assembled using glue only.

**176-4020** Cantilever **59.95**
Around since the early 1900s, cantilever-style signal bridges are still in use in some places where they have yet to be replaced by modern, safer designs. This all-metal signal based on a common Santa Fe/SP style used all over the country. The prototype is located in Fullerton, California along the BNSF mainline at a spot called "Basta".

IMPORTED FROM GERMANY BY WALTHERS

Brawa signals are made of brass (except as noted) and come fully assembled. The line features models of signals used by the German Federal Railways (DB) and include decals, where appropriate, to identify the signal type. Signals equipped with bulbs or LEDs can be wired to AC or DC transformers with a maximum output of 10 to 16V. For longer bulb life, 10 to 12V is recommended. Brawa relays #186-2760 or 2761 are designed for switching these signals and feature matching color-coded wiring.

# SIGNALS

**Limited Quantity Available On All Items**

## Color Light Signals

Most European State and private railways have begun replacing semaphores with color-light signals which display a variety of aspects. The signals have a built-in resistor for use with any AC or DC 14-16V power supply. Signals are approximately 3-1/2" high, unless noted.

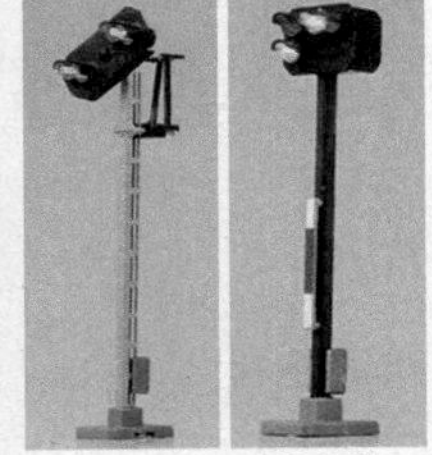

186-8808 186-8809

**186-8808** Distant Signal **26.99**

**186-8809** Trackside Stop Signal **26.99**
Approximately 2-1/2" high.

## LED Color Light Signals

**Limited Quantity Available On All Items**

Signals feature LEDs (Light-Emitting Diodes) and have a built-in resistor for use with any AC or DC 14-16V power supply. The low current draw (15mA from 14V supply) allows use of Brawa LED signals with transistor or integrated circuits. To install Brawa LED signals on benchwork, drill a 23/64" 9mm hole and simply press into place. Signals are approximately 3-1/2" high, unless noted.

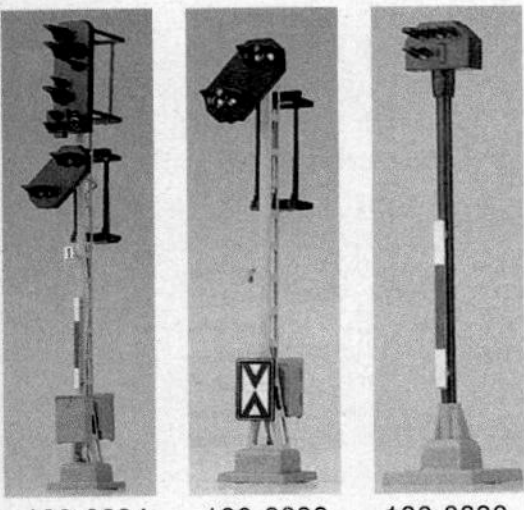

186-8834 186-8838 186-8839

**186-8834** Starter Signal w/Distant & Track Block Signal, 10 LEDs **79.99**

**186-8838** Distant Signal, 4 LEDs **44.99**
Distant signals give train crews advance warning of the next signal aspect.

**186-8839** Trackside Stop Signal, 4 LEDs **44.99**
Head: 4.8 x 7.2 x 1.8mm.

## Semaphore Signals

**Limited Quantity Available On All Items**

Semaphore signals were a common sight during the steam-era and are still in widespread service today in Europe. The moving signal arm adds realistic action to a layout, while providing a visual indication of the route setting. Signals are approximately 4" high.

**186-8932** Bavarian Stop Signal **47.99**

**186-8535** Repeater Signal w/Slow Memory Drive, 2 Aspect (Vr 0/2) **54.99**
Fixed disk, movable arm and one aspect.

**186-8930** Home Signal, 1-Arm (2 position) **47.99**

# CATENARY LIGHT

**186-5531** Catenary Light, Swiss Style **13.99**

# CROSSING SIGNALS

## Crossing Gate Set

**Limited Quantity Available**

**186-1194** Crossing Gate Set **295.99**
Set features two gates with slow memory drive for realistic gate action. Also includes four brass crossing signs, two street lights (#186-5496), road section, warning loudspeaker (#186-2650), crossing shanty, electronic control unit (#186-2765) for gates with outputs for bell and flasher unit (#186-6129), two magnets (#186-3543), four switches (#186-3530), two resistors (#186-6154) and a bell (#186-1141).

# TELEPHONE POLES

**Limited Quantity Available On All Items**

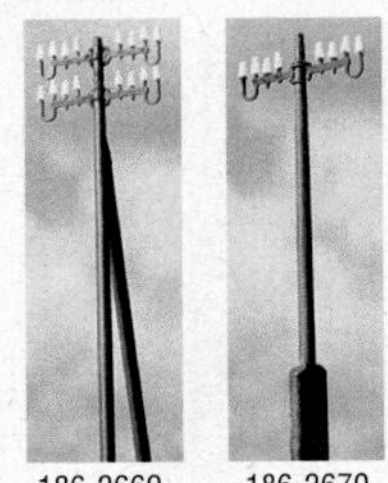

186-2669 186-2670

**186-2669** With Supports pkg(3) **24.99**
Approximately 3-1/4" high.

**186-2670** With Base Supports pkg(3) **25.99**
Approximately 3" high.

# HIGH TENSION TOWERS

**Limited Quantity Available On All Items**

Suitable for use in HO or N Scale, towers are made of metal. Approximate height 4" 10cm.

**186-2658** High Tension Tower **31.99**

**186-2659** High Tension Tower Set pkg(4) **122.99**
Set of four #186-2658 high tension towers with wires, warning globes and tension springs.

# RELAYS

## With Three Contacts

**186-2761 98.99**
Same as #186-2760, but with a third contact.

## With Two Contacts

**Limited Quantity Available**

**186-2760 66.99**
Precision relay for reliable switching of signals, electromagnetic and motor drives. Two separate inputs. Power supply 10 to 24V AC. Switching current max. 60mA. Contact load approximately 3A per contact. Voltage up to 24V AC or DC. Operated by momentary contact, track contact or reed contact.

# CLOCKS

Clocks are illuminated.

186-5260 186-5261

**186-5260** Platform Clock, 2" High **17.99**

**186-5261** Wall Clock **13.99**
Horizontal or vertical mounting. Frame diameter approximately 1/2".

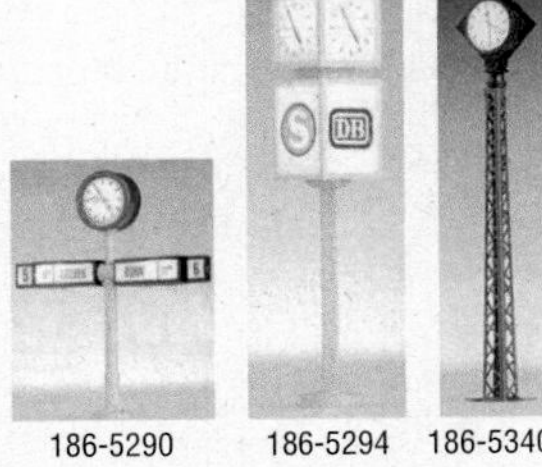

186-5290 186-5294 186-5340

**186-5290** Platform Clock w/Train Direction Signs, 2" High **27.99**

**186-5294** Clock w/DB/S Bahn Signs, 2-1/8" High **22.99**

**186-5340** Station/Yard Clock, 3" High **19.99**
With adjustable hands.

186-5361 186-5362 186-5366

**186-5361** Historic Wall Clock-Baden-Baden **20.99**
With adjustable hands.

**186-5362** Baden-Baden Clock w/3 Faces, 2-1/2" High **41.99**
With adjustable hands.

**186-5366** Berlin Stettin Station Clock, 3-1/4" High **28.99**
With adjustable hands.

186-5368 186-5495 186-5761

**186-5368** With Lattice Mast & Platform, 4-1/2" High **24.99**

**186-5495** Platform Light w/Clock, 2-3/4" High **26.99**

**186-5761** Kiosk w/Clock, 1-1/2" High **32.99**
With adjustable hands.

**186-5870** Station Clock pkg(2) **25.99**

# SIGNS

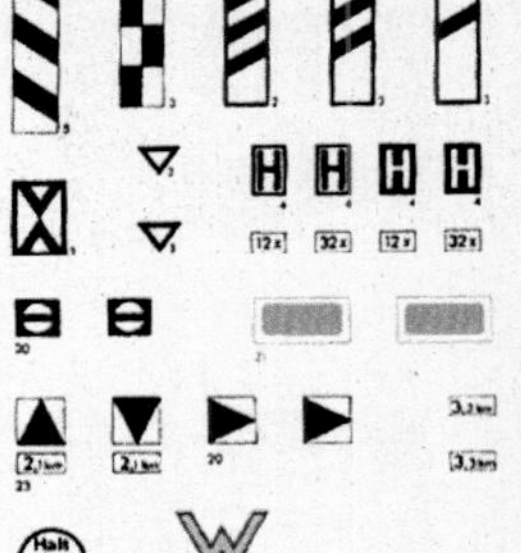

**Limited Quantity Available**

**186-8618** Advance Warning Signs **10.99**
Set includes all types of trackside signs used by the DB. Posts are molded in black plastic; signs are printed in full color with self-adhesive backing.

IMPORTED FROM GERMANY BY WALTHERS
Pre-wired plastic signals are assembled and ready to install.

## NEW PRODUCTS

### Signals

#### European Railroad Signals

Items listed below are available by Special Order (see Legend Page).

189-5820 189-5832 189-5833

**NEW 189-5820** Safety Signal Indicator w/2 LEDs **24.99**

**NEW 189-5832** Main Signal w/Pre-Warning Signal & 7 LEDs **46.99**

**NEW 189-5833** Departure Signal w/6 LEDs **35.99**

### Signs

#### Poster Sets 6.99 ea

Use these colorful German language advertising poster sets to add a touch of authenticity to your European-themed layout scenes. Sets include stands/pillars for some posters.

**NEW 189-1137** Brewery Posters pkg(70)

**NEW 189-1138** Modern Advertising Posters pkg(60)

### Flags

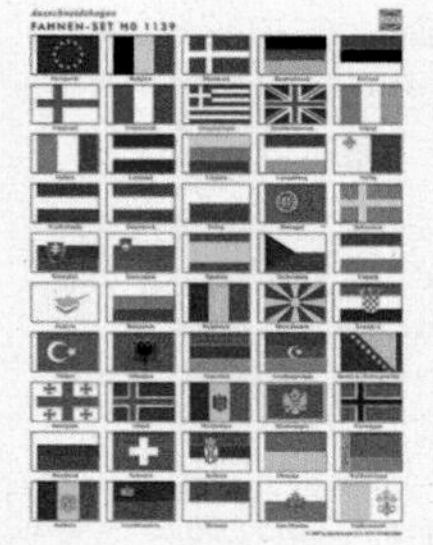

**NEW 189-1139** pkg(50) **11.99**
Two-sheet set includes over 50 European flags that can be placed back-to-back to make a two-sided flag. Also included are 10 tall flagpoles and 50 small flag bars for attachment to roofs and buildings.

## SIGNALS

189-5802 189-5803 189-5804

**189-5802** Blocksignal 2 LEDs **15.99**

**189-5803** Hauptsignal 4 LEDs **20.99**

**189-5804** Vorsingal 4 LEDs **22.99**

189-5806 189-5821 189-5822

**189-5806** Haupt/Vorsignal 8 LEDs **41.99**

**189-5821** Block Signal, 2 LEDs **22.99**

**189-5822** Main Signal, 3 LEDs **23.99**

Crossing Blinkers 189-5934

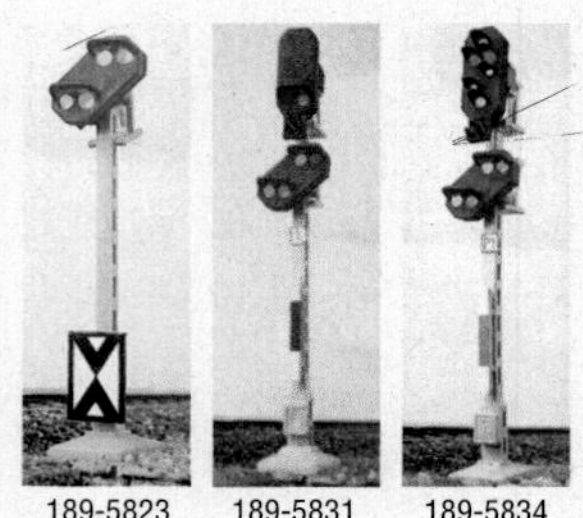

189-5823 189-5831 189-5834

**189-5823** Block/Warning Signal, 4 LEDs **29.99**

**189-5831** Block/Warning Signal, 6 LEDs **43.99**

**189-5834** Departure/Warning Signal, 10 LEDs **56.99**

Items listed below are available by Special Order (see Legend Page).

**189-5805** Block/Vorsignal 6 LEDs **36.99**

### Crossing Signals

Signals include control units.

**189-5300** Modern Crossing Gates w/Electronic Drive **76.99**

**189-5751** Crossing Blinkers w/Bell Sound **103.99**

**189-5913** 4-Pack w/Signs **43.99**

**189-5934** U.S. Style Crossing Blinkers **36.99**
Set includes two crossing signals and control unit.

**189-5966** Swiss Style pkg(2) **41.99**

Items listed below are available by Special Order (see Legend Page).

**189-5903** Crossing Blinkers **27.99**

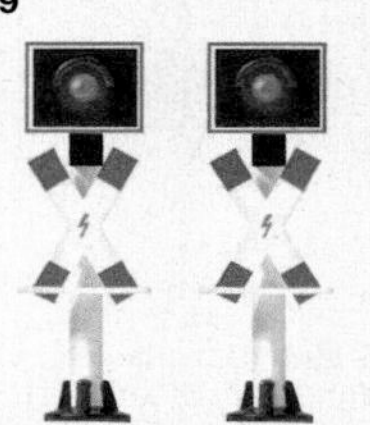

**189-5951** Blinking Crossing Warning (European) Pair **17.99**

**189-5968** Belgian Railways Crossing Flashers **41.99**

### Traffic Signals

Signals include control units.

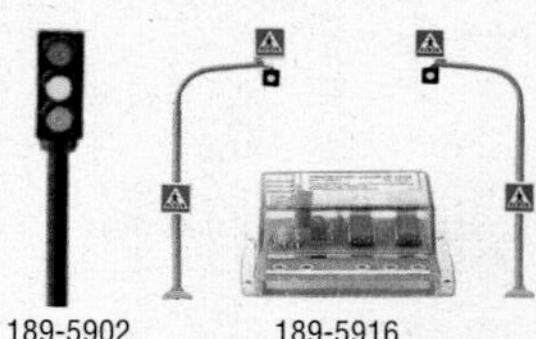

189-5902 189-5916

**189-5901** Traffic Signal Expansion Set **32.99**
Expansion set for 189-5902 (sold separately), includes two traffic signals.

**189-5902** pkg(2) **60.99**

**189-5916** Pedestrian Crossing Set pkg(2) **46.99**

### Barricades

**189-5450** American Construction Zone Blinkers **35.99**
Keep highway crews safe wit[h] this set of working constructi[on] flashers. Includes four stanchions (two of which are equipped with yellow LEDs) and a flasher control unit.

**189-5937** Construction Zone **35.99**
When it's time to repair city streets and sewers, keep motorists alert with these seven construction zone blinkers, four of which blink. Includes control unit.

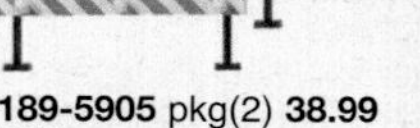

**189-5905** pkg(2) **38.99**
With control unit.

**189-6022** Guardrail & Speed Limit Set **6.99**

Items listed below are available by Special Order (see Legend Page).

**189-5907** Construction Zone Set pkg(7) **45.99**
Includes seven stanchion barricades (four with blinking lights) and control unit.

**189-6048** Road Construction Set **17.99**

IMPORTED FROM GERMANY BY WALTHERS

Pre-wired plastic signals are assembled and ready to install.

**189-5917** Construction Zone Set pkg(15) **77.99**
Includes 15 stanchion barricades (eight with blinking lights), three signs and control unit.

## Signal Kits

**189-5490** Compact Light **19.99**
Includes base, masts, LEDs and resistors to construct a pair of signals.

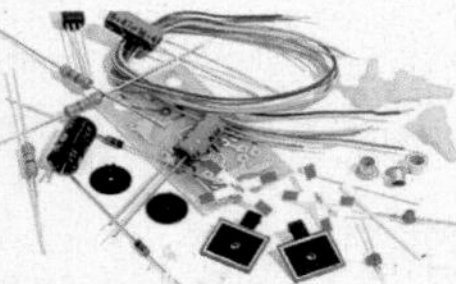

**189-5491** Modern Crossing Flasher **15.99**
Parts to construct a pair of contemporary German crossing flashers with red LEDs, signs, resistors, assembled circuit board and wiring.

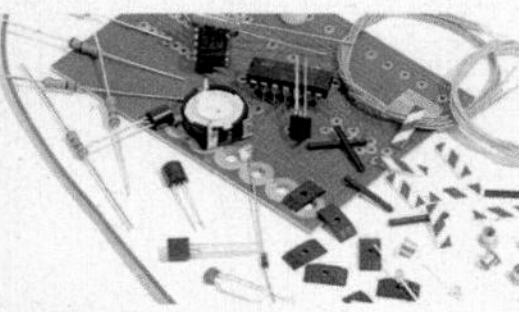

**189-5492** Highway Construction Barricades w/Flasher **27.99**
Kit includes parts for seven barricades, plus LEDs and flasher circuit to equip four barricades with flashing yellow lights.

# SIGNS

## Dry Transfer

Decal sets include rub-on pen.

**189-6024** German Federal Railways (DB) Logos **4.99**

**189-6035** Graffiti Detail Set **8.99**

# ADVERTISING SIGNS

**189-5920** Advertising Signs **79.99**
These flashing signs will bring life to the landscape of your railroad. Ready to use for connection to transformer 14-16V AC or DC.

**189-6002** Sign Set (German) **6.99**

## BAR MILLS

# BILLBOARD IN A BAG

This complete kit makes it easy-to-build four custom signs (depending on size and height) for your layout with 200 etched-brass letters.The kit also includes highly detailed injection-molded plastic supports and some basic graphics, along with ideas for making your own artwork. A set of nonworking lamps provides the finishing touch.

**171-35** N-HO Scale **17.95**

**171-36** HO-O Scale **19.95**

## CLEVER MODELS

# NEW PRODUCTS

## Sign Kits

Don't let your eyes fool you - all of the signs shown here are really made of paper! Easy to build and loaded with detail, each is precision printed with realistic colors and design elements already in place, on special high-strength cardstock. Simply cut, fold and glue to create affordable, beautiful 3-D models for your railroad.

## Palace Hotel

**NEW 217-1123 9.95**

## Deco Sheetmetal Sign Set

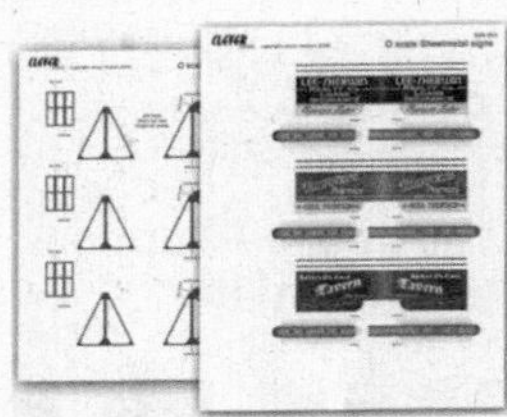

**NEW 217-1124 9.95**



Digitrax

# Plug 'N Play Signaling

## Digitrax Plug 'N Play Signaling

The Digitrax Plug 'N Play Signal system is the perfect way to add signaling to your layout. And whether you use DC or DCC controls, it will add a new dimension of realism to operations.
The SE8C Signal Decoder is the heart of the system, and can drive up to 32 signal heads using most popular signal types like bi-color LED searchlight types with two or three leads, or 3-LED heads with common anode or cathode. It can even drive B&O or Pennsy type heads with multiple indicators. Current resistors are built-in for setting LED brightness. The SE8C can also be used to drive 8 slow-motion turnout machines, such as Circuitron's Tortoise™ or eight semaphore signals driven by slow-motion turnout machines. The SE8C provides 16 inputs, eight control lines for local turnout control and eight occupancy sensor inputs.
A full line of accessory products let you use modular plug 'n play wiring and components to install a fully customizable signaling system on your railroad. The Signal Driver Cable Kits take the hassle out of running wires for your signal system. Signal Mast Base Kits, Terminal Mounting Strip Kits and Signal Hardware Mounting Kits make it easy to use either inexpensive circuit board type signals, or your own finely detailed signals with the system.

If you're using a computer to control your layout, the Digitrax Plug 'N Play Signaling System is a great way to add prototypical signaling to your railroad. If you're not using a computer, the SE8C Signal Decoder lets you manually operate signals on the layout from your throttle. With a computer and compatible software, you'll be able to realize the full potential of the Digitrax Plug 'N Play Signaling System.

**245-SE8C** Signal Decoder **125.00**

**245-SDCK** Signal Driver Cable Kit **19.99**

**245-SMHK** Signal Mounting Hardware Kit **9.99**

**245-TSMK** Terminal Strip Mounting Kit (2 Boards) **14.99**

**245-SMBK** Signal Mast Base Kit pkg(3) **14.99**

## COUNTRY TRAINS

## Road Signs 1.50 ea

Signs are printed in appropriate colors on glossy, coated cardstock. Two sheets included with each set.

**203-1** Street Corner, Road Signs & Construction (110 signs)

**203-2** Highway Signs (56 signs)

**203-3** Speed Limit, Railroad Crossing, Stop & Warning (72 signs)

**203-4** Railroad Track & Crossbucks (86 signs)

Items listed in blue ink may not be available at all times (see Legend Page).

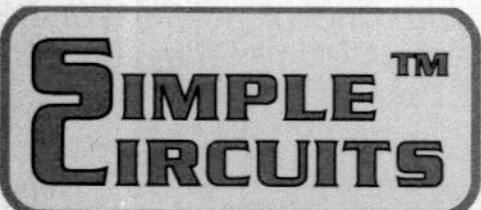


Easier connections, less costly, but still full-featured, circuits with the Simple Circuits™ designation are ideal for modelers interested in layout animation and a minimum investment of time and money.

## PRINTED CIRCUIT MOUNTING TRACK (PCMT)

**800-9506** PCMT, 6" **5.95**
Plastic assembly provides simple, snap-in mounting of all Circuitron printed circuit boards. Prepunched with mounting holes; can be mounted using screws, adhesive or double-backed tape. After PCMT is mounted, circuit boards simply snap into the track and can easily be removed for service.

## BLOCK OCCUPANCY DETECTION UNITS

### Optical Detectors

Tiny Opto-Sensors detect train movement. Sensors mount between the rails and activate circuitry when shaded by a passing train. Independent of track power, rolling stock requires no modifications. Sensors fit between HO Scale ties and may be ballasted over in most cases. Circuitry is extremely sensitive and will operate properly under very low levels of room light.

### BD-1 Optical Detectors

Positive indication whenever a section of a layout is occupied by rolling stock. Contains all circuitry to power two-color block signals at each end of the protected block. Will give proper indications if a train leaves a block by backing out. No modifications to rolling stock needed. Completely bi-directional. No additional driver boards or relays are needed. 250 mA output can power lamp or LED-type signals. Requires 6-20V DC input. Independent of track power. Compatible with radio or command control systems.

**800-5501** BD-1 Optical Detector **34.95**

**800-5521** BD-1HD Optical Detector **39.95**
Same as #800-5501, but with 500 mA. output.

### BD-2 Current Sensing Detection Unit

Detects current drawn by a locomotive or lighted piece of rolling stock. Unpowered equipment can be detected by using metal wheelsets with resistors connected across the insulator. Will directly drive two-color lamp or LED-type block signals. 250 mA output (500 mA. for BD-2HD). Circuit boards are designed for easy daisy-chain wiring of multiple blocks and will snap into a section of Printed Circuit Mounting Track. Requires 10-18V DC. Works in any scale and with most track power, systems including most forms of command control.

**800-5502** BD-2, 3 amp Capacity **22.95**

**800-5522** BD-2HD, 6 amp Capacity **29.95**

### BD-5 DCC Detector

Same speecifications as BD-2 above but provides complete isolation from the DCC track power. CANNOT be used with conventional DC track power.

**800-5505** BD-5 w/250mA Lamp Drive Capacity **19.95**

**800-5525** BD-5HD w/500mA Lamp Drive Capacity **24.95**

## GRADE CROSSING DETECTION UNITS

Specifically designed for use at grade crossings, using Opto-Sensors to detect the train. Output controls flashers, gates, bells, etc. Note: DT-1, DT-2, DT-3 and DT-5 Detection Units require an Alternating Flasher Unit (FL-2 or FL-3) to operate flashing lamps.

### DT-1 Detection Unit

**800-5201 34.95**
Detects train when an Opto-Sensor is covered. Senses track polarity and activates only the Opto-Sensors for the direction of travel. Always turns off after the last piece of rolling stock clears the crossing. Includes four Opto-Sensors. Note: DT-1 cannot detect a short train or loco if it falls between Opto-Sensors. Use in any scale with DC track power. Not ideal for DCC. 2 x 3" printed circuit board. 10-18V AC or DC input.

### DT-2 Detection Unit

**800-5202 46.95**
Full logic system duplicates prototype grade crossing action. Does not require sensor to stay covered to activate. Integrated memory keeps output "on" until last car clears the crossing. Activates whenever a train approaches from either direction. If train stops short then backs away, unit will detect that and turn output "off." Independent of train length - will detect a short train even if it falls between Opto-Sensors. Includes four Opto-Sensors. Not ideal for DCC. 3 x 3" printed circuit board. 10-18V AC or DC input.

### DT-3 Single-Direction Detection Unit

**800-5203 26.95**
Single-direction unit for crossings where bi-directional detection is unnecessary, such as a mainline with trains traveling in only one direction. Operates with any length train. Completely independent of track power. Use in any scale and with any form of track power including DCC. Requires 10-18V AC or DC input.

### DF-1 Detection With Flasher

**800-5250 39.95**
Single-direction grade crossing detector with alternating flasher on one circuit board. Operates with any length train. Independent of track power. Use in any scale and with any form of track power including DCC. Can power two 250 mA loads (5 grain-of-wheat lamps or 10 LEDs per side). 10-18V AC or DC input.

## GRADE CROSSING ANIMATORS

Complete, simple detection, Alternating Flasher and Tortoise™ gate driver circuitry on one board. For 2-rail DC or 3-rail AC track power in all scales.

### GA-1 Grade Crossing Animator

**800-5260 29.95**
Provided with two Opto-Sensors, the flasher outputs will be on when either is shaded. Drives LEDs or lamps (250mA per side). Also directly powers a Tortoise (not included) for gate activation. Does not detect short trains falling between sensors. One additional sensor can be added (see Accessories) but will reduce sensitivity. Adjustable for light intensity. Not for very low-light situations. 10-18V AC or DC input. Add DT-5 for additional track.

### GL-1 Grade Crossing Animator

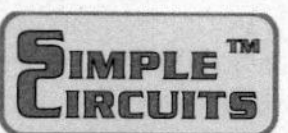


**800-5261 24.95**
Same as GA-1 but for 3-rail AC track power. Uses isolated outside rail for detection. No Opto-Sensors necessary. No light limitations. No detection unit needed for additional tracks.

Get Your Daily Dose of Product News at
**www.walthers.com**

## ROLLING STOCK DETECTION UNIT

### DT-4 Rolling Stock Detector

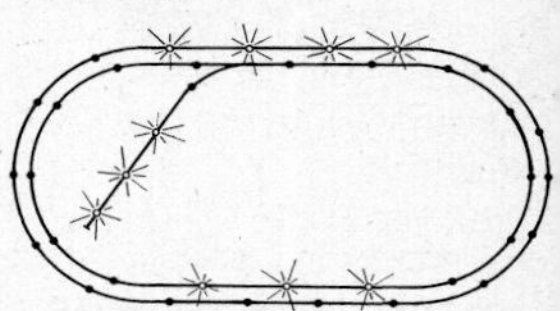

**800-5204 39.95**
Ideal for spotting a hidden train or piece of rolling stock. Four independent detection units combined onto one circuit board, can be used separately or together to control external devices. Supplied with four Opto-Sensors that mount between rails to detect movement. When train covers a sensor, the unit activates any connected DC accessory, such as an indicator light on a control panel. Independent sensitivity controls are provided for adjusting each Opto-Sensor to lighting conditions. Constructed on a 3 x 3" printed circuit board. Requires 10-18V DC. Independent of track power. Compatible with radio or command control systems.

## DRIVERS

### SD-1 Signal Driver

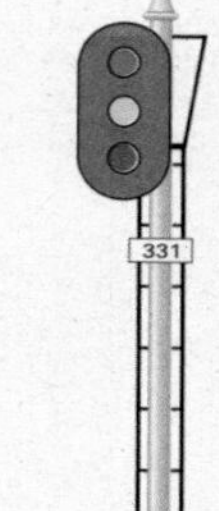


**800-5510 15.95**
Logic and output drivers to control any three-lamp, three-color block signal. Will power LED or lamp-type signals. LED type requires common positive (anode) connection of all LEDs. Detection circuits (such as BD-1) are needed for a minimum of three blocks to display all three aspects. 10-18V DC input.

### SD-2 3-Position Semaphore Driver

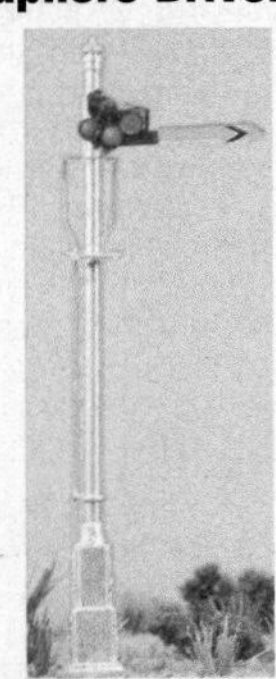

**800-5520 19.95**
Use with the Tortoise™ Switch Machine and an upper or lower quadrant semaphore-style signal. Includes all the logic circuitry to drive the signal to all three positions. Works with BD-1 or BD-2 Block Occupancy Detectors. A minimum of two blocks must have detectors installed for the SD-2 to indicate all three positions. Requires 10-18V DC power. See Crossing Signals section for Gate/Semaphore Activator.

### SD-3 Signal Driver

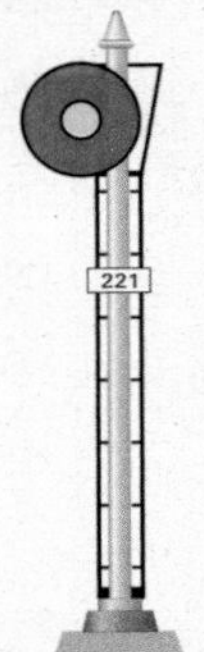


**800-5530 15.95**
Drives any single-target tri-color LED-type signal to red, green and amber aspects. Will not drive lamp signals. Amber hue fully adjustable. May be controlled by three-position switch or automatically by detection circuits such as BD-1 (minimum of 3 blocks required). 10-18V AC or DC.

## INTERFACE CIRCUITS 9.95 ea

Circuit boards change polarity so different electronic products can be used together.

800-5271 LT-1 Positive Logic Translator

800-5272 LT-2 Negative Logic Translator

## BLOCK SIGNAL ANIMATORS

Complete, simple detection, with timed three-color block signal animation. Signal turns red as train passes. After last car clears signals, adjustable time delay starts (up to 30 seconds). After time delay, signal then turns yellow. After another adjustable time delay, the signal goes back to green. For 2-rail DC or 3-rail AC track power in all scales.

### SA-1 Block Signal Animator

800-5540 22.95
For three-lamp (red, yellow and green) or LED-type signals and 2-rail DC track power. DCC compatible. LED-type signals require common positive (anode) connection of all LEDs. Provided with Opto-Sensor. Three outputs can control 250mA each. Adjustable for room-light intensity. 10-18V AC or DC input.

### SL-1 Block Signal Animator

800-5541 17.95
For 3-rail AC track power. All other specifications are the same as SA-1. Uses isolated section of outside rail for detection. No Opto-Sensors, adjustments or light limitations.

### SA-3 Block Signal Animator

800-5542 24.95
For Bi- or Tri-Color LED-type target signals and 2-rail DC track power. DCC compatible. Amber hue fully adjustable. Provided with Opto-Sensor. Output will drive only one LED. Adjustable for room-light intensity. 10-18V AC or DC input.

### SL-3 Block Signal Animator

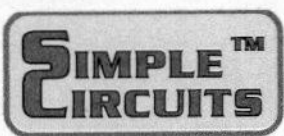


800-5543 19.95
For 3-rail AC track power. All other specifications are the same as SA-3. Uses isolated section of outside rail for detection. No Opto-Sensors, adjustments or light limitations.

## TRAIN CONTROL CIRCUITS

### AR-1 Automatic Reversing Circuit

**800-5400 44.95**
Changes direction when the Opto-Sensor is covered. Use for test track, window display, mine train or automatic reverse loop operation. Pushbuttons can be connected for manual reversing. Requires 12V DC power source. Constructed on 2 x 3" printed circuit board.

### AR-1CC Reverse Loop Controller

**800-5410 49.95**
Same as AR-1, but with four Opto-Sensors for automatic reverse loop switching on command control layout. Trains must be shorter than loop for proper operation.

### AR-2 Automatic Reverse With Adjustable Display

**800-5401 54.95**
Same as AR-1, but with adjustable delay to hold train at sensor before reversing. Adjustable delay from one second to over one minute. Can be connected to push-button or DT-4 to permit stops and delays without reversing. Requires 12-18V AC or DC power supply. Constructed on 3 x 3" printed circuit board.

### AS-1 Automatic Slowdown

**800-5601 18.95**
Slows train speed in a section of track. Bi-directional; use with AC or DC power. Output is continuously variable between 1/4 and 3/4 of the input voltage.

### TD-1 Time Delay Circuit

**800-5602 29.95**
Use with detection units for adjustable delay with self-contained relay on the output. Great for automatic stop at a station or siding. Time delay adjustable from 0 to over one minute. Requires 12V DC power supply.

## SOUND

### Bell Ringer Circuits

Connects to detection unit to simulate crossing bell. Rate and volume are adjustable. Designed for under layout mounting. Use with 10-18V AC or DC.

**800-5700** BR-1 w/2-1/2" Bell **45.95**

**800-5702** BR-2, w/Circuit Board **29.95**
Use any dual-coil electro-magnetic doorbell.

## ALTERNATING FLASHERS

Use to flash signals, emergency vehicle lights, signs and more.

### FL-2 Alternating Flasher

Flashes LEDs or lamps. Connects to Detection Units. Maintains constant flash rate. 1.5 x 3" printed circuit board. Requires 10-18V AC or DC input. 250 mA. output.

**800-5102** FL-2 **18.95**

**800-5122** FL-2HD **22.95**
Same as FL-2, but with 500 mA load capability per side. Adaptable for all scales.

### FL-3 Alternating Flasher

**800-5103 39.95**
Heavy-duty, with three control terminals and three outputs. Independent flashing at up to three locations. Outputs can control 250 mA. Can flash LEDs or lamps. 3 x 3" printed circuit board. 10-18V AC or DC input.

## CROSSING SIGNALS

### Gate Driver Circuit

800-5550 14.95
Use with detection circuits, alternating flashers, the Tortoise switch machine and Remote Signal Activator (#800-8100, sold separately) to automate crossbuck signals and gates with vertical-control wire actuators.

### Signal/Accessory Actuator w/Internal Drivers

**800-6200 39.95**
Same size and mounting as the TORTOISE™. 12-14 volts DC or DCC power supply. Compatible with most detection systems and all DCC systems that provide accessory address control. May also be controlled with panel switches. May be used for crossing gates or three-position semaphores in all scales with no additional drivers necessary. Adjustable speed. Use with #800-8100 Remote Signal Activator (sold separately). Other specifications same as TORTOISE™.

### SMAIL™ Value Packs

(Dealers Note: Items are not labeled for individual sale.)

**800-6206** pkg(6) **230.00**

**800-6212** pkg(12) **440.00**

### Terminal Blocks

Set of two screw-type terminal blocks that can be soldered to the SMAIL™ circuit board to allow easy under-layout connections.

**800-6301** Single **4.95**

**800-6306** pkg(6) **24.95**

**800-6312** pkg(12) **42.95**

### SMAIL™ w/Terminal Blocks

Includes factory installed screw-type terminal blocks for simple connections without soldering.

**800-6200TB 46.95**

(Dealers Note: Items are not labeled for individual sale.)

**800-6206TB** pkg(6) **270.00**

**800-6212TB** pkg(12) **520.00**

### Gate/Semaphore Actuator

Mounting bracket and mechanism utilize the TORTOISE™ or SMAIL™ (not included) and a special drive wire cable assembly to remotely actuate any crossing gate, train order or semaphore signal having a vertical control wire extending below the layout. Positive, adjustable stops are provided at both ends of travel. Can drive two cables from the one drive mechanism, if desired. Adjustable for all scales.

**800-8100** Drive Mechanism w/Cable & Actuator **10.95**

**800-8101** Extra Cable & Actuator **5.95**

## HIDDEN ACCESSORY SWITCHES

On-Off reed switches for strobe flashers, marker lights or other electrical accessories. Operated by holding a magnet near the loco or car. Nothing to detract from the look of the model. Kits contain a subminiature reed switch and a tiny bias magnet.

**800-9101** RS-1 Kit **5.95** Requires adjustment before mounting.

**800-9102** RS-2 Kit **7.95** Requires no adjustment.

**800-9100** Magnet **1.95**

**800-9103** Subminiature Slide Switch pkg(2) **2.95**

## TURNOUT CONTROL CIRCUITS

### Snapper Switch Machine Power Supply

**800-5303 29.95**
Solid state, provides positive power to dual-coil switch machines. Protects from burnout due to stuck pushbuttons, short circuits, etc. Operates off accessory terminals of power pack or transformer up to 25V. 24V input can activate five to ten coils simultaneously if connected to same control. Instant recycle time. Includes a section of Printed Circuit Mounting Track (PCMT).

### 3 AMP Diode

**800-9350** pkg(2) **1.95**
Heavy-duty, silicon rectifiers with 50V rating, axial leads and surge rating of 300 amps. Use in turnout control diode matrix with Snapper Switch Machine Power Supply (#800-5303, sold separately) or wire across a gap in the track to stop a train automatically.

### TC-1 Automatic Turnout Control

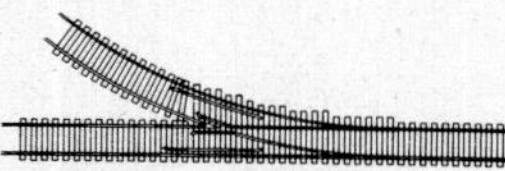

**800-5605 29.95**
Activates dual-coil switch machine when used with DT-4. Momentary pulse when detection unit is activated, protects from burnout. Can be used to control both directions. Requires 10-18V AC or DC input. The higher the voltage input, the greater the output power. Recycle time on each side is one to two seconds.

### TC-2 Turnout Direction Alternator

**800-5606 31.95**
Automatically alternates turnout direction when used with DT-4. Sends momentary pulse to one coil of the switch machine, throwing the turnout in one direction. Next activation throws it in the other direction. Allows train to travel alternate routes automatically. Requires 10-18V AC or DC input.

### TC-3 Automatic Tortoise Control

**800-5615 18.95**
Automatically activates Tortoise switch machine when used with detection unit. Two drive inputs control direction. Only momentary inputs are required; can be used for pushbutton or matrix control. Requires 12-18V DC.

### TC-4 Tortoise Direction Alternator

**800-5616 19.95**
Similar to #800-5606, but output is designed to drive the Tortoise switch machine. Requires 12-18V DC.

### ER-1 External Relay

**800-5604** SPDT **14.95**
Single pole, double throw, 6 amp relay mounted on a circuit board, with driver circuitry to be directly connected to the output of any detection unit. Provides high current, bi-directional contacts for train control. Ideal for use with Block Occupancy Detectors to power blocks for automatic train control. Requires 12V DC power supply.

### ER-2 External Relay

**800-5624** DPDT **18.95**
Double-pole, double-throw version of ER-1 with 2 amp rating.

### PB-1 Power Booster

**800-5603 14.95**
Connects directly to the output of any detection unit to raise load capacity to 1 amp DC. Can only be used for DC circuits. Up to 50 Power Boosters can be controlled by one detection unit. Requires 10-18V AC or DC input.

## POWER SUPPLIES

Most Circuitron accessories operate off AC or DC, but perform best with a DC supply. These units convert power from AC to DC, for improved operation and include a section of PCMT.

### PS-1 Converter

**800-5301** Filtered AC to DC Converter **14.95**
Maximum load capacity 1 amp, maximum input voltage 22V AC. Output is not regulated; voltage will vary depending upon input voltage and output load. (Requires transformer or power pack for AC input.)

### PS-2 Converter

**800-5302** Filtered & Regulated AC to DC Converter **22.95**

### PS-2A Converter & Regulator

**800-5305 26.95**
Self-contained AC to DC converter with adjustable output between 1.25 and 12V DC. Maximum continuous current output in excess of 1 amp. Ideal for powering any low current DC accessories, including 1.5V micro-lamps. AC or unfiltered DC input should be about 5-6V higher for maximum current output. Input voltage up to 22V, but may result in reduced current available at the output, particularly at lower voltage settings.

## ACCESSORIES

### In-Line Fuse Holder

**800-9601 2.00**
Accepts any standard length, 1/4" diameter fuse. With wire leads.

### Diodes

**800-9350** 3 amp pkg(2) **1.95**

**800-9351** 1 amp pkg(6) **1.95**

**800-9352** 6 amp pkg(2) **2.95**

**800-935012** 3 amp pkg(12) **6.95**

**800-935212** 6 amp pkg(12) **12.95**

### Opto-Sensors

For use with all Circuitron Detection Circuits. .185" diameter.

**800-9201** Single **3.95**

**800-9202** Two-Pack **7.50**

**800-9206** Six-Pack **19.95**

## LABELLE

### Burma Shave Signs pkg(6) 7.98 ea

The Burma Shave signs were roadside staples from the mid-1920s on. Usually in sets of six, these red-and-white signs were spaced around one hundred yards apart. The signs told a short but pointed story, with the last sign in the set always featuring the Burma Shave logo.

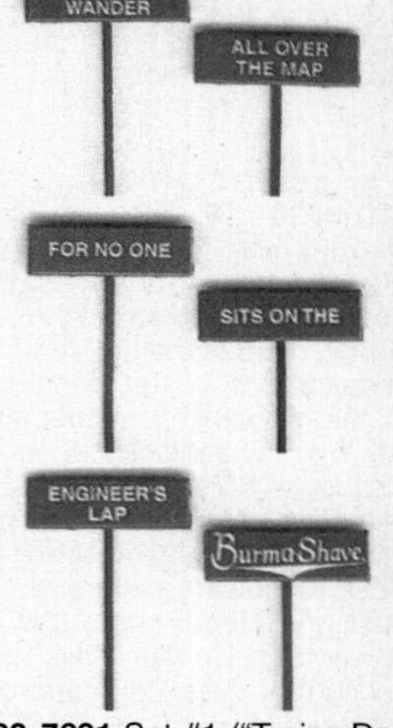


**430-7601** Set #1 ("Trains Don' Wander...")

**430-7602** Set #2 ("Trains Don' Whistle...")

**430-7603** Set #3 ("Approachec A Crossing...")

**430-7604** Set #4 ("Train Wrecks Few...")

**430-7605** Set #5 ("It's Trains, Not Girls...")

**430-7606** Set #6 ("As Fast Train Neared...")

## SIGN SOFTWARE

Easy-to-use software lets you print your own railside and street signs or classic advertisements in any scale. Print the signs and advertisements you need in the scale you need to add great detail to your layout. System requirements: PC running Windows 98/NT/ME/2000/XP/XP-Pro.

## NEW PRODUCTS

### The Advertiser

**NEW 266-A04 30.00**
Create signs for your structures and rolling stock. Hundreds of classic ads and many templates for creating your own storefront signs. Modify the existing advertising text with your text in the design screen. Resize your ads to fit your needs. Add great realistic detail to your models.

### Highway and Railway Sign Creator

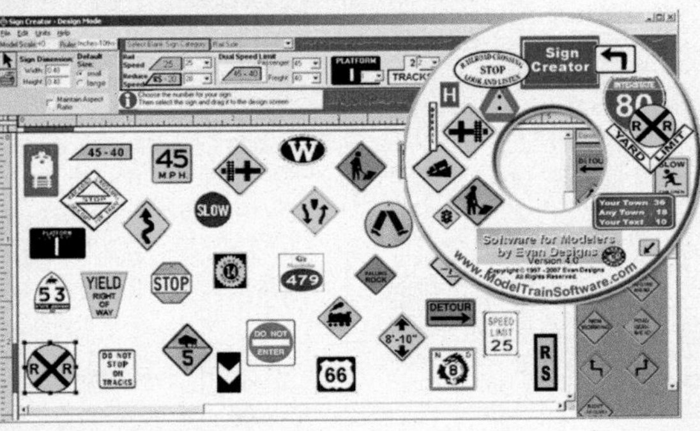


**NEW 266-A23 40.00**
Over 300 road and railway signs. Includes 50 state route highway signs and Canadian province signs, both past and present, that you can add your own route numbers to. Also includes 15 customizable Hazmat placards for box cars and tanker cars. Set road speed limits, bridge height and weight limits, platform numbers and number of tracks, passenger and freight car speed limits. Pre-built signs include stop signs, yield signs, railroad crossing, customizable construction signs, school crossings, directional signs, railroad engineer signs, warning signs and more. Signs automatically come into the design screen in your chosen scale. Print your signs on glossy or matte photo paper (sold separately).

## FALLER

IMPORTED FROM GERMANY BY WALTHERS

Assembled plastic models molded in realistic colors.

## CROSSINGS

**272-120171** Protected Level Crossing **229.99**
Features warning lights, 2 gates over the entire width of the road and gatekeeper's lodge. Operated when train triggers an optoelectronic sensor. Useable on all types of tracks and also suitable for Faller Car System. Measures: 9-7/8 x 7-1/8 x 2-3/4" 25 x 18 x 7cm

**272-120170** Small Grade Crossing w/Gates **21.99**
5-1/8 x 4-3/4" 13 x 12cm

**272-120172** Curved Grade Crossing w/Gates **28.99**
7-1/2 x 6-5/16" 19 x 16cm

**272-120173** Curved Grade Crossing w/Gates (Dummy) **28.99**
5-7/8 x 5-11/16" 15 x 14.5cm

**272-120174** Grade Crossing w/Gates **85.99**
8-5/8 x 10" 22 x 25.5cm

**272-180630** Crossing w/Warning Lights **42.99**

**272-180643** Grade Crossing w/Bells pkg(2) **49.99**
As soon as the signal flashes, the bell sounds. Comes with loudspeaker. 12-16V AC.

## SIGNS

### Railroad Signs

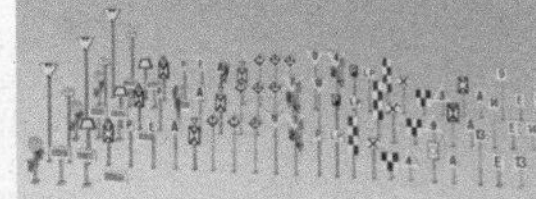

**272-120226** European Railroad Trackside Sign Set pkg(200) **27.99**

### Traffic Signs

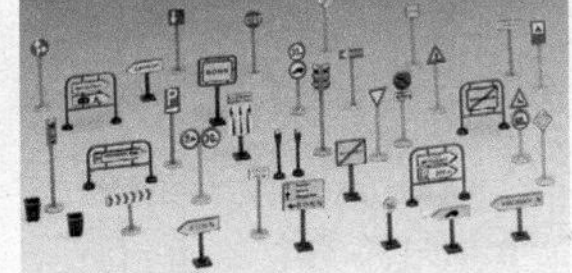

**272-180578** Traffic Signs **27.99**
City signs, direction signs, traffic signs and lights, parking meters and waste baskets.

**272-180594** German Traffic Signs 1948-1977 **16.99**

**272-180595** European Traffic Signs 1977-1985 **16.99**

For Daily Product Updates Point Your Browser to
**www.walthers.com**

## NOCH

IMPORTED FROM GERMANY BY WALTHERS

Molded in realistically colored plastic.

### Signs

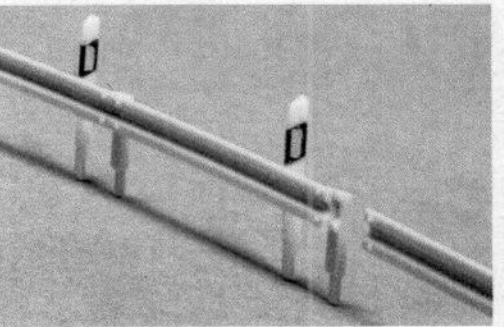

**528-60511** Crash Barriers **10.99**

**528-60521** Assorted Traffic Signs **15.99**

Item listed below is available by Special Order (see Legend Page).

**528-11290** Advertising Sign & Kiosk **12.99**

## RIX PRODUCTS

### Railroad Telephone Poles 4.99 ea

Two-piece plastic poles molded in realistic brown color. Any number of crossarms can be added to the poles. Notches are provided in the poles for easy assembly of the crossarms.

628-32 628-34

**628-30** 30' & 40' Poles pkg(36)

**628-31** Crossarms Only pkg(72)

**628-32** 2-Arm Poles pkg(18)

**628-34** 4-Arm Poles pkg(12)

**628-35** Clear Green Crossarms pkg(36)

**628-40** 40' Poles Only pkg(36)

These full-color posters and signs add color and life to layouts of any era. Printed on two 4 x 5-1/2" heavy paper sheets. Application and weathering instructions included.

## NEW PRODUCTS

### Signs

#### Advertising Posters & Signs 3.79 ea

**NEW 361-265** Turn of the Century III Signs 1890s-1920s

**NEW 361-266** Vintage Candy Poster/Signs 1930s-1950s

**NEW 361-267** 1950s Vintage Bus & Bus Depot Signs

## POSTERS & SIGNS

#### Consumer Products 3.79 ea

**361-182** 1940s & 1950s Household (41 Signs)

**361-185** 1940s-1960s Alcohol/ Tobacco/Chewing Gum (40 Signs)

**361-197** 1930s-1960s Vintage Soft Drink (72 Signs)

**361-282** 1940s & 1950s Consumer Products (42 Signs)

**361-297** 1930s-1950s Soft Drink Series II (44 Signs)

**361-322** 1930s-1950s Country Store

**361-406** Uncommon & Unusual Soft Drinks 1940s-1950s

#### Turn Of The Century 3.79 ea

**361-285** 1890s-1920s pkg(40)

**361-385** Series II 1890s-1920s

#### Waterfront/Marine 3.79 ea

**361-405** 1950s-1960s **3.49**

#### Feed & Seed 3.79 ea

**361-183** 1940s-1950s Farm Implement (54 Signs)

**361-383** 1950s-Present Grain Elevator (44 Signs)

#### Consumer Products 3.79 ea

**361-178** 1940s-1950s Paint & Consumer Signs pkg(54)

**361-422** Ice Cream/Soda Fountain Signs 40s-50s pkg(49)

**361-425** Unusual Soft Drink Signs 40s-50s pkg(40)

**361-426** Food & Household Product Signs 40s-50s pkg(37)

**361-427** Tobacco, Cigar & Beer Signs 30s-50s pkg(30)

**361-483** 1950s-Present Grain Elevator II (44 Signs)

#### Transportation 3.79 ea

**361-204** 1900s-1960s Vintage Motorcycle & Auto (63 Signs)

**361-283** 1940s-1950s Planes/ Trains/Industrial (55 Signs)

**361-304** Motorcycles 1920s & Up

**361-404** Auto 1940s-1950s

**361-407** Railroad, Railway Express Agency & Depot Signs 1940s-1960s

**361-408** Railroad Advertising Signs 1940s-1960s

#### Gas Stations 3.79 ea

**361-284** Series II 1940s-1960s (55 Signs)

**361-384** Series III 1930s-1960s

#### 1940s-1950s

**361-184** Gas Station & Oil (41 Signs)

**361-373** Oil & Tire Signs for Gas Station (49 Signs)

**361-488** Vintage Shell

#### 1930s-1950s

**361-372** Gilmore Gas Station (107 Signs)

**361-484** Texaco

**361-485** Mobil

**361-486** Sinclair

**361-487** Phillips

Assembled signals and accessories feature prepainted plastic parts.

**361-489** Vintage Flying "A"

### Road Signs 3.79 ea

**361-196** Danger/Warning (250 Signs)

**361-202** Uncommon Street & Parking (150 Signs)

### Saloon/Tavern Signs 3.79 ea

**361-332** Series 1 1900-1920

**361-333** Series 2 1930-1950

**361-362** 1940s-1950s (49 Signs)

## BILLBOARD SIGNS

### Transportation 3.79 ea

#### 1940s & 1950s Automobile

**361-172** Set #1 6 Signs

**361-173** Set #2 6 Signs

#### 1960s Automobile

**361-174** Set #1 5 Signs

**361-175** Set #2 5 Signs

#### 1940s Railroad Theme

**361-186** Set #1 6 Signs

**361-187** Set #2 6 Signs

#### 1940s Automobile

**361-188** Set #1 6 Signs

**361-189** Set #2 6 Signs



#### 1950s Auto & Transportation

**361-192** Set #1 6 Signs

**361-193** Set #2 6 Signs

**361-374** 1950s Vintage Bus Billboards (6 Signs)

#### 1970s Automobile

**361-272** Set #1 6 Signs

**361-273** Set #2 6 Signs

#### 1960s Automobile

**361-274** Set #1 6 Signs

**361-275** Set #2 6 Signs

**361-375** 6 Signs

### Tractor Billboards

**361-376** 1940s-1950s (6 Signs) 3.79

### Consumer Products 3.79 ea

#### 1930s-1960s Vintage Soft Drink

**361-198** Set #1 6 Signs

**361-199** Set #2 6 Signs

#### 1930s-1960s Vintage Tobacco

**361-212** Set #1 6 Signs

**361-213** Set #2 6 Signs

#### RC Cola Signs

**361-298** Set #1 6 Signs

**361-299** Set #2 6 Signs

## BILLBOARDS

### Telephone Pole Style

**361-176** pkg(2) **7.49**

Kit includes Northeastern basswood, six full-color auto billboard signs, four nonilluminated lamps per billboard, chain-link fencing and illustrated instructions.

### Sidewalk Lattice

**361-277 6.99**

Kit includes Northeastern basswood for four signs, eight full color billboard signs and molded plastic lattice.

### Fence Base

**361-276** pkg(2) **7.49**

Billboards feature movie stars promoting RC Cola.

## RIGHT-OF-WAY SIGNS

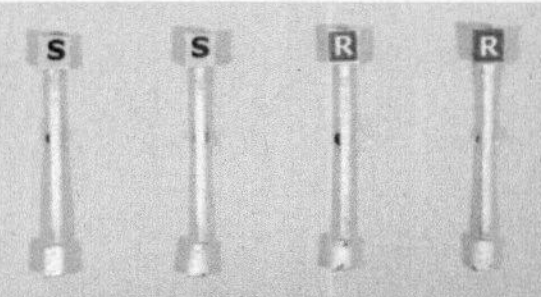

**361-830** Resume/Slow **4.49**

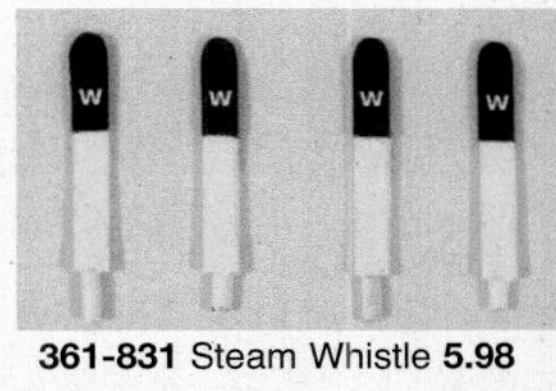

**361-831** Steam Whistle **5.98**

**361-832** Section (Post Style) **5.49**

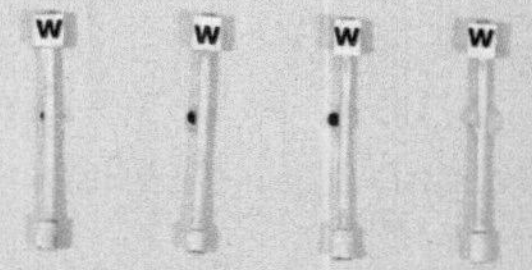

**361-833** Whistle **4.49**

**361-834** Switching Limit **4.98**

**361-835** Section (Pole Style) **5.49**

**361-836** Water One Mile **4.98**

**361-837** Junction One Mile **4.98**

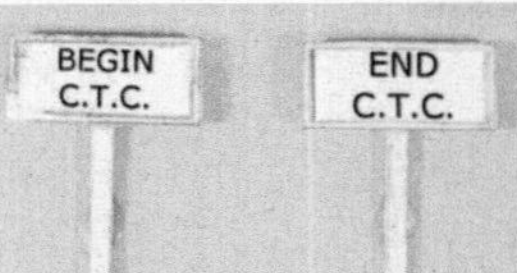

**361-838** Begin/End C.T.C. **4.98**

**361-839** Stop R.R. Crossing 400 Ft. **4.98**

**361-840** Begin/End Single Track **4.98**

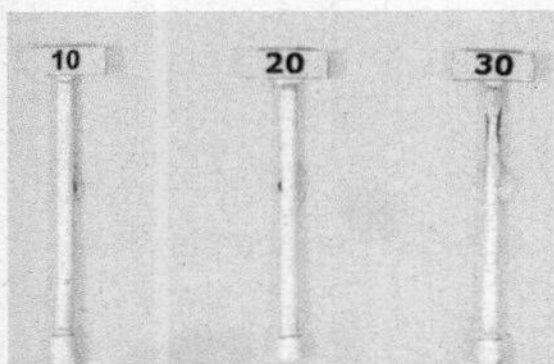


**361-841** Rectangle Speed (Slow Set) **4.98**

**361-842** Rectangle Speed (High Set) **4.98**

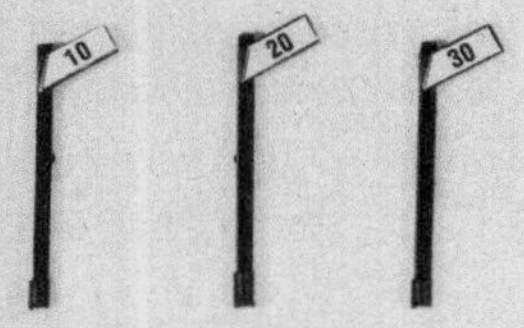


**361-843** Angled Speed (Slow Set) **4.98**

**361-844** Angled Speed (High Set) **4.98**

**361-845** Standard Railroad Crossbuck **5.98**

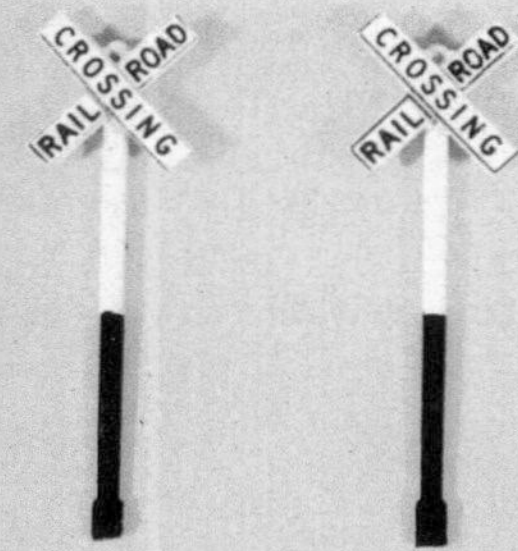


**361-846** Deluxe Railroad Crossbuck (Two-Tone) **6.98**

**361-847** Stop Drawbridge 400 Feet **4.98**

**361-848** Yard Limit **5.49**

## TRAIN ORDER SIGNAL

**361-252** Nonoperating **3.98**

### Catalog

**361-8 5.75**

## PASTIME HOBBIES & MINIATURES

## NEW PRODUCTS

### Signal Bridge Kits

Animate your layout with these signal bridge kits. Designed for easy construction, each includes precision laser-cut wood parts for the bridge framing and signal heads, along with all the LEDs and wiring needed to complete a working model.

**NEW 554-202** Double-Track **32.50**

**NEW 554-302** Cantilever **32.95**

Assembled, painted brass signals and lights are operating, handcrafted brass, unless noted.

## SIGNALS

### Block 15.50 ea (Unless Noted)

**490-1451** pkg(6) **5.95**
Three green and three red signal lights, and two relay cabinets.

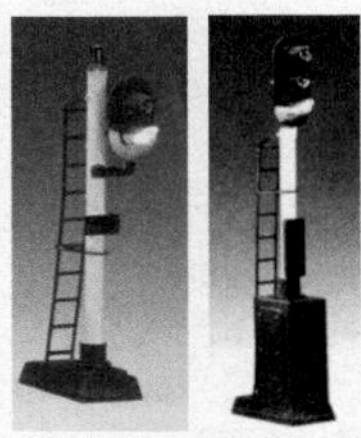

490-1675 490-1680

**490-1675** 2 Indication

**490-1676** 2 Indication w/Relay

**490-1677** 3 Indication

**490-1678** 3 Indication w/Relay

**490-1679** Target 3 Indication

**490-1680** Traffic 3 Indication

**490-1682** 2 Color w/Relay

### Miscellaneous

490-1681  490-1684

**490-1681** Crossing Signals pkg(2) **18.98**

**490-1684** North American Signal **15.50**

**490-1690** Relay **9.98**
Feeds control panel lamps and allows for selective power control for signals, lights and frogs.

## LIGHTS

### Surburban pkg(3) 8.98 ea

**490-593** Clear, 1-1/2"

**490-594** Frosted, 1-1/2"

### Boulevard pkg(3) 8.98 ea

490-499 490-500 490-595

**490-499** Square, Clear, 2"

**490-500** Round, Clear, 2"

**490-595** Round, Frosted, 2" Station Lamp

### Globe Post Lamp

**490-498** 2" pkg(3) **8.98**

### Traffic

Lights include four-way slide switch and red, green and amber bulbs. Painted and prewired.

490-596 490-597

**490-596** Standard pkg(2) **16.98**

**490-597** Two-Way **12.98**

**490-599** Left & Right **16.98**

**490-5961** Standard **12.98**

**490-5991** Right **12.98**

**490-5992** Left **12.98**

### Highway 8.98 ea

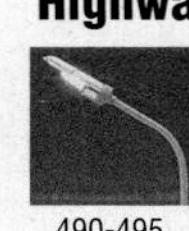
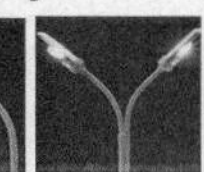

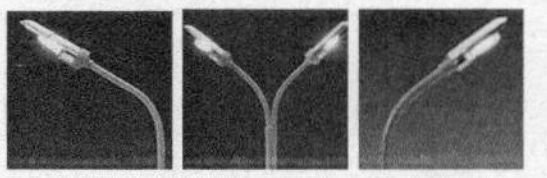

490-495 490-496 490-497

**490-495** Single, 4" pkg(3)

**490-496** Double, 4" pkg(2)

**490-497** Small Single, 2-1/4" pkg(3)

### Gas pkg(3) 8.98 ea

**490-493** Clear, 1-1/2"

**490-494** Frosted, 1-1/2"

### Clock

**490-598** Lighted, 2-Sided pkg(2) **9.98**

Latest New Product News Daily! Visit Walthers Web site at **www.walthers.com**

## SIGNS

### Billboards

**490-700** With Light pkg(2) **9.9**

**490-701** Running Billboard **32.98**
Features 28 LED running lights.

**490-703** Running Billboard w/Base **32.98**
Features 28 LED running lights.

### Gas Station Signs pkg(2) 8.98 ea

Illuminated brass parts.

**490-704** Shell

**490-705** Exxon

**490-706** Gulf

### Movie Posters pkg(8) 8.98 ea

**490-702** 1924-1940 Era

**490-7021** 1940-1960 Era

### Telephone Poles

**490-1452** pkg(12) **5.98**

### Road & Rail Signs

**490-1454** pkg(24) **5.98**

LIGHT WORKS USA™
By Miller Engineering

# ELECTROLUMINESCENT SIGN KITS

Each sign is made of special plastic that's only .008" thick for a near scale appearance. The sign is coated on one side with phosphor, which glows when current is applied. This produces a soft, neon-like light that's bright enough to be seen under regular room lights, but generates no heat. Each kit comes with an assembled 3V power supply, which requires two AAA batteries, not included. Complete instructions cover all of the steps needed for installation and operation.

## NEW PRODUCTS

### Animated Signs

Suitable for HO and O Scales.

**Goodyear**

4-7/16 Wide x 2-7-/8" Tall

**NEW 502-2381** **32.95**
This billboard is a replica of the original that still exists in Akron, Ohio. Letters light up and chasing lights blink around the sign.

**Breyers**

Building not included

**NEW 502-2581** **45.95**
4-1/8 Wide x 4-3/16" Tall
The word "Breyers" lights up sequentially followed by "Ice" and "Cream". This 8-channel sequencing sign can be mounted atop a building or flush mounted on a building for a different look. Limited run.

**Dr. Pepper**

**NEW 502-2681** **32.95**
A great companion to H&C coffee #7881 (sold separately), this sign features letters that light up with chasing lights circling the outside.

**Bowling Alleys**

**NEW 502-7081** **32.95**
4-3/8 Wide x 1-5/8" Tall
Letters light up and bowling ball and pins are animated.

**Rexall**

Building not included

**NEW 502-7581** **45.95**
4-1/4 Wide x 3-7/8" Tall
The word "Rexall" lights up sequentially followed by "Parker" and "Drugs". Can be mounted two ways - as a rooftop billboard or flush against the side of a building for a completely different look. 8-channel sequencing. Limited run.

**Stan's Drive-In**

**NEW 502-7681** **45.95**
2-1/8 Wide x 3-7/8" Tall
This double-sided sign is designed to be free standing. A replica of an original at a 1949 car hop in Fresno, CA, the letters and car hop's outline light up. Animated chase lights flash around the word "Stan's".

**Animated Barber Pole**

**NEW 502-8082** Medium **36.95**
1-1/2" Tall
This true 3-D barber pole is fascinating to watch.

### Lighting Accessories

**Chase Light Experimenter's Kit**

**NEW 502-2505** **32.95**
Contains two 8-3/4" EL lamps with two rows of chasing dots per strip. Several chase patterns included. Strips can be cut to length. Also includes one rectangular EL lamp as an additional light source. Requires 4.5V DC. Great for marquees, signs and special effects!

### Desk Top Neon™ 32.95 ea

Perfect for the collector, these popular signs are encased in a handsome display case. These ready-to-operate signs replicate the original designs and animation. Distinctive boxes outline the history. Feature on/off switch and factory-installed batteries. Optional AC adapter sold separately. Measures: 4 x 3-1/2 x 6"

**NEW 502-1250** Las Vegas

**NEW 502-1450** Front Car Wash Sign

# MULTI-GRAPHIC ANIMATED WALL-MOUNTED SIGN KITS

These lighted signs add realism to any storefront. Each includes colorful graphic overlays for six businesses that provide full-color lighted lettering; plug-and-play electronics, on-off switch and battery holder that uses three AAA batteries (sold separately). Larger signs are suitable for HO and larger scales; smaller signs can be used in HO and N Scales. All are available in left- or right-handed orientations and are easily mounted to the front of your storefronts. Suitable for steam or diesel eras.

### Curved-Arrow Series #1

Sign features animated chase lights and arrow.

**1-1/8" Tall 26.95 ea**

**502-65811** Left
**502-65812** Right

### Downtown Businesses Series #1

Sign features animated chase lights and arrow.

**Large 2-1/4" Tall 26.95 ea**
**502-66811** Left
**502-66812** Right

**Small 1-1/2" Tall 24.95 ea**
**502-66821** Left
**502-66822** Right

### Downtown Businesses Series #2

Sign features animated rays.

**Large 2-13/32" Tall 26.95 ea**
**502-67811** Left
**502-67812** Right

**Small 1-1/2" Tall 24.95 ea**
**502-67821** Left
**502-67822** Right

LIGHT WORKS USA™
By *Miller Engineering*

### Hotel/Motel Series
Signs feature animated chase lights and arrow.

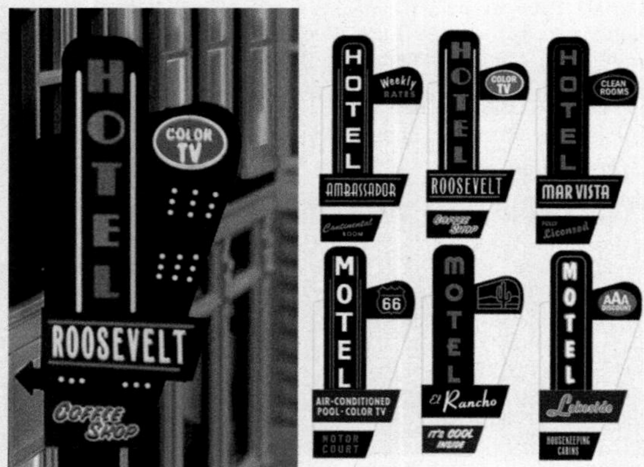


**Large 2-1/4" Tall 26.95 ea**
**502-68811** Left
**502-68812** Right

**Small 1-1/2" Tall 24.95 ea**
**502-68821** Left
**502-68822** Right

### Fan Series
Sign features animated curved fan of lights.

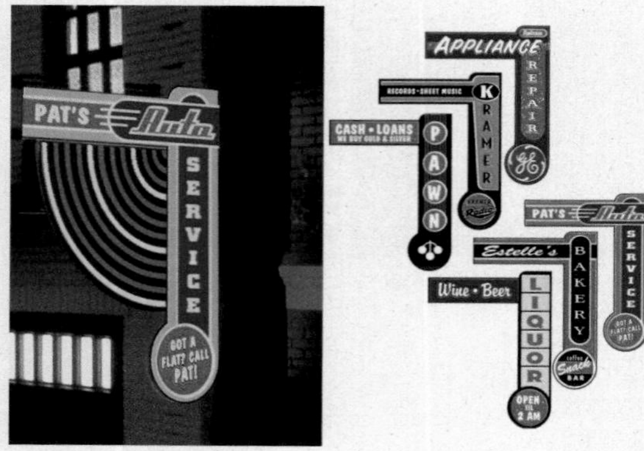


**Large 2" Tall 26.95 ea**
**502-69811** Left
**502-69812** Right

**Small 1-5/16" Tall 24.95 ea**
**502-69821** Left
**502-69822** Right

**NEW 502-1460** Back Car Wash Sign

**NEW 502-1650** Citgo

**NEW 502-1750** H&C Coffee

**NEW 502-1850** Dr Pepper

### AC Adapter

**NEW 502-4800** 4.5V AC Adapter **6.95**

## ANIMATED BILLBOARDS

Add authenticity to your layout's skyline. These animated billboards feature lighted "neon" lettering, moving graphics and simulated black supporting structure. All are wafer thin, but rigid enough to be freestanding. Each includes plug-and-play electronics, on-off switch and battery holder that uses three AAA batteries (sold separately). Large billboards are suitable for HO and larger scales; medium billboards can be used in N and HO Scales.

### Atlas Moving & Storage

**502-2081 32.95**
3-27/32" Wide x 2-3/8" Tall
The latitude lines are animated.

See What's Available at
**www.walthers.com**

### Shell

**502-7781 49.95**
4-1/2" Wide x 8-3/8" Tall
The original billboard was built in 1933 and later moved to its current location in Cambridge, MA. This eight-channel sequencing sign would be a real showpiece on any layout! The word "SHELL" lights up sequentially with the yellow shell border animated. Comes with photo etched stainless steel supports. Limited run.

### H&C Coffee

**502-7881 32.95**
3-5/16" Wide x 4" Tall
A beloved Roanoke Valley landmark built in 1946, the restored sign was moved to Shenandoah Hotel. Letters, cup and coffee pot are lit and the pouring coffee is animated.

### White Fuel

**502-7981 32.95**
3-13/32" Wide x 3-13/16" The original sign dates back to the 1930s when it sat atop the Westminster Hotel in Boston, MA. It was demolished in the 1970s. Letters are lit and animated dots emerge from the derrick.

### Blue Diamond Mfg. Co.

**502-8581** 3.75 x 3"
9.4 x 7.5cm **32.95**
Background is animated.

### Sandpiper Lounge

**502-8681** 2.7 x 3.5"
6.8 x 8.8cm **32.95**
"Open" flashes and bubbles in glass are animated.

### Citgo

**502-8781** 3.8 x 2.5"
9.5 x 6.3cm **32.95**
Background and Triangle are animated.

### Rylies Radio Repair

**502-8881** 3.84 x 3.37"
9.6 x 8.4cm **32.95**
Dots between tube's "anode" and "cathode" are animated.

### Galaxy Drive-In

**502-8981 32.95**
4" Wide x 2-3/4" Tall
Rings, planet and arrow are animated.

### Galaxy Tool & Die

**502-9081 32.95**
4" Wide x 2-3/4" Tall
Rings, planet and arrow are animated.

LIGHT WORKS USA™
By *Miller Engineering*

## MULTI-GRAPHIC ANIMATED ELECTROLUMINISCENT SIGN KITS

Animated electroluminiscent sign kits include peel-and-stick graphics that allow you to customize them for a variety of businesses. Kits include battery holder and all necessary electronics for plug-and-play installation. Signs require three AAA batteries (not included).

### Oval w/6 Overlays

**502-7181** Large 4" Tall **32.95**
**502-7182** Medium 2-5/8" Tall **28.95**

### Vertical w/6 Overlays

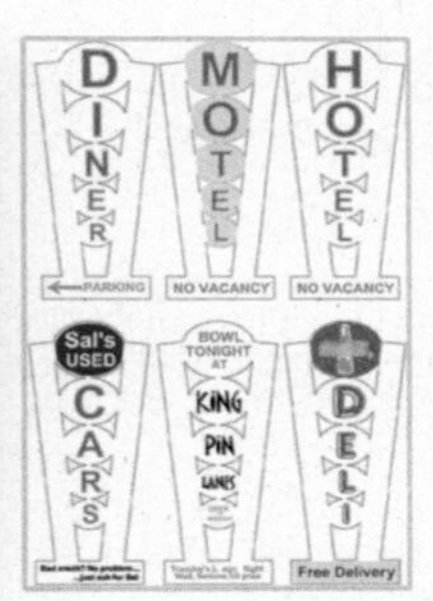


**502-7282** Medium 3" Tall **28.95**

### Round w/6 Overlays

**502-7382** Medium 3-1/4" Tall **28.95**

### Animated Arrow w/7 Overlays

**502-7482** Medium 3-3/4" Tall **28.95**

### Standard Plumbing Supply

Building not included

**502-9181** 1-3/4 x 3-1/2" **26.95**
Faucet turns on and off, water drops cascade down.

### City Light & Power

Features lighted bulb and lettering, animated wire to bulb.

**502-9281** Large 3-3/4 x 2-7/8" **32.95**

**502-9282** Medium 2-1/2 x 1-7/8" **25.95**

### I.C. Sparks

Features animated welding torch and flying sparks.

**502-9381** Large 4-1/4 x 2-3/8" **32.95**

**502-9382** Medium 2-1/2 x 1-7/8" **25.95**

### Patriot Flag Co.

Features animated flag.

**502-9481** Large 2-1/8 x 3-5/16" **32.95**

**502-9482** Medium 1-1/2 x 2-5/16" **26.95**

### Arctic Refrigeration

Thermometer moves down as icicles grow longer.

**502-9581** Large 4 x 2-5/8" **32.95**

**502-9582** Medium 2-13/16 x 1-13/16" **26.95**

### Polar Ice

Background features animated falling snow.

**502-9681** Large 3-13/16 x 2-1/2" **32.95**

**502-9682** Medium 2-5/8 x 1-3/4" **26.95**

### Noise-R-Us

Background features animated fireworks.

**502-9781** Large 2-1/8 x 3-5/16" **32.95**

**502-9782** Medium 1-1/2 x 2-5/16" **26.95**

### DeKays Dental Supply

Toothpaste tube squeezes out toothpaste.

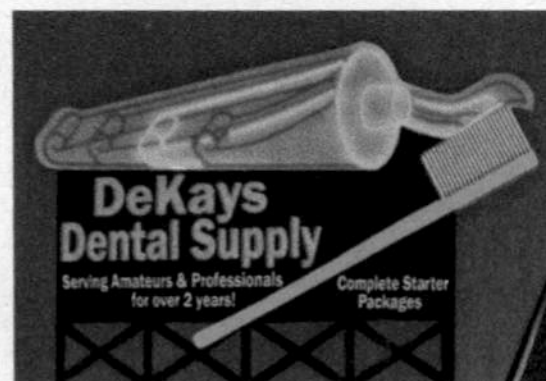


Building not included

**502-9881** Large 3-11/16 x 2-1/2" **32.95**

**502-9882** Medium 2-5/8 x 1-3/4" **26.95**

## ANIMATED ROADSIDE BILLBOARDS

These kits include an etched stainless steel support structure. Unpainted metal parts are simply folded together and glued using cyanoacrylate (CA) cement.

### Gulf

**502-8181 42.95**
4-5/16" Wide x 5-13/16" Tall
Features illuminated letters; "Gulf" letters light up sequentially.

### Amtrak

**502-8281 42.95**
4-5/16" Wide x 5-1/8" Tall
Features animated arrow and illuminated white and red letters.

### Elephant Car Wash

**502-8381 42.95**
4-5/16" Wide x 6" Tall
Features illuminated letters and animated spray from elephant's trunk.

### Union City Speedway

**502-8481 42.95**
4-5/16" Wide x 5-3/32" Tall
Features illuminated letters; car tires and road markers are animated.

LIGHT WORKS USA
By Miller Engineering

### Sherwin Williams

**502-9981 32.95**
4" Wide x 1-29/32" Tall
Covers the Earth.

## WALL-MOUNT SIGNS

Kits are designed to mount through a slot in your structure's wall.

### Amtrak 26.96 ea

1-39/64" Wide x 45/64" Tall

Features illuminated letters and animated arrow.

**502-64811** Left Hand

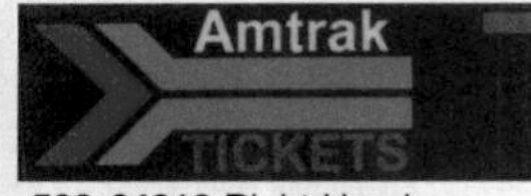


**502-64812** Right Hand

## ELECTRO-LUMINESCENT SIGN KITS

Left and right version may be mounted together to create a sign that lights on both sides.

### Bentens Bar & Grill

**502-12011** Medium, Left **14.95**
**502-12012** Medium, Right **14.95**
**502-12021** Small, Left **13.95**
**502-12022** Small, Right **13.95**

### Cafe

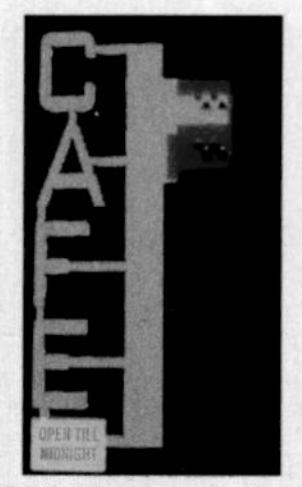


**502-13011** Large, Left **16.95**
**502-13012** Large, Right **16.95**

### Hotel

**502-14011** Large, Left **16.95**
**502-14012** Large, Right **16.95**

### Star Drug 14.95 ea

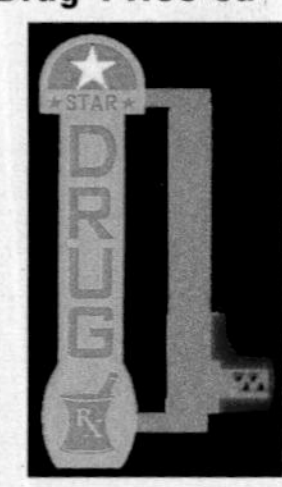


**502-31021** Medium, Left
**502-31022** Medium, Right

### Mid State Bank 14.95 ea

**502-14411** Medium, Left
**502-14412** Medium, Right

### Open

**502-36011** Large, Left **15.95**
**502-36012** Large, Right **15.95**
**502-36021** Medium, Left **14.95**
**502-36022** Medium, Right **14.95**

### Pawn Shop

**502-37011** Large, Left **15.95**
**502-37012** Large, Right **15.95**
**502-37021** Medium, Left **14.95**
**502-37022** Medium, Right **14.95**

### Pizza (Round)

**502-38011** Large, Left **15.95**
**502-38012** Large, Right **15.95**

### Theater

**502-41011** Large, Left **16.95**
**502-41012** Large, Right **16.95**
**502-41021** Medium, Left **15.95**
**502-41022** Medium, Right **15.95**

## Horizontal

Horizontal signs are designed to mount on a roof or wall.

### Gilmor Hotel

**502-1801** Large **17.95**

### Diner

**502-1901** Large **17.95**

### Hotel

**502-2101** Large **14.25**

### Ambassador Hotel

**502-5201** Large **19.95**

### Union Station

**502-5601** Large **22.95**
**502-5602** Medium **17.95**
**502-5603** Small **14.95**

### Parkway Diner

**502-2801** Large **19.95**

### Hotel Belmont

**502-2901** Large **17.95**
**502-2902** Medium **14.95**

### Clock

Left and right are the same.

**502-3201** Large **13.95**
**502-3202** Medium **12.95**

## ANIMATED ELECTRO-LUMINESCENT SIGN KITS

These signs are created with the same EL material as the non-animated signs, with all the benefits and more. Each kit is pre-programmed with 36 different chase patterns. Each pattern has its own action. Once a pattern is chosen, it is stored in memory and is remembered each time the sign is turned on again. The patterns can be changed over and over again.

## Vertical

### Cafe & Arrow

**502-13811** Large, Left **22.95**
**502-13812** Large, Right **22.95**
**502-13821** Medium, Left **20.95**
**502-13822** Medium, Right **20.95**



### Hotel

**502-14811** Large, Left **22.95**
**502-14812** Large, Right **22.95**
**502-14821** Medium, Left **20.95**
**502-14822** Medium, Right **20.95**

### Animated Theater Sign

**502-41811** Left **23.95**
**502-41812** Right **23.95**
72 electroluminescent lights scroll around the theater sign. 41 different chase patterns. Comes ready to run. .015" thick.

### O'Malley's Bar

**502-54811** Large, Left **22.95**
**502-54812** Large, Right **22.95**
**502-54821** Medium, Left **21.95**
**502-54822** Medium, Right **21.95**

## Horizontal

### Cafe

**502-1781** Large **22.95**
**502-1782** Medium **20.95**

### Diner

DINER

**502-1981** Large **22.95**
**502-1982** Medium **20.95**

LIGHT WORKS USA
By Miller Engineering

### Hotel

**502-2181** Large **22.95**

**502-2182** Medium **20.95**

### Blue-Star Diner

**502-5581** Large **22.95**

**502-5582** Medium **21.95**

### Shamrock Hotel

**502-6181** Large **22.95**

**502-6182** Medium **21.95**

## LIGHTING ACCESSORIES

### EL Experimenter's Kits

Turn your ideas into working models with these complete accessory kits. The heart of each set is a specially designed, wafer-thin electroluminiscent (EL) lamp. It's easily cut and can be used to make several lamps. The sets also come with a ready-to-use power supply and an assortment of color overlays for special effects. A detailed instruction book provides tips and ideas for using EL lamps.

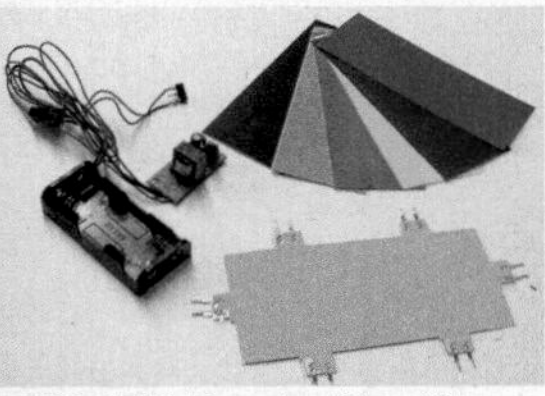

**502-2501** Regular Sign Kit **22.95**
1-45/64 x 3-3/4" Makes up to six signs.

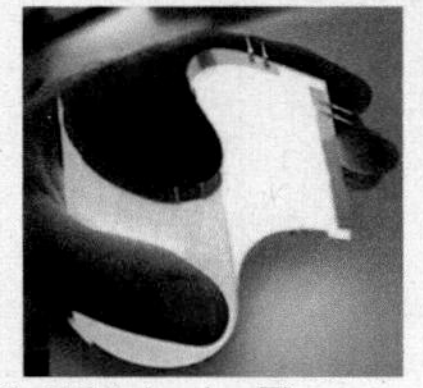

**502-2504** Jumbo EL Experimenter's Kit **32.95**
4 x 6" Makes up to 14 signs.

**502-2502** Animator's Kit **28.95**
Contains all the same features of non-animated kit with the addition of being able to create animation. Includes 36 pre-programmed chase patterns. Each chase pattern has five channels, meaning you can light up to five segments.The last chase pattern picked will be remembered when the unit is turned on again. Chase patterns can be changed over and over again.

### Color Overlay Set

**502-2601** Small **6.95**

**502-2602** Large **10.95**

### Electroluminiscent Lamp Only

**502-4301** Small 1-3/4 x 3-3/4" (white) **15.95**

**502-4401** Small 1-3/4 x 3-3/4" (red) **16.95**

### Chase Light Driver Circuit

**502-2702 15.95**
Same circuit used in 502-2502. Includes AA battery holder.

### Flasher Unit

**502-4701 5.95**
Converts any of the electro-luminescent sign kits into flashing signs. Flashes at a fixed rate of 1/2 second on and 1/2 second off.

### Electroluminescent Wire Kit 22.95 ea

EL wire is a very robust material that produces a soft neon-like glow, can be bent to almost any shape, with a diameter of .090". EL wire produces no heat and is perfect for illuminating the perimeter of buildings or hard to reach places where lighting is desired. It can also be easily cut to length. Each kit comes with a three foot length of EL wire and driver board. Requires soldering to hook up wire to the included driver circuit.

502-25031

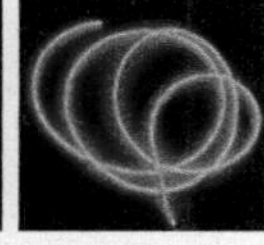

502-25032

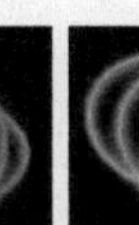

502-25033

502-25034

**502-25031** White

**502-25032** Red

**502-25033** Blue

**502-25034** Green

### Marquee Chase Light Kit

**502-875052 32.95**
Includes a special white LED and 60 fiber optic strands to simulate moving lights found on theaters everywhere. All electronics come fully assembled and are powered by a 9V battery, not included. Kit also comes with step-by-step instructions.

### Miniature Fluorescent Lamps

Kits consist of two fluorescent lamps and one driver circuit. Lamps are extremely bright, produce very little heat and have a life of over 15,000 hours. All lamps have a diameter of .160" and require a constant 12V DC source. Lamps should not be run with less than 12V.

**502-712** AC Flourescent Lamp Adaptor 12V (Runs 6 lamps, sold separately) **16.95**

**502-713** 5" Flourescent Lamp Extension Cable **2.25**

**502-719** Flourescent Lamp Mounting Kit (For use w/1 lamp, sold separately) **2.50**

**502-721** 2" Lamp w/Driver Circuit **19.95**

**502-722** 2" Dual Lamps w/Driver Circuit **24.95**

**502-741** 4" Lamp w/Driver Circuit **19.50**

**502-742** 4" Lamp w/Driver Circuit pkg(2) **22.95**

**502-781** 8" Lamp w/Driver Circuit **19.95**

**502-782** 8" Lamp w/Driver Circuit pkg(2) **24.95**

## BILLBOARD SUPPORT

**502-990 7.50**
Includes an etched stainless steel support structure. Unpainted metal parts are simply folded together and glued using cyanoacrylate (CA) cement.

### Photo Etch Supports

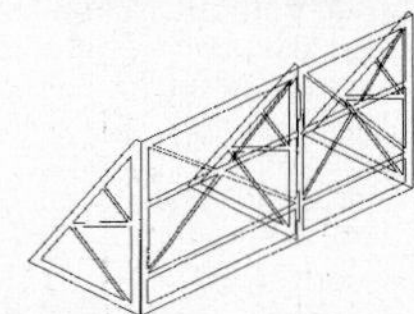

**502-4501** Large **10.95**
Support for large, horizontal electro-luminescent lamps.

**502-4502** Medium **10.95**
Support for medium, horizontal electro-luminescent signs.

### Wall Adapter

**502-4801** 3-Volt **6.95**
Eliminates the need for a battery pack. Will run up to five signs. For non-animated signs only.

## CATALOG

**502-1 3.00**
Handy book includes full-size printouts of all simulated neon signs and dimensions for all structures.

## CONVERTER MODULE FOR ANIMATED SIGNS

**502-4804 12.95**
An input voltage from 5 to 17 volts, AC or DC, will produce a 4.5 volt output. Converter Module can connect up to six Miller Engineering animated neon signs. Maximum current draw is 500ma.

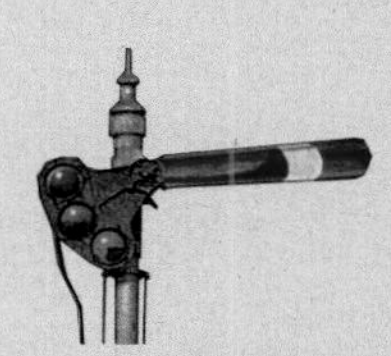

### Look Out For The Cars

With a wide variety of signals and signs available for all eras, detailing grade crossings is easier than ever. Like any right-of-way detail, grade crossings can add an extra bit of authenticity to your layout. Here's a bit of information about typical installations.

As you drive along any highway in the U.S., you'll know a crossing is on the horizon when you pass the circular yellow advance warning sign placed several hundred feet before the tracks. As you approach the tracks, you'll often see "RR XING" pavement markings too.

Now that you're at the tracks, there are many different kinds of signals in use, the most common being a pair of crossbucks. Depending on road and rail traffic, funding sources and local laws, flashing lights, gates, overhead lights, bells, median strips, stop or yield signs and even red strobes may be present. Along the tracks, a relay cabinet and storage battery box is usually just off the edge of the roadway.

During the steam era, there were many kinds of crossing signals. Wig-wags, Grizwold signals with rotating stop signs and others were also used. Many busy crossings rated a flagman stationed in a nearby shanty who manually lowered gates and flagged down motorists.

## NEW PRODUCTS

### Signal House/Mast Combinations

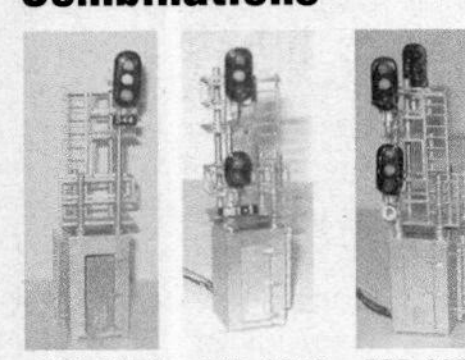
525-1071 525-1072 525-1073

**NEW 525-1071** 3-Light 1 Pair **45.99**

**NEW 525-1072** 2-Light **49.99**

**NEW 525-1073** Bi-Directional D-Type 3-Head **55.99**

## SIGNALS

All brass construction, assembled, painted and lighted.

### Position Lights

**525-1040** PRR 8-Light **39.99**

**525-1041** PRR Position Light w/Absolute Stop **39.99**

**525-1210** B&O Color Position **29.99**

**525-1270** N&W 2-Light **19.99**

### Semaphores

**525-1000** 3-Light Upper Quadrant **37.99**

**525-1010** 2-Light Lower Quadrant **29.99**

### Ground Type Dwarf

525-1100

525-1110

**525-1100** 2-Light **11.99**

**525-1110** 3-Light **12.99**

**525-1130** 3-Light Left-Hand Ground **12.99**

**525-1140** 3-Light Right-Hand Ground **11.99**

### Upper-Quadrant Semaphores w/3V Bulb 29.99 ea

Signals come pre-wired with a 3V bulb and necessary dropping resistor attached. Activation can be accomplished via the brass rod in the pole and protruding from the base. Both are compatible with the activation system from Circuitron (sold separately).

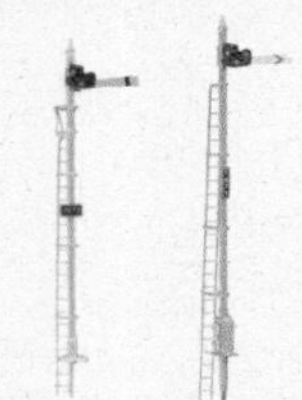
525-1002 525-1003

**525-1002** 3-Light Upper Quadrant No Relay Cabinet

**525-1003** 3-Light Upper Quadrant w/Relay Cabinet Base

### D-Type Color Lights

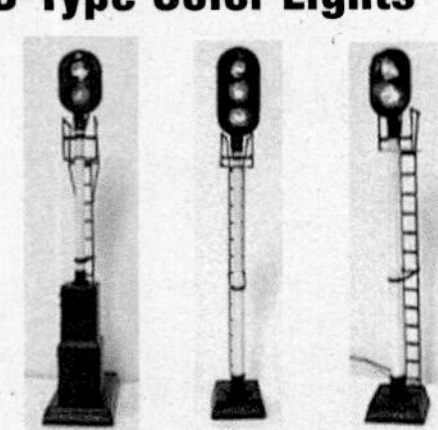
525-1020 525-1031 525-1081

**525-1020** 2-Light w/Relay Base **19.99**

**525-1023** 3-Light w/Relay Base **19.99**

**525-1031** 3-Light Board (black) **18.99**

**525-1032** 3-Light Board (silver) **18.99**

**525-1033** Double Board 3 Over 3 **31.99**

**525-1038** Double Board 3 Over 2 **29.99**

**525-1081** 2-Light Board (black) **17.99**

**525-1082** 2-Light Board (silver) **17.99**

**525-1088** Double Board 2-Over-2 **29.99**

**525-1089** 1-Light Double Board 1 Over 1 **29.99**

### G-Type Tri-Color

**525-1060** Double Target 3 Over 3 Light **29.99**

### G-Type w/LEDs

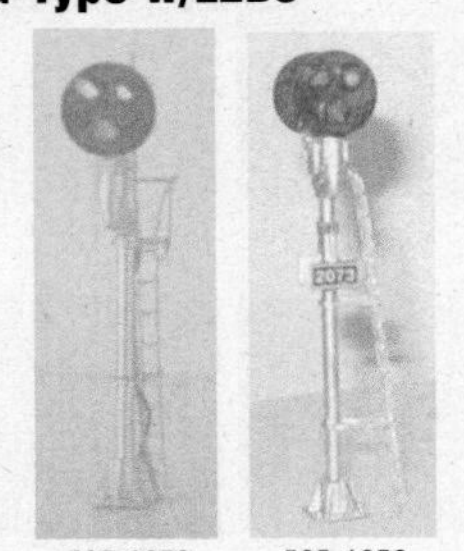
525-1053 525-1056

**525-1053** Single Head **32.99**

**525-1054** Double Head **36.99**

**525-1056** Bi-Directional Heads **36.99**

### Signal Heads w/LEDs

Heads include mountings for use on signal bridges and other structures.

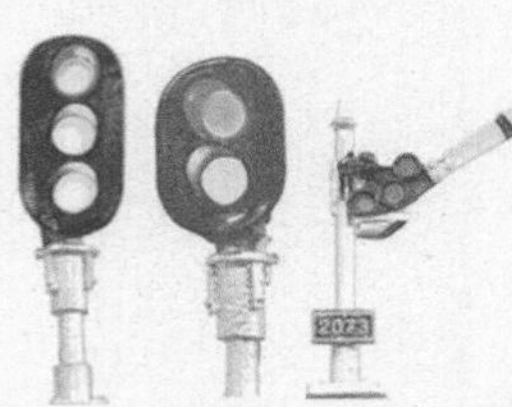
525-1036 525-1083 525-1004

**525-1036** D-Type 3 Light **17.99**

**525-1055** G-Type 3 Light **19.99**

**525-1083** D-Type 2 Light **14.99**

**525-1004** Upper-Quadrant Semaphore **19.99**

### Target

Signals exact scale. All brass with bi-color LEDs.

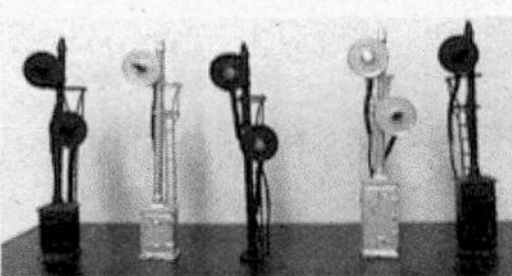

**525-1341** Single Target Silver **19.99**

**525-1342** Single Target Black **19.99**

**525-1343** Single Target Silver Low Cabinet **22.99**

**525-1346** Single Target Black High Cabinet **22.99**

**525-1347** Double Target Silver **24.99**

**525-1348** Double Target Black **24.99**

**525-1349** Double Target Silver Low Cabinet **26.99**

**525-1350** Double Target Black Low Cabinet **26.99**

**525-1351** Double Target Silver High Cabinet **26.99**

Items listed below are available by Special Order (see Legend Page).

**525-1344** Single Target Black Low Cabinet **22.99**

**525-1345** Single Target Silver High Cabinet **22.99**

**525-1352** Double Target Black High Cabinet **26.99**

### SA Searchlight

**525-1220** Triple Single Target **19.99**

### Ground Dwarf Signals 15.99 Pair

Exact scale, all brass, painted, with LEDs.

**525-1290** Silver w/Red LED

**525-1291** Black w/Red LED

**525-1292** Silver w/Green LED

**525-1293** Black w/Green LED

**525-1294** Silver w/Amber LED

**525-1295** Black w/Amber LED

### Train Order

**525-1150** 3-Light **25.99**

### Signal Disc Heads-Brass

**525-4103** 3-Light Board **2.59**

**525-4104** PRR 8-Light **5.59**

**525-4106** 3-Light Target **2.99**

**525-4107** Small Single Target **2.49**

**525-4108** 2-Light Board **2.49**

**525-4122** Single Target **2.49**

**525-4130** N&W 2-Light **2.29**

### Signal Accessories - Brass

**525-1337** Relay Cabinet-Silver Low pkg(2) **6.99**

**525-1338** Relay Cabinet-Black Low pkg(2) **6.99**

**525-1339** Relay Cabinet-Silver High pkg(2) **6.99**

**525-1340** Relay Cabinet-Black High pkg(2) **6.99**

### Blue Flags & Signs

**525-1308** pkg(18) **19.95**
Set includes 18 different safety signs; all brass, painted and lettered. Features mounting for rail head and ground. Includes stop, men-at-work, safety first, danger and more.

## SIGNAL BRIDGE

Injection-molded plastic kits.

### Standard Two Track

**525-4009** Silver

**525-4010** Black

### Cantilever

**525-4001** 1-Track Silver **17.99**

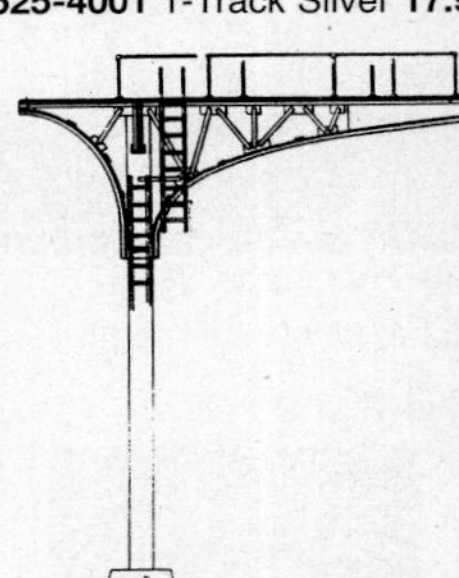

**525-4002** 1-Track Black **17.95**

**525-4003** 2-Track Silver **19.95**

**525-4004** 2-Track Black **19.95**

### I-Beam

**525-4006** I-Beam 2 Track **13.95**

### 2-Target Signal Masts 24.99 ea

All-brass signal masts for mounting on signal bridges and other structures. Assemblies include bi-polar/bi-color LEDs.

**525-1303** Black

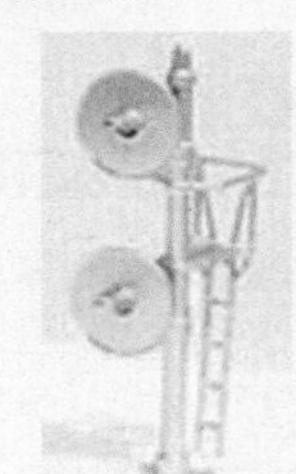

**525-1304** Silver

## CROSSINGS & CROSSING SYSTEMS

Signals are all brass, Exact-Scale painted and lettered. All gates swing freely but are not motorized. Signals work with most flasher circuits (sold separately).

### Crossing Gates 27.95 (1 Pair)

525-1171

**525-1170** "A" Arm Red & White

**525-1171** "A" Arm Black & White

**525-1172** Bar Arm Red & White

**525-1173** Bar Arm Black & White

## N.J. International

### Pedestal Type 1 Pair 45.99

Pedestal-type crossing gates feature LEDs facing both directions.

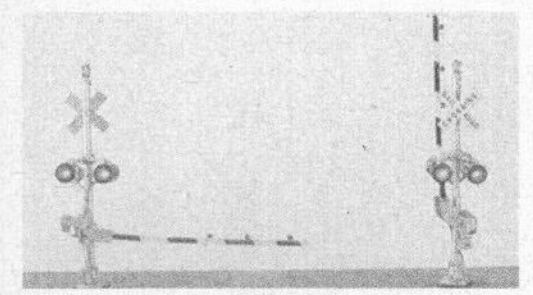

**525-1164** Red/White Arm

**525-1165** Black/White Arm

### Crossbucks w/Gate & LEDs 39.95 (Pair)

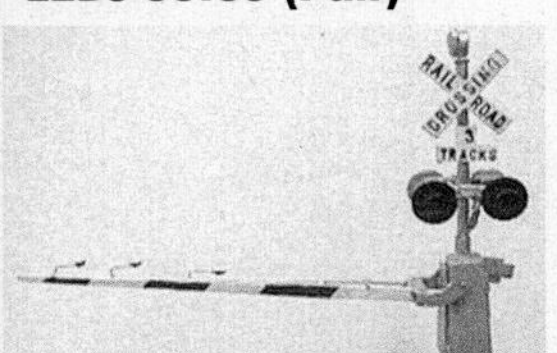

**525-1160** "A" Arm Red & White

**525-1161** "A" Arm Black & White

**525-1162** Bar Arm Red & White

**525-1163** Bar Arm Black & White

### Modern Over-Road Grade Crossing

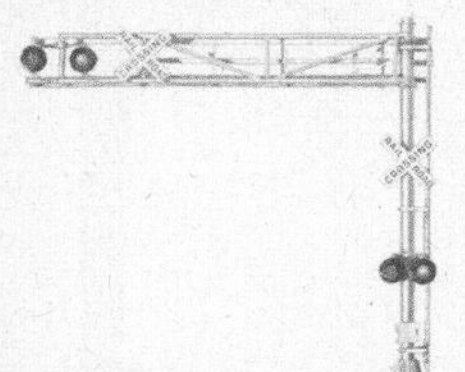

**525-1191** Single Pole Short Arm **59.99**

### Crossbucks

**525-1095** 1 Pair **29.95**
With LEDs facing both directions.

### Wig Wag Crossings

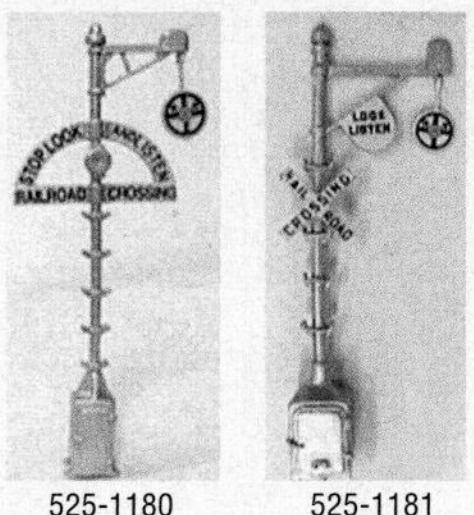

525-1180 525-1181

**525-1180** Wig Wag pkg(2) **25.95**

**525-1181** UP Type Wig Wag pkg(2) **29.95**

### Crossbuck w/Bulbs & Lenses

**525-1090** Crossbuck **16.99**

**525-1190** Over the Road **38.99**

### Crossing Flashers

**525-8020** Flasher Module **19.99**

**525-8109** Flasher & HO Crossbuck **36.99**

## SIGNS

Each sign features all-brass construction and predrilled flat base with hole for mounting with a track nail or spike.

### Crossing Signs pkg(2) 9.99 ea

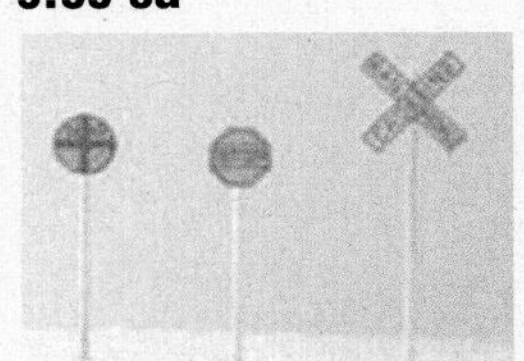

**525-1240** Round Advance Warning pre-1950s pkg(2)

**525-1250** Railroad Stop Sign (yellow & black)

**525-1260** Crossbucks 90° Angle



## STREET LIGHTS

**525-1980** Street Lights w/Simulated Cast-Iron Post (green) pkg(3) **8.99**

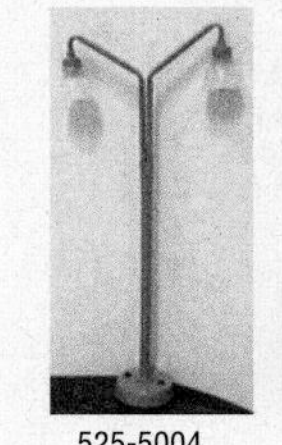

525-5004 525-5005

**525-5003** Boulevard Light, Single Arm **11.99**

**525-5004** Boulevard Light Double Arm **15.99**

**525-5005** Street Light **9.99**

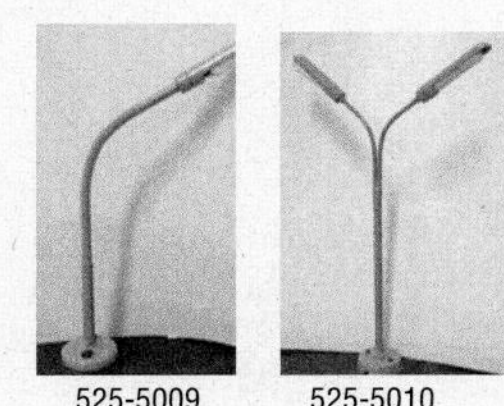

525-5009 525-5010

**525-5009** Boulevard Lamp **9.99**

**525-5010** Boulevard Light, Double Arm **14.99**

**525-5013** Double-Arm Street Lamp **13.99**

## TRAFFIC LIGHT

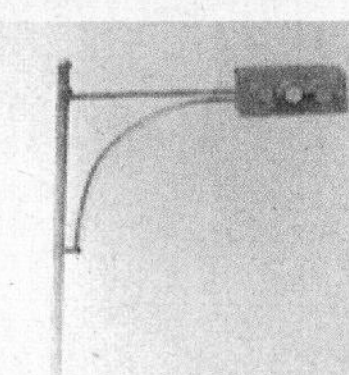

**525-1978 15.99**

## TOWERS

### Metal

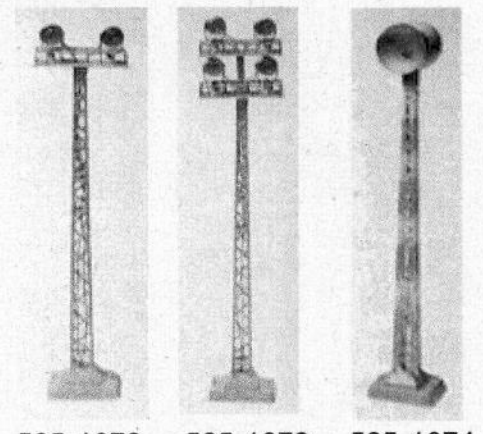

525-1972 525-1973 525-1974

**525-1972** Twin Searchlight **16.99**

**525-1973** Quad Searchlight **20.99**

## ACTIVATION SYSTEM

### Servo Master Activation System

Servo-Master activation system works with crossing gates and semaphores. Each system is capable of operating two crossing gates with flashing lights or two semaphores.

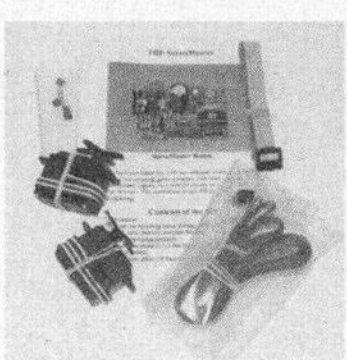

**525-8000 119.99**

**NEW 525-8001** Expander Kit **59.99**

**NEW 525-8002** Grade Crossing Flasher Controller **55.99**

## LINESIDE SIGNAL CABINET

**525-1359** pkg(2) **9.99**
All-brass kit features doors that open. Use at any location where signals are located for added realism.

### Plastic

**525-1974** Microwave Dish Antenna (plastic) **13.99**

## SCALE STRUCTURES LIMITED

### Billboards pkg(2) 17.95 ea

Kits include wood and metal parts, plus assorted four-color signs.

**650-1108** 1920s

**650-1155** #2

## PIKESTUFF

### Crossbucks

**541-1017** pkg(4) **4.25**
Set includes plastic molded parts, decals and assembly instructions.

## PREISER

IMPORTED FROM GERMANY BY WALTHERS

Items listed in blue ink may not be available at all times (see Legend Page).

## NEW PRODUCT

### Signs

**NEW 590-31018** Emergency/ Construction Barriers & Signs **17.99**

### Signs

Sign kits include styrene masts and adhesive signs.

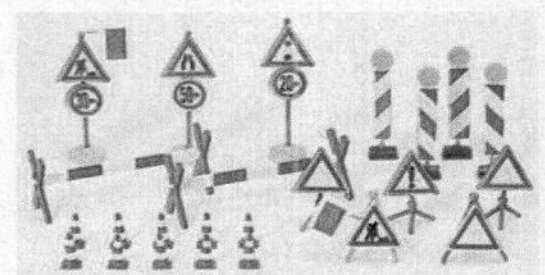

**590-17176** Traffic & Construction Signs **23.99**

**590-17208** Advertising Boards **8.99**

**590-18203** Sign Assortment pkg(40) **13.99**

# SIGNALS, DETECTION UNITS & SIGNS

Flexible system of signal heads, LEDs and accessories can be used to create a variety of working signals. All parts are molded in black styrene and can be illuminated using LEDs or fiber optics.

## SIGNALS

Each kit builds a complete signal with target, mast, ladder, base and finial. Small LEDs and resistors also included.

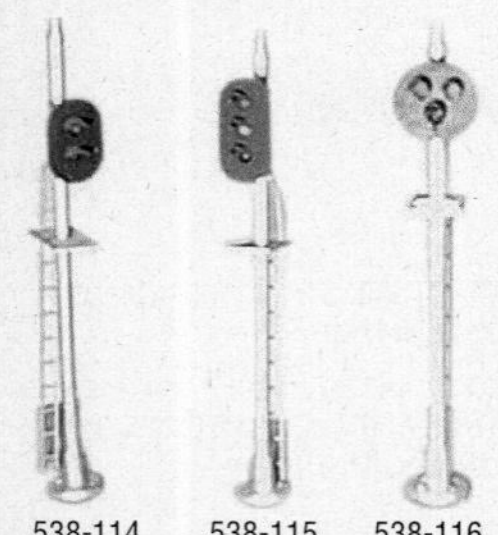

538-114 538-115 538-116

**538-114** Two Light **9.95**

**538-115** Three Light **10.95**

**538-116** Three Light, Circular **10.95**

538-117 538-120

**538-117** PRR Intermediate **17.95**

**538-118** PRR Absolute **17.95**

**538-120** UP/DRGW Hooded **10.95**

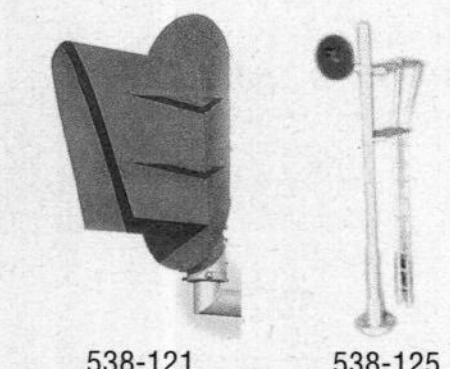

538-121 538-125

**538-121** UP/DRGW Hooded Targets Only pkg(3) **5.95**

**538-125** Single **10.95**

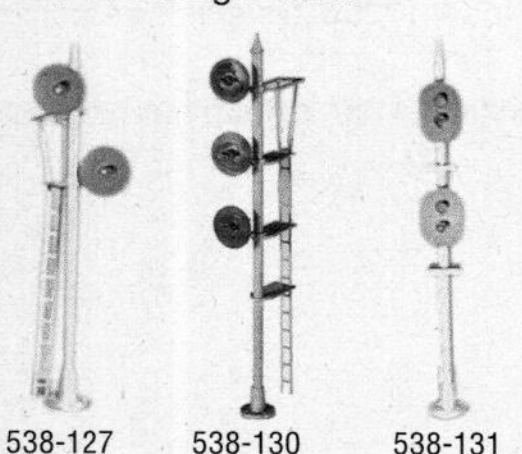

538-127 538-130 538-131

**538-127** 2 Target Single **16.95**

**538-130** Triple Target Single **19.95**

**538-131** 2 Over 2 **15.95**

538-132 538-133 538-134

**538-132** 3 Over 2 **16.95**

**538-133** 3 Over 3 **17.95**

**538-134** 3 Over 3, Circular **17.95**

### Dwarf Signals

Signals change to colors shown when polarity is reversed. Great for use as turnout indicators.

Single Lite Double Lite

**Single Lite pkg(2) 8.95 ea**
538-122 Red/Green

**538-135** Red/Yellow

**Double Lite pkg(2) 7.50 ea**
**538-123** Red/Green

**538-136** Red/Yellow

### Dwarf Turnout Indicators

**538-140** pkg(10) **27.95**
Single two-color (red/green) LED with three leads.

### Assembled Block Signals

Ready for service anywhere along your line, these signals come fully assembled and complete with bi-color (red/green) LEDs. Can be operated with any detection system designed for LEDs. Poles are finished in silver, with black targets, like those used on most prototype roads.

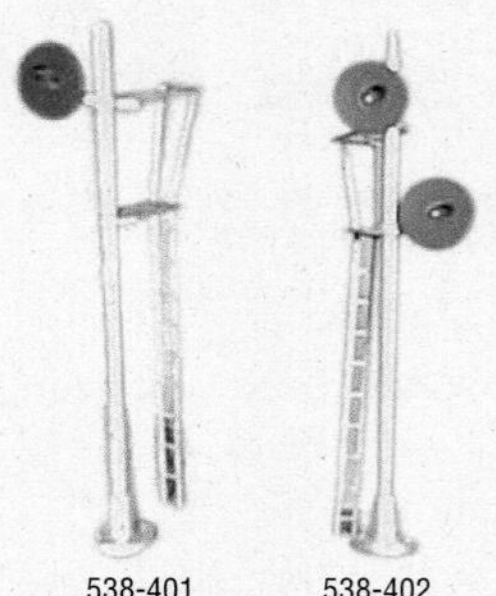

538-401 538-402

**538-401** Single Target **21.95**

**538-402** Double Target **31.50**

### "Searchlight" Signal Light Targets

Each set includes three heads with brackets and finials. Based on prototype introduced in 1920s and still in use on many railroads.

**538-102** Single pkg(3) **3.95**

**538-103** Double pkg(3) **4.50**

**538-104** Triple pkg(3) **4.50**

### Crossing Flashers

**538-113** pkg(2) **17.95**
Easy-to-build with targets, crossbucks, base, mast, red LEDs and decals.

### Crossbucks

**538-112** pkg(4) **4.95**
Each package includes two each of two different size crossbucks.

### "Position Light" Signal Heads

Commonly used by eastern railroads, these signals were introduced in 1915 and use lights in various positions to prevent misreading signals. Each includes accessories.

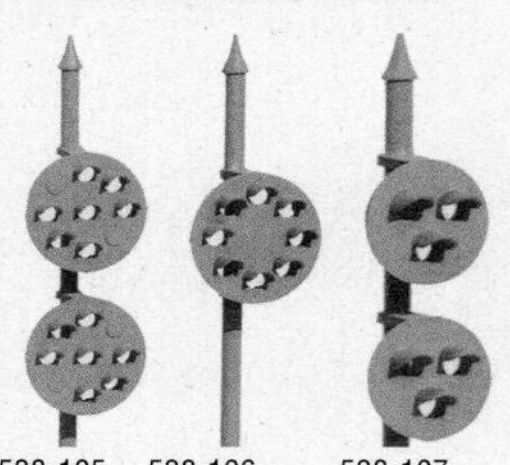

538-105 538-106 538-107

**538-105** PRR/N&W pkg(6) **7.95**

**538-106** B&O pkg(3) **5.95**

**538-107** NYC/ROCK pkg(3) **4.50**

### Signal Hook-up Wire

**538-304** 28 Gauge **2.95**

### Sampler Set

**538-108 7.95**
Includes one of each type of signal head (seven different types), with bases, walkway grating, brackets and more.

### LEDs

Correct sizes for press fit into signal heads.

**.088" Square pkg(3) 3.50 ea**

**538-109** Green

**538-110** Red

**538-111** Yellow

**1/8" (3mm)**
**538-137** Red pkg(6) **3.50**

**538-138** Green pkg(6) **3.50**

**538-139** Yellow pkg(6) **3.50**

**538-141** White pkg(3) **5.95**

**Bi-Color**
**538-126** Red/Green pkg(2) **4.95**
Changes color when polarity is reversed, measures 1/8" 3mm.

## SIGNAL BRIDGES

### With Pennsylvania Position Lights

**538-150** 2 Track **22.95**

**538-153** 4 Track **24.95**

### With Union Switch & Signal 1-, 2- & 3-Light Targets

**538-151** 2 Track **22.95**

**538-154** 4 Track **24.95**

Prototype Photo Shown

### With Semaphores

**538-152** 2 Track **24.95**

**538-155** 4 Track **27.95**

### Cantilevered Signal Bridges

**538-101** C&O **17.95**
Prototype at Peach Creek, West Virginia. Can be installed on single or double track. Includes wire handrails and assembly instructions.

**538-99** UP/DRGW **23.95**
Includes hooded UP targets, LEDs and resistors.

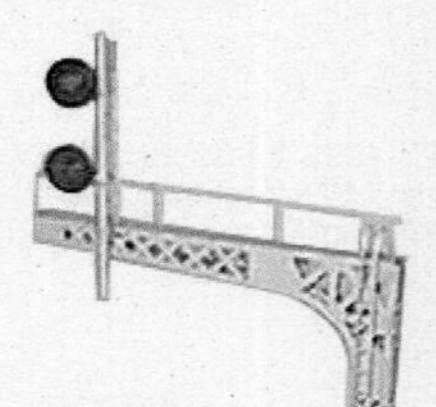

**538-129** Single Searchlight Bridge Unit **12.95**
Kit includes mast and LEDs to add single searchlight to any signal bridge.

## S&S Hobby Products
*"Realism in Model Railroading"*

### Road Sign Kits
Kits include etched brass signs, steel posts and color decals.

**643-300** Stop Sign Set pkg(12) **8.99**
Includes four Stop signs, two Railroad Crossing signs, two Pedestrian Crossing signs, plus one each 25, 35, 45 and 55 MPH speed limit sign.

**643-301** Route Sign Set pkg(10) **6.99**
Includes two each: Slippery When Wet, Soft Shoulder, No Parking, Do Not Stop on Tracks and Route (with decals to select your own route numbers).

**643-302** Interstate Sign Set pkg(10) **7.99**
Includes two each: Train Station, Bus Stop, Yield, Do Not Enter and Interstate (with decals to select your own interstate numbers).

**643-303** Street Sign Set pkg(10) **7.99**
Includes two each: Fallout Shelter, No U Turn, No Passing, Truck Route and Stop Ahead.

**643-304** Smokey Sign Set pkg(8) **8.99**
Includes two each: Smokey Bear, Deer Crossing, National Forest and Falling Rock.

## TOMAR INDUSTRIES

Assembled signals are painted and wired with bulbs or LEDs and feature brass construction. Complete instructions included.

## NEW PRODUCTS

### Dwarf Searchlights
**NEW 81-875sl** Single (silver) **10.30**

**NEW 81-875bl** Single (black) **10.30**

**NEW 81-876sl** Double (silver **13.50**

**NEW 81-876bl** Double (black) **13.50**
Union Switch & Signal Searchlights

**NEW 81-872** Single Head **31.75**

**NEW 81-873** Double Head **41.75**

**NEW 81-874** Offset Double Head **42.75**

### Order Board
**NEW 81-890** US&S Lower Quadrant Train Order Board **57.25**

### B&O Signals
#### Color Position Lights
**NEW 81-880** Three Aspect **38.60**

**NEW 81-886** Four Aspect **44.05**

## SIGNALS

### C&O-Style Signals

81-845CO 81-850CO

**81-845CO** Upper-Quadrant Train Order Board **57.70**

**81-850CO** Three-Light Dwarf Signal **11.50**

**81-866CO** Two-Head, Three-Light Vertical Signal **48.25**

### Signals w/Snow Hoods
**81-8561** Three-Light Vertical **23.50**

**81-8571** Two-Light Vertical **21.55**

**81-8661** Two Head, Three-Light over Three-Light Vertical **45.10**

**81-8671** Two Head, Three-Light over Two-Light Vertical **41.50**

## SWITCH STANDS

81-851 81-848

**81-851 15.25**
Finished in black with red and green lenses, red and white target blades. Illuminated with 1.5V bulb, rotates 360°.

**81-848** 90° Operator **7.30**
Assembled, links switch machine to switch stand. Indexes to 90°.

### Dwarf Signals
Feature black finish.

**81-847** Two Light **9.80**
Yellow over red.

**81-852** Two Light **9.80**
Green over red.

**81-850** Three Light **11.50**
Red, yellow and green LEDs.

### Searchlight Signals
Three colors from one LED.

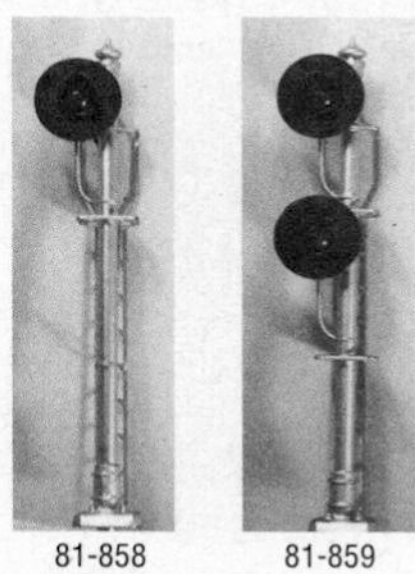
81-858 81-859

**81-858** Single Head **29.15**

**81-859** Double Head **38.70**

**81-861** Triple Head **57.70**

### Semaphore Signals
**81-842** Double-Headed Semaphore **48.45**
Features 1.5V lamps with green-yellow-red lens and two three-position arms.

**81-843** 3-Color Searchlight Train Order Signal **38.80**

**81-844** Lower-Quadrant Train Order Board **52.45**
Features a 1.5V lamp with red-red-green lens and a three-position arm.

**81-845** Assembled Upper Quadrant Train Order Board **52.45**

**81-853** 3-Position Semaphore **26.20**
1.5V bulb.

**81-854** 3-Position Semaphore **28.35**
With relay box base, 1.5V bulb.

**81-860** Assembled Lower Quadrant Semaphore w/Relay Base **28.35**

### Vertical Signals
**81-843** Assembled Train Order **38.80**

**81-856** Three Light w/LEDs **21.90**

**81-857** Two Light **19.90**

**81-866** Two Head 3 Light **43.00**

**81-867** Two Head **39.35**

### Three-Position Blade Signal Mechanism
**81-870 44.65**
For use with three-position semaphores and train order boards. Kit contains Tortoise Switch Machine, Remote Signal Activator and Card Connector with Circuit Board. One kit is needed for each signal arm.

### Flasher Unit

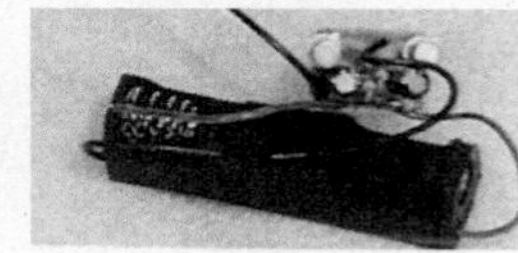

**81-823 10.50**

### Signal Resistors Kit pkg(2) .30 ea
Signal resistors for Tomar signals using LEDs. Resistors limit the current to the LEDs, allowing usage of higher supply voltage than the LED rating.

**81-864390** Green

**81-864560** Yellow

**81-8641500** Red

### Crossing Signals
**81-862** Without Gate pkg(2) **49.30**
Features operating LEDs.

**81-863** With Gates pkg(2) **157.45**
Features four LEDs: two to the front, and two to the back.

### Railroad Crossbucks
Completely assembled, painted and decaled solid brass signs.

**81-868** pkg(2) **12.10**

**81-869** With Track Numbers pkg(2) **13.15**

### Signal Ladder
**81-899** 12" pkg(2) **10.45**

### Target Signals
**81-855** With LEDs **21.90**

**81-865** Two Head **43.00**

### Semaphore Arms 8.30 ea
**81-6066** Upper Quadrant Pointed Blade 3-Color w/Front Painted Yellow w/Black Stripe

**81-6067** Upper Quadrant Square Blade 3-Color w/Front Painted Red w/White Stripe

**81-6070** Lower Quadrant (red-red-green) w/Front Painted Red w/White Stripe

**81-6071** Lower Quadrant Arms "Fishtail"

**81-6072** Lower Quadrant Arms Pointed

### Train Order Signal Arms 8.30 ea
**81-6068** Upper Quadrant (red-yellow-green) w/Front Painted Red w/White Stripe

**81-6069** Lower Quadrant (red-red-green) w/Front Painted Solid

## SELLEY FINISHING TOUCHES

### Burma Shave Signs 4.30 ea
Sets include cast-metal sign posts and self-adhesive Burma-Shave signs printed in red and white.

1941-1949
HO

| REMEMBER THIS | WHISTLE BECAUSE |
|---|---|
| IF YOU'D BE | THEY'RE SCARED |
| SPARED TRAINS DON'T | Burma-Shave |

675-6282

**675-6281** 1930s Era

**675-6282** 1940s Era

**675-6283** 1950s Era

Daily New Product Announcements! Visit Walthers Web site at
**www.walthers.com**

## STEWART PRODUCTS

### Clearance Guard Kits

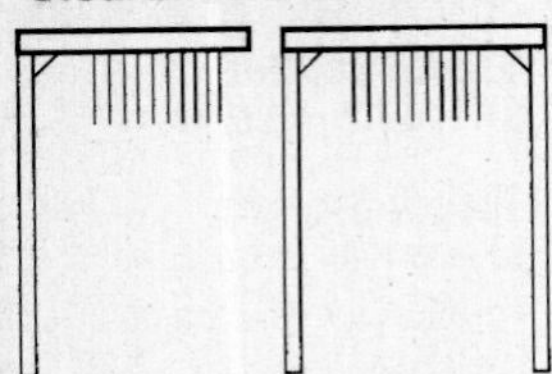


**683-128** Single Post **8.95**

**683-129** Double Post **9.40**

### Sign Kits 4.15 ea

**RR Speed Limit Signs**

**683-859** Square pkg(6)

**683-860** Diamond pkg(6)

## WOODLAND SCENICS

### Street & Traffic Light Set

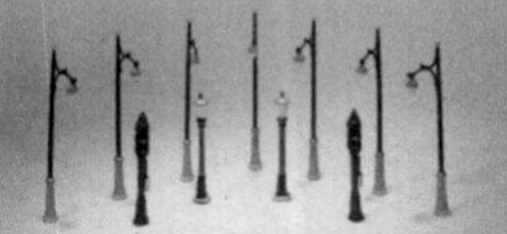

**785-248 7.98**
Detailed white metal castings. Set includes two traffic lights, seven tall single arm lights and two short street lights.

## TR HOBBY PRODUCTS

## NEW PRODUCTS

### Fiber Optic Signals

Fiber optics transmit light from base-mounted bulbs to show the proper indications. Plastic and metal construction. Fully assembled, wired and ready to install.

**NEW 183-221** Two-Light Standard **12.95**

**NEW 183-222** Two-Light Dwarf **11.95**

**NEW 183-231** Three-Light Standard **13.95**

**NEW 183-232** Three-Light Dwarf **11.95**

**NEW 183-233** Three-Light Target **13.75**

### LED Signals

**NEW 183-224** Two-Light Standard **12.75**

**NEW 183-225** Two-Light Dwarf **11.75**

**NEW 183-226** Two-Light Target **12.95**

**NEW 183-234** Three-Light Standard **13.25**

**NEW 183-235** Three-Light Dwarf **12.95**

### Jewels pkg(12) 2.10 ea

Without backing.

**755-56** Clear

**755-57** Red

**755-58** Green

**755-59** Yellow

### Lanterns

Lost-wax brass castings.

**755-86** Switch Stand Kit **4.25**
Includes one lantern casting and four jewels (two red and two green).

**755-95** Illuminated **11.35**
1.5V kit. Adaptable to various colors and scales.

### Marker Lights

Lost-wax brass castings.

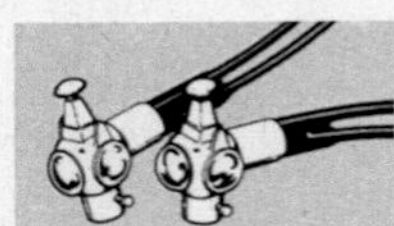

**755-64** 1 Pair **17.70**
1.2V kit with lights installed. Includes assorted transparent colored jewels.

### Switch Stand

Lost-wax brass castings.

**755-89** Non-illuminated Kit **8.90**

Models and Photo by Howard Dwyer

With a sound all its own, Island Central's 80-ton Shay roars and rumbles downhill with a work train in tow. While the old engine puts on a mighty good show, local fishermen know its arrival is likely to scare all kinds of critters away from the tracks and down into the deep woods on the other side of the river. Today it's momma bear and her cubs who are heading for safety downstream where they won't be bothered by the either the local anglers or the railroad.

Finding a level route for the tracks could be quite a challenge for early railroad builders, who often found it convenient to follow riverbanks, where the water had long ago cut away any top soil and other obstacles. Adding this kind of scene to his layout, Howard Dwyer of Farmingville, New York, started construction with Enviro-Tex water. The lush growth alongside the tracks was modeled with a variety of material from Woodland Scenics and Scenic Express. A Bachmann Spectrum Shay powers the train, and the cars were built from an old MDC 3-in-1 kit (out of production).

Whether your railroad runs through towering mountains, arid deserts or past miles of lush farmland, re-creating the scenery found alongside the line is easy with the wide range of modern materials available. Inside this section, you'll find all kinds of ground cover, foliage, trees, water and much, much more to make your work fast and fun.

# INSTANT HORIZONS™

MANUFACTURED BY WM. K. WALTHERS, INC.

Freight Yards
949-711

Hotel/Business
949-712

The Docks
949-713

Drywash Desert
949-705

Saguaro Desert
949-706

Sierra Boomtown
949-701

Tall Timber
949-702

Eastern Foothills
949-715

Prairie/Grain Elevator
949-709

Take your layout beyond the basement with panoramic mountains, deserts, big cities and more, in full-color. Instant Horizons and Instant Buildings are a complete background system, expanding your perception of distance, adding miles of scenery to your layout. Perfect for every era, they can be mixed and matched to show an ever changing landscape. Easily added to layouts that are "finished" or under construction, complete instructions are included in each set. All scenes are scaled for use with HO models, but are easily used with larger scales to create a feeling of greater distance. Measures 24 x 36".

## INSTANT HORIZONS BACKGROUND SCENES

**8.98 ea**

### City Scenes

Busy industrial and commercial scenes are perfect for rail yards, terminals and big city skylines.

**949-711** Freight Yards

**949-712** Hotel/Business

**949-713** The Docks

### Desert

With little vegetation and distant foothills, these scenes capture the look of the southwestern US. For variety, several transition scenes are designed especially for use with these views.

**949-705** Drywash Desert

**949-706** Saguaro Desert

### Mountain Scenes

From foothills to snow capped peaks, put your layout in a mountain setting with any of these scenes.

**949-701** Sierra Boomtown (Gold Rush)

**949-702** Tall Timber

**949-715** Eastern Foothills

# INSTANT HORIZONS™

## Rural Scenes

Fewer details and plenty of sky add miles of scenery and a wide, open look to any layout.

**949-709** Prairie/Grain Elevator

**949-710** Whistle Stop

## Transition Scenes

These special views smooth the transition between different kinds of scenery, creating a more natural and realistic change.

**949-703** Mountain to Desert

**949-704** Desert to Mountain

**949-707** Desert to Country

**949-708** Country to Desert

**949-714** Country to Eastern Foothills

**949-716** Country to City

**949-717** City to Country

Scenes can be arranged side by side for a panoramic background. All Instant Horizons are drawn so they can easily be combined for a realistic transition between different kinds of scenery.

Whistle Stop
949-710

Country to Desert
949-708

Mountain to Desert
949-703

Country to Eastern Foothills
949-714

Desert to Mountain
949-704

Country to City
949-716

Desert to Country
949-707

City to Country
949-717

# *Instant Buildings©*

MANUFACTURED BY WM. K. WALTHERS, INC.

## INSTANT BUILDINGS

### 8.98 ea

Put more scenery in less space combining Instant Buildings with Instant Horizons™. These printed buildings fit between actual structures and scenes, smoothing the transition from foreground to backdrop. Where space is limited, or to hide seams, glue Instant Buildings on the scene. For a 3-D effect, arrange Instant Buildings in tiers and elevate structures at the rear to add depth. Or, mount the buildings on a sheet of styrofoam and cut out small angles and openings using a hot wire cutter. Each includes complete instructions. (Some sets include additional details, not illustrated.) All Buildings are scaled for use with HO models, but are easily used with larger scales to create a feeling of greater distance.

**949-722** Back Street Structures
Tallest Building: 6" 15cm
Longest Building: 12-1/2" 31.25cm
Rear views of older brick structures, just like you see beside the tracks in most big cities. Use with 949-711 Freight Yards, 949-712 Hotel/Business, 949-713 The Docks.

**949-723** Old West Frontier
Tallest Building: 10-1/4" 25.6cm
Longest Building: 15" 37.5cm
A collection of wooden and brick businesses, right out of the old west. Use with:
949-701 Sierra Boomtown, 949-702 Tall Timber, 949-703 Mountain to Desert, 949-705 Dry Wash Desert, 949-706 Saguaro Desert, 949-707 Desert to Country.

**949-724** Industrial District
Tallest Building: 7" 17.5cm
Longest Building: 15" 37.5cm
Large industrial structures, with a variety of interesting roof-top vents, smokestacks and more.
Use with: 949-711 Freight Yards, 949-712 Hotel/Business, 949-713 The Docks.

**949-725** Main Street Stores
Tallest Building: 6" 15cm
Longest Building: 13" 32.5cm
Brick storefronts, suitable for scenes from the 1890s to the present. Use with: 949-709 Prairie/Grain Elevator, 949-710 Whistle Stop, 949-711 Freight Yards, 949-712 Hotel/Business.

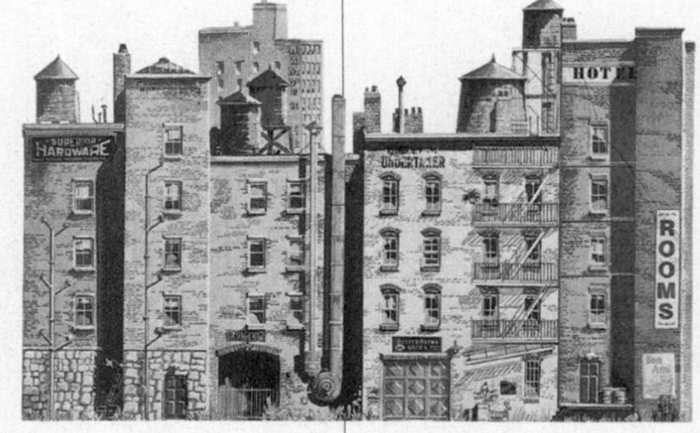

Back Street Structure Buildings
949-722

Old West Frontier Buildings 949-723

Industrial District Buildings
949-724

Main Street Store Buildings 949-725

Division of
Wm.K.Walthers, Inc.

433-1983 433-1992

433-1984 433-1988

# NEW PRODUCTS

## SceneMaster™ Trees

- Ready to Use
- Intricately Molded Branches
- Ultra-Fine Flock Foliage
- Removable Bases

### Apple Trees

- Great for Rural or City Scenes
- Includes "Fruit"

**NEW 433-1983** 3" Tall pkg(4) **8.98**

### Barren Trees

- Perfect for Late Fall or Winter Scenes
- Great Start for Making Your Own Trees

**NEW 433-1984** 3" Tall pkg(4) **8.98**

**NEW 433-1985** 5" Tall pkg(4) **10.98**

**NEW 433-1986** 6" Tall pkg(2) **10.98**

### Evergreen Trees

- Great for Holiday Layouts

**NEW 433-1987** 2" Tall pkg(5) **8.98**

**NEW 433-1988** 5" Tall pkg(4) **8.98**

**NEW 433-1989** 7" Tall pkg(3) **10.98**

### Pruned Trees

- Great for Residential Areas
- Perfect for City Parks
- Four Different Sizes to Choose From

**NEW 433-1992** 2-1/2" Tall pkg(4) **8.98**

**NEW 433-1993** 3-1/2" Tall pkg(3) **8.98**

**NEW 433-1994** 4-1/2" Tall pkg(3) **9.98**

**NEW 433-1995** 6" Tall pkg(3) **9.98**

### 8" Trees

433-1991 433-1996

**NEW 433-1991** Green pkg(2) **12.98**

**NEW 433-1996** Brown pkg(2) **12.98**

# TREES

Trees are assembled, self-standing, appropriately colored. Sizes are approximate.

### Autumn & Spring pkg(4) 8.00 ea

**433-1903** Autumn 3"

**433-1922** Autumn 4"

**433-1926** Spring 4"

### Blue Spruce

**433-1952** 5-1/2" pkg(2) **8.00**

### Deciduous 8.00 ea (Unless Noted)

433-1924 433-1925

**433-1924** White Birch 4" pkg(4)

**433-1925** Poplar 4" pkg(4)

433-1950 433-1971

**433-1950** Redwood 5-1/2" pkg(2)

**433-1971** Oak 6-1/2" pkg(2) **13.50**

### Evergreens pkg(4) 8.00 ea (Unless Noted)

433-1941 433-1907

433-1923 433-1972

**433-1941** Small - 2" pkg(4)

**433-1907** 3" pkg(4)

**433-1923** 4" pkg(4)

**433-1972** 6-1/2" pkg(2) **13.50**

### 3" Fruit pkg(4) 8.00 ea

433-1908  433-1909

**433-1908** Apple

**433-1909** Orange

### Shade Trees pkg(4) 8.00 ea (Unless Noted)

433-1940 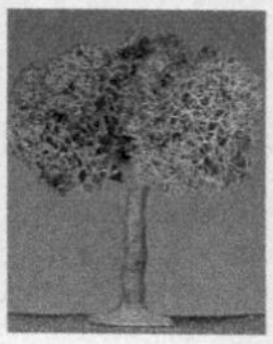 433-1902

433-1921  433-1951

**433-1940** 2" pkg(4)

**433-1902** 3" pkg(4)

**433-1921** 4" pkg(4)

**433-1951** 5-1/2" pkg(2)

### Summer Shade pkg(4) 8.00 ea

433-1910  433-1927

**433-1910** Small

**433-1927** Large

### Winter

Flocked to simulate snow on branches.

433-1901  433-1970

**433-1901** Small 3" pkg(4) **8.00**

**433-1970** Big 8-1/2" pkg(2) **13.50**

Division of Wm. K. Walthers, Inc.

## SCENEMASTER™ TREES (W/ BENDABLE ARMATURES)

Give outdoor scenes a burst of realism and beauty with SceneMaster trees. Each tree is individually handcrafted and finely detailed through realistic forms, colors and sizes. Each tree features bendable armatures, giving modelers a wide variety of shaping options.

433-1974

433-1975 433-1976

### Elm

**433-1974** Small pkg(3) **9.25**

**433-1977** Medium pkg(4) **10.00**

**433-1980** Large pkg(3) **11.00**

### Maple

**433-1975** Small pkg(4) **9.25**

**433-1978** Medium pkg(3) **10.00**

**433-1981** Large pkg(3) **11.00**

### Oak

**433-1976** Small pkg(4) **9.25**

**433-1979** Medium pkg(3) **10.00**

**433-1982** Large pkg(3) **11.00**

## GROUND COVER

### Shaker Container Counter Display

**Limited Quantity Available**

**433-1040 148.50**
Includes three each #433-1041, 1042, 1043, 1044, 1045 and 1046.

### Lichen

**Shaker Containers 2oz 8.25 ea**

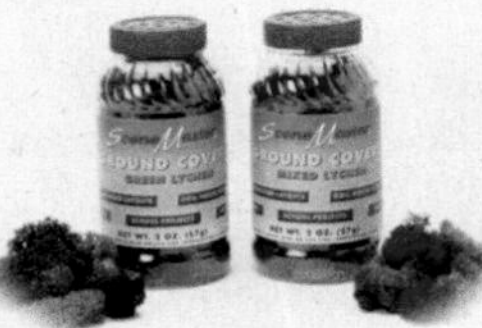

**433-1041** Mixed Colors

**433-1042** Green

### Ground Foam

**Shaker Containers 4.6oz 8.25 ea**

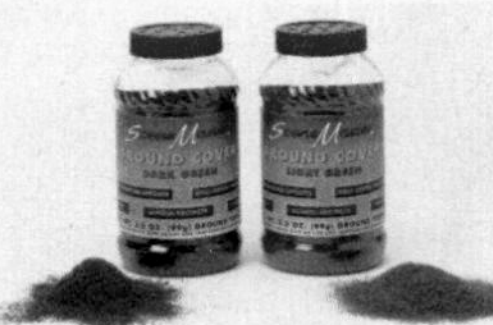

**433-1043** Dark Green

**433-1044** Light Green

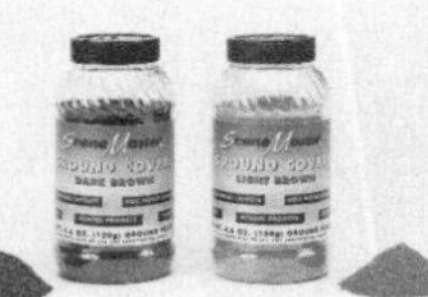

**433-1045** Dark Brown

**433-1046** Light Brown

### Ballast

1104 1105 1106

**433-1104** Ballast/Gray 15oz **5.00**

**433-1105** Coal 15oz **5.00**

**433-1106** Gravel 15oz **5.00**

New Arrivals Updated Every Day! Visit Walthers Web site at **www.walthers.com**

# Make It Fast, Fun & Affordable with SceneMaster Grass Mats

**EASY TO APPLY**

## *Instant Greenery for Your Scenery!*

- **More Affordable – *LOWER PRICES!***
- **Perfect for Quick Scenery Projects**
- **Part of the Complete SceneMaster Line**
- **Easily Cut & Shaped**
- **Works in Any Scale**
- **Nonmagnetic**
- **2 Handy Sizes**
- **Realistic Texture**

### Velour Soft Grass Mat

**433-1153** Small Roll 30 x 99" **14.99**

### SceneMaster Grass Mats

**433-1151** Flocked **5.98**
Small Roll 50 x 33" 0.8 x 1.27m

**433-1156** Flocked **9.98**
Large Roll 50 x 99" 1.27 x 2.5m

**Covers Standard 4 x 8' Plywood Sheet Without Cutting!**

Dealers MUST order in multiples of 12

## TUNNELS

Tunnels are lightweight, durable foam and are finished in realistic colors.

**433-1304** Straight **9.98**
Dealers MUST order in multiples of 12

**433-1305** Large Straight **14.98**
Dealers MUST order in multiples of 6

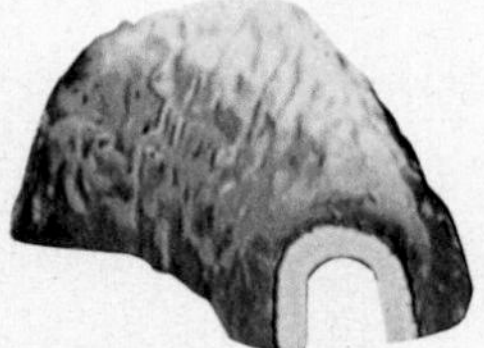

**433-1306** Curved **19.98**
Dealers MUST order in multiples of 6

## ACCESSORIES

### Landscaping Cement

**433-1403 15.50**
Clean, nontoxic, non-flammable adhesive. Dries hard and clean on almost any surface. Resealable 1 pint can.

### Mountain Paper

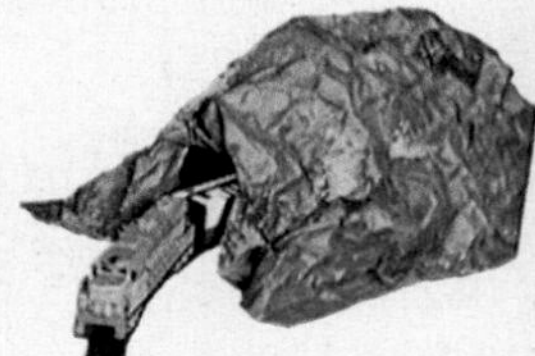

**433-1157 7.00**
Ready-to-use mountain paper can be used to create scenes, mountains and tunnels. Just wet, shape and install as desired. The paper is finished in a realistic color and is reusable. Measures 24 x 72".

Division of
Wm. K. Walthers, Inc.

## SCENEMASTER SCENE ESSENTIALS

- Ready to Use
- Figures, Vehicles & Accessories
- Assembled & Painted
- Fit Popular Modeling Eras

### Farm Set

**433-1321 11.98**
Includes a stake truck, tractor, windmill, 2 hand-painted people, 3 hand-painted animals and a watering trough.

### Construction Set

**433-1322 11.98**
Includes a construction crane, dump truck, air compressor, 3 barricades, 4 hand-painted workers and large sign.

### Campground Set

**433-1323 11.98**
Includes 6 hand-painted figures, a campfire, 2 pick-up trucks, 2 rowboats, 3 pup tents, 2 large tents and park entrance gate with sign.

### Car Lot Set

**433-1324 11.98**
Includes 3 autos, office building, a hand-painted figure, power poles with pennants and large sign.

### Roadwork Set

**433-1675 11.98**
Includes 3 hand-painted figures, 3 barriers, dump truck, 12 painted barrels, air compressor and road grader.

### Farm & Field Set

**433-1676 11.98**
Includes 2 hand-painted figures, 2 pigs, 2 sheep, tractor (molded in color w/hand-painted details), pick-up truck, wagon (attaches to tractor) and storage shed.

### City Set

**433-1677 11.98**
Includes 4 hand-painted figures, 6 fire hydrants, taxi, delivery truck and billboard sign.

### Loading Dock Set

**433-1678 11.98**
Includes 2 hand-painted figures, 4 painted barrels, 3 stacks of crates, truck, 2 forklifts and 4 pallets.

### School Days Set

**433-1679 9.75**
Includes 4 hand-painted children and a decorated school bus.

### Cops & Robbers Set

**433-1680 9.75**
Includes 2 hand-painted officers, 2 hand-painted bad guys and a decorated police cruiser.

AMACO

## MOLDING MATERIAL

### Instant Paper Mache

Dry powder mixes with water, ready to use in 15 to 20 minutes. Material is nontoxic. Dries white, can be painted with any type of paint when dry.

**126-41810** 1lb **6.79**

**126-41811** 5lbs **23.99**

### Sculptamold®

White, nontoxic powder material mixes with water, sets in 30 minutes without shrinking. Clings to most clean surfaces and can be applied over forms without cracking.

**126-41821** 3lbs **6.49**

**126-41822** 25lbs **42.49**

**126-41823** 50lbs **78.99**

### Casting Compound

**126-52761** 5lbs **12.49**
When mixed with water and poured into a form, compound sets hard in a few minutes. Cast pieces and molds are white, fine-textured and durable.

### Crea-Stone

**126-53401** Natural Color 25lbs **56.49**
Dry powder mixes with water to make castings or moldings. Can be sculpted and carved for long periods if kept moist.

### Plasterform™

**126-50081** 6.4oz **4.49**
In a few simple steps, you can have easy-to-make scenic landscapes, model train dioramas, mountains and sculptures.
4 x 180" roll

### Mix-A-Mold

Nontoxic material for creating molds using 3-D objects. Picks up every detail of original. Powder mixes with water and molds are ready in two minutes.

**126-75541** 8oz **12.49**

**126-75542** 2-1/2lbs **38.49**

### Mountain Building Kit

**126-41820** U Build The Mountain Kit **17.49**
Kit includes a 2lb bag of Sculptamold, measuring cup, craft stick, mixing bag and instructions.

### Rubber Latex

**126-89915** 16oz **14.49**
Use to make your own custom molds for casting scenery, small parts and other hobby or craft items.

## WIREFORM®

Each sheet measures 16 x 20".

### Wireform Expandable Modeling Mesh

Mini-packs ideal for detailed projects on your layout.

**126-50004** Contour Aluminum 1/16" Pattern **6.99**

**126-50005** Sparkle Aluminum 1/8" Pattern **6.99**

**126-50006** Diamond Aluminum 1/4" Pattern **6.99**

**126-50007** Impression Copper 1/8" Pattern **9.49**

**126-50008** CopperForm Copper 1/4" Pattern **9.49**

### Wireform Woven Modeling Mesh

**126-50023** Modeler's Aluminum **14.49**
The woven wires create a structural grid, assuming different textures when shaped. Includes two sheets of 16 x 20" wiremesh.

COLOR-RITE

## ROCK MOLDS

### Rock Molds 5.50 ea

Made of soft vinyl for the "Wet Method" of applying rock castings. Each mold allows unlimited variations, using finger and thumb pressure. Almost indestructible, will not lose detail with use. Unconditional, free, lifetime replacement guarantee by Color Rite.

**211-802** 3-1/2 x 3-1/2"

**211-803** 6 x 2-1/2"

**211-804** 4 x 4-1/4"

**211-805** 8 x 3-1/2"

**211-806** 4-1/4 x 2-1/2"

**211-807** 4-3/4 x 3-1/2"



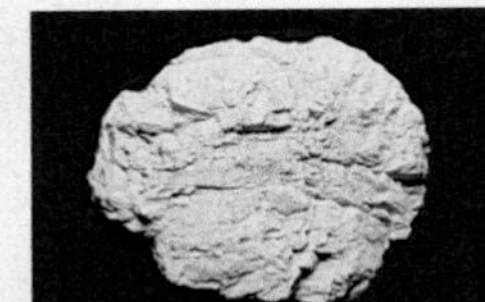

**211-808** 6-1/2 x 4-1/4"

**211-809** 5 x 3-1/2"

### Rock Mold Sets

**211-801** 8 Mold Set **39.95**
Includes one each #802 - 809.

**211-810** 5 Mold Set (Large) **39.95**
Bigger molds cover large area in less time. Molds are 6 x 6-1/2" to 6-1/2 x 8" in area and 1/2" deep.

## WATER

### Waterfall Kit

**211-701 6.95**
Easy way to model realistic waterfalls. Heat-sensitive plastic is easily cut, and can be shaped using hot water. Material is semi-transparent; spray paint the back to model water of any color. 62' high by 26' wide (HO Scale).

## COLORING

### Color Pigments 3oz 4.95 ea

Pure Paint Pigments are the only coloring recommended for mixing with plaster for "zip-texturing" or hard shell scenicking.

Some pigments shown not available.

**211-303** Burnt Sienna
**211-304** Raw Sienna
**211-305** Burnt Umber
**211-306** Raw Umber

### Rock & Earth Stains 4oz. 2.79 ea (Unless Noted)

Acrylic base stains for recreating Nature's coloring on exposed rock. Highly concentrated, will not fade like water colors.

**211-402** Yellow Ochre
**211-403** Burnt Sienna
**211-404** Raw Sienna
**211-405** Burnt Umber
**211-406** Raw Umber
**211-407** Lamp Black
**211-408** Ultra-Marine Blue
**211-401** Assortment **17.95**
One each #402-408.

A.I.M. Products are cast in high-density plaster to give maximum strength and stain absorption. This process is exclusive with A.I.M. Products.

## SPRAY CAN REPLACEMENT VALVES

**110-908** pkg(10) **4.69**
Replace clogged valves for most hobby, household and craft brands.

## WEATHERING POWDERS

### Approx. 1oz 5.50 ea (Unless Noted)

Self-adhesive powders are easily applied to get that rusty, dusty, grimy look. Will not rub off like chalk.

**110-3101** White

**110-3102** Grimy Black

**110-3103** Medium Earth

**110-3104** Dirty Yellow

**110-3105** Dark Rust

**110-3106** Light Rust

**110-3107** Dark Earth

**110-3108** Medium Rust

**110-3110** Medium Gray

**110-3111** Dark Gray

**110-3112** Brick Red

**110-3113** Dusty Brown

**110-3100** Assortment 1 Each #3101-3107, 3110 pkg(8) **36.95**

## WALLS

Overall height 3-5/8", overall width 5-5/8", overall thickness 3/4" (unless noted).

**110-106** Cut Stone pkg(2) **10.95**

**110-107** Fieldstone pkg(2) **10.95**

**110-108** Random Stone pkg(2) **10.95**

**110-114** Poured Concrete pkg(2) **10.95**

**110-122** Wood Outside Braced pkg(2) **9.95**

**110-127** Concrete Board – Formed pkg(4) **9.95**
1-3/4 x 4" 4.3 x 10cm

**110-139** Log **11.95**
5 x 7" 12.5 x 17.5cm

**110-140** Fractured Rock – Large **11.95**
6 x 12" 15 x 30cm

**110-141** Log Cribbed – Large **11.95**
6 x 12" 15 x 30cm

**110-142** Jurassic **9.95**
Features exposed dinosaur bones in rock wall.

**110-702** Staggered Wall-Split Stone pkg(2) **10.95**

**110-706** Interlocking Wall-Split Wall pkg(2) **10.95**

### Pre-Finished Walls pkg(2) 13.95 ea

Stained in authentic color, these models are ready to add to your trackside scenery.

**Split Stone**

**110-802** Staggered Wall

**110-806** Interlocking Wall

**Retaining Walls**

**110-506** Cut Stone

**110-514** Poured Concrete

## WING WALLS

### pkg(2) 10.95 ea (Unless Noted)

Height: high end 3-1/2", low end 2"; width 5-5/8", thickness 3/4".

**110-105** Random Stone

**110-115** Poured Concrete

**110-123** Wood Outside Braced

**110-126** Poured Concrete Board – Formed

**110-929** pkg(2) **8.95**
For bridge abutments #110-92, sold separately.

### Pre-Finished 13.95 ea

Height: high end 3-1/2", low end 2"; width 5-5/8", thickness 3/4".

**110-502** Cut Stone

**110-515** Poured Concrete

**110-803** Split Stone

## TUNNEL PORTALS

### Pre-Finished

**Single Track 12.95 ea (Unless Noted)**

**110-510** Cut Stone **10.95**

**110-516** Concrete – Grooved Face

**110-517** Concrete – Plain Face

**110-533** Lough

**110-810** Split Stone **13.95**

**Double Track**

**110-511** Cut Stone **13.95**

**110-534** B&O **13.95**

### Unfinished

**110-710** Split Stone **10.95**

### 3/4" Thick Portals

**Single Track 9.95 ea (Unless Noted)**

Overall height 5-1/4", overall width 6-1/4".

**110-109** Blasted Rock **10.95**

**110-110** Cut Stone **10.95**

**110-112** Random Stone

**110-116** Groove Face

**110-117** Plain Face

**110-119** Concrete Lined

**110-120** Blasted Rock, HOn3

**110-121** Wood Outside Braced

**110-128** Poured Concrete Board – Formed

**110-130** Eroded Limestone

**110-131** Granite Gingerbread

**Double Track 10.95 ea (Unless Noted)**

Overall height 5-5/8", overall width at base 7-1/2".

**110-111** Cut Stone

**110-113** Random Stone

**110-129** Poured Concrete Board – Formed

**110-132** Granite Face

**110-133** Modern Concrete **9.95**

**110-134** Concrete

## BRIDGES

**110-927** Cut Stone Arch **17.95**
9 x 3" 22.5 x 7.5cm

## VIADUCT

**110-926** Cut Stone **44.95**
18-1/2 x 8" 46.2 x 20cm
Two-span viaduct includes abutments, center pier and wing walls.

## BRIDGE ABUTMENTS

Overall height 5-3/4", width at base 4", overall thickness 3/4" (unless noted). Numbers 110-124 and 125 are designed to fit Micro-Engineering structures #255, 501-504, 507 and 508.

**110-100** Cut Stone pkg(2) **10.95**

**110-101** Fieldstone pkg(2) **10.95**

**110-102** Cut Stone pkg(2) **10.95**

**110-103** Fieldstone pkg(2) **10.95**

**110-104** Random Stone pkg(2) **10.95**

**110-118** Concrete pkg(2) **10.95**

**110-124** Poured Concrete Board – Formed pkg(2) **10.95**

**110-125** Pier w/Cutwater **17.99**

**110-135** Pier **13.95**

**110-136** Cutwater Only pkg(2) **10.50**

**110-137** Pylon Bent Footing pkg(4) **9.95**

**110-138** Double Wide pkg(2) **13.95**

**110-501** Cut Stone Pre-Finished pkg(2) **13.95**

**110-518** Poured Concrete Pre-Finished pkg(2) **13.95**

**110-718** Split Stone **11.95**

**110-818** Split Stone Pre-Finished **14.95**

## PIERS

### 38' Tall Split Stone

**110-735** Standard **14.95**
**110-835** Pre-Finished **17.95**

## CUTWATER

**110-736** Split Stone Standard pkg(2) **11.50**

**110-836** Split Stone Pre-Finished pkg(2) **14.50**

## SCENERY SOLUTIONS

These easy-to-use products are compatible with one another. Using them in combination will give models a rundown rusty look.

### 16oz ea 9.95

**110-901** Quick Age
Gives building and rolling stock an old gray look. Spray on and let dry. Add more coats until desired effect is seen.

**110-902** Real Rust
Produces a rusty orange color. Great for rust streaks on tanks, tenders, etc.

**110-903** Real Rust, Dark
Get the effect of older rust. Apply Real Rust over this and great multi-colored rusted model.

**110-906** Grungy Grimy Black
Will make models look dirty and grimy. Great for engines, running gear, smokestacks, etc.

**110-907** New Fresh Rust
Create rust streaks of that fresh orange rust color from recent scratches in metal.

## SIGNS

### "Faded Glory" Series Weathered Vintage Signs/Posters 3.95 ea

**110-3001** Set #1

**110-3002** Set #2

**110-3003** Set #3

**110-3004** Set #4

**110-3005** Set #5

**110-3006** Set #6

**110-3007** Set #7

**110-3008** Set #8

**110-3009** Set #9

**110-3010** Set #10

**110-3011** Set #11

**110-3012** Set #12

**110-3013** Set #13

**110-3014** Set #14

**110-3015** Set #15

**110-3016** Set #16

**110-3017** Set #17

**110-3018** Set #18

## ROCKS

**110-500** 1lb **13.95**
Assorted rock castings, about 9 castings per package.

## SCENIC DETAILS

**110-904** Advertising **5.95**

## NEW PRODUCT

### Fence

**NEW 150-774** Hairpin-Style Fencing **4.25**
Features loop pickets and spear finials. Easy-to-assemble fencing requires no glue or cement.

### Fences 4.25 ea

Parts are molded of styrene in appropriate colors. Figures sold separately.

**150-776** Picket Fence & Gate-White 6'

**150-777** Rustic Fence & Gate-Brown 6'

### Telephone Poles

**150-775** Telephone Poles pkg(12) **4.25**
Styrene parts, molded in appropriate colors.

## Weathering Solutions 7.59 ea

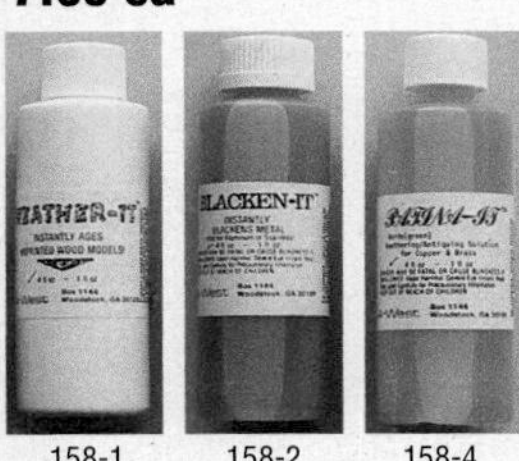

158-1 158-2 158-4

Instructions are included with all of our weathering solutions and they are useful for a variety of effects whose exact applications are limited only by the users' imaginations.

Customers have won modeling awards with and written articles about these products. These weathering solutions have also been credited in several magazine spreads and covers. Each solution comes in a 4oz bottle.

**158-1** Weather-It
Gives unpainted wood a gray, aged look. Not a paint or stain. Use for old paint effects and realistic plaster "concrete" too.

**158-2** Blacken-It
Works on most metals, not a paint. Conducts electricity, can be soldered.

**158-4** Patina-It
Produces shades of blue/green on copper, brass and bronze. Not a paint. Also for Corrode-It technique on white metal, producing a pewter-gray/black patina. Also blackens stainless steel when Blacken-It #158-2 (sold separately) doesn't work.

### Using A-West Products

The following is an example of how each of the above products were used in the creation of a realistic wood trestle. To begin with, all wood parts were weathered with Weather-It, giving them the look of having endured many years of nature's hardships.

The truss rods, represented by copper wire, were treated with Blacken-It. This turned the normal copper wire into the black rods that are seen on such structures. Patina-It was then used on the small details of cast white metal which were used for turnbuckles, nuts and washers on the truss rods. This allowed the parts to take on the gray/black color as seen on prototype trestles. Blacken-It could also be used in place of Patina-It, depending on the look the modeler is trying to achieve. When all is said and done, a simple kit has been transformed into a true-to-life replica by the simple use of weathering solutions.

A • M • S • I
SCALE MODEL SUPPLIES

## Ground Cover

Natural, realistic foam ground cover is ideal for adding color and variety to any scene.

### Earth Colors 1 oz 4.99 ea

**Spring Green**
**137-401** Fine
**137-402** Medium

**Yellow Green**
**137-411** Fine
**137-412** Medium

**Ochre Green**
**137-421** Fine
**137-422** Medium
**137-423** Coarse

**Olive Green**
**137-431** Fine
**137-432** Medium

**Grass Green**
**137-441** Fine
**137-442** Medium

**Conifer Green**
**137-451** Fine
**137-452** Medium

**Dirt Brown**
**137-461** Fine

**Gray Green**
**137-471** Fine
**137-472** Medium

**Straw**
**137-491** Fine

**Aspen Gold**
**137-511** Fine
**137-512** Medium

**Leaf Green**
**137-541** Fine

**Spruce Green**
**137-551** Fine
**137-552** Medium

**Eucalyptus**
**137-561** Fine

**Dust**
**137-571** Fine

**Apple Green**
**137-611** Fine
**137-612** Medium

**Hunter Green**
**137-651** Fine

### Flower Colors 1/2 oz 3.49 ea

**137-10801** White
**137-10811** Delphinium
**137-10812** Violet
**137-10825** Cherry Red
**137-10827** Wisteria

### Textures 1 oz 4.99 ea

Premixed in combinations of green and ready to apply as foliage, grass or ground cover.
**137-1109** Lawn
**137-1206** Light Tree
**137-1207** Medium Tree

### Wisteria Vine Kit

**137-90670 26.99**

### Finished Hedge pkg(4) 19.98 ea

Ready to use, natural variegated exterior.
**137-80110** 1/2 x 1"
**137-80120** 1/4 x 1/2"

# NEW PRODUCTS

## SceneScapes™ Trees

SceneScapes trees feature realistic colors and and are suitable for any layout. Each tree features a removable base so you can make them freestanding on your layout surface or remove the base and plant them for more durability. Each package includes trees of varying heights in the specified size range.

### Conifers pkg(6) 7.95

**NEW 160-32001** Pines 5-6"

**NEW 160-32002** Snow-Covered Pines 5-6"

**NEW 160-32003** Conifers 5-6"

**NEW 160-32004** Spruce 5-6"

**NEW 160-32005** Cedar 5-6"

### Deciduous pkg(3) 8.95

**NEW 160-32006** Deciduous 3-4"

**NEW 160-32007** Walnut 2-1/2 to 3-1/2"

**NEW 160-32008** Elm 3-4"

**NEW 160-32009** Sycamore 3-4"

**NEW 160-32010** Aspen 3-4"

**NEW 160-32011** Maple 3-4"

# SCENERY ACCESSORIES

## Fences

**160-42100** pkg(24) **6.50**

## Telephone Poles

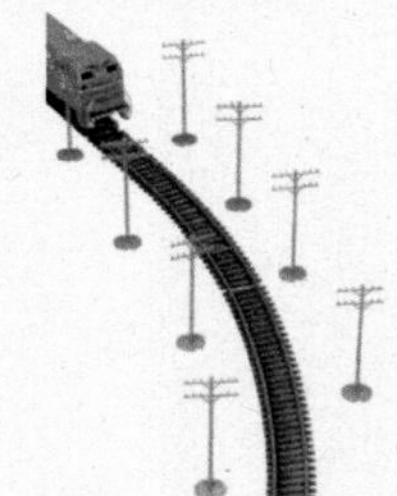

**160-42102** pkg(12) **6.50**

## Park Items 6.50 ea

**160-42209** City Park Accessories

**160-42213** Picnic Set
Includes picnic tables, trash cans, an outdoor fireplace, protective awning and a water pump.

**160-42214** Playground Equipment
Youngsters will enjoy their time on a variety of playground equipment. Set includes a slide, seesaw, swingset and merry-go-round.

**160-42215** Swimming Pool & Accessories
Cool off on a hot summer day by setting up a swimming pool in your layout's park. Includes a pool with ladder and diving board, lifeguard chair, round picnic table with umbrella, four chairs, a table and a protective awning.

**160-42218** Center Square Monument
Plaque commemorates lives lost in battle.

# Better Fields Begin with Busch

BUSCH

Follow any railroad line through rural areas and you'll find plenty of variety in the fields on either side of the tracks. Cornfields, vineyards, grain fields and sunflowers have always been a challenge to model—until now. Busch scenery makes planting realistic cash crops on your pike easier than ever. Easy-to-build plastic kits feature parts molded in appropriate colors and complete instructions. Simply build and plant!

**Corn Field** 189-1202 13.99

**CHOOSE FROM THESE REALISTIC CROPS:**

**Grape Vines**
189-1200 16.99

**Pumpkin Patch**
189-1201 10.99

**Wheat Field**
189-1204 14.99

**Roses**
189-1205 10.99

**Tulips**
189-1206 10.99

**Oxeye Daisies**
189-1207 10.99

IMPORTED FROM GERMANY BY WALTHERS

# NEW PRODUCTS

## Trees

### Pine Trees pkg(2)

**NEW 189-6141** 5-1/8 & 5-3/4" 13 & 14.5cm Tall **16.99**

**NEW 189-6142** 5-3/4 & 6-5/16" 14.5 & 16cm Tall **18.99**

**NEW 189-6143** 7-1/4 & 7-11/16" 18.5 & 19.5cm Tall **22.99**

**NEW 189-6144** 6-7/8 & 8-1/4" 17.5 & 21cm Tall **23.99**

## Field Crops

### Hops

**NEW 189-1215 16.99**
This discinctive-looking crop will add authenticity to any rural scene. Each kit includes enough molded-plastic hop plants to make a field 3-15/16 x 3-15/16 x 2-3/8" 10 x 10 x 6cm. Kit includes plants and poles.

### Barley

**NEW 189-1216 14.99**
Easy to use kit includes enough material to "plant" an area 3-15/16 x 3-15/16" 10 x 10cm. Barley stalks measure about 3/4" 2cm tall and each planting strip has about 50 stalks.

## Garden Plants

### Flower Pot Set w/Flowers

**NEW 189-1209 14.99**
Set includes parts for 20 flower pots and includes roses, daisies, lupin and dahias.

### Tomatoes & Cucumbers

**NEW 189-1214 10.99**
Kit includes parts for six tomato plants and six cucumber plants, all about 1" 2.5cm tall.

### Lupine pkg(16) 10.99 ea

**NEW 189-1217** Wild Varieties

**NEW 189-1218** Garden Varieties

### Dahlias

**NEW 189-1219** pkg(120) **10.99**

### Flower Pots

**NEW 189-1230 16.99**
Includes four potted plants, bucket and spade packaged in a transparent display box.

### Tulips & Oxeye Daisies

**NEW 189-1231 16.99**
Includes two rows each of tulips and oxeye daisies and a wheelbarrow packaged in a transparent display box.

### Sunflowers & Roses

**NEW 189-1232 16.99**
Set includes 12 sunflowers with bases, two rose bushes and hand water pump, packaged in a clear display box.

## Ground Cover

### Expandable Foliage Pads 4.99 ea

Through a special manufacturing process, each 5-29/32 x 9-27/32" 15 x 25cm foliage pad incorporates micro flocking into a sheet which can be stretched or cut to fit your scene. This material is great for adding over existing scenery for extra detail.

**NEW 189-7341** Spring Green

**NEW 189-7342** Medium Green

**NEW 189-7343** Dark Green

### Gravel 9oz 300ml 5.99

**NEW 189-7526** Park Path/Beach

**NEW 189-7527** Forest/Field Gravel

### Thinning Grass Pads

Simulate realistic grassy fields with bare patches with these easy-to-use ground cover pads. Each features grass flocking attached to a transparent base with the grass blades standing on end. The material can be cut to fit your required area and cemented on top of existing soil ground cover so the dirt shows through in the barren areas. Each pad measures: 8-1/4 x 11-11/16" 21 x 29.7cm.

**NEW 189-1301** Dry Grass **20.99**

**NEW 189-1302** Spring Grass **20.99**

**NEW** Hops 189-1215

**NEW** Barley 189-1216

**NEW 189-1303** Summer Grass **20.99**

**NEW 189-1304** Late Summer Grass **20.99**

**NEW 189-1305** Late Summer/ Early Autumn Grass **28.99**

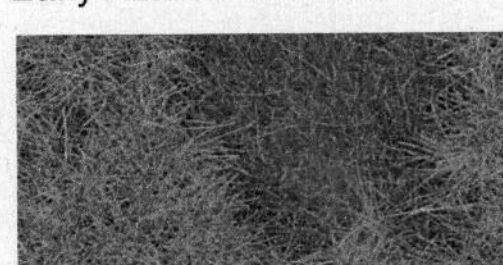

**NEW 189-1306** Late Spring/ Early Summer Grass **30.99**

**NEW 189-1307** Spring Meadow Grass **30.99**

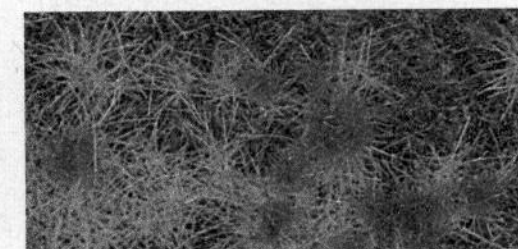

**NEW 189-1308** Edge of Forest Grass **37.99**

**NEW 189-1309** Heathland Grass **37.99**

**NEW 189-1310** Harvested Cornfield **33.99**

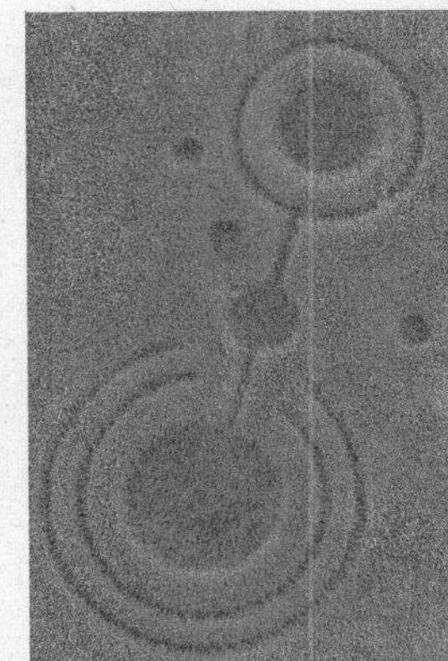

**NEW 189-1311** Grain Field w/Crop Circle **37.99**

**NEW 189-1312** Marsh/Pond w/Grass & Reed Shoreline **37.99**

IMPORTED FROM GERMANY BY WALTHERS

## Forest/Meadow Starter Set

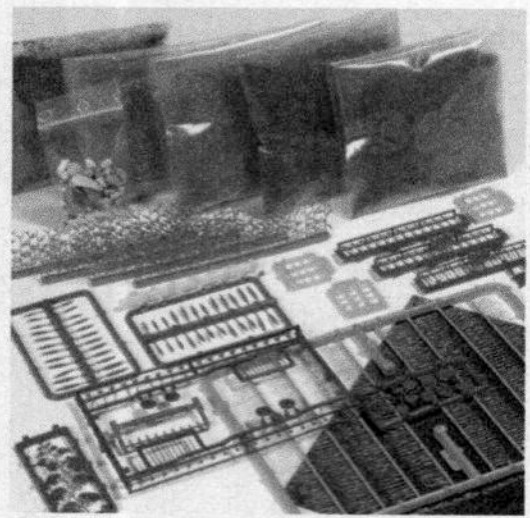

**NEW 189-6043 28.99**
This kit comes with everything you need to create realistic meadow and forest lands. Included is an illustrated step-by-step guide and all the materials you need to add ground cover, soil, grasses flowers, details such as mushrooms and lupine, reeds, a pond surface sheet and more.

## Printed Ballast/ Crushed Stone Sheet

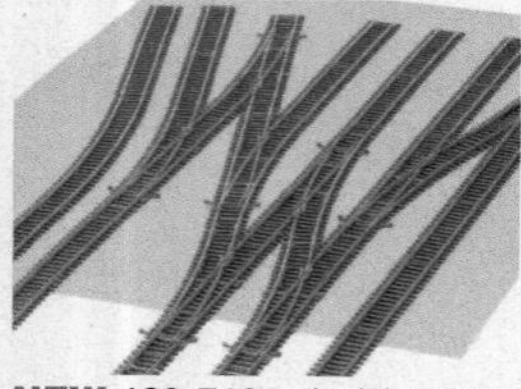

**NEW 189-7181** pkg(2) **5.99**
26-3/4 x 19-1/4" 68 x 49cm

Use this printed ballast sheet underneath turnouts and other movable track pieces. Its color matches Busch ballast #189-7127, sold separately.

## Hedges

**NEW 189-7150** Green
25-13/32 x 13/32" 100 x 1cm
**5.99**

**NEW 189-7151** Green
59 x 11/16" 150 x 1.8cm **9.99**

**NEW 189-7152** Blooming
4-1/8" 10.5cm **7.99**

## Scenery Base Construction Components

Busch scenery construction components allow easy construction of lightweight, sturdy corrugated cardboard scenery base for your layout. Strong plastic "honeycomb" connectors hold corrugated cardboard sheets together and allow you to create flat surfaces and angled bevels. Once you've settled on your final configuration, simply glue the cardboard to the connectors and secure it in place. Add a realistic contour to your landscape by filling the spaces around the cardboard sheets with layers of foam sheets. Glue the sheets to the cardboard base and let dry. Create a realistic ground contour by shaping the sheets with a knife or rasp and finish it by adding ground cover and scenery details.

**NEW 189-7206** 15 Connectors & 5 Cardboard Sheets **33.99**
Sheets measure:
16-1/2 x 11-11/16 x 5/16"
42 x 29.7 x .8cm

**NEW 189-7207** Cardboard Sheet **14.99**
Sheets measure:
35-7/16 x 23-5/8 x 5/16"
90 x 60 x .8cm

**NEW 189-7208** Foam Sheets **46.99**
Sheets measure 19-11/16 x 9-27/32" 50 x 25cm and each pack includes two 25/32" 2cm thick sheets and one each 2" 5cm and 3-1/8" 8cm thick sheets.

## Complete Miniature Scenes

Sets include vehicles, figures and scenery accessories to create a scenario on your layout.

**NEW 189-7623** Merry Christmas XI "High Flyer" **33.99**

**NEW 189-7624** Halloween 6 **33.99**

**NEW 189-7673** Flower Power **26.99**

**NEW 189-7680** Kindergarden **23.99**

**NEW 189-7681** Swimming Pond **23.99**

**NEW 189-7700** Beer Delivery Truck at Gas Pump **19.99**

**NEW 189-7701** Bank Robbery **25.99**

**NEW 189-7702** Hippies Camping **29.99**

**NEW 189-7703** Beer Garden **21.99**

# SCENERY STARTER SETS

## Basic Scenery Starter Set

**189-7189 18.99**
This easy-to-use kit will walk you through the basics of landscaping your layout. Kit includes trees, foliage, ground cover, stones, a field fence and instructions.

**NEW** Forest/Meadow Starter Set 189-6043

**NEW** Scenery Base Construction Components 189-7206

**189-7191 48.99**
Learn the basics of adding scenery to your layout. Set includes foliage, trees, sand, water paper, asphalt roadway, road signs, bicycles, a motor scooter, an automobile and more.

# TREES

## Apple Trees pkg(2)

**189-6628** 1-13/16" 45mm pkg(2) **5.99**

**189-6848** 2-15/16" 7.5cm **5.99**

**189-6858** 4-11/32" 11cm **7.99**



## Ash

**189-6957** 5-7/8" 15cm pkg(2) **9.99**

**189-6967** 7-1/16" 18cm **9.99**

## Beech

**189-6779** 8-13/32" 210mm **14.99**

IMPORTED FROM GERMANY BY WALTHERS

## Birch

**189-6776** 8-13/32" 210mm **14.99**

**189-6936** 3-1/2" 9cm pkg(2) **5.99**

**189-6946** 4-1/2" 11.5cm pkg(2) **6.99**

**189-6956** 5-7/8" 15cm pkg(2) **9.99**

**189-6966** 7-1/16" 18cm **9.99**

## Red Beech

**189-6758** 5-7/8" 15cm pkg(2) **11.99**

**189-6958** 5-7/8" 15cm pkg(2) **9.99**

**189-6968** 7-1/16" 18cm **9.99**

## Beech

**189-6939** 3-1/2" 9cm pkg(2) **5.99**

**189-6949** 4-1/2" 11.5cm pkg(2) **6.99**

**189-6959** 5-7/8" 15cm pkg(2) **9.99**

**189-6969** 7-1/16" 18cm **9.99**

## Blooming Trees pkg(2)

**189-6252** Small 2-13/16" 7cm Tall **2.99**

**189-6253** Medium 3-5/8" 9cm Tall **3.99**

**189-6254** Large 4-3/16" 10.5cm Tall **4.99**

**189-6813** Red 1-3/8" 3.5cm **3.99**

**189-6843** 2-15/16" 7.5cm **5.99**

**189-6853** 4-11/32" 11cm **7.99**

## Chestnut

**189-6771** 8-13/32" 210mm **14.99**

**189-6961** 7-1/16" 18cm **9.99**

## Deciduous Tree Assortment

**189-6484** Spring Trees pkg(16) **18.99**
Includes a variety of trees from 2-13/16-5" 7cm-12.5cm tall.

**189-6487** pkg(25) **27.99**

**189-6741** 4 Deciduous Trees & Benches **20.99**
4-1/2" 11.5cm
Includes one each birch, beech, poplar and weeping willow plus two benches.

**189-6751** Trees & Bushes Set **24.99**
5-7/8" 15cm
Includes one each birch, poplar and beech and two bushes.

## Deciduous/Pine Assortment

**189-6490** pkg(35) **24.99**

## Forest Trees

**189-6489** Mixed Assortment pkg(24) **31.99**

## Fruit Trees

**189-6641** Fruit Tree Scene **17.99**
3" 7.5cm
Includes one each heart cherry, green apple, yellow plum and plum, plus well pump and scarecrow.

**189-6651** Fruit Trees & Stand **17.99**
4-3/8" 11cm
Includes 3 fruit trees, wood fruit stand and meadow fence.

**189-6817** 1-3/8" 3.5cm pkg(2) **3.99**

**189-6847** 2-15/16" 7.5cm pkg(2) **5.99**

**189-6857** 4-11/32" 11cm pkg(2) **7.99**

## Pine Tree Assortments

**189-6470** pkg(15) **13.99**
Includes three each: 2-1/2, 3 and 3-1/2" (60, 75, 90mm) and two: 2, 4-1/2 and 5-1/2" (50, 110, 135mm).

**189-6471** pkg(30) **24.99**
Includes six each: 2-1/2, 3 and 3-1/2" (60, 75, 90mm) and four each: 2, 4-1/2 and 5-1/2" (50, 110, 135mm).

**189-6472** pkg(60) **46.99**
Includes 12 each: 2-1/2, 3 and 3-1/2" (60, 75, 90mm) and eight each: 2, 4-1/2 and 5-1/2" (50, 110, 135mm).

## Forest Set

**189-6478** **24.99**
2 - 4-3/8" 5 - 11cm

Includes everything you need to create a small pine forest scene: 20 trees, 3 extra trunks for tall trees, 2 wood piles, footbridge and ground cover.

**189-6497** pkg(50) **24.99**

**189-6498** pkg(20) **9.99**
Trees range in height from about 1-1/2-3-1/2" 40-90mm.

**189-6499** pkg(100) **39.99**
Trees range in height from about 2-1/2-4-1/2" 60-110mm.

Deciduous/Pine Assortment 189-6490

Pine Tree Assortment 189-6499

**189-6412** Serbian Pines 3-13/32-5-5/8" 8.5-14cm Tall pkg(20) **23.99**

**189-6466** Snow Covered Pines 2-3/8-5-3/8" 6-13.5cm Tall pkg(20) **22.99**

**189-9740** Pine Set pkg(20) **16.99**

## Pine Trees w/Roots

**189-6475** pkg(10) **10.99**
Includes two each: 2-1/2, 3-1/2 and 4-1/2" (60, 90, 110mm), three 3" (75mm) and one 5-1/2" (135mm).

**189-6476** pkg(20) **19.99**
Includes four each: 2-1/2, 3-1/2 and 4-1/2" (60, 90, 110mm), six 3" (75mm) and two 5-1/2" (135mm).

**189-6477** pkg(40) **36.99**
Includes eight 2-1/2, 3-1/2 and 4-1/2" (60, 90, 110mm), twelve 3" (75 mm) and four 5-1/2" (135mm).

**189-6577** pkg(40) **24.99**
1-3/16 to 2-3/16" 30-60mm.

## Poplars

**189-6229** Poplars pkg(10) **13.99**
Includes six 4-13/16" 12cm and four 3-13/16" 9.5cm tall trees.

**189-6933** 3-1/2" 9cm pkg(2) **5.99**

**189-6943** 4-1/2" 11.5cm pkg(2) **6.99**

**189-6953** 5-7/8" 15cm pkg(2) **9.99**

IMPORTED FROM GERMANY BY WALTHERS

### Spruce

These super detailed trees feature lifelike drooping branches, delicate construction from the root to the crown of tree, simulated needles created using special micro fibers trunks with authentic grain and fine root system. Even tiny cones are supplied that can be glued to the larger trees.

#### Full-Trunk pkg(2)

**189-6131** 2-3/16" 5.5cm **8.99**

**189-6132** 2-3/4" 7cm **10.99**

**189-6133** 3-1/2 & 4-3/4" 9 & 12cm **13.99**

**189-6134** 6-11/16 & 7-11/16" 17 & 19.5cm **17.99**

**189-6492** pkg(35) **22.99** 2 - 4-3/8" 5-11cm

#### High-Trunk pkg(2)

**189-6136** 5-1/8" 13cm **12.99**

**189-6137** 6-5/16 & 6-7/8" 16 & 17.5cm **13.99**

**189-6138** 7-1/4 & 7-11/16" 18.5 & 19.5cm **14.99**

**189-6411** pkg(10) Serbian Spruces **16.99**

### Weeping Willows

**189-6650** 4-13/16" 120mm pkg(2) **14.99**

## PLANTS

### Grapevines

**189-1200** pkg(80) **16.99**
Set up a vineyard on your layout with these detailed grapevines. Each vine features 15 hanging bunches of grapes and over 100 realistic leaves. Each package includes enough material for 80 vines and includes baseplates for an approximately 15-3/4" 40cm long line of vines.

### Pumpkin Patch

**189-1201** pkg(80) **10.99**
Grow Jack-O'-Lanterns on your layout! Each package includes 80 pumpkins in various sizes and eight 1-5/8" 4cm vines with realistic leaves and tendrils.

### Cornfields

**189-1202 14.99**
Finally, here's a solution for modeling one of the most common trackside crops. Each corn field set includes 400 1" 2.5cm tall molded corn stalks; simply place them on the base strips and build up a field to fit your scene. Each stalk contains up to eight leaves and two ears. The set contains enough stalks to make a 39-3/8" 100cm square field, plus flocking for the tassels. a base plate and flocking for tassels.

### Mushrooms & Ferns

**189-1203 10.99**
Add detail to your forest floors, gardens and grassy scenes with these realistic plants. Each set includes materials for 20 ferns and 28 mushrooms of varying sizes and colors.

## WHEAT FIELDS

**189-1204 14.99**
Here's a crop that'll be at home on any layout in any era! Grain is grown in every region, and is the reason why many railroad lines were built. Now adding realistic grain fields to your railroad is easier than ever! These wheat stems feature fine leaves and thickened heads that simulate a variety of grains. Approximately 50 plants are attached to each soil strip, so that planting a large field is easy. Golden colored to represent crops near harvest, these wheat fields are also ideal for use as as dry grass along railway embankments, walls, fences etc. Each package includes: 39-3/4" 100cm sq. wheat field equal to over 5000 3/8" 1cm-high plants!

## FLOWERS

### Roses

**189-1205** pkg(120) **10.99**
Kit includes parts for 120 rose plants in five different colors and 20 dirt piles on which they can be arranged.

### Tulips

**189-1206** pkg(120) **10.99**
Kit includes parts for 120 tulip plants in five different colors and ground plates.

### Oxeye Daisies

**189-1207** pkg(120) **10.99**
Kit includes parts for 120 Oxeye Daisy plants in white and yellow, plus ground plates.

### Flower Box Set

**189-1208 9.99**
Kit includes six flower boxes with white, pink, red and blue flowers.

## GARDEN POND SET

**189-1210 16.99**
Add realistic ponds to gardens, parks and other scenes. This unique set includes pond surfaces complete with water lilies and Koi fish printed on rippled, shiny plastic that looks like real water when placed on your layout. Simply cut the material to fit and customize the scene with water lilies, printed additional fish, shoreline stones and other supplied details.

IMPORTED FROM GERMANY BY WALTHERS

## Flowerpots and Potted Plants

**189-1211 24.99**
Whether you're setting up a garden center, adding landscaping around city buildings or simply detailing a park or neighborhood scene, this set is just the thing you need. This kit includes over 40 plants and park trees, pots, garden advertising posters with stands, a garden cart, pile of topsoil, tools and more. Use it in a single scene or spread it around for added realism on your pike.

## Hay and Straw Bales and Rolls

**189-1212 13.99**
Perfect for any rural or farm scene, these bales and rolls are perfect for adding detail to fields and barn scenes. Set includes 18 hay bales, six haystacks and 16 rolled bales of straw.

## Cabbage and Lettuce

**189-1213 11.99**
Kit includes eight each red cabbage, white cabbage, cauliflower, broccoli and 16 heads of lettuce.

## Sunflowers

**189-6003** pkg(60) **10.99**
Add a sunflower field to your pike with this set. Includes 60 sunflowers and base.

# ROCK CASTINGS

**189-7497** Rock Assortment **43.99**
Add jagged outcroppings to your peaks and valley walls with these ready-to-use rock castings.

# SNOW

**189-7171** Snow Powder 500g **8.99**

# PRINTED SURFACE SHEETS

Decor sheets are printed on thin cardboard for flexibility. Simply use compatible glue to affix to streets, walls and more to simulate terra cotta tiles, weatherbeaten asphalt and more. Each measures 8-1/4 x 5-13/16" 21 x 14.8cm.

## pkg(2) 2.99 ea

**189-7413** Antique Flagstone Plaza

**189-7414** Rustic Flagstone Plaza

**189-7415** Weathered Industrial Stone Wall

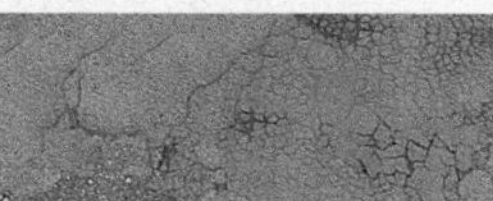

**189-7416** Weathered Asphalt Tarmac

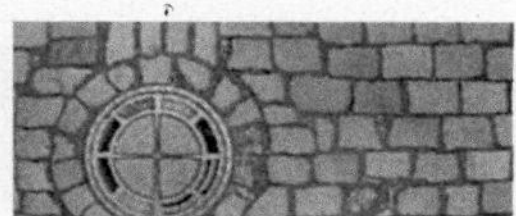

**189-7417** Cobblestone Street

**189-7418** Sidewalk Plate

**189-7419** Wood Boards (bright)

**189-7420** Wood Boards (weathered)

# WATER

**189-7180** Foil/Paper **9.99**
18 x 14" 45 x 35cm

**189-7426** Sheet **2.99**

## Aqua Model Water

**189-7589** 3-3/4oz **8.99**
Create water scenes on your layout with this tough, viscous liquid. Apply a thin layer to your prepared stream or riverbed; apply multiple layers for deeper water. Dries clear with rippling.

## Garden Pond Set

**189-1210 16.99**
Add realistic ponds to gardens, parks and other scenes. This unique set includes pond surfaces complete with water lilies and Koi fish printed on rippled, shiny plastic that looks like real water when placed on your layout. Simply cut the material to fit and customize the scene with water lilies, printed additional fish, shoreline stones and other supplied details.



# GROUND COVER

## Grass Flocking 2.99 ea

**189-7110** Dark Green

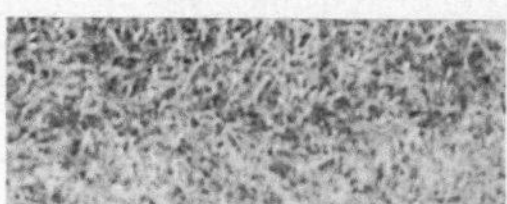

**189-7111** Spring Green

## Micro-Flocking 15oz 500ml 3.99 ea

Use this extra-fine flocking to simulate fall leaves on trees or wisps of dry grass.

**189-7324** Tan
**189-7325** Orange-Brown
**189-7326** Reddish Brown

## Flocking 2.99 ea

**189-7331** Spring Green
**189-7332** Medium Green
**189-7333** Dark Green
**189-7337** Light Green

## Foam Scatter Material

Ground foam in a variety of colors and textures, suitable for trees, weeds, grass and other plants.

### Fine 6.99 ea

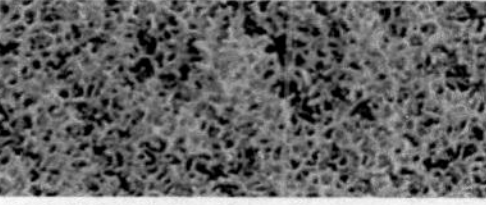

**189-7311** Spring Green

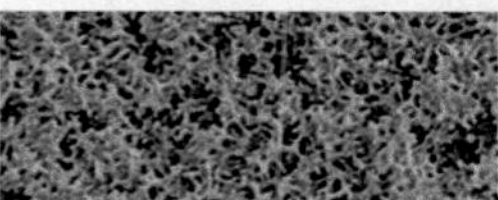

**189-7312** Medium Green

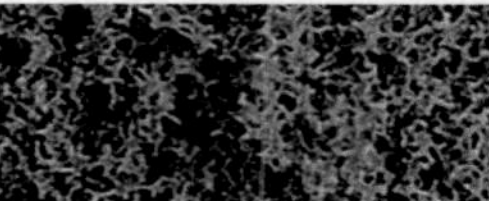

**189-7313** Dark Green

**189-7314** White

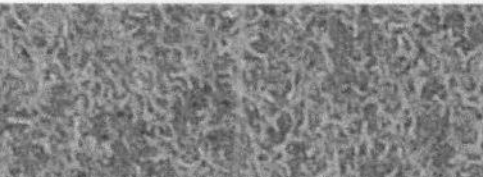

**189-7315** Rose

IMPORTED FROM GERMANY BY WALTHERS

### Coarse 5.99 ea

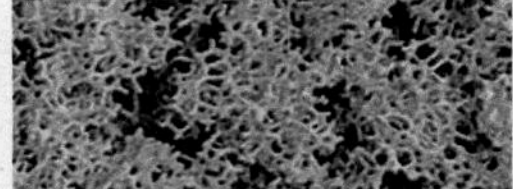

**189-7317** Light Green

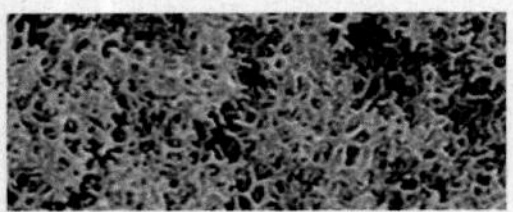

**189-7318** Medium Green

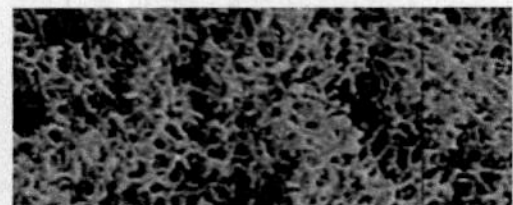

**189-7319** Dark Green

### Scatter Material

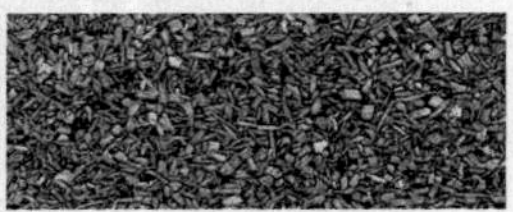

**189-7051** Forest Green **1.99**

### Forest Ground Cover

10oz 300ml Packages

**189-7528** Deciduous Forest **5.99**

**189-7529** Coniferous Forest **5.99**

### Micro Flocking 3.99 ea

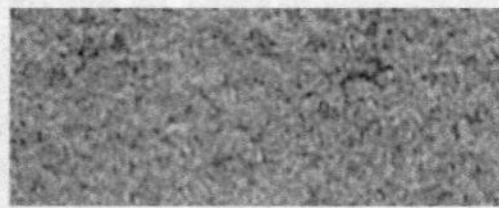

**189-7321** Spring Green

**189-7322** Medium Green

**189-7323** Dark Green

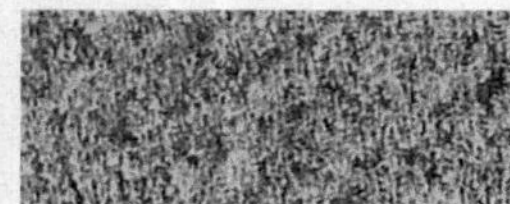

**189-7327** Light Green

### Track Ballast 2.99 ea (Unless Noted)

**189-7069** Gray **2.49**

**189-7513** Crystalline Gray

**189-7514** Terra Cotta

**189-7515** Natural White

**189-7517** Beige/Brown

### Wild Grass Material 3.99 ea

Extra large, 6mm.

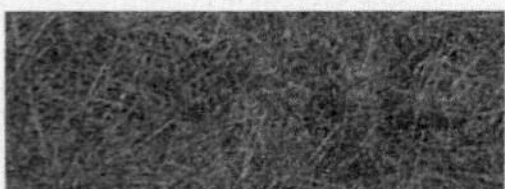

**189-7370** Dark Green

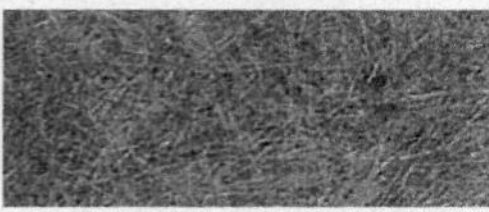

**189-7371** Spring Green

**189-7372** Grain Field

## SCENERY MATS

### Mustard Field Mat

**189-7184 17.99**
7-3/32 x 11-13/32" 18 x 29cm

Drive along any highway in springtime and you'll see endless fields of bright yellow flowers. This new scenic mat makes adding this detail to your layout easy. Simply cut to fit your scene and affix with compatible glue.

### Wild Grass Mats

Longer material is ideal for modeling fields, pastures, meadows and more.

### Mini Grass Mats

15-1/2 x 10-5/8" 39.5 x 27cm

**189-7291** Assortment of (30) Green **84.99**

**189-7292** Assortment of (16) Long Wild Grass **74.99**

**189-7293** Spring Green **8.99**

### Small 10.99 ea

Each measures 20 x 16" 50 x 40cm.

**189-7210** Light Green

**189-7211** Dark Green

**189-7214** Corn Field

### Large 28.99 ea

Each measures 32 x 32" 80 x 80cm.

**189-7215** Light Green

**189-7216** Dark Green

**189-7219** Corn Field

### Plowed Field Mat

**189-7182** pkg(2) **6.99**
19 x 11" 48 x 28cm

### Flowering Meadow Mats

Each 11-13/32 x 7-1/16" 29 x 18cm sheet features a field with specific kinds of wildflowers. Simply cut to fit your available space.

**189-7185** Poppy Field **17.99**

**189-7186** Thistle Field **17.99**

### Large Grass Mats

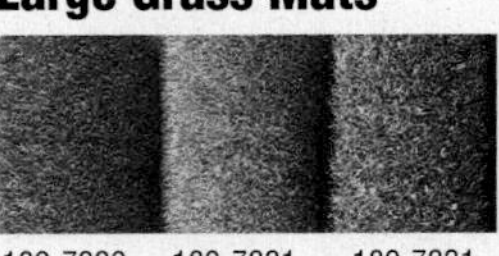

189-7220 189-7221 189-7231

**189-7220** Dark Green **14.99**
40 x 32"

**189-7221** Spring **14.99**
40 x 32"

**189-7224** Autumn-Brown **14.99**
31-1/2 x 39-3/8" 80 x 100cm

**189-7231** Spring **29.99**
79 x 32"

**189-7256** Brown **9.99**
30 x 28" 75 x 70cm

**189-7261** Self-Adhesive Backed Spring Green **35.99**
40 x 32" 150 x 100cm

**189-7270** Dark Green **28.99**
60 x 40" 150 x 100cm

**189-7271** Spring **28.99**
60 x 40" 150 x 100cm

### Grain Field & Reeds 125g

**189-7375 8.99**
Ideal for modeling dried fields of grain, reeds or tall grasses. Strands are approximately 4.4cm long.

## MODELER'S SAND

Great for modeling dirt or gravel roads with truck or tire tracks, this material retains its shape when it hardens. Just mix with water, apply it to your scenery base and add your choice of textures, such as tire tracks, by rolling or molding them into the surface. When dry, Modeler's Sand has a natural, sandy look and can be remoistened for reuse or modification.

### 500g 7.99 ea (Unless Noted)

**189-7553** Light Green

**189-7554** Dark Green

## SCENIC MATERIALS

### Scenery Mortar/Plaster

**189-7193** Natural Sand 35oz 1kg **12.99**
High-quality cellulose spackling compound features a plastic additive that retains fine detail. Busch Scenery Plaster remains workable for approximately 30 minutes—great for carving details into rock molds and more. Once dry it does not shrink, warp and can be worked like wood.

### Mixing Cup

**189-7205 1.99**
Flexible mixing bowl for mixing plaster, paper mache and other materials. To clean, simply crack out dried material by flexing bowl.

## ROADWAY

**189-9710** Asphalt 48" Straight 2-Lane (Asphalt Gray w/White Markings) **7.99**

### Flexible Roadway

**189-1105** Asphalt w/Potholes **7.99**
2-5/8 x 39" 6.6cm x 1m

IMPORTED FROM GERMANY BY WALTHERS

**189-6031** Old Town Street **12.99**
78-3/4 x 3-9/64" 2m x 8cm

**189-6032** Paved Area **4.99**
7-7/8 x 6-19/64" 20 x 16cm

**189-6033** Asphalt Country Road (With White Stripe) **6.99**
39-3/8 x 2-19/32" 1m x 6.6cm

**189-6034** Asphalt Country Road (Unmarked) **6.99**
39-3/8 x 2-19/32" 1m x 6.6cm

**189-6037** Cobblestone Street **7.99**
39-3/8 x 2-19/32" 1m x 6.6cm

**189-6038** Town Street w/Sidewalk **9.99**
39-3/8 x 4-11/32" 1m x 11cm

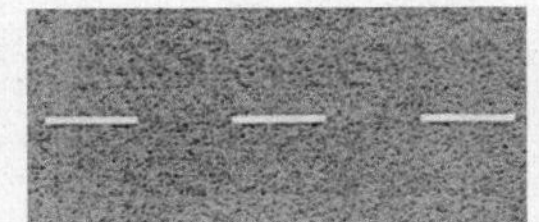

**189-6039** Tarmac (Chip-Seal) Road **7.99**
39-3/8 x 3-9/64" 1m x 8cm

**189-7074** Intersection w/Pedestrian Crossing **10.99**
For use w/8cm-wide streets.

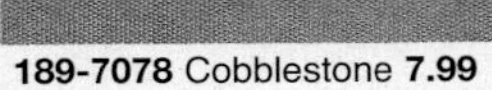

**189-7078** Cobblestone **7.99**

**189-7082** Bicycle Path **6.99**
14.5mm (5/8") wide, printed in gray/red with bicycle symbol.

**189-7084** Flexible Field Path **5.99**
23mm (1") wide.

**189-7085** Asphalt **9.99**
22 x 13" 56 x 33cm

**189-7086** Asphalt - Wide **11.99**
22 x 73"

**189-7090** Asphalt Tape - Double-Faced **15.99**

**189-7093** Country Asphalt **7.99**

**189-7098** Street Curve 120mm **8.99**

## Sidewalk Sheet

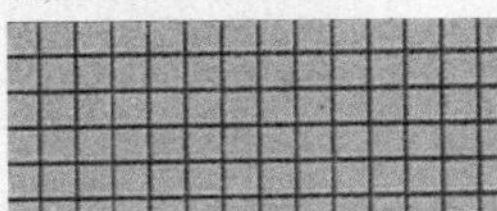

**189-7094** pkg(6) **4.99**
8-1/2 x 6" 21 x 15cm

## Parking Lots 4.99 ea

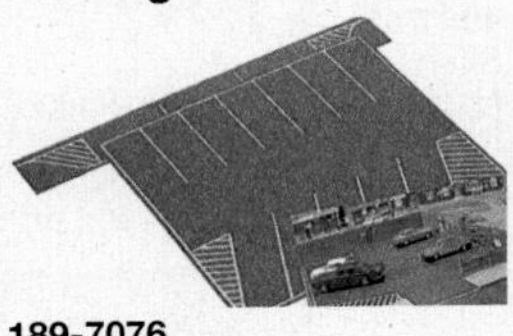

**189-7076**
8 x 6-1/2" 20 x 16cm

**189-9713** Asphalt Gray w/White Markings

## Curved Roads

**189-1103** Curve **7.99**
7-5/8" 19cm

**189-9711** 2-Lane Semi-Circle (Asphalt Gray w/White Markings) **8.99**

## Intersections

**189-9712 10.99**
Features white crosswalks and stop lines. Asphalt-gray color.

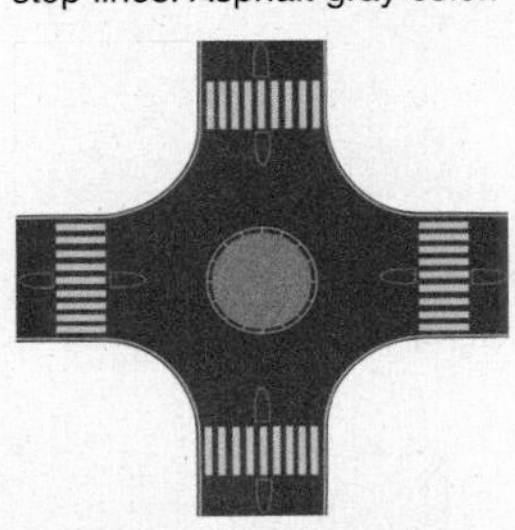

**189-1101** 4-Way Roundabout/ Traffic Circle **15.99**
12 x 12" 30 x 30cm

**189-1104** 4-Way Intersection w/Sidewalks **17.99**

## Mortar 9.99 ea

Self-adhesive putty can be used to create all kinds of scenic formations. Mix one part mortar with one part water, knead into a pasty dough and apply. Stays workable for up to four hours, dries completely in two days. Package includes 17-1/2oz (500g).

**189-7590** Rocks (Gray)

**189-7591** Soil (Tan)

See What's Available at

**www.walthers.com**

# TUNNEL PORTALS

## "Ice" Tunnel Portals

Modern designs are based on portals used on the German Railways Inter City Express (ICE) line.

**189-7020** Single Track **9.99**

**189-7021** Double Track **11.99**

**189-7028** Double Track "Montabaur" **15.99**

## Tunnel Portals w/Wings 11.99 ea

**189-7022** Single Track

**189-7023** Double Track

## Single-Track Tunnel Portals

**189-7024** Less Liner Holder pkg(2) **3.99**

**189-7026** With Liner Holder pkg(2) **3.99**

## Double-Track Tunnel Portals

**189-7027** pkg(2) **4.99**

# LIGHTED SCENIC DETAILS

**189-5404** Graves w/Lamps **28.99**
Includes four graves with LED lamps and an angel statue.

**189-5407** Campfire & Grill **35.99**
You almost smell the steaks cooking! Includes a brick fire pit with campfire, which is illuminated by two lamps and an electronics circuit. The grill is complete with small sausages and steaks. Includes wood table, two wood seats and six stumps which can be used as additional seating.

**189-5408** Summer Night Party Set **31.99**
Features a garland with 12 colored lights, two wooden masts, four benches and two tables.

**189-5409** Christmas Tree w/7 Yellow Lights **26.99**

**189-5410** Christmas Tree w/Lights **26.99**
2" 5cm Tall. Includes seven miniature LEDs. 14-16V.

IMPORTED FROM GERMANY BY WALTHERS

**189-5450** Construction Zone pkg(4) **35.99**
Contains four stantions (two blinking) and control unit.

**189-6021** Railroad/Highway Grade Crossing (European Style) **17.99**
Includes two gates, highway sections and warning signs.

**189-6465** Winter Set **18.99**
Includes 10 white trees, snowman, aviary and snow powder.

**189-9719** Modern Highway Guardrail Set (silver) **6.99**
36" 90cm.

**189-9730** Construction Site Blinkers **34.99**
Warn oncoming vehicles of road work ahead with these construction site blinkers. Seven stations (four of which blink), control unit and traffic signs are included.

## MINIATURE SCENES

These collectible miniatures look great on your layout or on display. Fully assembled with figures and scenery material, most also include a vehicle and accessories. For safe, dust-free display, each comes in a clear plastic box with base.

**189-5420** Grill Truck **35.99**
Includes grill truck with interior LED illumination and transparent display counter, tables, benches, menu boards and signs.

**189-5425** Caravan Cuties **38.99**
Aluminum travel trailer equipped as a rolling "love nest." Includes illuminated sign, interior light and female figure.

**189-6004** Winter Set Kit **10.99**
Includes snowboards, carving ski, roof rack, roof-top carrier and snowman.

**189-6011** Windsurfer Kit **10.99**
Includes four boards, sails, mast, riggs and vehicle roof rack.

**189-6049** Cemetery **28.99**
This highly detailed scene pays honor to those who have recently passed away. All details needed to make this realistic scene are included.

**189-7622** Joe The Sprayer **14.99**
Graffiti "artist" tags a wooden fence. Includes van, painter and decorated wooden fence.

**189-7636** Dinosaur Escape! **16.99**
Prehistoric beasts push their way out of a cage, terrifying the man standing on the other side.

**189-7646** Fairy Tale Wedding **33.99**

**189-7648** Speed Trap **18.99**
Includes radar unit, officer and three-wheel truck w/load.

**189-7649** Wedding Day **30.99**
Includes Benz 1886 Motorwagen, bride, groom and ornate fence.

**189-7650** Halloween II **27.99**
This hot rod hearse will get you to the cemetery in a hurry! Includes hearse street rod, Grim Reaper, iron fence, coffin and more.

**189-7652** Lure of the Deep **16.99**
Includes diver, mermaid, kelp and more.

**189-7654** Merry Christmas VIII **27.99**
Perfect for tackling any kind of winter weather, the new Santamobile guarantees that the gifts will be delivered on time! Includes the vehicle, woman driver figure and small snow-covered tree.

**189-7655** Merry Christmas IX **33.99**
Includes Santa, female helper, truck, snowman and tree.

**189-7658** Halloween 5 **32.99**

Cemetery 189-6049

**189-7659** Merry Christmas X **33.99**

**189-7662** Rest In Peace **8.99**
Includes six graves with flowers and one fountain.

**189-7665** Forest Cruiser **29.99**

**189-7666** Animal Banquet **30.99**

**189-7668** The Slow Apprentice **18.99**
New mechanic learns the tricks of the trade. Includes auto, lift, welding tanks and figures.

**189-7669** Admiring the Scenery **17.99**
Nudist colony scene includes two nude figures and one observer, air mattress, fence with knothole, bicycle and tree.

**189-7670** Traveling Light **25.99**
Includes vintage auto, two figures, nostalgic advertising pillar, dog and luggage.

**189-7671** Sobriety Checkpoint **22.99**
Includes auto, two figures and signs.

**189-7672** "Wild Boar" **20.99**

**189-7673** Flower Power **26.99**
Includes VW Beetle with "Flower Power" graphics, two nude "Flower Children" figures and sunflowers.

**189-7674** Streetball (Basketball) **15.99**
Includes basketball hoop, ball, trash can, two figures and sign.

**189-7676** Hearse Breakdown **25.99**

**189-7677** BSE Free Zone **16.99**
Includes police car, police officer, farmer, cow and sign.

**189-7678** "Fallen Down" **23.99**

IMPORTED FROM GERMANY BY WALTHERS

**189-7690** Spring Feelings **11.99**
Includes a blooming tree, figure, bull and a section of rail fence.

### Labyrinth Garden Scene

**189-7153 21.99**
7-7/8 x 7-7/8" 20 x 20cm

Create a garden maze with this set. Includes three trees, angel statue, well with pump and benches.

## SCENIC DETAILS

**189-1130** Advertising Posters (German) **7.99**

**189-1131** Building Details **15.99**
Includes vents, clocks, satellite dishes, signs and more.

**189-1132** Assorted Freight Loads **8.99**
Includes pallets, crates, barrels and more.

**189-1134** Beverage Cases **11.99**
Visit any large retailer or gas station/convenience store and you'll find sodas and more displayed outside next to the building walls. This set includes 80 beverage bins (16 each in green light blue, beige and red), a cooler and German language wall signage (some of which is usable on U.S.-themed layouts).

**189-1135** Nostalgic Scene with Advertising Pillars **13.99**
Set includes nostalgic posters in German, iron-and-brick fencing and park benches.

**189-1136** Refuse Set **11.99**
Perfect for back alleys and streets, set includes 16 refuse containers in assorted colors (garbage, bio-waste, old paper, etc.), 12 refuse bags, three trash receptacles, sand piles with wheelbarrows and various tools.

**189-1150** Summer & Fall Figures **19.99**
Includes mermaid, scarecrow, grim reaper w/casket and tombstone.

**189-1151** Winter Figures **19.99**
Includes Santa, helper, angel and snowman.

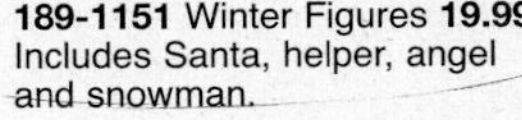

**189-6010** Bridge & Swans **18.99**

**189-6026** Campsite w/Tents **16.99**
Includes four tents with partial interiors, a folding table and stool, a life boat and air mattresses.

## FENCES

### 6.99 ea (Unless Noted)

**189-1016** Concrete Wall **13.99**
1/2" 1.2cm wide x 1-3/8" 3.5cm high sections; overall length 22-7/16 57cm.
Makes a great border/prison wall when used with 189-1015 Watch Tower (sold separately).

**189-1017** Chain-Link Fence **11.99**
1" 2.5cm high x 37-13/32" 95cm long.
Includes 24 round fence posts and two gates.

**189-6007** Picket Fence Set
48" with four gates.

**189-6008** Farm Field Fence Set (brown)
52" 130cm.

**189-6009** Garden Fence Set (white)

**189-6016** Wrought Iron w/Brick Posts **12.99**
25-5/8" 65cm

**189-6018** With Gates **7.99**
120cm+

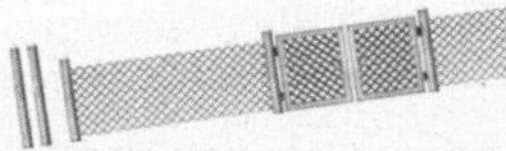

**189-6019** Chain-Link **7.99**
40" 100cm.

## WALLS

**189-6014** Stone w/Metal Gate **10.99**

## FLEXIBLE WALL SHEETS

Precolored, self-adhesive wall sheets are made of embossed foam material for extra realism. Stick them on building sides or other smooth surfaces to add realistic texture and color. Can be weathered with chalks.

**189-7401** Tile Gray **7.99**

**189-7402** Even Brick Brown **5.99**

**189-7403** Natural Stone **5.99**

### Plastic Sheets pkg(2) 2.49 ea

**189-7035** Interlocked Stone
**189-7036** Hex Stone
**189-7037** Random Stone
**189-7038** Cut Stone
**189-7039** Wood Planking

## WALL CARDS

### 2.99 ea

**189-7421** Layered Stone

**189-7422** Natural Stone

**189-7423** Sandstone

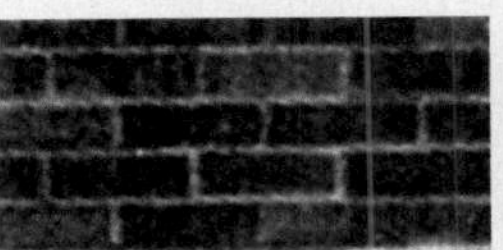

**189-7424** Dark Brick

**189-7425** Red Brick

IMPORTED FROM GERMANY BY WALTHERS

# BACKGROUND SCENES

## CD-ROM

Create and print your own background scenes using the images on this CD. Features a variety of elements including structures and landscapes. Structures are photographed frontally and can be printed out in any scale and mounted on cardboard to make a variety of affordable backdrops. Images are in JPEG and PSD format for use with photo editing applications such as PhotoShop, PhotoPaint, CorelDraw and others. Requires a IBM-compatible PC running Windows 95 or higher. (German language).

**189-2870** Backgrounds for Model Railroads 2 CD Set **33.99**

**189-2867** North German Backgrounds **17.99**

**189-2868** Alpine Backgrounds **17.99**

Item listed below is available by Special Order (see Legend Page).

**189-2869** Dutch Backgrounds **17.99**

## Preprinted Backgrounds 15.99 ea

Add realistic background scenes to your layout with these photo-quality scenes. Backgrounds include elements at each end that allow them to be placed end-to-end along your layout backdrop. Each background measures 78 x 13-3/8" 198 x 34cm and can be used as a basis for further customizing by gluing on printed elements from the Backgrounds for Model Railroads CD 189-2870.

**189-2871** Forest Background

**189-2872** Hilly Landscape

**189-2873** Village

**189-2874** Old City

USA Backgrounds 2CD Set 189-2866

Hilly Landscape 189-2872

Village 189-2873

Old City 189-2874

## Day and Night Backgrounds 15.99 ea

Want to add a background scene that simulates both daylight and night lighting conditions? These unique backgrounds are printed on translucent material that allows you to use them two ways. When lit with conventional room lighting, they offer a photo-realistic background scene. To simulate a nighttime scene, simply mount the scene in a frame with a light box behind it (both sold separately) and the scene is magically transformed. The translucent base is printed with a pattern that allows bright light to shine through only in selected places such as through windows and on streetlights. The rest of the scene gets its depth from the remaining shadows. Each scene measures 77-15/16" x 13-3/8" 198 x 34cm.

189-2875 River #1

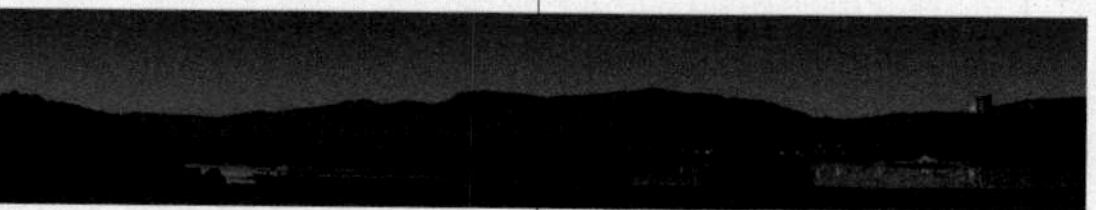

189-2876 River #2

189-2877 City #1

189-2878 City #2

# AM MODELS

## Rocks

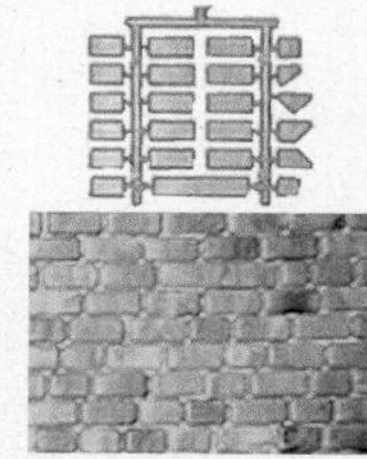

**129-502 2.95**
Molded in various shapes and colors, enough to cover 10 square inches.

## Fences

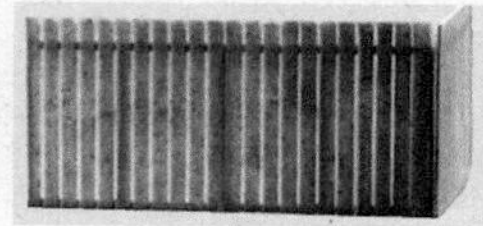

**129-503** pkg(4) **2.95**
Includes four sections, each eight scale feet long.

# CM SHOPS, INC.

## Tunnel Portals

Full-size modern-style portals designed to clear today's larger rolling stock, such as double-stack and auto rack cars. Molded in concrete colored plastic, which is easily painted or weathered.

### Arched Opening

**12-2001** Single Track **6.75**

**12-2002** Double Track **7.75**

### Square Opening

**12-2011** Single Track **6.75**

**12-2012** Double Track **7.75**

# BRAWA

LIEBE ZUM DETAIL

IMPORTED FROM GERMANY BY WALTHERS

## WALLS

Additional wall sections for use with #186-2880 (sold separately).

### Arched Retaining Walls pkg(2) 5.99 ea

6 x 4".

**186-2865** Gray - 4 Arches

**186-2866** Brick Red- 4 Arches

**Limited Quantity Available**
**186-2860** Gray - 6 Arches

### Under-Viaduct Storefronts

**186-2880 18.99**
Berlin Stadbahn railroad arches with shops. Plastic kits are molded in appropriate colors. With 2 arch sections; approximately 3 x 8-1/2". Arches are about 4-1/4" long.

### Arch w/Recess

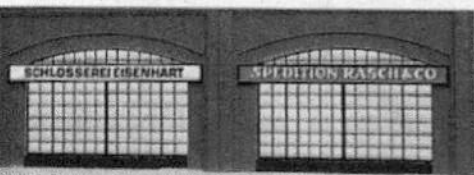

**186-2881** Arcade Wall pkg(2) **16.99**

### Arch w/Enclosed Windows

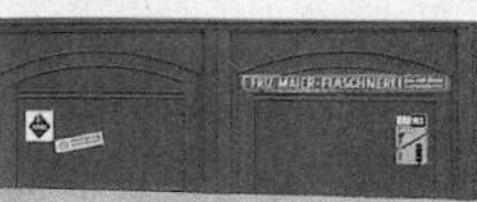

**186-2882** Arcade Wall pkg(2) **16.99**

All Chooch Enterprises scenery products are handcast resin, prepainted and weathered.

# TUNNEL PORTALS

## Single Track 8.99 ea

**214-8320** Concrete
4.5 x 4.4"

**214-8321** Cascade
5 x 4.9"

**214-8340** Cut Stone
4.5 x 4.5"

**214-8360** Random Stone
5 x 4.75"

## Double Track 8.99 ea

**214-8330** Concrete
6.6 x 5.25"

**214-8350** Cut Stone
6.5 x 5.4"

**214-8370** Random Stone
6.5 x 5.25"

# BRIDGE ABUTMENTS

## Single Track 9.99 ea

Fits Central Valley Rigid Truss Bridge (#210-1902), sold separately.

**214-8440** Cut Stone
3.5 x 3.75"

**214-8460** Cut Stone Tapered
5 x 3.75"

## Double Track

**214-8450** Cut Stone **9.99**
3.5 x 3.75"

For Daily Product Updates Point Your Browser to
**www.walthers.com**

# BRIDGE PIERS

For Central Valley Bridge.

**214-8430** Cut Stone (Pointed End) **9.99**
4.75 x 1.12 x 3.75"

**214-8431** Cut Stone Rectangular **9.99**
4 x 1.25 x 3.75"

## Double Track

**214-8432** Cut Stone Double-Pointed Bridge Pier **14.99**
5.75 x 2 x 3.75"

# WALLS

## Stepped Walls 8.99 ea

**214-8400** Cut Stone
6.6 x 3.75"

## Interlocking Retaining 7.99 ea

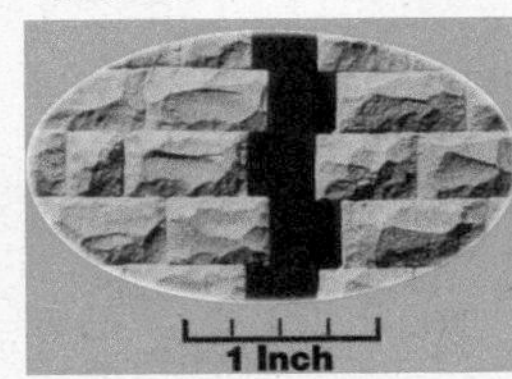


Diagram reflects size of interlocking retaining walls.

### Random Stone

**214-8300** Small
6.75 x 3.6"

**214-8302** Medium
7 x 3.4"

Cut Stone Bridge Pier (Pointed End) 214-8430

Cut Stone Stepped Wall 214-8400

Random Stone Tunnel Portal 214-8360

**214-8304** Large
6.75 x 3.4"

### Cut Stone

**214-8310** Small
6.75 x 3.4"

**214-8312** Medium
6.75 x 3.5"

**214-8314** Large
6.75 x 3.5"

## NEW PRODUCTS

### Laser-Cut Wood Grade Crossings

### Curved pkg(2) 6.00 ea

**NEW 184-125** 15" Radius

**NEW 184-126** 18" Radius

**NEW 184-127** 22" Radius

**NEW 184-128** 24" Radius

**NEW 184-129** 30" Radius

**NEW 184-130** 36" Radius

## STREET/HIGHWAY DETAILS

### Pre-Assembled Road Barricades pkg(2) 7.00 ea

**184-161** Modern (orange & white)
Includes "Road Closed" sign.

**184-1612** Older Style (black & white)

### Manhole Covers & Storm Drains

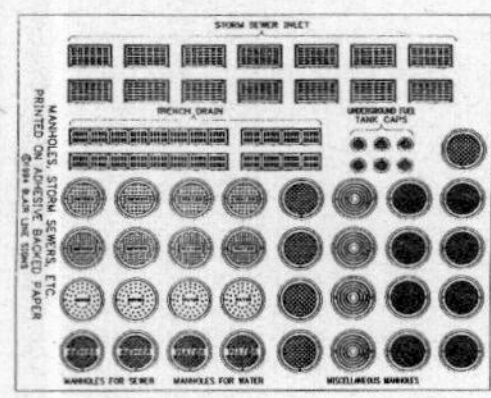

**184-162 4.00**
Printed on adhesive-backed paper. Features cut, peel-and-stick installation.

## LASER-CUT GRADE CROSSINGS

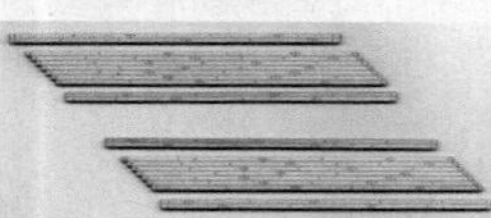

**184-132** Laser-Cut Wood Grade Crossings – Angled Left pkg(2) **7.00**

**184-134** Laser-Cut Wood Grade Crossings – Angled Right pkg(2) **7.00**

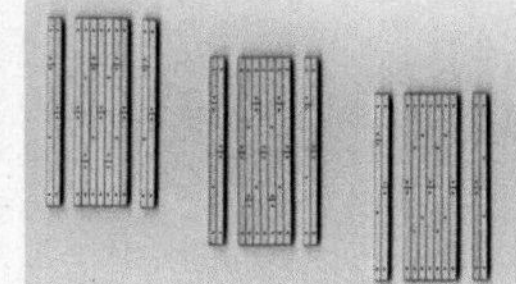

**184-133** Laser-Cut Wood Grade Crossings – One Lane pkg(3) **6.00**

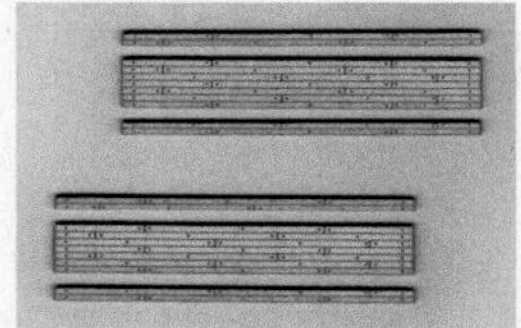

**184-165** Two-Lane pkg(2) **6.00**
Each highway grade crossing is fully assembled and ready to paint/stain and install.

## CENTRAL VALLEY

### Fence & Railing Assortment

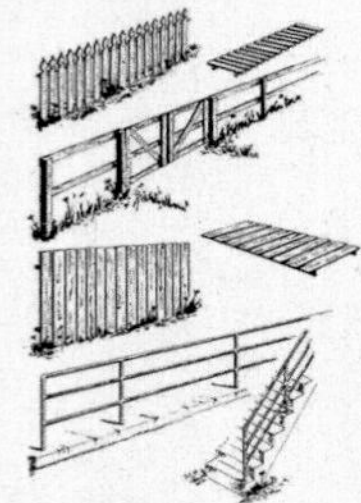

**210-1601** pkg(4) **5.98**
Includes four "sprues" of five styles of fencing material, enough for approximately 24 inches of each style, including gates. Styles include: 3' scale high pickets with gate, 4' scale post and rail with gate, 6' scale vertical board with gate, 3' scale welded pipe and 3' welded pipe for 45° stairsteps.

### Steps & Ladders

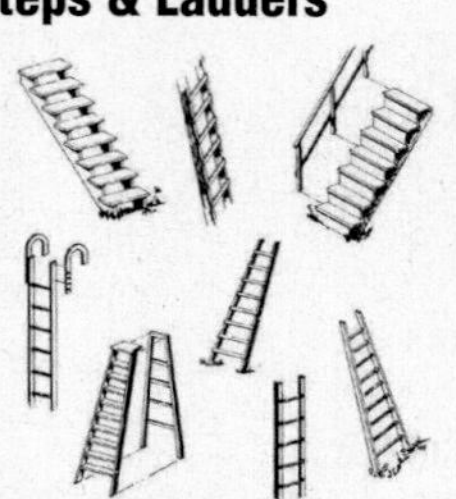

**210-1602** pkg(4) **5.98**
Second in this series of products, the package includes four "sprues" of ten different step and ladder materials. Includes 24" open riser stair, 24" closed riser stair, 24" wood ladder stock, 24" steel ladder stock, four-piece 10 foot step ladder, four pairs of steel ladder loops, four-piece wood ladder, four-piece wood ladder-slat, eight-piece freight car ladder and 24" wood stair railing.

## B.T.S.

*Better Than Scratch!*

These Craftsman Kits feature precision laser-cut basswood and plywood. They are engineered for easy assembly.

## ONE-NITERS

There are many structures that are more complex than a simple detail casting, and much less work than the easiest small building kit. These One-Niter kits can be finished in just one evening of model building.

### Board Fence

Each contains 90 scale feet of fence.

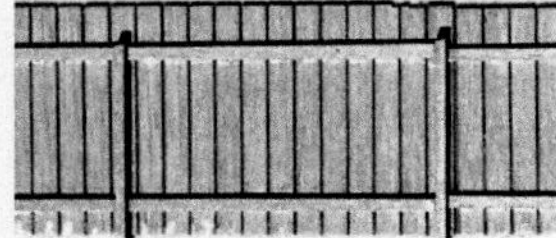

**464-23014** 6' Height **6.95**

**464-23019** 9' Height **9.95**

### Benches

**464-23011** Workbench pkg(2) **5.95**

**464-23012** Bench pkg(2) **4.95**

### Cable Reel

**464-23003** 4' Diameter pkg(4) **6.95**

### Chairs

**464-23006** Rocking Chair pkg(4) **4.95**

**464-23016** Wood Chair - Straight pkg(4) **4.95**

**464-23017** Captain's Chair pkg(4) **4.95**

### Crossbucks

**464-23001** pkg(4) **8.95**

### Logger/Picnic Table

**464-23018 4.95**

### Oil Drum Rack w/Drums

**464-23000** pkg(2) **8.95**

## "ONE HOLER" OUTHOUSE KITS 6.95 ea

**464-23004** Standard Type w/Flat Roof, Positionable Doors pkg(2)

**464-23005** Peaked Roof, Positionable Doors for Ladies (Crescent Moon) & Gentlemen (Star) pkg(2)

### Pallets

**464-23013** pkg(16) **4.95**

### Wood Ladders

**464-23015** pkg(4) **7.95**

### Gas Station Details

**464-20711** Hydraulic Auto Hoist **4.50**

**464-20712** Gas Tank Filler Vent Pipe **1.25**

**464-20774** Detail Set **24.95**
Complete with color decals, two oil bunkers with crank arms, two filler vent pipes for simulated underground storag tanks, air compressor, inner tube test tank, concrete lube pad, pump island, vehicle lift, two gas pumps and more.

## MISCELLANEOUS

**464-23007** Clothes Line pkg(4 **5.95**

**464-23008** Upright Piano **5.95**

**464-23020** Heavy Duty Sawhorse pkg(4) **4.95**

## NEW PRODUCTS

### Scenic Details

**NEW 176-4102** Large Electrical Box **7.75**
This kit makes a perfect detail along mainlines or near industrial yard buildings and yard offices.

**NEW 176-4111** Portable Toilet (pkg 2) **8.45**
Sporting events, construction sites, fairgrounds and other places where there's no permanent plumbing are ideal spots to set this detailed model. Engineered using prototype dimensions, this model is fully assembled and molded in color.

**NEW 176-4107** Concrete K-rail Barrier (pkg 8) **7.45**
These portable concrete barriers are a common sight around government buildings, private security companies, rail yards, construction sites and more. This detailed plastic part is molded in color so it will add instant realism to your scene.

**NEW 176-4108** Concrete Car Stop (pkg 20) **5.95**
A perfect way to detail parking lots, this plastic part is molded in a light gray color that can be painted for additional uses such as 5-minute parking, etc.

### Fences

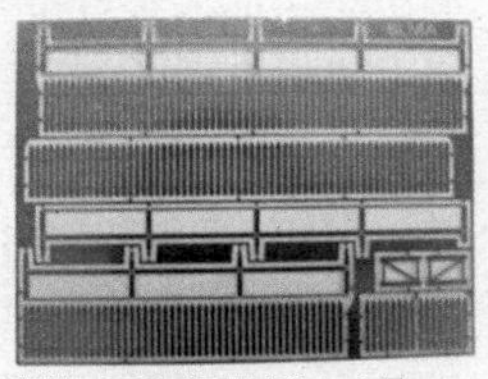

**NEW 176-4200** Picket Fence **18.75**
Now it's easy to add a charming picket fence to your residential scenes. Each etched-metal kit features detailed fencing with pointed tops and support stringers that are cemented to the back; once assembled the fence has a thin profile and pins for mounting the fence to holes drilled in your layout base. Also included are two positionable gates. Meaures over 70 linear scale feet.

**NEW 176-4210** Chain Link Fence **19.50**
Featuring near-scale dimensions, this realistic fencing comes complete with plastic rods to simulate fence posts. Package includes mounting poles and over 110 linear scale feet of 6' tall fencing.

## GRADE CROSSINGS

**176-4105** Concrete **7.50**
Plastic injection-molded parts are easy to assemble. Simply paint and drop into place. Crossing is .06" thick allowing easy installation on Code 83 track. Adding a shim will raise crossing to correct level for Code 100 rail. Based on a prototype in La Habra, California, it's ideal for 1970s to present layouts.

**NEW 176-4106** Rubber Grade Crossing **7.50**
Molded in black plastic, this accurately detailed model is easy to install and will work on Code 60 and larger track. It's a perfect fit for layouts from the 1980s to today. Each package makes a crossing approximately 5" in length.

ETI ENVIRONMENTAL TECHNOLOGY, INC.

## MOLDING MATERIALS

### Casting Resin w/Catalyst

Water clear, shelf life of approximately nine months, (longer if stored at cool temperatures.)

**207-34016** 16oz **21.39**

**207-34032** 32oz **29.90**

**207-34128** 1gal **81.90**

### EasyCast

Two part, low odor clear casting epoxy. Compatible with transparent dyes.

**207-33008** 8oz **10.29**

**207-33016** 16oz **17.00**

**207-33032** 32oz **27.95**

**207-33128** 1gal **85.55**

### Casting Resin

Less catalyst.

**207-175** 16oz **17.15**

**207-183** 32oz **25.45**

**207-191** 1gal **81.35**

**207-46388** Catalyst 1/2oz **4.85**
Needed to cure (harden) resin, for use with #s 175, 183 and 191.

### Envirotex Lite

Pour-on plastic material dries to a hard, clear finish.

**207-2007** 4oz **6.98**

**207-2008** 8oz **10.29**

**207-2016** 16oz **17.00**

**207-2032** 1qt **27.95**

**207-2064** 1/2gal **50.45**

**207-2128** 1gal **85.55**

### Liquid Latex Rubber

**207-779** Mold Builder 16oz **12.19**
For mold making.

### Mixing Cup Set

**207-1013 6.29**
6 disposable cups, stirring paddles and 3 craft brushes.

### Polymer Coatings

Simply mix, measure and pour these decoupage resins to create realistic water. Low odor, low heat and nonflammable. Includes resin and hardener.

**207-27** Ultra-Glo 8oz **10.29**

**207-35** Ultra-Glo 16oz **17.00**

### Transparent Dye 1oz 5.30 ea

Add for see-through color in resin.

**207-46430** Blue

**207-46432** Green

**207-46436** Amber

**207-46440** Pearl

## CITY CLASSICS

### Modular Retaining Walls

**195-601** pkg(2) **9.98**
Hold back those hillsides with City Classics modular retaining walls. Based on poured-concrete walls used along railroads and highways, these walls feature injection-molded styrene plastic parts molded in a realistic concrete color. Each package includes two three-panel wall sections each measuring 8-9/16" long x 3-1/4" tall, plus an additional concrete pilaster. Wall sections may be easily combined without cutting for additional length or may be cut using a razor saw if desired.

For Daily Product Updates Point Your Browser to

**www.walthers.com**

## CAMPBELL SCALE MODELS

### Tunnel Portal

**200-351** Timber **24.84**
11-1/2 x 5"
Can be used as O Scale mine portal.

### Ground Cover 7.59 ea

**200-793** Decomposed Granite Ballast
7oz per package.
**200-795** Coal
For tenders, gondolas and hopper loads.

### Miscellaneous

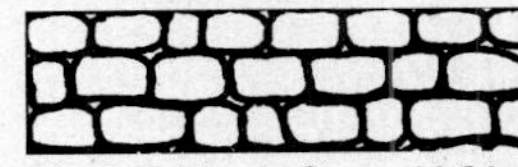

**200-810** Plastic Stone **11.21**
5-3/8 x 17-1/4"
Clear plastic. Model random stone foundations, retaining walls, etc.

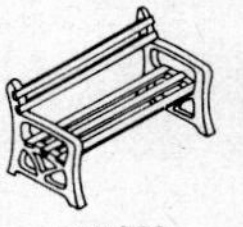

200-930

200-931

**200-930** Park Bench pkg(4) **4.89**

**200-931** 48-Star Flag & Pole **4.49**

# FALLER

IMPORTED FROM GERMANY BY WALTHERS
Creating realistic scenery is fast and fun with the complete Faller line. No matter what kind of terrain you're creating, you'll find trees, groundcover and many other easy-to-use materials that produce realistic miniature scenes.

## NEW PRODUCTS

### Premium Trees

Plant a forest or an orchard. Shade a roadside or line a field with these realistic specimens.

**NEW 272-181210** Birch 5-1/8" 13cm **15.99**

**NEW 272-181211** Alder 5-1/2" 14cm **16.99**

**NEW 272-181212** Oak 3-7/8" 10cm **16.99**

**NEW 272-181213** Apple 3-3/16" 8cm pkg(2) **16.99**

**NEW 272-181214** Cherry 3-3/16" 8cm pkg(2) **16.99**

**NEW 272-181215** Small Alder 3-3/16" 8cm pkg(2) **16.99**

**NEW 272-181216** Sycamore 3-3/8" 8.5cm pkg(2) **16.99**

**NEW 272-181217** Leafless 2-3/4 & 4-3/4" 7 & 12cm pkg(2) **16.99**

**NEW 272-181218** Deciduous 2-3/16" 5.5cm pkg(5) **16.99**

**NEW 272-181229** Arborvitae 1-9/16" 4cm pkg(6) **11.99**

**NEW 272-181376** Weeping Birch 3-1/2" 9cm pkg(3) **11.99**

**NEW 272-181383** Black Poplar 4-3/4" 12cm pkg(4) **10.99**

**NEW 272-181384** Black Poplar 4-1/8" 10.5cm pkg(6) **11.99**

### Shrubs

**NEW 272-181230** Bushes 1-9/16" 4cm pkg(3) **12.99**

**NEW 272-181240** Property Line Trees & Bushes 4-3/4" 12cm pkg(5) **33.99**

### Ground Cover

Natural stone material in various sizes and colors. Perfect for ballast, rock outcroppings and other areas where loose stone accumulates.

#### 10-1/2oz 300g

**NEW 272-171690** Gray-Green 2-5mm **6.99**

**NEW 272-171691** Beige 2-5mm **6.99**

#### 1lb 4oz 650g

**NEW 272-171695** Dark Gray 0.5-1mm **11.99**
Especially for Marklin C-Track.

**NEW 272-171696** Beige-Brown 0.5-1mm **11.99**

**NEW 272-171697** Beige-Brown 0.2-0.6mm **11.99**

**NEW 272-171698** Medium Green 0.2-0.6 **11.99**

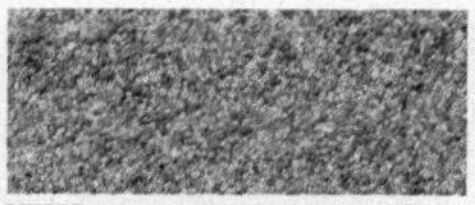

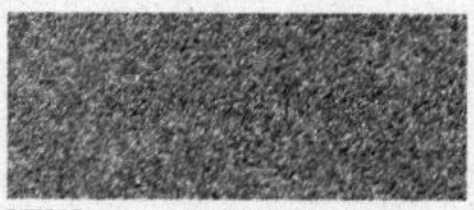

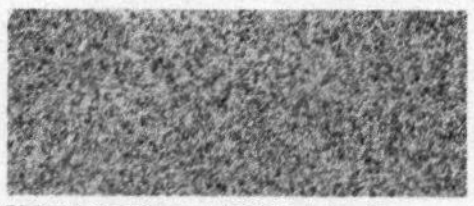

### Fences

The Faller 2007 fence concept kits offer even more diversity for your layout. Choose from many new styles and colors. Measurement shown is total length.

**NEW 272-180401** Two-Rail 42-1/2" 108cm **8.99**

**NEW 272-180402** Picket & Lattice 42-1/2" 108cm **8.99**

**NEW 272-180403** Iron Railing 71-5/8" 182cm **8.99**

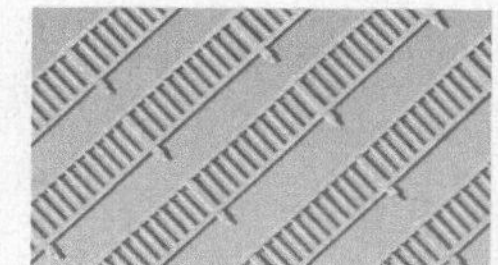
**NEW 272-180404** Two-Rail w/Posts 56-11/16" 144cm **8.99**

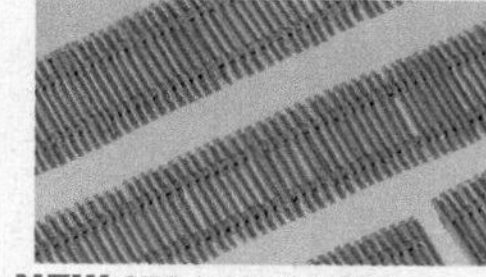
**NEW 272-180405** Slat 31-1/4" 79.4cm **8.99**

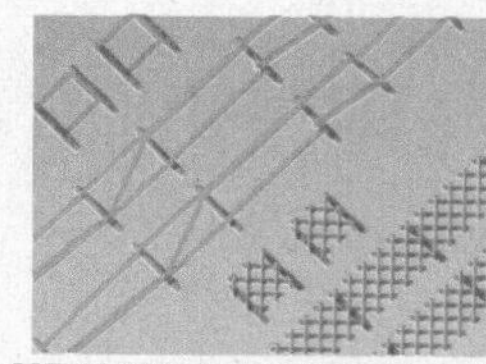
**NEW 272-180406** Garden & Field 92-15/16" 236cm **8.99**

**NEW 272-180407** Lattice Tw Rail 92-7/8" 108cm **8.99**

**NEW 272-180408** Bonanza 53-1/8" 135cm **8.99**

**NEW 272-180409** Fence System (Assorted Fence Part **8.99**

**NEW 272-180410** Garden Fence w/Gate 55-1/8" 140cm **8.99**

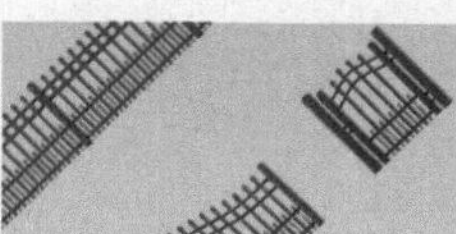
**NEW 272-180411** Iron Garde Fence 55-1/8" 140cm **8.99**

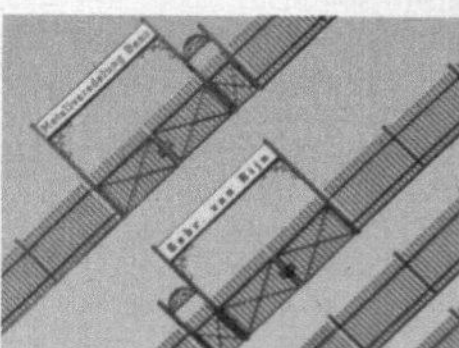
**NEW 272-180412** Iron Fence w/Gate 49-15/16" 104cm **8.99**

**NEW 272-180432** Iron Fence w/Concrete Posts **13.99**

**NEW 272-180433** Industrial Metal Fence **13.99**

**NEW 272-180434** Farmyard Fence System in Two Heights **13.99**

# FALLER

IMPORTED FROM GERMANY BY WALTHERS

## Miniature Scenes

These small scenes capture memorable moments of real life in miniature. The sets make it easy to bring life to any layout and are ideal for collectors.

**NEW 272-154110** Under The Pergola **25.99**
Peaceful scene includes a courting couple, pergola, bench, a tub of flowers and a tree.

**NEW 272-154111** Japanese Garden At the Zoo **25.99**
This delightful zoo scene includes two children, a colorful peacock, an information panel and a barrel with flowers and bushes.

**NEW 272-154112** Boy Scouts At the Campfire **25.99**
Two boy scouts are taking a rest on the rocks after a busy day camping. Includes two figures, campfire, a stack of wood and a tree.

**NEW 272-154113** Actors & Audience **25.99**
The audience is caught up in the drama in this open-air theater scene. Set includes four actors, three spectators and stage scenery.

**NEW 272-180548** Hiker Accessories **30.99**
Wanderers in the wilderness will appreciate these details. Package includes a shelter, footpath signs, a wooden bridge, footbridge and information panel.

## Scenic Details

Finish off your scene or create a new one with these great detail sets.

**NEW 272-180545** Interior Building Details **30.99**
Bring your interiors to life with this set of furniture and accessories. Contains pieces to finish off offices, living areas, bedrooms, kitchens and hallways. Room lighting w/three LEDs is also included.

**NEW 272-180546** Garden Design Elements **22.99**
Add charm to residential or commercial gardens. Set includes plant tubs, trellises and pergolas partially finished with etched-wire filigree.

**NEW 272-180549** Construction Site Details **33.99**
There's always lots of activity and lots of stuff around a construction site. Complete your building site scene with these details. Set includes concrete mixer, scaffolding w/safety net, trash containers and more.

**NEW 272-180553** Modern Bus Shelter **25.99**
These clear contemporary structures will give your bus riders a sheltered place to wait till their bus comes along. There's also parking for bicyclists. Set includes open and closed shelters, bicycle stands and bicycles.

**NEW 272-130525** Stable Interior Equipment **42.99**
Add realism to the inside of a barn or stable with this kit. Includes stable partitions, bright interior lighting and hay racks with skewed rungs to feed farm animals. Ideal accessory for Breeding Farm #272-130520 (sold separately).

**NEW 272-130526** Mangers **21.99**
Two Each: 1-1/2 x 1-3/16 x 1-3/8 & 1-1/4 x 1-1/8 x 1-5/16"
3.9 x 3 x 3.5 & 3.1 x 2.9 x 3.3cm

Feed the sheep, goats, cows, cattle and horses with these covered feed troughs. Kit includes two each of two different styles.

**NEW 272-180550** Soccer Playground **39.99**
9-1/4 x 6-1/2 x 1-3/16"
23.5 x 16.5 x 3cm

Here's everything you need to host the home team at a soccer tournament on your layout. Includes printed lawn, two goals, two board walls and five figures.

# TREES

## Premium Series Trees

**272-181301** Fir 5-1/8" 13cm pkg(2) **16.99**

**272-181302** Fir 5-1/8" 13cm pkg(2) **16.99**

**272-181303** Fir 8-1/4" 21cm **16.99**

**272-181304** Fir **16.99**

**272-181305** Fir pkg(2) **19.99**

**272-181306** Fir pkg(3) **17.99**

**272-181311** Spruce 4-11/32" 11cm pkg(2) **16.99**

**272-181312** Spruce 5-29/32" 15cm pkg(2) **16.99**

**272-181313** Spruce 7-7/8" 20cm pkg(2) **16.99**

**FALLER**

IMPORTED FROM GERMANY
BY WALTHERS

**272-181315** Larch **16.99**

**272-181316** Larch pkg(2) **17.99**

**272-181317** Larch HO/N pkg(2) **16.99**

**272-181320** Horse Chestnut 5-3/16" 13cm **9.99**

**272-181321** White Birch 3-3/16" 8cm pkg(3) **12.99**

**272-181322** Plane Maples 4" 10cm pkg(2) **11.99**

**272-181323** Gray Alders 4" 10cm pkg(2) **11.99**

**272-181324** Common Maples 3-3/16" 8cm pkg(3) **12.99**

**272-181325** White Birch 3-3/16" 8cm pkg(3) **12.99**

**272-181326** Rowan 3-3/16" 8cm pkg(3) **12.99**

**272-181327** Pollard Willow 2-13/16" 7cm pkg(2) **12.99**

**272-181329** Assorted Approximately 2-3/4" 7cm pkg(5) **12.99**

**272-181330** Lime 6" 15cm **11.99**

**272-181331** Ash 8" 20cm **15.99**

**272-181332** Black Alder 4-3/8" 11cm pkg(3) **14.99**

**272-181333** White Birch 4-3/8" 11cm pkg(3) **14.99**

**272-181334** White Birch 5-5/8" 14cm **11.99**

**272-181335** Plane Trees 5-5/8" 14cm pkg(2) **12.99**

**272-181336** Apple w/Fruit 3-11/32" 8.5cm pkg(2) **11.99**

**272-181337** Mountain Ash w/Fruit 5-1/2" 14cm **11.99**

272-181340 272-181341

**272-181340** Swamp Cypress 7-3/16" 18cm pkg(3) **16.99**

**272-181341** Lombardy Poplar 6-13/16" 17cm pkg(3) **16.99**

**272-181342** Trembling Poplar 6-11/16" 17cm pkg(3) **16.99**

**272-181343** Horse Chestnut 7-7/8" 20cm pkg(3) **15.99**

**272-181344** Blossoming Lime 7-7/8" 20cm **15.99**

**272-181345** Red Beech **12.99**

**272-181348** Blue Spruce 5-1/8" 13cm pkg(2) **19.99**

**272-181349** Blue Spruces 2 to 2-3/4" 5-7cm pkg(3) **17.99**

FALLER

IMPORTED FROM GERMANY BY WALTHERS

## Top Series Trees

**272-181364** Beech 7-1/8" 18cm pkg(2) **16.99**

**272-181365** Ash 5-1/2" 14cm pkg(2) **15.99**

**272-181367** Ash 6" 15cm **15.99**

**272-181368** Column Shaped Beech 6-3/8" 16cm **15.99**

**272-181369** Pines 6-3/8" 16cm **11.99**

**272-181370** Pines Set #2 4" 10cm **11.99**

**272-181371** Fruit Trees 2-3/8" 4cm **11.99**

**272-181372** White Birches 5-3/16" 13cm pkg(3) **12.99**

**272-181373** Holm Oaks 4-3/8" 11cm pkg(2) **15.99**

**272-181374** Hornbeams 4" 10cm pkg(3) **15.99**

**272-181375** Bushes 2" 5cm pkg(2) **11.99**

**Limited Quantity Available**

**272-181363** Elm Tree 6-1/4" 16cm **14.99**

## Tree Kits

**Limited Quantity Available**

**272-181382** With Flocking Material 15 Sets **18.99**

## Mixed Forest pkg(15)

For use in HO or N Scales.

**272-181497** Approximately 4" 10cm **32.99**

## Deciduous

**272-181405** 2 Birch & 2 Poplar 2-13/16" 7cm Tall **10.99**

**272-181412** Small 2-1/2" pkg(4) **9.99**

**272-181410** Large 5-1/4" pkg(3) **10.99**

**272-181413** Small 2-1/2" pkg(4) **9.99**

**272-181416** Medium 4-1/4" pkg(4) **10.99**

**272-181488** Small 2-3/8" pkg(6) **10.99**

**272-181453** Large 5-1/2" pkg(2) **12.99**

**272-181455** Beech pkg(4) **12.99**

**272-181459** Poplars HO/N pkg(4) **10.99**

**272-181470** Trees 5" 13cm pkg(14) **33.99**

**272-181471** Small 1-3/16- 2-3/8" 3-6cm pkg(15) **28.99**

**Limited Quantity Available**

**272-181452** Beech 8" 20cm Tall **14.99**

## Oak

**272-181450** Large Oak 6-5/8" **12.99**

**272-181483** Small Oaks 4-1/4" pkg(2) **18.99**



## Fruit 10.99 ea (Unless Noted)

**272-181361** 4-3/8" 11cm pkg(3) **12.99**

**272-181400** Large 4-1/2" Without Fruit pkg(3)

**272-181401** Medium 3-1/4" Without Fruit pkg(3)

**272-181402** Small 2-1/2" Without Fruit pkg(4)

**272-181403** Apple 3-1/4 to 4" pkg(3)

**272-181406** Cherry pkg(3)

**272-181407** Small 2-1/3" w/Fruit pkg(4)

**272-181408** Medium 4-1/4" Rowan w/Fruit pkg(3)

**272-181414** Small 1-3/16 to 2-3/8" pkg(5)

**272-181445** Fruit Trees 10cm pkg(4) **12.99**

**272-181484** Lime 6-13/32" 16cm Tall **12.99**

**Limited Quantity Available**

**272-181360** 3-5/8" 9cm pkg(3) **11.99**

## Weeping Willow

**272-181424** Medium 3-7/8" pkg(2) **12.99**

## FALLER

IMPORTED FROM GERMANY BY WALTHERS

**Birch 10.99 ea (Unless Noted)**

**272-181423** 3-1/2" pkg(4)

**272-181422** Medium 4-1/4" pkg(4)

**272-181420** Medium 5-1/8" pkg(3)

**272-181457** 6-3/4" **12.99**

**272-181415** 1-3/4" Mini pkg(5) **9.99**

**272-181486** Small 2-3/16" pkg(5)

**Limited Quantity Available**

**272-181456** Assorted 4-1/2" pkg(3) **8.99**

**Beech**

**272-181454** 7" 18cm pkg(2) **10.99**

**Poplar**

**272-181362** 5-5/8" 14cm pkg(3) **12.99**

**272-181421** 6" 15cm pkg(4) **16.99**

**272-181425** Large 5-1/4" pkg(3) **10.99**

**272-181426** White 5-1/2" pkg(4) **12.99**

**272-181487** Small 2-1/2" pkg(5) **10.99**

**Limited Quantity Available**

**272-181460** Black, Medium pkg(4) **9.99**

**Flowering**

**272-181475** Forsythia -Yellow Flowers pkg(6) **10.99**

**Chestnut**

**Limited Quantity Available**

**272-181463** Large 6-3/4" **11.99**

**Tree Assortments**

**272-181491** Deciduous 4" 10cm Tall pkg(15) **26.99**

**272-181493** Silver Firs 2 to 4-13/16" 5 to 12cm Tall pkg(40) **49.99**

**272-181495** Mixed Forest Trees 3-5/8 to 6" 9 to 15cm Tall pkg(15) **32.99**

### Evergreens

**Blue Spruce**

**272-181429** Tall Spruce w/Root Detail Each 7-13/64 to 8" 18 to 20cm Tall pkg(6) **19.99**

**272-181432** Blue Spruce pkg(3) **10.99**
One medium 4-1/2" and two large 5-1/2".

**Colorado Spruce**

**272-181439** 5 Each: 3-1/2, 4-3/4 & 6" pkg(15) **19.99**

**Tamarack 10.99 ea**

**272-181437** Assorted 4-1/2" pkg(3)

**272-181438** Small 3-1/2" pkg(4)

**Pine 10.99 ea**

**272-181433** Large Fir 4-1/2" pkg(3)

**272-181436** Medium 4" pkg(3)

**272-181434** Small Fir 2" pkg(5)

**272-181431** Medium Fir 3-3/4" pkg(4)

**272-181430** Large Fir 5-1/2" pkg(3) **10.99**

**272-181441** Nordic Pine 5 1/4" pkg(3) **10.99**

**272-181462** Nordic 3" 8cm pkg(4) **10.99**

**272-181428** pkg(3) **10.99**

**Pine Assortments**

**272-181440** 10 Each: 1-1/4, 2 & 2-3/4" pkg(30) **19.99**

**272-181464** Fir, Assorted pkg(50) Sizes Ranging From 4 to 6" **33.99**

**272-181465** Fir, Assorted pkg(25) Sizes Ranging From 4-3/4 to 6-1/2" **27.99**

## PREMIUM SCENERY MATERIALS

**Natural Blossoms pkg(100)**

**272-171830** White **13.99**

**272-171831** Yellow **13.99**

**272-171832** Red **15.99**

**272-171833** Lilac **15.99**

**Natural Shrubs .7oz 20g**

**272-171834** Yellow **9.99**

**272-171835** Wine Red **9.99**

**272-171836** Blue Blooming **9.99**

**272-171837** Light Green **8.99**

**272-171838** Dark Green **8.99**

**Plants**

**272-171839** Green Climbers pkg(20) **6.99**

## HEDGES

**272-181350** Light Green pkg(3) **10.99**

**272-181352** Blooming - Red pkg(3) **10.99**

**272-181356** Light Green pkg(4) **10.99**

**272-181358** Blooming - Red pkg(4) **10.99**

**272-181398** Light Green pkg(3) **9.99**
4 x 3/8 x 3/8" 10 x 1 x 1cm

**272-181399** Flowering Yellow pkg(3) **9.99**
4 x 3/8 x 3/8" 10 x 1 x 1cm

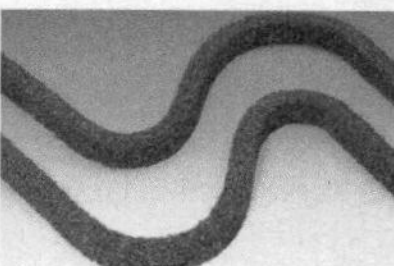

**272-181449** Small 19" pkg(2) **9.99**

**272-181448** Medium 19" pkg(2) **9.99**

**272-181489** Long - pkg(3) **12.99**
20 x 1" 50 x 1 x 2.7cm

## SHRUBS

**272-181366** 1-1/8" 3cm pkg( **15.99**

**272-181474** Assortment pkg(12) **17.99**

**272-181476** Red Flowers pkg(6) **10.99**

**272-181478** Blooming 1-1/2" pkg(6) **10.99**

**272-181479** Green 1-1/2" pkg(6) **10.99**

**272-181443** Large Bushes pkg(3) **9.99**

**272-181468** Shrubs 1-13/16" 4.5cm Tall pkg(6) **12.99**

**Limited Quantity Available**

**272-181381** 15 Kits **18.99**
With flocking material.

**HO/N pkg(4) 10.99 ea**

**272-181395** w/Red Flowers

**272-181396** w/Yellow Flowers

**272-181397** Light Green

IMPORTED FROM GERMANY BY WALTHERS

# VINES

**272-181490** Vineyard w/Poles pkg(36) **19.99**
Complete vineyard with foliage and poles, each about 1-1/4" 3cm tall.

# GROUND COVER

## Foliage 12.99 ea

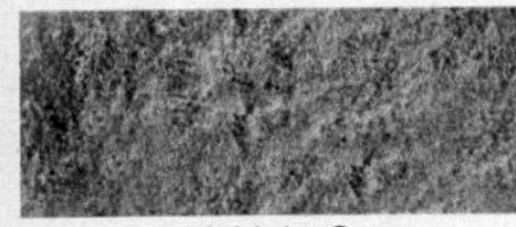

**272-181390** Light Green

**272-181391** Dark Green

**272-181392** Medium Green

## Ground Cover Material 4.99 ea (Unless Noted)

**272-170701** Black (45g) **2.49**
**272-170712** Spring Green (120g)
**272-170713** Forest Green (120g)
**272-170714** Flowery Meadow (120g)

## Flock 3.49 ea

### Fine .88oz

**272-170756** Spring Green
**272-170757** Dark Green

**Limited Quantity Available**

### 2.99 ea (Unless Noted)

### Medium .53oz

**272-170758** Spring Green
**272-170759** Dark Green

### Coarse .53oz

**272-170760** Spring Green
**272-170761** Dark Green,
**272-170762** Multicolor **3.49**

## Meadow Grass 14.99 ea

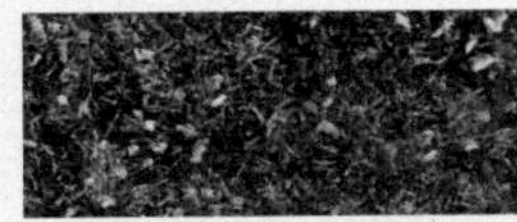

**272-181393** Medium Green

**272-181394** Mixed Green

## Lichen

**272-170730** 5 Assorted Colors 2.8oz **11.99**

## Scatter Material

1oz packages.

**272-170702** Spring Green **2.49**
**272-170703** Forest Green **2.49**
**272-170710** Meadow Green **2.49**
**272-170725** Grass Fiber **6.99**
**272-170726** Grass, Dark Green **6.99**
**272-170727** Dark Brown **6.99**

**272-170716** Marsh Reeds pkg(20) **11.99**

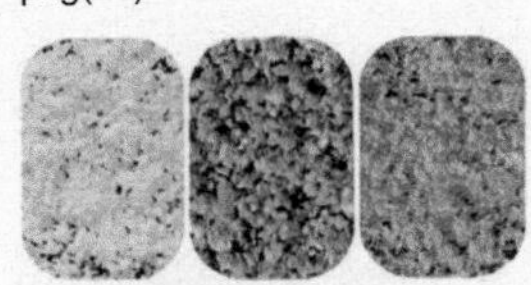

**Limited Quantity Available**

**272-170707** Yellow **1.99**
**272-170717** Flower Decor **10.99**
**272-170708** Light Blue **1.99**
**272-170709** Flower Red **1.99**

Daily New Arrival Updates! Visit Walthers Web site at **www.walthers.com**

## Scenery Assortments

**272-170735** Winter Scene Making Set **42.99**
Set includes enough material to completely cover an area about 39-1/4 x 39-1/4" 100 x 100cm or three to four houses and some trees. Comes complete with detailed instructions, six trees, spatula and large and small icicles.

**Limited Quantity Available**

**272-180503** 4-1/2oz **9.99**
Uncolored.

## Ground Mats

### Light Green

**272-180766** Small **13.99**
40 x 30" 100 x 75cm
**272-180767** Medium **26.99**
40 x 60" 100 x 150cm
**272-180769** Large **45.99**
40 x 100" 100 x 250cm

**Limited Quantity Available**

### Meadow Green

**272-180781** Small **13.99**
40 x 30" 100 x 75cm
**272-180782** Medium **26.99**
40 x 60" 100 x 150cm
**272-180783** Large **44.99**
40 x 100" 100 x 250cm

### Dark Green

**272-180770** Small **13.99**
40 x 30" 100 x 75cm
**272-180771** Medium **26.99**
40 x 60" 100 x 150cm
**272-180773** Large **45.99**
40 x 100" 100 x 250cm

## Flowering Meadow

**272-180774** Small **13.99**
40 x 30" 100 x 75cm
**272-180775** Medium **26.99**
40 x 60" 100 x 150cm
**272-180777** Large **45.99**
40 x 100" 100 x 250cm

## Mini Ground Mats pkg(2) 4.49 ea (Unless Noted)

15-3/4 x 11-5/8" 40 x 29.5cm

**272-180787** Light Green

**272-180788** Dark Green

**272-180789** Flowery Meadow

**272-180791** Wild Grass Light Green **4.99**

**272-180792** Wild Grass Dark Green **4.99**

**272-180793** Cornfield **6.99**

## Ballast Mats

Measures 40 x 30" 100 x 75cm.

**272-180778** Gray Mat **11.99**
Use for yards, parking lots etc.

**272-180785** Dark Brown **11.99**

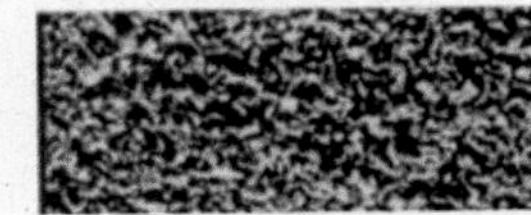

**272-180786** Light Brown **11.99**

## Grass 7oz 13.99 ea

Makes neat, easy work of applying grass. Includes shaker, ready for use.

**272-170752** Light Green
**272-170753** Dark Green
**272-170754** Meadow Flowers

## Grass Shaker Refills 3-1/2oz 11.99 ea

**272-170736** Light Green
**272-170737** Dark Green

## Soil 1oz 2.49 ea

**272-170704** Plowed Field
**272-170705** Sand Brown

## Coal

**272-170723** 140 grams **4.99**

## Rocks 3.49 ea

8-3/4oz (250g).

**272-170741** Natural Gray

**272-170742** Dark Brown (Soil)
**272-170740** Slate, Natural
**272-170743** Slate, Gray
**272-170744** Quartz

**272-170745** Quarry Stones - Gray Granite
**272-170747** Beach Pebble, Beige

## Rock Walls 21.99 ea

Realistic texture and hand-painted to enhance detail, each section is made of polyurethane foam and is easily cut to fit your layout

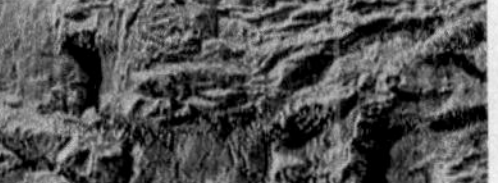

**272-170793** Gneiss

**272-170794** Stratified Rock

## Ballast

**272-170706** Gray 1.58oz **2.49**
**272-170720** Gravel Brown 1.6oz **4.99**
**272-170721** Brown/Gray **4.99**
**272-170722** Gravel, Stone Gray **4.99**
**272-170731** Dark Brown 10.5oz **8.99**
**272-170732** Light Brown 10.5oz **8.99**
**272-170751** Track (Brown) 24oz **19.99**

FALLER

IMPORTED FROM GERMANY BY WALTHERS

## BUILDING MATERIALS 2.29 ea

Embossed panels are preprinted in appropriate colors. Panels measure: 9-7/8 x 4-7/8" 25 x 12.5cm.

Dealers MUST order in multiples of 10.

**272-170600** Sidewalk

**272-170601** Cobblestone

**272-170602** Natural Stone Ashlars

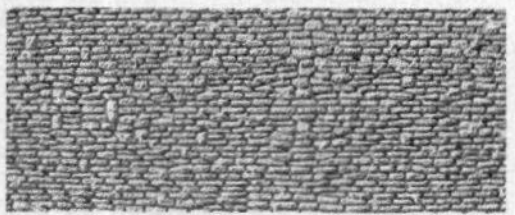
**272-170603** Natural Stone

**272-170604** Cut Stone-Brown

**272-170607** Glazed Brick

**272-170608** Red Brick

**272-170609** Roman Cobblestones

**272-170610** Natural Stone

**272-170611** Wallboard Sandstone (red)

**272-170613** Cut Stone-Red

**272-170617** Cut Stone-Basalt

**272-170618** Cut Stone-Slate

**272-170620** Cut Stone-Limestone

## DECORATIVE SHEETS & TILES

**272-144091** Plain Concrete Slab **8.99**

**272-144090** Reinforced Concrete Slab **8.99**

### pkg(2) 7.99 ea (Unless Noted)

**272-170802** Natural Stone Sheet
37 x 12 x .4cm

**272-170803** Brick Sheet
37 x 12 x .4cm

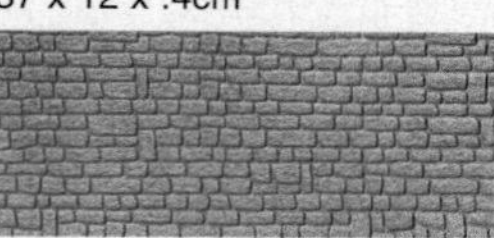
**272-170804** Natural Cut Stone
37 x 12 x .4cm

**272-170805** Stretching Masonry (gray)
14-3/4 x 5 x 1/4"
27 x 12.5 x .6cm

**272-170806** Sandstone (red)
14-3/4 x 5 x 1/4"
27 x 12.5 x .6cm

**272-170807** Base Plate (gray) **7.99**

**272-170834** Wall Still Tiles
37 x 12 x .4cm

**272-170860** Natural Stone **8.99**

**272-170861** Natural Stone Ashlars **8.99**

**272-170862** Rock Structure **8.99**

**272-170863** Profi Stretching Masonry **8.99**

**Limited Quantity Available**

**272-170847** Cornice Stone Sandstone **6.99**
1/6" .4cm thickness.

## PREMIUM SCENERY CASTINGS

These detailed scenery features are cast in rigid foam and are precolored. Easily cut with a hobby knife or saw, so blending into your scenery is quick and easy.

### Tunnel Portals

**272-171820** Single Track w/Annexed Rock Wall **21.99**
9-27/32 x 7-1/2 x 1-3/4"
25 x 19 x 4.5cm

**272-171821** Double Track w/Annexed Rock Wall **25.99**
12-19/32 x 8-15/32 x 2"
32 x 21.5 x 5cm

### Walls

**272-171810** Rock #1 **21.99**
9-1/16 x 9-1/16 x 2"
23 x 23 x 5cm

**272-171811** Rock #2 **21.99**
9-1/16 x 9-1/16 x 2"
23 x 23 x 5cm

**272-171812** Rock #3 **21.99**
12-3/16 x 6-5/16 x 2-3/4"
31 x 16 x 7cm

### Rock Casting

**272-171813** Rocky Peak **13.99**
5-29/32 x 3-15/16 x 4-11/32"
15 x 10 x 11cm

## ARCADES

### Natural Stone

**272-170835 15.99**
14-3/4 x 5 x 1/2"
37 x 12.5 x 1.3cm

**272-170838** With Round Arch (gray) **15.99**
14-3/4 x 5 x 1/2"
37 x 12.5 x 1.2cm

**272-170890** With Cornice Stones **16.99**
14-3/4 x 5 x .1/2"
37 x 12.5 x 1.3cm

**272-170895** With Pillars **7.99**

### With Round Arch

44-1/2 x 5 x 1/2"
111.2 x 12.5 x 1.2cm

**272-170839** Right Slope (gray) **28.99**

**272-170840** Left Slope **28.99**

**272-170893** Profi Ashlars w/Rocks & Squared Arch **23.99**

**272-170897** Concrete Arches w/Cornice Stones **15.99**
14-1/2 x 5 x 1/2"
37 x 12.5 x 1.2cm

**272-170898** Natural Stone Arches **16.99**
14-1/2 x 5 x 1/2"
37 x 12.5 x 1.3cm

### Sandstone Red 13.99 ea

**Limited Quantity Available**

**272-170841** With Round Arch
14-3/4 x 5 x 1/6"
37 x 12.5 x 1.2cm

**272-170844** With Recessed Arcades
14-3/4 x 5 x 1/2"
37 x 12.5 x 1.2cm

## GALLERY

### 20.99 ea

**272-170894** Profi Natural Stone Ashlars

**272-170891** Natural Stone

**272-170892** Natural Stone Ashlars

## WALLS

**272-170899** Natural Stone Retaining Wall pkg(2) **16.99**
9 x 6-3/8 x 3/8"
23 x 16.2 x 1cm

IMPORTED FROM GERMANY
BY WALTHERS

## LANDSCAPE PAPER

**Limited Quantity Available**

**272-170666** Gray Crepe Paper **10.99**
Use to model a variety of surfaces, such as lightly eroded rocks, roadways, stream beds and many other applications. Sheet measures 60 x 30" 150 x 75cm.

## WIRE MESH

**272-170665** Aluminum Screening **28.99**
Flexible and easily formed as a base for mountains, hills and other scenic formations. Measures 40 x 32" 100 x 80cm.

## TUNNEL PORTALS

Tunnel portal kits are precolored plastic and include numbered instructions.

### Single Track

**272-120558** Low Clearance - Steam Era **8.99**
2-3/4" 7.2cm clearance.

**272-120559** High Clearance - Steam Era **11.99**
Optional cap for 3-31/2" or 4" (9 or 9.8cm) clearance.

**272-120561** Low Clearance for Steam Era pkg(2) **6.99**
2-3/4" 7.2cm clearance.

**272-120563** High Clearance for Catenary pkg(2) **6.99**
3-3/4" 8.5cm clearance.

**272-170830** For Steam & Catenary Operation **9.99**
6-3/4 x 5-3/4 x 1/3"
17 x 14.3 x .9cm

**272-170880** Natural Stone Ashlars **10.99**
6-3/4 x 5-1/4 x 2/5"
17 x 13.2 x 1cm

### Double Track

**272-120564** Kylburg **22.99**
4" 10cm clearance. This ornate entry is based on an actual portal in use at Kylburg. It can be used with steam or electric locos.

**272-120565** Steam & Catenary Operation pkg(2) **7.99**
4" 10cm clearance.

**272-120566** Portal Set pkg(2) **15.99**
4" 10cm clearance.

**272-170831** For Steam & Catenary Operation **11.99**
9-1/4 x 6-1/4 x 1/3"
23 x 15.7 x .9cm

**272-170881** Natural Stone Ashlars **12.99**
9-1/4 x 5-3/4 x 2/5"
23 x 14.5 x 1cm

### Tunnel Accessories

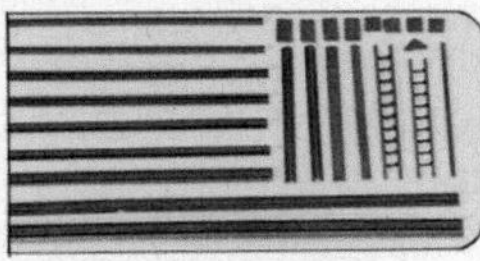

**272-120540** Assorted Structural Sections **13.99**

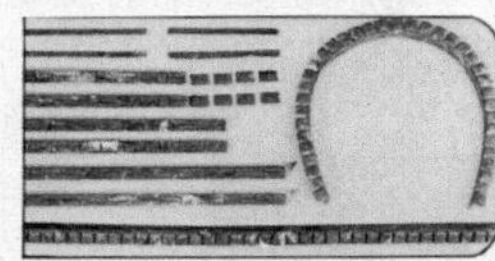

**272-120550** Facing Strips **15.99**

**272-170886** Tunnel Tube Rock Structure **4.99**
14-3/4 x 8 x .08"
37 x 20 x .2cm

## GLUE

Colofix glues are tinted and dry to the color listed. Ideal for use with various shades of ground cover, grass and ballast.

272-170660 272-170661

**272-170660** Colofix-Brown 9.2oz **11.99**

**272-170661** Colofix-Green 9.2oz **11.99**

**272-170662** Colofix-Gray 7.5oz **9.99**
Packaged in a special applicator for use with track.

**272-180501** Colofix Wood Compound-White **10.99**
White wood cement, dries clear and is perfect for applying scenery material.

## BACKGROUND SCENES

Each scene is a full color photo, printed on several paper panels.

**272-180511** Black Forest-Baar Extension **46.99**
Set of four panels can be used to enlarge #180514 (sold separately) to the right or left as desired. 155-3/16 x 26" 388 x 65cm total length. Panels can also be used alone.

Black Forest-Baar Extension Scene 272-180511

Neuschwanstein Scene 272-180512

Karwendelgebirge Scene 272-180513

Schwarzwald-Baar Scene 272-180514

Lowenstein Scene 272-180515

Oberdorf Scene 272-180516

Oberdorf Expander Scene 272-180517

**272-180512** Neuschwanstein **33.99**
Two sections, totaling 10'-8" x 40" 320 x 100cm.

**272-180513** Karwendelgebirge **33.99**
Two sections, totaling 10'-8" x 40" 320 x 100cm.

**272-180514** Schwarzwald-Baar **46.99**
Four sections totaling 12'-9" x 26" 388 x 65cm.

**272-180515** Lowenstein **33.99**
Three sections totaling 9'-8" x 17-3/4" 290 x 45cm.

**272-180516** Oberstdorf **33.99**
Three sections totaling 9'-8" x 17-3/4" 290 x 45cm.

**272-180517** Oberstdorf Expander Scene **33.99**
Three-part expander scene use with #180516 to increase overall length to about six yards (5.8 meters).

FALLER

IMPORTED FROM GERMANY BY WALTHERS

## PLASTER CLOTH

A neat and easy way to create hills and other landscapes. Special cloth is pretreated with plaster. Dip in water and apply. Rolls include 80" of cloth.

**272-170663** 4" Wide **9.99**

**272-170664** 8" Wide **13.99**

## PAINT

Water-based acrylic paint can be thinned with water.

**272-170796** Granite Rock Paint 3.5oz 118ml **15.99**
Adds realistic coloring to rock surfaces.

**272-180507** Roadway Paint 7.5oz 250ml **11.99**
Realistic asphalt color for highways, parking lots, driveways or other paved surfaces.

Item listed below is available by Special Order (see Legend Page).
**272-170797** Sand Ground Paint 3.5oz 118ml **15.99**
Perfect for country roads, beaches or other sandy areas.

## FILLER MATERIAL

**272-170654** Terrain Filler Putty 17.5oz 500g **12.99**
Dark gray powder mixes with water for easy-to-use putty. Make rocks and other terrain, or spread smooth to model roads.

**272-180500** Filler **12.99**
Build all kinds of realistic roads and terrain with this material. Filler is self-adhesive and easy to use. Ideal for constructing your own road surfaces for the Faller car system.

**Limited Quantity Available**

**272-170655** Terrain Filler-Brown 17.5oz 500g **10.99**
Realistic brown color is perfect for rock and landscape formations. Material is self-adhesive and designed for ease of use.

## FENCES & GATES

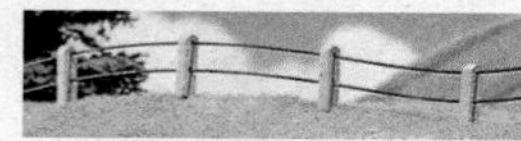

**272-180518** Iron Fence w/Concrete Posts **16.99**
12 wire sections each 8" 20cm and 80 concrete posts.

**272-180520** Metal Industrial Fencing **16.99**

**Limited Quantity Available**

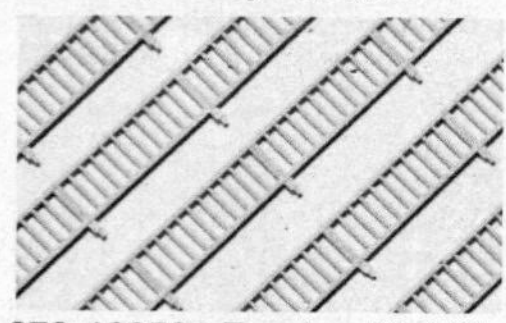

**272-180524** Fencing 57-1/2" pkg(8) **14.99**

**272-180526** Assorted Fences 7" pkg(10) **14.99**

**272-180532** Wall Fence **21.99**

### Garden Fences

**Limited Quantity Available**
**272-130361** **8.99**
62 sections of assorted styles of modern fencing.

## ROADWAY

### Concrete

Printed, self-adhesive two-lane sections with realistic concrete gray color and white markings.

**272-170621** 90° Curves pkg(4) **14.99**

**272-170622** Straight w/White Markings **10.99**
40 x 3-13/64" 100 x 8cm

**272-170623** Straight - No Markings **7.99**
40 x 3-13/64" 100 x 8cm



### Flexible

**272-180591** Roadway Markings **5.99**

**272-170650** 2-Lane Flexible - w/Markings **10.99**
3 x 3"

**272-170651** 2-Lane Flexible - Less Markings **7.99**
3 x 3"

**272-170652** Roman Stone **8.99**
2 x 3"

### Parking Space Markings 10.99 ea

4 x 2-1/2".

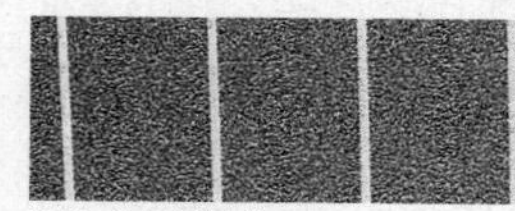

**272-170648** Square

**272-170649** Diagonal

### Cobblestone Pavement

**272-170646** Square **14.99**
Self-adhesive material with realistic color. Measures 19-3/16 x 9-5/8" 48 x 24cm.

**272-170647** Arch **10.99**
Self-adhesive material with realistic color. Measures 4 x 2-13/16" 10 x 7cm.

**272-170825** **7.99**
Foamed polyester material is easily cut thanks to thin construction. Measures 14-3/4 x 8 x .08" 37 x 20 x .2cm.

**272-170826** Roman **7.99**
Foamed polyester material is easily cut thanks to thin construction. Measures 14-3/4 x 8 x .08" 37 x 20 x .2cm.

## MINIATURE SCENES

**272-180563** Modern Bicycle Shelter **25.99**
Comes with 12 bicycles in assorted colors. Measures: 2-3/8 x 2-1/6 x 1-1/8" 6 x 5.2 x 2.8cm

**272-180564** Beer Garden **68.99**
Includes tables, chairs, entrance sign, umbrellas, beer stand, lighted garland and more.

**272-180682** Worker w/Operating Pneumatic Hammer **59.99**
Includes compressor, small building site and electronic 12-16V control unit.

**272-180683** Operating Bulldozer **59.99**
Includes 12-16V driving motor, building site and other details.

**272-180575** Barbecue Site **28.99**
3 x 2" 7.8 x 5.4cm

Includes wooden hut with benches, tables and stools, open and stone fireplaces and pile of firewood. A smoke generator can be fitted into the stone fireplace to bring the scene to life.

**272-180576** Playground Equipment **20.99**
Complete with slide, swings, merry-go-round, sandbox, jungle gym, pipes and more.

**272-180681** Lawn Mower w/Motor **85.99**
The lawn mower is run by a 16V AC motor. Features an operating figure, garden with meadow, and a garage.

**272-180684** Road Roller With Drive **56.99**
Roller comes to life with a 12-16V AC drive motor (undercarriage mount) and moves slowly back and forth on the roadway.

**Limited Quantity Available**

### Castle Ruins

**272-170851** Fleckenstein Castle Ruin **37.99**
10 x 6-5/8 x 8"
25 x 16.5 x 20cm

Includes two colored, prefabricated parts.

## SCENIC DETAILS

**272-130283** Boats and Windsurfing Boards pkg(21) **16.99**

**272-180560** Straw-Bale Figures **25.99**

**272-180561** Hay-Harvest **25.99**

FALLER

IMPORTED FROM GERMANY BY WALTHERS

**272-180562** Silo & Straw Bales **9.99**

**272-180569** Garbage Can Assortment pkg(10) **12.99**
Cans come in various styles in blue, brown, green and gray.

**272-180519** Stairway Set **25.99**

**272-180573** Picnic Accessories **21.99**
Includes two tables, benches, stools, fountain and wood pile to finish any park scene.

**272-180566** Inn & Stop Signs **25.99**
Includes 44 various brass-etched signs, with designs on both sides.

**272-180568** Park Benches **11.99**

**272-180579** Tables & Chairs **10.99**
Assortment with four tables and 24 chairs. Ideal for pubs and outdoor restaurants.

**272-180588** Freight Load **13.99**
Assorted barrels, crates and other details, less building and figures.

**272-120142** Trackside Accessories **27.99**

**272-130358** Party Tents & Furniture **9.99**

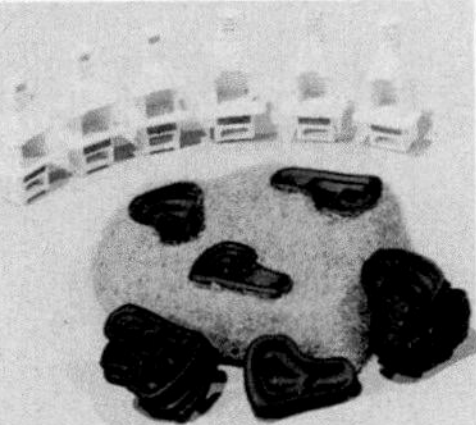

**272-130359** Garden Grills & Ponds **11.99**
A modern touch for today's back yards. Includes six barbecue grills and seven plastic pond forms

**272-180571** Garden Chairs w/Tables pkg(45) **10.99**
Set includes 36 chairs and nine tables, perfect for detailing picnic areas, beer gardens or restaurants.

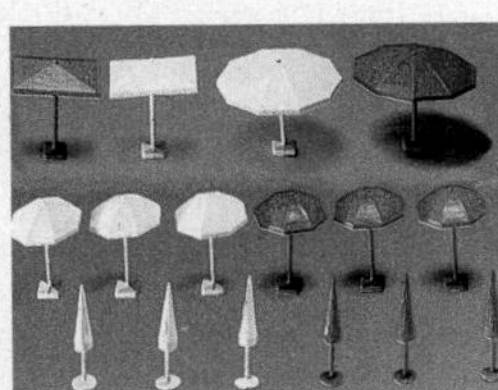

**272-180572** Parasols pkg(16) **10.99**
Various sizes of garden umbrellas.

**272-180577** Adventure Playground **21.99**
Superdetail a park with this assortment of equipment, including a wooden train, tower, teeter-totter, sandbox, benches and more.

**272-180585** Town Accessories **27.99**

**272-180584** Two Bicycle Stands & 16 Bikes **27.99**
2-1/4 x 1-1/8" 5.9 x 2.7cm
2 x 5/8" 5.1 x 1.7cm

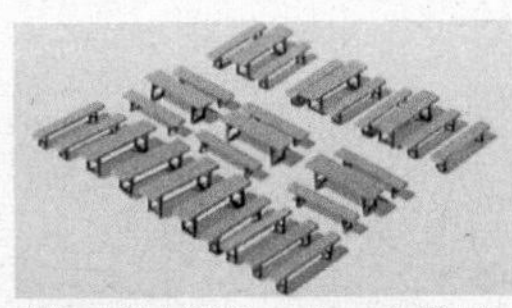

**272-140449** Benches & Tables **27.99**
Includes 30 tables & 60 benches.

## LIGHTING

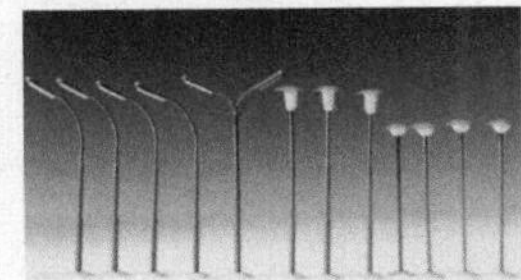

**272-180625** Nonworking Street Lamp Set pkg(56) **16.99**
Decorate your downtown, station platform, city park or subdivision with these detailed plastic lamps. Set includes six different styles and a total of 56 lamps in all. Plastic parts, cannot be converted to working models.

## STATUES

**272-180557** Mozart 250th Anniversary Of Mozart's Birth **21.99**

**272-180558** Goethe & Schiller **16.99**
2-3/16 x 1-3/8 x 3"
5.5 x 3.5 x 7.5cm

**272-180559** Frederick the Great **25.99**
2-3/8 x 1-9/16 x 4-1/8"
6 x 4 x 10.5cm

## FOUNTAINS

**272-130232** Ornamental Fountain **21.99**
4-1/2 x 4-5/16" 11.5 x 11cm

**272-180581** Fountain w/Figure. Nonoperating **15.99**
1-5/8 x 1-5/8" 4.3 x 4.3cm

## WATER

**272-170791** Lake Construction Kit **15.99**
21-1/4 x 10-1/4" 53 x 26cm

Includes rippled plastic sheet for realistic wave surface, which can be painted or use the blue paper (included) for coloring. Easily cut and shaped.

**272-171814** Waterfall **32.99**
Use with Quarry Pond (#272-171815, sold separately).

6-3/8 x 2-5/16 x 11-13/16"
16.2 x 5.9 x 30cm

**272-171815** Quarry Pond **33.99**
Use with Waterfall (#272-171814, sold separately).

8-7/8 x 7-7/8 x 2-3/8"
22 x 20 x 6cm

## WATER PUMP

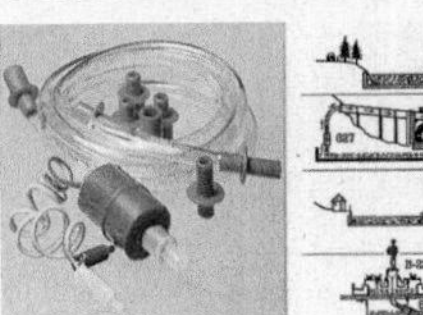

**272-180627** Water Pump & Accessories **39.99**
Pump real water anywhere on your layout. Includes 12-16V AC electric pump, 36" 90cm PVC hose and two connecting pieces, plus detailed instructions.

# Grand Central Gems inc.

## TREES

Perfect for foreground scenes, dioramas and displays, these trees are hand-made from natural materials to capture the correct shape, foliage and colors of actual trees. Fully assembled and ready to install, several different types are available in a wide range of sizes, suitable for most scales.

Spruce Pine

### Pines

**Medium - 5" Tall**
**295-T1** pkg(20) **20.00**
**295-T4** pkg(4) **5.00**

**Large - 7" Tall**
**295-T2** pkg(10) **15.00**
**295-T5** pkg(3) **5.00**

**Larger - 9" Tall**
**295-T8** pkg(7) **20.00**

**Small - 3" Tall**
**295-T3** pkg(50) **38.00**
**295-T6** pkg(6) **5.00**

**Extra Large - 11" Tall**
**295-T7** pkg(3) **15.00**

### Spruce

**295-T9** Medium - 5" Tall pkg(20) **20.00**

### Aspens

**Medium - 5-7" Tall**
**295-T10** pkg(4) **16.00**
**295-T11** pkg(10) **35.00**

**Small - 2-4" Tall**
**295-T12** pkg(15) **30.00**

### Fall Aspens

**Medium - 5-7" Tall**
**295-T13** pkg(4) **16.00**
**295-T14** pkg(10) **35.00**

**Small - 2-4" Tall**
**295-T15** pkg(15) **30.00**

### Oaks

**Medium - 5-7" Tall**
**295-T16** pkg(4) **16.00**
**295-T17** pkg(4) **35.00**

**Small - 2-4" Tall**
**295-T18** pkg(15) **30.00**

### Fall Oaks

**Medium - 5-7" Tall**
**295-T19** pkg(4) **16.00**
**295-T20** pkg(10) **35.00**

**Small - 2-4" Tall**
**295-T21** pkg(15) **30.00**

### Fruit Trees

**Small - 3-5" Tall pkg(5) 30.00 ea**

295-T22

295-T23

**295-T22** Orange
**295-T23** Apple
**295-T24** Grapefruit

### Palms

**Medium, 5-7" Tall pkg(2) 20.00 ea**
**295-T26** Fan Palm
**295-T25** Mexican Palm

### Juniper Pines

**295-T27** Small - 2-4" Tall pkg(15) **20.00**

### Sage Oaks

**Summer 30.00 ea**
**295-T28** Small - 3-4" Tall pkg(5)
**295-T29** Medium - 5-7" Tall pkg(3)
**295-T30** Large - 8-10" Tall pkg(2)
**295-T31** Extra-Large - 11-12" Tall

**Fall 30.00 ea**
**295-T32** Small - 3-4" Tall pkg(5)
**295-T33** Medium - 5-7" Tall pkg(3)
**295-T34** Large - 8-10" Tall pkg(2)
**295-T35** Extra-Large - 11-12" Tall

### Lodgepole Pine Trees 30.00 ea

**295-T36** Small - 3-5" Tall pkg(5)

**295-T37** Medium - 5-7" Tall pkg(3)

**295-T38** Large - 10-12" Tall pkg(2)

**295-T39** Extra-Large - 18-22" Tall

### Rock Molds

Add realistic rock cliffs, walls and other formations to your scenery with these one-piece rubber molds.

**295-RM1** Small **10.00**
**295-RM2** Medium **15.00**
**295-RM3** Large **20.00**

Aspens - Medium - 5-7" Tall pkg(4) 295-T10

Fruit Trees - Grapefruit 295-T24

Sage Oaks - Medium 295-T29

Lodgepole Pine Trees - Small - 3-5" Tall pkg(5) 295-T36

## CLEVER MODELS

## NEW PRODUCTS

### Fence Kits

Don't let your eyes fool you - the fences shown here are really made of paper! Easy to build and loaded with detail, each is precision printed with realistic colors and design elements already in place, on special high-strength cardstock. Simply cut, fold and glue to create an affordable, beautiful 3-D model for your railroad.

**NEW 217-1121** Plank Board **9.95**

**NEW 217-1122** White Wood **9.95**

## DETAIL ASSOCIATES

### Background Rail Scenes 6.98 ea

Create a unique backdrop for your layout, module or diorama with Rail Scenes. Printed modules can be joined in any order, creating a unique scene. Each measures 8-1/2 x 22" 21.25 x 55cm.

**229-7501** City
**229-7502** Downtown
**229-7504** Lumber Yard
**229-7505** Estuary
**229-7506** Tank Farm
**229-7507** Oil Fields
**229-7508** Farm Town
**229-7509** Land
**229-7510** Woods
**229-7512** Mountains

### Instruction Manual

**229-7550 4.98**
38-page illustrated booklet contains instructions for creating backdrops, shows possible combinations and suggestions for details. Measures: 11 x 8-1/2".

## FRENCHMAN RIVER MODEL WORKS

## NEW PRODUCTS

### Sidewalks

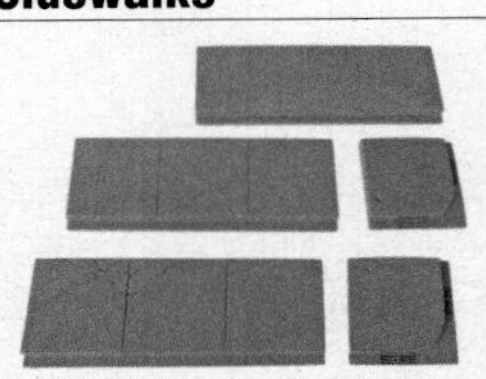

**NEW 267-4** Big City 5-Piece Set **8.75**
Cast resin set includes two corners with storm drains, one straight section, one straight section with manhole cover and one driveway section. Loads of detail including gutters cast in place will make city scenes come to life. HO scale dimensions are approximately 9' (not including the gutter) wide and 27' long per section.

**NEW 267-5** Small Town 5 Piece Set **6.50**
Cast resin set consists of two corners, one straight section, one straight section with manhole cover and one driveway section with gutters cast in place. HO scale dimensions are approximately 4' (not including the gutter) wide and 27' long per section.

## LABELLE INDUSTRIES

## LICHEN

### 1.5oz 1.99 ea

**430-5001** Light Green
**430-5002** Dark Green
**430-5003** Gray
**430-5004** Fall Red
**430-5005** Fall Yellow
**430-5006** Mixed Colors
**430-5007** Sunset Orange

### 4oz 4.99 ea

**430-5101** Light Green
**430-5102** Dark Green
**430-5103** Gray
**430-5104** Fall Red
**430-5105** Fall Yellow
**430-5106** Mixed Colors
**430-5107** Sunset Orange

## GRS Micro Liting™

### Miniature Scenes

All scenes include a Micro-Flamemaker kit, plus instructions for wiring, installation and painting. 6-20V AC/DC.

**296-2000** Hobo Camp w/Working Fire **39.95**
A pair of hobos camp for the night, heating a can of beans over a small fire. Complete kit with detailed scene casting, two soft-metal tote sticks and two painted hobos.

**296-2001** Prospector's Camp w/Working Fire **49.95**
A content prospector warms himself by the fire while his trusty mule grazes nearby. Complete kit includes detailed scene casting, several soft-metal accessories, and painted prospector and mule.

Info, Images, Inspiration! Get It All at
**www.walthers.com**

## HEICO-MODELL

IMPORTED FROM GERMANY BY WALTHERS

Kits feature precolored laser-cut parts and instructions.

## PLANTS

### Reeds

**335-67407** Natural pkg(25) **18.99**

**335-67408** Green pkg(25) **19.99**

### Flowers

**335-67409** Sea Roses **17.99**

### Ferns

**335-67410** pkg(6) **17.99**

### Cacti

**335-67412** pkg(6) **17.99**

### Kohlrabi

**335-67413** pkg(6) **17.99**

## HELJAN

### Scenic Accessories 5.98 ea

**322-501** Park Benches pkg(15)

**322-502** Barrels, Cases & Ladders pkg(28)

**322-503** Telephone Booth pkg(3)

**322-512** Telephone Poles pkg(10)

**322-513** Modern Street Lights Nonworking pkg(12)

**322-520** Assorted Fences 72-3/4" 181.8cm pkg(12)

**Limited Quantity Available**
**322-522** Stairway pkg(4)

## TREES

### Tree Assortments 23.99 ea

Assortments include shade, birch, cedar, oak, ash, maple, evergreen, juniper, fir, forest pine and hedgerows. Each assortment includes trees in various heights (as noted) which can be used in any scale. Trees are fully assembled, with plastic trunks and realistic foam foliage.

**338-301** Small Trees 1-1/2 - 3-1/2" pkg(40)

**338-302** Small Trees 2 - 3-1/2" pkg(40)

**338-303** Medium Trees 2-1/2 - 4" pkg(30)

**338-304** Medium Trees 3-5" pkg(24)

**338-305** Medium Trees 2-1/2 - 5" pkg(12)

**338-306** Small Pines 2 - 3-1/2" pkg(30)

**338-307** Large Pines 4-7" pkg(12)

**338-308** Large Trees 4-7" pkg(12)

**338-309** Small Pines 1-1/2 - 3" pkg(100)

An entire forest in a single set! Great for use by themselves, or combine with larger trees to model a variety of scenes. Pines are fully assembled, ready for use on your layout.

## JOE'S MODEL TRAINS

## NEW PRODUCTS

### Real Rocks Ballast

**12.95 ea**

Ballast your tracks like the prototype with real rock. This imported quartz stone aggregate features uniform roundness and no trash particles. Prototypical colors, size and weight. Each clear plastic bottle w/ easy-pour spout contains 8 oz.

350-121 350-122 350-123

**NEW 350-120** Black
**NEW 350-121** Dark Gray
**NEW 350-122** Light Gray
**NEW 350-123** Limestone
**NEW 350-124** Earth Blend

## HIGHBALL PRODUCTS

## GROUND COVER

### Ballast

**1lb 6.99 ea**

Genuine limestone.

**330-220** Limestone
**330-221** Light Gray
**330-222** Dark Gray
**330-223** Black
**330-224** Cinder
**330-225** Brown
**330-226** Light Gray/Dark Gray Blend

**5lbs 34.95 ea**

**330-2205** Limestone
**330-2215** Light Gray
**330-2225** Dark Gray
**330-2235** Black
**330-2245** Cinder
**330-2255** Brown
**330-2265** Light Gray/Dark Gray Blend

### Coal 8.99 ea

**330-130** Stoker 1-3" 14oz
**330-131** Egg 2-5" 14oz
**330-132** Lump-Small 6" 14oz
**330-133** Lump-Large 14oz
**330-134** Dust 5oz

### Grass 3oz 8.99 ea

Regular and electrostatic, can be used in Noch grass applicator #528-5018, sold separately.

**330-160** Green - Regular - Static
**330-161** Light Green - Regular - Static
**330-162** Green - Fine
**330-163** Light Green - Fine
**330-164** Moss Green - Regular - Static

### Scenic Rock 1lb 8.99 ea

**330-150** Sand-White
**330-151** Stone
**330-152** Small Stone
**330-153** Iron Ore
**330-154** Sand-Brown

### Earth 3oz 8.99 ea

**330-170** Light Brown - Regular
**330-171** Light Brown - Fine
**330-172** Dark Brown - Regular
**330-173** Dark Brown - Fine
**330-174** Top Soil
**330-175** Red

### Miscellaneous

**330-400** Sawdust Pack 4oz **20.95**
Six assorted packs of sawdust.
**330-510** Dirt 12oz **8.99**
Real dirt, specially processed for model scenery.
**330-520** Gravel 1lb **8.99**

## MR MOTION

Put life and action into your scenery with this animation module, designed for easy installation, and adaptable to a wide range of projects.

## NEW PRODUCT

### Swing Module

**NEW 454-33041 40.00**
Operates any swinging object to which a small magnet can be attached. Easily mounted under your benchwork, simply use the module as guide for cutting a mounting hole. Unit operates on 18V AC and the swinging speed is adjustable.

New Arrivals Updated Every Day! Visit Walthers Web site at **www.walthers.com**

## INTERNATIONAL HOBBY CORP.

### Accessories

**348-4** Farm Accessory Set **2.49**

### Roadway 1.49 ea

**348-8** Pavements (8 Straight, 2 Corner)

**348-10** Road Sections (5 Straight, 1 Curved)

### Village Accessories

**348-222** Village Green Accessories **1.99**

## MILLER ENGINEERING

### Fencing

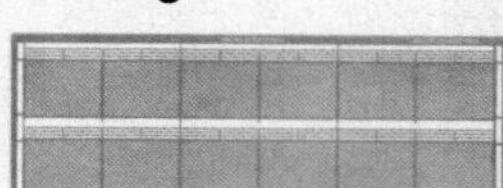

**502-87985** Chain-Link Fence **22.95**
Etched stainless steel fencing features the typical diamond mesh pattern and includes three-strand barbed wire on top. Includes template to simplify drilling mounting holes.

# kibri®

IMPORTED FROM GERMANY BY WALTHERS

## NEW PRODUCTS

### Accessory Sets

**NEW 405-8661** Straw Rolls pkg(10) **25.99**
11/16 x 1/2" 1.7 x 1.3cm

**NEW 405-8662** Crates On Pallets **25.99**

**NEW 405-8663** Assorted Logs **33.99**
For Sawmill #405-9854, sold separately.

## ACCESSORY SETS

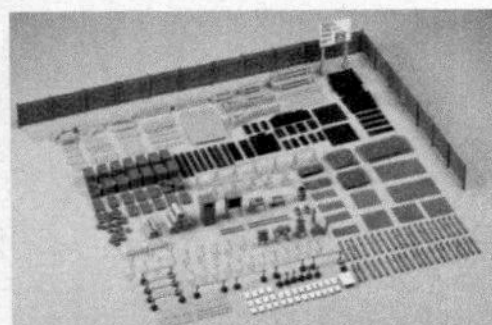

**405-8538** Construction Site Accessories **89.99**

**405-8539** Construction Site Accessories w/Building Fence **53.99**

**405-8646** Luggage Transporter Assortment **29.99**

**405-8607** Assorted Loaded Pallets pkg(13) **29.99**

**405-8647** Small Load Containers **27.99**

**405-8648** Assorted Disposable Containers **25.99**

**405-8650** Containers for Special Transport **94.99**

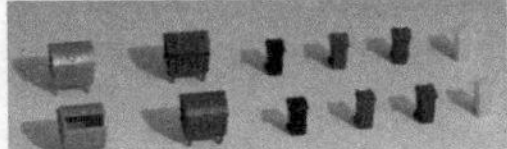

**405-8656** Garbage Cans **16.99**

**405-8102** City Street Assortment **25.99**

**405-8108** Station Detail Set **27.99**
Includes modern covered waiting shelter (great for a bus stop too), bike rack, sign boards, posters, benches, luggage, baggage cart and four nonworking lamp posts.

**405-8313** Construction Yard Assortment **45.99**
Includes barrels, boxes, dump truck, four telephone poles, dumpsters, shed, fences, walls and more.

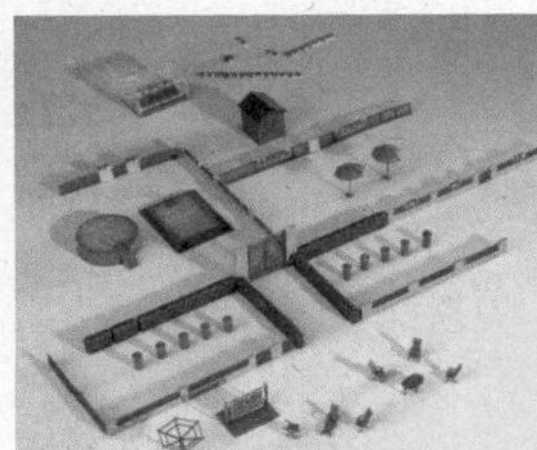

**405-8333** Garden Accessories **54.99**

**405-8528** Dockside Accessories **23.99**

**405-8614** Covered & Open Swimming Pools w/Backyard Accessories **29.99**

**405-8628** Transport Accessories Set **36.99**
Includes crates, boxes, skids & forklift.

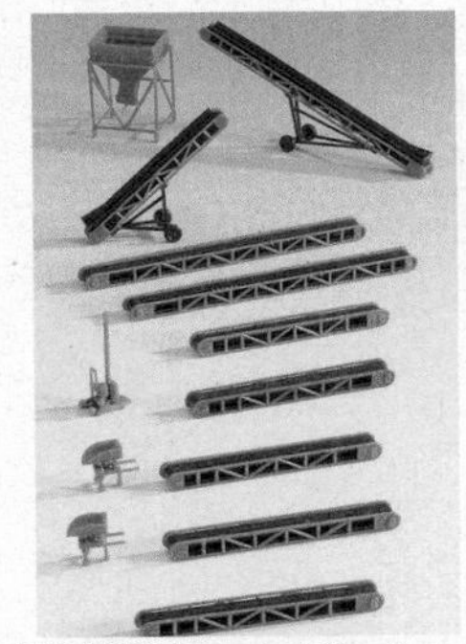

**405-8606** Assorted Coaling Accessories pkg(13) **24.99**

**405-8608** Marketplace Accessories **30.99**
Includes picnic tables, patio tables, bike rack and booths.

**405-9386** Assorted Oil Drums pkg(24) **13.99**

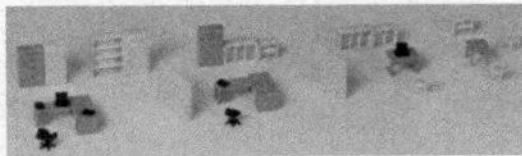

**405-8654** Office Furniture **16.99**

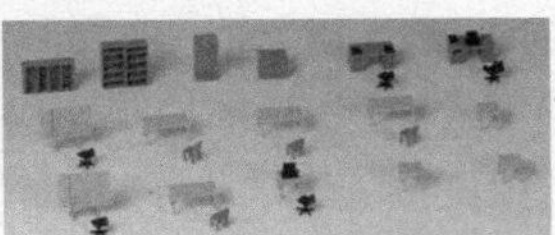

**405-8655** Office Furniture for Technicians **16.99**

Items listed below are available by Special Order (see Legend Page).

**405-8611** Assorted Station Accessories **30.99**

**405-9562** Service Information Figure Boards pkg(4) **20.99**

## BUILDING MATERIALS

Sheets are molded in appropriately colored plastic. Each sheet is 8 x 4-3/4".

### Brick 6.99 ea

405-4122

405-4124

**405-4122** Red
**405-4124** Cobblestone

**405-4125** Cobblestone w/Grooves for Track
**405-4147** Brown

### Concrete 6.99 ea

405-4123

405-4128

**405-4123** Concrete (light gray)
**405-4128** Concrete Slab 5 x 8"

**405-4148** Concrete 20 x 21cm

### Roof Sections 6.99 ea

**405-4116** Tile (brown)

405-4140

405-4142

**405-4140** Flat Tile (red)
**405-4142** Round Tile (red)

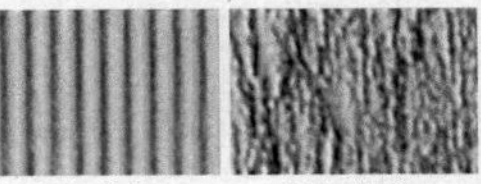

405-4143 405-4139

**405-4143** Corrugated Metal (light gray)
**405-4139** Thatched (tan)

**405-4144** Slate Tile

### Stone 6.99 ea

405-4119

405-4121

**405-4119** Cut Stone (beige)
**405-4121** Natural (gray)

**405-4145** Smooth Cut Stone (beige)

## FENCES

**405-8603** Mesh Fencing 118" 3m (green) **24.99**

**405-8605** Mesh Fencing 118" 3m (gray) **24.99**

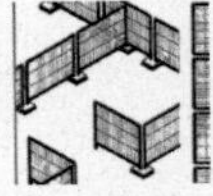

**405-8649** Fence 4' 125cm long **24.99**

kibri

IMPORTED FROM GERMANY BY WALTHERS

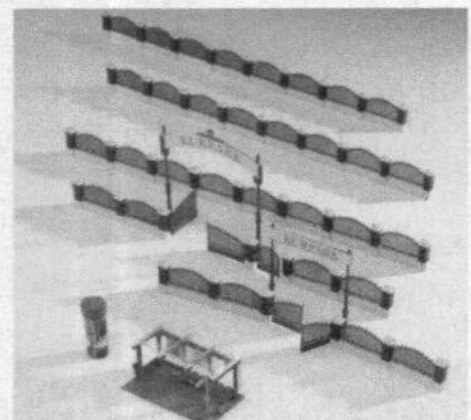

**405-8601** Fence For English Garden (green) **30.99**

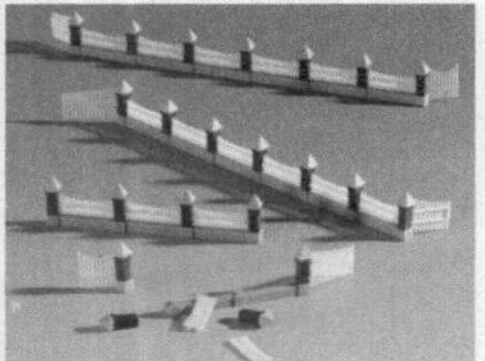

**405-8630** Wood Paling Fence w/3 Double Gates (30" 77cm) **16.99**

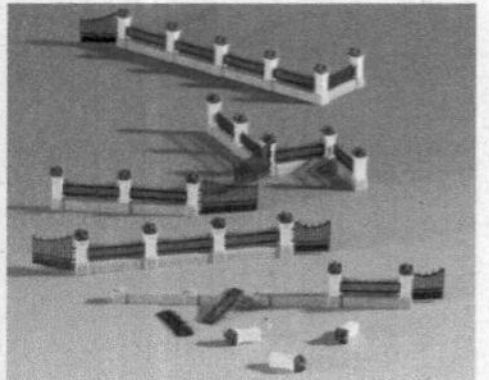

**405-8631** Wrought Iron Fence w/3 Double Gates (30" 77cm) **16.99**

## FLOWERS

**405-8106** Assorted Flowers & Window Boxes pkg(57) **9.99**

## ROCKS

**405-4112** pkg(10) **29.99**
Gray molded plastic.

## PAVEMENT

**405-4127** Paving for Dockside Crane **5.99**
7-7/8 x 4-3/4" 20 x 12cm

**405-8629** Sidewalk Pavement 100" 252cm / 67" 168cm **16.99**

## TUNNEL PORTALS

### Single Track

**405-4101** 2-3/4" pkg(2) **9.99**

Items listed below are available by Special Order (see Legend Page).

**405-4103** 2-3/4" w/Tunnel Tube **9.99**

**405-4105** 8-7/8" w/Tunnel Tube **10.99**

## WALLS

### Avalanche Wall Section

**405-4110** 8" length **7.99**

### Wall Sections 6.99 ea

Plastic sheets measure 4 x 7-3/4".

405-4118 405-4120

**405-4118** Cut Stone
**405-4120** Random Cut Stone

## WATER

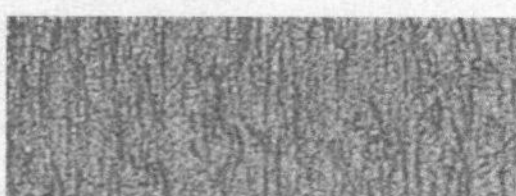

**405-4126** **6.99**
Sheet measures 5 x 8".

Mountains in Minutes™
I.S.L.E. LABORATORIES

Turn empty areas of your layout into detailed scenes in minutes. Foam castings are made of rigid urethane and prepainted. Finished models are lightweight and highly detailed.

## CULVERTS

**473-204** pkg(4) **8.99**
Approximately 4-1/8 x 7/8 x 3/4". Molded in rigid plastic foam.

## MOLDING MATERIAL

### Latex Mold Compound

**473-704** Quart Bottle **20.98**
**473-705** Pint Bottle **11.49**

### Model Landscape Kit

**473-701** **55.99**
A complete set to make your own foam castings and rubber molds. Perfect for use in the field, using real rocks as masters. Includes one pint each of polyfoam "A" and "B" latex mold compound and mold release.

### Mold Release

**473-706** 2oz Bottle **3.29**

### Polyfoam Refills 23.98 ea

Each can includes two pints (32oz) of liquid.

**473-702** Part "A"
**473-703** Part "B"

## ROCK

### Embankment

**473-820** **20.98**
Measures 15 x 6-1/2" 38 x 16cm. Easily cut with serrated or hobby knife.

### Mountains

Adaptable to various scales, mountains feature sheer walls molded from actual rock surfaces and are handpainted.

**473-855** Small **23.98**

**473-860** Medium **59.98**
Premolded rigid foam mountain in variable color and detail of natural rock. Templates provided for easy carving of optional-size tunnel openings. 10 x 18 x 20" 254 x 470 x 508mm.

**473-880** Front **104.98**

### Natural Rock Castings 20.98 ea (Unless Noted)

Foam duplicates of actual rocks. Use as masters to produce duplicate castings with Mountain In Minutes Polyfoam, or cut and fit into your layout. Each casting comes with instructions and painting tips. Castings measure 12 x 12" 30.5 x 30.5cm.

473-801

473-802

**473-801** Agawa Canyon Wall
**473-802** Kitanning Slope

473-803

473-804

**473-803** Royal Gorge
**473-804** Colorado Red Rock

**473-501** Flexrock Rock Canyon Wall **19.98**

**473-502** Flexrock Rock Embankment Wall **19.98**
**473-503** Flexrock Rock Gorge **19.98**

Latest New Product News Daily! Visit Walthers Web site at
**www.walthers.com**

## TUNNEL PORTALS

### 8.99 ea

Tunnel portals are molded in rigid plastic foam, with two-tone, golden-brown and burnt-umber finish. The Brick Portal is surrounded by a mixture of boulders and stratified rock. The rough-hewn Cut Stone Portal is set back into a sheer rock wall. The Wolfe's Cove Portal is a scale model of a Canadian Pacific portal of concrete with wooden snow doors, also surrounded with stratified rock. The Hoosac Tunnel Portal will allow for double track.

**473-101** Brick 6-1/4 x 7-1/4"

**473-102** Cut Stone 6 x 7-1/4"

**473-103** Wolfe's Cove 6 x 7-3/4"

**473-104** West Face-Hoosac Tunnel 6 x 7"

## WALLS

### Cut Stone Wall

**473-824** 11-1/2 x 7" **10.99**

### Cut Stone Wall W/Staircase

**473-821** 10 x 3-1/2" **8.99**

### Log Cribbing

**473-822** **8.99**
Used for reinforcing, embankments or holding steep banks. Measures 8" long x 3-1/2" high.

## NEW PRODUCTS

### Preformed Ponds 10.00 ea

Now it's easy to add a pond or lake to your layout. These preformed shapes are made of durable styrene. A stencil profile included allows you to prefit the form to your layout. Paint, add details like weeds, docks and stones and pour in Magic Water #100, sold separately. After 12 to 16 hours form can be tilted to create ripples and waves.

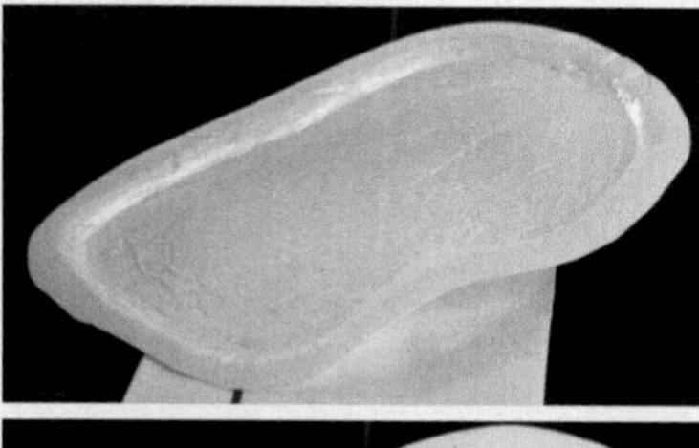

**NEW 754-102** Magician Lake 14 x 9"

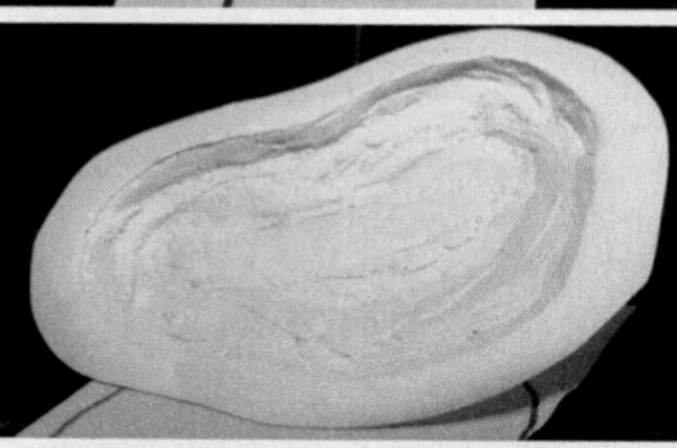

**NEW 754-103** Little Pawpaw 11 x 8"

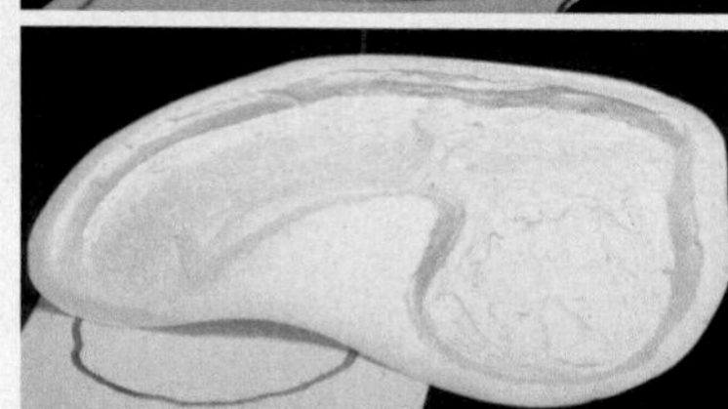

**NEW 754-104** Crooked Lake 14 x 11"

### Magic Water™

**754-100 29.95**
From a mud puddle to an ocean harbor, this unique two-part resin product makes it easy to model water on any layout or diorama. Simple to use, complete instructions include project ideas and modeling tips. Each 18 ounce box covers up to 300 square inches when poured 1/8" deep, but can be poured as deep as you like without layering. You can also tint Magic Water with inks, oil based paints, enamels and more for additional realism. It cures without heat so it's safe for use on wood, foam, plastic surfaces and painted wood, and has no annoying odor or dangerous fumes. Average curing time is 24 hours, so you can easily add details without creating bubbles or tease the surface to model waves and ripples. Once set, it dries crystal clear and isn't affected by temperature, and won't yellow, shrink, bubble or crack. It has an indefinite shelf life, so left over material won't dry out or "go bad" after opening. Finished water can be cleaned with anti-static plastic cleaner (sold separately).

DIVISION OF LEISURETIME PRODUCTS

### Roadways 6.79 ea (Unless Noted)

Thin precut material with realistic black/brown color and authentic markings. Will lie flat without adhesive, but can be glued for permanent scenery.

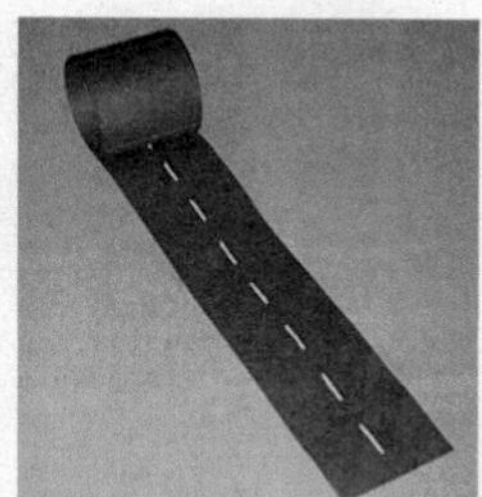

**406-201** Straight Passing Zone 9'

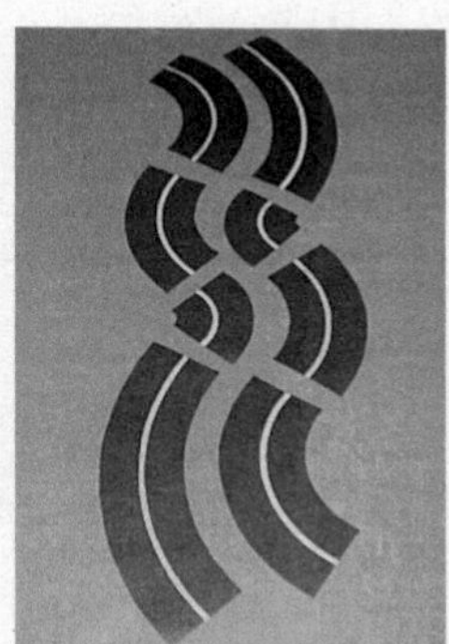

**406-203** Curved Roadway 6'

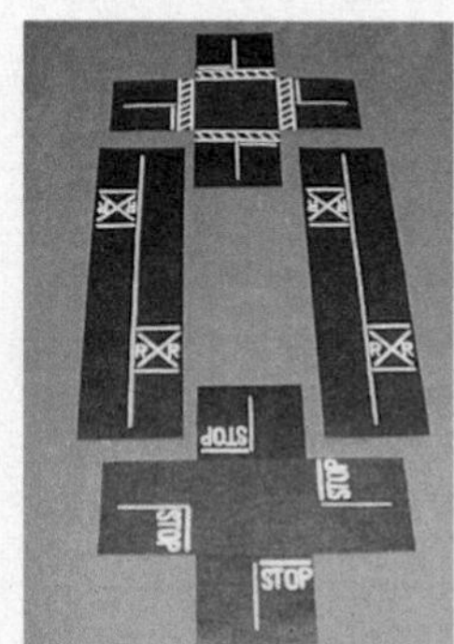


**406-205** Railroad Crossing & Intersection pkg(2)

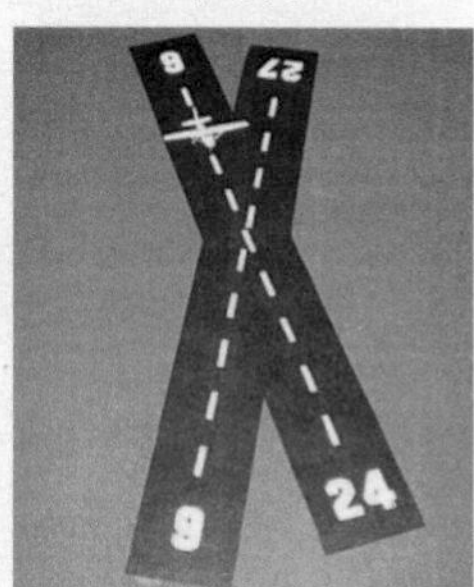


**406-209** Airport Runways 3' pkg(2) **7.79**

## GRASS MAT

**490-172** Velour Grass Mat 54 x 99" **21.98**

## TREES 17.99 ea

These architectural trees are fully assembled, making them ready for quick placement on your layout. Trees vary in height from 4-1/2 to 5-3/4" in each package (unless noted).

**490-1411** Medium Green (Spring) pkg(14)

**490-1413** Dark Green (Summer) pkg(14)

**490-1415** Green Pine (Winter) pkg(14)

**490-1417** Rust (Autumn) pkg(14)

**490-1425** 5-1/2" 14cm

## ACCESSORIES

**490-547** 54" Picket Fence **6.98**

**490-548** 54" Iron Fence **6.98**

**490-550** Garage Sale Furniture **9.50**

## NEW PRODUCT

### Automobile Junk Scrap Yard Pile

**NEW 493-2106 10.99**
5-1/2 x 3-1/2"

Prepainted, cast-resin, layout-ready scrap pile is ideal for your auto junk yards.

## JUNK PILES 10.99 EA

Prepainted cast-resin junk piles are ideal for adding realism to your scenes and cars.

**493-2101** City Junk Pile
Measures approximately
3-3/4 x 3-1/4" 9.5 x 8.3cm

**493-2102** Railroad Junk Pile
Measures approximately
4-3/4 x 3-1/4" 12.1 x 8.3cm

**493-2103** Shredded Scrap Metal Pile
Measures approximately
4-1/4 x 3-1/4" 10.8 x 8.3cm

## GONDOLA LOAD

**493-2104** Shredded Scrap Metal Load **9.49**
Prepainted resin load fits PROTO 2000™ 52'6" Gondola; can be trimmed to fit other cars.

Add a finishing touch of realism to railroad scenes with these detailed, one-piece castings. Each is hand-cast from a very strong gypsum material that picks up fine details much like dental plaster. Most items come handpainted to bring out the many details, and there's a selection of unpainted kit items for "do-it-yourselfers", too.

## Banded Lumber Stacks pkg(2) 5.70 ea

Fast and easy way to load box cars, trucks or bins at lumber yards. (Cars shown not included; loads shown sold separately.)

**506-130** Red Ends

**506-140** Green Ends

**506-141** Plain Ends

**506-142** Blue Ends

**506-143** Orange Ends

## Brick & Stone Culverts 9.18 ea

**506-430** Red

**506-431** Gray

## Bridge Abutments pkg(2) 8.63 ea

**506-920** Red

**506-921** Gray

## Brick Chimneys

One-piece casting eliminates problems of hiding seams so common with multiple-piece plastic and resin kits. A quick and easy upgrade for other manufacturer's kits or to finish scratchbuilt models. Each chimney stands 8-1/2" 21.2cm tall.

### Square w/Ladder 31.86 ea

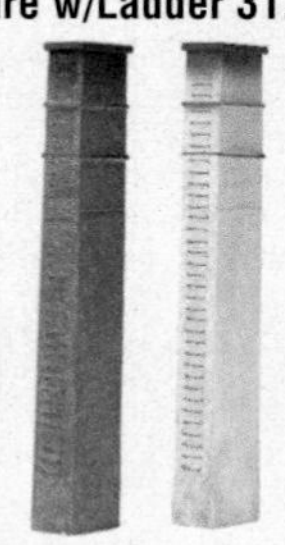

**506-670** Red

**506-680** Yellow

### Round 24.30 ea

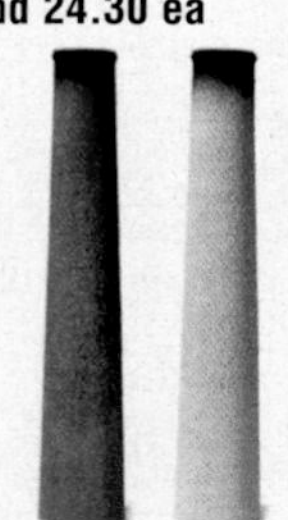

**506-840** Red

**506-850** Yellow

## 55-Gallon Oil Drums

Each set includes four different colors of drums.

**506-160** Stacked pkg(4) **5.70**

**506-560** On Pallets pkg(4) **5.67**

## Hay Bales

**506-1690** pkg(5) **4.09**

## Loading Ramps

**506-170** Wooden End-Of-Track Style **6.99**

**506-180** Wood & Stone Trackside Style **6.99**

**506-200** Coal Trestle Unloading Ramp **11.34**

## Matching Tunnel Portals & Wing Walls

## 7.44 ea

### Concrete Style #1

**506-690** Single Track Portal

**506-700** Straight Wing Wall

**506-710** Angle Wing Wall - Right Hand

**506-711** Angle Wing Wall - Left Hand

### Concrete Style #2

**506-1480** Straight Wing Wall

**506-1490** Angle Wing Wall - Right Hand

**506-1491** Angle Wing Wall - Left Hand

**506-1500** Single Track Portal

## Material Piles

**506-4** Woodchips **4.86**

**506-5** Coke **5.70**

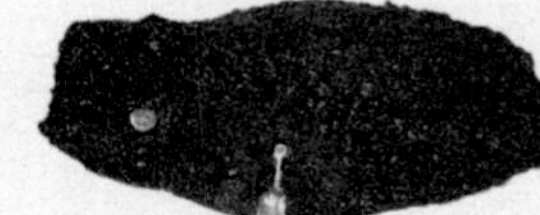

**506-6** Coal w/Bucket & Shovel **6.21**

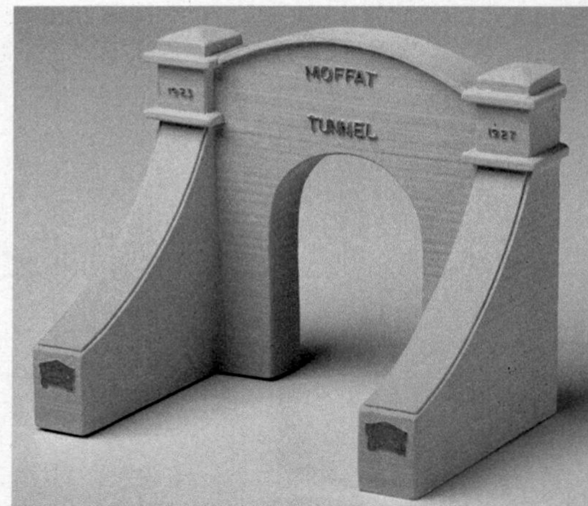


Moffat Tunnel West Portal 506-1271

Moffat Tunnel East Portal 506-1270

**506-7** Firewood **5.70**

**506-110** Junk Pile w/Weeds **6.87**

**506-120** Broken Drainage Tiles & Blocks pkg(4) **5.70**

**506-150** Railroad Ties pkg(2) **5.70**

## Moffat Tunnel Portals 38.88 ea

**506-1270** East Portal
8-1/2" 21.2cm wide
9-1/2" 23.7cm tall
1-1/4" 3.1cm deep

**506-1271** West Portal
5-3/4" 14.3cm wide
5" 12.5cm tall
4-1/2" 11.2cm deep

## Oil Storage Tanks 8.52 ea

**506-800** Black

**506-801** Silver

## Palletized Materials pkg(4) 5.67 ea

**506-540** Concrete Block - Banded

**506-550** Cinder Block - Banded

**506-570** Sacks - Not Banded

### Drain Tiles

Banded on pallets.

**506-500** Red

**506-510** Yellow

### Bricks

Banded on pallets.

**506-520** Red

**506-530** Yellow

### Piers

Each section measures 6-3/4" 16.8cm long.

**506-810** Normal **6.47**
1-7/8" 4.6cm Tall

**506-811** High Tide **7.02**
1-1/2" 3.7cm Tall

**506-812** Low Tide **7.02**
2-1/4" 5.6cm Tall

## Pilings

### Rotted Wood

**506-820 7.02**

### Railroad Tie

**506-830 7.02**

### Dolphin

**506-1590** Single Cluster **5.94**

### Steel

**506-2010 7.55**
1-7/8" 4.6cm Tall;
6-7/8" 17.1cm Long

## Retaining Walls

### Stone

**506-210** Large Stones (Interlocking) pkg(2) **11.34**

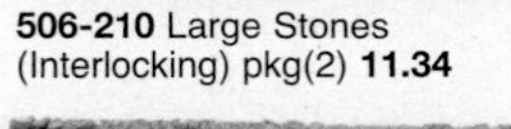

**506-450** Smaller Stones **5.94**

### Run-Down Brick 4.86 ea

**506-440** Red

**506-441** Gray

### Cut Stone w/Drain Pipes 5.94 ea

**506-460** Red

**506-461** Gray

For Up-To-Date Information and News Bookmark Walthers Web site at
**www.walthers.com**

## Small Dam

**506-470** With Flowing Water Detail **8.52**

## Stacked Drain Tiles pkg(6) 4.86 ea

**506-480** Red

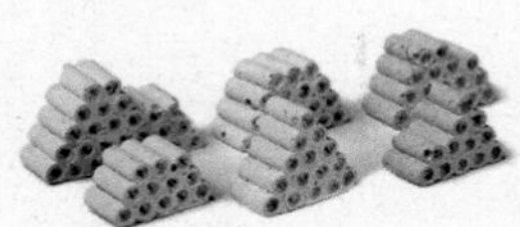

**506-490** Yellow

## Stone Bridge Pier Set pkg(3) 43.04 ea

Each set includes three graduated piers measuring 3-1/2, 5-1/2 and 8-1/2" (8.7, 13.7 and 21.2cm) tall in the same color.

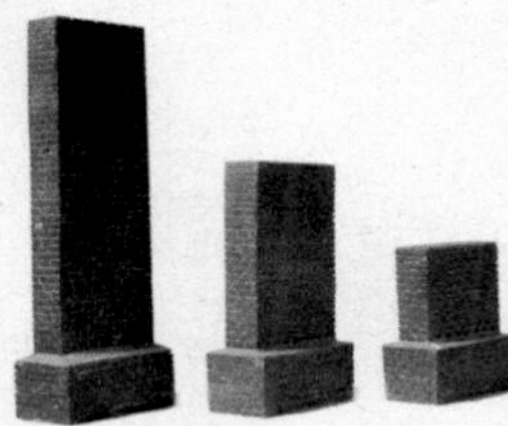

**506-1420** Red

**506-1425** Gray

## Individual Stone Bridge Piers

Parts match items in set #1420 but are sold as individual items.

### Red

**506-1421** 8-1/2" 21.2cm Tall **21.05**

**506-1422** 5-1/2" 13.7cm Tall **12.95**

**506-1423** 3-1/2" 8.7cm Tall **11.87**

### Gray

**506-1426** 8-1/2" 21.2cm Tall **21.05**

**506-1427** 5-1/2" 13.7cm Tall **12.95**

**506-1428** 3-1/2" 8.7cm Tall **11.87**

## Stone Center Bridge Piers

### Single Track 12.95 ea

**506-1540** Red

**506-1541** Gray

### Double Track 22.67 ea

**506-1640** Red

**506-1641** Gray

## Tree Stumps (Assorted Sizes)

**506-2** pkg(12) **5.89**

**506-3** Very Large pkg(6) **4.81**

## Unpainted Mr. Plaster Kits

Unpainted, unassembled kits.

### Chimneys 2.70 ea

506-1600 506-1610 506-1650

**506-1600** 1/4 x 1/4 x 1-1/2" .625 x .625 x 3.7cm

**506-1610** 1/4 x 1/4 x 1-1/2" .625 x .625 x 3.7cm

**506-1650** 1/4 x 1/4 x 3-1/2" .625 x .625 x 8.7cm

### Foundations

**506-1700** Stone Sections pkg(2) **4.85**

### Palletized Materials pkg(6) 4.30 ea

**506-930** Bricks

**506-940** Blocks

**506-950** Tiles

**506-960** 55-Gallon Drums

**506-970** Sacks

### Viaduct Footings pkg(2) 4.05 ea

Fits Micro Engineering Viaduct Towers, sold separately.

**506-1400** Stone

**506-1410** Concrete

### Wooden Crates pkg(3) 4.86 ea

**506-1450** Assorted Sizes

**506-1580** Large

# Grass So Realistic You'll Almost Want To Water It!

Tired of ground cover materials that add color to your layout scenes but don't appear to have the right texture? Here's an easy way to add grass to your layout that looks so realistic you'll swear it's alive.

The Noch Gras-Master® makes it easy to use static electricity to make Static Grass stand on end just like the real thing. Noch Static Grass material accepts a static electrical charge very easily, Gras-Master takes advantage of this and provides the necessary charge to position individual strands of flocking as they're shaken from the applicator bottle. When they hit freshly applied glue or cement, they stick to the surface on-end. The result is a grass carpet—grass fibers stand almost vertically on the terrain—just like real grass!

Noch Gras-Master includes an applicator cup with strainer lid and two special strainer grates to handle different lengths of Static Grass, an alligator clip for the electrical ground and a 9V battery.

**528-60130 Gras-Master $189.99**

IMPORTED FROM GERMANY BY WALTHERS

## NEW PRODUCTS

### Fences

**14.99 ea**

**NEW 528-13100** Residential Fence w/Gate & Posts
33 x 1-7/32" 84 x 3.1cm

**NEW 528-13110** Palisades
38-3/16 x 11/16" 97 x 1.8cm

**NEW 528-13120** Ornamental
31-7/8 x 9/16" 81 x 1.4cm

**NEW 528-13130** Wrought Iron w/Posts
31-1/8 x 5/8" 79 x 1.6cm

**NEW 528-13140** Wrought Iron
32-9/32 x 13/16" 82 x 2cm

**NEW 528-13150** Garden
32-9/32 x 19/32" 82 x 1.5cm

### Laser-Cut Kits

### Residential Fences 18.99 ea

**NEW 528-13350** Berlin w/Gate
4-15/16 x 1-1/4" 12.5 x 3.2cm

2 Door Sections, 2 Fence Sections, 10 Posts

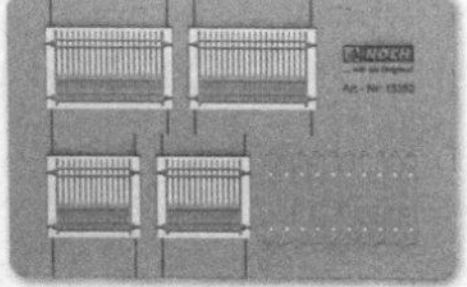

**NEW 528-13352** Berlin
3-15/16 x 25/32" 10 x 2cm

4 Fence Sections, 10 Posts

**NEW 528-13360** Hessen w/Gate
18.2 x 1.7cm

2 Door Sections, 1 Garden Gate, 4 Fence Sections, 10 Posts

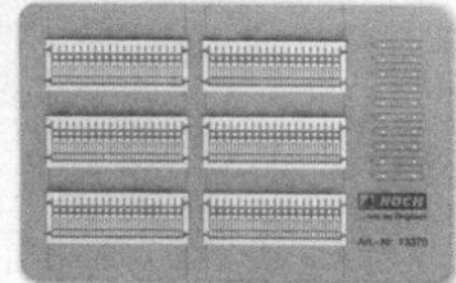

**NEW 528-13370** Sauerland w/Gate
8-3/4 x 1/2" 22.2 x 1.2cm

6 Fence Sections, 10 Posts

### Drain Covers

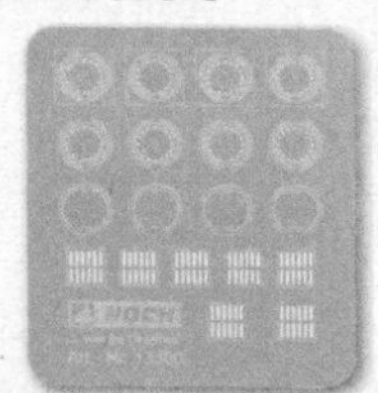

**NEW 528-13300** 5 Different Types pkg(19) **18.99**

### Molded-Foam Rocks

**25.99 ea**

Lightweight, weatherproof and easy to use, these molded foam pieces are ideal for creating rock faces and mountains on your layout.

**NEW 528-58451** Granite pkg(5)

**NEW 528-58452** Sandstone pkg(6)

**NEW 528-58453** Slate pkg(4)

### Miniature Scenes

**NEW 528-11344** Lakeside Playground **14.99**
Includes 2 figures, 1 dog & accessories.

**NEW 528-11385** Biker Meeting **21.99**
Includes 4 figures, 2 motorcycles, 2 cows & accessories.

**NEW 528-11387** Mini Petting Zoo **21.99**
Includes 4 figures, 5 animals & accessories.

**NEW 528-11475** Firefighters At Work **18.99**
Includes 3 firemen, 1 concession stand & accessories.

**NEW 528-11524** Street Cafe **21.99**
Includes street vendor carts, 3 figures & accessories.

**NEW 528-11525** Motorcycle Accident **21.99**
Includes 3 figures, advertising kiosk, motorcycle & more.

**NEW 528-11535** Fishermen **21.99**
Includes 3 figures & accessories.

**NEW 528-11733** Nudist Beach **21.99**
Includes 4 figures, 1 dog & accessories.

### Scenic Accessories

**NEW 528-14811** Campsite w/Tents **19.99**
Includes inflatable boat, picnic table, chairs and rotisserie w/chicken.

**NEW 528-14842** Post Office Equipment **19.99**
Includes mailboxes, bicycles, bike trailer and handcarts.

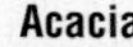

**NEW 528-14874** Funeral **19.99**
Includes coffins, headstones, cart w/coffin and garlands.

## TREES

### Deciduous

#### Acacia

**528-20810** 6-3/16" 16cm **34.99**

**528-25850** 5-29/32" 15cm **12.99**

#### Alder

**528-21755** 7-1/8" 18cm **14.99**
**528-25855** 7-7/8" 20cm **12.99**

#### Apple

**528-25113** Green 3-1/8" 8cm pkg(3) **12.99**

#### Ash

**528-21650** Mountain Ash ("Bird Berry") 4-1/2" 11.5cm **7.99**

#### Beech

**528-21690** 5-1/8" 13cm **11.99**

**528-21730** 5-1/2" 14cm **11.99**

**528-25170** 5-1/8" 13cm pkg(2) **12.99**

#### Birch

**528-25120** 3-1/8" to 3-15/16" 8 to 10cm pkg(3) **12.99**

**528-21640** 4-1/2" 11.5cm **7.99**

#### Chestnut

**528-21800** 7-5/8" 19.5cm **12.99**

#### Elm

**528-25180** 5-1/8" 13cm pkg(2) **12.99**

#### Fruit 7.99 ea

**528-21550** Green 3" 7.5cm

**528-21560** w/Fruit 3" 7.5cm

**528-21570** Blooming 3" 7.5cm

**528-21580** Cherry 3" 7.5cm

**528-21600** Pear - Green 4-1/2" 11.5cm

#### Horse Chestnut

**528-25895** 6-5/16" 19cm **12.99**

IMPORTED FROM GERMANY BY WALTHERS

### Lime 12.99 ea

**528-25880** 6-5/16" 19cm

**528-25110** Green 3-1/8" 8cm pkg(3)

**528-25111** White Blossoms 3-1/8" 8cm pkg(3)

**528-25112** Pink Blossoms 3-1/8" 8cm pkg(3)

### Maple

**528-25150** 3-1/2" 9cm pkg(3) **13.99**

### Marsh Oak

**528-20830** 7-13/16" 20cm **35.99**

**528-25865** 7-7/8" 20cm **12.99**

### Nut

**528-21710** 5-1/2" 14cm **11.99**

### Oak

**528-20820** 6-5/8" 17cm **35.99**

**528-21768** With Treehouse, Swing & 2 Children **41.99**

**528-25860** 6-5/16" 16cm **12.99**

**528-21680** 4-3/4" 12cm **7.99**

### Pine

**528-25160** 4-3/4" 12cm pkg(3) **13.99**

### Plum

**528-25100** Green 3-1/8" 8cm pkg(3) **12.99**

**528-25101** With Blossoms 3-1/8" 8cm pkg(3) **12.99**

### Poplar

**528-25140** 4-3/4" 12cm pkg(3) **13.99**

### Summer Lime

**528-20840** 7-13/16" 20cm **37.99**

### Weeping Willow

**528-21770** 4-3/8" 11cm **11.99**

**528-25130** 3-1/8" 8cm pkg(3) **13.99**

## Super Trees

These deluxe models are fully assembled, with a highly detailed plastic form and realistic colors of foliage. Can be used for very large HO trees, or with larger scales.

### Fir

**528-21890** 8-3/4" 22cm **14.99**

528-21900  528-21905

**528-21900** 10" 25.5cm **16.99**

**528-21905** 6-3/4" 15cm **14.99**

**528-21910** 8-3/4" 20cm **16.99**

**528-25210** Northern Firs 5-1/8" 13cm pkg(2) **16.99**

For Daily Product Updates Point Your Browser to

**www.walthers.com**

**528-25230** 3-1/8 – 3-7/8" 8-10cm pkg(5) **11.99**

**528-25430** 1-3/8 – 2-3/8" 3.5-6cm pkg(5) **11.99**

**528-26322** pkg(10) **20.99**
Six each 6-11/16" 16.7cm tall, and four each 7-7/8" 19.7cm tall.

### Pines

**528-11911** Lighted Tree w/Couple On Bench **33.99**

**528-26328** Assorted Winter 3-1/8 – 5-7/8" 8-15cm pkg(25) **34.99**

**528-42528** Assorted Winter Pines 1-3/8 – 2-3/8" 3.5-6cm pkg(25) **27.99**

### Spruce

**528-21955** 8-3/4" 20cm **14.99**

**528-21960** 9-1/2" 24cm **16.99**

**528-25240** 3-1/8 – 3-7/8" 8-10cm pkg(5) **11.99**

**528-26327** pkg(10) **21.99**
Six each 6-11/16" 16.7cm tall, and four each 7-7/8" 19.7cm tall.

**528-28220** 5-1/8" 13cm **7.99**

**528-25440** 1-3/8 – 2-3/8" 3.5-6cm pkg(5) **11.99**

**528-28200** Weathered 5-1/8" 13cm **5.99**

### Boxed

Trees come in a clear display package.

528-21971  528-21981

**528-21971** Palm 5-7/8" 15cm **14.99**

**528-21981** Palm 7-1/2" 19cm **16.99**

## Tree Assortments

**528-23100** Nature Tree Kit **24.99**

Includes an assortment of natural tree armatures ranging in size from 1-1/2 to 7-5/8" 3.8 x 19.1cm tall. For added realism, trees can be sprayed with adhesive and sprinkled with foliage to simulate leaves. Usable for any scale

### Light & Dark Green Deciduous

3-1/2 to 5-7/8" 9 to 15cm tall

**528-26301** Set of 25 **32.99**

**528-26401** Set of 10 **13.99**

### Spring Trees

3-1/2 to 5-15/16" 9 to 15cm Light green with white and red blossoms.

**528-26306** Set of 25 **34.99**

**528-26406** Set of 10 **14.99**

IMPORTED FROM GERMANY BY WALTHERS

## Mixed Forest
3-1/2 to 5-15/16" 9 to 15cm

**Deciduous and Model Firs**

**528-26311** Set of 25 **32.99**

**528-26411** Set of 10 **13.99**

### Conifers
**528-26320** Model Fir 3-7/8 – 5-7/8" 10-15cm pkg(25) **32.99**

**528-26321** Fir 2-3/8 - 6-11/16" 6-17cm pkg(50) **59.99**

**528-26325** Spruce Trees 3-1/8 – 5-7/8" 8-15cm pkg(25) **34.99**

**528-26340** Long Stem Firs 5-1/8 – 7-7/8" 13-20cm pkg(25) **32.99**

**528-26420** Model Fir Trees 4-6" 10-15cm pkg(10) **13.99**

**528-26425** Model Spruce Trees 4-6" 10-15cm pkg(10) **14.99**

**528-26440** Fir 5-1/8 - 7-3/32" 13-18cm pkg(10) **13.99**

### Spruce
**528-26326** 2-3/8 - 6-11/16" 6-17cm pkg(50) **62.99**

### Snow Fir

**528-26428** 3-5/32 - 5-29/32" 8-15cm pkg(10) **14.99**

### Hedges 9.99 ea
Dress up yards and gardens with decorative hedges. Each package contains 19-5/8" 50cm of flexible hedge material; measurements below show cross-section dimensions.

**528-21512** Light Green 5/8 x 3/8" 1.5 x .8cm

**528-21514** Dark Green 5/8 x 3/8" 1.5 x .8cm

**528-21516** Dark Red 5/8 x 3/8" 1.5 x .8cm

**528-21522** Light Green 3/8 x 1/4" 1 x .6cm

**528-21524** Dark Green 3/8 x 1/4" 1 x .6cm

**528-21526** Dark Red 3/8 x 1/4" 1 x .6cm

### Bushes

**528-25400** 1-9/16" 2cm pkg(24) **11.99**

### Vines

**528-25405** 3/4" 4cm pkg(3) **11.99**

## GROUND COVER

### Grass Mats 12.99 ea (Unless Noted)
Ready-to-use mats are available in many colors and textures to simulate natural ground cover. Grass mats are made with static grass, so that the blades are standing.

**528-110** Spring 39-3/8 x 29-1/2" 100 x 75cm

**528-120** Autumn 39-3/8 x 29-1/2" 100 x 75cm

**528-240** Meadow 47-1/4 x 23-5/8" 120 x 60cm (Cows and trees sold separately.)

**528-280** Summer Meadow 14-1/4 x 23-5/8" 120 x 60cm

**528-300** Spring Meadow **52.99** 94-1/2 x 47-1/4" 240 x 120cm

**528-8330** Flowering **2.99** 14-1/4 x 23-5/8" 120 x 60cm

### Large Grass Mats 35.99 ea (Unless Noted)
78-3/4 x 39-3/8" 200 x 100cm

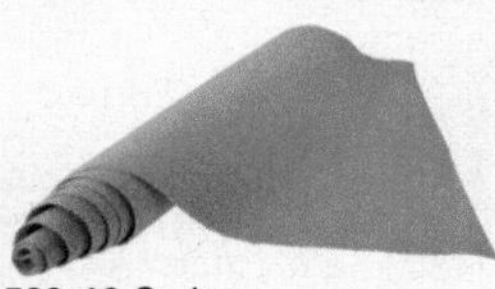

**528-10** Spring

**528-11** Flowering

**528-12** Summer

**NEW 528-20** Spring Meadow, Medium Green 300 x 100cm **56.99**

### Static Grass Applicator

**528-60130** Gras-Master® **189.99**

This handy tool makes grass flocking stand up on end like the prototype. Simply follow the directions to electrically polarize grass material as you apply it. The unit includes an applicator cup with strainer lid, alligator clip for electrical ground and 9V battery.

### Static Grass

**528-230** Dark Green Meadow **12.99**

### 3/4oz 20g 2.99 ea
**528-8300** Spring Green

**528-8310** Light Green

**528-8320** Dark Green

**528-8340** Brown

### 3-1/2oz 100g 11.99 ea

**528-50190** Light Green

**528-50200** Dark Green

**528-50210** Spring Green

### Terrain Mat Surfacer
**528-60920 9.99**

### Wild Grass
**528-7070** Field & Wild Grass Assortment w/Glue pkg(11) **37.99**

### Field Grass 1-1/2oz 42.5g 10.99 ea
Grass in approximately .2" .5cm tall.

**528-7082** Light Green

**528-7084** Mid Green

**528-7086** Ochre

**528-7088** Golden Brown

### Foliage 12.99 ea
9-5/8 x 6" 24 x 15cm

**528-7121** Beige

**528-7122** Light Green

**528-7124** Bright Green

**528-7126** Dark Green

**528-7312** Light Green

**528-7314** Mild Green

**528-7316** Dark Green

### Flock Foliage 12.99 ea
Package contains enough material to cover a 9-5/8 x 6" 24 x 15cm area.

**528-7160** Olive Green

**528-7162** Light Green

**528-7164** Medium Green

**528-7166** Dark Green

### Reed Assortment

**528-7060** Green, Beige, Brown **13.99**

## FLOCKING

### Wild Grass 1-3/4oz 50g 11.99 ea

**528-7101** Beige

**528-7102** Light Green

**528-7106** Dark Green

### Fine 3/4oz 20g 4.99 ea
**528-7200** Olive Green

**528-7202** Light Green

**528-7204** Medium Green

**528-7206** Dark Green

**528-7221** Beige

**528-7223** Light Brown

**528-7225** Medium Brown

**528-7227** Dark Brown

**528-7302** Light Green

**528-7304** Mid Green

**528-7306** Dark Green

## SCATTER MATERIAL

### Leaves 1-3/4oz 50g 5.99 ea

**528-7140** Olive Green

**528-7142** Light Green

**528-7144** Medium Green

**528-7146** Dark Green

IMPORTED FROM GERMANY BY WALTHERS

**528-7148** Yellow

**528-7149** Red

**528-8350** Forest 3/4oz 20g **4.99**
Combination of materials, ideal for blending with grass mats and other scenery.

### Flower Petals

**528-7170** Heath, Poppy, Dandelion, White **13.99**

### Meadow Flora

**528-7172** Olive, Green, Light Brown, Reddish Brown **13.99**

## LICHEN

### 1-1/4oz 35g Packs 3.99 ea

**528-8600** Stone Gray

**528-8610** Assorted Green

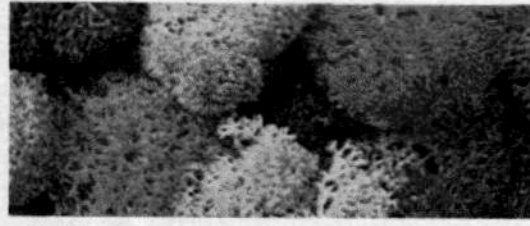

**528-8630** Autumn Mix

### 2-5/8oz 75g Packs 7.99 ea

**528-8620** Autumn Mix

**528-8621** Light & Dark Green

### 1-1/2oz 42g Packs 1.99 ea

**528-8400** Flower Red

**528-8410** Light Green

**528-8420** Dark Green

**528-8440** Brown

**528-8450** Mountain Grass

**528-8460** Gray

**528-8470** Forest

### 5-3/4oz 165g Packs 6.99 ea

Each color comes in a reclosable plastic bag for easy storage.

**528-8401** Summer Flowers

**528-8411** Alpine Meadow (Light Green)

**528-8421** Dark Green

**528-8441** Brown

**528-8461** Gray

## NATURAL STONE

### 2.99 ea

Use this natural stone as track ballast, in freight car loads or to detail your scenery. Each package contains 8-3/4oz 250g of material.

528-9202

528-9204

528-9205

**528-9202** Coal, Coarse

**528-9204** Gray, Fine

**528-9205** Gray, Coarse

528-9214

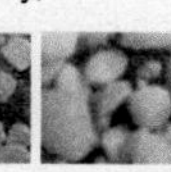

528-9216

**528-9214** Gravel (gray)

**528-9216** Gravel (beige)

528-9224

528-9226

**528-9224** Rocks, Medium

**528-9226** Rocks, Large

## APPLICATORS

**528-8099** Multi-Purpose (For Leaves & Grass) **3.99**

Simply fill with your favorite flock and puff it onto wet adhesive on your layout. Puffing action helps make grass stand up with a static charge.

## WATER

### Water-Drops®

Water-Drops water material is easy to use and produces a realistic surface. Simply melt in a cup immersed in boiling water until soft. If color is to be used, the color is also melted into the material. Then pour onto a scenicked riverbed or pond and allow to cool.

**528-60855** Clear 8oz 250g **19.99**

**528-60856** Clear 8oz 250g & 1oz Each (blue, green & brown) **29.99**

**528-60872** Water Effects 4.2oz 125ml **11.99**

### 2K Water Gel

Mix equal parts Water Gel components and pour into a pre-scenicked riverbed or pond. Colors can be added during mixing.

**528-60870** Clear 3.3oz 100ml **47.99**

**528-60875** Water Coloring Set **24.99**
Includes 3.3oz 100ml of clear acrylic and .3oz 10ml blue, green and brown color concentrates.

### Sea Mats

Boat & Accessories Not Included

**528-60850** 16-1/8 x 10-1/4" 41 x 26cm **10.99**

**528-60851** 29-1/2 x 19-5/8" 75 x 50cm **27.99**

**528-60860** Wild Water Set **13.99**
Includes 1-3/4oz 50g multi-colored pebbles and 5/8 fl oz 20ml bottle each: blue paint and transparent blue gloss.

## SNOW

**528-8750** Powdered Snow 8-3/4oz 250g **11.99**

**528-8100** Dispenser Bottle **5.99**
Hand-held bottle with sprinkler opening, allows for precise application in small area. Can be used with various materials.

**528-61130** Cement for Grass 7-1/2oz 250ml **10.99**

**528-61164** Snow Crystals 4-1/2oz 150ml **13.99**

## ROADWAYS

**528-58300** Subway Crossing 5 1/2 x 4 3/8" 14 x 11cm **10.99**

**528-60470** Highway 39-3/8" 1m pkg(2) **11.99**

**528-60540** Street Markings . Transfers. 7-7/8 x 3-7/8" 20.5 x 10cm **10.99**

**528-60550** Parking Lot, Gray pkg(2) **10.99**
Adhesive backed with printed parking spaces. Includes four plastic parking meters. 3-7/8 x 7-7/8" 10 x 20cm.

### Flexible Roadway

Noch Flexible Roadways are made of a special crepe paper which can be curved to fit your scenes. Each package of self-adhesive roadway contains two 39-3/8" 1m rolls, each representing approximately one-lane width of driving surface (unless noted).

**528-60410** Blacktop **9.99**

**528-60430** Cobblestone **9.99**

**528-60440** Old-Town **9.99**

**528-60450** Pavement 1/2" 1.2cm Wide **9.99**

**528-60451** Bike Path 1/2" 1.2cm Wide **9.99**

**528-60480** Country 1/2" 1.2cm Wide **7.99**

---

Got a Mouse? Click Walthers Web Site at

**www.walthers.com**

**528-60490** Highway **13.99**

**528-60610** Roadway, Country **13.99**

**528-60570** Sheet Paved 7-7/8 x 3-7/8" 20 x 10cm **10.99**

**528-60620** Pavement **7.99**

**528-60726** Sidewalk **7.99** 1 x 39-3/8" 2.5cm x 1m

**528-60728** Bicycle Path **5.99** 5/8 x 39-3/8" 1.5cm x 1m

### Flexible Rubber Roadways

Noch Flexible Rubber Roadways are self-adhesive and can be curved to fit your scenes. Roads feature pre-printed lane markings and come in two-lane width, 39-3/8" 1m rolls. Curves are preprinted on appropriate material matching the roads, and can be cut and stretched to fit your needs.

**528-60700** Highway Asphalt 3-1/8" 8cm Wide **9.99**

**528-60701** Highway Curve Asphalt 3-1/8" 8cm Wide pkg(2) **12.99**

**528-60703** Highway (gray) 3-1/8" 8cm Wide **9.99**

**528-60704** Highway Curve (gray) 3-1/8" 8cm Wide pkg(2) **12.99**

**528-60706** Country Road Asphalt 2-5/8" 6.6cm Wide **9.99**

**528-60707** Country Road Curve Asphalt 2-5/8" 6.6cm Wide pkg(2) **11.99**

**528-60709** Country Road (gray) 2-5/8" 6.6cm Wide **9.99**

**528-60710** Country Road Curve (gray) 2-5/8" 6.6cm Wide pkg(2) **11.99**

IMPORTED FROM GERMANY
BY WALTHERS

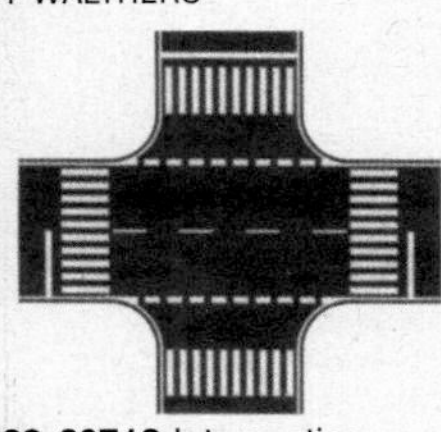

**528-60712** Intersection, Asphalt 8-5/8 x 8-5/8" 22 x 22cm **12.99**

**528-60714** Intersection, Gray 8-5/8 x 8-5/8" 22 x 22cm **12.99**

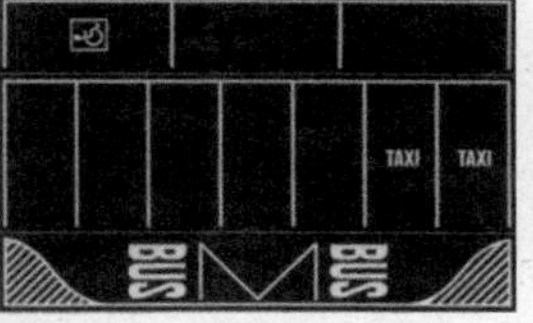


**528-60718** Parking Spaces, Asphalt 8-5/8 x 5-1/2" 22 x 14 cm pkg(2) **12.99**

**528-60720** Parking Spaces, Gray 8-5/8 x 5-1/2" 22 x 14 cm pkg(2) **12.99**

**528-60722** Cobblestone Sheet 39-3/8 x 2-5/8" 100 x 6.6cm **9.99**

# FENCES

## 12.99 ea (Unless Noted)

**528-13050** Stable 1/2 x 39" 1.3 x 97.5cm

**528-13060** Abandoned 5/8 x 35-7/8" 1.6 x 89.7cm

**528-13090** Yard 3/8 x 37-3/8" .9 x 93.4cm

**528-13095** Rural 53 Sections 114-3/16" 290cm **17.99**

## Field 12.99

**528-13010** Field Round Timber 3/8 x 39" .9 x 97.5cm

**528-13020** 3/8 x 35-7/8" .9 x 89.7cm

## Pasture 12.99

**528-13030** 3/8 x 39" .9 x 97.5cm

**528-13040** 1/2 x 39" 1.3 x 97.5cm

## Garden 12.99 ea (Unless Noted)

**528-13070** 3/8 x 35-7/8" .9 x 89.7cm

**528-13080** Garden 1/2 x 38-1/4" 1.3 x 95.6cm

**528-13096** Garden 72 Sections 106-5/16" 270cm **17.99**

# WALLS

## Residential 29.99 ea

**528-13202** Church Walls 4-11/16 x 15/16" 12 x 3.3cm

**528-13204** Country House Walls 4-11/16 x 13/16" 12 x 2cm

**528-13208** Garden Walls 4-11/16 x 1/2" 12 x 1.3cm

**528-13210** Villa Walls 4-11/16 x 1/2" 12 x 1.3cm

**528-13212** Villa Wall Set w/Stairs & Round Arch

## Hard Foam Walls

Detailed, hard-foam walls come pre-weathered and ready to use.

### Stone

**528-58100** 9-1/4 x 4-7/8" 23.5 x 12.5cm **12.99**

**528-58200** Long 25-5/8 x 4-7/8" 65 x 12.5cm **37.99**

**528-58110** Retaining Wall 10-1/4 x 4-1/2" 26 x 11.5cm **12.99**

**528-58115** Retaining Wall Long 25-5/8 x 4-1/2" 65 x 11.5cm **37.99**

**528-58120** Arcade 10-1/4 x 4-1/2" 26 x 11.5cm **12.99**

**528-58125** Arcade Long 25-5/8 x 4-1/2" 65 x 11.5cm **37.99**

**528-58160** Natural Stone 9-1/4 x 4-7/8" 23.5 x 12.5cm **12.99**

**528-58090** Arcade w/Natural Rock in Arches 13 x 4-7/8" 33 x 12.5cm **29.99**

### Quarrystone

**528-58250** 9-1/4 x 4-7/8" 23.5 x 12.5cm **12.99**

**528-58255** Long 25-5/8 x 4-7/8" 65 x 12.5cm **37.99**

**528-58260** Open Arcade 10-5/8 x 3-7/8" 27 x 10cm **16.99**

**528-58148** Smooth-Face 9-1/4 x 4-15/16" 23.1 x 12.3cm **12.99**

**528-58149** Smooth-Face Extra Long 25-5/8 x 4-15/16" 64.1 x 12.3cm **37.99**

# WATCHTOWER

Pieces come prepainted in realistic colors.

**528-58340** 3-5/32 x 2-3/8 x 5-1/8" 7.9 x 5.9 x 12.8cm **25.99**

# TUNNELS

Add mountains to your layout in minutes with these tunnels. Noch tunnels are fully assembled and feature molded-in detail with realistic decoration and applied grass.

**528-2120** Single Track **13.99** 9-13/16 x 7-1/2 x 7-1/16" 25 x 19 x 18cm

**528-2200** With Creek **26.99** 13-3/8 x 10-5/8 x 6-1/4" 34 x 27 x 16cm

**528-2220 32.99** 13-3/8 x 10-1/4 x 7-1/2" 34 x 26 x 19cm

**528-2221** Single Track, Straight **20.99** 13-3/8 x 9-7/8 x 7-1/2" 34 x 25 x 19cm

**528-2430 36.99** 11-13/16 x 11 x 6-11/16" 30 x 28 x 17cm

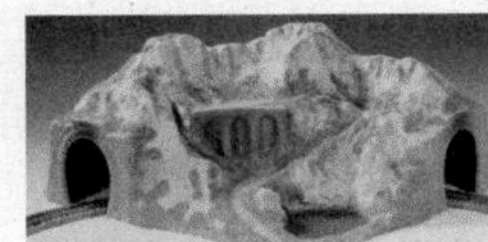

**528-5130** Single Track, Curved **32.99** 16-1/8 x 14-5/8 x 7-7/8" 41 x 37 x 20cm

**528-5170** Single Track, Curved **42.99** 16-1/8 x 14-5/8 x 8-5/8" 41 x 37 x 22cm

**528-5180** Curved Track **39.99** 16-7/8 x 16-1/8 x 9" 43 x 41 x 23cm

# TUNNEL PORTALS

Tunnel portals are made of hard foam material with realistic colors and textures.

## ICE - Style Concrete

**528-58040** ICE - Concrete Tunnel Portal **19.99**

## Smoothface Quarrystone

**528-58140** Single Track **15.99** 6-5/16 x 4-3/4" 15.8 x 11.9cm

**528-58141** For Single-Track Tunnel Portal #528-58140, Sold Separately pkg(2) **7.99** 3-1/2 x 3-3/16" 8.8 x 8cm

**528-58144** Double Track **19.99** 12-5/8 x 6-5/16" 31.6 x 15.8cm

**528-58145** For Double-Track Tunnel Portal #528-58144, Sold Separately pkg(2) **12.99** 5-1/2 x 3-9/16" 13.8 x 8.9cm

## Quarrystone

**528-58247** Single Track **16.99**

**528-58248** Double Track **16.99**

**528-58290** Modern Street Portal **15.99**

# ROCK

Use these hard-foam rocks to add realistic outcroppings and peaks to your mountain scenes. Each casting is appropriately colored.

**528-58448** Arlberg pkg(3) **35.99** Size range: 3-7/8 x 3-1/8 x 2-3/4" to 5-1/2 x 3-1/2 x 2-3/4" 10 x 8 x 7cm to 14 x 9 x 7cm

**528-58450** Tirol pkg(3) **35.99** Size range: 4-3/4 x 2-3/8 x 3-1/2" to 5-7/8 x 2-3/4 x 4-3/4" 12 x 6 x 9cm to 15 x 7 x 12cm

IMPORTED FROM GERMANY BY WALTHERS

**528-58454** Widderstein **29.99**
7-1/2 x 5-7/8 x 8-1/4"
19 x 15 x 21cm

**528-58455** Mittagspitze **29.99**
10-5/8 x 6-3/4 x 6-3/4"
27 x 17 x 17cm

### Foam Rock Formations 25.99 ea

Highly detailed, hard foam castings can be used as a single piece, or easily cut with a saw to fit your layout. Foam material is molded in realistic colors, and is easily painted to match existing scenery, or model different types of rock. Models are less figures, vehicles, trees and other details.

**528-58470** Granite Panel
12-5/8 x 6-1/4" 32 x 16cm
Use randomly with other scenery, or join several to form a continuous wall.

**528-58480** Schichtgestein
13-3/8 x 8-5/8" 34 x 22cm
Rocky plate with partial grass.

### Cork Rock Sections

**528-8810** Small 2-3/4oz 80g **9.99**
**528-8820** Large 6-1/4oz 180g **17.99**
Chunks of cork, ideal for stratified rock formations.

### Plastic Stone Sheets 2.49 ea

12-5/8 x 5-7/8" 32 x 15cm

528-57510 528-57520

**528-57510** Granite
**528-57520** Dolomite

528-57530 528-57550

**528-57530** Basalt
**528-57550** Brick

528-57560 528-57570

**528-57560** Square Stone
**528-57570** Sandstone

### Large Plastic Stone Sheets 5.99 ea

25-1/8 x 5-7/8" 64 x 15cm
**528-57700** Granite
**528-57710** Dolomite
**528-57720** Basalt
**528-57730** Brick

## STYRO-FLEX WALLS & TUNNEL PORTALS

Styro-flex foam tunnel portals and wall sections feature cut-stone surface detail that's easy to weather to match your scenery. Simply cut the material to fit your scene with a sharp hobby knife (sold separately) to install realistic tunnel portals, retaining walls, arcades and more while training the look of structures that were built at the same time.

### Sandstone Walls

#### Walls

**528-58074** 13-13/64 x 4-7/8" 33.5 x 12.5cm **16.99**
**528-58075** 26-13/32 x 4-7/8" 67 x 12.5cm **33.99**

#### Retaining Walls

**528-58076** 13-13/64 x 4-7/8" 33.5 x 12.5cm **18.99**
**528-58077** 26-13/32 x 4-7/8" 67 x 12.5cm **37.99**

#### Arcade Retaining Walls

**528-58078** 13-13/64 x 4-7/8" 33.5 x 12.5cm **18.99**
**528-58079** Extra Long 26-13/32 x 4-7/8" 67 x 12.5cm **37.99**

**Limited Quantity Available**

**528-57970** Slight-Arch Arcade Wall (beige) 13-25/32 x 4-15/16" 35 x 12.5cm **19.99**

### Sandstone Tunnel Portals

Catenary Compatible

**528-58071** Single Track 5-5/16 x 5-1/8" 13.5 x 13cm **13.99**

**528-58072** Double Track
8-13/64 x 5-11/16"
21 x 14.5cm **15.99**

## PROFI-PLUS SCENIC COMPONENTS

Profi-Plus walls and tunnel portals are made of rigid foam castings that feature exceptional detail. Each piece is cut with a sharp hobby knife or razor saw (sold separately) to fit your scenes. No painting is necessary and components are easily weathered using weathering powders or compatible paints.

### Tunnel Portals

Catenary compatible.

**528-58051** Single Track (gray) 5-5/16 x 5-1/8" 13.5 x 13cm **13.99**

**528-58052** Double Track (gray) 8-1/4 x 5-11/16" 21 x 14.5cm **15.99**

### Walls & Arcades

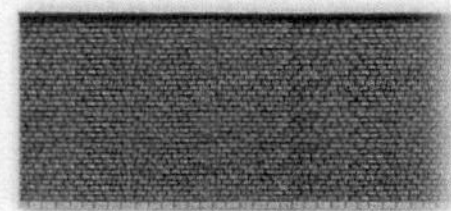

**528-58054** Wall (gray) 13-3/16 x 4-59/64" 33.5 x 12.5cm **16.99**

**528-58055** Extra Long Wall (gray) 26-3/8 x 5-1/8" 67 x 12.5cm **33.99**

**528-58056** Retaining Wall (gray) 13-3/16 x 4-59/64" 33.5 x 12.5cm **18.99**

**528-58057** Extra Long Retaining Wall (gray) 26-3/8 x 5-1/8" 67 x 12.5cm **37.99**

**528-58058** Arcade Wall (gray) 13-3/16 x 4-59/64" 33.5 x 12.5cm **18.99**

**528-58059** Extra Long Arcade Wall (gray) 26-3/8 x 5-1/8" 67 x 12.5cm **37.99**

### Plaster Cloth

**528-60982** Plaster Cloth Rolls pkg(4) **24.99**
Includes four 118-1/8" 300cm rolls in assorted widths: two 5-11/16" 14.5cm, one 3-3/4" 9.5cm and one 2-3/8" 6cm wide.

## MICRO PAINT ROLLER

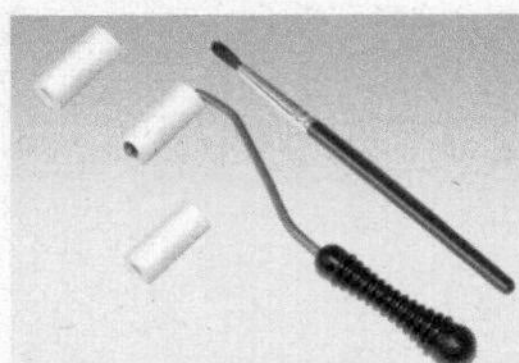

**528-60142** 7/8" 2.29cm wide **31.99**
**528-60143** Replacement Rollers pkg(3) **8.99**

## MINIATURE SCENES

Put life in your layout with this assortment of figures and accessories. Each item is prepainted, ready to install.

**528-10870** Patio Umbrella Set **8.99**
**528-10900** Well **8.99**
**528-10910** Outdoor Privy **8.99**

528-10920 528-10930

**528-10920** Roofed Shrine **8.99**
**528-10930** Feeding Hut w/Hay **8.99**
**528-10940** Hunter's Lookout w/Ladder **8.99**

**528-10970** Wild Water Scene w/Bridge **8.99**
**528-11340** Graves pkg(5) **14.99**

**528-11362** Lumberjacks (3 figures & accessories) **14.99**

**528-11382** Picnic (3 figures, 3 animals & accessories) **14.99**

**528-11472** Swineherd (3 figures, 4 animals & accessories) **18.99**
**528-11493** Nature Calls (2 figures, 1 animal & accessories) **18.99**

**528-11522** In The City Park (3 figures, 2 motorbikes, 1 bicycle & accessories) **18.99**

**528-11542** Flower Stand Scene **21.99**

**528-11570** Building Site **21.99**
Includes two workers, outhouse and accessories.

**528-11580** Playground Equipment **18.99**

**528-11590** Playground **27.99**

**528-11641** Tennis Match **27.99**
Comes with court, three figures and accessories.

**528-11682** Foal Pasture (5 animals, 1 tree & accessories) **18.99**

**528-11692** Rural Scene (3 figures, 1 animal & accessories) **21.99**

IMPORTED FROM GERMANY BY WALTHERS

**528-11700** Campers & Tents **21.99**

**528-11732** At the Lake (4 figures, 2 bicycles, 3 lounge chairs & accessories) **21.99**

**528-11742** Cattle Drive (3 figures, 3 animals & accessories) **21.99**

**528-11912** White Christmas (Illuminated Christmas Tree, Santa Claus & accessory) **33.99**

**528-11942** Coach Trip (3 figures, 4 animals & accessories) **27.99**

**528-11972** Wooden Wagon w/Horses **27.99**

**528-60580** Tennis Court w/Fence **16.99**

**Limited Quantity Available**

**528-11370** Country Yard Set **14.99**

## SCENIC ACCESSORIES

### 17.99 ea (Unless Noted)

All parts are handpainted for added realism.

**528-10880** Watering Trough **8.99**

**528-11200** Park Benches pkg(10) **14.99**

**528-14801** Beer Garden

**528-14802** Barbecue Party

**528-14803** Ice-Cream Parlor Accessories

**528-14804** Market Accessories includes fruit & vegetable stands **19.99**

**528-14806** Construction Site

**528-14807** Beach Accessories

**528-14808** Garden Plot Accessories **19.99**

**528-14809** Playground Accessories

**528-14810** Train Station Includes luggage, baggage cart, backpacks, waiting room seat for four, small signboard.

**528-14815** Auto Workshop Includes welding torch cart, hand truck, dolly, floor jack, tires and more.

**528-14820** Auto Workshop & Lift Includes four tires, dolly, work cars, tool chest, two drums and more.

**528-14830** Stable Includes wood dolly, five crates, barrel, wooden cart, doghouse, saddle and more.

**528-14831** Farm Accessories

**528-14840** Locomotive Shop

**528-14841** Freight Yard Accessories

**528-14845** Industrial Tools

**528-14847** Benches **10.99**

**528-14850** Workshop

**528-14870** Christian Symbols

**528-14871** Gravestones

**528-14872** Gravestones & Statues **19.99**

**528-14873** Tombstones

**528-14880** Fountains

**528-14881** Fountains



## NuComp Miniatures

All accessories are unpainted. Other details and items shown in pictures are not included.

### Scenic Details

**534-87502** Wood Piles pkg(2) **2.00**

**534-87503** Fire Hydrants pkg(2) **2.00**

**534-87506** Air Conditioners pkg(2) **1.50**

**534-87507** Garbage Cans pkg(2) **2.00**

**534-87508** Swimming Pool **3.00**

**534-87509** Mail Boxes pkg(4) **1.50**

**534-87510** Dog House **2.50**

**534-87204** 2 Lawnmowers & 2 Pop Machines **4.00**

**534-87206** Row Boat w/Oars **6.00**

**534-87504** Lawn Mowers pkg(2) **2.00**

**534-87505** Pop Machines pkg(2) **2.00**

### Accessory Pack

**534-87501 12.00**
Includes one each lawnmower, pop machine, fire hydrant, woodpile, doghouse, window air conditioning unit and rowboat, and two garbage cans.

### Tree Stumps

**534-87205** pkg(12) **3.00**

## NEW LONDON INDUSTRIES

### Background Scene Stencils 9.98 ea

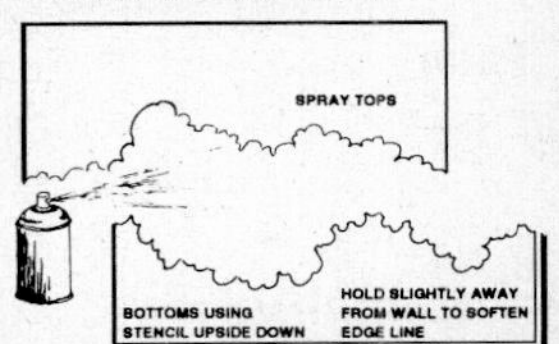


Create a unique background scene. Stencils are cut from heavy cardstock and can be used over and over. May be used for various scales. Includes instructions.

**519-1** The Clouds pkg(4)

**519-2** The Mountains pkg(4)

**519-3** The City pkg(4)

**519-4** The Details pkg(2) Two fine-cut cloud stencils, ideal for adding extra detail to #519-1 and for smaller scales near the horizon.

**519-5** The Hills pkg(4)

**519-6** The Mountains II

### Scenery Video

**519-10** "The Sky's the Limit" **19.98**
Explains and demonstrates the techniques of making a background scene using stencils.

# TREES

Fully assembled, ready for planting.

## Armatures

Bare plastic forms are ideal for winter scenes or detailing with foliage, sold separately.

**570-94031** 1-1/4" pkg(5) **7.85**
**570-94032** 2" pkg(5) **9.20**
**570-94033** 3" pkg(5) **10.55**
**570-94034** 4" pkg(4) **10.55**
**570-94035** 6" pkg(2) **9.20**
**570-94036** 8" pkg(2) **9.20**

## Poplar

Fully assembled, with twisted wire form and mixed green foliage.

**570-94021** 1/4" pkg(5) **8.95**
**570-94022** 1/2" pkg(5) **9.95**
**570-94023** 1-1/2" pkg(5) **10.95**
**570-94024** 1-7/8" pkg(5) **12.95**
**570-94025** 2-5/8" pkg(5) **17.95**
**570-94026** 3-1/2" pkg(4) **21.95**
**570-94027** 4-3/4" pkg(3) **18.95**
**570-94028** 6-3/4" pkg(2) **18.95**

## Palm

Easily bent for natural, curved appearance.

**570-94061** 1-1/4" pkg(5) **8.95**
**570-94062** 1-1/2" pkg(5) **9.95**
**570-94063** 1-5/8" pkg(2) **6.95**
**570-94064** 2-3/8" pkg(2) **8.95**
**570-94065** 3-7/8" pkg(2) **11.95**
**570-94068** 5" pkg(2) **13.95**
**570-94066** 6" **10.95**
**570-94067** 9-1/2" **13.95**

## Econo Palm Trees 10.95 ea (Unless Noted)

**570-94262** 2" pkg(4)
**570-94263** 3-1/2" pkg(3)
**570-94264** 5" pkg(2)
**570-94265** 7" pkg(2)
**570-94266** 12" **7.95**

## Sycamore

Fully assembled with etched brass form, painted brown and flocked.

**570-94101** 1/4" pkg(5) **9.95**
**570-94102** 1/2" pkg(5) **11.95**
**570-94103** 3/4" pkg(5) **14.95**
**570-94104** 1" pkg(4) **14.95**
**570-94105** 1-3/8" pkg(4) **16.95**
**570-94106** 1-7/8" pkg(3) **16.95**
**570-94107** 2-1/4" pkg(2) **13.95**
**570-94108** 2-7/8" **7.95**
**570-94109** 3-1/4" **8.95**
**570-94110** 3-7/8" **10.95**
**570-94111** 4-7/8" **12.95**

## Elm

Each pack includes a mix of up to five different shades of green foliage.

**570-94001** 1/4" pkg(5) **5.95**
**570-94002** 1/2" pkg(5) **8.95**
**570-94003** 7/8" pkg(5) **9.95**
**570-94004** 1-1/8" pkg(5) **10.95**
**570-94005** 1-1/4" pkg(5) **10.95**
**570-94006** 1-1/2" pkg(5) **11.95**
**570-94007** 1-7/8" pkg(5) **12.95**
**570-94008** 2-1/4" pkg(4) **13.95**
**570-94009** 2-3/4" pkg(4) **17.95**
**570-94010** 3-1/2" pkg(3) **15.95**
**570-94011** 4-3/4" pkg(3) **16.95**
**570-94012** 6-1/4" pkg(2) **16.95**
**570-94013** 7" pkg(2) **18.95**

## Fir

Each pack includes a mix of dark and medium green shades.

**570-94041** 1/2" pkg(5) **8.95**
**570-94042** 3/4" pkg(5) **10.95**
**570-94043** 1-1/4" pkg(5) **11.95**
**570-94044** 2" pkg(5) **12.95**
**570-94045** 2-7/16" pkg(5) **14.95**
**570-94040** 3-3/4" pkg(3) **7.95**
**570-94046** 4" pkg(4) **19.95**
**570-94047** 4-7/8" pkg(3) **19.95**
**570-94048** 6-3/4" pkg(2) **17.95**

## Spruce

**570-94170** 3" pkg(3) **7.95**

## Econo Pine Trees

**570-94080** 5/16 to 11/32" pkg(22) **7.85**
**570-94081** 9/16 to 13/16" pkg(10) **5.95**

## Christmas Trees

**570-94082** 2-3/8" pkg(3) **8.95**
**570-94083** 3-3/4" pkg(3) **10.95**
**570-94084** 4-5/8" pkg(3) **11.95**

## Pro Roundhead Trees

**570-94121** 1" pkg(5) **18.95**
**570-94122** 1-1/2" pkg(4) **18.95**
**570-94123** 2" pkg(3) **18.95**
**570-94124** 2-1/2" pkg(3) **21.95**
**570-94125** 3" pkg(2) **19.95**

## Pro Willow Trees

**570-94131** 2" pkg(2) **9.95**
**570-94132** 1-1/2" pkg(2) **13.95**
**570-94133** 3" pkg(2) **19.95**

## Pro Jacaranda Trees

**570-94141** 1-1/2" pkg(4) **18.95**
**570-94142** 2" pkg(3) **17.95**
**570-94143** 2-1/2" pkg(3) **21.95**

## Pro Lombardy Trees

**570-94151** 1-1/2" pkg(3) **11.95**
**570-94152** 2-1/4" pkg(3) **11.95**
**570-94153** 3-1/2" pkg(3) **18.95**
**570-94154** 4-1/2" pkg(2) **18.95**

## Pro Pine Trees

**570-94161** 1-1/2" pkg(4) **16.95**
**570-94162** 2-1/2" pkg(2) **13.95**
**570-94163** 4" pkg(2) **18.95**
**570-94164** 5" pkg(2) **26.95**

## Tree Trunks

Adds realistic detail and stability to plastic trees, or use alone to model stumps. Simply press wire trunk of tree into place. Molded in brown styrene.

**570-94092** Fits Medium Tree pkg(5) **2.95**
**570-94093** Fits Large Fir/Poplar pkg(3) **2.30**

# CACTUS

## Saguaro

**570-94052** 1" pkg(5) **13.20**
**570-94053** 1-3/16" pkg(4) **14.50**
**570-94054** 2" pkg(2) **14.50**
**570-94056** 2-1/2" pkg(4) **4.40**

## Prickly Pear

**570-94071** 1/2" pkg(18) **3.85**
**570-94072** 3/4" pkg(20) **5.00**
**570-94073** 1-3/8" pkg(16) **6.50**

## Econo Saguaro Cactus

**570-94251** 1-1/4" pkg(6) **4.75**
**570-94252** 2" pkg(5) **5.90**
**570-94253** 3-1/2" pkg(4) **6.95**
**570-94254** 4" pkg(3) **7.55**
**570-94255** 4-1/2" pkg(3) **7.95**

# GROUND COVER

**570-94435** Fine Light Green 50g **7.50**
**570-94436** Fine Medium Green 50g **7.50**
**570-94437** Fine Dark Green 50g **7.50**

## Gravel 8oz 2.60 ea

**570-94501** Extra Fine Mixed
**570-94502** Fine Mixed
**570-94503** Super Fine Mixed

## 10oz 5.20 ea (Unless Noted)

**570-94512** Super Fine Beige **6.55**
**570-94513** Super Fine Gray **6.55**
**570-94514** Fine Beige
**570-94515** Fine Gray
**570-94516** Fine Brown
**570-94517** Fine Red
**570-94518** Fine Black
**570-94519** Fine White

## Ballast

**570-94505** Super Fine Black 8oz **2.60**

## Blossom Foam 8g 4.60 ea

### Extra Fine

**570-94482** Burgundy
**570-94483** Red
**570-94484** Dark Pink
**570-94485** Purple
**570-94486** Blue
**570-94487** Yellow
**570-94488** White

### Fine

**570-94481** Pink

## Ground Foam

Use to model grass, weeds, foliage and more.

### Extra Fine 7.50 ea

**570-94471** Spring Green
**570-94472** Grass Green
**570-94473** Evergreen
**570-94476** Burnt Green
**570-94477** Light Green
**570-94478** Dark Ground
**570-94479** Straw

### Fine 6.55 ea

Each package contains 1oz of ground foam.

**570-94401** Spring Green

**570-94402** Grass Green

**570-94403** Conifer Green

**570-94404** Olive Green

**570-94405** Gold Straw

**570-94406** Dark Earth

### Medium 6.55 ea

Each package contains 20g of ground foam.

**570-94411** Spring Green
**570-94412** Grass Green
**570-94413** Conifer Green
**570-94414** Olive Green
**570-94415** Gold Straw
**570-94416** Dark Earth

### Coarse 6.55 ea

Each package contains 20g of ground foam.

**570-94421** Spring Green
**570-94422** Grass Green
**570-94423** Conifer Green
**570-94424** Olive Green
**570-94425** Gold Straw
**570-94426** Dark Earth

## Mass Planting

**570-94561** 1/4 x 12 x 24" **18.50**
**570-94562** 3/8 x 12 x 24" **21.15**
**570-94563** 1/2 x 12 x 24" **23.80**

## Turf Matting

**570-94568** Grass Green, 27 x 36", .4mm Thick **16.95**

# VINES

**570-94280** 8 x 4" **16.95**

# BUSHES & HEDGES

## Bushes

**570-94381** 1-1/2 x 2" pkg(2) **7.85**
**570-94382** 2-1/2 x 1-3/4" pkg(2) **10.55**
**570-94383** 2 x 3" pkg(2) **13.15**
**570-94384** 4 x 2" pkg(2) **15.80**
**570-94385** 4-1/2 x 1-3/4" pkg(2) **18.40**
**570-94386** 7 x 2" pkg(2) **21.05**
**570-94387** 9 x 2" pkg(2) **25.05**

### Manicured Foam Bushes 5.60 ea

**570-94377** 1 x 5/8" pkg(3)
**570-94378** 1-1/2 x 3/4" pkg(2)
**570-94379** 1-1/2 x 1-1/2" pkg(2)
**570-94380** 1-1/2 x 1-1/2" (round) pkg(2)

### Bushes

**570-94595** 2 x 1" **9.50**
**570-94596** 3 x 1-1/2" **9.95**

### Manicured Foam Hedges

**570-94586** 12 x 3/16 x 1/4" **5.00**
**570-94587** 12 x 1/4 x 3/8" **5.50**
**570-94588** 12 x 3/8 x 5/8" **7.00**
**570-94589** 12 x 3/8 x 1" **7.95**
**570-94590** 12 x 1 x 1-1/2" **8.95**
**570-94598** 12 x 1-1/2 x 3" **12.95**

## CRATERS

**570-91695** Moon/Bomb Craters pkg(2) **9.75**
An easy way to create realistic landscapes for science fiction or military dioramas.

## BUILDING MATERIALS

### Rock & Stone Sheets pkg(2) 9.75 ea

7 x 12" patterned sheets are vacuum-formed styrene .020" thick.

**570-91559** Stone Wall

**570-91561** HO Coursed Stone

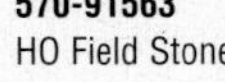
**570-91563** HO Field Stone

**570-91570** HO Rock Embankment

**570-91581** HO Random Stone

**570-91582** HO Polished Stone

**570-91590** HO Dressed Stone

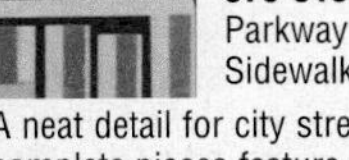
**570-91690** Parkway Sidewalks
A neat detail for city streets, complete pieces feature grass parkway with realistic concrete curb and 30' of straight sidewalk. Also includes two corners and two driveways.

### Brick pkg(2) 9.75 ea

**570-91605** Rough Brick .150"

**570-91611** .145"

### Stucco 16.95 ea

Measures 24 x 14"
**570-91771** Smooth
**570-91772** Coarse

### Dressed Stone/Block

**570-91774** 24 x 7 x 1-3/4" **9.95**

**570-91620** Concrete Block .175" pkg(2) **9.75**

### Roof Shingles

7x 12" vacuum-formed styrene sheet .020" thick.

**570-91630** Asphalt Gray .125 Spacing pkg(2) **9.75**

### Dollhouse Materials

#### 1" Square Tiles pkg(48) 10.95 ea

**570-91906** Beige
**570-91907** Blue

#### Sheet 7 x 12" 15.95 ea

**570-91916** Beige
**570-91917** Blue

## WATER

7 x 12" clear, 6 x 9" blue plastic sheets with patterned surfaces.

### Calm/Shallow

**570-91801** Blue **6.20**
**570-91811** Clear **8.95**

### Agitated/Shallow

**570-91802** Blue **6.20**
**570-91812** Clear **8.95**

### Choppy/Deep

**570-91803** Blue **6.20**
**570-91813** Clear **8.95**

### Stormy/Deep

**570-91804** Blue **6.20**
**570-91814** Clear **8.95**

### Waterfalls 6.55 ea

#### Blue

**570-94611** 1-5/8 x 8-1/2"
**570-94616** 1-5/8 x 5-1/4"

#### Clear

**570-94612** 1-5/8 x 8-1/2"
**570-94617** 1-5/8 x 5-1/4"

## CELLULAR FOAM

A lichen-type ground foam for modeling tree foliage and brush. Won't dry out.

### Medium 7.50 ea

Each package contains 20g of ground foam.
**570-94450** Green Mix
**570-94451** Spring Green
**570-94452** Grass Green
**570-94453** Evergreen
**570-94454** Sugar Maple Mix
**570-94455** Autumn Mix
**570-94456** Leaf Green
**570-94458** Mint Green

Cellular Foam listed below is available by Special Order (see Legend Page).
**570-94457** Bright Green

### Fine 7.50 ea

Each package contains 20g of ground foam.
**570-94460** Green Mix
**570-94468** Mint Green Green
**570-94469** Autumn Gold
**570-94470** Autumn Red

Cellular Foam listed below is available by Special Order (see Legend Page).
**570-94461** Spring Green
**570-94462** Grass Green
**570-94463** Evergreen
**570-94465** Autumn Mix
**570-94466** Leaf Green
**570-94467** Bright Green

### Mixed 7.50 ea

Each package contains 50g of ground foam.
**570-94445** Dark Cedar Mix
**570-94446** Lush Green Mix

Cellular Foam listed below is available by Special Order (see Legend Page).
**570-94441** Light Green Mix
**570-94442** Medium Green Mix
**570-94443** Dark Green Mix

## ROADS

Ideal for modeling all types of paved surfaces. Choose from printed paper or Flex Mat with finely ground aggregate surface.

### Asphalt

**570-91791** Black 24 x 7" **9.95**
**570-91792** Black 24 x 14" **16.95**

**570-94535** Paper 11-3/4 x 26-3/4" **5.25**

### Concrete

**570-91793** Gray 24 x 7" **9.95**
**570-91794** Gray 24 x 14" **16.95**
**570-94536** Paper 11-3/4 x 26-3/4" **5.25**

**Limited Quantity Available**
**570-94552** Roadway Kit **24.60**

## FENCES

### Chain Link

**570-90451** Mesh & Rod 48" **9.40**
Includes two strips of precut fencing, which measure 1-1/8" tall by 24" long, plus five 15" lengths of plastic rod for posts.

### 4-Bar Horizontal

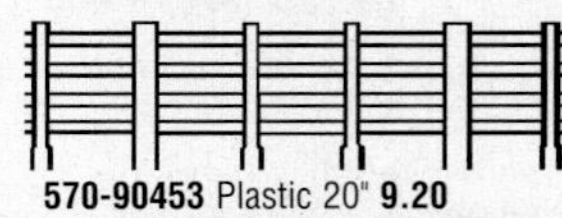
**570-90453** Plastic 20" **9.20**

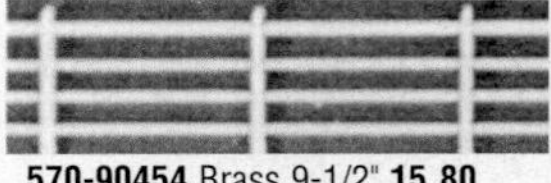
**570-90454** Brass 9-1/2" **15.80**

### Picket

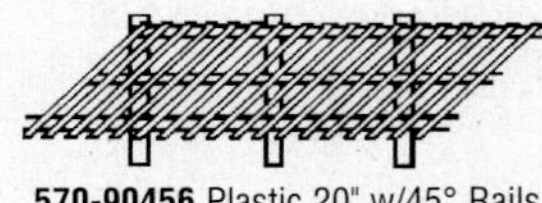
**570-90456** Plastic 20" w/45° Rails **10.55**
**570-90458** 75" Long **17.10**

**570-90460** Plastic 20" w/Vertical Rails **9.20**

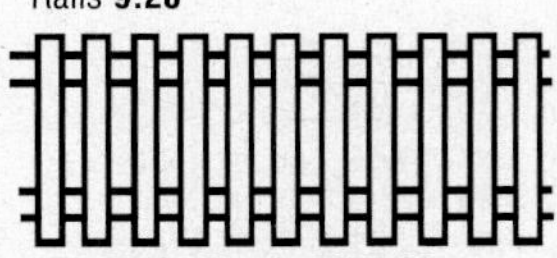
**570-90464** Plastic 28" **7.85**
**570-90466** Styrene Plastic 20" **7.85**
**570-91457** 5/8 x 8" **6.70**

### Cross Design

**570-91455** 1/2 x 8" **6.70**

### Fence Details

#### Vertical Bar - Lattice Trim

**570-91451** 1 x 8" **6.70**
**570-91452** 5/8 x 8" **7.80**

#### Lattice

**570-90918** 4-1/2 x 2-1/2" with 3/8" Pattern Spacing **4.95**
**570-90919** 3-5/8 x 2" with 3/8" Pattern Spacing **4.50**



New Rail Models

## SCENIC ACCESSORIES

Easy-to-build kits feature unpainted laser-cut wood parts.

**501-33001** Picnic Table Kit (Makes 4 Tables) **9.95**

**501-33002** Bench & Trash Receptacle (Makes 2 Each) **9.95**

**501-33005** Peel and Stick Ultra Shingles, Shake pkg(2) **9.95**
Each sheet measures 24 x 53 scale feet.

**501-33008** Plywood Loads pkg(16) **27.95**

**501-33009** 4 x 8' Plywood Sheets pkg(25) **4.95**

## NEAL'S N-GAUGING TRAINS

## NEW PRODUCTS

### Scenic Details

**NEW 530-339** Etched-Metal Ivy Vines (Unpainted) **24.95**
**NEW 530-340** Agricultural Hardware **24.95**
Includes mangers, troughs, electrical fenceposts, etc.
**NEW 530-217** Sailing Dingy w/Furled Sail - Painted **11.95**
**NEW 530-218** Row Boat - Painted **10.95**

ORIGINAL **Preiser**

IMPORTED FROM GERMANY BY WALTHERS

# NEW PRODUCTS

## Scenic Accessories

### Statues 4.99 ea

590-29073 590-29076 590-29077

**NEW 590-29073** Religious Statue

**NEW 590-29076** Lady Justice Statue

**NEW 590-29077** Venus Statue

# SCENIC ACCESSORIES

## Carts, Forklifts

**590-17103** Handcarts (Assorted) pkg(8) **13.99**

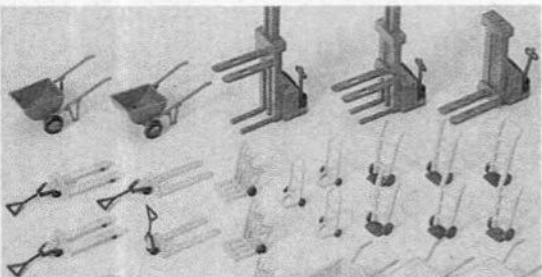

**590-17107** Fork Lifts, Wheelbarrows pkg(26) **31.99**

**590-17112** Postal Carts **23.99**

**590-17224** Grocery Carts, Unpainted pkg(10) **12.99**

## Construction Site Details

**590-17177** Concrete Mixer, Tool Kit **23.99**

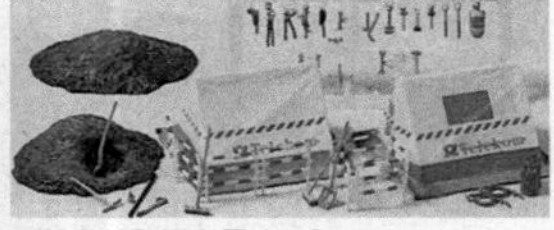

**590-17179** Telephone Construction Set **24.99**

**590-17180** Scaffolding Kit **14.99**

## Emergency Equipment

**590-31020** Chemical Protection Equipment **9.99**

**590-31021** Paramedics Accessories **9.99**

## Fences

**590-17604** Shepherds Fences **8.99**

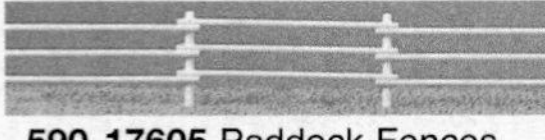

**590-17605** Paddock Fences **8.99**

**590-18337** Barbed Wire/ Stakes Kit **13.99**

## Industrial Details

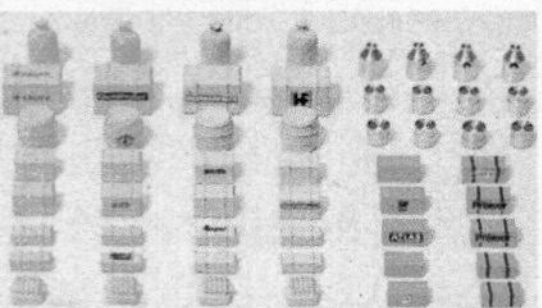

**590-17100** Cargo Kit pkg(90) **13.99**

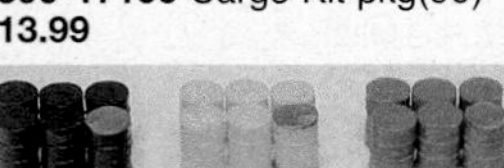

**590-17101** Metal Drums pkg(30) **13.99**

**590-17102** Sacks pkg(60) **13.99**

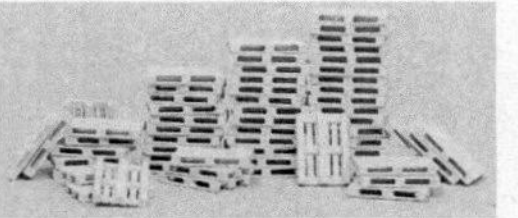

**590-17104** Pallets pkg(60) **13.99**

**590-17105** Beer Barrels & Crates w/Bottles **13.99**

**590-17110** Lattice Box, Pallets, Crates pkg(38) **39.99**

**590-17111** Cargo Accessories **39.99**

**590-17113** Plastic Boxes Kit **13.99**

**590-17114** Cable Roll and Transport Box **14.99**

**590-17501** Fruit & Vegetable Boxes **20.99**

**590-17502** Baskets Fruit/Vegetables **17.99**

## Railroad Details

**590-17005** Luggage Assortment pkg(90) **13.99**

**590-17007** Luggage **4.99**

**590-17175** Accessories for Track Workers **21.99**

## Recreation & Sports

**590-17161** Bicycles w/Trailer Kit pkg(4) **14.99**

**590-17163** Bicycle Stand, Bicycles, Trailer **8.99**

**590-17200** Park Benches (unpainted) pkg(24) **13.99**

**590-17201** 8 Tables & 48 Chairs w/Umbrella **13.99**

**590-17209** Garden Umbrellas Multi-Colored pkg(5) **13.99**

**590-17213** German Mailboxes, Telephone Booths **9.99**

**590-17219** Banquet Tables & Chairs pkg(12) **14.99**

**590-17220** Tableware & Food for Tables **18.99**

**590-17308** Beach Chairs, Lounges & Huts pkg(18) **21.99**

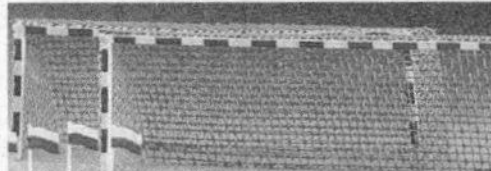

**590-17325** Soccer Goals **7.99**

**590-17500** Market Stalls & Sunshades **20.99**

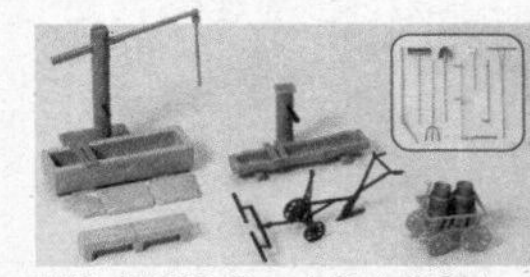

**590-17600** Rural Detail Set **23.99**
Includes water pump with trough, horse-drawn plow, cart and tools.

**590-24705** Dance Floor, Less Figures **23.99**

## Roadway

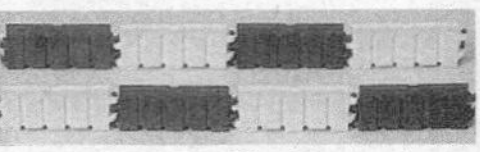

**590-17178** Traffic Control Accessory Kit **13.99**

**590-18200** Curb Set 38 Pieces **9.99**

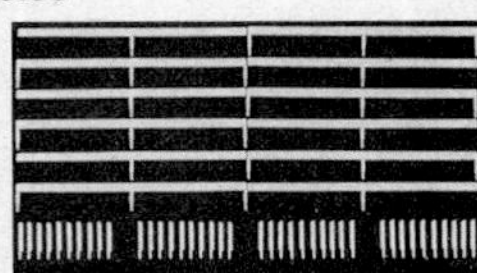

**590-18202** Guardrail Set 40 Pieces **9.99**

**590-18325** Concrete Slabs Kit **13.99**

**590-25175** Barriers Kit **13.99**

## Statues

**590-10525** Statue Assortment **13.99**

**590-29035** Kneeling Statue **4.49**

**590-29054** Standing Statue **4.49**

## Trees

**590-18600** Palm Trees pkg(4) **18.99**
Easy-to-assemble, appropriately colored plastic.

Tunnel portals and accessories are odorless urethane castings in a natural "smoky gray" color, which can be used as-is or painted.

## TUNNEL PORTALS

### Single Track

**483-101** Timber **11.50**
4-1/4 x 4"  11 x 10.5cm

**483-103** Random Stone **11.50**
4-3/4 x 5"  11.5 x 13cm

**483-105** Cut Stone **11.50**
4-3/4 x 5"  11.5 x 12.5cm

**483-113** Concrete **11.50**
4-3/4 x 4-3/4"  11.5 x 11.5cm

**483-117** Blasted Rock Rough Square **14.00**
6-1/2 x 5-1/4"  16.3 x 13.1cm

**483-118** Blasted Rock Rough Round **14.00**
6-1/2 x 5-1/4"  16.3 x 13.1cm

**483-119** Blasted Rock Smooth Square **14.00**
6-3/4 x 5-1/4"  16.9 x 13.1cm

**483-120** Blasted Rock Smooth Round **14.00**
6-1/4 x 5-1/4"  15.6 x 13.1cm

### Double Track 14.00 ea

483-104

**483-102** Timber
4-3/4 x 7"  11.5 x 17.5cm

**483-104** Random Stone
4-3/4 x 7"  11.5 x 17.5cm

**483-106** Cut Stone
4-3/4 x 7"  11.5 x 17.5cm

**483-114** Concrete
4-3/4 x 6"  11.5 x 15.5cm

### Auto Portals 9.25 ea

**483-180** Modern Concrete

**483-181** Old Concrete

**483-182** Random Stone

## WALLS

### Retaining Walls 8.50 ea (Unless Noted)

**483-110** Timber
6-1/4 x 3-1/2"  15.5 x 8.5cm

**483-111** Random Stone
6-1/4 x 3-1/2"  15.5 x 8.5cm

**483-112** Cut Stone
6 x 3-1/2"  15 x 8.5cm

**483-116** Concrete
3-1/2 x 6-1/4"  8.8 x 15.6cm

**483-137** "Broken Face" Granite Block **14.00**
8 x 4-1/8"  20 x 10.3cm

### Tunnel Abutments pkg(2) 14.00 ea

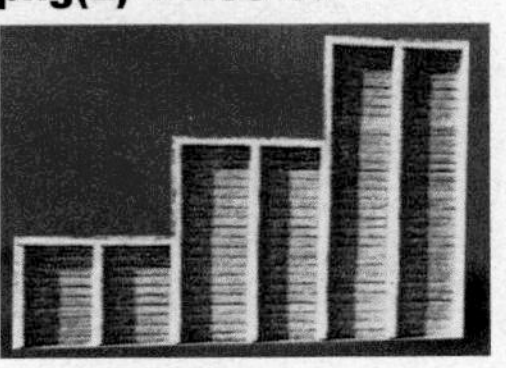

**483-107** Timber
6-3/4 x 4-1/2"  17 x 11.5cm

**483-108** Random Stone
4-1/2 x 6"  11.3 x 15cm

**483-109** Cut Stone
5-3/4 x 4-3/4"  14.5 x 11.5cm

**483-115** Concrete
4-1/4 x 6-1/4"  10.6 x 15.6cm

### Single Deck Bridge Abutments 14.00 ea

**483-140** 4' Timber w/Rock Base pkg(2)
1 x 4-3/4"  2.5 x 11.9cm

**483-141** 15' Timber pkg(2)
3/8 x 3"  .9 x 7.5cm

**483-142** 30' Random Stone

**483-143** 30' Cut Stone
4 x 3-3/4"  10 x 9.4cm

**483-144** 30' Old Concrete
4-1/4 x 4-3/4"  10.6 x 11.9cm

**483-145** 30' Smooth Concrete
4 x 3-3/4"  10 x 9.4cm

### PILLARS

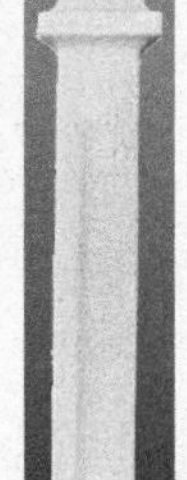

**483-138**
"Broken Face" Granite Block
pkg(2) **10.00**
Scale 33-1/2'. Compliments wall #483-137 (sold separately).

## BRIDGE PIERS

### Single Deck 21.00 ea (Unless Noted)

**483-130** 33' Random Stone
4-5/8 x 4-1/8"  11.6 x 10.3cm

**483-131** 33' Cut Stone
4-1/2 x 3-3/4"  11.3 x 9.4cm

**483-132** 30' Old Concrete
4-1/4 x 4-1/8"  10.6 x 10.3cm

**483-133** 35' Smooth Concrete
5 x 4-3/4"  12.5 x 11.9cm

**483-134** 22' Granite Block Trestle Tower Footing 14.00

### "Broken Face" Granite Block Series

Each pier measures a scale 34-1/2'.

**483-135** Oval w/Cap **35.00**
5-1/4"  13.1cm high

**483-136** Rectangular w/Cap **40.75**

## CULVERTS

### pkg(2) 9.25 ea

**483-122** Random Stone, 48"
2 x 1 x 1-5/8" deep
5 x 2.5 x 4cm

**483-150** Random Stone Double Pipe, 48"
4-5/8 x 1-1/4"  11.6 x 3.1cm

**483-123** Cut Stone, 8' Arch
Sides measure 1-3/8 x 1"
3.4 x 2.5cm; center measures
2-3/8 x 1-3/4"  5.9 x 4.4cm

**483-124** Concrete, 8' Arch
Sides measure 1-3/8 x 1"
3.4 x 2.5cm; center measures
2-3/8 x 1-3/4"  5.9 x 4.4cm

**483-125** Concrete, 36" Double Pipe
2 x 1-1/4"  5 x 3.1cm

**483-126** Concrete, 2 - 6' Rectangular
2-3/8 x 1 x 1-3/8" deep
5.9 x 2.5 x 3.4cm

### Culvert Walls

**483-127** 20' Single Bridge **12.75**
3-5/8 x 1-3/4 x 3" deep
9.1 x 4.4 x 7.5cm

**483-128** 20' Double Bridge **15.50**

## FIELDS

Each field measures
5-3/8 x 8-1/2"  13.4 x 21.3cm

**483-701** Plowed **12.75**

**483-702** Disked **12.75**

## SCRAP PILE

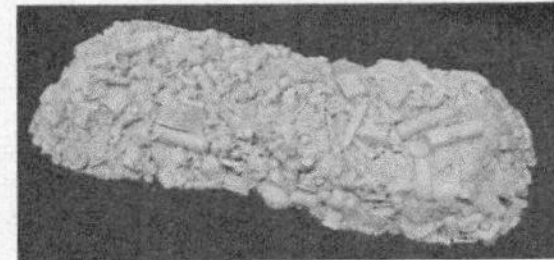

**483-703**  **22.50**

## PIKESTUFF

### Culverts

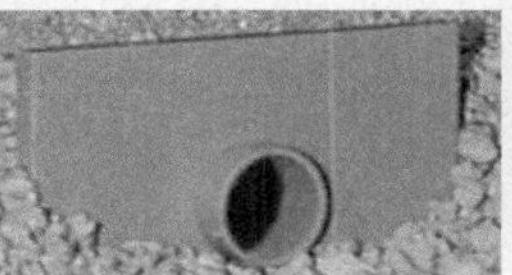

**541-2** Concrete 2 x 1"
5 x 2.5cm pkg(2) **2.50**
Molded gray plastic. Use as a bridge-type culvert or at the base of a hill emptying into a creek, river or drainage ditch.

## S&S HOBBY PRODUCTS

### Roadway

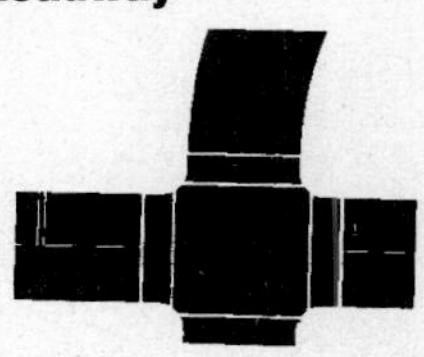

**643-305** E-Z Streets Kit **9.99**
Add paved roads to every part of your layout with this easy to use kit. Printed on waterproof styrene, kit includes six 12" straight sections (two with railroad crossing lines), curves and an intersection with crosswalk lines.

### Etched Brass Road Stencils 4.49 ea

643-1

643-2

643-3

**643-1** Stop Ahead
**643-2** R/R Crossing
**643-3** 25 MPH Street

## SCALE SCENICS

DIVISION OF CIRCUITRON

### Safety Pylons

**652-3506** Safety Pylons pkg(24) **4.95**
Bright orange plastic, great detail for construction scenes.

Scenic Express produces a wide variety of trees, ground cover and other scenery materials suitable for use in HO and other scales.

## NEW PRODUCTS

### Flock & Turf™ Ground Cover

#### Adirondack Blends

A forest floor in a bottle, these blends feature all the textural elements found on the forest floor including grasses, leaves, bushes, dirt, dead fall and mosses. Scatter them liberally to simulate a thick, natural look. Use the dark blend to make the deep parts of your forests seem even deeper.

**32oz Shaker Containers 6.98 ea**

**NEW 653-897B** Green

**NEW 653-898B** Dark

**1/2 Gallon Containers 12.98 ea**

**NEW 653-897C** Green

**NEW 653-898C** Dark

#### Dead Fall Blend

This all-in-one forest scatter debris is ideal for simulating a very coarse dead-fall forest floor. The blend features scale grasses, dried leaves, weeds, reeds, sticks, twigs, scrub brush and dead-fall logs. It's also suitable for use with S and O Scale scenes.

**NEW 653-896B** 32oz **6.98**

**NEW 653-896C** 1/2 Gallon **12.98**

## TREES

### SuperTrees™ Starter Kit

**653-220 41.98**

Includes everything you need to start making realistic trees immediately. Components include a sampler pack of SuperTree material to make 15-18 trees, 4oz concentrated matte medium, two 32oz shakers of Flock & Turf™ green base color, seven 2oz highlight and autumn portions of Flock & Turf, two 5oz Assorted Noch Leaf Flake Flock, a SprayMister® sprayer, four pairs of self-closing tweezers, two foliage collection and storage trays, sturdy carrying case and complete illustrated instructions.

### SuperTrees

Natural tree armature material captures the airy look of the real thing. Just add Flock & Turf foam materials to simulate leaves.

**653-214** 1/4 Bushel **24.98**
Yields about 30-35 trees ranging from 5 to 8" tall. Ideal for all scales.

**653-215** Super Value Case **110.49**
Yields about 200-300 trees ranging from 5 to 8" tall. Perfect for big projects and club layouts.

### SuperSage™

Natural tree armature material.

**653-240** Value Pack **24.98**

**653-243** Starter Kit **41.98**

Item listed below is available by Special Order (see Legend Page)

**653-242** Super Value Case **110.49**

See What's Available at

**www.walthers.com**

## FLOCK & TURF GROUND COVER

### Green Tones

Fine materials are great for simulating grass and other ground cover. Coarse materials are ideal for unkempt grass, small bushes or tree foliage.

#### Light Green Fine

**653-801B** 32oz **6.98**
**653-801C** 64oz **12.98**
**653-801D** 5gal **118.49**

#### Light Green Coarse

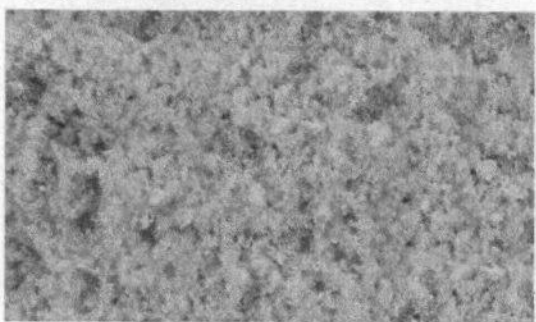

**653-802B** 32oz **6.98**
**653-802C** 64oz **12.98**
**653-802D** 5gal **118.49**

#### Spruce Green Fine

**653-803B** 32oz **6.98**
**653-803C** 64oz **12.98**
**653-803D** 5gal **118.49**

#### Spruce Green Coarse

**653-804B** 32oz **6.98**
**653-804C** 64oz **12.98**
**653-804D** 5gal **118.49**

#### Grass Green Fine

**653-805B** 32oz **6.98**
**653-805C** 64oz **12.98**
**653-805D** 5gal **118.49**

#### Grass Green Coarse

**653-806B** 32oz **6.98**
**653-806C** 64oz **12.98**
**653-806D** 5gal **118.49**

#### Spring Green Fine

**653-810B** 32oz **6.98**
**653-810C** 64oz **12.98**
**653-810D** 5gal **118.49**

#### Spring Green Coarse

**653-811B** 32oz **6.98**
**653-811C** 64oz **12.98**
**653-811D** 5gal **118.49**

#### Burnt Green Fine

**653-812B** 32oz **6.98**
**653-812C** 64oz **12.98**
**653-812D** 5gal **118.49**

#### Burnt Green Coarse

**653-813B** 32oz **6.98**
**653-813C** 64oz **12.98**
**653-813D** 5gal **118.49**

#### Forest Green Fine

**653-815B** 32oz **6.98**
**653-815C** 64oz **12.98**
**653-815D** 5gal **118.49**

#### Forest Green Coarse

**653-816B** 32oz **6.98**
**653-816C** 64oz **12.98**
**653-816D** 5gal **118.49**

#### Hazy Green Fine

**653-817B** 32oz **6.98**
**653-817C** 64oz **12.98**
**653-817D** 5gal **118.49**

#### Hazy Green Coarse

**653-818B** 32oz **6.98**
**653-818C** 64oz **12.98**
**653-818D** 5gal **118.49**

#### Conifer Green Fine

**653-820B** 32oz **6.98**
**653-820C** 64oz **12.98**
**653-820D** 5gal **118.49**

#### Conifer Green Coarse

**653-821B** 32oz **6.98**
**653-821C** 64oz **12.98**
**653-821D** 5gal **118.49**

#### Moss Green Fine

**653-822B** 32oz **6.98**
**653-822C** 64oz **12.98**
**653-822D** 5gal **118.49**

### Moss Green Coarse

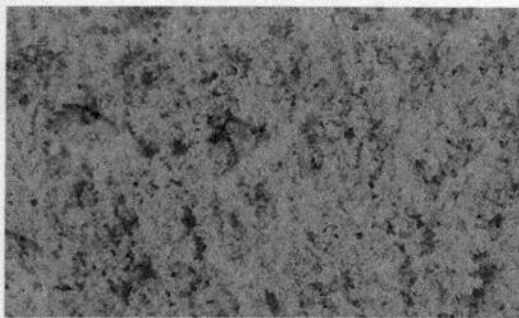

**653-823B** 32oz **6.98**
**653-823C** 64oz **12.98**
**653-823D** 5gal **118.49**

### Sage Green Fine

**653-824B** 32oz **6.98**
**653-824C** 64oz **12.98**
**653-824D** 5gal **118.49**

### Sage Green Coarse

**653-825B** 32oz **6.98**
**653-825C** 64oz **12.98**
**653-825D** 5gal **118.49**

## Brown Tones

Ideal for simulating a variety of earth colors.

### Light Brown Fine

**653-830B** 32oz **6.98**
**653-830C** 64oz **12.98**
**653-830D** 5gal **118.49**

### Light Brown Coarse

**653-831B** 32oz **6.98**
**653-831C** 64oz **12.98**
**653-831D** 5gal **118.49**

### Yellow Clay Fine

**653-835B** 32oz **6.98**
**653-835C** 64oz **12.98**
**653-835D** 5gal **118.49**

### Yellow Clay Coarse

**653-836B** 32oz **6.98**
**653-836C** 64oz **12.98**
**653-836D** 5gal **118.49**

### Georgia Clay Fine

**653-840B** 32oz **6.98**
**653-840C** 64oz **12.98**
**653-840D** 5gal **118.49**

### Georgia Clay Coarse

**653-841B** 32oz **6.98**
**653-841C** 64oz **12.98**
**653-841D** 5gal **118.49**

### Soil Brown Fine

**653-845B** 32oz **6.98**
**653-845C** 64oz **12.98**
**653-845D** 5gal **118.49**

### Soil Brown Coarse

**653-846B** 32oz **6.98**
**653-846C** 64oz **12.98**
**653-846D** 5gal **118.49**

### Dark Brown Fine

**653-850B** 32oz **6.98**
**653-850C** 64oz **12.98**
**653-850D** 5gal **118.49**

### Dark Brown Coarse

**653-851B** 32oz **6.98**
**653-851C** 64oz **12.98**
**653-851D** 5gal **118.49**

### Desert Dust Fine

**653-855B** 32oz **6.98**
**653-855C** 64oz **12.98**
**653-855D** 5gal **118.49**

### Desert Dust Coarse

**653-856B** 32oz **6.98**
**653-856C** 64oz **12.98**
**653-856D** 5gal **118.49**

## Autumn Tones

Bring fall trees to life with this selection of oranges and reds.

### Early Autumn Blend Coarse

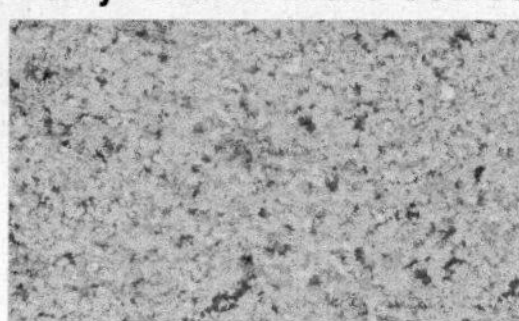

**653-870B** 32oz **6.98**
**653-870C** 64oz **12.98**
**653-870D** 5gal **118.49**

### Autumn Glory Blend Coarse

**653-871B** 32oz **6.98**
**653-871C** 64oz **12.98**
**653-871D** 5gal **118.49**

Scenic Express Flock & Turf scenic foam textures are perfect for a variety of uses including ground cover, tree foliage, bushes and dirt. Plenty of colors are available, each in convenient 32oz shaker dispenser and 64oz jars. For big jobs or club-sized layouts 5-gallon containers are available by Special Order (see Legend Page).

### Aspen Yellow Fine

**653-872B** 32oz **6.98**
**653-872C** 64oz **12.98**
**653-872D** 5gal **118.49**

### Aspen Yellow Coarse

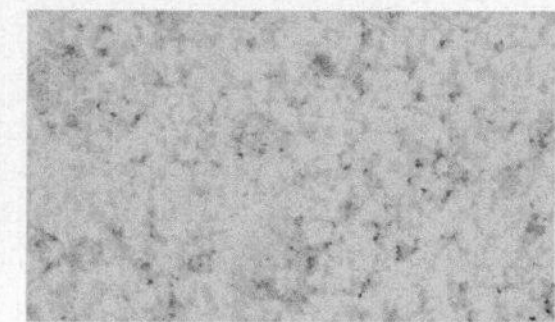

**653-873B** 32oz **6.98**
**653-873C** 64oz **12.98**
**653-873D** 5gal **118.49**

### Autumn Gold Fine

**653-874B** 32oz **6.98**
**653-874C** 64oz **12.98**
**653-874D** 5gal **118.49**

### Autumn Gold Coarse

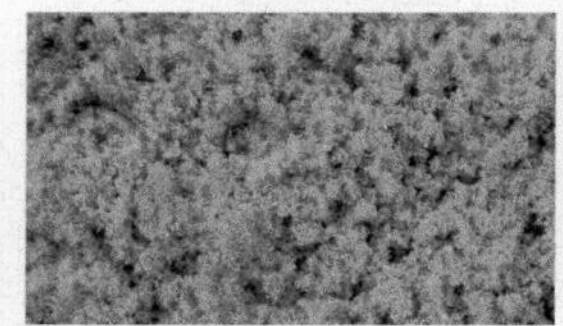

**653-875B** 32oz **6.98**
**653-875C** 64oz **12.98**
**653-875D** 5gal **118.49**

### Burnt Orange Fine

**653-876B** 32oz **6.98**
**653-876C** 64oz **12.98**
**653-876D** 5gal **118.49**

### Burnt Orange Coarse

**653-877B** 32oz **6.98**
**653-877C** 64oz **12.98**
**653-877D** 5gal **118.49**

### Red Autumn Fine

**653-878B** 32oz **6.98**
**653-878C** 64oz **12.98**
**653-878D** 5gal **118.49**

### Red Autumn Coarse

**653-879B** 32oz **6.98**
**653-879C** 64oz **12.98**
**653-879D** 5gal **118.49**

## Blends
Save time mixing colors with these blends. Each includes fine, coarse or a mixture of both as appropriate.

### Grass Turf Blend

**653-880B** 32oz **6.98**
**653-880C** 64oz **12.98**
**653-880D** 5gal **118.49**

### Summer Lawn Blend

**653-881B** 32oz **6.98**
**653-881C** 64oz **12.98**
**653-881D** 5gal **118.49**

### Scrub Lawn Blend
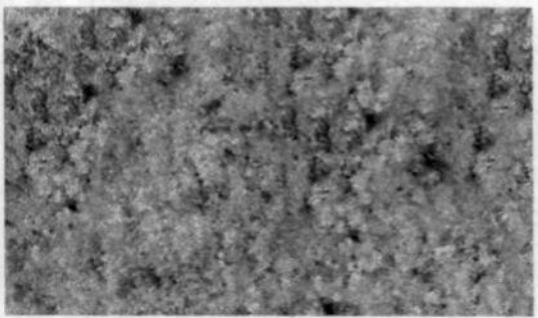

**653-882B** 32oz **6.98**
**653-882C** 64oz **12.98**
**653-882D** 5gal **118.49**

### Conifer Floor Blend

**653-883B** 32oz **6.98**
**653-883C** 64oz **12.98**
**653-883D** 5gal **118.49**

### Alpine Meadow Blend

**653-884B** 32oz **6.98**
**653-884C** 64oz **12.98**
**653-884D** 5gal **118.49**

### Forest Floor Blend

**653-885B** 32oz **6.98**
**653-885C** 64oz **12.98**
**653-885D** 5gal **118.49**

### Farm Pasture Blend

**653-886B** 32oz **6.98**
**653-886C** 64oz **12.98**
**653-886D** 5gal **118.49**

### Swampy Bog Blend

**653-887B** 32oz **6.98**
**653-887C** 64oz **12.98**
**653-887D** 5gal **118.49**

### Dark Humus Blend

**653-888B** 32oz **6.98**
**653-888C** 64oz **12.98**
**653-888D** 5gal **118.49**

### Earth Blend

**653-889B** 32oz **6.98**
**653-889C** 64oz **12.98**
**653-889D** 5gal **118.49**

For Daily Product Information Click
**www.walthers.com**

## Flock&Turf™ 6-Packs 38.98 ea
Each includes six 32oz bottles of Flock&Turf.

**653-900** Green Tones
Includes one each: Light Green Fine, Grass Fine, Forest Coarse, Hazy Green Fine, Spruce Coarse and Conifer Fine

**653-910** Brown Tones
Includes one each: Light Brown Fine, Soil Fine, Desert Sand Coarse, Georgia Clay Coarse, Yellow Clay Coarse and Dark Brown Fine

**653-920** Blended Textures
Includes one each: Summer Lawn, Alpine Meadow, Farm Pasture, Forest Floor, Conifer Floor, and Swampy Bog

**653-930** Autumn Tones
Includes one each: Aspen Yellow Coarse, Burnt Orange Fine, Autumn Gold Fine, Autumn Red Fine, Early Autumn Blend and Autumn Glory Blend

## Flowers

### Flower Material Sets 6.98 ea
Brightly colored fine Flock&Turf foam material is perfect for adding flowers to plants. Sets include four 2oz bags of flower material.

653-890 653-891 653-892

**653-890** Spring Flowers (Lavender, Pink Petunia, Buttercup & Orange Blossom)

**653-891** Summer Flowers (White Mums, Pink Peony, Bluebell & Red Rose)

**653-892** Autumn Flowers (Autumn Yellow, Marigold, Red Maple & Leaf Brown)

### Flowering Vine Kit
**653-501 6.98**

## Flock&Turf Accessories

### 20oz Shaker Bottles
Extra bottles for storing your own custom blends. Includes 2 labels.

**653-226 3.49**

### Matte Medium
**Prepared**
Ready for use, this liquid can be brushed or sprayed and will not yellow with age. Apply it to your scenery base or tree armatures and apply Flock & Turf.

**653-10** 16oz **4.98**
**653-20** 1gal **20.98**

**Concentrated**
Mix with 4 parts water for use.
**653-30** 16oz **9.49**
**653-31** 1gal **56.98**

### SprayMister
**653-23** 24oz **4.98**
No-clog spray head is ideal for use with matte medium.

## PLASTERS
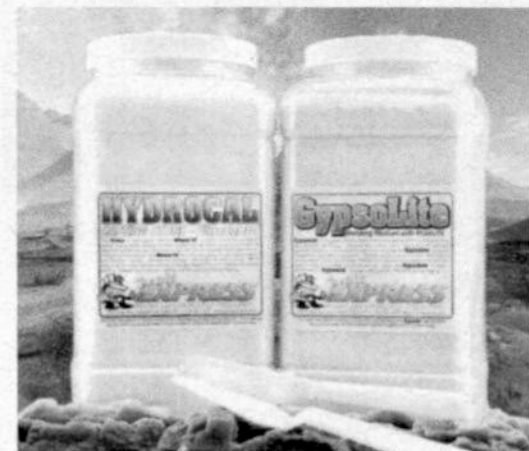


### Hydrocal
**653-40** 8lb **10.98**
Ultracal 30 is ideal for making castings with fine detail. When cured it is 5-1/2 times harder than regular casting plaster.

### Gypsolite™
Has a long working time and has Pearlite to give a gritty effect to castings. Also great for blending rock castings or as a scenery base when brushed on in thin layers. Can be mixed to any consistency.
**653-50** 5lb **10.98**
**653-51** 20lb **29.98**

### Plaster Cloth
Simply cut, dip in water and apply to your layout base or mountain framework to create a durable landscape shell. Cures in minutes.

#### PlasterWrap™

**653-60** 8" x 15' Roll **6.49**

#### PlasterSplint™
Same material as PlasterWrap, but comes in 5 x 30" sheets.
**653-62** pkg(50) **29.98**

## GLYCERINE

Keep lichen from drying out by spraying it with glycerine. Can also be used to help refresh other scenery materials. Includes complete instructions.
**653-70** Concentrate 16oz **6.49**
**653-71** Concentrate 64oz **28.98**

## FIGURE ADHESIVE

**653-140** MiniHold 2oz **3.49**
Warmth activated wax holds figures and details in place without damaging scenery or equipment. Cleans off with rubbing alcohol.

# Timberline Scenery Co., LLC

Bring new realism to your railroad with this line of realistic trees, ground cover, foliage and other scenery products.

## ROCK RITE

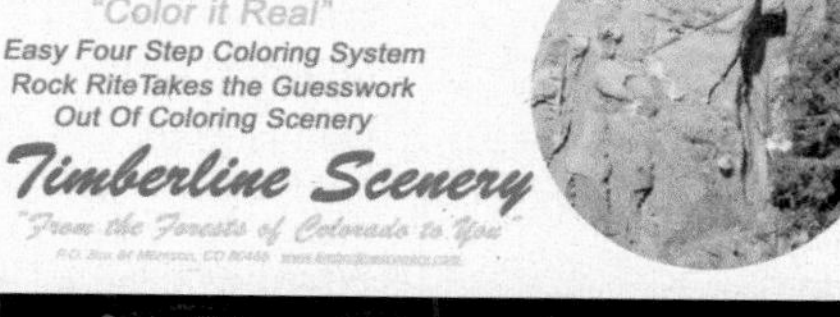

**NEW 710-8470** Rock Rite Kit pkg(4) **19.95**
This easy, four-step water-based coloring system takes the guesswork out of creating realistic scenery. Specially formulated to color plaster rock castings or carvings. Kit includes four 1 oz bottles; one each tan, red, brown, dark brown and black.

## TREES

Create a realistic forest in any scale with these detailed tree replicas. Each is hand-built one at a time, to ensure the highest quality and that no two are ever identical. Pine trees (conifers) are available with real wood trunks for dioramas or foreground, or with wire forms for backgrounds and scenes requiring many trees. All leafed (deciduous) trees feature real wood trunks.

Deep Woods Green Trees

Pine Tree Assortment

### Conifers w/Wire Form Trunks

**Northwoods Green**
**710-101** 1/2-2" 1.25-5cm pkg(6) **7.69**
**710-102** 2-4" 5-10cm pkg(3) **7.69**
**710-103** 4-6" 10-15cm pkg(2) **7.69**
**710-104** 6-9" 15-22.5cm **8.69**
**710-105** 9-11" 22.5-27.5cm **9.69**

**Deep Woods Green**
**710-106** 1/2-2" 1.25-5cm pkg(6) **7.69**
**710-107** 2-4" 5-10cm pkg(3) **7.69**
**710-108** 4-6" 10-15cm pkg(2) **7.69**
**710-109** 6-9" 15-22.5cm **8.69**
**710-110** 9-11" 22.5-27.5cm **9.69**

**Lodge Pole Green**
**710-111** 1/2-2" 1.25-5cm pkg(6) **7.69**
**710-112** 2-4" 5-10cm pkg(3) **7.69**
**710-113** 4-6" 10-15cm pkg(2) **7.69**
**710-114** 6-9" 15-22.5cm **8.69**
**710-115** 9-11" 22.5-27.5cm **9.69**

**Deadwood Brown**
**710-116** 1/2-2" 1.25-5cm pkg(6) **7.69**
**710-117** 2-4" 5-10cm pkg(3) **7.69**
**710-118** 4-6" 10-15cm pkg(2) **7.69**
**710-119** 6-9" 15-22.5cm **8.69**
**710-120** 9-11" 22.5-27.5cm **9.69**

**Timberline Green**
**710-121** 1/2-2" pkg(6) **7.69**
**710-122** 2-4" pkg(6) **7.69**
**710-123** 4-6" pkg(2) **7.69**
**710-124** 6-9" **8.69**
**710-125** 9-12" **9.69**

### Pine Trees w/Real Wood Trunks

**Northwoods Green**
**710-1102** 2-4" 5-10cm pkg(3) **8.69**
**710-1103** 4-6" 10-15cm pkg(2) **8.69**
**710-1104** 6-9" 15-22.5cm **10.69**
**710-1105** 9-11" 22.5-27.5cm **11.69**

**Deep Woods Green**
**710-1107** 2-4" 5-10cm pkg(3) **8.69**
**710-1108** 4-6" 10-15cm pkg(2) **8.69**
**710-1109** 6-9" 15-22.5cm **10.69**
**710-1110** 9-11" 22.5-27.5cm **11.69**

**Lodge Pole Green**
**710-1112** 2-4" 5-10cm pkg(3) **8.69**
**710-1113** 4-6" 10-15cm pkg(2) **8.69**
**710-1114** 6-9" 15-22.5cm **10.69**
**710-1115** 9-11" 22.5-27.5cm **11.69**

**Deadwood Brown**
**710-1117** 2-4" 5-10cm pkg(3) **8.69**
**710-1118** 4-6" 10-15cm pkg(2) **8.69**
**710-1119** 6-9" 15-22.5cm **10.69**
**710-1120** 9-11" 22.5-27.5cm **11.69**

**Timberline Green**
**710-1122** 2-4" pkg(6) **8.69**
**710-1123** 4-6" pkg(2) **8.69**
**710-1124** 6-9" **10.69**
**710-1125** 9-12" **11.69**

**Assortments**
**710-190** Without Trunks 1/2-6" 1.25-10cm pkg(17) **34.95**
**710-1190** With Real Wood Trunks 1/2-6" 1.25-10cm pkg(11) **34.95**

### Deciduous w/Real Wood Trunks

**Summer Leaves**
**710-201** 2-4" 5-10cm pkg(3) **8.69**
**710-202** 3-5" 7.5-12.5cm pkg(2) **8.69**
**710-203** 6-9" 15-22.5cm **11.69**

**Spring Green**
**710-204** 2-4" 5-10cm pkg(3) **8.69**
**710-205** 3-5" 7.5-12.5cm pkg(2) **8.69**
**710-206** 6-9" 15-22.5cm **11.69**

**Late Autumn**

**710-190** Alpine Forest 1/2-6" 1.25-10cm pkg(20) **34.95**
**710-207** 2-4" 5-10cm pkg(3) **8.69**
**710-208** 3-5" 7.5-12.5cm pkg(2) **8.69**
**710-209** 6-9" 15-22.5cm **11.69**

**Fall Splendor**
**710-210** 2-4" 5-10cm pkg(3) **8.69**
**710-211** 3-5" 7.5-12.5cm pkg(2) **8.69**
**710-212** 6-9" 15-22.5cm **11.69**

**Autumn Gold**
**710-213** 2-4" 5-10cm pkg(3) **8.69**
**710-214** 3-5" 7.5-12.5cm pkg(2) **8.69**
**710-215** 6-9" 15-22.5cm **11.69**

**Harvest Dawn**
**710-216** 2-4" 5-10cm pkg(3) **8.69**
**710-217** 3-5" 7.5-12.5cm pkg(2) **8.69**
**710-218** 6-9" 15-22.5cm **11.69**

**October Orange**
**710-219** 2-4" 5-10cm pkg(3) **8.69**
**710-220** 3-5" 7.5-12.5cm pkg(2) **8.69**
**710-221** 6-9" 15-22.5cm **11.69**

**Indian Summer**
**710-222** 2-4" 5-10cm pkg(3) **8.69**
**710-223** 3-5" 7.5-12.5cm pkg(2) **8.69**
**710-224** 6-9" 15-22.5cm **11.69**

### Fruit Trees

**Lemon**
**710-225** 2-4" 5-10cm pkg(3) **8.69**
**710-226** 3-5" 7.5-12.5cm pkg(2) **8.69**
**710-227** 6-9" 15-22.5cm **11.69**

**Orange**
**710-228** 2-4" 5-10cm pkg(3) **8.69**
**710-229** 3-5" 7.5-12.5cm pkg(2) **8.69**
**710-230** 6-9" 15-22.5cm **11.69**

**Apple**
**710-231** 2-4" 5-10cm pkg(3) **8.69**
**710-232** 3-5" 7.5-12.5cm pkg(2) **8.69**
**710-233** 6-9" 15-22.5cm **11.69**

**Assortments pkg(11) 34.95 ea**
Trees measure 2-5" 7.5-12.5cm in each assortment.
**710-290** Summer Grove
**710-291** Autumn Grove

## GROUND COVER

### Forest Floor

This special blend of fine texture foliage and real wood deadfall adds overall depth to ground cover. Each comes in a resealable bag.

**20 Cubic Inch Bag 3.19 ea**
**710-400** Forest Floor

**710-403** Deep Forest Floor

**710-406** Mountain Meadow

**710-409** Spring Mountain Meadow

**60 Cubic Inch Bag 8.49 ea**
**710-60400** Forest Floor
**710-60403** Deep Forest Floor
**710-60406** Mountain Meadow
**710-60409** Spring Mountain Meadow

## Timberline Scenery Co., LLC

### Foliage 20 Cubic Inch Bag 2.99 ea

Diverse colors and textures great for scenic detailing! Comes in resealable bags.

**Alpine Green**
**710-301** Fine
**710-302** Medium
**710-303** Coarse

**Mid-Summer Green**
**710-304** Fine
**710-305** Medium
**710-306** Coarse

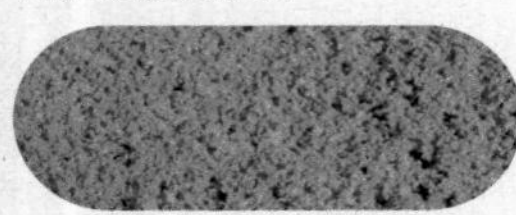

**Spring Meadow Green**
**710-307** Fine
**710-308** Medium
**710-309** Coarse

**Sage Brush Blue**
**710-310** Fine
**710-311** Medium
**710-312** Coarse

**Bristlecone Green**
**710-313** Fine
**710-314** Medium
**710-315** Coarse

**Mojave Sand**
**710-316** Fine
**710-317** Medium
**710-318** Coarse

**Pine Cone Brown**
**710-319** Fine
**710-320** Medium
**710-321** Coarse

**Winter Wheat**
**710-322** Fine
**710-323** Medium
**710-324** Coarse

**Tumbleweed Tan**
**710-325** Fine
**710-326** Medium
**710-327** Coarse

**Autumn Gold**
**710-328** Fine
**710-329** Medium
**710-330** Coarse

**Santa Fe Sunburst**
**710-331** Fine
**710-332** Medium
**710-333** Coarse

**October Orange**
**710-334** Fine
**710-335** Medium
**710-336** Coarse

**Cherokee Sunrise**
**710-337** Fine
**710-338** Medium
**710-339** Coarse

**Indian Paint Brush**
**710-340** Fine
**710-341** Medium
**710-342** Coarse

**Cherry Blossom Pink**
**710-343** Fine
**710-344** Medium
**710-345** Coarse

**Cimarron**
**710-346** Fine
**710-347** Medium
**710-348** Coarse

**Lilac**
**710-349** Fine
**710-350** Medium
**710-351** Coarse

**Wild Flowers**
**710-352** Fine
**710-353** Medium
**710-354** Coarse

**Forest Glen**
**710-355** Fine
**710-356** Medium
**710-357** Coarse

**Lost Canyon Sage**
**710-358** Fine
**710-359** Medium
**710-360** Coarse

### Foliage 60 Cubic Inch Bag 7.89 ea

All the same great colors and features of regular Ground Cover, but with three times more material for larger scenery projects.

**Alpine Green**
**710-60301** Fine
**710-60302** Medium
**710-60303** Coarse

**Mid-Summer Green**
**710-60304** Fine
**710-60305** Medium
**710-60306** Coarse

**Spring Meadow Green**
**710-60307** Fine
**710-60308** Medium
**710-60309** Coarse

**Sage Brush Blue**
**710-60310** Fine
**710-60311** Medium
**710-60312** Coarse

Forest Floor/Ground Cover

**Bristlecone Green**
**710-60313** Fine
**710-60314** Medium
**710-60315** Coarse

**Mojave Sand**
**710-60316** Fine
**710-60317** Medium
**710-60318** Coarse

**Pine Cone Brown**
**710-60319** Fine
**710-60320** Medium
**710-60321** Coarse

**Winter Wheat**
**710-60322** Fine
**710-60323** Medium
**710-60324** Coarse

**Tumbleweed Tan**
**710-60325** Fine
**710-60326** Medium
**710-60327** Coarse

**Autumn Gold**
**710-60328** Fine
**710-60329** Medium
**710-60330** Coarse

**Santa Fe Sunburst**
**710-60331** Fine
**710-60332** Medium
**710-60333** Coarse

**October Orange**
**710-60334** Fine
**710-60335** Medium
**710-60336** Coarse

**Cherokee Sunrise**
**710-60337** Fine
**710-60338** Medium
**710-60339** Coarse

**Indian Paint Brush**
**710-60340** Fine
**710-60341** Medium
**710-60342** Coarse

**Cherry Blossom Pink**
**710-60343** Fine
**710-60344** Medium
**710-60345** Coarse

**Cimarron**
**710-60346** Fine
**710-60347** Medium
**710-60348** Coarse



**Lilac**
**710-60349** Fine
**710-60350** Medium
**710-60351** Coarse

**Wild Flowers**
**710-60352** Fine
**710-60353** Medium
**710-60354** Coarse

**Forest Glen**
**710-60355** Fine
**710-60356** Medium
**710-60357** Coarse

**Lost Canyon Sage**
**710-60358** Fine
**710-60359** Medium
**710-60360** Coarse

## TIMBERLINE BASE COAT

### 16oz Bottle 6.98 ea

**710-8400** Forest Floor
**710-8403** Deep Forest Floor
**710-8406** Mountain Meadow

## WEATHER-RITE

**710-808** 8oz **7.98**
Make your models look like they've spent years outside with this handy weathering solution. Perfect for aging ballast, wood, plaster, metal and much more. Ready to use with no thinning, it's easily applied with brush or eyedropper.

## ADHESIVE

**710-816** Timberline Adhesive 16oz **5.49**
Ready to use right from the bottle, this water-soluble adhesive is perfect for securing ballast or ground covers. Can be applied by brushing or spraying and dries clear.

# VOLLMER

IMPORTED FROM GERMANY BY WALTHERS

## NEW PRODUCTS

### Flowers

**12.99 (Unless Noted)**

**NEW 770-5116** Asters (red)

**NEW 770-5117** Asters (dark blue)

**NEW 770-5125** Tulips (white)

**NEW 770-5126** Meadow w/Assorted Varieties **19.99**

### Miniature Scene

**NEW 770-2606** Bruno Lives On **26.99**
Vollmer makes a donation to the World Wildlife Federation (WWF) for each miniature scene sold. Set includes 1bear, 1 hunter, 1 hunting stand kit, 2 demonstrators, 1 photographer.

## FLOWERS

**12.99 ea**

### Tulips

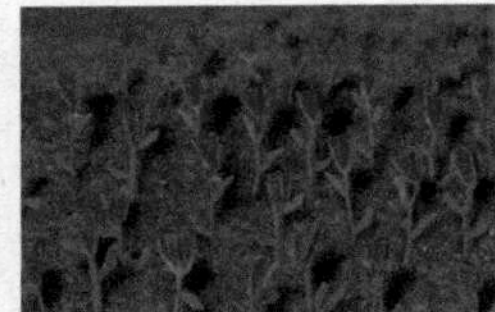

**770-5121** Red

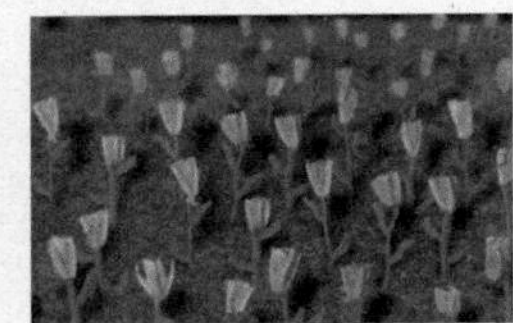

**770-5122** Yellow

### Daffodils

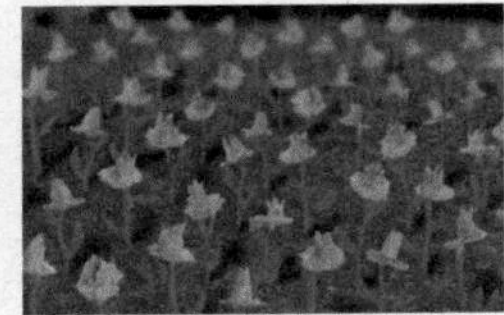

**770-5123** Yellow

### Ox-Eyes

**770-5124** White Ox

## SCENERY ACCESSORIES

**770-5021** Structural Shapes **13.99**

**770-3668** Adventure Playground **24.99**

**770-5131** Postal Accessories **11.99**

**770-5136** Turnout Scenic Accessories **15.99**

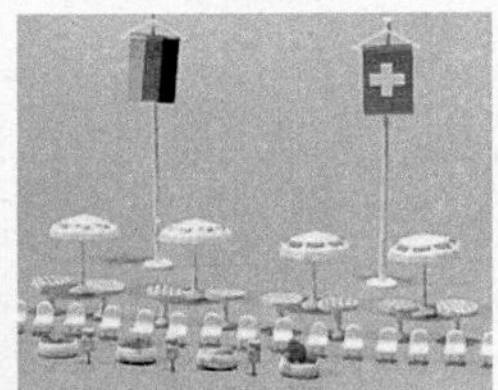

**770-5142** Round Tables & Chairs **14.99**

**770-5143** Rectangular Tables & Chairs **14.99**

**770-5241** Brick Piles & Pipe **10.99**
1/2 x 1/4 x 1/4" 11.5 x 7 x 7mm

**770-5242** Wooden Cases pkg(10) **10.99**

**770-5705** Loading Gauge & Water Spout **18.99**
Column: 2-1/2 x 1 x 3"
6.2 x 2.5 x 7.5cm
Gauge: 2-3/4 x 13/32 x 2-1/2"
7 x 1 x 6.5cm

**770-5742** Bicycle Stands pkg(3) **19.99**

**770-6524** Water Column Only **12.99**
2-1/2 x 1 x 2-3/4"
6 x 2.4 x 7.2cm

### Outdoor Farmer's Market

**770-5141 29.99**
Set is complete with snackbar trailers, tables, umbrellas, tents and other details.

### Party Tents

**770-5130 11.99**
1-13/32 x 1-13/32 x 1-5/8"
3.5 x 3.5 x 4cm

## ROADWAY

### Foil

770-6012 770-6020 770-6021

**770-6012** Cobblestone 40 x 3-13/64" **11.99**

**770-6020** Road 39 x 3" **8.99**

**770-6021** Street 39 x 3" **10.99**

**770-6022** Cobblestone 39 x 3" **10.99**

### Parking Lots 11.99 ea

Self-adhesive foil. Each measures 40 x 2-13/32" 100 x 6cm.

**770-6014** With Straight Stalls

**770-6015** With Diagonal Stalls

## BACKGROUND SCENES

Full-color photographic backgrounds, printed on heavy paper.

**770-6105** Clouds 112 x 32" 280 x 80cm **40.99**

**770-6109** Achtergrond 112 x 32" 280 x 80cm **48.99**

**770-6110** Foothills & Mountain Scene **40.99**
(2 sections) 112 x 20"
280 x 50cm

**770-6111** Alpenvorland 10 x 2' 300 x 60cm **44.99**

**770-6112** Background Clouds 108 x 20" 270 x 50cm **37.99**

## GROUND COVER

**770-5240** Gravel **7.99**

## BUILDING MATERIALS

**pkg(5) 35.99 ea**
Each plastic sheet measures 4-1/2 x 8-1/2".

**770-6024** Natural Stone

**770-6025** Wood Shingles

**770-6026** Red Tile

770-6027 770-6028

**770-6027** Corrugated Iron

**770-6028** Brick

**770-6029** Tar Paper

**770-6030** Slate

**770-6031** Stone Wall

**770-6032** Tile

### Stone Pattern Embossed Paper pkg(10) 27.99 ea

Embossed paper can be used as pavement or building materials. Less adhesive. Each sheet measures 10 x 5" 25 x 12.5cm.

**770-6041** Cobblestone

**770-6042** Red Brick

**770-6043** Brown Stone

**770-6045** Gray Sandstone

**770-6048** Granite

**770-6053** Design Pavement

**770-6054** Concrete Stone

**770-6055** Natural Stone

**770-6056** Random Cobblestone

**770-7369** Porphyry

### Walls pkg(10) 27.99 ea

10 x 5" 25 x 12.5cm.

**770-6039** Gneiss

**770-6040** Granite

### Wall Sections

**770-4508** Retaining Wall pkg(5) **41.99**
Molded of appropriately colored plastic. 36 x 41-1/2" 90 x 104cm.

## VOLLMER

### FENCES

**14.99 ea (Unless Noted)**

**770-5007** Iron (black)

**770-5008** Iron (silver)

**770-5009** Chain Link **20.99**

**770-5011** Fence

**770-5012** Meadow

**770-5013** Garden

**770-5014** Factory

**770-5015** Hoarding

**770-5016** Wooden

**770-5017** Paling

**770-5018** Diamond Pattern

**770-5133** Ornate **16.99**
Approximately 39" 97.5cm long.

### TUNNEL PORTALS

**770-2501** Single Track pkg(2) **8.99**
Cut stone, maximum clearance, 3-1/2" 9cm.

**770-2502** Double Track pkg(2) **10.99**

**770-2503** Double Track pkg(2) **11.99**
Cut stone, maximum clearance, 3-3/4" 9.5cm.

**770-2504** Single Track Rhine Valley **10.99**
5-5/8 x 5-5/8" 14 x 14cm

770-2505

770-2506

**770-2505** Double Track Rhine Valley **12.99**
8-13/16 x 5-13/16"
22 x 14.5cm

**770-2506** Double Track Moseltal **12.99**
8-13/16 x 5-17/32"
22 x 13.8cm

### CAMPFIRE

**Campfire with Flickering Light**
**770-3667 14.99**

### ARCADES

**770-4505** Gray Stone **10.99**

### TELEPHONE POLES

**770-6010** Single Pole pkg(12) **13.99**

**770-6011** Double Pole pkg(12) **13.99**

## SMALLTOWN U.S.A.

### Sidewalks

**699-7000** pkg(6) **4.99**
Finish your city scene with these plastic sidewalk sections. Each piece measures 10 scale feet by 40 scale feet long.

## Terrain For Trains
### By American Plastics

Take the work out of layout building with these molded plastic layouts – perfect for folks with limited space, or anyone living where the mess and noise of traditional layout building could pose problems. All of the scenic forms, including rocks, streams, roads, mountains and railroad right-of-way are molded in place. Simply glue the four interlocking layout sections together, no major tools are needed, and complete instructions are provided. Support risers are included that install on the underside of the layout, providing support and creating a firm structure. Then add track, trains, structures and other scenery details (all sold separately) to complete construction. The basic layout weighs about 32 pounds, so it's easy to move or store between operating sessions. Forms are available prepainted to speed construction, or unpainted so you can match your favorite scenes.

### LAYOUT TERRAIN FORMS

#### Timber Ridge

Combining mainline running for two trains on upper and lower levels with plenty of industrial sidings, this layout offers loads of operating fun in an area of only 5 x 8' - just the right size to fit a ping pong table. Designed for use with Atlas Code 83 or 100 track; minimum curve radius is 18".

**146-4005** Painted **749.99**

Item listed below is available by Special Order (see Legend Page).
**146-4000** Unpainted **589.99**

Layout forms are unassembled and unpainted; track, trains structures and other accessories shown sold separately.

#### Tunnel Addition

Take your Timber Ridge layout (sold separately) to a new level with this molded plastic mountain that includes openings for two tunnels. Simple to install with no layout modifications required.

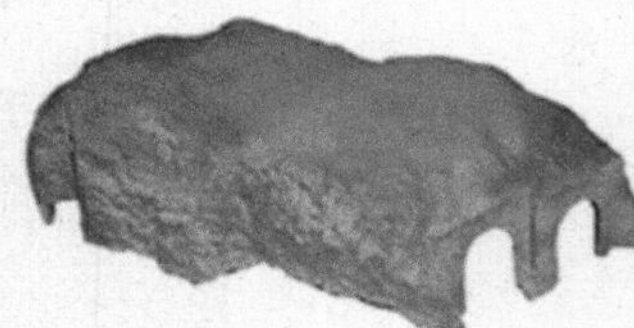

**146-4015** Painted **119.99**

**146-4010** Unpainted **84.99**

## SUBTERRAIN® FOAM PRODUCTS

**The Revolutionary Layout System for beginners or experienced modelers.**

- **No Expensive Power Tools**
- **No Dusty Mess**
- **No Complicated Calculations**

**CREATE THE IDEAL BASE FOR REALISTIC SCENERY IN JUST FIVE EASY STEPS...............YOU CAN DO IT!**

Install Risers wherever track will be laid. This raises the track level to the height of the Risers, causing surrounding areas to be lower. You can quickly and easily make creeks and other low-lying areas without cutting into the layout base.

### Risers*

**785-1406** 1/2" pkg(4) **5.98**
**785-1414** 3/4" pkg(4) **6.49**
**785-1407** 1" pkg(4) **6.98**
**785-1408** 2" pkg(4) **9.29**
**785-1409** 4" pkg(2) **9.29**

Use at least 2" Risers to elevate track, 4" Risers give maximum elevation for steep relief. 1/2" and 1" Risers* are generally used with Incline Starters to create varying grades. Each piece is 2-1/2" wide x 24" long.

*Woodland Scenics Patented Product

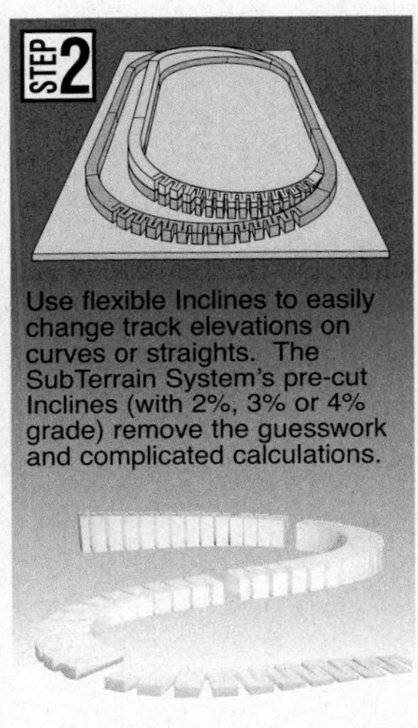


Use flexible Inclines to easily change track elevations on curves or straights. The SubTerrain System's pre-cut Inclines (with 2%, 3% or 4% grade) remove the guesswork and complicated calculations.

### Incline Sets*

Stack the pre-cut Inclines on top of Risers* for quick and easy elevation changes. Each piece is 2-1/2" wide and 24" long.

**785-1410** 2% pkg(8) **15.98**
Elevates your track 4" in 16'.

**785-1416** 3% pkg(6) **13.98**
Elevates your track 4-1/2" in 12'.

**785-1411** 4% pkg(4) **10.98**
Elevates your track 4" in 8'.

### Incline Starters*

Can be used alone or with sets to start your track on an incline. Each piece measures 2-1/2" wide x 24" long.

**785-1412** 2% pkg(8) **5.98**
Eight identical pieces that raise the elevation 1/2".

**785-1415** 3% pkg(6) **5.98**
Six identical pieces that raise the elevation 3/4".

**785-1413** 4% pkg(4) **5.98**
Four identical pieces that raise the elevation 1".

*Woodland Scenics Patented Product

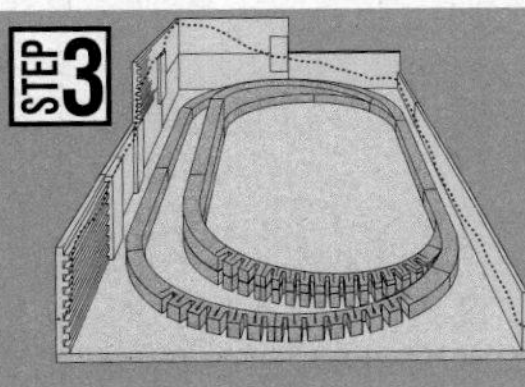


Install interlocking Profile Boards with matching Connectors to make a sturdy layout perimeter that can easily be cut with the Hot Wire Foam Cutter or a hobby knife to conform to any profile desired.

### Profile Boards

**785-1419** (2 Connectors and 2 Boards) **7.98**

Profile Boards are used around the perimeter of your layout to define the contours. Their special interlocking design allows them to be stacked and locked together. Each board is 8" high and 24" long.

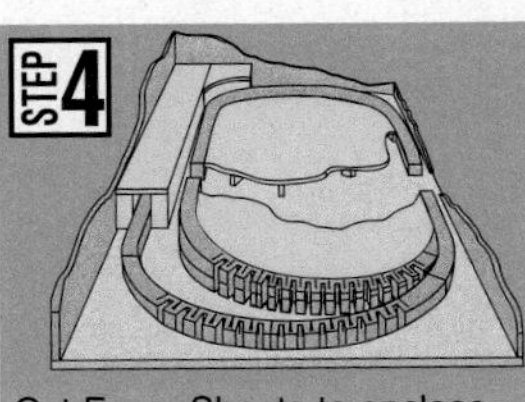


Cut Foam Sheets to enclose tunnels, create interior terrain profiles and form level, elevated areas for buildings and towns.

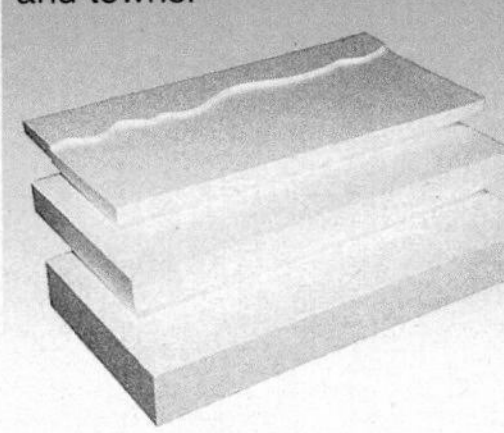

### Foam Sheets

**785-1422** 1/4" pkg(4)* **13.96**
**785-1423** 1/2" pkg(4)* **15.92**
**785-1424** 1" pkg(4)* **19.16**
**785-1425** 2" **7.98**
**785-1426** 3" **11.98**
**785-1427** 4" **14.98**

Use Foam Sheets to create elevated flat areas for towns, tunnels and contour supports. The 1/4" can be bent to a tight radius. Each piece 12" x 24".
*Sold in package quantities only.

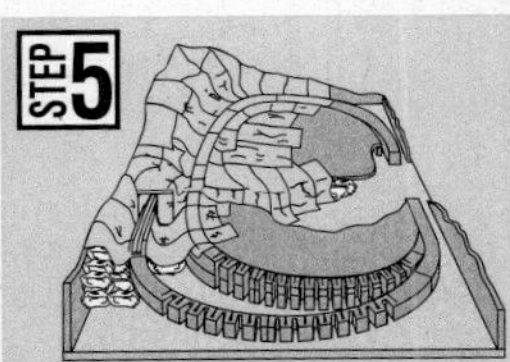


Form terrain with newspaper wads and cover with Plaster Cloth that has been dipped in water. The Plaster Cloth will dry to a hard shell without adding any plaster. Install the Track-Bed.

### Plaster Cloth

**785-1203 8.79**

A simple, convenient, and lightweight way to create a durable terrain shell or base. Just wad newspaper and stack to form the desired shape. Dip Plaster Cloth in water. Lay over newspaper wads. Plaster Cloth will dry to a hard shell without adding any plaster. 8" wide x 15' long (10 sq. ft.).

## SUBTERRAIN LEARNING AIDS

785-1400

785-1401

### How To Video 24.98 ea

**785-1400** DVD
**785-1401** VHS

Approximately 60 minutes. A step-by-step video that shows you how to build a model railroad layout with the revolutionary SubTerrain Layout System.

### How To Manual

**785-1402 7.98**

An illustrated how-to manual that teaches you how to create the ideal base for scenery and landscaping in five easy steps. 101 pages with 43 illustrations and 160 photos.

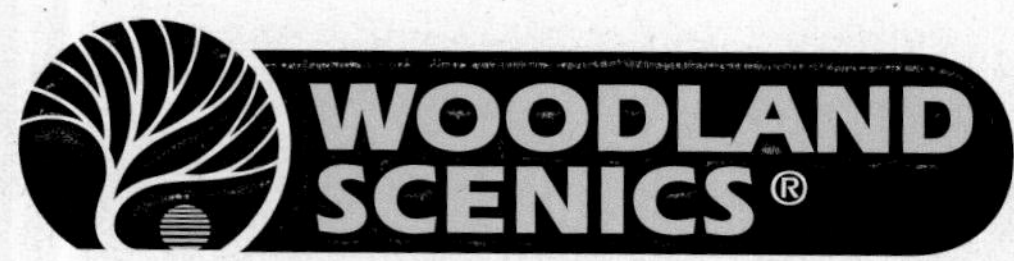


## ACCESSORIES

All of these accessories are available to help you successfully build your SubTerrain Layout.

### Foam Pencils

**785-1431 4.79**

Foam Pencils have special lead that allows you to draw on foam without causing any damage. The colors will not bleed through paint or other coverings. Each package contains 2 red and 2 black pencils.

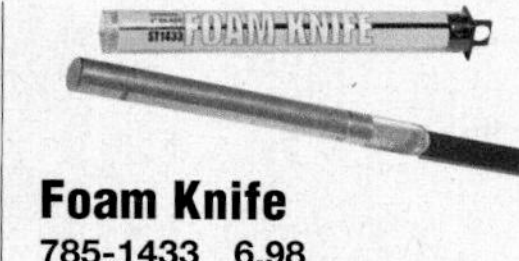

### Foam Knife

**785-1433 6.98**

The Foam Knife comes with a 2" replaceable blade that is ideal for cutting thick pieces of foam.

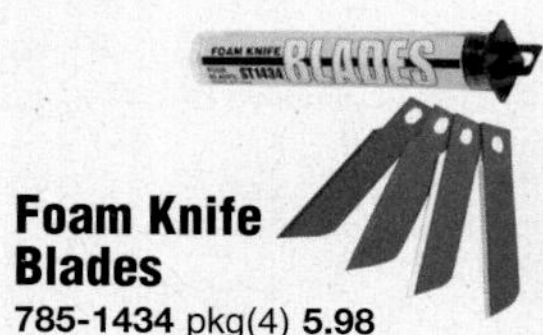

### Foam Knife Blades

**785-1434** pkg(4) **5.98**

### Flex Paste

**785-1205**

16 fl oz **14.98**

A specially formulated, non-cracking modeling paste. Use for a filler, surfacer or primer on styrofoam.

### Foam Tack Glue

**785-1444** 12 oz **10.98**

This specially formulated glue is high-tack and effective on most materials. Use as a contact cement whenever bonding two large surfaces.

### 2" Foam Nails

**785-1432** pkg(75) **4.98**

Use Foam Nails to temporarily pin track, foam or other products to your layout.

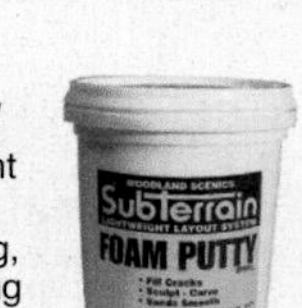


### Foam Putty

**785-1447** 1 pint **8.49**

A non-shrinking, lightweight filling material that has the same characteristics as foam. Fill cracks and gaps then sand.

### Low Temp Foam Glue Gun

**785-1445 16.98**

The Glue Gun with the Low Temp Glue Sticks operates at a temperature that will not damage foam and bonds instantly.

### Low Temp Foam Glue Sticks

**785-1446**

pkg(10) **5.98**

10" Sticks.

### Plaster Cloth

**785-1203 8.79**

A simple, convenient, and lightweight way to create a durable terrain shell or base. Just wad newspaper and stack to form the desired shape. Dip Plaster Cloth in water, lay over newspaper and allow to dry. A quick, no mess scenery base. Includes 8" wide x 15' long (10 sq. ft.) roll.

### Hot Wire Foam Cutter 39.98 ea

The Hot Wire Foam Cutter has adjustable collars allowing for clean, accurate cuts in foam. Woodland Scenics recommends using this tool only with SubTerrain white foam, which has no toxic fumes. Use only special Nichrome replacement wire, listed below.

**785-1435** 120V - North America

**785-14401** 230V - Europe

**785-14402** 240V - United Kingdom Only

**785-14403** 230V or 240V - Plug for Australia/New Zealand

### 4' Foam Cutter Replacement Wire

**785-1436 2.29**

Special Nichrome wire retains an even temperature required to cut Woodland Scenics foam products. Use only with Hot Wire Foam Cutter #1435, (sold separately).

### Foam Cutter Bow & Guide

**785-1437 7.98**

This Bow Attachment adds versatility to the Hot Wire Cutter. Attach the guide to make precise angle cuts (handle not included).

## COMPLETE ROAD SYSTEM

Making roads, parking lots or any asphalt or concrete surface has never been easier than with the Woodland Scenics Road System. Use directly on any clean hard surface.

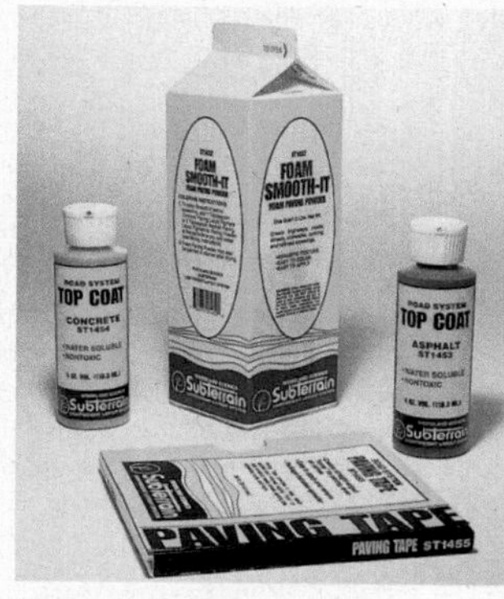


### Paving Tape

**785-1455** 1/4" x 30' **6.98**

An adhesive backed foam tape that is used to outline streets, roads and sidewalks, fill with Smooth-It, sold separately. A spreader is included.

### Smooth-It

**785-1452** 1 qt **5.29**

Mix with water and apply directly to any hard surface. Smooth-It is a plaster material that is used to smooth rough spots, create streets, roads and parking lots.

### Top Coat 4.49 ea

**785-1453** Asphalt 4 oz

**785-1454** Concrete 4 oz

Two realistic Top Coat colors are available: Asphalt and Concrete. Use full strength or thin with water.

**STEP 1**

Draw road and apply Paving Tape.

**STEP 2**

Fill and spread Smooth-It.

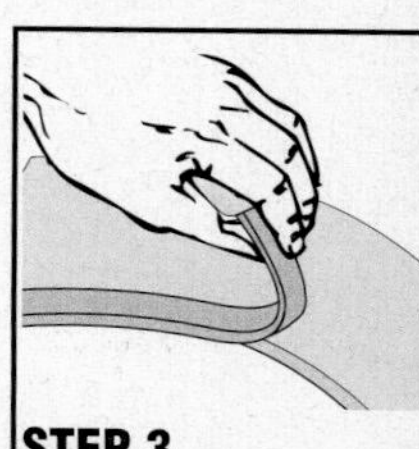

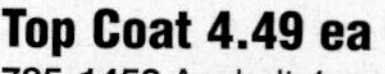

**STEP 3**

Remove Paving Tape.

## TRACK-BED

### HO Scale Strips, Rolls and Sheets.

- Quieter Operation (Sound Deadening Material)
- Smoother Operation (Cushions Vibrations)
- Easier to Use (Tack or Glue Down, Flexible, No Soaking, Compatible with Cork, Won't Dry Out or Crumble
- Better Value (Higher Quality. . . Lower Cost)

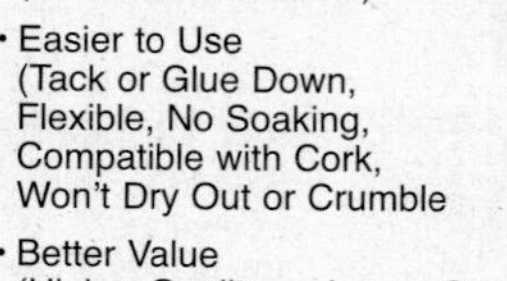

### Track-Bed Strips

Each piece is 2' (60cm) long.

**785-1461** Bulk Pack pkg(36) **28.47**

**785-1471** Standard Pack pkg(12) **9.49**

### Track-Bed Roll

**785-1474** 24' (720cm) Long **9.49**

Same great material in a continuous roll for almost seamless installation.

### Track-Bed Sheets

All sheets are 5mm thick; use in yards, stations or other areas.

**785-1470** 5 x 24" (12.5 x 60cm) pkg(6) **13.49**

**785-1477** 12 x 24" (30 x 60cm) pkg(6) **4.29**

## PORTALS AND RETAINING WALLS

### 8.69 ea (Unless Noted)

Tunnel Portals and Retaining Walls are high density Hydrocal* castings that are easy to stain with Earth Color Liquid Pigments and are available in concrete, cut stone, random stone and timber styles. Retaining Walls come in three sections per package. Each section can be used alone or installed adjacent to another in an endless chain fashion. They can be cut to varying heights to accommodate the adjoining terrain.
* Hydrocal is a product of US Gypsum.

**785-1252** Concrete - Single

**785-1253** Cut Stone - Single

**785-1254** Timber - Single

**785-1255** Random Stone - Single

**785-1256** Concrete-Double 9.29

**785-1257** Cut Stone - Double 9.29

**785-1258** Concrete pkg(3)

**785-1259** Cut Stone pkg(3)

**785-1260** Timber pkg(3)

**785-1261** Random Stone pkg(3)

## CULVERTS

### pkg(2) 7.79 ea

Culverts are also high density Hydrocal castings. There are two culverts per package.

**785-1262** Concrete

**785-1264** Random Stone

**785-1263** Masonry Arch

**785-1265** Timber

## Talus 3.59 ea

Natural rock debris usually occurs near rock faces and outcroppings, near culverts and portals and in creeks and ditches. For super detailing add Talus to models in appropriate areas with white glue. Intermix grades, blend shades, and even stain your own to match rock castings with Woodland Scenics Earth Colors. 12 oz bags.

**FOUR COLORS** | **FOUR GRADES**

Buff

Fine

Brown

Medium

Gray

Coarse

Natural

Extra Coarse

| COLOR | FINE | MED. | COARSE | EXTRA COARSE |
|---|---|---|---|---|
| **Buff** | 785-1270 | 785-1271 | 785-1272 | 785-1273 |
| **Brown** | 785-1274 | 785-1275 | 785-1276 | 785-1277 |
| **Gray** | 785-1278 | 785-1279 | 785-1280 | 785-1281 |
| **Natural** | 785-1282 | 785-1283 | 785-1284 | 785-1285 |

## Coal

Mine Run Coal

Lump Coal

**785-92** Mine Run Coal 6 oz vol. Unsorted **3.79**

**785-93** Lump Coal 6 oz vol. 4" or greater in (scale) diameter **3.79**

## Ballast 3.79 ea (Unless Noted)

## 32 oz Ballast Shaker 9.98 ea

Woodland Scenics now offers its realistic colors and textures of ballast in standard Bags with 18 cubic inches, or 32 oz Shakers that hold 50 cubic inches and allow easy application and storage.

Iron Ore

Dark Brown

Brown

Buff

Light Gray

Gray

Cinders

Blended Medium Gray

| COLOR | | FINE | MEDIUM | COARSE |
|---|---|---|---|---|
| **Iron Ore** | Bag | 785-70 | 785-77 | 785-84 |
| **Dark Brown** | Bag | 785-71 | 785-78 | 785-85 |
| **Brown** | Bag | 785-72 | 785-79 | 785-86 |
| | 32 oz Shaker | 785-1372 | 785-1379 | 785-1386 |
| **Buff** | Bag | 785-73 | 785-80 | 785-87 |
| | 32 oz Shaker | 785-1373 | 785-1380 | 785-1387 |
| **Light Gray** | Bag | 785-74 | 785-81 | 785-88 |
| | 32 oz Shaker | 785-1374 | 785-1381 | 785-1388 |
| **Gray** | Bag | 785-75 | 785-82 | 785-89 |
| | 32 oz Shaker | 785-1375 | 785-1382 | 785-1389 |
| **Cinders** | Bag | 785-76 | 785-83 | 785-90 |
| | 32 oz Shaker | 785-1376 | 785-1383 | 785-1390 |
| **Blended Medium Gray** | | | | |
| | 24 oz. Vol | 785-94 7.98 | | |
| | 32 oz Shaker | 785-1393 | 785-1394 | 785-1395 |

Fine

Medium

Coarse

**SCALE REFERENCE CHART: BALLAST**

| SCALE | FINE | MEDIUM | COARSE |
|---|---|---|---|
| Z | 2.2"-7.3" | 7.3"-11" | 11"-18.3" |
| N | 1.6"-5.3" | 5.3"-8" | 8"-13.3" |
| HO | .9"-2.9" | 2.9"-4.3" | 4.4"-7.2" |
| S | .6"-2.1" | 2.1"-3.2" | 3.2"-5.3" |
| O | .5"-1.6" | 1.6"-2.4" | 2.4"-3.9" |
| 1 | .3"-1" | 1.1"-1.6" | 1.6"-2.6" |
| G | .24"-.8" | .8"-1.2" | 1.2"-1.9" |

# SCENIC CEMENT

**785-191** 16 fl oz **6.49**
Water-soluble, nontoxic, ready to-use for Ballast, Turf and more. Dries to a clear, matte finish. Apply with Scenic Sprayer (sold separately) or brush on.

# SCENIC SPRAYER

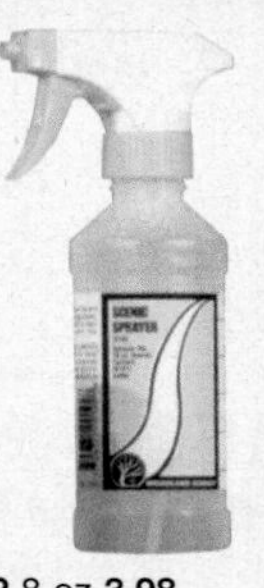

**785-192** 8 oz **3.98**
Nozzle is adjustable from a very fine mist to a steady stream. May be used to spray water, diluted Earth Colors Liquid Pigment.

# CANISTER SHAKER

**785-194** 32 Ounces Volume **3.98**
A multi-purpose container used to store and organize landscape products. Comes with dual-purpose cap; one side serves as a shaker, the other is for accessing larger quantities.

**785-199** Pack of Six **19.98**
Empty containers in a storage tray. Great way to organize your landscape products.

## PREMIUM TREES

Fully assembled, Premium Trees are works of art that replicate real live trees. Each is handcrafted. The design of the branch and leaf structure easily identifies each tree type. The tree trunks are textured to look like real bark. Each tree has a planting pin so it's easy to add to new or existing scenery. Three different package sizes are available, with trees ranging from 1-3/4 (4.4cm) to 5-3/4" (14.6cm) tall. All sizes shown are approximate heights.

### Birch

**785-1601** 4" **12.98**

### Dead Elm

**785-1602** One Each 3-1/4 & 2-1/4" **11.98**

### Sycamore

**785-1603** One Each 3 & 2-1/4" **14.98**

**785-1609** 4" **12.98**

### Maple

**785-1604** Fall - One Each 3-1/4 & 2-1/2" **14.98**

**785-1610** 4-1/2" **13.98**

**785-1614** Dead - 4" **13.98**

### Paper Birch 12.98 ea

**785-1605** One Each 1-1/2, 2-1/4 & 2-3/4" **12.98**

**785-1616** 4"

### Oak

**785-1606** 3" **10.98**

**785-1620** 5" **18.98**

### Locust

**785-1607** One Each 1-3/4 & 2-3/4" **12.98**

### Sweetgum

**785-1608** 4" **12.98**

### Poplar

**785-1611** One Each 3-1/2, 4 & 4-1/2" **15.98**

See What's New and Exciting at

**www.walthers.com**

### Aspen

**785-1612** One Each 2-1/4 & 2-3/4" **11.98**

### Beech 16.98 ea

**785-1613** Fall - 4"

**785-1615** 4"

### Royal Palm

**785-1617** One Each 4-1/2, 3 & 4" **19.98**

### Basswood

**785-1618** 4" **14.98**

### Juniper

**785-1619** One Each 5-1/4, 2-1/2 & 3" **19.98**

### Spruce

**785-1621** One Each 5 & 4" **17.98**

### Walnut

**785-1622** 4" **18.98**

### Hickory

**785-1623** 5-3/4" **18.98**

### Pine

**785-1624** One Each 5-1/4 & 4" **17.98**

# TREES

## Ready Made Realistic Trees

There are 25 different packages of trees for variety. Each tree is hand crafted; individually shaped and uniquely foliated. No two trees are exactly the same. These treees are ready to use right out of the package. Realistic Trees lend authenticity to a layout or diorama. Natural colors and realistic texture duplicate nature and blend with other Woodland Scenics landscaping products.

## Deciduous Fall Trees

**785-1540** Fall Mix 1.25"-3" pkg(9) **14.49**

**785-1541** Fall Mix pkg(6) 3"-5" **16.49**

## Pines

**785-1560** Conifer Green 2.5"-4" pkg(5) **8.49**

**785-1561** Conifer Green 4"-6" pkg(4) **8.49**

**785-1562** Conifer Green 6"-7" pkg(3) **9.98**

**785-1563** Conifer Green 7"-8" pkg(3) **11.49**

## Deciduous Trees

**785-1501** Medium Green .75"-1.25" pkg(8) **7.29**

**785-1502** Medium Green 1.25"-2" pkg(5) **7.29**

**785-1503** Light Green 2"-3" pkg(4) **7.98**
**785-1504** Medium Green 2"-3" pkg(4) **7.98**
**785-1505** Dark Green 2"-3" pkg (4) **7.98**

**785-1506** Light Green 3"-4" pkg(3) **9.49**
**785-1507** Medium Green 3"-4" pkg(3) **9.49**
**785-1508** Dark Green 3"-4" pkg(3) **9.49**

**785-1509** Light Green 4"-5" pkg(3) **9.98**
**785-1510** Medium Green 4"-5" pkg(3) **9.98**
**785-1511** Dark Green 4"-5" pkg(3) **9.98**

**785-1512** Light Green 5"-6" pkg(2) **9.49**
**785-1513** Medium Green 5"-6" pkg(2) **9.49**
**785-1514** Dark Green 5"-6" pkg(2) **9.49**

**785-1518** Medium Green 7"-8" pkg(2) **14.49**

**785-1515** Light Green 6"-7" pkg(2) **10.98**
**785-1516** Medium Green 6"-7" pkg(2) **10.98**
**785-1517** Dark Green 6"-7" pkg(2) **10.98**

**785-1519** Medium Green 8"-9" pkg(2) **16.49**

## Ready Made Trees Value Pack 26.98 ea

Nine different Value Packs contain deciduous or pine trees ranging in size from 3/4" to 8". Quantities vary according to size. Mixed green, conifer or fall colors.

Mixed Green

Fall Colors

Conifer Colors

### Green Deciduous

**785-1570** .75"-2" Mixed Green pkg(38)

**785-1571** 2"-3" Mixed Green pkg(23)

**785-1572** 3"-5" Mixed Green pkg(14)

### Fall Deciduous

**785-1575** .75"-2" Fall Colors pkg(38)

**785-1576** 2"-3" Fall Colors pkg(23)

**785-1577** 3"-5" Fall Colors pkg(14)

### Pines

**785-1580** 2.5"-4" Conifer Colors pkg(33)

**785-1581** 4"-6" Conifer Colors pkg(24)

**785-1582** 6"-8" Conifer Colors pkg(12)

## Kit Form "Realistic Trees" 15.98 ea (Unless Noted)

Six selections of tree kits in deciduous or conifer styles ranging in size from 3/4" to 8" give you the opportunity to make easy and truly unique trees for your layout. Create the armature shape you want then add as much or as little foliage as desired. Easy for beginners.

785-1111

### Green Deciduous

| | | | |
|---|---|---|---|
| **785-1101** | .75"-3" | ABC | Mixed Green pkg(36) |
| **785-1102** | 3"-5" | ABC | Mixed Green pkg(14) |
| **785-1103** | 5"-7" | ABC | Mixed Green pkg(7) |
| **785-1111** | .75"-3" | B | Medium Green pkg(21) **12.49** |
| **785-1112** | 3"-7" | B | Medium Green pkg(6) **12.49** |

785-1105

### Pines

| | | | |
|---|---|---|---|
| **785-1104** | 2.5"-4" | D | Conifer Colors pkg(42) |
| **785-1105** | 4"-6" | D | Conifer Colors pkg(24) |
| **785-1106** | 6"-8" | D | Conifer Colors pkg(16) |
| **785-1113** | 2.5"-6" | E | Forest Green pkg(24) **12.49** |

A Light Green

B Medium Green

C Dark Green

D Conifer Colors

E Forest Green

## Fine-Leaf Foliage* 12.98 ea

Great for modeling bushes, saplings, trees, shrubs and hedges. Fine detail is superb and adds realistic dimension. Color-fast and available in six realistic colors. 75 cu. in.

**785-1130** Dark Green

**785-1131** Medium Green

**785-1132** Light Green

**785-1133** Olive Green

**785-1134** Dead Foliage

**785-1135** Fall Mix

* Woodland Scenics Patented Products

## TREE KITS

With Woodland Scenics Kits, no two trees need ever look alike because you design each tree! You bend the branches and shape the tree. You position the Foliage. Try using different colors of Foliage with varied placement for realism and variety.

### Three Basic Steps

Bend and twist the soft metal armature to a realistic shape. Stretch out the Foliage until thin and lacy. Apply Foliage to tree and glue.

### Stumps 4.29 ea

**785-31** Cut Stumps pkg(14)

**785-32** Broken Stumps pkg(14)

### Small Tree Kits 8.98 ea

Each tree kit contains two to five bendable metal trunk castings with bark texture; pre-colored, non-metallic Foliage material; and easy to follow instructions. These are highly detailed, extremely versatile trees, designed to lend realism and variety to any layout.

**785-11** Forked Tree 2-1/4" pkg(4)

**785-13** Straight Trunk 2-1/2" pkg(5)

**785-18** Double Forked 3-1/2" pkg(2)

**785-21** Gnarled 4-1/2" pkg(2)

**785-12** Ornamental 2-1/2" pkg(5)

**785-14** Softwood Pine 3-1/4" pkg(5)

**785-20** Columnar Pine 4-1/2" pkg(4)

**785-19** Shade Tree 4" pkg(2)

**785-17** Shag Bark 3-1/2" pkg(3)

**785-22** Dead Trees pkg(5)

### Large Tree Kits 14.98 ea

These soft white metal tree kits provide realism for the special scenes in your layout.

**785-23** Pine Trees Approx. 6-9" Tall pkg(5)

**785-25** Hardwood Trees Approx. 5-1/2 to 6-1/2" Tall pkg(3)

**785-27** Pine Forest Approx. 2-4" Tall pkg(24)

**785-24** Hedge Row Scene 24-30" long. Contains: 18 trees, 6 bushes, 3 colors Foliage, 2 colors Turf.

**785-26** Big Old Trees Approx. 7 to 7-1/2" Tall pkg(2)

**785-28** Hardwood Forest Approx. 2-4" Tall pkg(24)

### Complete Landscape Kit

**785-926 34.98**
Contains: 18 trunks (2-4" tall), 3 packs Foliage, 7 stumps, 2 packs Green Blend Turf, 3 packs accent Turf.

### Tree Armatures 11.98 ea

Tree armatures are bendable plastic and hold their shape once twisted into a new position. Each has a base pin for easy planting on your layout. Choose from four sets of deciduous and two sets of pine trees, which include a variety of types and sizes in each package.

**Deciduous**

**785-1120** .75"-2" Pack of 114
**785-1121** 2"-3" Pack of 57
**785-1122** 3"-5" Pack of 28
**785-1123** 5"-7" Pack of 12

**Pines**

**785-1124** 2-1/2"-4" Pack of 70
**785-1125** 4"-6" Pack of 44

# GROUND COVERS

## Clump-Foliage*

Clump-Foliage is a patented foliage product available in one or three quart bags in six realistic colors. Use as Ground Cover, Bushes, shrubs, and tree foliage. Previously available in Realistic Tree Kits only.

### Burnt Grass

**785-181** 3 Quart **14.49**

### Light Green

**785-182** 3 Quart **14.49**
**785-682** 1 Quart **5.79**

### Medium Green

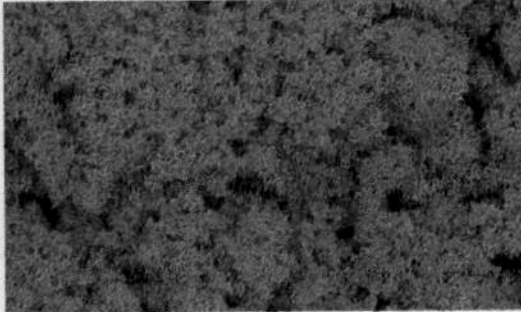

**785-183** 3 Quart **14.49**
**785-683** 1 Quart **5.79**

### Dark Green

**785-184** 3 Quart **14.49**
**785-684** 1 Quart **5.79**

### Conifer Green

**785-185** 3 Quart **14.49**

### Autumn Mix

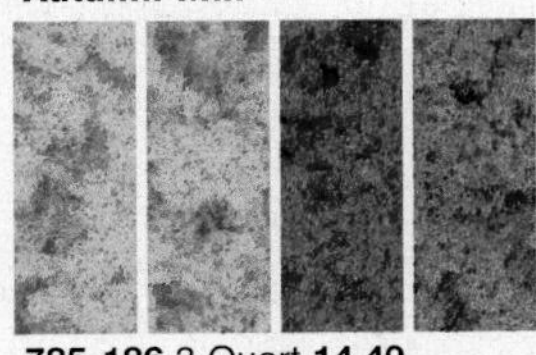

**785-186** 3 Quart **14.49**

*Woodland Scenics Patented Product

## Lichen

This natural product blends in a limitless variety of colors and textures when combined with Woodland Scenics Turf and Foliage lines. Two package sizes and several colors offer variety and economy.

### Spring Green

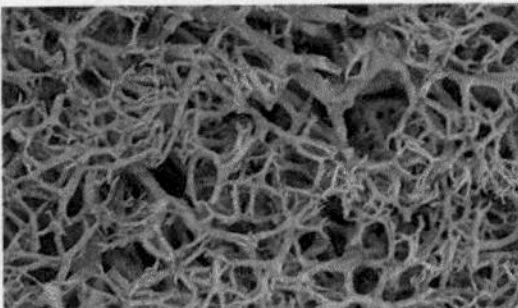

**785-161** 1-1/2 Quart **6.98**

### Light Green

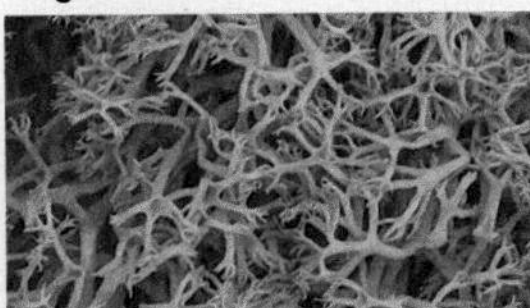

**785-162** 1-1/2 Quart **6.98**

### Medium Green

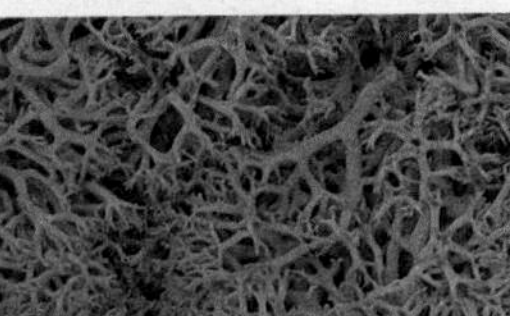

**785-163** 1-1/2 Quart **6.98**

### Dark Green

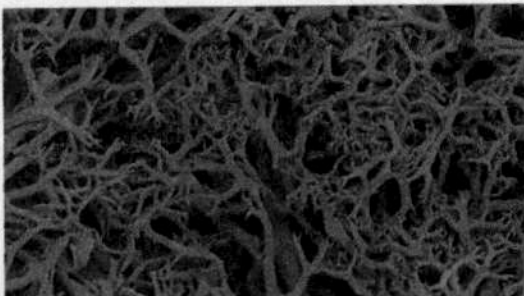

**785-164** 1-1/2 Quart **6.98**



### Autumn Mix

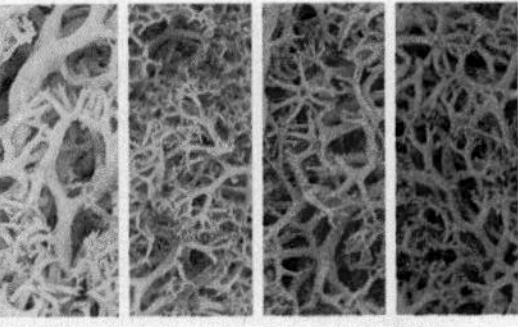

**785-165** 1-1/2 Quart **6.98**

### Natural

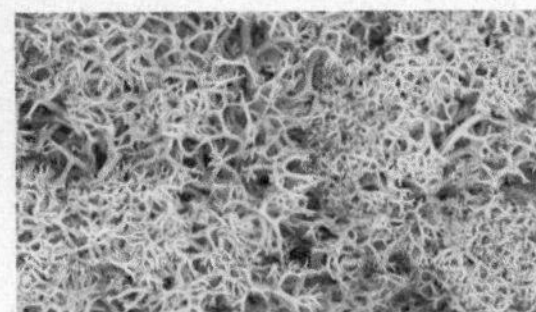

**785-166** 1-1/2 Quart **6.98**

### Light Green Mix

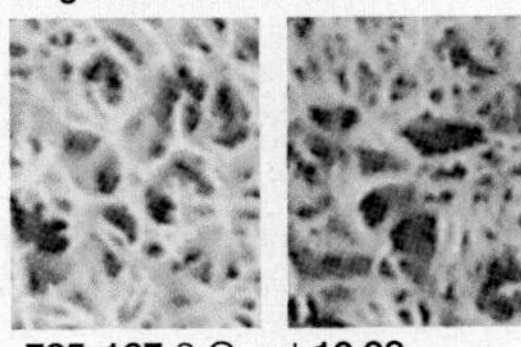

**785-167** 3 Quart **12.98**

### Dark Green MIx

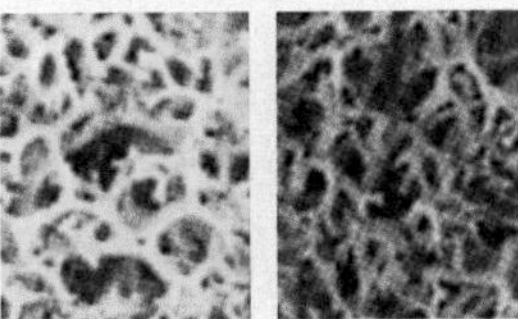

**785-168** 3 Quart **12.98**

## Field Grass

An extremely fine natural hair product that models tall grass, field grass and weeds. Easy to follow instructions. Available in four realistic colors.

### Natural Straw

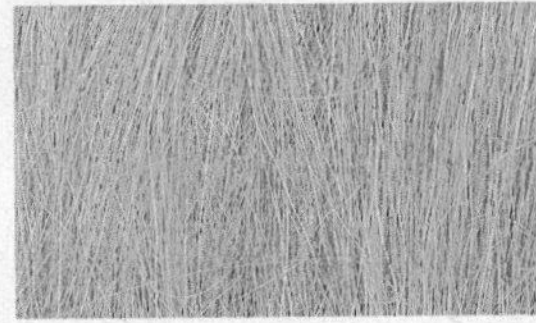

**785-171** 8 gr. **3.49**

### Harvest Gold

**785-172** 8 gr. **3.49**

### Light Green

**785-173** 8 gr. **3.49**

### Medium Green

**785-174** 8 gr. **3.49**

## Static Grass Flock

Create realistic three-dimensional grass in any scene with this special material. When applied, Static Grass Flock has a tendency to stand up, so the grass looks more like the real thing. Available in six realistic colors which can be mixed and matched to create a variety of vegetation. Each comes in a 32 oz shaker with a sifter top for easy application and storage.

### Wild Honey

**785-631** 32 oz **9.98**

### Harvest Gold

**785-632** 32 oz **9.98**

### Burnt Grass

**785-633** 32 oz **9.98**

### Light Green

**785-634** 32 oz **9.98**

### Medium Green

**785-635** 32 oz **9.98**

### Dark Green

**785-636** 32 oz **9.98**

# TURF

## Blended Turf

Turf is a ground foam material for modeling grass, dead grass, and various types of plant life. Easy to apply, Turf is available in a variety of colors and sizes that allow you to create combinations and textures for any season in any scale.

### Green Blend

**785-49** 54 cu. in. **6.98**
**785-1349** 32 oz Shaker **9.79**

### Earth Blend

**785-50** 54 cu. in. **6.98**
**785-1350** 32 oz Shaker **9.79**

## Fine Turf

### Soil

**785-41** 18 cu. in. **3.59**
**785-1341** 32 oz Shaker **9.79**

### Earth

**785-42** 18 cu. in. **3.59**
**785-1342** 32 oz Shaker **9.79**

### Yellow Grass

**785-43** 18 cu. in. **3.59**
**785-1343** 32 oz Shaker **9.79**

### Burnt Grass

**785-44** 18 cu. in. **3.59**
**785-1344** 32 oz Shaker **9.79**

### Green Grass

**785-45** 18 cu. in. **3.59**
**785-1345** 32 oz Shaker **9.79**

### Weeds

**785-46** 18 cu. in. **3.59**
**785-1346** 32 oz Shaker **9.79**

## Landscape Accessories

**785-47** Fruit-Apples (red) & Oranges **3.49**

**785-48** Flowers (4 Colors) **3.49**

## Coarse Turf

### Earth

**785-60** 18 cu. in. **3.59**

### Yellow Grass

**785-61** 18 cu. in. **3.59**
**785-1361** 32 oz Shaker **9.79**

### Burnt Grass

**785-62** 18 cu. in. **3.59**
**785-1362** 32 oz Shaker **9.79**

### Light Green

**785-63** 18 cu. in. **3.59**
**785-1363** 32 oz Shaker **9.79**

### Medium Green

**785-64** 18 cu. in. **3.59**
**785-1364** 32 oz Shaker **9.79**

### Dark Green

**785-65** 18 cu. in. **3.59**
**785-1365** 32 oz Shaker **9.79**



### Conifer Green

**785-1366** 32 oz Shaker **9.79**

### Fall Yellow

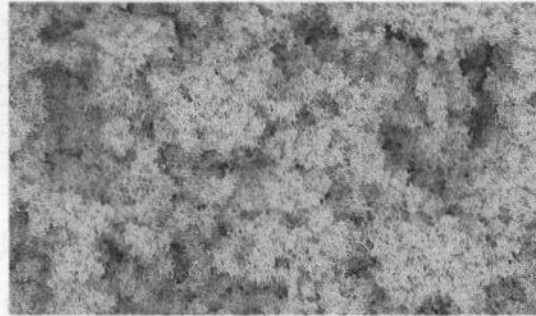

**785-1353** 32 oz Shaker **9.79**

### Fall Orange

**785-1354** 32 oz Shaker **9.79**

### Fall Red

**785-1355** 32 oz Shaker **9.79**

### Fall Rust

**785-1356** 32 oz Shaker **9.79**

## Foliage Clusters*

A specially produced ground foam cluster for bushes, undergrowth and foliage. Use as is or break into smaller clusters. Each 45 cubic inches.

### Light Green

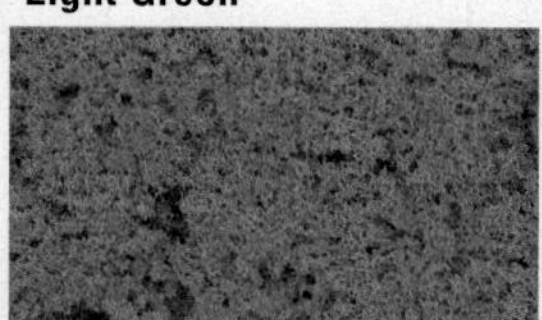

**785-57** 45 cu. in. **7.98**

### Medium Green

**785-58** 45 cu. in. **7.98**

### Dark Green

**785-59** 45 cu. in. **7.98**

*Woodland Scenics Patented Product

# FOLIAGE

Foliage can be used for trees, vines, weeds, bushes, or any other low growth. Simply stretch foliage material to desired density and apply. Each 60 sq. inches.

### Light Green

**785-51** 60 sq. in. **3.98**

### Medium Green

**785-52** 60 sq. in. **3.98**

### Dark Green

**785-53** 60 sq. in. **3.98**

### Conifer Green

**785-54** 60 sq. in. **3.98**

### Early Fall Mix

**785-55** 60 sq. in. **3.98**

### Late Fall Mix

**785-56** 60 sq. in. **3.98**

# REALISTIC WATER

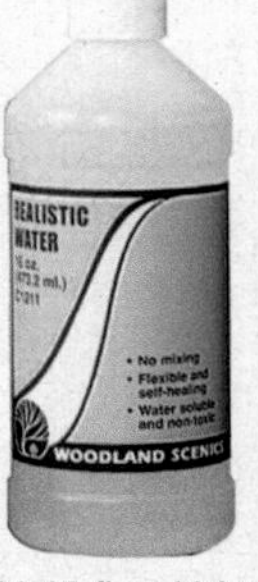

**785-1211** 16 fl oz Volume **15.98**
Use for modeling various bodies of water such as lakes rivers, ponds, creeks and streams. This ready-to-use water is flexible, self-leveling and will not dry hard or brittle. Self-healing characteristics make it an ideal choice for dioramas or modules that are handled often.

# WATER EFFECTS

**785-1212** 8 fl oz **12.98**
Use to model impressions of moving water such as waterfalls, rapids, ripples, waves and water rings. Ready to use right from the bottle, material is flexible and easy to use. Will not dry hard or brittle, is nontoxic and water-soluble.

## UNDERBRUSH*

Available in six realistic colors and great for making small trees too!

### Olive Green

**785-134** 12 oz **3.98**
**785-1634** 32 oz Shaker **11.49**

### Light Green

**785-135** 12 oz **3.98**
**785-1635** 32 oz Shaker **11.49**

### Medium Green

**785-136** 12 oz **3.98**
**785-1636** 32 oz Shaker **11.49**

### Dark Green

**785-137** 12 oz **3.98**
**785-1637** 32 oz Shaker **11.49**

### Forest Green

**785-138** 12 oz **3.98**
**785-1638** 32 oz Shaker **11.49**

### Forest Blend

**785-139** 12 oz **3.98**
**785-1639** 32 oz Shaker **11.49**

## BUSHES*

Available in six realistic colors and great for making hedges, bushes, shrubs and trees.

### Olive Green

**785-144** 12 oz **3.98**
**785-1644** 32 oz Shaker **11.49**

### Light Green

**785-145** 12 oz **3.98**
**785-1645** 32 oz Shaker **11.49**

### Medium Green

**785-146** 12 oz **3.98**
**785-1646** 32 oz Shaker **11.49**

### Dark Green

**785-147** 12 oz **3.98**
**785-1647** 32 oz Shaker **11.49**

### Forest Green

**785-148** 12 oz **3.98**
**785-1648** 32 oz Shaker **11.49**

### Forest Blend

**785-149** 12 oz **3.98**
**785-1649** 32 oz Shaker **11.49**

*Woodland Scenics Patented Product

## LEARNING AIDS . . . YOU CAN DO IT

### Woodland Scenics Learning Kits 13.98 ea

**Rock Faces**
**785-951**
Teaches you how to make and color realistic rock formations.

**Road System**
**785-952**
Learn to add roads and pavement to any layout.

**Trees**
**785-953**
Shows you how to make and add trees to your layout.

**Landscaping**
**785-954**
Teaches you how to use the complete line of Woodland Scenics ground covers and foliage products.

**River/Waterfall**
**785-955**
Learn how to create the illusion of deep water and make a river with a waterfall. Includes Earth Colors Liquid Pigments, Realistic Water, Water Effects, Talus, Plaster Cloth, Green Blend Turf, Scenic Glue and applicator.

**Scenery Details**
**785-956**
Learn simple techniques to detail your layout. Includes Dead Fall, Fine Turf, Bushes, Underbrush, Fine-Leaf Foliage, Field Grass, Flowering Foliage, Poly Fiber and Scenic Glue.

## DETAILS

### Soft Flake Snow Shaker

**785-140**
**9.98**
This realistic, easy-to-use snow is available in a 32 oz Shaker with a sifter top. Perfect for adding either light dustings or heavy drifts.

### Dead Fall

**785-30** .5 oz Weight **3.98**
A natural ready-to-use product for modeling fallen or standing dead trees and stumps, as well as modeling forest floor debris.

## POLY FIBER

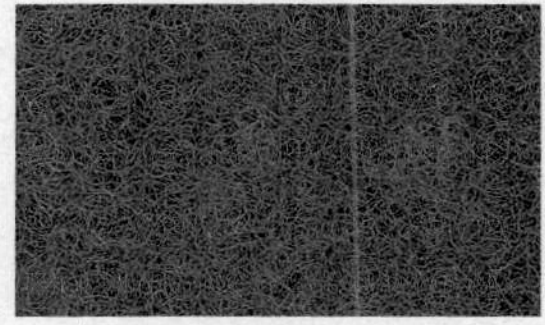

**785-178** Green **2.98**
A synthetic fiber intended for use with ground foam to create undergrowth, vines, and economical trees.

## FLOWERING FOLIAGE 3.39 ea

A great way to model wildflowers or create flowering bushes and add a splash of color anywhere on your layout. Available in two colors; Purple and Yellow. Use for modeling flowerbeds along the railroad tracks, in fields, on hillsides or around buildings. Covers 100 sq. in.

**785-176** Yellow

**785-177** Purple

## ADHESIVES

### Hob-e-Tac®

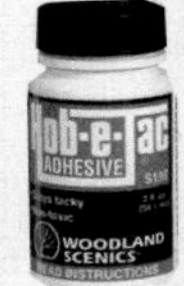


**785-195** 2 oz **5.49**
Multi-purpose, water-soluble, high-tack adhesive. Perfect for making trees. Should be used as a contact adhesive.

### Scenic Glue

**785-190** 8 fl oz **6.49**
Formulated especially for model landscaping. Dries clear with a matte (flat) finish, is flexible and leaves no residue. Use to attach various Foliage, Bushes, Underbrush and Lichen. Does not become brittle after drying.

### Scenic Cement

**785-191** 16 fl oz **6.49**
Water-soluble, non-toxic, ready-to-use for Ballast, Turf and more. Dries to a clear, matte finish. Apply with Scenic Sprayer (sold separately) or brush on.

## THE COMPLETE TERRAIN SYSTEM

Woodland Scenics Terrain products are a complete system for beginners and craftsmen alike. The Terrain System has all the products needed to make earth contour models that reflect any type of terrain. The system includes Lightweight Hydrocal, Mold-A-Scene, Plaster Cloth, E-Z Water, Flex Paste, Latex Rubber, Tunnel Portals, Retaining Walls, Culverts, Talus, Tunnel Liner Form, Earth Color Liquid Pigments, Scenic Sprayer, Rock Molds and The Scenery Manual. Each product has easy to follow instructions.

### E-Z Water

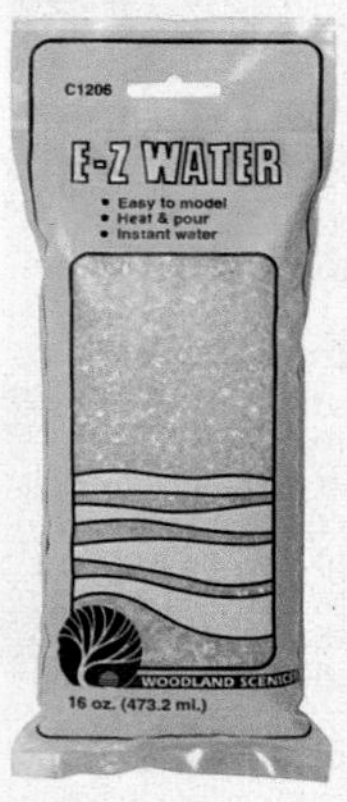


**785-1206** 16 oz **10.49**
This heat activated water modeling material has been developed for the special needs of the scenery modeler. Melt on stove and pour.

See What's Available at

**www.walthers.com**

### Tunnel Liner Form

**785-1250 4.79**
Easy way to cast realistic rock walls and ceilings to detail the interior of single or double track tunnels.

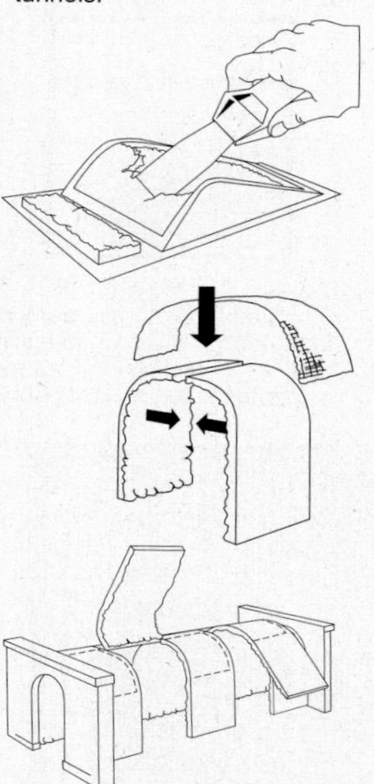

### Pigments 5.29 ea (Unless Noted)

#### Earth Colors Liquid Pigments

Use the eight different colors of Earth Colors Liquid Pigment to stain rocks, terrain, and plaster castings. They are water soluble and can be diluted and blended in limitless combinations. Extremely concentrated for economical use. 4 oz each. (Photo shows plaster rock castings, stained with color.)

**785-1216** White

**785-1217** Concrete

**785-1218** Stone Gray

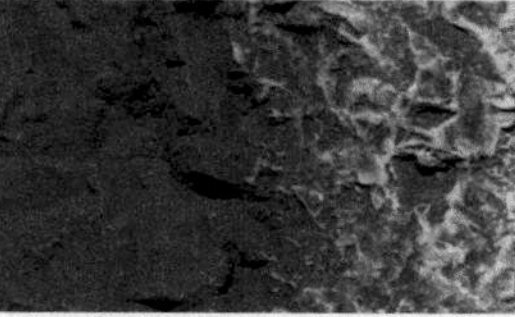

**785-1219** Slate Gray

**785-1220** Black

**785-1221** Raw Umber

**785-1222** Burnt Umber

**785-1223** Yellow Ocher

#### Undercoat Pigments 6.98 ea

Formulated for use under Green Blend and Earth Blended Turf (785-49 and 78 50) to provide a base color. These two colors of Liquid Pigment can also be used fo rocks and plaster castings. Extremely concentrated. 8 oz each. (Photo shows plaster rock castings, stained with color.)

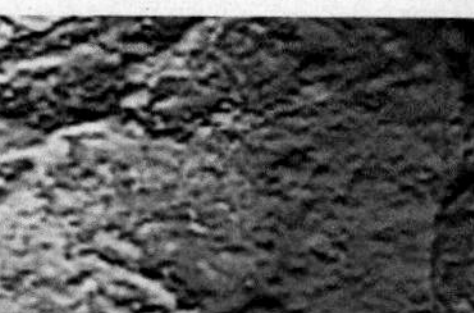

**785-1228** Green Undercoat

**785-1229** Earth Undercoat

### Earth Color Kit

**785-1215** Earth Color Kit **18.98**
A simple system for staining rocks, terrain and plaster castings such as portals. Beginners get quality results. The Earth Color Kits include instructions, applicator, palette and eight 1 oz bottles each of Earth Color Liquid Pigment (White, Concrete, Stone Gray, Slate Gray, Raw Umber, Burnt Umber, Yellow Ochre).

## READYGRASS® VINYL MAT*

These high-quality grass mats can be used as-is, or mounted to plywood. They're great for model railroads, school projects, arts and crafts, gaming, military models, architectural models, collectible houses, slot cars and much more. The special vinyl back can easily be shaped with the Heat Tool (#785-5162) and newspaper wads to form hills, mountains and valleys. The turf is also removable and leaves a hard, smooth surface that's perfect for roads, sidewalks, parking lots (easily modeled with the Road Kit #785-5151) or building placement. By removing turf and using the Water Kit (#785-5153), you can add rivers, streams, lakes and ponds. Choose from three mat sizes; Large 50 x 100" (125 x 250cm), Small 33 x 50" (82.5 x 125cm) or the Project Sheet 14-1/8 x 12-1/2" (35.6 x 31.2cm) in four different colors.

### Spring Grass

**785-5121** Large **24.98**
**785-5131** Small **9.98**
**785-5141** Project Sheet **2.98**

### Green Grass

**785-5122** Large **24.98**
**785-5132** Small **9.98**
**785-5142** Project Sheet **2.98**

### Forest Grass

**785-5123** Large **24.98**
**785-5133** Small **9.98**
**785-5143** Project Sheet **2.98**

### Summer Grass

**785-5124** Large **24.98**
**785-5134** Small **9.98**
**785-5144** Project Sheet **2.98**

## READYGRASS ACCESSORIES

### Road Kit

**785-5151 10.98**
Complete kit with everything needed to make roads, sidewalks and parking lots.

### Landscape Kit

**785-5152 14.98**
Includes everything needed - Foliage, Bushes, Shrubs and adhesive - to enhance a 4' x 8' area.

### Water Kit

**785-5153 10.98**
Everything needed to model a pond, stream, river or lake in one complete kit.

### Tree Kit

**785-5154 19.98**
A complete kit with everything you'll need to make 27 deciduous and pine trees for a 4' x 8' area. Trees range in height from 2-1/2 to 6" (5 to 15.2cm).

### Mat Adhesive

**785-5161 6.98**
Use for permanent or temporary mounting of ReadyGrass Mats on any surface; can also be used for mounting puzzles and posters to art board.

### Heat Tool

**785-5162 24.98**
Use with ReadyGrass vinyl mats to form hills, mounds and valleys.

*Patent Pending

### ReadyGrass Accessories

**Attach Mat with Mat Adhesive**

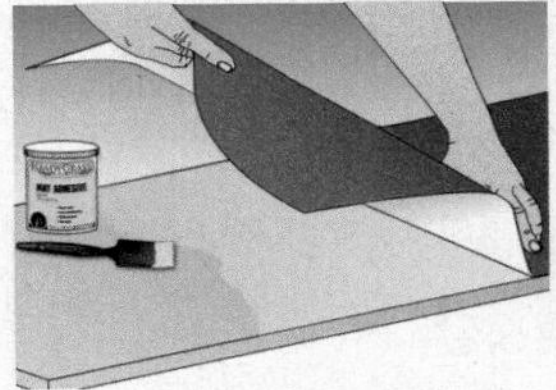

Glue to any surface with Mat Adhesive.

**Form Hills with Heat Tool**

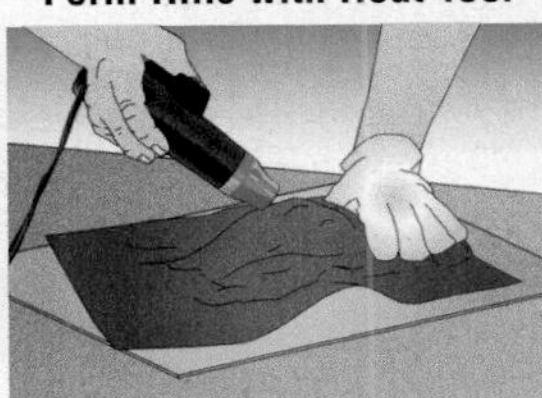

Form hills over newspaper wads with Heat Tool.

**Make Roads and Sidewalks with Road Kit**

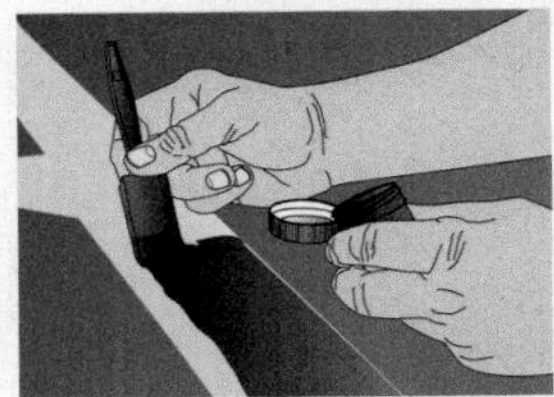

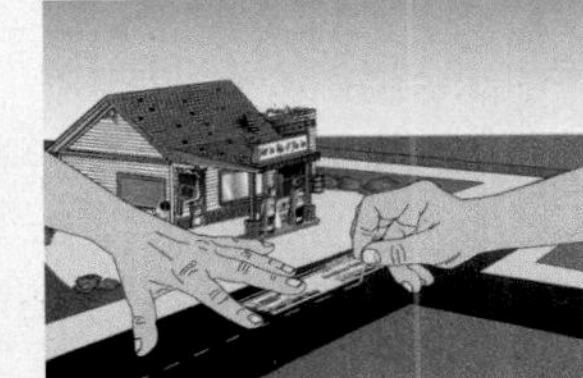

Wet area, scrape off turf, then paint. Detail road and parking lot with Striping Pin.

**Add Water with Water Kit**

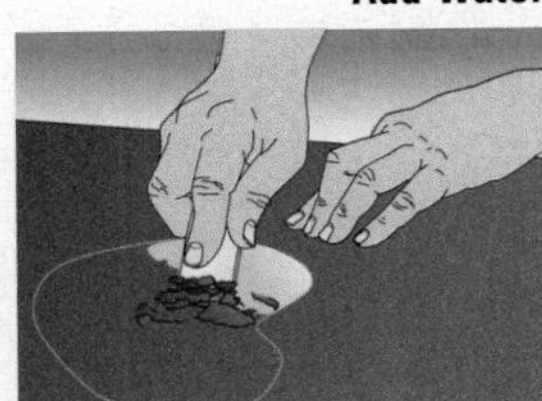

Wet area, scrape off turf, then paint. Pour water.

**Add Trees with Tree Kit**

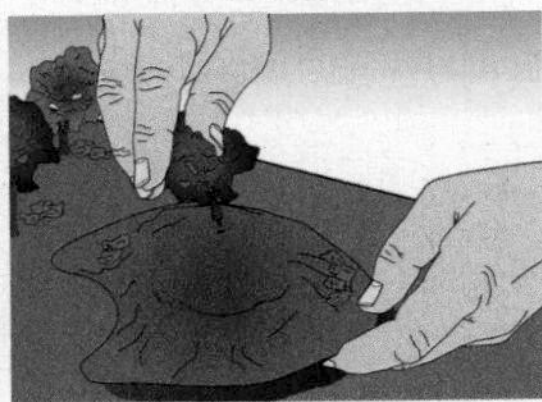

Make and plant trees.

**Add Landscaping with Landscape Kit**

Add bushes and highlights.

## PLASTER

### Plaster Cloth

**785-1203** 15 ft roll **8.79**
A simple, convenient, and lightweight way to create a durable terrain shell or base. Just wad newspaper and stack to form the desired shape. Dip Plaster Cloth in water, lay over newspaper and allow to dry. A quick, no mess scenery base. Includes approximately 10 square feet of cloth.

### Lightweight Hydrocal*

**785-1201** 1/2 gal **9.49**
A specially formulated new Lightweight Hydrocal for terrain model builders. Lightweight Hydrocal is nearly half the weight of Hydrocal, goes almost twice as far, and is the tough, quick setting product.

*Hydrocal is a product of U.S. Gypsum

### Latex Rubber

**785-1204** 16 fl oz **13.98**
Make your own rock molds with this ready to use Latex Rubber. It is formulated to reproduce fine detail and to be durable.

### Mold-A-Scene Plaster

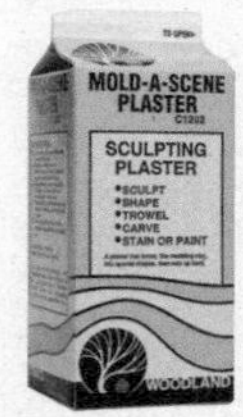


**785-1202** 1/2 gal **9.49**
Mold-A-Scene is a plaster material that can be shaped without a mold like modeling clay. Its longer setting time allows a scenery modeler to add terrain contours to new or existing scenery.

### Flex Paste

**785-1205** 16 fl oz **14.98**
Use this as a flexible, non-cracking coating over Styrofoam or as a road base for concrete or asphalt modeling.

## ROCK MOLDS

**7.79 ea (Unless Noted)**

Highly detailed, flexible, and durable rock molds. Use to cast small boulders, rock outcroppings, top rock for fields and creeks, or make entire rock faces by combining castings produced with these molds.

**785-1230** Outcroppings

**785-1231** Surface Rocks

**785-1232** Boulders

**785-1233** Embankments

**785-1234** Random Rock

**785-1235** Laced Face Rock

**785-1236** Classic Rock

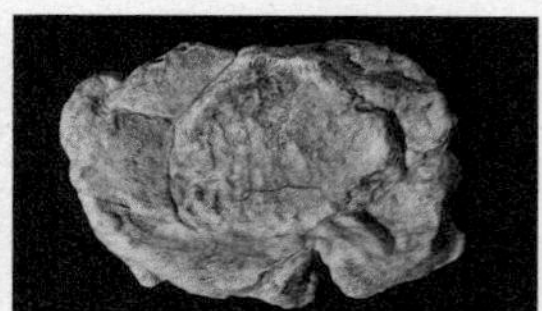
**785-1237** Wind Rock

**785-1238** Weathered Rock

**785-1239** Strata Stone

**785-1240** Rock Mass

**785-1241** Layered Rock

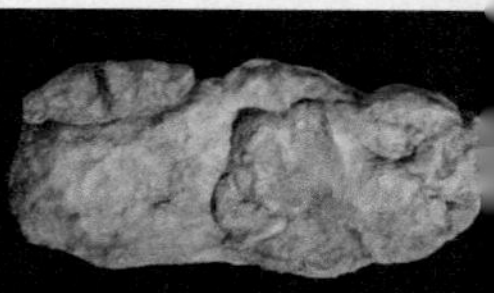
**785-1242** Washed Rock **8.79**

**785-1243** Base Rock **8.79**

**785-1244** Facet Rock **8.79**

## MINI-SCENE®

### 13.98 ea (Unless Noted)

These kits contain everything required to build Mini-Scenes, including pewter castings, landscape materials and instructions. (Less paint and glue). Mini-Scene kits can be finished in pewter or painted as realistic miniatures. They can be built as a complete HO scene for display, or added to your layout.

**785-101** Abandoned Log Cabin

**785-102** Moonshine Still

**785-103** The Windmill

**785-104** The Hunter

**785-105** The Sign Painter

**785-106** The Tack Shed

**785-107** Tommy's Treehouse

**785-108** Outhouse Mischief

**785-109** Ernie's Fruit Stand

**785-110** Saturday Night Bath

**785-111** Floyd's Barber Shop

**785-112** Tractor Pit Stop

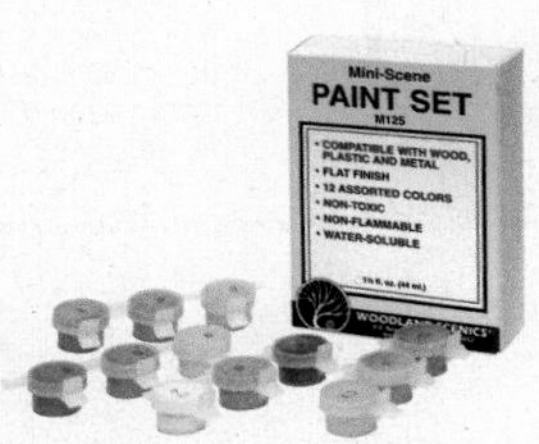


**785-125** Paint Set **6.98**

**785-126** Pewter Patina Finish **2.29**

**785-127** Display Dome with Base **11.49**

## COMPLETE SCENE KITS 31.98 ea

Nearly any model railroad can be improved with the addition of one or more of the Complete Scene Kits. The kits contain highly detailed castings plus all other materials needed to build one of the three scenes pictured (except paint and glue). All are HO scale and can be assembled in several different ways to fit the available space.

**785-130** Smiley's Tow Service (7" x 9")
Includes: Basswood building and fence, seven trees (with two colors of Foliage), four different colors of grass and soil, three colors of Foliage for bushes and weeds, and over 60 white metal castings including tires, concrete blocks, fuel tanks, oil drums, firewood, mail box, man and several other assorted pieces including junk pile.

**785-131** Maple Leaf Cemetery (8" x 11")
Includes: Basswood tool shed and fence rail, eight trees (with two colors of Foliage), four colors of grass and soil, two colors of Foliage for bushes and weeds, and over 40 white metal castings including stone fence posts and walls, gates, two men, a central monument and 28 tombstones with names.

**785-132** Memorial Park (8" x 14")
Includes: Shelter House, basswood fence, nine trees (with two colors of Foliage), four colors of grass and soil, two colors of Foliage for bushes and weeds, and over 40 white metal castings including bar-b-q ovens, tire swing, teeter-totter, picnic tables, people, trash cans and park swing.

## SIMPLIFY LAYOUT BUILDING WITH THE RIVER PASS SYSTEM

River Pass is a complete 4' x 8' HO layout kit available in three easy kits. Each kit interfaces with the others, but can be used separately. Kits #1 and #2 can also be adapted to N or O Scale. River Pass teaches you how to build a complete layout from start to finish. No dusty mess, expensive power tools or complicated calculations are required. It has been designed for expansion and includes detailed plans and instructions. And you'll save money when purchased as a kit. When River Pass is complete, you'll not only have a great layout but the knowledge and skill to build more.

Layout shown with all three River Pass kits, each sold separately. Track and trains not included.

### River Pass Layout Kit

**785-1484 379.00**
This kit features the SubTerrain System and includes Risers, Inclines, Profile Boards, Foam Sheets, Plaster Cloth, Tunnel Portals, Culverts and Earth Color Liquid Pigments. Complete plans and detailed instructions are also included to make building a complete terrain base easy.

### River Pass Building Kit

**785-1487 210.00**
Set includes 15 architecturally realistic building kits, over 225 detailed accessories, 20+ different posters and signs, in one money-saving package. Also includes a suggested street plan with detailed instructions. Easy to assemble and fun to make.

### River Pass Scenery Kit

**785-1488 229.98**
Kit includes Realistic Water, Water Effects, Dead Fall, Flowering Foliage, various foliages including Fine Leaf Foliage, Underbrush and Bushes, trees, several landscape adhesives and applicators, Rock Molds, Talus, Ballast, Road System, and Paint. Complete plans and detailed instructions are included.

### River Pass Track Pack

**150-578 71.50**
This Atlas track pack gives you all the track components required for the Woodland Scenics 4' x 8' River Pass Layout (sold separately) in one convenient pack. The track in this pack features realistic brown ties and Code 83 rail, matching the track described in the Woodland Scenics layout instructions.

## MOD-U-RAIL® SYSTEM

Build the layout of your dreams – one module at a time! This space-saving system lets you build individual modules at your own pace. There are two kits available, the Straight and Corner Module Kits.

Guidelines for creating your own track plan are provided and the system assembles without power tools or complicated calculations – and best of all, there's no dusty mess!

Even the landscape material is included to make trees, ballast track, and create beautiful ground cover using various colors and sizes of turf and foliage. Simply add your choice of track, structures and vehicles (all sold separately).

Each Kit includes bolts and two connector plates so you can bolt your modules end-to-end. You can buy the Connector Plate Set (785-4780, 10.98) which allows you to connect your modules together side-to-side or end-to-end. It includes four connector plates and hardware.

### Straight Module Kit

**This module is for the straight portion of your layout. It can be bolted to another straight or to a corner module.**

**785-4801** Straight Module **129.98**
Measures approximately 18 x 36" 45 x 90cm.

### Corner Module Kit

**This module also makes a square and can be used as a curve for your layout. Track can be placed anywhere. This module bolts to another corner or to a straight module.**

**785-4802** Corner Module **149.98**
Measures approximately 36 x 36" 90 x 90cm.

### Connector Plate Set

**785-4780 10.98**
Expand the possibilities of your Mod-U-Rail layout with this set. Special connectors allow modules to be bolted together side-by-side, so you can easily create a larger area as needed. Complete with connectors, bolts and wing nuts.

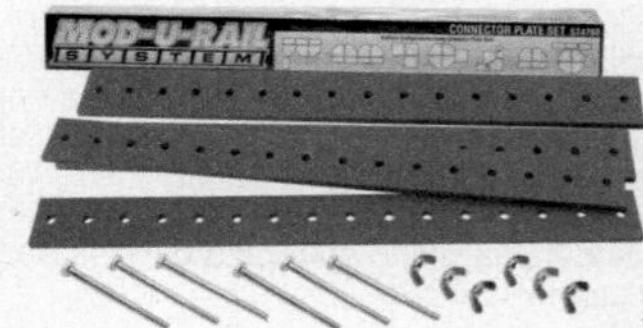

## GRAND VALLEY HO SCALE LIGHTWEIGHT LAYOUT KIT

**NO POWER TOOLS • NO DUSTY MESS • NO CALCULATIONS • ANYONE CAN DO IT**

**785-1483** 4' x 8' **498.00**
Building your first HO Scale layout will be a snap with this 4' x 8' 120 x 240cm foam base with a preprinted track plan. Complete set comes with foam Risers, Inclines and Profile Boards, Plaster Cloth, rock faces, Tunnel portals, turf, ground cover, trees, road system kit and Track-Bed™ to complete scenery construction. No power tools are needed and easy-to-follow instructions are included.

### Grand Valley Track Pack

**150-589 82.50**
Atlas Grand Valley Track Pack includes all the Code 83 track, switches, bridges and rail joiners needed to build a railroad on the 4 x 8' Grand Valley HO Scale Layout from Woodland Scenics (#785-1483, sold separately).

Buildings, vehicles, figures, track and trains shown in all photos are sold separately.

## THE SCENERY KIT

Whether beginner or expert, with this kit modelers learn scenery techniques that dramatically improve their skills...in just hours! A 10" x 18" diorama displays your favorite rolling stock or engine when finished.

You Will Learn To:

- Make Trees, Create Mountains, Build Rolling Terrain, Stain Rocks Realistically, Plant Grass, Weeds & Bushes, Install Track & Ballast.
- Includes a piece of HO track, but N scale can be substituted
- All scenery materials included...even paint and hardboard base (Everything!)

**785-927** If purchased separately $61.00. Suggested retail only **59.98**

## THE MOUNTAIN VALLEY SCENERY KIT

Once tracks are in place, use the Mountain Valley Scenery Kit to transform that basic 4' x 8' sheet of plywood into a three-dimensional sceniced layout. It includes everything needed to add trees, grass, weeds, rocks, mountains, tunnels, ballast and more to a layout. Use your HO Scale track plan or ours. Step-by-step instructions make this kit fun and easy!

**785-928** $104 value if items purchased separately, only **84.98**

## BOOKS, VIDEOS & CATALOGS

### The Clinic Video 24.98 ea

785-970

785-990

**785-970** DVD

**785-990** VHS
Learn by watching the professionals demostrate landscaping and terrain modeling techiques. In this video, you'll see just how easy it is. 1 hour and 15 minutes.

### Model Railroad Scenery Made Easy Video 24.98 ea

785-973

785-993

**785-973** DVD

**785-993** VHS
A comprehensive, detailed account of scenery modeling. Provides helpful information for modelers of any skill level, and shows how to do scenery the easy way. Approximately 60 minutes.

### SubTerrain: Build a Layout Fast & Easy 24.98 ea

785-1400

785-1401

**785-1400** DVD

**785-1401** VHS
A step-by-step video that shows you how to build a model railroad layout with the revolutionary Sub Terrain Layout System. Approximately 60 minutes.



### The Scenery Manual

**785-1207 10.98**
Fully-illustrated, with new spiral binding, teaching manual, developed by the experts on model scenery.

### Buyer's Guide

**785-100 2.50**
Full-color, 80-page guide to Woodland Scenics products.

### SubTerrain Manual

**785-1402 7.98**
An illustrated how-to manual that teaches you how to create the ideal base for scenery and landscaping in five easy steps.

Here's a complete line of products designed to make building dioramas, arts & crafts, or special projects fast, fun and affordable! Easy to use, the kits are great for all kinds of modeling projects or for learning new scenery skills. And they're perfect for school assignments on any subject (all items are non-hazardous and conform to ASTM D-4236). Each product includes instructions, tips and techniques for unlimited possibilities, and you'll learn how to modify their uses to fit your project.

## NEW PRODUCTS

### Diorama Kits

These four Diorama Kits include everything you need to create your own diorama scenery for any locale in this world (or out of this world!). Use your imagination and the materials supplied to make any diorama you want (project bases shown are each sold separately).

#### Basic Diorama Kit

**NEW 785-4110 16.98**
Includes a ReadyGrass® Sheet for an instant, flat grassy flat area suitable for buildings or other habitats. Bushes, grasses and flowers are also included to customize and complete the scene.

#### Mountain Diorama Kit

**NEW 785-4111 19.98**
Learn to make and color rock formations of all kinds including mountains, volcanoes, hills, caves, erosion or any land contours with rock outcroppings. Includes earth-colored paint, grasses, bushes, soils, vines and rock debris.

#### Desert Oasis Diorama Kit

**NEW 785-4112 16.98**
Create a desert oasis, or landscape a Mission, balmy beach or other tropical location. Includes palm trees, desert vegetation, short and tall grasses, flowers, sand rocks and vines.

#### Water Diorama Kit

**NEW 785-4113 19.98**
Make and color still or moving water such as lakes, rivers or waterfalls. Includes earth-colored paint, short and tall grasses, bushes and vines to landscape the banks of your waterway.

### Accents

**8.98 ea**

#### Foliage & Grasses

**NEW 785-4120**
Add short and tall grasses, weeds, bushes, shrubs, hedges, ivy and flowering plants, plus roads and paths.

#### Rock Making Kit

**NEW 785-4121**
Use this kit to create lava flows, make and color rocks, make creek banks, outcroppings, cliffs and plaster castings for any diorama or display.

#### Ripplin' Water Kit

**NEW 785-4122**
Make realistic looking waterfalls, rapids, splashes, waves, rivers, lakes, ponds, streams, beaches and pools - any still or moving water!

#### Winter Effects

**NEW 785-4123**
Model winter weather conditions on any diorama such as snowdrifts, a light dusting of snow, icicles, glaciers and more.

#### Desert Plants

**NEW 785-4124**
These plants look so real you want to touch them! Add cacti, tumbleweeds, short and tall grasses, weeds, scrub brush, ivy, vines, and others kinds of desert flora to your diorama.

### Trees

**8.98 ea**

Fully assembled trees feature removable bases, and can be used to model almost any location in the world. Easily modified by bending branches and removing small bits of foliage.

**NEW 785-4150** Deciduous; 2 - 2-1/2" 5 - 6.3cm Tall pkg(4)

**NEW 785-4151** Conifer; 4 - 5-1/2" 10.1 - 13.9cm Tall pkg(4)

**NEW 785-4152** Palm; 4 - 5" 10.1 - 12.7cm Tall pkg(6)

**NEW 785-4153** Fall; 3 - 3-1/2" 7.6 - 8.8cm Tall pkg(4)

## ReadyGrass® Sheets

**3.98 ea**

Add realism to any landscape. Attach to Project Base (sold separately) or flat surface with Sticky Bond™ (sold separately). Scrape off Turf to add water areas, roads and sidewalks. Measures 10-3/4 x 16-1/4" 27.3 x 41.2cm

**NEW 785-4160** Summer Grass
Use to create late summer or arid climate grasses.

**NEW 785-4161** Green Grass
Use to create early summer or wet climate grasses.

**NEW 785-4162** Desert Sand
Use to create late desert or arid climates, beaches or shorelines.

## Project Base & Backdrop

Bases double as shadowboxes, built-in placard for labeling. Backdrops are provided to add backgrounds and horizons or labeling the parts of your project.

**NEW 785-4165** Large
12-1/2 x 18" 31.7 x 45.7cm
**7.98**

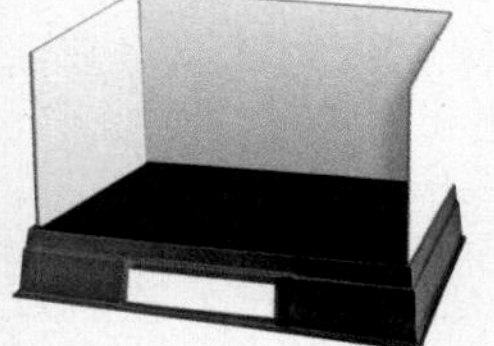

**NEW 785-4166** Small
9-1/2 x 12-1/2" 24.1 x 31.7cm
**5.98**

## ShowBox™

**NEW 785-4167 4.98**
Base Project Area:
8-1/2 x 13 x 4-1/2"
21.5 x 33 x 11.4cm;
Overall Size: 10 x 13 x 4-1/2"
25.4 x 33 x 11.4cm

Compact size is perfect for shoebox dioramas, displays and more. Simply build your scene inside, and decorate the bright white outside. Made of durable materials and includes labels for project identification.

## Project Accessories

### Project Glue

**NEW 785-4142**
3 oz Plastic Bottle
**3.98**
Use this multi-purpose, water-soluble adhesive to attach trees, bushes, paper and more to dioramas or displays. Safe for kids.

### Sticky Bond™

**NEW 785-4143**
2 oz Plastic Bottle
**3.98**
This contact adhesive is perfect for a wide range of jobs, such as attaching ReadyGrass sheets to Project Bases (both sold separately).

### Project Book

**NEW 785-4170 9.98**
Here are 84 pages of great ideas for making dioramas, displays, or other projects using Scene-A-Rama products. Lots of easy tips and techniques, with colorful illustrations and photos too!



## Building & Structure Kit

**NEW 785-4130 9.98**
Make buildings, structures, geometric shapes and more with the materials, tips and techniques included in this kit.

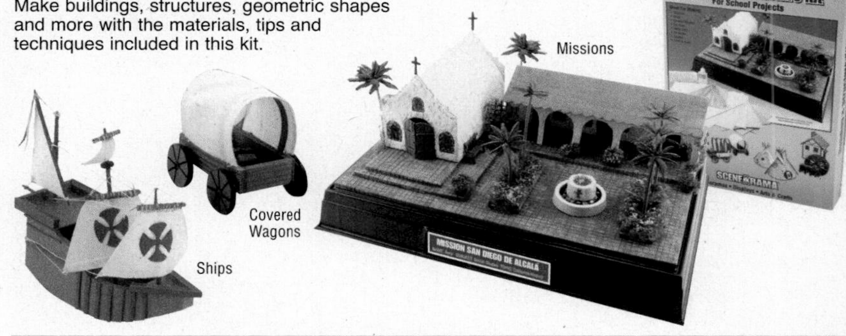


## Sculpting Kit

**NEW 785-4131 8.98**
Use these unique sculpting materials, tools, tips and techniques to create figures animals, and all kinds of shapes for any project.

## Horizon & Detail Kit

**NEW 785-4132 8.98**
Learn to make horizons and backgrounds for your projects. Includes background patterns, plus materials for lettering and labeling project parts.

## Plaster Cloth

**NEW 785-4140 7.98**
Use this special cloth to make hard land surfaces, masks and more. Forms over any shape.

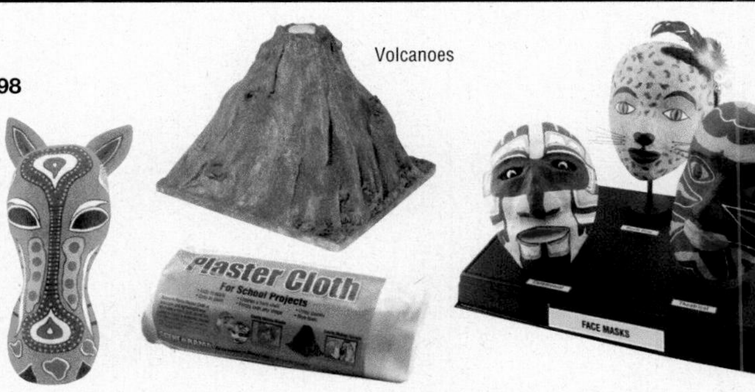


## Casting Plaster

**NEW 785-4141 3.98**
Cast rocks, fossils, animal tracks and more. Use with any mold or impression, or to model cave formations and lava flow.

2008
HO
Model Railroad
Reference Book

Photo by Randy Pepprock

# STRUCTURES

Busted! It's funny how a simple scene like this can create so much interest and tell such a complete story. Starting with the Liquor Store from the Downtown Deco Addams Ave. Part Five kit Randy Pepprock painted, detailed and weathered this scene to perfection. One of the reasons it looks so realistic is because the main structure already has so much detail cast right into the walls – cracked stucco, chipped and missing bricks and general aging. All of the master pattern work is hand carved, brick by brick, stone by stone for maximum realism and complete, easy to understand painting and weathering instructions are included with each kit. Downtown Deco kits will have your guests saying "Wow! Does that ever look like the real thing!"

Several elements help tell the story in this scene. First is the location. Right off you can tell it's the bad part of town. With signs advertising Beer, Wine, Lottery Tickets and Western Union there's no mistaking this joint for an upscale store. Security bars on the windows (custom made by Tichy Train Group) add even more realism, as does the corroding stucco and brick. For the final bit of story telling, the bad guys are getting searched and cuffed by a couple of Metropolis' finest.

Tell your own story by creating a scene around a structure where people work, live, shop or relax. From small city newsstands to huge industrial complexes and cozy Victorian houses to modern hi-rises, this section offers a wealth of structures that are ideal for your layout. Get started quickly with a fully assembled model or choose from a variety of kits for every skill level from beginner to expert.

75
WALTHERS
1932-2007
WE'RE JUST GETTING STARTED

# All-New Structures to Complement your *Hiawatha* Collection

**Designed Especially for the New Hiawatha**
**Illustrated Instructions • Use on any Layout**
**Detailed Plastic Parts • Easy to Build**

Complete the scene on your layout with these Milwaukee structures alongside your new fleet of Hiawatha streamliners! Based on several historic railroad structures that served the Milwaukee Road in its namesake city, these HO Scale kits capture the look of the prototypes in a size that fits most layouts. See the Passenger Cars Section for complete details on the all-new Hiawatha cars & locos!

**NEW** *Limited-Run Milwaukee-Style Station & Train Shed Kit*
*933-2943 $249.98 Fall 2007 Delivery*

*Built-Up Yard Office*
*933-2830 $29.98 In Stock*

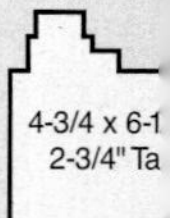

**NEW** *Freight House & Freight Office Combo*
*933-2950 $49.98 Spring 2008 Delivery*

**NEW** *Train Shed Only Kit*
*933-2949 $99.98 Winter 2007-08 Delivery*

*Built-Up Walthers Water Street Building*
*933-2814 $39.98*
*Fall 2007 Delivery*

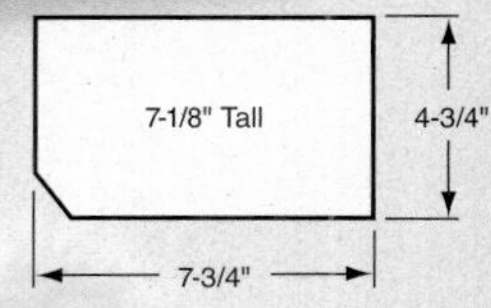

**NEW** *Freight Office Kit*
*933-2953 $31.98 Spring 2008 Delivery*

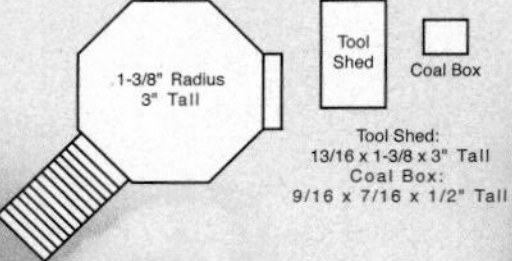


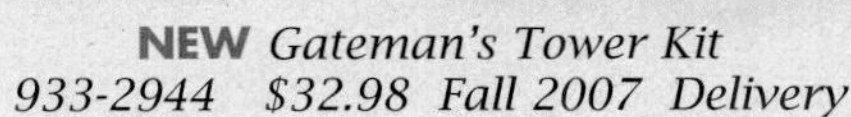

**NEW** *Gateman's Tower Kit*
*933-2944 $32.98 Fall 2007 Delivery*

**NEW** *Freight House Kit*
*933-2954 $29.98 Spring 2008 Delivery*

Photos show preproduction models, details and colors may vary.

# Bring Today's Grain Industry to Your Railroad

**Cornerstone Series® Kits**
- Mix & Match to Model an Entire Operation
- Puts Maximum Detail in Minimum Space
- Completely New Models
- Fits 1970s to Present
- Highly Detailed Plastic Parts
- Adaptable to Many Other Industries
- Complete Instructions

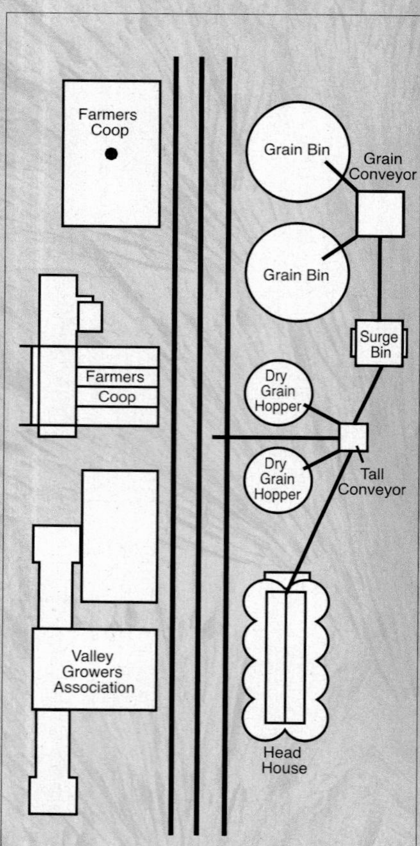


**HO Head House**
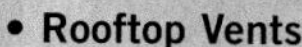
933-2942 $44.98
Winter 2007-08 Delivery
Prototypes house grain-lifting & distribution augers located at the top of storage silos.
- Easy Upgrade for ADM® Elevator (#933-3022 sold separately)
- Truck Dock w/Overhead Doors
- Safety Railings
- Separate Windows & Doors
- Rooftop Vents

ALL NEW KITS

**HO Surge Bin**
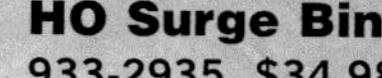
933-2935 $34.98
Fall 2007 Delivery
Prototype gravity-feeds wet grain into dryer.
- Fine "Corrugated Metal" Details
- "Steel" Supports and Crossbraces
- Use with Grain Dryer (#933-3128, sold separately)
- Safety Cage Ladders

# with this Complete Series of All-New Kits

**HO Conveyors ("Leg")**
**933-2936 $39.98 Fall 2007 Delivery**

Prototypes, known as "legs," lift wet and dry grain (a typical operation has two or more, each dedicated to incoming and outbound grain) using an endless bucket conveyor; grain is then gravity-fed to bins through supply piping.

- **Must-Have for Modern Operations**
- **Fits Any Complex**
- **Adjustable Height**
- **Conveyor Details**
- **Motor & Belt Drive Details**
- **Safety Cage Ladders w/See-Through Platforms**
- **Authentic Ground-Level U-Trough Augers**
- **Overhead Piping**

**HO Wet/Dry Grain Bin**
**933-2937 $44.98**
**Winter 2007-08 Delivery**

Prototypes used for either wet or dry grain storage.

- **Fine "Corrugated Metal" Details**
- **"Steel" Supports and Crossbraces**
- **Safety Cage Ladders**
- **One-Piece Roof**

**HO Detail Kits** ***(Photo-Etched Brass)***

- **Near-Scale Thickness for Ultimate Realism**
- **Easily Assembled, Painted & Installed**

**HO Conveyor Bridge & Support Tower** 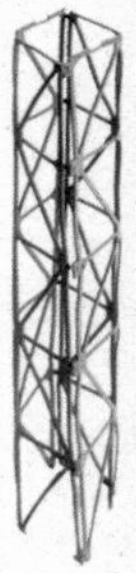
**933-2940 $29.98**
**Winter 2007-08 Delivery**

Prototypes connect storage bins and provide access to trough auger conveyors used in place of overhead pipes.

- **Build One Tall or Two Short Towers**
- **Use with Wet/Dry Grain Bin**
- **Fine Handrails & Trusses**
- **See-Through Walkways**

**HO Platforms & Stairways**
**933-2939 $19.98**
**Winter 2007-08 Delivery**

- **Super Details for Conveyor & Grain Bin**
- **Near-Scale Railings & Platforms**
- **Fine Handrails & Trusses**
- **Open Stairways**

**HO Caged Ladders & Safety Cages** 
**933-2956 $19.98**
**Winter 2007-08 Delivery**

- **Thin Cross Section**
- **Build With or Without Security Gates**
- **Easily Cut to Fit**
- **Used on Many Modern Buildings**

**HO Support Trusses for Guywires & Piping** 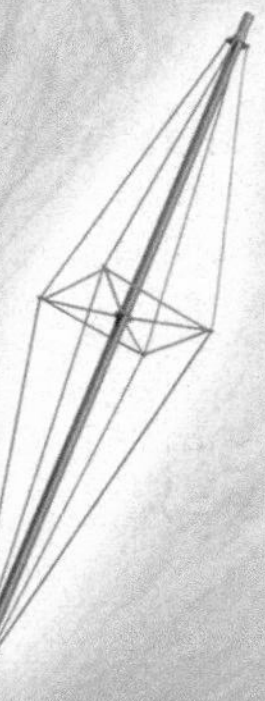
**933-2955 $19.98**
**Winter 2007-08 Delivery**

Prototypes support overhead pipes and prevent them from bending under load.

- **Quick & Easy to Assemble**
- **Mix & Match Parts for Authentic Detail**
- **Fits Overhead Piping in #933-2936 (sold separately)**

# Built-ups

## IMPERIAL FOODS

**NEW 933-2852 44.98**

**Winter 2007-08 Delivery**
10-1/2 x 8" 26.6 x 20.3cm

- Instant Fun & Realism
- Fits any Railroad, any Era
- Hand-Weathered
- Separate Details for Easy Customizing
- Fully Assembled
- Fits Steam or Diesel Eras
- Perfect for any Industrial Area
- Detailed Brickwork
- Front Loading Dock
- Molded in Authentic Colors

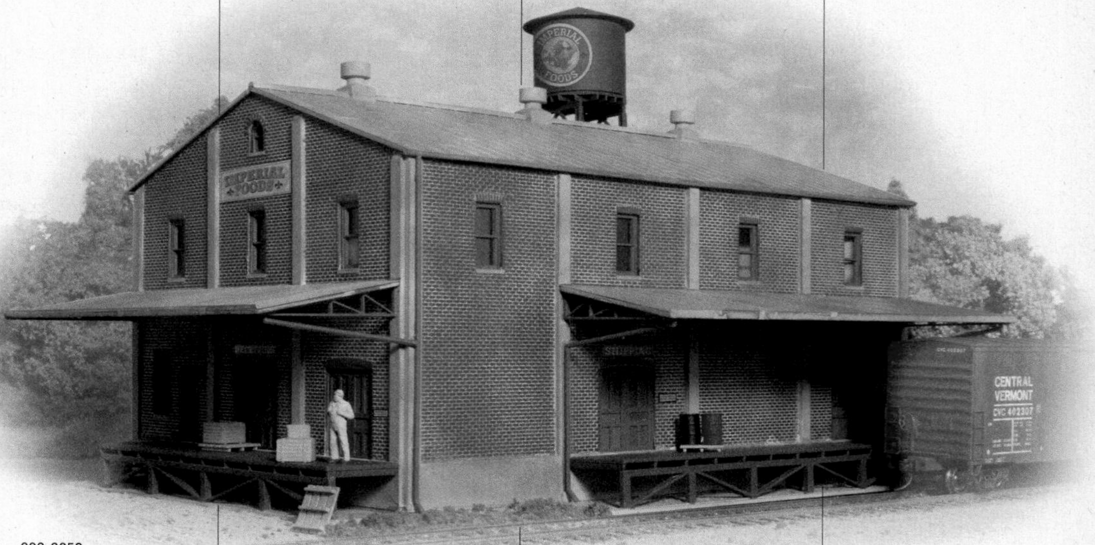

933-2852

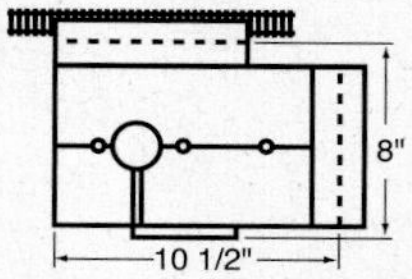

8"
10 1/2"

## WASHINGTON SALVAGE YARD

**NEW 933-2928 44.98**
Main Building:
8-3/8 x 9-1/4 x 3-1/2"
21.2 x 23.4 x 8.8cm

Scale: 8-5/8 x 1-7/8"
21.9 x 4.7cm

- Great for Modern Businesses
- Brick Office & Metal Garage
- American Prototype
- Use from 1960s to present

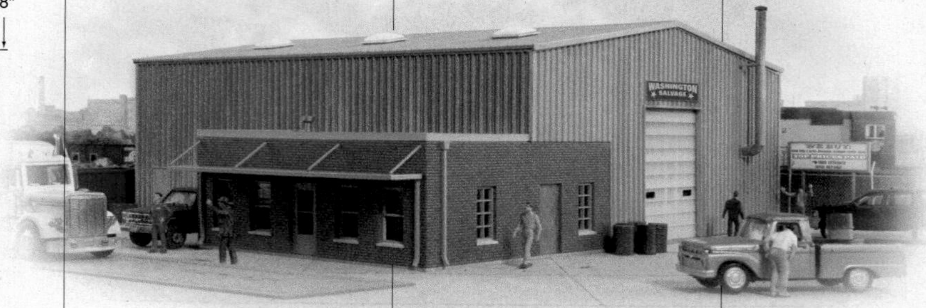

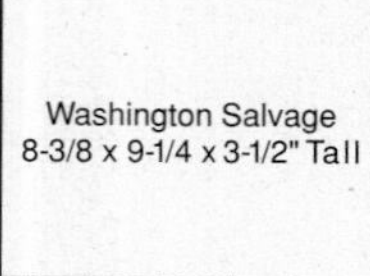


933-2928

## THROUGH PLATE-GIRDER BRIDGE

**NEW 933-2948 19.98**

- Build as Single or Double Track
- Fits Steam or Diesel Era
- North American Prototype
- Matches Bridge from Art Deco Highway Underpass (933-3190, sold separately)

933-2948

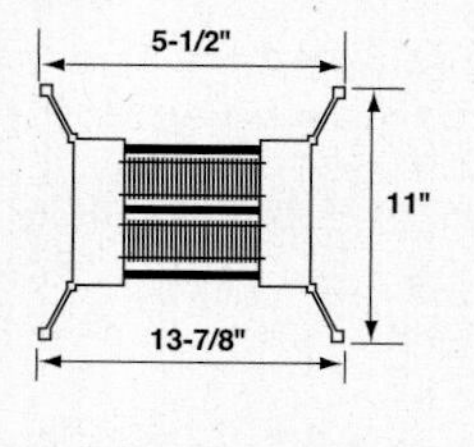




## YMCA BUNKHOUSE

**Winter 2007-08 Delivery**
**NEW 933-2951 44.98**

- All-New Kit
- Neat Addition to Yard & Terminal Scenes
- American Prototype
- Fits early 1900s to Present
- Detailed Brick Work
- "Stone" Trim
- Use as Bank, Police Station, or City Hall too!
- Decal Signs

933-2951

*Building on the Power of Your Imagination™*

# Create the Structures You've Been Dreaming of!

- Design and Build any Industry
- Easy Assembly & Customizing
- Molded in Colors
- American Prototype
- Fits Popular Eras
- Reclosable Packages
- Illustrated Instructions & Tips

- New Window Style
- Authentic Detail for Period Structures

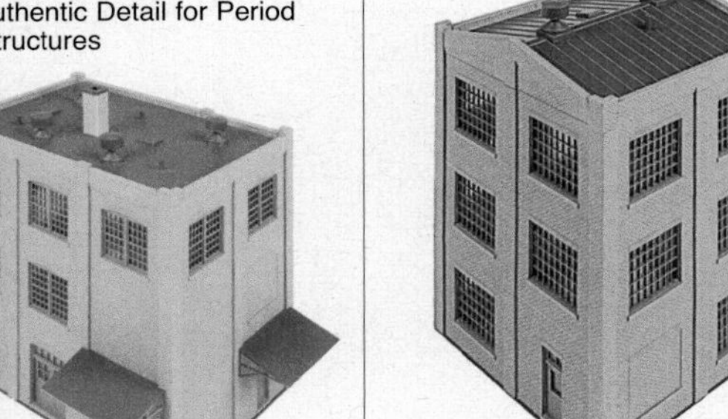

## Small Walls with Single Large Arched Windows

933-3731 9.98

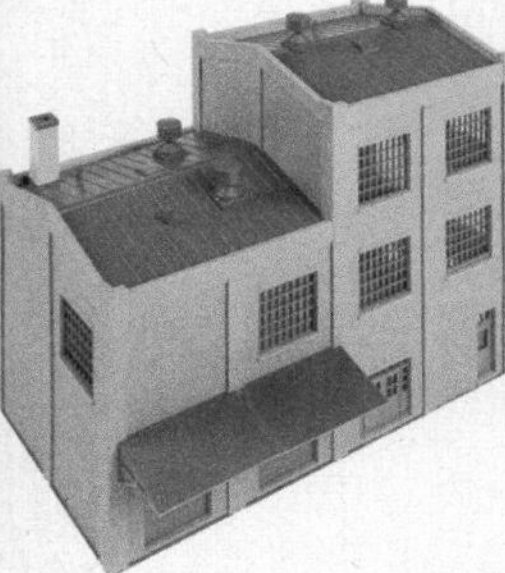

## Small Walls with Large Metal Sash Windows

933-3732 9.98

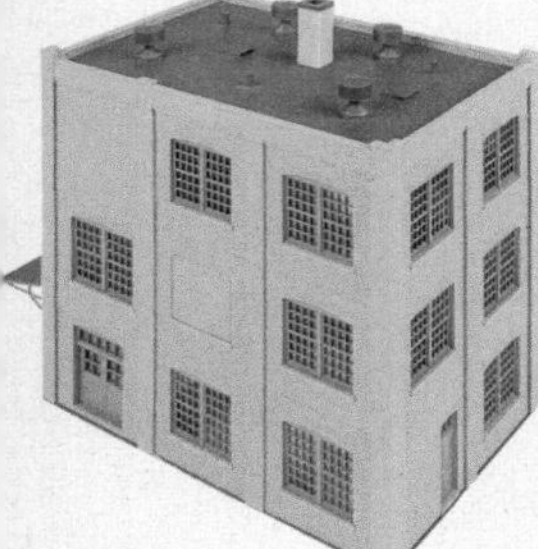

## Large Walls with Single Large Arched Windows

933-3734 9.98

## Large Walls with Large Metal Sash Windows

933-3735 9.98

## Quality Investment Casting

933-3751 29.98

- Includes Modernized "Steel" Building Facade
- "Glass Block" Front Windows
- Perfect for Post-40s Layouts
- Engineered for Easy Assembly & Customizing
- Decal Signs for Businesses & Industries
- North American Prototype

## Modular Decal Set

934-1030 14.98

- Adds that Final Touch of Realism
- Specially Designed For Modular System
- Variety of Signs & Business Names Included
- Use with Most Buildings

## Fire Escape Sets 9.98 ea

933-3729 Vintage Set

933-3736 Modern Set

- Must-Have Detail for City Buildings
- Vintage Style for Period Scenes
- Modern Style Perfect for Post-War Scenes
- Includes Fire Escapes to Serve Four Stories
- Structure Mounting Template Included
- Fits any Large Structure

## Empire Leather Tanning

933-3798 149.98

- Four Complete Structure Kits
- Build as Complete Complex or Individual Structures
- Customize with Cornerstone Modulars Parts
- Decal Signs for 4 Different Industries
- Smokestack & Water Tanks Included
- American Prototype
- Fits Popular Modeling Eras
- Parts Molded in Appropriate Colors
- Complete Instructions

## Industrial Tanks Detail Set

933-3197 9.98

- Parts for Six Complete Tanks:
  - 3 Horizontal Styles
  - 3 Vertical Styles
- "Concrete" Supports
- Detailed Manways
- Easy to Assemble

## 3-IN-1 BUILDING SET

Basic Rectangle...

Small One- and Two-Story...

or Expanded "L"

933-3750 29.98

- Builds One of Three Different Variations
- Fits Any Era
- Doors, Windows, Walls & Roofs Included
- Add Custom Names to Your Industries – Special Decal Set Inside!

Take your finished building to a new level of realism with custom decal signs! This kit includes a special set of decals that makes it easy to model typical factory lettering from different eras. Just cut the backgrounds to fit — complete instructions are included — and mix and match to create one-of-a-kind decals for your new industry.

## 3-IN-1 BUILDING SET #2

Two-Story Office w/Large Loading Addition...

Two-Story Office w/Modernized Front & Twin Garage Bay...

or Two-Story Factory w/Modernized-Front Office Addition.

933-3752 39.98

- Builds One of Three Different Structures
- Customize to Fit Your Layout
- New Doors, Windows, Walls, Modernized Fronts & Roofs Included

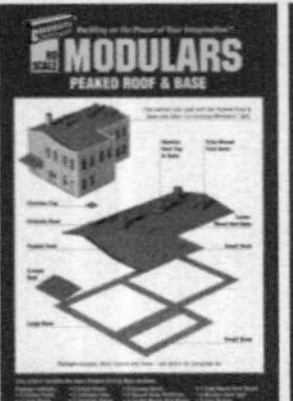

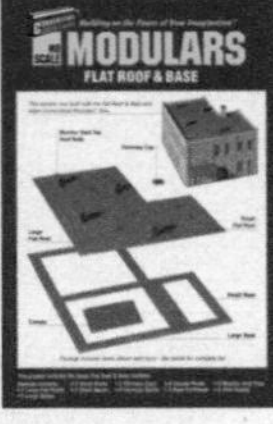

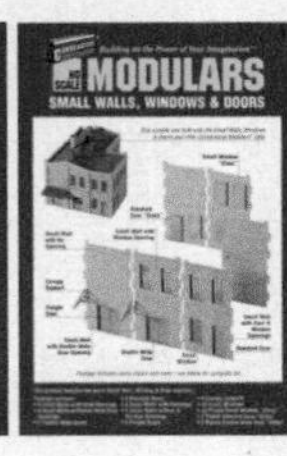


**Peaked Roof & Base**
933-3720 9.98

**Flat Roof & Base**
933-3721 9.98

**Small Walls, Windows & Doors**
933-3722 9.98

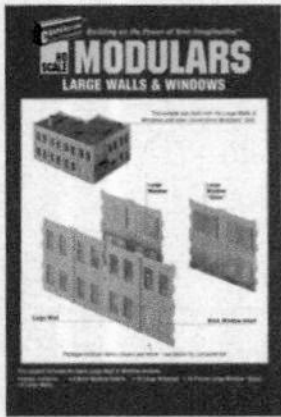

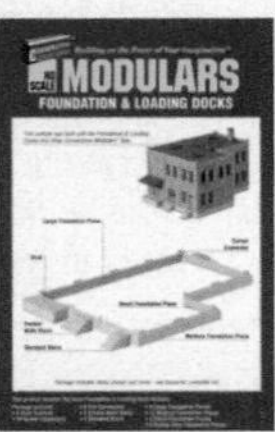

**Large Walls & Windows**
933-3723 9.98

**Foundation & Loading Docks**
933-3724 9.98

**Wall Columns & Caps**
933-3725 9.98

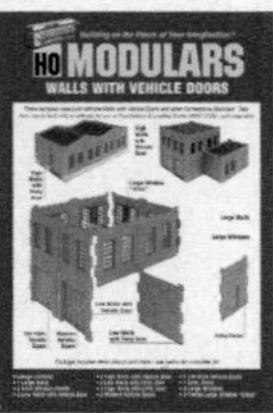

**Large Door Wall Section**
933-3727 9.98
- Clears HO Freight Cars
- Great for Heavy Industry
- Authentic Roll-Up "Metal" Door
- Build Door Open or Close

**Walls with Vehicle Doors**
933-3730 9.98
- Drive-In Door for Autos or Trucks
- Build With or Without Foundations

**Roof Details**
933-3733 9.98
- Makes Buildings More Realistic
- 10 Different Vent Styles

If you would like to download a Modular Planning Template, go to:

http://www.walthers.com/exec/page/ho_n_modulars

## Congratulations Contest Winners!

CORNERSTONE SERIES HO MODULARS

***Thanks to everyone who entered!***
***Here are the winners of the Modular Modeling Contest.***

### First Prize Winner

Mike Gilbert of Mooresville, NC
Entry: Monks Paper Goods — New England Mill

"This model represents an old New England mill with a siding."

Typical of early factories built on odd shaped lots, Mike made angled pilasters by sanding flat columns, then joining them with plastic cement. Walls were painted with Polly Scale Oxide Red, and detailed with Roberts Brick Mortar Formula.

### Second Prize Winner

John McHugh of Onalaska, WI
Entry: La Crosse Freight House

"Built in 1879 as a freight house, this building is now home to one of La Crosse's premiere restaurants."

John removed window mullions to match those on the actual building; the cupola and entrance are also made from Modulars windows. Photos of actual signs were sized to fit. And like the prototype, a retired heavyweight car is displayed out front.

### Third Prize Winner

Kurt Wamser of Pewaukee, WI
Entry: Circus Winter Quarters

"My latest project started with a need to store my circus wagons."

With workshops, storerooms and offices, Kurt's plan gradually evolved into a complete winter quarters. Test fitting each building revealed where details could be added for visual interest. The roof of the wagon barn is removable so models can be stored inside.

# TRAINLINE®
**by WALTHERS**

Make your railroad look real in minutes with assembled and decorated structures! These beautifully decorated buildings feature colorful applied signs; storefronts include factory-installed windows with realistic preprinted signs and banners.

## UNITED TRUCKING TERMINAL

**931-804 22.98**

## WALLSCHLAGER MOTORS

**931-805 24.98**

## GEMINI BUILDING

**931-806 24.98**

## 10TH WORLD COMICS

**NEW 931-807 21.98**

3 x 4 x 4-3/8"
7.6 x 10.1 x 11.1cm

## KATIE'S CANDY CREATIONS

**NEW 931-808 24.98**

2-1/2 x 3-1/2 x 3-3/8"
6.3 x 8.8 x 8.5cm

## BATEMAN VACATIONS & TRAVEL

**NEW 931-809 29.98**

5 x 8-1/4 x 4"
12.7 x 20.9 x 10.1cm

## ELECTRICAL POLE SET

**931-803 6.98**

- Realistic Detail for any Railroad
- "Wood" Poles, Transformers

# Fill Out Your Trackside Scenes with these Ready-to-Use Structures and Accessories

931-804

931-805

931-806

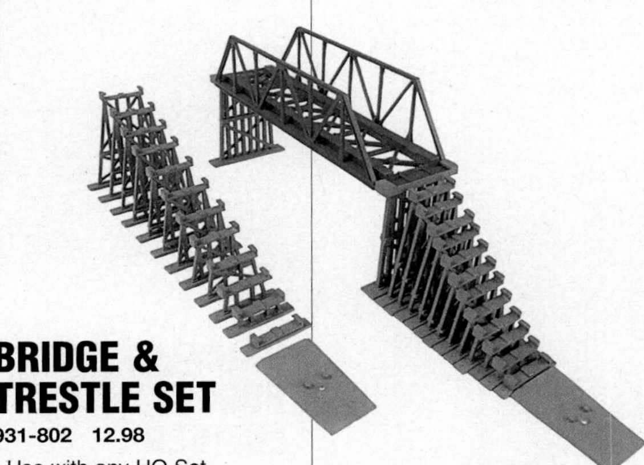

## BRIDGE & TRESTLE SET

**931-802 12.98**

- Use with any HO Set

931-807

931-808

931-809

For Up-To-Date Information and News Bookmark Walthers Web site at

**www.walthers.com**

**Built-ups**

## STEEL WATER TANK

933-2832 19.98

- Classic Steam-Era Design
- Fine Rivet Details
- Perfect for Service Facility Scenes
- Includes Two Water Columns, Two Pallets, Three 55 Gal. Drums, and Vendor Applied Signage

## TRACKSIDE & YARD BUILDINGS

933-2845 44.98

- Two Different Trackside Shanties
- Use Together or Apart
- Authentic Weathering
- Adaptable to Numerous Uses
- Ballast, Figures & Other Details Included

## ELEVATED CROSSING TOWER WITH GATES

**34.98 ea**

**933-2833** Yellow Ochre & Oxide Brown

**933-2834** Cream & Railroad Green

**933-2835** Two-Tone Gray

- All-New Model
- Three Colors Match Trackside Buildings
- Authentic Weathering
- Fits Steam & Diesel Layouts
- Detailed "Wooden" Walls
- Includes Two Nonoperating Crossing Gates, Figures & Other Accessories

## INTERLOCKING TOWER

**24.98 ea**

**933-2837** Yellow Ochre & Oxide Brown

**933-2838** Cream & Railroad Green

**933-2839** Two-Tone Gray

- Three Colors Match Trackside Buildings
- Fits Steam & Diesel Layouts
- Detailed Stairs & Control Rods
- Includes Two Preiser Figures, three 55 Gal. Drums, Two Pallets, and Vendor Applied Signage

CITY NEWS

BOB'S News & Magazine

2-1/4" — 2-1/4" Tall — 1-1/8"

3-1/8" — 1-1/5" Tall — 1-1/8

## NEWSSTANDS

933-2846 39.98

- Great Detail for City Street Corners
- Two Different Styles Included
- Authentic Weathering
- Freestanding & Lean-to Styles
- Signboards & Awnings
- Printed Newspapers, Magazines & Other Accessories

933-2832

933-2845

5-3/4 x 3-1/2" 3-1/2" Tall | 5-3/4 x 3-1/2" 2-3/4" Tall

933-2834

## SPOONER SASH & DOOR

933-2847 39.98

- Large Vehicle Doors
- Oversized Multi-Pane Windows
- Authentic Weathering
- Suitable for Many Types of Businesses
- Vehicles, Figures & Other Details Included\

9-1/2 x 4-3/4" 4-1/4" Tall

4" Tall — 1-1/8" — 3"

933-2838

## DRUMLIN FOREST LUMBER

933-2844 44.98

- Corrugated "Metal" Exterior
- Two Different Buildings
- Use Together or Separately
- Realistic Weathering
- Figures, Forklift, Pallets & More Included

5-3/4 x 3-1/2 x 3-1/2" Tall | 4-3/4 x 4" 3" Tall

## CLARKESVILLE DEPOT

49.98 ea

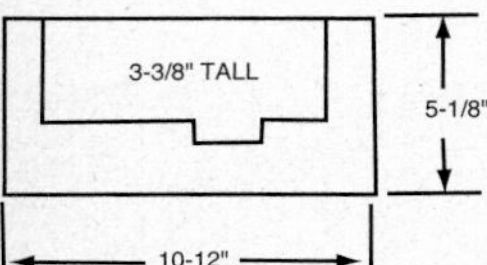


**933-2841** Yellow Ochre & Oxide Brown

**933-2842** Cream & Railroad Green

**933-2843** Two-Tone Gray

- Includes Two Park Benches, One Contemporary Soda Machine, One 50s Era Soda Machine, Four Preiser Figures, Three Trash Cans, One Baggage Cart, Baggage Set, and Vendor Applied Signage

## PELLA BRICK DEPOT

**933-2831  54.98**

- Unique Brick Design
- Stained Glass Transom Decals
- Authentic Design & Detail
- Rock Island Prototype

## PALACE THEATER

**933-2817  99.98**

- Classic American Design
- Ready to use in any city scene
- Lighted marquee with animated chase lights,
- Lighted name sign
- Lighted entry with windows
- Colorful front wall panels
- Self-cling letters – show your favorite movies
- Assembled electronics with transformer and plug-in power cable

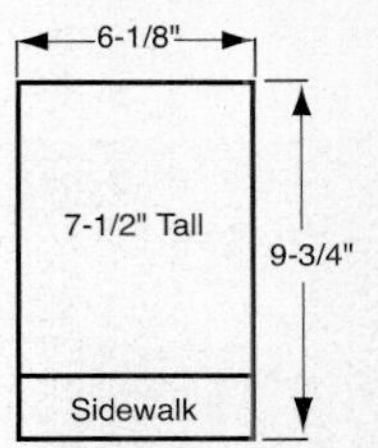


Get Your Daily Dose of Product News at

**www.walthers.com**

## ROUTE 66 MOTEL

**933-2822  79.98**

- Fully assembled
- Working "neon" sign complete with chase lights,
- Separate office with working sign and interior light,
- Two guest cabins

## MOTEL CABIN

**933-2824  19.98**

- Matches cabins in 933-2822
- Great for company towns at mines or logging camps

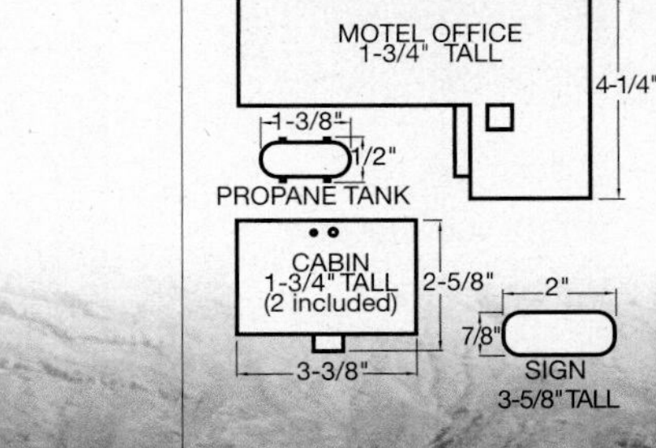

# Built-ups

9-3/8 x 7-1/8"
4-15/16" Tall

## DAYTON MACHINE CO.

**933-2823 39.98**

- Layout-ready
- Use alone or in a larger complex
- Fits popular eras
- Working light.
- Small size fits odd-shaped lots
- Customize with modern metal or wooden door - both included
- Colorful Sign Decals

## WOOD WATER TANK

**29.98 ea**

**933-2813** Yellow Ochre

**933-2819** Cream

**933-2820** Gray

**933-3531** Kit Version (gray)

- Must-have for steam-era layouts
- Fully assembled
- Choose three different colors — matches other Trackside buildings
- Detailed "wooden" support timbers
- Moveable spout

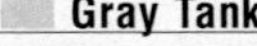

Gray Tank

Yellow Ochre Tank

Cream Tank

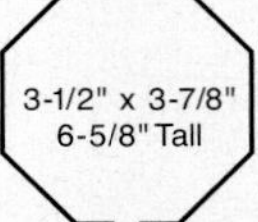

3-1/2" x 3-7/8"
6-5/8" Tall

For Up-To-Date Information and News Bookmark Walthers Web site at

**www.walthers.com**

933-2825 Black

933-2826 Silver

## CITY WATER TOWER 29.98 ea

**933-2825** Black

**933-2826** Silver

- Use from 1900s - Present
- Perfect detail for large industry
- Layout-ready in black or silver
- Features conical roof, caged ladder, latticework legs and concrete base.
- Alphabet decals to personalize your model

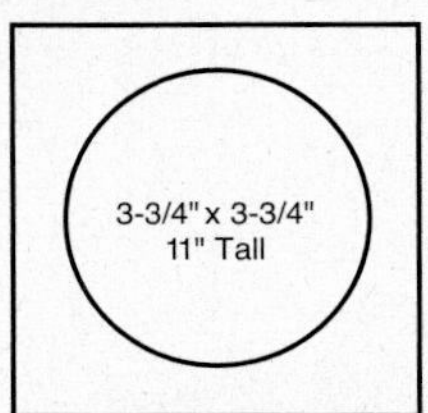

3-3/4" x 3-3/4"
11" Tall

## FIRE CO. NO. 4

**933-2809 39.98**

- Typical American Design
- Use from early 1900s to today
- Fits big city or small town
- Customize with "wood" or modern "metal" doors
- Realistic decals

9-1/2" Tall
4-7/8"
8"

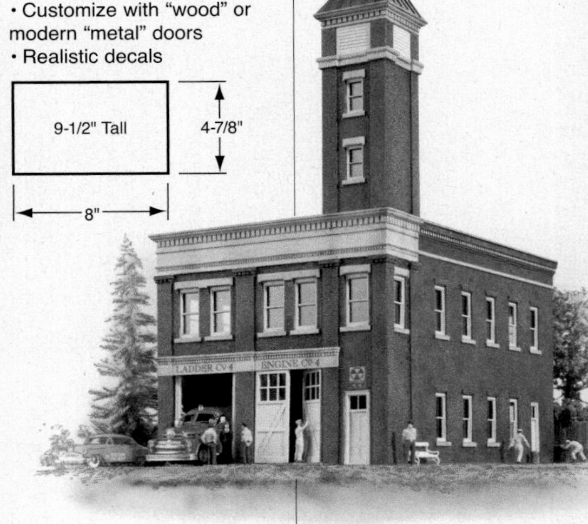

## MELISSA'S EASTSIDE DELI

**933-2815 29.98**

- Fully assembled
- Detailed trim molded in color with handpainted insets
- Working interior light
- Handsome upstairs bay window
- Large ground-floor windows.
- Hanging sign with colorful stickers for five additional businesses.

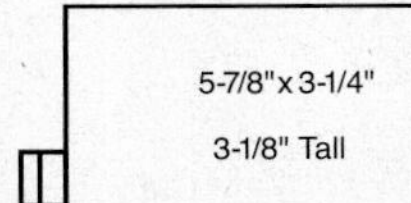

5-7/8" x 3-1/4"
3-1/8" Tall

## SILVER DOLLAR CAFE

**933-2816 29.98**

- Fully assembled
- Detailed trim molded in color with handpainted insets
- Working interior light
- Hanging sign with colorful stickers for five additional businesses.

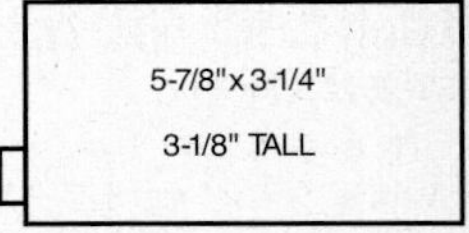

5-7/8" x 3-1/4"
3-1/8" TALL

Both Melissa's East Side Deli and the Silver Dollar Cafe come with these six colorful signs so you can model different businesses in seconds!

**Built-ups**

## TRACKSIDE STRUCTURES SETS

- Make authentic scenes in minutes
- Typical American designs
- Fits 1880s to the 1970s
- Three matching buildings and accessories in each set
- Matching buildings available separately

### 3-Piece Sets With Accessories 29.98 ea

Includes Interlocking Tower, Speeder Shed with Unpowered Speeder Replica Crossing Shanty and Two Positionable Crossing Gates.

**933-2800** Yellow Ochre Siding w/Brown Trim

**933-2803** Cream Siding w/Railroad Green Trim

**933-2810** Two-Tone Gray

**933-3530** Kit Version (gray)

### Individual Buildings

**Yellow Ochre With Oxide Brown Trim**

**933-2801** Speeder Shed & Speeder **19.98**

**933-2802** Crossing Shanty w/2 Positionable Gates & 6 Utility Poles **14.98**

**Cream & Railroad Green**

**933-2804** Speeder Shed & Speeder **19.98**

**933-2805** Crossing Shanty w/2 Positionable Gates & 6 Utility Poles **14.98**

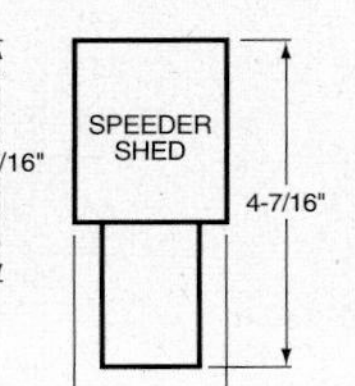

**Two-Tone Gray**

- Gray Siding
- Gray Trim
- Yellow Ochre Siding
- Oxide Brown Trim
- Cream Siding
- Railroad Green Trim

A Track Bumper is included with Speeder Shed

Speeder Shed with Unpowered Speeder 933-2804

Interlocking Tower from 933-2803

933-2802 Shows Positionable Gate and two of the different kinds of poles which are included in this set.

## GOLDEN VALLEY DEPOT

### 29.98 ea

- Perfect small town station
- Fully assembled
- Includes nonworking train order signal
- Authentic "herringbone" brick platform
- Working light
- Decal signs
- Colors match other Trackside Built-Ups

**933-2806** Yellow Ochre w/Oxide Brown Trim

**933-2807** Cream w/Railroad Green Trim

**933-2808** Two-Tone Gray

**933-3532** Kit Version (gray)

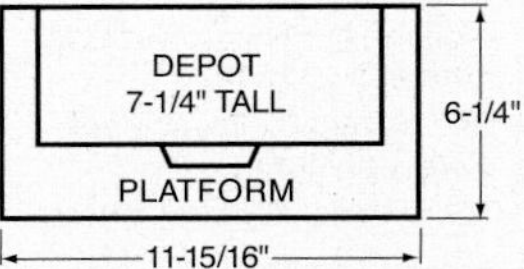

## GOLDEN VALLEY FREIGHT HOUSE

### 29.98 ea

**933-2821** Yellow Ochre w/Oxide Brown Trim

**933-2827** Cream w/Railroad Green Trim

**933-2828** Light Gray w/Dark Gray Trim

**933-3533** Kit Version (gray)

- Fully assembled
- Detailed "wooden" siding
- Name signs match with Golden Valley Depot.
- Colors match other Trackside Built-Ups

Freight House
3-1/4" Tall

# Gold Ribbon Series™: Add These Easy-to-Build, Highly Detailed Structures to Your Layout in Minutes

## Now Include Interior Lighting!

### Vintage Styling and Detail, Snap-Together Construction

- Simple snap-together assembly
- Perfect for layouts, dioramas or Christmas villages.
- Main parts molded in appropriate colors
- No painting needed
- Scale windows molded in color over clear glazing
- Colorful Decals
- Printed signs and interior detail sheets
- Working lights
- Complete instructions
- Fits all popular modeling eras

All parts feature alignment tabs for easy, snap-together assembly.

Two-color molding allows detail, depth and contrast without painting.

Snap-in windows with molded mullions and glass eliminate the spread of glue onto window panes.

## J.C. LANDRY FEED & SUPPLY

933-3619 29.98

- Great Business for Rural Scenes
- Receiving Dock & Door on Back Wall
- Ornate "False Front"

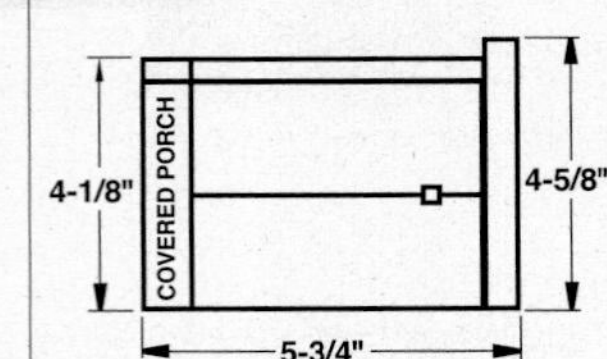

## POST ROAD PET SUPPLY

933-3620 34.98

- Fits Any Business District

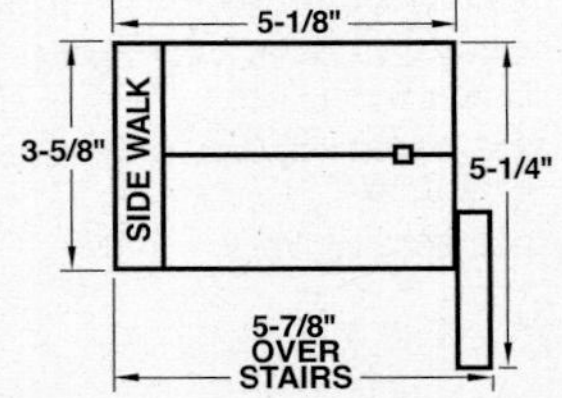




## ELECTRICORP SUPPLY

933-3611 39.98

- Builds into a typical electrical contractor's supply yard
- Main storage building features double-wide door and loading dock
- Small office/ warehouse
- Overhead crane
- Cable reels, utility poles and more included
- Colorful printed signs
- Working interior light

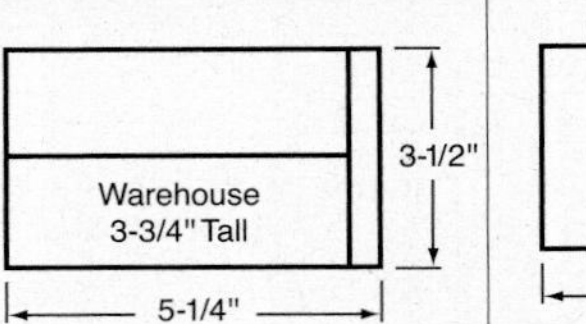


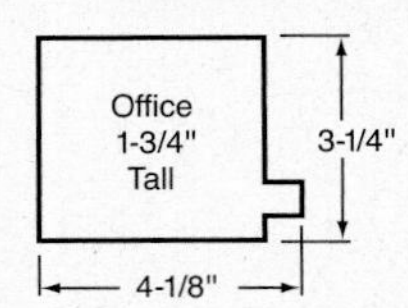


## ROCKY POINT LIGHTHOUSE W/WORKING LIGHTS

933-3603 49.98

- Working lights in tower and Keeper's cottage
- Use as as a collectible, or layout building
- Tower looks like real stucco
- Keeper's cottage has "wood" siding
- Separate doors and clear "glass" windows

Easy-To-Build Premium HO Scale Structure Kits

## ALL NEEDS INSURANCE AGENCY

**933-3617 44.98**

- Quick and easy way to detail any business block.
- Main office on ground floor
- Large vertical windows for extra character.
- Fits the middle of any commercial block
- Complete with bay window, cornice trim, chimneys and more.

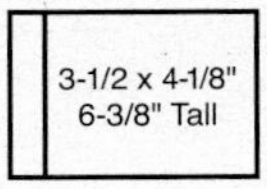

3-1/2 x 4-1/8"
6-3/8" Tall

## ROBERT'S USED BOOKS

**933-3615 29.98**

- Great addition to any model Main Street
- Fine brick detail
- Authentic arched windows
- Separate cornice molded in color.

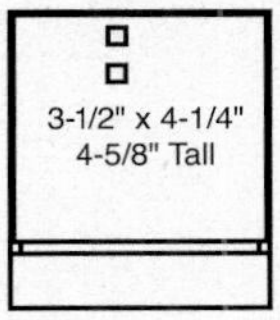

3-1/2" x 4-1/4"
4-5/8" Tall

## BAUER FAMILY PHARMACY

**933-3618 29.98**

- Ground-floor storefront
- Large horizontal windows
- Separate entrance for the second story
- Superb front cornice detail
- Includes chimneys and tarpaper roof

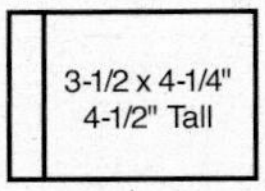

3-1/2 x 4-1/4"
4-1/2" Tall

## THE DAILY EXAMINER

**933-3616 54.98**

- Great addition to any business district
- Big three-story building
- Designed especially for right-hand corner lots
- Side and front entrances
- Elaborate cornice trim on three sides

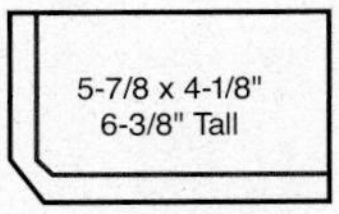

5-7/8 x 4-1/8"
6-3/8" Tall

Easy-To-Build Premium HO Scale Structure Kits

## WORTHINGTON HOTEL

**933-3609 59.98**

- Captures the look and feel of a hotel built prior to 1900
- Features decorative cornice, angled corner and separate side entrance
- Designed to fit on a city corner
- Realistic decals

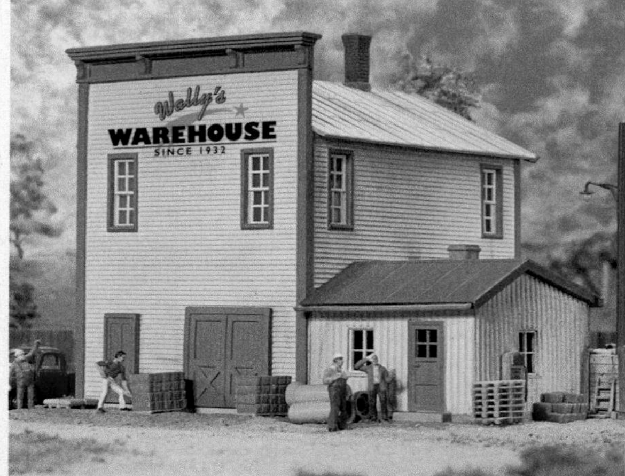


## WALLY'S WAREHOUSE

**933-3605 29.98**

- Use for almost any business
- Classic American design
- Highly detailed parts capture the look of wood construction
- Decal signs for several small businesses

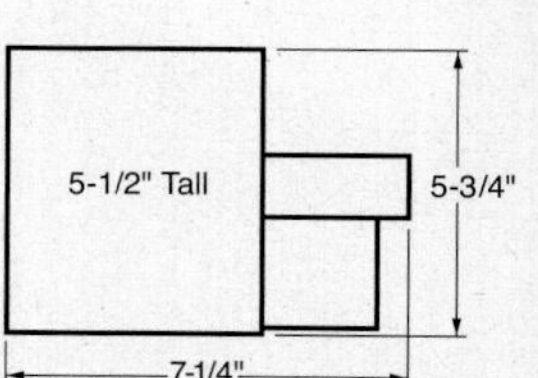


## LAKE FOREST COTTAGE

**933-3608 24.98**

- Perfect summer home
- Use on any layout in any era
- Fits big city neighborhoods.
- Great for company towns serving factories, mines or other industries.
- Includes trellis, table, umbrella, hedgerows, window boxes, chairs, printed interior scenes and interior light.

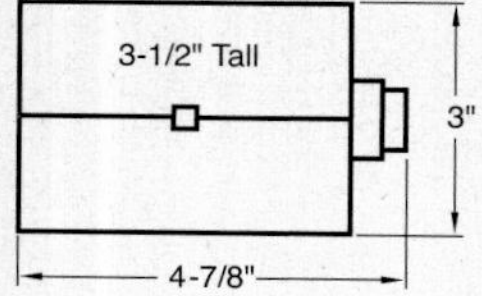


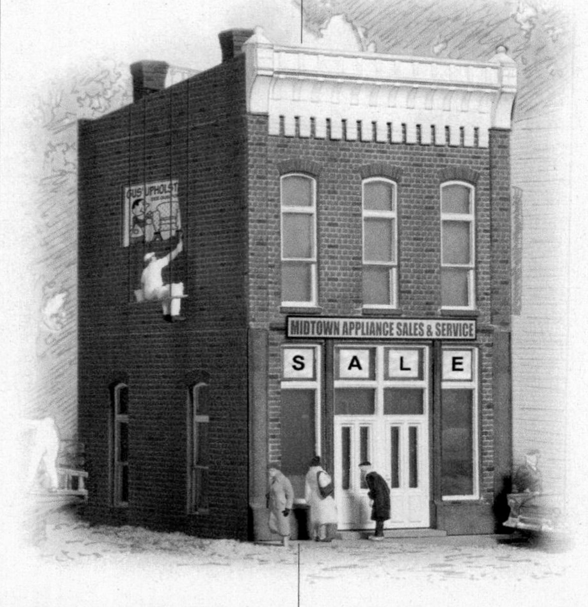


## MIDTOWN APPLIANCE SALES & SERVICE

**933-3614 29.98**

- Authentic American design
- Big double doors
- Large front windows

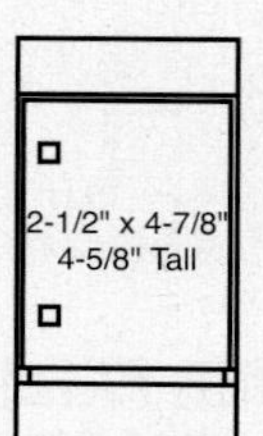

## SMITH'S GENERAL STORE

933-3604 29.98

- Perfect for small town or country crossroads.
- Ornate bay window
- Tall "false front" wall
- Printed interior detail sheets
- Colorful decal signs
- One-piece, open stairway
- Interior light.

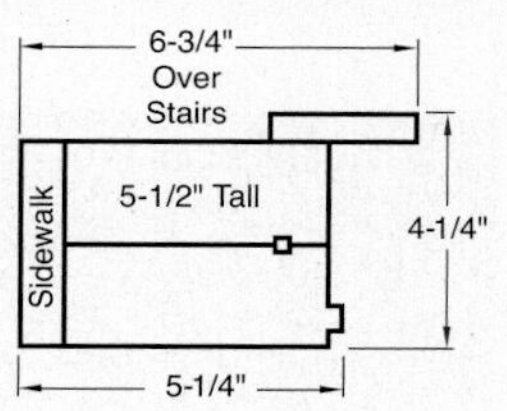

## COTTAGE GROVE SCHOOL

933-3607 29.98

- Patterned after typical rural wooden schoolhouses
- Bell tower
- "Stone" foundation with basement windows
- Realistic decals
- Interior Light

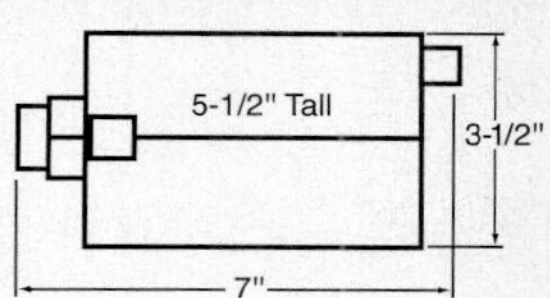


## BENSON'S FIVE & DIME

933-3613 29.98

- Patterned after stores found across America
- Exterior stairway to the second-story
- Realistic decals
- Printed drapes

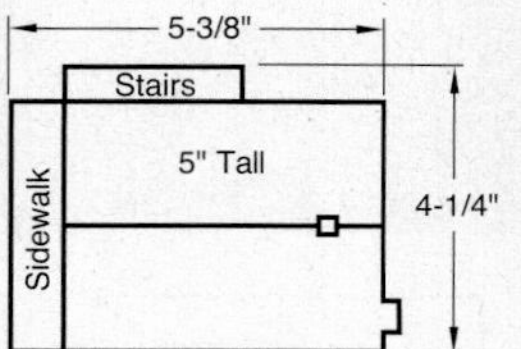

See What's Available at

**www.walthers.com**

## RIVER ROAD MERCANTILE

933-3600 29.98

- Realistic "wood" detailing
- Printed interior scenes,
- Colorful decal signs
- Interior light

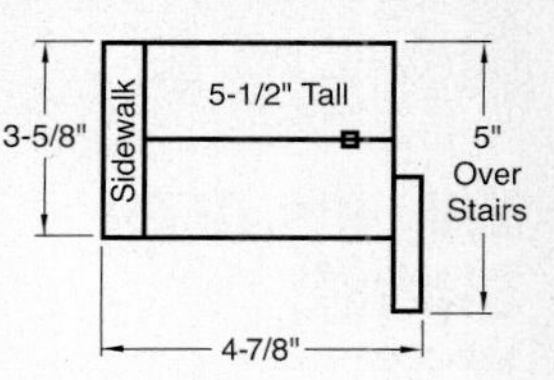

## COTTAGE GROVE CHURCH

933-3606 29.98

- Perfect for any village or rural area
- Traditional tall steeple and arched windows
- "Stone" foundation with basement windows
- Simulated stained-glass window decals
- Interior light
- Sign decals

Includes decals for simulated stained glass windows.

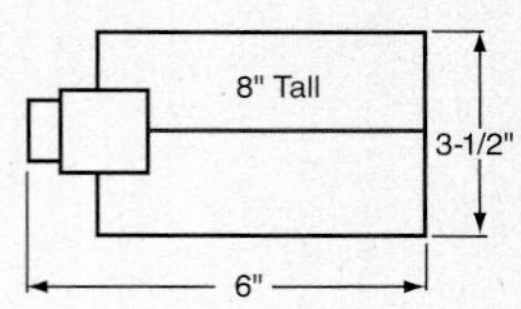

## WILLOW GLEN BRIDGE

933-3602 24.98

- Use with any rural road
- Detailed "wood" beams and boards
- Realistic "stone" abutments
- Easily added to new layouts, or blended with existing scenery.
- Colorful decal signs from different eras

## 109 ELM STREET

933-3612 34.98

- Right at home in any setting
- Early 20th century styling fits steam- or diesel-era layout
- Wrap-around porch with detailed railing and spindles
- Interior light
- Separate one-car garage with opening doors

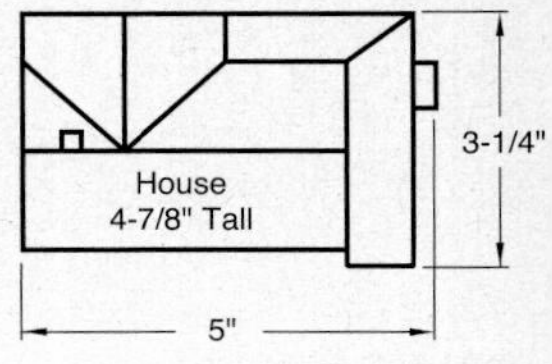

## AUNT LUCY'S HOUSE

933-3601 29.98

- Fits city or country scenes
- Traditional two-story design
- Turned "wood" railings and eave trim.
- Elegant shingled gables
- Inviting front porch
- Printed interior details including curtains
- Interior light

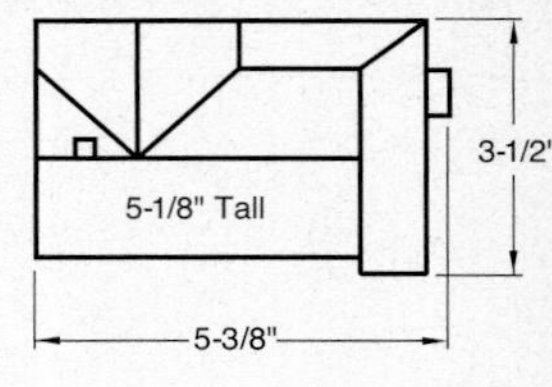


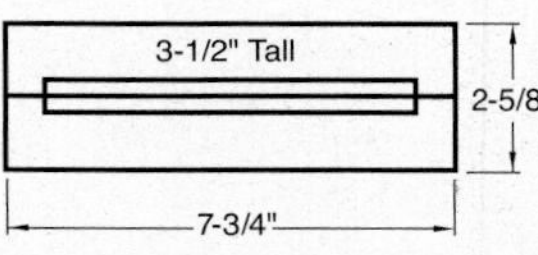

## Building An Engine Servicing Facility Diorama

Engine service facilities are some of the most popular features of any layout. And since most of us have more engines than any other model, we often build terminals to store and display our collections.

In the real world though, they served a more important purpose taking care of the many mechanical needs of the iron horse.

We wanted to share some of what we learned about the prototypes—and overcome the notion that you need a lot of space to do it right.

### Getting Started

We built our base from a 2" thick sheet of foam insulation.

We used a wide selection of readily available products including Walthers Code 83 Track, Woodland Scenics and Highball scenery materials, as well as Floquil paints, Preiser figures and more.

The finished scene includes everything you'd find in a prototype terminal and measures just over 4 x 8'. As you plan your terminal, remember that real railroads faced the same space problems modelers do, resulting in a great variety of sizes and shapes. And you can arrange the various buildings as needed. These factors allow you to easily add a terminal to existing scenery, or build a small extension for one. And, since these facilities were beehives of activity, a terminal scene would make a great theme for a layout in a limited space.

### A Trip Down the Service Tracks

Keeping steam locos ready for the road was a big job. After each trip, they had to be refueled, cleaned, oiled and inspected. This work (called "turning") was done at engine terminals.

While each railroad had its own ideas about the "correct" way, most followed a step-by-step sequence.

### Coming Clean

The first stop was usually the ash pit to "clean the fire." On coal-fired engines, ashpan was emptied to keep air flowing through the grates. With tons of ash and cinder dropped each day, the pits had to be emptied regularly. But cinders made ideal ballast and fill so they were recovered from the pit. Ash hoists made quick work of the job. A large bucket in the pit held the hot ash. When cool, a winch pulled the loaded bucket up a dump tower, where it was unloaded into a waiting gondola.

### Fill 'er Up

As bigger engines outpaced the capacity of existing coaling towers, many roads began building large towers to refuel engines at busier terminals. In addition to coal, tenders would be topped off with water. Roads that used oil for fuel built storage tanks and trackside oil columns.

### Get a Grip!

Big engines carried tons of sand for traction on slick rails. But it had to be dry. Wet or "green" sand arrived in gondolas, and was shoveled into a wooden storage bin. From there, workers loaded it into special stoves in the drying house. When dry, it was screened to remove debris, then lifted by compressed air into a trackside tower.

Since diesels also needed sand, these structures remained in service years after the last steamer was retired.

### Taking Turns

Because steam locos were built to run facing forward, they had to be turned around for their next trip. For many roads, the length of the turntables dictated the maximum size of new engines. And if larger locos were ever needed, older turntables had to be replaced.

### A Room with a View

Roundhouses were used to inspect and service locos under cover. Most of the work was done up front, so it was common for locos to face the wall.

And if the brakes should fail or the throttle slip, it was better to crash through the windows than into the turntable pit!

ENGINE SERVICING FACILITY

While engines started growing early in the 20th century, no one foresaw the giants that were in service by the 1940s. And as traffic increased, some roads opted to add and extend a few stalls. Longer stalls were normally reserved for these behemoths.

### Keeping 'em Moving

Steam locos were complex machines, and all it took was one bad part to sideline an engine. Many roundhouses had a machine shop. The roundhouse stall next door was often fitted to assist the shop with heavy jacks and cranes for removing and replacing parts. And many shops had a through track so a loco could be moved inside for work.

*This view shows some of the "secrets" of construction. The roundhouse footprint is open so the building can be put in the exact spot every time. While the turntable pit is secured to the base, the Bridge is removable. For a module or portable display, being able to remove large and potentially fragile pieces greatly simplifies transporting the unit.*

*For portability, we split our diorama base in two. Here, construction has just started on the "second half." The pink foam surface has been painted a gray-black so any chips won't show the original color below. The Backshop has been set in place temporarily so tracks can be positioned.*

*This view shows a fraction of what you can do in an area measuring just 4 x 8'. We left room between buildings for photography, but you could easily compress this to fit.*

*George substituted rolled roofing and heavily weathered this otherwise stock Modern Coaling Tower kit (#933-2903), which serves the new engine terminal in the city of Fillmore.*

## Take a look at the engine facilities on the Franklin & South Manchester – all built from Walthers kits!

One of the best-known free-lanced layouts, the HO Scale Franklin & South Manchester is the work of master modeler George Sellios. In recent years, he has been expanding his already large and incredibly detailed railroad.

Part of this ongoing project includes a new city yard at Fillmore, which required construction of a large engine terminal. Work began about the same time that Walthers Engine Service Facility series was released, and George found that several of the kits were just what he had in mind.

George was kind enough to send some "in progress" photos taken by Richard Josselyn, which we are very happy to share here with you!

*With tons of cinders to move each day, you can bet the workers at Fillmore were mighty glad to see this Cinder Conveyor and Ash Pit (#933-3181) being built! George built the majority of the kit as it comes right out of the box, but scratchbuilt a new machinery house using cardstock covered with corrugated metal panels.*

*Campbell shingles and a new wood ladder were the only changes made to this Wood Water Tank kit (#933-3531). Most viewers who see the heavily weathered model can't believe it's really made of plastic!*

This scene incorporates the Modern Roundhouse, one Add-On Stalls kit, Machine Shop and Modern 130' Turntable.

## MODERN ROUNDHOUSE

**933-2900 59.98**

- American prototype
- Holds engines up to 125 scale feet long
- Includes stall add-on for engines up to 145 scale feet long
- Modular design - easily expanded to a full circle
- Compact 10° stall spacing
- Interior & exterior brick detail
- Fine window details
- Floor inspection pits
- Decal signs

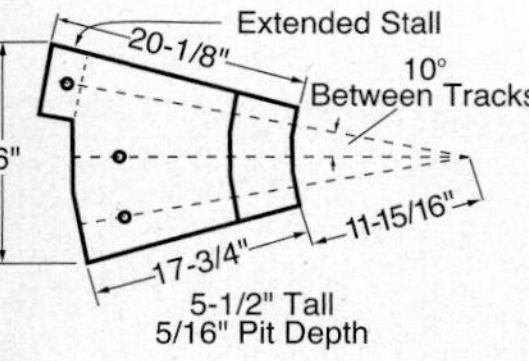

**Roundhouse Figure Set**

**590-1010249 19.98**

- 10 Different Figures
- Hand-Painted In Authentic Colors
- Realistic Poses
- Ready To Use

## MODERN ROUNDHOUSE ADD-ON STALLS

**933-2901 49.98**

- Matches Roundhouse 933-2900
- Holds engines up to 125 scale feet long
- Includes stall add-on for bigger engines up to 145 scale feet long
- Compact 10° stall spacing
- Interior & exterior brick detail
- Fine window details
- Floor inspection pits
- Decal signs included

## MACHINE SHOP

**933-2902 44.98**

- Build as free-standing or attached building
- Authentic brick detail
- Attached boiler house
- Build with roll-up doors open or closed
- Matches Roundhouse & Roundhouse Add-on
- Authentic American design
- Slotted floor accepts popular rail sizes
- Decal signs

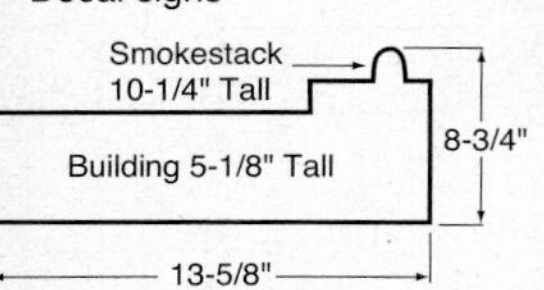

## SAND HOUSE & TOWERS

**933-3182 29.98**

- Brick drying house
- Detailed "wooden" storage bin
- Early & late style towers included
- Realistic piping
- Decal signs

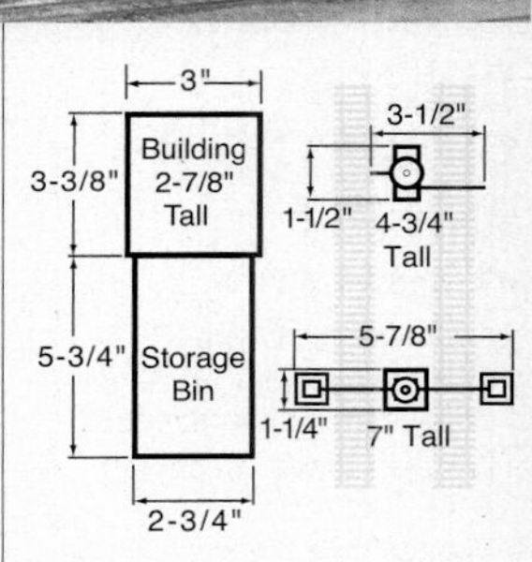

## MODERN 130' TURNTABLE

**933-2829 299.98**

- Fully assembled
- Programmable indexing for up to 60 positions
- Motorized gear drive
- Detailed and hand-weathered one-piece pit
- Holds engines up to 130 scale feet long
- Authentic bridge with separate arch
- Decal signs

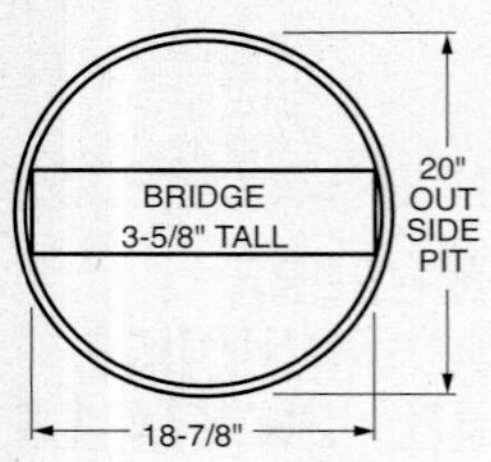

## MODERN COALING TOWER

**933-2903 54.98**

- Authentic American prototype
- Serves 3 tracks
- Coal delivery shed
- Loaded with separate details
- Decal signs

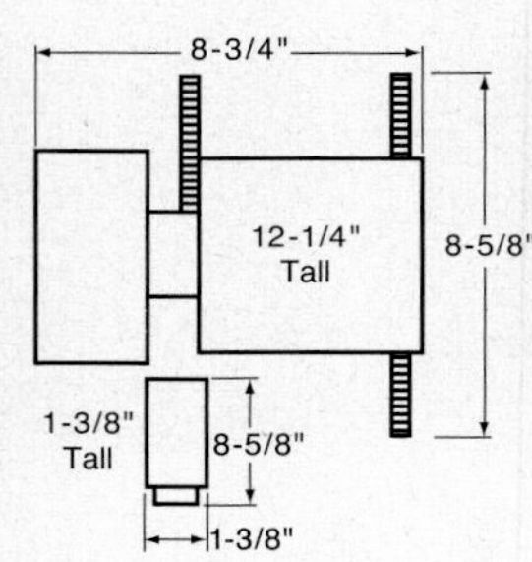

## CINDER CONVEYOR & ASH PIT

**933-3181 24.98**

- American prototype
- Compact size for maximum detail in minimum space
- Detailed tower, machinery shed & pit
- Positionable bucket & dump chute
- Decal signs

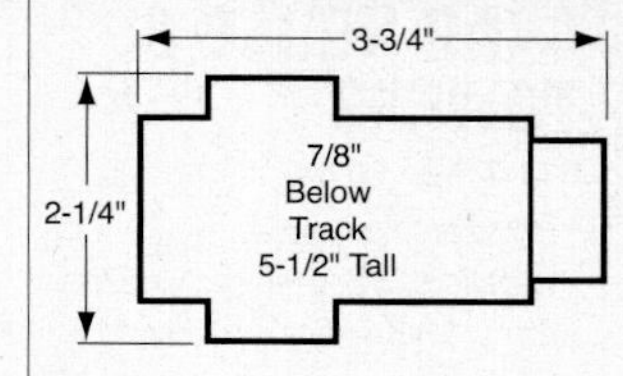


Got a Mouse? Click Walthers Web Site at

**www.walthers.com**

## 90' TURNTABLE

**933-2840 299.98**

- Fully Assembled
- Programmable indexing for up to 60 positions
- Motorized Gear Drive
- Authentic American Design
- Weathered One-Piece Plastic Pit
- Holds Engines up to 12-3/8" Long
- Detailed Bridge with Arch
- Complete Instructions

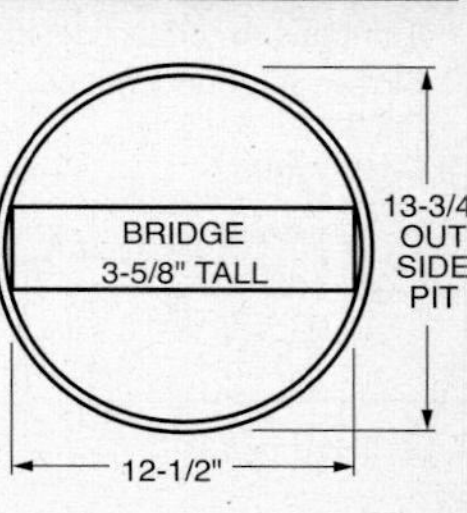

## DIESEL HOUSE

**933-2916 69.98**

- All-New Model
- Use with other Engine Service Facility Structures
- Interior Inspection Pits, Platforms & Craneway
- Use with Classic or Modern Power
- Hold Locos up to 17" Long

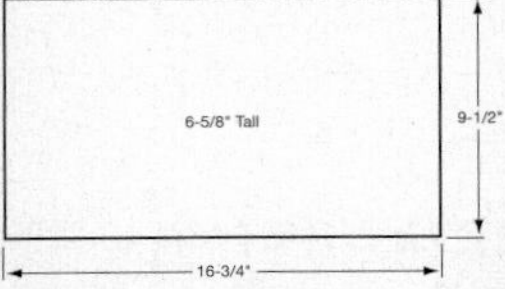

## TRACK SCALES

**933-3199 24.98**

- Builds One of Two Versions: Flat or Peaked Roof Light or Heavy-Duty Scale
- Simulated Turnouts for Scale Tracks Included
- Track Alignment Guides on Base
- Easily Added to Your Layout
- Great for Yards & Heavy Industries

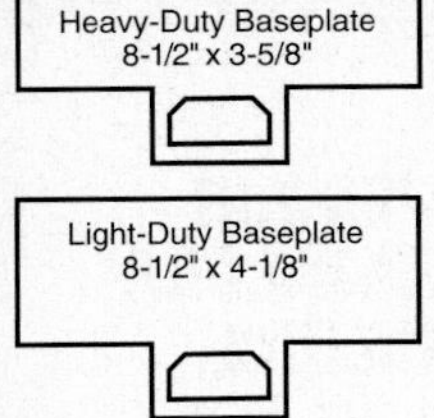

Flat Roof 933-3199

Peaked Roof 933-3199

## DIESEL FUELING FACILITY

**933-2908 24.98**

- Prototypes Introduced in the 1940s
- Authentic Detail for Engine Terminals
- Builds a Typical Two-Track Fueling Facility
- Storage Tank, Fuel Crane, Water Crane, Pump House & Tank Car Unloading Rack Included
- Catch Pans for Contemporary Railroads Too

5 x 2-3/4" Storage Tank
Unloading Rack 1/2 x 3/4 x 2-7/8" Tall
Circuit Box
Pump House
Fueling Crane
Water Crane
Cement Berm 11 x 7"

## ROUNDHOUSE

**933-3041 39.98**

- American style
- Traditional two-level roof
- Separate clerestory windows and smokejacks
- 23 large windows
- Holds engines up to 13" long
- Compact 10° stall spacing
- Modular design for easy expansion up to a full circle

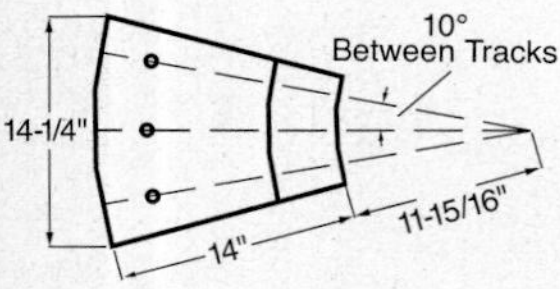


## 90' TURNTABLE

**933-3171 39.98**

- Pit diameter: 13-3/16" 33 cm
- Holds locos up to 12-3/8" 30.9 cm long
- Fits most layouts
- One-piece pit for drop-in mounting.
- Easily motorized with Motorizing Kit #933-1050, sold separately.
- Complete hook-up instructions.
- Detailed bridge with operator's cab, handrails and arch

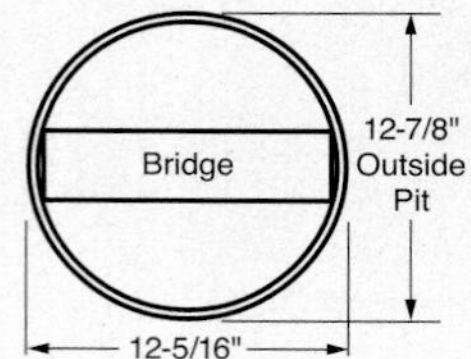

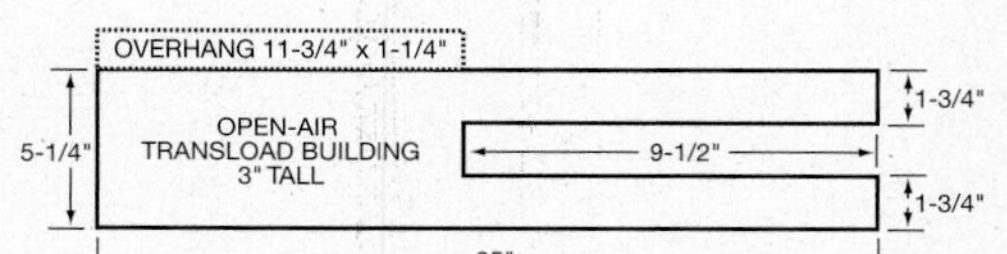


## OPEN AIR TRANSLOAD BUILDING

**933-2918 39.98**

- Authentic Post-War Design
- Raised Docks for Road/Rail Service
- Main Office/Covered Loading Area

## MOTORIZING KIT

**933-1050 19.98**

- Fits various Walthers models
- Low-speed motor for smooth, realistic operation.
- Complete hook-up instructions.

## HEAVY DUTY CRANE

**933-3150 12.98**
11 x 2-3/8 x 2-5/16"
27.3 x 5.7 x 6.5cm

- Finishing touch for Backshop (#933-3039, sold separately).
- Packed with prototype details
- Decal signs
- Easily adapted to big industrial buildings

## ENGINE HOUSE/CARSHOP DETAIL KIT

**933-3512 19.98**

- Dress-up any shop scene
- Finely detailed resin castings
- Overhead crane, forge smoke stack, two small sheds, three ash cans, three 55-gallon drums, awning, a bin, waybill/mail box, phone/electrical box and fuel oil tank included

## CONCRETE COALING TOWER

**933-3042 39.98**

- Typical American design
- Perfect for smaller terminal scenes
- Covered pit, machinery house, lifting equipment and chutes to serve two tracks
- Realistic concrete & steel detailing
- Decal signs

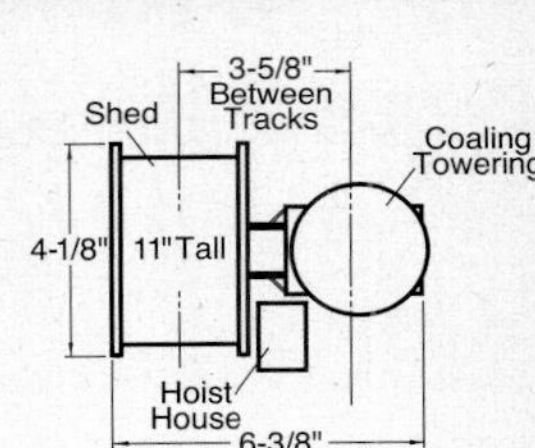

## "WOOD" COALING TOWER

**933-2922 49.98**

- Detailed Parts Simulate Timber Construction
- Use with other Engine Service Facility Structures
- Must-Have For Steam-Era Layouts

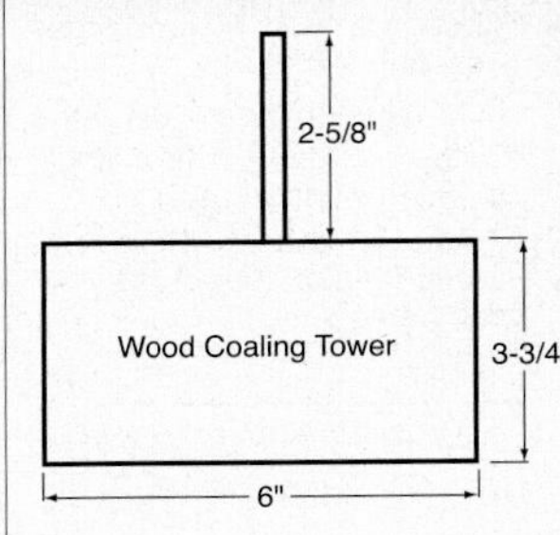

## 2-STALL ENGINE HOUSE & ACCESSORIES

**933-3007 32.98**

- Great for small terminals
- Movable doors
- Separate windows
- Pillar crane
- Parts to extend one track through building.
- Holds Engines up to 11-5/8" long

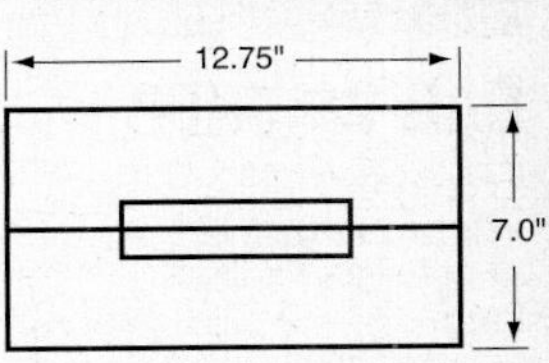


See What's Available at

**www.walthers.com**

## CITY STATION

**933-2904 44.98**

- Focal point of a city scene
- Typical of larger, fancier stations
- Covered end platform
- Attached baggage room
- Perfect for steam-or diesel-era
- Easily expanded with Wood Station Shed & Platform (#933-3188, sold separately)

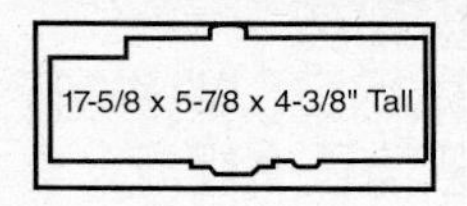

## WOOD STATION SHED & PLATFORM

**933-3188** pkg(4) **24.98**

- Typical "umbrella-style" shelter
- Used at stations large and small
- Great addition to suburban operations, small towns or big cities
- Looks great with City Station (#933-2904, sold separately)
- Modular design for easy expansion
- Build as a freestanding structure or attach to station building with special roof section included in kit

5-5/8 x 2-3/8 x 2-3/8" Tall

## CAR WASHER

**933-3186 19.98**

- Great for Post-War Passenger Facilities
- Based on six-brush washers favored by many roads
- Complete with large brushes, simulated motor drives, sprayer and rinse nozzles, washer control house and detailed base with drains

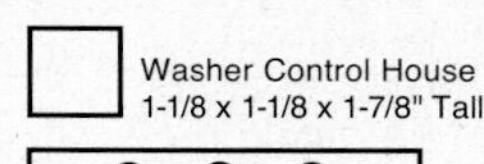


## BUTTERFLY-STYLE STATION PLATFORM SHELTERS

**933-3175** pkg(4) **24.98**

- Found at big cities and outlying suburbs
- Parts for four complete platforms
- Modular design
- Underground "subway" stairways included
- "Wooden" walkway crossings between tracks
- Four platform benches
- Detailed "steel" columns and platform signboards
- Perfect for use with Union Station (#933-3094, sold separately)

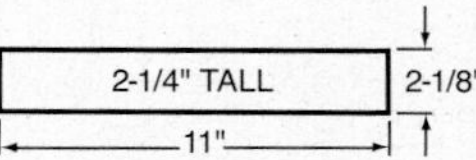


## RAILWAY EXPRESS AGENCY (REA) TRANSFER BUILDING

**933-3095 44.98**

- Modular design, for easy customizing
- Brick construction & large windows
- Fits any era from the 1900s to the present
- Decals for various eras

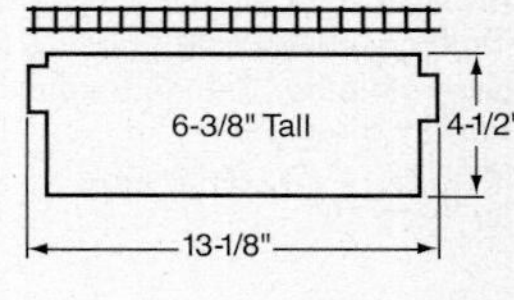

## UNION STATION

**933-3094 59.98**

- Puts big detail in a small space
- American prototype
- Classic design fits steam- or diesel-era
- Nonworking clock
- Realistic cut stone detailing
- Separate doors and windows
- Molded-in cut lines to simplify customizing
- Rooftop skylights & vents
- End-door canopies
- Realistic decals

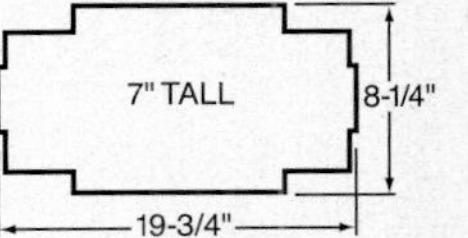

## MISSION-STYLE DEPOT

**933-2920 39.98**

- All-New Model
- Santa Fe Prototype
- Great Addition to Southwestern Layouts
- Simulated Stucco Finish
- Tile Roof
- Matching Mission Style Freight House (#933-2921) Available Separately

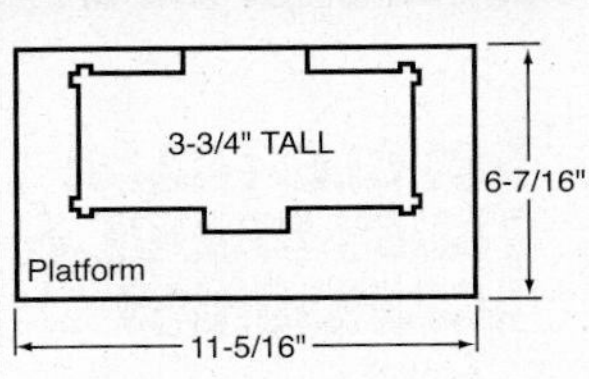

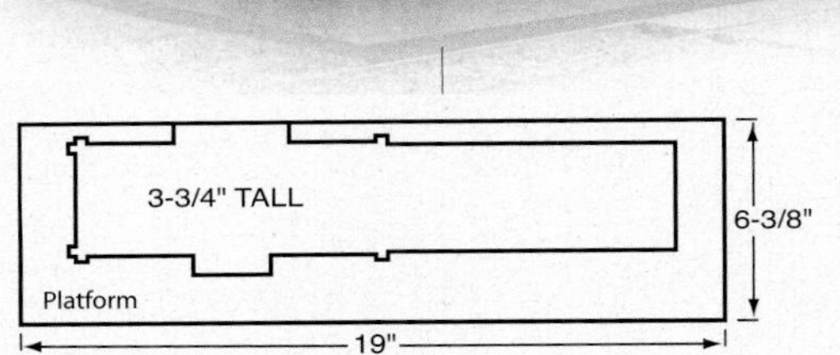


## MISSION-STYLE DEPOT W/ FREIGHT HOUSE

**933-2924 54.98**

- All-New Model
- Santa Fe Prototype
- Great Addition to Southwestern Layouts
- Simulated Stucco Finish
- Tile Roof

## MISSION-STYLE FREIGHT HOUSE

**933-2921 29.98**

- All-New Model
- Santa Fe Prototype
- Great Addition to Southwestern Layouts
- Simulated Stucco Finish
- Matching Mission-Style Depot (#933-2920) Available Separately

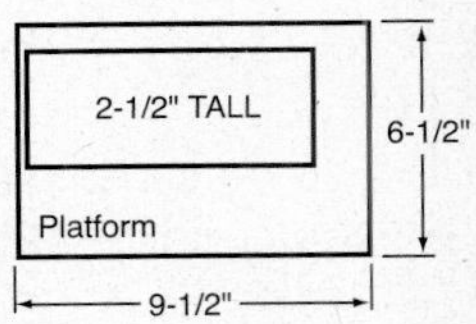

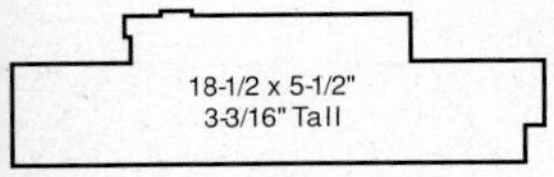

18-1/2 x 5-1/2"
3-3/16" Tall

## WHITEHALL STATION

**933-2932 44.98**

- Whitehall, Wisconsin, Prototype
- Similar to Small Town Stations Across U.S.
- Fits 1900s to Present
- Authentic "Brick" Exterior
- Covered Platforms on Two Sides
- Attractive Curved Windows & Gabled Roof

## SINGLE-TRACK TRUSS BRIDGE

**933-3185 24.98**

- Most common bridge used by railroads
- Realistic trusses, chords and bridge shoes
- Safety sign and graffiti decals
- Fits all popular eras
- Clears taller modern cars

SINGLE-TRACK TRUSS BRIDGE
5" TALL
3-1/4"
20"

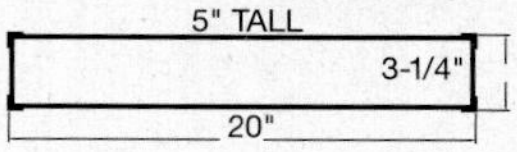

**Make your bridge installation easier with these scenic accessories!**

**933-1040** Abutment **9.98**

**933-1041** Bridge Pier **12.98**

**933-1042** Abutment Wings pkg(2) **7.98**

## DOUBLE-TRACK TRUSS BRIDGE & ACCESSORIES

**933-3012 21.98**

- Typical of steel bridges found throughout North America.
- Trusses, chords and bridge shoes
- Safety sign and graffiti decals
- Steam-era prototype (some modern cars will not clear)

### Wing Walls

**933-1042** pkg(2) **7.98**
Measures: 3-3/4 x 3-3/8"
9.5 x 8.6cm

- Simulates retaining walls used with abutments on many bridges
- Includes two one-piece resin wings
- Each measures 3-3/8" high and 3-3/4" wide at the base.
- Adaptable to many HO bridges

### Bridge Abutment

**933-1040 9.98**
Measures: 5-5/8 x 4 x 1/2"
14.3 x 10.2 x 1.3 cm

- Matches width of #933-3012 adaptable to many models
- One-piece resin casting
- One abutment is required for each end of the bridge

### Bridge Pier

**933-1041 12.98**
Measures: 5-3/8 x 1-1/8 x 3-3/8
13.7 x 2.9 x 8.6cm

- Adaptable to many bridge models
- One-piece casting
- Matches height of Bridge Abutment and Wings

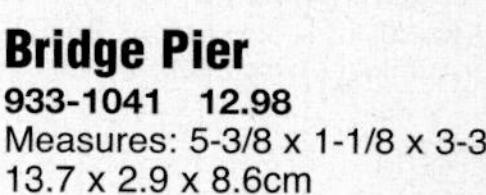

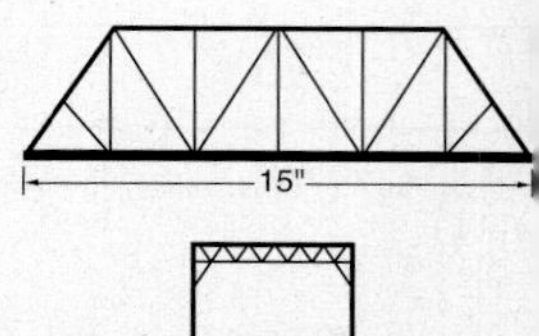


### Bridge Track

**948-899 19.99**

- Designed for Truss Bridge (#933-3012, sold separately)
- Adaptable to most HO bridge kits
- Code 83 outer main rails with Code 70 inside guard rails
- Correct bridge ties
- Measures 19-11/16" (#933-3012 requires two sections for double track.)

## SWING BRIDGE

**933-3088 64.98**

Finished model measures:
27 x 6-3/8 x 7-9/16"
69 x 16.2 x 19.3cm

Additional measurements:

10" clear channel on either side of center pier

2-5/8" Rail height above water

7-9/16" Overall height above water

2-1/16" Track center spacing

6-3/8" Abutment width

8-1/4" Center pier width

- Movable structure
- Warren truss-style swing bridge with plate girder deck
- Includes 196' "steel" span, "concrete" center pier, abutments and operator's cabin
- Patterned after early-1900s prototype
- Clears most modern equipment
- Motorize for realistic movement with #933-1050 sold separately

## MOTORIZING KIT

**933-1050 19.98**

- Fits various Walthers models
- Low-speed motor for smooth, realistic operation
- Complete hook-up instructions

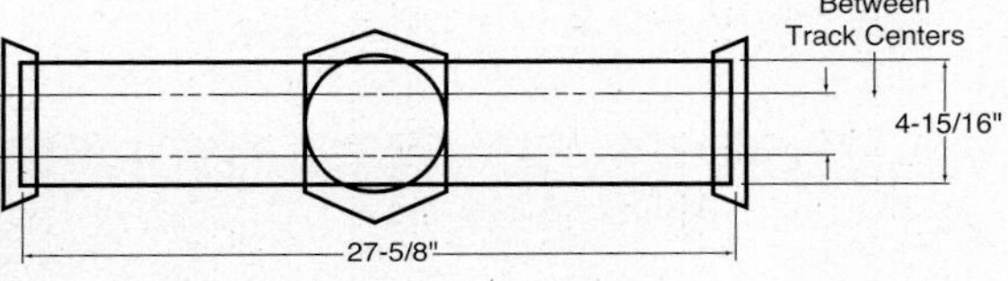

## 1/2-METER BRIDGE TRACK

**948-886 18.98**

- Detailed, closely spaced bridge ties and stringers with simulated wood grain and bolt detail
- Guard rails run the entire length
- Two 60mm end sections with "V" guard rail ends and standard ties included
- Double-Track Swing Bridge, requires three sections and some track cutting is necessary

## TRESTLE W/STEEL DECK GIRDER BRIDGE

**933-3147 24.98**

Each single-track trestle with deck girder bridge measures: 15-1/2" long with 3-1/2" deck girder bridge section, 3" wide at the bottom of the tallest girder, 4" tall.

- Build with or without girder bridge
- Two complete trestle/girder bridges per kit
- Combine parts for more detailing options
- Combine both trestles to span gaps up to 31" long
- Place side by side for double track
- Easily cut to fit
- Perfect for use in any era
- Optional deck girder bridge

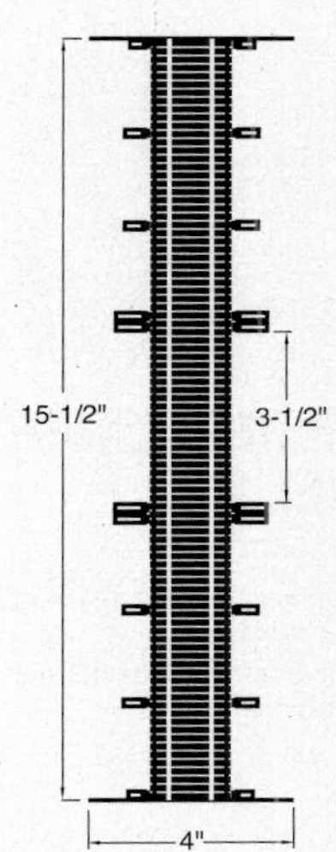


4" Tall (Dimensions for each of the sections)

Photography and diorama base by Ken Patterson.

Pre-production models shown; some details may vary. Colors shown are painted by modeler; paint not included. Figures, vehicles, railroad equipment, scenery and other accessories sold separately.

## ART DECO HIGHWAY UNDERPASS

**933-3190 24.98**

- All-New Model
- Unique Styling & Details
- Fits Single- or Multiple-Track Lines
- Detailed Deck
- Use from 1930s to Present Day
- Found in All Parts of the U.S.

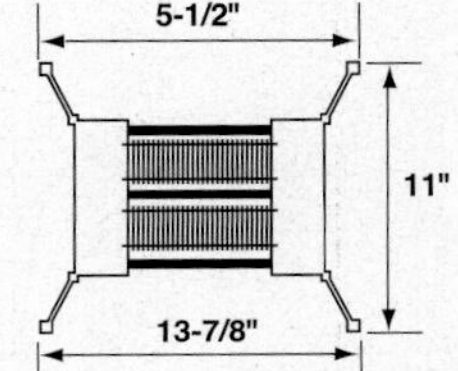


**2-1/4" - Track height from street**

**3" - Overall height**

## GOLDENFLAME FUEL CO.

933-3087 49.98

- Features three bunker-style coal silos.
- Includes two oil tanks and pump house
- Combined office/scalehouse
- 160 scale feet of "wood" fence
- Portable car unloader and conveyor
- Colorful decals
- Easily arranged to fit small or odd-shaped spaces

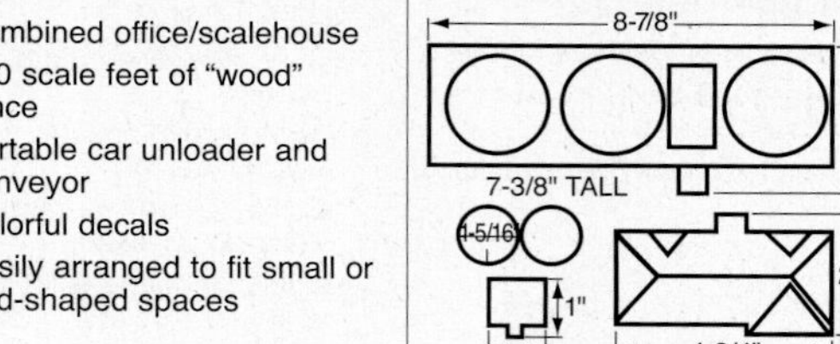
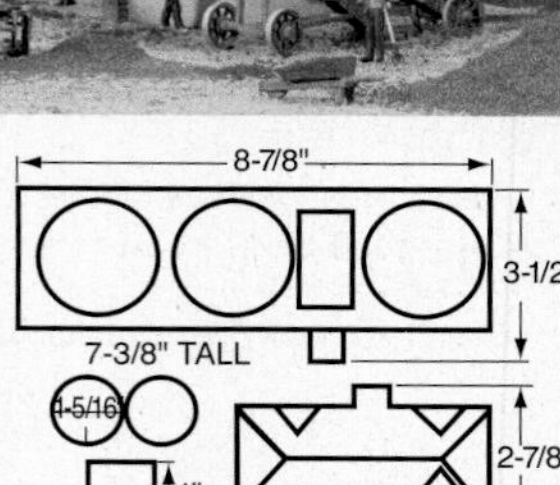

## O.L. KING & SONS COAL YARD & ACCESSORIES

933-3015 24.98

- Features elevated trestle-style unloading ramp
- Complete with brick office, fencing, shed, decals and instructions

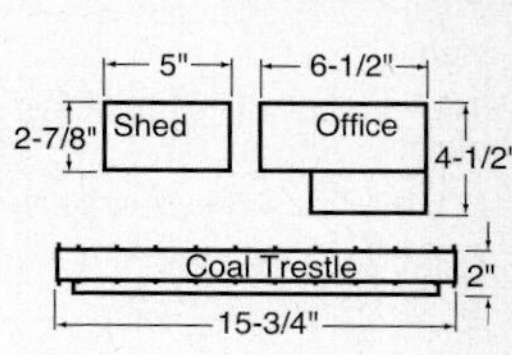

## OLD TIME COAL CONVEYORS

933-3520 9.98

- Make any spur suitable for unloading hopper cars
- Use for gravel, sand, grain, fertilizers, coal and other materials
- Includes three unloaders and three conveyors

## WESTERN COAL FLOOD LOADER

933-3089 39.98

- Great loading point for modern unit coal trains
- Roof-top machinery
- Modular conveyor (matching sections available separately in kit #933-3518)
- Stackable silo sections build tall or short structure

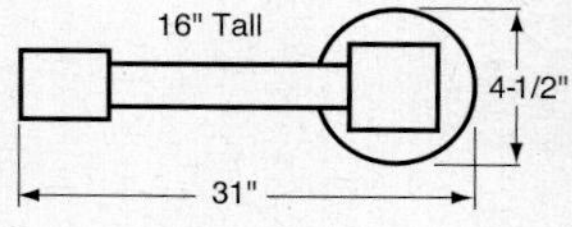
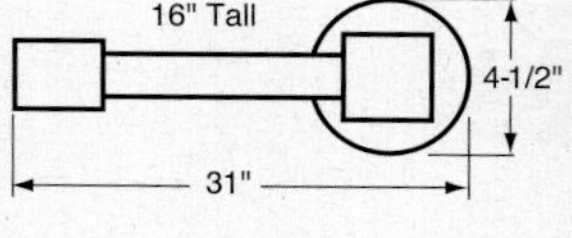

## MODERN CONVEYORS

933-3518 12.98

- Includes 21" of conveyors and supports
- Matches Conveyor parts in #933-3089, sold separately

## NEW RIVER MINING COMPANY & ACCESSORIES

933-3017 36.98

Main Building:
12-1/2 x 9 x 9-3/8"
31.2 x 22.5 x 23.2cm

- Early 1950s style loader
- Typical of facilities in all parts of the country
- Includes main building, truck loading facility and conveyors
- Separate windows and door

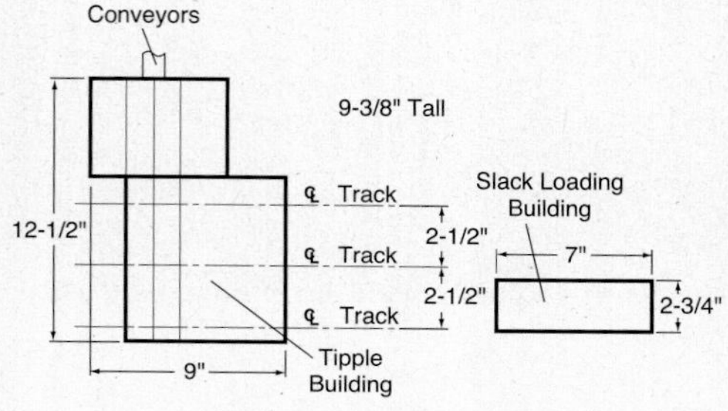

## GAS PLANT

**933-2905 59.98**

- Excellent Brick Detail
- Arched Windows with Thin Profile Frames
- Large Exterior Tanks, Typical of Modernized Operations
- Used to Cool & Clean Raw Gas – A Must Have for any Facility

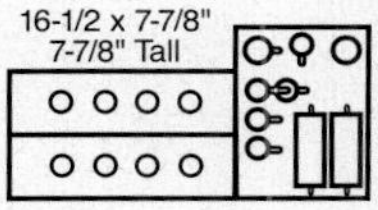

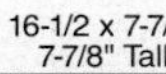


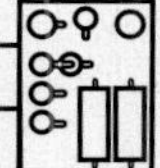

## GAS STORAGE TANK

**933-2907 49.98**

- Used by the Prototype to Store & Pressurize Gas
- Intricate Detail with Easy Construction
- Signature Structure of any Gas Works
- Perfect for Period City Scenes
- Detailed "Steel" Trusses
- American Prototype

## COKE RETORT

**933-2910 79.98**

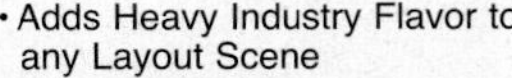

- Adds Heavy Industry Flavor to any Layout Scene
- Modernized with Overhead Coal Bunker
- Authentic Oven Details
- Covered Conveyor Included
- First Step in Prototype Process where Coal was Baked to Produce Gas

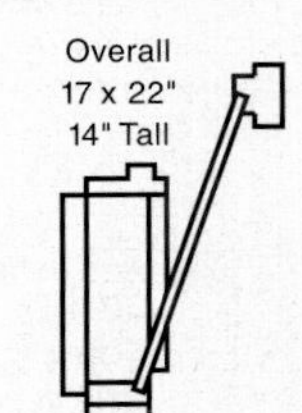

## BRIDGE CRANE

**933-2906 59.98**

- Build in one of four different lengths; 22", 24", 28", 31"
- Detailed "Steel" Truss Work
- Positionable Trolley with Clamshell Bucket
- Used on the Prototype to Unload Coal from Ships
- Use at a Coal Pier or Steel Works
- Operator's Cab

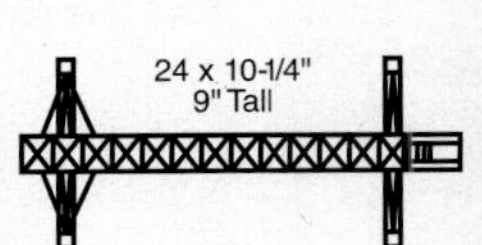

**High-Voltage Transmission Towers**
933-3121 15.98
- Add realism to modern skylines
- Includes four easy-to-build towers
- Molded-on eyelets for "wire" (sold separately)

**Transformer**
933-3126 11.98
- Great flat car load
- Neat detail around the Northern Light & Power Powerhouse (#933-3021, sold separately)

**Electric Utility Pole Set**
933-3101 9.98
- 24 easy-to-assemble power poles, with insulators, nonilluminated street lights and realistic "wire"

## NORTHERN LIGHT & POWER POWERHOUSE & ACCESSORIES
933-3021 32.98
- Brick main building
- Large smokestack
- Coal dump pit
- Separate doors, roof and windows with clear "glass"
- Decal signs and billboard included

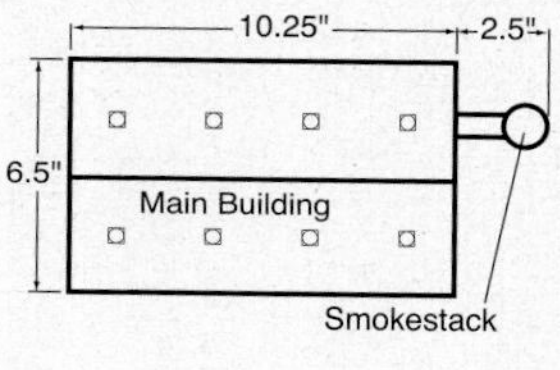

## NORTHERN LIGHT & POWER SUBSTATION & ACCESSORIES
933-3025 26.98

Baseplate: 8-1/2 x 12-1/2"
- Includes all the details of the prototype
- Transformers
- Chain-link fence
- Warning signs and billboard decal included

## NORTHERN LIGHT & POWER INTERIOR
933-3130 9.98
- Complete with boiler walls, generators and turbines (Overhead Traveling Crane, #933-3102, sold separately)

## BLACK GOLD ASPHALT - HOT MIX PLANT

933-3085 59.98

- Highly detailed
- Includes oil tanks, conveyors, three-bay mixing bin with conveyor, furnace with ductwork, rotary mixing kiln, piping, double loading silos
- Colorful decal sign

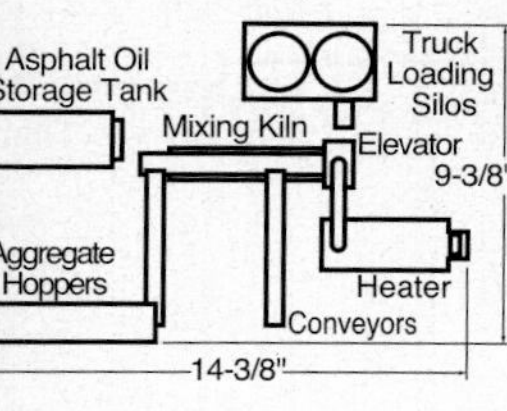

## MEDUSA CEMENT COMPANY & ACCESSORIES

933-3019 32.98

- Great addition to any industrial district
- Eight tall storage silos
- Conveyor tower
- Rail car unloading shed.
- Separate roll-up doors roof-top piping, railing and dust collectors

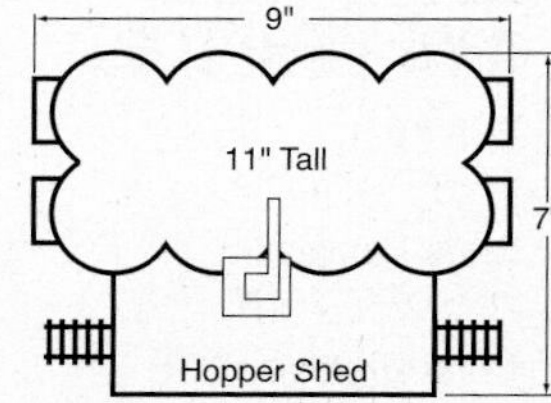

## GLACIER GRAVEL

933-3062 39.98

Unique design simulates stone crusher/washer

- Great for any quarry
- Detailed parts capture the look of concrete and steel
- Main building holds two tracks
- Conveyors included — matching sections (#933-3149) available separately

### Conveyors

933-3149 pkg(3) 8.98

- Matches conveyors included in #933-3062, sold separately

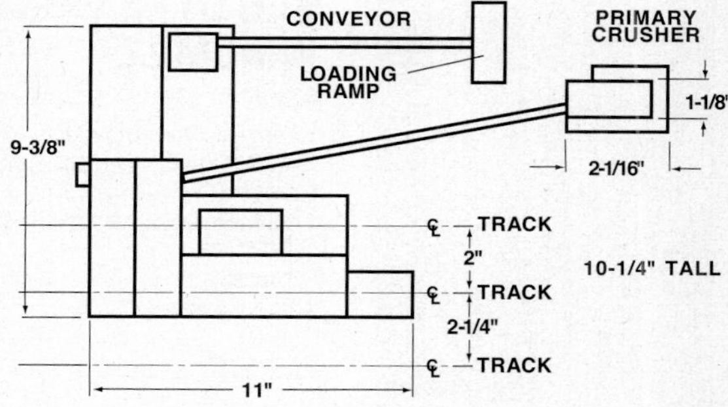

## BULK TRANSFER CONVEYOR

933-3519 29.98

- Add a hopper car unloading point to your pike
- Includes under-track pit, stairway, conveyor, wheeled rotary conveyor, drive motor details, track grate, and corrugated metal office
- Realistic decals

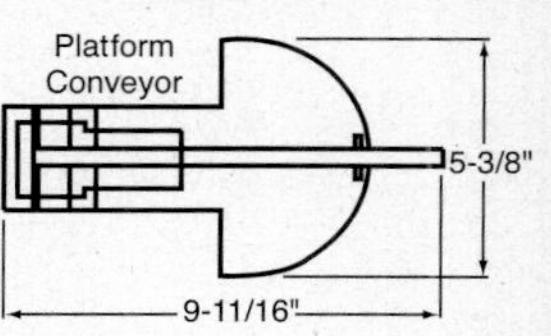

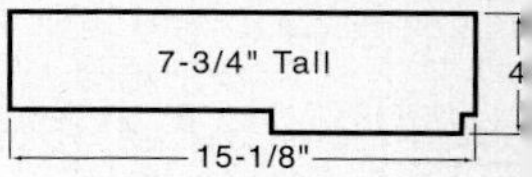

## FARMERS COOPERATIVE RURAL GRAIN ELEVATOR

933-3036 27.98

- Colorful signs
- Period styling
- Use from the 1800s to the present
- Includes main elevator, storage building and scalehouse
- Realistic "wood" detail.
- Separate doors and windows

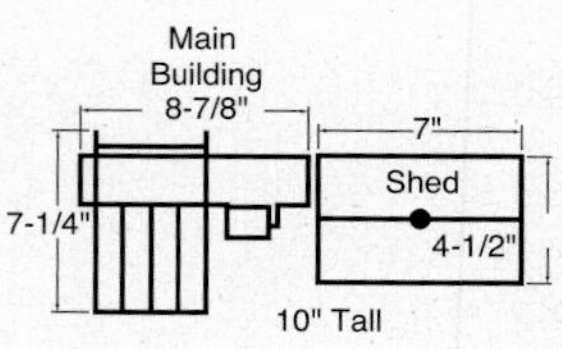


## VAN DYKE FARM WINDMILL

933-3198 24.98

- Familiar Farm Structure
- Adjustable to Four Different Heights
- "Cement Base" with "Wood" Well Cap
- Realistic 10' Diameter Blade
- Two Windmills Included

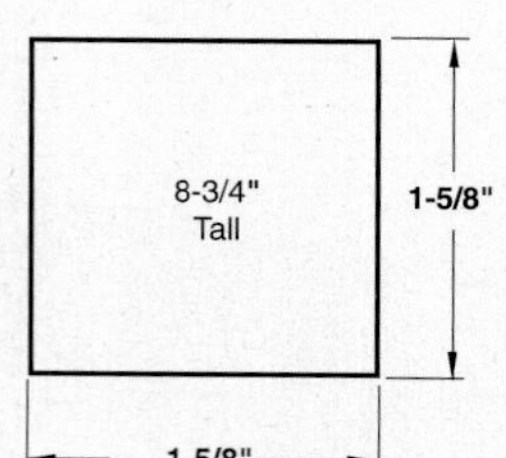


## SUNRISE FEED MILL

933-3061 24.98

- Authentic "wooden" drop siding
- Large roof-top dust collector
- Rail and truck/wagon unloading docks
- Colorful decals

7-3/4" Tall

15-1/8"

## GRAIN HANDLING EQUIPMENT AND VEHICLES

**Grain Bin**
933-3123 14.98

**Grain Conveyor**
933-3124 14.98

**Grain Dryer**
933-3128 9.98

## VALLEY GROWERS ASSOCIATION

933-3096 36.98

- Simulated metal siding
- Perfect for steam- and diesel-era layouts
- Positionable sliding doors
- Office building
- "Wood" grain bin
- Realistic decals

A segmented trackside loading pipe is included so you can simulate loading box cars or covered hoppers.

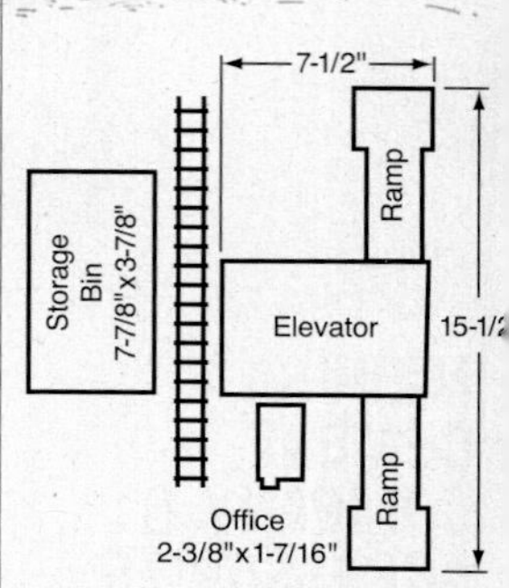

## RED WING FLOUR MILL

**933-3026 34.98**

- Modern concrete building
- Truck and rail loading facilities
- Blowers and vents
- Separate doors and windows
- Full-color decal signs

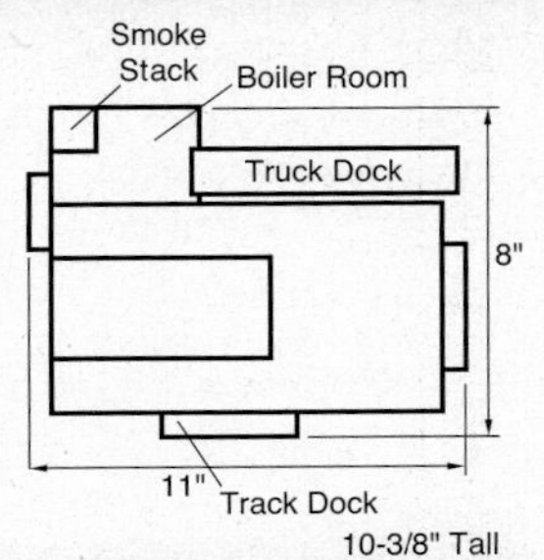

## ADM® GRAIN ELEVATOR & ACCESSORIES

**933-3022 32.98**

- Includes elevator, eight storage silos, dust bins, head house and sheds for rail and trucks
- Full-color ADM logos
- Billboard sign decals

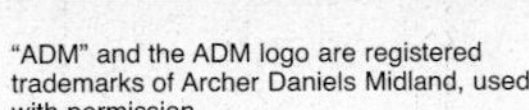
"ADM" and the ADM logo are registered trademarks of Archer Daniels Midland, used with permission.

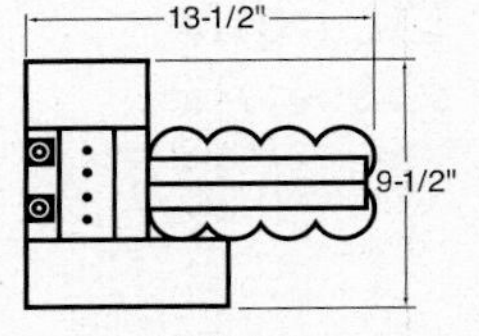

PRAIRIE STAR ELEVATOR 10" TALL
6"
6-3/4"

## PRAIRIE STAR ELEVATOR

**933-2927 34.98**

- Detailed "Wood" Walls
- Unique Large Capacity Building
- Perfect for Any Grain Handling Operations
- Use with Flour Mill Building (#933-2914) Sold Separately

## PRAIRIE STAR MILLING

**933-2914 64.98**

- Early 20th Century Design
- Use for Almost any Industry
- Authentic Styling & Trim
- One-Piece Smokestack
- Use with Flour Mill Elevator (#933-2927) Sold Separately

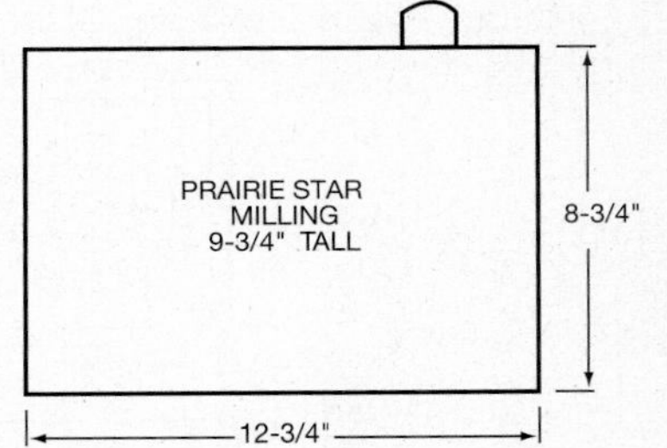

## COLUMBIA FEED MILL

**933-3090 36.98**

- Authetic gambrel-roof
- Separate two-story clapboard storage building with angled end wall
- Two concrete loading docks
- Realistic decals

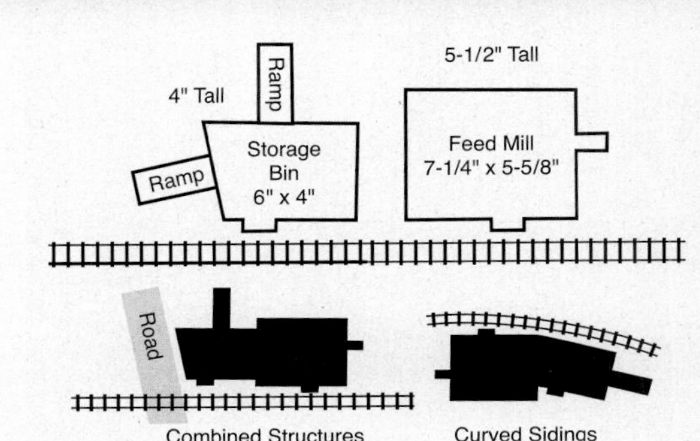


See What's Available at

**www.walthers.com**

## INTERSTATE FUEL & OIL

**933-3006 32.98**

- Fits cities and towns
- Easily arranged to fit available space
- Includes horizontal and vertical storage tanks, piping, pump house with header stand, truck loading rack and corrugated metal office
- Includes gas pump, oil drums and other details

933-3168

933-3167

## OIL STORAGE TANKS

**32.98 ea**

**933-3167** Wide

**933-3168** Tall

- Simulates 500,000-gallon tank
- Stairway molded to fit
- Includes modular berms and crossover stairways
- Colorful decals

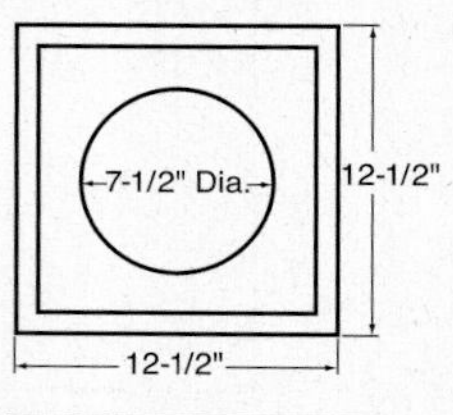


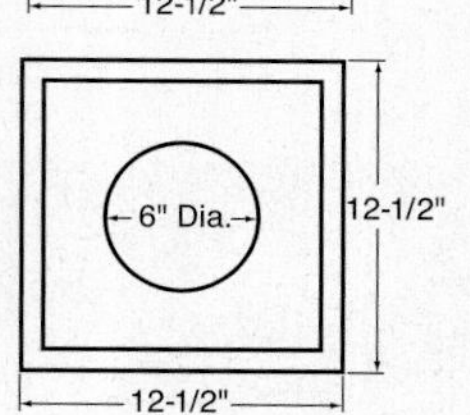


## MOTORIZING KIT

**933-1050 19.98**

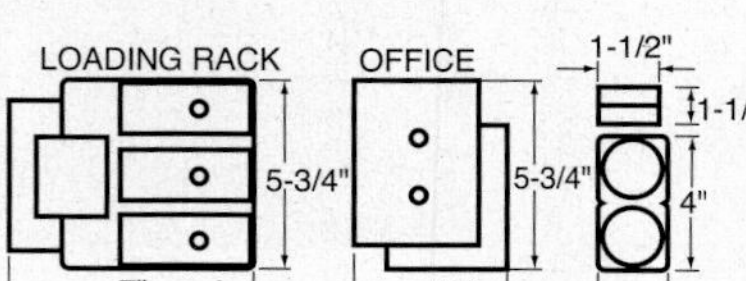


## OIL LOADING PLATFORM

**933-3104 11.98**

- Serves two tracks
- Complete with piping, nozzles, platforms and stairway
- Safety sign decals

Photo shows two kits combined to build a longer platform.

## REFINERY PIPING KIT

**933-3114 11.98**

- Give refinery scenes the busy look of the prototype
- Adaptable to other industries
- Includes overhead supports, angles and more
- Modular design

## PIPING KIT

**933-3105 10.98**

- Add individual pipelines to refinery scenes
- Adaptable to many large industries.
- Includes angles, elbows, tees, straight pipes, valves and more

## TRUCK LOADING RACK

**933-3169 29.98**

Finished model measures:
7 x 3-1/2 x 3-3/16"
17.8 x 8.9 x 8.1cm

- Includes piping, rack and awning

## MCGRAW OIL COMPANY

**933-2913 34.98**

- Four Vertical Tanks
- Two Brick Pumphouses
- Tank Car Unloading Rack
- Detailed Berms
- Colorful Decals for Several Dealerships

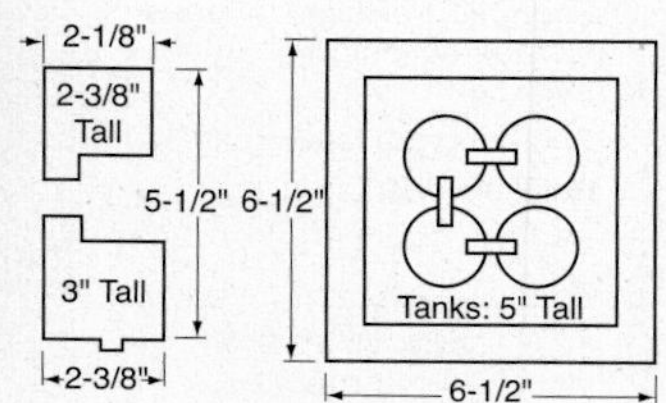

## OIL PUMP

**933-3170 24.98**

- Used in oil fields across the continent.
- Includes drive motor mounting bracket and gears for the addition of the Motorizing Kit
- Animate with Motorizing Kit 933-1050 (sold separately)
- Chain link fencing
- Colorful signs

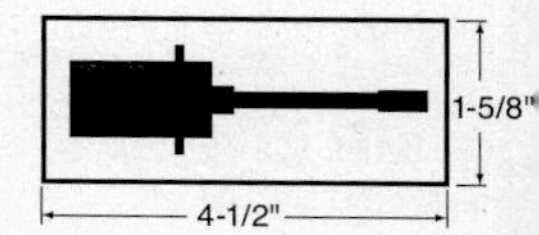

## CLAYTON COUNTY LUMBER

**933-2911 34.98**

- Four Complete Buildings — Use Together or Separately
- Authentic Corrugated Metal Detailing
- Angled Wall fits Inside or Outside of Curved Siding
- Perfect for Steam- or Diesel-Era Scenes
- Signs for Several Businesses Included

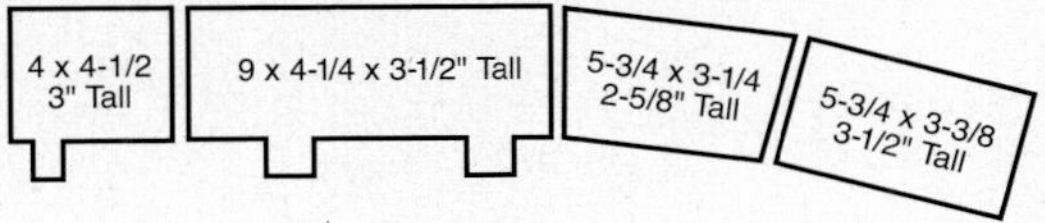

## SAWMILL OUTBUILDINGS

**933-3144** Set of Four **39.98**

- Four complete kits including Log Debarker, Wood Chipper, Rail Car Loader and Truck Woodchip Loader
- Comes complete with gravity-feed storage bin and blower details.

## MOUNTAIN LUMBER COMPANY SAWMILL

**933-3058 69.98**

- Includes Sawmill Building, Log Conveyor, Sawdust Burner, and Powerhouse
- Canopied area for timber sorting
- "Board & batten" siding and "corrugated metal" roofing

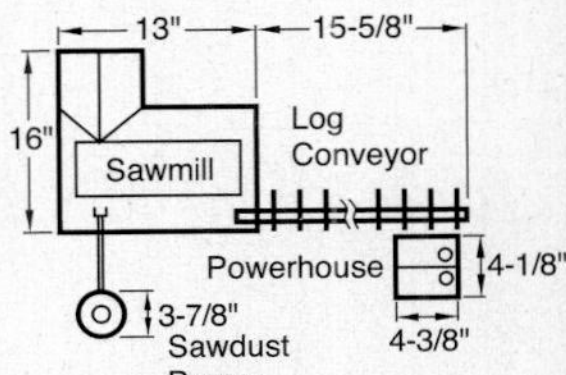


Tallest Item 8-1/2"

## WALTON & SONS LUMBER COMPANY

**933-3057 39.98**

- Found in every town
- Fits almost any available space
- Build one large covered or two open storage buildings
- Separate main office
- Colorful sign decal

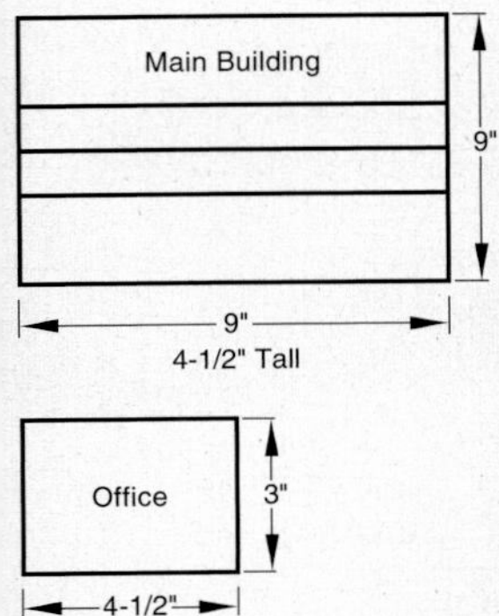


## LOG UNLOADER

**933-3146 19.98**

- Perfect for small logging operations
- Positionable trolley and lifting arms
- Use with Mountain Lumber Company Sawmill (933-3058)

## STERLING CONSOLIDATED DAIRY

**933-3799 179.98**

- Five Complete Structure Kits
- Build as Complete Complex or Individual Structures
- Smokestack, Water Tower & Coal Dump Included
- Decal Signs for Different Industries

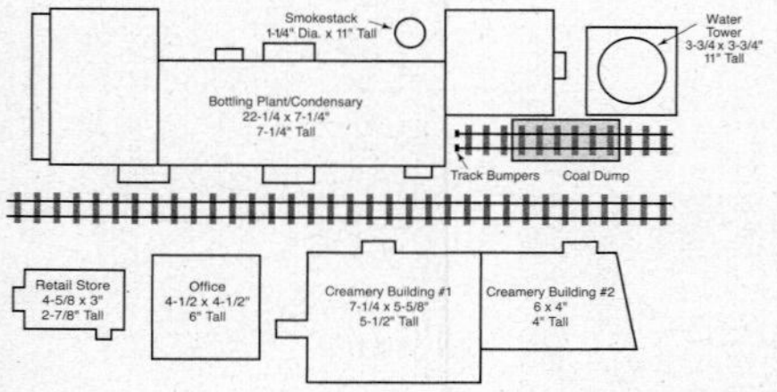

Smokestack 1-1/4" Dia. x 11" Tall
Water Tower 3-3/4 x 3-3/4" 11" Tall
Bottling Plant/Condensary 22-1/4 x 7-1/4" 7-1/4" Tall
Track Bumpers
Coal Dump
Retail Store 4-5/8 x 3" 2-7/8" Tall
Office 4-1/2 x 4-1/2" 6" Tall
Creamery Building #1 7-1/4 x 5-5/8" 5-1/2" Tall
Creamery Building #2 6 x 4" 4" Tall

## CO-OP STORAGE SHED

**933-3529 19.98**

- Great accessory for trackside businesses
- Fits any siding in any era
- Includes box car and truck loading doors
- Realistic printed signs

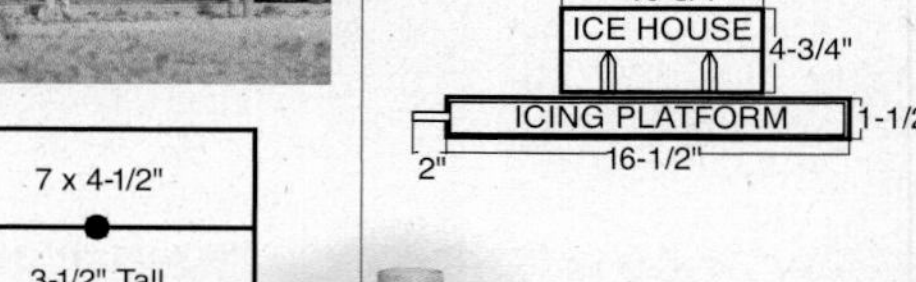

## ICE HOUSE AND ICING PLATFORM

**933-3049 30.98**

- Includes detailed Ice House and modular Icing Platform
- Add-on details include an optional platform roof, roof vents and 24 ice blocks

## VALLEY CEMENT

**933-3098 69.98**

- Everything to model a complete industry in one kit
- Fits steam- or diesel-era
- Includes bulk material storage building, corrugated-metal processing structures, concrete silos with attached hopper car loading facility, tall smokestack and covered conveyors.
- Rotary kiln is easily motorized with Walthers Motorizing Kit, 933-1050 (sold separately)



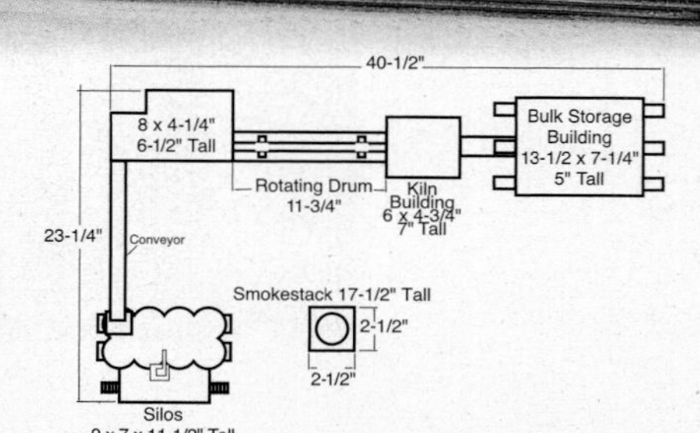

## EMD 567 PRIME MOVER

**933-3119 4.98**

- Easy to build
- A great detail for the shop floor or as a car load

## MAGIC PAN BAKERIES

**933-2915 54.98**

- Contemporary Industrial Structure
- Fits Any Region
- Separate Main Building, Storage Silos & More
- Easily Arranged to Fit Available Space

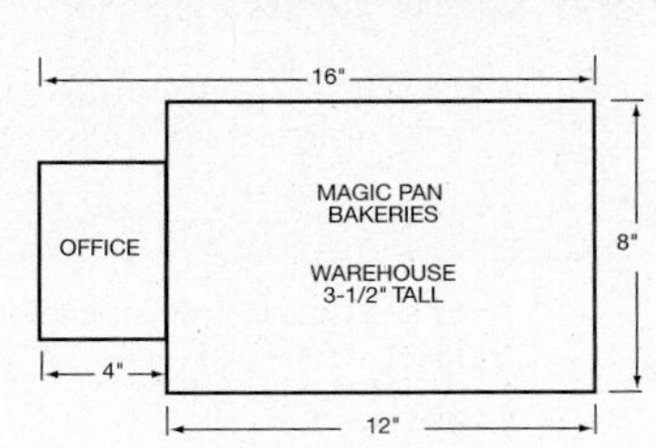


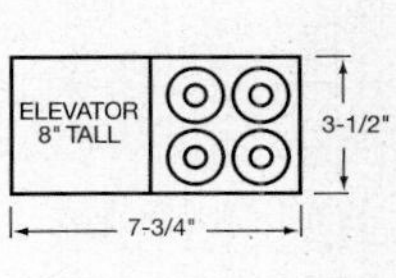

## LAKEVILLE WAREHOUSING

**933-2917 44.98**

- Perfect for Contemporary Industrial Parks
- Use for Any Type of Warehouse Operations
- Authentic 10' Dock Doors

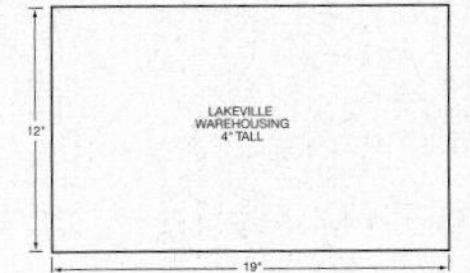

## OVERHEAD TRAVELING CRANE

**933-3102 14.98**

- Positionable bridge and covered motor housing
- Use with your industries, scrapyards, steel mills and railroad shops
- Includes Operator's cab with "glass," hoist hooks and a nonworking electromagnet

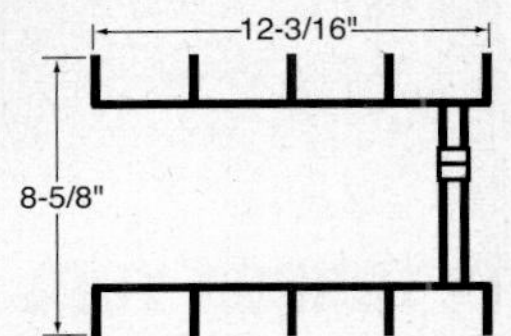

## GREATLAND SUGAR REFINING

**933-3092 54.98**

- Fits layouts spanning 1900s to 1980s
- Includes three-story processing plant, boilerhouse and warehouse
- Special track insert included to simulate beet dump
- Colorful sign decals

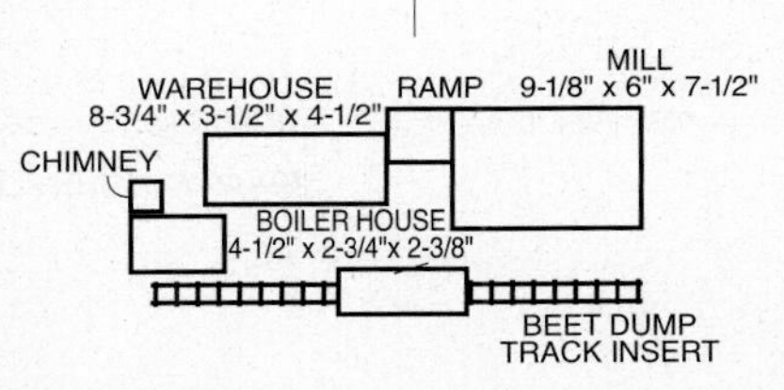

## VALLEY CITRUS PACKERS

**933-2926 39.98**

- Fits Steam- or Diesel-Era
- Authentic "Wood" Construction
- Unique Trackside Industrial Structure

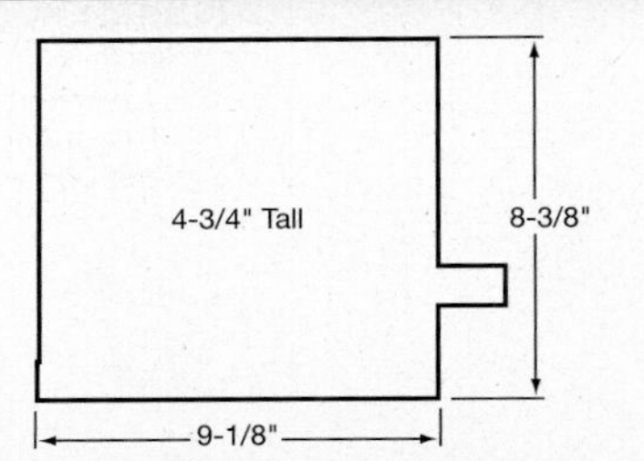

## AMERICAN HARDWARE SUPPLY

933-3097 49.98

- Fits layouts covering the early 20th century to the present
- Easy to modify with included optional loading doors, windows and solid brick panels
- Modular design makes it easy to combine kits
- Includes a concrete railroad loading dock
- Colorful signs for a variety of businesses

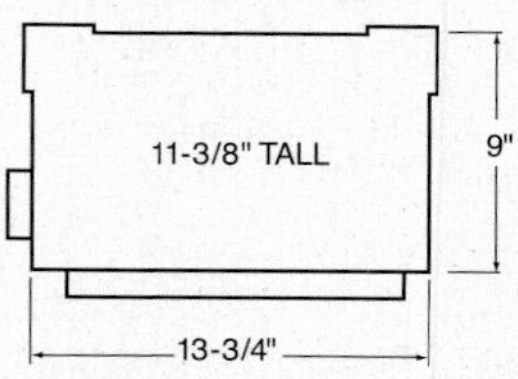

## PETERSON TOOL SPECIALTIES

933-3091 49.98

- Includes ground-level truck freight doors (with a sloped ramp) and conventional raised dock doors the same height as a trailer floor
- Features "steel" and "concrete" construction
- Modular design makes it easy to combine kits
- Colorful signs

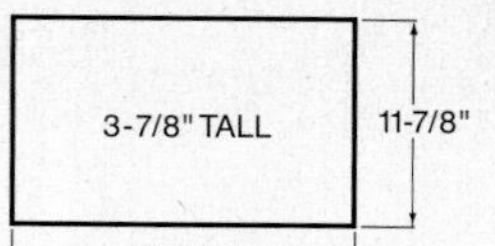


## OLD TIME COAL CONVEYORS

933-3520 pkg(3) 9.98

- Suitable for unloading bulk materials from hopper cars
- Use for unloading coal, grain fertilizer, gravel, sand and other products

## ROLLING MILL

933-3052 49.98

- Use with steel works or as large modern factory building
- Modular design
- Optional cut-out end doors and walls
- Baseplate includes simulated rails
- Includes both full-length monitor-type and individual round roof vents

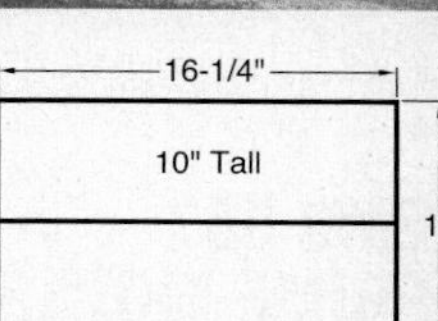

## MIDSTATE MARBLE PRODUCTS

933-3073 39.98

- Includes detailed main building, overhead crane with craneway supports, bridge and operator's cab, positionable derrick and machine house
- Other uses include a carshop for a shortline, logging or industrial railroad; a heavy equipment garage; a maintenance building for trucks or buses; a wagon works; or a machine shop

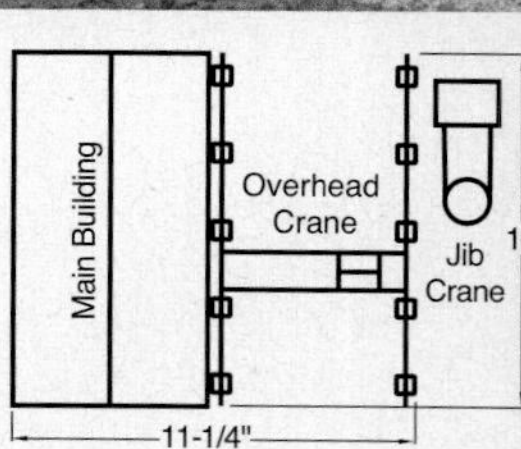


Main Building: 4 1/2" Tall

## TEAM TRACK

RETIRED MODEL

**933-3166** Basic Kit Only
**29.98**
Some details shown not included.

- Versatile kit that works with any HO Scale depot or freight station, and most industries
- Includes small clerk's office, positionable gantry crane, a large ramp, a portable conveyor, 160' of wood fencing, other small details and realistic decals

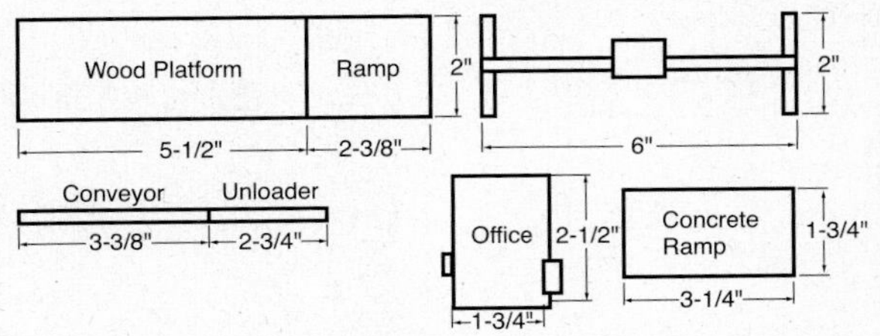

## CHAMPION PACKING COMPANY

**933-3048 44.98**

- Includes multi-story building with elevated cattle chute, attached office, power plant, roof-top details and four dressed beef
- Colorful decals

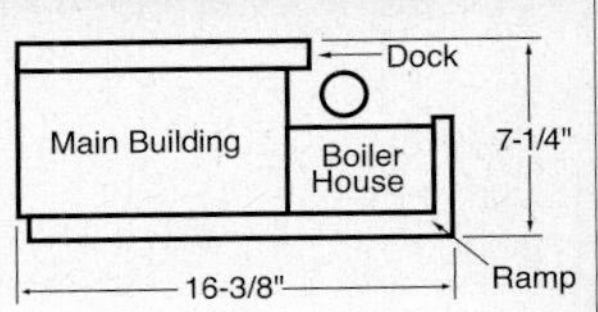


## BEEF CATTLE

**933-3143** pkg(16) **6.98**

- Features 16 Hereford steers in realistic poses

## STOCKYARD

**933-3047 24.98**

- Includes detailed parts for two pens with loading chutes, which align with 40' stock cars, plus a lean-to for shelter or feeding

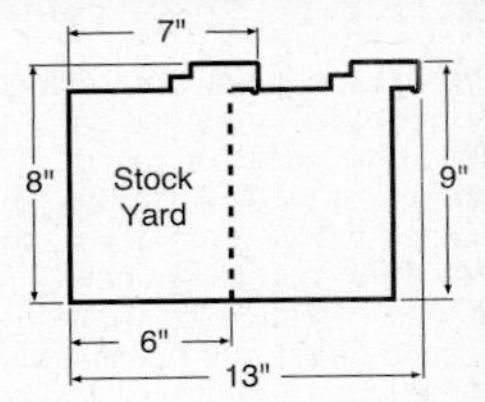

## FREIGHT HOUSE DETAILS

RETIRED MODEL

**933-3513** Complete Set **19.98**

- Highly detailed resin castings
- Includes a pair of tow motors, five freight wagons, two pallet jacks, two platform scales and three hand trucks

## BACKGROUND BUILDING KITS

- Add New Dimensions To Your Background Scenes
- Create Complete Industries In Less Than 6"
- Great For scenes With Limited Room
- Molded Cut Lines For Simple Customizing
- Fits Most Popular Modeling Eras

Finally! There's a quick, affordable way to add scenery anywhere space is limited - without the added time and trouble of kitbashing!

Background Building Walls let you use that last little bit of space to create a realistic background for any industrial area. These kits can be used on the edge of your benchwork, along a shelf or modular layout and in dioramas. Once installed, they provide a smooth, realistic transition between 3-D foreground scenes and printed or painted backgrounds. (Check out the complete listing of Instant Horizons™ printed backgrounds in the Scenery Section for more ideas on creating a backdrop for your layout.)

Based on popular Cornerstone Series® structures, you can build them stock or easily customize them. Each has scribed cut lines molded on the inside so you can cut new angles or reduce the width to fit your pike. Each building also comes with a variety of add-on details, a partial roof and colorful sign decals.

## IMPERIAL FOODS

**933-3184 24.98**

- Based on a typical early-1900s structure
- Includes the brick packing house front with canopied loading dock, rooftop water tank and realistic decals

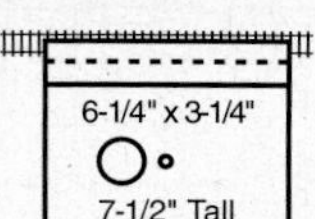

## TOMASO'S MARKET

**933-3179 21.98**

- Features a three-story brick storefront with parts molded in appropriate colors plus realistic decals

4-1/8 x 2-1/2"
6-1/2" Tall

## COMMISSARY/ FREIGHT TRANSFER

**933-3173 29.98**

- Includes canopied loading dock and decal signs

6-1/8" Tall
12-5/8"

## CENTENNIAL MILLS

**933-3160 24.98**

- Building Back
- Includes a covered loading dock, fire escape ladder and wall-mounted dust collectors

8-7/16" Tall
10"

## RIVER CITY TEXTILES

**933-3178 34.98**

- Represents the loading-dock side of an early-1900s curtain-wall factory or warehouse building
- Details include rooftop water tank, elevator headhouse and decals for several business names.
- Sectional main wall allows you to combine kits for a longer background building

12-7/8" x 2-3/8"
11-1/8" TALL

## ARMSTRONG ELECTRIC MOTORS

### Building Back

**933-3172 32.98**

- Includes the railroad side of a typical brick curtain-wall factory building with large, multi-paned windows and a canopied trackside loading dock for box cars
- Modular wall sections make it easy to customize to fit on your layout or module
- Components in this versatile kit can make one of the following structures of your choice:

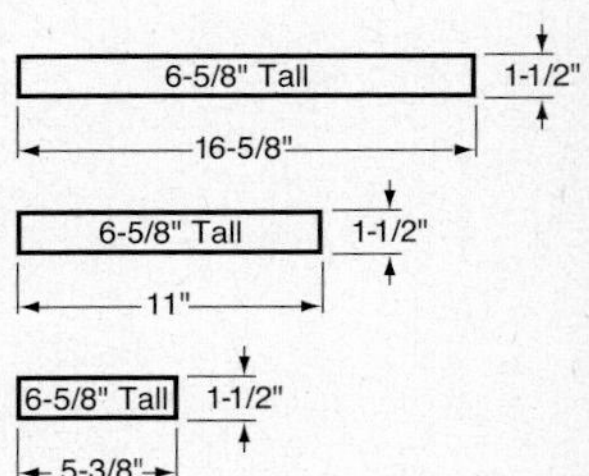

## SHOP BUILDING NO. 1

### Building Back

**933-3165 29.98**

- Use as a steel fabricator, warehouse, assembly plant or any commercial building you can imagine
- Inside spur allows you to lay track into the building for the perfect way to access hidden storage/staging tracks or simulate loads-in/empties-out operations

7" Tall
3-1/4"
11-9/16"

Heritage Furniture Building Back
933-3164

Shop Building No. 1 Building Back
933-3165

## HERITAGE FURNITURE

### Building Back

**933-3164 29.98**

- Great by itself or as a warehouse for a larger plant.
- Features a covered freight car loading dock

9" Tall
4-3/4"
11-3/8"

## PARKVIEW TERRACE APARTMENTS

### Building Back

**933-3176** Brown w/Light Gray Trim **29.98**

**933-3177** Tuscan w/Dark Green Trim **29.98**

- Appropriate for the steam-era through the present
- Easily shortened using cut lines molded on the inside
- Each building comes with a variety of add-on details, a partial roof and colorful decals

6" TALL
2-3/16"
7-3/4"

## FIREPROOF STORAGE & TRANSFER

933-3189 24.98

- Fits All Popular Eras
- Separate Doors & Windows
- Use for Any Business

12-1/4 x 7/8 x 7-1/4" Tall

## PLANT NO. 4 BACKGROUND BUILDING

933-3183 24.98

6 x 2-1/4 x 7-1/2" Tall

- Adds Big City Detail to Limited Layout Space
- Use as Stand Alone Detail or with Additional Background Buildings
- Fits All Popular Modeling Eras
- Realistic Decal Signs

## AUTO PLANT

933-3191 Windowed Walls **29.98**

933-3192 Solid Walls **29.98**

- Available in Two Styles
- Perfect for Contemporary Industrial Parks
- Model Any Modern Industry

19 x 1-1/8 x 4" Tall

## ARROWHEAD AL

933-3193 24.98

- Fits Steam- or Diesel-Era Layouts
- Separate Loading Docks

4-5/8" Tall
2-
12-1/4"

## THE BRALICK BUILDING

**933-3099 39.98**

- Looks great in a post-1970s business district
- Includes modern windows, wall inserts to close off the loading dock area and a rooftop water tank support (the complete water tank is also included)
- Colorful signs for easy customizing

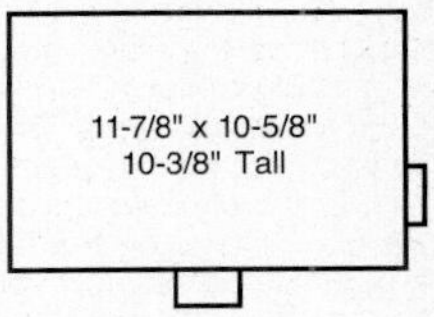

11-7/8" x 10-5/8"
10-3/8" Tall

## MODERN WATER TOWER

**933-3528 17.98**

- Features body with realistic weld lines, plus a service door entrance and overflow pipe at the base.
- Decals for three different town names

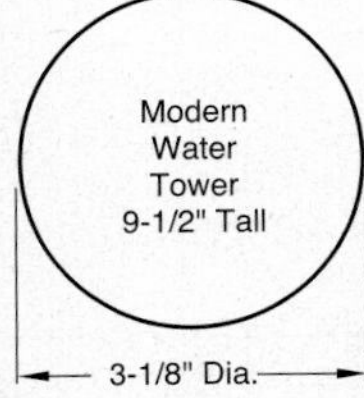


## AL'S VICTORY SERVICE STATION

**933-3072 21.98**

- Build this kit three ways! Steam, classic diesel or modern era
- Includes gas pumps for 1930- 40s, 1950-60s and 1970-80s
- Two different styles of signs
- Includes colorful decals

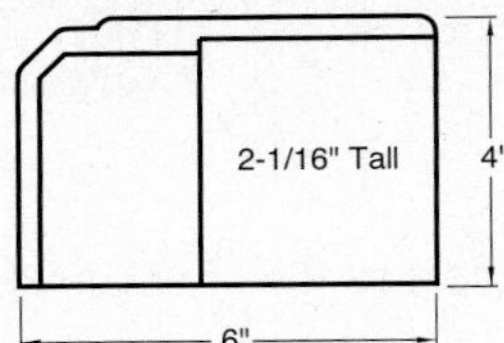

## GAS STATION DETAIL KITS

**RETIRED MODEL**

**20.98 ea**

**933-3501** Vintage
**933-3502** Modern

*WALTHERS EXCLUSIVE*

## 1940S PD K103 INTERCITY GREYHOUND BUS

**21.98 ea**

**221-32101** New York City
**221-32102** Los Angeles
**221-32103** Chicago
**221-32104** Blank
**221-32105** Union Pacific

## SILVER SPRINGS TERMINAL

**933-2934 39.98**

- All-New Model
- Typical of Bus Stations in Small Cities or Towns
- Fits 1940s to Present
- Authentic "Brick" Exterior
- Covered Boarding Area
- Colorful Signs

## WELCOME TO MAIN STREET USA

Every town has a Main Street USA. And everyone has memories of the Main Street in his or her hometown. It might be the ice cream parlor where you had your first triple scoop cone, or the dime store you rode your bike to on Saturdays for baseball cards. Now you can recapture the excitement and nostalgia of Main Street on your layout with the Cornerstone Series® "Main Street USA" collection.

Each kit is easy to build, with styrene parts molded in colors, including a roof and numerous details. All of the architectural features such as trim, windows and doors, are molded in place to speed construction. Each kit also includes full-color decals with a wide range of business names so you can build a custom structure, or model several versions of the same kit.

### Don's Shoe Store

**933-3000 14.98**

Dimensions: 2-1/2 x 3-1/2 x 3-3/8" 6.2 x 8.7 x 8.2cm

### State Line Farm Supply

**933-2912 34.98**

- One-Piece Front Wall w/Optional Windows & Doors
- Two Rear Walls w/Large Doors or Windows
- Separate "Wood" Loading Ramp
- Decals for Additional Businesses
- Oil & Fuel Tanks Included

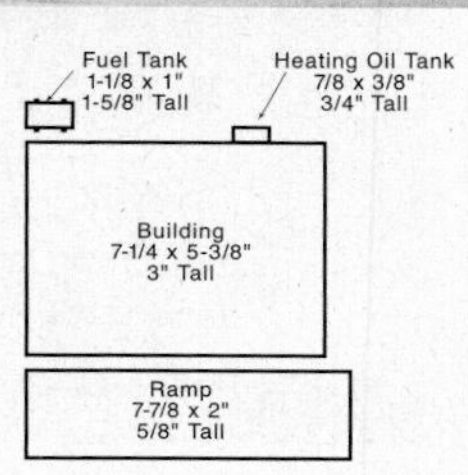

### Bill's Glass Shop

**933-3002 14.98**

This three-story brick building has plenty of space for a growing HO Scale business. The upper floors can be rented out for additional offices or apartments.

Dimensions: 3 x 4 x 4-3/8" 7.5 x 10 x 16.7cm

### Adam's Ribs Restaurant

**933-3034 17.98**

From the turn of the century to the present, buildings like this have been an integral part of many neighborhoods. The kit is ideal for any busy street corner and includes a distinctive corner tower/entryway.

Dimensions: 5-1/2 x 3 x 6" 13.7 x 7.5 x 15cm

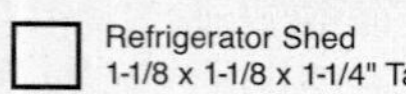

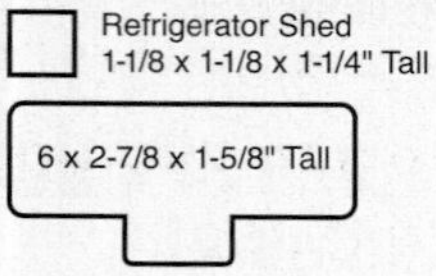

### Miss Bettie's Diner

**933-2909 29.98**

- Complete Interior with Tables, Stools & Counter
- Great for Layouts from the 40s to the Present
- Authentic "Stainless Steel" Construction
- Outdoor Refrigerator Shed
- Colorful Signs

## JIM'S REPAIR SHOP

**933-3527 19.98**

- Makes a great storefront, rural factory, restaurant, bait shop and more
- Includes realistic decals

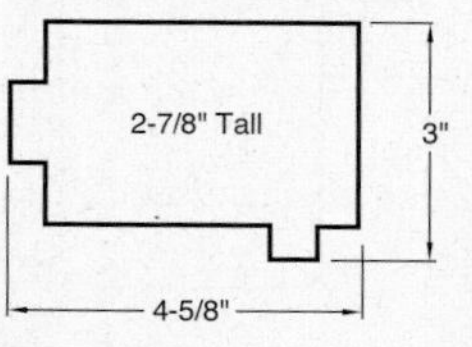

### Bailey Savings & Loan

**933-3031 29.98**

- Easy-to-build
- Realistic cut stone stone facade
- Authentic Beaux arts architectural styling
- Suitable for steam- or diesel-era layouts
- Parts molded in realistic colors

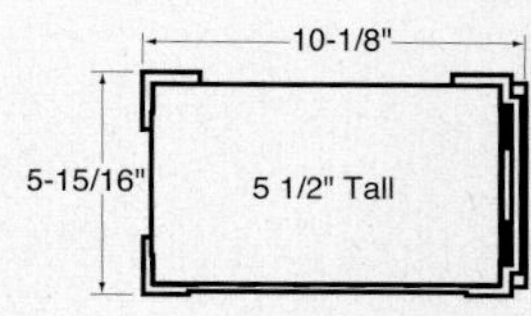

## Western Avenue Fire Station

**933-3037 17.98**

- Perfect for early 1900s through today
- Includes a special set of fire station decals

Dimensions:
4-1/4 x 6-3/4 x 5-3/4"
10.6 x 16.8 x 14.3cm

## White Tower Restaurant

**933-3030 14.98**

Dimensions: 4-5/8 x 3 x 2-7/8"
11.5 x 7.5 x 7cm

## Southtown HI-FI

**933-2919 24.98**

- All-New Model
- Parts for Original or Brick Storefront Versions
- Authentic Design and Details
- Unique Addition to any Post-War Business District

Original: 6-9/16 x 2-3/4" x 1-3/8" Tall
Brick Storefront: 6-11/16 x 2-13/16" x 2-/16" Tall

## Merchant's Row I

**933-3028 29.98**
Five different stores in one complete structure.

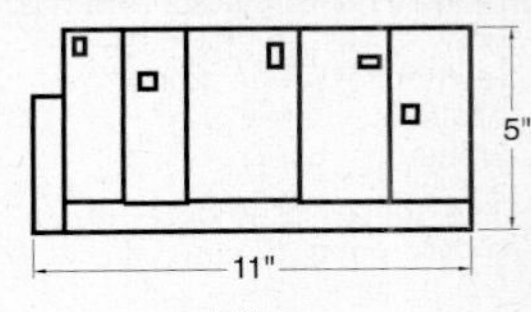


4" Tall

## Merchant's Row II

**933-3029 29.98**
Three storefronts, highlighted by an elaborate corner building with turret.

10-1/2"
5-13/16"
6 1/4" Tall

## Merchant's Row III

**933-3064 19.98**
Based on a real building in eastern Ohio, with three small businesses under one roof.

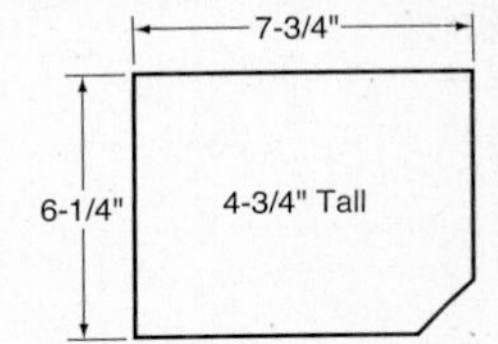

## STREET SYSTEMS

### 12.98 ea

Walthers street system makes quick and easy work of modeling everything from busy downtowns, to tree-lined residential areas, to narrow alleyways in the grimy industrial district.

The secret is the detailed plastic parts, that install just like sectional track. Glue the sections together. Add sidewalks, curbs and other details. Weather for more realism (if desired) and install on your layout. #933-3139 and #933-3138 include approximately 25" (63cm) of roadway. Parts for one complete intersection, sidewalks, curbs, driveway and alley entrances, plus complete instructions are included.

Straight sets include eight sections of straight streets only and one set of curbs.

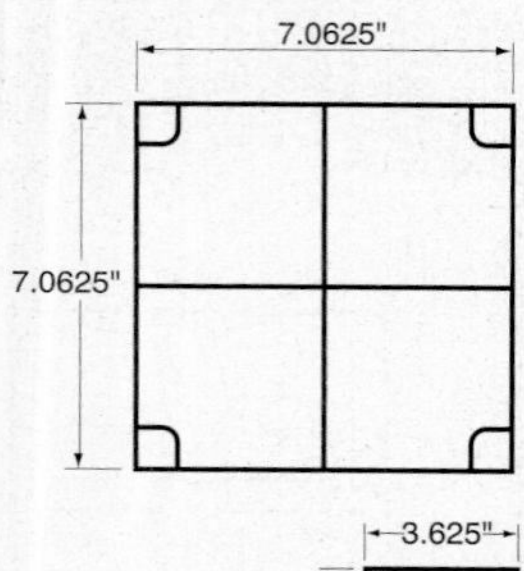


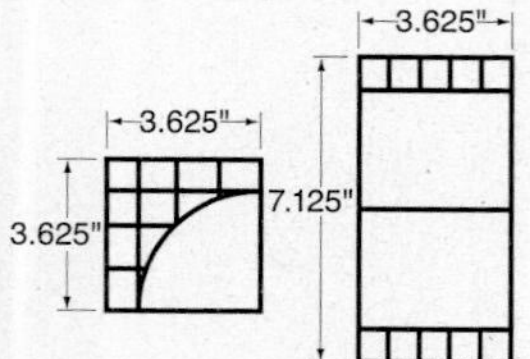


### Concrete

**933-3138** Full Set **12.98**

**933-3155** Straight Sections Only **11.98**

- Perfect for modern steam-era highway, or a modern stretch of road
- Features realistic texture and center crown for ultimate realism

### Brick

**933-3139** Full Set **12.98**

**933-3156** Straight Sections Only **11.98**

- Authentic detail for steam-era street scenes or older parts of a modern city
- Simulated brick-by-brick construction

### Asphalt 12.98 ea

**933-3194** Full Set

**933-3195** Straight Sections Only

- Realistic Color & Texture
- Includes Curves, Straights, Sidewalks & More
- Compatible with Other Street System Products
- Assembles like Sectional Track
- Build Realistic Roads in Minutes

### Street Track Insert Set

**933-3140 19.98**

- Sized to fit Code 83 track
- Includes straight sections, plus pieces for 15, 18 and 22" radius curves and parts to fit #4 and 18" radius turnouts
- Simulated concrete detail matches Walthers Street System kits #933-3138 (Concrete) or #933-3139 (Brick), both sold separately

### Grade Crossing

**933-3137 6.98**

- Detailed parts replicate rubber mat style
- Use on large and small railroads
- Ideal for use with Code 83 track

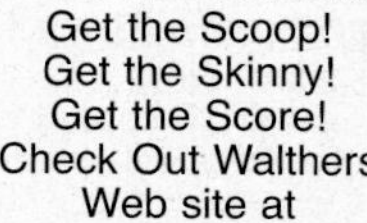

### Street System - Arched Road Bridge

**933-3196 24.98**

- Use with Brick, Concrete or Asphalt Street System
- Fine Railings & Details
- Fits Steam-Era to Present D

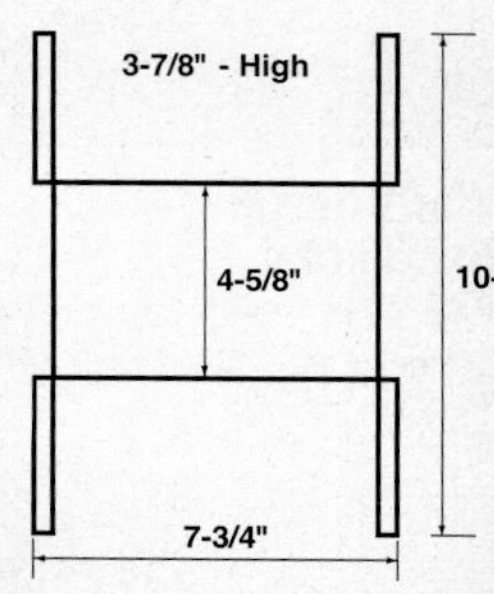

# INDUSTRIAL DETAILS

- Easy-to-build kits
- Plastic parts molded in colors, or detailed resin castings you can paint yourself
- Complete instructions included

## Track Bumpers

**933-3511** pkg(12) **9.98**

- Easy-to build kits feature plastic parts molded in realistic color
- Simply snap into place when complete

## Cargo Set

**590-17100 13.99**

Keep your loading docks busy with this assortment of boxes, barrels, sacks, milk cans, labels and more.

## Oil Drum & Figure Set

**933-3100 11.98**

- Includes 36 oil drums (six each molded in red, silver, blue, yellow, green and black) plus three hand-painted figures and a two-wheel freight dolly

## Wall-Mount Dust Collectors

**933-3510 9.98**

- Highly detailed resin castings

## Wood Water Tanks

**933-3507** pkg(3) **9.98**

- Parts for three complete tanks
- Detailed plastic parts look like real wood and are molded in colors.
- Separate roof and supports are also included

## Chain-Link Fence

**933-3125 11.98**

- Styrene poles, gates and details.
- Fine mesh chain-link material included
- Builds about 80" of fence
- Combine kits for longer areas

## One-Piece Brick Smokestack

**933-3728** Set of 2 **15.98**

- Used at all kinds of industries
- Fits steam- and diesel-eras
- Molded in one piece — no seam to hide
- Optional baseplate and trim ring
- Fine brick detail
- Molded in realistic color
- Easy upgrade for many structure kits

## City Accessory Package

**933-3535 9.98**

- Realistic Details
- ATMs, Fire Hydrants, Bike Racks, Parking Meters & More
- Resin & Etched-Metal Parts

COMING SOON!

**Spring 2008 Delivery**

## Inter-Track Fencing

**NEW 933-2952 24.98**

- Photo-Etched Brass Parts
- Near Scale Thickness
- Includes Fencing, Gates & Brackets
- Build w/Gates Open or Closed
- Great Detail for City Station Scenes

## Wooden Fencing

**933-3521** pkg(3) **10.98**

- Highly detailed plastic parts feature realistic wood grain
- Includes three 15" 37.5cm long sections

## Industrial Tank Set

**933-3514 10.98**

- Great for rooftops or alongside a factory building
- Includes a pair of vertical tanks with connecting piping, a wall-mount tank with regulator/compressor detail, a small horizontal tank with piping (that can be run to the ground or into a building) and a large horizontal storage tank with pedestals

## Yard Office

**933-3517 11.98**

- Includes corrugated guard shack, positionable gates, stop and other warning signs too
- Great for busy parking lots, rail yards, intermodal terminals, steel works, auto plants, military installations or other major industry

## Brick Sheets pkg(4) 9.98 ea

Plastic sheets match style and color of brick in Cornerstone Series® kits. 4 x 9.5" 10 x 23.75cm 1mm thick.

**933-3522** Light Brick Red

**933-3523** Dark Brick Red

**933-3524** Dark Cream

## Safety Cage Ladders & Wall Vents

**933-3515** 5 Each **9.98**

- Great for modernizing older buildings or detailing contemporary structures
- Includes five complete ladder and cage assemblies and five wall-mounted vents

## Dumpster Set

**933-3516** pkg(8) **11.98**

- Great detail for the back alley of any commercial area, industrial district, railroad shop, school
- Includes two large roll-off dumpsters, two medium roll-off bodies and four scrap metal slide-off dumpsters.

## Industrial Substation

**933-3506 20.98**

- Includes three transformers, distribution rack with detailed insulators and fencing
- Major parts are detailed resin castings

Division of
Wm. K. Walthers, Inc.

These easy-to-build structures feature plastic parts molded in colors and hand-painted details.

Trackside Shanties 433-1348

Scene Maker Expander Set 433-1739

Woodlawn Police Station 433-1382

## SCENE MAKER EXPANDER SET

**433-1739 38.00**
Includes trees, building kit, passenger station, utility poles and vehicles.

## STATIONS & PLATFORMS

### Train Station

**433-1347 8.75**
2 x 11-5/8" 5.1 x 29.5cm

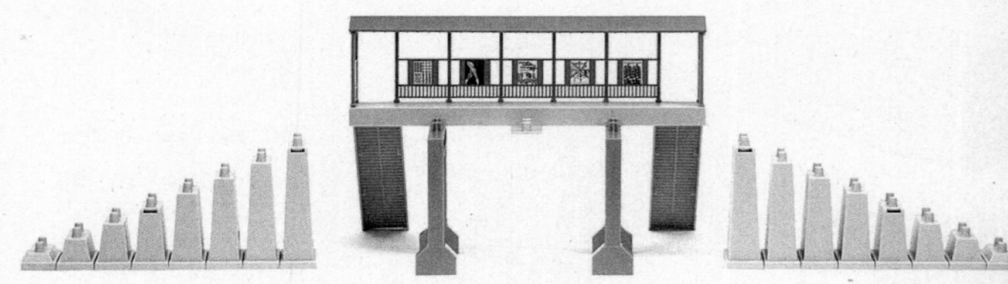

Snap-Loc Elevated Commuter Passenger Station 433-1376

Snap-Loc Commuter Passenger Station 433-1381

### Snap-Loc® Passenger Station

**433-1352 10.75**

### Snap-Loc Elevated Commuter Passenger Station

**433-1376** With 18 Piers **27.00**

### Snap-Loc Commuter Passenger Station

**433-1381 10.75**

## YARD EQUIPMENT & FACILITIES

### Trackside Shanties

**433-1348 8.75**
Includes one of each: Line Shack (2 x 2-1/4" 5.1 x 5.9cm), Switchman's Shanty (1-5/8 x 2-1/8" 4 x 5.5cm) and Whistle Stop (2 x 2-1/4" 5.1 x 5.9cm).

## RURAL BUILDINGS

### Snap-Loc Stock Pen

**433-1378 13.00**
5-7/8 x 5-7/8" 14.9 x 14.9cm

For Daily Product Updates Point Your Browser to
**www.walthers.com**

### Western Homestead

**433-1338 15.25**
7-3/4 x 5-1/2" 19.7 x 14cm

## HOUSES

### House Lighting Kit

**433-1205 4.75**
Working lights will add drama and action to your entire layout, and this economical kit makes it easy to install lighting in almost any building. It's completely assembled, with screw-type bulb, socket with hook-up wires and a plastic mounting base, which can be nailed to your layout surface, or glued inside your buildings.

## CITY BUILDINGS

### Downtown Business Center

**433-1373 13.50**
6-1/4 x 8-3/8 x 4-1/2"
15.6 x 20.9 x 11.2cm

Revitalize your downtown with this new building. The first floor is home to an Italian restaurant, a phone communications company and a barber shop, while the upstairs is leased to a bowling alley. Realistic signs, a chimney and a roof-mounted air conditioner are all included.

### Woodlawn Police Station

**433-1382 13.50**
6-1/4 x 8-3/8" 15.9 x 21.3cm

### Hampden Fire Engine House #46

**433-1390 13.50**
6-1/4 x 8-3/8" 15.9 x 21.3cm

## TANKS & TOWERS

433-8304 433-8305

### Flashing Light Storage Tank

**433-8304 16.25**
2-7/8" 7.3cm square
With blinking light and graffiti decals.

### Lighted Yard Tower

**433-8305 16.25**
2-7/8" 7.3cm square
Includes working light.

Division of Wm. K. Walthers, Inc.

## CHURCHES

**Town Church**
**433-1350 8.75**
5 x 6" 12.8 x 15.3cm

## BUSINESSES

**Ace Super Market**
**433-1330 13.50**
5-1/2 x 9-3/8 x 3-1/2"
13.7 x 23.7 x 8.7cm

Part of the urban landscape for decades, convenience stores like this can be found in virtually any town. Detailed model is complete with ads for the windows, a full interior with shelves, cash registers and an ice machine, plus phone booth and a loading door in the rear.

**Mt Vernon Manufacturing Co.**
**433-1337 15.25**
8-1/4 x 5-1/2" 21 x 14cm

Modular design allows for easy kitbashing.

**Belvedere Downtown Hotel**
**433-1339 15.25**
5-1/2 x 2-1/2" 14 x 64cm

**General Store**
**433-1351 8.75**
6 x 4-7/8" 15.2 x 12.4cm

**Kentucky Fried Chicken® Drive-In**
**433-1394 13.50**
8-3/8 x 4-1/4" 21.3 x 10.8cm

## INDUSTRIAL

**National Oil Co.**
**433-1331 13.50**
5-1/2 x 4-1/2 x 2-3/4"
13.7 x 11.2 x 6.8cm

Storage tanks like these can be found at lots of industries, railroad shops, or alongside bulk oil dealers. Kit includes two storage tanks which can be positioned together or used separately, a pump house, barrels, tools and wood stacks.

**Coaling Tower**
**433-1377 28.00**

**Supply House**
**433-1398 28.00**

For Up-To-Date Information and News Bookmark Walthers Web site at
**www.walthers.com**

**Operating Gravel Unloader w/Dump Car**
**433-8204 18.00**
6-5/8 x 5-1/2" 16.8 x 14cm
Includes gravel.

**Operating Logging Mill**
**433-8311 40.50**
12 x 7-3/4" 30.5 x 19.7cm

Includes dump car, logs and log pond.

## BRIDGES & VIADUCTS

**Bridge & Trestle Set**
**433-8202 11.50**

**Arch Span Bridge**
**433-8207 20.50**
18-5/8 x 5-1/4" 46.6 x 13.1cm

## TRAIN SET EXPANDER VALUE PACKS

Detailing your layout has never been easier! A complete railroad setting in one box – from structures to rolling stock, from figures to vehicles!

**Railroad Corral**
**433-1743 35.25**
Includes stock pen, train station, stock car, railroad signs, farm workers and cows.

Ace Super Market 433-1330

Kentucky Fried Chicken® Drive-In 433-1394

## POWER-LOC™ OPERATING ACCESSORIES

Make any model railroad more fun with these working structures! Models are designed for Power-Loc track-and-roadbed system, but are compatible with standard track.

433-8214

433-8306

**Bridge/Pier Set**
**433-8214 17.50**

**Operating Coal Tipple**
**433-8306 22.75**
Includes hopper, scale coal and a handy pick-up tray to catch spills.

433-8307

433-8308

**Gravel Unloader**
**433-8307 18.00**
A detailed plastic building hides the mechanical dump, which you control with a lever. Complete with operating dump car and simulated gravel load, plus gravel storage bin.

**Log Dump Station**
**433-8308 18.00**
Car loads of lumber arrive and drop logs for the mill at this busy siding. Includes a small building, lever dump, working log dump car, logs and storage bin.

# FALLER

IMPORTED FROM GERMANY BY WALTHERS

## NEW PRODUCTS

### Ready-Made Models

Ready for your layout, Faller's fully assembled models feature the same fine details and weathering as their kits but without all the work. Just unwrap, install and enjoy!

### Stations & Platforms

#### Waldbrun Station

**NEW 272-193099 61.99**
9-7/16 x 5 x 5-5/16"
24 x 12.5 x 13.5cm

A cast-iron roofed platform accents this typical brick station that makes a great addition to any town.

### Yard Equipment & Facilities

#### Mittelstadt Yard Tower

**NEW 272-193120 33.99**
3-5/16 x 2-7/16 x 4"
8.3 x 6.2 x 10.1cm

Multi-paned windows, a brick exterior and an outside staircase are featured in this two-story tower.

#### Goods Depot

**NEW 272-193154 44.99**
8-1/4 x 3-1/4 x 3-1/2"
20.9 x 8.2 x 9cm

Rustic wooden freight house features a trackside loading dock and a covered open area for outside storage.

#### Engine House

**NEW 272-193161 75.99**
12 x 6-7/16 x 5-7/16"
30.5 x 16.4 x 13.8cm

Nicely detailed two-stall engine house is painted and weathered for instant realism.

### Rural Buildings

#### Falkeneck Hunter's Lodge

**NEW 272-193385 85.99**
7-3/8 x 5-5/16 x 8-7/8"
18.8 x 13.4 x 22.5cm

A drawbridge entrance leads to this country castle. The impressive building features half-timbered upper stories, towers and verandas and balconies for relaxing.

### Houses

#### Rural Half-Timbered House

**NEW 272-193270 66.99**
5-3/16 x 3-13/16 x 3-1/2"
13.2 x 9.7 x 9cm

Wooden shutters, flower-filled window boxes and a covered porch give this cottage a cozy feel.

#### Boarding House

**NEW 272-131332 34.99**
4-9/16 x 4-3/16 x 5-1/8"
11.6 x 10.6 x 13cm

City residents will find a charming place to live in this three-story residence that features a small attached one-stall garage with a rooftop deck.

#### Black Forest House

**NEW 272-131333 34.99**
5-3/16 x 5-5/8 x 4"
13.2 x 14.3 x 10.2cm

Create a delightful country scene in minutes with this chalet-style home that comes with its own fountain and a small milk house.

### Churches

#### Village Church

**NEW 272-131321 39.99**
5-3/16 x 2-13/16 x 9"
13.1 x 7.2 x 22.8cm

This charming church features a tall steeple with a clock and an onion-shaped spire.

### Industrial

#### Cement Works

**NEW 272-193474 68.99**
8-1/8 x 3-1/2 x 8-7/8"
20.7 x 9 x 22.5cm

Model is complete with an office building, a supply silo and a passageway for truck loading.

Cement Works 272-193474

Goods Shed 272-120248

### Kits

Easy-to-build kits feature prototypically colored plastic parts, great details, printed signs and fully illustrated step-by-step instructions.

### Stations & Platforms

#### Gera-Liebschwitz Station

**NEW 272-110117 119.99**
3 x 7-1/2 x 6-5/16"
7.5 x 19 x 16cm

Traditional-style cinder-block station features two-story main building with adjoining goods shed and waiting room.

#### Loading Gauge & Milk Platform

**NEW 272-120227 25.99**

Loading Gauge: 2-3/8 x 1-3/16 x 2-5/16" 6 x 3 x 5.8cm

Platform: 6-7/8 x 1/2 x 1/2" 17.3 x 1.4 x 1.3cm

This non-operating model checks the weight and width of freight cars right on the track. Kit includes a loading platform with 20 milk pails.

### Yard Equipment and Facilities

#### Electric Engine Shed

**NEW 272-120217 136.99**
14-3/16x 10 x 4-1/2"
36.1 x 25.2 x 11.3cm

Accommodates three tracks and handles engines up to 12-3/16" 310mm in length. Catenary operation is possible. Modular design allows expansion with additional kits, sold separately. Doors can open and close with the addition of Door Drive Unit #272-180624, sold separately.

#### Door Drive Unit

**NEW 272-180624 59.99**
Opens and closes the doors of the Electric Engine Shed #272-120217 and Breeding Farm #272-130520, each sold separately. Manual pushbutton operation.

#### Goods Shed

**NEW 272-120248 42.99**
8 x 6-1/8 x 4-1/8"
20.5 x 15.5 x 10.5cm

This wooden goods shed has sliding freight doors and a natural stone foundation. It's ideal for 1920s to 40s layouts.

FALLER

IMPORTED FROM GERMANY BY WALTHERS

## Rural Buildings

### Campground Set

**NEW 272-130501 85.99**

Visitor Center: 9-7/8 x 5-7/16 x 3-1/8" 25 x 13.8 x 7.9cm

Basic campground set includes an entrance gate, visitor center with restaurant, two camping trailers, two tents, camp furniture and a garden umbrella.

### Campground Add-On Set

**NEW 272-130502 59.99**

Shower Building: 4-1/2 x 3-7/8 x 2-3/8" 11.3 x 9.9 x 6cm

Snack Bar: 3-3/16 x 3-3/16 x 2-1/16" 8 x 8 x 5.2cm

Bicycle Shelters: 2-5/16 x 1-1/16 x 1-1/16 & 2 x 11/16 x 1" 5.9 x 2.7 x 2.7cm & 5.1 x 1.7 x 2.6cm

Give your campers more amenities to enjoy with this add-on set. Goes great with Campground Set #272-130501, sold separately.

### Camping Trailer Set

**NEW 272-130503 51.99**

Set of four trailers includes multi-colored awnings for each trailer and camping furniture.

### Camping Tent Set

**NEW 272-130504 33.99**

Set includes six tents in different colors, two party tents and a variety of camp furniture.

### Boy Scout Camp

**NEW 272-130551 51.99**

This commemorative set includes large group tents, small tents, a campfire with flickering red light, benches, tables, stools and eight boy scout figures in uniform.

### Breeding Farm

**NEW 272-130520 85.99**

House: 5 x 4-15/16 x 3-1/2" 12.7 x 12.6 x 8.8cm

Barn: 10-7/16 x 5-13/16 x 3-11/16" 26.5 x 14.7 x 9.3cm

Barn Door: 1-9/16 x 2" 4 x 5cm

Includes a farmhouse and a barn. Sliding doors on both sides of the barn can be activated with Door Drive Unit #272-180624 and interior can be finished with Stable Interior Equipment #272-130525, each sold separately. Compatible with Faller Car System vehicles, also sold separately.

### Implement Shed

**NEW 272-130521 56.99**

10-1/2 x 5-5/16 x 3-5/8" 26.6 x 13.4 x 9.2cm

This open-sided shed helps protect agricultural equipment, vehicles and other farm equipment from the elements.



## Houses

### Solar House

**NEW 272-130302 59.99**

7-7/8 x 7-13/16 x 4-13/16" 20 x 19.9 x 12.2cm

The home features a lean-to roof, a balcony with etched-metal railing and open light-filled rooms. Interior can be finished with #272-180545, sold separately.

### House Under Construction

**NEW 272-130307 42.99**

4-3/4 x 3-1/2 x 2-3/16" 12 x 9 x 5.5cm

The foundation, basement and first-floor decking are finished and the exterior walls are going up for the new house on the block. Kit includes common building site accessories.

### House w/Graffiti

**NEW 272-130416 51.99**

7-7/8 x 4-3/8 x 5-11/16" 20 x 11.2 x 14.5cm

Next to this renovated house is an empty lot surrounded by a fence that connects to the garage. Both the fence and garage are covered with graffiti.

## City Buildings

### Martin Luther House

**NEW 272-130408 119.99**

8-5/8 x 5-7/16 x 7-3/16" 21.8 x 13.8 x 18.4cm

One of the most picturesque and oldest half-timbered buildings in Eisenach, the Martin Luther House is currently a museum.

Gas Station w/Repair Shop 272-130349

### Book Shop & Townhouse

**NEW 272-130453 59.99**

5-7/16 x 4-15/16 x 6-7/8" 13.7 x 12.5 x 17.5cm

This multi-story townhouse features a bookstore and an open passageway to the back courtyard on the ground floor.

### The Grape

**NEW 272-130454 42.99**

7-1/2 x 4-3/16 x 6-7/8" 19 x 10.7 x 17.5cm

A small wine bar occupies the first floor of this three-story townhouse.

### Kebap's Corner

**NEW 272-130455 64.99**

8-1/4 x 7-1/2 x 7-5/16" 21 x 19 x 18.5cm

Neighborhood residents get together for gyros and more at Kebap's Corners located on the first floor of this four-story corner townhouse.

### Townhouse Under Renovation

**NEW 272-130456 51.99**

5-3/8 x 6-11/16 x 6-5/16" 13.6 x 17 x 16cm

Renovations are in full swing on this townhouse that features a passageway to the back yard. Complete the scene with Construction Site Details #272-180549, sold separately.

## Tanks & Towers

### Water Tower

**NEW 272-120213 59.99**

5-5/8 x 5-5/8 x 12-5/16" 14.3 x 14.3 x 31.2cm

Based on a tower in Weimar, Germany, model features circular brick base and polygonal top.

## Churches

### Small Town Church

**NEW 272-130239 51.99**

7-7/8 x 4-5/8 x 10-5/8" 20 x 11.8 x 27cm

Cozy church features cinder-block exterior with slender spire, stone bas-relief trim and "stained glass" windows.

## Businesses

### Gas Station w/Repair Shop

**NEW 272-130349 68.99**

10-5/16 x 6-1/2 x 3-1/16" 26.2 x 16.5 x 7.7cm

Fill 'em up and fix 'em or junk them—this full-service station can take complete care of your HO vehicles. For added realism, there's a hand-painted and fully assembled base plate with a junk auto scene.

IMPORTED FROM GERMANY BY WALTHERS

## Workshop w/Truck Junkyard

**NEW 272-130350 68.99**
7-5/16 x 4-1/2 x 3-3/4" 18.5 x 11.5 x 9.5cm / 6-7/8 x 3-7/8 x 1-3/16" 17.5 x 10 x 3cm

The hand-painted kit comes with a fully assembled base plate featuring a detailed truck scrap yard.

## Modern Car Dealership

**NEW 272-130338 339.99**
13-13/16 x 9-11/16 x 5-7/8"
35.2 x 24.6 x 14.9cm

Car buffs won't want to miss this limited-edition model. This full-service dealership includes a sales and consulting area with an information counter and a complete shop with equipment. Vehicles are presented on a rotating turntable with motor. Specially designed lighting and a functioning car lift with motor as well as interior equipment and decoration parts are included. Comes with electronic controller to activate turntable, car lift and lights. Compatible with Faller Car System, sold separately.

## Car Lift Drive

**NEW 272-180623 68.99**
Operates lift for Car Dealership #272-130338, sold separately.

## Attractions

## Penguin Zoo Exhibit

**NEW 272-130562 67.99**
8-7/8 x 6-1/8 x 2"
22 x 15.5 x 5cm

With their tuxedo-like "coats", waddling walk and ability to "fly" underwater, penguins are a major attraction at any zoo. This model features a painted and weathered fenced outdoor enclosure, a pool for swimming (water not included), penguin figures and an adjoining shelter.

Modern Car Dealership 272-130338

## Polar Bear Zoo Exhibit

**NEW 272-130563 67.99**
7-11/16 x 6-11/16 x 2"
19.5 x 17 x 5cm

Fuzzy white polar bears climb on the "ice" and cool off in the water in this hand-painted and weathered outdoor enclosure with sea ice landscape, a water basin and a family of polar bears. Animate the scene with Synchronous Motor kit #272-180629, sold separately and the standing bear will knock at the hanging play barrel.

## Red Deer Game Enclosure

**NEW 272-130564 42.99**
10-5/8 x 7-1/8 x 1-9/16"
27 x 18 x 4cm

Kit includes an open-sided shelter building, hay bales, a feed manager, fencing and a herd of red deer.

## Hagenbeck Zoo Entrance

**NEW 272-130561 64.99**
9-7/16 x 2-7/16 x 4-1/16"
24 x 6.2 x 10.3cm

An ornate entrance adorned with filigree iron gates, animal sculptures and warrior statues welcomes visitors to Tierpark Hagenbeck in Hamburg, Germany. This faithful reproduction of the famous zoo features handpainted figures, cast-metal gates and many fine details.

## Jena Planetarium

**NEW 272-130939 99.99**
11 x 9-7/16 x 6"
28 x 24 x 15cm

An imposing entrance, voluminous dome and circular colonnade highlight this painted and weathered building. The structure is modeled after the Zeiss planetarium in Jena. Built in the 1920s, it's the oldest planetarium still in operation in the world.

## Carnival

## Children's Merry-Go-Round

**NEW 272-140329 49.99**
5 x 4-1/2" 12.5 x 11.5cm

Round and round they go, riding motorcycles, horses, tigers and cars. No carnival would be complete without its merry-go-round. The kit comes with a 12-16V AC motor to power the ride.

## Ghost Temple Roundabout

**NEW 272-140427 254.99**
4-3/16 x 7-1/8 x 7-1/4"
36 x 18 x 18.3cm

Only those with nerves of steel can ride the Ghost Temple. Elaborately decorated, this ride will be the star attraction at any fair. Innovative technology ensures a smooth and scary ride for your HO fairgoers. The model comes with a lighting system and 12-16V AC drive motor.

Hagenbeck Zoo Entrance 272-130561

Jena Planetarium 272-130939

## Fairground Booths

**NEW 272-140446 42.99**
3-11/16 x 1-13/16 x 2-1/2" 9.3 x 4.6 x 6.3cm / 3-7/8 x 1-3/4 x 2-11/16 10 x 4.4 x 6.8cm

Try your luck at the Ducky Pond or Fishing Game. These two easy-to-play games are popular with fairgoers of all ages.

## Log Ride Replacement Parts

**NEW 272-190430 33.99**
Allows you to easily replace worn parts of Pirate's Island Wildwater Log Ride #272-140430, sold separately. Includes two complete lifts without motor, decorative parts and installation instructions.

## Go-Kart Racing

## Metallic Go-Kart w/Driver

**NEW 272-141011 39.99**
Add more racers to your go-kart track, #272-140333 or 141000, each sold separately. Includes a driver figure and one fully assembled racing cart painted in a bright metallic color. (Colors may vary).

## Go-Kart Set

**NEW 272-141012 85.99**
Bump up the competition at your go-kart track, #272-14033 or 141000, each sold separately. Set includes two fully assembled vehicles with drivers and a starter figure with checkered flag all packaged in a sturdy storage box.

# FALLER HISTORY CERAMIC BUILDINGS

## Signal Box

**272-131315 33.99**
6 x 2-3/8 x 4-3/8"
15 x 6 x 11cm

This slender structure will slide right between the tracks.

IMPORTED FROM GERMANY BY WALTHERS

### Gatekeeper's Lodge
**272-131316 33.99**
3-7/8 x 3-1/2 x 3-3/16"
10 x 9 x 8cm

Charming stucco and brick building is perfect for level crossings.

### Rural Fire-Brigade House
**272-131320 37.99**
5-1/8 x 3-7/8 x 5-1/2"
13 x 10 x 14cm

Small firehouse features a hose-drying tower at the top.

### Railway Station
**272-131310 51.99**
9-7/16 x 4-11/32 x 4-1/2"
24 x 11 x 11.5cm

### Hip-Roof House w/Delicatessen
**272-131330 35.99**

### Franconian Half Timbered House w/Toy Shop
**272-131331 37.99**

## STATIONS & PLATFORMS

### Falkenwalde Station
**272-110106 63.99**
11-7/16 x 6 x 3-34"
29 x 15 x 9.6cm

Typical small-town station featuring clinker brick half-timbered construction, entrance area with double door and loading platform annexed on one side.

### Bad Durkheim Station
**272-110109 134.99**
19-11/16 x 11 x 7-1/2"
50 x 28 x 19cm

Classic mainline station features two wings joined by a central section. Station has wide entrance areas on the street and a covered platform trackside.

### Prussian Railway Lodge
**272-120224 23.99**
3 x 2-13/16 x 2-7/16"
7.5 x 7.1 x 6.2cm

Classic red brick lodge is ideal for gatekeepers and numerous other uses.

### Friedrichshohe Passenger Station w/Covered Platform & Built-on Freight Depot
**272-110110 85.99**
16 x 6" 40.7 x 15.6cm

### Bonn Passenger Station
**272-110113 169.99**
27-1/2 x 6-1/4" 70 x 16cm

This classic station is based on the prototype at Bonn, Germany.

### Trossingen Station
**272-110114 134.99**
14-3/16 x 7-1/2 x 9-5/8"
36 x 19 x 24.5cm

This 1898-built station still stands on the Schwarzwald-Baar-Kreis. The painted and weathered kit is based on the original, non-modernized structure.

### Loading Ramp w/Crane
**272-120231 27.99**
13-1/4 x 4-1/16 x 4-1/16"
33.6 x 10.3 x 10.3cm

### DB Information/ Ticket Kiosk
**272-120234 27.99**
Patterned after typical DB automatic ticket machines and information kiosks used throughout Germany.

### Storage Depot
**272-120249 42.99**
6-1/2 x 4-3/8 x 2-27/32"
16.5 x 11.1 x 7.2cm

Includes opening doors and cargo loads.

### Working Goods Shed
**272-120250 119.99**
11-5/8 x 6 x 5-1/8"
29.5 x 15.3 x 13cm

This animated wooden freight house comes painted and weathered. Watch as two workers load cargo aboard the open box car. Cannot be used with other freight cars. Includes motor, figures and cargo.

### Country Station
**272-110092 28.99**
8 x 4-1/8" 20.3 x 10.4cm

### Blumenfeld Wayside Station
**272-110097 47.99**
9-1/4 x 5-1/4" 24 x 13.5cm

Suitable for use with TT Scale.

### St. Niklaus Station
**272-110098 68.99**
12-3/8 x 5 x 4-3/4"
31 x 12.7 x 12cm

Based on a station in Switzerland, this preweathered building includes a goods shed, loading ramp and dead-end sidings.

### Waldbrunn Station
**272-110099 51.99**
9-5/8 x 5 x 5-3/8"
24 x 12.5 x 13.5cm

This typical preweathered brick station features a roofed platform of cast-iron construction.

### Lutzen Station
**272-110103 68.99**
16-11/64 x 5-3/8 x 6"
40.4 x 13.4 x 15cm

### Guglingen Station
**272-110107 68.99**
12-1/16 x 5-1/4"
30.8 x 13.5cm

### Burgschwabach Station
**272-110108 119.99**
14-3/8 x 8-5/8 x 7-1/2"
36 x 21.5 x 18.9cm

Station features waiting rooms on the main floor, a roofed platform across the building front and annexed terraces on the upper floor.

### Talheim Rural Station
**272-110105 51.99**
9-7/16 x 4-1/2" 23.9 x 11.5cm

### Neufeld Station
**272-131288 28.99**

### Schwarzburg Station
**272-110116 136.99**
19 x 7" 47.6 x 17.5cm

### Freight Station
**272-120155 33.99**
7-9/16 x 4-1/4" 19.2 x 10.8cm

### Bonn Passenger Station Canopy
**272-120180 63.99**
11-7/8 x 7" 30.2 x 17.8cm

### Platform Lighting
**272-120183** For Passenger Station #272-120180, sold separately **22.99**

IMPORTED FROM GERMANY BY WALTHERS

## Covered Platform
**272-120181 32.99**
13 x 3-1/2" 33.8 x 9.2cm

Platform with passenger exit. Suitable for all track.

## Platform Accessories
**272-120182 25.99**

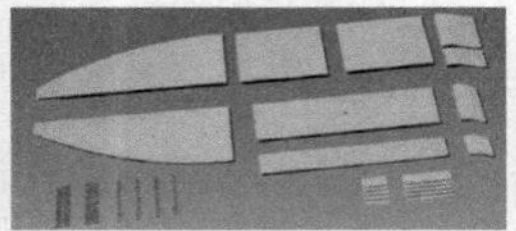

## Assorted Level Platforms
**272-120184 27.99**

## Platform Accessories
**272-120186 21.99**
For use with platform #272-120199 and ICE platform extension #272-120195, each sold separately. Includes billboards, timetables, benches, waste baskets, clock and train target indicators.

## ICE Platform Extension
**272-120195 25.99**
6 x 3-3/4 x 1/2"
15 x 9.5 x 1.2cm

Roofless extension for the ICE platform.

## Glass-Covered Platform
**272-120187 28.99**
19-1/4 x 2-1/8" 48.8 x 5.3cm

## Platform
**272-120201 27.99**
15 x 3 x 3" 37.5 x 7.6 x 7.4cm

For use with Platform w/Drive #272-120200 (sold separately).

## Modern German Railroad Station Information/ Bulletin Boards
**272-120194** pkg(6) **16.99**
Contemporary sculpture signs attract attention in any station scene. Includes two each in red, blue and yellow, with assorted schedules and other stick-on signs.

## Glass Train Shed w/Accessories
**272-120188 39.99**
19-1/4 x 2-1/8" 48.8 x 5.3cm

## Platform Extensions

**272-120197** For Covered Platform #272-120199, sold separately **51.99**
19-1/2 x 1-1/2 x 2-5/8"
48.6 x 3.8 x 6.7cm

**272-120203** For Passenger Station Platform #272-120191 (sold separately) **37.99**
16-3/4 x 2 x 2-5/8"
42 x 4.8 x 6.7cm

## Covered Platforms
**272-120204 28.99**
14-3/8 x 3-1/4 x 2-3/8"
36 x 5.6 x 6cm

Designed for use with the Waldbrunn Station #272-110099 (sold separately). Preweathered platforms feature cast-iron construction and a clock and train target.

## Covered Platform
**272-120189 27.99**
11-1/2 x 2-1/4" 29.5 x 5.3cm

Suitable for use with all track.

## Roofed Platform
**272-120190 21.99**
7-1/8 x 2-7/8" 18 x 7.2cm

## Passenger Station Platform
**272-120191** pkg(2) **49.99**
11-7/8 x 1-7/8" 30.2 x 4.8cm

## Roofed Platform w/Accessories
**272-120192 21.99**
17-3/4 x 1-7/8" 45 x 4.8cm

## Wayside Station
**272-110091 16.99**
4-7/8 x 3-3/16" 12.4 x 8.1cm

## S-Bahn Railway Station
**272-120119 85.99**
28-13/16 x 8 x 8"
72 x 20 x 19.8cm

Platform buildings and an underground passage that can be reached by stairway add to the realistic detail. Bridge parts and columns are identical to the S-Bahn Railway Bridge #272-120551, sold separately.

## Platform w/Drive
**272-120200 102.99**
15 x 3 x 3" 37.5 x 7.6 x 7.4cm

Six figures included with the platform can move across the walkway, thanks to a built-in drive mechanism that animates this railway platform.

## Bus Stop Shelters
**272-180587** Set of Two **20.99**
2-3/8 x 1-5/16 x 1-1/2"
6 x 3.3 x 3.8cm
2-13/16 x 1 x 1-7/16"
7 x 2.5 x 3.6cm

Simulating wooden construction, the kit includes parts for two complete buildings.

## Modern Intercity Express (ICE) Train Platforms
**272-120193 66.99**
27-13/64 x 3-5/8 x 2-13/32"
68 x 9.2 x 6.2cm

Ideal for any contemporary station scene. Simulated steel and glass roof construction, complete with signs.

## Platform Extension
**272-120185 25.99**
Extensions for use with covered station platform #272-120181 (sold separately).

## Mittelstadt Passenger Station
**272-110115 111.99**
17-1/2 x 6-1/4" 44.6 x 16cm

This nicely sized passenger depot can easily be adapted to a layout or module.

## Neustadt Weinstasse Station
**272-110111 238.99**
31-11/16 x 11 x 10-3/4"
79.2 x 27.5 x 26.8cm

This impressive turn-of-the-century station is still serving the city of Neustadt. Special edition model includes interior details, opening doors, decorative trim and many other features. Its many windows make it a natural for lighting.

**Limited Quantity Available**

## Susch Station
**272-110101 56.99**
13-3/8 x 6 x 4-5/8"
33.5 x 15 x 11.5cm

Based on a typical Swiss station, this preweathered building features a ridge roof and deeply recessed windows and doors.

**Limited Quantity Available**

## Outhouse
**272-130953 20.99**
3-1/4 x 3 x 2-3/4"
8.2 x 7.6 x 7.1cm

Lavatory is designed with railroad station exteriors in mind! Constructed with panels protecting entrance vision on each side.

FALLER

IMPORTED FROM GERMANY BY WALTHERS

# YARD EQUIPMENT & FACILITIES

### Store Shed
**272-120251 24.99**
7-3/8 x 3-3/8 x 1-3/4"
18.8 x 8.5 x 4.4cm

This practical wooden shed has a flat roof and open and closed shelters for vehicles and equipment. Combine several models for a larger structure.

### Workers Barracks
**272-120252 25.99**
5-15/16 x 2-13/16 x 1-13/16"
15.1 x 7.2 x 4.6cm

Designed for the construction crew, this structure is ideal for building sites and other business uses.

### Ash Pit & Hoist
**272-120221 49.99**
-3/4 x 3-15/16 x 3-3/32"
7.2 x 10 x 10.4cm

Painted and weathered kit.

### Inspection Pits
**272-120136** pkg(2) **39.99**
3-1/2 x 5-3/4" 34.4 x 14.7cm

Rails are molded on baseplate.

### Three Trackside Shanties
**272-120140 21.99**

### German Railways Service Station
**272-120196 28.99**
8 x 3-3/4 x 1-1/2"
20.1 x 9.4 x 3.9cm

Features an oil tank, pump, switchgear, floor section and service building.

### Gantry Crane
**272-120127 23.99**
5-3/16 x 2 x 3-13/16"
13 x 5.4 x 9.5cm

Timber construction adds to the realistic look of this model.

### Engine Driver's Cabin
**272-120133 21.99**
1-1/4 x 1-1/8" 3.2 x 2cm

### Small Coaling Station
**272-120131 32.99**
8-1/4 x 3-1/8" 21 x 8cm

Includes positionable crane with bucket and coal storage bins.

### Compressor Housing & Accessories
**272-120139 44.99**
3-5/8 x 2-1/8" 9.4 x 5.6cm
3 x 3-5/8" 7.6 x 9.3cm

This small facility is used to clean the flues and fireboxes of steam locos. A shed with compressor, sand blasting frame and fire cleaning tools with rack are included.

New Arrivals Updated Every Day! Visit Walthers Web site at
**www.walthers.com**

### Freight House
**272-120150 64.99**
9-3/4 x 5-5/8" 24.8 x 14.4cm

### Storage Shed w/Loading Crane
**272-120152 33.99**

### Freight Depot
**272-120154 39.99**
8-1/4 x 3-7/16" 21 x 8.8cm

### Duderstadt Enginehouse
**272-120160 85.99**
12-1/4 x 7-1/4" 31 x 18.5cm

### 2-Stall Enginehouse
**272-120161 64.99**
8-1/4 x 6-1/8" 21 x 15.7cm

### Overhead Crane
**272-120164 27.99**
5-3/8 x 1-1/4" 13.7 x 3cm

### Two-Stall Engine Shed
**272-120165 68.99**
14-1/4 x 7-7/8 x 5-1/4"
35.5 x 19.5 x 13cm

### Engine Shed
**272-120168 51.99**
10-7/8 x 5 x 3-13/16"
27.2 x 12.7 x 9.5cm

Doors open and close automatically as engines roll in or out. Features detailed brick and half-timber construction, holds locos up to 9-3/16" 23cm long.

Overhead Crane 272-120164

3-Stall Roundhouse - Long 272-120177

Two-Stall Engine Shed 272-120165

### Three-Stall Roundhouse
**272-120176 85.99**
13-1/2 x 16" 34 x 40cm

Matching structure for #272-120175 (sold separately), can also be used by itself. Will hold engines up to 8-3/4" 22cm long.

### Roundhouse w/Water Supply
**272-120175 119.99**
13-1/2 x 2" 34 x 5cm

Separate office building also houses a water tank. Doors automatically open and close as engines arrive and depart. Will hold engines up to 8-3/4" 22cm long.

### Three-Stall Roundhouse - Long
**272-120177 111.99**
16 x 13-1/2 x 5"
40 x 34 x 12.5cm

Holds locos up to 9-3/16" 23cm long.

### Small Engine Shed w/House
**272-131287 28.99**

IMPORTED FROM GERMANY BY WALTHERS

### Gantry Crane
**272-120162 66.99**
13-3/8 x 2-1/4" 34 x 5.8cm

The kit can be built with a hook, a clamshell bucket or logging hooks. The crane cab can be rotated 360° degrees; use motor #272-180629, available separately, for remote control or operate manually.

### Small Coaling Station
**272-120147 33.99**
8-1/8 x 3-1/8" 20.7 x 8cm

### Coal Lift
**272-120220 34.99**
3-5/8 x 1-5/8 x 5-1/4"
9 x 4 x 13.2cm

Used to load steam engines with coal. This preweathered lift includes an attached motor frame.

### Small Line House
**272-120225 32.99**
Includes a transformer station, oil pump station, inspection trolley and various direction boards and accessories. Preweathered.

### Freilassing Roundhouse
**272-120218 171.99**
20-3/4 x 14 x 5"
52 x 35 x 12.5cm

This preweathered, five-stall roundhouse allows for engines with an overall length of 12-1/2" 30cm. Each stall is at a 7.5° angle. Roundhouse doors can be operated by a special mechanism.

### Service Area Materials Store
**272-130972 57.99**
9 x 8-3/4 x 6"
22.8 x 21.8 x 13.9cm

## RURAL BUILDINGS

### Beekeeper's Stand
**272-130378 27.99**
Stand: 2-3/8 x 1-5/8 x 2-7/16"
6 x 4.1 x 6.2cm
Hive hut: 1-3/4 x 1-1/4 x 1-7/8"
4.4 x 3.2 x 4.7cm

### Black Forest Farm
**272-130365 79.99**
10-5/8 x 9-7/16 x 5-11/16"
27 x 24 x 14.5cm

### Bakehouse, Chapel, Utility Shed
**272-130379 51.99**
Bakehouse: 2-23/32 x 2-1/16 x 2-5/32" 6.9 x 5.2 x 5.5cm
Chapel: 2-5/32 x 2-1/16 x 3-19/32" 5.4 x 5.1 x 9.1cm
Utility Shed: 4-13/32 x 3-1/2 x 2-1/4" 11.2 x 8.3 x 5.8cm

Painted and weathered kit. Perfect for use with the Black Forest Farm #272-130365, sold separately.

### Village Smithy
**272-130203 33.99**
4-1/2 x 4-7/8 x 4-3/4"
11.3 x 12.2 x 11.8cm

### Rural Fire Station
**272-130268 33.99**
5-1/8 x 4" 13 x 10cm

### Farm Buildings w/Details
**272-130276 51.99**
6-3/8 x 3-7/8" 16.2 x 9.8cm
3-3/4 x 2-1/16" 9.6 x 5.3cm
5-3/8 x 3-7/8" 13.7 x 9.8cm

### Hunter's Lookout
**272-130290 20.99**
1-9/16 x 1-3/16" 4 x 3cm

### Log Barn
**272-130294 20.99**
4-3/16 x 2-1/4" 10.6 x 5.7cm

### Log Cabin
**272-130299 18.99**
3-1/4 x 30" 8.2 x 7.6cm

Old Coal Mine 272-130470

### Hay Sheds
**272-130334** pkg(2) **27.99**
3 x 2-1/2" 7.5 x 6.5cm

### Farm
**272-130370 102.99**
8-3/4 x 13-1/4" 22.5 x 34cm

Includes half-timber farmhouse, shed for sheep, barn, pig sty with fence, dog house and manure wagon.

### Lower-Saxon Farmhouse
**272-130371 51.99**
4-1/4 x 7" 11 x 17.5cm

### Wooden Hut
**272-130947 23.99**
4 -3/8 x 2-7/8" 11.1 x 7.2cm

### Forest Log Cabin
**272-130293 20.99**
3-7/16 x 2" 8.7 x 5.1cm

### Old Coal Mine
**272-130470 51.99**
16-9/64 x 14-9/16 x 7-1/2"
41 x 37 x 19cm

### Watermill
**272-130225** With Pump **85.99**
9-1/2 x 5-1/8" 24 x 13cm

### Black Forest Farmyard w/Accessories
**272-130366 85.99**
10-13/16 x 9-5/8 x 6-1/4"
27 x 24 x 15.6cm

### Operating Sawmill
**272-130229 118.99**
13-3/4 x 8 x 5-3/4"
34.5 x 20 x 14.5cm

Features a water wheel driven by a 12-16V AC motor. The motor also operates the saw frame.

## HOUSES

### Villa
**272-130364 68.99**
7 x 5-3/4" 17.5 x 14.5cm

IMPORTED FROM GERMANY BY WALTHERS

## World's Largest Cuckoo Clock

**272-130389 119.99**
4-5/16 x 3-3/4" 11 x 9.5cm

Constructed by Joseph Dubold, in the style of a traditional home, the building houses the world's largest cuckoo clock. The working model is complete with battery-powered clock mechanism, which includes the cuckoo and its familiar song. There is also an electric motor to drive the waterwheel.

## Rural Half-Timbered House

**272-130275 59.99**
6-1/2 x 4 x 4-5/8"
16.5 x 10.2 x 11.8cm

A masonry lower story and projecting second-floor balconies add interest to this cozy home.

## Rosenstrabe 2 House

**272-130320 49.99**
4-15/16 x 4-3/8 x 4-13/16"
12.5 x 11 x 12.3cm

Features cream-colored plaster walls, shutters, balconies and a big dormer window. Matches #272-130321, sold separately.

## Rosenstrabe 3 House

**272-130321 49.99**
4-15/16 x 4-3/8 x 4-13/16"
12.5 x 11 x 12.3cm

Multiple dormers, a tile roof and shutters make this a charming residence. Goes with #130320 (sold separately).

## Half-Timbered House

**272-130266 64.99**
6-1/2 x 4 x 4-11/16"
16.6 x 10.3 x 11.9cm

This painted and weathered kit features a brick basement and entrance with exterior stairway.

## Relief Town Houses pkg (2)

Perfect for tight spaces, these thin-profile models will add visual depth to your city scenes.

**272-130435** Three-Story **68.99**
4-15/16 x 2-3/16 x 7-1/2"
12.5 x 5.6 x 19cm
4-15/16 x 2-1/8 x 7-1/4"
12.5 x 5.5 x 18.4cm

**272-130436** Four-Story **68.99**
4-15/16 x 1-13/16 x 9"
12.6 x 4.6 x 23cm
4-15/16 x 2-3/16 x 8-3/4"
12.6 x 5.6 x 22.3cm

## Town House Under Demolition

**272-130466 59.99**
8-1/2 x 4-1/2 x 6"
21.5 x 11.5 x 15.2cm

This painted and weathered kit includes the remains of the facade on the old structure, a rubble heap, temporary fencing, a Wiking excavator and single axle trailer, and assorted junk.

## One-Family House

**272-130207 32.99**
4-5/8 x 3-3/4 x 4-5/8"
11.5 x 9.5 x 11.5cm

## White Plaster House w/Tile Roof

**272-131209 25.99**
3-5/8 x 3-3/8" 9.3 x 8.6cm

Assembled.

## Goethestrasse 88 Town House

**272-130918 78.99**
6-1/2 x 5 x 10-3/4"
16.4 x 14.8 x 27cm

## Beige Plaster House

**272-131205** Assembled **25.99**
3-5/8 x 3-3/8" 9.3 x 8.6cm

## Gatekeeper's House

**272-120132 21.99**
3-7/8 x 2-15/16" 9.8 x 7.5cm

## House w/Dormer

**272-130200 16.99**
3-17/32 x 3-1/8" 9 x 8cm

## 1-1/2 Story House

**272-130205 16.99**
5-3/16 x 3-1/4" 13.2 x 8.3cm

## Chalet w/Porch

**272-130204 16.99**
3-15/16 x 3-1/4" 10 x 8.3cm

## Development Houses 13.99 ea

**272-131223** With Dormer

**272-131224** With Extension

## Half-Timbered Black Forest House

**272-130369 85.99**
10-7/8 x 9-5/8 x 6-5/8"
27 x 24 x 16.5cm

Features a projected roof, side entrance and typical accessories. Preweathered.

## Summer Houses

**272-130208** pkg(3) **21.99**
1-7/16 x 1-7/16 x 1-9/32"
3.6 x 3.6 x 3.2cm
2-11/64 x 1-31/32 x 1-9/32"
5.4 x 4.9 x 3.2cm
2-13/32 x 2-1/8 x 1-9/32"
6 x 5.3 x 3.2cm

These tiny timber homes are great for tourist cabins, roadside motels, backyard playhouses and hundreds of other uses around your layout.

## House w/Balcony

**272-130209 16.99**
4 x 3-3/4" 10.1 x 9.5cm

## House w/Red Roof

**272-131228 13.99**

## Detached House

**272-130214 27.99**
3-1/2 x 2-13/16" 9.1 x 7.2cm

## House w/Balcony

**272-131225 13.99**

## Timbered House w/Garage

**272-130215 27.99**
4-7/8 x 2-13/16" 12.6 x 6.2cm

## One-Family House

**272-130221 20.99**
3-3/4 x 3-1/2" 9.3 x 8.7cm

IMPORTED FROM GERMANY BY WALTHERS

**Half-Timbered House**
**272-130222 20.99**
3-3/4 x 3-1/2" 9.3 x 8.5cm

**One Family House w/Half-Timber Framing**
**272-130257 32.99**
4-5/8 x 3-13/16 x 4-5/8"
11.5 x 9.5 x 11.5cm

**Half-Timbered Chalet**
**272-130277 25.99**
4-1/2 x 3-3/8" 11.5 x 8.7cm

**Rural Half-Timbered House**
**272-130270 56.99**
5-1/4 x 3-7/8 x 3-5/8"
13.2 x 9.7 x 9cm

**Half-Timbered Two-Family House**
**272-130259 32.99**
5-5/8 x 4-15/64 x 5-13/32"
14 x 10.6 x 13.5cm

Perfect duplex for any residential area. Designed for easy construction, ideal for first-time kit builders. Complete with decorating accessories.

**Two-Family Brick House Under Construction**
**272-130263 49.99**
8-13/32 x 6-31/64 x 5-13/64"
21 x 16.2 x 13cm

Complete scene in one kit. Includes scaffolding, old cement mixer and cement silo.

**House**
**272-130280 33.99**
4-5/8 x 4-1/2" 11.7 x 11.5cm

Includes stork's nest.

**Boathouse & Boat**
**272-130284 18.99**
3-5/8 x 2-23/32" 9.2 x 6.9cm

**Rosel Guest House**
**272-130286 28.99**
3-15/16 x 3-3/8" 10 x 8cm

**Large Mountain Chalet**
**272-130287 28.99**
5 x 3-3/4" 12.7 x 9.3cm

**Small Mountain Chalet**
**272-130297 25.99**
4-11/16 x 3-7/8" 11.9 x 9.9cm

**Romantic Single Family Home**
**272-130301 33.99**
5 x 5" 12.7 x 12.6cm

**House Under Construction**
**272-130303 33.99**
4-11/16 x 3-1/2" 12 x 9cm

**Kristall House**
**272-130306 33.99**
6-5/8 x 5-11/16 x 3-13/16"
16.6 x 14.2 x 9.5cm

**Familia House**
**273-130397 28.99**
5 x 5 x 3-1/2"
12.5 x 12.5 x 8.75cm

**Building Shell w/Scaffolding**
**272-130309 30.99**
5-1/8 x 4" 13 x 10cm

**North German One-Family House**
**272-130310 30.99**
4-3/4 x 6-3/8 x 4-3/8"
12 x 16 x 11cm

**Bergisches Land House**
**272-130311 30.99**
6-1/2 x 4-5/8 x 5"
16.3 x 11.6 x 12.6cm

**Brilliant House**
**272-130395 28.99**
5-13/16 x 5 x 3"
14.5 x 12.7 x 7.7cm

**Turkis House**
**272-130396 28.99**
8-13/64 x 5-11/64 x 3-13/32"
20.5 x 12.9 x 8.5cm

This model home (prototype built by Weberhaus) comes with a two-car garage with roof-top deck, covered entry and many other fine details.

**Corner House w/Toy Shop**
**272-130411 39.99**
3-1/4 x 2-1/2" 8.4 x 6.4cm

**House w/Wine Shop**
**272-130413 44.99**
3-1/2 x 2-15/16" 9.1 x 7.5cm

**Two Flats w/Lower Shops**
**272-130414 47.99**
3-5/16 x 2-1/2" 8.4 x 6.4cm
3-1/2 x 3" 9.1 x 7.5cm

**Cottages**
**272-180590** pkg(4) **31.99**

**Schwabentor Townhouse**
**272-130424 56.99**
6 x 3-9/16" 15 x 9cm

**Urban Dwelling House**
**272-130425 33.99**
3 x 3-1/8" 7.5 x 8cm

**Stucco Timbered House**
**272-131207 25.99**
3-5/8 x 3-3/8" 9.3 x 8.6cm

Assembled.

IMPORTED FROM GERMANY BY WALTHERS

**Brick/Timbered House**
**272-131208 25.99**
3-5/8 x 3-3/8" 9.3 x 8.6cm
Assembled.

**Relief Houses**

**272-130430** pkg(6) **99.99**
This row of six space-saving houses are perfect for the edges of your layout.)

**272-130433** pkg(2) **51.99**
6 x 1-3/4 x 2-1/4"
15 x 4.3 x 5.5cm
Add-on homes for use with other Faller relief houses #272-130430, 130431 and 130432, each sold separately.

**Goethestrasse 63 Town Corner House**
**272-130906 64.99**
4-7/8 x 4-1/2 x 8-5/8"
12.2 x 11.2 x 21.7cm

**Goethestrasse 73 Town Corner House**
**272-130907 61.99**
4-7/8 x 4-1/2 x 7-3/8"
12.2 x 11.2 x 18.5cm

**4-Story Town Angle House**
**272-130919 75.99**
10 x 8-1/4 x 9"
25 x 20.5 x 22.5cm
Features stuccowork design, garage entry and a ground-level pub.

**Relief Houses pkg(2) 39.99 ea**
Use together, or with #272-130430, sold separately.
**272-130431** Cream
**272-130432** Beige

**Gate Keeper's House**
**272-120130 21.99**
4 x 3-5/8 x 3-3/8"
10 x 9 x 8.4cm

**Black Forest House**
**272-130367 59.99**
6-5/8 x 4-13/32 x 4-1/2"
16.5 x 11 x 11.3cm

**Falkeneck Hunter's Lodge**
**272-130385 76.99**
7-3/8 x 5-1/4" 18.8 x 13.4cm
Includes wooden draw bridge and walkway.

**House Under Construction**
**272-130246 16.99**
2-15/16 x 2-3/4" 7.5 x 7.1cm

**L-Shaped Bungalow**
**272-130398 28.99**
6-3/16 x 5-13/16 x 3"
15.5 x 14.5 x 7.5cm

**Limited Quantity Available**

**One-Family House w/Balcony**
**272-130313 28.99**
4-5/8 x 4-3/8 x 5-1/8"
11.7 x 11 x 12.8cm

**Two-Family Stucco House**
**272-130248 27.99**
5-5/8 x 3-5/8 x 5-13/32"
14 x 9.2 x 13.5cm

**3-Story Town Angle House**
**272-130921 65.99**
10 x 8-1/4 x 7-3/4"
25 x 20.5 x 19.5cm

**North German Town House**
**272-130993 43.99**
10 x 7-5/8 x 11-1/4"
25.2 x 19.2 x 28cm

**One-Family House**
**272-130206 26.99**
5-1/2 x 4-1/4 x 4-2/3"
14 x 10.5 x 11.6cm
Includes a clothesline and a fenced front garden.

**Basic Village Set**
**272-130255 91.99**
Here's everything you need to build a small village in one complete set! Including three Cape Cod homes and a small church, the set also features an assortment of fir trees and a playground which is detailed with teeter-totters, a swing set and more.

## CITY BUILDINGS

**Angle Townhouse**
**272-130452** w/Scaffolding **64.99**
7-1/8 x 7-1/8 x 7-7/8"
18 x 18 x 17.5cm
Scaffolding parts included. 45 degree adjoining angle.

**Erich Kastner Classical Secondary School**
**272-130923 111.99**
8-7/8 x 9-1/4 x 10-13/16"
22.5 x 23.5 x 27.4cm
Bring back those warm and wonderful memories of school days with this classic building. Features oriel and sandstone-framed entry door.

**Rainbow Nursery School**
**272-130938 119.99**
10-13/16 x 10 x 9-11/16"
27.5 x 25.5 x 24.5cm
The days of paste, crayons and sandboxes come to life with this half timbered home that houses a large nursery school on the main level. Courtyard fencing and play equipment are included.

**Bus Shed**
**272-130970** w/Vehicle **85.99**
10-5/16 x 8-3/8 x 4-13/16"
26.2 x 21.5 x 12.3cm
Four large bays accommodate the buses of the local public transportation system.

**Three-Story Apartment Building**
**272-130442 85.99**
14-3/8 x 6-1/2 x 7-7/8"
36.6 x 16.6 x 20cm

## FALLER

IMPORTED FROM GERMANY BY WALTHERS

### Paradise Bar
**272-130445 68.99**
7-3/16 x 4-13/16 x 8-3/16"
18.3 x 12.5 x 20.8cm

### Alfredo's Pizzeria
**272-130446 64.99**
5-11/16 x 4-13/16 x 8-1/16"
14.5 x 12.5 x 20.5cm

### Zur Krone Inn w/Beer Garden
**272-130314 32.99**
6-9/16 x 4-1/8 x 3-15/16"
16.7 x 10.5 x 10cm

### Modern Fire Station
**272-130989 85.99**
17-3/8 x 8-1/4 x 15-23/64"
44.1 x 21 x 39cm

Includes three-stall garage, hose-drying/observation tower and commander's building.

### Newspaper & Waffle Stands
**272-130211** pkg(2) **23.99**
Newstand: 3-1/4 x 2" 8.5 x 5cm
Waffle Stand: 2-3/4 x 1-1/2"
6.8 x 3.8cm

Great detail for parks, city streets, fair scenes and more.

### Two Town Houses w/Shop
**272-130418 59.99**
4-3/4 x 5-7/8" 12 x 14.9cm

### Town House w/Shops
**272-130421 51.99**
3-3/4 x 6-1/2" 9.7 x 16.5cm

Entrance to hair salon and pub, both of which are located on the ground floor of this building.

### City Optical House w/Shop
**272-130426 37.99**
3 x 3-1/8" 7.5 x 8cm

Combines a ground floor optical center with upstairs apartment. Features half-timber framing.

Get Daily Info, Photos and News at
**www.walthers.com**

### Lindau Town Hall
**272-130902 111.99**
8-3/8 x 7-5/8 x 9-7/8"
21 x 19 x 24.5cm

Based on an existing town hall in Lake Constance, featuring elaborate paintings on the front and rear sides of the building.

### Bad Liebenstein Post Office
**272-130903 94.99**
8-5/8 x 6-1/4 x 7-5/8"
21.5 x 15.7 x 19cm

Based on an existing building, this charming post office features finely worked half-timbered construction and laterally built-on tower.

### Four-Face Clock Tower w/Newsstand
**272-180583 32.99**
2 x 2" 5.2 x 5.2cm

### Allmannsdorf Town Hall
**272-130427 85.99**
7 x 6-3/8 x 9-3/16"
17.5 x 16 x 23cm

Based on a prototype at Allmannsdorf.

### 4-Story Corner Townhouse - #62 Gothe Street
**272-130916 64.99**
4-5/8 x 4 x 8-13/16"
11.5 x 10 x 18.5cm

A classic addition to your busy downtown, with first-floor shops and upstairs apartments or offices. Easily Americanized to fit your favorite modeling era.

### 3-Story Corner Townhouse - #70 Gothe Street
**272-130917 61.99**
4-5/8 x 4 x 7-13/32"
11.5 x 10 x 18.5cm

Great addition to any business district and easily Americanized to fit the scene.

### St. Martin's City Gate
**272-130922 73.99**
4-3/8 x 3" 11.2 x 7.8cm

### Post Office
**272-130933 68.99**
7-5/8 x 7-13/16 x 8-5/8"
19 x 19.5 x 21.5cm

Handsome three-story structure includes large front stairway, positionable entryway doors and a large loading platform to handle trucks.

### Fire/Rescue Station
**272-130991 99.99**
14-11/16 x 6-13/16 x 8-13/32"
36.7 x 17 x 21cm

### Fire Station
**272-130985 85.99**
7-5/8 x 5 x 11-3/8"
19.2 x 12.5 x 28.5cm

Features an annexed tower and two stalls. Preweathered.

### Schillerstrasse City Block
**272-130925 171.99**
15-1/4 x 4-1/4" 38.9 x 11cm

### Lila Eule Nightclub
**272-130440 94.99**
10 x 8-3/4 x 8-3/8"
25 x 22 x 21cm

For the discriminating modeler, here's a multi-story, preweathered building for a red-light district! Features figures outside the building, as well as in the windows!

FALLER

IMPORTED FROM GERMANY BY WALTHERS

## Burning Tax Office

**272-130441 97.99**
7-3/4 x 5-3/8 x 7-3/8"
19.5 x 13.3 x 18.5cm

The facade of this preweathered burning building is blackened by smoke and fire! Features a special 16V smoke generator, flashing lights and smoke oil to refill the generator.

## Goethe Street Townhouses

**272-130915** pkg(4) **171.99**
28-13/16 x 5 x 9-13/16"
72 x 12.5 x 24.5cm

The kit includes parts for four complete buildings, dating from about 1929. Build them right from the box for steam-era layouts, or weather and customize them to fit a modern setting.

## Park Hotel

**272-130934 85.99**
10-13/32 x 9-5/8 x 9-13/32"
26 x 24 x 23.5cm

## 1950s Building Set

**272-130965 154.99**
Includes a plumber's workshop with accessories, backyard auto repair shop, ruined townhouse with rubble heap, a ruined wall, demolition excavator and ARAL gas station. Preweathered.

## Small Town Hall w/Clock Tower

**272-130924 58.99**
8 x 5-3/8 x 9-5/8"
20 x 13.3 x 24cm

This three-story building features a large entrance portal, window decorations, and a small clock tower.

## Old-Town Peel Towers

**272-130403 39.99**
1-5/8 x 1-5/8 x 5"
4 x 4 x 12.5cm
5-13/32 x 2 x 5"
6 x 5 x 12.5cm

Use these towers to add corners to your walled city. Includes one each 45° and 90° towers, which can be used with kits #272-130401, 272-130402 and 272-130404 (all sold separately).

## Old-Town Walls

**272-130404 28.99**
6-1/8 x 2-13/16 x 5"
15.3 x 3.7 x 12.5cm

Highly detailed wall sections, for use with kits #272-130401, 272-130402, and 272-130403, all sold separately.

## North German Storehouse 41.99 ea

**272-130996** Red Brick
5-5/8 x 3-5/8 x 9"
14.2 x 9 x 22.5cm

## Mittelstadt Apartments

**272-130926** pkg(2) **68.99**
5-5/8 x 3-1/8" 14.5 x 8cm

## Village Inn

**272-130269 33.99**
5-5/8 x 5-5/8" 14.5 x 14.5cm

This charming inn is the perfect place to hold a wedding reception or other celebration. The building is complete with an outdoor bandstand plus tables and chairs.

## Old Town Wall Set

**272-130401 169.99**
Re-create a medieval city for an amusement park, diorama, adventure/war game or European city scene. Basic kit includes old town wall with attached half-timber house, wall with stairway, wall with battlements, two peel towers and city gate with an attached house (both with entrances). This starter set can be expanded and customized with kits #272-130402, 130403 and 130404, all sold separately.

## 7-Story Office Building

**272-130932 154.99**
10-13/32 x 8-11/64 x 13-13/16"
26 x 20.4 x 34.5cm

Great addition to any modern city or suburban skyline, includes "mirrored glass" for offices with clear glass to showcase the elevator (nonworking) and stairway details on each floor.

# TANKS & TOWERS

## Block Post

**272-120117 23.99**
4-3/4 x 3-1/8 x 4-3/4"
12 x 7.8 x 12cm

## Signal Tower Accessories

**272-120118 15.99**
Furnish the interior of any signal tower with these devices, typical of any tower.

## Small Signal Tower

**272-120123 38.99**
5-3/8 x 1-7/8 x 4-7/16"
13.6 x 4.7 x 11.3cm

## Mittlestadt Signal Tower

**272-120120 30.99**
3-3/16 x 2-1/2" 8.4 x 6.4cm

## Sanding Tower

**272-120138 21.99**
1-3/8 x 1-3/8" 3.7 x 3.7cm

Includes hopper and ramp.

## Water Tower

**272-120143 39.99**
Radius: 3-7/8" 10cm
Height: 9-1/2" 24.2cm

IMPORTED FROM GERMANY BY WALTHERS

**Small Windmill w/Motor**
**272-130376 85.99**
4-1/2 x 4-1/2 x 10-1/4"
11.5 x 11.5 x 26cm

Includes 12-16V AC motor to move the sails at realistic slow speeds.

**Brick Signal Tower**
**272-120121 33.99**
5-1/4 x 3-1/4 x 4-3/4"
13 x 8 x 12cm

The building itself is brickwork, while the upper portion of the tower is adorned with a half-timbered design.

**Brend Observation Tower**
**272-130386 39.99**
2 x 11" 5.2 x 28cm

A narrow, two-story observation tower of natural stone, with an outside stairway on the lower area and an observation platform above

**Oil Tank w/Gasoline Pumps & Hoses**
**272-130948 23.99**
3-3/4 x 1-11/16" 9.6 x 4.3cm

**Town Gas Cylinder**
**272-130471 63.99**
6-17/32" Diameter x 6-11/16" High 16.6cm Diameter x 17cm High

**Klingentor Old City Gate**
**272-130405 85.99**
9-13/64 x 3-13/16 x 17-1/8"
23 x 9.5 x 42.8cm

**Old-Town Tower House**
**272-130402 39.99**
4 x 2-3/32 x 8-5/8"
10 x 5.2 x 21.5cm

**Neustadt Overhead Signal Tower**
**272-120124 68.99**
11-3/32 x 6-3/4 x 8-3/8"
28 x 16.8 x 21cm

The kit includes interior details for the tower and provides clearance of 3-3/16" 80cm without tracks installed. Model is based on a prototype at Neustadt/ Weinstrasse.

**Overhead Signal Tower**
**272-120125 54.99**
7 x 6-5/8" 18 x 17cm

**Two-Story Signal Tower**
**272-131220 13.99**

**Castle Tower Ruins**
**272-130285 28.99**
5-11/16 x 3-1/8" 14.5 x 8cm

New Arrivals Updated Every Day! Visit Walthers Web site at
**www.walthers.com**

**Windmill w/Motor**
**272-130233 76.99**
4 x 3-1/2" 9.8 x 8.8cm

Powered model includes 12-16V AC motor to turn the blades.

**Observation Tower**
**272-130291 23.99**
4-1/2 x 2-1/2" 11.5 x 6.5cm

**Nordex Wind Generator**
**272-130381 44.99**
2 x 2 x 13-3/16" 5 x 5 x 33cm

Based on a prototype installed in the Black Forest in 1996, it's typical of modern units seen around the world. Includes 12-16V AC motor and three-blade propeller.

**Bielefeld Water Tower**
**272-120166 54.99**
3-1/2 x 3-1/2 x 9-3/4"
9 x 9 x 24.5cm

Can be used in service areas or as the main water supply for a small town. Features a masonry entrance area, clinker tower and spherical water holder.

**Limited Quantity Available**

**Kleinau Signal Tower**
**272-120126 48.99**
7 x 5-3/8 x 4-3/4"
17.5 x 13.3 x 11.8cm

## CHURCHES

**Chapel w/Wayside Crosses**
**272-130235 30.99**
2-5/8 x 2-3/16 x 4"
6.5 x 5.5 x 10cm

Nestled high on a mountainside, this charming Swiss chapel includes wayside crosses, typically found alongside the path.

IMPORTED FROM GERMANY BY WALTHERS

**Small Village Church**
**272-130236 27.99**
4-3/4 x 2-3/4" 12 x 5.5cm

**Chapel**
**272-130234 16.99**
2 x 2-3/8" 5 x 6cm

**Mountain Chapel**
**272-131229 13.99**

**St. Bernhard Chapel**
**272-130237 33.99**
4 x 2-1/2 x 4-5/8"
9.8 x 6.1 x 11.6cm

**Church**
**272-130238 40.99**
5-13/16 x 3-1/2" 14.8 x 8.8cm

**Village Church**
**272-130241 85.99**
9-5/16 x 5" 24 x 12.9cm

**Mountain Chapel**
**272-130242 23.99**
3-13/16 x 2-5/8 x 4-3/16"
9.5 x 6.5 x 10.5cm

**Town Church w/Twin Steeples**
**272-130905 111.99**
13-5/8 x 5-5/8 x 14"
34 x 14 x 35cm

Kit includes optional spires (or "onion" domes) as well as tower crosses and stained "glass" windows.

**Bell Chimes**

**272-180642 85.99**
Features five different bell chime sounds. 12-16V AC. For use with Faller churches in HO, N and TT Scales.

**Mountain Chapel**
**272-130243 20.99**
2-3/4 x 2-3/4" 7.1 x 7.1cm

**Village Church**
**272-130240 37.99**
4-3/4 x 4" 12 x 10.2cm

Features a single bell tower with a traditional steeple. Suitable for use with TT Scale.

## BUSINESSES

**Aldi Supermarket**
**272-130339** South/North **47.99**
10-1/2 x 7-3/16 x 3-3/8"
26.6 x 18.4 x 8.6cm

This store features a delivery area, glass-front entrance and shopping carts. Stop by and save on groceries.

**Zur Linde Rural Restaurant**
**272-130428 85.99**
8-7/16 x 5-13/16 x 5-1/2"
21.4 x 14.7 x 14cm

Stairs attached to one side of this half-timbered restaurant allow customers to enjoy the outdoor eating area.

**Gas Pumps w/Service Bay**
**272-130346 21.99**
4-7/8 x 2-1/2" 12.4 x 6.3cm

**BP Gas Station**
**272-130347 33.99**
7-11/16 x 3-5/8 x 2-3/32" 19.2 x 9 x 5.5cm

This 1950s vintage station projected a clean, modern image to motorists. The large windows showcase the office details, while pumps and signs are provided for the canopy.

**Gas Station w/Car Wash**
**272-130296 44.99**
Car Wash: 4 x 3-13/16 x 1-5/8" 10 x 9.5 x 4.9cm
Office: 3-3/8 x 1-13/16 x 2" 8.5 x 6.5 x 3.9cm
Pump Island: 3-3/8 x 1-13/16 x 2" 8.4 x 4.5 x 5cm

**Gas Station w/Service Bay**
**272-130345 44.99**
6-1/4 x 3-5/8" 15.8 x 9.6cm

**Drive-In Movie**
**272-130340 549.99**
What Friday night was complete without a trip to the local drive-in? Re-live those teenage days on your layout. Includes viewing area, concession stand, marquee and 7" LCD screen that can be plugged into a regular VCR or DVD player.

## FALLER

IMPORTED FROM GERMANY BY WALTHERS

### Burnt-down Zur Sonne Restaurant

**272-130429 51.99**
5-3/8 x 4-11/16 x 4-11/16"
13.6 x 11.9 x 11.9cm

Add smoke and flashing lights (not included) for more added realism.

### Townhouse with Pub

**272-130447 64.99**
5-5/16 x 5 x 7-7/8"
13.5 x 12.5 x 20cm

This multi-story residence has a fully equipped pub on the first floor.

### Allianz Tea & Spices Townhouse

**272-130448 64.99**
7-1/4 x 5 x 8-3/16"
18.3 x 12.5 x 20.8cm

Sweet aromas drift across the street from the tea and spice shop on the ground floor of this structure. The building also houses an insurance company.

### Belaria Cinema

**272-130449 64.99**
5-11/16 x 6-7/8 x 7-7/8"
14.5 x 17.5 x 20cm

Come and see all your favorite old movies at this small-town cinema.

### Dr. Pohl Lawyer's Office

**272-130450 64.99**
5-11/16 x 5-1/2 x 7-7/8"
14.5 x 14 x 20cm

This typical townhouse has a lawyer's office on the main level and moveable windows.

### Dold Town Butcher's Shop

**272-130451 64.99**
5-11/16 x 5 x 8"
14.5 x 12.5 x 20.5cm

Fresh chicken, steaks and pork chops are custom-cut for your dinner at this local butcher shop. Includes interior equipment.

### Fontanella Ice Cream Parlor

**272-130931 33.99**
4-5/8 x 4-1/2 x 5-1/2"
11.7 x 11.4 x 13.8cm

Quench that desire for cool, refreshing ice cream inside this parlor, which is on the main level of a small-town house.

### Grocer's Shop & House

**272-130278 42.99**
8 x 6 x 4-9/32"
20 x 15 x 10.7cm

### Grain Store w/Accessories

**272-130333 25.99**
3-1/2 x 3-1/8" 9 x 8cm

### Mini Market

**272-130342 58.99**
7-3/4 x 7-3/4" 19.8 x 19.8cm

Shopping will be easy in this modern mini-mart which features a complete interior with shelves, merchandise and cash registers. For added realism, the sign on the roof can be made to rotate with motor #272-180629 (sold separately).

### Monastery Tavern

**272-131284 28.99**

### Small Greenhouse

**272-130213 30.99**
3-5/8 x 1-7/8" 9.2 x 4.7cm 2-3/4 x 1-5/8" 7.1 x 4.2cm

### Garden Center

**272-130253 59.99**
Includes house, three greenhouses, two hot beds, straw mats and accessories.

### Building Contractor's Office & Garage

**272-130971 75.99**
Office w/3-Stall Garage: 8-3/64 x 4-21/64 x 3-7/16"
20.1 x 10.8 x 8.6cm
Covered Shed: 14-13/16 x 8-21/64 x 3-23/32" 37 x 20.8 x 9.3cm

The garage features rolling shutter doors. A separate three-stall covered shed with no doors is also provided to store additional vehicles or materials. All three buildings can be used by themselves.

### Newsstands

**272-120135** pkg(2) **21.99**
Round: 2-3/4 x 1-9/16"
7 x 4cm
Square: 1-15/16 x 1-15/16"
5 x 5cm

### Auto Service/Factory

**272-130946 32.99**
6-1/4 x 3-5/8" 15.8 x 9.6cm

### Small Food Stand

**272-130212 21.99**
3-1/8 x 3" 8 x 7.7cm

FALLER

IMPORTED FROM GERMANY BY WALTHERS

## Pharmacy w/Multi-Story House

**272-130417 51.99**
4-1/2 x 3-3/4" 11.6 x 9.6cm

## Transformer Station

**272-130958 59.99**
Includes insulators, transformers and power lines.

## Krone Inn w/Beer Garden

**272-130415 51.99**
4-1/2 x 5 x 6"
11.6 x 13 x 15cm

## Wood Carver's Shop & Residence

**272-130281 51.99**
6 x 5-13/64 x 4-13/32"
15 x 13 x 11cm

A fun structure for any tourist town served by your railroad. Authentic Alpine styling with beautifully printed signs on the walls, bay window and a special set of interior details for the display window from Preiser.

## Edelweise Retirement Home

**272-130282 42.99**
6-13/64 x 6 x 4-1/8"
15.5 x 15 x 10.3cm

Kit features authentic Alpine styling and is complete with colorful wall "paintings" already printed in place. Open-air terrace includes benches and parasols.

**Limited Quantity Available**

## Hairdressing Salon

**272-130341 29.99**
7-11/16 x 5 x 5-5/16"
19.5 x 12.8 x 13.5cm

The ground floor of this one-family house has a fully-equipped hair salon complete with all interior details. Kit comes with a high-quality Wilkinson Quattro Safety Razor for your personal use.

## Television Tower Restaurant

**272-130969** Rotating Cafe, Beacon & Motor **159.99**
8-13/16 x 7-3/16 x 36"
22 x 18 x 90cm

There's a ground-floor restaurant, open observation decks, a rotating restaurant and a detailed antennae at the very top. Includes a motor drive for the restaurant, and flashing red lamp.

## Building Market

**272-130356 85.99**
23-1/2 x 22 x 6-1/2"
4.66 x 13 x 8.7cm

Set up the fencing to display the large inventory of building accessories available at the market! Also comes with a flat sales building and open storage shed.

## Kowalski Haulage Contractor

**272-130964 74.99**
14 x 10-3/8 x 4-1/4"
35 x 26 x 10.5cm

Perfect for any period layout where horse-drawn carriages and wagons are a staple! Features various buildings and accessories to complete the scene.

# INDUSTRIAL

## Municipal Gas Works Plant Stadtisches Gaswerk

**272-130472 102.99**
11-13/16 x 6-1/2 x 12-19/32"
30 x 16.5 x 32cm

## Fuel Depot

**272-130942 25.99**
4-9/16 x 3-15/16 x 2-1/4"
11.6 x 10 x 5.7cm

Includes three vertical and three horizontal storage tanks.

## Cement Works

**272-130474 59.99**
8-1/8 x 3-1/2 x 8-7/8" 20.7 x 9 x 22.5cm

Full-service cement business complete with office building, storage silos and passage for truck loading.

## SP Injection Molding Workshop

**272-130475 154.99**
14-3/4 x 8-5/8 x 5-1/8"
37.5 x 21.8 x 13cm

Includes office building, "glass" windowed work area, raw material silos and separate cooling plant. Injection molding machines include two functioning units with a red fault indicator.

## Diesel Oil Facility

**272-120145 21.99**
4-1/8 x 1-3/8" 10.5 x 3.5cm

## Sanding Facilty

**272-120146 39.99**
6 x 2-1/8" 15.5 x 5.5cm
1-1/2 x 1-1/2" 3.7 x 3.7cm

Includes sanding tower, sand house and bag of sand.

## Lumber Assortment

**272-180589 13.99**

## Loading Crane

**272-120129 16.99**
1 x 3-1/4" 2.6 x 8.3cm

Nonworking model.

## Building & Civil Engineering Construction Site

**272-130984 339.99**
This 2004 exclusive numbered model features three Wiking machines, a Brekina MAN dump truck, two construction site trailers, control panel for performing and controlling movement cycles and plenty of site details.

FALLER

IMPORTED FROM GERMANY BY WALTHERS

### Cinder Removal Facility
**272-120149 68.99**
13-1/2 x 5-3/4" 34.4 x 14.7cm

### Scrap Dealer
**272-130962 51.99**
9-3/8 x 8-3/4 x 4-1/4"
23.6 x 21.9 x 10.5cm

Includes fencing and positionable building gates.

### Sedlicek & Sohn Bell Foundry
**272-130968 68.99**
9-5/8 x 6-3/4 x 6-5/8"
24 x 17 x 16.7cm

An industrial plant for bell-making Preweathered.

### Hexenloch Mill
**272-130388 99.99**
9-3/4 x 4-3/4" 24.7 x 11.9cm

This working model includes an electric motor that turns the waterwheels in opposite directions, like the prototype.

### Gütermann Knitting Mill
**272-130979 136.99**
15-13/64 x 7-3/4 x 12-13/16"
38 x 19.3 x 32cm

The kit includes a loading ramp, a tall smokestack and a variety of period details.

### Coaling Station
**272-120148 115.99**
13 3/8 x 10-3/4"

Kit is complete with a large gantry crane, equipped with a clamshell bucket.

### Small Shed
**272-120151 25.99**
4-3/4 x 3" 12 x 6.7cm

### Minehead w/Winch House
**272-130945 78.99**
10-1/4 x 6-7/8" 26 x 17.5cm

Powering underground conveyors, the winch house is an essential part of any mining operation. The kit is complete with a minehead building and the winch can be powered with an electric motor #272-180629, available separately.

### Swivel Water Spout
**272-120137** pkg(2) **30.99**
3 x 9/16" 7.8 x 1.5cm

Includes external heater device and two gully covers.

### Back Shop
**272-120159 68.99**
10-3/8 x 6"

This brick structure features one stall, large smokestack and lots of details.

### Diesel Fuel Facility
**272-120157 51.99**
8-7/8 x 4-7/8" 22.5 x 12.4cm

### Double Silo
**272-120167 33.99**
3 x 6" 7.8 x 14.8cm

### Timber Yard
**272-130288 21.99**
5-1/8 x 3-1/2" 13 x 9cm

### Coal Chips
**272-170724 4.99**
These specially designed chips look like real coal but can be used without the mess.

### Old Concrete Mixing Plant
**272-130951 58.99**
6 x 4-5/8 x 9"
15.5 x 11.5 x 22.5cm
5-13/32 x 3-13/64 x 1-17/32"
13.5 x 8 x 3.8cm

### Old Stone Crushing Plant
**272-130961 44.99**
8 x 7-13/64 x 6"
20 x 18 x 15cm

### Old-Time Factory
**272-130980 115.99**
20-1/8 x 6-7/8" 51.2 x 17.3cm

A covered loading ramp and large smokestack (which can be fitted with a smoke generator) are included.

### Brewery
**272-130960 63.99**
6-15/16 x 6-1/2"
17.6 x 16.5cm

### Heating & Power Plant
**272-130982 68.99**
9 x 8-1/4" 23 x 21cm

## BRIDGES & VIADUCTS

### Viaduct Piers
**272-120479** Tall 7-13/64" 18cm pkg(3) **25.99**

For Marklin C track. Use with 272-120477 & 272-120478, sold separately.

### Fishbellied Bridge
**272-120496 45.99**
18-5/8 x 3-3/8 x 3-1/4"
47.2 x 8.5 x 8.2cm

This upside-down arch-supported bridge features two straight track beds and two bridge heads. Can be used with all model tracks.

### Arcades In Track Bed
**272-120486 34.99**
14-1/4 x 5 x 3-1/2"
35.8 x 12.8 x 8.7cm

Two-track arcades can be used with any type of track. Features closed brickwork arch.

### Steel Bridge
**272-120487 34.99**
Two-track steel bridge features a supporting pillar substructure. Can be used with all types of track.

### Two-Track Viaduct Bridge
**272-120485 85.99**
For use with all track. Includes track bed, high pillars and two bridge heads. Track bed height: 9-3/8" 23.4cm; inside radius: 14-3/8" 36cm; outside radius: 17.5" 43-3/4cm.

IMPORTED FROM GERMANY BY WALTHERS

## Railway Bridge
**272-120483 25.99**
12 x 2-7/8 x 4"
29.8 x 7.2 x 9.8cm

Comes with two bridge heads and one track bed.

## Two-Track Viaduct Bridge
**272-120488 76.99**
15 x 6 x 10-1/2"
37.6 x 15 x 26.2cm

Comes with track bed and high piers.

## Parapets
**272-120489** pkg(2) **31.99**
6-3/4 x 2-1/2 x 5-2/3"
16.8 x 6 x 14.2cm

For use with Two-Track Viaduct Bridge #272-120488, sold separately.

## Lifting Bridge w/Drive
**272-120490 119.99**
18 x 7-1/4 x 6-3/8"
45 x 18 x 16cm

This preweathered railway bridge features a 12-16V AC drive motor for lifting and lowering the bridge section.

## Railway-Road Bridge
**272-120491 51.99**
13-3/8 x 5-5/8 x 5"
33.5 x 14 x 12.5cm

## Bietschtal Bridge
**272-120535 119.99**
43-13/16 x 3-13/16 x 8-13/16" 109.5 x 9.5 x 22cm

This impressive steel span, an authentic replica of the Biestchtal bridge, is perfect for carrying your line across a river or other natural obstacle. Prototype is located on the south side of the Lotschberg tunnel. Use with any type of track.

## 4-Track Concrete Foot Bridge
**272-120179 33.99**
13-1/8" 33 x 19.5cm

The basic kit will cross four tracks and additional kits can be combined to build a longer bridge.

## Covered Footbridge
**272-120198 40.99**
Overall: 11 x 7-13/16 x 5-3/16"
27.3 x 19.5 x 13.8cm
Clearance: 3-3/4" 9.3 cm

Two-level open stairways lead to an enclosed walkway that can span up to four tracks. Plenty of room underneath for steam-era models or modern double-stacks, bi-level cars or electrified equipment.

## Railroad Girder Bridge
**272-120560 39.99**
15-13/64 x 3-13/64 x 5-17/32"
38 x 8 x 13.8cm
Clearance: 1-13/16" 4.5cm

## Arch Bridge
**272-120536 34.99**
14-1/4 x 2-1/2 x 4-3/4"
36 x 6.5 x 11.9cm

## Deck Arch Bridge
**272-120541 33.99**
14-1/4 x 2-1/2 x 4-3/4"
36 x 6.5 x 11.9cm

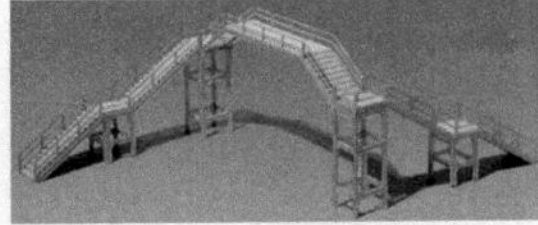

## 2-Track Steel Foot Bridge
**272-120178 28.99**
7 x 4-3/4" 18 x 11.9cm

## Girder Bridge
**272-120534 22.99**
7 x 4-3/4" 18 x 11.9cm

## Concrete Bridge Piers
**272-120538** pkg(18) **25.99**
For #120534, 120536 and 120541.

## Stone Arch Bridge
**272-120533 51.99**
14 x 1-3/4" 36 x 4.4cm

Several bridges can be built and interconnected with each other.



## Bridges & Accessories For Marklin C Track

### Up & Over Bridge Set 85.99 ea

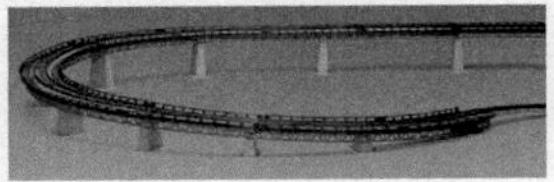

272-120470 272-120471

**272-120470** Outside Circle-Large Radius 360mm
**272-120471** Inside Circle-Smaller 17-1/2" 43.7cm Radius
Smaller radius allows you to build another bridge inside of #272-120470, sold separately.

### Bridge Piers pkg(6)
For use with #272-120470, 120474 and 120475, all sold separately.

272-120472 272-120473

**272-120472** Graduated **14.99**
From 5/8 to 3" 1.5 to 7.5cm tall.

**272-120473** Tall **14.99**
Each stands 3" 7.5cm tall, and includes a 21/64" 0.8cm cap which locks into Bridge Track Beds (sold separately).

### Bridge Track Bed 11.99 ea
Matching parts that can be used to customize #272-120470 and 120471, each sold separately.

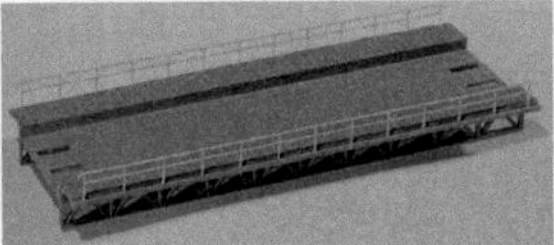

272-120474 272-120475

**272-120474** Straight 7-1/2" 18.9cm tall
**272-120475** Curved 14-13/32" 36cm Radius
**272-120476** Curved 17-1/2" 43.7cm Radius

### Viaduct Top Sections 21.99 ea
Sections stand 2-5/8" 6.5cm tall.

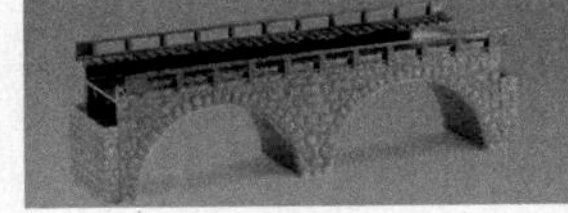

272-120477 272-120478

**272-120477** Straight 7-1/2" 18.9cm Long
**272-120478** Curved 14-13/32" 36cm Radius

**Limited Quantity Available**

## Canal Bridge
**272-120492 20.99**
5-3/8 x 2-3/8 x 3-1/4"
13.4 x 6 x 8cm

## Straight Bridge Section
**272-120553 11.99**
7" 18cm long.

# CASTLES

## Lichtenstein Castle
**272-130245 51.99**
5-1/2 x 2-15/16" 13.3 x 7.5cm

This imposing castle is specially designed for use as a backdrop building. The finished model is slightly smaller than HO Scale, so it will not overwhelm surrounding scenery.

FALLER

IMPORTED FROM GERMANY BY WALTHERS

## Rabenstein Castle

**272-130244 68.99**
11-3/8 x 8 x 8-3/8"
28.5 x 19.9 x 21cm

This spacious medieval castle features a tower, dwelling wing and premise-enclosing wall. Note: castle does not conform to HO Scale, but is suggested for use as a background building to indicate distance.

# CARNIVAL

## RIDES

### Power Tower

**272-140325** Operating Ride **256.99**
9-7/8 x 8-3/8 x 27"
25 x 21.5 x 68.5cm

Travel up to a dizzying height followed by a moment of hesitation and then a fast free fall. The WORKING model is equipped with a 12-16V AC/DC drive motor.

### Faller 20th Anniversary Edition Wild Mouse Roller Coaster

**272-140425 256.99**
21-3/4 x 9-11/16 x 13"
55.2 x 24.6 x 33cm

This working model features four cars that are lifted and sent careening around a twisting, turning track, through the "Cat's Mouth" tunnel and back to the base station. Also includes working lights, ticket shanty and signs. Preiser figures shown sold separately. Special lighting unit included requires a 5V power source.

Break Dancer No. 1 Roundabout
272-140461

Pirate's Island Wildwater Log Ride
272-140430

### Octopussy Roundabout

**272-140426 214.99**
9-13/16 x 10-1/4 x 5-5/8"
25 x 26 x 14.2cm

Model features five rotating arms that move up and down and tilt, all controlled by the drive system.

### Circus World Roundabout

**272-140331 133.99**
6-11/16 x 5-5/16 x 2"
17 x 13.5 x 5cm

### Chair-O-Plane

**272-140315 102.99**
8 x 8" 20 x 20cm

The operating model features 12 seats and brightly colored roof panels, motor and lighting for night scenes.

### Jupiter Ferris Wheel

**272-140470 323.99**
11-1/4 x 8-7/8 x 20-3/4"
28 x 22 x 52cm

This colorful carnival ride features 36 illuminated cars, "Jupiter" lettering, ticket booth and supporting pillars with illuminating option. Bring this great ride to life with the 16V AC motor.

### Ferris Wheel Lighting Kit

**272-140471 254.99**
For use with Jupiter Ferris Wheel #272-140470, sold separately. Will bring all the lighting elements of the wheel to life, from the 36 separate cars to the "Jupiter" lettering to the front supporting pillars. Comes with power supply.

### Undulation Roundabout

**272-140317 308.99**
12-5/8 x 8 x 6-5/8"
31.5 x 20 x 16.5cm

Carousel-type ride has swings suspended from chains that swing outward as the ride circles about! The 12-16V DC/AC motor brings the ride to life, lifting and lowering the roof for the swings to spin! Includes rows of double seats and a ticket booth.

### Break Dancer No. 1 Roundabout

**272-140461 102.99**
Sixteen colorful gondolas spin riders on four turntables. Set also comes with two ticket booths. Can motorize with 12-16V AC motor #272-180629, sold separately.

Jupiter Ferris Wheel 272-140470

Undulation Roundabout 272-140317

### Pirate's Island Wildwater Log Ride

**272-140430 299.99**
21-3/16 x 17 3/16 x 8 7/16"
53 x 43 x 21cm

The log boats race along the course on real water, powered by two water pumps that keep the water jetting along. Two motor lifts carry the logs up the hills where they soon shoot down the steep inclines. Includes everything you need to recreate a thrilling water ride. Motors and pumps each require 12-16V AC.

### Pit's Steep Face Show

**272-140330 134.99**
7-1/8 x 6-5/8 x 5"
17.8 x 16.7 x 12.5cm

Three motorcycles drive around the steep-face circle, thanks to the drive motor and 16V AC/DC control unit. Includes a colorful trailer.

FALLER

IMPORTED FROM GERMANY BY WALTHERS

### Top Spin

**272-140431 205.99**
9-5/8 x 9-5/8 x 8-9/16"
24 x 24 x 21.4cm

Model comes with two drive motors (operates from any 12-16V AC power source) that turn the large arms and the gondola just like the real ride! Complete with background panels, ticket booth and detailing accessories.

### Ferris Wheel

9 x 7-1/2 x 22-3/8"
22.5 x 18.7 x 56cm

This is a must for every county fair, carnival or amusement park scene! This kit includes over 275 parts, molded in 10 different colors. Unpowered Ferris Wheel can be powered with Electric Motor #272-180629 and lighted with Lighting Set #272-180635, each sold separately.

**272-140312** Unpowered Ferris Wheel **119.99**
**272-180635** Lighting Set For Ferris Wheel **59.99**
**272-180636** Replacement Bulbs pkg(6) **23.99**
**272-180629** Electric Motor **33.99**
**272-180628** High Power Motor **39.99**
Reversible, 4/15 RPM, produces 35% more power than #272-180629.

### Music Express Roundabout

**272-140437 119.99**
Jump in and hang on as the Music Express whirls your car around at super speed! Includes 20 colored cars, chrome-plated parts, 12-16V AC motor and lighting.

### Swingboats

**272-140318 82.99**
7-3/8 x 4" 18.4 x 9.8cm

Includes motor to move boats back and forth. Special feature on motor makes red lamps flash on and off (requires Lighting Kit #272-180671, sold separately.

### Top In Dodgem Car Ride

**272-140435 186.99**
15-5/8 x 7-13/16 x 4-13/16"
39 x 19.5 x 12cm

An exact replica of the Mack original. Twelve dodgem cars bump about, thanks to a hidden magnet drive powered by a 12-16V AC motor. The ride features detailed decoration, a raised platform and ticket booth.

### Jungle Train Carousel

**272-140433 119.99**
8-21/64 x 7-31/32 x 3-3/4"
20.8 x 19.9 x 9.3cm.

The 20 gondolas included on this WORKING ride spin forward and backward, thanks to a hidden drive motor included with the kit (requires 12-16V AC power supply).

### Flipper Roundabout

**272-140439 119.99**
10-3/8 x 9" 26 x 22.5cm

Twelve colorful gondolas spin around at breathtaking speed, with the rotating table rising and falling at the same time. Complete with motor, background scene and ticket booth. Can be illuminated with Lighting Kit #272-180671 (sold separately).

### Big Dipper Roller Coaster

**272-140451 248.99**
28-5/8 x 17-1/8 x 16-3/8"
71.5 x 43 x x 41cm

Fully functional roller coaster has a 12-16V DC or AC motor that pulls cars up to the top of the run, where their own momentum carries them around the track with the help of ball bearings.

## CONCESSIONS & GAMES

### Mouse Circus & Hamburger Stand Fairground Booths

**272-140319** pkg(2) **46.99**
Mouse Circus: 3-1/4 x 1-5/8 x 2-1/4" 8 x 4 x 5.5cm;
Hamburger Stand: 6 x 2 x 3-1/8" 15 x 5.2 x 7.8cm

### Midway Booths

**272-140320** pkg(2) **27.99**
3-7/8 x 1-1/4" 9.6 x 3.2cm

### Pizza & Popcorn Stands

**272-140324** pkg(2) **32.99**
3-3/4 x 2-3/8" 9.4 x 6.1cm
2-3/4 x 1-5/8" 7 x 4.1cm

### Candy & Crepes Stands

**272-140453** pkg(2) **27.99**
1-7/8 x 1-7/8" 4.5 x 4.5cm

Midway Booths 272-140320

Pizza & Popcorn Stands 272-140324

Candy & Crepes Stand 272-140453

Funfair Stands 272-140462

Food Booths 272-140455

### Funfair Stands

**272-140462** pkg(2) **32.99**
Hat Toss: 2-1/2 x 1-1/2 x 2"
6.4 x 3.9 x 5cm
Maize Man:
2-1/2 x 1-1/2 x 3-5/8"
6.3 x 3.9 x 9.1cm

Two colorful booths to delight young and old along your model midway!

### Food Booths

**272-140455** pkg(2) **32.99**
Liven up any midway with this set. One sells fruit drinks, while the other is an Asian food stand.

## FALLER

IMPORTED FROM GERMANY BY WALTHERS

### Roundabout Bar Refreshment Stand

**272-140322 37.99**
6-1/4 x 3-3/8 x 3"
15.5 X 8.3 X 7.4 cm

Complete with high tables, stools and decorative material.

### Sylter Backfischrutsche Shop

**272-140352 41.99**
2-1/2 x 2-1/2 x 4-1/4"
6.4 x 6.4 x 10.7cm

Fish is fried in the lighthouse, then slides down a stainless-steel chute into the salesroom below.

### Fairground Booths

**272-140457** pkg(2) **23.99**
2-1/2 x 2 x 2-3/8"
6.5 x 4 x 5.5cm

Your layout just won't be complete without the familiar site of these gaming booths, common at fairs and carnivals across the land.

### Two Fair Booths

**272-140465 19.99**
Visit the American ice cream stand and the garlic baguette seller!

### Midway Food & Game Stands

**272-140464** Set of Two **32.99**
Mr. Hot Dog:
2-1/2 x 1-5/8 x 2-3/8"
6.4 x 4 x 5.9cm
Power Ball Toss:
2-11/16 x 1-3/4 x 3-27/32"
6.7 x 4.3 x 9.6cm

Kits are complete with printed signs. Preiser figures shown not included.

### Game Booths

**272-140452 42.99**
10-1/8 x 2-1/4" 25.3 x 5.5cm

### Midway Food Stands

**272-140463** pkg(2) **30.99**
Puschmann's Kitchen:
3-49/64 x 2-17/32 x 3-17/32"
9.4 x 6.3 x 8cm
Pineapple Fruit Stand:
1-31/32" x 1-7/8 x 2-31/64"
4.9 x 4.7 x 6.2cm

Set includes parts for two complete kits.

### Vehicles

**272-140468** Fairground Van Set **44.99**
Includes two luggage vans and two lavatory units.

## GO-KART RACING

### Paris-Dakar Race

**272-140333** Go-Kart Ride **272.99**
17-1/8 x 8-7/8 x 6-7/8"
43.5 x 22 x 17.5cm

Spectators are spellbound watching the speedy go-karts whiz around the circuit of this two-level track. 16V AC transformer needed to operate the ride is not included. Additional go-karts #272-141010 are available separately.

### Go-Kart Circuit

**272-141000 272.99**
16-1/2 x 11-15/16 x 5/8"
42 x 30.2 x 1.5cm

Capture the fun and excitement of a racetrack. Two go-karts race side-by-side around this sinuous two-lane circuit. Kit comes with roadway borders, tire piles and two controllers. 16V DC transformer not included. Additional go-karts #272-141010 available separately.

### Go-Kart

**272-141010** Assorted Colors **33.99**
Fully assembled vehicle with driver for use with racing circuits #272-14033 and 272-141000, each sold separately.

### Conti Tower

**272-141070 33.99**
11-11/16 x 3-3/16 x 7-5/16"
29.8 x 8 x 18.5cm

This slim tower with six attached garages is the ideal staging area for go-kart races. Features spectators terraces and printed signs. Use with racing circuit #272-14101, sold separately.

Go-Kart Racing Paris-Daker Race 272-140333

Go-Kart Circit 272-141000

### Start/Finish Terraces

**272-141071 39.99**
7-7/8 x 3-3/16 x 6-3/8"
20 x 8.1 x 16.2cm -
10 x 6.2 x 5.9cm

Race fans want to be at the heart of the action and this two-level grandstand fills the bill. Place at the start/finish line of go-kart circuit #272-141000, sold separately.

### Rotunda Cafe

**272-141072 27.99**
4-15/16 x 3-1/2 x 3-1/2"
12 x 9 x 9cm

Even die-hard race fans need food and drink. But they won't miss any of the action while enjoying a snack in this see-through round restaurant. Designed to match go-kart circuit #272-141000, sold separately.

## FRENCHMAN RIVER MODEL WORKS

## NEW PRODUCT

### Awning Kit

**NEW 267-201 9.50**
Add realistic awnings cut to the exact size of storefront or standard windows on any building with this simple kit. Includes over 159 scale feet of awning fabric in green, red, black and white, plus over 318 scale feet of support wire and easy instructions.

Designed for ease of construction, all Laserkit® structures feature precision laser-cut basswood and plywood parts that assemble much like plastic kits. Unless noted, all kits feature peel and stick assembly windows with positionable sashes, doors, trim and roofing material. All walls and major assemblies have tab-and-slot construction. Kits may also include white metal and acrylic detail parts.

## NEW PRODUCTS

### Stations & Depots

**UP Standard Single Story Depot**
**NEW 152-182 89.95**
10 x 3-1/2 x 2-1/2" 25.4 x 8.9 x 6.4cm

Patterned after a standard UP design, this wooden depot is similar to station buildings used across the continent.

**PRR MO Tower**
**NEW 152-185 TBA**
4-1/2 x 2-5/8 x 4-1/2"
10.7 x 6.6 x 11.4cm

**PRR 1911 Standard Watch Box**
**NEW 152-186** pkg(2) **23.95**
1 x 3/4 x 1-1/2"
2.5 x 1.9 x 3.8cm

**PRR 1879 Standard Watch Box**
**NEW 152-187** pkg(2) **22.95**
1 x 3/4 x 1-1/2"
2.5 x 1.9 x 3.8cm

**ATSF Standard Telephone Booths**
**NEW 152-183** pkg(3) **19.95**
Each: 3/4 x 3/4 x 1-1/2"
1.9 x 1.9 x 3.8cm

### Houses

**The Drinkwater Place**
**NEW 152-184 39.95**
3 x 5 x 4-1/4"
7.6 x 12.7 x 10.8cm

Based on a typical North American family farm house, this 1920s-era home looks great on steam- and diesel-era layouts.



## STATIONS & PLATFORMS

**Illinois Central Type B Depot**
**152-124 39.95**
3 x 4-1/4" 7.5 x 10.6cm

**Union Pacific Standard 24 x 64' Depot Oregon Shortline Version**
**152-127 89.95**
10 X 3-1/2 x 2-1/3"
8.4 x 17.1cm

**Atlantic Coast Line Depot**
**152-130 79.95**
13 x 5 x 3-1/2"
32.5 x 12.5 x 8.7cm

**Great Northern Depot**
**152-133 69.95**
8-1/4 x 4-1/8 x 3-1/4"
20.6 x 10.3 x 9.3cm

**Southern Pacific Standard No. 22 Depot**
**152-134 129.95**
Station building alone:
11 x 3-1/2 x 4-1/2"
27.5 x 8.7 x 11.2cm
Loading dock adds 5" (12.5cm) to length, 1" (2.5cm) to width.

**Springfield Depot**
**152-138 44.95**
5-1/2 x 2-1/4 x 2-1/2"
13.8 x 5.6 x 6.3cm

**Southern Pacific Combination Type 23 Depot w/Dock**
**152-150 109.95**
16 x 4-3/4 x 3-1/2" 40 x 11.9 x 8.8cm

**SP Two Story Combination Depot Type 22**
**152-176** Left Hand **129.95**
11 x 3-1/2 x 4-1/2" 27.9 x 8.9 x 11.4cm

**New Freedom, Pennsylvania Depot**
**152-141 84.95**
13 x 5 x 3-3/4"
32.5 x 12.5 x 9.3cm

**New Haven Wethersfield Depot**
**152-148 59.95**
6-1/4 x 3-1/2 x 3-1/2"
15.6 x 8.7 x 8.7cm

**Northern Pacific Class A Depot**
**152-149 84.95**
10-1/2 x 3 x 3-1/2"
26.2 x 7.5 x 8.7cm

**Ilinois Central Type A Depot**
**152-177 39.95**
5 x 2-3/4 x 2-1/4"
12.7 x 7 x 5.7cm

**Freight House**
**152-701 39.95**
8 x 4 x 3-1/2"
20 x 10 x 8.8cm

**Box Car Depot Set**
**152-717 39.95**
Each measures:
5 x 1-1/4 x 1-1/2"

Includes two structures.

**Santa Fe Depot #3**
**152-801 84.95**
8-3/4 x 4-1/8 x 3-1/4"
21.8 x 10.3 x 9.3cm

**ATSF #1 Standard One-Story Depot**
**152-802 54.95**
5-1/2 x 2-1/4 x 2-1/2"
14 x 5.7 x 6.4cm

### ATSF #5 Standard One-Story Depot

**152-805 129.95**
15-1/2 x 4-1/8 x 3-1/4"
39.4 x 10.5 x 8.3cm

### Dolores Depot

**152-803 129.95**
9-1/2 x 4 x 4"
24.1 x 10.2 x 10.2cm

### Strong Depot

**152-804 69.95**
6 x 3 x 5" 15.2 x 7.6 x 12.7cm

## YARD EQUIPMENT & FACILITIES

### Railroad Supply Building

**152-118 34.95**
4-7/8 x 2-5/8" 12.1 x 6.5cm

### Pennsylvania Tool House

**152-131 19.95**
3 x 2-1/4 x 2" 7.5 x 5.6 x 5cm

### CB&Q Standard Tool House

**152-163** pkg(2) **19.95**
2 x 1-3/4 x 1-1/2"
5.1 x 4.5 x 3.8cm

### 85' Wood Roundhouse

**152-170** Two Stall **129.95**
12" 30.5cm Long,
6" 15.2cm High, 8" 20.3cm
Wide at rear of building.

**152-171** Center-Stall Add-on
**49.95**

**152-172** Four Stall **204.95**
12" 30.5cm Long, 6" 15.2cm High, 14-1/2" 36.8cm Wide at rear of building.

**152-173** Six Stall **284.95**
12" 30.5cm Long, 6" 15.2cm High, 14-1/2" 55.9cm Wide at rear of building.

### Pump House

**152-158 12.95**
1-1/2 x 1-1/2 x 5"
3.7 x 3.7 x 12.5cm

A companion structure to kit #154 Water Tank.

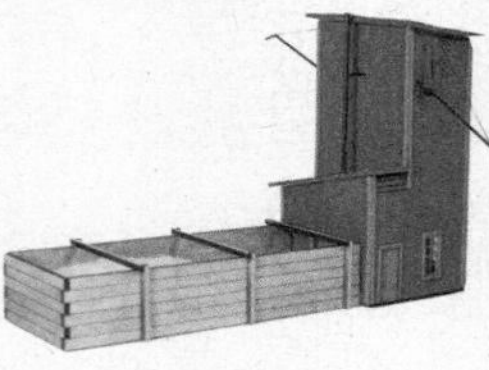

### Railroad Sandhouse

**152-162 34.95**
7-5/8 x 2-1/2 x 5"
19.4 x 6.4 x 12.7cm

### Single-Stall Engine House

**152-708 52.95**
9 x 5 x 4" 22.5 x 12.5 x 10cm

### Santa Fe Structures

Based on ATSF standard drawings. All kits feature 100% laser-cut parts with Tab & Slot construction and Peel & Stick components. All kits also include door hasps with open and close switch locks.

### Yard Closets (Outhouses)

**152-167** Single Stall pkg(2)
**8.95**
5/8 x 5/8 1-1/4"
1.5 x 1.5 x 3.1cm

**152-168** Double Stall pkg(2)
**9.95**
1-1/8 x 5/8 x 1-1/4"
2.8 x 1.5 x 3.1cm

### Houses

**152-169** Standard Section Tool House **11.95**
2 x 1-3/4 x 1-3/4"
5 x 4.3 x 4.3cm

**152-174** Signal Maintainer's House w/Motor Car Stall **12.95**
3 x 2 x 1-3/4" 7.5 x 5 x 4.3cm

Kit includes one-piece roof, door roller mounts, door rail with mounting hardware, roof flashing and more.

**152-175** Signal Maintainer's House – No Motor Car Stall
**11.95**
2 x 1-3/4 x 1-3/4"
5 x 4.3 x 4.3cm

## RURAL BUILDINGS

### Sonny's Shack

**152-705 22.95**
4-1/2 x 2-1/2 x 1-3/4"
11.2 x 6.2 x 4.3cm

### Elevated Warehouse

**152-706 34.95**
4-3/4 x 2-1/2 x 2-1/2"
11.8 x 6.2 x 6.2cm

### Midwest Farm Combo

**152-178 129.95**
Country Barn: 7-1/2 x 5-1/2 x 5-3/4" 19.1 x 14 x 14.6cm
Two-Story Farmhouse: 4-3/4 x 4-1/2 x 4-1/4" 12.1 x 11.4 x 10.8cm
Sonny's Shack: 4-1/2 x 2-1/2 x 1-3/4" 11.4 x 6.4 x 4.4cm

This cost-saving combo includes the Country Barn, the Two-Story Farmhouse and Sonny's Shack to build a typical Midwestern family farm scene.

### Feeder Barn

**152-711 29.95**
7 x 4-3/4 x 3-1/2"
17.5 x 11.8 x 8.7cm

### Country Barn

**152-119 79.95**
7-1/2 x 5-1/2" 18.8 x 13.8cm

## HOUSES

### Mrs. Williams House

**152-126 44.95**
6 x 3-3/4" 15 x 9.3cm

### Two-Story Section House

**152-128 44.95**
3-3/4 x 4-1/2 x 3"
9.7 x 11.5 x 7.5cm

### One-Story Section House

**152-129 29.95**
5-3/4 x 2-1/2 x 2-1/2"
14.4 x 6.3 x 6.3cm

### 1-1/2 Story House w/Porch - 139 Maple Street

**152-139 34.95**
3-1/2 x 3 x 2-1/2"
8.7 x 7.5 x 6.2cm

### Two-Story Farm House w/Front Porch

**152-140 46.95**
4-3/4 x 3-1/4 x 4-1/4"
11.8 x 8.1 x 10.6cm

### Old Man Dan's House

**152-151 44.95**
4 x 4 x 2-1/4"
10 x 10 x 5.6cm

### Long Bell Lumber Co. Skid Shacks

**152-710** pkg(3) **24.95**
2-1/2 x 1-3/4 x 1-1/2"
6.2 x 4.3 x 3.7cm

**Railroad Rooming House**
**152-713 59.95**
11-1/2 x 2 x 3"
28.7 x 5 x 7.5cm

## TANKS & TOWERS

**Interlocking Tower N&W "Forest"**
**152-132 52.95**
2-1/4 x 1-3/4 x 4"
12.5 x 6.2 x 10.6cm

**Burlington (CB&Q) "Wood Tower"**
**152-160 44.95**
6 x 1-3/4 x 3-1/2"
15 x 4.3 x 8.7cm

**50,000 Gallon Railroad Water Tank**
**152-154 59.95**
3-1/2 x 3-1/2 x 4-1/2" 8.9 x 8.9 x 11.4cm

**Yard Office**
**152-709 29.95**
2-1/2 x 1-3/4 x 3"
10 x 4.3 x 7.5cm

**Interlocking Tower**
**152-702 29.95**
2-1/4 x 1-3/4 x 4"
5.6 x 4.3 x 10cm

**Wood Water Supply Tank w/Pump House**
**152-720 29.95**
Tank: 2-1/2 x 2 x 6"
Pump House: 1-3/4 x 1 x 1-1/2"

## CITY BUILDING

**Hillview Volunteer Fire Company**
**152-147 44.95**
2-3/4 x 3-3/4 x 4-3/4"
6.8 x 9.3 x 11.8cm

## BUSINESSES

**Dill's Market**
**152-122 22.95**
4-1/4 x 3" 10.6 x 7.5cm

**Corydon General Store/ Post Office**
**152-123 44.95**
5 x 3-1/4 x 3"
12.5 x 8.6 x 7.5cm

**Ellington's Mercantile**
**152-135 44.95**
6-1/2 x 6 x 3-1/2"
16.2 x 15 x 8.7cm

**Springfield Cafe**
**152-136 32.95**
4-1/2 x 2-1/4 x 3"
11.3 x 5.6 x 7.5cm

**Windsor Hotel**
**152-143 59.95**
3-1/2 x 6-1/2 x 4-1/2"
8.8 x 16.3 x 11.3cm

**Millennium Series – Dabler Mill & Supply**
**152-2001 279.95**
18 x 12 x 9" 45 x 30 x 22.5cm

A multi-level, multi-roof-angle structure featuring laser-cut wood, fake "rolled asphalt brick siding," exposed cast white metal "drive gear and chain" on the grain elevator housing, grain dryer, enclosed rail car unloading area with adjoining outdoor dock, office, storage shed, exterior stairs, ventilators with individual tabbed slats, numerous smokejacks and chimneys, signage, and detail parts including a window air conditioner, gas pumps, scales and much more. Construction is AMB's tab and slot with peel and stick windows, doors, roofing and "brick" siding.

**Martinsburg Coal Mine #1**
**152-164 62.95**
10 x 9 x 5" 25.4 x 22.9 x 12.7cm

Includes hoist house with attached changing room, headframe with loading house and tailings trestle. Coal chutes provided for both railcar and truck loading.

**152-165** 12" Trestle Extension for #152-164 **16.95**

**A.C. Brown Manufacturing Company**
**152-715 104.95**
12 x 6-1/4 x 5-1/4"

**Nine Mile House & Tavern**
**152-145 69.95**
4 x 5 x 4-1/2"
10 x 12.5 x 11.2cm

**Polar Bear Café**
**152-714 44.95**
4 x 4 x 3"
10.2 x 10.2 x 7.6cm
Includes cast-resin polar bear statue, metal detail parts and color signs.

## INDUSTRIAL

**Farmer's Grain & Stock Co.**
**152-115 54.95**
9 x 5 x 7"
22.5 x 12.5 x 17.5cm

**Silex Elevator**
**152-121 44.95**
4-1/2 x 5-1/2 x 7-3/4"
11.2 x 13.8 x 19.4cm

**Glenwood No. 2 Oil Derrick**
**152-716 82.95**
9 x 4-1/2 x 15"
22.5 x 11.2 x 37.5cm
Designed for use with Walthers HO Scale Oil Pump. 100% laser-cut with several outbuildings, stairs and a platform.

**Alton Grain Elevator**
**152-166 69.95**
6-1/2 x 5-1/2 x 10-1/2"
16.2 x 13.7 x 26.2cm

**Coldwater Coal Company**
**152-181 79.95**
This structure is typical of small community material yards where local townspeople and businesses purchased heating coal and other commodities such as gravel and sand. The kit includes a yard office with truck scale, storage bins, 120 scale feet of wood fencing and a coal trestle based on a PRR prototype.

**F. Bruckner Woodworking**
**152-719 34.95**
7 x 4-1/4 x 3"
17.5 x 10.6 x 7.5cm

**Mittco-Hornkohl Manufacturing Co.**
**152-721 49.95**
10-1/4 x 5-1/4 x 2-3/4"
25.6 x 13.1 x 6.8cm

## RAIL-MARINE

**NYC Harbor Barge Style #1**
**152-8001 129.95**
14 x 4 x 3"
35.6 x 10.2 x 7.6cm

**Bump-End Barge**
**152-8000 119.95**
14 x 4 x 3"

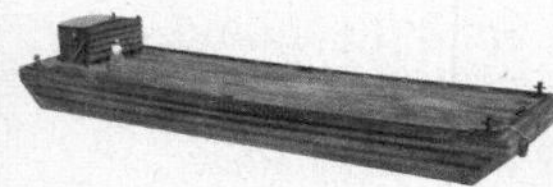

**Cabin Scow Barge**
**152-8003 79.95**
14 x 4 x 3" 35 x 10 x 7.5cm



## LASERKIT® XPRESS

Priced under 16.95 so you can put multiples of these products on your layout, these kits are designed to be simple enough for the first time modeler to complete assembly in under two hours.

**Branchline Station**
**152-790 13.95**
3 x 2-1/4 x 2"
7.6 x 5.7 x 5.1cm

**Crossroads Church**
**152-791 15.95**
4 x 2 x 3-1/2" 10.2 x 5.1 x 8.9cm

**Gandy Dancer's Shack**
**152-792 11.95**
3-1/2 x 1-1/2 x 1-1/2"
8.9 x 3.8 x 3.8cm

**McCormac's Dry Goods**
**152-793 16.95**
5 x 2-1/2 x 3"
12.7 x 6.4 x 7.6cm

**The Loft Barn**
**152-794 14.95**
2-1/2 x 3-1/4 x 3"
6.4 x 8.3 x 7.6cm

**One Car Garage**
**152-796 10.95**
2 x 2-1/2 x 1-3/4"
5 x 6.4 x 4.4cm

**Gas Station**
**152-797 16.95**
2-1/4 x 1-1/4 x 2-1/4"
5.7 x 3.2 x 5.7cm
Includes cast white-metal pumps and base.

**Company House**
**152-798 11.95**
2-3/4 x 2-1/2 x 2"
7 x 6.4 x 5cm

**Small False Front Store**
**152-799 10.95**
1-1/2 x 2-1/2 x 2"
3.8 x 6.4 x 5cm

## CATALOG

**Catalog**
**152-99999** HO **2.00**

These HO craft train kits feature cardstock or metal construction (as noted). Mat board is printed or embossed to simulate brick, concrete block, board and batten, clapboard or stucco. These kits also include stripwood for bracing and trim. Corrugated metal buildings require soldering skills. Kits include signs and detail parts. Interiors and lighting are included with some models.

Items listed in blue ink may not be available at all times (see Legend Page).

## STATIONS & PLATFORMS

**Modern Station**
700-503 9.63
4-1/2 x 7" 11.5 x 8cm

**Standard Station**
700-504 14.03
4 x 6" 10 x 15.3cm

**Combination Town Depot 40.15 ea**
6 x 12-1/2" 15.3 x 32cm

Southern Pacific Type 22. Figures not included.

**700-7002** Gray

Items listed below are available by Special Order (see Legend Page).

**700-7001** Orange

**700-7003** Red

## YARD EQUIPMENT & FACILITIES

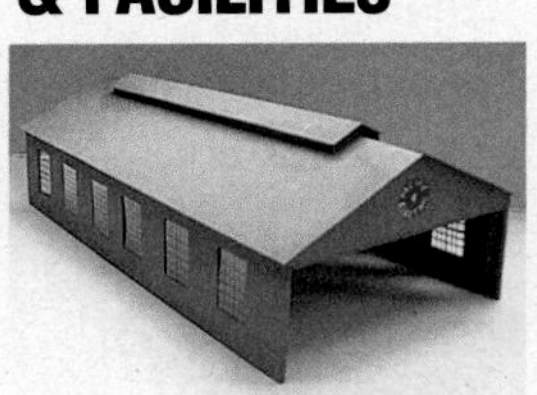

**3-Track Car Barn-Metal**
700-20 28.05
17 x 16" 18 x 40.5cm

**3-Stall Roundhouse-Metal**
700-8 34.65
12 x 12" 30.5 x 30.5cm

Items listed below are available by Special Order (see Legend Page).

**3 Extra Stalls for Roundhouse-Metal**
**700-8243 22.28**

**1 Extra Stall for Roundhouse-Metal**
**700-8241 9.35**

**Brick Car Barn**
700-21 2-Track 30.80

## CITY BUILDINGS

**Fire Station #9**
**700-3080 30.75**
3-1/2 x 6-1/8 x 3-7/8"
8.8 x 15.3 x 9.7cm

This two-story brick firehouse comes with two equipment bays, a hose tower, signs, flagpole and American flag. Choose from two different door styles (round-top swing-out or flat-top roll-out) to customize the design.

## BUSINESSES

**Old Town Buildings**
700-571 pkg(3) 31.08
2-1/4 x 4" 5.7 x 10cm
5-3/4 x 5" 14.7 x 12.8cm
4-1/4 x 5-1/2" 10.8 x 14cm

**Your Hobby Shop**
**700-71 21.45**
5-1/2 x 6" 14 x 15.3cm

Item listed below is available by Special Order (see Legend Page).

**Illuminated Sign for Hobby Shop**
**700-7112 4.35**

**Sunkist Citrus Exchange**
700-83 19.53
4-1/2 x 6-1/2" 11.5 x 16.5cm

"Stucco" mat board. Includes dock.

**Old Town Lodgings**
**700-572 21.73**
3-1/4 x 4" 8.3 x 10cm
4 x 4-7/8" 10 x 12.5cm

## INDUSTRIAL

**Buckhorn Mine Ore Plant-Metal**
700-4 28.55
6 x 16" 15.3 x 40.5cm

**Black Bart Mine & Shaft-Metal**
700-5 17.55
3 x 7" 7.5 x 18cm

**Red Lake Hillside Mine-Metal**
**700-6 18.54**
5 x 7" 12.8 x 17.8cm

For hillside construction.

**Grain Elevator-Metal**
**700-12 28.05**
5 x 5" 12.8 x 12.8cm

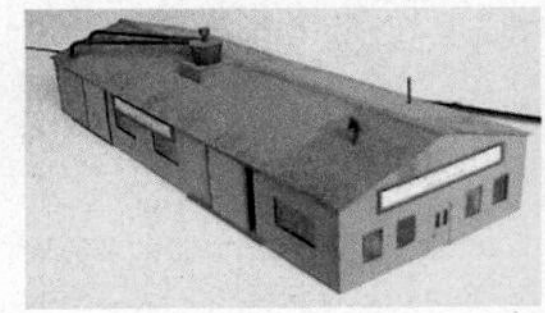

**Furniture Factory-Metal**
700-1 21.45
4-1/2 x 12" 11.5 x 30.5cm

**Mining Company Mill-Metal**
**700-18 13.20**
4 x 6" 10 x 15.3cm

**Lumber Company Store & Shed**
700-562 20.85

**Scale Lumber Package**
**700-565 6.33**

**American Chemical & Potash Co. & Annex-Metal**
700-22 Main Plant 37.40
700-23 Annex 42.90
6 x 14" 15 x 35cm

**Mining Hoist House-Metal**
**700-17 13.20**
3 x 5" 7.5 x 12.8cm

**Pacific Foundry-Metal**
700-19 13.20
5 x 8" 12.8 x 20.5cm

### Electronics Plant

700-74 18.43
5-1/4 x 11" 13.5 x 28cm

### Lumber Rack & Office

700-561 18.65

### Millard's & Sons Industrial Office Building

**700-1699 14.03**
3 x 6" 7.6 x 15.2cm

This small corrugated metal structure is suitable for use as a mining office, small manufacturing shop or an outbuilding for an industrial spread. Includes plastic windows and sign.

Item listed below is available by Special Order (see Legend Page).

### G&H Sugar Elevator

**700-2698 35.20**
6-1/2 x 12-1/2" 16.5 x 31.8 cm

Modeled after a G&H facility in City of Industry, California, this corrugated metal kit features plastic doors, window frames and stairs.

## SIGNS

### Wood Billboard

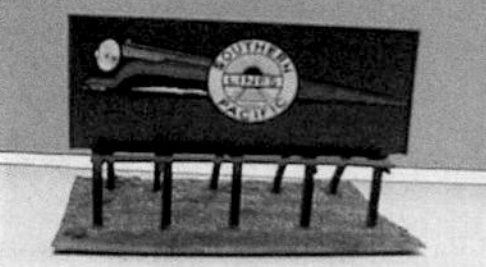

**700-89** With Four-Color SP "Daylight" Sign **8.78**

## NEW PRODUCTS

### Diesel Service Equipment

**NEW 147-5500 29.95**
Get your diesel servicing facilities up and running right away! Set includes a fully assembled and painted Sand Tower and two Fuel Cranes; both feature positionable parts for display alongside your favorite locos.

## YARD EQUIPMENT & FACILITIES

### Synder Fuel Crane

**147-5200** 2 Kits **5.95**

## TANKS & TOWERS

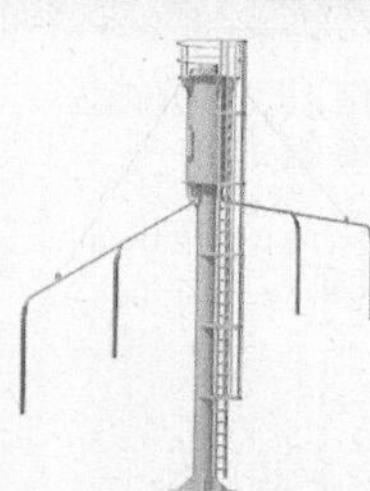

### Diesel Sanding Tower

**147-5100 12.95**

## STACKERS

### Chassis Stackers

**147-5300** pkg(2) **9.95**
Holds 18 van container chassis each.

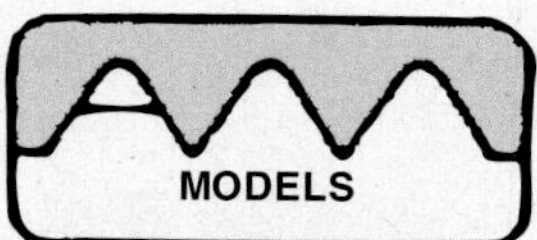

These smaller buildings add realism to any railroad. Each is designed for easy construction with injection-molded parts.

## STATIONS & PLATFORMS

### Freight Station

**129-104 5.10**
1-1/2 x 2-1/16" 4 x 5.2cm

### Freight Platform

**129-107 4.35**
2-1/4 x 5-1/2" 5.6 x 13.9cm

### Freight Station

**129-108 8.80**
2-1/2 x 2-1/4" 6.2 x 5.6cm

### Long Freight Station

**129-110 8.80**

### Hamelton Freight Station

**129-111 14.65**



## YARD EQUIPMENT & FACILITIES

### Trackside Shanty

**129-101 2.20**
5/8 x 3/4" 1.5 x 2cm

### Shanty

**129-102 4.35**
1 x 1" 2.5 x 2.5cm

Prototype located in Hudsonville, Michigan, next to the C&O tracks.

### Williamsburg Yard Office

**129-103 5.10**
1-1/2 x 2-1/16" 4 x 5.2cm

### Workshed

**129-106 8.80**
1-1/2 x 4-3/4" 4 x 12cm

### Bunkhouse

**129-109 5.10**
2-1/4 x 2-1/4" 5.6 x 5.6cm

129-112 129-113

### Small Shanties

5/8 x 3/4" 1.6 x 1.9cm

**129-112** With Windows **2.95**

**129-113** Without Windows **2.20**

### Garage

**129-114 5.80**
2-1/2 x 2-1/4" 6.2 x 5.6cm

Clapboard siding, includes doors and windows.

### Storage Shed

**129-115 5.10**
2-1/2 x 2-1/4" 6.2 x 5.6cm

Clapboard siding, includes large sliding door, no windows.

## TANKS & TOWERS

### Tower

**129-105 5.10**
1 x 1-1/2" 2.5 x 4cm

## BRIDGES & VIADUCTS

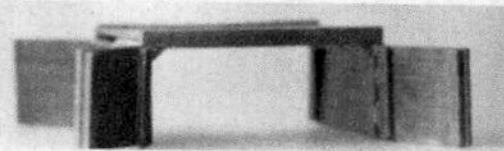

### Simple Beam Bridge

**129-301 2.95**
4" x 1-9/16" 10 x 4cm;
4" 10cm tall

### Short Trestle Bridge

**129-302 5.10**
2-1/4 x 1-1/4" 5.7 x 3.2cm

### Long Trestle Bridge

**129-303 6.65**

Start a construction boom on your layout with the Atlas line of trackside structures and accessories! Based on authentic American prototypes, the kits are molded in realistically colored styrene. The kits also include easy-to-follow instructions, decals and printed window glazing where appropriate.

## NEW PRODUCT

### Garage

### Barb's Bungalow Garage Kit

**NEW 150-730** pkg(2) **39.95**
Laser-cut wood kit is a typical one-car garage featuring roll-up wooden doors, multi-pane windows, hip roof and block foundation. Kit features precision laser-cut micro plywood parts and complete instructions for easy assembly. Architecture matches Barb's Bungalow, but is perfect for use in any 1930s or later neighborhood.

## TANKS & TOWERS

### Elevated Gate Tower

1-1/4 x 2" 3.1 x 5cm
**150-701** Kit **7.25**
**150-601** Assembled **14.25**

### Water Tower

3-1/8 x 3-1/4" 7.8 x 8.2cm
**150-703** Kit **9.25**

### Signal Tower

2-5/8 x 3-1/8" 6.5 x 14cm
**150-704** Kit **9.25**
**150-604** Assembled **18.75**

## YARD EQUIPMENT & FACILITIES

### Trackside Shanty

2-1/4 x 3-1/8" 5.7 x 8cm
**150-702** Kit **7.25**
**150-602** Assembled **14.25**

### Turntable Motor Drive Unit

**150-304 25.75**
Belt-driven for quiet operation.

### 3-Stall Roundhouse

**150-709 27.95**
14-3/8 x 15 x 4-5/8" 35.9 x 37.5 x 11.5cm

Now there's an HO Scale roundhouse sized to correctly fit the ever-popular Atlas Turntable! This structure features three stalls spaced at 15 degree angles, perfectly matching the alignment of the #150-305 Turntable (sold separately).

Detailed plastic parts are molded in colors, so no painting is required. The sturdy construction features brick detail, stall doors which can be positioned open or closed, a separate office section which can be added in multiple locations, and two different styles of roof ventilators. Plus, the building features a modular design, so several kits can be combined to construct a larger structure up to a full circle.

### Telephone Shanty & Pole

1-1/2 x 3" 3.8 x 7.5cm
**150-705** Kit **4.95**
**150-605** Assembled **10.95**

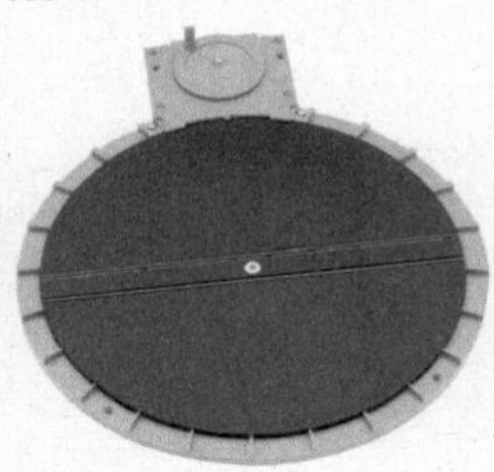

### Turntable

**150-305 25.75**
Fully assembled, 9" diameter turntable has the ability to stop at 21 positions, 15° apart. Geneva movement locks table in exact position every time. Simulated wood brown turntable deck and concrete pit ring. Surface mount; no cutting necessary. Manual crank operation; can be easily motorized for remote control operation with the #304 Turntable Drive Unit, sold separately.

## BRIDGES & VIADUCTS

### Pier Set

**150-80 14.95**
Includes 46 stone masonry piers (graduated in height) one pier girder and snap-in shims.

### Bridge Piers

3" 7.5cm
**150-81** pkg(4) **3.95**

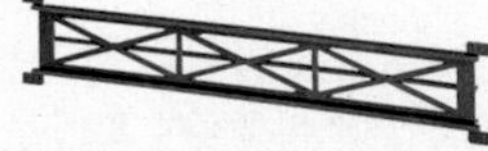

### Pier Girders

**150-82** pkg(4) **2.95**

### 65' Deck Truss Bridge w/Nickel-Silver Rail 5.95 ea

9" 23cm
**150-591** Code 83
**150-884** Code 100

### 65' Warren Truss Bridge w/Nickel-Silver Rail 5.95 ea

9" 23cm
**150-590** Code 83
**150-883** Code 100

See What's Available at

**www.walthers.com**

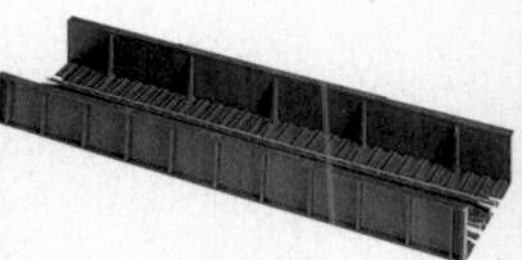

### 65' Thru Plate Girder Bridge w/Nickel-Silver Rail 5.95 ea

Comes assembled.
9 x 2-5/8" 23 x 6.5cm
**150-592** Code 83
**150-885** Code 100

Erie 150-890

NYC 150-891

ATSF 150-893

### Girder Bridge w/Decorated Plate 10.95 ea

Based on a common prototype, these detailed bridges with Code 100 track are decorated with well-known roadnames.

**150-890** Erie (black, white)
**150-891** NYC (silver, black)
**150-892** DRGW (silver, black)
**150-893** ATSF (black, white)
**NEW 150-894** D&H (black)
**NEW 150-895** DL&W (black)
**NEW 150-896** NH (black)
**NEW 150-897** NKP (black)
**NEW 150-898** SP (silver)
**NEW 150-899** UP (silver)
**NEW 150-70000000** CNW (green, yellow)
**NEW 150-70000001** GN (black, white)
**NEW 150-70000002** N&W (black, silver)
**NEW 150-70000003** PRR (black, white)
**NEW 150-70000004** WM (silver, black)

## GARAGE

### Micro-Plywood Garage Kit

**NEW 150-740** pkg(2) **39.95**
Designed to complement Kate's Colonial Home, this laser-cut wood kit is an ideal addition to any neighborhood scene. The kit features unpainted wood parts and comes with complete instructions.

## HOUSES

### Lovely Ladies Home Series™

This series of popular catalog homes from the 1920s feature clapboard siding, rain gutter and downspout detail, brick chimney, window glazing and Bilco® cellar doors.

Colors May Vary

**Kate's Colonial Home**

The assembled model measures 4-1/4 x 5-5/8 x 5-1/8" 10.6 x 14.1 x 12.8cm

**150-711** Kit **21.95**

**150-611** Assembled **38.50**

**Kim's Classic American Home**

**150-713** Kit **21.95**

The latest release in the Lovely Ladies Home Series™, this kit's features include a front porch with lattice detail and shingle detail on the upper half. The finished model measures approximately 6.3 x 3.3 x 4.5" 15.8 x 8.3 x 11.3cm.

Colors May Vary

**Barb's Bungalow**

Features shingle roofing. The assembled model measures 6-1/4 x 3 x 2-3/4" 15.8 x 7.6 x 7cm.

**150-612** Assembled (colors may vary) **38.50**

**150-712** Kit (off-white, Brick Red, tan) **21.95**

## STATIONS & PLATFORMS

**Passenger Station**

4-1/8 x 9" 10.3 x 22.5cm

Includes one station platform.

**150-706** Kit **11.95**

**150-606** Assembled **32.95**

**Station Platform**

2-1/8 x 6-1/2" 5.4 x 16.3cm

**150-707** Kit pkg(2) **5.75**

**150-607** Assembled **16.50**

**Maywood Station**

This model is a full scale replica of a depot built by the New Jersey Midland Railroad (predecessor to the present-day New York Susquehanna & Western Railway) at Maywood, NJ in 1872. Stations built to a similar Victorian-era design could be found in small towns and suburbs of larger cities on railroads across the US. The restored prototype for this model still stands today, and like similar vintage depots across the continent, houses a small museum. This detailed model features separate window glazing, a separate platform base with brick pattern, roof finials, benches, non-operating lamps under roof overhang, separate "hairpin" style track fence and separate freight platform railing, plus decals for various station names. The finished model measures: 9-1/4 x 4-1/4 x 3" and is available as a kit or assembled in three different color schemes.

**Kit**

**150-720** Tan w/Brown Trim **24.95**

**Assembled 39.95 ea**

**150-6201** Tan w/Brown Trim

**150-6202** Gray w/Maroon Trim

**150-6203** Pale Green w/Dark Green Trim

## BUSINESSES

**Roadside Restaurant**

5-5/8 x 8-3/4" 14.3 x 21.9cm

**150-760** Kit **11.95**

**150-660** Assembled **32.95**

**Refreshment Stand**

3-3/8 x 4-1/4" 8.4 x 10.7cm

**150-715** Kit **6.95**

**150-615** Assembled **14.25**

## INDUSTRIAL

**Lumber Yard & Office**

3-3/4 x 8-1/2" 9.5 x 21.3cm

Mill lumber (#150-791) sold separately.

**150-750** Kit **11.50**

**150-650** Assembled **27.50**

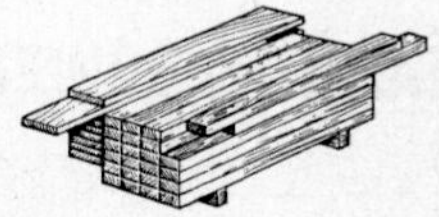

**Scale Lumber**

**150-791 4.25**

Easy-to-build kit features stacks of lumber, molded in realistic color of plastic.

## CHURCH

**19th Century Church**

9-1/2 x 4-3/4 x 10-3/4"
23.8 x 11.9 x 26.9cm

A charming addition to any community, based on an actual structure. Molded in blue and white ABS plastic, no painting is needed. Requires ABS cement for assembly (sold separately).

**150-708** Kit **27.95**

**150-608** Assembled **54.95**

Bachmann Plasticville® USA structures are perfect for adding a slice of small-town realism to your model railroad. Plasticville USA Built-Ups are assembled, layout-ready versions of Plasticville USA kits. Kits are molded in color and complete instructions are included. Assembly requires glue for plastic, sold separately.

Plasticville USA Built-Ups

## Plasticville USA Built-Ups

## STATIONS & PLATFORMS

### Freight Station w/Platform Station
**160-45006** Assembled **30.00**

**160-45171** Kit **12.00**
2-3/8 x 4-3/4" 12.1 x 6cm

### Suburban Station
**160-45173 12.00**
1-7/8 x 5-1/2" 14 x 4.8cm

### Platform
**160-45194 13.00**
2-1/8 x 7" 5.5 x 18cm

### Lighted Freight Station
**160-46216 22.00**
5-1/2 x 9-1/2" 14 x 24.1cm
Preassembled.

### Passenger Station w/Light
**160-46217 22.00**
5-3/8 x 9-3/8" 13.7 x 23.8cm
Preassembled.

## YARD EQUIPMENT & FACILITIES

### Signal Bridge
**160-45001** pkg(2) **32.00**

### Storage Building w/Steam Whistle Sound
**160-46209 29.00**

**160-45009** Railroad Work Sheds Assembled pkg(2) **30.00**

## RURAL BUILDINGS

### School House
6 x 7-1/8" 15.3 x 4.8cm
**160-45133 10.00**

**160-45011** School House Assembled **25.00**

### Dairy Barn
**160-45007** Assembled **26.00**

**160-45151** Kit **11.00**
2-1/2 x 3-1/2" 6.4 x 9cm

### Farm Building w/Animals
**160-45152 11.00**

## HOUSES

### Cape Cod Style House
**160-45131 10.00**
1-7/8 x 3" 4.8 x 7.5cm

### Ranch Style House
**160-45154 11.00**
2-1/4 x 5-1/2" 5.7 x 14cm

### House Under Construction
**160-45004** Assembled **26.00**

**160-45191** Kit **13.00**
2-7/8 x 5-1/4" 7.3 x 13cm

Split Level House

### Split Level House
**160-45005** Assembled **30.00**

**160-45213** Kit **15.00**
2-7/8 x 6-1/8" 7.3 x 15.5cm

### Contemporary House
**160-45432 17.00**
2-7/8 x 8-3/4" 7.3 x 22.3cm

## CITY BUILDINGS

### Post Office
**160-45144 10.00**
2-1/8 x 4-5/8" 5.5 x 11.8cm

### Police Station
**160-45145 10.00**

## CHURCHES

### Cathedral
**160-45192 13.00**

**160-45012** Cathedral Assembled **25.00**

## TANKS & TOWERS

### Switch Tower
**160-45132 10.00**
1-5/8" 4.2cm square

Gas Station 160-45174

Motel w/Swimming Pool 160-45214

### Water Tank

**160-45008** Assembled **22.00**
**160-45153** Kit **11.00**
3-1/4" 8.2cm diameter.

### Coaling Station

**160-45002** Assembled **28.00**
**160-45211** Kit **15.00**
3-3/8 x 3" 8.6 x 7.6cm

### Oil Tanks

4-3/4" 12.1cm diameter.

**With Diesel Horn**
**160-46208 29.00**

**With Blinking Light**
**160-46212 19.00**

## BUSINESSES

### Super Market

**160-45141 10.00**
2-1/8 x 4-5/8" 5.5 x 11.8cm

### 5 & 10 Store

**160-45142 10.00**
2-1/8 x 4-5/8" 5.5 x 11.8cm

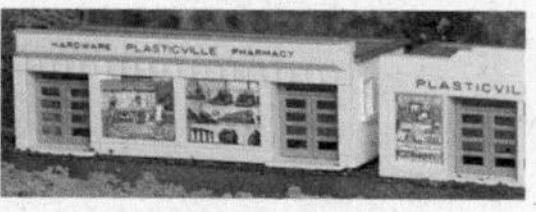

### Hardware Store

**160-45143 10.00**
2-1/8 x 4-5/8" 5.5 x 11.8cm

### Gas Station

**160-45174 15.00**

**160-45013** Gas Station Assembled **30.00**

### Motel w/Swimming Pool

**160-45214 15.00**
4-1/8 x 12-3/4" 10.5 x 32.4cm

### Drive-In Hamburger Stand

**160-45434 17.00**

## BRIDGES & VIADUCTS

### Pedestrian Foot Bridge

**160-45003** Assembled **26.00**
**160-45172** Kit **12.00**

### Covered Bridge

**160-45010** Assembled **25.00**

## BROADWAY LIMITED

### SWITCH TOWER

Based on typical wooden structures that guarded busy yard throats and highway crossings, this layout-ready model is packed with detail. Made of heavyweight etched-brass parts and features interior detailing and window glazing. Handpainted in a typical railroad color scheme.

Preproduction Model Shown

**187-162** Green **29.99**

Hot New Products Announced Daily! Visit Walthers Web site at **www.walthers.com**

## ALEXANDER SCALE MODELS

DIVISION OF TOMAR INDUSTRIES

### STATIONS & PLATFORMS

**120-7200** NYC Fairbanks-Morse Coaling Station 2-1/2 x 3-1/4" **TBA**

**120-7622** Freight Station NYC **TBA**

**120-7631** Flagstop Station PRR **TBA**

### YARD EQUIPMENT & FACILITIES

**120-6031** Switch Stand Hi-Level **TBA**

**120-7445** Loading Rack 8-3/4 x 3/4" **TBA**

**120-7519** Brownhoist Little Hook **26.20**

### RURAL BUILDINGS

**120-7750** Morse Lake Country School **TBA**

### HOUSES

**120-7558** Haunted House **TBA**

### TANKS & TOWERS

**120-7443** Oil Tank & Rack Parkersburg **TBA**

**120-7444** Oil Tank **TBA**

**120-7880** Interlocking Tower B&O **TBA**

### INDUSTRIAL

**120-7488** Oil Drilling Rig **TBA**

**120-7514** Stiff Leg Derrick **23.65**

## BLMA MODELS

### NEW PRODUCTS

### Modern Yard Office

**NEW 176-4300 29.95**
6-3/4 x 2-3/4"
This fully assembled plastic model features installed window glass and numerous other details. The modern design fits 1970s to today and is perfect for rail yards, construction sites, city dumps and more.

### Radio Antenna Tower

**NEW 176-4101 44.95**
Towers like this serve as a vital link between train crews, dispatchers and other yard personnel. Standing at over 70 scale feet (9-1/2"), this kit includes all the antennas featured on the prototype. It makes a great addition to any rail yard scene.

### 150' Truss Bridge 325.00 ea

Fully assembled brass model is based on a 150-foot long UP mainline bridge in southern California's Afton Canyon. The prototype was built in 1938 to span a narrow section of the Mojave River and serves as a link between Los Angeles, Salt Lake City and points east. Carefully recreated by hand, the highly detailed model features accurate dimensions, rivet details and more.

**NEW 176-5000** Silver
**NEW 176-5001** Black

### Cell Phone Antenna Tower

**176-4100 19.95**
A must for any modern layout, this kit is based on a common prototype used throughout the country. Main structure is etched brass and stainless steel with etched ladder, cast metal antennas by Details West and plastic mounting pole.

Create detailed scenes along your right-of-way with this selection of structure kits. Each model features wood parts that are precision-cut and/or etched with a laser. The result is a highly detailed building that assembles much like a plastic kit. Complete instructions are included to make construction quick and easy.

## NEW PRODUCTS

### Businesses

**Bud Smiley's Gas Stop**

**NEW 171-102** **44.95**
Perfect for your streetside scenes, this model includes vintage gas pumps, a pump island, storage tank, a complete set of signs and other details.

**Mortimer Stiph's Caskets & Headstones**

**NEW 171-122** With Accessories **44.95**
Complete with caskets, a wagon, tombstones and more, this little kit will work both on and away from the track.

**Capt. Jack's Boat & Bait House**

**NEW 171-892** **77.95**
Sure to become an anchor business along your waterfront, Capt. Jack's includes cast-metal boats and details, etched-brass lobster traps, a roof stencil sign and complete instructions.

**Four Finger Tony's**

**NEW 171-112** Wholesale Meat & Butcher Shop w/Accessories **89.95**

About 5 x 9" 12.7 x 22.8cm

Combining a retail storefront with a warehouse operation this kit has it all, from the sides of hanging beef down to the fresh produce displayed on the street.

### Bar Mills Basics

**NEW 171-662** The Fishing Shack At Cozy Cove **22.95**
Great addition to any pier or harbor scene, features "split-shingle" siding on one part of the building.

**NEW 171-672** The Busted Knuckle Garage **19.95**

**NEW 171-792** Twin Crossing Shacks **19.95**
Includes 2 buildings, 2 crossings and 4 crossbucks.

## BRIDGES

**Low Boy Trestle Kit**

**171-404** **13.95**
This modular kit is typical of trestles found along just about every American rail line. The versatile design lends itself to customizing. When assembled, the model is about 6" 15cm long, but each section is slotted so you can easily combine several kits to build a longer structure. All parts are laser-cut and notched to speed assembly. Track not included.

**The Stanley Stove Company**

**NEW 171-972** **67.95**
Whether along the tracks or a highway, this business will add character to your scenes. Kit includes an etched-stone foundation, enclosed exterior staircase, building side extension, cast-metal details, signs and instructions.

**The Gravely Building**

**NEW 171-882** **89.95**
Approximately 6-3/4 x 4-3/4"
A complete business block in a single kit, with numerous details and signs. (Photo shows S Scale model; truck shown not included.)

"THE GREAT LITTLE KIT..."
Bar Mills
SCALE MODEL WORKS
"FROM THE GREAT STATE OF MAINE"

**The Shack Pack**
171-992 pkg(3) 37.95
Three highly detailed structures complete with white metal detail castings, signs, fencing, and a custom-printed "Mail Pouch Tobacco" dry-transfer.

## BUSINESSES

**Earl's Oil**
171-802 44.95
Includes fencing, tanks, billboards, signs, white metal details and lampheads.

**Tylick Tool Company**
171-812 139.95
Includes two buildings, one with a recessed freight car door, the other with a truck loading dock, plus an overhead walkway and crane. Metal castings and dry transfer signs are included.

**Mooney's Plumbing Emporium**
171-822 64.95
This small manufacturing facility comes with a billboards, castings and "Insta-Fence."

**Rusty's Radiator Co.**
171-832 37.95
Typical of an old-time radiator shop, this small structure is perfect for any layout. Kit includes cast-metal details and signs.

**Shipyard Brewing Company**
171-852 99.95
9 x 3-1/2 x 9"

False-front kit features plastic windows, a "diamond pattern" self-stick roof, white metal castings, a roof sign, and a detailed cupola.

**Waterfront Willy's/ Trackside Jack's**
171-922 54.95
Improve any commercial district with this versatile building. A complete set of pilings is included to support the structure over water, or shorten them for a hillside location. Laser-cut "cedar shake" shingles and windows (which can be built open or closed), optional doors and shutters, plus a set of white metal detail parts are included.

**Saulena's Tavern**
171-932 57.95
A classic design that fits most modeling eras, complete with metal details, awnings, signs, and a corner sidewalk.

**Majestic Hardware**
171-942 89.95
Includes double laminated roofing, stencils so that the roof can be lettered with actual paint (instead of decals or dry-transfers), over 30 white-metal castings and laser-cut windows.

## STATIONS & PLATFORMS

**Whistle Stop Junction**
171-911 47.95
Kit features laser-etched siding that shows fine details right down to individual nail holes! A set of white metal castings is also included.

## RURAL BUILDINGS

**Collard's Creek Series**
Many of us spent vacations in small cabin camps like the one. The kits can be used for stand-alone scenes or combined for a larger camp. Kits feature unpainted laser-cut wood, metal and plastic parts, full-color signs, fine details and complete instructions.

**Cabins at Collard's Creek**
171-862 37.95
Includes three guest cabins. Great for use with #171-872 (sold separately).

## Wicked Wanda's

**171-962 57.95**
This laser-cut structure can serve as a freight-transfer facility, a small trackside industry or as its namesake "Wicked Wanda's...the Friendliest House in Town." Kit is complete with laser-cut windows and doors, graphics and white metal details.

## Booty Corner

**171-982 119.95**
Features pre-printed storefront windows and "Buster's Barber Shop" with a little newsstand. Also included are fire escapes, awnings, fruit crates and more. Second-story windows can be adjusted to be modeled opened or closed.

## Swanson's Lunch Counter

**171-952 27.95**
Features white metal castings, laser-cut self-stick interior rafters, shingles, signs and fine-precision pre-etched details.

## Collard's Creek Motor Park

**171-872 44.95**
Includes the office and one guest cabin. Expand your cabin camp with #171-862 (sold separately).

# "THE 1-KIT"

**171-32 34.95**
Create one-of-a-kind buildings for your railroad with this unique product. The "1-Kit" provides basic basswood parts that can be modified in an almost endless variety of ways to scratchbuild just about any kind of wooden structure. You can also adapt them or combine them with wood, metal and plastic parts from other kits

# BAR MILLS BASICS

Bar Mills Basics kits make it easy to add a structure, complete with signs and details, to your layout even if you've never built a laser-cut wood kit. Each includes unpainted laser-cut wood parts for easy assembly, appropriate cast-metal details, full-color signs and complete instructions.

**171-702** Twin Utility Sheds **21.95**

**171-712** Furlow Freight & Transfer **22.95**

**171-722** Revelia Shipping & Storage **22.95**

**171-732** Miracle Chair Company **22.95**

**171-742** HJ Simpson Feed & Seed **22.95**

**171-752** Zack's Shack **17.95**

**171-772** Magee's Tire Service **21.95**

# COVERED STAIRWELLS

**171-405** pkg(2) **14.95**
A neat detail that can to quickly improve and detail almost any commercial, residential or industrial building in any era.

# WEATHERING POWDER SET

**171-45** Rust pkg(4) **9.95**
Includes four shades of rust-colored pigment.

# SIDEWALKS

**NEW 171-682 11.95**
Kit includes 300 scale feet of sidewalks complete with laser-etched curb lines and cracks. Parts are made of special heavy, textured stock and are layout ready.

# BAGGAGE CARTS

**NEW 171-782** Twin REA Baggage Carts pkg(2) **8.95**
Laser-cut wood kit includes unpainted parts for two complete baggage wagons.

# FENCE

## Insta-Fence

**171-42 7.95**
Includes about 160 scale feet of fencing, complete with signs.

# LOBSTER TRAPS

**171-47** pkg(8) **12.95**
Kit features etched-metal parts for extra realism and easy assembly.

# STREET ELEVATORS

**171-401** Two Complete Elevators & Door Sets **8.95**
Sidewalk elevators served all types of businesses by providing a quick and easy way to deliver packages and merchandise into store basements. This kit is based on elevators still in production today, and features photo-etched brass parts for a near-scale appearance. The elevators can be modeled with doors open or closed.

Laser-Art Structures by Branchline Trains

Laser-Art building kits include precision laser-cut wood and plastic parts. Easy peel-and-stick construction speeds assembly.

# NEW PRODUCTS

## Stations & Platforms

### Canaan Union Station

**NEW 181-659 299.99**
22 x 20 x 7" 55.8 x 50.8 x 17.7cm

The Canaan, Connecticut, Union Station was built in 1872 at the junction of the Central New England and Housatonic railroads (both later part of the New Haven). A major architectural landmark, it stood intact and essentially as built until 2001 when it was severely damaged by arson. Thanks to a grass roots local effort, the station is currently undergoing a complete restoration.

This kit depicts the station circa 1940 - the plan has been modified slightly to accommodate a 90° diamond crossing (the original is at about an 85° angle) but can be modified for those that want to portray it accurately and lay their own track - based on plans provided by the restoration firm along with copies of the original plans and information provided by the New Haven Railroad Historical and Technical Association. Kit includes wood, resin and photo-etched parts, Grandt Line baggage carts, appropriate signs and posters and much more.

**NEW 181-660** Backwoods Junction Station **43.99**
This compact station is based on the 2' narrow gauge Wiscasset, Waterville and Farmington Railway's Wiscasset, Maine, station. Its compact size makes it perfect for use as a commuter or flag stop station nearly anywhere.

## Rural Buildings

**NEW 181-644** Schoolhouse **41.50**
3 x 9 x 4" 7.6 x 22.8 x 10.1cm

This kit is a typical classic schoolhouse and includes a cast resin bell for the tower.

## Houses

### Company Houses

In the late 1800s and early 1900s mining and railroad companies often built company towns using standard house plans, to provide convenient, affordable housing for employees. Many can still be seen in ex-company towns throughout the country.

**NEW 181-605** #1 **34.98**
3-1/2 x 6 x 4"
8.8 x 15.2 x 10.1cm

This basic single-family design is the most compact of the group. It features three bedrooms upstairs with a kitchen, dining room and living room downstairs.

Get Daily Info, Photos and News at

**www.walthers.com**

Marilyn's Bar & Grill 181-645

**NEW 181-606** #2 **44.98**
3-1/2 x 6 x 4"
8.8 x 15.2 x 10.1cm

Larger than house #1, this plan is for a larger family or group. It has four bedrooms upstairs with a kitchen, dining room and living room with a separate entrance hall downstairs.

**NEW 181-607** #6 **47.98**
3-1/2 x 6 x 4"
8.8 x 15.2 x 10.1cm

A two family duplex design, with housing for two families or groups under one roof. Each half contains three bedrooms upstairs with a large kitchen, a living room and a washroom downstairs. Each half of the house has its own entrance and stairway.

**NEW 181-604** Callahan House **44.98**
7 -1/2 x 4 x 2-1/2"
19 x 10.1 x 6.3cm

Complete with an attached garage, this home is a perfect addition to any layout.

**NEW 181-610** Maxwell Cape House **39.98**
5 x 3-1/2 x 3"
12.7 x 8.8 x 7.6cm

Perfect for any residential are similar homes can be found just about anywhere.

**NEW 181-611** Madison Cape House **39.98**
5 x 4-1/2 x 3"
12.7 x 11.4 x 7.6cm

Homes like the Madison were built during the post-WWII housing boom. Classically styled yet modern, these sma capes dot the landscape from coast to coast. Can be built with or without roof dormers.

**NEW 181-617** Oxford House **66.98**
5 x 4 x 3" 12.7 x 10.1 x 7.6cm

Latest in a series of catalog homes of the 1920s, the "Oxford" was featured by Harris, McHenry and Baker of Elmira, New York, in their 192 catalog. Kit includes resin planter boxes for the side porch (not shown).

## Businesses

**NEW 181-645** Marilyn's Bar & Grill **128.99**
6 x 7 x 4-1/2"
15.2 x 17.7 x 11.4cm

Typical of similar businesses found in communities throughout the country, kit Includes signs and awnings.

Laser-Art Structures by Branchline Trains

NEW **181-646** Burger Stand **9.95**
Classic small roadside stand is typical of many burger eateries and suitable for just about any layout. Kit includes appropriate signs and picnic tables.

NEW **181-694** Crosby's Coal **7.98**
x 2-1/2 x 5"
0.3 x 6.3 x 12.7cm
Based on a prototype in Danby, Vermont, on the Rutland Railroad. Built in 1914, the building still stands today. Similar coal dealers could be found throughout the country. Kit includes pre-cut wood parts with one-piece resin foundation, decal signs and more.

## Bridge

NEW **181-672** Shoreham Covered Bridge **143.98**
2 x 3 x 4"
0.4 x 7.6 x 10.1cm
Located on the Rutland Railroad's Addison branch, this classic Howe truss covered bridge was built in 1897 and served as a railroad bridge until 1951. Today it has been restored and is part of a rails-to-trails footpath. Kit inlcudes pre-cut wood parts with see-through side panels, tie rods, nut-bolt-washer castings and more.

## Rocky Point Light House

NEW **181-695** **124.95**
Perfect for any waterfront scene, this handsome kit combines laser-cut, resin and photo-etched parts. For more realism, it can be illuminated with the Flasher Circuit #186-696, sold separately.

NEW **181-696** Light House Flasher Circuit **29.98**
Make the Rocky Point Light House (#181-695, sold separately) more realistic with this custom-made circuit that mimics the circling effect of a real light house beacon.

## STATIONS & PLATFORMS

**181-661** Cannondale Train Station **59.99**
7 x 2-1/2 x 3-1/2"
17.7 x 6.3 x 8.8cm
Built by the New Haven railroad on its Danbury branch just north of Wilton, CT, this classic small town station design is complete with waiting room, baggage room and operator's bay window.

**181-662** Flag Stop Station **25.75**
2-1/2 x 3 x 2" 6.3 x 7.6 x 5cm
Kit includes appropriate signs and coal bin.

**181-663** Centre Hall Station - PRR **77.98**
6-1/2 x 2 x 2" 16.5 x 5 x 5cm
The prototype was built in 1884 on the Lewisburg & Tyrone Railroad, later part of the PRR. The kit is based on the 1940s appearance.

**181-665** Santa Fe #4 Station **71.75**
12 x 4-1/2 x 3"
30.4 x 11.4 x 7.6cm
A standard design used at several locations across the system. Add a freight platform to this model using kit #181-666 (sold separately).

**181-666** Santa Fe #4 Platform **31.98**
16 x 4-1/2" 40.6 x 11.4cm
Designed for use with #181-665 sold separately.

**181-667** Munnsville Station **69.50**
15 x 3 x 3-1/2"
38.1 x 7.6 x 8.8cm
A New York, Ontario & Western prototype; kit includes signs and milk cans.

**181-668** Laura Station **48.99**
7 x 5 x 3" 17.7 x 12.7 x 7.6cm
Santa Fe standard design used system-wide, kit includes main building and attached loading dock.

**181-670** NYC Woodard Station **63.50**
6 x 2 x 2-1/2" 15.2 x 5 x 6.3cm

## YARD EQUIPMENT & FACILITIES

**181-671** Shed Pack **37.98**
Includes Telephone Booth, Telegraph Office, Tool/Hand Car Shed & Crossing Shanty Houses

**181-683** Engine House **94.98**
10-1/2 x 6 x 4"
26.6 x 15.2 x 10.1cm
Based on a Central Vermont prototype, this model is generic enough to be usable anywhere in the country. Kit includes interior wall bracing, full floor, positionable windows and doors (can be modeled open or closed), resin smoke jack and more.

Rocky Point Light House 181-695

Engine House 181-683

The Barn 181-650

## RURAL BUILDINGS

**181-650** The Barn **93.50**
5 x 8-1/2 x 5-1/2"
12.7 x 21.5 x 13.9cm
This barn will fit right into a rural layout of almost any era.

### Farmhouses

**181-652** Deluxe w/Gingerbread Trim **94.95**

**181-653** Original - No Trim **74.98**

### Outbuildings

**181-651** Farm Set **45.50**
Includes Barn, Large Shed, Smokehouse, Chicken Coop & Outhouse

Laser-Art Structures by Branchline Trains

## HOUSES

### Historic Homes

**181-602** Dwight Eisenhower Boyhood Home **73.98**
This modest home in Abilene, Kansas, belonged to the Eisenhower family from 1898 until 1946. Ike lived there from age 8 until he left for West Point in 1911. Preserved as it was in 1946, the home is the centerpiece of the Eisenhower Center and Library. Kit includes resin chimneys.

**181-603** Ronald Reagan Boyhood Home **85.98**
5-1/2 x 7-1/2 x 5"
13.9 x 19 x 12.7cm

Based on his boyhood home in Dixon, Illinois, where the family lived for three years. The prototype is preserved as it would have looked in 1920 when the Reagan family lived there.

**181-626** The Lincoln House **149.98**
5-1/2 x 7-1/2 x 5"
13.9 x 19 x 12.7cm

Based on plans from the National Park Service, kit portrays the house as it was when Lincoln was president. Features photo-etched porch railings and includes gutters, downspouts, shutters and fence.

### Victorian Classics

**181-600** Dubois House **110.50**
Ornate Queen Anne-style houses like this were built throughout the continent between 1880 and WWI. Kit includes laser-cut gingerbread trim, peel-and-stick windows, shutters, stonework and roofing material.

**181-601** Tower House **74.98**
5 x 3-3/4 x 6"
12.7 x 9.5 x 15.2

Based on an 1878 catalog design by Palliser, Palliser & Co, Architects of Bridgeport Connecticut, this home offered "...a comfortable, convenient cottage home of six rooms, with tower, which is designed to command a view of the surrounding country where erected. Cost, $1,700".

**181-618** Woodward House **54.98**
3-1/2 x 4-1/2 x 4-1/2" 8.8 x 11.4 x 11.4cm

A colorful home with arched trim on the porch and the front dormer.

### Catalog Homes

**181-619** Thelma House **34.95**
6 x 6 x 5-1/2"
15.2 x 15.2 x 13.9cm

A typical catalog house with a covered corner front porch, that will fit in almost anywhere across the country.

**181-620** Stoddard Catalog House **64.98**
5 x 3-3/4 x 6"
12.7 x 9.5 x 15.2cm

Based on the 1925 catalog plans of Harris, McHenry and Baker of Elmira, NY.

**181-621** Albion Catalog House **54.98**
4 x 6 x 4-1/2"
10.1 x 15.2 x 11.4cm

**181-622** Whitehall Catalog House **54.98**
4-1/2 x 6 x 5"
11.4 x 15.2 x 12.7cm

Based on a home in the 1927 Sears catalog, the kit price of $1,863.00 included all lumber, millwork, trim, cupboards, doors, windows, hardware, gutters and downspouts - even paint and varnish. For an additional $112.00 buyers could add oak doors, trim and floors for living and dining room, and maple floors in kitchen and bathroom. (Garage sold separately.)

**181-623** Suburban House **39.98**
4 x 5-1/2 x 4"
10.1 x 13.9 x 10.1cm

Based on a plan shown in the 1917 Aladdin catalog.

**181-624** Drayton House **19.98**
2-3/4 x 4 x 2"
6.9 x 10.1 x 5cm

Based on a plan shown in the 1917 Aladdin catalog.

Garage sold separately.

**181-625** The Finley House **39.98**
5 x 5 x 3-1/4"
12.7 x 12.7 x 8.2cm

Based on a plan shown in the 1917 Aladdin catalog.

**181-627** Beverly 2-Family House **59.98**
4 x 8-1/2 x 4-3/4"
10.1 x 21.5 x 12cm

Based on a design in the 1917 Aladdin catalog. It offered two complete apartments, each with its own entrance.

The Lincoln House 181-626

Dubois House 181-600

**181-628** The Stanley **34.95**
A typical catalog home with a front porch, the Stanley would fit in almost anywhere across the U.S.

**181-629** The Lasalle **49.98**
4 x 6 x 4-1/2"
10.1 x 15.2 x 11.2cm

Based on a home in the 1926 Sears catalog, the LaSalle looked like a single family home but included a second floor apartment for extra income.

**181-634** Wenonah House **58.98**
6 x 4-1/2 x 4-1/2"
15.2 x 11.4 x 11.4cm

Built from a typical 1920s pla book, large windows let in plenty of light.

**181-636** Avon House **57.50**
5 x 5 x 3-1/2"
12.7 x 12.7 x 8.8cm

Laser-Art
Structures
by Branchline Trains

**181-638** Row House w/Optional Detail Parts **39.98**
Patterned after wooden row houses seen throughout the continent. Kit includes parts for one house plus optional trim details so you can build several unique versions.

**181-639** Tucson House **34.98**
This compact design can fit on any layout. Complete the scene with the matching Tucson Garage, #181-637 sold separately.

## Garages & Sheds

**181-633** Tool Shed **13.99**

**181-635** Residential Set **21.98**
1 Each Garden Shed, 1-Stall Garage & Outhouse

**181-637** The Tucson Garage **22.50**

**181-664** Patterson Garage **19.50**

### Bennett Company Garages

These structures were named after popular cars of the day.

**181-630** Buick Garage **17.99**

**181-631** Cadillac Garage **22.99**

**181-632** Hudson Garage **17.99**

## BUSINESSES

**181-640** Dubois Store **99.98**
7-1/2 x 8-1/2 x 4-1/4"
19 x 21.5 x 10.7cm

Based on a prototype built in the 1880s, stores like this can be found all over the continent.

**181-641** Dubois Store Interior Kit **36.50**
Complete with shelves and goods, as well as a restaurant interior with tables, chairs, counters and more. Also includes color signs.

**181-643** Roscoe Store **89.98**
6 x 6-1/2 x 6"
15.2 x 16.5 x 15.2cm

This classic small store once stood across the tracks from the O&W station in Roscoe, New York.

**181-654** Majestic Theatre **99.95**
7 x 5-1/2 x 3"
17.7 x 13.9 x 7.6cm

This classic is typical of those found in communities throughout the country. Includes a collection of vintage movie posters and marquee signs to help draw in the crowds!

**181-687** Gas Station **50.99**
9-1/2 x 7 x 4-1/2"
24.1 x 17.7 x 11.4cm

This canopy-style station was a common design used by many companies. Kit includes 1930s and 1940s-50s gas pumps

**181-691** Dan's Welding & Fabrication **54.99**
6 x 4 x 3-1/2"
15.2 x 10.1 x 8.8cm

Kit includes resin chimneys. It's perfect for a small space on your layout.

## CHURCHES

**181-642 67.50**
6 x 6-1/2 x 6"
15.2 x 16.5 x 15.2cm

## TOWER

**181-669** Ellinor Tower **59.98**
Standard ATSF design.

Valley Fuel & Supply 181-693

## INDUSTRIAL

**181-680** Creamery **63.98**
5 x 4 x 4"
12.7 x 10.1 x 10.1cm

Before Interstates, local farmers would deliver cans of Bessie's best to the local creamery for storage and rail shipment to city distributors.

**181-681** Ice House **37.50**
Provided storage for the block ice used in reefers and in creameries.

**181-682** Meat Packing Plant **94.98**
11-1/2 x 7-1/2 x 4-1/2"
29.2 x 19 x 11.4cm

Based on a typical wood meat packing plants frequently seen in the east.

**181-684** County Feed **79.98**
6-1/2 x 3-1/2 x 5"
16.5 x 8.8 x 12.7cm

**181-685** Caldwell Tool & Die **79.98**
7-1/2 x 6 x 5"
19 x 15.2 x 12.7cm

**181-686** Flour Mill **49.98**
This kit could easily represent a number of other industries.

**181-688** Weimers Mill **109.98**
6 x 5 x 8"
15.2 x 12.7 x 20.3cm

Features a water wheel.

**181-689** Grain Elevator **43.98**
4 x 4-1/2 x 6-1/2"
10.1 x 11.4 x 16.5cm

Includes grain elevator/loader, loading shed and small office/store room.

**181-692** Geo. A. Nickels Milling & Feed **67.50**
6 x 4 x 3-1/2"
15.2 x 10.1 x 8.8cm

Use as a feed mill or any light industry, includes signs.

**181-693** Valley Fuel & Supply **134.99**
11 x 12 x 8"
27.9 x 30.4 x 20.3cm

Features a trackside loading dock and two coal silos. Includes signs.

BRAWA
LIEBE ZUM DETAIL

IMPORTED FROM GERMANY BY WALTHERS
These detailed structures feature metal, plastic and wood parts, and require only minor assembly or installation. Powered models require a 14-16V DC power supply, or can be converted for AC power using Bridge Rectifier #2185 (sold separately).

## CABLEWAYS

These working models look great on mountain ranges. Each is complete with drive cable, mechanism and cars. Systems can be expanded with additional cable and pylons, as well as other accessories listed with the various sets. The speed can be controlled with Brawa controllers #6149 or 6150 (sold separately). Structures to house the cable mechanisms are also available separately.

### Nebelhorn Cableway

**186-6340** Without Buildings
**289.99**
Features two lighted cars with motor-driven rotating base, middle mast (11" 28cm), hauling and bearer cable drive for the mountain station and rope guide on the valley side.

### Nebelhorn Buildings

**186-6341** Mountain & Valley Buildings for Nelbelhorn Cableway
**114.99**
The perfect way to hide the electrical accessories for the Nebelhorn Cableway (#186-6340, sold separately). Mountain Station measures 6-9/16 x 6-13/16" 16.7 x 17.3cm; Valley Station measures 5-5/16 x 6-15/16" 13.5 x 17.6cm.

Titlis Cableway 186-6330

### Titlis Cableway

**186-6330 426.99**
Offering breathtaking views of the Alps, the prototype is located in Engelberg and climbs nearly 10,000 feet on its 45 minute trip. During the journey, the cabin rotates, offering an ever-changing view of the area. This superb replica will be a hit in any scene. The set comes with a cabin, which has a rotating floor like the real one, plus summit and valley mechanisms, drive motors and a speed control.

### Center Pylon

**186-6283 29.99**
Matches pylon in set #6280, to support a longer cableway. About 7-1/2" 190mm tall.

### Station Buildings

**186-6290** pkg(2) **41.99**
House your summit and valley cable mechanisms inside these structure kits. Parts for two complete buildings are provided. Summit station measures about 5 x 7-1/2" 165 x 125mm while the Valley station is approximately 4-1/2 x 6" 155 x 125mm.

Kanzelwandbahn Cableway Set 186-6280

### Kanzelwandbahn Cableway Set

**186-6280 249.99**
Complete with both valley and summit cable mechanisms, six cars, a center pylon that's about 7-1/2" 190mm tall and drive cables.

### Extra Cabin w/Figure 14.99 ea

**186-6281** Red

**186-6282** Blue

### Drive Support Cables (35.5'/10m)

**186-6241 10.99**

**Limited Quantity Available**

### Spare Drive Cable

**186-6292 7.99**
Approximately 11 yards of cable, for use with #6280, 6210, 6270 and 6560.

For Daily Product Updates Point Your Browser to
**www.walthers.com**

### Replacement Motors For Cableways

**186-9713 29.99**
For cableways made after September, 1992.

## STATIONS & PLATFORMS

### Platform Edges

**186-2869 9.99**
Includes four straight section (8-5/16" 208mm long), four ramps (3" 78mm long) and tw transition sections (2" 52mm long). Use Brawa building material sheets for platform surface (sold separately in Scratchbuilding Supplies).

## CREATIVE MODEL ASSOCIATES

Add the finishing touch to you layout with these easy-to-buil plastic kits. Each is finely detailed and comes with complete instructions.
Visit Walthers Web site at www.walthers.com for a complete listing of Creative Model Associates products.

363-1001

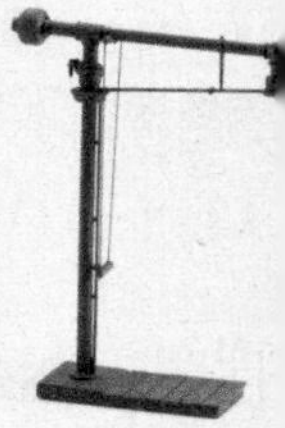

363-1002

### Mail Crane

**363-1001 5.95**
Includes one-piece arm with mail pouch molded in place.

### Oil Column

**363-1002 6.95**
Refuel oil-burning steamers a this detailed column.

### Telltale

**363-1004** pkg(2) **4.95**
For safe operation near overhead obstacles.

# B.T.S.

*Better Than Scratch!*

These Craftsman Kits feature precision laser-cut basswood, plywood and/or styrene parts. They are engineered for easy assembly. Kits include one or all of the following: white metal castings, brass details, figures, color signs and detailed instructions.

## NEW PRODUCTS

### Railroad Facilities

**Signal Maintainer's Storage**
**NEW 464-26511 39.95**

### Bridges

**Cheat Run Trestle**
**NEW 464-27142** HO **22.95**
13 x 27"
**NEW 464-27143** HOn3 **22.95**
12 x 27"

## CABIN CREEK SERIES

**Rural Church**
**464-27232 39.95**
3-5/16 x 7-11/16"

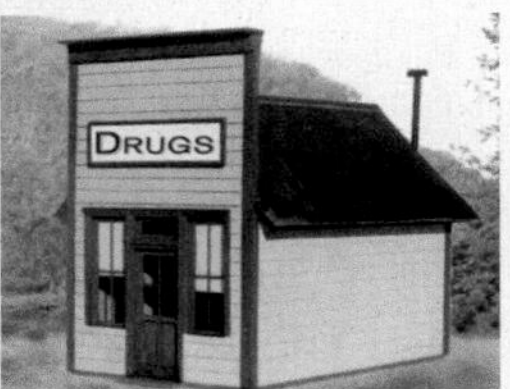


**Small Store**
**464-27225 23.95**
1-5/8 x 2-11/16"

**Singer Watch Repair**
**464-27234 26.95**
14 x 27" 35.6 x 68.6cm

**East End Grocery**
**464-27226 39.95**
2-3/8 x 4-11/16"

**Post Office**
**464-27233 26.95**
2-3/16 x 3-1/2"

**Boot Repair**
**464-27230 23.95**
2 x 3-5/16"

**Greeley's Place**
**464-27227 18.95**
2-3/16 x 2-3/8"

Info, Images, Inspiration! Get It All at
**www.walthers.com**

**Flagstop Station**
**464-27400 34.95**
5-1/2 x 2-5/8"

**Slade's Office**
**464-27430 24.95**
3 x 3-5/16"

**Clegg's Cabin**
**464-27470 14.95**
1-11/16 x 2-11/16"

**Cleator's Gas**
**464-27410 29.95**
3 x 1-1/2"

**Elliott & Sons Supply**
**464-28106 139.95**
8-3/16 x 5-1/2"

## GOIN' HOME SERIES

**Junior's Shiner**
**464-27405 32.95**
4-5/8 x 3"

**Pritchard's Barn**
**464-27420 39.95**
5 x 2-1/2"

**Babe's Diner**
**464-27440 49.95**
6-13/16 x 2-11/16"

**Willet's Supply**
**464-27435 49.95**
6-3/16 x 3-5/16"

**The Shanty**
**464-27110 49.95**
5 x 6-13/16"

**Shotgun House**
**464-27300 26.95**
**464-27301** 3-Pack **69.95**
2-5/16 x 7-1/8"

**Tobacco Barn**
**464-27304 29.95**
5 x 2-1/2"

**Anderson Pulpwood Yard**
**464-27480 59.95**
3-5/16 x 5-1/2"

**Best Auto Garage**
**464-27415 69.95**
3-13/16 x 4-1/8"

# B.T.S.
*Better Than Scratch!*

## HOUSING

**#110 Second Street**
**464-27700 39.95**
2-3/8 x 5-1/2"

## WESTERN

**Buck's Dynamite Building**
**464-27455 31.95**
3-3/16 x 2-3/16"

**Red Eye Saloon**
**464-27460 21.95**
2 x 3-3/8"

**Kee's Chinese Laundry**
**464-27465 23.95**
3 x 3-3/8"

## RAILROAD FACILITIES

**LCL Ramp**
**464-27509 16.95**
1-1/2 x 4-1/2"

**W&W Iams Station**
**464-27600 49.95**
6 x 3-13/16"

**Freight House**
**464-27500 69.95**
3-11/16 x 11"

**Tool Storage Shed**
**464-27112 13.95**
1-5/8 x 2"

**Crossing Shanty**
**464-27111 14.95**
1-5/8 x 2"

**Team Track Office**
**464-27107 14.95**
1-5/8 x 2"

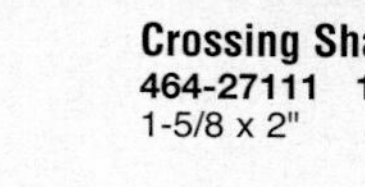

**Utility Building Combo**
One each of 27107, 27111, 27112 above.
**464-27116 39.95**

**W&W West Amity Station**
**464-27603 34.95**
3 x 3-5/16"

**W&W Deer Lick Station**
**464-27601 44.95**
2 x 7"

**NKP Green Springs Station**
**464-27162 49.95**
3 x 7"

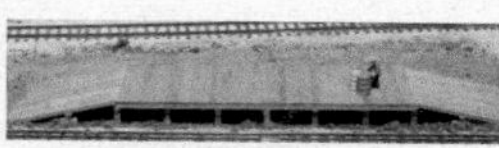

**Loading Dock**
**464-27506 15.95**
2-3/16 x 11-11/16"

**Single-Stall Switcher Shed**
**464-27502 59.95**
2-13/16 x 9-5/8"

**NG Box Car Storage Shed**
**464-27507 19.95**
1 x 2-5/8"

**DT&I Station**
3 x 6-3/16"

**464-27119** Waiting Room on Left **49.95**

**DT&I Station**
3 x 6-3/16"

**464-27118** With Waiting Room On Right **49.95**

**MoW Shed**
**464-27501 24.95**
3 x 4"

**Handcar Shed**
**464-27503 29.95**
2-3/8 x 2-11/16"

**E.B.T. Coles Station**
**464-27124 29.95**
3-1/2 x 4-1/8"

**E.B.T. Saltillo Station**
**464-27123 59.95**
6-5/16 x 6"

## WAR BETWEEN THE STATES SERIES

### 40' Long Wood Rick

**464-27800** Covered **29.95**

**464-27801** Open **19.95**

## BRIDGES

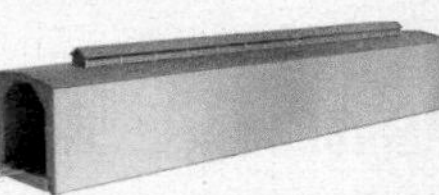

**East Tennessee & Western North Carolina Howe Thru-Truss Covered Bridge**
**464-27140** HOn3 **89.95**
18 x 118 Scale Feet

**Ballasted Deck Trestle**
**464-27103 24.95**
2 x 6-13/16"

## LOGGING

**Logging Bunkhouse**
**464-27425** pkg(3) **29.95**
3 x 1-13/16"

**Camp Reynolds Cookhouse**
**464-27475 49.95**
6-13/16 x 5"

**Coyote Draw Engine House, HOn3**
**464-27445 79.95**
6-13/16 x 8"

**Backwoods Engine House, HOn3**
**464-27450 59.95**
4 x 6-13/16"

IMPORTED FROM GERMANY BY WALTHERS
Easy-to-build structure kits by Busch feature detailed, injection-molded plastic parts molded in appropriate colors, plus realistic German-language signage as appropriate. Models are based on prototypes found throughout the world, making them suitable for North American-style layouts by simply adding your own English signs or decals (sold separately).

## NEW PRODUCTS

### Houses

#### Summer Cottages 29.99 ea

These wood cottages will look great in the mountains or along a lake or river. The buildings feature parts molded in colors and feature a removable roof that reveals an interior stone floor and fireplace. 4-5/16 x 3-1/2 x 2"  11 x 9 x 5cm

**NEW 189-1080** Blue
**NEW 189-1081** Green
**NEW 189-1082** White
**NEW 189-1083** Red
**NEW 189-1084** Yellow

### City Buildings

#### Mobile Police Station in Converted Containers

**NEW 189-1058  29.99**
This mobile police station kit includes two converted shipping containers with windows and details, electrical cabinet, floodlight, radio antenna, interior furniture, 24 barricades, police truck and other details.

### Businesses

#### Casino/Gaming Hall

**NEW 189-1003  43.99**
4-13/32 x 3-3/8 x 3-3/16"  11.2 x 8.6 x 7.8cm

This gaming house adds a touch of glitz to any modern layout scene. Kit includes interior light to accentuate the German language wall signs and graphics

#### Beer Garden

**NEW 189-1046  33.99**
This Beer Garden Set is just the thing for any festival setting. The set includes two concession stands, 14 tables, 28 benches, two umbrellas, four nonworking lamps, a signpost with sign, two grilles and more. Figures sold separately.

#### Fischer Beverage Store

**NEW 189-1047  26.99**
4-11/32 x 3-1/8 x 2-3/8"  11 x 8 x 6cm

This converted gas station office is now the best place in town to buy beverages. This easy-to-build kit includes the main structure, interior details, shopping carts, signage (in German) and more.

#### Tire Service Center

**NEW 189-1062  43.99**
This service center brings a typical business to any comemrcial district. Kit includes a converted gas station office building with a converted container on the rear that shelters the service bay, and includes a weathered Volvo tow truck, tire stacks, tools, shop details and German signs.

#### Campground

**NEW 189-6044  33.99**
Set includes a welcome kiosk, 15 typical tents, chairs, campfire, converted container with restrooms, life boat, wood pile, garbage cans, wastebaskets, standing tables, beverage crates, and more.

## HIGH-RISE OFFICE BUILDINGS

Modular high-rise buildings can be built to any number of stories using add-on story kits. Basic office building kit includes six floors and includes entry doors and outdoor canopy. Add-on floor kits include two floors.

#### Basic Kit 126.99 ea

7-11/16 x 7-11/16 x 11-13/32"
19.5 x 19.5 x 29cm

**189-1006** Gold
**189-1008** Copper

#### Add-On Floors 41.99 ea

7-11/16 x 7-11/16 x 3-3/4"
19.5 x 19.5 x 9.5cm

**189-1007** Gold
**189-1009** Copper

## INDUSTRIAL

#### Timber Shop

**189-6047  20.99**

## BUSINESSES

### Gas Station

**189-1005 43.99**
Designed by Dutch architect W. Dudok, its modern architecture allows the model to be used on any post-1950s layout. Suitable for a major highway or in a small town, the 2-part gas station building can be set up back-to-back, side-by-side or as two free-standing structures. The buildings also make great concession stands, workshops, or retail stores. Kit includes gasoline pumps, prototypical signage and interior accessories.

## TANKS & TOWERS

### Watch Tower

**189-1015 29.99**
Observation tower kit based on those used on the former East German Republic's borders. Includes border fence and printed sheet of typical German-language signs that may be cut and used. The detailed assembly instructions include other building suggestions. The concrete pole consists of stackable rings allowing for variation in the tower height and making the kit also suitable for TT scale. Overall height approximately 6-1/2" 16.5cm.

### Florist Shop

**189-1049 35.99**
This small flower shop adds character to any scene. This detailed scene includes planters and flower boxes with realistic roses, tulips, daisies, sunflowers, etc., as well as tables, benches, trash cans, various tools and more.

### Cell Phone Towers

**189-1021 32.99**
Maximum Height:
12-5/8" 32cm

Kit comes complete with fence and numerous individual parts including several different styles of antennae and satellite dishes that you can add as you please to make each tower unique. Also included is a switching gear cabinet, signal box and a sturdy base with stairs.

### Transmitter Tower

**189-5965 52.99**
14-3/4" 37cm

Modernize communications on your layout with this modern radio tower. To protect aircraft, there are three LEDs at the top of the tower which flash in sequence. Model is fully assembled, ready to install.

## BRIDGES & VIADUCTS

### Pedestrian Stone Bridge

**189-6041 15.99**

## RURAL BUILDINGS

### Forest Set

**189-6042 35.99**
Create a local recreation area with log cabin and accessories. The kit includes a typical forest cabin (kit) of dark wood, 2 wood tables with 4 chairs fashioned from trunks, 12 dowels for use as seating or fencing, 2 waste receptacles, 4 large information boards (e.g. for forest education exhibits), 6 signposts, 2 wood barriers to control access to the forest trail, fodder crib, stand, different forest animals (squirrel, owl, rabbit, woodpecker), wood fence, wood trunks and roots, timber bridge, 3 woodpiles, well, outhouse, pond foil and signs and displays.

### Log Cabin

**189-1035 23.99**
4-3/8 x 3-5/8 x 2"
11.1 x 9.2 x 5cm

Kit for a super-detailed cabin built from light-colored pine based on a structure from the Black Forest. The door and the windows can positioned either open or closed.

Trailer Park 189-1054

Swimming Pool 189-1025

Stadium 189-1051

Top View of the Stadium

IMPORTED FROM GERMANY BY WALTHERS

### Tennis Court w/Grandstand

**189-1056 30.99**
7-7/8 x 8-1/4" 20 x 21cm

Includes playing fields with white lines, grandstand, referee's high seat, net, fence with gate, scoreboard, and advertising banners.

### Fenced Basketball Court

**189-1057 25.99**
8-11/16 x 5-15/16" 22 x 15cm

Includes a base plate, two nets with stands, two exercise bars and a fence with gates.

### Christmas Fair Street Scene

**189-1059 28.99**
Includes four concession stands, Christmas tree lot with eight firs, cashier's booth, tables, beer kegs, snowman figure and more.

## PORTABLE BUILDINGS

Special events, construction sites and other nonpermanent installations often require temporary structures. Special modular buildings, based on shipping containers, allow structures to be assembled on site. Busch container buildings can be used as offices, medical clinics, schools, shops, banks or in any setting where temporary office space is required.

**189-1031** Container Set pkg(6) **22.99**
Kit includes two each container buildings in red, blue and white. Use them individually or combine them for larger complexes.

### Building Construction Site

**189-1053 45.99**
Includes a three-dimensional ground plate with excavation, three container-based site offices with stairs, construction truck, about 23-5/8" 60cm of wood fencing, 9-7/8" 25cm of wire-mesh fencing, electrical cabinets, portable toilet, stacks of wood, wooden boxes, wheelbarrow, tools and more.

### Trailer Park

**189-1054 32.99**
This complete kit contains everything needed to create a realistic trailer park, campground or RV park scene. Includes kits for 2 "Airstream" style campers plus camp table, stools, campfire, wooden booth, enclosure, 3 fir trees, fence and printed sheets with various camping and national park signs.

**189-1030** Container Railway Station **59.99**
8-5/8 x 4-1/2 x 3-1/8"
21.9 x 11.3 x 8cm

Based on a temporary depot building used for three years while the venerable Manheim, Germany, station was being renovated. Kit includes 16 container sections, parts for the glass-enclosed central hall and signs.

## SPORTS & RECREATION

### Swimming Pool

**189-1025 45.99**
7-1/8 x 5-1/8 x 3-1/8"
18 x 13 x 8cm

Winter or summer, day or night, this indoor swimming pool is great for year round entertainment. Features a large pool with ladders and diving boards, separate entrance area and changing rooms. Upstairs there's a gallery cafeteria with standing tables, paper plates, garbage can, beverage cans, bottles and more.

### Gymnasium

**189-1026 95.99**
8-7/8 x 7-7/8 x 3-9/64"
22.5 x 20 x 8cm

Perfect for year-round use, this modern sports hall will add realism to any layout. Includes floor, interior grandstand/ concession stand and enclosed building entrances.



### Glider Field w/Accessories

**189-1050 35.99**
Here's a hangout for your layout's pilots. Kit includes two gliders, container control tower, field signs and markers, windsock and mast, and vehicle.

### Stadium

**189-1051 52.99**
Maximum Size: 19-5/8 x 13"
50 x 33cm

Add a sports complex to your layout with this kit. Includes bleachers, fencing and nets, picnic tables, ticket booth, storage container, lawn surface mat, lunch stand and 12 unpainted soccer player figures. There's also a practice/exercise field with pylons and gates.

### Sales Stands

**189-1055 13.99**
Wooden sales booths with cases and bottles are perfect for use as fruit vendor's stands, carnival and event food and drink booths, or news stands. Kit includes two booths, crates, bottles and printed signs in German. Ideal addition to the Busch Christmas Market 189-1059, sold separately.

CAD design and laser cutting produce a kit with all the precision of a plastic kit, but with all the advantages of wood. Walls, roofing, doors, windows and trim are laser-cut and ready to assemble. Models are highly detailed, easy to build and look great, too!

## NEW PRODUCT

### Stations & Platforms

#### Santa Fe 6-Room Section House

**NEW 184-194 59.95**
6-3/4 x 3-27/64"

These houses were provided to station agents, section foremen and their families in remote locations. Often, more than one were erected at these "company" neighborhoods. Even if you are not modeling the Santa Fe, this model looks great in any residential neighbrhood.

## INDUSTRIAL

#### Cash Mine Works Ore House

**184-186 129.95**
7-1/2 x 8-1/2" 18.7 x 21.3cm

Inspired by a model of the Silver King Ore House in Park City, Utah, this classic building is a great addition to any mine scene. The kit captures all of the flavor of the real thing, with its varied roof lines, exposed structural framing and covered loading areas that serve two tracks. Designed for easy construction, it includes laser-cut walls with tab and slot connections, doors, window frames, trim, floor, roofing and structural frames.

#### Warehouse Backdrop Building

**184-192 94.95**
13 x 2 x 7" 32.5 x 5 x 17.5cm

Three-story wood-sided warehouse and storage building with covered wood loading dock and rooftop sign. Includes laser-etched nail holes on aged clapboard siding, positionable windows, lampshades, exhaust fans, crates, pallets and a do-it-yourself rooftop sign to make your own custom factory name.

## BUSINESSES

#### General Store

**184-180 34.95**
3-3/4 x 5-1/4" 9.3 x 13.1cm

Kit features such great laser-cut details as walls, windows, floors, doors and back porch addition. Also comes with a chimney, peel-n-stick trim and roofing, full-color signs and a wall sign decal.

#### Dari-King Drive-In Restaurant

**184-182 33.95**
4 x 5" 10 x 12.5cm

Before the modern style of fast-food restaurants, the drive-in was the most convenient way to get a quick meal. Bring retro styling and a touch of nostalgia to your HO layout with this eatery. Attract customers with a laser-cut roadside sign that will catch any motorist's eye. Also includes a large selection of full-color signs.

#### Ernie's Gas Station

**184-181 39.95**
2-3/4 x 1-3/4" 6.8 x 4.3cm

Based on a gas station in Carthage, Missouri, this kit includes laser-cut walls, doors, window frames, trim, floor, roofing and sign frames. Also comes with gas pumps and island, chimney, tire display, soda machine, a roadside sign and a variety of colorful decals and signs to change the look of the station exterior.

Fireworks Stand

Totem Pole Trading Post

#### Roadside Tourist Trap

**184-170 33.95**
5 x 3-1/4" 12.5 x 8.1cm

This fun and easy-to-build kit includes one laser-cut wood structure, and full-color signs for four different businesses: Fireworks Stand, Totem Pole Trading Post, Reptile Ranch and Hollywood Wax Museum. Also includes a sheet of advertising signs.

### Drive-In Theatre
**184-168 24.95**
A fun way to bring back old memories, and sure to be a conversation piece on your layout! Kit includes laser-cut tower, frame and ticket booth; pre-printed plastic screen and fence; three different marquees; and 17 movie signs from the 1930s to the 1990s. The space-saving design fits against a backdrop or wall, or build it with a parking lot and display HO Scale vehicles (not included)!

### Clark Oil Gas Station
**184-187 38.95**
Office: 4 x 3" 10 x 7.5cm

Based on the popular station design of the 1950s (which can still be seen today), this kit features laser-cut exterior and interior walls, doors, window frames, trim, floor, roofing and sign frames. Other details include gas pumps and island, chimney, soda machine, signs and billboards.

### Fred & Red's Cafe
**184-190 31.95**
2 x 4-1/2" 5 x 11.2cm
Long before look-alike fast food chains, small roadside cafes like these catered to travelers and truck drivers along the nation's major two-lane highways. Here and there, a few still survive today. Packed with details, the kit includes a laser-cur floor, aged sidewalks, and exterior walls feature laser-etched nail holes. Plastic windows are included, along with signs, burglar bars, lampshades, a cast metal smokejack, plus laser-cut "OPEN" and "EAT" signs for the finishing touch.

## STATIONS & PLATFORMS

### C&O Railway Depot
**184-185 69.95**
2-3/4 x 7" 6.8 x 17.5cm

This combination passenger/freight depot will fit any railroad. Kit features peel-n-stick doors, windows, roofing and trim. Also includes a cast chimney and signs, as well as laser-cut window "glass" and interior walls.

### Boston Depot
**184-193 54.95**
Small combination depot based on Missouri Pacific prototype in Boston, Missouri. Includes peel-n-stick hex shingles.

### Gerald Depot
**184-195 69.95**
3-5/16 x 6-3/4" 8.3 x 16.9cm

Combination depot with a pagoda style roof. Similar styling to the Leeton Depot (#184-188), but in a bigger structure. Includes signs and chimney.

### Blairstown 2-Story Depot
**184-178 49.95**
8 x 2-3/4" 20 x 6.9cm

Combination depot with board and batten siding. In remote locations, the second floor was used as living quarters for the station agent. The one story addition serves as the freight and baggage room.

### Leeton Depot
**185-188 69.95**
Main Building: 3-5/16 x 5-1/2"; Ramp:1 x 3-1/4"

Pagoda-style or flared roofs were found on the depots used by several railroads. The prototype for this model was the Rock island station at Leeton, Mo., but it's typical of stations found all over America. As-built, the depot had a loading ramp, and parts are included to model this feature if desired. Signs and a chimney are also included.

## YARD EQUIPMENT & FACILITIES

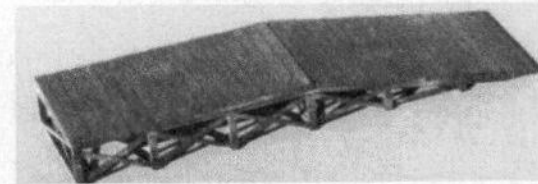

### Wood Loading Ramp
**184-174 16.95**
5-1/2 x 1-3/8" 13.8 x 3.4cm

### Section Car Toolhouse
**184-175 16.95**
2-1/8 x 1-3/4" 5.3 x 4.4cm

This structure was a common trackside storage building in every railroad town or city in the United States and Canada.

### Truck Dump
**184-177 19.95**
4 x 1-3/4" 10 x 4.4cm

Found everywhere coal, stone and other minerals were mined and transported by truck and loaded on railcars.

### Coal Storage House
**184-183 15.95**
1-3/8 x 1-3/8" 3.4 x 3.4cm

Coal houses were used to store coal used as heating fuel for depots, towers and other railroad facilities.

### Scale House
**184-184 15.95**
3/4 x 1-3/4" 1.9 x 4.3cm

The scale house was common in railroad yards, mining regions or industrial areas.

## HOUSES

### One-Car Garage
**184-173 16.95**
2-3/4 x 1-3/4" 6.9 x 4.4cm

### Company House
**184-176 26.95**
3-1/2 x 2" 8.8 x 5cm

Company houses were found in many coal-mining towns and timber camps. Would also make an excellent sharecropper's home, hillbilly shanty or "house on the wrong side of the tracks."

## BRIDGES & VIADUCTS

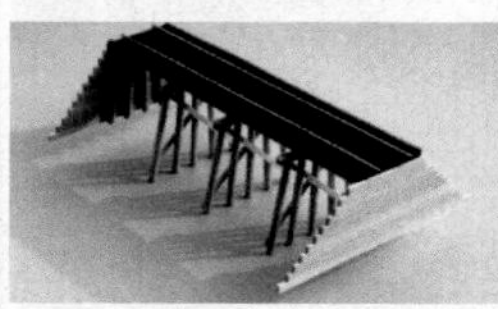

**Common Pile Trestle**
**184-167 21.95**
6" long x 2" tall
15cm long x 5cm tall

**Laser-Cut Pile & Frame Trestle**
**184-171 27.95**
6" long x 2" tall
15cm long x 5cm tall

## CHURCHES

**Wood Frame Church**
**184-169 39.95**
4-7/8 x 3 x 6"
12.2 x 7.5 x 15cm

## RURAL BUILDINGS

**Tom's Corn Crib**
**184-191 21.95**
2-1/4" 5.6cm Diameter
2-1/2" 6.2cm Tall

Used to air-dry corn this model captures all the intricate detail of the eight-sided original, which still stands in Kansas, in an easy-to-build kit.

Cibolo Crossing

These craft train kits include detailed plaster walls with beveled corners for easier assembly. Doors and windows are cast in place, and stripwood is provided for window sashes.

## BUSINESSES

**Menard Wool & Mohair**
**231-8 34.95**
3-1/2 x 7-1/2" 9 x 18.5cm

Includes plastic windows. Prototype in Menard, Texas.

**Alamosa Oil Service**
**231-9 34.95**
4-1/2 x 5" 12 x 13cm

Includes plastic windows. Prototype in Alamosa, Colorado.

**Blacksmith Shop**
**231-14 21.95**
4 x 4" 10 x 10cm

Wooden building. Includes plastic windows and preweathered wood.

## TANKS & TOWERS

231-24 231-25

**Tapered, 9' Diameter Water Tank w/Tower**
**231-24 22.95**
1-3/8 x 3-7/8" 3.5 x 10cm

Includes rod banding. Water tanks can be built with tower, or free-standing as a roof-top detail. Kits feature preweathered wood parts.

**Straight, 6' Diameter Water Tank w/Tower**
**231-25 20.95**
1-1/4 x 4-5/8" 3 x 11.5cm

Includes hoop banding.

## INDUSTRIAL

**Salida Coal Company**
**231-1 34.95**
3-3/4 x 8-3/4" 9.5 x 22cm

Includes dry transfer sign.

**Salida Coal Bins**
**231-2 19.95**
2-1/2 x 10-1/2" 6 x 26.5cm

Wood kit with plastic details.

**Salida Machine Shop**
**231-3 22.50**
3-1/4 x 3-1/4" 9 x 9cm

**Dynamite Igloos**
**231-4** pkg(3) **14.95**
2-1/2 x 1-3/4" 6.4 x 4.5cm

One-piece Hydrocal® castings.

231-6 231-7

**70' Square Brick Chimney**
**231-6 11.95**

**70' Octagonal Brick Chimney**
**231-7 11.95**
1-1/2 x 9-5/8" 3.8 x 24.4cm

Smokestacks are one-piece plaster castings with realistic brick detail.

**Lighted Mine Tunnel w/Mirror**
**231-20 29.95**

CON-COR

**Moxam Soap Works**
**222-1714 13.98**

**Yardmaster's Office**
**222-9032 8.98**

**Engine Crew Shanty**
**222-9033 8.98**

**Summer Stock Theater**
**222-9035 14.98**

**Bridge & Trestle Set**
**222-9039 14.98**

**Welding Shop**
**222-9059 12.98**

**Cambria Fuel Depot**
**222-9061 17.98**

**Cambria Fuel Tanks**
**222-9062 16.98**

**Cambria Fuel Rack**
**222-9063 16.98**

**Cambria Tire Repair Shop**
**222-9064 15.98**

**Star Glass Co. Five Story Chimney**
**222-9071 16.98**
2 x 2 x 10" 5 x 5 x 26cm

## DOVER PUBLICATIONS

Visit Walthers web site at www.walthers.com for a complete listing of Dover Publications products.

## NEW PRODUCTS

**Cut-Out Structure Kits**

**241-23536** Early New England Village **9.95**

**NEW 241-73407** Ferris Wheel **6.95**

**241-23736** Western Frontier Town **8.95**

**241-23849** Victorian Houses **9.95**

# Campbell Scale Models

These craft train kits feature precision-cut wood, "profile shingles," molded plastic windows and doors, vents, signs, corrugated aluminum siding, etc., as needed. Each kit includes templates and complete instructions.

## STATIONS & PLATFORMS

### Skull Valley Station
**200-367 80.79**
3-7/8 x 10-1/4" 9.52 x 26.3cm

### Quincy Station
**200-402 97.41**
5-1/8 x 12" 13.1 x 30.6cm

### Freight House & Passenger Station
**200-442 45.02**
3-1/16 x 3-3/8" 7.8 x 6.8cm

### LCL Freight Station
**200-353 43.64**
3-1/2 x 7" 8.7 x 17.5cm

Includes ramp.

### Wayside Freight Station
**200-361 52.38**
2-7/8 x 6-5/8" 7.62 x 16.8cm

### Passenger Shelter
**200-362 40.48**
2 x 9-7/8" 4.5 x 24.8cm

### Kiowa Junction Station
**200-423 73.37**
2-7/8 x 7-1/2" 7.3 x 19.2cm

Prototype in Junction, Kansas.

### Large Freight Station
**200-447 89.59**
5-3/4 x 10-5/8" 14.6 x 27cm

South Pacific Coast Railroad prototype.

## YARD EQUIPMENT & FACILITIES

### Portable Bunkhouses
These kits are designed to introduce modelers to craft train kit construction. The buildings feature simple design and fewer parts, making them ideal for beginners. Kits include precut wood with plastic castings for the windows and details. 1-1/4 x 3" 3.2 x 7.7cm.

**200-230 "A" 12.65**

**200-231 "B" 13.80**

### Supply Shed & Single Handcar House
**200-370 45.20**
Shed: 2-1/2 x 5-1/4" 6.3 x 13.3cm
House: 2 x 3-7/8" 5 x 10.1cm

### Windy Gulch Engine House
**200-389 87.69**
3 x 12" 7.6 x 30.4cm

### Quincy Speeder Shed & Ice House
**200-403 41.29**
Shed: 2 x 3" 5.1 x 7.7cm
Ice House: 1-3/4" 4.5cm

### Kiowa Trackside Details #1
**200-425 44.28**
3-9/16 x 6" 9 x 15.2cm

### Kiowa Trackside Details #2
**200-426 46.58**
3-9/16 x 6" 8.9 x 15cm

**Sand House**
200-358 60.38
3 x 8" 7.6 x 20.3cm

**Engine House**
200-401 94.88
6-3/4 x 11" 17.2 x 28cm

**Traveling Crane**
200-404 45.20
1-5/8 x 6-1/8" 4 x 15.6cm

**Fuel Oil Dock**
200-405 65.38
Each: 3 x 1-5/8" 7.5 x 4cm

## RURAL BUILDINGS

**Sheriff's Office**
200-364 45.89
3-1/2 x 5" 8.9 x 12.7cm

**Stockpens w/Double Chutes**
200-437 43.64
10-1/2 x 1" 26.7 x 27.9cm

**Grain Storage Bin**
200-449 56.24
3-5/8 x 7-1/2" 9.2 x 18.5cm

**Cattle Loading Pens**
200-781 20.70
7-7/8 x 5-3/4" 20.3 x 14.6cm

House Shown At Right Not Included.

**Barn**
200-382 57.21
4-1/8 x 6-3/4" 10.4 x 17.1cm

See What's Available at
**www.walthers.com**

The "Norm's Landing" complex, pictured above, consists of the following kits: Fishing Pier #200-392, Boat Shop #200-396, and Ice House & Cafe #200-397.

**Fishing Pier**
200-392 75.61
Pier: 7-1/2x 10" 19 x 25.4cm Ramp: 2-1/2 x 10" 6.3 x 25.4cm
Float: 4 x 7-1/8" 10.1 x 18cm

**Boat Shop**
200-396 75.61
3-1/2 x 6-1/4" 8.9 x 15.8cm

**Ice House & Cafe**
200-397 70.09
Ice House: 2-1/2 x 4-1/4"
6.3 x 10.8cm
Cafe: 3-1/2" Square
8.9cm Square

**Shed Under Construction & Double Handcar House**
200-368 43.64
Shed: 2-1/2 x 5-1/4" 6.3 x 13.3cm
House: 3-1/8 x 3-7/8" 7.9 x 9.8cm

## HOUSES

**Gran'Ma's House**
200-387 91.08
House:
5 x 5-1/4"
12.7 x 13.3cm
Garage:
2-1/2 x 1-3/4"
6.3 x 4.5cm

**Abandoned House**
200-393 53.88
4 x 4-1/2" 10.1 x 10.8cm

**Picken's Place**
200-395 52.73
4 x 4-1/2" 10.1 x 10.8cm
1-5/8 x 1-5/8" 4.2 x 4.2cm

## CITY BUILDINGS

**1875 Fire House**
200-355 46.58
2-3/4 x 3-5/8" 7 x 9.2cm

**Iowa School House**
200-369 65.49
2-3/4 x 4-1/2" 7 x 10.8cm

**Carsten's Flop House**
200-413 108.79
3-3/4 x 6" 9.5 x 15.2cm

**Summer Bandstand**
**200-383 53.19**
3-1/2 x 3-1/2" 8.8 x 8.8cm

**Breckenridge Fire House**
**200-441 82.92**
5 x 6-1/4" 13 x 16cm

Prototype in Breckenridge, Colorado, until 1941.

**Post Office**
**200-446 43.64**
2-1/2 x 5-7/8" 6.5 x 15cm

## CHURCHES

**Community Church**
**200-359 76.99**
3-1/4 x 7-5/8" 8.3 x 19.3cm

With "stained-glass" windows.

## TANKS & TOWERS

**Timber Oil Derrick**
**200-354 58.94**
3-3/4 x 9" 9.5 x 22.8cm

**Water Tank**
**200-356 65.49**
4" 10.1cm Square

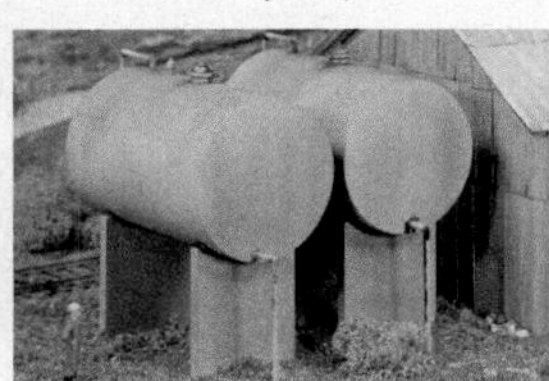

**18' Horizontal Tanks**
**200-407** pkg(2) **37.95**
Each: 3-3/4 x 1-5/8"
9.5 x 4cm

**24' Horizontal Tanks**
**200-408** pkg(2) **37.95**
Each: 3-3/4 x 1-5/8"
9.5 x 4cm

**Pump House**
**200-360**
**38.70**
2-3/4 x 3-1/4"
6.9 x 7.6cm

**Loading Tanks**
**200-410 43.93**
4-1/8 x 2-1/8" 10.5 x 5.5cm

Vertical tanks with small loading rack.

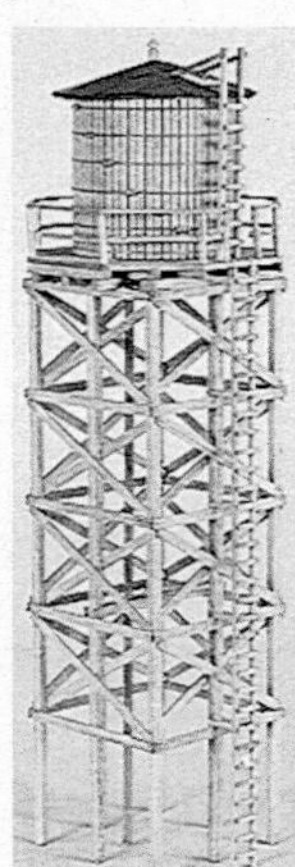

**Water Tower**
**200-453 45.43**
1-5/8" 4.2cm Square

**Plastic Windmill**
**200-1604 6.90**

**Square Water Tower**
**200-421 43.64**
3 x 3-1/4" 7.5 x 8.5cm

**Branchline Water Tank & Tool House**
**200-372 45.31**
Tank: 2 x 3-1/2" 5 x 9cm
Tool House: 3/5 x 1-1/2" 1.5 x 3.8cm

**Northern Water Tank**
**200-376 65.49**
4" 10.1cm Square 6-1/2" 16.3cm Tall

**Kiowa Tower**
**200-424 61.24**
2-5/16 x 6-1/8" 13.5 x 15.5cm

## BUSINESSES

**Campbell Supply Company**
**200-363 66.30**
4 x 10" 10.1 x 25.4cm

**Kee Ling Laundry & Cigar Store**
**200-365 64.34**
Cigar Store: 2-11/16 x 3-3/16"
7 x 8.3cm
Shelter: 2 x 9-7/8" 5 x 25.4cm

**W. T. Stephenson Drug Company & Barber Shop**
**200-366 64.34**
Drug Co.: 3-1/2 x 3-3/16"
8.9 x 17.8cm
Barber Shop: 2-3/8 x 3"
5.8 x 8.9cm

**Matthew's Mercantile**
**200-371 66.53**
3 x 3-1/2" 7.6 x 8.9cm

**Susannah's Frocks**
**200-375 66.53**
3-1/4 x 4" 8.3 x 10.1cm

**Seebold & Sons Manufacturing Company**
**200-377 66.53**

**Sherry's Scarlet Slipper Saloon**
**200-378 76.99**
Saloon: 4-1/4" 10.8cm Square
Frame: 2-1/8 x 4"
5.3 x 10.1cm

**Columbia Gazette Office**
**200-380 47.84**
4 x 5" 10.1 x 12.7cm

**Bret's Brewery**
**200-385 88.55**
5-1/2 x 10-1/2" 13.9 x 26.6cm

**Marjorie's Millinery**
**200-390 52.73**
3-1/8 x 2-7/8" 7.9 x 7.3cm

**Doctor's Office**
**200-398 75.61**
3-5/8 x 5" 9.5 x 12.7cm

**M.E. Nelson Livestock Company**
**200-400 70.15**
7-1/2 x 14" 19 x 35.5cm

**Dewitt's Depository**
**200-412 76.42**
3 x 7" 7.6 x 17.7cm

**Montgomery Feed & Seed**
**200-419 94.99**
3-1/4 x 9" 8.3 x 22.8cm

**Richmond Barrel Manufacturing Company**
**200-422 73.37**
3-1/4 x 6-5/8" 8.3 x 16.8cm

**Carriage Works**
**200-430 66.53**
3-3/4 x 4-3/4" 9.6 x 12.1cm

**Produce Shed**
**200-379 78.95**
4 x 16" 10.1 x 40.6cm

**Schrock's Meat Co.**
**200-411 108.79**
3-11/16 x 11-1/16" 9.8 x 28.1cm

**Santangelo Fruit Co.**
**200-420 94.59**
4-7/8 x 9-1/2" 12.4 x 23.5cm

**Tobacco Shop**
**200-434 47.38**
2-3/4 x 3-7/8" 7 x 9.9cm

**Assay Office/ Clothing Store**
200-431 49.85
3-3/4 x 4-7/8" 9.6 x 12.5cm

**Corrugated Warehouse**
200-373 46.58
3 x 5-3/4" 7.6 x 14.6cm

**Cabinet Makers Shop**
200-443 66.41
5 x 7-3/8" 12.7 x 18.7cm

**Cordage Works**
200-455 69.86
5-3/8 x 6-3/8" 13.6 x 16.1cm

**Gunsmith Shop**
200-456 53.19
3-1/4 x 5-5/8" 8.2 x 14.4cm

**Frederick J. Hamilton Dinghies Ltd.**
200-394 87.29
3-3/4 x 8-3/4" 9.5 x 22.1cm

**Grain Elevator**
200-384 77.17
3-1/2 x 10-1/2" 8.9 x 26.6cm

## INDUSTRIAL

**Mine Head Frame**
200-352 47.44
3-3/4 x 11-1/2" 9.5 x 29.2cm

**Oil Compound House (Including Dock)**
200-409 48.70
4 x 5-1/2" 10.2 x 14cm

**Coaling Station**
200-357 78.49
5 x 6" 12.7 x 15.2cm

**Silver Spur Mine**
200-388 85.10
Shaft House: 4-1/2 x 6-1/2" 10.8 x 16.5cm
Tunnel & Tipple: 1-3/4 x 3-3/4" 4.5 x 9.5cm

**Ayres Chair Factory**
200-391 91.08
6-3/4 x 7-1/4" 17.1 x 18.4cm

**Saez Sash & Door Machine Shop, Shed & Hopper**
200-417 103.73
6 x 12" 15.6 x 27.9cm

**Idaho Springs Mine**
200-433 51.18
Main Structure: 3 x 3-3/8" 7.7 x 8.6cm Trestle: 12-1/2" 31.8cm

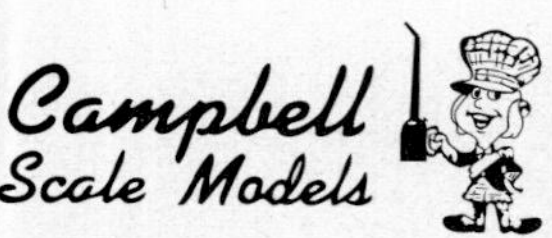

**Farm Co-Op Creamery**
**200-418 84.41**
9-1/2 x 5-5/8" 24.2 x 14.3cm

**Abandoned Freight Warehouse**
**200-427 42.32**
3-5/8 x 4-5/8" 9.3 x 11.9cm

**Ten Stamp Mill**
**200-428 66.30**
7-7/8 x 7-1/4" 20 x 18.5cm

**Iron Foundry**
**200-444 68.31**
4-3/8 x 9-5/8" 11.1 x 24.5cm

**The Blacksmith Shop**
**200-461 45.08**
3 x 5-1/8" 7.7 x 13cm

**Grist Mill**
**200-374 64.06**
3-1/4 x 4-1/2" 8.3 x 10.8cm

**Quick's Coal**
**200-386 94.88**
Yard: 3 x 8" 7.6 x 20.3cm
Office: 2 x 3-1/2" 5 x 8.9cm

**Oil Warehouse & Office**
**200-406 65.38**
4-1/8 x 8-1/4" 10.5 x 21cm

**Saez Sash & Door Mill House & Loft**
**200-416 95.34**
5-5/8 x 10" 14.3 x 25.4cm

**Red Mountain Mine**
**200-429 90.56**
9-9/16 x 5-3/8" 23.9 x 13.4cm

**King's Cannery**
**200-439 107.53**
6-3/4 x 12-1/2" 17.2 x 31.8cm

Santa Fe prototype from Irvine, California.

**Ore Bin**
**200-438 53.76**
3-7/8 x 3" 9.9 x 7.7cm

Campbell Scale Models

## BRIDGES & VIADUCTS

**50' Ballasted Deck Pile Trestle (Less Ties)**
**200-301 29.84**
6-7/8 x 3" 17.3 x 7.6cm

**50' Open Deck Pile Trestle**
**200-302 29.84**
6-7/8 x 3" 17.3 x 7.6cm

**70' Curved Trestle**
**200-303 43.64**
15-1/4 x 1-3/8" 38.7 x 3.5cm

**Howe Truss Bridge**
**200-305 65.49**
14-1/2 x 3-1/8" 36.8 x 7.6cm

**Covered Bridge**
**200-306 71.99**
14-5/8 x 3-1/4" 37.2 x 8.2cm

**110' Tall Curved Trestle**
**200-304 57.21**
15-1/4 x 1-3/8" 38.7 x 3.5cm

**Wharf**
**200-307 71.99**
22-3/8 x 5-1/4" 56.6 x 13.3cm

**144-216' Tall Timber Trestle**
**200-751 64.00**
20 x 29" 50.8 x 73.6cm

**50' Deck Timber Bridge**
**200-761 54.68**
14" 35.5cm

**70' Thru Timber Bridge**
**200-762 58.19**
14 x 3-3/4" 35.5 x 9.5cm

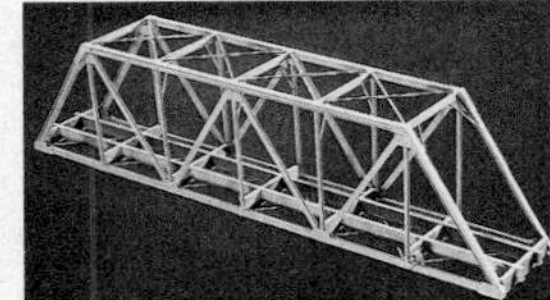

**125' Single Track Truss Bridge**
**200-763** Less Ties **50.89**
17-1/4 x 3" 40.2 x 7.6cm

**125' Double Track Truss Bridge**
**200-764 57.44**
16-7/8 x 3-3/8" 35.8 x 12cm

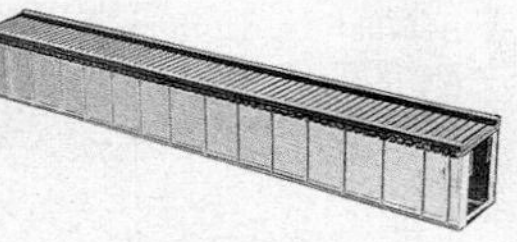

**70' Deck Plate Girder Bridge**
**200-765 41.52**
9-5/8 x 1-3/8" 24.4 x 3.5cm

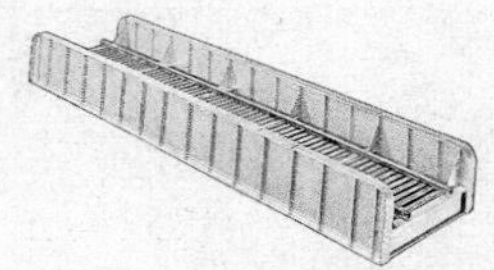

**70' Thru Plate Girder Bridge**
**200-766 43.30**
9-5/8 x 2-1/2" 24.4 x 5.2cm

For Up-To-Date Information and News Bookmark Walthers Web site at
**www.walthers.com**

CM CLASSIC MINIATURES

DIVISION OF TAURUS PRODUCTS

Wood kits feature template construction, Kappler and Northeastern lumber, roofing material, plastic and metal cast details. Visit Walthers Web site at www.walthers.com for a complete listing of Classic Miniatures structures.

### Stations & Platforms

**Ophir Depot**
**225-31156 56.00**
29 x 68'

**Laws Depot**
**225-31415 59.00**
40 x 115'

**SP Sparks Depot**
**225-31905 37.00**
30 x 38'

**SP Engine House**
**225-32401 35.00**
17 x 60'

### Yard Equipment & Facilities

**Branchline Oil Facility**
**225-38926 37.00**
12 x 24'

### Houses

**Queen Anne Cottage**
**225-38903 44.00**
27 x 34'

**Winters Mansion**
**225-38908 48.00**
50 x 80'

**Red Light District**
**225-38910** pkg(5) **28.00**
Each building is 11 x 18'.

**Columbia Miner's Cabin**
**225-38918 28.00**
15 x 28'

### City Buildings

**Fraternity Hall**
**225-38902 27.00**
26 x 39'

**Montezuma Post Office**
**225-38917 34.00**
25 x 44'

### Churches

**Bodie Church**
**225-38914 34.00**
29 x 45'

### Businesses

**Wells Fargo & Co. Office**
**225-38905 26.00**
17 x 39'

CENTRAL VAL

## BRIDGES & VIADUCTS

**150' Pratt Truss Bridge**

**210-1902 39.95**
20-5/8" 52.5cm

Single-track bridge features a removable upper truss, premolded bridge ties and extra-long girder components. Ties accept Code 70 or 83 rail, easily modified for Code 100 rail.

### Plate Girder Bridges

**Single Track**

**210-1903 14.95**
10" 25.5cm long,
2-1/2" 6.35cm wide.

72', one-piece floor and bridge tie sections. Prototypically correct rivet detail on all sides of the girder sections.

**Double Track**

**210-1904 21.95**
10" 25.4cm long,
4-3/4" 9.5cm wide.

### Box Girder Sections

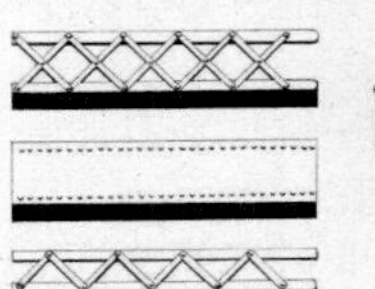

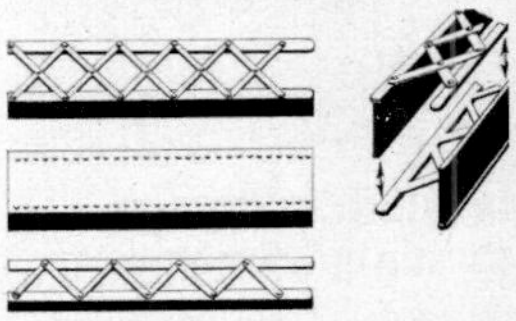

**210-19025** 5-7/8" pkg(5) **11.95**

### Plate Girder Section

**210-19031** 10" Long pkg(2) **5.98**

### Bridge Tie Sections

**210-19032** 10" Long pkg(2) **8.95**

**210-190210** 3-1/4" Long pkg(10) **11.95**

...ready in ..., on special high-strength cardstock. Simply cut, fold and glue to create affordable, beautiful 3-D models for your railroad.

## NEW PRODUCTS

### Rural Buildings

**Roadside Stand**
**NEW 217-1101 10.95**
Down on the farm or serving as a shanty on your railroad, this handsome blue clapboard building has a lot of possibilities. Screened windows provide a view of the printed interior details!

### Houses & Garages

**2-Bay Stone Block Garage**
**NEW 217-1102 10.95**

**Insulbrick Storage Building/Garage**
**NEW 217-1103 10.95**
An asphalt sheet material popular in the late 40s and 50s, Insulbrick was easily nailed over any existing building; the colorful brick patterns offered a quick and affordable way to improve the looks of the structure. Many are still standing today though a little worse for wear, like this model that features heavily distressed Insulbrick siding.

**...age ...rage**
**... 10.95**
...ucked along a city alley, this building is a great way to detail a small space. Model features yellow/tan clapboard siding.

**Brick Garage with Shed**
**NEW 217-1112 14.95**
Give a big city neighborhood real character with this brick garage, based on an actual building in the Rogers Park area of Chicago. Perfect for any kind of small business or light industrial shop, the kit includes parts for two different roofs, several types of doors and a small shed.

**3 Complete Houses**
**NEW 217-1114 29.95**

### Stations & Platforms

**Small Town Depot**
**NEW 217-1116 39.95**
Back when life centered on the comings and goings of the railroad, fancy structures like this were important to small towns along the line. This typical combination station has a freight room at one end, a waiting room at the other and the agent/operator's office in the middle. With its ornate roof and end trim, it's perfect for any line that wants to make a good impression on passengers and shippers.

### Shiner

**NEW 217-1128** pkg(3) **9.95**

### Towers

**Octagonal Gateman's Tower**
**NEW 217-1105 14.95**
Sitting above busy city streets, a single crossing watchman could easily lower and raise several sets of pneumatic crossing gates from the comfort of this tower. Based on a Milwaukee Road design used in many locations from the 1920s on, it's easily used on any railroad.

### Industrial

**Small Forge Building**
**NEW 217-1106 24.95**
Here's a shop building that will look right as almost any small industry. The large rooftop window bay can be used as is, shortened or left off entirely to change the look and feel of the finished model. A tall freight door on one side, along with a sheet metal roof, vents and blowers are included. Several buildings can easily be combined to make a bigger structure if desired.

**Furniture Factory**
**NEW 217-1107 24.95**
This wood frame factory is typical of many small, backwoods industries. The model features very distressed red painted clapboard siding for an aged look that fits into any era.

**Turbine House**
**NEW 217-1108 24.95**

**Quonset Hut**
**NEW 217-1110** 1 Each Clean & Weathered Styles **14.95**
Sold as surplus after WWII, these pre-fab metal buildings found new uses as everything from small businesses to private homes! Kit includes two complete huts, one that's painted white with slight weathering and one that's heavily rusted. An optional side loading bay, dormers and a roll-up steel door are included for easy customizing.

**Steel Utility Building w/Shed**
**NEW 217-1111 14.95**
Roof Overhang: 38'6" x 26'3"

Any business or industry that needs storage space will find plenty in this handsome building. Windows, along with a garage door and shed are included that can be added wherever you need them.

**Plant #2**
**NEW 217-1115 24.95**
Perfect for odd-shaped layout spaces, this triangular factory is a great addition to any industrial area. Based on several late 40s-vintage buildings in and around Evanston, Illinois, it features a 40' rail loading dock, a truck bay and an attached cinderblock garage.

**Sheet Metal Storage Building**
**NEW 217-1117 10.95**
Roof Overhang: 38'6" x 26'3"

This small building works great as part of a larger complex or by itself. It features large industrial windows and the walls are covered with standing seam steel sheets.

**5-Story Brick Warehouse**
**NEW 217-1119 27.95**
Give any industrial area a realistic look and feel with this big building. Great as a stand-alone structure or combined with others (easily kitbashed to make larger or smaller buildings as well as background flats too), it features five detailed stories, along with two truck bays and two railcar loading doors.

**Timber Loading Ramp**
**NEW 217-1125 9.95**
Overall: 18'6" x 8'3" x 4'; Flat Deck 7'9" from End, Slope about 20" Tall

Moving heavy loads from freight cars to trucks will be a snap with this model on your industrial sidings. It features a worn wood deck supported by heavy timbers, so it's perfect for any industry.

### Businesses

**The Mercantile**
**NEW 217-1113 14.95**
Perfect for tight spaces, this triangular business building features a covered stairway entrance, plus a heavy-timber loading ramp, plus two styles of loading dock doors Designed for easy construction, this kit is a great introduction to modeling with paper.

**Jefferson Ice Co.**
**NEW 217-1118 24.95**
The local ice company was a fixture in towns large and small, supplying ice for home and commercial use. This model is an exact duplicate of the Des Plaines, Illinois, prototype.

# The Ride Of Your Life!

Based on the classic wooden coasters once found at every amusement park, this kit builds into a fully operational HO Scale model! It's designed for continuous operation as an accessory on a layout – and it's sure to grab viewers' attention whenever it's running.

Young and old alike will marvel at the exciting operation as the three-car train climbs the lift hill, then speeds around the tracks on gravity power – just like its full-sized counterpart.

Modeled after the timeless and classic lines of a real wood coaster, the kit was designed by actual roller coaster engineers with an incredible level of detail. Designed for easy construction, most of the pre-colored plastic parts simply snap together, however some gluing is needed. Trains roll on precision brass wheels for consistent operation. The electric lift motor operates on the 12V accessory outlet on your transformer. Measuring just 12 x 27" when completed, the kit adds loads of detail and animated action to a small layout space.

Future items planned for the model include working brakes for two-train operation, a lighting kit and a sound module!

**The Comet Roller Coaster**
199-WC002 169.95

**Lighted Sign Adds to the Fun!**
199-WC0010 29.95
This animated neon sign is sure to bring back memories for anyone who ever loved riding the roller coasters of yesteryear! Custom-made especially for this kit, the unit is fully assembled and easily installed.

# CITY CLASSICS

Photos by John Polyak and Flinchbaugh Photography. These easy-to-build kits capture the look of various styles of architecture and are ideal for steam-or diesel-era layouts. Kits feature injection molded, plastic parts, styrene roof material, clear window glazing and easy-to-follow instructions.

## BUSINESSES

### 1930s Crafton Avenue Service Station

**195-108 17.98**
5 x 3" 25.4 x 12.7cm
Includes the station building, gas island with nonworking lamp, two different pump styles, two different sign posts and heads, soda and ice machines, oil and tire displays plus printed signs for a number of different oil companies.

### Route 22 Diner

**195-110 17.98**
6-1/2 x 4" 16.5 x 10cm
The easy-to-build plastic kit includes the "stainless steel" diner, a concrete block kitchen addition, a free-standing sign and easy to follow instructions.

### West End Market

**195-114 18.98**
This model is based on typical corner grocery stores in use from the 1940s to the present—perfect for use on steam- or diesel-era layouts. On your layout, this detailed model can be used as any kind of retail store, restaurant or auto showroom. Includes decals and full-color window signs.

### Carson Street Rail/Truck Terminal

**195-107 12.98**
8-1/2 x 6" 21.6 x 15.2cm
A small building that's perfect for a variety of small industries.

### Carnegie Street Manufacturing Building

**195-109 17.98**
10 x 5" 25.4 x 12.7cm
A common small industrial building that may be built a variety of ways using the extra parts.

### Forbes Ave. Pharmacy

**NEW 195-115 TBA**

## CITY BUILDINGS

Kits 101, 102, 105, and 106 do not include signs shown.

### Grant Street Iron Front Building

**195-101 18.98**
5-1/4 x 3-1/2" 13.4 x 8.9cm
Accurately captures the look of an ornate cast iron facade that was common during the late 1800s.

### Penn Avenue Tile Front Building

**195-102 18.98**
5-1/4 x 3-1/2" 13.4 x 8.9cm
This unique style of architecture using terra cotta blocks will stand out among dark masonry buildings and brighten up your towns at the same time!

### Baum Boulevard Art Deco Building

**195-105 18.98**
5-1/4 x 3-1/2" 13.4 x 8.9cm
This seldom modeled art deco style building will really stand out on your layout! The unique modular front makes kitbashing easier than ever.

### East Ohio Street Building

**195-106 18.98**
5-1/4 x 3-1/2" 13.4 x 8.9cm
A classic structure that may be found in just about every city and town! Features a modular front that makes it easy to combine additional kits to get larger buildings.

## WALLS & WINDOWS 4.00 ea

Items #201-207 can be used with the basic Smallman Street Warehouse (#103) to build a larger or customized structure.

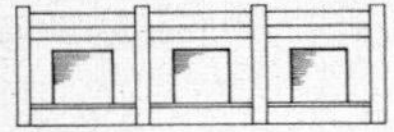

### Long Lower Walls w/Doors

**195-201** pkg(2)

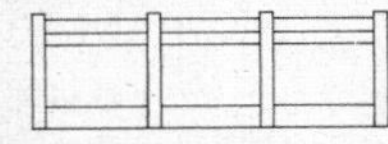

### Long Lower Walls Less Doors

**195-202** pkg(2)

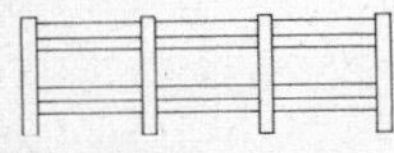

### Long Upper Walls

**195-203** pkg(2)

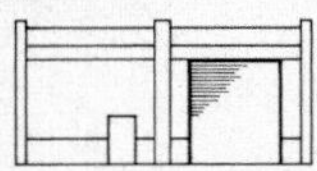

### Short Lower Walls w/Doors

**195-204** pkg(2)

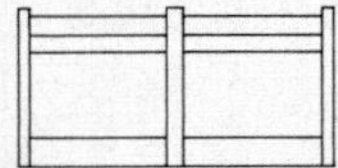

### Short Lower Walls Less Doors

**195-205** pkg(2)

### Short Upper Walls

**195-206** pkg(2)

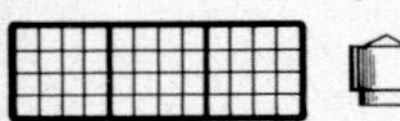

### Factory Windows & Roof Vents

**195-207**
Set includes 10 windows and two roof vents.

## HOUSES

### Railroad Street Company House

In the 1880s two-story wooden company houses began popping up all around North America. Many of them are still around today. Out-of-the-way businesses such as mining companies, lumber mills, and sometimes even factories in industrial districts, built structures like these to house the workers in their employment. Because these businesses had such a large number of workers, numerous company houses were often needed. Perfect for detailing any layout, these structures will give your HO Scale workers a lovely place to live! Each kit includes parts to build one Company House, including rear addition and outhouse (not visible in picture).

**195-111 18.98**

**195-112** 3-Pack **49.98**

### Robert's Road Mobile Home

**195-113 14.98**
This 1950s style mobile home looks great on any layout from the transition-era to the present. Whether a part of a trailer park, out in the back woods or anywhere you like, this easy-to-build kit offers character and detail for your layout. Model can be built as a permanent structure with skirting or on wheels as a highway vehicle.

## INDUSTRIAL

### Smallman Street Warehouse

**195-103 20.98**
8-1/2 x 6" 21.6 x 15.2cm

Ideal for just about any era being modeled. Add extra stories with #104 Two Story Add-On Kit.

### Two-Story Add-On Kit

**195-104 11.98**
For Smallman Street Warehouse #195-104, sold separately.

## STRUCTURE DETAILS

WINDOW DRESSINGS
BY CITY CLASSICS

The perfect finishing touch for City Classics and other buildings, these preprinted window treatments make adding realism to your buildings as easy as cutting them out and installing them. Each set features razor-sharp printing on clear PVC plastic glazing (pictures here are shown on black for clarity). Each set features typical period fonts that look like real handpainted lettering from specified eras. Some window treatments are designed to fit specific buildings, all sold separately.

### Window Treatments

#### 40s-50s Window Signs 6.98 ea

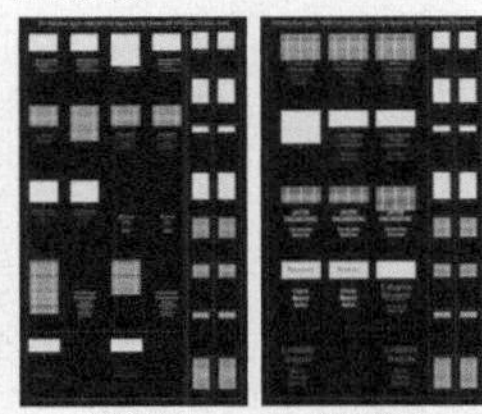

195-701 195-702

**195-701** For 101 Grant St. #195-101

**195-702** For 102 Penn Ave. #195-102

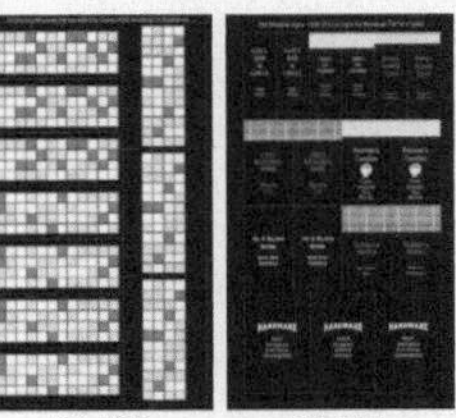

195-703 195-704

**195-703** For Smallman St. Warehouse #195-103

**195-704** For Windows 3/8 to 1" Wide

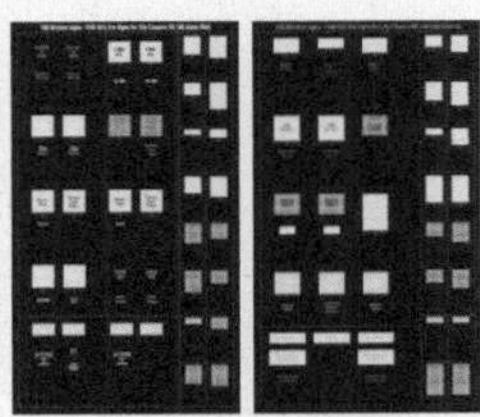

195-705 195-706

**195-705** For 105 Baum Blvd. #195-105

**195-706** For 106 East Ohio St. #195-106

#### Curtains & Blinds 6.98 ea (Unless Noted)

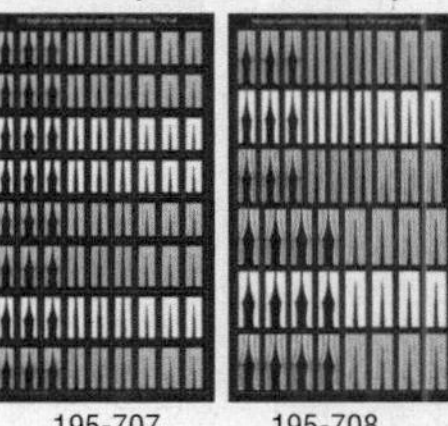

195-707 195-708

**195-707** Small Curtains 1/4" Wide x 13/16" Tall pkg(70)

**195-708** Large Curtains 5/16 or 3/8" Wide x 1-1/8" Tall pkg(50)

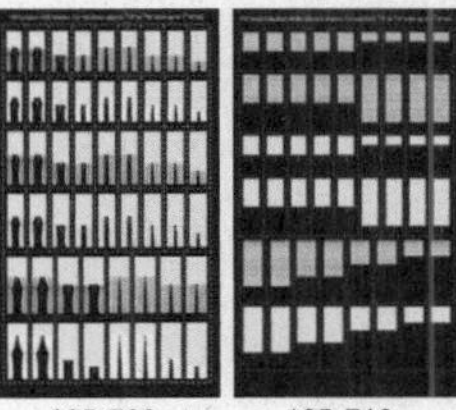

195-709 195-710

**195-709** Curtains w/Shades 1/4 to 3/8" Wide x 1-1/8" Tall pkg(50)

**195-710** Small & Medium Venetian Blinds & Pull Shades 1/4 to 3/8" Wide x 1-1/4" Tall pkg(50)

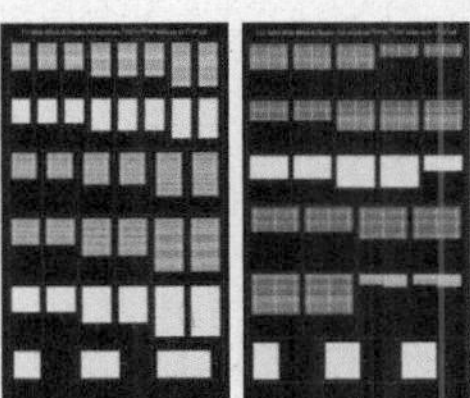

195-711 195-708

**195-711** Wide Venetian Blinds & Pull Shades 7/16 to 9/16" Wide x 1-1/4" Tall pkg(36)

**195-712** Extra-Wide Venetian Blinds & Pull Shades 3/4 to 15/16" Wide x 1-1/4" Tall pkg(25)

**195-713** Includes one of each set 195-707 to 712 **40.00**

## SIGNS 3.00 ea

### Window Signs

These paper signs are the perfect for adding that touch of realistic detail to your buildings' windows.

**195-5011** Eating & Drinking Establishments
**195-5012** Business Establishments

### Outdoor Advertising Signs

**195-5013** Beverage Advertising
**195-5014** Gasoline & Auto Repair
**195-5015** Food Advertising
Over 35 signs in various sizes covering all types of food advertising.
**195-5016** Miscellaneous Advertising
40 signs advertising a variety of subjects - clothing, candy, pharmaceuticals, home repairs, etc.

## DPM GOLD KITS

Gold Kits are plastic kits with numerous detailed accessories and Dry Transfer Decals included.

### Popa Weelie's Saloon And Dew Duck'n Cafe

**243-407 69.98**
10-1/2 x 6" 26.6 x 15.2cm

Hang out with your gang at Popa Weelie's Saloon and Dew Duck'n Cafe. These classic biker bars fit any era and look great in older parts of town. The set includes two structure kits plus over 80 detailed accessories including 10 different stock and chopper motorcycles and much more. You also get custom Dry Transfer signs for the finishing touch.

### Harlee & Sons Cycle Shop

**243-406 59.98**
11-3/4 x 6-7/8" 27.9 x 17.4cm

More than just another model, this kit builds an entire scene! The combination sales and service building doubles as a gas station and looks great along industrial or commercial streets. A chainlink fence and 40 metal detail parts (including a mean ol' junk yard dog) are included to complete the scene (people not included).

### Coal River Passenger & Freight Depots

**243-405 59.98**
15-9/16 x 6-3/8" 39.5 x 16.1cm

Two complete buildings with molded-in architectural details and more than 40 white metal castings (people and vehicles not included).

### Emery Lane

**243-404 54.98**
8 x 12-1/2" 20.3 x 31.7cm

Two different Victorian houses with over 90 metal castings (people not included).

### Entertainment District

**243-403 59.98**
9-1/4 x 5-1/2" 23.4 x 13.9cm

Two different buildings and over 80 metal castings. Includes 16 full-color posters, billboard, 2 marquees, canopy and signs, search light, street lights, Dry Transfer Decals and more (cars and people not included).

### Whitewater Brewing Co.

**243-402 69.98**
6 x 9-1/2" 15.2 x 24.1cm

With Dry Transfer Decals, smokestack, loading dock and over 50 white metal castings including beer kegs, crates, louvered wall fan and more (truck, cars and people not included).

### Drywell Inks

**243-401 59.98**
13-3/4 x 7" 34.9 x 17.7cm

With storage tank, awnings, Dry Transfer Decals and over 30 detailed metal castings (truck, cars and people not included).

## 100 SERIES KITS

#100 Series plastic kits include authentically detailed walls plus roof, clear window material and complete instructions. Architectural details are molded in place for easy assembly in minutes. Use any plastic model cement solvent and paint. Figures, vehicles, decals not included.

## STATIONS & PLATFORMS

### Freight Depot

**243-107 16.98**
5-3/4 x 4-3/4" 14.5 x 12cm

See What's Available at
**www.walthers.com**

## BUSINESSES

### Kelly's Saloon

**243-101 15.98**
2-3/4 x 4" 7 x 10.2cm

### B. Moore Catalog Showroom

**243-104 16.98**
4-3/4 x 5" 13 x 12.9cm

**Skip's Chicken and Ribs**
**243-105 15.98**
2-3/4 x 4" 7 x 10.2cm

**Carol's Corner Cafe**
**243-113 16.98**
4-1/4 x 2-3/4" 11 x 7cm

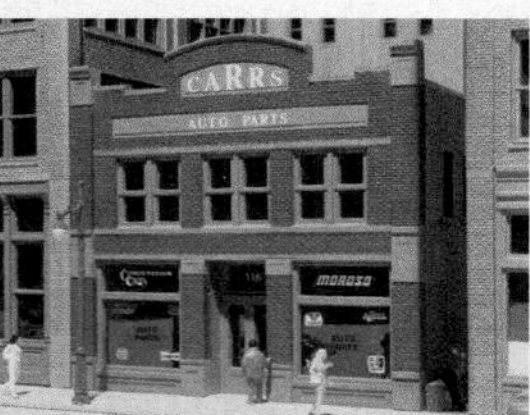


**Carr's Parts**
**243-116 16.98**
4-3/4 x 3-3/4" 12 x 9.5cm

## INDUSTRIAL

**Cutting's Scissor Co.**
**243-103 16.98**
7-1/4 x 3" 18.5 x 7.7cm

**Laube's Linen Mill**
**243-106 16.98**
6-3/4 x 3-1/4" 17.2 x 8.4cm

## HOUSES

**Townhouse #1**
**243-109 15.98**
2-1/2 x 4-1/4" 6.4 x 11cm

**Townhouse #2**
**243-110 15.98**
2-1/2 x 4-1/4" 6.4 x 11cm

**Townhouse #3**
**243-111 15.98**
2-1/2 x 4-1/4" 6.4 x 11cm

**Three Townhouse Flats (Fronts Only)**
**243-114 14.98**
2-1/2 x 4-7/8" each
6.4 x 12.2cm

## CITY BUILDINGS

**Goodfellows Hall**
**243-108 16.98**
6-1/4 x 4-3/4" 16 x 12cm

Hot New Products Announced Daily! Visit Walthers Web site at
**www.walthers.com**

**M.T. Arms Hotel**
**243-119 26.98**
7-3/4 x 2-3/4" 20 x 7cm

## BUSINESSES

**Robert's Dry Goods**
**243-102 15.98**
4-1/2 x 3-3/4" 11.5 x 9.5cm

**City Cab Co.**
**243-112 16.98**
6-1/4 x 5-3/4" 16 x 14.5cm

**The Other Corner Cafe**
**243-115 16.98**
4-3/4 x 3" 12 x 7.7cm

**JC Nickels**
**243-117 16.98**
6-3/4 x 4" 17 x 10.2cm

**1st National Bank**
**243-118 16.98**
3 x 4-1/2" 7.7 x 11.5cm

**Front Street Building**
**243-120 16.98**
5-3/4 x 4" 14.7 x 10.2cm

**Seymour Block**
**243-121 18.98**
7 x 3" 18 x 10.2cm

## INDUSTRIAL

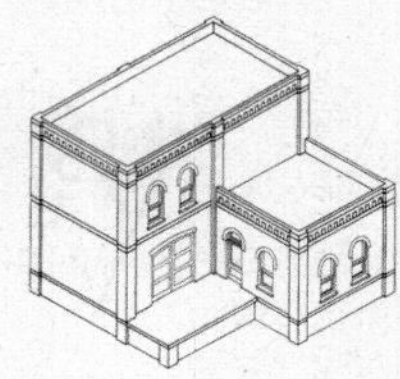

**Three-in-one Kit**
**243-351** 120 Pieces **39.98**
Complete either of two buildings up to 8-1/2 x 6" (21.9 x 15.4cm) or a 23" (59cm) long 3-D "flat."

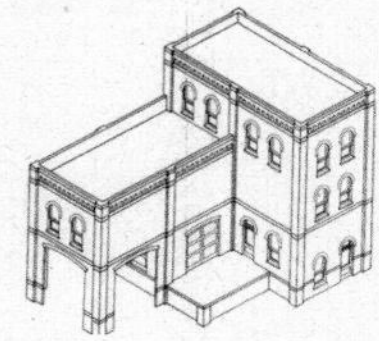

**Four-in-one Kit**
**243-352** 175 Pieces **42.98**
Complete any of three buildings up to 7-1/2 x 8-1/2" (19 x 21.9cm) or a 17" (41.9cm) long 3-D "flat."

## Fedups Freight Co.

**243-354 49.98**
19-3/4 x 8-3/4" 50 x 22.2cm

A shipping and receiving center with an action-oriented focal point.

Authentic detail and architecture are portrayed in this DPM downtown scene.

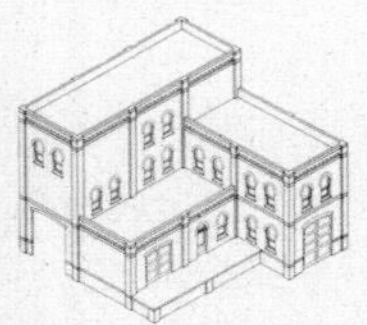

## Four-in-one Kit

**243-353** 213 Pieces **49.98**
Complete any of three buildings up to 11-1/2 x 8-1/2" (29 x 21.9cm) or a 20" (50.5cm) long 3-D "flat."

## Tera Surplus Window Warehouse

**243-355 49.98**
8-3/4 x 11-1/2" 22.2 x 29.5cm

An industrial/warehouse structure with a high profile.

## Powerhouse

**243-356 49.98**
11-1/4 x 5-3/4" 30 x 14.9cm

An industrial structure with dramatic 3-story windows.

# CATALOG

## Structure Catalog

**243-13 1.95**
A complete listing of all HO, N and O Scale kits, shown in full color.

# 200 SERIES KITS

#200 Series kits make painting optional because the walls are one color, doors and windows another. These plastic kits include detailed walls and separate window and doors. Roof, clear window material and complete instructions are also included. Use plastic model cement or solvent. Figures, vehicles, decals not included.

# CITY BUILDINGS

## Walker Building

**243-204 15.98**
3 x 4-1/4" 7.7 x 10.7cm

# BUSINESSES

## Schultz's Garage

**243-201 16.98**
3 x 4-3/4" 7.7 x 12.2cm

## Pam's Pet Shop

**243-202 15.98**
2-1/8 x 3" 5.4 x 7.7cm

# INDUSTRIAL

## C. Smith Packing House

**243-203 16.98**
4-3/4 x 5-3/8" 12.2 x 14.8cm

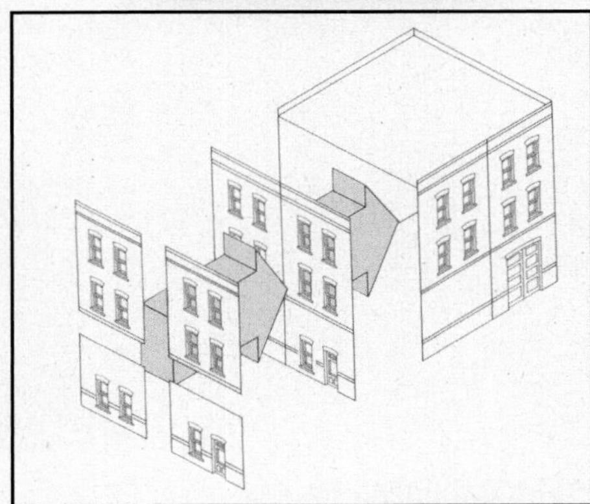

# MODULAR BUILDING SYSTEM

## UNLIMITED BUILDING OPTIONS

Interchangeable plastic wall sections make it possible to create buildings of any size, shape and height. Build a variety of styles - whatever you want or need.

- One-story building - use street or dock level wall sections and cornice.
- Two-story building - use street or dock level wall sections, top with one story wall sections and cornice.
- Three-story building - use street or dock level wall sections, top with two story wall sections and cornice.
- More stories - add additional wall sections to create as many stories as desired.

Packages include four identical wall sections with pilasters, plus doors, windows and clear window material where needed. All sections are the same width (2-3/4" 7cm) and color. Cornice packages include eight sections of Cornice with Cornice pilasters, Dock Riser Wall packages include eight Dock Riser Wall sections with Dock pilasters. Powerhouse Window packages include two two-story windows and four walls. Packages are 5.98 - 6.98 each. Designer Bulk Packs are an economical way to purchase modular wall sections for your own designs (see next page).

### Dock Level Wall Sections 6.98 ea (Unless Noted)

**243-30105** Dock Level Arched Entry

**243-30103** Dock Level Arched Window

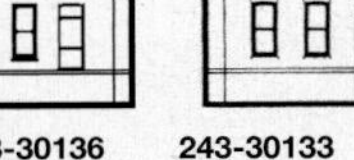

**243-30136** Dock Level Rectangular Entry

**243-30133** Dock Level Rectangular Window

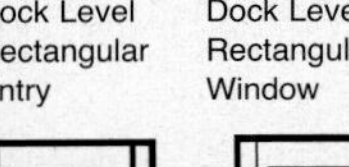

**243-30143** Dock Level Victorian Window

**243-30163** Dock Level 20th Century Window

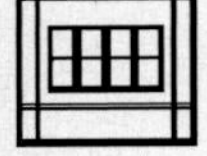

**243-30172** Dock Level Steel Sash Entry

**243-30173** Dock Level Steel Sash Window

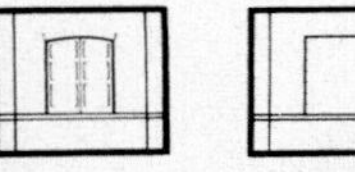

**243-30106** Dock Level Freight Door

**243-30135** Dock Level Overhead Door

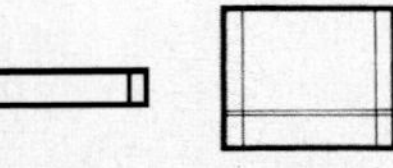

**243-30115 5.98** Dock Riser Wall (8 per package)

**243-30104 5.98** Street/Dock Level Blank Wall

### Street Level Wall Sections 6.98 ea (Unless Noted)

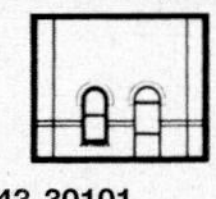

**243-30101** Street Level Arched Entry

**243-30131** Street Level Rectangular Entry

**243-30134** Street Level Rectangular Window

**243-30141** Street Level Victorian Entry

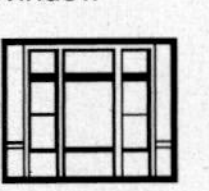

**243-30142** Street Level Victorian Window

**243-30161** Street Level 20th Century Entry

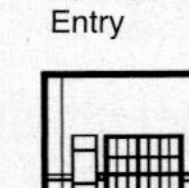

**243-30162** Street Level 20th Century Window

**243-30171** Street Level Steel Sash Entry

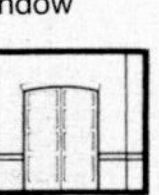

**243-30102** Street Level Freight Door

**243-30132** Street Level Overhead Door

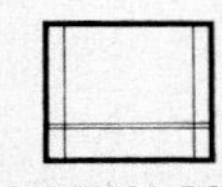

**243-30107 5.98** Street Level Open Arch

**243-30104 5.98** Street/Dock Level Blank Wall

### Two-Story Wall Sections 6.98 ea (Unless Noted)

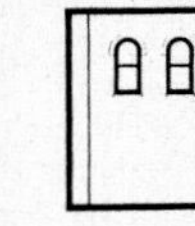

**243-30108** Two-Story Arched 4 Window

**243-30109** Two-Story Arched 2 Window (HIGH)

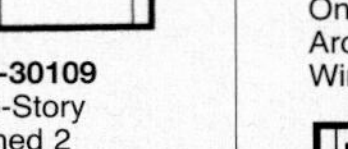

**243-30110** Two-Story Arched 2 Window (LOW)

**243-30138** Two-Story Rectangular 4 Window

**243-30139** Two-Story Rectangular 2 Window (HIGH)

**243-30137** Two-Story Rectangular 2 Window (LOW)

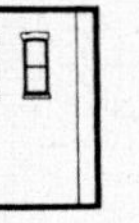

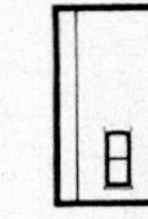

**243-30144** Two-Story Victorian Window

**243-30164** Two-Story 20th Century Window

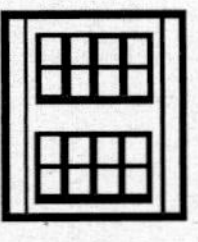

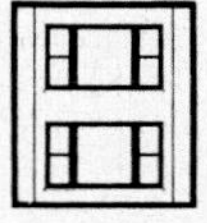

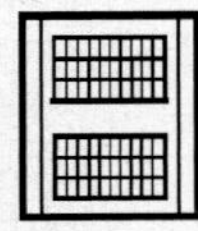

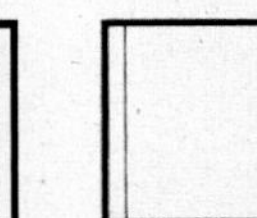

**243-30174** Two-Story Steel Sash Window

**243-30111 5.98** Two Story Blank Wall

### One-Story Wall Sections 6.98 ea (Unless Noted)

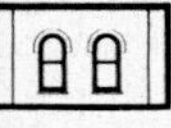

**243-30112** One-Story Arched Window

**243-30130** One-Story Rectangular Window

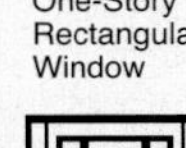

**243-30147** One-Story Victorian Window

**243-30167** One-Story 20th Century Window

**243-30175** One-Story Steel Sash Window

**243-30113 5.98** One-Story Blank Wall

### Cornices pkg(8) 5.98 ea

**243-30117** Cornice - Plain

**243-30114** Cornice - Fancy

### Powerhouse Window

**243-30118 6.98** Powerhouse Window (2 per package)

### Roof And Trim Kit

**243-30190 5.98**
For modular buildings, this plastic kit includes styrene roof material, brick detailed parapet wall trim and styrene supports for "inside" corners. Assorted roof vents and hatches suitable for all buildings are also included. They all add fine detail and realism to building tops.

### Planning Packet

**243-30191 1.98**
Pre-plan buildings with paper mock-ups. The HO scale Planning Packet contains full-sized drawings of wall sections. To use, make photo copies of wall sections, cut out the wall sections you want and arrange into walls. Tape walls on cardboard, cut out cardboard and tape together to form a three-dimensional paper mock-up. Modify mock-up until it is satisfactory, then purchase the required wall sections to construct your building.

### HO Scale Modular Learning Kit

**243-360 10.98**
Learn the techniques for building with DPM's Modular System components. Complete instructions and planning packet show you how to do it. The result is this 5-3/4 x 3" (14.8 x 7.7cm) building with a variety of uses on your HO layout. Kit includes decals, roof and clear window material. Use any plastic model cement or solvent. Figures and vehicles not included.

## DESIGNER BULK PACKS

Designer Bulk Packs each feature one of the five different architectural styles represented in the modular system. Each pack contains plans for three specific buildings and all plastic modular parts needed to finish any one of the three. Styrene roof material, clear window material, complete instructions, building plans and painting and weathering tips are included. Use plastic model cement or solvent. Note: Designer Bulk Packs provide approximately 40% in savings over buying modular parts in separate packages. Figures, vehicles, decals not included.

### Arched Window Industrial Building

**243-361 49.98**
Arched Window Industrial Buildings embody classic architectural features. Designed for factory, warehouse or institutional usage, they endure in every skyline.

### Rectangular Window Industrial Building

**243-362 49.98**
Rectangular Window Industrial Buildings premiered in the late 1800s. Popular as factories, warehouses and institutional buildings, they maintain their profiles in cities and towns today.

### Victorian Style Storefront Building

**243-363 49.98**
Victorian Style Storefront Buildings characterize the ornate style of the 19th Century. Retail stores commonly occupy the street level while the upper floors function as offices, showrooms, and department stores.

### Twentieth Century Storefront Building

**243-364 49.98**
Twentieth Century Storefront Buildings enhance the marketplace with dignified style. The upper floors accommodate offices, showrooms, and financial institutions, while large display windows at street level attract customers to the retail activity within.

### Steel Sash Industrial Building

**243-365 49.98**
Steel Sash Industrial Buildings gained popularity early in the 20th Century. Larger windows provide energy conserving light to the workplace while multiple panes of glass supported by steel framework create an open feeling.

Add character to urban areas along your railroad with this series of structure kits. The models feature detailed walls made of cast Hydrocal, plastic windows and doors, along with full-color signs and awnings. Each can be assembled with basic hobby tools, and easy to understand step-by-step instructions walk you through construction, from gluing the kit together to final painting and weathering.

## NEW PRODUCTS

### Skid Row Part Two

**NEW** **244-1032** **69.95**
7 x 8"

This neat looking two-building set features all-new Hydrocal® castings, plastic doors, windows and fire escapes as well as full-color signs and some really interesting brick textures. There's even a wall with a "ghost" building indicating where an adjacent structure was torn down years ago. Also includes a bag of trashcans and junk.

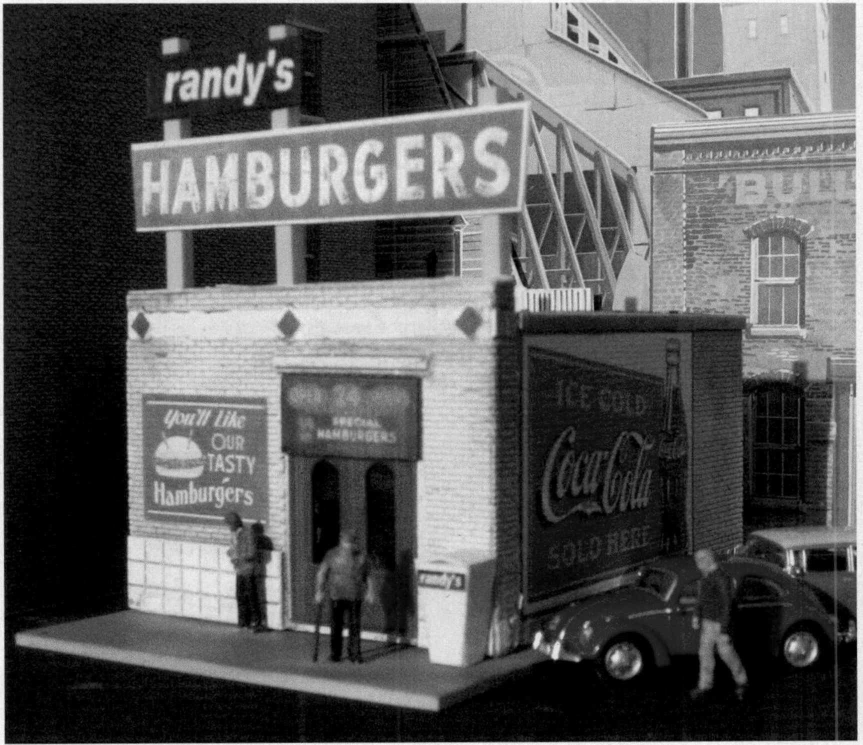


### Randy's Burgers

**NEW** **244-1038** **34.95**
3 x 4"

Everyone likes a good burger and this little shack would look good crammed into a tiny downtown lot or alongside some rural road. Classic Americana at its best, kit includes detailed Hydrocal castings, laser-cut wood door and full-color signs.

### Skid Row Part Three

**NEW** **244-1033** **49.95**
3-1/2 x 6"

The slightly smaller companion to Skid Row Part Two, this building is absolutely packed with charm. There's a funky covered fire escape stairwell complete with pre-rusted corrugated material, full-color signs, a recessed entranceway and a few trash cans to round out the scene. The very narrow profile of this structure just begs to have it tucked tightly into a busy urban scene.

## Kitty Korner

**NEW** 244-1035 34.95
3 x 5"

What downtown area would be complete without a gentlemen's club? Kit includes full-color signs and complete painting and aging instructions. Guaranteed to be an attention getter!

## Sidewalks

### Old Brick

**NEW** 244-1039 24.95
5-1/2 x 1-9/16 x 1/8"

These rustic, old brick sidewalks cast in Hydrocal are just packed with detail. The master patterns were hand built one HO scale brick at a time for maximum realism. Kit includes about three feet of sidewalks, corners along with complete painting, fitting and finishing instructions. A neat detail that is usually only seen on the very best of layouts.

### Weathered

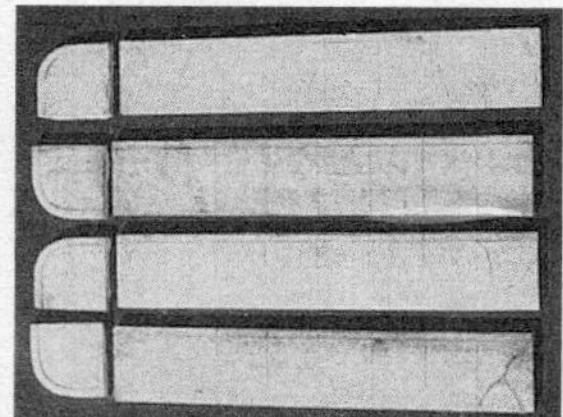

**NEW** 244-1036 24.95
6 x 1-1/8 x 1/8"

Includes enough Hydrocal sidewalks to cover about four feet on your layout. Great detail carved right in. Comes with painting, fitting and finishing instructions.

## Burgess Manufacturing

**NEW** 244-1037 89.95
12 x 7"

The fine modeler, Tony Burgess, helped master these patterns and the end result is spectacular. This wonderfully cluttered lineside industry would look great along any weed-covered siding. Kit includes beautifully detailed Hydrocal castings, plastic doors and windows, full-color original signs, a whole bag of detail castings to "junk" up your scene and complete finishing instructions. Includes both structures that can be placed separately.

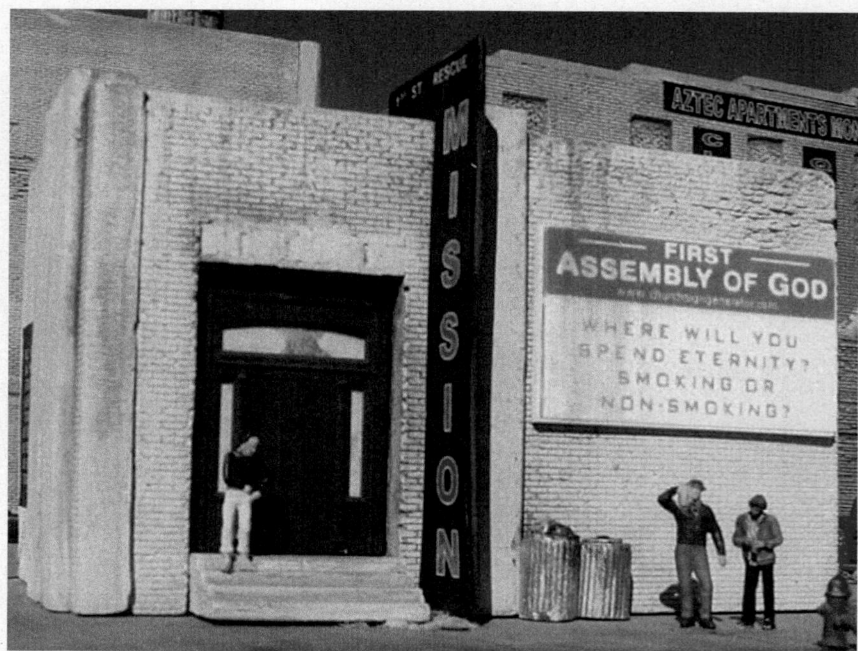


## Rescue Mission

**NEW** 244-1034 34.95
3 x 5"

Even those down on their luck need a place to get off of their feet and enjoy a bite to eat. Typical of rescue missions, the sign says, "Where will you be spending eternity, smoking or nonsmoking?" Kit features Hydrocal castings, plastic doors and windows.

## DOWNTOWN DECO

Fallberg Station 244-1004

Coin Laundry 244-1028

Bingo's Pool Hall 244-1029

Grimm's Funeral Home 244-1030

Blair Ave. Part One 244-1005

Blair Ave. Part Two 244-1031

### Fallberg Station

**244-1004 39.95**
3 x 4" 7.5 x 10cm

Perched high in a mountain pass... dozing out its last days in a sleepy tank town... brand-new and serving an up-and-coming farm community.... No matter how you envision it, this tiny station fits easily into any layout. It's based on a design by John Olson and includes a stone loading dock to handle freight shipments. The kit consists of cast Hyrdocal® plaster walls and includes plastic doors and windows. Includes pre-aged corrugated roofing material from Paper Creek.

### Coin Laundry

**244-1028 34.95**
6 x 6" 10 x 10cm

Like many city buildings, this structure has had many owners and many uses over the years. Its classic Art Deco styling still shines through, making it standout from other businesses along the block. The kit features a smooth brick front with rough brick sides and back wall. Colorful signs are included.

### Bingo's Pool Hall

**244-1029 34.95**

Next to the depot or the barbershop, the local pool hall was often the best hang-out for the men in towns large and small. This little structure is a real eye-catcher and the side walls feature a neat cracked stucco over brick finish, captured in detailed Hydrocal castings. The elaborate front wall is a one-piece resin casting. Rounding out the model are full-color signs, a trash can and junk.

### Grimm's Funeral Home

**244-1030 109.95**
5 x 7"

Tall spires, multiple gables, a "widow's peak" railing and spooky gargoyle skulls cast into the upper window boxes combine to form an eerie structure that will add a unique touch to any layout. A few bats perched on high complete the scary scene. Build it as a creepy funeral home, haunted house or even a well-kept mansion. This finely detailed kit features Hydrocal plaster walls, plastic doors and windows and laser cut paper shingles for the roof.

### Blair Avenue - Part 1

**244-1005 49.95**
4 x 6" 10 x 15cm

Turn the "wrong-side-of-the-tracks" into everyone's favorite part of town with this set of neat commercial structures. Based on actual buildings, the kit includes both the Photo Studio and Chinese Restaurant, with detailed castings that capture the look of the prototype's old stone and brick construction.

### Blair Ave. Part Two

**244-1031** Johnny Stechino's & Big Ed's **59.95**
8-1/2 x 5-1/2"

Here's a cool-looking structure with something for everyone. The exterior of this two-building set features old brick, cracked stucco, old clapboard and a corrugated aluminum shed. The peaked roof and tall stone chimney add even more character. Customers have their choice of home-style Italian cuisine at Johnny Stechino's or crispy barbecue at Big Ed's. Great graphics for both eateries are included. Kit has Hydrocal plaster walls, plastic doors and windows and full-color paper signs and awnings.

DOWNTOWN DECO

Part 4 244-1025

Part 5 244-1027

# ADDAM'S AVENUE

Typical of the older buildings that are now on the "wrong side of the tracks" in larger cities, this series includes five different kits that can be used alone or grouped together.

## Part 1

**244-1000 49.95**
5 x 9" 5.2 x 22.5cm

This seedy looking block of stores includes a Pawn Shop, Liquor Store, Tattoo Parlor and Bar.

## Part 2

**244-1002 49.95**
10 x 5" 25 x 5.2cm

This rundown looking block features a Massage Parlor, Bail Bondsman, Nightclub and Mexican Grocery. Perfect for any Railroad Avenue scene!

## Part 3

**244-1003 49.95**
5 x 5" 5.2 x 5.2cm

This typical skid row/downtown hotel includes the "Palace Hotel & Card Room", "Red's Bar" and the "Downtown Apartments."

## Part 4

**244-1025 59.95**
14 x 6" 35 x 15cm

In addition to the highly detailed Hydrocal castings, this kit also feaures Mt. Albert Scale Lumber for the fence, Paper Creek aged corrugated roofing for the shed, Tichy windows, a Rix Products storefront, a laser-cut "Auction" stencil, full-color signs (including the large pin-up art for the "Bottoms Up Bar"), a laser-cut roof, new detail castings (boxes, crates, junk, etc.), microshredded newspaper for "street debris," a full-color billboard, tarpaper roofing, awnings and more.

## Part 5

**244-1027 59.95**
6-1/2 x 12" 16.2 x 30cm

This neat set of three buildings has a bit of everything — right down to a place to buy beer and lottery tickets! The walls feature loads of detail and simulate cracked stucco as well as old and new brick. Lots of little things, like fire escapes and security bars for windows, along with full-color signs and complete instructions round out this block that's seen its better days.

Part 1 244-1000

Part 2 244-1002

Part 3 244-1003

Model a variety of authentic railroad structures with these craft train kits, which are complete with scale lumber, plastic and/or metal castings, signs and instructions.

## YARD EQUIPMENT & FACILITIES

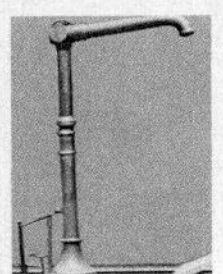

**Water Crane**
**254-17 9.95**
7/8 x 1-5/8"
2.3 x 4.2cm

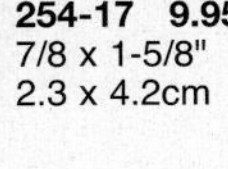

**Water Column**
**254-27 3.95**

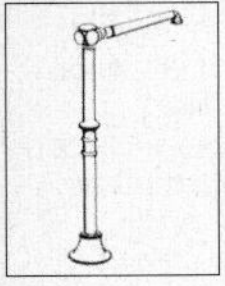

**Cleanout Rack**
**254-39 7.50**
3/4 x 1/16"
2 x .2cm

**Coal Loader**
**254-41 19.95**
5-1/8 x 1-5/8" 9.5 x 4.2cm

**Jib Crane**
**254-68 11.95**
2-3/4 x 3/4"
7 x 2cm

**Fleming Mail Catcher**
**254-70 6.50**
1/4 x 7/8"
.7 x 2.3cm

**Overhead Crane**
**254-72 11.95**
2-3/4 x 3"
7 x 7.7cm

## TANKS & TOWERS

**Q&TL Water Tank**
**254-28 18.95**
Unique Quincy & Torch Lake prototype.

## BUSINESSES

**The Newspaper Office**
**254-56 21.95**
3-5/8 x 3-1/2" 9.2 x 9cm

Easy to assemble. Includes laser-cut walls, white metal detail parts, plastic windows and doors.

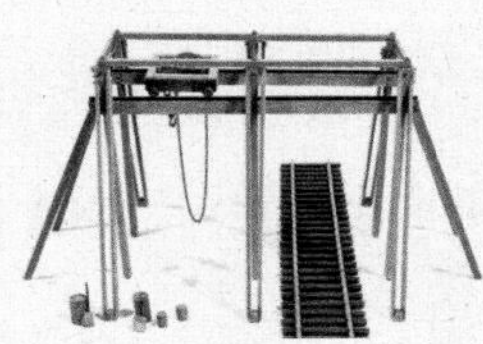

**Traveling Crane**
**254-73 16.95**
4-1/2 x 3-5/8" 11.5 x 9.2cm

**D&RG Ore Loading Ramp**
**254-125 19.95**
Based on a Rio Grande prototype located on Marshall Pass, this HO Scale kit features precut wood parts.

## INDUSTRIAL

**Gravity Stamp**
**254-35 14.95**
1-5/8 x 1"
4.2 x 2.5cm

**Ashpit**
**254-40**
**26.95**
3-3/4 x 2-5/8"
9.5 x 6.7cm

See What's Available at
**www.walthers.com**

## RURAL BUILDINGS

**Handcar Shed Kits 29.95 ea**
Both sheds include handcar kits. 2 x 3" 5 x 7.7cm.

**254-29** HOn3

**254-32** HO

**Goose/Gander Outhouses**
**254-120 10.95**
Two laser-cut outhouses and Trout Lake station signs.

**Water Tanks 49.95 ea**
4-1/4 x 4-1/2" 11 x 11.5cm

**254-59** DRGW, HOn3

**254-67** Standard, HO

**Extra Spout Kit**
**254-66 4.95**
1-1/2 x 5/8" 4 x 1.7cm

For use with water tank kits #59 or 67 listed above.

**RGS Trout Lake Water Tank**
**254-119**
**49.95**
3-3/4" 9.5cm diameter

Grand Central Gems inc.

## TRESTLE PARTS

Creating realistic wooden trestles is easy with this assortment of parts made from real wood. Each piece comes fully assembled and stained in a realistic weathered creosote color, ready to install in new or existing scenery.

**Bents pkg(5)**

**295-TB1**
Small **10.00**

**295-TB2**
Medium **15.00**

**295-TB3**
Large **15.00**

**295-TB4**
Extra-Large
**20.00**

**12" Bridge Deck**

**295-TB5** With Blackheads **20.00**
Use for short trestles or as the end pieces of longer structures.

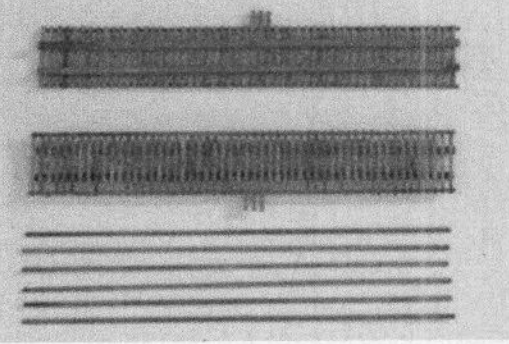

**295-TB6** With Stringers pkg(2)
**25.00**
Use as intermediate sections on long trestles. Cut in small sections to make curved truss deck.

## DEPOTS BY JOHN

DETAILED REPLICAS IN SCALE

Please visit Walthers web site at www.walthers.com for a complete listing of all available items from Depots By John.

## STATIONS & PLATFORMS

**Country Depot**
**87-110 43.95**
2-1/2 x 5-1/2" 6.3 x 13.8cm

**D-3 Depot**
**87-131 15.95**

**Passenger Platform Shelter**
**87-120** 12" **18.95**

## YARD EQUIPMENT & FACILITIES

**Fairbanks-Morse Scalehouse**
**87-114 9.95**

**Garage/Trackside MOW Building**
**87-122 9.95**

**Interurban Electrical Substation**
**87-136 36.95**

## RURAL BUILDINGS

**2-Hole Outhouse**
**87-132 3.99**

## HOUSES

### Windy City Series Houses

**Bungalow #1**
**87-301 44.95**
3 x 5-1/4" 7.5 x 13.1cm

**Bungalow #2**
**87-302 54.95**
3 x 7" 7.5 x 17.5cm

**Victorian Cottage**
**87-303 44.95**
3 x 6-1/2" 7.5 x 16.3cm

**2-Flat**
**87-304 64.95**
3 x 7-3/4 x 4-1/2"
7.5 x 19.4 x 11.3cm

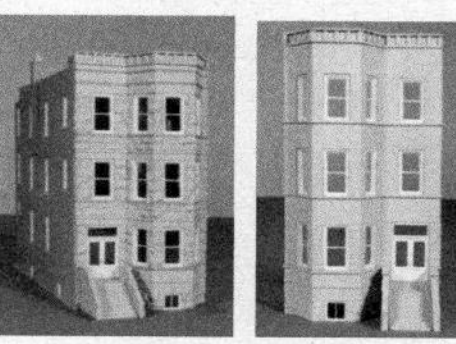

87-305 87-306

**3-Flats 74.95 ea**
3 x 9-1/4 x 5-3/4"
7.5 x 23.1 x 14.4cm
**87-305** Rough Stone
**87-306** Smooth Stone

## CITY BUILDINGS

### Rear Facades

87-307 87-308

**87-307** 2-Flat **21.95**
**87-308** 3-Flat **24.95**

## PHONE BOOTHS
**pkg(2) 5.95**

87-117 87-118 87-119 87-116

**87-116** NKP
**87-117** IC
**87-118** MILW
**87-119** ATSF

Create great detail for your layout in any scale with these easy to use software titles. Choose from a large variety of ready to print designs to make your layout unique. Never have your model buildings all look the same, or look like someone else's. System requirements: PC running Windows NT/ME/2000/XP/XP-Pro/Vista.

## BUILDING SOFTWARE

### Brickyard

**266-A33 15.00**
This program allows you to print full sheets of bricks and stones in any scale for modeling walls, foundations, bridge abutments and more. Program includes 20 different brick and stone patterns.

### Stained Glass

**266-A41 15.00**
Add color and variety to all types of structures with this unique software program that allows you to scale, arrange and print over 45 different stained glass images. Shapes include rectangle, round and half-round.

### Model Builder

Building constructed using printouts from Model Builder software

**266-A51 45.00**
Create realistic structure and backdrops in any scale. Twenty-five-plus different texture categories, over 400 images in all. Image categories include: brick, siding, cement, wood, slate and asphalt roofing, rusty metal, trim, storefronts, factory and residential windows and doors, utilities and more. Images can be stretched, tiled, arranged and overlapped to create unique structures. Also included: scaleable building plans and illustrated manual with project ideas.

### Window Designer

**266-A12 40.00**
End the vacant building look. Print window treatments, text, silhouettes and artwork for every building window on your layout. Window templates provided for many popular manufacturer's N Scale and larger buildings, or you can lay out your own custom arrangements. Simply print out your finished designs on transparency or vellum (one sheet of each included to get you started) and install.

### Toolkit "Lite"

**NEW 266-A101 95.00**
This software collection includes our most popular programs for making and adding detail to structures: The Advertiser, Model Builder and Window Designer. Model Builder and Window Designer are described above. See the Signals section of this book for a description of The Advertiser.

### Complete Toolkit

**NEW 266-A102 155.00**
The complete collection of Evan Designs software on one CD. This software collection includes: Model Builder, The Advertiser, Highway and Railway Sign Creator, Window Designer, Brickyard and Stained Glass. Also included are useful scratch building materials and a printer variety pack of 10 sheets of specialty papers, two sheets of decal paper, two sheets of Architectural Chipboard, two sheets of Gatorfoam, a Fire Pack LED light kit and a Welding Pack LED kit.

Take your layout, module or diorama to a new level of realism with these laser-cut structure kits. Every detail of the prototype is carefully captured, and all parts are laser-cut to ensure accuracy and ease of assembly. Interlocking walls and bases keep parts aligned. Doors and windows are separate pieces and can be positioned open or closed. All kits include complete instructions; larger structures include scaled full elevation drawings.

## NEW PRODUCTS

### Stations & Platforms

#### Junction City Depot

**NEW 292-13371 129.99**
10-1/8 x 5-15/16 x 3-1/2"

Based on the SOO/MILW joint depot built in 1896 in Junction City, Wisconsin, this kit features a detailed interior and exterior with positionable windows, operable doors, removable roof and more.

#### Milk Station

**NEW 292-12571 24.99**
3-5/16 x 1-1/4 x 2-3/16"

This small station will look great along a siding in a rural area.

### Yard Equipment & Facilities

#### PRR J Tower

**NEW 292-1340 109.99**
4-1/4 x 3-7/16 x 5-7/8"

The prototype was built in 1885 for the Cumberland Valley and Northern Central Railway busy crossing at the PRR Enola yard. Both railroads later became part of the PRR. Kit includes detailed stair, interior trim, positionable windows, operable doors, removable roof and more.

#### Speeder Shed

**NEW 292-1249 17.99**
2 x 2-7/16 x 1-7/16"

Here's a place to store those gasoline inspection cars, tools and more along your railroad.

#### Yard Office

**NEW 292-1255 12.99**
3-5/16 x 2-5/8 x 1-7/8"

No yard would be complete without an office to house all the yardmaster and all the paperwork.

### Rural Buildings

#### Outhouse

**NEW 292-1145** pgk(2) **9.99**
13/16 x 13/16 x 1-1/8"

Before there was indoor plumbing there were outhouses and these detailed models are typical of those found throughout the countryside.

#### Windmill

**NEW 292-1229 39.99**
1-15/16 x 2-3/4 x 8-5/8"

A familiar sight on farms across the country, this model comes complete with a positionable mechanism.

### Houses

#### Farm House

**NEW 292-1346 69.99**
5-9/32 x 5-9/16 x 4-7/16"

Featuring a covered front porch for relaxing on Sunday afternoons, this home is typical of those found on farms across the country.

#### Apollo Residence

**NEW 292-14301 89.99**
5-5/8 x 5-1/4 x 4-3/8"

Here's a charming home that will fit right into an established neighborhood. Kits features laser-etched beadboard siding and includes operable windows and doors.

#### Club House

**NEW 292-12611 9.99**
1-3/16 x 15/16 x 7/8"

Any group of kids would love to call this place their own. No adults allowed!

#### Tree House

**NEW 292-12612** w/Ladder **9.99**
15/16 x 1 x 3"

A favorite of children everywhere, this treetop refuge has a ladder that can be pulled up to keep out intruders.

#### Dog House

**NEW 292-1159** pkg(2) **5.99**
15/32 x 25/32 x 1/2"

The family pet will have a nice place to live in this tiny home.

#### 1-Car Garage

**NEW 292-1247 19.99**
2-5/8 x 3-1/2 x 2-1/16"

#### 2-Car Garage

**NEW 292-1248 29.99**
4-3/8 x 3-3/8 x 3"

### Businesses

#### Lou's Drive-In

**NEW 292-1311 59.99**
4 x 12 x 2-5/8"

Stop by this roadside stand on a hot summer day and cool off with a frosty mug of root beer. This detailed replica will be at home on any post 50s layout.

### Recreational

#### Swimming Platform

**NEW 292-1266 14.99**
1-5/16 x 1-3/4 x 1/2"

Platforms like these are often seen just off shore from cottages or resorts on inland lakes. They give swimmers a destination and a place to rest.

#### Boathouse

**NEW 292-1464 139.99**
6-15/16 x 7-11/16 x 5-1/4"

Relive those lazy summer days cruising on the lake or sipping a cool beverage on the upstairs porch while watching water skiers and fishermen with this bungalow-style boathouse.

#### 38' Boat

**NEW 292-1465 29.99**
1-3/8 x 5-1/4 x 1-1/16"

This classic cabin cruiser will look great docked at your Boathouse #292-1464 (sold separately).

## STATIONS & PLATFORMS

#### Peru, Iowa, Depot

**292-1315** Chicago Great Western Prototype **49.99**
5 x 4-1/8 x 2-15/16"

Local folks in any small town would be mighty proud to have this fine depot. The kit includes 132 laser-cut pieces, but the intricate wall trim is actually done as one piece with corners, casing, base and frieze boards. The kit also comes with laser-cut parts to build four benches, sign backer with printed signs, laser-cut window glazing, sheet material to model rolled roofing, and a laser-etched chimney with cap. The roof is removable so you can add your own interior details if desired.

#### Elmhurst Depot

**292-1332 99.99**
7-7/16 x 4-3/4 x 3"

Based on a Chicago Great Western prototype located along the mainline in Elmhurst, Illinois, this finely detailed structure is typical of other wood depots found throughout the Midwest.

#### Sturtevant, Wisconsin, Depot

**292-1514** Milwaukee Road Prototype **134.99**
11-15/16 x 11-15/16 x 4-3/4"

One of the most handsome of all Milwaukee Road depots, this elaborate structure was built at the intersection of two routes at Sturtevant, Wisconsin, where it still stands today. The kit features over 400 laser-cut parts, plus 165-laser cut tabbed shingles and roof cap to finish the removable roof. Separate windows, doors, corbels, trim, columns, signs and a host of other details are all included, along with complete illustrated instructions, roof alignment grid and jigs to simplify assembly.

GCLaser

### PRR Passenger Shelter

**292-1250** Circa 1911 **12.99**
1-5/8 x 2-1/8 x 2-1/8"

This simple shelter protected passengers from the rain, wind and elements while they waited for the train to arrive. These small structures were placed at whistle or flag stops on lightly used routes where there weren't enough passengers to build a full-size depot.

### Stock Loading Ramp

**292-1225 19.99**
3-9/16 x 7/8 x 2-1/16"

It's easy to herd those cattle and other livestock into waiting stock cars with this wooden ramp.

### Concrete Ramp

**292-1142 9.99**
3-3/4 x 1-1/4 x 9/16"

### Icing Platform

**292-13061 69.99**
21-7/8 x 2-9/16 x 2-5/8"

In the days of ice-cooled reefers, large docks like these were often seen at the edges of yards and along the mainline. Kit includes 17 laser-cut bent assemblies with sway braces, a laser-etched deck with wheel tracks for ice carts, plus three ladders, railings, stairs, braces and spacers.

## RURAL BUILDINGS

### Tool Shed

**292-1201 13.99**
2-3/8 x 1-15/16 x 1-5/8"

Great for use down on the farm or trackside as a railroad shanty. Kit consists of 38 laser-cut pieces and includes a small outside tool/coal box.

### Country Market

**292-1209 23.99**
3-1/16 x 3-3/8 x 1-11/16"

A great detail for modern layouts, you'll find everything from fresh fruit to vegetables sold in roadside stands like this. The kit includes 78 laser-cut parts including display table and four produce containers, printed signs and more.

### Silo

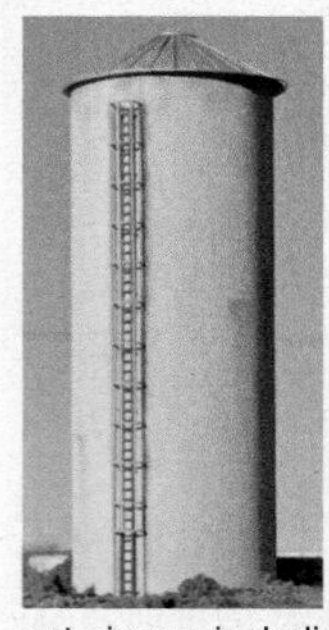

**292-1312 33.99**
3-9/16 x 3-1/16 x 8-1/8"
Keep your livestock fed year 'round with this neat structure on your scale farm. The kit consists of 23 laser-cut pieces, including the dryer house which is laser-etched to simulate brick construction. A ladder with enclosure, assembly jig and one-piece conical roof are all included.

For Daily Product Updates Point Your Browser to
**www.walthers.com**

### County Co-op

The perfect trackside business for any small town, this big elevator/feed mill is typical of designs found all over the United States. With over 400 laser-cut parts and rolled roofing, the kit also comes with chimney, vents, an etched floor with grate detail, platforms, loading ramps, door and window awnings, chimney and more. The model can be built as one large or two separate structures as desired.

**292-1420 99.99**
10-1/2 x 6-3/16 x 9-1/2"

**292-14202** Mirror Image w/o Office **69.99**

**292-14203** Co-op w/o Office **69.99**
5-3/4 x 8-1/2 x 9-7/16"

### Auction House

**292-15211 289.99**
13-25/32 x 15-21/32 x 3-3/8"

Reserve a spot at the front of your layout for this amazing model so visitors can see and appreciate every single detail! While it includes over 1100 parts, a 40-page, illustrated booklet of step-by-step instructions is included so you can build the model easily and at your own pace. There's a complete set of fencing along with positionable ramp chutes, and an assembly fixture makes construction of the bleacher seating easy. The model comes with a pre-textured base, and pre-cut bases are provided for all wall and fence locations. (Be sure to check out the Cattle Truck Body kit (292-12232, listed in the Parts Section for another great accessory for this structure!)

### Auction House Add-On

13-25/32 x 5-1/2 x 3-3/8"

**292-15212** Auction House Add-On **99.99**
Adds an additional 40 lineal feet.

### Storage Shed

**292-11391** w/Board & Batten Vertical Siding **12.99**
1-7/8 x 2-1/8 x 1-7/16"

This basic structure can serve a variety of purposes on the farm, in a back yard or trackside.

### Barn Under Construction

**292-14282 199.99**
7-7/8 x 5-1/8 x 5-3/8"

Bring back the days of old-fashioned barn raisings when everyone in the community pitched in to help new settlers get started. The tradition of these one or two day events continues on in some parts of the U.S. and rural Canada.

### Completed Barn

**292-14283 199.99**
7-7/8 x 5-1/8 x 5-3/8"

This large barn is typical of those found on farms throughout the country. It's the finished version of #292-14282 (sold separately).

### Small Cabin

**292-11601 19.99**
1-7/8 x 2-1/8 x 1-7/16"

Tuck this cozy cabin deep in a wooded area as a hideaway for hunters or hikers. Includes printed shingle siding. Modeler may choose location and quantity of windows.

## BUSINESSES

### M&J Service Station

**292-1305 79.99**
9-13/16 x 7-1/16 x 2-9/16"

You'll find lots of ways to use this building along your layout. With appropriate vehicles and figures (sold separately) it will make a great used car dealership, body shop, trucking terminal garage and much more. Walls and chimney are laser-etched to simulate cinder block construction. Both rolled roofing and gravel are included to model the pitched and flat roofs. Includes 57 laser-cut parts.

## BRIDGES

### Covered Bridge

**292-1318 72.99**
3-15/16 x 16-3/16 x 2-5/8"

A reminder of long-ago days, this handsome model adds a neat detail to rural scenes. Perfect for period layouts or as a restored structure in a modern setting, the kit is fully detailed inside and out. Laser-etched decking, railings, walls and roof sections, along with joists with phosphor-bronze guy wires are all included. Includes over 100 laser-cut parts in all.

## BILLBOARD SUPPORTS

Each: 4-9/16 x 15/16 x 2-3/4"

A neat detail by itself, or add your own signs for the finishing touch. Modern billboard kit consists of 13 laser-cut pieces and includes five sway braces and trussed supports, plus a catwalk. An optional sheathing panel is also included.

**292-11031** Single **12.99**

**292-11032** 3-Pack **37.99**

# GRANDT LINE

Easy-to-build kits feature finely detailed parts made of injection-molded styrene.

## YARD EQUIPMENT & FACILITIES

### Contemporary Relay Houses

**300-5910** pkg(2) **6.00**
These pre-fabricated steel-designed buildings were used from the early 1940s to present times. Set contains two styles: 8 x 6' and 6 x 6".

### Standard Section Tool House

**300-5905 6.75**
Crews used these handy buildings to store all kinds of tools and supplies, as well as track inspection cars. This kit represents a pre-fabricated steel design, used system-wide on the Rio Grande starting around 1940. Still in use today, its styling is typical of similar buildings used on many roads. The kit features detailed plastic parts and the large doors can be built in the open or closed position.

## HOUSES

### Reese Street Rowhouses

**300-5903** pkg(3) **26.95**
Total Area: 10 x 5"
26.2 x 12.5cm

Based on actual row houses built in Silverton, Colorado. These small homes are perfect for any area. Includes parts for three complete buildings. Windows and doors are separate parts. Four different eave trims are included. Extra details include three outhouses, interior floors and three lengths of boardwalk.

### No Problem Joe's

**300-5906 26.95**
This structure is based on the still-standing home of "No Problem Joe," a local fix-it man in Aspen, Colorado. Ski-lift operators often called Joe to correct problems that threatened operation. Joe was always able to rectify the crisis, swearing there was "no problem." Model is constructed of styrene components and can be built on a 7 x 3.6" footprint. Kit contains a main house with front porch, coal shed and outhouse.

## INDUSTRIAL

### Wentamuck Mine

**300-5902 25.95**
Total Area: 4-1/2 x 9"
11.2 x 22.5cm

Typical of small "new venture" mines that appeared in Colorado and Nevada around 1910.

### The Silverton Ore Chute

**300-5904 22.00**
2 x 3" 5 x 7.6cm

Located on the south side of the tracks at Silverton, Colorado, this ore chute makes an interesting addition to any HO Scale line. Built sometime in the late 1930s or early 1940s, the prototype was served by trucks and used to load box cars with high-grade ore, which required more protection in transit. The complete kit is molded in styrene with a high level of detail. Designed for easy construction, the ore chutes and cribing can be configured to fit your available space. The model includes a complete set of optional stairs and railings which can be arranged as needed to add character to the finished model, or left off to match the appearance of the actual structure.

Latest New Product News Daily! Visit Walthers Web site at
**www.walthers.com**

### East Terrible Mill & Mining Co.

**300-5901 29.95**
7-1/2 x 7-1/8" 19 x 18cm

This ten-stamp mill complex is typical of many built in the 1890s. Features separate doors and windows.

Warehouse #300-5908 Now Sold Separately

### Midwest Petroleum Distributors

**300-5907 32.00**
Typical throughout the United States from the 1920s to the present. Features pumphouse, three storage tanks, loading rack, fire hose box and gas pumps. Finely detailed. 7 x 9", or configure to your needs.

### Corrugated Iron Warehouse Kit

**300-5908 26.95**
4-3/4 x 6-1/4" 11.9 x 15.7cm

Based on a prototype facility located in Placerville, California, the design of this structure is common to industrial sites from the 1920s to today. Building features two sliding warehouse doors and an office that opens out onto the loading platforms. The risers can be left off so structure can sit directly on the ground. Windows and doors are molded separately.

# GRANDT LINE

## BUSINESSES

### Second Class Saloon
**300-5900 22.00**
4-3/4 x 3-1/8" 12 x 8cm

Includes Thin Film® decals, five-color signs printed on cardstock, barrels and more.

### The Gomez Store
**300-5909 35.00**
This general store is typical of many structures found along the highways throughout the United States from the 1920s to present times. The prototype was located in Pagosa Junction, Colorado. Extra details include gas pump, signage and barrels.

### Valley Feed & Seed
**300-5911 27.50**
Typical of many structures found in agricultural communities in the U.S. from the 1920s to the present.

## INDUSTRIAL

### Warehouse Kits
### 19.95 ea
Models measure
4-3/8 x 8-1/4" 10.9 x 20.6cm.

**Dual-Bay**
**326-6320** Sand
**326-6321** Gray

**Single-Bay**
**326-6322** Sand
**326-6323** Gray

### Office Buildings
### 19.95 ea
Buildings measure
8-1/4 x 8-1/4" 20.6 x 20.6cm.
**326-6324** Light Brown
**326-6325** Gray

### Dealership Buildings
### 19.95 ea
Buildings measure
8-1/4 x 8-1/4" 20.6 x 20.6cm.
**326-6326** Light Brown
**326-6327** Gray

Single-Bay Warehou
326-6323; Dealership Building 326-63

Light Brown Office Buildi
326-63

Dual-Bay Warehouse 326-6320;
Office Building 326-6324

Light Brown Dealership Buildi
326-63

# GEM CITY AMUSEMENTS

## TENTS
Kits are made of fabric and come complete with precut poles, braided "rope" and brass eyelets. Instructions with diagrams and placement templates are also included.

### Full Circus Set
**294-8901 199.95**
Includes a Big Top, Entrance Marquee, Menagerie and Side Show tents. To help set things up, a videotape of instructions is included.

### Big Top & Entrance Marquee
**294-8902 114.95**
For building a smaller circus scene or diorama.

Big Top & Entrance Marquee
294-8902

### Accessory Tents
**294-8903 99.95**
Four accessory tents with hip and gable roofs. These tents can be used for the horse tents, cookhouse, dining tent, dressing tent or other tents.

### Giant Big Top Tent
**294-9704 179.95**
The tent needed for a real-size circus model. Room for a three-ring circus with plenty of space for acts and seating. Requires set-up space of 20 x 38".

# Great West Models, Inc.

MADE IN THE USA

Easy-to-build plastic kits. Create-A-Scene details shown in some photos are sold separately. Industrial buildings are based on modern concrete "tip-up" style buildings.

## NEW PRODUCTS

### Structures

#### Ajax Plumbing Supply

**NEW 24-509 22.99**
9-1/4 x 5-7/8 x 2-1/2"

A great building for any type of trackside company. Includes one railcar and two truck dock doors.

#### Twin Cities Distribution

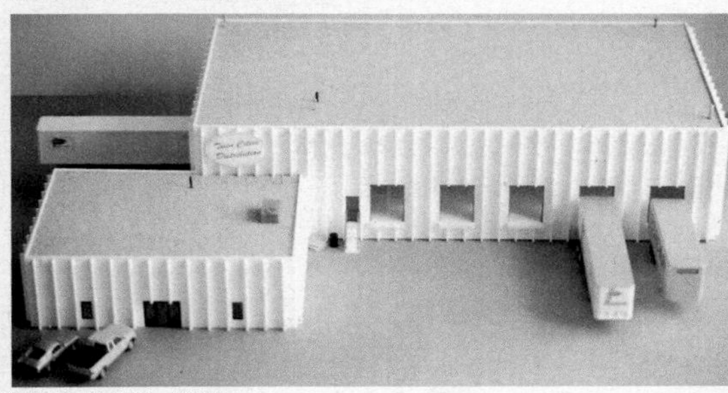

**NEW 24-510 66.99**
21-1/2 x 15 x 4-1/8"

If you're looking for a trackside building to show off your tractors and trailers, this is it! Includes two railcar dock doors on the back side and and several truck dock doors on the front and side.

### Assorted Warehouse Details

**24-314** Includes Pallet Jack, Pallets, Feed Bags, Seed Bags & Signs **9.98**
**NEW 24-317** Pallets w/Feed & Seed Bags pkg(3) **9.98**
**NEW 24-318** Pallets w/Medium & Large Boxes pkg(3) **9.98**

#### Star Manufacturing

**24-104 30.99**
14-3/4 x 7-1/8 x 4-1/8"

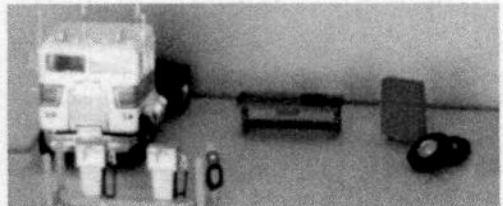

#### Tractor/Trailer Details

**24-315 23.95**
Tool chest and base, workbench, two fuel pumps and island, grinder, air pump and hose, 12 building protectors, four-way wrench, two tires, two wheels and signs.

#### Fuel Island

**24-316 9.95**
Includes island, two fuel pumps, 55-gallon trash drum and signs.

#### Angled Acme Dist.

**24-500 25.99**
11-1/2 x 7-1/8 x 4-1/8"

#### Allied Chemicals

**24-501 27.99**
10-1/2 x 10-1/2 x 4-1/8"

## INDUSTRIAL

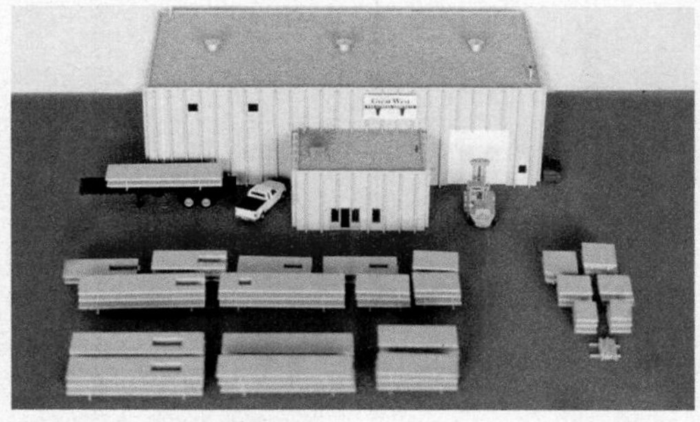

#### Great West Pre-Stress

**24-507 58.99**
14-3/4 x 10-1/2 x 4-1/8"

A perfect building for your cement, gravel and sand hoppers. Kit includes buildings and over 60 wall panels for the yard. Put flatbed trailers in yard for loading. Signs included.

#### Detroit Motors/Railcar Rebuilders

**24-508 66.99**
27 x 19-1/4 x 4-1/8"

A great structure to model a semi manufacturing plant to display your favorite semis, or a farm tractor and implement plant to display your new farm equipment. Ideal for railcar rebuilders; inside railcar unloading, outdoor freight car dock, two outgoing doors for railcars or semis or tractors, and two tractor/trailer docks. Signs included.

#### All American Tractor & Trailer

**24-502 29.99**
11-1/2 x 9-1/4 x 4-1/2"

A great structure to use as a backdrop for your tractor and trailer collection. Can also be used as intermodal maintenance facility.

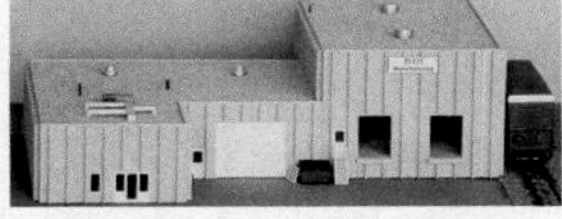

#### Ellis Manufacturing

**24-503 35.99**
14-3/4 x 12-3/4 x 4-1/8"

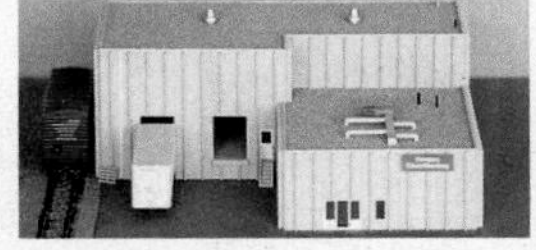

#### Fergus Distributing

**24-504 36.99**
14-3/4 x 11-1/2 x 4-1/8"

Similar to #24-505 except smaller.

#### Golden Foods

**24-505 45.99**
21-1/2 x 11-1/2 x 4-1/8"

This structure is made to have two service sidings along with two truck docks and is ideal for shelf or modular layouts.

#### Valley Feed & Seed

**24-506 27.99**
13-3/4 x 10-1/2 x 4-1/8"

A perfect structure to use with your grain cars. Use in a country or downtown setting with or without your favorite grain elevator. Signs included.

#### Matrix Components

**24-105 33.99**
16 x 9-1/4 x 4-1/8"

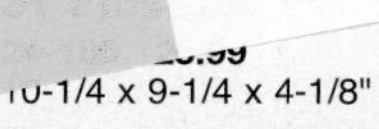

10-1/4 x 9-1/4 x 4-1/8"

Same as #105, but without one-story office area.

#### Mitchell's Machine Service

**24-102 20.99**
8 x 6 x 4-1/8"

#### Stan's Fabricating

**24-101 18.99**
7 x 5 x 4-1/8"

A slightly smaller version of #102.

#### Acme Distributing

**24-103 24.99**
9-1/8 x 7-1/8 x 4-1/8"

A slightly larger version of #102.

#### Riteway Engineering

**24-108 17.99**
5-7/8 x 7 x 2-1/2"

#### Winslow Construction Co.

**24-109 18.99**
7 x 9-1/4 x 2-1/2"

Front View

Back View

#### One-Story Office/ Warehouse

**24-110 20.99**
11-3/8 x 6 x 2-1/2"

# YARD EQUIPMENT & FACILITIES

### Engine/Car Shop

**24-107 27.99**
9-1/4 x 11-1/2 x 4-1/8"

# HOUSES

All house and garage kits feature numerous choices of door and window locations to suit your particular layout.

### The Neighborhood

**24-1111 44.99**
Includes three houses, two single-car garages and one double-car garage.

### Garage Kits

**24-1010** Single Door, 2 Car w/Gable Roof **12.99**

24-1020

24-1030

**24-1020** Double-Door, 2 Car w/Gable Roof **12.99**

**24-1030** Single Door, 2 Car w/Hip Roof **12.99**

**24-1040** Single Door, 1 Car w/Gable Roof pkg(2) **14.99**

### House Kits 12.99 ea

Kits are complete with chimney, one door and three windows.

24-1060

24-1070

**24-1060** Hip Roof

**24-1070** Gable Roof

# BUSINESSES

### Gas Station & Repair Garage

**24-1100 27.99**
Includes add-on details and signs.

### Gas Station Only

**24-1090 22.99**
Includes add-on details and signs.

### Garage Only

**24-1080 12.99**

### Roadside Motel Cottages

**24-1050** pkg(4) **26.99**
Includes add-on details, makes a great steam- or early diesel-era motel, too!

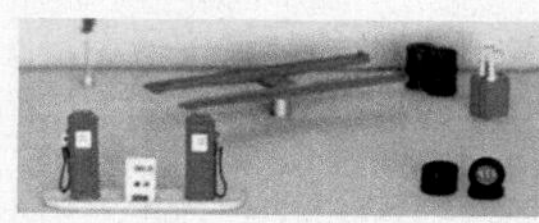

### Old Style Gas Station Details 22.98 ea

Includes island, two pumps, oil can rack, two oil bunkers, five tires, two 55-gallon drums, one car lift, one tire pump and signs.

**24-3131** Lesters & Phillips

**24-3132** Lesters & Shell

**24-3133** Lesters & Mobil

**24-3134** Lesters & Sinclair

### 1960s-1980s Gas Station Details 23.98 ea

Includes island, two gas pumps, mechanic tool chest and base, work bench, car hoist, tire rack, seven tires, signs, tire pump and hose.

**24-3135** Wes's & Gulf

**24-3136** Wes's & Esso

**24-3137** Wes's & Mobil

**24-3139** Wes's & Sinclair

# CREATE-A-SCENE

**24-301** House Details **7.98**

**24-302** Roof Details **14.98**
Small air conditioning unit, assorted ductwork, large evaporation cooler and assorted vents.

**24-303** Roof Details **14.98**
Medium air conditioning unit, large evaporative cooler, "J" vent, assorted vents and two small evaporation coolers.

**24-304** Roof Details **17.98**
Large air conditioning unit, small air conditioning unit, assorted ductwork, "J" vent and assorted vents.

**24-305** Warehouse Details **14.98**
Dumpster, large gas meter, fire plug, parking and dock bumpers, building protector posts and industrial electric meter.

**24-306** Assorted Warehouse Details **8.98**

**24-310** Assorted Roof Details **12.98**
Assorted duct work, small air conditioning unit, one large and one small domed vent, and five assorted vents.

**24-311** Assorted Roof Details **12.98**
One small evaporative cooler and 13 large and small assorted vents.

**24-312** Assorted Roof Details **12.98**
Two small evaporative coolers, nine assorted vents and two (one large and one small) roof or wall exhaust blowers.

### Fence

**24-309** 150' Metal Chainlink Fencing **24.95**

### Assorted Industrial Signs 3.95 ea

Each colored sheet has assorted warning, parking, and company signs.

**24-400** Set #1

**24-401** Set #2

**24-402** Set #3

## Roof Toppers

Make your buildings stand out with these arched and flat tar-paper styrene roofs. Add Create-A-Scene evaporative coolers and vents to Roof Toppers and really detail a roof.

### Roof Toppers 5.25 ea

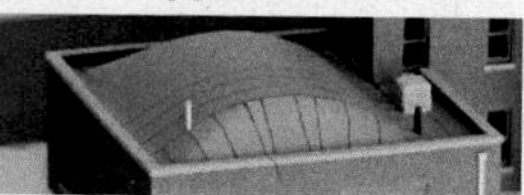

**24-901** For City Classics #107 (sold separately)

**24-902** For City Classics #109 (sold separately)

**24-903** For Design Preservation Models #112 (sold separately)

**24-904** Universal for Flat Roofs

**24-905** Fits Walthers Wallschlager Motors (#933-3004, sold separately)

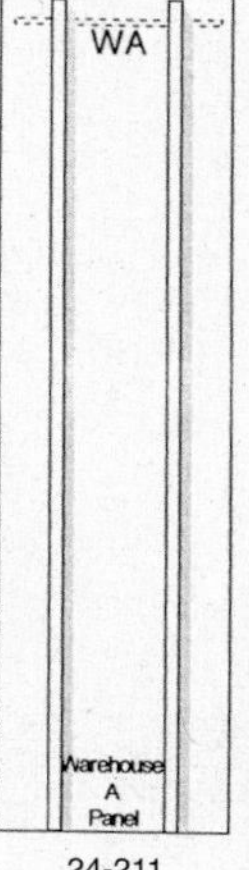

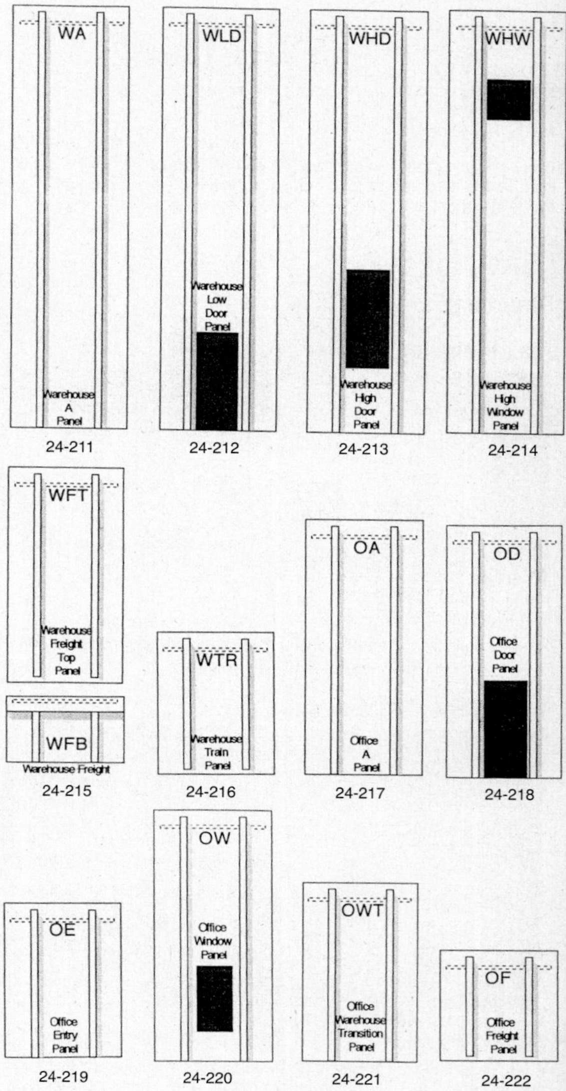

24-211

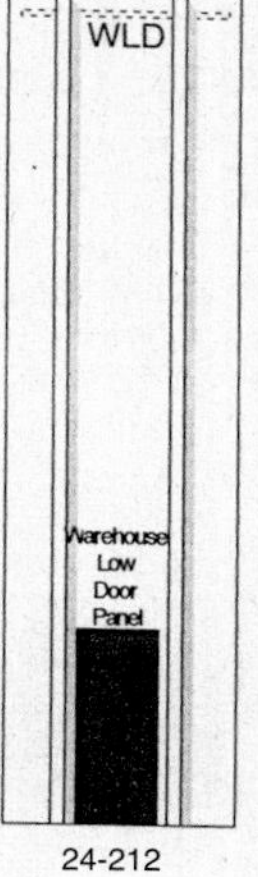

24-212

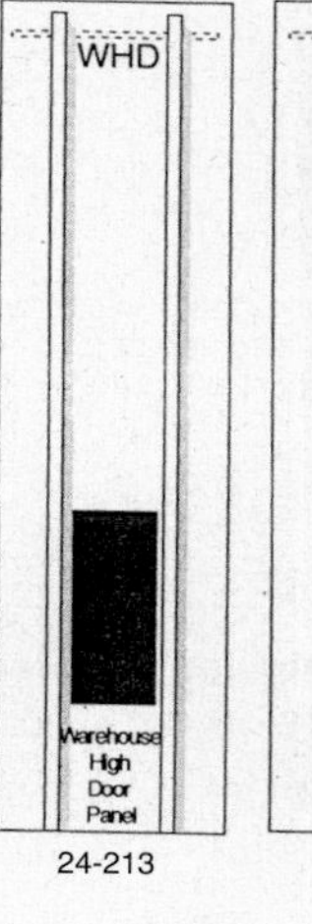

24-213

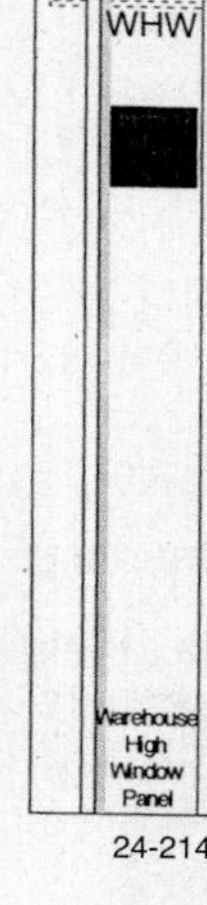

24-214

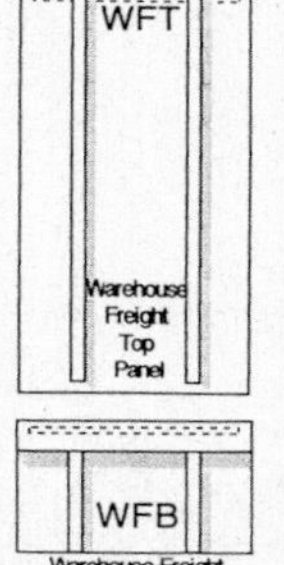

24-215

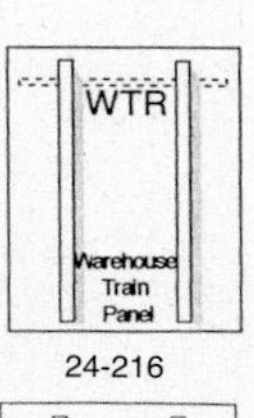

24-216

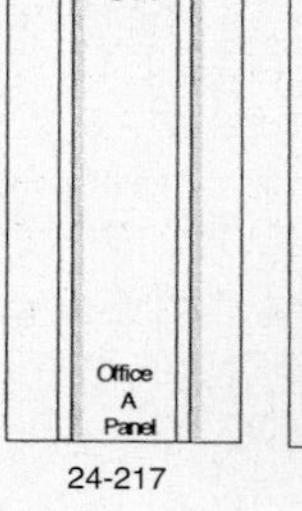

24-217

24-218

OE
Office Entry Panel
24-219

24-220

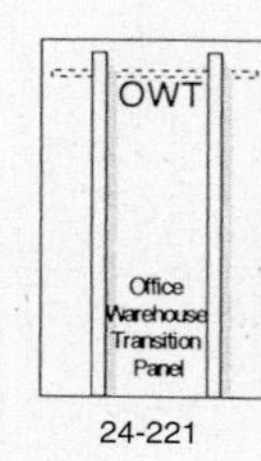

24-221

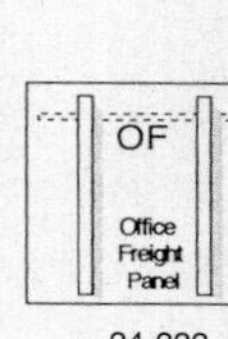

24-222

### Modular Wall Panels System

Expand, customize stock kits, or create your own structures with these easy-to-assemble panels. Panels are same as those included in modern concrete buildings.

**24-211** 4 Warehouse A Panels **4.50**

**24-212** 4 Warehouse Low-Door Panels, 2 Solid Doors, 2 Window Doors **4.50**

**24-213** 4 Warehouse High-Door Panels, 2 Solid Doors, 2 Window Doors **4.50**

**24-214** 4 Warehouse High-Window Panels, 4 Windows **4.50**

**24-215** 3 Each Warehouse Freight Top Panels, Warehouse Freight Bottom Panels, Freight Door Frames, Freight Doors **4.75**

**24-216** 4 Warehouse Train Panels, 2 Train Door Frames **3.50**

**24-217** 4 Office A Panels **3.50**

**24-218** 4 Office Door Panels, 2 Solid Doors, 2 Window Doors **3.50**

**24-219** 4 Office Entry Panels, 4 Office Entry Doors **3.50**

**24-220** 4 Office Window Panels, 4 Windows **3.50**

**24-221** 6 Office/Warehouse Transition Panels **3.50**

**24-222** 2 Each Office Freight Top Panels, Freight Door Frames, Freight Doors **3.50**

**24-223** 2 Stairs, 4 Railings **3.25**

**24-224** Instruction & Panel Copy Sheet **.75**

**24-225** Styrene Sheet, 3 x 3 Window Glass, 2 Scuppers, 2 Downspouts **4.25**

Get Daily Info, Photos and News at
**www.walthers.com**

Guts, Gravel & Glory
GGG
Scenic Railroad Supplies

Add a variety of small commercial and industrial buildings to your layout with these kits. Walls are Hydrocal® plaster castings, which capture fine details. Separate Grandt Line windows and wood parts are also provided.

## RURAL BUILDINGS

**Ertner's Feed & Grain**
308-105 21.60
6-1/4 x 4-1/4" 15.9 x 10.8cm

**Clairmont, Texas Jail**
308-110 19.20
4-1/4 x 3-1/4" 10.8 x 8.3cm

**Schacht's Shack (Dog House)**
308-115 18.00
2-1/4 x 5" 5.6 x 12.5cm

**Prichett Mountain Tattler**
308-117 13.20
2 x 3-1/2" 5.1 x 8.9cm

**Howard Farm Barn**
308-121 16.20
4 x 5" 10.2 x 12.7cm

**Martin's Pole Barn**
308-123 10.20
2-3/4 x 2" 6.9 x 5.1cm

**d'Orsey Gas Station w/Pit 1930s**
308-126 30.00
2-7/8 x 4-3/4" 7.3 x 12.1cm

**Grease Pit for Gas Station, 1930s**
308-127 8.40
1-1/4 x 4-3/4" 3.2 x 12.1cm

**John Hall Feed & Silage**
308-136 42.00
3-1/2 x 4-3/4" 8.9 x 12.1cm

**Reed's Crib & Carriage**
308-137 78.00
7 x 16-1/2" 17.8 x 41.9cm

**E.D. Smith Cabinetmaker**
308-139 42.00
5 x 9-1/2" 12.7 x 24.1cm

**Copeland Leather & Boot Company**
308-140 54.00
7 x 7" 17.8 x 17.8cm

## HOUSES

**Shotgun House**
308-111 12.60
4-1/2 x 1-3/4" 11.4 x 4.4cm

**Cromwell's Cabin**
308-114 14.40
2-1/8 x 3-1/4" 5.4 x 8.3cm

**Bueerman's Cottage**
308-118 13.20
2-5/8 x 2-3/8" 6.7 x 6cm

**Farmer's Sod House**
308-160 13.20
5-1/2 x 3" 13.8 x 7.5cm

## BUSINESSES

**Edward's Place**
308-101 10.20
3-1/2 x 2" 8.9 x 5.1cm

**Payne's Clock Works**
308-102 13.20
2-1/2 x 2" 6.4 x 5.1cm

**Wu Tang Laundry & Drugs**
308-104 14.40
3 x 2-3/8" 7.6 x 6cm

**Motte's Mining Supply**
308-112 11.40
3 x 2" 7.6 x 5.1cm

**Paquette Hardware**
308-116 16.20
2-1/4 x 4-1/2" 5.7 x 11.4cm

**Wisby's Grocery**
308-122 14.40
3 x 2-1/2" 7.6 x 6.4cm

**Baker's Pool Hall**
308-128 16.20
2-1/4 x 5" 5.7 x 12.7cm

**Burrus Livery**
308-130 16.20
3-1/2 x 5-1/4" 8.9 x 13.3cm

**Orr's Broken Butt Cafe**
308-131 14.40
2-1/8 x 3-1/2" 5.4x 8.9cm

**Wally's Hot Dog Haven**
308-161 13.20
2-3/8 x 2-1/2" 6 x 6.4cm

**Kyle's Koffee Shoppe**
308-162 13.20
2-1/2 x 2-1/2" 6.4 x 6.4cm

**Robbie's Burger Roost**
308-163 13.20
5-11/16 x 2-9/16" 14.4 x 6.5cm

**Jack's Saddle Shop**
308-170 21.60

**Brent's Powder & Shot**
308-171 28.80

**Greer's Butcher Shop**
308-172 21.60

## INDUSTRIAL

**J. Lott Welding & Blacksmith**
308-106 14.40
4-1/4 x 2-3/4" 10.8 x 6.9cm

**McCartney's Mill Engine House**
308-125 36.00
6-3/8 x 11" 16.2 x 27.9cm

**Burkholtz's Ten Stamp Mill**
**308-132 36.00**
3-3/4 x 9" 9.5 x 22.9cm

**S. Kaulman Ice Plant**
**308-135 42.00**
6-1/2 x 11-1/2" 16.5 x 29.2cm

**Bob's Liquor & Libations**
**308-138 132.00**

**Grimes Mill Complex**
**308-146 131.90**
14 x 10" 35.6 x 25.4cm

**Miner's Half Dugout**
**308-156 12.00**
2-1/2 x 3" 6.4 x 7.6cm

**Fanny Rawlin's Mine**
**308-157 78.00**
7 x 12" 17.8 x 30.5cm

**Clear Grit Mine**
**308-167 133.20**
16 x 16" 40 x 40cm

**Welch's Dairy & Feed Mill**
**308-168 54.00**

**Ferrie's Machine Shop**
**308-169 48.00**
12-1/4 x 6-1/4" 31.1 x 15.9cm

## FUNARO & CAMERLENGO

Craft Train Kits feature thin, flexible styro-urethane castings with architectural details cast in place, stripwood and wire. Important Note: This listing includes items which are available by special order only. Please see the Legend Page for information, and visit www.walthers.com for a complete listing of in-stock and special order products.

**Standard Tool Houses**
**279-16** SP pkg(2) **15.99**

**Company House**
**279-6 15.99**
3-3/4 x 3-5/8" 9.5 x 9.2cm

See What's Available at
**www.walthers.com**

These Craft Train kits feature wood parts, with pewter details and complete instructions.

## HOUSES

**Section House**
**261-214 69.95**
House your railroad workers along the track.

## TANKS & TOWERS

**Branchline Water Tank**
**261-513 29.95**

## BRIDGES & VIADUCTS

All trestle bridges measure 3-1/8 x 11-1/8" 8 x 28.3cm.

**Gully Trestle**
**261-504 26.95**

**Ravine Trestle**
**261-514 34.95**

## LOGGING BUILDINGS

**Logging Camp Car Kit**
**261-212 44.95**
Wood kit is based on the St. Paul & Tacoma Lumber Company camp car. Comes with complete interior detail.

## BUSINESSES

**Dollar Brothers Motor Express**
**261-207 69.95**
Perfect for any versatile and busy spot on your pike. Can accommodate train traffic on one side and wagon/truck freight on the other.

**Pool Hall**
**261-211 59.95**
3 x 3-1/4" 7.5 x 9cm

Give the people on your layout a place to relax! This laser-cut kit features real cedar shingles and complete interior detail.

**1930s Gas Station**
**261-206 40.95**
3 x 4" 7.5 x 10.2cm

In the steam era, service stations like this could be found along many state and county highways. This detailed kit comes with two gravity-feed gas pumps, plus tires, tools and welding equipment for making repairs.

Make your layout scenes more realistic with this detailed model. Craft Train kit consists of photo-etched metal parts that capture many fine details and are near scale thickness to produce a highly realistic model.

## ELEVATED RAILROAD WATCHMAN'S TOWER

Automobile shown sold separately; see the complete line in the Vehicles Section.

**462-3047 40.95**
A common sight along busy railroad lines from the 1870s to the 1960s, elevated crossing shanties like this were installed near stations and streets where the watchman needed a better view of approaching trains and traffic.

Since the towers were highly visible to the traveling public, they were well maintained and painted in the standard color schemes for stations. Interior furnishings were spartan, with a stove and chair for the watchman, along with pneumatic or manual controls to raise and lower nearby crossing gates. In later years, electrical switches were added to activate crossing flashers.

This detailed replica is typical of towers used on many lines and comes complete with staircase, handrails and stovepipe stack.

# Put Real-World Action in Your Intermodal Terminal

For the first time, you can actually load and unload HO Scale intermodal trains like the prototype! As trains arrive, the lights can be turned on, the crane moved alongside each car, the lifting trolley extended, turned and lowered, and containers moved to and from road, rail or ship - all with the touch of a few buttons. Powered by small, rugged motors mounted right inside the model and a precision drive system like those found in today's finest model locomotives, the crane responds to the controls as smoothly and realistically as the prototypes.

- ***Fully Assembled Working Model!***
- Easy to Set-Up & Operate – Step-By-Step Instructions Included
- Working Cab and Gantry Floodlights
- Handles any Model Container
  Other manufacturer's models require Container Conversion Adapters #322-858906, sold separately.
- Modular Baseplate for Easy Expansion
- Precision Drive System
- Built-In DCC Decoder with Adjustable CVs
- Easy-to-Use Controller Handles up to 3 Cranes
- Can be Operated from your Home Computer or Joystick (both sold separately)
- Easy to Add to Your Layout
- See this amazing model in action at walthers.com!

**NEW Operating Container Crane**
**HO Scale | 322-89001 | $750.00**

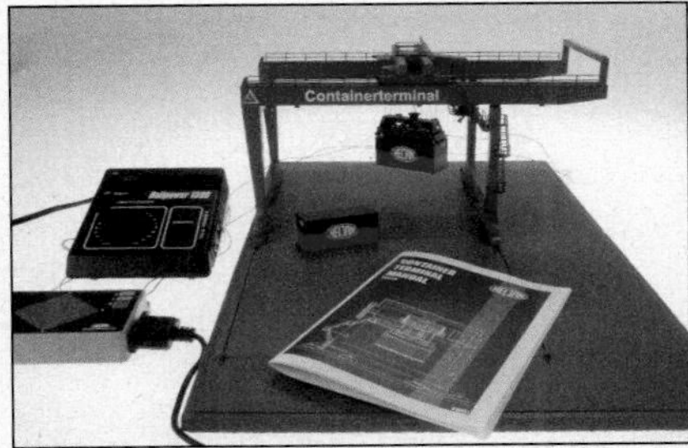

## Customize Your Crane with these Accessories

**20' Containers with Metal Adapters**
**322-858903 $19.98**
Set of four 20' corrugated side box containers decorated for Heljan.

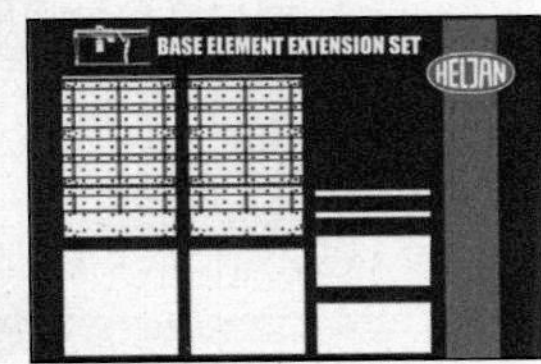


**Base Extension Set**
**322-858904 $54.98**
Matching base plates let you extend the area served by the Container Crane.

**Track Extension Kit**
**322-858905 $19.98**
Expand rail operations with this set of two "paved" HO Scale track sections and eight rail connectors.

**Container Conversion Adapters 322-858906 $7.98**
Set of five magnet adapters to convert other manufacturer's containers for use with the Container Crane.

IMPORTED FROM DENMARK BY WALTHERS
These easy-to-build kits consist of prototypically precolored plastic parts and complete instructions. Kits are European prototypes. With minor modifications most can be easily Americanized.

## NEW PRODUCTS

### Operating Container Crane

**NEW 322-89001 750.00**
Base measures 13-3/16 x 22-13/16" 33 x 57cm

Combining a full range of prototype movement, smooth operation, easy assembly, DCC-compatibility and modular design, this incredible working HO Scale model opens new areas for realistic modeling and operations.

### 20' Containers w/Adapters

**NEW 322-858093** pkg(4) **19.98**

Ready to use with #89001, sold separately.

### Container Conversion Adapters

**NEW 322-858096** pkg(5) **7.98**

Use with any container to convert it for use with #89001.

### Base Extension Set

**NEW 322-858904 54.98**

Matching base plates to build a larger working area for #89001, sold separately. Includes two Central sections each 13-3/16 x 18-1/8" 33 x 45.2cm long, two track sections each 9-1/16" 22.6cm long, eight rail connectors, 16 screws and four fittings.

### Track Externsion Set

**NEW 322-858905** pkg(2) **19.98**

Matching "paved" track sections.

## STATIONS & PLATFORMS

### Small Brick Station

**322-130 13.98**
7-5/8 x 3 x 4-13/64"
19 x 7.7 x 10.5cm

### Spanish Style Station

**322-152 24.98**
9 x 7-5/8 x 3-5/8"
22.5 x 19 x 9cm

### Container Terminal

**322-1716 24.98**
8 x 10 x 7-5/8"
20 x 25 x 19cm

### Freight Loading Accessories

**322-1733 7.98**

### Modern Passenger Station

**322-120 24.98**
19-1/5 x 5-1/5 x 4"
48 x 13 x 10cm

### 2-Story Brick Station

**322-153 24.98**
9-7/8 x 5-7/8" 25 x 15cm

### Wayside Station

**322-156 19.98**
8-13/64 x 2-13/16 x 2-5/8"
20.5 x 7 x 6.5cm

### Station

**322-157 19.98**
19 x 6-5/8 x 3-13/16"
47.5 x 16.5 x 9.5cm

### Smith's Creek Station

**322-913 28.98**
11 x 5-1/8 x 3-15/16"
28 x 13 x 10cm

### Country Station

**322-1712 19.98**
9-5/8 x 3-13/16 x 4-13/32"
24 x 9.5 x 11cm

### Auto Unloading Ramp

**322-1717 14.98**
12 x 4 x 4-3/5"
30 x 10 x 11.5cm

**NEW** Operating Container Crane 322-89001

### Brick Station - 1910 Era

**322-1750 23.98**
13 x 4-3/4" 32.5 x 11cm

### Railroad Station

**322-1752 25.98**
15-3/4 x 6-5/8" 40 x 17cm

### Long Passenger Platform

**322-1753 14.98**
18-3/4 x 2-3/4" 47.5 x 7cm

### Small Freight Station

**322-1760 8.98**
4 x 2-3/4" 10 x 7cm

## YARD EQUIPMENT & FACILITIES

### Walthers Turntable Drive

**942-472 29.98**
Motorize your Walthers N Scale (#933-3203) or Heljan HO Scale Turntable (#322-804) with this easy conversion kit. Includes one RPM 12V DC motor, motor support bracket, mounting hardware and instructions. Complete unit mounts out of sight below the turntable pit.

### 3-Stall Roundhouse

**322-802 44.98**
15-5/8 x 16 x 4-3/4" 39 x 40 x 12cm

For a larger facility, an add-on kit (#322-803) is available.

### 3-Stall Add-On (for Roundhouse #322-802)

**322-803 39.98**
Includes three extra stalls and a rear extension to hold locomotive up to 19-1/4" in length.

### Manual Turntable

**322-804 34.98**
Kit is typical of a steam-era turntable but many are used to turn diesels today.

### Brick Engine House 2-Stall

**322-842 35.98**
15-5/8 x 9-5/8 x 5-5/8"
39 x 24 x 14cm

### Diesel Service Facility

**322-1711 18.98**
12-13/16 x 2 x 3-5/8"
32 x 5 x 9cm

### Yard Tower - 1910 Era

**322-1751 8.98**
3-1/2 x 2-1/2 x 4-3/4"
12.5 x 5 x 9.5cm

### Modern Yard Tower

**322-1754 10.98**
4-7/8 x 2-1/2" 9 x 6.5cm

### Sand & Coaling Complex

**322-111 32.98**
11-5/16 x 4-15/16 x 9-1/4"
28.7 x 12.5 x 23.5cm

### Diesel Fueling Rack

**322-112 22.98**
26-1/8 x 6-1/16 x 2-3/4"
66.4 x 15.4 x 7cm

### Diesel Sanding Rack

**322-113 27.98**
25-3/16 x 5-7/8 x 7-3/16"
64 x 15 x 18.2cm

Get Daily Info, Photos and News at
**www.walthers.com**

## RURAL BUILDINGS

**Danish Farm**
**322-204 12.98**
8-1/4 x 4-15/16 x 2-3/4"
21 x 12.5 x 7cm

**Dairy Plant**
**322-207 16.98**
7-1/8 x 4-3/4 x 6-1/4"
18 x 12 x 16cm

**Watermill**
**322-1771 10.98**
4-1/2 x 3-5/16" 11.5 x 8.5cm

**Farm House**
**322-1791 15.98**
7-1/16 x 4-7/8" 18 x 12.5cm

## HOUSES

**Country Home**
**322-139 14.98**
5-3/16 x 4-3/16 x 4"
13 x 10.5 x 10cm

**Street Houses**
**322-155** pkg(2) **12.98**
3-3/8 x 2" 8.5 x 5cm

**Half-Timbered House**
**322-203 10.98**
5-5/8 x 3 x 2-5/8"
14 x 7.5 x 6.5cm

**Small Brick House**
**322-211 9.98**
3-5/8 x 4 x 3-13/64"
9 x 10 x 8cm

**Tract House w/Terrace**
**322-213 9.98**
4 x 3-1/2" 18 x 12cm

**Hans Christian Andersen House**
**322-220 9.98**
4-5/16 x 4" 11 x 10cm

**American Farm House**
**322-301 11.98**
4-1/8 x 3" 10.5 x 7.5cm

**Terrace Houses**
**322-1706** pkg(2) **15.98**
8-3/8 x 7-5/8 x 4-7/16"
21 x 19 x 11cm

**Weekend Cottage (2-In-1 Kit)**
**322-350 9.98**
2-1/4 x 3-1/8" 5.8 x 8cm
2-1/4 x 2-7/8" 5.8 x 6.8cm

**Tract House**
**322-1772 10.98**
4 x 3-3/8 x 2" 10 x 8.5 x 5cm

**2-Story House w/Balcony**
**322-1779 13.98**
6 x 4-13/16 x 3-3/5"
15 x 12 x 8.5cm

**House w/Garden**
**322-1781 11.98**
5-13/16 x 3-3/8 x 2-5/8"
14.5 x 8.5 x 6.5cm

**Modern House w/Garage**
**322-1783 11.98**
9 x 4-13/16 x 7-5/8"
22.5 x 12 x 19cm

**Cottage**
**322-1792 11.98**
8-5/8 x 3-3/16 x 1-5/8"
21.5 x 8 x 4cm

**Modern House w/Carport**
**322-1793 16.98**
7-5/8 x 7-3/16 x 3-3/16"
19 x 18 x 8cm

**Ranch House w/Attached Garage**
**322-218 14.98**
10-5/8 x 6-5/16" 27 x 16cm

**Old Suburban House**
**322-1773 10.98**
4 x 3-5/8 x 2-3/8" 10 x 9 x 6cm

**American Weekend Cottage**
**322-217 9.98**
7-1/16 x 3-15/16" 18 x 10cm

**Modern 2-Story House**
**322-1794 16.98**
6-1/8" 15.5cm square

**House Against City Wall**
**322-1797 18.98**
4-1/2 x 3-3/8" 11.5 x 8.5cm

## CITY BUILDINGS

**City Hall**
**322-907 29.98**
10-1/4 x 6-5/16 x 6-5/16"
26 x 16 x 16cm

**Bar & Beauty Salon w/Apartments**
**322-465 14.98**
4 x 2-1/2" 10 x 6.5cm

**Limited Quantity Available**

**Fire Station**
**322-1703 19.98**
12-13/16 x 6-3/16 x 5-5/8"
32 x 15.5 x 14cm

**Museum**
322-1799 19.98

**Customs House**
322-2019 24.98
11-1/2 x 9-13/64 x 4-13/32"
28.7 x 23 x 11cm

## TANKS & TOWERS

**Old Windmill**
322-201 11.98
4" 10cm square

**Wooden Water Tank - Canadian**
322-1001 19.98
4 x 4 x 6-3/16"
10 x 10 x 15.5cm

**Overtrack Switch Tower**
322-1757 16.98
6-3/8 x 4 x 5-3/16"
16 x 10 x 13cm

**High Tension Tower**
322-2014 pkg(3) 15.98
3/8 x 1-3/16 x 8-1/2"
1 x 3 x 21.7cm

## CHURCHES

**Village Church**
322-202 13.98
6-3/16 x 3-5/8 x 5-3/16"
15.5 x 9 x 13cm

**Country Church**
322-713 14.98
7-5/8 x 3-5/8 x 4-13/16"
19 x 9 x 12.5cm

## BUSINESSES

**Roadside Inn**
322-206 14.98
7-1/8 x 4-1/8 x 3-1/2"
18 x 10.5 x 9cm

**General Store**
322-208 16.98
6-3/4 x 4-3/4 x 3-3/8"
17 x 12 x 8.5cm

**Drug Store**
322-461 13.98
2-3/4 x 2-3/8 x 5-1/2"
7 x 6 x 14cm

**Small Retail Store**
322-462 12.98
2-3/8 x 2-3/16 x 4-1/8"
6 x 5.5 x 10.5cm

**Wood Railroad Hotel - 1900 Era**
322-820 21.98
5-1/16 x 5-5/16" 13 x 13.5cm

**Brick Storefront Buildings**
322-902 33.98
9 x 7-7/8 x 4-5/16"
23 x 20 x 11cm

**Ice Cream & Woolworth Stores**
322-904 33.98
9-7/8 x 9 x 4-3/4"
25 x 23 x 12cm

**Limited Quantity Available**

**Gas Station**
322-908 24.98
7-7/8 x 7-1/16 x 3-15/16"
20 x 18 x 10cm

**Movie Theater**
322-909 32.98
7-1/16 x 9 x 4-3/4"
18 x 23 x 12cm

**Drug Store**
322-911 31.98
7-1/16 x 9 x 4-3/4"
18 x 23 x 12cm

**Edison's Laboratory**
322-915 24.98
15-5/8 x 4-3/8 x 4-3/16"
39 x 11 x 10.5cm

**Self-Service Store**
322-1702 15.98
5-13/16 x 8 x 2-5/8"
14.5 x 20 x 6.5cm

**Synagogue**
322-1000 19.98
9-13/16 x 10-13/16 x 7-5/8" 24.5 x 27 x 19cm

Raised brick detailing, simulated beveled-glass windows, decorative window frames, a varied roofline and a rooftop balcony are just some of the exquisite details on this HO kit from Heljan. This structure is based on a historic building still in use in New York, this early-1900s structure also makes a great mansion, apartment, private school or upscale office. The kit features easy construction with only a small amount of gluing necessary, making it suitable for modelers of any skill level.

**Shopping Center w/5 Stores**
322-1775 21.98
6-3/4 x 5-7/8" 17 x 15cm

**Modern Gas Station**
322-1776 11.98
6 x 4 x 2-13/64"
15 x 10 x 5.5cm

**The Old Inn**
322-1777 12.98
7 x 4-5/8 x 3-3/8"
17.5 x 11.5 x 8.5cm

**Appliance Warehouse**
322-1780 13.98
8-3/16 x 4-3/8 x 3-3/16"
20.5 x 11 x 8cm



## INDUSTRIAL

**Brewery Malt House**
322-807 56.98
26 x 7-5/8 x 22"
65 x 19 x 55cm

**Island Creek Coal Co.**
322-1708 21.98
9-1/4 x 6-7/8 x 6-3/32"
23.5 x 17.5 x 15.5cm

**Grain Elevator**
322-806 29.98
14-3/16 x 6-5/16 x 12-3/16"
36 x 16 x 31cm

**Power Station**
322-2018 21.98
5-1/2 x 5-1/8 x 3-3/8"
14 x 13 x 8.5cm

**Palumbo Cement Works**
**322-1715 25.98**
8-1/2 x 4-3/4 x 6-11/16"
21.5 x 12 x 17cm

## BRIDGES & VIADUCTS

**Road Bridge Overpass**
**322-102 9.98**
9-1/2 x 2-3/8 x 3-3/4" 5 x 10cm

**British Pedestrian Overpass**
**322-715 11.98**
9-1/4 x 5-1/4 x 4-3/4"
23 x 13 x 12cm

**Pedestrian Overpass**
**322-1736 9.98**
9-1/2 x 2-1/2" 24 x 6.5cm

**Stone Bridge Pier (2-In-1 Kit)**
**322-1765 7.98**
3-13/64 1-13/64 x 3-13/64"
8 x 3 x 8cm

**Timber Trestle**
**322-174 26.98**
Larger trestle used for main or branch line operations. Molded in dark brown plastic. Its modular design can be used to arrange the various pieces to fit your scenery.

**Tunnel Portals**
**322-1759 10.98**
19-5/8 x 1-7/16 x 5-3/8" 49 x 3 x 13.5cm

Assembled resin structures are ready for your layout.

## NEW PRODUCTS

**Tom's Quonset Hut 15.00 ea**
**NEW 353-6100** New
**NEW 353-6101** Rusty

**Stengel's Barn**
**NEW 353-6102 18.00**

**1st Street Church**
**NEW 353-6103 20.00**

**Diner**
**NEW 353-6104 20.00**

**Firehouse**
**NEW 353-6105 20.00**

**Farm Buildings**
**NEW 353-6106 11.00**
Includes three buildings, one dog house and one trough.

**Gas Station**
**NEW 353-6107 27.00**

**New England Ranch House**
**NEW 353-6108 20.00**

**Ranch House**
**NEW 353-6109 20.00**

**Supermarket**
**NEW 353-6110 24.00**

**Switch Tower**
**NEW 353-6111 16.00**

**Levittown**
**NEW 353-6112** Model A **18.00**
**NEW 353-6113** Model B **18.00**
**NEW 353-6114** Model C **20.00**
**NEW 353-6115** Model D **20.00**

Build realistic industrial areas for your layout with this line of detailed kits, suitable for many modeling eras. Kits feature detailed urethane castings (water towers consist of molded plastic parts) and are designed for easy construction. Important note: This listing includes items which are available by special order only. Please see the Legend Page for information, and visit www.walthers.com for a complete listing of in-stock and special order products.

## YARD EQUIPMENT & FACILITIES

**Roundhouse**
**411-104** Three-Stall **66.95**
15-1/2 x 8-1/2"

American design features 20 windows, three smokejacks and detailed doors for each stall.

**Add-On Stall**
**411-105** For #411-104 **19.95**
Matches parts from #104 (sold separately); several stalls can be combined to build a larger roundhouse.

## INDUSTRIAL

**General Lighting & Power Plant**
**411-107 144.95**
6-1/2 x 23-1/2"; includes coal ramp 5-1/2 x 12"

**General Light & Power Sub Station**
**411-110 36.95**
8 x 5"

**Acme Nuts & Bolts**
**411-802 36.95**
18 x 5 1/4 x 9"

## WATER TANKS

**18.95 ea**
Typical of tanks built for cities, industries and other facilities, these easy to build kits feature injection molded plastic parts.

**Ellipsoidal**
**411-126** 66' Tall

**1900s Vintage**
**411-127** 74' Tall

**1930s Vintage**
**411-128** 69' Tall

## HI-TECH DETAILS

## CONCRETE PHONE BOOTH

**331-8000** SP **3.95**

These easy-to-build kits feature pre-colored molded plastic parts, with base and concrete sidewalks, trim details and clear plastic windows (unless noted).

## STATIONS & PLATFORMS

**Rico Station**
348-807 17.98

**Mainline Station**
348-3502 16.98

**Freight Station w/Loading Platform**
348-3505 17.98

**Freight Station**
348-3510 15.98

**Large Equipment Shed**
348-9 2.49

**Mobile Office Site**
348-223 .99

**Truck Terminal**
348-47758 14.98

**Gantry Crane**
348-7777 13.98

**Trackside Sandhouse**
348-7763 12.98

## HOUSES

**Colonial House**
348-4945 10.98

**Aunt Millie's House**
348-47776 15.98

**Stockyard**
348-7781 13.98

**Kavanaugh**
348-1001 15.98

**Queen Ann**
348-1002 15.98

**Steiner**
348-1003 15.98

**Victorian**
348-1005 15.98

**Victorian Assortment**
348-10091 pkg(5) 79.90

**Huntington**
348-1007 19.98

**Stevenson**
348-1009 19.98

**Baldwin**
348-10011 19.98

**Vanderbilt**
348-1008 19.98

**Pullman**
348-10010 19.98

**Colonial House Assortment**
348-10089 pkg(5) 99.98

**Ranch House**
348-4944 10.98

## RURAL BUILDINGS

**Greenhouse**
348-5 1.99

**Farmhouse**
348-7 2.49

**Farm Silo**
348-225 1.49

**Legal & Professional Office**
348-10026 18.98

**The South Street Smoke Shop**
348-10015 24.98
Includes wooden Indian.

**Rita's Antiques**
348-10016 24.98
Includes roof-top shed.

**Grant Cary's Apothecary**
348-10018 24.98

## CITY BUILDINGS

**County Court House**
348-805 16.98

**Store & Auto Repair**
348-3504 22.98

**Ice Cream Parlor & Boarding House**
348-3507 20.98

**1st National Bank**
348-10025 16.98

**Ma's Place**
348-47779 13.98

**Fast Photo**
348-10044 12.98

**Charisma Dress Shop**
348-10045 12.98

**Dino's Pizza Parlor**
348-10046 12.98

**Health Aids**
348-10048 12.98

**Shopping Center Assortment**
348-100100 pkg(5) **64.90**
Includes one each: 10044, 10045, 10046 and 10048, as well as a card shop not available separately in this Reference Book.

## BUSINESSES

**Old Time Gas Station**
348-712 13.98

**Service Station**
348-3509 19.98

## CHURCHES

**Colonial Church**
348-804 15.98

## INDUSTRIAL

**Cement Plant w/Platform**
348-2 4.99

**Cannery**
348-7002 8.98

**Water Bridge**
348-5006 18.98

## BRIDGES & VIADUCTS

Buildings Not Included With Pier

### Heavy Duty Pier
348-5501 12.98

### Expansion Packs 2.98 ea
348-5513 Wide Pier
348-5514 Narrow Pier
348-5515 Track Pier

## SNAP-EAZE SERIES

"SNAP-EAZE" kits feature snap-together construction. No glue required.

### Stations & Platforms

Switch Tower
348-4102 14.98

### Churches

Country Church
348-4105 5.98

### Chemical Processing Plant
348-7006 13.98
Includes a tank house, mineral processing unit with drying vat, machinery house, digester vat, reagent and reactant tanks, vertical storage tank and enclosed process control section. Comes with tank house interior details, color signs and complete instructions.

### Concrete Mixing Plant
348-5007 29.98

### Novelty Iron Works
348-5047 19.98

Buildings Not Included With Pier

### Large Transfer Pier
348-5505 12.98

## BROWNSTONE POLYBAG KITS

### Abercrombie Mansion
348-19 9.98

### Reagan Mansion
348-20 9.98

### Morgan Mansion
348-21 9.98

### Carrington Mansion
348-22 9.98

## MASTERPIECE SERIES

Easy-to-build kits, construction time varies with kit size.

### Houses

3 Houses Under Construction
348-711 11.98

### City Buildings

Society Hill Townhouse
348-809 17.98

### Industrial

Transformer Plant
348-2015 14.98

Sand & Fueling Depot
348-3506 15.98

## CIRCUS RIDES

Customize your midway with these easy-to-build plastic ki[ts]. Models are molded in colors and include full-color printed signs. Each can be built as a working model, using motorizing kit #348-5190 (sold separately).

### Swinger

348-5113 16.98
Hanging seats spin out and u[p] the faster the ride turns.

### Falling Star

348-5117 17.98
Platform rises, falls and turns just like the real thing.

### Sea Dragon

348-5118 17.98
Colorful ship sweeps back an[d] forth.

## Spider
**348-5125 17.98**
Six spinning arms, each with twin cars.

## Octopus
**348-5124 17.98**
With eight spinning arms.

## Sky Wheel Double Ferris Wheel
**348-5112 17.98**
When motorized, the two smaller wheels turn as they rotate around the larger axis. Stands about 12" tall.

## Thunder Bolt

**348-5119 19.98**
Cars rise up as they swing around the central column.

## Motorizing Kits
**348-5190** Deluxe, For Rides **7.98**

**348-5198** Battery Box w/Switch & Wiring Harness **2.98**

# CONCESSIONS & GAME BOOTHS

## Carnival/Rail Ticket Office
**348-4407 1.98**

# CENTER STREET SERIES

Center Street Series buildings look great on any main street. Most come with interiors and lighting. Parts are molded in colors with lots of detail.

## Bridges & Viaducts

### Crossover Signal Bridge
**348-47767 13.98**
Keep trains moving safely. Bridge also has pedestrian walkway for those busy mainlines in urban areas.

## Stations & Platforms

### Arlee Station
**348-47761 11.98**
A typical small town or suburban station, combining passenger and freight operations. Complete with bay window and attached platform.



## Industrial

### Machine Shop
**348-47764 12.98**
A perfect small industry, use as part of a larger complex or by itself.

## Tanks & Towers

### Water Tower
**348-47769 9.98**
A must for steam-era operations. Wooden tank with spout and other details.

## Businesses

### Barber Shop & Chinese Laundry
**348-47771 17.98**
A great business complete with chairs, counters and cash register.

### Howard Johnson's Restaurant
**348-47754 17.98**
An authentic replica of the famous roadside stop.

### Drug Store & Camera Shop
**348-47772 16.98**
Two stores in one, with booth-style seats, camera on tripod, movie projector and counters.

## International Hobby Corp.

**Joe's Fruit Store & Dentist Office**
**348-47797 15.98**
Detailing is a snap as this kit includes 24 crates of produce.

**Honest Sam's Used Car Lot**
**348-47796 16.98**
Honest Sam won't steer you wrong! Just look at those shiny cars out front, included for the showroom or the lot.

**Loew's Movie Theatre**
**348-47799 17.98**
An ornate old-time structure, complete with a big three-sided marquee, a ticket booth and a fire escape - everything you need but the popcorn.

**Furniture Store**
**348-47774 15.98**
A full inventory of lamps, chairs, tables, a bedroom set, grandfather clock and more.

## JV MODELS

SCALE KITS FOR THE DISCERNING MODELER

Wood Craft Train Kits with metal or plastic parts.

### STATIONS & PLATFORMS

**Victoria Station**
**345-2025 39.98**
Scale 23 x 56'

### YARD EQUIPMENT & FACILITIES

**Haliburton Engine House**
**345-2024 37.98**
Scale 23 x 79'

**Section Tool House**
**345-2005** pkg(2) **21.98**
2 x 4-1/8" 4.5 x 9.5cm

**Motor Car House**
**345-2006** pkg(2) **21.98**
2 x 4-1/8" 4.5 x 9.5cm

**Bunkhouses Or Line Storage Shed**
**345-2011** pkg(2) **23.98**
Scale 10 x 20'

### RURAL BUILDINGS

**Farm Silo**
**345-2000 19.98**
Scale 18 x 44'

**Gabled Roof Dairy Barn**
**345-2001 31.98**
5-1/4 x 10-1/2" 13.3 x 26.5cm

**Watson's Siding**
**345-2020 43.98**
Scale 40 x 30'

### BUSINESSES

**Roadside Fruit Stand & Bait Shop**
**345-2004 16.98**
2-3/4 x 7-1/4" 7 x 18.2cm

### TANKS & TOWERS

**Forest Ranger Tower**
**345-2002 29.98**
3 x 3" 7.5 x 7.5cm

**Sand Tower & Drying House**
**345-2008 36.98**
5-3/8 x 6-1/8" 13.5 x 13.3cm

345-2013 345-2029

**Mainline Wood Water Tower**
**345-2013 33.98**
Scale 28 x 56'

**Branchline Wood Water Tower**
**345-2012 29.98**
Scale 22 x 42'

**40-Ton Coaling Tower**
**345-2029 33.98**
Scale 16 x 16 x 65'

### INDUSTRIAL

**Boyd Logging Camp**
**345-2018 63.98**
Scale 50 x 85'
Includes eight structures.

**Ward's Salvage**
**345-2022 41.98**
Scale 50 x 60'

**Alden Farms Stockyard**
**345-2028 37.98**
Scale 80 x 120'

**Burnt River Mining Co**
**345-2019 41.98**
Scale 23 x 15'

**Pontypool Farm Suppl**
**345-2023 43.98**
Scale 57 x 24'

**Austinburg Lumber Ya**
**345-2031 47.98**
Scale 64 x 92'

**Lucas Sawmill**
**345-2021 59.98**
Scale 50 x 95'

### BRIDGES & VIADUCTS

**Wood Timber Trestle**
**345-2014 49.98**
18" long x 16" high.

**Curved Wood Trestle**
**345-2016 62.98**
36" long x 16" high.

### SMALL BOAT LANDING

**345-2003 19.98**
2-3/4 x 7-1/4" 7 x 18.2cm

### LUMBER LOAD

**345-2010** Kit pkg(3) **21.98**

### CATALOG

**345-8400 2.00**

This line of craft train laser-cut wood kits features precut Northeastern siding and Grandt Line windows/doors, with illustrated instructions.

## Business

### D.C. Cochran Confectionery

**NEW 361-471 44.95**
3-3/8 x 5-1/2" 8.6 x 14cm
This vintage candy store comes complete with a roof billboard, cast metal details and full-color signs.

## STATIONS & PLATFORMS

### East Junction Yard Office

**361-451 19.95**
2-3/4 x 1-1/2"
This small wood building will make a great yard office or crew shanty in any steam or diesel-era scene. The laser-cut wood kit includes plenty of details, realistic roofing and complete instructions.

### Purity Milk Platform

**361-461 22.95**
5-1/2 x 1-3/8"
This detailed, laser-cut wood kit includes a typical elevated platform, shanty, cast-metal details, signs and complete assembly instructions.

### Suds Bucket

**361-361 42.95**
5-3/4 x 3-1/2"
Features two girder roof billboards, over a dozen new cast detail parts, three of JL's own classic 1947 motorcycles, and over 50 full-color signs.

### Wilbur Shaw's Speed Shop

**361-371 42.95**
10 x 3-7/8"

### McLeod Super Service

**361-311 37.95**
6 x 3-3/4"
Kit features over 60 full-color signs, a fence-base billboard, cast metal details and two prepainted and labeled custom barrels.

### Saw Pit Store

**361-321 37.95**
Over 20 cast metal details and plastic accessories, detatched garage, Socony Vacuum shield sign, a pair of custom prepainted barrels, 185 color country store posters/signs.

### McSoreley's Old Ale House

**361-331 49.95**
7-3/8 x 3-1/4" 18.4 x 8.1cm
Kit includes 40 cast metal details and plastic accessory parts, custom-designed full color signs, with a detailed roof and a rear add-on section.

### East Junction Section House

**361-261 22.95**
5-3/8 x 2-7/8" 13.4 x 7.2cm

### McDougall Telegraph Office

**361-271 19.95**
3-1/4 x 2-7/8" 8.1 x 7.2cm

## TANKS & TOWERS

### Avon St. Elevated Crossing Tower

**361-241 22.95**
Includes pre-bent rail support truss, Central Valley steps, railings and Campbell shingles.

### Bagwell Junction Tower

**361-291 39.95**
2-3/8 x 1-7/8 x 3-3/8"
5.7 x 4.5 x 8.4cm
Features laser-cut shingles, Central Valley steps and railings, a separate storage shed, nonoperating train order signal, seven relay/ phone boxes, train order hoop stand, battery cellar and extra rail fencing.

**Vic's Auto Alignment**
**361-161 26.95**
7-3/4 x 3-3/4" 19.4 x 9.4cm

**Pickard Motors**
**361-171 44.95**
11-1/2 x 8-1/2" 28.8 x 21.3cm

**Fryxell Feed & Seed**
**361-181 37.95**
4-1/2 x 4-1/4" 11.2 x 10.7cm

**Storm Lake Mobil Service**
**361-431 39.95**
9 x 9" (Includes area for pump island)

**F.S. Jones Painting**
**361-441 23.95**
4-3/4 x 1-3/4"
F.S. Jones Painting is typical of small wooden business buildings from the early 1900s. This detailed kit features a diminutive wooden structure, concrete loading dock and plenty of full-color signs.

## YARD EQUIPMENT & FACILITIES

**Trackside Jamboree**
**361-231 29.95**
Large Building: 3-3/4 x 1-1/2" 9.5 x 3.7cm
Small Building: 2-5/8 x 1-3/4" 6.4 x 3.2cm

Over 20 Grandt Line windows, doors and accessories, including standard gauge Fairmont pushcar, pallets and junk are included.

## INDUSTRIAL

**Brookside Ice House**
**361-191 36.95**
5-3/8 x 9"
13.6 x 22.5cm

**Ice Blocks**
**361-205** pkg(25) **2.89**

**Industrial Pillar Crane & Dock**
**361-391 26.95**

**Limited Quantity Available**

**Hubermill Warehouse**
**361-121**
**36.95**
9-1/4 x 3"
23 x 7.5cm

## ICE FISHING SHACKS

**Woebegone Winter Detail Set**
**361-453 18.95**
Features two unique ice fishi houses, vintage snowmobile, toboggan, and a riding mowe with a snowblower attachmen

## BUSINESSES

**Val's Hamburgers**
**361-131 26.95**
5 x 3" 12.5 x 7.5cm

**LaBosky's Motorcycle Repair**
**361-141 34.95**
5-3/4 x 4-1/2" 14.3 x 11.2cm

**Woody's**
**361-211 39.95**
5-1/2 x 3" 12.5 x 7.5cm

**Bertani's Billiards**
**361-351 54.95**
7-1/4 x 3-1/2" 18.1 x 8.8cm

Bertani's features multi-angled roofs, Central Valley stairs/ railings, cast metal details, a sheet of full-color signage and "Small Town" injection-molded street-level storefront walls.

## Brownie's Northside Service

**361-341 39.95**
Kit features gravity-feed and electric pumps that allow modelers to help determine the service station's appropriate era. In addition, 217 gas station signs allow you to decide if your station is affiliated with Shell, Texaco or Flying A.

## Kilborn Marine Sales

**361-381 48.95**
Includes two main buildings: a sales office and a workshop/marine service station. Details include two fishing boat, motor and trailer sets and loads of other marine details. Also includes over 75 color vintage marine signs and a pair of large billboards.

## Schmiege's Little Dutch Store

**361-411 46.95**
5-3/4 x 4-1/8"

Laser cut country store features loads of details, signs, and accessories. (Vehicles and figures sold separately.)

## Picorelli's Ice Cream Parlor

**361-421 64.95**
5-7/8 x 3-3/4"

Laser-cut kit features girder roof billboard and wall billboard (ice cream sundae). Detail parts include plastic fences, ladders, fire escapes and telephone pole. Also, includes many cast-metal detail parts and tricycle ice cream motorcycle.

## KEYSTONE LOCOMOTIVE WORKS

Craft train kits feature wood construction, with injection molded styrene and cast metal details.

### Stations & Platforms

**Passenger Shelter**
**395-117 17.95**

### Industrial

**Danby Saw Mill**
**395-111 29.95**
7 x 7" 18 x 18cm

Includes logs and other details.

**Kindling Wood Factory**
**395-124 48.95**
3 x 3" 7.6 x 7.6cm
7 x 4" 18 x 10.3cm

Double kit, with Sawing Building connected to Drying Building.

## MOUNTAINS IN MINUTES

## BRIDGES & VIADUCTS

**Bridge Abutments**
**473-825** pkg(2) **10.99**
3-1/2 x 8-3/4" 9 x 22.5cm

**Multi Scale Arch Bridge**
**473-826 16.49**
1-3/4 x 11-7/8" 4.5 x 30cm

For HO or N Scales.

**Multi Scale Viaduct**
**473-827 31.98**
8 x 21" 20 x 44cm

Use with HO, O or N Scales.

## New Rail Models

## NEW PRODUCTS

### 1920s Bungalow

**NEW 501-13017 47.95**
3-1/2 x 5-1/4" 8.8 x 13.3cm

Small homes like this can still be found near the tracks in many cities and towns. Sold as a kit and shipped by box car, the prototype of this model was designed by the Gordon Van-Tine Company, of Davenport, Iowa. This model is designed for easy construction with peel and stick Ultra Shingles and a Grandt Line chimney. Self-adhesive concrete block is included for the foundation, with cast "concrete" front stairs. The model can be built with a removable roof to add an interior or lighting (both sold separately) if desired. Complete photo-illustrated instructions are also included. To complete your scene, add the 1920s Garage Kit (#501-13006, sold separately.)

### Joe's Shack

**NEW 501-13019 TBA**
A great way to detail any empty lot along your line, this building makes a great bunkhouse, fishing cabin in the woods, or other small house. The model can be built with a removable roof to detail the porch or add lighting (both sold separately) if desired.



## STRUCTURES

### Laser-Cut Wood Kits

These detailed kits feature precision-cut wood parts and each includes peel-and-stick roofing material.

**A-Frame Cabin w/Deck**

**501-13003 42.95**
A great structure for any mountain or resort scene, this cabin is based on prototypes seen everywhere. Includes peel-and-stick Ultra Shingles™

**Classic 1920s Garage**

**501-13006 22.95**
Based on typical one-car garages used across the continent, thousands of these structures still stand in neighborhoods coast to coast. Includes peel-and-stick Ultra Shingles.

**Bingen Loading Warehouse**

**501-13007 79.95**
Add this unique trackside warehouse to your diesel-era layout. Makes a great stand-alone structure or use several near a lumber or plywood mill to create a bustling trackside scene. Includes peel-and-stick tar paper roofing.

**Log Scaling Platform**

**501-13010 45.95**
Log scaling platforms are where a value is placed on truckloads of freshly cut logs. Often located near sawmills to measure incoming logs, this model is closely based on the facility at the Hull Oaks Lumber Co. in Dawson, OR, but is similar to those in use at many other sawmills.

kibri®

IMPORTED FROM GERMANY BY WALTHERS

**NEW** Garden Houses 405-8659

## NEW PRODUCTS

### Yard Equipment & Facilities

**Water House w/Movable Water Spout**
**NEW 405-9327 24.97**
4-3/4 x 3-1/2 x 4-3/8"
12 x 9 x 11cm

**Water Tower w/Water Spout**
**NEW 405-9328 33.99**
4-3/8 x 9-7/16"
11 Dia x 24cm High

**Signal Tower w/Track Overpass**
**NEW 405-9329 74.99**
17 x 9-7/8 x 7-1/8"
43 x 25 x 18cm

### Houses

**Garden Houses 23.99 ea**
7-7/8 x 4-3/4 x 2"
20 x 12 x 5cm

**NEW 405-8658** w/Brown Fence

**NEW 405-8659** w/Green Chain Link Fence

**NEW 405-8660** w/Silver Chain Link Fence

**Markgrafler Village House**
**NEW 405-8742 28.99**
4-3/4 x 4-3/8 x 4-3/4"
12 x 11 x 12cm

**Half-Timbered House in Markgrafler**
**NEW 405-8745 24.99**
4-1/8 x 3-7/8 x 5-5/16"
10.5 x 10 x 10.5cm

**Schwabisches Farmhouse**
**NEW 405-8746 36.99**
6 x 4-3/4 x 5-1/8"
15 x 12 x 13cm

**Markgrafler Village Set**
**NEW 405-8747 107.99**
Includes #s 405-8742, 8743, 8745 & 9363, also sold separately.

**Half-Timbered House in Munsterland**
**NEW 405-8919 40.99**
5-1/2 x 4-3/4 x 5"
14 x 12 x 12.5cm

**Die Schatulle House in Munsterland**
**NEW 405-8920 34.99**
4-3/8 x 3-7/8 x 5-1/8"
11 x 10 x 13cm

**NEW** KFZ-Service Tire Workshop 405-8542

**Half-Timbered House in Munsterland**
**NEW 405-8923** Green & White **28.99**
4-3/8 x 3-7/8 x 3-13/16"
11 x 10 x 9cm

### City Buildings

**Markgrafler City Hall**
**NEW 405-8743 33.99**
4-3/4 x 3-1/2 x 7-1/2"
12 x 9 x 19cm

**Hotel Rossle in Markgrafler**
**NEW 405-8744 33.99**
3-7/8 x 3-7/8 x 5-5/16"
10 x 10 x 13.5cm

See What's Available at
**www.walthers.com**

### Churches

**Westerwald Church**
**NEW 405-9765 68.99**
9-7/16 x 6-3/8 x 8-7/8"
24 x 16 x 22cm

**Brick Wall**
**NEW 405-8657 23.99**
For Westerwald Church #405-9765, sold separately.

**Westerwald Church w/Wall**
**NEW 405-9766 82.99**
Includes #s 405-9765 & 9766

### Businesses

**Aral Gas Station**
**NEW 405-8541 28.99**
7-7/8 x var x 1-13/16"
20 x var x 4.5cm

**KFZ-Service Tire Workshop**
**NEW 405-8542 51.99**
12-13/16 x 4-1/2 x 3-1/2"
32.5 x 11.5 x 9cm

**Pharmacy in Munsterland**
**NEW 405-8921 28.99**
4-3/8 x 3-7/8 x 3-13/16"
11 x 10 x 9cm

IMPORTED FROM GERMANY BY WALTHERS

### Drugstore in Munsterland
NEW 405-8922 28.99
4-3/8 x 3-7/8 x 3-13/16"
11 x 10 x 9cm

### Dress Shop
NEW 405-8924 57.99
3-7/8 x 3-7/8 x 8"
10 x 10 x 20.5cm

### Half-Timbered Prussian Building
NEW 405-8925 57.99
3-7/8 x 3-7/8 x 8"
10 x 10 x 20.5cm

### Optician
NEW 405-8926 57.99
4-1/2 x 3-7/8 x 6-1/2"
11.5 x 10 x 16.5cm

### Men & Women's Clothing Shop
NEW 405-8927 57.99
4-1/2 x 3-7/8 x 7-11/16"
11.5 x 10 x 19.5cm

### Half-Timbered Resin Set
NEW 405-8928 207.99
Includes #s 405-8924, 8925, 8926 & 8927.

### Half-Timbered Building Set In Munsterland
NEW 405-8929 119.99
Includes #s 405-8919, 8922, 8923 & 9369.

### Beverage Market
NEW 405-9215 38.99
6-11/16 x 4-3/4 x 3-1/2"
17 x 12 x 9cm

## Industrial

### Truck Garage w/Opening Doors
NEW 405-8540 24.99
6-11/16 x 4-3/4 x 3-1/2"
17 x 12 x 9cm

### Overhead Log Crane
NEW 405-8543 88.99
6-11/16 x 17-5/16 x 7-1/2"
17 x 44 x 19cm

### Trackside Warehouse w/Platform
NEW 405-9214 60.99
15-1/2 x 7-1/2 x 5-11/16"
39.5 x 19 x 14.5cm

### Herbede Factory Complex
NEW 405-9849 366.99
Includes #s 405-9846, 9847 & 9848.

### Sawmill
NEW 405-9852 64.99
24-7/16 x 6 x 4-3/4"
62 x 15 x 12cm

### Sawmill Set
NEW 405-9854 171.99
Includes #s 405-9852, 8543 & 8663.

### Schawarz Concrete Works
NEW 405-9930 84.99
7-1/8 x 5-1/8 x 10-13/16"
18 x 13 x 27.5cm

### Schwarz Concrete Works Double Silos
NEW 405-9931 16.99
3 x 1-3/8 x 6" 7.5 x 3.5 x 15cm

### Schwarz Concrete Works Fuel Tank
NEW 405-9932 13.99
4-3/8 x 4-1/8 x 1-9/16"
11 x 10.5 x 4cm

NEW Herbede Factory Complex 405-9849

NEW Schawarz Concrete Works 405-9930

## Bridges

### Pedestrian Overpass
NEW 405-9330 25.99
8-1/4 x 8-1/4 x 4-3/4"
21 x 21 x 12cm

## 30 YEAR KIBRI ANNIVERSARY SPECIALS

### Containers/Work Offices
405-8627 pkg(6) 32.99

### Wood Yard
405-8804 61.99
13-5/8 x 7-3/16 x 5-3/8"
34 x 18 x 13.5cm

### Euro Transport Co. w/Accessories
405-9205 108.99
12-5/8 x 6-13/16 x 5-3/16"
31.5 x 17 x 13cm

IMPORTED FROM GERMANY BY WALTHERS

**Construction - Cement Works**
**405-9804 36.99**
5-5/16 x 3-3/4 x 8-15/32"
13.5 x 9.5 x 21.5cm

**Gravel Works**
**405-9805 54.99**
10-13/16 x 4-13/16 x 8-3/8"
27 x 12 x 21cm

**Emergency - Fire Station w/2 Trucks**
**405-9207 119.99**
7-3/8 x 6-3/8 x 6-3/16"

## STATIONS & PLATFORMS

**Railway Station**
**405-9315 49.99**
with Next Door Building
6-7/8 x 5-1/2 x 5-5/16,
5-1/8 x 2-3/8 x 2-3/4"
17.5 x 14 x 13.5cm,
13 x 6 x 7cm

**Valley Gatekeeper**
**405-9320 31.99**
5-1/8 x 4-11/32 x 3-3/8";
4-3/4 x 2-3/8 x 2-3/8"
13 x 11 x 8.5cm; 12 x 6 x 6cm

**Shed**
**405-9321 39.99**
12 x 5 x 4-11/32"
30.5 x 12.8 x 11cm

**Original Shed**
**405-9322 44.99**
13-3/16 x 5-11/16 x 4-1/2"
33.5 x 14 x 11.5cm

**Oberried Station Lvon**
**405-9370 62.99**
12-5/8-21-7/8", B 6-5/16",
H 5-1/2" 32-55.5. B 16, H 14cm

**Calw Station**
**405-9371 98.99**
21-11/16 x 6-5/16 x 6-5/16"
55 x 16 x 16cm

**Solis Station**
**405-9372 50.99**
13-3/16 x 5-1/2 x 4-1/2"
33.5 x 14 x 11.5cm

**Bonn Station**
**405-9373 167.99**
38 x 10 x 6-7/8"
99 x 25.5 x 17.5cm

**Frasdorf Station**
**405-9374 61.99**
12-7/16 x 7-5/16 x 4-3/4"
31.5 x 18.5 x 12cm

**Tubbergen Station**
**405-9375 62.99**
17-3/16 x 6-1/8 x 6-1/8"
43.6 x 15.5 x 15.5cm

**Beckingen Station**
**405-9376 44.99**
8-1/4 x 4-1/2 x 3-7/8"
21 x 11.5 x 10cm

**Lehmberg Depot**
**405-9312 153.99**

**Kreutztal Depot**
**405-9313 79.99**

**Feldafing Station**
**405-9366 109.99**
64 x 19 x 17cm

**Furstenberg Station**
**405-9367 83.99**
42 x 15 x 14cm

**Eschborn Station**
**405-9368 53.99**
34 x 13 x 14.5cm

**Schapen Station**
**405-9369 36.99**
15 x 7 x 11cm

**Platform**
**405-9566 56.99**
121.5 x 5.5 x 6cm

**Stgt Rohr Local Station**
**405-9362 32.99**
7-13/16 x 4-3/8 x 3"
19.5 x 11 x 7.5cm

**Barenthal Station**
**405-9363 52.99**
7-13/16 x 5-5/8 x 6"
19.5 x 14 x 15cm

Item listed below is available by Special Order (see Legend Page).

**Modern German Subway (S-Bahn) Stop Nurnberg Street**
**405-9563 54.99**

**Reischelsheim Station**
**405-9492 45.99**
9-1/2 x 5-1/2" 24 x 14cm
Includes an attached freight shed.

**Platform Extensions**

**Detmold**
**405-9543 20.99**

**Platform Extensions**
**405-9545** For #405-9547 & 9555 **16.99**

Item listed below is available by Special Order (see Legend Page).

**Langwied**
**405-9541 20.99**

**Burg-Spreewald Statio**
**405-9509 53.99**
10 x 6-3/8 x 8"
25 x 16 x 20cm
Includes ornate waiting area and decorative turret.

Item listed below is available by Special Order (see Legend Page).

**Station Building**
**405-9491 45.99**

**Dettingen Station**
**405-9507 57.99**
13-5/8 x 4-13/16 x 6"
34 x 12 x 15cm
Upstairs living quarters, passenger waiting room and a freight house are combined into a single building.

kibri®

IMPORTED FROM GERMANY BY WALTHERS

**Langenthal Station**
405-9504 54.99
17-1/8 x 5-1/2" 43 x 14cm

**Sulsberg Platform**
405-9556 42.99
40-5/8 x 1-1/2 x 2-3/8"
101.5 x 3.8 x 6cm
Modern design with large glass shelter and loads of details.

**Hofheim Platform**
405-9558 30.99
26-5/8 x 1-1/2 x 2-3/8"
66.5 x 3.8 x 6cm
Includes "glass" shelter, nonworking lamps, signs and other details.

Item listed below is available by Special Order (see Legend Page).

**Blankenberg Station**
405-9529 155.99
17-7/16 x 6-3/16 x 6-3/16"
43.6 x 15.5 x 15.5cm

## YARD EQUIPMENT & FACILITIES

**Track Construction Building**
405-9323 76.99
9-11/16 x 9 x 8-15/32"
24.5 x 23 x 21.5cm
(vehicles sold separately)

**Track Repair Building**
405-9324 76.99
13-1/2 x 10 x 4-15/16"
34.5 x 25.5 x 12.5cm
(vehicles sold separately)

**Track Repair Railroad Assortment**
405-9325 142.99
9-11/16 x 9 x 8-15/32",
13-1/2 x 10 x 3-15/16"
24.5 x 23 x 21.5cm,
34.5 x 25.5 x 12.5cm
Includes #s 405-9323 & 9324
(vehicles sold separately)

**Railway Administration Building**
405-9314 63.99
21 x 12 x 15cm

**Lineside Building w/Hut**
405-9349 16.99
18 x 6.5 x 8cm

**Bonn Train Shed**
405-9565 66.99
43 x 22 x 13.8cm

**Railroad Tie Track Bumper**
405-9311 9.99
5.5 x 4.5 x 3cm

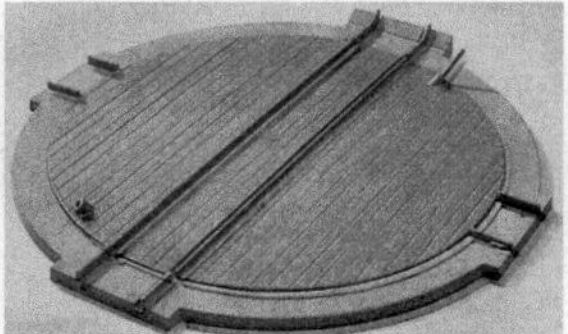

**Turntable**
405-4130 9.99
4-3/4 x 4-3/4" 12 x 12cm

Item listed below is available by Special Order (see Legend Page).

**3-Track Locomotive Shed**
405-9352 62.99
13-5/8 x 7 x 4-13/32"
34 x 17.5 x 11cm

**Railway Office Building**
405-9354 53.99
6 x 6-5/8 x 6-13/64"
15 x 16.5 x 15.5cm

**Single-Stall Engine House**
405-9436 41.99
7-7/8 x 4-3/4" 20 x 12cm

Items listed below are available by Special Order (see Legend Page).

**Railway Office Building w/3-Track Shed**
405-9350 105.99
Includes one each of kits #405-9354 and 9352.

**Locomotive Repair Shed**
405-9438 57.99
10-1/4 x 5-7/8" 26 x 15cm



Item listed below is available by Special Order (see Legend Page).

**Burg-Spreewald Freight Shed**
405-9459 30.99
6 x 4-3/16 x 2-5/8"
15 x 10.5 x 6.5cm

**Freight House w/Loading Dock**

405-9462 79.99
18-1/2 x 5-1/2" 47 x 14cm

**Limited Quantity Available**

**Freighthouse w/Concrete Loading Platform**
405-9302 119.99
20 x 12 x 14-13/16"
50 x 30 x 12cm

## RURAL BUILDINGS

**Farm in Simmentaler**
405-8807 51.99
7-7/8 x 5-1/2 x 3-1/2"
20 x 14 x 9cm

**Farm in Emmental**
405-8808 68.99
7-5/16 x 11-5/8 x 5-5/16"
18.5 x 29 x 13.5cm

**Mountain House in Palu**
405-8809 33.99
6-11/16 x 4-3/4 x 3"
17 x 12 x 7.5cm

**Mountain House in Fextal**
405-8810 36.99
6-1/8 x 5-15/16 x 3-1/2"
15.5 x 15 x 9cm

**Mountain Hotel in Steinbock**
405-8811 33.99
6-5/16 x 5-15/16 x 3-11/16"
16 x 15 x 9.5cm

**Mountain House in Sils**
405-8812 33.99
6-5/16 x 5-1/8 x 3-7/8"
16 x 13 x 10cm

**Barn with Fence**
405-8814 31.99
5-15/16 x 4-3/8 x 3-5/32"
15 x 11 x 8cm

**Large Shed with Small Stables**
405-9098 40.99
5-15/16 x 4-1/8 x 3-3/8"
15 x 10.5 x 8.5cm

**Farm House**
405-9099 83.99
31 x 13.5 x 13cm

kibri®

IMPORTED FROM GERMANY
BY WALTHERS

**Barnhouse**
**405-8045 53.99**
7-13/64 x 5-13/32 x 5-13/64"
18 x 13.5 x 13cm

Items listed below are available by Special Order (see Legend Page).

**Black Forest Farm House**
**405-8074 57.99**
8 x 6" 20.5 x 15cm

**Barn w/Hayloft**
**405-8035 34.99**
2-5/8 x 2-13/64 x 3-5/8"
6.5 x 5.5 x 9cm

## HOUSES

**Poststrabe House**
**405-8735 27.99**
5-1/8 x 3-7/8 x 5-1/2"
13 x 10 x 14cm

**Talstrabe House**
**405-8736 27.99**
6-5/16 x 5-5/16 x 4-15/16"
16 x 13.5 x 12.5cm

**Gruenlicht House**
**405-8737 32.99**
5-15/16 x 5-5/16 x 5-1/2"
15 x 13.5 x 14cm

**Family House with Garage**
**405-8738 36.99**
4-3/4 x 4-3/8 x 4-3/4",
3-5/16 x 1-13/16 x 2"
12 x 11 x 12cm,
8.3 x 4.5 x 5.1cm

**Family House**
**405-8739 36.99**
5-1/2 x 4-3/4 x 3-78",
3-5/16 x 1-13/16 x 2"
14 x 12 x10cm,
8.3 x 4.5 x 5.1cm

**Chalet in Brienz**
**405-8805 29.99**
4-3/4 x 3-1/2 x 2-3/4"
12 x 9 x 7cm

**Chalet in Sigriswil**
**405-8806 33.99**
1-3/8 x 3-7/8 x 3-1/2"
3.5 x 10 x 9cm

**House with White Roof in Davos**
**405-8815 36.99**
3-11/16 x 4-15/16 x 3-11/16"
9.5 x 12.5 x 9.5cm

**House with Red Roof in Davos**
**405-8816 36.99**
5-11/16 x 5-1/2 x 3-11/16"
14.5 x 14 x 9.5cm

**House with Black Roof in Davos**
**405-8817 36.99**
4-3/8 x 4-3/4 x 3-11/16"
11 x 12 x 9.5cm

**Bichelberg House**
**405-8822 39.99**
5-1/2 x 4-1/2 x 4-3/8"
14 x 11.5 x 11cm

**Alpenblick House**
**405-8823 39.99**
5-1/2 x 4-1/2 x 4-3/8"
14 x 11.5 x 11cm

**Half-timbered House in Urach**
**405-8908 40.99**
4-1/2 x 3-3/8 x 5-1/8"
11.5 x 8.5 x 13cm

**Double Half-timbered House in Urach**
**405-8909 48.99**
5-5/16 x 3-11/16 x 5-1/2"
13.5 x 9.5 x 14cm

**House in Nurtinen**
**405-8913 36.99**
4-3/8 x 2-3/4 x 4-1/8"
11 x 7 x 10.5cm

**Bahnhofstrabe House**
**405-8740 22.99**
4-3/8 x 3-15/32 x 4-3/16"
11 x 8.8 x 10.6cm

**Wiesengrund House**
**405-8741 17.99**
3/8 x 3-5/32 x 3-1/2"
11 x 8 x 9cm

Items listed below are available by Special Order (see Legend Page).

**Kreuzstrasse Single Family House w/Shop**
**405-8720 14.99**
3/16 x 3-13/16 x 3-3/16"
10.5 x 9.5 x 8cm

**Untere Aue Single Family House**
**405-8721 14.99**
4-3/16 x 3-13/16 x 2-13/16"
10.5 x 9.5 x 7cm

**Haus Gretel Brick House**
**405-8722 16.99**
11 x 9.5 x 9cm

**Riedelstrabe Duplex House**
**405-8723 16.99**
10.5 x 9.5 x 10cm

**Half-Timbered House**
**405-8728 27.99**
13.7 x 10.5 x 12.8cm

**Detached House**
**405-8729 22.99**
10 x 9 x 10cm

**House w/Gable Roof**
**405-8730 22.99**
10 x 9 x 11cm

**Prinzenhofstrasse House**
**405-8321 30.99**
4 x 4 x 4-5/8"
10 x 10.5 x 11.5cm

## kibri®

IMPORTED FROM GERMANY
BY WALTHERS

### Bussardstrasse House
**405-8323 44.99**
5-13/16 x 4-3/16 x 4-3/16"
14.5 x 10.5 x 10.5cm

Item listed below is available by Special Order (see Legend Page).

### Amseliweg House
**405-8325 50.99**
6-3/16 x 4-3/16 x 3-5/8"
15.5 x 10.5 x 9.5cm

### Villa w/Garage
**405-8331 54.99**
10 x 7 x 3-7/16"
25 x 17.5 x 8.5cm

### Cloppenburg House
**405-8332 34.99**
7-3/16 x 5-3/16 x 3-5/8"
18 x 13 x 9cm

### Elchbaussee Villa w/Garage
**405-8334 36.99**
3-13/32 x 4-3/16 x 3-13/32"
8.5 x 10.5 x 8.5cm

### Verkehrsamt Alpine House
**405-8021 34.99**
4-13/64 x 3-13/64 x 2-13/16"
10.5 x 8 x 7cm

Item listed below is available by Special Order (see Legend Page).

### Ahornboden House
**405-8015 34.99**
4-13/16 x 4-13/16 x 3-13/32"
12 x 12 x 8.5cm

### Lindenstrase Detached House
**405-8710 25.99**
5-5/8 x 4-13/16 x 4"
14 x 12 x 10cm

### Bergwald House
**405-8712 27.99**
4 x 3-5/8 x 4-3/8"
10 x 9 x 11cm

### Amselweg Flats
**405-8713 25.99**
4 x 3-5/8 x 4" 10 x 9 x 10cm

### Factory Street House
**405-8716 27.99**
5-3/16 x 4 x 5-5/8"
13 x 10 x 14cm

### Maybach House
**405-8717 27.99**
6-5/8 x 5-3/16 x 4-5/8"
16.5 x 13 x 11.5cm

### Borgis Street House
**405-8718 32.99**
6 x 5-7/16 x 5-5/8"
15 x 13.5 x 14cm

Item listed below is available by Special Order (see Legend Page).

### Gletscherblick House
**405-8019 36.99**
3-13/16 x 4 x 3-13/32"
9.5 x 10 x 8.5cm

Item listed below is available by Special Order (see Legend Page).

### Stucco House w/Mansard Roof
**405-8160 27.99**
4-13/16 x 4-3/8" 12 x 11cm

### Brewery Guest House
**405-8197 54.99**
9 x 7" 22.5 x 17.5cm

## CITY BUILDINGS

### Sauerland City Hall
**405-8395 49.99**
6-1/8 x 5-1/8 x 10-13/16"
15.5 x 13 x 27.5cm

### Construction Site
**405-8537 62.99**
7-7/8 x 7-1/8 x 7-1/8"
20 x 18 x 18cm

Construction Site 405-8537

Hotel Sonne in Tolz 405-8819

### Post Office in Munderkingen
**405-8734 44.99**
9-1/4 x 4-3/8 x 6-5/16"
23.5 x 11 x 16cm

### Public Library in Tolz
**405-8818 43.99**
5-5/16 x 6-3/8 x 6-5/16"
13.5 x 16.2 x 16cm

### Hotel Sonne in Tolz
**405-8819 48.99**
5-5/16 x 6-3/8 x 6"
13.5 x 16.2 x 15.4cm

### Sportshouse in Tolz
**405-8820 43.99**
5-5/16 x 6-3/8 x 5-11/16"
13.5 x 16.2 x 14.5cm

### Pharmacy in Tolz
**405-8821 39.99**
5-5/16 x 6-3/8 x 4-15/16"
13.5 x 16.2 x 12.5cm

### Country City Hall in Machingen
**405-8906 39.99**
4-1/2 x 4-3/8 x 7-1/8"
11.5 x 11 x 18cm

## kibri®

IMPORTED FROM GERMANY
BY WALTHERS

**City Hall in Urach**
**405-8907 58.99**
5-11/16 x 4-1/8 x 7-7/8"
14.5 x 10.5 x 20cm

**Fountain in Urach**
**405-8910 16.99**
2-3/8 x 2-3/8 x 2-3/4"
6 x 6 x 7cm

**Venezia Cafe in Herrenberg**
**405-8911 40.99**
4-3/8 x 3-1/2 x 4-15/16"
11 x 9 x 12.5cm

**Schaferlies Inn in Urach**
**405-8912 36.99**
3-7/8 x 3-5/32 x 5-1/2"
10 x 8 x 14cm

**City Wall with Framework Tower in Weil**
**405-8914 38.99**
11-7/6 x 3-7/8 x 9-7/8"
29 x 10 x 25cm

**City Wall with Round Tower in Weil**
**405-8915 38.99**
9-7/8 x 5-5/16 x 10-5/8"
25 x 13.5 x 27cm

**City Wall with Small Garden in Weil**
**405-8916 29.99**
13-7/16 x 1-3/8 x 4-1/8"
34 x 3.5 x 10.5cm

**Oberes Tor in Weil**
**405-8917 40.99**
3-1/2 x 2-3/8 x 8-15/32"
9 x 6 x 21cm

**Eckhaus Diplomat Villa in Bonn**
**405-9100 58.99**
5-5/16 x 5-5/16 x 7-1/8"
13.5 x 13.5 x 18cm

**Townhouse with Turret in Bonn**
**405-9101 44.99**
3-7/8 x 5-5/16 x 7-1/8"
10 x 13.5 x 18cm

**Townhouse in the Park in Bonn**
**405-9102 44.99**
3-5/32 x 5-5/16 x 7-1/8"
8 x 13.5 x 18cm

Hot New Products Announced Daily! Visit Walthers Web site at
**www.walthers.com**

**Townhouse with Studio in Bonn**
**405-9103 44.99**
3-1/2 x 5-5/16 x 6-7/8"
9 x 13.5 x 17.5cm

**Firehouse in Bahlburg-Lune**
**405-9210 39.99**
4-3/8 x 4-3/8 x 6-11/16"
11 x 11 x 17cm

**THW Maintenance Garage**
**405-9211 87.99**
28-3/8 x 15-3/4" 72 x 40cm

**Government Building with Railroad Crossing**
**405-9847 81.99**
8-7/8 x 5-15/16 x 11-13/16"
22 x 15 x 30cm

**Government Building with Workshop**
**405-9848 162.99**
10-13/16 x 5-15/16 x 8-7/8"
27 x 15 x 22cm

Venezia Cafe in Herrenberg
405-8911

**Townhouse with Covered Passage**
**405-8375 36.99**
9.3 x 9.3 x 15.5cm

**City Residence**
**405-8377 41.99**
10.5 x 10.5 x 19cm

**Gernsbach City Residence**
**405-8379 50.99**
11 x 12 x 24cm

**Leer Town Hall**
**405-8381 90.99**
30 x 22.5 x 35cm

**Ballhausplatz Townhouse**
**405-8383 60.99**
13.5 x 12 x 18.9cm

**Postplatz Townhouse**
**405-8384 56.99**
13.5 x 12 x 19.4cm

## kibri®

IMPORTED FROM GERMANY BY WALTHERS

**Elbenplatz Townhouse**
**405-8385 56.99**
16 x 16.8 x 18cm

**Schillerplatz Townhouse**
**405-8387 48.99**
16 x 16.5 x 15.5cm

**Sachsenplatz Townhouse**
**405-8388 48.99**
16 x 16.5 x 15.5cm

**Corner Terrace Houses**
**405-8390 60.99**
12 x 12 x 17.5cm

**City Hall w/Fountain**
**405-8900 63.99**
12.5 x 14 x 25cm

**Miltenberg Gatehouse**
**405-8901 41.99**
14 x 13.5 x 16cm

**Half-Timbered House w/Bay Windows**
**405-8902 50.99**
15 x 10 x 20cm

**Half Timbered House On Market Square**
**405-8903 36.99**
10.5 x 8 x 16.5cm

**Half-Timbered Corner House**
**405-8904 54.99**
15 x 13.5 x 16cm

**Town Square Fountain**
**405-8905 16.99**
6 x 6 x 7cm

**Brick Corner Building**
**405-8315 51.99**
5-5/8 x 4 x 4-11/16"
14 x 10 x 11.6cm

Item listed below is available by Special Order (see Legend Page).

**Limburgstrasse Apartment Building**
**405-8365 101.99**
10 x 4-3/16 x 4-15/16"
25 x 10.5 x 12.3cm

**Information Stand**
**405-8618 24.99**

**Alexander Place 7-Story Modern Office Building**
**405-8398 155.99**
8 x 7-3/16 x 9-5/8"
20 x 18 x 24cm

**Europanhaus Tower Block Modern 10-Story Office Building**
**405-8399 197.99**
8 x 7-3/16 x 13-1/8"
20 x 18 x 32.8cm

**Terrace House w/Tower**
**405-8294 86.99**
11 x 9-1/2" 27.6 x 23.5cm

## TANKS & TOWERS

**Gantry Covered Loading Crane**
**405-9316 40.99**
4-3/4 x 1-31/32 x 5-1/8"
12 x 5 x 13cm

**Geislingen/Steige Signal Tower**
**405-9317 40.99**
5-11/16 x 3-1/2 x 5-1/2"
14.5 x 9 x 14cm

**Ottbergen Signal Tower**
**405-9318 35.99**
8-7/8 x 2-3/8 x 5-1/8"
22 x 6 x 13cm

**Langenstein Block Signal Station**
**405-9319 26.99**
3-7/8 x 3-1/2 x 4-15/16"
10 x 9 x 12.5m

**Chimney**
**405-8633** 29cm
**12.99**

**Hamm Signal Tower**
**405-9310 54.99**
28 x 10 x 16.5cm

# kibri

IMPORTED FROM GERMANY BY WALTHERS

**Single Fuel Storage Tank**
**405-9830 32.99**
18 x 14 x 13cm

**Twin Fuel Storage Tanks**
**405-9832 37.99**
26 x 15 x 13cm

**Distribution Filling Tanks**
**405-9834 42.99**
18 x 9 x 8cm

**Allendorf Signal Tower**
**405-9483 49.99**
4-5/8 x 3 x 3-5/8"
11.5 x 7.5 x 9cm

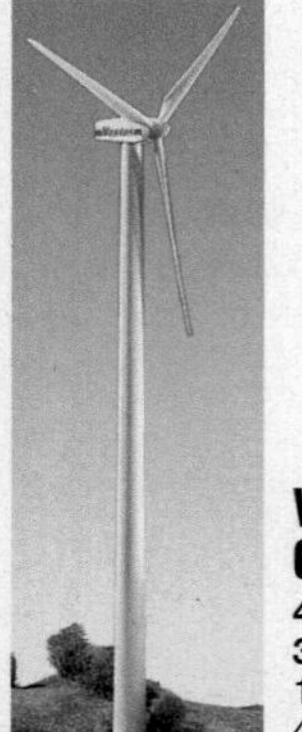

**Wind Generator**
**405-8532**
**36.99**
17-5/8"
44cm high

**High-Tension Electrical Towers**
**405-8533** pkg(4) **32.99**
1-5/8 x 1-5/8 x 11-13/16"
4 x 4 x 29.5cm

**Electric Tower Under Construction Set**
**405-8534 90.99**
Includes one each #405-8533 and 13001.

**Wind Generator Under Construction**
**405-8535 188.99**
Includes one each #405-8532 and 13005.

**Oil Storage Tanks w/Truck Filling Rack**
**405-9835 45.99**
6-3/8 x 3-13/16 x 3"
16 x 9.5 x 7.5cm

**Colbe Signal Tower**
**405-9488 40.99**
6-1/2 x 2-3/4" 16.5 x 7cm

**High Voltage Transmission Towers**
**405-9842** pkg(4) **30.99**

**Transformers**
**405-9844** pkg(2) **24.99**

Items listed below are available by Special Order (see Legend Page).

**Marbach Signal Tower**
**405-9477 34.99**
4-13/16 x 2-3/16 x 4-3/8"
12 x 5.5 x 11cm

**Country Signal Tower**
**405-9486 36.99**

Distribution Filling Tanks 405-9834

Oil Storage Tanks w/Truck Filling Rack 405-9835

Outdoor Chapel w/Accessories 405-9780

## CHURCHES

**Chapel in Saas-Grund**
**405-8813 36.99**
6-11/16 x 4-3/4 x 7-1/8"
17 x 12 x 18cm

**White Church with Red Roof**
**405-9002 44.99**
9-7/8 x 6-5/16 x 7-7/8"
25 x 16 x 20cm

**Church in Chiemgau**
**405-9763 34.99**
11-13/16 x 4-3/8 x 11-13/16"
30 x 11 x 30cm

**Church in Ramsau**
**405-9770 58.99**
11-13/16 x 4-3/8 x 11-13/16"
30 x 11 x 30cm

**Outdoor Chapel w/Accessories**
**405-9780 29.99**
2-3/8 x 2-3/8 x 3-7/8"
6 x 6 x 10cm

**St. Veith Vicarage**
**405-8711 25.99**
5-3/16 x 4 x 5-5/8"
13 x 10 x 14cm

kibri®

IMPORTED FROM GERMANY BY WALTHERS

**Roman Catholic Church**
**405-9760 120.99**
12-1/4 x 7-1/2 x 14-1/8"
31 x 19 x 36cm

With its twin spires, fine brickwork and "stained glass" windows, this is an impressive model from any angle.

**St. Veith Village Church**
**405-9761 32.99**
5-1/8 x 3-3/4 x 10-1/4"
13 x 9.5 x 26cm

**Village Church**
**405-9772 54.99**
8-7/8 x 5-3/4 x 11"
22 x 14.5 x 28cm

Item listed below is available by Special Order (see Legend Page).

**Kuehtzagl Miniature Chapel**
**405-9781 16.99**
2 x 1-5/8" 5 x 4cm

## BUSINESSES

**Nikis Beauty Salon in Dusseldorf**
**405-8391 88.99**
5-1/8 x 6-5/16 x 7-7/8"
13 x 16 x 20cm

**Stadthaus Pizzeria in Dusseldorf**
**405-8392 58.99**
3-1/2 x 3-1/2 x 7-7/8"
9 x 9 x 20cm

**Stadthaus Cafe in Dusseldorf**
**405-8393 51.99**
3 x 3-1/2 x 8" 7.5 x 9 x 20.5cm

**Stadthaus Boutique in Dusseldorf**
**405-8394 44.99**
3-1/2 x 3-1/2 x 6-1/8"
9 x 9 x 15.5cm

**Publishing House**
**405-8382 50.99**
12 x 12 x 17.5cm

**Chemist Shop**
**405-8386 48.99**
13.5 x 12 x 15.5cm

**Food Stand w/Accessories**
**405-8619 24.99**

Item listed below is available by Special Order (see Legend Page).

**Gas Station w/Tow Truck**
**405-8704 116.99**
7-3/16 x 4-13/16 x 2-13/16"
18 x 12 x 7cm

**Modern Gas Pump Island**
**405-8705** SB-Tankstelle **36.99**
7-3/32 x 4-23/32 x 2-3/4"
18 x 12 x 7cm

Roman Catholic Church 405-9760

Container Crane 405-8530

Items listed below are available by Special Order (see Legend Page).

**Forester's Lodge**
**405-8072 45.99**
6 x 4-1/2" 15 x 11.5cm

**Market Place Terrace House**
**405-8296 62.99**
6-1/2 x 6-3/4" 16 x 16.8cm

See What's New and Exciting at
**www.walthers.com**

## INDUSTRIAL

**Over-Track Dockside Crane**
**405-8510 66.99**

**Container Crane**
**405-8530 88.99**
12-13/16 x 6-7/8 x 6-11/16"
32 x 17.5 x 17cm

**Coal Building**
**405-8536 63.99**
10-5/8 x 5-15/16 x 3-11/16"
27 x 15 x 9.5cm

IMPORTED FROM GERMANY
BY WALTHERS

## Garage
**405-9212 68.99**
13-7/16 x 6-7/8 x 4-3/8"
34 x 17.5 x 11cm

## Operating Yard
**405-9213 63.99**
27-9/16 x 23-5/8" 70 x 60cm

## Cement Storage Building
**405-9820 84.99**
7-1/8 x 5-1/8 x 10-13/16"
18 x 13 x 27.5cm

## Brewery in Rheinfelden
**405-9825 96.99**
8-1/4 x 8-7/8 x 10-1/4"
21 x 22 x 26cm

## Storage and Delivery Building in Rheinfelden
**405-9826 96.99**
11-1/4 x 7-11/16 x 6-5/16"
28 x 19.5 x 16cm

## Tower with Machine Shop
**405-9845 99.99**
11-13/16 x 4-3/4 x 14-1/2"
30 x 12 x 37cm

## Motor and Belt
**405-8653 37.99**
For Use with Tower and Machine Shop #9845 (sold separately)

## Herbede Boiler Factory
**405-9846 162.99**
23-5/8 x 4-3/4 x 14-1/2"
60 x 12 x 37cm

## Town House w/Factory Annex
**405-8389 72.99**
13 x 17.5 x 18.5cm

## Thatched Watermill
**405-9157 59.99**
18 x 13.5 x 13cm

## Boiler House w/Chimney
**405-9821 41.99**
18 x 15 x 37cm

## Warehouse
**405-9208 54.99**
29 x 12 x 19cm

## Factory w/Annex
**405-9813 63.99**
28 x 17 x 16cm

## Grunderzeit Factory Building
**405-9814 101.99**
27 x 25 x 22cm

## Toolshed For Lift Truck
**405-9815 45.99**
21.5 x 11 x 8cm

## Interior of Sawmill
**405-9816 90.99**
60 x 17 x 11cm

## Timber Yard & Crane
**405-9817 46.99**
26 x 3.5 x 13.5cm

## Complete Factory
**405-9819 233.99**
Includes 1 each: 9813, 9814, 9815, 9821, 9822

Herbede Boiler Factory 405-9846

Distribution Fuel Depot Set 405-9836

## Distribution Fuel Depot Set
**405-9836 108.99**
Includes 1 each: 9830, 9832, 9834 & 8225 Fencing

## Wooden Toy Factory
**405-9806 138.99**
11-13/16 x 11-13/16 x 6-1/2"
30 x 30 x 16.5cm

## Fratelli Knitwear Factory
**405-9807 181.99**
18-13/16 x 12-13/16 x 6-3/8"
47 x 32 x 16cm

## Zwirn Spinning Mill
**405-9808 30.99**
9-5/8 x 5 x 3-13/16"
24 x 12.5 x 9.5cm

## Siux Shoe Factory
**405-9810 258.99**
23-3/16 x 6-13/16 x 8-13/16"
58 x 17 x 22cm

## Galaxy Spectacle Works
**405-9811 123.99**
8 x 8 x 8-13/16"
20 x 20 x 22cm

Items listed below are available by Special Order (see Legend Page).

## Transformer Station
**405-8500 34.99**
1-13/16 x 1-5/8 x 5"
4.5 x 4 x 12.5cm

kibri

IMPORTED FROM GERMANY BY WALTHERS

**Electric Substation w/Transformer & High-Tension Towers**
**405-8531 136.99**
16 x 8" 40 x 20cm

**Lifting Equipment Set w/Crane**
**405-8101 29.99**
Give any industrial scene a lift with this set of accessories. Includes a small winch-type of crane for the finishing touch.

**Garage**
**405-8136 42.99**
12-5/8 x 4-3/8" 32 x 11cm

**WLZ Farm Supply Elevator/Warehouse**
**405-9408 86.99**
14 x 5-5/8 x 10"
35 x 14 x 25cm

Transform any rural siding into a busy spot with this big farm supply building. It includes a tall grain elevator, offices and a warehouse for all types of agricultural needs.

**Warehouse**
**405-9404 86.99**
49-1/4" 124cm

Items listed below are available by Special Order (see Legend Page).

**Modern Factory Building**
**405-9793 50.99**
10-13/32 x 5 x 3"
26 x 12.5 x 7.5cm

**Electrical Substation**
**405-9840 133.99**
20 x 10-13/32" 50 x 26cm

## BRIDGES & VIADUCTS

**Bascule Bridge**
**405-9708 30.99**
19.5 x 9 x 9cm

**2-Track Steel Footbridge**
**405-9301 54.99**
9-3/16 x 8 x 4-13/16"
23 x 20 x 12cm

## WINDMILLS

**Auf Fehmarn Windmill**
**405-9150 27.99**
12 x 10.5 x 21cm

**Hammarlunda Windmill**
**405-9151 72.99**
14 x 11.5 x 35cm

## LIGHTHOUSES

**Lighthouse On The Elbe**
**405-9152**
Without Light
**22.99**
16cm high

**Lighthouse On Hiddensee**
**405-9153 72.99**
7.6 x 20.6 x 22.5cm

## CASTLES

**Grafeneck Castle**
**405-9001 90.99**
19-3/16 x 11-3/16 x 13-3/16"
48 x 28 x 33cm

**Falkenstein Castle**
**405-9010 136.99**
18-7/8 x 11 x 13"
48 x 28 x 33cm

Built in the 13th century, this castle was restored in 1905 and remains a favorite with tourists. The model is nicely detailed, with rough stone and timber construction.

Rear (For Rail Traffic) 533-8710021

Front (For Trucks) 533-8710022

## INDUSTRIAL

**Warehouse #2**
**533-871002 73.98**
45 x 45 x 5-1/2"
112.5 x 112.5 x 13.8cm

Great structural details like skylights, darkened windows and a front porch area will make this warehouse a standout in any industrial park. Constructed of a high-density, gray-colored styrene, this warehouse features three sizes of freight doors, 30 skylights (molded in white styrene), two sizes of sidewalks and more.

**Background Warehouses**
Place at the back of your layout to create the illusion of more businesses! Each kit (a background model of Warehouse #2, #533-871002, sold separately) includes two side walls and three front walls.

**533-8710021** Rear (For Rail Traffic) **34.98**

**533-8710022** Front (For Trucks) **38.95**
Can service 12 trucks at one time.

## EXPANSION PACKS

Create or grow distinct structures with a variety of wall expansion packs.

**533-871** Rear Walls **18.98**
Contains almost 30" of rear walls and three rail doors.

**533-872** Front Walls **22.98**
Contains almost 20" of front walls and 12 truck doors.

**533-873** Side Walls **18.98**
Contains almost 40" of side walls and four stairs.

**533-874** Entrance Ways **19.98**
Includes one 10" front entrance wall, tinted window glass, front walkway with two sizes of sidewalk, large access door and ramp.

**533-875** Roof Sections pkg(4) **9.50**
Contains four specially cut 10 x 10" sections of .040" thick styrene.

Add a slice of authentic American flavor to any scene with this line of laser-cut kits. The selection includes five different types of barns, plus colorful billboard signs designed especially for them, pre-1950s houses, and a wide selection of historic railroad structures based on prototype plans. Each kit consists of laser-cut wood parts and includes complete instructions.

## NEW PRODUCTS

### Railroad Buildings

#### PRR-Style Wooden Tower

**NEW 511-964HO 44.98**
2 x 3"

Towers like this were common along the Pennsy and this model is similar to one known as Jack's Tower. Kit includes laser-cut shingles, milled wood trim and plywood walls, roof, trim and windows. Tab and slot construction speeds assembly.

#### M&StL Class 1 Station

**NEW 511-980HO 47.98**
This style depot was built at eleven locations along the M&StL in Minnesota, Iowa and South Dakota.

### Rural Building

#### Sugar Shack

**NEW 511-204HO 29.98**
Each spring sap from maple trees is gathered and brought to the Sugar House for processing into maple syrup. Built in 1980 to preserve the history of the process and show visitors how maple syrup is made, the prototype of this structure is located in Geauga County, Ohio.

### Details

#### Picnic Table

**NEW 511-015HO** pkg(6) **8.98**
Great addition to parks, back yards or town squares. Figure shown not included.

#### Grandstand

**NEW 511-020HO** Medium **15.98**
2-1/4 x 5"

This easy to build kit includes two sets of stairs, handrails and a laser-cut jig to speed assembly.

## BARNS

### 16.98 Each

Add color and charm to rural scenes with these models, typical of various styles of barns found on farms everywhere.

#### Type #1

**511-101HO**
2-3/4 x 4-1/4 x 3"

#### Type #2

**511-102HO**
4-1/2 x 4-1/2 x 3"

#### Type #3

**511-103HO**
4-1/2 x 4-1/2 x 2-1/2"

#### Type #4 with Small Addition

**511-104HO**
3-1/4 x 3-1/2 x 2-1/2"

#### Type #5

**511-105HO**
2-3/4 x 3-1/2 x 2-3/4"

## BARN DECALS

### 2.00 ea

Classic, full-color re-creations of actual billboards seen on barns across the Southern states for decades. Sized to fit Barn kits 1-5, sold separately, adaptable to other models.

#### Mail Pouch Tobacco

**511-MPD1HO**
Straight Name – White & Yellow

**511-MPD2HO** Stacked Name – White & Yellow

**511-MPD3HO** Straight Name – Red, Yellow, White

#### Rock City

**511-RCD1HO** See Beautiful Rock City

**511-RCD2HO** ... You See the Best

**511-RCD3HO** ... Atop Lookout Mountain

**511-RCD4HO** ... See 7 States

**511-RCD5HO** See Beautiful Rock City To-Day

#### Kentucky Club Pipe Tobacco

**511-KCD1HO** It Never Tires Your Taste

#### Eat More Possum!

**511-EPD1HO** At Joe's Diner

#### Old Loyalty Cigarette Tobacco

**511-OLD1HO** Big Bag & Papers 5 Cents

## RAILROAD BUILDINGS - B&O

#### Office Building

**511-201HO 12.98**
Designed from actual B&O plans, this small structure is perfect as a yard office or flag stop station, but can easily be adapted for other uses. Finished model is at home on layouts from the late 1800s to the present.

#### Passenger Shelter

**511-901HO 15.98**
This was a standard design found in many locations. This kit includes three benches and features laser-cut plywood, basswood and shingles.

#### Benches

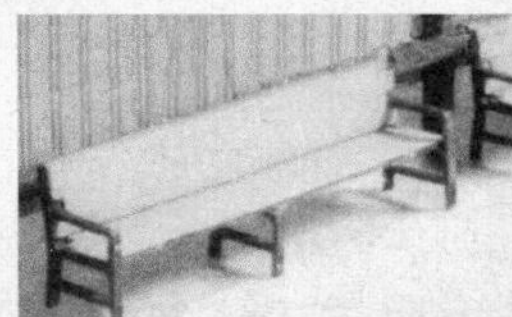

**511-10HO 2.49**

#### Winton Place Station

**511-902HO 48.98**
Laser-cut construction of basswood and plywood parts. Also included are laser-cut roofing, benches and printed, accurate signage.

#### Baggage Building

**511-903HO 13.98**
Designed after the prototype at Winton Place, this kit is the right size to go on just about any layout and can substitute for many different types of buildings. Like the real building, there is a small indent in the wall for the call box used by the local cab company and the remains of what used to be a side baggage door. The kit consists of laser-cut plywood walls, with laser-cut battens that apply in four sheets instead of individually, and laser-cut shingles.

## Octagonal Crossing Shanty

**511-904HO 15.98**
This kit makes a fine looking crossing shanty that will fit just about any layout scene from 1870 to the 1950s. The prototype was located close to the Winton Place Station. The kit is made up of finely laser-cut and engraved plywood of differing thickness, tarpaper roofing and a cast metal smoke pipe.

# RAILROAD BUILDINGS - C&O

## Standard Stations

To reduce costs, many railroads designed standard station buildings. To meet local needs, the basic structure could easily be modified as needed, but common elements (such as doors, trim, window style etc.) were retained to give each a "family" appearance that instantly identified the owner. These authentic replicas of C&O stations present three variations of the same design.

**511-941HO** Standard #1 **44.98**
This medium sized combination station is typical of those built for bigger towns, where more space was needed to handle freight and/or passenger traffic.

**511-942HO** Standard #2 **49.98**
This larger version of the Standard #1 depot features a larger area to handle freight or baggage.

**511-943HO** Standard #3 **39.98**
This small town station has a tiny waiting room, office and freight/baggage room under one roof.

## Small Buildings

**511-944HO** pkg(3) **26.98**
Great details to complete any station or yard scene; set includes outhouse, motor car shed and a small section house.

## Quinnimont Cabin

**511-945HO 54.98**
Quinnimont, West Virginia, was a busy coal hub where the Piney Creek and Laurel subdivisions joined the New River division mainline. This distinctive telegraph and yard office building, known as "QN Cabin" for its telegraph call, survived into the 1980s.

## Durbin Station

**511-946HO 54.98**
Based on the historic station at Durbin, West Virginia.

# RAILROAD BUILDINGS - PRR

## Class A Station

**511-961HO** Standard #3 **46.98**
Measures 16 x 40 Scale Feet

The Class A passenger and freight station, built between 1887 and 1906, was found in scores of towns served by the Pennsy. Laser-cut slate shingles and injection-molded chimney are included, and the kit is engineered with tab and slot construction, along with many other time-saving features.

## Section House

**511-962HO 13.98**
Measures 12' 4" x 16' 4" Scale

The 1st class section house was found almost everywhere along Pennsy rails from 1899 to the end of the railroad. They were used by section gangs to house handcars, track tools, and the foreman's office Laser-cut plywood model faithfully follows the prototype and is based on tracing #8140.

## Watch Box 3-Pack

**511-963HO 16.98**
Each Measures 6 x 6 Scale Feet

Watch boxes were found at street crossings and railroad yards (as shelters from the elements for switchmen and brakemen) from 1887 onward. These very accurate models capture the known variations. Kits contain laser-cut plywood walls, trim, and windows, plus injection-molded smoke jacks and laser-cut tarpaper roofing material. Each kit contains enough parts to make three watch boxes; walls are interchangeable so you can model variations.



# RAILROAD BUILDINGS - ATSF

## Sandhouse

**511-990HO 84.98**
Based on Santa Fe's sand house in San Bernardino, California, as it appeared in the late 40s and 50s after it was expanded and adapted for sanding diesel locos as well as steam. Similar sand houses were used throughout the system, though there were differences in each. The kit includes materials for the main building, the sand bin, and the trestle leading to the bin. Walls are cut from thin plywood that resists warping and still makes for a very durable model. Ladders, windows, glazing, roofing material and a door are cut specifically for the kit. Wire is included for modeling the sanders, which requires some soldering. The kit also includes Tichy nut-bolt-washer castings, light fixtures and a track bumper, along with a custom fire extinguisher casting, made especially for this model.

# RAILROAD BUILDINGS - CENTRAL OF GEORGIA

## Standard Station

**511-910HO 39.98**
This standard Class C style depot was found throughout the south, but is typical of small town depots everywhere. Kit was produced from actual company architectural drawings.

# RAILROAD BUILDINGS

## Universal Building

**511-202HO 29.98**
Measures 24 x 32 scale feet

This building is a natural on any layout in any era. Use it as a local business, a railroad structure, or whatever your heart desires. The two-sided dock can be installed along any wall or converted to a double-length dock.

# COMMERCIAL BUILDINGS

## Rabbit Hash General Store

**511-203HO 39.98**
Based on an actual store founded in 1831 and still in use today, this little retail establishment serves the tiny hamlet of Rabbit Hash, Kentucky. Kit consists of laser-cut plywood, basswood, roofing and injection-molded chimney parts. Two laser-cut benches and stair sets with railings are also included. Two front signs from different eras that are accurate for the building are provided, along with extra advertising signs. The model can be built on stilts like the prototype or flat on the ground. A six-page instruction manual is included along with several reference photos of the prototype.

# PRE-1950s HOUSES

## White Residence

**511-301HO 29.98**
This two-story house features laser-cut, three-tab shingles, windows that can be positioned open or closed, and dormers that can be positioned where you'd like, or left off if desired.

## Greene Residence

**511-302HO 29.98**
Perfect addition to any subdivision, many homes of this type are still standing today.

## NEW PRODUCT

### Bridge

### Merchant Street Bridge

**NEW 493-2009 39.95**
8 x 12 x 2-3/4"

This ornate 1920s-30s concrete highway underpass kit features pedestrian sidewalk passageways. Parts include nine high-density gypsum castings, laser-cut wood sidewalks and printed signage. Railroad equipment and track, figures and vehicles not included.

## YARD FACILITIES

### White Rock Freight House

**493-2201 41.95**
Laser-cut wood structure kit with cast metal scenery parts, corrugated metal roof and wood dock.

### Smith Lake Freight House

**493-2202 36.95**
Laser-cut wood structure kit with cast metal scenery parts, tarpaper roof and wood dock.

### Wood Loading Ramp

**493-2203 11.99**
6-3/4 x 1-3/8 x 5/8"
12.7 x 7.6 x 3.7cm

Laser-cut basswood railroad loading ramp is ideal for use at team tracks and small businesses.

## BUSINESSES

### Jurgen's Junk Yard

**493-2204 55.95**
Building: 5-1/8 x 4-1/2 x 2-3/4"
38.4 x 11.4 x 7cm
Yard Area: 4-1/2 x 5"
11.4 x 12.7cm

A perfect addition along any spur, this detailed kit includes a laser-cut wood Quonset hut with wood facade, corrugated metal roofing material, white-metal castings designed by Monroe Models, resin scrap metal junk pile, fencing and signs. Includes complete assembly and finishing instructions.

## BRIDGES AND VIADUCTS

Monroe Models bridges feature realistic high-density gypsum castings. All are easily assembled using wood glue or ACC. Paint them using any water-based hobby paints. Kits come packaged in strong corrugated-cardboard boxes and include instructions with assembly diagrams.

### Stone Arch Bridge

**493-2001 29.95**
11-1/2 x 7-1/2 x 3"
29.2 x 19.1 x 7.6cm

This single-track bridge features six castings in a highly detailed cut-stone pattern. Includes front and back arch, as well as all four wing walls.

### Concrete Bridge

**493-2002 29.95**
9-1/4 x 3 x 3"
23.5 x 7.6 x 7.6cm

Based on a simple, single-track cast-concrete bridge, this kit features wood details cast in place. Includes three piers, two abutments, bridge deck and road signs for a highway running under the bridge.

### Art Deco Bridge

**493-2003 36.95**
5-1/2 x14 x 3-9/16"
14 x 35.6 x 9.1cm

Featuring Art Deco styling, this double-track bridge includes seven castings; four wing walls, two abutments and the bridge deck. Also included are cast white-metal bridge railings and height restriction warning signs for a road running under the bridge.

### Country Road Bridge

**493-2007 44.95**
Measures: 13-1/2 x 3-1/4 x 4-1/8" 34.3 x 8.3 x 10.5cm;
Underpass Opening:
2-1/2 x 3-5/16" 6.4 x 8.4cm

Laser cut plywood and basswood parts. Includes signs for the bridge and roadway.

### Culverts

Like a bridge, these quality high-density gypsum castings create a "see through" space. Realistic eight scale foot interior included. Single or double track capable.

### Modern Concrete Box Culvert

**493-2021 12.99**
7 x 1-1/2 x 1-1/4"
17.8 x 3.8 x 3.2cm

### Concrete-Arch Culvert

**493-2022 12.99**
5 x 3 x 1-7/16"
12.7 x 7.6 x 3.7cm

Jurgen's Junk Yard 493-2204

Wood Loading Ramp 493-2203

Country Road Bridge 493-2007

Stone Arch Bridge 493-2001

Concrete Bridge 493-2002

Art Deco Bridge 493-2003

## TALL STEEL VIADUCTS

Customized 255-75515

Tall steel viaducts are some of the most spectacular and interesting types of bridges. They are used by railroads to span wide and/or deep valleys, often replacing wooden trestles. The popular HO and HOn3 tall steel viaducts are available in three base kits, three length extension kits, a height extension kit which adds a 4th and 5th story, and a tower kit. The various kits allow you to design and build your own custom bridge of any length from one to five stories high, with full towers or bents, and straight or curved. A new ten-page instruction sheet with over 35 photos and illustrations is included. These bridges are beautifully detailed and are often the centerpiece structure on modelers' layouts.

### 210' Tall Steel Viaduct, Standard Bridge

Three 50' spans, two 30' spans and two towers 29" Long x 10-3/4" High.

**255-75515** HO **51.65**

**255-75517** HOn3 **60.45**
Includes Code 55 Bridge-Flex Trak.

### 150' Tall Steel Viaduct, Standard Bridge

Five 30' spans and and two towers, 20-3/4" Long by 10-3/4" High.

**255-75514** HO **47.25**

**255-75516** HOn3 **53.85**
Includes Code 55 Bridge Flex-Trak.

### 150' Tall Steel Viaduct, Light Weight w/Bents

Three 50' spans and two three-story bents, 20-3/4" Long by 10-3/4" High.

Customized 255-75540

**255-75513** HO **29.65**

**255-75540** HOn3 **36.25**
Includes Code 55 Bridge Flex-Trak.

### 210' Tall Steel Viaduct, Low Bridge w/Bents

Seven 30' spans, six 1, 2 or 3-story bents. 29" Long by 10-5/8", 7-1/2" or 4-1/4" High.

**NEW 255-75550** HO **55.95**

**NEW 255-75551** HOn3 **64.75**
Includes Code 55 Bridge Flex-Trak.

### Tall Steel Viaduct Length Extension Kits

Use these kits to add length to your Tall Steel Viaduct bridge kits to form custom bridge lengths. The Bridge Connector kits are used for connecting two Tall Steel Viaduct bridge kits together to form a bridge more than twice as long.

**255-75524** HO 80' Length Extension **24.15**
One 50' span, one 30' span and one tower.

**255-75525** HO 60' Length Extension **21.95**
Two 30' spans and one tower

**255-75526** HO 30' Bridge Connector **17.55**
One 30' span and one tower.

**255-75527** HOn3 80' Length Extension **28.55**
One 50' span, one 30' span and one tower. Includes Code 55 Bridge Flex-Trak.

**255-75528** HOn3 60' Length Extension **26.35**
Two 30' spans and one tower. Includes Code 55 Bridge Flex-Trak.

**255-75529** HOn3 30' Bridge Connector **19.75**
One 30' span and one tower. Includes Code 55 Bridge Flex-Trak.

### Tall Steel Viaduct Height Extension Kit

**255-75546 25.25**
Adds one or two stories to base of two towers. 3-1/4 or 6-1/2" height increase. For use with HO and Hon3 Scales.

### Tall Steel Viaduct Tower or Two Three-Story Bents

**255-75169** HO-HOn3 **13.15**
4-1/2 x 4-1/2" Base x 10" High

## THROUGH-GIRDER BRIDGES

These kits contain all the details and interior structure found on prototype bridges such as lateral bracing, crossbeams with knee braces, stringers, rivet plates, bridge shoes and extensive molded-in detail including rivet heads. HO Code 83 Bridge Flex-Trak is included with each kit. the bridges can be modeled with square or rounded ends on the girders—both types are found on the prototype. They can also be modeled as open-deck and ballasted-deck bridges using the "concrete" deck included in each kit. Additional Through-Girder Bridges and/or Deck Girder Bridges can be combined, along with Bridge Supports #255-80175 to form longer custom bridges.

### 50' Single Track

**255-75520 13.95**
6-7/8" Long x 3/4" Track Height

### 50' Double Track

**255-75521 20.95**
6-7/8" Long x 3/4" Track Height

### 100' Single Track

**255-75522 23.75**
Includes bridge support legs, 13-3/4" Long x 3-7/8" Track Height

### 100' Double Track

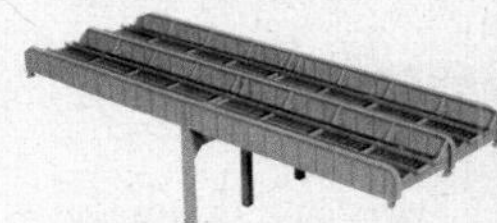

**255-75523 38.60**
Includes bridge support legs, 13-3/4" Long x 3-7/8" Track Height

### 110' Combination Bridge

**255-75530 35.15**
Two 30' Deck Girder spans, one 50' Through-Girder span and two bridge supports, 15" Long x 3-7/8" Track Height

### 160' Combination Bridge

**255-75532 42.45**
Two 30' Deck Girder spans, two 50' Through-Girder spans and three bridge supports, 22" Long x 3-7/8" Track Height

### Bridge Support

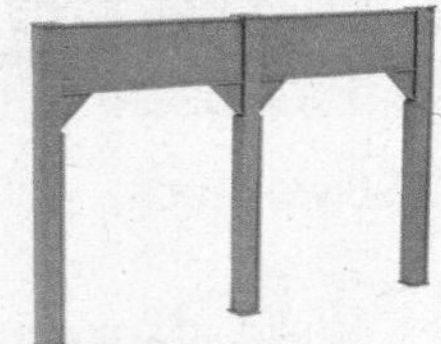

**255-80175 9.70**
Kit makes two single-track or one double-track support, 3-3/8" high.

## MODERN STRUCTURES

The Modern Structures series of buildings represents typical modern metal buildings used for light manufacturing or warehousing. Buildings are easy to assemble. pre-colored injection-molded kits. Scored lines molded on the back side of wall panels allow for optional window and door locations. Plastic and white-metal detail parts are included.

### Murphy Manufacturing

**255-55004 18.20**
4-1/8" Wide x 9-3/8" Long

### Transworld Truck Terminal

**255-55005 20.95**
4-1/8" Wide x 13-3/8" Long

### Petroff Plumbing Supply

**255-55006 20.95**
8-3/8" Wide x 9-3/8" Long

## CITY VIADUCTS

City viaducts were constructed in many American cities in the early twentieth century where elevated track was needed by railroads or mass transit systems in congested city areas. Many of the prototype viaducts are still in use today making these HO kits suitable for turn of the century through modern-era layouts. City Viaduct kits follow prototype construction by incorporating scale-size moldings of the lattice work, angle irons, cross beams, lateral bracing, X bracing and many rows of rivet heads. All kits fit HO track.

Customized 255-75512

### 90' Single Track

**255-75509 25.20**
Three 30' spans and one tower, 12-3/8" Long x 4-1/8" High

### 90' Double Track

**255-75510 39.95**
Six 30' spans and one tower, 12-3/8" Long x 4-1/8" High

### 150' Single Track

**255-75511 39.95**
Five 30' spans and two towers, 20-5/8" Long x 4-1/8" High

### 150' Double Track

**255-75512 61.55**
Ten 30' spans and two towers, 20-5/8" Long x 4-1/8" High

### City Viaduct Tower

**255-75168 8.35**
4-3/8" Long x 2-1/4" Wide 3-3/8" High

## SMALL BUSINESSES

Small buildings are some of the most common structures found on model railroad layouts. Their small size adds "clutter" and they are easily modified to a different look. Plastic and white-metal detail parts are included.

### Groger's Grocery

**255-70604 18.20**
5" Wide x 5" Long including lean-to and boardwalk. Includes signs, awning, lean-to and clutter parts.

### Small Shed

**255-70605 6.35**
1-3/8" Wide x 2-1/8" Long

## RURAL BUILDING

### Outhouse

**255-80172** Plastic Kit **3.20**
Figure not included.

## DECK GIRDER BRIDGES

Deck girder bridges are used by prototype railroads more frequently than any other type of bridge. They span everything from ditches to small rivers. These kits include X braces, lateral braces, rivet plates, bridge shoes and extensive molded-in detail including rivet heads. The Open-Deck bridges include Bridge Flex-Trak while the modeler's regular ballasted track runs across Ballasted-Deck Bridges.

255-75506/255-75505

255-75501/255-75502

### Deck Girder Bridges, Open Deck

**255-75505** HO 85' **14.95**
11-5/8" Long x 1-5/8" High
Includes Code 83 Bridge Flex-Trak

**255-75501** HO 50' **10.25**
6-7/8" Long x 1-1/4" High
Includes Code 83 Bridge Flex-Trak

**255-75502** HO 30' **9.25**
4-1/8" Long x 1" High
Includes Code 83 Bridge Flex-Trak

**255-75503** HOn3 50' **10.25**
6-7/8" Long x 1-3/8" High
Includes Code 55 Bridge Flex-Trak

**255-75504** HOn3 30' **9.25**
4-1/8" Long x 1-3/8" High
Includes Code 55 Bridge Flex-Trak

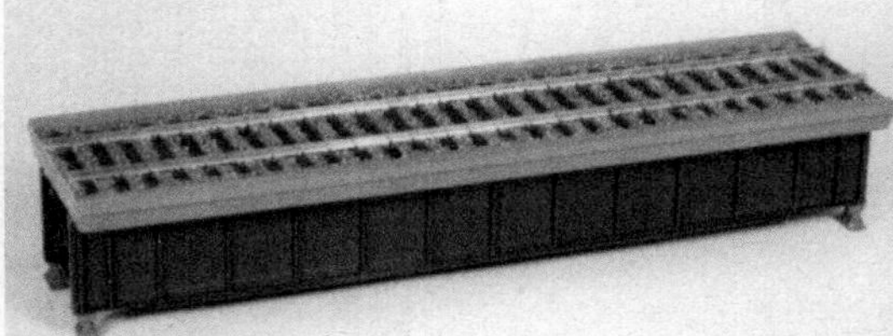

255-75507 Track Not Included

### Deck Girder Bridges, Ballasted Deck

**255-75506** HO 85' **15.70**
11-5/8" Long x 1-5/8" High
Includes concrete deck.

**255-75507** HO 50' **10.75**
6-7/8" Long x 1-3/8" High

**255-75508** HO 30' **9.70**
4-1/8" Long x 1-1/8" High

By Miller Engineering

Capture the look of classic American buildings for your layout with this series of easy-to-build kits. Models consist of very fine photo-etched brass and stainless steel parts that assemble in layers, producing detailed 3-D structures. Each comes complete with step-by-step, easy to follow instructions. Figures, vehicles and other details shown in photos are not included.

## BUSINESSES

### The Parkway Diner

**502-871001 69.95**
6-5/16 x 4-13/32" 15.7cm x 11cm

A great detail for busy streets from the 40s to the present. Made of real stainless steel with art deco style, just like the prototypes!

### Parkway Diner Interior Details & Lighting Kit

**502-871015 39.95**
Transform the Parkway Diner (502-871001, sold separately) with this exciting accessory. Includes a full interior complete with counter, tables, benches, stools and more!

### City Scoop

**502-871002 58.95**
3-5/8 x 3-3/4" 9.3cm x 9cm

The perfect place to spend those hot summer nights, hanging out with the classic car club or your buddies from school. Photo-etched stainless steel construction provides super realism. Colorful sign decals are included for the finishing touch.

### Gulf Gas Station

**502-879300 89.95**
6-1/8 x 3-5/8" 9 x 15.2cm

Turn any empty corner into a superdetailed scene with this art deco style station. Licensed, HO Scale replica of the original Gulf design, reproduced in photo-etched brass. Complete with authentic decals and painting tips.

### Gulf Gas Station Lighting Kit

**502-879310 39.95**
Kit includes six custom-cut electroluminescent lamps for lighting the interior and all signs of the Gulf Gas Station (#879300), sold separately.

### Pink Elephant Car Wash

**502-879600 89.95**
8-1/8 x 5" 20.3 x 12.5cm

This 1950s era car wash is produced from etched stainless steel and is complete with decals and painting tips.

### Gazebo

**502-871004 29.95**
A shady spot in the backyard of the "Victoria" (sold separately) or an attraction in a small city park. This Victorian-era structure features turned brass posts for more realism.

## HOUSES

### The Victoria

**502-876060 129.95**
4-13/16 x 3-13/16"
12 x 9.5cm

Kit is produced from photo-etched brass and includes turned brass porch posts and easy-to-follow detailed instructions.

## CITY DETAILS

### Garbage Can Kit

**502-871400** pkg(2) **7.95**
Contains parts to build two garbage cans.

### Newspaper Stand Kit

**502-871410** pkg(2) **9.95**
Kit contains one each of the newspaper stands pictured. Figure not included.

### Picnic Tables

**502-879440** pkg(4) **11.95**
The perfect detail for a backyard or a park scene. Includes parts for four picnic tables.

### Phone Booth Kit

**502-879550 8.95**

## CATALOG

**502-1 3.00**
Handy book includes full-size printouts of all simulated neon signs and dimensions for all structures.

## BRIDGE & TRESTLE KITS

Skill Level 1 kits are designed for first-time builders (a few parts need cutting and fitting) and can be assembled with basic hobby tools. Skill Level 2 kits are for builders with some experience shaping, cutting or fitting parts and include assembly jigs to simplify some steps. All kits feature micro-cut basswood parts, many of which are precut and/or shaped. A variety of details are included. Each kit comes with a multi-page, step-by-step instruction manual with tips for installing the finished model on your layout, as well as customizing ideas.

SKILL 1 LEVEL

**Silver Creek Timber Bridge**
**472-3050 22.99**
10-3/8 x 2-9/16 x 2" 26.3 x 6.5 x 5.1cm

SKILL 2 LEVEL

**Canyon City Trestle**
**472-3051 49.99**
14 x 6 x 3-3/8" 35.5 x 15.2 x 8.6cm

SKILL 2 LEVEL

**Eagle Pass Truss Bridge**
**472-3053 44.99**
11-7/8 x 2-5/32 x 3-1/2" 30.1 x 5.4 x 8.9cm

SKILL 2 LEVEL

**Fox River Thru-Truss Bridge**
**472-3054 54.99**
11-7/8 x 2-5/32 x 3-1/2" 29.7 x 5.4 x 8.8cm

*Information* STATION

### Adding Lights Inside Structures

Few things add life to your buildings like lights. A warm glow from a farmhouse or bright lights of a warehouse interior give your scenes realism and implied action.

Adding lights to buildings is easy, and these tips can make illuminated structures look better.

Paint the interior black or a dark color to reduce or eliminate light showing through the plastic.

Place the lights high in the ceiling. Most interiors have overhead lighting; especially commercial or industrial buildings. By putting the lights above the windows, you can't see the bulbs and won't have to model individual fixtures.

Light blocks for simulating darkened rooms can be made by placing black or dark colored paper or cardboard behind a few windows. On multi-story buildings, you may have to make "floors" with additional sheets of paper.

Don't forget exterior lights on buildings. Industrial buildings often have lamps mounted above doors and houses have porch lights. Commercial buildings such as storefronts and train stations may also have illuminated signs including neon signs hanging in the windows.

Make sure bulbs don't make contact with building walls or roof sections. Some bulbs give off enough heat to melt or warp plastic parts.

Easy-to-build kits include pre-colored plastic parts and step-by-step instructions. Built-ups are lighted and include two figures.

# BUILDING KITS & BUILT-UPS

## Stations & Platforms

**Covered Passenger Walkway**
**490-402** Four-track Kit **22.98**

**Switching Station**
**490-403** Kit **18.99**

**Station & Freight Shed**
**490-427** Kit **26.98**

**490-570** Built Up **33.98**

**Whistle Stop Station**
**490-444** Kit **16.98**

**490-562** Built Up **20.98**

**Blue Coal Depot**
4 x 6-1/2" 10.2 x 16.5cm

**490-453** Kit **25.98**

**490-673** Built Up **29.98**

**Two Station Platforms**
**490-478** pkg(2) **21.98**
Each: 2 x 14" 5.5 x 36cm

**2-Story Railroad Station**
**490-480** **26.98**
9-1/2 x 5" 24 x 12.5cm

**Port Chester Station**
**490-542** Kit **24.98**
5-3/8 x 12-3/8"
13.7 x 31.6cm

**Silverado Station**
**490-605** Kit **24.98**
4-1/4 x 6-1/2" 11 x 16cm

**Redwood Station**
**490-564** Built Up **31.98**

## Yard Equipment & Facilities

**3 Trackside Buildings**
**490-437** Kit **18.99**

**490-643** Built Up **17.98**

**Trackside Maintenance**
**490-408** Kits pkg(3) **18.98**
Storage Shed:
1-3/4 x 2" 4.5 x 5.1cm

Transformer Box:
1-1/4 x 2" 4.5 x 5.1cm

Shed w/Extension:
3 x 8" 7.6 x 20.3cm

**Loco Maintenance Building**
**490-553** Kit **23.98**

**490-629** Built Up **31.99**

**Offices and Shed**
**490-650** Built Up **26.99**

**Tank Crew Office & Union Building**
**490-697** Built Up **27.98**

## Rural Buildings

**Hunter's Log Cabin**
**490-434** Kit **13.98**

**490-640** Built Up **16.98**

**Old Storage Shed**
**490-435** Kit **12.98**

**490-641** Built Up **16.98**

**Lumber Shed**
**490-436** Kit **15.98**

**490-642** Built Up **17.98**

New Arrivals Updated Every Day! Visit Walthers Web site at

**www.walthers.com**

**Ranger Lookout w/Trees**
**490-438** Kit **12.98**

**490-644** Built Up **16.98**

**Fisherman's Cabin**
**490-439** Kit **13.98**

**490-645** Built Up **16.98**

**Deluxe Barn Kit**
**490-482** Kit **21.99**

**490-592** Built Up **28.98**

**Barn**
4-5/16 x 5-1/2" 11 x 14cm

**490-601** Kit **21.99**

**490-567** Built Up **27.98**

## Houses

**Rooming House**
**490-426** Kit **20.98**
6-1/4 x 6-1/2" 16 x 16.5cm

**Farm House**
**490-433** Kit **22.98**
3 x 7" 7.7 x 17.7cm

**Delta Fraternity House**
**490-456** Kit **24.98**
3-1/2 x 7" 9 x 17.5cm

**2 Twin Cape Cod Houses**
**490-479** Kits pkg(2) **21.98**
3-3/4 x 5" 9.5 x 12.5cm

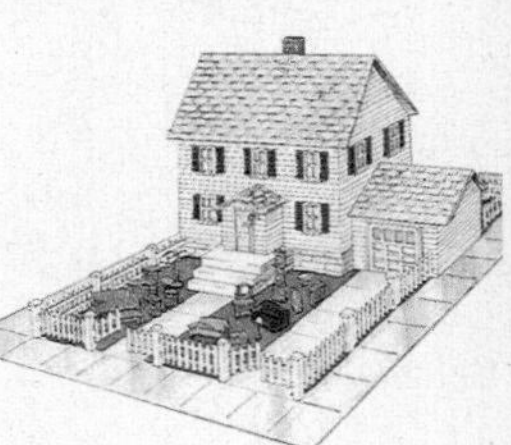

**Moving In House**
**490-484** Kit **21.99**
7-1/2 x 9" 19 x 23cm

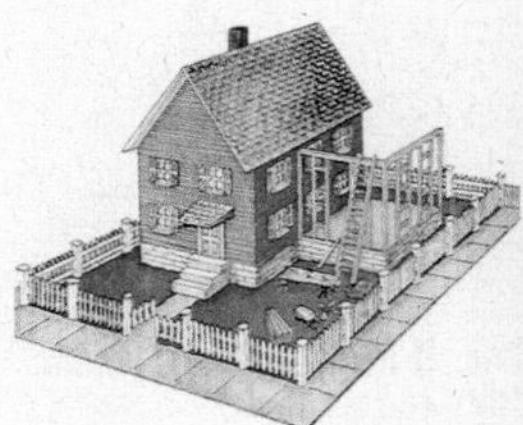

**The Grabitski House**
**490-485** Kit **21.99**
7-1/2 x 9" 19 x 23cm

**Mr. Rogers' House**
**490-585** Built-Up **24.98**
4 x 4-1/2" 10.2 x 11.4cm

**Haunted House**
**490-486** Kit **21.99**

**490-586** Built Up **24.98**
7-1/2 x 9"  19 x 23cm

**Grandma's House**
7-1/2 x 9"  19 x 23cm

**490-487** Kit **21.99**

**490-587** Built Up **24.98**

**Sullivan House**
7-1/2 x 9"  19 x 23cm

**490-488** Kit **21.99**

**490-588** Built Up **24.98**

**Mr. & Mrs. Diggers House**
**490-489** Kit **21.99**
7-1/2 x 9"  19 x 23cm

**Simpson's House**
**490-589** Built Up **24.98**

**Bella's Farm House**
**490-490** Kit **21.99**
7-1/2 x 9"  19 x 23cm

**Jordan's House**
**490-590** Built Up **24.98**

## City Buildings

**Town Hall**
**490-400** Kit **27.98**

**Fire House w/2 Engines**
**490-409** Kit **21.98**
4-1/2 x 5-1/4"  11.5 x 13.5cm

**Urban Renewal Project**
**490-579** Built Up **26.98**
4-1/2 x 9-1/4"  11.4 x 23.5cm

**Pure Water Supply Co.**
**490-415** Kit **23.98**

**490-563** Built Up **28.98**

**Building On Fire**
**490-569** Built Up **28.98**
2-3/4 x 6"  7 x 15.2cm

**Western Union Office**
**490-452** Kit **25.98**
4-1/2 x 6-1/2"  11.5 x 16.5cm

**Marryin' Sam's Chapel**
**490-457**  **24.98**
3-1/2 x 7"  8.8 x 17.8cm

**IRS on Fire**
**490-470** Kit **51.98**

**Ace Hardware**
**490-577** Built Up **27.98**
3-1/2 x 7"  9 x 17.7cm

**Building Under Demolition**
**490-469** Kit **24.98**
4-1/2 x 8-1/2"  11.5 x 21cm

**Cathy's Flower Shop**
**490-545** Kit **17.98**
3-3/8 x 7-3/8"  8.6 x 18.9cm

**Globe News & Printing**
6-3/4 x 9-1/4"  17 x 23.5cm

**490-477** Kit **21.98**

**490-578** Built Up **27.98**
Hand-weathered.

**Little Red School House**
**490-604** Kit **20.98**
3-1/2 x 5-1/2"  8.9 x 14cm

**Building Interior & Lighting Kit**
**490-602**  **15.98**
Includes three interior lights with wire, sockets and bulbs, plus assorted furniture.

## Tanks & Towers

**Water Tank w/Shed**
Tank: 3-1/2 x 4"  9 x 10.4cm
Shed: 1-3/4 x 2"  4.5 x 5.4cm

**490-428**  Kit pkg(2) **19.98**

**490-561** Built Up **23.98**

**Interlocking Tower**
**490-481** Kit **18.98**

**Trackside Yard Tower**
**490-551** Kit **13.98**

**490-627** Built Up **16.99**

**Industrial Water Tower**
**490-552** Kit **13.98**

**490-628** Built-Up **16.99**

**3500-Gallon Tanks**
**490-1455** pkg(4) **10.98**

**Motorized Windmill**
**490-404** Kit **39.98**

**Radio Tower**
**490-696** Built Up **27.98**

## Businesses

**Johnny's Shrimp Shack**
**490-401** Kit **14.98**

**Billy's Auto Body**
**490-414** Kit **21.98**

**490-575** Built Up **26.98**
5 x 6"  12.5 x 15.4cm

**Bob's Hot Dog Stand**
2-1/2 x 4-1/4"  6.5 x 10.8cm

**490-441** Kit **17.98**

**490-573** Built Up **19.98**

**Citibank 27.98 ea**
3-5/8 x 8-1/4"  9.2 x 21cm

**490-675** Built Up

## Industrial

**Hoffa Cement Factory**
490-297 Kit 26.99
490-670 Built Up 37.98

**Hoffa Sand Bunker**
490-299 Kit 21.99
490-671 Built Up 30.99

**Grading Tower**
490-301 Kit 26.99
490-647 Built Up 37.99

**Silo & Transporter**
490-302 Kit 24.98

**Unloading Crane**
490-303 Kit 24.98

**Grain Depot**
490-305 Kit 26.98

**Grain Silos**
490-307 Kit 26.99

**Tank Filling Station**
490-309 Kit 19.98

**Oil Facility Office**
490-310 Kit 19.98

**Fertilizer Bunker w/Fertilizer**
490-313 Kit 20.98

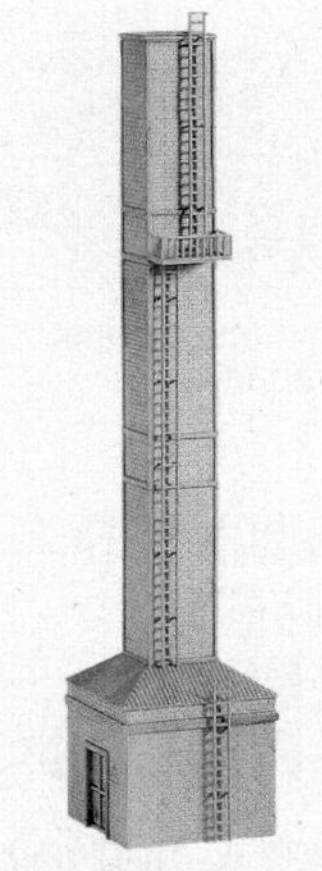

**Factory Smoke Stack**
490-312 Kit 15.98

**Old Coal Mine**
490-316 Kit 38.98

**Coaling Station**
6 x 6"  15.3 x 15.3cm
490-410 Kit 27.98
490-560 Built Up 34.98

**Interstate Freight**
3-1/2 x 7"  8.4 x 18cm
490-411 Kit 21.98
490-574 Built Up 26.98

**City Power Station No. 15**
490-416 Kit 19.98

**Natural Gas Supply Co.**
490-417 Kit 20.98

**Builders Depot**
490-418 Kit 21.98

**Durkin Pickle Factory**
490-576 Built Up 26.98

**Rail Crane**
490-424 Kit 19.98
3 x 9-1/2"  7.7 x 24cm

**Power Station**
490-443 Kit 16.98
490-580 Built Up 21.98

**Brewery**
490-451 Kit 27.98

**Heinz Pickle Factory**
490-465 27.98
5-1/2 x 12"  14 x 30.5cm

**Dual Loco Shed**
490-541 Kit 23.98

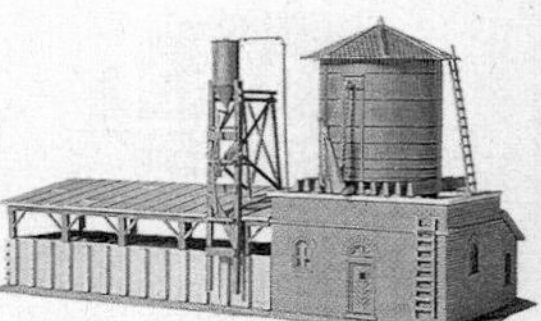

**Steam Locomotive Supply Depot**
490-617 Kit 23.98
490-572 Built Up 31.98

**Lumber Yard**
4 x 6"  10 x 15cm
490-407 Kit 24.98
490-674 Built Up 28.98

## Bridges & Viaducts

**Trestle Bridge 15-Piece Set**
490-79 Kit 5.50

**Over & Under Pier Set**
490-99 Kit 6.50

**Truss Bridge**
490-102 Kit 6.50

**Blinking Bridge**
490-111 Kit 7.50

**High Trestle Bridge**
490-112 Kit 11.98

### Girder Bridges 6.50 ea
Models are fully assembled with realistic, brown painted ties, colorful railroad logos and two figures.

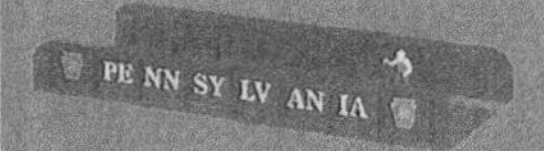


490-121

**490-120** ATSF

**490-121** PRR

**490-123** Amtrak

**490-122** Unlettered

### Loading Bridge
**490-300** Kit **26.99**

**490-646** Built Up **37.99**

### Railroad Signal Bridge
**490-419** Kit **7.98**
4 x 5-1/2" 10.2 x 14cm

### Loading Bridge
**490-646** Built Up **37.99**

# KITS W/FIGURES

## Stations & Platforms

### Station Platform
**490-616** Kit **20.98**

**490-583** Built Up **24.98**

## Yard Equipment & Facilities

### Twin Loco Shed
**490-611** Kit **23.98**
10 x 6-13/16" 25.7 x 17.4cm

## Churches

### Church
7-1/2 x 9" 19 x 22.9cm

**490-613** Kit **21.98**

**490-582** Built Up **24.98**

## Tanks & Towers

### Deluxe Gas Tank Kits 24.98 ea
**490-618** Shell

**490-619** Gulf

# BUILT-UPS

## Houses

### Ma's Place
**490-672 27.98**

## Military

### Quonset Hut
**490-669** With Vehicles and Figures **27.98**

### Tents 25.00 ea
With vehicles and figures

**490-665** Olive

**490-666** Desert

### U.S. Army Water Tower
**490-632 15.98**

### Army Motor Pool
**490-667 37.98**

### Army Munition Depot w/2 Minitanks
**490-668 37.98**

# ASSEMBLED & LIGHTED BUILDINGS W/2 FIGURES

## Stations & Platforms

### Durango Station Platform
**490-566 29.98**
4-1/4 x 6-3/4" 10.6 x 16.8cm

### Chester Station
4 x 7-3/4" 11 x 9.7cm.

**490-676** Built Up **25.98**

### Farmingdale Freight Station
**490-694** Built Up **28.98**

## Rural Buildings

### Fruit Stand
5 x 5" 12.5 x 12.5cm.

**490-682** Built Up **24.98**

## City Buildings

### Post Office
**490-677** Built Up **33.98**

### Rileys Building
2-3/4 x 6" 7 x 15cm

**490-680** Built Up **28.98**

### Leviton Office
**490-769 26.98**

### Nick's Pickles
3-1/2 x 6" 9 x 15.2cm

**490-681** Built Up **29.98**

### Embassy
**490-684** Built Up **32.98**

## Businesses

### Aces Hardware/Barber Shop
**490-678** Built Up **37.98**

### Grocery & Antiques
**490-679** Built Up **37.98**

### Shell Station w/Tanker
**490-688** Built Up **38.98**

## Industrial

### Dual Loco Shed
**490-685** Built Up **32.98**

## Houses

### Sinatra's House
**490-584 24.98**
2-5/8 x 5-1/2" 6.7 x 14cm

### House On Fire
**490-568 27.98**

## Tanks & Towers

490-630 490-631

### Water Tower
**490-630 13.98**

### Search Tower
**490-631 13.98**

### Deluxe Shell Tank Ltd.
**490-565 36.98**
6-1/2 x 6-1/2" 16.2 x 16.2cm

### Gulf Gas Tank
**490-571 36.98**

### Signal Tower
**490-683** Built Up **23.98**

## Assembled & Lighted Buildings w/2 Figures & Truck

**Exxon Station**
**490-689 38.98**

**Thru-Way Truck Stop**
**490-767 37.98**

**D&S Wire & Cable Co.**
**490-770 34.98**

**American Foundry Co.**
**490-771 37.98**

**West End Shopping Center**
**490-772 37.98**

MODEL RAILSTUFF
REALITY BY THE CARLOAD

Add a finishing touch of realism to your railroad scenes with these detailed, one-piece castings. Each is hand-cast from a very strong gypsum material that picks up fine details much like dental plaster. Items are handpainted to bring out the many fine details.

## Brick/Tile Kilns 37.80 ea

5" 12.5cm diameter

**506-650** Red

**506-660** Yellow

## Coke Ovens

### "Beehive" Or "Bell" Style

2-1/4 x 1-3/8" 5.6 x 3.4cm

**506-630** Intact pkg(4) **32.35**

**506-640** Collapsed pkg(4) **31.86**

### Oven Fronts Only pkg(2) 9.72 ea

Use to model early battery type ovens.

**506-580** Closed

**506-590** Open

## Brick Chimneys

One-piece casting eliminates problems of hiding seams so common with multiple-piece plastic and resin kits. Great detail for any small industry. Each chimney stands 8-1/2" 21.2cm tall.

### Square w/Ladder 31.86 ea

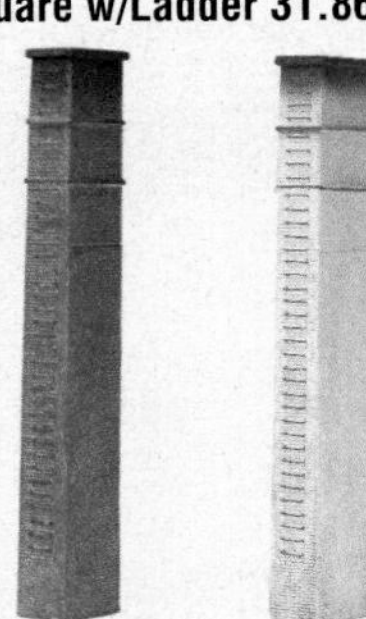

**506-670** Red

**506-680** Yellow

### Round 24.30 ea

**506-840** Red

**506-850** Yellow



## N.J. INTERNATIONAL

Easy-to-build kits feature plastic and etched-metal parts as noted.

### Tanks & Towers

**525-1970** Oil Derrick **9.99**

### Maintenance Platform Kits

With etched see-through stainless steel walkways and stair treads.

**525-4020** 68' Platform pkg(2) **21.95**

**525-4021** 102' Platform pkg(2) **27.95**

**525-4022** 136' Platform pkg(2) **31.95**

**525-4023** 68' Handrail Kit **4.99**

**525-4024** 68' Walkway **10.99**

## OREGON RAIL SUPPLY

# STATIONS & PLATFORMS

### Menomonee Falls Depot

**538-501 44.95**
16 x 5" 40.6 x 12.7cm

Easy-to-build plastic kit, molded in color.

*Information* STATION

### That Family Look

On many railroads, building, locomotive, car design and paint scheme standards were applied to the entire system. In many places, just standing along the tracks you could tell which railroad you were on without ever seeing a train. Examples include the Western Pacific's turquoise-painted lineside signals and relay boxes; on the Milwaukee Road's many "D" series depots and matching speeder sheds, and Santa Fe's station signs that featured mineral red post and a white sign with black lettering supported by curved metal brackets.

Buildings on many lines were built to standard plans and architectural style, with only the size of the structure tailored to fit the location and use. Stations, towers, crossing shanties, dispatcher telephones and speeder sheds usually all wore the same color scheme. Through standardization, the railroads cut costs through volume purchases of materials and reduced design and planning time. For modelers and observers, the result was an unmistakable family look to most railroads' rights-of-way.

Adding matching structures along your line, along with other "system unique" details, makes adding a "railroad" feeling to your layout easy. Just place buildings with "company" color schemes, such as Cornerstone Series® Built-ups railroad structures, all up and down the length of your railroad. Using more than one of each building will enhance the family look of your road's right-of-way scenes.

IMPORTED FROM GERMANY BY WALTHERS
All structures are molded in appropriately colored plastic.

## NEW PRODUCTS

### All-In Diorama Sets

Diorama sets include decorated molded-foam base, figures and accessories.

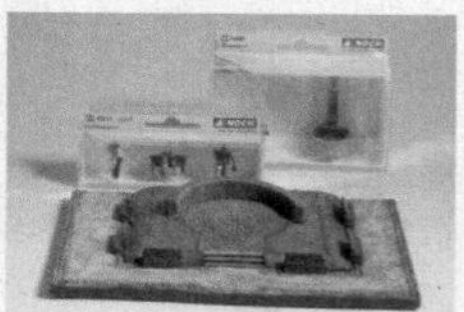

**NEW 528-65502** City Park **56.99**
6-11/16 x 4-3/4 x 11/16"
17 x 12 x 1.8cm

Add this small park to your layout in minutes. The hand-painted molded foam base features a path, benches and an elevated section for a fountain. Set includes two fountains and three courting couples.

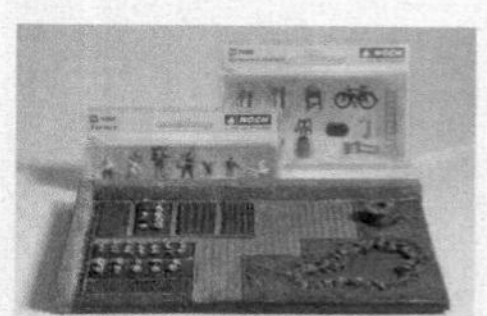

**NEW 528-65504** Garden Plot **56.99**
6-11/16 x 4-3/4 x 5/8"
17 x 12 x 1.5cm

**NEW 528-65506** Wood Storage Yard **56.99**
6-11/16 x 4-3/4 x 5/8"
17 x 12 x 2.5cm

### Molded-Foam Structures

Add a touch of old-world realism to your layout with these ready-to-use hard-foam structures. Each is detailed, weathered and decorated to look like ruins.

**NEW 528-58606** Church Ruin **94.99**
11-7/16 x 8-7/8 x 7-1/8"
29 x 22.5 x 18cm

**NEW 528-58607** Cloister **46.99**
7-5/16 x 6-11/16"
18.5 x 17 x 7.5cm

**NEW 528-58608** Church Steeple **94.99**
6-11/16 x 6-3/8 x 11" 17 x 16 x 28cm

## ALL-IN DIORAMA SETS

### Weathered 189.99 ea

Sets include buildings, figures, scenery accessories and fences. Components are realistically weathered.

**528-65010** Mountain Farm
10-3/16 x 8-1/8 x 3-7/8" - 3-1/2 x 2-3/8 x 2-1/8" 26 x 20.5 x 10cm - 9 x 6 x 5.4cm

**528-65012** Mountain Inn
9-13/16 x 8-1/8 x 3-1/2"
25 x 20.5 x 9cm

**528-65014** Horse Yard
9-5/8 x 8-1/8 x 3-1/2" - 3-1/2 x 2-13/32 x 2-1/8" 24.5 x 20.5 x 9cm - 9 x 6 x 5.4cm

## BRIDGES & VIADUCTS

### Quarrystone Viaduct

**528-58660 81.99**
Maximum dimensions:
14-3/4 x 1-5/8 x 9-7/8"
37.4 x 4 x 25.1cm

This tall, cut-stone viaduct captures the look of heavy stone construction. Made of dense urethane foam, it's easily cut to fit your scene using a fine-toothed saw, and several kits can be combined to create a longer bridge. The kit includes one single-track viaduct; extra piers are sold separately.

**528-58661** Extra Cut-Stone Pier for Viaduct **9.99**
1-3/8 x 2-3/4 x 6"
3.4 x 7.1 x 15.2cm

**528-58664** Curved Viaduct 14-7/64" Radius (gray) **44.99**
13-3/16 x 4-59/64"
33.5 x12.5cm
This modular curved quarrystone viaduct can be expanded to fit your layout. Each section is 30° of a complete circle (12 sections make a complete circle). Base piers are 6" 15.5cm tall by 2-51-64" 7.1cm wide at the base; the entire viaduct stands 9-7/8" 25.1cm at full height. These products are designed as companion pieces to the Quarrystone Viaduct (#528-58660, sold separately).

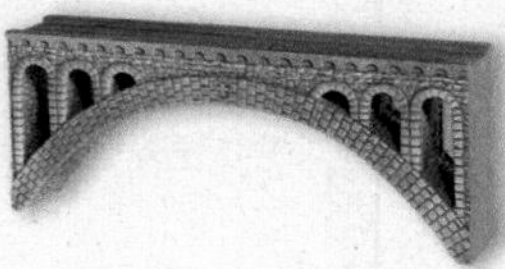

### "Rhone" Viaduct

**528-58670 59.99**
15 x 6" 37.6 x 15cm

### "Achtobel" Stone-Arch Bridge

**528-58690 29.99**
9 x 2-13/16 x 2-15/16"
22.5 x 7 x 7.3cm

### Small Foot Bridges

**528-11050** pkg(4) **12.99**

### Girder Bridge

**528-21310 31.99**
14 x 1-3/4" 36 x 4.5cm high

Wood Storage Yard 528-65506

### Thru Truss Bridge

**528-21320 31.99**
14 x 2-1/4" 35.6 x 5.7cm

### Truss Bridge

**528-21330 17.99**
7 x 2-1/4" 17.8 x 5.7cm

### Straight Steel Bridge

**528-21340 11.99**
7 x 2-1/4" 17.8 x 5.7cm

### Curved Steel Bridge

**528-21350 11.99**
7 x 2-1/4" 17.8 x 5.7cm

### Bridge Piers

528-21410 528-21400

**528-21400** 1-1/8" 3cm pkg(5) **2.99**
Realistic detail for any Noch bridge.

**528-21410** 1/4" .5cm **1.99**
Can be used with #528-21400 to build a higher pier.

### Double Bridge Piers

**528-21420 18.99**
3-3/4" 9.4cm high

## CASTLE RUINS

**528-58600 51.99**
7-1/8 x 5-1/2 x 4-3/4"
18 x 14 x 12cm

### Christmas Mangers 56.99 ea

**528-58581** Oriental
5-7/8 x 3-13/16 x 3-13/16"
15 x 9.6 x 9.6cm

**528-58582** Rock
6-1/2 x 4-5/8 x 3-7/8"
16.5 x 11.8 x 9.8cm

These small trackside structures are easy to assemble laser-cut kits that feature multiple use buildings that can be placed in nearly any small area on your layout. Kits do not include detailing parts.

## NEW PRODUCTS

### Yard Equipment & Facilities

**Yard Office**
**NEW** 520-40025 32.50
3 x 4-1/4"

Standing up on stilts, the yard office features a slightly pitched roof, staircase and assembled laser-cut shingle roofing.

### Business

**Angelo's Place**
**NEW** 520-40026 37.75
3-5/8 x 3-3/4"

Angelo's Place is the quintessential wood-framed neighborhood restaurant. This diminutive kit includes assembled laser-cut shingle roofing, awnings and signs.

## STATIONS & PLATFORMS

**Passenger Shelter**
520-40001 9.15

**Freight Depot**
520-40003 26.50

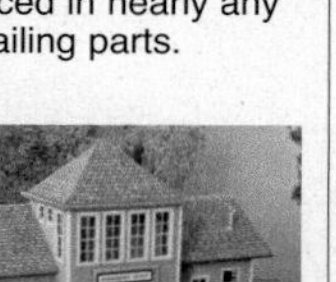

**Barnsboro Depot**
520-40022 59.80
Measures about 3-1/2 x 8-3/4"
8.8 x 21.9cm

## YARD EQUIPMENT & FACILITIES

**Motor Car Shed**
520-40004 10.55

**Storage Shed**
520-40002 11.95

**Watch Box**
520-40005 pkg(2) 8.05

**Yard Storage**
520-40008 20.75

## RURAL BUILDINGS

**Dairy Barn**
520-40009 23.05

**Cupola**
520-40010 8.05

## TANKS & TOWERS

**Watch Tower**
520-40006
10.55

## BUSINESSES

**First National Bank & Trust Co.**
520-40021 27.25
Measures about 2-7/8 x 6-3/4"
7.2 x 16.9cm

**Old Fashioned General Store**
520-40024 57.70
Measures about 5 x 8"
12.7 x 20.3cm

## CITY BUILDINGS

**Earl Smallshaw's Tenement Row**
520-20108 pkg(3) 138.95

**Springfield Fire Station**
520-40023 57.70
Measures about 4-7/8 x 5-1/8"
12.2 x 12.8cm

Earl Smallshaw's Tenement Row 520-20108

Feed & Grain Storage 520-40016

Sam Cahoon's Fish Pier 520-20109

Box & Crate Factory 520-40015

## INDUSTRIAL

**Feed & Grain Storage**
520-40016 76.15

**Sam Cahoon's Fish Pier**
520-20109 111.95
Model is based on a Dave Frary original and adds a neat touch to any waterfront area.

**Box & Crate Factory**
520-40015 46.15

**Tool & Die Shop**
520-40013 42.65

## Valley Hardware & Plumbing Supply

**520-40017 46.15**
Footprint is 3-3/4 x 4-7/8".

## Farm & Garden Supply

**520-40018 72.75**
Measures about 4-5/16 x 8-1/4"
10.8 x 20.6cm.

## Sheet Metal Shop

**520-40019 46.15**

## Transfer Station

**520-40020 27.25**

# BRIDGES & VIADUCTS

## Railroad Covered Bridge

**520-40014 46.15**

Create exacting replicas of railroad and trackside buildings. Kits feature laser-cut micro-plywood for superior durability and resistance to warping. Tab and slot construction reduces errors and produces a sturdier model. Self-stick windows, doors, glazing and trim pieces are provided, along with numerous laser-etched architectural details and full-color roofing material. All kits feature illustrated step-by-step instructions with scale drawings and assembly photos. Many kits also feature custom-made castings from Fine-N-Scale and P&D Marsh of England.

# NEW PRODUCTS

## CNJ Two-Story Station

**NEW 716-40008 124.95**

## AR Tower

**NEW 716-40009 109.95**
7-1/4 x 3 x 4"
18.4 x 7.6 x 10.2cm

Based on AR ("Allegheny Ridge") Tower in Gallitzin, Pennsylvania. Put into service on October 2, 1909 it was primarily used to protect the loop track for helpers heading back to Altoona. AR was closed in 1995 and operations were then remotely controlled from Harrisburg. Kit features self-adhesive styrene American Bond brick and slate pieces. The foundation is made of Taskboard® wood fiber material. A prototype color photo sheet is included as a reference for coloring and "modernizing" the structure.

## Waterville Freight House

**716-40005 89.95**
4-1/2 x 4-1/2 x 9"
11.4 x 11.4 x 22.9cm

This complete trackside operation includes scenic details, an interior loading platform, full-color roofing, window glazing numerous castings and Model Builder's Supply Line styrene brick material with self-stick adhesive.

## MG Tower

**715-40007 109.95**
8 x 4 x 6" 20.3 x 10.2 x 15.2cm

Based on the Mid-Grade (MG) interlocking tower that stands alongside the former Pennsy mainline near Horseshoe Curve. The kit includes laser-cut wood parts, and Model Builder's Supply Line styrene brick material with self-stick adhesive.

## Waterville Switchman's Shanty

**716-40006 15.95**
2 x 1-1/2 x 2"
5.8 x 3.81 x 5.8cm

## Alto Tower

**716-40002 89.95**
6 x 4 x 6" 15 x 10 x 15cm

Based on the tower that still protects the mainline in Altoona. Model has been back-dated to look as it probably did during its golden years.

Descriptions of the standard Pennsy paint scheme for this type of structure are included, along with recent photos to build a modern version. Instructions include elevation and floor plan drawings, techniques and in-progress assembly photos.

## Branchville Station

**716-40003 89.95**
10-1/2 x 5 x 3-1/2"
26.2 x 12.5 x 8.7cm

Based on the station that once stood at the terminus of the Delaware, Lackawanna & Western's Sussex Branch in Branchville, New Jersey.

## Williamstown Coal

**716-40004 159.95**
10 x 7 x 8" 25 x 17.5 x 20cm

Based on a pair of structures that still stand in Williamstown, Massachusetts, similar dealerships were found all over America. The kit is complete with wooden silos made from "bubble-free" resin castings and elevator housing, realistic chutes and metal details. Complete instructions feature scale drawings and plenty of assembly tips. Detail parts are also included.

# NuComp Miniatures

Seen all over North America, these mobile home kits and accessories offer great detail for any modern layout. The cast polyurethane resin kits are available in a set to build a complete trailer park, or as individual kits. Kits can be painted using water based acrylic paints. Figures, details and accessories shown in pictures are not included.

## HOUSES

**Mobile Home w/Porch #1**
**534-871002 18.00**
9-3/8 x 1-3/4" 23.4 x 4.3cm

**Mobile Home #1**
**534-871003 18.00**
7-1/2 x 1-1/2" 18.7 x 3.7cm

**Mobile Home w/Tip Out (Enclosed Entry)**
**534-871005 19.00**
7-7/8 x 1-1/2" 19.8 x 3.7cm
Tipout: 3-1/8 x 1" 7.9 x 2.5cm

**Mobile Home #2**
**534-871006 18.00**
7-1/2 x 1-1/2" 19 x 3.8cm

**Mobile Home w/Porch #2**
**534-871007 18.00**
7-1/4 x 1-1/4" 18.4 x 3.2cm

**Single Wide Mobile Home**
**534-871004 14.00**
7 x 1-1/4" 18.4 x 3.2cm

**Double Wide Mobile Home**
**534-871041 20.00**
7 x 3-1/2" 17.8 x 8.9cm

### 1950s Era House Trailer/Mobile Home Kits 16.00 ea (Unless Noted)

This trailer is modeled after a typical 1950s travel trailer. It can be modeled in transit or as a stationary mobile home. Each measures 4 x 1" 10 x 2.5cm.

**534-871008** Style #1 4 x 1" 10.1 x 2.5cm

**534-871009** Style #2 4 x 1" 10.1 x 2.5cm

**534-871010** Super **17.00** 6 x 1-1/16" 15.2 x 2.7cm

## NuComp Miniatures

**534-871011** Deluxe **17.00**
5-5/8 x 1-1/8" 14.3 x 2.9cm

**534-871012** Large
4-1/8 x 1-1/16" 10.5 x 2.7cm

**534-871013** Midsized
3-3/8 x 1" 8.8 x 2.5cm

## GARAGE

**534-87213 14.00**
3-1/4 x 2" 8.1 x 5cm

## BUSINESSES

### Mobile Home Utility/Office Trailer

**534-871001 14.00**
3-1/2 x 1-1/2" 8.7 x 3.7cm

## TRAILER PARKS

**534-87101 115.00**
Creating a trailer park scene has never been easier! Now you can build a complete trailer park with a single, convenient kit. Set includes six trailer kits: one each of #871001-871003 and 871005-871007, as well as a Work Shed (#87212), Tree Stumps (#87205), two lawn mowers and two pop machines (#87204)

**534-87150 115.00**
Includes six 1950s-style trailer kits, (871008, 871009, 871010, 871011, 871012 and 871013) work shed, tool shed, two lawnmowers, two pop machines and 12 tree stumps. Other scenery shown in photo is not included.

## SHEDS

These small sheds look great in the vicinity of any home, be it mobile or otherwise.

**534-87212** Work Shed **14.00**
2-3/4 x 2" 6.8 x 5cm

**534-87210** Tool Shed **9.00**
1-3/8 x 1" 3.4 x 2.5cm

PECO

IMPORTED FROM GREAT BRITAIN BY WALTHERS

# YARD EQUIPMENT & FACILITIES

Accessories Shown Not Included

### Overhead Traveling Crane

**552-546 56.99**
A great addition to any freight yard for transferring containers from freight cars to vehicles.

### Locomotive Inspection Pits 15.99 ea

These versatile inspection pits can be placed near any engine depot or servicing sheds. The kit is made up of six pit sections, which can extend up to 11.7" 29.7cm long. Also includes end steps, two plate walkways and rail to slide in the rail chairs after completing the pit.

**552-SL8356** Code 83

**552-121128** Code 100

**552-121129** Code 75

# INDUSTRIAL

### Half-Relief Warehouse & Mill

**552-207 20.99**
This die-cut structure features a group of industrial buildings that can be used as a backdrop, or multiple kits can be used together to produce whole buildings. Easy-to-build kit features a variety of extras, including windows, brick card, doors, window arches and roof tiles. Comes with assembly instructions.

### Industrial Buildings

**552-219 23.99**
Based on an early 20th-century design, this light industrial building can be used for any type of factory. This die-cut building includes clear glazing for windows, pre-cut components, various business signs and step-by-step instructions.



ORIGINAL Preiser

IMPORTED FROM GERMANY BY WALTHERS

# CIRCUS STRUCTURES

**Limited Quantity Available**

### Circus Decals

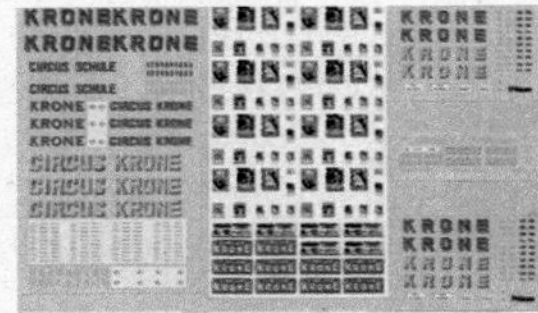

**590-21049** Krone **17.99**

### Circus Tent & Accessories

**590-21045** Circus Tent Set **227.99**
Features 19-1/4" (480mm) diameter big top that's 6-3/8" (160mm) high, plus a transparent insert to protect interior of big top from dust when open for display. Also includes a horse tent (15-1/4 x 6 x 3" 380 x 150 x 75mm), open animal tent (14-3/4 x 4-3/8 x 3" 370 x 110 x 75mm), entrance and restaurant tents, baseplate with preformed benches and 18-3/8" (460mm) diameter ring, tent poles, entrance stairways, signs, tent rigging and more. Tents are preformed plastic.

**590-21048** Accessories for Krone Circus Tent **33.99**
Includes seats, lights, poles, posters, hand trucks, wheelbarrows, pitchforks, shovels and more.

### Game Booths

**590-24693** China Game **46.99**

**590-24694** Shooting Gallery **46.99**

**590-24700** Hammer Game **24.99**

China Game 590-24693

Circus Tent Set 590-21045

Shooting Gallery 590-24694

These craft train kits feature molded plastic parts with separate doors and windows. All wall sections are molded without window or door openings, enabling you to add them where you want. Easily kitbashed or combined with more kits to build a larger structure.

## STATIONS & PLATFORMS

### Rail/Truck Transfer Facility
**541-100 22.95**

## YARD EQUIPMENT & FACILITIES

### Modern 1 or 2 Stall Engine House
**541-8 19.95**
5-1/2 x 11" 14 x 28cm

### Modern Small Engine House
**541-5000 11.25**
4-3/16 x 8-5/16" 10.5 x 21cm

### Loading Docks & Ramp
**541-17 5.25**
Includes ramp and four modular docks, each scale 40' long, 10' wide and 5' 3" tall.

### Atkinson Engine Facility
**541-5007 21.95**

### Small Yard Office
**541-5 5.95**
1-5/8 x 1-1/4" 4.2 x 3.2cm

### Wood Handcar Shed
**541-6 5.50**
1-5/8 x 1-1/4" 4.2 x 3.2cm

### Yard Office
**541-16 9.95**
Includes material to build one of three heights; 12', 18', 22' x 40' scale feet.

### Yard Office Kit
**541-162 9.95**

## CITY BUILDINGS

### Add-on Office Showroom
**541-11 8.50**

### Fire Station 13.95 ea
**541-19** Blue

**541-191** Green

**541-192** Red
7 x 5-1/2" 17.5 x 12.5cm

This modern building will be the pride of your small town volunteers. Features three apparatus bays and comes in your choice of red, green or blue.

### Modern 2-Story Office Building
**541-5002 11.45**

## BUSINESSES

### Auto Repair Shop
**541-9 17.95**
3-1/2 x 8-1/4" 9 x 21cm

### Shop w/Add-on Office
**541-15 22.95**
70 x 80 scale feet.

### Milton A. Corporation
**541-104 34.95**
4-1/8 x 8-1/4" 10.3 x 20.6cm
9-3/4 x 11 x 7"
24.3 x 27.5 x 17.5cm

This kit includes a rail car-height door for inside unloading, with freight doors for outside truck and railroad service. Versatile design uses parts from other kits, and can be arranged to fit just about any space.

## INDUSTRIAL

### Diamond Tool & Engineering Co.
**541-18 14.95**
5-1/2 x 8-1/4" 14 x 21cm

### Machine Tool Center
**541-101 20.95**
Includes one each: Smalltown, USA Hardware Kit, USA Sidewalks Kit, Three Size Yard Office and Loading Docks.

### Multi-Purpose Steel Building
**541-5005 13.25**

### U&K Plastics
**541-102 22.95**
Includes a factory that's 70' wide by 60' deep, plus an attached two-story office that measures 50' wide by 40' deep. All wall sections are molded in "Monsoon Green" so no painting is needed. Also includes concrete parking barriers for the employee lot.

Yard Office 541-16

Fire Station 541-19

Auto Repair Shop 541-9

Shop w/Add-On Office 541-15

Milton A. Corporation 541-104

Modern 2-Story Office Building 541-5002

**The Warehouse**
**541-4 15.95**
4-1/8 x 8-1/4" 10.8 x 21cm

**Retail/Warehouse Center**
**541-7 21.95**
4-1/4 x 8-1/4" 10.8 x 21cm
Includes outdoor sign and decals for a variety of stores.

**Distribution Center**
**541-10 15.95**
9-5/8 x 5-1/2" 24.5 x 14cm

**Tri-Star Industries 16.95 ea**
**541-20** Blue

**541-201** Green
9-5/8 x 8-1/4" 24.5 x 21cm

**Piping & Mechanical Contractors**
**541-103 21.95**

**Contractors Building**
**541-5006 13.95**

**Motor Freight Terminal**
**541-5001 13.95**
4-3/16 x 11-1/8" 10.5 x 28cm

## ADD-ON WALL SECTIONS

**For Most Kits**
**541-14 4.50**
20 scale feet long.

**Extension Kits 4.50 ea**
**541-141** Green

**541-142** Red
Make virtually any of the modern metal buildings larger. Includes two wall sections molded in color, plus white roof and other details.

## SELLEY FINISHING TOUCHES

## YARD EQUIPMENT & FACILITIES

**Old Time Crossing Shanty**
**675-604 17.90**
Easy-to-build kit features cast metal construction. Measures 11/16 x 11/16 x 1" 1.2 x 1.2 x 2.5cm.

## RURAL BUILDINGS

**Rural Outhouse**
**675-607 8.70**
Includes occupant, half-moon door and mail-order catalog.

# Plastruct

These craft train kits feature a variety of plastic shapes and parts and are complete with construction plans.

## STATIONS & PLATFORMS

**Service Platforms**
570-1010 pkg(2) 15.60
3-1/2 x 1" 9 x 2.5cm

## YARD EQUIPMENT & FACILITIES

**Twin Lamp Posts**
570-1012 pkg(4) 7.80
6-1/4" high, nonoperating.

**Gas Pumps**
570-94872
pkg(3) 4.65

**Sand Tower**
570-1011 12.25
1 x 6-3/4" 2.5 x 17.2cm

Includes material for concrete slabs, walkways, etc.

## TANKS & TOWERS

**Electrical Towers & Oil Wells**
570-1005 24.60
Contains enough material to build either one oil well derrick or one each of the transmission towers.

**Welded Steel Water Tank**
570-1009 26.80
3-1/2" 9cm diameter

100,000 gallon, used during the last days of steam.

**Twin Bulk Oil Storage Tanks**
570-1014 19.00
2-1/4 x 5-1/4" 5.7 x 13.3cm

**Oil Storage Tank**
570-1015 16.75
2-1/4 x 3-1/4" 5.7 x 8.3cm

For expanding your refinery, tank farm or bulk oil distribution center.

**Utility Water Tower**
570-1016 19.00
2 x 2 x 15"
5.08 x 5.08 x 38.1cm

A must for all modern industries. Adjustable height.

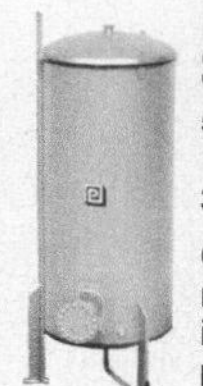

**Propane Storage Tank**
570-1017 12.25
1-1/2 x 5"
3.81 x 12.7cm

Can be used at refineries, large industries or propane distributors.

**Side-By-Side Vertical Tanks**
570-1018 27.95
3" 7.62cm tall,
1-1/2" 3.81cm diameter.

Use as chemical tanks or silos.

**Twin LP Gas Storage Tanks**
570-1019 20.10
1-1/2" 3.81cm diameter,
10" 25.4cm long.

**Silos & Grain Elevators**
570-1025 55.95
Tanks: 3 x 7" 7.6 x 17.7cm

Office: 3-1/8 x 2-1/8"
7.9 x 5.4cm

Elevator: 3/4 x 1 x 15"
1.9 x 2.54 x 38.1cm

Typical of smaller facilities, includes three silos, headhouse and small office building.

**Spherical Storage Tank**
570-1026 23.45
3 x 3-1/2" 7.6 x 8.9cm

**External Floating Roof Tank**
570-1027 36.90
5 x 4" 12.7 x 10.1cm

**Cone Roof Elevated Water Tank**
570-1028 26.95
Probably the most common style of water tower found in industrial settings.

**2" Oil Tank**
570-94876 pkg(2) 4.30
45/64" 1.27cm tall,
2" 5.08cm diameter.

**3-1/2" Tower**
570-94893 6.60

**5-1/2" Tower**
570-94892 7.30

**8" Tower**
570-94891 8.30

**Water Tanks**
O.D. = Outside Diameter

570-94884 1/4" O.D. .6cm
pkg(8) 3.30

570-94883 1/2" O.D. 1.2cm
pkg(4) 3.65

570-94882 1" O.D. 2.5cm
pkg(2) 4.65

570-94881 1-3/4" O.D. 4.5cm
4.65

## INDUSTRIAL

**Petro/Chemical Refinery**
570-1008 89.55
20 x 24" 51 x 70cm

Includes piping, angles, valves, tanks and other details.

**Steel Mill Fakefront**
570-1030 49.95
22 x 3 x 12" 56 x 7.5 x 30cm

**Sintering Plant Fakefront**
570-1031 59.95
30 x 18 x 7"
76.2 x 45.7 x 17.8cm

Three kits in one; Sintering Processing Building, Materials Bunker and Blower Assembly. Can be modified to fit many other industrial facilities.

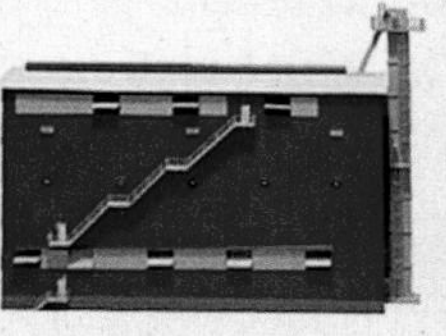

**Lime Building**
570-1032 39.95
18 x 12-1/2 x 5"
4.57 x 31.75 x 12.7cm

Replica of a lime processing building used by Copper Smelting. May be modified to fit many other industrial facilities.

## BRIDGES & VIADUCTS

**Simple Span Bridge**
570-1001 17.85
15-1/8" 38.4cm

**Truss Bridge**
570-1002 23.45

**Old Time Moving Bridge**
570-1007 27.95
24" long, 13-1/2" wide over piers.

## Rail Town Model Railroad Supplies

Add a modern look anywhere along your railroad with these easy to build kits. Based on contemporary structures that can be found in cities and towns of every size, these easy-to-build kits feature pre-colored plastic parts, decals and complete instructions.

## NEW PRODUCTS

### "Lock-It-Up" Two-Unit Storage Facility 14.99 ea

Includes parts for two units, each about 2 x 5-3/4" 5 x 14.6cm

**NEW 632-2901** Medium Blue

**NEW 632-2902** Red/Orange

**NEW 632-2903** Yellow

Everybody needs more space these days, and these self-storage units make a great addition to modern layouts. Parts for two complete units are provided, which can be arranged to fit small or odd-shaped spaces just like the prototypes. Each includes doors on both sides of the building, gutters, down spouts, a rooftop ridge vent, and curbs around the door entries. Roll-up doors come with and without padlock details (to model a few units that are available for rent) plus lift handles and frames. The entry door has a small handle, and both the door and window also have frames. For more detail, there's a large sign complete with post and base. Decals are included for window blinds and typical small window signs, along with the large "Lock-It-Up" lettering for both sides of the street sign.

### Spherical Water Tower 14.99 ea

Base Diameter: 3" 7.6 cm

Sphere Diameter: 4" 10.1cm
9-3/4" 24.7 cm Tall

**NEW 632-2904** Sky Blue

**NEW 632-2905** White

Modeled after modern water towers found all over the country, this kit is the perfect size for most layouts. Realistic details include an entry door, and mounting nuts around the base flange. A special decal set includes additional door details, a window and a No Trespassing sign. Designed for easy assembly, the parts are pre-colored and complete instructions are included.

## SHEEPSCOT SCALE PRODUCTS

This line of craft train kits takes structure modeling to a new level of detail. Kits include Northeastern lumber and siding, Grandt Line windows, doors and other details (as appropriate), Evergreen styrene, metal castings from Model Masterpieces and Alloy Forms, as well as the firm's own roofing material (simulating asphalt shingles), photo-etched brass and cast-metal detail parts.

## PHOTO-ETCHED BRASS MODELS

Made from solid sheets that are just 0.012" thick, easily soldered or assembled with adhesive of your choice.

### Tanks & Towers

**Radio/High Tension Tower**
**668-75008 10.00**
Includes two cast insulators, measures 52' tall and 20' wide at base. Leave the top in place and build a 62' tall radio tower. Includes microwave dish and open grid antenna.

**Windmill**
**668-75011 15.00**
A common sight on farms before rural electricity, the windmill was used to pump water.

### Industrial

**Pump House**
**668-75010 15.00**
This unique design eliminates stone joints by bending the walls from the front. Two choices for the brick ends are included, and the bricks are exactly to scale. Separate doors, windows, frames and sashes simplify painting. Measures 12 x 17 scale feet.

## STATE TOOL & DIE CO.

## STATIONS & PLATFORMS

**Passenger Shelter**
**661-525 12.40**
Assembled structure.

## YARD EQUIPMENT & FACILITIES

**Railroad Privy**
Standard design features detailed plastic parts and basic instructions. Can also be used as a small storage shed.

**661-500** Single Kit **3.95**

**661-5003** Set of 3 **8.95**

Get the Scoop!
Get the Skinny!
Get the Score!
Check Out Walthers Web site at
**www.walthers.com**

## TICHY TRAIN GROUP

Kits are injection-molded styrene.

## YARD EQUIPMENT & FACILITIES

**Handcar Shed**
**293-7011 9.50**
1-5/8 x 2-11/16" 4.1 x 6.8cm

**Coaling Tower Lift Mechanism**
**293-8008 20.00**

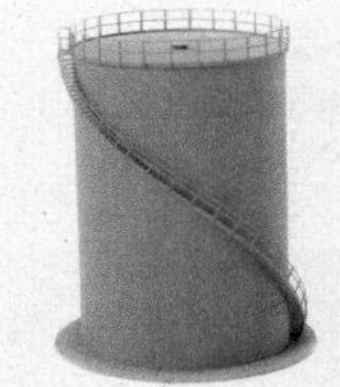

**Oil Tank**
**293-7013 15.00**

Recreate many of the structures seen along US railroads with these easy-to-build plastic kits. Detailed styrene parts are molded in realistic colors.

## HOUSES

### One-Story House w/Side Porch
**628-203 11.95**
3-1/2 x 3-7/8" 9 x 9.9cm

### One-Story House w/Front Porch
**628-202 11.95**
3 x 4-3/8" 7.7 x 11.2cm

Each house kit features white weatherboard walls, red brick foundations, brown asphalt roofing and clear windows.

### Porch Kit
**628-204 5.99**
1/2 x 1" 1.3 x 2.5cm

Includes brick porch, steps, doors, porch floor, gable and porch roof.

### One-Story House
**628-201 10.95**
3 x 3-7/8" 7.7 x 9.9cm

## TANKS & TOWERS

### Water/Oil Tank Flat Top

**628-500** 29' **8.99**

**628-501** 43' **11.99**

**628-502** 60' **15.99**

### Water/Oil Tank Peak Top

**628-503** 29' **8.99**

**628-504** 43' **11.99**

**628-505** 60' **15.99**

### Water/Oil Tank Ladder Kit
**628-506 2.49**

### Big Blue Storage Silo
**628-510 11.99**
A great storage system for farm or industry, measures a scale 24' diameter by 49' tall (at eave).

### Elevated Tank
**628-520 9.99**

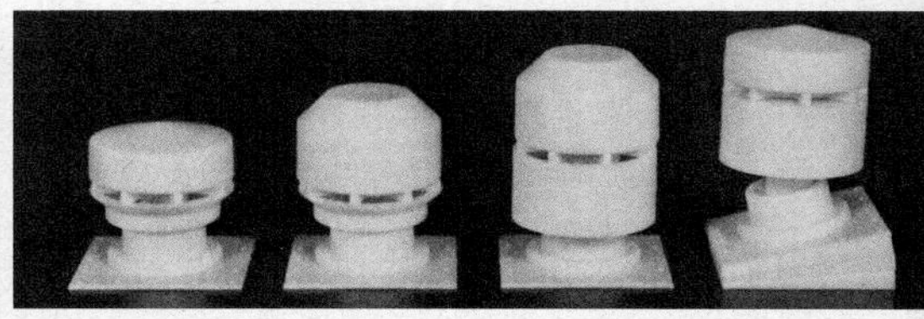

### Roof Vents
**628-610 6.95**
Realistic detail for the most-seen part of model industrial buildings the roof! Includes separate bases, spacers and vent bodies to mak eight vents (four of one and four of another, in five possible combinations).

## INDUSTRIAL

### Quonset Hut
**628-410 11.99**
Built by the thousands during WWII, these pre-fab metal buildings found all sorts of post-war uses. Kit includes one complete building. Measures a scale 24 x 26 x 12' and features pre-cut door and window openings.

### Grain Bins 30° Peaked Top
Typical of steel bins found on farms and at elevators to store all types of grains. Each section consists of six bands, which are stacked to various heights. Kits include parts to build the height shown. Also includes door, vents, dryer, chutes and grain head. All parts are molded in realistic galvanized color.

**628-304** 33' Tall **13.99**

**628-305** 44' Tall **16.99**

### Galvanized Color Grain Bin Roofs 3.49 ea
**628-356** 15° Pitch

**628-357** 30° Pitch

### Grain Bin Detail Parts
**628-358 3.49**
Includes door, vents, dryer, chutes and grain head. Use with any grain bin kit.

### Grain Bin Extension
**628-354 4.99**
Three complete bin sections, add up to 30' to #304 or #305.

### Grain Elevator
**628-407 17.99**
Detailed replica of the pipes and machinery used to move grain from bins, great for use with #304 or #305. Includes ladders with safety cages, platforms, chutes and tubes. Can be built in scale 10' increments, up to 90' tall.

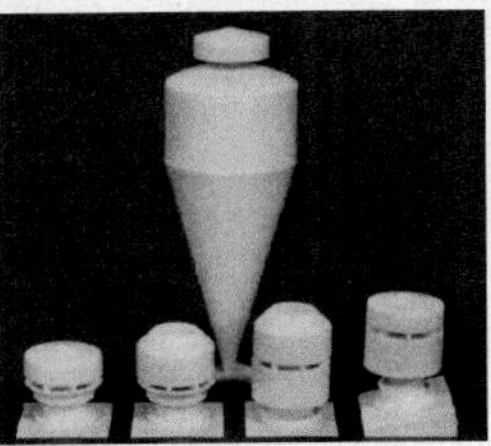

## Cyclones & Vents

**628-611 11.95**
This set includes the large cyclone type dust collectors that are mounted on the roofs and walls of many manufacturing plants, along with the vents found in kit #610.

# BRIDGES & VIADUCTS

## 1930s Overpass Railings

**628-104** pkg(4) **4.99**

## Beams

**628-105** pkg(10) **4.99**

## Modern Median Divider

**628-115** pkg(4) **4.99**
Individual parts match those used in the overpass kits.

## Modern Railings

**628-114** pkg(4) **4.99**

## Roadway

**628-106** pkg(4) **4.99**

## Rural Wooden Overpass

**628-200 13.98**
Great detail for rural right-of-way, typical of crossings built for farm roads.

# STONE CULVERTS

**628-651** Small Cut **8.95**

**628-652** Large Cut **11.95**

## Vintage Highway Overpasses

These vintage highway overpass kits model concrete bridges built in the 1930s and 1940s, which are still used today. All parts are molded in realistic concrete color. Each overpass section is a scale 50' long and 25' wide. Modular design and interlocking parts make it easy to build longer overpasses.

**628-101** 50' **6.99**

**628-102** 50' w/Pier **11.95**

**628-103** 150' w/4 Piers **34.95**
Kit includes three overpass kits and four piers.

## Vintage Highway Pier

**628-100 4.99**

## Modern Highway Overpasses

These overpass kits feature details to match newer construction. Each overpass section is a scale 50' long and 25' wide. Modular design and interlocking parts make it easy to build longer overpasses.

**628-111** 50' **7.99**

**628-112** 50' w/Pier **11.95**

**628-113** 150' w/4 Piers **34.95**
Kit includes three overpass kits and four piers.

## Wrought Iron Highway Overpass

These kits are modeled after bridges built to span over railroad tracks. Overpasses consist of 50 foot spans which interlock together so that any length bridge can be built. The piers are designed to be adjustable so that raising or lowering the bridge for different heights is quick and easy.

**628-121** 50' **6.99**

**628-122** 50' w/Adjustable Pier **11.95**

**628-123** 150' w/Four Adjustable Piers **34.95**
Kit includes three overpass kits and four adjustable piers.

## Wrought Iron/Concrete Railings

**628-124** 50' pkg(4) **4.99**

# TRIX

## Gantry Crane

**441-T66105 621.95**
14-3/16 x 14-3/16 x 10-5/8" 36 x 36 x 27cm

Add realism to any dockside, steel mill, or heavy transloading scene with this full-featured, working model. The Gantry Crane offers you two ways to lift cargo—a diecast metal hook is shipped with the model, or you can add the supplied electromagnet. Hook-up is easy: the model is powered by the 14V AC terminals on your power pack. The model features digital control and includes a controller that allows you to control all the crane's functions individually. The crane bridge is driven by two powerful motors and the motorized cab is capable of rotating 360°—perfect for moving objects just like the real thing! Other features include a working spotlight and a supplied base plate that you can add onto so the model can cover more territory. The base plate is designed to fit the track spacing system for Märklin C or Trix two-rail C Track. Clearance between the running rails is 9-1/8" 23.25cm.

The charm and attention to detail of yesteryear can be part of your layout with this line of kits. Each structure consists of wood and cast metal parts, numerous add-on details and complete instructions. Instant Kit 1400/1500 series buildings are constructed of resin castings and include various add-on details and full-color printed signs.

PLEASE NOTE: The entire line of SS Ltd. furniture, detail parts and other items, which are listed in their catalog, #650-9999, are available by special order through your dealer.

Items listed in blue ink may not be available at all times (see Legend Page).

## STATIONS & PLATFORMS

**Victorian Station w/Interior**
650-1115 144.95

**Grizzly Flats Depot**
650-1147 40.95

**Freight Transfer Platform**
650-1148 15.95

**Gothic Crossing Shanty**
650-1153 12.95
Metal kit.

**Columbia Depot**
650-1404 34.95

## YARD EQUIPMENT & FACILITIES

**Telephone Shack**
650-1107 6.95

**Flue Rack & Fire Stand**
650-1109 17.95

**Robertson Cinder Conveyor**
650-1110 28.95

**110'-130' Turntable**
650-1124 71.95

**70'-90' Turntable**
650-1126 61.95

**Board & Batten Crossing Shanty**
650-1151 12.95

Powerhouse 650-1519

Dorothy's Home 650-1125

**Victorian Crossing Shanty**
650-1152
12.95
Metal kit.

**Rio Grande Car Repair Barn**
650-1158 89.95
Prototype at Durango, Colorado, kit is based on the building as it appeared circa 1938.

**Trackside Shanties**
650-1422 pkg(3) 21.95

**The Powerhouse**
650-1519 91.95
With covered siding.

## RURAL BUILDINGS

**Hometown Gazebo**
650-1154 31.95

**Country Corn Crib**
650-1156 24.95

## HOUSES

**Dorothy's Home**
650-1125 81.95
Whether modeled as a brand new Victorian building, or a freshly restored home on a modern layout, this is the kind of house you'll wish YOU coul live in! Features elegant perio details, a spacious porch, detailed brickwork and loads of metal castings.

## CITY BUILDINGS

**New York Brownstone**
650-1103 36.95

**San Francisco Apartment**
650-1104 36.95

**Chicago Townhouse**
650-1105 36.95

**Corner Drug Store**
650-1111 71.95

**San Francisco Office Building**
650-1113 51.95

**San Francisco Office Building - Walls Only**
650-1150 pkg(2) 5.95

**Quincy Street**
650-1539 61.95

**The Store**
650-1118 91.95

**1880 Union Hotel**
650-1149 61.95

**Miners Union Hall**
650-1502 31.95

**Municipal Building**
650-1530 61.95

**Burlington Street**
650-1534 49.95

**Art Deco Movie Theater**
650-1536 51.95

**Birthplace of Model Railroader**
650-1543 36.95

**Des Plaines Avenue**
650-1545 36.95

For Up-To-Date Information and News Bookmark Walthers Web site at
**www.walthers.com**

## TANKS & TOWERS

**Oil Tanks**
650-1112 36.95

**T.W. Snow Coaling Tower**
650-1116 71.95

**Twin Water Tanks**
650-1145 45.95

**Steel Water Tank**
650-1424 21.95

**Wood Branchline Water Tank**
650-1443 21.95

## BUSINESSES

**1929 Gas Station**
650-1101 31.95

**Halloway's Plumbing Supply**
650-1410 21.95

**Dixie's Diner**
650-1415 21.95

**Rick's Place**
650-1525 24.95

**1940s Gas Station**
650-1531 51.95

**Reggie's Veggie Market**
650-1437 23.95

**Smiley's Place**
650-1537 14.95

**White Tower Restaurant**
650-1540 31.95

**Brach's Candy Company**
650-1556 71.95

**Automobile Junk Yard**
650-8016 19.95

## INDUSTRIAL

**Boiler House**
650-1102 71.95

**Tool House & Pillar Crane**
650-1106 31.95

**Pillar Crane & Platform**
650-1120 18.95

**Oil Loading Facility**
650-1123 29.95

**Timber Gantry**
650-1146 61.95

**Maple Valley Coal & Ice**
650-1416 18.95

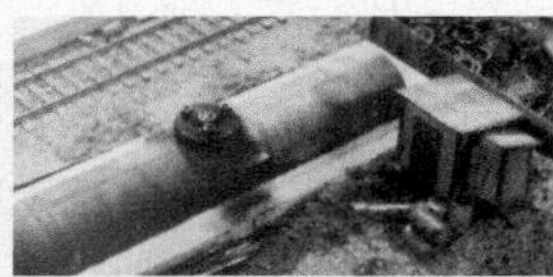

**Below Ground Storage Tank Facility**
650-1417 21.95

**The Country Garage**
650-1418 23.95

**Track Gang Baggage House**
650-1419 18.95

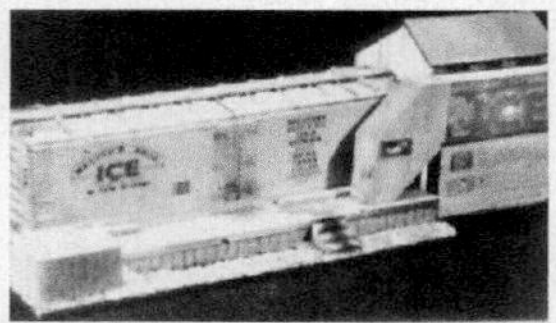


**Meltnick's Ice Station**
650-1423 23.95

**Purina Grain Loader**
650-1441 26.95

**Concrete Loading Dock & Ramp**
650-1446 12.95

**Jennings Lumber Co.**
650-1117 224.95
The only thing this kit needs is the smell of fresh-cut sawdust! A miniature masterpiece, the model is packed with detail inside and out. The exterior includes a variety of roof vents, cyclone dust collector with wooden storage tank and water barrels for fire protection. Inside, there's a complete set of belt-driven machinery and furniture for the offices.

**Toadsuck Canning Company**
650-1157 174.95
Fresh as the catch of the day, this local cannery really adds "flavor to your entire layout. This dockside industry is a natural for a busy rail siding, bringing in tin cans, paper labels and parts for the machinery. Empty cars can be reloaded with canned goods for distant markets. Lots of neat wood, resin and metal parts provide hours of construction fun.

**Wischer's Washer Company**
650-1523 51.95

**Wood Loading Dock & Ramp**
650-1447 12.95

**J.E. Work's Gravel Yard**
650-1449 23.95

**Oil Storage Tank Facility**
650-1455 21.95

**Fountain Brewery**
650-1510 71.95

**Tickners Watchworks**
650-1524 41.95

**VFWD Pumping Station**
650-1527 51.95

**Victoria Falls Transfer Co.**
650-1533 49.95

**Broken Back Mines**
650-8075 21.95

**V & T Jib Crane**
650-9126 34.95

## BRIDGES & VIADUCTS

**Deck Bridge**
650-1144 2 Kits 31.95

**Dinky Creek Bridge**
650-1127 49.95



## SUPER KITS

650-1001 Baker Street Super Kits 199.95
Includes one each of kit #1101, 1103, 1104, 1105, and 1108. Includes detail castings.

## INSTANT KIT SERIES

This series of kits feature cast resin walls, add-on details, printed signs and complete instructions.

**Concrete Loading Dock**
650-1405 11.95

**McHugh's Hardware Store**
650-1453 26.95

**Ruston Shanties**
650-1451 18.95

Item listed below is available by Special Order (see Legend Page).

**Hillside Oil Facility**
650-1412 21.95

## CATALOG

650-9999 4.00

J.E. Work's Gravel Yard 650-1449

Victoria Falls Transfer Co. 650-1533

Deck Bridge 650-1144

Dinky Creek Bridge 650-1127

Division of **Rix Products**

Create a custom business district with these easy-to-build plastic kits. Each series has a common front wall, which can be painted and detailed for variety. Side walls feature different window and door locations, so models can be used on right or left corners, or in the middle of a block. Small size fits most layouts, and kits can be used in different time periods by adding appropriate signs and other details (sold separately). Parts are molded in appropriate colors.

## CITY BUILDINGS

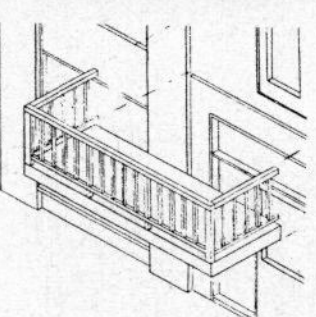

**Balcony Kit**
**699-6 2.49**

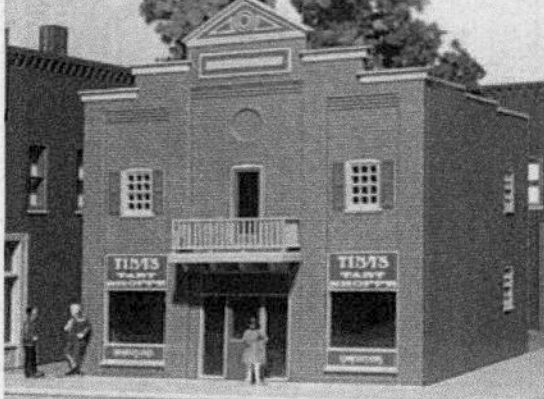

**Tina's Tart Shop**
**699-6000 11.95**
4 x 4-1/8" 10 x 10.3cm

**Mike's Market**
**699-6001 11.95**
4-3/4 x 2-3/4" 11.9 x 6.9cm

**Tony's Gym**
**699-6002 11.95**
4-3/4 x 2-3/4" 11.9 x 6.9cm

**Jessica's Salon**
**699-6003 11.95**
4-3/4 x 2-3/4" 11.9 x 6.9cm

**Madelene's Deli**
**699-6004 11.95**
4-3/4 x 2-3/4" 11.9 x 6.9cm

**Dime Store & Office**
**699-6005 11.95**
4 x 4-1/8" 10 x 10.3cm

**Hardware Store**
**699-6006 11.95**
4 x 4-1/8" 10 x 10.3cm

**Cab Company**
**699-6007 11.95**
4 x 4-1/8" 10 x 10.3cm

**Freight Office**
**699-6008 11.95**
4 x 4-1/8" 10 x 10.3cm

**Roy's Fix-It Shop**
**699-6009 11.95**
4-3/4 x 2-3/4" 11.9 x 6.9cm

**Sally's Antiques**
**699-6010 11.95**
4-3/4 x 2-3/4" 11.9 x 6.9cm

**John's Place**
**699-6011 11.95**
2-3/4 x 5" 7 x 12.8cm

Left-hand corner building.

**Furniture Showroom**
**699-6015 15.95**
9-1/2 x 4-1/8" 24.2 x 10.5cm

Here's a big building that's right at home in your business district! Typical of large stores, it might be a department store, furrier or perhaps a small factory with a showroom. The finished model includes the large display windows and recessed entry and measures 69 scale feet across the front by 30 scale feet deep.

**Vivian's Family Shoe Store**
**699-6013 11.95**
2-3/4 x 5" 7 x 12.8cm

**Old Indian Tobacco Shop**
**699-6014 11.95**
2-3/4 x 5" 7 x 12.8cm

**'lorist's Office**
**99-6016 11.95**
x 4-1/8" 10 x 10.3cm

**rug Store**
**99-6017 11.95**
-1/8 x 4-1/8" 10.5 x 10.5cm

**'arcel Delivery Service**
**99-6018 11.95**
-1/8 x 4-1/8" 10.5 x 10.5cm

**lelen's Country Kitchen**
**99-6012 11.95**
2-3/4 x 5" 7 x 12.8cm

**Cycle Repair Shop**
**699-6019 11.95**
4-1/8 x 4-1/8" 10.5 x 10.5cm

**Kevin's Toy Store**
**699-6021 11.95**
4-3/4 x 2-3/4" 11.9 x 6.9cm

**Bonnie B. Boutique**
**699-6022 11.95**
4-3/4 x 2-3/4" 11.9 x 6.9cm

**Hal's Hobbies**
**699-6023 11.95**
4-3/4 x 2-3/4" 11.9 x 6.9cm

Right-hand corner building.

**Buck's Book Shop**
**699-6024 11.95**
4-3/4 x 2-3/4" 11.9 x 6.9cm

**Freytag's Furnace Co.**
**699-6025 11.95**
4-3/4 x 2-3/4" 11.9 x 6.9cm

**Appliance Mart**
**699-6020 15.95**
5-1/4 x 5" 13.4 x 12.8cm

## TALLTOWN BUILDINGS

Make your city skyline more realistic with really tall buildings! They're easy to create from these complete kits, or design your own using the four different modules. Parts are made of plastic.

**Vicky's Fashions**
**699-6027 34.50**
You'll find the latest styles in this big five-story store. A prime location for a department store or any commercial venture.

**Rusty's Graphic Arts**
**699-6028 17.50**
7-7/8 x 4-13/16" 20 x 12.2cm

Perfect for revitalizing any downtown,Rusty modernized the storefront by adding larger windows and a four-door entry. The kit includes TallTown modules for the brick walls, windows and doors, plus Evergreen stock to build up the the framing for the new windows.

**Rogy's**
**699-6030 17.50**
9-1/2 x 4-1/8" 23.7 x 10.3cm

Shop for a work of art to decorate your home, or the materials you need to create one at this big double store. A great addition to the business district, the structure features an as-built upper floor with brick walls and older style windows, while the first floor has been modernized. The kit includes injection molded brick walls, along with four TallTown modules and Evergreen strip and sheet styrene. Construction is similar to other kits in the series, but the modernized front needs to be built up from the Evergreen materials.

Smalltown USA
Division of Rix Products

# TALLTOWN MODULES

**Pkg(6) 4.00 ea**
Use these modules in an endless variety of ways to create custom high-rise buildings for your city scene.

**699-7001** #1 Four Doors

**699-7002** #2 Four Windows-Equal Panes

**699-7003** #3 Two Small End-Two Large Middle Windows

**699-7004** #4 Four Large Pane Windows

# WALLS

### Front Wall w/Recessed Entry
**699-1** **2.25**

### Front Wall w/Flush Entry
**699-2** **2.25**

### Front Wall w/Corner Entry
**699-3** **2.45**

STEWART PRODUCTS Since 1950

These HO Scale, craft train kits consist of diecast, stamped and formed metal parts and vinyl tubing, as noted. Complete instructions included.

# YARD EQUIPMENT & FACILITIES

### Service Track Structures

**683-101** Water Column **9.40**
1/2 x 3/4" 1.3 x 2cm

**683-100** Fuel Column **9.40**
1/2 x 1-1/2" 1.3 x 3.8cm

**683-102** Sand Tower **13.60**
3/4 x 3-1/2" 2 x 9cm

**683-103** Sand, Fuel & Water Column Set **26.20**
3/4 x 5/8" 1.9 x 1.6cm

### Diesel Oil Storage Tank Center & Pump House
**683-107** **20.95**
1-1/4 x 4" 3.2 x 10.2cm

### Watchman's Shanty
**683-108** **9.40**
1-1/4 x 1-1/2" 3.2 x 3.8cm
Includes figure and super details.

### Trackside Shanty W/Stove
**683-116** **9.40**
1 x 1" 2.54 x 2.54cm

### Crew Shelter
**683-117** **9.40**
1 x 1-3/8" 2.54 x 3.4cm

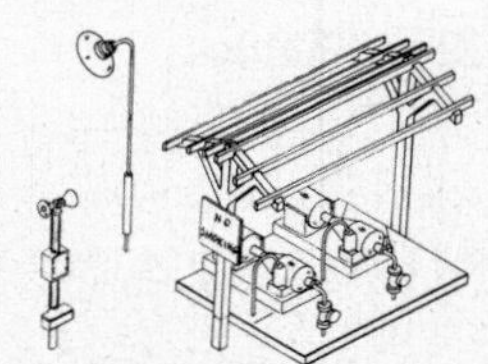

### Oil Pump & Shelter
**683-215** **15.75**
1 x 1-3/8" 2.5 x 3.5cm

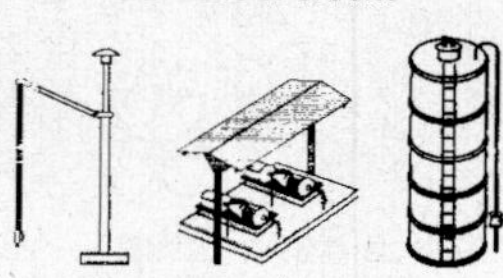

### Branchline Fueling Facility Kit
**683-300** **28.30**

### Branchline Watering Facility Kit
**683-301** **20.95**

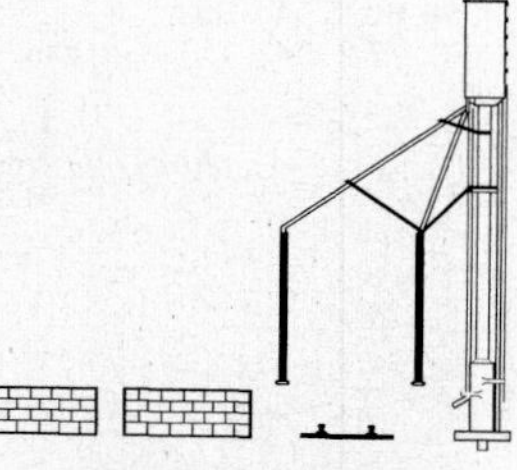

### Branchline Sanding Facility Kit
**683-302** **17.80**

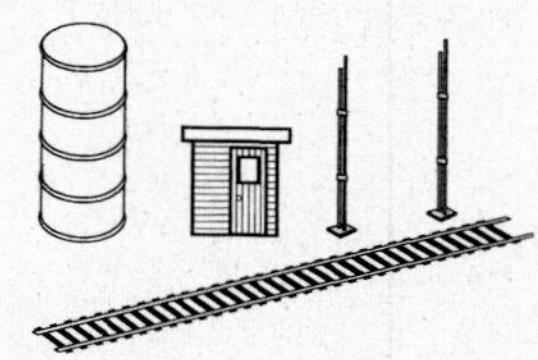

### Branchline Cattle Spraying Facility
**683-304** **17.80**
Includes spraying stands, pumphouse and water tank.

# TANKS & TOWERS

### Double Track Diesel Sand Tower Kit
**683-114** **15.70**
4-7/8" 12.3cm tall

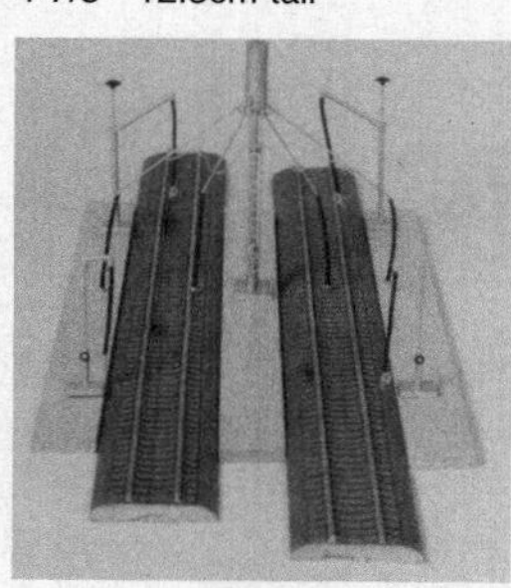

### Double Track Diesel Sand Tower, Fuel & Water Columns
**683-115** **38.80**
3/4 x 5/8 x 4-7/8"
1.9 x 1.6 x 12.3cm

### Refinery Type Pressure Tank
**683-216** **10.50**
7/8 x 2-1/2" 2.2 x 6.3cm

### Tank Extension Sections
**683-217** For 683-216 (Sold Separately.) pkg(4) **7.30**

### Diesel Oil Storage Tank
**683-218** **11.50**
7/8 x 2-1/2" 2.2 x 6.3cm

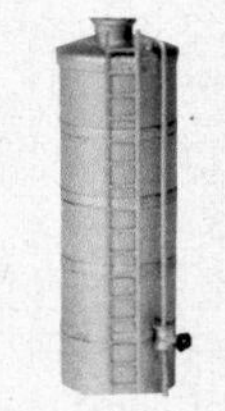

### Vertical Oil Storage Tank
**683-219** **10.50**
7/8 x 2-1/2" 2.2 x 6.3cm

SUNCOAST MODEL
Division of JV Models

Craft train kits include styren and color-coded wood parts.

# STATIONS & PLATFORMS

### Freight Station
**690-3030** **38.98**
3-1/4 x 6-1/2" 8.3 x 16.5cm

# YARD EQUIPMENT & FACILITIES

### Yard Office
**690-3040** **38.98**
4 x 8" 10.2 x 20.3cm

### Fairbanks-Morse Automatic Coaling Station
**690-3080** **25.98**
4 x 18" 10.2 x 45.7cm

### Icing Platform
**690-3020** **47.98**
4 x 18" 10.2 x 45.7cm

### Icing Platform Extension Kit
**690-30201** Adds 18" **23.98**

# TANKS & TOWERS

### Branch Line Water Tower
**690-3010** TBA

### 200-Ton Coaling Tower
**690-3070** TBA

# INDUSTRIAL

### Logging Camp
**690-3050** **39.98**
8-1/2 x 11" 21.5 x 28cm

### Concrete Grain Elevator
**690-3060** **49.98**
9-1/2 x 13" 24.1 x 33cm

### Grain Elevator Extension Kit
**690-30601** Adds 4 silos **25.9**
4 x 3-5/8" 10.2 x 9.2cm

# trident

IMPORTED FROM AUSTRIA BY WALTHERS

## MILITARY STRUCTURES

Resin structure castings.

**Observation Post**
729-99001 5.99

**Large Atlantic Wall Bunker**
729-99002 13.99

**Ruined Mansion**
729-99003 21.99

**Russian Eastern Front ("Stalin Line") Machine Gun Bunker**
729-99004 24.99

**Russian Farmhouse - Intact (Kate)**
729-99005 37.99

**Ruined Industrial Smokestack**
729-99006 24.99

**Stone Bridge - Intact**
729-99007 31.99

**Destroyed Russian Farmhouse**
729-99008 37.99

**Open Wooden Shed**
729-99009 29.99

**Light Anti-Aircraft Gun Emplacement**
729-99010 39.99
Gun sold separately.

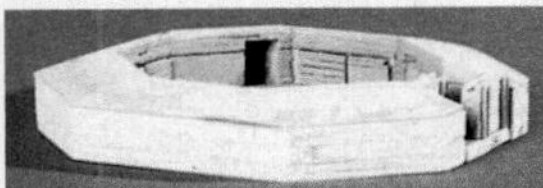

**Heavy Anti-Aircraft Gun Emplacement**
729-99011 57.99
Gun sold separately.

**WWII Bunker Flank Protection 57.99 ea**

729-99012 Right

729-99013 Left

**R67 Bunker w/Pl Turret**
729-99014 19.99

**Army Barracks**
729-99015 49.99

**R28 Artillery Observation Post**
729-99016 72.99

**Machine Gun Pillbox**
729-99017 25.99

See What's Available at
**www.walthers.com**

**R58C Machine Gun Bunker - Tobruk**
729-99018 24.99

**Limited Quantity Available**

**M262 Fire Control Bunker**
729-99019 168.99

**R23 Concrete Machine Gun Bunker**
729-99020 109.99

**Tank Service/ Undercarriage Access Ramps**
729-99021 18.99

**R 20 PAK-Bunker**
729-99022 Anti-Tank Gun Emplacement **104.99**

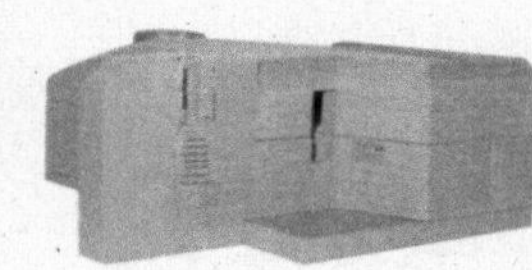

**R 632 Bunker**
729-99023 With 3-Embrasured Turret **113.99**

**Russian Church**
729-99024 45.99

**Bell Tower**
729-99025 For Russian Church **48.99**
Shown with #729-99024, sold separately.

**Mosque**
729-99026 38.99

**R 10 Machine Gun Bunker**
729-99027 89.99

**Minaret**

729-99028 TBA

**Arabian House I**

729-99029 35.99

**Arabian House II**

729-99030 29.99

# VOLLMER

IMPORTED FROM GERMANY BY WALTHERS
Vollmer models are easy-to-build plastic kits. Detailed, injection-molded parts come molded in appropriate colors. While most are based on European prototypes, many are easily Americanized simply by adding English signs or decals (sold separately).

## NEW PRODUCTS

### Bridges

These layout-ready all-metal bridges are based on typical prototypes used across the globe. Each model comes completely assembled and decorated.

**Arch Bridge**
**NEW 770-2560 69.99**
19-11/16 x 2-1/4 x 4-3/4" 50 x 5.8 x 12cm

**Truss Bridge**
**NEW 770-2561 39.99**
7-1/16 x 2-1/4 x 1-7/8" 18 x 5.8 x 4.8cm

**Through-Truss Bridge**
**NEW 770-2562 43.99**
8-1/4 x 2-1/4 x 3" 21 x 5.8 x 7.5cm

**Double-Track Arch Bridge**
**NEW 770-2565 69.99**
11-13/16 x 4-5/16 x 3-13/16" 30 x 11 x 9.7cm

### Yard Equipment & Facilities

**Wood Shanty**
**NEW 770-5713 35.99**
6-5/16 x 2-3/8 x 3-5/32" 16 x 6 x 8cm

**1-Stall Brick Engine House**
**NEW 770-5763 50.99**
12-5/8 x 3-3/4 x 4-5/8" 32 x 9.5 x 11.8cm

### City Building

**Parking Garage**
**NEW 770-3804 101.99**
15 x 7-1/2 x 7-1/16" 38 x 19 x 18cm

### Industrial

**Klimperle & Co. Piano Factory**
**NEW 770-5613 116.99**
14-1/2 x 6-1/2 x 5-7/8" 37 x 16.5 x 15cm

### Stations & Platforms

**Altenkirchen Station**
**NEW 770-3506 162.99**
22-1/4 x 7-1/16 x 5-1/2"
56.5 x 18 x 14cm

**Altenburg Station**
**NEW 770-3509 96.99**
14-3/16 x 7-1/16 x 5-1/2"
36 x 18 x 14cm

### Businesses

**Utzelbrutzel Snack Ba**
**NEW 770-5151 28.99**
3-1/2 x 3-3/8 x 2-3/4"
9 x 8.5 x 7cm

**Flower Shop**
**NEW 770-5152 29.99**
5-1/8 x 3-15/16 x 2-3/4"
13 x 10 x 7cm

**Strawberry Kiosk**
**NEW 770-5153 28.99**
2 x 2 x 1-3/4" 5 x 5 x 4.5cm

**Petting Zoo**
**NEW 770-3789 49.99**
6-1/2 x 6-1/8 x 6-1/2"
16.5 x 15.5 x 16.5cm
Includes sheep, cows, horses
1 pig and 1 goat.

# VOLLMER

IMPORTED FROM GERMANY BY WALTHERS

## STATIONS & PLATFORMS

**Spatzenhausen Station**
**770-3501 73.99**
13.3 x 5.4 x 4.9"
33.8 x 13.7 x 12.5cm

**Moritzburg Station**
**770-3502 162.99**
21-13/64 x 6 x 7-13/64"
53 x 15 x 18cm
Complete with attached station platform, signs and much more.

**Kitzlingen Station**
**770-3503 79.99**
13-5/8 x 5-7/16 x 6"
34 x 13.5 x 15cm

**Kleckersdorf Station**
**770-3504 75.99**
12-7/16 x 4-1/8 x 5-7/16"
31 x 10.3 x 13.5cm

**Waldbronn Station**
**770-3505 82.99**
12-1/2 x 6" 31 x 15cm

**Bad Wimpfen Station**
**770-3508 126.99**
14-3/32 x 7-9/32 x 7-9/32"
35.8 x 18.5 x 18.5cm

**Neuffen Passenger Station**
**770-3510 103.99**
16-1/8 x 5-3/8 x 5-1/2"
41 x 13.5 x 16.5cm

**Wildbach Station**
**770-3512 83.99**
13-5/8 x 6-13/16 x 6-1/8"
34 x 17 x 15.3cm

**Swiss Darligen Station**
**770-3515 79.99**
13-1/2 x 5-1/4"
34.5 x 13.5cm

**Laufenmuhle Station**
**770-3518 79.99**
10-13/16 x 6-13/32 x 4-31/32"
27 x 16 x 12.4cm

**Tonbach Station**
**770-3524 63.99**
13.3 x 5.4 x 4.9"
33.8 x 13.7 x 12.5cm

**Bad Berg Station**
**770-3526 54.99**
9-5/8 x 4-13/16 x 4-13/32"
24 x 12 x 11cm

**Covered Platform**
**770-3534 36.99**
14-5/8 x 1-7/8 x 2-3/4"
37 x 4.8 x 7cm

**Rheinburg Station Platform**
**770-3535 42.99**
14-13/16 x 2-5/8 x 2-3/8"
37 x 6.5 x 6cm

**Seeburg Station Platform**
**770-3536 52.99**
38-3/8 x 2-5/8 x 2-3/8"
96 x 6.5 x 6cm

**Covered Platform**
**770-3537 29.99**
14-5/8 x 1-3/8 x 2-5/8"
37 x 3.4 x 6.7cm

**Station Platform Neuffen**
**770-3539 21.99**
17-1/8 x 1-3/8 x 3-1/8"
43.6 x 3.5 x 8cm

**Baden Station Platform**
**770-3562 86.99**
44-13/16 x 2-11/64 x 3-13/32"
112 x 5.4 x 8.5cm

**Casino Loyale**
**NEW 770-6007 162.99**
15-15/16 x 6-11/16 x 8-11/16" 40.5 x 17 x 22cm
Kit includes Vollmer playing cards and instructions.

**Steam-Era Station Platform Hall**
**770-3545 52.99**
14-3/16 x 5-5/8 x 4-13/64"
37 x 14 x 10.5cm
A smaller version of kit #3546.

**Service Platform**
**770-3558 22.99**
35-1/4 x 1-1/8 x 1/4"
29 x 10 x 9cm

**Platform w/Cover**
**770-3559 73.99**
40-1/2 x 1-7/8 x 2-5/8"
102 x 4.8 x 6.6cm

**Baden-Baden Station**
**770-3560 168.99**
30-3/4 x 6-1/4 x 7-7/8"
78 x 16 x 20 cm
Matching platforms (#770-3559) are available for modeling the complete station scene.

**Nordstadt Station**
**770-3561 92.99**
21-1/4 x 6-1/4 x 6-1/4"
54 x 16 x 16cm

**Freight Shed w/Crane & Ramp**
**770-5701 54.99**
11-3/8 x 3-7/8 x 3-1/2"
29 x 10 x 9cm

**Freight Station**
**770-5715 69.99**
15 x 5-1/8 x 5-3/8"
38 x 13 x 13.5cm

## YARD EQUIPMENT & FACILITIES

**Spatzenhausen Train Crew Terminal**
**770-3507 45.99**
6.3 x 4.1 x 4.9"
16 x 10.5 x 12.5cm

**Railway Workshop**
**770-5603 27.99**
4-3/8 x 2-1/4 x 2-1/4"
11 x 5.8 x 5.8cm

## VOLLMER

IMPORTED FROM GERMANY BY WALTHERS

**Workshop**
770-5612 32.99
5-1/8 x 2-3/4 x 4-3/8"
13 x 7 x 11cm

**Pumphouse w/Loco Water Spout**
770-5708 47.99
5-1/2 x 1-5/8 x 4-5/8"
13.8 x 11.5 x 4cm

**Loading Gauge, Water Spout & Coaling Station**
770-5711 59.99

**Loco Station Einsatzleitung**
770-5712 52.99
5-11/16 x 3-5/8 x 5-7/16"
14.2 x 9.1 x 13.5cm

**Coal Loader w/Crane**
770-5714 51.99
9-1/4 x 4-1/8 x 6-1/2"
23.5 x 10.5 x 16.5cm

**Coal Bunker**
770-5719 42.99
5-5/8 x 2-1/2" 13 x 6 x 6.5cm

**Scale House**
770-5721 18.99
1-3/4 x 1-3/8 x 1-3/4"
4.5 x 3.5 x 4.6cm

**Signal Box Overhead 2-Track**
770-5726 60.99
9-5/16 x 2-3/4 x 7-1/16"
23.6 X 7 X 18cm

**Shanty**
770-5728 23.99
3-1/2 x 2-3/4 x 1-3/4"
9 x 7 x 4.5cm

**Signal Box Nurnberg**
770-5732 37.99
5-1/8 x 2-1/4 x 4-5/8"
13 x 5.8 x 11.8cm

**Cinder Conveyor**
770-5741 38.99
2-9/16 x 1-9/16 x 4-3/16"
6.5 x 4 x 10.6cm

**Corrugated Huts**
770-5743 pkg(3) 24.99
2-1/6 x 1-1/16 x 1-5/16"
5.2 x 2.8 x 3.3cm

**Engine Cleaning Plant**
770-5747 29.99
4-7/8 x 1-3/16" 12.5 x 3.2cm

**Engine Repair Stage**
770-5749 14.99
4-3/4 x 25/32 x 1-3/4"
12 x 2 x 4.4cm

**Single-Engine Shed**
770-5750 50.99
6-1/8 x 4-7/8 x 3-1/2"
15.5 x 12.5 x 9cm

**2-Stall Engine Shed**
770-5752 84.99
12 x 7-5/8 x 3-1/2"
30.5 x 19.5 x 9cm

**Locomotive Shed**
770-9112 40.99

**2-Stall Engine House**
770-5753 89.99
12-7/16 x 8-7/16 x 5-1/2"
31 x 21 x 13.8cm

**Three-Stall Roundhouse**
770-5754 142.99
13 x 19-5/8 x 4-7/8"
33 x 50 x 12cm

With a 15 degree angle between bays, the round house can be used with various turntables. Locos up to 11-3/8" long can be stored inside.

**Six-Stall Roundhouse**
770-5758 228.99
16-1/8 x 35 x 5-1/8"
41 x 89 x 13cm

**4-Stall Engine Shed**
770-5759 147.99
12-13/16 x 13-13/64 x 5-5/8"
32 x 33 x 14cm

**KOF Engine Shed**
770-5761 29.99
2-3/4 x 1-5/8" 6.7 x 4cm

**Single-Stall Engine House**
770-5762 52.99
12-19/32 x 5 x 4-5/8"
32 x 12.6 x 11.8cm

**Electric Engine Shed**
770-5765 84.99
13-13/64 x 6 x 4-13/32"
33 x 15 x 11cm

**Signal Box "Lehmen"**
770-5769 27.99
3-7/16 x 2-7/16 x 3-15/16"
8.5 x 6 x 9.8cm

**Covered Locomotive Sand Storage Bin**
770-5771 34.99

**Bucket Coal Loader**
770-5773 For Small Steam Locos 23.99
3-49/64 x 31/32 x 3-1/8"
9.4 x 2.4 x 7.8cm

**Engine Shed**
770-9110 40.99
6-1/2 x 5" 16 x 12.5cm

VOLLMER

IMPORTED FROM GERMANY
BY WALTHERS

## RURAL BUILDINGS

### Grain Mill
**770-3687 59.99**
5-13/32 x 5-15/16 x 5-13/64"
16 x 14.8 x 13cm

### Alpine House/Farm
**770-3705 71.99**
7-1/4 x 5 x 3-1/2"
18.5 x 12.8 x 9.2cm

### Farmhouse
**770-3717 48.99**
5-1/8 x 3-15/16 x 4-23/32"
13 x 10 x 12cm

### Farm
**770-3720 103.99**

### Farm House w/Barn
**770-3721 56.99**
6-13/16 x 4-13/16 x 4-13/16"
17 x 12 x 12cm

### Beehives with Shed
**770-3725 18.99**
2-1/2 x 1-31/32 x 1-7/8"
6.3 x 4.9 x 4.7cm

### Stable w/Pigeon Loft
**770-3726 45.99**
5-1/2 x 3-1/8" 14 x 8cm

### Farmyard Accessories
**770-3729 23.99**
Includes well, pump, rubbish dumps and duck house.

### House w/Barn
**770-3731 49.99**
4-7/8 x 2-3/4 x 4-3/4"
12.5 x 7 x 12cm

### Goat Shed
**770-3737 47.99**
5-19/32 x 3-15/16 x 3-3/4"
14.2 x 10 x 9.5cm

### Pig Barn
**770-3740 39.99**
6-1/8 x 3-3/4 x 2-13/32"
15.5 x 9.5 x 6.1cm

### Stable
**770-3741 20.99**

### Shepherd's Carriage
**770-3742 20.99**

### Silos
**770-3743** pkg(2) **16.99**
Great for grain or feed storage, these silos are natural additions to any barn or farmhouse scene.

### Farmhouse w/Shed
**770-3744 59.99**
8-3/8 x 5 x 4-7/8"
21 x 12.5 x 12cm

### Sheep Farm

**770-3746 56.99**
6.3 x 5.7 x 4.1"
16 x 14.5 x 10.5cm

### Mountain Road Scene
**770-3835 153.99**

### Hunting Cabin
**770-3855** With Wolf & 7 Goats
**39.99**
4-13/32 x 3-13/32 x 2-3/32"
11 x 8.5 x 5.2cm

### Farm Equipment Repair Shop
**770-3682 60.99**
6-3/8 x 4-3/4 x 4-3/4"
15.8 x 12 x 12cm

## HOUSES

### Gatekeeper's Home
**770-3528 34.99**
3-41/64 x 2-31/64 x 2-31/32"
9.1 x 9.2 x 7.4cm

### Gatekeeper's House
**770-3529 58.99**
3-37/64 x 2-7/16 x 2-29/32
13.2 x 9.5 x 11.5cm

### Garden Houses
**770-3640** pkg(2) **24.99**
Whether you call them garden houses, planting sheds or outbuildings, these tiny houses are just the place to hang out on a nice day. In many German cities, townsfolk rent oddly-shaped plots of vacant land for gardens. They often put up small sheds to store their gardening and picnic supplies. On North American layouts, these buildings make great backyard sheds.

### Timber-Framed Duplex with Garage
**770-3641** pkg(2) **39.99**
4-13/64 x 4-5/8 x 5-13/64"
10.5 x 11.5 x 13cm

### Duplex with Garage
**770-3642** pkg(2) **39.99**
4-13/64 x 4-5/8 x 5-13/64"
10.5 x 11.5 x 13cm

### House
**770-3670** Tan **27.99**
2 x 3-5/16 x 5-5/16"
5.2 x 8.3 x 13.3cm

### House
**770-3671** Yellow **27.99**
2 x 3-5/16 x 5-5/16"
5.2 x 8.3 x 13.3cm

### Half-Timbered House
**770-3672** White **27.99**
2 x 3-5/16 x 5-5/16"
5.2 x 8.3 x 13.3cm

VOLLMER

IMPORTED FROM GERMANY BY WALTHERS

**Half-Timbered House**
**770-3673** Gray **27.99**
2 x 3-5/16 x 5-5/16"
5.2 x 8.3 x 13.3cm

**House Under Construction**
**770-3689 42.99**
4-23/32 x 4-1/2 x 4-11/32"
12 x 11.5 x 11cm

**Mountain Cottage**
**770-3701 29.99**
4-3/4 x 5-3/8 x 3"
12.5 x 13.5 x 7.5cm

**Alpine House-Chalet Style**
**770-3702 29.99**
6-1/8 x 4-3/8 x 3"
15.5 x 11 x 7.5cm

**Vampire Villa**
**770-3679 92.99**
4-13/16 x 4-13/16 x 5-13/16"
12 x 12 x 14.5cm

From the boarded-up windows to the eerie red light that flickers inside, this old house is sure to give you the creeps! And for more frightening fun, a blanket of fog can be generated using Smoke Unit #770-4114 (sold separately).

**Smoke Generator for #3679**
**770-4114 48.99**

**Alpine Lodge**
**770-3708 28.99**

**Lake Shore House**
**770-3711 38.99**
7-5/8 x 4-3/4 x 3-3/8"
19.5 x 12 x 8.5cm

**Ranch Style House**
**770-3712 29.99**
5-7/8 x 4-3/8 x 2-1/2"
15 x 11 x 6.5cm

**Country House**
**770-3713 29.99**
5-1/8 x 5-1/8 x 2-3/4"
13 x 13 x 7cm

**White House w/Gray Trim**

**770-3715 40.99**
4.5 x 3.5 x 5.5"
11.5 x 9 x 14cm

**Beige House w/Brown Trim**

**770-3716 40.99**
4.5 x 3.5 x 5.5"
11.5 x 9 x 14cm

**House w/Garage**
**770-3718 30.99**
4-1/2 x 4-3/4 x 3-1/2"
11.5 x 12 x 8.8cm

**Bungalow**
**770-3719 30.99**
5-1/8 x 4-3/4 x 2-7/8"
13 x 12 x 7.3cm

**House w/Bakery**
**770-3724 36.99**
4-3/4 x 4-3/4 x 3-1/8"
12 x 12 x 8cm
4-3/4 x 3 x 2-1/8"
12 x 7.5 x 5.5cm

**House On Fire**
**770-3728 60.99**
4-3/4 x 3-1/2 x 5-3/4"
12 x 9 x 14.5cm

**Smoke Generator**
**770-4113 32.99**
For #s 3728 and 3729.

**One-Car Garage/Shed**
**770-3766 18.99**
3-3/16 x 1-3/4 x 2-5/64"
8 x 4.4 x 5.2cm

**Mansion**
**770-3775 158.99**
12-3/8 x 4-1/4 x 8-1/16"
31.5 x 10.8 x 20.5cm

**Forester's House**
**770-3792 59.99**
5-1/2 x 4-1/2 x 5"
14 x 11.5 x 12.5cm

**Birthplace of Pope Benedict XVI**
8-5/8 x 7 x 4-5/8"
22 x 17.5 x 11.6cm
**770-3828** Kit **60.99**
**770-3829** Assembled **76.99**

**Alpine Chalet with Carport**
**770-3846 52.99**
6-13/16 x 4-13/32 x 3-5/8"
17 x 11 x 9cm

**House Of The Witch**
**770-3851 48.99**
4-11/64 x 3-27/32 x 3-21/64"
10.4 x 9.6 x 8.3cm

**2-Story Cottage**
**770-3853** With Little Red Riding Hood & Wolf Figures **39.99**
5 x 4-13/32 x 3"
12.5 x 11 x 7.5cm

**Single Car Port w/Shed**
**770-5127 16.99**
3-1/16 x 2-11/16 x 1-9/16"
7.8 x 6.9 x 4cm

**Double Car Port w/Shed**
**770-5128 16.99**
2-9/16 x 2-3/16 x 1-3/8"
6.5 x 5.5 x 3.5cm

**House w/Vineyard**
**770-5129 35.99**

VOLLMER

IMPORTED FROM GERMANY
BY WALTHERS

## CITY BUILDINGS

### Old Fire Station
**770-3776 84.99**
Main Building:
8-1/16 x 5 x 6-3/32"
20.5 x 12.6 x 15.5cm

Hose-Drying Tower:
2-5/32 x 2-5/32 x 7/8"
5.5 x 5.5 x 20cm

### Burning Revenue (Tax) Office
**770-3785 126.99**
10-7/16 x 4-1/8 x 7-9/32"
26.5 x 10.5 x 18.5cm

### 5-Story Corner Building Castle Avenue #1
**770-3811** Red Brick **83.99**
5-5/8 x 5-5/8 x 9-13/64"
14 x 14 x 23cm

### 4-Story Corner Apartment House Castle Avenue #3
**770-3813** Yellow/Brown **69.99**
4-13/32 x 4-21/64 x 7-13/16"
11 x 10.8 x 19.5cm

### 4-Story House at The Park Castle Avenue #5
**770-3815** Two-Tone Gray **69.99**
4-13/32 x 4-21/64 x 7-13/16"
11 x 10.8 x 19.5cm

### 3-Story Corner Building
**770-3816 60.99**
5-1/2 x 5-1/4 x 7"
14 x 13.4 x 17.8cm

### Main Street
**770-3820 194.99**
Includes 1ea #'s 3816, 3817, 3818 & 3819.

### Council Office
**770-3832 57.99**
5-3/16 x 4-5/8 x 6-5/64"
13 x 11.6 x 15.2cm

### Village Fire Station
**770-3751 59.99**

### Police Station
**770-3763 59.99**

Latest New Product News Daily! Visit Walthers Web site at
**www.walthers.com**

### Station Road Value Set
**770-3675 174.99**
Includes 1 each #s 3669, 3670, 3671, 3672, 3673 and 3674.

### Furstenberg City Hall
**770-3690 83.99**
9-13/32 x 4-13/64 x 8-13/64"
23.5 x 10.5 x 20.5cm

### Police Station w/Jail
**770-3693 83.99**
7-3/4 x 5-1/2" 19.5 x 14cm

### Police Station
**770-3747 52.99**
1-3/64 x 5-5/8 x 3-13/32"
3 x 14 x 8.5cm

### Old Time Post Office
**770-3748 49.99**
4 x 4-3/4 x 7-1/2"
10 x 12 x 19cm

### Fire Station w/Tower
**770-3752 60.99**
4-3/4 x 4-3/4 x 8-5/8"
12 x 12 x 22cm

### Maintenance Depot
**770-3756 39.99**
5-1/2 x 3-1/8 x 6-5/8"
14 x 8 x 17cm

### Ornamental Fountain
**770-3758 21.99**
2-1/8 x 2-1/8 x 5-3/4"
5.5 x 5.5 x 14.5cm

### Modern Fire Station
**770-3759 91.99**
12.5 x 6 x 9.5
32 x 15 x 24cm

Three structures (main building, lobby/office and six-story hose tower) are included and can be arranged in a variety of ways.

### Playground
**770-3665 17.99**

### City Hall
**770-3760 121.99**
7-1/8 x 4-3/4 x 11-1/4"
18 x 12 x 28.5cm

Features ornate clock tower and solid, stone construction

### Fire Station 112
**770-3761 60.99**
Main Building:
5-13/64 x 5-5/8 x 4"
13 x 14 x 10cm;

Hose Tower:
2-13/32 x 2-13/32 x 5-13/64"
6 x 6 x 13cm

### Public Restrooms
**770-3762 21.99**
2 x 2 x 2-3/8"
5.1 x 5.1 x 6cm

### Post Office
**770-3765 113.99**
8-1/4 x 6-1/2" 21 x 16.6cm

### Red Cross Center
**770-3764 59.99**
7 x 5-15/16 x 5-1/8"
17.6 x 14.8 x 12.8cm

### Set Of Three Apartments
**770-3780 158.99**
Kit includes one each of #3777, 3778 and 3779.

## VOLLMER

IMPORTED FROM GERMANY
BY WALTHERS

**Classic Style Building w/Cafe**
**770-3770 62.99**
4-3/4 x 4 x 7-3/4"
12 x 10 x 19.6cm

**Public Record Office**
**770-3773 62.99**
4-3/8 x 7 x 8"
11 x 10.8 x 20.5cm

**Modern Office Building**
**770-3800 69.99**
5-1/2 x 5-1/2 x 7-7/8"
14 x 14 x 20cm

**Modern Apartment Building**
**770-3801 69.99**
6 x 4-9/16 x 7-7/8"
15.2 x 11.5 x 20cm

**Transformer House**
**770-5535 25.99**
2-1/8 x 2-1/8 x 5"
5.4 x 5.4 x 12.6cm

## TANKS & TOWERS

**Water Tower**
**770-5710 52.99**
4-5/16 x 9-7/8" 11 x 25cm

**Ornate Water Tower**
**770-5704 50.99**
3-5/8 x 3-5/8" 9 x 9cm

**Spherical Gas Storage Tank**
**770-5529 35.99**
3-13/16 x 3-29/64 x 6"
9.5 x 8.6 x 15cm

**Diesel Tank**
**770-5530 33.99**
7-21/64 x 5-11/16 x 3-13/16"
18.3 x 14.2 x 9.5cm

Includes valves, piping, vents, safety cage ladder and more.

**Gera Water Tower**
**770-5707 50.99**
4 x 4-13/32 x 10-13/32"
10 x 11 x 26cm

**Coaling Tower**
**770-5720 84.99**
7-5/8 x 7-23/64 x 5-5/8"
19 x 18 x 14cm

**Interlocking Yard Tower**
**770-5731 35.99**
5-1/8 x 2 x 5-1/8"
13 x 5 x 13cm

**Fellbach Signal Tower**
**770-5734 49.99**
6 x 2-13/64 x 6-13/16"
15 x 7 x 17cm

**Stuttgart Signal Tower**
**770-5735 81.99**
9-7/16 x 6 x 6-13/16"
26.3 x 15.2 x 17cm

**Interlocking Tower**
**770-5737 25.99**
3-1/2 x 2 x 3-3/8"
9 x 5 x 8.5cm

**Signal Tower**
**770-5738 60.99**
6-1/4 x 3" 15.5 x 7.5cm

**Haunted Rothenberg Tower**
**770-3900 54.99**
3-1/2 x 3-1/2 x 14-1/2"
9 x 9 x 36.5cm



## CHURCHES

**Altbach Half-Timber Church**
**770-3768 81.99**
7-13/16 x 5-5/8 x 12"
19.5 x 14 x 30cm

**Cathedral**
**770-3739 136.99**
11-3/4 x 5-3/8 x 15-3/4"
30 x 13.5 x 40cm

For extra realism, full-color stained glass "windows," printed on translucent paper, are included. For a more detailed scene, the Cathedral Steps (#770-3738) can be added.

**Cathedral Steps**
**770-3738 29.99**
16-1/2 x 7-7/8 x 1/2"

**St. Andrew's Church**
**770-3709 70.99**
7-1/4 x 5-1/2" 18.5 x 14cm

VOLLMER

IMPORTED FROM GERMANY
BY WALTHERS

## ALPINE BUILDINGS

**Schweineberg Church**
**770-3710 60.99**
7-13/32 x 3-7/8 x 6-13/32"
18.5 x 9.7 x 16cm

**Ludwig Huber Butcher's Shop**
**770-3836 35.99**
4-13/16 x 4 x 3-13/16"
12 x 10 x 9.5cm

**Trachten Hallhuber Boutique**
**770-3837 35.99**
4-13/16 x 4 x 3-13/16"
12 x 10 x 9.5cm

**Restaurant Gasthhaus zum Ochsen**
**770-3838 35.99**
4-13/16 x 4 x 3-13/16"
12 x 10 x 9.5cm

**Village Set with Church**
**770-3839 147.99**
Includes one each church#3710 and 3836, 3837, 3838.

## BUSINESSES

**Chinese Restaurant**
**770-3817 54.99**
5 x 4-3/4 x 6-7/16"
12.6 x 12 x 16.4cm

**Bed & Breakfast**
**770-3818 50.99**
5 x 4-3/4 x 6-7/16"
12.6 x 12 x 16.4cm

**Law Office**
**770-3819 50.99**
5 x 4-5/16 x 6-7/16"
12.6 x 11 x 16.4cm

**Open-Air Market Hall/Pavillion**
**770-5608 76.99**
10 x 11-13/32 x 4"
25 x 28.5 x 10cm

**Village Inn**
**770-3637 62.99**
7-13/16 x 5 x 6"
19.5 x 12.5 x 15cm

**Burger King**
**770-3632 71.99**
7-7/8 x 5-3/4" 20 x 14.8cm

**Restaurant**
**770-3645 58.99**
6 x 5-13/64 x 5-13/16"
15 x 13 x 14.5cm

**Shoe Shop**
**770-3646 42.99**
4-13/64 x 3-1/4 x 5-1/2"
10.5 x 8.2 x 13.8cm

**Plumber's Shop**
**770-3648 42.99**
4-13/64 x 3-1/4 x 5-1/2"
10.5 x 8.x13.8cm

**Sports Shop**
**770-3651 42.99**
4-13/64 x 3-1/4 x 5-1/2"
10.5 x 8.2 x 13.8cm

**Market Street**
**770-3655** pkg(3) **116.99**
Features kits #3651, 3652 and 3653.

**A Walthers Exclusive**

**Porsche Dealership**
**770-5606** Assembled **101.99**
10-5/8 x 7-1/2 x 3-1/8" 27 x 19 x 8cm

**Disco Casablanca**
**770-3656 63.99**
8 x 5-5/8 x 3-5/8"
20 x 14 x 9cm

**Aldi Supermarket**
**770-3658 56.99**
8 x 5-15/16 x 1-3/16"
20 x 14.8 x 3cm

**Supermarket**
**770-3660 62.99**
16.8 x 14cm

**Lidl Supermarket**
**770-3662 56.99**
8 x 5-15/16 x 3-5/8"
20 x 14.8 x 9cm

**Station Restaurant**
**770-3663 62.99**
7-3/4 x 4-3/4" 19.8 x 12cm

**Rebmann Winery**
**770-3686 62.99**
8-15/32 x 5-1/2 x 4-23/32"
21.5 x 14 x 12cm

**Butcher's Shop**
**770-3674 42.99**
4-5/8 x 3-13/16 x 6"
11.5 x 9.5 x 15cm

**Adler Inn w/Beer Garden**
**770-3736 62.99**
8-1/4 x 5-1/8" 21 x 13cm

**Cafe**
**770-3676 62.99**
5-1/8 x 4-1/2" 13 x 11.5cm

# VOLLMER

IMPORTED FROM GERMANY BY WALTHERS

**Winery Festival**
**770-3680 52.99**
6-1/4 x 5-1/2" 16 x 14cm

Includes an outdoor serving area with benches, wine press and wooden storage barrel.

**Boutique**
**770-3694 66.99**
7-1/2 x 5-5/16" 19 x 13.5cm

**Liquor Store**
**770-3697 79.99**
8-1/16 x 5-1/8" 20.5 x 13cm

**Savings Bank**
**770-3698 81.99**
7-7/8 x 5-7/8 x 5-7/8"
19.5 x 14 x 14.5cm

**Alpine Restaurant**
**770-3706 62.99**
6 x 5-7/8 x 4"
17.8 x 15 x 11.5cm

**Vintner's Lodge**
**770-3732 49.99**
4-3/4 x 3-1/2 x 5-3/4"
12 x 9 x 14.5cm

**Restaurant Rebstock**
**770-3745 57.99**
5-11/16 x 4-5/8 x 5-3/4"
14.2 x 11.6 x 14.4cm

**Village Inn Rathskeller**
**770-3754 67.99**
4-3/4 x 4-3/4 x 5-3/4"
12 x 12 x 14.5cm

**Gas Station**
**770-5744 33.99**
3-3/8 x 4 x 1-3/4"
8.5 x 10 x 4.3cm

**4-Story Bank Building**
**770-3771 62.99**
4-1/8 x 3-5/8 x 7-3/4"
10.5 x 9.3 x 19.7cm

**4-Story Hotel**
**770-3772 62.99**
4-3/8 x 3-3/4 x 8-3/4"
11 x 9.5 x 22cm

**Black Forest Inn**
**770-3707 59.99**
5-1/4 x 4-1/2 x 4-7/10"
13.4 x 11.4 x 11.8cm

**City Hotel**
**770-3782 79.99**
5-3/8 x 5-1/16" 13.8 x 13cm

**Restaurant**
**770-3788 66.99**
4-5/8 x 4-5/8" 11.5 x 11.5cm

**Bookstore**
**770-3842 52.99**
3-7/8 x 3-3/8 x 5-5/8"
10 x 8.5 x 14.5cm

**Food Vendor Stands**
**770-5144 19.99**
2-13/32 x 1-5/8 x 1-13/32"
6 x 4 x 3.5cm

Each is complete with converted trailer and colorful signs.

**Restaurant**
**770-3781 79.99**
6-1/16 x 4-11/16" 15.5 x 12cm

**Country Inn w/Beergarden**
**770-3833 66.99**
19.4 x 11.6 x 12.2cm

**Max Ziegler Boat Rentals**
**770-5120 37.99**
5-13/16 x 3-5/8 x 2-5/8"
14.5 x 9 x 6.5cm

**Braustuberl Country In**
**770-3845 68.99**
8-13/64 x 5-13/64 x 3-13/16"
20.5 x 13 x 9.5cm

**Repair Shop**
**770-5602 31.99**
5-1/8 x 3-15/16 x 2"
12.8 x 9.8 x 5cm

**Topferei Pottery Store**

**770-5596 65.99**
7.7 x 4.9 x 4.1"
19.5 x 12.5 x 10.5cm

## INDUSTRIAL

**Hammermill**
**770-5598 65.99**
8.9 x 5.7 x 5.1"
22.5 x 14.5 x 13cm

**Contractor's Yard**
**770-5600 81.99**

**Container Crane**
**770-5620 126.99**
11-13/16 x 9-1/8 x 8-7/8"
30 x 23.2 x 22.5cm

## VOLLMER

IMPORTED FROM GERMANY
BY WALTHERS

### Construction Cars
**770-5722** pkg(2) **29.99**

### Overhead Gantry Crane
**770-5774 29.99**
5 x 2-13/64 x 4-13/32"
12.5 x 5.5 x 11.4cm

### Gantry Crane
**770-5625 42.99**
12-19/32 x 9-21/32 x 5-7/8"
32 x 24.5 x 15cm

### Oil Refinery
**770-5525 73.99**
5-7/8 x 3-7/8 x 9-1/4"
15 x 10 x 23.5cm

### Factory on Fire
**770-5601 89.99**
13-3/8 x 5-1/2 x 11-3/16"
34 x 14 x 30cm

Includes two red flashing lamps to simulate flames, collapsed wall and burned roof, plus debris.

### Sawmill
**770-3797 109.99**
13-1/8 x 5-1/2" 33 x 14cm

### Sawmill
**770-3799 76.99**
5.1 x 5.1 x 5.5" -
3.9 x 39.4 x 7.3"
13 x 13 x 14cm -
10 x 100 x 18.5cm

### Brewery w/Interior
**770-5609 89.99**
16-3/8 x 5-1/2" 41.5 x 14cm

### 2-Story Factory Building
**770-5610 40.99**
5-1/8 x 2-3/4 x 5-1/8"
13 x 7 x 13cm

### Substation or Annex Office
**770-5614 19.99**
2-3/8 x 2-3/4 x 2-3/4"
6 x 7 x 7cm

### Boiler House
**770-5617 58.99**
10 x 5-13/64 x 12"
25 x 13 x 30cm

### Radsatzdreherei Wheel Repair Shop
**770-5618 40.99**
5-13/64 x 3-5/8 x 5-5/8"
13 x 9 x 14cm

### Workshop
**770-5619 32.99**
5-13/64 x 3-13/32 x 4-13/64"
13 x 8.5 x 10.5cm

### Coal Bins
**770-5717 12.99**
4-13/32 x 1-13/32 x 15/16"
11 x 3.5 x 2.3cm

### Overhead Crane
**770-5624 52.99**
10 x 4-3/4 x 6-1/2"
25.5 x 12 x 16.5cm

### Overhead Crane
**770-5727 31.99**
5-5/8 x 2-5/16 x 4-13/16"
14 x 5.8 x 12cm

Includes positionable trolley and more.

### Road Sign Depot
**770-5778 36.99**
5-1/8 x 3-15/16 x 2"
12.8 x 9.8 x 5cm

### Smoke Stack Only
**770-6017 14.99**

Boiler House 770-5617

Workshop 770-5619

Smoke Stack Only 770-6017

## VOLLMER

IMPORTED FROM GERMANY BY WALTHERS

## BRIDGES & VIADUCTS

### Overpass Bridge
**770-2544 16.99**
4-13/16 x 2-27/32 x 1-31/64"
12 x 7.1 x 3.7cm

### Viaduct Enlargement
**770-2512 19.99**
4 x 2-5/8 x 5-3/4"
10.2 x 6.5 x 14.3cm

Matches the brick construction of #2513, allows for easy expansion of the viaduct, sold separately.

### Truss Bridge
**770-2545 34.99**
10-5/8 x 3 x 2-5/16"
27 x 7.5 x 5.8cm

### Viaduct
**770-2513 51.99**
12-1/4 x 2-5/8 x 5-3/4"
30.6 x 6.5 x 14.3cm

This detailed brick viaduct is ideal for a steam- or diesel-era right-of-way. It can be lengthened with #770-2512 and #770-2529 (both sold separately).

### Covered Bridge
**770-2515 39.99**
8-13/16 x 3-1/8 x 3-5/8"
22 x 7.8 x 9cm

### Foot Bridge
**770-5709 39.99**
10 x 8-1/4" 25 x 21cm

### Bridge Piling
**770-2529 7.99**
Matches pilings included with kit #2513, for use with kit #2512, sold separately.

### Gray Brick Bridge
**770-2551 54.99**
15-3/4 x 3-1/32 x 4-1/64"
40 x 7.7 x 10.2cm

### Halle Viaduct
**770-2550 73.99**
28-13/16 x 2-13/16 x 9-13/64"
72 x 7 x 23cm

### Piers
**770-4004** pkg(10) **40.99**
9-1/2" 24cm high

Used to support track ramps. May be cut to shorter lengths.

### Arcades
**770-4500** Brown Brick **57.99**

### Railings
**770-5000** pkg(20) **19.99**
3-1/2" 9cm long

## CAMPER

**770-5147 25.99**
2-13/32 x 1-5/8 x 1-13/32"
6 x 4 x 3.5cm

## SKATEBOARD PARK

**770-3610 24.99**
Features assorted ramps.

## CASTLE

**770-3910 253.99**
13-3/4 x 11-3/4" 35 x 30cm

## RIDES & ACCESSORIES

Each kit is easy to build and molded in realistic colors, so no painting is needed.

### Roundabout Ride
**770-3622 52.99**
7-3/8 x 6-3/8 x 4-1/2"
18.5 x 16 x 11.2cm.

You can build this colorful roundabout as a static model, or add motor #4200 (available separately) for a working ride!

### Swingboat Ride
**770-3620 52.99**
7-1/4 x 4-5/8 x 5-1/4"
18 x 11.6 x 13.2cm.

The kit can be built for display, or powered with motor #4200 (available separately) to animate your scene.

### Ghost Train
**770-3627 63.99**
7-3/4 x 4-1/2 x 3-7/8"
20 x 11.5 x 10cm.

For added excitement, there's a special electronic sound unit that produces eerie noises.

### Tent
**770-3623 37.99**
7-1/4 x 4-3/4 x 3-3/8"
18 x 12 x 8.5cm

### Game Booths
**770-3625** pkg(2) **22.99**
Kit includes parts to build a toy lottery and a plant lottery. Full color panels make these eye–catching models for any miniature midway.

### Fair Assortment

**770-3626 174.99**
Includes two game booths, Swingboats, Roundabout and tent kits.

Latest New Product News Daily! Visit Walthers Web site at
**www.walthers.com**

# BUILT-N-READY® STRUCTURES

These pre-assembled, hand-painted and fully detailed structures are great for detailing cities, towns and villages in a just a few minutes.

## STATIONS & PLATFORMS

### Dansbury Depot

**785-5023 59.98**
7-1/2 x 5-1/8 x 4" 19 x 13 x 10.1cm
Complete with high platform, non-working train order signal and other details.

## HOUSES

### Granny's House

**NEW 785-5027 59.98**
5 x 4 x 2-5/8" 12.7 x 10.1 x 6.6cm
Perfect for a small town or older city residential area, the large front porch has plenty of toys to keep the grandkids busy.

## BUSINESSES

### Fill 'er Up & Fix'er Up

**785-5025 59.98**
6 x 5-3/8 x 2-5/8" 15.2 x 13.6 x 6.6cm
Once a common sight on many highways, this structure is complete with office and service bays, signs, gas pumps and much more.

### Lubener's General Store

**785-5021 49.98**
4-1/2 x 3-3/4 x 4-1/8" 11.4 x 9.5 x 10.4cm
Ready for business and complete with awnings, signs, and sidewalk displays.

### Harrison's Hardware

**785-5022 49.98**
4-1/8 x 2-3/4 x 4-1/8" 10.4 x 6.9 x 10.4
Great addition to any street scene, complete with colorful signs, merchandise displays and a dumpster.

### Corner Emporium

**785-5024 49.98**
4-1/8 x 2-3/4 x 4-1/8" 10.4 x 6.9 x 10.4cm
Home to three different businesses, complete with signs and loads of details.

## INDUSTRIAL

### Clyde & Dale's Barrel Factory

**785-5026 69.98**
7 x 9 x 7-1/2" 17.8 x 22.9 x 19.1cm
A great trackside customer for a railroad, includes rooftop water tank, beer barrels, vents and more.

## TRACKSIDE SCENES

Designed specifically for modelers who want fine quality craftsmanship, intricate detail, and authenticity. These are not just models of a single item, but of a complete scene. Each kit contains over 70 highly detailed white metal castings, trees, Turf, Foliage, and all the accessories necessary to complete a scene covering up to 200 square inches.

### Possum Hollow

**785-151 31.98**
An abandoned caboose has been converted to a home for a rural family. The piles of accumulated junk add to that backwoods atmosphere of the scene.

### Caboose & Sand Facility

**785-152 31.98**
This is a common sight found around railroad yards. The sand tower supplies the locomotives' needs while the storage shed keeps cabooses well stocked.

### Otis Coal Company

**785-153 39.98**
Private coal companies like this were found along spur lines throughout the United States. Such facilities served as the links between the long coal trains and the consumer.

### Tie & Plank Mill

**785-154 39.98**
Steam powered sawmill... a small industry with lots of possibilities for your layout.

## COMPLETE SCENES 31.98 ea

Kits contain highly detailed castings plus all other materials needed to build a scene, except paint and glue. Scenes can be assembled in several different ways to fit available space.

### Smiley's Tow Service

**785-130** 7" x 9"
Kit includes: basswood building and fence, seven trees (with two colors of Foliage), four different colors of grass and soil, three colors of Foliage for bushes and weeds, and over 60 white metal castings including tires, concrete blocks, fuel tanks, oil drums, firewood, mail box, man and several other assorted pieces including junk pile.

### Maple Leaf Cemetery

**785-131** 8" x 11"
Kit includes basswood tool shed and fence rail, eight trees (with two colors of Foliage), four colors of grass and soil, two colors of Foliage for bushes and weeds, and over 40 white metal castings including stone fence posts and walls, gates, two men, a central monument and 28 tombstones with names.

### Memorial Park

**785-132** 8" x 14"
Kit includes shelter house, basswood fence, nine trees (with two colors of Foliage), four colors of grass and soil, two colors of Foliage for bushes and weeds, and over 40 white metal castings including bar-b-q ovens, tire swing, teeter- totter, picnic tables, people, trash cans and park swing.

## SCENIC DETAILS

### Stations & Platforms

**Flag Depot**
785-239 15.98

### Yard Equipment & Facilities

**Trackside Scale**
785-231 7.98

**Diesel Fuel Facility**
785-232 7.98

### Rural Buildings

**Aermotor Windmill**
785-209 7.98

Smokehouse
785-213 9.98

3 Outhouses & Man
785-214 9.98

Chicken Coop
785-215 9.98

Tool Shed
785-216 9.98

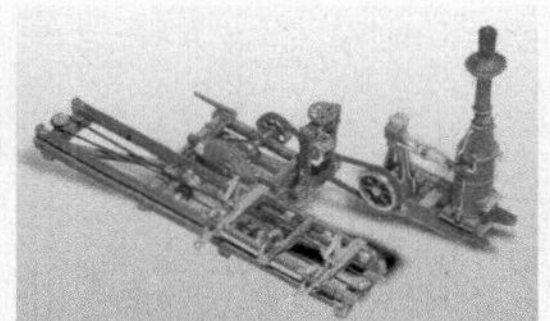

Rural Sawmill
785-243 9.98

## Tanks & Towers

Branch Line Water Tower
785-241 15.98

Three Fuel Stands
785-212 7.98

## Businesses

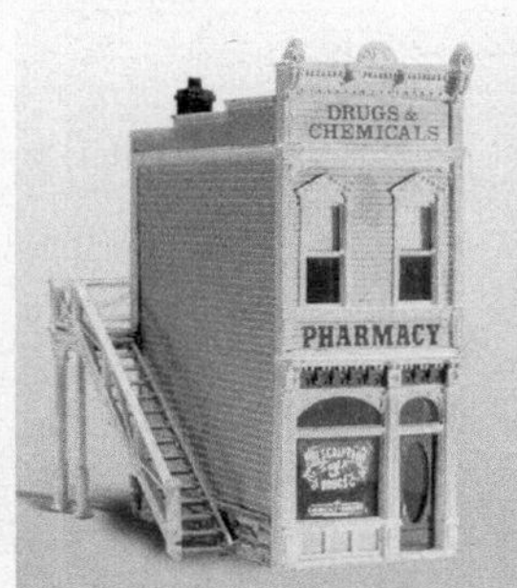


Pharmacy
785-221 15.98

Doctor's Office & Shoe Repair
785-224 15.98

Ice House
785-219 15.98

Daniel's Outfitters
785-220 15.98

Ticket Office
785-222 15.98

Rocky's Tavern
785-238 15.98

Gas Station
785-223 15.98

Tucker Brothers Machine Shop
785-240 15.98

## Miscellaneous

Gazebo
785-236 9.98

## SCENIC DETAILS®

### 5.98 ea (Unless Noted)

**785-201** Tombstones - Assorted Shapes & Sizes pkg(20)

**785-202** Trackside Junk Piles

**785-203** Assorted Crates, Barrels & Sacks

**785-204** Assorted Skids

**785-205** Assorted Junk Piles

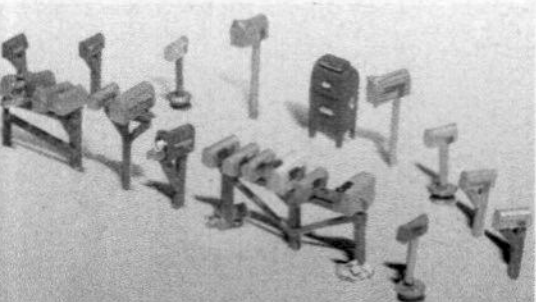

**785-206** Assorted Rural & City Mailboxes

**785-225** Industrial Junk Piles

**785-229** Steam Engine & Hammer Mill **7.98**

**785-230** Assorted Vending Machines (Ice, Soda, Gum, Popcorn) pkg(8) **7.98**

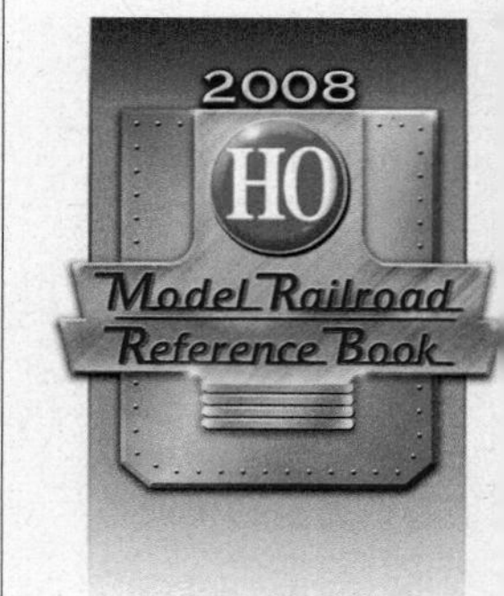

# MAGIC OF MODEL RAILROADING

**Models and Photo by Lou Sassi, Charlton, NY**

Passengers have a fine view of the surrounding country from atop the Saul High Trestle. Conductors on day trains make it a point to announce the approaching viewpoint, which has long been a favorite of hikers, campers and photographers in the region. Of course riders only have a few minutes to enjoy the scenery as the train passes, but on a clear day like this, it's a high point of any trip.

Working downgrade towards Adams, ten-wheeler #74 rumbles along with a two-car local in tow on this spectacular scene by Lou Sassi of Charlton, New York.

We'd love to see your layout, module or diorama here next year and invite you to submit photos for our "Magic of Model Railroading" Photo Contest.

Our first place winner receives $250, second wins $100 and third place gets $75. All published Honorable Mentions receive $25 and a copy of the Walthers Reference Book. Color slides or high resolution digital images are preferred, but prints can also be submitted — please see walthers.com for full details. Please include a brief description (typed or printed please!) of the scene, along with the correct spelling of private roadnames, town names and the name of the photographer if different from your own.

PRINT YOUR NAME AND ADDRESS ON EACH SLIDE OR PRINT. Please limit your submissions to your 10 best photos.

Deadlines will be announced at walthers.com and in Walthers publications. Please mail slides to:

**ATTN: SLIDES FOR CATALOG**
**C/O Wm. K. Walthers, Inc.**
**PO Box 3039**
**Milwaukee, WI 53201-3039**

# FIRST PLACE AWARD - $250

**Models and Photo by Howard Dwyer, Farmingville, NY**

Midday on Bleecker Street finds a utility worker taking a break to watch the S-2 switcher pass beneath him, pushing a flat car loaded with debris from a nearby urban renewal project. It's another busy day in downtown East Utica on Howard Dwyer's Island Central Railroad. The switcher is from Atlas and the flat car is from Athearn. City Classics and Downtown Deco structures were used to create this aging, rundown section of town.

**Models and photo by Volker Lange, Grosspoesna, Germany**

Whether you call it a "tankola" or "gondank," this cut-down tank car makes a great car for moving material around the scrapyard. Volker Lange patterned the model after a prototype car he saw at a scrap dealer in Richmond, California. The car began life as a Walthers model.

**Models by Vic Roman, Schenectady, NY**
**Photo by Bill McChesney, Niskayuna, NY**

Steaming impatiently, Niagara #6024 waits for the highball alongside the Union Station in downtown Albany, New York. The growl of EMD F3s rings over the station tracks as a freight wheels through, en route to the Maiden Lane swing bridge and the Rensselear Yard. We're trackside on Vic Roman's New York Central Hudson Division. Soon to be heading west for Chicago, the 4-8-4 is a Broadway Limited Model. The F units ride on Stewart drives and feature Highliner shells. The city scene was built with a variety of kitbashed Bachmann, DPM and Walthers kits.

**Models & photo by Alden Armstrong, Grand Junction, CO.**

Just like lots of kids who grew up loving trains, Alden Armstrong was introduced to railroading by his father. On weekends, his dad took him down to the Santa Fe tracks to see the trains and wave to the engineer as the train rolled past. The engineer of this Sunset Santa Fe 2-8-2 doesn't look like he'll wave back at first, but decides he can't disappoint the child sitting on his dad's shoulder. The photo was taken on a diorama and the figures are by Preiser.

**Models and photo by Richard Bailey, Cartersville, GA**

The reefers have just been iced and loading is complete at the Beanfield siding. In minutes the carloads of fresh bananas will be on their way to grocery stores across the country. The locomotive is a PROTO 2000, rolling stock is from Intermountain and Roundhouse, the track is Atlas and the vehicle is from Wheel Works. Products from Woodland Scenics were used to create the scenery and the structure is from Sheepscot.

**Models by Gilles Mallet and Pierre Dion; Photo by Pierre Dion, Montreal, Canada**

A Central Vermont northbound freight is taking a detour over Boston & Maine track on its way to Bellows Falls powered by a CNR F7A and a CVR Geep. The action takes place on the Vermont & Essex Club layout. The bridge was built by Gilles Mallet who also weathered the Geep. Pierre did the landscaping using products from Woodland Scenics and Scenic Express.

**Models by Vic Roman, photo by Bill McChesney, Schenectady, NY**

On a late afternoon the famous 20th Century Limited heads east through the unsavory part of Albany, its two-tone gray nose just visible between businesses. The train skirts the old commercial district, home to several taverns and the focus of local law enforcement who try to keep crime to a minimum. The action takes place on Vic's NYC Hudson division layout. The loco is a PROTO 2000 model, structures are a mix of Walthers Cornerstone Series®, Bar Mills, Fine Scale Miniatures, Design Preservation Models and Heljan kits, all constructed and customized for the scene.

**Models and photo by Steve McIver, Feasterville Trevose, PA**

Just 23 miles from its namesake city, the minesweeper U.S.S. Weston loads up on supplies at Port Weston. The crowded harbor is just as busy as the double-track Weston & Matherly mainline that separates it from the W&M's south yard. On the mainline, an EMD FP7 races past with the daily Weston Rocket. The action takes place on Steve's late 1950s freelanced railroad in the northeast. The pier terminal is a Walthers Cornerstone Series® model, the minesweeper is from Lindbergh, the dockyard switcher is Rivarossi, the FP7 is Atlas, the crane is from Model Power and the passenger cars are Walthers.

**Models and photo by Erik Block, Antwerpen, Belgium**

A hot summer afternoon near the border of Arizona and New Mexico is not a good place for your Chevy to break down. This driver tries to flag down a passing car for help. The prospects look good because the other car will have to stop at the crossing for the oncoming train. The locomotive is a PROTO 2000 model.

MAGIC OF MODEL RAILROADING

**Models and photo by Jim Bzdawka, Milwaukee, WI**

It's early morning in downtown Newport and the residents are busy choosing fresh produce a local farmer is selling in front of the grocery store. The action takes place in the late 1950s on Jim's fictional Sauk Co. Shortline. Vehicles are Classic Metal Works, figures are Woodland Scenics and the structure is Walthers Cornerstone Series Merchants Row II.

**Models and photo by Jim "Mitch" Mitchell, Grand Junction, CO**

Wherever there's construction you'll find a gravel company spur. Cherokee Ridge Gravel is a perfect example—it's in the heart of an area where there's a construction boom. Currently, the business receives several cars of crushed stone each week, a rotary sorter in the yard sorts the different kinds of rock into bins. Jim built Cherokee Ridge Gravel with a Cornerstone Series Bulk Transfer Conveyor. The ballast hoppers are also from Walthers.

**Models and photo by Brian & Dave Morris, Grand Junction, CO**

Amid the smoke and steam of the mill, a Baldwin S-12 hauls a couple of slag cars toward the furnaces for reloading. Rolling past the coke ovens, the slag pots are still smoldering as they rock and roll along the rough track. Brian and Dave created this scene with Walthers Cornerstone Series steel industry kits and rolling stock. The loco is from Athearn.

**Models & photo by Alden Armstrong, Grand Junction, CO.**

Lompoc, California was a favorite spot of Alden Armstrong's family. The nearby fields were full of flowers grown for seed. In summer when all the flowers were in bloom it was a spectacular sight. In this scene near Lompoc, an SP freight train slides past the brightly colored flower fields that are carefully being tended by a group of workers. Figures are by Preiser and the flowers are Woodland Scenics.

**Models and photo by Greg Drewiske, Wisconsin Rapids, WI**

A northbound Tomahawk Southern freight rolls past one of several power plants along the busy line. Serving a paper-producing region, the TSRR handles coal, forest products and related traffic for the Wisconsin River Valley. The Atlas GP40 has been enhanced with parts from Details West and Detail Associates. It's rolling past structures made by Walthers and Rix. A Busch signal protects drivers and a Preiser pedestrian on the Walthers Street System roads. The rest of the scenery features materials by Woodland Scenics, Super Trees and Highball.

**Models and photo by Paul Cyr, Frenchville, ME**

The local led by GP7 #68 is pulling into Madawaska Brick & Block to pick up an empty coal hopper before heading back to Madawaska. The GP7 is Atlas, the hopper is Stewart, the cement storage tanks are a heavily modified Walthers Medusa Cement kit and the storage shed is scratchbuilt with Evergreen and Plastruct plastic sheets.

**Models and photo by Bob Boudreau, New Bruswick, Canada**

Nighttime is a quiet time at the engine house of Lomax Lumber Company but work on the Mack 18-ton diesel switcher must go on. Bob scratchbuilt the engine house with Northeastern stripwood and covered it with typing paper he painted black. The switcher is from Jordan, the fueling rack on the left is Woodland Scenics and most of the junk is from Keystone Models.

**Models by Tom Bielefeld, Dave Watkins & Susan Anderson, photo by Tom Bielefeld, Tucson, AZ**

Drums and horns herald the arrival of the marching band strolling down Elk Avenue in Crested Butte, Colorado during their weekly practice session. The buildings are replicas of ones that still exist in Crested Butte. City Hall houses the town council and fire department and the Elkhead got its name from the world record elk antlers the two men are carrying into the hall. Tom scratchbuilt both buildings and kitbashed Spritzlers Pool Hall from a Walthers kit. Wagons and vehicles were assembled by Dave Watkins from Jordan Highway Miniatures kits. Figures are Preiser and the background mural was painted by Susan Anderson. It's all on the HOn3 gauge operating layout in the Crested Butte Mountain Heritage Museum.

**Models and photo by Jeff Hauser, Troy, MI**

C&O #3024 hauls a string of empty coal cars through the tunnel and across the bridge as it rolls through the mountains of West Virginia. The rumble of the train blends with the roar of the waterfall below. The crew has many miles to go today but the beautiful mountain scenery is a sweet reward. The GP30 is a PROTO 2000 model with weathering using A.I.M. powders. The tunnel, bridge abutments and scenery are from Woodland Scenics and the bridge is from Vollmer. Jeff created the waterfall with Woodland Scenics Water Effects.

**Models and photo by Fred Lagno, Queenstown, MD**

Bathed in low fall sunlight, an Allegheny Central local eases past an old house in Ogdensburg as it heads for the Greenway Cement Co. It's said that the president of a local coal company once lived there and counted the coal hoppers as they rolled by. Today, the line only makes it as far as the cement company. The caboose is a PROTO 2000 model and the scenery features natural materials.

**Models and photo by Richard Bailey, Cartersville, GA**

Somewhere between St. Jude and Eastown, the locals are having a real time of it trying to get through a heavy snowfall. Only the IHC steamer is running on time to make sure everything gets delivered before the sun fully sets on this snowy day. The structures are JL Innovative Design and Campbell Scale Models products, the truck is from Wheel Works and the track is Atlas. Plain old baking soda was used for the snow and the rest of the scenery is from Woodland Scenics.

**Models and photo by Bob Boudreau, New Bruswick, Canada**

The passing of Fundy Northern Railroad's Climax #6 disturbs the tranquility of the log pond just as a fisherman launches his boat for a quiet day of fishing. The Climax loco is a Bachmann model and the log cars are by Roundhouse. Bob scratchbuilt the covered bridge with Northeastern stripwood and Campbell shingles. The rowboat is from Campbell, the figure from Preiser and the scenic materials from Woodland Scenics. Bob added the smoke and steam digitally using Paint Shop Pro.

**Models and photo by Paul Cyr, Frenchville, ME**

In northern Maine, the end of September is potato picking time. School lets out for two weeks so the kids can pick potatoes for the farmers. It's hard work but the kids don't mind because to them being outdoors is a lot more fun than school any day. Plus, they earn some money to spend on their favorite hobby – model railroading. The GP7 is Atlas, scenery is Woodland Scenics and the structures are Dyna Models (now out of production).

**Models and photo by Fred Lagno, Queenstown, MD**

Looking east down Route 40 the only activity on this fall afternoon is the passing of a school bus and a work van. The tall grain bins of West Maryland Grain cast shadows across the highway in the late afternoon sunlight. Chase's Garage on the left is a scratchbuilt model and the Bins are a mix of Walthers Cornerstone Series and Rix kits.

**Models and photo by Jeff Hauser, Troy, MI**

Jane watches a box car get spotted at the warehouse while she waits for the #12 bus. The streetlights lit up early and Jane is anxious for the bus to arrive. She certainly doesn't want to get stuck in this part of town after dark so she's careful to avoid eye contact with the customer at Bukowski Liquors. The liquor store is part of Addams Avenue Part One by Downtown Deco, the streetlight is a Walthers built-up and the switcher is by BLI. Figures and the road are Woodland Scenics, the fire hydrant is from JL Innovative and the vehicles are by Classic Metal Works.

**Models and photo by Alex Mantle, Buffalo, WY**

Chicago Denver & Northern RS-3 #102 spots a Rock Island box car at Johnson and Sons Freight House while a few employees take a breather out back. CD&N #102 is a custom-painted Atlas loco and the car is from Athearn. A Design Preservation Models building sits along Walthers and Shinohara track. Scenery is a mix of Woodland Scenics materials, vehicles are by Busch and Alloy Forms and the figures are from Preiser.

**Models and photo by Bill McChesney, Niskayuna, NY**

Running downhill with a clean stack, a long B&M freight with doubleheaded 2-8-0 and 2-6-0 locomotives soars across a valley on a tall steel viaduct. Bill McChesney painted and detailed the brass locos. The bridge is by Micro Engineering and scenery is a mix of AMSI, Woodland Scenics and natural materials.

**Models and photo by Ken Kirkwood, Yucaipa, CA**

Painters are hurrying to finish the trimwork, and the second-floor rooms are still undone. They'll have to get a move on as the grand opening of Stonehaven's new five-and-dime is scheduled for next Saturday. The store is by Design Preservation Models, the painters are from Preiser and Woodland Scenics and the vehicles are Jordan and On-Trak Model Products.

**Models and photo by Ron Foreman, Glendale, CA**

Now that #2 has backed onto the bridge, her crew will have to wait for some "muscle" to arrive to head in the right direction. Those scalawag roustabouts employed by the D.G.&H. are probably hiding out in one of the town's many saloons avoiding work on this raw, dreary day. Ron scratchbuilt the turntable.

**Models and photo by Alberto Franchi, Prato, Italy**

Spring grasses are getting tall in northern Ontario where an Ontario Northland local bounces across a rural grade crossing. By the end of summer, the grass will be so tall that even the tire ruts in the road will be hidden. This photo diorama features Micro Engineering track, Noch and Woodland Scenics scenery materials, Highball ballast and Rix and Pikestuff details. Painting and weathering was accomplished using Floquil and Tamiya paints and powdered coffee. The loco is an Overland brass import and the hopper is from Intermountain, detailed with Plano parts.

**Models and photo by Jim Bzdawka, Milwaukee, WI**

Comin' round the bend on this sunny autumn afternoon is the Sauk Co. Shortline's last freight of the day. The engineer keeps a close eye on the wandering hobo who will probably try to hop onto one of the empty box cars he's hauling today. Luckily it's a straight track up ahead so the engineer should have a view all the way back to the caboose. On Jim Bzdawka's late 1950s layout, the Sauk County Shortline relies on leased and used equipment from other railroads. The loco is a Bachmann Spectrum while the figure and most of the scenery are from Woodland Scenics.

**Models and photo by Mark Pitanza, Old Bridge, NJ**

Believe it or not, many institutions once received coal by rail to feed their powerplant boilers. On Staten Island, the Mount Loretto orphanage was the last customer on its namesake branch. One of the sisters has brought a few of the children to see the last train pull the last car off the coal trestle in this 50s-era scene. Marc built this diorama depicting the final days of the branch. The loco is a custom painted Atlas unit and the car is a PROTO 2000 model. The bridge is scratchbuilt, the scenery features Woodland Scenics products and the figures are by Preiser.

MAGIC OF MODEL RAILROADING

**Models by Mike Budde and Vic Smith, and photo by Vic Smith, Bridgeton, MO**

This motorist got a little too close to the tracks and suffered the consequences. His prized Mustang is smashed and he's off to the hospital. Some nearby workers take a break to watch the action as the police call for a tow truck. Meanwhile the freight rolls overhead with, of all things, a load of brand new cars. Mike Budde created the smashed Mustang by hand forming aluminum foil around a stock Busch vehicle.

**Models and photo by Paul Backenstose, Dowington, PA**

The action is heavy at Ridgely Yard near Cumberland, Maryland, as arriving and departing freights roll past each other doing their part on the "middleman of the Alphabet Route". It's just another typical day along the Western Maryland Railway.

**Models and photo by Ken Kirkwood, Yucaipa, CA**

Some turn-of-the century railroads afforded tourists a unique way to enjoy their scenic routes. "Gravity" cars, akin to the modern roller coaster, would allow passengers to coast gently downhill, the speed controlled by an ever-alert brakeman and handbrake. Like many a prototype, Ken's Ma and Pa K gravity car has made an impromptu stop in the woods for a photo opportunity. The gravity car is scratchbuilt, passengers are by Preiser and scenery materials are from Noch, AMSI and Scenic Express.

**Models by Graham Hoffman, Plymouth WI and photo by Cal Krasonya**

Hunters in the background hold their fire as Beaver Falls and Mudd River Land and Lumber Co. Class B two-truck Climax No. 7 totes a Barnhardt log loader and logging caboose past the deer stand. The loco is a Bachmann Spectrum® model and rolling stock is by IHC and Kadee. The diminutive train is headed back to camp on the Plymouth Model Society's layout.

**Models and photo by Ken Kirkwood, Yucaipa, CA**

Ma and Pa K Heisler #3 prepares to take the last train of the day up the steep slope of Mount McKinley. Passengers will be treated to some terrific twilight views of the valley below as they climb to the resort at the summit. The loco is a Rivarossi model, the figures are Preiser and the scenery is Noch, AMS and Scenic Express. Both the enginehouse and water tower are scratchbuilt.

**Models and photo by Ken Nelson, Scotia, NY**

Fast freight NJ-51 blasts across the river behind a trio of GP30s. Purchased in the 60s to handle a traffic boom, the units are still at work doing what they do best—hauling heavy trains. The three locos are PROTO 2000 models and the bridge is scratchbuilt.

**Models and photo by Paul Backenstose, Dowington, PA**

Travel back in time to August 12, 1955 as Western Maryland Railway AJ12 exists Brush Tunnel on its way east to Cumberland, Maryland. Just behind is the wave of the future – TOFC flats on one of their early runs.

**Models and photo by Neil Schofield, Seekonk, MA**

Ahh, the good old days when CP RS-18s and C424s ruled CP operations in Vermont's Northeast Kingdom. With a few shorts blasts of the horn, a northbound CP freight crosses an inlet of Lake Memphramagog and enters North Newport on Neil Schofield's HO Scale layout set in the summer of 1980. Both locomotives are heavily modified Atlas engines painted and detailed for specific prototypes. The residence is a modified Model Power kit with various Woodland Scenics and Scenic Express scenery items used to complete the scene.

**Models and photo by Ron Foreman, Glendale, CA**

Purchased from the Denver & Rio Grande as a T-12, 4-6-0 "Virginia" is at present the narrow gauge D.G.&H.'s only working engine. Number 1, an 0-6-0 was stolen from the shops before it could be put into service and delivery of 2-4-0T #3 from the Porter Co. is delayed due to a strike. Former Rio Grande Southern Mogul #4 is being rebuilt so it's up to #2 to shoulder the burden and deliver the kind of service customers expect. Engine #2 is a brass import with mico-motor and gearhead, altered details, paint and a loyal crew. The homebuilt 4-wheel tender was substituted for the T-12's 8-wheel one to fit the 51-foot turntable.

# FIGURES

Models and Photo by Alden Armstrong

Bell ringing, engine #2746 wastes no time backing down the main after cutting off from its local run. The "Coast Daylight" is a bit late, but due along shortly. To help get the train back on time, the station crew has already spotted baggage wagons of express and mail on the platform.

While they may not move without your help, figures still tell an important story anywhere along your railroad. Alden Armstrong of Grand Junction, Colorado, used a number of Preiser figures to round out the station scene. You'll also find a crew on duty in the cab of #2746, which is a Sunset brass import. Finishing touches around the platforms include baggage wagons built from Jordan kits.

Bringing any area of your layout to life is a quick and easy project with the wide range of figures you'll find on the pages that follow.

Division of
Wm. K. Walthers, Inc.

## Animals 10.25 ea

**433-1603** Barnyard Animals pkg(7)
Includes four 3-1/4" fence sections.

**433-1605** Cattle pkg(6)

## Pedestrians 10.25 ea

**433-1604** City People pkg(7)

**433-1606** Standing pkg(6)

**433-1607** Sitting pkg(6)
Includes two park benches.

**433-1609** Walking pkg(8)

**433-1610** Townspeople pkg(8)

## Workers pkg(6) 10.25 ea

**433-1608** Farmers

**433-1611** Railroad Workers

**433-1630** Police Officers

**433-1631** Firefighters

**433-1684** Railroad People

Barnyard Animals 433-1603

City People 433-1604

Sitting People 433-1607

Walking People 433-1609

Farmers 433-1608

Railroad Workers 433-1611

Railroad People 433-1684

Get the Scoop!
Get the Skinny!
Get the Score!
Check Out Walthers
Web site at

**www.walthers.com**

# ATLAS

Unpainted plastic figures.

## Animals 4.25 ea

**150-778** Cows & Horses pkg(12)

**150-779** Sheep (12 white, 1 black)

## People

**150-793** Undecorated Figures pkg(24) **4.25**

# INTERNATIONAL HOBBY CORP.

All figures are handpainted plastic.

## American Firemen

**348-4260** 3 w/Hose, 3 w/Ax **2.98**

**348-4261** 6 Firemen, 2 Extinguishers, Stretcher, Bullhorn, Ax & Hose **3.98**

Handpainted plastic figures.

## Railroad Personnel pkg(6) 7.50 ea

**160-42333** Train Crew

**160-42334** Work Crew

**160-42341** Train Work Crew

## Passengers pkg(6) 7.50 ea

**160-42330** Waiting

**160-42342** Sitting

## Pedestrians pkg(6) 7.50 ea

**160-42331** Sitting People

**160-42332** Standing People

**160-42339** People at Leisure

## Animals

**160-42201** Cows & Horses pkg(12) **6.50**

## Miscellaneous

**160-42335** Old West People pkg(6) **7.50**

# FALLER

IMPORTED FROM GERMANY BY WALTHERS

## NEW PRODUCTS

### Animals 15.99 ea

**NEW 272-154007** Fallow & Red Deer pkg(12)

**NEW 272-154008** Eight Goats & Seven Pigs

**NEW 272-154009** Alpine Mountain Goats (Four Chamois & Six Ibex) pkg(10)

### Pedestrians

**NEW 272-150907** Passers-By V **15.99**

### Working People

**NEW 272-151051** Construction Workers **15.99**

### Sports & Recreation 15.99 ea

**NEW 272-151052** At the Kiosk

**NEW 272-151053** Fun At the Campground

**NEW 272-151054** Merry Drinkers

**NEW 272-151055** Wanderers

**NEW 272-153025** Boy Scouts

**NEW 272-153050** Fairground Figures #1

**NEW 272-153051** Fairground Figures #2

**NEW 272-153052** Fairground Figures #3

### Animals 15.99 ea

**272-154001** Sheep w/Shepherd & Dog

**272-154002** 4 Brown Horses & 4 Brown Cows

**272-154003** Black Spotted Cows pkg(8)

**272-154004** Cows, Brown Spotted

**272-154005** Horses pkg(7)

**272-154006** Storks in Nests pkg(11)

### Firemen 15.99 ea

**272-151006** Firemen w/Accessories

**272-151036** With Orange Uniforms

**272-151037** With Blue Uniforms

### Pedestrians pkg(8) 15.99 ea (Unless Noted)

**272-150501** Passengers 1

**272-150502** Passengers 2

**272-150503** Passengers 3

**272-150504** Passengers 4

**272-150701** Sitting Persons 1

**272-150702** Sitting Persons 2

**272-150703** Sitting Persons 3

**272-150704** Sitting Persons IV

**272-150901** Passers-By 1

**272-150902** Passers-By 2

**272-150903** Passers-By 3

**272-150904** Passengers w/Dog

**272-150906** Travelers in a Hurry w/Luggage

**272-151021** Bride & Bridegroom

**272-151022** Children On The Road pkg(7)

**272-151023** Playing Children

**272-151025** Passengers On Stairs

**272-151027** Red Cross w/Wounded

**272-151028** Guys At The Station

**272-151029** Accident Scene

**272-151031** Playing Children

**272-151034** Young People w/Cell Phones

**272-151035** In Supermarket

**272-151043** Wedding Guests

**272-157102** Groups of Seated People

**272-157230** Wedding Figures

### pkg(36) 52.99 ea

**272-153001** Sitting People

**272-153002** Passengers/ Passers-By

### Farmers pkg(8) 15.99 ea (Unless Noted)

**272-151007** Farm Hands

**272-151008** Potato Harvesters

**272-151009** Grain Harvesters

**272-153004** Farm People/ Animals pkg(36) **52.99**

### Railroad Personnel 15.99 ea

**272-151000** Tracklayers pkg(8)

**272-151002** Railway Staff pkg(8)

**272-151003** Railway Staff w/Dog pkg(9)

**272-151004** Engine Drivers pkg(8)

**272-151005** Railroad Switch Crew pkg(8)

**272-151017** Track Layers pkg(8)

**272-151050** Track Layers

IMPORTED FROM GERMANY BY WALTHERS

**Working People 15.99 ea**

**272-150905** Businessmen

**272-151001** Transport Workers w/Cargo

**272-151010** Gas Station Workers pkg(8)

**272-151011** Construction Workers/Carpenters pkg(8)

**272-151012** Street Cleaners/ Workers pkg(7)

**272-151013** Various Occupations pkg(8)

**272-151014** Washday w/Clothesline

**272-151015** Market Day w/Fruit Stand

**272-151018** Policemen, Period V pkg(8)

**272-151026** Garden Workers

**272-151032** Bus/Truck Driver/ Forwarder

**272-151033** Driver/Transport Workers

**272-151038** At the Blacksmiths

**272-151041** Lumberjacks pkg(6)

**272-151042** Sales Personnel pkg(8)

**272-151044** Policemen w/Dog pkg(7)

**272-151045** Municipal Road Workers (European) pkg(8)

**272-151046** Painters w/Accessories pkg(7)

**272-151047** Radar Traffic Control

**272-151048** Mowing the Lawn

**272-151049** Bricklayers & Painters w/Ladders

**Sports & Recreation 15.99 ea (Unless Noted)**

**272-151016** Fairgoers/ Salesmen pkg(8)

**272-151019** Resting Persons w/Deck Chairs pkg(8)

**272-151020** At The Pool/On The Beach pkg(8)

**272-151030** Beachgoers

**272-151024** Hunters/ Lumbermen/Deer pkg(9)

**272-151039** Hunting Men

**272-151040** People at the Open-Air Swimming Pool Restaurant

**272-153003** Fairgoers

**272-153005** Marching Band In Uniform **25.99**

**272-153006** Fairgoers pkg(36) **52.99**

**272-153020** Soccer Players & Referee - White & Black Uniforms **26.99**

**272-153021** Soccer Players & Referee White & Red Uniforms **26.99**

**272-153022** Tennis Players

**272-153023** Kayakists w/Kayaks

**272-153024** Tournament Riders

**272-155407** Bathers I

IMPORTED FROM GERMANY BY WALTHERS

**Steam/Early Diesel Era Engineer & Fireman Sets 6.49 ea**

Figures are molded in plastic, fully painted and include one engineer and one fireman per set.

**430-7001** Slouching & Leaning

**430-7002** Waving & Sitting

**430-7004** All Four Unpainted

**Contemporary Diesel Engineer & Fireman Sets 6.49 ea**

**430-7008** Waving & Sitting

**430-7009** Slouching & Leaning

**Yard Crew**

**430-7010** pkg(4) **9.98**

**KIBRI**

IMPORTED FROM GERMANY BY WALTHERS

**People Assortments**

**405-8114** Seated Passengers pkg(30) **16.99**

**NEW PRODUCTS**

**Painted Figures**

Cast-metal figures come decorated and ready for placement on your layout.

**NEW 530-233** Painters pkg(3) **14.95**

**NEW 530-234** Garbage Men w/Trash Cans **14.95**
Includes three figures and two garbage cans.

**NEW 530-219** Wild Birds **11.95**
Includes heron, owl, woodpecker and more.

**NEW 530-225** Cats pkg(6)

**NEW 530-232** Assorted Wild Animals pkg(5)

**PAINTED FIGURES**

**530-220** Swans pkg(2) **11.95**

**530-221** Seagulls **11.95**

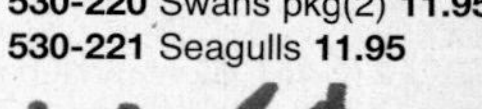

**530-224** Squirrels (gray) pkg(5) **9.95**

**530-224R** Squirrels (red) pkg(5) **9.95**

**530-226** Young Man w/Airplane **14.95**

**530-227** Young Man w/Boat **14.95**

**530-228** Ducks pkg(6) **9.95**
In a row, swimming

**530-229** Chickens pkg(6) **9.95**

**530-230** Rooster **4.95**

## Railroad Personnel pkg(6) 7.98 ea

**490-5700** Track Laying Crew

**490-5701** Work Crew

**490-5704** Train Crew

**490-5709** Station Crew

**490-5714** Work People
**490-5739** Railroad Staff

## Working People 7.98 ea

**490-5747** Utility Workers
**490-5748** Masons & Bricklayers
**490-5773** Service Staff
**490-5775** Shepherd & Sheep

**490-5781** Farmer's Market

**490-5782** County Road Workers
**490-5785** Postal Workers

## Passengers pkg(6) 7.98 ea

**490-5702** Station

**490-5703** Sitting

**490-5706** Sitting

**490-5707** Station

**490-5708** Standing
**490-5725** Sitting w/Bench & Dog

## Action pkg(6) 7.98 ea

**490-5711** Hunters
**490-5715** Farm Action People

**490-5746** Sportsmen

## Prisoners 7.98 ea

**490-5783** Black & White Stripes

**490-5784** Orange

## Animals pkg(6) 7.98 ea

**490-5726** Assorted Livestock

**490-5731** Cows & Calves (black & white)
**490-5732** Cows & Calves (brown)
**490-5734** Deer
**490-5742** Cows & Calves (brown & white)
**490-5776** Horses

## Unpainted Figure Sets pkg(72) 10.98 ea (Unless Noted)

**490-5772** **8.50**
**490-5790** Rail & Road Workers
**490-5791** Sitting People w/Benches
**490-5792** Standing People
**490-5793** Animals

## Military pkg(6) 7.98 ea

**490-5693** Figures Standing (Olive)
**490-5694** Figures Sitting (Olive)
**490-5695** Figures Standing (Desert)
**490-5696** Figures Sitting (Desert)

## Recreation 7.98 ea

**490-5740** Beach Figures
**490-5751** Bicycle & Scooter

**490-5752** Hikers
**490-5766** Tennis Players

## Pedestrians pkg(6) 7.98 ea

**490-5697** Fat People
**490-5705** Town People

**490-5716** Steam-Era People

**490-5717** Street People
**490-5718** Young Women w/Children & Strollers
**490-5721** Commuters
**490-5722** Children Playing
**490-5724** Going To The Train
**490-5735** Market People
**490-5736** Tourists
**490-5745** Walking
**490-5749** People Waving
**490-5774** Kissing Couples
**490-5779** Traveling Figures

**490-5780** Women on the Move
**490-5786** City Park People
**490-5787** Homeless People
**490-5788** Crime Scenes
**490-5789** People Eating

## Religious 7.98 ea

**490-5720** Deacon & His Flock
**490-5737** Pastor & Congregants w/Pulpit
**490-5741** Marriage

## Fire Fighters

**490-5738** New Firemen **7.98**

## Miniature Scenes

Some Included Figures Not Shown

**490-5712** Winter 3/4" Tall pkg(6) **7.98**

**490-5710** Figures & Accessory Set **14.98**
Includes six figures, four benches, three fire hydrants, three mailboxes and three trash cans.

For Up-To-Date Information and News Bookmark Walthers Web site at **www.walthers.com**

## PLASTRUCT

### Business Figures

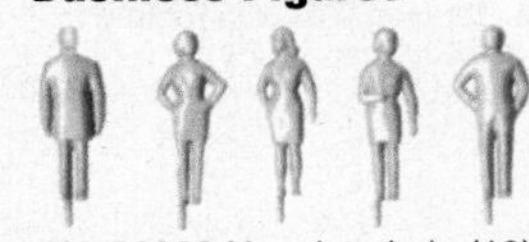

**570-93322** Unpainted pkg(10) **14.50**

### City Figures

**570-93389** Painted pkg(6) **9.95**
**570-93333** Unpainted pkg(6) **5.95**

**570-93390** Painted pkg(6) **9.95**
**570-93340** Unpainted pkg(6) **5.95**

### Family Figures

**570-93357** Painted pkg(9) **9.40**

### Industrial Figures

**570-93302** Male Reaching 1:32 pkg(2) **4.25**
**570-93304** Male Reaching 1:16 pkg(2) **4.30**
**570-93312** Male Standing 1:32 pkg(2) **4.25**
**570-93314** Male Standing 1:16 pkg(2) **4.30**

## WIKING

## NEW PRODUCTS

Add life to your layout by placing these painted figures behind the wheel of your vehicles.

### Vehicle Drivers

**pkg(10) 11.99 ea**

**NEW 781-1603** Tractor Drivers w/Suspenders
**NEW 781-1604** Tractor Drivers
**NEW 781-1605** Modern Convertible Drivers

## SELLEY FINISHING TOUCHES

Unpainted metal.

### Animals

**675-158** Trough & 6 Pigs **3.60**
**675-161** Cows pkg(6) **4.00**
**675-162** Bull, Cow & Calf **4.00**
**675-163** Horses pkg(6) **4.20**
**675-178** Dog & Hydrant **2.40**
**675-297** Chickens pkg(12) **3.60**
**675-454** Horse & Colt **3.00**
**675-456** Elephant **2.30**
**675-457** Giraffe **2.30**
**675-458** Camel **2.30**
**675-459** Elk **2.30**
**675-520** Lion **2.40**

### Railroad Personnel

**675-81** Steam Train Crew pkg(3) **2.60**
**675-139** Man w/Wheelbarrow **2.60**
**675-231** Drivers pkg(3) **2.60**
**675-289** Road Gang Working pkg(5) **8.30**
**675-294** Brakeman, Crewman pkg(6) **3.00**
**675-647** Diesel Train Crew pkg(3) **2.60**
**675-701** Handcar Man **2.00**

### Miscellaneous

**675-160** Cowboy & 2 Horses **5.10**
**675-662** Hobos & Dog pkg(5) **3.30**
Includes four figures and dog.
**675-700** Drunk Leaning On Lamppost **2.00**
**675-6571** Prospector w/Burro **5.10**
**675-6572** Prospector w/2 Burros **6.30**

# Merten M:

IMPORTED FROM GERMANY BY WALTHERS
Bring layout scenes to life with these detailed plastic people. Molded in life-like poses and prepainted, they're ready for all sorts of jobs and leisure activities on your layout.

## NEW PRODUCTS

### Sports & Recreation

**NEW 447-2462** Miniature Golf Players w/Clubs & Fairways **10.99**

### Pedestrians 10.99 ea

**NEW 447-2554** Casual Passers-by
**NEW 447-2555** City Passers-by

Ice-Cream Seller On The Beach w/Bathers 447-2552

Bathers Sitting & Lying 447-2553

Storks w/Two Nests 447-764

Children Playing 447-2197

Singles #1 447-2286

Old-Time People Set #2 447-2162

Downhill Skiers-Men 447-2144

Downhill Skiers-Women 447-2150

Water Skiers-Men 447-2168

### Animals 10.99 ea

**447-724** Geese on Land pkg(12)
**447-764** Storks w/Two Nests pkg(7)

**447-2411** Fallow Deer (Small) pkg(12)

**447-2549** Apes (black & orange) pkg(9)

### Children

**447-2197** Playing pkg(7) **10.99**

### Passengers pkg(6) 10.99 ea

**447-2286** Singles #1

**447-2292** Groups #1

**447-2295** Singles #2

**447-2301** Groups #2

**447-2399** Chubby Singles pkg(7)

**447-2400** Chubby Groups pkg(3)

**447-2525** Standing, Waving Partial Figures
For use in passenger cars, buses, or automobiles with limited interior clearance.

**447-2546** Females pkg(6)

**447-2528** Seated #1

**447-2539** Waiting Passengers w/Luggage

**447-2547** Male Passengers w/Baggage

**447-2550** Passengers w/Luggage Cart

### Emergency Services pkg(6) 10.99 ea

**447-982** First Aid Workers #1

**447-988** First Aid Workers #2

**447-2246** Policemen

**447-2252** Traffic Policemen

**447-2371** German Fire Fighters-Set #1 (1950s)

**447-2377** German Fire Fighters-Set #2 (1950s)

**447-2383** American Fire Fighters #1

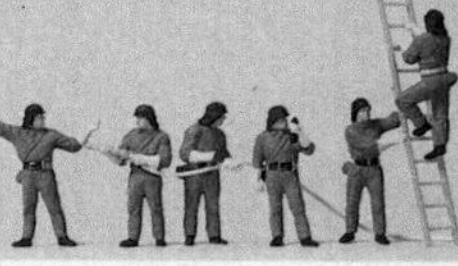

**447-2545** German Firemen w/Ladder

### Old-Time People pkg(6) 10.99 ea

**447-2156** Set #1
**447-2162** Set #2

### Sports & Recreation 10.99 ea

**447-2552** Ice-Cream Seller On The Beach w/Bathers
**447-2553** Bathers Sitting & Lying

**447-948** Swimmers Set #1

**447-954** Swimmers-Seated & Laying Down

**447-960** Swimmers-Standing in Groups pkg(3)

**447-967** Wedding Guests
**447-2144** Downhill Skiers-Men
**447-2150** Downhill Skiers-Women
**447-2168** Water Skiers

**447-2174** Musicians on the Beach

**447-2209** Organ Grinder & Audience pkg(5)

## Merten M:

IMPORTED FROM GERMANY BY WALTHERS

**447-2215** Ice Skaters-Set #1

**447-2221** Ice/Figure Skaters 3 Pair

**447-2227** Ice Skaters-Paired Couples 3 Pair

**447-2349** Joggers-Men

**447-2355** Joggers-Women

**447-2361** Vacationers Reclining in Chaise Lounges

**447-2398** Happy Drunks

**447-2485** Men Running Hurdles (8 Figures; 80 Hurdles)

**447-2486** Women Running Hurdles (8 Figures; 80 Hurdles)

**447-2490** Tennis Players (4 Players, 2 Ball Boys, 1 Official)

**447-2498** Soccer Players pkg(11)

**447-2499** 2 Soccer Goals, 6 Corner Flags, 1 Referee & 2 Linesmen

**447-2500** Canoeists & Kayakers pkg(4)

**447-2502** Pasers-By #2

**447-2524** Standing People at Beach Snackbar

**447-2526** Nude Swimmers-Standing Females

**447-2527** Nude Swimmers-Females Undressing

**447-2533** Family On The Nudist Beach pkg(7)

**447-2540** Youths w/Phones

**447-2543** Family Get-Together

**447-2544** Wanderers/Hikers

### Hunters pkg(6) 10.99 ea

**447-2120** Paired-Carrying Game

**447-2126** Single-Carrying Game

### Pedestrians 10.99 ea

**447-2180** Pedestrians #1 pkg(6)

**447-2186** Pedestrians w/Umbrellas/Rain Coats pkg(6)

Ice Skaters-Set #1 447-2215

Ice/Figure Skaters 447-2221

Joggers-Men 447-2349

Joggers-Women 447-2355

Happy Drunks 447-2398

Men Running Hurdles 447-2485

Tennis Players 447-2490

Soccer Players 447-2498

Soccer Goals, Flags & Judges 447-2499

Canoeists & Kayakers 447-2500

Standing People at Beach Snackbar 447-2524

Youths w/Cell Phones 447-2540

Family Get-Together 447-2543

Wanderers/Hikers 447-2544

Paired-Carrying Game 447-2120

Pedestrians w/Umbrellas 447-2186

Beatniks 447-2397

**447-2191** School Children-Walking pkg(7)

**447-2397** Beatniks-Young People pkg(6)

**447-2551** Passers-by w/Stroller

## Merten

IMPORTED FROM GERMANY BY WALTHERS

### Railroad Figures pkg(6) 10.99 ea

**Track Repair Crews**

**447-876** #2

**447-882** #3

**447-886** #4

**Railroad Personnel**

**447-908** #1

**447-914** #2

**447-2268** #3

**447-2280** #5

**447-2530** East German State Railways (DR) Staff w/Passengers pkg(6)

### Travelers pkg(6) 10.99 ea

**447-806** Women

**447-812** Men

**447-818** Groups pkg(2)

**447-820** Pairs pkg(3)

**447-853** Seated Women

**447-859** Seated Men

**447-865** Seated Groups pkg(2)

**447-867** Seated Pairs pkg(3)

**447-971** Running Women

**447-2132** Skiers in Winter Clothes Carrying Skis & Luggage

**447-2519** Seated Passengers

**447-2523** Foreign Travelers

**447-2516** Walking

Track Repair Crew #2 447-876

Track Repair Crew #3 447-882

Railroad Personnel #1 447-908

Railroad Personnel #2 447-914

Railroad Personnel #3 447-2268

Railroad Personnel #5 447-2280

Men Travelers 447-812

Seated Women 447-853

Seated Men 447-859

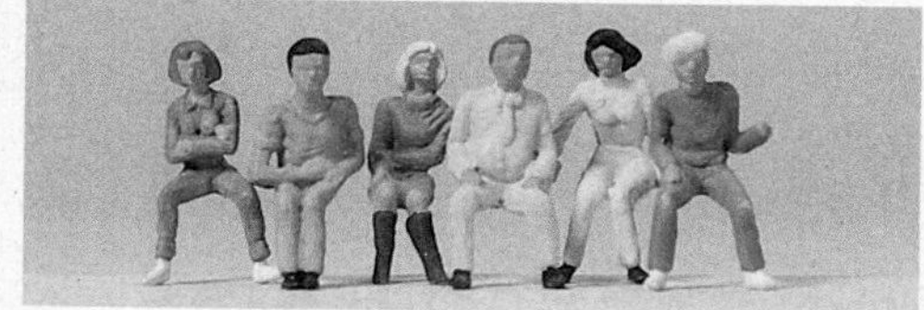

Seated Passengers 447-2519

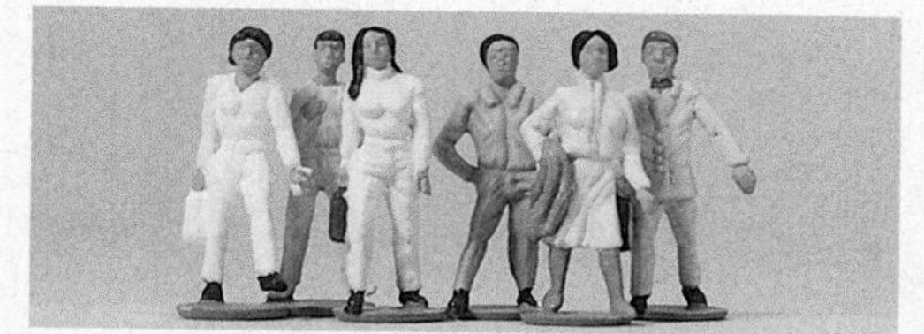

Travelers Walking 447-2516

Street Vendors 447-800

Foresters & Shepherds 447-891

Harvesters #1 447-902

Harvesters #2 447-920

Harvesters #3 447-926

Auto Mechanics 447-2331

### Workers pkg(6) 10.99 ea

**447-800** Street Vendors

**447-889** Blacksmiths (4) & Horses (2)

**447-891** Foresters & Shepherds pkg(5)

**447-896** Farm Workers

**447-902** Harvesters #1

**447-920** Harvesters #2

**447-926** Harvesters #3

**447-2234** Workers Loading #1

**447-2240** Workers Loading #2

**447-2313** Fruit Stand Vendors & Shoppers w/Bananas

**447-2319** Women Hanging Laundry pkg(5)

**447-2325** Gas Station Workers/Mechanics

**447-2331** Auto Mechanics

# Merten

MPORTED FROM GERMANY
Y WALTHERS

47-2337 **Cement Workers**
47-2343 **Construction Workers**
47-2403 **Shepherd w/Dog & 8 Sheep**

**47-2510** Gardeners

**47-2521** People Recycling Glass & Paper

**47-2522** Truck Drivers/ Helpers
**47-2542** Family Working In Yard pkg(5)

## Figure Accessories 10.99 ea

**447-2454** Playground Equipment #1

**447-2455** Playground Equipment #2

## ECONOMY FIGURE SETS

### 7.99 ea

Same detailed plastic figures, but with simplified painting. Great for backgrounds, interiors, or scenes where a large number of figures are needed at a lower cost.

**447-5001** Travelers

**447-5002** Seated People Set #1

**447-5003** Seated People Set #3

**447-5004** Standing People

**447-5005** Automobile Drivers

**447-5006** People Exercising

**447-5007** Skateboarders & Rollerbladers

**447-5008** People Dumping Trash

**447-5009** Truck Drivers

**447-5010** Restaurant Staff

**447-5012** Fire/Rescue Dive Crew

**447-5013** Fire/Rescue Dive Crew in Boat

**447-5014** Gardeners-Set #1

**447-5015** Gardeners-Set #2

**447-5016** Foreign Passers-By

**447-5017** Travelers w/Baggage

**447-5020** Modern German Firefighters pkg(6)

**447-5021** Street Pedestrians pkg(6)

**447-5022** Emergency Team w/Stretchers & 1 Patient pkg(6)

**447-5023** Passengers Seated pkg(6)

**447-5024** German Federal Railways (DB) Personnel-Standing pkg(6)

**447-5025** Traffic Policemen pkg(6)

**447-5026** Shepherd w/Dog & Sheep pkg(10)
**447-5030** Maid w/Pigs

Construction Workers 447-2343

Shepherd w/Dog & 18 Sheep 447-2403

Family Working In Yard 447-2542

Maid w/Pigs 447-5030

Horses 447-5018

Wild Boars 447-5028

**447-5031** Shepherd Boy w/Goats

## Animals 7.99 ea

**447-5018** Horses (brown)

**447-5019** Cows (black & white)

**447-5027** Deer (Buck, Doe & 8 Fawns)
**447-5028** Wild Boars

**447-5029** Deer (Roes)

ORIGINAL **Preiser**

IMPORTED FROM GERMANY BY WALTHERS
Hand painted, lightweight plastic figures in action poses.

## NEW PRODUCTS

### Moving Figures 43.99 ea

14-16V AC/DC.

**NEW 590-27001** German Platform Agent w/Flag

**NEW 590-27002** Roadworker w/Flag

**NEW 590-27003** Officer w/Signaling Disc

### Individual Figures

### Railroad Personnel

**NEW 590-28090** Track Worker w/Pick **4.49**

### People Working

590-28080 590-28082

**NEW 590-28080** Chimney Sweep w/Ladder **4.49**

**NEW 590-28082** Sign Painter **4.99**

**NEW 590-28083** Post Office Worker w/Cart **6.49**

590-28086 590-28094

**NEW 590-28086** Camera Man w/Movie Camera **4.99**

**NEW 590-28094** Secretary At Her Desk **6.49**

590-29081 590-29082

**NEW 590-29081** Mime Artist **4.49**

**NEW 590-29082** Pop Singer **4.99**

### People At Home

**NEW 590-28085** Woman Mowing the Lawn **4.99**

**NEW 590-28087** Woman Taking a Shower **6.49**

**NEW 590-28089** Woman Doing Her Hair **4.49**

**NEW 590-28093** Man Shaving **4.49**

### Pedestrians

590-28079 590-28081

**NEW 590-28079** Woman Pushing Child in Stroller **6.49**

**NEW 590-28081** Shopaholic w/Loaded Cart **4.99**

590-28092 590-28095

**NEW 590-28092** Punk Rocker w/Mohawk **4.49**

**NEW 590-28095** Graffiti Artist **6.49**

### Sports & Recreation

**NEW 590-28078** Man Pulling Child on Sled **6.49**

590-29080 590-29083

**NEW 590-29080** Jockey On Horse **4.99**

**NEW 590-29083** Pop Fan **4.49**

### Police

**NEW 590-28088** Task Force Officer **4.99**

### Wedding

**NEW 590-28091** Wedding Couple **6.49**

### Fantasy

590-29072 590-29074

**NEW 590-29072** Female Artist w/Bunny Ears **4.49**

**NEW 590-29074** Vampire **4.99**

Roadworker w/Flag 590-27002

US Railway Workers pkg(6) 590-10547

Road Workers w/Accessories 590-10546

590-29075 590-29078

**NEW 590-29075** Female Vampire **4.99**

**NEW 590-29078** Devil **4.99**

**NEW 590-29079** Demonic Creature **4.99**

### Figure Sets

### Railroad Personnel

**NEW 590-10547** US Railway Workers pkg(6) **19.99**

**NEW 590-14035** Track Workers pkg(5) **9.99**

**NEW 590-14036** Track Workers w/Ties pkg(6) **9.99**

### Passengers

**NEW 590-10540** Travelers w/Luggage **17.99**

**NEW 590-10544** Travelers A Personnel w/Elderly pkg(6) **19.99**

**NEW 590-14038** Travelers I Winter Clothing pkg(6) **9.99**

**NEW 590-14043** Walking Travelers Wearing Coats pkg(6) **9.99**

**NEW 590-14044** Standing Travelers Wearing Coats pkg(6) **9.99**

### People Working

**NEW 590-10542** Bricklayers w/Accessories **23.99**

**NEW 590-10546** Road Workers w/Accessories **23.99**

**NEW 590-10555** Miners w/Masks pkg(6) **21.99**

ORIGINAL **Preiser**

IMPORTED FROM GERMANY
BY WALTHERS

**NEW 590-14039** Cattle At Market w/Figures pkg(5) **9.99**

**NEW 590-28084** Dock Workers w/Cart **7.99**

**NEW 590-30449** Farm Wagon w/Baskets, Horses & Figures **33.99**

**NEW 590-30494** Moving Wagon w/Figures, Horses & Accessories **41.99**

## Sports & Recreation

**NEW 590-10538** At the Campsite/Beach pkg(11) **23.99**

**NEW 590-10545** Railfans w/Cameras pkg(6) **19.99**

**NEW 590-10551** Open Air Concert pkg(11) **23.99**

**NEW 590-10552** Hunters w/Rifles pkg(6) **23.99**

**NEW 590-10553** At The Barbecue pkg(12) **23.99**

**NEW 590-10554** Birthday Party Goers pkg(12) **23.99**

**NEW 590-33246** Barbecue At The Campsite **31.99**

## Pedestrians

**NEW 590-10529** Assorted Babies pkg(9) **12.99**

**NEW 590-10541** Passers-By pkg(7) **17.99**

**NEW 590-10548** Passers-By pkg(7) **17.99**

**NEW 590-10550** Pregnant Women pkg(5) **19.99**

**NEW 590-14037** Passers-By In Winter Clothing pkg(6) **9.99**

**NEW 590-14041** Walking Women w/Children pkg(6) **9.99**

**NEW 590-14042** Walking Passers-By Wearing Coats pkg(6) **9.99**

## Emergency Personnel

**NEW 590-10543** Paramedics w/Injured Person **21.99**



# INDIVIDUAL FIGURES

## Railroad Personnel

**590-28000** Conductor w/Arm Raised **4.49**

590-28002 590-28003

**590-28002** Platform Dispatcher w/Signal Paddle **4.99**

**590-28003** Platform Dispatcher **4.99**

590-28008 590-28009

**590-28008** Modern Switchman w/Safety Vest **4.49**

**590-28009** Modern Switchman w/Safety Uniform - Raised Arm **4.49**

**590-28010** Modern Switchman w/Safety Jacket - Hat Off **4.99**

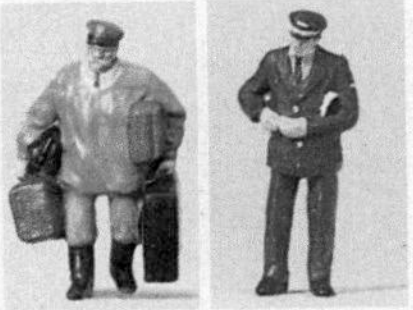

590-28013 590-28034

**590-28013** Porter w/Luggage **4.99**

**590-28034** Conductor Checking Ticket **4.49**

Railfans w/Cameras pkg(6) 590-10545

At The Barbecue pkg(12) 590-10553

590-28038 590-28039

**590-28038** Engineer **4.49**

**590-28039** Fireman **4.49**

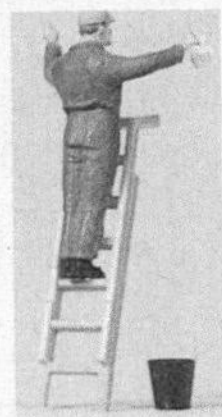

**590-28048** Passenger Car Window Washer w/Ladder **4.99**

**Limited Quantity Available**

590-28001 590-28051

**590-28001** Railway Employee **3.99**

**590-28051** Railway Official **3.99**

590-28004 590-28005

**590-28004** Conductor **3.99**

**590-28005** Lady Platform Dispatcher **3.99**

590-28011 590-28007

**590-28011** Railway Policeman **4.49**

**590-28007** Female Railway Official (blue dress) **3.99**

## Passengers

590-28014 590-28015

**590-28015** Priest In A Hurry **4.49**

**Limited Quantity Available**

**590-28014** Man w/Luggage **3.99**

## People Working 4.49 ea (Unless Noted)

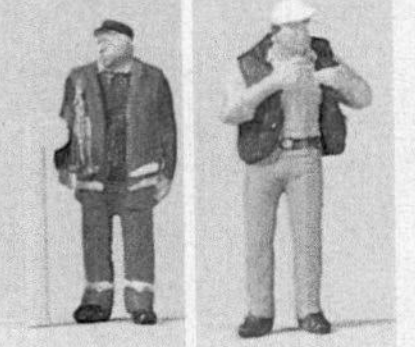

590-28030 590-28032

**590-28030** Safety Guard **4.99**

**590-28032** Trucker

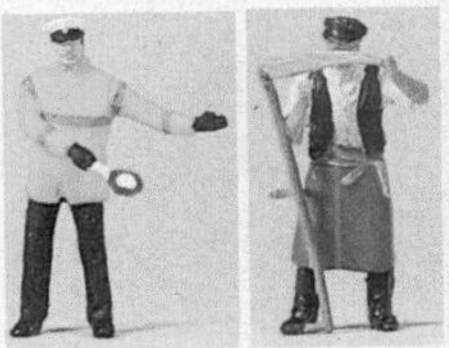

590-28033 590-28041

**590-28033** Toll Collector **4.99**

**590-28041** Farmer With Scyth

ORIGINAL **Preiser**

IMPORTED FROM GERMANY BY WALTHERS

590-28042 590-28044

**590-28042** Inquiry Clerk
**590-28044** Waiter

590-28049 590-28050

**590-28049** Cleaning The House

**590-28050** Landscape Painter **4.99**

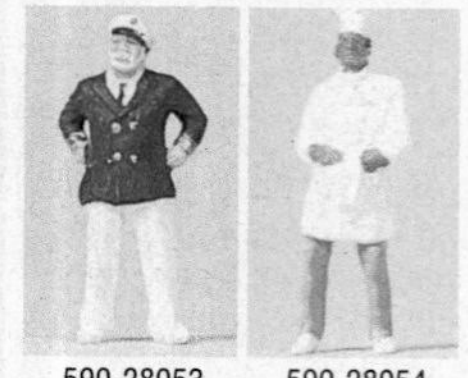
590-28053 590-28054

**590-28053** Captain

**590-28054** Chef de Cuisine

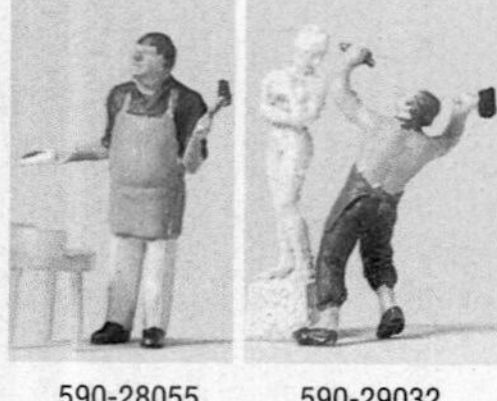
590-28055 590-29032

**590-28055** Hobby Cook

**590-29032** Sculptor With Sculpture **6.49**

**590-28069** Photographer **4.99**

590-28074 590-28075

**590-28074** Maid

**590-28075** Ice Cream Man w/Cart **6.49**

**590-29033** Nude Female Model

590-29034 590-29046

**590-29034** Alpine Horn Blower

**590-29046** Criminal

590-29049 590-29051

**590-29049** Man Carrying Sandwich Board Sign **4.99**

**590-29051** Sheriff "5 To 12"

590-29053 590-29057

**590-29053** Saxophone Musician

**590-29057** Playing The Accordion

**590-29058** Artist **4.99**

**590-29059** Female Nude Model

**590-29067** Standing Guitar Player

## Sports & Recreation

**590-28043** Hunter **4.49**

**590-28052** Angler In a Boat **6.49**

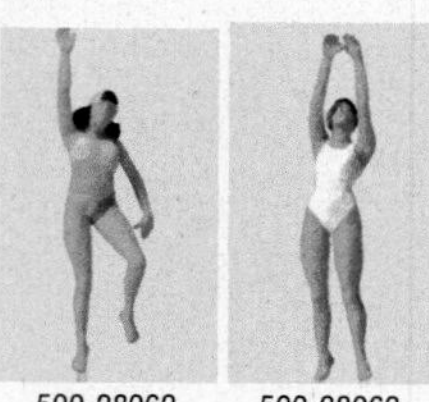
590-28062 590-28063

**590-28062** Female Beach Volleyball Player **4.99**

**590-28063** Female Beach Volleyball Player in White Swimsuit **4.99**

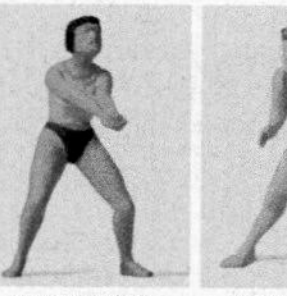
590-28064 590-28065

**590-28064** Beach Volleyball Player **4.99**

**590-28065** Volleyball Player #2 **4.99**

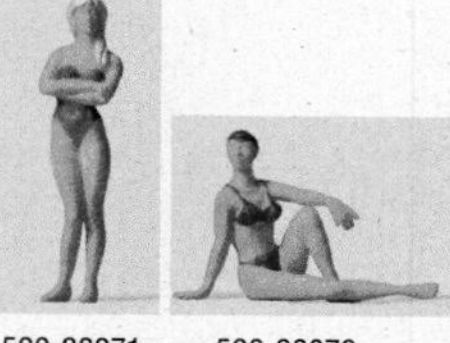
590-28071 590-28072

**590-28071** Standing Female Swimmer **4.49**

**590-28072** Seated Female Swimmer **4.49**

**590-28073** Reclining Female Swimmer **4.49**

**590-28077** Standing Female Sunbather **4.49**

590-29005 590-29006

**590-29005** Sumo Wrestler **4.49**

**590-29006** Golf Player **4.49**

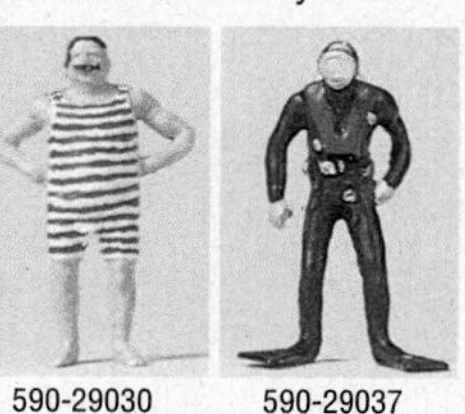
590-29030 590-29037

**590-29030** Enjoying a Swim **4.99**

**590-29037** Scuba Diver **4.49**

**590-29048** Sun Bathing Nude Figure **4.99**

**590-29056** Old Shatterhand Figure **4.49**

590-29061 590-29066

**590-29061** Majorette #1 **4.99**

**590-29066** Majorette #2 **4.99**

**590-29064** Mandy, Standing Cowgirl **4.49**

**590-29065** Cowboy on Horse **6.49**

**Limited Quantity Available**

590-29007 590-29008

**590-29007** American Footba Player Throwing Ball **4.49**

**590-29008** Baseball Batter **4.49**

**590-29009** Baseball Pitcher **4.49**

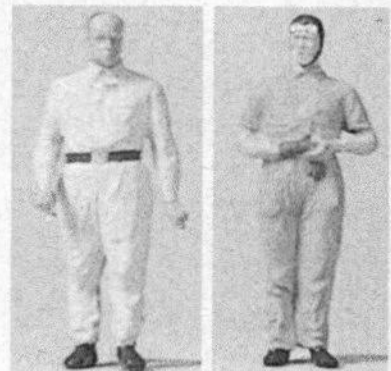
590-29042 590-29043

**590-29042** After The Race **3.9**

**590-29043** Before Starting Th Race **3.99**

## Pedestrians

590-28016 590-28019

**590-28016** Man Reading Newspaper **4.99**

**590-28019** Man w/Broken Le **4.49**

590-28021 590-28023

**590-28021** Photographer **4.99**

**590-28023** Mother w/Child **4.9**

# ORIGINAL Preiser

IMPORTED FROM GERMANY BY WALTHERS

590-28031 590-28035

**590-28031** Happy Homecoming (Couple) **6.49**

**590-28035** Small Man - Big Words **4.99**

**590-28036** Man With Cart **6.49**

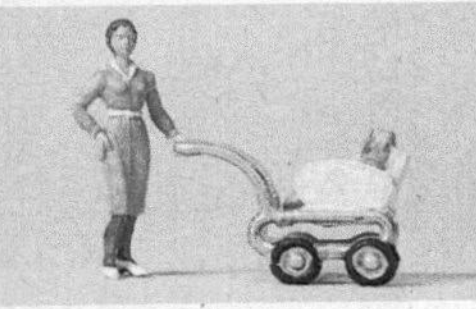

**590-28037** Woman w/Baby Carriage **4.99**

590-28040 590-28045

**590-28040** Where's The Ticket? **4.49**

**590-28045** Wine Connoisseur **4.49**

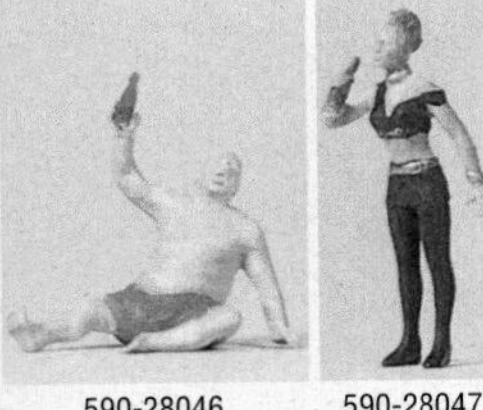

590-28046 590-28047

**590-28046** Enjoying Wine **4.49**

**590-28047** Female Punk **4.49**

590-28056 590-28057

**590-28056** Nun **4.49**

**590-28057** Monk **4.49**

**590-28058** At The Doctor **6.49**

590-29039

**590-29039** Man w/I Love You Signboard **4.99**

**590-29045** Taking A Bath - Female Nude **4.49**

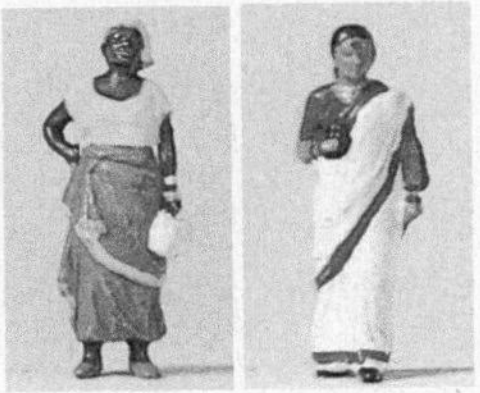

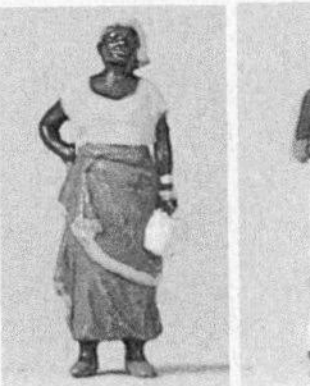

590-29047 590-29050

**590-29047** African Woman **4.49**

**590-29050** Indian Woman w/Sari **4.49**

**590-29052** Japanese Woman w/Kimono **4.49**

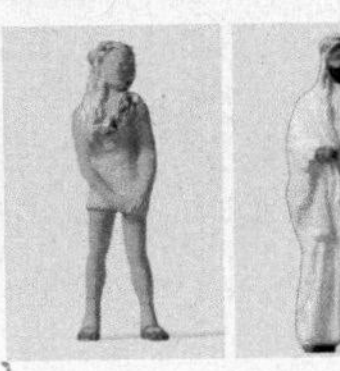

590-29060 590-29062

**590-29060** Young Woman Standing **4.49**

**590-29062** Sheik **4.49**

**Limited Quantity Available**

**590-28020** Woman Passer-By **3.99**

590-28026 590-28059

**590-28026** Artist **4.49**

**590-28059** Do Not Disturb **3.99**

## Police

**590-28012** Modern German Policeman w/Safety Vest **4.99**

590-28070 590-29068

**590-28070** German Federal Police **4.49**

**590-29068** Italian Police Officer Circa 1985 **4.99**

590-28069 590-29070

**590-29069** French Constable **4.49**

**590-29070** British Policeman **4.49**

**590-29071** Berlin Policeman Circa 1900 **4.99**

## Wedding

**590-28029** Bride & Groom **6.49**

## Circus

590-29000 590-29001

**590-29000** Man Selling Balloons **6.49**

**590-29001** Clown w/Umbrella **6.49**

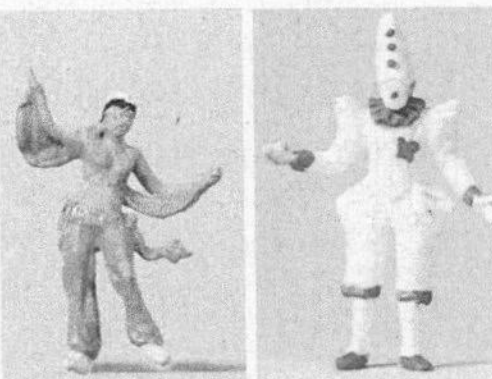

590-29002 590-29038

**590-29002** Charming Lady Dancer **4.49**

**590-29038** Clown **4.49**

590-29041 590-29044

**590-29041** Bear Trainer w/Bear **6.49**

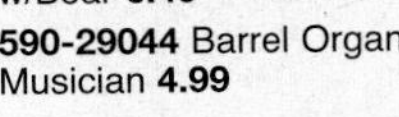

**590-29044** Barrel Organ Musician **4.99**

590-29055 590-29063

**590-29055** Female Snake Charmer **4.49**

**590-29063** Circus Ring Master/Announcer **4.49**

## Holiday

590-29026 590-29027

**590-29026** Girl - Santa's Helper #1 **4.49**

**590-29027** Santa w/Sack of Gifts **4.99**

590-29028 590-29029

**590-29028** Girl - Santa's Helper #2 w/Sack of Gifts **4.99**

**590-29029** Santa Claus - Long Coat **4.49**

## Historic Dress

590-29031 590-29040

**590-29031** Native American "Winnetou" **4.49**

**590-29040** Native American "Nscho-Tschi" **4.49**

590-29018 590-29019

**590-29018** King Ludwig II **4.99**

**Limited Quantity Available**

**590-29019** Man Wearing Swiss National Costume of Canton Uri **4.49**

ORIGINAL Preiser

IMPORTED FROM GERMANY BY WALTHERS

**Limited Quantity Available**

590-29020 590-29021

**590-29020** Woman Wearing Swiss National Costume of Canton Uri **4.49**

**590-29021** Woman Wearing German National Costume of Gutachtal **3.99**

590-29022 590-29023

**590-29022** Man Wearing German National Costume of Gutachtal **4.49**

**590-29023** Man Wearing German National Costume of Urach **3.99**

590-29024 590-29025

**590-29024** Woman Wearing German National Costume of Urach **4.49**

**590-29025** Man Wearing German National Costume of Spree Forest **3.99**

## Religious

590-28060 590-29061

**590-28060** Pope Benedict XVI **4.99**

**590-28061** Protestant Sister w/Child **6.49**

590-28066 590-29067

**590-28066** Altar Boy Carrying Cross **4.99**

**590-28067** Altar Boy Carrying Holy Water **4.49**

590-28068 590-29076

**590-28068** Altar Boy Carrying Incense **4.49**

**590-28076** Priest Wearing a Cassock **4.49**

## Fantasy 4.49 ea (Unless Noted)

**590-29003** Exotic Female Dancer w/Top Hat

590-29004 590-29010

**590-29004** Grim Reaper w/Sickle

**590-29010** Angel Statue

**590-29012** Mermaid #1

**590-29013** Mermaid w/Mirror

**590-29014** Mermaid w/Hair Adornment

**590-29015** Walking Female Elf/Pixie

**590-29016** Seated Female Elf/Pixie

**590-29017** Standing Female Elf/Pixie

## Miscellaneous

590-28027 590-28028

**590-28027** Politician Konrad Adenauer **4.49**

**590-28028** Politician Ludwig Erhard **4.99**

# FIGURE SETS

## Vintage 17.99 ea (Unless Noted)

**590-12045** Vintage Passengers 1847 pkg(13) **33.99**

**590-12046** Vintage Engine Crew w/Standing Passengers pkg(6)

**590-12102** Firemen pkg(6) **14.99**

**590-12129** Standing Cyclists pkg(7) **19.99**

**590-12130** Prussian RR Personnel pkg(6)

**590-12131** Passers-By & Police pkg(6)

**590-12132** Family Walking pkg(6)

**590-12133** Passengers, Men pkg(6)

**590-12134** Bavarian RR Personnel pkg(6)

**590-12135** People Bathing pkg(6)

**590-12136** Passengers, Sitting On Platform pkg(6)

# COMPLETE YOUR SCENES WITH THESE CUSTOM FIGURE SETS

Improve dull dioramas and lifeless layouts in minutes with custom figure sets available from Walthers. Many are exclusives, which feature special groups of figures and custom painting to complement our structure, passenger car and vehicle kits.

Each figure is molded in a realistic pose and hand-painted to bring out its unique character. Choose from figures for a variety of eras and occupations.

# WALTHERS EXCLUSIVE SETS

**590-1010248** United States WWII - Army Personnel for Troop Sleeper pkg(6) **15.98**
Detail period station scenes with this set of figures. Includes three soldiers in World War II dress uniforms with duffel bags, one office in dress uniform, MP and Pullman Porter.

**590-1010249** Engine Servicing Facility Series - Roundhouse Figu Set pkg(10) **19.98**

## Passenger Sets pkg(36) 36.98 ea

### WALTHERS US EXCLUSIVE

Add hustle and bustle to station scenes with these sets of Preiser figures. Crowds of travelers outside Walthers Union Station (933-3094) or the Butterfly Style Station Platforms (933-3175) will be easy to model with the Standing/Walking Passengers. And trains c Walthers cars will take on a new level of detail with Seated Passengers on board.

Molded in plastic to capture fine details and hand-painted for more realism, each set includes 36 figures. And best of all, they're affordably priced so you can populate an entire scene.

**590-1014008** Standing/Walking Passengers for Platform

**590-1014009** Seated Passengers

ORIGINAL **Preiser**

IMPORTED FROM GERMANY BY WALTHERS

**590-12137** People, Sitting On Platform pkg(7)

**590-12138** Travelers & Passers-By pkg(6)

**590-12139** Passers-By pkg(6)

**590-12176** Passers-By pkg(6)

**590-12184** Passers-By Wearing Winter Clothes pkg(6)

**590-12193** At the Grocer's pkg(7)

**590-12194** Women & Children pkg(6)

**590-12195** People At Christmas Fair pkg(6)

**590-12196** Wilhelm II Era pkg(6)

**590-12197** Passers-By Wearing Winter Clothes pkg(6)

**590-12198** Postal Officials pkg(5)

**590-24608** Group From Spreewald pkg(6) **33.99**

**Limited Quantity Available**

**590-12187** Seated Firemen pkg(6) **20.99**

## Railroad Personnel

**590-10010** RR Workers pkg(6) **13.99**

**590-10011** German Railway Personnel pkg(6) **13.99**

**590-10012** Station Personnel #2 pkg(5) **14.99**

**590-10019** Japanese RR Personnel pkg(6) **14.99**

**590-10031** Track Workers pkg(5) **13.99**

**590-10086** French Train Crewmen pkg(6) **14.99**

**590-10087** Swiss Railway Personnel pkg(6) **14.99**

**590-10213** Netherlands RR Personnel pkg(6) **19.99**

**590-10236** 1989 RR Personnel pkg(6) **14.99**

**590-10237** 1989 Train Personnel pkg(6) **14.99**

**590-10238** Italian RR Workers pkg(6) **17.99**

**590-10244** Belgian Railway Personnel pkg(6) **19.99**

**590-10245** Railway Workers pkg(6) **14.99**

**590-10375** Railway Personnel pkg(6) **17.99**

**590-10407** Modern Swiss Railroad Personnel pkg(7) **19.99**

**590-10409** Railway Workers pkg(7) **17.99**

**590-10410** Railway Workers Great Britain pkg(6) **19.99**

Track Workers 590-14403

**590-10416** German Federal Railway Personnel pkg(6) **17.99**

**590-10418** Track Workers w/Tools pkg(6) **19.99**

**590-10444** Track Workers w/Accessories pkg(6) **21.99**

**590-10452** Transition-Era Crew pkg(6) **15.99**
A complete crew for any passenger train of the 1940s to the 1960s.

**590-10490** Tram Staff pkg(6) **17.99**

**590-10535** Railroad Workers w/Welding Equipment **19.99**

**590-14018** Railway Shunters DB pkg(6) **9.99**

**590-12191** Engine-Driver/ Stoker pkg(5) **17.99**

**590-14011** Station Personnel pkg(6) **9.99**

**590-14012** German RR Personnel DB pkg(6) **9.99**

**590-14013** Railway Yard Workers pkg(6) **9.99**

**590-14014** Steam Engine Crew pkg(6) **9.99**

**590-14017** Track Workers pkg(6) **9.99**

**590-14033** Track Workers pkg(6) **9.99**

**590-14105** Railway Shunters pkg(6) **9.99**

**590-14141** Train Personnel DB 1989 pkg(6) **9.99**

**590-14403** Track Workers pkg(24) **31.99**

**590-20261** Circus Workers **19.99**

**590-20264** Circus Workers w/Driver **19.99**

## Passengers

**590-10020** Passengers pkg(6) **13.99**

**590-10021** Seated Persons pkg(6) **12.99**

ORIGINAL **Preiser**

IMPORTED FROM GERMANY BY WALTHERS

**590-10027** Seated On Benches pkg(6) **14.99**

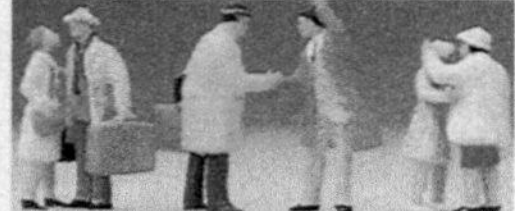
**590-10028** Arriving pkg(6) **14.99**

**590-10029** Departing pkg(7) **14.99**

**590-10103** Seated Diners pkg(6) **13.99**

**590-10114** Waiting pkg(6) **14.99**

**590-10115** Standing pkg(6) **14.99**

**590-10123** Teens Walking pkg(6) **14.99**

**590-10281** Travelers w/Luggage pkg(6) **14.99**

**590-10298** Railway, Seated pkg(7) **13.99**

**590-10299** Seated pkg(8) **15.99**

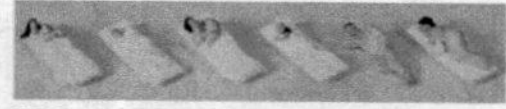
**590-10300** Sleeping pkg(6) **17.99**

**590-10327** Passengers Hurrying pkg(6) **15.99**

**590-10351** Industrial, Sitting pkg(6) **17.99**

**590-10379** Passengers On Platform pkg(6) **17.99**

**590-10380** Businessmen pkg(6) **17.99**

**590-10381** Businessmen w/Coats pkg(6) **17.99**

**590-10382** Passengers w/Steward pkg(6) **17.99**

**590-10384** Sitting On Bus #1 pkg(8) **15.99**

**590-10385** Sitting On Bus #2 pkg(8) **15.99**

**590-10386** Sitting On Bus #3 pkg(12) **17.99**

**590-10387** Seated Couples pkg(4) **15.99**

**590-10391** Passengers Sitting/Eating pkg(8) **15.99**

**590-10402** Nuns w/Luggage pkg(6) **17.99**

**590-10403** Standing Travelers w/Luggage, Set #1, Era III pkg(6) **17.99**

**590-10406** With Bus Driver pkg(7) **17.99**

**590-10412** Seated Travelers pkg(6) **17.99**

**590-10413** Foreign Travelers pkg(6) **17.99**

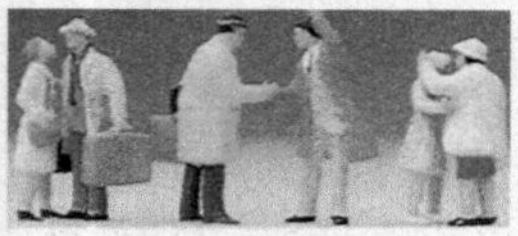

**590-10417** Railroad Passengers w/Accessories pkg(6) **19.99**

**590-10434** Sitting Travelers pkg(6) **17.99**

**590-10459** Travelers w/Luggage Carts pkg(8) **21.99**

**590-10465** Travelers Pushing Cart & Wheelchair #1 **21.99**

**590-10470** Travelers Pushing Cart & Wheelchair #2 pkg(6) **21.99**

**590-10504** Standing pkg(6) **17.99**

**590-10505** Walking w/Luggage pkg(7) **17.99**

**590-10506** Seated pkg(6) **17.99**

**590-10511** Walking Passengers **17.99**

**590-10513** At The Platform **19.99**

**590-10537** Seated Passengers **17.99**

**590-14000** Walking Passengers pkg(6) **9.99**

**590-14004** Seated Passengers w/Bench pkg(6) **9.99**

**590-14019** Travelers w/Luggage pkg(6) **9.99**

**590-14020** Passengers pkg(6) **9.99**

**590-14027** Passengers w/Bags pkg(6) **9.99**

**590-14028** Arriving pkg(6) **9.99**

**590-14029** Travelers Standin pkg(6) **9.99**

**590-14068** Travelers Hurryin **9.99**

**590-14070** Walking Railway Travelers **9.99**

**590-14071** Waiting Travelers At The Platform **9.99**

**590-14072** Seated Railway Travelers **9.99**

**590-14088** Waiting Passengers **9.99**

**590-14104** Passengers pkg(6 **9.99**

**590-14123** Teenage Passengers pkg(6) **9.99**

**590-14133** Passengers pkg(6, **9.99**

**590-14142** Passengers **9.99**

**590-14145** Seated Passenger pkg(6) **9.99**

ORIGINAL Preiser

IMPORTED FROM GERMANY BY WALTHERS

**590-14400** Seated w/Cargo pkg(48) **56.99**

**590-14401** Standing/Walking pkg(24) **31.99**

**590-14404** Bus Driver, Passengers pkg(26) **31.99**

**590-14406** Railway Shunters pkg(24) **31.99**

## People Working

**590-10539** People On the Farm **21.99**

**590-14081** People Working in the Garden **9.99**

**590-14083** People on the Farm #2 **9.99**

**590-14084** Seated Workers **9.99**

**590-10037** Crane Operators pkg(6) **13.99**

**590-10220** Construction Workers pkg(10) **23.99**

**590-10251** Bricklayers/ Accessories **17.99**

**590-10338** Construction Workers Eating Lunch **23.99**

**590-14128** Crane Personnel pkg(6) **9.99**

**590-10347** Street Repair Crew w/Accessories pkg(4) **33.99**

**590-10374** Telephone Workers w/Tent **33.99**

**590-10420** Modern Workmen w/Warning Vests pkg(6) **19.99**

**590-10423** Modern Workmen w/Outdoor Gear pkg(6) **19.99**

**590-10432** German Technical Services 1999 Set #1 pkg(5) **23.99**

**590-10433** German Technical Services 1999 Set #2 pkg(5) **23.99**

**590-10445** City Workers w/Accessories pkg(4) **23.99**

**590-10457** Federal Technical Emergency Service Workers (1950) pkg(6) **19.99**

**590-10458** Federal Technical Workers (1990) pkg(6) **21.99**

Bus-Driver, Passengers 590-14404

Railway Shunters 590-14406

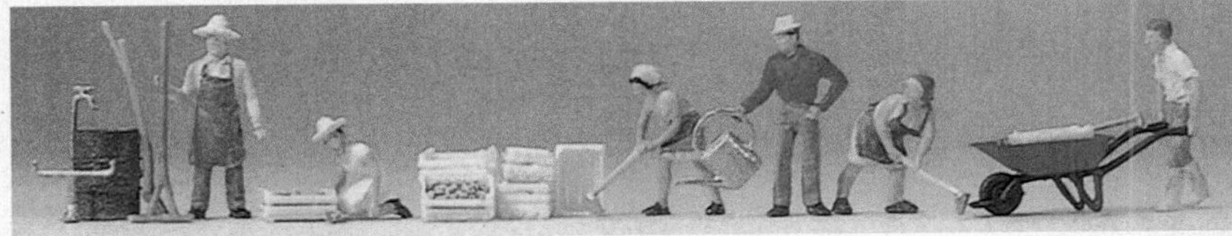

Gardeners & Accessories 590-10046

Cattle Traders 590-10048

Farm Set w/Animals & Accessories 590-13001

**590-10461** Workers w/Picks & Shovels pkg(5) **19.99**

**590-10350** Industrial/Dock Workers pkg(6) **17.99**

**590-10352** Merchant Sailors Ashore pkg(6) **17.99**

**590-10353** Ship Crewmen pkg(6) **17.99**

**590-14147** Loading Dock Crew pkg(5) **9.99**

**590-10248** German Postal Workers **15.99**

**590-10422** Policemen Era III pkg(6) **19.99**

**590-14146** Policemen Era III pkg(6) **9.99**

**590-10419** Policemen w/Warning Vests & Accessories pkg(4) **23.99**

**590-10405** Street Car Crew w/Pedestrians pkg(7) **19.99**

**590-10040** Farm Workers #1 pkg(6) **14.99**

**590-10044** Farm Workers #2 pkg(5) **15.99**

**590-10045** Harvest Workers pkg(6) **17.99**

**590-10295** Farm Workers pkg(6) **17.99**

**590-10404** 2 Swiss Dairymen w/3 Cows pkg(5) **33.99**

**590-10046** Gardeners & Accessories pkg(6) **21.99**

**590-10048** Cattle Traders **17.99**

**590-13001** "Super Set" Farm Set w/Animals & Accessories pkg(60) **99.99**

ORIGINAL **Preiser**

IMPORTED FROM GERMANY BY WALTHERS

**590-10463** Gardeners pkg(5) **21.99**

**590-10464** Hobby Gardeners pkg(5) **21.99**

**590-10477** Paint Crew pkg(5) **19.99**

**590-10478** Paint Crew w/Ladders & Accessories pkg(5) **21.99**

**590-10495** Lumberjacks w/Logs pkg(5) **21.99**

**590-10497** Scaffolders pkg(6) **17.99**

**590-10498** Craftsmen w/Tools pkg(5) **17.99**

**590-14031** Mechanics pkg(6) **9.99**

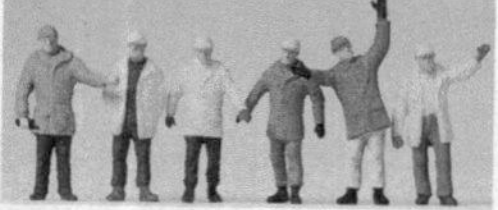
**590-14034** Workers In Protective Clothing pkg(6) **9.99**

**590-14040** Farm Workers pkg(6) **9.99**

**590-14129** At The Mill pkg(6) **9.99**

**590-10036** Truck Drivers Standing pkg(6) **13.99**

**590-10038** Truck Drivers pkg(6) **13.99**

**590-10328** Tractor Drivers **21.99**

**590-14009** Truckers pkg(6) **9.99**

**590-14127** Standing Truckers pkg(6) **9.99**

**590-10014** Different Professions pkg(5) **13.99**

**590-10016** Delivery Men w/Loads pkg(6) **14.99**

**590-10042** Lumberjacks pkg(6) **14.99**

**590-10105** Steeplejacks pkg(6) **14.99**

**590-10243** Craftsmen pkg(5) **19.99**

**590-10294** Stock Workers **23.99**

**590-10373** Mechanics pkg(6) **13.99**

**590-10376** Carpenters **21.99**

**590-14016** Delivery Men w/Loads #2 pkg(6) **9.99**

**590-14130** Mechanics pkg(6) **9.99**

**590-14149** Cleaning Crew pkg(5) **9.99**

**590-10466** Men Planting Trees pkg(4) **21.99**

**590-10210** Innkeeper/Waiter/ Waitress pkg(5) **17.99**

**590-10275** Baker Krause **15.99**

**590-10329** Cooks pkg(5) **17.99**

**590-10330** Cooks At The Buffet pkg(5) **17.99**

**590-10348** Pantomime In Cafe pkg(5) **23.99**

Paint Crew w/Ladders & Accessories pkg(5) 590-10478

Worker On Ladder Putting Up Poster, Trailer 590-10526

**590-10369** Street Cafe pkg(5) **23.99**

**590-10367** At The Restaurant pkg(5) **19.99**

**590-10377** Bakery pkg(6) **23.99**

**590-14131** In Front Of A Hotel pkg(6) **9.99**

**590-14148** Figures Standing At Window pkg(6) **9.99**

**590-10089** Photographers pkg(6) **15.99**

**590-10062** TV/Movie Crew pkg(5) **15.99**

**590-10106** Artists/Models/ Nudes pkg(6) **15.99**

**590-10421** Film Crew pkg(4) **23.99**

**590-10050** Women Hanging Laundry pkg(5) **14.99**

**590-10059** Housewives Working pkg(6) **15.99**

**590-14050** Women Hanging Laundry **9.99**

**590-10491** Belgian Railway Personnel **19.99**

**590-10512** Surveyors **21.99**

**590-10518** Paramedics **23.99**

**590-10526** Worker On Ladder, Putting Up Poster, Hoarding, Trailer **23.99**

ORIGINAL **Preiser**

IMPORTED FROM GERMANY BY WALTHERS

**590-13003** Shepherd w/Flock & Accessories **84.99**

**590-14062** Workers Standing **9.99**

**590-14063** Workers Walking **9.99**

**590-14064** Workers w/Knit Caps **9.99**

**590-14075** Workers **9.99**

## Spectators

**590-10025** Seated pkg(6) **12.99**

**590-10297** Seated Youths pkg(6) **13.99**

**590-10346** Night People pkg(7) **21.99**

**590-10365** Female Commuters pkg(6) **19.99**

**590-10366** Male Commuters pkg(6) **19.99**

**590-10368** Tourists, Waiter, Artist **23.99**

**590-14025** Seated pkg(6) **9.99**

**590-10455** Guide w/Tourists pkg(7) **17.99**

**590-10467** Sightseers pkg(6) **17.99**

**590-10468** City Sightseers pkg(7) **17.99**

**590-14095** Seated Persons pkg(6) **9.99**

**590-14143** Spectators pkg(5) **9.99**

**590-14079** Spectators **9.99**

## Vendors

**590-10052** Market Stalls **33.99**

**590-10053** Food Vendors/Cart **33.99**

See What's Available at

**www.walthers.com**

**590-10056** Flower Stand/ Customers **17.99**

**590-10337** Market Stall **17.99**

## Sports & Recreation

**590-10528** People Playing Beach Volleyball **23.99**

**590-10530** Standing Children Playing **19.99**

**590-10531** Trainspotters **19.99**

**590-14082** Mountain Climbers **9.99**

**590-14080** Standing Photographers **9.99**

**590-10070** Bathers Standing pkg(6) **12.99**

**590-10071** Bathers Reclining pkg(6) **12.99**

**590-10072** Family w/Boats **13.99**
Includes 3 figures and 3 boats.

**590-10074** Roller Skaters & Skateboarders pkg(6) **15.99**

Shepherd w/Flock & Accessories 590-13003

**590-10496** Inline Skaters pkg(7) **17.99**

**590-10107** Nude Sunbathers pkg(6) **15.99**

**590-10211** Fun At The Beach pkg(6) **13.99**

**590-10249** Divers pkg(6) **17.99**

**590-10283** Family At Beach pkg(6) **15.99**

**590-10306** Swimming People pkg(6) **13.99**

**590-10307** Children at Pool pkg(8) **13.99**

**590-10308** Children/Teens at Pool pkg(7) **13.99**

**590-10309** Bathers pkg(6) **14.99**

**590-10424** Sunbathers Eating pkg(6) **19.99**

**590-10426** Speedboat Driver & Passengers pkg(6) **17.99**

**590-10427** 3 Beach Huts w/Figures pkg(3) **33.99**

**590-10428** Beachgoers Sitting & Standing pkg(6) **21.99**

**590-10429** Sunbathers On Lounges pkg(6) **23.99**

**590-10430** Tourists Resting On Folding Chairs pkg(6) **23.99**

**590-10431** Sunbathers On Folding Chairs pkg(6) **23.99**

**590-10438** Sunbathers & Beach Hut pkg(7) **21.99**

**590-10439** Nude Bathers w/2 Lounges pkg(8) **21.99**

**590-10312** Cross Country Skiers pkg(6) **15.99**

**590-10314** Figure Skaters **15.99**

**590-10313** Down Hill Skiers pkg(6) **15.99**

**590-10315** Skaters pkg(6) **15.99**

**590-10316** Skiers pkg(7) **17.99**

**590-10077** Men Fishing pkg(6) **15.99**

ORIGINAL Preiser

IMPORTED FROM GERMANY BY WALTHERS

**590-10113** Hikers pkg(6) **15.99**

**590-10190** Mountain Climbers pkg(6) **15.99**

**590-10260** Boy Scouts pkg(6) **15.99**

**590-10296** Backpackers pkg(6) **21.99**

**590-10441** Hikers At Water Pump pkg(7) **23.99**

**590-10442** Hikers Resting pkg(6) **21.99**

**590-10443** Hikers At Spring pkg(6) **23.99**

**590-14413** Strollers, Hikers, Backpackers pkg(24) **31.99**

**590-10081** Cyclists w/Hercules pkg(3) **23.99**

**590-10091** Bike Riders w/Bikes pkg(6) **19.99**

**590-10125** Mopeds w/Riders pkg(3) **23.99**

**590-10126** Motorbikes w/Riders pkg(3) **23.99**

**590-10128** Motor Bikes & Rider Set **23.99**

**590-10120** Couples Dancing pkg(3) **14.99**

**590-10240** Bavarian Folk Dancers pkg(6) **17.99**

**590-10241** Folk Dancers pkg(6) **17.99**

**590-24607** Bavarian Group pkg(6) **23.99**

**590-10078** Tennis Players pkg(6) **15.99**

**590-10075** Soccer Team pkg(12) **23.99**

**590-10231** Golfers pkg(6) **17.99**

**590-10349** Students/Artists In Cafe **23.99**

**590-10110** Boys & Girls pkg(6) **14.99**

**590-10500** Riders w/Horses #1 pkg(5) **19.99**
Includes two horses and three people.

Strollers, Hikers, Backpackers 590-14413

Bike Riders w/Bikes 590-10091

Soccer Team 590-10075

**590-10501** Riders w/Horses #2 pkg(5) **19.99**
Includes two horses and three people.

**590-10502** At The Riding School #1 **19.99**

**590-10503** At The Riding School #2 **19.99**

**590-10508** Lawn Bowling Players pkg(6) **17.99**

## Cyclists 13.99 ea (Unless Noted)

**590-10515** Cyclists Waiting At The Railroad Crossing **17.99**

**590-17161** Bicycles w/Trailer Kit pkg(4) **14.99**

Cyclists w/Bicycle Trailer pkg(4) 590-10507

**590-10333** Cyclists pkg(3)

**590-10336** Cyclists pkg(3)

**590-25001** Team B-White pkg(3)

**590-10507** Cyclists w/Bicycle Trailer pkg(4) **23.99**

**590-25004** Team A-Yellow pkg(3)

**590-25006** Team C-Blue pkg(3)

**590-25086** Racing Bicycles Kit **17.99**

## Pedestrians

**590-10527** Standing Couples with Dog **15.99**

**590-10533** Protestant Sisters with Children **17.99**

**590-10536** Seated Grandfather with Children **17.99**

For Daily Product Updates Point Your Browser to

**www.walthers.com**

ORIGINAL Preiser

IMPORTED FROM GERMANY BY WALTHERS

**590-14085** Female Commuters on Way to Train **9.99**

**590-14086** Male Commuters on Way to Train **9.99**

**590-14087** Walking Workers **9.99**

**590-10022** Passers-By pkg(6) **13.99**

**590-10024** Group of Women pkg(6) **13.99**

**590-10026** Railfans, Standing pkg(6) **13.99**

**590-10051** Women & Children On Benches pkg(6) **13.99**

**590-10095** Seated pkg(6) **14.99**

**590-10096** Seated #2 pkg(6) **14.99**

**590-10097** Seated #3 pkg(6) **14.99**

**590-10103** Seated Diners #2 pkg(6) **13.99**

**590-10116** Walking Passers-By pkg(6) **14.99**

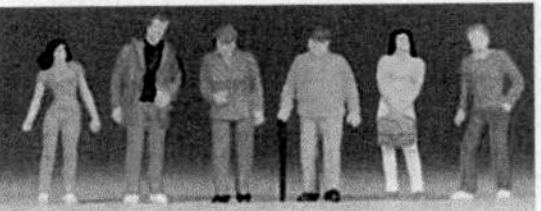
**590-10117** Standing pkg(6) **14.99**

**590-10118** Walking pkg(6) **14.99**

**590-10119** Standing pkg(6) **14.99**

**590-10121** Shopping pkg(6) **14.99**

**590-10122** Group Of Girls pkg(6) **14.99**

**590-10124** Senior Citizens pkg(6) **14.99**

**590-10180** Couples Seated **14.99**

**590-10181** School Children pkg(7) **14.99**

**590-10183** Teens pkg(7) **14.99**

**590-10258** Girls pkg(7) **14.99**

**590-10278** Family Picture pkg(6) **14.99**

**590-10279** Family In City pkg(6) **14.99**

**590-10280** Alpine Family pkg(6) **14.99**

**590-10282** Family Sitting pkg(6) **17.99**

**590-10284** Family Walking pkg(6) **15.99**

**590-10291** Teenagers pkg(7) **14.99**

**590-10305** Fashion Boutique **33.99**

**590-10310** Krause Family In Winter pkg(6) **17.99**

**590-10325** Shopping Promenade pkg(3) **15.99**

**590-10326** Passers-By Hurrying **15.99**

**590-10332** People Seated pkg(6) **15.99**

**590-10343** Travelers **15.99**

**590-10344** School Crossing **17.99**

**590-10378** Passers-By w/Policemen pkg(6) **15.99**

**590-10388** Dressing **17.99**

**590-10400** Standing Commuters pkg(6) **19.99**

**590-10401** Nun w/Small Children pkg(7) **17.99**

**590-14003** Boys & Girls pkg(6) **9.99**

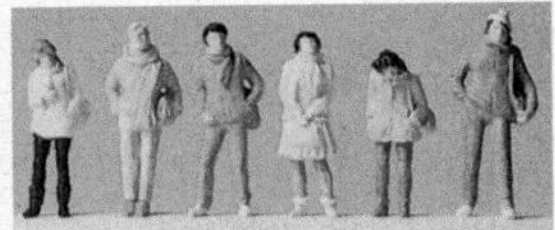
**590-14005** Youths pkg(6) **9.99**

**590-14006** Teenagers pkg(6) **9.99**

**590-14007** Children pkg(7) **9.99**

**590-10408** Standing Travelers w/Luggage, Set #2, Era III pkg(6) **17.99**

**590-10411** Business Commuters pkg(6) **17.99**

**590-10414** People Waiting for Bus pkg(6) **21.99**

**590-10415** Parents & Grandparents w/Children pkg(6) **17.99**

**590-10447** Oktoberfest Goers #1 Seated At Tables pkg(6) **23.99**

**590-10448** In The Beer Garden #1 Seated At Tables pkg(6) **23.99**

**590-10449** Oktoberfest Goers #2 Seated At Tables pkg(6) **23.99**

**590-10450** In The Beer Garden #2 Seated At Tables pkg(6) **23.99**

**590-10451** Passers-By Waiting pkg(6) **17.99**

ORIGINAL Preiser

IMPORTED FROM GERMANY BY WALTHERS

**590-10454** Passers-By pkg(6) **19.99**

**590-10456** Demonstrators w/Signs pkg(8) **28.99**

**590-10462** American Pedestrians #1 pkg(5) **19.99**

**590-10469** Passers-By & Wheelchair pkg(5) **21.99**

**590-10471** American Pedestrians #2 pkg(6) **19.99**

**590-10473** Punk Rockers pkg(6) **23.99**

**590-10474** People Sitting On Stairs pkg(6) **19.99**

**590-10475** Street Scene pkg(5) **19.99**

**590-10476** School Children pkg(6) **17.99**

**590-10479** Elderly Being Pushed In Wheelchairs pkg(6) **21.99**

**590-10488** People w/Grocery Carts pkg(6) **21.99** Includes three carts and three figures.

**590-10492** Going Shopping w/Carts pkg(5) **21.99**

**590-10493** Mothers w/Children In Strollers & Grandparents **21.99**

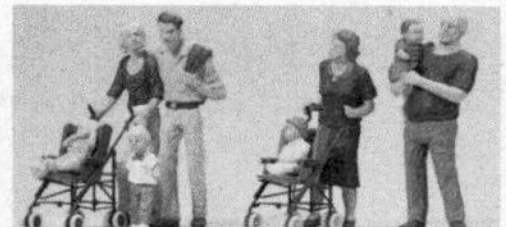

**590-10494** Parents w/Children & Strollers **21.99**

**590-10509** Swiss National Costume of Canton Uri pkg(6) **23.99**

**590-14001** Passers-By pkg(6) **9.99**

**590-14002** Standing Passers-By pkg(6) **9.99**

**590-14022** Passers-By pkg(6) **9.99**

**590-14023** Passers-by w/Policeman pkg(6) **9.99**

**590-14101** Seated Persons #1 **9.99**

**590-14124** Passers-By pkg(6) **9.99**

**590-14125** Passers-By pkg(5) **9.99**

**590-14126** Children pkg(6) **9.99**

**590-14132** Climbing Stairs pkg(6) **9.99**

**590-14134** Passers-By pkg(6) **9.99**

**590-14135** Passers-By pkg(6) **9.99**

**590-14136** Shopping pkg(6) **9.99**

**590-14137** Passers-By pkg(6) **9.99**

**590-14138** Seated Couples pkg(6) **9.99**

**590-14402** Crowd of 36 **46.99**

**590-14139** Children pkg(6) **9.99**

**590-14416** Assorted Seated People pkg(48) **56.99**

**590-10514** Walking Couples **19.99**

**590-10516** Walking Travelers #1 **17.99**

**590-10517** Walking Travelers #2 **19.99**

People Sitting On Stairs 590-10474

Street Scene 590-10475

School Children 590-10476

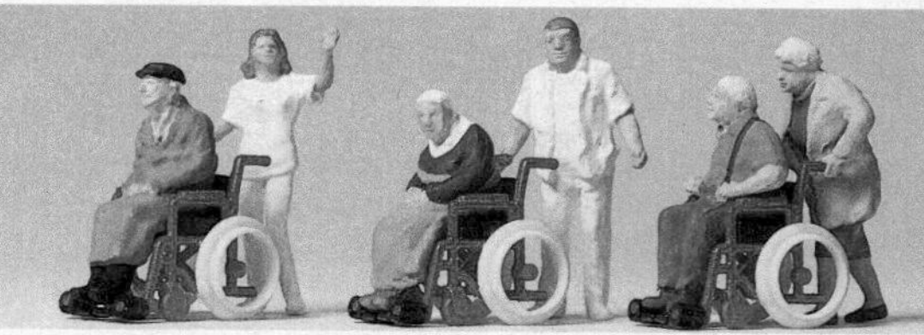

Elderly Being Pushed In Wheelchairs 590-10479

People w/Grocery Carts 590-10488

Crowd of 36 590-14402

**590-10519** Funeral, Protestant **19.99**

**590-10520** Funeral, Catholic **19.99**

**590-10521** Funeral Attendants **17.99**

**590-10522** Seated Woman, Baby Carriages, Benches **21.99**

ORIGINAL Preiser

IMPORTED FROM GERMANY BY WALTHERS

**590-10523** Waiting Persons At The Telephone Box **23.99**

**590-10524** Seated Travelers **23.99**

**590-13002** On Streets & Squares **169.99**

**590-14065** Young Passers-By **9.99**

**590-14066** Young Ladies **9.99**

**590-14067** Passers-By **9.99**

**590-14069** Passers-By Wearing Coats **9.99**

**590-14073** Seated Persons **9.99**

**590-14074** School Children **9.99**

**590-14076** Spectators **9.99**

**590-14077** Wanderers **9.99**

Pedestrians 590-14412

Funfair Visitors 590-14414

**590-14078** Jogging **9.99**

**590-14412** Pedestrians pkg(36) **46.99**

**590-14414** Funfair Visitors pkg(30) **38.99**

**Limited Quantity Available**

**590-16800** WWII Civilians Waving pkg(5) **12.99**

## Emergency

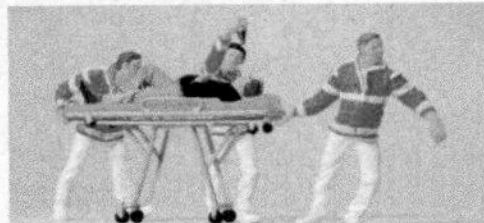

**590-10532** Paramedics with Stretcher **23.99**

**590-10534** Travelers Aid **21.99**

## Police & Firefighters

**590-10389** German Mounted Police In Summer Uniform pkg(2) **21.99**

**590-10390** German Mounted Police pkg(2) **21.99**

**590-10396** US SWAT Team pkg(6) **19.99**

**590-10397** US Mounted Police pkg(2) **21.99**

**590-10398** Italian Mounted Police pkg(2) **23.99**

**590-10399** German Mounted Police 1960 pkg(2) **21.99**

**590-10435** Republican Guards on Horseback pkg(2) **23.99**

**590-10460** Republican Guards on Horseback w/Flag-Bearer pkg(2) **23.99**

**590-10392** German Riot Police w/Shields At Side pkg(6) **23.99**

**590-10393** German Riot Police w/Shields Up pkg(6) **23.99**

On Streets & Squares 590-13002

**590-10394** German Border Guards **19.99**

**590-10395** German Riot Police w/Shields Down pkg(6) **23.99**

**590-10446** German SWAT Team (GSG9) pkg(6) **21.99**

**590-10064** Traffic Police pkg(6) **15.99**

**590-10175** Motorcycle Police pkg(5) **17.99**

**590-10191** French Police w/Motorcycles **19.99**

**590-10340** German Police pkg(6) **17.99**

**590-10341** French Police pkg(6) **17.99**

**590-10370** Policemen, USA pkg(6) **19.99**

**590-10371** Policemen, Great Britain pkg(6) **19.99**

**590-10396** US SWAT pkg(6) **19.99**

**590-14008** Policemen **9.99**

ORIGINAL Preiser

IMPORTED FROM GERMANY BY WALTHERS

**590-25108** French Police pkg(6) **17.99**

**590-10214** Firemen pkg(6) **14.99**

**590-10230** Austrian pkg(6) **17.99**

**590-10232** French w/Modern Helmet pkg(6) **17.99**

**590-10242** Firemen in Action pkg(6) **15.99**

**590-10342** German Firemen pkg(6) **17.99**

**590-10486** German Firefighters-Technical Support Personnel pkg(5) **23.99**

**590-10489** Police On Motorcycles pkg(3) **33.99**

**590-10510** Firefighters in HAZMAT Suits pkg(6) **17.99**

**590-14200** Firemen #1 pkg(6) **9.99**

Wedding Guests 590-14415

**590-14201** Firemen #2 pkg(6) **9.99**

**590-14202** Firemen #3 pkg(6) **9.99**

**590-14203** Firemen #4 pkg(6) **9.99**

**590-14204** Firemen #5 pkg(6) **9.99**

**590-14205** Firemen #6 pkg(6) **9.99**

**590-14206** Firemen #7 pkg(6) **9.99**

**590-14207** Firemen Seated pkg(6) **9.99**

**590-10100** Emergency Doctors w/Motorcycle pkg(5) **23.99**

**590-10101** Emergency Team pkg(6) **12.99**

## Wedding Groups

**590-10057** Protestant pkg(6) **14.99**

**590-10058** Catholic pkg(6) **14.99**

**590-10331** Wedding Guests pkg(6) **17.99**

**590-10339** Bride/Groom/ Guests pkg(6) **15.99**

**590-10436** Formal Guests pkg(6) **17.99**

**590-10437** Guests On Folding Chairs pkg(6) **23.99**

**590-10440** Guests At Buffet pkg(6) **21.99**

**590-14057** Protestant pkg(5) **9.99**

**590-14058** Catholic pkg(5) **9.99**

**590-14415** Wedding Guests pkg(24) **31.99**

Police On Motorcycles 590-10489

## Bands

**590-10206** Tyrolean #1 pkg(6) **19.99**

**590-10207** Tyrolean #2 pkg(6) **19.99**

**590-10250** Bavarian Band pkg(12) **33.99**

**590-24602** Band pkg(11) **33.99**

## Circus Figures

**590-10109** Concession Workers & Customers pkg(6) **15.99**

**590-20254** Magician, Clowns, Acrobats pkg(8) **33.99**

**590-20258** Clowns **33.99**

**590-20259** Seated Circus Band **23.99**

**590-20260** Sea Lions w/Tamer **14.99**

**590-20261** Circus Workers **19.99**

**590-20262** Circus Workers pkg(6) **19.99**

**590-20263** Circus Workers pkg(6) **19.99**

**590-20264** Circus Workers w/Driver **19.99**

**590-20381** Performing Lions pkg(3) **12.99**

**590-20382** Horses pkg(6) **23.99**

## ORIGINAL Preiser

IMPORTED FROM GERMANY BY WALTHERS

**590-20257** Girl w/Monkeys **15.99**

**590-20388** Monkeys **12.99**

**590-24652** For Merry-Go-Round #590-24650 (sold separately) pkg(6) **14.99**

**590-24656** Weight Lifter, Sword Swallower, Stilt Walker **33.99**

**590-24659** Selling Balloons **23.99**

**590-24660** For Swings #590-24658 (sold separately) pkg(6) **14.99**

**590-24661** Ice Cream Stands **30.99**

**590-24662** For Shooting Gallery #590-24694 (sold separately) pkg(6) **15.99**

**590-24663** Circus Goers pkg(7) **17.99**

**590-24664** For Chairoplane pkg(6) **14.99**

### Holiday

**590-30448** Horse Drawn Sleigh, Father Christmas, Parcels **33.99**

Railroad Personnel, Travelers & Passers-By 590-13000

### Miscellaneous

**590-10198** Franciscan Friars pkg(6) **17.99**

**590-14015** Motorists pkg(6) **9.99**

**590-24604** Figures In National Costumes pkg(6) **21.99**

**590-13000** Railroad Personnel, Travelers & Passers-By pkg(100) **169.99**

**590-24606** Figures In Carriage **33.99**

**590-24653** Fair Musicians **23.99**

### Animals

**590-10150** Horses pkg(6) **14.99**

**590-10151** Donkeys pkg(3) **12.99**

**590-10156** Horses pkg(5) **15.99**

**590-10169** Assorted Birds **19.99**

**590-14150** Horses pkg(5) **9.99**

**590-14407** Horses pkg(26) **39.99**

Hot New Products Announced Daily! Visit Walthers Web site at

**www.walthers.com**

**590-14155** Cows pkg(5) **9.99**

**590-14408** Cows Black & White pkg(30) **39.99**

**590-14409** Cows Brown & White pkg(30) **39.99**

**590-14160** Shepherd w/Sheep pkg(8) **9.99**

**590-14161** Sheep pkg(18) **9.99**

**590-14162** Goats & Hogs pkg(10) **9.99**

**590-14165** Cats & Dogs pkg(12) **9.99**

**590-14168** Chickens pkg(18) **9.99**

**590-10179** Stags & Does pkg(6) **14.99**

**590-14178** Reindeer #2 pkg(6) **9.99**

**590-14179** Deer pkg(5) **9.99**

**590-10166** Turkey/Peacock pkg(4) **15.99**

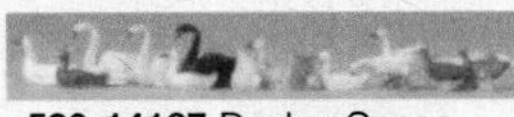

**590-14167** Ducks, Geese, Swans pkg(16) **9.99**

**590-20379** Lions pkg(3) **12.99**

**590-20380** Tigers pkg(3) **12.99**

Girl w/Monkeys 590-20257

Monkeys 590-20388

Assorted Birds 590-10169

Horses 590-14407

Cows Black & White 590-14408

Cows Brown & White 590-14409

Chickens 590-14168

**590-20383** Camels pkg(6) **17.99**

**590-20384** Polar Bears pkg(4) **13.99**

**590-20385** Giraffes pkg(2) **13.99**

**590-20386** Brown Bears pkg(4) **13.99**

**590-20387** Zebras pkg(4) **13.99**

**590-20389** Llamas pkg(3) **12.99**

Preiser

IMPORTED FROM GERMANY BY WALTHERS

**590-20391** Buffalo pkg(4) **17.99**

**590-20392** Kangaroos pkg(3) **12.99**

**590-20393** Moose pkg(3) **15.99**

**590-14411** Sheep pkg(60) **25.99**

**590-20394** Reindeer pkg(6) **19.99**

**590-20395** Seals **12.99**

**590-20397** Camels pkg(3) **15.99**

**590-20398** Penguins pkg(6) **12.99**

## Unpainted Figure Sets

**590-10483** Seated Driver & Crew pkg(8) **23.99**

**590-10484** German Firefighters Arriving At Scene pkg(5) **23.99**

**590-10485** German Firefighters Putting Out Fire pkg(5) **23.99**

**590-10487** Engineers/Pump Operators At Engine pkg(5) **23.99**

**590-16325** Railroad Personnel & Travelers pkg(120) **31.99**

**590-16326** Trades People pkg(120) **31.99**

**590-16327** Figures & Animals pkg(120) **31.99**

**590-16328** Sitting People pkg(120) **31.99**

**590-16329** Firemen w/Accessories pkg(42) **13.99**

**590-16337** Passengers & Passers-by pkg(120) **31.99**

**590-16339** Firemen pkg(60) **15.99**

**590-16342** Fair/Visitors/ Showman pkg(60) **19.99**

**590-16343** Passers-By/ Spectators pkg(130) **31.99**

**590-16345** Uniformed People Combination Kit **15.99**

**590-16346** Sport & Leisure pkg(80) **26.99**

**590-16347** Winter pkg(65) **26.99**

**590-16348** At Goods Shed **19.99**

**590-16349** Seated Passengers pkg(36) **12.99**

**590-16350** Assorted Police pkg(21) **19.99**

**590-16351** Modern German Firefighters pkg(20) **15.99**

**590-16352** At The Train Station pkg(120) **31.99**

**590-16353** Bavarian Band pkg(18) **19.99**

Railroad Personnel & Travelers 590-16325

Figures & Animals 590-16327

Firemen w/Accessories 590-16329

Firemen 590-16339

Fair/Visitors/ Showman pkg(60) 590-16342

Sport & Leisure pkg(80) 590-16346

At The Train Station pkg(120) 590-16352

Unpainted Country Figures (52 People & 50 Animals) pkg(102) 590-16354

**590-16354** Unpainted Country Figures (52 People & 50 Animals) pkg(102) **31.99**

**3590-16400** Adam & Eve Combination Kits pkg(26) **21.99**

**590-16568** Women Working in Ruins pkg(7) **9.99**

## CATALOG

**590-93037 14.99**

Buffalo 590-20391

Sheep 590-14411

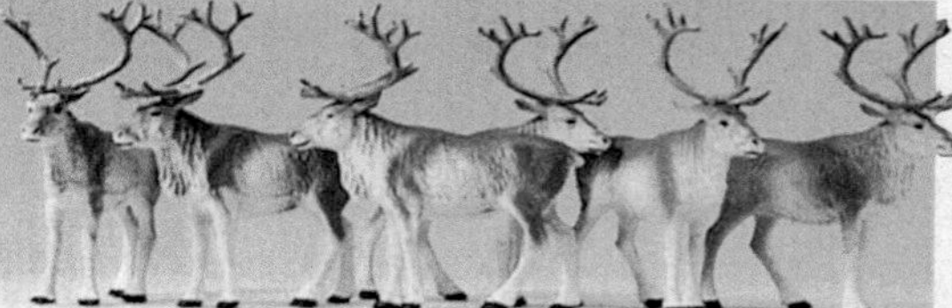

Reindeer 590-20394

Seals 590-20395

# VOLLMER

IMPORTED FROM GERMANY BY WALTHERS
Each plastic figure is molded in a realistic pose and painted in a simplified scheme.

## NEW PRODUCTS

### Figures

**NEW 770-2293** German Railway Personnel DB pkg(6) **13.99**

**NEW 770-2294** Delivery Men w/Loads pkg(6) **14.99**

**NEW 770-2295** Police Women & Men pkg(6) **15.99**

**NEW 770-2296** Workers w/Hard Hats pkg(6) **18.99**

**NEW 770-2298** Track Maintenance Gang pkg(6) **20.99**

**NEW 770-2299** Standing Passengers pkg(6) **16.99**

**NEW 770-2300** Passengers w/Luggage pkg(6) **16.99**

**NEW 770-2301** Jogging Group pkg(6) **13.99**

## FIGURES

### Animals 12.99 ea (Unless Noted)

**770-2217** Horses pkg(4)

**770-2220** Deer (brown) 1 Stag, 1 Doe & 3 Fawns

**770-2258** Farm Animals **13.99**

**770-2261** Horses w/Foal **7.99**

### Pedestrians pkg(5) 12.99 ea (Unless Noted)

**770-2202** Walking Pedestrians

**770-2211** Seated Travelers

**770-2213** Foreign Travelers pkg(15) **56.99**

**770-2221** Hunter w/2 Dogs & 5 Rabbits

**770-2227** Standing Male Passengers

**770-2228** Travelers w/Luggage

**770-2229** Shoppers

**770-2232** Standing Passengers pkg(24) **42.99**

**770-2236** Tourist w/Packages pkg(24) **43.99**

**770-2249** People Sitting on Bench **13.99**

**770-2250** Tyrolean Band **15.99**

**770-2265** Popes, Nuns & Monks pkg(6) **17.99**

**770-2266** Kindergarten & Children **23.99**

**770-2277** School Children w/Book Bags **13.99**

**770-2207** People Standing on Station Platform #2

### Railroad Personnel pkg(5) 12.99 ea

**770-2208** Switch Crew

**770-2212** Track/Shop Crew

**770-2234** Railroad Track Gang pkg(24) **44.99**

**770-2240** Modern Construction/Railroad Workers

**770-2245** Porters/Red Caps w/Luggage

### Working People pkg(5) 12.99 ea (Unless Noted)

**770-2205** Farm Hands

**770-2215** German Firemen Set #1

**770-2216** German Firemen Set #2

**770-2222** Girl w/Flock of 8 Geese pkg(9)

**770-2223** Shepherd w/Dog & 6 Sheep pkg(8)

**770-2237** Road Building Gang

**770-2238** Farmers & Wives on the Field **13.99**

**770-2246** Boy w/Goats **11.99**

**770-2247** Farmer w/Pigs **11.99**

**770-2257** On the Farm w/Fowl **20.99**

**770-2268** Forest Worker

**770-2269** Inside Gardener

**770-2274** Police **13.99**

**770-2276** Medical Crew **13.99**

### Recreation

**770-2225** Rowboats w/Figure pkg(3) **14.99**

**770-2226** Wanderers/Hikers pkg(5) **14.99**

**770-2275** Hikers w/Packs pkg(5) **13.99**

### Unpainted Figures

**770-2231** Sheep pkg(24) **14.99**

**770-2233** Standing Passengers pkg(24) **20.99**

**770-2235** Horses & Cows pkg(24) **20.99**

**770-2256** Unpainted Assorted Figures pkg(60) **23.99**

Scenic Accents are colorful, action-packed HO scale figures, animals and accessories. They are superbly sculpted and hand painted. Their fine features add realism needed to bring any layout to life. Scenic Accents set the scene.

Scenic Accents Glue

**785-198** 1 fl. oz **4.29**
Specially formulated to attach Scenic Accents or any type of figure or detail to a layout or diorama. Figures can be positioned without waiting for glue to dry. And since it stays tacky, they can be placed in one position, picked up and moved to another without regluing at any time. Accent Glue leaves no puddles or residue. It's water-soluble and a small brush applicator is included.

Gentle Grips

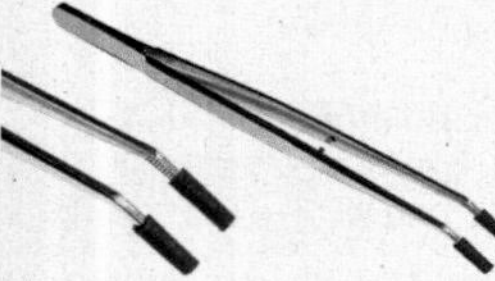

**785-200** Tweezers w/Cushion Tips **5.98**
These unique tweezers are perfect for handling Scenic Accents or any type of figure or detail. Protective tips prevent damage while curved ends and special non-slip thumb and forefinger grips help you hang on to small items. Longer length lets you reach into any area with- out damaging nearby details.



## ECONOMY FIGURE PACKS

**99.98 ea**

Populate your layout, at an affordable price, with these little works of art! Each package includes over 100 pieces, enough to detail multiple scenes.

Assorted Farm Set **785-2051**
Assorted Worker Set **785-2052**
Assorted Figure Set **785-2053**

## NEW PRODUCTS

### Figure Sets

**NEW** Family Fishing 729-1923 **15.98**

**NEW** People on Benches 785-1924 **10.98**

**NEW** Sermon on the Crate 785-1925 **11.98**

**NEW** Shootin' Hoops 785-1926 **15.98**

**NEW** One Man Crew 785-1927 **13.98**

**NEW** Garage Treasures 785-1928 **13.98**

## FIGURE SETS

Pedestrians 785-1821 **9.49**

Policemen 785-1822 **9.49**

Dock Workers 785-1823 **10.98**

Ordinary People 785-1824 **9.49**

Window Shoppers 785-1825 **8.49**

City Workers 785-1826 **10.98**

People & Pets 785-1827 **9.49**

Roofers 785-1828 **10.98**

People Sitting 785-1829 **9.49**

Kids at Play 785-1830 **9.49**

Active People 785-1831 **8.49**

Moms & Kids 785-1832 **8.98**

Lovers 785-1833 **8.49**

Sitting & Waiting 785-1834 **8.49**

Professionals 785-1835 **9.49**

Tourists 785-1836 **8.49**

General Public 785-1837 **8.98**

People Talking 785-1838 **8.49**

Commuters 785-1839 **8.49**

Travelers 785-1840 **9.49**

Dogs & Cats 785-1841 **10.49**

Chestnut Horses 785-1842 **9.49**

Hereford Cows 785-1843 **9.49**

Livestock 785-1844 **9.49**

Full Figured Folks 785-1845 **10.49**

Recreational People 785-1846 **9.49**

Train Personnel 785-1847 **10.49**

Checker Players 785-1848 **10.49**

Rebels 785-1849 **9.49**

Road Crew 785-1850 **9.49**

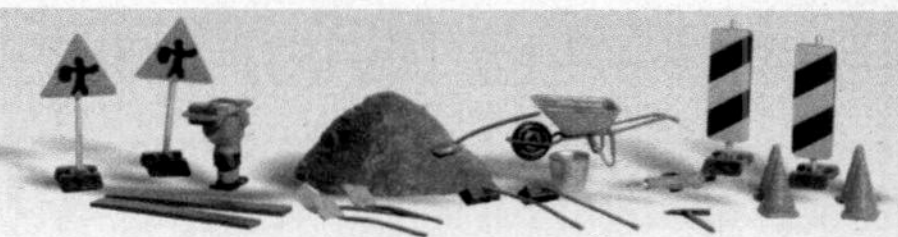
Road Crew Details 785-1851 **10.49**

Assorted Junk 785-1852 **11.49**

Sun Bathers 785-1853 **9.49**

Assorted Skids 785-1854 **11.49**

Assorted Crates 785-1855 **11.49**

Tombstones 785-1856 **11.49**

Farm People 785-1857 **10.49**

Chain Gang 785-1858 **10.49**

Train Mechanics 785-1859 **10.49**

Hobos 785-1860 **10.49**

Bus Stop People 785-1861 **9.49**

Farm Horses 785-1862 **9.49**

Holstein Cows 785-1863 **9.49**

Hampshire Pigs 785-1864 **10.49**

Track Workers 785-1865 **10.49**

Engineers 785-1866 **10.49**

Factory Workers 785-1867 **10.49**

Graveside Service 785-1868 **10.49**

Baseball Players #1 785-1869 **10.49**

Baseball Players #2 785-1870 **10.49**

Welders & Accessories 785-1871 **11.49**

Bystanders 785-1872 **9.49**

Passengers 785-1873 **9.49**

Casual People 785-1874 **9.49**

People & Pesky Raccoons 785-1875 **10.49**

Lumberjacks 785-1876 **10.49**

Shoe Shiners 785-1877 **10.49**

Gone Fishing 785-1878 **11.49**

Park Benches 785-1879 **9.49**

Game of Horseshoes 785-1880 **10.49**

Spectators 785-1881 **11.49**

Firemen to the Rescue 785-1882 **11.49**

Surveyors 785-1883 **11.49**

Deer 785-1884 **10.49**

Black Bears 785-1885 **9.49**

2nd Shift Workers 785-1886 **9.49**

Dairy Farmers 785-1887 **11.49**

Farm Animals 785-1888 **9.49**

Horseback Riders 785-1889 **10.49**

Painters 785-1890 **11.49**

Children 785-1891 **9.49**

Uniformed Travelers 785-1892 **10.49**

Accident Waiting to Happen 785-1893 **11.49**

Snowball Fight 785-1894 **11.49**

Youth Football Players 785-1895 **15.49**

Farmers Market 785-1896 **13.49**

Beekeepers 785-1897 **11.49**

Rail Workers 785-1898 **11.49**

Ice Skaters 785-1899 **11.49**

Couples in Coats 785-1900 **10.49**

Masonry Workers 785-1901 **12.49**

Jug Band 785-1902 **11.49**

Rabbit Hunt 785-1903 **11.49**

Bicycle Buddies 785-1904 **15.49**

Dog Wash 785-1905 **12.98**

Newsstand 785-1906 **11.98**

Golfers 785-1907 **10.98**

Sixteen Passengers 785-1908 **15.98**

Depot Workers & Accessories 785-1909 **12.98**

Fly Fisherman 785-1910 **11.98**

Workers w/Forklift 785-1911 **12.98**

Goodbye People 785-1912 **8.98**

People Walking 785-1913 **8.98**

Auto Mechanics 785-1914 **10.98**

Lawn Workers 785-1915 **10.98**

Park Bums 785-1916 **12.98**

Campers 785-1917 **12.98**

Canoers 785-1918 **12.98**

Smoke Jumpers (Forest Fire Fighters) 785-1919 **12.98**

Picket Line 785-1920 **12.98**

Playtime 785-1921 **12.98**

Senior Citizens 785-1922 **9.98**

## METAL FIGURE KITS

Each kit features unpainted castings, assembly required.

Farmer, Plow, Disc & Horse 785-210 **7.98**

Assorted Cats & Dogs w/Man 785-226 **5.98**

The Bare Hunter 785-227 **5.98**

# MILITARY

Models and Photo by Mellow Mike

An army may still travel on its stomach, but for the heavy mechanized forces of today, long distance journeys are usually easier to make by train. En route to an embarkation point a pair of Heavy Expanded Mobility Tactical Trucks — "Hem-tets" for short — are ready to move out aboard a Trailer Train flat car under the fading light of a chilly winter sunset.

The trucks are reworked Roco models hand-painted with Testors colors in the three-tone camouflage used on National Guard equipment. They're loaded aboard a modified Walthers 89' flat car, built by Mike of Spokane Valley, Washington. The deck of the car was reworked with ratchet troughs for chains and wood planking, modeled with Evergreen styrene. Mike painted the car, adding the various patches of fresh paint often seen on TTX equipment, and completed the model with Micro Scale decals.

Capture the drama and heritage of the world's military equipment, figures and many other accessories, which you'll find on the pages of this section.

TRAINLINE®
by WALTHERS

US Army GP9M Diesel & Caboose
931-701

81' 4-Truck Depressed Center Flat Car
932-5622

## POST-1945 – UNITED STATES

### Railroad Equipment

- Unique Addition to Any Collection
- Based on Equipment Now in Service
- Fully Assembled
- Working Knuckle Couplers

### Loco & Caboose Set

**931-701** US Army (red, yellow) GP9M Diesel #4600; Caboose #909 **39.98**

- Powered GP9M Diesel
- Working Headlight
- Diecast Metal Frame
- Powerful Five-Pole Motor with Flywheel
- Matching Wide-Vision Caboose

### 81' 4-Truck Depressed Center Flat Car

**932-5622** Department of Defense **29.98**

- Based on actual Department of Defense Cars
- Fully Assembled
- Diecast Metal Body for Outstanding Performance.

## WORLD WAR II – UNITED STATES

### Tanks

**675-288** "Sherman" **6.90**
Makes an ideal flat car load that adds realistic detail and extra weight without extra work. Unpainted, cast metal kit is designed for easy construction.

## MOTORCYCLES

**361-907** U.S. Military Set pkg(3) **9.99**
Unfinished, white-metal kit

Get the Scoop!
Get the Skinny!
Get the Score!
Check Out Walthers Web site at
**www.walthers.com**

IMPORTED FROM GERMANY BY WALTHERS

## NEW PRODUCT

### US Air Force Post-1945

**NEW 189-44010** Dodge Power Wagon 4x4 Pick-Up **14.99**

## MODERN GERMAN ARMY

Busch vehicles come completely assembled, ready for use on your layout or diorama.

### Automobiles 16.99 ea

**189-48949** Smart City Coupé Bundeswehr

**189-49503** Smart Forfour Subcompact Bundeswehr

### Multicar

**189-42203 15.99**

## UNITED NATIONS

**189-43002** Toyota Land Cruiser UN **14.99**

## POST-1945 - UNITED STATES

### Armored Vehicles

**218-V003** LAV M1117 ASV-150 4-Wheel "Guardian" Armored Car - Military Police Security Unit **24.00**

**218-V011** M-48 AVLB Armored Vehicle Launched Bridge **51.00**

## WORLD WAR II - GERMANY

### Aircraft

#### Jet Fighters

**218-A001** Messerschmidt Me 262 Jet "Schwalbe" (Swallow) **33.00**

**218-A002** Heinkel He 162 "Salamander" **27.00**

**218-A005** Arado Ar 234 "Blitz" (Lightning) Jet Bomber **36.00**

**218-A006** Junkers Ju88 **39.00**

**218-A007** Heinkel He 111 **39.0**

**218-A009** Fiesler Fi 56 "Storch" (Stork) Observation/ Spotter Light Plane **30.00**

### Focke-Wulf Fw 190 27.00 ea

**218-A003** A8 "Zerstbrern" Bomber Interceptor

**218-A004** 190 D-9 "Dora" Interceptor

IMPORTED FROM THE CZECH REPUBLIC BY WALTHERS
Expand your collection of World War II models for display or gaming with this line of kits. Each includes highly detailed resin parts, decals and detailed instructions with painting information.

## Armor

### Medium Tank 21.00 ea

**218-V004** Panzer II

**218-V030** Flakzwilling (Krupp) Panther G w/Twin 55mm Anti-Aircraft Cannon

**218-V031** Panther G w/Gerat 58 55mm Anti-Aircraft Cannon

### Self-Propelled Gun

**218-V002** Panzer III Chassis w/SiG 33 150mm Howitzer **16.50**

### Artillery

**218-V001** SiG 33 150mm Field Howitzer **15.00**

### Armored Vehicles

**218-V005** Bergepanther Armored Recovery Vehicle on Panzer D Chassis **27.00**

### Remote Controlled Armored Mines

**218-V006** Goliat (Goliath) Wire-Guided, Miniature Tracked Carrier pkg(4) **16.50**

**218-V007** Springer Radio-Guided, Medium Tracked Carrier pkg(2) **13.50**

### Borgward IV Radio-Guided Tracked Carrier

**218-V008** Model A pkg(2) **13.50**

**218-V009** Model B **13.50**

**218-V017** Bergepanzer III Armored Recovery Vehicle On Panzer III Chassis **18.00**

**218-V021** Self-Propelled Gun Sturmgeschutz III Model A (Early Version) **19.50**

**218-V033** Half-Track SdKfz 7/3 Feuerleitpanzer (Flamethrower) w/Trailer **27.00**

**218-V039** Military - Former German Army WWII - Tank Destroyers (Resin & Plastic Kits) SdKfz 184 Early Model "Ferdinand" **27.00**

**218-V040** Trailer Light Trailer w/Fi 156 "Storch" (Stork) Light Aircraft **42.00**

### Rockets

**218-V012** Meilerwagen 3-Axle Heavy-Duty Trailer **39.00**
This heavy-duty transporter carried the V2 to the firing site after the warhead was attached.

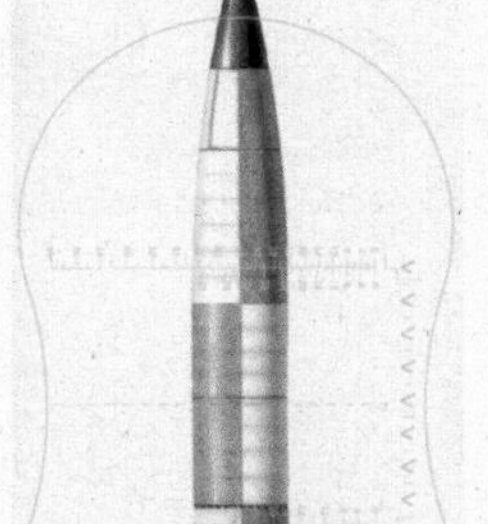

**218-V013** V2A4 Ballistic Missile **27.00**

**218-V014** Hanomag Heavy-Duty Tractor **30.00**
Adapted from a Civilian vehicle, this powerful 100 horsepower truck was used for various towing jobs, and was usually seen moving loaded Meilerwagen trailers (sold separately).

### Half-Tracks

**218-V033** SdKfz 7/3 Feuerleitpanzer (Flamethrower) w/Trailer **27.00**

### Trailers

**218-V041** SdAnH. 13 w/PS Motor Boat **19.00**

**218-V044** Searchlight **12.00**

**218-V046** Fuel Tank **4.50**

**218-V047** Air Compressor **9.00**

### Staff Car

**218-V042** Mercedes 1500A **20.00**

**218-V043** Commander Caravan **15.00**

### Surface-to-Air Anti-Aircraft Missiles 32.00 ea (Unless Noted)

**218-V054** Wasserfall (Waterfall) w/Launching Ramp **19.00**

**218-V055** Enzian (Duck) w/Launching Ramp

**218-V056** Rheintocher (Rhine Maiden) w/Launching Ramp

**218-V057** Feuerlilie (Tiger Lily) w/Launching Ramp

## POST-1945 - GERMANY

### Tanks

**218-V019** M48 (US M8A1) w/Bulldozer Blade **33.00**

**218-V020** M48A2 GA2 w/105mm Gun **24.00**

### Armored Vehicles

**218-V018** M-1 Panther II w/Mine Detonation Roller **27.00**

**218-V032** Leopard I Training Vehicle (Schulpanzer) **21.00**

### Heavy Trucks

**218-V045** Faun L1212 w/50-Ton Tank Transport Trailer **65.00**

### Engineer Equipment

**218-V060** Mine-Laying Trailer **14.00**

## WORLD WAR II – SOVIET UNION

### Armored Rail Equipment

**218-R001** Draisine MBW-2 Armored Railcar **54.00**
Unpowered model based on pre-war design.

**218-R004** Soviet Draisine "Krasnaja Zvezda" **42.00**

## POST-1945 - SOVIET UNION

### Tanks

**218-V016** T-55 w/Mine Detonation Roller **30.00**

**218-V015** T-55A **24.00**

**218-V010** T-55 AM2 "Kladivo" (Modernized w/Czech-Built Fire Control System) **33.00**

### Armored Vehicles 33.00 ea

**218-V022** T-55 BREM Armored Repair & Recovery Vehicle (VT-55)

**218-V027** Self-Propelled Gun "Akatsiya" (Akacia) 2S3 152mm Howitzer

## BRIDGES

**218-V050** Wooden Plate **42.00**

**218-V051** Boat Bridge **12.00**

## STAR DUST PIGMENTS

Create a wide range of dusty and dirty or metallic finishes for any kind of models with this line of pigment powders. Can be dusted on right out of the bottle or mixed with acrylic thinner for washes or airbrushing.

### Weathering Colors 4.60 ea

**218-1** Dark Rust

**218-2** Light Rust

**218-3** Sandy Dust

**218-4** Vietnam Earth

**218-5** Dark Earth

**218-6** Dark Dust

**218-7** Light Dust

**218-8** Light Earth

**218-9** Brick Dust

**218-10** Black Smut

**218-11** White

**218-12** Black

**281-13** Dirty White

### Metallic Colors 5.50 ea

**218-51** Bronze

**218-52** Copper

**218-53** Gold

**218-54** Aluminum

**218-55** Brass

IMPORTED FROM SPAIN BY WALTHERS

Fully-assembled, plastic models from World War II and the post-war era.

## WORLD WAR II – UNITED STATES

### Tanks

**265-4012** M4 "Sherman" **4.99**

### Armored Vehicles

Shown Painted & Detailed

**265-4002** M8 "Greyhound" Armored Car w/37mm Cannon **3.99**

### Trucks 4.99 ea (Unless Noted)

**265-2056** GMC Personnel Carrier

**265-2057** GMC Cargo/ Personnel Carrier w/Canvas Covered Bed

**265-2058** GMC Water/Fuel Tank Truck

**265-4036** DUKW "Duck" Amphibious 6x6 **6.99**

## POST-1945 – UNITED STATES

### Tanks 4.99 ea

**265-4003** M48 "Patton II"

**265-4008** M47 "Patton"

**265-4014** M41 "Walker Bulldog"

### Armored Vehicles 4.99 ea

**265-4018** M42 Self-Propelled Anti-Aircraft Gun

**265-4019** M40 Self-Propelled Howitzer

**265-4030** T235 Self-Propelled Howitzer

**265-4031** T245 Self-Propelled Howitzer

**265-4032** Armored Recovery Vehicle w/Crane

**265-4033** T198 Self-Propelled Howitzer

### Trucks

**265-4007** Jeep Cabover Pick-Up **2.49**

**265-4027** M35 2-1/2-Ton 6x6 "Honest John" Missile Launcher **6.99**

## WORLD WAR II – GERMANY

### Tanks 4.99 ea

**265-4009** Panther

**265-4010** Tiger

**265-4039** Panzer III

### Artillery

**265-4006** Light Cannon **2.49**

## POST-1945 – GERMANY

### Tanks

**265-4040** Panzer P111 **4.99**

## WORLD WAR II – ENGLAND/GREAT BRITAIN

### Tanks 4.99 ea

**265-4004** Centurion

**265-4043** Matilda MKII

### Trucks

**265-4023** Military Land Rover **2.49**

**265-4044** Slava Ambulance **3.99**

**265-4045** Large Military Land Rover **3.99**

## WORLD WAR II – SOVIET UNION

### Tanks

**265-4001** T-34 Tipo Standard **4.99**



## POST-1945 – SOVIET UNION

### Tanks 4.99 ea

**265-4013** T54

**265-4020** PT-76 Light Amphibious Tank

**265-4029** "Stalin"

### Armored Vehicles

**265-4021** BTR50 Personnel Carrier **4.99**

## POST-1945 – FRANCE

### Tanks

**265-4011** AMX 13 **3.99**

**265-4017** EBR75 8-Wheeled Tank **3.99**

**265-4038** AMX **4.99**

## POST-1945 – SPAIN

### Trucks

**265-4035** TT90.25 Cargo Carrier **4.99**

FALLER

IMPORTED FROM GERMANY BY WALTHERS

# POST-1945 GERMANY

## Structures

**Military Base**
**272-144020** Set #1 - 1 each #144021, 144031, 144041 **136.99**
Create a complete base of operations for your favorite branch of service with this set. You'll get a Barracks (#272-144041), Guard Shack with Entry Gate (#272-144021) and a 3-Stall Vehicle Shed (#272-144031) to start construction. Each building is also available as a separate kit, so it's easy to build a bigger base.

**Officers' Mess**
**272-144044 59.99**
8-23/32 x 7-3/8 x 5-31/32" 21.8 x 18.4 x 14.9cm

Officers assigned to your camp will feel right at home enjoying their meals in this handsome building. It features large windows and an enclosed entryway.

**Small Barracks**
**272-144034 23.99**
4-7/16 x 2-7/8 x 2-1/8"
11.1 x 7.2 x 5.3cm

This versatile hut features a roofed entrance, plank and tarred-felt covered roof.

**Above-Ground Storage Building**
**272-144056 39.99**
5-3/64 x 4-13/32 x 2"
12.6 x 11 x 5cm

This fuel storage facility features a protective screen and panel facing. Two storage tanks are housed inside the facility.

**Ammunition Storage Boxes**
**272-144055** pkg(6) **13.99**
1-29/64 x 41/64 x 47/64"
3.6 x 1.6 x 1.8cm

A must-have for secure storage of rounds on any range where live-fire exercises are underway. Set of six storage boxes adds a neat detail to camp street scenes, too.

**Barracks Main Entrance**
**272-144022 30.99**
4-59/64 x 1-29/64 x 3-57/64"
12.3 x 3.6 x 9.7cm
2-17/32 x 2-3/32 x 1-31/64"
6.3 x 5.2 x 3.7cm

Secure entry into your installation with this impressive main gate structure. The set includes a main entry with a simulated sliding gate, a check-point entrance on one side and a separate guard room.

**Camp Fence**
**272-144023 23.99**
62" 155cm

Maintain a secure perimeter around any facility with this masonry fence with built-in steel railings. Matches style of Barracks Main Entrance #272-144022, (sold separately).

**Soldiers' Quarters/Barracks**
**272-144041 85.99**
14-31/64 x 4-13/64 x 6-59/64"
36.2 x 10.5 x 17.3cm

From boot camp to duty station, any HO Scale soldier will appreciate these barracks. The three-story building is highly detailed and includes bars for the ground-floor windows. Several kits can be used together to create a typical large company area and parade ground.

**Heavy Equipment Service/Inspection Pit & Ramps**
**272-144025 21.99**
15-3/32 x 2-9/16 x 1" 37.7 x 6.4 x 2.5cm

Provide easy access to the underside of any vehicle with this facility in your motor pool area. Includes large drive-on ramps with open center pit. Add figures, vehicles and a few accessories to create a great mini-scene in minutes!

**Motor Pool Gas Pump Island & Accessories**
**272-144024 16.99**
7-13/16 x 1-17/32 x 1-21/64" 19.5 x 3.8 x 3.3cm

Complete with four fuel pumps, oil barrels and a small shelter.

**3-Stall Vehicle Shed w/Open Front**
**272-144031 32.99**
7-5/8 x 6-5/64 x 2-59/64" 19 x 15.2 x 7.3cm

Keep your armor and other vehicles running and ready for inspection with these buildings on your military base. Modern design features an open front to showcase your collection, while modular assembly makes it easy to place several kits side-by-side to build a bigger motor pool.

**Motor Pool Sheds**
**272-144033** 3-Stall Repair Shed **49.99**
13-5/8 x 4-21/64 x 3-13/32" 34 x 10.8 x 8.5cm

Features modular construction, positionable folding doors and simulated exhaust fans.

FALLER

IMPORTED FROM GERMANY BY WALTHERS

### Headquarters Building

**272-144042 56.99**
7-1/2 x 4-1/4 x 8-1/8"
18.8 x 10.6 x 20.3

A must-have for any major installation, this building is complete with double front doors, attic louvers and window grates for a secure area on the ground floor.

### Infirmary/Ambulance Station

**272-144043 76.99**
14-9/16 x 4-1/4 x 5-17/32"
36.4 x 10.6 x 13.8cm

Locate your Medical Corps staff in this two-story facility, which includes larger entry doors, attic louvers and more.

### Guard Shack w/Entry Gate

**272-144021 42.99**
5-9/32 x 2-7/8 x 2-1/8"
13.2 x 7.2 x 5.3cm

Limit access to your military base with this kit protecting every entrance. Kit includes main guard building, two roadway security gates, two guard shacks, wide sliding-style gate for roadway, personnel entrance gate, concrete fence posts, 8-13/32" 21cm of mesh material for chain link fencing and two flag poles.

### Obstacle Course

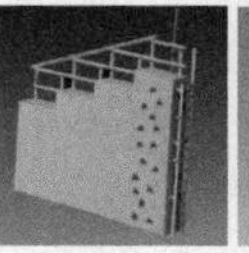

Obstacle Wall — Hand-Over Hand Climbing Obstacle

Net Wall — Balance Beam

Rope Bridge

Concrete Climbing Tower

Balance Beams

Inclined-Ascent Obstacles

Sewer Pipe Obstacle

Hand-Over-Hand Climbing Wall

**272-144046** With 10 Different Stations **85.99**
Includes rope bridge, hand-over-hand climbing obstacle, obstacle wall with stepping stones, net wall, hand-over-hand climbing wall, sewer pipe obstacle, two balance beams between two steel towers, balance beam, concrete climbing tower and an inclined-ascent obstacle.

### Accessories

**272-144058** Hospital Tents pkg(3) **25.99**
These Medical Corps tents (one large and two small) are decorated with large red and white emblems. Includes camp beds and stretchers.

**272-144057** Field Tents (undecorated) pkg(6) **16.99**
Assortment of four different sizes.

**272-144080** Set #1 **11.99**
Includes barrels, boxes and pushcarts.

**272-144081** Set #2 **23.99**
Contains observation towers, auxiliary terrain steps, obstacles and ladders.

## NATO/MODERN GERMAN ARMY

### Figures 15.99 ea (Unless Noted)

Plastic figures are molded in realistic poses with superb details. Uniforms are similar to those used by the United States and NATO in this period, but are easily customized with paint to model World War II U.S. forces.

**272-156001** Soldiers on the Parade Ground pkg(8)

**272-156002** Soldiers on Guard Duty pkg(8)
Set of Military Police and Traffic Control Officers.

**272-156003** Soldiers in the Field pkg(8)
With full field gear, carrying various small equipment and weapons.

**272-156004** Soldiers on the March pkg(8)
Seven are wearing berets, and one is carrying a steel helmet

**272-156005** Combat Infantry pkg(8)

**272-156006** Paratroopers & Gear pkg(8)

**272-156007** Maintenance Personnel pkg(8)

**272-156008** Marching Infantrymen pkg(8)

**272-156009** Tank Drivers pkg(12) **26.99**
Figures are partial for mounting in tank hatches.

**272-156010** Soldiers, Standing

**272-156011** Marching Infantrymen

**272-156012** Paratroopers, Standing

**272-156013** Ground Crew

**272-156014** Soldiers in Rubber Boats

**272-156015** Soldiers in Training

**272-156016** Pilots pkg(8)

**272-156017** Drivers pkg(8)

**272-156018** Motorcyclists w/Motorcycles pkg(3)

**272-156019** Soldiers at Railway Station

## MODERN ERA

### Structures

### Tracked Vehicle Washing Facility

**272-144027 37.99**
8 x 5-5/8 x 2-1/2"
20 x 14 x 6.3cm

### Barracks Building

**272-144035 25.99**
6 x 2-7/8 x 2-1/16"
15 x 7.2 x 5.2cm

Line several barracks side by side to create an ambulance station or classrooms.

### Vehicle Shed

**272-144036 46.99**
9-1/4 x 6-3/8 x 3-1/4"
23 x 16 x 8cm

Place several sheds side-by-side to store your entire military fleet!

### Workshop for Commercial Vehicles

**272-144037 49.99**
10-3/8 x 5 x 2-3/8"
26 x 12.4 x 6cm

This repair shop features six gates and movable folding doors.

FALLER

IMPORTED FROM GERMANY BY WALTHERS

### Fuel Depot
**272-144038 25.99**
4-3/8 x 3-7/8 x 2-3/4"
11 x 9.7 x 6.8cm

This overhead fuel depot features three horizontal and three vertical fuel tanks.

### Military Fire Station
**272-144039 90.99**
21-3/8 x 8-3/8 x 11-1/4"
53.5 x 21.1 x 28cm

Features a commander's building, three-stall garage with movable rolling shutter doors, two separate garages and hose tower.

### Fire Garage
**272-144040 33.99**
8-1/2 x 8-1/2 x 2-3/8"
21.2 x 21.2 x 6cm

Add an extra three stalls to the Military Fire Station (#272-144039, sold separately).

### Airfield Control Tower Building
**272-144047 112.99**
15-7/16 x 7-1/16 x 11-5/8"
38.5 x 17.6 x 29cm

Based on an existing tower on the Otto Lilienthal barracks, this building houses an air traffic controller station and service, offices, canteen, weather station and classrooms.

### Helicopter Hangar
**272-144048 166.99**
21-5/8 x 15-3/16 x 5-3/16" 54 x 38 x 13cm

The perfect add-on building to the Airfield Control Tower Building (#272-144047, sold separately). Building features side-annexed vehicles shelter with telescopic gates, staff and storeroom, sliding gates, roof position lamps, floor lighting and typical accessories.

### Emergency Exits
**272-144053** pkg(4) **16.99**
1 x 1 x 5/8" 2.2 x 2.2 x 1.6cm

For use with subterranean bunkers and shelters.

### Shooting Range
**272-144051 51.99**
Observation Tower: 5 x 2-3/4 x 7-5/32" 12.7 x 7 x 18.2cm
Shed: 7-13/32 x 3-11/32 x 1-3/4" 18.8 x 8.5 x 4.4cm

Keep troops in practice at the shooting range. Includes a tower for observing tank and armor maneuvers and a storage building.

### Drinking Water Plant
**272-144052 23.99**
Pumphouse: 1-21/32 x 1-31/32 x 3" 4.2 x 5 x 7.6cm
Filling Station: 1-1/2 x 1-1/16 x 13/16" 3.8 x 2.7 x 2.1cm

This freshwater tapping point includes two filling stations and a separate pumphouse.

## Accessories

### Sandbags
**272-144059** pkg(200) **16.99**

### Outdoor Boot Washing Station
**272-144054 13.99**
3-1/16 x 1-1/12 x 3/4"
7.6 x 3.7 x 1.9cm

Your soldiers can give their boots a shine at this cleaning station, based on an infantry school design in Hammelburg.

### Barbed Wire Barriers
**272-144060** pkg(15) **25.99**
These anti-personnel obstacles consist of wooden barriers and barbed wire coils.

## Signboards

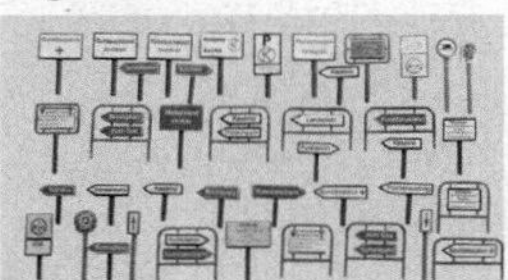

**272-144061 16.99**

kibri

IMPORTED FROM GERMANY BY WALTHERS
Modernize your collection of German Army equipment with these highly detailed, plastic kits. Designed for easy construction, each comes with illustrated instructions and all parts are sequentially numbered to simplify assembly. Most parts are molded in Dark Green (unless noted) with other details in appropriate colors. All kits are complete with optional add-on parts and decals for superdetailing if desired.

## POST-1945 – GERMANY

### Trucks

**405-18266** Magirus Jupiter Cargo/Personnel Carrier w/Cover **36.99**

Item listed below is available by Special Order (see Legend Page).

**405-18087** Jupiter 7t KHD 6x6 Tractor w/Hoist **36.99**

### Emergency Vehicles

**Limited Quantity Available**

**405-18000** KHD "Jupiter" FlKfz 3800/4000 Foam & Water Fire Truck **38.99**

### Engineer-Construction Equipment

**405-18089** Kaelble Wheel Loader w/Bucket & Forklift **54.99**

**405-18090** Bomag Surface Compacter/Roller **45.99**

**Limited Quantity Available**

**405-18002** Liebherr LR 631 Crawler Tractor w/Front End Loader **24.99**

**405-18004** Construction Site Office Trailers pkg(2) **21.99**

**405-18008** Zettelmeyer Wheeled Front End Loader **37.99**

**405-18018** Mercedes 4x4 Tractor w/Mower & Hay Baler **39.99**

**405-18022** Mercedes 4x4 Industrial Tractor w/Front End Loader **37.99**

### Railroad Equipment

Item listed below is available by Special Order (see Legend Page).

**405-18088** Unimog Hy-Rail Flatbed (Nonpowered) w/Flat Car & Pontoon Load **69.99**

# HEISER'S MODELS

Recreate motorized equipment of the world's armies from 1930-1950 with this line of highly detailed kits. Ideal for flat car loads or details outside factories and camps on period layouts, or as displays in parks or Veteran's Memorials in the present. Small size is ideal for collecting and wargaming as well. Kits feature parts molded in resin, as well as plastic or metal (as noted), and some use a combination of materials.

Important Note: This listing includes items which are available by special order only. Please see the Legend Page for information, and visit www.walthers.com for a complete listing of in-stock and special order products.

Items listed in blue ink may not be available at all times (see Legend Page).

## WORLD WAR II – UNITED STATES

### Light Tanks

**M3/M5 "Stuart" 11.99 ea**

Introduced in the 1930s, Stuarts served as scouts and infantry support tanks in Europe and the Pacific. Small size makes an ideal flat car load, typically three were carried per car. Kits include plastic accessory parts sprue with Pioneer tools, .50 and .30 caliber machine guns, and gas and water cans.

**323-307** M3 w/Welded Cupola

**323-311** M5A1-Early Production w/Lengthened Turret

Shown Assembled, Painted & Detailed

**323-312** M5A1-Later Production w/Lengthened Turret

Items listed below are available by Special Order (see Legend Page).

Shown Assembled, Painted & Detailed

**323-309** M3A3 w/Lengthened Turret

**323-310** M5 w/Cylindrical Turret

### Medium Tanks

**M4 Series "Sherman"**

As the limitations of the M3 series became increasingly obvious, work began on an improved version, resulting in the M4 "Sherman." Armed with a single 75mm cannon in a rotating turret atop the hull, the M4 became the backbone of American armored forces in World War II. They later served in the Korean War and were also sold to many other countries, where they were used until the 1970s.

**323-2335** M4A1 Very Early Production w/Cast Hull **10.50**
Plastic kit with resin parts.

**323-2336** M4A1 Early Production w/Cast Hull **9.50**
Plastic kit with resin details.

**323-2337** M4 Early Production w/Welded Hull **9.50**
Plastic kit with resin details.

**323-2338** M4 Mid-Production w/Welded Hull **8.50**
All plastic kit.

**323-2339** M4A1 Mid-Production w/Cast Hull **8.50**
All plastic kit.

**323-2340** M4A3 Early Production w/Welded Hull **8.50**
All plastic kit.

**323-2341** M4 Early Production Composite Hull **10.50**
Plastic kit with resin upper body piece.

**323-2342** M4 (105) w/105mm Howitzer & 47° Hull Front **10.50**
Resin kit with plastic parts.

**323-2345** M4A2 Mid-Production w/Diesel Engine & Welded Hull **9.50**
Plastic kit with resin upper body piece.

**323-2346** M4A2 Late Production w/47° Angled Front, Diesel Engine & Welded Hull **9.50**
Plastic kit with resin upper body piece.

**323-2353** Late Production M4 w/Composite Hull & 75mm Gun Turret **11.00**

**323-2358** M4A4 w0/Welded Hull & 75mm Gun Turret **11.00**
Resin kit with plastic parts.

Items listed below are available by Special Order (see Legend Page).

**323-2343** M4A1(75)W w/75mm Gun Turret **10.00**

**323-2362** M4A6 w/Welded Hull, 75mm Gun, Lengthened Hull & Tracks **16.50**

### Heavy Tanks

**"Pershing" 16.99 ea**

Introduced in January, 1945 these experimental models were America's first true heavy tanks. They proved highly effective and production continued after World War II. Widely used in the Korean War, Pershings were also sold to other free-world countries. Kits include plastic accessory part sprue.

**323-352** M26 w/Standard 90mm Gun

**323-353** M45 w/105mm Howitzer

### Armored Vehicles

**M8**

**323-101** Howitzer Motor Carriage **11.99**
Open-topped, self-propelled 75mm howitzer on the M5A1 light tank chassis.

**"Lee" Armored Recovery Vehicles 22.99 ea (Unless Noted)**

**323-331** M31 Riveted Hull

Shown Assembled, Painted & Detailed

**323-332** M31B1 Welded Hull

Item listed below is available by Special Order (see Legend Page).

**323-333** M33 (Ex-M31) Prime Mover Towing Vehicle **17.99**

**Half-Tracks pkg(2) 11.99 ea (Unless Noted)**

Kits include plastic sprue and one open and one closed (canvas covered) vehicle.

Shown Assembled, Painted & Detailed

**323-24** M2

**323-25** M3

**323-27** M2A1

**323-28** M3A1

**323-30** M3A1 pkg(2) **13.99**
Two open vehicles with mine racks.

**81mm Mortar Carrier 11.99 ea**

Include plastic sprue.

**323-26** M21 on M3 Half-Track Chassis

**323-29** M4 on M2 Half-Track Chassis

**White**

**323-23** M3A1 Scout Car pkg(2) **11.99**
Includes plastic sprue and one openand one closed vehicle.

### Medium Trucks

**Dodge WC-Series 3/4 Ton 4x4**

**323-50** WC-54 Ambulance **13.99**

**323-51** Command Car, WC56 (No Winch) & WC57 (w/Winch) **15.99**

**323-52** "Beep" WC51 (No Winch) or WC51M/G (No Winch, with Machine Gun) **15.99**

**323-53** "Beep" w/Winch, WC52 & WC52M/G with Machine Gun **15.99**

# HEISER'S MODELS

## Heavy Trucks

### GMC 6x6 2-1/2 Ton Cargo/ Personnel Carrier pkg(2) 15.99 ea

Kits include one each open and closed bed trucks; both with hollow cabs.

**323-151** Long Bed

**323-152** Short Bed

### Dodge WC-Series 1-1/2 Ton 6x6 Cargo/Personnel Carrier 21.99 ea

This larger carrier, based on the WC series and sharing many of the same parts, was introduced later in the war when the US increased the size of rifle squads from eight to 12 troops.

**323-153** WC62 (No Winch)

**323-154** WC63 (With Winch)

**323-155** WC63M/G (With Winch & Machine Gun)

### Diamond T 980

**323-177** M19 Tank Transporter **37.99**
Includes M20 Prime Mover and M9 45-Ton Low-Bed Trailer.

## Trailers

**323-184** 1-Ton Cargo Carrier pkg(6) **11.99**
Includes two each; open with box load and canvas covered.

# WORLD WAR II – ENGLAND/UNITED KINGDOM

## Light Tanks

### Vickers Mark VI Series pkg(2) 19.99 ea

As technology improved between the wars, light tanks evolved into fast machine gun carriers designed to smash enemy defenses. Introduced in 1936, the Mark VI was the last and heaviest of this series and sported several improvements. Armament consisted of a .50 and a .303 caliber machine gun. When World War II began in 1939, the Mark VI made up the bulk of British armored forces. Serving in France, Egypt, Greece, Crete, Malta and Persia, they were finally withdrawn from front line service in 1942; surviving vehicles were reassigned to training units.

**323-206** Mark VI A
The return roller was moved on this model, which was otherwise identical to the Mark VI.

**323-207** Mark VI B
The most common and widely used version, this model was fitted with a cylindrical cupola on the turret to improve the commander's field of vision. The turret also received a Bren anti-aircraft gun mount.

**323-208** Mark VI C
This final version had the cupola replaced by two domed hatches, and the engine cover had only a single inlet louver. A deflector plate was often added in front of the driver's vision hatch to reduce the chance of a hit from a ricochet. Main armament consisted of a Besa 15mm machine gun (some carried a 7.92mm as their main gun), and a .303 caliber or 7.92mm machine gun.

## Cruiser Tanks

British development of a "fast" tank to fit between light and heavy infantry tanks. With light armor and small gun, they were quick to become obsolete.

### "Crusader" 19.99 ea (Unless Noted)

**323-221** I w/2 Pounder Gun

**323-222** II w/2 Pounder Gun

**323-223** II CS w/3" Howitzer

**323-224** III & III CS w/57mm (6 Pounder) Gun or 3" Close-Support Howitzer **21.99**

## Medium Tanks

**323-325** M3 "Grant" **15.99**
Variant of the US-built M3 "Lee" with British-designed turret.

**323-2359** "Sherman Firefly" **11.00**
M4A4 Sherman with modified turret to mount 17 pounder gun. Resin kit with plastic parts.

**323-2363** M4 "Firefly" w/Composite Hull, Large Hatch, 17 Pounder Gun in Modified Turret **12.50**

Items listed below are available by Special Order (see Legend Page).

**323-225** "Cromwell IV" w/75mm Gun **14.99**

**323-226** "Cromwell IV" w/95mm Howitzer **14.99**

**323-227** "Challenger" w/17 Pounder Gun **14.99**
A modified version of the Cromwell, fitted with a heavier gun.

Vickers Mark VI A
323-206

Vickers Mark VI B
323-207

Vickers Mark VI C
323-208

## Armored Vehicles

### Mortar Carrier w/3" Mortar

**323-203** Universal Mortar Carrier pkg(2) **15.99**

## Light Trucks

### Morris-Commercial C8/GS 4x4

This all-purpose transport served with virtually all of the United Kingdom forces and was adapted from earlier models first developed in the 1930s. The short wheelbase (about 8') required a small cab to provide maximum cargo space.

**323-230** Truck Only pkg(2) **19.99**
Can be built with sides open or closed.

## Artillery 18.99 ea

**323-231** "Portee" Transport w/2-Pounder Anti-Tank Gun

**323-2331** Two-Pounder (40mm) Anti-Tank Gun pkg(2)
Developed in the mid-30s, the unique three-legged carriage allowed the road wheels to clear the ground so the gun could quickly be traversed in any direction.

# WORLD WAR II – BELGIUM

Item listed below is available by Special Order (see Legend Page).

**323-700** T-15 Carden-Loyd M1934 (British supplied) w/13.2mm Machine Gun pkg(2) **18.99**

Morris-Commercial C8/GS 4x4 Truck
323-230

# WORLD WAR II – FRANCE

## Light Tanks

All light tank kits include French cupola and parts to model captured tanks in German service.

### Renault 14.99 ea

**323-756** R35; 1930s, w/Short Barrel 37mm Gun

**323-757** R39; 1930s, w/Long Barrel 37mm Gun

### Hotchkiss 14.99 ea

**323-758** H35; 1930s, w/Short Barrel 37mm Gun

**323-759** H39; 1930s, w/Long Barrel 37mm Gun

## Medium Tanks

**323-760** Char SOUMA S-35 w/47mm Gun **13.99**
Entering service in 1936, the S-35 became the standard medium tank of the French army. Around 500 were built before the French surrender in 1940.

## Heavy Tanks

**323-766** Char B1-bis **16.99**
Introduced in 1936, this heavy tank saw service until the fall of France in 1940. Model includes APX4 Turret with 37mm cannon and hull-mounted 75mm SA 35 cannon.

## HEISER'S MODELS

# WORLD WAR II – SOVIET UNION

### Light Tanks

**T-60 pkg(2) 18.99 ea**
In 1941 and 1942, over 6,000 were produced.

Items listed below are available by Special Order (see Legend Page).
**323-260** Early Production
**323-261** Mid Production
**323-262** Late Production w/Uparmored Turret

### Heavy Tanks

**KV-85**

323-251 17.99
This lighter and faster version of the KV-1s carried a heavier 85mm cannon and was introduced in September/October of 1943. It served as a fill-in model until the formidable JSII was ready for service.

**"Joseph Stalin" 16.99 ea**
Entering service in late 1943, this heavy tank was fitted with a huge 122mm cannon to counter the threat of new German designs. Some were still in service into the late 1970s.

**323-252** JSII

**323-253** JSII-m

# WORLD WAR II – GERMANY

### Light Tanks

**Panzer I Series 13.99 ea (Unless Noted)**
Panzer I and II kits have been improved with new tracks, turret hatches and detail parts.
**323-401** PzIA w/Two Machine Guns in Turret

Items listed below are available by Special Order (see Legend Page).
**323-403** Command Unit (SdKfz 256) **11.99**
Built on IA or IB chassis, but with a fixed cupola housing a single machine gun and additional radio equipment.
**323-4021** PZIB Early Production
**323-4022** PzIB Late Production

**Panzer II Series 11.99 ea**
A larger (10-ton) and better armed (20mm cannon and machine gun) model than the IA, that entered service from 1937-40.

**323-405** PzIIF Version

Items listed below are available by Special Order (see Legend Page).
**323-4041** PzIIA w/Early Turret
**323-4042** PzIIB or PzIIC w/Late Turret

### Medium Tanks

**PzKpfw 35C 739(f)**
Item listed below is available by Special Order (see Legend Page).
**323-761** Captured French S-35 w/German Modified Cupola **13.99**

**Panzer V 13.99 ea**
The Panzer V family of tank kits has been improved with new tracks, turret hatches and detail parts.

Items listed below are available by Special Order (see Legend Page).
**323-412** A w/Side Skirts
**323-413** PzVA w/Side Skirts & Zimmerit
**323-414** G w/Exposed Tracks
**323-4161** G w/Side Rail, Skirts & Zimmerit
**323-4162** PzVG Late w/Raised Fans, Small Grilles & Side Skirts

### Armored Vehicles

**Jagdpanther Heavy Tank Destroyer 13.99 ea**
Built on the Panther V chassis and equipped with the fearsome 88mm cannon.

Items listed below are available by Special Order (see Legend Page).
**323-417** Early Production w/1-Piece Gun Barrel, Early Style Rear Deck and Side Skirts
**323-418** Late Production w/2-Piece Gun Barrel, Raised Fan & Side Skirts
**323-419** Late Production w/2-Piece Gun Barrel, Raised Fan, Zimmerit & Side Skirts

### Self-Propelled Guns

**323-451** Panzerjager I Anti-Tank Gun on Panzer IB Chassis w/47mm Cannon **11.99**

**323-472** "Bison" on Pz38(t) Chassis - Type H w/Center-Mount 150mm Cannon **13.99**

**323-473** "Grille" (Cricket) on Pz38(t) Chassis - Type M w/Rear-Mount 150mm Cannon **13.99**

**323-480** "Wespe" (Wasp) SdKfz 124 w/105mm Howitzer on Panzer II Chassis **15.99**

Item listed below is available by Special Order (see Legend Page).

**323-471** "Bison" PzIB w/150mm Cannon **16.99**

### Munitions Carriers 12.99 ea

**323-481** For "Wespe" (Wasp) on Panzer II Chassis

Item listed below is available by Special Order (see Legend Page).

**323-474** Type M for "Grille" (Cricket) on Pz38(t) Chassis

### Half-Track Armored Vehicles

**323-513** SdKfz 252 Ammo Carrier w/Ammo Trailer **13.99**

**323-549** SdKfz 10 1-Ton Soft Skin **20.99**

Item listed below is available by Special Order (see Legend Page).

**323-514** SdKfz 253 Artillery Observation Vehicle **11.99**

**SDKFZ 250/9 Recconnaissance Half-Tracks**

323-517 Late Production Vehicle & Turret w/20mm Cannon & Machine Gun 13.99

**Opel "Maultier" Half-Tracks**

**323-550** SdKfz 4/1 Armored Rocket Launcher **16.99**

**323-552** 3-Ton, Soft-Skin Cargo Carriers (1 Each Open & Canvas Covered) pkg(2) **18.99**

Items listed below are available by Special Order (see Legend Page).

**323-551** SdKfz 4 Armored Ammo Carrier **14.99**

323-553 SdKfz 3 Soft-Skin Field Radio Unit 14.99

### Half-Track Armored Personnel Carriers

**SdKfz 250**
Items listed below are available by Special Order (see Legend Page).
**323-509** One Each Open & Closed Top pkg(2) **12.99**
**323-510** w/Open Tops pkg(2) **13.99**
**323-511** w/Open Tops & Side Storage Boxes pkg(2) **13.99**

### Artillery

**sIG 33 150mm Heavy Infantry Gun pkg(2) 21.99 ea**

**323-493** Wood Spoke or Steel Rubber Tired Wheels for Motorized Towing

Item listed below is available by Special Order (see Legend Page).
**323-492** Wood Spoke or Steel Wheels for Horse-Drawn Towing

**Nebelwerfer Towed Rocket Launcher pkg(4) 19.99 ea**
Items listed below are available by Special Order (see Legend Page).
**323-494** 150mm w/6 Launch Tubes
**323-495** 210mm w/5 Launch Tubes

### Trucks

**Opel "Blitz" (Lightning) 1-Ton**

**323-575** Cargo Trucks (1 Each Open & Canvas Covered) pkg(2) **16.99**

## HEISER'S MODELS

# WORLD WAR II – ITALY

### Light Tanks

Item listed below is available by Special Order (see Legend Page).

**323-813** L6-40 1940-1945 w/20mm BREDA Gun **18.99**

### Medium Tanks

**323-814** M11/39 1939-1942 w/Hull Mounted 37mm Gun & Machine Gun Turret **16.99**

**323-815** M13/40 1940-1942 w/Full Fenders & 47mm Gun Turret **13.99**

Item listed below is available by Special Order (see Legend Page).

**323-816** M13/40 1940-1942 w/Half Fenders & 47mm Gun Turret **13.99**

### Self-Propelled Guns

**323-812** L40-47/32 w/47mm Cannon on L6 Light Tank Chassis pkg(2) **17.99**

**323-820** M40-75/18 w/Half Fenders & 75mm Cannon **13.99**

**323-821** M40-75/18 w/Full Fenders & 75mm Cannon **13.99**

Autoblinda AB 40 w/Twin Machine Gun Turret 323-801

Lancia 3/Ro 323-835

### Armored Cars

Items listed below are available by Special Order (see Legend Page).

**323-801** Autoblinda AB 40 w/Twin Machine Gun Turret **12.99**

**323-802** Autoblinda AB 41 w/20mm Gun Turret **13.99**

### Heavy Trucks

**323-835** Lancia 3/Ro pkg(2) **24.99**

With a superb diesel engine, plus good towing and payload capacities, this heavy truck was put to work towing artillery and transporting tanks and it could also carry 40 fully equipped soldiers.

### Trailers

**323-836** Viberti M Type Tank/ Cargo Transport pkg(2) **21.99**

This sturdy trailer was used to carry medium tanks and Semovente self-propelled guns; all four sidewalls were hinged to speed loading/ unloading. Kit includes parts for two complete trailers.

# WORLD WAR II – JAPAN

### Medium Tanks

**323-857** Type 89 "CHI-RO" w/57mm Cannon & Two 6.5mm Machine Guns **13.99**

Item listed below is available by Special Order (see Legend Page).

**3323-858** "CHI-HA" w/57mm Cannon, Rail Radio Antenna & Two 7.7mm Machine Guns **13.99**

### Armored Vehicles

**323-890** 6-Wheel Armored Car; Naval Late Series **12.99**



## MICROSCALE®

# DECALS

# AMERICAN CIVIL WAR 1861-65

### Flags 6.00 ea

**460-871175** Battle Flags & Unit (Regimental Colors) Flags

**460-871176** Confederate National Flags 1861-65

**460-871177** Confederate States Army Battle & Unit Flags

### Railroad Equipment 6.00 ea

**460-871168** Steam Locos Striping Set #1

**460-871172** US Military Railroad Freight & Passenger Cars 1861-65

**460-871173** Western & Atlantic Steam Locos 1860-66

**460-871174** Western & Atlantic Freight & Passenger Cars 1861-65

# POST-1945 – UNITED STATES

### Railroad Equipment

Railroads have always been looked upon by the military as strategic assets. Over the years, they've carried troops, weapons, supplies and ammunition. Today, they still carry vital supplies across the land; they're also used on bases for hauling materials and supplies between interchanges with mainline railroads and base operations.

**460-4391** U.S. Army Transportation Corps Mini-Cal 1940+ **3.60**

In the 1940s, the U.S. Army Transportation Corps applied a standardized lettering scheme to all of its locomotives. This set includes circular USATC logos, yellow scare striping, numbers and painting instructions.

**460-4278** U.S. Army Reserve 1205th Transportation Railway Operating Battalion 1990+ **3.60**

At present, the US Army Reserve has two active Railway Operations Battalions whose primary mission is handling ammunition and supplies at bases and port facilities. This set includes lettering for the low-nose Geeps currently assigned to the 1205th Transportation Railway Operating Battalion (United States Army Reserve). The set also includes a variety of special markings and a complete painting and lettering diagram.

### Vehicles

Suitable for all types of wheeled or tracked vehicles including tanks, trucks, armored vehicles and more from the 1940s to the present. Includes various sizes of white stars with and without white surrounds, Regimental and Battalion code identification letters (AA, AB etc.), Company Code identifications (AM, AW, CON, etc.) plus other assorted USA and numbers in white. Also includes circular yellow panels and black numbers for bridging weight (maximum vehicle weight in tons).

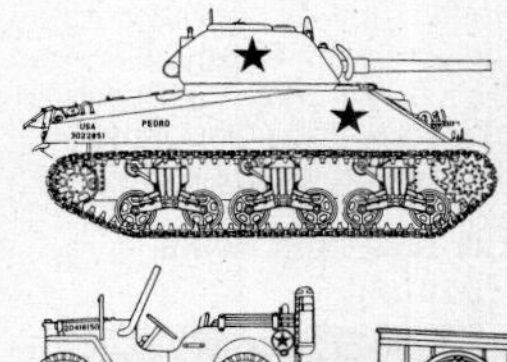

**460-4279** HO Scale Mini-Cal **3.60**

**460-604279** N Scale **4.80**

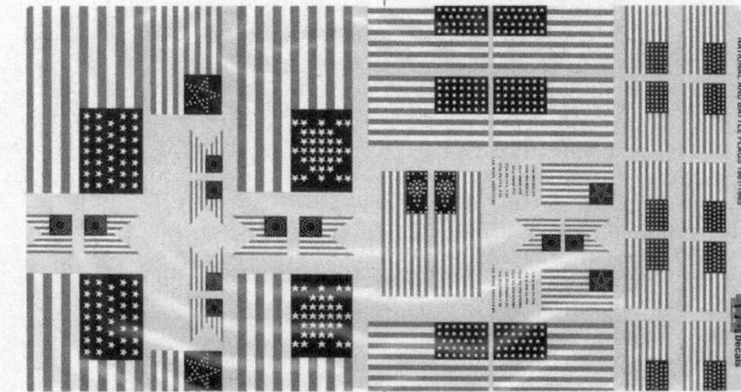

Battle Flags & Unit (Regimental Colors) Flags 460-871175

Turn your basic models into masterpieces with the tips and ideas featured in these how-to books. From beginner to advanced modeler, you'll find great suggestions and practical advice on assembling, detailing and painting military models that can be used in any scale.

In addition to the titles shown here, Kalmbach offers a complete selection of how-to books on building all types of models, scenery and more. Be sure to see the complete listing in the Books, Videos & Railroadiana section.

## BOOKS

FineScale Modeler

### How-To

#### Modeler's Guide to Realistic Painting & Finishing

**NEW 400-12257 16.95**
Perfect for the beginning plastic modeler who wants to learn more advanced techniques, this photo-driven guide includes an introduction to airbrushing and sections on brush painting, dry-brushing, applying washes and pastel chalk weathering. Softcover, 80 pages, 200 color photos, 10 illustrations, 8-1/4 x 10-3/4".

#### The Basics of Scale Modeling

**400-12251 16.95**
Beginning scale modelers are full of questions: What tools do I need? What glue works best? How do I put a model together? How are decals applied? Modelers will find the answers to these questions and more compiled in this book. Softcover, 80 pages, 230 color photos, 10 illustrations, 8-1/2 x 10-3/4".

#### Easy Scale Modeling

**400-12259 7.95**
Simple techniques, detailed photos and easy-to-follow diagrams get new modelers started. Offers basic information on assembling, painting, finishing and displaying scale models. Softcover, 16 pages, 64 color photos, 8-1/2 x 10-3/4".

### Figures

#### How To Paint Realistic Military Figures

**400-12240 21.95**
Covers military figures and horses from medieval times to Desert Storm. Softcover, 96 pages, 120 color and 75 B&W photos, 8-1/4 x 10-3/4".

### Armor

#### How To Build Armor Dioramas

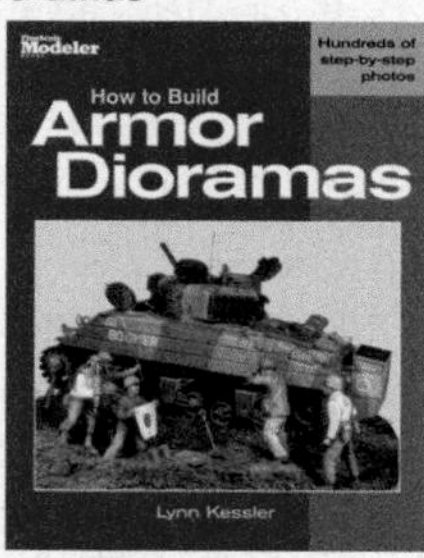


**400-12239 22.95**
Learn the steps to building detailed armored vehicles. Then get tips on the best ways to display your new models. Also includes great tips on figure modeling, kit assembly and finishing details. Softcover, 112 pages, 300 color photos, 8-1/4 x 10-3/4".

### Aircraft

#### Building and Displaying Scale Modeling Aircraft

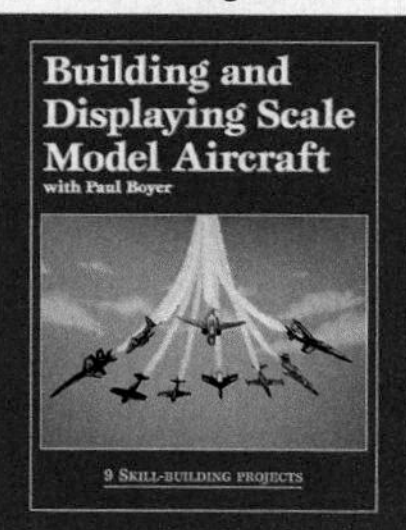


**400-12151 12.95**
Teaches basic aircraft modeling preparation and assembly techniques. Includes suggestions for painting and decaling with special attention to creative displays and mounting tips for finished projects. Softcover, 88 pages, 50 color and 110 B&W photos, 8-1/4 x 10-3/4".

#### Modeling Classic Combat Aircraft

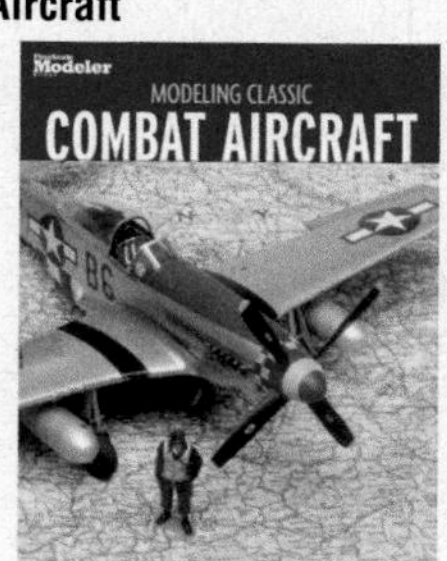


**400-12255 21.95**
Learn to build, paint and finish military aircraft models from WWII to today. Over 15 projects are featured, including the P-51 Mustang, F-18 Sabre, the A-7D Corsair, the B-17 Flying Fortress, and more. Compiled from the pages of FineScale Modeler magazine and edited by Mark Thompson. Softcover, 96 pages, 300 color photos, 8-1/4 x 10-3/4".

#### Classic Combat Aircraft

**NEW 400-12431** Vol. 2 **18.95**
Learn to build, modify, detail and paint these legendary WWII warbirds. Eighteen illustrated projects include the P-51 Mustang, P-47 Thunderbolt, B-17 Flying Fortress as well as Axis aircraft like the Bf 109 and Stuka. Introduction by Paul Boyer. Softcover, 96 pages, 300 color photos, 8-1/4 x 10-3/4".

### Ships

#### Basics Of Ship Modeling

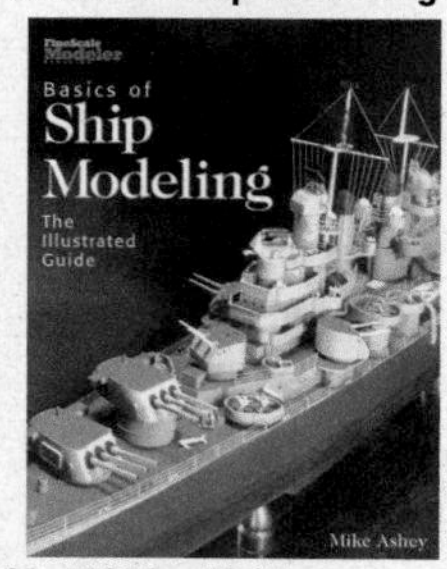


**400-12220 19.95**
Step-by-step photos guide you from basic assembly techniques to painting and weathering, detailing, masking and displaying your model ships. Softcover, 112 pages, 25 color and 400 B&W photos, 8-1/4 x 10-3/4".

### Dioramas

#### How To Build Dioramas

**400-12136** 2nd Edition **24.95**
With this newly updated book, making realistic dioramas has never been easier. Includes new projects and photos, along with tips on weathering, painting, detailing and more. Softcover, 144 pages, 290+ photos, 41 illustrations, 8-1/4 x 10-3/4".

### Airbrushing

#### Airbrushing Basics

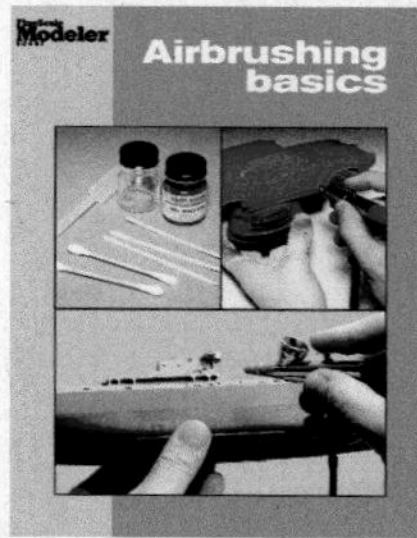


**400-12430 7.95**
Learn airbrushing tips and techniques from the experts! This booklet provides a clear guide on getting the most out of your airbrush, including proper cleaning and maintenance techniques. Softcover, 16 pages, 45 color photos, 5 illustrations, 8-1/4 x 10-3/4".

#### How To Use An Airbrush

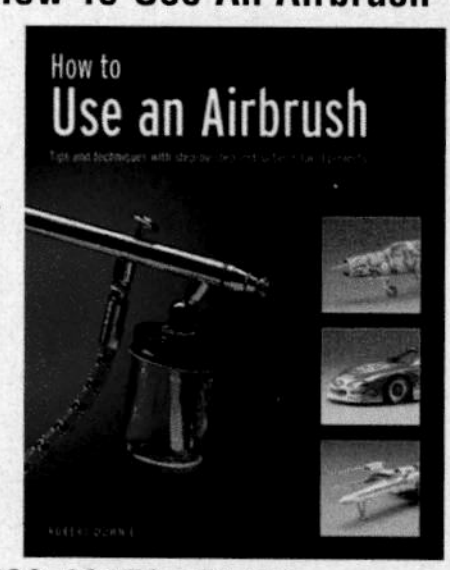


**400-12173 21.95**
Learn how to achieve special airbrushing effects on a variety of plastic models. Eleven projects teach the basics of realistic finishes, camouflage, weathering and other special effects for scale plastic modeling. Softcover, 96 pages, 196 color photos, 8-1/4 x 10-3/4".

# POST-1945 – UNITED STATES

## Vehicles

### Trucks

**490-30006** Kenworth Tow Truck **15.98**
Fully-assembled from diecast and plastic parts. Full cab interior with driver, positionable boom and more.

## Freight Cars - U.S. Army w/Load

All models are assembled and ready to run. Each includes a Model Power flat car loaded with the minitank or vehicle listed.

### Olive Drab 17.98 ea

**490-8450** With "Long Tom" Howitzer

**490-8455** With Patton Tank

### Camouflage

**490-8456** With 20' Container & Patton Tank **18.98**

### Additional Army Rail Equipment 17.99 ea (Unless Noted)

**490-6953** Flat Car w/Tractor & 50' Trailer

**490-9159** Flat Car w/Road Grader

**490-9160** With M47 Patton Tank

**490-9162** Hidden "Q Gun Box Car"

**490-9163** Big Thunder Railway Gun

**490-9164** Exploding Box Car
Car "explodes" when hit by missile.

**490-9165** Extended Vision Caboose **8.98**

**490-9181** Flat Car w/Launcher & 3 Missiles

## Passenger Cars

**490-9895** 67' Harriman Coach **17.98**
Ready-to-run model.

## Railroad Equipment - U. S. Air Force w/Load 16.98 ea (Unless Noted)

Models are decorated in U.S. Air Force Colors of blue and white.

**490-91611** Searchlight Command Center Car

**490-91621** Tank Buster Hidden Gun Car

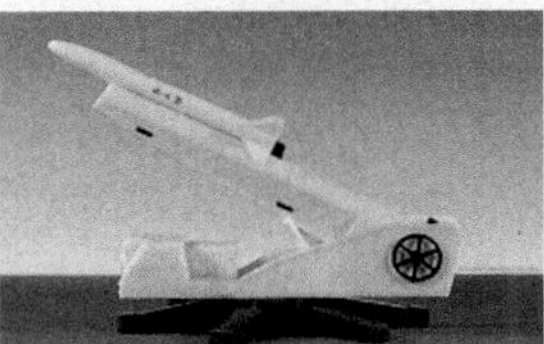

**490-91641** Missile Launcher w/Planes & Missiles

**490-91661** Tank Car **9.98**

# MILITARY ACTION SERIES

## Freight Cars

### Flat Cars

**490-8664** U.S. Army Searchlight Car w/2 Figures **13.98**

**51'**

**490-8652** With Low Boy Transport **15.98**

**490-8655** With Bradley Tank & Gas Tank **17.98**

**490-8657** With Missile Launcher & Troop Carrier **17.98**

**490-8658** With Electrical Cable Spool Trailer **17.98**

**490-98653** With Truck Equipment Mover **15.98**

**490-98662** With Two Army Truck Cabs **19.98**

**Limited Quantity Available**

**490-8650** With Lift Truck **15.98**

**40'**

**490-8656** With Howitzer Tank **15.98**

**490-8659** Depressed Metal w/Truck Cab **17.98**

**490-8660** Depressed Metal w/Rocket Fuel Tank **17.59**

**490-8661** With Handrails & Tow Truck **17.98**

**490-98654** With Abrams Tank **15.98**

**490-98661** With Handrails & Tow Truck **17.98**

**490-98659** Depresssed Metal w/Truck Cab **17.98**

**490-98660** Depressed Metal w/Rocket Fuel Tank **17.59**

**Limited Quantity Available**

**490-8651** With Troop Carrier **15.98**

### 40' Tank Car

**490-98663** US Army **9.98**

## Passenger Cars

**490-9896** U.S. Army Hospital & Troop Carrier **17.98**

## Assembled Structures

Detail your military installation in minutes! These buildings come fully assembled and painted with interior light and two figures.

**490-632** Water Tower **15.98**

**490-633** US Army Searchlight **13.98**

**490-669** Quonset Hut w/Figures & Vehicles **27.98**

**490-667** Motor Pool **37.98**

**490-668** Army Munitions Depot w2 Mini-Tanks **37.98**

# Preiser

ORIGINAL Preiser

IMPORTED FROM GERMANY BY WALTHERS

Items listed in blue ink may not be available at all times (see Legend Page).

Guard Battalion pkg(21) 590-16593

Soldiers Holding Draft Horses w/2Figures & 6 Horses 590-16597
Figures Shown Painted

Modern Infantry - Standing pkg(16) 590-16529
Figures Shown Painted

## NEW PRODUCTS

### Post-1945 Germany

#### Unpainted Figures

**NEW 590-16593** Guard Battalion pkg(21) **23.99**

### World War II Germany

#### Motorcycles

**NEW 590-16563** Zundapp KS 750 Motorcycle w/Sidecar pkg(3) **19.99**

**NEW 590-16572** BMW R 12 Motorcycle pkg(3) **19.99**

#### Horse-Drawn Transport

**NEW 590-16570** Hf 1 Field Wagon w/2 Figures & 2 Horses **19.99**

**NEW 590-16588** Horse-Drawn Field Wagon w/2 Figures & 2 Horses **19.99**

#### Artillery

**NEW 590-16582** 2cm Flakvierling 38 Anti-Aircraft Gun w/SdAnh 52 Trailer **15.99**

**NEW 590-16591** 3.7cmPAK L/45 In Action w/Gunners **21.99**

#### Unpainted Figures

**NEW 590-16585** Infantry Riflemen w/Mortar & Horse **23.99**

**NEW 590-16592** Infantry Riflemen In Winter Uniforms w/If 8 Carts **23.99**

**NEW 590-16594** Joining The Chow Line Field Kitchen w/6 Figures **21.99**

**NEW 590-16596** Bicycle Unit Cycling & Walking w/6 Figures & 6 Bicycles **23.99**

**NEW 590-16597** Soldiers Holding Draft Horses w/2Figures & 6 Horses **13.99**

**NEW 590-16598** Motorcycle Crew w/BMW R 12 Motorcycles **21.99**

## WORLD WAR II – UNITED STATES

### Unpainted Figures

**590-16521** US Army Air Corps/Air Force - Standing pkg(12) **8.99**
Easily painted for other branches of service with appropriate colors, see the Paint & Paint Supplies Section.

## POST-1945 – UNITED STATES

### Unpainted Figure Sets

**590-16529** Modern Infantry - Standing pkg(16) **9.99**

**590-16533** Modern Infantry pkg(12) **8.99**

**590-16548** Tank Crewmen pkg(16) **8.99**

**590-16567** Tank Crew pkg(8) **7.99**

## AMERICAN CIVIL WAR – 1861-1865

### Confederate Army

**590-12051** Marching Infantry pkg(6) **21.99**

**590-12053** Confederate Flag Group pkg(4) **23.99**
Set includes one each: mounted officer, infantryman, flag bearer and drummer.

### Union Army

**590-12050** Marching Infantry pkg(6) **21.99**

**590-12052** Union Flag Group pkg(4) **23.99**
Set includes one each: mounted officer, infantryman, flag bearer and drummer.

## WORLD WAR II – GERMANY

### Armored Vehicles

#### SD.KFZ/251 (All-Purpose) Series Half-Tracks

Models are fully assembled plastic.

**590-16516** 251/1 Armored Personnel Carrier w/Machine Gun **14.99**

**590-16517** 251/3 Armored Field Radio Unit **15.99**

**590-16518** 251/7 Armored Engineering Unit **15.99**

**590-16522** 251/2 Armored Mortar Carrier **15.99**

**590-16523** 251/9 Kanonenwagen (Gun Cart) w/7.5cm **15.99**

**590-16544** SdKfz 11 Half-Track - Engineer Version **24.9**

**590-16554** Sd.Kfz Half-Track 251/21 Model C w/2cm Anti-Aircraft Gun **18.99**

**590-16555** 251/1 Model C "Stuka on Foot" Rocket Launcher **18.99**

**590-16556** 251/10 Model C Platoon Leader Vehicle w/Anti Tank & Machine Guns **18.99**

**590-16559** Sd.Kfz Half-Track 251/8 Model C Armored Ambulance **18.99**

**590-16560** Sd.Kfz Half-Track 251/1 Model C Armored Troop Carrier Desert Sand **12.99**

ORIGINAL Preiser

IMPORTED FROM GERMANY BY WALTHERS

## Artillery

Plastic kits.

**590-16513** Horse-Drawn 105mm Field Gun w/Cassion & Crew **30.99**
This impressive kit is suitable for display or war games. Includes six-horse hitch with three outriders, one mounted rider, a four-man crew, 105mm cannon and ammunition cassion.

**590-16527** 10.5cm Light Field Howitzer LeFH 18 M & Ammunition Limber **21.99**

**590-16534** 10.5cm LeFH 18/40 Howitzer **19.99**
A complete Gun Crew is available separately in set #590-16537.

**590-16535** PAK 40 7.5cm Anti-Tank Gun **19.99**
Can be used with optional Gun Crew #590-16539, sold separately.

**590-16549** 3.7cm PAK L/45 Anti-Tank Gun pkg(2) **13.99**

**590-16565** 2cm Flak 38 Anti-Aircraft Gun w/SdAnh 51 Trailer **13.99**

**590-16566** 60cm Anti-Aircraft Search Light w/SdAnh 51 Trailer **13.99**

**590-16581** 7.5cm le IG 18 Deployed for Action **7.99**

## Trucks

**590-16538** SdKfz.11 Half-Track Heavy Tractor w/Canvas Covered Bed (Plastic Kit) **24.99**

**590-16552** Kfz. 70 3-Axle Personnel Carrier **20.99**

**590-16553** Kfz. 69 6x4 Artillery Tractor w/3.7cm PAK L/45 Anti-Tank Gun **25.99**

**590-16561** Sd.Kfz Half-Track Type 11 3-Ton Open Version **24.99**

**590-16562** Sd.Kfz Half-Track Model 11 3-Ton Closed Version **24.99**

**590-16584** Krupp Kfz 83 w/Generator & 60cm Anti-Aircraft Searchlight on SdAnh 51 Trailer **25.99**

## Trailers

**590-16574** vSdAnh51 w/Muntions & Tools pkg(2) **13.99**

**590-16576** Small Arms Ammunition Carts, 2 Horses & 3 Figures (Unpainted) **17.99**

## Horse-Drawn Transport

**590-16507** Field Kitchen w/2-Horse Hitch & Driver (Unpainted) **19.99**

**590-16512** Supply Wagon **19.99**
Unassembled plastic kit. Includes handpainted four-horse hitch, two outriders and driver figure.

## Painted Figures

### Refugees

**590-16802** Exclusive Series Refugees **33.99**

### Panzergrenadier - Mechanized Infantry

Perfect for detailing Sd.Kfz Half-Tracks, trucks or other open vehicles.

**590-16876** Seated (5) & Standing (1) Soldiers pkg(6) **23.99**

**590-16877** Seated Infantry w/Rifles pkg(6) **23.99**

**590-16878** Dismounting - Action Poses pkg(6) **33.99**

### Panzer Crews 23.99 ea

**590-16882** Standing Commanders - Full Figures pkg(6)

**590-16883** Crew Reloading pkg(6)

**590-16884** Assorted Crewmen pkg(6)

**590-16885** Making Repairs pkg(6)

### Combat Infantry

**590-16875** Marching Infantry w/Field Equipment pkg(6) **38.99**

**590-16879** Advancing w/Weapons pkg(6) **33.99**

Horse-Drawn 105mm Field Gun w/Cassion & Crew 590-16513

Supply Wagon 590-16512

Infantry at Rest pkg(12) 590-16501
Figures Shown Painted

**590-16880** Firing Weapons pkg(6) **33.99**

**590-16881** Resting pkg(6) **35.99**

### Motorcycle Troops

**Two Zundapp KS 750 Cycles w/Sidecars**

**590-16571** w/Six Figures Standing at Attention **15.99**

**590-16575** w/Five Riding Figures **15.99**

**590-16580** w/Three Figures Pushing and 1 Standing w/ Binoculars **15.99**

## Unpainted Figure Sets

**590-16500** Tank Crewmen At Rest pkg(20) **9.99**

**590-16501** Infantry at Rest pkg(12) **8.99**

**590-16502** Luftwaffe Pilots & Ground Crew pkg(26) **15.99**

**590-16503** Luftwaffe Paratroopers, Pilots & Ground Crew pkg(40) **15.99**

**590-16504** Armored Infantry (Panzergrenadiers) pkg(16) **8.99**

**590-16515** Panzer (Tank) Crews pkg(20) **9.99**

Preiser

IMPORTED FROM GERMANY BY WALTHERS

**590-16519** Walking Infantry pkg(12) **8.99**
Figures shown painted.

**590-16520** Mechanized Infantry pkg(20) **9.99**
Includes seated and standing figures, designed for use with SdKfz Half-Tracks, sold separately.

**590-16528** Armored Infantry - Dismounting pkg(12) **8.99**

**590-16536** General, Runner & Radio Operators pkg(4) **6.99**

**590-16537** Gun Crew for leFH 18 Howitzer pkg(7) **6.99**
Designed for use with Howitzer #590-16534, sold separately, listed under Artillery.

**590-16539** Gun Crew for PAK 40 Anti-Tank Gun pkg(5) **4.99**
Designed for use with #590-16535, sold separately, listed under Artillery.

**590-16540** Mortar Crew pkg(5) **7.99**

**590-16541** Fighting Mortar Crew pkg(5) **7.99**

**590-16542** Home Leave pkg(6) **6.99**

**590-16547** Horse- & Hand-Drawn Infantry Carts w/3 Soldiers **9.99**
Figures shown painted.

**590-16557** Advancing Panzergrenadiers pkg(12) **8.99**

**590-16558** Civilian Refugees w/Luggage pkg(7) **9.99**

**590-16573** Riflemen in Formation pkg(36) **10.99**

**590-16577** Two Guards Escorting 17 Russian Prisoners **12.99**

## Detail Parts

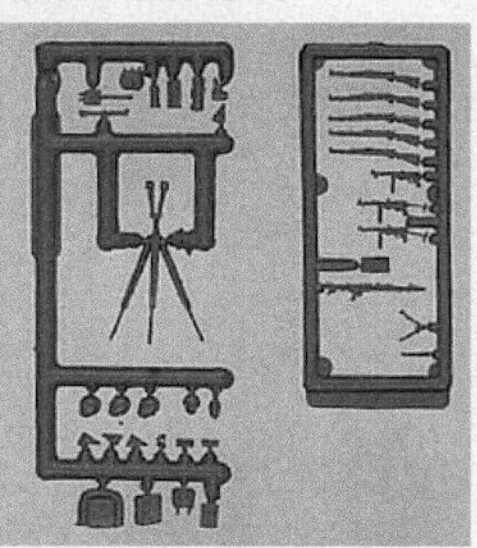

**590-18357** Weapons & Gear Assortment #1 **4.99**

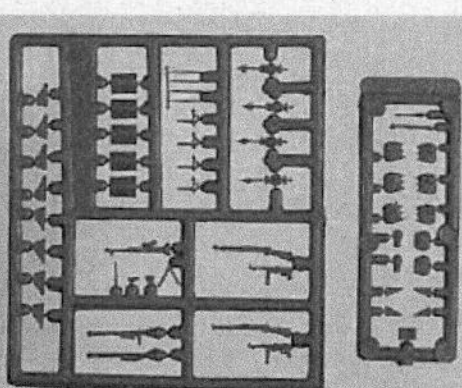

**590-18358** Weapons & Gear Assortment #2 **4.99**

**590-18359** Folding Lawn Chairs **4.99**

# POST-1945 – GERMANY

## Federal German Border Guard (BGS)

### Motorcycles

**590-18362** Military-Style w/Saddlebags **8.99**

Soldiers Walking & Standing pkg(39) 590-16543

## Trucks

**590-37017** Mercedes L508 Van **18.99**

**590-37010** Mercedes 3-Way Dump Truck **26.99**

## Painted Figure Sets

**590-13256** 61-Piece Air Force Marching Band **329.99**

**590-13257** 83-Piece Army Marching Band **419.99**

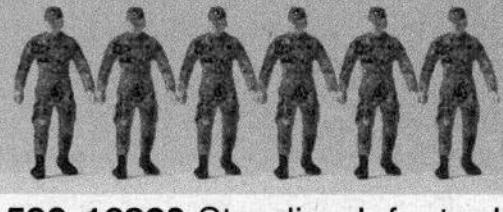

**590-16830** Standing Infantry In Camouflage w/Field Caps - No Rifle or Gear pkg(6) **26.99**

**590-16831** Standing Infantry In Camouflage w/Green Beret - No Rifles or Gear pkg(6) **26.99**

**590-16832** Military Police - Field & Duty Uniforms pkg(6) **31.99**

**590-16833** Military Police On Motorcycles pkg(3) **33.99**

**590-16834** Soldiers On Motorcycles pkg(3) **23.99**

**590-16835** Seated Drivers, Full Figures pkg(6) **19.99**

Riflemen in Formation pkg(36) 590-16573

Two Guards Escorting 17 Russian Prisoners 590-16577

83-Piece Army Marching Band 590-13257

**590-16836** Soldiers On Parade Ground, Dress, Fatigue & Duty Uniforms pkg(6) **23.99**

**590-16837** Engineers In Coveralls pkg(6) **19.99**

**590-16839** Soldiers Standing w/Cap - Battledress Camouflage pkg(6) **26.99**

**590-16840** Soldiers Standing w/Beret - Coat & Battledress Camouflage pkg(6) **26.99**

**590-16841** Soldiers Standing at Attention w/Red Beret - Battledress Camouflage pkg(6) **26.99**

**590-16842** Soldiers Standing at Ease w/Cap - Coat & Battledress Camouflage pkg(6) **26.99**

### Limited Quantity Available

**590-13258** 51-Piece Military Band pkg(51) **261.99**

## Unpainted Figure Sets

**590-16506** Assortment: Riflemen, Armored Infantry, Engineers & Military Policemen pkg(50) **10.99**

**590-16508** Paratroopers & Accessories pkg(30) **8.99**

**590-16510** Assortment: Sentries, Tank Crew, Drivers pkg(18) **8.99**

**590-16531** Wiesel (Weasel) Armed Fighting Vehicle Crew Half-Figures pkg(12) **6.99**
Partial figures for mounting in open hatches on Roco LLPz Wiesel Armored Fighting Vehicles (#625-710, 711 or 864, all sold separately).

**590-16543** Soldiers Walking & Standing pkg(39) **17.99**

# ORIGINAL Preiser

IMPORTED FROM GERMANY BY WALTHERS

**590-16550** 51-Piece Band w/Instruments **33.99**

51-Piece Band w/Instruments 590-16550

Russian Guards Infantry Circa 1942, Combat Poses pkg(18) 590-16505

**590-18366** Seated Passengers pkg(12) **4.99**
Partial figures for use in automobile or truck interiors.

## Detail Parts

**590-18338** Guard Tower **30.99**

**590-18339** Sentry Gate Post **8.99**

**590-18350** Wooden Supply Crates **4.99**

**590-18351** Steel 55-Gallon Drums **4.99**

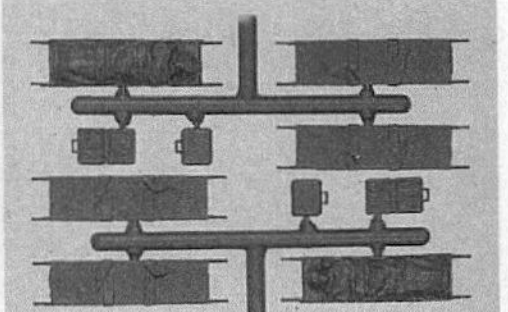

**590-18352** Assorted Stretchers **4.99**

**590-18353** Pallet Jacks & Pallets **4.99**

**590-18354** "Powered" Hand Freight Truck **4.99**

**590-18355** Drill Press & Lathe **4.99**

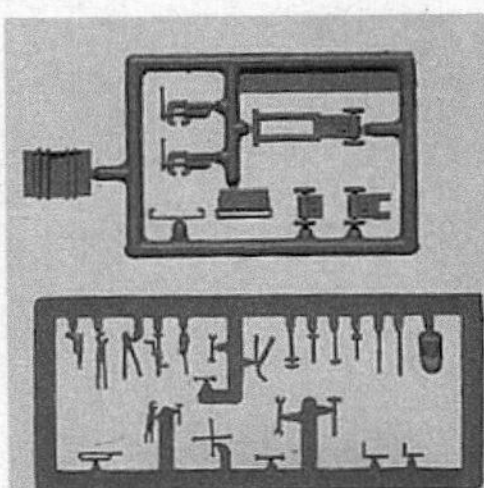

**590-18356** Hand Tools **4.99**

**590-18360** Trailer-Mounted Air Compressor **8.99**

**590-18361** Steel Storage Chests **4.99**

Marine Light Infantry pkg(11) 590-16569

Two Guards Escorting 17 German Prisoners 590-16578

**590-18363** Steel Parts Storage Baskets **4.99**

**590-18364** Portable Generators **4.99**

**590-18365** Modern Weapons & Gear Set #3 **4.99**

**590-18367** Raft w/Oars & Life Jackets **4.99**

New Arrivals Updated Every Day! Visit Walthers Web site at

**www.walthers.com**

## WORLD WAR II – SOVIET UNION

### Unpainted Figure Sets

**590-16505** Russian Guards Infantry Circa 1942, Combat Poses pkg(18) **8.99**

**590-16526** Infantry/ Riflemen at Rest pkg(10) **8.99**

**590-16530** Infantrymen & Partisans 1942-43 pkg(12) **8.99**

**590-16545** Armored Infantry Riflemen Riding Tank pkg(12) **9.99**

**590-16546** Tank Crew pkg(10) **8.99**

**590-16569** Marine Light Infantry pkg(11) **7.99**

**590-16578** Two Guards Escorting 17 German Prisoners **12.99**

## *Information* STATION

### The Great Locomotive Chase

During the Civil War, a small group of Union soldiers decided to use the railroad as an attempt to gain dominance over the Confederacy. Their 1822 battle became known as the Great Locomotive Chase, led by the command of James Andrews.

A band of 22 Union spies decided to stop supplies going to Confederate troops. To do this, they stole the General, a locomotive owned by the Western and Atlantic Railroad. The plan was to move north along the railroad's line and destroy bridges, track, telegraph lines and tunnels in their path.

But the crew of the General did not take the theft lying down. Finding their locomotive stolen while they stopped for breakfast, the conductor and engineer took it upon themselves to bring this theft to a quick end. First pursuing the criminals on foot, they soon procured a handcar and maintenance crew to aid in their efforts. Soon, the crew was able to secure a number of locomotives to engage in the chase.

The chase continued on, as the Union renegades dropped crossties from the engine, released box cars to stop their capture, and set cars afire in the hopes of destroying bridges. But the General eventually reached its limits, and the engine was unable to continue on. The main targets of the Union Army were never destroyed. The bandits escaped, but were eventually rounded up by the Confederate Army. Of the 22 men involved in the railroad chase, 14 were sent to prison, while eight, including James Andrews, were hung and buried in an umarked grave.

# trident

IMPORTED FROM AUSTRIA BY WALTHERS

## NEW PRODUCTS

### Resin Kits

### Modern US/NATO

"Stryker" Armored Fighting Vehicles

Prototype Photo Shown

**NEW 729-87090** M1126 Infantry Carrier Vehicle **TBA**

Prototype Photo Shown

**NEW 729-87091** M1133 Medical Evacuation Vehicle (Armored Ambulance) **TBA**

#### Trailers

Prototype Photo Shown

**NEW 729-81019** M871 22-Ton 2-Axle Flatbed (Composite Kit) **TBA**

Prototype Photo Shown

**NEW 729-87089** M1101 High Mobility 3/4-Ton Cargo Trailer **TBA**

### United States Marine Corps

#### Trucks

Prototype Photo Shown

**NEW 729-87088** Medium Tactical Vehicle Replacement (MTVR) MK36 Semi-Tractor **57.99**

### World War II - Former German Army

#### Medium Tanks

Prototype Photo Shown

**NEW 729-87082** PzKpfw III/SdKfz 141/1 Model L **TBA**

#### Armored Vehicles

Prototype Photo Shown

**NEW 729-87083** Sturmgesschutz - StuG III/SdKfz 142 Model F **TBA**

#### Half-Tracks

Prototype Photo Shown

**NEW 729-87084** SdKfz 10 lZgKw Artillery Tractor **TBA**

### Modern Austrian Army

#### Armored Infantry Fighting Vehicle

Prototype Photo Shown

**NEW 729-87085** Steyr 4K4FA/A1 G2 AIFV **47.99**

Prototype Photo Shown

**NEW 729-87086** Steyr "Ulan" **53.99**

Prototype Photo Shown

**NEW 729-87087** Steyr "Pandur II" 8x8 **TBA**

### Plastic Models

### World War II - Former German Army

#### Light Tanks SdKfz 121/PzKpfw II

**NEW 729-90330** Model B (sand) **15.99**

**NEW 729-90330G** Model B (gray) **21.99**

**NEW 729-90332** Model C (sand) **21.99**

**NEW 729-90332G** Model C (gray) **21.99**

**NEW 729-90333** Model A (sand) **21.99**

**NEW 729-90333G** Model A (gray) **21.99**

**NEW 729-90334** Model F (sand) **22.99**

**NEW 729-90334G** Model F (gray) **22.99**

#### SdKfz 250 Series Half-Tracks

**NEW 729-90331** 250/9 nA w/Old Open Turret & 20mm Kwk 38 Cannon **18.99**

#### SdKfz 251 Series Half-Tracks

**NEW 729-90190A** 251/8 Model D Armored Ambulance **15.99**

### Modern Canadian Army

#### Light Trucks

**NEW 729-90351** Military Police Chevrolet Suburban **16.99**

## RESIN KITS

### World War II – United States

#### Armored Vehicles 48.99 ea

**729-87045** Tank Destroyers M18 Hellcat

**729-87046** M39 Armored Utility Vehicle (Troop Transport/Gun Tractor on M18 Hull)

#### LCVP Landing Craft

**729-87065** LCVP; Landing Craft - Vehicle, Personnel **54.99**

#### Small Boats

**729-87070** LCM(3) - Landing Craft, Mechanized **69.99** (Nonpowered Resin Kit) **69.99**

### World War II – Germany

#### Heavy Tanks 44.99 ea

**729-87001** Porsche Design Kpz Maus (Mouse) w/150mm Cannon

**729-87004** Army Design Kpz E-100 (Development Series 100) w/Anti-Aircraft Cannon

**Limited Quantity Available**

**729-87002** Porsche Design Maus (Mouse) Anti-Aircraft Unit

**729-87003** Army Design Kpz E-100 (Development Series 100) w/170mm Cannon

#### Armored Vehicles 38.99 ea (Unless Noted)

**729-87007** Tank Destroyer SdKfz 162(V) JgdPz IV Guderian's Ente (Guderian's Duck) w/75mm L48 Gun

**729-87008** Self-Propelled Gun Stug IV G w/75mm Gun, Saukopf (Pig Head) Mantlet & Double Muzzle Brake

**729-87009** Self-Propelled Gun SdKfz 166 Sturmpanzer IV Brummbar (Grizzly Bear) w/150mm L/12 Howitzer

**729-87010** Self-Propelled Gun SdKfz 165 Hummel (Bumble Bee) w/150mm Howitzer **46.99**

**729-87011** Heavy Tank Destroyer SdKfz 164 Nashorn (Rhino) w/88mm Cannon **46.99**

**729-87012** Munitions Carrier for Hummel

**729-87013** Tank Recovery Vehicle Bergepanzer IV

## trident

IMPORTED FROM AUSTRIA BY WALTHERS

**729-87014** Tank Destroyer JgdPz IV A Intermediate Production Model

**729-87015** FlakPz IV Ostwind (East Wind) w/3.7cm Flak 43 Anti-Aircraft Cannon **44.99**

**729-87016** FlakPz Wirbelwind (Whirlwind) w/Quad 2cm Anti-Aircraft Cannon **44.99**

**729-87017** SdKfz 9 18-Ton FAMO Heavy Half-Track Troop Transporter/Artillery Tractor w/Canvas Cover **51.99**

**729-87018** SdKfz 9 18-Ton FAMO Heavy Half-Track Bzgkw Tank Recovery Vehicle w/Rear Bracing Spade **51.99**

**729-87019** SdKfz 9 18-Ton FAMO Heavy Half-Track SdKfz 9m w/Canvas Cover **51.99**

**729-87021** SdKfz 9 18-Ton FAMO Heavy Half-Track 9/1 Mobile Crane **51.99**

**729-87022** SdKfz 9 18-Ton FAMO Heavy Half-Track Transport w/Mounted 88mm Flak 36 Anti-Aircraft Gun **54.99**

**729-87030** Self-Propelled Gun Gerat 040 Heavy Siege Mortar "Karl" w/60cm Barrel **119.99**

**729-87031** Self-Propelled Gun Gerat 041 Heavy Siege Mortar "Karl" w/54cm Barrel **119.99**

**729-87032** Munitions Carrier/ Loader for "Karl" Heavy Siege Mortars **51.99**

**729-87040** Half-Track SdKfz 6 Zgkw 5t Towing Unit **39.99**

**729-87051** Half-Track SdKfz 6/2 w/Anti-Aircraft Gun **54.99**

**729-87056** Artillery Tractor Magirus Raupenschlepper Ost (Crawler Tractor East) w/Open Bed **37.99**

**729-87057** Self-Propelled Gun Raupenschlepper Ost (Crawler Tractor East) w/7.5 Anti-Tank Gun **40.99**

**729-87058** Artillery Tractor Raupenschlepper Ost (Crawler Tractor East) Ambulance **37.99**

### SdKfz Series Half-Tracks

**729-81014** 250/8 nA, Self-Propelled Gun (Composite Kit) **27.99**

**729-81015** 251/6 Type A Armored Command/Radio Vehicle (Composite Kit) **TBA**

**729-81016** 250 w/5cm Pak 38 Anti-Tank Gun (Composite Kit) **35.99**

**729-81017** 252 Ammo Carrier **36.99**

### Amphibious Vehicles

**729-87023** Landwasser-schlepper - LWS (Land-Water Tractor) **51.99**

### Artillery

**729-87066** 5cm Pak 38, Anti-Tank Gun **21.99**

**729-87071** 7.5cm Pak 97/38 - Anti-Tank Gun **20.99**

### Trucks

**729-87005** Kfz 18 sPkw w/Raised Canvas Top **27.99**

**729-87006** Kfz 31 Ambulance **29.99**

**729-87027** Steyr 1500 Late Production Version 1945 **28.99**

**729-87047** Bussing-NAG 4500 Cargo/Personnel Transport **54.99**

**729-87048** Bussing-NAG Mobile Crane **58.99**

**729-87049** Bussing-NAG Repair Unit **56.99**

**729-87050** Bussing-NAG w/Anti-Aircraft Cannon **74.99**

**729-87052** Faun 900 Lkw 9t **56.99**

**729-87053** Faun 900 Tank Transporter **56.99**

**Limited Quantity Available**

**729-87033** Bussing 900 w/Anti-Aircraft Cannon **43.99**

### Trailer

**729-87020** Heavy-Duty Trailer Special Type 116 8-Wheel Heavy Tank Transport Flatbed **51.99**

**729-87055** Sonderanhanger 115 **40.99**

## Post-1945 – United States

### Armored Vehicles

**729-87028** Self-Propelled Howitzer M-44 w/155mm Cannon **42.99**

**729-87029** Self-Propelled Howitzer M-52 w/105mm Cannon **42.99**

**729-87041** M88A2 Hercules Armored Tank Recovery Vehicle **51.99**

**729-87044** Self-Propelled Howitzer M109A6 Paladin w/155mm Cannon **51.99**

### Artillery

**729-87067** M198 155mm Howitzer FG **29.99**

## Modern US/NATO

### Hawk MIM-23B Improved Missile Launch/Control System

**729-87073** M78 Launcher w/3 Surface-to-Air Missiles **33.99**

**729-87074** M501 Loader **27.99**

**729-87075** M390C Transport Platform w/3 Surface-to-Air Missiles **33.99**

**729-87076** AN/MPQ-51 Range Only Radar **TBA**

**729-87077** AN/MPQ-55 Acquisition Radar **30.99**

**729-87078** AN/MPQ-46 Target Illuminator Radar **TBA**

**729-87079** AN/MPQ-35 Target Acquisition Radar **43.99**

**729-87080** AN/MSQ-110 Information Co-Ordination Center **TBA**

**729-87081** AN/TSW-11 Battery Control Center **26.99**

## US Marine Corps

### Light Armored Vehicle (LAV)

**729-81018** Air Defense Version - LAV-AD **32.99**

IMPORTED FROM AUSTRIA BY WALTHERS

### Medium Trucks

Prototype Photo Shown

**729-87072** MTVR Mk23 (Medium Tactical Vehicle Replacement) 6x6 Cargo Truck **57.99**

## Post-1945 – Germany

### Trucks

**729-87034** Faun SLT 56t 4-Axle Cabover Tractor w/6-Axle Flatbed Trailer **121.99**

**729-87054** German Federal Army Faun L912/45 Zgkw **56.99**

### Engineer Equipment 38.99 ea

**729-87042** Ahlmann SLT 56t Closed Cab Heavy Forklift

**729-87043** Steinbock FUG Front-End Wheel Loader

## World War II – Great Britain

### Light Tanks

**729-87060** "Matilda II" A12 Mk II (Resin Kit) **48.99**

### Medium Tanks

**729-87061** "Churchill" Mk IV (Resin Kit) **49.99**

**729-87062** "Churchill Crocodile" Flamethrower w/Trailer **61.99**

### 15-CWT Medium Trucks

**729-87059** Cargo/Personnel Carrier **33.99**

**729-87063** LW (V) Field Radio Unit **34.99**

**729-87064** Machinery Truck **36.99**

## Modern Austrian Federal Army

### Self-Propelled Guns

**729-87069** Steyr SK105A2mod. Kurassier Self-Propelled Anti-Tank Gun **51.99**

### Armored Vehicles

**729-87068** Steyr 4K4FA/A1-G1 Armored Personnel Carrier **47.99**

# FULLY ASSEMBLED PLASTIC MODELS

## World War II – Germany

### Tanks 19.99 ea (Unless Noted)

**729-97007** "Panther" Model A **20.99**

**729-97008** "Panther" Model D

**729-97010** "Panther" Model F

**729-97027** "Panther" Model G

### Armored Vehicles 19.99 ea (Unless Noted)

**729-97011** Sd.Kfz 173 "Jagdpanther" Armored Anti-Tank Gun

**729-97012** FlaZwilling 341 "Coelian" Armored Anti-Aircraft Gun

**729-97025** SdKfz 179 Panzer "Panther" Armored Recovery Repair Vehicle **20.99**

**729-97026** "Sturm Panzer" (Storm Panther) Assault Gun/Mortar Carrier

**729-97028** PzBeobwg "Panzer" (Panther) Armored Reconnaissance Unit

### SdKfz 250 Series Half-Tracks 15.99 ea (Unless Noted)

**729-90246** 250/1 Armored Personnel Carrier – Early Model **14.99**

Faun SLT 56t 4-Axle Cabover Tractor w/6-Axle Flatbed Trailer 729-87034

**729-90247** 250/7 Self-Propelled Mortar Carrier - Early Model

**729-90248** 250/1 Armored Personnel Carrier - Late Model

**729-90249** 250/3 Armored Radio/Command Unit - Early Model

**729-90267** 250/5 Armored Observation Vehicle

**729-90267G** 250/5 Armored Observation Unit (gray)

**729-90268** 250/10 w/3.7cm Pak Anti-Tank Gun

**729-90268G** 250/10 w/3.7cm Pak Anti-Tank Gun (gray)

**729-90269** 250/11 w/Anti-Tank Gun **16.99**

**729-90269G** 250/11 w/Anti-Tank Gun (gray) **16.99**

**729-90306** 250/9 Self-Propelled Gun (sand) **18.99**

**729-90306G** 250/9 Self-Propelled Gun (gray) **18.99**

**729-90324** 250/3 Armored Combat Recon Vehicle

**729-90325** 250 Anti-Tank Gun **16.99**

**729-90326** 250/3 Armored Command Reconnaissance Vehicle

**729-90327** 250/7 Self-Propelled Mortar Carrier

**729-90328** 250/9 w/Open Turret & 20mm Kwk 38 Cannon **18.99**

**729-902461** 250/1 Armored Infantry Carrier **14.99**

**729-902471** 250/7 Armored Mortar Carrier **15.99**

**729-902491** 250/3 Armored Radio/Command Unit **15.99**

### SdKfz 251 Series Half-Tracks 16.99 ea (Unless Noted)

**729-90090** 251/1 Armored Infantry Carrier **15.99**

**729-90091** 251/2 Armored Mortar Carrier **15.99**

**729-90092** 251/9 Self-Propelled Gun **15.99**

**729-90127** 251/7 Armored Engineer Carrier **15.99**

**729-90128** 251/16 Armored Flamethrower

# trident

IMPORTED FROM AUSTRIA BY WALTHERS

**729-90129** 251/21 Self-Propelled Anti-Aircraft Gun

**729-90155** 251/1 Armored Rocket Launcher ("Stuka on Foot")

**729-90156** 251/10 Armored Infantry Carrier **15.99**

**729-90189** 251/17 Self-Propelled Anti-Aircraft Gun

**729-90190** 251/8 AMR Armored Ambulance **14.99**

**729-90304** 251/23 Type D Self-Propelled Gun **17.99**

**729-90305** 251/1 Self-Propelled Anti-Tank Gun **16.99**

**729-90329** 251/23 Late Model D w/Open Top Turret & 20mm Kwk 38 Cannon **19.99**

**729-900901** 251/1 Armored Infantry Carrier – Camouflage **23.99**

**729-900921** 251/9 Self-Propelled Gun – Camouflage **24.99**

## SdKfz 253 Series Half-Tracks

**729-90270** 253/5 Armored Personnel Carrier w/Enclosed Body **16.99**

## Conversion Parts for SdKfz Series Half-Tracks

Half-tracks are sold separately.

**729-96018** "Uhu" (Giant Owl) 2' 60cm Infra-Red Searchlight for SdKfz 251/20 **14.99**

**729-96024** 7.5cm Pak 40 Anti-Tank Gun for SdKfz 251/22 **17.99**

**729-96025** 7.5cm Stu. K 37 L/24 Anti-Tank Gun for SdKfz 251/9 **13.99**

**729-96026** 2cm Anti-Aircraft Cannon for SdKfz 251/17 **19.99**

**729-96031** Telephone Cable Laying Equipment for SdKfz 251/11 **6.99**

## Motorcycles 9.99 ea

**729-90124** NSU "Kettenkraftrad" HK-101 Half-Track Motorcycle

**729-901241** NSU HK-101 Half-Track Motorcycle

## Light Artillery

**729-96042** 4.7cm Festungspak (t) Anti-Tank Gun **TBA**

## Structures

Models are resin castings.

**729-99001** Observation Post **5.99**

**729-99002** Large Atlantic Wall Bunker **13.99**

**729-99004** Machine Gun Bunker **24.99**

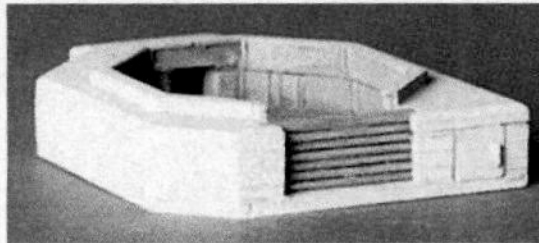

**729-99010** Light Anti-Aircraft Gun Emplacement (Gun Sold Separately) **39.99**

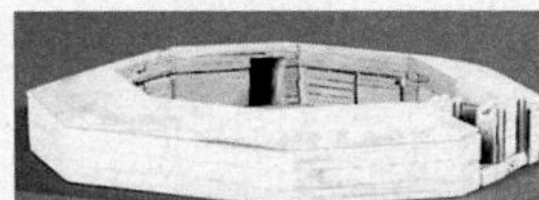

**729-99011** Heavy Anti-Aircraft Gun Emplacement (Gun Sold Separately) **57.99**

**729-99012** Right Flank Protection Bunker **57.99**

**729-99013** Left Flank Protection Bunker **57.99**

See What's Available at

**www.walthers.com**

251/10 Armored Infantry Carrier
729-90156 Shown Assembled & Painted

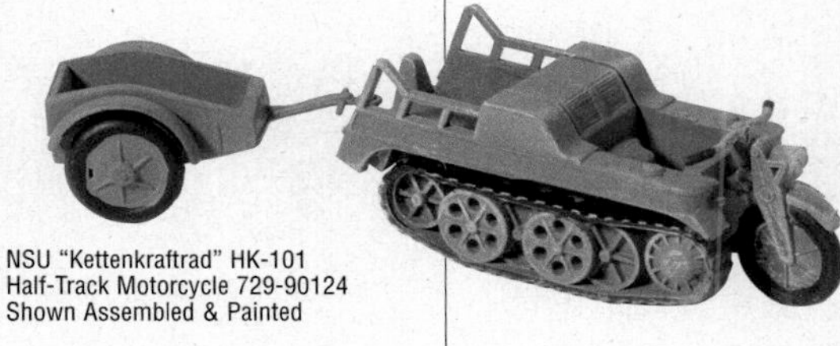

NSU "Kettenkraftrad" HK-101 Half-Track Motorcycle 729-90124 Shown Assembled & Painted

**729-99014** R67 Bunker w/PI Turret **19.99**

**729-99015** Army Barracks **49.99**

## R28 Artillery Observation Post

**729-99016 72.99**

## Machine Gun Pillbox

**729-99017 25.99**

## R58C Machine Gun Bunker - Tobruk

**729-99018 24.99**

## M262 Fire Control Bunker

**Limited Quantity Available**

**729-99019 168.99**

IMPORTED FROM AUSTRIA BY WALTHERS

### R23 Concrete Machine Gun Bunker

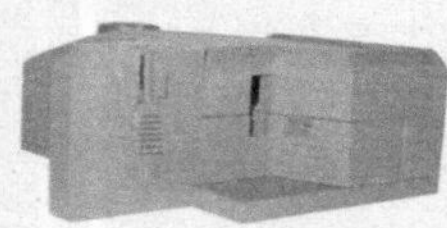

**729-99020** **109.99**

### R 20 Pak Bunker

**729-99022** Anti-Tank Gun Emplacement **104.99**

### R 632 Bunker

**729-99023** w/3 Embrasure Turret **113.99**

### Bell Tower for Russian Church

**729-99025** **48.99**
Use with #729-99024, sold separately.

### Mosque

**729-99026** **38.99**

### R 10 Machine Gun Bunker

**729-99027** **89.99**

**729-99028** Minaret **TBA**

**729-99029** Arabian House I **35.99**

**729-99030** Arabian House II **29.99**

## Anti-Tank Obstacles

**729-96019** Hedgehog Type 1 pkg(5) **10.99**

**729-96020** Hedgehog Type 2 pkg(5) **10.99**

**729-96021** Dragon's Teeth pkg(4) **13.99**

**729-96022** Jack Type pkg(5) **11.99**

## Accessories

**729-96023** Road Blockade **11.99**

**729-96035** Road Block Type 2 - Steel Gate for Streets **17.99**

## Post-1945 – United States

### Armored Vehicles - United States Marine Corps

**729-90013** LAV-CC Armored Command/Communications Unit (green) **13.99**

**729-90027** LAV-R Armored Recovery Vehicle w/Boom Crane (green) **13.99**

**729-97004** M873 Crawler Tractor & Personnel Trailer **18.99**

### Landing Vehicle, Tracked (LVT) Assault Amphibian Vehicles

**729-97001** Personnel Type 7, Model A1 (AAVP7A1) w/Machine Guns **18.99**

**729-97002** Command Type 7, Model A1 (AAVC7A1) **18.99**

**729-97020** Personnel Type 7, Model A1 (AAVP7A) **21.99**

**729-97023** Command Model 7A1 (AAVC7A1) **19.99**

915 Conventional 3-Axle Tractor w/M872 3-Axle Flatbed Trailer 729-90028

**729-97024** Recovery Vehicle Model 7A1 (AAVR7A1) **19.99**

### Trucks

**729-90003** M1009 Utility Truck/Staff Transport Vehicle (Chevrolet Blazer) **11.99**

**729-90004** M1008 Open Troop Carrier (Chevrolet Pick-Up) **12.99**

**729-90005** M1008 Cargo Carrier w/Canvas Cover (Chevrolet Pick-Up) **11.99**

**729-90006** M1028 Field Radio Unit (Chevrolet Pick-Up, green) **12.99**

**729-90007** M1010 Ambulance (Chevrolet Pick-Up Cab) **12.99**

**729-90028** 915 Conventional 3-Axle Tractor w/M872 3-Axle Flatbed Trailer **26.99**

**729-90043** M915 3-Axle Conventional w/MILVAN 20' Container Chassis & Reefer **26.99**

**729-90051** M915 Convention[al] 3-Axle Semi Tractor (No Trailer) **17.99**

**729-90053** M915 3-Axle Wrecker w/Towing Gear **17.99**

**729-90066** Chevrolet Personnel Van **13.99**

**729-90083** Chevrolet Cargo Van **14.99**

**729-90086** M1078 2-1/2-Ton Single Axle Flatbed MTV w/Canvas Cover **18.99**

**729-90087** M1083 5-Ton Dual-Axle Flatbed w/Cover **18.99**

**729-90112** US Navy Shore Patrol/Security Chevrolet Personnel Van **13.99**

## trident

IMPORTED FROM AUSTRIA BY WALTHERS

**729-90125** M1079 2-1/2Ton Flatbed MTV w/S-280 Shelter Load **20.99**

**729-90144** M915A1 Conventional 3-Axle Tractor w/M872 Flatbed Trailer & Two 20' Containers **31.99**

**729-90177** Ford Expedition Military Police **16.99**

**729-90205** Ford F-350 Utility Pickup w/4-Door Crew Cab **16.99**

**729-90224** M1079 LMTV Mobile Shop Van **20.99**

**729-90244** M1080 Single-Axle Flatbed **19.99**

**729-90250** Kosovo Peace-Keeping Forces KFOR M915A1 3-Axle Conventional Tractor w/M872 3-Axle Trailer & 2 Containers **31.99**

**729-90322** M915 Conventional 3-Axle Tractor w/M872 3-Axle Flatbed Trailer & 2 Forklifts **44.99**

**729-90323** M1009 Chevy Suburban - Military Police **15.99**

**Limited Quantity Available**

**729-90217** M1078 2-1/2 Ton Cargo/Troop Transport w/Canvas Cover **16.99**

### MTV Series Heavy Trucks

**729-81005** M1089 5-Ton Capacity 3-Axle 6x6 Wrecker **61.99**

**729-81006** M1090 3-Axle, 6x6, 5-Yard Capacity Dump Truck **34.99**

**729-81008** M1088 MTV 5-Ton, 3-Axle, 6x6 Semi Tractor **41.99**

### Heavy Trucks

**729-81010** M1074 Palletized Load System 5-Axle Tractor **TBA**
Use with M1076 Trailer #729-81011, sold separately.

**729-81012** M920 4-Axle Semi Tractor **TBA**

#### Conversion Parts

**729-96027** Conversion Parts for HEMTT Truck M984A1 Recovery Unit **20.99**

**729-96028** Conversion Parts for HEMTT M983 Truck Tractor w/Fifth Wheel **10.99**

### M1031 US Air Force Utility Trucks 11.99 ea

**729-90017** Maintenance

**729-900171** Red

**729-900172** Blue

**729-900173** Yellow

#### Trailers

**729-81009** M1082 LMTV Single-Axle 2-1/2 Ton Trailer **17.99**
Use with LMT Series Trucks, sold separately.

**729-81011** M1076 3-Axle Wagon-Type Flatbed **TBA**
Use with M1074 Tractor #729-81010, sold separately.

**729-81013** M1095 MTV 2-Axle Flatbed (Composite Kit) **25.99**

**729-90068** M872 3-Axle Flatbed (No Tractor) **18.99**

**729-90069** M872A3 3-Axle Flatbed w/Sidewalls (No Tractor) **23.99**

**729-90079** MILVAN 2-Axle 20' Container Chassis w/Box Container **18.99**

**729-90181** MILVAN 20' Single-Axle Container Chassis w/20' Box Container **18.99**

#### Fork Lift

**729-90084** MHE237 Fork Lift **16.99**

#### Artillery

**729-90025** M119 105mm Light Field Gun **9.99**

#### Emergency Equipment

**729-90110** Air Force Fire Chief #1 Chevrolet Suburban **13.99**

**729-90111** Fire Chief Chevrolet Suburban **14.99**

**729-90018** Air Force Fire Dept. Command Unit; Chevrolet Suburban (Lime Yellow) **12.99**

**729-90044** Ambulance w/Chevrolet Pickup Cab **14.99**

**729-901111** Assistant Fire Chief Chevy **14.99**

#### Accessories

**729-90126** S-280 Shelter **6.99**

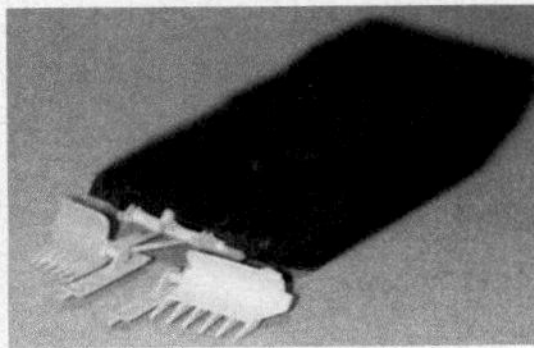

**729-96015** Anti-Tank Mine Plow for M1 "Abrams" Tanks **19.99**

**729-96016** Multiple Launch Rocket System (MLRS) Reload **17.99**

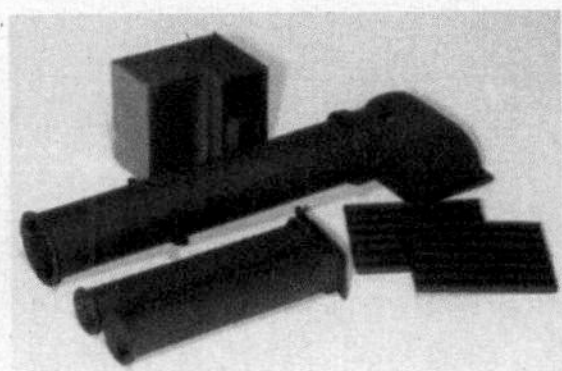

**729-96017** "Snorkel" Amphibious Conversion Kit For M1A1 "Abrams" Tanks **10.99**

**729-99021** Tank Service/ Undercarriage Access Ramps **18.99**

**729-96037** Tools **6.99**

**729-96038** Radio Equipment **6.99**

**729-96039** Tires 11mm **6.99**

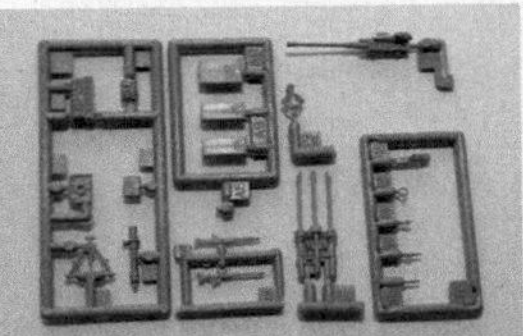

**729-96040** Weapons Set **6.99**

**920-96041** Fording Kit (Extended Air Intakes) for M4 "Sherman" Tank (Sold Separately) **5.99**

### Post-1945 – Germany

#### Trucks

**729-97003** BV206D Crawler Tractor & Trailer Personnel Carrier **18.99**

### World War II – Soviet Union

#### Structures

Models are resin castings.

**729-99003** Ruined Mansion **21.99**

**729-99005** Intact Farmhouse **37.99**

**729-99006** Ruined Industrial Smokestack **24.99**

**729-99007** Intact Stone Bridge **31.99**

**729-99008** Destroyed Russian Farmhouse **37.99**

**729-99009** Open Wooden Shed **29.99**

trident

IMPORTED FROM AUSTRIA BY WALTHERS

## Post-1945 – Austria

### Trucks

**729-90019** MAN/OAF F8 Low-Side Dump Truck (green) **14.99**

## Recent Conflicts – Austria

### Trucks

**729-81007** STEYR 12M18 Cargo/Personnel Carrier w/Covered Bed **34.99**

**Limited Quantity Available**

### Bosnian Peace-Keeping Mission

**729-900191** AN/OAF F8 5 Ton Truck (Olive Green, white) w/IFOR Markings **9.99**

## Post-1945 – Italy

**729-970031** Personnel Transport BV206D Crawler Tractor & Personnel Trailer **28.99**

## United Nations

**729-90245** M1008 Personnel Transport (Chevrolet Blazer) **12.99**

**729-90251** M1078 Single-Axle Covered Flatbed **18.99**

**729-970032** Personnel Transport BV206D Crawler Tractor & Personnel Trailer **28.99**

# UNPAINTED METAL KITS

## World War II – United States

### Armored Vehicles

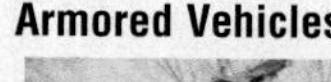

**729-80200** Self-Propelled Gun M7B2 Priest **34.99**

### Trucks

**729-80106** CCKW 353 w/Le-Roi Construction Air Compressor **35.99**

## World War II – Germany

### Armored Vehicles

**729-80178** Sd.Kfz 10/4 w/Flak 38 Self-Propelled Anti-Aircraft Half-Track **35.99**

**729-80179** Sd.Kfz 10 Heavy Artillery Tractor Half-Track **27.99**

**729-80189** Sd.Kfz 222 Armored Personnel Carrier w/Light Cannon **34.99**

**729-80198** Self-Propelled Gun SdKfz 124 Wespe (Wasp) **34.99**

### Artillery

**729-80186** 2cm Flak 38 Anti-Aircraft Gun **19.99**

**729-80190** 3.7cm Flak 36 Anti-Aircraft Gun **22.99**

### Trucks

**729-80180** Kfz 15 mPkw Command Car w/Top Down **27.99**

**729-80188** Steyr 1500A sPkw Personnel Carrier **27.99**

**729-80194** Kfz 1 IPkw Command Unit Vehicle **28.99**

**729-80195** Kfz 2 Pkw Field Radio Unit **28.99**

**729-80196** Kfz 2/40 IPkw Infantry Troop Vehicle **28.99**

**729-80197** Kfz 17 mPkw Field Radio Unit **29.99**

**729-80199** Kfz. 70 Krupp-Protze Tractor (3-Axle Personnel/Cargo Carrier) **34.99**

## Post-1945 – United States

### Trucks

**729-80141** M998 "Hummer" 1-Ton Multi-Purpose Vehicle **22.99**

**729-80144** M715 Cargo Carrier (American Motors/ Jeep Pick-Up Truck) **23.99**

**729-81001** M1070 HET 4-Axle Conventional Truck Tractor **71.99**

**729-81002** M1000 5-Axle Heavy-Duty Flatbed **47.99**

### Artillery

**Hawk Missile System MIM-23B**

**729-80081** M78 Launcher w/3 Surface-to-Air Missiles **28.99**

**729-80082** M501 Loader **21.99**

**729-80083** M390C Transporter w/3 Surface-to-Air Missiles **27.99**

**729-80084** AN/MPQ-51 Range Only Radar **28.99**

**729-80085** AN/MPQ55 Acquisition Radar **28.99**

**729-80086** AN/MPQ46 Target Illuminator Radar **29.99**

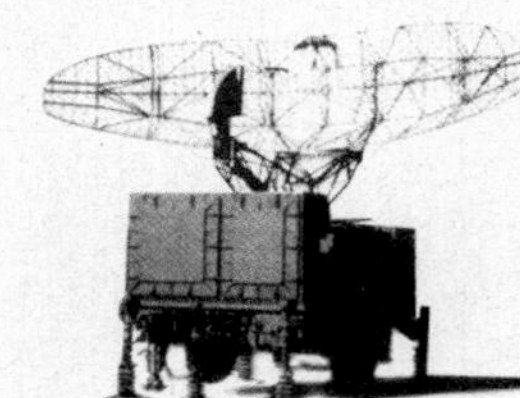

**729-80087** AN/MPQ35 Target Acquisition Radar **35.99**

**729-80088** AN/MSQ110 Information Co-Ordination Center **28.99**

**729-80089** AN/MS43 Missile Test Shop **14.99**

**729-80090** AN/TSW11 Battery Control Center **21.99**

**729-80091** HF45D Generator **11.99**

## Post-1945 – Germany

### Artillery

**729-80158** Rhinmetall Anti-Aircraft Gun MK20 RH202 **23.99**

## World War II – Soviet Union

### Artillery

**729-80181** 76.2cm Anti-Tank Gun **18.99**

trident

IMPORTED FROM AUSTRIA BY WALTHERS

## Post-1945 – Soviet Union & Warsaw Pact

### Tanks

**Limited Quantity Available**

**729-80043** T-72 w/125mm Cannon **29.99**

**729-80131** T-80 ERA w/125mm Cannon & Reactive Armor **31.99**

### Armored Vehicles

**729-80041** BRDM2 Armored Reconnaissance Vehicle **29.99**

**729-80042** BRDM-2 AT5 Anti-Tank Guided Weapon Vehicle **31.99**

**729-80156** BMD-2 Infantry Fighting Vehicle **33.99**

**729-80157** BMP-3 Armored Personnel Carrier **34.99**

**729-80174** BRDM-2 "Gaskin" Self-Propelled Anti-Aircraft Missile Launcher **34.99**

**Limited Quantity Available**

**729-80031** MT-LBW Troop Transporter/Artillery Tractor **25.99**

**729-80049** BTR-70 Armored Personnel Carrier **29.99**

**729-80064** BTR-60PA Armored Personnel Carrier **29.99**

**729-80093** SA-13 TELAR 1 Anti-Aircraft Vehicle w/"Strela 10" Missiles **31.99**

### Trucks

**729-80175** ZIL-157 Truck Tractor **34.99**

**Limited Quantity Available**

**729-80165** UAZ-452 Personnel Van **22.99**

## Post-1945 – England/ Great Britain

### Trucks

**729-80167** Bedford MK 4-Ton Flatbed Cargo Carrier **34.99**

**729-80168** Land Rover 109 Armored Personnel Carrier **30.99**

**729-80184** Bedford MK 4-Ton Single-Axle Flatbed w/Crane **34.99**

**729-80192** Land Rover 90 Pick-Up w/Canvas Covered Bed **27.99**

**729-80193** Land Rover 110 Cargo Van **28.99**

**Limited Quantity Available**

**729-80173** Land Rover 101FC Single-Axle Flatbed **26.99**

**729-80182** Land Rover 127 Single-Axle Flatbed **24.99**

## Post-1945 – Austria

### Armored Vehicles

**729-80170** STEYR "Pandur" Armored Personnel Carrier **34.99**

**Limited Quantity Available**

**729-80171** STEYR "Ulan" Armored Infantry Fighting Vehicle **30.99**

### Artillery

**729-80159** "Super Fledermaus" (Super Bat) Fire Control Radar System **36.99**

## Post-1945 – France

### Armored Vehicles

**729-80161** AMX-10P Armored Infantry Fighting Vehicle w/20mm Cannon **34.99**

**729-80164** Panhard Armed Reconnaissance Vehicle **26.99**

## Israeli Defense Force (IDF)

### Armored Vehicles

**729-81003** Armored Personnel Carrier "Achzarit" Heavy Infantry Assault Vehicle **44.99**

**729-81004** Armored Personnel Carrier "Classical" M113 **52.99**



### Conversion Parts

**729-96029** Conversion Parts Blazer Armor for M60 Tanks **8.99**

**729-96030** Conversion Parts Armored Recovery Unit (Crane, Tank Parts) for M113 Armored Personnel Carrier **10.99**

## Post-1945 – Switzerland

### Armored Vehicles

**729-80169** MOWAG Self-Propelled Guided Anti-Tank Rocket Launcher **34.99**

**729-80176** MOWAG "Piranha" Armored Personnel Carrier **35.99**

**729-80183** MOWAG Armed Reconnaissance Vehicle **33.99**

## CATALOG

**Limited Quantity Available**

**729-94000** 2004/2005 Vehicle Catalog **10.99**

# MONEY-SAVING SETS FOR YOUR MILITARY MODELING AND COLLECTING

Shown Assembled & Painted

trident

## Panzers On The Prowl

The Panzer was one of the finest medium tanks of World War II and was used by many of Germany's top tank aces. Introduced to counter the threat of the Russian T-34, the Model D was the first to see full production in 1942-43. An important offshoot of the Panzer was the Jagdpanzer (Hunting Panther) Tank Destroyer. This was a completely up-to-date, purpose-built vehicle fitted with a fixed 88mm cannon. German engineers produced a wide range of vehicles and one of the most unique was the "Kettenkraftrad," or tracked motorcycle, used as small tractor/prime mover. This Trident set includes one each of the Panzer Model D, SdKfz 173 "Jagdpanzer" and NSU HK-101 "Kettenkraftrad." Each model comes partially assembled from plastic parts and includes a variety of add-on details with basic installation instructions.

**5-7292 German Set #6**
Panzers on the Prowl

**Retail Value: $39.97**

**Your Cost: $19.98**

Set Includes One Each:

**729-97008** Panzer Model D

**729-97011** SdKfz 173 "Jagdpanzer" Armored Anti-Tank Gun

**729-90124** NSU HK-101 Ha Track Motorcycle "Kettenkraftrad"

TL-DECALS

trident

IMPORTED FROM AUSTRIA BY WALTHERS

Turn your military models into superdetailed replicas with these authentic period markings. Printed in authentic colors each decal is actual size, so there's no clear film around the edges to spoil the realism of your finished equipment.

A great value, each set will allow you to complete several projects with full markings.

## WORLD WAR II – UNITED STATES

**729-1282** US Army First Armored Division ("Old Ironsides"), 37th Regiment, 1st Battalion, B Co. **19.99**

**729-1420** White Stars – Standard Vehicle Recognition Markings **19.99**
Includes six sizes of white stars with solid, broken and bar surrounds. Standard marking for all US Army vehicles from the 1940s to the present. Also includes two large 50-star US flags in full-color.

### Post-1945 – United States

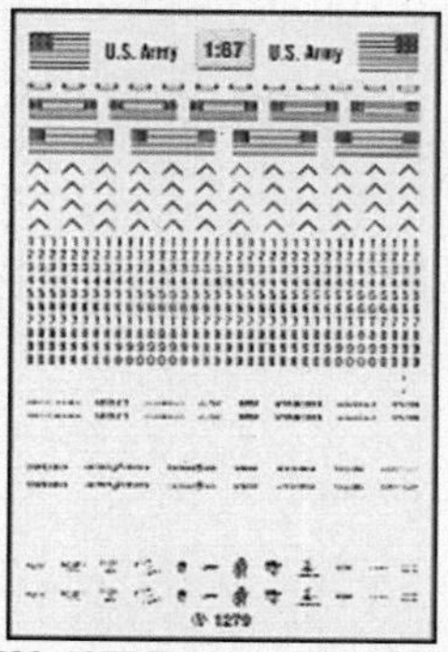


**729-1279** Tactical Markings & Numbers in Black for Vehicles Painted Sand/Tan **19.99**

**729-1425** US Army 1945+ Various Markings for Wheeled & Tracked Vehicles **19.99**

### 1st Armored Division "Old Ironsides" 19.99 ea

**37th Regiment, 1st Battalion**

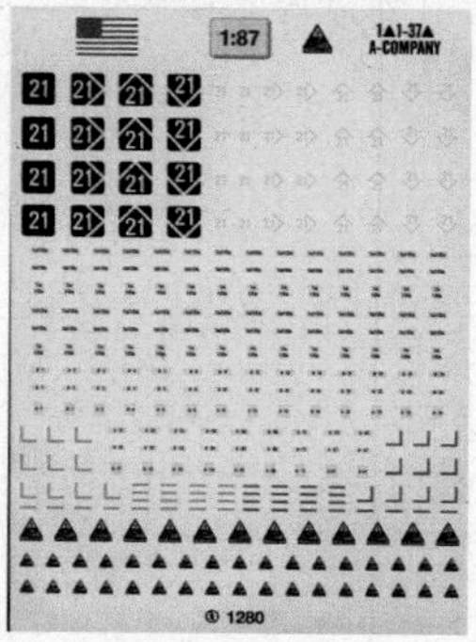


**729-1280** A-Company

**729-1281** Headquarters Company

**729-1283** C-Company

**1st Squad, 1st Cavalry Regiment**

**729-1285** A-Troop

**729-1286** B-Troop

**729-1287** C-Troop

**729-1288** HHT-Troop

## WORLD WAR II – GERMANY

### Decals 19.99 ea (Unless Noted)

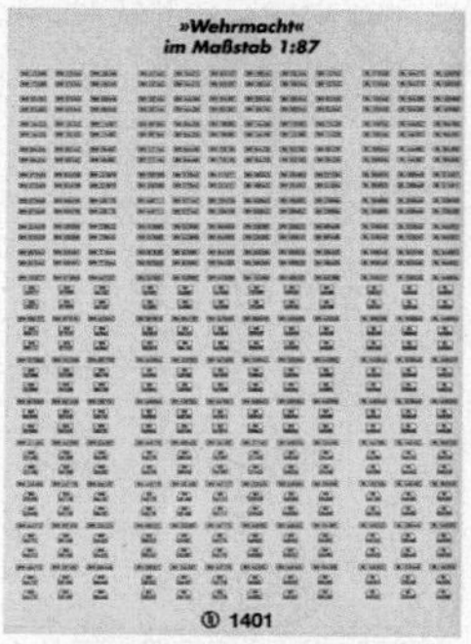


**729-1401** Wehrmacht (WM, WH & WL Prefixes) License Plates for Motor Vehicles

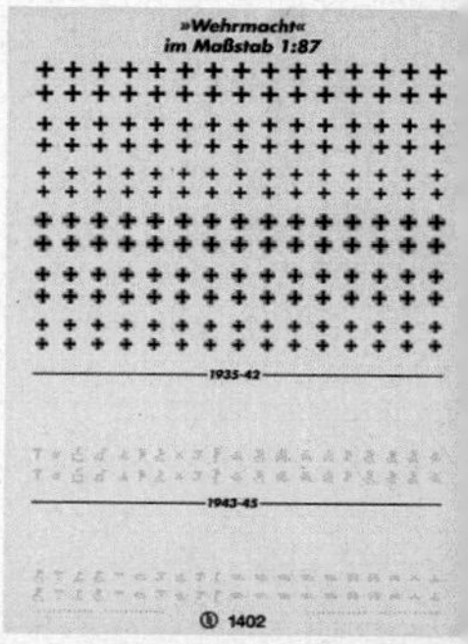


**729-1402** Balkenkreuze (Bea Cross) & Tactical Emblems Vehicle Recognition Markings Middle to Late War
Includes solid black and white surround Balkenkreuze insign plus a variety of German tacti pictograph symbols (used to identify the type of service to which the vehicle was assign which are correct for equipme from 1935-42 and 1943-45 in white and yellow.

See What's New and Exciting at

**www.walthers.com**

TL-DECALS

trident

MPORTED FROM AUSTRIA BY WALTHERS

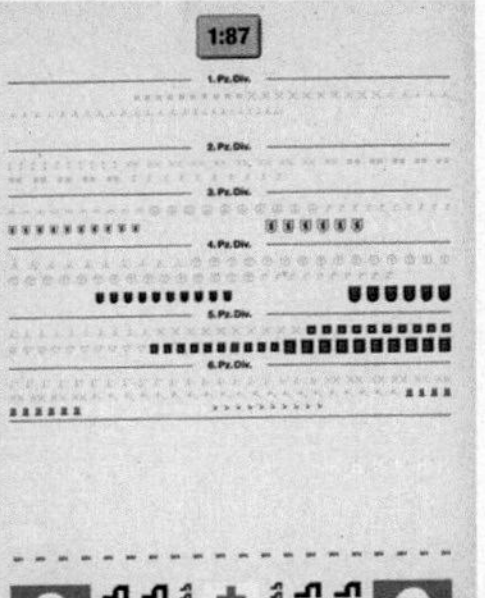

**729-1403** Panzer (Armor) 1st o 6th Division Insignia
This set includes standard Wehrmacht markings, plus personalized crew markings including girl's names and white victory rings (a series of small lines painted on the barrel of tank cannons to show how many enemy tanks had been knocked out by the crew). Includes a single Medical Corps red cross flag, plus two large and two small German flags used for air recognition.

**729-1404** State Police Schutzstaffel - SS) Vehicle Markings **17.99**

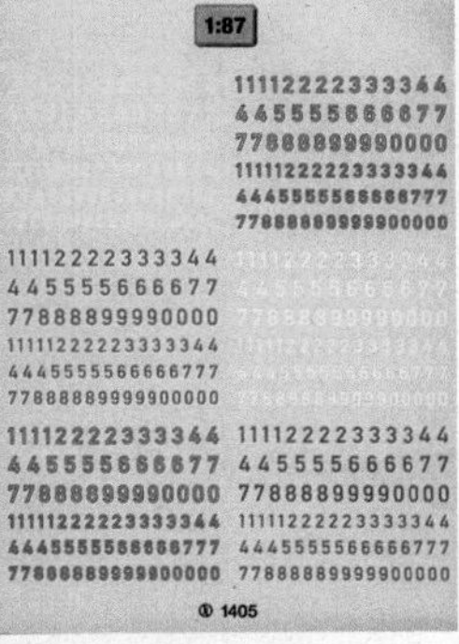

**729-1405** Panzer (Armor) Division Turret Number Jungle (Assorted Colors)
These large identification numbers were painted on tanks in the later years of the war. Surprisingly, they were done in highly visible bright colors, often with a contrasting border to make them stand out even more! While they actually identified the vehicle by company and battalion, they also made the tank more recognizable to friendly forces in the heat of comb.

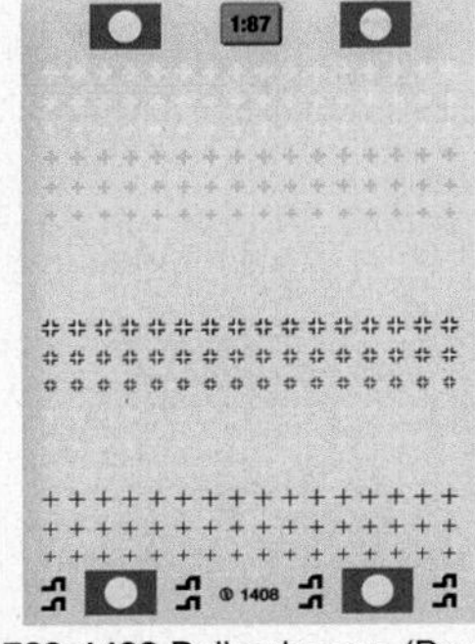

**729-1408** Balkenkreuze (Beam Cross) Variations - Vehicle Recognition Markings – Early War Years
This set includes various Balkenkreuze emblems in solid white and yellow, and in black with white outlines as used during the early war years on most equipment. Includes four German flags used for air recognition.

**729-1411** 7th-12th Panzer Division Tactical Emblems & Insignia (white, black, yellow)

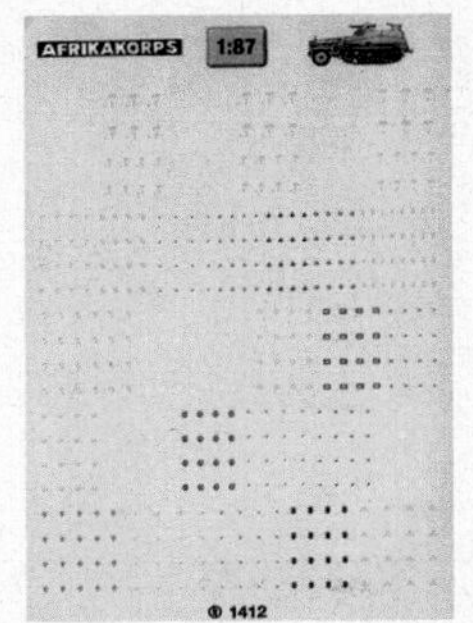

**729-1412** Afrika Korps **22.99**
Various tactical markings for half-tracks in yellow, red, black and white, plus the unique palm tree emblems in two sizes, printed in yellow and white.

**729-1413** Tank Turret Numbers (white) **18.99**

**729-1414** Turret Numbers
Various turret numbers in white for 1st through 9th Regiment, 1st and 2nd Division and 1st and 5th Company. **18.99**

**729-1415** 12" 30cm Tall Tank Turret Numbers w/White Outline - Companies 2-4 **18.99**

**729-1416** 12" 30cm Tall Tank Turret Numbers w/White Outline - Companies 6-8 **18.99**

**729-1417** Later Style Panzer Division Tactical Markings

**729-1418** Tactical Markings for 13th-19th Panzer Divisions

**729-1419** Markings for 20th - 26th Panzer Divisions

**729-1426** 3rd, 10th, 15th, 16th, 18th & 20th Panzergrenadier Division Emblems

**729-1441** Medical Corps
Includes Red Cross markings in various sizes, plus tactical markings for vehicles and related field signs.

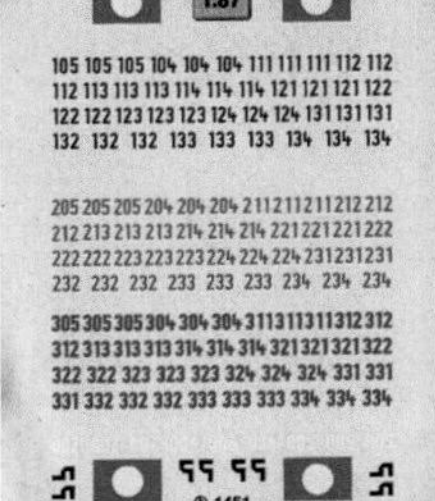

**729-1451** 101st Panzer Squadron (Units w/"Tiger" Tanks) Turret Numbers **17.99**
Assorted markings, plus four German flags used for air recognition.

**729-1454** 506th Heavy Tank Unit Markings (Tiger Tanks) Company 1 & 2 **17.99**

**729-1455** 506th Heavy Tank Unit Markings (Tiger Tanks) Company 3 & 4 **17.99**

**729-1461** Afrika Korps 1941-43 Markings for Rommel's 250/3 Half-Track "Greif," and 501st (second company, first and second platoons) and 504th (second company, first, second and third platoons) heavy tank battalions.

**729-1473** 506th Heavy Tank Unit Markings (Tiger Tanks) Company 1 & 2 Small Turret Numbers 6" 15cm for Tanks (black) **16.99**

**729-1474** Turret Numbers - 24" 60cm Tall (black, red) **16.99**

**729-1475** Turret Numbers - 18" 45cm Tall (black, red) **16.99**

**729-1476** Tank Turret Markings – White with Red Border **16.99**
Includes various markings measuring 30 & 40cm (12 & 16" tall.

**729-1479** Aircraft Markings Balkenkreuze and small swastika recognition markings.

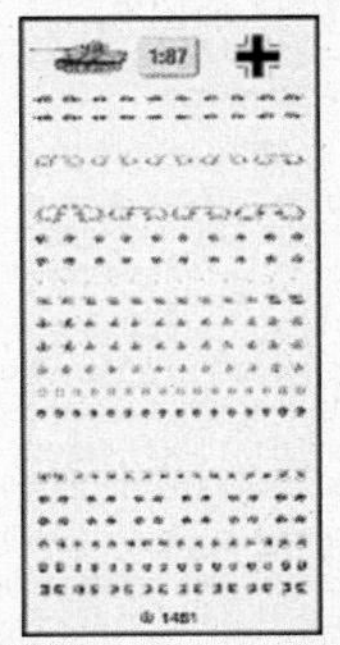

**729-1481** Insignia for Armored Companies Equipped w/Tiger Tanks **17.99**

**729-1482** Insignia for Various Armored Regiments **17.99**

**Limited Quantity Available**

**729-1427** Improvised Signs - Multicolor Field & Highway Route Markings

**729-1440** Tactical Markings for Army Supply Companies **16.99**

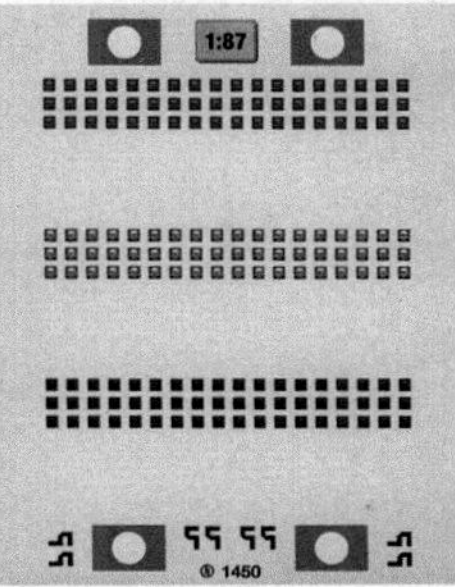

**729-1450** 192nd Assault Gun Squad Markings **17.99**
Assorted markings plus four German flags used for air recognition.

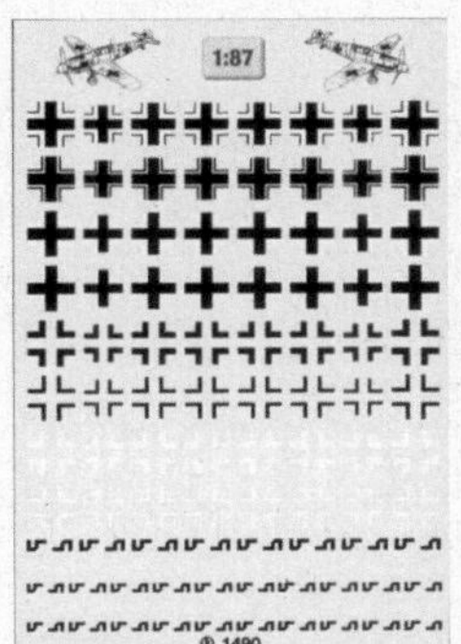

**729-1490** Balkenkreuze & Small Swastika Recognition Markings

## POST-1945 – GERMANY

### Decals

**729-1121** Eiserne Cross - Vehicle Recognition Markings **17.99**
Modern markings for a variety of equipment.

**729-1159** Tactical Symbols (white) MLC (yellow & black) w/Modern "Iron Cross" Insignia **17.99**

**729-1161** Medical Corps Insignia (red crosses) & Vehicle Markings **16.99**

**729-1166** Regimental Insignia for 363th Panzer, 352nd Grenadier & 115th Artillery **19.99**

**729-1167** NATO Warning Panels/Plates **17.99**
Convoy Starts/Ends signs and explosives placards in various sizes and colors

**729-1168** Barracks Signs - Tannenberg & Husaren **17.99**

**729-1170** Army Helicopters **19.99**
Includes numbers, national insignia and flags, plus safety/warning markings in color.

**729-1171** Tactical Markings for Armored Unit Vehicles **16.99**

**729-1173** Tactical Insignia for Armored Unit Vehicles **16.99**

**729-1174** Tactical Markings for 100th Air Defense Brigade **16.99**

**729-1268** Warning Signs & Markings for Heavy Transport Unit **17.99**

**729-1269** Maintenance Equipment Markings - Assorted Colors **17.99**

**729-1271** NATO "KFOR" Kosovo Peace-Keeping Forces - TFF & TFH **17.99**

**729-1272** International Security Assistance Force (ISAF; Afghanistan) & UN Insignia **17.99**

**729-1273** Recognition Symbols & Numbers for Maneuvers/ Excercises **17.99**

**Limited Quantity Available**

**729-1264** Markings for 93rd Panzer Training Battalion – Munster **16.99**

**729-1265** Markings for 92nd Panzergrenadier Battalion – Munster **16.99**

**729-1266** Insigina, Markings & Emblems for 64th Tank Battalion **17.99**

**729-1169** Barracks & Base Signs **17.99**

**729-1175** Air Force Tactical Markings **16.99**

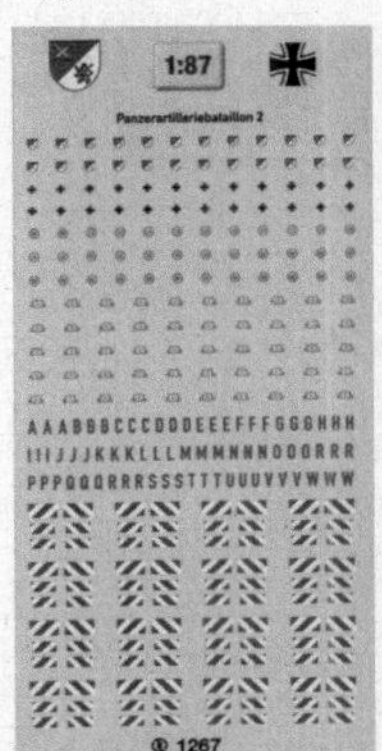

**729-1267** 2nd Panzer Artillery Battalion **17.99**

**729-1270** 35th Airborne Regiment CH-53 Helicopter Markings **15.99**

**729-1290** German National Guard (NVA) Insignia, Vehicle License Plates, Tactical Markings & Numbers **17.99**

### White Tactical Markings 16.99 ea

**Limited Quantity Available**

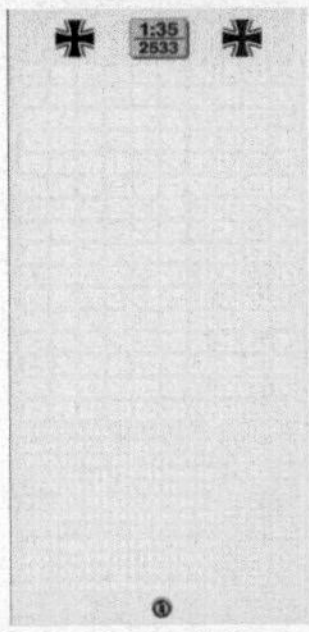

**729-2533** Tanks & Armored Infantry Units

IMPORTED FROM AUSTRIA BY WALTHERS

**729-2534** Medical & Infantry Units

### Emergency Vehicles – Technical Help Services 16.99 ea

A branch of the German armed forces, the Technical Help Service (THW) operates as a specialized Engineering unit, and also assists civilian authorities during natural disasters.

**Limited Quantity Available**

**729-1191** New Design, White Markings

**729-1192** New Design, Blue Markings

### Decals

**Limited Quantity Available**

**729-1136** International (IFOR) and Somalian (SFOR) Forces **13.99**

**729-1162** Kosovo Forces (KFOR) **9.99**

## WORLD WAR II – BRITAIN

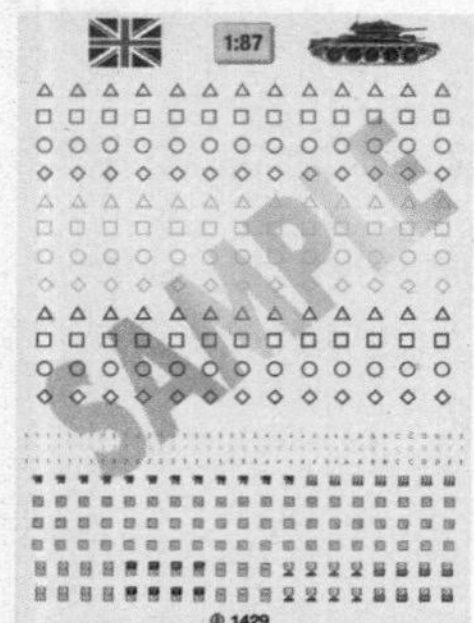

**729-1429** Tactical Markings & Vehicle Recognition Insignia **19.99**

**729-1430** Division Insignia for Indian, Australian, New Zealand & South African Units **19.99**

**729-1157** Army Vehicle Markings **19.99**

## WORLD WAR II – SOVIET UNION

### Decals 19.99 ea

**729-1422** Insignia & Slogans
A variety of typical Soviet markings including six sizes of red stars, two sizes of white stars, 14 different patriotic slogans in red and white, assorted squadron animal insignias and two sizes of hammer and sickle insignia in yellow and red.

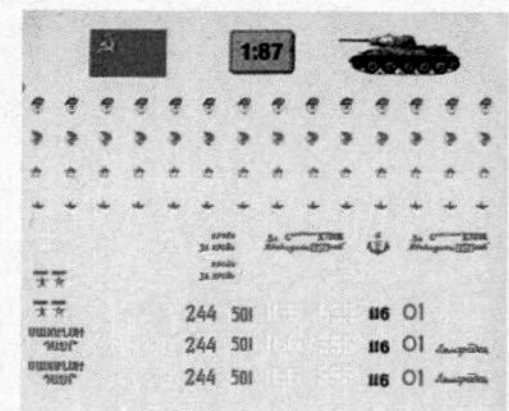

**729-1424** Turret Numbers, Insignia & Slogans
Tactical markings, unit insignia and patriotic slogans in red, white and yellow.

## POST 1945 – SOVIET UNION & WARSAW PACT

### Decals 19.99 ea

**729-1291** Insignia, License/Number Plates & Turret Numbers for Tanks

**729-1292** National Flags & Insigna for Poland, Bulgaria, Czechoslovakia, Ukraine

## NORTH ATLANTIC TREATY ORGANIZATION – NATO 1999-PRESENT

**729-1165** Fuel Tanker Vehicle Markings/Warnings & Placards **17.99**

**Limited Quantity Available**

**729-1163** NATO (Large & Small) & Member Nation's Flags (Small) **16.99**

## RED CROSS – MEDICAL CORPS

### Decals

**729-1421** Universal Red Cross Emblems **13.99**
Used to identify Medical Corps equipment and facilities throughout the 20th century, includes red cross emblems in seven different sizes on square, white backgrounds.

## WORLD WAR II – ITALY

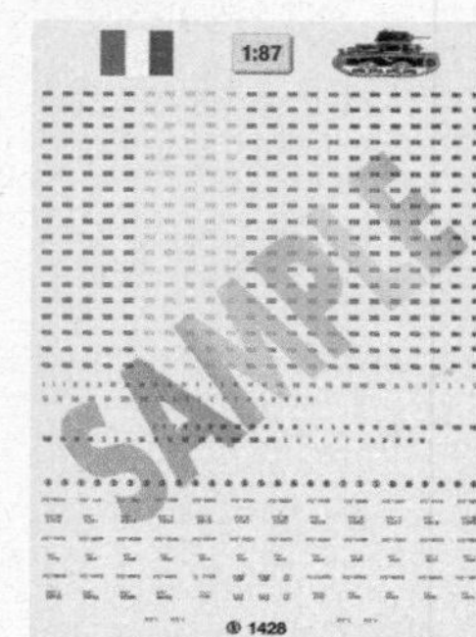

**729-1428** Tactical Markings & Vehicle Recognition Symbols **19.99**

## POST-1945 - SWITZERLAND

**729-1154** Army Vehicle Insignia, Markings & Signs **19.99**

## OTHER ARMIES POST 1945

### Decals 19.99 ea (Unless Noted)

**729-1151** Austrian Federal Army Markings

**729-1155** French Army Bridging plates, tactical markings, convoy warning signs and license plates.

**729-1156** Canadian Army National insignia (large black maple leaf, plus small red and white maple leaf), bridging plates and tactical markings.

**729-1423** France Early Tank Markings (red, white, blue, yellow)

**Limited Quantity Available**

**729-1152** Royal Belgian Army Vehicle insignia, "scare stripes" bridging plates, tactical markings and license plates. **16.99**

## MISCELLANEOUS

**729-1172** Assorted Modern Armies Flags & KFOR Markings for Kosovo Peace-Keeping Forces **16.99**

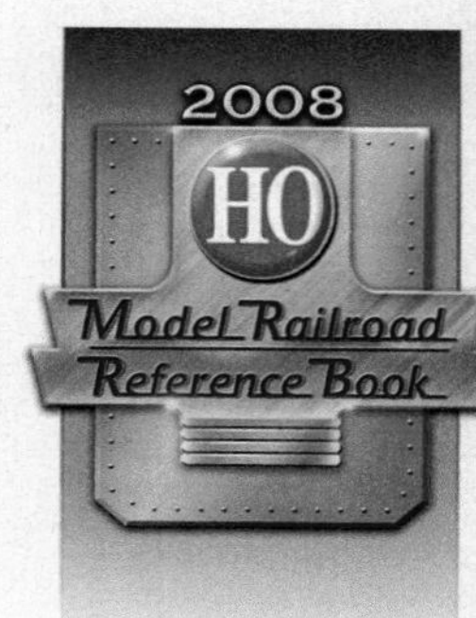

# VEHICLES

Models by Gilles Mallet, Pierre Dion and Vermont & Essex Club members, Photo by Pierre Dion

Kids are already grumbling about the start of school as the first fall colors blaze across northern New England. The very last of the summer tourists are already heading south. Most who stop for gas can't pass up one last chance to take home a freshly-baked pumpkin pie, some Maine potatoes or maple sugar candy, all made and grown right on the farms down the highway. Mom and dad know they have a long drive ahead, but the kids have already drifted off to sleep as the station wagon works a little harder to get the rented trailer up the hill ahead.

This charming scene is featured on the Vermont & Essex club layout. Member Gilles Mallet built the Gulf gas station from a Micro Structures kit. The car leaving town is from Woodland Scenics, as are the details and shoppers that make up the Farmer's Market in the station parking lot. Dad couldn't wait to rent one of those new camping trailers this year, and this model is from Busch. Pierre Dion, who also took the photo, completed the scenery with a variety of Woodland Scenics foliage and other products.

From horse-drawn wagons to modern grocery-getters, you can set the time and place of the streets and highways of your layout with the many different kinds of vehicles you'll find parked on the pages just ahead.

# WALTHERS

## RESIN VEHICLE KITS

- Easy-to-Build
- Detailed Bodies
- Open Windows
- Basic Interior

### Automobiles

**933-4001** Checker Marathon Taxi **8.98**

### Farm Machinery

**933-4016** Modern Farm Tractor **8.98**

**933-4008** Grain Truck **12.98**

### Trucks

**933-4012** Logging Truck **19.98**

**933-4013** Wood Chip Truck **19.98**

**933-1035** Wood Chip Truck Load **2.98**

**933-4014** Pulp Wood Truck **19.98**

**933-1036** Pulp Wood Truck Load **6.98**

**933-4002** Divco Milk Truck **8.98**

**933-4003** 1941 Pick-Up **8.98**

**933-4011** Model R Dump Truck **12.98**

## PLASTIC VEHICLE KITS

### Construction Equipment 24.98 ea

**933-3142** Terex Heavy Dump Truck

**933-3162** Komatsu Heavy-Duty R992 Wheel Loader on Rubber Tires (Safety Yellow, black) **34.98**

### Delivery Vans

**933-1591** With Gold Lettering Decals **6.98**

**933-1590** Undecorated **4.98**

### Farm Machinery

**933-1047** Combine **32.98**
Includes small grain and corn heads.

## TRAILERS

### 26' Parcel Trailers 4.98 ea

**933-1581** Parcel Van w/Decals

**933-1580** Undecorated

### 48' Stoughton Semi Trailers 5.98 ea

**933-1901** XTRA Intermodal (white)

**933-1904** J.B. Hunt (white)

**933-1906** Schneider (white)

**933-1907** Strick Lease (white)

**933-1908** Tip Lease (white)

**933-1909** Schneider (orange)

**933-1919** BNSF

**933-1922** Ryder

**933-1925** Werner

**933-1900** Undecorated

### 53' Stoughton Van Trailers 6.98 ea

**933-1453** Swift

**933-1454** Bison

**933-1455** Yanke

**933-1459** Klyson

**933-1460** J.B. Hunt

**933-1461** Schneider

**933-1462** MS Carriers

**933-1450** Undecorated

### Extendable Container Chassis

**933-3110** pkg(2) **8.98**

## CONTAINER CRANES

### Mi-Jack Translift Intermodal Crane

**933-3122 21.98**

- Adjustable Parts
- Magnets Hold Containers without Gluing
- Authentic Decals
- Complete Instructions

### Kalmar Container Crane

**933-3109 19.98**

- Molded in Safety Yellow
- Authentic Decals
- Complete Instructions

## CONTAINERS

- Available in 20, 28, 40 and 48' Lengths
- Great Loads or Terminal Details
- Prepainted & Assembled

### 20' Ribbed-Side Container 4.49 ea

**933-1751** Maersk

**933-1752** K-Line

**933-1753** Hanjin

**933-1754** Evergreen

**933-1755** Genstar

**933-1756** OOCL

**933-1757** Mitsui OSK

**933-1758** Triton

**933-1759** Nedlloyd

**933-1761** CP Ships

**933-1762** CAST

**933-1763** American President Lines (APL)

**933-1764** Flexi-Van

**933-1765** NOL

**933-1766** NYK

**933-1767** Hamburg Sud

**933-1768** XTRA International

**933-1769** UASC

**933-1750** Undecorated

### 20' Tank Container 4.98 ea

**933-1951** ATSF

**933-1952** UP

**933-1953** SEACO

**933-1954** TransAmerica

**933-1955** K&W Alaska

**933-1957** Tiphook

**933-1961** Bond

**933-1962** Vanhool

**933-1963** Hoyer

**933-1964** Stolt

**933-1966** Miller

**933-1950** Undecorated

### 20' Corrugated-Side Containers 4.98 ea

Corrugations run uninterrupted for the entire length of the box

**933-2001** Maersk-Sealand

**933-2002** K-Line

**933-2003** XTRA

**933-2004** Genstar

**933-2005** OOCL

**933-2006** Gateway

**933-2007** Triton

**933-2008** Tiphook

**933-2009** P&O

**933-2010** SEACO

**933-2011** Tex

**933-2012** Yang Ming

**933-2000** Undecorated

### 40' High-Cube Container 4.49 ea

**933-1701** Maersk

**933-1702** APL

**933-1703** Evergreen

**933-1704** K-Line



**933-1705** Hapag-Lloyd

**933-1706** Matson

**933-1707** ITEL

**933-1708** CAST

**933-1709** CP Ship

**933-1710** OOCL

**933-1711** Hyundai

**933-1712** Hanjin

**933-1713** TransAmerica

## WALTHERS

933-1714 Genstar
933-1715 XTRA
933-1716 Tropical
933-1717 P&O
933-1718 Nedlloyd
933-1719 Yang Ming Line
933-1720 Columbus Line
933-1721 Crowley
933-1700 Undecorated

### 40' Reefer Container 4.98 ea

933-1851 K-Line
933-1852 Sea-Land
933-1853 TransAmerica
933-1854 Evergreen
933-1855 Maersk
933-1856 APL
933-1857 Dole
933-1858 Hyundai
933-1861 NYK
933-1862 P&O
933-1863 Cosco
933-1864 Trans Ocean
933-1850 Undecorated

### 40' Hi-Cube Corrugated-Side Containers 4.98 ea

933-2051 APL
933-2052 K-Line
933-2053 Hyundai
933-2054 Genstar
933-2055 SEACO
933-2056 Hapag-Lloyd
933-2057 OOCL
933-2058 PO Nedlloyd
933-2059 Maersk-Sealand
933-2060 Triton
933-2061 Capitol
933-2062 Uniglory
933-2050 Undecorated

### 48' Stoughton Ribside Exterior Post Container 4.98 ea

933-1805 NS
933-1816 EMP
933-1817 ATSF

933-1818 BN America
933-1819 J.B. Hunt®
933-1820 APL
933-1821 NACS
933-1823 UP
933-1849 Undecorated

### 48' Stoughton Smoothside Container 4.98 ea

933-1801 CP/US Service
933-1802 CN Laser
933-1803 BN America
933-1806 APL

933-1807 Conquest
933-1808 Genstar
933-1809 CSX/SL
933-1810 XTRA
933-1811 ATSF
933-1812 SP
933-1814 ITEL
933-1813 UP/Genstar
933-1815 J.B. Hunt
933-1800 Undecorated

Daily New Arrival Updates! Visit Walthers Web site at
**www.walthers.com**

LIFE-LIKE PRODUCTS®

Division of Wm. K. Walthers, Inc.

## SCENEMASTER VEHICLES

### 9.00 ea

### Automobiles

**433-1616** Coupe Cars pkg(4)

**433-1623** American Automobiles pkg(4)

**433-1624** American Automobiles pkg(4)

**433-1694** Hearse

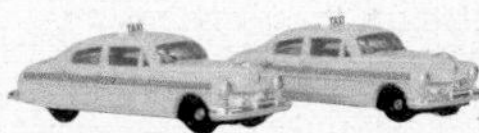

**433-1699** Taxi pkg(2)

### Buses

**433-1637** School Bus **9.00**

### Construction Equipment 9.00 ea

**433-1619** Forklift w/Crates & Barrels **9.00**

**433-1638** Road Grader

**433-1639** Cement Mixer

### Emergency Vehicles

**433-1693** Ambulance

**433-1695** Emergency Medical Services

**433-1696** Police Wrecker

**433-1697** Fire Chief Cruiser pkg(2)

**433-1698** Police Cruiser pkg(2)

### Farm Machinery

**433-1625** Plow & Planter

**433-1626** Disc & Wagon

**433-1627** Tractors (green, red)

### Trucks

**433-1613** Pickup Trucks pkg(4)

**433-1617** Dump Trucks pkg(2)

**433-1618** Stake Trucks pkg(2)

**433-1640** Fuel Tank Truck

**433-1642** Coal Truck w/Moveable Bed

**433-1643** Tow Truck w/Swinging Hook

**433-1644** Box Truck

**433-1645** Milk Truck

Items listed in blue ink may not be available at all times (see Legend Page).

## AUTOMOBILES & LIGHT TRUCKS
### 7.95 ea (Unless Noted)

#### Buick

**119-2031** 1949 Roadmaster

**119-2033** 1953 Skylark Convertible w/Continental Spare

#### Cadillac

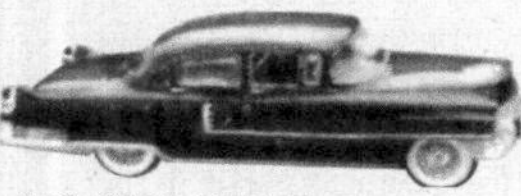

**119-2024** 1955 Fleetwood

**119-2032** 1959 Eldorado Convertible

#### Chevrolet

**119-2008** 1957 Bel-Air Sports Coupe w/Engine **8.95**

**119-2019** 1950 4-Door Fastback

**119-2020** 1955 Bel-Air 2-Door

**119-2025** 1953 Corvette

**119-2029** 1955 Nomad Wagon

**119-2037** 1953 Bel-Air

**119-2039** 1959 Impala Convertible

**119-2045** 1959 El Camino Pickup

#### De Soto

**119-2018** 1949 4-Door

#### Ford

**119-2021** 1956 Pickup **8.95**

**119-2022** 1956 Thunderbird w/Roof Porthole

**119-2030** 1948 Convertible w/Engine **8.95**

**119-2038** 1955 Thunderbird Without Roof Porthole

**119-2041** 1951 Panel Delivery Truck **8.95**

**119-2042** 1956 Pickup w/Camper **9.95**

**119-2043** 1956 Pickup w/Rack & Utility Boxes **9.95**

#### Hudson

**119-2023** 1949 4-Door

#### Mercury

**119-2028** 1949 Two-Door

#### Plymouth 1941 Coupe

**119-2026** Less Engine

**119-2027** With Engine **8.95**

#### Studebaker

**119-2040** 1949 Starline

## CIRCUS

#### Circus Tent Van

**119-7077** Mack Circus Tent Van **24.95**
1930s Mack (CJ) universal tractor with dual axle, canvas circus van and spoke wheels. Kit consists of unpainted white-metal parts. Also includes styrene, brass and rubber details.

## EMERGENCY VEHICLES

#### Diamond REO/Pierce 26.95 ea

**119-7032** CRV-18 Heavy Rescue Unit

**119-7036** Suburban Pumper

#### Ford/Pierce

Models feature Ford truck cabs with Pierce Fire Apparatus bodies.

**119-7007** LN Pumper **31.95**

**119-7029** LN Suburban Pumper **31.95**

**119-7031** LNT CRV-18 Heavy Rescue Unit **26.95**

**119-7038** LNT 2500-Gallon Tanker **26.95**

#### LN9000

**119-7069** Suburban Pumper **31.95**

**119-7071** CRV-18 Heavy Rescue Vehicle **26.95**

**119-7073** 2500-Gallon Tanker, Tandem Axle **26.95**

#### LS/LS9000/LTS 31.95 ea (Unless Noted)

**119-7025** LS Pumper

**119-7030** LS Suburban Pumper

**119-7072** LS9000 2500-Gallon Tanker **26.95**

#### Mack B42/B61 Pumper 31.95 ea

**119-3035** Closed Cab

**119-3136** Open Cab

#### Mack CF

**119-7017** 2- or 4-Door Pumper **31.95**

**119-7040** 2500-Gallon Tanker **26.95**

**119-7042** CRV-18 Heavy Rescue Unit **31.95**

**119-7043** 2- or 4-Door Cab Chassis w/Spoke Wheels **24.95**

#### Equipment Bodies

**119-3086** Generic Fire Pumper Body **20.95**
Adaptable to various truck kits, complete with ladders, hose reels and other details.

**119-7035** Pierce Pumper for Extended Chassis **20.95**

**119-7046** FDNY (New York City) Pumper Body **21.95**

**119-7092** Pierce Pumper **21.95**

**119-7093** Pierce CRV-18 Heavy Rescue Vehicle **10.95**

**119-7094** Pierce 2500-Gallon Tanker **21.95**

## HEAVY TRUCKS

All kits except #2044 include plastic wheels and vinyl tires.

#### Autocar

Models feature disc wheels.

**119-3100** Tractor **19.95**

**119-3101** Dump Truck w/12' Heil Dump Bed **24.95**

**119-3116** "Constructor" Dump Truck w/Curved-Side Body **24.95**

**119-3162** "Constructor" Off-Road Tractor **19.95**
Builds single- or dual-axle version.

**119-7001** Dump Truck-Large Body **26.95**

**119-7053** "Constructor" w/Closed Roll-Off Trash Compactor Body **24.95**

**119-7088** "Constructor" w/Roll-Off Trash Compactor Body & Disc Wheels **24.95**

#### Chevrolet

**119-2044** 1955 2-Ton Stake Truck **11.95**
All metal kit.

#### Diamond Reo 24.95 ea (Unless Noted)

Models feature spoked wheels.

**119-3114** Tractor **19.95**

**119-3134** 14' Dump Body

**119-3145** 7' Heil Dump Body

**119-3148** Flatbed **23.95**

**119-7033** Dump Truck w/Curved-Side Body

**119-7050** Fuel Oil Tank Truck

#### Ford

All models feature disc wheels.

#### LNT

**119-3042** Tri-Axle w/12' Heil Dump Body **24.95**

**119-3117** Dump Truck w/Curved-Side Body **22.95**

**119-3135** Dual-Axle Tractor w/Dual Exhaust, Round Fuel Tanks **19.95**

#### LTS

**119-3151** Dump Truck w/Curved-Side Body **23.95**

**119-7020** Dual-Axle Tractor w/Dual Exhaust, Round Fuel Tanks **19.95**

**119-7022** Dump Truck w/20' Dump Bed **26.95**

**119-7021** Dump Truck w/12' Heil Dump Bed **24.95**

ALLOY FORMS

## LN 9000

**119-7056** Dual-Axle Dump Truck w/12' Heil Dump Body **24.95**

**119-7075** Dual-Axle Tractor w/Dual Exhaust, Round Fuel Tanks **19.95**

## LS 9000

**119-7063** Dual-Axle Tractor w/Round Fuel Tanks **26.69**

**119-7066** Boom/Block Truck **24.95**

## GMC Astro Universal Tractor

### Sleeper Cabs - Dual Axle

**119-3012** Single Exhaust, Square Fuel Tanks, Dual Axle **19.95**
Models include sleeper cab, air cleaner and disc wheels.

### Short Cabs

Kits include dual exhaust, round fuel tanks, and spoke wheels.

**119-3022** GMC Astro w/16' Van **24.95**

**119-3025** Dual Axle **19.95**

## Mack

### B42/B61 Universal Tractor 24.95 ea (Unless Noted)

Models feature spoke wheels.

**119-3001** Flatbed Truck w/Stakes **23.95**

**119-3007** Short Refrigerated Van Truck

**119-3009** Concrete Block Truck w/Boom

**119-3018** Ribbed Side Van

**119-3019** Dump Truck w/Curved-Side Dump Body

**119-3023** Fuel/Water Tanker

**119-3027** Box Van w/24' Riveted Smooth Side Body

**119-3028** Dual-Axle Dump Truck w/Heil Dump Bed

**119-3034** Tri-Axle Dump Truck w/12' Heil Dump Bed

**119-3138** Tractor Only **19.95**

**119-3049** Dual-Axle Dump Truck w/12' Heil Dump Bed

### B71

Models feature disc wheels.

**119-3008** Dump Truck w/Curved-Side Body **24.95**

**119-3137** Tractor **19.95**

**119-3139** Tractor w/Three-Axle Heavy Duty Flatbed **23.95**

### DM-800 Offset Cab Tractor 19.95 ea

**119-3011** R-800

**119-7052** With Spoke Wheels

## 1930s Mack Trucks

### BM/BQ

All models feature spoke wheels.

**119-3020** Tank Truck **22.95**

**119-3031** Single Axle Tractor **19.95**

**119-3106** Van **24.95**

**119-3107** Stake Truck **23.95**

**119-3164** Dump Truck w/Curved Body **24.95**

**119-7078** Oil Tanker w/Five-Dome Fuel Oil Tank **24.95**

**119-7079** Heavy Duty Wrecker **24.95**

**119-7081** Single-Axle Tractor w/Two Double-Bottom Tank Trailers **31.95**

**119-7085** Van w/16' Riveted Smooth-Side Body **24.95**

**119-7086** Dual-Axle Oil Tanker w/Five-Dome Tank **24.95**

### 1933 CJ

Models feature spoke wheels.

**119-3021** Tank Truck **22.95**

**119-3104** Van **24.95**

**119-3105** Stake Truck **23.95**

**119-3146** Tractor Only **19.95**

**119-3147** Oil Truck w/Five-Dome Tank Body **24.95**

**119-3163** Dump Truck w/Curved Body **24.95**

**119-7076** City Fuel Oil Truck **24.95**

**119-7077** Circus Canvas (Tent) Truck **24.95**

## Trailers 24.95 ea (Unless Noted)

**119-3017** 45' Heavy-Duty Lowboy Trailer w/Spoke Wheels

**119-3029** 30' Open Frame Logging Trailer w/Spoke Wheels

**119-3110** 30' Tri-Axle Dump Trailer w/Spoke Wheels

**119-3149** 45' Ribbed Sided Van w/Spoke Wheels

**119-3154** 37' Depressed Center w/Spoke Wheels

**119-7010** 22' Dump Trailer w/Disc Wheels

**119-7015** 22' Dump Trailer w/Bogie w/Disc Wheels **28.95**

**119-7074** UPS-Type Over-the-Road Trailer

**119-7091** 30' Open Frame Trailer pkg(2)

**119-7095** 24' Riveted Side Van w/Spoke Wheels



## Trailers - Container Transport

Kits feature spoke wheels. Trucks not included.

**119-7018** 20' pkg(2) **21.95**

**119-7019** 40' pkg(2) **24.95**

## Truck Bodies

**119-3024** 24' Riveted Smooth-Side Van **20.95**

**119-3151** LS Dump Truck w/Dual Exhaust **23.95**

**119-3155** 20' Coal/Gravel Dump **20.95**

**119-3156** 1930s Delivery Van **10.95**

**119-3157** 1930s 20' Canvas Top Van **15.95**

**119-3158** 1930s Round Tanker **6.95**

**119-3159** 1930s City Fuel Oil Delivery Tank **10.95**

**119-3160** Sloped/Curved Tanker **10.95**

**119-3183** Heavy-Duty Flatbed w/Side Stakes **6.95**

**119-3184** Curved Side Dump **8.95**

**119-7034** Short Refrigerated Van **10.95**

**119-7047** 7' Heil Dump **8.95**

**119-7048** 11' Heil Low-Side Dump **8.95**

**119-7051** 12' Heil Dump **8.95**

**119-7054** Trash Compactor **10.95**

**119-7080** Heavy-Duty Ribbed-Side Dump **10.95**

**119-7082** 5-Dome Fuel Oil Tank **10.95**

**119-7084** 16' Riveted Smooth-Side Van **10.95**

**119-7089** 1930 Mack Wrecker **10.95**

**119-7090** 14' Ribbed-Side Dump **10.95**

**119-7096** Boom/Block Flatbed **10.95**

**119-7097** Ribbed-Side Van **10.95**

**119-7099** Light-Duty Flatbed pkg(2) **10.95**

**119-7098** Heavy-Duty Flatbed pkg(2) **10.95**

## Truck Loads

**119-8022** Logs - Stack of 3 **11.95**

**119-8050** Banded Lumber pkg(4) **11.95**

**119-8052** Covered Machinery/ Lumber pkg(3) **12.95**

**119-8082** Wooden Crates (6 Large, 6 Small) pkg(12) **9.95**

## Custom Finishing

All products are unpainted metal kits.

Please visit Walthers Web site at www.walthers.com for a complete listing of all available items.

## TRUCKS

### Truck Body Kits

Cab and chassis not included.

**247-5010** Logging Truck Body w/Cherry Picker **39.95**
Fits Atlas #150-1220 series, sold separately.

## CONSTRUCTION EQUIPMENT

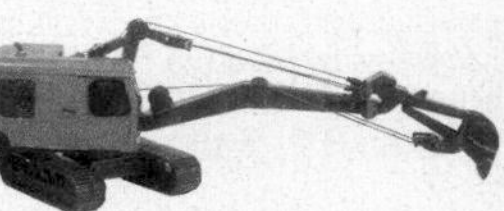

**247-5012** Cable-Operated Backhoe Excavator **62.95**
Features a swiveling cab; fully detailed cab interior with pedals, levers and seat; tilting elevation column; raising and lowering boom; and dipperstick with bucket. Includes cables and window glazing.

## STREET SWEEPER

**247-7092** 3-Wheel Road Curb Sweeper **42.95**

## TRAILERS

### Logging Trailers

**247-5008** 40' w/Working Tag Axle **24.95**

**247-5009** Tag-Along 2-Axle Type **16.95**

## BACHMANN

### Automobiles

**160-42206** Automobile Set pkg(6) **6.50**
Preassembled in appropriately colored plastic with painted details.

Capture the look of today's intermodal equipment for railroad or highway with these easy-to-build plastic kits, accessories and decals.

# TRAILER KITS

## 28' Wedge Trailer

**116-50500** Roadway Express **11.95**

## 28' Parcel Trailer

Drop-style "pup" parcel transport trailer. Easy-to-assemble kit includes undecorated, one-piece plastic body with separate floors, vinyl tires, wheels and mud flaps.

**116-50113 7.50**

**116-50512** With Parcel Decal **9.75**

**116-50513** With RPS Decal **9.75**

## Trailer Dolly

**116-50114** Parcel **3.95**
Allows two 28' parcel vans to be operated as "doubles."

## 28' Wedge Trailer

This is an exact replica of the Pines 28' Wedge Trailer. This model has a highly detailed one-piece body, roll-up style rear door, separate floor, landing gear, suspension, separate wheels and vinyl tires.

### Undecorated 9.25 ea

**116-50129** Ribbed
**116-50130** Smooth

### Trailers w/Decals 11.25 ea (Unless Noted)

116-50514, 116-50516

**116-50514** Smooth w/Yellow Transit Decals (New 1997 Scheme)

**116-50516** Smooth w/Yellow Transit (Early) Decals

116-50518, 116-50519, 116-50517

**116-50517** Smooth w/Roadway Express Decals

**116-50518** Smooth w/Roadway Decals

**116-50519** Ribbed w/Roadway Decals **11.95**

## 28' Wedge Trailer Parts

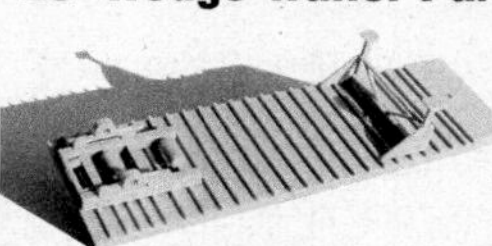

**116-50147** Trailer Suspension **3.50**

**116-50148** Trailer Floor **3.00**

## 53' Duraplate Trailer

Wabash National led the market with this 53' plate trailer. Now with the introduction of the uniquely designed and manufactured 53' Duraplate composite wall trailer, Wabash National is in the lead again. A-Line brings this unique trailer to life in HO Scale with exacting detail from manufacturers' blueprints. Available in two sidewall configurations, this highly detailed kit includes unpainted one-piece body with separate suspension wheels, landing gears and separate doors.

### Undecorated Trailer 10.95 ea

**116-50520** All Buttons

**116-50521** No Buttons

### Undecorated Trailer w/Decals 14.95 ea

Decals include tractor markings.

**116-50532** Schneider

**116-50533** Werner

## 53' Trailer Accessories

**116-50132** 53' Trailer Floor (Use for Bowser Trailer & Kitbashing) **3.00**

**116-50133** Wabash Landing Gear **3.75**

**116-50134** Trailer & Container Tie Down Button Covers (etched brass) pkg(48) **3.00**

**116-50300** Rib Masking Tape **3.25**
Precut to exact size (.080 x .360") makes detail quick and easy. Just paint trailer silver, tape side ribs, apply finish color and remove for perfect detailing every time.

## 53' Plate Trailer

One of the most distinctive trailers on the rail or road today. Wabash National 53 x 102' Plate Trailers are used by Schneider, Werner, Heartland and others. Easy-to-assemble kit includes one-piece body with separate floor suspension wheels and landing gear.

### Undecorated 9.50 ea

**116-50127** All Button

**116-50140** No Button

**116-50141** Partial Button

### Undecorated Trailers w/Decals 14.95 ea

**116-50550** Schneider

**116-50551** Werner

### Painted White w/Silver Ribs 15.95 ea (Unless Noted)

Includes decals.

**116-50501** No Decals **13.95**

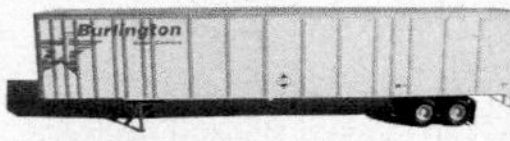

**116-50502** BN Decal (blue, red)

**116-50503** BN Decal (blue, black)

**116-50504** Alpis Decals

**116-50505** Heartland Decals

## 53' Reefer Trailer

This distinctive 7-1/2 corrugation side Utility Reefer Trailer is tooled from the original blueprints. Exquisite detail down to the last rivet. New utility landing gear, separate rear (swing style) door. Available with or without reefer and fuel tanks.

### Undecorated

**116-50154** Without Reefer & Tanks **10.95**

**116-50507** With Reefer & Tanks **12.95**

### With Decals 16.95 ea

116-50511

**116-50508** Werner

**116-50509** Stevens Transport

**116-50510** Market Transport

**116-50511** CR England

### Swing Reefer Door

**116-50157** pkg(2) **3.50**

## Fruehauf 40' "Z" Van pkg(2) 13.50 ea

One of the most widely used trailers in piggyback and road service, prototypes remained in production for years. Kits are molded in aluminum with separate tires, wheels, doorbars and other details. Each includes two undecorated trailers, complete instructions and list of correct decals.

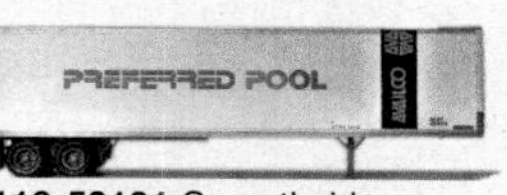


**116-50101** Smoothside
Later style, manufactured from 1979 to 1986.

**116-50102** Beaded Side
Manufactured from 1965 to 1978.

## 5' Van Extension

An easy conversion kit to model 40' trailers rebuilt into 45' units. This was a common method of extending the life of older trailers from about 1981 to 1984, and many are still in use. Use kit #50101, or complete conversion with trailer and extension #50116.

**116-50115** Extension Kit Only **3.25**

**116-50116** 40' Van w/Extension **10.00**

## Miscellaneous Trailers

All items listed are "Trucks N Stuff"

**116-101** Bottom-Dump Dirt Double Trailer w/Working Gates **12.95**

**116-105** 24' Flatbed Doubles Set (unpainted) **12.95**

**116-106** 24' Outside-Frame Flatbed Doubles w/Grain Hoppers **12.95**

**116-109** 28' 6" Hi-Cube Intermodal Smoothside Van **6.50**

**116-111** 48' Spread-Axle Flatbed **12.95**

**116-118** 53' Reefer Van w/Reefer Unit Undecorated **8.95**

**116-119** 53' Rivet-Side Dry Van Undecorated **8.95**

# DECAL SETS

A-Line decals are custom-designed to be prototypically correct and give excellent detail to all models. These decals are unique: they have more detail, different numbers and many decals will do one or more tractors and trailers per package.

## Safety Stripes

**116-50162** Red & White **3.50**
Improve visibility of any trailer preprinted in the right colors and size.

## 28' Parcel Decals 3.50 ea

Decals for one trailer only.

**116-50160** Parcel

**116-50161** RPS

## 28' Wedge Decals

Most contain decals for multiple tractors and trailers.

116-50203

116-50211  116-50221

116-50212

116-50213

**116-50203** Roadway & Roadway Express **5.85**
Decals are longer to fit correctly over ribs.

**116-50211** Yellow **4.85**

**116-50212** SAIA-28', 45', 48' & Bobtail **4.85**

**116-50213** G.O.D. 28', 48' **4.8**

**116-50221** Yellow (new '97) **4.85**

## Parcel Equipment

**116-50200** 28' Trailer, Container, Chassis, Tractor & Dolly **4.85**
**116-50201** 40' Drop Trailer, 45' Trailer, 48' Martrac Trailer **4.85**

## 53' Duraplate Trailer Decals

Includes tractor markings.
**116-50185** Schneider **4.50**
**116-50186** Werner **4.50**

## 53' Reefer Trailer Decal 4.85 ea

**116-50214** Werner
**116-50215** CR England
**116-50216** Stevens

**116-50220** Market Transport

## 53' Plate Trailer Decals 3.50 ea (Unless Noted)

Most contain decals for tractors and trailers.
**116-50163** Schneider **4.50**
**116-50164** Werner **4.50**
**116-50166** Burlington (blue, red)
**116-50167** Heartland
**116-50183** Burlington (blue/black)
**116-50184** Alpis

# FUEL TANKS

## Large Capacity pkg(4) 3.80 ea

**116-50107** Long
Contains two 150-gallon tractor fuel tanks and two 60" refrigerator fuel tanks.
**116-50108** Short
Contains two 120-gallon tractor fuel tanks and two 47" refrigerator fuel tanks.

## Large, Medium, Small Capacity pkg(8) 3.95 ea

Kits include parts to make small, medium and large tanks.
**116-50124** Tractor
**116-50125** Reefer Trailer

Decal 116-50167
Decal 116-50163
Decal 116-50164

# LANDING GEAR

## pkg(2) 3.75 ea (Unless Noted)

Common styles, molded in down position (trailers on flat cars or parked). Includes instructions to modify parts for up position (hitched to tractors). Each includes two sets of gears, with cross support and crank, molded in plastic.

116-50145
(Shown w/Fuel Tanks #116-50125)

**116-50111** Trailmobile
**116-50133** Wabash
**116-50144** Pines
**116-50145** Utility
**116-50030** Modern Square Pads **3.50**
**116-50031** Old-Style w/Wheels **3.50**

## Large Trailer Details

Ideal for superdetailing Accurail® or McKean 45', Walthers 48' or Bowser 53' trailers.

116-50122, 116-50142

**116-50122** Sliding Tandem Assembly (Leaf Spring) **3.75**
**116-50142** Air Hose-Trailer pkg(6) **3.25**
Use anywhere hose detail is needed.

# TRACTOR PARTS

**116-50008** Fifth Wheel Upgrade Kit **3.00**
**116-50020** COE Airdam pkg(2) **3.98**
**116-50021** Sleeper Wing pkg(2) **2.50**
**116-50050** Budd 2-Hole Front Wheels for Semi Tractors **3.50**
**116-50104** Vinyl Tires **4.50**
Contains 24 tires, use on virtually any model.

**116-50120** Delrin Vehicle Windshield Wipers pkg(8) **3.25**
**116-50123** Record/Document Boxes **3.25**
**116-50131** Tie-Down Chain (12") **3.50**
A must for holding open loads securely in place on flatbed trailers.

## Tractor Truck Sleepers 2.95 ea (Unless Noted)

**116-50010** Small – Short
**116-50011** Small – Tall
**116-50012** Large Flat Top
**116-50013** Small w/Window
**116-50014** Small w/Airdam
**116-50015** KW w/Airdam
**116-50016** Aero. Max w/Airdam
**116-50017** Small w/Wing **4.75**
**116-50018** Pete w/Wing **4.75**
**116-50019** Mack
**116-50020** COE Airdam pkg(2) **3.98**
**116-50021** Sleeper Wing pkg(2) **2.50**

## Mirrors

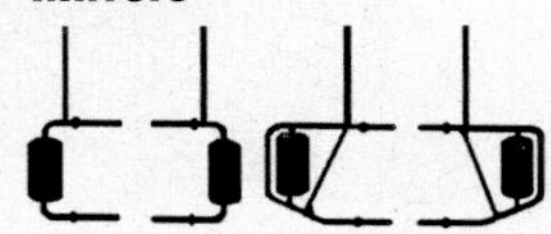

116-50152 116-50153

**116-50152** Straight pkg(4) **3.75**
**116-50153** Curved pkg(4) **3.75**
**116-50034** Mirrors Plastic Straight 5 Pair **4.95**

## Mud Flaps pkg(16) 3.25 ea

**116-50005** Plastic (white)
**116-50117** Vinyl (black)
**116-50118** Plastic (black)

## Reefer Units 3.95 ea (Unless Noted)

Highly detailed and true-to-prototype, these parts are a neat detail to convert box vans, trailers or containers into refrigerated units. Includes fuel tanks.

### Thermo King

**116-50135** Modern **6.59**
**116-50136** Old Style
**116-50137** Nose & Underbody

### Carrier

**116-50138** Old Style
**116-50139** Modern



## Trailer Dress-Up Kits 3.95 ea

Kits include four wheels, eight tires, two mud flaps, two axles, one adapter tube and one mud flap bracket.
**116-50119** Spoke Wheels
**116-50121** 2-Hole Disc Wheels

## Trailer Floors

**116-50132** 53' **3.00**
Fits A-Line, Bowser and Walthers.
**116-50159** 45' & 48' Universal Trailer Floor & Sliding Tandem **3.25**
Fits Front Range, McKean, Accurail, Walthers and Atlas.
**116-50002** 53' Universal Floor & Suspension **3.25**
Great for kitbashing.

## Tractors 10.95 ea

**116-50602** Roadway (color only)

## Rear Trailer Doors pkg(2) 3.50 ea

**116-50007** Swing Plate
**116-50110** Roll-Up 96" Wide
**116-50156** Roll-Up 102" Wide
**116-50157** Swing Reefer

## Front Tractor Wheels

Authentic replicas of wheels found on modern American trucks.

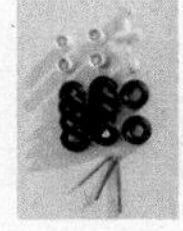

116-50105

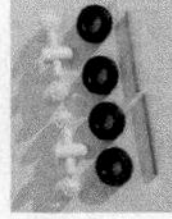

116-50106

**116-50105** Two-Hole Disc **4.50**
Includes two front and four driving (dual) wheels, 10 tires and axles.
**116-50106** Ten-Hole Front Wheels **3.50**
Includes four wheels, four tires and axles.

## Wheelsets

### 10-Hole Wheels & Tires

**116-50070** Includes 2 Front, 4 Rear Chrome **6.95**

### Early Dayton Spoke Wheels & Tires

**116-50071** Includes 2 Front, 2 Rear **4.85**

### 6-Hole Disc Wheels & Tires 4.85

Includes 2 front, 2 rear
**116-50072** 6 Lug
**116-50073** 10 Lug Includes 2 Front, 4 Rear **6.50**

### Mack Spoke Wheels & Tires

**116-50074** Includes 2 Front, 4 Rear **6.95**
**NEW 116-50076** Includes 2 Front, 4 Rear Mack Spoke 10-Hole (plain) **6.50**

### 5-Hole Disc Wheels & Tires

**116-50075** Includes 2 Front, 2 Rear (10 Lug) **6.95**

## Trailer Detail Kits

**116-50003** Upgrade Kit 2- Hole Disc Wheel **4.50**
**116-50103** Upgrade Kit-Spoke Wheels **4.50**
New tires, wheels and axles for two trailers, adaptable to virtually any model.
**116-50004** 2-Hole Disc Wheels/Axles pkg(8) **3.50**

**Limited Quantity Available**
**116-50151** Spoke Wheels and Axels pkg(8) **3.50**

## Trailer Parts

All items listed are "Trucks N Stuff"
**116-102** 2-Hole Rims w/Tires (white) **6.50**
**116-104** Trailer Dollies Complete Unit **4.95**
**116-107** Modern-Style Trailer Landing Legs pkg(2) **3.50**
**116-108** Fenders w/Mud Flaps(Over-Axle Mounting) pkg(2) **3.50**
**116-110** Trailer Subframes w/Mud Flaps(Over-Axle Mounting) pkg(2) **3.50**
**116-123** Rope Boxes pkg(4) **3.50**

Bright Russet Red 150-30000005

1914 18/32 w/Top Down 150-99087015

Specter Linens 150-99087062

Red 150-99087081

Skytint Blue 150-99087120
Color Shown Not Available

1996 Ford Taurus Medium Willow Green 150-1272

Ford F-150 Pick-Up Truck 150-1250

# NEW PRODUCTS

## Automobiles

### 1978 Ford® Fairmont Sedan 10.95 ea (Unless Noted)

**NEW 150-30000004** Black

**NEW 150-30000005** Bright Russet Red

**NEW 150-30000006** Dark Blue Metallic

**NEW 150-30000007** Light Chamois

**NEW 150-30000008** Silver Metallic

**NEW 150-30000003** Undecorated **8.95**

## Masterpiece Automotive Replicas

These accurate models feature collector's quality detail and authentic paint colors where applicable.

### Austro Daimler 16.95 ea

**NEW 150-99087010** 1914 18/32 w/Top Up

**NEW 150-99087015** 1914 18/32 w/Top Down

**NEW 150-99087020** 1908 28/35 w/Maja Engine

### White Walk-In Van 16.95 ea (Unless Noted)

**NEW 150-99087061** Miracle Bakery

**NEW 150-99087062** Specter Linens

**NEW 150-99087060** Undecorated **14.95**

### 2007 Jeep® Wrangler® Unlimited 4-Door 15.95 ea

**NEW 150-99087080** White

**NEW 150-99087081** Red

**NEW 150-99087082** Jeep Green

### 1936 Chrysler® Airflow Imperial Eight 15.95 ea

**NEW 150-99087120** Skytint Blue

**NEW 150-99087121** Harvard Maroon

**NEW 150-99087122** Gunmetal Gray

### Master Line® 48' Pines Trailers 13.95 ea (Unless Noted)

All decorated trailers are white with the indicated color graphics and markings.

**NEW 150-20000038** CSX #613055 (blue, black)

**NEW 150-20000039** CSX #613179 (blue, black)

**NEW 150-20000040** CSX #613800 (blue, black)

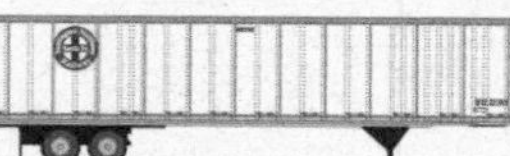

**NEW 150-20000041** BNSF #221759 (blue, green)

**NEW 150-20000042** BNSF #221805 (blue, green)

**NEW 150-20000043** BNSF #221963 (blue, green)

**NEW 150-20000044** TIP Intermodal #228018 (red, black)

**NEW 150-20000045** TIP Intermodal #228061 (red, black)

**NEW 150-20000046** TIP Intermodal #228067 (red, black)

**NEW 150-20000047** Thoroughbred Distribution (NS) #613274 (black)

**NEW 150-20000048** Thoroughbred Distribution (NS) #613550 (black)

**NEW 150-20000049** Thoroughbred Distribution (NS) #613856 (black)

**NEW 150-20000050** Redon #229025 (black)

**NEW 150-20000051** Redon #624805 (black)

**NEW 150-20000052** Redon #814378 (black)

**NEW 150-20000037** Undecorated **9.95**

# AUTOMOBILES

### 1996 Ford Taurus 9.50 ea (Unless Noted)

Add modern vehicles to your highways with these 1996 Ford Taurus Four-Door Sedans. Cars come completely assembled and feature clear window glazing and black tires.

**150-1271** Moonlight Blue

**150-1272** Medium Willow Green

**150-1273** Charcoal Green

**150-1274** Rose Mist

**150-1275** Toreador Red

**150-1276** Vibrant White

**150-1277** Ebony

**150-1278** Iris Frost

**150-1279** Light Saddle

**150-1280** Midnight Red

**150-1281** Pacific Green

**NEW 150-1283** Taxi

**150-1270** Undecorated **6.50**

# TRUCKS

## Ford F-150 Pick-Up Trucks

Models feature side mirrors.

### With Standard Sides

**Solid Colors 9.95 ea (Unless Noted)**

**150-1241** Black

**150-1243** Pacific Green

**150-1244** Dark Red

**150-1245** Tan

**150-1240** Undecorated **6.95**

**Two-Tone Colors 10.95 ea**

**150-1247** Green & Tan

**150-1248** Red & Tan

### With Flared Sides 9.95 ea

**150-1261** Black

**150-1263** Pacific Green

**150-1265** Tan

**Limited Quantity Available**

**150-1266** White

## Ford LNT9000 Tractor 8.95 ea

Based on the common prototype of the 1984 Ford LNT9000 tractor, each features details including seats, steering wheels and rubber tires. This is an officially licensed Ford product.

**150-1221** Black

**150-1222** Dark Blue

**150-1223** Medium Blue

**150-1224** Green

**150-1228** Yellow

## 45' Pines Trailer 14.95 ea (Unless Noted)

Each 45' Pines trailer includes two landing gears (fully extended or retracted,) rubber tires and prototypical lettering schemes and numbers.

**150-1200** Undecorated **9.95**

**Limited Quantity Available**

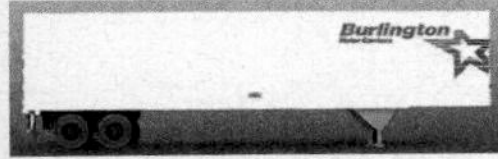


**150-12012** Burlington Motor Carriers #2 **12.95**

**150-12014** Burlington Motor Carriers

**150-12034** CSX #4 **11.95**

**NEW 150-12055** NS #235222 **11.95**

**NEW 150-12056** NS #235298 **11.95**

**NEW 150-12104** BN #931374 (Cascade Green) **11.95**

**NEW 150-12144** ATSF #25148 (white, blue) **11.95**

**NEW 150-12201** Kankakee, Beaverville, & Southern #UPSZ 852071 (white, black)

**NEW 150-12202** Kankakee, Beaverville, & Southern #UPSZ 852123 (white, black)

**NEW 150-12203** Redon #REDZ 930256 (grey, black, green, white)

**NEW 150-12204** Redon #REDZ 930313 (grey, black, green, white)

**NEW 150-12205** ATSF #SFTZ 630288 (white, blue)

**NEW 150-12206** ATSF #SFTZ 730135 (white, blue)

**NEW 150-12207** Transamerica #REAZ 638400 (white, black, red, blue)

**NEW 150-12208** Transamerica #REAZ 638453 (white, black, red, blue)

**NEW 150-12209** UP #230111 (white, black)

**NEW 150-12210** UP #230259 (white, black)

**NEW 150-12211** Vermont Railway #VTRZ 738164 (white, green, black)

**NEW 150-12212** Vermont Railway #VTRZ 738225 (white, green, black)

**NEW 150-12213** Xtra #CFKZ #250513 (white, red, yellow, black)

**NEW 150-12214** Xtra #CFKZ #251954 (white, red, yellow, black)

**NEW 150-12217** Kankakee, Beaverville & Southern #634037 (white, black, green) **11.95**

**NEW 150-12218** Kankakee, Beaverville & Southern #634292 (white, black, green) **11.95**

**NEW 150-12222** Transamerica #REAZ 654624 (white, black, red, blue) **11.95**

**NEW 150-12224** Vermont Railway #VTRZ 236471 (white, green) **11.95**

**NEW 150-12226** Xtra #653641 (white, red, yellow, blue) **11.95**

## 20' TANK CONTAINER TRAILERS

**147-7710** Yellow **8.95**
Includes UP decals, with trailer parts molded in yellow.

**147-7720** Blue **8.95**

**147-7800** BNSF Tank Container & Chassis Kit **12.95**

**147-7810** UP Tank Container and Trailer **12.95**

### Trailer Details

**147-7715** Fender & Walkway Kit **2.95**

## EXTENDIBLE CHASSIS KITS

Extendible Chassis Kits
147-7730 and 7740 shown; container sold separately.

### Single Chassis 7.50 ea

**147-7730** Yellow - OOCL & UP

**147-7740** Black - APL, Maersk, Matson, Evergreen, Genstar, Flexi-Van

### Three-Packs 17.95 ea

**147-7733** Yellow - OOCL & UP

**147-7743** Black - APL, Maersk, Matson, Evergreen, Genstar, Flexi-Van

### Container Chassis Decals

**147-6230** For Walthers Container Chassis **3.50**

NEW SUPPLIER

## NEW PRODUCTS

### Fresh Cherries™ American Autos

Set the scene on 1970s and 80s era layouts with this collection of affordable, assembled American autos! Based on work-a-day "grocery getters," these were the cars seen everywhere, from city freeways to small town side streets. Each comes fully assembled from diecast parts with a full interior, window glazing (some have open driver's-side windows), chrome parts as appropriate, and rubber tires, plus each is prepainted in a variety of authentic colors (actual color may vary from models shown). All models come on a display base so they're ideal for collections too.

### American Motors Corp. 4.50 ea

**NEW 467-8002** 1974 Gremlin

**NEW 467-8003** 1978 Pacer

**NEW 467-8007** 1974 Hornet

### Ford 4.50 ea

**NEW 467-8001** 1977 Pinto

**NEW 467-8004** 1981 Escort

**NEW 467-8005** 1984 Tempo

**NEW 467-8008** 1971 Mustang Sportsroof

### Mercury

**NEW 467-8006** 1975 Bobcat **4.50**

### Forgotten Classics

**NEW 467-73960** pkg(6) **19.99**
Detail a street in seconds with this set of six cars including a '77 Pinto, '74 Gremlin, '78 Pacer, '81 Escort, '84 Tempo and '75 Bobcat.

IMPORTED FROM GERMANY BY WALTHERS

Highways and streets come to life instantly with these detailed models of American and European vehicles. All types of cars, trucks, buses and emergency equipment are offered. Each is fully assembled from plastic parts, with authentic markings where appropriate. Check out the models with working lights for your layout or collection too!

## NEW PRODUCTS

Vehicles denoted as CMD Collection feature handpainted detailing and fine printing for added realism.

### Automobiles

#### Audi

**NEW 189-49220** A4 Sedan **13.99**

**NEW 189-49222** A4 Limousine Fahrschule **16.99**

**NEW 189-49270** A6 Avant **13.99**

#### Benz-Patent

**NEW 189-40003** 1886 Motorwagen w/Display Box **28.99**

#### Borgward

**NEW 189-43151** Isabella Cabrio Rhein Tour Koblenz w/Display Box **33.99**

#### Ford

**NEW 189-47409** Probe 24 V Ninja **13.99**

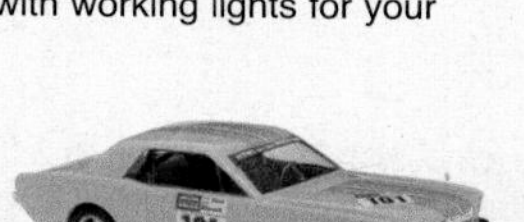

**NEW 189-47557** Ford Mustang Historic Tour #101 **18.99**

#### Mercedes-Benz

**NEW 189-41558** 170V Sternquell **13.99**

**NEW 189-43605** C-Klasse Elegance CMD **21.99**

**NEW 189-43610** C-Klasse Avantgarde CMD **21.99**

**NEW 189-44806** 300 Konrad Adenauer w/Display Box **26.99**

**NEW 189-46300** GL-Klasse Avantgarde CMD **14.99**

**NEW 189-46810** W123 T Modell Rhein-Tour Koln w/Display Box **33.99**

**NEW 189-46853** W123 Rhein-Tour Manheim w/Display Box **33.99**

**NEW 189-46854** W123 Limo w/Camper Trailer **26.99**

**NEW 189-49700** R Klasse Standard **14.99**

#### Messerschmitt

**NEW 189-48806** KR 200 Kundendienst **12.99**

#### Morgan

**NEW 189-47110** Plus 8 Cabrio Rhein Tour Bingen **33.99**

#### Multicar

**NEW 189-42206** DB Bahnsteigreinigung **18.99**

#### Opel

**NEW 189-42100** Kadett C **18.99**

**NEW 189-42104** Kadett C Rhein Tour Mainz **33.99**

#### Renault

**NEW 189-46506** 4CV St. Raphael **16.99**

**NEW 189-46507** 4CV Ricard **16.99**

**NEW 189-46508** 4CV Cinzano **16.99**

#### Smart

##### Fortwo

**NEW 189-46105** 2007 Coupe CMD **21.99**

**NEW 189-46185** Gold Smart **21.99**

**NEW 189-46186** Sternquell **16.99**

**NEW 189-48965** Towing & Salvage Service (German) **19.99**

**NEW 189-48992** Flowers **18.99**

**NEW 189-48993** Hessischer Rundfunk **16.99**

**NEW 189-48996** Scratch Black **14.99**

**NEW 189-1133** Tarp-Covered Fortwo pkg(6) **9.99**
Six tarps molded to look like covered Smart Fortwos. Park them on streets or in driveways, or use them as a load on an auto rack car or truck.

##### Fortwo Cabrio

**NEW 189-46175** 2007 Cabrio CMD **21.99**

**NEW 189-48974** Zebra **13.99**

##### Forfour

**NEW 189-49504** Blaupunkt **17.99**

##### Roadster

**NEW 189-49304** Collector's Edition (silver, graphite) **16.99**

**NEW 189-49307** MB Stern **16.99**

#### Tempo

**NEW 189-40647** Dreirad Hanseat Castrol Oil **11.99**

IMPORTED FROM GERMANY BY WALTHERS

## Emergency Vehicles

### Automobiles

#### Audi

**A4 Avant**

**NEW 189-49273** Feuerwehr Kaufbeuren **20.99**

**A6**

**NEW 189-49603** Sedan Bavarian Police **21.99**

**NEW 189-49652** Avant Notarzt Schwelm **20.99**

#### Ford

**Crown Victoria**

**NEW 189-49017** Baltimore Police **13.99**

**NEW 189-49018** Baltimore Sheriff **13.99**

#### Mercedes-Benz

**C-Klasse**

**NEW 189-49169** Feuerwehr Hamiln Limited Edition w/Display Box **31.99**

**E-Klasse**

**NEW 189-49457** T-Model DRK Reutlingen **19.99**

**NEW 189-49460** T-Model Admont Fire/Rescue **21.99**

**NEW 189-49461** T-Model Police (German) **18.99**

**NEW 189-49462** Feuerwehr Trier (German) **19.99**

**W123**

**NEW 189-46851** Baden-Wurttemberg Police **19.99**

**NEW 189-46852** Feuerwehr Bremen **19.99**

#### Opel

**NEW 189-42103** Kadett C Feuerwehr Dortmund **19.99**

#### Smart

**Fortwo**

**NEW 189-48966** Ordnungsamt (City Services, German) **16.99**

**NEW 189-48988** Wien Police (German) **19.99**

**NEW 189-48989** Feuerwehr Lindau (German) **18.99**

### Trucks

#### American-LaFrance

**NEW 189-46026** Pumper Baltimore City Fire Department **28.99**

**NEW 189-46027** Ladder Truck Baltimore City Fire Department **39.99**

#### Ford

**NEW 189-41826** E-350 Baltimore City Ambulance **19.99**

#### Mercedes-Benz

**NEW 189-40782** LP809 Aerial Ladder Truck Bad Camberg Fire Brigade **19.99**

#### Multicar

**NEW 189-42204** Berufsfeuerwehr Brandenburg **18.99**

### SUVs

#### Mercedes-Benz

**NEW 189-48522** M-Klasse Notarzt Nordvorpommern **19.99**

**NEW 189-48540** M Klasse First Responder FW Helfendorf (Metallic) **21.99**

### Vans

#### Dodge

**NEW 189-44655** Ram Van Baltimore City Fire Department **16.99**

#### Mercedes

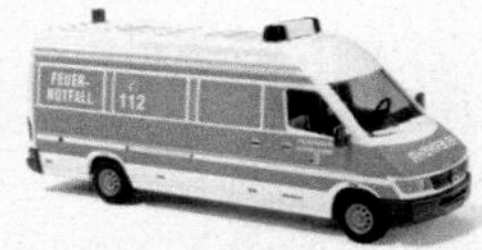

**NEW 189-47835** Sprinter Van Dusseldorf Fire Brigade Emergency **16.99**

#### Peugeot

**NEW 189-47386** Boxer BRK Wasserwacht **16.99**

**NEW** Ford Crown Victoria Baltimore Police 189-49017

**NEW** Ford Crown Victoria Baltimore Sheriff 189-49018

**NEW** American-LaFrance Pumper Baltimore City Fire Department 189-46026

**NEW** American-LaFrance Ladder Truck Baltimore City Fire Department 189-46027

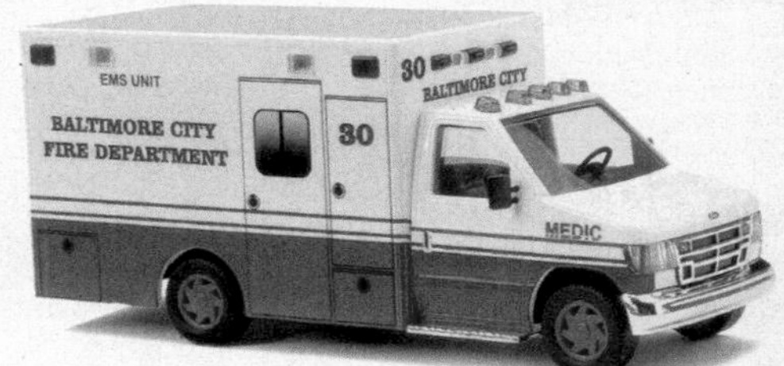


**NEW** Ford E-350 Baltimore City Ambulance 189-41826

**NEW** Dodge Van Ram Van Baltimore City Fire Department 189-44655

IMPORTED FROM GERMANY BY WALTHERS

## Trailer

**NEW 189-44915** German Police **11.99**

## Buses

### GMC TDH-5301 "Fishbowl" City Bus

**NEW 189-44504** Teen Pregnancy Information Campaign Bus **41.99**

**NEW 189-44533** Edmonton, Alberta w/Environment Conservation Graphics **43.99**

**NEW 189-44534** Baltimore, MD **43.99**

## Racing Cars

### Auto Union

**NEW 189-46904** Type C #18 Eifelrennen 1936, Bernd Rosemeyer w/Display Box **23.99**

### BMW

**NEW 189-40304** 3.5 CSL Rennwagen #42 **33.99**

**NEW 189-40305** 3.5 CSL #43 **33.99**

### Mercedes-Benz

**NEW 189-47007** Silberpfeil W196 #8 Grober Preis v Holland 1955, J.M.Fangio **23.99**

## Taxis

### Citroen

**NEW 189-48009** DS 19 Taxi **13.99**

### Mercedes-Benz

**NEW 189-48542** M-Klasse Taxi **15.99**

### Smart

**NEW 189-48997** City Coupe Taxi **18.99**

## Trucks

### Chevrolet

#### 1950 Pickup

**NEW 189-48222** Aspinwall, Pennsylvania, Department of Public Works **15.99**

**NEW 189-48224** Louis Diner w/Motorcycle **24.99**

**NEW 189-48200128** With Motorcycle Unlettered (black, orange) **24.99**

### Iveco

**NEW 189-47920** Daily Sternquell **21.99**

**NEW 189-47975** Daily Claus' Fruits & Vegetables w/Load **18.99**

### Mercedes-Benz

**NEW 189-40783** LP809 Beverage Truck Sternquell **18.99**

**NEW 189-41556** 170V Pick-Up w/Load Basinus Quelle Mineral Water **13.99**

### Monster Trucks

**NEW 189-48984** Smart Forfun **33.99**

### Toyota

#### Land Cruiser

**NEW 189-43005** Zebra **18.99**

**NEW 189-43006** Weathered w/Roof Rack **23.99**

**NEW 189-43007** With Rooftop Tent **24.99**

#### Land Cruiser HZJ

**NEW 189-43500** HZ J 78 (white) **16.99**

**NEW** GMC Fishbow City Bus Teen Pregnancy Information Campaign Bus 189-44504

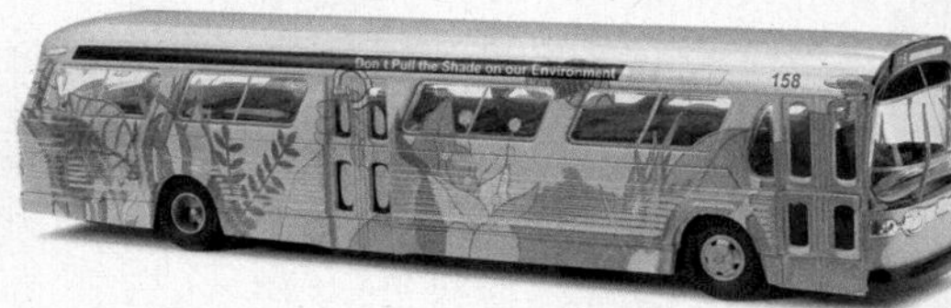

**NEW** GMC Fishbow City Bus Edmonton, Alberta w/Environment Conservation Graphics 189-44533

**NEW** GMC Fishbow City Bus Baltimore, MD 189-44534

**NEW** Toyota Land Cruiser Weathered w/Roof Rack 189-43006

**NEW** Motorcycles Trike w/Trailer & Motorcycle 189-1152

## Vans

### Citroen

**NEW 189-41954** H Van Orangina **13.99**

**NEW 189-41955** H Van Du Tilleul **13.99**

### Fiat

**NEW 189-47334** Ducato Spielothek **15.99**

### Motorcycles

**NEW 189-1152** Trike w/Trailer & Motorcycle **24.99**

### Trailers

**NEW 189-44980** Aluminum Camping Trailer **16.99**

IMPORTED FROM GERMANY BY WALTHERS

## Farm Equipment

### Tractors

#### Fortschritt

**NEW 189-42801** ZT 300 NVA **22.99**

**NEW 189-42810** ZT 303 **21.99**

**NEW 189-42820** Fortschritt/Hangtraktor ZT 305 **23.99**

**NEW 189-42830** ZT 304 w/Sternquell Trailer **26.99**

### Trailer

**NEW 189-44916** Anhänger LPG **9.99**

### Vehicles w/Working Lights

**NEW 189-5640** Mercedes-Benz M Klasse **23.99**

**NEW 189-5654** Chevrolet Caprice (Metallic) **22.99**

**NEW 189-5655** Chevy Blazer SUV **22.99**

## AUTOMOBILES

### 3 Packs 19.99 ea

**189-5994** European 1950s

**189-5995** European 1960s

**189-5996** European 1980s

**189-5997** American 1950s

**189-6000** European 1930s

**189-6001** American 1970s Includes Dodge Monaco four-door sedan, Cadillac limousine and Trans-Am two-door hardtop.

### Audi A4

**189-49200** 4-Door Sedan **11.99**

**189-49225** 2005 A4 4-Door Sedan **19.99**

**189-49250** 2001 Avant A4 Station Wagon **10.99**

**189-49255** 2001 Avant A4 Station Wagon (Metallic) **19.99**

**189-49275** 2005 Avant Station Wagon **19.99**

### A6

**189-49600** 2005 4-Door Sedan **14.99**

**189-49601** DVS Quattro (Metallic) **19.99**

**189-49605** 4-Door Limousine **21.99**

**189-49650** Avant **13.99**

**189-49655** Baujahr 2004 CMD Collection **21.99**

### BMW

**189-40200** 1938 327 2-Door Hardtop Coupe **20.99**

**NEW** Trailers Aluminum Camping Trailer 189-44980

**NEW** Chevy Blazer SUV 189-5655

#### 1938 327 2-Door

**189-40201** Hardtop Coupe **15.99**

**189-40255** 1938 327 Convertible w/Top Down **20.99**

#### 3.5 CSL 2-Door

**189-40300** Black **22.99**

**189-40301** White **22.99**

### Borgward

#### 1958 Isabella

**189-43100** 1957 Isabella 2-Door Hardtop Coupe **13.99**

**189-43101** Coupe (metallic paint) **14.99**

**189-43102** Isabella 2-Door Hardtop Coupe **13.99**

**189-43150** 2-Door Convertible **13.99**

### Bentley

**189-44411** Convertible Coupe, Top Down **9.99**

### Benz-Patent

**189-40002** Bertha Benz at the Drugstore **25.99** Includes 1886 Benz-Patent Motorwagen, figure, sign and display case.

### Buick

**189-44706** 1950 Sedan Limousine **11.99**

**189-44719** Crazy Car **14.99**

IMPORTED FROM GERMANY BY WALTHERS

**Limited Quantity Available**

**189-44717** 1952 2-Door Hardtop Street Rod **11.99**

## Cadillac

### 1952 Coupe Deville

**189-43416** 2-Door Hardtop **11.99**

### 1959 EL Dorado Two-Door

**189-45110** Pink **11.99**

### 1970 "Woody" Station Wagon

**189-42906 13.99**

**189-42909** 1970 Station Wagon Harvey's Charter Fishing Boats **18.99**

## Chevrolet

### 1957 Bel Air

**189-45003** Coupe **12.99**

**189-45007** Convertible - Top Down **12.99**

**189-45014** Crazy Car "Royal Toy" **14.99**

### Caprice

**189-47601** 1995 Classic **10.99**

### 1956 Corvette

**189-45405** Convertible–Top Up **12.99**

**189-45406** Convertible w/Top Down **13.99**

**189-45407** Convertible w/Top Up "American Graffiti" **13.99**

## Citroen

### AX

**189-45602** Two-Door Hardtop w/Sunroof **7.99**

### DS 19

**189-48000** Plain **11.99**

**189-48001** Two-Color **12.99**

## Dodge

### Monaco

**189-46603** Four-Door Sedan **10.99**

## Fiat

### 500 F 2 door

**189-48700** 1965 **11.99**

**189-48705** 500 "Fiat" **12.99**

## Ford

### Crown Victoria

**189-49000** Sedan (red) **11.99**

### 1935 Eifel Convertible

**189-41201** Top Down **10.99**

### Escort

**189-45700** Four-Door Hardtop **8.99**

**189-45707** Two-Door Convertible-Top Down, Metallic **11.99**

### 1964 Mustang 12.99 ea (Unless Noted)

**189-47500** Convertible-Top Down

**189-47501** Convertible-Top Up

**189-47507** Convertible "Stars & Stripes" **14.99**

**189-47550** 2-Door Hardtop **13.99**

### Probe

**189-47403** Metallic **11.99**

### 1956 Thunderbird Convertible 11.99 ea

**189-45210** Top Down

**189-45211** with/Top Up

## Horsh

**189-41309** 853 Convertible **13.99**

## MG Midget TC

**189-45907** Convertible **13.99**

1950 Buick Limousine 189-44706

1957 Bel Air Convertible 189-45007

Ford 2-Door Hardtop 189-47550

## Mercedes-Benz

### 170V

**189-41409** Four-Door Sedan **8.99**

### 300 SL

**189-40800** Coupe **9.99**

**189-40508** 170S Convertible (top up) **11.99**

### 1960s 300 Limousine 220 SE

**189-40420** Four-Door Hardtop w/Closed Sunroof **10.99**

### 1977 W 123

**189-46800** T-Model Station Wagon **11.99**

**189-46805** T-Model Station Wagon (metallic blue) **21.99**

**189-46855** W123 CMD Collection **21.99**

### A-Klasse

**189-48600** Classic **10.99**

**189-48601** Avantgarde w/Ope Sunroof (Metallic Blue) **12.99**

### C-Klasse

**189-49100** 2000 W203 4-Doo Sedan (blue) **11.99**

**189-49120** 4-Door Sedan **19.99**

**189-49155** T-Model Station Wagon "Designo Line" **20.99**

IMPORTED FROM GERMANY BY WALTHERS

### CLK Cabrio

**189-49400** 2003 Convertible w/Top Down **12.99**

**189-49405** 2003 Convertible **21.99**

### E-Klasse

**189-49450** 2003 T-Model Station Wagon **11.99**

**189-49455** 2003 T-Model Station Wagon **20.99**

### GL Klasse

**189-46305** CMD Collection **21.99**

### M-Klasse

**189-48530** 4-Door **12.99**

**189-48535** Restyled 2001 M-Class ML 500 4-Door (metallic paint, chrome trim) **21.99**

**189-48570** ML 55 AMG SUV **13.99**

**189-49805** 2005 CMD Collection **20.99**

**189-49810** 2005 W164 **14.99**

### R Klasse

**189-49705** CMD Collection **21.99**

## Messerschmitt

### Kabinroller KR 200 3-Wheeler 11.99 ea (Unless Noted)

**189-48800** 1955 KR 200 **10.99**

**189-48803** "Castrol"

**189-48804** Kabenroller KR 200 3-Wheel Subcompact "Just Married"

**189-48805** 1955 KR 200 "Kabinenroller" Subcompact 3-Wheeler "Franck"

## Morgan Plus 8 11.99 ea

**189-47104** Metallic

**Limited Quantity Available**

**189-47107** "Rallye" Race Car

## NSU

**189-48400** 1965 TT Two-Door Hardtop **9.99**

## Opel

**189-42050** 1967 Commodore 4-Door Sedan (metallic) **13.99**

**189-42105** 1977 Kadett C CMD Collection **18.99**

**189-42000** Rekor D Model C 1966 4-Door Sedan **12.99**

**189-41100** 1938 Olympia Two-Door **10.99**

## Plymouth

**189-46651** Fury 4-Door Sedan **10.99**

## Pontiac

### 1973 Firebird Trans Am

**189-41705** 2-Door Hardtop **11.99**

**189-41706** Crazy Car w/Hood Scoop **11.99**

## Puch

### Steyr Puch 500

**189-48750** **11.99**

**189-48755** 500 EHW Elfisches Hilfswerk Limited-Edition Diorama **26.99**

## Renault

**189-42500** R5 **7.99**

**189-46500** 1946 4 CV 4-Door Compact Sedan **11.99**

**189-46501** 4CV 2-Door Sedan Delivery "Arbeille" **14.99**

**189-46504** 4CV 2-Door Sedan Delivery "Picon" **14.99**

**189-46505** 4CV Postes **14.99**

## Rolls Royce

**189-44415** Silver Cloud III, Metallic **12.99**

## Smart

### City Coupe

**189-48900** **11.99**

**189-48901** 2-Door Subcompact **12.99**

**189-48902** 2002 "Facelift" **12.99**

**189-48907** With Bike Rack & Bike **13.99**

**189-48918** Subcompact 2-Door Hardtop City Coupe w/Ski Rack, Skis & Snowman **13.99**

**189-48923** "Der Flotter Feger" City Sanitation Vehicle **15.99**

**189-48925** "Numeric Blue" **16.99**

**189-48936** Street Cleaning Vehicle (German) "Mist Mobil" **20.99**

IMPORTED FROM GERMANY BY WALTHERS

### City Coupe 18.99 ea (Unless Noted)

**189-48940** Conny's Party Service

**189-48944** With "Clevertrailer" **19.99**

**189-48945** Schweizer Zoll

**189-48948** "Herzen" w/Trailer & Heart Locket **24.99**

**189-48949** Bundeswehr (Metallic) **16.99**

**189-48950** Stork Funeral Service (German) **16.99**

**189-48951** "Fulda Reifen"

**189-48954** Swisscom w/Clevertrailer **24.99**

**189-48955** "Sinalco" 100th Anniversary w/Trailer **24.99**

**189-48960** German Post Express **16.99**

**189-48961** Pizzaladen w/Clevertrailer **25.99**

**189-48962** Streckenerkundung

**189-48964** Circus Roncalli **16.99**

**189-48967** Mr. Brown Coffee-Drink **16.99**

### Fortwo Cabrio Convertible

**189-48970** 1999 2-Door Subcompact Convertible w/Top Down (gray, black) **12.99**

**189-48971** Förstina-Sprudel **17.99**

**189-48972** "Trio Trans" **16.99**

**189-48973** Top Down **16.99**

**189-48975** Top Down Scharr **16.99**

### Crossblade Convertible

**189-48985** 2002 w/Open Cockpit **14.99**

**189-48986** "Overnight" **19.99**

**189-48963** ProChrist Mobil **17.99**

**189-48969** "Fusball" (Soccer/Football) **14.99**

**189-48987** Fleurop **16.99**

### 2003 Roadster

**189-49300** Convertible w/Top Down (red, black) **14.99**

Toyota Land Cruiser J4 Hardtop
189-43000

**189-49302** Metallic **16.99**

**189-49303** Crazy Car Metallic **18.99**

**189-49305** Top Down **23.99**

**189-49350** Coupe (yellow, black) **14.99**

**189-49351** "Smart" **18.99**

**189-49352** Coupe "Europcar" Metallic **16.99**

**189-49355** Hardtop **23.99**

**Limited Quantity Available**

**189-49301** "Party" **16.99**

### 2004 Forfour

**189-49500** Silver, Gray **14.99**

**189-49505** 4-Door Hardtop **21.99**

### Tempo

**189-40644** Dreirad "Honig-Lieferwagen" w/Cover and Barrel Load **11.99**

### Toyota

**1960 Land Cruiser J4**
**189-43000** Hardtop **22.99**

### Volvo

**189-43906** 544 Two-Door Hardtop **12.99**

## BIKES & SCOOTERS

**189-6013** 2 Vespa Scooters, 6 Bikes & 2 Bike Riders **10.99**

IMPORTED FROM GERMANY BY WALTHERS

# BUSES

## GMC TDH-5301 "Fishbowl" City Bus

Introduced in 1959, these buses were popular with transit agencies across North America. Many of these veterans still haul passengers in city service or for private operators.

**189-44500** Green **29.99**

**189-44501** Red **29.99**

**189-44503** Niagara Express **33.99**

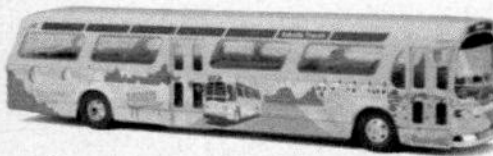

**189-44530** Oakville (Ontario) **43.99**

**189-44531** Markham (Ontario) **43.99**

**189-44532** Santa Monica (California) **41.99**

**189-44552** York Bus Service **34.99**

## Mercedes-Benz

**189-41035** Swiss Postal Bus (PTT) **16.99**

**189-41045** Mercedes Benz O-3500 Travel Bus **14.99**

See What's Available at

**www.walthers.com**

## Renault

**189-47200** R312 Paris 13. Version **35.99**

# CONSTRUCTION EQUIPMENT

**189-47332** Wide Load Escort Fiat Ducato Van w/Reflective Warning Signs **15.99**

# EMERGENCY VEHICLES

## Fire Department Set

Item listed below is available by Special Order (see Legend Page).

**189-49924** Berlin City **47.99**
Includes one each: VW Passat Wagon, Iveco Daily Van and Mecedes LP 809 Equipment Truck with authentic Berlin markings, in a special presentation box.

## Audi

### A4

#### 4 Door Sedan

**189-49201** Audi A4 4-Door Sedan Bavarian Police **11.99**

**189-49205** German Red Cross **12.99**

**Limited Quantity Available**

**189-49203** Bayern, Germany, Police Department **16.99**

#### Avant Station Wagon

**189-49262** Malteser Notarzt (German) **18.99**

**189-49271** BRK Notarzt (German) **22.99**

**189-49272** Feuerwehr Idar-Oberstein **18.99**

**Limited Quantity Available**

**189-49251** 4-Door Hatchback Polizei Bayern **11.99**

**189-49252** Baden Württemberg, Germany, Police Department **16.99**

**189-49264** Fire (German) **15.99**

#### 2005 A6 4-Door Sedan

**189-49602** Safety Car **21.99**

## Chevrolet

### Caprice 4-Door Sedan

**189-47621** "Area 51 Police" w/Alien Figure **13.99**

**189-47623** San Francisco Police Dept. D.A.R.E Unit **15.99**

**189-47626** Honolulu, Hawaii Police **14.99**

GMC TDH-5301 Fishbowl City Bus Niagara Express 189-44503

**189-47627** Goderich (Ontario) Police **14.99**

**189-47682** Iowa State Patrol #23 (silver) **12.99**

**189-47684** Massachusetts State Police (two-tone blue) **12.99**

**189-47685** Arkansas State Police (white) **12.99**

**189-47686** Maine State Police **12.99**

**189-47688** Louisiana State Police No. 39 **13.99**

**189-47689** Alabama State Trooper **13.99**

**189-47690** Vermont State Police **13.99**

**189-47691** North Carolina Highway Patrol **14.99**

**189-47692** Washington State Patrol **14.99**

**Limited Quantity Available**

**189-47625** York Fire Dept. **11.99**

### Blazer 4-Door SUV

**189-46405** With Horse Trailer NYPD **21.99**

## Chrysler

### Voyager Minivan

**189-44621** "Stadtfeuerwehr Attnang" (Fire Dept.) **16.99**

**189-44654** Fire Dept. (German) **14.99**

## Dodge

### Monaco 4-Door Sedan

**189-46675** Idaho State Patrol **13.99**

## Ford

### Crown Victoria 12.99 ea (Unless Noted)

**189-49010** Sheriff D.A.R.E. Unit **15.99**

**189-49015** Springfield Police **14.99**

IMPORTED FROM GERMANY BY WALTHERS

**189-49016** Molalla Police (Oregon) **14.99**

**189-49075** Wisconsin State Patrol #22

**189-49077** Montana Highway Patrol (dark blue)

**189-49079** North Dakota State Police

**189-49080** Wyoming Highway Patrol

**189-49081** South Carolina Highway Patrol No. 36

**189-49082** Kentucky State Police No. 38

**189-49083** New Mexico State Police No. 40

**189-49085** West Virginia State Police **13.99**

**189-49086** Connecticut State Police **13.99**

**189-49087** Rhode Island State Police **13.99**

**Limited Quantity Available**

**189-49014** Grand Prairie, Texas, Police **13.99**

## E-350 Ambulance

**189-41812** Mercy Medical Services Paramedic **16.99**

**189-41818** Plano, Texas Fire Rescue **21.99**

**Limited Quantity Available**

**189-41819** German Red Cross, Fulda District **19.99**

## Mercedes-Benz

### 170V 4-Door Sedan

**189-41421** Berlin Fire Brigade **10.99**

**189-41422** Heppenheim Fire Dept. (German) **13.99**

### A-Klasse

**189-48616** AvD Metallic **19.99**

### C-Klasse

**Sedan**

**189-49108** German Police Rhineland-Palatinate **17.99**

**189-49110** Berlin Police (German) **18.99**

**189-49111** Police (German) **17.99**

**T-Model Station Wagon**

**189-49156** Autobahnpolizei **17.99**

**189-49163** Green, Metallic Silver **16.99**

**189-49164** T-Model Station Wagon German Red Cross **14.99**

**Limited Quantity Available**

**189-49151** T-Model Station Wagon Wurttemberg Police **14.99**

**189-49157** Lippstadt Fire Dept. **13.99**

**189-49165** Dornier Werksfeuerwehr **15.99**

### E Klasse

**189-49454** Berlin Police (German) **20.99**

**189-49458** German Red Cross Emergency Doctor **20.99**

**189-49463** Technical Help Service (German) **16.99**

**Limited Quantity Available**

**189-49456** Hamburg Germany Police (Metallic Silver, blue) **17.99**

### M-Klasse

**Limited Quantity Available**

**189-48520** Dinslaken Fire Notarzt (German) **17.99**

**189-48534** Malteser Emergency Services **16.99**

### W123 4-Door Station Wagon

**189-46806** Baden Württemberg Police **16.99**

**189-46809** Fire Pfungstadt **16.99**

### Sprinter Van

**Limited Quantity Available**

**189-47829** ITW Thuringen **15.99**

**189-47830** WMF (German) **13.99**

## Plymouth

### Fury

**189-46654** Niagara Falls Fire **14.99**

## Puch

**189-48750** Steyr Puch 500 Feldbach, Austria Fire Brigade **11.99**

**189-48756** 500 Gendarmerie **13.99**

## Smart

### 2-Door City Coupe

**189-48929** Hamburg Police **17.99**

**189-48933** English Police **17.99**

**189-48939** "First Responder" **16.99**

IMPORTED FROM GERMANY BY WALTHERS

**189-48959** City Coupe Technical Help Service (THW) **14.99**

**189-49502** Forfour First Responder **18.99**

**Limited Quantity Available**

**189-48922** City Coupe 2-Door ASB **15.99**

## Buses

### GMC TDH-5301 Fishbowl City Bus 38.99 ea

**189-44550** City of York Fire Dept. (FDNY)

**189-44551** York Police Dept. (NYPD)

## Fire Apparatus

### American LaFrance

**189-46024** Pumper Niagara Falls Fire Dept. **25.99**

**189-46025** Aerial Ladder Niagara Falls Fire Dept. **38.99**

## Trucks

### Chevrolet

#### Blazer SUV

**189-46414** Niagra Emergency Service Paramedic **16.99**

Pumper Niagara Falls Fire Dept.189-46024

Aerial Ladder Niagara Falls Fire Dept.189-46025

**189-46415** Niagra Falls Police Dept. **15.99**

### Dodge

**189-44007** Power Wagon 4x4 Pickup Fire Dept. **21.99**

### Ford

#### E-350 Ambulance

**189-41823** Pikesville Volunteer Fire Co. **24.99**

**189-41824** EMS Niagara **19.99**

### Mercedes

**189-40728** LP809 "BRK Einsatzleitung" **22.99**

#### M Klasse SUV

**189-48521** DRK Rettungshundestaffel (German Red Cross) **19.99**

Hot New Products Announced Daily! Visit Walthers Web site at

**www.walthers.com**

**189-48539** Laege Ambulanz (German) **23.99**

### Toyota

#### Land Cruiser

**189-43001** Corpo de Bombeiros **16.99**

**189-43003** Fanzosische Fire Dept. (German) **16.99**

**Limited Quantity Available**

**189-43004** Macau Police (German) **18.99**

## Vans

### Mercedes

#### Sprinter

**189-47831** Katastrophenschutz **16.99**

**189-47836** Katastrophenschutz FW Wuppertal **16.99**

## SPECIAL VALUE PRICING

### Chevrolet

#### Caprice 4-Door Sedan

**189-47683** Minnesota State Patrol #25 (maroon) ~~**12.99**~~ **5.99**

**189-47687** New Hampshire State Police ~~**12.99**~~ **5.99**

#### Blazer

**189-46409** Alaska State Patrol ~~**12.99**~~ **6.99**

### Ford

#### Crown Victoria

**189-49071** Utah Highway Patrol ~~**12.99**~~ **3.99**

**189-49073** South Dakota Highway Patrol ~~**12.99**~~ **5.99**

**189-49074** Arizona State Patrol #24 ~~**12.99**~~ **3.99**

**189-49076** Mississippi Highway Patrol (gray) ~~**12.99**~~ **5.99**

**189-49078** Maryland State Police #30 ~~**12.99**~~ **5.99**

## TRAILERS

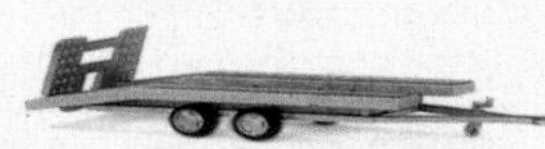

**189-44903** Tandem for Auto Transport **6.99**

**189-44914** "Comfort" Travel Trailer **9.99**

**189-44951** Glider w/Trailer **9.99**

**189-44970** Single Axle **6.99**

**189-44981** Airstream Trailer "Nestlé Scholler" **16.99**

## RACING CARS

### Auto Union

**189-46903** 1936 Auto Union Type C #4 Nuremberg Winner **24.99**

### BMW

**189-40302** 3.5 CSL 2-Door #30 **32.99**

### Ford

#### 1964 Mustang 2-Door Hardtop

**189-47551** 2003 Historic Tour #95 **18.99**

**189-47552** 2003 Historic Tour #96 **16.99**

**189-47553** 1964 Mustang Hardtop 2003 Historic Tour **18.99**

IMPORTED FROM GERMANY BY WALTHERS

**189-47554** 2003 Historic Tour #92 **21.99**

**189-47555** Indianapolis 500 Pace Car **14.99**

**189-47556** 2003 Historic Tour #100 **20.99**

## Mercedes

### SSK

**189-48306** 1928 2-Door Coupe w/Top Down **23.99**

## NSU

**189-48406** 1000 TTS "Trofeo Florio" Start-Nr. 73 **15.99**

## Volvo

**189-43908** 544 Historische Tourenwagen Trophy, Start-Nr. 72 **20.99**

**Limited Quantity Available**

**189-43907** 1958 544 2-Door Hardtop East African Safari #1 **21.99**

## TAXIS

**189-42006** Opel Rekord C 4-Door Sedan Taxi **12.99**

**189-46808** Mercedes W123 Taxi (German) **14.99**

**189-49152** Mercedes C-Class T-Model 4-Door Station Wagon/Hatchback **12.99**

**189-49254** Audi A4 Avant 4-Door Hatchback Wagon **13.99**

**189-49459** E Klasse T Model Station Wagon Taxi **17.99**

## TRUCKS

## Chevrolet

### S-10 Blazer SUV

**189-46401** 1998 **13.99**

**189-46410** 1998 Blazer w/Surfboard & Metallic Paint **14.99**

**189-46412** Continental Air Transport **17.99**

**189-46413** Florida Fish & Wildlife Commission **16.99**

### 1950 Pickup

**189-48200** Standard **12.99**

**189-48214** Esso w/Fuel Tank **13.99**

**189-48216** 1950 Pick-Up/Tow Truck w/Winch Stockton Towing Service **16.99**

**189-48217** 1950 Covered Flatbed w/Pick-Up Cab Mobil "Flying Horse" **13.99**

**189-48219** 1950 Pickup Beverage trade w/Beer Case Load **15.99**

**189-48220** 1950 Stakebed Fruit Company w/Pumpkins **14.99**

**189-48221** Blumen Studio Schmitt (Schmitt Flower Shop w/Plants) **20.99**

**189-48223** Schlachterei Lieben **15.99**

## Dodge

### 1945-68 Power Wagon 4 x 4

**189-44000** Standard Pick Up **13.99**

**189-44001** Farm Truck Stakebed **14.99**

**189-44005** Power Wagon 4 x 4 Tree Farm w/Tree Load **16.99**

Standard 1950 Pick Up 189-48200

1950 Stakebed Fruit Company w/Pumpkins 189-48220

Dodge Power Wagon 4 x 4 Pick Up 189-44000

Dodge Power Wagon 4 x 4 Farm Truck Stakebed 189-44001

**189-44006** 1945-68 Power Wagon 4 x 4 Stakebed **16.99** Includes cornstalks and scarecrow.

**189-44008** Canadian Fargo Railroad Inspection w/Flanged Wheels **14.99**

**189-44009** Pickup Stillwater Garage **16.99**

**189-44011** Stakebed Farm Truck w/Hay Load (Weathered) **16.99**

## Ford

**189-41850** E-350 Delivery Box Truck **14.99**

### 1931 Model AA

Based on the one-ton truck chassis, these delivery vehicles were a favorite with many businesses.

Various Colors

**189-47700** Plain **12.99**

**189-47721** 1-Ton Panel Truck Hearse w/Chrome Rims **13.99**

IMPORTED FROM GERMANY BY WALTHERS

**189-47722** Model AA England Apple Service **13.99**

**189-47723** 1931 Model AA 1-Ton Panel Truck Eisenbahn Expressgut (German Railway Express) **12.99**

## Iveco

**189-47918** Daily Griechische Spezialitaten **18.99**

## Mercedes

### 170 V

**189-41557** 170V "Fernmeldedienst" **11.99**

## Mercedes Benz

### LP809

**189-40726** Lumber Flatbed "Karl Schaffert" **14.99**

**189-40729** LP809 "Rene Strickler" **22.99**

### M Klasse

**189-48537** SUV Schutz & Rettung Zurich **20.99**

## Monster Truck

**Limited Quantity Available**

**189-46616** Dodge Monaco Sedan on Truck Chassis "Bloodhound" **21.99**

**189-46407** Blazer "The Viper" **19.99**

## Multicar

**189-42200** Flatbed **11.99**

**189-42201** Public Utilities **13.99**

**189-42202** Police Sachsen-Anhalt **16.99**

**189-42205** Snowplow **18.99**

## Peugeot

**189-42322** Revillard Garage **10.99**

## Tempo

**189-40641** 3-Wheeler Dreirad Shell Motor Oil (red, yellow) **12.99**

**189-40646** "Ella's Flower Power" **15.99**

## UFO

**189-1010** UFO Flying Saucer **49.99**
From the deepest corners of outer space comes an out-of-this-world UFO. The craft features working lights, and includes five alien figures. Dimensions: 6 x 2" 15 x 5cm.

# VANS

## Citroen Model H

**189-41909** Metallic **9.99**

**189-41952** "Posterijen" **13.99**

**Limited Quantity Available**

**189-41950** Esso Motor Oil **11.99**

Voyager 189-44600

## DKW 3=6

**189-40911** Delivery Van "Esso" **11.99**

**189-40913** DKW Kundendienst **11.99**

**189-40914** Gasolin (German) **12.99**

**189-40915** Bus **12.99**

## Dodge 1990 Minivans

**189-44600** Voyager **11.99**

**189-44650** Ram (black) **11.99**

**Limited Quantity Available**

**189-44619** Plymouth Voyager "Woody" **13.99**

## Fiat

**189-47333** Ducato Delivery Van "Galbani" **15.99**

## Mercedes

**189-41550** 170V Delivery Van "Texaco" **11.99**

### Sprinter

**189-47832** Circus Krone **13.99**

**189-47834** Circus Knie **16.99**

## Plymouth

**189-44614** 1990 Voyager (red) **12.99**

## Renault

**189-45500** Van **8.99**

IMPORTED FROM GERMANY BY WALTHERS

# FARM MACHINERY

## Tractors

**189-42800** Fortschritt ZT300 Enclosed Cab **21.99**

# MOTORCYCLE

**189-40150** Single Motorcycle **10.99**

# VEHICLES W/WORKING LIGHTS

## Automobiles 20.99 ea (Unless Noted)

A bright spot on any highway, day or night. Models feature working head and tail lights, powered by miniature bulbs. Models and electrical equipment are fully assembled, just connect to 14-16V DC or AC power.

**189-5625** Mercedes C-Class T-Model Station Wagon Polizei (police) **38.99**

**189-5645** A-Klasse

**189-5648** Ford Crown Victoria 4-Door Sedan

**189-5650** Mercedes Benz C-Class 4-Door Sedan

**189-5651** Audi A4 4-Door Sedan

**189-5652** Mercedes C-Class T-Model Station Wagon w/Working Headlights

**189-5653** Audi A4 Avant Station Wagon w/Working Headlights

## Emergency Vehicles

These eye-catching models are sure to stop traffic with their working lights! Models come fully assembled with miniature blue or red lamps, flasher circuit and wiring. Simply hook up to 14-16V AC or DC power.

### American La France

**189-5604** Pumper (Red Lamps) **41.99**

**189-5605** Ladder Truck (Red Lights) **55.99**

### Mercedes

**189-5608** MB Fire Truck w/Ladder **37.99**

## Trucks

**189-5643** 1950 Chevrolet Pick-Up (Head & Tail Lights) **20.99**

## Vans 20.99 ea

A bright addition to any scene, Models feature working head and tail lights powered by miniature bulbs. Models and electrical equipment are fully assembled. Connect to 14-16V DC or AC power.

**189-5647** Chrysler/Dodge Caravan Mini-Van

# VEHICLE ACCESSORIES

## Body Panel Set

**189-48991** Smart Body Panel Set (red, yellow) **5.99**

## Tire & Axle Set

Sets include three pairs of tires and three axles.

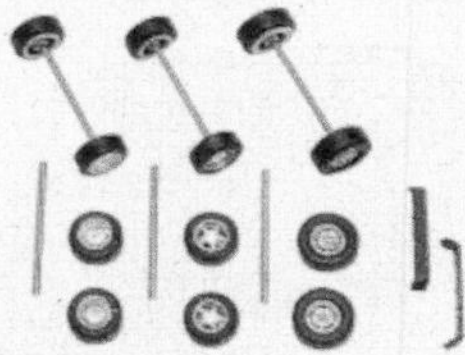

**189-49950** Sport (Includes 2 spoilers) **6.99**

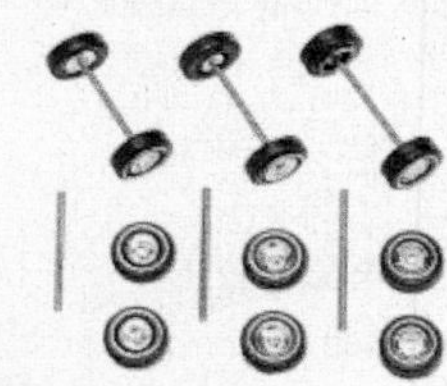

**189-49951 8.99**

Motorcycle 189-40150 (Single Motorcycle)

1950 Chevrolet Pick-Up 189-5643

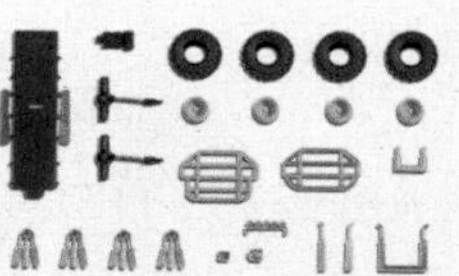

**189-49966** Monster Truck Parts **8.99**
Includes large wheels and tires, grille guards, lift kits and exhaust pipes.

## American Emergency Vehicles 6.99 ea

Convert HO Scale models into police or fire department vehicles with these accessories. Lights are molded in red or blue plastic and are nonworking.

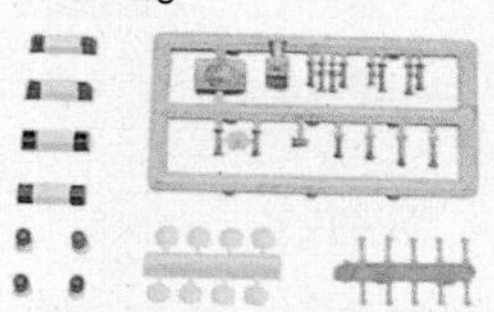

**189-49960** Europe

**189-49961** Modern American

**189-49962** 1950s-Present

Older warning lights, sirens, early light bars and air horns, which can be adapted to vehicles from the 1950s to the present.

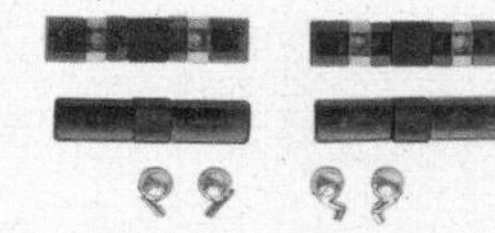

**189-49963** Modern Vehicles Set #2
Contemporary lightbars and spotlights.

## Display Boxes

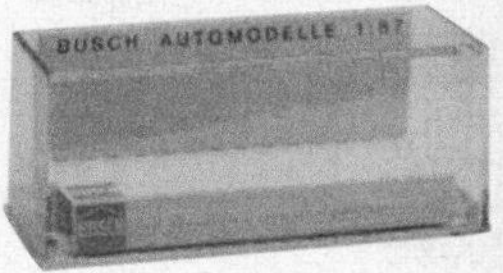


**189-49970** Clear Plastic **2.49**
3 x 1-1/8 x 1-3/8"
7.6 x 3 x 3.4cm
Here's the perfect way to showcase your Busch vehicles! Great protection from dust and curious fingers. Stackable, clear plastic box comes with cardboard base insert.

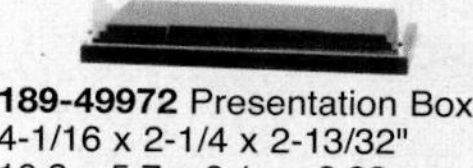

**189-49972** Presentation Box
4-1/16 x 2-1/4 x 2-13/32"
10.3 x 5.7 x 6.1cm **6.99**

**189-49971** Smart Tower Box
2-1/4 x 1 x 1"
5.2 x 2.5 x 2.5cm **2.49**

## Add-On Accessories

**189-49968 11.99**
Includes surfboards, Bicycles, Rafts, Luggage Racks and more.

Street scenes come to life in seconds with these fully assembled, licensed replicas of American autos and trucks! Great for steam-, transition- and diesel-era layouts, the selection includes popular models from the 1940s to the 70s, which also look great as restored collector cars in modern scenes. Off the layout, the small size is ideal for collecting and display. The highly detailed diecast bodies are painstakingly finished in official factory paint colors. Next, they're pad printed to capture other details like chrome trim and graphics.

Each model has a full interior, plus there's an opening hood to showcase all the HO horsepower in the authentically detailed engine. The models also feature plated parts to simulate chrome hubcaps, wheels, grilles and bumpers. Clear plastic windows and lights, as well as real rubber tires complete the standard equipment on every model. Colors may vary.

## NEW PRODUCTS

### Automobiles 12.00 ea

#### 1959 Ford Fairlane 4-Door Sedan

**NEW 221-30192** Turquoise

**NEW 221-30193** Torch Red

**NEW 221-30194** Raven Black

**NEW 221-30195** Yellow Cab w/Nonworking Roof Light

**NEW 221-30206** Police

#### 1936 Ford Fordor Sedan

**NEW 221-30196** Black

**NEW 221-30197** Poppy Red

**NEW 221-30198** Washington Blue

**NEW 221-30199** Yellow Cab w/Nonworking Roof Light

**NEW 221-30205** Police

### Trucks

#### IH R-190 Tractor/Trailer Sets 17.50 ea

**NEW 221-31147** RISS

**NEW 221-31149** Carling's Black Label Lager

#### White WC Tractor/Trailer Sets 17.50 ea

**NEW 221-31146** Del Monte

**NEW 221-31148** Safeway Foods

#### IH R-190 Refrigerated Delivery Truck

**NEW 221-30204** Borden's 13.00

#### 1954 Ford F-350 9' Express Box 1-Ton Pickup 13.00 ea

**NEW 221-30200** Raven Black

**NEW 221-30201** Vermillion

**NEW 221-30202** Sheridan Blue

**NEW 221-30203** Meadow Green

#### 1954 Ford F-350 Pickup Truck

**NEW 221-30207** UP

**NEW 221-30208** PRR

**NEW 221-30209** NYC

**NEW 221-30210** ATSF

### Trailers pkg(2) 19.00 ea

#### AeroVan

**NEW 221-31150** UP

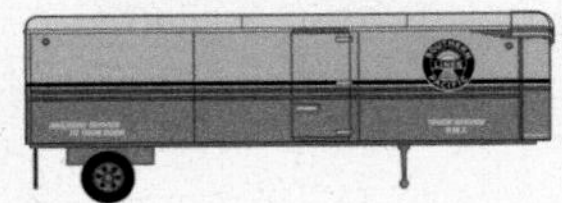

**NEW 221-31151** SP

## BUSES

### Walthers Exclusive!

Just the thing for adding realism to the Cornerstone Series® Silver Springs Terminal bus station and highway scenes. Patterned after the GM PD 4103 design from the 40s, these sleek buses were used across the continent into the 60s and 70s. Each model features exquisitely detaied plastic and diecast parts, flush-mounted window glazing with realistic frame decoration, full interiors, rubber tires and realistic painting and printing. Cities shown are printed in the destination sign board.

#### 1940s PD 4103 Intercity Bus 21.99 ea

**221-32101** Greyhound New York City

**221-32102** Greyhound Los Angeles

**221-32103** Greyhound Chicago

**221-32104** Greyhound Blank Destination/Sign Board

**221-32105** Union Pacific

**NEW** 1959 Ford Fairlane 4-Door SedanYellow Cab 221-30195

**NEW** 1936 Ford Fordor Sedan 221-30197

**NEW** IH R-190 Tractor/Trailer 221-31149

## AUTOMOBILES

Colors may vary from those shown.

**11.00 ea**

### 1978 Chevrolet Impala 4-Door

**Limited Quantity Available**

**221-30163** Dark Brown Metallic

**221-30170** Dark Blue Metallic

**221-30184** Carmine Red

**221-30185** Light Blue Metallic w/Black Vinyl Roof

### 1967 Ford Custom 500 4-Door

**Limited Quantity Available**

**221-30160** burgundy metallic

**221-30169** green metallic

**221-30182** dark green

**221-30183** Pebble Beige w/Black Vinyl Roof)

## EMERGENCY VEHICLES

**11.00 ea**

### Chevrolet

**Limited Quantity Available**

**221-30168** 1978 Impala Fire Chief

### Ford

**Limited Quantity Available**

**221-30167** 1967 Custom 500 Fire Chief

## TAXIS

**Limited Quantity Available**

**221-30158** 1967 Ford Custom 500 4-Door **11.00**

## TRUCKS

### Tractor/Flatbed Trailer Sets 16.50 ea

**International R-190 w/Flatbed**

**221-31122** Roadway

**221-31123** Pacific-Intermountain-Express (P-I-E)

**221-31124** ICX

**White WC22 w/Flatbed**

**221-31125** US Steel National Tube Co.

### Tractor/32' Covered Wagon Trailer Set 16.50 ea

**International R-190**

**221-31128** Roadway

**221-31129** Pacific-Intermountain-Express (P-I-E)

**White WC22**

**221-31130** Wayne Feeds

**221-31141** US Steel American Sheet Steel Co.

**221-31142** Ralston Purina **17.50**

### Tractor/32' Aerovan Trailer Set 16.50 ea

**International R-190**

**221-31133** Navajo

**221-31135** Consolidated Freightways

**White WC22 16.50 ea**

**221-31134** Spector

**221-31136** Yale Transport

### WC22 Tractor/32' Aerovan Reefer Trailer 16.50 ea

**221-31139** Carnation (white)

**221-31140** A&P Grocers (red)

### Aerovan Trailer Set 17.50 ea

**221-31143** Kroger

**221-31144** Railway Express Agency

**221-31145** Coles Express

### International Harvester 1954 R-190 Semi Tractor

**16.50 ea**

**with 32' Fruehauf® Aerovan™ Trailer**

**Limited Quantity Available**

**221-31101** Hennis

**221-31102** Roadway

**221-31103** P-I-E

**221-31114** Eastern Motor Express

**221-31115** Illinois California Express

**w/32' Aerovan Reefer**

**Limited Quantity Available**

**221-31120** Swift's Premium

**221-31121** Sealtest

New Arrivals Updated Every Day! Visit Walthers Web site at

**www.walthers.com**

## Semi Tractors

### White WC22 Mustang 11.00 ea

**221-31137** Red No Lettering

**221-31138** Green No Lettering

### 1954 IH R-190 11.00 ea

**Limited Quantity Available**

**221-31108** Chicago Express

**221-31109** Mid-States

**221-31110** Cooper-Jarrett

**221-31118** Pennsylvania Railroad Merchandise Service

**221-31119** Santa Fe Railroad Express Service

**221-31111** Red Undecorated

**221-31112** Green Undecorated

**221-31113** White Undecorated

### White WC22 Delivery Trucks 11.00 ea (Unless Noted)

**221-30187** Kraft Refrigerated Van

**221-30188** Nabisco Delivery Van

**221-30189** Flatbed Red No Lettering

**221-30190** Falstaff Beer **13.00**

**221-30191** CP **13.00**

### International Harvester R-190 Express Van

**Single Axle 11.00 ea**

**Limited Quantity Available**

**221-30164** NYC

**221-30165** PRR

**221-30166** ATSF

**221-30172** Ice Delivery

**221-30173** A&P Grocery

**221-30174** United States Mail

**221-30175** B&O

**221-30176** CB&Q

**221-30177** NKP

**221-30181** Sears

**Double Axle 11.00 ea**

**221-30156** Refrigerator Swift's Meats

**221-30171** Armour Star

**221-30178** Red Cab, White Body, No Lettering

**221-30179** Dark Green Cab, Silver Body, No Lettering

**221-30180** Yellow Cab, Silver Body, No Lettering

### Flat Bed 11.00 ea

**Limited Quantity Available**

**221-30157** Flatbed

**221-30186** Builder's Supply

## TRAILERS

### 32' Covered Wagon Trailer Set pkg(2) 16.50 ea

**221-31131** Red No Lettering

**221-31132** Green No Lettering

### 32' Flatbed Trailer Set pkg(2) 16.50 ea

**221-31126** Red No Lettering

**221-31127** Green No Lettering

### 32' Fruehauf Aerovan Trailer 2-Pack 16.50 ea

**Limited Quantity Available**

**221-31104** Chicago Express

**221-31105** Mid-States

**221-31106** Cooper-Jarrett

**221-31116** Pennsylvania Railroad Merchandise Service

**221-31117** Santa Fe Railroad Express Service

**221-31107** Undecorated

## AUTOMOBILES

### pkg(3) 6.98 ea (Unless Noted)

**223-4002** Lamborghini

**223-4004** Ferrari Testarossa

**223-4005** Ferrari F-40

**223-4006** 1963 Corvette **7.98**

**223-4032** Porsche 356B Convertible (silver)

**223-4033** Porsche 356B Convertible (green)

**223-4034** 1966 Porsche 911 (yellow)

**223-4035** 1966 Porsche 911 (red)

**223-4036** 1950s BMW Limousine (ivory)

**223-4037** 1950s BMW Limousine (black)

## BUSES 14.98 EA

**223-1043** U.S. Army

**223-1044** Camp Woebegon

**223-1045** Washington High School

**223-1046** Good Shepherd Church

## CONSTRUCTION EQUIPMENT

### Redi-Mix Concrete Trucks 18.98 ea

**223-4002023** Material Service

**223-4002024** Tri-County Redi-Mix

**223-4002025** American Redi-Mix

**223-4002027** Granite

**223-4002028** Aztec

**223-4002029** Undecorated Kenworth Style

**223-4002030** Undecorated Mack Style

### Dump Trucks 13.98 ea

**223-1015** Terra

**223-1064** Cleveland Wrecking Company

**223-1065** Cambria City Iron Works

**223-4002032** Department of Highways

**223-1067** Undecorated Mack Style

## TRUCKS

### Moving Vans 13.98 ea (Unless Noted)

**223-1021** Collins

**223-1062** Chapparal Van Lines

**223-1072** National Van Lines

**223-1098** Graebel Moving Company **14.98**

### 20' U-Haul Moving Trucks 13.98 ea

**223-7007** Vermont (Skiers)

**223-7009** Utah (Dinosaurs)

**223-7011** Kentucky (Race Horses)

**223-7012** Massachusetts (Boston Marathon)

**223-7013** Tennessee (Country Western)

**223-7015** Oklahoma (Pioneers)

**223-7016** South Dakota (Mount Rushmore)

**223-7018** Rhode Island (Sailing Boat)

### 28' Vans 13.98 ea

**223-1087** Perkins Furniture

**223-1090** Pelican Sourdough Bread

### Special Edition Christmas Trucks 14.98 ea

**223-1995** Candy Canes

**223-1997** Christmas Brew

## SEMIS

### Tractor Trailers

**223-1006** Log Truck **15.98**

**233-10061** Log Load **2.99** For #223,1006, sold separately.

**223-1022** Weaver Popcorn **9.98**

**223-1054** LaBelle Lubs Oil Tanker **9.98**

**223-1069** Vita Fresh Fresh Juice **13.98**

**223-1070** Quad Graphics **14.98**

**223-1071** Huckleberry Farms **14.98**

**223-1074** Hawkeye Trucking **13.98**

**223-1075** Auto Zone **14.98**

**223-1077** Freight Train Trucking **13.98**

**223-1080** Syndicate Sales Group **13.98**

**223-1096** Hickman Eggs **13.98**

**223-1097** Dulin Date Gardens **14.98**

**223-1099** Mrs. Smith's **13.98**

**223-1100** River City Produce **14.98**

**223-1102** GATTO Industrial Platers **14.98**

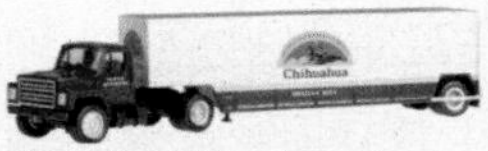

**223-8701** Chihuahua Beer **15.98**

**223-4002019** Star Glass Company **13.98**

**223-4009301** Shell Oil **15.98**

**223-4009303** Truckstops of America **15.98**

**223-4009304** w/40' ACL Trailer **12.98**

**223-4009306** Syndicate Sales w/40' Trailer **13.98**

**223-4009501** Interpolmer **13.98**

**223-4009502** Fireman's Fund **14.98**

**223-4009506** Krogel Freight Systems **13.98**

**223-4009507** Timely Transportation **13.98**

**223-4009601** T600A Ashley w/48' Trailer **15.98**

**223-4009602** Monogram **15.98**

**223-4009603** Hapag Lloyd w/Container **13.98**

**223-4009607** Jack Grey w/Dump Trailer **13.98**

**223-4009701** Jim Palmer Trucking **15.98**

**223-4009801** Quad Graphics/Package Direct **15.98**

### Tractors

**223-132000** Freightliner Standard Sleeper Cab **8.98**

**223-232000** GMC/Chevy Bison Conventional **6.98**

**223-751000** Light Duty **8.98**

### Trailers

#### 40' pkg(2) 10.98 ea

**223-8115** Rio Grande

**223-8139** NP

**223-8140** N&W

**223-8141** WP

**223-8142** B&O

#### 45' pkg(2) 11.98 ea

**223-8201** Nitrol

**223-8202** Crab Orchard & Egyptian Railway

**223-8203** Texas-Mexican Lines

**223-8204** Cornucopia

**223-8205** CP Rail

**223-8206** Seaboard System

**223-8207** BN

**223-8208** UP "Flag"

**223-8209** Lynden Transport w/Alaska Map

**223-8210** Illinois Central Gulf

**223-8211** BN "Expediter"

**223-8212** Prefered Pool

**223-8213** Shippers Co-Op

**223-8214** BN "Innovation"

## CONTAINERS

### 45' Ribbed Side

**223-8355** Model Railroader 60th Anniversary (white) **6.98**

**223-8350** Undecorated pkg(2) **9.98**

### 40' Smooth Side pkg(3) 9.98 ea

**223-8401** OOCL

**223-8403** Showa Container Line

**223-8400** Undecorated

### 45' Ribbed Side

**223-8450** Undecorated pkg(2) **8.98**

### 48' Ribbed Side

**223-8503** CP **5.98**

**223-8508** XTRA Intermodal **5.98**

**223-8500** Undecorated **4.98**

### 48' 4.98 ea

**223-8554** BN America

**223-8555** Itel

**223-8559** NS Triple Crown

**223-8550** Undecorated

### Bulktainers 7.98 ea

**223-8331** UP

**223-8332** Sealand

## CIRCUS VEHICLES

### Trailers pkg(2) 10.98 ea

**223-8134** 28' Midway

**223-8135** 40' Midway

**223-8136** 40' Royal American Shows

**223-8146** 40' Barnum

**223-8147** 45' Barnum

### Water Tanker

**223-8137** Royal American Shows pkg(2) **10.98**

For Daily Product Information Click **www.walthers.com**

FIRST GEAR®

Tackling tough layout construction jobs, heading down the line as a flat car load, or on display, these HO Scale models of authentic International Harvester equipment come fully assembled from diecast metal parts to capture every detail.

## NEW PRODUCTS

### TD-15 Crawler/Dozer

**35.95 ea**

The perfect size for many jobs, these models are complete with the sweep Roll Over Protective Structure (ROPS) and rear-mounted winch.

**NEW 283-800310** Yellow

**NEW 283-800313** Forestry Division (red)

### 560 Wheel Loader

**35.95 ea**

These big loaders are perfect for moving all kinds of loose materials at mines and construction sites. The model measures just over 4" long and features a positionable bucket that can be raised, lowered and tilted like the real thing. Riding on free-rolling wheels, the front features articulated steering, and the rear wheels oscillate just like the real machine. An incredibly detailed engine and operator's cabin round out these replicas.

**NEW 283-800311** Yellow & White

**NEW 283-800315** Sunrise Mining (white, black)

### 175 Crawler w/4-in-1 Bucket & Ripper

**35.95 ea**

With its special 4-in-1 bucket, a 175 crawler could handle dozer work as well as excavating and loading chores. This authentic model includes a positionable bucket, along with a rear-mounted ripper.

**NEW 283-800312** US Forest Service (yellow)

**NEW 283-800314** Yellow

## TD-25 CRAWLER/ DOZER

**35.95 ea**

This heavy-duty crawler is fully loaded with Roll-Over Protective Structure (ROPS) with see-through mesh screen, segmented, moveable tracks, a functioning semi-U blade with working cylinders, a poseable ripper attachment, and a complete operator's control center with instrument console, foot pedals, gear selector, steering levers and textured step pads.

**283-800303** Yellow

**283-800307** Forestry Division (red)

**283-800309** Municipal Services (Lime Green)

Boley
Where the action is!®

## U.S. FOREST SERVICE

**185-302255** 8500 GMC Topkick Crew Bus **11.99**

ENHANCED!
**185-403255** INT'L 4900 Crew Cab Brush Engine **9.99**

**185-457055** 7000 Series INT'L Crew Cab **10.99**

**185-417055** 4300 INT'L Crew Cab Brush Truck **10.99**

**185-240455** 1:72 Ford F-150 **7.99**

ENHANCED!
**185-205955** Crew Cab Brush Engine **10.99**

ENHANCED!
**185-450355** INT'L 7000 Brush Patrol **10.99**

ENHANCED!
**185-450955** 7000 Series INT'L Water Tender with Pump **10.99**

ENHANCED!
**185-402155** INT'L 4900 2 Door Brush Engine **9.99**

**185-451055** 7400 INT'L Crew Bus **10.99**

**185-310155** 1:72 GMC Sierra **7.99**

**185-302055** GMC 3-Axle Fire Tanker **11.99**

## UNITED STATES BUREAU OF LAND MANAGEMENT

**185-457288 10.99**

**185-450988 10.99**

**185-450388 10.99**

### INT'L 4300 2DR COMMERCIAL PUMPER

**185-412411 10.99**

**185-412471 10.99**

**185-412478 10.99**

**185-412417 10.99**

## CALIFORNIA DIVISION OF FORESTRY

- Area - 32,000,000 million acres.
- Vehicles - 1300 + pieces of fire apparatus.
- Personnel 5000 full time & seasonal firefighters. Plus 5000 volunteer personnel.
- Fire Stations - 634 State & Contract Stations.

These awesome stats reflect the largest state fire agency in the USA and one of the largest in the world.

Dept 1-87 is proud to present an "Enhanced" product line with CDF logo and markings.

ENHANCED!
**185-402171** White/Red **9.99**

**185-450911** Red/Red **10.99**

**185-457217** Red/White **10.99**

ENHANCED!
**185-205971** White/Red **10.99**

**185-302111** Red/Red **11.99**

**185-240411** Ford F-150 **7.99**

**185-417017** Red/White **10.99**

ENHANCED!
**185-450371** White/Red **10.99**

**185-310111** GMC Sierra **7.99**

**185-451017** Red/White **10.99**

### INT'L 4300 SERIES 3-Axle Tankers With Pumps

**185-412671 10.99**

**185-412611 10.99**

**185-412678 10.99**

**185-302071 11.99**

**185-302078 11.99**

**185-220071** White/Red **12.99**

**185-220011** Red/Red **12.99**

**185-220077** White/White **12.99**

## SPARTAN Custom Cab Attack Tanker

**185-220111** Red/Red **12.99**

**185-220178** White/Yellow **12.99**

**185-220171** White/Red **12.99**

**185-412277** White/White **9.99**



* Ladder Full Extension Not Shown

**185-220271** White/Red **12.99**

## SPARTAN QUINT With Top Mount Pump & 2 Section Ladder

* Ladder Full Extension Not Shown

**185-220278** White/Yellow **12.99**

**185-413611** Urban Search & Rescue **10.99**

**185-413037** Black/ White **9.99**

**185-413137** Black/White **9.99**

**Limited Quantity Available**

**185-402311** Crew Cab Fire Utility Stake Bed **7.99**

**185-250217** 1993 Seagrave Crew Cab Pumper JB 30 CK - Numbered, FDNY Specifications Limited-Run w/Special Display Box **14.99**

**185-250278** Seagrave Custom Pumper White/Yellow With Red Reflective Stripe **14.99**

**185-250211** Seagrave Custom Pumper Red/Red **14.99**

**185-250417** Seagrave 7400 Commercial Engine **12.99**

**185-250311** Seagrave GMC Commercial Pumper **12.99**

**185-300627** **9.99**
**185-301927** **10.99**

**185-300637** **9.99**
**185-301937** **10.99**

## Dept 1-87 Salutes America With This Patriotic Stars & Stripes Detailed Paint Scheme

**185-450312** Stars & Stripes **12.99**

**185-220411** HAZ-MAT **12.99**

* Graphics May Differ

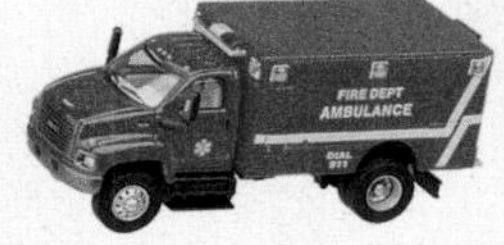

**185-301511** **10.99**

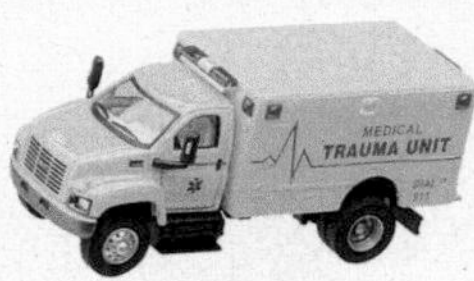

**185-301588** **10.99**

**185-301592** **10.99**

**185-301577** **10.99**

**185-2089** Chicago Police Car **3.99**

**185-417287** Yellow/ White **10.99**

**185-417387** Yellow/ White **10.99**

**185-457387** Yellow/ White **10.99**

**185-457213** Black/Red **10.99**

**185-220013** Black/Red **12.99**

**185-401013** Black/Red **9.99**

**185-457313** Black/Red **10.99**

**185-220313** Heavy Rescue **12.99**

* Graphics May Differ

185-401011 9.99

185-401078 9.99

185-401071 9.99

185-205977 10.99

185-205911 10.99

**185-412111** 10.99
**185-412155** Green **10.99**
**185-412171** Red/White **10.99**

**185-402271** 4900 Early Style INT'L Modular Box Ambulance **9.99**

For Daily Product Information Click
**www.walthers.com**

**EMERGENCY SERVICES**

185-2071 10.99

**185-403211** Rescue SCBA Pumper **9.99**

185-2070 10.99

ENHANCED!
185-450311 10.99

185-302011 11.99

**185-417088** Airport RIV Unit **10.99**

185-417011 10.99

185-417211 10.99

185-417217 10.99

185-457317 10.99

185-457411 10.99

185-417317 10.99

185-457417 10.99

185-402411 9.99

185-402478 9.99

185-402417 9.99

185-402471 9.99

185-417311 10.99

FIRST ALARM FIRE SERIES

## Fire House

1930'sstyle 2-bay fire Satation Feature

- Opening Doors
- Imitated "Glass" Windows
- Hose Drying Tower

**NEW 185-2602** Midwest Style Fire House with Gray Brick, White Trim & Red Equipment Bay Doors **29.99**

**NEW 185-2603** Traditional "Red" Brick Fire House with Gray Trim & Red Bay Doors **29.99**

185-402611 9.99

185-402671 9.99

185-402678 9.99

**185-412576** White/Silver **8.99**
**185-412556** Green/Silver **8.99**
**185-412517** Red/White **8.99**
**185-412537** Black/White **8.99**

**185-411216** Red/Silver **8.99**
**185-411286** Yellow/Silver **8.99**

**185-411226** Blue/Silver **8.99**

**185-411396** Orange/Silver **8.99**
**185-411311** Red/Red **8.99**
**185-411326** Blue/Silver **8.99**

**185-411377** White/White **8.99**
* Load not included

## INTERNATIONAL® 4300 SERIES

### Truck

**185-410216** Red/Silver **8.99**
**185-410277** White/White **8.99**
**185-410288** Yellow/Yellow **8.99**
**185-4102BN** Brown/Brown **8.99**

**185-410366 8.99**

### Collectible Candy Trucks

**185-410200** 4 Assorted **10.99**

**185-413422** Blue **9.99**
**185-413488** Yellow **9.99**
**185-413411** Red **9.99**

**185-413477** White **9.99**

## INTERNATIONAL® 4300 SERIES

### Service Truck

**185-412399** Orange **8.99**
**185-412377** White **8.99**

**185-410796 8.99**
**185-410717 8.99**
**185-410726 8.99**

**185-410777 8.99**

**185-410588** Yellow **8.99**
**185-410517** Red/White **8.99**
**185-410599** Orange **8.99**

**185-410576 8.99**

**185-411596** Orange/Silver **8.99**
**185-411517** Red/White **8.99**
**185-411566** Silver/Silver **8.99**

**185-412855 8.99**
**185-412877 8.99**

**185-412812 8.99**

* Load not included

**185-412788 8.99**

**185-412799 8.99**

**185-411127** Blue/White **9.99**
**185-411177** White/White **9.99**

**185-411116** Red/Silver **9.99**

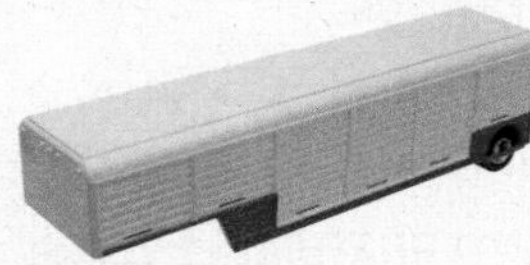

**185-20641 7.99**
**185-20648 7.99**
**185-20649 7.99**
**185-20642 7.99**
**185-20647 7.99**

## SCHOOL BUS

Chassis + Body All Die-Cast Construction Excellent Detail Working Features

Working Guide Rod

Working Flip-out stop sign

**185-420088** CE Series School Bus. Made by IC Corporation. (IC Corporation is a wholly owned subsidiary of International Truck and Engine) **14.99**

**185-420078** CE Series School Bus. Yellow/White **14.99**

**185-41011** Red **6.99**
**185-41012** Blue **6.99**
**185-41013** Black **6.99**
**185-41017** White **6.99**
**185-41019** Orange **6.99**

**185-41002** Blue **6.99**
**185-41001** Red **6.99**
**185-41003** Black **6.99**
**185-41007** White **6.99**
**185-41009** Orange **6.99**

**185-412916** Yellow/Silver **14.99**
**185-412986** Red/Silver **14.99**
**185-412976** White/Silver **14.99**
**185-412966** Silver/Silver **14.99**

## TOW TRUCKS

**185-302672 14.99**

**185-302688 14.99**

**185-413511 14.99**

**185-413577 14.99**

**185-451437 14.99**

**185-451427 14.99**

## INTERNATIONAL® 4300 SERIES

### Tree Service Truck

**185-413300** Blue **10.99**
**185-413377** White **10.99**

**185-413388** Yellow **10.99**

**185-413311** Red/Yellow **10.99**

## INTERNATIONAL Altec 4300 SERIES

### City Power + Light Truck

185-413288 10.99

185-413211 10.99

185-413277 10.99

185-413200 10.99

## INTERNATIONAL®/Altec 7000 SERIES

### Line Maintenance Truck

185-451277 10.99

185-451200 10.99

185-451288 10.99

185-451211 10.99

## INTERNATIONAL® 4300 SERIES

### Service Truck

185-417588 City Services 8.99

185-417577 Contractor Services 8.99

185-417599 Road/Highway Dept. 8.99

185-417488 County City Services 8.99

185-417477 8.99

185-417499 Highway Dept. 8.99

185-411499 8.99

185-4114BL 8.99

## INTERNATIONAL 7000 SERIES

### Severe Service Trucks

185-457588 Closed Stake Bed Maintenance. 9.99

185-457688 City Crew Dump 9.99

185-450799 Orange 9.99

185-450777 White 9.99

185-450788 Yellow 9.99

185-450599 9.99

185-450588 Yellow 9.99

## INTERNATIONAL® 70000 SERIES

### Service Truck

185-457699 County/State Road Dept. 9.99

185-457677 Contractor Services White 9.99

185-457599 Highway Dept. 9.99

185-457577 White 9.99

## INT'L 7000 2-Axle Snow Plows With Spreaders

185-450100 9.99

185-450111 Red 9.99

185-450188 Yellow 9.99

185-450199 Orange 9.99

## Stakebed Truck

185-450211 Red 9.99

185-450277 White 9.99

185-450288 Yellow 9.99

## INT'L 7000 3-Axle Flatbed Truck

185-450036 Black/Silver 9.99

185-450077 White/White 9.99

185-450016 Red/Silver 9.99

## INT'L 7000 3-Axle Roll On & Off Dumpster

185-450855 Green 9.99

185-450877 White 9.99

185-450812 Red/Blue 9.99

185-451153 Green/Black 9.99

185-451163 Silver/Black 9.99

185-451186 Yellow/White 9.99

185-450416 Red/Chrome 14.99

185-450476 White/Chrome 14.99

185-450466 Sliver/Chrome 14.99

185-450486 Yellow/Chrome 14.99

Boley
Where the action is!®

## NT'L 7000 4-Axle Cement Mixer

85-450616 Red/Silver 9.99
85-450677 Red/White 9.99
85-450617 White/White 9.99

85-450686 Yellow/Silver 9.99

85-451388 Yellow 9.99
85-451322 Blue 9.99
85-451377 White/Red 9.99

85-451311 9.99

GMC

## MC —Topkick Tree Service Truck

85-302400 Blue 10.99
85-302477 White 10.99
85-302488 Yellow 10.99

**185-302411** Red/Yellow **10.99**

**185-301755** Green **9.99**
**185-301777** White **9.99**

**185-301771** **9.99**

**185-300576** White **9.99**
**185-300516** Red **9.99**
**185-300526** Blue **9.99**
**185-300536** Black **9.99**

**185-300316** Red **9.99**
**185-300336** Black **9.99**
**185-300356** Green **9.99**
**185-300377** White **9.99**

**185-300117** Red/White **9.99**
**185-300136** Black/Silver **9.99**
**185-300156** Green/Silver **9.99**
**185-300177** White/White **9.99**
**185-300196** Orange/Silver **9.99**

**185-300287** Yellow/White **9.99**
**185-300216** Red/White **9.99**
**185-300277** White **9.99**
**185-301712** Blue **9.99**

**185-300888** Yellow **9.99**
**185-300817** Red **9.99**
**185-300899** Orange **9.99**
**185-301712** **9.99**

**185-301699** **10.99**

**185-301677** **10.99**

**185-301688** **10.99**

## Beverage Truck

**185-302511** Red **9.99**
**185-302588** Yellow **9.99**
**185-302577** White/Red **9.99**

**185-302522** Blue **9.99**

**185-300720** Blue **9.99**
**185-300711** Red **9.99**
**185-300777** White **9.99**
**185-300799** Orange **9.99**

**185-300926** **9.99**
**185-300911** Red **9.99**
**185-300977** White **9.99**
**185-300988** Yellow **9.99**

**185-301499** **9.99**
**185-301400** Blue **9.99**
**185-301488** Yellow **9.99**

**185-301399** Orange **10.99**
**185-301317** Red/White **10.99**

**185-301326** Blue/Silver **10.99**
**185-301377** White/White **10.99**

**185-301016** **9.99**
**185-301076** **9.99**

**185-301088** **9.99**
**185-301099** **9.99**

## 2003 GMC TOPKICK 3-Axle Coal Dump Truck

**185-301116** **9.99**
**185-301163** Silver Cab, Black Body **9.99**
**185-301173** White Cab, Black Body **9.99**

**185-301126** Blue Cab, Silver Body

**185-300417** Red/White **9.99**

**185-300436** Black/Silver **9.99**

## 3-Axle Generic Commodities Tanker Trucks

**185-301226** Blue/Silver **10.99**
**185-301276** White/Silver **10.99**
**185-301286** Yellow/Silver **10.99**

For Daily Product Information Click
**www.walthers.com**

IMPORTED FROM SPAIN BY WALTHERS
Vehicles are molded in appropriately colored plastic, with painted details. Markings may vary from what is shown in Reference Book. Visit walthers.com for a complete listing of Eko vehicles.

## AUTOMOBILES

### Citroen 2.49 ea
**265-2021** 2 CV
**265-2027** DS 19
**265-2034** 2 CV Truck
**265-2048** AMI
**265-2076** Break

### Fiat 2.49 ea
**265-2031** 600 Multipla
**265-2062** Seat 850

**265-2065** Seat 124

### Ford 1.99 ea

**265-2044** Thunderbird

**265-2071** Zephyr

**265-2073** Comet

**265-2079** Falcon

### Jaguar 2.49 ea (Unless Noted)
**265-2098** E Coupe
**265-2100** Racer
**265-2106** Mark Nine **3.49**

### Jeep 2.49 ea (Unless Noted)

**265-2008** Pickup Truck

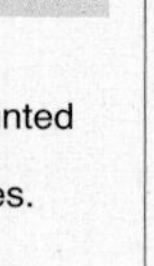

**265-2078** Wagon **3.49**

### Land Rover

**265-2077** Rover 3/L **2.49**

**265-2116** Safari **3.49**

### Mercedes Benz 2.49 ea

**265-2003** 300

**265-2010** 190SL
**265-2011** 190SL Coupe

**265-2012** 190 SL Passenger
**265-2049** Racer

### Miscellaneous 2.49 ea
**265-2002** BMW 501

**265-2042** De Soto Diplomat

**265-2043** Plymouth Suburban

**265-2045** Chevrolet El Camino
**265-2050** Simca Sedan 1000

**265-2063** Dodge Dart
**265-2081** DAF Coupe

**265-2084** Volvo Sport

**265-2089** Morris Mini

**265-2109** Borgward Isabella

**265-2124** Skoda Coupe

### Opel 2.49 ea

**265-2004** 1954 Kapitan

**265-2039** Rekord

**265-2040** Station Wagon

### Renault 1.99 ea

**265-2025** Dauphine
**265-2047** 4-L Station Wagon
**265-2051** Florida

**265-2064** R-8

### Seat 1.99 ea

**265-2006** Sedan 1400

**265-2032** Sedan 1400C
**265-2036** Coupe 600

**265-2037** Seat 1400 Panel Truck

### Studebaker

**265-2070** Hawk **1.99**

### Family Cars 2.49 ea

**265-2009** Convertible Cabriolet

**265-2099** Karmann Ghia

**265-2030** Microbus **2.49**

## BUSES
**265-2088** Mercedes Microbus **3.49**
**265-2117** Chausson Motor Bus **8.99**

## CAMPERS
**265-2022** 2-Wheel Camping Trailer **2.49**

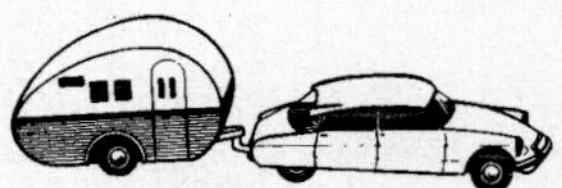

**265-2059** Citroen DS-19 w/Trailer **4.99**

**265-2060** Fiat 1800 w/Trailer **4.99**

**265-2061** Vehicle w/Trailer **4.99**

## EMERGENCY VEHICLES
**265-2019** Fire Truck w/Ladde **5.49**
**265-2029** Ford Ambulance **2.49**

## TRUCKS

### Ford

**265-2013** Flatbed **4.99**

**265-2014** Flatbed w/Canvas Top **4.99**

**265-2020** Gas Oil Tank Truck **5.49**

### Magirus
**265-2024** Tank Truck **5.49**

### Thames 5.49 ea

**265-2119** Flatbed Truck
**265-2120** Soda Delivery Truck

**265-2121** Beer Delivery Truck

### Sava
**265-2123** Garbage Truck **5.49**

### Miscellaneous
**265-2067** Barreiros Van **5.49**

**265-2090** Panel Truck Furgon **3.49**

# FALLER

IMPORTED FROM GERMANY BY WALTHERS

## NEW PRODUCTS

### Nonpowered Vehicles

**NEW 272-120228** Horse-Drawn Wagon & Railroad Ties **33.99**
Worn-out railroad ties are being hauled away from the track after new ones were installed. Set includes wagon, horses and loose railroad ties.

**NEW 272-130527** Wagon w/Advertising Sign **16.99**
This hay wagon comes complete with a billboard for advertising events and products. Place it at the edge of a farm field along a country road.

**NEW 272-154022** Manure Wagon **33.99**
Haul manure from the barn with this old-style wagon. Set includes one wagon, two horses and one figure.

**NEW 272-154023** Lumber Wagon **33.99**
Move logs from forest to rail with this horse-drawn wagon. Set includes one lumber wagon, two horses and one figure.

Get Daily Info, Photos and News at

**www.walthers.com**

### Car System

These moving vehicles will add a new dimension of realism to your railroad. Start-sets, vehicles, control units and numerous accessories are available so you can design a car system to suit your layout.

### Start-Sets

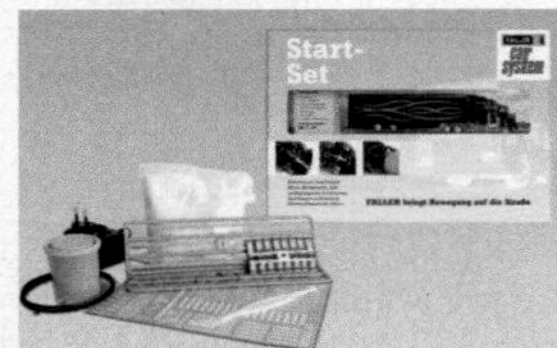


**NEW 272-161518** Kenworth Truck **169.99**
Keep vehicles on the move with this set. Cab features a traction engine. To operate with the trailer a minimum radius of 6" 15cm is required.

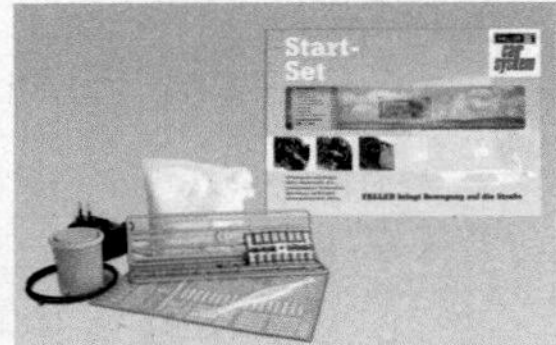


**NEW 272-162003** Magirus Eckauber Lf 16 Fire Brigade **169.99**
This limited edition set features a handmade fire truck, battery charger, special guide wire, roadway, markings, paint and detailed assembly instructions.

### Vehicles

#### Buses

**NEW 272-161413** Setra S 315 Urban Bus **196.99**
Realistic interior and exterior lighting make this city bus a great addition to the downtown area of your Faller car system layout. Batteries are included.

**NEW 272-161612** Setra S 315 Auto-Hummel **135.99**

#### Cars

**NEW 272-161525** Trabant 601 S Universal **135.99**

**NEW 272-161526** Volkswagen Beetle w/Oval Rear Window **135.99**

**NEW 272-161527** Mercedes Benz C-Class **135.99**

**NEW 272-161528** Volkswagen Golf IV **135.99**

#### Farm Equipment

**NEW 272-161536** MF Tractor w/Trailer **152.99**

#### Vans & RVs

**NEW 272-161537** Volkswagen T1 B Campers w/Telescoping Roof **135.99**

#### Emergency Equipment

**NEW 272-161542** Mercedes Benz Sprinter Polizei w/Flashing Light **139.99**

**NEW 272-161578** Mercedes Benz Atego RLFA 2000 AT Rosenbauer Fire Brigade Truck w/Flashing Light **162.99**

Starter Set w/MB Actros Tank Truck 272-161516

Starter Set w/Ford Transit Van Brekina 272-161513

#### Construction Equipment

**NEW 272-161568** MAN F 2000 Side-Tip Dump Truck **143.99**

#### Trucks

**NEW 272-162044** Mercedes Benz Ackermann Moving Van Carl Balke **169.99**

**NEW 272-162045** Mercedes Benz SK Truck **139.99**

### Control Unit

**NEW 272-161679** All-Purpose Switching Unit **51.99**
Allows you to control up to three car system drive units including door drive unit #272-180624 (sold separately). Makes automating sequences easier and comes with detailed instructions.

## CAR SYSTEM

### Start-Sets

Add a new dimension of realism to your railroad, as vehicles move along streets and highways under their own power! Includes battery charger, special guide wire, roadway filler, roadway markings, roadway paint, crash barriers, marker posts and detailed assembly instructions.

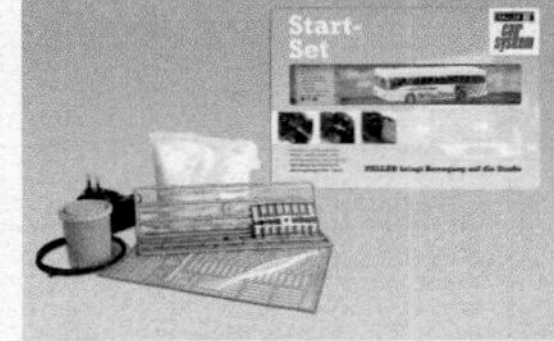


**272-161508** MB O 405 School Bus **119.99**

**272-161516** MB Actros Tank Truck **186.99**

**272-161512** Mercedes SK Truck Herpa **119.99**

**272-161513** Ford Transit Van Brekina **119.99**

**272-161514** City Tourist Mini-Train **171.99**

FALLER

IMPORTED FROM GERMANY BY WALTHERS

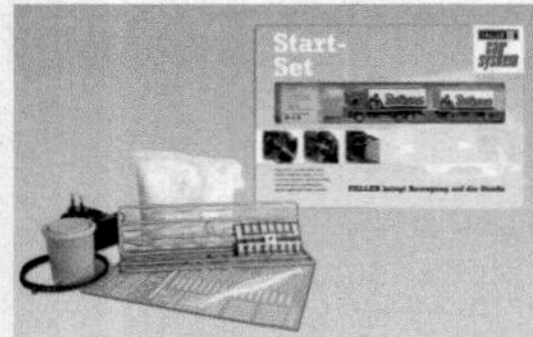

**272-161517** MB Actros Road Train **154.99**

### Battery Operated

Coach and two non-rechargeable batteries included.

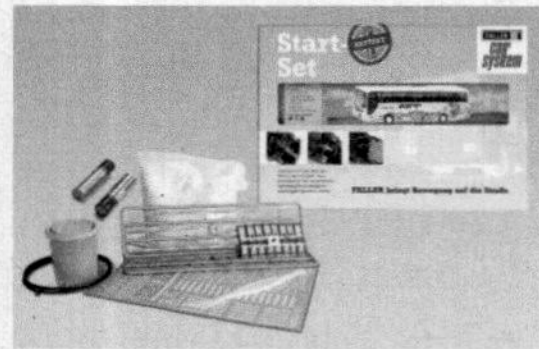

**272-161402** MAN Coach **102.99**

### Roadway

Offers complete design flexibility, so you can build wide or narrow streets, curves, moderate grades, straights, one-way streets, freeways or virtually any other modern road. Each set includes self-adhesive road surface in realistic colors, diecut cardboard base sections and guide wire. Base pieces interlock like a jigsaw puzzle, so installation is fast and easy. For custom applications, you can cut the various pieces to fit, or just install the guide wire in new or existing streets.

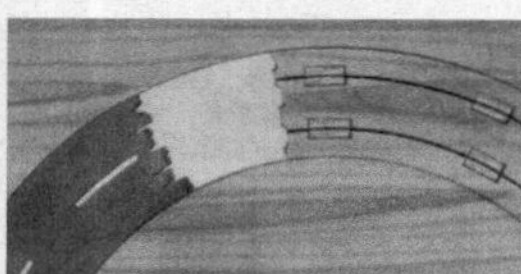

**272-161660** Curves 2-Lane Small pkg(6) **33.99**
Includes two 90° and four 45° curved sections. Radius is about 8-1/2" 212mm.

**272-161661** Intersection **33.99**
Includes special intersection piece, plus four straight sections. Measures 5-7/8 x 5-7/8" 15 x 15cm.

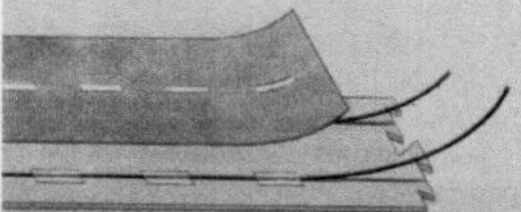

**272-161650** Straight **33.99**
Includes six straight two-lane roadway sections, each 12" 30cm long.

**272-161657** Railroad Crossing **13.99**
Specially cut and marked roadway surfaces, plus a track filler piece allow Car System vehicles to cross tracks. Works with most track systems.

**272-161677** Junction Branch-off **33.99**

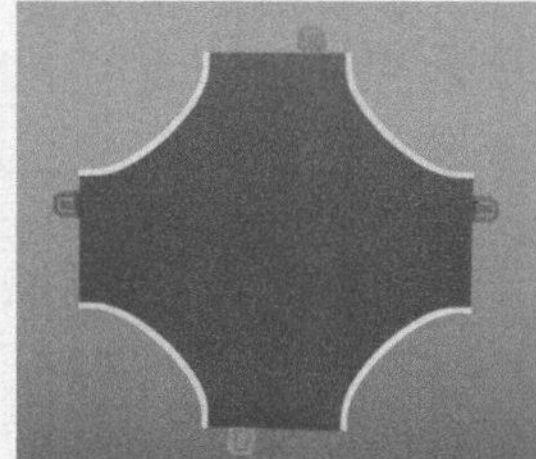

**272-161823** Big Crossing **89.99**

### Roadway Details

**272-180506** Roadway Paint 7-1/2oz 250ml **11.99**
Special formula for use with Car System roadways, dries to a realistic grayish-black.

**272-180591** Roadway Markings **5.99**
Self-adhesive rub-on transfer lines, arrows and more, all in white.

**272-180592** Crash Barriers **13.99**
Includes 32 lane marker posts and 32" 80cm of crash barrier.

**272-161674** Parking Space **28.99**
15V DC connection.

### Control Units

**272-161668** Rectifiers **33.99**
For use with connecting stops, junction or parking lots. Connect to a 16V AC terminal on the transformer.

**272-161678** Distance Control **94.99**
This state-of-the-art control system brings vehicles to a timer-adjusted hold-up for a following vehicle at a crosswalk.

### Diverging Route Switches

**272-161676** Electro-Mechanical **33.99**

**272-161677** Electrical **33.99**
Use these switches with #161662 (sold separately) to route vehicles straight ahead or onto a diverging route. Requires 12-16V DC or AC power; can be used on right or left.

**272-161675** Stop Section **25.99**
Brings vehicles to a stop automatically, great for all kinds of special effects. Permanent electro-magnet operates reed switches on all vehicles. Operates on 12-16V DC.

### Traffic Lights

**272-161655** Signals w/Switch pkg(2) **119.99**
A great accessory for use with #161661,(sold separately) operates up to four signals through the full sequence of green-yellow-red and brings vehicles to a safe stop in both directions! Includes fully assembled micro-processor to control electronics, operates on 12-16V AC or DC.

**272-161656** Traffic Lights - Less Switch pkg(2) **63.99**
Additional signals for use with #161655 (each sold separately.)

### Truck Rail Roll-On/Off

Add a working intermodal ramp to your Car System equipped layout with this exciting accessory. Trucks actually pull onto flats and drive ahead, coming to a stop on the empty car. At the end of the line, simply switch the motor back on with an electromagnet hidden under the tracks and trucks drive off under their own power! Magnets are designed to fit Marklin or Fleischmann flat cars, (sold separately.) Complete ramp requires one each #161680 and 161681.

**272-161680** Basic Car Conversion Set **166.99**
Includes one flat car conversion set (two permanent magnets, one for each end of the car), contact wire and two electromagnets. For intermediate size flats. Designed for use with ramp (#272-161682, sold separately.)

**272-161681** Rail Roll-On/Off Add-On Set **85.99**
Additional magnets and accessories to convert Intermediate flats. Includes one car insert with two magnets, contact wire and two electromagnets.

**272-161682** Loading Platform Only **25.99**
Installs in minutes, allows trucks to drive directly onto flat cars. For use with Marklin K or M Track (M Track requires transition piece from M to K track) or Fleischmann. Designed for use with Basic Set #272-161680, sold separately.

### Bus Stop

**272-161671** **154.99**
Animate your city streets or rural roads with this kit. Includes special controls which allow a bus (sold separately) to turn off the main road, come to a stop, then pull back onto the highway.

### VEHICLES

Car System vehicles are fully assembled, with a can type motor, and built-in reed switch for use with accessories. Power is supplied by a pair of rechargeable ni-cad batteries. A built-in socket allows batteries to be charged in the vehicle. (Charging time is about seven hours, and vehicles will operate for many hours on a full charge.) Riding on rubber tires, each vehicle actually steers as it moves around corners. The front axle has a fully operational linkage and a strong magnet that follows the hidden guide wire. (Colors and markings of vehicles may vary from what is shown).

#### Automobile

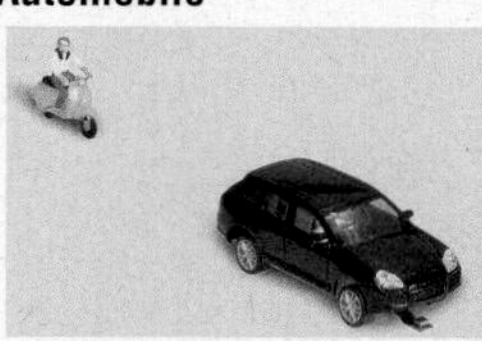

**272-161534** Porsche Cayenne w/Scooter **145.99**

#### Trucks

**272-161569** Iveco Cement Mixer **154.99**

**272-161573** Mercedes Benz Atego DLK 23/12 w/Electronic Flasher **166.99**

**272-161574** Mercedes Benz Actros M Milk Tank Trailer Truck **150.99**

**272-161575** MB Actros Tanker **147.99**

**272-161576** MB Actros Semi Rothaus **150.99**

**272-161577** MB Actros w/Log Trailers w/Flashing Light **154.99**

Item listed below is available by Special Order (see Legend Page).

**272-161570** MAN Dump Truck (Wiking) **145.99**

#### Farm Tractor

**272-161535** Deutz Tractor **145.99**

#### Vans & RVs

**272-161529** Porsche Cayenne w/Caravan **136.99**

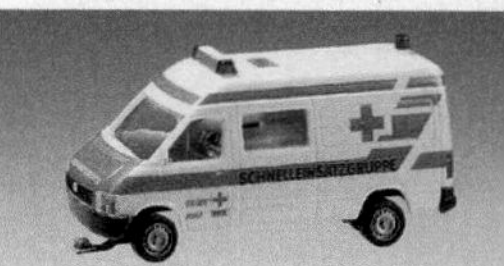

**272-161538** Volkswagen LT2 RTW No Electronic Flasher **145.99**

**272-161539** Volkswagen Karmann Mobile Home **145.99**

**272-161540** MB Sprinter Fire Brigade **145.99**

# FALLER

IMPORTED FROM GERMANY BY WALTHERS

**272-161541** MB Sprinter 60 Years Faller Model World **145.99**

**272-161649** MB Sprinter Spedition Effinger (white) **119.99**

## Accessories

**272-161690** Battery Charge Unit for Car System 110V **33.99**

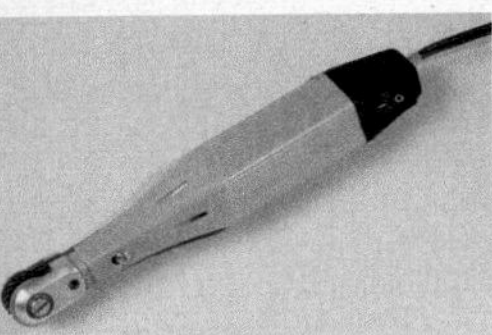

**272-161669** Groove Cutter **179.99**
Made especially for laying the contact wire in Faller Car Systems. 12V DC electrical connection.

**272-161670** Guide Wire 33' 9.9m **16.99**

## Scene Sets

**272-161673** Construction Site **188.99**
Everything you need to create the illusion of a roadwork team is included in this functioning construction site. Set includes two 16V traffic lights with switchgear, warning lights and traffic cones, barrier with flashing lights, traffic signs and an electronic control with adjustable flash-sequence speed.

Preiser/Wiking Deutz Tractor 272-161535

**Limited Quantity Available**

**272-161672** Gas Station **136.99**
Fill 'er up! This colorful gas station allows your Car System Vehicles (sold separately) to get ready to head out on the Autobahn! Includes one electronic control section, three control sensors, one stop, one electronic junction, and detailed mounting instructions.

## Play Street Series

Designed for faster and easier set-up than the standard system roadways, Play Streets come fully assembled with built-in connectors and are molded in a realistic asphalt color with white markings. Simply connect sections together to create a custom roadway in minutes. Hidden guide wires in each section are perfectly aligned to direct the steering magnets on the bottom of all battery powered Car System vehicles (sold separately).

**272-161801** Mercedes Bus **238.99**
Includes bus, battery charger and roadway oval (two 8" 20cm) straight stop switch.

### Roadway Sections

**272-161810** Straights 8" 20cm **20.99**

**272-161811** Assorted Short Straights **20.99**
Includes two each 4" 10cm & 2" 5cm long sections.

**272-161815** 45° Curves pkg(2) **20.99**

**272-161825** Turn-Around 15-1/2 x 11 x 1/3" 39 x 27.5 x .8cm **39.99**

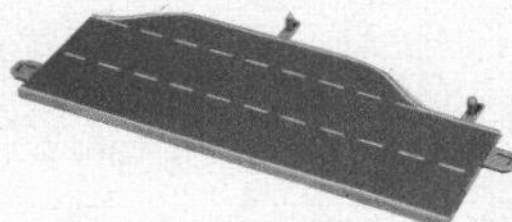

**272-161826** Turnout 14 x 5-3/4 x 1/3" 35 x 14.5 x .8cm **39.99**

**272-161812** Short Straights 7" pkg(2) 17.5cm **20.99**

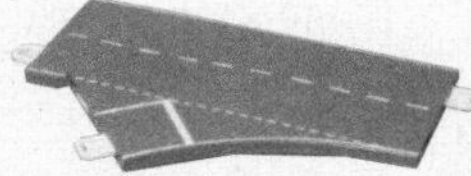

**272-161820** Left Turn Off 12" 30cm **39.99**

### Intersections

Each measures 8 x 8" 20 x 20cm.

**272-161822** Standard **20.99**

**272-161850** With Built-in Start-Stop Mechanism **38.99**

# NON POWERED VEHICLES

## Boats

**272-131005** Motor Cargo Barge **33.99**

**272-131006** River Cargo Boat with Dwelling Cabin **37.99**

## Wagons 33.99 ea

**272-154020** Haulage Cart

**272-154021** Horse-Drawn Wagon

# EVERGREEN HILL DESIGNS

# BULLDOZER

**261-508** RD-8 Caterpillar **34.95**
Unpainted metal kit.



## *Information* STATION

### Weathering Cars

Next time you're out and about, check out the cars on the road. They're not usually all that clean, many are dull and faded and, unless you live in areas without a lot of snow or rain, many have rusted parts showing.

For added realism, weather your automobiles. Add dust effects by brushing on powdered chalks or drybrushing some light paint streaks along the bottom of the doors and rear fenders to simulate road grime ad dust. Older cars may appear more weatherbeaten; for these cover the entire vehicle with a light coat of dusty colored chalk, along with a small amount of chalk which roughly matches the vehicle color to simulate oxidized paint. Mask off the windows and spray on a dulling coat which is compatible with the materials and paint on the vehicle.

Another easy way to make autos on your pike more realistic is to add battle scars. Accidents, weather and flat tires take their toll on cars and trucks. Try repainting an occasional door or fender in primer gray or another vehicle color. If your car has whitewall tires, paint one all black. And, don't forget rusty body rot around the wheel wells, easily added by drybrushing on some dark oxide paint.

Unpainted pewter kits feature high quality castings.

## AUTOMOBILES

**284-63001** 1932 Ford Hot Rod w/Figures **19.95**

## FARM EQUIPMENT

Unpainted kits; color refers only to prototype manufacturer.

### "Red"

**284-60001** 1950s "Red" Farm Tractor w/Farmer **12.95**

**284-60002** 1950s "Red" Manure Spreader **14.95**

**284-60003** "Red" 3-Bottom Plow **14.95**

**284-60005** 1950s "Red" Super M-TA w/Front Loader & Farmer **19.95**

### "Green"

**284-60004** 1960s "Green" 4020 Farm Tractor w/Farmer **14.95**

**284-60007** 1960s "Green" 4020 Tractor w/237 Corn Picker & Farmer **29.95**

**284-60010** "Green" F145H 5-Bottom Plow **19.95**
Use with "Green" 4020 Tractor (#284-60004), sold separately.

**284-60006** 1940s "Green" 12-A Grain Harvester **24.95**

### Ford

**284-60009** Ford 8N Tractor w/2 Bottom Plow, Scraper Blade & Farmer Figure **19.95**

### Wagons 12.95 ea

**284-60008** Bin Wagon

**284-60012** Hay Wagon

## CONSTRUCTION EQUIPMENT

**284-61001** Bobcat w/Operator Figure **12.95**

**284-61002** Light Utility Trailer **9.95**

**284-61003** Front End Loader w/Operator Figure **24.95**

**284-61004** 1940s Tractor w/Logging Arch & Operator Figure **39.95**

**284-61005** Log Loader w/Operator Figure **24.95**

**284-61006** 1940s Bulldozer w/Operator Figure **39.95**

**284-61007** Forklift w/Operator Figure **14.95**

**284-61008** Road Grader w/Operator Figure **39.95**

**284-61009** Material Handler w/Operator Figure **24.95**

**284-61010** Backhoe w/Operator Figure **29.95**

**284-61011** 1940s Tracked Crawler **24.95**

**284-62001** 50-Ton Low Boy Trailer **19.95**

*Information*
STATION

### Where are Carfloats and Carferries Used?

Carfloats and carferries were often the only way for some railroads to cross bodies of water. Quicker and cheaper than constructing a bridge they were used almost everywhere, including as an interim measure until a bridge was designed and built.

Carfloats, or car barges were simply pushed along by a railroad-owned or contracted tugboat, often with a tall cab so the pilot could see over the freight cars. Major areas which saw extensive carfloat use include New York Harbor and along the Hudson River; Philadelphia, Baltimore, New Orleans, San Francisco, Seattle and Vancouver.

Carferries, which unlike carfloats are self propelled, saw extensive use along the Great Lakes, especially along all coasts of Michigan; as well as in eastern Canada, Florida, along the Gulf Coast, across the Mississippi River, in the Puget Sound near Seattle, at Vancouver and Alaska.

Many smaller carfloat and carferry services operated everywhere from the forests of Louisiana on several logging lines, to the many lakes in southern British Columbia where CP and CN had a series of isolated branches connected only by carfloats.

By adding a carfloat to your layout, you can simulate an offline connection to another railroad or branch line. For prototypical operations, they represent an interchange for moving freight cars off the layout. They don't take up much room either, making them easy to add. All you need is a carfloat apron, a small yard and a carfloat or carferry.

Set the scene on your highways with these assembled, plastic models based on European and American prototypes. Each is finely detailed with interiors, rolling wheels and "glass." Many are offered in either a standard or a brighter metallic paint scheme. High Tech models feature opening hoods and detailed engines; some also feature metal chassis.

# NEW PRODUCTS

## American Trucks

### International Harvester

**NEW 326-6140** Beverage Truck (Undecorated) **11.95**

### Kenworth

**NEW 326-6228** W-900 w/Sleeper & Elliptical Tanker Royal American Shows **12.95**

### Tractor Only

#### Heavy Haul Pacific Short Chassis

**NEW 326-15252** Undecorated **6.50**

**NEW 326-15253** Painted **7.50**

## European Automobiles

### Audi

#### A8 Sedan w/Redesigned Grille

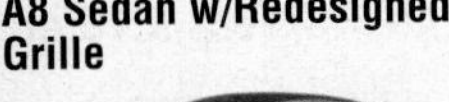

**NEW 326-23368** Standard Paint **10.95**

**NEW 326-33367** Metallic Paint **11.75**

#### A3 2-Door Hardtop

**NEW 326-23375** Standard Paint **10.75**

**NEW 326-33374** Metallic Paint **10.95**

#### Ur-Quattro 2-Door Hardtop "25 Quattro Years"

**NEW 326-33336** Metallic Paint **10.95**

#### A3 Sportback 4-Door Station Wagon

**NEW 326-46596** Audi Mobile Service **16.50**

### BMW

#### Z4 Convertible Roadster

**NEW 326-23320** Standard Paint **10.95**

**NEW 326-33329** Metallic Paint **11.75**

#### 7 Series 4-Door Sedan

**NEW 326-23344** Standard Paint **10.75**

**NEW 326-33343** Metallic Paint **10.95**

#### 3 Series Sedan

**NEW 326-23351** Standard Paint **10.75**

**NEW 326-33350** Metallic Paint **10.95**

#### 3-Series T 4-Door Station Wagon

**NEW 326-23429** Standard Paint **10.50**

**NEW 326-33428** Metallic Paint **11.25**

#### X5 Sport Utility

**NEW 326-23696** Standard Paint **10.75**

**NEW 326-33695** Metallic Paint **11.75**

#### 760 Li Sedan

**NEW 326-23740** Standard Paint **10.75**

**NEW 326-33749** Metallic Paint **11.75**

### Mini

#### Mayfair 2-Door Compact

**NEW 326-23689** Standard Paint **10.75**

**NEW 326-33688** Metallic Paint **11.75**

### Opel

#### Kadett E Gt Sedan

**NEW 326-23719** Standard Paint **9.95**

**NEW 326-33718** Metallic Paint **10.75**

### Volkswagen

#### Scirocco I 2-Door Hardtop

**NEW 326-23443** **9.75**

## European Construction Equipment

### Litronic

**NEW 326-151689** PR 734 Bulldozer w/Ripper **35.95**

## Emergency

### Ambulances

#### Mercedes

**NEW 326-47418** Sprinter German Red Cross **19.25**

### Fire Dept. Vehicles

#### Mercedes Atego Sedan Cab Pumper

**NEW 326-47401** Dietenhofen Fire Department **25.75**

**NEW 326-47449** 20/16 **26.50**

### Police Vehicles

#### Mercedes E-Class Sedan

**NEW 326-47456** Lower Saxony **15.75**

### Emergency Vehicle Accessories

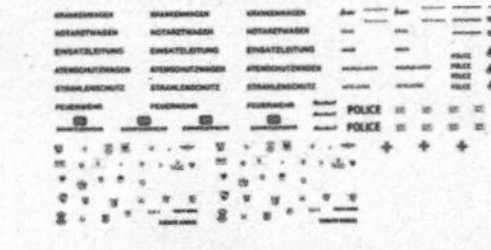

**NEW 326-50074** Fire Truck Decals **5.95**

**NEW 326-50821** Fire Dept. Rescue Boat, Hose, Lights & Tools **11.95**

**NEW 326-51163** Fire Truck Accessories **13.50**

**NEW 326-51408** Techno Design "V" Lightbar (Nonworking w/Blue Lamps) **8.50**

**NEW 326-51736** Portable Fire Pump **10.75**

## Military

### Modern German Army - Automobiles 15.75 ea

**NEW 326-47425** Mercedes E-Class Sedan Military Police

**NEW 326-47432** BMW 3 Series Sedan

## European Trucks

### DAF

**NEW 326-153300** Cf 85 Cabover w/Dry Bulk Tank Freund **39.25**

### MAN

**NEW 326-153355** Tga LX Cabover w/Dry Bulk Tank Melmer **36.75**

**NEW 326-153362** Tga Xlx Cabover w/4-Axle Flatbed **48.50**

**NEW 326-153478** Tga Xxl Cabover w/Matching 2-Axle Trailer **36.75**

## Mercedes

### Actros 36.75 ea (Unless Noted)

**NEW 326-153324** L w/3-Axle Curtain Side Trailer Wandt

**NEW 326-153348** Lh w/3-Axle Curtain Side Trailer Oppel/Air

**NEW 326-153379** L w/Roll-On/Off Container Wandt

**NEW 326-153409** S w/Roll-On/Off Dumpsters Hochtief

**NEW 326-153485** Beverage Truck & 2-Axle Trailer Hauff Braeu **37.75**

### Atego

**NEW 326-149334** Boom Truck **23.95**

## Renault Premium Cabover

**NEW 326-153270** w/3-Axle Tanker Shell **35.25**

**NEW 326-153287** w/3-Axle Curtain Side Trailer Bolk **38.50**

## Scania R TL Cabover

**NEW 326-153294** w/4Axle Canvas Side Trailer Hoevelmann **36.75**

**NEW 326-153416** Heavy-Duty Tractor w/12 Axle Flatbed Hochtief **40.50**

**NEW 326-153461** Heavy-Duty Tractor w/4-Axle Lowboy Riwatrans **51.95**

## Volvo

**NEW 326-153249** Fh Gl Truck, Dolly & Reefer Trailer Alex Andersen **45.25**

## Tractors Only

### MAN

**NEW 326-153447** F8, F90 & F2000 Set **58.50**

### Mercedes

**NEW 326-153454** Sk88, S, Sk94 w/Dual Drive Set **58.50**

### Renault

**NEW 326-153423** Magnum Cabover **17.75**

### Scania

**NEW 326-153225** Scania R TL & Volvo Fh Gl Xl Set **47.25**

## European Vans

### Volkswagen T4 Camper 11.95 ea

**NEW 326-63523** Olive Green

**NEW 326-63524** Light Blue

## Trailers

**NEW 326-5317** 40' 3-Axle Flatbed **8.95**

**NEW 326-5318** 3-Axle 48' Flatbed **8.95**

**NEW 326-5350** Round 3-Axle Chemical Tanker **10.95**

**NEW 326-5351** 2-Axle Elliptical Tanker w/Lift Axle **10.95**

**NEW 326-5353** Tri-Axle Elliptical Tank Trailer **10.95**

**NEW 326-51576** 2-Axle Utility Trailer (Use w/Cars, SUVS or Pickups) **7.95**

**NEW 326-76210** 45' 3-Axle Container Chassis w/Container **12.95**



## Private Collection

### European Automobiles

#### BMW Alpina 23.95 ea

**NEW 326-101769** B12

**NEW 326-101776** B6

### European Trucks 79.75

**NEW 326-120944** Mercedes Actros Reefer Henglein-Pizza

## Magic Series

### European Automobiles pkg(2) 7.25 ea

**NEW 326-451550** Ford Taunus P5 Sedan

**NEW 326-451574** Opel Rekord Station Wagon

**NEW 326-451598** DKW Junior 2-Door Hardtop

**NEW 326-451604** NSU TT 2-Door Hardtop

**NEW 326-451611** Porsche 914 2-Door

**NEW 326-451628** Renault R16 Sedan

**NEW 326-451567** Audi 100 L Sedan

**NEW 326-451581** Audi 60 Avant Station Wagon

### European Trucks 11.95 ea

**NEW 326-451147** Mercedes Actros LH w/Canvas Side Trailer Stroh Rum

**NEW 326-451666** Scania TL Schumacher

## Automobile Accessories

**NEW 326-50951** Towing Hitc **7.95**

## Truck Accessories

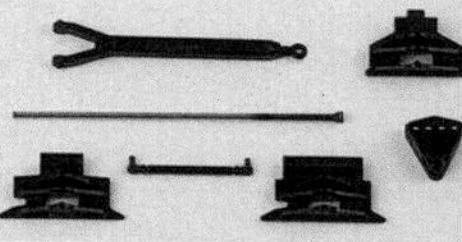

**NEW 326-51811** Push & Pul Bars **12.95**

**NEW 326-51828** Covered Flatbed Ballast Carrier for Heavy Tractor pkg(2) **9.95**

### For Mercedes

**NEW 326-51842** Mudguards Skirts for Actros Tractors pkg(3) **9.25**

**NEW 326-52320** Heavy-Duty Towing Rig for Titan pkg(2) **11.25**

### Heavy-Duty Winch For MAN Tractors 9.75 ea

**NEW 326-51798** Winch Only pkg(2)

**NEW 326-51804** w/Dual Exhaust & Warning Lights (Nonworking)

## Hiab Hydraulic Crane 9.25 ea

**NEW 326-51484** w/Small Loading Hook

**NEW 326-51491** w/Timber/Pulpwood Grapple

**NEW 326-51507** w/Pallet Fork

## Hypoid Axles pkg(8) 9.25 ea

**NEW 326-52504** Silver Plastic

**NEW 326-52511** Painted Silver

## Grille w/Nonworking Flashers 10.50 ea

**NEW 326-52528** For Mercedes-Benz Sprinter

**NEW 326-52535** For Volkswagen Crafter

# AUTOMOBILE SETS

**326-6319** Econo Vehicle Set pkg(96) **199.00**
Set of 96 (eight types) of American models from 1948 to 1965.

# AMERICAN AUTOMOBILES

## Buick

**326-22026** Grand National 2-Door Hardtop – Standard **9.50**

## Chevrolet 9.50 ea

**326-21982** 1957 Bel Air

**326-21968** 1963 Stingray Corvette 2-Door Hardtop – Standard

**326-21999** ZR1 Corvette - Standard

**326-32049** 1985 Camaro

## Chrysler

### Grand Cherokee

**326-6187** All-Terrain **8.25**

## Ford

**326-21975** AC Cobra **9.50**

**326-22019** 1969 Mustang **9.50**

**326-22033** 1989 Thunderbird 2-Door Hardtop – Standard **9.50**

## Pontiac

**326-22002** Grand Prix **9.50**

# EUROPEAN AUTOMOBILES

## Audi

### A3 Compact 2-Door Hardtop

**326-23306** Sportback **10.25**

**326-33305** Sportback (metallic) **10.95**

### 2-Door Convertible w/Top Down

**326-23061** Standard **10.25**

**326-33060** Metallic **10.95**

## BMW

### 1 Series

**326-23290** Sedan **10.25**

**326-33299** Sedan (metallic) **10.95**

### 320i

**326-23436** 320i 2-Door Hardtop **10.95**

### 1602

**326-22309** Standard **9.50**

### 5 Series Sedan

**326-23191** Standard **10.25**

**326-33190** Metallic **10.95**

**326-23269** Four Door Wagon **10.25**

**326-33268** Four Door Wagon (metallic) **10.95**

### 502

**326-22279** 4-Door Sedan **9.50**

### M3 2-Door Convertible w/Top Down

**Limited Quantity Available**

**326-22996** Standard **10.25**

**326-32995** Metallic **10.95**

### 3-Series Compact

**Limited Quantity Available**

**326-33015** Metallic **10.95**

### 6 Series

**326-23245** Convertible **10.25**

**326-33244** Convertible (metallic) **10.95**

### 3.0 CSI

**326-22811** 4-Seat Coupe 1970s Model **9.50**

### X5 4.4i 4-Door New Design "Sports Activity Vehicle"

**326-22842** Standard **10.25**

**326-32841** Metallic **10.95**

### 3 Series Touring Station Wagon - 1999 Model

**Limited Quantity Available**

**326-22873** Dark Blue Standard **10.25**

**326-32872** Aquagreen Metallic **10.95**

### Z4 2-Door Coupe w/Top Down

**Limited Quantity Available**

**326-23122** Standard (red) **10.25**

**326-33121** Metallic **10.95**

### Z8 Convertible

**326-22897** Standard **12.75**

**326-32896** Metallic **13.50**

### 6 Series Coupe

**326-23238** Standard **10.25**

**326-33237** Metallic **10.95**

## Citroen

### 2CV

**326-152181** 2CV w/Mobile Home Trailer & Peter Lustig Figure **47.25**

**326-20817** Sedan Charleston **9.75**

**326-20824** Standard **8.95**

## Fiat

### 124 Spider

**326-22354** Standard **9.50**

## Ford

### Escort 1 Two-Door Hardtop 9.50 ea

**326-22767** Early European Production Model

**326-22774** Racing Version

**326-33398** Taunus 1600 Coupe (Metallic Paint) **9.95**

## Jaguar

**326-32018** E Type **9.50**

## Mercedes

### SLK

**326-23252** Roadster Convertible w/Top Down **10.25**

**326-33251** Roadster Convertible w/Top Down **10.95**

### SL 2-Door Convertible w/Top Down

**326-23078** Standard **10.25**

**326-33077** (Metallic Paint) **10.95**

### 280SL

**326-22859** 2-Door Convertible w/Top Down 1970-89 Model **9.50**

## 300 SL

**Limited Quantity Available**

**326-32025** Gull Wing Coupe **9.50**

### CLK

### E Class 4-Door Sedan (2003 Model)

**326-23177** Standard **10.95**

**326-33176** Metallic **11.75**

### SLR McLaren 2-Door

**326-23207** Standard **12.75**

**326-33206** Metallic **13.50**

### T Class 4-Door Compact Sedan

**326-23405** Standard Paint **10.50**

**326-33404** Metallic Paint **11.25**

### CLS Coupe

**326-23313** Standard Paint **10.75**

**326-33312** Metallic Paint **10.95**

### S-Class 4-Door Sedan

**326-23412** Standard Paint **10.50**

**326-33411** Metallic Paint **11.25**

### 300 GE SUV

**326-23467** w/Open Roof - Off Road **14.50**

### CL Coupe

**Limited Quantity Available**

**326-22880** Standard **10.25**

### C-Class Elegance

**Limited Quantity Available**

**326-32957** Metallic **10.95**

## Mini-Cooper

### S 2-Door Hardtop

**326-23115** Standard **10.95**

**326-33114** Metallic **11.95**

### Mini Cooper S 2-Door Hardtop 19.75 ea

Features a flag graphic on the roof.

**326-101523** Canada

**Limited Quantity Available**

**326-101561** Mexico

### 2-Door Compact - New Body Style

**326-23023** Standard **10.95**

**326-33022** Metallic **11.95**

### Facelift

**326-22330** Folding Top Open, Standard **10.95**

## Rover Mini Cooper

**Limited Quantity Available**

**326-23276** Convertible w/Top Down **10.95**

**326-33275** Convertible w/Top Down (metallic) **11.95**

## Opel

### Safria 4-Door Station Wagon

**326-22729** Standard **10.25**

**326-32728** Metallic **10.95**

## Porsche

### 356B Cabriolet

**326-22286** Standard **9.50**

### 911

**326-22408** 1966 Standard **9.50**

**326-22835** Turbo 996 - Latest Body Style - Standard **10.25**

**326-32834** Turbo 996 - Latest Body Style - Metallic **10.95**

### 2001 911 Targa 2-Door Hardtop

**326-23030** Standard (black) **10.25**

**326-33039** Metallic (silver) **10.95**

### Carrera S 4

**326-30601** Metallic **9.50**

## Renault

### R4

**326-20190** Sedan **8.50**

### Twingo Compact Coupe

**326-21517** Top Open **8.95**

### Alpine A 110

**326-22828** 2-Door Hardtop **9.50**

### Leon 4-Door

**326-23474** Standard Paint **10.50**

**326-33473** Metallic Paint **11.25**

3-Axle Straight Truck w/Dump Bed 326-6297

T-600 Work Force 3-Axle Tractor w/20-Wheel Lowboy Heavy-Duty Flatbed Trailer 326-6302

## Trabant

### 601S

**326-20763** **8.75**

**326-20770** Universal Wagon **8.75**

**326-23450** 601 w/Luggage Standard Paint **12.95**

## Triumph

### TR 3

**326-22316** Standard **9.50**

## Volga

**326-23283** M 21 Four-Door Sedan (black) **9.50**

## Volkswagen

### Beetle

**326-22361** '69 Standard **9.50**

### Golf II GT I

**326-30519** 2-Door Compact – Metallic **9.50**

For Up-To-Date Information and News Bookmark Walthers Web site at

**www.walthers.com**

### Golf IV

**326-32575** 4-Door-Metallic **10.95**

### Karmann Ghia II

**326-23382** 2-Door Hardtop **9.50**

### Passat

### T4 Mini Van

**326-42406** California Coach-Pop-Up Camper **14.50**

## Wartburg

### 1985 4-Door Sedan

**326-22903** 353 **10.25**

# CONSTRUCTION EQUIPMENT

## International Harvester

**326-6297** 3-Axle Straight Truck w/Dump Bed **11.95**

## Kenworth

**326-6302** T-600 Work Force 3-Axle Tractor w/20-Wheel Lowboy Heavy-Duty Flatbed Trailer **24.95**

**326-6307** Dump Truck With 4 Resin Port-A-Potties (red cab, gray bed, blue Port-A-Potties) **15.95**

**326-6305** T-600 w/3-Axle Drop Deck **15.95**

**326-6311** T-600 3-Axle Conventional w/26' 2-Axle Gravel Dump Trailer (red & black w/silver) **14.95**

**326-6358** T-600 w/2-Axle Dump Trailer, 12' Drawbar w/Dolly & 26' 2-Axle Dump Trailer **21.95**

**326-6359** W-900 w/12' Drawbar & 3-Axle Dump Trailer **19.95**

## Liebherr

**326-148122** Front End Loader L580 **38.95**

**326-148931** Crawler Excavator R954 **46.95**

**326-150231** Liebherr LTM 1045/1 3-Axle Truck Crane **62.95**

**326-149921** L580 Front-End Loader "Coming to America" (red, white, silver, blue graphics) **49.95**

**326-150910** Breur & Wasel **64.75**

### R954 Litronic

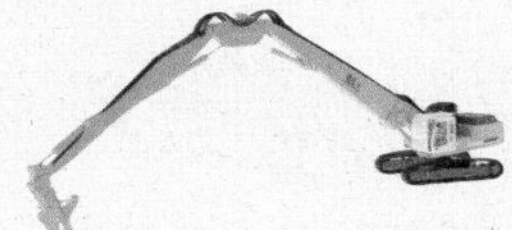

**326-152006** Crawler w/90' Demolition Boom **47.25**

## Mack

**326-6301** CH 603 Work Force 3-Axle Tractor (Anti-Glare Hood) w/2-Axle 36' Dump Trailer **15.95**

**326-6304** Truck w/2-Axle 102" Wide Drop Deck **15.95**

## MAN

### TG-A

**326-148603** XXL Lowboy Semi-Trailer w/Drop Deck **38.95**

## Mercedes-Benz

### Atego

**326-150804** Omni Dump Truck **16.75**

### Axor

**326-150903** Street Sweeper **23.25**

**326-151450** Concrete Mixer **23.95**

**326-151733** Dump Truck w/3-Axle Flatbed **35.25**

**326-152068** w/Nooteboom Teletrailer Flatbed **47.25**

### Actros

**326-150774** LH w/Flatbed & I-Beam Load **38.50**

**326-151788** M 3-Axle Cabover w/2-Axle Concrete Mixer Trailer **23.95**

**Limited Quantity Available**

**326-151443** 2002 S 4-Axle Dump Truck - Schmitt-Peterslahr **21.75**

## Kenworth

**326-6252** Conventional Heavy-Haul Dump Truck **10.95**

## Peterbilt

**326-6275** 359 w/Extended Chassis & XL Cement Mixer (red & black striped cab w/red mixer drum) **17.95**

### Scania

**326-150897** R 3-Axle Cabover Dump Truck **20.75**

**326-151894** 2004 Hauber w/Dump Trailer **25.75**

## White Road Commander

**326-6298** Cabover Dump Truck (yellow cab, silver body) **10.95**

## Trailers

**326-52368** w/Lane Closure Warning Sign **15.25**

# EMERGENCY VEHICLES

## BMW

**326-45711** 5 Series Station Wagon Brandenburg Police (silver, blue) **14.95**

**326-46244** X5 SUV German Red Cross Rheinfelden (DRK) **15.95**

**326-46770** X5 3.0 Diesel SUV Pinneberg EMS Emergency Doctor **15.50**

**326-46794** 1-Series 4-Door Hatchback Schwerin **20.75**

**326-46848** 5-Series Stationwagon Operations Control Unit **14.50**

**326-46381** 5-Series Touring Station Wagon, Berlin Autobahn Police (silver, green) **14.95**

**Limited Quantity Available**

**326-45865** 3-Series Compact "Offenbach Fire Chief" **14.25**

**326-46299** X5 SUV Samur Rescue Service (silver, red, yellow) **23.25**

**326-46480** 3 Series T Station Wagon Bavarian Police (silver, green) **14.75**

**326-46619** X3 S SUV Offenbach Inspection Unit **15.75**

## DAF

**Limited Quantity Available**

**326-45674** 65CF Cabover "Snorkel" Telescoping Rescue Platform (red, white) **25.50**

## EMO Ground Search

**326-6221** Jeep **12.50**

## Ford

**326-46374** Galaxy Mini Van German Auto Club (ADAC) (black, yellow w/Nonworking Lightbar) **17.50**

**Limited Quantity Available**

**326-450330** Straight Truck Blood Donor **15.95**

## International

**326-6246** Straight Truck Mobile Police Station **15.95**

## Jeep Grand Cherokee 10.95 ea

**326-6243** U.S. Forest Services (dark green)

**Limited Quantity Available**

**326-6244** Police (white, red & blue stripes, blue lettering, nonworking lightbar)

## Liebherr

**326-150972** LTM 1045/1 3-Axle Truck Crane **64.75**

## MAN

**326-46534** M2000 Evo LF 20/16 Sedan Cab Pumper Wiesbaden **25.50**

**Limited Quantity Available**

### LE 2000

**326-46589** HLF 20/16 Sedan Cab Pumper - Berlin **25.50**

**326-46664** LF 20/16 Sedan Cab Pumper - Kassel **26.25**

**326-45988** LE2000 Cabover w/Ruthmann Telescoping Tower Ladder TK 310 (red, white, yellow) **25.50**

**326-46077** LE2000 Sedan Cab LF 16/12 Pumper (red, white, yellow) **24.50**

**326-46169** M2000 DLK 23/12 Rearmount Aerial Ladder Truck (red, yellow, white, silver) **27.95**

## Mercedes

**326-43960** T2 Vario/Ziegler TSF-W Sedan Cab-Fire Dept. **20.75**

**326-45551** E-Class 4-Door Sedan North Rhine-Westphalia (white, blue) **12.75**

**326-45971** E Class 4-Door Sedan Fire Chief's Car (red, yellow stripe) **12.75**

**326-46121** Luxemburg Red Cross Rescue Dog Squad (white, blue, red) **17.50**

**326-46145** MB Vito Personel Van & 2-Axle Trailer; DRK - German Red Cross **26.25**

**Limited Quantity Available**

**326-45742** Vito Personnel Van THW Buehl (white, blue lettering) **12.75**

## Mercedes

**326-46275** Binz A w/Body **22.25**

**326-46305** Sprinter Van Samur Rescue Service **30.75**

**326-46350** Atego RW2 Rescue Unit (red, silver, yellow) **23.75**

**326-46466** Atego LF 20/16 Sedan Cab Pumper (red, yellow, white) **25.50**

**Limited Quantity Available**

**326-46268** T2 Armored Truck Prodiac (gray, green) **18.95**

**326-46329** Sprinter Crew-Cab Pickup Wiesbaden Fire Dept. **17.50**

**326-46435** Axor TLF 24/50 Pumper **25.50**

**326-46473** Vito Personnel Van Bremen Fire Dept. Emergency Doctor (red, white) **18.25**

### B-Class 4-Door Hatchback

**326-46985** Emergency Doctor **15.95**

### Sprinter

**326-46817** German Red Cross Kernen **17.25**

**326-46718** German Red Cross Ode-Spree District **17.50**

**326-46633** Crew Cab Covered Flatbed - Duesseldorf **17.50**

### Actros - 2002

**326-46732** S HLF Auxiliary Fire Tender **25.50**

### Atego

**326-46466** LF 20/16 Sedan Cab Pumper **25.50**

**326-46855** L32 Rear-Mount Aerial Ladder - Naila **27.25**

**Limited Quantity Available**

**326-46671** LF 20/16 Pumper/Equipment Truck - Essen **34.50**

### T2 Vario Box Van

**326-46060** LRF Rescue Unit **18.25**

### 2003 Binz A

**326-46824** Ambulance - Herne **22.95**

**Limited Quantity Available**

**326-46565** RW2 Rescue Unit w/Optional Raft & Equipment Box - Dusseldorf **24.75**

**326-46435** TLF 24/50 Pumper w/Tank **25.50**

**326-46763** Bremen **17.25**

**326-46473** Bremen Fire Dept. Emergency Doctor **18.25**

**326-46541** w/Single-Axle Box Trailer **27.95**

## Opel

### Zafira Mini-Van

**326-46626** Malteser Rescue Service **15.75**

**326-46886** Essen **15.95**

## Scania

**326-46695** R Roll-On/Off HAZMAT Unit Carrier **23.95**

## Volkswagen

### T3 Van

**326-46213** Hamburg Fire Dept. (red, yellow) **15.95**

### T4 Van

**326-46190** Wiesbaden Fire Dept. (orange, white) **15.95**

**326-46749** Duesseldorf **15.95**

# POLICE VEHICLES

## BMW

### 3-Series T Stationwagon

**326-46923** w/Nonworking Hella Lightbar **15.25**

**Limited Quantity Available**

**326-46480** Bavarian Police **14.75**

### 5-Series T Stationwagon

**326-46558** Berlin Police Dept. **15.75**

**326-46756** Brandenburg Police **14.75**

## Volga

### M 21 4-Door Sedan

**326-46725** East German Police **13.95**

**326-47005** Czechoslovakian Secret Police **12.95**

## Wartburg

### 1966 353 4-Door Sedan

**326-46701** Volkspolizei **13.95**

# TECHNICAL RESCUE SERVICE (THW)

## Mercedes Benz

### Sprinter

**326-46961** Crew Cab Covered Flatbed - Bad Essen **15.25**

# MILITARY

## Modern German Army (BW)

### Personnel Vans - BW Fuhrpark Service (Motor Pool)

**326-46787** Mercedes Vito **13.95**

Get Your Daily Dose of Product News at

**www.walthers.com**

**326-46657** Opel Zafira **14.50**

## Engineering Equipment

**326-151962** Liebherr L580 Front-End Loader **47.25**

# LIGHT TRUCKS

## European

### Mercedes

**Limited Quantity Available**

**326-42246** T2 Van Unpainted **8.95**

# BUSES

**326-6100** School Bus **14.95**

## Setra

**Limited Quantity Available**

**326-6257** S215 HDH North American Style Tour Bus (metallic gray) **15.95**

# SPORTS UTILITY VEHICLES (SUVs)

## BMW

**326-23221** X3 Standard **10.25**

**326-33220** X3 Metallic **10.95**

**326-6268** Security Vehicle (white w/red & blue markings) **10.95**

## Porsche Cayenne 4-Door

### Turbo 4x4

**326-23153** Standard **10.25**

**326-33152** Metallic **10.95**

### S Hardtop

**326-23146** Standard **10.25**

**326-33145** Metallic **10.95**

# TRUCKS–AMERICAN SEMIS

Includes matching tractor and trailer unless noted.

**American**
326-6262 Log Truck w/Log Picker **19.95**

**Limited Quantity Available**
326-450350 Pacific Tank Truck **15.95**

**3-Axle Container Chassis**
326-5315 40' **4.95**
326-5316 48' **5.50**

**3-Axle Flatbed 8.95 ea**
326-5317 40'
326-5318 48'

**Ford**
326-6162 Aeromax w/36' Dump Trailer **13.95**
326-6205 L-9000, Doubles, Ford Motorcraft **14.95**
326-6316 Aeromax 3-Axle Conventional w/Sleeper w/45' Full-Frame, Tri-Axle Curtain Wall Van (blue tractor) **19.95**
326-6295 L9000 3-Axle Conventional Tractor w/48' Box Van Trailer - Preston The 151 Line **14.95**

326-6360 L-9000 w/2 Container Chassis, Dolly & 40' Box Containers - Undecorated **21.95**
326-450370 S Series 2-Axle Garbage Truck (orange cab, white body) **15.95**

**GMC General**

326-6053 Overnite–Doubles **16.95**

**International (Navistar)**
326-6206 26' Straight Truck **10.95**

**Beverage Trucks**

326-6135 Taylor & Bates w/Trailer **14.95**

**Freightliner**

326-6353 Cabover w/Sleeper & Asphalt Tank Trailer **21.95**
326-15248 FLB 86 3-Axle Cabover w/Fairings & Airdam (undecorated) **8.95**
326-146869 FLB 86 3-Axle Cabover Tractor w/Sleeper - Standard Model **15.95**
326-146876 FLB 86 3-Axle Cabover w/Sleeper & Roof-Mounted Airdam **15.95**

**Limited Quantity Available**

326-6350 FLB 86 Cabover w/48' Box Van Trailer Weyerhaeuser **15.95**

**Kenworth**

326-6114 Dump Trailer **14.95**
326-6156 T600 w/48' Flatbed **15.95**
326-6195 W-900 w/48' Flatbed **17.95**
326-6230 T-600 Aerodyne Hill Transport **16.95**
326-6232 T-600a w/Aero-sleeper & 45' Van Trailer Southwestern **16.95**
326-6237 With Aerosleeper; B-Train Elliptical Tank Trailer Doubles **29.95**
326-6263 T-600 w/40' & Two 27' Van Trailers **25.95**
326-6306 W-900 Conventional Long Chassis/Flat Top Sleeper w/48' 3-Axle Drop Deck Trailer & Old Fire Truck Load **17.95**
326-6314 W-900 3-Axle Conventional w/Dual 48' Vans & 2-Axle Converter Dolly **19.95**
326-6332 W-900 With 2-Axle Logging Bunk **15.95**
326-6331 W-900 With Sleeper & 2 3-Axle Container Chassis w/48' Box Containers; A-Train Doubles **19.95**
326-6347 W-900 w/Skirted Chassis, Tool Box & 48' Livestock Trailer (white Tractor, black Trailer) **17.95**
326-6348 T-600 w/48' Livestock Trailer (blue Tractor, red Trailer) **17.95**

326-6356 T-600 Flat Top w/Bulk Tank **23.95**
326-25289 T-600 w/Sleeper & Long Flatbed (white) **9.50**
326-25290 T-600 Flatbed w/Sleeper Painted **9.95**

Kenworth (W-900 3-Axle Conventional w/Dual 48' Vans & 2-Axle Converter Dolly 326-6314

**Mack**

326-6071 CH 603 Tractor w/Walinga Bulk Feed Trailer Undecorated **16.95**
326-6224 Short Tractor w/Double Trailers N.Y.C.E. **15.95**
326-6313 CH 603 3-Axle Conventional w/Dual 3-Axle Hi-Boy Flatbed Trailers & 3-Axle Converter Dolly **19.95**
326-6328 CH 613 3-Axle Conventional w/Sleeper w/Two 48' Tri-Axle Vans B Train Doubles (Undecorated) **19.95**
326-6349 With 48' Livestock Trailer (gray Tractor, silver Trailer) **17.95**
326-450320 3-Axle Straight Truck – CH Cab w/Utility Body **15.95**

**Peterbilt**
326-6247 3-Axle Cabover w/Sleeper w/Two 27' Van Trailers Action Express (white, red & blue lettering) **16.95**

326-6255 362E 3-Axle Cabover w/45' Bottom-Dump Canvas Covered Grain Trailer **19.95**
326-6269 Flatbed w/3-Cargo Box Load & HIAB Hoist **24.95**
326-6329 362 Cabover w/Sleeper w/Two 27' Box Van Trailers - A Train Doubles **18.95**

326-6361 362E Cabover w/3-Axle Double Drop Deck Flatbed **19.95**
326-35232 With New Sleeper, Skirted Chassis **9.95**
326-35233 With New Sleeper, Skirted Chassis, Painted **10.95**

**White Road Commander**
326-450340 Single-Axle Oil/Fuel Delivery Tank Truck (yellow, no lettering) **15.95**

**Tractors**
Kits are fully assembled and include chrome add-ons, such as airhorns, grab irons and mirrors.

L9000 3-Axle Conventional Tractor w/48' Box Van Trailer - Preston The 151 Line 326-6295

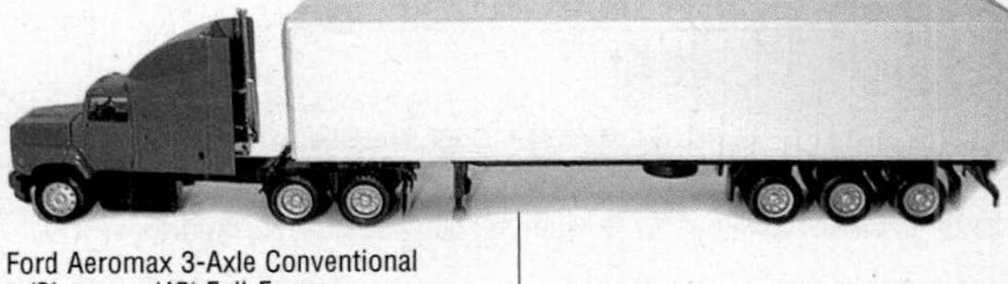

Ford Aeromax 3-Axle Conventional w/Sleeper w/45' Full-Frame, Tri-Axle Curtain Wall Van 326-6316

Peterbilt Flatbed w/3-Cargo Box Load & HIAB Hoist 326-6269

**Unlettered**
Cabs are painted in various colors, with no markings.
326-6226 International/Navistar U-Haul Type Box Van **10.95**

326-6310 Peterbilt 362 E 3-Axle Cabover w/Airdam (white, unpainted) **9.95**
326-15233 Peterbilt **7.50**
326-15235 GMC General **7.50**
326-15241 Ford L-9000 Short, Painted **9.95**
326-15264 Mack-No Sleeper **8.50**

326-15265 Mack CH603 w/Small Retro-fit Air Shield **9.50**

326-15277 Freightliner 3-Axle Conventional No Sleeper - Undecorated **7.95**

326-15278 Freightliner 3-Axle Conventional No Sleeper - Painted **8.95**
326-15290 Kenworth T-600 **9.95**
326-15297 International 2-Axle **8.50**
326-25233 Peterbilt Tractor w/Sleeper **7.95**
326-25235 GMC General w/Sleeper **7.95**
326-25236 White Road Commander 2-Axle **6.95**
326-25237 White Road Commander 3-Axle **7.50**
326-25238 Freightliner Medium Cab **8.95**
326-25239 Freightliner Supercab **8.95**
326-25241 Ford Aeromax w/Sleeper Painted **9.25**
326-25247 Freightliner FLB 86 Cabover w/Sleeper 3-Axle, No Airdam **8.95**
326-25248 Freightliner FLB 86 Cabover w/Sleeper 3-Axle w/Airdam & Fairings **9.95**
326-25249 Freightliner FLB 86 Cabover w/Sleeper 2-Axle, No Airdam **8.95**
326-25252 Freightliner Classic **10.95**

326-25264 Mack 613 w/Sleeper **9.50**

**326-25277** Kenworth W-900 Skirted Chrome Chassis w/Toolbox - Undecorated **9.95**

**326-25281** Kenworth W-900 w/Round Top Sleeper - Undecorated **7.95**

**326-25282** Kenworth W-900 w/Round Top Sleeper - Orange **8.95**

**326-25289** Kenworth T-600b Conventional w/Sleeper & Dual Rear Axles - Unpainted (white) **9.50**

**326-35235** Kenworth W-900 3-Axle Conventional w/60" Aerodyne Sleeper & Extended Chassis - Painted **10.95**

**326-35290** Kenworth T-600 Aero Sleeper **10.95**

### Peterbilt 359 Conventional

Includes long chrome chassis, toolbox bull bar and sleeper.

**326-25279** Undecorated **10.95**

**326-25280** Blue **11.95**

**326-144872** Peterbilt 2-Axle Conventional w/New Sleeper, Chromed Skirts & Airfoil **15.95**

**326-146180** Peterbilt 3-Axle Cabover w/Sleeper (black, chrome) **15.95**

**326-149686** Kenworth 3-Axle Conventional w/Aerodynamic Chassis & Large Sleeper **17.75**

### Undecorated

Cabs are white plastic with no markings.

**326-15232** Peterbilt **6.50**

**326-15234** GMC General **6.50**

**326-15236** Freightliner 2-Axle **6.50**

**326-15237** Freightliner 3-Axle **6.50**

**326-15238** Freightliner w/Sleeper **7.95**

**326-15239** Freightliner w/Long Sleeper **7.95**

**326-15240** Ford L-9000 Short Cab **8.95**

**326-15246** Peterbilt 362E Cabover Dual Axle w/Sleeper **7.95**

**326-15263** Mack-No Sleeper **7.95**

**326-35234** Kenworth W-900 X-Large Sleeper (Undecorated - white) **9.95**

**326-15289** Kenworth T-600 **8.95**

**326-25232** Peterbilt Tractor w/Sleeper **7.25**

**326-25234** GMC General-Short Wheelbase w/Sleeper-White **7.25**

**326-25240** Ford Aeromax w/Sleeper **8.50**

**326-25251** Freightliner Classic **9.95**

**326-25263** Mack 613 w/Sleeper **8.95**

**326-35232** Peterbilt w/New Sleeper & Skirted Chassis **9.95**

**326-35233** Peterbilt w/63" Sleeper & Skirted Chassis **10.95**

**326-35289** Kenworth T-600 Aero Sleeper **9.95**

**326-450020** Mack 603/613 3-Axle **9.95**

**326-450030** Mack 603/613 2-Axle w/Single Idler Axle **9.95**

**Limited Quantity Available**

**326-6337** Freightliner 3-Axle Supercab (Cabover) Tractor Only Painted w/White Airdam **9.95**

### Painted 8.95 ea

**326-25246** Peterbilt 362E Cabover Dual Axle w/Sleeper

### W-900

**3-Axle Conventional, Short Chassis**

**326-15275** Unpainted **7.95**

**326-15276** Painted (orange or green) **8.95**

**3-Axle Conventional, Long Chassis w/Chromed Air Deflector Wing**

**326-25275** Unpainted **8.95**

**326-25276** Painted (orange or green) **9.95**

## EUROPEAN TRUCKS

### BUSSING

**326-152167** 8000 Covered Flatbed w/3-Axle Flatbed Trailer - Wandt **34.95**

### DAF

**Limited Quantity Available**

**326-147668** CF Cabover Box Van & Matching 2-Axle Trailer w/Roll-On/Off Box Body CargoLine (red, black, white) **34.95**

### HENSCHEL

**326-152150** HS 140 Covered Flatbed w/3-Axle Flatbed Trailer **34.95**

### KRUPP

**Titan**

**326-150934** Covered Flatbed w/3-Axle Trailer **31.95**

**326-152174** BV Avral **23.95**

### MAN

**326-146265** TG-A XXL 2-Axle Cabover Tractor Only (blue) **17.75**

**326-146838** E2000 Evo 4-Axle Heavy-Duty Tractor Only **21.75**

Painted (orange or green) 326-25276

**326-148627** TG-A XL 4-Axle Heavy Duty Tractor w/Techno Design 8000 Warning Light (Light Blue) **25.50**

**326-151993** Kuebler **39.25**

**Limited Quantity Available**

**326-120432** TG-A XXL Safeliner "Friedenstruck" w/Special Paint & Graphics **78.95**

### Mercedes

**326-148849** Actros L 2-Axle Cabove w/sleeper & separate grille (red) **17.75**

**326-149334** Atego Cabover Flatbed w/Snorkel "Cherry Picker" Basket (orange) **23.95**

**326-150187** Actros M 2-Axle Cabover (red) w/3-Axle Kogel Dump Trailer (silver) **23.95**

**326-150460** 2002 Actros LH 3-Axle Cabover w/Sleeper & Air Dam **17.75**

**326-150538** Actros S Cabover 4-Axle Dump Truck **23.25**

**326-150651** Actros Titan 4-Axle Tractor **25.50**

**326-150675** Axor HD 2-Axle Cabover w/Airdam **17.75**

**326-151139** Kuehne & Nagel **34.95**

**326-151320** Ottensmann **34.95**

**326-151597** Schenker Stinnes **35.50**

**Limited Quantity Available**

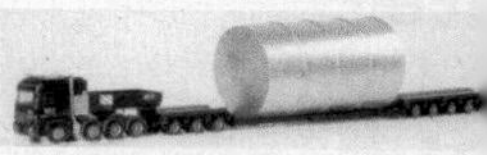

**326-149624** Actros SLT 4-Ax Heavy Tractor w/8-Axle Lowboy Flatbed & Tank Loac Kuehne & Nage **50.95**

**326-149914** Actros L 2-Axle Cabover w/3-Axle Canvas Side Trailer - Huppe (black, white, red) **33.50**

**326-150415** Mercedes S 2-Axle Cabover w/3-Axle Tar Trailer Hoyer (gray, white, re **38.95**

### Renault Magnum

**Limited Quantity Available**

**326-148269** 2-Axle Cabover w/Skirted 3-Axle Euro Box Va Trailer "TIP/CTR" (blue, silve yellow) **34.25**

### Scania

**326-150422** 2004 R Topline 2-Axle Cabover w/Sleeper & Airdam **17.75**

**326-150545** R Highline 2-Axl Cabover w/Airdam **17.75**

**326-150705** R Cabover Stak Truck w/Rear Loading Crane 2-Axle Flatbed Trailer **38.50**

**326-151115** 2-Axle w/Airdam (Tractor Only) **17.75**

**326-151726** 3-Axle Topline w/ Sleeper & Airdam (Tractor Only) **17.75**

**Limited Quantity Available**

**326-150453** 2004 R Topline 2-Axle Cabover w/3-Axle Euro Box Reefer Trailer Kleiner Feigling/Behn Originale **37.95**

Model R

326-151764 Cabover (Tractor Only) 16.75

**Limited Quantity Available**

326-149778 TL HD Cabover Box Van & Matching Trailer Worms (blue, red, white) 33.50

## Tractors

### DAF

326-148924 Body Style 95XF SSC 2-Axle Cabover w/Sleeper (orange) 17.75

### MAN

326-148108 TG-A XXL 3-Axle Cabover w/Sleeper - 2002 Restyling 17.75

### Mercedes

326-148795 Actros LH 2-Axle Cabover (blue) 17.75

326-151436 Tractor Only 17.75

### Volvo

326-149204 FH 12 2-A 2-Axle Cabover 17.75

326-149365 Volvo FH 12 GL 2-Axle Cabover w/Airdam 17.75

For Daily Product Updates Point Your Browser to

**www.walthers.com**

# PRIVATE COLLECTION VEHICLES

Models feature chrome rims, wipers, window frames, ornamental fittings and lettering, design stripe, plus chrome embossed or painted rearview mirrors.

## Automobiles

### Audi

326-100939 S2 Coupe (red) 17.95

### BMW

326-101127 Z3 M-Coupé 22.95

**Limited Quantity Available**

326-101134 3 Series Sedan 1998 Model 20.75

### Daimler Chrysler

326-101455 Maybach 57 4-Door Luxury Sedan (Two-tone light & dark green) 27.95

### Mercedes

**Limited Quantity Available**

326-101066 SLK Roadster 20.75

## SUVs

### DAF

326-110266 CF Tractor 26.95

## Trucks

### Fulda

326-120319 3-Axle Streamlined Cabover Promotional Truck w/Special 3-Axle Trailer 87.95

### Mercedes

326-110280 Actros LH 2-Axle Cabover 26.95

# MAGIC SERIES EUROPEAN TRUCKS

Made of diecast metal and plastic.

## MAN TG-A XXL w/3-Axle Euro Box Trailer 11.95 ea

326-451239 2-Axle Cabover Pedigree Dog Food w/Yellow Lab (yellow)

326-451260 Nippon (red, white, yellow, brown)

### Mercedes

326-451253 Actros LH 2-Axle Cabover w/3-Axle Euro Box Trailer - Mr. Tom (tan, red, yellow) 11.95

**Limited Quantity Available**

326-451222 Actros LH 2-Axle Cabover w/3-Axle Euro Box Van - Whiskas Cat Food w/Kittens (purple) 11.95

### Scania

326-451024 TL 2-Axle Cabover w/3-Axle Box Van Trailer - Wirtz 11.95

326-451246 TL HD 2-Axle Cabover w/3-Axle Euro Box Trailer - Trill w/Parakeet Art (green) 11.95

# TRAILERS

## American

326-5271 40' Reefer 6.75

326-5272 40' Dry Van 6.50

326-5273 27' Trailer 4.50

326-5274 Converter Dolly 2.50

326-5275 Elliptical Tank Trailer 9.50

326-5276 40' Flatbed 7.95

326-5280 40' Reefer Container 4.95

326-5281 36' Dump Trailer 6.75

326-5282 Walinga Feed Tank Trailer 9.50

326-5283 48' Electronics Van 6.75

326-5287 Chemical Tank Trailer, Round 9.50

326-5288 27' Dump Trailer 6.75

326-5291 48' Container & Trailer 9.25

326-5292 48' Container 5.50

326-5294 48' Flatbed 8.95

326-5300 Dual Axle Trailer Chassis 2.95

326-5301 Single Axle Trailer Chassis 2.00

326-5303 40' Container Chassis 4.25

326-5304 48' Container Chassis 4.25

326-5312 48' Van 6.75

326-5320 45' Container – Undecorated 5.50

326-5331 48' Spread-Axle Drop Deck Trailer w/Toolbox 8.95

326-5332 48' Tri-Axle Drop Deck Trailer w/Aluminum Deck 8.95

326-5340 36' Tri-Axle Dump Trailer 8.50

326-5362 3-Axle 48' Double Drop Deck Flatbed 9.95

326-5363 Dual Spread Axle Double Drop Deck 9.95

326-52382 2-Axle Box Trailer - Herpa on Tour 11.95

326-52221 Single Axle Covered Light Trailer; Use w/Car or Truck 7.95

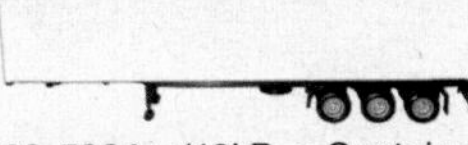

326-5364 w/48' Box Container 9.95

326-5365 w/40' Box Container 8.95

326-75657 Glass Transport 13.95

326-75664 Curtain Van (white) 14.75

326-75671 Asphalt Tank 14.75

326-75695 Jumbo Box 13.50

326-75787 5-Axle Modular Lowboy Flatbed Adapted For Large Tanks 20.95

326-75824 Bulk Tanker 60 Cubic Meters Undecorated (white) 15.75

326-75848 3-Axle Bulk Dry Lading Tank Trailer 13.50

326-75886 Euro Reefer 3-Axle Semi Trailer 13.50

326-75954 3-Axle Curtain Side w/Open Curtain 13.50

326-75985 40' High-Cube Container w/3-Axle Chassis 12.75

326-75992 4-Axle Euro Canvascover Trailer 11.95

326-76005 4-Axle Hi-Boy Flatbed w/Side Stakes 13.75

326-76012 3-Axle Gasoline Tanker 14.75

326-76036 Carnehl 2-Axle Dump Trailer 11.95

326-76050 3-Axle Nooteboom Teletrailer 23.25

326-75893 Lowliner Curtainside 3-Axle Canvas Trailer 13.50

326-460000 27' 2-Axle Van (Unpainted) 6.95

326-460010 2-Axle Converter Dolly 4.95

326-460050 48' 3-Axle Van (unpainted) 9.95

326-460060 48' 2-Axle w/Idler (Tag) Axle (unpainted) 9.95

326-460070 48' Dual Spread Axle Van (unpainted) 9.95

### 48' Livestock Trailers 9.95 ea

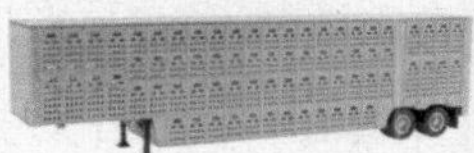

326-5354 Silver

326-5355 Black

326-5356 Red

## European

326-75350 Euro-Box 13.50

326-75404 Euro Canvas 13.50

326-75565 Canvas Cover w/Working Doors 15.75

326-75602 3-Axle Dump (unpainted) 12.50

326-75619 3-Axle Round Tank Trailer 14.75

326-75626 2-Axle Dump (unpainted) 11.95

**326-75909** 3-Axle, 55 Cubic Meter Capacity Dry Bulk Tank Trailer **13.50**

**326-146470** Goldhofer 5-Axle Heavy-Duty Lowboy Flatbed **19.95**
Use with 3-Axle Heavy Haul truck, sold separately.

# VANS

## Mercedes

**Limited Quantity Available**

**326-6312** Step Van Parcel Service **8.50**

### Viano

**326-23214** Standard **10.95**

### Sprinter

**Limited Quantity Available**

**326-46114** Cargo DHL (yellow, red) **16.75**

**326-46879** Wide Load Escort - Bruns **21.75**

**326-46978** Crew Cab Covered Flatbed - Colonia **19.95**

**326-46992** Crew Cab w/Glass Transport Body **19.25**

### Vito

**326-46015** Mini Bus (red) **11.25**

**Limited Quantity Available**

**326-46008** Cargo (green) **11.25**

## Peugeot

**326-23481** 806 w/Trailer & Peugeot 205 Turbo 2-Door Hatchback **27.95**

## Volkswagen

**326-6266** California Coach w/Pop-Up Tent **10.95**

**326-6357** T4 Van Camper - "Sunset in Arizona" **13.50**

**326-63524** Volkswagen T4 Camper (light blue) **11.95**

# VEHICLE ACCESSORIES

**326-51262** Sport Rims for Passenger Cars **15.25**

**326-50234** Fuel Tanks & Exhaust **9.95**

**326-52306** Taxi Signs pkg(20) **8.50**

## Containers

**326-75732** 20' Tank Containers pkg(2) **15.25**

**326-75749** 40' Bulkhead Flatbed Containers pkg(2) **10.95**

**326-75756** 20' Extended End Tank Containers pkg(2) **15.25**

## 40' Dry Bulk Pressurized

**326-76043** Bruhn Spedition (Truck or Train) **11.95**

**326-76067** Bruhn Spedition - Train Only **11.95**

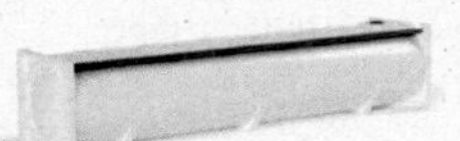

**326-75978** Undecorated (Truck or Train) **9.25**

## 30' Dry Bulk Pressurized 11.95 ea

**326-76029** Europool (Truck or Train)

**326-76074** Europool - Train Only

## 20' Box

**326-76104** Hamburg Süd pkg(2) **17.25**

## Interchangeable Boxes pkg(2) 17.75 ea

**326-76081** DHL - For Trains Only

**326-76098** Wandt - For Trains Only

## Steering Kits

Includes tie rods, spindles and pins to convert fixed front axles into positionable type for more realism.

**326-50517** Construction Equipment **6.50**

**326-50333** Trucks **6.50**

## Tow Bars

**326-52191** pkg(12) **8.50**

## Truck Accessories

**326-5313** All-Purpose Fifth Wheels pkg(10) **5.50**

**326-5314** Airfoils (silver) pkg(5) **4.25**

**326-5322** Tractor-Mounted Hoist w/Working Hydraulics **6.95**

**326-5324** Coe Airdam (3 Pieces) **4.50**

**326-5326** Extended Tractor Chassis for Kenworth W-900 or Peterbilt (chrome plated) **5.95**

**326-5333** 20' Single-Axle Container Chassis **3.50**

**326-5334** Mirror Package **1.75**

**326-5342** Kenworth Conversion Kit for W-900 Tractor (sold separately) **3.50**
Includes New Grille w/Removable Bug Screen, Dual Aircleaners and New Dual Exhaust.

**326-5343** Chrome-Plated Air Foils pkg(5) **5.75**

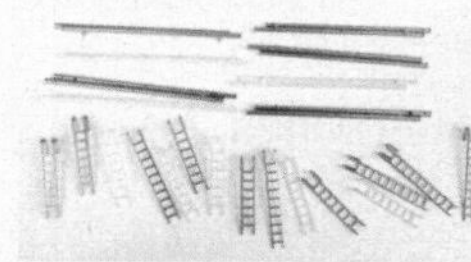

**326-5357** Assorted Ladders (15) & Pipes (8) **5.75**

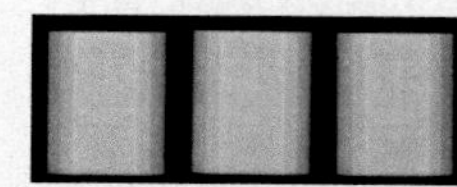

**326-5369** For Trailer or Straight Truck pkg(3) **2.95**

**326-5358** Truck Tires pkg(50) **4.95**

**326-5360** Air Deflectors for Front of Trailer pkg(3) **5.95**

**326-5361** 3-Axle Trailer Chassis pkg(2) **6.95**

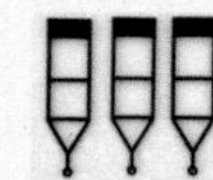

**326-5367** 12' Drawbars pkg(3) **4.95**

**326-5368** Passenger Van Tires pkg(10) **5.75**

**326-51002** Trim Panels **12.95**

**326-51101** Warning Systems **8.50**

**326-51118** Aerodynamics Package for 1994 Mercedes Sk **9.25**

**326-51170** Aerodynamic Package for Scania SL **8.75**

**326-51200** Undercarriage Protection **9.25**

**326-51217** Undercarriage Protection Set #2 **9.25**

**326-51286** 6- & 10-Cylinder Truck Engine **6.50**

**326-51378** Mudguards for Semi Tank Trailer **6.25**

**326-51385** Cow Catcher for MB Actros L **10.75**

**326-51392** Cow Catcher for MB Actros Lh **10.75**

**326-51422** Nose-Mounted Carrier Reefer Units pkg(3) **9.25**

**326-51446** Front End Guard w/Bumper for Scania Tractor **10.75**

**326-51453** Converter Dolly - 2-Axle Fifth Wheel Platorm **11.95**

**326-51538** Front End Guard for MAN TG-A XXI Tractors **10.75**

**326-51583** Full-Width Mud-flaps for Trucks & Trailers **12.95**

**326-51606** Rear Full-Width Bumper for Heavy-Duty Flatbed Trailer **10.75**
Fits Trailer Assemblies #326-51613 and #326-51620, each sold separately.

**326-51613** 2-Axle Heavy-Dut Trailer Conversion Units Heavy-Duty Trailer Tailboard Loader for #326-51637, sold separately **10.75**

**326-51620** 3-Axle Heavy-Dut Trailer Conversion Units Heavy-Duty Trailer Tailboard Loader for #326-51637, sold separately **12.50**

**326-51637** Heavy-Duty Traile Tailboard Loader & Swan-Nec **13.50**

**326-51644** Dump Box for 3-Axle Trucks **10.75**

**326-51651** Dump Box for 4-Axle Trucks **10.75**

**326-51668** Dump Box for 2-Axle Trailer **10.75**

**326-51675** Dump Box for 2-Axle Dump Semi-Trailer **12.50**

**326-51682** Side Impact Protection Barrier for Euro Trailer pkg(6) **7.95**

**326-51712** Cement Mixer Tan & Mount for 3-Axle Trucks **10.75**

**326-51859** Heavy-Duty Towin Conector for MAN E2000 **7.75**

**326-51866** Conversion Grilles w/Nonworking Blue Lights for Mercedes Sprinter pkg(8) **10.50**

**326-51873** Heavy-Duty Bumper w/Towing Connector for Mercedes Actros **11.25**

**326-51880** Heavy-Duty Towin Package for MAN TG-A **9.75**

**326-51897** Front End Guard & Bumper for MAN TGA **10.75**

**326-51903** Horns, Loudspeakers & Roof Rack **10.50**

**326-51910** Parts For Modular Lowboy Flatbed **6.95**

**326-51927** Roof Lights For All Tractor Cabs **8.95**

**326-51934** Telescoping Tank Adapter for Modular Lowboy Flatbed Trailer **13.95**

326-51941 Schmitz Truck/Trailer Rear Bumpers pkg(6) **11.75**

326-51958 Roof-Top Warning Sign For BF3 (2 Pieces) **12.50**

### M2000 Grille w/Nonworking Blue Flashers 10.50 ea

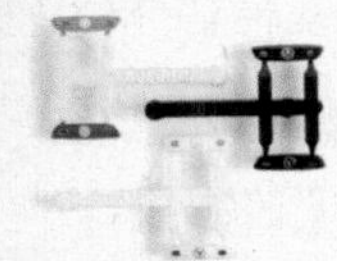

**326-52351** Mercedes Vito

**326-52344** MAN M2000

### Semi-Tractor Air Conditioners pkg(4)

**326-52207** White **11.25**

**326-52214** 1 Each Red, White, Blue & Black **7.95**

### Truck Parts

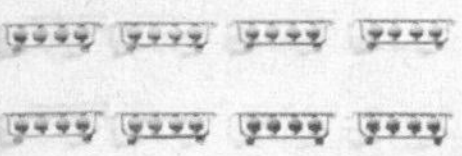

**326-52245** Bumper-Mounted Road/Fog Lights (Chrome Plated) **7.25**

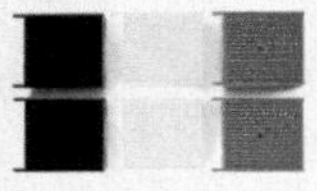

**326-52290** Pallet Boxes pkg(6) **9.95**

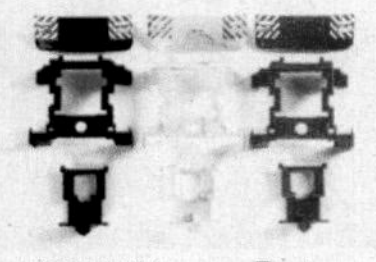

**326-52238** Heavy-Duty Bumpers for MAN TG-A **11.95**

### Trailer Details

**326-5302** Landing Gear **.60**

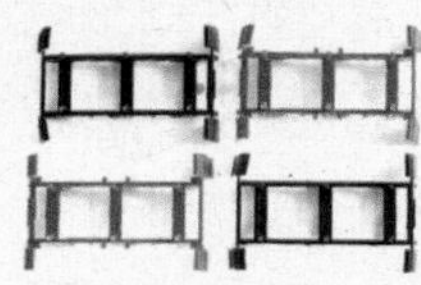

**326-52313** Trailer Chassis for Low Liner **8.50**

### Landing Gear - Trailer Support Wheelsets

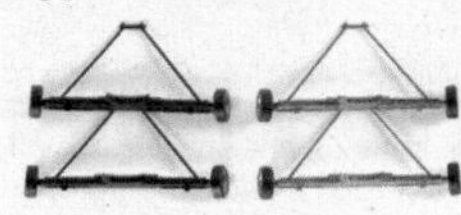

**326-52276** For tank Trailers **9.75**

### Undercarriage Protection Set

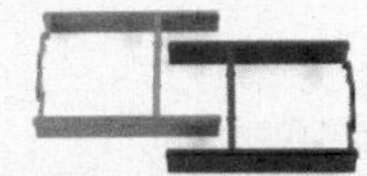

**326-52375** #1 **10.50**
**326-51217** #2 **9.25**

### Two-Axle Trailers

**326-51576** Utility (Use w/Cars, SUVS or Pick-Ups) **7.95**

### Thermo-King Reefer Units 9.25 ea

**326-51743** Rounded, Nose Mount

**326-51750** Underframe Mount

### Frigoblock

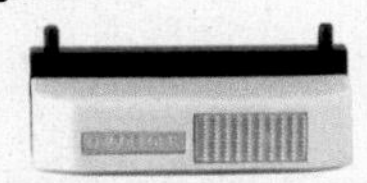

**326-5359** Frigoblock w/Mounting Plates pkg(3) **2.50**

**326-51767** Reefer Unit, Underframe Mount **9.25**

**326-51965** Side-Mount Guard For Semi Trailers **9.25**

**326-52047** Cow Catchers for 2002 Mercedes Actros L pkg(3) **10.75**

**326-52054** Cow Catchers for 2002 Mercedes Actros LH pkg(3) **10.75**

### Truck Loads

**326-50555** Cable Drums **6.50**

**326-75916** Large Container for Heavy Haul Trailer **12.50**

**326-75930** Bulk Tank **5.25**

**326-75947** Boiler **12.50**

**Limited Quantity Available**

**326-75923** Large Diameter Tank **5.25**

### Warning Lights 6.50 (Unless Noted)

**326-50159** Orange **7.95**

**326-50425** Hella Warning Light/Siren (blue)

**326-50494** Light Bars (red, blue & amber)

**326-50814** Hella Lite-Bar (blue & amber)

**326-52146** Hella RTK-6 Nonworking, Blue Lamps, White Base **8.50**

**326-52153** Hella RTK-6 Nonworking, Orange Lamps, White Base **8.50**

### Techno Design (Nonworking) 8.50 ea

**326-51699** 8000 Lightbar for Trucks (Blue Lamps)

**326-51705** 8000 Lightbar for Cars (Blue Lamps)

**326-51774** Amber Lightbar for Automobiles

**326-51781** Amber Lightbar for Trucks

### Wheels & Tires

**326-5335** Dayton Truck Wheels; 2 Front Single & 10 Rear Duals w/Tires (silver) pkg(12) **5.75**

**326-5336** Budd Truck Wheels; 2 Front Single & 10 Rear Duals w/Tires (chrome) pkg(12) **5.75**

**326-5337** Budd Truck Wheels; 2 Front Single & 10 Rear Duals w/Tires (silver) pkg(12) **5.75**

**326-5338** Low Profile Trailer Wheels & Tires pkg(6) **4.95**

**326-50197** Truck 6-Spoke **6.50**

**326-50357** Bus **8.50**

**326-50531** Chrome Truck Wheels **10.50**

**326-50920** Set of 3 Fifth Wheels **9.75**

**326-51033** 2-Part Wheels **9.75**

**326-51040** 2-Part Wheels #2 **8.75**

**326-51279** Special Wide Tires & Rims for Front Axle **8.75**

**326-51347** Special Wide Front Tires & Wheels for Trucks **9.75**

**326-51521** Wide Front Tires & Chrome Wheels for Trucks **10.50**

**326-51545** Front Tractor Tires w/Chrome Wheels & Metal Axles **9.75**

**326-51552** Low Profile Semi Tractor Tires (Wheels, Tires & Axles - Singles & Duals) **6.50**

**326-51569** Wheelsets (Tire, Wheel & Steel Axle) for Mega Trailer **6.50**

**326-51972** Red Wheelsets For Heavy-Haul Trailer pkg(10) **9.95**

**326-51989** Blue Wheel Sets For Heavy-Haul Trailer pkg(10) **9.95**

**326-52009** Dual Chrome Wheels w/Tires, Red Hubs & Axles (8 Sets) **10.50**

**326-52016** Trailer Tires w/Chrome Wheels, Red Hubs & Axles (9 Sets) **10.50**

**326-52023** Chrome Dual Wheels w/Black Hubs, Tires & Axles (8 Sets) **10.50**

**326-52030** Chrome Wheels w/Black Hubs & Axles for Trailers (9 Sets) **10.50**

**326-51996** Wide Front Tires, Axles & Red Hubs (8 Sets) **9.50**

**326-52139** Super Wide **11.95**

### Hypoid Axles 8-Sets 10.50 ea

**326-52399** Red

**326-52337** Chrome & Black

### Lowliner Wheels & Tires

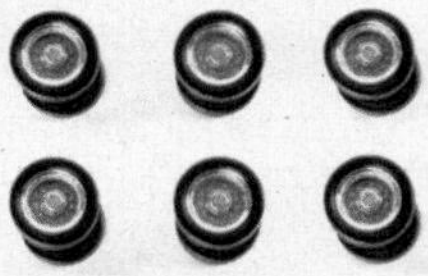

**326-52283** Chrome pkg(9) **10.50**

**326-52252** Chrome & Red pkg(9) **10.50**



### Wheels w/Tires 11.95

Customize your trucks with these wheels featuring different brands of tires. Each set includes six axles with preprinted tires.

**326-52108** Fulda

**326-52115** Bridgestone

**326-52122** Continental

**326-52160** Pirelli

**326-52177** Michelin

**326-52184** Dunlop

## STARTER SETS

### 199.00 ea

**326-149464** Gas Station #1; w/Roadway, Building Set & 5 Vehicles

**326-149655** Gas Station #2

**326-151580** Construction Company; 5 Vehicles, Building Materials & Paving

**Limited Quantity Available**

**326-149488** Trucking Company; 3 Trucks, 2 Cars, Warehouse & Roadway

International Hobby Corp.

Assembled, appropriately colored plastic vehicles, unless noted.

## AUTOMOBILES

**348-816** 1940-50s Style pkg(4) **4.98**

**348-1720** Assorted Classic Cars pkg(6) **7.98**
Diecast metal body with plastic details and underframe.

**348-1721** Assorted Classic Trucks pkg(6) **9.98**

## BUSES

**348-11** 1940s Style **1.49**

## CONSTRUCTION EQUIPMENT

**348-140** Front End Loader w/Blade **1.49**

**348-150** Front End Loader w/Bucket **1.49**

**348-160** Cement Mixer **1.49**

**348-226** Road Roller **1.49**

**348-4220** Road Grader (yellow) **2.98**

Semi Trucks Super Star 348-1725

Semi Trucks Top Express 348-1729

## EMERGENCY VEHICLES

### Fire Engines

**348-4200** Pumper (red) **5.98**

**348-4210** Ladder Truck (red) **5.98**

## FARM MACHINERY

**348-3** Harvester **1.49**

## TRACTOR/TRAILERS

**348-190** Oil Tanker w/40' Oil Tank **1.99**

**348-210** 40' **1.99**

## TRUCKS

### Cabover Trucks 1.49 ea

**348-130** Large Open Bed

**348-170** Delivery

### Semi Trucks 1.98 ea

**348-1725** Super Star

**348-1729** Top Express

### U-Haul® Trucks 3.98 ea

348-1130

**348-1011** Alabama
**348-1111** Hawaii
**348-1112** Idaho
**348-1113** Iowa
**348-1114** Illinois
**348-1119** Maine
**348-1122** Michigan
**348-1124** Mississippi
**348-1125** Missouri
**348-1126** Montana
**348-1134** North Dakota
**348-1135** Ohio
**348-1144** Utah
**348-1145** Vermont
**348-1146** Virginia
**348-1147** Washington

### Miscellaneous

**348-12** Tow Truck **1.49**

**348-180** Livestock Transporter **1.49**

**348-200** Flatbed w/Tank Container **1.99**

## VANS

**348-4222** International Box Van Kit pkg(2) **3.98**

## VEHICLE SET

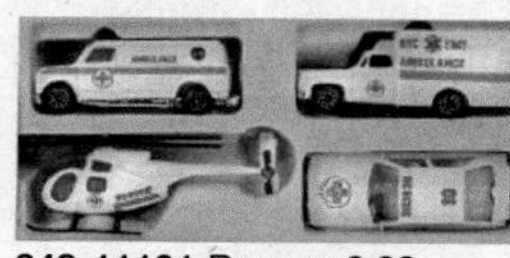

**348-11101** Rescue **3.98**

## SCALE STRUCTURES LIMITED

### Truck Bodies

**650-2477** Roll-Off Trash Body Kit **8.95**

### Construction Equipment

**650-9120** Ford Inspection Car **27.95**

**650-9121** Wood Mine Car **11.95**

**650-9122** Electric Mine Loco **13.95**

**650-9123** Side Dump Mining Car **11.95**

SELLEY Finishing Touch

Kits are easy-to-build and feature cast metal constructi

## CONSTRUCTION EQUIPMENT

**675-146** Forklift Truck **2.30**

## FARM MACHINERY

### Implements

**675-157** Wagon **5.10**

**675-228** Tractor-Drawn Harro **2.60**

### Platform Tractor

**675-147** Platform Mule **2.30**

### Tractors 3.60 ea

**675-226** #2

**675-227** #1

## HY-RAIL INSPECTION CAR

**675-642** Crazy Inspection Car **7.20**

# JORDAN
HIGHWAY MINIATURES

"Highway Miniatures" are detailed replicas of American vehicles from the steam era. Parts are molded in colors. Kits include step-by-step instructions and are easy to build. However, most include very small parts, so some modeling experience is helpful.

## NEW PRODUCTS

### Construction Equipment

#### Steam Crane

**NEW 360-304** Erie B-2 Steam Crane **24.95**

## AUTOMOBILES

### Essex

**360-222** 1926 Two-Door Hardtop **5.95**
First popular priced closed car.

### Ford

**360-213** 1925 Roadster or Pick-Up **5.95**
Can be built as a Roadster or Pick-Up with top up or down.

**360-217** 1929 Model A Station Wagon **6.95**

**360-225** 1940 Standard V-8 Sedan **7.95**
Includes optional engine assembly for "hood up" scenes.

**360-226** 1920 Model T Sedan **7.95**

**360-236** 1928 Model A Sedan **7.95**

**360-241** 1914 Model T Touring Car **9.95**

### Hot Rods 7.95 ea

**360-242** Roadster

**360-243** Coupe

### Oldsmobile

**360-228** 1904 Railroad Inspection Car & Curved Dash Auto **6.95**
Includes parts for both vehicles.

## BUSES

**360-229** 1934 Ford 21 Passenger Bus **7.95**

**360-244** 1940s City Transit Bus **11.95**

## CIRCUS

### Water Truck

**360-232** Mack Water Truck **8.98**
Includes decals for red or white version.

### Calliope Truck

**360-233** Air Calliope Truck **7.95**

### Popcorn Wagon

**360-235** 1913 Popcorn Wagon w/Horses **7.95**

## CONSTRUCTION EQUIPMENT

### Steam Shovel

**360-303** Erie B-2 Model **24.95**

## EMERGENCY VEHICLES

**360-208** 1913 Ford Model T Pumper **5.95**

**360-220** 1923 Mack Aerial Ladder **10.95**

**360-221** 1927 Ahrens Fox Pumper **7.95**

Beer Wagon 360-105

Stage Coach 360-234

**360-237** 1924 American LaFrance Pumper **8.95**

## FARM MACHINERY

### 1920 Fordson Tractors 4.95 ea

**360-218** Farm–Steel Wheels w/Cleats

**360-219** Industrial–Hard Rubber Tires

## HORSE-DRAWN WAGONS

**360-101** Light Delivery **5.95**

**360-102** Standard Delivery **5.95**

**360-103** Brougham **5.95**

**360-104** Buckboard pkg(2) **5.95**

**360-105** Beer Wagon w/8 Horses **10.95**

**360-106** Hearse w/Figure & 2 Horses **7.95**

**360-107** Farm Wagon **6.95**

**360-108** Buggy w/Horse & Driver **6.95**

**360-234** Stage Coach **9.95**

## BAGGAGE WAGON

**360-301** With Bags pkg(2) **4.95**

See What's Available at
**www.walthers.com**

# JORDAN
HIGHWAY MINIATURES

## TRUCKS

### Ford 7.95 ea

#### Model A

**360-240** 1928 Pick-Up

#### 1929 Model AA One-Ton

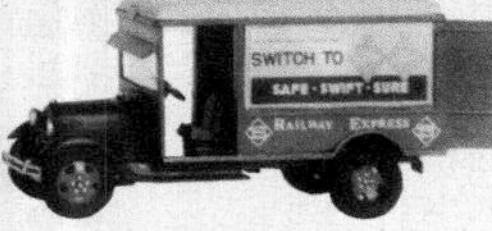


**360-214** Railway Express Agency

**360-239** Tank Truck w/Period Oil/Gas Cans

#### Model TT One-Ton

**360-238** 1923 Stake Truck

#### Model T 6.95 ea

**360-207** 1911 Delivery Truck

**360-215** 1925 Mail Truck

**360-216** 1925 Panel Truck

### 1923 Mack "Bulldog" Trucks 8.95 ea

**360-209** Stake Truck

**360-210** Dump Truck

**360-212** Tank Truck

**360-227** Mack Hi-Lift Coal Dump Truck

### Packard

**360-231** 1922 Stake Truck **7.95**



# JL INNOVATIVE DESIGN

Unfinished, cast-metal kits.

## NEW PRODUCT

### Boat

**NEW 361-458** Vintage Pontoon Boat, Trailer & Accessories **15.95**

### Golf Cart

**NEW 361-459** With Bags pkg(2) **10.99**

## AUTOMOBILES

### Racing Cars & Accessories

Easy-to-assemble cast metal kits modeled after a late 50s-early 60s front-engine rail dragsters and trailers.

**361-901** 1930s pkg(2) **10.99**

**361-920** Vintage Dragster **9.98**

**361-921** Vintage Dragsters pkg(2) **18.95**

**361-922** Vintage Dragster/Trailer/Tools Set **16.49**
Kit includes one cast metal dragster, one vintage wood deck trailer, plus tool boxes, tires, jack and gas can accessories. Figures not included.

**361-923** Vintage Wood-Deck Tandem Trailers pkg(2) **8.49**

## CONSTRUCTION EQUIPMENT

**361-900** Pelican-Style Vintage Street Sweeper **19.95**

### Cushman Utility Trucks

**361-924** Trucksters pkg(2) **9.49**

**361-925** Deluxe Truckster Set pkg(2) **10.99**

## MOTORCYCLES

### Classic 1947 Model Sets

**361-902** 1 Stock, 1 w/Saddlebags pkg(2) **5.99**

**361-903** 1 Stock & 1 Tricycle Servi-Car pkg(2) **6.79**

**361-904** 1 w/Saddlebags, 1 w/Sidecar pkg(2) **7.49**

**361-905** 1 Stock, 1 w/Service Sidecar Box pkg(2) **7.99**
Includes details such as a gas can, tool box and spare tire.

**361-906** 1 Stock, 1 w/Fuel Tank Sidecar pkg(2) **6.99**

**361-908** U.S. Mail/Fanny Farmer w/Enclosed Sidecar pkg(2) **8.99**

## OUTDOOR EQUIPMENT

**361-452** Lawnmowers **5.99**
Kit features parts to make one riding lawn mower and one gas push-style mower. Also includes labeling for vintage riding mower brands.

**361-453** Woebegone Winter Detail Set **18.95**
Features two unique ice fishing houses, vintage snowmobile, toboggan, and a riding mower with a snowblower attachment.

**361-454** Vintage Snowmobile **4.98**

**361-455** Fishing Boat w/Motor & Trailer **8.98**
Includes vintage fishing boat, outboard motor, gas can and trailer.

**361-456** Deluxe Boat, Motor & Trailer w/Marine Accessories **15.95**
Includes vintage fishing boat, two outboard motors, gas can, trailer oars, life vests, life rings, mushroom anchors and gas can to round out your scene.

### Military

See the Military Section for the complete listing of JL Innovative Design Military Motorcycles.

# kibri®

IMPORTED FROM GERMANY BY WALTHERS
Based on vehicles in service around the world, these easy-to-build kits feature parts molded in realistic colors. All parts are numbered to follow step-by-step, illustrated instructions in each kit. Many also include self-adhesive safety signs, names (German text) and other markings.

## NEW PRODUCTS

### Recreational Vehicles

**NEW 405-14977** Unimog Unicat RV **51.99**

### Construction Equipment

#### Cranes

**NEW 405-11286** Liebherr 934 w/High Profile Cab & Bucket **49.99**

**NEW 405-13034** Liebherr 1400 8-Axle Truck Crane w/Telescoping Boom **121.99**

**NEW 405-14979** Unimog Flatbed w/Atlas Crane **42.99**

**NEW 405-15705** Loading Crane Set **25.99**
Includes one each: Meiller, Palfinger, Epsilon, Atlas

#### Schwarz Concrete Series

**NEW 405-15200** Asphalt Stripping Machine Schwarz **76.99**

**NEW 405-15201** Mercedes Actros Cabover w/2-Axle Flatbed & Crane Load **51.99**

**NEW 405-15202** Atlas 4-Wheel Excavator **44.99**

**NEW 405-15203** O & K Grader 18-8 **36.99**

**NEW 405-15204** Faun Wheel Loader **29.99**

**NEW 405-15205** Liebherr 631 Front End Loader on Crawler Chassis **49.99**

**NEW 405-15206** Mercedes 4x4 Tractor w/Lime Spreading Trailer **42.99**

**NEW 405-15207** HAMM Rubber Wheel Compactor **42.99**

**NEW 405-15208** Liebherr LTM 1050/3 Truck Crane **39.99**

**NEW 405-15209** DAF 3-Axle Tractor w/3-Axle Dolly & Concrete Beam Load **44.99**

**NEW 405-15210** 3-Axle Truck Crane **42.99**

**NEW 405-15211** DAF 3-Axle Dump Truck 2-Axle Trailer **42.99**

**NEW 405-15212** HAMM Vibratory or Sheepsfoot Surface Compactor **36.99**

**NEW 405-15213** Mercedes 4x4 Tractor w/Vibratory Compactor **38.99**

**NEW 405-15214** Unimog Flatbed w/Pump & 3-Axle Tank Trailer **27.99**

### Tractors

**NEW 405-12269** Mercedes 4x4 Tractor w/Front Forklift & 2-Axle Flatbed Trailer w/Lumber Load **50.99**

**NEW 405-12270** Fendt 926 Tractor w/Twin Tires **42.99**

**NEW 405-12272** Fendt 936 als "Black Edition" Tractor **44.99**

### Construction Sets

**NEW 405-13802** European Construction Equipment Set pkg(6) **328.99**
Includes #405-13578, 13579, 13580, 13581, 13582 & 13034

### Logging Equipment

**NEW 405-12271** MAN Log Truck w/Log Crane **45.99**

**NEW 405-12995** Sawmill Vehicle Set **172.99**
Includes 14054, 12227, 12245, 12247, 14642 & 12262

### Emergency Equipment

#### Police & Fire

**NEW 405-18268** Mercedes Actros 3-Axle Dumpster Carrrier w/Dumpster **32.99**

**NEW 405-18269** MAN Tarp-Covered Flatbed **28.99**

**NEW 405-18270** Unimog Off-Road Forest Fire Pumper **51.99**

**NEW 405-18469** MAN Tarp-Covered Flatbed **38.99**

**NEW 405-18470** Unimog Off-Road Forest Fire Pumper **25.99**

#### Technical Help Services (THW)

**NEW 405-18471** Magirus 2-Axle Tarp Covered Flatbed THW (blue) **29.99**

**NEW 405-18472** Mercedes 2-Axle Cabover w/3-Axle Heavy-Haul Flatbed Trailer THW (blue) **29.99**

**NEW 405-18473** Faun Wheel Loader THW (blue) **27.99**

### Fork Lifts

**NEW 405-11756** Small Forklift (red) **21.99**

### Trucks

**NEW 405-13584** Kaelble ZG W2A 130 Cabrio DR (German State Railways, 1939) **36.99**

**NEW 405-14666** Mercedes 4-Axle Cabover Wrecker **39.99**

**NEW 405-14667** Mercedes Actros Box Van & Trailer w/Forklift **47.99**

kibri®

IMPORTED FROM GERMANY BY WALTHERS

**NEW 405-14668** Mercedes Actros Flatbed w/Matching 2-Axle Flatbed Trailer (Less Load) **45.99**

**NEW 405-14978** Unimog w/Line Spreader Body **49.99**

**NEW 405-14980** Unimog German Postal Service Roll On/Off Container Carrier **32.99**

**NEW 405-15010** Mercedes SK 3-Axle Garbage Truck **45.99**

## Tractor/Trailer Rigs

**NEW 405-13578** Mercedes SK 4-Axle Tractor w/Crane, 5-Axle Lowboy Flatbed & Portable Office **40.99**

**NEW 405-13579** Mercedes Actros 3-Axle Tractor w/Crane & 3-Axle Lowboy Flatbed w/Load **40.99**

**NEW 405-13580** DAF 3-Axle Box Van w/4-Axle Flatbed Trailer & Heavy Forklift **65.99**

**NEW 405-13581** MAN 4-Axle Heavy-Duty Tractor w/6-Axle Flatbed Trailer & Load **49.99**

**NEW 405-13582** Mercedes SK 4-Axle Heavy-Duty Tractor w/5-Axle Low Boy Trailer **49.99**

**NEW 405-13583** 20-Axle Self-Propelled Carrier w/Transformer (Nonworking) **99.99**

**NEW 405-14064** Mercedes Actros 3-Axle Flatbed w/Crane & Matching 2-Axle Flatbed Trailer **42.99**

**NEW 405-14663** Magerius Duetz Fuel Delivery Truck w/Matching 3-Axle Tank Trailer ARAL **38.99**

**NEW 405-14664** Mercedes 2-Axle Cabover w/3-Axle DOLL Tank Trailer ARAL **39.99**

**NEW 405-14665** MAN 4-Axle Oil Tanker ARAL **16.99**

## Trailers

**NEW 405-15706** European Trailer Set pkg(3) **42.99**

**NEW 405-15707** European Open Trailer Set pkg(3) **37.99**

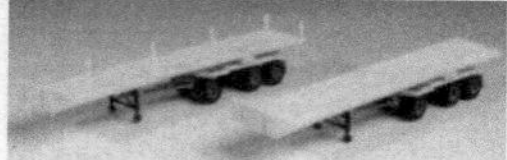

**NEW 405-15708** DOLL Flatbed pkg(2) Undecorated **51.99**

**NEW 405-15709** Langendorf Glass Transporter, 1 Open, 1 Closed **56.99**

**NEW 405-15710** 3-Axle Covered Flatbed pkg(2) **27.99**

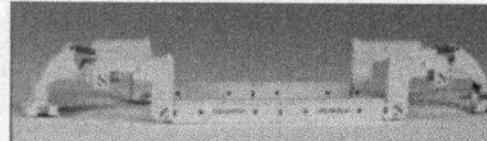

**NEW 405-15713** Large Boiler Transport **31.99**

**NEW 405-15714** Small Boiler Transport **28.99**

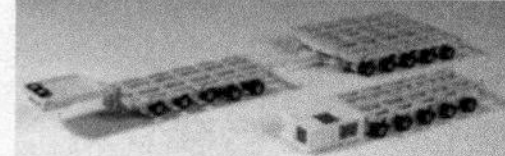

**NEW 405-15715** Heavy-Duty Modular Flatbed **42.99**

**NEW 405-15717** Bridge Section for Heavy-Duty Low Loader **24.99**

# 30 YEAR KIBRI ANNIVERSARY SPECIALS

## Construction Equipment

**405-11452** Kaelble Loader w/Attachments **36.99**

**405-11653** Pavement Remover **76.99**

## Compactor

**405-11553** HAMM Sheep's Foot Compactor **19.99**

Got a Mouse? Click Walthers Web Site at
**www.walthers.com**

Item listed below is available by Special Order (see Legend Page).

**405-14607** Dumpster Carrier w/Dumpsters **36.99**

## Cranes

**405-11751** Intermodal Equipment Kalmar Forklift Type **42.99**

**405-13010** FAUN Salvage Crane **27.99**

**405-13011** Liebherr 3-Axle Crane **30.99**

**405-13012** Liebherr 1120 Telescoping Crane w/Extended Jib **36.99**

## Excavators

**405-11264** Liebherr 922 w/Attachments **23.99**

**405-11265** Menck Tracked w/Shovel Bucket **41.99**

**405-11451** Zettelmayer Heavy-Duty w/Accessories **30.99**

## Grader

**405-11651** O&K **25.99**

## Tractors

**405-13528** Kaelble w/Tarp **15.99**

**405-13529** FAUN w/Low Loader - Bauman **25.99**

**405-13531** FAUN **16.99**

## Trucks

**405-14022** Articulated Dump Truck **23.99**

**405-14025** Mercedes Articulated Sand/Gravel Truck Meiller **16.99**

Items listed below are available by Special Order (see Legend Page).

**405-13530** Mercedes 3-Axle Heavy-Duty Tractor & Trailer **36.99**

**405-13532** MAN 3-Axle Heavy-Duty Tractor w/Crane **24.99**

## Emergency Equipment

### Ford

**405-18255** FK 2500 Fire Van **23.99**

kibri®

IMPORTED FROM GERMANY
BY WALTHERS

### Technical Help Service (THW)

**405-18456** Amphibious "Duck" DUKW 6x6 Truck **27.99**

**405-18457** 3-Axle Dump Truck **19.99**

**405-18458** Mercedes Dump Truck w/Flatbed Trailer **27.99**

Items listed below are available by Special Order (see Legend Page).

**405-18455** Mobile Excavator **30.99**

**405-18459** Mercedes Mountain Crane **23.99**

### Farm Machinery

#### Tractors

**405-12234** Farm Machinery Mercedes Tractor w/Vacuum Tanker **27.99**

### Tractor/ Trailers

#### DAF

**405-14620** DAF Articulated Truck - Kibri **16.99**

#### MAN

**405-14611** MAN 4-Axle Tanker SHELL **16.99**

**405-14612** MAN 2-Axle Tractor Schenker **20.99**

#### Mercedes

**405-14609** Mercedes Articulated Tanker DB ESSO **16.99**

**405-14610** Mercedes Roundnose Tractor w/Tanker Trailer ARAL **16.99**

**405-14613** Mercedes Articulated Beverage Truck Schenk **20.99**

## BOATS

**405-8135** Pontoons w/Bridge Sections **39.99**

**405-8520** Modern Push/Pull Tug Boat **36.99**
7-1/4 x 2-1/2 x 3-13/16"
18.2 x 6.2 x 9.5cm

**405-8522** Container Barge/Lighter **30.99**
11-13/64 x 3-5/8 x 1"
28 x 9 x 2.3cm

**405-8524** Bulk Material Loading Barge **30.99**
11 x 3-5/8 x 1-1/8"
27.5 x 9 x 2.8cm

**405-9154** Fire Boat **32.99**

**405-9155** Shrimp Boat **32.99**

**405-9156** Barge w/Excavator **59.99**

**405-9158** Canal/River Passenger Boat **32.99**

### Assorted Boats 16.99 ea

**405-9159** (4) Rowboats, (2) Motorboats, (2) Sailboats

**405-9160** (2) Sailboats, (1) Motor Launch, (1) Workboat

## CONSTRUCTION EQUIPMENT

### City Services Equipment

**405-15004** Unimog w/Boom Mounted Brush Cutter **45.99**

**405-15005** Unimog Flatbed w/Cherrypicker Boom & Basket **45.99**

**405-15006** Actros Cabover Truck 3-Axle Snow Plow w/Blade & Salt/Sand Spreader **49.99**

**405-15007** Fendt 926 Tractor w/Snow Plow Blade & Salt/Sand Broadcast Spreader **39.99**

**405-15009** MAN Garbage/Dump Truck **44.99**

### Cement Trucks

**405-14405** MAN **27.99**

### Compactors

**405-11556** HAMM w/Rubber Tires **42.99**

**405-11557** HAMM w/Rubber Tires **42.99**

**405-11558** BOMAG BS180 w/Steel Wheels **54.99**

### Cranes

**405-11752** Kalmar Container Crane w/Trailer Lifting Arms **62.99**

**405-11991** Liebherr Tower Crane **45.99**

**405-13026** 10-Axle Heavy Truck Crane **57.99**

**405-13027** 4-Axle Truck Crane **47.99**

**405-13028** 3-Axle Truck Crane **31.99**

**405-13029** 2-Axle Truck Crane Baumann (cream, red) **35.99**

**405-13030** LTM 1050/3 3-Axle Truck Crane (blue, white) **44.99**

**405-13032** LTM 1025 2-Axle Truck Crane **36.99**

kibri®

IMPORTED FROM GERMANY BY WALTHERS

**405-13033** LTM 1800 Heavy-Duty Telescoping Boom w/Jib **154.99**

**405-11253** 974 Tracked Crane w/Pile Driver Attachment **79.99**

**405-13005** LTM 1400 Mobile Crane w/Jib Extension **159.99**

Item listed below is available by Special Order (see Legend Page).

**405-13001** LTM 1600/2 Mobile Crane **86.99**

**405-13013** Twin Jib Lattice Crane w/Crawler Tracks **181.99**

**405-13014** Demag HC 665 6 Axle Crane "A. Scholpp" **123.99**

**405-13015** Liebherr LTM 1025 2-Axle Mobile Crane **36.99**

**405-13016** Liebherr LG 1800 "Spacelifter" **209.99**

**405-13533** Gottwald Baldwins Telescopic Crane Transport **36.99**

**405-13018** Gottwald AK 850 **107.99**

**405-13019** MAN **45.99**

**405-13021** Demag AC 665 (Telescoping) **90.99**

**405-13025** MAN w/Quick Assembly Crane **50.99**

Item listed below is available by Special Order (see Legend Page).

**405-13004** MAN 3-Axle House Conversion Type **45.99**

**405-13020** LTM 1050/3 - Breuer **42.99**

**405-13022** LTR 1800 **212.99**

**405-13023** LTM 1400 **119.99**

**405-13024** LTM 1030/2 **36.99**

## Crane Transport Set

**405-13801** Gottwald AK 850 Crane Transport Set Set of seven kits includes crane as rigged for highway transport and six support trucks to move the boom and other equipment. **334.99**

## Accessories

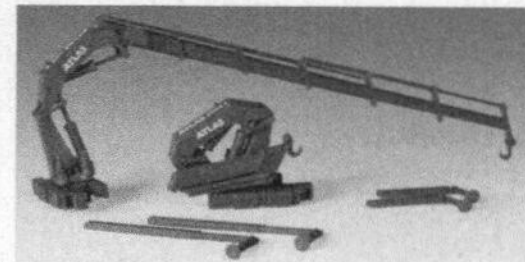

**405-10988** Atlas Loading Crane & Equipment (red, white) **20.99**

## Dump Trucks

**405-14048** DAF ZM Dump Truck **36.99**

**405-14050** Meiller Dump Truck **32.99**

**405-14051** MAN Dump Truck **26.99**

**405-14052** Dump Truck with Trailer **36.99**

**405-14058** Terex Dump Truck **35.99**

**405-11656** Kaelble **24.99**

**405-14038** Terex Heavy-Duty **36.99**

**405-14040** MAN Cabover w/Trailer **27.99**

## Magirus

**405-14031** Dump Truck Gray, Red **30.99**

**405-14032** Dump Truck Yellow Black **30.99**

## Mercedes

**405-14053** Gravel Truck **26.99**

**405-14057** Gravel Truck **26.9**

**405-14029** 2-Axle w/Trailer Orange **36.99**

**405-14030** 2-Axle **30.99**

**405-14039** Mercedes Cabover w/Trailer **32.99**

## Excavators

**405-11266** Sersa **45.99**

**405-11269** Atlas Mobile Excavator **45.99**

**405-11275** Terex-Atlas Excavator **44.99**

# kibri

IMPORTED FROM GERMANY BY WALTHERS

**405-11276** Atlas Excavator **44.99**

**405-11279** Hydraulic Excavator w/Derrick **68.99**

**405-11280** Cable Operated Excavator w/Slotted Arm **82.99**

**405-11281** Fox Excavator with Low & High Driver **25.99**

**405-11453** JCB 4 CX Excavator Loader 4 x 4 x 4 **41.99**

**405-11456** FAUN F1310 Wheel Loader **27.99**

## Komatsu 68.99 ea

**405-11354** D575 A-2 Bulldozer

**405-11454** WA800-2 Wheel Loader

## Liebherr

**405-11267** 974 w/Long Arm & Shovel **45.99**

**405-11270** 974 Excavator **39.99**

**405-11271** 974 w/Hammer Attachment **45.99**

## Liebherr

**405-11272** 974 w/High Shovel **42.99**

**405-11273** 974 w/Shovel **42.99**

**405-11274** 934 **49.99**

**405-11277** 922 w/Shovel **70.99**

**405-11278** 922 Excavator w/Deep Shovel **70.99**

**405-11282** 934 Excavator with Gripper **49.99**

**405-11285** R 934 Hydraulic Excavator **49.99**

**405-11353** 931 Bulldozer **29.99**

## Menck 44.99 ea

**405-11283** M154 Dragline Excavator

**405-11284** Excavator with Deep Bucket

## Front End Loaders

**405-12206** JCB w/Rear Wood Grapple **45.99**

**405-11255** Zettelmayer w/Snowblower **45.99**

## Richard Mayer Series

**405-11351** Liebherr Type 631 on Crawler Tracks "Mayer" **27.99**

Items listed below are available by Special Order (see Legend Page).

**405-14006** Mercedes SK 2-Axle Cabover w/2-Axle Dump Trailer **27.99**

**405-14007** Mercedes Actros 2-Axle Cabover w/3-Axle Gooseneck Equipment Trailer **32.99**

## Road Surfacing

**405-11650** O&G Road Grader Type G16-8 **36.99**

**405-11554** Hamm Vibrating Roller **32.99**

**405-11555** Hamm "Sheepsfoot" Material Compacter **16.99**

**405-11657** Wirtgen Asphalt Remover **75.99**

**405-11658** Demag DF120P Paving Machine **30.99**

**405-11659** Wirtgen Asphalt Cutter **75.99**

**405-11662** O&K Grader **35.99**

**Limited Quantity Available**

**405-11552** Bomag Surface Compacter w/Material Spreader **47.99**

## Shovels

## Liebherr

**405-11254** Liebherr Tracked Excavator w/Drag-Line & Bucket **86.99**

**405-11261** 934 Liebherr Jib Excavator w/Outriggers **53.99**

**Limited Quantity Available**

**405-11252** Liebherr 922 4-Wheel Excavator **31.99**

## Tractors

**405-14407** Fendt 926 w/Rear Stacker **43.99**

**405-13573** Kaelble 3-Axle Tractor Z6W 2A130 **36.99**

kibri®

IMPORTED FROM GERMANY BY WALTHERS

**405-11989** Mercedes 4x4 w/Machinery **44.99**

**405-12262** Mercedes w/Front End Loader & Backhoe **48.99**

**405-12246** Fendt 926 w/Front Loader & Rear Winches **36.99**

**405-12257** Mercedes 4x4 w/Cement Trailer **34.99**

**Limited Quantity Available**

**405-12254** Mercedes 4x4 w/Front Loader & Rear Winches **34.99**

## Trucks

### Unimog

**405-12259** Water Sprayer w/Tank **44.99**

**405-12222** w/Two 4-Axle Sugar Beet Trailers **42.99**

**405-14986** With Adjustable Height Body **32.99**

**405-14987** With Adjustable Height Open Body **30.99**

Item listed below is available by Special Order (see Legend Page).

**405-14988** Tanker **29.99**

**405-14997** With Snow Blower & Plow Combination - Schmid **44.99**

### MAN

**405-14402** 3-Axle Dump Truck w/Trailer **42.99**

**405-14403** 3-Axle Dumpster Carrier w/Trailer & Dumpsters **42.99**

### Mercedes

**405-13031** Actros 3-Axle Cabover Cherrypicker w/Telescoping Boom **50.99**

**405-14055** SK HD ZM Silo Container **28.99**

**405-14056** Actros ZM Pointed Silo Container **27.99**

**405-14059** Truck with Pointed Silo Container **27.99**

**405-14060** Atlas Truck with Long Bed & Derrick **31.99**

**405-14061** Concrete Pump **44.99**

**405-14062** Actros Cement Mixer **31.99**

**405-14655** SK HD Concrete Mixer **34.99**

**405-14656** Tank Car & Trailer **34.99**

**405-14657** Actros Tankcar **32.99**

**405-14660** Silo Truck with Trailer **31.99**

**405-14400** Actros Cabover 3-Axle Dump Truck **32.99**

**405-14404** Actros w/ 2 Dumpsters **42.99**

**405-14999** Actros Tow Truck Masterlift **37.99**

**405-15001** w/Snow Plow **40.99**

Items listed below are available by Special Order (see Legend Page).

**405-14008** Actros Flatbed w/Crane & Trailer Palfinger **36.99**

### Komatsu

**405-11660** Heavy-Duty 785-5 **49.99**

### Magirus

**405-14054** w/ Long Road Transport **42.99**

**405-18091** BW 2 Axle A6500 Tank Truck **42.99**

### Scania

**405-14049** Silo Carrier **28.99**

## Site Trailers

**405-11999** Forestry Container & Site Office Trailer Set **36.99**

## Construction Equipment Set

Item listed below is available by Special Order (see Legend Page).
**405-14021** Construction Equipment Set **79.99**

## Accessories

Item listed below is available by Special Order (see Legend Page).
**405-15700** Office, Flatbed & 2 Roll-On/Off Containers **34.99**

# EMERGENCY VEHICLES

## Police & Fire

**405-14649** Mercedes SK Recovery Vehicle **36.99**

**405-14650** MAN Recovery Vehicle **39.99**

**405-18265** Unimog Mini-Pumper w/Front Pump & Wate Tank **31.99**

**405-18267** Unimog Flatbed w/Optional Water Tank, 2-Axle Flatebd & Forklift **49.99**

**405-18853** Unimog Flatbed w/Loading Crane, 2-Axle Trailer & Security Perimeter Fence **49.99**

**405-18062** Magirus Crane Truck Fire Dept. 3-Axle Crane w/Clear Roof Turret **34.99**

**405-18651** Magirus Jupiter Malteser Rescue Service (gold red) **42.99**

**405-18652** German Red Cross (DRK) SK Cabover w/Trailer **32.99**

kibri®

IMPORTED FROM GERMANY BY WALTHERS

## Technical Help Service (THW) Equipment

A branch of the German government, this agency is responsible for heavy construction projects, including road and bridge repairs, during wartime or natural disasters. All equipment is painted in a distinctive blue scheme.

**405-18465** 4-Axle Truck Crane (blue, white) **46.99**

**405-18466** Unimog Flatbed w/Brush Cutter **36.99**

**405-18467** Unimog Field Generator/Light Plant w/Light Mast **33.99**

**405-18468** Mercedes Cabover Covered Flatbed w/Matching 2-Axle Trailer **27.99**

**405-18452** Mercedes 2-Axle Cabover w/3-Axle Heavy-Haul Flatbed Trailer **36.99**

**405-18453** FAUN Wheel Loader **27.99**

**405-18454** MAN Cabover w/3-Axle Canvas Side Trailer **32.99**

Item listed below is available by Special Order (see Legend Page).

**405-18451** Magirus 2-Axle Tarp Covered Flatbed **39.99**

# FARM MACHINERY

## CLAAS

**405-12263** Combine w/Corn & Small Grain Heads, Head Transport Trailer **66.99**

**405-12264** Jaguar Forage Harvester w/Corn, Hay & Small Grain Heads **66.99**

**405-12218** Jaguar Harvester w/Camper 330 Cutter **54.99**

**405-12258** Claas Xerion **48.99**

**405-11176** "Jaguar" 880 Forage Harvester w/Corn Head **42.99**

**Limited Quantity Available**

**405-12217** Jaguar Harvester w/Small Grain Head **47.99**

**405-12224** Jaguar 900 Combine w/Champion 4500 Cutter Attachment **47.99**

**405-12997** CLAAS Lexion Combine w/Grain Head, Unimog Euro II Flatbed Truck & Trailer **71.99**

## Harvesting Equipment

**405-12256** Zettelmayer Bale Loader **38.99**

## Tractors

### Fendt

**405-12209** Vario 926 w/6-Bottom Reversing Plow **45.99**

**405-12238** Vario w/Lowloader & Hay Bales **81.99**

Item listed below is available by Special Order (see Legend Page).

**405-15003** Vario w/Rear Snow Plow Attachment **38.99**

**405-12265** Vario Favorit 926 **36.99**

**405-12266** w/Kemper Uni Trans UT 18000 2-Axle Trailer **51.99**

**405-12268** Vario 936 **44.99**

**Limited Quantity Available**

**405-12216** Tractor w/Tree Planter Attachment **31.99**



### Lanz

**405-12267** Bulldog D 8506 w/Sun Shade **32.99**

**405-12221** Bulldog Tractor - No Roll-Over Protection Structure **32.99**

**405-12226** Tractor w/Carnival Float **42.99**

**405-12235** Bulldog w/Hay Cart **42.99**

**405-12236** w/Hay Wagon **42.99**

**405-12255** Bulldog **36.99**

### Mercedes

**405-12261** 4x4 w/Optional Dual Tires **53.99**

**405-12228** 4x4 Tractor w/Front Mower & Hay Baler **45.99**

**405-12229** 2-Axle Cabover w/3-Axle Flatbed Trailer & CLAAS Round Baler Load **45.99**

**405-12239** w/Cattle Trailer **50.99**

**405-12240** w/Winch & Wood Chopper **36.99**

**405-12253** 4x4 w/Crop Spraying Equipment **33.99**

## Wagons

**405-12996** Wagon Set **42.99**

**405-15702** Modern Flatbed Hay Trailers pkg(2) **30.99**

**405-15703** Old-Time Manure, Hay and Grain Wagons **32.99**

## Farm Implements

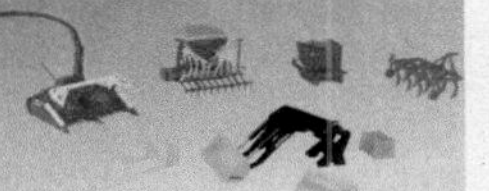

**408-10910** Tractor Mounted Tool Set pkg(8)
Includes Forage Harvester, Grain Drill, Cultivator, Dump Box, Fork Lift Blades, Loader, Mower/Conditioner and Counterweights. **27.99**

Item listed below is available by Special Order (see Legend Page).

**408-10908** Trailer Set pkg(3)
Includes bale throw wagon, dump trailer and liquid manure tank trailer. **27.99**

**Limited Quantity Available**

**405-12215** Soil Compacter, Manure Spreader & Tractor-Mounted Accessories **37.99**

kibri

IMPORTED FROM GERMANY BY WALTHERS

## Unimog Trucks

**405-12241** Unimog Euro II w/Mower & Trailer **44.99**

**405-12243** Unimog Euro II w/Plow & Ballast Weight **45.99**

**Limited Quantity Available**

**405-12242** Unimog Euro II w/Dethatcher **45.99**

# FORK LIFTS

**405-11754** Steinbock Fork Lift w/Safety Cage **9.99**

**405-11750** Kalmar LMV Forklift **29.99**

# INTERMODAL EQUIPMENT

## Containers

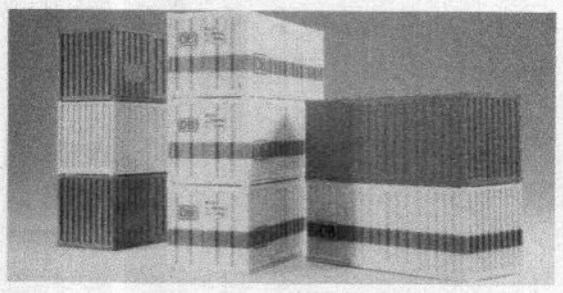

**405-10924** 20' Box Type Set pkg(8) **23.99**
Includes four United German Railways (DB-AG) units in current scheme, plus four additional containers in different colors.

**405-10922** 40' Box Type Set pkg(6) **27.99**
Includes six containers in different colors.

# TRACTOR/ TRAILER RIGS

**405-13007** Gottwald Breuer Telescopic Crane Transport Convoy **483.99**

## DAF

**405-14645** w/Box Trailer **32.99**

**405-14646** FT 280 DFS Double Luggage **29.99**

**405-14648** ZM Cab w/Low Loader & Bullock **44.99**

**405-14638** w/Curtain Sided Trailer **27.99**

## Kaelble

**405-13559** w/Coal Trailer **34.99**

**405-13560** w/Canvas-Covered Trailer **32.99**

**405-13570** 3-Axle Conventional w/16-Wheel Railroad Car Transport & Beer Car Load **54.99**

## Magirus

**405-14047** Tanker - Shell **38.99**

**405-14614** DAF Tarpaulin Truck **27.99**

## MAN

**405-13571** 3-Axle Flatbed w/5-Axle Flatbed Trailer **38.99**

**405-13576** MAN 3-Axle Cabover w/Baldwins 3-Axle Container Chassis **36.99**

**405-14661** MAN HD Semitrailer **33.99**

**405-12248** Animal Transporter & Trailer w/12 Cows **45.99**

**405-12249** 2-Axle Flatbed w/Cattle Trailer **45.99**

**405-13561** Heavy-Duty 4-Axle Cabover w/3-Axle Lowboy Trailer - Felbermayer **45.99**

**405-13562** 3-Axle Cabover w/Doll Bridge Trailer **32.99**

**405-13564** 4-Axle Heavy-Duty Caboverw/Goldhofer Platform Trailer **33.99**

**405-14632** 2-Axle Cabover w/Refrigerated Trailer **36.99**

**405-14633** 3-Axle Refrigerated Box Van & Trailer **34.99**

**405-13534** 3-Axle Cabover w/6-Axle Flatbed Trailer Baldwins **36.99**

**405-13536** 3-Axle Cabover w/6 Axle Flatbed Trailer Grohmann Attollo **36.99**

**405-13541** 3-Axle Cabover w/Low Side Trailer **36.99**

**405-14617** High-Roof Cabover w/3-Axle Reefer Box Trailer **27.99**

**405-18092** 3-Axle Cabover w/2 Axle Trailer UN (white) **32.99**

Item listed below is available by Special Order (see Legend Page).

**405-13540** 3-Axle Cabover w/Low Loader Trailer Schmidbauer **44.99**

## Mercedes

**405-13572** Canvas Covered Cabover Flatbed w/Matching 3-Axle Trailer **30.99**

**405-13574** 4-Axle Heavy-Duty Tractor w/5-Axle Flatbed Trailer **51.99**

**405-13575** Heavy-Duty 3-Axle Cabover w/3-Axle Bridge Transport Flatbed **45.99**

**405-13577** 4-Axle Heavy-Duty Tractor w/5-Axle Flatbed Traile **33.99**

**405-14639** SK Double Trailer Truck **32.99**

**405-14640** 1632 Double Traile Truck **32.99**

**405-14641** SK ZM Cab with Long Flatbed **36.99**

**405-14642** 1632S Cab with Long Flatbed **36.99**

**405-14643** SK Tractor with Fla Semitrailer **29.99**

**405-14644** 1632S Wackenhut Tractor w/Flat Semitrailer **29.9**

**405-14647** SK ZM Cab w/Low Loader **44.99**

**405-14654** Actros ZM Goldhofer Low-Loader **32.99**

**405-14662** Actros Cab with Double Trailers **27.99**

**405-13547** Tractor w/Low Loader Trailer Scheuerle **45.9**

**405-13548** 3-Axle Cabover w/Lowboy Flatbed Trailer - Scheuerle **45.99**

## kibri

IMPORTED FROM GERMANY BY WALTHERS

**405-13551** Heavy-Duty Cabover w/ 6-Axle Flatbed **53.99**

**405-13552** Heavy-Duty Cabover w/8-Axle Flatbed **45.99**

**405-13553** Heavy-Duty Cabover w/5-Axle Lowboy Flatbed **45.99**

**405-13554** Heavy-Duty Cabover w/Goldhofer 5-Axle Flatbed **45.99**

**405-13555** Cabover w/Container & 3-Axle Chassis **45.99**

**405-13563** w/Doll Long Load Transporter **27.99**

**405-13565** 2-Axle Cabover w/Covered Trailer **27.99**

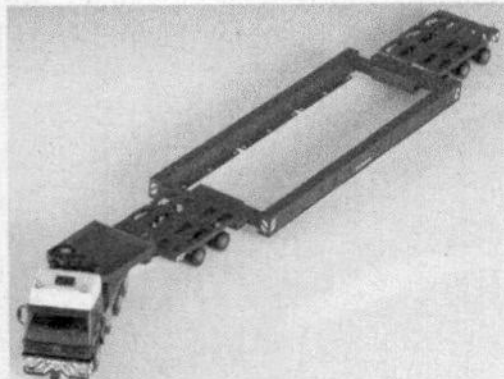
**405-13566** 4-Axle Heavy-Duty Caboverw/Wide Load Trailer **79.99**

**405-13568** 4-Axle Heavy-Duty Cabover w/6-Axle Lowboy Flatbed **45.99**

**405-14041** Actros w/Heavy Haulage Trailer **45.99**

**405-14042** 2-Axle Cabover w/Dry Bulk Trailer **22.99**

**405-14043** 2-Axle Round Hood Conventional w/Dry Bulk Trailer **27.99**

**405-14634** 2-Axle Cabover w/Two Flatbed Trailers **50.99**

**405-14637** Actros w/Low Loader Trailer & 2 Fork Lifts **48.99**

**405-13535** 4-Axle Cabover w/Rear Steering Trailer Schmidbauer KG **36.99**

**405-13537** SK 4-Axle Cabover w/Platform Trailer Grohmann Attollo **33.99**

**405-13539** 3-Axle Cabover w/Low Loader Trailer Schenker **42.99**

**405-14616** Actros w/ 3-Axle Trailer **33.99**

**405-14618** 2-Axle Cabover w/3-Axle Box Trailer **27.99**

**405-14619** 3-Axle w/Container Trailer **36.99**



Items listed below are available by Special Order (see Legend Page).

**405-13538** Actros 3-Axle Cabover w/Low Loader Trailer Grohmann Attollo **36.99**

### Actros 2-Axle

**405-14602** Cabover w/3-Axle Flatbed & Liebherr Wheeled Shovel **79.99**

### 4-Axle Heavy Tractors

**405-13508** With 10-Axle Flatbed & Machinery Load DB Cargo - Kit **88.99**

Item listed below is available by Special Order (see Legend Page).

**405-13514** SK w/11-Axle Heavy-Duty Flatbed Trailer & Rail Tamper Load **246.99**

**405-13518** With Nooteboom 6-Axle Flatbed Low-Loader Trailer **49.99**

**405-13526** With 10-Axle Gooseneck Flatbed & Large Crate Load - Kit **88.99**

## TRAILERS

**405-14658** Circus Trailer **44.99**

**405-14659** Unimog Circus Wagon with Front Loader **62.99**

**405-15704** House Trailers pkg(2) **32.99**

**405-13544** 4-Axle Low Loader & 3-Axle TSS Low Loader pkg(2) **42.99**

**405-13545** Doll Vario Extendible Trailers pkg(2) **53.99**

**405-14033** Meiller Dump Trailers pkg(2) **30.99**

**405-14034** Meiller 2-Axle Dump Trailer **23.99**

**405-14035** Meiller Gravel Tipper **23.99**

**405-14046** DryBulk & Cement Silo Flatbed Trailers **27.99**

**405-15701** Nooteboom 6-Axle Low Loader Flatbed trailers pkg(2) **54.99**

## TRUCKS

**405-14063** Magirus Deutz 230 D 26 AK w/Trailer **48.99**

**405-14651** DAF Cab with Two Trailers **31.99**

**405-14652** Actros Cab with Semi Trailer **34.99**

**405-14653** MAN HD Cab with Double Trailer **30.99**

**405-13567** Kaelble Tractor Unit **32.99**

**405-14631** MAN Oil Tanker **24.99**

**405-16304** Mercedes Tractor Unit **36.99**

### Unimog

**405-14981** w/Post Trailer **34.99**

**405-14982** w/Works Trailer **41.99**

**405-14983** w/Sprayer Attachment **45.99**

**405-14984** w/Attachments **50.99**

**405-14985** w/Animal Feed Trailers **45.99**

### Heavy-Duty Tractors

**405-13550** FAUN 3-Axle **22.99**

kibri®

IMPORTED FROM GERMANY BY WALTHERS

**405-13557** Mercedes 4-Axle **34.99**

**405-13558** MAN 4-Axle **34.99**

## Faun

**405-13542** Heavy-Duty Tractor Bauman **23.99**

## Unimog

**405-14989** Euro II Flatbed Street Sweeper w/Cleaning Brushes **65.99**

**405-14990** Euro II Flatbed w/Fork Lift Attachment & 2-Axle Trailer **54.99**

## MAN

**405-13543** 4-Axle Heavy-Duty Tractor w/Generator **33.99**

## Truck Loads

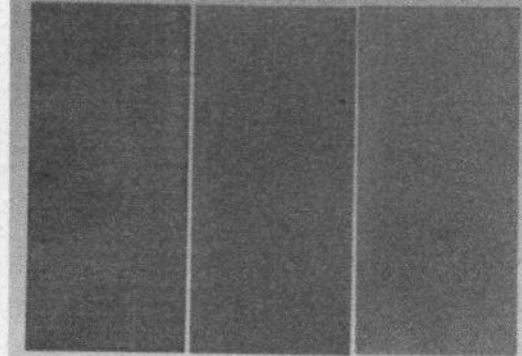
**405-11984** Sheet Metal pkg(3) **13.99**

## LOGGING EQUIPMENT

**405-12260** Mercedes 4x4 Tractor w/3-Axle Log Trailer **48.99**

**405-12202** Heavy-Duty Wheel Loader - Kaelble w/Timber Grapple & Logs **54.99**

**405-12244** Euro II w/Wood Trailer & Loader **54.99**

**405-12245** Mercedes 4x4 Tractor w/Log Trailer **36.99**

**405-12247** Mercedes Short Wood Transporter w/Crane **34.99**

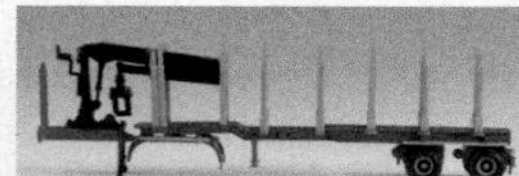
**405-12250** Doll Long Skeleton Trailer **27.99**

**405-12251** Doll Long Skeleton Trailer w/Crane **29.99**

## FRENCHMAN RIVER MODEL WORKS

## NEW PRODUCTS

### Boat Kits

Capture the look of classic vessels for your harbor with these detailed resin and metal kits that fit popular modeling eras. All models (except the 18' Utility Boat) feature waterline hulls (flat bottoms) to simplify adding them to new or existing scenes. See the Parts section for additional boat details.

**NEW 267-81** 56' Fishing Boat Kit **57.50**
Every wood plank shows off screw holes, wood grain and "character," which are complemented by the detailed anchor winch and boom winch. The fish wells and the cabin can be placed fore or aft — with two kits, you can build a pair of distinctly different fishing boats for the same scene. Kit includes detailed resin castings, Britannia metal detail parts, and comes complete with brass anchor chain, fishnet material, rigging line, colored marker/navigation lights and photo-etched brass detail parts that include a variety of fish species for your catch, anchors, boat hooks and more. Completed kit measures 7-3/4" 19.6cm long.

**NEW 267-91** 34' Lobster Boat Kit **37.00**
Detailed resin castings, rope and laser-cut lobster traps make this a realistic and complete model that would look great docked next to a fishing pier with a lobsterman unloading his catch of the day. Completed kit measures 4-1/2" 11.4cm long.

**NEW 267-101** 34' Steam Launch Kit **34.50**
With its vertical steam boiler, firewood stack and many other realistic details, this model would look great ferrying supplies or passengers across your harbor or up river to your logging camp. Kit includes detailed resin castings and Britannia metal detail parts. Completed kit measures 4-1/2" 11.4cm long.

**NEW 267-111** 68' Steam Freighter Kit **80.50**
These small but rugged freighters, called Clyde Puffers, were built from the 1850s through 1920 to carry freight into and around the coastal waterways of Scotland, but similar vessels could be found on many waterways. Kit consists of many highly detailed resin castings, Britannia metal detail parts, set of photo-etched brass detail parts, rope, chain, pulleys and much more. Completed kit measures 9-1/4" 24.1cm long.

**NEW 267-121** 18' Utility Boat Kit **11.50**
This open utility boat is a perfect fishing boat along the waterfront, lake or river; similar boats were often carried aboard larger vessels as work boats. Kit comes with a detailed resin full hull and Britannia metal outboard motor. Completed kit measures 2-3/4" 6.9cm long.

**NEW 267-131** 45' Harbor Tug Boat Kit **43.75**
The prototypes of this tug were designed and built for the US Army Transportation Corps. in the early 1950s. It was diesel powered and small enough to maneuver around crowded, busy ports. This detailed kit includes resin castings, Britannia metal detail parts, rope, anchor, chain and tire bumpers. Completed kit measures 6-1/4" 15.8cm.

### Multi-Scale Pier Kit

**NEW 267-191** **28.75**
Typical wooden pier seen on ocean fronts, lakes, rivers or anywhere you need to dock your boat. Realistic deck planks and pilings cast in place. One piece casting...all that's required is minimal clean up, painting, weathering and you're ready to add it to your layout! HO Scale dimensions: 90' long by 15' wide. The deck is 7' above the water.

New Arrivals Updated Every Day! Visit Walthers Web site at
**www.walthers.com**

Items listed in blue ink may not be available at all times (see Legend Page).

## PAINTED & ASSEMBLED AUTO CARRIERS

### 199.95 ea

Made of brass & plastic, each holds nine automobiles (sold separately).

**Allied Systems**
**437-5030** Cab #5275
**437-5031** Cab #5888

**Hadley Auto Transport (blue & white rig)**
**437-5032** Cab #9461
**437-5033** Cab #9882

## TRUCKS

### Ford Flatbed Lumber Truck w/20' Flatbed 17.95 ea (Unless Noted)

Kits features Herpa Ford L9000 assembled truck cab, door decals and a photo-etched grill for protecting the cab's rear window. Door decals are included (with permission from Walthers and Atlas) for the Walthers "Walton & Sons" lumber yard and the Atlas "Hillside Lumber" yard to match the graphics in these kits, making them perfect accessories.

**437-5200** Black
**437-5201** Red
**437-5202** Gray
**437-5203** Payless Cashways **18.95**
Features a special red truck frame.

### Ford L9000 w/Stake Bed

**Kits 18.95 ea**
**437-7001** w/Black Bed
**473-7000** w/Undecorated Gray Bed

**Assembled 29.95 ea**
**437-7100** UP MOW
**437-7101** BNSF MOW

## TRACTOR/ TRAILERS

### Mack Tractor w/Wilson Grain Trailer Purina Mills

**Assembled 42.95 ea**
**437-6011** Cab #9011245
**437-6012** Cab #9011795

## TRAILERS

### 40' Trailmobile Flatbed Trailer

**Kits 15.95 ea (Unless Noted)**

Each easy-to-build kit includes a laser-cut wood deck, plus two optional styles of bulkheads. You can also build a straight flatbed with no bulkhead. The kits offer a choice of round dollies or flat feet for the landing gear.

**437-5000** Standard (red)
**437-5009** Black
**437-5010** Construction (yellow)
**437-5011** UP (Tuscan Red)

**437-5012** BN (green)
**437-5013** ATSF (white)
**437-5014** US Army (green)

**437-5015** Viking Freight (blue)
**437-5016** GN (green)
**437-5017** Strick Lease (red)

**437-5018** JB Hunt (orange)

**437-5019** MP (silver)

**437-5020** Rock Island (red)
**437-5021** D&H (gray) **16.95**
**437-5001** Undecorated (gray)

Allied Sytems Auto Carrier 437-5030

Hadley Auto Transport Auto Carrier 437-5033

40' Trailmobile Flatbed Trailer 437-5010

40' Trailmobile Flatbed Trailer 437-5013

Ford Flatbed Lumber Truck 437-5203

Ford L9000 w/Stake Bed 437-7001

### Assembled 21.95 ea

**437-5025** Assembled, Standard (red) **21.95**

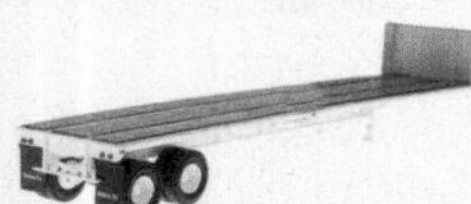

**437-5026** ATSF (white) **21.95**

**437-5027** UP

**437-5028** Construction Yellow

**437-5029** Black

## 50' Barrett Livestock Trailers

Authorized replicas are based on one of the most common designs in use. Photo-etched stainless steel sides, provide the realism of scale thickness and see-through walls.Use with any HO Scale semi-tractor. Decals included.

### Kits 24.95 ea

**437-4105** Early Style, Two-hand Hole

**437-4205** Modern Style, Four-hand Hole

**437-4305** Hog & Sheep, Early Style, Triple Deck, Three Hand Hole

**437-4405** Hog & Sheep, Current Style, Triple Deck, Four Hand Hole

### Assembled 44.95 ea

**437-4125** Early Style, Two-hand Hole

**437-4225** Modern Style, Four-hand Hole

**437-4325** Hog & Sheep, Early Style, Triple Deck, Three Hand Hole

**437-4425** Hog & Sheep, Current Style, Triple Deck, Four Hand Hole

## Wilson Grain Trailer

Constructed of molded aluminum, this grain trailer features Air Ride suspension. Kits can be built with the tarp open or closed.

**437-6000** With Light Blue Tarp **19.95**

**437-6001** With Black Tarp **19.95**

**437-6002** With Light Blue Tarp & Prepainted White Panels **21.95**

**437-6003** With Black Tarp & Prepainted Black Panels **21.95**

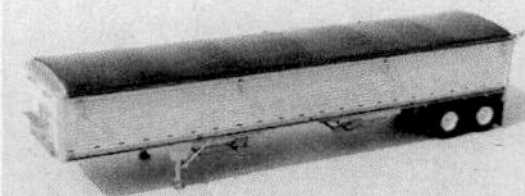

**437-6004** With Dark Blue Tarp **21.95**

**437-6005** With Dark Blue Tarp & Prepainted White Panels **21.95**

### Assembled 29.95 ea

**437-6006** With Black Tarp & Black Panels

**437-6007** w/Dark Blue Tarp & Prepainted Panels (white)

**437-6008** With Black Tarp & White Panels

**437-6009** With Blue Tarp & Black Panels

**437-6010** w/Light Blue Tarp & Prepainted Panels (white)

**437-6013** Purina Mills **31.95**

## Truck Bodies

### Stake Bed Only 9.95 ea

**437-7021** Black

**437-7023** Red

**437-7020** Undecorated Gray

## 20' Lumber Truck Bed Only 9.95 ea

**437-5210** Black

**437-5211** Red

**437-5212** Gray

40' Trailmobile Flatbed Trailer (Assembled) 437-5025

Wilson Grain Trailer 437-6000

Purina Mills 437-6013

Wilson Grain Trailer 437-6005

50' Barrett Livestock Trailer (Assembled) 437-4125

## TRAILER ACCESSORIES

### Trailmobile Details 2 Sets 4.50 ea

**437-12105** Wood Decking
Laser-cut wood decking.

**437-12106** Detail Sprue
Includes tool box, bulkheads, landing gear and tire rack.

### Trailer Suspension

**437-12107** Air Ride (blak)
2 Sets **4.50**

**437-12110** Air Ride Trailer Suspension Silver (Silver)
2 Sets **4.50**

### Working Pintle Hitch

**437-12113** Black, Delrin® plastic **4.50**

### Load Tie Downs

**437-12108** 4.50

### Trailer Wheels 4.50 ea

#### With Tires

Each package comes with 16 tires, eight wheels and four axles.

**Spoked Wheels**

Includes eight spoked-style wheels, 16 tires and four axles.

**437-12001** White

**437-12002** Black

**437-12003** Aluminum

**2-Hole Wheels**

**437-12103** White

#### Without Tires

Each package comes with 16 wheels and eight axles.

**437-12004** White

**437-12006** Aluminum

Item listed below is available by Special Order (see Legend Page).
**437-12005** Black

### Tires

**437-12104** pkg(24) **4.50**

### Trailer Mud Flaps pkg(12) 4.50 ea

**437-12013** White

**437-12014** Black

### Marker & Tail Light Lenses 4.50 ea

Each package features two sets and features 12 tail lights and 48 marker lights.

**437-12015** Red

**437-12016** Amber

**437-12017** Clear

**437-12018** Blue

**437-12019** Green

**437-12020** With Stainless Steel Frame Trim

## VEHICLE DECALS

**437-30029** For Kibri Komatsu
Each package includes two decal sheets.

**437-12021** For Lumber Truck **4.50**
Includes Trussway, Boise Cascade and Weyerhauser

**437-12046** For GHQ Model of Bobcat Skid Steer **8.00**

**437-30029** For Kibri Komatsu D575-A Super Dozer **9.95**

**437-30030** For Walthers or Kibri Komatsu WA800 Wheel Loader **9.95**

**437-30031** For Kibri Komatsu H785 or 330M Mine Truck **9.95**

**437-30032** Converts Kibri HD785 Komatsu to Dresser 330 M. Includes decals for Dresser 150T Dump Trailer. **9.95**

## VEHICLE ACCESSORIES

**437-30013** Pads for Construction Crane Stabilizers **6.95**

**437-30024** Replacement Rough Terrain Tires for Norscot Grader pkg(6) **4.95**

Latest New Product News Daily! Visit Walthers Web site at **www.walthers.com**

## MICRON ART

Add a new level of realism to your railroad with these detailed kits. Perfect for period layouts, they also add a touch of nostalgia to modern scenes. Each kit consists of photo-etched metal parts that capture many fine details and are near-scale thickness to produce a highly realistic model.

## HORSE-DRAWN VEHICLES

**462-3069** 1889 Four-Passenger Sleigh **22.95**

**462-3073** 1905 Express Delivery Wagon **25.95**

## AUTOMOBILES

### Ford Model T

**462-3021** 1911 Touring Car **45.00**
Includes removable top made of real cloth.

### Oldsmobile

**462-3029** 1904 Runabout **35.00**
Introduced in 1897, these tiny Runabouts were America's first popular priced car.

## BAGGAGE CART

**462-3037** Brass pkg(2) **22.95**
Detail your station scene, yard buildings or the front lawn of a railfan's home on your layout with this delightful kit. Revised model has improved axles and now includes two steamer trunks and suitcases. Made of photo-etched brass, the kit builds two complete carts.

## EMERGENCY VEHICLES

**462-3039** 1914 Knox Chemical Fire Engine **64.95**
Sure to be the pride of any department, this exquisite model is perfect for period scenes or as a restored rig in the present day. Incredible detail includes spoked wheels, rubber tires, steering wheel, seat, side lamps, ladders, bell, folded hose load, chemical tank, extinguishers, horn, siren, headlamps and a spotlight. The kit also comes with jewels for the lamps and full-color, illustrated instructions.

## TRUCKS

### Ford

**462-3017** 1913 Model T Delivery Van **35.00**
A favorite with stores of every kind, these delivery vans mounted a roomy body on the popular and affordable Model T chassis. Owners used them as rolling billboards, painting elaborate advertising on the sides.

**462-3019** 1923 Model T Stake Bed w/Loads **35.00**
Perfect for hauling chores at the factory or down on the farm. Includes parts to build a load of boxes.

**462-3057** 1925 Model TT 1-Ton Steel Body w/Closed Cab **36.50**
While 1925 marked the introduction of Ford's first factory-built pickups, this heavy-duty version was a glimpse of the future with its larger payload capacity, all-steel construction and enclosed cab.

# MODEL POWER MINIS

Fully painted 1/87 Scale precision diecast models feature rubber tires, accurate wheels, full interior and separately applied details. Includes stackable display box.

### Alfa Romeo 4.98 ea

**NEW 490-19355** 1972 1300 Spider Jr

**NEW 490-19375** 156 GTA Street Version

**NEW 490-19385** 147 GTA Street Version

### Audi 4.98 ea

**490-19080** A-4 Convertible (silver)

**490-19150** TT Roadster (silver)

### BMW 4.98 ea

**490-19040** 3-Series Convertible (black)

**490-19050** M3 Coupe (white)

**490-19060** 7-Series (black)

**490-19110** Z8 Convertible (red)

**490-19140** Z3 Convertible (blue)

**NEW 490-19320** 2003-4 Z-4 Cabrio

**NEW 490-19325** 2004 5 Series

**NEW 490-19330** 2004 X-5 Truck

### 1953 Cadillac Eldorado 5.49 ea

**NEW 490-19233** Baby Blue w/White Interior

**NEW 490-19234** Pink w/White Interior

**NEW 490-19235** Black w/Red Interior

**NEW 490-19243** Gold w/Black Interior

### Chevrolet

#### 1955 Belair 4.98 ea

**NEW 490-19236** Green, Cream

**NEW 490-19237** Red, White

**NEW 490-19238** Blue, White

**NEW 490-19239** Black, White

**NEW 490-19241** Purple, White

#### 1969 SS 396 Camaro 04.98 ea

**NEW 490-19251** Green

**NEW 490-19252** Yellow

**NEW 490-19253** Red

#### 1957 Corvette 4.98 ea

**NEW 490-19257** Red, White

**NEW 490-19258** Blue, White

**NEW 490-19259** Yellow, White

### 2003 Dodge Viper RT 10 4.98 ea

**NEW 490-19280** Blue

**NEW 490-19281** Red

### Ford

#### 2005 Crown Victoria

**5.49 ea**

**490-19390** White w/Police Lights

**490-19391** White w/Black Interior

**490-19392** Black w/Tan Interior

**5.98 ea**

**490-19393** Taxi

**490-19394** New York Police Department

**490-19395** New York State Police

**490-19396** California Highway Patrol

**490-19397** Texas State Police

**490-19398** Illinois State Police

**490-19399** Florida State Police

#### 1956 F-100 Pickup 5.49 ea

**NEW 490-19230** Black

**NEW 490-19231** Red

**NEW 490-19232** Light Tan

#### 1964 Mustang 5.49 ea

**NEW 490-19244** Blue

**NEW 490-19245** White

**NEW 490-19246** Red

**NEW 490-19247** Green

#### 2003-4 Thunderbird 4.98 ea

**NEW 490-19270** Red

**NEW 490-19271** Aqua

**NEW 490-19272** Silver

#### 1963 Thunderbird 5.49 ea

**NEW 490-19248** Red

**NEW 490-19249** Black

**NEW 490-19250** White

#### 1965 Shelby Cobra 4.98 ea

**NEW 490-19224** Blue w/White Stripes

**NEW 490-19225** White w/Blue Stripes

**NEW 490-19226** Red

**NEW 490-19227** Black w/Gold Stripes

**NEW 490-19228** Silver w/Black Stripes

### 1961 Jaguar 4.98 ea

**NEW 490-19430** XKE

**NEW 490-19435** XJS

### 2006 Lamborghini 4.98 ea

**NEW 490-19380** Gallardo Coupe (yellow)

**NEW 490-19381** Gallardo Coupe (orange)

**NEW 490-19382** Gallardo Coupe (blue-green)

**NEW 490-19386** Murcielago (dark gray)

### Mercedes Benz 4.98 ea (Unless Noted)

**490-19005** E Class

**490-19010** C Class Sport Coupe (silver)

**490-19020** CLK Coupe (black)

**490-19070** SLK Convertible (silver)

**490-19100** S Class (silver)

**490-19120** 500SL Convertible (black)

**490-19190** 300SL Gullwing Coupe (silver)

**490-19210** 300SL Convertible (silver)

**490-19240** Snowplow (orange, silver) **6.98**

**NEW 490-19310** 2000 E Class T Model

**NEW 490-19315** 2003 CLK Cabrio

**NEW 490-19365** 2002 ML Class Truck

**NEW 490-19400** 1963 L319 Cargo Van

#### Sprinter Van

**NEW 490-19219** EMS **5.98**

**490-19220** Yellow

**490-19221** White

**490-19222** Tan, White

**NEW 490-19223** Fed Ex Ground **5.98**

**NEW 490-19401** Santa's Gift Delivery **TBA**

### Mini Cooper 4.98 ea (Unless Noted)

**490-19130** Yellow w/Black Roof

**490-19131** Blue w/Black Roof

**490-19132** Red w/Black Roof

**NEW 490-19133** Blue w/White Roof & American Flag **TBA**

### 1969 Oldsmobile 442 5.49 ea

**NEW 490-19254** Gold w/Black Stripes

**NEW 490-19255** White w/Gold Stripes

**NEW 490-19256** Red w/Black Stripes

### 2002 Pontiac Firebird 4.98 ea

**NEW 490-19290** Black

**NEW 490-19291** Gold

### Porsche 4.98 ea

**490-19030** 911 Carrera Convertible (red)

**490-19090** Boxter (black)

**490-19180** 356B Convertible (red)

**NEW 490-19340** 2003-4 Cayenne Turbo Truck

**NEW 490-19350** 2003-4 Carrera GT

### Volkswagen 4.98 ea

**490-19170** Beetle (tan)

**490-19171** Beetle (Mint Green)

**490-19172** Beetle (red)

**490-19200** Karmann Ghia Coupe (tan)

**NEW 490-19335** 2004 Beetle Convertible

**NEW 490-19345** 2003-4 Toureg

**NEW 490-19370** Beetle RSI

### With Camping Trailers 6.98 ea

**490-19660** VW Beetle

**490-19670** VW Karmann Ghia

**490-19680** VW Bus

**490-19690** Porsche 356B

# AIRCRAFT

### Helicopters

**490-8224** Red **10.98**

# TRACTOR/ TRAILERS

### Short Haul Without Sleeper

#### With Box Trailer 16.98 ea (Unless Noted)

**490-15000** Trail Rail Service

**490-15001** B&O

**490-15002** Western Express

**490-15003** Pacific Fruit Express/UP/ATSF **17.98**

**490-15004** CR

**490-15005** SP Pig **17.98**

#### With Tank Trailer 16.98 ea

**490-16000** Water

**490-16001** Exxon

**490-16005** General Cesspool

**490-16006** Red/Silver

**490-16007** Sunoco

**490-16008** Shell

#### With Flatbed Trailer

**490-19000** Blue **16.98**

**490-19001** Red, Black **16.98**

**490-19002** D&S w/Wire Cables **18.45**

#### With Two 20' Containers 16.98 ea

**490-22000** K-Line Evergreen (white)

**490-22001** US Mail-US Army (blue truck)

**490-22002** Federal Express-Pennsy

**490-22003** ATSF-CP (black truck)

#### With Round Tank 16.98 ea

490-24002

**490-24000** Compressed Gas

**490-24001** Medical Waste

**490-24002** U.S. Army

**490-24003** Unlettered (silver)

### Long Haul w/Sleeper

#### With Box Trailer 16.98 ea

**490-17000** Candy Apple Red Baron

**490-17001** Black

**490-17002** White

**490-17003** Co-Op Shippers

**490-17004** Preferred Pool

**490-17005** WP Road Rail **17.98**

**490-17006** CP

**490-17007** Federal Express

**490-17009** US Mail Eagle (silver, blue, red)

**490-17010** Bud of California

**490-17011** CN Route – Leaf

490-18000 ATSF
490-18001 Pennsy
490-18002 UP
490-18003 Boston & Maine
490-18004 N&W
490-18005 NYC
490-18006 CR
490-18007 CP Rail

### With Moving & Racing Trailer 16.98 ea

490-21000 Black w/Chrome
490-21001 White w/Chrome
490-21002 Racing Dynamics Systems
490-21003 Bekins
490-21004 Dutch Masters

### With Refrigerator Trailer 16.98 ea

490-23000 Banana
490-23001 Fresh Farms Dairy
490-23002 USDA Meat
490-23003 Union Ice
490-23004 Unlettered (metallic blue)

### With Round Tank 16.98 ea

490-25000 Orange Juice
490-25001 Milk
490-25002 Unlettered (white)

## TRUCKS

### Diecast Wrecker Trucks 15.98 ea

490-3001 Mom's Towing
490-3002 Blue Angel Towing
490-3003 Red Devil Towing
490-30006 U.S. Army
490-30004 Unlettered (white)
490-30005 Unlettered (black)

### Dump Trucks 15.98 ea

Paint Color Shown Not Available

490-31001 Public Utility Corp.
490-31002 Department of Parks
490-31003 City of Hillsdale
490-31004 Town of Farmingdale
490-31000 Unlettered (yellow)

### 18' Metal Straight Trucks 15.98 ea

490-32001

490-32000 US Express Mail w/Eagle
490-32001 Federal Express
490-32003 Goodyear
490-32004 Unlettered (white)

### 17-18' Metal Refrigerator Trucks 15.98 ea

490-32101 Medowbrook Milk Co.

490-32103 Pabst Blue Ribbon Beer
490-32105 Washington Apples
490-32100 Undecorated (white)

### 18' Metal Box Truck w/Wood Chipper 23.98 ea (Unless Noted)

490-36100 Woody's Tree Service (yellow) 23.98
490-36000 White
NEW 490-37000 Town of Farmingdale

## TRAILERS

### Metal Wood Chippers 9.98 ea

490-26000 Yellow
490-26001 Red
490-26002 Blue

MOTORART collectible models

Modernize any construction site with this line of highly detailed models, based on popular European prototoypes. Each comes fully assembled from diecast and plastic parts, with many positionable features.

## NEW PRODUCTS

### European Construction Equipment

### Volvo

**NEW** 495-13040 L150C Wheel Loader **22.95**

**NEW** 495-13041 L180HL High Lift Log Handler w/Grapple **22.95**

**NEW** 495-13043 EC210 Excavator on Crawler Chassis **22.95**

**NEW** 495-13045 EW180B Excavator on Wheels **29.95**

**NEW** 495-13086 BL71 Backhoe Loader **31.95**

Daily New Arrival Updates! Visit Walthers Web site at
**www.walthers.com**

### EC240B Excavator on Crawler Chassis 24.95 ea

**NEW** 495-13088 Yellow

**NEW** 495-13340 Silver

### A40D Articulated Off-Road Dump Truck

**NEW** 495-13042 Yellow **24.95**
**NEW** 495-13351 Limited Edition Blue **31.95**

### Wheel Loader w/Attachments 49.95 ea

Includes Bucket, Timber Grapple, Fork Lift & Boom.

**NEW** 495-13094 L60E

**NEW** 495-13096 L70E

**NEW** 495-13098 L90E

### 4-Pack

**NEW** 495-13144 **89.95**
Includes A40D Dump Truck, Wheel Loader, Back Hoe & Excavator.

### JCB

**NEW** 495-13136 3CX Backhoe Loader **31.95**

**NEW** 495-13138 JS220 Excavator on Crawler Chassis **31.95**

### European Trucks

### Volvo FH12 Cabover w/3-Axle Curtain Trailer 16.95 ea

**NEW** 495-13079 Black

**NEW** 495-13083 Gray

**NEW** 495-13090 Blue

### Volvo FH Cabover w/3-Axle Lowboy Trailer 49.95 ea (Unless Noted)

**NEW** 495-13147 Gray w/Volvo A40D Articulated Dump Truck Load

**NEW** 495-13148 Gray w/Volvo L150C Wheel Loader Load

**NEW** 495-13149 Gray w/Volvo A40B Excavator Load
**NEW** 495-13383 Fire Red, No Load **24.95**

These officially licensed die-cast scale model replicas are great additions to layout scenes and make superb flat car loads as well as display models. Each is made from the original blueprints of the real-life machine to ensure a truly authentic reproduction. Fully assembled and finished in official colors, the models also feature many moving and/or positionable parts.

## NEW PRODUCTS

### Construction Equipment

#### Cat® Diesel No.12 Motor Grader

**NEW** 526-55173 23.95

#### Caterpillar® M318D Wheel Excavator

**NEW** 526-55177 22.95

#### CP-563E Padfoot Drum Vibratory Soil Compactor

526-55156

## CONSTRUCTION EQUIPMENT

### CAT® Construction Equipment 22.95 ea

**526-55107** 315C L Hydraulic Excavator A showpiece in any scene, this authentic model features a moveable boom, stick and bucket. The rubber tracks are also moveable. Cab can be rotated a full 360° on the chassis and features clear windows to show off the interior detail.

**526-55108** D5M LGP Track - Type Tractor w/Dozer Blade Rugged addition to any construction scene, the blade can be angled left or right. The rubber tracks are moveable, and the cab has full interior detail.

**526-55109** 966G Series II Wheel Loader
This hard-working model can put in a full day on the job with rolling wheels that are fitted with rubber tires that match the actual tread design! The rock bucket is moveable and the boom can be raised or lowered. Like the real machine, this replica has articulated steering and oscillating rear wheels.

**526-55127** 160H Motor Grader From building new highways to moving snow, these hard working graders are a familiar part of modern construction sites. The model features moveable drawbar, circle and moldboard for blade positioning, front axle and steering articulation, oscillating tandem left and right rear wheels, and a rear ripper scarifier that raises and lowers. It's finished with authentic paint and graphics.

**526-55130** 730 Articulated Truck
Features include an articulated hitch, movable hydraulic dump box, rolling wheels with authentic tire tread design, interior cab detail and working rear suspension.

**526-55156** CP-563E Padfoot Drum Vibratory Soil Compactor Features include articulated steering, forward rotating drum, rolling rear wheels with authentic tire tread pattern, front leveling blade raises and lowers and clear windows with interior cabin detail.

526-55107

526-55108

526-55109

526-55127

526-55130

# NORSCOT®
SCALE MODELS

526-55134

526-55141

526-55146

526-55155

## CAT® Construction Equipment

**526-55134** 627G Wheel Tractor Scraper **22.95**
Features tandem engine scraper, drop-down scraper bowl, operating ejector, rotating apron, articulated steering, tires with actual tread design and clear windows with interior cab detail.

**526-55155** CS-563E Smooth Drum Vibratory Soil Compactor **22.95**
Features include articulated steering, forward rotating drum, rolling rear wheels with authentic tire tread pattern and clear windows with interior cabin design.

**Limited Quantity Available**

**526-55141** 730 Articulated Truck with Klein Water Tank **12.95**

**526-55146** 966G Series II Forest Machine **12.95**



www.cat.com

## CASE® Construction Equipment

**526-21001** 340 Articulated Truck **20.95**

**526-21002** 580 Super M Series 2 Backhoe Loader **20.95**

**526-21003** 721D Wheel Loader **20.95**

**526-21004** CX330 Excavator **20.95**

# FARM EQUIPMENT

## CLAAS Farm Machinery 20.95 ea

**526-56016** CLAAS LEXION 580 Combine

**526-56017** CLAAS JAGUAR 900

**NEW 526-56020** CLASS ARES 657 ATZ

Forage Harvester CLAAS, LEXION and JAGUAR are trademarks of CLAAS KGaA mbH.

**NEW** CLAAS ARES 657 ATZ 526-56020

526-21001

526-21002

526-21003

526-21004

IMPORTED FROM GERMANY BY WALTHERS

Models are assembled of appropriately colored plastic.

## NEW PRODUCTS

### Vehicles

#### Baggage Cart

**NEW 528-16772** Electric Baggage Cart (Unpowered) Includes figure, boxes and luggage. **12.99**

#### Farm Equipment

Tractors 12.99 ea

**NEW 528-16750** Two Wheel Tractor w/Figure

**NEW 528-16754** Narrow Gauge Tractor w/Figure

#### Construction Equipment

**NEW 528-16762** Mini Excavator w/Figure **12.99**

## BOATS

**528-10710** Sailboats **9.99**

**528-11210** Sailboat w/Fisherman **12.99**

**528-11250** Sailboat w/Figure **14.99**

**528-11260** Row Boat w/2 People **14.99**

#### Background Boat Kits

N Scale models.

**528-35710** Tug Boat **43.99**

**528-35720** Coal Barge **33.99**

**528-35730** Assembled Motor Barget **35.99**

**528-35740** Motor Tank **38.99**

**528-35750** Pilot Boat **43.99**

## WAGONS

#### Horse-Drawn Wagons 23.99 ea (Unless Noted)

**528-16700** Landau (coach w/top down) w/2-Hourse Team & Driver

**528-16701** Beer Wagon w/4 Horse Hitch & 1 Figure **27.99**

**528-16702** Flatbed on Rubber Tires w/2 Horse Hitch & Standing Figure

**528-16703** Box Wagon w/2 Horses & 1 Figure

**528-16704** Box Wagon w/2 Oxen & 1 Standing Figure

on-trak model products

These period trucks and trailers will set the scene on your layout. Each craft train kit features unpainted white metal parts and styrene, wire and wood details.

Important Note: This listing includes items which are available by special order only. Please see the Legend Page for information, and visit www.walthers.com for a complete listing of in-stock and special order products.

## CONSTRUCTION EQUIPMENT

**786-5107** International Concrete Mixer **21.95**

**786-5108** Iroquois Steam Road Roller **20.45**

## FARM MACHINERY

**786-5201** JI Case Steam Tractor **83.95**

## TRUCKS

#### Kleiber

**786-5098** Flatbed Truck **21.95**

**786-5099** Flatbed w/Details **22.45**

#### Gerlinger Lumber Carrier

**786-5109** **24.95**

#### 1924 Mack "AC"

**786-5129** Flatbed **19.95**

**786-5134** Tank Truck (round) **21.95**

**786-5136** Long Chassis **19.95**

**786-5137** Wrecker **22.95**

**786-5146** Semi w/Fruehauf Van Trailer **27.95**

**786-5403** Railtruck Flatbed **22.95**

#### 1926 White

**786-5050** Cab & Chassis-No Body, Long Wheelbase **14.95**

**786-5051** Flatbed-Long Wheelbase **16.95**

**786-5055** Log **20.95**

**786-5056** Produce **19.95**

**786-5065** Delivery Van **20.95**

**786-5066** Semi Tractor Short Wheelbase **14.95**

PIRATE MODELS LTD.

IMPORTED FROM GREAT BRITAIN BY WALTHERS

## BUSES

Cast metal, craft train kits are based on popular city and cross-country buses. All models are less seats, interior details and decals.

#### Bluebird

**559-355** 1975 School Bus **77.69**

#### Eagle 79.99 ea

**559-3512** 05 Interstate

**559-3513** 05 Combo

**559-3514** 10 Interstate/ Suburban

#### Flxible 79.99 ea

**559-358** Grumman-Flxible 870

**559-3511** Flxible Metro

#### GMC 79.99 ea

**559-353** PD4903/4905A Coach

**559-357** 5909/12 Transit

**559-359** RTS Mark 3 Coach

**559-3510** RTS Mark 4

#### Mack

**559-354** 1930 AB Interstate Coach **69.99**

#### Renault 77.69 ea

**559-356** IN6C Paris

**559-3516** 1935 TN4H Paris Closed Platform

**559-3517** 1935 TN4H Paris Closed Side Entrance

**559-3518** 1934 K63C Paris Open Platform

**559-3519** 1934 K63C Paris Closed Side Entrance

#### Transit 79.99 ea

**559-351** 40' 53SER

**559-352** 4502/7

Daily New Arrival Updates! Visit Walthers Web site at

**www.walthers.com**

ORIGINAL Preiser

IMPORTED FROM GERMANY BY WALTHERS
These easy to build, highly detailed vehicles are ideal for collecting or use on layouts. Models feature realistic plastic parts molded in color, interior details, "glass" mirrors, wheels and much more. All are complete with assembly instructions. Some models are also available assembled, as noted.

Items listed in blue ink may not be available at all times (see Legend Page).

## NEW PRODUCTS

### Construction Equipment

**NEW 590-38041** Hanomag R55 Tractor w/Driver & Meier Coal Wagon **26.99**

### Emergency Vehicles

**NEW 590-33245** Social Services Car w/2 Figures **15.99**

## AUTOMOBILES

### Mitsubishi

**590-33243** Mitsubishi Pajero w/Trailer "White Beauty Riding School" w/Horse & 2 Figures **31.99**

## BOATS

**590-17304** Speed Boats pkg(2) **24.99**

## CONSTRUCTION EQUIPMENT

### Magirus

**590-31311** F 200 D 26 AK 6x6 w/3-Way Dumpbed Schmitt **28.99**

### MAN

**590-31300** Municipal Three-Way Dump Truck **30.99**

### Mercedes

**590-35014** LA 1924 Dump Truck **30.99**

## EMERGENCY VEHICLES

### Airport Vehicle Trucks

#### Faun FLF80/200

**590-35008** Assembled **39.99**

#### Mercedes

**590-31163** FTLF8000 Berlin Airport **28.99**

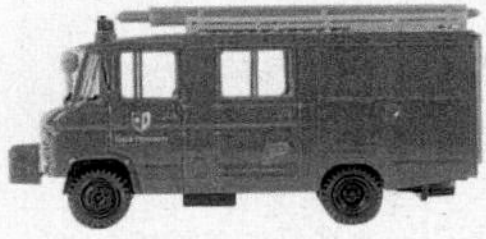

**590-35027** LF 8 408 D Equipment Van **20.99**

### Horse-Drawn Fire Equipment 33.99 ea (Unless Noted)

Models are fully assembled, based on German prototypes, but similar to equipment used in other countries.

**590-30425** Hand Pumper

**590-30426** Water Wagon

**590-30427** "Flying Squad" Personnel Wagon

**590-30428** Steam Pumper **41.99**

**590-30429** Coal Tender

### Mercedes

**590-31116** Meiller Multi-Purpose Truck w/4 Bodies **33.99**
Includes office, tall dumpster, low-side flatbed and equipment bodies.

**590-31128** F-16-2 Compartment Pumper **26.99**

**590-31144** AF/36 Hose Carrier **23.99**

**590-31180** LA 1924 w/Simon Snorkel **37.99**

**590-31207** Fire Dept. Dump Truck **28.99**

**590-31211** Mercedes 508 Technical Rescue Service Set pkg(4) **48.99**
This set includes two crew-cab equipment trucks and two personnel van kits. One pair is molded in orange, the other in the traditional blue.

**590-31230** LF16 Squad Tender **30.99**

**590-31246** LAF1113 Hose Carrier **30.99**

**590-35013** Sedan Cab Pumper **31.99**

Mitsubishi Pajero w/Trailer 590-33243

Technical Rescue Service 590-31211

**590-35019** Truck-Mounted Light Plant **26.99**

**590-35021** LF8 Pumper **20.99**

**590-35022** LF16 Pumper - Frankfurt Fire Dept. **33.99**

**590-37020** L508D Police Bus **19.99**

**Limited Quantity Available**

**590-35003** DLK 23-12 Ladder-Assembled **32.99**

**590-31178** TLF 24/50 Tank Pumper **28.99**

**590-31182** 1017 Rescue Unit w/Crane **33.99**

**590-31248** TLF16 Tank Pumper **30.99**

**590-31252** RW1 Rescue Unit **30.99**

**590-31280** LF16TS Squad Tender/Pumper **31.99**

**590-35011** O 309 Command Van-Assembled **18.99**

**590-35018** GW Breath Care **19.99**

Mercedes Emergency Equipment listed below are available by Special Order (see Legend Page).

**590-31172** TLF 48/50-5 Tank Pumper **39.99**

**590-35000** F-16-2 Compartment Pumper Assembled (red) **28.99**

**590-35001** TLF16 Pumper-Assembled **28.99**

**590-35004** Clean-Up Unit w/Meiler Dumpster-Assembled **23.99**

**590-35015** Equipment Truck w/Crew Cab & Covered Bed **21.99**

ORIGINAL Preiser

IMPORTED FROM GERMANY BY WALTHERS

**590-35026** Mercedes 408 D Fire Dept. Squad Truck **20.99**

## Magirus

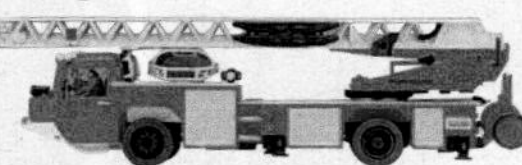

**590-31134** DLK23 Ladder (red) **39.99**

**590-31202** F200D Water Tanker **28.99**

**590-31204** F200D Rescue Squad **28.99**

**590-31218** 150D 10FA Pumper **26.99**

**590-31259** Hose Truck SW 2000 **30.99**

**590-31261** TroTLF16 w/Sedan Cab **30.99**

**590-31272** M125A LF 16TS **30.99**

**590-31265** F 150 D 10 w/Extension Ladder **46.99**

**590-31276** M125A Hose SW2000 **30.99**

**590-31292** 200 D16 Articulated Elevated Platform **39.99**

**590-35016** F200 Pollution Control Equipment Truck **28.99**

**Limited Quantity Available**

**590-31260** F200D 16A Water Container ZB6 **30.99**

**590-31263** LF 16 Sedan Cab Pumper On Mercury 150 A Chassis **30.99**

**590-31308** Fire Dept. Tools & Gear Truck **30.99**

**590-35012** DLK 23-12 Ladder **41.99**

## MAN

**590-31201** Flatbed w/Crane **28.99**

**590-31298** HA LF Pumper **33.99**

**590-31302** 1 Tender HA LF **33.99**

**590-35005** HA LF Pumper-Assembled **28.99**

**590-35007** Tool & Gear Carrier-Assembled **30.99**

MAN Emergency Equipment listed below is available by Special Order (see Legend Page).

**590-35006** Tender HA LF-Assembled **31.99**

## Ziegler

**590-31254** Hose Trailer **13.99**

**590-35010** 2B/2C w/Hose Trailer **15.99**

**590-31112** Firefighting Trailer **10.99**

## Emergency Vehicle Accessories

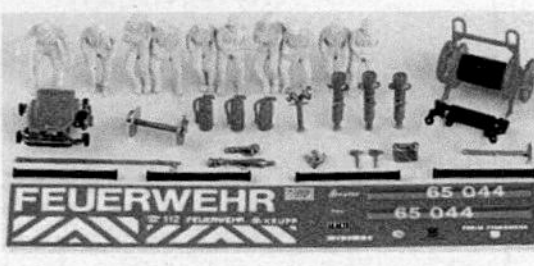


**590-31010** Seated Firemen, Hose Reels, Nozzles, Lettering **15.99**

**590-31114** Foam Sprayer & Water Cannon Trailers pkg(2) **10.99**

**590-31152** CO2 & Pressure Suction Container For #31116 **23.99**

**Limited Quantity Available**

**590-31213** Loading Platform **7.99**

## Technical Help Service (THW)

Models feature parts molded in blue.

### Mercedes

**590-31168** 911A Fire Truck w/Interior **28.99**

**590-37000** 911A Fire Truck Assembled-Less Interior **30.99**

**590-37007** L 407D Medical Van Assembled **28.99**

Mercedes Technical Help Service Equipment listed below are available by Special Order (see Legend Page).

**590-37001** LA1113B Assembled **30.99**

**590-37002** LA113 Assembled **23.99**

### Magirus

**590-31306** Tool & Gear Truck **30.99**

Hose Truck SW 2000 590-31259

TroTLF16 w/Sedan Cab 590-31261

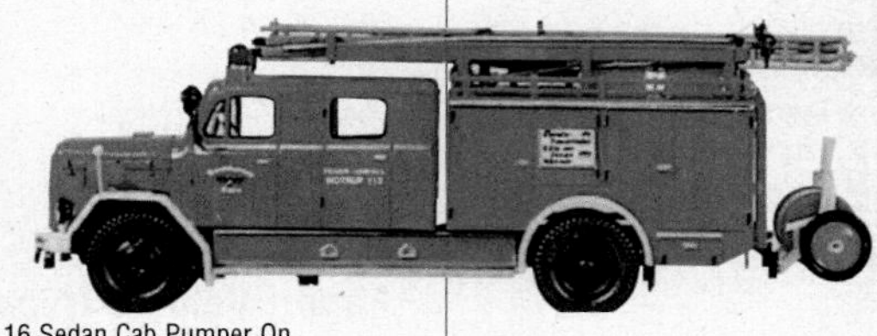

LF 16 Sedan Cab Pumper On Mercury 150 A Chassis 590-31263

**Limited Quantity Available**

**590-31307** Generator Truck **27.99**

# FARM EQUIPMENT

## Animal-Drawn

**590-30431** Farmer w/Horse-Drawn Plow **33.99**

**590-30443** Cow Drawn Sickle Bar w/Farmer **33.99**

## Implements

**590-17601** Shepherd's Trailer Kit **8.99**

**590-17918** Manure Spreader, Trailer & Plow **21.99**

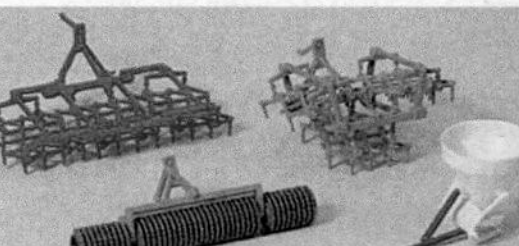

**590-17919** Drag Disc, Harrow & Manure Spreader **19.99**

## Tractors

**590-17927** Tractor Special Implement **21.99**

**590-17928** Tool Carrier w/Fork Lift **23.99**

**590-17929** Farm Tractor w/Roller **19.99**

**590-17933** Tool Carrier Tractor w/Cab & Sprayer **23.99**

IMPORTED FROM GERMANY BY WALTHERS

**590-17934** Farm Tractor (red) **13.99**

**590-17935** Tractor w/Potato Planter & 3 Figures **28.99**

### Deutz

**590-17913** Tractor w/Mower-Assembled **13.99**

**590-17914** Tractor w/Wagon-Assembled **19.99**

**590-17920** Tractors pkg(2) **23.99**

### Deutz D6206 Tractor Kits

**590-17922** With Shovel & Fork **26.99**
Can be built with or without roll-over protective structure.

**590-17923** With Enclosed Cab & Snow Plow **21.99**

**590-17924** With Enclosed Cab, Shovel & Fork **21.99**

**590-17930** Deutz D 6206 w/Mower **23.99**

Farm Tractor w/Roller 590-17929

**590-17937** w/Single Axle Trailer Carrying Manure Tank **20.99**

### Hanomag R55

**590-17915** Farm Tractor-Assembled **15.99**

**590-17916** Forestry Model w/Winch-Assembled **15.99**

**590-21000** Closed Cab Assembled **17.99**

**590-24679** Set of 2 **24.99**
Includes parts to build two complete tractors, one with roll-over protective structure, the other with fully enclosed cab.

### Lanz

**590-17921** Farm Tractor-Assembled **17.99**

**590-17925** D2416 w/Sickle Bar Mower **17.99**

### Trailers

**590-17917** Single-Axle Dump & Tank Trailers pkg(2) **17.99**

### Horse-Drawn Wagons

**590-30445** Beer Wagon w/2 Horse Team **37.99**

**590-30446** Horse-Drawn Wagon w/Tarp & 2 Figures **33.99**

**590-30450** Closed White Marriage Coach w/4 Figures Assembled **33.99**

**590-30451** Open White Marriage Coach w/4 Figures Assembled **33.99**

**590-30452** Closed Taxi w/3 Figures Assembled **33.99**

**590-30462** 1890s Beer Wagon **33.99**

**590-30434** Flatbed Wagon w/Driver, Horses & Cargo **33.99**

**590-30435** Liquid Manure Wagon w/Driver, Team & Wooden Tank **33.99**

**590-30436** Hay Rack w/Horses, Driver & Helper **31.99**

**590-30437** Beer Wagon w/Horses Lowenbrau **69.99**

**590-30438** Beer Wagon w/Horses Spatenbrau **69.99**

Farm Tractor 590-17930

Tool Carrier w/Fork Lift 590-17928

Tool Carrier Tractor w/Cab & Sprayer 590-17933

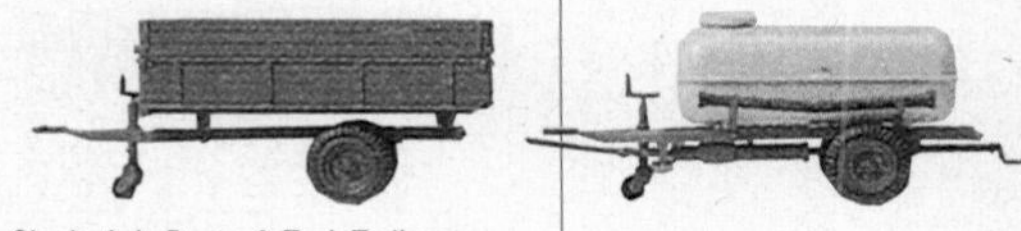

Single-Axle Dump & Tank Trailers 590-17917

Flatbed Wagon 590-30434

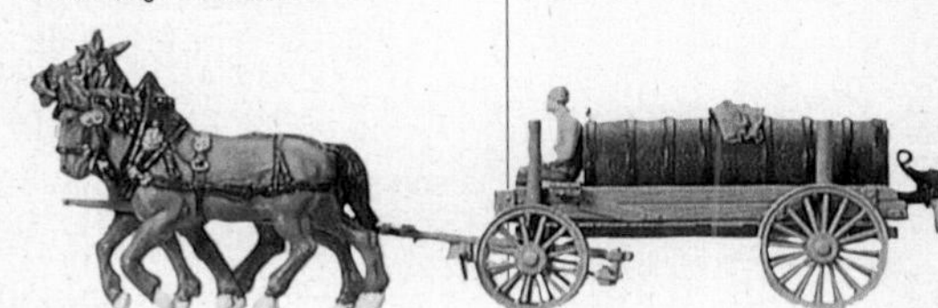

Liquid Manure 590-30435

# Preiser

ORIGINAL Preiser

IMPORTED FROM GERMANY BY WALTHERS

**590-30465** Log Wagon w/Driver & Load **33.99**

**590-30468** Ore Wagon w/Driver & Horses Assembled **24.99**

**590-30470** Cargo Wagon w/Horses Assembled **30.99**

**590-30472** Hay Wagon w/Driver & Load Assembled **30.99**

**590-30474** Manure Wagon w/Driver Load & Ox **30.99**

**590-30477** Hay Wagon w/Driver & Load **33.99**

## TRUCKS

### Mercedes

**590-37018** 508 Road Maintenance Truck **19.99**

**590-38036** 508D Transporter (dark gray) **15.99**

Hay Rack 590-30436

### Truck Accessories

**590-17202** Waste Container/Dustbin **14.99**

## CIRCUS VEHICLES

### Wagons

**590-20005** Wagon Set (undecorated), Kit pkg(3) **39.99**

**590-20006** Equipment Wagon Set (undecorated), Kit pkg(4) **39.99**

**590-20007** Animal Wagon Set (undecorated), Kit pkg(3) **39.99**

**590-20008** Wagon Set (undecorated), Kit pkg(3) **39.99**

**590-21016** Baggage Wagon **21.99**

**590-21018** Animal Wagon-Closed **23.99**

**590-21019** Animal Wagon-Open **23.99**

**590-21020** Krone Equipment Wagon **23.99**

**590-21021** Krone Equipment Caravan **23.99**

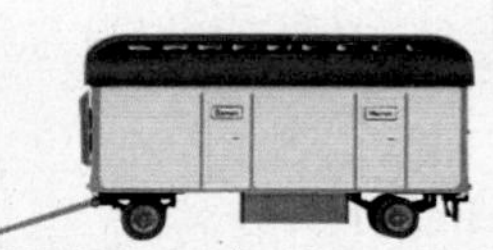

**590-21025** Toilet Wagon **23.99**

**590-21030** Krone Electronic Wagon **23.99**

**590-21031** Krone Cashier's Wagon **33.99**

**590-21032** Krone 5-Compartment Personnel Trailer **33.99**

**590-21050** Personnel Carrier w/3 Compartments Trailer **33.99**

**590-21051** Equipment Trailer & Extending Trailer **33.99**

**590-21052** Equipment Trailer & Restroom Trailer **33.99**

Item listed below is available by Special Order (see Legend Page).

**590-21017** Krone Baggage Wagon w/Windows **21.99**

### Tractors

**590-24679** Hanomag R55 (white), Kit pkg(2) **24.99**

Lowenbrau Beer Wagon 590-30437

Spatenbrau Beer Wagon 590-30438

Wagon Set 590-20005

Equipment Wagon Set 590-20006

Animal Wagon Set 590-20007

Wagon Set 590-20008

Personnel Carrier w/3 Compartments 590-21050

Equipment Trailer & Extending Trailer 590-21051

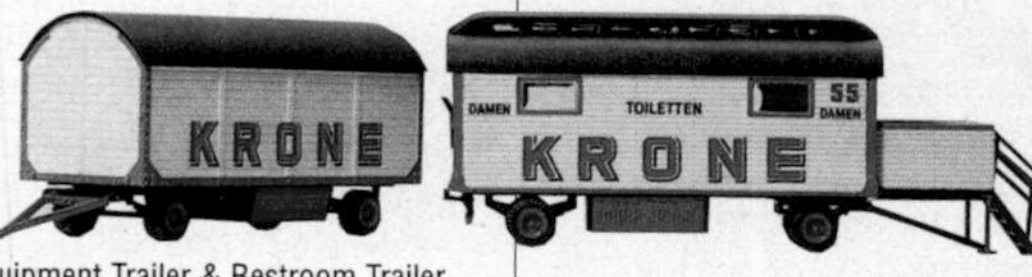


Equipment Trailer & Restroom Trailer 590-21052

Hanomag R55 590-24679

# RICKO™

Set the scene on layout streets with this line of HO Scale replicas, featuring classic and contemporary vehicles. Fully assembled from detailed plastic parts, they're ideal for layouts and dioramas, and will stand out in any collection of automobile miniatures.

## AMERICAN AUTOMOBILES

### Cadillac

**2003 Sixteen Concept Car 13.98 ea**

636-38357 Black
636-38457 Metallic Red

**2003 Escalade ESV 13.98 ea**

636-38358 Black
**NEW** 636-38458 White

**1934 V16 Aerodynamic Coupe 15.98 ea**

636-38360 Dark Blue
**NEW** 636-38460 Black

### Chrysler

**2006 PT Cruiser 11.98 ea**

636-38361 Blue
**NEW** 636-38461 Silver

**2005 300C SRT8 11.98 ea**

636-38362 Black
**NEW** 636-38462 Silver

**2005 Crossfire**

**Coupe 11.98 ea**

636-38365 Graphite
**NEW** 636-38465 Sapphire Silver

**Roadster 13.98 ea**

636-38376 Graphite
636-38476 Sapphire Silver

### Dodge

**2007 Caliber 11.98 ea**

636-38369 Inferno Red
**NEW** 636-38469 Sunburst Orange
**NEW** 636-38569 Bright Silver Metallic
**NEW** 636-38669 Black Clearcoat

### Ford

**2005 GT40 13.98 ea**

636-38371 Black
**NEW** 636-38471 Red
**NEW** 636-38571 White
**NEW** 636-38671 Yellow

### Lincoln

**1963 Continental Convertible Sedan 15.98 ea**

636-38322 Yellow - Top Down
**NEW** 636-38422 Black - Top Down

**1931 Model K Convertible Sedan 15.98 ea**

636-38363 Black - Top Down
**NEW** 636-38381 Black - Top Up
**NEW** 636-38463 Blue - Top Down
**NEW** 636-38481 Blue - Top Up
**NEW** 636-38563 Green - Top Down
**NEW** 636-38581 Green - Top Up
**NEW** 636-38663 Wine Red, Ivory - Top Down
**NEW** 636-38681 Wine Red, Ivory - Top Up

**2005 Mustang GT**

**Coupe 13.98 ea**

636-38370 Blue
**NEW** 636-38470 Silver

**Convertible 13.98 ea**

636-38374 Red - Top Down
**NEW** 636-38382 Red - Top Up
**NEW** 636-38474 Yellow - Top Down
**NEW** 636-38482 Yellow - Top Up

## EMERGENCY - POLICE VEHICLES

**Dodge 2006 Charger 13.98 ea**

636-38368 Special Service Police (black, white)

**NEW** 636-38468 Sheriff

## EUROPEAN AUTOMOBILES

### Ford

**1986 RS200**

**NEW** 636-38321 Rally 13.98
**NEW** 636-38337 White 11.98
**NEW** 636-38437 Black 11.98

### Audi

**1936 Wanderer W25 Roadster**

**NEW** 223-38349 Green - Top Down 15.98

### Horch

**1935 Pullman 851 15.98 ea**

**NEW** 636-38309 Black
**NEW** 636-38409 Moss Green

**1939 930V Cabriolet 15.98 ea**

**NEW** 636-38352 Black - Top Down
**NEW** 636-38380 Black - Top Up
**NEW** 636-38452 Red, Black - Top Down
**NEW** 636-38480 Red, Black - Top Up
**NEW** 636-38552 Blue, Black - Top Down
**NEW** 636-38580 Blue, Black - Top Up
**NEW** 636-38652 Black, Ivory - Top Down
**NEW** 636-38680 Black, Ivory - Top Up

### Mercedes-Benz

**1938 770 W07 Limousine**

**NEW** 636-38375 Emperor Hirohito's Limousine (maroon) 15.98

**1927 630K**

**NEW** 636-38378 Red - Top Up 15.98
**NEW** 636-38578 Ivory - Top Up 15.98

### Maserati

**2002 Coupe 11.98 ea**

**NEW** 636-38305 Dark Gray
**NEW** 636-38405 Dark Red

**2003 Quattroporte 11.98 ea**

**NEW** 636-38306 Metallic Gray
**NEW** 636-38406 Silver

**2002 Spyder 11.98 ea**

**NEW** 636-38307 Silver - Top Down
**NEW** 636-38407 Blue - Top Down

### Porsche

**1955 550 Speedster 13.98 ea**

**NEW** 636-38367 Silver
**NEW** 636-38467 Red

Seaport Model Works creates a line of marine components for model railroads. They specialize in products such as fishing boats, ferries and generic boat parts (see the Super Detailing Parts section of this Reference Book for a complete listing to marine parts available through Walthers). Components are made from polyurethane resin, metal or wood.

## NEW PRODUCT

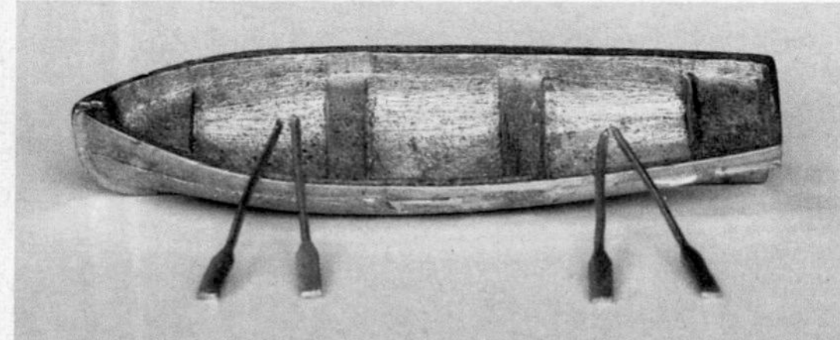

**NEW 663-P81HO** Metal Utility Boat w/ Oars 2-3/4" **8.95**

## BARGE

**663-M44HO** 43' Barge w/Square Bow **16.95**

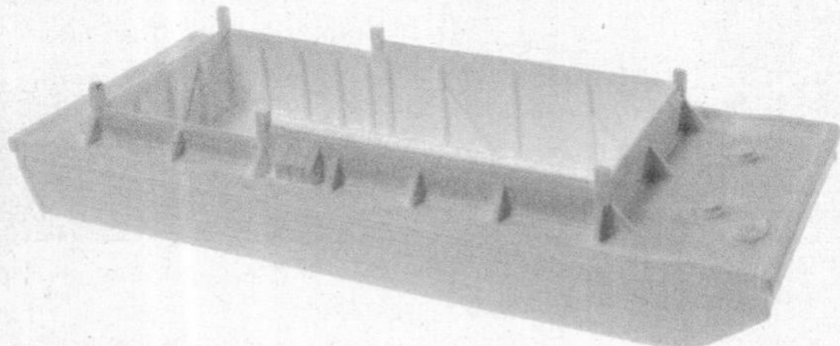

**663-M96HO** Square Front Barge Assembled **34.95**
Fully assembled and highly detailed, this version includes hatches, coiled lines, toolbox, interior framing detail and more.
Measures 8 x 3-11/16"; scale 59 x 27'

## HULLS ONLY

**663-M45HO** 46' Schooner/Sloop **16.95**
Measures 6-3/8 x 2-1/16" Long

## BOATS

**663-H115HO** 63' Sardine Carrier **49.95**
The handsome vessel is typical of the sardine/coastal freight carriers, trawlers and draggers common on both east and west coasts from the 1920s to the present. Waterline model (flat bottom) incorporates many features of the prototypes. Designed for easy assembly with superb detail, the kit includes both resin and metal castings. Measures 8-1/2" Long

**663-H116HO** 78' Steam Tug "Exeter" **94.95**
This freelance design incorporates features from many similar vessels to capture the look of a typical prototype. When complete, it represents a wooden-hulled steam tug built for railroad carfloat service, but boats of this type were also the "jack of all trades," with small passenger and freight cabins behind the deckhouse. Designed for easy construction — no shipbuilding skills required — the waterline (flat bottom) model features a resin hull with numerous quality castings and fittings, as well as drawings and instructions. Measures 10-1/2" Long

**663-M46HO** 41' Coaster/Fishing Boat **16.95**
Measures 5-9/16 x 1-1/4" Long

**663-M48HO** 63' Sardine Carrier Hull **25.95**
Measures 8-1/2 x 2" Long

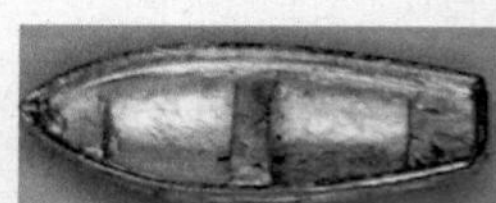

**663-P21HO** Small Boat w/Oars pkg(2) **3.95**
Measures 1-1/2" 3.7cm Long.

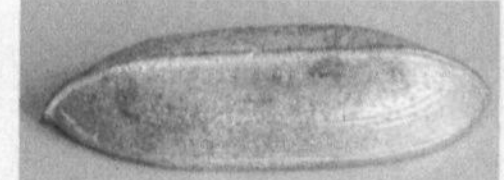

**663-P72HO** Small Life Boat **4.95**
Measures 2" long, 3/4" wide and 3/8" tall 5 x 1.8 x .9cm

See What's Available at
**www.walthers.com**

# trident

IMPORTED FROM AUSTRIA BY WALTHERS

Modernize your layout with these civilian vehicles, based on American prototypes, and military equipment from the US and other countries. All 90000 series models are assembled plastic with clear "glass" and full interiors. The 80000 series models are craft train kits, featuring detailed metal castings.

## NEW PRODUCTS

### Emergency

#### Ambulances

##### Chevrolet

**NEW 729-90352** Falck **18.99**

**NEW 729-90077A** Chicago **17.99**

**NEW 729-90105A** Chicago EMS; Pickup Cab **16.99**

#### Fire Dept. Vehicles

##### Chevrolet Suburban

**NEW 729-90064A** Fire Dept. of New York (FDNY) Fire Chief **16.99**

#### Police Vehicles

##### Chevrolet Box Van 18.99 ea

**NEW 729-90335** Tennessee Highway Patrol

**NEW 729-90347** US Secret Service

##### Chevrolet Pickup w/Special Body 17.99 ea

**NEW 729-90336** Virginia State Police

**NEW 729-90338** California Highway Patrol Bomb Squad

**NEW 729-90341** Missouri State Highway Patrol Explosives Disposal

##### Chevrolet Blazer

**NEW 729-90339** California Highway Patrol **17.99**

##### Chevrolet Suburban

**NEW 729-90343** Kentucky State Police **17.99**

**NEW 729-90348** US Secret Service **16.99**

**NEW 729-90350** Royal Canadian Mounted Police D.A.R.E. Unit **18.99**

##### Chevrolet Van

**NEW 729-90342** Maine State Police **16.99**

##### Ford Crewcab Pickup 17.99 ea (Unless Noted)

**NEW 729-90337** Utah Highway Patrol

**NEW 729-90340** Alabama State Trooper

**NEW 729-90349** Toronto Police **16.99**

### Vans

##### Chevrolet 16.99 ea (Unless Noted)

**NEW 729-90344** Allied Van Lines **14.99**

**NEW 729-90345** American Air Lines

**NEW 729-90346** Steelcase Van Lines

### Trucks

##### Ford F-350 Crew Cab Pickup 15.99 ea

**NEW 729-900785** Metallic Black

**NEW 729-900786** Metallic Silver

## BUSES & TAXIS

**729-90071** "Air Shuttle Service" **15.99**

**729-90076** Safe Line School Bus **15.99**

**729-90116** Chevy Suburban School Bus **14.99**

**729-90167** Taxi Yellow Cab **13.99**

## CONSTRUCTION EQUIPMENT

**729-90055** MAN F8 16.192 FAK Dump Truck **17.99**

**729-90094** Heavy-Duty Forklift **16.99**

**729-97013** All-Terrain Crawler Tractor & Trailer Hagglunds "Schwarzbau" (Schwarz Moonlight Builders) **18.99**

## EMERGENCY

### AMBULANCES

##### Chevrolet Suburban

**729-90060** Airport **15.99**

##### Chevrolet Pick-Up Cab w/Box Body 16.99 ea (Unless Noted)

**729-90061** Rescue

**729-90105** Emergency Medical Service

**729-90107** New York City EMS **17.99**

**729-90119** Technical Response Team

**729-900631** Advanced Life Support Unit

##### Chevrolet Van Cab w/Box Body 16.99 (Unless Noted)

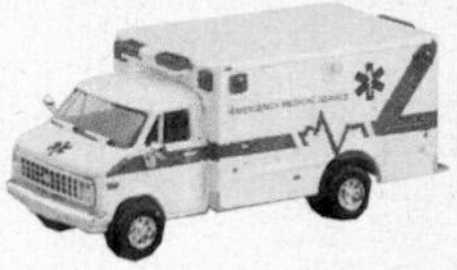

**729-90077** Emergency Medical Service

**729-90130** Mercy Paramedic

**729-90182** G.G.D. **15.99**

**729-90191** German Red Cross - Fulda **15.99**

**729-90203** GB Paramedics **20.99**

##### Chevrolet Van 17.99 ea (Unless Noted)

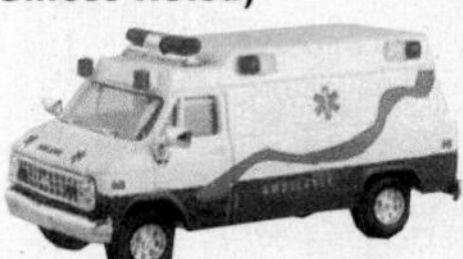

**729-90065** Paramedics

**729-90100** Metropolitan Ambulance **16.99**

trident

IMPORTED FROM AUSTRIA BY WALTHERS

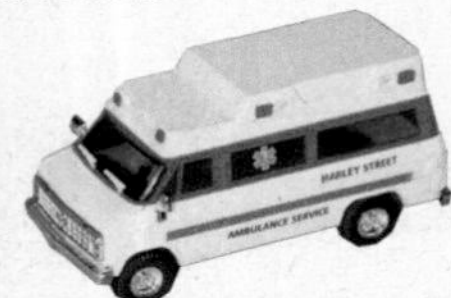

**729-90196** Harley Street Ambulance **16.99**

**729-90223** Israeli Ambulance

**729-90289** Israeli Ambulance **16.99**

**729-90290** German Baby Ambulance

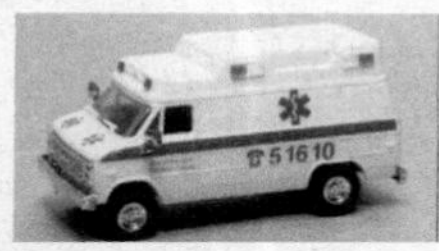

**729-90291** Krankentransport (Patient Transport) Leipzig

**Limited Quantity Available**

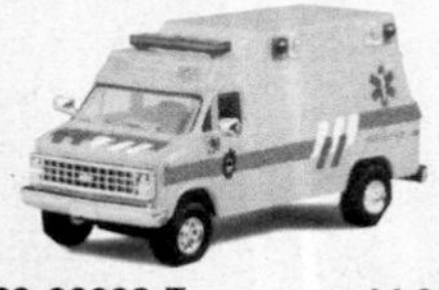

**729-90098** Emergency **14.99**

## Fire Dept. Vehicles

### Chevrolet Vans 16.99 ea (Unless Noted)

**729-90197** New York City Fire Dept. FDNY High Rise Unit

**729-90210** SDA 102 Fire Stockholm

**729-90292** Chicago Fire Dept. Air Mask Service

**729-90294** Freiwillige Feuerwehr - FFW Floing **14.99**

**729-90315** Toronto Fire Dept. **16.99**

### Chevrolet Pick-Up Cab w/Special Body

**New York City Fire Dept. (FDNY)**

**729-90139** Hazardous Materials Operations Unit **17.99**

**729-90140** Ambulance (red, white) **17.99**

**729-90170** Recuperation and Care (RAC) Equipment Truck **16.99**

**729-90198** Flatbed Stake Truck **16.99**

**Brush (Off-Road) Fire Pumper 17.99 ea**

**729-901631** White

**729-901632** Red

**Rescue Pumper 15.99 ea**

**729-901171** White

**729-901172** Red

**729-901173** Lime Green

**"Scat" Mini-Pumper 16.99 ea**

**729-90062** Red

**729-900621** White

**729-900622** Lime Green

### Chevrolet Van Cab w/Box Body

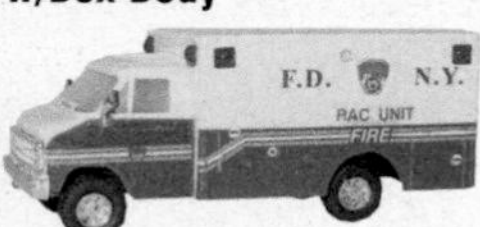

**729-90221** New York City Fire Dept. (FDNY) Recuperation and Care (RAC) Unit **17.99**

### Chevrolet Suburban 15.99 ea (Unless Noted)

**729-90064** New York City Fire Dept. (FDNY) Chief **16.99**

**729-900541** EMS Supervisor

**729-900581** Airport Fire Command "Florian 1"

### Pick-Up Mini Pumpers 16.99 ea

**729-90225** Chevrolet - Indianapolis Fire Dept.

**729-90264** Ford F-350 Quad Cab

## Motorcycles

**729-90204** NSU HK-101 Half Track w/Trailer **10.99**

### Ford Crewcab Pick-Up 16.99 ea

**729-90312** Rigaud Fire Dept.

**729-90319** Bell Helicopter Fire Dept.

## Police Vehicles

### Chevrolet Vans 14.99 ea (Unless Noted)

**729-90120** Polis

**729-90135** New York State Trooper

**729-90152** Treasury Dept. Explosive Investigation Bureau of Alcohol/Tobacco/Firearms

**729-90164** Wichita, Kansas, Police Field Sobriety/Breath Alcohol Testing

**729-90171** Police S.W.A.T. Unit **15.99**

**729-90185** New Jersey State Police Traffic Education Unit

**729-90201** Massachusetts State Police **17.99**

**729-90220** Tennessee Highway Patrol

**729-90203** Albany, NY, Police "D.A.R.E." Unit **20.99**

**729-90231** Indiana State Police

**729-90255** Colorado State Patrol

**729-90258** Montana Highway Patrol Commercial Motor Vehicle Inspection Unit

**Limited Quantity Available**

**729-90131** Dutch Traffic Police **15.99**

### Chevrolet Van 16.99 ea

**729-90277** Washington State Patrol

**729-90298** Federal Bureau of Investigation

**729-90310** Zurich Swilzerland Police **16.99**

**729-90311** Missouri Highway Patrol Crime Scene Investigation Unit **17.99**

**729-90314** Quebec Police Dept. **16.99**

**729-90317** Ontario Police **16.99**

### Chevrolet Van with 1-Ton Body 17.99 ea (Unless Noted)

**729-90178** Michigan State Police

**729-90209** Virginia State Police Crime Scene Investigation Unit **16.99**

**729-90218** Massachusetts State Police

**729-90238** Metro Police D.A.R.E. Unit

## trident

IMPORTED FROM AUSTRIA BY WALTHERS

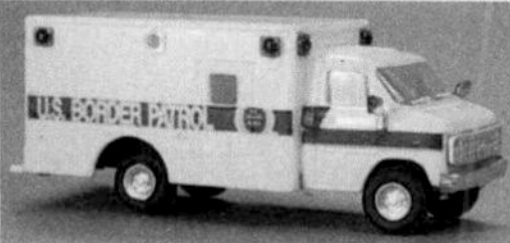


**729-90239** US Border Patrol

**729-90275** Alaska Dept. of Public Safety

**729-90279** Connecticut State Police

**729-90283** Maryland State Police

**729-90300** Police Special Response Team

**729-90303** Drug Abuse Resistance Education (D.A.R.E.) Unit

**729-90318** Ontario Police (white) **16.99**

### Chevrolet Pick-Up with Special Body 17.99 ea (Unless Noted)

**729-90147** Los Angeles Beach Patrol **14.99**

**729-90161** Washington Prison Unit **16.99**

**729-90188** New Jersey State Police Bomb Squad **14.99**

**729-90232** Colorado State Patrol Hazardous Materials Enforcement & Response Unit

**729-90234** Kansas Highway Patrol

**729-90235** South Carolina Highway Patrol

**729-90254** Massachusetts State Police

**729-90256** New Mexico State Police

**729-90281** Oregon State Police

**729-90285** Georgia State Patrol

**729-90307** Baton Rouge, LA, Service Unit

**729-90313** Quebec Police Dept. (white)

**729-90321** New Hampshire State Police **19.99**

### Chevrolet Tow Truck

**729-90262** US Border Patrol **17.99**

**729-90237** Washington Metro Police **16.99**

### Chevrolet Pick-Up

**729-90173** North Carolina Highway Patrol **17.99**

**729-90183** Ohio State Highway Patrol **15.99**

**729-90194** Arizona Highway Patrol **14.99**

### Chevrolet Suburban 16.99 ea (Unless Noted)

**729-90136** Colorado State Patrol

**729-90141** Navajo Nation Police

**729-90179** Louisiana State Police

**729-90193** US Border Patrol **15.99**

**729-90195** White Settlement Police

**729-90199** Park Ranger

**729-90227** South Dakota Highway Patrol

**729-90228** Wisconsin State Patrol

**729-90253** Massachusetts State Police **17.99**

**729-90278** Oklahoma Highway Patrol

**729-90316** Ontario Police

### Chevrolet Blazer 17.99 ea (Unless Noted)

**729-90133** Florida Highway Patrol

**729-90137** Colorado State Patrol **16.99**

**729-90148** Los Angeles Beach Patrol **14.99**

**729-90162** Nevada Highway Patrol

**729-90168** Alaska State Trooper **16.99**

**729-90172** North Carolina Highway Patrol

**729-90207** Maryland State Police

**729-90211** North Dakota Highway Patrol

**729-90229** Idaho State Police **16.99**

**729-90233** Massachusetts State Police

**729-90295** US Border Patrol **16.99**

**729-90308** Royal Canadian Mounted Police **16.99**

**729-90320** Vermont State Patrol **19.99**

**729-90273** US Sheriff **13.99**

### Chevrolet - New York City Police Dept. (NYPD) Vehicles

**729-90096** Van - Personnel Transport **15.99**

**729-90097** Van - Cargo Transport **15.99**

**729-90106** Blazer - Park Police **14.99**

**729-90108** Blazer - Patrol Unit **15.99**

**729-90215** Pick-Up w/Box Body - Radio Emergency **15.99**

**729-90240** Van - Emergency Service **16.99**

**729-90263** Van - Detective Bureau Crime Scene Unit **16.99**

## trident

IMPORTED FROM AUSTRIA BY WALTHERS

**729-90301** City of New York (NYPD) Technical Assistance Response Unit **17.99**

**729-90302** New York Canine Unit **16.99**

**729-90293** City of New York (NYPD) Police Ambulance **16.99**

### Ford Pick-Up Police Vehicles

**729-90208** Extended Cab Pick-Up State Park Police **17.99**

**729-90216** Oregon State Police **17.99**

**729-90219** Iowa State Trooper - Crewcab **17.99**

**729-90241** Police D.A.R.E. Unit - F-350 Quad Cab **17.99**

**729-90257** Pennsylvania State Police - F-350 Quad Cab **16.99**

**729-90274** Alaska State Trooper **16.99**

**729-90276** Missouri State Highway Patrol **16.99**

**729-90280** Maine State Police **16.99**

**729-90282** Massachusetts State Police **17.99**

**729-90284** Minnesota State Police **16.99**

### Royal Canadian Mounted Police (RCMP) Vehicles 16.99 ea (Unless Noted)

**729-90259** Ford F-350 Quad Cab Pickup

**729-90260** Chevrolet Suburban Patrol Unit

**729-90261** Chevrolet 1-Ton Box Van **17.99**

**729-90296** Chevrolet Personnel Van

**729-90297** Drinking & Driving Unit - Chevrolet Box Van **17.99**

**729-90299** Ambulance - Chevrolet Van **17.99**

### Police Dept. All-Terrain Crawler Tractor & Trailer

**729-90200** Massachusetts State Police **21.99**

### Technical Help Service - THW

**Limited Quantity Available**

**729-90070** MAN F8 Dump Truck w/Crane **15.99**

### All-Terrain Crawler Tractor 18.99 ea

**729-97005** All-Terrain Crawler Tractor & Trailer ALR Communal

**729-97006** With Cargo Trailer w/Crane - Eutin

**729-97014** With Personnel Trailer

**729-97015** With Construction Trailer w/Crane

# MILITARY VEHICLES

See the Military Section for the complete listing of Trident Military Vehicles.

# TRUCKS

## Chevrolet

### Delivery Truck - Pickup Cab w/Special Body 13.99 ea

**729-901541** White

**729-901542** Blue

**729-901543** Red

**729-901544** Green

### Full Size Blazer 11.99 ea

**729-90001** Blue w/White Rear Roof

**729-900012** Blue

**729-900013** Blazer Yellow w/Black Hard Top

### Fleetside Long Box Pickup 11.99 ea

**729-90008** White

**729-900081** Red

**729-900082** Gray

### Chevrolet 4-Wheel Drive Pickup 10.99 ea

**729-90002** White

**729-90002S** Black

**729-90002Y** Yellow

### Nine Passenger Suburban 12.99 ea (Unless Noted)

**729-900141** Red

**729-900142** White

**729-900143** Black

**729-900591** Two-Tone Red **14.99**

### Chevrolet Suburban

**729-90271** Airport Runway Escort "Follow Me" Unit **16.99**

### Chevrolet Tow Truck

**729-90272** Ariks Towing **17.99**

### Pickup w/Stakebed Body 14.99 ea

**729-901531** White

**729-901532** Blue

**729-901533** Red

**729-901535** Yellow

### Step Side 4x4 Pickup 10.99 ea (Unless Noted)

**729-90115** Stripe Graphics **14.99**

**729-900151** Red

**729-900152** White

### Tow Truck 16.99 ea (Unless Noted)

**729-90222** Chevy Dept. of Transportation Tow Truck **17.99**

**729-90287** Greg's Garage Tow Truck

**729-900721** White

**729-900722** Red

**729-900723** Blue

**729-900724** Yellow

## Ford

### 1-Ton Delivery Trucks

**729-90113** Furniture & More **14.99**

**729-90121** U Drive Truck Rentals **15.99**

**729-901011** Unlettered-White **13.99**

**729-901012** Unlettered-Blue **13.99**

**729-901013** Unlettered-Gray **13.99**

### Ford F-350 Crew Cab Pick-Up 16.99 ea

**729-900781** White

**729-900782** Red

**729-900783** Blue

**729-900784** Yellow

## Tractor-Trailers

### 3-Axle Conventional w/Airdam, No Sleeper

**729-90243** With 3-Axle Flatbed Trailer & Two 20' Box Containers **31.99**

### CCC 3-Axle Conventional

**729-90151** w/3-Axle Heavy-Duty Flatbed Trailer **29.99**

**729-90157** w/Single-Axle Container Chassis & 20' Reefer Container Peninsula Creamery **28.99**

## trident

IMPORTED FROM AUSTRIA BY WALTHERS

# VANS

### Chevrolet

**Sport Van 13.99 ea (Unless Noted)**

**729-90242** Sportvan w/American Flag Graphics **17.99**

**729-900411** White

**729-900412** Red

**729-900413** Blue

**729-900414** Green

**Cargo Van 13.99 ea (Unless Noted)**

**729-900461** White

**729-900462** Red

**729-900463** Blue

**729-900464** Yellow

**729-900465** Green

**729-90074** "TNT" **15.99**

**729-90075** "Rockway" **15.99**

**729-90102** DHL Worldwide Express Delivery **14.99**

**729-90114** Opel Racing Team **15.99**

**729-90123** U Drive Truck Rentals **15.99**

**729-90142** TV/Radio Station Remote Broadcast Truck w/Roof Satellite Dish **16.99**

**729-90143** Camper w/Roof Luggage Rack **16.99**

**729-90146** Yellow Cab **14.99**

**729-90169** United Van Lines **14.99**

**729-90180** Wells Fargo **15.99**

### Cargo Vans 16.99 ea

**729-90286** Express Mail

**729-90288** Ryder

# VEHICLE ACCESSORIES

**729-90186** 20' Container Set 2 Box Vans, 1 Reefer Unit **17.99**

**729-96011** Towing Device **5.99**

**729-96013** Portable Fire Pump w/Booster Hose Reels **7.99**

**729-96032** Cab Air Conditioners **7.99**

**729-96033** Fire Truck Parts; Hard Suction Hoses, Ladders & More **7.99**

**729-96034** Tow Truck Bed, Winch & More **7.99**

**729-96036** Roof Racks & Ladders **6.99**

**729-97009** 20' Containers **11.99**

### Emergency Lights – Nonworking

**729-96012** Set #2 - One each Red, Blue & Clear **5.99**

## SCALE SCENICS

DIVISION OF CIRCUITRON

Easy-to-build white metal kits include detailed parts and assembly instructions.

### Construction Equipment

**652-3502** Cement Mixer **8.95**

**652-3515** Fork Lift Truck **6.95**

These gasoline-powered fork lifts are found outside all types of industries. Includes several pallets.

### Conveyor

**652-3508** 2-Wheel Belt Conveyor **9.95**

## TRUCKS-N-STUFF

For a complete listing and availability of all Trucks-N-Stuff products, visit www.walthers.com.

# SEMIS

American prototype models include tractor and trailer, which are fully assembled (tractors include separate mirrors which must be installed by the modeler), and finished in colorful schemes.

### w/53' Van

**Freightliner Columbia 12.99 ea**

**734-3152** Knight Transportation

**734-3154** Swift Transportation

**NEW 734-3156** Swift Transportation Owner/Operator Division (blue cab)

**Volvo 670 12.99 ea**

**734-3150** Knight Transportation

**Limited Quantity Available**

**734-3151** Swift Transportation

**Volvo 780 12.99 ea**

**734-3153** Knight Transportation

**734-3155** KKW Trucking

## VOLLMER

IMPORTED FROM GERMANY BY WALTHERS

# TRAILERS

**770-5145** Camping Trailers pkg(2) **21.99**

These small travel trailers are natural additions to any campground or beach scene.

New Arrivals Updated Every Day! Visit Walthers Web site at **www.walthers.com**

IMPORTED FROM GERMANY BY WALTHERS

From the farm to downtown, this large selection of vehicles makes it easy to detail the scene. Choose autos from Audi to Volvo, buses, trucks, vans and recreation vehicles as well as construction, emergency and farm equipment. Each item is preassembled in appropriately colored plastic. (Markings and colors may vary from photos.)

## NEW PRODUCTS

### Audi

**NEW 781-6603** Q7 w/Horse Trailer **39.99**

**NEW 781-13240** A4 Cabrio (blue) **22.99**

**NEW 781-13302** Q7 (green metallic) **22.99**

**NEW 781-13401** TT Coupe (red) **22.99**

**NEW 781-13403** TT Coupe (Deep Sea Blue) **22.99**

**NEW 781-13440** TT Roadster (blue) **24.99**

### Borgward

**NEW 781-82336** Isabella Coupe **16.99**

### Citroen

**NEW 781-80708** ID 19 (yellow) **11.99**

**NEW 781-80908** 2 CV (dark yellow) **10.99**

### Ford

**NEW 781-80004** 17 M Taxi **15.99**

### Mercedes Benz

**NEW 781-13839** A-Classe 3-Door (blue) **22.99**

**NEW 781-21904** E-Klasse (beige metallic) **18.99**

**NEW 781-22106** CLK (blue metallic) **18.99**

**NEW 781-82405** 220 S (white) **14.99**

### Opel

**NEW 781-79916** Commodore Coupe **19.99**

**NEW 781-80408** GT (light blue) **13.99**

**NEW 781-82707** Manta A **13.99**

**NEW 781-84703** Rekord A Sedan **18.99**

**NEW 781-85001** 1956 Caravan (blue) **11.99**

**NEW 781-85002** 1956 Caravan (red) **12.99**

### Volkswagen

#### Old Beetle

**NEW 781-81007** Pink **10.99**

**NEW 781-79401** 1200 Cabrio w/Top Down **14.99**

**NEW 781-79440** 1200 Limousine (silver) **14.99**

#### New Beetle

**NEW 781-3513** Green **12.99**

#### Box Wagon

**NEW 781-79740** T1 **16.99**

#### Caddy

**NEW 781-27502** Candywhite **19.99**

#### California T5

**NEW 781-27303** w/Bicycle **26.99**

#### Eos

**NEW 781-6201** Candywhite **22.99**

**NEW 781-6202** w/Top Down (Midnight Blue) **22.99**

**NEW 781-6239** Gray **22.99**

**NEW** Old Beetle Volkswagen 781-81007

**NEW** Audi Q7 w/Horse Trailer 781-6603

**NEW 781-6240** Wheatbeige **19.99**

#### Golf

**NEW 781-6104** V (Candywhite metallic) **18.99**

#### Karmann Ghia

**NEW 781-80508** Coupe **13.99**

#### Passat

**NEW 781-6503** Variant w/Roof Box **26.99**

**NEW 781-6502** Variant Station Wagon (blue) **19.99**

#### Phaeton

**NEW 781-5906** Green **19.99**

**NEW 781-5907** 4-Door Sedan (white) **19.99**

#### Touran

**NEW 781-30540** Blue **24.99**

#### Touareg

**NEW 781-6040** Red **22.99**

#### Multivan

**NEW 781-30804** Wheatbeige **18.99**

### Sets

**NEW 781-91806** Mercedes Benz A160, Porsche Boxter, Volkswagen New Beetle pkg(3) **16.99**

### Buses

**NEW 781-73109** Double Decker Bus D89 (yellow) **38.99**

**NEW 781-79910** Pullman Bus w/Roof Rack **19.99**

WIKING

## Construction Equipment

**NEW 781-66007** Excavator (red) **14.99**

**NEW 781-84402** Hanomag Tractor Caterpillar K55 **18.99**

**NEW 781-86638** Kaelble Dump Truck (blue) **26.99**

**NEW 781-89703** Menck Excavator (blue) **32.99**

**NEW 781-89802** Ruthemeyer Road Roller **18.99**

## Trailers

**NEW 781-38240** Joskin Vacuum Tank **22.99**

**NEW 781-38805** Krampe 2-Axle Dump Trailer (red) **16.99**

## Emergency Equipment

### Aircraft

**NEW 781-2207** Police Helicopter (blue) **38.99**

### Magirus

**NEW 781-86111** Mobile Command Unit (red) **28.99**

### MAN

**NEW 781-60602** TGL Fire Engine Truck **31.99**

**NEW 781-61401** TGL Compactline Pumper **32.99**

**NEW 781-70602** Police Bus (green) **39.99**

### Mercedes Benz

**NEW 781-32103** Sprinter RTW Rescue Van **22.99**

**NEW 781-79913** L 1413 Salzburg Airport Crash Truck **22.99**

### Opel

**NEW 781-86112** 1956 Caravan Fire Engine (red) **13.99**

**NEW 781-86411** Rekord A German Police **23.99**

### Rosenbauer

**NEW 781-62601** Panther 6x6 Airport Crash Truck (gray, red) **49.99**

**NEW 781-62602** Panther 6x6 Berlin Airport Fire Brigade **49.99**

### Volkswagen

**NEW 781-10427** German Police (green & white) **26.99**

**NEW 781-10428** Touran German Police **24.99**

**NEW 781-10429** Passat Variant German Police **26.99**

**NEW 781-10432** T5 Police (white w/blue stripe) **28.99**

**NEW 781-10433** Touran Police Car (blue, silver) **26.99**

**NEW 781-86110** T1 Personnel Van (red) **18.99**

**NEW 781-86113** T1 w/Trailer Fire Department (red) **19.99**

**NEW 781-86114** 1960s T1 Personnel Van **18.99**

**NEW 781-86410** T1 Police Box Wagon **19.99**

### Sets

**NEW 781-62502** Fire Engine Set **44.99**

## Farm Machinery

### Tractors

**NEW 781-87101** Eicher-Konigstiger (blue) **19.99**

**NEW 781-87102** Eicher-Konigstiger w/Loader **23.99**

**NEW** Ferguson TE Tractors 781-89201

**NEW 781-87139** Eicher-Konigstiger w/Sickle Bar Side Cutter & Driver **19.99**

**NEW 781-87140** Eicher-Konigstiger w/Roll-Over Protective Structure **18.99**

**NEW 781-87202** Eicher-Konigstiger w/Frontloader **20.99**

**NEW 781-89201** Ferguson TE (gray) **12.99**

## Trucks

### Bussing

**NEW 781-84905** BS 16 **33.99**

### MAN

**NEW 781-63604** TGL ADAC Flatbed Tow Truck **31.99**

**NEW 781-67203** TGA M w/Meiller Roll-Off-Skip Loader **26.99**

**NEW 781-67504** TGL Cabover Flatbed w/Loading Crane **23.99**

**NEW 781-67803** TGA M Truck w/Trailer **29.99**

**NEW 781-67904** TGA 3-Axle Dumpster Carrier **24.99**

### Mercedes Benz

**NEW 781-63803** Econic Garbage Truck (orange) **28.99**

### Krupp

**NEW 781-79915** 806 w/Trailer **34.99**

**NEW 781-89103** Titan **38.99**

**NEW 781-89104** Titan **31.99**

**NEW 781-89137** Titan Friedrich Butzke GMBH **39.99**

## Tractor/Trailers

**NEW 781-53814** Steyr ST-A XXL Container Truck w/Pottinger Container **44.99**

**NEW 781-52903** MB Actros 2-Axle Cabover w/4 Axle Low Floor Van Trailer 2WIN **46.99**

**NEW 781-57107** MB Actros w/Nord-Sud Trailer **46.99**

**NEW 781-57309** MAN TGL XXL w/Demountable Bodies **42.99**

**NEW 781-85139** Kaelble 3-Axle Heavy-Duty Conventional w/6-Axle Heavy-Duty Flatbed Trailer (yellow) **55.99**

**NEW 781-89138** Krupp Titan Conventional w/Single Axle Fulda Box Trailer **32.99**

IMPORTED FROM GERMANY BY WALTHERS

## Recreational

**NEW 781-9702** Volkswagen Touareg w/Trailer & Boat (white) **38.99**

**NEW 781-79736** 1960s Volkswagen T1 Camper w/Luggage Rack **18.99**

**NEW 781-79738** Volkswagen T1 w/Boat on Top (orange, cream) **18.99**

**NEW 781-79739** Volkswagen T1 Box Wagon w/Dinghy **16.99**

## Vans

**NEW 781-79701** Volkswagen Delivery Van w/Rooftop Advertising Sign (green, orange) **18.99**

**NEW 781-79702** Volkswagen T1 w/Signboard (red, yellow) **23.99**

# AUTOMOBILES

## Audi

**781-13201** A4 2-Door Convertible w/Top Down (green) **22.99**

## Borgward

**781-82337** Isabella Coupe **13.99**

## Citroen

**Limited Quantity Available**

**781-80707** ID 19 4-Door Sedan (Red w/black top) **10.99**

See What's Available at

**www.walthers.com**

## Ford

**781-81104** 17M (sand, black) **12.99**

**781-82106** Capri 2-Door Fastback **12.99**

## Lloyd Alexander

**Limited Quantity Available**

**781-80638** 2-Door Hardtop **12.99**

## Mercedes Benz

### CLK

**781-6302** With Dormobile **32.99**

**781-22104** Gray/Beige Metallic **18.99**

**781-22105** Silver Metallic **18.99**

### A-Class

**781-13801** 5-Door Compact **19.99**

**781-13840** Hatchback **19.99**

**Limited Quantity Available**

**781-14917** Taxicab (cream) **19.99**

### S-Class

**781-15939** 4-Door Sedan **16.99**

### 220 S

**Limited Quantity Available**

**781-82404** 4-Door Sedan (Pearl White) **13.99**

### 280

**781-83436** SL Coupe **14.99**

### 300

**781-83605** 4-Door Sedan (red) **13.99**

## Mitsubishi

**781-26304** Montero/Pajaro Metallic Wheat Beige **9.99**

## Opel

**781-82705** Manta A **11.99**

**781-80405** GT-2 2-Door Hardtop **12.99**

**781-80407** GT (black) **12.99**

**781-84702** Rekord A 4-Door Sedan (gray) **16.99**

## Volkswagen

### "Old" Beetle

**781-831** Post Office **5.99**

**781-80204** w/Top Down **6.99**

**781-81006** Hardtop **10.99**

**NEW** Volkswagen Touareg w/Trailer & Boat (white) 781-9702

**NEW** Volkswagen T1 Box Wagon w/Dinghy 781-79739

Touraeg With Trailer & Boat 781-9701

**Limited Quantity Available**

**781-83007** Hardtop (Light Blue) **5.99**

### New Beetle

**781-3202** Convertible w/Driver & Top Down **16.99**

**781-3240** Convertible (yellow) **14.99**

**781-3512** Yellow **12.99**

**781-6340** w/Dormobile Single-Axle Camping Trailer **31.99**

### Golf

**781-6102** V (gray) **18.99**

**781-6103** V 4-Door Hatchback (Blue Graphite) **18.99**

**781-6140** Plus (Shadow Blue) **18.99**

### Jetta

**781-6701** 4-Door Sedan (Shadow Blue) **19.99**

### Karmann Ghia

**781-80506** Karmann Ghia Convertible (gray, white, black) **13.99**

### Multivan

**781-30802** Ravenblue Metalic **18.99**

**781-30803** 7-Passenger (Green Metallic) **18.99**

IMPORTED FROM GERMANY BY WALTHERS

**Passat**

**781-6401** Limousine (Arctic Blue Silver Metallic) **19.99**

**781-6501** Variant 4-Door Station Wagon (Granite Green) **19.99**

**Phaeton**

**781-5904** 4-Door Sedan **19.99**

**Polo**

**781-3440** Blue Metallic **18.99**

**Touran**

**781-7807** 4-Door Hatchback ADAC (German Auto Club) **24.99**

**781-30502** Silver **18.99**

**Touraeg**

**781-6003** With Roof Case **19.99**

**781-6005** Red **18.99**

**781-9701** With Trailer & Boat **33.99**

**781-6002** With Surfboard (Metallic Green) **19.99**

**Volvo**

**781-83904** PV 544 2-Door Fastback (green) **13.99**

**Limited Quantity Available**

**781-83903** PV 544 2-Door Hardtop (black) **12.99**

## BUSES

**781-73108** Double Deck D89 Traditionsbus Berlin **49.99**

## CONSTRUCTION EQUIPMENT

**781-663** Still R70-25 Forklift **6.99**

**781-66401** Still R 70-16 Forklift **7.99**

Different Color Shown

**781-65004** Road Roller (black/gray) **9.99**

**781-65505** Bulldozer w/Cab **8.99**

**781-65802** Mini Tracked Excavator HR 18 (white) **23.99**

**781-66602** 2-Axle Trailer For Mini Excavator w/Ramps (tan) **10.99**

**781-65840** Mini-Excavator w/Hydraulic Jackhammer & 2-Axle Transport Trailer **31.99**

**781-66006** Excavator **14.99**

**781-65107** Liebherr Wheel Loader **12.99**

**781-66101** Atlas 2005 M Wheeled Excavator (orange) **29.99**

**781-67802** MAN TGA M 3-Axle Cabover w/2-Axle Dump Trailer **32.99**

**781-86639** Kaelble Conventional 2-Axle Dump Truck (yellow) **26.99**

**781-86640** Krupp Titan 3-Axle Conventional **26.99**

**781-86802** Gmeinder-Kaelble PR 610 Bulldozer (yellow, blue) **8.99**

**781-84440** Hanomag K55 Crawler Tractor **18.99**

**781-84401** Hanomag 1950s-Era K55 Crawler Tractor **16.99**

**781-63203** Brandt Crane (gray, blue cab, red crane) **46.99**

Menck Excavator 781-89702

1950s-Era Hanomag K55 Crawler Tractor 781-84401

**781-65739** HakoStreet Cleaner – Hako Citymaster 300 **22.99**

**781-65740** Hako Citymaster 300 Street Sweeper **19.99**

**781-65301** Hako Wheel Loader Kramer 280 (yellow, gray) **22.99**

**781-50505** MercedesTractor w/6-Axle Lowboy Flatbed, Bulldozer & Front End Loader **49.99**

**781-89702** Menck Excavator **32.99**

**781-39204** Unimog 1700 w/Trailer & Scaffolding Load (Cream, Beige) **16.99**

**781-40503** Unimog U 140 Tractor w/Asphalt Boiler **14.99**

**781-37601** Unimog U 400 Dark Green **9.99**

**781-64640** Unimog U 400 Truck w/Front-Mount Street Sweeper (orange, silver) **34.99**

### Trailers

**781-66502** For Roll-Off Skip Loaders **10.99**

**781-60008** Rosenbauer Tunnellufter (red) **18.99**

## EMERGENCY VEHICLES

**Aircraft**

**781-2206** Police Helicopter **38.99**

**All-Terrain Vehicle**

**781-60007** 6-Wheel w/Driver & Equipment **22.99**

IMPORTED FROM GERMANY BY WALTHERS

### DLK

**781-61903** Fire Brigade 23-12 (Iveco EuroFire) **28.99**

**Econic 39.99 ea**
Rear-mount aerial ladder with rescue bucket.

**781-61504** 30 PLC
**781-61540** 30 PLC

### Iveco

**781-60109** Daily Cargo Van Fire Brigade Geratewagen Gefahrgut (red, yellow) **22.99**

**781-61103** LF 16/12 Fire Brigade SedanCab Pumper w/Special Graphics (German) **32.99**

### MAN

**781-62540** TG-A M Roll Off Container Truck **32.99**

**781-62302** Eurofire RW 2 Fire Dept. Rescue Truck **23.99**

### Magirus

**781-86109** Mercur Single-Axle Covered Flatbed (red, gray) **29.99**

**781-86502** DRK German Red Cross Pumper (cream, red) **27.99**

**DL 25 h**

**781-86240** Fire Brigade (German) **36.99**

**TLF16 Sedan Cab Pumper 28.99 ea**
**781-86339** Type 1

**781-86340** Type 2

**DL 25 h Rear-Mount Aerial Ladder 36.99 ea**

**781-86237** Type 1

**781-86238** Type 2
**781-86239** Type 3

### Mercedes

**781-616** Pumper **12.99**

**781-32102** Sprinter Rescue Van (yellow, red) **22.99**

**781-60108** A Class 4-Door Compact Sedan (red w/yellow lettering) **26.99**

**781-61702** Atego DLK 23-12 Fire Brigade w/Rear Mount Aerial Ladder **32.99**

**781-62501** Atego Cabover w/Roll-On/Off Command Module - Atemschutz (Respiratory Protection Unit) **34.99**

**Limited Quantity Available**

**781-10420** Police **17.99**

### Opel

**LF 8**

**781-86201** Aerial Ladder Truck (German) **10.99**

**781-86301** With Trailer (German) **11.99**

### Rosenbauer

**781-61301** Tunnel Rescue Unit **38.99**

**781-62240** TLF Pumper **29.99**

**781-61201** RLF 2000 AT **36.99**

### Unimog

**781-622** TLF 8/18 Fire Water Truck **10.99**

**781-86107** U 411 w/Snowplow **18.99**

### Volkswagen

**781-7111** Tourareg SUV Rescue Vehicle (white, fluorescent yellow) **24.99**

**781-10426** Passat 4-Door Sedan Polizei (blue, silver, white) **26.99**

**781-10425** Touareg Police (green, gray) **24.99**

**Limited Quantity Available**

**781-7109** 2002 Emergency Doctor (German) **20.99**

### Technical Help Service (THW)

**781-69308** Kramer 280 Wheel Loader **23.99**

**781-69309** Volkswagen T5 Transport Van **22.99**

**781-87040** Unimog 411 **14.99**

**781-87401** Magirus TLF 16 Pumper **29.99**

**781-87402** Magirus (blue) **29.99**

Latest New Product News Daily! Visit Walthers Web site at **www.walthers.com**

## FARM MACHINERY

### Tractors

**781-386** Deutz Enclosed Cab **7.99**

**781-88101** Deutz 1950s/60s (Styled, No Cab) **12.99**

**781-87702** Fahr **10.99**

**781-37701** Fendt Favorit 716 Vario **22.99**

**781-37740** Fendt 711 Vario w/Cab & Widetrack High Flotation Tires **23.99**

**781-37301** Fendt Vario 930 **24.99**

**781-37940** Fendt 926 With Haybale Grabber **23.99**

**781-87201** Hanomag WD **16.99**

WIKING

IMPORTED FROM GERMANY BY WALTHERS

781-88501 Hanomag R 16 **16.99**

**781-88002** Lanz Bulldog **8.99**

**781-88401** Man 4R3 **18.99**

**781-88402** Man 4R3 w/Sickle Bar Mower **22.99**

**781-38503** Massey-Ferguson MF 8280 **24.99**

**781-38540** Massey-Ferguson MF 8280 w/Front Loader (red) **26.99**

**781-39501** MDT Garden-Type Riding Lawn Mower **13.99**

**781-87802** Porsche **10.99**

**781-87501** Schluter Super 1250 VL Tractor (red) **18.99**

## HARVESTING EQUIPMENT

**781-38940** CLAAS Combine w/Corn Head **52.99**

**781-87003** Unimog 411 w/Sickle Bar Mower (black) **16.99**

**781-88901** Horse-Drawn Rake **18.99**

**781-88902** Tractor w/Rake **23.99**

### Trailers

**781-39601** Massey-Ferguson MF187 Rectangular Hay Baler **18.99**

**781-39602** Fendt 1290 S Hay Baler (green, black) **34.99**

**781-86902** Farm Trailer **8.99**

**781-89302** Open-Side Hay Wagon w/Rubber Tires and 2-Horse Team **19.99**

**781-89301** Open Sided Wagon w/Tractor **23.99**

**781-38100** Haywagon **5.99**

**781-38140** Pottinger Hay Loader "Jumbo" (red, yellow) **18.99**

**781-38201** Vacuum **7.99**

**781-38701** Claas Dump **14.99**

**781-38841** With Hay Bales **7.99**

**781-39001** For Combine Cutting Head **10.99**

**781-86901** European Agricultural Trailer (green) **8.99**

**781-38802** Joskin Fertilizer Spreader **16.99**

**781-38803** Joskin 2-Axle Hay Trailer w/Stake Bed **10.99**

**781-38804** Joskin 2-Axle Dump Trailer **14.99**

**781-88701** Fortuna Manure Spreader **9.99**

**781-88740** Fortuna Light-Duty Flatbed Trailer **8.99**

### Accessories

**781-1402** Large Tire Set for Fendt Favorit 716 Vario Tractor **13.99**

**781-39401** Hay Rake **16.99**

**781-88801** Fertilizer Spreader **9.99**

**781-38301** Claas Front Mount Hay Cutter for Tractor **7.99**

**781-38401** Claas Rollant 250 Round Hay Baler **13.99**

**781-38340** Claas Rotary Mower Attachment **11.99**

**781-37801** Lemken Reversible Plow **9.99**

## TRUCKS

### Bussing

**781-88607** 8000 Box Vanw/Matching 3-Axle Trailer – Fulda **38.99**

**781-84939** BS 16 L w/3 Axle Trailer (blue, orange) **34.99**

**781-84903** BS 16 L With Trailer Veltins **38.99**

**Limited Quantity Available**

**781-84940** BS 16 L - Herforder Bier **32.99**

### Krupp Titan

Covered Flatbed w/Matching Trailer

**781-85140** w/4-Axle Flatbed Trailer (yellow) **55.99**

**781-89140** Stiebel Eltron (blue) **39.99**

**781-89102** Blue **78.99**

### Magirus

**S 7500**

**781-85505** 1950s-Era Fulda Tires **31.99**

### Mercur

**781-84802** Open Beverage Truck Frucht Limonade **31.99**

**781-84840** Open Beverage Truck Herforder Bier **34.99**

**781-85506** (blue) **31.99**

**781-85540** Beer Truck Malz-Vollbier **28.99**

IMPORTED FROM GERMANY BY WALTHERS

### MAN

**781-52704** TBA XXL w/Container Chassis Wandt Spedition Transportberaung **39.99**

**781-57106** w/Trailer Stiebel Eltron **34.99**

**781-59803** w/Trailer & Container 17111 Transit Transport & Logistik **39.99**

**781-67903** TG-A M Dumpster Carrier **24.99**

**Limited Quantity Available**

**781-67304** Dump Truck (blue) **7.99**

### Mercedes

**781-56103** Atego Box Van w/Trailer "Staatl. Fachingen" **40.99**

**781-63940** Atego Garbage Truck **31.99**

**781-67202** Actros Cabover 3-Axle Roll-On/Off Open Container Carrier - Meiller (beige) **26.99**

**781-63904** Garbage Truck (white) **22.99**

**Limited Quantity Available**

**781-56401** Cattle Truck w/Trailer **23.99**

**781-63802** Econic Refuse Truck (light blue) **19.99**

**781-52902** Actros With 3-Axle Trailer "Spedition Schober" **39.99**

### Peterbilt

**Limited Quantity Available**

**781-457** 2632 Double-Bottom **9.99**

### Scania

**781-53807** 144 2-Axle Cabover w/3-Axle Box Van - Victorinox (full-color scene w/Swiss Army knife & watch) **46.99**

### Steyr

**781-53813** S-TA XXII 2-Axle Cabover w/3-Axle Box Van Trailer Wanner (pink, blue) **42.99**

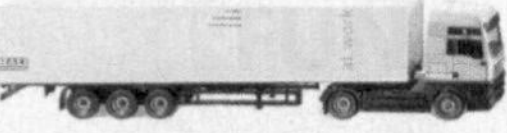

**781-53810** ST-A XXL 2-Axle Cabover w/3-Axle Box Van Trailer - Koffer "FUN at Work" **44.99**

### Unimog

**781-37202** U 40 (grass green) **26.99**

**781-37401** 1700 Flatbed **11.99**

## ALL-TERRAIN VEHICLE

**781-2301** 4x4 w/Driver (blue, black) **19.99**

## RECREATIONAL VEHICLES

**781-9240** Caravan T@B Camping Trailer "Tequila Sun" **19.99**

## TRAILERS

**781-87903** 2-Axle Type **5.99**

**781-66601** 2-Axle Flatbed Trailer w/Ramps **10.99**
For Mini-Excavator #781-65801 (sold separately).

**781-87940** Single Axle **6.99**

The Wheel Works

A DIVISION OF MICRO ENGINEERING

These kits are made of highly detailed white metal parts.

## AUTOMOBILES

### 1932 Ford 12.80 ea

**778-96105** Roadster (Top Down)

**778-96106** Roadster (Top Up)

**778-96121** Victoria Sedan

**778-96122** Coupe

**778-96130** Station Wagon

## FARM MACHINERY

### Tractors

**778-96115** Ford **9.35**

Panel Truck 778-96102

## TRUCKS

**778-96157** Terminal **17.10**

### Rail Truck 17.10 ea

**778-96111** HOn3

**778-96113** HO

### 1934 Ford

**778-96101** Pickup **12.80**

**778-96102** Panel Truck **13.40**
See large photo at top. Decals not included.

**778-96103** Stake Truck **17.45**
Includes decals.

**778-96108** Cab & Chassis **12.80**

**778-96109** Small Stake Truck **12.80**
Features plastic stake bed.

**778-96112** Log Truck **21.55**
Includes logs.

**778-96114** REA Panel Truck **18.80**
Includes decals.

**778-96117** Service Truck **15.30**

**778-96127** Flatbed Truck **13.40**

**778-96128** Flatbed w/Tractor **21.55**

**778-96129** Dump Truck **14.10**

For Up-To-Date Information and News Bookmark Walthers Web site at

**www.walthers.com**

AutoScenes have been finely crafted and custom painted for ultimate realism. These AutoScenes are exact 1:87 HO scale models. They add color, interest and authenticity to any layout or diorama. More than just a vehicle, each includes figures and accessories that capture the feel of the 40s and 50s era.

## NEW PRODUCTS

**NEW 785-5545** Rusty Springs Furniture (Mid 50s Box Van w/2 Figures & Couch) **27.98**
Two of Rusty's guys get ready to carry a couch up the ramp to the Rusty Springs Furniture truck.

**NEW 785-5546** Pit Stop (50s 2-Door w/Open Trunk, 3 Figures & Cooler) **17.98**
This mom and pop (with a bottle of pop!) have pulled over to let Junior do his business. Who hasn't seen this scene?

**NEW 785-5547** Hitchin' a Ride (40s Roadster w/2 Figures) **15.98**
This cutie is hitchin' more than a ride and the guy is all-too-happy to help her out!

**785-5537** Cop'n A Kiss (Late '40s Roadster w/3 Figures) **15.98**

**785-5538** Henry's Haulin' (Mid '50s Stakebed w/Figure & Accessories) **21.98**

**785-5539** Peter's Painting ('50s Delivery Van w/Figure & Ladders) **16.98**

**785-5541** Ike's Ice Cream Truck ('50s Delivery Van w/4Figures) **23.98**

**785-5542** Ma & Pa's Trailer Haven (2-Wheel Camper, 2 Figures, Dog & Accessories) **24.98**

**785-5543** Shove It or Leave It (Late '50s
2-Door Hardtop, 2 Men Pushing & Driver) **15.98**

**785-5521** Hall & Duke (Late '50s Pickup w/Driver & Dog) **14.49**

**785-5522** Billy Brown's Coupe ('50s 2-Door, Top Up w/Driver) **13.49**

**785-5523** Felix Fix-A-Flat (Late '50s 2-Door Hardtop, Tire Changer & Lady) **15.49**

**785-5525** Family Vacation (Mid '50s Station Wagon w/Luggage, Mom, Dad & Kids) **16.49**

**785-5526** Lubeners Loading (Mid '50s 2-Door w/Open Trunk, 2 Figures & Luggage) **15.49**

**785-5527** Roger's Rag Top (Late '40s 2-Door Coupe w/Top Down & Driver) **13.49**

**785-5529** Mickey's Milk Delivery ('50s Delivery Van w/Milkman & Lady Customer) **16.49**

**785-5530** Spoonin'-N-Croonin' (Early '50s Coupe w/Two Teenagers) **14.49**

**785-5531** Rusty's Regret (Late '50s 2-Door Hardtop in Bad Shape) **12.49**

**785-5533** Suds & Shine (Early '40s 2-Door Hardtop w/3 Figures) **15.49**

**785-5540** Getaway Gangsters (Late '40s Squad Car, Early '40s Coupe & 4 Figures) **26.98**

**785-5544** To The Lake ('50s 2-Door Hardtop, Boat, Trailer & 2 Figures) **24.98**

**785-5524** Wayne Recker's Tow Service (Late '50s Wrecker, Auto & 2 Figures) **27.49**

**785-5528** Willie's Warning (Early '50s 2-Door w/Driver & Late '40s Squad Car w/Officer) **25.49**

**785-5532** Thompson's Travelin' Trailer (Mid '50s Station Wagon w/2-Wheel Camper) **25.49**

**785-5536** Cruisin' Coupes (1 Each Early '50s w/Top Up & Early '40s Hardtop) **23.49**

**785-5534** Pickem' Up Truck (Mid '50s 1/2-Ton Pickup w/Driver) **13.49**

**785-5535** Sunday Drive (Late '40s Roadster w/Top Down & Two Couples) **15.49**

## SCENIC DETAILS®

Easy-to-assemble kits are unpainted, soft metal castings and include complete instructions.

### Trucks

#### 1914 Diamond T 9.98 ea

**785-217** Service Truck (w/Winch & Dry Transfer Lettering)

**785-218** Grain Truck

#### Diamond T 10.98 ea

**785-242** Tank Truck

**785-244** Flatbed & Tractor

#### Federal

**785-247** 1-1/2 Ton Dump Truck **10.98**

### Construction Equipment

**785-233** Bulldozer w/Blade **9.98**

**785-234** Motor Grader **9.98**

**785-235** Track Type Loader **9.98**

**785-237** Insley Model K Backhoe (on Crawler Chassis) **15.98**

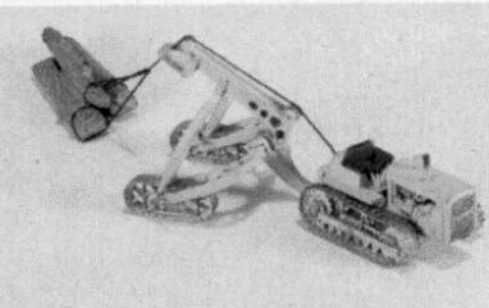

**785-246** Hyster Logging Cruiser and Tractor (Crawler Tractor w/Tracked Log Carrier) **14.98**

### Farm Machinery 7.98 ea

Tractors are based on an American prototype and come in original (unstyled; built 1934-38) with metal wheels or later versions (styled; built from 1938-47) with "rubber" tires.

**785-207** Disc & Tractor (1938-1946) (Styled w/Drag Disc)

**785-208** Seeder & Tractor (Styled w/Four-Row Planter)

**785-211** Two Tractors (Unstyled on Steel Wheels) pkg(2)

### Motorcycles

**785-228** Motorcycles and Sidecar (Set of 2) **5.98**
Includes parts for two complete bikes, plus a sidecar that can be added if desired.

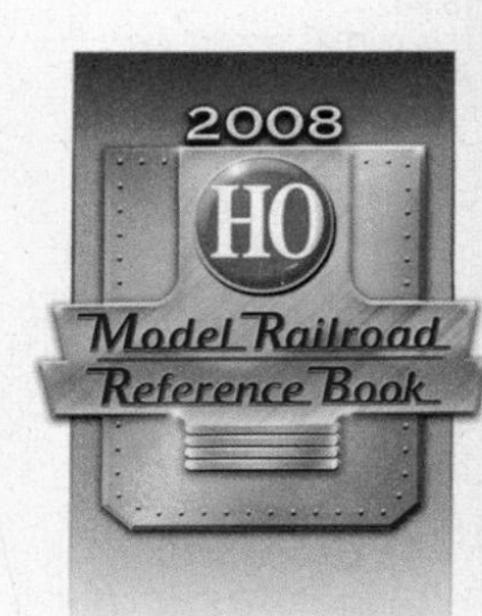

# HO RACING

This is what it all comes down to. For the past 499 miles, you've made split-second decisions, watched traffic ahead, listened for any sign of engine or tire failure, steered clear of others who weren't so lucky and kept the throttle on the floorboards, hitting over 200mph! You shift and accelerate hard coming out of turn three and up ahead, the familiar swirl of black and white flags means the end is just a seconds away!

Who will be the winner of today's event? That's up to you - but it doesn't hurt to have a little luck and skill with you as you climb behind the wheel! For flat-out family fin, nothing can match the excitement of HO Scale Road Racing from Life-Like! You can drive everything from licensed replicas of your Favorite NASCAR® teams, to today's barely street-legal Tuners! And with the wide selection of sets, you'll find a course that can challenge your skill with every new race. Lots of accessories are also available to expand your sets and keep your cars in top condition.

Swing down pit row and turn into the pages ahead for a complete look at the exciting line-up of Life-Like Road Racing!

Division of
Wm.K.Walthers, Inc.

## NEW PRODUCTS

### HO Scale Slot Car Racing

#### California Freestyling - Electric Skateboard Set

**NEW** 433-9067 74.99
Now with Bilingual instructions and packaging in English and Spanish. Grab your board and hang on for awesome action with this set that includes two huge vert ramps and a special 360-degree loop! Two skateboarders race down and around over 15' 4.5m of slot track - and a special feature lets you go forward or backwards for wicked stunts on elevated tracks, dips and switchbacks. Complete set includes two skateboarders, track, bridges, a tune-up kit and instructions.

#### Chevy® vs Ford® Racing Rivals

**NEW** 433-9058 79.99
Now with Bilingual instructions and packaging in English and Spanish. Side by side, the FedEx® #11 Chevy and Ameriquest® #16 Ford duke it out for top honors in this all-new set. Hang on as you race to the finish around 20' 6m of hairpin turns, lightning-fast straights, a cyclone curve and a dangerous squeeze track! A lap counter records the winner, and the set also comes with guard rails, flags, a tune-up kit and complete instructions.

#### Downtown Drifters

**NEW** 433-9059 79.99
Now with Bilingual instructions and packaging in English and Spanish. The hottest thing on the highway comes to HO Road Racing in this awesome set featuring customized Honda® Civic Si tuners! These barely street-legal rides are totally tricked out with super-powerful, road-gripping magnets, low-rider chassis for ultimate handling, and wide rear tires that send them red-lining to nearly 1000 scale miles per hour! A special tune-up kit keeps them running at peak performance. With nearly 17' 5.1m of twisting curves, two crossing tracks for full-throttle lane-changes, over-and-under bridges and many other accessories, this set will put any racing fan to the ultimate driving test!

California Freestyling 433-9067

Chevy vs Ford Racing Rivals 433-9058

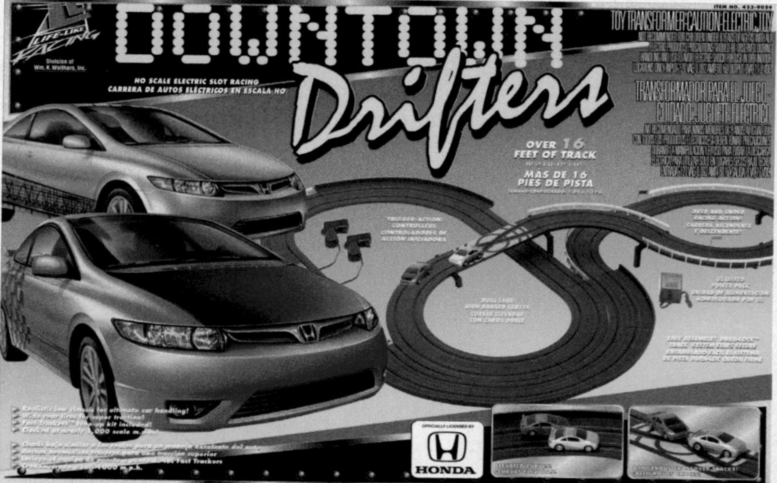


Downtown Drifters 433-9059

Division of
Wm. K. Walthers, Inc.

## HO SCALE SLOT CAR RACING

### urbo Blaster

**33-9011 109.99**

'here's fierce competition ahead as two of racing's most ecognizable cars clash on 35 feet of curving track. Colors fly as ne Kellogg's racer rounds the hairpin curves in a blur of blue and ellow. Closing the gap, the Lowe's car streaks by in a haze of gray nd blue. The wall climb adds the ultimate feature to this bi-level onfiguration. Officially licensed by NASCAR®. Set includes one Kellogg's #5 racer, one Lowe's #48 racer, one printed power track vith two trigger-action controllers, one UL listed power pack, one bstacle track, two 9" crossovers, 14 9" radius curves, six 9" straight tracks, four loop tracks, two loop cradles, one 9" lap counter, four 6" straight tracks, seven 15" straight tracks, 14 guardrails, 12 bridges, four stacking bridges, colorful flags, une-up kit and illustrated instructions. Set-up size: 79 x 39.5"

### Super Action Speedway

**433-9012 149.99**

"Super" is the only way to describe the intense action of this awesome 45-foot course! Two officially licensed NASCAR® vehicles maneuver elevated hairpin curves, huge straightaways, dizzying cyclone curves and a 360° loop! There are two lane change tracks for near-miss excitement and a dual lane lap counter to tally the winner. Set includes one Home Depot #20 racer, one DeWalt #17 racer, one power track with two trigger-action controllers, one UL listed power pack, two 9" crossovers, 26 9" radius curves, two 9" straight tracks, 12 loop tracks, two loop cradles, one 9" lap counter, three 6" straight tracks, seven 15" straight tracks, 26 guardrails, 18 bridges, seven stacking bridges, colorful flags, tune-up kit and illustrated instructions. Set-up size: 8' x 4'4"

### Championship Four Lane Speedway

**NEW 433-9046 169.99**

Rev up for 40+ feet 12.9+m of excitement times four! This set features four lanes of side-by-side racing, high velocity hairpin turns, two dual lane lap counters and a 6'6" 1.98m high speed straightaway. Drivers must maneuver carefully and quickly through four tricky cross tracks or face a major pile-up on the raceway! Track can be set up as two separate courses, or one course for two vehicles. Four NASCAR® favorites: Office Depot® #99, Dodge® Dealer #9, FedEx® #11 and Interstate Batteries #18 are included.

Turbo Blaster 433-9011

Super Action Speedway 433-9012

Championship Four Lane Speedway 433-9046

Division of
Wm.K.Walthers, Inc.

## HO SCALE SLOT CAR RACING

### Mustang Challenge

**433-9007 59.99**

America's love affair with the Ford® Mustang® comes to HO Scale racing with this fantastic new road course. There's plenty of room to put those ponies through their paces around and down 11' 3.3m of track (measures 46 x 32" 115 x 80cm when assembled) that includes a cyclone curve and a lap counter to record the winner. Set is complete with two Mustang racers and many other accessories.

### Turbo Stockers

**NEW 433-9056 49.99**

Go racing with Scott Riggs and J.J. Yeley! Battling side by side, the Valvoline® #10 and Interstate Batteries® #18 scream down the straight-aways and into the curves on this exciting 8-1/2' 2.5m figure 8 track. To add to the fun, the set includes a special power track emblazoned with the familiar NASCAR® logo, bridges, flags and many other accessories are included.

### NASCAR® Champions

**433-9010 89.99**

It's NASCAR excitement at its best on this action-packed 23' course. Two detailed NASCAR® champions, the DuPont® #24 and the Lowe's® #48, face a challenging skid track, crossovers and lightning fast straightaways. A dual lane lap counter determines who is the true NASCAR® champion! Set includes one Lowe's racer, one DuPont racer, one UL listed power pack, one printed power track with two trigger-action controllers, one 9' dual lap counter, one 15" skid track, two 9" cross tracks, 16 9" radius curves, one 6" straight track, three 9" straight tracks, six bridges, 16 guardrails, NASCAR flags and poles, tune-up kit and illustrated instructions. Set-up size: 60 x 49"

Mustang Challenge 433-9007

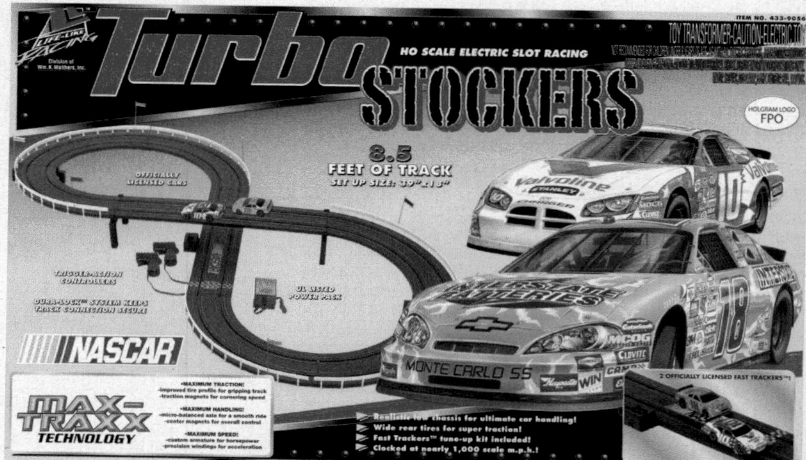


Turbo Stockers 433-9056

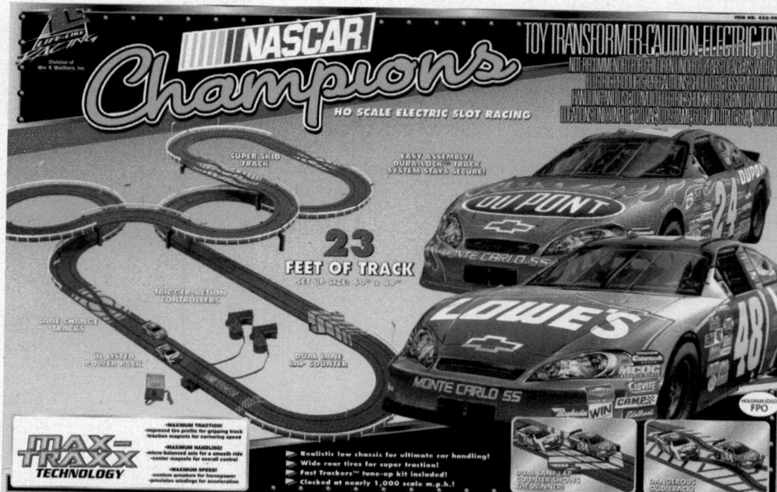


NASCAR Champions 433-9010

Latest New Product News Daily! Visit Walthers Web site at

**www.walthers.com**

Division of
Wm.K.Walthers, Inc.

# HO SCALE SLOT CAR RACING

## Raceway 400

**NEW 433-9057 74.99**

Hang on for twisting, turning flat-out fun on two levels as Tony Stewart challenges Kasey Kahne! This set provides 15-1/2' 4.7m of exciting curves and straight-aways where the Home Depot® #20 and Dodge® Dealer #9 cars set a blistering pace. Accessories in this set include a lap counter to keep track of the leader, a special power track printed with the NASCAR® logo, bridges, colorful flags, and much more.

## Dodge® Charger Challenge

**433-9449 49.99**

Dodge Chargers speed on this 8-1/2 foot figure-8 track. Life-Like's exclusive Dura-Lock connecting system makes this track a snap to assemble and helps maintain maximum electrical conductivity for awesome speed and performance. Set includes two Dodge Chargers, one UL listed power pack, one printed power track with two trigger-action controllers, six 9" radius curves, one 6" straight track, one 15" straight track, six guardrails, four bridges, 14 flags and banners, tune-up kit and illustrated instructions. Set-up size: 39 x 18"

## Demolition Derby

**433-9490 69.99**

Two special demolition cars move backwards and forwards, crossing lanes and hurling through the intersection, trying to crush the competition. A collision in just the right way can pop the trunk or bust up the hood. When the red engine light flashes, your car is wrecked! Cars snap back together instantly. Set includes two Demolition Derby Fast Trackers, one power track with two reverse-action controllers, one UL listed power pack, two crossover tracks, one intersection track, six 9" radius curves, four 6" straight tracks, one 9" straight track, six guardrails, tune-up kit and illustrated instructions. Set-up size: 56 x 26.5"

Raceway 400 433-9057

Dodge Charger Challenge 433-9449

Demolition Derby 433-9490

Division of
Wm. K. Walthers, Inc.

# HO SCALE SLOT CAR RACING

## Renegade Racers Sprint Car Racing

**433-9695 69.99**

It's racing action like you've never seen before as two authentic Sprint-style stock cars hurl around the curves of this 14-foot bi-level course. With aerodynamic construction and powerful Fast Trackers motors, these winged racers mimic the blistering speeds and furious action of professional sprint car renegades, while traction magnets provide driver control. A dual lane lap counter tallies the winner. Set includes two authentic sprint car racers, one UL listed power pack, one printed power track with two trigger-action controllers, one 9" dual lane lap counter, ten 9" radius curves, two 15" straight tracks, eight bridges, 10 guardrails, tune-up kit and illustrated instructions. Set-up size: 58 x 34"

## Ford® VS. Chevy® Super Truck Challenge

**433-9486 49.99**

The Ford F-350 Truck competes head-to-head against the Chevy Silverado in this classic figure-8 set. The layout features 8-1/2 feet of track, including hairpin curves, speed-building straightaways and over-under action. Set includes two Fast Trackers™, one UL listed power pack, one printed power track with two trigger-action controllers, six 9" radius curves, one 6" straight track, one 15" straight track, four bridges, six guardrails, colorful flags, tune-up kit and illustrated instructions. Set-up size: 39 x 18"

## Speedway Showdown

**NEW 433-9068 59.99**

Experience flat-out racing action as you test your skills at the throttle of the Irwin® #26 or the Dodge #19® racer! This fast-paced course features 11' 3.3m of cyclone curves, hairpin turns, over and under levels, and a tricky crash track for amazing near misses. To add to the fun, bridges, flags, a tune-up kit and many other accessories are included.

433-9695

Renegade Racers Sprint Car Racing 433-9695

Ford vs. Chevy Super Truck Challenge 433-9486

Speedway Showdown 433-9068

Division of
Wm.K.Walthers, Inc.

## FAST TRACKERS

Fast Trackers were rated first in speed and cornering when tested against all popular national slot car brands. Maxx Traxx technology offers maximum traction, handling and speed. Cars feature improved tire profile for gripping track, traction magnets for cornering speed, micro-balanced axle for a smooth ride, center magnets for all-over control, custom armature for horsepower and precision windings for acceleration.

### NASCAR 19.98 ea

**433-9034** Lowe's #48

**433-9036** Home Depot® #20

**433-9037** Interstate Batteries® #18

**NEW 433-9047** Ameriquest® #16

**NEW 433-9048** FedEx® #11

**NEW 433-9049** Irwin® #26

### Twin Packs 34.98 ea (Unless Noted)

**433-9031** Kellogg's® & Dupont Racers

**433-9032** Office Depot® & DeWalt® Racers

**433-9040** Ford® Fusion® vs. Chevy® Monte Carlo SS **29.98**

**433-9042** Kasey Kahne Dodge #9

**433-9043** Jeremy Mayfield Dodge #19

**433-9044** Scott Riggs Dodge Valvoline #10

### Assortment

**NEW 433-9050 239.76**
Includes two each of #9034, 9036, 9037, 9047, 9048, 9049

433-9849

### Fast Tracker 19.98 ea

**NEW 433-9041** Ford® Mustang GT

**NEW 433-9070** 2006 Honda® Civic Si Tuner

**433-9754** Chevy Silverado

**433-9793** Dodge Charger

**433-9794** Ford F350

### Renegade Racers Sprint Cars 19.98 ea

**433-9846** #53

**433-9847** #21

**433-9849** #18

**433-9850** #77

433-9847

433-9034

433-9047

433-9036

433-9037

433-9048

433-9049

433-9031

433-9032

433-9040

433-9042

433-9043

433-9044

433-9041

433-9070

See What's New and Exciting at
**www.walthers.com**

Division of
Wm.K.Walthers, Inc.

## DURA-LOCK TRACK

Add to the excitement of your HO scale racing set with extra track, curves and crossovers. Track features a patented side-locking system that locks securely in place for continuous electrical conductivity.

### Adapter Track 8.25 ea

**433-9931** Life-Like to AFX®
Includes two 6" straight tracks & two 3" adapters

**433-9932** Life-Like to Tyco®
Includes two 6" straight tracks & two 3" adapters

**433-9933** Life-Like to Tyco to AFX
Includes four 3" adapters

### Crossover Track

**433-9925** 9" pkg(2) **8.25**

### Intersection Track

**433-9898** **13.00**

### Skid Track

**433-9926** 15" pkg(1) **8.75**

### Straight Track pkg(2)

**433-9930** 9" **8.25**

**433-9934** 15" **11.00**

### Radius Curves

**433-9927** 9" Radius Curve pkg(2) **8.25**

**433-9928** 12" Radius Banked Curve pkg(4) **13.00**
Includes four pieces of track and three curve clips

### Bridges

**433-9920** Bridges pkg(2) **8.25**

### Lap Counter

**433-9923** 9" Dual Lap Counter **13.00**
Allows you to quickly determine the race winner.

## ACCESSORIES

### Tune-Up Kit

**433-9915** Master Tune-Up Kit **7.00**
Keeps your cars and track in tip-top shape.

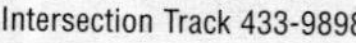
Intersection Track 433-9898

433-9932

433-9931

433-9930

433-9933

433-9934

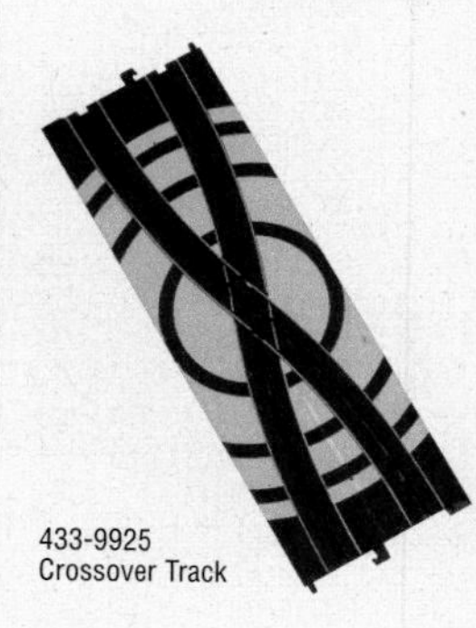
433-9925
Crossover Track

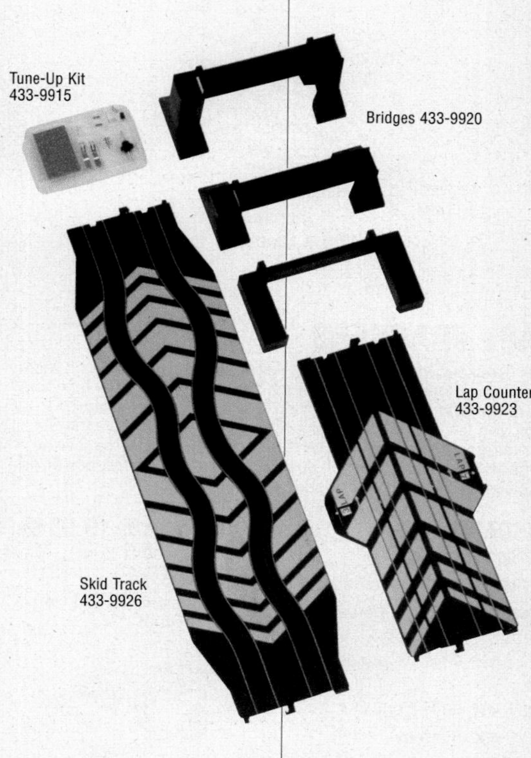
Tune-Up Kit
433-9915

Bridges 433-9920

Lap Counter
433-9923

Skid Track
433-9926

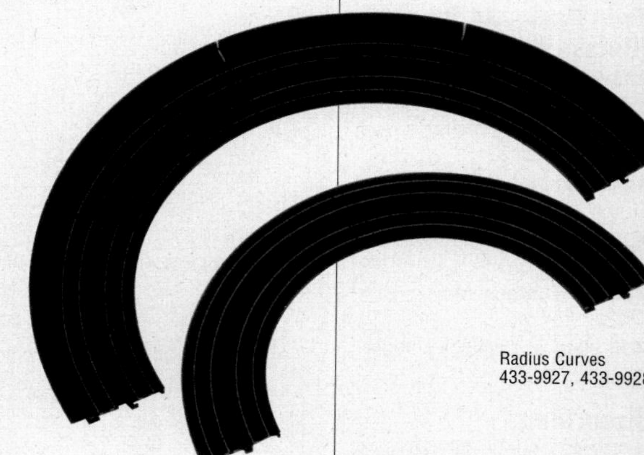
Radius Curves
433-9927, 433-9928

# LIGHTING

Models and Photo by Ron Foreman

Fragile as slivers of glass, long fingers of moonlight slide down the mountain and over the roofs and hills of Gold Mine Gap. A shrill whistle floats for miles in the chilly autumn air, signaling the arrival of the night train. The last of the harvest is coming in from local farms and ranches. And it won't be long before tenderfoots and folks who don't like snow will be moving south. After a long, hot summer, that warm engine cab feels pretty good tonight, and a swirl of smoke from the caboose stove hints at cold weather yet to come.

It's a beautiful night along the DG&H, a freelance western narrow gauge line built by Ron Foreman of Glendale, California. The warm glow of oil lights spills over the right-of-way from the caboose, while up ahead the headlight burns brightly to fill in the shadows.

Since the days of the first miniature bulbs, modelers have come up with ingenious ways to add working headlights, markers, structure lighting and much more to their layouts. The old stand-bys are still here, along with a new generation of even smaller LEDs and other electrical supplies that breath new life into any models. Check out the complete selection in this section for new modeling ideas!

## WALTHERS

### PASSENGER CAR INTERIOR LIGHTING KITS

Relive the romance of train travel day or night with these easy-to-add lighting sets. Fully assembled and designed for easy snap-in mounting, each features three bulbs and a light dispersion bar that provides uniform light. Sets are designed to fit in the indicated passenger cars. Each kit includes step-by-step instructions for removing car roof and adding lighting unit.

#### Walthers Passenger Cars

Lighting sets for Walthers passenger cars utilize the electrical contacts built into the car end, eliminating the need for additional wiring.

**933-1049** Budd & Pullman-Standard Cars **10.98**

**933-1058** Pullman-Standard Bilevel Cars **10.98**
Fits Commuter Coaches (932-6250 series) and Cab Cars (932-6260 series).

**933-1065** Budd Dome Cars **12.98**

**933-1083** Santa Fe Pleasure Dome **12.98**
Fits #s 932-9006, 932-9021 or 932-9020.

**933-1084** DCC Version for Budd & Pullman-Standard Cars **7.98**

**933-1087** DC Version for Heavyweights **10.98**

**933-1088** DCC Version for Heavyweights **7.98**

#### Rivarossi Passenger Cars

Complete kits include detailed instructions, metal truck sideframes and electrical components needed to light the car interior.

**933-1051** Streamlined Cars **15.98**
Fits -2003 and later Smoothside Coach, 10-6 Sleeper or Diner.

**933-1052** Streamlined Domes **17.98**
Fits -2003 and later Smoothside Dome, Dome-Lounge or Dome-Observation.

**933-1075** For Coach & Combine w/4-Wheel Trucks **17.98**

**933-1076** For Baggage Car & Railway Post Office w/6-Wheel Trucks **17.98**

### SOCKETS

**Limited Quantity Available**

**942-350** pkg(6) **4.98**

#### Hook-Up Wire

**Limited Quantity Available**
**942-414** 6', 4 Colors **2.49**

### BULBS

#### 16V, .100 Amp Mini-Bulb pkg(3) 4.98 ea

For longer bulb life, our 16V bulbs can be operated from a 12V power supply.

**Limited Quantity Available**

**942-3495** Green

**942-3496** Red

#### 1.5V, .83 Amp Micro Bulb

**Limited Quantity Available**

**942-433** Clear **5.98**

#### 1.5V, .83 Amp Grain-O-Rice pkg(3) 4.98 ea

**Limited Quantity Available**
**942-435** Clear

#### 6V Grain-O-Wheat

**Limited Quantity Available**
**942-441** Clear pkg(2) **2.98**

#### 16V, .100 Amp Grain-O-Wheat pkg(3) 4.98 ea (Unless Noted)

**Limited Quantity Available**

**942-3451** Amber

**942-3455** Green

**942-3456** Red

#### 16V, .100 Amp Sub-Miniature Bulb

**942-365** Clear pkg(3) **6.98**

#### Cornerstone Series® Building Replacement Bulb

**942-473** pkg(5) **4.98**
Replacement bulb fits lighting unit in Walthers O Scale structures kits, and HO Gold Ribbon Series™ buildings, adaptable to other uses.

Division of Wm.K.Walthers, Inc.

#### Bulbs 4.75 ea

**433-1213** Lamp Bulb pkg(3)
For use with Operating Crossing Gate #433-1808, sold separately. Screw-in style, 14V AC or DC.

433-1215

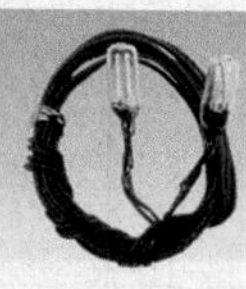

433-1217

**433-1215** With Wired Socket pkg(2)
14V AC or DC.

**433-1217** Grain Of Wheat pkg(2)
For use with Gas Light #433-1257 and Highway Light #433-1705, each sold separately.

#### House Lighting Kit

**433-1205** With Base **4.75**
All-purpose house light is pre-wired for easy operation. Use lamp bulb #433-1213, sold separately, as replacement bulb.

## ATLAS

#### Layout Wire 6.95 ea

20 gauge standard copper, 50' spool.

**150-315** Black

**150-316** Red

**150-317** Green

**150-318** Yellow

**150-319** Blue

#### 5-Conductor Ribbon Wire

**150-312** pkg(50') **18.95**
Wire matches what is included in all Atlas HO and N Scale switches. Can be used for any scale.

Daily New Arrival Updates! Visit Walthers Web site at
**www.walthers.com**

## ACCURATE LIGHTING

**Limited Quantity Available On All Items**

### DIESEL LOCOMOTIVE LIGHTING SYSTEM

#### Forward/Reverse Lighting

**144-50212** Directional Lighting For Kato GP35 **35.95**

Pro Line Series system realistic directional lighting is installed in series with the locomotive's motor and operates at full intensity before unit moves. Includes necessary bulbs/lenses and hardware to complete installation.

### HOOKUP WIRE

#### 24 Gauge Multi-Stranded Wire pkg(50') 6.95 ea

Ideal as jumpers from bus line to track sections.

**144-241** White

**144-244** Green

## BACHMANN

#### Electrical Accessories

#### Mini Electric Water Pump

**160-42219** **13.00**

#### Interior Lighting Kit w/Wire

**160-42240** pkg(2) **6.50**

# MOTORS

## Flat Can Motors

High-quality, precision-built can motors with low current draw, excellent torque, smooth low-speed characteristics and extremely consistent performance.

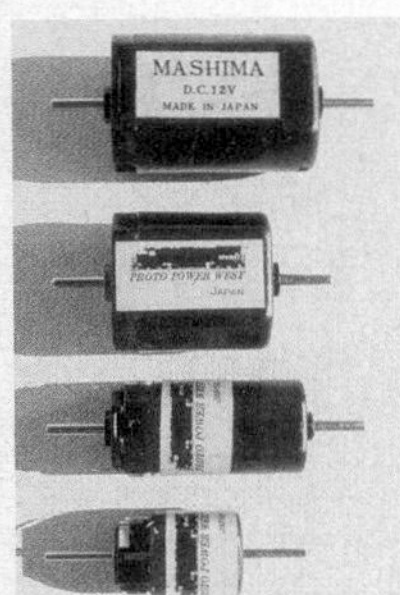


### 5-Pole Skewed Armature 2.0mm Shafts 37.95 ea

**116-40321** 18 x 33mm, DS, 8,500 RPM

**116-40322** 18 x 24mm, DS, 9,200 RPM

### 5-Pole 1.5mm Shaft

**116-40323** 12 x 20mm, DS, 17,000 RPM **34.95**

### 5-Pole, 2.0mm Shaft

**116-40324** 16 x 30mm, DS, 11,000 RPM **34.95**

### Holland Micro Motor

**116-30321 34.95**
For repowering wider-bodied HO Scale diesels.

## Motor Mount Tape

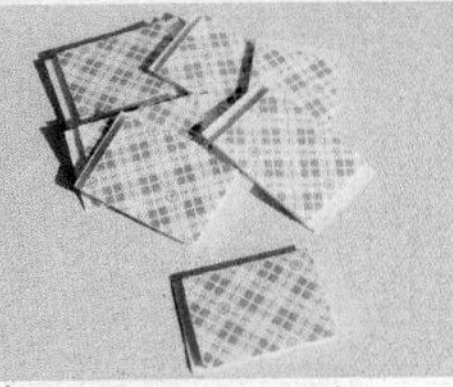

**116-12020** pkg(8) **3.25**
Two-sided foam tape.

## Electrical Hook-Up Kit

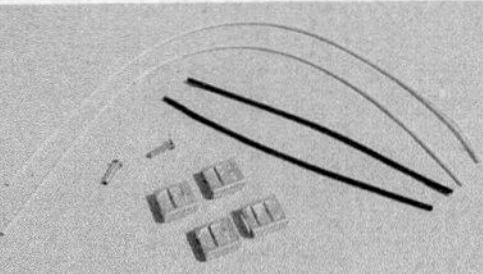

**116-12040 3.50**
For upgrading electrical connections on stock Athearn Locos. Also for installing can motors in Athearn and other locos. Will complete two locos.

## Hook-up Wire

**116-12041** pkg(2') **3.25**
Very fine, white, flexible, multi-stranded hook-up wire for all repowering jobs.

## Repowering Parts

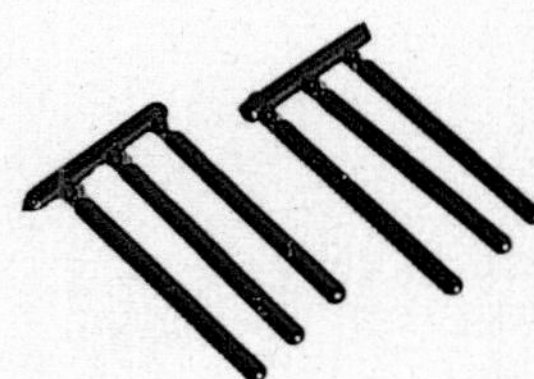

**116-12052** Long Spline Shafts pkg(6) **3.25**
Longer than standard Athearn shafts, can be cut to any length.

**116-12053** Brass Sleeves pkg(4) **5.95**
2mm inside diameter x 3/32" 2.4mm outside diameter.

**116-12054** Ball Couplings pkg(6) **3.25**
Fits Athearn 2mm shaft.

**116-12055** Ground Eyelets (Brass) pkg(20) **3.25**

## Locomotive Repowering Kits 45.95 ea

For Athearn and most other diesels. Kits include can motor, brass flywheels, wiring hardware and instructions.

**116-70321** Basic 4- & 6- Axle Diesels
Motor measures 18 x 33mm.

**116-80321** Diesel Switchers
18 x 33mm motor, tapered #20021 flywheels.

**116-90321** Short Wheel Base Diesel/Steam Loco
18 x 24mm motor, fits Athearn GP38, GP40 & GP50; also can be used for steam locomotive repowering.

### With Cradle Weights 50.95 ea

**116-12600** Athearn SD40-2, T-2, C44-9-W, AC4400

**116-12601** RPP GP60, B, M, GP40X

**116-12602** RPP SD60, SD45-2, SD90MAC, Athearn F59PH

**116-12605** Athearn GP38, 40, 50, 60, AMD-103

**116-12607** Athearn SD-9, SD45, UC, E-Units, F-45, FP45, SDP45

## Universal Coupling Assortment

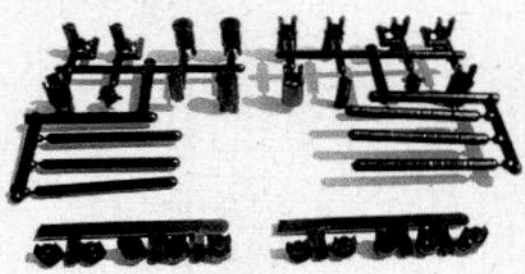

**116-12030 6.50**
26-piece kit includes assorted male and female universal joints and various length spines, all cast in Delrin®. Enough parts to retrofit two brass or plastic locomotives.

## Universal Coupling Kit

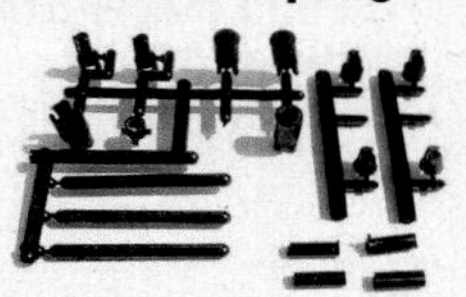

**116-12031 7.25**
28-piece kit includes two 4 x 3/32" diameter steel shafts with plastic splines and universal joint components (enough parts to retrofit two brass or plastic locomotives).

## Flywheels 7.95 ea (Unless Noted)

Precision machined from brass stock, flywheels are drilled and reamed for slip fit on drive shaft and secured with flywheel cement (#116-20010, sold separately), for easy positioning and removal if necessary. Each pack includes two flywheels, with Athearn style ball couplings installed and complete instructions. Dimensions shown are outside diameter, length and shaft size. Possible applications are listed with each item.

**116-20004** 1" x 1/2" x 3.0mm pkg(2)
Micro or Holland can motor fits Athearn F7, PA, F & FP45, Cary F & E, Train Miniature FA, Bachmann F9, Model Power/AHM E and most units with wide hoods.

**116-20006** 21/32" x 11/16" x 2.0mm pkg(2)
Flat can motor fits narrow hood units; Atlas, Athearn/GSB SD40-2, SD40T-2, Mantua GP20, Bachmann GP30, DD40X, BQ23-7, AHM RS-2, SD40. Fits on stock motored Atlas units. Also fits narrow hood brass imports and plastic diesels.

**116-20013** 11/16" x 3/8" x 2.4mm
Can motor in Athearn S12, SW1500 and most short wheelbase locomotives.

**116-20021** 11/16" x 3/8" x 2.0mm pkg(2) **8.95**
Flat can motor fits Athearn S12, SW1500 and most narrow hood units with short wheelbase, AHM ALCO 1000. Can also be used for steam locomotive repowering.

**116-20040** Bowser Trolley Flywheel Kit
Kit includes single flywheel, coupling set and installation instructions.

## Flywheel Cement

**116-20010 3.95**
.5ml., .02 fl. oz. Enough for multiple flywheel applications.

## Motor Mount Cradle Weights 5.50 ea (Unless Noted)

Unique system for adding weight and mounting motor. Custom-shaped lead weight is designed to fit many popular units. Easy to install: puts weight where you want it in the base of chassis; motor is fixed to cradle with silicon or double stick tape.

### Athearn

**116-12400** SD40-2, SD40T-2, C44-9W, AC4400

**116-12403** GP35, GP30, GP20

**116-12404** F7

**116-12405** GP38-2, GP40-2, GP50, GP60, AMD-103

**116-12407** SD45, UC, E-Unit F45, FP45, SDP45, SD9, RPP C30-7/C32-8

**116-12410** UB

**116-12413** Trainmaster

### Rail Power Products

**116-12401** GP60, GP60B, GP60M, GP40X

**116-12402** SD60, SD45-2, SD90MAC

**116-12406** 8-40CW, 9-44CW

**116-12409** SD9

**116-12410** CF7, 8-40B

**116-12411** SD38, 40, 45

### Front Range

**116-12412** GP7/9

### Walthers/Train Miniature

**116-12408** FA

### Repowering Book

**116-12051 9.95**
Describes the use of many A-Line repowering products.

# GRANDT LINE

## Universal Joints

**300-7009** .093" Set, pkg(2) **3.00**

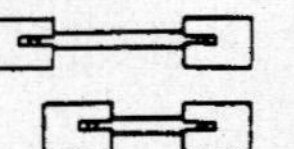

**300-7011** .079" Set, .600" to 1.00" pkg(4) **3.50**

**300-7004** Bores 3mm & 3/32" pkg(2) **3.00**

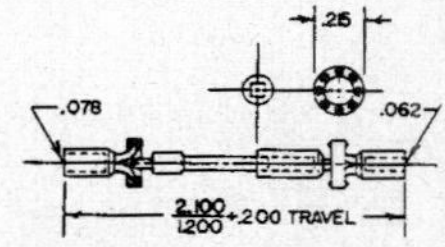


**300-7039** Climax Set, Delrin **5.75**

**300-7010** .078" 2mm, Delrin pkg(2) **3.00**

**300-7012** Bore w/Cross-Box **5.95**

**300-7013** Bore w/U-Joint **9.25**

## Sprockets

**300-70082** 8 Teeth, .371" Diameter **2.50**

**300-70122** 12 Teeth, .535" Diameter **2.50**

**300-70202** 20 Teeth, .848" Diameter **3.00**

## Miscellaneous

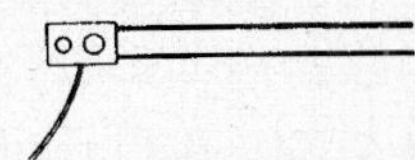

**300-7005** Electrical Pick-Up Shoe for Loco Drivers **6.75**

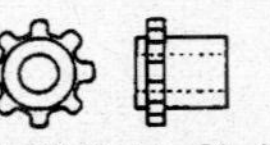

**300-7006** Delrin Chain & 8-Tooth Sprocket **11.00**

**300-7008** Flexible Delrin Shaft Coupling pkg(2) **3.95**
3/32" and .078" bores.

**300-70001** Delrin 6" Chain **8.25**

# Street Lights for North American-Style Layouts

Whether you're modeling bustling big city scenes or Main Street U.S.A., Brawa Pin-Socket System lights make adding realistic lighting to your scenes fast and easy. Following the supplied instructions, simply drill a hole in your layout base, insert the socket base and hook up to your transformer's AC accessory terminals or a separate 16V AC power supply. Plug the lights in and you're done. Pin-Socket System lights feature bases that can tilt a few degrees, lessening the chance of damage should they get slightly bumped while you're working on the layout or rerailing cars. Based on North American prototypes, each is compatible with other Brawa Pin-Socket System components.

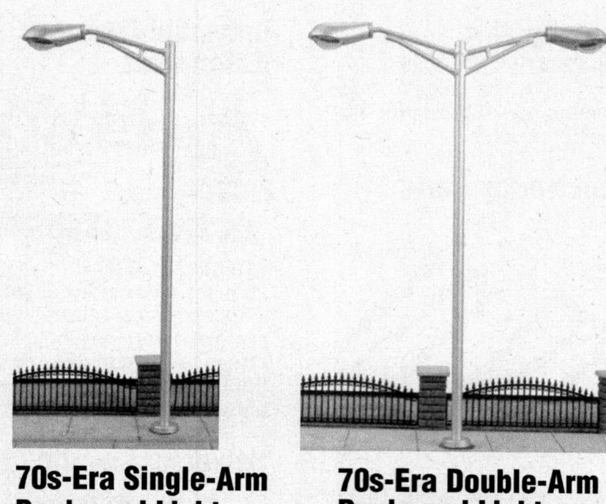

**70s-Era Single-Arm Boulevard Light**
186-5824 19.99

**70s-Era Double-Arm Boulevard Light**
186-5825 26.99

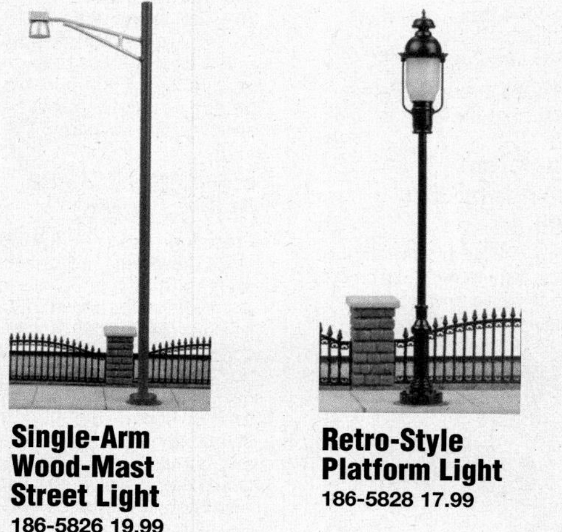

**Single-Arm Wood-Mast Street Light**
186-5826 19.99

**Retro-Style Platform Light**
186-5828 17.99

**Cast-Iron Style Street Light w/Decorative Frosted Globe**
186-5827 15.99

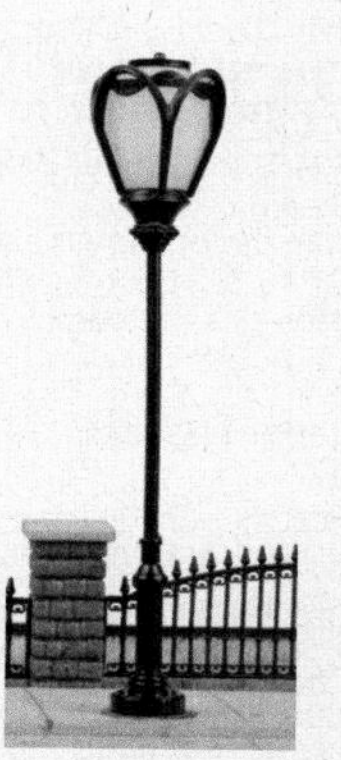

**Retro-Style "Gas" Street/Park Light**
186-5829 17.99

## *Easy to Use Pin-Socket System allows lights a bit of "give" when bumped.*

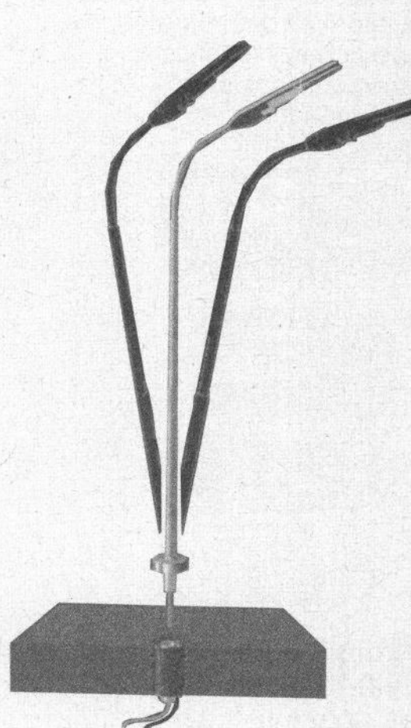

Pin-Socket System sockets have a built-in spring action that allows lights to pivot a few degrees. This way, if you bump them during an operating session or while working on the layout, they won't snap off.

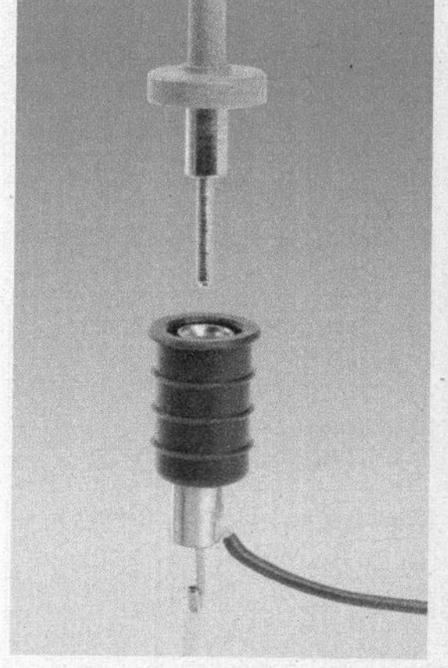

Easy-to-install sockets have two power wires. Ridges on the side of the socket housing keep it mounted firmly in your layout base. All Pin-Socket System lights use the same plug and socket, so it's easy to change lights whenever you want.

IMPORTED FROM GERMANY BY WALTHERS
Brawa offers a comprehensive line of electrical accessories, lighting equipment and wire suitable for use with all model railroad systems.

## NEW PRODUCTS

### Lights

#### Pin-Socket System LED Streetlights

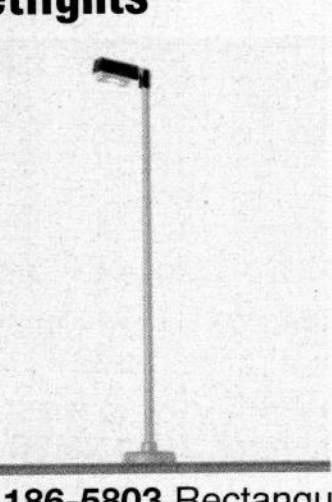

**NEW 186-5803** Rectangular-Head Light 4-1/2" 11.5cm pkg(2) **TBA**

**NEW 186-5833** Baden-Baden Gas Light 2" 5cm pkg(2) **TBA**

**NEW 186-5834** Gas Light 2" 5cm pkg(2) **TBA**

### Interior Lights

**NEW 186-3415** Interior Building Lights w/Plastic Bases pkg(6) **7.99**

See What's New and Exciting at
**www.walthers.com**

### Wiring Accessories

#### Lighting Connection Set

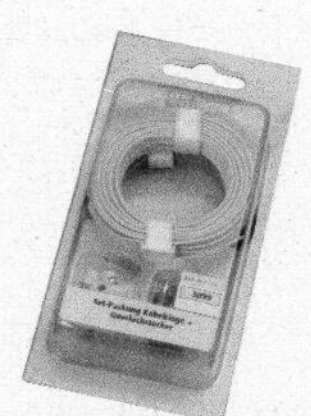

**NEW 186-3099 10.99**
Includes 33' 10m of brown and yellow wire and six yellow and brown plugs.

## LIGHTS

Lights are made of brass (with plastic parts where appropriate), fully assembled and ready to install. Lamps can be powered from an AC or DC transformer with a maximum output of 16V.

### Pin Socket System

The Brawa Pin Socket System is quick and easy to add to your layout. Just drill a hole for the socket, hook up the wires and plug the light into the socket. Each light is interchangeable and the sockets are spring loaded, allowing for ten degrees of play which gives these lights a bend but don't break feature.

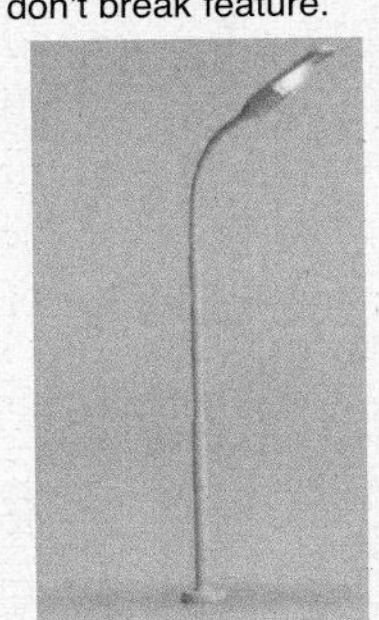

**186-5800** Elliptical pkg(3) **39.99**

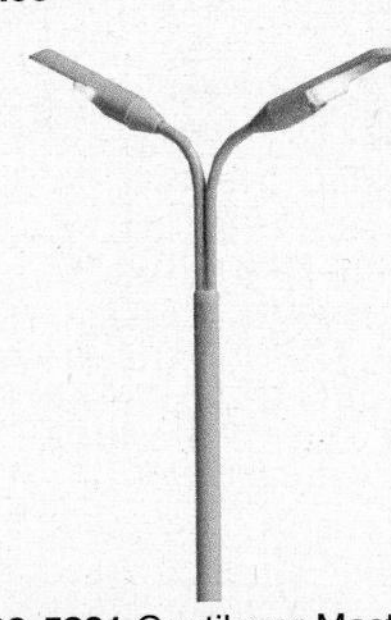

**186-5801** Cantilever Mast pkg(2) **32.99**

**186-5802** Brandenburg pkg(3) **39.99**

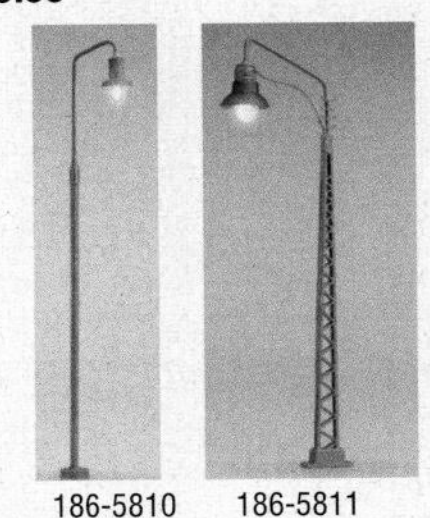

186-5810 186-5811

**186-5810** Station Light pkg(3) **34.99**
**186-5811** Grid Mast Light pkg(3) **45.99**

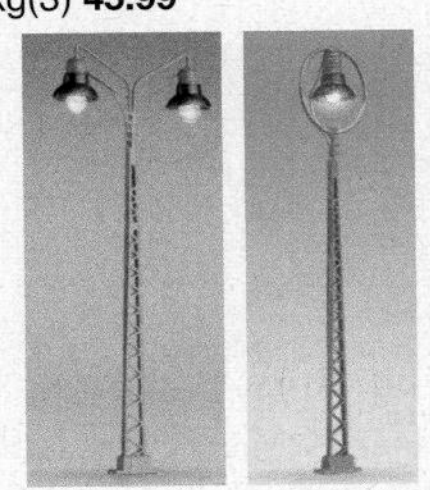

186-5812 186-5813

**186-5812** Grid Mast Light pkg(2) **38.99**
**186-5813** Lattice Pole w/Ring pkg(2) **31.99**

186-5814 186-5820

**186-5814** Lattice Narrow Square Pole pkg(2) **30.99**
**186-5820** Park Light pkg(3) **35.99**

186-5821 186-5830

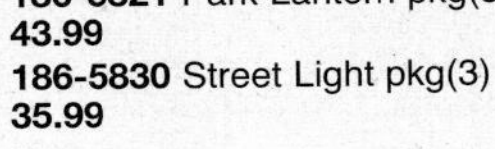

**186-5821** Park Lantern pkg(3) **43.99**
**186-5830** Street Light pkg(3) **35.99**

186-5831 189-5832 186-5840

**186-5831** Street Light pkg(3) **42.99**
**186-5832** Cast-Iron Street Light pkg(3) **35.99**
**186-5840** Wooden Mast Light pkg(3) **42.99**

**186-5841** Wooden Mast Light pkg(2) **39.99**

**186-5850** Platform Light pkg(3) **34.99**

**186-5860** Floodlight pkg(2) **52.99**

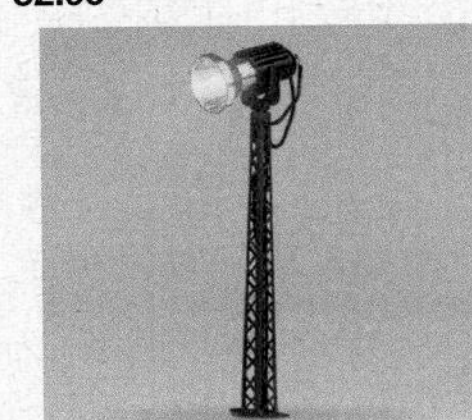

**186-5861** Floodlight pkg(2) **34.99**

**186-5863** Vertically Hinged Spotlight **27.99**

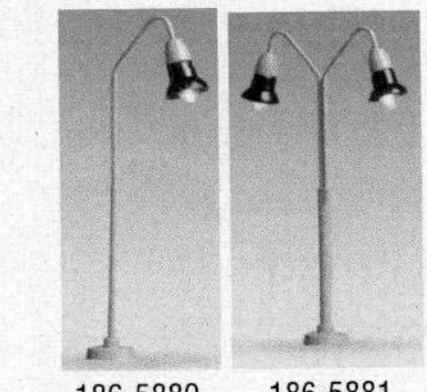

186-5880 186-5881

**186-5880** Curved Arm pkg(3) **33.99**
**186-5881** Twin Curved Arm pkg(2) **30.99**

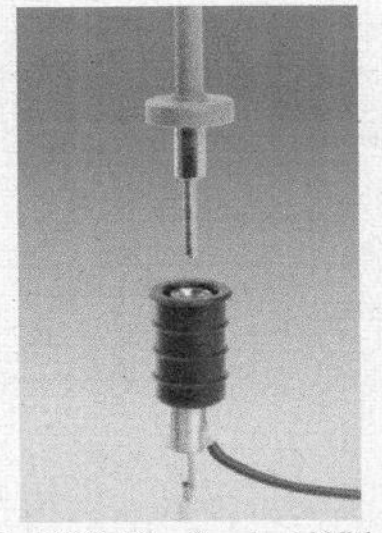

**186-5890** Pin Socket Without Light pkg(5) **11.99**

**186-5891** Station Set w/2 Lattice-Mast Lights, 2 Station Lights & Station Clock **62.99**
**186-5892** Pin-Socket Light Set **60.99**
2 Curved Mast Lights, 2 Park Lanterns & 1 Spotlight

### Station Lights

186-5040 186-5050 186-5175

**186-5040** St. Pauli Streetlight 2-1/16" High **16.99**
**186-5050** Station Light, 4-1/2" High **14.99**
**186-5175** Waiblingen, 2-1/2" High **16.99**

186-5176 186-5271 186-5272

**186-5176** Stettin Station-Berlin, 3" High **23.99**
**186-5271** One Arm w/Wooden Mast, 3" High **22.99**
**186-5272** Two Arm w/Wooden Mast, 3" High **27.99**

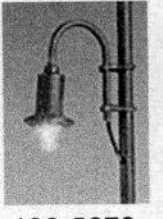

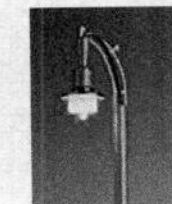

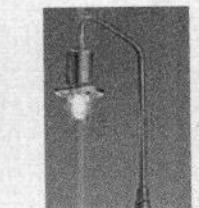

186-5273 186-5276 186-5451

**186-5273** Tall Goose Neck, 4" High **21.99**
**186-5275** With Wood Mast, 3-1/4" High **16.99**
**186-5276** With Wood Mast-Birkenau, 5-1/2" High **14.99**
**186-5451** Tall Station Light, 5" High **20.99**

IMPORTED FROM GERMANY BY WALTHERS

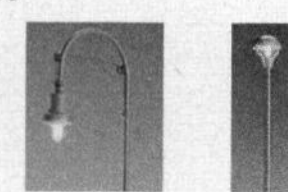

186-5453 186-5454 186-5458

**186-5453** Station Forecourt, 3" High **16.99**

**186-5454** Depot Light, 4" High **29.99**

**186-5458** With Wood Mast, 6-1/2" High **14.99**

186-5459 186-5518 186-5525

**186-5459** With Wood Mast, 6-1/2" High **16.99**

**186-5518** With Lattice Mast, 5" High **22.99**

**186-5525** Depot Light-Munich, 3-1/2" High **26.99**

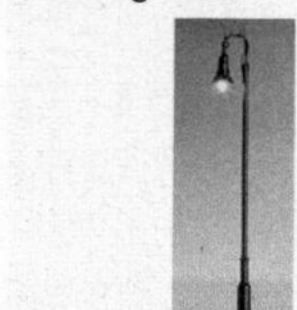

**186-5527** Depot Light-Frankfurt, 3-1/2" High **13.99**

**186-5842** Wooden Mast Light **42.99**

**Limited Quantity Available**

**186-5472** Station Light **13.99**

## Platform Lights

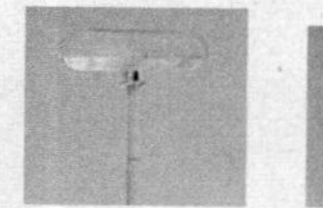
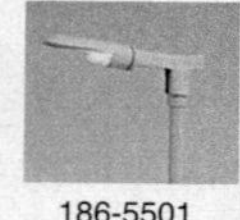

186-5499 186-5501

**186-5499** Modern, 2-3/4" High **14.99**

**186-5501** Single Arm, 2-3/4" High **11.99**

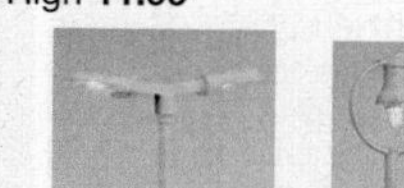
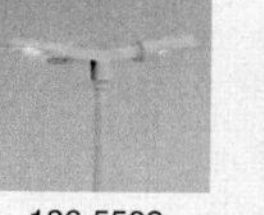

186-5502 186-5504

**186-5502** Double Arm, 2-3/4" High **17.99**

**186-5504** Ring Post, 3-1/2" High **16.99**

**186-5851** Platform Light pkg(3) **34.99**

**186-5852** Platform Light 2-Arm pkg(2) **30.99**

## Catenary Tower Lights

Lights fit Vollmer, Marklin and Sommerfeld towers.

186-5534 186-5535

**186-5534** Single Add-On Light **9.99**

**186-5535** Twin Add-On Light **14.99**

## Under-Roof Mounted Lights

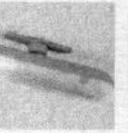

186-5320 186-5536 186-5537

**186-5320** Under Roof Mount, 1" Long **12.99**

**186-5536** Under Roof Mount **10.99**

**186-5537** Under Roof Mount, 3/4" Long **9.99**

## Wall-Mounted Lights

186-5352 186-5353 186-5356

**186-5352** Hanging **11.99**

**186-5353** Old Time **11.99**

**186-5356** Baden-Baden **21.99**

186-5357 186-5358

**186-5357** Nuremburg **12.99**

**186-5358** Wall Light **13.99**

## Lattice Mast Lights

186-5450 186-5460

**186-5450** Single Arm, 5" High **12.99**

**186-5460** Double Arm, 5" High **17.99**

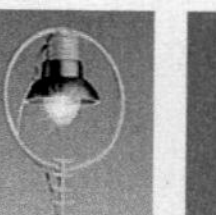

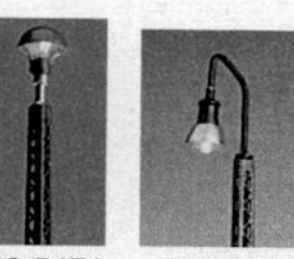

186-5470 186-5471 186-5505

**186-5470** Ring Post, 5" High **14.99**

**186-5471** Yard Light 5-11/32" High **21.99**

**186-5505** Narrow Rectangular Mast, 6" High **21.99**

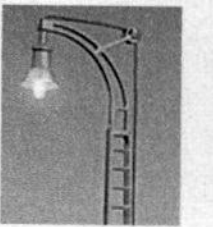
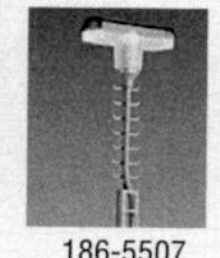

186-5506 186-5507

**186-5506** Flat Design, 6" High **22.99**

**186-5507** Flat Light, 5" High **21.99**

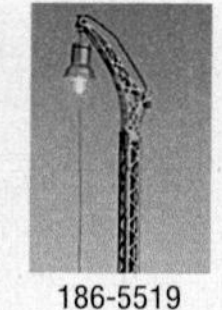

186-5509 186-5519

**186-5509** Narrow Rectangular Mast, 6" High **23.99**

**186-5519** Single Arm, 6" High **23.99**

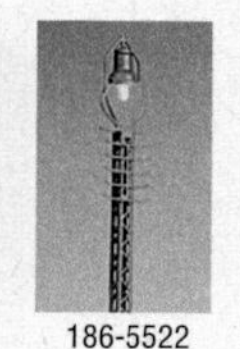

186-5520 186-5522

**186-5520** Two Arm, 6" High **31.99**

**186-5522** Ring Post, 5-1/2" High **18.99**

**186-5815** Lattice Mast Light pkg(2) **30.99**

## Park Lights

186-5001 186-5100 186-5230

**186-5001** Park Light, 2-1/2" High **14.99**

**186-5100** Park Light, 2-1/2" High **14.99**

**186-5230** Modern Park Light, 2" High (black) **11.99**

## Historic Park Lights

186-5092 186-5171 186-5220

**186-5092** Oldtime Park Light, 1-1/2" High **13.99**

**186-5171** Five Arm, 3-1/2" High **49.99**

**186-5220** Three Arm, 3-1/2" High **31.99**

186-5222 186-5223 186-5224

**186-5222** Double Arm, 3-1/2" High **29.99**

**186-5223** Triple Arm, 3-1/2" High **37.99**

**186-5224** Six Arm-Baden Baden, 3" High **89.99**

186-5225 186-5226 186-5253

**186-5225** Single Arm, 3-1/2" High **22.99**

**186-5226** Double Arm, 3-1/2" High **30.99**

**186-5253** Park/Street Light-Round, 1-21/32" High **13.99**

**Limited Quantity Available**

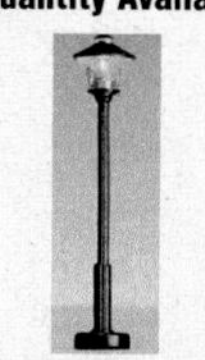

**186-5093** Park/Street Light, 1-3/8" High **11.99**

## Street Lights

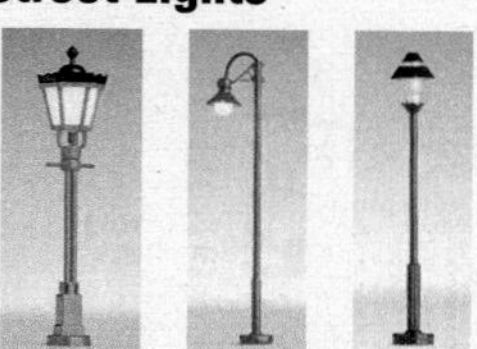

186-5000 186-5005 186-5007

**186-5000** Old Street Lamp, 2-1/2" High **11.99**

**186-5005** Urbach, 2" High **11.99**

**186-5007** Bad Homburg, 1-3/4" High **12.99**

186-5013 186-5172 186-5173

**186-5013** Wernigrode Street Light **11.99**

**186-5172** Nuremberg, 2" High **18.99**

**186-5173** Nuremberg, 4-Arm 2-1/2" High **37.99**

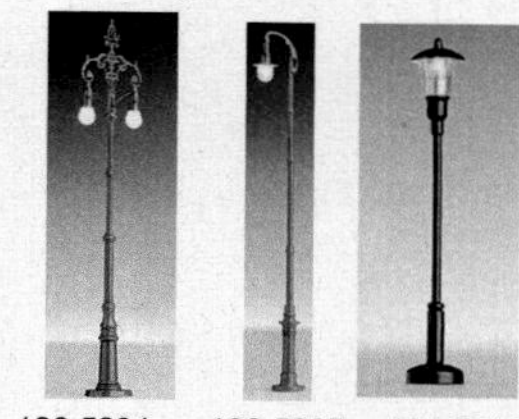

186-5204 186-5205 186-5210

**186-5204** Cologne Boulevard Light, 6-1/4" High **47.99**

**186-5205** Munich Boulevard Light, 4-3/4" High **16.99**

**186-5210** Modern Street Light, 2-1/2" High (black) **16.99**

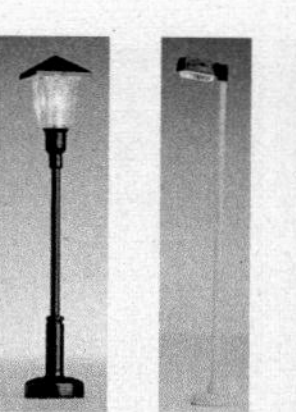

186-5240 186-5280 186-5515

**186-5240** Modern Street Ligh 2-1/2" High (black) **16.99**

**186-5280** Rectangular Head, 4-1/2" High **10.99**

**186-5515** Twin Rectangular Head, 4-1/2" High **16.99**

186-5020 186-5400 186-5410

**186-5020** Curved Mast-Single Arm, 4" High **14.99**

**186-5400** Curved Mast-Doubl Arm, 4-1/2" High **22.99**

**186-5410** Curved Mast-Triple Arm, 5" High **36.99**

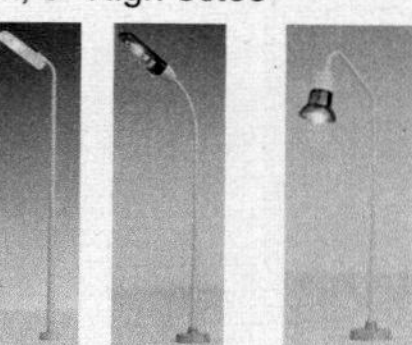

186-5452 186-5510 186-5512

**186-5452** Rail Yard Single Arm, 4-1/2" High **13.99**

**186-5510** Curved Mast-Single Arm, 5" High (yellow light) **11.99**

**186-5512** Curved Mast-Single Arm, 4" High **11.99**

**Limited Quantity Available**

186-5008 186-5101 186-5041

**186-5008** Lunen-Rye Market, 1-3/4" High **11.99**

**186-5101** Stuttgart Rosenstein Park Lamp **11.99**

**186-5041** Berlin City Streetligh **17.99**

**186-5514** Curved Mast-Double Arm, 5" High (yellow light) **14.99**

IMPORTED FROM GERMANY
BY WALTHERS

# LIGHTING

## Bulb Accessories

**186-3400** Building Light **1.99**
Plastic with brass socket (male) and 16" brown and yellow leads 16V. Two (female) plastic plugs for simple hook up.

**186-3422** Screw Metal Base w/2 Connectors Size E5.5 pkg(10) **7.99**

**186-5513** Curved Mast-Double Arm, 4" High **17.99**

## Historic Street Lights

This model is based on an actual German streetlamp as restored to its original appearance.

**186-5174** Berlin-Charlottenburg, 4-1/2" High **25.99**

## Modern Street Lights

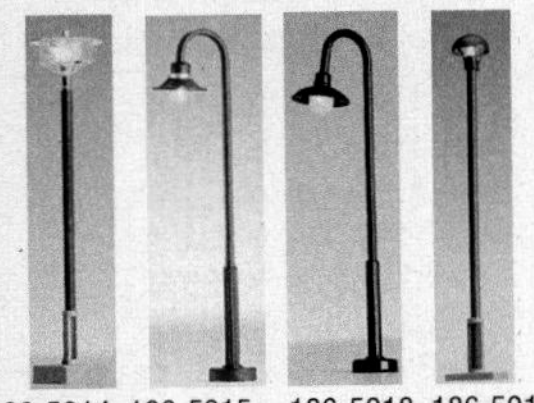

186-5014 186-5015 186-5018 186-5019

**186-5014** Street Light, 2-1/8" High **14.99**
**186-5015** Neuss, 1-3/4" High **14.99**
**186-5016** Munich, 2" High **13.99**
**186-5018** Harz, 3-1/2" High **11.99**
**186-5019** Modern, 3-15/16" High **14.99**

## Gas Lights

186-5010 186-5180 186-5190

**186-5010** Gas Light, 2" High **13.99**
**186-5180** Gas Light, 2-1/2" High **16.99**
**186-5190** Gas Light, 2" High **11.99**

186-5200 186-5201 186-5202 186-5203

**186-5200** Old Gas Light, 2" High **16.99**
**186-5201** Gas Light-Baden Baden, 2" High **16.99**
**186-5202** Gas Light-Hamburg, 2" High **17.99**
**186-5203** Gas Light-Stuttgart, 4" High **22.99**

## Floodlights

Floodlights pivot horizontally and vertically.

186-3278

186-5370

**186-3278** Spare Bulb pkg(2) **8.99**
**186-5370** Spotlight **11.99**
Approximate dimensions: 3/4 x 5/8 x 1/2"; pivots vertically.

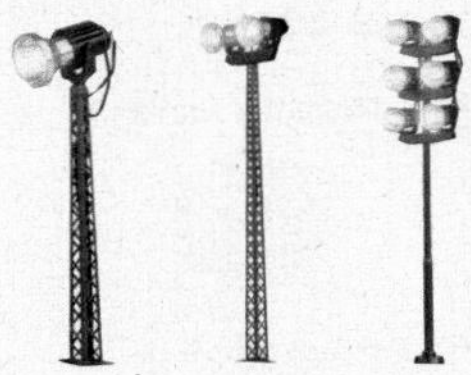

186-5581 186-5582 186-5583

**186-5581** Single Light, 3-1/4" High **16.99**
**186-5582** Double Light, 5-1/2" High **28.99**
**186-5583** Six Light, 6" High **50.99**
**186-5862** Floodlight 4-Arm **64.99**
**186-3433** E10 Screw Base, Raised pkg(10) **10.99**

### Limited Quantity Available

**186-3423** Recessed Base w/Bracket Size E5.5 pkg(10) **10.99**
**186-3424** E5 Screw Base, Raised pkg(10) **9.99**

## Festoon Bulb

**186-3250** Frosted 16V 30mA pkg(2) **6.99**
**186-3276** Candle Bulb, Amber pkg(4) **6.99**
Fits socket size E5.5, 19V, 65mA.
**186-3277** Candle Bulb, Clear pkg(4) **6.99**
Fits socket size E5.5, 19V 65mA.

**186-3278** Reflector Bulb, Clear pkg(2) **8.99**
80mA, 1 watt, approximate total length is 3/4", 16V.

## Fits E10 Size Sockets

**186-3330** 3.5V Clear, 200mA pkg(4) **5.99**
**186-3331** 19V Clear, 100mA pkg(4) **7.99**
**186-3332** 3.5V Red, 200mA pkg(4) **5.99**
**186-3333** 19V Red, 100mA pkg(4) **7.99**
**186-3335** 3.5V Green, 100mA pkg(4) **7.99**

## Grain-of-Wheat Bulb

16V, 30mA, unless otherwise noted.
**186-3254** Clear pkg(2) **5.99**
2 exposed electrodes, 16V, 35mA.
**186-3286** Short, Green pkg(2) **7.99**
**186-3287** 2-Wire, Clear **4.99**
**186-3288** Clear for #5760, 14V, 40mA **4.99**
**186-3291** Clear for Z Lights, 10V, 30mA pkg(2) **3.99**
**186-3293** Clear, 1 Black Wire **3.99**
**186-3290** Spare Bulb for Z Lights pkg(2) **5.99**
two exposed electrodes, clear, 10V, 30mA.
**186-3292** Miniature Bulb **3.99**
two electrodes for #7942; 1.5V 15mA. Connect only through resistor.
**186-3267** Micro Bulb, Clear, 3V pkg(2) **7.99**

## LEDs

Connect only through 1000 Ohm resistor.
**186-3295** Yellow, 2mm pkg(2) **2.99**
**186-3296** Red, 2mm pkg(2) **2.99**
**186-3297** Red, 1mm pkg(2) **6.99**
**186-3339** For Marklin Loco pkg(4) **5.99**

### Limited Quantity Available

**186-3298** Red, 3mm pkg(2) **5.99**
Miniature type for #4806. Approximate size 1/4 x 5/32".

## LED Panel Light 7.99 ea

Each LED features a built-in ballast resistor. Each 1/4" diameter, installed depth 1". 14-16V.

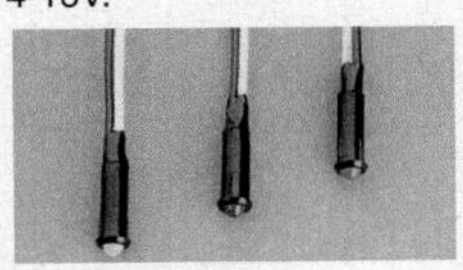

**186-3481** Yellow
**186-3482** Red
**186-3483** Green

## Lilliput Bulb

**186-3263** 24V, Clear pkg(2) **8.99**

## 16V, 35mA pkg(2)

**186-3271** Clear **4.99**
**186-3272** Red **5.99**
**186-3273** Green **5.99**
**186-3274** Yellow **5.99**

## Miniature Bulb pkg(2) 7.99 ea (Unless Noted)

14V, 30mA; for Brawa metal signals.
**186-3259** Clear **6.99**
**186-3260** Yellow
**186-3261** Red
Item listed below is available by Special Order (see Legend Page).
**186-3262** Green

## Mini Pin Terminal Strip

**186-3091** **6.99**
20 contacts that can be separated at any point; for use as pin and tubular socket. Spacing 1" 2.54mm, for all systems.

## Passenger Car Lighting

Items listed below are available by Special Order (see Legend Page).

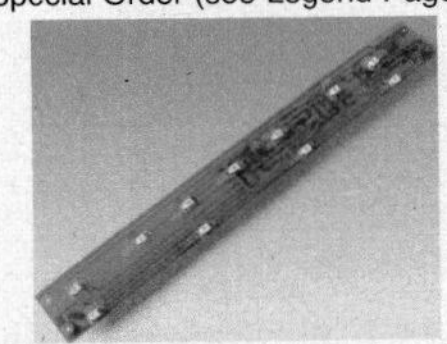

**186-2204** Passenger Coach Lighting **34.99**
**186-2201** Lighting For 4-Axle Passenger Cars **27.99**

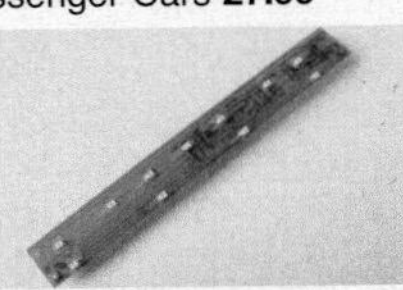

**186-2202** Lighting Board For D-Train Cars #2440-2443 **55.99**
**186-2220** AC Pick-up For 2-Axle Passenger Car #s 2150-2153 **12.99**
**186-2221** AC Pick-Up For 4-Axle Passenger Cars **12.99**

## Push-In Bulb

**186-3340** Clear pkg(4) **5.99**
For Marklin, 19V, 50mA.
**186-3341** Red pkg(4) **5.99**
For Marklin, 19V, 50mA.
**186-3342** Green pkg(4) **5.99**
For Marklin, 19V, 50mA.
**186-3343** Clear pkg(4) **5.99**
Marklin, new pattern with locating lugs; 19V, 50mA.
**186-3345** Clear pkg(4) **5.99**
For Trix, 14V, 50mA.
**186-3251** Clear pkg(2) **6.99**
3 x 2.55, 16V, 30mA.

## Push-In Panel Lights

For control panels and other installations where small diameter indicator lamps are needed. Units feature heat-resistant black plastic body with colored cap, nickel plated mounting ring, long life bulb and 6" leads. Fits mounting hole of 3/16". 12-14V, 60mA.
**186-3465** Blue **13.99**
**186-3469** White **13.99**

### Limited Quantity Available

**186-3461** Amber **12.99**
**186-3462** Red **12.99**
**186-3463** Green **12.99**

## Replacement Bulb For Telephone Booth

**186-3268** Clear, 3V **4.99**

## Screw Panel Light pkg(2) 8.99 ea

Size E5.5 for use on control panel. Current draw 50mA at 14-16V.

### Limited Quantity Available

**186-3449** White

## Special Bulbs pkg(2) 4.99 ea

With two electrodes. Replacement bulb for Brawa HO and N plastic signals made before 1981. 16V, 30mA.

### Limited Quantity Available

**186-3257** Green
**186-3258** Yellow

## Threaded Spherical Bulb pkg(4) 5.99 ea (Unless Noted)

Fits E5.5 size sockets.
**186-3300** 1.5V Clear, 100mA, 5mm
**186-3301** 3.5V Clear, 200mA, 5mm
**186-3302** 6V Clear, 100mA, 5mm
**186-3303** 14V Clear, 50mA, 5mm
**186-3304** 19V Clear, 60mA, 5mm
**186-3310** 19V Red, 50mA, 5mm
**186-3311** 19V Yellow, 50mA, 5mm
**186-3275** 19V Clear, 50mA,
**186-3316** 3.5V Clear, 200mA, 8mm
**186-3318** 14V Clear, 50mA, 8mm
**186-3319** 19V Clear, 50mA, 8mm **4.99**
**186-3325** 1.5V Clear, 100mA, 8mm

### Limited Quantity Available

**186-3307** 19V Clear, 50mA, 5mm **5.99**
**186-3322** 19V Green, 50mA, 8mm **5.99**

IMPORTED FROM GERMANY BY WALTHERS

## Miscellaneous Bulbs

**186-3264** Screw-In Bulb for #4621 & 4591 pkg(2) **6.99**

**186-3289** For Z Spotlight, 6V pkg(2) **2.99**

**186-3279** Valve Base 16V Clear pkg(2) **5.99**

**186-3337** Flat Top 19V Red pkg(4) **8.99**

**186-3338** Replacement Bulb For Marklin #60008 pkg(4) **7.99**

**186-3348** Mini Bayonet Bulb, 14V **2.99**

## 19V Tubular Bulb

**186-3282** 32mm pkg(2) **5.99**
**186-3283** 42mm pkg(2) **6.99**

# ELECTRICAL ACCESSORIES

## Adjustable Resistor

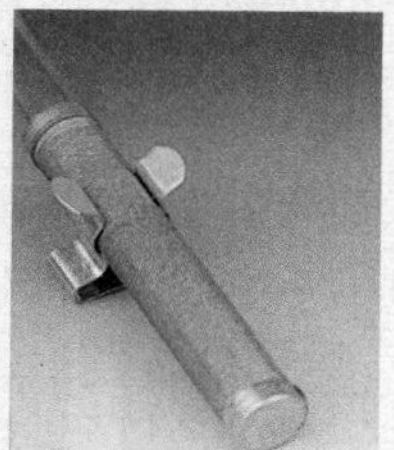

**186-6154 21.99**
Adjustable output clip. Reduces train speed for slow-running train blocks. 0-100 ohms; 1/4 x 2".

## Bridge Rectifier

**186-2185 13.99**
3/4 x 1/2 x 1/4", 10-16V, 1A.

## Distributor

Several distributors can be connected to supply more accessories.

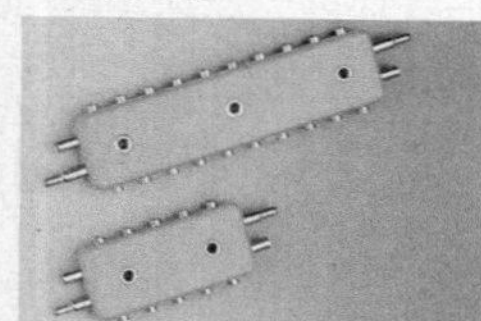

**186-2591** 5-Way, 2-Pole **8.99**
**186-2592** 10-Way, 2-Pole **11.99**

## Illuminated Push-Button 11.99 ea

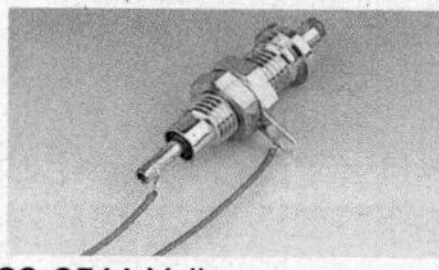

**186-3511** Yellow
**186-3512** Red
**186-3513** Green
**186-3519** White

## Magnetic Reed Switch

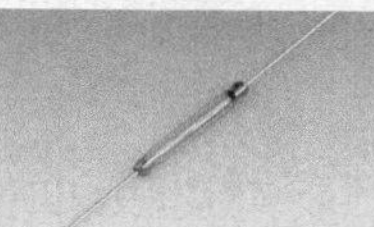

**186-3530** Inert Gas-Filled Tube Contact **4.99**
Contact load is 0.5A capacity, 3/4 x .1".

## Magnets

**186-3543** Bar Magnet **3.99**
For use with #3530; 1/4 x 1/2" (6 x 12 x 4mm).

## Momentary Contact Push-Button pkg(2) 8.99 ea (Unless Noted)

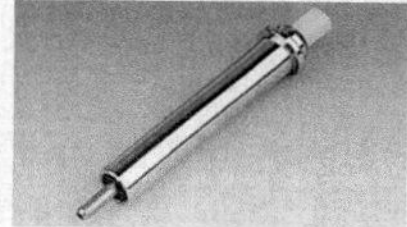

**186-3501** Yellow **9.99**

**Limited Quantity Available**
**186-3502** Red
**186-3505** Blue
**186-3508** Black
**186-3509** White

## Non-Illuminated Push-Button

1/4" diameter.
**186-3478** Black **8.99**
**186-3479** White **8.99**

**Limited Quantity Available**
**186-3471** Yellow **7.99**
**186-3472** Red **7.99**
**186-3473** Green **7.99**
**186-3475** Blue **7.99**

## Push-Buttons

**Limited Quantity Available**
**186-3573** Push-Button 3/4" pkg(4) **6.99**
**186-3500** Panel, Nickel-Plated **5.99**
Multi-purpose on/off switch with retaining clip. 1/4 x 1-1/2".

## Relays

Relays feature matching color-coded wiring for Brawa signals and accessories. Units may be operated manually or automatically with reed switches.
**186-2761** Triple 10-24V AC **98.99**

**Limited Quantity Available**
**186-2760** Double 10-20V AC **66.99**

## Screw Terminal Strip

**186-3094 3.99**
12-way, 4" long.

## SPST Panel Push-Button Switch w/Nut

**186-3524** pkg(2) **2.99**
Base approximately 1 x 1/2"; threaded neck length is approximately 1/2".

## Toggle Switch - On/Off

220 V/2A.
**186-3520** Single-Pole **11.99**

**Limited Quantity Available**
**186-3574** Tumbler Toggle Switch 3/4" pkg(4) **6.99**

## Wire Holder

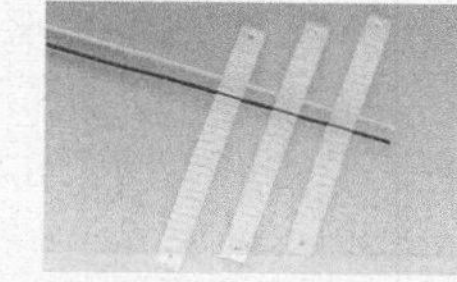

**186-3910** pkg(10) **5.99**
Holds up to 25 wires or leads securely.

# PLUG & SOCKET

## 30-Piece Set

**186-3071 11.99**
15 plugs, 15 sockets in five colors.

## 6-Pole Battery Cap Socket

**Limited Quantity Available**

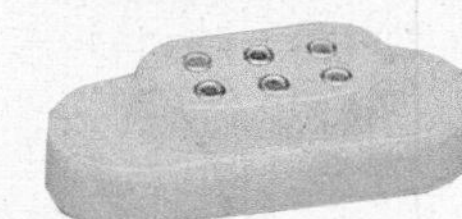

**186-3572 1.99**

## For Marklin

**186-3070 5.99**
8 crosshole plugs, 8 sleeves.

## Panel Sockets pkg(10) 37.99 ea (Unless Noted)

For use on control panels.

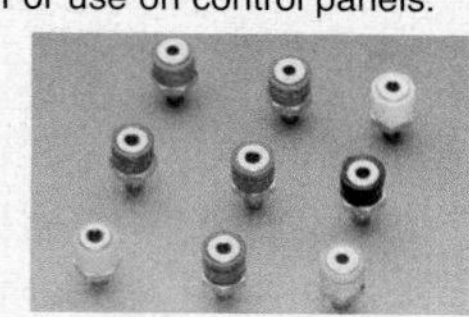

**186-3081** Yellow pkg(1) **3.99**
**186-3082** Red pkg(1) **3.99**
**186-3083** Green
**186-3084** Brown pkg(1) **3.99**
**186-3085** Blue
**186-3086** Orange
**186-3087** Gray
**186-3088** Black
**186-3089** White

## Round Plugs pkg(10) 3.99 ea

With crossover hole.
**186-3051** Yellow
**186-3052** Red
**186-3053** Green
**186-3054** Brown
**186-3055** Blue
**186-3056** Orange
**186-3057** Gray
**186-3058** Black
**186-3059** White

## Round Socket pkg(10) 3.99 ea

**186-3041** Yellow
**186-3042** Red
**186-3043** Green
**186-3044** Brown
**186-3045** Blue
**186-3046** Orange
**186-3047** Gray
**186-3048** Black
**186-3049** White

## 2-Pole Socket

**Limited Quantity Available**

**186-3570** pkg(5) **9.99**

# WIRE

## Fine Strand

Fine stranded copper wire, approximately .036" diameter. Maximum load 2.5A.

## 33' Roll 2.19 ea

Dealers must order in multiples of 10.
**186-3160** Purple
**186-3161** Yellow
**186-3162** Red
**186-3163** Green
**186-3164** Brown
**186-3165** Blue
**186-3168** Black

## 133' Roll 22.99 ea

**186-3222** Red
**186-3228** Black

## Multi-Conductor Flat Cable Hook-Up Wire

#24 solid copper wires in assorted colors, maximum load, 6A per wire.

**186-3139** #24 2-Conductor, pkg(164') White **18.99**

**186-3170** Brown/Yellow pkg(16') **3.99**

**186-3171** Brown/Yellow pkg(164') **25.99**

**186-3172** Blue/Yellow/Blue pkg(16') **5.99**
For use with Marklin.

**186-3173** Blue/Yellow/Blue pkg(164') **37.99**
For use with Marklin.

**186-3174** Yellow/Red/Blue pkg(16') **5.99**
For use with Marklin.

**186-3175** Yellow/Red/Blue pkg(164') **37.99**
For use with Marklin.

**186-3176** Gray/Violet/Blue pkg(16') **5.99**
For use with Arnold.

**186-3177** Gray/Violet/Blue pkg(164') **37.99**
For use with Arnold.

**186-3182** Blue/Yellow/Red/Green pkg(16') **6.99**

**186-3184** Five Conductor pkg(16') **7.99**

**186-3186** Blue/Brown/Yellow/Red/Green/Black pkg(16') **9.99**

**186-3188** Yellow/Brown/Red/Green/Blue/Gray/Black/White pkg(16') **12.99**

**186-3189** Same as #3188 pkg(164') **128.99**

**186-3230** #18 2-Conductor, Orange, White pkg(65') **29.99**

**186-3235** #18 3-Conductor, pkg(65') **42.99**
Yellow, white and green.

## Solid Strand

Solid Strand copper wire with PVC insulation. Max load 6A; length, 11 yards per coil, approximate diameter, .048".

## 33' Roll 2.29 ea

Dealers MUST order multiples of 10.
**186-3100** Purple
**186-3101** Yellow
**186-3102** Red
**186-3103** Green
**186-3104** Brown
**186-3105** Blue
**186-3107** Gray
**186-3108** Black
**186-3109** White

**Limited Quantity Available**
**186-3197** Brown **7.49**

## 328' Roll 18.99 ea

**186-3110** Purple
**186-3111** Yellow
**186-3112** Red
**186-3113** Green
**186-3114** Brown
**186-3115** Blue
**186-3117** Gray
**186-3118** Black
**186-3119** White

IMPORTED FROM GERMANY BY WALTHERS

### Switching-Circuit Wire .252mm x 25m 8.99 ea

**186-3210** Yellow
**186-3211** Red
**186-3212** Brown

### Wire Accessories

**186-3091** 20 Pin Miniature Connector **6.99**

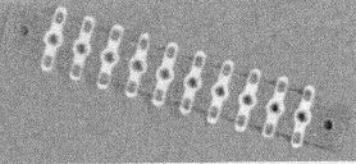

**186-3912** 10-Position **5.99**
**186-3913** Resistor 1000 ohm pkg(10) **2.99**
**186-3914** Terminal Strip, 30 Position **14.99**

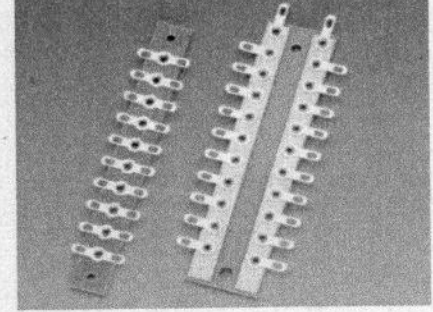

**186-3915** Soldering Plates 10 Terminal **10.99**
**186-3916** Soldering Plates 20 Terminal **18.99**

### #24 2 Conductor pkg(16') 2.29 ea

Dealers MUST order multiples of 10.
**186-3122** Red
**186-3123** Green
**186-3128** Black
**186-3129** White

## INTERNATIONAL HOBBY CORP.

### Lighting Kits

**348-4245** 4-Wheel pkg(12) **13.98**

**348-4246** 6-Wheel pkg(12) **16.98**

### Deluxe Motorizing Kit

**348-5190** For Circus Rides **7.98**

For Up-To-Date Information and News Bookmark Walthers Web site at
**www.walthers.com**

IMPORTED FROM GERMANY BY WALTHERS

Add electronic animation to your layout with these accessories. Each unit comes fully assembled, with bulbs and/or LEDs. Small component size is adaptable to most any HO scale building or vehicle.

### Light & Sound

**189-5755** Building Site w/Sound **179.99**

Items listed below are available by Special Order (see Legend Page).
**189-5750** Blue Blinker Set w/Sound **99.99**
Light and sound control unit with speaker and two bulbs.

**189-5923** Flashing Light Set w/Lamps & Circuit Boards for Vehicles (yellow) **28.99**

**189-49965** Vehicle Accessory Warning Set **6.99**

### Street Lamps

**189-8621** Old-Time Working (dark green) pkg(2) **27.99**
7-17/32" 18.8cm tall.

### LED

**189-5987** Standard LEDs 14-16V (white) pkg(2) **13.99**
White LEDs produce light approximating the glow of Xenon/Neon lamps.

### Blinker Sets

#### Two Alternating

**189-5935** With Blinker Control Blue **21.99**

**189-5918** Yellow **24.99**

**189-5919** Red **24.99**

### Emergency Lights

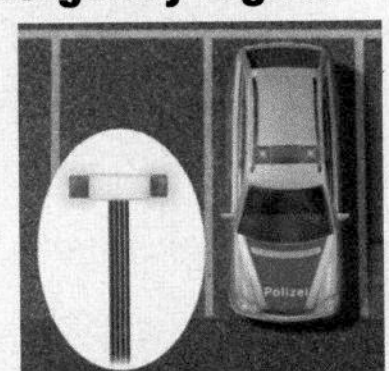

**189-5938** Blue Flashing Light Bar **28.99**
Add authenticity to any police or emergency vehicle with this kit. Includes rooftop light bar with two blue LEDs, flashing circuit and wire leads.

### Auto Lights

**189-5927** Headlights & Tail Lights **22.99**

### Timers

**189-5961** With Infra Red Unit **42.99**

**189-5963** Without Infra Red Unit **32.99**

### Switch Units

**189-5749** Random Electronic **70.99**

**189-5962** Standard Infrared Light **15.99**
Use with timer units #189-5961 and 189-5963, each sold separately.

### Cable Lamp w/250mm Of Cable 6.99 ea (Unless Noted)

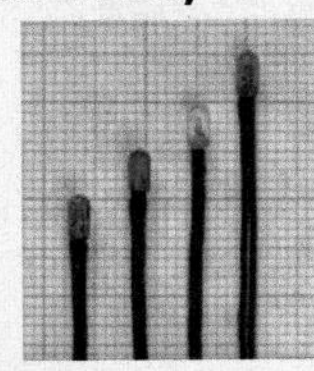

**189-4292** Amber 5V/60mA

**189-4293** Blue 5V/60mA

Items listed below are available by Special Order (see Legend Page).
**189-4290** Clear 16V/30mA **5.99**

**189-4291** Red 5V/60mA

**189-4294** Turquoise 5V/60mA

### Conductive Paint

**189-5900** Silver **13.99**
With the stroke of a brush, you have a painted line which will conduct electricity on plastic, wood, glass, etc. It can be painted over and still carry current.

### Scene Lighting

**189-5400** Luminous Advertising **29.99**
Includes eight LEDs and extra letters (dry decals). Perfect for advertising restaurants, clubs and more.

**189-5405** Flexible Light Band **30.99**
Features a string of 12 yellow LEDs. A nice addition to campsites or restaurants, or they can be used as Christmas lights.

**189-5408** Summer Night Party Set **31.99**
Everything you need for any backyard event. Complete with working string of colored lights (12 LEDs), two support poles, four benches and two tables.

**189-5409** Christmas Tree w/7 LEDs **26.99**
Fully assembled, snow-covered tree has seven yellow LEDs for a festive touch in any scene. Great accessory for Christmas villages too!

**189-5921** Flames **30.99**
Must be connected to 14-16V AC or DC power supply.

**189-5931** Electronic Welder **27.99**

Items listed below are available by Special Order (see Legend Page).
**189-5930** Blinking Trailer w/Control Unit **28.99**
Warn motorists of upcoming construction zones with this blinking trailer.

### Carnival Lighting

For use on carnival booths, rides and more. Each light strip measures 2-3/8 x 1/8" 60 x 3mm, and includes six LEDs. Control unit (14-16V AC or DC) also included.

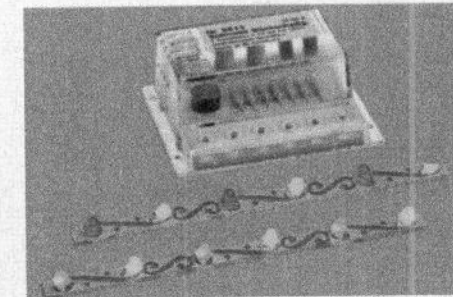

**189-5932** Blinking **34.99**

**189-5933** Constant **39.99**

### Structure Lights

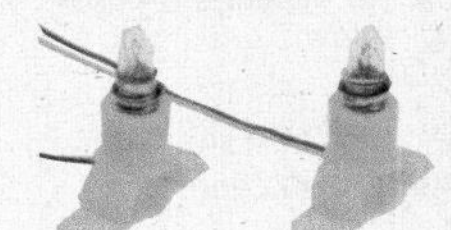

**189-4280** Building Interior Lights pkg(2) **2.99**
Fully assembled sockets with wire leads and replaceable bulbs.

**Relative intensity of Mitey Lites:**

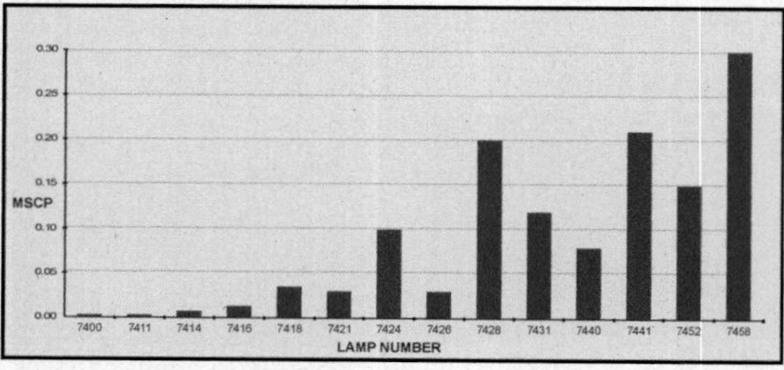


## Hyper-Brite LEDs

50 times brighter than general-purpose LEDs. 3mm diameter. For DC power. Includes limiting resistors for use with 12-16V supplies.

### 7501 White

Special resin reduces bluish output and provides incandescent look. Great for use as headlights.

**800-750101 3.95**

**800-750102** pkg(2) **6.95**

**800-750106** pkg(6) **12.95**

### 7502 Red

Diffused package for wide-angle viewing. Great for strobes, signals and traffic lights.

**800-750202** pkg(2) **3.50**

**800-750206** pkg(6) **6.95**

### 7503 Orange

Diffused package for wide-angle viewing. Great for strobes.

**800-750302** pkg(2) **3.50**

**800-750306** pkg(6) **6.95**

### 7504 Pure Green

Diffused package for wide-angle viewing. Intense deep green for signals or traffic light use.

**800-750402** pkg(2) **6.95**

**800-750406** pkg(6) **12.95**

### 7505 Blue

Diffused package for wide-angle viewing. Great for emergency vehicles.

**800-750502** pkg(2) **6.95**

**800-750506** pkg(6) **12.95**

### 7507 Yellow/Amber

Diffused package for wide-angle viewing. Deep yellow for signal or traffic light use.

**800-750702** pkg(2) **3.50**

**800-750706** pkg(6) **6.95**

## Lamps

### 7400 Sub-Micro

0.75mm diameter axial lead. 1.5 V, 18mA with 1" bare wire leads. Use for marker lights, number boards, step lights, etc.

**800-740002** pkg(2) **4.50**

**800-740006** pkg(6) **10.95**

**800-740012** pkg(12) **16.95**

**800-940012** Dropping Resistor For 12V pkg(10) **2.49**

**800-940016** Dropping Resistor For 16V pkg(10) **2.49**

### 7411 Standard Output

1.40mm diameter lens end, with 8" black stranded wires. 1.5V, 13mA.

**800-741102** pkg(2) **4.95**

**800-741106** pkg(6) **10.95**

**800-741112** pkg(12) **14.95**

**800-741125** pkg(25) **26.95**

**800-941112** Dropping Resistor For 12V pkg(10) **2.49**

**800-941116** Dropping Resistor For 16V pkg(10) **2.49**

### 7414 Medium Output

1.40mm diameter lens end with 8" black wire leads. 1.5V, 30mA. Ideal for headlights, mars lights, ditch lights, etc. to minimize total current draw.

**800-741402** pkg(2) **5.95**

**800-741406** pkg(6) **12.95**

**800-741412** pkg(12) **17.95**

**800-941412** Dropping Resistor For 12V pkg(6) **2.49**

**800-941416** Dropping Resistor For 16V **2.49**

### 7416 High Output

1.40mm diameter lens end, with 8" black wire leads. 1.5V, 60mA. Very bright! Use for headlights, etc.

**800-741602** pkg(2) **5.95**

**800-741606** pkg(6) **12.95**

**800-741612** pkg(12) **17.95**

**800-941612** Dropping Resistor For 12V pkg(6) **2.49**

**800-941616** Dropping Resistor For 16V pkg(6) **2.49**

### Colored Lamps

Same specifications as #7416 lamps. Use same dropping resistors as #7416. Ideal for warning lights, signals, signs and more.

**Set Of 2 5.95 ea**

**800-7416102** Orange

**800-7416202** Red

**800-7416302** Amber

**800-7416402** Green

**800-7416502** Blue

**800-7416702** Yellow

**Set Of 6 12.95 ea**

**800-7416106** Orange

**800-7416206** Red

**800-7416306** Amber

**800-7416406** Green

**800-7416506** Blue

**800-7416706** Yellow

### 7418 Very High Output

1.40mm diameter lens end, with 8" black wire leads. 3.0V, 26mA. Ideal for headlight, mars light, etc.

**800-741802** pkg(2) **6.95**

**800-741806** pkg(6) **13.95**

**800-741812** pkg(12) **16.95**

**800-941812** Dropping Resistor for 12V pkg(6) **2.49**

**800-941816** Dropping Resistor For 16V pkg(6) **2.49**

### 7421 Very High Output

1.70mm diameter lens end, with 8" black wire leads. 1.5V, 75mA. Extremely bright! Ideal for headlights, mars lights or ditch lights.

**800-742102** pkg(2) **6.95**

**800-742106** pkg(6) **13.95**

**800-942112** Dropping Resistor For 12V pkg(4) **2.49**

**800-942116** Dropping Resistor For 16V pkg(4) **2.49**

### 7424 Extra High Output

1.70mm diameter lens end with 8" black wire leads. 3.0V, 105mA. Extremely bright! Ideal for headlights, mars lights or ditch lights.

**800-742402** pkg(2) **6.95**

**800-742406** pkg(6) **13.95**

**800-942412** Dropping Resistor For 12V pkg(4) **2.49**

**800-942416** Dropping Resistor For 16V pkg(4) **2.49**

### 7426 Very High Output

2.4mm diameter lens end, with 8" black wire leads. 1.5V, 90mA. Extremely bright! Use for headlights, etc.

**800-742602** pkg(2) **5.95**

**800-742606** pkg(6) **12.95**

**800-942612** Dropping Resistor For 12V pkg(4) **2.49**

**800-942616** Dropping Resistor For 16V pkg (4) **2.49**

### 7428 Maximum Output

2.4mm diameter lens end with 8" black wire leads. 3.0V, 120mA. Extremely bright! Ideal for headlights, mars lights or ditch lights, etc.

**800-742802** pkg(2) **5.95**

**800-742806** pkg(6) **12.95**

**800-942812** Dropping Resistor For 12V pkg(4) **2.49**

**800-942816** Dropping Resistor For 16V pkg(4) **2.49**

### 7431 Very High Output

2.4mm diameter lens end, with 8" black wire leads. 12-14V, 50mA. Ideal for headlights in locomotives not equipped with constant lighting and for structure lighting.

**800-743102** pkg(2) **5.95**

**800-743106** pkg(6) **12.95**

### 7440 General Purpose

Long life miniature lamp. 3.0mm diameter with 12" wire leads. 14-16V, 30mA. Use for equipment and structure lighting.

**800-744006** pkg(6) **4.50**

**800-744012** pkg(12) **7.50**

**800-744025** pkg(25) **12.95**

### 7441 General Purpose

High-output version of 7440. 60mA. 2.5 times brighter. Other specs are the same.

**800-744106** Pkg(6) **5.50**

**800-744112** Pkg(12) **7.95**

**800-744125** Pkg(25) **13.95**

### 7452 Bi-Pin Style

3.0mm diameter with plug-in style, short, stiff leads. 5.0V, 60mA. Ideal replacement lam for LGB™ in-car and locomotive lighting applications.

**800-745202** pkg(2) **4.95**

**800-745206** pkg(6) **11.95**

**800-745212** pkg(12) **16.95**

### 7458 Bi-Pin Style

3.0mm diameter with plug-in style, short, stiff leads. 18-22V 45mA. Ideal replacement lamp for in-car and locomotive DCC lighting applications.

**800-745802** pkg(2) **4.95**

**800-745806** pkg(6) **11.95**

**800-745812** pkg(12) **16.95**

## LIGHTING SYSTEMS

Circuitron products are constructed on printed circuit boards and designed to moun by snapping into a section of Circuitron's PCMT (Printed Circuit Mounting Track). Solid-state integrated circuit technology. Connections to an Circuitron-printed circuit board can be made using .110" female solderless connectors or by soldering the leads directly to the terminals on the board. Complete instructions are included. One-year limited warranty.

### AW-1, AW-2 Arc Welde Circuits 19.95 ea

The AW-1 and AW-2 circuits utilize two lamps, one yellow and one blue, along with a circuit that provides a random flickering effect of the lamps. The result is a very convincing representation of an arc welder in operation. Require a 10-18V AC or DC input for proper operation. Adaptable for all scales.

**800-5841** AW-1
Includes micro-bulbs and is designed for direct viewing in all scales. A small wisp of cotton placed over the lamps will serve to diffuse the light and produce a very realistic smoke effect.

**800-5842** AW-2
Includes larger lamps and is designed to illuminate a window from within a structure. If the window is frosted to represent years of grime, the flickering effect is very realistic.

### Replacement Lamp Set pkg(2) 4.95 ea

**800-9342** AW-1
**800-9343** AW-2

## Basic Flashers

Simple, inexpensive circuits for flashing LEDs or lamps (sold separately).

**800-1601** Fixed Rate LED Flasher **12.95**

**800-1602** Fixed Rate Lamp (<250mA) Flasher **15.95**

**800-1603** Adjustable Rate & Duty Cycle Flasher for Lamp or LED (<250mA) **17.95**

## CF-1 Caboose Flasher 16.95 ea

Single rear facing bulb slowly flashes on and off. Includes CF-1 circuit board, sub-miniature LED and battery clip. A 9V battery provides about 100 hours of flashing.

**800-1200** Red

**800-1201** Yellow

## CL-1, CL-2 Chase Lights, 10-Step 39.95 ea

Ten-step sequence with one lamp lit at a time. Ideal for "moving" sign and marquee applications. CL-1 includes 10 micro-lamps (1.4mm dia.), perfect for the edge of signs. CL-2 includes 10 high-output 2.4mm lamps for direct viewing in larger scales or with 10 mil fiber optics. Both circuits provide adjustable step speed and operate off 10-18V AC or DC. An additional flasher output is provided to backlight a sign or marquee, and flashes at 1/10 the step speed. Fiber optics and sign material not included.

**800-5831** CL-1 w/Micro Lamps
**800-5832** CL-2 w/2.4mm Lamps

## Diodes

**800-9350** 3 Amp pkg(2) **1.95**

**800-9351** 1 Amp pkg(6) **1.95**

**800-9352** 6 Amp pkg(2) **2.95**

**800-935012** 3 Amp pkg(12) **6.95**

**800-935212** 6 Amp pkg(12) **12.95**

## DL-1 Ditch Lights

Alternately flashes two 1.7mm diameter, high-intensity, lens-end lamps (included) at a slow rate to simulate ditch lights. With the addition of a DPST or DPDT switch, the DL-1 circuit can be bypassed so the lights stay on. Requires 2.4-3.0V DC input from batteries, TP-2 #800-2002 or TP-3 #800-2003 Track Power Adapters (sold separately).

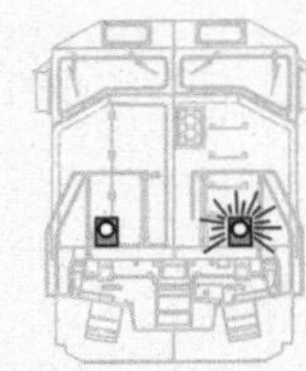

**800-1400** DL-1 Oscillating Ditch Lights **19.95**

**800-9123** Sub-Mini Slide Switch, DPDT pkg(2) **2.95**

**800-742402** Replacement Lamp Set for DL-1 pkg(2) **4.95**

## Emergency Flashers 17.95 ea

A low-cost circuit that alternately flashes two LEDs at a constant rate. Animate emergency vehicles, signs, barricades, towers, etc. Simple to install. Powered by a 9V battery or by using a PS-3.

**800-3002** .120" Red

**800-3003** .120" Yellow

**800-3022** .080" Red

**800-3023** .080" Yellow

## PS-3 Power Supply

**800-5304 14.95**
Designed to power the EF-1 Emergency Flasher in situations where battery operation is undesirable. Accepts AC or DC input of 10-18V and converts it to 9V DC.

## EOT/Fred Flashers 14.95 ea

Scale-size housing, easily mounted on any freight car. High-intensity LED slowly flashes a bright light rearward. Requires 3V input, easily obtained from two small batteries; the TP-1 Track Power Adapter, #800-2001, (sold separately) can be used if the car is equipped with track power pickups.

**800-1302** Red

**800-1303** Yellow

## Replacement Lamp Sets

**800-7416302** Firelites™ Flickering Flame Circuits Amber for FF-1 pkg(2) **4.95**

## FL-1 Strobe Flashers 16.95 ea

Bright flash, small package, battery operation. Long battery life; six months continuous operation from one AA alkaline cell. Will operate off hearing aid or watch cell. 1/2 x 3/4" high. HO 1.5V, O 3.0V, N 1.5V.

**800-1001** HO, Orange LED

**800-1002** HO, Red LED

**800-1003** HO, Yellow LED

**800-1011** O, Orange LED

**800-1012** O, Red LED

**800-1013** O, Yellow LED

**800-1021** N, Orange LED

**800-1022** N, Red LED

**800-1023** N, Yellow LED

## FLA Amtrak-Style Strobe Flasher

**800-1100 16.95**
Duplicates the action of twin Xenon strobes found on many Amtrak locos. Designed for mounting inside HO Scale dummy locos, uses 9V transistor type battery to provide approximately 100 hours of flashing. Twin white lamps flash brightly about once a second.

**800-9341** Replacement Lamp 0.1" dia pkg(2) **5.95**

## FLW White Strobes 18.95 ea

Bright white flash from small incandescent lamp (included). Battery or track power adapter powered. Same size as FL-1.

**800-1031** Bright 1.4mm Lamp, 1.5V

**800-1032** Very Bright 1.7mm Lamp, 3.0V

**800-1033** Extra Bright 2.4mm Lamp, 3.0V



## ML-1 Mars Light

**800-1500 19.95**
Realistic simulation of the gyrating beacon seen on many locos. Utilizing a special design, high-intensity lens end dual-filament, the ML-1 can be used in most HO locos. Uses 2.4-3.0V DC from batteries, #800-2002 TP-2 or the #800-2003 TP-3 Track Power Adapters (sold separately).

**800-9340** Replacement Dual Filament Lamp, 3V **2.95**

## ML-2 Mars Light

**800-1502 19.95**
Alternately flashes two 1.7mm diameter, high intensity, lens-end lamps (included) at a prototypical speed. Lamps may be mounted in dual headlight housings or side-by-side in larger headlight openings. Requires 2.4-3.0V DC input which can be provided by batteries, #800-2002 TP-2 or #800-2003 TP-3 Track Power Adapters (sold separately).

## Track Power Adapters

### TP-1

**800-2001 14.95**
Miniature voltage regulator can power any Circuitron LED-type Strobe Flasher or EOT flasher from track power. Can be used as a constant lighting unit in unpowered rolling stock. 35mA output will power two to three Strobes or EOT Flashers, LEDs with a 47 ohm resistor, one #7418 or two #7414 Mitey Lites™ (sold separately) wired in series. Bi-Directional, output will be present whether train is moving forward or backward. Can be used with DC, AC or Carrier Control systems. 0.3 x 0.3 x 0.8".

### TP-2

**800-2002 14.95**
Will power the ML-1 Mars Light and Strobe Flashers and also has outputs that will provide constant directional lighting. Fits most HO locos, can be used with motors drawing up to 1 amp.

### TP-3

**800-2003 16.95**
Adjustable output (1.5 or 3.0V DC). Ideal for constant lighting source in unpowered rolling stock. No ballast lamps or motors required. Will power Mars flasher in models driven by low current can motors. Works with all forms of track power. Max current output is 1/2 amp

## Opto-Sensors

.185" diameter. For use with all Circuitron Detection Circuits.

**800-9201** Single **3.95**

**800-9202** Set of 2 **7.50**

**800-9206** Set of 6 **19.95**

## PL-8, PL-12 Progressive Lamp Circuits

Create unique signs. Sequence for both circuits is the same, only the maximum number of letters (and lamps) is different. Can also light fewer letters. Lights each lamp in succession with all previous lamps remaining on until all lamps are lit. The speed is adjustable. All lamps remain on, then go out. Finally, all lamps come on, then go out. Time on/off is adjustable. The sequence automatically repeats. The PL-8 and PL-12 include 8 and 12 lamps respectively (12-18V, 3mm dia.) but other lamps may be substituted for specific application. Construction of the actual sign will depend upon application and is left to the modeler. The PL-8 and PL-12 require a 12V AC or DC supply for proper operation. Adaptable for HO and larger scales.

**800-5808** PL-8 **44.95**

**800-5812** PL-12 **54.95**

## SQ-8 Sequencing Strobe

**800-5838 39.95**
Provides a rapid sequencing of eight high-intensity white strobe lights (included). When the lamps are aligned, the effect is one of a light sweep from one end to the other. This type of lighting effect is commonly used near airports on the approaches, but can also be very effective on signs and other applications. Both the sweep speed and the delay between the sweeps are independently adjustable. Requires a 10-18V AC or DC input. For use with HO and larger scales.

## TL-1 Traffic Light Controller

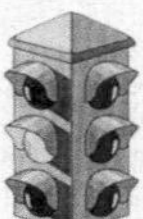

**800-5820 34.95**
Timing circuitry for standard traffic light. Outputs drive LED or lamp signals (not included). If LEDs are used, they must be common anode design. All four times are adjustable. Requires 10-18V AC or DC input. Red, yellow and green outputs provided for each direction (six total) and each can drive a 250mA maximum load. Adaptable for all scales.

# LIGHTING ACCESSORIES

## Adjustable Converter And Regulator

**800-5305** PS-2A **26.95**
A self-contained AC to DC converter with an adjustable voltage regulated output. The output voltage can be adjusted anywhere between 1.25 and 12V DC. Maximum continuous current output of the PS-2A is in excess of 1 amp. Ideal for powering any low current DC accessories including 1.5V micro-lamps. The AC or unfiltered DC input should be about 5-6V higher than the desired regulated output voltage to allow maximum current output. The input voltage may be as high as 22V, but this may result in reduced current available at the output, particularly at lower voltage settings.

## Battery Holders

For use with HO and O Scale Strobe Flashers.

**800-9611** AA, 1 cell, 1.5V **2.95**
**800-9612** AA, 2 cell, 3V **3.49**
**800-9613** AAA, 1 cell, 1.5V **2.95**
**800-9614** AAA, 2 cell, 3V **3.49**
**800-9615** N, 1 cell, 1.5V **2.95**
**800-9616** N, 2 cell, 3V **3.49**

## Heat Shrink Tubing 3.49 ea

Use to insulate and protect wire connections quickly and easily. Shrinks to half the listed diameter when heated with a match, soldering iron or heat gun.

**800-8703** 3/64" 1.191mm Diameter - 36" 0.9m Long
**800-8704** 1/16" 1.588mm Diameter - 36" 0.9m Long
**800-8706** 3/32" 2.381mm Diameter - 36" 0.9m Long
**800-8708** 1/8" 3.175mm Diameter - 30" 75cm Long
**800-8712** 3/16" 4.763mm Diameter - 30" 75cm Long
**800-8700** Assortment Includes 6" 15cm of each diameter from 3/64 to 3/16".

## Hidden Accessory Reed Switch Kits

A completely hidden switch for controlling strobe flashers, marker lights or other rolling stock electrical accessories. Reed switch kits are turned on and off simply by bringing an external magnet up to the outside of the locomotive or car body. No external projections detract from the appearance of the model. Kits contain a subminiature reed switch and a tiny bias magnet.

**800-9101** RS-1 **5.95**
Requires adjustment before mounting.

**800-9102** RS-2 **7.95**
Requires no adjustment.

**800-9100** External Magnet for Actuating Reed Switches **1.95**

**800-9103** Sub-Miniature Slide Switches SPDT pkg(2) **2.95**

## Miniature Switches

### Sub-Miniature Toggle Switches

Sub-Miniature Toggle Switches for panel mounting. 5 amp rating. Solder lug terminals. Chrome handle. 1/4" panel hole.

**800-911002** SPDT On-On pkg(2) **5.95**
**800-911006** SPDT On-On pkg(6) **15.95**
**800-911102** SPDT On-Off-On pkg(2) **6.95**
**800-911106** SPDT On-Off-On pkg(6) **18.95**
**800-911202** SPDT On-Off-On Momentary pkg(2) **7.49**
**800-911206** SPDT On-Off-On Momentary pkg(6) **19.95**
**800-912002** DPDT On-On pkg(2) **6.95**
**800-912006** DPDT On-On pkg(6) **18.95**
**800-912102** DPDT On-Off-On pkg(2) **7.49**
**800-912106** DPDT On-Off-On pkg(6) **19.95**
**800-912202** DPDT On-Off-On Momentary pkg(2) **7.95**
**800-912206** DPDT On-Off-On Momentary pkg(6) **20.95**
**800-9128** Red Plastic Sleeve for Handle pkg(6) **2.50**
**800-9129** Black Plastic Sleeve for Handle pkg(6) **2.50**

### Sub-Mini Slide Switches

**800-9103** SPDT pkg(2) **2.95**
**800-9123** DPDT pkg(2) **2.95**

### Pushbutton

800-9610 1.50

## Solderless Connectors 2.95 ea

Female .110" solderless connectors for all Circuitron printed circuit boards.

**800-9602** Non-Insulated pkg(8)
**800-9603** Insulated pkg(6)

## Ultrafine Hook-Up Wire 2.95 ea

Ultrafine stranded wire measures just 0.015" 0.397mm outside diameter. Vinyl insulation is easily stripped. Ideal for wiring locomotive lights, signals, signs and other small models. Each pack includes 10' 2.9m.

**800-8610** Black
**800-8612** Red
**800-8619** White

# LEDs

## .075" dia pkg(2) 2.95 ea

**800-9321** Orange
**800-9322** Red
**800-9323** Yellow
**800-9324** Green

## .125" dia pkg(2) 2.95 ea

Super-bright, diffused lens, ideal for strobe flashers, signs, signals and more.

**800-9301** Orange
**800-9302** Red
**800-9303** Yellow
**800-9304** Green
**800-9306** Red/Green, Bi-Color

## .200" dia pkg(2) 2.95 ea

**800-9311** Orange
**800-9312** Red
**800-9313** Yellow
**800-9314** Green
**800-9316** Red/Green, Bi-Color

## Fiber Optics

PMMA plastic fibers with a special fluoro-polymer coating. Light entering the end is transmitted along the length by internal reflection and exits the far end with very little loss in intensity. Use for signals, signs and special effects.

**800-8020** 0.020" dia 30' **7.95**
**800-8030** 0.030" dia 20' **7.95**
**800-8040** 0.040" dia 15' **8.95**
**800-8060** 0.060" dia 10' **8.95**

## Circuitron Catalog & Application Book #301

**800-9999** 60 pages **7.00**

# WIRING

## Miniature Wire

For connections where flat tape is not practical. 32 gauge.

**206-203** 2 Conductor Hookup pkg(25') **3.00**
Very fine, stranded, 25' shank.

**206-2032** 1 Conductor **1.98**
50' shank, white.

# LIGHTING

## Dropping Resistor

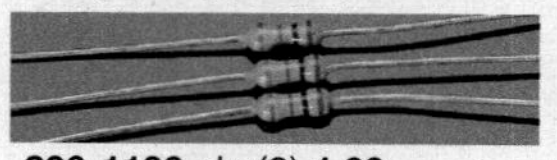

**206-1100** pkg(3) **1.30**
Used to directly connect 1.5V micro bulbs to a 12V source. A resistor must be connected to each bulb.

## Grain-Of-Wheat Bulbs

Bulbs consume between 50 and 60mA at 12V. Outside diameter approximately 1/8".

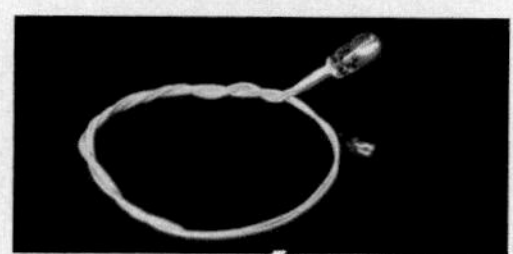

**206-10101** 12V w/1/8" Black Wire **1.25**
**206-10102** 16V w/8" White Wire **1.25**
**206-101011** 12V w/White Wire **1.59**
**206-101018** 3V w/8" White Wire **1.25**
**206-101021** 12V w/12" Brown Wire **1.30**
**206-101022** 12V w/18" Brown Wire **1.35**
**206-1010182** 3V w/8" Black Wire **1.49**
**206-10101822** 3V w/8" Black Wire pkg(100) **126.66**

## Screw Base Bulb

**206-10107** 12V **1.09**

## Bulb Socket

**206-10108** With 8" Black Wires **1.09**

## Grain-Of-Rice Bulbs

Bulbs consume between 35 and 45 mA at 12V. Outside diameter approximately 3/32".

**206-10106** 12V w/8" Black Wire **1.30**
**206-101020** 12V w/12" Brown Wire **1.59**
**206-101023** 12V w/8" Brown Wire **1.49**
**206-101062** 12V w/8" White Wire **1.30**
**206-101063** 16V w/8" Black Wire **1.30**

## Micro Bulbs 1.5V (1.4mm) 1.59 ea (Unless Noted)

**206-101013** With Black Wires
**206-101014** With White Wires
**206-101015** With Wire Terminals
**206-1010130** With Black Wire pkg(100) **135.15**

## Swivel Spotlight

**206-101010 3.25**
Miniature swivel spotlight features top-mounted 360° rotation and 180° side-to-side movement. Large size bulb has a highly focused lens for light concentration and will burn for 5000+ hours. Bulb snaps in and works on a 12V system. 7/8" long, 3/8" diameter.

# ACCESSORIES

## Wood Screws

**206-1045** #0 pkg(20) **1.80**
Measure 7/16" long x .060". Useful wherever small fasteners are required.

## Terminal Blocks

**206-1049** 2-Pole **3.75**
**206-10491** 4-Pole **4.10**
**206-10492** 6-Pole **4.39**
**206-10494** Terminal Block Jumpers 6-Pack **2.98**

## SUPER BRIGHT 100,000 HOUR LEDS

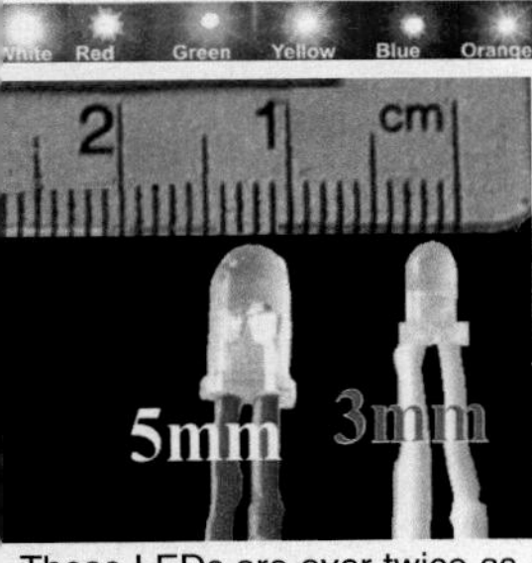


These LEDs are over twice as bright as comparable sized incandescent lights, with less than half the power consumption: only 20mA. All lights have water clear lens for truer colors. Each LED comes fully assembled and ready to hook up to any track power source.

## NEW PRODUCTS

### Solid LEDs pkg(5)

**Universal Input 5-19V**

**1.8mm 22.00 ea.**

**NEW 266-U11** Cool White
**NEW 266-U12** Blue
**NEW 266-U13** Red
**NEW 266-U14** Yellow
**NEW 266-U15** Green

**3mm 20.00 ea**

**NEW 266-U30** Warm White
**NEW 266-U31** Cool White
**NEW 266-U32** Blue
**NEW 266-U33** Red
**NEW 266-U34** Yellow
**NEW 266-U35** Green
**NEW 266-U36** Orange

**5mm 20.00 ea**

**NEW 266-U50** Warm White
**NEW 266-U51** Cool White
**NEW 266-U52** Blue
**NEW 266-U53** Red
**NEW 266-U54** Yellow
**NEW 266-U55** Green
**NEW 266-U56** Orange

**DC 4-13V**

**1.8mm 22.00 ea**

**NEW 266-DC11** Cool White
**NEW 266-DC12** Blue
**NEW 266-DC13** Red
**NEW 266-DC14** Yellow
**NEW 266-DC15** Green

**3mm 16.00 ea**

**NEW 266-DC30** Warm White
**NEW 266-DC31** Cool White
**NEW 266-DC32** Blue
**NEW 266-DC33** Red
**NEW 266-DC34** Yellow
**NEW 266-DC35** Green
**NEW 266-DC36** Orange

**5mm 16.00 ea**

**NEW 266-DC50** Warm White
**NEW 266-DC51** Cool White
**NEW 266-DC52** Blue
**NEW 266-DC53** Red
**NEW 266-DC54** Yellow
**NEW 266-DC55** Green
**NEW 266-DC56** Orange

### Bi-Directional 3mm Pre-Wired Red/Green LEDs

**NEW 266-BD1** Single **4.49**
**NEW 266-BD5** Set of 5 **20.00**

### Flashing LEDs pkg(5)

An integrated circuit creates the flash effect. Flash rate is slow, suitable for trains and warning beacons. No circuit board is needed. 1.5HZ flash speed.

**Universal Input 5-19V 22.00 ea**

**3mm**

**NEW 266-U31F** Cool White
**NEW 266-U32F** Blue
**NEW 266-U33F** Red
**NEW 266-U34F** Yellow
**NEW 266-U35F** Green

**5mm**

**NEW 266-U51F** Cool White
**NEW 266-U52F** Blue
**NEW 266-U53F** Red
**NEW 266-U54F** Yellow
**NEW 266-U55F** Green

**DC 4-13V 16.00 ea**

**3mm**

**NEW 266-DC31F** Cool White
**NEW 266-DC32F** Blue
**NEW 266-DC33F** Yellow
**NEW 266-DC35F** Green

**5mm**

**NEW 266-DC50F** Cool White
**NEW 266-DC52F** Blue
**NEW 266-DC53F** Red
**NEW 266-DC54F** Yellow
**NEW 266-DC55F** Green

### Fire Packs

LEDs flash at a random rate creating a realistic fire effect. Pack contains three different LEDs: one solid orange and one each flashing yellow and flashing red.

**DC 9.00 ea**

**NEW 266-DC3F** 3mm
**NEW 266-DC5F** 5mm

**Universal Input 12.00 ea**

**NEW 266-U5F** 5mm
**NEW 266-U3F** 3mm

### Welding Packs pkg(3)

These fully assembled lights are a combination of three LEDs: two flashing white and one solid blue. Varied flash rates give a realistically random effect. No circuit board needed.

**NEW 266-DC3W** 3mm DC **9.00**
**NEW 266-DC5W** 3mm Universal Input **12.00**

### Flashing LEDs pkg(5) 20.00 ea

Flashing LEDs have a built-in flashing circuit. They're ideal for warning signs, emergency vehicles and more.

**12V 5mm Diameter**

**266-BL213F** Red
**266-BL214F** Yellow

**12V 3mm Diameter**

**266-BL313F** Red
**266-BL314F** Yellow

**18V 5mm Diameter**

**266-BL213F18** Red
**266-BL214F18** Yellow

**18V 3mm Diameter**

**266-BL313F18** Red
**266-BL314F18** Yellow

## FALLER

IMPORTED FROM GERMANY BY WALTHERS

## LIGHTING

### Structure Light

**272-180670 1.99**
Set comes with bulb, lighting socket, cables and plugs.

### Micro Bulbs

**272-180677** White, 12-16V AC 35mA w/Wire Leads pkg(3) **6.99**

### 12-16V Grain-Of-Wheat Bulbs 3.49 ea

**272-180671** Clear
**272-180672** Red
**272-180673** Yellow
**272-180674** Green
**272-180676** Blue

### Platform Lighting

**272-180644 28.99**
Illuminate any HO or N Scale station platform with this 30cm assembly of six lamps.

### Flashing Lights

**272-180689** 16V AC (red) pkg(2) **8.99**

Latest New Product News Daily! Visit Walthers Web site at
**www.walthers.com**

## ELECTRICAL ACCESSORIES

### Plug Strip

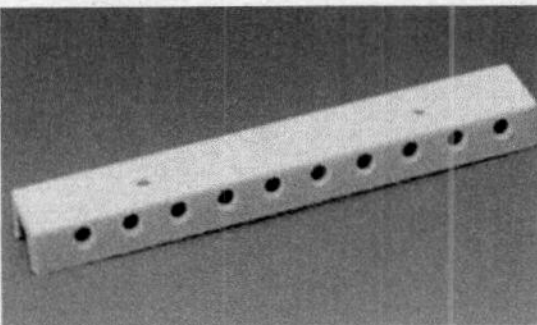

**272-180686 4.99**
Features 10 pairs of sockets.

### Synchronous Motors

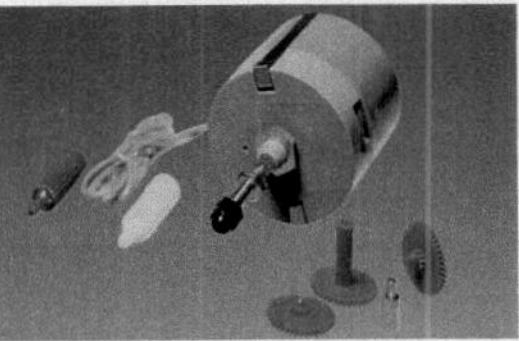

**272-180629 33.99**
Speed of 4/15 RPM. Revolves clockwise or counterclockwise. 16V AC.

**272-180628** Extra Power **39.99**
Provides 35% more power than #272-180629 for a variety of applications. Speed of 4/15 RPM, with reversible rotation. 12-16V AC, 60mA.

## KATO

**381-7502** Passenger Light Kit with White LED **17.00**
Recommended for use with DCC. Includes filter to alter lighting effect from white fluorescent to yellowish incandescent.

### Motors

**381-31500** HM 5 w/Double Shaft **19.98**
Excellent for repowering projects. 60mm overall length. Each shaft 11.6mm.

# LIGHTING KITS

## Electronic Lighthouse Beacon

Kit provides a realistic "rotating beam" effect with moving parts or mechanical assemblies. Bulb rapidly ramps up to full brightness, then slowly dims to give the illusion of a rotating beacon. This gives a more realistic look to any lighthouse, rather than using a permanent "on" or flasher-type bulb.

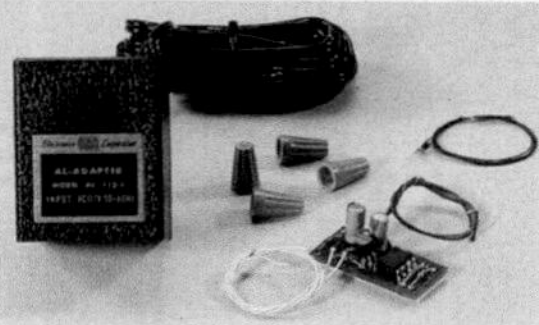

**296-1007** HO or N Scale **29.95**

**296-10071** O Scale **34.95**

**296-10072** 1/12 or G Scale **69.95**

## Litepac

Powers up to 25 1.5V, 15mA (400mA) micro bulbs on a layout diorama or module using any 4-20V AC power source. Unlike other AC transformers, the Litepac provides a fully regulated and filtered DC voltage that can extend bulb life up to 50%. A "Bulb Saver" circuit helps prevent harmful AC over-voltage conditions from destroying delicate 1.5V micro bulbs. Litepac comes fully assembled with built-in over-load protection, instructions and mounting hardware.

**296-125** 1.5V Converter/ Regulator **34.95**

**296-135** 1.5V Converter/ Regulator w/12-Pack #100 Micro-Bulbs **49.95**

## Micro Flamemaker

**296-1000 27.50**
Unit simulates flickering light produced by a small bonfire or campfire. 6-20V AC or DC. Use with all scales. 1 x 1 x 3/8" circuit board.

**296-205** Micro Flamemaker Replacement Bulbs **3.49**

## Slow Micro Flasher

**296-1001 27.50**
Consists of a 1 x 1" flasher board and two clear micro bulbs. Flash rate of four-second-on/two-second-off simulates flash rate on billboards, marquees and commercial signs. 12-20V AC/DC.

## Fast Micro Flashers 27.50 ea

Basically the same as #296-1001, but with flash rate of one-second-on and -off to simulate vehicle turn signals, traffic lights or road signals.

**296-1002** 2 Clear Bulbs

**296-10021** 1 Red Bulb, 1 Amber Bulb

## Micro Strobe

**296-1003 27.50**
Basically the same as #296-1001, but with a short, strobe-like flash every two seconds. Includes two strobe-blue micro bulbs. Use as tower warning lights, strobes or on emergency vehicles.

## Vehicle Lighting Kits

Kits come complete with assembled electronics, heavy-duty microbulbs, hardware and instructions. 6-20V AC or DC.

**296-1005** Rotating Beacon (red) **27.50**

**296-1011** Rotating Beacon (amber) **27.50**

**296-1008** Dual Litebar (2 red/ 2 blue) **39.95**

**296-1012** Basic Vehicle Lighting Kit **17.95**

## Super Flamemaker

**296-1004 27.50**
Unit simulates larger fires such as a working blast furnace or burning structure. Use in any scale. 16-20V AC. Circuit board, 1 x 1 x 5/8" high. Bulb assembly, 3/16" diameter x 7/8" long.

**296-300** Super Flamemaker Replacement Bulbs **2.95**

## Street Lights

296-302

296-303

**296-302** Frosted Globe Streetlight Kit **7.98**
Kit includes 1/16" diameter post adjustable to 12 HO Scale feet, 6mm frosted globe, #100 microbulbs and instructions. Use for N through S Scales.

**296-301** Frosted Globe Lamp **6.98**
Same as #296-302, except no brass tube included. Bulbs glued in globe.

**296-303** Oldtyme Gas Streetlight Kit **7.98**
Same as #296-302, except with tapered transparent lens and black plastic cap.

## Super Microbulbs 1.59 ea (Unless Noted)

These tiny light bulbs are perfect for use with signals, headlights or wherever space is limited. Bulbs work on 1.5V DC, draw 15mA of current and measure 1.4mm in diameter. Designed for long life.

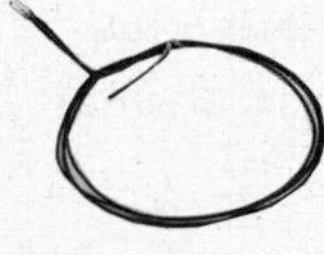

**296-100** Clear

**296-101** Red

**296-102** Green

**296-103** Amber

**296-104** Flame

**296-106** Strobe Blue

**296-10001** Clear pkg(25) **37.76**

## 3.0V Super GOR Bulbs 1.49 ea

Use wherever a larger, high-quality bulb is needed. Measures approximately .092" and draws 40 mA at 3.0V. 5,000 hours of life. The arc blue and rose bulbs are replacement bulbs for the #296-1013 Ultimate Arc Welder.

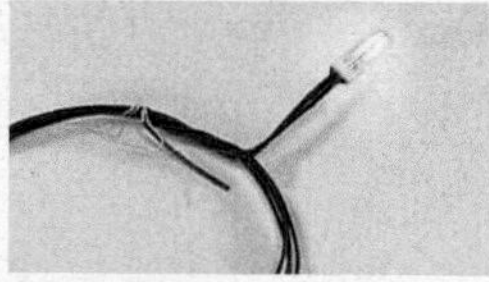

**296-501** Blue

**296-502** Rose

**296-503** Flame

**296-504** Clear

## Heavy Duty Fluorette Bulbs

Can be used to light interiors of buildings or passenger cars. 12-16V AC or DC.

**296-400** Frosted **1.69**

**296-401** Frosted pkg(6) **8.49**

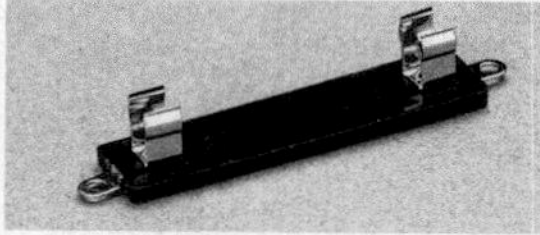

**296-402** Lamp Holder **2.19**

**296-403** Lamp Holder pkg(6) **11.00**

## Ultimate Microbulbs

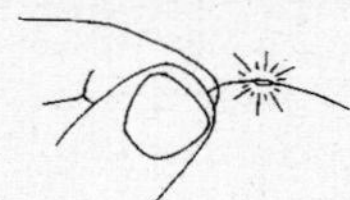

**296-500 2.39**
Can be used for working headlights, ditch, marker, or numberboard light on locos and caboose marker lights. Measures a mere 0.75mm in diameter and draws 15mA of current at 1.5V.

## Green Shade Lamp

**296-105 4.95**
Typical outdoor/security lamp, interior lighting for warehouse, roundhouse and engine repair shops, and is suitable for all types of buildings. Includes clear micro bulb, painted metal shade and instructions. HO and N Scales.

## 2-Pin Micro-Connector

Gold plated, assembled.

**296-906** With 5" Color-Coded Leads (1 Set) **4.95**

**296-907** Less Leads (2 Sets) **5.95**

## Ultimate Arc Welder

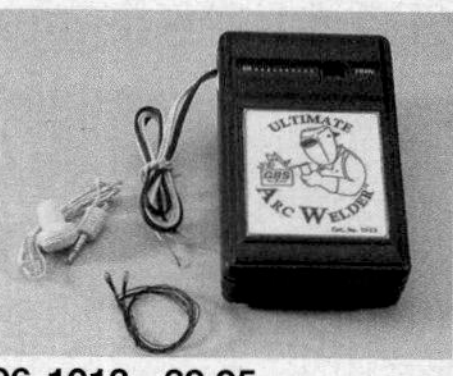


**296-1013 39.95**
Adjustable action and brightness to model the color and sporadic action of an actual arc welder. Great in railroad shops like Allied Rail Rebuilders. Includes assembled driver, blue- and rose-colored lamps (can be viewed directly or indirectly) and mounting Velcro for driver. 12-20V AC/DC required.

# MOTORS

## 1.5V DC Ultimate Micro Motor

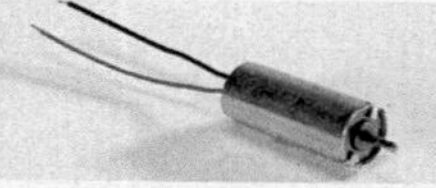

**296-600 19.95**
Motor: 0.28" dia., 0.67" long; Shaft: 0.038" (1.0mm) dia., 0.16" Long.

Perhaps the smallest electrical motor to be found in the model railroad industry. Not a toy motor; built for military standards. Use for static model aircraft, boats, working saw mills and conveyors. Draws 35mA at 1.5V DC, 120mA at 3.0V DC.

## Motor Controller

**296-601 27.50**
While this controller was designed especially for use with Micro Motor #296-600 (sold separately), it can work with any 1.5-3V motor that draws up to 300mA of current. Uses pulse modulation to create a wide range of speeds. Thermal limiting protects unit from damage if motor shorts or stalls.

# WIRE MANAGEMENT PRODUCTS

## Cable Clamps

Feature uncolored nylon.

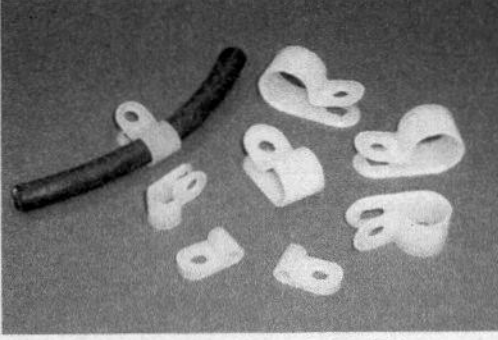

**357-1214** 1/8" Inside Diameter pkg(15) **1.85**

**357-1215** 1/4" Inside Diameter pkg(15) **1.85**

**357-1216** 3/8" Inside Diameter pkg(15) **2.15**

**357-1217** 1/2" Inside Diameter pkg(15) **2.95**

## Cable Tie Mounts pkg(15) 2.85 ea

These adhesive-backed cable tie mounts will secure cable ties to any clean, flat surface. Cable ties slide into any of the four sides for easy application. Feature uncolored nylon.

**357-1210** 1/2" Square

**357-1211** 3/4" Square

## Cable Ties

Nylon cable ties for wire organization and many other uses. Bent tip design for ease of insertion.

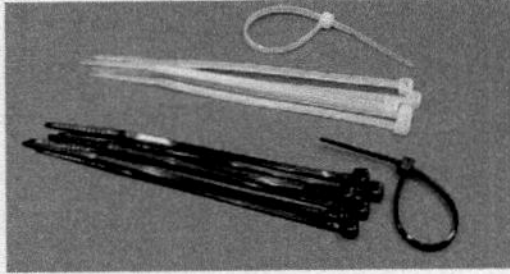

**357-1200** 4" Long, uncolored Nylon, pkg(100) **2.95**

**357-1201** 4" Long, Black Nylon, pkg(100) **3.25**

**357-1203** 5-1/2" Long, Mixed Colors Nylon pkg(100) **3.95**

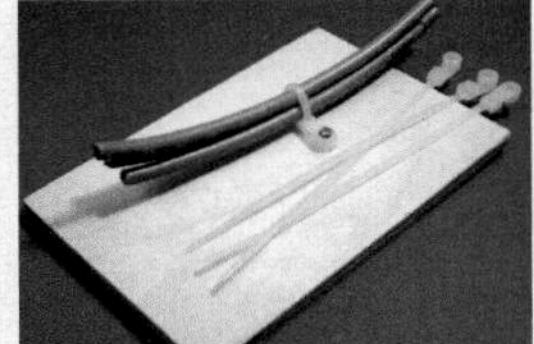

**357-1204** 4" long, Screw-Mount pkg(20) **4.95**

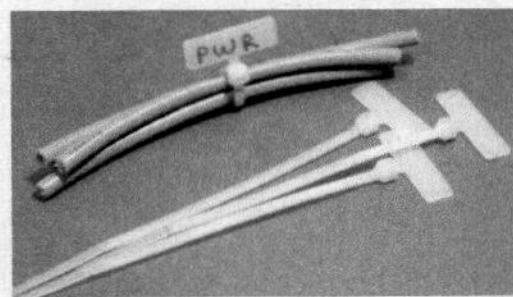


**357-1205** 4" long, Flag pkg(20) **4.95**

## Spiral Wire Wrap

Spiral polyethylene wrap organizes wires and cables. Simple to apply and very flexible, it also protects wire bundles from sharp edges and repeated handling. Solvent and abrasion resistant. Each package includes three three-foot sections of varying diameters for a total of nine linear feet. Bundling range 1/16 to 3". Multiple colors allow easy color coding of wire bundles.

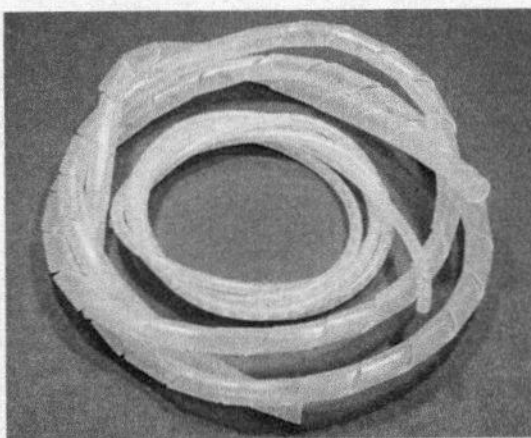

**357-1225** Natural Color, Mixed Diameters 1/8", 1/4" and 3/8" **5.95**

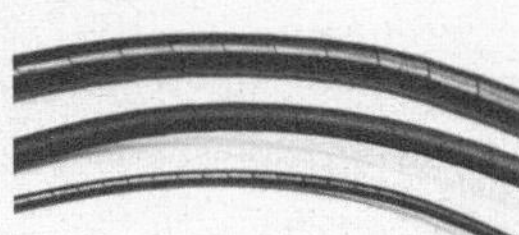

**357-1226** Red, Mixed Diameters 1/4", 3/8" and 1/2" **6.25**

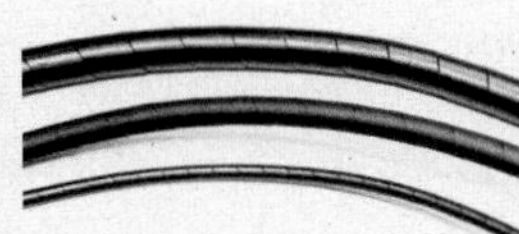

**357-1227** Black, Mixed Diameters 1/8", 1/4" and 3/8" **6.75**

## Terminal Block

**357-1209** 3-1/2" Long, 12-Position, 3 Amp **2.75**

## Test Clip Set

**357-1208 9.95**
Includes 10 24" long, 28-gauge alligator-clip leads in five colors.

## Wire Twist Locks

A simple and easy way to organize groups of wires or small cables. Can be untwisted and used again. Feature uncolored nylon.

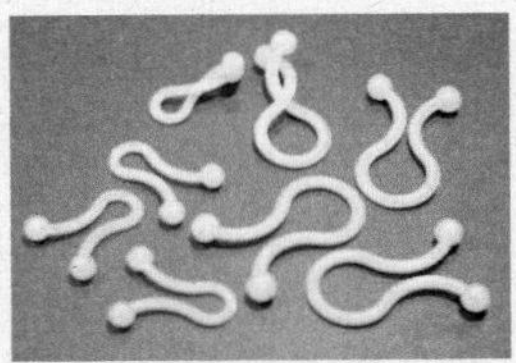

**357-1220** 1/4" Inside Diameter pkg(15) **1.85**

**357-1221** 1/2" Inside Diameter pkg(15) **2.45**

# WIRE

All purpose, color-coded, flexible pre-tinned wire.

**490-5201** 1 Conductor Red pkg(400') **24.25**

**490-5202** 2 Conductor Red, Black pkg(200') **27.50**

**490-5203** 3 Conductor Red, White, Black pkg(100') **24.24**

**490-5204** 4 Conductor Red, White, Yellow, Black pkg(100') **26.50**

**490-2301** 1 Conductor cd **2.39**

**490-2302** 2 Conductor cd **2.39**

**490-2303** 3 Conductor cd **2.39**

**490-2304** 4 Conductor cd **2.39**

**490-2310** 18 Gauge Wire 1 Conductor pkg(25') **3.29**

**490-2311** 18 Gauge Wire 2 Conductor pkg(12.5') **3.29**

**490-2299** 2 Spools #1 Conductor Wire, Extra Fine-2 Colors pkg(50') **2.39**

**490-5219** 18 Gauge 1 lead 250' **33.00**

**490-5220** 18 Gauge 2 lead 125' **35.00**

# BULBS

## 14V Grain of Sand pkg(3) 5.99 ea

**490-146** Clear, 1.2mm

**490-147** Red, 1.2mm

**490-148** Green, 1.2mm

**490-149** Amber, 1.2mm

## Grain of Rice

### 1.5V pkg(3) 4.49 ea

**490-152** Clear, 2.2mm

**490-153** Red, 2.2mm

**490-154** Green, 2.2mm

**490-155** Amber, 2.2mm

### 3V

**490-345** Clear, 150mA pkg(3) **4.39**

### 14V pkg(3) 4.49 ea

**490-252** Clear, 2.2mm

**490-253** Red, 2.2mm

**490-254** Green, 2.2mm

**490-255** Amber, 2.2mm

## Grain of Wheat

### 1.5V

**490-344** Pointed, 150mA pkg(3) **4.49**

### 3V pkg(3) 3.59 ea

**490-391** Clear, 3.2mm

**490-392** Red, 3.2mm

**490-393** Green, 3.2mm

**490-394** Amber, 3.2mm

### 14V pkg(3) 3.59 ea

**490-381** Clear, 3.2mm

**490-382** Red, 3.2mm

**490-383** Green, 3.2mm

**490-384** Amber, 3.2mm

## 14V Gas Pea Lamps pkg(2) 3.89 ea

**490-395** Clear, 6mm

**490-396** White, 6mm

## Headlights pkg(3) 4.49 ea

**490-340** 16V 70mA Wired Flat Head

**490-341** 14V 70mA Flat Head Screw

**490-342** 14V Oval Screw

**490-343** 14V Oval Bayonet

## Bayonet Base pkg(2) 3.29 ea (Unless Noted)

### 6V

**490-51960** #51 Clear

### 14V

**490-398** Pointed, w/14V G-O-W Bulbs pkg(3) **4.39**

**490-53961** #53 Clear

**490-53962** #53 Red

**490-257961** Clear

**490-257962** #257 Red

**490-363960** #363 Clear

### 18V

**490-1445960** #1445 Clear

## Building Lights

**490-491** Socket Stand & Bulb pkg(2) **3.99**

**490-492** 12V w/Screw Base pkg(6) **6.99**

**490-9898** Fire Lighting **6.50**

**490-10096** With Screw Base pkg(2) **3.89**

## Lamp Post Bulbs

**490-10095** pkg(2) **3.89**

## Screw Base pkg(2) 3.29 ea

### 14V

**490-1449960** #1449 Clear

**490-1449961** #1449 Red

**490-1449962** #1449 Green

**490-258960** #258 Clear

**490-430960** #430 Clear

**490-432961** #432 Clear

**490-432962** #432 Red

**490-461960** #461 Clear

### 18V

**490-1447960** #1447 Clear

## 1.5V Sub Mini

**490-145** Clear, 12.5mA pkg(3) **5.49**
Angel Hair 1.2mm.

## 3V Brite

**490-397** Clear, G-O-W pkg(3) **4.39**

## 14V Blinker pkg(2) 3.89 ea

Blinks after 20-second warm-up.

**490-10097** Clear, 250mA

**490-10098** Red, 250mA

**490-10099** Amber, 250mA

## Peel 'N Stick Bulbs

Clear, 12" leads.

### 12-16V

**490-510** Set of 4 **3.98**

**490-511** Set of 24 **16.98**

See What's Available at
**www.walthers.com**

# Miniatronics

"electronics for the hobbyist"

Miniatronics offers an extensive variety of electrical components, lamps, LEDs and special effects lighting units that are just the thing for adding realistic lighting to your layout. Most products are usable in any scale. Signs, street lamps and scale-specific products designed for HO are often appropriate for use in other scales as larger or smaller fixtures.

## INTERIOR CAR LIGHTING UNITS

For easy installation we have included one set of Phosphor Bronze Electrical Track Pickups and double sided mounting tape with each unit. If board is too long, one segment can be broken off to fit specific car.These units are voltage regulated and rectified and have the ability to run on AC or DC. 14VAC will work with DCC. 6VDC starts to light at 4-5 volts for those operating DC layouts. Maintains lighted mode for up to 4 minutes after power is turned off.

### Passenger 25.95 ea

**NEW 475-100YCL01** Passenger Car Yeloglo
Uses Yeloglo technology to simulate the look of incandescent bulbs for 1940 vintage and earlier. 7 LEDs. Draws 42mA of current.

**475-100ICL01** Passenger Car
Unit has 7 LEDs and draws a low 42mA of current. Three resistors let you dim light for sleeper cars.

### Caboose 22.95 ea

**NEW 475-100YCB01** Caboose Yeloglo
Uses Yeloglo technology to simulate the look of incandescent bulbs for 1940 vintage and earlier. 6 LEDs. Draws 36mA of current.

**NEW 475-100CB201** Caboose
Will fit most standard cabooses. 6 LEDs. Use for 1950s and later. Draws 36mA of current.

### Electrical Pickup

**NEW 475-5500104** Phosphor Bronze Electrical Track Pickup 2 sets **5.95**
With plastic trucks there is no place to solder, and using a screw does not work. The solution is to use wheel sets with metal axles and a pickup wire that rubs on the axle.

## ELECTRAK CLEANERS

Don't let grime or dirt slow down your railroad! Electrak Cleaners simplify track cleaning, especially in those hard-to-reach places. Works without abrasives, chemicals, rollers or pads while you run your trains. Safe for engines, wheels and DCC.

**475-PEC31** Electrak Clean III **99.95**
Trackside version with the same amazing cleaning power. Completely assembled and housed in a box. Unit uses high-energy impulses between the wheels and track. Not effective on pitted, rusted or warped tracks.

**475-PEC21** Electrak Clean II **119.95**
Electrak Clean II uses high-energy electrostatic impulses between its metal wheels and the tracks and is powered by track power. Housed in an Athearn F7B unit and equipped with McHenry knuckle couplers, simply push it with any loco.

## ELECTRICAL ACCESSORIES

### Micro Mini Connectors

Fully assembled with mated interlock assembly. Great for lighting, wiring, command control applications and special effects wiring. Connectors and attached wires have polarity markings for use as an indicator. Not recommended for powering rolling stock or other high-current applications. Rated at 1 amp.

**475-5000102** 2 Pin, 12" Flexible Leads 2 Sets **10.95**

**475-5000301** 3 Pin, 12" Flexible Leads 1 Set **9.95**

**475-5000401** 4 Pin, 12" Flexible Leads 1 Set **10.95**

**475-5050201** 2 Pin Waterproof; Rated 2AMP 1 Set **13.95**

### Power Distribution Block

**475-PDB1** 12 Position **19.95**
Hook up two wires from power source to the binding posts on a heavy-duty PC board. Can use either AC or DC power source. Prewired, rated @ 15 amps. Comes with mounting feet. Brings power to your accessories.

**475-PDB2** 24 Position **32.95**
Designed for maximum 24 accessories AC/DC. Rated at 15 amps.

### Switches

#### Magnetic Reed Switches

**475-3205805** With Matching Magnets pkg(5) **9.95**
These magnetically-activated switches make momentary contact when a magnet passes over them. Use them to trigger turnouts, signals or indicator lights on your layout.

#### Micro Leaf Switches

SPDT, 3A, 120V

**475-3401004** pkg(4) **6.95**

**475-3401008** pkg(8) **12.45**

#### Push Buttons

SPST momentary, normally open.

**475-3302502** 1/4" (1 red, 1 black) pkg(2) **5.25**

**475-3310004** 1/2" (2 red, 2 green) pkg(4) **7.85**

#### Six-Position Rotary Switch

**475-3562001 11.50**
Enclosed, two-pole with non-shorting contacts. 2.5 amps, includes knob. Good for switching blocks and throttles.

#### Sub-Miniature Latching Switch

**475-3301806** pkg(6) **7.30**
Single pole, single throw; rated 1 Amp 24V DC; 5/16" Diameter

#### Toggle Switches

**Sub Miniature**

DPDT, 3A, 120V, with solder lugs, 3/16" diameter threaded bushing mount.

**475-3610002** pkg(2) **5.95**

**475-3610005** pkg(5) **13.50**

**Miniature**

5A, 120V, with solder lugs, 1/4" diameter threaded bushing mount.

**SPDT**

**475-3621004** SPDT pkg(4) **7.50**

**475-3621008** SPDT pkg(8) **12.95**

**475-3622002** SPDT Center Off, Momentary/Spring Return pkg(2) **5.95**

**475-3622005** SPDT Center Off, Momentary/Spring Return pkg(5) **13.90**

**475-3623004** SPDT Center Off pkg(4) **11.50**

**475-3623008** SPDT Center Off pkg(8) **19.95**

**DPDT**

3625008 3626008 3627005

**475-3625004** DPDT pkg(4) **10.75**

**475-3625008** DPDT pkg(8) **17.95**

**475-3626004** DPDT Center Off pkg(4) **11.50**

**475-3626008** DPDT Center Off pkg(8) **19.95**

**475-3627002** DPDT Center Off, Momentary/Spring Return pkg(2) **6.50**

**475-3627005** DPDT Center Off, Momentary/Spring Return pkg(5) **14.95**

Single pole, single throw on/off switches; 5 amps, 120V.

**475-3620004** pkg(4) **6.50**

**475-3620008** pkg(8) **11.55**

#### Slide Switches

3805004 3810005 3820005

**475-3805004** Micro Miniature SPDT pkg(4) **4.25**

**475-3810005** Sub Miniature SPDT pkg(5) **3.95**

**475-3820005** Sub Miniature DPDT pkg(4) **4.25**

### Opto Sensors

**475-3900104** pkg(4) **9.45**
Light-sensitive Opto Sensors can be used wherever you need a detection device. Strategically placed sensor activates when light is blocked from the face. Requires an electronic circuit for activation.

### Terminal Block

**475-TB4** 2-3/16 x 7/8", 4-Screw Double Row pkg(3) **4.95**

**475-TB10** 10 Screw, Double Row pkg(3) **9.75**
4-1/2 x 7/8" 11.2 x 2.1cm.

### Heat Shrink Tubing

Shrinks to half its diameter to fit many irregular shapes.

**475-HST36410** 3/64" Size, 10' Long **7.95**

**475-HST10** 10' **7.95**
Five sizes included 3/64, 1/16, 3/32, 1/8 and 3/16"

### Capacitive Discharge Unit

**475-PDC1 32.95**
Fully assembled unit operates up to ten switch machines simultaneously. Easy to connect.

### Automatic Reversing Units

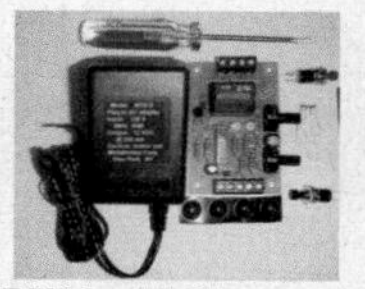

**475-RU11 45.95**
Automatically reverses from one point to another. Value-added package includes sensing device, push button switches, mounting feet, heat shrink tubing, transformer and screwdriver. 3 amps.

**475-RU21 99.95**
Easy way to automate trolleys, displays or other layouts. This unit will handle from two to five stops and stop time is adjustable. Unit operates under varied lighting conditions and includes self-adjusting sensors, which can be installed where needed. Value-added package is complete with 12-Volt transformer, 50' of 28 gauge, two-conductor wire, heat shrink tubing, and wood screws.

# Miniatronics
"electronics for the hobbyist"

## Transformers

**475-WT3** 3V DC @ 200mA **7.35**
Can run three electro-luminescent neon-like signs off one transformer!

**475-WT12** Regulated, 12V DC @ 1 Amp **17.95**
Good for any application that requires a regulated power source.

**NEW 475-WT16** Plug-In Wall Transformer **10.95**
Operates up to 25 Miniatronics 16V lampposts. 16AC @ 800mA.

**475-WT412** Filtered 12V DC, 400mA **9.45**
Use with Miniatronics Two Directional Lights, Light House Warning Beacon and other lighting effects. Can power from one to four units.

**475-WT1515** Regulated 1.5V DC @ 1.5 Amp **25.95**
Includes free 10 1.5V 15mA bulbs, will handle up to 100 1.5V 15mA bulbs.

## 8 OHM Speakers

**475-6007501** 3/4" Round x 3/16" High (Fits N & HO Scale) **4.95**

475-6007801 475-6011201

**475-6007801** 7/8" Round x 5/16" High (Fits HO, O, G & #1 Scales) **4.95**

**475-6011201** 1-1/8" Round x 9/16" High (Fits HO, O, G & #1 Scales) **4.95**

475-6011501 475-6011601

**475-6011501** 15mm x 25mm 1 Watt **9.95**

**475-6011601** 16mm x 35mm 1 Watt **9.95**

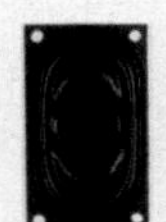

475-6012001 475-6012801

**475-6012001** 20mm x 35mm 1 Watt **9.95**

**475-6012801** 28mm x 40mm 2 Watts **10.95**

## Solder

### 60/40 Rosin Core Solder

Melting temperature 374 degrees Fahrenheit

**475-1064004** 4oz **7.60**

**NEW 475-1064016** 1lb **19.95**

**NEW 475-1064501** 1/2oz **1.85**

### Solder Paste

**NEW 475-1065002** 2 oz **2.78**
Cleans and pretins solder tip in preparation for next solder joint.

## LIGHTING

### Neon-Like Signs 16.95 ea

These fully assembled neon signs are designed to fit most structures. Requires 12V power source. Each measures 1-1/8 x 1-5/8". Signs can be made to flash by adding either of Miniatronics Variable Lamp Flashers #100N0101 or #100N0201, both sold separately.

**475-7501101** Beer On Tap (green)

**475-7501201** Café (violet)
**475-7501401** Ice Cream (white)
**475-7501501** Joe's Diner Home Cooking (red)
**475-7501601** Motel – No Vacancy (yellow)
**475-7501701** Open 24 Hours (red)
**475-7501801** Pizza (red)
**475-7502101** Christmas Tree Image (green)
**475-7503801** Pork Store (pink)
**475-7503901** Auto Repairs (green)
**475-7504101** Barber Shop (red)
**475-7504401** Optician (white)
**475-7504501** Train Store (red)
**475-7506101** Deli Cold Beer (yellow)
**475-7506201** Hot Coffee (orange)
**475-7506401** Keys Made Here (violet)
**475-7506501** Root Beer (white)

Items listed below are available by Special Order (see Legend Page).

**475-7501901** Shoe Repairs (green)
**475-7502001** Saloon Fine Food (orange)
**475-7502201** Happy Holidays (red)
**475-7502301** Merry Christmas (green)
**475-7502401** Season's Greetings (red)
**475-7503501** RX (white)
**475-7503601** Bakery (pink)
**475-7503701** Florist (violet)
**475-7504001** Liquors (pink)
**475-7504201** Hardware (orange)
**475-7504301** Pet Store (yellow)
**475-7504601** Bike Repairs (yellow)
**475-7504701** Beauty Parlor (pink)
**475-7504801** Fresh Fish (orange)
**475-7506001** Cigars (red)
**475-7506301** Hot Dogs (red)
**475-7506601** Shamrock Café (green)
**475-7506701** TV & Radio Repairs (red)

## Incandescent Lamps

All lamps have 8" insulated leads unless noted by an asterisk (*).

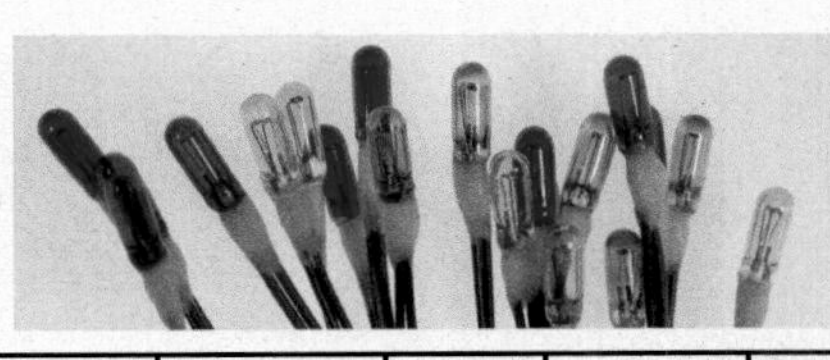

| COLOR | VOLTAGE | mA | mm Diameter | HOURS | PKG | PRICE | Item # |
|---|---|---|---|---|---|---|---|
| Clear-axial** | 1.5 | 20 | 0.75 | 1,000 | 10 | 15.75 | 1807510 |
| Clear | 1.5 | 15 | 1.2 | 500 | 10 | 10.75 | 1800110 |
| Clear | 1.5 | 15 | 1.2 | 500 | 20 | 18.45 | 1800120 |
| Assorted (4 of each)* | 1.5 | 30 | 1.2 | 1,000 | 20 | 20.95 | 18A0320 |
| Blue* | 1.5 | 30 | 1.2 | 1,000 | 10 | 11.95 | 18B0310 |
| Clear* | 1.5 | 30 | 1.2 | 1,000 | 10 | 11.95 | 18C0310 |
| Green* | 1.5 | 30 | 1.2 | 1,000 | 10 | 11.95 | 18G0310 |
| Red* | 1.5 | 30 | 1.2 | 1,000 | 10 | 11.95 | 18R0310 |
| Yellow* | 1.5 | 30 | 1.2 | 1,000 | 10 | 11.95 | 18Y0310 |
| Clear | 1.5 | 40 | 1.7 | 5,000 | 10 | 14.25 | 1870110 |
| Clear | 1.5 | 40 | 1.7 | 5,000 | 20 | 25.45 | 1870120 |
| Clear | 1.5 | 40 | 2.4 | 1,000 | 10 | 10.95 | 1820110 |
| Clear | 1.5 | 40 | 2.4 | 1,000 | 20 | 17.95 | 1820120 |
| Clear | 12 | 30 | 1.7 | 5,000 | 10 | 14.25 | 1871210 |
| Clear | 12 | 30 | 1.7 | 5,000 | 20 | 25.45 | 1871220 |
| Clear | 12 | 50 | 2.4 | 10,000 | 10 | 10.75 | 1801210 |
| Clear | 12 | 50 | 2.4 | 10,000 | 20 | 18.45 | 1801220 |
| Assorted (5 of each) | 12 | 50 | 2.4 | 10,000 | 20 | 20.95 | 18A1220 |
| Blue | 12 | 50 | 2.4 | 10,000 | 10 | 11.95 | 18B1210 |
| Green | 12 | 50 | 2.4 | 10,000 | 10 | 11.95 | 18G1210 |
| Red | 12 | 50 | 2.4 | 10,000 | 10 | 11.95 | 18R1210 |
| Yellow | 12 | 50 | 2.4 | 10,000 | 10 | 11.95 | 18Y1210 |
| Clear | 14 | 30 | 2.4 | 16,000 | 10 | 11.45 | 1801410 |
| Clear | 14 | 30 | 2.4 | 16,000 | 20 | 18.95 | 1801420 |
| Clear | 16 | 30 | 2.4 | 10,000 | 10 | 11.45 | 1801610 |
| Clear | 16 | 30 | 2.4 | 10,000 | 20 | 18.95 | 1801620 |
| Clear | 6 | 40 | 5.5 | 10,000 | 10 | 10.75 | 1801810 |
| Clear | 6 | 40 | 5.5 | 10,000 | 20 | 18.45 | 1801820 |
| Clear | 12 | 50 | 5.5 | 10,000 | 10 | 10.75 | 1802410 |
| Clear | 12 | 50 | 5.5 | 10,000 | 20 | 18.45 | 1802420 |
| Clear | 14 | 80 | 5.5 | 10,000 | 10 | 10.75 | 1802810 |
| Clear | 14 | 80 | 5.5 | 10,000 | 20 | 18.45 | 1802820 |

** Bare wire leads *12" Insulated wire leads

### Flashing Multi-Color Neon-Like Signs 22.95 ea

These flashing neon signs, feature a built-in mechanism that allows one part to flash alternately from the rest of the sign. Each runs off a 3V power source, and can be used with either batteries or a 3V DC transformer. 1-1/8 x 1-5/8".

**475-75E1101** Beer On Tap (green, yellow)
**475-75E1201** Café (pink, blue)
**475-75E1501** Joe's Diner Home Cooking (red, green)
**475-75E1601** Motel No Vacancy (red, blue)
**475-75E1701** Open 24 Hours (red, blue)
**475-75E4001** Liquors (blue, pink, yellow)
**475-75E4201** Hardware (red, yellow)
**475-75E4501** Train Store (red)

Item listed below is available by Special Order (see Legend Page).

**475-75E1801** Pizza (red)

## Miniatronics
"electronics for the hobbyist"

### Street Lights
Lampposts are scaled for use with HO Scale equipment and feature 16V 30mA, 5,000-hour average life bulbs unless noted.

**475-7200901** Gas Lamp, 2" 10cm Tall (black) **15.95**

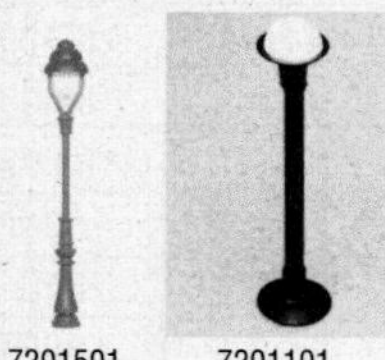

7201501 7201101

**475-7201501** Gas Lamp, 2-1/4" 5.6cm Tall (green) **15.95**

**475-7201101** Street Light, Half Globe, 12V 30mA Bulb, 1-7/8" 4.6cm Tall (black) **9.25**

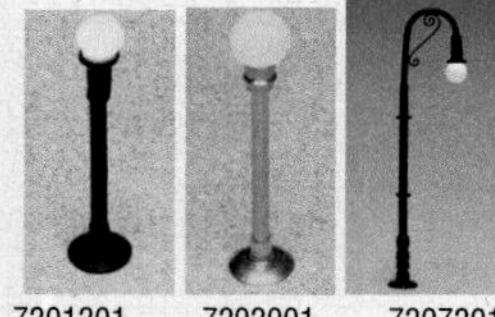

7201201 7202001 7207201

**475-7201201** Street Light, Full Globe, 12V 30mA Bulb, 1-3/4" 4.3cm Tall (black) **9.25**

**475-7202001** Park Lamppost (brass) 1-3/4" 4.3cm, 12V **9.25**

**475-7207201** Street Lamp (black) 2-1/2" 6.2cm **14.95**

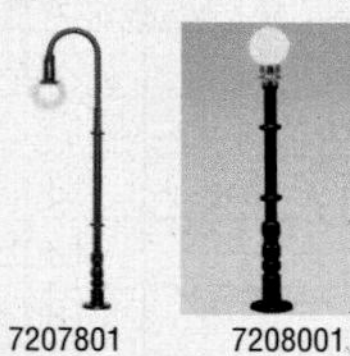

7207801 7208001

**475-7207801** Street Lamppost (black) 2-1/2" 6.2cm **14.95**

**475-7208001** Single Park Light (green) 2-1/4" 5.6cm **13.75**

**475-7208201** Double Park Light (green) 2-3/8" 5.9cm **19.25**

7208401 7208601

**475-7208401** Triple Park Light (green) 2-5/8" 6.5cm **23.95**

**475-7208601** Single Highway Light (gray) 2-3/4" 6.8cm **13.95**

7208801 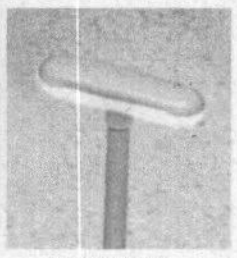 7209001

**475-7208801** Double Highway Light (gray) 2-3/4" 6.8cm **19.95**

**475-7209001** Dual Platform Light 2-7/8" 7.1cm **15.25**

7209601 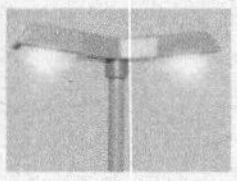 7209801

**475-7209601** Single Modern Lamppost (gray) 3-1/8" 7.8cm **13.95**

**475-7209801** Double Modern Lamppost (gray) 3-1/8" 7.8cm **20.95**

**475-7247201** Parking Field Light (Brass, without globe) 2-1/4" 5.6cm 12V **9.25**

475-7217201 475-7237201

**475-7217201** Parking Field Light (Brass) 2-1/4" 5.6cm 12V **9.25**

**475-7227201** Parking Field Light (black) 2-1/4" 5.6cm 12V **9.75**

**475-7237201** Parking Field Light (gray) 2-1/4" 5.6cm 12V **9.75**

### Lamp Shades

7210505 7211010

**475-7210505** With 12V 30mA Bulbs pkg(5) **11.95**

**475-7211505** With 1.5V 40mA Bulbs pkg(5) **11.95**

**475-7211010** Brass Lampshades Only pkg(10) **5.45**

**475-7231503** Painted Green w/White Interior (Bulbs included) pkg(3) **10.95**

### Outdoor Building Lights
Use these for the exterior of your structures.

**475-7200601** Decorative, Wall Mount **12.95**

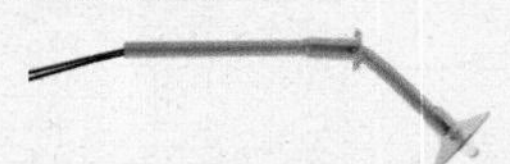

**475-7200702** Building/Billboard For Industrial Buildings pkg(2) **11.95**

### Platform Clock

**475-7211201** Double-Sided, Illuminated 16V **15.95**

### Spotlights

**475-7202801** Outdoor, Adjustable, 14-16V **15.45**

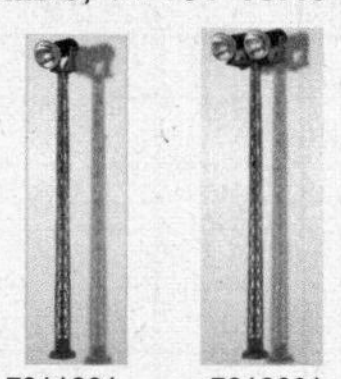

7211801 7212801

**475-7211801** Railyard Single Spotlight 5-1/2" 13.7cm **22.45**

**475-7212801** Railyard Double Spotlight 5-1/2" 13.7cm **30.45**

### String of Lights 23.95 ea

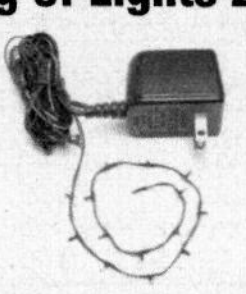

The 1.5V, 1.2mm diameter string of lights is fully assembled and connected to its own power source. String the lights around a building, used car lot or nursery; announce the grand opening of a store; use for platform light; string on a boat, theater or a Christmas tree!

**475-18WLT15** With 15 White Bulbs

**475-18XLT15** With 15 Colored Bulbs

### Light Emitting Diodes (LEDs)
A 470 ohm resistor is supplied with each LED.

#### Micro Mini 1/16" 1.5mm Diameter

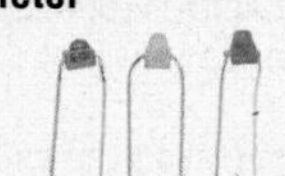

**475-1200018** 6 Each Red, Green & Yellow pkg(18) **9.95**

**475-1200112** Red pkg(12) **6.35**

**475-1200212** Green pkg(12) **6.35**

**475-1200312** Yellow pkg(12) **6.35**

#### Standard pkg(18) 7.95 ea
Six each red, green and yellow

**475-1203018** 1/8" 3mm Diameter

**475-1205018** 13/64" 5mm Diameter

#### White LEDs pkg(2) 7.95 ea
Must be used with a 560 ohm resistor, which is included with each package.

**475-1230002** 3mm Diameter

**475-1250002** 5mm Diameter

#### Blinker/Flasher Superbrite pkg(3) 5.50 ea

**3mm Diameter**

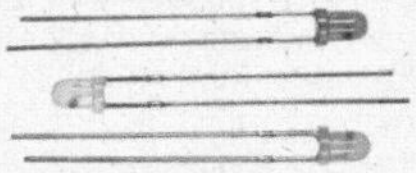

**475-1213003** One Each Red, Green & Yellow

**475-1213103** Red

**475-1213203** Green

**475-1213303** Yellow

**5mm Diameter**

**475-1215003** One Each Red, Green & Yellow

**475-1215103** Red

**475-1215203** Green

**475-1215303** Yellow

#### Bi-Directional Red/Green pkg(5) 4.75 ea

**1/8" 3mm Diameter**

**475-1222005** 2-Leg Style

**475-1223005** 3-Leg Style

**13/64" 5mm Diameter**

**475-1224005** 2-Leg Style

**475-1225005** 3-Leg Style

### Yeloglo LEDs
These LEDs feature a clear lens and combine the super-bright intensity of a white LED with the warm yellow glow of an incandescent lamp to make engine headlights more realistic. Choose from two different sizes. Two resistors for each LED are included in all sets.

#### Five-Pieces 8.95 ea

**475-1231005** 3mm Diameter

**475-1251005** 5mm Diameter

#### 10-Pieces 16.45 ea

**475-1231010** 3mm Diameter

**475-1251010** 5mm Diameter

### Yeloglo Ultra-Bright LED Headlights 14.95 ea
Operates on 4-16V DC.

**475-10031101** 3mm Diameter

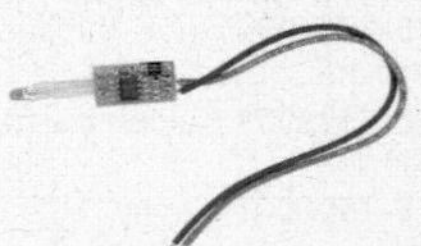

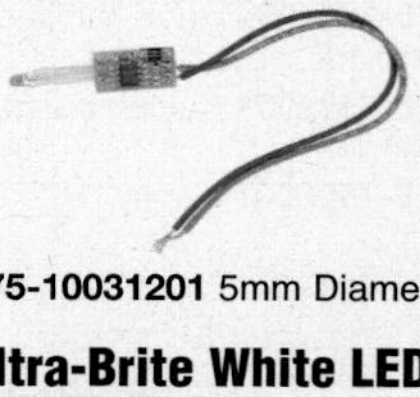

**475-10031201** 5mm Diameter

### Ultra-Brite White LED Headlight

**475-10030101** **17.55** Unit operates from track power or 4-16V DC. Board measures 5/16 x 5/8".

### Constant Lighting
Designed to fit in even the smallest of spaces, these units feature 12 inches of wire on a 1.5V bulb, and eight inches of wire for power hook-up. and a built-in surge protector.

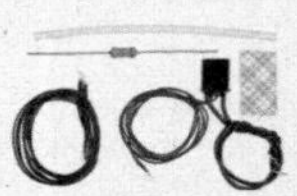

**475-CL01101** Forward Only **11.95**

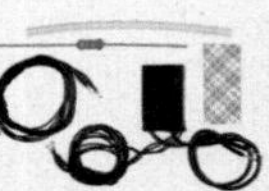

**475-CL01201** Forward/ Reverse **14.95**

**475-CL01301** Forward/ Reverse Dim (as in old steam engines) **14.95**

### Strobe Lights
Will operate on 9-14V AC/DC.

#### Single Simulated 13.95 ea

**475-100BS101** Blue

**475-100NS101** White

**475-100RS101** Red

**475-100YS101** Yellow

#### Dual Sychronized Simulate 15.95 ea

**475-100BS201** Blue

**475-100NS201** White

**475-100RS201** Red

**475-100YS201** Yellow

#### Alternating 19.95 ea

**475-100ABS01** Blue

**475-100ANS01** White

**475-100ARS01** Red

**475-100AYS01** Yellow

#### Adjustable 21.95 ea
Flash rate can be adjusted for variety of effects. Flash alternately or in unison. Operates on 9-14V AC/DC. Units now include bulbs

**Alternating Strobe**

**475-100AAB01** Blue

**475-100AAN01** White

**475-100AAR01** Red

**475-100AAY01** Yellow

**Dual Synchronized Strobe**

**475-100ADB01** Blue

**475-100ADN01** White

**475-100ADR01** Red

**475-100ADY01** Yellow

#### Adjustable 8-Position 34.95 ea
Rapid sequencing of pulsing strobe lights for emergency vehicles, road barricade or circus attractions. Operate on 9 14V AC/DC.

**475-1008CS01** Red & Yellow

**475-1008NS01** White

**475-1008RS01** Red

**475-1008YS01** Yellow

# Miniatronics
"electronics for the hobbyist"

Emergency Light Bars

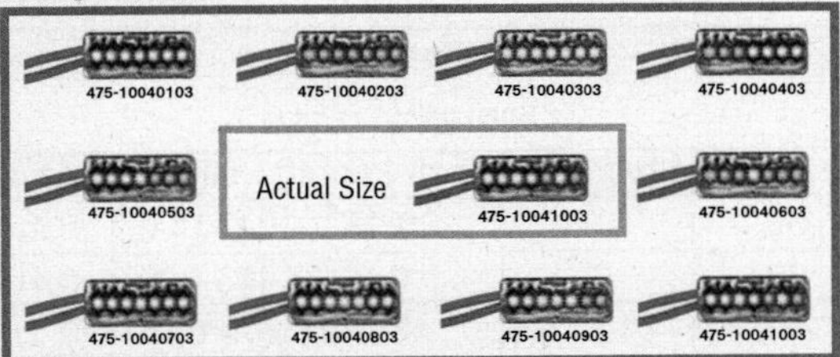


## Light Bars pkg(3) 19.95 ea

An easy way to add emergency lights to any police car, emergency vehicle or tow truck. PC board has seven LEDs in a chase pattern to add animation to any diorama.

**475-10040103** 7 Blue
**475-10040203** 7 Red
**475-10040303** 7 Yellow
**475-10040403** 3 Red, 4 Blue
**475-10040503** 3 Blue, 1 White, 3 Red
**475-10040603** 3 Red, 1 White, 3 Red
**475-10040703** 3 Blue, 1 White, 3 Blue
**475-10040803** 2 Blue, 3 White, 2 Blue
**475-10040903** 2 Blue, 1 White, 1 Yellow, 1 White, 2 Red
**475-10041003** 2 Blue, 1 Yellow, 1 Blue, 1 Red, 1 Yellow, 1 Red

## Flashers

Units require no assembly and will operate on any 9-14V AC/DC external power source.

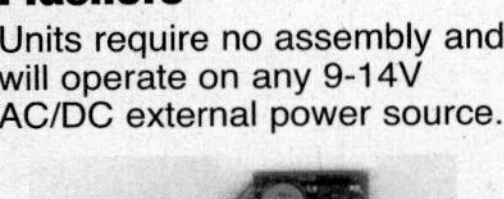

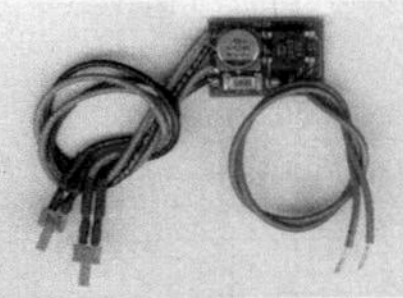

**475-10000201** Dual Emergency Flasher (red/red) **12.75**
Two red LEDs will flash alternately.

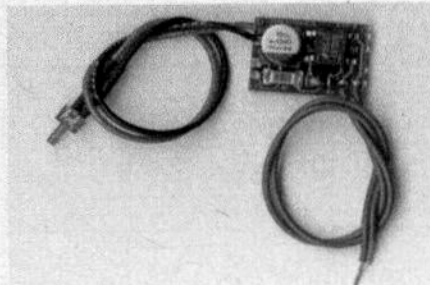

**475-10001101** Rear End Warning Flasher (red) **11.75**
Flasher can run directly off tracks.

## Incandescent Lamp Flashers

Control speed on these flashers with variable flash rates. Use with any 12-14V bulb NOT to exceed 100mA.

**475-100N0101** Single **17.95**
**475-100N0201** Dual **19.95**

## Mars Light, Adjustable

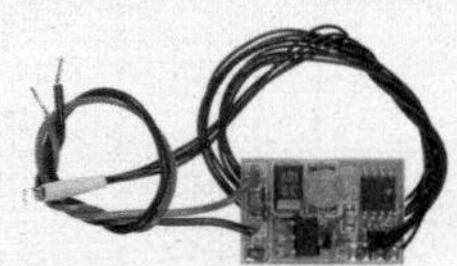

**475-100MAR01 34.95**
Fully assembled electronics board with two bulbs that create a gyrating "figure-eight" effect. Includes a clear lens and an adjustment tool. Operates on 4-16V DC.

## Ditch Lights

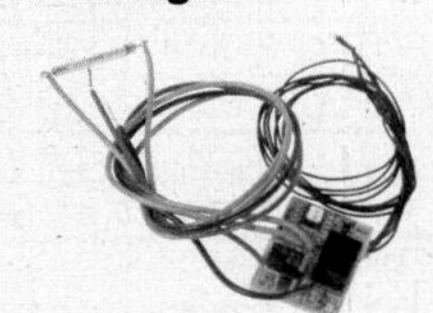

**475-10022001 34.95**
Capture the action of modern railroading with a fully-assembled PC board with reed switch and two incandescent lamps. Lamps come on at about 3V and remain on until the unit senses a hidden magnet, which causes them to alternately flash on and off until the unit senses a second magnet, which returns them to constant on. Includes eight bi-polar magnets, enough for four crossings, additional magnets are available separately.

## Ditch Light Magnets

**475-3701010** pkg(10) **9.45**
Bi-polar magnets for five crossings. For use with Ditch Lights #475-10022001, sold separately.

## Beacons

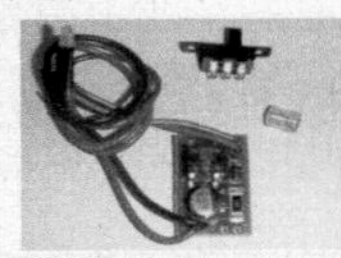

**475-10000101** Roof Top Flasher (amber) **11.75**
For use on diesel engines, roadway warning lights, tower signals or emergency vehicles.

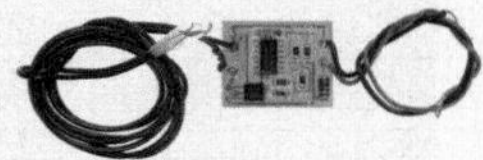

**475-100LHB01** Light House Warning **19.95**
Very bright white light will fit most HO Scale and larger lighthouses. **Requires filtered 12V DC power source.**

## Fire & Flame Effects

**475-10010101** Simulated Fire & Flame **23.95**
Create realistic fire scenes with state-of-the-art fire simulator, which features varying bursts of brightness for an authentic glow. Requires 12V DC power source.

**475-10020101** Arc Welding Light **29.95**
Create the illusion of scattered random lights in your auto repair shop, construction site or train yard maintenance shop. Requires 12V DC power source.

## Tower

**475-TW01101**
Brass Tower (Communications, Transmission or High Voltage Type) 4-3/4" 11.8cm High **12.45**

Use this etched brass tower as a tall industrial lamppost, as an antenna tower or as an electrical transmission tower. Add the Two Directional Light (#475-100NL101, sold separately) to simulate warning lights that automatically dim and brighten.

## Two-Directional Light

**475-100NL101 18.95**
Unit automatically dims and brightens, then repeats the sequence. Designed for use on Tower (475-TW01101, sold separately) and adaptable to other models. **Requires filtered 12V DC power supply.**

# WIRE

4812401 4818301 4856150

### 16 Gauge Flexible Single Stranded Conductor 50' 12.95 ea

**NEW 475-4856050** Black
**NEW 475-4856150** Blue
**NEW 475-4856350** Green
**NEW 475-4856550** Red
**NEW 475-4856750** White
**NEW 475-4856850** Yellow

### 16 Gauge Standard, Two Conductor, 50'

**475-4826050** Black/Red **25.95**

### 18 Gauge, Stranded, Single Conductor, 100' 30m 15.75 ea

**475-4818001** Black
**475-4818301** Green
**475-4818401** Orange
**475-4818501** Red
**475-4818601** White
**475-4818701** Yellow

### 22 Gauge, Stranded, Single Conductor, 100' 30m 8.95 ea

**475-4812001** Black
**475-4812201** Gray
**475-4812301** Green
**475-4812401** Orange
**475-4812501** Red
**475-4812601** Violet
**475-4812701** White
**475-4812801** Yellow

### 28 Gauge Flat, Stranded, 25' 7.5m

**475-4822825** Black 2 Conductor **8.45**
**475-4842825** Black 4 Conductor **12.75**

### 30 Gauge Ultra Flexible, Stranded, Single Conductor, 10' 3m 6.75 ea

**475-4813001** Black
**475-4813004** 2-1/2' Sections (1 each black, green, red, white)

### 30 Gauge Ultra-Flexible Standard, Single Conductor, 10' 6.75 ea

**475-48G3001** Green
**475-48R3001** Red
**475-48W3001** White

# CLIP-ON LAMP

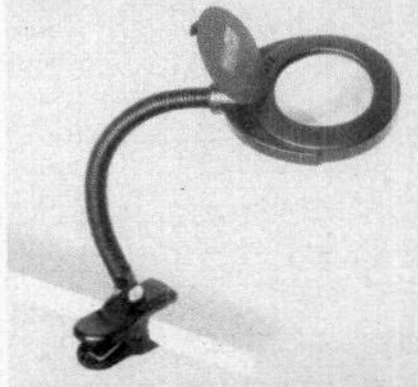

**475-10051801** Mini-Magnifying **36.95**
Magnifying lamp features a three-diopeter lens, swivel gooseneck and heavy-duty mounting clip.

# CATALOG

**475-2008** 2008 (Volume 10) **5.00**
This catalog gives detailed information on the Miniatronics line of premiere electronics circuits and lighting accessories.

# NorthWest Short Line

These high-precision, heavy-duty motors, with skewed five pole armatures, are suitable for all scales. They have a high efficiency (low battery drain) with high torque/speed characteristics, plus silent and maintenance free operation. Fully enclosed cylindrical type. Mounting screws (packed with motor) must not be inserted more than 2mm into motor case. Uses long life ceramic and ferrite magnets.

## Gearboxes Kits

### Mini Gearboxes 50-1 Ratio For HOn3, 1.5mm Input Shaft 34.95 ea (Unless Noted)

**53-1706** Accepts 2.4 Axle

**53-1716** Accepts 2.0 Axle

**53-1726** Accepts 1.5 Axle

**53-1736** Accepts 3.0 HOn3 Axle **36.95**

### Hi-Low Gearboxes 49.95 ea

For quiet HO Mallets and articulated locomotives. Features a quiet direct line drive system, molded of celcon acetal plastic with bronze worm shaft bearings, steel worm and machined brass gears. Eliminates noisy tower spur gears 2.4mm input shaft.

**53-1486** 28:1, 3mm Axle

**53-1496** 28:1, 1/8" Axle

**53-1586** 36:1, 3mm Axle

**53-1596** 36:1, 1/8" Axle

### Heavier-Duty .04 Module Series 49.95 ea

**53-2486** 28:1, 1/8" Axle

**53-2496** 28:1, 4mm – 5/32" Axle

Item listed below is available by Special Order (see Legend Page).
**53-2476** 28:1, 3mm Axle*

## Prime Mover Upgrade Kits 39.95 ea

For Athearn and other diesels, also large steam. 18 series for narrow hood diesels; 20 series for widebody diesels and steam. Feature a NWSL motor with pre-mounted flywheel (#53-1634 has two flywheels) and universal connectors that couple directly to gearing input shafts. High-efficiency premium motor provides slower, smoother speed, more power with lower amp draw and no need to re-gear.

**53-1624** 2032 F, PA (standard speed)

**53-1654** 1833 Switchers

**53-1674** For Athearn SD40, 1833 Motor, 2 Flywheels

## Motor Mount

**53-1996 1.00**
Sticky plastic for temporary attachment of parts and tools.

## Universal Driveline Coupler Sets

Ball-type universal driveline coupling for use as double universal or as two single joints. Sets with the same ball sizes may be combined to couple different shaft sizes. Easy to install press-fit or cup can be drilled and tapped for set screw. Made of acetal engineering plastic. 2.4mm fits 3/32". Refer to chart at right.

## Gearbox Input Shaft Conversion 6.00 ea

### For Double Idler & Direct Type .3 Mod

**53-1446** 2mm Input Shaft

**53-1456** 1.5mm Input Shaft

### For Idler .3 Mod

**53-1646** 2mm Input Shaft

**53-1656** 1.5mm Input Shaft

## Flatcan Motors 12V DC

Note: All dimensions on the chart are in millimeters. Double Shaft unless marked "S."

| Number | Price | Width | Length | Shaft Dia. | Shaft Length | RPM | Amps |
|---|---|---|---|---|---|---|---|
| 102539 | 34.95 | 10 | 25 | 1.2 | 15 | 7,000 | 0.06 |
| 183369 | 31.95 | 18 | 33 | 2.4 | 25 "S" | 8,800 | 0.09 |
| 183379 | 32.95 | 18 | 33 | 2.4 | 15 | 8,800 | 0.09 |

## 12V DC Round Can Motors

Note: All dimensions on the chart are in millimeters. Double Shaft unless marked "S."

| Number | Price | Dia. | Length | Shaft Dia. | Shaft Length | RPM | Amps |
|---|---|---|---|---|---|---|---|
| 163089 | 30.95 | 16 | 30 | 2 | 25 "S" | 15,000 | 0.10 |
| 163099 | 31.95 | 16 | 30 | 2 | 20 | 15,000 | 0.10 |
| 202759 | 31.95 | 20 | 26.5 | 2 | 15 | 9,800 | 0.11 |
| 203259 | 32.95 | 20 | 31.5 | 2 | 15 | 9,500 | 0.10 |
| 222439 | 26.95 | 22 | 24 | 2.4 | 18 | 10,500 | 0.16 |
| 223639 | 29.95 | 22 | 36 | 2.4 | 18 | 9,600 | 0.10 |
| 224059 | 29.95 | 22 | 40 | 2.4 | 18 | 9,600 | 0.10 |
| 223139 | 29.95 | 22 | 31 | 2.4 | 18 | 9900 | 0.15 |

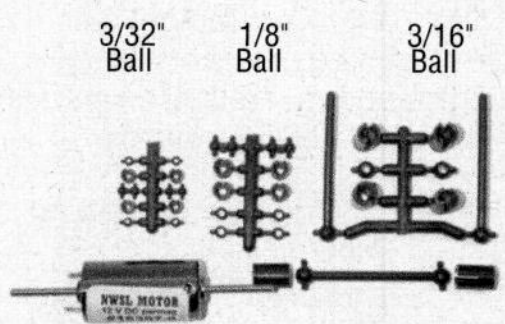


Universal Driveline Coupler 53-4806

## Gear Aligner Sets in 4 Sizes 8.95 ea

A gear truing tool designed to install and to check and minimize gear wobbling which can occur when installing gears on axles and shafts. Can sometimes straighten wobbling gear.

**53-314** For 2.0mm Axles & Shafts

**53-324** For 2.4mm (3/32") Axles & Shafts

**53-334** For 3.0mm Axles & Shafts

**53-384** For 1/8" Axles & Shafts

## Universal Driveline Couplers

Acetal engineering plastic; press-fit to shaft.

| No. | Primary Cups Shaft | Add'l Cups | Horned Ball Shaft | Ball Dia. | Price |
|---|---|---|---|---|---|
| 4806 | 1/8" | None | 2.4mm | 3/16" | 2.25 |
| 4816 | 2.4mm | None | 2.4mm | 3/16" | 2.25 |
| 4826 | 2.0mm | 1.5, 2.4mm | 2.0mm | 1/8" | 2.95 |
| 4836 | 1.5mm | 2.0, 2.4mm | 1.5mm | 3/32" | 2.95 |
| 4846 | 2.4mm | 2.4mm | 2.0mm | 1/8" | 2.95 |
| 4856 | 1.2mm | 1.5, 2.0mm | 1.5mm | 3/32" | 2.95 |
| 4866 | 3.0mm | None | 2.4mm | 3/16" | 2.25 |
| 4876 | 1.5mm | 1.5mm | 1.5mm | 3/32" | 2.95 |
| 4886 | 2.4mm | 2.0mm | 2.0mm | 1/8" | 2.95 |
| 4896 | 2.0mm | 2.0mm | 2.0mm | 1/8" | 2.95 |
| 4906 | 2.4mm | None | None | 3/16" | 3.95 |
| 4916 | 2.0mm | 2.4mm | None | 3/16" | 3.95 |
| 4926 | 2.0mm | 2.0mm | None | 3/16" | 3.95 |
| 4956 | 5/32" | 1/8" | 1/8" | 1/4" | 3.95 |
| 4966 | 5/32" | 3" | 1/8" | 1/4" | 3.95 |
| 4976 | 5/32" | 2.4mm | 1/8" | 1/4" | 3.95 |
| 4986 | 1/8" | 2.4mm | 1/8" | 1/4" | 3.95 |

## Gearboxes

Idler and standard gearboxes and a "high-rise" double idler to allow horizontal motor installation in the boiler. Power is transferred to driven axle via quiet, slow speed worm gears. Item with "†" is 36.95

| | .3 MOD Series | | | | | | | .4 MOD Series | | | | |
|---|---|---|---|---|---|---|---|---|---|---|---|---|
| | Light Duty | | Standard Duty | | | | | Heavy Duty | | | | |
| | 3.125:1 | 50:1 | 36:1 | | 28:1 | | | 28:1 | | 14:1 | 1.89:1 | 1:1 |
| Fits Axle Dia. | Transfer | Cmpd. | Idler | Direct | Dbl. Idler | Idler | Direct | Idler | Direct | Direct | Transfer | Transfer |
| 1.5mm | 2216 | 1726 | | | | | | | | | | |
| 2.4 - 3/32" | | 1706 | | | | 1466 | 1476 | | | 2136 | 2246 | 2236 |
| 3mm | | 1736† | 1506 | 1516 | 1366 | 1396 | 1406 | 2406 | 2416 | 2116 | | |
| 1/8" | | | 1536 | 1546 | 1416 | 1426 | 1436 | 2426 | 2436 | 2126 | | |
| 4 - 5/32" | | | | | | | | 2446* | 2456 | | | |
| Price | 29.95 | 34.95 | 34.95 | 29.95 | 36.95 | 34.95 | 29.95 | 34.95 | 29.95 | 29.95 | 34.95 | 34.95 |

Gearbox .3 MOD 53-1396

*Items with asterisk are available by Special Order (see Legend Page).

# NorthWest Short Line

## 72 DP Steel Worms

.1875 O.D. worms match worm gears listed at right.

**53-100006** 3/32" Bore **6.00**

**53-104006** 1.5mm Bore **6.50**

**53-105006** 2mm Bore **6.50**

## KMT Tower Gears .5 MOD 6.00 ea

2.4mm bore - found in KMT, Tenshodo and some other brass diesels. Not the same as Samhongsa tower gears.

| Brass | Delrin |
|---|---|
| **53-776096** 9T | **53-786096** 9T |
| **53-776106** 10T | **53-786106** 10T |
| **53-776116** 11T | **53-786116** 11T |
| **53-776126** 12T | **53-786126** 12T |
| **53-776136** 13T | **53-786136** 13T |
| **53-776146** 14T | **53-786146** 14T |
| **53-776156** 15T | **53-786156** 15T |
| **53-776166** 16T | **53-786166** 16T |
| **53-776176** 17T | **53-786176** 17T |
| **53-776186** 18T | **53-786186** 18T |
| **53-776196** 19T | **53-786196** 19T |
| **53-776206** 20T | **53-786206** 20T |
| **53-776216** 21T | **53-786216** 21T |
| **53-776226** 22T | **53-786226** 22T |
| **53-776236** 23T | **53-786236** 23T |
| **53-776246** 24T | **53-786246** 24T |
| **53-776256** 25T | **53-786256** 25T |
| **53-776266** 26T | **53-786266** 26T |

## Gear & Re-Gear Sets

### MDC Loco Regear Kits

**53-1786** 72:1 For Small Motor, 1.5mm Shaft **19.95**

**53-1796** 45:1 For Small Motor, 1.5mm Shaft **19.95**

**53-1806** 72:1 for Small Motor, 2.0mm Shaft **17.95**

**53-1816** 45:1 for Small Motor, 2.0mm Shaft **17.95**

**53-1826** 72:1 for Large Motor, 3/32" Shaft **17.95**

**53-1836** 45:1 for Large Motor, 3/32" Shaft **17.95**

### HOn3 MDC Loco Regear Kits

**53-1846 14.95**
Use existing motor.

**53-1896** For MDC HOn3 2-8-0 Consolidation Loco 1998 Redesign **24.95**

### Partial Re-Gear Kit For MDC Loco

**53-1866** 2-Truck Shay **19.95**

**53-1876** 3-Truck Shay **24.95**

**53-1886** Gear Upgrade Kit – Bull Gear **12.95**

### Brass 3.0mm Bore (.118") 72 DP 6.00 ea

| Number of Teeth | Spur Gear | Worm Gear | Reverse Worm Gear | O.D. |
|---|---|---|---|---|
| 15 | 177156 | 117156 | 147156 | 0.24 |
| 20 | 177206 | 117206 | 147206 | 0.306 |
| 24 | 177246 | 177246 | 147246 | 0.361 |
| 30 | 177306 | 117306 | 147306 | 0.444 |
| 36 | 177366 | 147366 | 147366 | 0.527 |
| 40 | 177406 | 117406 | 147406 | 0.583 |

### Brass 3/32" Bore (.0937") 72 DP 6.00 ea

| Number of Teeth | Spur Gear | Worm Gear | Reverse Worm Gear | O.D. |
|---|---|---|---|---|
| 10 | 170106 | 110106 | 140106 | 0.178 |
| 15 | 170156 | 110156 | 140156 | 0.24 |
| 20 | 170206 | 110206 | 140206 | 0.306 |
| 24 | 170246 | 110246 | 140246 | 0.361 |
| 30 | 170306 | 110306 | 140306 | 0.444 |
| 36 | 170366 | 110366 | 140366 | 0.527 |
| 40 | 170406 | 110406 | 140406 | 0.583 |

### Delrin® 3.0mm Bore (.118") 72 DP 6.00 ea

| Number of Teeth | Spur Gear | Worm Gear | Reverse Worm Gear | O.D. |
|---|---|---|---|---|
| 15 | 187156 | 127156 | 157156 | 0.24 |
| 20 | 187206 | 127206 | 157206 | 0.306 |
| 24 | 187246 | 127246 | 157246 | 0.361 |
| 30 | 187306 | 127306 | 157306 | 0.444 |
| 36 | 187366 | 127366 | 157366 | 0.527 |
| 40 | 187406 | 127406 | 157406 | 0.583 |

### Delrin 3/32" Bore (.0937") 72 DP 6.00 ea

| Number of Teeth | Spur Gear | Worm Gear | Reverse Worm Gear | O.D. |
|---|---|---|---|---|
| 15 | 180156 | 120156 | 150156 | 0.24 |
| 20 | 180206 | 120206 | 150206 | 0.306 |
| 24 | 180246 | 120246 | 150246 | 0.361 |
| 30 | 180306 | 120306 | *150306 | 0.444 |
| 36 | 180366 | 120366 | 150366 | 0.527 |
| 40 | 180406 | 120406 | 150406 | 0.583 |

### AHM (Rivarossi Circa 1960-1980)

**53-3016** 2-8-4 **9.95**

**53-3086** Mikado **10.95**

**53-3096** 0-4-0 & 0-6-0T **10.95**

**53-3106** USRA 0-6-0 **10.95**

**53-3126** 42% Reduction, AHM 0-8-0 **10.95**
Vertical motor shaft type only.

**53-3136** AHM 4-8-4 **10.95**

**53-3076** AHM Hudson, Pacific **10.95**

### Samhongsa

**53-3226** E-B 22T pkg(2) **10.95**

**53-3236** SD38-2 22T pkg(2) **10.95**

**53-3246** 22T pkg(2) **10.95**

**53-3256** 21T pkg(2) **10.95**

**53-3266** 25T pkg(2) **10.95**

**53-3276** 36T pkg(2) **10.95**

### Suydam

**53-3296** 10T x 6mm pkg(4) **14.95**

### Key/Samhongsa MR #7/ Cass #4 Shay

**53-3386** pkg(2) **10.95**

**53-3396** Feather River Shay (27T) **10.95**

### For WSM

**53-3056** 26T x 8.4mm Idler Gear Westside Models **6.95**

**53-3346** E-Unit **19.95**

### KMT Diesel Re-Gear Kit

See previous column for KMT Tower Gears.

**53-1006** 4-Axle **18.95**

**53-1016** 6-Axle **24.95**

### Thrust Washers

For miscellaneous fine tuning application. All slip fit dimensions listed.

**53-60005** Bronze Thrust & Spacer Washer Assortment pkg(104 Pieces) **13.95**

| Number | I.D. | O.D. | Thickness | Metal | Pkg | Price |
|---|---|---|---|---|---|---|
| 1004 | 3/32" | 3/16" | .005" | bronze | 10 | 0.99 |
| 11004 | 3/32" | 3/16" | .005" | bronze | 100 | 6.50 |
| 1034 | 3/32" | 3/16" | .010" | bronze | 10 | 0.99 |
| 11034 | 3/32" | 3/16" | .010" | bronze | 100 | 6.50 |
| 1064 | 1/8" | 3/16" | .010" | bronze | 10 | 0.99 |
| 11064 | 1/8" | 3/16" | .010" | bronze | 100 | 6.50 |
| 1084 | 2.0mm | 3.0mm | .010" | bronze | 10 | 0.99 |
| 11084 | 2.0mm | 3.0mm | .010" | bronze | 100 | 6.50 |
| 1094 | 2.0 | 3/16" | .010 | bronze | 10 | 0.99 |
| 11094 | 2.0 | 3/16" | .010 | bronze | 100 | 6.50 |
| 1104 | 1/16" | 3.0mm | .010" | bronze | 10 | 0.99 |
| 11104 | 1/16" | 3.0mm | .010" | bronze | 100 | 6.50 |
| 1119 | 1/16" | 3.0mm | .004" | bronze | 5 | 0.99 |
| 11114 | 1/16" | 3.0mm | .004" | bronze | 50 | 6.50 |
| 1124 | .064" | .120" | .020" | nylon | 5 | 0.99 |
| 11124 | .060" | .120" | .020" | nylon | 50 | 6.50 |
| 1134 | .220" | .099 | .015 | fiber | 5 | 0.99 |
| 11134 | .220" | .099 | .015 | fiber | 50 | 6.50 |
| 1144 | 3/32" | 1/4" | .016" | bronze | 10 | 0.99 |
| 11144 | 3/32" | 1/4" | .016" | bronze | 100 | 6.50 |
| 1164 | 4mm | 7mm | .010" | bronze | 5 | 0.99 |
| 11164 | 4mm | 7mm | .010" | bronze | 50 | 6.50 |
| 1174 | 5mm | 8mm | .010" | bronze | 5 | 0.99 |
| 1184 | 6mm | 9mm | .010" | bronze | 5 | 0.99 |
| 1204 | 2.0 | Terminal Wiring Solder Tabs | | bronze | 5 | 0.99 |
| 11204 | 2.0 | Terminal Wiring Solder Tabs | | bronze | 50 | 6.50 |

## NorthWest Short Line

### Speed Reduction Gear
**53-1206** Benson Shay 11smph **19.95**

**53-1216** B2, B3, Pacific Coast Shay 11smph **19.95**

**53-1296** B2, B3, Pacific Coast Shaft 22smph **19.95**

### PFM Shay 19.95 ea
**53-1246** (12T) 2.6mm Bore

**53-1266** (7T) 2.4mm Bore

**53-1276** (7T) 2.4mm Bore

### Samhongsa Diesel Replacement Gear pkg(2) 10.95 ea
**53-3336** 21T x 9.2mm Alco, SHS

**53-3356** 15T x 6.8mm Alco, SHS

### Idler Worm Gear pkg(2) 10.95 ea
**53-3366** Key/Samhongsa GP7 28T x 12mm

**53-3376** Samhongsa H15-44/ GP7, 23T

### Spur Gear For Samhongsa pkg(2) 10.95 ea
**53-3416** SD38-2, 14T

**53-3426** SD38-2, 15T

**53-3436** RSD-15/DL-600B, 15T

**53-3446** 20T

**53-3456** RSD-15/DL-600B, 21T

**53-3476** RS-3/RS-32, 21T

### Reverse Worm Gear pkg(2) 10.95 ea
**53-3486** For Hallmark Whitcomb, 25T

**53-3496** Hi-Angle For Samhongsa Diesels, 15T

### Spur Gear For Oriental/ Samhongsa
**53-3466** F3, 20T pkg(2) **10.95**

### 72 DP Worm Gear
**NEW 53-115306** Brass 2mm Bore 30T (RH) **5.00**

### KMT Tower Gear Service
**53-1056** **99.95**

### Flea II Drive Unit
**53-2056** Flea II #102039 Motor, 33"/88 Wheelset **59.95**
**53-2066** Flea II #102539 Motor, 33"/88 Wheelset **59.95**

**53-2076** Auxiliary Gearbox to Match Flea II (15:1) **8.50**
Less axle gear. See #53-20006 to order matching gear or wheelset.

## MISCELLANEOUS

### Shaft/Axle Stock 2.50 ea
Precision-ground steel rod for shafts, axles and worm shafts. Each package includes two 6" length.
**53-20154** O.D. 1.5mm

**53-20204** O.D. 2.0mm

**53-20244** O.D. 2.4mm
Often used in place of 3/32" in import models.

**53-20254** O.D. 2.5mm

**53-20304** O.D. 3.0mm
Used in place of 1/8" in import models and axles.

**53-20624** O.D. 1/16"

**53-20934** O.D. 3/32"
Common as motor shaft size.

**53-21254** O.D. 1/8"
Loco axles, some motor shafts in US models.

**53-20504** O.D. 5.0mm

**53-20584** O.D. 5.8mm

**53-20604** O.D. 6.0mm

**53-21564** O.D. 5/32"

**53-21874** O.D. 3/16"

**53-22504** O.D. 1/4"

Item listed below is available by Special Order (see Legend Page).
**53-20404** O.D. 4.0mm

### Axle Journal Flanged Bearings
**Brass pkg(8) 3.95 ea (Unless Noted)**
**53-3546** 3/32 x 1/8"

**53-3556** 9/64 x 5/32"

**53-3626** 1/8 x 5/32" 4mm **4.95**

**53-3666** 1/16" x 2.5mm

### Shaft Bearings
**Bronze pkg(2) 1.95 ea**
**53-3576** 1.5 x 4.0mm

**53-3586** 2.4 x 3.9mm

**53-3596** 2.0 x 3.9mm

**53-3606** 1.5 x 3.9mm

**53-3636** 1.5 x 2.5mm

**53-3646** 1.2 x 3.9mm

**53-3676** 1/8 x 3/16 x .315"

**53-3746** 1.2 x 2.5mm

**53-3756** 2.4mm x 3/16 x .130"

### Ball Bearings 9.95 ea
**53-3686** 1/8 x 5/16"OD x 9/64" pkg(2)

**53-3696** 3/32 x 3/16"OD x 1/16" Wide

### Pillow Block Style 3.95 ea
**53-3706** 2.4 Bore

**53-3726** 2.0 Bore

### Loco Driver Springs
4mm long springs with 2mm diameters.

**53-14004** Wimpy pkg(8) **2.45**

**53-14014** Light pkg(8) **2.45**

**53-14024** Medium pkg(8) **2.45**

**53-14104** Wimpy pkg(100) **12.95**

**53-14114** Light pkg(100) **12.95**

**53-14124** Medium pkg(100) **12.95**

### Fine Gauge Very Flexible Hook-Up Wire
**pkg(4') 1.45 ea (Unless Noted)**
**53-100019** 30 Gauge, 7-Strand, Black

**53-100029** 30 Gauge, 7-Strand, Red

**53-100039** 28 Gauge, 7-Strand, Black

**53-100049** 28 Gauge, 7-Strand, Red

**53-100059** 30 Gauge, 7-Strand, Brown

**53-100079** 29 Gauge 51 Strand, Superflex pkg(2) **1.95**

**Bulk pkg(50') 6.95 ea (Unless Noted)**
**53-990019** 30 Gauge, 7-Strand, Black

**53-990029** 30 Gauge, 7-Strand, Red

**53-990039** 28 Gauge, 7-Strand, Black

**53-990049** 28 Gauge, 7-Strand, Red

**53-990059** 30 Gauge, 7-Strand, Brown

**53-990079** 29 Gauge 51 Strand, Superflex **19.95**

### Press Fit Precision Flywheels
**53-4006** Brass, For 1.5mm Shaft, 10mm O.D. x 7mm Length **3.95**

**53-4016** Brass, For 1.5mm Shaft, 12mm O.D. x 7mm Length **3.95**

**53-4026** Brass, For 2mm Shaft, 16mm O.D. x 9mm Length **3.95**

**53-4036** Brass, For 2.4mm Shaft, 18mm O.D. x 11mm Length **4.95**

**53-4046** Brass, For 2.4mm Shaft, 25mm O.D. x 11mm Length **4.95**

**53-4056** Brass, For 2mm Shaft, 17mm O.D. x 11mm Length **4.95**

**53-4066** Brass, For 2.0mm Shaft, 18mm OD x 11mm Length **4.95**

**53-4086** Brass, For 1.5mm Shaft, 11mm O.D. x 7mm Length **3.00**

**53-4096** Brass, For 2.0mm Shaft, 11mm O.D. x 7mm Length **3.95**

**53-4116** Brass, For 1/8" Shaft, 28mm O.D. x 13mm Length **7.95**

**53-4126** Brass, For 1/8" Shaft, 38mm O.D. x 13mm Length **7.95**

**53-4156** Brass, For 5/32" - 4.0mm Shaft, 28mm O.D. x 13 Length **6.50**

**53-4166** Brass, For 5/32" - 4.0mm Shaft, 38mm O.D. x 13 Length **6.50**

**53-4176** Brass, For 5-32" - 4.0mm Shaft, 31mm - 1.25" O.D. x 16mm Length **7.50**

**53-4206** Brass, For 1.2mm Shaft, 10mm O.D. x 7mm Length **4.95**

**53-4216** Brass, For 1.2mm Shaft, 12mm O.D. x 7mm Length **4.95**

**53-4326** Slipfit, For 2mm Shaft, 16mm O.D. x 9mm Length **3.95**

New Arrivals Updated Every Day! Visit Walthers Web site at

**www.walthers.com**

## NOCH

IMPORTED FROM GERMANY BY WALTHERS

### Cable Holders

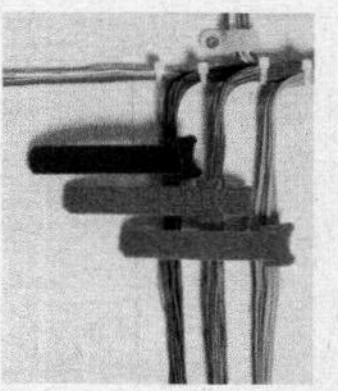

**528-60194** Cable Holders w/Velcro Fastening pkg(6) **6.9**
Includes 2 each red, green an black.

## LABELLE INDUSTRIES

### Light Bulbs
**Angel Hair**
**430-6451** Clear 1.5V pkg(3) **4.29**

**Grain-Of-Rice**
**430-6551** Clear 12-14V pkg(3) **3.79**

### Hook-Up Wire
Multi-strand, 33', 23 gauge.

**430-6001** Single-Conductor Black, Red, Green **3.99**

**30-6004** Four-Conductor Green, Yellow, Red, Blue **6.89**

Create a wide rage of special lighting effects for your motive power and other models with this line of LEDs and accessories.

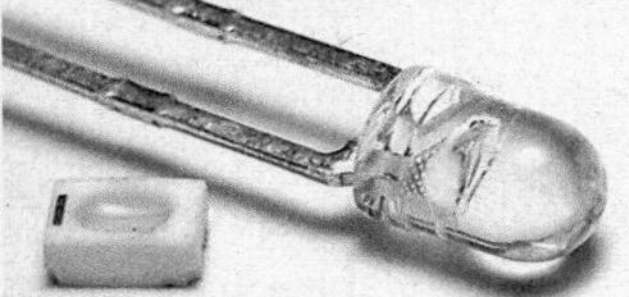

## NEW PRODUCTS

### Ultra-Miniature Lighting Effects Modules

#### Lighthouse Beacon Simulator

**NEW 514-N8035 12.95**
Generates slowly increasing and decreasing brightness of two alternating LEDs (white and green). The effect is timed to accurately represent the slowly rotating beacon in a lighthouse.

#### Marker Buoy Simulator

**NEW 514-N8036 12.95**
Creates a slowly increasing and decreasing intensity curve with a delayed dark period between cycles. This mimics channel and harbor buoys used from the late 1930's to present day. A second buoy (LED) can be connected which has a slightly offset starting time.

#### Early-era Flasher Simulator

**NEW 514-N8037 13.95**
Replicates older-style signal and warning flashers that used incandescent (filament) lamps to generate light. Typical flash rate of 3/4 second with an increasing and decreasing brightness curve. 3 outputs will each drive up to one pair of red and/or yellow LEDs. Outputs flash sequentially.

#### Early-era Alternating Flasher Simulator

**NEW 514-N8038 13.95**
Reproduces alternating flashes with increasing and decreasing brightness curves, as seen in the older incandescent lamp driven type crossbucks and early-era traffic signals. Will drive two pairs of series-wired red or yellow (or mixed) LEDs without additional circuitry.

#### Steam Loco Class Light Simulator

**NEW 514-N8039 14.95**
This simulator allows all three conditions (scheduled train - dark, second section following - green, extra train - white) to be easily controlled using only one input.

#### FRED (End of Train/EOT) Simulator

**NEW 514-N8040 12.95**
Produces a flash rate and duration that replicates the prototype and has a latching function that provides versatility for most applications whether battery or track powered. Small enough to hide anywhere.

#### Rotating Beacon Simulator 12.95 ea

**NEW 514-N8042**

**NEW 514-N8042A** For White LEDS
Reproduces a highly realistic simulation of a rotating beacon by sequencing 3 LEDs (sold separately) that are positioned to produce the effect. Timing closely replicates that of typical rotating beacons used by SP, WP, BN, and currently BNSF, as well as many emergency and utility vehicles.

#### Universal Strobe Simulator

**NEW 514-N8043 13.95**
Supports strobe effects for a wide range of locomotives, emergency vehicles and traffic situations. Strobe pulse occurs either once per second on all three outputs, or when the simulator input is grounded, on two outputs together and one output separately, alternating every 1/2-second.

#### Super-Incandescent High-Intensity LEDs - 2 x 3 mm

**NEW 514-N1022C2** pkg(2) **7.50**

**NEW 514-N1022C10** pkg(10) **35.00**

Identical to the 2 x 3 Super-incandescent LED except brightness is 880mcd minimum (very bright). Device voltage is slightly lower at 3.2-3.3 volts DC.

#### Micro Bridge Rectifier

Small enough to fit inside FDR's ear on a dime (.073 x .075"). It will rectify 140ma of current and handle up to 50-volts DC. With 12-volts as the source is can easily power 20 white LEDs.

**NEW 514-N302S2** pkg(2) **3.95**

**NEW 514-N302S10** pkg(10) **18.95**

#### DC Power Source

Get DC power from track power whether using analog or DCC! This tiny (.320 x .150") board has an ultra-low loss Schottky bridge and multi-layer 10uf filter capacitor with handy solder points, and an additional solder point for direct connection of an LED plus solder pads on the back for the LED's current protection/brightness control resistor. It will support up to 16V DC and rectify 200mA. Hookup wire included.

**NEW 514-N8101 3.95**

**NEW 514-N80105** pkg(5) **17.78**

## ULTRA-MINIATURE LIGHTING EFFECTS MODULES

Utilizing the industry's smallest microcontroller, these modules are smaller than any decoder, just .31 x .31 x .118". Designed specifically to provide realistic lighting effects using LEDs. Input voltage range 6-18VDC. Ideal for DCC applications. Extra input wires included. LEDs sold separately.

#### Mars Light Simulator

**514-N8031 12.95**
Provides a dazzling variable intensity output that represents the reflective bursts of a Mars Light. Truly eye catching.

#### Beacon Simulator

**514-N8032 12.95**
Provides a single repeating burst, increasing and decreasing in intensity to accurately represent roof beacons like those made by Prime and Federal used by most railroads.

#### Gyralight Simulator

**514-N8033 12.95**
Generates a varying (bell curve like) intensity to accurately represent Gyralight motion.

#### Ditch Light Module

**514-N8034 13.95**
Provides output for two LEDs, both on, then switches to alternating with realistic ramping of intensity when input is grounded (or activated by DCC function control).

## SUPER FLASHERS

Flashers automatically support all colors of 20mA LEDs with no additional resistors required. LED colors can even be mixed in the same circuit. Will drive multiple LEDs in series depending on power supply voltage. resistors can be added to on-board solder pads for LED brghtness control. 7-16V DC Less than 1" square. LEDs sold separately.

**514-N8011** Emergency Flasher **12.95**
Provides flashes in short bursts similar to lights used on emergency vehicles. Multiple LEDs can be wired in series.

**514-N8012** Signal Flasher **12.95**
Flashes like a typical stop/caution signal.

**514-N8013** Alternating Flasher **13.65**
Alternately flashes a pair of LEDs (or up to 4 pair depending on power source). Each light is on for 3/4 second, typical of grade crossings, school zones, etc.

**514-N8014** Variable-Rate Flasher **15.25**
Adjustable flash rate from 30 times per second to once every three seconds. On time and off time are equal (50% duty cycle).

**514-N8015** Variable-Rate Alternating Flasher **15.95**
Alternately flashes a pair of LEDs (or up to 4 pair depending on power source). Adjustable flash rate from 30 times per second to once every three seconds. On time and off time are equal (50% duty cycle).

## LED TESTER

Design allows any color LED to be tested. No need to worry about choosing the proper resistor to protect the LED. Simply snap the tester on a 9V battery and start testing. Includes spring-loaded contacts to hold wired LEDs.

**514-N8021 8.95**

## POWER SUPPLY

**514-N3512 15.95**
This power supply is fully filtered and regulated to within 3% over the fll range with no load to full load. It's protected against accidental shorting of the outputs and includes a EMI/RFI shield on the output cable. It's ideal for projects where highly regulated voltage is important. Includes a 6' 12V output cord.

## LEDS

#### Super-White LEDs - 2 x 3mm

Much smaller than the typical 3mm LED, this surface-mounted device (SMD) has a ceramic case with gold-plated solder pads on the back. Produces a very bright, pure white light output. Requires appropriate current limiting resistor, sold separately. Device Voltage: 3.6V DC, Current: 20 Ma, Average Life: 50-80,000 hours.

**514-N10212** pkg(2) **7.00**
**514-N102110** pkg(10) **32.50**

#### Super-Incandescent LEDs - 2 x 3mm

Identical to the 2 x 3 Super-White LED, except the warm light output color simulates an incandescent (filament) light source.
**514-N10222** pkg(2) **7.00**
**514-N102210** pkg(10) **32.50**

### Micro Super-White LEDs - 030 x .060"

Extremely small size of just .030 x .060 and very bright, pure white light output. Device Voltage: 3.3V DC, Current: 20 mA, Average Life: 50-80,000 hours.

**514-N10112** pkg(2) **4.95**
**514-N101110** pkg(10) **22.50**

### Micro Super Yellow-White LEDs

Identical to the Micro Super-White LED, except color output is a very warm, bright yellow-white that simulates the color of early incandescent or gas lighting; ideal for steam-era modelers.

**514-N10152** pkg(2) **4.95**
**514-N101510** pkg(10) **22.50**

### Micro LEDs in Colors - .030 x .060"

Pure colors to simulate signal and marker lights. Intensity can be adjusted by adding the appropriate resistor, sold separately.

#### Red

**514-N10125** pkg(5) **3.50**
**514-N101215** pkg(15) **9.45**

#### Yellow

**514-N10135** pkg(5) **3.50**
**514-N101315** pkg(15) **9.45**

#### Green

**514-N10145** pkg(5) **3.50**
**514-N101415** pkg(15) **9.45**

#### Blue

**514-N10165** pkg(5) **6.95**
**514-N101615** pkg(15) **19.45**

### Nano Super-White LEDs - .020 x .040"

Officially the smallest LED in the world! Though just .020 x .040" this tiny device is extremely bright. It produces a pure white color that can easily be tinted to a warmer hue if desired. Device Voltage: 3.3V DC, Current: 20 mA, Average Life: 50-80,000 hours.

**514-N10312** pkg(2) **6.75**
**514-N103110** pkg(10) **29.75**

### Nano LEDs in Colors .020 x .040"

Identical spectral hues to the Micro LEDs in colors and the same physical size as the Nano Super-White LED.

#### Red

**514-N10325** pkg(5) **3.95**
**514-N103215** pkg(15) **10.65**

#### Yellow

**514-N10335** pkg(5) **3.95**
**514-N103315** pkg(15) **10.65**

#### Green

**514-N10345** pkg(5) **3.95**
**514-N103415** pkg(15) **10.65**

## LIGHTING ACCESSORIES

### Wire

#### #38 Magnet Wire

**514-N5038** Red & Green; Each 100' **4.95**

Includes 100 feet each of red and green - the durable insulation is easily stripped as part of the tinning process.

#### Super-Flexible Insulated Electrical Wire - 5'

**514-N5029** #29 **4.50**

Contains 51 strands of #46 wire, will carry 600 mA.

**514-N5030** #32 **4.00**

Contains 18 strands of #44 wire, will carry 250 mA.

### Ultra-Miniature SPST Electrical Switch

This tiny switch measures just 1/4" in its longest dimension. It will carry 150 mA at 12 volts and is ideal for controlling lighting in rolling stock.

**514-N32002** pkg(2) **2.85**
**514-N320010** pkg(10) **13.25**

### Surface Mount (SMD) Resistors

These precision SMD resistors fit in the smallest spaces due to their flat shape and miniature size. Solder pads on each end are pre-tinned.

#### 1/8 Watt pkg(20) 1.65 ea

**514-NA60R4** 61 Ohm
**514-NA80R6** 81 Ohm
**514-NA1000** 100 Ohm
**514-NA1001** 1K Ohm
**514-NA1210** 121 Ohm
**514-NA1500** 150 Ohm
**514-NA1501** 1.5K Ohm
**514-NA1780** 178 Ohm
**514-NA2000** 200 Ohm
**514-NA2320** 230 Ohm
**514-NA2740** 274 Ohm
**514-NA3010** 301 Ohm
**514-NA3011** 3K Ohm
**514-NA5100** 510 Ohm
**514-NA5111** 5.11K Ohm

#### 1/4 Watt 20-Pack 1.65 ea

**514-NB1001** 100 Ohm
**514-NB3010** 301 Ohm
**514-NB3011** 3K Ohm
**514-NB3400** 340 Ohm
**514-NB3570** 357 Ohm
**514-NB4020** 402 Ohm
**514-NB4530** 453 Ohm
**514-NB5111** 5.11K Ohm
**514-NB5230** 523 Ohm

#### Assortments

**514-NX9V** 9 Volt pkg(150; 15 10-Packs) **9.85**
**514-NX12V** 12 Volt pkg(170; 17 10-Packs) **11.50**

### Tiny Bridge Rectifier – 1/2 Amp

Less than 1/4" square, this full-wave bridge will carry a full 1/2 Amp. It can easily drive 75 LEDs!

**514-N301S2** pkg(2) **1.85**
**514-N301S10** pkg(10) **8.40**

### 100uf Tantalum Capacitor

These tiny 16V DC capacitors can be "ganged" in parallel. Perfect for rolling stock lighting flicker control.

**514-N31006** pkg(6) **4.95**
**514-N310024** pkg(24) **17.80**

### HO Lampshades & Escutcheons

These aluminum lampshades and escutcheons have a very thin (.005") cross-section for prototypical appearance. The concave shape easily accepts many lighting products. Mounting holes are easily added.

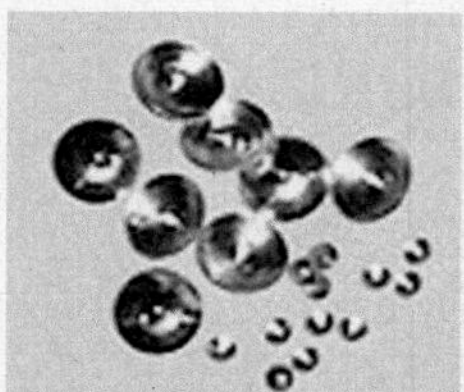

**514-N70058** 18" Lampshades pkg(8) **2.75**
**514-N70068** Escutcheons pkg(8) **1.50**

## SCALE SHOPS

Make your models more realistic with this assortment of miniature electronic supplies.

## CONNECTORS

Miniature size multi-pin connectors feature gold-plated contacts for reliable operation.

### Miniature

**649-3020** 2-Pin **1.98**
**649-3030** 3-Pin **2.49**
**649-3040** 4-Pin **3.49**
**649-3200** 20-Pin **15.98**

### Sub-Miniature

**649-3420** 2-Pin **2.49**
**649-3430** 3-Pin **3.49**
**649-3440** 4-Pin **4.49**
**649-3442** 20-Pin **20.98**

## DIODES

### 50 PIV

**649-4009** 3 amp pkg(3) **1.98**
**649-4010** 1 amp pkg(10) **1.49**

### Constant/Directional Lighting Diodes Kit

**649-7051** **2.98**

### LEDs

#### .085" dia x .115 High .98 ea

**649-5030** Red
**649-5031** Green

#### R-Y-G

**649-5049** 5mm Diameter **1.39**
**649-5110** Right Angle **.98**

#### 3mm dia pkg(2)

**649-5080** Red **.80**
**649-5090** Green **.80**
**649-5100** Yellow **.80**
**649-5105** Orange **.98**

#### 5mm dia pkg(2) .98 ea

**649-5106** Red
**649-5107** Green
**649-5108** Yellow
**649-5109** Orange

## PHOSPHOR BRONZE SHEETS

Sheets measure 1-5/8 x 6". Measurement indicates sheet thickness.

**649-8003** .003" **2.98**
**649-8008** .088" **3.98**

## SWITCHES

### Miniature Toggle

**649-4050** SPDT **2.79**

### SPDT Slides

**649-4052** Miniature **.98**
**649-4053** Sub-Miniature **1.69**

### Miniature Toggles

**649-4060** DPDT/CO **2.98**
**649-4070** DPDT **2.89**

## HEAT SHRINK TUBING

### pkg(12") Black

**649-4501** 3/64" Diameter **1.39**
**649-4502** 1/16" Diameter **1.49**
**649-4503** 1/8" Diameter **1.69**
**649-4504** 3/16" Diameter **1.89**
**649-4505** 3/32" Diameter **1.59**
**649-4600** Assortment **2.98**
4" of each listed above.

### pkg(12") Red

**649-4601** 3/64" Diameter **1.69**
**649-4602** 1/16" Diameter **1.49**
**649-4603** 1/8" Diameter **1.69**
**649-4604** 3/16" Diameter **1.89**
**649-4605** 3/32" Diameter **1.59**
**649-4700** Assortment **2.98**
4" of 3/64", 1/16", 1/8" and 3/16".

## VOLLMER

IMPORTED FROM GERMANY BY WALTHERS

### Lighting Strip

**770-6550** 2-Socket **14.99**

With over 25 years in the modeling industry, Ram Track produces a wide variety of lighting systems for your layout. These light and compact systems will run on either a 9V alkaline battery or a six-cell nicad. Systems are completely assembled and ready to install.

## LIGHTING

### Arc Welder

**616-137 29.95**
Equipped with a 3mm bright white LED, this unit produces a very realistic computer-controlled flash. Great detail for factories, garages, track repair scenes and more.

### Incandescent Lighting

#### Darkness-Sensing Structure Lights

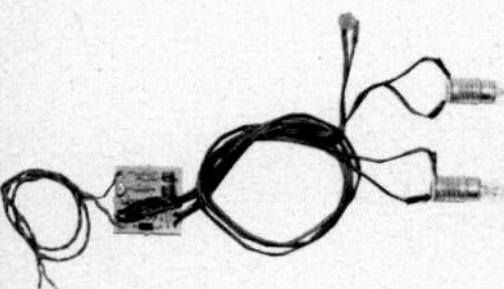

**616-86 19.95**
Adjustable-level, light-sensing circuit turns on two high-efficiency replaceable lamps. Requires 12-18V DC.

#### Oscillating Beacon/ Headlight

**616-134** Single Bulb **19.95**
Includes a 5/8 x 2-1/2" circuit board which operates from 5-24V. Includes two clear lenses, one 3/16" and one 1/4". Works on HO to G Scales.

#### Constant Oscillating Beacon/Headlight

**616-142 29.95**
Same features as #616-134 but has two mini nicad cells with circuitry for track/off track charging.

#### Constant Interior Lights

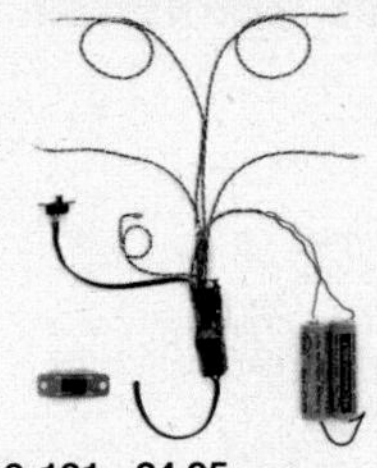

**616-131 24.95**
Lights can stay bright even if there is no power coming from railroad pick-ups. Four-bulb system includes two nicad cells with circuitry for track/off-track charging.

Item listed below is available by Special Order (see Legend Page).
**616-141** DCC **14.95**
Four mini bulbs provide uniform car interior lighting from standard track voltage.

#### Adjustable Strobe Lights

Perfect for engine mount or as an EOT device. Circuit board provides flash rate adjustment. Bulb is on a 12" lead. Each bulb includes two clear lens caps which can be used with O and G Scales.

**616-55** Single **19.95**

**616-56** Double **24.95**

#### Adjustable Revolving Beacons

Acts as an oscillating headlight, but it can also be used on an engine mount. Circuit board allows for adjustable revolving rate. Each bulb includes two clear lens caps for O and G Scales.

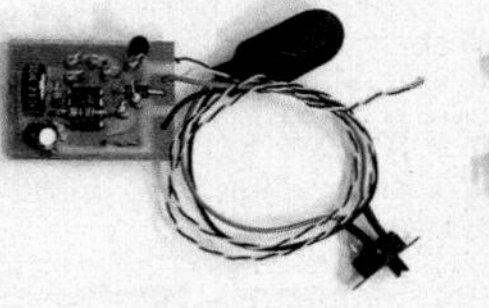

**616-57** Single **19.95**

**616-58** Double **24.95**

### LEDs (Track Powered)

#### Flashers

Offers single strobe effect from one LED. Complete and ready to install.

**616-91** Single (white) 3mm **14.95**

**616-92** Dual Flashing (white) 3mm **19.95**

**616-93** Single EOT Flashing (red) 3mm **9.95**

#### Super Brite Headlights

**616-115** Mini Single 3mm LED **12.95**

**616-116** Mini Dual 3mm LED **15.95**

**616-126** Single 3mm w/2 Lenses Up To 24V **19.95**

**616-127** Dual 3mm w/4 Lenses Up To 24V **24.95**

#### Steam-Era Headlight

An ultra-bright 1/8" 3mm LED provides the softer incandescent glow of a steam loco headlight. Includes 12" 30cm of high quality #30 flexible wire connected to 5/16 x 5/8 x 1" circuit board. System is complete and ready to install. Includes 3/16 and 1/4"s clear plastic lenses to accommodate most headlight openings.

**616-164** Low Voltage **11.95**

**616-165** High Voltage **14.95**

Same as #164, but designed to operate at up to 24V for DCC and G Scale.

Items listed below are available by Special Order (see Legend Page).

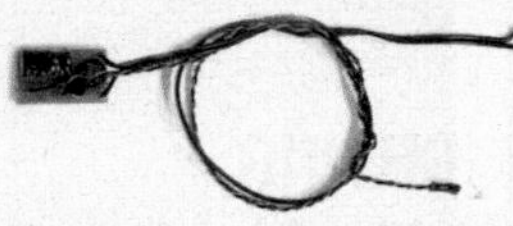

**616-109** Single 5mm LED **12.95**

#### Light Pipe

**616-110** Dual 5mm LED **15.95**

**616-101 9.95**
Bring lights to layout areas where traditional LED placement is not feasible. Includes 36" of .040" diameter fiber optic cable and shrink tubes to bring lighting to previously "light-deprived" areas.

#### Crossing Lights

**616-119 9.95**
Includes 3mm LED with two lens caps for larger scale. Module alternately flashes two red LEDS. Operates on 5-24V DC.

#### Ditch Lights

Alternately flashes two white 3mm LEDs, each on one foot of wire. Designed for low-voltage rail power. Adjustable flash rate options.

**616-118 24.95**

**616-128** Up To 24V **29.95**
Includes four lens cups

**616-138** Constant Ditch Lights **34.95**
Same features as #616-118 or 128, but has three mini nicad cells with circuitry for track/off track charging.

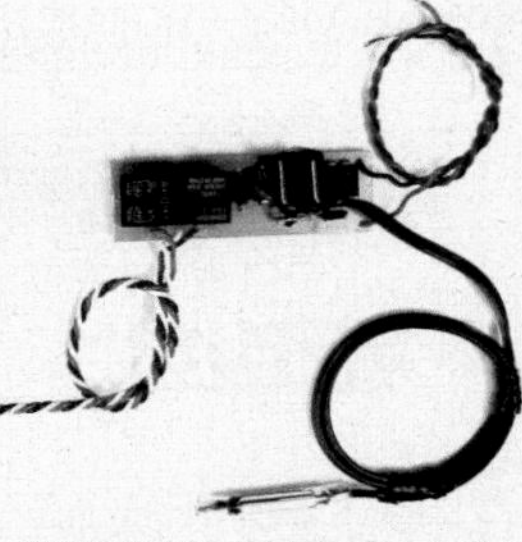

**616-177** Ditch Light Controller **19.95**
Specifically designed to give prototypical alternate flash or steady light operation, activated by track magnets. Instructions show simple hookup of the 3/4 x 2" circuit to Ram Track #616-118 or 128 Ditch Lights (both sold separately) but can also be adapted to other units.

#### Constant Headlight

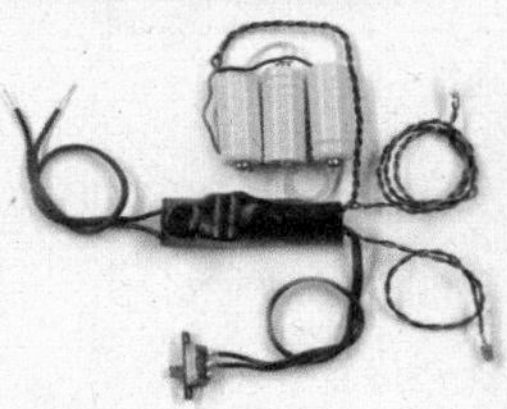

**616-135 24.95**
The single 3mm Ultra-Brite white LED of this system is powered by three mini "N" Nicad cells with a 1/2 x 2" circuit board for track or off-track charging. The headlight stays prototypically lit even when there is no power from the track. Includes 3/16" and 1/4" clear lenses.

#### Strobe Light

**616-176** Single Strobe **14.95**
24V w/3mm LED for DCC and G Scale uses.

#### Tube Lite

**616-183 14.95**
The 8 inch plastic tube glows like a flourescent tube and is lit by 2 white LEDs. The tube can be cut to length and color tinted. It can be track powered for on-board use or from 6 to 24 volts DC for trackside applications.

Info, Images, Inspiration! Get It All at
**www.walthers.com**

SOUNDTRAXX™

## MICROBULBS

Bright, long-lasting 1.5 Volt bulbs are an easy way to upgrade or replace existing lighting in locos when converting to DCC. Choose from two sizes to fit most applications.

#### .053" 1.3mm Diameter x .125" Long

**678-810022** Single **2.50**

**678-810023** 6-Pack **13.50**

#### .094" 2.5mm Diameter x .186" Long

Items listed below are available by Special Order (see Legend Page).
**678-810024** Single **2.50**

**678-810025** 6-Pack **13.50**

## INSULATIVE TUBING

Item listed below is available by Special Order (see Legend Page).
**678-810036** 24" Package **3.00**
24 gauge tubing for covering exposed component leads and wires.

## SHRINK TUBING

**678-810037** Assortment **6.00**
Provides 6" each of 1/16", 3/32", 1/8" and 1/4" diameter tubing, perfect for insulating solder connections.

## EXHAUST CAM SET

**678-810038 10.00**
An assortment of exhaust synchronization cams that can be mounted quickly and easily to the inside face of driver wheels, often without disassembly of the loco. Includes cams for 2-cylinder, shays and articulated engines. For N-Scale and larger. For use with Steam Sound Decoders.

## MICRO-MINI CONNECTORS

**678-810058** Micro-Mini Connectors pkg(10) **9.00**
Use these tiny connectors between loco and tender to make them easier to disconnect.

## RAPIDO TRAINS

### NEW PRODUCTS

**Passenger Car Lighting**

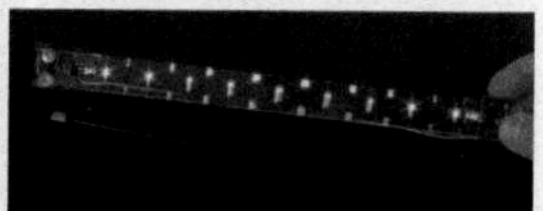

**NEW 606-102003** Easy-Peasy Passenger Car Lighting Set **15.95**
The "Easy-Peasy" Passenger Car Lighting Set contains all you need to add realistic lighting to your HO scale and S scale passenger cars: a lighting circuit and lightway, a Rapido Lighter, and two batteries. You turn the lights on and off by waving the Rapido Lighter over the roof of your passenger car. That's it. No soldering, no complex wiring, and no problems on DC or DCC. The "Easy-Peasy" Lighting Set can also be used in large scale cabooses, buses, trolleys, station platforms, etc.

**NEW 606-102000** Replacement Battery For Lighting Set pkg(4) **11.95**

## TAURUS PRODUCTS/ TROUT CREEK ENGINEERING

**Power Pickup**

**707-2001** Track Slider Power Pickup System pkg(4) **5.00**

## TOMAR INDUSTRIES

**Contact Wipers**

**81-825 6.75**
Package contains enough materials to make approximately eight wipers. Includes circuit board material, phosphor bronze, screws and hook-up wire.

## TR HOBBY PRODUCTS

### NEW PRODUCTS

**Electrical Accessories**

**LEDs**

**Dot Point 1.8mm pkg(4) 4.50 ea**

**NEW 183-247** Red

**NEW 183-248** Green

**NEW 183-249** Yellow

**Regular T-1 pkg(5) 4.65 ea**

**NEW 183-253** Red

**NEW 183-254** Green

**NEW 183-255** Yellow

**Resistors**

**NEW 183-260** 560 ohms pkg(5) **2.00**

**Fiber Optics**

**Fibers**

**NEW 183-701** 100' .010" **7.50**

**NEW 183-702** 30' .020" **6.50**

**NEW 183-703** 15' .030" **7.00**

**NEW 183-704** 15' .040" **7.00**

**NEW 183-700** Assortment **5.25**
Includes five feet each of .010, .020 and .030".

**Fiber w/Light Source 6.75 ea**

Includes two each of .020" and .030" optic fiber with bulb.

**NEW 183-711** Clear

**NEW 183-712** Green

**NEW 183-713** Red

**NEW 183-714** Yellow

**Multiple Light Source**

**NEW 183-715** For Multiple Fibers **11.95**
Does not include any fiber optic.

**Light Kits**

**NEW 183-532** Stars In Your Sky **45.00**
Place lighted stars in your HO backdrop skyline. Kit includes various sizes of fiber optic, light source and full instructions.

**NEW 183-535** Moon In Your Sky **12.00**

**NEW 183-720** Fiber Auto Headlight & Tail Light Kit **8.95**
Contains clear and red bulbs.

**NEW 183-721** Fiber Light Kit For Emergency Flashers **8.95**
Contains two red bulbs. Flasher not included.

## TRAIN TRONICS

### LIGHTING

**Chase Light**

**723-201 34.95**
Kit includes sign material, prebuilt circuit and fiber optics for a 36-light sign. Uses 12-16V DC power supply (not included).

## UTAH PACIFIC

**Constant Lighting Kits**

Reversing headlight and back-up light. Constant light for numberboards, cab lights, etc. Kit includes diodes and polarity board. Less light bulbs.

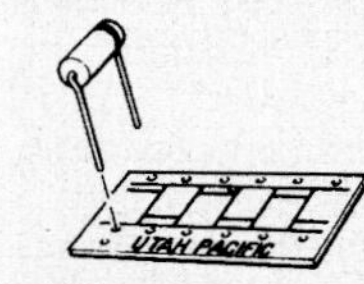


**755-96** Locomotive **8.50**

**755-66** Non-Directional **5.25**

## WIRE WORKS

### WIRE

Flexible, stranded wire is tinned for easy soldering.

**#22 Gauge**

**One Conductor - 50' 5.50 ea**

**851-122070500** Black

**851-122070501** Brown

**851-122070502** Red

**851-122070503** Orange

**851-122070504** Yellow

**851-122070505** Green

**851-122070506** Blue

**851-122070509** White

**One Conductor - 90' 9.00 ea**

**851-122070900** Black

**851-122070902** Red

**851-122070905** Green

**851-122070909** White

**Two Conductor - 30' 9.00 ea**

**851-222070300** Black/Red

**851-222070304** Yellow/Blue

**851-222070305** Green/Brown

**Three Conductor - 23' 9.00 ea**

**851-322070230** Black/Red/ Green

**851-322070234** Yellow/Blue/ White

**#20 Gauge**

To reduce voltage drop on HO layouts over 8'.

**One Conductor - 70' 9.00 ea**

**851-120100700** Black

**851-120100702** Red

**851-120100704** Yellow

**851-120100705** Green

**851-120100706** Blue

**851-120100709** White

**Two Conductor - 25'**

**851-220100250** Black/Red **9.00**

**Heat-Shrink Tubing 4.00 ea**

Packaged in 6" pieces, total length per package shown.

**851-21062** 1/16" (30")

**851-21093** 3/32" (30")

**851-21125** 1/8" (30")

**851-21187** 3/16" (24")

**851-21250** 1/4" (18")

# POWER SOUND SMOKE

Models and Photo by George Dutka

Steel beams groan a bit as the full weight of Central Vermont #4549 eases onto the trestle crossing the White River. Growling past their camera at a peaceful 10mph, there's little danger of scaring the fish, or the fisherman today! Once across, the local will soon be making better speed on its run to Bellows Crossing.

Serving George Dutka's White River Division, the loco is a sound and DCC-equipped Life-Like GP9, which sports added details and weathering.

From steam to diesel, you'll find the perfect sound effects, DC Controllers and other accessories here in the Power, Sound & Smoke Section.

## LIFE-LIKE®

Div. of Wm. K. Walthers, Inc.

### Smoke Fluid

**433-1414** 1oz **9.00**
Can be used in any smoke generator designed for petroleum-based smoke fluid.

## ALPINE DIVISION

### Innovator Walk-Around Throttle

Throttles offer smooth, slow operation as they contain an innovative feature called Log Precision Control. This feature effectively cuts the output voltage almost in half while allowing control from 270 potentiometers. Each contains a two-piece walkaround throttle with memory, forward and reverse, adjustable rate momentum and braking, low-level disappearing pulse for ultra slow motion, push-button acceleration and deceleration buttons, emergency stop button, speed switch, overload protection, power/overload indicator and two control modes (control knobs or push buttons).

No modifications to locomotives are required! A separate dedicated power transformer is supplied with each throttle. Comes complete with detailed instructions, one throttle jack, lead cables and a one-year warranty against defective materials and workmanship.

**700-1400** 2.5 Amps **137.95**

**700-3500** 4.0 Amps **164.95**

## ATLAS

### RIGHT TRACK™ POWER PACK

**150-311 44.95**
Features upgraded electronics for smooth operation, separate power and direction switches, overload indicator lamp, no pulse power to damage precision motors, UL/C-UL listed.

### DC SOUND CONTROLLER

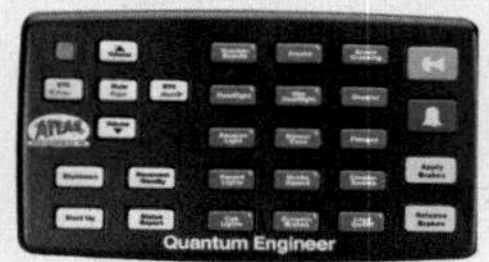


**150-325** Quantum Engineer™ Controller **64.95**
Allows DC users of Atlas Master Gold Series loco to control of all the QSI® Quantum System sound features. In addition to horn and bell sounds users can access a full range of sound and lighting effects. Also allows programming of features and more.Simply wire controller between a standard DC power pack and the track. Not suitable for older Quantum-equipped engines that do not have Quantum Analog Remote Control technology.

## BACHMANN

### Wall Pack w/Speed Controller

**160-44212 43.00**
Can be used with HO, N and On30 scale trains.

## BUSCH

IMPORTED FROM GERMANY BY WALTHERS

### SOUND SYSTEMS

#### American Railway Station

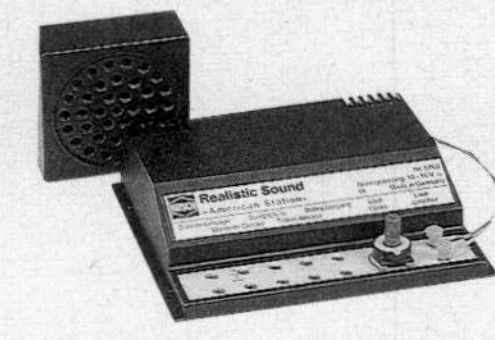

Item listed below is available by Special Order (see Legend Page).

**189-5768 149.99**
Realistic sounds, stored on a chip, create the atmosphere of a busy railway station. Sounds include Western bell, steam whistle, crossing bell, station voice announcement and "Tickets, please" voice announcement. Includes separate speaker; operates on 10-16V AC or DC.

#### City Sounds 149.99 ea

Items listed below are available by Special Order (see Legend Page).

**189-5764** Street Traffic

**189-5765** Church Bells

Daily New Arrival Updates! Visit Walthers Web site at

**www.walthers.com**

## FALLER

IMPORTED FROM GERMANY BY WALTHERS

### Smoke Generator

**272-180690** Smoke Generator Kit **42.99**

### Station Announcement Sound System

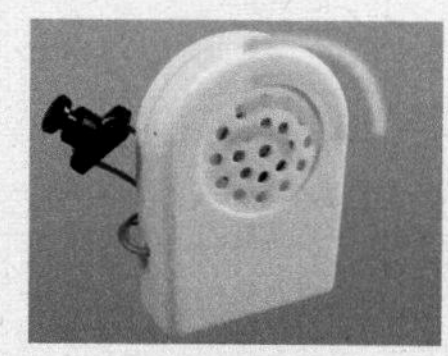

**272-180645 32.99**
This self-contained unit produces various station announcements (in German) for a 9-second duration when triggered by trains tripping a photoelectric sensor. Simply place it under your layout or inside your station building. Easy hookup to your power pack's 12-16V AC accessory terminal.

## MODEL POWER

### Smoke Fluid

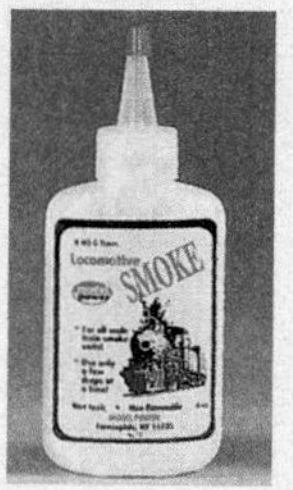


**490-12** 4oz **6.59**
For any scale of trains. Use only a few drops at a time. Nontoxic and non-flammable.

CIRCUITRON products are constructed on printed circuit boards that can be mounted on Printed Circuit Mounting Track Connections to Circuitron circuit boards can be made using .110" female solderless connectors or by soldering leads to terminals on the board. Solid-state integrated circuit technology. Complete instructions. One year limited warranty.

### SOUND SYSTEMS

#### Diesel Horn

**800-5701** DH-1 Diesel Horn **34.95**
Electronic multi-chime horn with speaker and push button. With external switches, unit can produce three different single-frequency or dual-chime tones, or a three-chime tone. Requires 10-18V AC or DC input.

800-9150

800-9610

**800-9150** Speaker 2-1/4" (8 ohm) **4.95**

**800-9610** Push Button **1.50**

#### Steam Sound

**800-9104** Spring Pickup Wire pkg(4) **2.00**
Four 3" lengths, 28 gauge (.0126") beryllium copper spring wire.

**800-9105** Sound System Synchronizing Insulation **3.00**

**800-9151** Speaker **9.95**
23mm (7/8") diameter, 3/8" thick high-output transducer.

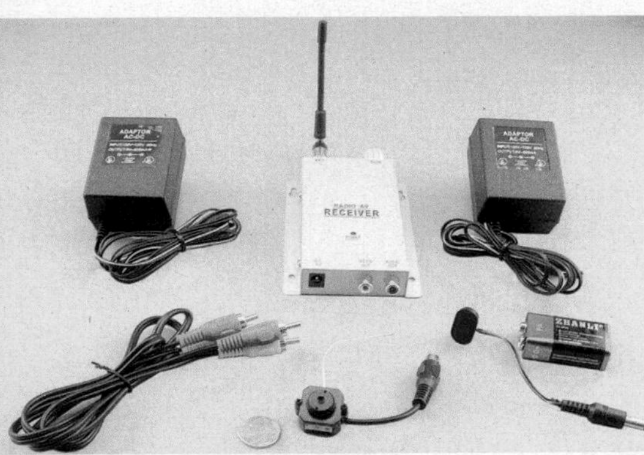
Train Remote View Camera System 227-56802

Original Train Engineer Walkaround Control 2-Piece Set 227-55470

# NEW PRODUCTS

## Train Engineer IV

The latest edition of the Train Engineer system eliminates the worry of clean track. Signal is transmitted via airwaves instead of through the track so it can run on battery or track power. Sound, all lighting functions and more can be operated from the handheld transmitter. Control up to 999 trains and accessories with one transmitter and identify every locomotive by both description and roadnumber. Innovative throttle allows easy and accurate operation. A graphic display walks you through all functions and a detailed manual is also included.

## Generation IV 900 MHZ On-Board Train Engineer

**NEW 227-57000** Train Engineer System **TBA**
Includes receiver and handheld transmitter.

**NEW 227-57001** Transmitter **TBA**

**NEW 227-57002** Receiver **TBA**

**NEW 227-57003** Receiver Pkg(6) **TBA**

**NEW 227-57074** Switch & Accessory Receiver **TBA**

**NEW 227-57075** Switch Control Receiver **TBA**

# THE TRAIN ENGINEER

Control your locomotives and accessories up to 300 feet away with this wireless FM radio control unit. The fully digital control works in all gauges and connects easily to your current power supply. Quick setup requires no loco modification. Features 256 steps for smooth speed control, adjustable momentum speed control and reverse timing for realistic starting and stopping. Safety pause when switching directions helps prevent motor wear. LED display shows which of the frequencies is in use and displays direction and relative speed of the train.

Handheld transmitter controls speed and direction by broadcasting a multi-directional, low-power FM signal (27 megahertz) to the receiver. Built-in Pulse-Code-Modulation (PCM) eliminates outside signal interference.

For easy remote control operations, add the Remote Accessory Unit #227-55474, sold separately, to run trackside turnouts, signals and lights with your Transmitter. Connect additional units to run up to 50 different accessories. For club or show layouts, or just running trains with another person, additional receivers #227-55471 and transmitters #227-55473 are available separately.

**227-55470** Original Train Engineer Walkaround Control 2-Piece Set **191.00**
Includes receiver and hand-held transmitter.

**227-55471** Original Train Engineer Additional Receiver Only **127.00**

**227-55473** Original Train Engineer Transmitter (27 Megahertz) **96.00**

**227-55474** Original Train Engineer Remote Accessory Controller **64.00**
Operates up to five lights, turnouts or accessories; additional units can be combined to control up to 50 accessories.

**227-55475** Original Train Engineer Accessory Receiver **69.00**
Designed for remote control of turnouts only. Operates up to five turnouts; additional units can be combined to control up to 50 turnouts.

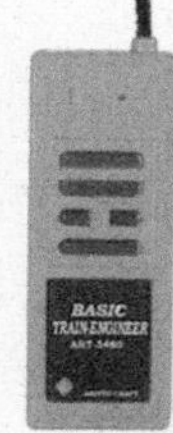

**227-55480** Basic DC/Train Engineer 2 Amp w/100' Range **87.00**
Simplified version of Train Engineer. A wireless radio control system for all DC electric trains. Includes one transmitter and one receiver.

**227-55491** On Board Receiver 75mhz **151.00**

**227-55499** Cooling Fan for Receiver **18.00**
Increases airflow to keep interior components of receiver (#227-55471; also included with #55470, both sold separately) cooler

**227-55495** Add-On Accessory Board **53.00**

# POWER PACKS

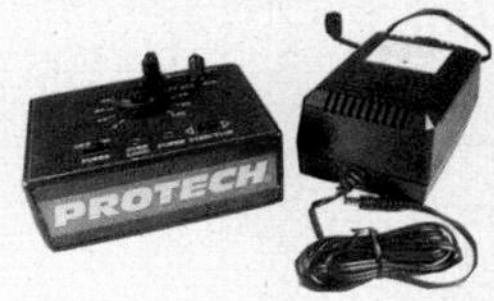


**227-5** ProTech Ultra HO 16V 2 Amp w/Switching Power Supply **20.00**

**227-55400** 1.8 Amp w/Pulse Width Control **58.00**
Perfect for those just starting out in the hobby. Features include 1.8 amp and directional control, auto electronic circuit protection, power and over current indicator lights, constant voltage pulse width speed control and automatic electronic momentum circuit for smooth operation.

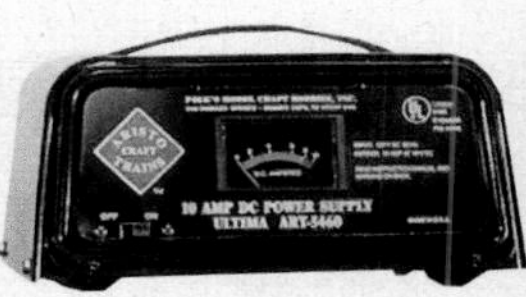


**227-55460** Ultima 10 Amp Linear **122.00**

**227-55401** Control Pack Adaptor For 10 Amp **69.00**
Convert your present power pack into a Pulse Width Control power pack. Features include directional control with Amp, auto electronic circuit protection, power and over-current indicator lights, constant voltage pulse width speed control and automatic electronic momentum circuit for smooth operation.

**227-55465** Switching DC Power Supply **179.00**
Works for both G and HO Scales. Supplies 22V DC at 13 amps for G Scale or 13.8V DC at 20 amps for HO Scale.

**227-55466** Regulated Switching 5-Amp, 221V Power Supply **116.00**

# TRAIN REMOTE VIEW CAMERA SYSTEM

**227-56802 105.00**
See what your railroad looks like from the engineer's point of view! With a camera slightly larger than the diameter of a quarter and only 3/4" deep, you can ride along with just about any loco. The camera broadcasts to the included receiver which is connected to a TV or VCR and you can watch all the action as if you were in the cab yourself.

System includes camera, microphone enclosed within camera case, receiver, 9V battery connector, a 36" two-wire A/V cable for easy positioning of receiver, 9V DC transformer for receiver and an 8V DC transformer for the camera.

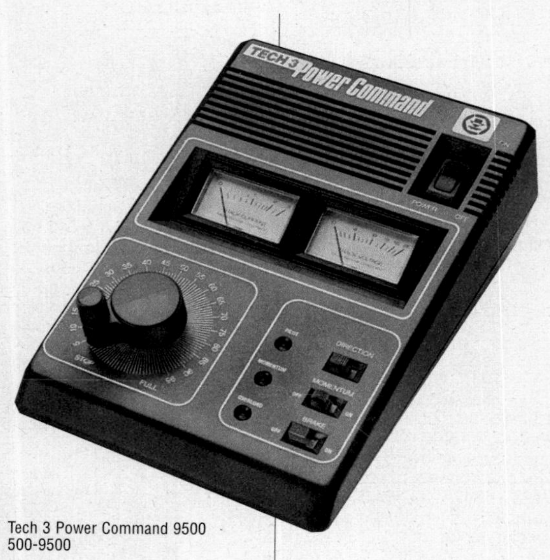


Tech 3 Power Command 9500
500-9500

Tech 4 220 w/16VA & Momentum
500-220

## POWER PACKS

### Tech 3 Power Command 9500

**500-9500** Power Command 9500 (30VA) **119.98**
Get maximum control: Ammeter and voltmeter let you monitor loco operation and identify problems before damage occurs. Achieve maximum realism: Advanced Proportional Tracking Control, momentum circuitry, plus braking and acceleration control make you feel like you're running a real locomotive. Available with 30VA of power, pack can run HO, N, G and other DC trains. Comes with Throttle Master control knob, 300° of control, thermostat protection, AC terminals for accessories and much more.

### Tech 4 Series

Accu-Tec technology provides the smoothest control available today. Most Tech 4 packs have nearly 25% more power than a comparable Tech II. In addition to the power, these durable packs are feature-rich and provide precise control.

**500-200** Tech 4 200 2/17VA **57.98**
This Tech 4 is perfect for upgrading any train set. Complete with sleek new design, improved features and powerful performance.

Tech 4 260 w/20VA & Momentum
500-260

**500-260** Tech 4 260 w/20VA & Momentum **79.98**
The Tech 4 260 is packed with power and all the features you need for a realistic operation, including Accu-Tec technology, PTC, precise momentum circuitry and braking with 25% more power than the comparable Tech II.

**500-220** Tech 4 220 w/16VA & Momentum **69.98**
The Tech 4 220 with Accu-Tec technology and Proportional Tracking Control provides instant response from locomotives throughout their entire speed range and automatically adjusts pulse characteristics to match the locomotive's motor. This Tech 4 has the power to upgrade train sets. Features momentum circuitry and braking control to make you feel as if you're running a real locomotive.

**500-280** Tech 4 280 Dual Power **79.98**
This Tech 4 has two units in one housing, controlling two trains in different blocks with common rail. With dual controls, Accu-Tec technology and Proportional Tracking Control, this Tech 4 provides power and precision in one convenient unit.

| PART NUMBER | DESCRIPTION | EXTENDED RANGE SPEED CONTROL | OVERLOAD LIGHT INDICATOR | DIRECTION CONTROL | ON-OFF SWITCH | MOMENTUM EQUIPPED | AMMETER AND VOLTMETER | POWER FOR AVERAGE TRAINS | FIXED 12V FOR DC EXPANSION |
|---|---|---|---|---|---|---|---|---|---|
| 500-200 | TECH 4 200 | • | | • | • | | | 4-5 | |
| 500-220 | TECH 4 220 | • | | • | • | • | | 4-5 | |
| 500-260 | TECH 4 260 | • | • | • | • | • | | 6-8 | |
| 500-280 | TECH 4 280 | • | | • | • | | | 2-4 | |
| 500-1300 | RAILPOWER 1300 | • | | • | • | | | 3 | |
| 500-1370 | RAILPOWER 1370 | • | | • | • | | | 4-5 | |
| 500-9500 | POWER COMMAND 9500 | • | • | • | • | • | • | 4-6 | • |

## Control Master 20

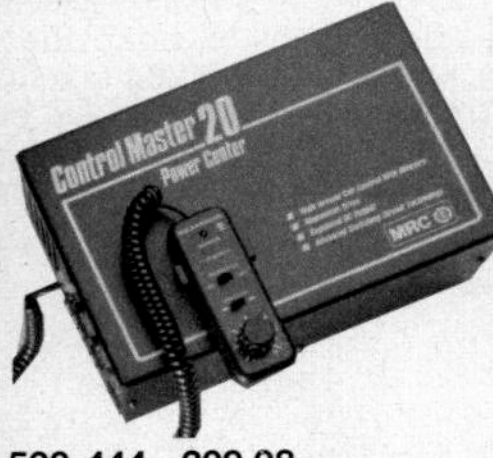


**500-444 209.98**
Handheld control with memory function. HO/N and G Scale. Terminals for ammeter and voltmeter hookup, filtered and regulated DC output, momen-tum circuitry, nudge switch control and a mode switch. 5.0 amps plus reserve power.

## Standard Power Packs

Maximum realism at an economical price. Check out the features on these durable power packs: extended range control throttle, master on-off switch, mainline direction switch and much more.

**500-1300** Railpower 1300 **34.50**
For use with HO, N and Z Scale trains. Total output 7VA on solid state circuitry, designed to deliver superior slow-speed acceleration for increased realism. Features a mainline direction switch, 300° speed control, circuit protection to guard against overload and more.

**500-1370** Railpower 1370 **139.98**
Power for up to five average HO trains! Solid state circuitry delivers 18VA output and superior slow-speed acceleration. Mainline direction switch, on-off switch, red LED pilot light, 300° speed control and circuit protection.

**500-6200** Trainpower 6200 **139.98**
Maximum power for G Scale, but also runs HO scale. Unit provides 60VA output power, plus 0-18.5V DC track voltage. Includes AC output for accessories, mode switch to select HO and N Scale or Large Scale, 300° throttle control and power monitor lamp. Delivers 3.6 amps of power to trains.

# SOUND SYSTEMS

## Symphony 77 Sound Station

**NEW 500-AA555 79.98**
Stand-alone sound system for all scales with digitally recorded sounds. This unit brings railroading to a new dimension of fun and enjoyment. Sounds include diesel idle and user-controllable rev-up, controllable steam chuff rate, rail clack, crossing bell, user-selectable horns and whistles. So versatile you can add sound on sound for added realism. Includes a two-way speaker system, handheld controller, five-watt amplifier and power supply.

## Sound Box

**NEW 500-1025 79.98**
Provides realistic synchronized sounds for both steam and diesel locomotives simply by choosing either mode. Additional accessory sounds for either mode and adjustable volume. Includes speaker for under layout mounting. Easy hookup to your current power pack and layout. Works with both DC and DCC.



## Blackbox

**NEW 500-1050 72.98**
DC users ... unlock the magic in your sound-equipped locomotives. No need for a sound activation box from every locomotive manufacturer. Works with an NMRA-compatible dual-mode decoder-equipped loco. Simple hookup between your power pack and track. Handheld unit lets you control speed, direction and all accessory sound functions available in the locomotive. 1.5 amp capacity.

## On-Board DC Sound Modules

These sound modules give DC users the sounds normally reserved for DCC users. Simply plugs into DCC-ready locomotives and you have on-board locomotive sound controlled by your present power pack. Includes NMRA eight-pin harness and nine-pin JST plug. Speaker also included. Enhance the accessory sounds in these modules with Blackbox #500-1050, sold separately. Sets come with handheld transmitter to control accessory sounds to complement the motor's synchronized sounds. Only one frequency available.

### With Transmitter 84.98 ea

**NEW 500-1000** Early EMD Diesel

**NEW 500-1007** Steam

### Without Transmitter 64.98 ea

Transmitter need to control accessory sounds.

**NEW 500-1001** Early EMD Diesel

**NEW 500-1008** Steam

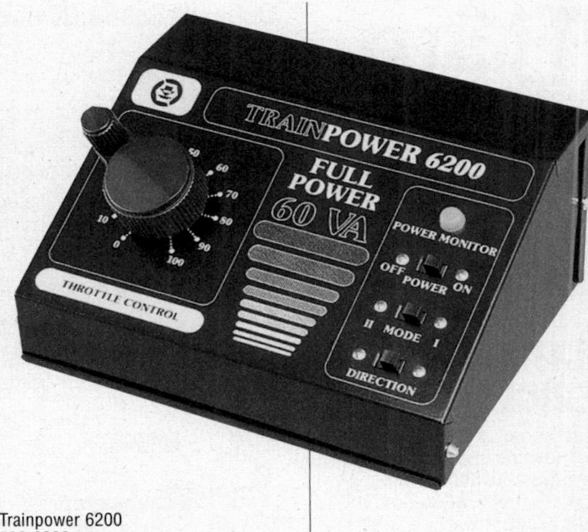


Trainpower 6200
500-6200

Railpower 1370
500-1370

# POWER SUPPLIES

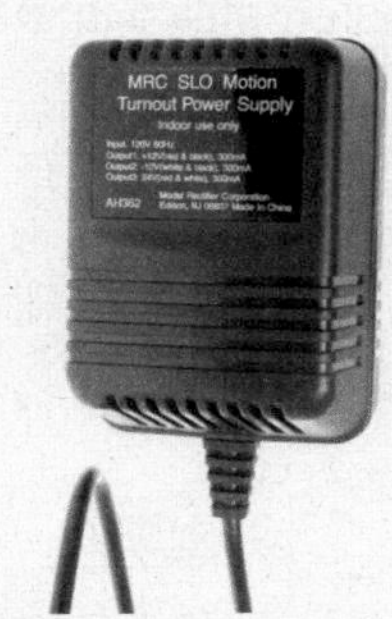


**500-AH362** Slow Motion Switch Machine Power Supply **35.98**
Designed to power all slow-motion (latching) switch machines where the power output must be +12V and –12VDC. Built to handle multiple switch machines. Good for all types of layout control.

# ACCESSORIES

**500-2040** Terminal Strip-Plain **6.98**

**500-2041** Terminal Strip-Wired **7.98**

**500-AT880** Universal Voltage Reducer **9.98**
Can be used with any power control (AC, DC or DCC), scale or gauge (but is especially useful in N Scale applications where top speeds are an issue). It lowers top voltage by approximately four volts. Installs in series between your power source and track.

# SWITCHES

**500-2001** SPST Slide **1.98**

**500-2003** DPDT Slide **3.98**

Ram Track manufacturers a variety of sound devices to provide accurate rendering of a variety of railroad sounds.

## DIGITAL SOUND DEVICES

These complete sound systems now include a train-actuated trigger switch and a speaker amplification box. All systems come with a 2" speaker, but can be replaced by a 1" speaker for onboard HO Scale use. 9-18V.

### Trackside Sound Devices 39.95 ea

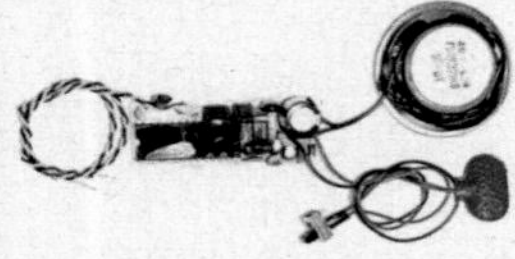

**616-77** Steam Calliope

**616-88** Conductor "All Aboard" Announcement

**616-89** Cattle Sounds

**616-103** Birds

**616-107** Factory Machinery

**616-108** Garage Sounds

**616-114** Crossing Bell

**616-139** Bell – Irregular Ring

**616-140** Bell – Regular Ring

**616-143** Telegraph

**616-148** Sawmill

**616-149** Summer Night

**616-150** Thunderstorm

**616-151** Horses

**616-153** Sheep

**616-154** Trolley Bell

**616-156** Crickets

**616-162** Haunted Sounds

**616-163** Barnyard Animals

Items listed below are available by Special Order (see Legend Page).

**616-104** City Traffic

**616-105** Construction Site

**616-106** Dock Side

**616-146** Honky Tonk Piano

**616-147** Blacksmith

**616-152** Pigs

**616-155** Interurban Horn

**616-157** Hobo Joe

### Onboard Sound Devices 39.95 ea

**616-72** Steam Whistle

**616-73** Diesel Horns

**616-75** Diesel Engine

**616-145** Track Click & Squeal

Items listed below are available by Special Order (see Legend Page).

**616-74** Engine Bell

**616-80** Old-Time Steam Whistle

### Rail Car Engine Sound

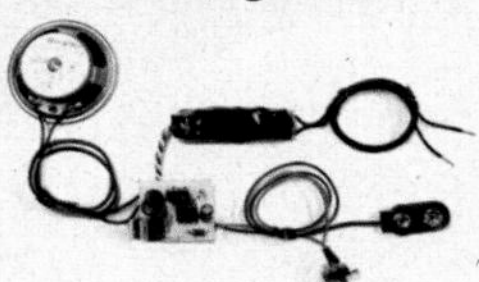

**616-180 39.95**
Bring your rail car alive with sound synchronized to speed, adjustable idle and max RPM. Compact system is easy to install and the included 2" speaker is easily replaced with a 1" (sold separately). Powered by 9V battery.

### A Hooga Horn

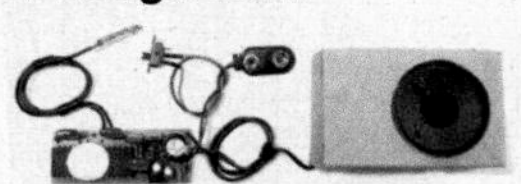

**616-181 39.95**
Add the sound of an old-fashioned car horn to your rail cars. Complete system includes a reed switch triggered by a magnet on the roadbed.

## ANALOG SOUND DEVICES

All systems come with speakers.

### Steam Engine Sounds 49.95 ea

Requires 9V battery power. By turning the axle on your engine, you can produce a steam chuff and hiss sound that is in perfect cadence with your engine's drive wheels. Size mentioned below indicates speaker size.

**616-51** 1"

**616-52** 2"

Item listed below is available by Special Order (see Legend Page).

**616-53** 3"

## CONTROL UNITS

### Xtra Control

**616-76 49.95**
This accessory radio system can turn on lights, sounds, horn, and operate multiple accessories without the use of a DCC system. Can be operated from 100 feet away. Mini-receiver requires 9-18V power supply.

### Station Stopper

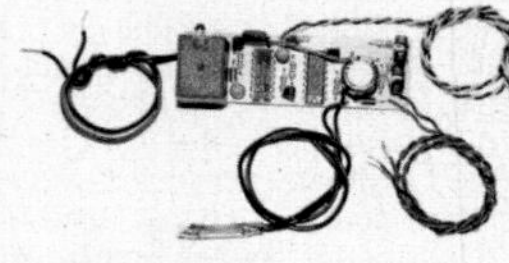

**616-85 34.95**
Train can be delayed for up to one minute.

## POWER SUPPLY DEVICES

### Power Source

**616-59** 9V Rail-Powered Source **14.95**
Will work with AC or DC powered trains (up to 28V), but is designed for use with 9V lighting and sound systems from RamTrack. Includes screw terminal strip for installation.

### Power Regulator

**616-87** 12V DC **24.95**
Provides a filtered, regulated, short circuit and thermally protected DC source to 1-1/2 amps from your power pack's AC source. Can be used to operate DCC accessories.

Get Your Daily Dose of Product News at

**www.walthers.com**

### Signal Driver

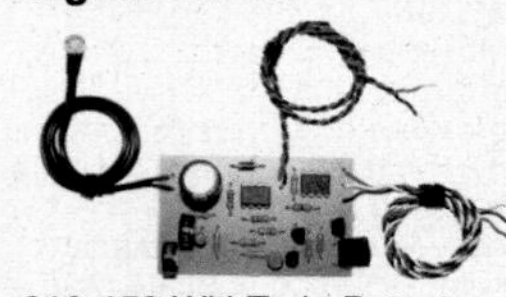

**616-158** WithTrain Detector **24.95**
This driver makes it easy to power any two-color signal (sold separately).

Unit will automatically turn on up to two bulbs or LEDs (up to 100ma) and is triggered by a photocell. In operation, the shadow of a passing train turns off the green light and turns on the red. Once the train passes, the signal can be set to stay red from two to 30 seconds, using the built-in adjustment on the circuit board. Fully assembled, the driver also includes an adjustable light sensor, resistors for use with LED signals, instructions, and a basic wiring diagram.

## SWITCHES

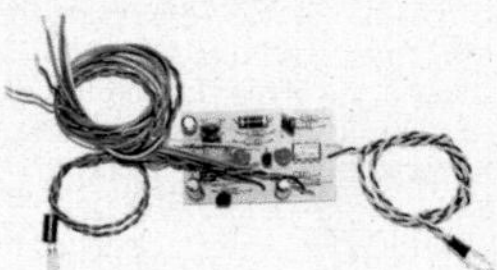

**616-102** Infra-Red **19.95**
1/2 amp, 5-24V DC. Motion-sensing infra-red system eliminates the need for magnets and minimal lighting. Can handle switching device up to 1/2 amp.

**616-111** Light-Activated **14.95**
1/2 amp, 5-24V DC. A small photo cell senses a passing train and switches devices up to 1/2 amp.

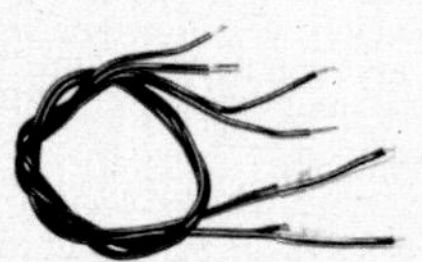

**616-112** Reed Switch & Magnets 2 Sets **9.95**
1" reed switch is triggered by a high-power, rare-earth magnet. Attached to 1' of wire.

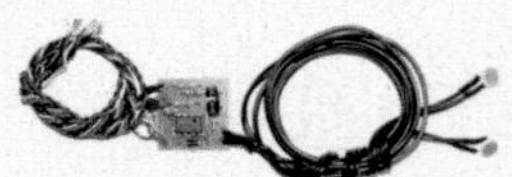

**616-117** Dual Sensor Light-Activated **24.95**
Two small photo cells sense a passing train and switch devices up to 1/2 amp. Perfect for activating a crossing signal.

### Latching Switch

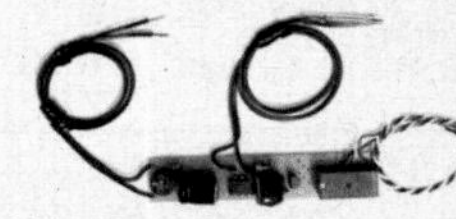

**616-173 19.95**
This on-board switch is activated by magnets to control the action of any on-board feature. Track powered, the 3/4 x 3" circuit has a DPDT relay capable of controlling up to three amps in a variety of configurations.

Item listed below is available by Special Order (see Legend Page).

**616-113** Tilt Switch **9.95**
Responds to random onboard motion. Mounted in rolling stock to randomly trigger devices.

## NEAL'S N GAUGING TRAINS

## NEW PRODUCT

### Power Supply

**NEW 530-1001** Transformer for DCC and/or Accessories **21.95**
3 Amp, Automatic Thermal Protection 16.5V AC 50VA

## NCE

## NEW PRODUCT

### Power Supplies

**NEW 524-224** P1018 Power Supply **89.95**
10 Amp, 15 volt AC power supply for the Power Cab™ system (sold separately) and other uses. Input 120VAC, output 13.5VDC.

2.4gHz Camera System 655-10008

## WIRELESS COLOR CAMERA SYSTEMS

Now you can get the thrill of seeing what it's like to "ride" inside your trains. The WirelessMicroColorCam produces a full-color image and is available with or without sound. The wireless signal range is 300 to 1000'—perfect for most home or club layouts. Tiny enough to be mounted on an N or HOn3 flat car or inside an unpowered HO locomotive (and it'll fit in a few powered units too). Each system includes the camera, wireless receiver, AC power supplies for the camera and receiver, TV/VCR hookup cables, nine volt battery clip for the camera, one nine volt battery and complete instructions. 2.4 gHz receivers cannot receive 1.2 gHz signals and vice-versa.

**NEW 655-10010** With Audio 2.4 ghz **99.95**

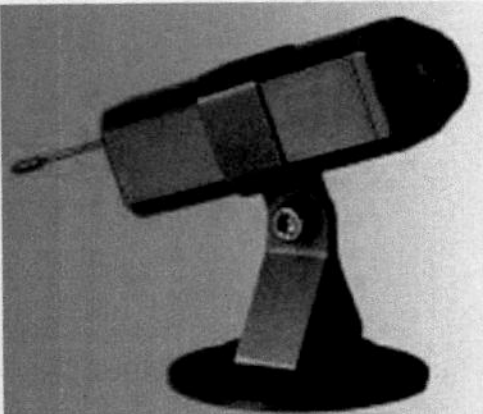

**655-10003** Rechargeable Single Camera With Audio 2.4 gHz **169.95**
Features built-in battery with five-hour recharge life. Also can operate on one of four channels so you can operate four systems at once. Includes recharger.

**655-10004** Two Camera System With Audio 2.4 gHz **199.95**
Double your fun with a two camera system. Switch between the two cameras with the button on the receiver or use the hand held TV-style remote. You can also program the receiver to automatically switch between the two cameras at a 7-8 second interval. The cameras have built-in microphones and mounting brackets so you can position them in your desired location.

### 2.4gHz Camera System

**655-10008** CCS-811T1 2.4 gHz w/Audio **149.95**
Perfect for adding a second camera-equipped train to your layout! This system has the same features as 655-10002, plus it includes two AC power supplies - one for the receiver and another for stationary camera operation. Also comes with a a camera mounting bracket, 9V battery clip and 9V battery for mobile camera operation.This system operates on 2.4 gHz and will not receive or interfere with 1.2 gHz cameras.

### Night Vision Camera System

**655-10009** CCS-812T **199.95**
Now you can see and hear in total darkness—perfect for simulated nighttime operations on your layout! It's also ideal for checking inside tunnel clearances on your layout and looking for hidden obstructions. Designed for indoor or outdoor use, the camera/transmitter is completely weather proof and has an unobstructed effective range of 100 meters or more between the camera and the receiver! The built in infrared LEDs will illuminate an area up to 23 feet from the camera. The camera view angle is 62 degrees. The camera can be operated from a 9 volt battery or for extended use a 9 volt AC power supply is included. It's also great as a security camera, for watching backyard critters at night or for night use on garden railroads.

**655-10005** 9V Battery Eliminator For DCC & BEC Control **29.95**
Use in place of battery for operation on DCC, TMCC and DCS layouts. Operates off track current or connection to function outputs on a DCC decoder.

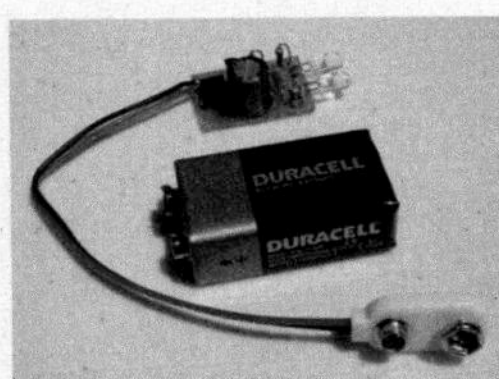


**655-10006** Super Bright White LED Light Board **29.95**
Light the way for your camera with this bright light board. Operates off a 9V battery or from any 5-18V AC or DC power source.

**655-10007** 9V AC Power Supply For Receivers or Cameras **12.95**

SEUTHE®

IMPORTED FROM GERMANY
BY WALTHERS

A quality line of smoke/steam generators for various foreign and domestic locomotives. Generators for structures and ships are also available.

## SMOKE & STEAM

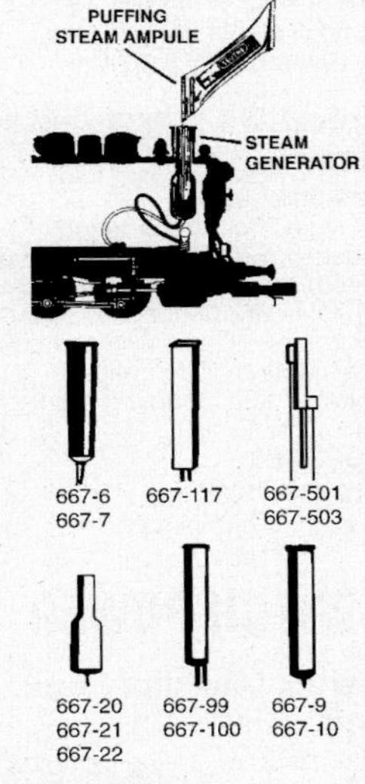


### Accessories

**667-101** Loco Smoke 10ml **5.99**
Bottle with filling tool.

**667-105** Neutral Steam Distillate, 50ml **10.99**

**667-106** Neutral Steam Distillate, 250ml **20.99**

**667-200** Steam Pipes pkg(6) **6.99**
For use with 667-10 Steam Generator.

### Smoke Generators

**667-5** 4-6V **27.99**
Smoke generator for ships and similar models.

**667-117** Smoke Chimney 16V **14.99**
For houses or buildings.

**667-117E** Chimney - Ready for Model Buildings **9.99**
No accessories included.

### Universal Smoke Generators 27.99 ea

**667-27** 10-16V

**667-28** 16-22V

### Steam Generators 27.99 ea

**667-6** Operating Voltage 14V
For model structures and factory chimneys as well as all O Gauge locomotives.

**667-7** Operating Voltage 16V
For model structures and factory chimneys as well as all O Gauge locomotives. Especially for Marklin 5700.

**667-9** Operating Voltage 14V
For Fleischmann 4170, 4175, 4177 and 4178; also, Marklin-Hamo DC (8335).

**667-10** Maximum 16V AC/DC
For Marklin 3046, 3047, 3048, 3084, 3085 and 3102; also Fleischmann and Liliput.

**667-11** Maximum 16V AC/DC
Same as #10 except for Marklin digital.

**667-12** Operating Voltage 16V
Same as #100 except for Marklin digital.

**667-20** Maximum 16V AC/DC
For Marklin 3083, 3091 and 3093; also, Hamo 8391, 8392 and 8393.

**667-21** Maximum 16V AC/DC
Universal type for all locomotives with metal bodies and extremely slim chimneys.

**667-22** Maximum 16V AC/DC
Universal type for all locomotives with plastic bodies and extremely slim chimneys.

**667-23** Maximum 16V AC/DC
Same as #22 except for Marklin digital.

**667-24** Maximum 16V AC/DC
Same as #20 except for Marklin digital.

**667-99** Operating Voltage 14V
For all types of locomotives with plastic bodies.

**667-100** Operating Voltage 16V
For all types of locomotives with plastic bodies.

### Super Smoke Units

**667-500** Ship Models/Large Chimneys **40.99**

**667-501** 12V w/Smoke Fluid **35.99**

**667-503** 16V w/Smoke Fluid **35.99**

### Supersteam Generator

**667-490** With Hose Connector **40.99**

**667-491** For Storage Vessels **35.99**

## SCALE SHOPS

### Voltrollers

Throttle/Knob Appearance May Vary

**1.5 Amp**

**649-1315** Walk-Around Throttle Kit **39.98**

**649-1316** Walk-Around Throttle, Assembled **69.98**

**649-1319** Panel Throttle Kit **19.98**

**3 Amp**

**649-1339** Panel Throttle Kit **29.98**

Items listed below are available by Special Order (see Legend Page).

**649-1335** Walk-Around Throttle Kit **49.98**

**649-1336** Walk-Around Throttle, Assembled **79.98**

**649-1338** Cabinet Throttle, Assembled **69.98**

## TRAIN TRONICS

## SOUND SYSTEMS

### Diesel Horn

**723-301** 3-Toned Diesel Horn Kit **27.95**

Kit includes push button speaker mounting clips and 3" speaker. To expand system add #723-415 speakers at various points around your layout. 6 to 16V AC/DC.

### Steam Whistle w/Diesel Horn

**723-305 89.95**

Provides both three-toned steam whistle with background steam hiss and three-chimed diesel horn. Kit contains solid-state prebuilt and tested circuit, push button, slide control, speaker and mounting clips.

### Speaker

**723-415 5.95**

8 ohm, 3" in diameter.

## SWITCH POWER

### Switch Machine Power Unit

Capable of operating up to 20 turnouts simultaneously, with positive snap-action. Operates any type of dual coil switch machine.

**723-603** Switchman Capacitive Discharge Unit **39.95**

**723-1801** AC Converter for Zero-1 **7.95**

**723-1804** Conductive Paint for Zero-1 **2.50**

Item listed below is available by Special Order (see Legend Page).

**723-1805** Power Booster for Zero-1 **99.95**

## VOLLMER

IMPORTED FROM GERMANY BY WALTHERS

### Smoke Unit

**770-1282** Smoke Generator **69.99**

For House on Fire #770-1280 (sold separately). Wisps of real smoke rise and float out of the building, producing a highly realistic scene. The unit comes fully assembled with hook-up wires.

**770-4112** Large Smoke Generator **50.99**

**770-4114** Smoke Generator **48.99**

Features a large tank for smoke-making. Includes enough fluid for 70 minutes of smoke.

**770-4116** Steam Distillate 250ml **23.99**

# COMMAND CONTROL

Models and Photo by Lou Sassi

Years of experience ride with you on every run. You know where the little hills are in the track that require just the slightest touch of sand to keep a heavy freight moving. You know where the low spots are that can make for a rough ride. Every smell, sound and vibration tells you something about how good, or bad, your engine is running today. Spotting the familiar white station at Hoosic Junction, you ease off the throttle and make your brake reduction, bringing the freight to a stop so slowly they can barely feel it in the caboose.

Time was when it took years of hands-on work and training to learn the ins and outs of being an engineer. You started out as a fireman, learning that important job first, before one day taking and passing the examinations that would promote you to the right-hand seat.

Today's modern electronic can't take you back in time, but thanks to the amazing level of realism that's possible with Command Control, you can get a feel for what it's like to be a working engineer. Inside this section you'll find a growing selection of throttles, decoders, sound accessories and much more that will help you take your entire railroad to a new level of realistic operation. Lou Sassi of Charlton, New York, posed a custom painted brass import of a Boston & Maine 2-8-0 along his layout for this photo.

# E-Z DOES IT!

## E-Z COMMAND®

### HO, N, and On30 Digital Command Control System

**$113.00**

Unsure about DCC? Bachmann invites you put your mind at ease with *E-Z Command,* the next step in digital command control. In partnership with Lenz Elektronik GmbH, Bachmann incorporates the latest digital technology to bring modelers a DCC system that is both easy to use and affordable. With a simplified programming process and intuitive controls, *E-Z Command* gives modelers digital mastery of speed, lighting, direction, and sound activation functions of multiple locomotives, employing plug-and-play compatibility with both existing DC systems and NMRA-compliant DCC railroads.

Also available are *E-Z Command Controller with DCC-Equipped Locomotive* sets that allow you to get your digital railroad up and running in no time. And an assortment of separate-sale HO scale *DCC On Board*™ locomotives round out Bachmann's digital line, with total lighting control, all-wheel drive, and 28-speed step decoders for smooth operation. So take it easy! Visit your local hobby retailer today to learn more about Bachmann's *E-Z Command* and *DCC On Board* locomotives.

- Easy and Affordable DCC
- Control Speed, Direction, Lighting, and Sound Activation
- 1 Amp Power Supply
- Plug-and-Play Compatibility
- Simple Programming on the Main
- Conforms to NMRA Standards
- DCC-Equipped Locomotives

*E-Z COMMAND®* CONTROL CENTER
Item No. 44902
**$113.00**

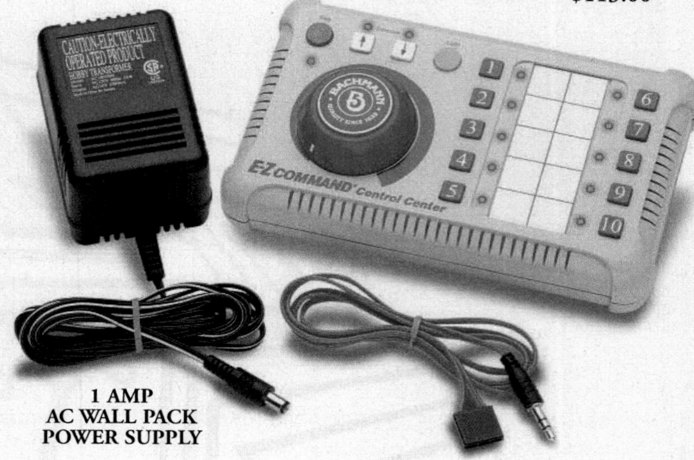


**1 AMP AC WALL PACK POWER SUPPLY**

**EMD GP40 CHESSIE**
Item No. 44905

**EMD GP40 SANTA FE**
Item No. 44904

**EMD GP50 NORFOLK SOUTHERN**
Item No. 44906

***E-Z COMMAND®***
*DCC System with DCC-Equipped Locomotive*

**$165.00 each**

***Features include:***

- DCC-equipped diesel locomotive
- *E-Z Command®* control center
- 1 amp AC wall pack power supply
- connects to any track system
- DVD format video instructions

An N scale version of our HO scale Santa Fe GP40 is shown for illustration purposes.

# E-Z COMMAND® SYSTEM

## Control System

**160-44902 113.00**
This DCC system, developed in conjunction with Lenz, allows modelers to digitally control speed, lighting and direction of multiple locomotives with simplified, one-button, main-track programming. The system features plug-and-play compatibility with all DC and DCC systems.

## Control System w/DCC-Equipped Locomotive

Each DCC-equipped diesel locomotive includes an E-Z Command control center and an AC wall pack power supply.

**EMD GP40 165.00 ea**
**160-44904** ATSF
**160-44905** Chessie
**160-44917** WM
**160-44918** CR
**NEW 160-44922** DRGW

**EMD GP50 High Hood**
**160-44906** NS **155.00**

**0-6-0 w/Tender 180.00 ea**
**160-44919** UP
**160-44920** GN
**160-44921** Unlettered

# E-Z COMMAND ACCESSORIES

## Walk-Around Companion

**160-44907 100.00**
Control multiple trains from convenient locations around your layout or coordinate independent operations between a primary and a secondary user. Features a plug-and-play connection to E-Z Command Control Center. It duplicates all locomotive addresses set on E-Z Command Control Center and allows simultaneous throttle control of several locomotives. Includes connector wires.

## Walk-Around Companion Connector Panel

**160-44908 38.00**
Used in conjunction with the Walk-Around Companion, multiple connector panels let you establish a series of control points virtually anywhere on the perimeter of your layout. Features plug-in ports and simple connections to all brands of track. Includes connector wires.

## Five-Amp Power Booster

**160-44910 250.00**
This device provides extra current to the track for the control of an increased number of DCC locomotives on your HO, N or On30 layout. Also appropriate for DCC decoder-equipped large scale locomotives.

## Automatic Reversing Loop Module

**160-44912 69.00**
Eliminates the complicated wiring previously needed to operate analog reverse-loop track layouts. The module senses train as it moves along the loop, automatically switching polarity to allow reverse loop control.

## E-Z Command DCC Decoders

### Turnout & Accessory Decoder

**160-44911 TBA**
Assume digital command of your entire layout with on/off control of turnouts, operating accessories and scenery elements.

### One-Amp Locomotive Decoders

Introduce your locomotives to the digital age with these basic one-amp decoders. E-Z Command decoders are compatible with NMRA compliant DCC systems. Features include: service mode decoder lock for main line programming, two- or four-digit addresses, advanced consisting and 28/128 speed steps. Decoders can control speed, direction and lighting functions and are offered in two versions with wire harnesses (for hard-wiring) or with eight-pin plug (for DCC-ready, NMRA socket-equipped locomotives).

EMD GP40 ATSF 160-44904

EMD GP40 Chessie 160-44905

EMD GP50 High Hood NS 160-44906

**160-44913** With Wire Harness **26.00**

**160-44914** With Wire Harness pkg(3) **76.50**

**160-44915** With NMRA Eight-Pin Plug **28.00**

**160-44916** With NMRA Eight-Pin Plug pkg(3) **82.00**

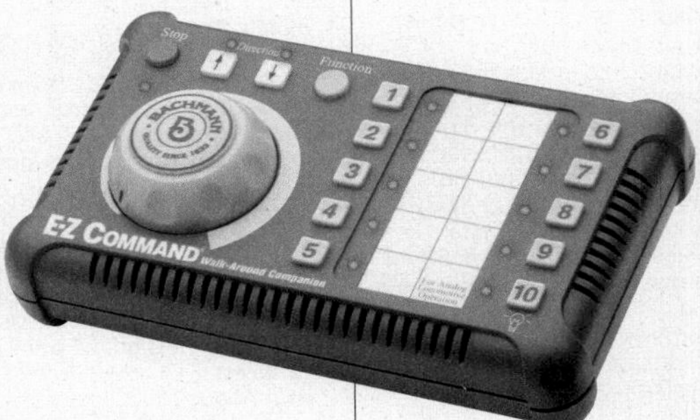

Walk-Around Companion 160-44907

Run your trains, not your track with the complete line of Digitrax Command Control Sets and components.

## Plug 'N Play Signaling

## DIGITRAX PLUG 'N PLAY SIGNALING

The Digitrax Plug 'N Play Signal system is the perfect way to add signaling to your layout. And whether you use DC or DCC controls, it will add a new dimension of realism to operations.

The SE8C Signal Decoder is the heart of the system, and can drive up to 32 signal heads using most popular signal types like bi-color LED searchlight types with two or three leads, or 3-LED heads with common anode or cathode. It can even drive B&O or Pennsy type heads with multiple indicators. Current resistors are built-in for setting LED brightness. The SE8C can also be used to drive 8 slow-motion turnout machines, such as Circuitron's Tortoise™ or eight semaphore signals driven by slow-motion turnout machines. The SE8C provides 16 inputs, eight control lines for local turnout control and eight occupancy sensor inputs.

A full line of accessory products let you use modular plug 'n play wiring and components to install a fully customizable signaling system on your railroad. The Signal Driver Cable Kits take the hassle out of running wires for your signal system. Signal Mast Base Kits, Terminal Mounting Strip Kits and Signal Hardware Mounting Kits make it easy to use either inexpensive circuit board type signals, or your own finely detailed signals with the system.

If you're using a computer to control your layout, the Digitrax Plug 'N Play Signaling System is a great way to add prototypical signaling to your railroad. If you're not using a computer, the SE8C Signal Decoder lets you manually operate signals on the layout from your throttle. With a computer and compatible software, you'll be able to realize the full potential of the Digitrax Plug 'N Play Signaling System.

**245-SE8C** Signal Decoder **125.00**

**245-SDCK** Signal Driver Cable Kit **19.99**

**245-SMHK** Signal Mounting Hardware Kit **9.99**

**245-TSMK** Terminal Strip Mounting Kit (2 Boards) **14.99**

**245-SMBK** Signal Mast Base Kit pkg(3) **14.99**

## STARTER SETS

### Zephyr Basic Digitrax Command Control Starter Set

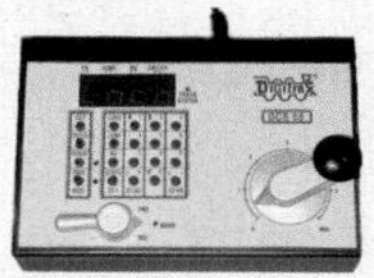

**245-ZEP 199.99**
An affordable entry into the world of DCC, this set is designed with the small layout in mind, but can easily grow if your railroad expands. Ideal for single or multiple operators, up to 10 additional throttles/operators can be accommodated. All-in-one unit incorporates throttle, command station and booster into an easy-to-use DCC controller. The Zephyr provides 128-step speed control, easy access to 10 functions that can be used for a multitude of special effects including sound (functions 0 through 8), constant brightness headlight on/off, direction control, access to four-digit addresses and turnout control. Set includes Zephyr DCS50 and power supply, decoder test kit, Zephyr Users Manual and Digitrax Decoder Users Manual. No decoder is included with this set, giving you the freedom to choose from Digitrax' wide variety of DCC decoders to fit your needs (decoders sold separately).

### Super Empire Builder Advanced Digitrax Command Control Starter Set

Advanced features provide easier, more prototypical operation. You spend lots of time making your locos look like the real thing, now make them run like the real thing, too!

Super Empire Builder delivers access to all Digitrax LocoMotion® System and FX³ System features including 128-step speed control and consist control, as well as access to four-digit addressing, turnout control, consisting, adjustable network synchronized fast clock and much more. The DT400 handheld walk-around dual throttle with full numeric keypad gives you control of two locos—you can run more than one train, control helpers, or handle multiple-unit operation on the head end. Backlit LCD display shows you train speed, direction, function status and more. The DT400 throttle even has a built in flashlight so you can read your paperwork in darkened layout rooms. Run up to 22 addresses with up to 22 operators with Super Empire Builder.

Super Empire Builder comes with a simple and intuitive Infra-Ready DT400 throttle that makes converting to wireless infrared operation as easy as adding IR Receiver UR90 or UR91 (sold separately). Also included is a DB150 Command Station/Booster with Intelligent Auto Reversing, UP5 LocoNet Panel, LT1 LocoNet Cable & Decoder Test Kit and easy-to-understand Super Empire Builder and Digitrax Decoder Users Manuals. Decoders not included.

The radio equipped version comes with the DT400R Radio Throttle and UR91 radio receiver. Approximate signal range is a 300' circle. Operates approximately 6-8 hours on fully charged NiCad batteries, 10-20 hours on alkaline batteries or can be run as a plug-in throttle with no batteries. (Please Note: Radio-equipped sets are available only in the US and Canada.)

**245-SEB** Super Empire Builder Advanced Starter Set **349.99**

**245-SEBRE** Radio-Equipped Super Empire Builder Advanced Starter Set **549.99**

Various decoders shown.

### Super Chief Premium Digitrax Command Control Starter Sets

Designed for the needs of any size home or club layout where operations are the key, the Super Chief Starter Set has more features than any other DCC set on the market. Large system command station has capacity for handling up to 120 addresses with up to 120 operators at a time. Super Chief gives you access to all Digitrax LocoMotion System and FX³ System features including four digit addressing, 128-step speed control, consist control, programming "on the fly," turnout control, adjustable network synchronized fast clock, and much, much more.

Your Super Chief has a separate programming output that allows for read back of programming information.

Super Chief sets come with a DT400 Infra-Ready throttle that makes converting to wireless operation as easy as adding the Infra-Red Receiver UR90 or UR91 (sold separately). The radio-equipped version comes with the DT400R Radio Throttle and UR91 radio receiver. (Please Note: Radio-equipped sets are available only in the US and Canada.)

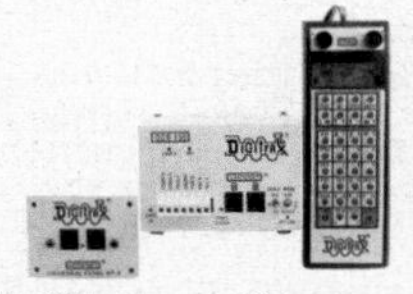

**245-SCF** Super Chief Premium Starter Set 5 Amps **449.99**

**245-SCF200** Super Chief Premium Starter Set 8 Amps **469.99**

**245-SCFRE** Radio-Equipped Super Chief Premium Starter Set 5 Amps **639.99**

**245-SCFRE200** Radio-Equipped Super Chief Premium Starter Set 8 Amps **659.99**

## MOBILE DECODERS

Digitrax mobile DCC decoders offer exciting DCC features at great low prices! All Digitrax decoders are rated for at least 1 amp for robust operation and long-term reliability. Available a variety of shapes and sizes to fit in almost any locomotive. Digitrax offers both traditional wired decoders as well as plug n' play decoders that make installation a snap. Visit Digitrax on the internet to determine which Digitrax decoder fits in your loco!

Digitrax decoders feature variable frequency Supersonic™ motor drive for quiet motor operation. They support all DCC standard programming methods. One-step decoder factory reset makes it easy to troubleshoot decoders. Motor isolation protection protects your investment in locos and decoders. Digitrax decoders support both two and four digit addressing and basic, advanced and universal consisting. They also have operations mode read-back capability so you can read back programming information while the decoder is on the main line.

Digitrax decoders are DCC compatible and can be used with any DCC compatible system.

## FX3 Function Systems

All Digitrax decoders are now FX3 capable. FX3 functions are fully remappable so they can be controlled by any function key on your system. Here's an example of remapping - a master light switch can be set to turn off all lights on a locomotive. Functions associated with advanced consists can be controlled too! FX or enhanced FX³ features. FX makes it easy to install prototypical lighting effects, like Mars lights, ditch lights and others, without having to buy and install an additional circuit board in your loco. All Digitrax decoders offer directional, constant-brightness headlights that can also be programmed for independent operation by the user. All Digitrax decoders offer full function re-mapping so you can choose which function (F0-F12) controls each function lead.

## The Digitrax LocoMotion® System

The Digitrax LocoMotion System gives you all the features and options you need to get the best operation possible from DCC equipped locos. All Digitrax mobile decoders come with 128-step speed control with torque compensation for smooth operation.

When you program the decoders, you can customize the momentum with acceleration and deceleration settings, set the normal direction of travel for your loco — long hood or short hood forward — just like the prototype. The switching speed feature gives you convenient, quick access to low speeds for switching operations.

With easy-to-set-up 3-step speed tables, you can determine the throttle response curve of each individual loco on the railroad. Your switchers run like switchers and your road engines run like road engines. Advanced 28-step speed table with 256 level resolution gives you even more precise control over how each loco responds to the throttle.

Premium decoders also include the Digitrax smooth, scaleable speed stabilization feature. You can further enhance your LocoMotion system by setting up this feature to compensate for the load on the loco to smooth out operation at very slow speeds and speed changes caused by track grade.

## These Tiny Decoders Handle One Full Amp!

**245-DZ143** Wired Decoder **34.95**

**245-DZ143PS** Decoder w/Medium DCC Plug on Short Harness **37.95**
This premium decoder will fit in those tiny spaces where nothing else will! Rated at one full amp for reliability in HO scale operation, these decoders are small enough to fit in N or Z scale engines. Measures .36 x .55 x .13" 9.1 x 13.9 x 3.2mm. Decoders are equipped for the Digitrax LocoMotion System with Scaleable Speed Stabilization, full FX³ features with four functions available, and transponding.

**245-DZ123** Wired Decoder **19.99**

**245-DZ123PS** Decoder w/Medium DCC Plug on Short Harness **22.99**
This full-featured, economy-priced decoder is the same size as DZ143. Includes the Digitrax LocoMotion System and standard FX features with two functions available.

## Our Most Popular HO Decoders With Nine-Pin Easy Connect Interface

Digitrax DH Series Decoders are recommended for most HO applications. The Digitrax nine-pin plug offers several different installation options to fit the needs of most HO modelers. Easy-connect plugs let you share decoders among several locos equipped with harnesses.

### DH123

1.5 amps (2.0 amps peak) approximate size .63 x 1.1 x .22" 16.0 x 27.9 x 5.6 mm. Low-cost DCC operation with Digitrax LocoMotion™ System and two Digitrax standard FX functions. Digitrax HO Easy-Connect nine-pin interface gives you many installation options.

**245-DH123D** Decoder w/Digitrax Harness **19.99**

**245-DH123P** Decoder w/DCC Medium Plug on Long Harness **22.99**

**245-DH123PS** Decoder w/DCC Medium Plug on Short Harness **22.99**

**245-DH123AT** Decoder w/Athearn Standard No-Solder Harness **24.99**

### DH163

Premium HO Decoder rated at 1.5 amps (2.0 amps peak), approximate size .63 x 1.1 x .22" 16.0 x 27.9 x 5.6 mm. Handles the Digitrax LocoMotion System with Scaleable Speed Stabilization, full FX³ features on six function leads and transponding.

**245-DH163D** Series 3 Decoder **29.99**

**245-DH163P** Decoder w/DCC Medium Plug on Long Harness **32.99**

**245-DH163PS** Decoder w/DCC Medium Plug on Short Harness **32.99**

**245-DH163AT** Decoder w/Athearn Standard No-Solder Harness **34.99**

### Accessories for DH Series Decoders

Accessory wire harnesses match those included with Digitrax DH series decoders. Extra harnesses allow you to share DH Series decoders among several locos in your fleet. Dummy plugs allow for non-DCC operation of harness equipped locomotives.

**245-DHWH** Digitrax Standard Wiring Harness 5 Pack **15.00**

**245-DHWHP** Digitrax Plug to DCC Medium Plug on 6" (long) Wire Harness **6.00**

**245-DHWHPS** Digitrax Plug to DCC Medium plug on 1.5" (short) Wire Harness **6.00**

**245-DHAT** Digitrax Plug to Athearn Standard No-Solder Harness **8.95**

**245-DHDP** Dummy Plug 5-pack for DH Harnesses **20.00**

### DH163IP-Integrated DCC Plug for Quick Installation in most HO Locos with Medium DCC Socket

Rated at 1.5 amps (2.0 peak) for HO locos. This premium-featured plug n' play decoder is equipped for use with the Digitrax LocoMotion System with Scaleable Speed Stabilization, full FX³ features with six functions available, and transponding. Approximate size .652 x .923 x .2" 16.5 x 23.4 x 5.1mm.

**245-DH163IP** Decoder w/Integral Medium DCC Plug **29.99**



## Plug N' Play Replacement Decoders for Kato, Atlas, Athearn Genesis & Life-Like

Designed to fit Kato, Atlas, Athearn Genesis, Life-Like and other diesels with circuit boards inside the loco, the DH1165 series decoders are rated at 1.5 Amp/2 Amp with 6 FX functions rated at 1/2 Amp and Sound Bug™ ready. The Sound Bug gives you the ability to plug in sound whenever you're ready. Purchase a DH165 decoder today and get "drop-in" type ease of installation, full FX3 features with six functions available and 1.5 amps of power. And when you're ready, purchase a Sound Bug module insert it into the decoder's sound socket and upgrade to realistic, downloadable sound.

### For Kato Locos

**NEW 245-DH165K0 27.99**

### For Kato SD40-2

**NEW 245-DH165K1 27.99**

### For Atlas Locos

**NEW 245-DH65A0 26.99**

### For Life-Like Locos

**NEW 245-DH165L0 26.99**

## Sound Bug Add-On to the 165 Series

**NEW 245-SFX004 49.99**
Sound generator module lets you add 4 bit/1 watt sound capability to DH 165xx-series decoders as well as stand-alone trackside sound.

## Function Decoders with Transponding

Various function decoders shown

Put more fun in your DCC operations with these tiny, function-only decoders. Use them to control lighting effects aboard your locomotives and other rolling stock. Approximate size is 0.461 x 0.31 x 0.161". Function decoders support two- and four-digit addressing and feature on/off functions or configurable strobe operation to simulate special lighting effects. TL1 supports F0 forward and reverse, it's great for adding a FRED at the end of the train. TF4 supports F0-F12, expanding the functions available for making loco lighting more realistic.

Programmable from DCC compatible programmers which can handle Digitrax transponding.

**245-TL1** Single Function Decoder w/Transponding **18.95**

**245-TF4** Quad Function Decoder w/Transponding **20.95**

## SOUND DECODERS

Add the dimension of authentic sound to your locomotive fleet with Digitrax Plug 'N Play Mobile Decoders with SoundFX™

### Lighting Function Decoder

**245-FN04K1 24.98**
This stand-alone function decoder is designed for use with the SDH104K1 SoundFX and LocoMotion Decoder. Features four functions with selectable outputs for controlling lighting functions. This alone is NOT a sound decoder, but is the function component of a sound decoder installation using a SoundFX decoder.

### SoundFX Decoders

Digitrax Plug 'N Play Mobile Decoders with SoundFX control locomotive motor and sound functions. Exciting new one-amp mobile decoder from Digitrax has all the LocoMotion features you've come to expect and SoundFX, too! Based on proven locomotive decoder technology, the decoder has preloaded sounds and can also handle downloadable sound. Supports the playable whistle feature with F2 key on DT400 throttles. Includes 28mm speaker. For complete control including lighting functions, use the FN04K1 Function Decoder with the SDH104 series decoder, or purchase the Combo Pack that includes the SoundFX decoder, 28mm speaker and FN04K1 lighting function decoder.

### Fits Kato AC4400

**245-SDH104K1A** Sound FX Decoder Only **64.98**

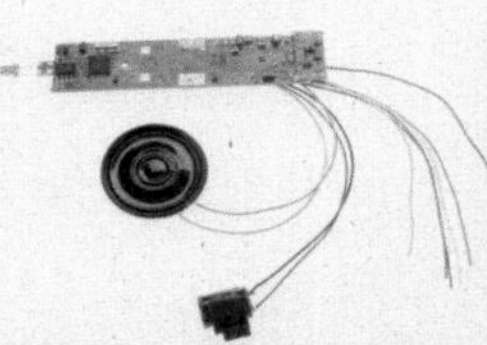

**245-SDH104K1AC** Combo Pack **79.98**

### Fits Kato SD38

**245-SDH104K1B** Sound FX Decoder Only **64.98**

**245-SDH104K1BC** Combo Pack **79.98**

### Fits Kato F40PH

**245-SDH104K1C** Sound FX Decoder Only **64.98**

**245-SDH104K1CC** Combo Pack **79.98**

## WIRE

**245-DCDRWIRE** Decoder Wire 9-Conductor 30 AWG - 10' **14.99**

## STATIONARY DECODERS

Designed to control turnouts and other accessories.

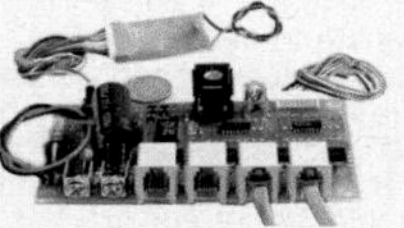

**245-DS44** Quad Stationary Decoder **39.99**
Control four slow-motion turnout machines. Quick set up for sequential addresses or set up for four independent addresses.

**245-DS51K1** For Kato Unitrack Turnouts **14.99**
Easy to use, cost-effective control for a single Kato Unitrack turnout or similar device. Rated at 1/2 amp. Great for HO and N Scale turnouts. Small size .319 x .509 x .152" 8.11 x 12.94 x 3.88mm.

**245-DS52** Dual Stationary Decoder **24.95**
Screw terminals make installation and set-up easy. Control two solenoid type turnout machines: two-wire bi-polar (Kato UnitrackSwitches, etc.) and/or three-wire (Peco, Atlas Snap Switches etc.). Addresses can be independent or sequential. For all scales up to 22V track power.

**NEW 245-DS64** 4-Output **59.99**
The DS64 Stationary Decoder allows you to install and operate up to four turnouts directly through any DCC system that has turnout control. Works with solenoid turnout machines and slow motion motors. Other features: easy to install, compatible with LocoNet, has an integral capacitor discharge, power from track or separate booster, buffered switch inputs and DCC compatible.

**245-DM1** Motor Adapter for DS54 **9.99**
In-line adapter modifies DS54 output to provide bi-polar drive current to run reversible DC motors, solenoid switches (like Kato & LGB turnouts), lamps and similar devices that draw up to 1/12 amp.

## THROTTLES

### Utility Throttles

These new throttles provide the optimum features requested for model railroad operation. The UT4 family integrates intuitive operation with rock solid design and low cost into a single, hand-held throttle featuring:

- 4-Digit Addressing
- Affordable Price
- Standard InfraReady
- UT4 upgradeable to UT4R radio version
- Functions F0-F12 for sound decoder operation
- Direction switch with center brake position
- Improved battery life
- Large knob for precise throttle control
- Automatic Selection and Speed matching features

**245-UT4** Standard **79.95**
**245-UT4R** Radio **129.99**

### Advanced Throttles

Digitrax user-friendly advanced throttles are designed for use with all LocoNet based systems; these dual control throttles offer tethered operation or wireless remote control with your choice of radio or infra-red signals.

With two sets of controls for locos, you can easily run two separate trains, multiple-unit lash-ups or mid- and end of train helpers. The dual controls make setting up and breaking up consists simple! Each throttle knob is a click encoder that rotates several times from zero to full speed. This gives you very fine speed control. Because it's an encoder, when you select a loco to run, the throttle knob will pick up the loco at its actual speed. You won't have to adjust the throttle knob to the speed of the loco on the track and if the loco is sitting still, it won't move until you turn the throttle knob. With the click encoder feature, single click the knob to recall locos previously in use and double click to reverse the loco you're running.

The multi-line, backlit LCD gives you all the information you need to run the railroad including controlling locos and turnouts, handling consist operations, programming locos and turnouts, controlling loco functions and setting up system parameters to customize your operation.

Units do not require batteries for tethered operation. For radio or infra-red operation, units use a 9V battery. When a battery is in use, they will operate for approximately 6-8 hours on fully-charged NiCad batteries or 10-20 hours on alkaline batteries. For radio operation, a UR91 Radio Receiver (sold separately) is available. For infra-red operation, one or more UR90 IR Receivers (sold separately) are needed.

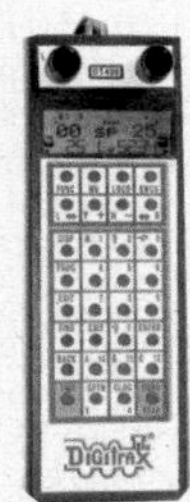

**245-DT400** Super Walk-Around IR **179.99**

**245-DT400R** Super Throttle Radio **229.99**
Full numeric keypad, single key controls for function control, MU operations, programming, editing and more. Controls functions 0-12.

Radio throttles have an approximate circular signal range of 300' 7.5m and operate in the 900Mhz band.

The antenna is located inside the case. Radio throttles have short cords to allow user to plug-in in case of emergency. Safety selection feature prevents more than one user from running the same loco. (Note: Radio control throttles are available only in the US and Canada.)

## WIRELESS SYSTEM RECEIVERS

UR90 and UR91 wireless receivers let you use your Digitrax Infra-Red or Radio Equipped Throttles (sold separately) as wireless throttles. You won't have to be plugged in to the layout to run your trains! Receivers look like other Digitrax Universal Panels and mount in the fascia of your layout. They connect quickly and simply to your existing LocoNet wiring. Each receiver supports approximately 10 throttles. Both types of receivers can be used at the same time on the layout. Normal tethered operation can also be used at the same time. UR90 and UR91 support all Digitrax IR or Radio equipped throttles including DT300, DT400, DT300R, DT400R, DT100IR and DT100R.

**245-UR90** Infra-Red Receiver **45.95**
Most layouts will need more than one receiver, as infra-red operation requires a line of sight signal. UR90 also includes one regular throttle jack for plugging in any Digitrax throttle. Digitrax IR throttles have a wide coverage area because they use dual LED emitters for better coverage. Requires 12V DC external power supply, use a single Digitrax PS12 power supply (sold separately) to power up to 10 UP and/or UR panels.

**245-UR91** Radio/Infra-Red Receiver **149.99**
Radio antenna is concealed under the layout. Most layouts need only one UR91, but some large areas may require a second unit to compensate for "dead" spots. UR91 also has an infra-red receiver and a regular throttle jack for plugging in any Digitrax throttle. PS12 power supply is included.

## AUTOMATIC REVERSING & POWER MANAGEMENT EQUIPMENT

### AR1 Single Automatic Reversing Section Controller.

**245-AR1 29.99**
Easy to use, works with any DCC layout. Use one or more AR1s to to make reverse loop and wyes work like the real thing. Each AR1 gives you cost-effective automatic contr of one reversing section without any manual switch operation — "Look Ma, no hands!"

### Quad Power Manager

**245-PM42** Quad Power Manager with Auto Reversing **79.95**
Get the benefits of sectioning your layout and auto reversing without additional boosters. PM42 has 4 levels of short circuit detection sensitivity settings so you can use it with a wide range of DCC equipment.

The PM42 lets you divide the output of a single booster into four sections for auto reversing, or to isolate areas o your layout so only an affectec area shuts down if a short circuit occurs. Each unit can run four sections from a single booster, in any combination of regular sections and auto reversing sections.

## Smart Booster w/Intelligent Autoreverse

Use to expand your Digitrax or other DCC systems. Additional units provide more power to run more trains, automate reverse loops and simplify electrical isolation of portions of your layout so a short circuit stops only one area. Automatically shuts down if command control drive signal is lost - layout will not convert to DC operation if a cable or connection is broken so trains won't "take-off" if they suddenly lose the DCC signal. Accepts 50/60Hz AC or DC from your current transformer, minimum input 12V AC or DC, maximum input 22V AC or 28V DC. Auto reset for overheating and short circuit protection, with unique "smart" protection that won't "weld" derailed locos to the track. Uses LocoNet Expansion Network for easy, reliable hook up and future system expansion. All connections are made with 6 conductor telephone jacks and wire.

Items listed below are available by Special Order (see Legend Page).

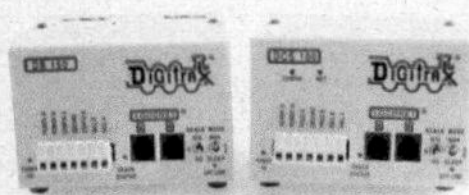

**245-DB150** 5 Amp/80 Watts **179.99**

**245-DB200** 8 Amp Booster **199.99**

## Command Station/ Booster

Operates as the command station (generates DCC packets that tell decoders what to do) and main system booster (receives the DCC signal from the Command Station, amplifies it and puts it on the track as the power that runs the locos) on a Digitrax LocoNet system, and accepts input from any Digitrax throttle, sold separately. Can also be used in conjunction with your computer if desired.

**245-DCS100** 5 Amp **285.00**

**245-DCS200** 8 Amp **305.00**

## Loconet Universal Interconnect Panels

**245-UP5** Universal Panel **16.95**
The UP5 has two RJ12 six-pin throttle jacks in the front for plugging in Digitrax walk-around throttles and two RJ12 six-pin expansion jacks on the back for hook up and expansion of LocoNet. An additional dual purpose RJ12 six-pin male connector is included on the side of the UP5 to allow for additional throttle jacks to be added or for branching the LocoNet network. Using six conductor telephone cable with RJ12 six-pin male connectors on each end, it's easy to daisy chain your network around the layout without hooking up a lot of wires. An indicator LED displays the power state of a local track section. In addition, the UP5 has a 2mm power supply jack. The UP5 gives your layout a professional look and provides a simple, cost effective way to add throttle jacks and expand your LocoNet wiring. Use a single PS12 power supply (sold separately) to power up to 10 UP and/or UR panels on your layout.

## Computer Interfaces

Item listed below is available by Special Order (see Legend Page).

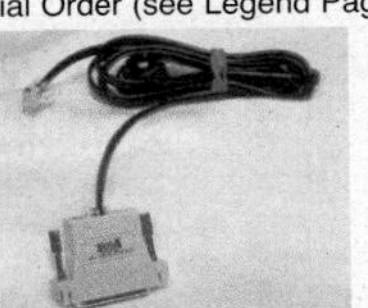

**245-MS100** RS232 Computer Interface **45.00**
Allows computers with an IBM-compatible COM, or RS232 communications port, monitor Digitrax LocoNet. Application software running in the computer can then interpret the activity on the LocoNet and report via a monitor. The MS100 is a signal-level translator between LocoNet and a 25 pin DB25 style RS232 port. As an example, you can set up a CTC-type panel which will respond to LocoNet messages. For IBM compatibles with 9-pin male DB9 type COM port connector.

## Power Supplies

**245-PS515** Ready to Run 15V AC, 5 Amps, 75VA Output **49.99**
Recommended for powering all Digitrax starter sets and accessories. Works for DC too!

Simply plug your PS515 into an appropriate wall outlet (AC120V 60Hz), attach the two output leads to your DCC Booster or other device that accepts up to 5 amps 15V AC.

Unit is overload protected.

**245-PS12** 12V AC Adapter **8.50**
Recommended for use with Digitrax accessories like UP3, BD46, UR90 and UR91.

**245-PS2012** 20 Amp **179.99**
Regulated power supply delivers more power with less heat for more efficient booster operation. Operate up to four five-amp boosters with the PS2012 supply. Scale selectable for use with N, HO or large scale. DC Ammeter. On/Off Switch. Integral cooling fan. Design coordinated for use with Digitrax products.



## OCCUPANCY DETECTORS

**245-BD4** Quad Occupancy Detector **29.95**
This unit provides cost-effective occupancy detection for four sections. Unit features outputs for panel-mounted LEDs (sold separately) to display occupancy. It will detect any powered loco, and unpowered rolling stock equipped with resistor wheelsets. Requires DS54 or SE8C, both sold separately, to transmit occupancy information to the LocoNet System.

**245-BDL168** For 16 Detection Sections **149.99**
Cost-effective occupancy detection for 16 detection sections. Add one or two RX4 Transponder Receivers (sold separately) and you can have Transponding in 8 zones. This means that you'll know when a detection section is occupied and the unique ID of all transponders in that section. Ops Mode Read Back lets you read back CV Values on any section of track that is set up for transponding with BDL168 and one or more RX4s. Unit also includes outputs for panel-mounted LEDs to display local occupancy and power zone status. Detects any powered loco, and unpowered rolling stock equipped with resistor wheelsets. Simply connect to LocoNet to transmit occupancy information to your LocoNet System.

## TRANSPONDING

Proven technology for bi-directional layout control! Does not require expensive modifications to your existing DCC system investment.

Track multiple locomotives and rolling stock as they move around your layout. Know the detection section and/or zone location and address of any specific locomotive or other rolling stock equipped with a trasnponding device. *Yes, now your dispatcher will be able to know "who you are and where you are!"*

Location and address information are updated constantly on LocoNet and can be displayed on a track diagram.

Transponding adds operations mode readback to your layout capabilities. This means you can read an CV from your decoders while on the layout.

Data received by the system from mobile decoders can be used for display, automation, aosund processing and much more.

Transponding allows you to automate staging yards and other operations.

You can use transponding devices in rolling stock in conjunction with transponding detectors on industry tracks to display the location of your freight cars.

Transponding will bring you an under layout system that will allow you to follow the locomotives around the layout based on transponding information received by the system.

You'll even be able to put transponders in other rolling stock and generate sounds like couplers, flat wheels etc. Wow!

The possibilites are endless! One person even said "It's like LoJack for your Locomotives!"

Transponders are incorporated into many Digitrax Premium Decoders. If you already have a DCC decoder (Digitrax or non-Digitrax) installed in a loco and you want to add a transponder, use TL1 or TF4 described above. These can also be used in nonpowered equipment like freight cars to provide transponding. Transponder equipped locos and rolling stock will not affect the operation of other command control systems that do not support transponding.

Transponder receivers are the track level component that you use to set up the track sections where you want transponding to be active. You won't need to equip every track section to have adequate coverage in most cases. Visit the Digitrax Web site at www.digitrax.com for some ideas on equipping your layout with transponding.

**245-RX4** Transponding Receivers 4-Zone Unit **49.99**

Important Note: This listing includes items which are available by special order only. Please see the Legend Page for information, and visit www.walthers.com for a complete listing of in-stock and special order products.

| | SET-100 | SET-90 | SET-LI |
|---|---|---|---|
| Command Station | LZV100 | LZV100 | LZV100 |
| Handheld included | LH100 | LH90 | none |
| Handheld style | Key Pad | Knob | PDA |
| Software upgradability | Yes | Yes | Yes |
| Maximum number of XpressNet devices | 31 | 31 | 31 |
| Number of locomotive addresses | 9999 | 9999 | 9999 |
| MU capabilities | 256 | 256 | 256 |
| Maximum number of locomotives/consists that can be controlled at one time | 256 | 256 | 256 |
| Number of functions | F0-F12 | F0-F12 | F0-F12 |
| Momentary functions | 12 | 12 (set up with LH100) | 12 |
| Power Station included | LZV100 | LZV100 | LZV100 |
| RailCom bit cutout | Yes | Yes | Yes |
| Amperage | 5 | 5 | 5 |
| Max number of additional Power Stations | 30 | 30 | 30 |
| Layout feedback | Yes | Yes | Yes |
| MSRP | $349.95 | $290.00 | $299.95 |

# DIGITAL PLUS STARTER SETS

Unleash the power of DCC with these professional grade NMRA DCC systems that are simple and intuitive to use, yet provide all the features advanced modelers want. These high-performance starter sets employ advanced and reliable technology, while simplifying user operations to make them friendly to any hobbyist. Sets also feature smart programming where you simply tell the system the locomotive address, and the system does all the work for you to set up the decoder. All systems have received NMRA Conformance Warrants.

**428-SET100 349.95**
The Set-100 Starter Set comes with an LH100 Dispatcher's handheld, a LZV100 command/power station, a complete easy-to-read-and-understand manual and a discount coupon for two decoders. This set is an excellent choice for most club and home layouts.

**428-SET90 290.00**
The Set-90 is identical to the Set-100 but comes with an LH90 Engineer's handheld instead of an LH100 handheld.

**428-SETLI 299.95**
A truly wireless computerized DCC system! Set LI contains an LZV100 command station/power station, an LI101 high-speed computer interface and the Loco Ce® software package. Requires user-supplied computer and wireless PDA.

# XPRESSNET COMPONENTS

The heart of the DIGITAL plus communication architecture is XpressNet, a high-speed, state-of-the-art, distributed multi-tier network. Each device on XpressNet contains a dedicated microprocessor that is responsible for providing its own unique user interface capabilities. This allows any certified XpressNet device to be used with your DIGITAL plus system.

XpressNet provides the peer-to-peer data exchange between each input device and from each input device to the DCC signal generator contained in the command station. The XpressNet network consists of a four-wire twisted pair connection. XpressNet may be up to 1000m (3300 feet) long and can support up to 30 simultaneous input devices. All Digital plus by Lenz XpressNet components are designed for upgradability. This allows the component to be upgraded with new software as it becomes available.

## Computer Interfaces

**428-LIUSB 154.95**
Device allows high-speed connection of your Digital Plus system to a computer. Includes USB connections, cables and a CD with sample demo programs.

**428-LI101F 99.95**
High-speed connection of your Digital Plus system to a computer. Data transfer rate from 19.2 Kbs to 115.2 Kbs, 9-pin SUB D jack, connecting cable and CD with several demo programs included.

## Command Station

**428-LZV100 199.95**
The LZV-100 integrated command station/power station has three micro processors for superior performance and operation, includes an LZ100 command station and a full 5 amp power station. Supports all forms of track wiring styles including common rail, two rail, and home return. Track voltage is fully programmable from 11 to 22 volts. Supports 31 XpressNet devices, has separate programming output and support for layout feedback. Plug-in screw terminals plus 5-pin DIN jack for direct connection of one handheld controller. Metal housing. 4-3/4 x 2-1/4 x 4-3/4".

## Throttles

**428-LH90** Engineer's Throttle (Knob-Based) **99.95**
Comes with a sensitive potentiometer, address selection for four-digit addresses, selectable 14, 28, or 128 speed control, F0-F8 functions, F0-F12 functions, center-off toggle switch for direction control and easy to read LED display. F1-F12 can be individually set to be momentary or latching per locomotive.

**428-LH100** Dispatcher's Throttle (Keypad-Based) **199.95**
For operation of locomotives, setting of turnouts, programming of decoders and configuring systems. Easy-to-read LCD display for operational instructions and display of locomotive address, direction, speed step and functions. Ability to control 13 locomotive functions (F0-F12), (Note: F1-F12 can be individually set to be momentary or latching per locomotive) plus keys for direction change, locomotive specific emergency stop and for general emergency stop.

## Programmer

**428-BLKBXPROG** Black Box Stand Alone Programmer **59.95**
Designed for users who desire a separate location for checking out installations and for programming. Allows programming of high inrush current sound decoders and access to all 1024 CVs. Requires external transformer for power and a handheld capable of programming such as Lenz Throttles #428-LH90 & #428-LH100 (each sold separately).

## XpressNet Phone Adapter

**428-XPA 62.95**
Provides affordable wireless control with fantastic range and no interference. Connect any cordless phone to the XPA, and connect the XPA to the XpressNet of your Digital Plus systems or XpressNet compatible systems. Allows for locomotive control, using the keys on your cordless phone. Now you can move freely around your system, be it inside your home or in the garden. Distance is determined by the specifications of the cordless phone, and can be up to 1000 feet. Allows for control of all 10,000 addresses, switch eight functions, and even control 1024 turnouts. And, if your phone supports it, you even have macros!

# IGITAL PLUS IMRA DCC ECODERS

l current Digital Plus ecoders have NMRA onformance and inspection arrants or have been ubmitted for NMRA testing.

ecoders are designed to rovide exceptionally smooth nd quiet operation of your odel railroad locomotive. All ecoders support 14/27, 28/55 128/256 speed steps (with ser-selectable speed table at is active in all modes), utomatic DC conversion (can e disabled), support for dvanced Consist Control, xtended four-digit addressing nd support for directional and dependent lighting that can e independently dimmed or onfigured with special lighting ffects that include Mars Light, iyro Light, Single Strobe or ouble Strobe. Four-function utput decoders also support ulsing and alternate blinking itch lights. Full support is rovided for all forms of service node programming as escribed in NMRA RP-9.2.3 nd operations mode programming as described in RP-9.2.1. ll Digital Plus locomotive ecoders comes with the ndustry's best "goof proof" warranty.

## unction Decoders

**28-LF101XF** Function-Only ecoder **22.95**
Six-function, ultra-thin decoder uitable for all scales from Z hrough Large Scale. Each unction has a current rating of 50mA. Can be configured to upport for all 13 NMRA DCC unctions. Special electronics or sophisticated direction-dependent lighting. Approximate size: 1 x 1/2 x 1/8".

## One-Amp Continuous Current Decoders

All decoders are designed for locomotives that have up to 1 Amp maximum continuous current. Equipped with four function outputs: one rated at 50mA, and three rated at 150mA each. Decoders all have extensive special lighting effects, including ditch light control.

**428-LE1014MP** Drive-Select w/NMRA Medium Plug **22.95**
User-selectable high-frequency motor control (Silent Drive) or Precision Glide Control. Ultra-thin profile. Approximate size: 1-1/2 x 5/8 x 1/5".

**NEW 428-STANDARDMP** Standard Decoder **29.95**
Ultra-thin, 1 Amp, three functions with Silent/Back EMF motor drive. Comes with NMRA 8-pin plug.

## High-Amperage Decoders

**428-LE1835W** Ultra Drive w/Wires **37.95**
1.8 amp decoder with high-frequency Ultra Drive Back EMF control for ultra-smooth precision control. Four function outputs and SUSI sound interface.

**428-LE1835MP** Ultra Drive w/NMRA Medium Plug **37.95**

# GOLD SERIES DECODERS

Revolutionizing DCC decoders for ultimate DCC control with three new technologies; asymmetrical DCC for sending location-specific commands, USP for eliminating dirty track problems, and RailCom allowing real-data transmission using NMRA standards.

**428-GOLDMINIW 54.95**
Measures: .43 x .35 x .11"
11 x 8 x 2.8mm

**428-GOLDMINID 54.95**
D version comes with the NEM651/NMRA Small plug.
Measures: .043 x .035 x .13"
11 x 9 x 33mm

## Gold JST Series Decoders 39.95 ea (Unless Noted)

1 Amp, advanced decoder, 4 functions, RailCom, SUSI interface, USP capable, silent-back EFM motor drive.

**428-GOLDJST** No Harness **36.95**
Measures: .91 x .66 x .1"
23 x 16.5 x 6.5mm

**428-GOLDJSTMP** NMRA Plug

**428-GOLDJSTWH** Wire Harness

**428-GOLDMAXI** Maxi **79.95**
3 Amps, Advanced Decoder, 8 Functions, RailCom, SUSI interface, USP capable

**428-GOLDSP** Gold Super Pack **94.50**
Includes Power1 presoldered onto the GOLD-JST decoder, LY011 and LY012 harnesses.

# SILVER SERIES DECODERS

Silver series incorporate the highest performance possible with Silent/Back EMF capacility and unparalleled short/overload protection.

**428-SLVRDIRECT 35.95**
1 Amp with integrated NMRA plug.

**428-SLVRMINIW 38.95**
.5 Amp continuous, advance decoder with Silent/Back EMF, with wires.

**428-SILVERMP 31.95**
Silver Series performance with integrated NMRA plug.

**NEW 428-SLVR21 35.95**
1 Amp with 21 pin plug.

# USP STORAGE MODULES

**428-POWER1 49.95**
This optional unit can be added to 428-Gold JST and GoldMINI decoders for onboard power supply to have uninterrupted performance on dirty track or locomotives with poor pick up. Features Lenz USP technology.

**NEW 428-POWER3 59.95**
Optional unit can be added to Gold Maxi for on-board power supply for uninterrupted performance on dirty track.

## Decoder Harnesses

**428-LY0115** Decoder Harness **12.00**
Designed for all decoders that support the nine-pin industry standard decoder socket. Install one decoder harness in each locomotive. Package includes five 200mm wire harnesses.

**428-LY0125** Decoder Harness w/NMRA Plug **25.00**
Designed for all decoders that support the nine-pin industry standard decoder socket. Each harness includes an NMRA medium eight-pin plug. Package includes five 88mm long harnesses.

## Digital Plus Modules

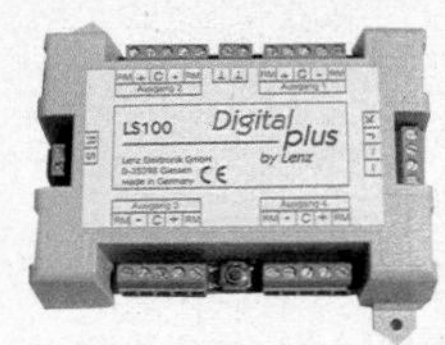


**428-LS100** With Connection To Feedback Bus **79.00**
Accessory decoder for connecting four turnouts with twin coil relays. Power supply may be either from a separate transformer or from the track power. Maximum current load of a single output is 0.75 continuous, peak 3A for maximum one second. Maximum total current load (as the sum of all outputs in use) 3.0A continuous.

## Asymmetrical DCC Block Section Modules

For sending specific location commands to components. Prerequisite for the use of BM1, BM2 and BM3 block section modules is the locomotive decoder from the GOLD series, or another decoder which supports asymmetrical DCC operation.

**428-BM1** For Red Signal Stop **11.95**

**428-BM2** For Red Signal Stop & "Caution" Yellow **44.95**
Easy control of the module using light signals and semaphore signals fitted with switches.

**428-BM3** For Red Signal Stop & "Caution" Yellow w/Block Control **54.95**
One module should be used for every block. Features two outputs to connect signals or other lights.

## Accessory Decoder

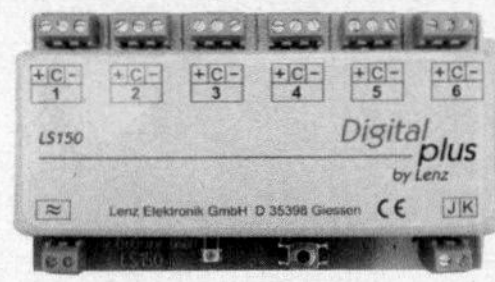


**428-LS150 49.95**
Controls up to six turnouts with twin coil or slow-motion switch machines. Does NOT include connection to the feedback bus on the LZV. Able to control snap or slow-motion switch machines.

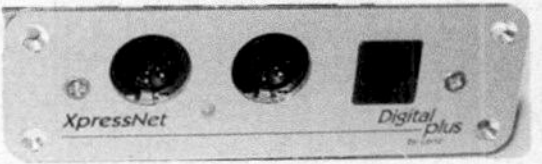


**428-LA152** XpressNet Panel Connector **22.95**
Faceplate with two Din plugs and one phone jack for easy XpressNET installations. Includes 21" cable with six pin RJ phone plugs.

**428-LA010** For Connecting Motor-Driven Turnouts or EPL Drives to Accessory Decoders LS100/LS110 **14.00**

**428-LR101** Feedback Module **52.00**
Sends the status of all feedback points to the command station.

**428-LB101** Occupancy Detector **19.95**
Provides information on track occupancy in combination with feedback module (428-LR101, sold separately). Features two independent detectors on one circuit board, maximum current load 3 Amp, all connectors designed as screw terminals.

**428-LK100** Automatic Reverse Loop Module **57.00**
Provides a simple way to travel through reverse loops in digital operation. Automatic changing of polarity when passing the isolation gaps of the loop, travel through loop without stopping or changing direction, regardless of the direction the loop is traversed, adjustable sensitivity depending on current needs of the layout. Maximum current load 3.5 Amp.

## DIGITAL PLUS POWER STATIONS

**428-LV102** 5 Amp Power Station **154.95**
Additional station can be connected to the Command Station (#428-LZV100, sold separately) to supply power to separate layout power districts. Features software-settable track voltage and opto-isolation.

## RAILCOM COMPONENTS

Advance DCC control for the advanced model railroader. RailCOM provides an open architecture for full bi-directional communication with your locomotive following the NMRA-proposed Recommended Practices. RailCOM provides the ability to detect the address of a locomotive when you first place it on the layout, the ability to detect the address of the locomotive upon entry to a detection zone, the ability to read any CV while on the mainline, the ability to track the locomotive as it moves over your layout, and the ability to stop a train in front of a red signal.

**428-LRC120** LED Display **60.00**
Allows for the display of locomotive's address.

## LOCOMOTIVES

Lenz locomotives come equipped with factory-installed DCC decoders and European-style NEM couplers. Locos can be used on standard DC or DCC systems.

### Steam Locomotives 290.00 ea

German 2-6-4 steam locomotive comes with factory-installed DCC decoder and sound system. Can be operated on digital or analog control and features load compensation.

**428-BR66**

**428-BR661** #001

**428-BR662** #002

### Diesel Locomotives

**428-V364** Series V36.4 "Ugly Entlien" **179.95**

**428-V3641** Series V36.4 "Ugly Entlien" w/Cupola **179.95**
During the 50s and 60s, this loco was the workhorse of the entire German Federal system (DB). This model has pickups on all wheels and a factory-installed back EMF (load compensation) decoder. It comes equipped with remote-controlled couplers that operate with the European standard handle coupler. Back EMF functions work in both DCC and traditional DC operation.

RAILNET SOLUTIONS, LLC MODEL RAILROAD NETWORK PRODUCTS

Simplify wiring and operating accessories along your Digitrax DCC-equipped layout with this family of ready-to-use stationary decoders. Each is designed for fast installation and includes an easy to use instruction sheet.

## DUAL SIGNAL DECODER

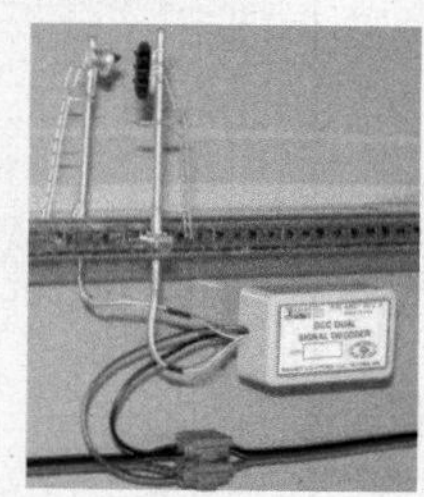

**621-64627 34.95**
Adding working signals to a Digitrax DCC-equipped layout will be fun and easy with this accessory unit. The decoder operates by "listening" to the rails, and lights each signal head corresponding to the patterns of block occupancy and turnout position messages it receives. Each Signal Decoder drives two signal heads (three LEDs each) and is compatible with most LED-type signals (sold separately). Fully assembled, the unit mounts under your benchwork using a self-adhesive patch (included). Simply connect two wires to your DCC cables and two 4-pin connectors to signal wires. Unit is adjusted by simply throwing turnouts and occupying blocks during an initial session and signals can be operating in half an hour. Other features include:

- Conforms to NMRA Standards.
- ABS (Automatic Block Signal) and CTC (Centralized Traffic Control) modes supported.
- Auto-detects Common Anode or Common Cathode LEDs.
- Wide Addressable Range: 0001 to 9983.
- Service-Mode and Ops-Mode Programming supported.
- Compatible with RR&Co, WinLok and other control software.
- Works great with #621 64802 Integrated Block Detector (sold separately.)
- Requires use of Railnet Translator (#621-646249 sold separately), one per layout.

## INTEGRATED BLOCK DETECTOR

**621-64802 19.95**
Simplifies installation and operation of block detection on your Digitrax™ equipped DCC layout. Detector actually monitors a block for occupancy and generates a LocoNet message in response. When locos, lighted cars or wheels equipped with resistors are detected, the "Block Occupied" LED turns on, and a LocoNet "Occupied" message is sent out. When the block clears, the LED turns off, and a "Clear" message is sent. Unit mounts under your benchwork and is easily added to new or existing layouts without complex wiring or soldering. Other features include:

- LocoNet Certified.
- Block Occupancy LED.
- Address Pushbutton.
- Wide Addressable Range: 0001 to 4096.
- Supports both Service-Mode and Ops-Mode Programming.
- Compatible with MS100, LocoBuffer, as well as RR&Co, WinLok and other train control software.
- Works great with #621-64627 Dual Signal Decoder sold separately.

## TRANSLATOR

**621-64629** Railnet Translator **16.95**
The Translator listens for LocoNet feedback messages from block detectors and switch machine decoders, and translates them for signal decoder operation. One required per layout. For use with Dual Signal Decoder (#612-64627 sold separately).



## HI-TECH

## DCC LIGHTING BOARD FOR 1.5 BULBS

**331-1000 14.95**
This 1.5V lighting circuit for DCC decoders provides voltage-dropping networks f four function outputs. Remov the guesswork of sizing resistors for dropping functio outputs to 1.5V for bulbs anc more. Also reduces the amo of wiring needed for lighting circuits making for a cleaner installation. Each circuit consists of a resistor and twc diodes to provide approxima 1.4V for each bulb. Measure 45/64" (.7") Diameter x 5/32" (.15) Thick.

DCC PECIALTIES .COM

# IEW PRODUCTS

## Stationary Decoders

### owershield X

he PSX series specifically ddresses the increased inrush ads (currents) that occur due large capacitors used for ound systems. This load ppears as a system short rcuit until the capacitors are harged. The logic in the PSXs etermines if the load is a true hort or just an inrush verload. Many improvements ere incorporated into this eries. Intelligent, solid-state, CC auto-reversers/breakers nd power district circuit reakers. No power supply eeded.

**IEW 246-PSXAR** With ntegrated Stall Motor Decoder **9.95**

**IEW 246-PSXARFB** With ntegrated Stall Motor Decoder Network Feedback **64.95**

**IEW 246-PSXARSC** With ntegrated Snap Coil Decoder **9.95**

**IEW 246-PSXARSCFB** With ntegrated Snap Coil Decoder Network Feedback **74.95**

### Block Control

DCC solid-state power district circuit breaker.

**NEW 246-PSX1** One Output **39.95**

**NEW 246-PSX2** Two Outputs **79.90**

**NEW 246-PSX3** Three Outputs **119.95**

**NEW 246-PSX4** Four Outputs **159.80**

## Block Detection Unit

### Block Watcher™

An intelligent block detector for all scales. Features all solid-state operation. No power supply needed.

**NEW 246-BLOCKWATCH** **29.95**

# PROGRAMMING BOOSTER

**246-PPX** PowerPax DCC Programming Booster **59.95**
Overcome programming problems with BLI, Soundtraxx and multiple decoder/loco combinations. Microprocessor controlled unit safely boosts and controls programming power to about 200 mA. When hooked up for programming, unit initially powers programming track to charge-up decoder components like capacitors that would otherwise reduce programming energy and cause a programming failure. Built-in circuit protection, with LED indicator, shuts down instantly in the event of an overload or short to protect the decoder and system programming circuits. Compatible with Broadway Limited locos, Digitrax, Lenz, MRC, NCE, TCS and Soundtraxx decoders in both single and dual decoder configurations and also works with programming software, RR&Co (Train Programmer) and JMRI (Decoder Pro), all sold separately.

# DCC POWER REGULATION & PROTECTION

## Onguard Auto-Reverser/Breakers

Protect your layout from short circuits and automate your reverse loops with the Onguard OG-AR DCC Auto-Reverser with integrated circuit breaker and the OG-CB power district circuit breaker. Each is rated at four amps and works without relays or a power supply. Simple screw terminals make them easy to add to existing wiring. Both are compatible with most DCC systems, however the Digitrax Zephyr and Atlas Commander do not have enough power to operate these units. Units are not for use with direct current (DC) applications.

**246-OGAR** Auto Reverser-Breaker **39.95**

**246-OGCB** Power District Circuit Breaker **29.95**

# DCC POWER SUPPLY

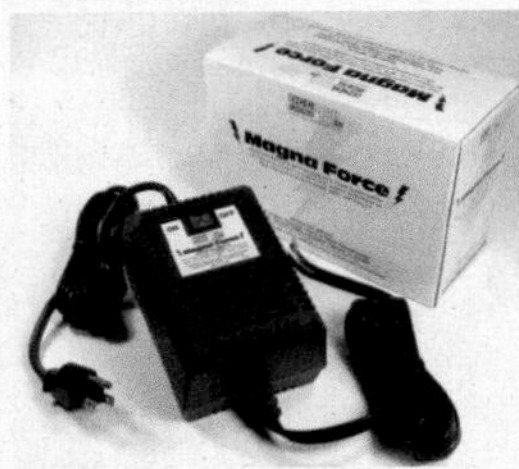


**246-MF615** Magna Force **44.95**
This advanced and affordable power supply was developed especially for DCC and can be used with Digitrax, Lenz, NCE and other systems. Features include grounded 16-gauge fail-safe, three wire input and output, illuminated rocker power switch, circuit breaker protection on output and a sealed, impact-resistant enclosure. Input: 120V AC 60HZ; Output 15V AC 6 AMP.

# STATIONARY DECODERS

## The "Hare"

Designed to drive the Tortoise Switch Machine (sold separately), this accessory decoder plugs directly on to the Tortoise – simply connect to track power using the two handy screw terminals and the unit is ready to use. The Hare is compatible with all DCC systems that support accessory operations. And, many advanced features are provided to enhance operation including:

- Auto Throw™ automatically throws points when train approaches against the points. Eliminates derailments, layout shorts, loco and scenery damage, and is ideal for difficult to reach turnouts and hidden staging. Works with both insul-frog and electro frog turnouts for Versions I and II.
- Smart Route™ sets up to 13 routes by simple address programming in addition to the primary decoder address. Each Smart Route can control an unlimited number of turnouts. Eliminates complicated programming, the need for computer operation or system macros.
- Smart Default Ops™ allows all Hare-controlled turnouts to move to a predetermined position when layout is powered up or to remain as last thrown. Eliminates possibly fouling the mainline when you power-up your layout.
- Operates LED turnout signals or remote panel LED indicators.
- Manual push button option for control panel operations.

PowerPax DCC Programming Booster 246-PPX

No Feedback 246-DSPHARE1

Rampmeter Digital Meter 246-RAMPMETER1

- System reset by simple CV programming. Resets to factory defaults.
- Digitrax LocoNet, NCE Cab Bus and Lenz Express Net feedback and position reporting options are supported by Version II (246-DSPHARE2).
- Automates reverse loop turnouts using Smart Throw.

**246-DSPHARE1** No Feedback **29.95**

**246-DSPHARE2** With Feedback **34.95**

## The "Wabbit"

Dual output stationary decoder has all the same patented exclusive features of its predecessor, the popular Hare.

**NEW 246-WABBIT** For DCC **29.95**

**NEW 246-WABBITFB** For DCC w/Feedback **39.95**

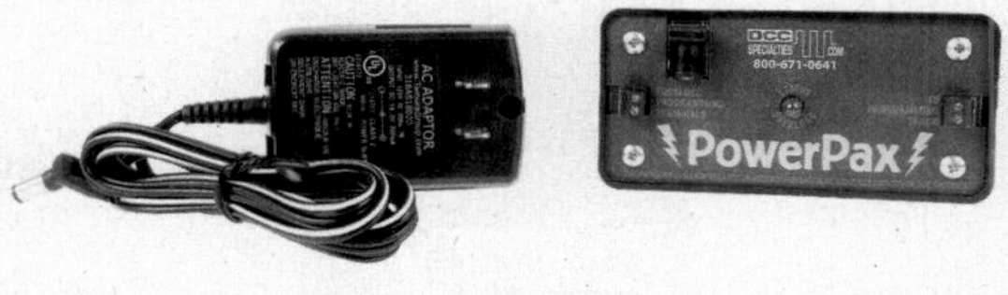

# RAMPMETER DIGITAL METER

Get accurate measurements of DCC, DC and AC volts and amps on your layout with these meters. Units are rated at 10 Amps and measure true RMS Volts/Amps, ± 2%. Compatible with all scales, adjustable contacts permit direct track voltage measurements; no batteries are needed for use with DCC systems. Use as a portable troubleshooting tool, or mount on control panel or fascia; rear screw terminals allow for easy connection to layout wiring.

**246-RAMPMETER1** No Enclosure **59.95**

**246-RAMPMETER2** Enclosed w/Clip Leads **89.95**

**246-RAMPMETER3** Enclosed w/Clip Leads & Battery Backup **99.95**

**246-RAMPMETERH** Enclosed w/Clip Leads & Battery Backup for High Voltage **119.95**

## NEW PRODUCTS

### LokSound V3.5 Sound Decoders

#### North American Diesels TBA ea

**NEW 397-72422** Alco 251 6 Cylinder, Non Turbo Charged, 3-Chime Air Horn

**NEW 397-72443** GE Cat. D17000 8 Cylinder, Non Turbo Charged, 1-Chime Air Horn

**NEW 397-72451** Baldwin 606/606NA, Non Turbo Charged, 2-Chime Air Horn

**NEW 397-72460** FM Trainmaster

#### GE 7FDL16A 16 Cylinder Turbo Charged

**NEW 397-72470**, Dynamic Brakes, Nathan 3-Chime Air Horn

**NEW 397-72471** Dynamic Brakes, Nathan 5-Chime Air Horn

**NEW 397-72472** Dynamic Brakes, Leslie 3-Chime Air Horn

**NEW 397-72473** Dynamic Brakes, Leslie 5-Chime Air Horn

#### Alco 539 6 Cylinder

**NEW 397-72494** 1-Chime Air Horn, Non Turbo Charged

**NEW 397-72495** 2-Chime Air Horn, Non Turbo Charged

#### EMD 16-710GB 16 Cylinder Turbo Charged

**NEW 397-82408** Dynamic Brakes, Nathan 3-Chime Air Horn

**NEW 397-82409** Dynamic Brakes, Nathan 5-Chime Air Horn

**NEW 397-82410** Dynamic Brakes, Leslie 3-Chime Air Horn

**NEW 397-82411** Dynamic Brakes, Leslie 5-Chime Air Horn

#### North American Steam TBA ea

**NEW 397-82450** Shay

**NEW 397-82451** Heisler

**NEW 397-84257** 0-6-0

**NEW 397-82458** 4-4-0 American

**NEW 397-82460** 2-8-0 Consolidation

**NEW 397-82461** 4-6-0

**NEW 397-82464** 2-8-8-2

**NEW 397-82465** 2-8-2

**NEW 397-82466** 2-6-0

**NEW 397-82467** 4-8-2

**NEW 397-82468** 2-10-0

### LokSound V3.5 Decoders 139.00 ea

Breathe new life into your roster with these decoders combining a full range of DCC operation with a programmable sound module and speaker. Sounds from a variety of actual steam, diesel and electric locos are available with more planned for future release.

With the LokSound Programmer (#397-53452 sold separately below) you can easily program your locos for maximum performance and add additional sounds using your home computer. A large 8 MBit memory allows for a wide range of complex sounds - up to 15 different sounds can be activated using your DCC function buttons. Four sound channels allow for realistic mixing and playback, with up to three sounds running simultaneously with the exhaust. Load-dependent sound (easily switched off if desired) lets you hear your engine working, and the sound can be synchronized with speed steps or external sensors (sold separately). Sound can be operated on DC layouts, or on DCC powered layouts running most popular systems.

Suitable for engines with DC, AC or coreless motors, each decoder has a pulse frequency of 32 KHz for super-quiet operation. Load compensation provides smooth operation uphill or down, while Dynamic Drive Control (back EMF) improves low speed performance. Additional control features include a Helper mode to mute bell and whistle, and Switcher mode to set half-speed for yard operations with the touch of a button. There are also four auxiliary inputs for lighting, smoke, automatic couplers or other special effects. Light brightness can be adjusted independently, or you can add special effects such as firebox flicker, Mars or Gyra-Lights, ditch lights, strobes and more. Function mapping can be allocated to any of 20 buttons, and functions can be combined for one-touch operation of sound and lighting at the same time. The units feature integrated function keys F13-F20 to meet current NMRA DCC standards. Built-in short circuit protection guards motors and decoders from potential problems.

#### Steam Sound Decoders

##### North American

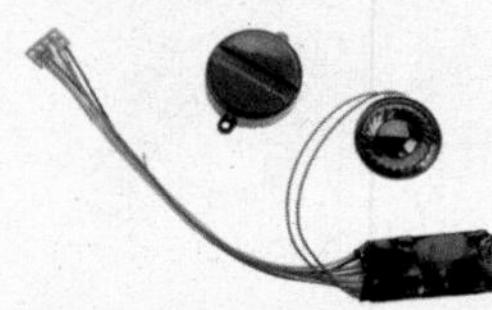

**397-82454** Big Boy 4-8-8-4

**397-82455** Mikado 2-8-2

##### European

**397-52401** 2 Cylinder Narrow Gauge - BR99

**397-52402** 3 Cylinder - BR 44, Belgian 25.021

**397-52403** 2/4 Cylinder - BR 01

**397-52404** BR 38, P8

**397-52405** BR 18, S 3/6

#### Diesel Sound Decoders

##### ALCO 244

**12 Cylinder w/Turbocharger**

**397-72400** WABCO A-2 Airhorn

**397-72403** Leslie S3 Airhorn

**16 Cylinder w/Turbocharger**
**397-72411** Leslie S3 Airhorn

##### EMD 567

**16-Cylinder - Non-Turbocharged**

**397-72427** Single-Chime

**397-72428** Single Chime w/Dynamic Brakes

**397-72429** Dual-Chime

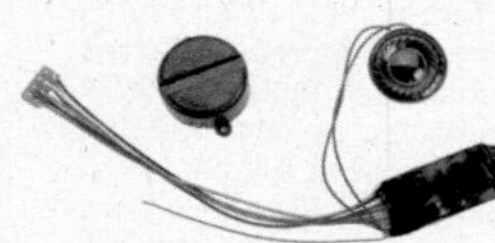

**397-72430** Dual-Chime w/Dynamic Brakes

**397-72432** Three-Chime w/Dynamic Brakes

**16-Cylinder - Turbocharged**

**397-72435** Five-Chime

**397-72436** Five-Chime w/Dynamic Brakes

**12-Cylinder**

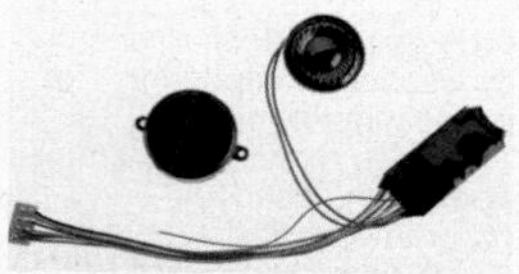

**397-72437** Single-Chime

**397-72438** Single-Chime w/Dynamic Brakes

##### EMD 645 - Turbocharged w/Dynamic Brakes

**397-72441** 16-Cylinder, 3-Chime

**397-72442** 20-Cylinder, 3-Chime

##### EMD 16-645E 16-Cylinder w/Dynamic Brakes

**397-72482** Nathan 3-Chime

**397-72483** Nathan 5-Chime

**397-72485** Leslie 5-Chime

##### EMD 12-710GB Turbocharged

**397-82400** 12-Cylinder, Nathan 3-Chime, Dynamic Brakes

##### EMD 16-710GB 16-Cylinder w/Dynamic Brakes

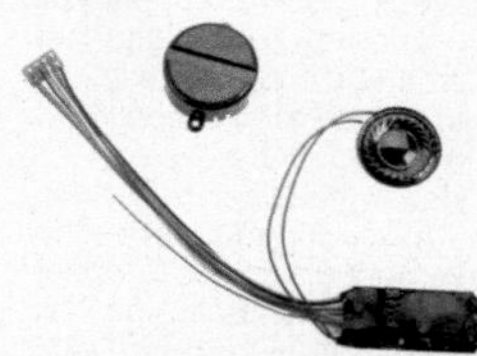

**397-82404** Non-Turbocharged, Nathan 3-Chime

**397-82405** Non-Turbocharged, Nathan 5-Chime

**397-82408** Turbocharged, Nathan 3-Chime

**397-82408** Turbocharged, Nathan 5-Chime

**397-82411** Turbocharged, Leslie 5-Chime

##### GE 7FDL16

16-Cylinder - Turbocharged

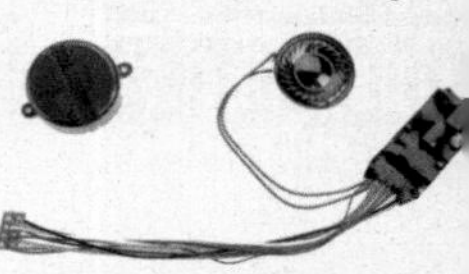

**397-72466** Nathan 3-Chime Horn, Dynamic Brakes

**397-72467** Nathan 5-Chime Horn, Dynamic Brakes

**397-72468** Leslie 3-Chime A Horn, Dynamic Brakes

#### European Diesels

**397-52433** BR 218

**397-52449** Multi-Unit ICE VT

**397-52459** V 120 DR "Taiga Drum"

#### Electrics

##### North American

**739-82469** Pennsylvania GG

##### European

**397-52461** E40

**397-52468** Re 460

### LokPilot V3.0 Standard DCC Decoder

**NEW 397-52610** With 8-Pin Plug **34.99**
For modelers using DCC without sound, the LokPilot provides a versatile decoder that's ideal for most motive power. Each unit automatically detects if used on DC or DCC systems. On DCC, the decoder will determine the number of speed steps and you can select any address up to 9999. A programmable speed curve allows precise adjustment. Function mapping can be assigned to any of 12 buttons in any combination, The units also support a wide range of lighting effects including Mars lights, ditch lights, Gyra-Lights, strobes and more, and lamp brightness is adjustable. Dynamic Drive Control (back EMF) improves low speed performance. Overload protection is provided for motor output and the four function outputs. 40KHz high frequency motor control provides smooth and quiet operation; output handles a maximum current of 1.1 Amps, functions are designed to handle .180mA each.

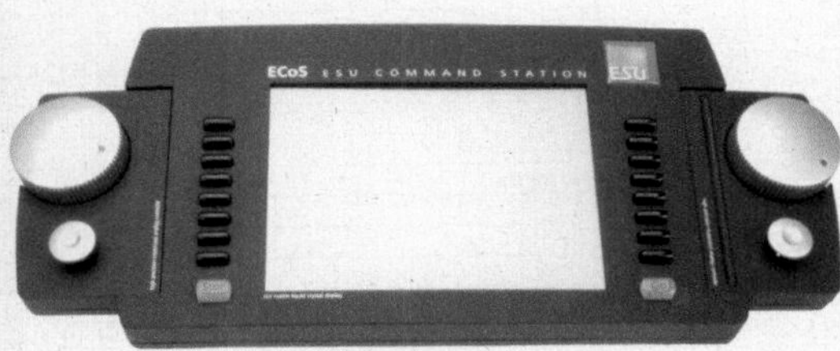

ECoS - ESU Command Station 397-50001

## LokSound Programmer

**397-53452 159.00**
Enjoy your LokSound equipped engines even more by adding or changing sounds and fine-tuning performance using this unit with your home computer. Easy to use with no prior knowledge of programming needed, the unit can be used with any PC with an audio card and a Windows® operating system. Just connect the programmer to your PC using the serial port or the USB adapter (included). Start the software then place a loco with a LokSound decoder on your programming track. The software automatically detects which type of decoder is installed and provides specific information; easy to follow on-screen graphics let you change loco address, speed steps, acceleration and deceleration, load control, speed curve and analog functions, assign function buttons for lighting effects and brightness, and all special settings. Plus, you can change or completely replace the current sounds with additional selections included on the software. You can also use your own recordings or choose from a wide range of downloads available on the LokSound Web-site. Unit is complete with power supply, serial cable, USB adapter, manual and CD.

## ECoS - ESU Command Station

**397-50001** Central Unit Digital Command Station **699.00**
The ECoS Command Station's extensive features include two cabs with motorized throttle knobs, eight function keys each and a two-axis, center-click joystick each. The large, white, background-illuminated LCD shows all informaiton in plain words. Each ECoS command station integrates a four-Amp steady-output booster and is supplied with a 90VA power supply.

# TRIX

Trix Mobile Station 441-T66920

## TRIX MOBILE STATION

**441-T66920 202.59**
The Trix System is a modular, expandable DCC system combined with a unique user-friendly operating concept. The Trix Mobile Station is a handheld DCC control unit that allows access of up to 20 decoder-equipped locomotives and operation of two or three locos simultaneously, depending on their current draw. It features locomotive selection from a writable locomotive database that lets you name your locos or use two-digit addresses. Nine buttons are included for additional functions. Function status is shown in the integrated graphic display through intuitive pictograms for locomotive selection from the database. The unit also features a locomotive selection button, menu button, and emergency stop button. Includes integrated connection cable with plug for connecting to DC – systems (via 60115 connection box). Dimensions: 6-1/2 x 2-23/32 x 1-3/8" 16.5 x 6.9 x 3.5cm.

Get Your Daily Dose of Product News at

**www.walthers.com**

## TRIX MOBILE STATION ACCESSORIES

### Decoder

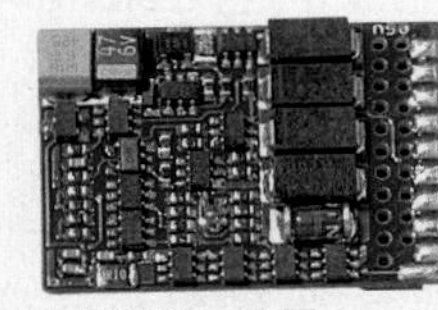

**441-T66839 47.35**
Receiver for all Trix H0 DC locomotives. Features a 21-pole connector and power consumption up to 1600mA (motor 1100mA; functions - 150mA each). Features include four switchable functions including lighting control and more, all of which can be centrally controlled via the Trix Mobile Station or a DCC Center. The decoder is capable of having maximum speed, acceleration rate, braking delay and motor control at different load conditions (e.g. ascending and descending grades) programmed in. In operation, the "function" and "f1" functions are switched on with analog direct current. All Trix locomotives with 21-pole connector are capable of having this decoder installed.

## Connectors and Power Supplies

**441-60055** Marklin Transformer 120V 60VA **138.69**
Power supply for Trix Mobile Station.

**441-60115** Marklin Connector Box **26.65**

**441-610479** Marklin Adapter Cable **10.49**

**441-610718** Marklin Cable to Transformer Connection 2-Pole **.95**

# DIGITAL COMMAND CONTROL (DCC)

## Prodigy Express System

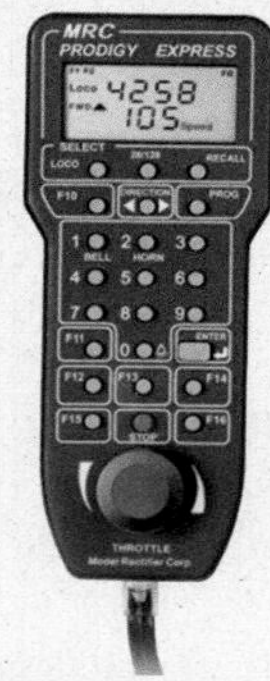

**500-1408 189.98**
So easy to use model railroaders can operate it without the need of instructions. Just enter the loco number (address) you wish to operate and move the throttle. It's intuitive. Programming is easy as well. Prodigy express is loaded with advanced features most beginner systems just don't have. An excellent way to get started in DCC! For a comparison between Prodigy Express and Prodigy Advance, see the chart at right.

- Easy hook up—two wires to the track and you're ready to go
- Large LCD screen that's easy to read and navigate
- Emergency stop button
- Two or four digit addressing (0-9999 addresses available)
- 28/128 speed steps for precise speed control
- Capable of 16 accessory functions
- Advance consisting
- Program all CVs with ease

## Prodigy Advance² DCC System

**500-1414 349.98**
Perfect for home or club layouts, Prodigy Advance supports up to 99 LCD-equipped, clearly labeled handhelds. Features include: two- or four-digit addressing, 14-28/128 selectable speed steps, easy programming and locomotive selection, program on the main, CV programming, advanced consisting and adjustable Fast Clock. NMRA functions to F28. Wireless ready.

## Prodigy Advance Accessories

### Prodigy Advance DCC LCD Walkaround

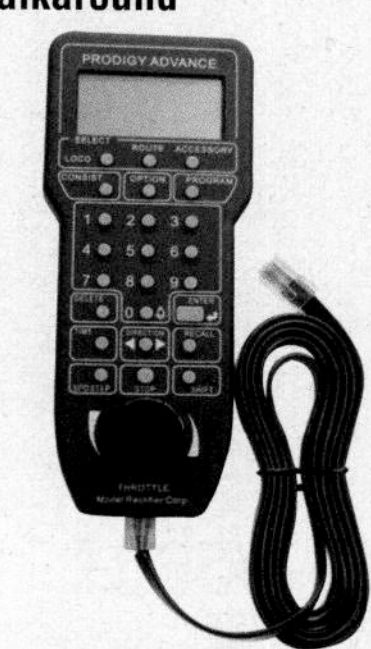

**500-1407 98.98**
Allows the Prodigy Advance user to add up to 98 more additional walkaround handhelds to the Prodigy Advance DCC system network. Easy to install around layout using Prodigy Advance Extension Plate #500-1501 nonpowered and #500-1502 powered, each sold separately.

### Prodigy Advance Extension Plate

**500-1501 33.98**
Simply install these ready-to-use plates around your layout and plug the handheld in. Each can control two handhelds. Equipped with 12" extension cables.

## Prodigy Advance Wireless

**NEW 500-1410 599.98**
Contains power supply, base unit with built-in receiver, handheld wireless (RF) transmitter. All the newest NMRA function up to F28. Duplex radio complete DCC system lets you program, acquire and run locomotives without a tethered throttle. Use multiple RF handhelds with three additional plugs for tethered throttles. Completely upgraded and upgradeable.

## Prodigy Wireless Conversion Set

**NEW 500-1412 298.98**
Contains one radio transmitter and one receiver that simply plugs into your Prodigy Express, Prodigy Advance (upgrades may be needed) and Prodigy Advance2. Duplex radio system lets you program, acquire and run locomotives without a tethered throttle, with all the functionality of a tethered throttle.

## DCC Decoders

### Sound Decoders

Each supports two or four-digit addressing, advanced consisting, accessory functions, programming on the main and 14, 28-128 speed steps. Each includes speaker.

**500-1626** Diesel Sound **79.98**
Diesel sound is synchronized to your locomotive. Other sounds include horn and bell.

**500-1629** Steam Sound **76.98**
Steam chuff is synchronized to your locomotive! Other sounds include long whistle, short whistle and bell.

### Snap-In Diesel Sound Decoders 49.98 ea

Replaces most Atlas, Athearn and Kato circuit boards. Multiple accessory sounds.

**500-1634** EMD Turbocharged

**500-1651** Non-Sound Decoder **24.98**
Two or four digit addressing, programming on the main four accessory functions. With 9-pin JST connection and NMRA 8-pin harness.

**500-AD360** Dispatcher Switch Machine/Accessory **17.98**
Operates both twin-coil and slow-motion switch machines or accessories. Red and green indicator LEDs included. Uses mobile decoder addresses. Works with any DCC system.

## Brilliance Sound Decoders

Brilliance DCC Sound Decoders offer a wide array of real sounds using MRC-developed wide-fidelity technology. Decoders measure just 1-13/16 x 11/16 x 1/4" 4.6 x 1.7 x .7 and use Back EMF technology to reduce decoder hum. Each supports four-digit addressing, 14-28/128 speed steps.

**Prodigy Advance² and Prodigy Express**

| | PRODIGY EXPRESS | PRODI ADVAN |
|---|---|---|
| 2 or 4 Digit Programming (*just plug in the #s and go*) | yes | yes |
| Choice of 14, 28 or 128 speed steps. | yes | yes |
| Program on the Main Track | yes | yes |
| Program on the Program Track | yes | yes |
| Program CVs | yes | yes |
| Advanced Consisting | yes | yes |
| Universal Consisting | no | yes |
| Number of Functions | 16 | 19 |
| Upgradable and Expandable+ | yes | yes |
| Plug and Play Technology* | yes | yes |
| Emergency Stop Button | yes | yes |
| Recall and Stack Features | yes | yes |
| Large LCD Display Screen | yes | yes |
| Power Output Capacity; Nominal | 1.6 amps | 4 amp |
| Number of Cab Jacks | 1 | 3 |
| System Adjustable | no | yes |
| Adjustable Fast Clock | no | yes |
| Accessory Decoder Operation | no | yes |
| Accessory Decoder Routing | no | yes |

**With MRC's patented "Plug and Play" technology, components from both DCC systems can be interchanged with each other with full compatibility.*

*+Prodigy Express is expandable to all of the features of Prodigy Advance, (over time and without the immediate cash outlay); both systems can expand to run up to 99 cabs. Both systems can have their respective outputs increased with the use of Prodigy Advance power boosters and powered extension plates.*

**500-1630** Steam **119.98**
Features include eight different synchronized steam chuffs, 10 different whistles, four different bells and control of 19 other sounds. Also provides functions for directional headlights. Includes a 28mm diameter speaker—perfect for installation in a tender.

**500-1631** Diesel **119.98**
Features include synchronized diesel engine sounds with eight notches, 10 types of horns, four different bell sounds and control of 19 other sounds. Also provides functions for directional headlights, marker lights, Gyralight and beacon. Includes a 28mm diameter speaker.

### Sheer Brilliance Mini HO Sound Decoders 84.98 ea

New small size, speaker included, two or four digit addressing, 1.5 amp capacity.

**500-1638** EMD Modern Large Diesel
Multiple horns and bells.

**500-1639** Steam
Synchronized chuff, multiple bells and whistles.

**500-1643** EMD Modern Switcher Diesel
Multiple bells and horns.

## Accessory Decoder w/4 Outputs

**500-1628 57.98**
Four decoders for the price of one. Controls twin-coil of slow-motion switch machines, building lights and signals. Has adjustable flash rates and switch machine throw rates. compatible with any DCC system that can program higher number CVs. (Not for use with Command 2000 or Prodigy DCC #AD150.)

## DCC Power Station 8

**500-AD501 179.98**
You can boost your DCC system up to eight powerful amperes with an easy hookup to run more trains or engines with bigger motors. Includes adjustable output voltage capability. Compatible with other DCC system brands. Simple hookup.

**500-1505** District Power Booster **159.98**
Provides 3.5 amps of power and circuit overload/short protection to your powered districts.

## DCC Auto Reverse

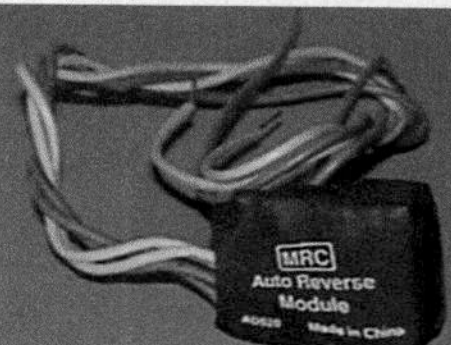


**500-AD520 39.98**
Automatically controls reverse loop circuits. Eliminates conventional block and switch systems. Simple hookup with two input and two output wires two amp rating. Works with all DCC layouts.

Build a complete operating system for your layout with this line of Digital Command Control (DCC) starter sets and accessories.

## NEW PRODUCTS

### DCC System Accessories

**NEW 524-28** DB3 3 Amp Generic Booster **79.95**
For more track power, add one or more DB3 boosters to your Smart Booster™ (sold separately). Can also be used with other DCC systems. Requires a power supply.

**NEW 524-223** USB Interface **49.94**
For computer programming and/or operation of Power Cab equipped layouts. Requires USB cable, computer and railroad computer program. Can also be used with Power Pro™ system to control trains, signals and/or accessories.

**NEW 524-226** Auto-SW™ **24.95**
Adds a separate program track to Power Cab™ system. Prevents accidental programming of ALL locos on your track when using Program Track mode. Automatically disconnects your main line when in Program Track mode but does not affect Program on Main. Compatible with all DCC systems.

**NEW 524-227** CP6 Circuit Protection **34.95**
Provides circuit protection for up to six sections of your railroad. Operates with any DCC system. Factory set to 1 Amp per section. Sections can be connected together for more power per section.

### CP6 Replacement Lamps pkg(6) 12.95 ea

**NEW 524-228** 1.75 Amp

**NEW 524-229** 1 Amp

**NEW 524-230** Mini Panel™ **49.95**
Build your control panels with greatly simplified wiring. Just connect pushbuttons to the Mini Panel and use to issue turnout routing macros, individual turnout commands by pushing one button. Set-up is easy, just plug in a Pro Cab™ (sold separately) and answer menu questions. For all NCE DCC systems.

**NEW 524-231** Packet Analyzer **49.95**
Use the Packet Analyzer and your computer to view DCC packets being sent by any DCC system. Selectively filter out idle, reset, accessory, function and/or speed packets. Information can be displayed in hexidecimal or our special "verbose" mode that makes it easy to decipher track activity. Requires PC, Mac or Linux computer with terminal program and 9-pin serial cable. Can also be used to monitor NCE Cab Bus activity.

### Silent Running™ Decoder

**NEW 524-139** Bachmann DCC-Equipped Diesel Replacement **19.95**
Four-function decoder is designed for smooth, quiet operation.

## POWER PRO STARTER SETS

User-friendly sets include everything to get two DCC controlled trains running (except power transformer). Choose standard plug-in or wireless radio cab. ProCab™ throttles walk you through operation with clearly labeled buttons and menu prompts in plain English on backlit LCD displays. Sets include ProCab throttle, Command Station with integral 5 amp power unit plus system reference manual with quick start guide.

### 5 Amp System

**524-1** PH-PRO Standard **529.95**

**524-2** PH-PRO-R Wireless w/916 MHz Radio & RB01 Base Station **699.95**

### Power Boosters

**524-3** PB105 5 Amp **159.95**
Delivers five full amps of voltage stabilized power; output is adjustable from 10 to 18 volts. Requires 14-16 volt transformer of 5 Amps or more.

**524-5** PB110 10 Amp w/Automatic Reverse Loop Capability **269.95**
Delivers 10 full amps of voltage stabilized power; output is adjustable from 12.5 to 20 volts. Requires 16-22 volt transformer of 10 Amps or more.

### Power Pro Command Stations

**524-8** CS02 Command Station Only (No Cab, Booster or Decoders) **239.95**

### Power Cab System™

**524-25 189.95**
A complete DCC starter system in the palm of your hand! Includes all the features of the NCE Powerhouse PH-PRO, but at a lower price. Operates up to 6 trains plus extra cabs. Wireless compatible. Includes 120/230V power supply.

### Smart Booster

**524-26 99.95**
Adds a 3 Amp booster to your Power Cab and support for additional cab, Wireless compatible.

### Wireless System Accessories

**524-23** RB02 Wireless Base Station **159.95**
Includes expansion ports for two RPT1 signal repeaters, sold separately.

**524-24** RPT1 Wireless Repeater **129.95**

### 10 Amp Systems for O/G Scales

**524-7** PH-PRO-R Powerhouse Pro w/916 MHz Radio & RB01 Base Station **849.95**

Item listed below is available by Special Order (see Legend Page).
**524-6** PH-10 Powerhouse Pro w/CS02, PB110, ProCab, D408SR Decoder, manual & wires **649.95**

For Daily Product Updates Point Your Browser to
**www.walthers.com**

## THROTTLES

### Deluxe Master ProCab

Deluxe cabs provide user-friendly access to advanced system features. Backlit LCD displays guide you through operations easily. Both a thumb wheel knob and repeating push buttons for speed control are provided. Control of single or multiple turnouts, animated accessories and lights is a snap. Recall button allows control of 1 to 6 trains per cab. The ProCab supports all DCC compatible sound units. All wireless (radio-control) systems operate at 916 MHz unless noted.

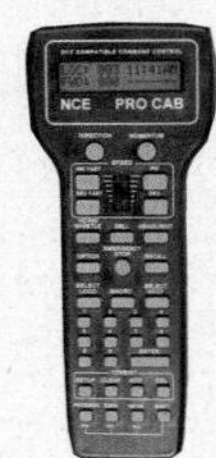

**524-10** ProCab Standard **159.95**

**524-11** ProCab-R Wireless **249.95**

### Engineer Cabs

These hand-held cabs are ideal for operating sessions. Each provides easy selection of locos/consists, single button operation of decoder functions, momentary HORN button, selection and control of individual turnouts or entire routes (via the MACRO key) and the unique OPTION button which can be programmed to act as any button you wish.

### Potentiometer Speed Control

Large control knob (300° rotation) provides smooth speed control. Can also be set to "Yard" mode so the speed knob acts as a "center off" speed control. Ideal for one-handed switching in the yard.

**524-12** CAB04p Standard Model **89.95**

**524-13** CAB04pr Wireless **179.95**

### Digital Encoder Speed Control

All the features of the CAB04 series plus the ability to control two trains. A large knob provides speed control through a digital encoder with adjustable "ballistic tracking;" the faster you turn the knob the faster speed will increase or decrease.

**524-14** CAB04e Standard w/2-Train Control **119.95**

**524-15** CAB04er Wireless w/2-Train Control **199.95**

### Speed Buttons Control

Push buttons feature adjustable automatic repeat rate from once every 4 seconds to as fast as 4 times per second. Just hold the button down and the speed changes smoothly from one speed step to the next as long as you hold the button.

**524-16** CAB05 Standard **89.95**

**524-17** CAB05r Wireless **179.95**

### 7' Coiled Cords for Cabs

**524-209** CoilcordRJ w/RJ12 (Telephone Type) Plug **9.95**

**524-210** CoilcrdDIN w/Molded Right Angle DIN Plug **10.95**

## SILENT RUNNING™ DECODERS

### 1-Amp

Sized to fit N Scale models, these smaller decoders can be adapted to some small HO Scale locos too.

**524-119** N12SR 2-Function **29.95**

**524-123** N12SRP 2 Function w/NMRA 8 Pin Plug **35.95**

**524-128** N14IP Plug In For Con-Cor PA-1, 4-8-4;. 4 Function **29.95**

**524-129** Z14SR 4 Function.57 x .34 x .125" w/Harness **34.95**

**524-130** Z14SRP 4 Function w/8 Pin NMRA Plug **39.95**

**524-131** N14SR Narrow; 4 Function, 4" Wire Harness **29.95**

**524-132** N14SRP Thin, 4 Function w/8 Pin NMRA Plug **35.95**

### 1.3-Amp

These decoders are built to eliminate annoying motor hum and buzz at slow speeds.

#### D13 Series

Includes three EFX function outputs; measures 1.65 x .63 x .12"

**524-100** D13SR Single **19.95**

**524-101** D13pack (Set of Four #524-100 Decoders) **74.95**

**524-102** D13SRP w/8 Pin NMRA Plug **25.95**

**524-121** #100 w/3 EFX function outputs pkg(10) **174.95**

**524-124** D13SRJ - 4 Function w/9 Pin Plug **19.95**

**524-125** D13SRJpack4 (Set of Four #524-124 Decoders) **74.95**

### D14 Series

**524-103** D14SRP **29.95**
Direct plug-in, with six EFX function outputs and NMRA 8-pin.

### D15 Series

With 6 EFX function outputs and nine-pin plug; measures 1.1 x .63 x.25"

**524-104** D15SR w/Harness **29.95**

**524-105** D15SRP w/NMRA Harness **35.95**

### D18 Series

**524-134** D18SR, 8 Function, NMRA 8-Pin Plug **29.95**

### DA Series

Solder-in, with 5 EFX outputs; for Kato drive & Athearn Genesis

**524-106** DA-SR Single **24.95**

**524-107** DApack (Four #524-106 Decoders) **89.95**

### Engine Decoders 29.95 ea

Designed especially for the engines listed.

**524-108** P2K-SR Direct Plug-In, 4 EFX Outputs for Life-Like GP7, 9, 30 & SD60

**524-109** KRS-SR Direct Plug-In, 4 EFX for Kato, Stewart & Intermountain

**524-110** SW9-SR 3 EFX for Life-Like SW8, SW9, SW900 & SW1200

**524-113** ATL-S4 Solder-In, 2 EFX Outputs for Atlas S1, S2, S3 & S4

**NEW 524-126** N12K0A
For Kato N Scale P-42, PA-1 & E-8. Golden glow LEDs are included and installed.

**NEW 524-143** N12K0B
For Kato N Scale F3A and B. Golden glow LEDs are included and installed.

**NEW 524-144** N12K0D
For Kato N Scale FB40H. Golden glow LEDs are included and installed.

### High Amp

**524-111** 4 Amp **69.95**
D408SR, 9 functions, for S, O & large scale

**524-112** 8 Amp **109.95**
D808, 30 amp stall, 8 EFX functions for USA trains, Charles Ro.

## SWITCH MACHINE DECODERS

**524-114** SWITCH-IT Stall Motor Type Machines **19.95**
Controls two Tortoise™, SwitchMaster™ or similar stall motor switch machines. Unit also remembers position of switches during a power failure. Supports accessory addresses from 1 to 2044. Each output of the decoder can have a completely different accessory address for easier operation.

**524-115** SNAP-IT For Twin Coil Type **19.95**

**524-116** Switch/Kat For Kato Unitrack Remote Switch **24.95**

**524-136** Switch 8 **59.95**
Controls eight Tortoise™ switch machines (sold separately).

## STRAIGHT CAB BUS CABLES

**524-213** 6 Wire **6.95**
RJ12-7, 7' RJ12 cable for UTP/DIN panel wiring.

**524-214** 7' Wire **7.95**
RJ12-12, 12' cable for UTP/DIN panel wiring.

**NEW 524-220** 6 Wire **22.95**
RJ12-40, 40' RJ12 cable for RPT1 wiring.

## BLOCK DETECTOR MODULE

**524-205** BD20 - .01 to 20 Amps **16.95**
Detects presence of train in block by the current it draws in a range from 0.01 to 20 amps. No electrical connection to track, simply route track feeder wire through holes in "tombstone" current transformer. Unit does not reduce track voltage or get hot. Easily connects to Auxiliary Input Unit (524-200, sold separately) or most commercial signal systems.

**524-200** AIU01 Auxiliary Input Unit (For Block Detection) **49.95**

**524-201** MACROPANEL For Turnout, or CTC Signal Control **69.95**
Issues Macro and CTC panel commands to signal, accessory (turnout) and auxiliary (lighting) decoders. 29 pushbutton inputs.

## CAB BUS FASCIA PANELS 19.95ea

**524-207** UTP Panel w/RJ12 (Telephone Type) Connectors

**524-208** DIN Panel w/DIN Connectors

## CIRCUIT BREAKER

**524-217** EB3 Triple-Output Circuit Breaker **54.95**

**NEW 524-225** EB1 Single Ouput Electronic Circuit Breaker **29.95**
Provides short circuit protection for a single power district. Can be used with any DCC command system rated at 3 to 10 Amps. With status LEDs and block detection.

## LEDS

**524-218** LED PACK 3mm Golden Glow LEDs pkg(10) **18.95**

## DECODER TEST KIT

**524-219** DTK **24.95**
A perfect companion for any DCC operation and layout. Self-contained unit allows you to program and test any decoder before it's installed in your loco. Can be used to test track power as well as accessory decoders and functions OF, OR, F1 and F2. Built-in indicator lights show Motor Forward or Reverse; add an optional motor (sold separately) for under-load testing.

## SIGNAL DECODER

**524-203** SIG-12 **39.95**
With occupancy detector, drives 2 signal heads.

## POWER SUPPLIES

**524-215** For PH-Pro Starter Sets **37.95**
P515, 15v AC, 5 amp.

**524-221** P114 Power Supply for Power Cab #524-25 (sold separately) **29.95**

**524-222** PCP Power Cab Power Panel **19.95**

## NMRA 8-PIN PLUGS

**524-211** Plug Pack pkg(10) **15.95**

### NEW RAIL MODELS

## NEW PRODUCTS

### Fascianomics™ Folding Drink & Tool Holder

Save your layout and models from the dangers of spilled liquids and drinks while you're working or operating with these adjustable, folding drink and tool holders. The width is adjustable to hold cans and larger drink cups, and the unit folds flat so it's out of the way when not in use. Each holder is made of ABS plastic with a black textured finish to match the Universal Throttle Pockets (sold separately). Perfect for use on your layout and in the crew lounge.

**NEW 501-40021** Single **12.95**

**NEW 501-400215** 5-Pack **49.95**

## UNIVERSAL THROTTLE POCKET™ 2

Keep throttles stored safely on your layout fascia during operating sessions with these handy holders. Made of tough ABS plastic, each simply screws in place and hold Atlas, CVP, Digitrax, Lenz, NCE and MRC throttles.

**501-40020** Single **11.95**

**501-400203** 3-Pack **29.95**

**501-4002010** 10-Pack **79.95**

## Information STATION

### Adding Decoders To Older Locomotives

While many locomotives now come with factory-installed decoders or simple connections to add one, older locomotives can also be converted to DCC.

Decoders are typically identified to scale (such as HO, N, etc.) to show which size models they fit and the current rating. You must make sure there's space inside the model for the decoder. The motor MUST be electrically isolated from the frame to electrical pickups - the motor must only receive power from the decoder.

Today, there are plenty of micro decoders, so finding one to fit shouldn't be a problem.

To prevent damaging the decoder, you must know the operating current, which is the amount of current needed to drive the motor and any accessories. Any mechanical problems (binding, lack of lubrication, etc.) should be corrected before installing a decoder, as they can raise the operating current.

You also need to determine the stall current, which is the amount of current drawn by the motor if stalled. Whenever you start an engine from a dead stop, the motor will pull almost as much current as it would if stalled. If the decoder isn't rated to handle this, the potential is there for damage.

# SOUNDTRAXX™

Bring a new dimensions of operation to your models with this line of digital sound decoders. Compatible with all DCC systems, choose from a wide range of assembled, drop-in units for steam and diesel locos, along with numerous accessories for custom conversions.

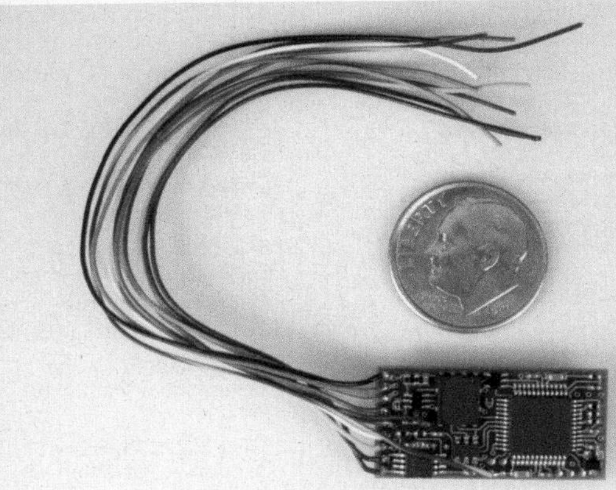

TSU-750 Micro-Tsunami Digital Sound Decoder

## NEW PRODUCTS

### TSU-750 Micro-Tsunami Digital Sound Decoder

**139.95 ea**

Adding sound in small engines is easy with these "micro" decoders that fit most HO and many N scale locos, with a stall current of 0.75 Amps. Each decoder combines a full-featured sound system, two Hyperlight lighting effects, a motor controller and a DCC decoder into a single, integrated unit compatible with the NMRA DCC Standards and Recommended Practices. These decoders can be used on "analog" layouts and controlled with a conventional power pack, though they really shine on DCC controlled layouts. At the Micro-Tsunami's core is a true 16-bit Digital Signal Processor, or DSP, capable of executing over 120 million instructions per second. With this level of performance, the Micro-Tsunami has 14 functions, over 22 individual sounds, and 4 special effects including the ability to alter the exhaust sound automatically in response to changes in the engine load. The motor controller has also been enhanced with high frequency PWM and load compensation. Only components available in highly miniaturized packages were selected for the Micro-Tsunami resulting in an overall size of just 1" long x 1/2" wide x 0.22" tall (2.5 x 1.2 x 0.5cm). Units work with standard 8 Ohm speakers, sold separately.

**NEW 678-826001** Light Steam
Eight whistles (C&S #74 (Road Mix & Yard Mix), Baldwin 2-8-0, Heisler, Westside Lumber Co. Shay #14, Peanut Whistle, DRGW Single Chime & RDG 6-Chime) and sounds for light steam engines such as a 4-4-0, 4-4-2, 2-6-0, 4-6-0, 2-8-0 and switchers.

**NEW 678-826002** Medium Steam
Eight whistles (Santa Fe Freight, B&O 3-Chime #74, PRR Banshee, Lehigh Valley, Nathan 5-Chime (Road & Yard Mix) & USRA 6-Chime) and sounds suitable for 4-6-2, 2-8-2, 4-6-4, 2-10-0 and others.

**NEW 678-826003** Heavy Steam
Whistles (SLSF #1522, N&W #1218, UP #4018 SP #4449 (whistle & horn) & USRA 6-Chime) and sounds for articulated and heavy steam engines such as 4-8-4, 2-10-2, 2-12-2, 2-8-8-2, 4-6-6-4 and others.

**NEW 678-826004** DRGW K Class
A collection of whistles and sounds commonly heard on K-Class Mikados. This decoder is also appropriate for other light and medium steam engines. Whistles included are: K-27 #463, K-36 #487, K-36 #488, K-36 #489, K-36 #489 (with broken chime) and K-37 #497.

**NEW 678-826005** SP Cab Forward
Classic SP whistles (and a few extra for variety including SP 6-Chime, SP #4449 Horn & Whistle, SLSF #1522, N&W #1218 and USRA 6-Chime) as well as the signature "aspirated" airpump.

**NEW 678-826016** DRGW Class C
Whistles and sounds commonly heard on C-Class Consolidations. This decoder is also appropriate for other light steam engines. Whistles included are: C-19 #340 (Yard & Road Mix), DRGW Single Chime, Westside Lumber Co. Shay #14 and Peanut whistle.

**NEW 678-826020** Light Logging
Whistles and sounds for geared and light logging engine such as the Shay, Climax, Heisler and other small engines. Whistles included are: Westside Lumber Co. Shay #14, Westside Lumber Co. Shay #12, Heisler, Peanut whistle and DRGW Single Chime.

## TSUNAMI® DIGITAL SOUND DECODERS®

This high-performance, onboard locomotive sound system combines a full-featured sound system, four Hyperlight lighting effects, a motor controller and a DCC decoder into a single, integrated unit. Compatible with NMRA standards and Recommended Practices, the Tsunami can also be used on DC layouts with a conventional power pack. At Tsunami's core is a true 16-bit Digital Signal Processor, or DSP, capable of executing over 120 million instructions per second. This provides 14 functions, over 22 individual sounds, and 4 special effects including the ability to alter the exhaust sound automatically in response to changes in the engine load.

Each Tsunami supports 7 bit address modes for compatibility with "simple" systems and allows for programmable acceleration, deceleration and starting voltage. The units also support 14 bit address modes for any loco number up to 9,999 and programming on the main.

Throttle features include 14, 28 and 128 step modes with smooth 128 speed step response in any mode. There are 15 pre-programmed speed tables and a user-programmable speed table is also provided. The units also feature high frequency silent motor drive and load compensation.

The sound system combines individual, adjustable volume control, a one watt audio amplifier, polyphonic sound processor, 16-bit audio processing, and a 7-band audio equalizer to produce high quality digital sound that includes playable whistle and reverb. Each is designed to use a standard 8 ohm speaker, sold separately.

Each unit can control 15 Lighting effects including "Rule 17" dimming, or automatic direction control.

### TSU-1000 1 Amp Digital Sound Decoders - Steam 119.95 ea

To take advantage of Tsunami's increased sample rate and dynamic range, all sound effects have been re-mastered and re-digitized for the best audio possible. New sounds include: multiple whistles so you can select the right sound for your model, plus a short whistle blast to produce a short, snappy toot required for many whistle signals. The dynamo effect has been improved to include the sound of the turbine windup when it is first turned on. Brake Squeal may be activated manually using a function key or automatically when the engine is slowed to a stop. The water stop effect can be activated with a function key whenever the engine is stopped and begins with the sound of the tender hatch being opened followed by the sound of water filling the tender. In all, each unit provides over 22 steam sound effects including bell, air pump, exhaust chuff, coupler, steam release, cylinder cocks, snifter valves, brake release, side rod clank, Johnson bar/power reverse, blower, injector, pop valve and Fireman Fred.

Tsunami Digital Sound Decoders are rated for the following loads:

Motor Stall Current: 1 Amp

Maximum Function Current: 100mA (each output)

Audio Amplifier: 1 Watt, 8 ohm load

Track Voltage: 27 Volts

Maximum Dimensions: 1.7 x 0.67 x 0.28"



**678-826101** Light Steam
For smaller locos including 4-4-0, 4-4-2, 4-6-0, 2-6-0, 2-8-0 and more; includes C&S #74 (Road and Yard mix), Baldwin Consolidation, Heisler, Westside Lumber Co. Shay #14, Peanut Whistle, DRGW Single Chime and Reading 6-Chime whistles.

**678-826102** Medium Steam
Whistles and sounds suitable for a 4-6-2, 2-8-2, 4-6-4, 2-10-0 and others. Whistles included are: ATSF Freight, B&O 3-Chime #74, PRR Banshee, Lehigh Valley Nathan 5-Chime (Road and Yard mixes) and USRA 6-Chime.

**678-826103** Heavy Steam
Suitable for bigger power from 4-8-4 to articulateds, whistles include Frisco #1522, N&W #1218, UP #4018 SP #4449 (whistle and single chime air horn) and USRA 6-Chime.

**678-826120** Light Logging Engines
Whistles and sounds for geared and light logging locomotives such as the Shay, Climax, Heisler and other small engines. Whistles included for Westside Lumber Co. Shay #14, Westside Lumber Co. Shay #12, Heisler, Peanut whistle and DRGW Single Chime.

**NEW 678-826105** SP Cab Forward
Includes classic SP whistles and the signature aspirated airpump. Additional whistles include SP 6 Chime, SP #4449 Whistle, SP #4449 Airhorn, SLSF #1522, N&W #1218 and USRA 6-Chime

### Rio Grande Narrow Gauge

These decoders provide common sounds of Rio Grande narrow gauge steam power.

**678-826104** K-Class 2-8-2
Includes whistles for K-27 #463, K36 #487, K36 #488, K-36 #489, K-36 #489 (with broken chime) and K-37 #497

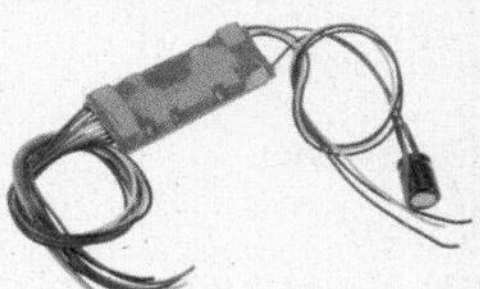

**678-826116** C-Class 2-8-0
Includes whistles for C-19 #340 (Yard and Road mix), DRGW Single Chime, Westside Lumber Co. Shay #14 and Peanut whistle.

# SOUNDTRAXX™

## PROGRAMMING TRACK BOOSTER

**678-829002** PTB-100 For All Decoders **59.95**
This handy tool lets you know if your decoder has received a programming instruction (or not!) using indicator lights on the circuit board. If your command station has problems reading CV data from some sound decoders that are otherwise working properly (responding to speed and direction commands), the problem may be due to incompatibilities between the electrical requirements of the sound decoder due to the added audio circuitry and the electrical characteristics of the programming track. This unit amplifies programming track signals to levels that work best with SoundTraxx Sound Decoders, and provides short circuit detection and some helpful diagnostics. The PTB-100 is not needed or recommended for use with the Zimo MX1 or the Lenz LVZ100.

## CD OWNER'S MANUALS

### FREE

Tips and techniques for successful installation of sound decoders in your models, now on CDs.

**NEW 678-140125** TSU-1000 Tsunami Decoders

**NEW 678-140127** LC Series Decoders

### Bipolar Capacitor

**678-810067** Bipolar Capacitor 33uF, 16V For DSXs, LC Decoders **0.75**

### Speakers

### 8 Ohm

**678-810053** 3/4" Diameter **9.95**

**678-810054** 1" Diameter **9.95**

**678-810055** 1-1/2" Diameter **8.95**

**678-810056** 2" Diameter **8.95**

**678-810057** 3" Diameter **8.95**

**678-810059** 4" Diameter **12.50**

**678-810078** Oval 1-1/8 x 1-9/16" **13.50**

**678-810083** 3/8" Diameter **9.95**

**678-810084** Oval 1-1/2 x 2-1/2" **15.25**

**678-810087** 2-1/2" Diameter **8.95**

**678-810089** 1/2" Diameter **9.95**

**678-810090** Oval 2 x 3-1/2" **16.50**

**678-810103** Oval 13/16 x 1-9/16" **13.50**

**678-810112** Oval 9/16 x 1" **13.50**

**678-810113** 8 Oval 5/8 x 1-3/8" **13.50**

### Wiring Harnesses 10.00 ea (Unless Noted)

### DSX

**678-810092** Steam **10.00**

**678-810093** Diesel **10.00**

### DSD

**678-810069** Power Wiring Harness **10.00**

**678-810097** DSD-100LC **6.00**

### Speaker Baffle Kits 3.65 ea

**678-810099** For Life-Like E Unit Diesels

**678-810100** For Life-Like ALCO PA & PB Diesels

**678-810101** For Stewart ALCO C628/630 Diesels

**678-810102** For Bachmann HO Shay

### Speaker Enclosures 3.00 ea

**678-810107** 3/8"

**678-810108** 1/2"

**678-810109** 3/4"

**678-810110** 1"

### Speaker Gasket Kits 1.50 ea

**678-810118** 3/4"

**678-810119** 1"

**678-810120** 20 x 40mm

**678-810121** 14 x 25mm

## DSD-101LC DIGITAL SOUND DECODERS

### 65.00 ea

These decoders combine a digital sound system, headlight and backup light, and a DCC decoder into a single, miniature electronic module. Each comes equipped with an NMRA-compatible 8-pin plug for easy installation.

### Steam

Add the speaker of your choice and enjoy three different whistles, bell, airpump, exhaust chuff sounds, plus, headlight and backup light, Rule 17 lighting or automatic direction control, and hyperlight effects.

**NEW 678-820111** Light

**NEW 678-820112** Medium

**NEW 678-820113** Heavy

### Diesel

Add the speaker of your choice and enjoy single-, three- or five-chime airhorns, bell, dynamic brakes, exhaust sounds, plus headlight and backup light, Rule 17 lighting or automatic direction control, and hyperlight effects.

**NEW 678-820120** EMD First Generation

**NEW 678-820121** ALCO

**NEW 678-820122** EMD Second Generation

**NEW 678-820124** EMD First Generation w/Canadian Airhorns

## DSD PLUG & PLAY DECODERS

### 70.00 (Unless Noted)

Easy to install decoders for many of today's most popular models. Each DSD installs inside your locomotive and integrates a full-featured digital sound system, sophisticated lighting effects and a DCC decoder into a single, miniature electronic module. Add the speaker of your choice and enjoy three different whistles or airhorns, bell, dynamic brakes, exhaust sounds, headlight and backup light, and Rule 17 lighting or automatic direction control.

### DSD-AT100LC Series for Atlas Diesels

**678-820040** EMD First Generation

**678-820041** EMD Second Generation

**678-820042** ALCO

**NEW 678-820043** GE **70.00**

**NEW 678-820044** Fairbanks-Morse **70.00**

See What's Available at

**www.walthers.com**

### DSD-LL110LC Series for Life-Like

**678-820070** EMD First Generation

**678-820071** EMD Second Generation

**678-820072** ALCO FA

**678-820080** USRA 0-8-0 **80.00**

## DSX DIGITAL SOUND DECODERS

### 85.00 ea

### Steam Engines

**678-824208** DRGW 2-8-2, K-27 Class No.463

**678-824215** Westside Lumber Co. Three-Truck Shay

**678-824218** Santa Fe 3751

Items listed below are available by Special Order (see Legend Page).

**678-824203** DRGW 2-8-2, K-36 Class No.484

**678-824206** DRGW 2-8-2, K-37 Class No.497

**678-824207** DRGW 2-8-2, K-28 Class No.473

**678-824209** East Broad Top 2-8-2

**678-824210** UP 4-6-6-4 Challenger #3985

**678-824211** SP 4-8-4 "Daylight" GS-4

**678-824212** N&W 2-6-6-4 Class A

**678-824214** British L-1 Class Tank

**678-824216** C-16

**678-824224** SLSF #1522 4-8-2 Mountain

### Diesel

**678-825202** EMD 1st Generation w/Leslie S3 Airhorn

**678-825214** ALCO w/Wabco E2 Airhorn

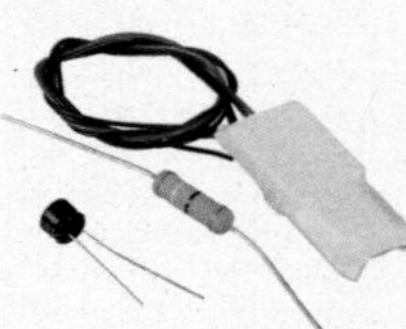

**678-825227** EMD 2nd Generation w/Nathan M3 Airhorn

**678-825250** Rio Grande Southern Galloping Goose

Items listed below are available by Special Order (see Legend Page).

**678-825201** EMD 1st Generation w/Wabco Airhorn

**678-825203** EMD 1st Generation w/Nathan K3 Airhorn

**678-825204** EMD 1st Generation w/Wabco E2 Airhorn

**678-825205** EMD 1st Generation w/Nathan M5 Airhorn

**678-825208** EMD 1st Generation w/Nathan P3 Airhorn

**678-825211** ALCO w/Wabco Airhorn

**678-825212** ALCO w/Leslie S Airhorn

**678-825213** ALCO w/Nathan K3 Airhorn

**678-825215** ALCO w/Nathan M5 Airhorn

**678-825218** ALCO w/Nathan P3 Airhorn

**678-825220** EMD 2nd Generation w/Leslie S5 Airhorn

**678-825222** EMD 2nd Generation w/Leslie S3 Airhorn

**678-825223** EMD 2nd Generation w/Nathan K3 Airhorn

**678-825226** EMD 2nd Generation w/Nathan K5 Airhorn

**678-825228** EMD 2nd Generation w/Nathan P3 Airhorn

**678-825230** GE w/Leslie S5 Airhorn

**678-825231** GE w/Wabco Airhorn

**678-825232** GE w/Leslie S3 Airhorn

**678-825234** GE w/Wabco E2 Airhorn

**678-825236** GE w/Nathan K5 Airhorn

**678-825238** GE w/Nathan P3 Airhorn

### Test Kit

**678-829001** Decoder Test Kit **3.00**

Upgrade your digital sound decodersfor added realism with these sound decoder upgrade components. Each upgrade chip is designed to replace the existing sound chip in existing QSI Quantum® sound decoders.

## NEW PRODUCTS

### Quantum Programmer

**NEW 601-QSISQP** Quantum Programmer **99.95**
Download sound files from your PC and program CVs. Interfaces between your PC and a program track which allows downloading software and new and future sounds into an upgraded Quantum Sound System without disassembling your locomotive. Includes Quantum CV Manager software that allows PC users to program and customize all the CVs graphically and effortlessly. Supports Operations Mode Programing (programming on the main) making it ideal for speed matching locos. Only compatible with Q1a Upgrade Chip (sold separately). Includes Quantum programmer, power supply, USB cable, software, installation guide and user manuals.

### Quantum Chip Upgrades 29.95 ea

Impressive performance upgrade adds many new features to your QSI-equipped DC (analog) and DCC locomotives. Accepts downloadable and future sounds. Can be installed without removing the memory chip.

**NEW 601-100** E7 1st Run, Leslie P3, w/o Mars Light, Trim Pot

**NEW 601-101** SW7/NW2, All Trim Pot

**NEW 601-102** SD40, Trim Pot

**NEW 601-103** Dash-8-40CW

**NEW 601-104** F7, Wab. E2, w/o Dynamic Brakes

**NEW 601-105** FM, Nathan M5, w/Mars Light

**NEW 601-106** FM w/o Mars Light

**NEW 601-107** E6 w/Mars Light & Leslie P3 Airhorn

**NEW 601-108** E6, No Mars Light, Leslie P3 Airhorn

**NEW 601-110** F7 w/WABCO E2 Airhorn

**NEW 601-111** SD24/26 w/Leslie S-3 3-Chime Airhorn

**NEW 601-112** GP9, Typhone A Single Chime

**NEW 601-113** RS10

**NEW 601-115** E3/E6 w/Mars Light & Leslie P3 Airhorn

**NEW 601-116** E3/E6, No Mars Light (Pot), w/Leslie P3 Airhorn

**NEW 601-117** E8/E9 w/Mars Light & WABCO E2 Airhorn

**NEW 601-118** E8/E9, No Mars Light, w/WABCO E2

**NEW 601-119** E7,Leslie P3, w/Mars Light, Reed Switch

**NEW 601-120** E7, Wab E2, No Mars Light, Reed Switch

**NEW 601-121** E3/E6 w/Mars Light, Reed Switch & Leslie P3 Airhorn

**NEW 601-122** E3/E6, No Mars Light, Reed Switch w/Leslie P3 Airhorn

**NEW 601-123** RS18

**NEW 601-124** U28B/U30B

**NEW 601-125** RSD-15

**NEW 601-126** Dash-8-40BW

**NEW 601-127** B23-7

**NEW 601-128** GE C30-7

**NEW 601-129** MP-15DC

**NEW 601-130** EMD GP20, Nathan M3 3-Chime

**NEW 601-131** AC6000

**NEW 601-132** Dash-8-40CW

**NEW 601-133** SW8 1st Generation

**NEW 601-134** SD40, Reed Switch

**NEW 601-135** E8/E9 w/Mars Light & WABCO E2 Airhorn

**NEW 601-136** E8/9, No Mars Light, w/WABCO E2 Airhorn

**NEW 601-137** RS27 Alco

**NEW 601-139** NSWR 620/720 w/Leslie S Airhorn

**NEW 601-140** EMD GP30, Leslie S3B 3-Chime

**NEW 601-143** F7, Wab. E2, w/Dynamic Brakes

**NEW 601-144** GP7 Phase 2 w/Dynamic Brakes, Leslie S3BJ Airhorn

**NEW 601-145** GP7 Phase II No Dynamic Brake, w/Leslie S3BJ Airhorn

**NEW 601-155** SW7/NW7, Reed Switch

**NEW 601-200** GG1, Trim Pot

**NEW 601-300** BLI Hudson, Trim Pot

**NEW 601-301** USRA Heavy or Light Mikado' Trim Pot

**NEW 601-302** M1A Mountain, Trim Pot

**NEW 601-303** On30-C/16 Standard, Trim Pot

**NEW 601-304** On30-C/16 Xmas

**NEW 601-305** ATSF 4-8-4 3751, Trim Pot

**NEW 601-306** PRR J1, Trim Pot

**NEW 601-307** UP 4-8-2 Mountain

**NEW 601-308** GN 700, SP&S

**NEW 601-309** PRR K4

**NEW 601-310** C&O T1 Texas

**NEW 601-312** N&W J 4-8-4

**NEW 601-313** NYC S1b 4-8-4

**NEW 601-315** USRA 0-8-0

**NEW 601-316** ATSF 3800 2-10-2/4

**NEW 601-317** 2-8-4 w/Mars Light

**NEW 601-318** 2-8-4 w/o Mars Light

**NEW 601-319** 0-6-0

**NEW 601-400** N&W Class A, Trim Pot

**NEW 601-401** PRR T1 Duplex, Trim Pot

**NEW 601-402** Challenger, Trim Pot

**NEW 601-403** SP AC4/AC5, Trim Pot

**NEW 601-404** USRA 2-8-8-2

**NEW 601-406** SP AC4/AC5, Reed Switch

**NEW 601-408** Y3, 2-8-8-2

**NEW 601-410** PRR T1 Duplex, Reed Switch

**NEW 601-500** Lionel Veranda Turbine, Pot LIO

**NEW 601-1001** E7 1st Run, New Horn, Wab E2, w/o Mars Light, Trim Pot

**NEW 601-1011** SW7/NW2, New Horn, All Trim Pot

**NEW 601-1021** SD40, New Horn, Trim Pot

**NEW 601-1031** Dash-8-40CW, New Horn

**NEW 601-1041** F7 w/o Dynamic Brakes, New Horn Leslie S3BJ3 Chime

**NEW 601-1042** F7 without Dynamic Brake NAT M5

**NEW 601-1051** FM w/Mars Light, New Horn

**NEW 601-1061** FM w/o Mars Light, New Horn

**NEW 601-1071** E6 w/Mars Light & WABCO E2

**NEW 601-1081** E6, No Mars Light, w/WABCO E2 Airhorn

**NEW 601-1101** F7 w/Nathan M5 Airhorn

**NEW 601-1111** SD24/26 w/Nathan M5 5-Chime Airhorn

**NEW 601-1112** SD24/26 w/Nathan K3 Airhorn

**NEW 601-1121** GP9, New Horn, Leslie SBJ-3

**NEW 601-1122** GP9 w/Nathan K3 Airhorn

**NEW 601-1151** E3/E6 w/Mars Light & WABCO E2 Airhorn

**NEW 601-1161** E3/E6, No Mars Light, Pot, w/WABCO E2 Airhorn

**NEW 601-1171** E8/E9 w/Mars Light w/Leslie P3 Airhorn

**NEW 601-1181** E8/E9, No Mars Light, w/Leslie P3 Airhorn

**NEW 601-1191** E7 New Horn Wab E2, w/Mars Light, Reed Switch

**NEW 601-1201** E7 New Horn, Wab E2, No Mars Light, Reed Switch

**NEW 601-1211** E3/E6 w/Mars Light, Reed Switch & WABCO E2 Airhorn

**NEW 601-1221** E3/E6, No Mars Light, Reed Switch, w/WABCO E2 Airhorn

**NEW 601-1241** U28B/U30B, New Horn

**NEW 601-1251** RSD-15, New Horn

**NEW 601-1261** Dash-8-40BW, New Horn

**NEW 601-1271** B23-7 Different Horn

**NEW 601-1281** GE C30-7 Different Horn

**NEW 601-1291** MP-15DC Different Horn

**NEW 601-1301** EMD GP20, Different Horn, Nathan M5 5-Chime

**NEW 601-1311** AC6000 Different Horn

**NEW 601-1321** Dash-8-40CW, New Horn

**NEW 601-1331** SW8 1st Generation, Same as 1330, Different Horn

**NEW 601-1341** SD40, Reed Switch, New Horn

**NEW 601-1351** E8/E9 w/Mars Light & Leslie P3 Airhorn

**NEW 601-1361** E8/E9, No Mars Light, w/Leslie P3 Airhorn

**NEW 601-1371** RS27 Alco Different Horn

**NEW 601-1401** EMD GP30, Different Horn, Nathan M5 5-Chime

**NEW 601-1431** F7 w/Dynamic Brakes, New Horn Leslie S3BJ3 Chime

**NEW 601-1432** F7 with Dynamic Brake, Nat M5

**NEW 601-1441** GP7 Phase 2 w/Dynamic Brakes, WP-3 Airhorn

**NEW 601-1451** GP7 Phase2, No Dynamic Brake, w/WP-3 Airhorn

**NEW 601-1551** SW7/NW2, Reed Switch, Different Horn

**NEW 601-3001** Hudson, Trim Pot, New Chuff

**NEW 601-3011** USRA Heavy Or Light Mikado, Trim Pot, New Whistle

**NEW 601-3021** M1A Mountain, Trim Pot, New Horn

**NEW 601-3031** On30-C/16 Standard, Trim Pot, New Chuff

**NEW 601-3051** ATSF 4-8-4 3751, Trim Pot, New Chuff

**NEW 601-3061** PRR J1, Trim Pot, New Chuff

**NEW 601-3071** UP 4-8-2 Mountain, New Chuff

**NEW 601-3091** PRR K4, New Chuff

**NEW 601-3101** C&O T1 Texas, New Chuff

**NEW 601-3121** N&W J 4-8-4, New Chuff

**NEW 601-3131** NYC S1b 4-8-4, New Chuff

**NEW 601-3151** USRA 0-8-0, New Chuff

**NEW 601-3161** ATSF 3800 2-10-2/4, New Chuff

**NEW 601-3171** 2-8-4 w/Mars Light, New Chuff

**NEW 601-3181** 2-8-4 w/o Mars Light, New Chuff

**NEW 601-3191** 0-6-0, New Chuff

**NEW 601-4001** N&W Class A, Trim Pot, New Chuff

**NEW 601-4031** SP AC4/AC5, Trim Pot, New Chuff

**NEW 601-4041** USRA 2-8-8-2, New Chuff

**NEW 601-4061** SP AC4/AC5, Reed Switch, New Chuff

**NEW 601-4081** Y3, 2-8-8-2, New Chuff

**NEW 601-999** Universal Chip takes any Q1a Upgrade

## Speakers

### Dream Speakers 8 ohm, 9.95 ea (Unless Noted)

#### Round

**NEW 601-TDS050** 0.50" Diameter 13mm

**NEW 601-TDS062** 0.62" Diameter 13mm **12.95**

**NEW 601-TDS075** 0.75" Diameter 20mm

**NEW 601-TDS100** 1.00" Diameter 26mm

**NEW 601-TDS110** 1.10" Diameter 26mm

**NEW 601-TDS120** 1.20" Diameter 30mm

**NEW 601-TDS125** 1.25" Diameter 32mm

#### Oval

**NEW** 601-TDSAOVAL Mini 14 x 24mm **12.95**

**NEW** 601-TDSBOVAL Small 16 x 35mm

**NEW** 601-TDSCOVAL Medium 20 x 35mm

**NEW** 601-TDSDOVAL Large 29 x 40mm **12.95**

#### High Base

**NEW 601-TDSHB106** 1.06" Diameter x .056" Height, Round Frame 27mm

**NEW 601-TDSHB110** 1.10" Diameter x 0.44 Height, Square Frame 28mm

## Enclosures

For round or oval speakers (sold separately).

### Round 8.95 ea (Unless Noted)

**NEW 601-TDSENC050** For 0.50" Speaker

**NEW 601-TDSENC062** For 0.62" Speaker

**NEW 601-TDSENC075** For 0.75" Speaker

**NEW 601-TDSENC100** For 1.00" Speaker

**NEW 601-TDSENC110** For 1.10" Speaker

**NEW 601-TDSENC120** For 1.20" Speaker

**NEW 601-TDSENC125** For 1.25" Speaker **11.95**

### Oval 11.95 ea

**NEW 601-TDSENCA** For Mini Oval Speaker

**NEW 601-TDSENCB** For Small Oval Speaker

**NEW 601-TDSENCC** For Medium Oval Speaker

**NEW 601-TDSENCD** For Large Oval Speaker

## Extractor Tool

**NEW 601-QSITOOL** PLCC Extractor Tool 9.95

# ADHESIVES

Models and Photo by David Temple

If you've ever had the pleasure of being downwind from a pickle factory on a hot summer day, you'll know why the engineer of #55 is getting a little fresh air outside of the cab! The strong aroma of vinegar lays heavy in the humid summer air, broken only by the soft coal smoke and what little breeze the slowly passing train can stir up. Those snow-capped mountains in the distance hint at the grades ahead, and the engineer is using just enough steam to get the Orbinas & Western local out of town.

One of the many shortlines with running rights on David Temple's Rio Verde in Roxboro, Quebec, #55 is the pride of the O&W and was kitbashed to fit a Mantua chassis. Faced with an odd-shaped layout corner, David turned the potential problem into a real showpiece with his scratchbuilt Peter Piper Pickle factory, constructed to fit using Northeastern lumber. A few Jordan vehicles rumble past as quickly as possibly, as they head for the main street of town.

Whether working with metal, plastics, scenery material and more, you'll find a wide range of suitable adhesives on the pages just ahead. And when your layout is up and running, there are all kinds of cleaners and lubricants to keep things in top shape.

# WALTHERS

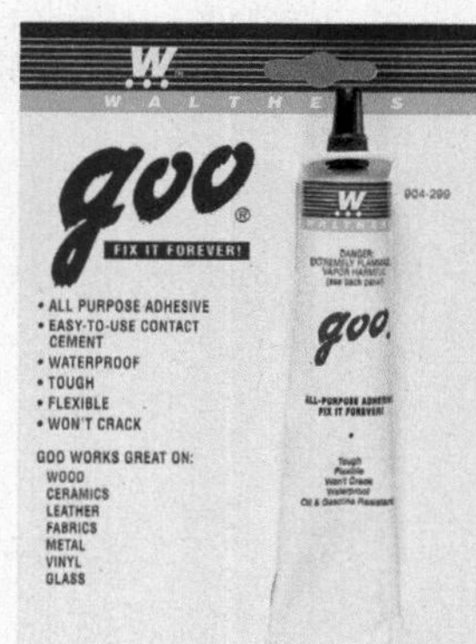


Goo® 904-299

## ADHESIVES

### GOO

**904-299** 1oz **2.98**

**•ALL PURPOSE ADHESIVE**
GOO is the permanent rubber base adhesive that grips most anything. It never lets go.

**•FAST-SETTING JOINTS**
Easy contact action opens new possibilities for fast-setting joints with any material.

Walthers GOO is the perfect adhesive for building or repairing jobs on your layout and around the house!

The easy contact action of GOO produces fast-setting joints with any material. GOO works with all types of metals (including steel, brass, aluminum, copper and others) plus items like wood, plastic, cardboard, china, leather, vinyl, ceramics, paper, concrete and many more, on any smooth or porous surface.

GOO is a permanent rubber-base adhesive that's shockproof, waterproof and crackproof–it's as flexible as rubber. Joints won't crack when flexed back and forth, won't break loose when the temperature changes and won't weaken when wet or damp. It sticks forever!

Dealers: MUST order in multiples of 6.

### Mikro Tip

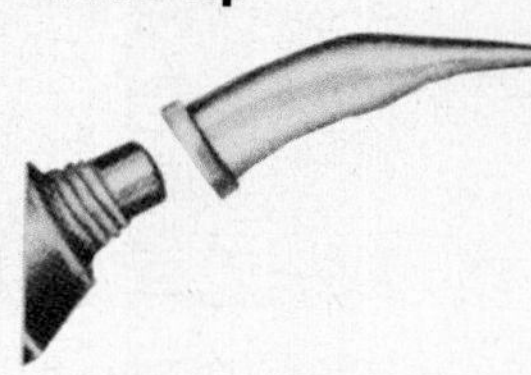

**904-302** pkg(10) **2.98**

### For Precision Gluing Fits Most Any Glue Tube

- Easily added to GOO Adhesive Tube
- Helps eliminate waste and mess
- Allows more precise application of glue
- Mounts on 3/16" diameter glue nozzle

## CLEANERS

### Bright Boy Abrasive Track Cleaner

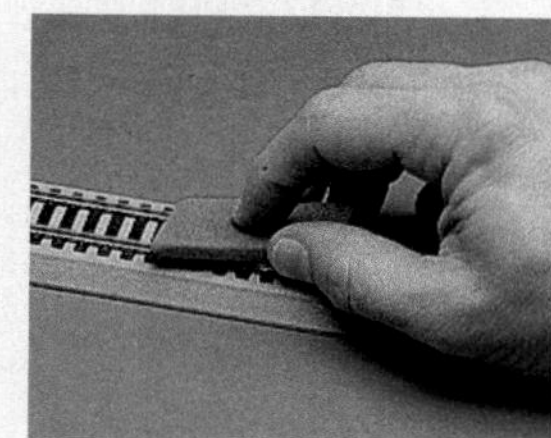

**949-521 5.98**
Improve the conductivity of your tracks by keeping them clean with easy-to-use Bright Boy!

## LIFE-LIKE®

Div. of Wm. K. Walthers, Inc.

### Maintenance Kit

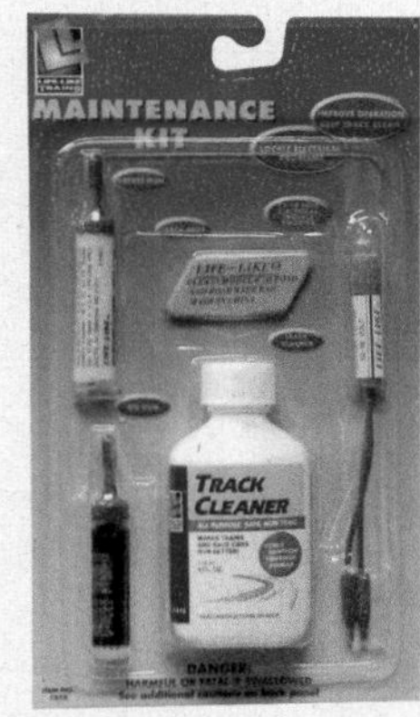


**433-1418 19.98**
Includes Grease Gun, Oil Gun, Track Cleaner, Track Brite and Trouble Shooter Circuit Tester.

### Track Cleaner

**433-1415** 8oz **9.50**

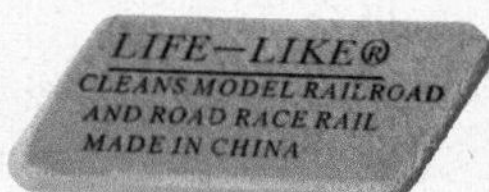


**433-1416** Track Brite **5.00**

See What's New and Exciting at
**www.walthers.com**

## A-LINE

### Flywheel Cement

**116-20010** .02 Fl. oz. **3.95**
Enough for multiple flywheel applications.

### Track Cleaning Pad Kit

**116-10003 4.95**
Easily converts most 40' box cars into track cleaning cars. Soft-abrasive pad wipes away built-up grime without scratching rail.

## ADAIR SHOPS

## NEW PRODUCTS

## PUTTY

### Model Railroad Body Putty Kit

**NEW 143-7007 7.74**
Non-toxic, solvent-free filler powder for general small seam filler use. Mixes with Weight Bond Glue included in kit and does not dry between uses. Accepts water-based and solvent paint.

## ADHESIVES

### Weight Bond™ Glue

Non-toxic, water-based glue is designed for use with Rite-Wey™ Weight kits (sold separately, see Parts Section for complete listing).

**143-7000** Single **5.14**

**143-7001** Two-Pack **9.10**

### Pink Sound Bond™ Glue

Great for general electronic uses including board mounting, sound system installations and sealing speakers and circuit boards. Simply apply over areas to be sealed. Dries pink.

**143-7002** Single **5.14**

**143-7003** Two-Pack **9.10**

### Adhesives

**130-1611** Clear Vinyl Cement 5/8oz Tube **2.00**
Crystal-clear cement for joining or mending rigid or flexible vinyl. Waterproof.

**130-154** EZ Mask 1oz Bottle **2.15**
Eliminate the use of messy tape with this brush-on, peel-off, water soluble masking liquid.

**130-157** Fas'N-All Adhesive/Sealant 1oz **2.55**
Rubber-based general purpose adhesive and sealant. Cured material is flexible, waterproof and shock absorbent.

**130-110** Pro Weld 2oz **3.10**
Clear, super fast plastic fusing adhesive bonds styrene, butyrate, ABS and acrylic.
Dealers: MUST order Dealer Pack of 12.

**130-126** Se•Cur•It 4oz **2.45**
Great for porous materials. Sandable resin glue will not stain and is nonflammable.

**130-1701** Safe Bond 5/8oz Tube **2.10**
Fast-drying, nontoxic adhesive for styrene plastics is designed for filling gaps in joints. Extra-fine-point application tip.

**130-160** Safe Weld 1oz Bottle **3.25**
Used for fusing styrene plastic this nontoxic solution includes an applicator brush.

**130-1521** Styrene Plastic Cement 5/8oz Tube **2.00**
Improved, fast-drying, more aggressive formula with super gap-filling qualities. Dries clear. Resistant to running.

**130-158** Tac-N-Place Adhesive 1oz **2.15**
Nontoxic, brush-on, pressure sensitive adhesive. For temporary or permanent joining of plastic, wood, paper, fabric, glass, foam and metal. Remains tacky.

### Liquid Cement

Waterproof cement mainly for use on wood but binds well to leather, canvas, metal, most fabrics and glass.

Dealers: MUST order Dealer Pack of 12.

**130-101** 1.8oz Tube **2.62**
**130-102** 3.2oz Tube **4.29**
**130-1511** 1oz Tube **2.15**

## ATLAS

# LUBRICANTS

Atlas lubricants are plastic compatible, making them ideal for use on all model railroad equipment.

### Gear Lubricant

**150-190 8.25**
Light grease ideal for gears in locos or accessories.

### Heavy-Duty Motor-Bearing Lubricant

**150-191 10.95**
Light oil for motor and gear bearings.

### Conducta Lube

**150-192 10.95**
Conductive liquid lubricant/cleaner for contact surfaces and bearings.

### Loco Track Maintenance Kit

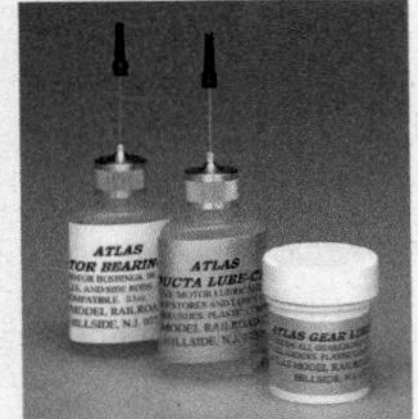

**150-193** pkg(3) **27.50**
One each of the lubricants listed above.

## A.J. FRICKO COMPANY

### Track & Wheel Cleaner

**274-10** Dr. Bonzola's Genuine Snake Oil 30ml **34.95**
The end of scrubbing rails! Keep electricity running to your cars with this greaseless track and wheel cleaner.

### Track & Motor Cleaner

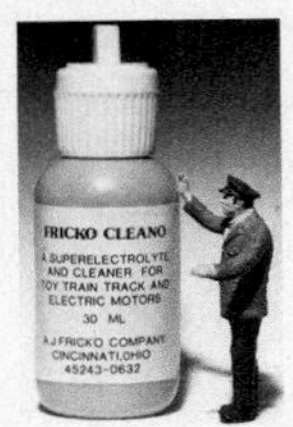


**274-8** Cleano 30ml **34.95**
Universal track and motor cleaner for layouts and locomotives. Just one drop per rail per 4 x 8' area remains effective for one year. Cleano will protect against rust even in the dampest basements.

## A-West

"On target for You!"

# STAINLESS NEEDLEPOINT APPLICATOR BOTTLES

Precision application of solvent, flux, paint, oil, glue, ink, cement, contact cleaner, fuel, ACC accelerators, ceramic decor, etc, etc. Length 1" or 4" snaps into bottle neck. Includes 1oz bottle, cap and cleaning wire.
o = outer diameter
i = inner diameter
f = relative flow rate

### 1" Needle 2.99 ea (Unless Noted)

**158-16** Blue .016o .008i 1f

**158-20** Yellow .020o .010i 2f

**158-25** Red .025o .013i 3f

**158-35** White .035o .023i 8f

**158-50** Black .050o .033i 17f

**158-65** Clear .065o .047i 35f

**158-73** Set #1 **6.59**
Includes tips for kit #s 16, 25, 50 and 1 bottle.

**158-76** Set #2 **12.19**
Includes tips for kit #s 16, 20, 25, 35, 50, 65 and 1 bottle.

### 4" Needle 3.99 ea

**158-164** Blue .016o .008i 1f

**158-204** Yellow .020o .010i 2f

**158-254** Red .025o .013i 3f

**158-354** White .035o .023i 8f

**158-504** Black .050o .033i 17f

**158-654** Clear .065o .047i 35f

# G-GUN

Makes it easy to apply grease, glue, putty or latex/plaster molding material to delicate or hard-to-reach places.

**158-900** 1/2oz **1.98**

**158-901** Jr. G-Gun pkg(2) **1.98**

## CGM ENTERPRISES

# INSTANT ADHESIVES (CYANOACRYLATES)

JET professional-grade CA glues feature a 12-month shelf life (usually more if refrigerated), comfortably shaped see-through bottles, clog-resistant caps, wide range of sizes and three viscosities to ensure the perfect bond characteristics. CAs are ideal for use on wood, metals, ceramics, rubber, most plastic, leather and some fabrics.

### Instant Jet™

Watery consistency produces the fastest set, penetrates and reinforces porous materials, provides an excellent corrosive-resistant finish, and is useful both for "tack" gluing and various final bonds.

**289-761** 1/4oz **2.99**

**289-762** 1/2oz **3.99**

**289-763** 1oz **6.49**

**289-764** 2oz **11.99**

### Super Jet™

Medium viscosity with exceptional strength and gap-filling capabilities, Super Jet is ideal for nearly all instant-bond situations. Recommended for all of the above uses, including hardwoods. Usually sets in 30-60 seconds. Also available in a no-spill, brush-on bottle.

**289-766** 1/4oz **2.99**

**289-767** 1/2oz **3.99**

**289-768** 1oz **6.49**

**289-769** 2oz **11.99**

**289-770** 4oz **19.99**

**289-771** Brush-On 1/2oz **4.99**

### Slow Jet™

The thickest version, Slow Jet provides maximum gap-filling, extra strength for laminations and high-stress areas, and allows a few extra seconds for repositioning.

**289-772** 1/2oz **3.99**

**289-773** 1oz **6.49**

**289-774** 2oz **11.99**

### Jet Set™ Pump

Jet Set is an accelerator for use with all brands of cyanoacrylate adhesives. Once pieces are properly positioned, this creates an instant bond.

**289-777** 2oz **5.99**

**289-778** Pump Refill 8oz **10.99**

### Jet De-Solv™

**289-781** 1oz **3.99**
Solvent used for removing Jet and other brands of CA. Excellent for clean-up, it may also be used to soften bonds, so that pieces may be separated.

### Jet Pak™ Cap & Tips

**289-789 3.99**
Includes a spare cap which fits all Jet CA bottles, five sizes of tips and 12" of capillary tubing.

### Jet™ Epoxy

Flexible, fuel-resistant, high-strength bonding in two workability formulas.

**289-791** 6 Minutes **11.99**
Workable for three to six minutes, and sets in 10-20 minutes.

**289-792** 20 Minutes **11.99**
Workable for 10-20 minutes, and sets in one to two hours.

### Jet™ Tips Extensions

**289-788** pkg(6) **1.99**
Six fine-bore extensions for precise application of JET cyanoacrylate glues.

## BACHMANN

Keep your track, rolling stock and motive power running in top condition with this line of high-grade lubricants.

### Lubrication

**160-99981** Conductive Contact Lube **13.00**
Designed for use with electric motor maintenance and track cleaning.

### Grease

**160-99982 13.00**
Heavy-duty grease is best used for applications requiring heavier viscosity materials.

### Oil 13.00 ea

**160-99983** Heavy Gear
Designed for use on bearings, draft gear boxes, motor bushings, side rods and valve gears.

**160-99984** Light Gear
Perfect for any shafts, gears, bolsters and bushings.

## CREST

### Crest Lube Conductive

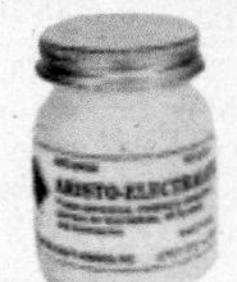

**227-29602 6.50**
Add extra conductivity and smooth operation to locomotives by adding to axle bearings and bushings.

### Crest Lube Oil

**227-29603 4.25**
Inhibits rust as well as prevents friction, heat and wear.

### Crest Smoke Fluid & Track Cleaner

**227-29601 4.00**
Keeps track and wheels clean for improved conductivity and engine performance. Also doubles as smoke fluid for the cleanest smoke around without the buildup.

## DR. MIKE'S MODEL-N' CRAFTER'S GLUE

### GLUE

Handle all types of hobby and household gluing chores with this line of Cyanoacrylate (CA) adhesives and accessories.

**352-200** Dr. Mike's Model-n' Crafter's Glue© 1/2 oz **12.95**
Make easy work of any project with this CA adhesive designed especially for models and crafts. It produces fast, strong bonds between all types of woods, plastics (including styrene, Delrin and ABS), metals, ceramics, rubber, glass and much more. It can also be used to glue dissimilar materials together such as Delrin to wood. And, the special formula doesn't evaporate in the container or clog the delivery tube — average shelf life after opening is 8 months or more at 70° or lower.

## FLOQUIL

### Polly Scale Plastic Cement

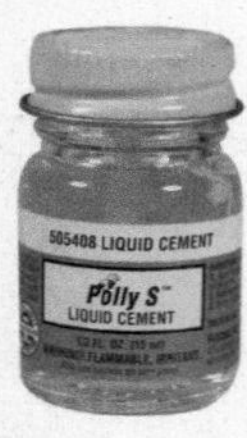


**270-505408** Liquid Cement 1/2oz 15ml **4.75**
Features applicator brush on cover.

## FALLER

IMPORTED FROM GERMANY BY WALTHERS

### NEW PRODUCTS

#### Cement, Cleaner & Lube Assortment

**NEW 272-170480**
Professional Assortment **33.99**
Includes Super EXPERT Cement, EXPERT Liquid Cement, Synthetic Gear Lube, Special Oiler and Cleaner Distillate in a convenient storage stand.

#### Cleaners

**NEW 272-170486** Cleaner Distillate **6.99**
Especially suitable for cleaning dirt on buildings, track, vehicles and more.

#### Plastic Cements

272-170490 272-170492

**272-170490** Super EXPERT Cement **6.79**
With special hollow needle and protective cap. Quicker, stronger bond. Dealers MUST order multiples of 24.

**272-170492** EXPERT Liquid **6.79**
With needle applicator. 25ml. Dealers MUST order multiples of 24.

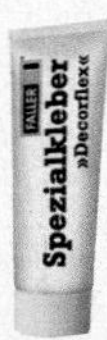


**272-170493** Decroflex **9.99**
An ideal adhesive for use with solvent-sensitive materials. 60g.

#### Lubricants

272-170488 272-170489

**272-170488** Synthetic Gear Lube 25ml **9.99**
Specially formulated for use on plastics, this long-lasting lubricant is acid-free to protect parts.

**272-170489** Special Oiler **9.99**
All-around oiler for small motors and gears. Resin and acid free. 25g.

Designed, Manufactured & Assembled entirely in the U.S.A.

### Lubricant

**380-231** Greas-Em Tube 5.5g **2.25**
A multi-purpose dry lubricant ideal for couplers, wheelsets and trucks, and many other applications.

## INTERNATIONAL HOBBY CORP.

### Track Cleaning Pads

**348-4398** pkg(6) **3.98**
Replacement pads for IHC Track Cleaning Car.

## MASCOT® PRECISION TOOLS

### Instant Adhesive

**230-752** 3g Tube .10 fl oz Gel **3.15**
High performance, extended range adhesive that bonds metal, plastic, rubber, ceramics and glass in seconds. Bonds colorless, eliminating the "white frosting" effect of other adhesives. No-drip formula fills gaps and is ideal for use on vertical surfaces.

## MISSION MODELS

### NEW PRODUCT

#### Precision Glue Tips

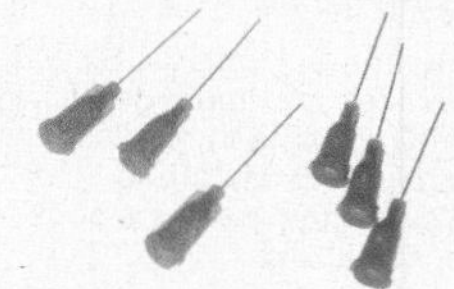

**NEW 466-MM13** 3 Each #27 & #25 Gauge **3.99**
Fits most CA bottles (designed especially for Zap products, sold separately) for precise application of CA and liquid cements. Includes six tips, three each of .025" and .027".

If it Moves - Lube it!©

For almost 50 years LaBelle lubricants have been the preferred choice by model railroaders and model train repairmen.

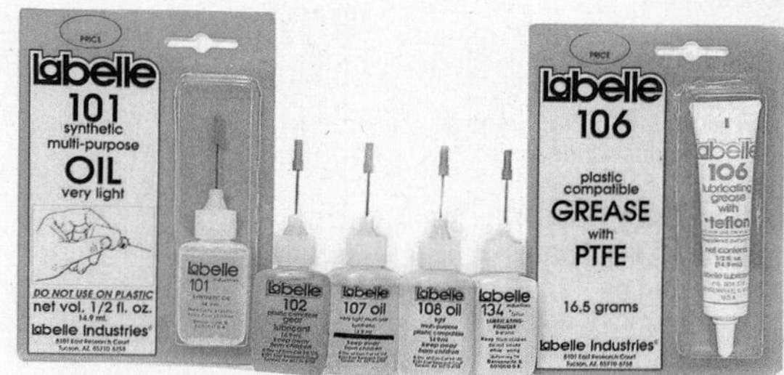


### NEW PRODUCTS

#### Cleaning System

**NEW 430-901** Labelle Cleaning System **TBA**
Includes cleaning liquid, solution compatible with electric motors, etc. and a variety of cleaning aids including cleaning pads, a gear tooth cleaning tool and more.

#### DVD

**NEW 430-951** How to Lubricate **14.98**
Shows how to lube your model trains, RC models, mechanical toys and collectibles using Labelle lubricants. Approximately 45 minutes.

#### Lubricants 5.89 ea

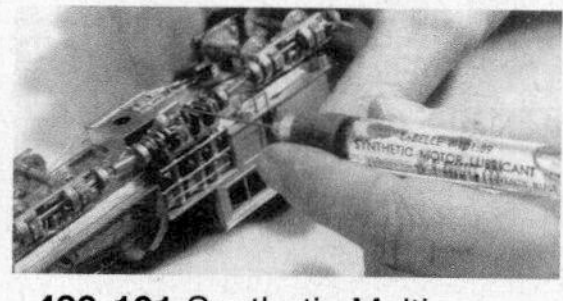

**430-101** Synthetic Multi-Purpose Oil 1/2oz
Very light oil for motors, bearings, etc. Natural penetrating action will usually free a "frozen" motor, will damage paints and some plastics.

**430-102** Plastic Compatible Gear Lubricant 1/2oz
A true gear oil. Should NOT be used on bushings, bearings, etc. Can be used on plastic.

**430-104** Synthetic Multi-Purpose Oil 1/2oz
Medium weight, non-gumming, long lasting. For small power tools, major appliances, etc. Will damage paints and some plastics.

**430-106** Plastic Compatible Grease w/PTFE (a close relative to Teflon™) 1/2oz
Compatible with other lubricants and can be applied over them if necessary. Non-staining, non-toxic.

**430-107** Plastic Compatible Motor Oil 1/2oz
Medium-weight lubricant for large-scale models with high-torque motors.

**430-108** Plastic Compatible Motor Oil 1/2oz
Lightweight lubricant for small locomotives with low- and medium-torque motors, precision instruments, sewing machines, etc. Will not harm plastics, painted surfaces. Non-staining.

**430-111** Racing Oil 1/2oz
For road race cars.

**430-134** Micro-Fine Powdered w/PTFE (a close relative to Teflon™)
A clean, white, dry, non-staining powdered lubricant. Will not harm plastics or paints. Use dry or add to oils or greases to make them "slipperier."

#### Lube Kits 17.49 ea

Sets includes extension needle adapter for those hard to reach places.

**430-1001** Kit #1
Includes one each of #s 102, 106 and 107.

**430-1002** Kit #2
Includes one each of #s 102, 106 and 108.

## MODEL POWER

### Track Cleaner
**490-14** 4oz **6.59**

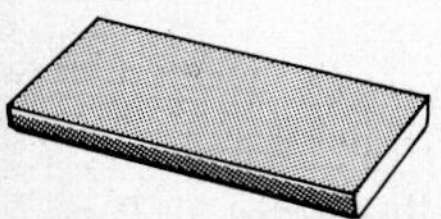

**490-250** Cleaning Block **3.25**
Blue ceramic stone.

## MICRO ENGINEERING CO.

### Pliobond® Adhesive
For gluing Delrin® track or hand-laid rail to ties.

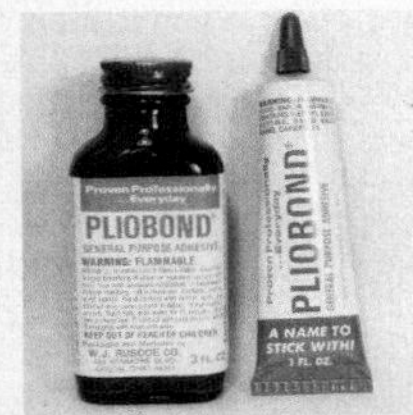


**255-49101** Brush Top Bottle 3oz **8.05**

**255-49102** Fine Tip Tube 1oz **5.35**

## MICROSCALE®

### Liquid Cement

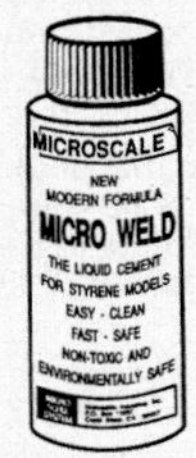


**460-109** Micro Weld-Plastic 1oz Bottle **2.50**
Colorless liquid plastic-fusing adhesive. Dissolves a thin layer of each surface to be joined and forms a welded joint.

**460-116** Micro Metal Foil Adhesive 1oz **2.50**
Bonds aluminum foil to models.

## NEW PRODUCTS

### Zap-O

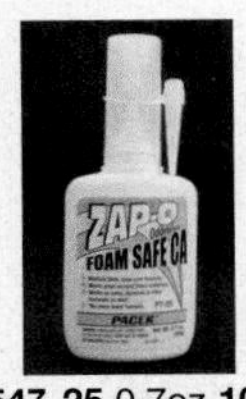


**NEW 547-25** 0.7oz **10.99**
Odorless foam-safe CA cures in 8 seconds.

### Zap Foam Safe Kicker

**NEW 547-28 6.39**
Accelerates cure time of CA glues. Safe on all types of foam.

## ADHESIVES

### Canopy Glue
**547-56** Bottle **3.79**
Works on balsa, plywood, plastics, film coverings, fiberglass and any primed or painted surfaces. Dries clear.

### Flex Zap

**547-454** 20g **7.99**
For use on fiberglass, carbon fiber and plywood. 10-15 second set time.

### Plasti-Zap

**547-442** 1/3oz **3.99**
Cyanoacrylate adhesive for assembly of plastic parts or kits. Will not attack painted surfaces, tacking cures in 10-20 seconds, full cure in 1-3 minutes. Can be removed with debonder or accelerated with ZIP-KICKER. Nonflammable, non-sniffable.

### Poly-Zap

**547-422** 1/2oz **5.69**
Glues and repairs Lexan®. Glues space-age plastics and nylon. Doesn't fog parts if glue is applied to film. Repairs EZ kits, too.

### Rail Zip

**547-452** 1oz **5.39**
Penetrates existing corrosion layers and restores electrical conductivity to the track. Also retards future corrosion. Nontoxic, safe for all metals and plastics.

### Slo-Zap CA-Slow Cure Adhesive

**547-443** 1oz **7.59**
High viscosity, slow cure cyanoacrylate adhesive. Adhesive has a 30-40 second positioning time and cures in 1-2 minutes. Surface sealing agent for cloth and porous surfaces. Bonds oily surfaces.

### Z-7 Debonder

**547-439** 1oz **4.29**
Waterbased material softens and removes cured cyanoacrylates, paint and hobby decals. Also removes ball point pen inks, permanent marker inks, typist correction fluid, nail polish and scuff marks from painted surfaces. Safe for most plastics.

### Zap-A-Gap
Cyanoacrylate adhesive bonds woods, veneers, cork, vinyl, fabrics, rubber, leather, plastics, metals, stone and porcelain. Also works on oily, fuel-soaked surfaces or prestained miniature pieces.

**547-425** 4oz **23.99**

**547-429** 2oz **12.49**

**547-431** 1oz **7.39**

**547-433** 1/2oz **4.39**

**547-435** 1/4oz **3.49**

### Zap
Very thin, penetrating, instant curing cyanoacrylate adhesive. Parts are held tightly together. Cures in 1-5 seconds. Bonds close-fitting balsa, cloth, all woods, veneers, plastics, metals, rubber, oily surfaces, etc.

**547-426** 4oz **23.99**

**547-428** 2oz **12.99**

**547-430** 1oz **7.39**

**547-432** 1/2oz **4.39**

**547-434** 1/4oz **3.49**

### Zap Gel
A form of thick CA, Zap Gel has the same great formula and is ideal for areas that will be under high stress or load-bearing parts. Concentrated formula will not run, even when applied on vertical surfaces.

**547-26** 20g **7.99**

**547-27** 3g **1.59**



### Zap-O

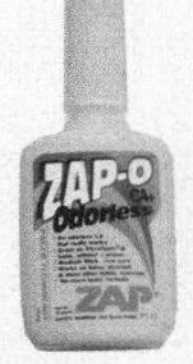


**547-25** 20g **10.99**
Odorless CA adhesive bonds balsa wood, plywood and fiberglass to Styrofoam without any primers. Bonds Styrofoam to Styrofoam without melting the foam.

### Z-Ends Dispensing Tips & Tubes
**547-441** pkg(10) **3.99**
Extra nozzle extension reaches into tight spots and has a molded ring for storage on bottle neck. 10 Z-Ends tips plus 10 teflon micro dropper tubes included.

### Zip-Kicker

**547-438** 2oz **6.39**
Accelerator forces immediate cure for all cyanoacrylates. Also expands gap filling ability, permits structural fillet forming and solves tough-to-bond combinations of materials.

## NGINEERING

### Low-Temp Silver-Bearing Solder

**514-N4200 1.95**
A unique blend of 62% tin, 36% lead and 2% silver alloy with a rosin flux core. The .020" diameter is well-suited for reaching tight spaces. Low melting point of 354-372°F 179-189°C makes it ideal for temperature-sensitive components. Includes dispenser tube.

## PECO

IMPORTED FROM GREAT BRITAIN BY WALTHERS

### Cleaner

**552-PL41** Abrasive Rubber Block Rail/Track Cleaner **6.99**

### Lubricant

**552-640** Electro Lube Cleaner & Oil **15.99**
Use to lube motors, gears, commutators and bearings. Pen-type applicator for reaching small parts. Safe for most plastics.

## PLASTRUCT

### Plastic Solvent Cement

Each cement is a colorless, liquid, plastic-fusing adhesive, and comes in a 2oz bottle.

570-2

570-3

570-4

**570-2** Plastic Weld **3.75**
Dissolves a thin layer of each surface to form a welded joint as strong as the surrounding area. Bonds styrene, ABS, butyrate and acrylics.

**570-3** Bondene **3.95**
Dissolves a thin layer of each surface to form a welded joint as strong as the surrounding area. Bonds styrene to styrene, ABS to ABS, and most other alike plastic combinations.

**570-4** Weldene **4.65**
Nontoxic. Instantly tacky, cures in hours. Provides a permanent bond. Environmentally friendly. Bonds styrene to styrene only.

## Satellite City "HOT STUFF"

### ACCELERATOR

**639-6** NCF Quick™ Aerosol Spray 6 oz **11.95**
Handy spray can is sealed, so it's always ready to use, and there's no evaporation loss. Stays active for up to three minutes. Works with all instant glues. Non CFC formula.

### ADHESIVES

#### Hot Stuff™

Cyanoacrylate, colorless, liquid instant adhesive bonds wood, glass, metal, leather, fabric, rubber and most plastics in five to ten seconds. Nontoxic.

**639-54** 2oz **9.95**
**639-58** 4oz **18.95**
**639-501** 1/2oz **3.60**
**639-502** 1/4oz **2.50**
**639-504** 1oz **5.75**

#### Super T™

Gap-filling clear cyanoacrylate glue with a cure rate of 10 to 25 seconds. Thick density makes it especially suitable for joining parts that don't fit perfectly.

**639-499** 4oz **18.95**
**639-505** 1oz **5.75**
**639-506** 1/2oz **3.60**
**639-507** 1/4oz **2.50**
**639-508** 2oz **9.95**

#### Special T™

Thick, clear, cyanoacrylate glue with a consistency five times that of SUPER T. Allows up to 50 seconds positioning time (most materials bond in 30 to 50 seconds).

**639-514** 4oz **20.95**
**639-515** 2oz **10.95**
**639-516** 1oz **6.50**

#### UFO™ Instant Glue

**Thin**
**639-519** 1oz **11.95**
Penetrating, odorless and no curing fumes. Instant clear glue for the cyano-sensitive modeler. Will not attack white foam, allows full joint coverage of all bonds.

**Thick**
**639-521** 1oz **11.95**
Odorless and no curing fumes. Ultra gap f0illing clear instant glue. Set time of 50 to 60 seconds. Use for assembly work.

#### Debonder Solvent

**639-512** Ultra Super Solvent 2oz **5.98**
Nitroparaffin based for cyanoacrylate/super glues.

## TENAX-7R

The Space Age Plastic Welder.

### Space Age Construction Kit

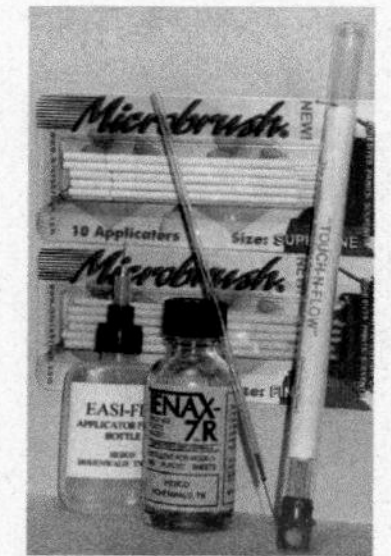


**731-8 17.99**
This new kit includes one bottle of Tenax-7R, one "Touch-N-Flow" liquid applicator, one "Easi-Fill" applicator filling bottle, one 10 unit packet of fine and one 10 unit packet of superfine "Microbrushes" and instructions.

### Plastic Welder

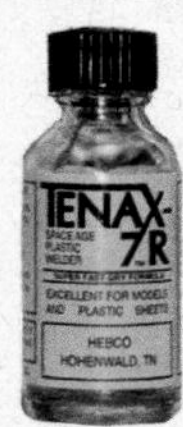


**731-7 3.99**
Tenax-7R causes plastic to become its own bonding agent. Works on styrene, butyrate, ABS and acrylic plastics. Apply Tenax-7R with a fine-hair bristled brush, a microbrush (#731-9,10, 11 & 12), or a Touch-N-Flow applicator (#232-711). Nonflammable, non-sniffable, non-sticky and leaves no residue. Tenax-7R bonds in seconds and dries in minutes.

Dealers MUST Order Dealer Pack of 12.

### Microbrush Cement Applicator Brushes pkg(10) 1.59 ea

Designed for use with liquid cement, the Microbrushes allow for precise control of cement application. Available in several sizes, they are perfect for touchup, polishing, working in limited space and for pinpoint cementing.

**731-9** Regular
**731-10** Fine
**731-11** Superfine
**731-12** Ultra Brush

## SQUADRON PRODUCTS

### PLASTIC PUTTY

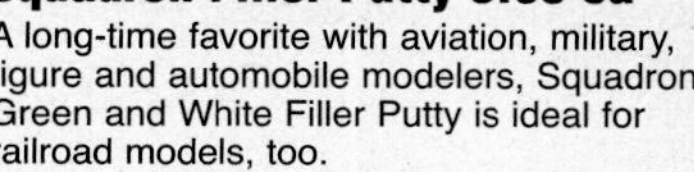

#### Squadron Filler Putty 3.50 ea

A long-time favorite with aviation, military, figure and automobile modelers, Squadron Green and White Filler Putty is ideal for railroad models, too.

Designed to quickly and easily fill gaps between plastic or metal parts, or repair surface scratches and nicks, the putty is fin grained (especially nice for small scale models) and quick-drying. Just apply, allow to dry for 30 minutes, then sand to final shape.

Each tube includes 2.3oz of putty, enough f several projects. Two different colors are offered to provide a suitable contrast on yo models. This makes it easier to sand just th areas that need to be filled without removin surrounding detail. Choose from white (whi is somewhat finer) for lighter-colored kits, o green for darker-colored kits.

**680-9055** Green (for Dark Color Plastics)
**680-9065** White (for Light Color Plastics)

## SCALE SCENICS

DIVISION OF CIRCUITRON

### Solder

**652-1502** pkg(10') **3.95**
Ultra-fine rosin core solder (.014" diameter), is electronics grade (60% tin, 40% lead). Ideal for soldering miniature circuits, detailing for brass models or to simulate scale size hose or piping.

For Up-To-Date Information and News Bookmark Walthers Web site at

**www.walthers.com**

## WELDBOND

### Weldbond

All-around wood glue, ballast cement, sealer, hardener, weather-proofer and more. Dries clear. Porous and non-porous applications. Safe to use. For ballast cement, mix one part Weldbond with two parts water.

A Weldbond application book i available at no charge. Please send a self-addressed stamped envelope to Walthers

**797-125** 4oz **3.49**
**797-185** 8oz **5.10**
**797-245** 12oz **6.89**
**797-795** 1/2gal **22.87**

Item listed below is available by Special Order (see Legend Page).
**797-1395** 1gal **38.11**

## ADHESIVES

Fast drying, non-yellowing cements.

### Plastic Cement

**704-3501** Tube 5/8oz **1.69**
Dealers MUST order Dealer Pack of 48.

**704-3502** Liquid–Bottle 1oz **2.99**
For clean, transparent plastic-to-plastic joints.
Dealers MUST order Dealer Pack of 12.

**704-3507** Liquid Cement w/Precision Applicator **4.49**
Dealers MUST order Dealer Pack of 6.

**704-3515** Clear Parts Cement 1oz **4.79**

**704-3521** Non-Toxic Tube 5/8oz **1.69**
For use by children.
Dealers MUST order Dealer Pack of 48.

### Wood Cement

**704-3503** Extra-Fast Drying 5/8oz **1.99**
Hot fuel proof.
Dealers MUST order Dealer Pack of 24.

### Plastic Putty

**704-3511** 5/8oz **2.19**
Can be used to fill, sculpture or redesign a surface.
Dealers MUST order Dealer Pack of 24.

### Cement Pen

**704-3532** 1/3oz **4.25**
Fast-drying, high-strength cement for plastic.

### Decal Setting Solution

**704-8804** 1/4oz Bottle **1.49**

### Gluing Tips

**704-8805** pkg(5) **1.99**
Fits most tubes of glue for precise glue application.
Dealers MUST order Dealer Pack of 12.

### Model Master Adhesives

**704-8872** Liquid **6.29**

## TIX

## SOLDER

•Indium-based solder

•Melts at 275° F (150° lower than lead-tin solders—with a much higher wetting ability)

Repairs to printed circuit boards are simple as the low melting point will not damage the board. Use with any flux, rosin, chloride or acid.

**118-1** 20 Sticks **12.60**

**118-2** 60 Sticks **35.90**

## FLUX

Works on most metals and alloys and may be used with any soft solder.

**118-3** 1/2oz **3.35**

**118-4** 2oz **5.25**

**118-5** 8oz **16.55**

Flux listed below is available by Special Order (see Legend Page).
**118-6** 16oz **26.55**

## ANTI-FLUX

Fast drying liquid inhibitor. Apply over area where solder is not wanted.

**118-7** 1/2oz **3.35**

**118-8** 2oz **5.25**

Anti-Flux listed below are available by Special Order (see Legend Page).
**118-9** 8oz **16.55**

**118-10** 16oz **26.55**

## NEW PRODUCTS

### Adhesives

### Elmer's® Stix-All Gel Cement

**NEW 790-E1011** 5/8oz **4.10**
Creates no-run, flexible bonds on multiple materials in hot and cold extremes, both indoors and outdoors. Ideal for gap filling and impact-resistant light repairs. Sets within 10 minutes, cures in 24 to 72 hours. Safe, non-toxic, dishwasher safe. Cleans up with soap and water before cure; mineral spirits after cure.

### Elmer's Super Fast Epoxy Cement

**NEW 790-E1009** 1oz. **4.10**
Fast curing for strong, rigid bonds on multiple materials, including wood, metal, plastic, glass, tile, marble. Bonds are resistant to heat, water, oil, gasoline. Sets within 5 minutes and cures fully within 24 hours. Cleans up with mineral spirits.

### Krazy Glue® All-Purpose Formula

Ultra-fast setting for rigid bonds on most surfaces, especially rubber and plastic type materials.

**NEW 790-KG58548MR** 2g **2.39**
One-drop applicator. Base holds tube upright for easy use.

**NEW 790-KG92548MR** 5g **3.75**
Brush applicator for hard-to-reach and large areas.

## ADHESIVES

### Elmers® Glue-All

All-purpose for light repair on a variety of materials.

**790-E381** 4oz **1.98**

**790-E383** 16oz **5.90**

### Elmers® Carpenter's® Interior Wood Glue

For soft and hard woods, particle board and porous materials. Indoor use only. Cleans up with soap and water when glue is wet; scrape and sand when glue is dry. Set time: 20 to 30 minutes.

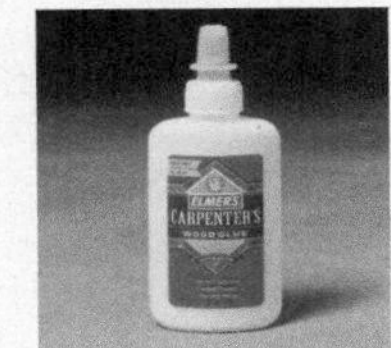

**790-E700** 4oz **2.77**

**790-E701** 7-5/8oz **4.04**

**790-E702** 16oz **6.89**

### ProBond® Interior/Exterior Wood Glue

**790-P9703** 12oz **5.00**
Superior shear strength (2,700PSI) for permanent bonds on a variety of woods. Interior/exterior formula creates a strong, water-resistant bond. Requires no mixing and is sandable and paintable. Easy water cleanup. Set time: 30 minutes.

### Krazy Glue® Advanced Formula 3.71 ea

Provides an extra-strength and durable shock-resistant bond. Precision applicator features an extended, no-clog tip with easy-open, easy-seal hanger cap. Gel formula for vertical applications. For use with rubber, plastic and metal. Holds in extreme heat up to 250 degrees.

**790-KG48348MR** Precision Tip 5g

**790-KG48448MR** Gel 4g

### Krazy Glue® Skin Guard Formula

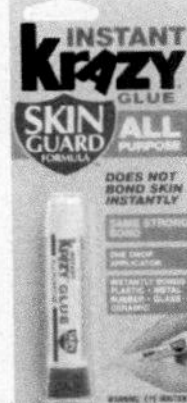


**790-KG78548R** 2g Tube **2.47**
Same strong bond as original Krazy Glue but WILL NOT instantly bond to skin. One-drop applicator is effective on plastic, metal, rubber, etc. Airtight, leak-proof case keeps glue from drying out.

**790-KG76648R** 2g Gel **2.88**
Convenient gel formula is ideal for non-horizontal surfaces, gluing up, down and sideways. WILL NOT bond skin instantly and forms a long-lasting instant bond with plastic, metal, rubber, glass and ceramic surfaces.

## Hob-E-Lube®

by Woodland Scenics®

## OILS & GREASE

Complete line of oils, greases and dry lubricants for model railroad equipment of any scale. All seven are paint and plastic compatible.

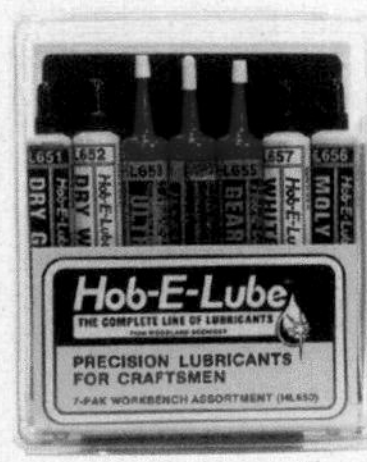


**785-650** 7-Pak Workbench Assortment **24.98**
Get all seven in one pack and save yourself more than seven dollars!

**785-651** Dry Graphite **4.49**
With Molybdenum. Does not attract dust and dirt.

**785-652** Dry White Lube w/Teflon* **4.49**
White, non-staining lube doesn't conduct electricity. Use on electrical switches, N & Z worm and gears.

**785-653** Ultra-Lite Oil **4.49**
Use with close tolerance precision parts.

**785-654** Lite Oil **4.49**
General purpose hobby lube, rust preventing.

**785-655** Gear Lube **4.49**
Tough, long-lasting lube with high adhesion to prevent dripping.

**785-656** Moly Grease **4.49**
With Molybdenum, covers entire surface and maintains high viscosity. Ideal for parts exposed to water.

**785-657** White Grease w/Teflon* **4.49**
Non-staining lube with corrosion protection and water-proof lubrication. Good for use outside.

* "Teflon" is a registered trademark of DuPont.

### Premium Oils

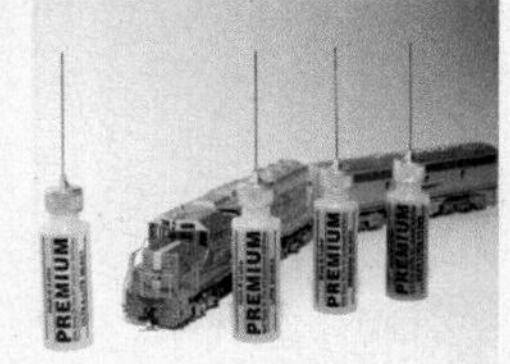

Premium Oils from Woodland Scenics are specially formulated for specific uses. All are paint and plastic compatible, and come in a needle applicator bottle for precise lubrication of small parts.

**785-661** Ultra-Lite Oil **7.49**
Contains proven anti-wear additives. Use on HO or smaller scales of model trains, precision instruments or where a light oil is needed.

**785-662** Lite Oil **7.49**
Multi-viscosity additives for trouble-free operation, even at extreme temperatures. Great for home and workshop applications.

**785-663** Medium Oil **7.49**
Prevents metal contact and surface scuffing. Specially formulated for use on R/C cars, airplanes, boats and HO Scale and larger model trains.

**785-664** Gear Lube **7.49**
A true gear lubricant, where tough, lasting gear oil is needed.

## ADHESIVES

### Mat Adhesive

**785-5161** 7 fl oz **6.98**
This adhesive allows you to permanently attach grass mats to any surface. Just brush Mat Adhesive on the back of grass mats and press onto surface.

Scenic Accents Glue

### Scenic Accents Glue

- For temporary or permanent placement of figures
- Stays tacky
- Removes easily
- Non-toxic

**785-198** 1 fl oz **4.29**
Created especially for use with Scenic Accents. Accent Glue is water-soluble, high-tack and easy to apply. Objects can easily be repositioned and removed. Simply brush on bottom of figure and allow glue to become tacky and clear (about 15 minutes). Position figure and press gently into place. To reposition the figure, simply lift and press into a different place. To remove adhesive, rub and pull off.

### Scenic Glue

**785-190** 8 fl oz **6.49**
Formulated especially for model landscaping. Dries clear with a matte (flat) finish and is flexible. Use to attach various foliage, Bushes, Underbrush and Lichen. Does not become brittle after drying.

### Scenic Cement

**785-191** 16 fl oz **6.49**
New and improved water-soluble, non-toxic, ready-to-use for Ballast, Turf and more. Dries to a clear, matte finish. Apply with Scenic Sprayer (sold separately) or brush on.

### Hob-e-Tac®

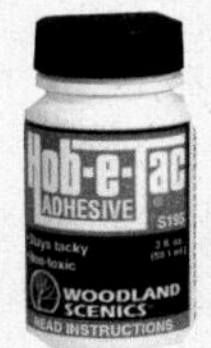


**785-195** 2 fl oz **5.49**
All purpose non-flammable, high-tack adhesive. For making trees and for attaching Field Grass. Can also be used as a contact adhesive.

### Foam Tack Glue

**785-1444** 12 fl oz **10.98**
This specially formulated glue is high-tack and effective on most materials. Use as a contact cement whenever bonding two large surfaces.

### Low Temp Foam Glue Sticks

**785-1446** pkg (10) **5.98**
Low Temp Foam Glue Sticks melt at a temperature that will not damage foam. Use with Low Temp Foam Glue Gun #785-1445, sold separately.

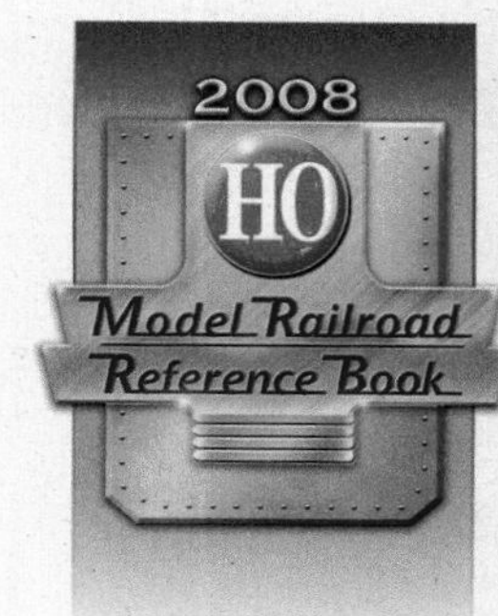

# PAINT

Models and Photo by Howard Dwyer

Hugging the banks of the river, freshly shopped Island Central #1160 is just a day or two out of the backshops. Better get pictures of the SW8 now, for a few more days of hard work like this will make quick work of that shiny finish!

Starting with a Broadway Limited engine, Howard Dwyer of Farmingville, New York, painted and decaled the switcher for his freelance shortline.

Whether bright and brilliant, or aged and worn, paint can transform even the simplest model. You'll find a great selection of colors and accessories to finish your next project in the pages of this section.

## WALTHERS

### Decal Setting Solution

**904-470** Solvaset 2oz 60ml **2.98**

Dealers MUST Order Multiples of 6.

Make decals snuggle down on any surface. Softens decal film so it stretches over surface details like rivets, seams and hinges. Eliminates air bubbles, white spots and draping without hiding detail.

### Masking Liquid

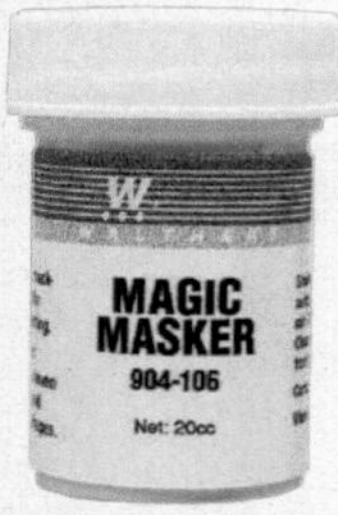


**904-106** Magic Masker 20cc **2.98**

Dealers MUST Order Multiples of 12.

An easy way to mask off small areas or odd shaped parts where tape won't work. Just brush it on and allow to dry. Then spray your color, let dry and peel off. Works on plastic, wood, metal, paint, doped surfaces, chrome and silver.

## SMP INDUSTRIES Accu-paint

Capture the color of railroading in the eastern U.S. with these paints. Matched to actual samples of prototype paint, they can be brushed or sprayed directly on wood, metals or plastics without the need for a barrier coat.

Please visit Walthers Web site at www.walthers.com for a complete listing of all available items.

Items listed in blue ink may not be available at all times (see Legend Page).

### Railroad Colors 1oz (30ml) 3.95 ea

**102-1** Stencil White
**102-2** Stencil Black
**102-3** Boston & Maine Blue
**102-4** Bangor & Aroostook Blue
**102-5** D&H Blue
**102-6** GTW
**102-7** CR Blue
**102-8** Vermilion
**102-9** Cornell Red
**102-10** Chinese Red
**102-11** CP Rail Action Red
**102-12** Oxide Brown
**102-13** Reefer Orange
**102-14** Socony Red
**102-15** Warm Orange
**102-16** NH Red-Orange
**102-17** CN Orange
**102-18** CN Red-Orange
**102-19** CN Yellow
**102-20** Medium Yellow
**102-22** Imitation Gold
**102-24** EL Yellow
**102-25** Hunters Green
**102-26** MEC Pine Green
**102-27** 401 Green
**102-28** Pullman Green
**102-30** CN Green
**102-31** Brunswick Green
**102-32** Jade Green
**102-34** EL Maroon
**102-35** Passenger Maroon
**102-36** Engine Maroon
**102-37** PRR Maroon
**102-38** CP Tuscan Red
**102-39** Alkyd Brown
**102-40** Aluminum
**102-41** Rich Gold
**102-43** CP Gray
**102-45** NYC Light Gray
**102-46** NYC Dark Gray
**102-47** D&H Gray
**102-48** EL Gray
**102-51** CP Rail Action Green
**102-52** CP Rail Action Yellow
**102-54** Rich Oxide Brown
**102-55** Erie Green
**102-56** Gray-Green
**102-57** Imitation Aluminum
**102-59** Iron Oxide
**102-60** Light Imitation Gold
**102-61** VIA Blue
**102-62** Weathered Black
**102-63** ATSF Warbonnet Blue
**102-64** ATSF Warbonnet Yellow
**102-65** SP Lark Dark Gray
**102-66** SP Scarlet
**102-67** UP/MILW Armour Yellow
**102-68** UP/MILW Harbor Mist Gray
**102-69** ATSF Warbonnet Red
**102-70** BN Green
**102-71** Illinois Central Gulf Orange
**102-72** DRGW Yellow
**102-73** Chessie Yellow
**102-74** Chessie Blue
**102-75** Southern Green
**102-78** NP Dark Green
**102-79** NP Light Green
**102-80** CSX Blue
**102-81** CSX Gray
**102-83** MILW Orange
**102-85** WP "New" Orange
**102-88** Penn Central Green
**102-89** CSX Buff
**102-90** BNSF Green
**102-91** BNSF Orange
**NEW 102-93** CNW Green
**NEW 102-94** CNW Yellow

### Paint Retarder

**102-97** 1oz (30ml) bottle **3.95**

### Primer

**102-98** Metal-Plastic 1oz (30ml) **3.95**
Special primer-sealer for use on plastics or metals.

### Thinner

Will not attack most modeling plastics.

**102-100** Bottle 1oz (30ml) **3.95**
**102-10016** Pint Can 16oz (480ml) **15.95**



## FALLER

IMPORTED FROM GERMANY BY WALTHERS

### Paint Marker Pens

**Limited Quantity Available**

**272-170690** Modeler's Color Pens pkg(6) **35.99**
Ideal for painting any kind of models. Water-based paints are opaque, economic and quick drying. Set includes red, yellow, orange, lavender, blue and green.

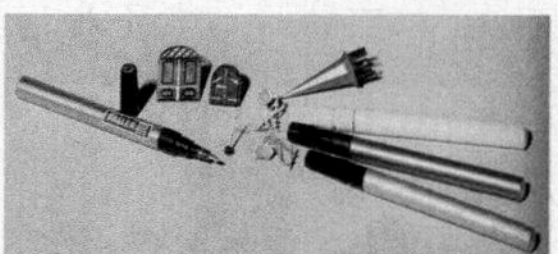

**272-170691** Metallic Paint Pens pkg(4) **31.99**
A fast and easy way to simulate a variety of natural metal finishes on your models. Includes white for base coat, plus gold, silver and copper. Colors are durable, permanent and quick drying.

### Patina Sets

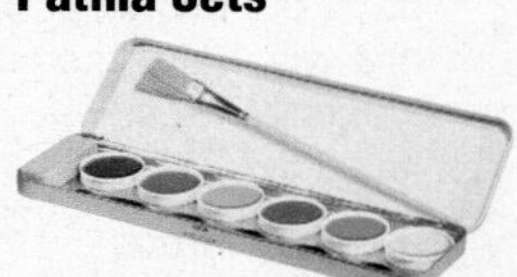

**NEW 272-170696** Patina Set **25.99**
Set of six water-soluble washable paints is ideal for adding patina to vehicles, bridges and buildings. Works especially well on plastic models. Includes applicator brush.

**272-170697 63.99**
Give any building exterior or scenery detail an aged appearance with this series of patina paints. This set includes six water-soluble acrylic paints, thinner and an applicator brush. Comes with instructions.

## GB ENGINEERING

### Work Holder

**298-600** Painting Handle **8.20**
Hold models securely and keep your hands clean while you paint. Works well with all types of models. "V"-shaped aluminum handle has foam pads on ends to prevent damage. Spring-loaded legs are adjusted with screw and nut to provide constant holding force. Secure grip lets you safely turn model to any position while airbrushing or spray painting.

## GYROS

### ARTIST'S RED SABLE WATER COLOR BRUSH SETS

**6.65 ea**

Perfect for arts, hobbies and all kinds of crafts, these high quality artist's brushes can also be used with oil, enamel, varnish and lacquer. After using with watercolors, clean with soap and water and shape to a point. If used with color or paint other than watercolor, clean brush with thinner and wash out thinner with soap and warm water and shape to a point. Allow brush to dry before reusing.

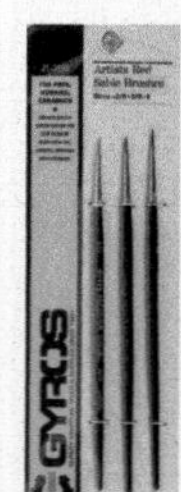


**321-211900** 3/0, 2/0 & 0
Smaller sizes provide good control for hobby, art or ceramic painting projects of all kinds.

**321-211910** 1, 3 & 5
This set includes a variety of sizes, perfect for painting models as well as art and craft projects.

**321-211920** 10/0, 5/0 & 4/0
Small sizes are ideal for fine detail painting of small parts, figures ands other miniatures.

Airbrushes, parts and accessories ideal for finishing all types of models, home, craft and art projects or professional painting and illustration. Brushes are equipped with spray head assembly and needle to produce one of three adjustable spray patterns.

**CAUTION**: For your safety, the use of a properly vented spray booth and a respirator which is paint mist and vapor compatible is strongly recommended when painting with an airbrush.

## AIRBRUSHES

### Hybrid Air Brush

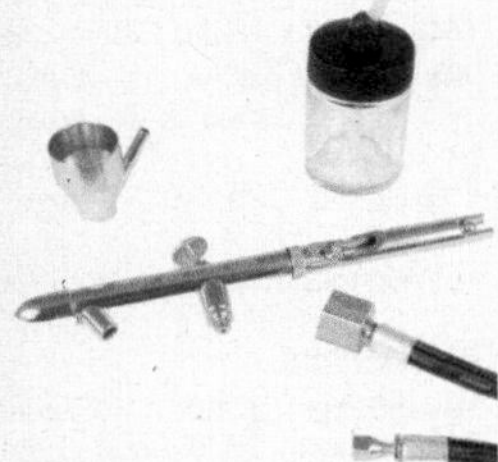

**165-31553 132.00**
Quality precision-crafted airbrush features a single-size paint tip, spray regulator, and needle that work with any properly reduced medium including acrylics, inks, enamels, stains and more. Suitable for many applications requiring a finer spray pattern. Includes one 1/4 oz color cup, 3/4 oz jar with adaptor and 6" braided hose.

### Model 100 Airbrush

Dual action, internal mix for fine detail work, each features: color cup or cavity, counter-balanced handle, self-lubricating Teflon® needle bearing and head seal, plus a non-slip, one-piece trigger that can be used in either hand.

Items listed below are available by Special Order (see Legend Page).

**165-100** Fine **109.00**
Model 100 Airbrush with fine needle and head, 1/16oz (2cc) color cup, protective cap, spare needle, wrench for head, hanger, instruction book and storage case.

**165-101** Medium **109.00**
Same as #165-100, with Medium needle and head.

**165-102** Gravity Feed - Fine **117.00**
Same as #165-100, but with gravity-feed color cup which holds 1/16oz (2cc).

### Model 100 LG Gravity Feed Airbrush Basic Sets 123.00 ea

For use with thinned artist acrylics and vinyls, and lighter viscosity materials.

Model 100 LG series airbrush with permanent top-mounted color cup and fitted cover (holds 1/3oz (10.5cc) of color), hanger, extra needle, wrench, protective cap and padded case.

**165-1005** Fine

Items listed below are available by Special Order (see Legend Page).
**165-1006** Medium

**165-1007** Heavy

### Model 100 SG Airbrush

Item listed below is available by Special Order (see Legend Page).
**165-1008** Extra Fine **109.00**
Includes Model 100 gravity feed airbrush with built-in fluid cavity. Designed to spray precise amounts.

### Model 150 Airbrush

Identical to Model 100, but uses jars or a removable color cup to hold paint.

#### Basic Sets 117.00 ea

Model 150 airbrush, attachable 3/4oz (22cc) and 2oz (60cc) paint jars with covers for big jobs, or force-fit color cup for smaller work, case, hanger, wrench, protective cap, self-lubricating Teflon needle bearing, head seal and siphon tube, plus non-slip, one-piece trigger.

**165-150** Fine

**165-153** Heavy

Item listed below is available by Special Order (see Legend Page).
**165-1501** Medium

#### Deluxe Sets

**165-152** Fine **157.00**
Fine head assembly and needle, 8' (2.45m) braided air hose, 1/4" pipe thread adapter (for use with compressor or CO2 tank), wrench for head, hanger, instruction booklet and wooden case.

**165-1507** Fine & Heavy **145.00**
Same as #165-152, but with fine and heavy head assemblies and needles, plus cardboard storage box.

### Crescendo Model 175 Airbrush

Bottom-feed, dual action, internal mix design.

#### Airbrush Only 102.00 ea

Items listed below are available by Special Order (see Legend Page).
**165-1754** Fine

**165-1755** Medium

**165-1756** Heavy

#### Basic Sets 123.00 ea

Items listed below are available by Special Order (see Legend Page).
Includes Model 175 airbrush, 1/4oz (7cc) metal color cup, 3/4oz (22cc) jar with adapter, 2oz (60cc) jar, spare needle, instruction book, protective cap, hanger and plastic case.

**165-1751** Fine

**165-1752** Medium

**165-1753** Large

#### Deluxe Set

**165-1757 145.00**
Crescendo 175 Airbrush with all three tips (fine, medium and heavy), spray regulators and needles, 8' (2.45m) braided air hose, 3/4oz (22cc) jar with adapter, two 2oz (60cc) paint jars, one 1/4oz metal paint cup, hanger, protective cap and instruction book.

### Model 200 Airbrush Sets

Single action delivers a pre-set amount of fluid.

#### Basic Set

**165-2001** Medium **78.00**
Model 200 airbrush, attachable 3/4oz (22cc) jar and 2oz (60cc) jar with cover, protective cap and wrench.

#### Deluxe Sets

**165-2003** Fine **95.00**
6' (1.83m) vinyl hose, Propel regulator, attachable 3/4oz jar, spare 3/4oz jar with cover and can of Propel.

**165-2005** Medium Only **89.00**
Includes: 6' (1.83m) vinyl airhose, Propel regulator, attachable and spare 3/4oz jars, one 2oz jar with cover and protective cap.

Item listed below is available by Special Order (see Legend Page).
**165-2004** Medium w/Compressor **358.00**
Model 1810 portable diaphragm compressor, 10' (3.05m) braided air hose, 1/4" pipe thread fitting (adapts brush to compressor or CO2 tank), attachable and spare 3/4oz jar, one 2oz jar with cover and protective cap.

#### Badger Detail Airbrush

**165-20020** Fine **86.00**
Set includes color cup, two mixing jars, Fast Blast adapter cap, wrench, instructions and black Badger airbrush case.

#### Gravity Feed Basic Set 76.00 ea (Unless Noted)

Identical to Model 200, but with permanently attached 1/16oz (2cc) color cup, ideal for smaller jobs. All sets include protective cap, wrench for head and storage case.

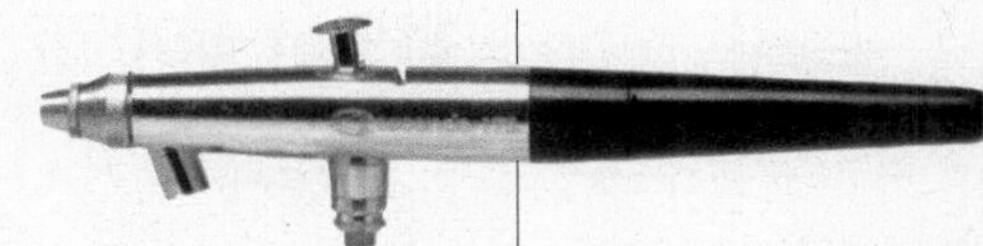

Crescendo Model 175 Airbrush 165-1754

Model 200 Airbrush 165-20020

Items listed below are available by Special Order (see Legend Page).
**165-2009** Fine

**165-20010** Medium

**165-20011** Fine w/Built-in Cavity **70.00**
Built-in color cavity holds enough color for small jobs.

### Model 200 Airbrush Accessories

Items listed below are available by Special Order (see Legend Page).
**165-41043** Guarded Regulator **7.30**

**165-51071** Replacement Head **12.20**

### Model 250 Airbrush Sets

Single action, external mix, bottom feed design. Spray pattern adjusts from 3/4" (18.9mm) to 2" (50.8mm).

#### Basic Sets

Model 250 airbrush with 3/4oz (22cc) jars and cover, 6' (1.83m) vinyl air hose and Propel regulator.

**165-2501** Boxed Set **27.00**

**165-2502** Carded Set **24.00**

**165-2503** Boxed Set w/Propel Can **35.00**

**165-2504** Large Capacity Set **37.00**
Same as #165-2503, with larger Model 250 Airbrush and attached 4oz (120cc) jar.

**165-2507** Basic Spray Gun Hobby Set **52.00**
Includes Model 250 airbrush with attached and spare 3/4oz (22cc) jars and cover, 6' (1.83m) vinyl air hose and Propel regulator, three hobby colors, mixing pipette, how-to book and instructions.

### Model 250 Accessories

**165-500012** 8' Vinyl Air Hose **7.50**

**165-500242** Cork Gasket **1.50**

### Model 350 Airbrush Sets

Single action, external mix, bottom feed design. Makes a larger dot spray pattern.

#### Basic Sets 56.00 ea

Include: Model 350 airbrush, 2oz (60cc) jar with cover, attachable 3/4oz (22cc) jar, wrench for head and instruction booklet, plus storage box.

**165-3501** Fine

**165-3504** Medium

#### Basic Sets w/Accessories

Both sets include 6' (1.83m) vinyl air hose and Propel regulator.

**165-3502** Medium **63.00**

**165-3503** Medium **70.00**
1/4oz (7cc) self-standing color cup and can of Propel.

#### Deluxe Sets

**165-35004** Model 350 Airbrush Set **98.00**
Includes three tips (fine, medium and heavy) and needles, attached 3/4oz (22cc) jar, 2oz (60cc) jar with cover, plus 8' (2.45m) braided air hose and 1/4" pipe thread fitting (converts airbrush for use with compressor or CO2 tank).

Item listed below is available by Special Order (see Legend Page).
**165-3506** Complete Craft Set **101.00**
Model 350 medium tip with attachable 3/4oz (22cc) jar, 6' (1.83m) vinyl air hose, Propel can and regulator, 3/4oz jar with cover, three reusable Mylar stencils, two sheets BriteWhite airbrush paper, five Air-Tex textile colors, one 1oz Air Tex cleaner, hanger and how-to booklet.

BADGER AIR-BRUSH CO.

## Model 360 Universal Airbrush

This unique dual-action design has a rotating front which allows a quick conversion from gravity to syphon feed or vice versa. Needle can be removed without taking the handle off. No additional tips are required to change spray patterns.

**165-3601** Airbrush w/Two 3/4oz Jars **185.00**

**165-3602** Airbrush Only **177.00**

## Model 400 Touch-Up Gun 155.00 ea

Fan control needle adjusts spray pattern from round to fan-shape.

**165-4001** Fine

**165-4002** Medium

**165-4003** Heavy

**165-4003** Heavy

## Anthem Series

Design features a thinner diameter needle; spray material without having to change spray heads. Body is a streamlined, lightweight design that provides exacting balance for easy operation and maximum user comfort.

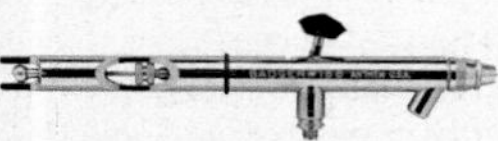

**165-1551** Anthem Airbrush Starter Set **124.00**
Includes 1/4oz cup, 3/4oz jar/adapter and 2oz jar.

**165-1557** Anthem Airbrush Complete Set **138.00**
Includes brush, hose, three jars with adapter, color cup, hanger and display box.

Item listed below is available by Special Order (see Legend Page).
**165-1552** Anthem Airbrush Only **102.00**

**165-1559** Anthem Airbrush w/Classic Wooden Storage Gift Case **160.00**

# SPRAY BOOTH

**165-1352** Hobby Spray Booth **306.80**
No more paint overspray or odors. Expanded design is easy to clean and features sturdy metal body, replaceable air filter, 165 cfm motor w/ 4' output adaptor. Measures: 17-1/2" wide x 14-1/2" tall x 9" deep.

**165-1362** Replacement Filter for #165-1352 **15.55**

# AIR COMPRESSORS

## Whirlwind 10 Air Compressor

**165-18010 193.00**
Diaphragm compressor never needs oil or lubrication. 1/10 HP, 2cfm, 30 PSI with on/off switch. Portable unit weighs just 9 pounds. Suction cup feet reduce compressor movement. Operates one airbrush.

## Thayer & Chandler Air Star V

**165-909 321.00**
Lightweight, quiet, 1/8-horsepower, automatic shut-off piston compressor with an adjustable air regulator and pressure gauge. Features include a built-in moisture filter and airbrush holder; on-off switch; and a maximum running pressure of 40 PSI. Maintenance and oil free. Measures 12 x 6 x 6".

## Silent Compressors

Powered by a highly efficient, oil-reciprocating piston motor, silent compressors feature automatic on/off pressure switch, thermal overload protection, adjustable air regulator, moisture trap, gauge for line pressure, pressure release safety valve, manual on/off valve and intake air filter.

Items listed below are available by Special Order (see Legend Page).

## Million-Air

**165-4801 748.00**
1/6th HP motor with .45 gallon (1.70l) tank which develops .70 CFM at 116 P.S.I. Operates up to two airbrushes.

## Billion-Air

**165-4802 891.00**
1/4 HP motor with 1.06 gallon (4.08l) tank which develops .90 CFM at 116 P.S.I. Operates up to three airbrushes.

## Trillion-Air

**165-4803 1049.00**
1/2 HP piston motor with 1.06 gallon (4.08l) tank which develops 1.75 CFM at 116 P.S.I. Operates up to five airbrushes.

## Cyclone I Air Compressor

**165-18012** Automatic Shut-Off **268.00**
1/12 HP, .80CFM, 25PSI

## Compressor Accessories

**165-50023** 1/4" Pipe Thread Fitting Adapter **4.15**
Adapts airhose to compressor or $CO^2$ tank.

**165-50051** Moisture Trap **50.65**
Air filter and water trap for air compressors.

**165-50054** Air Regulator Filter & Gauge Set **62.00**
For use with compressors. Allows easy adjustment of maximum air pressure, built-in filter traps moisture.

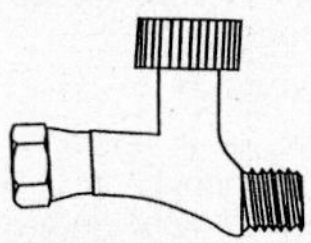

**165-502035** Mini Air Flow Regulator **12.20**
Chrome-plated regulator easily attaches to Badger diaphragm compressors. Easy to operate: the top adjustment screw increases and/or decreases air flow. Gauge not included.

Item listed below is available by Special Order (see Legend Page).
**165-50057** $CO^2$ Regulator & Gauge **109.20**
For use with $CO^2$ tanks only.

# AIRBRUSH ACCESSORIES

**165-121** Paint Mixer **12.00**
Requires two AA batteries, sold separately.

**165-126** Color Mixing Kit **.50**
Includes three mixing cups and stirring sticks.

**165-127** Spot Touch-up Prep Pen **8.55**

## Oil & Lubricant

**165-122** REGDAB™ Airbrush Lubricant 1oz (30cc) **5.10**
Maintains smooth trigger action and eliminates needle friction caused by dried paint.

**165-502019** Replacement Oil 22oz (.75l) **18.05**
Special lightweight oil for use in all silent compressors.

## Airbrush Holders

**165-125** Model 125 **26.75**
Heavy-duty unit holds two airbrushes; rotates, swivels and clamps on any surface up to 2" thick.

**165-50021** Airbrush Hanger **3.85**
Metal holder included with sets.

## Paint Filter

**165-502016 6.50**
For all airbrushes using jars or bottles. Micro screen mesh filter passes only particles which will flow through the airbrush.

## Color Cups 8.55 ea (Unless Noted)

**165-50047** 1/6oz (2cc) **8.45**

**165-50048** 1/8oz (3.5cc)
Self-standing, for Model 100 side-feed airbrushes. Screw-off bottom for easy cleaning.

**165-500482** 1/4oz (7cc)
Self-standing, fits 150 and 200 only.

**165-500483** 1/4oz (7cc)
Self-standing, fits 350 only.

## Cleaning Reamers

**165-50060** For Heads 100-200 **5.10**

**165-50061** 3-Cornered for Models 100 & 200 **6.45**

## Jars & Covers

### Fast Blast Airbrush Caps 3.20 ea

Easy-to-clean Fast Blast jar adapter caps can be used in place of existing jar adapter caps and match those now included in complete airbrush sets.

**165-50208** 1-5/16" 33mm

**165-51017** 25/32" 20mm
For 150/200 series airbrushes w/tube for 1oz jars

**165-51019** 25/32" 20mm
For 150/200 series airbrushes w/tube for 4oz jars

**165-51228** 1-1/8" 28mm
Fits Floquil jars.

### Jar Adaptors For 350 Series Airbrushes 3.20 ea

These jar adapters are direct replacements for metal jar adaptors and feature the correct 60° siphon tube angle.

**165-50308** 1-5/16" 33mm

**165-51018** Fits 1oz Air Opaque Jars

**165-51020** Fits 4oz Air Opaque Jars

See What's New and Exciting at
**www.walthers.com**

## Jar Adaptors For Models 200, 250, 350 and 150

**165-500052** 3/4oz (22cc) **1.50**

**165-500053** 2oz (60cc) **2.05**

## Badger Propel

**165-50002** 11oz (33ml) **9.70**

**165-50202** 17oz (51ml) **13.95**
Works with all types of airbrushes, requires regulator #165-50200 (sold separately).

## Propel Regulators

**165-50029** Tire Adapter **5.40**
Convert any spare tire into an air supply. Special fitting modifies Propel regulator #165-50200 (sold separately) to fit standard valve stem.

**165-50200** Complete Regulator **8.30**
Makes Propel last longer, regulates air pressure from ca at 10-50 P.S.I.

**165-50118** O-Ring Only **1.35**

Items listed below are availab by Special Order (see Legend Page).

**165-50117** Stem w/O-Ring **4.15**

**165-50119** Washer **1.35**

## Air Hoses

**165-502011** Braided w/Swivel Connections **18.60**
10' (3.05m) of heavy duty hos for use with compressors.

## Vinyl Airhoses

**165-50001** 5' **7.00**

**165-500011** 8' **11.10**
Flexible, lightweight, sturdy hose. With connectors at each end. Not recommended for us with compressors.

## 10' Re-Coil™ Hoses 20.95 ea

**165-504011** For Badger

Item listed below is available by Special Order (see Legend Page).
**165-504012** For Binks

## In-Line Moisture Filters

**165-502014** Filter Only **18.95**
For use with #165-50205 Air Hose Only.

**165-502025** With Hose **33.10**
Complete assembly with 10' (3.05m) braided air hose.

## Foto-Frisket Film

**165-600** pkg(10) **15.75**
Low tack, easy lift-off masking film.

## Respirators

**165-1902** Replacement Cartridge for #165-1901 **19.00**

**165-1903** Replacement Pre-Filter for #165-1901 **9.60**

Item listed below is available by Special Order (see Legend Page).

**165-1901** Double Cartridge Type **90.20**
Protects against paint mists and vapors.

BADGER AIR-BRUSH CO.

## AIR ABRASIVE GUNS

Removes rust or paint from metal, and roughs the surface for improved paint adhesion. **NOTE:** Use of wraparound safety goggles and a dust mask or respirator is recommended. Not for use by children.

**165-2601** Gun Only **35.00**
**165-2603** Starter Set **48.00**
Set includes: gun with attached 4oz (120cc) jar, 8' (240cm) hose and 12oz (336kg) net weight of aluminum oxide, face mask, Propel® and regulator.

## BOOKS

### How-To

**165-500** Hobby & Craft Guide to Airbrushing **7.90**
Includes instructions on preparation for painting, mixing paint, cleaning and maintenance. Softcover, 32 pages, over 130 full color illustrations, 8-1/2 x 11".
**165-505** Step by Step Modelers Guide to Airbrushing **11.65**
Painting models, figures and dioramas. Includes techniques from shadowing to mixing paint. Softcover, over 180 color photos, 32 pages, 8-1/2 x 11".

## MODELFLEX™ PAINT

Specially formulated for models, goes on super thin (.25 to .50 thousands) to color without hiding fine details. Non-toxic and with no foul odor, Modelflex cleans up with water and can be sprayed or brushed.

### Modelflex Sets 24.30 ea

**165-1701** Railroad Rolling Stock
One each: Engine Black, Reefer White, Reefer Gray, Reefer Yellow, Reefer Orange, Dark Tuscan Red, Light Tuscan Red.
**165-1702** Weathering & Railroad Off-Line
One each: Weathered Black, Antique White, Primer Gray, Concrete Gray, Sand, Signal Red, Light Green.
**165-1703** Railroad Private Colors
One each: Caboose Red, Rail Box Yellow, Mopac Blue, Pullman Green, Super Gloss Black, Maroon, Tuscan Red, ATSF Silver.
**165-1704** Military Colors
One each: Forest Green, Olive Drab, European Dark Green, Armor Sand, Field Drab, Medium Green, Camouflage Gray.
**165-1705** Gloss Auto Colors
One each: Black, White, Red, Blue, Brown, Yellow, Green

### Individual Paints 1oz (30cc) 3.60 ea

**165-1601** Engine Black
**165-1602** Reefer White
**165-1603** Grimy Black
**166-1604** Reefer Gray
**165-1605** Weathered Black
**165-1606** Antique White
**165-1607** Signal Red
**165-1608** Caboose Red
**165-1609** Reefer Orange
**165-1610** Reefer Yellow
**165-1611** Concrete Gray
**165-1612** Primer Gray
**165-1613** Dark Tuscan Oxide Red
**165-1614** Light Tuscan Oxide Red
**165-1615** Maroon Tuscan Oxide Red
**165-1616** Brunswick Green
**165-1617** Pullman Green
**165-1618** SOO Maroon
**165-1619** SOO Dulux Gold
**165-1620** Super Gloss Black
**165-1621** PRR Green
**165-1622** PRR Maroon
**165-1623** CNW Dark Green
**165-1624** UP Armor Yellow
**165-1625** UP Harbor Mist Gray
**165-1626** BN Green
**165-1627** NYC Gray Dark 1
**165-1628** NYC Gray Light 1
**165-1629** CR Blue
**165-1630** Sand
**165-1631** ATSF Red
**165-1632** ATSF Silver
**165-1633** ATSF Yellow
**165-1634** ATSF Blue
**165-1635** SP Lark Light Gray
**165-1636** SP Daylight Red
**165-1637** SP Scarlet Red
**165-1638** SP Daylight Orange
**165-1639** SP Letter Gray
**165-1640** SP Lark Dark Gray
**165-1641** SP Armor Yellow
**165-1642** MILW Orange
**165-1643** MILW Maroon
**165-1644** MILW Gray
**165-1645** MILW Brown
**165-1646** SOU Sylvan Green
**165-1647** Light Green
**165-1648** Weyerhauser Yellow Green
**165-1649** CSX Blue
**165-1650** Insignia Yellow
**165-1651** EL Gray
**165-1652** EL Yellow
**165-1653** EL Maroon
**165-1654** Rail Box Yellow
**165-1655** CNW Old Yellow
**165-1656** CNW Zeto Yellow
**165-1657** SOO Red
**165-1658** Amtrak Red
**165-1659** Amtrak Blue
**165-1660** B&M Blue
**165-1661** DRGW Orange
**165-1662** DRGW Gold
**165-1663** GN Big Sky Blue
**165-1664** GN Orange
**165-1665** GN Green
**165-1666** GTW Blue
**165-1667** C&O Enchantment Blue
**165-1668** C&O Yellow
**165-1669** B&O Royal Blue
**165-1670** CSX Gray
**165-1671** WC Maroon
**165-1672** WC Cream
**165-1673** IC Orange
**165-1674** IC Brown
**165-1675** GM&O Red
**165-1676** D&H Blue
**165-1677** NP Light Green
**165-1678** NP Yellow
**165-1679** Rock Island Blue
**165-1680** MKT Green
**165-1681** MKT Yellow
**165-1682** L&N Blue
**165-1683** L&N Gray
**165-1684** L&N Yellow
**165-1685** RDG Green
**165-1686** MP Blue
**165-1687** Missabe Road Maroon
**165-1688** Missabe Road Yellow
**165-1689** WP Orange
**165-1690** Penn Central Green
**165-16151** BNSF Green
**165-16152** BNSF Orange
**165-16153** CB&Q Chinese Red
**165-16154** CB&Q Gray
**165-16155** Wabash Blue
**165-16156** Wabash Gray
**165-16157** Frisco Orange
**165-16158** CP Action Yellow
**165-16159** CP Action Red
**165-16160** CP Tuscan Red
**165-16161** CP Yellow
**165-16162** CP Gray
**165-16163** CN Red #11
**165-16164** CN Green #11
**165-16165** CN Orange #10
**165-16166** CN Yellow #11
**165-16167** CN Gray #11
**165-16168** Trailer Train Yellow
**165-16169** MP Eagle Blue
**165-16170** MP Eagle Roof Gray
**165-16171** MP Eagle Gray
**165-16172** Rust
**165-16173** Mud
**165-16174** Earth
**165-16175** Rail Brown
**165-16176** Roof Brown
**165-16177** NH Hunter Green
**165-16178** NH Warm Orange
**165-16179** NH Imitation Silver
**165-16180** NH Pullman Green
**165-16181** NH Imitation Gold
**165-16182** NH Red-Orange
**165-16183** NH Socony Red
**165-16184** LV Cornell Red
**165-16185** SAL Pullman Green
**165-16186** ACL Imitation Aluminum
**165-16187** CNW Red
**165-16188** D&H Gray
**165-16189** B&M Maroon
**165-16190** B&O Dulux Gold
**165-16191** Pullman Harbor Mist Gray
**165-16192** WP Green
**165-16193** CB&Q Imitation Aluminum
**165-16194** CB&Q Red
**165-16195** BNSF Silver
**165-16196** BNSF Yellow
**165-16197** SP/ATSF Overland Light Gray
**165-16198** SP/ATSF Overland Dark Gray
**165-16199** Rock Maroon
**165-16200** Rock Red
**165-16201** Rock Aluminum White
**165-16202** John Deere Yellow
**165-16203** John Deere Green
**165-16204** Light Flesh
**165-16205** Medium Flesh
**165-16206** Dark Flesh
**165-16208** Metallic Gold

### Military Colors

**165-1691** Bomber Green
**165-1692** SAC Bomber Green
**165-1693** Bomber Blue
**165-1694** Field Drab
**165-1695** Green Drab
**165-1696** Olive Drab
**165-1697** Camouflage Gray
**165-1698** Camouflage Brown
**165-1699** Flat Gull Gray
**165-16100** Euro Dark Green
**165-16101** Medium Field Green
**165-16102** Forest Green
**165-16103** Armor Sand
**165-16104** Dark Green
**165-16105** Medium Green

### Gloss Colors

**165-16106** Black
**165-16107** White
**165-16108** Red
**165-16109** Orange
**165-16110** Blue
**165-16111** Green
**165-16112** Yellow
**165-16113** Brown
**165-16114** Silver
**165-16115** Midnight Blue
**165-16116** Deep Red
**165-16117** Bright Orange
**165-16118** Sunset Yellow

### Flat Colors

**165-16119** Flat Black
**165-16120** Flat White

### Clear Finish

**165-16601** Flat
**165-16602** Satin
**165-16603** Gloss

### Extender

**165-16600** Extender

### Marine Paints 1oz Bottles 3.60 ea

**165-16401** Anti-Fouling Red Oxide
**165-16402** Navy Red
**165-16403** Coast Guard Red
**165-16404** Coast Guard Orange
**165-16405** Deck Tan
**165-16406** Navy Brown
**165-16407** Quartermaster Brown
**165-16408** Navy Buff
**165-16409** Panama Buff
**165-16410** Navy White
**165-16411** Deck Green
**165-16412** Hull Black
**165-16413** Wrought Iron Black
**165-16414** Bulwarks Red
**165-16415** Caprail Green
**165-16416** Midship Blue
**165-16417** White
**165-16418** Slate Gray
**165-16419** Umber
**165-16420** Yellow Ochre
**165-16421** Hull Cream
**165-16422** Windjammer White
**165-16423** Windjammer Yellow
**165-16424** Windjammer Red
**165-16425** Windjammer Green
**165-16426** Windjammer Blue
**165-16427** Salmon Buff
**165-16428** Orange Ochre
**165-16429** Shipyard Rust
**165-16430** Shipyard Grimy Gray
**165-16431** Deck Red
**165-16432** Dark Deck Gray
**165-16433** Tug Light Blue
**165-16434** Tug Medium Blue
**165-16435** Tug Deep Blue
**165-16436** Tug Light Green
**165-16437** Tug Olive Green
**165-16438** Tug Orange
**165-16439** Tug Yellow
**165-16440** Tug Light Gray
**165-16441** Army Corps Engineer Buff
**165-16442** Golden Yellow
**165-16443** Bright Silver
**165-16444** #5 Standard Navy Gray
**165-16445** #20 Standard Deck Gray
**165-16446** 5-L Light Gray (Early 1941)
**165-16447** 5-0 Ocean Gray (Early 1941)
**165-16448** 5-D Dark Gray (Early 1941)
**165-16449** 5-H Haze Gray (Late 1941)
**165-16450** 5-0 Ocean Gray (Late 1941)
**165-16451** 5-S Sea Blue A (Late 1941)
**165-16452** 5-N Navy Blue (Late 1941)
**165-16453** Deck Blue 20B (Late 1941)
**165-16454** #82 Black (1943)
**165-16455** 5-P Pale Gray (1943)
**165-16456** 5-L Light Gray (1946)
**165-16457** Dull Coat
**165-16458** Matte Coat
**165-16459** Gloss Coat
**165-16460** Retarder

### Cleaner

**165-16606** 16oz **9.00**

## DECAL ACCESSORIES

### Decal Solutions 2.45 ea

Use these handy solutions to make decals adhere to your models like paint.
**165-16801** Setting Solution
**165-16802** Softening Solution
**165-16803** Liquid Decal Film
Allows you to create your own decals by brushing it on a flat clean surface, allow to dry, and draw or paint on your image. Also allows you to save old decals when brushed over an old decal, film seals and provides a new surface.

## ACCESSORIES

### Just-a-Dab Applicators

Flexible plastic applicators with textured shaft and micro-fibre heads for applying paints with accuracy. Washable and reusable.
**165-50560** Fine pkg(12) **2.15**
**165-50570** Regular pkg(12) **2.15**
**165-50580** Combo (9 Fine & 9 Regular) **3.20**

## CATALOGS

**165-BA2000** Catalog 2005 **N/C**
**165-BA200** Retail Price Guide 2005 **N/C**

## JOE'S MODEL TRAINS

## NEW PRODUCTS

### Detail/Decal Remover

**NEW 350-100** Gel Formula 2oz **10.95**
Cleanly fades or removes factory applied letters and numbers with minimal or no damage to underlying paint. Allows you to control what detail and how much is removed. Use on plastic, metal or wood. Not suitable for models that use the same ink/paint on both body and details.

### Rusty Rails Painter

This mini paint roller tool neatly paints rails without messy spraying or masking. Allows you to paint cross ties over loose or molded ballast and makes it easy to reach tight spots like switches or bridges. Roller is adjustable so you can paint rails, spikes and plates at the same time. Use your own thinned oil-base paints or Rusty Rails Custom Acrylic Paint. Painter includes paint jar with nickel plated brass paint tube, stainless steel screw axle, spacer and nut, and roller with two DuraLar™ solvent-resistant polyester disks installed. Includes five rollers, extra polyester disks and complete instructions

**NEW 350-101** HO, N & Z Scale Painter **14.95**

**NEW 350-102** O Scale Painter **14.95**

**NEW 350-103** Starter Kit **19.95**
Includes Rusty Rails Painter tool and two ounce bottle of Brown Rust acrylic paint.

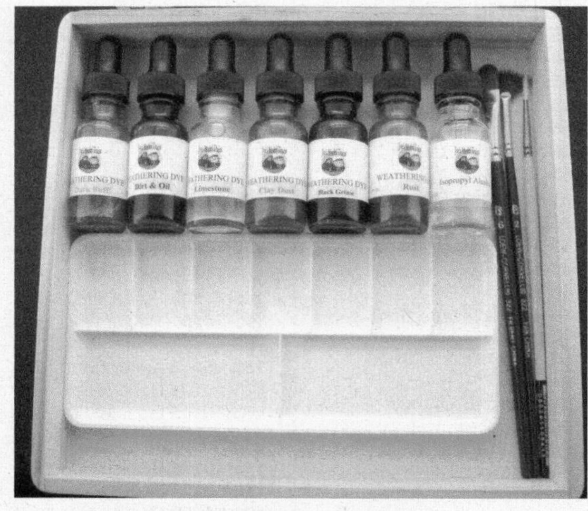

### Joe's Custom Weathering Dyes Kit

**NEW 350-112 39.95**
These water/alcohol soluble washes will adhere to any painted or bare surface, dry to a flat finish and won't easily rub off - making the model safe to handle. No sealer coat is required. Best of all, if you don't like the finish, the dye can be removed with dish detergent or modified with water or alcohol at any time! Complete set includes six custom colors, a plastic tray palette with wells for dispensing and mixing dyes and an unfinished wooden storage box with locking clasp. Brushes are not included. Box has styrofoam padding to hold contents in place and can be finished with your favorite railroad colors.

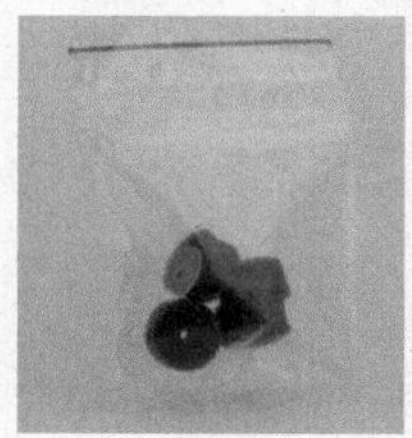

**NEW 350-109** Painter Rollers Only **3.95**

### Rusty Rails Custom Acrylic Paint 2 Ounce Bottles 6.95 ea

Flat acrylic enamel paint delivers a smooth flow with good adhesion to bare metal. Colors can be blended together for a custom look. Specially formulated for painting model railroad track. Designed especially for Rusty Rails Painter #350-101 (sold separately).

**NEW 350-105** Weathered Black

**NEW 350-106** Shale

**NEW 350-107** Dark Brown

**NEW 350-108** Brown Rust

### Joe's Custom Weathering Dye

Create a wide range of subtle weathering with these special dye colors. Won't harm paint finishes, dries flat and can be sprayed with an airbrush.

Offers superior adhesion even to glossy finishes. No sealer coat needed. Dye won't rub off when dry but is water or alcohol soluble at any time.

### One Ounce Bottles 8.45 ea

**NEW 350-113** Black Grime
**NEW 350-114** Limestone
**NEW 350-115** Clay Dust
**NEW 350-116** Dirt & Oil
**NEW 350-117** Rust
**NEW 350-118** Dark Buff

### Artist Mixing Palette

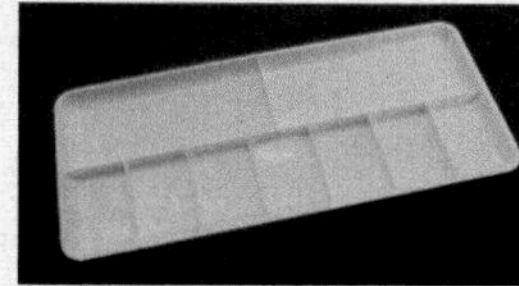

**NEW 350-119 3.95**
Plastic tray features seven wells for dispensing and mixing dyes and paint.

## MICROSCALE®

### Micro Liquid Decal Film

**460-117** 1oz (30ml) **2.50**
To make decals, brush super film on a flat clean surface, allow to dry and draw or paint on your image.

### Masking Liquid

**460-110** Micro Mask 1oz (30ml) **2.50**
Just brush on and allow to dry. Can be cut with hobby knife to create special effects. For use with solvent based paints (Micro Mask is water soluble).

### Decal Setting Solution 1oz (30ml) 2.50

These setting solutions soften decal film, allowing it to stretch over details for the most realistic appearance. Prevents air bubbles and results in an invisible carrier film, reducing silvering. Formulated especially for MicroScale decals, can be used with most other brands.

460-104

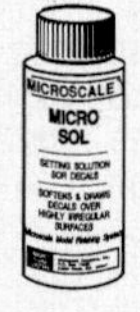


460-105

**460-104** Micro Set
Brush over area where decal is to be applied. Special wetting agents cut oils in new paint and strengthens adhesive on decal.

**460-105** Micro Sol
A stronger formula, for use on larger details or stubborn areas. Just brush on; actually makes decal part of the paint.

### Clear Finishes 2.50 ea

These water-clear, non-yellowing, acrylic resins adhere strongly to paint and plastics and hide decal film. Can be applied with a brush, or airbrushed (40lbs pressure recommended). Clean up with water.

**460-103** Micro Coat Flat
Dead-flat finish for a dirty, weathered or camouflaged look.

**460-106** Micro Coat Satin
Semi-gloss, for a less shiny or slightly dirty look.

**460-108** Micro Coat Gloss
Provides a smooth surface for decaling and produces a high-gloss "wet look" when dry.

### Adhesives 1oz (30ml) 2.50 ea

**460-109** Micro Weld Plastic Cement
Formulated for styrene, produces strong joints without crazing or warping thin parts. Nontoxic and environmentally friendly, mild flammability.

**460-114** Micro Krystal Kleer
Perfect for attaching clear parts. Dries clear, or tint with food coloring. Can be used to model window "glass" by applying a thin layer to window openings. Cleans up with water, waterproof when dry.

**460-115** Micro Liquitape
Holds parts securely, but allows you to remove and replace them over and over. Also for attaching patterns. Cleans up with water.

**460-116** Micro Metal Foil Adhesive

**CAUTION:** For your safety, the use of a properly vented spray booth and a respirator which is paint mist and vapor compatible is strongly recommended when painting with an airbrush.

## ROBART

### Paint Shaker

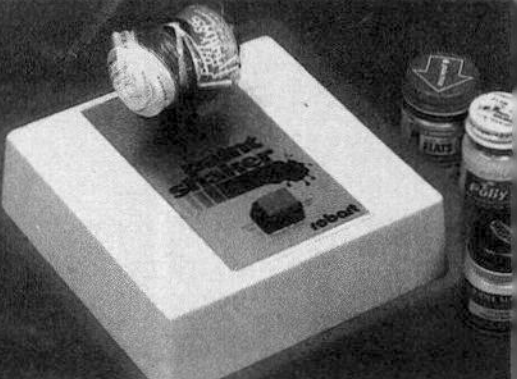

**547-411** Electrically Powered **39.50**
Keep your hobby paints mixed and ready to use. Great for mixing thinner and paint when airbrushing or blending custom colors. Eliminates messy stirring sticks and paint spills. Paint is shaken at 5,000 cycles/minute. Adjustable rubber strap holds all 1/4, 1/3, 1/2, 5/8 and 1oz bottles. Assembled and ready for use. Complete with transformer, plugs into any U.S. standard outlet (110V AC).

**547-415** Replacement Straps pkg(5) **5.70**
Adjustable replacement straps for shaker.

# iwata
Professional Airbrushes

## NEW PRODUCT
Item listed below is available by Special Order (see Legend Page).

### High Performance Plus Airbrush
**NEW 358-4001** HP-C Plus **265.00**
A practical choice for most users, this airbrush does it all from fine lines to backgrounds and the entire range of stippling effects. The larger 1/3oz 9ml gravity-feed cup and 0.3mm needle/nozzle configuration allow for use with most media. Features, dual-purpose cutaway pre-set hangle for easy clean up and precise paint flow, Teflon™ needle, redesigned gravity feed cups and single-piece auxiliary lever/needled chucking guide for easy assembly.

## AIRBRUSHES
iwata Revolution

Manufactured with the same high-quality materials as the rest of the Iwata line. These general-purpose, high-flow airbrushes are able to spray detail and background work, as well as a variety of different paint types. They feature a siphon feed assembly, a larger needle chucking nut for easy assembly, a trigger with an attached auxiliary lever to the needle chuck guide, and easy-to-replace internal Teflon needle packing for use with any types of solvent-based paints.

**385-R2001** Dual Action w/Hose **115.00**

Item listed below is available by Special Order (see Legend Page).

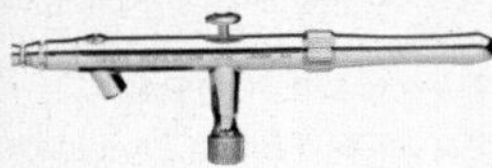

**358-R1000** Single Action **95.00**

## Eclipse
Eclipse multi-purpose, high-paint-flow, high-detail airbrushes offer versatile, reliable performance. Commonly used to spray premixed or heavier paints, they cover a wide range of uses and are well suited for uses demanding precise control of spray when applying moderate-to-large amounts of paint to a variety of surfaces and to various-sized areas. Eclipse airbrushes are easy to maintain and highly durable. Sets include airbrush, paint jar and braided hose.

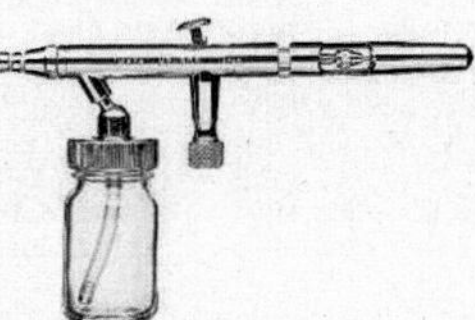

**358-2001** HP-BCS Set **157.00**
Bottom-feed with 0.5mm needle and nozzle combination.

Items listed below are available by Special Order (see Legend Page).
**358-HPCS** HP-CS **185.00**
Gravity-feed with .35mm needle and nozzle combination for fine-details and 1/3oz cup for easy clean up and efficient paint flow.

**358-HPSBS** HP-SBS **185.00**
Side-feed with 0.35mm needle and nozzle combination and the option of four cup sizes.

## AIRBRUSH ADAPTERS

### Airhose Adapters 8.50 ea
Allows conversion of most other manufacturers' airbrush hoses to be used with Iwata airbrushes.

**358-1001** Adapts Iwata Airbrushes to Paasche Airhoses

**358-1002** Adapts Iwata Airbrushes to Badger or Thayer & Chandler Airhoses

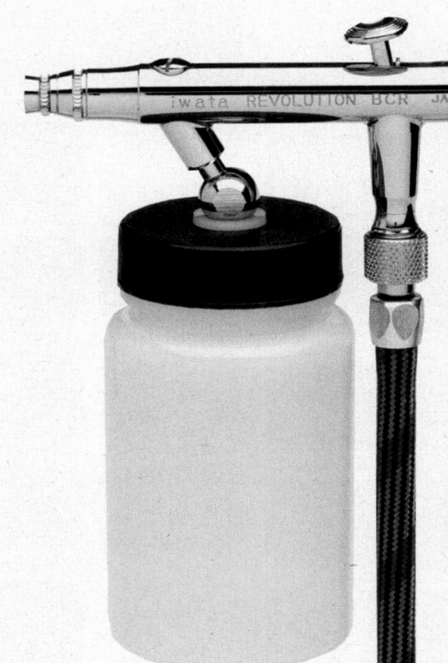


- **Precision Made**
- **One Needle/One Tip Does It All**
- **Get A Fine Line Up To A 2" Spray Pattern**
- **Easy To Use & Easy To Clean**

Revolution Airbrush Set 358-R2001

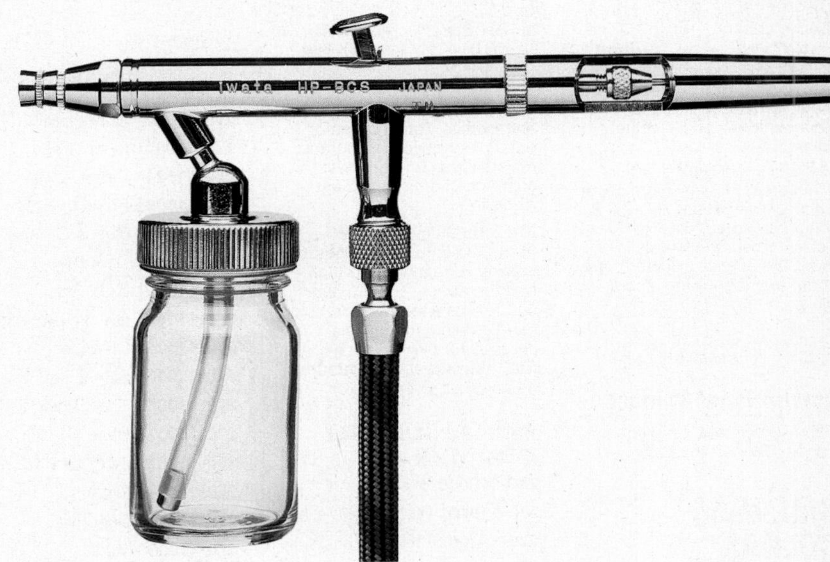


Eclipse Bottle Feed Airbrush Set 358-2001

## AIRBRUSH ACCESSORIES

### Braided Nylon Covered PVC Airhose
**358-10** For Iwata (10') **25.50**

### Handles
#### Single Cut
Item listed below is available by Special Order (see Legend Page).
**358-16191** For Eclipse Bottom Feed, Side Feed & Gravity Feed Airbrushes **23.00**

### Jars 6.00 ea
Jars are made of high-strength translucent plastic.

**358-14802** 2oz 56ml

Item listed below is available by Special Order (see Legend Page).
**358-14803** 3oz 84ml

# FLOQUIL®

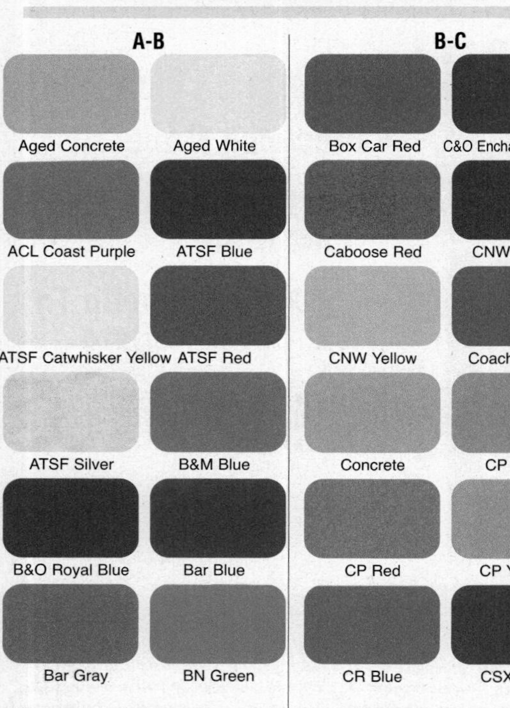


C-D

CSX Gray — CSX Tan

CSX Yellow — D&H Avon Blue

D&H Gray — Dark Green

Depot Buff — Depot Olive

Dirt — DRGW Building Brown

DRGW Building Cream — DRGW Freight Car Red

DRGW Orange — DRGW Yellow

Due to the printing process, the colors above are only representative of the actual colors.

Made especially for painting miniatures, Floquil colors cover without hiding detail. Floquil is solvent based, while Polly Scale™ colors are water-reducible acrylics. Dealers: Ask about merchandising display racks.

## NEW PRODUCT

### Acrylic Paint Thinner

**NEW 270-50496** Universal Acrylic Thinner 4oz **6.29**

## RAILROAD COLORS

**270-110001** Thinner-Brush Cleaner **4.49**
Only chemical compatible solvent for Floquil colors, can be used for thinning, mixing and cleaning equipment.

**270-110002** Retarder **4.49**
Slows drying time of solvent-based colors, for airbrushing and covering large areas.

**270-110003** Hi-Gloss **4.49**
Light amber-colored coating for indoor use. Heat, water and alcohol resistant. Dries in about four hours with an extremely high-gloss finish.

**270-110004** Crystal Cote **4.49**
Water-clear, quick-drying gloss and fixative. Use indoors or out; does not yellow. Durable, resists abrasion and most common chemicals except alcohol.

**270-110005** Glaze **4.49**
Amber-colored, semi-gloss coating. Use indoors or out. Dries in about 15-20 minutes and resists water, alcohol and most common chemicals. Can be used for priming, or mix with solvent-based colors for an eggshell finish.

### Railroad Colors 1oz (30ml) 4.49 ea

**270-110006** Dust
**270-110007** Rail Brown
**270-110009** Primer
**270-110010** Engine Black
**270-110011** Reefer White
**270-110012** Reefer Gray
**270-110013** Grimy Black
**270-110014** Railroad Tie Brown
**270-110015** Flat Finish
**270-110016** Aged Concrete
**270-110017** Weathered Black
**270-110020** Caboose Red
**270-110023** Flesh Tone Base
**270-110025** Tuscan Red
**270-110030** Reefer Orange
**270-110031** Reefer Yellow
**270-110033** Railbox Yellow
**270-110034** Brunswick Green
**270-110035** BN Green
**270-110040** Dark Green
**270-110041** Light Green
**270-110044** Depot Olive
**270-110045** Pullman Green
**270-110048** Coach Green
**270-110050** Dark Blue
**270-110051** Light Blue
**270-110056** GN Big Sky Blue
**270-110058** CR Blue
**270-110065** Signal Red
**270-110070** Roof Brown
**270-110073** Rust
**270-110074** Box Car Red
**270-110081** Earth
**270-110082** Concrete
**270-110083** Mud
**270-110084** Foundation
**270-110085** Antique White
**270-110086** Grime
**270-110087** Depot Buff
**270-110088** D&H Caboose Red
**270-110100** Old Silver (metallic)
**270-110101** Bright Silver (metallic)
**270-110103** Bright Gold (metallic)
**270-110104** Brass (metallic)
**270-110105** Copper (metallic)
**270-110108** Gun Metal (metallic)
**270-110119** Graphite (metallic)
**270-110130** SP Lettering Gray
**270-110131** SP Lark Light Gray
**270-110132** SP Lark Dark Gray
**270-110133** SP Armour Yellow
**270-110134** SP Daylight Orange
**270-110135** SP Daylight Red
**270-110136** SP Scarlet
**270-110144** Platinum Mist (metallic)
**270-110166** UP Armour Yellow
**270-110167** UP Harbor Mist Gray
**270-110168** UP Light Orange
**270-110174** SOU Green
**270-110175** SOU Freight Car Brown
**270-110176** ATSF Red
**270-110177** ATSF Blue
**270-110178** ATSF Yellow
**270-110179** ATSF Mineral Brown
**270-110180** BNSF Orange
**270-110181** BNSF Green
**270-110182** BNSF Yellow
**270-110183** RDG Green
**270-110184** Tuscan Red #2
**270-110186** Railroad Oxide Red
**270-110250** CN Orange #11
**270-110252** CN Gray #17
**270-110254** CN Yellow #12
**270-110256** CN Green #12
**270-110260** CNW Yellow
**270-110262** CNW Green
**270-110280** WC Gold
**270-110282** WC Maroon
**270-110310** TTX Yellow
**270-110320** MKT Green
**270-110330** NYC Jade Green
**270-110350** CSX Gray
**270-110352** CSX Blue
**270-110354** CSX Black
**270-110356** CSX Yellow
**270-110357** CSX New Image Blue
**270-110358** CSX New Image Gold
**270-110450** SOO Red
**270-110601** Zinc Chromate Primer

### Railroad Aerosols 3oz (150ml) 5.49 ea

Same colors, but in spray cans for covering large areas, or quick paint jobs.

**270-130004** Crystal Cote
**270-130007** Rail Brown
**270-130009** Primer
**270-130010** Engine Black
**270-130011** Reefer White
**270-130012** Reefer Gray
**270-130013** Grimy Black

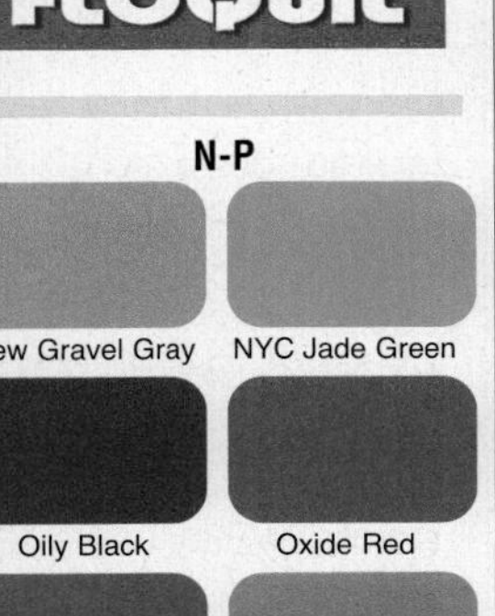


**N-P**

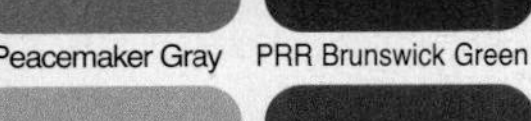
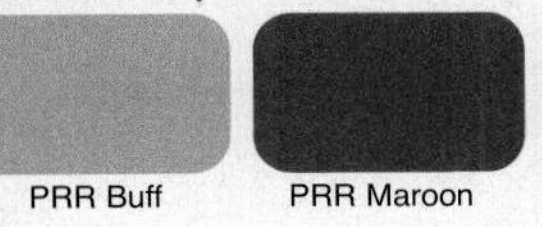

New Gravel Gray, NYC Jade Green, Oily Black, Oxide Red, Pacemaker Red, Penn Central Green, Peacemaker Gray, PRR Brunswick Green, PRR Buff, PRR Maroon

**P-R**

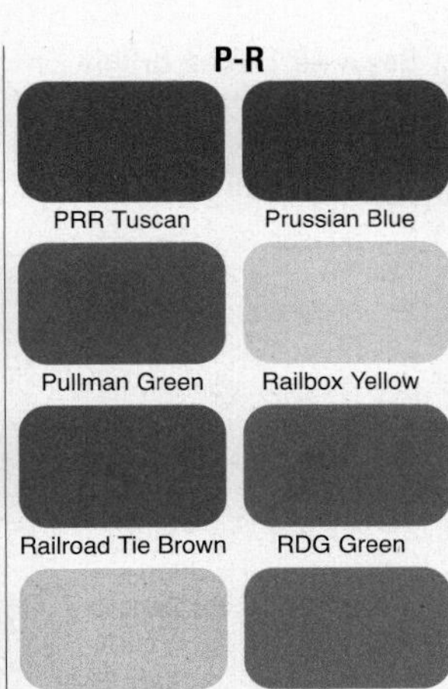

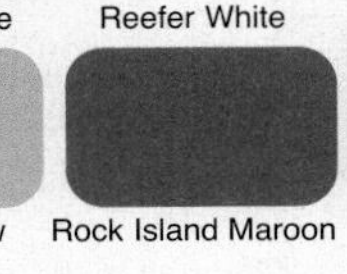

PRR Tuscan, Prussian Blue, Pullman Green, Railbox Yellow, Railroad Tie Brown, RDG Green, RDG Yellow, Reefer Gray, Reefer Orange, Reefer White, Reefer Yellow, Rock Island Maroon

**R-S**

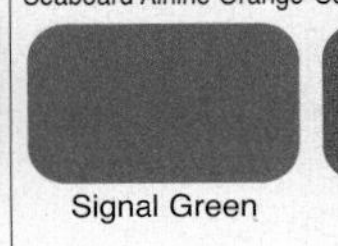
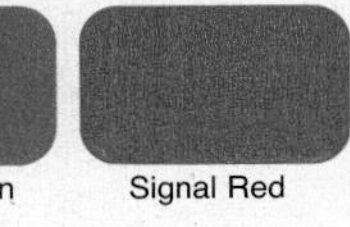

Roof Brown, Roof Red, Rust, Sand, SCL Caboose Car Orange, SCL Hopper Car Beige, SCL Hopper Car Yellow, Seaboard Airline Chinese Red, Seaboard Airline Orange, Seaboard Airline Yellow, Signal Green, Signal Red

**S**

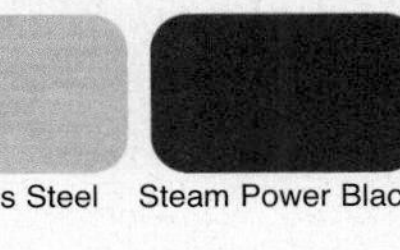

Signal Yellow, SOO Red, SOU Sullivan Green, SP Daylight Orange, SP Daylight Red, SP Lark Dark Gray, SP Lettering Gray, SP Scarlet, Special Oxide Red, St. Lawrence Blue, Stainless Steel, Steam Power Black

**T-Z**

Tarnished Black, TH&B Cream, TTX Yellow, Undercoat Light Gray, UP Armor Yellow, UP Dark Gray(184), UP Harbor Mist Gray, Utility Orange, Vermont Green, WC Maroon, Weyerhauser Green, Zinc Chromate Primer

**270-130015** Flat Finish
**270-130016** Instant Weathering
**270-130020** Caboose Red
**270-130025** Tuscan Red
**270-130030** Reefer Orange
**270-130031** Reefer Yellow
**270-130040** Dark Green
**270-130045** Pullman Green
**270-130048** Coach Green
**270-130050** Dark Blue
**270-130070** Roof Brown
**270-130074** Box Car Red
**270-130081** Earth
**270-130082** Concrete
**270-130101** Bright Silver (metallic)
**270-130601** Zinc Chromate Primer

### Aerosol Figure Primer 3oz 5.49 ea

Permanent, high-adherence primers resist chipping. Made especially for metal figures and miniatures, works well on most models. Fine pigments cover completely without filling in or hiding fine details. Can be used as a base under water- or solvent-based paints. Available in four colors to highlight detail and simplify application of finish coats. Dealers must order packs of three.

**270-330022** Figure Flat
**270-330009** Light Gray
**270-330010** Base Black
**270-330021** Base White

## ENAMELS

### Weathering Markers Pkg(3) 7.49

These new three-marker sets are ideal for quick, neat weathering applications.

**270-3801** Rail Brown, Railroad Tie Brown, Rust
**270-3802** Aged Concrete, Weathered Black, Roof Brown
**270-3803** Earth, Mud, Grime

## POLLY SCALE™

A comprehensive line of user-friendly acrylics, Polly Scale colors are water-reducible, odor-free and environmentally safe. A wide selection of railroad and military colors are available, excellent for plastics, metals and brass. Fine ground pigments cover without hiding surface details and the formula is self leveling. Easily brushed, drybrushed and airbrushed. Can be sprayed at low pressure. Use plain water for clean-up or thinning. All colors are intermixable with older Polly S paints.

### Railroad Colors 1/2oz (15ml) 3.99 ea

**270-404046** Atlantic Coast Line Purple
**270-404049** Maine Central Harvest Gold
**270-404052** Maine Central Pine Green
**270-404055** Toronto, Hamilton & Buffalo Cream
**270-404058** CP Yellow
**270-404061** CP Red
**270-404064** PRR Buff
**270-404067** TTX Yellow
**270-404070** Depot Olive
**270-404073** MOW Gray
**270-404076** Coach Green
**270-404079** Oxide Red
**270-404082** Roof Red
**270-404085** Signal Yellow
**270-404088** Signal Green
**270-404091** Signal Red
**270-404094** Utility Orange
**270-404097** Prussian Blue

### Railroad Colors 1oz (30ml) 4.99 ea

**270-414110** Steam Power Black
**270-414113** Reefer White
**270-414116** Reefer Gray
**270-414119** Reefer Orange
**270-414122** Reefer Yellow
**270-414125** Railbox Yellow
**270-414128** Caboose Red
**270-414131** Aged White
**270-414134** Undercoat Light Gray
**270-414137** Grimy Black
**270-414140** Tarnished Black
**270-414143** ATSF Silver
**270-414146** ATSF Catwhisker Yellow
**270-414149** ATSF Red
**270-414150** ATSF Blue
**270-414152** MILW Orange
**270-414155** MILW Maroon
**270-414158** MILW Gray
**270-414161** PRR Maroon
**270-414164** PRR Brunswick Green
**270-414167** PRR Tuscan
**270-414170** UP Armor Yellow
**270-414173** UP Dark Gray
**270-414176** UP Harbor Gray
**270-414179** SP Letter Gray
**270-414182** SP Lark Dark Gray
**270-414183** SP Scarlet
**270-414185** SP Daylight Orange
**270-414186** SP Daylight Red
**270-414188** CNW Green
**270-414191** CNW Yellow
**270-414194** D&H Avon Blue
**270-414197** D&H Gray
**270-414200** WC Maroon
**270-414203** GN Big Sky Blue
**270-414206** CR Blue
**270-414209** BN Green
**270-414212** SOO Red
**270-414215** CSX Yellow
**270-414218** CSX Gray
**270-414221** CSX Blue
**270-414222** CSX Tan
**270-414224** GN Orange
**270-414227** GN Empire Green
**270-414228** GN Glacier Green
**270-414230** Bangor & Aroostook Blue
**270-414233** Bangor & Aroostook Gray
**270-414236** EL Yellow
**270-414239** EL Gray
**270-414242** EL Maroon
**270-414245** Boston & Maine Blue
**270-414248** Rock Island Maroon
**270-414251** CP Gray
**270-414254** DRGW Orange
**270-414255** DRGW Cream
**270-414256** DRGW Brown
**270-414257** DRGW Yellow
**270-414258** DRGW Freight Red
**270-414260** C&O Enchantment Blue
**270-414263** Pacemaker Red
**270-414266** Pacemaker Gray
**270-414269** B&O Royal Blue
**270-414272** Dark Green
**270-414275** Roof Brown
**270-414278** Depot Buff
**270-414281** Box Car Red
**270-414284** Pullman Green
**270-414287** Vermont Green
**270-414290** Engine Black
**270-414293** Zinc Chromate Primer
**270-414296** Stainless Steel

FLOQUIL

270-414299 Flat Aluminum

270-414302 Sand

270-414305 Dust

270-414308 Dirt

270-414311 Earth

270-414314 Mud

270-414317 Concrete

270-414320 Aged Concrete

270-414323 Rust

270-414326 Oily Black

270-414329 Railroad Tie Brown

270-414332 New Gravel Gray

270-414350 Mineral Red

270-414352 Light Freight Oxide Red

270-414354 Special Oxide Red

270-414356 Grand Trunk Western Morency Orange

270-414358 Grand Trunk Western Blue

270-414360 LV Cornell Red

270-414362 Detroit, Toledo & Ironton Cherry Red

270-414364 St. Lawrence Blue

270-414366 Weyerhauser Green

270-414368 Penn Central Green

270-414370 NYC Jade Green

270-414372 Guilford Gray

270-414374 SOU Sylvan Green

270-414376 RDG Green

270-414378 RDG Yellow

270-414380 L&N Gray

270-414382 Seaboard Air Line Chinese Red

270-414384 Seaboard Air Line Yellow

270-414386 Seaboard Air Line Orange

270-414388 Seaboard Coast Line Hopper Car Beige

270-414390 Seaboard Coast Line Hopper Car Yellow

270-414392 Seaboard Coast Line Caboose Orange

270-414393 CSX New Image Blue YN3

270-414394 CSX New Image Gold YN3

270-414396 BNSF Heritage Orange

270-414397 BNSF Heritage Green

270-414398 BNSF Yellow

## Polly Scale Air/Armor Colors 1/2oz (15ml) 3.99 ea

Recreate equipment from World War I to the present. Matched to Army/Navy (A/N), Federal Standard 595 (FS) and German WWII (RLM orders) as noted. Colors marked * indicate an approximate match to the Federal Standard color listed.

270-505011 White (RLM 21 *37886)

270-505014 Scale Black (RLM 66 *36081)

270-505017 Yellow (RLM 04 *33538)

270-505020 Red (RLM 23 FS 31302)

270-505023 Dark Blue (RLM 24 *25053)

270-505026 Green (RLM 25 *34108)

270-505029 Doped Linen (*33727)

270-505032 Brown Drab PC-10 (FS 34098)

270-505035 German Mauve (FS 37144)

270-505038 FR/FOK Dark Green (FS 34096)

270-505041 FR Chestnut Brown (FS 20140)

270-505044 FR Beige (FS 33546)

270-505051 Light Blue (RLM 65 *35352)

270-505055 Black Green (RLM 70 *34050)

270-505056 Dark Green (RLM 71 *34083)

270-505059 Dark Gray (RLM 74 *36081)

270-505060 Gray Violet (RLM 75 *36152)

270-505061 Light Gray (RLM 76 *36473)

270-505070 Brown Violet (RLM 81 *34079)

270-505071 Dark Green (RLM 82 *34083)

270-505072 Light Green (RLM 83 *34138)

270-505075 Gray (RLM 02 *16165)

270-505080 US Olive Drab (A/N613 *33070)

270-505082 US Medium Green (A/N612 *34092)

270-505084 US Sand (A/N616 *30279)

270-505086 US Neutral Gray (A/N603 *36118)

270-505088 USN Blue Gray (*35189)

270-505090 USN Light Gray (A/N602 *36440)

270-505092 USN Sea Blue (A/N607 *35045)

270-505094 USN Intermedi-ate Blue (A/N608 *35164)

270-505096 US Interior Green (A/N611 *34089)

270-505098 US Olive Drab (*34088)

270-505110 Panzer Dark Gray (*36152)

270-505111 Panzer Dark Yellow (*33440)

270-505112 Panzer Red Brown (*30111)

270-505113 Panzer Olive Green (*34092)

## Polly Scale Model & Hobby Colors 1/2oz (15ml) 3.99 ea

Matched to Federal Standard 595 (FS) and German WWII (RLM orders) as noted. Colors marked * indicate an approximate match to the Federal Standard color listed.

270-505200 Rust (FS 30215)

270-505202 Dust (FS 37778)

270-505204 Grimy Black (FS 36081)

270-505205 Dirty White

270-505206 Mud (FS 33440)

270-505208 Dirt (FS 30095)

270-505210 Old Concrete (FS 30318)

270-505212 Flesh (*32648)

270-505214 Night Black (22) (FS 37038)

### U.S. Army Air Corps

270-505216 Blue (23) (*15102)

270-505218 Olive Drab (22) (FS 10118)

270-505220 Orange Yellow (4) (FS 13432)

### U.S. Army

270-505222 Khaki (*30219)

270-505224 Olive Drab (FS 34087)

### Soviet Union (USSR)

270-505226 Underside Blue (FS 15200)

270-505228 Light Earth Brown (FS 33434)

270-505230 Topside Green (FS 34201)

270-505232 Dark Topside Gray (FS 36176)

270-505234 Light Topside Gray (FS 36270)

### France

270-505236 Dark Blue Gray (FS 35164)

270-505238 Khaki (FS 34127)

270-505240 Earth Brown (*30140)

270-505242 Light Blue Gray (FS 36238)

### Royal Australian Air Force

270-505244 Earth Brown (FS 30099)

270-505246 Foliage Green (FS 34092)

270-505248 Sky Blue (FS 35550)

### Royal Air Force - Britain

270-505250 Dark Green (*34079)

270-505252 Dark Earth (*30118)

270-505254 Sky (Type "S" *34504)

270-505256 Ocean Grey (*35237)

270-505258 Sea Grey Med (FS 36293)

270-505260 Middlestone (*30266)

270-505262 Azure Blue (*35231)

270-505264 Extra Dark Sea Grey (*36118)

270-505266 Dark Slate Grey (*34096)

270-505268 P.R.U. Blue (*35189)

270-505270 Interior Grey Green (*34226)

### Imperial Japanese Army

270-505272 Green (*34098)

270-505274 Light Gray (*36628)

270-505276 Brown (FS 30108)

### Imperial Japanese Navy

270-505278 Green (*34058)

270-505280 Sky Gray (*36495)

270-505282 Deep Yellow (*33538)

### Italian

270-505284 Hazel Tan (*30219)

270-505286 Camo Brown 2 (FS 10076)

270-505288 Camo Green (FS 34227)

270-505290 Light Blue Gray 1 (FS 36307)

270-505292 Camo Yellow 2 (FS 33481)

270-505294 Camo Yellow 3 (FS 33434)

270-505296 Dark Olive Green 2 (FS 34052)

### Germany

270-505298 Uniform Gray (*34158)

270-505300 Dark Brown (RLM 61 - *30040)

270-505302 Green (RLM 62 *34128)

270-505304 Light Gray (RLM 63 - *36375)

270-505306 Light Blue (RLM 64 - *25414)

270-505308 Dark Olive Green (RLM 67 - *34151)

270-505310 Light Olive Green (RLM 68 - *34258)

270-505312 Light Tan (RLM 69 - *33695)

270-505314 72 Green (RLM 72 - *36081)

270-505316 73 Green (RLM 73 - *34064)

270-505318 78 Light Blue (RLM 78 - *35414)

270-505320 Sand Yellow (RLM 79 - *30215)

270-505322 Olive Green (RLM 80 *34083)

270-505324 Sky Green (RLM 84 - *34554)

### U.S. Navy

270-505326 Pale Blue Gray 5 (*36440)

270-505328 Light Gray 5L (*36373)

270-505330 Haze Gray 5H (*36251)

270-505332 Ocean Gray 50 (*36173)

270-505334 Navy Blue 5N (*36081)

270-505336 Deck Tan (FS 1735)

270-505338 Weathered Deck Blue 20-B (*36076)

### Israel - Early

270-505340 Camo Blue (*35053)

270-505342 Tan (*31433)

270-505344 Light Gray (*37722)

### Israel

270-505346 Gray (*36300)

270-505348 Khaki (*30277)

### NATO Tricolor

270-505350 Black (FS 37038)

270-505352 Brown (FS 30051

270-505354 Green (FS 34094

### Soviet

270-505356 Brown #2 (*32473)

270-505358 Green (*34226)

270-505360 Khaki #2 (*34088

270-505362 Sand (*33798)

270-505368 Warsaw Pact Gray Green (*34258)

### U.S. - Modern

270-505364 Desert Storm Sand (FS 33446)

270-505366 Earth Red (FS 30117)

270-505370 Olive Drab (FS 34087)

270-505372 Brown Special (FS 30140)

270-505374 Dark Ghost Gray (FS 36320)

270-505376 Light Ghost Gray (FS 36375)

270-505378 Dark Gull Gray (FS 36231)

270-505380 Light Gull Gray (FS 36440)

270-505382 Gunship Gray (FS 36118)

270-505384 Neutral Gray (FS 36270)

270-505386 Tan Special (FS 10400)

## FLOQUIL

**270-505388** Tac Dark Green (FS 34079)

**270-505390** Tac Mid-Green (FS 34102)

**270-505392** USTAC Tan

**270-505394** Tac Light Gray (FS 36622)

**270-505396** Light Blue (FS 35622)

## POLLY SCALE™ ACCESSORIES

### Clear Finishes 3.49 ea

**270-404100** Gloss

**270-404103** Satin

### Decal Setting Solutions 3.15 ea

**270-505401** Decal Softening Solution
A stronger solution, makes decals snuggle down in problem areas where surface detail is more pronounced.

**270-505403** Decal Solution Set
Softens decal film to hug surface details. Works fast.

### Plastic Cement

**270-505408** Liquid 1/2oz (15ml) **4.75**

### Plastic Prep

A pre-painting cleaner for use on plastics. Removes mold release, silicones, grease, etc. Leaves plastic clean, static-free and dust-free.

**270-546007** 8oz (240ml) **6.85**

### Mixing Bottles

Empty glass bottle with seals and lids. Ideal for mixing and storing custom colors or thinned paints for airbrushing.

**270-190231** 1/2oz (15ml) pkg(6) **5.94**

**270-190232** 1oz (30ml) pkg(6) **7.14**

## BRUSHES

Manufactured and designed especially for the demands of hobby painting, all brushes are hand-made from the finest materials. Natural hairs or synthetic fibers are set in seamless nickel ferrules.

### Red Sable

Prized for its ability to hold a needle point, found in detail and specific-use brushes.

### Round 6.89 ea (Unless Noted)

**270-201** #3 **8.49**

**270-202** #2

**270-203** #1

**270-204** #0

**270-205** 3/0

**270-206** 5/0

**270-207** 10/0

**270-208** 15/0

### Flat 8.49 ea (Unless Noted)

**270-209** #4 **8.99**

**270-210** #3

**270-211** #2

**270-212** #1

### Kolinsky Premium 8.49 ea

**270-101** #3

**270-102** #0

**270-103** 3/0

**270-104** 5/0

### Camel Hair

A blend of natural hairs obtained from various animals. Brushes are versatile and can be used with all types of colors.

### Lacquering Series

**270-501** 1" **8.49**

**270-502** 3/4" **6.89**

**270-503** 1/2" **5.25**

**270-504** 3/8" **5.25**

**270-505** 1/4" **5.25**

### Round Detailing Series

**270-506** #6 **5.25**

**270-507** #5 **5.25**

**270-508** #4 **5.25**

**270-509** #3 **5.25**

**270-510** #2 **2.49**

**270-511** #1 **2.49**

**270-512** #0 **2.49**

**270-513** 3/0 **2.49**

**270-514** 5/0 **2.49**



### Silver Fox 8.49 ea

Brushes feature synthetic fibers, designed to provide excellent performance and longer life, with performance qualities like red sable.

### Flat

**270-401** 1/4"

**270-402** #4

**270-403** #3

**270-404** #2

**270-405** #1

### Round

**270-406** #2

**270-407** #0

**270-408** 3/0

**270-409** 5/0

### Golden Fox

**270-301** #1 Round **6.89**

**270-302** #0 Round **6.89**

**270-303** 3/0 Round **6.89**

**270-304** 5/0 **6.89**

**270-305** 10/0 **8.49**

**270-306** 20/0 **8.49**

**270-307** 25/0 **8.49**

**270-308** #4 Flat **8.49**

**270-309** #2 Flat **8.49**

### Recommended Air Pressures & Thinning Ratios For Airbrushing

All measurements are approximate. Thinning ratio and pressure needed may vary, depending upon the type of finish required or brand of compressor.

### Always Test First!

Floquil solvent-based Model Railroad.

Thinning Ratio: 75% color, 5% glaze, 20% Thinner-Brush Cleaner. Approximate Pressure: 12-20lbs.

### Clear Coatings

Crystal-Cote Thinning Ratio: Usually none required, if needed use Airbrush Thinner. Approximate Pressure: 12-20 lbs.

### Polly Scale Colors

Thinning Ratio: 10-15% distilled water. Approximate Pressure: 15-20lbs.

**IMPORTANT**: For best results, it's imperative that your airbrush be cleaned thoroughly when you are done spraying to keep paint from drying inside and clogging the spray tip. This should be done immediately, especially when using acrylics, which set up faster than enamels and lacquers.

## Paasche Airbrush Co.

A complete line of airbrushes and accessories, suitable for all types of model painting, crafts and other hobbies, as well as fine art illustration.

Please visit Walthers Web site at www.walthers.com for a complete listing of all available items.

**CAUTION:** For your safety, the use of a properly vented spray booth and a respirator, which is paint mist and vapor compatible, is strongly recommended when painting with an airbrush.

## AIRBRUSHES

### Airbrush Card Set

Sets include one airbrush, wrench, air regulator valve, 6' hose assembly and color jar with cap.

**542-32** H Series **53.00**

Items listed below are available by Special Order (see Legend Page).

**542-49** F Series **52.00**

**542-51** VL Series **85.00**

### H Series Airbrushes 56.00 ea (Unless Noted)

This popular single-action, siphon-feed, external-mix airbrush is highly recommended for beginners. Sturdy and flexible, it can be adapted to practically any hobby use. Available in three sizes of spray patterns; each brush can be converted to another size with Aircaps and Color Adjusting Part, sold separately. Suitable for left- or right-hand users. Optional color cups and bottles are also available separately.

**542-26** Medium 1/32-1-1/4"

**542-27** Large 1/16-1-1/2"

**542-2001** 2000H Hobby Kit **67.00**
Includes single-action, internal-mix airbrush plus two 1/2oz bottle assemblies, air hose with coupling, airbrush hanger, adjusting wrench, Allen wrench and "22 Airbrush Lessons" book.

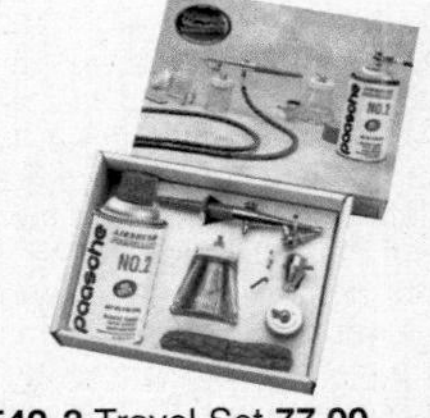

**542-3** Travel Set **77.00**
Includes large spray pattern, single-action airbrush, one 8oz (240ml) can of Propellant, bottle assembly, color cup, air hose, tank valve, "22 Airbrush Lessons" book and parts list.

### VLS

Item listed below is available by Special Order (see Legend Page).

**542-53** Swivel Set **115.00**
Identical to #52, but with a screw-on swivel airbrush connector.

### VL Series

### Airbrushes 91.00 ea

Items listed below are available by Special Order (see Legend Page).

Maximum versatility for virtually any hobby or craft painting project. Double-action, internal-mix, siphon-fed brush can spray fine lines or cover broad areas. Available in three sizes of spray patterns; each brush can be converted to another size with Aircaps and Color Adjusting Part, sold separately. Optional color cups and bottles are also available separately.

**542-46** Small 1/32-1"

**542-47** Medium 1/32-1-1/4"

**542-48** Large 1/32-1-1/2"

### Sets

**542-2002** Hobby Kit **94.00**
Small spray pattern airbrush, two 1/2oz bottle assemblies, air hose with coupling, airbrush hanger, adjusting wrench, Allen wrench and instructions are all included.

Paasche Airbrush Co.

## VSR

Item listed below is available by Special Order (see Legend Page).

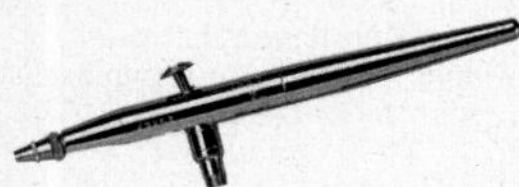

**542-55** VSR90#1 Set **115.00**
This gravity-feed, internal-mix, dual-action brush allows quick color changes using three different size cups, which are included. Cups attach to the top of the brush and swivel to left or right for a clear view of your work, or to fit either hand. Extra needle, aircap and tip are also included for use with heavier materials or broader coverage.

## VL SET

**542-52** Model VL Small Pattern **109.00**

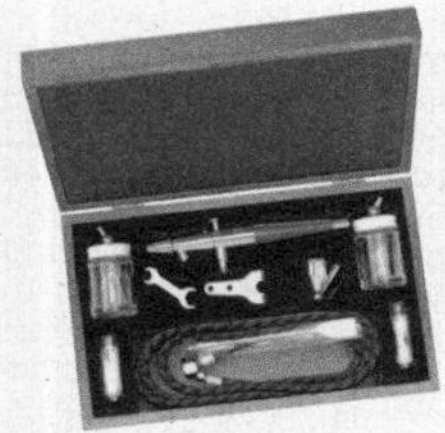

**542-54** Model VL In Wood Box **145.00**
Includes small spray pattern airbrush, plus spray assemblies and needles for medium and large (VL5) applications, 1/4oz (7cc) color cup, 3oz (90ml) and 1oz (30ml) bottle assemblies, 1oz (30ml) plain bottle and cap, hanger, wrench, air hose with couplings, head protector, instructions and parts list.

## H SET

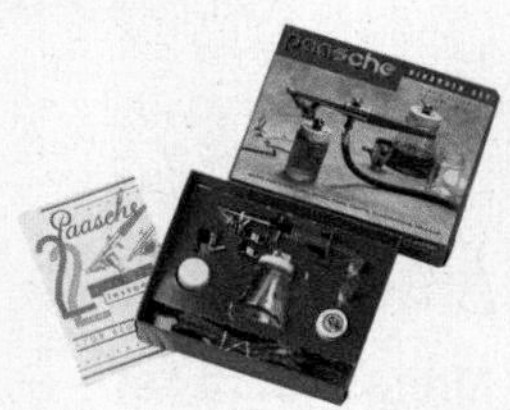

**542-31** Model H Small Pattern **85.00**
Includes small spray pattern, single-action airbrush, 1/4oz (7cc) color cup, 1oz (30ml) bottle assembly, 1oz (30ml) bottle and cap, color adjusting parts, hanger, wrenches, air hose with couplings, aircaps, "22 Airbrush Lessons" instruction booklet and parts list.

## MILLENNIUM

**542-99** Complete Set In Wood Box **145.00**
This double-action, internal-mix, siphon-feed brush features a thin barrel grip that allows for easy pullback of the needle mechanism to clear clogs. A rounded trigger button offers greater comfort and better control. Set includes Medium Airbrush (1/32-1-1/4" spray pattern), 1/4oz color cup, wrench, hanger, storage case and instructions.

## MINI SANDBLAST GUN

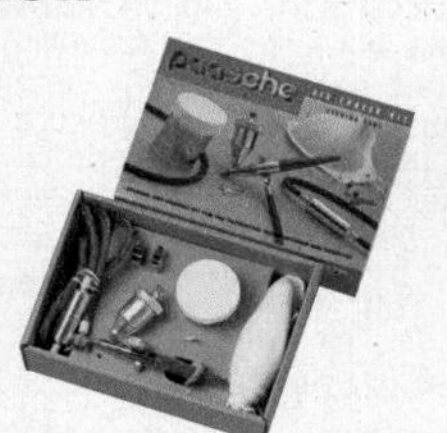

**542-19** Air Eraser Set **104.00**
Etch glass or remove paint and rust. Set includes air eraser, fast cutting compound, air hose with moisture trap, wrench, hanger and five disposable respirators.

### Fast Cut Compound

**542-1905** 5lb **17.00**

**542-1906** 6oz **3.95**

## AIRBRUSH PROPELLANT

Portable, disposable cans of airbrush propellant. Use when a compressor or electricity is not available. Provides air pressure for varying amount of time, depending on brush and type of work. Propellant has no CFCs which harm the ozone layer. To control the air volume between the can and the brush, use the Pressure Tank Valve, sold separately.

**542-6236** Large 11oz (330ml) **11.50**

**542-6238** Small 9oz (255ml) **8.50**

**542-1456** Pressure Tank Valve **7.20**
Use with #6236 or #6238. Controls air volume from tank to airbrush. All-brass construction.

## PAINTING SUPPLIES

### Air Hose

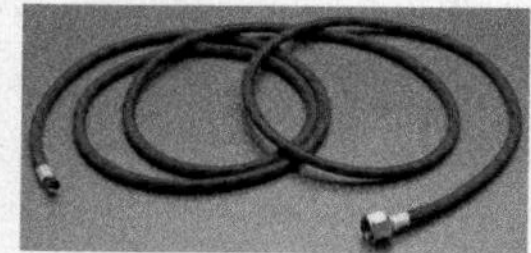

**542-2118** Braided w/Couplings **10.85**
1/8" (3.175mm) diameter, 8' (2.4m) long.

### Moisture Trap

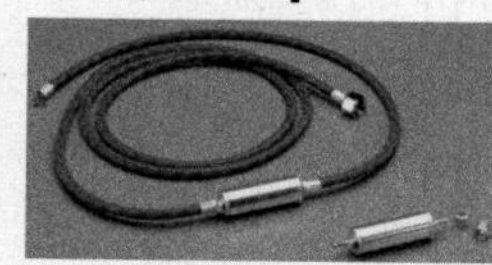

**542-6171 14.50**
Fits 1/8" (3.175mm) air hose to remove moisture from air.

### Regulator

**542-75** In-Line **32.00**
Low pressure unit has a 60 P.S.I. gauge and moisture drain. Easy adjustment of pressure and provides clean, dry air.

## SPRAY BOOTHS

**542-10000 289.00**
Paint safely by venting paint and fumes. Filter removes larger particles, but will not remove hazardous materials, so exhaust should be vented outside. Compact in size: 22" W x 20" D x 16" H and easy to assemble. Provides 80 to 100 LFM air movement. Complete with motor.

### Spray Booth Filters

**542-10001** Polyester **1.75**

**542-10002** Charcoal **5.35**

## REPLACEMENT PARTS & ACCESSORIES

### H Series Airbrushes

#### Aircaps 4.20 ea

**542-5516** For H#1

**542-5518** For H#3

**542-5519** For H#5

#### Color Adjusting Parts 10.95 ea

**542-5381** For H#1 Small

**542-5429** For H#3 Medium

**542-5433** For H#5 Large

#### Needles 6.95 ea

**542-5631** #1 Fine

**542-5633** #3 Medium

**542-5635** #5 Heavy

#### Tips 5.25 ea

**542-5621** For H#1 Small

**542-5623** For H#3 Medium

**542-5625** For H#5 Large

#### Miscellaneous

**542-5387** 1/4oz (7cc) Metal Color Cup **5.40**

**542-1455** "O" Ring pkg(6) **3.95**

### VL/SA Series Airbrushes

#### Aircaps 5.10 ea (Unless Noted)

**542-9561** For VL#1 Small

**542-9563** For VL#3 Medium

**542-9565** For VL#5 Large

#### Airtips 4.60 ea

**542-9553** For VL#1 Small

**542-9554** For VL#3 Medium

**542-9555** For VL#5 Large

#### Color Bottle Assemblies 5.10 ea

**542-9511** 1oz (30ml)

**542-9549** 3oz (90ml)

#### Color Cup

**542-9515** 1/4oz (7cc) **5.40**

#### Multihead Assemblies 12.50 ea

**542-9575** For VL#1 Small

**542-9576** For VL#3 Medium

**542-9577** For VL#5 Large

#### Replacement Needles 4.60 ea

**542-9578** For VL#1 Small

**542-9581** For VL#3 Medium

**542-9583** For VL#5 Large

#### Miscellaneous

**542-174** Finger Lever Assembly **7.40**

#### SA 2000 Needles 5.40 ea

(All other replacement parts for SA2000 are the same as the VL series.)

**542-2631** #1 Fine

**542-2633** #3 Medium

**542-2635** #5 Heavy

### Universal Parts

Parts fit all Paasche airbrushes.

#### Bottles

**542-5388** 3oz (90ml **1.45**

**542-5435** 1oz (30ml) **1.20**

#### Color Bottle Assemblies

**542-5383** 1oz (30ml) **5.10**

**542-5430** 3oz (90ml) **5.25**

#### Gaskets pkg(6) 3.95 ea

**542-3107** For 3oz Cup

**542-5007** For 1oz Cup

#### Instruction Book

**542-99999** 22 Airbrush Lessons for Beginners **2.00**
Teaches the basics of airbrush control along with the proper use of masks, stencils and frisket paper. Easy to follow with illustrated lessons. Included with brushes and sets.

#### Plain Covers .70 ea

Less gaskets.

**542-190** For 3oz Bottle

**542-191** For 1oz Bottle

## COMPRESSORS

**542-63** 1/10 Horsepower **119.00**
An economical unit with oil-less diaphragm, suitable for use with properly thinned fluids. Delivers up to 30 pounds of air and can be used with any airbrush. Equipped with three-wire cord. Delivers .5 CFM at 20 P.S.I. Weighs approximately 12lbs.

WOODLAND SCENICS®

## MINI-SCENE® PAINT SET

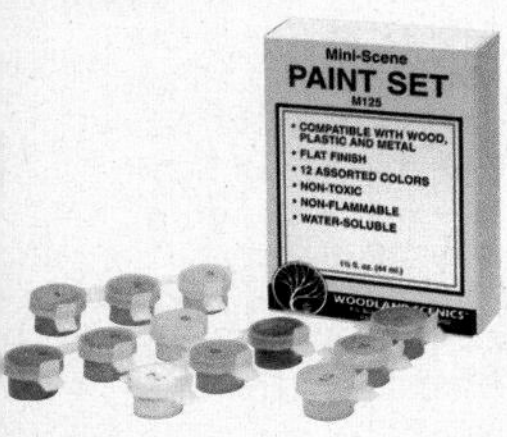


**785-125** Set of 12 **6.98**
For metal details. Set includes 12 assorted colors each 1-1/2 fluid ounces (44ml): red, yellow, blue, black, gray, white, cream, tan, rust, yellow ocher, brown and pewter. Paint is nontoxic, nonflammable and water-soluble.

## TOP COAT

### 4.49 ea

Use full-strength or dilute with water. Color highways, streets and sidewalks with Concrete Top Coat. For blacktop surfaces use Asphalt Top Coat.

**785-1453** Asphalt 4 fl oz
**785-1454** Concrete 4 fl oz

## PEWTER PATINA FINISH

**785-126** 7/8 fl oz (30ml) Bottle **2.29**
Gives any metal the look of a fine pewter casting. Great for figures or special effects. Dealers MUST order multiples of 5.

## EARTH COLOR KIT

**785-1215 18.98**
A simple system for staining rocks, terrain, and plaster castings such as portals. Beginners get quality results. The Earth Color kit includes instructions, applicator, palette and eight one Fluid ounce bottles each of Earth Color, Liquid Pigment (White, Black, Concrete, Stone Gray, Slate Gray, Raw Umber, Burnt Umber and Yellow Ochre).

## UNDERCOAT

### 8 Fluid Ounce Bottle 6.98 ea

Formulated for use under Blended Turf to provide a base color for terrain. Extremely concentrated.

**785-1228** Green

**785-1229** Earth

## MINI-SCENE® GLASS DISPLAY DOME

**785-127** with Plastic Base **11.49**
Perfect for protecting and displaying small scenes, figures and keepsakes. Features plastic base with separate clear glass dome; measures 3" 7.5cm in diameter.

For Daily Product Updates Point Your Browser to
**www.walthers.com**

## EARTH COLORS LIQUID PIGMENTS

### 4 Fluid Ounce Bottle 5.29 ea

Use these eight different pigments to stain rocks, terrain and other plaster castings. They are water-soluble and can be diluted and blended in endless combinations. Extremely concentrated for economical usage.

**785-1216** White

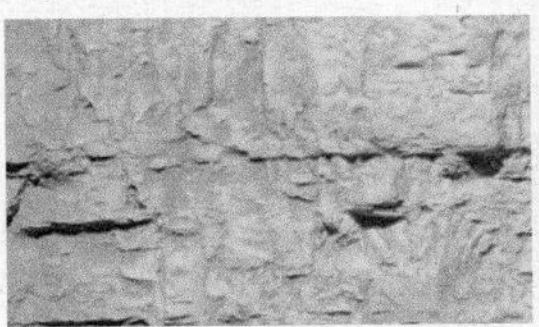
**785-1217** Concrete

**785-1218** Stone Gray

**785-1219** Slate Gray

**785-1220** Black

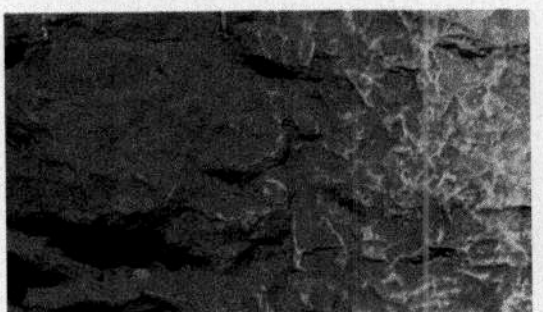
**785-1221** Raw Umber

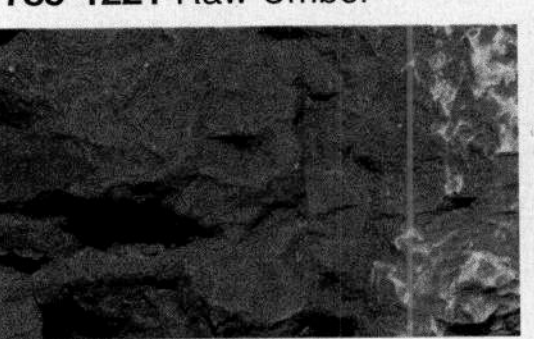
**785-1222** Burnt Umber

**785-1223** Yellow Ocher

# SCALECOAT

Scalecoat I and II and weathering colors also available in 1oz bottles. Please visit Walthers web site at www.walthers.com for a complete listing of all available products.

## SCALECOAT I

### Railroad Colors
### 2oz 60ml 4.19 ea

**640-10012** Locomotive Black (Low Gloss Finish)
**640-10022** Oxide Red (Low Gloss Finish)
**640-10032** Graphite & Oil (Low Gloss Finish)
**640-10052** Smoke Box Gray
**640-10062** Brunswick Green
**640-10082** D&H Yellow
**640-10092** D&H Blue
**640-10102** Black
**640-10112** White
**640-10122** Tuscan Red
**640-10132** Box Car Red
**640-10142** Caboose Red
**640-10152** Reefer Yellow
**640-10162** Reefer Orange
**640-10172** Pullman Green
**640-10182** Coach Olive
**640-10192** SOU Green
**640-10202** MOW Gray
**640-10212** Roof Brown
**640-10222** UP Yellow
**640-10232** Silver
**640-10242** ATSF Blue
**640-10252** GN Green
**640-10262** ATSF Red
**640-10272** IC Orange
**640-10282** SP Dark Gray
**640-10292** SP Scarlet
**640-10302** SP Daylight Orange
**640-10312** SP Daylight Red
**640-10322** UP Harbor Mist Gray
**640-10332** UP Dark Gray
**640-10352** CNW Canary Yellow
**640-10362** CNW Green
**640-10372** B&O Royal Blue
**640-10382** BN Green
**640-10402** DRGW New Orange
**640-10412** EL Gray
**640-10422** EL Maroon
**640-10432** EL Yellow
**640-10452** GN Empire Builder Green
**640-10462** GN Empire Builder Orange
**640-10472** Aluminum
**640-10602** NP Light Green
**640-10612** NP Dark Green
**640-10622** LV Cornell Red
**640-10632** D&H Gray
**640-10652** NYC Light Gray
**640-10662** NYC Dark Gray
**640-10692** CP Tuscan Red
**640-10752** CR Blue
**640-10762** CB&Q Chinese Red
**640-10772** RDG Green
**640-10782** BNSF Orange
**640-10792** BNSF Green
**640-10802** BNSF White
**640-10812** PRR Freight Car Red
**640-10822** N&W Red
**640-10832** MILW Orange
**640-10842** UP Hopper Car Gray
**640-10852** New UP Yellow
**640-10862** NH Hunter Green
**640-10872** Box Car Red #2
**640-10882** Box Car Red #3
**640-10892** CP Rail Bright Red
**640-10902** NH Orange
**640-10912** C&O Blue
**640-11122** Detail Black
**640-11192** Chessie Yellow
**640-11202** PRR Dark Tuscan
**640-11212** Metallic Smoke Box Gray

### Scalecoat Thinner

**640-10487** Can 8oz .24L **4.75**
**640-10499** Can 1qt .95L **9.95**
**640-10502** Bottle 2oz 60mL **2.79**

### Strippers

**640-10568** Paint Remover 16oz .47L **8.95**
**640-10599** Metal Stripper 32oz .48L Can **10.95**

### Coatings

#### Glaze 2oz 60ml 4.19 ea

**640-10512** Flat
**640-10522** Gloss
Semi-gloss finish, with less shine than actual paint finish.

#### Sanding Sealer

**640-10532** Wood Sealer 2oz 60mL **4.19**
**640-10572** Thinner 2oz 60mL Special formula, for use only with #53 Sanding Sealer. **2.79**

### Spray Cans
### 6oz 180ML 6.95 ea

**640-10016** Loco Black
**640-10026** Oxide Red
**640-10036** Graphite & Oil
**640-10056** Smoke Box Gray
**640-10066** PRR Green
**640-10086** D&H Yellow
**640-10096** D&H Blue
**640-10106** Black
**640-10116** White
**640-10126** Tuscan Red
**640-10136** Box Car Red
**640-10146** Caboose Red
**640-10156** Reefer Yellow
**640-10166** Reefer Orange
**640-10176** Pullman Green
**640-10186** Coach Olive
**640-10196** SOU Green
**640-10206** MOW Gray
**640-10216** Roof Brown
**640-10226** UP Yellow
**640-10236** Silver
**640-10246** ATSF Blue
**640-10256** GN Green
**640-10266** ATSF Red
**640-10276** IC Orange
**640-10286** SP Dark Gray
**640-10296** SP Scarlet
**640-10306** SP Daylight Orange
**640-10316** SP Daylight Red
**640-10326** UP Harbor Gray
**640-10336** UP Dark Gray
**640-10356** CNW Yellow
**640-10366** CNW Green
**640-10376** B&O Royal Blue
**640-10386** BN Green
**640-10406** DRGW New Orange
**640-10416** EL Gray
**640-10426** EL Maroon
**640-10436** EL Yellow
**640-10456** GN Empire Green
**640-10466** GN Empire Orange
**640-10476** Aluminum
**640-10606** NP Light Green
**640-10616** NP Dark Green
**640-10626** LV Cornell Red
**640-10636** D&H Gray
**640-10656** NYC Light Gray
**640-10666** NYC Dark Gray
**640-10696** CP Tuscan Red
**640-10756** CR Blue
**640-10766** CB&Q Chinese Red
**640-10776** RDG Green
**640-10786** BNSF Orange
**640-10796** BNSF Green
**640-10806** BNSF White
**640-10816** PRR Freight Car Red
**640-10826** N&W Red
**640-10836** MILW Orange
**640-10846** UP Hopper Gray
**640-10856** New UP Yellow
**640-10866** NH Hunter Green
**640-10876** Box Car Red #2
**640-10886** Box Car Red #3
**640-10896** CP Rail Bright Red
**640-10906** NH Orange
**640-10916** C&O Blue
**640-11126** Detail Black
**640-11196** Chessie Yellow
**640-11206** PRR Dark Tuscan
**640-11216** Metallic Smoke Box Gray

### Glaze 6.95 ea

**640-10516** Flat Glaze
**640-10526** Gloss Glaze

## SCALECOAT II

### Railroad Colors
### 2oz 60ml 4.19 ea

Matching colors formulated especially for use on plastics. Drying time can be decreased by adding Quick-Dry.

**640-20012** Locomotive Black
**640-20022** Oxide Red
**640-20032** Graphite & Oil
**640-20052** Smoke Box Gray
**640-20062** PRR Brunswick Green
**640-20082** D&H Yellow
**640-20092** D&H Blue
**640-20102** Black
**640-20112** White
**640-20122** Tuscan Red
**640-20132** Box Car Red
**640-20142** Caboose Red
**640-20152** Reefer Yellow
**640-20162** Reefer Orange
**640-20172** Pullman Green
**640-20182** Coach Olive
**640-20192** SOU Green
**640-20202** MOW Gray
**640-20212** Roof Brown
**640-20222** UP Yellow
**640-20232** Silver
**640-20242** ATSF Blue
**640-20252** GN Green
**640-20262** ATSF Red
**640-20272** IC Orange
**640-20282** SP Dark Gray
**640-20292** SP Scarlet
**640-20302** SP Daylight Orange
**640-20312** SP Daylight Red
**640-20322** UP Harbor Mist Gray
**640-20332** UP Dark Gray
**640-20352** CNW Yellow
**640-20362** CNW Green
**640-20372** B&O Royal Blue
**640-20382** BN Green
**640-20402** DRGW New Orange
**640-20412** EL Gray
**640-20422** EL Maroon
**640-20432** EL Yellow
**640-20452** GN Empire Builder Green
**640-20462** GN Empire Builder Orange
**640-20472** Aluminum
**640-20602** NP Light Green
**640-20612** NP Dark Green
**640-20622** LV Cornell Red
**640-20632** D&H Gray
**640-20652** NYC Light Gray
**640-20662** NYC Dark Gray
**640-20692** CP Tuscan Red
**640-20752** CR Blue
**640-20762** CB&Q Chinese Red
**640-20772** RDG Green
**640-20782** BNSF Orange
**640-20792** BNSF Green
**640-20802** BNSF White
**640-20812** PRR Freight Car Red
**640-20822** N&W Red
**640-20832** MILW Orange
**640-20842** UP Hopper Car Gray
**640-20852** New UP Yellow
**640-20862** NH Hunter Green
**640-20872** Box Car Red #2
**640-20882** Box Car Red #3
**640-20892** CP Rail Bright Red
**640-20902** NH Orange
**640-20912** C&O Blue
**640-21122** Detail Black
**640-21192** Chessie Yellow
**640-21202** PRR Dark Tuscan
**640-21212** Metallic Smoke Box Gray

### Scalecoat II Thinner

**640-20487** Can 8oz .24L **4.75**
**640-20499** Can 1qt .97L **9.95**
**640-20502** Bottle 2oz 60mL **2.79**

### Quick Dry

**640-10542** Quick-Dry 2oz 60mL **4.19**
Speeds drying time of Scalecoat colors on plastic and wood. Drying time varies.

### Spray Cans
### 6oz 180ML 6.95 ea

**640-20016** Loco Black
**640-20026** Oxide Red
**640-20036** Graphite & Oil
**640-20056** Smoke Box Gray
**640-20066** PRR Green
**640-20086** D&H Yellow
**640-20096** D&H Blue
**640-20106** Black
**640-20116** White
**640-20126** Tuscan Red
**640-20136** Box Car Red
**640-20146** Caboose Red
**640-20156** Reefer Yellow
**640-20166** Reefer Orange
**640-20176** Pullman Green
**640-20186** Coach Olive
**640-20196** SOU Green
**640-20206** MOW Gray
**640-20216** Roof Brown
**640-20226** UP Yellow
**640-20236** Silver
**640-20246** ATSF Blue
**640-20256** GN Green
**640-20266** ATSF Red
**640-20276** IC Orange
**640-20286** SP Dark Gray
**640-20296** SP Scarlet
**640-20306** SP Daylight Orang
**640-20316** SP Daylight Red
**640-20326** UP Harbor Gray
**640-20336** UP Dark Gray
**640-20356** CNW Yellow
**640-20366** CNW Green
**640-20376** B&O Royal Blue
**640-20386** BN Green
**640-20406** DRGW New Oran
**640-20416** EL Gray
**640-20426** EL Maroon
**640-20436** EL Yellow
**640-20456** GN Empire Builder Green
**640-20466** GN Empire Builder Orange
**640-20476** Aluminum
**640-20606** NP Light Green
**640-20616** NP Dark Green
**640-20626** LV Cornell Red
**640-20636** D&H Gray
**640-20656** NYC Light Gray
**640-20666** NYC Dark Gray
**640-20696** CP Tuscan Red
**640-20756** CR Blue
**640-20766** CB&Q Chinese Red
**640-20776** RDG Green
**640-20786** BNSF Orange
**640-20796** BNSF Green
**640-20806** BNSF White
**640-20816** PRR Freight Car Red
**640-20826** N&W Red
**640-20836** MILW Orange
**640-20846** UP Hopper Gray
**640-20856** New UP Yellow
**640-20866** NH Hunter Green
**640-20876** Box Car Red #2
**640-20886** Box Car Red #3
**640-20896** CP Rail Bright Red
**640-20906** NH Orange
**640-20916** C&O Blue
**640-21126** Detail Black
**640-21196** Chessie Yellow
**640-21206** PRR Dark Tuscan
**640-21216** Metallic Smoke Bo Gray

### Color Chart

NEW **640-S222** **No Charge**

See What's Available at **www.walthers.com**

Please visit Walthers Web site at www.walthers.com for a complete listing of all Tamiya paint, brushes and tools.

## NEW PRODUCTS

### Bottled Paint Stand w/4 Alligator Clips

**NEW 865-74077 24.00**
This rotating two-tier paint stand holds paints for easy access. The four supplied alligator clips also allow the unit to be used as a drying stand. (Paints not included).

### Masking Tape

### Tape w/Dispenser

Dimensions shown are tape width.

**NEW 865-87030** 6mm **4.70**
**NEW 865-87031** 10mm **4.80**
**NEW 865-87032** 18mm **6.00**

### Masking Tape Refills

**NEW 865-87033** 6mm **2.40**
**NEW 865-87034** 10mm **2.60**
**NEW 865-87035** 18mm **3.65**

## AIRBRUSH SYSTEM & ACCESSORIES

**865-74520 147.00**
The Spray-Work basic compressor with airbrush is capable of professional-quality paint application. Compressor output is 15psi and the airbrush is capable of spraying wide areas and lines down to about 1/8" 2mm. The kit includes the compressor, airbrush, and 17 and 40cc color cups. The compressor requires a 7.2 battery pack or suitable AC adaptor as a power source (not included).

## SPRAY-WORK PAINTING STAND SET

**865-74522 20.00**
Multi-purpose painting turntable includes four adjustable-width spring clips to hold models. Measures 6-5/16" 16cm diameter

## TAMIYA COLOR

Water-soluble acrylics, suitable for brushing or airbrushing.

### Acrylic 3/4oz (23ml) Bottles 2.80 ea (Unless Noted)

#### Gloss Finish

**865-81001** Black
**865-81002** White
**865-81003** Royal Blue
**865-81004** Blue
**865-81005** Green
**865-81006** Orange
**865-81007** Red
**865-81008** Lemon Yellow
**865-81009** Brown
**865-81010** Gun Metal
**865-81011** Chrome Sliver
**865-81012** Gold Leaf
**865-81013** Metallic Blue
**865-81014** Sky Blue
**865-81015** Light Green
**865-81016** Purple
**865-81017** Pink
**865-81028** Park Green
**865-81031** Titanium Gold **3.75**
**865-81032** Titanium Silver **3.75**
**865-81033** Bronze **3.75**
**865-81034** Metallic Brown **3.75**

#### Flat Finish

**865-81301** Black
**865-81302** White
**865-81303** Yellow
**865-81304** Yellow Green
**865-81305** Green
**865-81306** Copper
**865-81307** Red
**865-81308** Blue
**865-81309** Hull Red
**865-81310** Brown
**865-81311** Japan Navy Green
**865-81312** Japan Navy Gray
**865-81313** Japan Army Green
**865-81314** Japan Army Gray
**865-81315** Flesh
**865-81316** Aluminum
**865-81317** Sea Blue
**865-81318** Medium Blue
**865-81319** Sky Gray
**865-81320** Medium Gray
**865-81321** Sky
**865-81322** RLM Gray
**865-81323** Light Blue
**865-81324** Dark Gray
**865-81325** Light Sea Gray
**865-81326** Deep Green
**865-81327** Black Green
**865-81328** Dark Copper **3.75**
**865-81349** Khaki
**865-81350** Field Blue
**865-81351** Khaki Drab
**865-81352** Earth
**865-81353** Neutral Gray
**865-81354** Dark Sea Gray
**865-81355** Deck Tan
**865-81356** Metallic Gray
**865-81357** Buff
**865-81358** Olive Green
**865-81359** Desert Yellow
**865-81360** Dark Yellow
**865-81361** Dark Green
**865-81362** Olive Drab
**865-81363** German Gray
**865-81364** Red Brown
**865-81365** Field Gray
**865-81366** Light Gray
**865-81367** NATO Green
**865-81368** NATO Brown
**865-81369** NATO Black
**865-81370** Dark Green
**865-81371** Cockpit Green

### Clear Colors 3/4oz (23ml) Bottles 2.80 ea

Special clear tints can be used to create stained glass, turn signals, brake lamps, tinted automobile glass, warning lamps and more. Dries with a clear gloss finish.

**865-81019** Smoke
**865-81023** Clear Blue
**865-81024** Clear Yellow
**865-81025** Clear Green
**865-81026** Clear Orange
**865-81027** Clear Red

### Clear Finish 3/4oz (23ml) Bottles 2.80 ea

**865-81021** Flat Base
Mix with glossy paints to reduce their shine as needed.
**865-81002** Acrylic Clear

### Semi-Gloss Acrylic

**865-81018** Black **2.80**
3/4oz (23ml) bottle.

### Acrylic Thinner

**865-81020** Small (.69oz 23ml) **2.80**
**865-81030** Medium (1.2oz 40ml) **3.20**
**865-81040** Large (7-1/2oz 250ml) **7.50**

### Surface Primer

### Spray Cans 5.4oz 180ml 8.25 ea

Suitable for use on plastic and metal.

**865-87042** Gray
**865-87044** White

### Weathering Products

Adding realistic weathering to your models is as easy as brushing it on with these powders. Sets include three appropriate cakes for special effects such as caked-on mud etc. Mud and Snow Weathering Sticks feature a twist-out brush for easy application.

### Weathering Master Sets 9.25 ea

**865-87079** Set A (Sand, Light Sand, Mud)
**865-87080** Set B (Snow, Soot, Rust)
**865-87085** Set C (Orange Rust, Gun Metal, Silver)
**NEW 865-87088** Set D (Burnt Blue, red, Oil Stain)

### Weathering Sticks 4.40 ea

**865-87081** Mud
**865-87082** Snow
**NEW 865-87086** Sand
**NEW 865-87087** Light Earth

## PAINT BRUSHES

#### Fine-Point Brushes

Kolinsky pointed Sable hair pro modeling brushes feature durable bristles that naturally form a fine point even after frequent use. The handle has an ergonomic design that reduces hand strain during long periods of use.

**865-87071** #1 **23.00**
**865-87072** #0 **22.00**
**865-87073** #00 **21.50**
**865-87074** #000 **20.50**

### Horse Hair

**865-87013** #5 Flat **2.50**
**865-87014** #3 Flat **1.95**
**865-87015** #0 Flat **1.85**
**865-87016** Medium Pointed **2.50**
**865-87017** Small Pointed **3.50**

### Weasel Hair

**865-87018** Medium Pointed **6.75**
**865-87019** Small Pointed **5.75**

*Information*

### Painting Bricks

To start with, choose several color variations of the same basic color that you are going to use for your brick. Depending on the size of the building, five to eight different shades should suffice. Pick one hue as the base color and cover the entire wall with it. Then, using a very small brush, apply the different colors to individual bricks in a random pattern. This will create the realistic, haphazard designs seen on buildings in real life.

After all the bricks have been colored to you liking and are dry, apply an India ink wash. This causes the colors to fade somewhat while still retaining the common color variations. When dry, add a light coat of sealer.

To achieve the look of mortar between the bricks, apply a light or medium gray wash to the brick wall; be quite generous in the application and have many paper towels on hand. Wipe the excess wash off with the paper towels. What is left behind is the gray coloring in the recessed areas between the bricks.

One thing to remember is to use different base colors for different buildings. Buildings are generally built at different times by different contractors, so the supplies will not be the same.

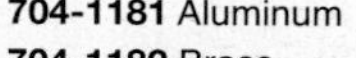

A complete line of colors for railroad, automobile and military modelers. Enamel, acrylic and lacquer formulas are available to meet your painting needs.

## ENAMELS

### Bottles - 1/4oz (7.5ml) 1.49 ea

All-purpose paints are fast drying, easy to apply, and can be used on many different surfaces. Colors are carefully controlled from batch to batch so that each bottle exactly matches the corresponding spray. Use on styrene, ABS plastic, wood, metal, leather, glass, wax and other materials. Colors dry fast to a hard gloss finish (unless noted).

Dealers MUST order multiples of 12.

**704-1103** Red
**704-1104** Dark Red
**704-1108** Light Blue
**704-1110** Medium Blue
**704-1111** Dark Blue
**704-1112** Pale Yellow
**704-1114** Yellow
**704-1116** Cream
**704-1124** Green
**704-1127** Orange
**704-1133** Light Brown
**704-1134** Purple
**704-1138** Gray
**704-1140** Brown
**704-1141** Wood
**704-1144** Gold
**704-1145** White Gloss
**704-1146** Silver
**704-1147** Black Gloss
**704-1149** Flat Black
**704-1150** Flat Red
**704-1151** Copper
**704-1152** Metallic Red

### Brush-On Metal Flake

**704-1529** Ruby Red
**704-1530** Jade Green
**704-1531** Burgundy Purple
**704-1539** Sapphire Blue
**704-1542** Lime Gold

### Military Flat Colors

**704-1162** Sky Blue
**704-1163** Battle Gray
**704-1164** Olive Drab Green
**704-1165** Army Olive
**704-1166** Military Brown
**704-1167** Desert Tan
**704-1168** White
**704-1169** Yellow
**704-1170** Light Tan
**704-1171** Beret Green
**704-1172** Sea Blue
**704-1180** Steel
**704-1181** Aluminum
**704-1182** Brass
**704-1183** Rubber
**704-1184** Zinc Chromate
**704-1185** Rust

## SPRAY ENAMELS

### 3oz (90ml) 4.49 ea

Matching colors for bottled colors in a handy spray can. Dries to hard gloss finish unless noted.

Dealers MUST order multiples of 3.

**704-1203** Red
**704-1204** Dark Red
**704-1208** Light Blue
**704-1210** Bright Blue
**704-1211** Dark Blue
**704-1214** Yellow
**704-1224** Green
**704-1226** Aircraft Gray
**704-1231** Bright Red
**704-1233** Flat Light Gray
**704-1234** Purple
**704-1237** Primer
**704-1238** Gray
**704-1240** Brown
**704-1241** Wood
**704-1244** Gold
**704-1245** White Gloss
**704-1246** Silver
**704-1247** Black Gloss
**704-1249** Flat Black
**704-1250** Flat Red
**704-1251** Copper
**704-1257** Transparent Blue
**704-1258** Flat White
**704-1261** Glosscote
**704-1265** Flat Olive Drab

### Spray Custom Colors

**704-1601** Candy Emerald Green
**704-1605** Candy Apple Red
**704-1607** Candy Hot Rod Red
**704-1617** Candy Grape
**704-1628** Competition Orange

### Spray Metal Flake

**704-1629** Ruby Red
**704-1630** Jade Green
**704-1631** Burgundy Purple
**704-1639** Sapphire Blue
**704-1642** Lime Gold

### Chrome Spray

**704-1290** Chrome Silver

### Automotive Enamels

**704-1801** Cherry Red
**704-1804** Blue Pearl Metallic
**704-1813** Black Pearl

## MODEL MASTER

### FS Enamels 1/2oz (15ml) Bottles 2.99 ea (Unless Noted)

FS Series colors match Federal Standard number indicated. Bottled paints are specially formulated for airbrushing, with popular colors also offered in spray cans.

Dealers MUST order in multiples of 6.

**704-1701** Military Brown (FS 30117)
**704-1702** Field Drab (FS 30118)
**704-1704** Armor Sand (FS 30277)
**704-1705** Insignia Red (FS 31136)
**704-1706** Sand (FS 33531)
**704-1707** Chrome Yellow (FS 13538)
**704-1708** Insignia Yellow (FS 33538)
**704-1709** Radome Tan (FS 33613)
**704-1710** Dark Green (FS 34079)
**704-1711** Olive Drab (FS 34087)
**704-1712** Field Green (FS 34097)
**704-1713** Medium Green (FS 34102)
**704-1714** Forest Green (FS 34127)
**704-1715** Interior Green (FS 34151)
**704-1716** Pale Green (FS 34227)
**704-1717** Dark Sea Blue (FS 15042)
**704-1718** Flat Sea Blue (FS 35042)
**704-1719** Insignia Blue (FS 35044)
**704-1720** Intermediate Blue (FS 35164)
**704-1721** Medium Gray (FS 35237)
**704-1722** Duck Egg Blue (FS 35622)
**704-1723** Gunship Gray (FS 36118)
**704-1725** Neutral Gray (FS 36270)
**704-1726** Light Sea Gray (FS 36307)
**704-1728** Light Ghost Gray (FS 36375)
**704-1729** Gloss Gull Gray (FS 16440)
**704-1730** Flat Gull Gray (FS 36440)
**704-1731** Aircraft Gray (FS 16473)
**704-1732** Light Gray (FS 36495)
**704-1733** Camouflage Gray (FS 36622)
**704-1734** Green Zinc Chromate
**704-1735** Wood
**704-1736** Leather
**704-1740** Dark Gull Gray (FS 36231)
**704-1741** Dark Ghost Gray (FS 36320)
**704-1742** Dark Tan (FS 30219)
**704-1744** Gold
**704-1745** Insignia White (FS 17875)
**704-1747** Gloss Black (FS 17038)
**704-1749** Flat Black (FS 37038)
**704-1764** Euro Dark Green (FS 34092)
**704-1768** Flat White (FS 37875)
**704-1772** Blue Angel Blue (FS 15050)
**704-1775** Fluorescent Red (FS 28915)
**704-1780** Steel
**704-1781** Aluminum
**704-1782** Brass
**704-1785** Rust
**704-1786** Medium Field Green (FS 34095)
**704-1787** Green Drab (FS 34086)
**704-1788** Euro 1 Gray (FS 36081)
**704-1790** Chrome Silver (FS 17178)
**704-1791** Navy Gloss Gray (FS 16081)
**704-1792** SAC Bomber Tan (FS 34201)
**704-1793** SAC Bomber Green (FS 34159)
**704-1794** Navy Aggressor Gray (FS 36251)
**704-1795** Gunmetal
**704-1796** Jet Exhaust
**704-2021** Tan (FS 20400)
**704-2022** International Orange (FS 12197 - Gloss)
**704-2023** Blue Angels Yellow (FS 13655 - Gloss)
**704-2024** US Army Helo Drab (FS 34031)
**704-2025** Marine Corps Green (FS 34052)

**704-2026** Dark Drab (B-52 FS 24091- Semi-Gloss)
**704-2027** Dark Green (B-52 FS 34096)
**704-2028** Willow Green (FS 14187 - Gloss)
**704-2029** Green (FS 34258)
**704-2030** True Blue (FS 15102 - Gloss)
**704-2031** Blue (FS 35109)
**704-2032** Bright Blue (FS 35183)
**704-2033** Blue (FS 35414)
**704-2034** Engine Gray (FS 36076)
**704-2035** Air Mobility Command Gray (FS 36173)
**704-2036** Dark Gray (F-15 FS 36176)
**704-2037** Flint Gray (FS 36314)
**704-2038** Light Gray (FS 36492)
**704-2039** Canadian Voodoo Gray (FS 16515)
**704-2040** Aircraft Interior Black (FS 37031)
**704-2041** Fluorescent Red-Orange (FS 28913-Semi Gloss)

### Figure Colors
Special flat colors for skin tones and uniforms.
**704-2001** Skin Tone-Light Base
**704-2002** Skin Tone-Dark Base
**704-2003** Skin Tone-Warm Tint
**704-2004** Skin Tone-Shadow Tint
**704-2005** Burnt Umber
**704-2006** Raw Umber
**704-2007** Burnt Sienna
**704-2008** Raw Sienna
**704-2009** British Crimson
**704-2010** Piping Pink
**704-2011** Cadmium Yellow Light
**704-2012** Cobalt Blue
**704-2013** Napoleonic Violet
**704-2014** German Uniform Feldgrau
**704-2015** Flat Clear Lacquer **3.99**
**704-2016** Semi-Gloss Clear Lacquer **3.99**
**704-2017** Gloss Clear Lacquer **3.99**
**704-2018** Thinner **3.99**

### Decal Solutions
**704-2145** Solvent
**704-2146** Setting

### World War II United States & Royal Air Force
**704-2048** RAF Azure Blue (ANA 609)
**704-2049** RAF Sky Type "S" (ANA 610)
**704-2050** Olive Drab (ANA 613)
**704-2051** Faded Olive Drab
**704-2052** RAF Middlestone (ANA 615)
**704-2053** Sand (ANA 616)
**704-2054** Dark Earth (ANA 617)
**704-2055** Navy Blue Gray
**704-2056** RAF Dark Slate Grey
**704-2057** RAF Ocean Gray
**704-2058** RAF Medium Sea Grey
**704-2059** RAF Dark Sea Gray
**704-2060** RAF Dark Green
**704-2061** RAF P.R.U. Blue
**704-2062** RAF Interior Green
**704-2063** RAF Trainer Yellow

### World War II Italian Colors
**704-2110** Sand
**704-2111** Dark Brown
**704-2112** Olive Green
**704-2113** Blue Gray

### World War II German Luftwaffe
These semi-gloss colors match the RLM specifications for camouflage colors used on German Aircraft during World War II.
**704-2071** Grun (RLM 02)
**704-2072** Gelb (RLM 04)
**704-2073** Rot (RLM 23)
**704-2074** Dunkelblau (RLM 24)
**704-2075** Dunkelbraun (RLM 61)
**704-2076** Grun (RLM 62)
**704-2077** Licthgrau (RLM 63)
**704-2078** Hellblau (RLM 65)
**704-2079** Schwarzgrau (RLM 66)
**704-2080** Schwarzgrun (RLM 70)
**704-2081** Dunkelgrun (RLM 71)
**704-2082** Grun (RLM 72)
**704-2083** Grun (RLM 73)
**704-2084** Graugrun (RLM 74)
**704-2085** Grauviolett (RLM 75)
**704-2086** Licthblau (RLM 76)
**704-2087** Hellblau (RLM 78)
**704-2088** Sandgelb (RLM 79)
**704-2089** Olivgrun (RLM 80)
**704-2090** Braunviolett (RLM 81)
**704-2091** Dunkelgrun (RLM 82)
**704-2092** Licthgrun (RLM 83)

### World War II German Panzer Colors
**704-2094** Schwarzgrau (1939-43 RAL 7021)
**704-2095** Panzer Dunkelgelb
**704-2096** Schokololaden-braun (1943 RAL 8017)
**704-2097** Panzer Olivgrun 1943
**704-2098** Afrika Khakibraun 1941 (RAL 7008)
**704-2099** Afrika Grunbraun 1941 (RAL 8000)
**704-2100** Signalbraun (RAL 8002)
**704-2101** Anthracitgrau (RAL 7016)
**704-2102** Afrika Braun 1942 (RAL 8020)
**704-2103** Afrika Dunkelgrau 1942 (RAL 7027)
**704-2104** Panzer Interior Buff-Semi-Gloss

### World War II French Colors
**704-2105** Dark Blue Gray
**704-2106** Khaki
**704-2107** Chestnut
**704-2108** Earth Brown
**704-2109** Light Blue Gray

### World War II Japanese Colors
**704-2114** Imperial Japanese Army Green
**704-2115** Imperial Japanese Army Light Gray
**704-2116** Imperial Japanese Navy Green
**704-2117** Imperial Japanese Navy Gray
**704-2118** Deep Yellow
**704-2119** Interior Metallic Blue

### World War II Russian Colors
**704-2120** Topside Gray
**704-2121** Underside Gray
**704-2122** Topside Green
**704-2123** Underside Blue
**704-2124** Earth Brown
**704-2125** Earth Gray
**704-2126** Topside Blue
**704-2127** Marker Red
**704-2128** Marker Yellow
**704-2129** Russian Armor Green

### Modern Russian Colors
All colors have a semi-gloss finish.
**704-2130** Flanker Pale Blue
**704-2131** Flanker Medium Blue
**704-2132** Flanker Blue/Gray
**704-2133** Fulcrum Gray
**704-2134** Fulcrum Gray/Green
**704-2135** Interior Blue/Green

### Modern Armor (Gulf War) Colors
**704-2136** US Army/Marines Gulf Armor Sand
**704-2137** British Gulf Armor Light Stone
**704-2138** Israeli Armor Sand/Gray

### Tint Whites
**704-2142** Flat White (FS 37295)
**704-2143** Semi-Gloss White (RLM 21)
**704-2144** Gloss White (FS 17295)

### Automotive Enamels
**704-2702** Arctic Blue Metallic
**704-2709** Light Ivory
**704-2710** Sand Beige
**704-2711** Anthracite Gray Metallic
**704-2712** Graphite Metallic
**704-2713** Black Metallic
**704-2714** German Silver Metallic
**704-2715** French Blue
**704-2716** British Green Metallic
**704-2717** Bright Yellow
**704-2718** Guards Red
**704-2719** Italian Red
**704-2720** Classic White
**704-2721** Classic Black
**704-2723** Turn Signal Amber
**704-2724** Stop Light Red
**704-2725** Header Flat White
**704-2726** Ford Engine Light Blue
**704-2727** Ford/GM Engine Blue
**704-2728** Pontiac Engine Blue
**704-2729** Oldsmobile Engine Blue
**704-2730** Chrysler Engine Blue
**704-2731** Chevy Engine Red
**704-2732** Chrysler Engine Red
**704-2733** Ford Engine Red
**704-2734** Silver Chrome Trim
**704-2735** Black Chrome Trim
**704-2736** Clear Top Coat
**704-2737** Gray Primer
**704-2738** Flat Interior Tan
**704-2739** Flat Interior Gray
**704-2740** Semi-Gloss Black
**704-2750** Plum Crazy
**704-2755** Hot Magenta
**704-2757** Panther Pink
**704-2764** Grabber Blue
**704-2765** Turquoise
**704-2767** Sublime Green
**704-2770** Go Mango

### Spray Enamels 3oz (90ml) 4.99 ea
Dealers MUST order multiples of 3.
**704-1910** Dark Green (FS 34079)
**704-1911** Olive Drab (FS 34087)
**704-1913** Medium Green (FS 34102)
**704-1917** Dark Sea Blue (FS 15042)
**704-1920** Intermediate Blue (FS 35164)
**704-1923** Gunship Gray (FS 36118)
**704-1926** Light Sea Gray (FS 37307)
**704-1929** Gloss Gull Gray (FS 16440)
**704-1930** Flat Gull Gray (FS 36440)
**704-1933** Camouflage Gray (FS 36622)
**704-1942** Dark Tan (FS 30219)
**704-1947** Gloss Black (FS 17038)
**704-1949** Flat Black (FS 37038)
**704-1950** Panzer Gray (FS 36076)
**704-1954** Light Earth (FS 30140)
**704-1955** Afrika Mustard (FS 30266)
**704-1972** Blue Angel Blue (FS 15050)
**704-1988** Euro 1 Gray (FS 36081)
**704-1992** SAC Bomber Tan (FS 34201)
**704-1993** SAC Bomber Green (FS 34159)
**704-1994** Navy Aggressor Gray (FS 36251)

### Automotive Colors
**704-2901** Silver Blue Metallic
**704-2902** Arctic Blue Metallic
**704-2905** Burgundy Red Metallic
**704-2909** Light Ivory
**704-2910** Sand Beige
**704-2913** Black Metallic
**704-2914** German Silver Metallic
**704-2915** French Blue
**704-2916** British Green Metallic
**704-2917** Bright Yellow
**704-2918** Guards Red
**704-2919** Italian Red
**704-2920** Classic White
**704-2921** Classic Black
**704-2922** Champagne Gold Metallic
**704-2936** Clear Top Coat
**704-2937** Gray Primer
**704-2938** Racing Orange
**704-2939** Racing Red
**704-2940** Racing Blue
**704-2942** 1950s Aqua
**704-2943** Bright White
**704-2944** Gloss Pearl Clear Coat
**704-2945** Turquoise Metallic
**704-2947** Deep Pearl Purple
**704-2948** White Primer
**704-2949** Transparent Black Window Tint
**704-2950** Plum Crazy
**704-2955** Hot Magenta
**704-2957** Panther Pink
**704-2964** Grabber Blue
**704-2965** Turquoise
**704-2967** Sublime Green
**704-2970** Go Mango

### Clear Finish - Enamel
**704-1960** Flat
**704-1961** Gloss

### Thinner - Enamel

Dealers MUST order multiples of 12.

**704-1148** 1/4oz (7.5ml) Bottle **1.49**

**704-1156** 1-3/4oz (52.5ml) Bottle **2.89**

### Paint Marker Sets pkg(3) 10.49 ea

#### Enamel

These easy-to-use, fast-drying markers provide a glossy appearance and are highly pigmented for superior coverage.

**704-25001** Gloss Black, Gloss White, Gloss Red

**704-25002** Flat Black, Gloss Blue, Gloss Yellow

**704-25003** Gloss Black, Gold, Silver

### Paint Markers 3.99 ea

Perfect for painting small parts, doing touch-up and more. Colors match PLA Enamels and sprays. Fast drying, with double chisel tip for fine lines or bold strokes. 1/3oz.

Dealers MUST order multiples of 6.

#### Enamel

**704-2503** Gloss Red
**704-2508** Gloss Light Blue
**704-2511** Gloss Dark Blue
**704-2514** Gloss Yellow
**704-2524** Gloss Green
**704-2527** Gloss Orange
**704-2538** Gloss Gray
**704-2540** Gloss Brown
**704-2544** Metallic Gold
**704-2545** Gloss White
**704-2546** Metallic Silver
**704-2547** Gloss Black
**704-2549** Flat Black
**704-2575** Fluorescent Red

### Model Master Metalizer Lacquer

Recreate virtually any natural metal finish on plastic models using these special lacquer colors. Designed for airbrush application only, colors are premixed in Buffing (which can be polished to various degrees of sheen) or Nonbuffing types.

#### Buffing 1/2oz (15ml) Bottle 3.49 ea

Dealers MUST order multiples of 6.

**704-1401** Aluminum Plate
**704-1402** Stainless Steel
**704-1403** Magnesium
**704-1404** Titanium
**704-1405** Gunmetal
**704-1406** Exhaust
**704-1412** Dark Anodonic Gray
**704-1415** Burnt Metal

#### Buffing Spray 3Ooz (90ml) 5.25 ea

Same great colors in easy to use spray cans.

Dealers MUST order multiples of 3.

**704-1451** Aluminum Plate
**704-1452** Stainless Steel
**704-1453** Magnesium
**704-1454** Titanium
**704-1455** Gunmetal
**704-1459** Metalizer Sealer

#### Nonbuffing 1/2oz (15ml) Bottle 3.49 ea

Dealers MUST order multiples of 6.

**704-1417** Brass
**704-1418** Aluminum
**704-1420** Steel
**704-1423** Gunmetal
**704-1424** Burnt Iron

### Metalizer Thinner & Sealer 3.99 ea

Special formulas for use with Metalizer colors. 1-3/4oz (52.5ml) bottle.

Dealers MUST order multiples of 12.

**704-1409** Sealer
**704-1419** Thinner

## PAINT SETS

**704-9120** Auto Detail **12.49**
Get a new model builder revved up for his or her first project with this set. Complete with six 1/4oz bottles of paint, 1/4oz bottle of thinner, paint brush, cement pen for clean and easy application of model glue and a handy storage tray.

**704-9121** Aircraft **12.49**
Make ready on the flight deck with this starter set! Comes with six 1/4oz bottles of paint, 1/4oz bottle of thinner, paint brush, cement pen to make gluing easier and a storage tray.

**704-9131** Military Flats **12.49**
Black, blue, gray, green, brown, tan, white and blue.

**704-9132** Fluorescent **10.49**

**704-9146** Promotional Paint Set **10.49**

**704-9116** Standard Finishing - Model Building **12.49**

### Acrylic Spray Sets

Sets include five 1/4oz nontoxic colors, 1/2oz primer, propellant and spray cap.

**704-9215** Model Car **19.99**

**704-9216** Military Aircraft **19.99**

**704-9135** Model Car Refill Set **12.99**

**704-9136** Model Aircraft Refill Set **12.99**

### Acrylic Pot Sets

Each includes a paint brush and mixing tray.

#### Hobby Craft

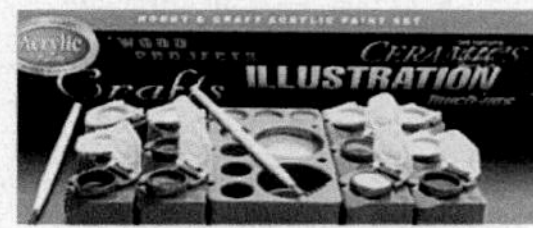

**704-9184** 12 Colors **6.85**

**704-9186** 18 Colors **7.99**

#### Model Car

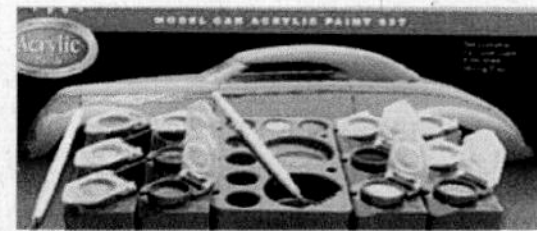

**704-9185** 12 Colors **6.85**

### Supplies Kit

**704-9111** Model Building Supplies Kit **10.49**
Drop cloth, three brushes, hobby knife, five gluing tips and five sanding films.

### Plastic Model Finishing Kits 23.99 ea (Unless Noted)

11 bottles of enamel, bottle thinner, tube plastic cement, putty, broad tip brush, fine tip brush, 1/4" (.6cm) brush, hobby knife, drop cloth, three gluing tips, five sanding films and plastic tray.

**704-9160** Flat
**704-9161** Gloss
**704-9115** Enamel Set - Small **10.49**
Red, yellow, blue, silver, white and black, plus brush.

### Clear Finish

#### Dullcote

A protective, transparent lacquer that dries dead flat without altering the color.

**704-1160** 1-3/4oz 52.5ml **2.89**
Dealers MUST order Dealer Pack of 12.

**704-1260** Spray 3oz 90ml **4.49**
Dealers MUST order multiples of 3.

#### Glosscote

Clear lacquer dries to a transparent, high-gloss protective finish that does not alter the color.

**704-1161** Bottle 1-3/4oz 52.5ml **2.89**
Dealers MUST order multiples of 12.

**704-1261** Spray 3oz 90ml **4.49**
Dealers MUST order multiples of 3.

### Lacquer Brush Cleaner

**704-1159** 1oz 30ml Bottle **2.89**
Use with Clear and Dull Coat.

Dealers MUST order multiples of 6.

### Decal Setting Solution

Softens decal film to conform to surface details.

**704-8804** 1/4oz 7.5ml **1.49**
Dealers MUST order Dealer pack of 12.

**704-1737** 1/2oz 15ml **2.99**
Dealers MUST order Dealer pack of 6

## PAINT BRUSHES

Applying colors, highlighting fine details, weathering, washes, drybrushing and mar other painting jobs are easy with this complete selection of brushes. Choose from natural and synthetic hairs in various shapes and sizes.

### Round 4.79 ea

**704-8731** #3
**704-8732** #0
**704-8733** #2

### Flat

**704-8734** 5/16" **4.79**

### Model Master

These top quality brushes help insure professional results. All Model Master brushes are made with solid birch handles and seamless nickel-plated ferrules.

Dealers MUST order multiples of 12.

#### Sable

**704-8841** #2 Red Sable Roun **5.79**
For fine detail work and pinpoint washes.

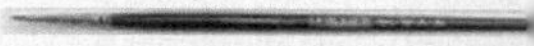

**704-8842** #3/0 Red Sable Round **5.25**
For precise, small scale work.

**704-8861** 1/2" Black Sable Fla **8.39**
For broad color applications and washes.

#### Camel

**704-8851** 3/8" Camel Hair Fla **7.89**
Soft, fine bristles designed for high-gloss finishes.

#### Synthetic

**704-8831** #2 Round **5.25**
Fine tip and good body, for painting small assemblies.

**704-8832** #0 Round **5.49**
Durable bristles and fine point are ideal for applying liquid cement.

**704-8833** 1/4" Chisel **7.39**
Use for blending, such as secondary camouflage patterns.

### Shed Proof Synthetic

Unique brushes feature nylon bristles stapled in the tip to keep them from falling out.

Dealers MUST order multiples of 12.

### Individual Brushes

**704-8701** Broad Tip **.99**

**704-8702** Fine Tip **.99**

**704-8705** 1/4" Tip **1.69**

### Sets

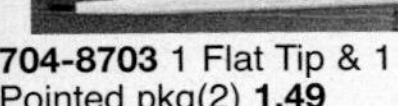

**704-8703** 1 Flat Tip & 1 Pointed pkg(2) **1.49**

**704-8704** 2 Flat & 1 Pointed pkg(3) **1.79**

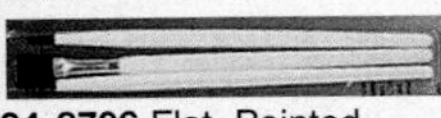

**704-8706** Flat, Pointed 1-1/4" Tips pkg(3) **1.99**

## AIRBRUSHES

**CAUTION:**
For your safety, the use of a properly vented spray booth and a respirator which is paint mist and vapor compatible is strongly recommended when painting with an airbrush.

### Testors Airbrush Sets

Use standard paint bottles to supply color and speed color changes. Spray width is adjusted by turning nozzle. Volume can be changed by raising or lowering bottle.

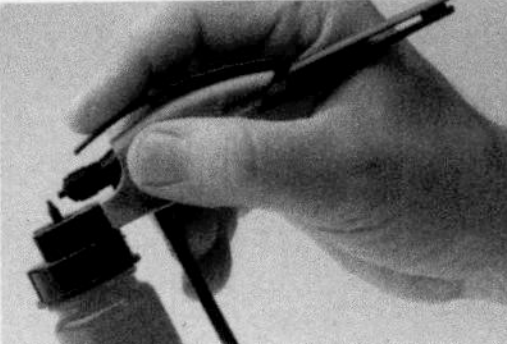

**704-8814** Multi-Purpose Paint Sprayer **17.99**
Perfect for covering large areas with almost any paint or stain. This external-mix, single-action sprayer comes with a 2oz bottle.

### Aztek Airbrushes

Easy to use and maintain. Available in both single- and dual-action, as well as internal or external mix. Bodies are acetal resin, which is impervious to solvents, lightweight and nearly unbreakable.

### External Mix

Fully assembled, single-action, with 6' air hose.

**Model 1220**

**704-2203** Set **29.99**

**704-2206** Set w/6oz Can Ozone-Safe Propellant **39.99**
Includes airbrush, two 1/2oz (15cc) bottles, 28mm quick change cap, compressor adapter and instructions.

**Model A270**

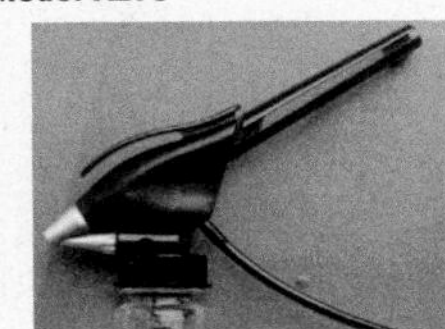

**704-2705** Set **49.99**

**704-2706** Set w/6oz Can Ozone-Safe Propellant **52.99**
Includes airbrush, 28 and 33mm bottle/cap assemblies, compressor adapter, instruction book and video.

**Model A320**

**704-3205** Set **64.99**

**704-3208** Set w/6oz Can Ozone-Safe Propellant **74.99**
Includes airbrush, general detail nozzle (.53mm), 28 and 33mm siphon caps and bottles, compressor adapter, video and instruction book.

### Internal Mix

Superb control, with interchangeable nozzles. Paint travels through the nozzle, not the body, so only the nozzles need to be cleaned. Gravity feed color cup can be positioned for right or left hand. Dual-action brushes are fully assembled and include air hose.

**Model A470**

**704-4702** Set w/Plastic Storage Case **119.95**

**704-4709** Set w/Wooden Storage Case **199.99**
Includes airbrush with 15' air hose, fine, medium and large nozzles, 2.5, 3 and 7.5cc gravity feed color cups, 28 and 33mm siphon bottles and caps, aircan hose adapter, instruction manual and video, plus storage case.

**Model A430**

**704-4305** Set w/Plastic Storage Case **99.95**

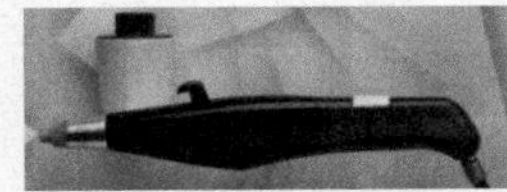

**704-4308** Set w/Wooden Storage Case **129.99**
Includes airbrush with 10' hose, general detail, medium coverage and large coverage nozzles, 7.5cc gravity feed color cup, 28 and 33mm siphon bottles and caps, instruction manual and video, plus storage case.

### Metal Airbrush Kits

**704-4809** With Wooden Storage Case **249.99**
Includes metal-body airbrush, hose, six nozzles, four paint cups, 28 and 33mm siphon cap and jars, cleaning tool, nozzle wrench and detailed instructional video.

### Complete Airbrush System

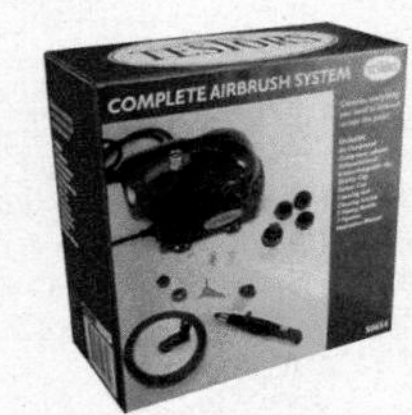


**704-50654** **229.99**
Includes double-action airbush and hose, general purpose nozzle, high flow nozzle, acrylic general nozzle, acrylic high-flow nozzle, 12cc gravity feed cup, 28mm siphon cap, four 1/2oz bottles, pipette, cleaning station, compressor adapter, blue-mini compressor, and instruction manual.

## AIR COMPRESSORS

### Aztek

**704-50201** AC100 **299.99**
Features 1/8 horsepower, 1.58 CFM, 35 P.S.I. maximum pressure, oil-less diaphragm, 1/4 NPS air hose fitting and an on/off switch. 110V, .8 amps.

**704-50202** AC200 **349.99**
Delivers up to 25lbs of air. Built-in moisture trap and pressure gauge. Rubber feet minimize vibration and noise with oil-less operation, fan cooling and built-in thermal protection switch. Two-year guarantee and10,000 hour service life.

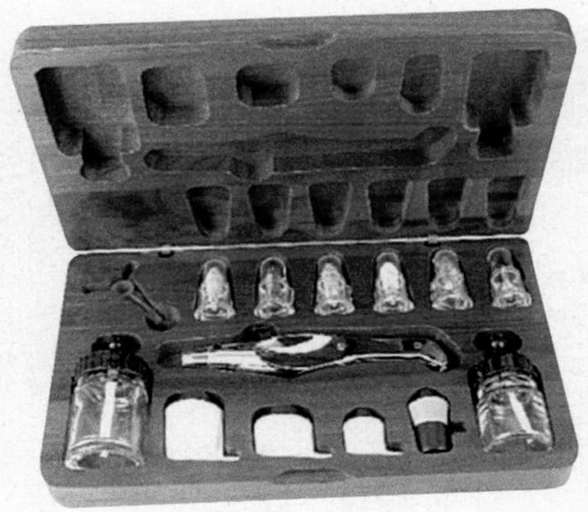

Metal Airbrush Kits With Wooden Storage Case 704-4809

Air Compressor Aztek AC100 704-50201

AC 500 Compressor 704-50205

**704-50205** AC 500 **399.99**
Features a pressure holding tank with an automatic pressure switch, allowing the unit to maintain constant pressure while reducing pulsing. Feature 1/8 horsepower, 1.58 CFM, 32 psi maximum pressure, an air pressure auto-shutoff switch, air pressure gauge and a pressure holding tank with a water drain valve. 110V, .08 amps; weight: 16-1/2lbs.

## Blue Mini Compressor

**704-50204 129.99**
Styled in an "ice blue" transparent case, this UL-approved, 110V mini compressor feature oil-less operation, 0.18 CFM, approximately 20psi, 6' power cord, and a fan-cooled motor.

Blue Mini Compressor 704-50204

# COMPRESSOR ACCESSORIES

## Regulator & Moisture Trap

**704-50680 99.99**
Built-in regulator to increase or decrease pressure. Moisture trap dries air. Fully assembled.

## Pressure Gauge

**704-50681 29.99**
Large, easy-to-read black and white markings. Fully assembled, fits most compressors.

## Spray Booth

**704-50210 599.99**
20W x 15D x 14H"
50 x 37.5 x 35cm
Powered fan collects overspray in three-stage filter system and vents vapors. Mounting brackets provided for additional lighting (sold separately).

# AIRBRUSH ACCESSORIES

## Air Hose 10'

**704-9311** Straight **16.99**
**704-9312** Coiled **25.99**

## Adapter

**704-9313** Air Can Hose Adapter **10.49**

## Siphon Caps & Bottles

**704-9314** 33mm **7.99**
**704-9319** 28mm **6.99**
**704-9326** Bottles 1/2oz pkg(2) **6.99**
**704-9327** Bottles 2/3ozpkg(2) **6.99**

## Aztek Nozzles 11.99 ea (Unless Noted)

**704-9304** Fineline (.30mm)
**704-9305** General Coverage (.40mm)
**704-9306** High Flow (.50mm)
**704-9342** General (.53mm)
**704-9343** Medium (.70mm)
**704-9344** Large (1.02mm)
**704-9302** Nozzle Set 4 Assorted **44.99**

## Acrylic Paint Nozzles 11.99 ea

**704-9307** .40mm Spatter
**704-9340** General (.30mm)
**704-9341** High Flow (.40mm)

## Cleaning Station

**704-9315** Airbrush Cleaning Station **34.99**
Convenient, environmentally sound way to clean your airbrush. Simply insert in the adjustable neck and spray. Solvent passes through the nozzle, then through a filter and is trapped in the jar.

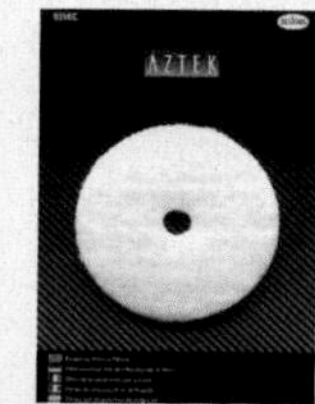


**704-9316** Replacement Filters for #9315 **13.99**

## Color Cups

**704-9308** 1.0cc Side Feed **3.69**
**704-9309** 2.5cc Side Cup **3.69**
**704-9310** 8.0cc Side Cup **4.75**
**704-9303** Color Cup Set **11.99**
**704-9346** 12cc Top Feed **4.75**

**704-9347** 3.0cc **3.69**
**704-9348** 7.5cc **3.69**
**704-9349** 12.0cc **4.75**

## Model Master

### Pipettes

**704-50642** pkg(6) **4.75**
Transfer color or thinner for mixing custom colors. Plastic, easy to clean and reusable.

### Masking

**704-50622** Modeling Tape **7.35**
1/2" x 20' 1.25cm x 6m
For sharp separations between colors. Light adhesive will not lift paint under normal use.

### Propellant

**704-8822** 15oz 450ml **14.99**
Ozone-safe air supply with fittings. For any airbrush designed to accept propellant cans.

## T-Connector

**704-50682 19.99**

Models and Photo by Fred Terrell

What does it take to keep a railroad running? Most folks would probably answer locomotives. Some would point out coal and water, for nothing would move without either of those. Others might point to passing freight cars as a source of revenue that makes it possible for the line to buy all of these important supplies and equipment. Outside of the folks who work there, very few shippers or the traveling public would even think about the backshops. But here, every piece of equipment from the simplest hand tools to the President's private car can be overhauled and returned to duty good as new.

Just about ready to return to duty, we're standing inside Fred Terrell's scratchbuilt machine shop for a look at an Athearn flat car. Spotted alongside the Atlas track, which runs through the building, you can see a wide range of machinery and other details made from K&S Tubing and Evergreen Styrene. A couple of Preiser figures are on hand to pose for the company photographer. The building is made from balsa wood, with plaster outer walls to simulate stonework. One wall and the roof can be removed to showcase the full interior.

Having the right tools for the jobs along your model railroad can keep things moving smoothly too! Whether you're working with small parts, cutting rail, scratchbuilding, soldering or hundreds of other jobs, you'll find a wide selection of helpful items inside this section.

## A.J. FRICKO COMPANY

Items listed below are available by Special Order (see Legend Page).

### Pinhole Lens For 35mm SLR Camera* 229.00 ea

Focusing pinhole lens with colens to overcome fuzziness.

*Must have a camera with removable lens. Pinhole lens fits onto a camera body.

Lens features:

- 0.018" diameter aperture
- 105 f/stop
- etched in stainless steel
- a much sharper image
- a brighter viewing screen
- a shorter exposure time
- depth of field from 1" to infinity

**274-842** Canon
Manual focus camera body.

**274-843** Konica

**274-844** Minolta
Manual focus camera body.

**274-845** Nikon
Either manual or auto focus camera body.

**274-846** Olympus

**274-847** Pentax K
Bayonet mount, also works for Ricoh.

**274-848** Pentax S
Universal screw mount for all screw mount body types.

**274-849** Yashica/Contax

**274-851** Minolta Maxxum

**274-852** Canon EOS

## ARISTO-CRAFT

### HO Stationary Rollers

Great for breaking in your new locomotive and testing all of its features. Rollers can also be used to troubleshoot mechanical problems and work in lubrication. Includes four roller sets.

**614-6 60.00**

**614-PLK50103** 3-Rail For Marklin Locos **60.00**

## CREATIONS UNLIMITED HOBBY PRODUCTS

## TOOLS

## FLEX-I-FILE™

Tough, flexible, polyester tapes, for wet or dry sanding, on lightweight, high-strength, anodized aluminum frames.

**232-700** Starter Set **10.95**
Includes frame and two each of polyester fine, medium and coarse tapes.

**232-123** Combo Set **16.95**
Includes frame with eight each fine, medium and coarse polyester tapes, plus one bonus tape on frame.

**232-301** 3-in-1 Set **24.95**
Includes three frames plus seven each fine, medium and coarse polyester tapes.

### Tool-Tender Plus

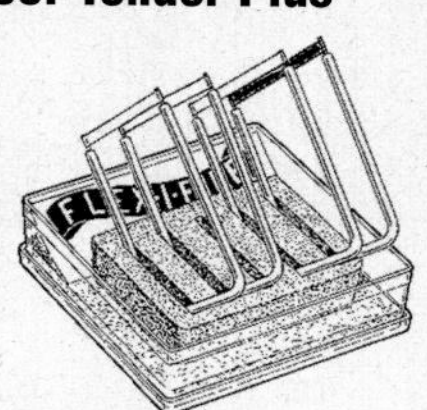

**232-401 37.95**
Five-place tool stand with four complete sets and room for five. Includes clear plastic storage case.

**232-400** Tool Stand Only **19.95**

### Replacement Polyester Sanding Tapes pkg(6) 2.59 ea

**232-150** Coarse

**232-280** Medium

**232-320** Fine

**232-600** X-Fine

## ABRASIVE SHEETS 4.29 ea

**232-801** Polyester Abrasive
Includes two sheets each of #150, 280, 320 and 600 grit.

**232-802** Ultra-Fine Finishing/ Polishing
Includes two sheets each of polyester abrasive #1000, 1500, 6000 and 10,000 grit.

## POLISHER

**232-3210** Triple Grit **3.39**
Three-in-one polisher/finisher.

## SCRIBES

### Scribe-N-Cut

**232-6087** Folding Knife **5.49**
Large blade is ideal for cutting big sheets of styrene and small vacuum-formed parts.

### Needle Point Scriber

**232-6114** Ultra-Fine w/2 Needle Points **9.25**
Includes two each coarse and fine needles.

**232-6115** Replacement Needles for #6114 pkg(3) **3.95**
Includes three each coarse and fine needles.

## FLEX-PAD

Flexible polyester sanders with angled end. Available in handy 1/2 x 6" sizes.

### Sets

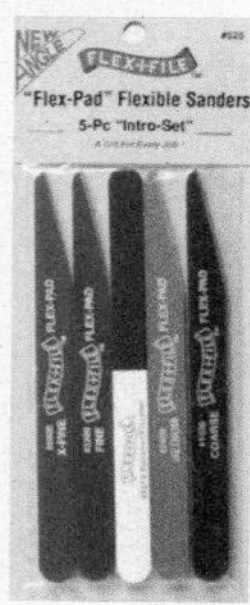


**232-525** Intro Set **16.49**
One each of above, plus triple-grit polisher.

**232-550** Flex Set **24.95**
Includes Flex-I-File with an assortment of polyester tapes and all 5 Flex-Pads.

### Individual Flex-Pad Files 2.98 ea

**232-1500** Coarse

**232-2800** Medium

**232-3200** Fine

**232-6000** X-Fine

## ADHESIVES

### A+B Epoxy

Hand-moldable epoxy ribbon. Easily carved and worked before curing; easy to sand, file and paint when dry.

**232-1** Putty Regular Gray 1lb **16.79**

**232-2** Fast Set Putty 8oz **16.29**

**232-5** Fast Set Paste 5oz **16.79**

## APPLICATORS

### Touch-N-Flow

**232-711 6.49**

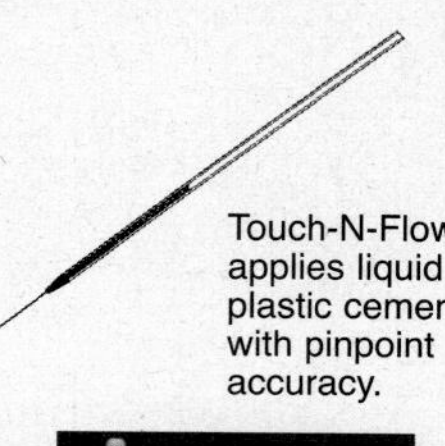

Touch-N-Flow applies liquid plastic cements with pinpoint accuracy.

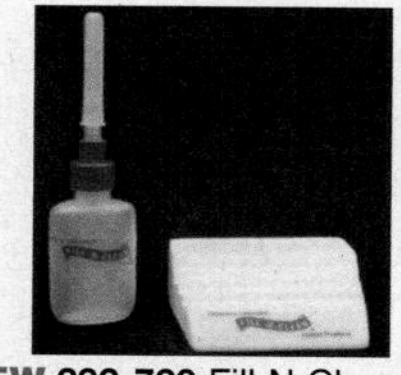

**NEW 232-720** Fill-N-Clean **14.95**
Accessory for 232-711; Includes squeeze bottle and base to hold bottle securely and keep it ready for use.

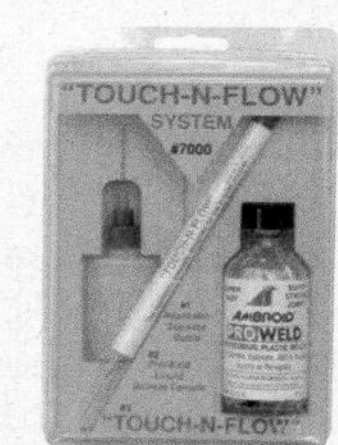


**232-7000** Touch-N-Flow System **16.79**
Bottle of ProWeld Cement, a Filler Bottle and the Touch-N-Flow. All in one package.

**232-715** Filler Bottle **6.49**

### Applicator Tool

**232-805** Cyanoacrylate Adhesive (CA) Applicator Tool **6.29**

### Applicator Bottles 6.49 ea

One-drop applicators for precise use of thin liquids.

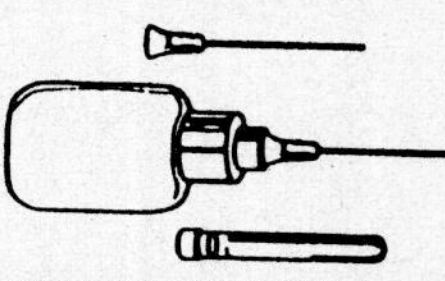

**232-6003** With 2 Tubes

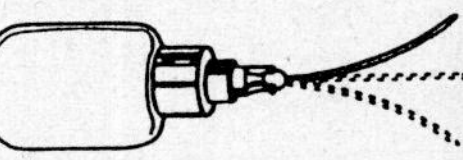

**232-6051** With "Flex" Tube
Good for filling Touch-N-Flow applicator.

## AIRBRUSH CLEANING KIT

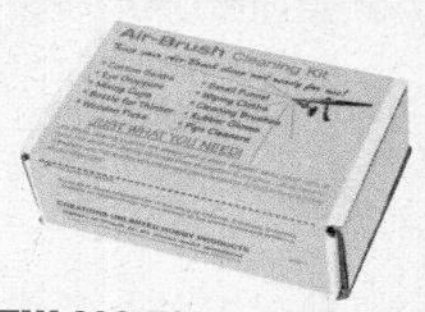

**NEW 232-7011 14.95**
Everything you need to keep your airbrush clean and working properly, in one handy package. Includes one each #7012 - 7020; also available separately.

### Cleaning Kit Accessories

**Cotton Swabs**
**NEW 232-7012** pkg(20) **1.50**

**Plastic Eye Droppers**
**NEW 232-7013** for Mixing Paint pkg(6) **2.99**

**Pipe Cleaners**
**NEW 232-7014** pkg(20) **2.49**

**Mixing Cups**
**NEW 232-7015** pkg(5) **1.29**

**Rubber Gloves**
**NEW 232-7016** One Size fits All **1.10**

**Small Funnel**
**NEW 232-7017 1.99**

**Squeeze Bottle**
**NEW 232-7018** For Thinner **4.99**

**Cleaning Brushes**
**NEW 232-7019** For Air-Brush pkg(6) **2.49**

**Wiping Cloths**
**NEW 232-7020** pkg(3) **1.99**

## MODEL DUSTING BRUSH

**232-8050** Brush Duster **4.99**

## OptiVISOR®

The OptiVISOR is a precision-made binocular magnifier that is worn on the head, leaving both hands free. Can be instantly tilted downward when needed and upward when not in use. Can be worn over regular prescription or safety glasses. Comes with dial, adjustable, conforming headband, high impact visor, genuine leather padded comfort band and optical glass lenses mounted in an interchangeable frame. Six lens powers available, plus an attachable auxiliary OptiLOUPE lens for additional magnification.

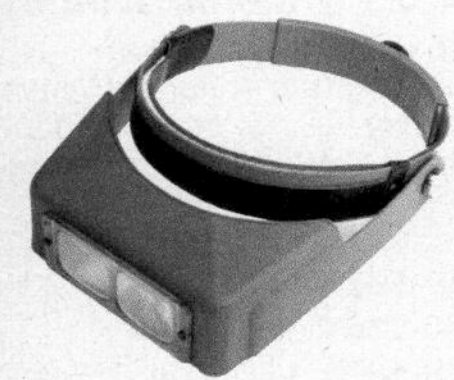

**240-402** 1-1/2x, 20" Focal Length **42.30**

**240-403** 1-3/4x, 14" Focal Length **42.30**

**240-404** 2x, 10" Focal Length **42.30**

**240-405** 2-1/2x, 8" Focal Length **42.30**

**240-407** 2-3/4x, 6" Focal Length **43.85**

**240-410** 3-1/2x, 4" Focal Length **43.85**
For extremely fine work.

## OptiVISOR LX 29.20 ea

Includes all the same great features of the regular OptiVISOR, except it has acrylic lenses instead of glass.

**240-15** 1-3/4x, 14" Focal Length

**240-16** 2x, 10" Focal Length

**240-17** 2-1/2x, 8" Focal Length

**240-18** 2-3/4x, 6" Focal Length

## OptiVISOR® Professional Set

**240-400** OptiVISOR Professional Series Set **259.09**
Includes an OptiVISOR, six lenses, OptiLOUPE®, VisorLIGHT® and carrying case.

## Accessories For OptiVISOR

### OptiLOUPE

**240-300 9.49**
Adds 2-1/2x to all other lenses.

### OptiVISOR Lens Plate 25.79 ea (Unless Noted)

**240-2** Lens Plate 2 For #402

**240-3** Lens Plate 3 For #403

**240-4** Lens Plate 4 For #404

**240-5** Lens Plate 5 For #405

**240-7** Lens Plate 7 For #407 **27.15**

**240-10** Lens Plate 10 For #410 **27.15**

### Replacement Lens Plate For Accursite/OptiVISOR LX Magnifiers 11.00 ea

**240-213** 1-3/4x, 14" Focal Length

**240-214** 2x, 10" Focal Length

**240-215** 2-1/2x, 8" Focal Length

### Visorlight

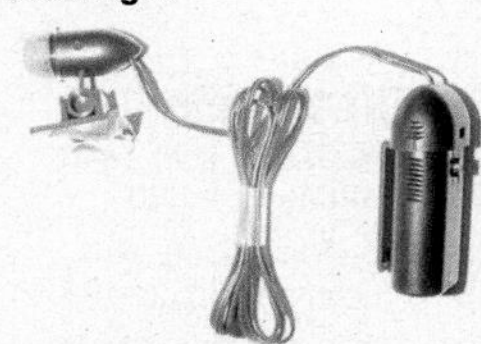

**240-6** With Battery Pack & 10" Cord. **23.49**

**240-42** With Battery Pack & 42" Cord **23.49**

**240-2204** Replacement Bulb **6.20**

## Flex Arm Magnifiers

### With Acrylic Lens

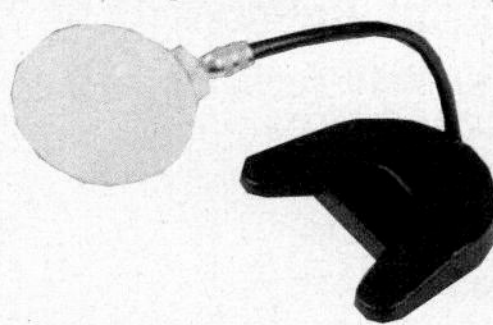

**240-204** Flex-A-Mag **28.70**
Features optical grade acrylic material which has been selected for its hard surface qualities as well as its refractive index. Weighted base.

### With Optical Glass Lens 91.35 ea

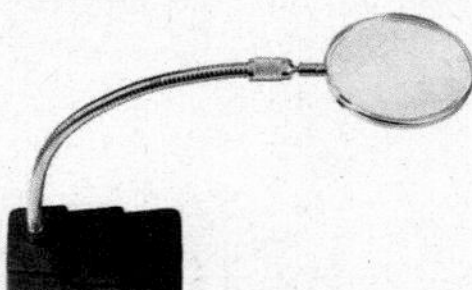

Item listed below is available by Special Order (see Legend Page).
**240-1043** 4" Round w/Clamp

## Optisight Magnifying Visor

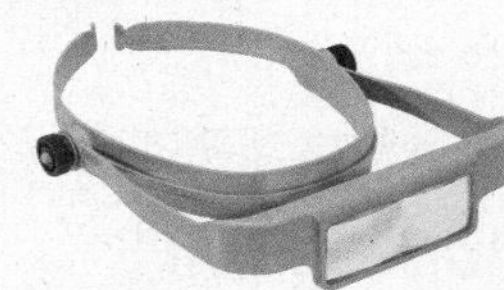

**240-600 27.60**
Visor tilts up for normal viewing, or down for magnification. Constructed of a high-strength plastic, the visor can be worn over prescription or safety glasses. Its state-of-the-art design shields out unwanted glare, so modelers can focus on the project in hand! Features a precision optical grade acrylic prismatic lens, and three interchangeable lens plates (3, 4 and 5).

## Ultra-Light Eyeglass Loupe

### Single 23.59 ea

**240-28** 10 Power

**240-29** 7 Power

**240-30** 5 Power

**240-31** 4 Power

**240-32** 3 Power

### Double 29.50 ea

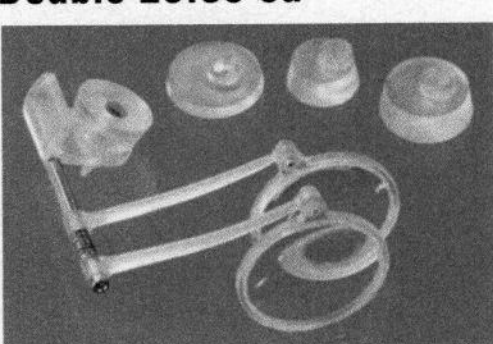

**240-33** 5 Power & 10 Power/ 15 Power Combined

**240-34** 4 Power & 10 Power/ 14 Power Combined

**240-35** 5 Power & 7 Power/ 12 Power Combined

Items listed below are available by Special Order (see Legend Page).
**240-36** 4 Power & 7 Power/ 11 Power Combined

**240-37** 3 Power & 7 Power/ 10 Power Combined

**240-38** 3 Power & 5 Power/ 8 Power Combined



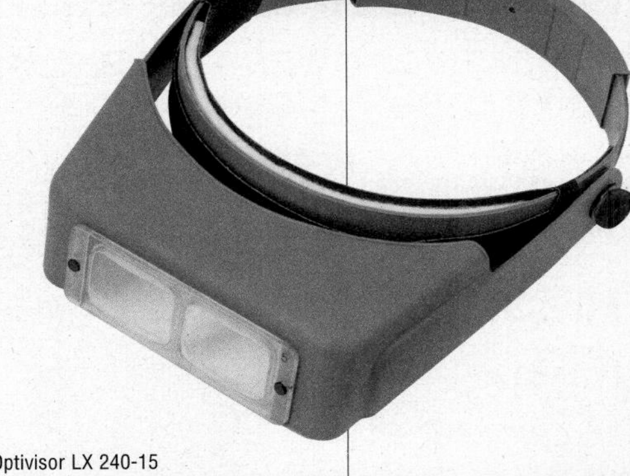

Optivisor LX 240-15

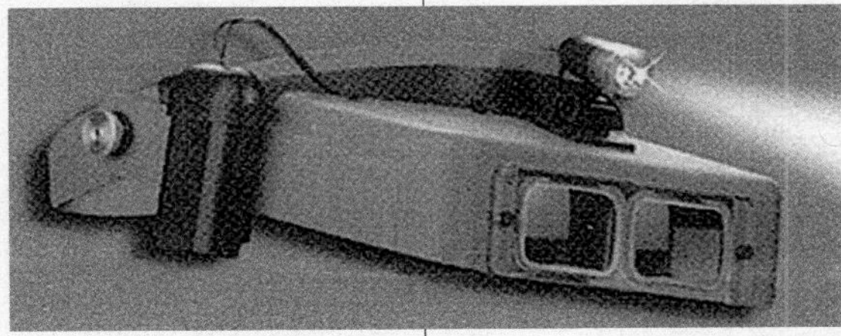

VisorLight 240-6
Shown with OptiVisor, Sold Separately

## Clip-On Binocular Magnifier 27.60 ea

Hands free magnification for detailed tasks. Lightweight frame can be used with frame included, or easily clipped onto most eyeglass frames. Pivots up when magnification is not needed. Relieves eye strain and increases accuracy.

**240-503** 1-3/4x, 14" Focal Length

**240-504** 2x, 10" Focal Length

**240-505** 2-1/2x, 8" Focal Length

**240-507** 2-3/4x, 6" Focal Length

## Pocket Magnifiers 6.90 ea (Unless Noted)

**240-703** 3x

**240-704** 4x

**240-705** 5x

**240-903** Single Fold 3x

**240-904** Single Fold 4x

**240-905** Single Fold 5x

**240-937** Double Fold 3/4/7x **8.30**

**240-949** Double Fold 4/5/9x **8.30**

## Classic Series Magnifiers

These lightweight, handheld magnifiers feature ABS plastic handles and acrylic lenses that are produced to high opthalmic standards.

**240-602** Round, 2-1/2" Lens, 6" Focal Length **9.69**

**240-603** Round, 3-1/4" Lens, 8" Focal Length **10.89**

**240-604** Round, 4" Lens, 9" Focal Length **12.15**

**240-624** Rectangular, 2 x 4" Lens, 9" Focal Length **12.15**

**240-625** Rectangular w/Bifocal, 2 x 4" Lens, 9" Focal Length **12.15**

# DREMEL®

## CREATIVE POWER TOOLS

Visit Walthers Web site at www.walthers.com for a complete listing of Dremel tools and accessories.

## DREMEL STYLUS

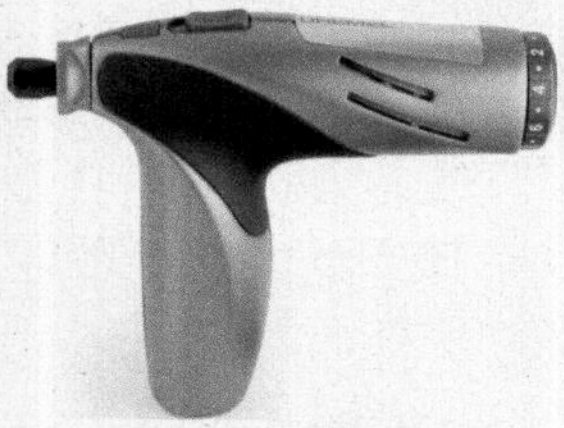

**250-110001 116.00**
7.2V lithium ion cordless rotary tool.

## EZ LOCK™ MANDREL SYSTEM

Simplifies accessory changes. One-piece mandrel design eliminates the need for a screw and screwdriver. Designed for reinforced cutting wheels and compatible with all Dremel rotary tools.

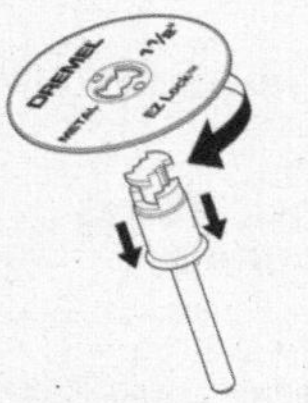

**250-EZ402** Mandrel **10.75**

**250-EZ456** 1-1/2" Diameter Cut Off Disks pkg(5) **11.39**

**250-EZ456B** 1-1/2" Diameter Cut off Wheels pkg(12) **24.98**

**250-EZ476** 1-1/2" Cut Off Wheels For Plastic pkg(5) **11.39**

**NEW 250-423E** Polishing Cloth **3.85**

**NEW 250-EZ406** EZ Lock Starter Kit **18.15**
Includes EZ402 mandrel and five EZ456 cut off disks.

## GLUE GUN

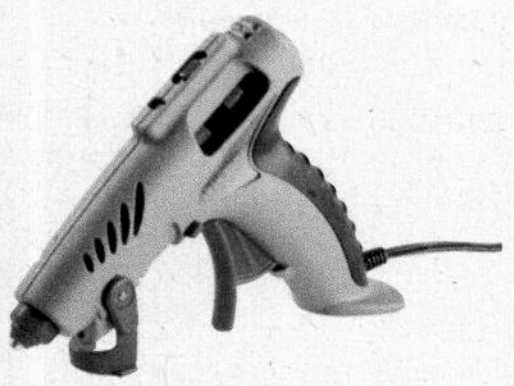

**250-120001 31.75**
Dual-heat gun features three interchangeable anti-drip tips, light, kickstand and wide base.

## MULTIPRO®

### Variable Speed MultiPro Kits

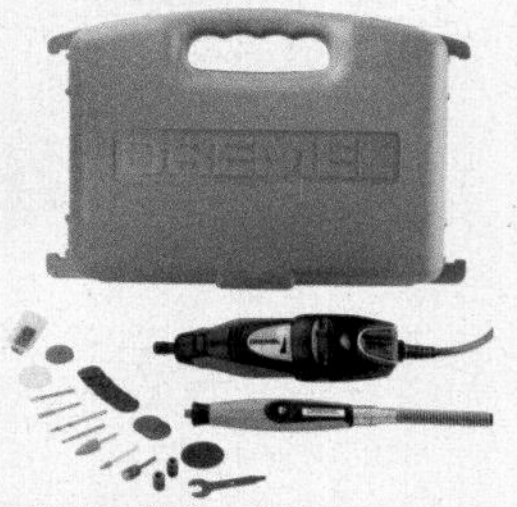

**250-300125 95.00**
Features everything necessary to grind, sharpen, drill, polish, sand and more. Kit comes with variable speed MultiPro tool, storage case, flex shaft attachment, Micro Case accessory organizer, 25 assorted accessories and 175+ Uses book.

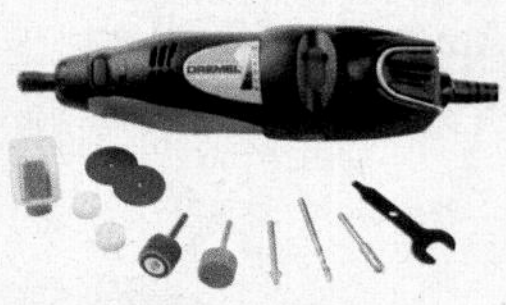

**250-300N10 89.40**
Ideal for the widest range of special do-it-yourself projects using various speed ranges for added versatility. Provides improved ergonomics, precision and control. Operates at 5,000-35,000 RPM. Includes MultiPro variable speed rotary tool, ten accessories and "Projects for the Imagination" book.

### Minimite

Cordless rotary tool with five accessories.

**250-750** MiniMite **42.50**

**250-755** MiniMite Removable Battery Pack **22.30**

**250-756** MiniMite Battery Charger **11.40**



### MultiPro Accessories

#### Work Station

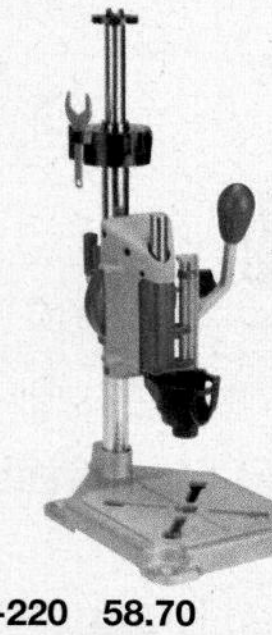

**250-220 58.70**
For models #275, 285 and 395. MultiPro not included.

## ACCESSORIES

### Multipro Chuck

**250-4486** Keyless, Knurled, 3-Jaw Chuck **12.25**
For quick bit changes. Not for use with cordless or Flex-Shaft tools.

### High Speed Steel Cutters w/1/8" Steel Shanks 5.85 ea

250-114

250-115

250-116

250-117

250-118

250-121

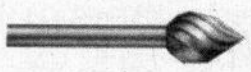
250-124

250-125

250-131

250-134

250-144

250-190

250-191

250-192

250-193

250-194

250-196

250-198

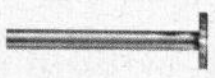
250-199

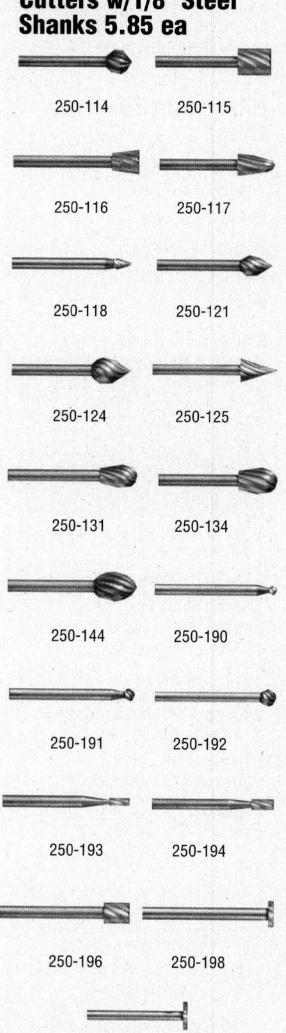

### Mandrels 2.95 ea

**250-401** Screw Mandrel
Used with polishing accessories, 1/8" shank.

**250-402** Mandrel
Used with wheels, sanding discs, polishing wheel, 1/8" shank.

### Small Engraving Cutters 2.95 ea

Quality cutters for detail engraving, carving, routing in wood, fiberglass, plastic and soft metals. Not for use with hardened materials. 3/32" shanks only.

**250-105** Circular-Tip, Small

**250-106** Medium

**250-107** Circular-Tip, Large

**250-108** Square-Tip, Small

**250-109** Square-Tip, Medium

**250-110** Square-Tip, Large

**250-111** Rectangular-Tip, Small

**250-112** Rectangular-Tip, Medium

**250-113** Rectangular-Tip, Large

### Tungsten Carbide Cutters 15.55 ea

1/8" shanks with maximum cutting head of 1/8".

**250-9931** Slim Taper

**250-9932** Ball Nose

**250-9933** Cylindrical

**250-9934** Wide Taper

**250-9935** Round

**250-9936** Wheel Shape (Rotor Saw)

### Cut-Off Wheels

**250-409** .025" Thick, 15/16" Diameter pkg(36) **5.90**

**250-420** Heavy Duty .40" Thick 15/16" Diameter pkg(20) **6.35**

**250-426** Super Duty pkg(5) **8.50**
Fiberglass (1-1/4" diameter), long lasting. Larger diameter for cutting thicker materials.

**250-540** 1-1/4 x 1/16" **4.40**
Cut-off, groove and trim metals, woods and ceramics. Use with Mandrel #402, sold separately.

### Chuck Collets

#### For Moto-Tools Series 2 Or Later 2.95 ea

**250-480** 1/8"

**250-481** 3/32"

**250-482** 1/16"

**250-483** 1/32"

### Grinding Wheel

**250-541** 7/8 x 1/8" **2.95**
Use for deburring, removing rust and general purpose grinding. Use with Mandrel #402, sold separately.

### Drum Sanders

#### 1/2" Diameter Drum Sande[rs] & Bands

**250-407** Drum Sander **4.00**

**250-408** Coarse Grit Sander Bands pkg(6) **2.95**

**250-432** Fine Grit Sander Bands pkg(6) **2.95**

#### 1/4" Diameter Drum Sande[rs] & Bands

**250-430** Drum 1/4" w/Coarse Band **4.00**

**250-431** Sander Bands 1/4" Coarse pkg(6) **2.95**

#### 3/8" Diameter Drum Sande[rs] & Bands

**250-439** 3/8" Drum Sander **4.00**

**250-440** 3/8" Sander Bands-Coarse pkg(6) **2.95**

#### Carbide Sanding Drum

**250-475** With Mandrel **17.79**

### Brass Brushes 3.90 ea

Brass brushes are non-sparking and softer than steel so they will not scratch softer metals. Use on gold, copper, brass and other precious metals.

**250-535** Wheel Shape

**250-536** Cup Shape

**250-537** End Shape

### Stainless Steel Brushe[s] 3.90 ea

Use on pewter, aluminum, stainless steel and other metals.

**250-530** Wheel Shape

**250-531** Cup Shape

**250-532** End Shape

### Brushes 2.95 ea

Not to be used over 15,000 RPM.

**250-403** Bristle 3/4"

**250-404** Bristle1/2"

**250-405** Bristle 1/8"

**250-428** Wire 3/4"

**250-442** Wire 1/2"

**250-443** Wire 1/8"

**250-424** Screw Mandrel Used with #427 polishing wheel, 1/8[" shank].

## ATLAS

### Snap Saw

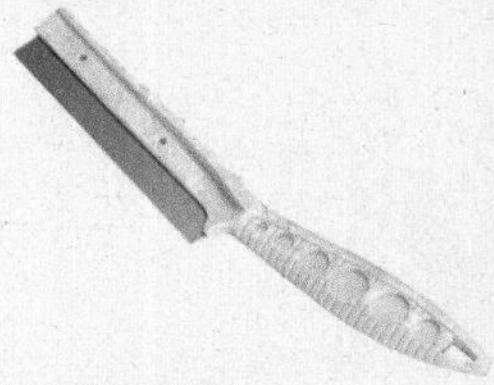

**150-400 3.25**

## NEW PRODUCTS

### Stainless Steel Hemostats

NEW **271-55530** 5" Curved Nose **6.84**

NEW **271-55531** 7-1/2" Curved Nose **13.19**

NEW **271-55532** 5-1/2" Deluxe Curved Nose w/Soft Handle **7.89**

NEW **271-55540** 5" Straight **5.84**

NEW **271-55541** 7-1/2" Straight Nose **13.19**

## AWL

**271-30604** Aluminum Handle Needle Point Hobby Awl **3.32**

## BURNISHERS

### Aluminum Handle

**271-30601** Ball Tip 1/16" **3.53**

**271-30602** Ball Tip 1/8" **3.53**

**271-30603** Spoon Tip 1/8" **4.28**

**271-30605** Burnishing Set **7.23** 4 Interchangeable Tips (1/32", 1/16", 1/8" & spoon)

**271-30606** Burnisher/Pounce Wheel **7.23**

**271-30609** Double Ended **6.42** 1/8" Ball & 1/8" Spoon Tips.

## CLAMPS

### Adjustable Plastic Clamps

**271-55663** Small **2.59**

**271-55664** Large **5.36**

## CUTTING MATS

### Self-Healing (Green)

**271-60000** 5-1/2 x 9" **6.29**

**271-60002** 8 x 12" **11.18**

**271-60003** 12 x 18" **18.89**

## CUTTING KITS

**271-90001** Precision Cutting Kit with K18 **16.81**

**271-90003** Mini Precision Cutting Kit with K1 **9.56**

## DRILLS

### Fine High Twisted Drills

**271-50050** #50 pkg(12) **11.23**

**271-50051** #51 pkg(12) **11.23**

**271-50052** #52 pkg(12) **11.23**

**271-50053** #53pkg(12) **11.23**

**271-50054** #54 pkg(12) **11.23**

**271-50055** #55 pkg(12) **11.23**

**271-50056** #56 pkg(12) **11.23**

**271-50057** #57 pkg(12) **11.23**

**271-50058** #58 pkg(12) **11.81**

**271-50059** #59 pkg(12) **11.81**

**271-50060** #60 pkg(12) **11.81**

**271-50061** #61 pkg(12) **11.81**

**271-50062** #62 pkg(12) **11.81**

**271-50063** #63 pkg(12) **11.81**

**271-50064** #64 pkg(12) **11.81**

**271-50065** #65 pkg(12) **11.81**

**271-50066** #66 pkg(12) **12.03**

**271-50067** #67 pkg(12) **12.03**

**271-50068** #68 pkg(12) **12.03**

**271-50069** #69 pkg(12) **12.03**

**271-50070** #70 pkg(12) **12.03**

**271-50071** #71 pkg(12) **12.03**

**271-50072** #72 pkg(12) **12.03**

**271-50073** #73 pkg(12) **12.03**

**271-50074** #74 pkg(12) **12.36**

**271-50075** #75 pkg(12) **12.36**

**271-50076** #76 pkg(12) **12.36**

**271-50077** #77 pkg(12) **12.36**

**271-50078** #78 pkg(12) **12.36**

**271-50079** #79 pkg(12) **12.36**

**271-50080** #80 pkg(12) **12.36**

## DRILL SETS

**271-55510** 20-Piece Drill Set #61-80, with Dome Stand **30.35**

**271-55520** Assorted Drill Set #52-67, pkg(6) **7.31**

**271-55521** Assorted Drill Set #53-67, pkg(12) **13.49**

## FILES

### 5-1/2" Long, Cut #2 Needle Files

**2.26 ea**

**271-55600** Square

**271-55601** Round

**271-55602** Three Square

**271-55603** Flat

**271-55604** Knife

**271-55605** Equaling

**271-55606** Half Round

### 5-1/2" Long, Cut #2 Needle File Sets

**271-55607** 12 Assorted Files in Pouch **22.58**

**271-55608** 4" Cut #2 Needle Files 12 Mini Files in Pouch **13.55**

**271-55667** 6 Assorted Set **11.97**

**271-55668** 6 Assorted Set w/Handle **14.51**

**271-70001** Aluminum File Handle w/6 Assorted Mini Needle Files **15.41**

## HAMMER

**271-55672** Swiss Style Mini Hammer **9.22**

## KNIVES

K1 Round Aluminum Handle Knife with Safety Cap

**271-15001** w/5 #20011 Blades **3.90**

**271-16001** Knife Only **2.36**

**271-19001** w/5 Assorted Blades **4.41**

### Light Duty

**271-16008** K8 Flat Yellow Handle **1.87**

NEW **271-16030** K30 Rite-Cut Non-Roll Plastic Handle Knife **1.77**

**271-16040** K40 Pocket Clip On Plastic Knife w/Twist On Safety Cap **3.21**

### K2 Medium Duty Round Aluminum Handle Knife w/Safety Cap

**271-16002** **3.21**

**271-19102** Tubed w/5 Assorted Blades **5.34**

### Heavy Duty

**271-16005** K5 Plastic Red Handle Knife w/Safety Cap **3.90**

**271-16006** K6 Hex Aluminum Handle Knife w/Safety Cap **6.61**

### K18 Grip-On Non-Roll Soft Handle Knife w/Safety Cap

**271-16018** **4.28**

NEW **271-16022** Green **4.28**

**271-19018** w/5 #20011 Blades **6.00**

### Retractable

**271-16047** Executive w/Clip **13.73**

**271-16048** Deluxe w/Clip **11.46**

## KNIFE SETS

**271-19062** Basic Knife Set **10.44**

**271-44082** Hobby Knife Set in Plastic Tray **17.14**

**271-44090** Professional Set in Plastic Tray **22.49**

**271-44200** Super Deluxe Knife Set In Vinyl Case **66.35**

**271-44282** Hobby Knife Set in Wooden Box **24.10**

**271-44283** Craftsman Set in Wooden Box **25.69**

**271-44284** Woodworking Set in Wooden Box **28.91**

**271-44285** Handyman Set in Wooden Box **25.28**

## KNIFE & BLADE HOLDER

**271-23111** Knife and Blade Holder **13.49**
Comes with 15 Super Sharp #11 Blades in a Safety Dispenser.

## MAGNIFIERS

### Deluxe Magna-Visor

**23.17 ea**

**271-70021** Gray

**271-70022** Black

### Magnifier w/Tweezer

**271-70040** 4-1/4" Magnifier w/Tweezer **4.69**

## MERCHANDISE DISPLAYS

Items listed below are available by Special Order (see Legend Page).

**271-60001** Miniature High Speed Twist Display 360 Pieces **333.99**

**271-77K01** K1 Light Duty Knife Display 60 Pieces **134.95**

**271-77K18** K18 Soft Grip Knife Display 36 Pieces **138.32**

**271-77K40** K40 Light Duty Pockit Clip Plastic Knife w/Twist Safety Cap Display 36 Pieces **106.83**

## MITRE BOXES

**271-55665** Mitre Box Only w/45 Degree Angle **9.28**

**271-55666** Mitre Box w/K5 Handle & Saw Blade **17.32**

## NAIL SETTER

**271-90002** Nail Setter **13.48**

## PIN VISES

**271-55661** Swivel Head Pin Vise **7.50**

**271-70005** Deluxe Pin Vise w/6 Assorted Drills **14.61**

**271-70023** 4" Double Ended Pin Vise Drill **7.42**

## PICK-UP TOOL

**271-70004** 5 Prong Pick-Up Tool **7.42**

## PLIERS

### Spring Loaded Soft Grip Pliers

**9.10 ea (Unless Noted)**

**271-55550** 4-1/2" Wire Cutter

**271-55560** 5" Needle Nose

**271-55561** 6" "Long" Needle Nose

**271-55570** 5" Flat Nose

**271-55580** 5" Needle Nose w/Side Cutter

**271-55590** 5" Bent Nose

**271-55591** 5" End Nipper

**NEW 271-55592** 5" Round Nose

**271-55594** Sprue Cutter (blue) **10.48**

**271-55595** Sprue Cutter (black) **10.48**

**271-70050** 4 1/2" Side Cutter **13.23**

**271-70051** 5 1/2" Serrated Long Nose w/Side Cutter **13.23**

**271-70052** 5 1/2" Smooth Jaw Long Nose **13.23**

**271-70053** 5 1/2" Smooth Jaw Flat Nose **13.23**

## POUNCE WHEELS

### Aluminum Handle 7.23 ea

**271-30606** With 1/4" Tip (18 Teeth/Inch)

**271-30607** With 7/16" Tip (18 Teeth/Inch)

**271-30611** With 5/16" Tip

## REPLACEMENT BLADES

### Light Duty

**Fit K1, K3, K17, K18, K30 & K40 Handles pkg(5)**

**271-20006** Stencil Edge Blade **2.01**

**271-20010** Curved Edge Blade **2.50**

**271-20011** Super Sharp Double Honed **1.71**

**271-20013** Fine Saw **3.00**

**271-20014** Assorted **1.95**

**271-20016** Stencil Edge **1.71**

**271-20017** Small Chisel **1.71**

**271-20021** Super Sharp Stainless Steel **2.07**

**271-22611** Super Sharp Double Honed pkg(100) **25.22**

**271-23010** Curved Edge Blade pkg(15) **6.53**

**271-23011** Super Sharp Double Honed pkg(15) **6.43**

**271-24017A** Narrow Chisel **3.32**

### Medium & Heavy Duty

**Fit K2, K5 & K6 Handles pkg(5)**

**271-20002** Super Sharp Straight Edge **2.07**

**271-20004** Assorted Heavy Duty **2.30**

**271-20015** Narrow Saw **4.87**

**271-20018** Large Chisel **2.07**

**271-20019** Sharp Edge Angled **2.07**

**271-20022** Curved Edge **2.63**

**271-20023** Double Edge Stripping **3.27**

**271-20024** Deburring **2.07**

**271-20025** Contoured **3.27**

**271-20026** Whittling **3.80**

**NEW 271-20027** Saw Blade **4.93**

**271-20028** Concave Carving Blade **3.27**

### Light & Heavy Duty Cutting Pull Out Saw Blades

**Fit K2, K5 & K6 Handles**

**271-30440** 3/4" Deep 42 Teeth/Inch **3.80**

**271-30450** 1" Deep 42 Teeth/Inch **4.02**

**271-30460** 1-1/4" Deep 24 Teeth/Inch **4.18**

**271-30470** 1-1/2" Deep 30 Teeth/Inch **4.93**

**271-30480** 2" Deep 16 Teeth/Inch **5.14**

**271-30490** 1-1/4" Deep 54 Teeth/Inch **4.18**

**271-30491** 1-1/2" Deep 54 Teeth/Inch **4.28**

### Fine Jeweler's Saw Blades 3.14 ea

**271-20510** #4/0 72 Teeth/Inch

**271-20520** #2/0 66 Teeth/Inch

**271-20530** #1/0 58 Teeth/Inch

**271-20540** #1 56 Teeth/Inch

**271-20550** #2 52 Teeth/Inch

**271-20560** #3 46 Teeth/Inch

### Utility Blades

**271-20065** Executive Retractable pkg(2) **3.43**

**271-20066** Deluxe Retractable pkg(2) **3.43**

**271-20080** Straight Edge pkg(5) **2.52**

## RULERS

### Scale Model Rulers

**12.14 ea**

**271-55778** 12" Deluxe Model Reference Rule

**271-55779** 12" Scale Model Reference Rule

## SANDING STICKS & BELTS

**8.60 ea (Unless Noted)**

**271-55678** Sanding Stick w/Extra Belt **6.41**

**271-55679** Assorted Sanding Belts pkg(5) **9.22**

**271-55680** #120 Grit Sanding Belts (red) pkg(5)

**271-55681** #240 Grit Sanding Belts (blue) pkg(5)

**271-55682** #320 Grit Sanding Belts (green) pkg(5)

**271-55683** #400 Grit Sanding Belts (yellow) pkg(5)

**271-55684** #600 Grit Sanding Belts (black) pkg(5)

**271-55685** #80 Grit Sanding Belts (gray) pkg(5)

## SAWS

### Razor Saw Set Handle

**271-55001** w/1 Blade **8.10**

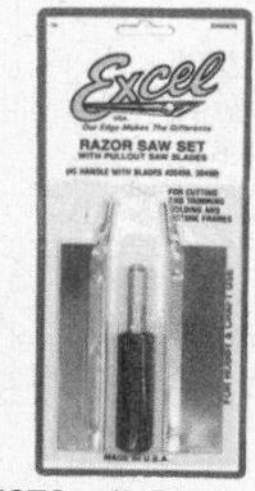


**271-55670** w/2 Blades **11.58**

### Jeweler's

**271-55671** Adjustable Jeweler's Saw 7-1/2 x 2-1/2" **15.67**

## SCISSORS

### Light Duty Stainless Steel

**5-1/2" Lexan 9.66 ea (Unless Noted)**

**271-55533** Curved

**271-55538** Straight

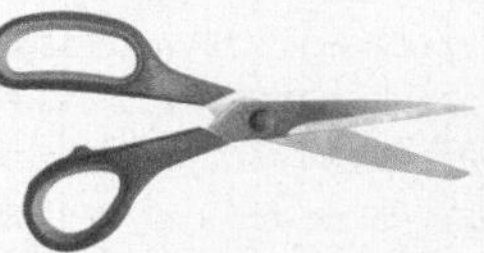

**271-55620** Grip-On Stainless Steel **5.50**

**271-55621** Comfort Grip Spring Action **9.37**

### Super Sharp

**NEW 271-55612** 4" **4.41**

**NEW 271-55615** 3-1/2" Straight **4.41**

## SCREWDRIVER SET

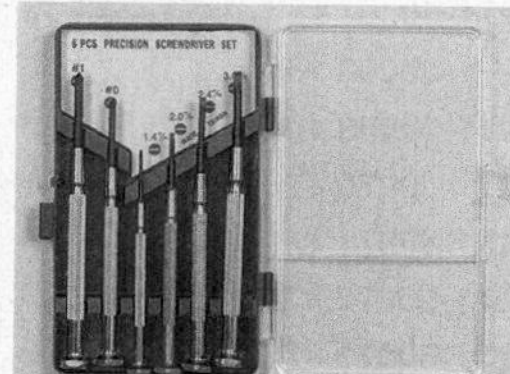


**271-55662** 6-Piece Precision Screwdriver Set **5.40**

## SCRIBES

### 5-1/2" Retractable Scribe

**14.46 ea**

**271-16049** .60"

**271-16050** .90"

## TOOL SETS

### Deluxe Wooden Boxed Tool Sets

**271-44286** Knife Tool Set **51.73**

**271-44287** Airplane Tool Set **51.73**

**271-44288** Dollhouse Tool Set **59.23**

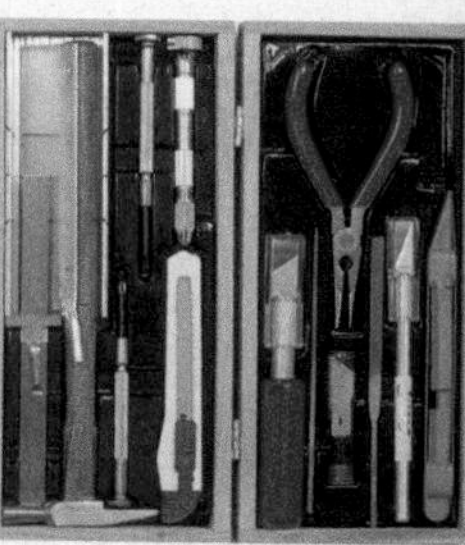

**271-44289** Railroad Tool Set **72.83**

**271-44290** Professional Set **28.38**

**271-44291** Ship Builder's Tool Set **66.94**

### Mini Tool Set

**271-60008** 21-Piece Mini Tool Set **19.86**

## TORCH

**271-80770** Butane Micro Torch **39.34**

## TWEEZERS

### Stainless Steel

**271-30410** 4-1/2" Curved Point **4.37**

**271-30411** 4-3/4" Slide Lock Pointed **4.86**

**271-30412** 4-3/4" Sharp Pointed **4.37**

**271-30413** 4-1/2" Pointed Self Closing **4.86**

**271-30414** 6-1/2" Large Self Closing **5.08**

**271-30415** 6" Curved Point **5.08**

**271-30416** 4-Piece Set **16.54**

**271-70025** 6" Helping Hand Tweezer **7.71**

## WORK HOLDER

**271-55674** Double Clip Extra Hands **16.99**

**271-55675** Double Clip Extra Hands w/Magnifier **20.08**

## ESCHENBACH

Hands-free magnification can be a big help when working with small parts or trying to read fine print. Ideal for all types of hobby and craft work, Eschenbach magnifiers come in a wide range of styles and levels of magnification. Each features precision made, highly polished, scratch-resistant PXM® lenses for a crystal clear view.

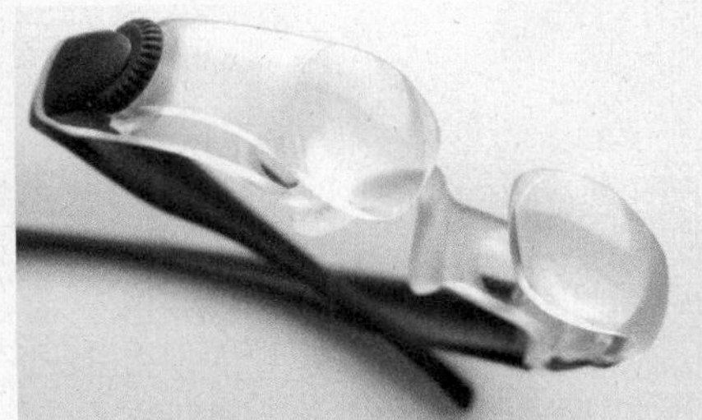

MAXDetail Glasses 281-16245

Binocular Clip-on Magnifier 281-164625

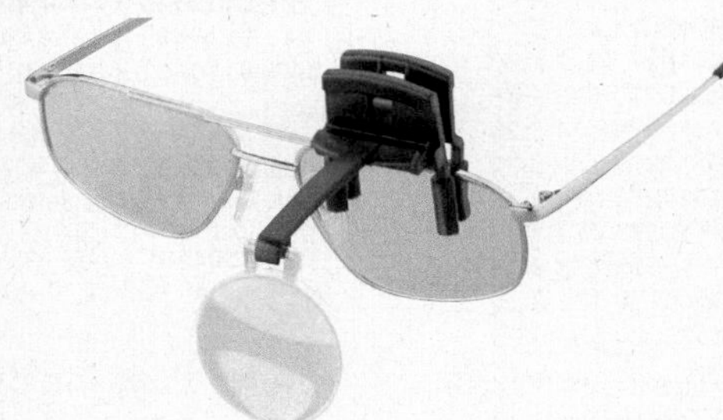

Monocular Clip-on Magnifier 281-164640

## NEW PRODUCTS

### MAXDetail Glasses

NEW 281-16245 2x Power, Focus Adjustable 159.98
Perfect for precision work of all kinds and reading, this magnifier is designed to be worn like a pair of glasses. It provides 2x magnification and can be adjusted so that each eye lens can be focused separately (±3 diopters) and will focus on near objects with working distances of 8 to 28" (20.3 - 71.1cm) depending on the eye.

### Clip-on Magnifiers

**99.98 ea**
These magnifiers offer modelers who wear glasses several choices for hands-free magnification. Lightweight and designed to fit most eyeglass frames (Bridge: 25mm, Jaws open 15mm) these magnifiers simply clip on to your frame, and feature protective rubber tips. When not in use, they can be flipped up and out of the way. In use, lenses are 2" from the eye, allowing for more comfortable working distances.

**Binocular**
**NEW 281-164617** 1.7x; 16" 40.6cm Working Distance
**NEW 281-164620** 2x; 10" 25.4cm Working Distance
**NEW 281-164625** 2.5x; 7" 17.7cm Working Distance
**NEW 281-164630** 3x; 6+" 15.24+cm Working Distance

**Monocular**
**NEW 281-164640** 4x; 2" 5cm Working Distance
**NEW 281-164670** 7x; 1-1/2" 3.8cm Working Distance

## FALLER

IMPORTED FROM GERMANY BY WALTHERS

### Abrasive Files

**272-170689** pkg(5) **10.99**
Five different grits from #80 to 120. Small size makes sanding and shaping metal, wood or plastic parts easy.

### Dust Brush

**272-170686 14.99**
This ideal modeling brush is great for removing dust from structures, vehicles, figures or any other detail work on your layout. Removes even the finest dust particles.

### Professional Tool Set

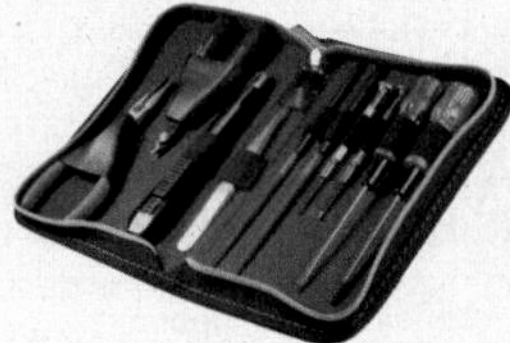

**272-170685 51.99**
This set contains one side cutter, one pair of pliers, one cutter knife, one pair of tweezers, two files and four screwdrivers, all in a handy storage case.

## BOWSER

## TOOLS

### Car Cradle

**6-22 12.59**
Shaped foam cradle gives you a gentle helping hand when working on the underside of your locos and cars. Cradle also has a compartment for holding small parts like screws, trucks, couplers etc.

## Kadee

Designed, Manufactured & Assembled entirely in the U.S.A.

## TOOLS

### Grippers

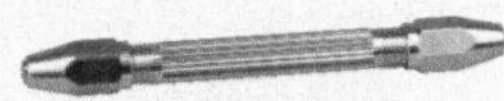

**380-239** Five-Prong Gripper **5.95**

### Pin Vise

**380-240** Double-Headed Pin Vise **5.95**

### Spring Pic/Uncoupler

**380-241** Dual Tool Manual Uncoupler/Spring Pic **1.95**
For manually uncoupling Scale, Standard and Shelf couplers. Blade end has a built-in spring pic.

### Tweezers

**380-1020** Coupler Tweezers **3.95**

### Trip Pin Pliers

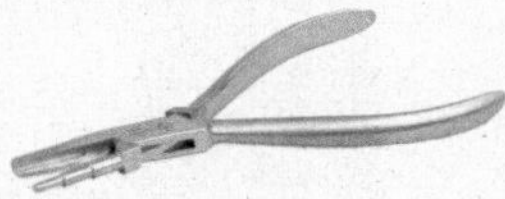

**380-237 12.35**
Special pliers for adjusting the height of coupler trip pins. Jaws of pliers are curved to conform to the correct bend in the trip pin and prevent kinking.

### Tap & Drill Sets

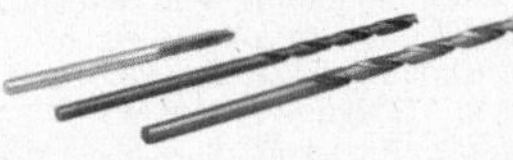

**380-246** 2-56 Tap, #43 & 50 Drills **5.95**
For 2-56 screw mounting most HO couplers and trucks.
**380-780** 0-80 Tap, #52 & 55 Drills **5.95**
For 0-80 and 0-48 screws used in the side lugs of the #4, 5, 9, 78, 234, 711 and 714 gear box.
**380-247** 1-72 Tap, #48 & 53 Drills **5.95**
**380-1059** 00-90 Tap, #62 & 56 Drills **6.25**

## K-TOOL™ MODELING TOOLS

### Grade Gauge

**211-150 14.95**
A must for anyone building or modifying a model railroad layout to quickly and accurately determine any track grade. Easy to use: attach to any standard 24" or 48" carpenter's level. Set gauge to desired incline percent. Lay on roadbed. Raise roadbed until bubble balances. Secure roadbed using standard construction practices.

### Miter Box

Cuts any angle from 0° to 60°, in 5° increments, right or left (plus 22-1/2°, half of 45°).

- Cutting depth 1/4" with razor blade (more with saw blade).
- Cuts all woods, plastics and thin wall metal tubing.
- Handle accepts "Zona" saw or single-edged razor blades (one of each included).
- Adjustable slide-stop for cutting many same-length pieces.
- 7-1/2 x 7-1/2" cutting surface.
- Lexan base with non-skid rubber feet.
- Designed for either right- or left-hand operation.

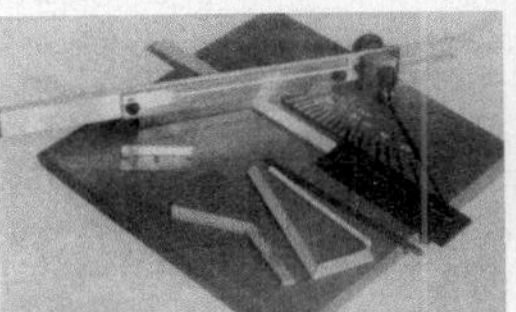

**211-2 32.95**
**211-21** Extra Handle for #2 **8.50**

## CIR-KIT CONCEPTS, INC.

### Mini Drill

**206-201 6.95**
High speed and hand operated; will drill small accurate holes in all types of material. 4-1/2" long, 3-to-1 ratio and accepts number size bits 61 through 80. Hollow handle stores your extra bits. #55 Bit (CK1025-4) included.

## Power Pro™ Rotary Tool Kits

Handle a wide range of chores around your layout, workshop, garage and home with these complete rotary tool sets. Variable speed makes it easy to cut, grind, polish and shape a wide range of materials. Each kit includes a holder to support the tool and a flex ible shaft for more precise control when doing fine work and an EZ-Lite™ that can be mounted directly onto the tool whenever you need to shine a bright light directly onto your work surface. Both kits come housed in a sturdy plastic storage case and includes a variety of attachments and accessories. Choose from a standard plug-in style or battery-powered cordless version for use almost anywhere.

**321-4010470** Variable Speed 1.2A Rotary Tool Kit **74.99**
Standard plug-in model features a powerful 1.2A electric motor to handle bigger jobs. Adjustable speed from 8,000 to 35,000 RPM with a separate on-off switch - letting you set and keep a desired speed. Also includes a flexible shaft, tool holder, cutting guide for more precise control of depth with clear visibility as well as an EZ-Lite and 85 accessories. Set is complete with 1/8, 3/32, 1/16 and 1/32" collets. 5 Year Manufacturer's Warranty.

**321-4010370** Cordless 9.6V Rotary Tool Kit **71.99**
Great for projects on the go! Set includes two battery packs, flexible shaft, E-Z Lite, charger and 50 accessories. Speed can be adjusted from 5,000 to 25,000 RPM. Includes 1/8 and 3/32" collets. 2 Year Manufacturer's Warranty

## Routers

**321-4620655** HSS Keyhole Slot Cutter **7.69**
5/16" head diameter, 1/8" shank, titanium-nitrite coated.

### Router Sets

These 1/8" shank routers feature a gold-colored titanium nitride coating, to extend tool life. For use with a drill press or a rotary tool with router attachment.

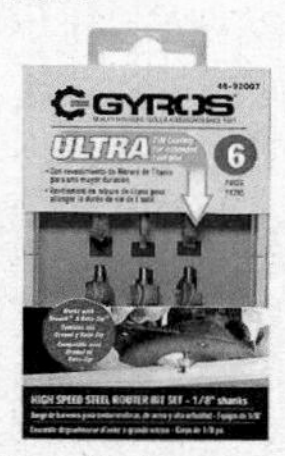


**321-4692007** pkg(6) **40.35**
Includes the following routers: 1/4" diameter beading, 1/8" diameter straight, 1/4" diameter straight, 3/16" diameter piloted cove, 1/8" diameter piloted rabbeting and 1/8" diameter piloted corner rounding.

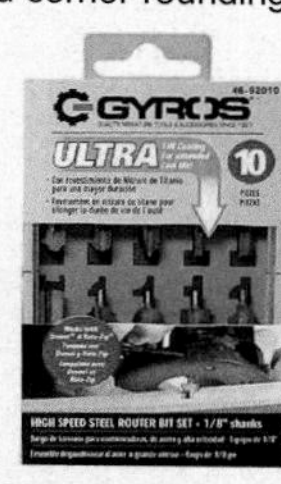


**321-4692010** pkg(10) **57.10**
Includes the following routers: 1/4" diameter beading, 1/4" diameter veining, 1/4" diameter V-groove, 1/8" diameter straight, 3/16" diameter straight, 1/4" diameter straight, 3/32" diameter piloted beading, 3/16" diameter piloted cove, 1/8" diameter piloted rabbeting and 1/8" diameter piloted corner rounding.

## Cutter Sets

**321-4692006** Titanium Nitride pkg(6) **23.98**
Set includes the following cutters: three cylindrical (1/8, 7/32 and 5/16" diameters), 1/4" diameter cone, 5/16" diameter tapered radius and 3/16" diameter ball.

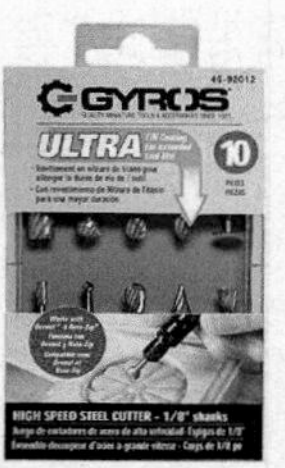


**321-4692012** Titanium Nitride pkg(10) **32.55**
Set includes the following cutters: two cylindrical (1/8 and 5/16" diameters), two ball (1/8 and 5/16" diameters), 1/4" diameter cone, 1/4" diameter tapered radius, 1/4" diameter oval, 3/8" diameter wheel, 1/4" diameter flame and 1/4" diameter inverted taper.

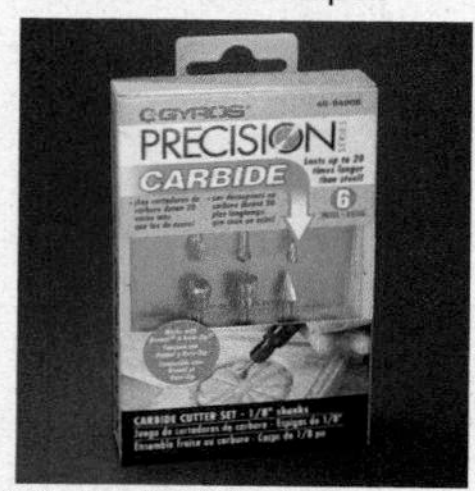


**321-4694006** Carbide pkg(6) **54.85**
Set includes the following cutters: three cylindrical (1/8, 7/32 and 5/16" diameters), 1/4" diameter cone, 5/16" diameter tapered radius and 3/16" diameter ball.

## Aluminum Oxide Abrasive Flap Wheels

For use on metal and wood. Polishes, sands, deburs, blends seams, removes old finish, rust and scale. With 1/8" shank.

### 3/8" Diameter x 3/8" x 1/8"

**321-1108003** 80 Grit **6.10**
**321-1112003** 120 Grit **6.10**
**321-1118003** 180 Grit **6.19**
**321-1124003** 240 Grit **6.29**

### 5/8" Diameter x 5/8" x 1/8"

**321-1108005** 80 Grit **6.10**
**321-1112005** 120 Grit **6.10**
**321-1118005** 180 Grit **6.19**
**321-1124005** 240 Grit **6.29**

### 3/4" Diameter x 3/4" x 1/8"

**321-1108007** 80 Grit **6.19**
**321-1112007** 120 Grit **6.19**
**321-1118007** 180 Grit **6.29**
**321-1124007** 240 Grit **6.35**

### 1-3/16" Diameter x 1-3/16" x 1/8"

**321-1108013** 80 Grit **6.35**
**321-1112013** 120 Grit **6.35**
**321-1118013** 180 Grit **6.45**
**321-1124013** 240 Grit **6.50**

## Drill Bits

### Carbon pkg(2)

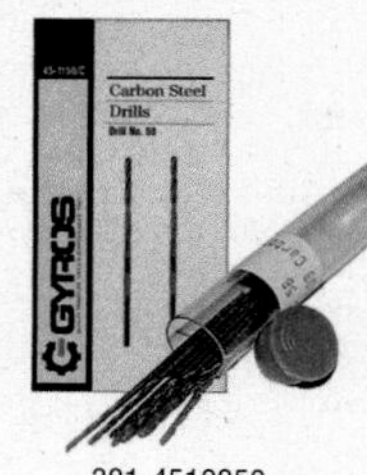


321-4510250

**321-4510250** #50 **2.69**
**321-4510251** #51 **2.69**
**321-4510252** #52 **2.69**
**321-4510253** #53 **2.69**
**321-4510254** #54 **2.69**
**321-4510255** #55 **2.69**
**321-4510256** #56 **2.69**
**321-4510257** #57 **2.69**
**321-4510258** #58 **2.85**
**321-4510259** #59 **2.85**
**321-4510260** #60 **2.85**
**321-4510261** #61 **2.85**
**321-4510262** #62 **2.85**
**321-4510263** #63 **2.85**
**321-4510264** #64 **2.85**
**321-4510265** #65 **2.85**
**321-4510266** #66 **2.85**
**321-4510267** #67 **2.85**
**321-4510268** #68 **2.85**
**321-4510269** #69 **2.85**
**321-4510270** #70 **2.85**
**321-4510271** #71 **2.85**
**321-4510272** #72 **2.85**
**321-4510273** #73 **2.85**
**321-4510274** #74 **3.35**
**321-4510275** #75 **3.35**
**321-4510276** #76 **3.35**
**321-4510277** #77 **3.35**
**321-4510278** #78 **3.35**
**321-4510279** #79 **3.35**
**321-4510280** #80 **3.95**

### High-Speed Steel pkg(2)

**321-4520250** #50 **3.00**
**321-4520251** #51 **3.00**
**321-4520252** #52 **3.00**
**321-4520253** #53 **3.00**
**321-4520254** #54 **3.00**
**321-4520255** #55 **3.00**
**321-4520256** #56 **3.00**
**321-4520257** #57 **3.00**
**321-4520258** #58 **3.25**
**321-4520259** #59 **3.25**
**321-4520260** #60 **3.25**
**321-4520261** #61 **3.25**
**321-4520262** #62 **3.25**
**321-4520263** #63 **3.25**
**321-4520264** #64 **3.25**
**321-4520265** #65 **3.25**
**321-4520266** #66 **3.25**
**321-4520267** #67 **3.25**
**321-4520268** #68 **3.25**
**321-4520269** #69 **3.25**
**321-4520270** #70 **3.25**
**321-4520271** #71 **3.25**
**321-4520272** #72 **3.25**
**321-4520273** #73 **3.25**
**321-4520274** #74 **3.85**
**321-4520275** #75 **3.85**
**321-4520276** #76 **3.85**
**321-4520277** #77 **3.85**
**321-4520278** #78 **3.85**
**321-4520279** #79 **3.85**
**321-4520280** #80 **4.50**

## Drill Sets

Each set includes #61-80 drill bits.

### Carbon

**321-4512010** Plastic Storage Dome **26.19**
**321-4512020** Metal Storage Box **21.05**

### High-Speed Steel

**321-4522010** **27.49**
20 high-speed drills sizes 61-80. Includes storage box with plastic dome.
**321-4522020** Metal Storage Box **23.19**

## Tungsten Steel Taps-Plug

**321-9110090** 00-90 **8.10**
**321-9110080** 0-80 **6.10**
**321-9110172** 1-72 **5.39**
**321-9110256** 2-56 **4.75**
**321-9110348** 3-48 **4.70**
**321-9110440** 4-40 **4.49**
**321-9110540** 5-40 **4.49**
**321-9110632** 6-32 **4.49**
**321-9110832** 8-32 **3.98**

## Tap Sets 24.69 ea

**321-9305102** Model Airplane One Each: #2-56, 3-48, 4-40, 6-32 & 8-32.
**321-9304101** Model Railroad One Each: #00-90, 0-80, 1-72 & 2-56.

## Swivel Head Pin Vise

**321-9701818** **9.15**
Holds drills, taps, reamers, etc, from 0 to 1/8" diameter. Steel, 3-5/8"' long. Includes 2 Collets.

## Adjustable Split Dies 13/16" dia. 17.35 ea (Unless Noted)

**321-9210090** 00-90 **18.59**
**321-9210080** 0-80
**321-9210172** 1-72
**321-9210256** 2-56
**321-9210348** 3-48
**321-9210440** 4-40
**321-9210540** 5-40
**321-9210632** 6-32

**321-9401728** Die Holder **10.10**

## ...p Wrench

**...1-9401710** #0-1/4" **16.20**

## ...azor Saws

**...21-8316008** Model Makers ...azor Saw **22.35**
...uts wood, plastic and brass ...ithout dulling. 9-1/4" overall ...ith hardwood handle and ...rass back. Cuts 3/4" deep, ...ith 60 teeth per inch. Blade is ...-1/4" long and .008" thin.
**...21-8416008** Replacement ...lade For #8316008 **14.95**
...eplaceable Blade can be ...eversed in the holder for ...elicate work requiring a pull ...troke.

## ...lexi-Blade Flush Cut Saw

**...21-8312320 33.45**
...eatures a double-edged ...recision blade with a unique ...hin and flexible design, perfect ...or cutting wood, plastic and ...oft metals. The result: easy, ...exible maneuvering, as well ...as clean trimming. Features 23 ...eeth per inch, .020" blade ...hickness, 4-3/4" blade length, ...-3/8" blade width, 1"overall ...ength.

## Gyrosguard™ Safety Guard Kits

Provides safety and protection when using most Dremel®- and Craftsman®-type hand-held motor tools. Each lightweight guard is shatter-resistant. Guard measures 2-3/4" long. Comes with mandrel and cutting accessory.

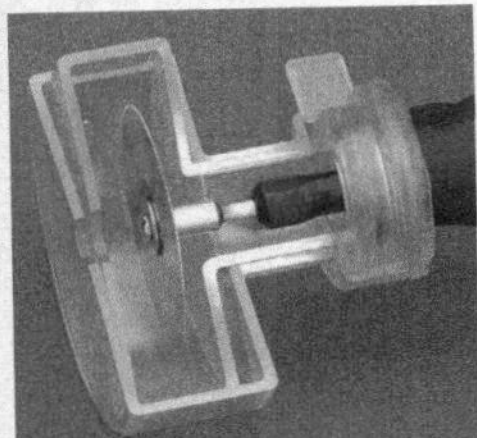

**321-5012510** 0-1-1/2" Diameter Capacity **20.59**
Kit includes 1 Fiber Disk™ and mandrel.
**321-5025010** 0-2-1/2" Diameter Capacity **25.75**
Kit includes 1 Fiber Disk™ and mandrel.

## Ratchet Drill/Vise

**321-9701837 16.05**
Tool can be used as pin vise or as hand drill by pushing the quick return center piece along the twisted bar. Holds drills 68-80.

## Fiber Disks

Cuts and grinds many materials, and resists breakage.

### Low Tensile

Can be used on glass, plastic, stone, ceramic, wood, aluminum, copper, brass and other low tensile strength materials. 1/8" hole use mandrel #321-8018100.
**321-1132102** 1" Dia x 1/32", 1/8" Hard pkg(2) **3.45**
**321-1132154** 1-1/2" Dia x 1/32", 1/8", Hard pkg(2) **3.89**

### High Tensile

Ideal on steel, steel alloys, hard bronze and other high tensile strength materials.
**321-1132156** 1-1/2" Dia x 1/32", 1/8" Hard pkg(2) **3.19**
1/8" hole, use with Mandrel (#321-8018100).
**321-1132208** 2" Dia x 1/32", 1/8" Hard pkg(2) **4.05**
1/8" hole, use with Mandrel #321-18100.

## Circular Saw Blades

Circular, tempered carbon steel blades, hollow-ground for superior performance with 1/8" hole. Use with mandrel #321-8018100. Dimension indicates diameter.

### Ultra-Fine Teeth

For wood, plastic and soft metal. Includes two washers.
**321-8110805** .005", 7/8" Diameter, 1/16" Hole, 120 Teeth **6.30**
**321-8210805** .005" w/Mandrel **8.75**

### Fine Teeth

**321-8110715** 3/4", 60 Teeth **11.95**
**321-8110815** 7/8", 80 Teeth **12.39**
**321-8111015** 1", 68 Teeth **12.89**
**321-8111215** 1-1/4", 80 Teeth **14.25**
**321-8111515** 1-1/2", 100 Teeth **16.05**
**321-8112015** 2", 140 Teeth **22.09**
**321-8211000** 1 Each of Thick & Thin 1" Diameter, 76 Teeth w/Mandrel pkg(2) **18.59**
**321-8210715** 3/4", 60 Teeth w/Mandrel **14.79**
**321-8210815** 7/8", 80 Teeth w/Mandrel **15.35**
**321-8211015** 1", 68 Teeth, w/Mandrel **15.85**
**321-8211215** 1-1/4", 80 Teeth w/Mandrel **17.19**
**321-8211515** 1-1/2", 100 Teeth w/Mandrel **18.98**
**321-8212015** 2", 140 Teeth w/Mandrel **25.19**

### Coarse Teeth

**321-8120715** 3/4", 36 Teeth **11.89**
**321-8121015** 1", 34 Teeth **12.89**
**321-8220715** 3/4", 36 Teeth w/Mandrel **14.79**
**321-8221015** 1", 34 Teeth w/Mandrel **15.85**

### Rip Saw Blades

With set teeth for fast, controlled, split-free cutting of all soft and hard woods. Ideal for plastics. Non-binding.
**321-8132018** Thin, Fine 2" x .018" w/140 Teeth **13.79**
**321-8232018** Same as #321-8132018 w/Mandrel **16.98**
**321-8131222** 1-1/4", 48 Teeth **11.05**
**321-8231222** 1-1/4", 48 Teeth w/Mandrel **13.79**
**321-8230821** 7/8" w/Mandrel, 36 Teeth pkg(2) **16.49**

## 1/8" Chucks

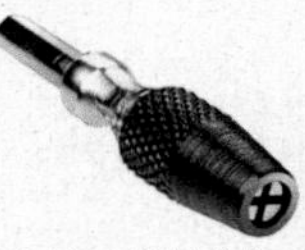

**321-4501801** Mini Adaptor Chuck Stainless Steel **6.95**
Collet capacity 0" to .0390" (drill #61-80). Used in hand or electric drills for fast accurate centering of 61-80 drill bits.

**321-4501819** Adaptor Chuck Stainless Steel **14.79**
For use with drills #42-80. The all-purpose chuck has two collets with range of .0-.094". Features a cross-drilled hole for easily tightening larger drills.

## Mandrels

Mandrels for saws and fiberglass reinforced cut-off wheels.

### 1/8" Shank

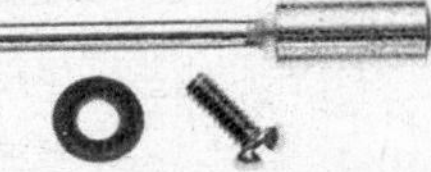

**321-8018100** Stainless Steel, 1/8" Screw **3.19**
**321-8018102** Nickel Plated Steel, 1/16" Screw **3.19**
**321-8018105** Stainless Steel 1/4" Screw **4.20**

## Mounted Wire Wheel

**321-1184285** Steel, 3/4" Diameter **3.00**

## 5-1/2" Files 1.25 ea

Dealers MUST order multiples of 12.
**321-4901261** Knife
**321-4901263** Square 
**321-4901266** Flat

## Needle File Sets

### Economy Needle File Set

**321-4901406** 5-1/2", 6-Piece **7.15**
One each #2 cut: knife, rat tail, equaling, square, half round and flat. Pouched.

### Giant Needle File Set

**321-4901407** 7", 5-Piece **13.29**
One each #2 cut: triangular, square, 1/2 round, round and equaling. Pouched.

### Superior Needle File Set

For all soft metals and wood. #2 cut, unless noted. Pouched.

**321-4901400** 5-1/2", 6-Piece **12.60**
**321-4901401** 5-1/2", 12-Piece **21.85**

## Rasp Sets

### Needle

**321-4901405** 6-Piece **16.15**
Coarse cut for plaster, wood plastic, stone and all soft materials, including wax. Includes square, equalizing, 1/2 round, 3 square, round and flat 5-1/2". Pouched.

### Curved

**321-4901485** 6-Piece **31.39**
Double-ended, 8", maintains a great finish. Pouched.

## Riffler Sets

Double-ended riffler files for wood, metal, plastic and stone. 6" long. Each tool has two shaped ends. All sets pouched.

**321-4901488** 6-Piece Set, Single & Double Cut **27.05**
**321-4901489** Mini 3-Piece Set, Medium Cut **17.05**

For Up-To-Date Information and News Bookmark Walthers Web site at
**www.walthers.com**

## Hobby Hand Brushes 3.65 ea

Fine wire brush cleans files, saws and drill bits. Removes rust, tarnish, dirt. 3/8", wire bristles, .005"; 8" overall. Smooth wood handle.

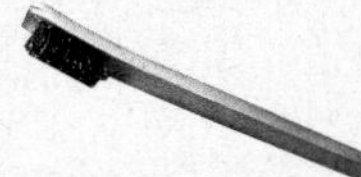

**321-2101822** Stainless
**321-2101824** Brass

## Mini-Vise

**321-9701827 9.15**
Clamp-on tiny diecast steel vise fits 3/4" table top. 7/8" opening.

## Mini-Pick 5 Piece Assortment

**321-7101840 25.39**
Stainless tiny picks, probes, scrapers, hooks. 6" long.

## Mini-Watchmakers Pliers Set

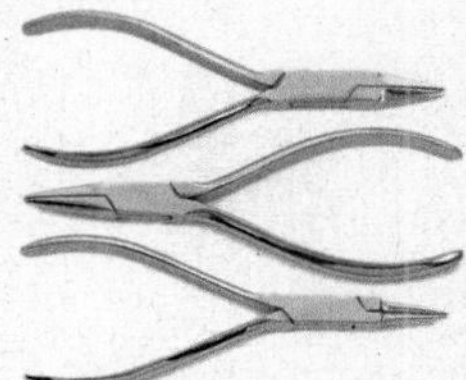

**321-7301333 22.40**
Smooth jaw, box joint, 4-1/2" set includes flat, round and chain.

## Tiny Tinsnip

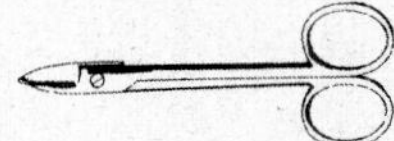

**321-7301830 6.85**
4-1/4", one serrated jaw.

GYROS

## Tweezers 6.35 ea

Swiss-style watchmakers tweezers. Nonmagnetic, stainless steel, fine point 4-5/8" long.

**321-9501741** Straight

**321-9501742** Curved

## Hemostats 8.19 ea

Use to grip, pull or clamp. Ideal for soldering, wire work and other modeling needs. 5-1/2" long.

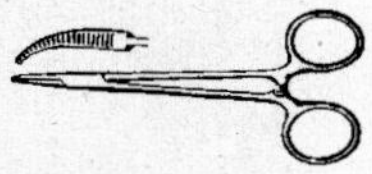

**321-9501820** Curved

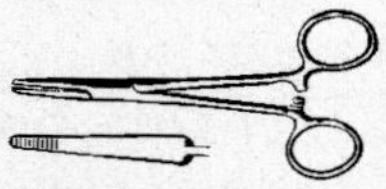

**321-9501821** Straight

## Propak Tool Sets

These kits provide an array of cutting accessories for most cutting needs.

**321-6111807** Fiber Disk (7 Pieces) **16.75**
Includes five disks ranging in size from 1" diameter to 2-1/2" diameter in all three formulations of LT (cuts glass, plastic, stone, ceramic, wood, aluminum, copper and brass), HT (cuts hardened and unhardened steel, steel alloys and hard bronze) and ST (cuts stainless steel, titanium, chrome). Two mandrels included.

**321-6111808** Fiber Disk (8 Pieces) **17.19**
Includes seven fiber disks ranging in size from 1" diameter to 1-3/4" diameter in formulations of LT, HT and ST.

## Calipers

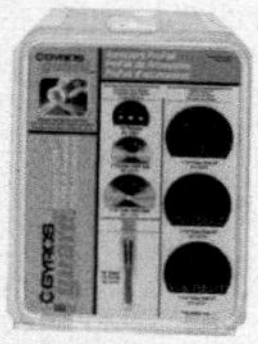

**321-6111817** Accessory (7 Pieces) **34.25**
Includes three circular saws (fine teeth 1-1/4" diameter, coarse teeth 1" diameter, and ripsaw 7/8" diameter), three fiber disks (one each LT, HT and ST, 1-1/2" diameter), and one mandrel.

GENERAL®

Measuring, marking and assembly tools for hobbyists, industry or specialty trades.

## Calipers

**285-143** 6" Digital **92.80**
Gives direct readings of 0.001" (0.1mm). Features include an adjustable zero, fiberglass-reinforced super polyamid, friction thumb roller and four-way measurement (outside, inside, depth and step).

**285-142** 6" Dial Caliper **37.59**
6" capacity in .01" and 64ths and mm. Adjustable zero for inside, outside, depth and step measurements.

**285-144** Metric Version of #142 **39.89**
Capacity 0-150mm by .01mm.

**265-145** 6" Dial Caliper **44.55**
Capacity 0-6". Readings in .001". Single revolution of dial is .100".

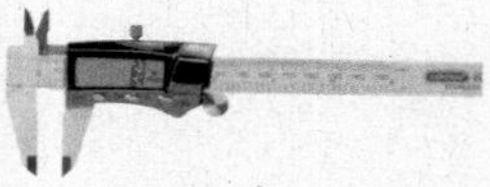

**NEW 285-147** Digital Fractional Caliper (metal) **44.95**

## Drill Accessories

**285-33** Drill Saw **4.30**
For handheld power drill or drill press.

## Drill Gauges

**285-13** #61-80 **16.45**

**285-15** #1-60 **13.90**

**285-24** Hobby 1/16 to 1/2" in 64ths **6.60**

**285-715** Reference Table **7.79**
Tap drill sizes and decimal equivalents.

## Files

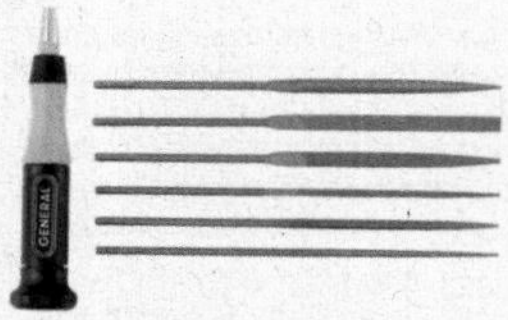

**NEW 285-707476** Swiss Pattern Needle File Set **13.29**
Six styles with case.

## Knives

**NEW 285-853** Utility Knife **5.45**
Includes three heavy-duty blades.

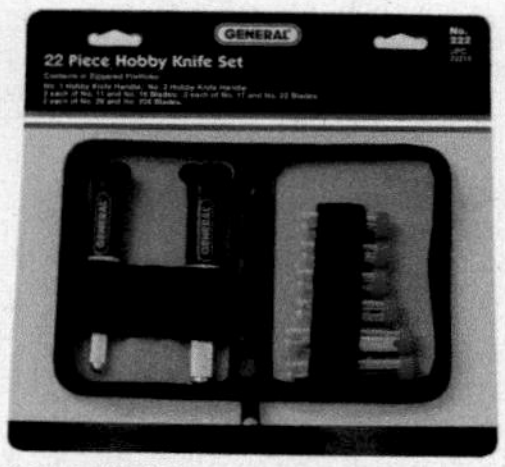

**285-75622** 22-Piece Hobby Knife & Blade Set **20.79**

## Mechanics Steel Squares

**285-2706** 6" **27.90**

## Nut Driver Set

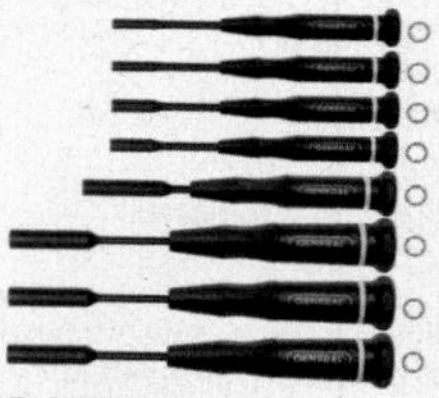

**285-67508B** 8-Piece Precision Set **35.80**
5/64, 3/32, 7/64, 1/8, 5/32, 3/16, 7/32, 1/4

## Oiler

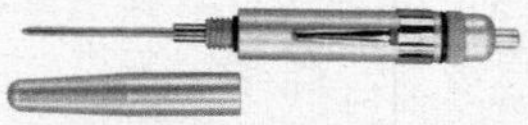

**285-589** Precision Oiler **10.55**

## Pick-Ups

**285-388** Mini **6.45**
Four-prong steel jaws retrieve small objects up to 1/2" 14mm. Tapered point for hard-to-reach work areas.

**285-396** Heavy-Duty **7.89**
With flexible 24" shaft and four-prong jaws.

## Punch

**285-70079** Automatic Center Punch **12.50**
Adjustable light to heavy stroke, single-handed operation. 5 x 1/2" body.

## Rules

### Multi Use Rule & Gauge

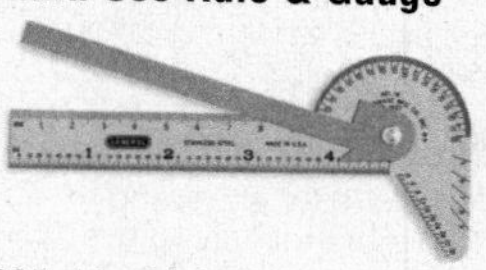

**285-16** **11.98**
4th rule in 64th and mm, drill point gauge, protractor, center finder for shafts and circles, circle divider, and tap-and-drill table for National Thread.

## Protractors

**285-17** Machinist/Mechanic **14.95**
0 to 180 square head, 6" adjustable arm. Made of steel.

**285-29** Woodworking Protractor/Angle Finder **5.25**
Measures outside, inside and sloped angles.

## Railroad Scale Rules

**285-1251** 12" **8.30**
12" flex model railroad rule. 1" wide with HO, S, O, N, MM, 64, graduations and decimal equivalent.

**285-1203** 12" Flexible Rule **7.65**
12" flex rule 15/32" wide with mm, .5mm, 32, 64 grads.

## Screwdrivers

### Pocket 4-in-1 Mini Screwdriver

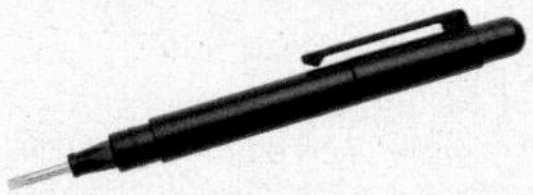

**285-744** **2.55**
Features two slotted tips (1/16 and 1/8") and two cross-point tips (#1 and #00). 5-1/8" overall closed length.

## Precision Screwdrivers

**285-612020** #00 Phillips **3.70**

**285-712010** #0 Phillips **4.15**

**285-712101** #1 Phillips **4.98**

**285-611078** 5/64 Slotted **3.70**

**285-611094** 3/32 Slotted **3.70**

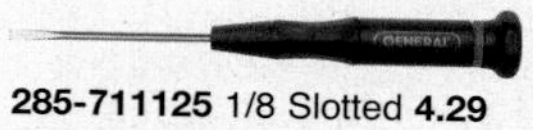

**285-711125** 1/8 Slotted **4.29**

**285-711140** 9/64 Slotted **4.50**

**285-711156** 5/32 Slotted **4.50**

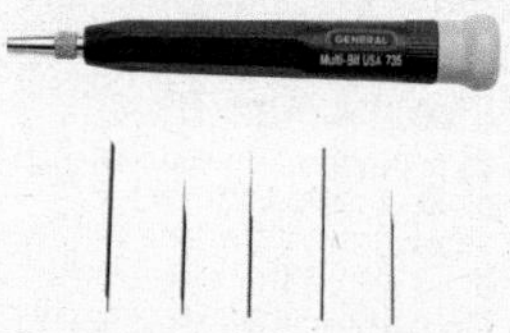

**285-735** 5-In-One Multi-Bit Precision Screwdriver **10.89**

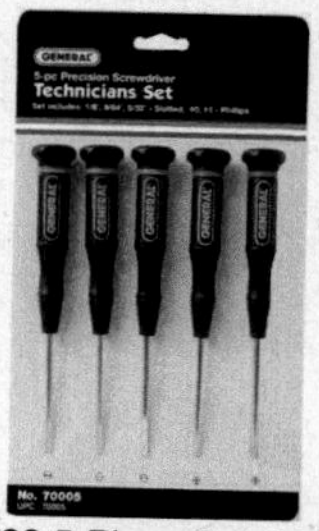

**285-700** 5-Piece Set **19.29**
Includes one each Precision Screwdrivers #701-703, 705 and 706.

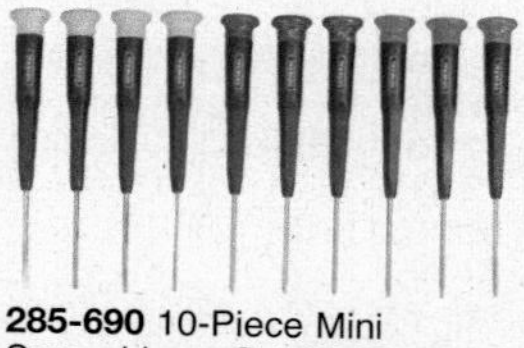

**285-690** 10-Piece Mini Screwdrivers Set **22.19**
Includes one each Slotted 3/64, 1/16, 5/64, 3/32. Phillips 000,00,0. Torx T6, T7, T8.

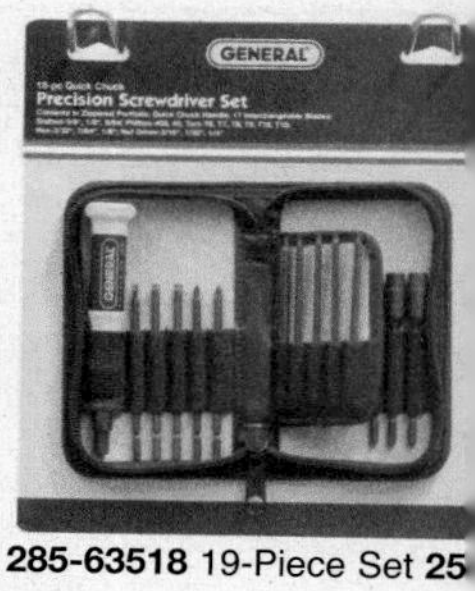

**285-63518** 19-Piece Set **25**

## Scriber

**285-81** Pocket Scriber **5.86**
3/8" diameter. Knurled body with reversible, hardened-ground point.

## Vises

### Pin Vises

**285-90** Pin Vise **14.49**
Nickel-plated body is hollow permit use of long rods, 3-3/ long with 5/16" body. Two double-ended collets, capac .0 to .125, .0 to 3.2mm.

**285-93** Heavy Duty Adjustab Pin Vise **13.95**
Holds small drills, wires, files etc. Three jaw-hardened stee keyless chuck, sturdy plastic handle. 6-7/8" overall length, 1" diameter. Capacity .040 to .250, 1mm to 6.4mm.

**285-92** Swivel Head Pin Vise **11.19**
Exceptional for delicate work Single collet made of harden tool steel. Large free-wheelin swivel head. 4" overall, 5/16" diameter body.

## Wire Stripper

**285-69** Dial Wire Stripper **10.85**
Set wire size on dial for exact stripping without the worry of damaging wire. Features viny cushion handles.

ENGINEERING

›ldering tools, various tool ›ts and accessory items for ›odel builders.

### djustable Threading ies 8.99 ea Jnless Noted)

gh speed, steel, 13/16" ameter dies with unified reads.

**70-415** 0-80
**70-416** 1-72
**70-417** 2-56
**70-418** 3-58
**70-419** 4-40
**70-420** Die Handle **12.70**
arbon steel, positive lock die ›ock handle.

### leedle File Set

**70-430** 6" pkg(10) **11.19**

### lex-I-Grit 2.75 ea

ealers MUST order dealer ack of 36 (all one number).

**70-4001** "A" Regular, ssorted Grits
or general purpose hobby anding, one sheet each: SIL 50 coarse grit, GAR 280 nedium grit, SIL 320 fine grit, L 400 extra-fine grit, AL 600 ltra-fine grit.

**70-4002** "B" Micro-Fine, ssorted Grits
or exceedingly high finishes. One sheet each: 23 micron silicon carbon, light gray; 23 micron aluminum oxide, tan; micron silicon carbide, dark gray. 0.5 micron chromium oxide, green; 1.5 micron cerium oxide, burnt orange. Micron = 1 millionth of a meter). Five 4 x 5-1/2" sheets per pack.

### Flex-I-Grit Sanding Sheets pkg(5) 2.75 ea

- Sand any surface: wood, plastic, metal, paint
- Fit to any shape; won't crack, peel or clog
- Flex to clean

Use over and over, wet or dry. Reusable abrasive coated polyester. Silicon carbide. Dealers MUST Order dealer pack of 36.

**370-4011** 150 Coarse
**370-4031** 320 Fine

### Hobby Drill

**370-6504 24.99**
This lightweight, powerful battery-operated drill is great for small jobs including drilling and embossing metal, etching metals and wood, sanding, tool sharpening and more. Comes in a cool camouflage color scheme and includes stylus, etching and drill bit, two sanding disks, and three different chucks.

### Hobby Hammer

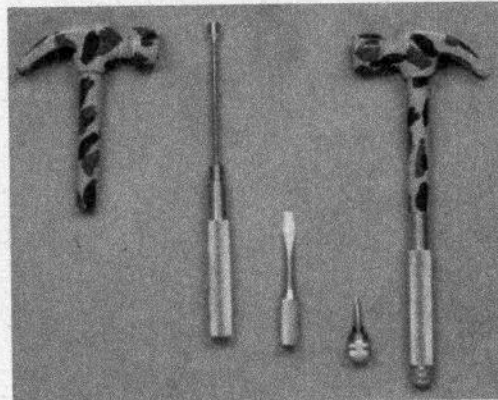

**370-6502 13.99**
Achieve professional results with this multi-use tool in a fresh, cool design. Features flat and Phillips head screwdrivers and strong steel hammer head. Extendable magnetic pickup gets into hard-to-reach places.

### Sandpaper

**370-476** Wet/Dry **1.79**
Contains three each: 180 coarse grit, 240 medium grit, 280 fine grit.

Dealers MUST order 24 packs.

### Saw

**370-295** Precision Metal Saw **9.99**
Designed for cutting tubing and small metal shapes of brass and copper. 52 teeth per inch for fine cutting.

### Soldering Gun

**370-1210** Electric Soldering Gun **24.99**
With tip, 110V, 100 watts.

### Soldering Iron

**370-300** With Tip, 30 Watts **9.99**

**370-311** Replacement Tips for #300 **3.90**

**370-910** Heavy Duty w/Tip, 60 Watts **9.79**

**370-911** Replacement Tips for #910 **3.90**

### Taps 5.49 ea (Unless Noted)

**370-435** 0-80
**370-436** 1-72
**370-437** 2-56
**370-438** 3-48
**370-439** 4-40
**370-434** Tap Handle **13.49**

### Tubing Bender Kit

**370-321 3.19**
Bend tubing in the following sizes: 1/16", 3/32", 1/8", 5/32" and 3/16" outside diameter.

### Tubing Cutter

**370-296 6.49**

### Wire Bender

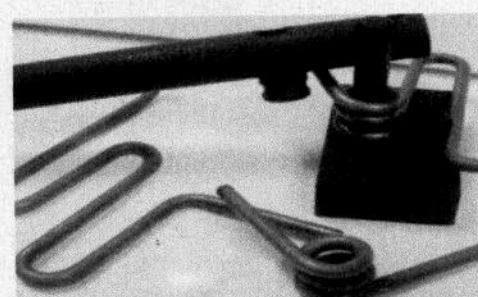

**370-326** Mighty Wire Bender & Coiler **27.99**
Bends 1/4" music wire and square or rectangular shaped metal. You can produce your own clamps, brackets, landing gear, hangers and more.

**370-323** Mini **12.99**
Bends music wire or brass wire diameters of 1/8" and smaller, as well as square- and rectangular-shaped metal.

## ERNST MANUFACTURING

### Hobby Trays

Each tray measures 1-1/2" deep.

**259-158** Regular 10-1/2 x 10-1/2" **3.95**
Stackable tray features 3" wide compartments.

**259-159** Deluxe 11 x 16" **5.95**
Features a variety of compartment sizes for unlimited storage versatility.

## NOVACON TOOLS

### NEW PRODUCT

### Quasar LS

**NEW 515-6010** LED Lighting System for Magnifying Visors **24.95**
Provides even lighting for OptiVISOR® magnifying visors (sold separately). Unit simply screws onto the lens plate with no modification needed. A small battery pack strapped to the headband supplies power to the lightweight LED board.

## Labelle industries

### NEW PRODUCTS

### Original Tippi Hot Wire Foam Cutter

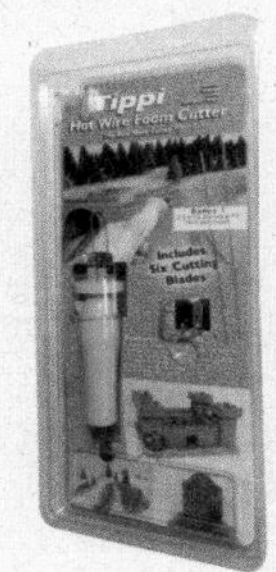

**NEW 430-284774 39.98**
Using the Original Tippi you can create custom brick and rock retaining walls, tunnel portals, secnic hills and rivers for only pennies of material instead of buyiing expensive factory pre-fab scenic features. Includes four cutting blades, two extra straight blades and complete instructions.

### Accessories

**NEW 430-284779** Copi Cutter Attachment **22.98**
For cutting thicker foam. Includes two blades and instructions.

**NEW 430-284780** B Wire pkg(5) **8.98**
Straight blades .045" Diameter.

**NEW 430-284781** Custom Blade Pack pkg(4) **16.98**
0.45 Diameter. Includes one each needle nose, square, round and detail blade.

**NEW 430-284782** .072 Fine Detail Blade Pack **14.95**
Includes one each square, needle nose, detail and .072 Diameter terrain cutter.

**NEW 430-284786** Wooden Foam Binding Rods pkg(100) **2.00**

### DVD

**NEW 430-284787** How to Create Scenic Effects Using the Original Tippi **14.98**
This instructional DVD includes ideas for train layouts, Christmas decorations, Dept. 56 collectible displays and much, much more. Approximately 45 minutes. Expected delivery Fall 2007.



### Klippie Light

**NEW 430-801 pkg(2) 4.49**
Illuminate tight and hard to reach areas with this tiny, high intensity LED light. It can easily be clipped to the bill of a cap or any stationary object for hands-free lighting on your work bench or layout. Comes with alligator clip base. A small ball socket provides rotation all directions. Batteries are included. Buy an extra set for your auto glove compartment.

## NMRA

### Standards Gauge 12.00 ea

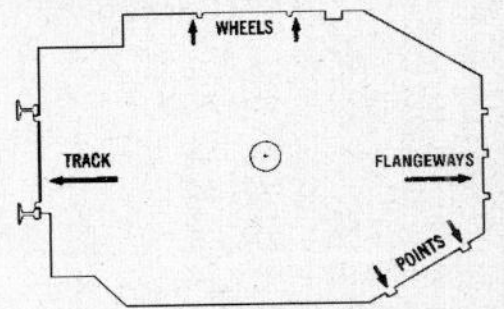


Designed and developed by the NMRA (National Model Railroad Association) Engineering Committee, this pocket-sized gauge enables you to check all important dimensions on your track and rolling stock as follows:

- Gauge of track and turnouts
- Flangeway depth and "check gauge"
- Clearance
- Height of loading platform and coupler

If cars do not run correctly, this gauge will pinpoint the trouble for you. Complete instructions come with each gauge.

**98-1** HO Standard Gauge
**98-2** HOn3 Standard Gauge
**98-5** O Standard Gauge
**98-6** On3/00 Standard Gauge
**98-7** Sn3 Standard Gauge
**98-8** N Standard Gauge

# MASCOT® PRECISION TOOLS

Mascot tools are quality engineered to give top performance and satisfaction.

## MOTORIZED HANDPIECE ACCESSORIES

### Adapter Chuck

**230-982 8.15**
The 3/32" shaft fits all portable electric rotary tools. Holds miniature drills from #80 (.014") to #43 (.089").

### Bur & Wheel Stand

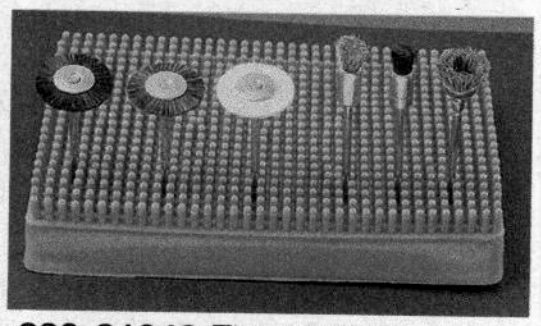

**230-81049** For 3/32" Shank Burs **5.99**
Holds all your shaft tools upright and ready for quick access.

### Cut Off Disks

**230-81030** 7/8" pkg(50) **10.50**
These high-speed resin-bonded, aluminum-oxide disks offer fast, cool and smooth cutting on all metal.

### Sander Set

**230-980 41.95**
Rotary Tool Accessory Kit (18 pieces) 1/8" and 1/32" shanks. Fits all electric portable rotary tools.

## PLIERS

### Joint Pliers 12.60 ea

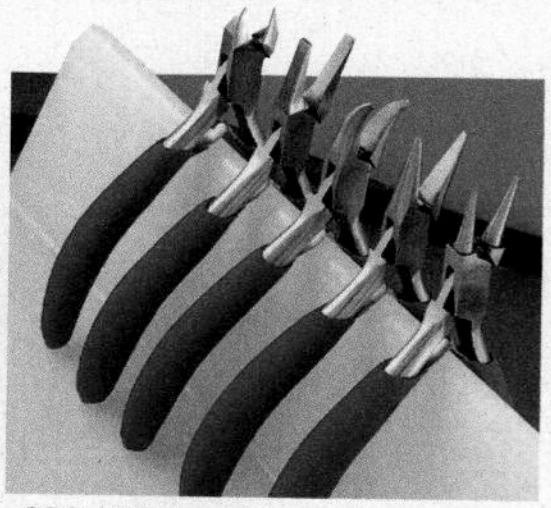

**230-480** Flat Nose
**230-481** Chain Nose
**230-483** Diagonal Cutters
**230-485** Bent Nose
**230-488** Round Nose

### Long Ranger Pliers 11.55 ea

These unique pliers have an extra long body that gets the user closer to the work than regular pliers. The hinged joint of the plier jaws is closer to the working end of the tool, giving the maximum possible holding power. Each has matte finish with closed-cell handle covers and leaf spring return.

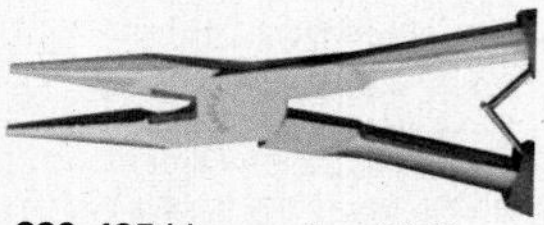

**230-495** Lineman's w/Cutter

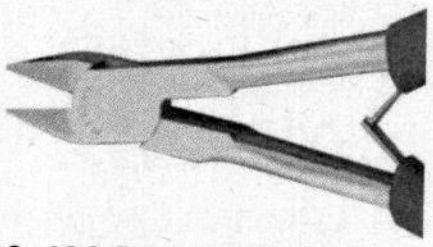

**230-496** Diagonal Cutters

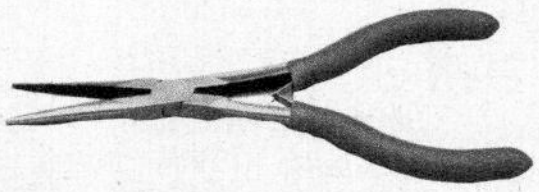

**230-498** Serrated Jawed Needle Nose

### Miniature Electronic Pliers 8.40 ea

Features double-leaf spring return for extra-smooth and quiet, nonbinding opening and closure.

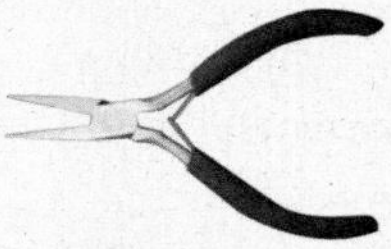

**230-380** Flat Nose

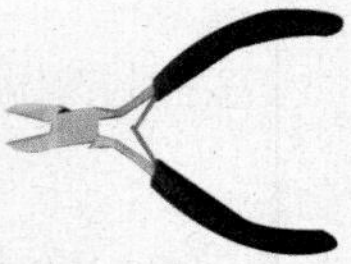

**230-383** Diagonal

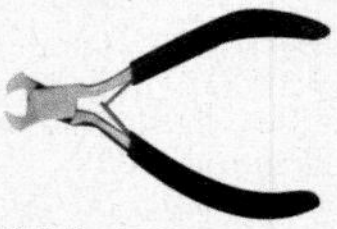

**230-384** End Nippers

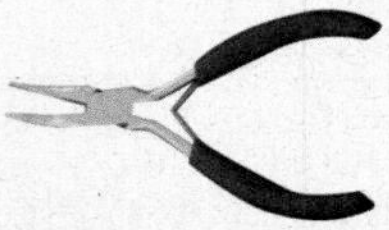

**230-385** Bent Needle Nose

**230-387** Needle Nose

### Miniature Pliers 5.25 ea (Unless Noted)

Each pliers offers a brushed satin finish and spring action return with a solid feel.

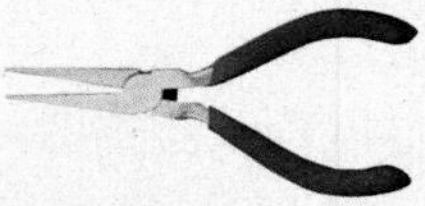

**230-370** Flat Nose

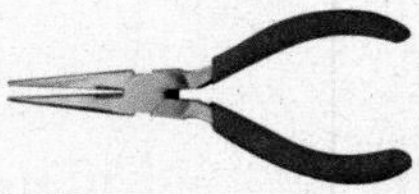

**230-371** Needle Nose

**230-373** Diagonal **10.80**

**230-374** End Nippers **10.80**

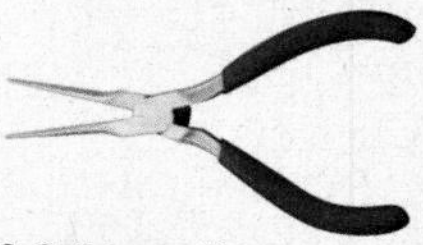

**230-376** Long Nose

### Premier Pliers

**230-400** Flat Nose **24.15**
**230-402** Needle Nose **26.25**
**230-403** Wire Cutter **31.50**

For Daily Product Updates Point Your Browser to
**www.walthers.com**

### Sprue & Fine Wire Cutting Pliers

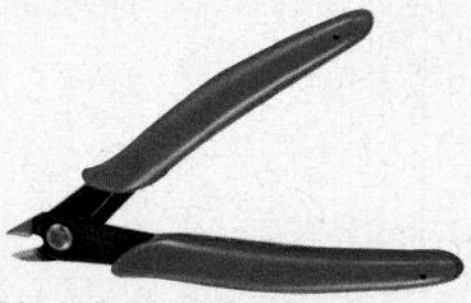

**230-450 11.30**
Features hardened, slim-line, razor-sharp jaws, cushion grips and is perfect for cutting sprue cleanly. Can also cut wire up to .40" 1mm.

## TWEEZERS

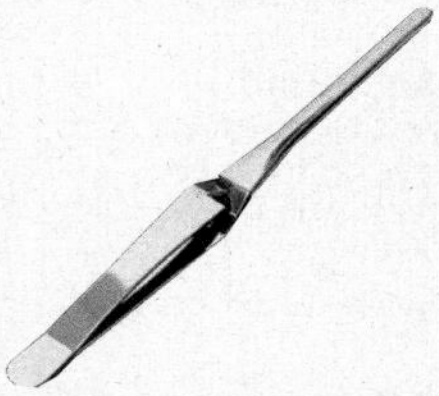

**230-500** Cross-Locking 6-3/8" **5.25**
Tips serrated for sure grip.

**230-501** Fine-Pointed 4-1/4" **19.95**
Sharp tips and light tension for fine work. Nickel-plated steel. Magnetic.

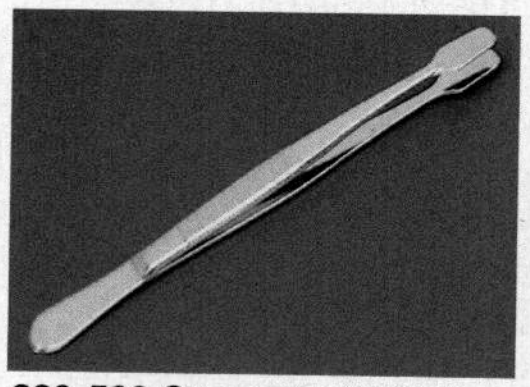

**230-503** Stamp 4-1/2" **3.70**
Smooth, wafer-thin points. Nickel-plated steel.

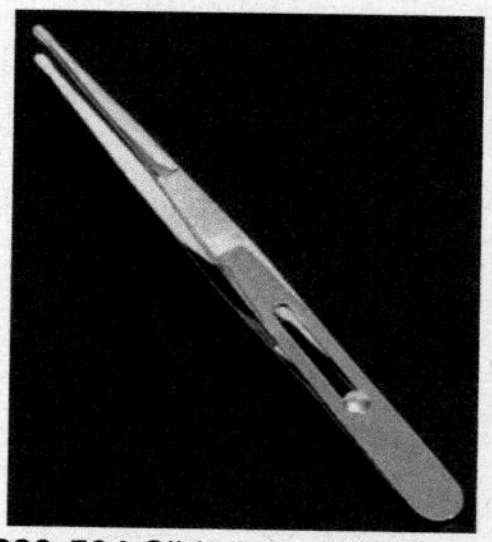

**230-504** Slide Lock 5-7/8" **8.15**
Thin serrated tips for firm grip, thin flat back permits holding tweezer vise. Chrome plated.

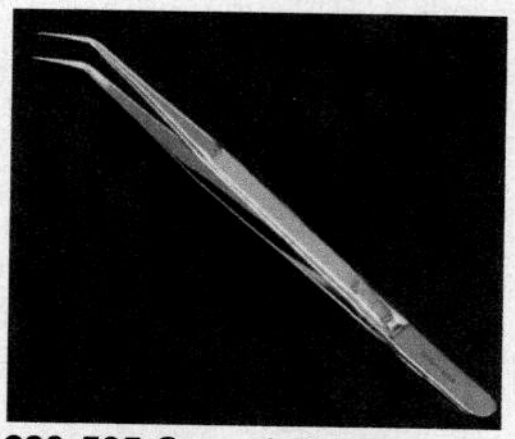

**230-505** Curved 6" **6.60**
Nickel-plated steel with slender tips, serrated for positive grip.

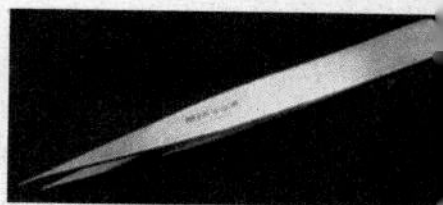

**230-506** Sharp Pointed 4-3
**5.80**

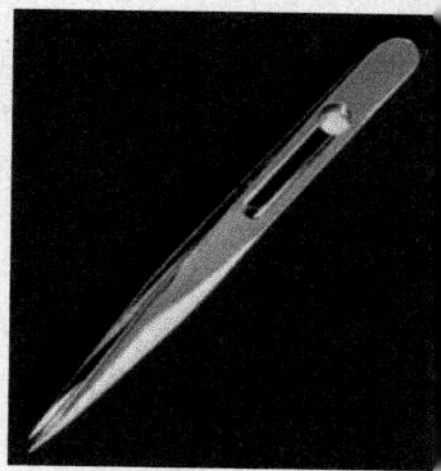

**230-507** Slide Lock 4-3/4" 6

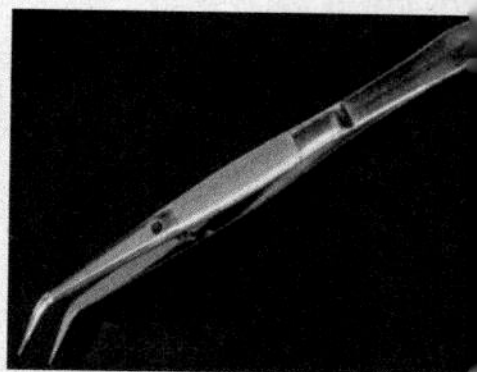

**230-508** Curved 4-1/2" **6.50**

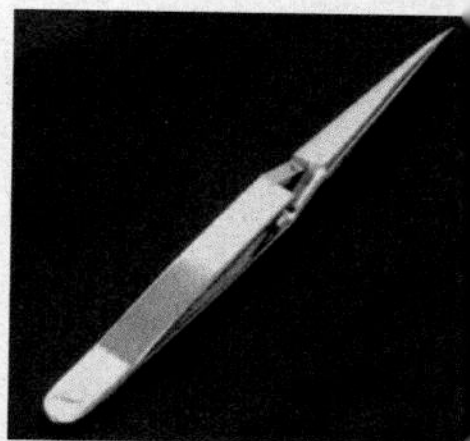

**230-509** Cross Lock 4-1/2" **5.80**

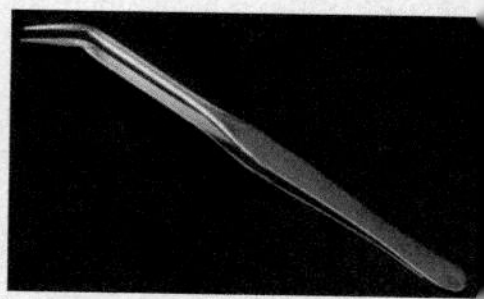

**230-510** Curved 6-7/8" **5.80**

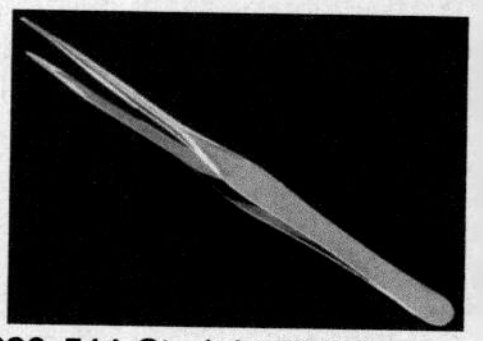

**230-511** Straight 7" **5.25**

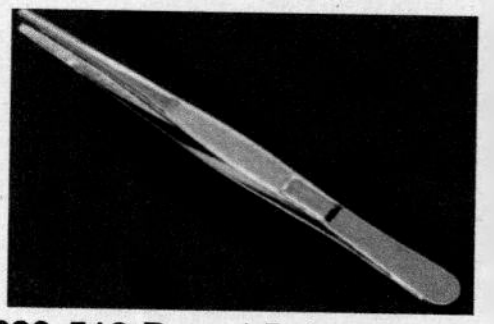

**230-512** Round Point 6" **5.25**

**230-515** Glass Filled Tweezer Non-Conductive/Anti-Magnetic **2.10**

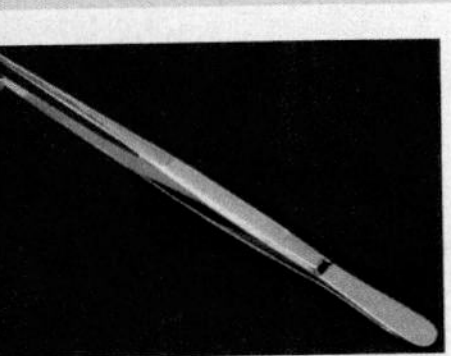

30-520 Retrieving 8" **8.35**

30-521 All Purpose Tweezer Set **23.95**
3/4" stamp, 4-1/2" sharp pointed, 6" retrieving, " curved, 6-1/2" curved and 1/2" self-closing.

30-530 Magnifying Tweezers .40

30-531 Decal Tweezers 4-1/2" **7.35**
Nickel-plated steel tweezers with thin, smooth spade points, angled to allow perfect placement of decals.

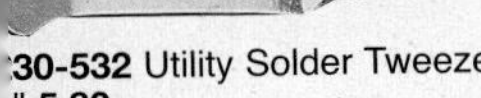

30-532 Utility Solder Tweezer " **5.80**

30-533 Slotted Tweezers 4" .35

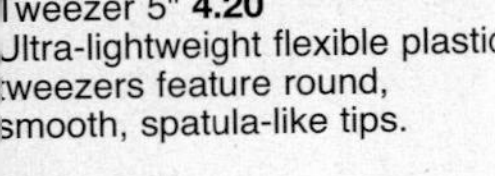

230-534 Soft Tipped Decal Tweezer 5" **4.20**
Ultra-lightweight flexible plastic tweezers feature round, smooth, spatula-like tips.

# KNIVES

## Knife Blades w/Safe Vial

### Blades for #230-1 Knife Handle

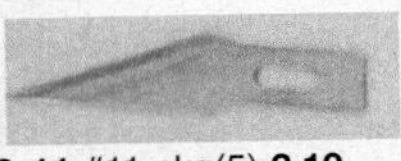

**230-11** #11 pkg(5) **2.10**

**230-16** #16 pkg(5) **1.95**

### Blades For #230-2, 230-5, 230-9 Knife Handles

**230-22** #22 pkg(5) **3.50**

**230-23** #23 pkg(5) **5.60**

**230-24** #24 pkg(5) **2.30**

**Limited Quantity Available**

**230-19** #19 pkg(5) **2.45**

### Mini Blades For #230-110 Knife Handles

**230-1101** pkg(5) **5.05**

## Knife Sets

### Deluxe Hobby-Craft Modelers Knife & Tool Set

**230-866 41.90**
Contains one each lightweight, medium weight, heavy-duty knife, hobby awl, miter box, razor saw, sander, screwdriver and 20 assorted blades.

### Precision Knife Set

**230-182 15.75**
Includes a lightweight, medium weight and heavy-duty knife plus a plastic storage tray.

### Deluxe Knife Set

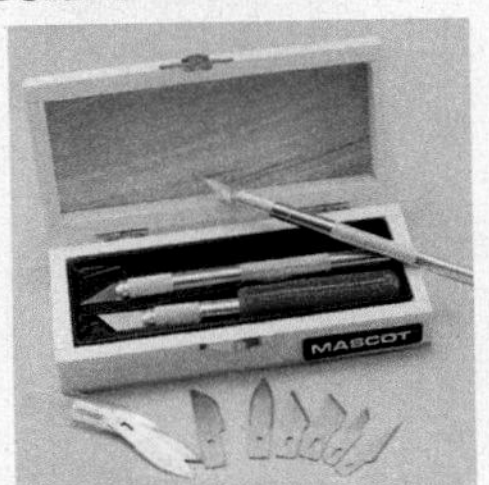

**230-865 19.70**
Same knives as #182 plus 10 assorted blades and wooden storage box.

## Modeling Knives

### #1 Lightweight w/Blade

**230-1 2.55**

**230-111** With 3 Blades **5.05**

### #2 Medium Weight w/Blade

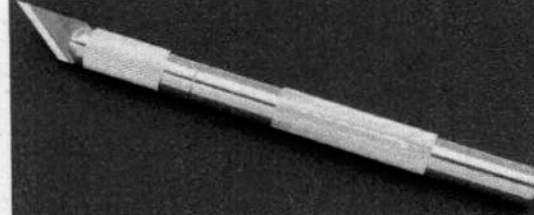

**230-2 3.80**

### #5 Heavy-Duty w/Blade

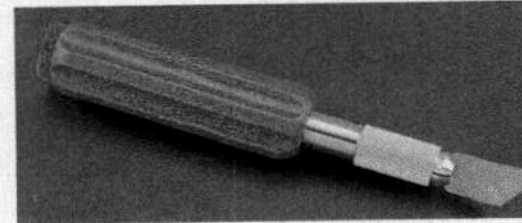

**230-5 4.40**

### Scalpel w/Blades

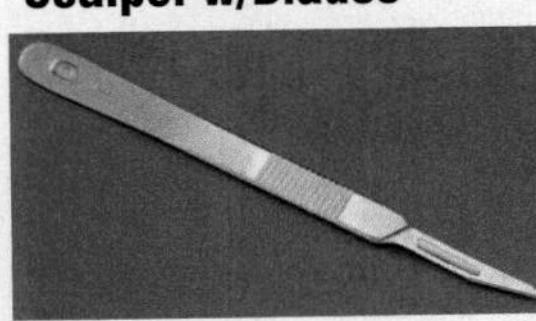

**230-30 5.25**
True medical-surgical instrument with slim-line, stainless-steel scalpel handle. Includes two German-engineered scalpel blades.

**230-3011** Replacement Blades pkg(5) **3.45**

# SAWS

## Hobby Saw w/Blades

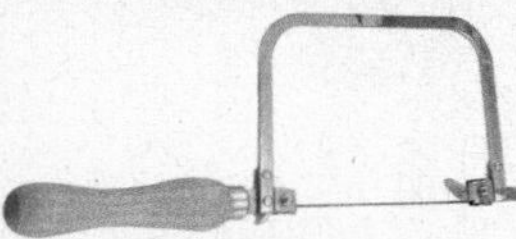

**230-99 10.50**
Holds blades securely. Offers rigidity for accurate cut. Includes 12 Swiss-made jeweler's saw blades.

## Jeweler's Saws

Includes 12 blades.

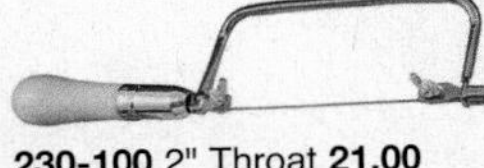

**230-100** 2" Throat **21.00**

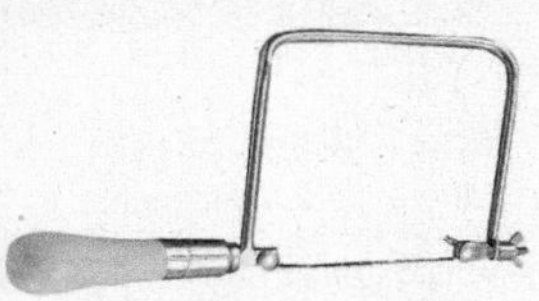

**230-103** 4" Throat **24.15**

### Jeweler's Saw Blades, Bulk Packs pkg(144) 27.25 ea

**230-120** Blade #3
**230-121** Blade #2
**230-122** Blade #1
**230-123** Blade #0
**230-124** Blade #2/0
**230-125** Blade #4/0

## Pocket Hacksaw

**230-1051** Blades For Pocket Hacksaw pkg(3) **2.70**

## Razor Saw Blade

**230-102** 1-1/4" **4.35**
Fits #2 and #5 handles.

# MITER BOXES

## Aluminum Miter Box

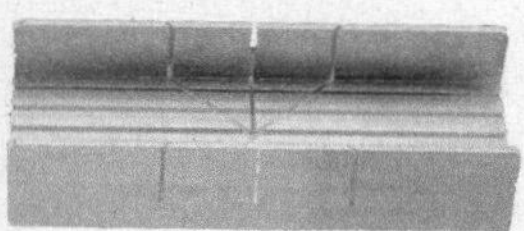

**230-206 8.40**
Just 5-1/2 x 2". Uses 1-1/4" blade, has two 45° slots and one 90° slot.

## Mini Miter Box

**230-208 5.25**

## Portable Bench Double Miter Box

**230-209 6.95**

# FILES

## Double End Scriber

**230-300** 7" **10.50**

## Individual Files 4.10 ea

**230-770** Flat
**230-771** Half Round
**230-772** Round
**230-773** Square

**230-774** Equaling

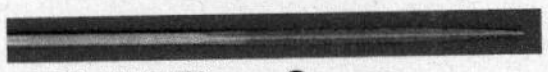

**230-775** Three-Square

## Reamers

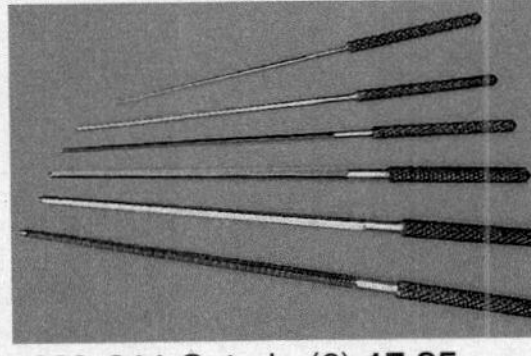

**230-311** Set pkg(6) **17.85**

## Swiss Single Cut Set

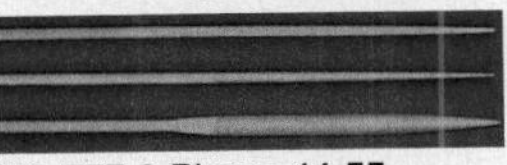

**230-777** 3 Pieces **11.55**
Includes three-square, round and half-round. 5-1/2" long.

**230-778** 6 Pieces **22.60**
Includes round, half-round, square, flat, three-square and equaling. 5-1/2" long.

## Utility File Set

**230-780** 6 Pieces **17.80**

# WOODWORKING TOOLS

## Burnishers 10.95 ea

**230-296** Curved Blade

## Scraper

**230-297 11.95**

## Woodcarving Knife Set

**230-860** 4 Pieces **64.95**
Finely balanced knives with alloy blades and wooden handles. Designed for carving, incising, shaving, splicing and notching.

## Wood Rasp Set

**230-779 59.95**
Equaling, flat, half-round, round and three-square. Overall 5-1/2" in length.

MASCOT® PRECISION TOOLS

### Woodworking Tool Sets Miniature

Both sets include one each of the following: a bent square chisel (7/32"), straight skew chisel (1/4"), straight small gouge (3/32"), bent large gouge (7/32") and a "V" parting tool (3/32").

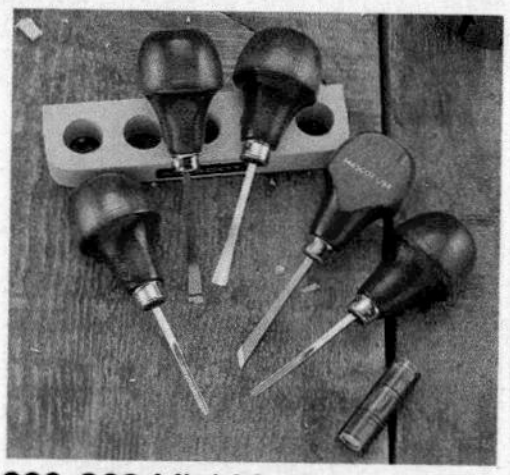

**230-863** Mini Mushroom **75.10**

**230-864** Mini Straight **69.95**

### Woodworking Tool Sets Standard

Each set has five basic shapes and you have a choice of palm-grip mushroom-shape handles (#862) or the conventional straight handle styling (#861). Both sets include one each of the following: a bent square chisel (5/16"), straight skew chisel (5/16"), straight small gouge (5/32"), bent large gouge (5/16") and a "V" parting tool (5/32").

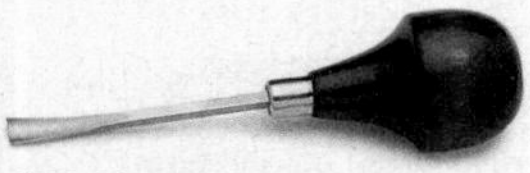

**230-861** Mushroom **69.95**

**230-862** Straight **72.95**

## JEWELER'S TOOLS

### Model Making

**230-463** Chamois Buff Set pkg(6) **10.50**

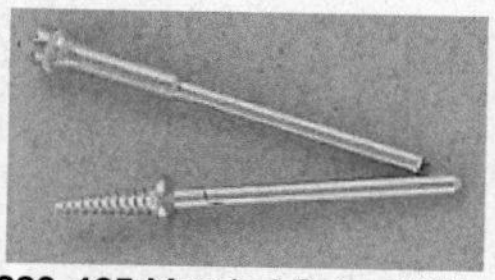

**230-465** Mandrel Set - 3/32" **4.20**

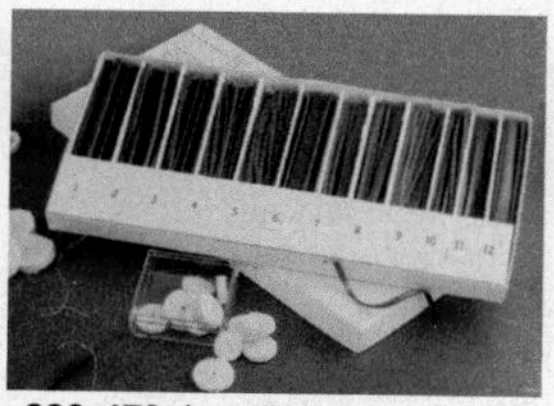

**230-470** Jeweler's Wax Set **18.95**

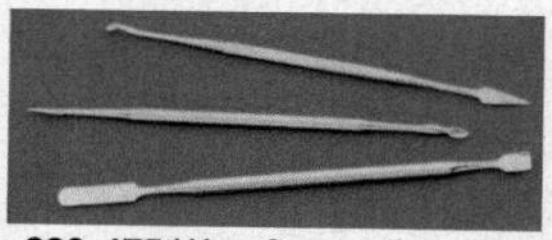

**230-475** Wax Carver/Spatula Set pkg(3) **10.50**

## DRILLS

**230-840** Mini Hand Drill **9.75**

**230-841** Spiral Drill **17.85**

### 12 Carbon Twist Drills

**230-178** **11.05**
Includes one dozen assorted drills from #50 to 80.

### Carbon Twist Drill Assortments

**230-86** 6 Carbon Twist Drills **6.30**
Assortment of the top six drill sizes preferred by hobbyists; 50, 56, 60, 65, 70 and 76.

### Carbon Twist Drills

Carbon twist drills are only available in packages of 12.

| pkg(12) 9.45 ea | pkg(12) 12.60 ea |
|---|---|
| **230-50** #50 | **230-68** #68 |
| **230-51** #51 | **230-69** #69 |
| **230-52** #52 | **230-70** #70 |
| **230-53** #53 | **230-71** #71 |
| **230-54** #54 | **230-72** #72 |
| **230-55** #55 | **230-73** #73 |
| **230-56** #56 | **230-74** #74 |
| **230-57** #57 | **230-75** #75 |
| **230-58** #58 | |
| **230-59** #59 | |
| **230-60** #60 | |

| pkg(12) 11.55 ea | pkg(12) 13.15 ea |
|---|---|
| **230-61** #61 | **230-76** #76 |
| **230-62** #62 | **230-77** #77 |
| **230-63** #63 | **230-78** #78 |
| **230-64** #64 | **pkg(12) 13.40 ea** |
| **230-65** #65 | **230-79** #79 |
| **230-66** #66 | **230-80** #80 |
| **230-67** #67 | |

### Pin Vises

**230-810** Double End **8.95**

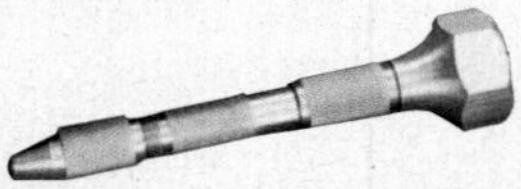

**230-811** Swivel Head **7.80**

**230-815** Slide Lock **9.95**

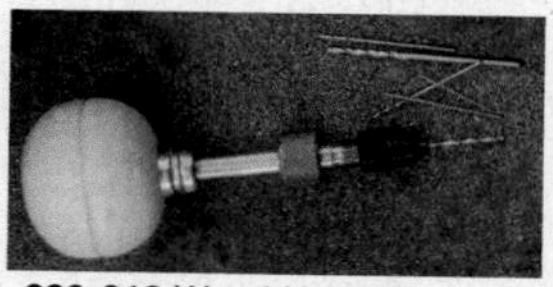

**230-812** Wood Head Pin Vise Drill Set **19.95**

**230-822** Pin Vise & Drill Set **13.55**

### Precision Drill Set

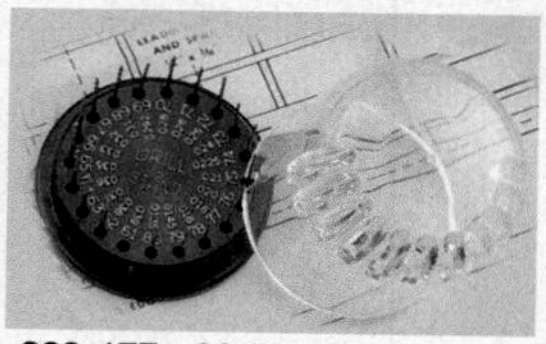

**230-177** **30.20**
#61-80 set (20 pieces) carbon drills with plastic case.

## CLAMPS

### File Block & Clamp

**230-150** **7.90**

### Mini Clamps pkg(2)

Made of rigid, high-impact, nylon-filled plastic, these clamps are lightweight and virtually indestructible.

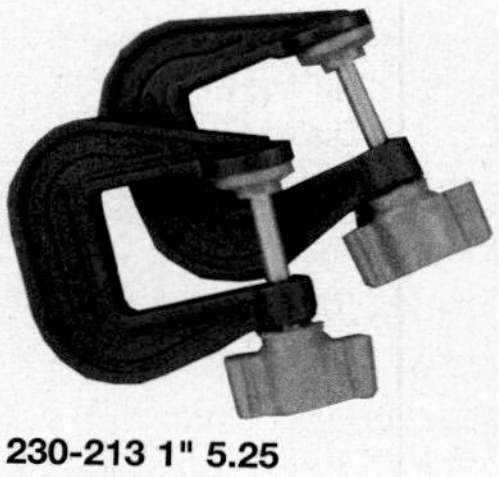

**230-213** **1" 5.25**

**230-214** **2" 6.30**

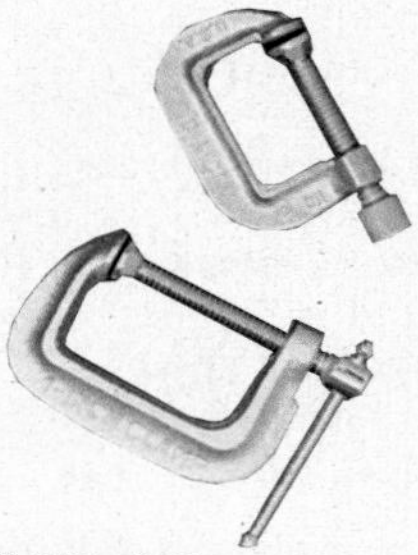

**230-210** **9.95**
Includes 1" and 3/4".

### Non-Mar Wedge Clamp

**230-202** **12.60**
Leather-lined jaws grip securely without marring. Resin body.

### The Third Hand

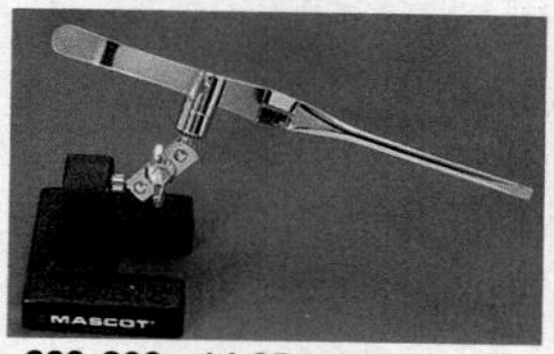

**230-200** **14.65**
Tweezer-mounted work positioner.

### Twin Grip Positioner

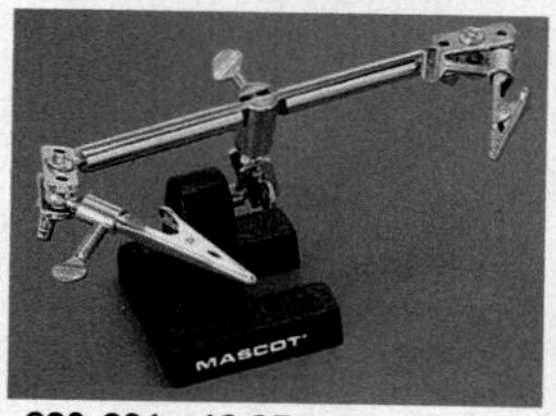

**230-201** **19.95**

### Twin Grip w/Magnifier

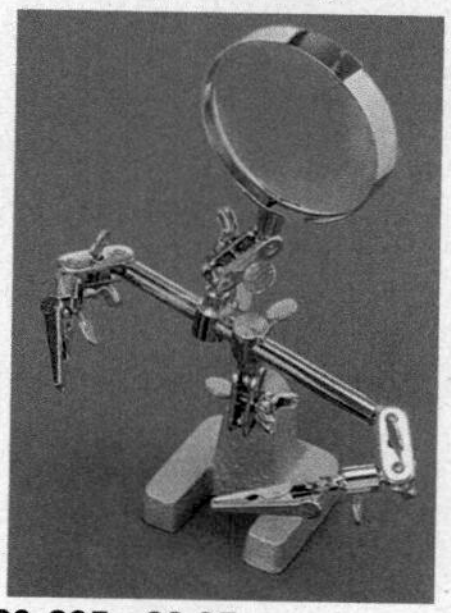

**230-205** **22.05**

### Wood Handle Hand Vise

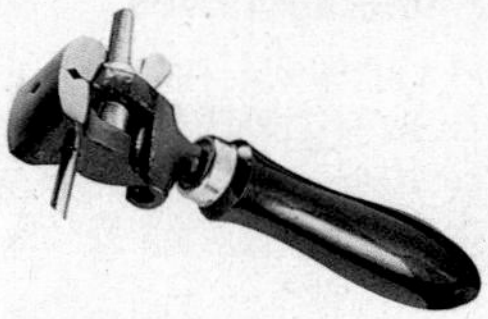

**230-199** **12.60**

## MAGNIFIERS

**230-899** Spectacle Loupe (
**5.25**
Loupe fits securely to right
left lens. Flips out of way fo
convenience. Scratch-proof
plastic-coated clip. Lightwei

**230-900** Eyepiece (2.5x) **7.9**

**230-901** Pocket (10x) **11.55**

**230-903** With Case (4x & 5x)
**13.65**

**230-904** Dual Focus Magnifie
**7.95**

**230-909** Bench Magnifier (3x)
**24.15**

**230-910** Binocular (2.5x) **19.4**

**230-999** Lighted Head Band Magnifier **39.99**

## MALLETS & HAMMERS

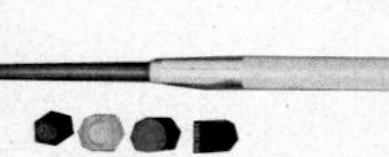

30-600 Mascot Multi Hammer w/6 Heads 13.65

30-601 Swiss Style Watchmakers Hammer 8.40
Double-faced head is only 2-1/4" long with flat and chisel faces. Forged head mounted on a hardwood handle. Overall length 8".

230-602 Brass Mallet 10.50
Overall length is 9" with 2" head.

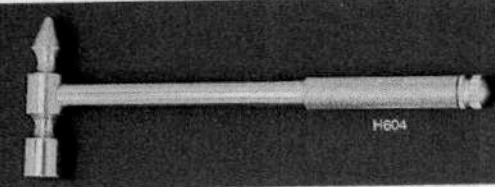

230-603 Mallet w/Interchangeable Face 18.40
Includes brass, fiber and nylon faces. Overall length is 9" with 2" head. Comes with wrench for changing faces.

### Hammer/Screwdrivers Set

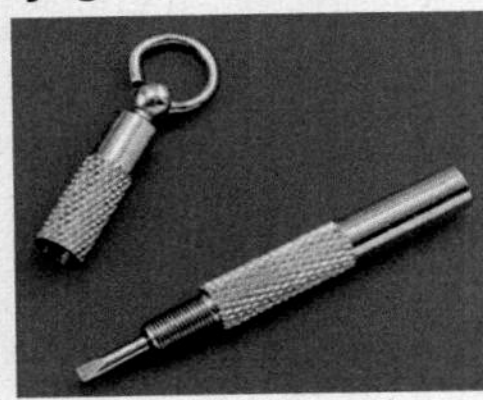

230-604 5 Pieces 16.75

## SCREWDRIVERS

### Eyeglass Screwdriver

230-804 2.25

### Metric Screwdriver Set w/2 Phillips

230-853 6 Pieces 5.95

### Precision Screwdriver Set

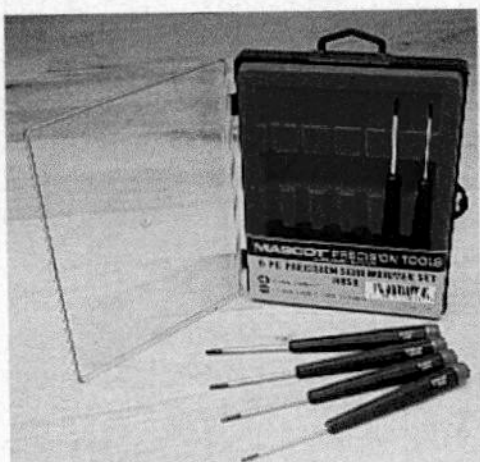

230-850 6 Pieces 18.90
This one-of-a-kind set features non-rolling handles with contoured swivel heads, shafts made of molybdenum steel (hardened and chrome plated for strength and torque) and precision ground tips for sure fit and absolute control. Includes four slotted heads (1.5 x 50mm, 2 x 50mm, 3 x 50mm) and two Phillips head sizes (00 x 50mm, 0 x 50mm) and a handy hard-plastic carrying case.

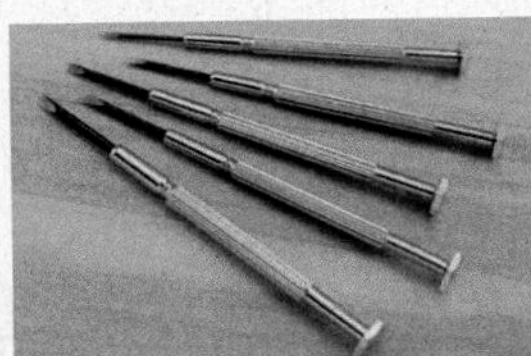

230-855 5 Pieces 14.95
Nickel plated, with swivel heads. 3" to 3-5/8" length, sizes .048" to .085". Blades permanently fixed in handles.

### Reversible Blade Screwdrivers

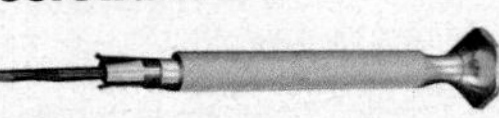

230-800 Flat Head 7.50
Blade has 1/16" and 3/32" ends with swivel head.

### Screwdriver Sharpener

230-847 10.50
Spring-action device holds screwdriver firmly in place while rolled over sharpening stone (stone not included)

## MISCELLANEOUS

### Blower

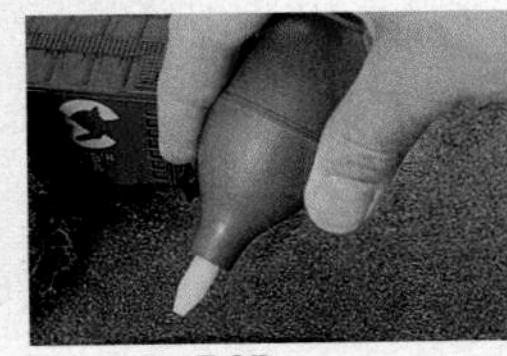

230-915 7.35

### Dental Probes

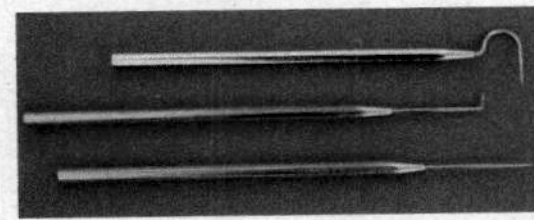

230-303 Set(3) 7.60

### Electrician Scissors

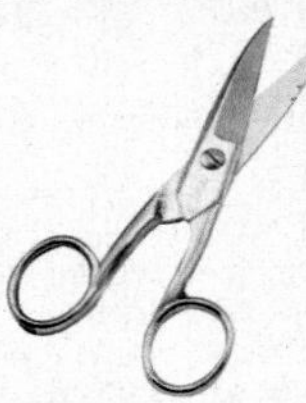

230-163 13.15
Double-plate, chrome-over-nickel with notches for stripping wire. 5" long.

### Gear Pullers

230-220 Stationary 17.95
230-221 Adjustable 24.95

### Hemostats 8.30 ea

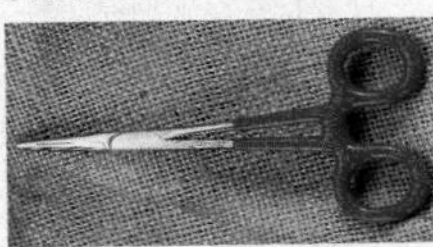

230-340 Straight Blade

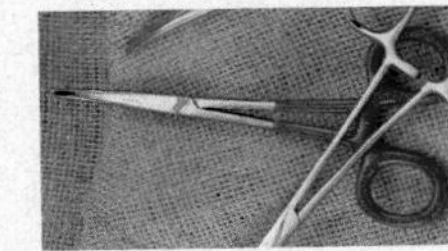

230-341 Curved Blade

Latest New Product News Daily! Visit Walthers Web site at
**www.walthers.com**

### Inspection Mirrors

1" diameter, stainless-steel mirrors mounted in 8" long handle.

**Limited Quantity Available**

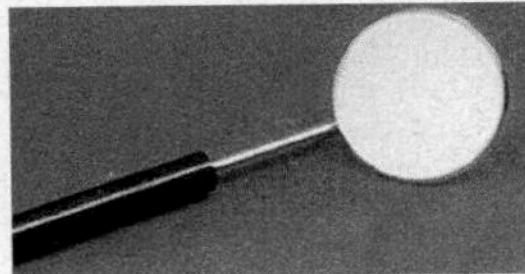

230-905 Plain Mirror 8.95

### Micro Cleaner Set

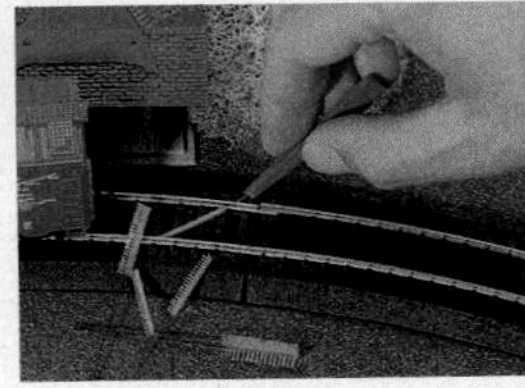

230-700 6.30
Assortment of five micro-cleaning wire brushes in sizes .09", .12", .15", .18" and .30". Includes a separate handle that will accommodate all but the largest brush. Packed in a reusable plastic vial.

### Miniature Open-End Wrench Set

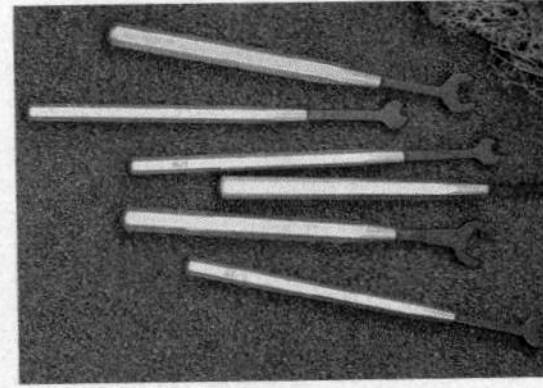

230-856 17.60
Sizes include 3/32", 1/8", 5/32", 3/16", 1/4" and 5/16".

### Mini-Automatic Punch

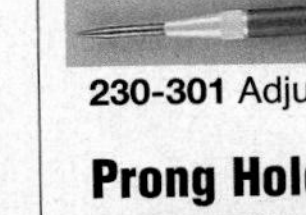

230-301 Adjustable 22.35

### Prong Holders

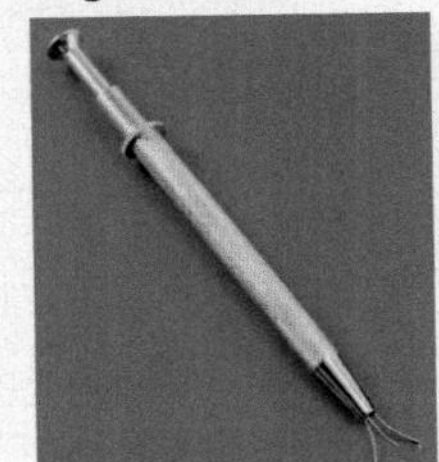

230-203 3 Prongs 6.30

230-204 4 Prongs 6.85

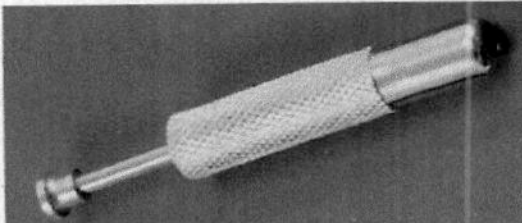

230-2031 Mini 3 Prong 5.99

### Rulers

#### 6" Metric/English

230-710 2.85

#### 12" Model Railroad Scale

230-711 9.45
Scale conversions for HO, O and S Gauges.

### Steel Scratch Brush

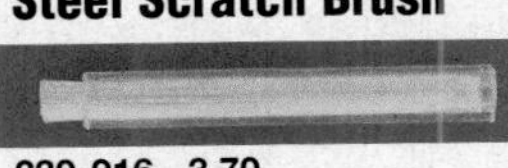

230-916 3.70
Hundreds of applications. Features straight steel wire tightly packed in vinyl sleeve that can be peeled away as brush wears.

### Titanium Solder Pick

230-917 10.95
Use to move solder to and from desired spot.

### Track Cleaners

230-970 Track & Tool Cleaning Tablet 7.95

### Mascot Hobby Tool Catalog

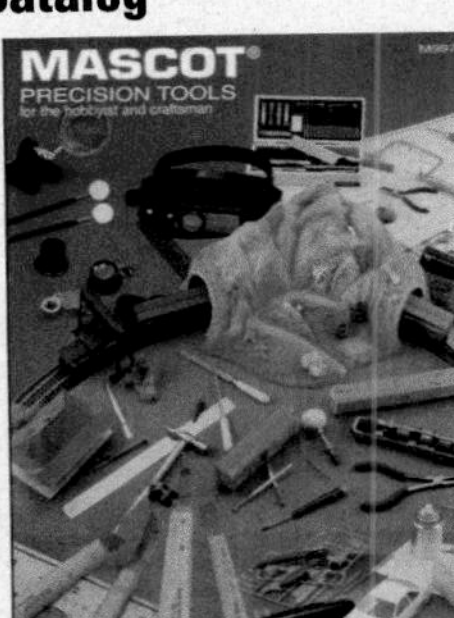


230-997 N/C

MIDWEST PRODUCTS CO., INC.

## NEW PRODUCTS

### Super Sanders 11.99 ea

These long-lasting sanders are easy to use thanks to a lightweight plastic design that minimizes hand cramping. They're also easy to clean - just brush the tungsten carbide pad with a brass wire brush. Perfect for wood, metal, plastic, foam and many more surfaces.

**NEW 472-1130** Fine Grit #150

**NEW 472-1131** Medium Grit #80

**NEW 472-1132** Coarse Grit #60

### Easy Ultimate Cutter

**472-1134 25.99**
The perfect tool for making multiple cuts on one particular angle. Features a self-indexing, movable fence with seven popular angles (from 45 to 135°). Cuts wood strips up to 1/2" thick. Features a no-slip rubber grip and a safety lock handle.

### Hobby & Craft Square

**472-1123 5.29**
A ruler, square, protractor and more: all in one convenient tool! Constructed from a sturdy plastic, this square reads both English and Metric measurements.

### Scale Lumber Gauge

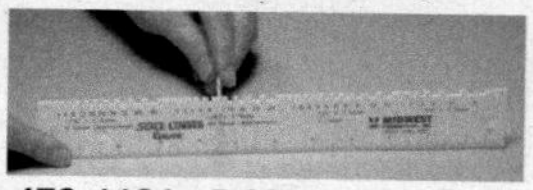

**472-1124 5.29**
For quick and accurate sizing and identifying of Basswood Scale Lumber, designed exclusively by Midwest Products. Features built-in strip identification gauge in O, HO and N Scales. Also features a built-in 12" ruler with English and Metric measurements. Made from rugged plastic.

### Hobby & Craft Ruler

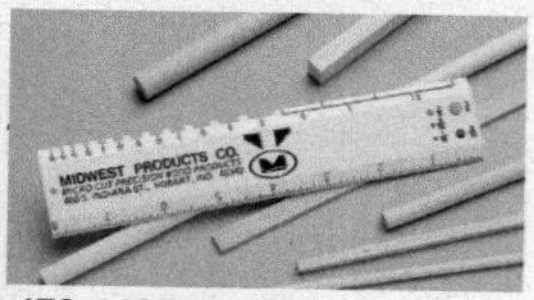

**472-1125 3.11**
Rugged plastic ruler features slots to measure thickness from 1/16" to 1/2", and holes from 1/16" to 1/4" – perfect for dowels or rods! Measures up to eight standard inches.

### Easy Cutter

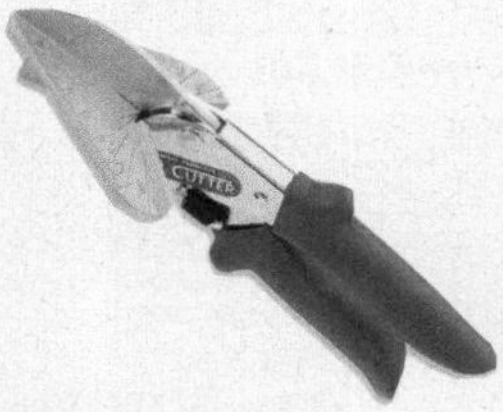

**472-1126 22.49**
A perfect tool for cutting small wood strips to length accurately and quickly. Features a diecast angle plate for making accurate angle cuts.

**472-1127** Replacement Blade For Easy Cutter **7.25**

### Super Easy Cutter

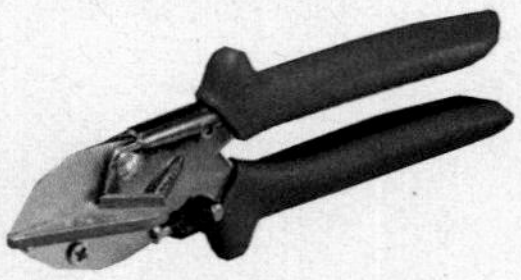

**472-1128 18.49**
A perfect cutter for small hands! Makes clean cuts through basswood strips and hardwood dowels up to 1/4" thick. Also an excellent tool for making angle cuts and 45° bevels.

MISSION MODELS

Take on tough modeling tasks with this line of tools. Ideal for all kinds of modeling, these unique items are precision engineered and manufactured to provide years of service.

## NEW PRODUCTS

### Panel Scriber Set

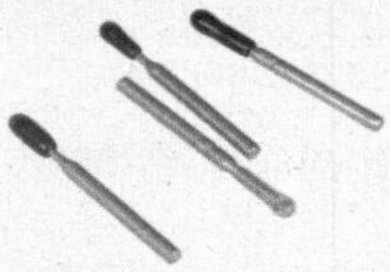

**NEW 466-MM12** Set of 4 **19.99**
Designed to fit the MM-09 Micro Chisel (sold separately) and machined from hardened stainless steel, this unique design allows you to replicate accurate, square panel lines in all kinds of scale models. These razor-sharp long lasting scribers will cut through styrene plastic with ease along with resins, epoxy, putties, and more. Includes pointed tip for scribing templates, plus, .005, .0075 and .010" tips for precision control and accurately sized lines; each tip features a marker ring indicating size.

### Precision Glue Tips

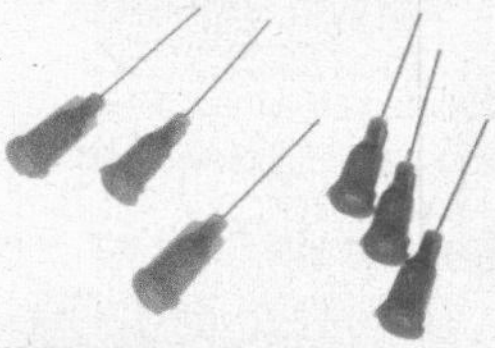

**NEW 466-MM13** 3 Each #27 & #25 Gauge **3.99**
Fits most CA bottles (designed especially for Zap products, sold separately) for precise application of CA and liquid cements. Includes six tips, three each of .025" and .027".

### Etch Mate™ Photo Etch Bending Tool

**NEW 466-MIO21** Etch Mate 3C **59.99**
Make straight, square folds in photo-etched parts for any scale with this upgraded version of the popular Etch Mate. This handy tool now includes a three-clamp system for additional gripping pressure when you need it. Measuring just 6-1/2 x 3-1/2" (16.2 x 8.7cm), the base is now made of composite material to reduce weight and features a non-reflective surface. The upper folding head is spring loaded and reversible, and now features a different shape with outboard, adjustable clamps. Folding blades now come in Safety Orange to provide high contrast and better visibility while bending parts.

### Folding Blades for Etch Mate 3C

**NEW 4566-MIO22** Set of 3 **5.99**
Safety Orange folding blades as included with the Etch Mate 3C (#MIO21, sold separately). Package includes two short and one long blade; can also be used with the original Etch Mate.

### The Grabhandler™

**466-MM06 69.00**
Make custom grab irons and handrails from 1/16 to 1-1/2" long quickly, easily and accurately with this handy tool. Unlike pliers, the Grab Handler provides exact spacing for perfect results every time, and a simple screw handle can be tightened to hold material securely. The unit will handle rods, tubes, flat stock and wire made of soft or hard metals without damage. Made of carbon steel, the tool has a black oxide finish to prevent corrosion and is fully indexed with English and Metric dimensions.

### Multi Tool™

**30.00 ea**
Designed to bend photo-etched parts, this handy tool lets you create accurate and efficient radii up to 360 degrees for a wide range of small details. Made of machined aluminum and too steel, with laser-marked sizir index in both English and Metric sizes.

**466-MM07** Small
For use with smaller parts, handles the following sizes: .375"/9.53mm, .325"/8.26mm .275"/6.99mm, .225"/5.72mm .175"/4.45mm, .100"/2.54mm .047"/1.20mm.

**466-MM08** Large
For use with larger parts, handles the following sizes: .500"/12.70mm, .350"/8.89mr .300"/7.62mm, .250"/6.35mm .200"/5.08mm, .125"/3.18mm .063"/1.60mm.

### Micro Chisel

Perfect for removing molded on details, cleaning seam line sculpting and much more, the Micro Chisel is designed to g into hard to reach areas and remove as much or as little material as needed. Available in two sizes, each features a stainless steel handle with rubber grip. The chisel tip is produced from hardened spring steel and honed to a fine razor-sharp cutting surface; tips are removable and replaceable using the bui in set screw.

The Micro Chisel will cut through, both hard and soft plastics, resins, plaster, all putties, epoxy putties, wood, soft white metal and similar materials. NOTE: Tips are extremely sharp and safety glasses should always be wor when using these tools.

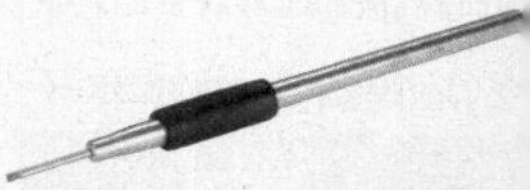

**466-MM09** 2mm Tip **14.99**

**466-MM10** 1mm Tip **11.50**

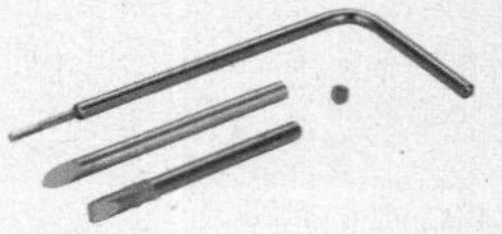

**466-MM11** 2mm Tip Set; Flat & Angled Blades, Allen Wrench **8.50**

See What's Available at

**www.walthers.com**

# NorthWest Short Line

## The Quarterer

53-444 39.95
For quartering or quarter checking of drivers up to 1" O.D. on 1/8" or 3.0mm axles. Permits quartering either right or left lead. Wheel is pressed onto axle while wheelset is still securely held in tool to avoid possibility of slippage. Can be used to compare quartering of existing drivers. Includes operating instructions and two index pins (crank pin substitutes). Requires .100" space on each side of gear to fit driver into tool.

## Professional Quartering Tools

All-metal, precision-machined quartering tool with no axle diameter or bearing (space) restriction.

53-644 HO, On3 & S Scale Size Locomotives **135.95**

**53-674** O & Large Scale Size Locomotives **185.95**

## The Puller

53-454 9.95
A rigid, precision tool for removing wheels, drivers and gears from axles and shafts. Made for HO Scale modeling, but handles larger and smaller scales. Capacity: axles 1/16" to 1/8"; drivers, wheels and gears up to 1-5/8" O.D. Maximum press depth 1". Puller comes complete with two press screws, V-plate, Allen wrench and operation suggestions. Allen wrench not usually needed, finger pressure being adequate in most cases.

## V-Plate

**53-45074** V For Puller **1.25**

## The Puller II

53-554 9.95
This Puller provides greater depth of press. It can remove gears from a shaft with a distance of 1-5/8" 4cm from the face of the gear to the shaft end. Wheels up to 1-1/4" 3.1cm (Scale 55" in O; 33" in #1) can be pressed from their axles. Great for repairs or rebuilding in smaller scales and repowering slot or RC cars, too.

## V-Plate

**53-45104** For Puller II **.95**

## The Puller III

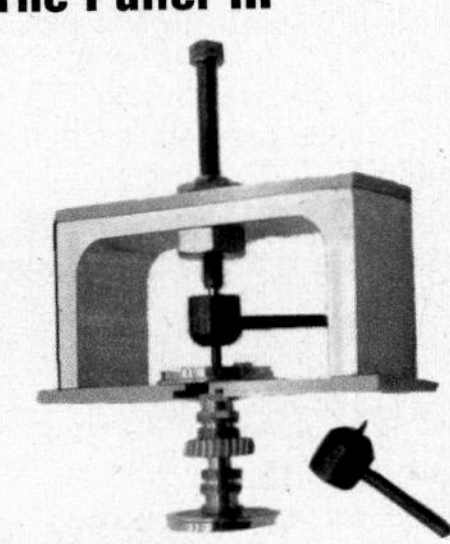

53-654 44.95
A large, heavy-duty, precision machined Puller with tool steel reinforcement and puller plate for those heavy and larger scale jobs found in O and G Scale modeling work. Use for removing wheels, drivers and gears from axles and shafts. Works on the principle of pressing the shaft out of the gear, wheel, etc. Takes axles/shafts from 3/32" to 1/4"; drivers, wheels and gears up to 2-1/4"; outside maximum press depth is 1". Includes allen wrench, 3/32" tip press screw, 1/4" puller plate (removable) and operating suggestions.

## Press Screws 2.50 ea

Optional for use with thumb screw head (will not accept Allen wrench). For 454, 554, 654.

**53-45314** 1/16" Tip

**53-45324** 3/32" Tip

**53-45334** Cone Tip

**53-45344** Flat Tip
Will accept Allen wrench.

**53-45354** Bored 3/32" Puller Press Thumbscrew

**53-45364** Bored 1/16" 1.5mm Puller Press Thumbscrew

## Precision Press Tools

### Individual Press Tools pkg(2) 9.95 ea

**53-45404** 1mm

**53-45424** 1.2mm

**53-45444** 1.5mm

**53-45464** 2.4mm

## Professional Precision Press Tool Sets

**53-45394** Complete Set pkg(4) **34.95**
Includes one each press tools #53-45404, 45424, 45444 and 45464.
Use with the Puller (#53-454), Puller II (#53-554), Puller III (#53-654) and the Puller IV (#53-754), each sold separately. Press tools ensure accurate alignment while pressing smaller shafts and eliminate torque problems inherent in pressing with a screw-based gear puller. Each set consists of a short, hardened steel pin mounted in a mandrel press for loosening gears, and a hardened steel pin fitted in a mandrel press to "break" the shaft free of the gear. The mandrel includes a "stabilizer" bar to remove rotational force when pressing, for consistent alignment and less chance of damage. The tools can also help in the accurate assembly of short, small shafts with gears and wheels.

## The Bender

53-484 39.95
Press bending brake to bend brass or other light sheet metals up to 90° (depends on how far you tighten press screws) up to 3" bend length, up to .020" half-hard brass capacity. Depth guide permits duplication of bend placement on stock being bent. Includes reversible die operation suggestions and alternate urethane die material.

## The Chopper

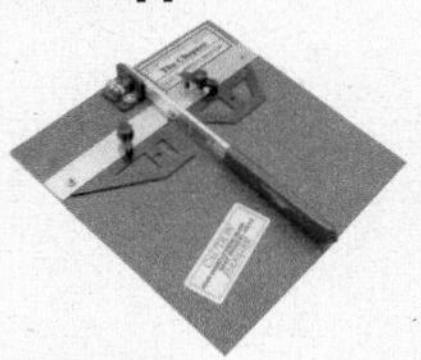

53-494 29.95
Heavy-duty strip wood length cutter. Also can do mitre cuts (guides for 30, 45, 60 and 90? included). Adjustable guide location permits setting any cut length up to 3-1/4" for exactly duplicate cut pieces–for car decking, ties, trestle building, etc. A extra blade and operating suggestions included. No special blades needed, uses single-edge razor blades. Also cuts styrene and other model-making plastics. Safety top keeps handle from slipping or raising dangerously high.

**53-49154** Extra Blades pkg(8) **1.50**

## The Chopper II

53-694 44.95
All-metal, heavier duty precision-cutting tool includes replaceable cutting mat for continuing cleaner cuts. The mat is manufactured to be repositioned as it wears and can be easily replaced as needed. It also features rigid aluminum handle and base, mitre guides for 30, 45, 60 and 90° angles, and a safety stop. With its compact 7 x 7" size, The Chopper II can cut wood and styrene strip material up to 1/8".

**53-69054** Replacement Cutting Mat For Chopper II **3.95**

## Chopper III

53-594 39.95
Heavy-duty wide base version of the Chopper allows easier handling of long pieces of material. Chopper III provides for installation of up to three handles, permitting multiple set-ups. Includes one handle only, additional handles are available (see #49144 below). The 18" wide base provides a sturdier, larger work area. The safety top keeps handle from slipping or raising dangerously high.

**53-49144** Extra Handle **17.95**
For Choppers #s 494 and 594 (sold separately)

## Sanding Sticks w/2 Belts 3.75 ea

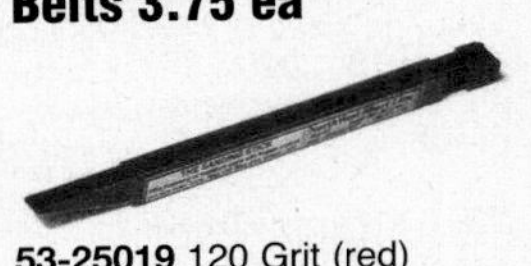

**53-25019** 120 Grit (red)

**53-25029** 240 Grit (blue)

**53-25039** 320 Grit (green)

**53-25049** 400 Grit (yellow)

**53-25059** 600 Grit (black)

## Replacement Belts For Sanding Sticks pkg(2) 1.75 ea

**53-28069** For #25019

**53-28079** For #25029

**53-28089** For #25039

**53-28099** For #25049

**53-28109** For #25059

## The Duplicutter II

53-624 36.95
Designed for working with styrene or other plastic sheet material (scribing, squaring and cutting to size), but can also be used with thin sheet wood and locomotive window "glass" to cut duplicate shape panes. Accepts sheets up to 8" wide. Includes scribing tools (single-edge razor blade).

## The True-Sander

53-574 36.95
Combination holding jig and sanding block for finishing and squaring off stripwood and strip styrene.

## Drill & Tap Sets Tap, Tapdril, Clearance Drill

**53-30505** 1/6-60W Each **19.95**

**53-30605** 1.0mm x 0.25 Each **13.95**

**53-30625** 1.2mm x 0.25 Each **13.95**

**53-30645** 1.4mm x 0.3 Each **11.75**

**53-30675** 1.7mm x 0.35 Each **11.25**

**53-30705** 2.0mm x 0.4 Each **11.00**

**53-30765** 2.6mm x 0.45 Each **10.25**

**53-30805** 3.0mm x 0.5 Each **10.25**

See metric screws and nuts in Scratch Building Supples section of the Reference Book.

## The Sensipress+ Miniature Arbor Punch Press

53-504 99.95
Now finely finished with tool holder overarm to keep tools together. Use the press for assembling parts, wheels, etc. and as a gear puller to disassemble. Can give a sensitive touch as well as supply up to 250 lbs of pressure. Reversible 3/8" ram is flat on one end and bored 3/16" on the other so you can interchange various tools. Ram set screw retains the tool. 3/32" tip for gear and wheel pulling is included. Gibbed and adjustable overarm for precision alignment.

NorthWest Short Line

## Sensipress+ Punch Adapter

**53-50014 3.50**
Fits Sensipress+ ram to hold round hole punches (below). Punches up to 1/8" holes easily in brass and styrene; larger holes may exceed tool capacity depending on material and thickness. You can "nibble" your way with adjacent punching to make car window openings, etc. Includes ram adapter. Punches and dies available separately (see below).

## Round Hole Punches & Dies For Sensipress+ 7.50 ea (Unless Noted)

### Punches

**53-50104** 1/16"

**53-50124** 5/64"

**53-50144** 3/32"

**53-50164** 1/8"

### Dies

**53-50114** 1/16"

**53-50134** 5/64"

**53-50154** 3/32"

**53-50174** 1/8"

## Accessories For Sensipress+ 1.95 ea (Unless Noted)

**53-50504** Oversize 1/2" OD Tool

**53-50514** Blank Flat End Tool **.95**

**53-50524** 1/16" Diameter Tip

**53-50534** 3/32" Diameter Tip

**53-50544** Cone End, Concave

**53-50564** Bored 2.0mm Tool

**53-50594** Interchange Tool Set **14.95**
Accessory tools - set of nine pieces.

**53-50604** Heavy Duty "V" Plate **3.50**

Items listed below are available by Special Order (see Legend Page).

**53-50554** Bored 1.5mm Both Ends

**53-50574** Bored 3/32" Tool

**53-50584** Bored 1/8" Tool

## The Riveter+

Shown Attached To Sensipress (Sold Separately)

**53-514 59.95**
Riveter+ attaches to Sensispress+ (sold separately) to provide accurate, precision control of rivet embossment location. Comes with .015" (1-1/2" HO) rivet-embossing punch and die. Tool enables straight, accurate "rivet" spacing. Advance knob is calibrated in .001" increments.

## Optional Embossing Punches & Dies For Riveter+

### Punches

**53-51004** Universal **3.50**

**53-51104** .010" **5.00**

**53-51154** .015" **5.00**

**53-51204** .020" **4.00**

**53-51304** .030" **4.00**

**53-51404** .040" **4.00**

**53-51504** .050" **4.00**

### Dies

**53-51114** .010" **5.00**

**53-51164** .015" **5.00**

**53-51214** .020" **4.00**

**53-51314** .030" **4.00**

**53-51414** .040" **4.00**

**53-51514** .050" **4.00**

## Rivet Embossing Punch/Die Set For Riveter+

**53-51014 34.95**
Includes one each to the following sizes of punches and dies: .010", .020", .030", .040" and .050" and a universal punch.

## The Aligner Gear Alignment Tools 8.95 ea

Installing a gear squarely (without wobble) on a shaft or axle is tedious and sometimes unsuccessful. This tool will "square-up" and salvage most problem gears in place.

**53-314** For 2.0mm Axle

**53-324** For 2.4mm or 3/32" Axle

**53-334** For 3mm Axle

**53-384** For 1/8" Axle

NGINEERING

## MICRO CLIPS W/SMOOTH JAWS

**514-N440010** pkg(10) **2.75**
These handy copper-plated clips are ideal for holding small parts like Ngineering LEDs during soldering, but have hundreds of uses in model making. 5-Amp current rating.

## EASY-REACH CURVED TIP SYRINGE

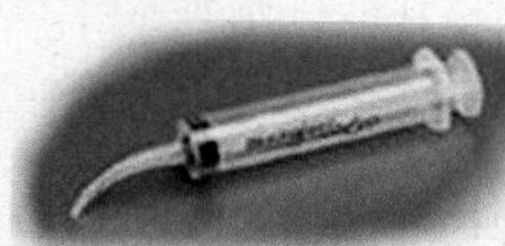

**514-N4310 1.85**
This is the Monoject® #412, with a long, curved tip that allows easy access in tight places. The small tip opening of just .028" diameter provides precise dispensing control. It can be used with a wide variety of materials including glues, caulking, oils, grease, cleaners, soldering flux and more. Holds up to .4 ounces 12cc of material to handle big jobs or for more work time between refills.



OLFA®

*Best made cutting tools in the world®*

Perfect for any hobby, household repairs or on the job, OLFA® offers a complete line of professional cutters, knives, blades and accessories. Lifetime warranty on all products.

Please visit www.walthers.com for a complete listing of in-stock and special order products.

## CUTTERS

### Plastic/Laminate

These special cutters produce a very fine score line allowing for the precise breaking of plastics. Each features a tungsten blade with two additional blades stored in the handle.

**540-5012** Heavy-Duty **10.49**
Features a reversible tungsten blade.

## COMPASS

**540-9911 10.49**
Perfect for model making, Extra blades can be stored in handle. Cuts circles up to 6" 15cm in diameter.

## KNIVES

### Heavy-Duty

**540-9046** Handsaver Heavy-Duty Cutter **9.49**
Heavy-duty utility knife with stainless steel blade channel, ratchet wheel blade lock and stainless steel snap-off blade.

### Standard

**540-5001** Standard Type **3.29**
Perfect for light-duty cutting jobs. Features slide lock, pocket clip and built-in blade snapper.

**540-5019** Auto-Lock Stainless Steel Professional Knife **8.49**
Auto-locking blade slide, stainless steel handle and built-in safety blade snapper. For left- or right-handed users.

## SELF-HEALING CUTTING MATS

Mats are double-sided with green base color and yellow grid lines (straight and common angles) on one side for easy measurement and cutting, solid green on opposite for general cutting.

**540-9952** Small **3.49**
6 x 8" 15 x 20cm

**540-9880** Medium **15.49**
12 x 18" 30 x 45cm

*Informatio*

STATIO

### Handy Tools for Superdetailing

Some modelers find that kitbuilt or layout-ready models don't offer them the degree of individuality they desire for their layout. These hobbyists often create one-of-a-kind models that reflect their own creative ideas, or are closer to an existing prototype. But super-detailing and kitbashing require certain tools for the job; here are a few suggested tools and their uses.

Modifications range from simply replacing molded-on grab irons and ladders with separate ones, to complete rebuilding using parts of several cars. While these changes may sound difficult, using the right tools for the job can make the job go smoothly.

On plastic locomotives, rolling stock, vehicles and structure parts, molded-on features can be removed with a sharp hobby knife fitted with a chisel-shaped blade. Curved riffler files are a smart buy for removing details in recessed areas where a chisel blade won't reach. Use fine sandpaper to remove any trace of the old details.

If you're going to shorten or combine car or structure parts, you'll need a good hobby (or razor) saw. These tools, along with a miter box, will help you get accurate cuts without leaving a rough edge or a broad kerf.

Many small detail parts like grab irons and stirrups are designed to be mounted in new holes, drilled into the model. A set of small drill bits and a pin vise will make this job a breeze.

Look through the pages of the Tools Section of this Reference Book to see what other tools you can use for turning kits or ready-to-run cars into unique models. You might be surprised at what you find!

# PANAVISE®

## Work Holders

PanaVise work holder tool systems are very versatile. All movements are controlled by the variable-pressure knob, making it possible to move the work to any desired position.

Model not included

**550-201** PV Jr. Work Vise **3.99**

**550-203** PV Jr. Vise Head **0.99**

**550-301** Standard PanaVise **44.99**
Standard height base and vertical jaw vise head with nylon jaws.

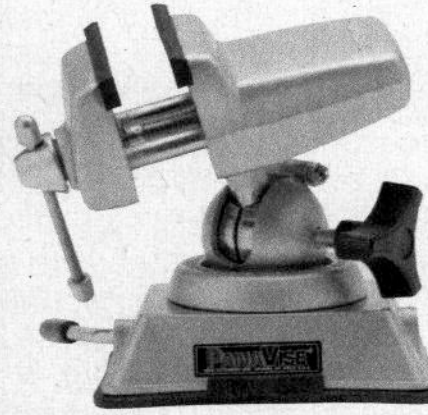

**550-381** Vacuum Base PanaVise **57.99**
Vacuum base and vertical jaw vise head with nylon jaws included.

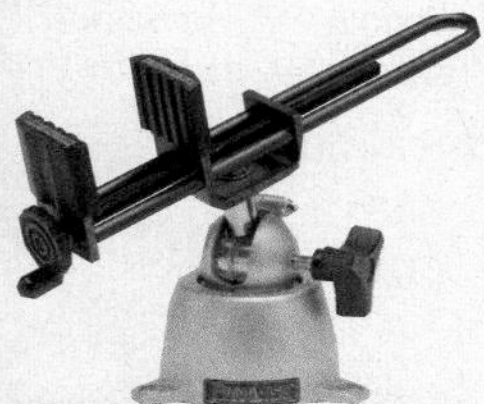

**550-396** Wide-Opening Head PanaVise **53.99**
Standard height base and wide opening jaw vise head #366 with Neoprene jaw pads.

## Heads

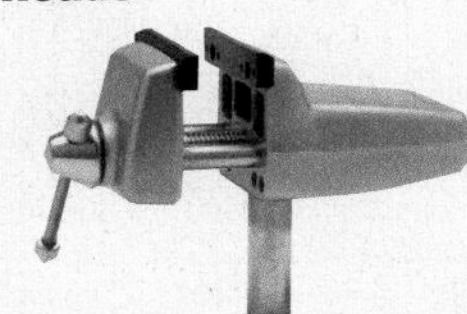

**550-303** Original Vise Head **24.99**
Nylon jaws. Fits #300 Series bases.

**550-304** Low Profile Vise Head **32.99**
Steel jaws. Fits #300 Series bases.

**550-315** Circuit Board Holder **32.99**
Complete with 14" cross-bar. Fits all #300 Series bases. Ideal for holding box cars for lettering.

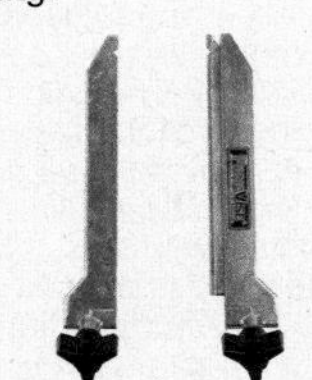

**550-316** Extra Arms 1 Pair **19.99**
For #315 circuit board holder.

## Crossbars

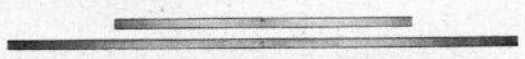

**550-318** 14" Cross Bar **5.99**
For #315 circuit board holder (lengths to 30" on special order).

**550-31822** 22" **7.99**
For #550-315.

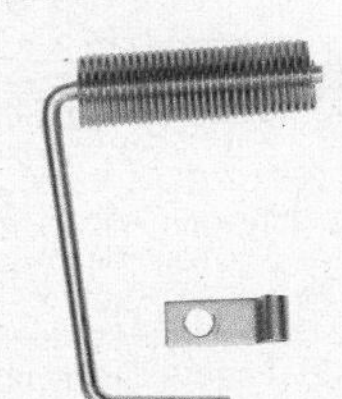

**550-358** Universal Holder **21.99**

**550-366** Wide Opening Head **33.99**
Wide opening head features Neoprene jaw pads. Fits all #300 Series bases.

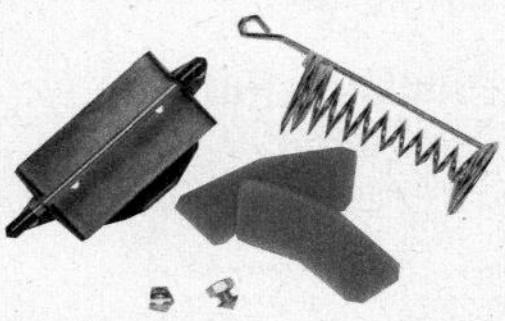

**550-371** Solder Station **11.99**
Solder and iron holder attach to #312 and all bases (except #380), to bench, wall or free standing. Includes two sponges and mounting screws.

**550-376** Extra Wide Opening **45.99**
Self-centering double action jaws (opens to 9") and reversible jaw pads. Fits #300 Series bases. Base not included.

## Bases

**550-300** Standard Height (Original) **20.99**

**550-305** Low Profile **20.99**

**550-380** Vacuum PanaVise Base **33.99**

## Accessories

### Replacement Jaws

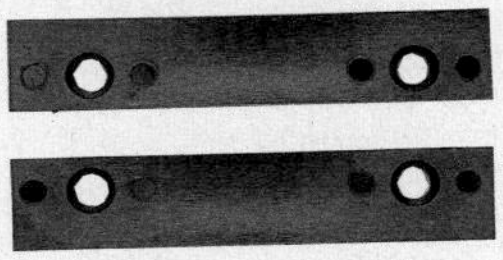

**550-343** Nylon Jaws w/Screws 1 Pair **2.79**
For #303 and #304 heads.

**550-344** Grooved Nylon Jaws w/Screws 1 Pair **3.79**
With horizontal groove, for #303 and #304 heads.

**550-346** Deluxe Neoprene Jaw Pads for #366 1 Pair **2.99**

**550-352** Teflon Jaw w/Screws **11.99**
For #303 and #304.

**550-353** Plated Steel Jaws w/Screws 1 Pair **6.49**
For #303 and #304.

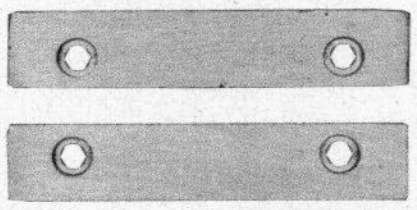

**550-354** Brass Jaws w/Screws 1 Pair **8.49**
For #303 and #304.

## Fixturing Heads

**550-337** Fixturing Head Face Plate **18.99**
Fits all #300 Series bases.

## Mountings

**550-308** Mounting Plate, Weighted **29.99**
Complete with mounting holes and mounting screws, for #300 and #305 bases.

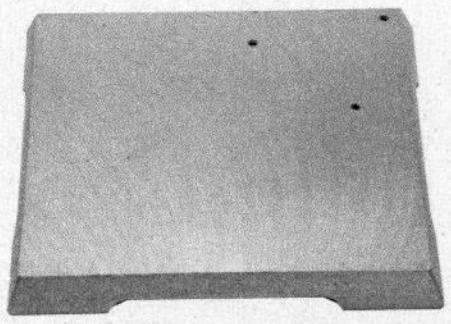

**550-310** Surface Plate **94.99**
Blanchard ground, with mounting holes for #300 and #305 bases with mounting screws.

**550-312** Tray Base Mount **19.99**
Handy small parts tray, mounts to bottom of bases. Includes mounting screws, for #300 and #305 bases.

## Miscellaneous

**550-319** Circuit Board Replacement Knobs pkg(4) **3.99**

Items listed below are available by Special Order (see Legend Page).

## PANAPRESS

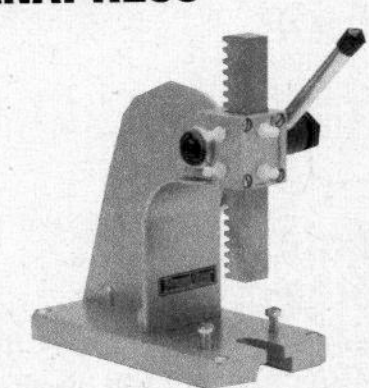

**550-502** Precision Panapress **119.99**
Although it weighs less than 6 pounds and stands only 7" high, this hand arbor press exerts pressure up to a quarter-ton. Ideal for pressing bearings, sleeves or collars, forming and assembling small parts, punching, riveting, broaching, staking and dozens of other operations.
Arbor and table-plate diecast of high strength Zamak III.
Operating mechanism of hardened and ground steel.
Ram is reversible.

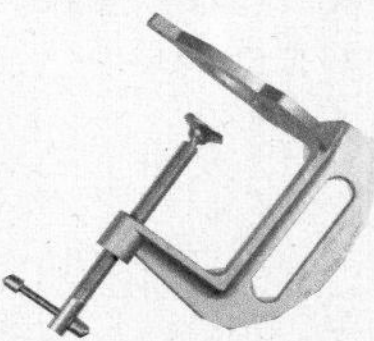

**550-311** Bench Clamp **39.99**
Complete with mounting screws, for #300 and #305 bases.

**550-350** Multi-Purpose Work Center **83.99**
Wide opening head, standard base and tray base mount with 6 trays for small parts and tools.

## RIBBONRAIL

### Work Cradles

Hold your favorite models safely and securely while detail painting, decaling or making repairs. Made of Alclad aluminum, these easy-to-assemble holders are adjustable and padded to protect the finish of your work.

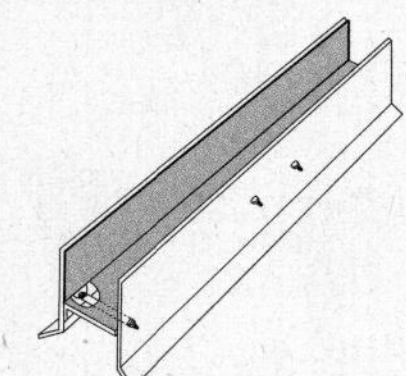

**170-55** 12" **12.95**

**170-1155** 6" **7.5**

## ROBART

### Carbide Cutters 7.95 ea

Tungsten carbide cutters on 1/8" steel shanks for all woods, fiberglass and plastics.

### Disc Cutter

**547-4651** Coarse Grit

### 1/4" Rod Cutter

**547-4631** Coarse Grit

### 3/8" Ball Cutter

**547-4611** Coarse Grit

### Cone Cutter

**547-4602** Fine Grit

Items listed below are available by Special Order (see Legend Page).

### 1/4" Ball Cutter

**547-4621** Coarse Grit

**547-4622** Fine Grit

## SHERLINE

Items listed below are available by Special Order (see Legend Page). Please visit Walthers web site at www.walthers.com for a complete listing of all available items.

### Mill

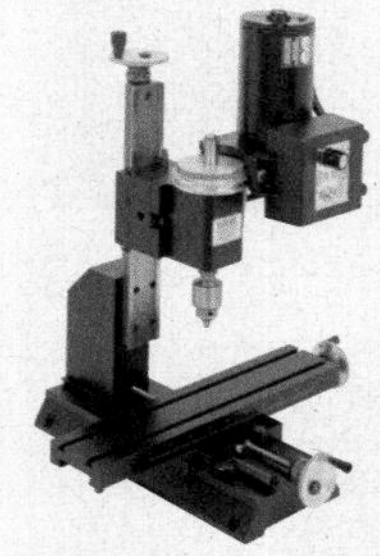

**677-5400** Deluxe Mill Package 5400A English **1020.00**
Includes 1/4" drill chuck, headstock spacer block, adjustable zero handwheels, laser-engraved scales and 11 accessories.

### Lathes & Attachments

**677-4000** 3.5 x 8" Lathe English **575.00**
"A" package w/accessories.

**677-40001** 3.5 x 8" Lathe #4000 English **675.00**
With 2-1/2" 3-jaw chuck and 1/4" drill chuck.

**677-44001** 3.5 x 17" Lathe #4400 Metric **800.00**
With adjustable zero handwheels, 3-1/8" 3-jaw chuck and 3/8" drill chuck.

### Book

**677-5301** Book - Tabletop Machining **40.00**
8.5 x 11" 350 pages, color.

Got a Mouse? Click Walthers Web Site at

**www.walthers.com**

## SQUADRON PRODUCTS

# HAND TOOLS

All tools are made from stainless steel.

### Precision Putty Applicator

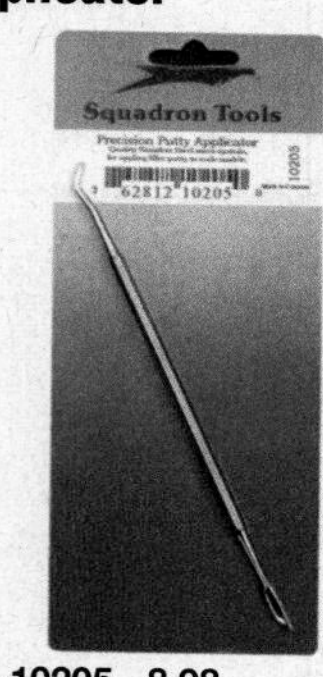


**680-10205 8.98**
Features specially designed blades for applying filler putty on scale models.

### Scribing Tool

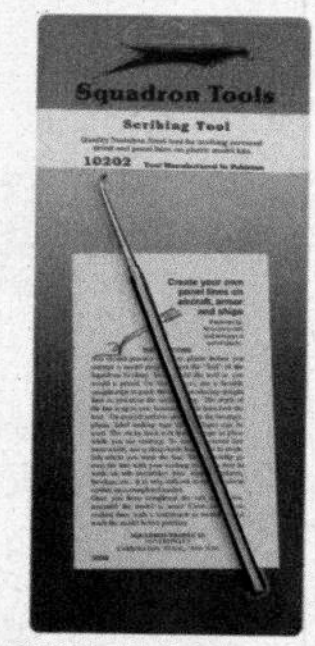


**680-10202 9.98**
Used for scribing recessed detail and panel lines on plastic model kits.

### Seam Scraper

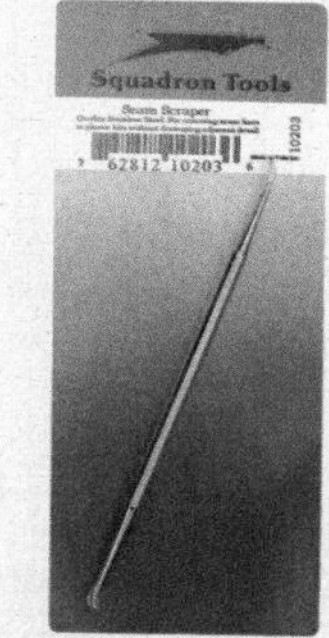
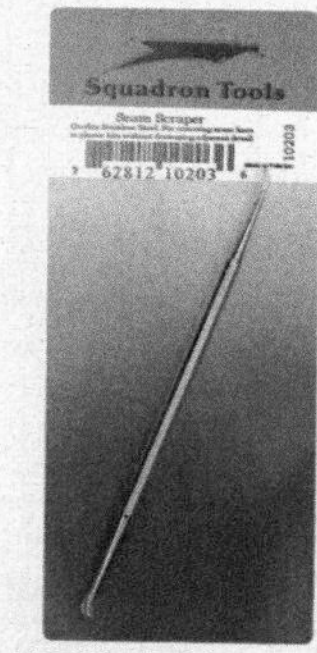


**680-10203 9.98**
For removing seam lines in plastic kits without destroying adjacent details.

### Adjustable Hand-Held Vise

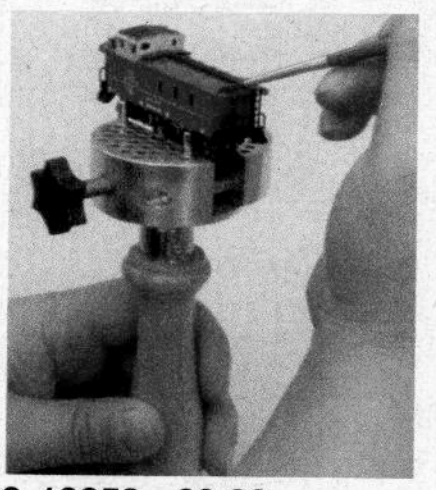

**680-10253 29.98**
Provides a secure grip for odd-shaped or sized parts. Simply insert the four pins as needed in the openings in the metal head, place model between pins and tighten. Large wooden handle provides comfortable grip and allows you complete access to your project from any direction. Additional pins (#680-10254) are available separately.

### Replacement Pins

**680-10254** pkg(4) **1.98**
Set of four pins for use with Adjustable hand-Vise #680-10253, sold separately.

## TL MARSHALL CO.

# FOAM CUTTERS

A must-have for every modeler's toolbox, these knives allow you to cut high density foam with ease, speed and accuracy. The rigid blade can plunge into the foam without bending or warping to cut concave terrain like riverbeds, caves and tunnels. Use the edge of the blade to cut fine lines and the flat of the blade to smooth foam corners. Cutting foam with heat leaves a finished foam edge without messy airborne particles to clean up.

**715-12050** Crafter's Hot Knife **69.95**
Has an operational time of 5-10 minutes before shutting down to cool. The "Deadman's switch" shuts the knife off automatically when set down.

**715-12051** PRO-1 **89.95**
Heavy-duty knife allows you to score and cut a wide variety of foam with ease. Features a heavy-duty stainless steel blade that heats evenly under your control and can stay hot for up to five hours. Also includes a sled that allows you to consistently cut to a specified depth. Features an on-off switch for continuous cutting (knife will stay hot when turned on, even when set down).

## TRIX

### Locomotive Wheel Cleaning Brush

**441-66602 28.49**
This easy-to-use brush clea wheels for improved conductivity and preventing radio/television interference. Two-rail DC.

## TAMIYA

# NEW PRODUCT

### Work Station w/Magnifying Lens

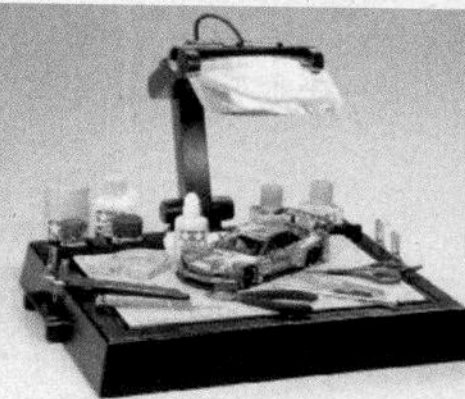

**NEW 865-74064 117.00**
Base Measures:
16-15/16 x 14-3/16 x 2-3/4" 43 x 36 x 7cm
Magnifying Lens:
5-7/8 x 3-15/16" 15 x 10cm

This work stand is specifically designed with modelers in mind. Six white LED lights illuminate a work area with a frame designed to accept an A4-sized (8-1/4 x 11-11/16" 21 x 29.7cm) cutting mat. A large adjustable 2X magnifyir lens gives you a good look at your project, and five parts-holder clips on each side, fou bottle holders, three brush holders and a decal water tra help keep your workspace organized.

### Decal Scissors

**865-74031 22.50**
Coated with a special material to resist sticking to adhesives when cutting decals and stickers. Sharp, fine blades allow for delicate work.

**ecal Applicator ystem**

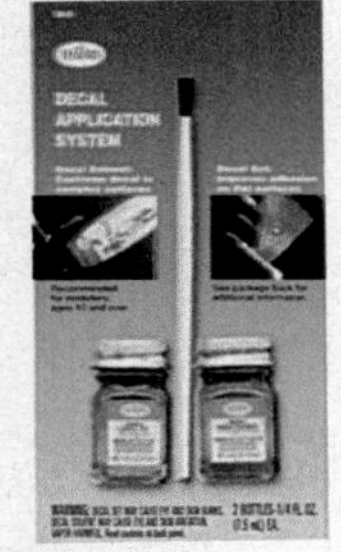

**04-8809 3.69**
ystem helps decals conform o difficult shapes through mproved adhesion. System ncludes two bottles of decal olution and one brush.

**rop Cloth**

**704-8803 4.49**
24 x 36" sheet is impervious to most solvents.

**Hobby Knives**

Specially designed for building plastic kits. Blade can be resharpened.

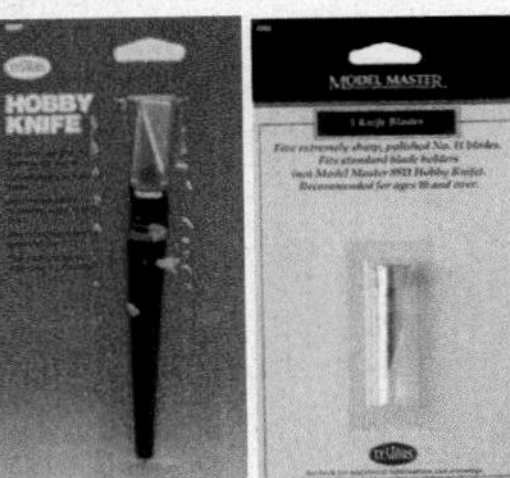

704-8801 704-8816

**704-8801** Hobby Knife **1.99**
Dealers MUST Order Packs of 12.

**704-8816** Knife Blades pkg(5) **4.75**

**704-8830** Hobby Knife w/5 Blades pkg(5) **4.75**

**Needle File Set**

**704-50630 15.99**

**Pin Vise**

**704-50629 15.99**
With six drill bits.

**Sandpaper**

**704-8802 2.99**
These hobby sanding films are washable, flexible, reusable and tough. Five grades: coarse, medium, fine, extra-fine and ultra-fine.

**Sprue Cutters**

**704-50628 16.99**

**Tweezers**

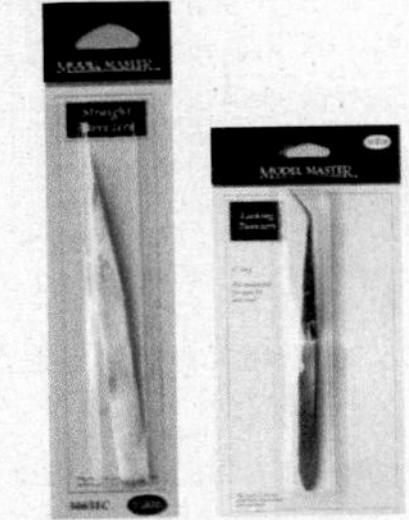

704-50631 704-50632

**704-50631** Straight **6.29**

**704-50632** Lock **6.29**

XURON CORP.

## SHEARS

These high-precision shears have a special ultra-tapered shape that provides a simple way to quickly and cleanly cut in hard-to-reach areas. Perfect for cutting sprue and wire.

**791-90001** Premium Quality Shear - Oval Head **20.49**

**791-90005** Premium Quality Shear - Tapered Head **20.49**

**791-90006** Shear - Tapered Head with Wire Retainer **22.49**

**791-90026** Crafter's Shear **14.49**

**791-90028** Track Cutter **14.49**

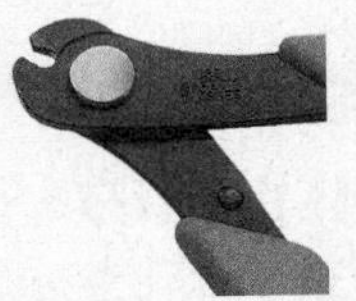

**791-90033** Hard Wire & Cable Cutter **17.49**

**791-90036** Ultraflush Cutting Shear **11.49**

**791-90039** High Precision Shear **11.49**

**791-90043** Angled High Precision Shear **17.49**

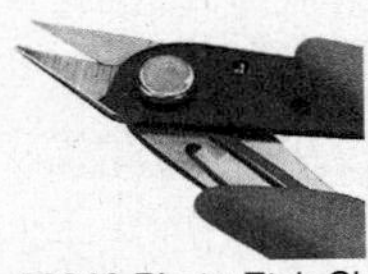

**791-90046** Photo Etch Shear **16.49**

**791-90137** Track Cutter for MarklinTrack **18.49**

## SCISSORS

**791-90118** Modeler's **18.99**
This handy stainless-steel scissors easily cuts mylar, fabric, styrene, soft aluminum or brass sheet stock.

**791-90128** High Durability **22.49**
These user-friendly scissors are designed to cut through tough Kevlar fibers, but can be used to trim photo-etched parts and carbon fiber strips. Feature high carbon steel blades and serrations on one edge.

## PLIERS

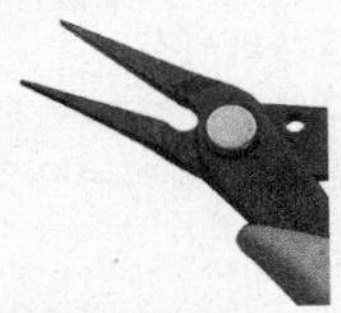

**791-90065** Tweezernose™, Smooth **18.99**

**791-90066** Tweezernose, Serrated **18.99**

**791-90075** Longnose, Smooth **11.99**

**791-90122** Round Nose **15.49**

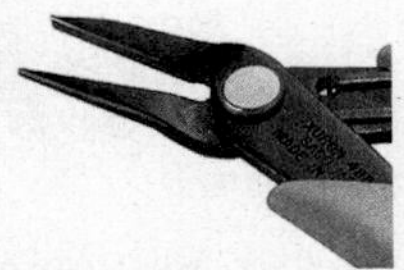

**791-90123** Combination Tip **15.49**

**791-90124** Split Ring **13.99**

**791-90125** Micro Former **16.99**

## STAINLESS STEEL TWEEZERS

**25.99 ea**

High-quality, Swiss-manufactured, electronic-grade tweezers manufactured from anti-magnetic, anti-acid stainless steel.

**791-90107** Tapered, Extra Fine Tips

**791-90108** Precise, Thin, Curved Tips

Items listed below are available by Special Order (see Legend Page).

**791-90105** Precise, Straight Tips

**791-90109** Rounded, Straight Tips

**791-90113** Precise, Very Strong

## TOOL KITS

**791-90119** Modeler's **49.99**
Includes #90039 high-precision shear, #90065 Tweezernose pliers and #90118 modeler's scissors in a durable tri-fold pouch.

**791-90120** Railroader's **47.00**
Features the #90028 Xuron track cutter, #90039 high-precision shear and #90066 serrated Tweezernose pliers in a tri-fold fabric pouch.

## DISPENSING BOTTLES

**4.49 ea (Unless Noted)**
Polyethylene bottles with stainless-steel dispensing tubes for controlled dispensing of a wide variety of liquids, including solvents. 2oz.

**791-90115** 0.010" ID Needle

**791-90116** 0.020" ID Needle

**791-90117** 0.040" ID Needle

**791-90114** 2oz Dispensing Bottle Nozzle Spout **2.49**

# X-ACTO®

Designed for artists, crafters and hobbyists. X-ACTO began producing precision knives and tools in 1935. Included are cutting tools and accessories, drills, tweezers, pliers, files, woodcarving sets and other craft tools that are ideal for miniature work.

## KNIVES

### X-2000™ Precision Knives 6.38 ea

This safer stylish knife offers anti-roll design, no-slip grip, center barrel blade release for fast and easy blade changing, greater stability, snap-on safety cap and comes in colors. Comes with No. 11 Fine Point Blade.

**790-3722** Cranberry

**790-3723** Blue

**790-3724** Black

### Hobby Knives

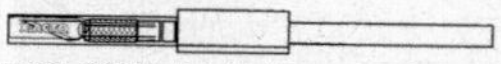

**790-3021** #1 Knife w/Safety Grip **4.12**
Includes #11 blade and tri-angular safety grip to prevent rolling.

**790-3201** #1 Light Duty Knife **3.05**

**790-3311** #1 Knife w/5 #11 Blades **5.30**

**790-3601** #1 Knife w/Safety Cap **3.58**

**790-3295** X-Calibre Retractable Knife **14.19**
Executive design with metal pocket clip. Balanced, lightweight; perfect for most light duty cutting.

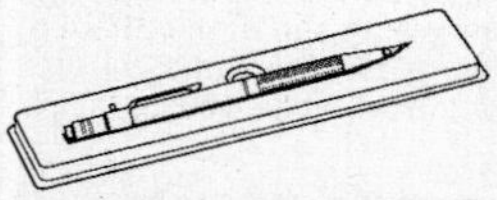

**790-5095** X-Calibre RT Set **18.16**
Stainless steel blade retracts with pushbutton pocket clip.

**790-3209** 9RX Knife **11.52**

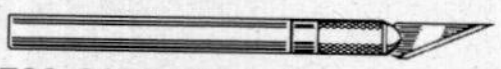

**790-3202** #2 Medium Duty Knife **4.34**

**790-3602** #2 Knife w/Safety Cap **5.46**

**790-3203** Gripster Soft Grip #3 Pen-Knife **6.06**

**790-3205** #5 Heavy Duty Knife **5.73**

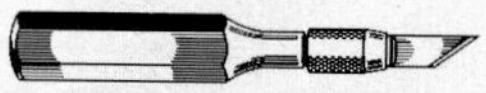

**790-3206** #6 Heavy Duty Knife **9.37**
Contoured aluminum handle; includes No. 24 Deburring Blade.

**790-3241** Craft Swivel Knife **8.52**
The perfect precision tool for all light-duty cutting.

**790-3261** Soft Grip Woodcarving Knife **9.59**

**790-3628** Gripster Knife **5.09**
With safety cap, assorted colors. Rubberized barrel anti-roll design.

### Compass and Swivel Knife

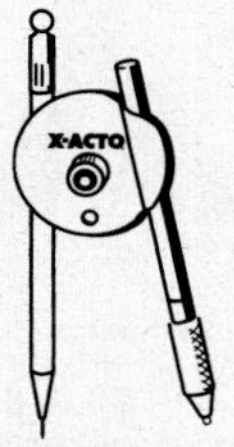


**790-7753 10.35**
For cutting circles up to 12" in lightweight materials, paper and film. Use with ballpoint pen, pencil or scriber.

### Utility Knives & Accessories

**790-3008** #8R Utility Knife **2.00**
Compact with lightweight plastic handle, adjustable cutting depth and retractable, reversible blade.

**790-3208** #8R Retractable Utility Knife **2.14**
Cycolac handle with 2 blades.

**790-3246** Snap-Off Blade Knife **8.57**

**790-3272** Plastic Retractable Utility Knife **6.38**

**790-3274** Metal Retractable Utility Knife **9.11**

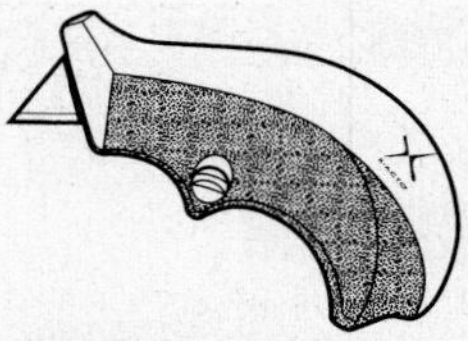

**790-3275** Ergo Utility Knife **8.56**
Assorted colors.Dual design for cutting or scraping.

**790-7747** Board Cutter **17.09**
Contoured shape and soft grip allow perfect 90° cuts through mat board and foam board up to 1/2" thick, and cuts precise 45° bevel with special adapter.

## SAWS

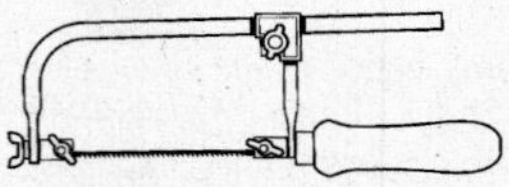

**790-7043** Jeweler's Saw w/Blade **35.29**

### Razor Saw Sets

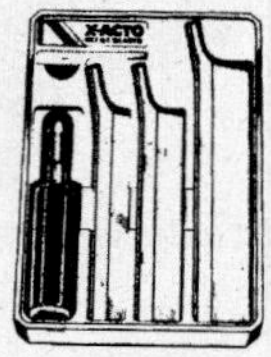


**790-75310** Razor Saw & Knife Set **18.18**
#5 Handle, 234, 235 and 236 blades, #15 keyhole saw blade and 5 knife blades.

**790-75300** #5 Handle Set **9.90**
Includes #234 and #235 blades.

**790-75350** Extra-Fine Set **8.85**

## MITRE BOXES

**790-75320** Mitre Box Set Carded **18.79**
Contains aluminum mitre box #7533, #236 razor saw blade and #5 handle. For use with #236 blade only.

**790-75330** Mitre Box Only, Carded **9.90**
Extruded aluminum, 6" long, 3/4 x 1-3/4" capacity. Grooves on base to hold wood, etc., from 1/16 to 1/4".

## TRIMMER

**790-2605** 6" Mini Trimmer (red) **10.70**
Precision trimmer is ideal for photos, paper and other craft materials.

## TOOL SETS

### Knife Sets

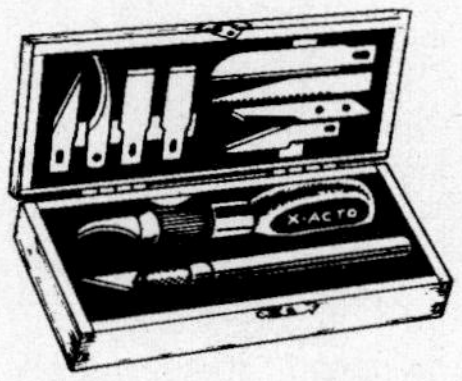


**790-5028** Carded Do-It-Yourself Set **26.73**
#2 and woodcarving knives, plus 8 assorted blades.

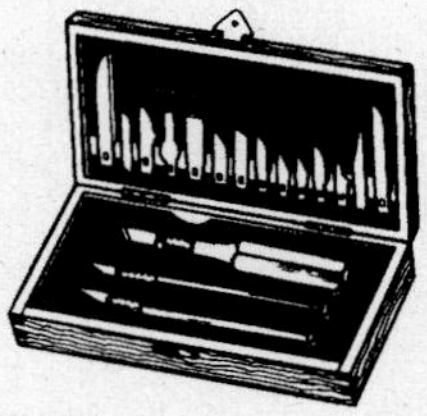

**790-5083** Deluxe Knife Set **35.30**
#1, #2 and #6 knives plus 14 assorted blades.

**790-5096** Scrapbooking Knife Set **21.41**

**790-5211** Knife Set #51 **5.30**
#1 knife with 5 assorted blades.

**790-5212** Knife Set #52 **7.45**
#2 knife with 5 assorted blades.

**790-5262** Double Knife Set #62 **13.12**
#1 and #2 knives with 10 assorted blades.

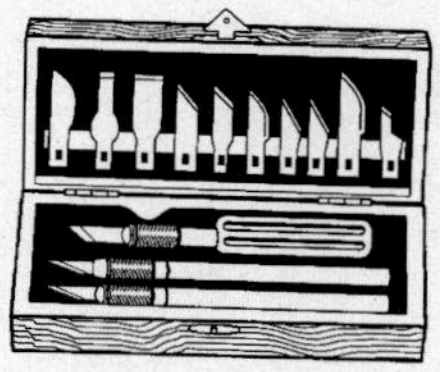

**790-5282** Carded Knife Chest #82 **24.10**
#1, #2 and #5 knives plus 10 assorted blades.

### Home/Office Cutting Sets

Carded sets include self-healing cutting mat and knife.

**790-7768 10.66**
Includes 4 x 7-1/2" gray mat, #1 knife w/safety cap & five #11 blades.

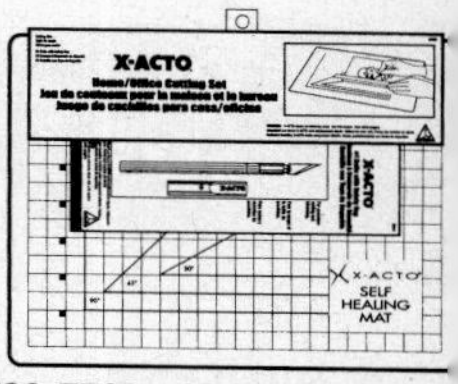


**790-7769 14.99**
Includes 9 x 12" gray mat ar
#1 knife w/safety cap.

### Carving Tool Sets

**790-5175** Carving Chest **36.**
Deluxe woodcarver set. #5 handle with 5 assorted blade two 3" blades, 6 gouges and routers.

**790-5177** Woodcarving Set Basic **19.82**
#5 handle with 6 gouge-blad 4 regular blades and two 3-inch blades.

**790-5179** Carving Tool Set **38.51**
Six hardwood-handled chisel

**790-5224** Standard Woodcarving Set **26.73**
For narrow cuts, deep cross cuts, leveling, whittling, gene carving, initial shaping and outlining in wood. Includes # Knife with blades 19, 15, 18, 22, 24, 26 and A, B, C, D, E and F gouges.

### Knife & Tool Sets

**790-5076** Basic Craft Tool Se **36.37**

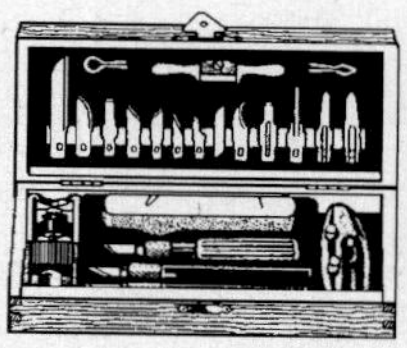

**790-5086** "The Crafter" Tool Set **53.51**
#1, #2 and #5 knives and assortment of blades, gouger, routers, plus plane, sander, spoke shave and balsa stripp in a wood chest.

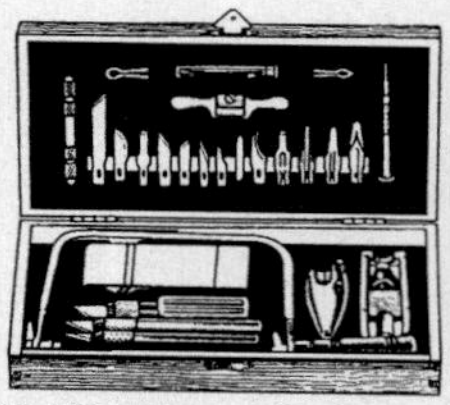

**790-5087** Deluxe Craft Tool Set **78.15**
Complete assortment of knives, blades and tools including coping saw, block plane, sander, jeweler's screwdriver, spoke shave, balsa stripper, pin vise, 3 drill bits, 4 gouges, 2 routers and 9 assorted blades.

# X-ACTO®

## BLADES

### Knife Blades

**790-2** #2 Blade pkg(5) **2.50**
Sharp angle precision cutting of medium to heavyweight materials. Fits knife handles 2, 2SGK, 5, 6 and woodcarving handle.

**790-202** Carded pkg(5) **2.58**

**790-402** Carded Safety Dispenser pkg(15) **6.96**

**790-208** Carded pkg(5) **2.68**

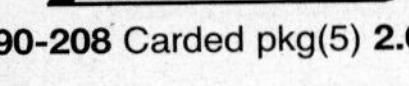

**790-209** #9RX Carded pkg(5) **7.45**
For light-duty stencil and frisket cutting. Also used as a lifter. Fits knife handle #9XR.

**790-210** #10 Blade Carded pkg(5) **3.75**
For general cutting, light carving and slicing. Fits handles 1, 1SGK, Super No. 1 X-Press, Gripster, Cut All and #3 Pen.

**790-610** Bulk Pack pkg(100) **64.22**

**790-11** #11 Blade pkg(5) **2.41**
Sharp angle for delicate, precision cutting, trimming and stripping. Fits knife handles 1, 1SGK, Super No. 1 X-Press, Gripster, Cut All and #3 Pen.

**790-211** Carded pkg(5) **2.41**

**790-411** Carded Safety Dispenser pkg(15) **5.89**

**790-611** Bulk Pack pkg(100) **33.15**

**790-291** Broad Tip #11 pkg(5) **2.68**
Modified blade provides a stronger, more flexible point.

**790-212** Carded pkg(5) **9.11**
For delicate paper cutting, stenciling and carving. Fits knife handles 1, 1SGK, Super No. 1 X-Press, Gripster, Cut All and #3 Pen.

**790-213** #13 Blade pkg(5) **3.75**
For precision cutting of plastics, balsa and thin metals. Fits knife handles 1, 1SGK, Super No. 1 X-Press, Gripster, Cut All and #3 Pen.

**790-215** #15 Keyhole Saw Blade pkg(5) **7.45**
For small interior cuts. Fits knife handles 2, 5, 6 and woodcarving handle.

**790-216** Carded pkg(5) **2.41**
For stenciling, etching and scoring and printed circuit boards. Fits knife handles 1, 1SGK, Super No. 1 X-Press, Gripster, Cut All and #3 Pen.

**790-616** Bulk Pack(100) **33.10**

**790-217** Carded pkg(5) **2.41**
For precision wood chiseling with 1/4" chisel. Fits knife handles 1, Super No. 1 X-Press, Gripster and Cut All.

**790-218** Carded pkg(5) **2.68**
For deep cross and smooth chiseling of wood with 1/2" surface. Fits handle #2.

**790-219** Carded pkg(5) **2.68**
For light chiseling, shaping, deburring and trimming. Fits handles 2 and 2SGK.

**790-222** Carded pkg(5) **4.66**

**790-223** #23 Blade Carded pkg(5) **9.37**
For corner cuts & tight spaces.

**790-224** Carded pkg(5) **2.41**
For close corner cuts on templates and mats, deburring, stripping and gasket cutting. Fits handles 2 and 2SGK.

**790-225** Carded #25 Blade pkg(5) **8.30**
For heavy-pressure cutting, whittling, carving and trimming. Fits handles 2 and 2SGK.



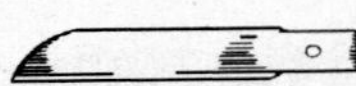

**790-226** #26 pkg(5) **5.30**
Blade 2-5/16" cutting edge for general purpose whittling and trimming. Fits handle #2.

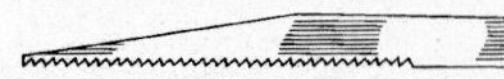

**790-227** #27 pkg(5) **6.70**
Blade for general purpose cutting of lightweight and medium woods. 3" length allows deeper cuts. Fits handle #2.

**790-228** Carded pkg(5) **12.59**
For whittling, leather and linoleum. Fits handles 2 and 2SGK.

**790-245** Craft Swivel Knife Blade pkg(2) **3.16**
Designed to rotate 360° for easy cutting of curves and circles in lightweight materials.

**790-243** Heavy-Duty Snap-Off Blades pkg(5) **3.75**

**790-292** Heavy Duty Utility pkg(5) **3.21**
For #3272 and 3274. For cutting mats, carpeting, wallboard, wallpaper, tile, plastic and wood.

**790-295** X-Calibre RT Knife Blade pkg(5) **8.03**
For fine cutting, trimming paperwork and stenciling. Stainless steel resists corrosion, won't rust.

**Limited Quantity Available**

**790-28** #28 pkg(5) **11.50**

**790-9** #9RX Blade pkg(5) **6.95**

### Stainless Steel Blades

**790-221** Carded pkg(5) **2.68**

**790-421** Carded Safety Dispenser pkg(15) **7.77**

**790-621** Bulk pkg(100) **41.73**

### Blade Assortment #1

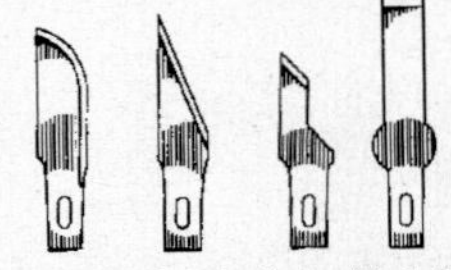

**790-231** Carded pkg(5) **2.58**
Includes two #11 and one each of #s 10, 16 and 17.

### Blade Assortment #2

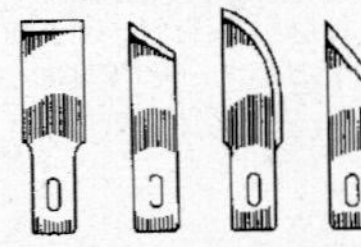

**790-232** Carded pkg(5) **3.48**
Includes blades 18, 19, 22 and two 24s.

### Razor Saw Blades

#### #234 Razor Saw Blade

**790-234** Fine Saw Blade **3.48**
For delicate sawing, cutting circuit boards, model construction and shaping balsa wood. Cutting edge 4-1/2" long, 3/4" deep.

#### #235 Razor Saw Blade

**790-235** Medium Saw Blade **3.38**
For delicate sawing, cutting circuit boards, model construction and shaping balsa wood, cutting fiberglass, plastic, narrow gauge tubing, metals and railroad tracks. Cutting edge 4-1/2" long, 1" deep.

#### #236 Razor Saw Blade

**790-236** Coarse Saw Blade **3.75**
For coarse sawing of wood, plastic, fiberglass, metals and moldings. Cutting edge 5-1/2" long, 1-1/4" deep.

**790-239** Extra Fine Saw Blade **3.75**
For delicate sawing work in confined space, cutting circuit boards, model construction, shaping balsa wood, cutting fiberglass, plastic, metals and railroad tracks. Cutting edge 5-1/2" long, 1-1/4" deep.

### Jeweler's Saw Blades pkg(12) 7.45 ea

For #7043 saw.

**790-746** #6/0 Extra Fine Cut

**790-752** #2/0 Fine Cut Single Edge Razor Blades

**790-270** pkg(5) **2.31**

**790-670** pkg(100) **16.02**

### Carving Blades 4.02 ea

**790-103** Convex pkg(2)
For carving cylindrical shapes, rug cutting and linoleum cutting.

**790-104** Concave, 3/4" Radius pkg(2)
For general carving.

**790-105** Concave, 1-3/8" Radius
Initial shaping and carving.

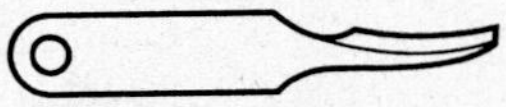

**790-106** Concave Carving Blade pkg(2)

## PRECISION TOOLS

### Routers

**790-135** Routers Assortment pkg(4) **11.52**
Fits knife handles #5 and #6. For carving out grooves, hollows and recesses.

### File Sets

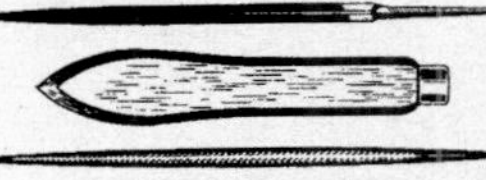

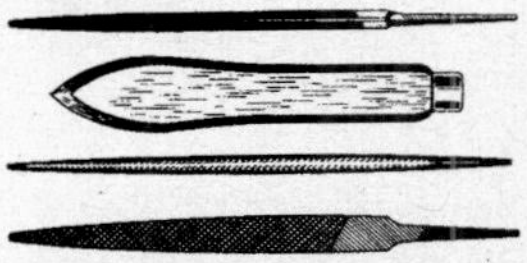

**790-73580** File Set **11.50**
Includes 3 files and handle.

**790-73610** Needle File Set w/Handle Carded **21.39**

### Hand Drill Pin Vise

**790-73220** Double-Ended Hand Drill Pin Vise **6.00**
Contains chucks that will accept #49-#80 bits.

**790-7144** **11.50**
Carded set includes double-ended pin vise, bit guard and three assorted drill bits (1.35-7.3mm)

### Twist Drills

**790-6409** Drills 55-80 Assorted pkg(12) **16.00**

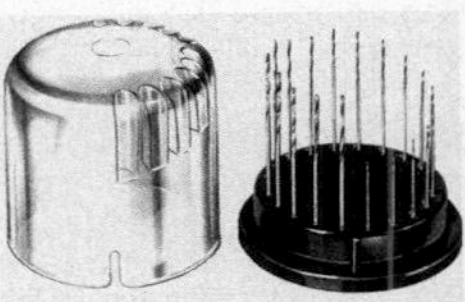

**790-6412** Drill Stand Set **34.25**
With 20 drills 61-80, stand and cover.

### Tweezers 5.15 ea

**790-73360** Soldering Tweezer 4-1/2"
Medium sharp points.

**790-73430** Angular Tweezer
Fine serrated points.

### Soldering Iron

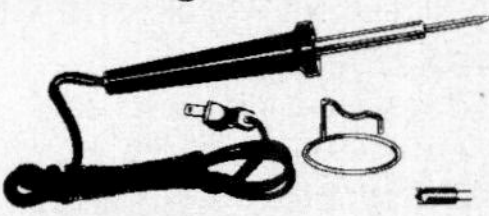

**790-73780** Soldering Iron 110V **18.79**
With tip and hot knife blade.

### X-Tra Hands

Double alligator spring clamps and double ball joints hold work firmly.

**790-75140** Double **15.55**

**790-75170** With 2x Magnifier **18.79**

## X-ACTO

### Vise
**790-73700** Mini Vacu-Vise **10.35**

### Clamps
**790-7004** Large Clamp, Plastic pkg(2) **8.10**
7-1/4" long with 2-1/16" throat.

**Limited Quantity Available**
**790-7450** Mini "C" Clamp Assortment pkg(3) **8.00**

### Screwdrivers

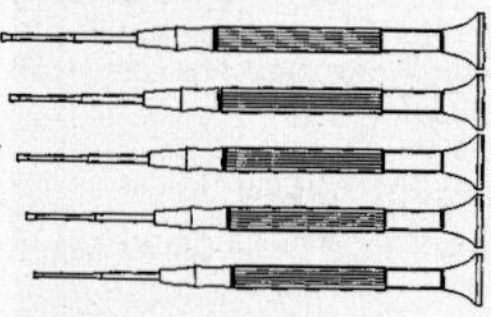

**790-7068** Jeweler's pkg(5) **10.95**

### Self-Healing Mat
One-inch grid pattern, 3mm thickness, non-slip bottom.

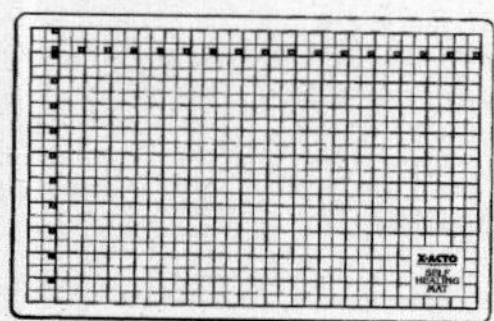

**790-7760** 8-1/2 x 12" (gray) **14.51**

**790-7761** 12 x 18" (gray) **17.10**

**790-7764** 9 x 12" (Translucent White) **14.51**

**790-7765** 12 x 18" (Translucent White) **17.10**

**790-7766** 18 x 24" (Translucent White) **41.55**

### Hobby Rulers 8.50 ea

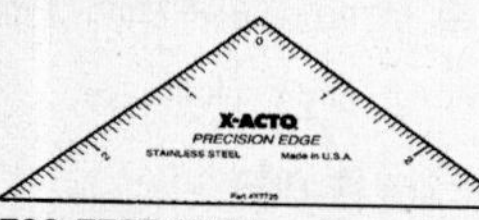


**790-7725** 3" Triangle, Inches Only

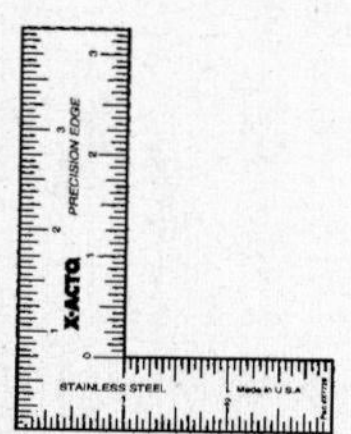

**790-7726** 3 x 4" Square, Inches Only

### Miscellaneous

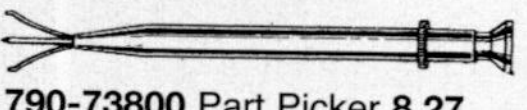

**790-73800** Part Picker **8.27**

## WOODLAND SCENICS®

### Low Temp Foam Glue Gun

**785-1445 16.98**
The Glue Gun with the Low Temp glue sticks operates at a temperature that will not damage foam.

**785-1446** pkg(10) **5.98**
10" glue sticks.

### Hot Wire Foam Cutter

**785-1435 39.98**
The Hot Wire Foam Cutter has adjustable collars allowing for clean, accurate cuts in foam. Attach the Guide for more precise cutting. The Bow attachment adds versatility to the Hot Wire Cutter. Woodland Scenics recommends using only on SubTerrain white foam which emits no toxic fumes. Use only special Nichrome replacement wire.

### Foam Cutter Replacement Wire
**785-1436** 4' **2.29**

### Foam Cutter Bow & Guide

**785-1437 7.98**
This accessory increases the versatility of the Hot Wire Foam Cutter (785-1435, sold separately), allowing cuts in material from 1/4 to 5" thick, or cuts at precise angles.

### Foam Knife

**785-1433 6.98**
The Foam Knife comes with a 2" replaceable blade that is ideal for cutting thick pieces of foam.

### Foam Knife Blades

**785-1434** pkg(4) **5.98**

## 4 In 1 Saw Set

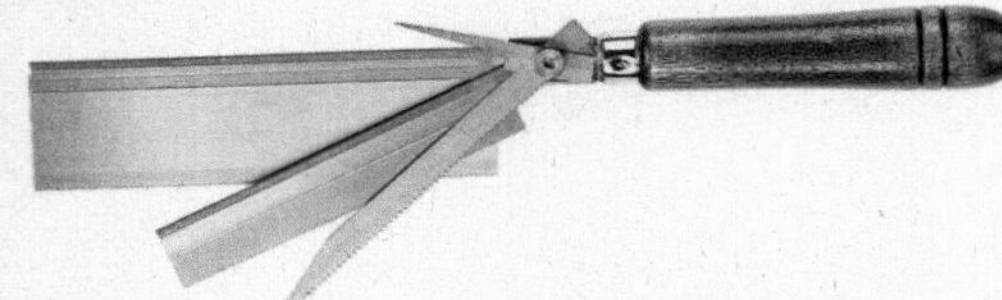

**795-35140 8.90**
Versatile set for all kinds of cutting. Includes four interchangeable blades that attach with a wing nut and screw.

## 4 In 1 Replacement Blades

**795-36406** Keyhole Saw Blade (Pull Style) pkg(3) **2.10**

**795-36408** Keyhole Saw Blade (Push Style) pkg(3) **2.10**

**795-36458** Saber Saw Blade **.95**

**795-36050** Razor Saw Blade, 7/16" Cutting Depth **1.60**

**795-36555** Razor Saw Blade, 1-3/16" Cutting Depth **1.60**

## Mini Miter Box w/Saw

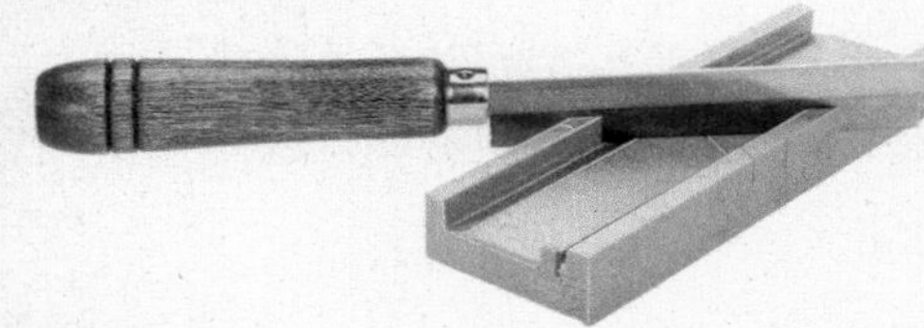

**795-251 9.50**
Combination saw and miter box (w/#200 saw).

**795-250** Miter Box Only **4.95**
Designed to fit all razor-type saws. Adjustable stop and beveled channel.

## Thin Slot Miter w/Thin Gauge Saw

**795-35241** Saw & Miter Box Set **22.50**
Aluminum miter box with unique narrow slots to maintain accurate cuts. Cuts material up to 2" wide and 7/8" thick at 90, 45 and 30° angles. Comes with 42 TPI razor saw.

**795-37240** Thin Slot .014" Miter Box Only **14.90**

**795-37245** Medium Slot .025" Miter Box Only **14.90**

## Retractable Knife Set

**795-39850 4.95**
Knife with #11 blade in handle and five additional #11 blades.

## Soft Grip Knife

**795-39910** With Fine Point Blade **4.50**
Put an end to blisters with the Soft Grip Knife. The soft grip handle provides extra comfort and control, and features an anti-roll design. Perfect for cutting wood, paper, plastic film, balsa wood, vinyl, foamboard and rubber.

**795-39920** Set Includes 4 Extra Blades **5.95**

## Ultra Thin Saws 5.50 ea

The thinnest razor saws available with ultra thin .008" thick blades. #150 is ideal for super fine cuts in wood and plastic without splitting or ragged edges. #200 offers longer wear in metal cutting applications. Both have shorter cutting depths plus steel backs for greater blade stability.

**795-150** 42 TPI

**795-200** 32 TPI

**795-35050** 52 TPI

## 24 TPI Woodcraft Saw

**795-300 6.50**
.015" thick blade, 6-1/2" long, 7/8" cutting depth.

## 32 & 42 TPI Universal Saws

**795-500 6.50**
A good all-purpose saw. .010" thick blade, 6-1/2" long, 1-3/16" cutting depth.

**795-35550** Extra Fine Cuts **6.50**
A good all-purpose saw for model and miniature making and smooth precision cuts in balsa and other wood, plastic, copper or brass.

## Saber Saw Set

**795-450 6.90**
.022" thick blade, 4-1/2" long, 3/8" wide. Ideal for large inside cuts and for cutting through thick material. Set also includes #36408 "push" and the #36406 "pull" miniature keyhole saber blades.

## Finger Sanders

**795-37795** 1-1/2" **5.00**

**795-37790** 3/4" **3.90**

**795-37794** Master Set **13.20**

## Adjustable Jeweler's Saw

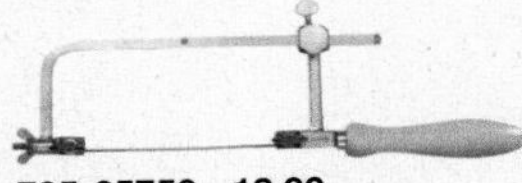

**795-35750 12.90**

## Jeweler's Saw Blades pkg(12) 3.90 ea

**795-36475** .019 x .0095" x 61 TPI

**795-36476** .020 x .010" x 56 TPI

**795-36480** .028 x .013" x 43 TPI

## Junior Hack Saw

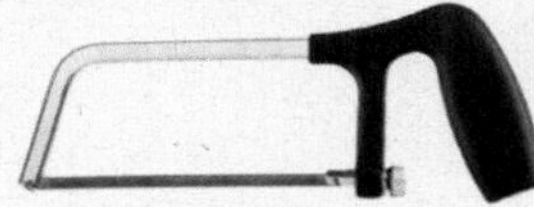

**795-650 10.50**
Has a well balanced and sturdy, solid, metal frame with comfortable handle grip. Several different blades can be easily inserted and tightened securely in this frame using the tensioning screw.

## Hobby Clamps Berna Assemblers®

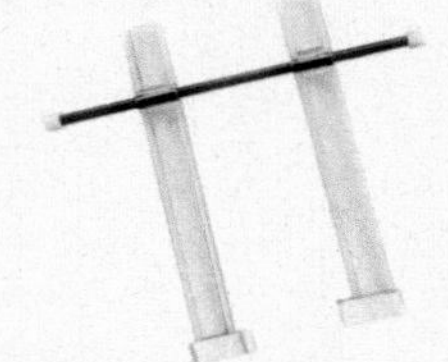

**795-38710 5.20**
Assembled, 3" beam with 3" jaws.

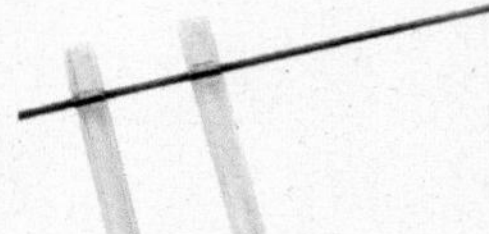

**795-38720 6.20**
8" beam with 3" jaws.

## Hobby Clamp Assortment

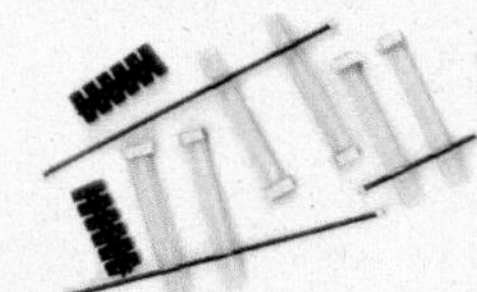

**795-38725** Hobby Clamp Assortment **17.50**
Includes two 8", one 3" clamps and Connector Strip.

## Spiral Hand Drill w/Spring

**795-37160 8.75**
For use with small, wire sized drills from #80 to #70. Push ring down to turn drill. Spring return makes drilling easier and faster.

## Swivel Head Pin Vise

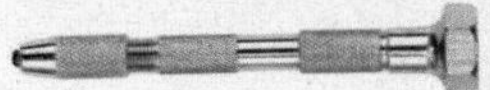

**795-37140 6.90**
Comes with two double-ended collets in the handle with 0 to .125" range. Holds any small tool with round shank: drills, burs, reamers, taps, needles, scribers, etc.

## Tool Holder w/Two Chucks

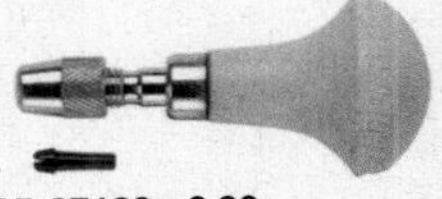

**795-37130 6.90**
Includes two collets with capacity range of 1/64" to 3/32" diameter. Ideal for use with small tools including: chisels, files, reamers, beading tools, burs and gravers.

## Hanging Drill Set

**795-37150** 20 Pieces **25.95**
Contains high speed twist drills in wire gauge #61 through #80, one each. For use in above tools.

## Tweezer Set

**795-37540 20.90**
A selection of five quality tweezers for handling small objects. Includes one each of fine point, flat blade, slide lock, curved point and cross locking tweezers.

## 3" Triangle

**795-37433 6.95**
Made from .022" thick stainless steel.

## L-Square 3 x 4"

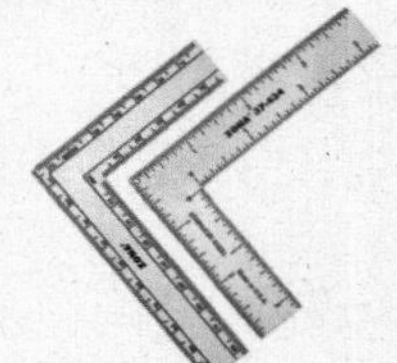

**795-37434 6.95**
Made from .022" thick stainless steel.

2008
HO
Model Railroad
Reference Book

# SCRATCH BUILDING

Models and Photo by Gerry Gilliland

One last meeting with the bookkeeper at the bank pretty much decided the fate of the old mill. Any profits were long gone, despite every effort to drum up business. Things started to go down some years ago, and from then on, only the most needed repairs were made until there wasn't any money left for those either. Well now that the bank and the sheriff have served their papers, maybe things can get going again. A few ads in some of the county newspapers, a good harvest, and a little luck might just turn things around once more.

Things are pretty quiet around this old mill building constructed by Gerry Gilliland of Rothesay, New Brunswick. An aging Maritime Lumber box car provides some company for the old building, at least until the pigeons return for the night. Both of these models were completely scratchbuilt for this scene. Northeastern lumber, Campbell corrugated roofing and Grandt Line windows were all used in the construction of the mill. Trees from Scenic Express were used, along with plenty of Woodland Scenics materials for the underbrush and weeds that complete the look and feel of the entire scene.

Whether it's a prototype for a complex kit that just isn't available, or something special to set your layout, or perhaps just one small area apart, scratchbuilding offers plenty of fun modeling. Find some plans or photos to get started, and complete your bill of materials with the many different types of wood, plastic and metal products you'll find inside this section.

# WALTHERS

A complete range of miniature wood, machine and nylon screws, plus hex nuts and washers in assorted sizes are available. (Machine and wood screws may be brass or brass plated.)

### SIZE INFORMATION

| Size | 00-90 | 0-80 | 1-72 | 2-56 |
|---|---|---|---|---|
| Screw Body Diameter | .047 | .060 | .073 | .086 |
| Clearance Drill Number | 55 | 52 | 48 | 43 |
| Tap Drill Number | 61 | 55 | 53 | 50 |
| Hex Head Across Flat | .078 | .097 | .109 | .123 |
| Height | .042 | .042 | .055 | .064 |
| Round Head Diameter | .089 | .108 | .136 | .164 |
| Height | .041 | .047 | .055 | .065 |
| Flat Head Diameter | .089 | .108 | .136 | .164 |
| Height | .024 | .035 | .043 | .051 |

## HARDWARE

### Brass Washers pkg(16) 2.98 ea

**947-1270** #00
(O.D.=105" I.D.=060" .020" Thick)

**947-1271** #0
(O.D.=125" I.D.=068" .020" Thick)

**947-1272** #1
(O.D.=156" I.D.=084" .025" Thick)

**947-1273** #2
(O.D.=188" I.D.=094" .025" Thick)

### Flat-Head Brass Machine Screws 2.98 ea

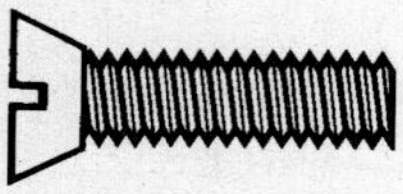

**00-90**
**947-1042** 3/16 x .047" pkg(12)
**947-1043** 1/4 x .047" pkg(12)
**947-1045** 3/8 x .047" pkg(12)
**947-1046** 1/2 x .047" pkg(10)

**0-80**
**947-1052** 3/16 x .060" pkg(16)
**947-1053** 1/4 x .060" pkg(16)
**947-1055** 3/8 x .060" pkg(12)
**947-1056** 1/2 x .060" pkg(10)

**1-72**
**947-1062** 3/16 x .073" pkg(16)
**947-1063** 1/4 x .073" pkg(16)
**947-1065** 3/8 x .073" pkg(12)
**947-1066** 1/2 x .073" pkg(10)

**2-56**
**947-1072** 3/16 x .086" pkg(16)
**947-1073** 1/4 x .086" pkg(16)
**947-1075** 3/8 x .086" pkg(12)
**947-1076** 1/2 x .086" pkg(10)

### Hex-Head Brass Machine Screws 2.98 ea

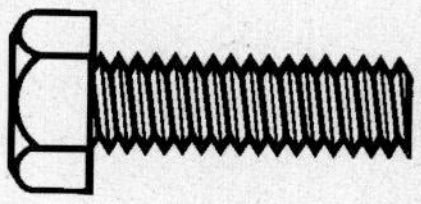

**00-90**
**947-1122** 3/16 x .047" pkg(12)
**947-1123** 1/4 x .047" pkg(12)
**947-1125** 3/8 x .047" pkg(12)
**947-1126** 1/2 x .047" pkg(10)

**0-80**
**947-1132** 3/16 x .060" pkg(12)
**947-1133** 1/4 x .060" pkg(12)
**947-1135** 3/8 x .060" pkg(12)
**947-1136** 1/2 x .060" pkg(10)

**1-72**
**947-1142** 3/16 x .073" pkg(12)
**947-1143** 1/4 x .073" pkg(12)
**947-1145** 3/8 x .073" pkg(12)
**947-1146** 1/2 x .073" pkg(10)

**2-56**
**947-1152** 3/16 x .086" pkg(12)
**947-1153** 1/4 x .086" pkg(12)
**947-1155** 3/8 x .086" pkg(12)
**947-1156** 1/2 x .086" pkg(10)

### Hex Nuts pkg(12) 2.98 ea

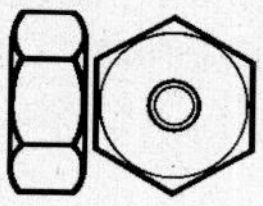

**Brass**
**947-1250** 00-90 (.040 x 5/64")
**947-1251** 0-80 (.050 x 5/32")
**947-1252** 1-72 (.062 x 7/64")
**947-1253** 2-56 (.072 x 1/8")

**Nylon**
**947-1255** 2-56 (.075 x 3/16")
**947-1256** 4-40 (.100 x 1/4")

### Round-Head Brass Machine Screws 2.98 ea

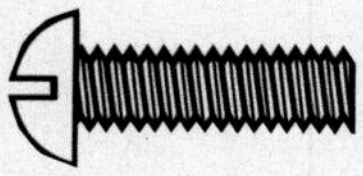

**00-90**
**947-1002** 3/16 x .047" pkg(12)
**947-1003** 1/4 x .047" pkg(12)
**947-1005** 3/8 x .047" pkg(12)
**947-1006** 1/2 x .047" pkg(10)

**0-80**
**947-1012** 3/16 x .060" pkg(16)
**947-1013** 1/4 x .060" pkg(16)
**947-1015** 3/8 x .060" pkg(12)
**947-1016** 1/2 x .060" pkg(10)

**1-72**
**947-1022** 3/16 x .073" pkg(16)
**947-1023** 1/4 x .073" pkg(16)
**947-1025** 3/8 x .073" pkg(12)
**947-1026** 1/2 x .073" pkg(10)

**2-56**
**947-1032** 3/16 x .086" pkg(16)
**947-1033** 1/4 x .086" pkg(16)
**947-1035** 3/8 x .086" pkg(12)
**947-1036** 1/2 x .086" pkg(10)

### Round-Head Nylon Machine Screws pkg(12) 2.98 ea

**947-1163** 1-72 1/4 x .073"
**947-1177** 2-56 5/8 x .086"
**947-1188** 4-40 3/4 x .112"

### Self-Tapping #2 Sheet Metal Screws pkg(24) 2.98 ea

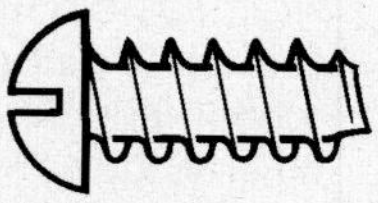

**947-1189** 3/16 x .088"
**947-1190** 1/4 x .088"
**947-1191** 1/2 x .088"

### Wood Screws - Brass or Brass-Plated pkg(24) 2.98 ea

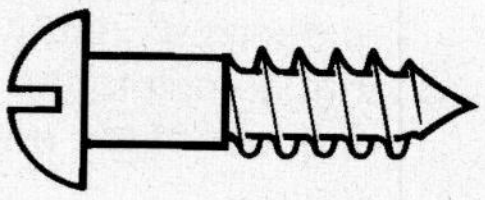

**#0**
**947-1195** 3/8 x .060"

**#1**
**947-1196** 3/8 x .073"
**947-1197** 1/2 x .073"

**#2**
**947-1198** #2 3/8 x .086"
**947-1199** #2 1/2 x .086"

## TOOLS

### Drill Bits pkg(2)

**1.98 ea**
**947-43** .089"
**947-48** .076"
**947-50** .070"
**947-52** .064"
**947-53** .060"
**947-55** .052"
**947-56** .047"
**947-57** .043"
**947-58** .042"
**947-60** .040"

**2.29 ea**
**947-61** .039"
**947-62** .038"
**947-63** .037"
**947-64**. 036"
**947-65** .035"
**947-66** .033"
**947-67** .032"
**947-68** .031"
**947-69** .0292"
**947-70** .028"
**947-71** .026"
**947-72** .025"
**947-73** .024"
**947-74** .0225"
**947-75** .021"
**947-76** .020"
**947-77** .018"
**947-78** .016"
**947-79** .0145"
**947-80** .0135"

### Drill Set & Accessories

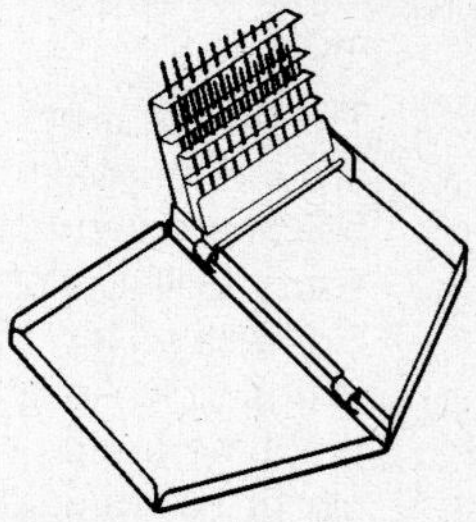

**949-659** Set of 20 Bits w/Case **18.98**
in a metal case.

**949-660** Drill Case Only **4.98**

### Pin Vise

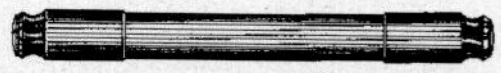

**949-664** Double Ended **9.98**
Includes two single end collets. Holds bits from #42 to #70.

### Tap & Die Holder

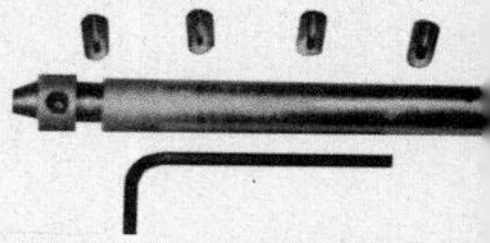

**949-663** Tap Holder **17.98**
Includes storage case, holde Allen wrench and collets for 00-90, 0-80, 1-72 and 2-56 taps.

### Taps 3.98 ea

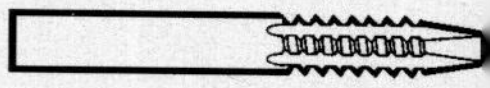

**947-1301** 00-90
**947-1302** 0-80
**947-1303** 1-72
**947-1304** 2-56

### Work Holder

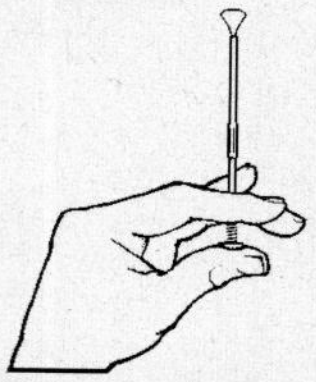

**949-519** Screw Sticker **5.98**
Get a firm grip on tiny screws parts and more. One-handed operation makes the miniatur fingers an extension of your own.

### Wrenches 3.98 ea

Will fit brass hex nuts and hex head screws.

**947-1321** #00
**947-1322** #0
**947-1323** #1
**947-1324** #2

**949-662** Wrench Set pkg(4) **15.98**
Includes one each #1321-1324.

## POURABLE METAL

### Temp-Low™

**949-525** 3oz (84g) **5.98**
Melt in hot water (158° to 190° F). Pour in without fear o unsoldering detail. Make custom castings in cardboard, rubber or plaster molds. Makes a great filler to support tubing while bending.

# WALTHERS

## ADHESIVE

### Fix It Forever with GOO®!

**904-299** GOO Adhesive, Large Tube 1oz **2.98**

### •All Purpose Adhesive

GOO is the permanent rubber base adhesive that grips most anything. It never lets go.

### •Fast-Setting Joints

Easy contact action opens new possibilities for fast-setting joints with any material.

GOO is the perfect adhesive for building or repairing jobs on your layout and around the house!

The easy contact action of GOO produces fast-setting joints with any material. GOO works with all types of metals (including steel, brass, aluminum, copper and others) plus items like wood, plastic, cardboard, china, leather, vinyl, ceramics, paper, concrete and many more, on any smooth or porous surface.

GOO is a permanent rubber base adhesive that's shockproof, waterproof and crack proof–it's as flexible as rubber. Joints won't crack when flexed back and forth, won't break loose when the temperature changes and won't weaken when wet or damp. It sticks forever!

Dealers MUST order multiples of 6.

## PAINTING ACCESSORIES

### Masking Liquid

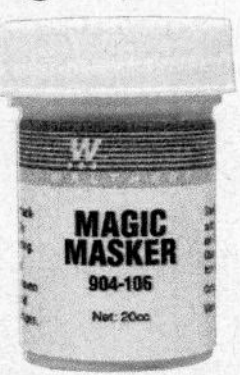


**904-106** Magic Masker (20cc) **2.98**
Get professional results when covering odd shaped or small areas, such as windows, without the time and trouble of cutting and fitting tape. Brush it on and allow to dry. Then spray your color, let dry and peel off. Works on plastic, wood, metal, paint, chrome and silver.

Dealers MUST order multiples of 12.

### Decal Setting Solution

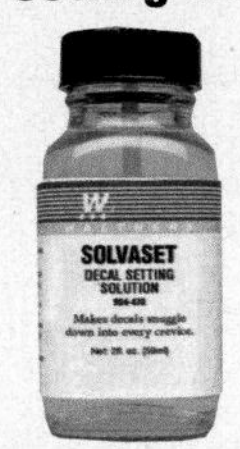


**904-470** Solvaset 2oz **2.98**
Softens decal film so it snuggles down on surface, details Eliminates air bubbles, white spots and draping.

Dealers MUST order multiples of 6.

Daily New Arrival Updates! Visit Walthers Web site at

**www.walthers.com**

## ALPINE DIVISION SCALE MODELS

Items listed in blue ink may not be available at all times (see Legend Page).

### Aluminum Paper

**700-1001** Corrugated, 4 x 11-1/2" pkg(6) **4.02**

### Tin Siding Sheets

**.010" Corrugated**

**700-100** 4 x 12" pkg(6) **8.25**

**700-101** 2 x 12" pkg(6) **5.50**

**.010" Plain**

**700-102** 4 x 12" pkg(6) **6.05**

**90° Angle**

**700-104** 1/8 x 12" pkg(6) **4.13**

## AMACO

### ARTEMBOSS® METAL SHEETS

Embossing foil sheets are made of soft metal so they're easy to emboss yet hold their shape. Emboss them with the Amaco Stylus Tool (sold separatley) or hand tools and textured surfaces. Use these sheets to make embossed metal details such as rivet strips, tin-panel roofing for building interiors, decorative door panels, roof flashing and more. Each sheet measures 9-1/4 x 12" 23.1 x 30cm and includes a wooden embossing stick, decorative craft patterns and instructions.

**126-50063** Pewter Medium **10.49**

**126-50064** Brass Light **7.65**

**126-50065** Copper Medium **7.45**

**126-50066** Copper Light **6.49**

**126-50067** Aluminum Medium **5.45**

**126-50068** Aluminum **4.95**

**126-50114** Matte Black **5.95**

**126-11107P** Stylus Tool Set **3.39**

IMPORTED FROM GERMANY BY WALTHERS

### PLASTIC SHEETS

**4.99 ea**

Ideal for all kinds of scratchbuilding projects, each pack includes two sheets measuring 4 x 6". Thickness varies from .031 to .039".

186-2800 186-2801

**186-2800** Wood Flooring (Dark Brown)

**186-2801** Wood Flooring (Natural Finish)

186-2805 186-2806

**186-2805** Cobblestones

**186-2806** Historic Cobblestones (gray)

186-2810 186-2815

**186-2810** Curved Cobblestones

**186-2815** Random Stone Paving

186-2825 186-2826

**186-2825** Masonry Slabs (Sandstone)

**186-2826** Masonry Slabs (Brick Red)

186-2827 186-2830

**186-2827** Brick Wall Sheet

**186-2830** Sidewalk Paving

186-2835 186-2840

**186-2835** Ribbed Metal Sheet (silver)

**186-2836** Ribbed Metal Sheet (black)

**186-2840** Window Glazing

186-2845 186-2850

**186-2845** Artificial Paving Stone

**186-2850** Sheet Piling

186-2855 186-2856

**186-2855** Corrugated Metal Sheet (gray)

**186-2856** Corrugated Sheet (translucent)

**186-2867** Wall Tiles (Brick Red)

### TUBING/RODS

Brass tube and angles are 12" long unless noted; dimensions shown are external diameter x wall thickness in millimeters.

Dealers MUST order multiples of 10.

**Limited Quantity Available on All Items**

#### Angle

**186-3764** 4.0 x 4.0 x 0.50 **5.45**

#### Square Tube

**186-3722** 4.0 x 4.0 x 0.30 **2.90**

## B.T.S.

### Shingles

Laser-cut shingles are peel and stick for easy installation. Each package contains two sheets of shingles which cover approximately 14 square inches.

**464-21000** Random Cedar **4.00**

**464-21004** Octagonal **4.00**

**464-21006** Diamond **4.00**

**464-21008** Saw Tooth **4.00**

**464-21010** Three Tab **3.50**

**464-21012** French Diamond **3.50**

# CLEVER models

Create custom models with realistic detail quickly and easily with these preprinted paper sheets. Easily adapted to a wide range of models, each is printed in full-color on high quality, self-adhesive paper. Each sheet measures 8-1/2 x 11" 21.5 x 27.9cm overall, but the actual useable area is slightly less.

## NEW PRODUCTS

### Self-Adhesive Flat Sheets

**3.00 ea**

#### Brick

217-104

217-105

**NEW 217-104** Medium Brick w/Dark Mortar

**NEW 217-105** Old Brick (Needs Tuckpointing)

217-106

217-112

**NEW 217-106** New Brick (Companion to Old Brick)

**NEW 217-112** Red

217-120

217-121

**NEW 217-120** Light Brick

**NEW 217-121** Virginia City Brick (light color, dry appearance)

#### Contemporary Factory Brick

217-118

217-119

**NEW 217-118** Brown w/Dark Mortar

**NEW 217-119** Yellow w/Dark Mortar

#### Clapboard Siding

217-115

217-116

**NEW 217-115** Faded Yellow

**NEW 217-116** Green

**NEW 217-117** Tan

#### Distressed Clapboard Siding

217-101

217-102

**NEW 217-101** Blue, Gray

**NEW 217-102** Tan

**NEW 217-114** Red

#### Cinderblock

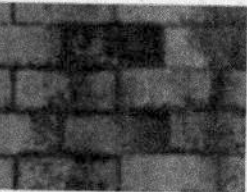
217-111

217-127

**NEW 217-111** Lightly Distressed

**NEW 217-127** Gray

**NEW 217-128** Tan

#### Concrete

217-129

217-130

**NEW 217-129** Light

**NEW 217-130** Medium

**NEW 217-131** Dark

#### Corrugated Fiberglass Panels

217-134

217-135

**NEW 217-134** Green & White 8-1/2 x 11" Panels

**NEW 217-135** Individual Green Panels 8-1/2 x 11"

**NEW 217-136** Individual White Panels 8-1/2 x 11"

#### Corrugated Steel

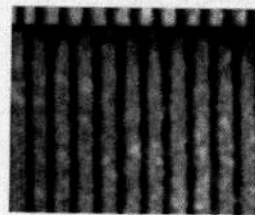
217-103

217-132

**NEW 217-103** Moderate Rust

**NEW 217-132** Clean

**NEW 217-133** Very Rusty

#### Insulbrick (Asphalt Faux Brick)

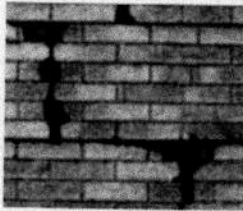
217-122

217-123

**NEW 217-122** Distressed

**NEW 217-123** Brown

217-124

217-125

**NEW 217-124** Gray

**NEW 217-125** Red

#### Industrial/Factory Windows

**NEW 217-167**

#### Shingles

##### Wood

**NEW 217-107** Weathered

##### Asphalt

217-108

217-137

**NEW 217-108** Brown

**NEW 217-137** Red

217-138

217-139

**NEW 217-138** Dark Gray

**NEW 217-139** Brown

**NEW 217-140** Green

**NEW 217-155** Diamond Pattern (red)

##### Shake Shingle

**NEW 217-141** Tan, Gray

#### Stone Block

**NEW 217-163** Dark Gray

#### Standing Seam Steel Panel

**NEW 217-145**

#### Terracotta

**NEW 217-159** Green & White Building Facade

**NEW 217-162** Coping

#### Tarpaper

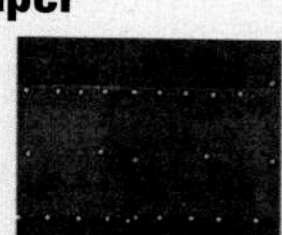

**NEW 217-147** Rolled w/Nail Heads

##### Distressed

**NEW 217-113** Vertical

**NEW 217-148** Horizontal

#### Walls

**NEW 217-110** Limestone Block

**NEW 217-156** Brick w/Concrete Pilasters & Windows

**NEW 217-157** Brick w/Concrete Pilaster Only

**NEW 217-160** Brick & Stone Arch Retaining Wall

**NEW 217-161** Glass Factory Wall w/Random Color Panes

**NEW 217-164** Rectangular Stone Wall (tan)

##### Industrial Wall

**NEW 217-159** Type D; Cinderblock & Fiberglass w/Roll-Up Door

**NEW 217-166** Type C; Brick & Steel Siding, Roll-Up Door, No Windows

**NEW 217-168** Type A; Brick, Steel Siding & Fiberglass

**NEW 217-169** Type B; Brick, Steel Siding, & Glass Factory Windows

#### Welded Steel Plate

217-143

217-144

**NEW 217-143** Light Weathering

**NEW 217-144** Dark Weathering

#### Wood

217-126

217-142

**NEW 217-126** Weathered Board & Batten (From Virginia City)

**NEW 217-142** Interior Studs & Plywood

**NEW 217-149** Wood Underlay (Used under siding & roofing material)

**NEW 217-152** Wood Decking (gray for platform & flooring)

**NEW 217-154** Distressed Barn Siding

**NEW 217-165** 12" Board w/Nail Holes - Vertical

#### Wood Planks

**NEW 217-150** Gray

**NEW 217-151** White

**NEW 217-109** 10" Wide

**NEW 217-153** Distressed (brown)

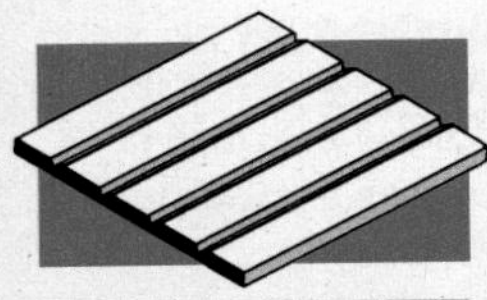

Styrene is one of the most common modeling plastics. It can be used to simulate concrete, metal or wooden surfaces and is easily cut and sanded to virtually any shape. When cutting sheets, simply score with a sharp knife, then "break" on the scored line. Small strips and very thin sheets can be cut through. Parts can be joined with plastic solvents, while epoxies and CA adhesives can be used to join painted parts or other materials. Before brush painting with Floquil, Scalecoat or other lacquers, a primer coat of Floquil Barrier or Scalecoat Shieldcoat should be applied to prevent the paint from "attacking" the plastic.

## SIDING

Duplicate many common types of building siding with these opaque white sheets. Each is pre-scribed to match different widths of lumber.

### V-Groove

Used on freight and passenger cars, railroad, commercial and residential buildings. Many 19th- and early 20th-century structures had panels of v-groove siding applied in horizontal, vertical and diagonal patterns, or in combination with clapboard and novelty siding for decorative effects. Part dimension indicates spacing.

#### 6 x 12" Sheet 4.59 ea

**.020" Thick**

**269-2025** .025"
**269-2030** .030"
**269-2040** .040"
**269-2050** .050"
**269-2060** .060"
**269-2080** .080"
**269-2100** .100"
**269-2125** .125"

**.040" Thick**

**269-4030** .030"
**269-4040** .040"
**269-4050** .050"
**269-4060** .060"
**269-4080** .080"
**269-4100** .100"
**269-4125** .125"
**269-4188** .188"
**269-4250** .250"

See What's Available at
**www.walthers.com**

#### 12 x 24" Sheets 14.99 ea

**.020" Thick**

**269-12025** .025"
**269-12030** .030"
**269-12040** .040"
**269-12050** .050"
**269-12060** .060"
**269-12080** .080"
**269-12100** .100"
**269-12125** .125"

**.040" Thick**

**269-14030** .030"
**269-14040** .040"
**269-14050** .050"
**269-14060** .060"
**269-14080** .080"
**269-14100** .100"
**269-14125** .125"
**269-14188** .188"
**269-14250** .250"

### Novelty

Many buildings of the mid-19th to early-20th century used novelty siding, also known as shiplap or drop siding. It consisted of overlapping boards, with a rabbet in the bottom of each board, overlapping in the round cove on the top of the board below. Part dimension indicates spacing.

#### 6 x 12 x.040" Sheet 4.59 ea

**269-4062** .060"
5-1/4 HO Scale inches, 9-1/2 N Scale inches.

**269-4083** .083"
7-1/4 HO Scale inches.

**269-4109** .109"
9-1/4 HO Scale inches.

**269-4150** .150"

#### 12 x 24 x .040" Sheet 14.99 ea

**269-14062** .060
**269-14083** .083
**269-14109** .109
**269-14150** .150

### Board & Batten

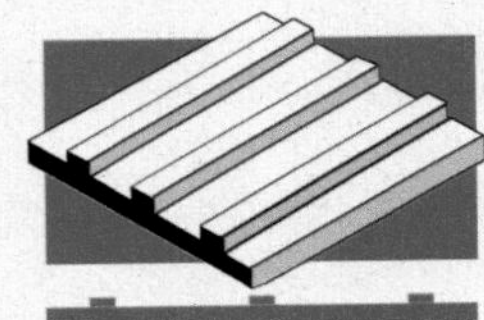

Part dimension indicates spacing. Sheets are .040" thick.

#### 6 x 12" Sheet 4.59 ea

**269-4542** .075"
**269-4543** .100"
**269-4544** .125"

#### 12 x 24" Sheet 14.99 ea

**269-14542** .075"
**269-14543** .100"
**269-14544** .125"

### Clapboard

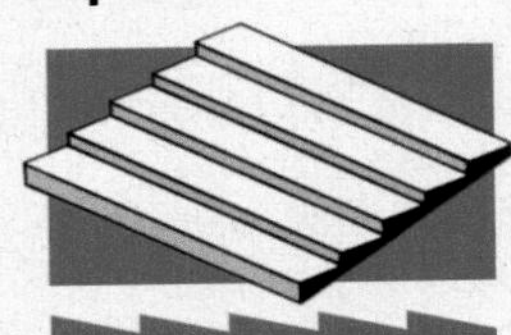

One of the most common sidings (often called lap siding), clapboard is a prominent feature of many wooden railroad buildings as well as city, town and farm structures of all kinds. Sheets are .040" thick. Part dimension indicates spacing.

#### 6 x 12" Sheet 4.59 ea

**269-4031** .030"
**269-4041** .040"
**269-4051** .050"
**269-4061** .060"
**269-4081** .080"
**269-4101** .100"

#### 12 x 24" Sheet 14.99 ea

**269-14031** .030"
**269-14041** .040"
**269-14051** .050"
**269-14061** .060"
**269-14081** .080"
**269-14101** .100"

### Corrugated Metal

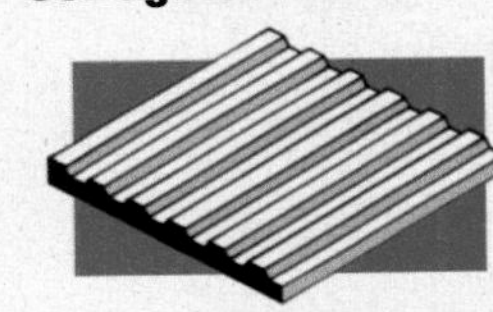

Part dimension indicates spacing. Sheets are .040" thick.

#### 6 x 12" Sheet 4.59 ea

**269-4525** .030"
**269-4526** .040"
**269-4527** .060"
**269-4528** .080"
**269-4529** .100"
**269-4530** .125"

#### 12 x 24" Sheet 14.99 ea

**269-14525** .030"
**269-14526** .040"
**269-14527** .060"
**269-14528** .080"
**269-14529** .100"
**269-14530** .125"

### Passenger Car

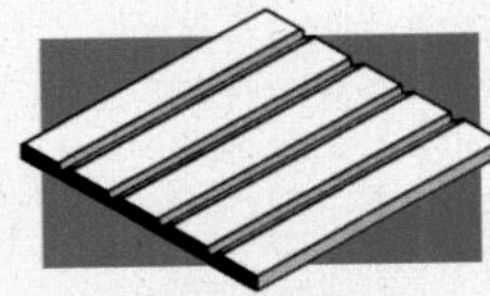

**269-3025** .030" **4.59**
Grooved with 2-1/4" scale spacing, thickness matches Grandt Line molded windows and doors. Each 6 x 12" sheet has grooves running the entire length to eliminate splicing.

### Freight Car 4.59 ea

Grooved with 3-1/4" scale spacing. Each 6 x 12" sheet has grooves running the entire length to eliminate splicing.

**269-2020** .020" N
**269-2037** .020" HO
**269-4037** .040" HO

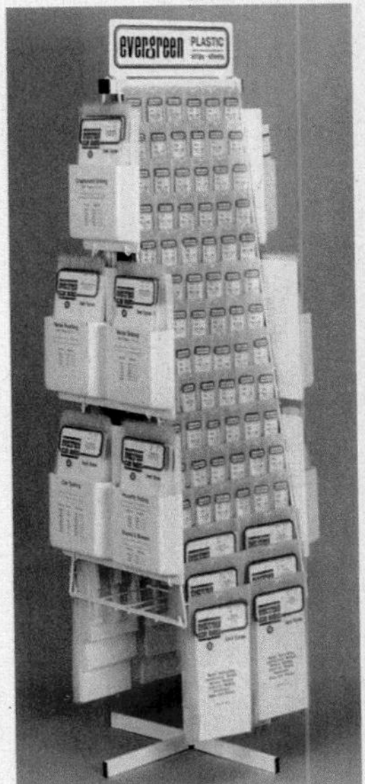

## STRIPS

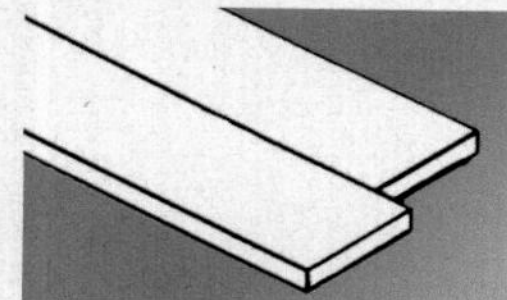

### Square 2.59 ea
**269-196** 3/16 x 3/16" pkg(4)
**269-199** 1/4 x 1/4" pkg(3)

### Dimensional
Opaque white strips.

### 14" Long 2.59 ea
**.010" Thick pkg(10)**
**269-100** .020"
**269-101** .030"
**269-102** .040"
**269-103** .060"
**269-104** .080"
**269-105** .100"
**269-106** .125"
**269-107** .156"
**269-108** .188"
**269-109** .250"

**.015" Thick pkg(10)**
**269-110** .020"
**269-111** .030"
**269-112** .040"
**269-113** .060"
**269-114** .080"
**269-115** .100"
**269-116** .125"
**269-117** .156"
**269-118** .188"
**269-119** .250"

**.020" Thick pkg(10)**
**269-120** .020"
**269-121** .030"
**269-122** .040"
**269-123** .060"
**269-124** .080"
**269-125** .100"
**269-126** .125"
**269-127** .156"
**269-128** .188"
**269-129** .250"

**.030" Thick pkg(10)**
**269-131** .030"
**269-132** .040"
**269-133** .060"
**269-134** .080"
**269-135** .100"
**269-136** .125"
**269-137** .156"
**269-138** .188"
**269-139** .250"

**.040" Thick pkg(10)**
**269-142** .040"
**269-143** .060"
**269-144** .080"
**269-145** .100"
**269-146** .125"
**269-147** .156"
**269-148** .188"
**269-149** .250"

**.060" Thick**
**269-153** .060" pkg(10)
**269-154** .080" pkg(10)
**269-155** .100" pkg(10)
**269-156** .125" pkg(10)
**269-157** .156" pkg(9)
**269-158** .188" pkg(9)
**269-159** .250" pkg(8)

**.080" Thick**
**269-164** .080" pkg(9)
**269-165** .100" pkg(8)
**269-166** .125" pkg(8)
**269-167** .156" pkg(8)
**269-168** .188" pkg(8)
**269-169** .250" pkg(7)

**.100" Thick**
**269-175** .100" pkg(8)
**269-176** .125" pkg(7)
**269-177** .156" pkg(7)
**269-178** .188" pkg(7)
**269-179** .250" pkg(6)

**.125" Thick**
**269-186** .125" pkg(6)
**269-187** .156" pkg(6)
**269-188** .188" pkg(6)
**269-189** .250" pkg(5)

### 24" Long 5.59 ea
**.040" Thick**
**269-344** .080" pkg(15)
**269-345** .100" pkg(15)
**269-346** .125" pkg(15)
**269-347** .156" pkg(14)
**269-348** .188" pkg(14)
**269-349** .250" pkg(14)
**269-350** .312" pkg(12)
**269-351** .375" pkg(10)
**269-352** .438" pkg(9)

**.060" Thick**
**269-353** .060" pkg(15)
**269-354** .080" pkg(15)
**269-355** .100" pkg(14)
**269-356** .125" pkg(14)
**269-357** .156" pkg(14)
**269-358** .188" pkg(12)
**269-359** .250" pkg(12)
**269-360** .312" pkg(10)
**269-361** .375" pkg(9)
**269-362** .438" pkg(8)
**269-363** .500" pkg(7)

**.080" Thick**
**269-364** .080" pkg(14)
**269-365** .100" pkg(12)
**269-366** .125" pkg(12)
**269-367** .156" pkg(11)
**269-368** .188" pkg(11)
**269-369** .250" pkg(10)
**269-370** .312" pkg(9)
**269-371** .375" pkg(8)
**269-372** .438" pkg(7)
**269-373** .500" pkg(5)
**269-374** .625" pkg(4)

**.100" Thick**
**269-375** .100" pkg(12)
**269-376** .125" pkg(11)
**269-377** .156" pkg(10)
**269-378** .188" pkg(9)
**269-379** .250" pkg(8)
**269-380** .312" pkg(7)
**269-381** .375" pkg(7)
**269-382** .438" pkg(6)
**269-383** .500" pkg(5)
**269-384** .625" pkg(4)
**269-385** .750" pkg(4)

**.125" Thick**
**269-386** .125" pkg(10)
**269-387** .156" pkg(9)
**269-388** .188" pkg(8)
**269-389** .250" pkg(7)
**269-390** .312" pkg(6)
**269-391** .375" pkg(6)
**269-392** .438" pkg(5)
**269-393** .500" pkg(4)
**269-394** .625" pkg(4)
**269-395** .750" pkg(3)

**.188" Thick**
**269-398** .188" pkg(6)
**269-399** .250" pkg(6)
**269-400** .312" pkg(5)
**269-401** .375" pkg(4)
**269-403** .500" pkg(3)
**269-404** .625" pkg(3)
**269-405** .750" pkg(2)

**.250" Thick**
**269-409** .250" pkg(5)
**269-410** .312" pkg(4)
**269-411** .375" pkg(3)
**269-413** .500" pkg(3)
**269-414** .625" pkg(2)
**269-415** .750" pkg(2)

### HO Scale pkg(10) 2.59 ea
Dimensions shown are HO Scale inches. Strips are 14" long, opaque white.
**269-8102** 1 x 2"
**269-8103** 1 x 3"
**269-8104** 1 x 4"
**269-8106** 1 x 6"
**269-8108** 1 x 8"
**269-8110** 1 x 10"
**269-8112** 1 x 12"
**269-8202** 2 x 2"
**269-8203** 2 x 3"
**269-8204** 2 x 4"
**269-8206** 2 x 6"
**269-8208** 2 x 8"
**269-8210** 2 x 10"
**269-8212** 2 x 12"
**269-8404** 4 x 4"
**269-8406** 4 x 6"
**269-8408** 4 x 8"
**269-8410** 4 x 10"
**269-8412** 4 x 12"
**269-8606** 6 x 6"
**269-8608** 6 x 8"
**269-8610** 6 x 10"
**269-8612** 6 x 12"

## STRUCTURAL SHAPES
14" actual length, molded in opaque white styrene.

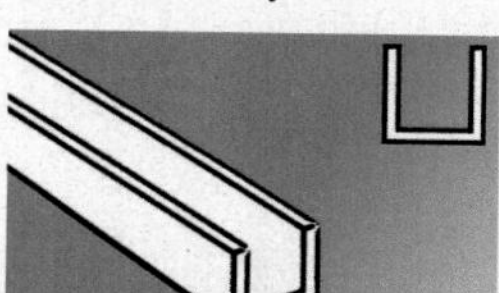

### Channels 2.59 ea
**269-261** .060" pkg(4)
**269-262** .080" pkg(4)
**269-263** .100" pkg(4)
**269-264** .125" pkg(4)
**269-265** .156" pkg(4)
**269-266** .188" pkg(3)
**269-267** .250" pkg(3)
**269-268** .312" pkg(3)

### I-Beams 2.59 ea
**269-271** .060" pkg(4)
**269-272** .080" pkg(4)
**269-273** .100" pkg(4)
**269-274** .125" pkg(4)
**269-275** .156" pkg(3)
**269-276** .188" pkg(3)
**269-277** .250" pkg(3)
**269-278** .312" pkg(2)
**269-279** .375" pkg(2)

### H-Columns 2.59 ea
**269-281** .060" pkg(4)
**269-282** .080" pkg(4)
**269-283** .100" pkg(4)
**269-284** .125" pkg(3)
**269-285** .156" pkg(3)
**269-286** .188" pkg(3)
**269-287** .250" pkg(2)

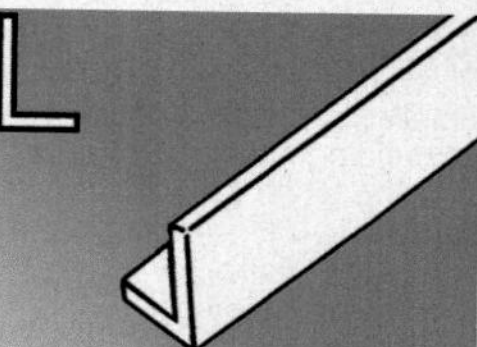

### Angles 2.59 ea
**269-291** .060" pkg(4)
**269-292** .080" pkg(4)
**269-293** .100" pkg(4)
**269-294** .125" pkg(3)
**269-295** .156" pkg(3)
**269-296** .188" pkg(3)
**269-297** .250" pkg(2)

## ROD & TUBING
Each piece molded in white styrene.

### 14" Long 2.59 ea
**269-217** Rod & Tube Assortment pkg(7)

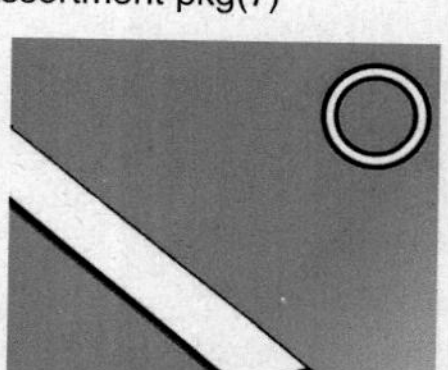

**Round**
**269-210** .030" pkg(10)
**269-211** .040" pkg(10)
**269-212** .080" pkg(6)
**269-213** .100" pkg(5)
**269-214** .125" pkg(4)
**269-218** .020" pkg(10)
**269-219** .025" pkg(10)
**269-220** .035" pkg(10)
**269-221** .047" pkg(10)
**269-222** .062" pkg(8)

evergreen scale models

### Round Tubing
**269-223** .093" pkg(6)
**269-224** .125" pkg(5)
**269-225** .156" pkg(4)
**269-226** .187" pkg(4)
**269-227** .219" pkg(3)
**269-228** .250" pkg(3)
**269-229** .281" pkg(3)
**269-230** .312" pkg(3)
**269-231** .344" pkg(2)
**269-232** .375" pkg(2)
**269-234** .438" pkg(2)
**269-236** .500" pkg(2)

### Half-Round
**269-240** .040" pkg(5)
**269-241** .060" pkg(5)
**269-242** .080" pkg(4)
**269-243** .100" pkg(3)
**269-244** .125" pkg(3)

### Quarter Rounds
**269-246** .030" pkg(5)
**269-247** .040" pkg(5)
**269-248** .060" pkg(4)
**269-249** .080" pkg(3)
**269-250** .100" pkg(3)

### Square Tubing
**269-252** .125" pkg(3)
**269-253** .187" pkg(3)
**269-254** .250" pkg(2)
**269-255** .312" pkg(2)
**269-256** .375" pkg(2)

### Rectangular Tubing
**269-257** .125 x .250" pkg(3)
**269-258** .187 x .312" pkg(2)
**269-259** .250 x .375" pkg(2)

### 24" Long Round Tubing 5.59 ea
**269-423** .093" pkg(9)
**269-424** .125" pkg(8)
**269-425** .156" pkg(7)
**269-426** .187" pkg(6)
**269-427** .219" pkg(6)
**269-428** .250" pkg(5)
**269-429** .281" pkg(5)
**269-430** .312" pkg(5)
**269-431** .344" pkg(4)
**269-432** .375" pkg(4)
**269-434** .438" pkg(3)
**269-436** .500" pkg(3)

## STYRENE SHEETS
Part dimension indicates thickness.

### White

#### 6 x 12" 2.99 ea
**269-9008** Assortment
Includes one each .010, .020 and .040".
**269-9009** .005" pkg(3)
**269-9010** .010" pkg(4)
**269-9015** .015" pkg(3)
**269-9020** .020" pkg(3)
**269-9030** .030" pkg(2)
**269-9040** .040" pkg(2)
**269-9060** .060"
**269-9080** .080"

#### 8 x 21" 12.00 ea (Unless Noted)
**269-9101** .010" pkg(8)
**269-9102** .015" pkg(6)
**269-9103** .020" pkg(6)
**269-9104** .030" pkg(4)
**269-9105** .040" pkg(3)
**269-9106** .060" pkg(2)
**269-9107** .080" pkg(2) **9.99**
**269-9108** .125"

#### 11 x 14" 21.60 ea
**269-9210** .010" pkg(15)
**269-9215** .015" pkg(12)
**269-9220** .020" pkg(12)
**269-9230** .030" pkg(8)
**269-9240** .040" pkg(6)
**269-9260** .060" pkg(4)
**269-9280** .080" pkg(3)

#### 12 x 24" Multi-Packs 32.40 ea (Unless Noted)
Dealers MUST order in these quantities.
**269-19010** .010" pkg(15)
**269-19015** .015" pkg(12)
**269-19020** .020" pkg(12)
**269-19030** .030" pkg(8)
**269-19040** .040" pkg(6)
**269-19060** .060" pkg(4)
**269-19080** .080" pkg(3)
**269-19100** .100" pkg(2) **27.00**
**269-19125** .125" pkg(2)

### Clear

#### 6 x 12" 3.59 ea
**269-9005** .005" pkg(3)
**269-9006** .010" pkg(2)
**269-9007** .015" pkg(2)

#### 12 x 24" 32.40 ea
**NEW 269-19005** .005" .13mm pkg(10)
**NEW 269-19006** .010" .25mm pkg(6)
**NEW 269-19007** .015" .38mm pkg(5)

### Black

#### 8 x 21" 20 x 52.5cm 12.00 ea (Unless Noted)
**269-9111** .010" pkg(8)
**269-9113** .020" pkg(6)
**269-9114** .030" pkg(4)
**269-9115** .040" pkg(3)
**269-9116** .060" pkg(2)
**269-9117** .080" pkg(2) **15.00**

#### 6 x 12" 15 x 30cm 3.59 ea
**269-9511** .010" pkg(4)
**269-9513** .020" pkg(3)
**269-9514** .030" pkg(2)
**269-9515** .040" pkg(2)
**269-9516** .060"
**269-9517** .080"

### Sheet Assortment
**269-9002** Odds & Ends **6.59**
A scratchbuilder's delight – a 1/2lb (8oz) of sheet plastic in various thicknesses and lengths.

## TILES
Scribed in squares to represent flooring. Opaque white sheets are .040" thick.

#### 6 x 12" 4.59 ea
**269-4501** 1/16" Square
**269-4502** 1/12" Square
**269-4503** 1/8" Square
**269-4504** 1/6" Square
**269-4505** 1/4" Square
**269-4506** 1/3" Square
**269-4507** 1/2" Square

#### 12 x 24" 14.99 ea
**269-14501** 1/16" Square
**269-14502** 1/12" Square
**269-14503** 1/8" Square
**269-14504** 1/6" Square
**269-14505** 1/4" Square
**269-14506** 1/3" Square
**269-14507** 1/2" Square

## SIDEWALKS
Opaque white sheets are .040" thick, scribed in squares, just paint and cut to model sidewalks.

#### 6 x 12" Sheet 4.59 ea
**269-4514** 1/8" Square
**269-4515** 3/16" Square
**269-4516** 1/4" Square
**269-4517** 3/8" Square
**269-4518** 1/2" Square

#### 12 x 24" Sheet 14.99 ea
**269-14514** 1/8" Square
**269-14515** 3/16" Square
**269-14516** 1/4" Square
**269-14517** 3/8" Square
**269-14518** 1/2" Square

## LADDER KIT
**269-201** HO Scale (1/87) **2.59**
Features slotted stringers, makes 24" of ladder.

## STANDING SEAM ROOFING

#### 6 x 12" Sheet 6.59 ea
With seam strips, measures .040" thick.
**269-4521** 3/16" Square
**269-4522** 1/4" Square
**269-4523** 3/8" Square
**269-4524** 1/2" Square

## BOOKS

**269-14** Styrene Modeling **14.95**
88 pages.

**269-48** Floor Rack Add-On Book Pocket **89.70**
Includes six copies of Styrene Modeling (#269-14), 12 product lists and a wire pocket.



GCLaser

## NEW PRODUCTS

### Ridge Caps 3.99 ea
For use with Shingles (sold separately below). Covers 36 linear inches.

#### 3-Tab
**NEW 292-111313** Black

**NEW 292-111314** Brown
**NEW 292-111315** Green
**NEW 292-111316** White

#### Diamond

**NEW 292-111317** Black
**NEW 292-111318** Brown
**NEW 292-111319** Green
**NEW 292-111320** White

#### Scalloped
**NEW 292-111321** Black
**NEW 292-111322** Brown
**NEW 292-111323** Green
**NEW 292-111324** White

## ROOF SHINGLES
Put a new roof on any model. Sets include six matching laser-cut sheets plus instructions and drawings. Enough material to cover 84 square inches.

### 3-Tab pkg(6) 17.99 ea
**292-11131** Black

**292-11132** Brown
**292-11133** Green
**292-11134** White

### Diamond 17.99 ea

**292-11135** Black
**292-11136** Brown
**292-11137** Green
**292-11138** White

### Scalloped 21.99 ea
**292-11139** Black
**292-111310** Brown

**292-111311** Green
**292-111312** White

Precut metal strips and shapes can be used for a variety of custom building applications in any scale. Most items are available as single pieces (first price shown) or in multi-packs (second price).

NOTE: Tubing size indicates outside diameter. Dealer displays available, call for information.

Dealers MUST order dealer packs.

# TUBES & TUBING

## Assorted Tubing

**370-707** Sizes & Shapes **15.95**
A large assortment of brass, copper and aluminum tubing and shapes.

## Aluminum

### 12" Round
### .014" Wall Thickness

**370-1008** 1/16" pkg(3) **1.49** pkg(15) **7.45**
**370-1015** 3/32" pkg(3) **1.59** pkg(15) **7.95**
**370-1022** 1/8" pkg(3) **1.79** pkg(15) **8.95**
**370-103** 5/32" **.89** pkg(12) **10.68**
**370-104** 3/16" **.89** pkg(12) **10.68**
**370-105** 7/32" **.99** pkg(10) **9.90**
**370-106** 1/4" **.99** pkg(10) **9.90**
**370-107** 9/32" **1.09** pkg(8) **8.72**

### .035" Wall Thickness

**370-3030** 3/16" **1.89** pkg(6) **11.34**
**370-3031** 1/4" **1.99** pkg(4) **7.96**
**370-3032** 5/16" **2.19** pkg(4) **8.76**
**370-3033** 3/8" **2.39** pkg(3) **7.17**
**370-3034** 7/16" **2.99** pkg(3) **8.97**
**370-3035** 1/2" **3.19** pkg(2) **6.38**

### .049" Wall Thickness

**370-3060** 3/16" **2.19** pkg(5) **10.95**
**370-3061** 1/4" **2.49** pkg(4) **9.96**
**370-3062** 5/16" **2.79** pkg(4) **11.16**
**370-3063** 3/8" **3.49** pkg(3) **10.47**

### 12" Square

**370-3010** 3/32 x 3/32" **1.29** pkg(7) **9.03**
**370-3011** 1/8 x 1/8" **1.39** pkg(6) **8.54**
**370-3012** 5/32 x 5/32" **1.59** pkg(6) **9.54**
**370-3013** 3/16 x 3/16" **1.59** pkg(5) **7.95**
**370-3014** 7/32 x 7/32" **1.69** pkg(5) **8.45**
**370-3015** 1/4 x 1/4" **2.99** pkg(5) **14.95**

### 35" Streamline

**370-1100** 1/4" **3.59** pkg(5) **17.95**
**370-1101** 5/16" **3.59** pkg(5) **17.95**
**370-1102** 3/8" **3.99** pkg(4) **15.96**
**370-1103** 1/2" **5.09** pkg(4) **20.36**
**370-1104** 5/8" **5.99** pkg(3) **17.97**
**370-1105** 3/4" **6.79** pkg(2) **13.58**

### 36" Round

**370-1108** 3/32" **1.79**
**370-1109** 1/8" **1.99**
**370-1110** 5/32" **2.09**
**370-1111** 3/16" **2.19** pkg(6) **13.14**
**370-1112** 7/32" **2.29** pkg(6) **13.74**
**370-1113** 1/4" **2.39** pkg(5) **11.95**
**370-1114** 9/32" **2.59** pkg(5) **12.95**
**370-1115** 5/16" **2.79**

#### .016" Wall Thickness

**370-9409** 3/8" **3.79** pkg(4) **15.16**
**370-9411** 7/16" **4.59** pkg(3) **13.77**
**370-9413** 1/2" **5.19** pkg(3) **15.57**
**370-9415** 5/8" **5.99** pkg(2) **11.98**

#### .035" Wall Thickness

**370-9309** 3/16" **4.99** pkg(6) **29.94**
**370-9311** 1/4" **5.19** pkg(6) **31.14**
**370-9313** 5/16" **5.79** pkg(5) **28.95**
**370-9315** 3/8" **5.99** pkg(4) **23.96**
**370-9317** 7/16" **6.79** pkg(4) **27.16**
**370-9319** 1/2" **7.19** pkg(4) **28.76**

## Copper

### 12" Round

**370-1176** 1/16" pkg(3) **1.79** pkg(15) **8.95**
**370-1186** 3/32" pkg(3) **2.09** pkg(15) **10.45**
**370-119** 5/32" **.99** pkg(12) **11.88**
**370-120** 1/8" **.99** pkg(12) **11.88**

### 36" Round

**370-9509** 5/32" **3.29** pkg(8) **26.32**
**370-9511** 3/16" **5.39** pkg(7) **37.73**
**370-9513** 7/32" **5.99** pkg(6) **35.94**
**370-9515** 1/4" **6.59** pkg(5) **32.95**

## Brass

### 12" Square

**370-1497** 1/16" pkg(2) **2.09** pkg(10) **10.45**
**370-1503** 3/32" pkg(2) **2.39** pkg(10) **11.95**
**370-151** 1/8" **1.49** pkg(12) **17.88**
**370-152** 5/32" **1.59** pkg(10) **15.90**
**370-153** 3/16" **1.69** pkg(6) **10.14**
**370-154** 7/32" **1.79** pkg(6) **10.74**
**370-155** 1/4" **1.99** pkg(6) **11.94**

### 12" Rectangle

**370-262** 3/32 x 3/16" **2.69** pkg(4) **10.76**
**370-264** 1/8 x 1/4" **3.29** pkg(4) **13.16**
**370-266** 5/32 x 5/16" **3.39** pkg(4) **13.56**
**370-268** 3/16 x 3/8" **3.49** pkg(4) **13.96**

### 12" Hexagon

**370-271** 3/32" **1.39** pkg(8) **11.12**
**370-272** 1/8" **1.59** pkg(7) **11.13**
**370-273** 5/32" **2.59** pkg(6) **15.54**
**370-274** 3/16" **2.69** pkg(5) **13.45**

### 12" Streamline

**370-122** Small **1.99** pkg(4) **7.96**

### 12" Round

**370-1251** 1/16" pkg(3) **2.19** pkg(15) **10.95**
**370-1268** 3/32" pkg(3) **2.29** pkg(15) **11.45**
**370-127** 1/8" **.99** pkg(15) **14.85**
**370-128** 5/32" **1.19** pkg(12) **14.28**
**370-129** 3/16" **1.39** pkg(12) **16.68**
**370-130** 7/32" **1.49** pkg(10) **14.90**
**370-131** 1/4" **1.69** pkg(8) **13.52**
**370-132** 9/32" **1.89** pkg(8) **15.12**
**370-133** 5/16" **2.09** pkg(6) **12.54**
**370-134** 11/32" **2.29** pkg(6) **13.74**
**370-135** 3/8" **2.39** pkg(6) **14.34**
**370-136** 13/32" **2.59** pkg(4) **10.36**
**370-137** 7/16" **2.69** pkg(4) **10.76**
**370-138** 15/32" **2.79** pkg(4) **11.16**
**370-139** 1/2" **2.99** pkg(4) **11.96**
**370-140** 17/32" **3.19** pkg(3) **9.57**
**370-141** 9/16" **3.39** pkg(3) **10.17**
**370-142** 19/32" **3.49** pkg(2) **6.98**
**370-143** 5/8" **3.69** pkg(2) **7.38**
**370-144** 21/32" **3.89** pkg(2) **7.78**

### 36" Round

#### .014" Wall Thickness

**370-1143** 1/16" **2.29**
**370-1144** 3/32" **2.39**
**370-1145** 1/8" **2.69**
**370-1146** 5/32" **3.19**
**370-1147** 3/16" **3.69**
**370-1148** 7/32" **4.19** pkg(6) **25.14**
**370-1149** 1/4" **4.89** pkg(5) **24.45**
**370-1150** 9/32" **5.39** pkg(5) **26.95**
**370-1151** 5/16" **5.89** pkg(4) **23.56**
**370-1152** 11/32" **6.39** pkg(4) **25.56**
**370-1153** 3/8" **6.99** pkg(3) **20.97**
**370-9109** 13/32" **8.99** pkg(4) **35.96**
**370-9111** 7/16" **9.59** pkg(4) **38.36**
**370-9113** 15/32" **9.99** pkg(4) **39.96**
**370-9115** 1/2" **10.59** pkg(4) **42.36**
**370-9117** 17/32" **11.79** pkg(3) **35.37**
**370-9119** 9/16" **12.49** pkg(3) **37.47**
**370-9121** 19/32" **12.99** pkg(3) **38.97**
**370-9123** 5/8" **13.59** pkg(3) **40.77**
**370-9125** 21/32" **14.49** pkg(2) **28.98**

#### .029" Wall Thickness

**370-9209** 1/4" **7.69** pkg(5) **38.45**
**370-9211** 5/16" **10.49** pkg(5) **52.45**
**370-9213** 3/8" **12.09** pkg(4) **48.36**
**370-9215** 7/16" **14.39** pkg(4) **57.56**
**370-9217** 1/2" **17.09** pkg(4) **68.36**
**370-9219** 9/16" **20.09** pkg(3) **60.27**
**370-9221** 5/8" **20.79** pkg(2) **41.58**
**370-9223** 11/16" **21.29** pkg(2) **42.58**
**370-9225** 3/4" **21.99** pkg(2) **43.98**

## Stainless Steel

### 12" Round

**370-7111** 1/8" **3.29** pkg(10) **32.90**
**370-7113** 3/16" **3.79** pkg(8) **20.32**
**370-7115** 1/4" **4.19** pkg(6) **25.14**
**370-7117** 5/16" **4.69** pkg(4) **18.76**
**370-7119** 3/8" **5.19** pkg(3) **15.57**
**370-7121** 7/16" **5.79** pkg(2) **11.58**
**370-7123** 1/2" **6.49** pkg(2) **12.98**

### .36", .028" Wall Thickness

**370-9617** 5/16" **12.49** pkg(4) **49.96**
**370-9619** 3/8" **13.99** pkg(4) **55.96**
**370-9621** 7/16" **15.59** pkg(3) **46.77**
**370-9623** 1/2" **17.49** pkg(3) **52.47**

# RODS

## 12" Solid Aluminum

**370-3040** 1/32" pkg(3) **1.29** pkg(18) **7.74**
**370-3041** 1/16" pkg(3) **1.49** pkg(18) **8.94**
**370-3042** 3/32" **.89** pkg(10) **8.90**
**370-3043** 1/8" **.99** pkg(10) **9.9**
**370-3044** 3/16" **1.19** pkg(8) **9.52**
**370-3045** 1/4" **1.69** pkg(6) **10.14**
**370-3046** 5/16" **2.09** pkg(4) **8.36**
**370-3047** 3/8" **2.59** pkg(4) **10.36**
**370-3048** 1/2" **3.59** pkg(3) **10.77**

## 12" Brass

**370-1596** .020" pkg(5) **1.29** pkg(25) **6.45**
**370-1602** 1/32" pkg(5) **1.29** pkg(25) **6.45**
**370-1619** 3/64" pkg(4) **1.29** pkg(20) **6.45**
**370-1626** 1/16" pkg(3) **1.39** pkg(15) **6.95**
**370-163** 3/32" **.79** pkg(16) **12.04**
**370-164** 1/8" **1.19** pkg(10) **11.90**
**370-165** 5/32" **1.59** pkg(8) **12.72**
**370-166** 3/16" **2.09** pkg(5) **10.45**
**370-1671** .114" pkg(2) **2.19** pkg(10) **10.95**
**370-1688** .081" pkg(3) **2.09** pkg(15) **10.45**
**370-1695** .072" pkg(3) **1.59** pkg(15) **7.95**

## 12" Stainless Steel

**370-7131** 1/16" **1.59** pkg(8) **12.72**
**370-7133** 3/32" **2.09** pkg(6) **12.54**
**370-7135** 1/8" **1.29** pkg(10) **12.90**
**370-7137** 3/16" **1.99** pkg(8) **15.92**
**370-7139** 1/4" **3.09** pkg(6) **18.54**
**370-7141** 5/16" **4.09** pkg(5) **20.45**
**370-7143** 3/8" **5.09** pkg(4) **20.36**
**370-7145** 7/16" **6.29** pkg(3) **18.87**
**370-7147** 1/2" **7.99** pkg(2) **15.98**

ENGINEERING

## 36" Brass

**370-1160** 1/16" **2.59** pkg(5) **12.95**

**370-1161** 3/32" **2.29** pkg(5) **11.45**

**370-1162** 1/8" **3.29** pkg(5) **16.45**

**370-1163** 5/32" **4.29** pkg(5) **21.45**

**370-1164** 3/16" **5.99** pkg(5) **29.95**

**370-1165** 1/4" **9.99** pkg(4) **39.96**

**370-1166** 5/16" **15.69** pkg(3) **47.07**

## MUSIC WIRE 36"

**370-497** .039" pkg(4) **1.89**

**370-498** .015" pkg(5) **1.99**

**370-499** .020" pkg(5) **1.99**

**370-500** .025" pkg(5) **1.89**

**370-501** .032" (1/32") pkg(4) **1.79**

**370-502** .047" pkg(4) **2.09**

**370-503** .055" pkg(5) **1.89**

**370-504** .062" (1/16") pkg(5) **2.09**

**370-505** .078" pkg(3) **2.19**

**370-506** 3/32" pkg(2) **2.29**

**370-507** 1/8" **1.29** pkg(9) **11.61**

**370-508** 5/32" **1.59** pkg(7) **11.13**

**370-509** 3/16" **2.09** pkg(4) **8.36**

**370-510** 7/32" **2.89** pkg(4) **11.56**

**370-511** 1/4" **3.39** pkg(3) **10.17**

**370-512** 9/32" **5.09** pkg(3) **15.27**

## SHEETS

### Strip & Sheet Assortment

**370-727 9.99**
Brass, copper and aluminum strips and sheets in a variety of thicknesses, widths and lengths.

### Corrugated-Metal Siding

These corrugated sheets are perfect for simulating metal building siding and roofing on HO Scale structures.

### Aluminum

5 x 7" .002" thick

**370-16130** Corrugated .03" Spacing pkg(2) **4.39**

**370-16132** Corrugated .060" Spacing pkg(2) **4.29**

**370-16134** Crimped .187" Spacing pkg(2) **4.29**

### Copper

5 x 7" .003" thick

**370-16140** Corrugated .03" Spacing pkg(2) **5.59**

**370-16142** Corrugated .060" Spacing pkg(2) **5.49**

**370-16144** Crimped .187" Spacing pkg(2) **5.49**

### Expandable Wire

Each sheet comes in a 12 x 24" roll.

**370-6094** Aluminum **12.50**

**370-6095** Copper (Small Holes) **17.00**

**370-6096** Designer Copper **20.00**

**370-6097** Brass **19.00**

### Tin

Each sheet measures .016" thickness.

**370-6505** 5 x 7" **3.49**

**370-6510** 6 x 8" **4.39**

**370-6512** 8 x 10" **5.89**

**370-6515** 9 x 12" **6.99**

**370-6520** 12 x 18" **9.99**

### Copper

Each sheet measures .013" thickness.

**370-6525** 5 x 7" **6.49**

**370-6530** 6 x 8" **8.79**

**370-6532** 8 x 10" **13.59**

**370-6535** 9 x 12" **17.99**

**370-6540** 12 x 18" **31.29**

### Clear Plastic

9 x 12", flexible and clear as glass. Vacuum formable.

**370-1301** .010" **3.59** pkg(10) **35.90**

**370-1304** .015" **3.99** pkg(10) **39.90**

**370-1306** .030" **3.59** pkg(10) **35.90**

### Aluminum

Each piece measures 6 x 12"; dimension shown is thickness.

**370-3070** .064" **6.99**

**370-3071** .090" **9.99**

**370-3072** .125" **12.99**

### Brass

Each sheet measures 6 x 12".

**370-16402** .010" **5.49**

**370-16404** .016" **7.49**

**370-16405** .020" **9.79**

**370-16407** .032" **13.99**

**370-16408** .040" **18.99**

**370-16409** .064" **26.99**

### Metal

4 x 10"

**370-250** .005" Brass **2.19** pkg(6) **13.14**

**370-251** .010" Brass **2.19** pkg(6) **13.14**

**370-252** .015" Brass **3.99** pkg(6) **23.94**

**370-253** .032" Brass **7.49** pkg(3) **22.47**

**370-254** .008" Tin **1.39** pkg(6) **8.34**

**370-255** .016" Aluminum **1.49** pkg(6) **8.94**

**370-256** .032" Aluminum **1.89** pkg(6) **11.34**

**370-257** .064" Aluminum **3.19** pkg(6) **19.14**

**370-258** Assorted Brass **3.59** pkg(6) **21.54**

**370-259** .025" Copper **6.99** pkg(3) **20.97**

### 12 x 30" Foils

**370-6005** .002" Brass **12.50**

**370-6010** .005" Soft Brass **15.50**

**370-6015** .003" Copper **14.00**

**370-6020** .005" Soft Copper **16.00**

**370-6025** .005" Aluminum **6.90**

**370-6030** .002" Stainless Steel **12.50**

### Phosphor Bronze

**370-15053** 5 x 7" **4.19**
.016" thickness.

### Stainless Steel

Each sheet measures 6 x 12".

**370-7181** .010 **5.49**

**370-7183** .018 **6.19**

**370-7185** .028 **7.69**

## STRIPS

### Brass

#### 12"

**370-230** .016 x 1/4" **.69** pkg(20) **13.80**

**370-231** .016 x 1/2" **.79** pkg(15) **11.85**

**370-232** .016 x 1" **1.29** pkg(10) **12.90**

**370-233** .016 x 3/4 **.89** pkg(10) **8.90**

**370-234** .016 x 2" **1.79** pkg(5) **8.95**

**370-235** .025 x 1/4" **.79** pkg(15) **11.85**

**370-236** .025 x 1/2" **.99** pkg(10) **9.90**

**370-237** .025 x 1" **1.89** pkg(6) **11.34**

**370-238** .025 x 3/4" **1.09** pkg(6) **6.54**

**370-239** .025 x 2" **3.69** pkg(3) **11.07**

**370-240** .032 x 1/4" **.89** pkg(15) **13.35**

**370-241** .032 x 1/2" **.99** pkg(10) **9.90**

**370-242** .032 x 1" **1.69** pkg(5) **8.45**

**370-243** .032 x 3/4" **1.39** pkg(6) **8.34**

**370-244** .032 x 2" **3.29** pkg(3) **9.87**

**370-245** .064 x 1/4" **1.19** pkg(8) **9.52**

**370-246** .064 x 1/2" **1.79** pkg(4) **7.16**

**370-247** .064 x 3/4" **2.59** pkg(3) **7.77**

**370-248** .064 x 1" **3.39** pkg(2) **6.78**

**370-249** .064 x 2" **6.29** pkg(3) **18.87**

#### 36"

**.015" Wall Thickness**

**370-9709** .016 x 1/4" **1.99** pkg(5) **9.95**

**370-9712** .016 x 1/2" **2.49** pkg(5) **12.45**

**370-9715** .016 x 1" **4.39** pkg(5) **21.95**

**370-9718** .032 x 1/4" **2.39** pkg(5) **11.95**

**370-9721** .032 x 1/2" **4.19** pkg(5) **20.95**

**370-9724** .032 x 1" **7.39** pkg(5) **36.95**

**370-9727** .064 x 1/4" **4.19** pkg(4) **16.76**

**370-9730** .064 x 1/2" **7.69** pkg(3) **23.07**

**370-9733** .064 x 1" **14.79** pkg(3) **44.37**

**370-9736** .090 x 1/4" **7.29** pkg(4) **29.16**

**370-9739** .090 x 1/2" **11.49** pkg(3) **34.47**

**370-9742** .090 x 1" **20.99** pkg(3) **62.97**

### Stainless Steel 12"

**370-7151** .010 x 1/2" **.59** pkg(16) **9.44**

**370-7153** .010 x 3/4" **.79** pkg(12) **9.48**

**370-7155** .010 x 1" **.99** pkg(8) **7.92**

**370-7157** .018 x 1/2" **.79** pkg(10) **7.90**

**370-7159** .018 x 3/4" **.99** pkg(8) **7.92**

**370-7161** .018 x 1" **1.19** pkg(6) **7.14**

**370-7163** .028 x 1/2" **.89** pkg(8) **7.12**

**370-7165** .028 x 3/4" **1.19** pkg(6) **7.14**

**370-7167** .028 x 1" **1.49** pkg(4) **5.96**

## SPECIAL SHAPES PRODUCTS

These 12" structural shapes are ideal for a variety of modeling projects: bridges, box cars, handrails, catenaries, architecture, kitbashing and more.

### Round Tubing

.006" wall.

**370-15035** 1/32" **2.19**

**370-15036** 3/64" pkg(2) **1.99**

**370-15037** 1/16" pkg(2) **1.39**

### Round Wire pkg(3) 1.59 ea

**370-15044** .010"

**370-15045** .016"

### Brass

#### Angles

**370-15001** 1/32" **1.89**

**370-15003** 1/16" **2.69**

**370-15005** 1/8" **3.49**

#### H Columns

**370-15008** 1/16" **2.59**

**370-15010** 1/8" **3.89**

#### I Beams

**370-15013** 1/8 x 1/16" **3.29**

**370-15014** 3/16 x 3/32" **4.69**

#### C Channels

**370-15015** 1/16 x 1/32" **1.99**

**370-15017** 1/8 x 1/16" **2.59**

#### Flat Bars

**370-15019** 1/64 x 1/32" pkg(2) **1.09**

**370-15020** 1/64 x 1/16" pkg(2) **1.09**

**370-15021** 1/64 x 3/32" pkg(2) **1.19**

**370-15022** 1/64 x 1/8" **1.09**

**370-15023** 1/64 x 3/16" **1.09**

**370-15024** 1/32 x 1/16" pkg(2) **1.29**

**370-15025** 1/32 x 3/32" **1.19**

**370-15026** 1/32 x 1/8" **1.19**

#### Square Bars

**370-15047** 1/32" pkg(2) **1.49**

**370-15049** 1/16" pkg(2) **1.49**

**370-15052** 1/8" **2.09**

## ETCHED MESH

### 7.75 ea

1-7/16 x 7".

### Square Fine

**370-2701** 1/32"

**370-2702** 3/64"

**370-2703** 1/16"

**370-2704** 5/64"

**370-2705** 3/32"

**370-2706** 1/8"

### Diamond

**370-2707** 1/64"

**370-2709** 3/64"

**370-2710** 5/64"

**370-2711** 3/32"

**370-2712** 1/8"

### Square Heavy

**370-2714** 3/64"

**370-2715** 1/16"

**370-2716** 5/64"

**370-2717** 1/8"

### Metal Sheets

**370-15054** Copper 5 x 7" .016" Thick **5.79**

**370-15055** Tin 5 x 7" .016" Thick **3.19**

### Mesh Sheets

**370-15056** Copper 5 x 12" **5.79**

**370-15057** Aluminum 5 x 12" **4.19**

### Foil Combo

**370-15058** .005" pkg(3) **5.79**

## TRUSS

**370-2718 7.75**

## TRUSS TYPE GIRDERS

### 7.65 ea pkg(4) 30.60

**370-2777** Cross Braced On 2 Sides
**370-2778** Cross Braced On 1 Side
**370-2779** Single Cross Braced On 2 Sides
**370-2780** Single Cross Braced On 1 Side
**370-2781** Cross Braced on 4 Sides

## JV MODELS

### Dimensional Brick Building Material pkg(3) 7.59 ea

Each package includes three sheets measuring 4-3/4 x 8-1/2".

**345-8451** Colonial Red
**345-8452** Dirty City Brick
**345-8453** Stone Gray
**345-8454** New Brick

### Paper Wall Material

**345-8411** Brown Brick pkg(3) **5.59**
Brick wall or foundation material. 14-1/2 x 7-1/2" sheets.

### Catalog

**345-8400 2.00**

Designed, Manufactured & Assembled entirely in the U.S.A.

### Acetal Screws

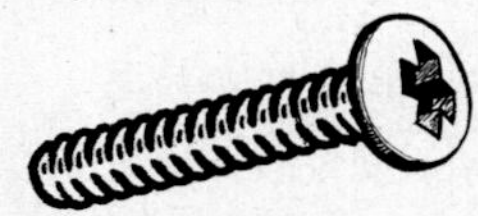

**380-256** Round head 1/2" Insulating Screws pkg(12) **1.80**

### Stainless Steel Hardware pkg(12)

**0-80**
**380-1640** Nuts **2.95**
**380-1641** Washers **2.75**

**Round Head Screws**
**380-1643** 1/8" **2.95**
**380-1646** 1/4" **2.95**
**380-1648** 3/8" **2.95**
**380-1649** 1/2" **3.30**

**1-72**
**380-1680** Nuts **3.25**
**380-1681** Washers **3.10**

**Round Head Screws**
**380-1683** 1/8" **3.25**
**380-1686** 1/4" **3.25**
**380-1688** 3/8" **3.25**
**380-1689** 1/2" **3.30**

**2-56**
**380-1700** Nuts **3.25**
**380-1701** Washers **3.15**

**Round Head Screws**
**380-1703** 1/8" **3.25**
**380-1706** 1/4" **3.25**
**380-1708** 3/8" **3.25**
**380-1709** 1/2" **3.25**
**380-1710** 5/8" **3.45**
**380-1711** 3/4" **3.30**

For Up-To-Date Information and News Bookmark Walthers Web site at
**www.walthers.com**

A complete selection of stripwood and scale lumber, cut to match common construction sizes. Check out Walthers Web site at www.walthers.com for a complete listing of scale lumber products, as well as stripwood and structural accessories.

## SCALE LUMBER

### 12" Length 2.75 ea

Dimensions are in HO Scale inches, (1 x 2", etc.) with actual length of 12". Also available in 24" lengths, for $2.95 each

**1"**
**385-200** x 2" pkg(11)
**385-201** x 3" pkg(11)
**385-202** x 4" pkg(10)
**385-203** x 6" pkg(10)
**385-204** x 8" pkg(9)
**385-205** x 10" pkg(8)
**385-206** x 12" pkg(7)
**385-207** x 14" pkg(7)
**385-208** x 16" pkg(6)
**385-209** x 18" pkg(6)
**385-210** x 20" pkg(6)
**385-212** x 24" pkg(6)

**2"**
**385-213** x 2" pkg(14)
**385-214** x 3" pkg(14)
**385-215** x 4" pkg(14)
**385-216** x 6" pkg(14)
**385-217** x 8" pkg(11)
**385-218** x 10" pkg(11)
**385-219** x 12" pkg(10)
**385-220** x 14" pkg(10)
**385-221** x 16" pkg(10)
**385-222** x 18" pkg(10)
**385-223** x 20" pkg(10)
**385-224** x 22" pkg(8)
**385-225** x 24" pkg(8)

**3"**
**385-226** x 3" pkg(14)
**385-227** x 4" pkg(14)
**385-228** x 6" pkg(12)
**385-229** x 8" pkg(12)
**385-230** x 9" pkg(10)
**385-231** x 12" pkg(10)
**385-233** x 10" pkg(10)
**385-234** x 14" pkg(10)
**385-235** x 16" pkg(10)
**385-236** x 18" pkg(10)
**385-237** x 20" pkg(10)

**4"**
**385-238** x 4" pkg(14)
**385-239** x 6" pkg(12)
**385-240** x 8" pkg(11)
**385-241** x 10" pkg(11)
**385-242** x 12" pkg(10)
**385-243** x 14" pkg(10)
**385-244** x 16" pkg(8)
**385-245** x 18" pkg(8)
**385-246** x 20" pkg(8)
**385-247** x 22" pkg(8)
**385-248** x 24" pkg(6)

**6"**
**385-249** x 6" pkg(12)
**385-250** x 8" pkg(11)
**385-251** x 10" pkg(10)
**385-252** x 12" pkg(9)
**385-253** x 14" pkg(9)
**385-254** x 16" pkg(9)
**385-255** x 18" pkg(8)
**385-256** x 20" pkg(8)
**385-257** x 22" pkg(6)
**385-258** x 24" pkg(6)

**8"**
**385-259** x 8" pkg(10)
**385-260** x 10" pkg(9)
**385-261** x 12" pkg(9)
**385-262** x 14" pkg(8)
**385-263** x 16" pkg(6)
**385-264** x 18" pkg(6)
**385-265** x 20" pkg(6)
**385-266** x 22" pkg(6)
**385-267** x 24" pkg(6)

**10"**
**385-268** x 10" pkg(9)
**385-269** x 12" pkg(8)
**385-270** x 14" pkg(8)
**385-271** x 16" pkg(8)
**385-272** x 18" pkg(6)
**385-273** x 20" pkg(6)
**385-274** x 22" pkg(6)
**385-275** x 24" pkg(6)

**12"**
**385-276** x 12" pkg(7)
**385-277** x 14" pkg(6)
**385-278** x 16" pkg(6)
**385-279** x 18" pkg(6)
**385-280** x 20" pkg(6)
**385-281** x 22" pkg(6)
**385-282** x 24" pkg(6)

*Information* STATION

### History's Greatest Showman

Known as one of history's greatest showmen, P.T. Barnum had a personal history as interesting as the circus itself. Phineas Taylor Barnum began his professional career not with the circus, but with a New York City general store in 1826. But it was only a few years later when his love of showmanship began to guide his career choice.

Soon after his marriage in 1829, he began touring the country with a variety of entertainers. He also opened a museum in New York City to display a wide variety of unusual attractions. Some of these eccentric exhibitions included: 161-year-old nurse Joice Heth, "The Feejee Mermaid," and General Tom Thumb.

But it wasn't until 1860 that his tour of oddities became known as a circus: P. T. Barnum's Grand Traveling Museum, Menagerie, Caravan and Circus. It soon became known (by Barnum's own promotion) as "The Greatest Show On Earth." And it wasn't until 1887 that he partnered with James Bailey to create the Barnum and Bailey Circus. (After Bailey's death, the name was purchased by the Ringling brothers and is still used to this day.)

Barnum was always conscious of his public persona. He published his autobiography, The Life Of P.T. Barnum, Written By Himself in 1854. And he made sure the New York Sun ran his obituary before his death so he could read what would be said about him. The headline read: "Great And Only Barnum – He Wanted To Read His Obituary – Here It Is."

Create unique models for your layout with this selection of precut wood strips, shapes, dowels and more.

## BALSA

### Strips

All items are 36" long.

**472-6022** 1/16 x 1/16" pkg(60) 14.40

**472-6024** 1/16 x 1/8" pkg(57) 16.53

**472-6025** 1/16 x 3/16" pkg(36) 14.40

**472-6026** 1/16 x 1/4" pkg(30) 13.80

**472-6029** 1/16 x 1/2" pkg(24) 16.56

**472-6033** 3/32 x 3/32" pkg(48) 13.92

**472-6038** 3/32 x 3/8" pkg(20) 13.80

**472-6044** 1/8 x 1/8" pkg(36) 14.40

**472-6045** 1/8 x 3/16" pkg(36) 16.56

**472-6046** 1/8 x 1/4" pkg(30) 17.10

**472-6048** 1/8 x 3/8" pkg(20) 15.00

**472-6049** 1/8 x 1/2" pkg(15) 13.50

**472-6055** 3/16 x 3/16" pkg(25) 12.75

**472-6056** 3/16 x 1/4" pkg(20) 13.80

**472-6066** 1/4 x 1/4" pkg(20) 15.80

**472-6068** 1/4 x 3/8" pkg(15) 14.55

**472-6069** 1/4 x 1/2" pkg(12) 15.60

**472-6088** 3/8 x 3/8" pkg(12) 15.60

**472-6099** 1/2 x 1/2" pkg(9) 18.99

### Sheets

**472-6102** 1/16 x 1" pkg(20) 24.80

**472-6104** 1/8 x 1" pkg(20) 29.60

**472-6105** 3/16 x 1" pkg(10) 19.90

**472-6106** 1/4 x 1" pkg(10) 24.90

**472-6302** 1/16 x 3" pkg(20) 31.60

**472-6303** 3/32 x 3" pkg(20) 39.80

**472-6304** 1/8 x 3" pkg(20) 45.80

**472-6305** 3/16 x 3" pkg(10) 27.90

**472-6306** 1/4 x 3" pkg(10) 34.90

**472-6402** 1/16 x 4" pkg(20) 48.80

**472-6403** 3/32 x 4" pkg(15) 42.75

**472-6404** 1/8 x 4" pkg(15) 46.65

**472-6405** 3/16 x 4" pkg(10) 39.20

**472-6406** 1/4 x 4" pkg(10) 47.10

**472-6602** 1/16 x 6" pkg(10) 39.80

**472-6603** 3/32 x 6" pkg(10) 44.80

**472-6604** 1/8 x 6" pkg(10) 55.10

**472-6605** 3/16 x 6" pkg(5) 29.80

## BASSWOOD

### Strips

All items are 24" long.

**472-4022** 1/16 x 1/16" pkg(60) 13.20

**472-4024** 1/16 x 1/8" pkg(48) 13.44

**472-4026** 1/16 x 1/4" pkg(42) 17.64

**472-4029** 1/16 x 1/2" pkg(24) 17.04

**472-4033** 3/32 x 3/32" pkg(60) 17.40

**472-4044** 1/8 x 1/8" pkg(48) 13.92

**472-4045** 1/8 x 3/16" pkg(36) 14.40

**472-4046** 1/8 x 1/4" pkg(30) 14.40

**472-4049** 1/8 x 1/2" pkg(15) 14.10

**472-4050** 5/32 x 5/32" pkg(36) 14.40

**472-4055** 3/16 x 3/16" pkg(36) 15.84

**472-4058** 3/16 x 3/8" pkg(20) 15.60

**472-4059** 3/16 x 1/2" pkg(15) 15.60

**472-4066** 1/4 x 1/4" pkg(20) 14.60

**472-4068** 1/4 x 3/8" pkg(16) 15.84

**472-4069** 1/4 x 1/2" pkg(12) 14.88

**472-4077** 5/16 x 5/16" pkg(18) 15.84

**472-4088** 3/8 x 3/8" pkg(15) 17.85

**472-4099** 1/2 x 1/2" pkg(10) 19.20

### Sheets

All items are 24" long.

**472-4102** 1/16 x 1" pkg(15) 17.85

**472-4103** 3/32 x 1" pkg(15) 19.50

**472-4104** 1/8 x 1" pkg(15) 22.20

**472-4105** 3/16 x 1" pkg(10) 18.20

**472-4106** 1/4 x 1" pkg(10) 21.10

**472-4301** 1/32 x 3" pkg(15) 22.35

**472-4302** 1/16 x 3" pkg(15) 22.95

**472-4303** 3/32 x 3" pkg(15) 26.55

**472-4304** 1/8 x 3" pkg(15) 30.60

**472-4305** 3/16 x 3" pkg(10) 24.90

**472-4306** 1/4 x 3" pkg(10) 29.90

**472-4308** 3/8 x 3" pkg(5) **19.95**

**472-4309** 1/2 x 3" pkg(5) **29.95**

**472-4401** 1/32 x 4" pkg(15) 37.35

**472-4402** 1/16 x 4" pkg(15) 36.45

**472-4403** 3/32 x 4" pkg(15) 38.40

**472-4404** 1/8 x 4" pkg(15) 43.50

**472-4405** 3/16 x 4" pkg(10) 33.50

**472-4406** 1/4 x 4" pkg(10) 40.90

### Flooring/Siding

3 x 24". Measurement indicates spaced groove.

**pkg(15) 33.60 ea**

**472-4440** 1/4"

**472-4441** 3/8"

**472-4442** 1/2"

**pkg(10)**

**472-4434** 1/16 x 1/32" **23.30**

**472-4435** 3/32 x 1/32" **23.30**

**472-4436** 1/8 x 1/32" **23.30**

**472-4437** 1/16 x 1/16" **23.30**

### Corrugated Siding pkg(10) 28.60 ea

3 x 24".

**472-4490** 1/32" Spacing

**472-4491** 1/16" Spacing

### Clapboard Siding

Measurement indicates spacing.

**3 x 24" pkg(10)**

**472-4448** 1/16" **28.60**

**472-4449** 3/32" **28.60**

**472-4450** 1/8" **26.80**

**472-4451** 1/4" **29.10**

**472-4452** 3/8" **29.10**

**472-4453** 1/2" **29.90**

### Board & Batten Siding pkg(10) 27.50 ea

1/16 x 3 x 24".

**472-4444** 1/16"

**472-4445** 3/32"

## ARCHITECTURAL SCALE LUMBER

All items are 11" long.

**472-8000** .0208 x .0208" pkg(17) **2.44**

**472-8001** .0208 x .0312" pkg(17) **2.44**

**472-8002** .0208 x .0416" pkg(17) **2.44**

**472-8003** .0208 x .0625" pkg(15) **2.44**

**472-8004** .0208 x .0833" pkg(15) **2.44**

**472-8005** .0208 x .1041" pkg(15) **2.44**

**472-8006** .0208 x .125" pkg(15) **2.44**

**472-8016** .0416 x .0416" pkg(15) **2.44**

**472-8017** .0416 x .0625" pkg(15) **2.44**

**472-8018** .0416 x .0833" pkg(15) **2.44**

**472-8019** .0416 x .1041" pkg(15) **2.44**

**472-8020** .0416 x 125" pkg(15) **2.44**

**472-8021** .0208 x .1664" pkg(15) **3.29**

**472-8022** .0208 x .208" pkg(14) **3.29**

**472-8023** .0208 x .250" pkg(10) **3.29**

**472-8024** .0416 x .1664" pkg(15) **3.29**

**472-8025** .0416 x .208" pkg(14) **3.29**

**472-8026** .0416 x .250" pkg(10) **3.29**

**472-8027** .0833 x .0833" pkg(15) **3.29**

**472-8028** .0833 x .125" pkg(12) **3.29**

**472-8029** .125 x .125" pkg(12) **3.29**

**472-8030** .125 x .1664" pkg(9) **3.29**

**472-8031** .1664 x .1664" pkg(9) **3.29**

**472-8032** .208 x .208" pkg(5) **3.29**

## DOWELS

Measurement indicates diameter.

### 12" Long

**472-7903** 1/16" **20.40**

### Hardwood 36" Long

**472-7904** 1/8" pkg(45) **15.30**

**472-7905** 3/16" pkg(36) **19.80**

**472-7906** 1/4" pkg(30) **20.10**

**472-7907** 5/16" pkg(25) **20.25**

**472-7908** 3/8" pkg(20) **20.60**

**472-7909** 1/2" pkg(12) **18.84**

## SUPER SHEETS

Custom-build your projects with these 7.6 x 12.6" sheets available in white styrene, clear PVC, clear polyester, colored PVC, white PVC foam, clear Lexan, mirror gold and silver styrene.

### White Styrene

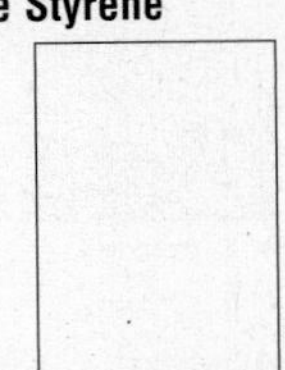

**472-60101** 0.015" 0.30mm pkg(4) **3.96**

**472-60102** 0.020" 0.50mm pkg(4) **4.76**

**472-60103** 0.030" 0.75mm pkg(4) **5.96**

**472-60104** 0.040" 1.00mm pkg(4) **7.16**

**472-60105** 0.060" 1.50mm pkg(4) **8.76**

**472-60106** 0.080" 2.00mm pkg(4) **10.76**

**472-60107** 0.118" 3.00mm pkg(4) **15.16**

MIDWEST PRODUCTS CO., INC.

### Clear PVC

**472-60201** 0.005" 0.15mm pkg(4) **4.36**

**472-60202** 0.010" 0.25mm pkg(4) **5.96**

**472-60203** 0.015" 0.40mm pkg(4) **6.36**

### Clear Polyester

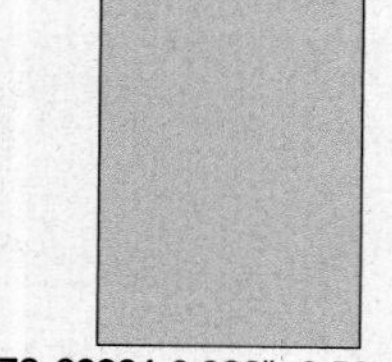

**472-60301** 0.020" 0.50mm pkg(4) **8.36**

**472-60302** 0.030" 0.75mm pkg(4) **10.36**

**472-60303** 0.040" 1.00mm pkg(4) **13.16**

**472-60304** 0.060" 1.50mm pkg(4) **18.36**

**472-60305** 0.080" 2.00mm pkg(4) **21.96**

**472-60306** 0.118" 3.00mm pkg(4) **32.36**

**472-60307** 0.177" 4.00mm pkg(4) **43.16**

### Clear, Colored PVC

Each sheet is 0.010" or 0.23mm thick.

**pkg(4) 7.96 ea**

**472-60401** Yellow
**472-60402** Orange
**472-60403** Red
**472-60404** Brown
**472-60405** Green
**472-60406** Blue

### White PVC Foam

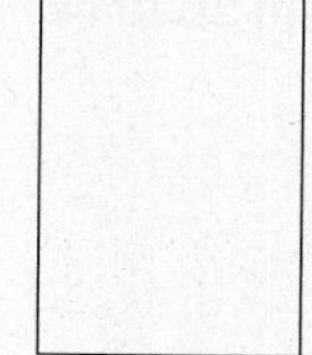

**472-60501** 0.080" 2.00mm pkg(4) **14.76**

**472-60502** 0.118" 3.00mm pkg(4) **17.96**

**472-60503** 0.156" 4.00mm pkg(4) **23.16**

**472-60504** 0.197" 5.00mm pkg(4) **28.76**

**472-60505** 0.236" 6.00mm pkg(4) **35.56**

### Clear Polycarbonate

**472-60601** 0.040" 0.15mm pkg(4) **15.98**

**472-60602** 0.060" 0.15mm pkg(2) **21.98**

**472-60603** 0.080" 0.15mm pkg(2) **23.98**

**472-60604** 0.118" 0.15mm pkg(2) **35.98**

### Mirror Gold Styrene

**472-60701** 0.040" 1.00mm pkg(4) **23.96**

**472-60702** 0.080" 2.00mm pkg(4) **31.96**

### Mirror Silver Styrene

**472-60801** 0.040" 1.00mm pkg(4) **23.96**

**472-60802** 0.080" 2.00mm pkg(4) **31.96**



## Hob-Bits®

by Woodland Scenics®

Hob-Bits® – High quality brass machine screws, nuts and washers in four different sizes and four different styles. Hob-Bits tools include wrenches, taps and dies for all four sizes.

### Fillister Head Screws

**00-90 pkg(5) 2.19 ea**
**785-821** 1/8 x .046"
**785-822** 1/4 x .046"
**785-823** 3/8 x .046"
**785-824** 1/2 x .046"

**0-80 pkg(5) 2.19 ea**
**785-825** 1/8 x .058"
**785-826** 1/4 x .058"
**785-827** 3/8 x .058"
**785-828** 1/2 x .058"

**1-72 pkg(5) 2.19 ea**
**785-829** 1/8 x .072"
**785-830** 1/4 x .072"
**785-831** 3/8 x .072"
**785-832** 1/2 x .072"

**2-56 pkg(5) 2.19 ea**
**785-833** 1/8 x .085"
**785-834** 1/4 x .085"
**785-835** 3/8 x .085"
**785-836** 1/2 x .085"

### Flat Head Screws

**00-90 pkg(5) 2.19 ea**
**785-841** 1/8 x .046"
**785-842** 1/4 x .046"
**785-843** 3/8 x .046"
**785-844** 1/2 x .046"

**0-80 pkg(5) 2.19 ea**
**785-845** 1/8 x .058"
**785-846** 1/4 x .058"
**785-847** 3/8 x .058"
**785-848** 1/2 x .058"

**1-72 pkg(5) 2.19 ea**
**785-849** 1/8 x .072"
**785-850** 1/4 x .072"
**785-851** 3/8 x .072"
**785-852** 1/2 x .072"

**2-56 pkg(5) 2.19 ea**
**785-853** 1/8 x .085"
**785-854** 1/4 x .085"
**785-855** 3/8 x .085"
**785-856** 1/2 x .085"

### Hex Head Screws

**00-90 pkg(5) 2.19 ea**
**785-861** 1/8 x .046"
**785-862** 1/4 x .046"
**785-863** 3/8 x .046"
**785-864** 1/2 x .046"

**0-80 pkg(5) 2.19 ea**
**785-865** 1/8 x .058"
**785-866** 1/4 x .058"
**785-867** 3/8 x .058"
**785-868** 1/2 x .058"

**1-72 pkg(5) 2.19 ea**
**785-869** 1/8 x .072"
**785-870** 1/4 x .072"
**785-871** 3/8 x .072"
**785-872** 1/2 x .072"

**2-56 pkg(5) 2.19 ea**
**785-873** 1/8 x .085"
**785-874** 1/4 x .085"
**785-875** 3/8 x .085"
**785-876** 1/2 x .085"

### Round Head Screws

**00-90 pkg(5) 2.19 ea**
**785-801** 1/8 x .046"
**785-802** 1/4 x .046"
**785-803** 3/8 x .046"
**785-804** 1/2 x .046"

**0-80 pkg(5) 2.19 ea**
**785-805** 1/8 x .058"
**785-806** 1/4 x .058"
**785-807** 3/8 x .058"
**785-808** 1/2 x .058"

**1-72 pkg(5) 2.19 ea**
**785-809** 1/8 x .072"
**785-810** 1/4 x .072"
**785-811** 3/8 x .072"
**785-812** 1/2 x .072"

**2-56 pkg(5) 2.19 ea**
**785-813** 1/8 x .085"
**785-814** 1/4 x .085"
**785-815** 3/8 x .085"
**785-816** 1/2 x .085"

### Hex Nuts

**pkg(5) 2.19 ea**
**785-881** 00-90
**785-882** 0-80
**785-883** 1-72
**785-884** 2-56

### Washers

**pkg(5) 2.19 ea**
**785-891** 00-90
**785-892** 0-80
**785-893** 1-72
**785-894** 2-56

## TOOLS

### Dies 49.98 ea
**785-877** 00-90
**785-878** 0-80
**785-879** 1-72
**785-880** 2-56

### Taps 6.98 ea
**785-895** 00-90
**785-896** 0-80
**785-897** 1-72
**785-898** 2-56

### Wrenches 6.98 ea
**785-885** 00-90
**785-886** 0-80
**785-887** 1-72
**785-888** 2-56

## SCALE SCENICS

DIVISION OF CIRCUITRON

### Flat Wire

**652-1504** Nickel Silver **2.95**

Used for simulating strapping. Measures .010 x .030". Package contains 5' 150cm of wire.

### Micro-Mesh

Lightweight, non-woven, raised diamond pattern mesh. easures just .005" thick.

3 x 6" 7.5 x 15cm.

Shown Actual Size

**652-3500** Aluminum **4.95**

**652-3501** Brass **5.95**
May be soldered.

All items are prepackaged and available only in the quantities shown.

# LUMBER

## 11" Long 2.35 ea

Large dimension is height, small dimension is thickness. Decimals are actual size.

### 1 HO Scale Inch
(Actual size .012")
**521-3001** x 2" (x .024") pkg(14)
**521-3002** x 3" (x .036") pkg(14)
**521-3003** x 4" (x .048") pkg(14)
**521-3004** x 6" (x .072") pkg(12)
**521-3005** x 8" (x .096") pkg(12)
**521-3006** x 10" (x .120") pkg(12)

### 2 HO Scale Inches
(Actual size .024")
**521-3010** x 2" (x .024") pkg(14)
**521-3011** x 3" (x .036") pkg(14)
**521-3012** x 4" (x .048") pkg(14)
**521-3013** x 6" (x .072") pkg(12)
**521-3014** x 8" (x .096") pkg(12)
**521-3015** x 10" (x .120") pkg(12)
**521-3016** x 12" (x .144") pkg(10)

### 3 HO Scale Inches
(Actual size .036")
**521-3020** x 3" (x .036") pkg(14)
**521-3021** x 4" (x .048") pkg(14)
**521-3022** x 6" (x .072") pkg(12)
**521-3023** x 8" (x .096") pkg(12)
**521-3024** x 10" (x .120") pkg(12)
**521-3025** x 12" (x .144") pkg(10)

### 4 HO Scale Inches
(Actual size .048")
**521-3030** x 4" (x .048") pkg(12)
**521-3031** x 6" (x .072") pkg(12)
**521-3032** x 8" (x .096") pkg(12)
**521-3033** x 10" (x .120") pkg(12)
**521-3034** x 12" (x .144") pkg(12)

### 6 HO Scale Inches
(Actual size .072")
**521-3040** x 6" (x .072") pkg(12)
**521-3041** x 8" (x .096") pkg(10)
**521-3042** x 10" (x .120") pkg(10)
**521-3043** x 12" (x .144") pkg(10)

### 8 HO Scale Inches
(Actual size .096")
**521-3050** x 8" (x .096") pkg(10)
**521-3051** x 10" (x .120") pkg(10)
**521-3052** x 12" (x .144") pkg(10)

### 10 HO Scale Inches
(Actual size .120")
**521-3060** x 10" (x .120") pkg(10)
**521-3061** x 12" (x .144") pkg(8)

### 12 HO Scale Inches
(Actual size .144")
**521-3070** x 12" (x .144") pkg(8)

# STRIPWOOD

Each basswood piece is 24" 60cm long. Large dimension indicates thickness, small dimension indicates width.

## 1/32" Thick
**521-70120** x 1/32" pkg(10) **2.50**
**521-70122** x 3/64" pkg(10) **2.50**
**521-70123** x 1/16" pkg(10) **2.50**
**521-70124** x 5/64" pkg(10) **2.90**
**521-70125** x 3/32" pkg(10) **2.90**
**521-70126** x 1/8" pkg(10) **2.90**
**521-70127** x 5/32" pkg(10) **3.30**
**521-70128** x 3/16" pkg(10) **3.30**
**521-70130** x 1/4" pkg(10) **4.10**
**521-70131** x 5/16" pkg(10) **4.30**
**521-70132** x 3/8" pkg(10) **5.90**
**521-70134** x 1/2" pkg(10) **6.90**
**521-70135** x 3/4" pkg(10) **6.95**
**521-70136** x 1" pkg(5) **4.35**
**521-70137** x 2" pkg(5) **7.20**
**521-70138** x 3" pkg(2) **3.96**
**521-70139** x 4" pkg(2) **5.27**

## 3/64" Thick
**521-70161** x 3/64" pkg(10) **3.20**
**521-70162** x 1/16" pkg(10) **3.20**
**521-70163** x 5/64" pkg(10) **3.20**
**521-70164** x 3/32" pkg(10) **3.20**
**521-70165** x 1/8" pkg(10) **3.20**
**521-70166** x 5/32" pkg(10) **3.85**
**521-70167** x 3/16" pkg(10) **3.85**
**521-70169** x 1/4" pkg(10) **4.90**
**521-70171** x 3/8" pkg(10) **6.10**
**521-70173** x 1/2" pkg(10) **7.10**
**521-70174** x 3/4" pkg(10) **7.20**
**521-70175** x 1" pkg(5) **4.55**
**521-70176** x 2" pkg(5) **8.65**
**521-70177** x 3" pkg(2) **5.65**
**521-70178** x 4" pkg(2) **5.85**

Item listed below is available by Special Order (see Legend Page).
**521-70170** x 5/16" pkg(10) **5.90**

## 1/16" Thick
**521-70180** x 1/16" pkg(10) **3.20**
**521-70181** x 5/64" pkg(10) **3.20**
**521-70182** x 3/32" pkg(10) **3.20**
**521-70183** x 1/8" pkg(10) **3.68**
**521-70184** x 5/32" pkg(10) **3.90**
**521-70185** x 3/16" pkg(10) **4.10**
**521-70187** x 1/4" pkg(10) **5.20**
**521-70188** x 5/16" pkg(10) **5.40**
**521-70189** x 3/8" pkg(10) **6.90**
**521-70191** x 1/2" pkg(10) **7.85**
**521-70192** x 3/4" pkg(10) **9.65**
**521-70193** x 1" pkg(5) **6.15**
**521-70194** x 2" pkg(5) **8.75**
**521-70195** x 3" pkg(2) **4.65**
**521-70196** x 4" pkg(2) **5.95**

## 5/64" Thick
**521-70198** x 5/64" pkg(10) **3.30**
**521-70199** x 3/32" pkg(10) **3.75**
**521-70200** x 1/8" pkg(10) **3.75**
**521-70201** x 5/32" pkg(10) **4.00**
**521-70202** x 3/16" pkg(10) **4.25**
**521-70204** x 1/4" pkg(10) **5.15**
**521-70205** x 5/16" pkg(10) **5.75**
**521-70206** x 3/8" pkg(10) **7.25**
**521-70208** x 1/2" pkg(10) **7.90**
**521-70211** x 2" pkg(5) **8.95**
**521-70212** x 3" pkg(2) **4.95**
**521-70213** x 4" pkg(2) **6.75**

Items listed below are available by Special Order (see Legend Page).
**521-70209** x 3/4" pkg(10) **9.50**
**521-70210** x 1" pkg(5) **6.20**

## 3/32" Thick
**521-70215** x 3/32" pkg(10) **3.75**
**521-70216** x 1/8" pkg(10) **3.75**
**521-70217** x 5/32" pkg(10) **3.75**
**521-70218** x 3/16" pkg(10) **4.35**
**521-70220** x 1/4" pkg(10) **5.15**
**521-70221** x 5/16" pkg(10) **6.25**
**521-70222** x 3/8" pkg(10) **7.65**
**521-70224** x 1/2" pkg(10) **8.50**
**521-70225** x 3/4" pkg(10) **9.65**
**521-70226** x 1" pkg(5) **6.45**
**521-70227** x 2" pkg(5) **9.15**
**521-70228** x 3" pkg(2) **4.95**
**521-70229** x 4" pkg(1) **3.75**

## 1/8" Thick
**521-70231** x 1/8" pkg(10) **3.80**
**521-70232** x 5/32" pkg(10) **4.70**
**521-70233** x 3/16" pkg(10) **4.95**
**521-70235** x 1/4" pkg(10) **5.80**
**521-70236** x 5/16" pkg(10) **6.30**
**521-70237** x 3/8" pkg(10) **7.90**
**521-70239** x 1/2" pkg(10) **10.10**
**521-70240** x 3/4" pkg(10) **12.50**
**521-70241** x 1" pkg(5) **6.85**
**521-70242** x 2" pkg(5) **9.95**
**521-70243** x 3" pkg(2) **5.50**
**521-70244** x 4" pkg(1) **4.10**

## 5/32" Thick
**521-70246** x 5/32" pkg(5) **2.60**
**521-70247** x 3/16" pkg(5) **2.75**
**521-70249** x 1/4" pkg(5) **3.15**
**521-70250** x 5/16" pkg(5) **3.85**
**521-70251** x 3/8" pkg(5) **3.95**
**521-70253** x 1/2" pkg(5) **5.30**
**521-70254** x 3/4" pkg(5) **6.55**
**521-70255** x 1" pkg(2) **3.05**
**521-70256** x 2" pkg(2) **4.85**
**521-70257** x 3" pkg(2) **5.60**
**521-70258** x 4" pkg(1) **4.10**

## 3/16" Thick
**521-70260** x 3/16" pkg(5) **3.15**
**521-70262** x 1/4" pkg(5) **3.45**
**521-70263** x 5/16" pkg(5) **3.95**
**521-70264** x 3/8" pkg(5) **4.95**
**521-70266** x 1/2" pkg(5) **5.70**
**521-70267** x 3/4" pkg(5) **6.65**
**521-70268** x 1" pkg(2) **3.20**
**521-70269** x 2" pkg(2) **4.80**
**521-70270** x 3" pkg(2) **6.00**
**521-70271** x 4" pkg(1) **4.50**

## 1/4" Thick
**521-70285** x 1/4" pkg(5) **4.10**
**521-70286** x 5/16" pkg(5) **4.30**
**521-70287** x 3/8" pkg(5) **5.30**
**521-70289** x 1/2" pkg(5) **6.70**
**521-70290** x 3/4" pkg(5) **6.80**
**521-70291** x 1" pkg(2) **4.10**
**521-70293** x 3" pkg(2) **6.75**
**521-70294** x 4" pkg(1) **5.15**

Item listed below is available by Special Order (see Legend Page).
**521-70292** x 2" pkg(2) **5.40**

## 5/16" Thick
**521-70296** x 5/16" pkg(5) **5.40**
**521-70297** x 3/8" pkg(5) **6.60**
**521-70299** x 1/2" pkg(5) **7.10**
**521-70300** x 3/4" pkg(5) **8.35**
**521-70301** x 1" pkg(2) **3.75**
**521-70303** x 3" pkg(2) **8.15**

Item listed below is available by Special Order (see Legend Page).
**521-70302** x 2" pkg(2) **5.95**

## 3/8" Thick
**521-70306** x 3/8" pkg(5) **6.55**
**521-70308** x 1/2" pkg(5) **6.95**
**521-70309** x 3/4" pkg(5) **8.50**
**521-70310** x 1" pkg(2) **4.10**
**521-70311** x 2" pkg(2) **6.65**
**521-70312** x 3" pkg(2) **8.10**

## 1/2" Thick
**521-70323** x 1/2" pkg(2) **3.70**
**521-70324** x 3/4" pkg(2) **4.00**
**521-70325** x 1" pkg(2) **4.65**
**521-70326** x 2" pkg(2) **9.10**
**521-70327** x 3" pkg(2) **12.75**

## 3/4" Thick
**521-70330** x 3/4" pkg(2) **4.40**
**521-70331** x 1" pkg(2) **5.75**
**521-70332** x 2" pkg(1) **5.20**
**521-70333** x 3" pkg(1) **8.35**

## Bulk Pack - 50 Pieces
Each piece is 24" 60cm long.
**521-120** 1/32 x 1/32" **10.50**
**521-123** 1/32 x 1/16" **10.50**
**521-125** 1/32 x 3/32" **12.50**
**521-126** 1/32 x 1/8" **12.50**
**521-161** 3/64 x 3/64" **13.00**
**521-180** 1/16 x 1/16" **13.00**
**521-183** 1/16 x 1/8" **15.00**
**521-231** 1/8 x 1/8" **16.50**

# SCRIBED SHEATHING

## pkg(2) 6.95 ea

First dimension indicates scribe spacing, second is thickness. Each item is 24" long and 3-1/2" wide.
**521-70350** .025 x 1/32"
**521-70351** 1/32 x 1/32"
**521-70353** 3/64 x 1/32"
**521-70354** 1/16 x 1/32"
**521-70355** 3/32 x 1/32"
**521-70356** 1/8 x 1/32"
**521-70357** 3/16 x 1/32"
**521-70358** 1/4 x 1/32"
**521-70359** 3/8 x 1/32"
**521-70360** 1/2 x 1/32"
**521-70361** Random x 1/32"
**521-70362** .025 x 1/16"
**521-70363** 1/32 x 1/16"
**521-70365** 3/64 x 1/16"
**521-70366** 1/16 x 1/16"
**521-70367** 3/32 x 1/16"
**521-70368** 1/8 x 1/16"
**521-70369** 3/16 x 1/16"
**521-70370** 1/4 x 1/16"
**521-70371** 3/8 x 1/16"
**521-70372** 1/2 x 1/16"
**521-70373** Random x 1/16"

## 6" WIDE SIDING

Each sheet measures 24" long, 6" wide and 1/8" thick.

### Conventional Clapboard 7.25 ea

**521-6510** 1/16" Spacing
**521-6512** 3/32" Spacing
**521-6511** 1/8" Spacing

### Aged Clapboard 7.25 ea

**521-6504** 1/16" Spacing
**521-6505** 3/32" Spacing
**521-6507** 1/8" Spacing

### Board & Batten 7.25 ea

**521-00450** 1/16" Spacing
**521-00451** 1/8" Spacing
**521-00452** 3/16" Spacing
**521-00449** 1/4" Spacing

### Scribed Sheathing 7.25 ea

**521-6506** 1/16" Spacing
**521-6509** 3/32" Spacing
**521-6508** 1/8" Spacing

## SIDING

### Clapboard pkg(2) 6.95 ea

Dimension indicates lap spacing. Each item is 24" long and 3-1/2" wide.
**521-70375** 1/32"
**521-70377** 3/64"
**521-70378** 1/16"
**521-70379** 3/32"
**521-70380** 1/8"
**521-70381** 3/16"
**521-70382** 1/4"
**521-70383** 3/8"
**521-70384** 1/2"

### Board & Batten pkg(2) 6.95 ea

Dimension indicates cap spacing.
**521-70402** 1/16"
**521-70403** 3/32"
**521-70404** 1/8"
**521-70405** 3/16"
**521-70406** 1/4"
**521-70407** 3/8"
**521-70408** 1/2"
**521-70409** 3/4"

### Imprinted Concrete pkg(2) 6.95 ea

**521-70415** 1/16"
**521-70417** 1/8"
**521-70418** 3/16"

### Corrugated pkg(2) 6.95 ea

Dimension indicates corrugation spacing.
**521-70424** .40"
**521-70426** 1/16"
**521-70436** 3/32"
**521-70437** 1/8"

### Steel pkg(2) 6.95 ea

**521-70347** HO Steel Siding
**521-70349** O Steel Siding

### Siding Packs pkg(2) 3.79 ea

Each pack includes two pieces of scale lumber 3 x 11".

#### Board & Batten

**521-6006** 3/32"
**521-6007** 1/8"
**521-6008** 3/16"

#### Clapboard

**521-6001** 1/16"
**521-6002** 3/32"
**521-6003** 1/8"

#### Corrugated

**521-6020** 1/16"
**521-6021** 3/32"
**521-6022** 1/8"

#### Scribed

Dimensions show distance between scribes and material thickness.
**521-6010** 1/32-1/32"
**521-6011** 1/16-1/32"
**521-6012** 3/32-1/32"
**521-6013** 1/8-1/32"
**521-6015** 1/16-1/16"
**521-6016** 3/32-1/16"
**521-6017** 1/8-1/16"

## STRUCTURAL SHAPES

### Angles

#### 22" Multi-Packs

**521-70499** 1/32" pkg(5) **4.70**
**521-70500** 3/64" pkg(5) **4.70**
**521-70501** 1/16" pkg(5) **5.10**
**521-70502** 5/64" pkg(5) **5.10**
**521-70503** 3/32" pkg(5) **5.10**
**521-70504** 1/8" pkg(5) **5.65**
**521-70505** 5/32" pkg(5) **6.20**
**521-70506** 3/16" pkg(5) **6.20**
**521-70507** 1/4" pkg(5) **6.45**
**521-70508** 5/16" pkg(2) **3.20**
**521-70509** 3/8" pkg(2) **4.35**
**521-70527** 1/2" pkg(2) **5.15**

### Channels

#### 22" Multi-Packs

**521-70540** 1/16" pkg(5) **5.10**
**521-70541** 5/64" pkg(5) **5.10**
**521-70542** 3/32" pkg(5) **5.10**
**521-70543** 1/8" pkg(5) **5.65**
**521-70544** 5/32" pkg(5) **6.20**
**521-70545** 3/16" pkg(5) **6.20**
**521-70546** 1/4" pkg(5) **6.45**
**521-70547** 5/16" pkg(2) **3.20**
**521-70548** 3/8" pkg(2) **4.35**
**521-70549** 1/2" pkg(2) **5.30**

### Corner Posts

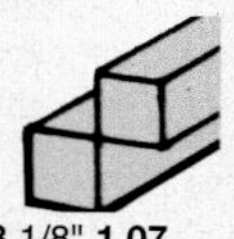

**521-593** 1/8" **1.07**
**521-595** 3/16" **1.18**

### H Columns

#### 22" Multi-Packs

**521-70550** 1/16" pkg(5) **5.10**
**521-70551** 5/64" pkg(5) **5.10**
**521-70552** 3/32" pkg(5) **5.10**
**521-70553** 1/8" pkg(5) **5.65**
**521-70554** 5/32" pkg(5) **6.20**
**521-70555** 3/16" pkg(5) **6.20**
**521-70556** 1/4" pkg(5) **6.45**
**521-70557** 5/16" pkg(2) **3.20**
**521-70558** 3/8" pkg(2) **4.35**
**521-70559** 1/2" pkg(2) **5.30**

### I Beams

#### 22" Multi-Packs

**521-70560** 1/16" pkg(5) **5.10**
**521-70561** 5/64" pkg(5) **5.10**
**521-70562** 3/32" pkg(5) **5.10**
**521-70563** 1/8" pkg(5) **5.65**
**521-70564** 5/32" pkg(5) **6.20**
**521-70565** 3/16" pkg(5) **6.20**
**521-70566** 1/4" pkg(5) **6.45**
**521-70567** 5/16" pkg(2) **3.20**
**521-70568** 3/8" pkg(2) **4.35**
**521-70569** 1/2" pkg(2) **5.30**

### Tees

**521-70510** 3/64" pkg(5) **4.70**
**521-70511** 1/16" pkg(5) **5.10**
**521-70512** 5/64" pkg(5) **5.10**
**521-70513** 3/32" pkg(5) **5.10**
**521-70514** 1/8" pkg(5) **5.65**
**521-70515** 5/32" pkg(5) **6.20**
**521-70516** 3/16" pkg(5) **6.20**
**521-70517** 1/4" pkg(5) **6.45**
**521-70518** 5/16" pkg(2) **3.20**
**521-70519** 3/8" pkg(2) **4.35**
**521-70525** 1/32" pkg(5) **4.70**

### Zees

#### 22" Multi-Packs

**521-70520** 3/64" pkg(5) **4.70**
**521-70521** 1/16" pkg(5) **5.10**
**521-70523** 3/32" pkg(5) **5.10**

## MOULDINGS

All items are 24" 60cm long unless noted.

### Cove

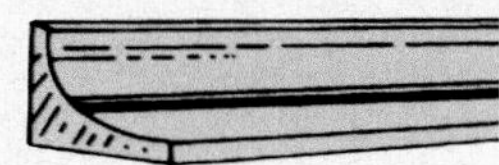

**521-91** 1/16" **.91**
**521-92** 5/64" **.91**
**521-93** 3/32" **.91**
**521-94** 1/8" **.95**
**521-95** 5/32" **1.00**
**521-96** 3/16" **1.00**
**521-98** 1/4" **1.16**

### Double Bead

**521-871** 1/8" **1.04**
**521-872** 3/32" **.91**
**521-873** 5/64" **.91**
**521-874** 1/16" **.91**
**521-875** 3/64" **.84**

### Half Round

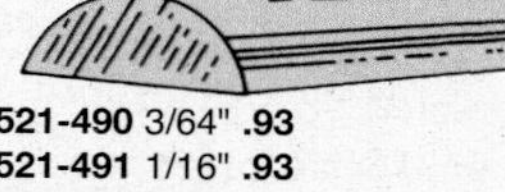

**521-490** 3/64" **.93**
**521-491** 1/16" **.93**
**521-492** 5/64" **.93**
**521-493** 3/32" **.93**
**521-494** 1/8" **.1.04**
**521-495** 5/32" **1.16**
**521-496** 3/16" **1.16**
**521-498** 1/4" **1.26**

### Quarter Round

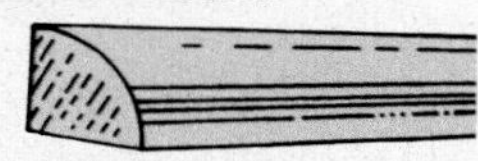

**521-570** 3/64" **.84**
**521-571** 1/16" **.84**
**521-572** 5/64" **.84**
**521-573** 3/32" **.84**
**521-574** 1/8" **.94**

### Round

**521-485** 3/64" **.84**
**521-486** 1/16" **.91**
**521-487** 5/64" **.91**
**521-488** 3/32" **.91**
**521-489** 1/8" **.1.04**

## MODEL RAILROAD CAR PARTS

### Roofs & Floors

**521-682** Clerestory Passenger Roof **5.25**
**521-692** Passenger Floor **2.05**

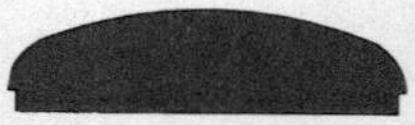

**521-702** Streamline Roof **3.9**

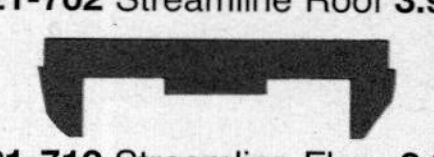

**521-712** Streamline Floor **3.9**

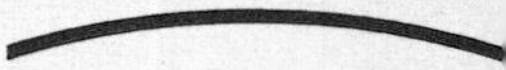

**521-642** Hollow Caboose Roo **2.50**

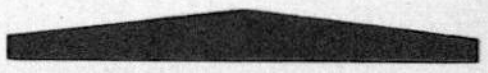

**521-652** Inner Roof **2.50**

**521-662** Freight Floor **2.45**

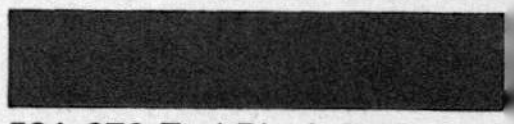

**521-672** End Block **2.50**

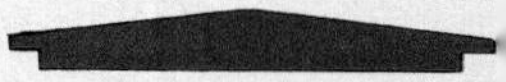

**521-602** Overhanging Roof **3.95**

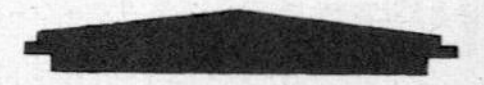

**521-612** Recessed Roof **3.95**

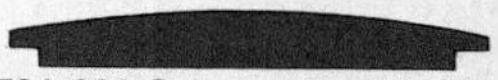

**521-622** Caboose Roof **3.95**

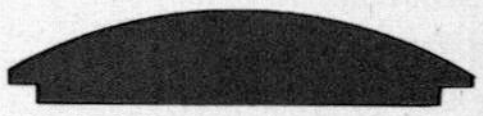

**521-632** Refrigerator Roof **3.9**

Miscellaneous

**521-722** Coach Siding **1.50**

**521-732** Solid Sill - Freight **.95**
**521-742** Grooved Sill **1.20**

**521-752** Fish Belly **1.00**
**521-762** Passenger Center Sil **1.85**

**521-772** Roofwalk **.45**

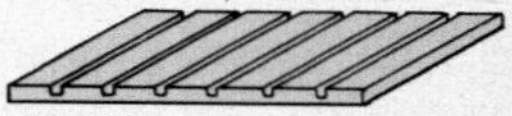

**521-782** Lateral Roofwalks pkg(12) **.55**

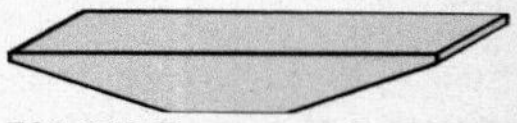

**521-802** Passenger Car Bolsters 1 Pair **.60**

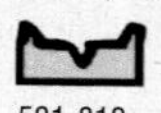


**521-812** Window Molding **.80**
**521-822** Corner Post **.60**

**521-832** Belt Rail **.55**
**521-842** Threshold **.60**

NorthWest Short Line

# METRIC SCREWS

## Nickel-Plated Screws .95 ea

### Flat Head

**53-11535** 1.4 x .3 x 3mm pkg(8)

**53-11545** 1.4 x .3 x 4mm pkg(8)

**53-11565** 1.4 x .3 x 6mm pkg(8)

**53-11995** 1.7 x .35 x 16mm pkg(8)

**53-12255** 2 x .4 x 5mm pkg(8)

**53-12755** 2.6 x .45 x 5mm pkg(10)

**53-12295** 2 x 18 x .4mm pkg(6)

### Pan Head

**53-11035** 1 x .25 x 3mm pkg(6)

**53-11045** 1 x .25 x 4mm pkg(6)

**53-11075** 1 x .25 x 7mm pkg(6)

**53-11235** 1.2 x .25 x 3mm pkg(6)

**53-11245** 1.2 x .25 x 4mm pkg(6)

**53-11255** 1.2 x .25 x 5mm pkg(6)

**53-11425** 1.4 x .3 x 2mm pkg(8)

**53-11435** 1.4 x .3 x 3mm pkg(8)

**53-11445** 1.4 x .3 x 4mm pkg(8)

**53-11465** 1.4 x .3 x 6mm pkg(8)

**53-11505** 1.4 x .3 x 10mm pkg(8)

**53-11725** 1.7 x .35 x 1.8mm pkg(8)

**53-11755** 1.7 x .35 x 5mm pkg(8)

**53-11885** 1.7 x .35 x 18mm pkg(8)

**53-12035** 2 x .4 x 3mm pkg(10)

**53-12045** 2 x .4 x 4mm pkg(10)

**53-12055** 2 x .4 x 5mm pkg(10)

**53-12065** 2 x .4 x 6mm pkg(10)

**53-12085** 2 x .4 x 8mm pkg(10)

**53-12105** 2 x .4 x 10mm pkg(8)

**53-12125** 2 x .4 x 12mm pkg(8)

**53-12635** 2.6 x .45 x 3mm pkg(10)

**53-12645** 2.6 x .45 x 4mm pkg(10)

**53-12655** 2.6 x .45 x 5mm pkg(10)

**53-12665** 2.6 x .45 x 6mm pkg(10)

**53-12685** 2.6 x .45 x 8mm pkg(10)

**53-12705** 2.6 x .45 x 10mm pkg(10)

**53-12755** 2.6 x .45 x 5mm pkg(10)

**53-13055** 3 x .5 x 5mm pkg(10)

**53-13105** 3 x 10 x 5mm pkg(10)

## Set Screws pkg(6) .95 ea

**53-16725** 1.7 x .35mm Steel

**53-16835** 2 x .4 x 3mm

**53-216415** 1.4 x 1.5 x .3mm

**53-216725** 1.7 x 2 x .35mm

**53-216845** 2 x 4 x .4mm

## Plastic Insulating Pan Head Screws pkg(4) .95 ea

**53-51745** 1.7 x 4 x .35mm

**53-52055** 2 x 5 x 4mm

## Nylon Screws pkg(6) .95 ea

### Fillister Head

**53-41745** 0-80 x 1/8"

**53-41765** 0-80 x 1/2"

### Flat Head

**53-42245** 0-80 x 9/32"

**53-42365** 1-72 x 7/16"

**53-42455** 2-56 x 3/8"

### Pan Head

**53-41165** 0-90 x 1/2"

**53-41265** 0-80 x 3/8"

**53-41365** 1-72 x 1/2"

**53-41475** 2-56 x 1/2"

## Black-Plated Pan Head Screws pkg(8) .95 ea

**53-211425** 1.4 x .2 x 3mm

**53-211435** 1.4 x .3 x 3mm

**53-211445** 1.4 x .4 x 3mm

**53-211455** 1.4 x .5 x 3mm

**53-211465** 1.4 x .6 x 3mm

**53-211485** 1.4 x .8 x 3mm

**53-211725** 1.7 x .25 x 35mm

**53-211745** 1.7 x .4 x 35mm

**53-212045** 2 x .4 x 4mm

**53-212065** 2 x .6 x 4mm

**53-212085** 2 x .8 x 4mm

**53-212105** 2 x .10 x 4mm

**53-212685** 2.6 x .8 x 45mm

## Sheet Metal Screws

**53-18065** 2 x 6mm pkg(8) **.95**

# NICKEL-PLATED BRASS HEX NUTS .95 ea

**53-10105** 1 x .25mm pkg(6)

**53-10125** 1.2 x .25mm pkg(6)

**53-10145** 1.4 x .3mm pkg(8)

**53-10175** 1.7 x .35mm pkg(8)

**53-10205** 2 x .4mm pkg(8)

**53-10265** 2.6 x .45mm pkg(8)

**53-10305** 3 x .5mm pkg(8)

See Drill and Tap Sets in Tools Section.

# ASSORTMENTS

Assortments include a complete set of available items in size indicated. Great for the workbench so you don't have to stop work to find an oddball screw or nut.

## Metric Fastener Assortments

Assortments come in handy clear plastic snap-pack boxes for easy access.

**53-61005** 1mm & 2mm pkg(47) **7.95**

**53-61405** 1.4mm pkg(121) **15.95**

**53-61705** 1.7mm pkg(71) **9.95**

**53-62005** 2mm pkg(143) **17.95**

**53-63005** 2.6mm & 3mm pkg(113) **11.95**

## Washer Assortments

**53-60005** Bronze Thrust & Space Washer Assortment pkg(104) **13.95**

See the complete listing of Northwest Short Line washers in the Lighting - Electrical - Motors section of this book.

# STAINLESS STEEL TUBING

Laser-welded stainless steel, plug-drawn for increased density, smoothness and straightness, with no visible seams. Easily formed and cut, all sizes are supplied in 9" lengths.

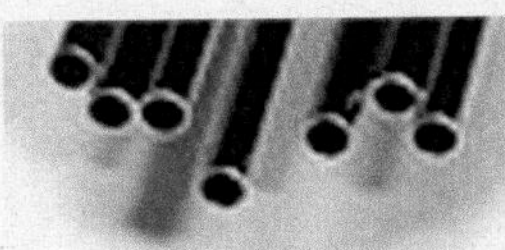

## .018" Outside Diameter — .002" Thick Wall

**514-N20182** pkg(2) **3.95**

**514-N20184** pkg(4) **7.25**

## .025" Outside Diameter - .003" Thick Wall

**514-N20252** pkg(2) **3.75**

**514-N20254** pkg(4) **6.85**

## .032" Outside Diameter - .0025" Thick Wall

**514-N2032U2** pkg(2) **3.85**

**514-N2032U4** pkg(4) **6.95**

## .032" Outside Diameter — .006" Thick Wall

**514-N20322** pkg(2) **3.40**

**514-N20324** pkg(4) **6.35**

## .042" Outside Diameter — .0035" Thick Wall

**514-N20422** pkg(2) **5.35**

**514-N20424** pkg(4) **9.95**

## .050" Outside Diameter — .004" Thick Wall

**514-N20502** pkg(2) **5.35**

**514-N20504** pkg(4) **9.75**

## .065" Outside Diameter — .005" Thick Wall

**514-N20652** pkg(2) **5.65**

**514-N20654** pkg(4) **10.50**

## .095" Outside Diameter — .005" Thick Wall

**514-N20952** pkg(2) **5.95**

**514-N20954** pkg(4) **10.95**

# STRAIGHTENED STAINLESS STEEL WIRE

## .004" Diameter

**514-N210410** pkg(10) **3.65**
Straight within .002" over total 9" length — ultra thin!

## .012" Diameter

**514-N211210** pkg(10) **2.25**
Straight within .010" over total 9" length.

# .005" THICK PLATE GLASS 2.75 EA

This super-flat borosilicate glass has superior strength and is ideal for any model windows where a realistic appearance is desired. Simply scribe and snap to size, glue in place with any adhesive.

**514-N70038** .85 x .85" pkg(8)

Truck Shown Not Included

**514-N70044** .85 x 1.70" pkg(4)

## ASSEMBLED SHINGLE SHEETS

Scratchbuilding shingle roofs has been made easier thanks to Northeastern Scale Models. Shingle sheets feature laser-cut paper shingle strips assembled into 3-1/2 x 8" 8.8 x 20cm sheets that are easily to cut to fit your model. Sheets are available in single- and two-sheet packs in a variety of colors and styles.

### Single Sheets 7.95 ea

**520-50001** Gray Slate

**NEW 520-50005** Gray Fishscale

**NEW 520-50007** Gray Random

**NEW 520-50009** Sienna Random

**NEW 520-50011** Terra Cotta Fishscale

**NEW 520-50013** Charcoal

**NEW 520-50015** Dark Green

### Two-Sheet Packs 13.95

**520-50003** Gray Slate

**NEW 520-50004** Green Slate

**NEW 520-50006** Gray Fishscale

**NEW 520-50008** Gray Random

**NEW 520-50010** Sienna Random

**NEW 520-50012** Terra Cotta Fishscale

**NEW 520-50014** Charcoal

**NEW 520-50016** Dark Green

## NEW PRODUCTS

### MODEL BUILDER'S SUPPLY LINE™

### Styrene Building Sheets HO/N pkg(2) 19.95 ea

11 x 14 x .020"
27.5 x 35 x .005cm

These crisp and well defined, textured sheets are available in many different surfaces. The large sheet size helps you avoid unsightly seams on large projects and, because it's styrene, it's easy to apply. These sheets are produced in a neutral white.

**NEW 716-50001** Modern Brick

**NEW 716-50002** British Bond Alternate Row On-End

**NEW 716-50003** Flemish Bond Alternate Brick On-End

**NEW 716-50004** Brick Arches & Columns

**NEW 716-50005** Concrete Block

**NEW 716-50006** Ceramic Tile/Paving Stones

**NEW 716-50007** Small Welded Plate

**NEW 716-50008** Large Welded Plate

**NEW 716-50032** Lakes & Rivers

**NEW 716-50033** American Bond - 6th Row on End

**NEW 716-50034** Slate Roofing

### Taskboard®

This durable, lightweight wood fiberboard is available in several thicknesses, and is great for simulating concrete or stucco walls, building parts and more. It's also ideal for making major structure components to which brick or other textured surfaces will be laminated. Unlike wood, it can be shaped and bent into curved walls with the use of hot steam or water. Taskboard also sands smoothly and is easily cemented with white glue.

### 10 x 15" Sheets

#### 1/16" Thick

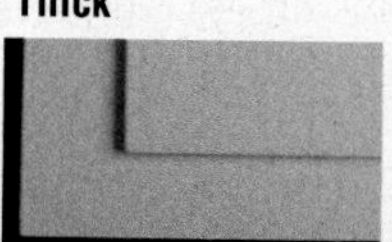

**NEW 716-50037** 2-Pack **9.95**

**NEW 716-50039** 4-Pack **12.95**

#### 3/32" Thick

**NEW 716-50038** 2-Pack **10.95**

**NEW 716-50039** 4-Pack **13.95**

## BUILDING MATERIAL

### Cap Tiles

**541-1008** For Concrete Sheets **2.25**

### Concrete Block Walls 2.75 ea

Molded in gray plastic, use to create warehouses, gas stations, garages and other concrete structures. Measurement in HO scale feet.

**541-1004** 14-1/2 x 28' pkg(4)

**541-1005** 14-1/2 x 18-1/2' pkg(4)

**541-1006** 14-1/2 x 9-1/4' pkg(8)

### Prefab Steel Warehouse Walls

**541-1011** Two Wall Panels & Downspouts (18 x 80' scale feet) **4.75**

**541-1012** Peaked End Panels pkg(2) **4.25**

**541-1013** Two Roof Panels & Supports (15 x 80' scale feet) **4.75**

### Shingles

**541-1007** Panels (7-3/16 x 2-1/32") pkg(2) **3.00**

**541-1015** Roof (5 x 8") **4.25**

### Siding

**541-1014** Board & Batten (5 x 8') **4.25**

## Information STATION

### Working With Styrene

Styrene has different needs from modelers than other plastics. Evergreen Scale Models has offered these helpful hints to make working with styrene an easy process:

To cut styrene, score the sheet with a sharp knife and break the sheet on the scored line. Thinner sheets or strips can be cut with a razor blade or sharp knife.

Styrene parts are joined together by bonding with a solvent, making it different than using wood or other materials. Apply a solvent to the joint (like cyanoacrylate or plastic cement) and the surfaces will bond themselves together.

Create the look of wood grain to the styrene surface by rubbing course sandpaper over the styrene in the direction of the grooves. You can create a more weathered appearance by wiggling the sandpaper slightly.

If simulating a wood or metal sheen, then spray painting is the best way to coat the styrene. Styrene works well with all types of modeling paint.

Your weathering options are limitless with styrene. Mud can be created by using the same base paint color. Pastel chalk or dyes can also create a weathering effect.

# Plastruct

For a complete listing of Plastruct products, visit Walthers website at www.walthers.com.

## ABS PLASTIC

Stronger than styrene, ABS is ideal for all types of model building, especially architectural models, or items subject to frequent handling. For easy identification, Plastruct ABS products are molded in gray.

### ABS Sheet

Each sheet measures 7 x 12", thickness shown.

**570-91001** .010" pkg(5) **4.50**
**570-91002** .020" pkg(5) **5.75**
**570-91003** .030" pkg(4) **5.60**
**570-91004** .040" pkg(3) **5.95**
**570-91005** .060" pkg(2) **5.35**
**570-91006** .080" pkg(2) **7.05**
**570-91007** .100" pkg(2) **8.55**
**570-91008** .125" pkg(2) **10.65**

### ABS Strip Stock

Each piece measures 1-1/4 x 24", thickness shown.

**Concrete**
**570-90361** .020" pkg(5) **6.95**
**570-90362** .030" pkg(4) **5.95**

**Steel**
**570-90365** .020" pkg(5) **6.95**
**570-90366** .030" pkg(4) **5.95**

### ABS Rod

Each solid piece is 15" long, outside height and width shown.

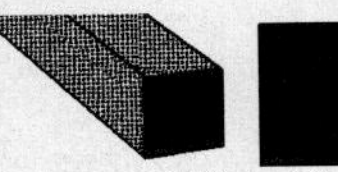

**570-90351** 1/8" pkg(5) **5.75**
**570-90352** 1/8 x 1/4" pkg(5) **6.50**

### ABS Rectangular & Square Tubing

Each piece is 15" long, height and width shown.

**570-90221** 1/4 x 3/16" pkg(6) **6.05**
**570-90222** 5/16 x 1/4" pkg(5) **6.00**
**570-90223** 3/8 x 1/4" pkg(5) **7.00**

**570-90201** 1/8" pkg(7) **6.40**
**570-90202** 3/16" pkg(6) **6.35**
**570-90203** 1/4" pkg(5) **6.50**
**570-90204** 5/16" pkg(4) **5.75**
**570-90205** 3/8" pkg(4) **6.75**

### Butyrate Round Tubing

Each piece is 15" long, outside diameter shown.

**570-90101** 3/64" Wire pkg(15) **6.50**
**570-90102** 1/16" Wire pkg(12) **5.75**

**570-90103** 3/32" pkg(10) **5.75**
**570-90104** 1/8" pkg(10) **6.25**
**570-90105** 3/16" pkg(9) **6.95**
**570-90106** 1/4" pkg(7) **6.75**
**570-90107** 5/16" pkg(6) **6.95**
**570-90108** 3/8" pkg(5) **7.00**

### Insert Wire For Butyrate Round Tubing

Brass wire for 3/32" or 1/8" Butyrate tube, adds stiffness and allows bending to almost any configuration.

**570-90121** For 3/32" Tube .045" Outside Diameter pkg(10) **5.25**
**570-90122** For 1/8" Tube .058" Outside Diameter pkg(10) **5.75**

### Butyrate Half-Round Profile

Each piece is 15" long, outside diameter shown.

**570-90171** 3/16" pkg(4) **5.60**
**570-90172** 1/4" pkg(4) **5.75**
**570-90173** 5/16" pkg(4) **5.95**

### ABS Structural Shapes

#### Angles

Height and length shown.

**570-90001** 3/64 x 10" pkg(10) **5.75**
**570-90002** 1/16 x 10" pkg(10) **6.25**
**570-90003** 3/32 x 15" pkg(8) **6.15**
**570-90004** 1/8 x 15" pkg(7) **6.40**
**570-90005** 3/16 x 24" pkg(5) **6.50**
**570-90006** 1/4 x 24" pkg(4) **5.75**
**570-90007** 5/16 x 24" pkg(4) **6.95**
**570-90008** 3/8 x 24" pkg(3) **6.20**

#### I Beams

Height and length shown.

**570-90021** 1/16 x 10" pkg(10) **6.25**
**570-90022** 3/32 x 10" pkg(8) **5.75**
**570-90023** 1/8 x 15" pkg(7) **6.40**
**570-90024** 3/16 x 24" pkg(5) **6.50**
**570-90025** 1/4 x 24" pkg(4) **5.75**
**570-90026** 5/16 x 24" pkg(4) **6.75**
**570-90027** 3/8 x 15" pkg(5) **6.50**
**570-90028** 7/16 x 15" pkg(4) **5.60**
**570-90029** 1/2 x 15" pkg(4) **6.55**
**570-90030** 9/16 x 15" pkg(4) **7.15**
**570-90031** 5/8 x 15" pkg(3) **6.20**

#### Channels

Height and length shown.

**570-90041** 1/16 x 10" pkg(10) **6.25**
**570-90042** 3/32 x 10" pkg(8) **6.15**
**570-90043** 1/8 x 15" pkg(7) **6.40**
**570-90044** 3/16 x 15" pkg(5) **5.25**
**570-90045** 1/4 x 24" pkg(4) **5.60**
**570-90046** 5/16 x 24" pkg(4) **6.75**

#### H Columns

Height and length shown.

**570-90061** 1/16 x 10" pkg(8) **6.55**
**570-90062** 3/32 x 15" pkg(6) **5.75**
**570-90063** 1/8 x 15" pkg(5) **5.25**
**570-90064** 3/16 x 24" pkg(4) **5.95**
**570-90065** 1/4 x 15" pkg(5) **5.75**
**570-90066** 5/16 x 15" pkg(5) **6.50**
**570-90067** 3/8 x 15" pkg(4) **5.55**

#### Handrails

**570-90471** N Scale 3-5/8" pkg(2) **2.25**
**570-90472** HO Scale 6" pkg(2) **2.75**
**570-90473** O Scale 24" **4.65**
**570-90474** G Scale 24" **5.10**
**570-90476** 1/16" Scale 24" **6.25**

#### Handrail Stanchion

**570-90479** **10.50**

#### Tees

Height and length shown.

**570-90081** 3/64 x 10" pkg(10) **6.25**
**570-90082** 1/16 x 10" pkg(8) **5.75**
**570-90083** 3/32 x 15" pkg(8) **6.55**
**570-90084** 1/8 x 15" pkg(7) **6.75**
**570-90085** 3/16 x 24" pkg(5) **7.00**
**570-90086** 1/4 x 24" pkg(4) **6.55**

#### Ladder

**570-90421** N Scale 3" Long pkg(2) **2.25**
**570-90422** HO Scale 5" Long pkg(2) **2.75**
**570-90423** O Scale 15" Long pkg(2) **5.65**
**570-90424** 3/8 x 39/64 x 15" pkg(2) **6.35**
**570-90425** 1/2 x 3/4 x 15" pkg(2) **7.05**
**570-90426** 3/4 x 1-3/32 x 15" pkg(2) **7.75**

#### Ladders w/Safety Cage

**570-90431** HO Scale 5" Long **4.30**
**570-90432** O Scale 12" Long **7.30**
**570-90433** G Scale 1" Long **8.55**

#### Stairs

**570-90441** N Scale 3" Long pkg(2) **3.25**
**570-90442** HO Scale 5" Long pkg(2) **4.05**
**570-90433** O Scale 12" Long **8.55**

#### Stairways

**570-90445** 13/32 x 1-1/8 x 12" **5.60**
**570-90446** 13/32 x 1-5/16 x 12" **5.95**
**570-90449** 13/16 x 2-3/32 x 12" **7.30**
**570-90450** 13/16 x 2-15/32 x 12" **7.60**

#### Stair Rails

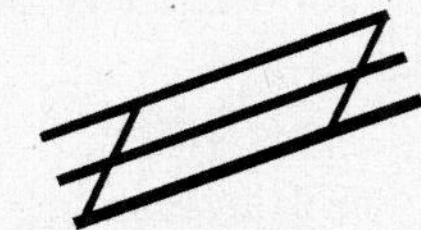

**570-90481** N Scale 3-5/8" Long pkg(2) **2.25**
**570-90482** HO Scale 6" Long pkg(2) **2.75**
**570-90483** O Scale 24" Long **4.65**
**570-90484** 1-5/16" **5.10**
**570-90486** 2-21/32" **6.25**

#### Railings pkg(2)

**Vertical**
**570-90491** 1/4" **3.25**
**570-90493** 3/8" **3.70**
**570-90494** 9/16" **4.05**
**570-90496** 3/4" **4.50**
**570-90497** 1-3/16" **4.75**
**570-90498** 1-9/16" **5.05**
**570-90499** 2-3/8" **5.35**

**Diagonal**
**570-90492** 9/32" **3.50**
**570-90495** 9/16" **4.25**

#### Open Web Truss

**Warren Style 2**
**570-90401** 1/8 x 6" pkg(2) **4.20**
**570-90402** 3/16 x 6" pkg(2) **4.75**
**570-90403** 1/4 x 6" pkg(2) **5.50**
**570-90404** 3/8 x 6" pkg(2) **6.20**
**570-90405** 1/2 x 12" pkg(2) **6.95**
**570-90406** 5/8 x 12" pkg(2) **7.75**
**570-90407** 3/4 x 12" pkg(2) **8.55**
**570-90408** 1 x 12" pkg(2) **9.25**

**Warren Style 1**

**570-90411** 1/8 x 3" pkg(2) **6.20**
**570-90412** 13/64 x 3" pkg(2) **6.80**
**570-90413** 9/32 x 5" pkg(2) **7.20**
**570-90414** 13/32 x 7" pkg(2) **7.80**
**570-90415** 1/2 x 9" pkg(2) **8.25**
**570-90416** 5/8 x 11" **4.65**
**570-90417** 3/4 x 11" **5.05**
**570-90418** 1 x 11" **5.55**

## ACRYLIC PLASTICS

Plastruct Acrylic products are crystal clear unless noted.

### Acrylic Balls

Measurement indicates diameter.

**570-92001** 1/8" pkg(10) **2.75**
**570-92002** 5/32" pkg(10) **2.75**
**570-92003** 3/16" pkg(10) **2.75**
**570-92004** 1/4" pkg(10) **3.25**
**570-92005** 9/32" pkg(10) **3.75**
**570-92006** 5/16" pkg(10) **3.75**
**570-92007** 3/8" pkg(10) **4.25**
**570-92008** 7/16" pkg(10) **4.75**
**570-92009** 1/2" pkg(10) **4.75**
**570-92010** 5/8" pkg(10) **6.25**
**570-92011** 3/4" pkg(5) **6.50**
**570-92012** 7/8" pkg(3) **5.30**
**570-92013** 1" pkg(2) **4.50**
**570-92014** 1-1/4" pkg(2) **4.35**

### Acrylic Cubes

Use for modern buildings, sculpture or craft projects.

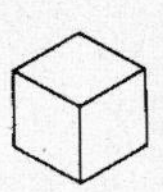

**570-92021** 1/4" pkg(10) **4.25**
**570-92022** 3/8" pkg(10) **4.75**
**570-92023** 1/2" pkg(10) **6.25**

Cubes listed below are available by Special Order (see Legend Page).

**570-92024** 5/8" pkg(5) **3.75**
**570-92025** 3/4" pkg(5) **5.25**
**570-92026** 1" pkg(3) **5.30**
**570-92027** 1-1/4" **4.65**

### Acrylic Domes

A one-piece, easy way to model ends of oil, water, gas or food storage tanks. Outside diameter shown.

**Elliptical**

**570-95741** 3/8" pkg(5) **2.00**
**570-95742** 7/16" pkg(5) **2.00**
**570-95743** 1/2" pkg(5) **2.25**
**570-95744** 9/16" pkg(5) **2.25**
**570-95745** 5/8" pkg(5) **2.75**
**570-95746** 3/4" pkg(5) **3.00**
**570-95747** 7/8" pkg(5) **3.50**
**570-95748** 1" pkg(5) **3.75**
**570-95749** 1-1/8" pkg(5) **4.00**
**570-95750** 1-1/4" pkg(5) **4.75**
**570-95751** 1-1/2" pkg(5) **6.50**
**570-95755** 2" pkg(2) **5.05**
**570-95759** 3" pkg(2) **7.85**
**570-95763** 4" **6.10**
**570-95767** 5" **7.65**
**570-95771** 6" **9.25**

**Hemispherical**

**570-95841** 3/8" pkg(5) **2.00**
**570-95842** 7/16" pkg(5) **2.00**
**570-95843** 1/2" pkg(5) **2.25**
**570-95844** 9/16" pkg(5) **2.75**
**570-95845** 5/8" pkg(5) **3.00**
**570-95846** 3/4" pkg(5) **3.50**
**570-95847** 7/8" pkg(5) **3.75**
**570-95848** 1" pkg(5) **4.00**
**570-95849** 1-1/8" pkg(5) **4.50**
**570-95850** 1-1/4" pkg(5) **5.25**
**570-95851** 1-1 /2" pkg(5) **8.25**
**570-95855** 2" pkg(2) **5.55**
**570-95859** 3" pkg(2) **9.05**
**570-95863** 4" **6.55**
**570-95867** 5" **8.45**
**570-95871** 6" **10.80**

**Plastruct**

### Acrylic Rod
All pieces are 17-1/2" long unless noted.

**Solid Round**
Simulate bracing, wiring, cabling, piping, conduit or use anywhere round stock is needed. Outside diameter shown.

**570-90291** 1/16 x 8-1/2" Long pkg(40) **7.75**
**570-90292** 1/8 x 8-1/2" Long pkg(30) **7.85**
**570-92031** 1/16" pkg(20) **7.75**
**570-92032** 1/8" pkg(10) **5.15**
**570-92033** 3/16" pkg(5) **3.25**
**570-92034** 1/4" pkg(5) **4.20**
**570-92035** 5/16" pkg(5) **6.50**
**570-92036** 3/8" pkg(3) **5.60**
**570-92037** 7/16" pkg(2) **4.65**
**570-92038** 1/2" pkg(2) **5.75**
**570-92039** 9/16" **4.00**
**570-92040** 5/8" **5.25**
**570-92041** 3/4" **6.60**

**Half-Round**
Extruded in crystal clear acrylic. Outside diameter shown.

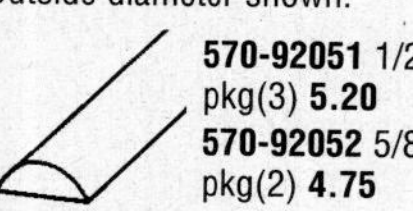

**570-92051** 1/2" pkg(3) **5.20**
**570-92052** 5/8" pkg(2) **4.75**
**570-92053** 3/4" **3.95**
**570-92054** 1" **5.95**

**Square**
Width and height shown.

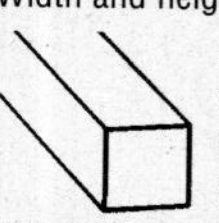

**570-92061** 1/8" pkg(10) **6.25**
**570-92062** 3/16" pkg(5) **5.75**
**570-92063** 1/4" pkg(3) **4.40**
**570-92064** 3/8" pkg(2) **4.25**
**570-92065** 1/2" **4.00**
**570-92066** 5/8" **6.95**
**570-92067** 3/4" **9.25**

**Rectangular**
Extruded in crystal clear acrylic. Width and height shown.

**570-92071** 5/8 x 1/8" pkg(3) **4.25**
**570-92072** 3/4 x 3/16" pkg(2) **4.65**
**570-92073** 1/4 x 17-1/2" pkg(2) **5.05**
**570-92074** 1 x 1/4" **4.30**
**570-92075** 3/4 x 1" **9.90**

**Spiral**

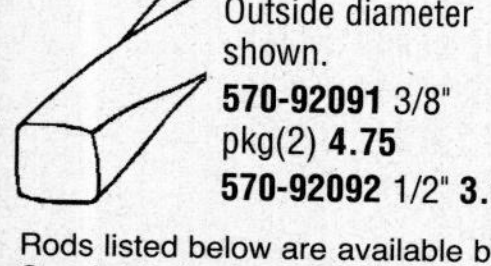

Outside diameter shown.
**570-92091** 3/8" pkg(2) **4.75**
**570-92092** 1/2" **3.65**

Rods listed below are available by Special Order (see Legend Page).
**570-92093** 5/8" **5.00**
**570-92094** 3/4" **7.30**
**570-92095** 1" **9.95**

### Acrylic Tubing
All pieces are 15" long. Outside dimensions shown.

**Round**

**570-90131** 3/32" pkg(10) **5.75**
**570-90132** 1/8" pkg(10) **6.30**
**570-90133** 3/16" pkg(7) **5.40**
**570-90134** 1/4" pkg(5) **4.75**

**Square**

**570-90241** 1/8" pkg(5) **5.80**
**570-90242** 3/16" pkg(5) **6.50**
**570-90243** 1/4" pkg(4) **5.60**

### Clear Sheet
**Butyrate & Acrylic**
Each sheet measures 7 x 12", dimension shown is thickness.

**570-91204** .040" Butyrate pkg(2) **7.75**
**570-91206** .060" Acrylic **7.95**

**Copolyester**
Each sheet measures 7 x 12", dimension shown is thickness.
**570-91251** .030" pkg(3) **7.25**
**570-91252** .040" pkg(2) **6.35**
**570-91253** .060" pkg(2) **9.25**

### Ladder Clips

**570-95435** Fits Ladder #90423 (O) pkg(5) **2.50**
**570-95437** Fits Ladder #90425 (G) pkg(5) **3.00**
**570-95438** Fits Ladder #90426 (1/16) pkg(5) **3.50**

### Fluorescent Acrylic Sheet pkg(2) 5.60 ea
Sheets are 12 x 7 x .010".

**570-91301** Blue
**570-91302** Green
**570-91303** Red
**570-91304** Yellow

### Fluorescent Acrylic Rods

**Blue**
**570-90251** 1/16 x 10" pkg(10) **4.75**
**570-90252** 3/32 x 10" pkg(8) **5.60**
**570-90253** 1/8 x 10" pkg(7) **6.40**
**570-90254** 5/32 x 10" pkg(5) **6.25**
**570-90255** 5/32 x 20" pkg(3) **7.55**
**570-90256** 1/4 x 20" pkg(2) **9.75**
**570-90257** 3/8 x 20" **9.25**

**Green**
**570-90261** 1/16 x 10" pkg(10) **4.75**
**570-90262** 3/32 x 10" pkg(8) **5.60**
**570-90263** 1/8 x 10" pkg(7) **6.40**
**570-90264** 5/32 x 10" pkg(5) **6.25**
**570-90265** 5/32 x 20" pkg(3) **7.55**
**570-90266** 1/4 x 20" pkg(2) **9.75**
**570-90267** 3/8 x 20" **9.25**

**Red**
**570-90271** 1/16 x 10" pkg(10) **4.75**
**570-90272** 3/32 x 10" pkg(8) **5.60**
**570-90273** 1/8 x 10" pkg(7) **6.40**
**570-90274** 5/32 x 10" pkg(5) **6.25**
**570-90275** 5/32 x 20" pkg(3) **7.55**
**570-90276** 1/4 x 20" pkg(2) **9.75**
**570-90277** 3/8 x 20" **9.25**

**Yellow**
**570-90281** 1/16 x 10" pkg(10) **4.75**
**570-90282** 3/32 x 10" pkg(8) **5.60**
**570-90283** 1/8 x 10" pkg(7) **6.40**
**570-90284** 5/32 x 10" pkg(5) **6.25**
**570-90285** 5/32 x 20" pkg(3) **7.55**
**570-90286** 1/4 x 20" pkg(2) **8.25**
**570-90287** 3/8 x 20" **9.75**

## CEMENT

### Plastic Solvent Cements
Plastic-fusing adhesive 2oz bottle.

570-2

570-3

570-4

**570-3** Bondene **3.95**
Bonds most alike plastic combinations.
**570-4** Weldene **4.65**
A non-toxic adhesive for bonding styrene to styrene ONLY. Dealers must order in multiples of 12.
**570-2** Plastic Weld **3.95**
This adhesive bonds styrene, ABS, butyrate, and acrylics.

## CLEAR COPOLYESTER PLASTIC

### Skylights
**Square Pyramid**
**570-93001** 1/4" pkg(2) **5.35**
**570-93002** 3/8" pkg(2) **5.55**
**570-93003** 1/2" pkg(2) **5.75**
**570-93004** 5/8" pkg(2) **6.25**
**570-93005** 3/4" pkg(2) **6.55**
**570-93006** 1" pkg(2) **7.05**

**Square Dome**
**570-93011** 1/4" pkg(2) **5.35**
**570-93012** 3/8" pkg(2) **5.55**
**570-93013** 1/2" pkg(2) **5.75**
**570-93014** 3/4" pkg(2) **6.35**
**570-93015** 1" **7.35**
**570-93016** 2" **6.60**

**Barrels**
**570-93031** 1/4 x 1/2" pkg(2) **5.55**
**570-93032** 1/4 x 3/4" pkg(2) **6.15**
**570-93033** 1/4 x 1" pkg(2) **6.55**
**570-93034** 3/8 x 3/4" pkg(2) **7.25**
**570-93035** 1/2 x 1" **4.10**
**570-93036** 1/2 x 1-1/2" **4.50**
**570-93037** 3/4 x 1-1/2" **5.05**
**570-93038** 1 x 2" **5.45**
**570-93039** 1 x 3" **5.95**
**570-93040** 1 x 4" **6.60**
**570-93041** 1-1/2 x 2" **5.60**
**570-93042** 1-1/2 x 3" **6.10**
**570-93043** 1-1/2 x 4" **6.60**

## STYRENE PLASTIC
Molded in white, unless noted. Bonds with most styrene cements. Accepts most acrylic paints; a primer coat is recommended. Dealers MUST order in multiples as shown.

### Strips, Rods & Sheets
**Styrene Strips pkg(10) 2.75 ea (Unless Noted)**
Each piece is 10" long, unless noted. Width and height shown.

**570-90710** .010 x .020"
**570-90711** .010 x .030"
**570-90712** .010 x .040"
**570-90713** .010 x .060"
**570-90714** .010 x .080"
**570-90715** .010 x .100"
**570-90716** .010 x .125"
**570-90717** .010 x .156"
**570-90718** .010 x .187"
**570-90719** .010 x .250"
**570-90721** .020 x .030"
**570-90722** .020 x .040"
**570-90723** .020 x .060"
**570-90724** .020 x .080"
**570-90725** .020 x .100"
**570-90726** .020 x .125"
**570-90727** .020 x .156"
**570-90728** .020 x .187"
**570-90729** .020 x .250"
**570-90732** .030 x .040"
**570-90733** .030 x .060"
**570-90734** .030 x .080"
**570-90735** .030 x .100"
**570-90736** .030 x .125"
**570-90737** .030 x .156"
**570-90738** .030 x .187"
**570-90739** .030 x .250"
**570-90743** .040 x .060"
**570-90744** .040 x .080"
**570-90745** .040 x .100"
**570-90746** .040 x .125"
**570-90747** .040 x .156"
**570-90748** .040 x .187"
**570-90749** .040 x .250"
**570-90754** .060 x .080"
**570-90755** .060 x .100"
**570-90756** .060 x .125"
**570-90757** .060 x .156"
**570-90758** .060 x .187"
**570-90759** .060 x .250"
**570-90765** .080 x .100" **3.25**
**570-90766** .080 x .125" **3.25**
**570-90767** .080 x .156" **3.25**
**570-90768** .080 x .187" **3.25**
**570-90769** .080 x .250" **3.25**
**570-90776** .100 x .125" **3.25**
**570-90777** .100 x .156" **3.25**
**570-90778** .100 x .187" **3.25**
**570-90779** .100 x .250" **3.25**
**570-90787** .125 x .156" **3.75**
**570-90788** .125 x .187" **3.75**
**570-90789** .125 x .250" **3.75**
**570-90798** .156 x .187" pkg(5) **1.75**
**570-90799** .156 x .250" pkg(5) **1.75**
**570-90809** .187 x .250" pkg(5) **2.25**
**570-90641** .020 x 1-1/4 x 24" pkg(5) **5.00**
**570-90642** .030 x 1-1/4 x 24" pkg(5) **5.75**

**Round Rod**
Each piece is 10" long, outside diameter shown.

**570-90849** .015" pkg(10) **2.75**
**570-90850** .010" pkg(10) **2.75**
**570-90851** .020" pkg(10) **2.75**
**570-90852** .025" pkg(10) **2.75**
**570-90853** .030" pkg(10) **2.75**
**570-90854** .035" pkg(10) **2.75**
**570-90855** .040" pkg(10) **3.25**
**570-90856** .045" pkg(10) **3.25**
**570-90857** .050" pkg(10) **3.25**
**570-90858** .060" pkg(10) **3.25**
**570-90859** .080" pkg(5) **1.75**
**570-90860** .100" pkg(5) **2.00**
**570-90861** .125" pkg(5) **2.00**
**570-90862** .156" pkg(5) **2.50**
**570-90863** .187" pkg(5) **2.75**
**570-90864** .250" pkg(5) **3.00**

**Half-Round Rod**
Each piece is 10" long, outside diameter shown.

**570-90879** .030" pkg(10) **2.75**
**570-90880** .040" pkg(10) **3.25**
**570-90881** .060" pkg(10) **3.25**
**570-90882** .080" pkg(10) **3.75**
**570-90883** .100" pkg(10) **3.75**
**570-90884** .125" pkg(5) **2.00**
**570-90885** .156" pkg(5) **2.50**
**570-90886** .187" pkg(5) **2.75**
**570-90887** .250" pkg(5) **3.00**

**Square Rod**
Each piece is 10" long, height and width shown.

**570-90709** .010" pkg(10) **2.75**
**570-90720** .020" pkg(10) **2.75**
**570-90730** .030" pkg(10) **2.75**
**570-90740** .040" pkg(10) **2.75**
**570-90750** .060" pkg(10) **2.75**
**570-90760** .080" pkg(10) **3.25**
**570-90770** .100" pkg(10) **3.25**
**570-90780** .125" pkg(10) **3.75**
**570-90790** .160" pkg(5) **1.75**
**570-90800** .190" pkg(5) **2.50**
**570-90810** .250" pkg(5) **3.00**

**Quarter-Round Rod**
Each piece is 10" long, height and width shown.

**570-90891** .030" pkg(10) **2.75**
**570-90892** .040" pkg(10) **3.25**
**570-90893** .060" pkg(10) **3.25**

**570-90894** .080" pkg(10) **3.75**
**570-90895** .100" pkg(5) **2.00**
**570-90896** .125" pkg(5) **2.00**

### Triangular Rod

Each piece is 10" long, height and width shown.

**570-90841** .030" pkg(10) **2.75**
**570-90842** .040" pkg(10) **3.25**
**570-90843** .060" pkg(10) **3.25**
**570-90844** .080" pkg(10) **3.75**
**570-90845** .100" pkg(5) **2.00**
**570-90846** .125" pkg(5) **2.00**

### Hexagonal Rod

**570-90871** .020" pkg(10) **2.75**
**570-90872** .030" pkg(10) **2.75**
**570-90873** .040" pkg(10) **3.25**
**570-90874** .060" pkg(10) **3.25**
**570-90875** .080" pkg(10) **3.75**
**570-90876** .100" pkg(5) **2.00**
**570-90877** .125" pkg(5) **2.00**

### Clear Sheet

**570-91201** .010" pkg(3) **5.60**
Measures 7 x 12", dimension shown is thickness.

### White Sheet

Each sheet measures 7 x 12", dimension shown is thickness.

**570-91101** .010" pkg(8) **4.20**
**570-91102** .020" pkg(7) **4.95**
**570-91103** .030" pkg(5) **4.50**
**570-91104** .040" pkg(4) **4.75**
**570-91105** .060" pkg(3) **5.45**
**570-91106** .080" pkg(2) **4.75**
**570-91107** .100" pkg(2) **6.15**
**570-91108** .125" pkg(2) **7.85**

### Colored Sheet 5.35 ea

Each sheet measures 7 x 12", .020" thick.

**570-91151** Red pkg(2)
**570-91161** Beige pkg(2)
**570-91171** Gray pkg(2)

## Styrene Tubing

Each piece is 15" long.

### Round

Outside diameter shown.

**570-90603** 3/32" pkg(15) **5.75**
**570-90604** 1/8" pkg(10) **4.25**
**570-90605** 3/16" pkg(8) **3.75**
**570-90606** 1/4" pkg(7) **4.30**
**570-90607** 5/16" pkg(6) **4.55**
**570-90608** 3/8" pkg(5) **4.25**

### Square

Height and width shown.

**570-90621** 1/8" pkg(7) **4.30**
**570-90622** 3/16" pkg(6) **4.25**
**570-90623** 1/4" pkg(5) **3.75**
**570-90624** 5/16" pkg(5) **4.50**
**570-90625** 3/8" pkg(4) **3.95**

### Rectangular

Height and width shown.

**570-90631** 1/4 x 3/16" pkg(5) **3.75**
**570-90632** 5/16 x 1/4" pkg(5) **4.50**
**570-90633** 3/8 x 1/4" pkg(4) **3.95**

## Styrene Structural Shapes

### Angles

**570-90501** 3/64 x 10" pkg(10) **4.25**
**570-90502** 1/16 x 10" pkg(10) **4.75**
**570-90503** 3/32 x 15" pkg(8) **4.95**
**570-90504** 1/8 x 15" pkg(7) **5.00**
**570-90505** 3/16 x 24" pkg(5) **4.75**
**570-90506** 1/4 x 24" pkg(5) **5.25**
**570-90507** 5/16 x 24" pkg(4) **5.15**
**570-90508** 3/8 x 24" pkg(4) **5.60**

### I-Beams

**570-90511** 1/16 x 10" pkg(10) **4.25**
**570-90512** 3/32 x 10" pkg(10) **4.75**
**570-90513** 1/8 x 15" pkg(8) **4.95**
**570-90514** 5/32 x 15" pkg(6) **4.55**
**570-90515** 3/16 x 24" pkg(5) **4.75**
**570-90516** 1/4 x 24" pkg(5) **5.25**
**570-90517** 5/16 x 24" pkg(4) **5.15**
**570-90518** 3/8 x 15" pkg(5) **4.00**
**570-90519** 7/16 x 15" pkg(5) **4.75**
**570-90520** 1/2 x 15" pkg(4) **4.55**
**570-90521** 9/16 x 15" pkg(3) **3.80**
**570-90522** 5/8 x 15" pkg(3) **4.10**

### Channels

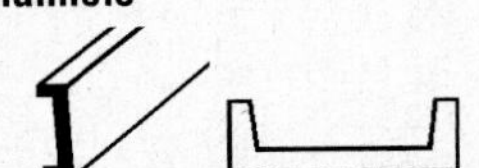

**570-90531** 1/16 x 10" pkg(10) **4.25**
**570-90532** 3/32 x 10" pkg(10) **4.75**
**570-90533** 1/8 x 15" pkg(8) **4.95**
**570-90534** 5/32 x 15" pkg(6) **4.55**
**570-90535** 3/16 x 15" pkg(5) **4.50**
**570-90536** 1/4 x 24" pkg(5) **5.25**
**570-90537** 5/16 x 24" pkg(4) **5.15**

### Deep Channels

**570-90581** 1/16 x 10" pkg(10) **4.25**
**570-90582** 3/32 x 10" pkg(10) **4.75**
**570-90583** 1/8 x 15" pkg(8) **4.95**
**570-90584** 3/16 x 15" pkg(5) **4.00**
**570-90585** 1/4 x 24" pkg(5) **5.25**

### H Columns

**570-90541** 1/16 x 10" pkg(10) **4.25**
**570-90542** 3/32 x 15" pkg(10) **5.75**
**570-90543** 1/8 x 15" pkg(8) **5.00**
**570-90544** 5/32 x 15" pkg(6) **4.55**
**570-90545** 3/16 x 24" pkg(5) **5.00**
**570-90546** 1/4 x 15" pkg(5) **3.75**
**570-90547** 5/16 x 15" pkg(5) **4.75**
**570-90548** 3/8 x 15" pkg(4) **4.55**

### Tees

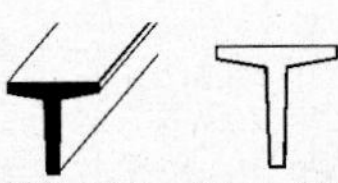

**570-90561** 3/64 x 10" pkg(10) **4.25**
**570-90562** 1/16 x 10" pkg(10) **4.75**
**570-90563** 3/32 x 15" pkg(8) **4.95**
**570-90564** 1/8 x 15" pkg(7) **5.00**
**570-90565** 3/16 x 24" pkg(5) **4.75**
**570-90566** 1/4 x 24" pkg(5) **5.25**

### Zees

**570-90591** 1/16 x 10" pkg(10) **4.75**
**570-90592** 3/32 x 10" pkg(9) **5.15**
**570-90593** 1/8 x 15" pkg(8) **5.75**
**570-90594** 3/16 x 15" pkg(5) **4.00**
**570-90595** 1/4 x 24" pkg(5) **5.25**

### Plastic Letters 7.95 ea

**570-96001** 5/64"
**570-96002** 5/32"

### Balcony Railings pkg(2)

Molded in brown.

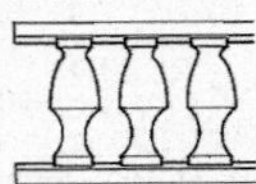

**570-90901** N Scale 6-1/2" **6.40**
**570-90902** HO Scale 6-1/2" **7.10**
**570-90903** O Scale 6-1/2" **7.60**
**570-90904** Victorian Style Railing/Trim 1/4 x 3 1/2" **3.35**

### Ladders

**570-90671** N Scale 3" pkg(2) **1.95**
**570-90672** HO Scale 5" pkg(2) **2.25**

### Handrails pkg(2)

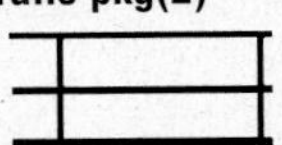

**570-90681** N Scale 3-5/8" **2.00**
**570-90682** HO Scale 6" **2.25**

### Stairs pkg(2)

**570-90661** N Scale 3-5/8" **1.95**
**570-90662** HO Scale 5" **2.55**

### Open Web Trusses

**Warren Style 2**

**570-90651** 1/8 x 6" pkg(2) **3.40**
**570-90652** 3/16 x 6" pkg(2) **3.95**
**570-90653** 1/4 x 6" pkg(2) **4.35**
**570-90654** 3/8 x 6" pkg(2) **5.05**
**570-90655** 1/2 x 12" pkg(2) **5.75**
**570-90656** 5/8 x 12" pkg(2) **6.50**
**570-90657** 3/4 x 12" pkg(2) **7.35**
**570-90658** 1 x 12" pkg(2) **8.35**

**Pratt Style**

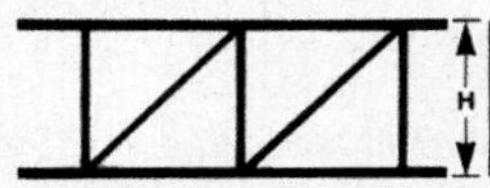


**570-90921** 1/4 x 4" pkg(2) **4.75**
**570-90922** 5/16 x 4" pkg(2) **5.05**
**570-90923** 7/16 x 7" pkg(2) **5.35**
**570-90924** 43/64 x 7" pkg(2) **5.80**
**570-90925** 27/32 x 8" pkg(2) **6.35**
**570-90926** 1-1/4 x 7" pkg(2) **7.15**
**570-90927** 1-5/8 x 8" pkg(2) **8.25**

**Cellform Style**

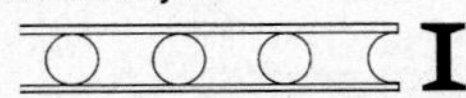

**570-90931** 1/8 x 4" pkg(2) **5.05**
**570-90932** 7/32 x 4" pkg(2) **5.35**
**570-90933** 5/16 x 4" pkg(2) **5.55**
**570-90934** 13/32 x 4" pkg(2) **5.75**

### Stair Rails pkg(2)

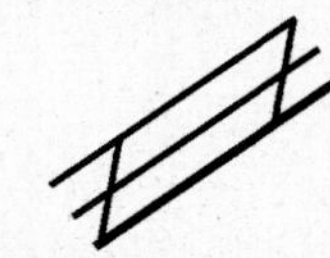

**570-90691** N Scale 3-5/8" **1.95**
**570-90692** HO Scale 6" **2.25**

### Lattice

**570-90918** 4-1/2 x 2-1/2" w/ 3/8" Pattern Spacing **4.95**
**570-90919** 3-5/8" x 2" w/ 1/8" Pattern Spacing **4.50**

### Staircase

**570-90948** Spiral **7.30**
**570-90954** Custom 7 x 12" **7.90**
**570-90961** Custom Spiral 2-1/4 x 13/32 x 5/64" **9.20**

### Steps/Louvers

Vacuum-formed or injection-molded, dimensions shown indicate width and length.

**570-90951** N Scale 34° 3-7/8 x 2-1/8" **4.65**
**570-90956** N Scale 17° 3-7/8 x 2-1/8" **3.00**
**570-90952** HO Scale 34° 3-7/8 x 2-1/8" **5.60**
**570-90957** HO Scale 17° 3-7/8 x 2-1/8" **3.25**
**570-90953** O Scale 34° 7 x 12" **7.90**

### Wood Sheet Planking

Measurement next to part number indicates spacing.

**12 x 7" 30 x 17.5cm pkg(2)**

**570-91535** .0625" **9.75**
**570-91536** .125" **9.75**
**570-91762** 1/16" **9.95**

**24 x 7" 60 x 17.5cm 9.95 ea**

**570-91761** 1/16" pkg(2)
**570-91763** .078" pkg(2)
**570-91764** 1/8" pkg(2)

## PATTERNED SHEETS

Vacuum formed from .020" styrene. Scales shown indicate relative size. Sheets measure 12 x 7" unless noted, dimension shown is the size of an individual object in the pattern.

### Brick

**570-91611** .145" (HO) pkg(2) **9.75**
**570-91608** .062" (N) pkg(2) **9.75**
**570-91609** .100" (TT) pkg(2) **9.75**
**570-91613** .187" (O) pkg(2) **9.75**
**570-91616** .375" (G) 24 x 7" **9.95**
**570-91601** .730" (1/12) 24 x 7" **9.95**

### Brick Relief

**570-91603** .720" (1/12) **14.95**
Includes two sets of arches, sills and corners. Use with Brick Sheet 570-91601, sold separately. Sheet measures 24 x 7".

### Rough Brick

**570-91605** .150" (HO) pkg(2) **9.75**
**570-91606** .200" (O) pkg(2) **9.75**
**570-91604** .400" (G) pkg(2) **9.75**
**570-91616** .400" (G) 24 x 7" **9.95**
**570-91607** .800" (1/12) 24 x 7" **9.95**

### Concrete Block

**570-91620** .175" (HO) pkg(2) **9.75**
**570-91621** .325" (O) pkg(2) **9.75**
**570-91624** .650" (G) pkg(2) **9.75**
**570-91618** .650" (G) 24 x 7" **9.95**
**570-91622** 1.30" (1/12) 24 x 7" **9.95**

### Flooring pkg(2) 9.75 ea (Unless Noted)

**Planking**

**570-91531** .078" (HO)
**570-91530** .039" (N)
**570-91532** .120" (O)
**570-91533** .210" (G)
**570-91766** .210" (G) Single Sheet 24 x 7" 60 x 17.5cm **9.95**

### Square Tiles

For use with all scales.

**White**

**570-91540** .050"
**570-91541** .055"
**570-91543** .075"
**570-91539** .125"
**570-91542** .180"
**570-91544** .235"
**570-91545** .485"
**570-91546** .960"

**Red**

**570-91749** .125"
**570-91750** .050"
**570-91751** .055"
**570-91752** .180"

## Plastruct

570-91753 .075"
570-91754 .235"
570-91755 .485"
570-91756 .960"

Clear
570-91741 .055"
570-91743 .075"
570-91739 .125"
570-91742 .180"
570-91744 .235"
570-91745 .485"
570-91746 .960"

### Roofing 9.75 ea (Unless Noted)

**Asphalt Shingle**

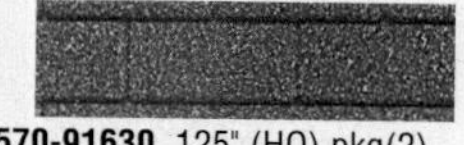

570-91630 .125" (HO) pkg(2)
570-91631 .250" (O) pkg(2)
570-91633 .475" (G) pkg(2)
570-91642 .475" (G) 24 x 7" **9.95**
570-91636 .980" (1/12) 24 x 7" **9.95**

**Ribbed Metal pkg(2)**

570-91511 .093" (HO)
570-91512 .200" (O)
570-91513 .287" (G)

**Scalloped Tile**

570-91650 .125" (HO) pkg(2)
570-91651 .250" (O) pkg(2)
570-91654 .375" (G) pkg(2)
570-91643 .375" (G) 24 x 7" **9.95**
570-91653 .785" (1/12) 24 x 7" **9.95**

**Spanish Tile**

570-91638 .087" (HO) pkg(2)
570-91640 .048" (N) pkg(2)
570-91637 .125" (O) pkg(2)
570-91632 .250" (G) pkg(2)
570-91619 .250" (G) 24 x 7" **9.95**
570-91639 .500" (1/12) 24 x 7" **9.95**

**Wood Shake Shingles**

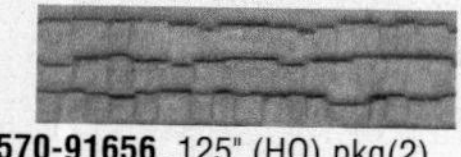

570-91656 .125" (HO) pkg(2)
570-91655 .250" (O) pkg(2)
570-91659 .375" (G) pkg(2)
570-91644 .375" (G) 24 x 7" **9.95**
570-91658 .750" (1/12) 24 x 7" **9.95**

**Ridged Clay Tile pkg(2)**

570-91665 .110" (HO)
570-91666 .220" (O)

### Siding pkg(2) 9.75 ea (Unless Noted)

For use with all scales.

**Clapboard Siding**

570-91550 .062"
570-91551 .125"
570-91552 .187"
570-91554 .250" 11 x 7"
570-91558 .250" 22 x 7" **9.95**
570-91556 .312" 11 x 7"
570-91769 .312" 22 x 7" **9.95**
570-91767 .375" 24 x 7" **9.95**
570-91768 .375" 14 x 24" **16.95**

**Corrugated Siding**

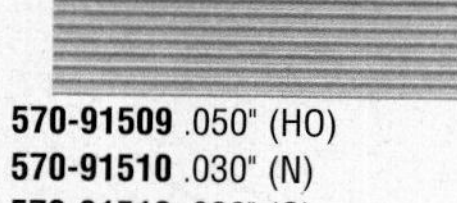

570-91509 .050" (HO)
570-91510 .030" (N)
570-91519 .080" (O)
570-91520 .125" (1/32) 11 x 7"
570-91521 .187" (G) 11 x 7"
570-91522 .250" (1/16) 11 x 7"

### Stone pkg(2) 9.75 ea (Unless Noted)

**Dressed Stone/Block**

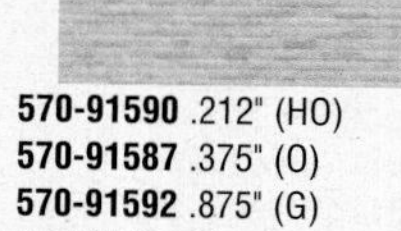

570-91590 .212" (HO)
570-91587 .375" (O)
570-91592 .875" (G)
570-91774 24 x 7 x 1-3/4" **9.95**

**Interlocking Paving**

570-91670 .082" (HO)
570-91671 .150" (O)
570-91672 .350" (G)
570-91645 .350" (G) 24 x 7" **9.95**
570-91673 .650" (1/12) 24 x 7" **9.95**

**Random/Field Stone**

570-91581 .170" (HO)
570-91580 .240" (HO)

**Random Coursed Stone**

570-91561 .312" (HO)
570-91562 .100" (N)
570-91560 .450" (O)

**Field Stone**

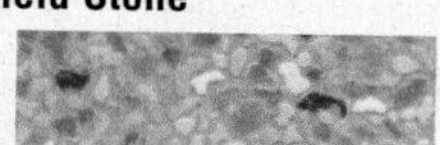

570-91563 .250" (HO)
570-91565 .325" (O)
570-91564 .575" (G)
570-91583 .750" (1/12) 24 x 7" **9.95**

**Round Field Stone**

570-91591 .810" (1/12)

**Random Polished**

570-91582 .225" (HO)
570-91584 .125" (N)
570-91588 .312" (O)
570-91589 .375" (G)
570-91615 .375" (G) 24 x 7" **9.95**
570-91586 1" (1/12) 24 x 7" **9.95**

**Patio Stone**

570-91593 .750" (G)

**Stone Wall**

570-91559 .310" (All)

**Rock Embankment**

570-91570 .125" (HO)
570-91571 .225" (O)

**Stucco Wall**

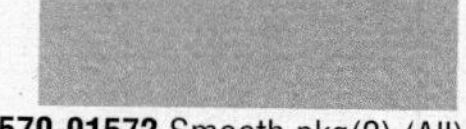

570-91572 Smooth pkg(2) (All)
570-91573 Coarse pkg(2) (All)

### Safety Tread

**Checker Plate**

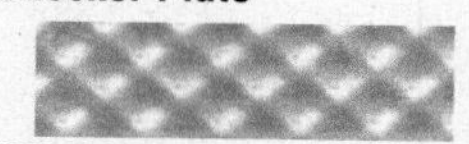

570-91680 .125" (HO) Clear pkg(2) **9.75**

**Tread Plate pkg(2) 6.25 ea (Unless Noted)**

570-91681 .100" (HO) pkg(2) **9.75**
570-91701 .035" (Z) 3-7/8 x 2-1/4"
570-91702 .055" (N) 3-7/8 x 2-1/4"
570-91703 .200" (O) 3-7/8 x 2-1/4"
570-91704 .280" (G) 3-7/8 x 2-1/4"

**Double Diamond Plate pkg(2) 10.75 ea**

570-91682 .150" (G)
570-91683 .187" (1/16)



**Single Diamond Plate pkg(2) 10.75 ea**

570-91687 .030" (HO)
570-91684 .050" (O)
570-91686 .125" (1/16)

**Rubber Tread pkg(2)**
3-7/8 x 2-1/4"

570-91711 .070 (O) **6.25**
570-91712 .140 (G) **6.25**
570-90125 3/64" pkg(25) **11.85**
570-90126 1/16" pkg(25) **13.20**
570-90127 3/32" pkg(25) **15.20**
570-90128 1/8" pkg(25) **17.20**

## CORK SHEETS

570-94571 12 x 12 x 1/16"
30 x 30cm x 1.5mm **5.60**

## MIRROR SHEETS

### 4 x 12" pkg(2) 16.80 ea

570-91360 Silver
570-91361 Bronze
570-91362 Gold
570-91363 Copper
570-91364 Smoke Gray
570-91365 Brass
570-91366 Blue
570-91367 Green
570-91368 Pink
570-91369 Violet

### 12 x 12" pkg(2) 22.40 ea

570-91370 Silver
570-91371 Bronze
570-91372 Gold
570-91373 Copper
570-91374 Smoke Gray
570-91375 Brass
570-91376 Blue
570-91377 Green
570-91378 Pink
570-91379 Violet

## TUBE FITTINGS & ACCESSORIES

Parts are molded in Butyrate (white or gray) or ABS plastics as noted.

### Column Base Mounts pkg(5)

570-95411 Fits 570-90063 **2.75**
570-95412 Fits 570-90064 **3.00**
570-95413 Fits 570-90065 **3.50**
570-95414 Fits 570-90066 **3.75**
570-95415 Fits 570-90067 & 7/16" **4.00**
570-95416 Fits 1/2 & 9/16" **4.25**

Mounts listed below are available by Special Order (see Legend Page).
570-95417 Fits 5/8 & 3/4" **4.75**

### Column Blocks pkg(5)

570-95401 Fits 570-90205 **2.50**
570-95403 Fits 1/2" **3.00**
570-95404 Fits 9/16" **3.75**
570-95405 Fits 5/8" **4.00**
570-95406 Fits 3/4" **3.75**

Block listed below is available by Special Order (see Legend Page).
570-95402 Fits 7/16" **2.75**

### Couplings pkg(5)

Clear Butyrate plastic.

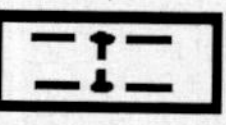

570-95081 Fits 570-90101 **2.00**
570-95082 Fits 570-90102 **2.00**
570-95083 Fits 570-90103 **2.25**
570-95084 Fits 570-90104 **2.25**
570-95085 Fits 570-90103 **2.00**
570-95086 Fits 570-90104 **2.00**
570-95087 Fits 570-90105 **2.25**
570-95088 Fits 570-90106 **2.25**
570-95090 Fits 570-90108 **2.75**

Coupling listed below is available by Special Order (see Legend Page).
570-95089 Fits 570-90107 **2.75**

### Elbows

White Butyrate plastic

**90° Elbows pkg(5)**

570-95001 Fits 570-90103 **2.00**
570-95002 Fits 570-90104 **2.25**
570-95003 Fits 570-90105 **2.25**
570-95004 Fits 570-90106 **2.50**
570-95005 Fits 570-90107 **2.50**
570-95006 Fits 570-90108 **2.75**

**90° Female Elbows pkg(5)**

570-95041 Fits 570-90103 **2.00**
570-95042 Fits 570-90104 **2.25**
570-95043 Fits 570-90105 **2.25**
570-95044 Fits 570-90106 **2.50**
570-95045 Fits 570-90107 **2.50**
570-95046 Fits 570-90108 **2.75**

**45° Elbows pkg(5)**

570-95021 Fits 570-90103 **2.00**
570-95022 Fits 570-90104 **2.25**
570-95023 Fits 570-90105 **2.25**
570-95024 Fits 570-90106 **2.50**
570-95025 Fits 570-90107 **2.50**
570-95026 Fits 570-90108 **2.75**

**45° Female Elbows pkg(5)**

570-95061 Fits 570-90103 **2.00**
570-95062 Fits 570-90104 **2.25**
570-95063 Fits 570-90105 **2.25**
570-95064 Fits 570-90106 **2.50**

## Plastruct

**570-95065** Fits 570-90107 **2.50**
**570-95066** Fits 570-90108 **2.75**

### Five Diameter Bends pkg(5)

**570-95101** Fits 570-90105 **2.75**
**570-95102** Fits 570-90106 **3.25**
**570-95103** Fits 570-90107 **3.50**
**570-95104** Fits 570-90108 **3.75**

### Three Diameter Bends pkg(5)

**570-95111** Fits 570-90105 **2.75**
**570-95112** Fits 570-90106 **3.00**
**570-95113** Fits 570-90107 **3.25**
**570-95114** Fits 570-90108 **3.50**

### Flanges pkg(5)

White Butyrate plastic.

**570-95171** Fits 570-90101 **2.00**
**570-95172** Fits 570-90102 **2.00**
**570-95173** Fits 570-90103 **2.00**
**570-95174** Fits 570-90104 **2.25**
**570-95175** Fits 570-90105 **2.25**
**570-95176** Fits 570-90106 **2.50**
**570-95177** Fits 570-90107 **2.50**
**570-95178** Fits 570-90108 **2.75**

### Light Shades pkg(5)

Molded in Green ABS plastic, with open center for mounting.

**570-95901** 5/16" O.D. **2.25**
**570-95902** 7/16" O.D. **2.75**
**570-95903** 5/8" O.D. **3.00**
**570-95904** 15/16" O.D. **3.50**

### Manways pkg(3)

Molded in Gray ABS plastic.
O.D. = Outside diameter.

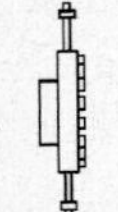
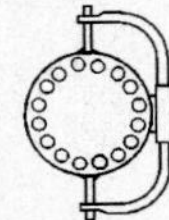

**570-95641** 13/16" O.D. **2.75**
**570-95642** 1-1/16" O.D. **3.85**
**570-95643** 1-1/2" O.D. **4.85**

### Motors pkg(3)

Molded in Green ABS plastic.

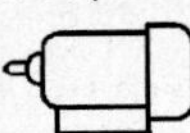

**570-95911** 3/8" **2.75**
**570-95912** 1/2" **3.05**
**570-95913** 5/8" **3.50**
**570-95914** 3/4" **3.95**

### Motor & Pump Sets

Each set includes a nonoperating motor, pump and base plate. Molded in Gray and Green ABS.

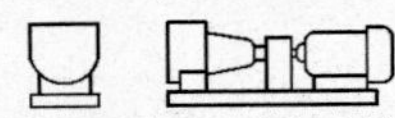

**570-95922** 1-1/16 x 1/4 x 1/2" **3.65**
**570-95923** 1-9/16 x 3/8 x 5/8" **4.00**
**570-95924** 1-5/8 x 1/2 x 5/8" **4.30**
**570-95929** 2-7/32 x 5/8 x 3/4" **5.60**

### Nozzles pkg(5)

Gray ABS plastic.

**570-95602** Fits 570-90102 **2.00**
**570-95603** Fits 570-90103 **2.50**
**570-95604** Fits 570-90104 **2.50**
**570-95605** Fits 570-90105 **2.75**
**570-95606** Fits 570-90106 **2.75**
**570-95608** Fits 570-90108 **3.00**

Nozzels listed below are available by Special Order (see Legend Page).
**570-95601** Fits 570-90101 **2.00**
**570-95607** Fits 570-90107 **3.00**

### Reducers pkg(5)

White Butyrate plastic.

#### Concentric

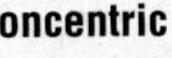

**570-95132** Reduces 90104 to 90103 **2.25**
**570-95133** Reduces 90105 to 90103 **2.50**
**570-95134** Reduces 90106 to 90104 **2.50**
**570-95135** Reduces 90106 to 90105 **2.75**
**570-95136** Reduces 90107 to 90105 **2.75**
**570-95137** Reduces 90107 to 90106 **3.25**
**570-95139** Reduces 90108 to 90107 **3.50**

#### Eccentric

**570-95161** Reduces 90105 to 90103 **2.25**
**570-95162** Reduces 90606 to 90604 **2.50**
**570-95163** Reduces 90607 to 90605 **2.75**
**570-95164** Reduces 90608 to 90606 **3.25**

### Rings pkg(5)

Molded in Gray ABS plastic.

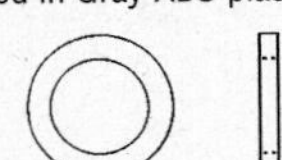

**570-95621** Fits 3/8" **2.00**
**570-95622** Fits 7/16" **2.25**
**570-95623** Fits 1/2" **2.75**
**570-95624** Fits 9/16" **3.00**
**570-95625** Fits 5/8" **3.50**
**570-95626** Fits 3/4" **3.75**
**570-95627** Fits 7/8" **4.00**
**570-95628** Fits 1" **4.50**
**570-95629** Fits 1-1/8" **4.75**
**570-95630** Fits 1-1/4" **5.00**

### Stub-In Tees pkg(5)

White Butyrate plastic.

**570-95221** Fits 570-90105 **2.25**
**570-95222** Fits 570-90106 **2.25**
**570-95223** Fits 570-90107 **2.50**
**570-95224** Fits 570-90108 **2.50**

### Tees pkg(5)

White Butyrate plastic.

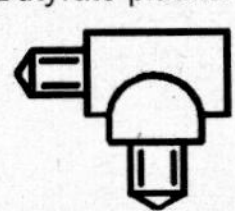

**570-95201** 3/32" **2.00**
**570-95202** Fits 570-90104 **2.25**
**570-95203** Fits 570-90105 **2.25**
**570-95204** Fits 570-90106 **2.50**
**570-95205** Fits 570-90107 **2.50**
**570-95206** Fits 570-90108 **2.75**

### Snap-On Tees pkg(5)

White Butyrate plastic.

**570-95241** Fits 570-90101 **1.75**
**570-95242** Fits 570-90102 **1.75**
**570-95243** Fits 570-90103 **2.00**
**570-95244** Fits 570-90104 **2.00**
**570-95245** Fits 570-90105 **2.25**
**570-95246** Fits 570-90106 **2.25**
**570-95247** Fits 570-90107 **2.50**
**570-95248** Fits 570-90108 **2.50**

### Lateral Tees pkg(5)

**570-95271** 1/16" **2.50**
**570-95272** 3/32" **2.75**
**570-95273** 1/8" **3.00**
**570-95274** 3/16" **3.50**

### Tube Caps pkg(5)

White Butyrate plastic.

**570-95301** Fits 570-90103 **2.00**
**570-95302** Fits 570-90104 **2.25**
**570-95303** Fits 570-90105 **2.25**
**570-95304** Fits 570-90106 **2.75**
**570-95305** Fits 570-90107 **2.75**
**570-95306** Fits 570-90108 **3.00**

### Support Triangles pkg(5)

**570-95421** 1/4" **1.45**
**570-95422** 3/8" **1.45**
**570-95423** 1/2" **1.45**
**570-95424** 5/8" **1.75**
**570-95425** 3/4" **1.75**
**570-95426** 7/8" **2.00**
**570-95427** 1" **2.00**

### Valves

#### Check Valves pkg(5)

**570-95482** To Fit Tube #2 **2.25**
**570-95483** To Fit Tube #3 **2.50**
**570-95484** To Fit Tube #4 **2.50**
**570-95485** To Fit Tube #6 **2.75**
**570-95486** To Fit Tube #8 **2.75**
**570-95487** To Fit Tube #10 **3.25**
**570-95488** To Fit Tube #12 **3.50**

#### Gate Valves pkg(5)

Gray Butyrate plastic.

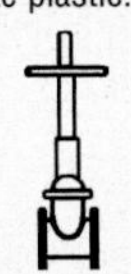

**570-95501** Fits 570-90101 **2.25**
**570-95502** Fits 570-90102 **2.25**
**570-95503** Fits 570-90103 **2.50**
**570-95504** Fits 570-90104 **2.50**
**570-95505** Fits 570-90105 **2.75**
**570-95506** Fits 570-90106 **2.75**
**570-95507** Fits 570-90107 **3.25**
**570-95508** Fits 570-90108 **3.50**

#### Control Valves pkg(5)

Gray Butyrate plastic.

**570-95521** Fits 570-90101 **2.25**
**570-95522** Fits 570-90102 **2.25**
**570-95523** Fits 570-90103 **2.50**
**570-95524** Fits 570-90104 **2.50**
**570-95525** Fits 570-90105 **2.75**
**570-95526** Fits 570-90106 **2.75**

#### Angle Valves pkg(5)

Gray Butyrate plastic.

**570-95532** Fits 570-90102 **2.00**
**570-95533** Fits 570-90103 **2.50**
**570-95534** Fits 570-90104 **2.50**
**570-95535** Fits 570-90105 **2.75**
**570-95536** Fits 570-90106 **2.75**

#### Relief Valves pkg(5)

**570-95541** Fits 570-90101 **2.25**
**570-95542** Fits 570-90102 **2.25**
**570-95543** Fits 570-90103 **2.50**
**570-95544** Fits 570-90104 **2.50**
**570-95545** Fits 570-90105 **2.75**
**570-95546** Fits 570-90106 **2.75**

#### Plug Valves pkg(5)

Gray Butyrate plastic.

**570-95551** Fits 570-90102 **2.25**
**570-95552** Fits 570-90103 **2.50**
**570-95553** Fits 570-90104 **2.50**
**570-95554** Fits 570-90105 **2.75**
**570-95555** Fits 570-90106 **2.75**

### Support Clips pkg(5)

Gray Butyrate plastic.

**570-95561** Fits 570-90101 **1.75**
**570-95562** Fits 570-90102 **1.75**
**570-95563** Fits 570-90103 **2.00**
**570-95564** Fits 570-90104 **2.00**
**570-95565** Fits 570-90105 **2.25**
**570-95566** Fits 570-90106 **2.25**
**570-95567** Fits 570-90107 **2.50**
**570-95568** Fits 570-90108 **2.50**

### Support Flanges pkg(5)

**570-95582** 1/16" **1.50**
**570-95583** 3/32" **1.75**
**570-95584** 1/8" **1.75**

### Saddles pkg(5)

**570-95661** Fits 570-90106 **1.75**
**570-95662** Fits 570-90107 **2.00**
**570-95663** Fits 570-90108 **2.00**
**570-95664** Fits 7/16" **2.25**
**570-95665** Fits 1/2" **2.25**
**570-95666** Fits 9/16" **2.75**
**570-95667** Fits 5/8" **2.75**
**570-95668** Fits 3/4" **3.00**
**570-95669** Fits 7/8" pkg(3) **1.70**
**570-95670** Fits 1" pkg(3) **2.00**
**570-95671** Fits 1-1/8" pkg(3) **2.15**
**570-95672** Fits 1-1/4" pkg(3) **2.30**

### Flat Caps

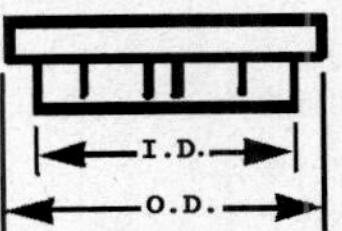


**570-95701** 1/14" pkg(5) **2.00**
**570-95707** 3/4" pkg(5) **2.25**

### Handwheels

**570-95589** pkg(4) **3.30**

### Wheels

**570-95591** 1/4" pkg(10) **2.25**
**570-95592** 3/8" pkg(10) **2.25**
**570-95593** 1/2" pkg(10) **2.95**
**570-95594** 5/8" pkg(5) **1.50**
**570-95595** 3/4" pkg(5) **1.50**
**570-95596** 7/8" pkg(5) **1.75**
**570-95597** 1" pkg(5) **1.75**
**570-95598** 1-1/8" pkg(5) **1.75**

### 45° Stub Tees pkg(5)

**570-95261** Fits 570-90105 **2.25**
**570-95262** Fits 570-90106 **2.50**
**570-95263** Fits 570-90107 **2.50**
**570-95264** Fits 570-90108 **2.75**

2008
HO
Model Railroad
Reference Book

# PARTS

Models and Photo by Gary Hoover

If you grew up in a small town, the most exciting part of your day was the sound of every far-away whistle. A fast bike ride out to your favorite spot, and you were sure to be rewarded with a friendly toot or wave from the passing train crews. Just down the line from Sullivan's curve, there's plenty of entertainment for young railfans as a venerable 2-10-2 begins the uphill shove behind an eastbound freight, while a set of F7s growl westward.

The glorious days of summer live on along Gary Hoover's "Santa Fe 1951" layout in Florissant, Missouri. The westbound is headed up by Stewart Fs, finished with Polly Scale paint and lettered with Micro Scale decals. The steamer and caboose are both imported brass models. To build the Santa Fe-style switch stand, Gary combined parts from Utah Pacific and Details West. Figures from Woodland Scenics and Preiser enjoy the passing trains. Other details along the right-of-way include Rix poles and a Walthers Code 83 turnout.

From complete scene to a single model, small details really make a big difference! Finding the right parts to add those extra touches of realism is easy with the wide selection of items you'll find on the following pages.

## WALTHERS

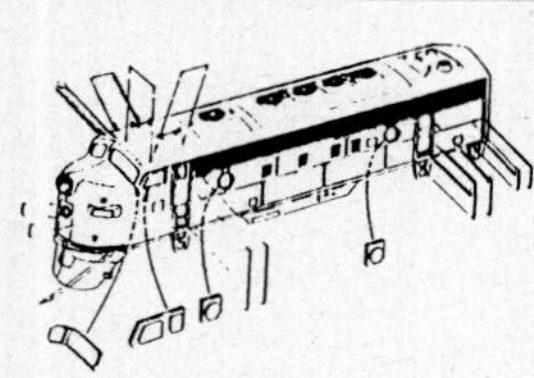

### F Unit Super Detailing Kit

**933-822** 51 Pieces **5.98**
Dress up F7 and F9 A and B units with this superdetailing kit. Designed especially for Athearn Blue Box and Ready-To-Roll™ Fs, the kit contains enough parts for one A and one B Unit, including clear plastic windshield, windows and port holes, pre-formed wire grab irons and two clear plastic headlight lenses. Complete instructions and placement diagram included.

## AM MODELS

Parts are molded in brown plastic (unless noted).

### Doors & Windows 2.20 ea

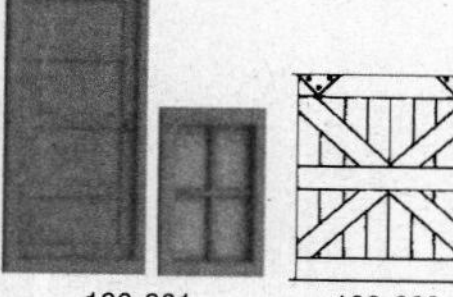
129-201 129-203

**129-201** Doors & Windows Includes four doors and 12 windows.

**129-203** Freight Doors pkg(4)
Molded in white plastic.

### Pallets & Skids

**129-50112** pkg(12) **2.20**

**129-50136** pkg(36) **5.10**

**RIVAROSSI LOCOMOTIVE PARTS ARE AVAILABLE WHILE SUPPLIES LAST**

All Rivarossi locomotives come complete with instructions featuring an exploded view of the loco with parts labeled with item numbers that correspond with the following list. All items listed below are currently available from Walthers, but are not stocked in the Walthers warehouse. Walthers orders them directly from Rivarossi and ships them as soon as they are received.

## HEISLER LOCO PARTS 50.00 ea (UNLESS NOTED)

### Parts For #5461 - McCloud River

**635-L7045461CA** Cab Assembly & Fuel Bunker For #R5461

**635-L7045461SS** Complete Boiler Assembly for #R5461

### Parts For #5462 - Georgia Pacific

**635-L7045462CA** Cab Assembly w/Fuel Bunker for #R5462

**635-L7045462SS** Complete Boiler Assembly for #R5462

### Parts For #5463 - Pacific Lumber

**635-L7045463CA** Cab Assembly w/Fuel Bunker for #R5463

**635-L7045463SS** Complete Boiler Assembly for #R5463

### Parts For #5464 - Ohio Match Co.

**635-L7045464CA** Cab Assembly w/Fuel Bunker for #R5464

**635-L7045464SS** Complete Boiler Assembly for #R5464

### Parts For #5465 - Coos Bay Lumber Co.

**635-L7045465CA** Cab Assembly w/Fuel Bunker for #R5465

**635-L7045465SS** Complete Boiler Assembly for #R5465

### Parts For #5466 - West Side Lumber Co.

**635-L7045466CA** Cab Assembly w/Fuel Bunker for #R5466

**635-L7045466SS** Complete Boiler Assembly for #R5466

### Parts For #5467 - Weyerhaeuser Timber Co.

**635-L7045467CA** Cab Assembly w/Fuel Bunker for #R5467

**635-L7045467SS** Complete Boiler Assembly for #R5467

### Parts For #5468 - St. Regis Paper Co.

**635-L7045468CA** Cab Assembly w/Fuel Bunker for #R5468

**635-L7045468SS** Complete Boiler Assembly for #R5468

### Parts For #5469 - Cass Scenic Railway

**635-L7045469CA** Cab Assembly w/Fuel Bunker for #R5469

**635-L7045469SS** Complete Boiler Assembly for #R5469

### Weights

**635-L70PV5468Z** Tender Weight - 3-Truck Models Only **30.00**



## ACCURAIL®

Molded plastic parts can be adapted to all types of kits or scratchbuilt models.

## FREIGHT CAR DETAILS

### ACF Hopper

**112-118** Hatches & Outlets **1.49**

### Doors pkg(4) 1.49 ea

#### Plug

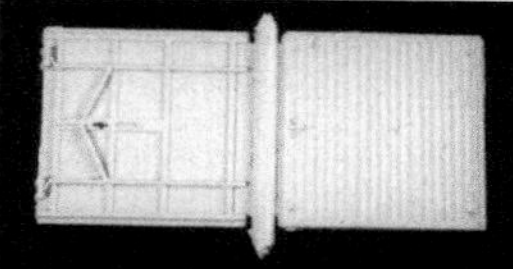

**112-110** 10' w/Standard Youngstown

**112-115** 8'

#### PS-1

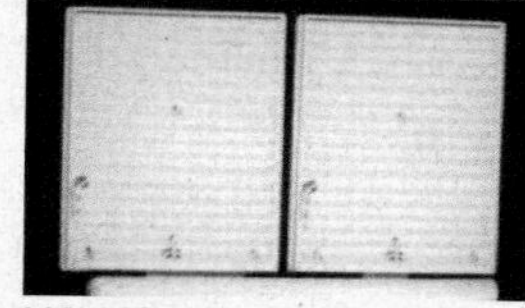

**112-112** 8'

**112-116** 6'

#### Superior Panel

**112-113** 6'

**112-114** 7'

#### Youngstown

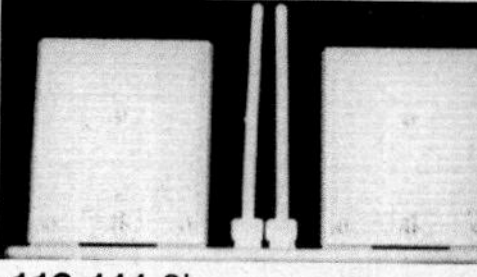

**112-111** 8'

### Dummy Couplers

**112-109** For Unit Trains pkg(12) **2.49**

### Grade Crossing Mat

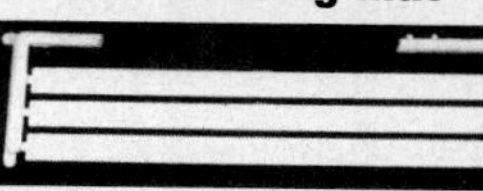

**112-117** Modern Rubber Styl 6 Pieces **1.99**

### Steel Roof

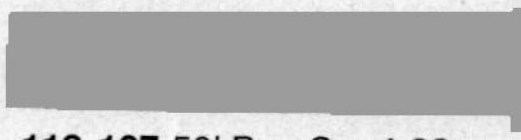

**112-107** 50' Box Car **1.98**

### TOFC Flat Car

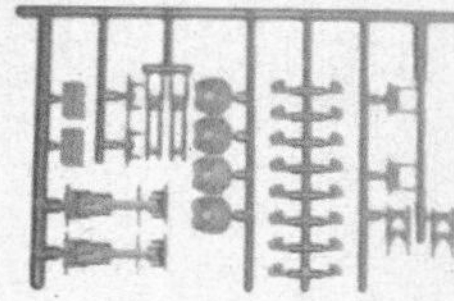

**112-119** Hitches & Details **1.9**

### Underframes

**112-105** 40' Fishbelly **2.98**

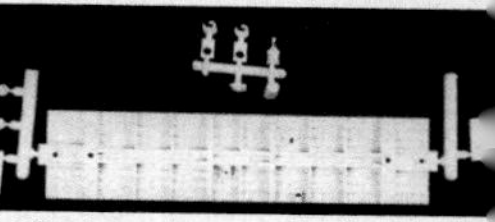

**112-106** 40' Steel **2.98**

**112-120** 50' Box Car w/Details **3.98**

# DETAIL PARTS

### Chain
**119-1000** 24" Copper (36 Links Per Inch) **3.95**

### Junk Yard Details
**119-2046** Junk Autos pkg(5) **8.95**
Five different disabled car bodies to create an auto wrecking yard, or smash and stack to use as flat car or truck loads.

# VEHICLE DETAILS

### Auto Parts
**119-2035** Engine Kits pkg(3) **7.45**

**119-2047** Assorted Auto Parts pkg(7) **7.45**

**119-2051** Brass Airplane Hood Ornament pkg(6) **4.35**

**119-2052** Window Glass for Chevy Coupe (Clear Plastic) pkg(2) **2.95**

**119-2053** White Walls for Autos (Decal) pkg(12) **4.35**

**119-2054** Generic Steering Wheels pkg(12) **4.35**

### License Plates pkg(12) 4.35 ea
**119-2050** 1950

**119-2055** 1955

**119-2056** 1956

**119-2057** 1957

**119-2058** 1948

**119-2059** 1959

**119-2060** 1941

**119-2061** 1951

**119-2062** 1949

**119-2063** 1953

### Truck Parts

#### Bogies 4.45 ea
**119-3122** With Offset Springs & Tires

**119-3123** With Centered Springs & Tires

#### Bumpers 3.45 ea
**119-3161** Front, Off-Road (2 Types) for Ford Trucks 2 Pair

**119-3167** Rear Drop Step for Trailers/Flatbeds pkg(2)

**119-3169** Front For GMC Astro 2 Pair

**119-3171** Heavy-Duty Front (2 Types) for Diamond Reo/ Autocar 2 Pair

#### Cab Details

**119-3004** Air Deflector pkg(3) **3.45**

**119-3065** Mack Bulldog Radiator Caps (Brass) pkg(6) **3.45**

**119-3069** 1/4 Tractor Fenders pkg(2) **2.45**
Mount in front of dual wheels.

**119-3074** Air Dam for Cab Roof pkg(3) **3.45**

**119-3081** Sun Visors Mack B42/61/71 pkg(3) **2.45**

#### Cab Seats 2.45 ea
**119-3058** Standard pkg(2)

**119-3059** Modern Hi-Back Type pkg(2)

**119-3071** Truck Seat Bench Type

#### Decals
**119-3053** For Mack & GMC pkg(2) **3.45**

#### Exhaust Pipes & Accessories
**119-3046** Dual for Mack H-60 **2.45**

**119-3054** Dual for Mack B-42/61/71 pkg(2) **3.45**

**119-3056** Dual for Ulrich Kenworth **3.45**

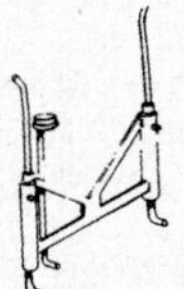

**119-3057** Dual w/Air Cleaner for Athearn Freightliner **2.45**

**119-3063** Dual w/"Snorkel" Air Cleaner for GMC **2.45**

**119-3062** Single Pipe/Air Cleaner pkg(2) **2.45**

**119-3180** Stacks (3 Types) for Autocar, Diamond Reo, Ford pkg(6) **3.45**

#### Fire Truck Parts
**119-3052** Spotlights w/Brackets pkg(2) **3.45**

**119-3087** Fire Pumper Detail Set **7.45**
Includes two hose reels with stand, two cluster hose connections and two extinguishers.

**119-3099** Update Detail Parts/Fire Trucks **3.45**

**119-3172** Rectangular Light Bars pkg(6) **3.45**

**119-3173** Detail Kit **7.45**
Includes 3 and 5" hose fittings, hose guides and water cannon. Enough parts for two trucks.

**119-3174** Ladders (Large & Small) 2 Sets **3.45**

**119-3175** Hoses-Single, Double & Triple 2 Sets **3.45**

#### Fifth Wheel Dolly
**119-3078** Tandem Axle **7.95**

**119-3079** Single Axle pkg(2) **7.45**

**119-3182** Dual Axle pkg(2) **7.45**

#### Gas & Air Tanks
**119-3050** GMC Astro Rectangular w/Recessed Steps pkg(2) **3.45**

**119-3051** GMC Astro Cylindrical pkg(2) **3.45**

**119-3067** Mack B-42/61 w/Step pkg(2) **2.45**

**119-3082** Ford "L" Round w/Steps pkg(2) **2.45**

**119-3085** Air Tank w/Mounting Bracket pkg(4) **3.45**

**119-3090** Autocar Rectangular **3.45**

**119-3124** Air Tank-Long Frame pkg(4) **3.45**

#### Lights 3.45 ea
**119-3093** Torpedo Running Lights pkg(2)

**119-3094** Headlight - Autocar Style pkg(4)

**119-3095** Tail Lights/Tractors pkg(2)

**119-3096** Tail Lights/Trailers pkg(2)

#### Mirrors pkg(2) 2.45 ea
**119-3055** Mack DM 800-Etched Brass

**119-3060** GMC (plastic)

**119-3066** Etched Brass (Mack B & Ford LNT/LTS)

**119-3098** Etched Brass (Autocar)

#### Refrigeration Units
**119-3080** Trailer pkg(2) **3.45**

### Truck Accessories
**119-3010** Sleeper Box **3.45**

**119-3037** Bed Stakes (Plastic) **3.45**

**119-3038** Wheel Bogies **3.45**

**119-3064** Athearn Tractor Detail Kit **3.45**

**119-3068** Mud Flaps pkg(4) **2.45**

**119-3070** Fender for Dual Axles Set **3.45**

**119-3073** Handle-Brass pkg(6) **3.45**

**119-3075** Lumber Headache Rack pkg(2) **3.45**

**119-3076** Radiator Guards for Tractors pkg(3) **2.45**

**119-3077** Jack Stands for Trailers - Wheel Type pkg(2) **2.45**

**119-3088** Tri-Axle Conversion Kit **7.45**

**119-3089** Loading Boom & Cradle **5.45**
Converts flatbed to concrete block truck.

**119-3091** Air Cleaner-Horizontal pkg(4) **3.45**

**119-3092** Power Steering Oil Cooler/Lubrifiner Filter pkg(4) **3.45**

**119-3097** Air Horns pkg(6) **2.45**

**119-3118** 5th Wheel Plate & Base pkg(2) **2.45**

**119-3120** Hose & Cable Rack pkg(4) **3.45**

**119-3121** Standard Differential & Drive Shaft pkg(3) **3.45**

**119-3127** Air Horns-Short Single pkg(6) **3.45**

**119-3129** Spare Tire Holder w/Cover pkg(3) **3.45**

**119-3130** Spare Tire Holder-No Cover pkg(3) **3.45**

**119-3132** Mack Air Cleaner pkg(4) **3.45**

**119-3165** Generic Steering Wheels pkg(6) **3.45**

**119-3166** Heavy-Duty Winch for Flatbeds pkg(2) **3.45**

**119-3167** Bumper pkg(2) **3.45**
Rear drop step type for flatbeds or trailers.

**119-3168** Spare Tire Holder & Cover **3.45**

**119-3170** Arched Front & Rear Springs w/Differential 2 Sets **3.45**

**119-3176** Detail Kit for B Series Macks **7.45**
Includes air horns, air cleaner, Bulldogs, battery box, exhausts and gas tanks.

**119-3177** Head & Tail Lights for 1930s Trucks (2 Types) 2 Sets **3.45**

**119-3178** Pistons for Dump Body/Trailer 2 Sets **3.45**
Includes two each, small medium and large sizes.

**119-3179** Flat Rear Springs w/Differential For Dump or Flatbed Trailers pkg(2) **3.45**

### Truck Tires 3.45 ea
**119-3061** Large pkg(10)

**119-3072** Small pkg(10)

**119-3133** Spare Tires pkg(4)

### Ulrich Upgrade Kits 7.45 ea (Unless Noted)
Sets include mirrors, wheel rims, tires and axles. Metal, plastic and brass parts.

**119-3005** Kenworth Tractors

**119-3006** All Trailers

#### Mack Tractors
**119-3002** Single-Axle **6.45**

**119-3003** Dual-Axle

### Wheel Sets 3.45 ea
Includes wheels, axles, tires and hubs.

**119-3119** Duals pkg(4)

**119-3039** Budd Disc

**119-3040** 6 Spoke

**119-3045** Low Boy

Suitable for detailing structures and other models.

### Caboose Interior

**700-421** **7.15**

### Crates

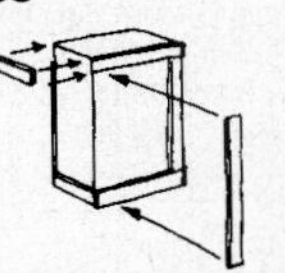

**700-512** Wood Platform Crates Kit **2.75**

### Freight Car Load
**700-431** Flat Car Crate Load **3.41**
Two large and one small machinery crates.

### Neoprene "O" Ring Drive Belt pkg(6) 5.78 ea
**700-1179** 1/2"

**700-1180** 9/16"

### Pacific Electric Decals 3.30 ea

**700-121** 15/16" pkg(4)

**700-122** 1-7/8" pkg(2)

### Pacific Electric Pilots
**700-185** Standard Wood **3.41**

### Structural Details
Item listed below is available by Special Order (see Legend Page).

**700-120** Station Shed Support **9.63**

### Vents

**700-113** Cast "A" pkg(12) **3.80**

#### Miscellaneous
Items listed below are available by Special Order (see Legend Page).

**700-177** Dynamotor/ Compressor (brass) **2.75**

**700-173** Motor Pulley Twin Groove pkg(3) **4.95**

Adair Shops™ **ADAIR SHOPS™**

*Weight Upgrade Kits for Contemporary Model Railroad Car Kits*

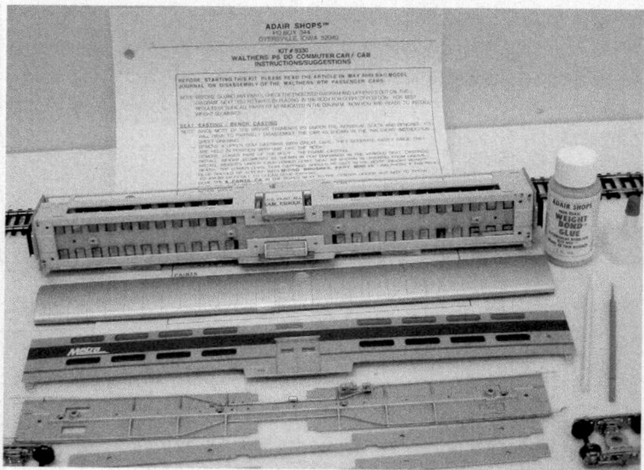

Improve the operation of your freight and passenger car fleet with Rite-Wey™ weight kits. Most can be installed so the weights are virtually invisible, so they're perfect for assembled models or kits, including box cars with open doors and/or hatches, many open cars or models with lights, interiors or circuit boards. Each weight kit consists of precut and finished segments made of a nontoxic industrial lead alloy. Each piece fits a specific location in or under the car with no cutting or sanding needed. Simply glue the pieces in place to bring the car up to or beyond NMRA weight standards quickly and easily without disturbing any details. Kits are available in two versions: Standard for normal applications, or the heavier Heavy Weight series — cars equipped with Heavy Weight kits should be coupled next to your motive power. For best results on wood, metal or plastic models, nontoxic, water-based Weight Bond™ Glue is recommended for a strong, permanent installation.

# RITE-WEY™ WEIGHT UPGRADE KITS

## Accurail

### Regular Weight 5.14 ea (Unless Noted)

**143-1010** 40' PS-1 3400 Series Steel Box Car

**143-1014** 50' Plug Door 5000 Series Steel Box Car

**143-1018** 50' AAR Double-Door Boxcar

**143-1022** 50' Welded Double-Door Box Car

**143-1026** 40' Wood Reefer

**143-1030** 50' Exterior Post Box Car

**143-1034** 40' Wood Stock Car, 4000/4700 Series

**143-1037** 40' Stock Car, 4000/4700 Series

**143-1040** 40' Wood Box Cars; 4000 & 4700 Series

**143-1046** 2-Bay Hoppers

**143-1053** 40' Plug Door Box Car; 3000 Series

**143-1056** 40' Wood Door Box Car; 7100 Series w/Modified Frames

**143-1059** 40' Single Sheathed Box Car; 7100 Series

**143-1062** 89' TOFC Flat Car **7.74**

**143-1065** Bi-Level Auto Rack (32 parts) **7.74**

**143-1068** Tri-Level Auto Rack (32 parts) **7.74**

**143-1071** Bi- & Tri-Level Auto Racks - Under Floor Mount **2.02**

**143-1074** 3-Bay ACF Centerflow Hopper

**NEW 143-1076** Triple Hopper

### Heavy Weight 6.37 ea

**143-1052** 2-Bay Hopper

**NEW 143-1077** Triple Hopper

## Accuready

**NEW 143-1080** 3-Bay Hopper Slope Sheet Set **3.84**

## Athearn

### Regular Weight 5.14 ea (Unless Noted)

**143-10** 40 or 48' Trailer

**143-15** 86' Hi-Cube Box Car

**143-22** 85' Flat Car

**143-29** 50' Old Style Piggyback Flat Car

**143-36** 50' Box Car

**143-40** 50' Plug Door Box Car (Modern Billboard)

**143-44** Express & Plug Door Reefers

**143-48** 50' Covered Gondola

**143-53** 40' Flat Car

**143-61** 50' Flat Car

**143-68** 40' Pulpwood Rack Car

**143-75** 40' Hi-Cube Box Car

**143-82** 40' AAR Box Car

**143-93** 50' P-S 5344 Box Car; 5 Ounce Weight

**143-98** 50' Box Car; 5 Ounce Weight

**143-102** 50' Plug Door Insulated Box Car; 5 Ounce Weight

**143-106** Crane Tender/Work Caboose

**143-108** 62' Tank Car

**143-113** 42' Chemical Tank Car

**143-117** 34' Steel Side 2-Bay Hopper

**143-123** 34' Composite Side 2-Bay Hopper

**143-129** 34' Wood Side 2-Bay Hopper

**143-135** 34' Offset Side 2-Bay Hopper

**143-141** 40' Open-Top Quad Hopper

**143-146** 54' P-S Covered Hopper

**143-150** 55' ACF Center Flow Hopper - Assembled Cars

**143-154** 40' Stock Car

**143-158** All Streamline Passenger Cars

**143-164** All Standard Steel Pullman Passenger Cars

**143-172** Gunderson Husky-Stack Car

**143-173** 40' Steel Reefer

**143-177** 40' Banana Reefer

**143-181** Wide Vision Caboose

**143-183** Heavy Duty Flat Car

**143-186** Standard Steel Railway Post Office

**143-188** Cupola Caboose

**143-190** Bay Window Caboose

**143-192** Bombardier Commuter Car/Cab **7.74**

**143-196** 57' Mechanical Reefer

**143-3120** 50' Hi-Cube Box Car

### Heavy Weight 6.37 ea (Unless Noted)

**143-14** 40' or 48' Trailer **4.90**

**143-35** 50' Old Style Piggyback Flatcar

**143-39** 50' Box Cars

**143-43** 50' Plug Door Box Car - Modern Billboard

**143-47** 50' Express & Plug Door Reefers

**143-52** 50' Covered Gondola

**143-60** 40' Flat Car

**143-67** 50' Flat Car

**143-74** 40' Pulpwood Rack Car

**143-81** 40' Hi-Cube Box Car

**143-88** 40' AAR Box Car

**143-97** 50' P-S 5344 Box Car; 6.2 Ounce Weight

**143-101** 50' Box Car; 6.2 Ounce Weight

**143-105** 50' Plug Door Insulated Box Car; 6.2 Ounce Weight

**143-107** Crane Tender/Work Caboose

**143-112** 62' Tank Car

**143-116** 42' Chemical Tank Car

**143-185** Heavy Duty Flat Car

## Athearn Impack

### Regular Weight

**143-200** Outer (End Car of Multi-Unit Set) One Unit **3.84**

**143-212** Inner (Middle Cars of Multi-Car Sets) One Unit **3.84**

**143-170** Outer (End Car of Multi-Unit Set) 2 Units **7.67**

**143-171** Inner (Middle Cars of Multi-Unit Set) 3 Units **11.51**

## Athearn RTR

**NEW 143-208** 28' Trailer pkg(2) **5.14**

**NEW 143-210** 85' Flat Car (New Style) **5.14**

**NEW 143-215** 65' Mill Gondola Load (Painted) **7.74**

**NEW 143-240** 20' Container pkg(3) **5.14**

**NEW 143-236** 40' Container pkg(2) **5.14**

**NEW 143-238** 45' Container pkg(2) **5.14**

**NEW 143-216** 48' Container pkg(2) **5.14**

**NEW 143-231** 53' Stoughton Container **3.84**

**NEW 143-250** 55' ACF Center Flow Hopper **5.14**

**NEW 143-232** 40' Gondola Painted Floor For Athearn or MDC **3.84**

**NEW 143-7716** 2-Bay Hopper Slope Sheet Set **3.84**

**NEW 143-223** 40' 3-Bay Hopper Slope Sheet Set **3.84**

**NEW 143-218** 4-Bay Hopper Slope Sheet Set **3.84**

**NEW 143-228** Heavy 40' 3-Bay Hopper Slope Sheet Set **3.84**

**NEW 143-89** Bethgon **3.84**

**NEW 143-203** Heavy Bethgon **3.84**

## Atlas 3.84 ea

**NEW 143-6225** GSC Pulpwood Flat Car

**NEW 143-6228** Coalveyor

**NEW 143-6231** Heavyweight 2-Bay Hopper Slope Sheet Set

**NEW 143-6234** Regular Weight 2-Bay Hopper Slope Sheet Set

## Bachmann

### Regular Cars 5.14 ea (Unless Noted)

**NEW 143-9036** 3-Bay 100-Ton Hopper

**NEW 143-9037** Ore Car **3.84**

**NEW 143-9038** Humane Livestock Car **3.84**

**NEW 143-9039** Stock Car

**NEW 143-9040** 40' Quad Hopper **3.84**

**NEW 143-9044** Flat Car

**NEW 143-9046** Amfleet Coach, Café

**NEW 143-9047** ATSF 85' Full Dome

## Spectrum 5.14 ea

**NEW 143-2800** Heavyweight Coach

**NEW 143-2801** Heavyweight Observation

**NEW 143-2802** Heavyweight Dining Car

**NEW 143-2803** Heavyweight Combine

**NEW 143-2804** Heavyweight Pullman

## Bowser

### Regular Weight 5.14 ea (Unless Noted)

**143-4051** 50' PRR K-9 Stock Car

**143-4054** 40' PRR K-9 Stock Car

**143-4057** PRR GS 40' Gondc

**143-4060** F-30a 50' Flat Car

**143-4063** 100-Ton 45' 3-Bay Hopper

**143-4069** PRR H-21A 4-Bay Hopper

**143-4075** H-21 Hopper w/Clamshell Doors

**143-4081** PRR H-22a Hopper Car

**143-4087** H-22 70-Ton Hoppe Car

**143-4093** GLa 2-Bay Hopper

**NEW 143-4102** 4-Bay Hoppe Slope Sheet Set **3.84**

**NEW 143-7741** GLa 2-Bay Hopper, Long Interior Style Slope Sheet Set **3.84**

## Central Valley

### Stock Cars

Sets include construction jigs.

**143-8011** Regular Weight **6.44**

**143-8012** Heavy Weight **7.67**

## Branchline

### Regular Weight 5.14 ea

**143-1101** 50' AAR Box Car

**143-1103** 40' Plug Door Box Car

**143-1105** 50' Plug Door Box Car

**143-1107** 40' AAR Box Car

**143-1110** Heavyweight Pullman (NMRA + 1.1oz)

### Heavy Weight

**143-1111** Heavyweight Pullman - NMRA+ 1.9oz **6.35**

## Con-Cor

### Regular Weight 5.14 ea

**143-3600** 12 Panel Greenville 100-Ton Coal Hopper

**143-3606** 15 Panel Greenville 100-Ton Coal Hopper

**143-3612** 54' Mill Gondola

### Passenger Cars 5.14 ea

**NEW 143-3615** 72' Coach, Baggage, RPO, Diner

**NEW 143-3617** 70' Baggage Corrugated

**NEW 143-3618** 85' Coach, Dome, Sleeper, Diner

**NEW 143-3621** 85' Observation

**NEW 143-3622** 72' Dome

**NEW 143-3623** 72' Observation

**NEW 143-3624** 85' Observation, Dome

**NEW 143-3625** 85' Budd Dome

Adair Shops ADAIR SHOPS™
Weight Upgrade Kits for Contemporary Model Railroad Car Kits

### HC

**Regular Weight 5.14 ea**

**143-8060** Smooth Side/ Corrugated Side Baggage

**143-8061** Smooth Side/ Corrugated Side Coach

**143-8062** Smooth Side/ Corrugated Side Dining Car

**143-8063** Smooth Side/ Corrugated Side Observation

**143-8064** Smooth Side/ Corrugated Side Combine

**143-8065** Smooth Side/ Corrugated Side Railway Post Office

**143-8066** Smooth Side/ Corrugated Side Sleeper

**143-8067** Smooth Side/ Corrugated Side Vista Dome

**143-8068** Heavyweight Baggage

**143-8069** Heavyweight Coach

**143-8070** Heavyweight Combine

**143-8071** Heavyweight Diner

**143-8072** Heavyweight Observation

**143-8073** Heavyweight Baggage/Railway Post Office

**143-8074** Heavyweight 8-1-2 Sleeper

**143-8075** Heavyweight 12-1 Sleeper

### Intermountain

**Regular Weight 5.14 ea (Unless Noted)**

**143-2022** 60' PS-1 Single Door Box Car

**143-2026** National Steel Cylindrical Hopper

**143-2037** ACF Center Flow 2-Bay Hopper

**143-2041** USRA Composite Gondola

**143-2048** 4750 Cubic Foot 18-Rib 3-Bay Hopper

**143-2052** 60' Wood Deck Flat Car **7.74**

**NEW 143-2055** Bathtub Gondola

**Heavy Weight**

**143-2047** USRA Composite Gondola **6.37**

### LBF/E&C

**Regular Weight 5.14 ea**

**143-4151** Woodchip Car

**143-4155** 50' AC&F Hi-Cube Box Car

**143-4159** 50' AC&F Santa Fe Double-Door Box Car

**143-4163** Boeing Skybox Flat Car

**143-4167** 52'6" Greenville Mill Gondola 1900 Series

**143-4173** Johnstown Coalporter (Improved)

**143-4178** 65' Mill & General Purpose Gondolas

**143-4181** High Capacity Woodchip Cars

**Heavy Weight 6.37 ea**

**143-4154** Woodchip Car

**143-4158** 50' AC&F Hi-Cube Boxcar

**143-4162** 50' AC&F Santa Fe Double-Door Box Car

**143-4166** Boeing Aircraft Parts Box & Flat Car

**143-4172** Johnstown Coalporter - Old Style

**143-4184** High Capacity Woodchip Car

### Miscellaneous

**Regular Weight**

**143-1401** Electroten - Talgo Lounge **2.95**

**143-1402** Electroten - Talgo End/Cab Car **2.95**

**143-1403** Electroten - Talgo Coach **2.95**

**NEW 143-7721** Accurail/Walthers USRA 55-Ton 2-Bay Hopper Slope Sheet Set **3.84**

**143-8011** Central Valley - Stock Car (Includes Construction Jigs) **6.44**

**143-8031** LaBelle - Passenger Cars **5.14**

**Light Weight**

**143-8035** LaBelle - Passenger Cars (Wood Construction) **5.14**

**Heavy Weight 6.44 ea (Unless Noted)**

**NEW 143-7726** Accurail/Walthers USRA 55-Ton 2-Bay Hopper Slope Sheet Set **3.84**

**143-8021** ERM - Eel River Models - 62' 10-1/2" Insulated Box Car w/Construction/ Assembly Jigs

**143-8022** ERM - Eel River Models - 62' 10-1/2" Beer Car w/Construction/Assembly Jigs

### PROTO 2000™

**Regular Weight 5.14 ea (Unless Noted)**

**143-1151** 50' 50-Ton AAR Standard Flat Car

**143-1155** 52'6" Drop End Mill Gondola

**143-1159** 50-Ton War Emergency Hopper

**143-1164** 8,000-Gallon Type 21 Tank Car

**143-1167** PS-2CD Covered Hopper

**NEW 143-1170** 10,000 Gallon Tank Car

**NEW 143-1173** War Emergency Hopper Slope Sheet Set **3.84**

### Red Caboose

**Regular Weight 5.14 ea**

**143-2200** Composite Side Drop Bottom Gondola, Sugar Beet Gondola With or Without Side Extensions

**143-2206** General Service Steel Side Gondola

**143-2212** Meat Reefer

**143-2215** 40' Standard AAR Single or Double-Door Box Car

**143-2218** 100-Ton Coil Car - Assembled

**143-2222** 100-Ton Evans Coil Car w/Load - Assembled

**143-2225** 42' Fishbelly Flat Car

**143-2231** 53'6" Flat Car w/Wood Deck - Fits Assembled or Kit Versions

### Roundhouse/MDC

**Regular Weight 5.14 ea (Unless Noted)**

**NEW 143-234** 50' Mill Gondola Painted Floor **3.84**

**143-3000** 40' Gondola

**143-3004** Bulkhead Flat Car

**143-3009** 50' Modern Gondola

**143-3014** Old-Time Tank Car

**143-3026** 60' Flat Car

**143-3031** 52' 5-Bay Rapid Discharge Coal Hopper

**143-3038** Black Mesa 52' 5-Bay Rapid Discharge Hopper

**143-3045** Offset Ballast Hopper

**143-3049** Ribbed Ballast Hopper

**143-3055** 40' 3-Bay Ribbed Hopper

**143-3059** 2-Bay Covered Hopper

**143-3062** 50' Thrall Gondola

**143-3068** 50' Bathtub Gondola

**143-3074** 36' Old-Time Stock Car

**143-3077** 30' Flat Car or Gondola

**143-3080** Old-Time Side Door Caboose

**143-3082** 30' Outside Braced Wood Caboose

**143-3083** 3-Window Caboose

**143-3084** 30' Side Door Open End Caboose

**143-3085** Old-Time Overton Combine

**143-3088** 30' Side Door Blind End Caboose

**143-3089** 30' Small Side Door Caboose

**143-3090** 30' 3-Window Steel Caboose

**143-3091** 60' Harriman Passenger Cars

**143-3094** 26' Caboose - All Styles

**143-3097** 30' Modern Tank Car **3.84**

**143-3101** 22' Ore Car - Taper Side

**143-3105** AAR 40' Box Car

**143-3108** Pullman Palace Observation

**143-3114** 3-Bay Offset Side Hopper

**NEW 143-3116** 50' Plug Door Box Car

**NEW 143-3117** 50' Express Reefer

**NEW 143-3118** 3-Bay Hopper Slope Sheet Set **3.84**

**NEW 143-3129** 50' Overland Car

**Heavy Weight 6.37 ea (Unless Noted)**

**143-3008** Bulkhead Flat Car

**143-3013** 50' Modern Gondola

**143-3017** Old Time Tank Car

**143-3018** 50' Tank Car

**143-3022** 50' Tank Car

**143-3030** 60' Flat Car

**143-3037** 52' 5-Bay Rapid Discharge Coal Car

**143-3044** Black Mesa 52' 5-Bay Rapid Discharge Coal Car

**143-3087** Old Time Overton Combine

**143-3110** 50' FMC Covered Hopper/Grain Car - 3520 Series

**NEW 143-3126** 3-Bay Hopper Slope Sheet Set **3.84**

### Stewart Hobbies

**Regular Weight 5.14 ea (Unless Noted)**

**143-4000** Fishbelly 55-Ton 6 Panel 2-Bay Hopper

**143-4005** Offset 70-Ton 9 Panel Triple Hopper

**143-4010** H-39 70-Ton 12 Panel Triple Hopper

**143-4015** 70-Ton AAR/NYC 14 Panel Triple Hopper

**143-4020** G39B 77-Ton Ore Car

**NEW 143-4025** 3-Bay Hopper Slope Sheet Set **3.84**

**NEW 143-7711** 2-Bay Hopper, Short Interior Style Slope Sheet Set **3.84**

**NEW 143-7746** 2-Bay Hopper, Long Interior Style Regular Slope Sheet Set **3.84**

**NEW 143-7751** 2-Bay Hopper, Long Interior Style Heavy Slope Sheet Set **3.84**

### Tichy Train Group

**Regular Weight 5.14 ea (Unless Noted)**

**143-1201** 53' GSC Commonwealth Flat Car

**143-1205** 40' Pulpwood Flat Car

**143-1208** USRA 55 Ton Twin Hopper

**143-1212** 52' War Emergency Gondola - Kit

**143-1216** 52' War Emergency Gondola - Assembled

**NEW 143-7731** USRA 55-Ton 2-Bay Hopper, Long Interior Style Slope Sheet Set **3.84**

**Heavy Weight**

**NEW 143-7736** USRA 55-Ton 2-Bay Hopper, Long Interior Style Slope Sheet Set **3.84**

### Walthers

**Regular Weight 5.14 ea (Unless Noted)**

**143-4251** 45' or 48' Stoughton Van Trailers

**143-4258** 89' Flat Car - 6 Ounce Weight

**143-4264** 89' Auto Rack

**143-4268** 65' Mill Gondola

**143-4272** 70' Thrall Double Stack - Single Unit Car

**143-4276** 52' Thrall Gondola

**143-4279** Plain Kit Interior Floor **3.84**

**143-4282** Russell Snowplow

**143-4284** 46' 70-Ton USRA Gondola

**143-4288** Pullman-Standard 60' Auto Box Car

**143-4293** 40' Idler Flat Car (#933-968; Out of Production)

**143-4296** Pullman-Standard 89' Hi-Cube Box Car

**143-4299** Coke Car

**143-4301** Trinity RD-4 Coal Hopper

**143-4311** 40' Wood Door Grain Box Car

**143-4312** Bethgon **3.84**

**143-4322** 75' Early Piggyback Flat Car 1995

**143-4328** Stock Car

**143-4336** Spine Flat Car

**143-4339** 72' Center Beam Flat/Lumber Car

**143-4342** SP C-30-1 Wood Caboose

**143-4344** 30' Wood Caboose - 3 Window Offset Cupola, Ready-to-Run

**143-4346** UP CA-1 30' Wood Caboose

**143-4348** 25' Chesapeake & Ohio Style Wood Caboose; Ready-to-Run

**143-4350** 30' 4-Window Wood Caboose; Ready-to-Run

**143-4352** PS Double-Deck Commuter Cars **7.74**

**143-4355** 85' Budd 10-6 Sleeper; Ready-to-Run

**143-4356** 85' Budd 46 Seat Coach; Ready-to-Run

**143-4357** 85' Budd 52 Seat Coach; Ready-to-Run

**143-4358** 85' Budd Grill-Diner; Ready-to-Run

**143-4359** 85' Budd Lounge; Ready-to-Run

**143-4360** 85' Budd Tavern-Observation Car; Ready-to-Run

**143-4361** 85' Budd Dome Coach; Ready-to-Run

**143-4362** 73' Budd Baggage Car; Ready-to-Run

**143-4363** 63' Budd Railway Post Office Car; Ready-to-Run

**143-4364** Pullman Heavyweight 12-1 Sleeper; Ready-to-Run

**143-4365** 89' Auto Rack - Retro Weight For Completed Car

**143-4366** Pullman Heavyweight 14 Section Sleeper

**143-4367** 60' Heavyweight Baggage

**143-4368** 60' Heavyweight Railway Post Office

**143-4369** 60' Heavyweight Combine

**143-4370** 60' Heavyweight Coach

**143-4371** USRA 55-Ton 2-Bay Hopper

**NEW 143-7721** Gold Line 2-Bay Hopper Slope Sheet Set **3.84**

**NEW 143-4346** Front Runner w/Trailer

**NEW 143-4364** Heavyweight 12-1 Sleeper
**NEW 143-4365** Heavyweight 8-1-2 Sleeper
**NEW 143-4366** Heavyweight 14-Section Sleeper
**NEW 143-4367** 60' Heavyweight Baggage
**NEW 143-4368** 60' Heavyweight RPO
**NEW 143-4369** 60' Heavyweight Combine
**NEW 143-4370** 60' Heavyweight Coach
**NEW 143-4375** Ore Car **3.84**
**NEW 143-4378** PS-3 Coal Hopper
**NEW 143-4385** 84' Auto Rack **3.84**
**NEW 143-4389** Heavyweight Diner
**NEW 143-4390** Heavyweight Pair Coach
**NEW 143-4391** Heavyweight Observation
**NEW 143-4392** ATSF Caboose
**NEW 143-4394** SP Wood Caboose
**NEW 143-4396** Difco Dump Car **3.84**
**NEW 143-4400** 40' Container
**NEW 143-4401** 48' Container
**NEW 143-4403** Pulpwood Flat Car
**NEW 143-4406** 50' Flat Car
**NEW 143-4409** Center Beam Flat Car
**NEW 143-4412** 72' Centerbeam Flat Car w/Opera Window
**NEW 143-4415** Greenville Woodchip Hopper
**NEW 143-4420** Trainline 40' Offset Side Hopper
**NEW 143-4428** 53' Stoughton Trailer **3.84**
**NEW 143-4430** 40' Hi-Cube Container
**NEW 143-4431** 20' Container
**NEW 143-4432** 28' Container
**NEW 143-4433** 26' Parcel Trailer
**NEW 143-4434** GSC Commonwealth 53' Flat

### Heavy Weight 6.37 ea (Unless Noted)

**143-4257** 45' or 48' Stoughton Van Trailers
**143-4262** 89' Heavy Flat Car
**143-4267** 89' Auto Rack
**143-4271** 65' Mill Gondola
**143-4287** 46' 70-Ton USRA Gondola
**143-4305** Trinity RD-4 Coal Hopper (NMRA + 3 oz.) **5.14**
**143-4308** Trinity RD-4 Coal Hopper (NMRA + 3.3oz) **5.14**
**143-4317** Bethgon **3.84**
**143-4331** Stock Car
**NEW 143-4377** 2-Bay Hopper
**NEW 143-4418** Greenville Woodchip Hopper **6.44**

## Alexander scale models

DIVISION OF TOMAR INDUSTRIES

All parts are white metal castings.

### Chimneys

**pkg(2) 1.60 ea**
**120-2701** Fancy
**120-2705** Brick
**120-2706** Stone

### Coach Seats

**2.00 ea**
**120-3401** 2-Seater pkg(6)
**120-3402** 3-Seater pkg(4)
**120-3403** 4-Seater pkg(4)

### Doors

**3.15 ea (Unless Noted)**
**120-2401** Freight **1.40**
**120-2402** Freight **1.40**
**120-2403** Entry Door & Window pkg(3) **3.65**
**120-2404** Entry Door w/Transom pkg(4)
**120-2405** Entry Door 4-Panel pkg(4)
**120-2406** Double Entry Door pkg(2) **3.65**
**120-2407** Solid Panel Door pkg(4)
**120-2408** 3-Panel Door pkg(4)
**120-2409** 2-Window Door pkg(4)
**120-2410** 4-Panel Door pkg(4)
**120-2411** Door w/4-Pane Window pkg(4)

### Gates & Lattice

**120-2900** Lattice Material pkg(6) **2.65**
**120-3000** Fence Gate pkg(4) **2.95**

### Electrical

**120-801** Meter Box pkg(4) **1.40**

### Gears

**pkg(2) 1.60 ea (Unless Noted)**
**120-414** Large
**120-415** Small
**120-416** Pinion
**120-422** Small Fine Tooth **2.10**
**120-423** Large Fine Tooth

### Ghost town details

**120-1601** Ghost Town Railing pkg(6) **2.10**
**120-1602** Ghost Town Freight Door **1.05**
**120-1603** Tombstones pkg(12) **3.15**

### Hatches

**pkg(4)**
**120-4000** Ice Hatch Narrow Gauge **1.40**
**120-4002** Small **3.15**

### Lamps

**120-1800** Outside Kerosene Lamp pkg(6) **3.15**

### Locomotive Details

**120-2203** Diesel Awning pkg(2) **1.30**
**120-1301** Engineer & Fireman's Seat **2.65**

### Machine Tools

**120-2603** Lathe/Tool Makers **4.20**
**120-2604** Modern Drill Press Floor Model **1.60**
**120-2605** Pedestal Tool Grinder **1.05**
**120-2606** Bridgeport Vertical Milling Machine **4.20**

### Mine Equipment

#### Cars

**120-2801** Mine Latrine Car 2' Gauge **5.25**
**120-2821** Kanawha Mine Car **5.85**
**120-9801** Calico Mine Car 18" gauge **5.00**

#### Details

**120-2820** Jeffrey Mine Motor **7.20**
**120-9808** Pick & Shovel 2 ea **1.60**
**120-9809** Miner Mike **4.20**
**120-9810** Prospector Pete **4.20**

#### Track

**120-2804** Mine Track Straight pkg(4) **3.05**
**120-2805** Mine Track Curved pkg(4) **3.05**
**120-9803** Mine Track Curved 2" radius pkg(4) **4.20**
**120-9804** Mine Track Kick switch pkg(2) **4.20**
**120-9806** Mine Track Straight 18" Gauge Metal pkg(4) **4.20**

### Miscellaneous

**120-305** Yard Air Connection pkg(3) **4.00**
**120-410** Fire Extinguisher pkg(5) **3.15**
**120-430** Lufkin Oil Pump Unit **TBA**
**120-508** Marker Lights **3.25**
**120-3902** Sand House Spout **4.20**

### Plumbing Details

**120-408** Valve pkg(5) **3.15**
**120-409** Elbow pkg(5) **3.15**
**120-3301** Manhole Cover pkg(10) **3.15**
**120-3901** Water Tank Spout **1.60**

### Plug Doors

**pkg(2) 2.65 ea**
**120-301** Hi-Cube
**120-302** Youngstown
**120-303** 60' Auto Parts
**120-304** Superior

### Smoke Jacks & Vents

**pkg(4) 1.60 ea (Unless Noted)**
**120-901** Caboose
**120-2702** Side Mount **2.10**
**120-2703** Smoke Jack
**120-2704** Smoke Jack

### Stairs & Steps

**120-1201** Stair Riser pkg(6) **2.95**
**120-1202** Open Stair Section **2.30**
**120-1203** Short Stair Section **1.05**
**120-1204** Medium Stair Section **1.80**
**120-1205** Long Stair Section **3.15**
**120-1207** Short Step pkg(2) **1.30**

### Trackside Details

**120-1001** Order Board **3.15**
**120-1002** Train Order Board **3.15**
**120-2101** Ticket Window **3.15**
**120-3101** Ground Relay Box pkg(2) **1.30**
**120-3102** Instrument Case **2.85**
**120-3103** Signal Relay Equipment House **3.70**
**120-3104** Relay Enclosure **2.10**
**120-3105** Battery Box Double **2.30**
**120-3107** Electrical Switch Motor **3.15**
**120-3108** Circuit Controller pkg(10) **3.15**
**120-3109** Cable Junction Box **3.15**
**120-3110** Vault Cover **2.00**
**120-3111** Remote Signal Indicator pkg(3) **3.15**
**120-3112** Electrical Lock pkg(3) **3.15**
**120-3113** Equipment Base pkg(6) **2.95**
**120-3201** Scale Counter 200lb capacity pkg(4) **2.65**
**120-9500** Railway Mail Crane **6.30**
**120-9501** Hayes Derail Set **5.25**
**120-9511** Hayes Bumper **3.50**
**120-9515** ACI Car Counter **9.45**
**120-9805** Timber Car 18" Gauge **6.00**

### Telephone Shelters

**120-3114** Wooden **3.70**
**120-3115** Concrete **3.15**

### Vents

**120-701** Exhaust Fan **1.60**
**120-1701** Passenger Car **1.60**
**120-1900** Louvered **TBA**
**120-1901** Louvered pkg(4) **1.40**

## *Information* STATION

### The Second Lives of Containers

Container trains have been an important part of the railroad scene since the late 1950s. Millions are moved each year and over time older, smaller "boxes" are replaced by larger, newer ones. But what happens to retired containers? In many cases, the older containers are scrapped and the steel is recycled. But containers are sturdy — they have to endure the rigors of rail shipment and handling by crane operators. They're also relatively watertight and have large end doors, so they make excellent storage buildings.

Containers are readily available in every scale, so using them to add interest to your layout scenes is easy. Since the 80s, railroads have used them to store track materials and tools. They're easily moved, so they often accompany work crews at major track and construction projects. A few roads even use them as section houses and speeder sheds, positioning them with doors facing the tracks and speeder rails or old ties leading inside.

Outside of the railroad industry, farmers use them to shelter farm machinery, and homeowners in rural areas use them as garages for their cars. Contractors use them for storage at job sites, and a high school up the road from Walthers uses them next to the football field to store athletic equipment. Businesses and industries use them for all sorts of storage.

On your layout, as in the real world, painting them is up to you. Many are simply left in their previous owners' colors. Businesses paint them in their corporate colors. Some companies refurbish them by making them entirely watertight, adding roof vents and electrical conduits for interior lighting, and painting them into neutral colors. Some are even converted into temporary offices with the addition of a side door, windows and window air conditioners!

Add the finishing touch of realism to your models with this selection of white metal, wood, and plastic (as noted) parts.

Important Note: This listing includes items which are available by special order only. Please see the Legend Page for information, and visit www.walthers.com for a complete listing of in-stock and special order products.

# FREIGHT CAR DETAILS

## Caboose Parts

**152-226** Axle Generator pkg(2) **5.95**

**152-227** Modernization Kit Athearn Santa Fe Caboose **11.95**

**152-915** Caboose Grab Iron Bending Template **4.95**

### Athearn 34' Cupola Caboose Details

**152-340** Detail Set **12.95** Includes wood roofwalks, window glazing and screens for doors and windows. Based on ATSF prototype.

**152-341** Screen Door & Window Set **5.95**

**152-342** Wood Roofwalks **5.95**

**152-343** Window Set **4.95**

## Car Floors

Laser-cut flooring adds a level of realistic detail to open cars.

**152-233** Walthers 54' GSC Flat Car w/Bolt Holes **7.95**

**152-234** Walthers 54' GSC Flat Car Without Bolt Holes **4.95**

**152-320** Athearn 40' Flat Cars **4.95**

**152-321** Athearn 50' Flat Cars **4.95**

**152-322** Proto 2000™ Gondolas **4.95**

**152-323** Athearn Gondolas **4.95**

**152-324** MDC Gondolas **4.95**

**152-325** MDC 60' Flat Cars **5.95**

**152-326** Red Caboose 42' Flat Cars **5.95**

**152-328** InterMountain Flat Cars **5.95**

**152-329** Proto 2000 53' Flat Cars **5.95**

**152-330** Tichy War Emergency Gondola **4.95**

## Roofwalks 4.95 ea

**152-293** Athearn Box Car

**152-294** InterMountain Box Car

**152-296** Athearn 50' Box Car

**152-297** Walthers 50' Automobile Box Car

**152-299** Proto 2000 50' Box Cars

## Tack Boards

**152-298** For Freight Cars **2.95**

# WINDOW SETS

Easy to install flush-mounted window "glass" for your favorite locos and rolling stock. Clear plastic parts are laser-cut for precise fit and premasked on front and back for easy painting.

## Athearn 4.95 ea (Unless Noted)

American Model Builders 07HO Parts

**152-222** E & F Cab Unit Sun (laser-Cut heavy gray paper) pkg(4) **3.95**

**152-228** Scale F-Units **5.95** Correct-size windshields, engine requires modification.

**152-229** Semi-Scale F-Units Larger windshields fit standard Athearn opening.

**152-230** Modern GP & SD Locos

**152-231** SW7

**152-232** SW1000/1500

**152-235** GP7/9

**152-236** Wide Vision Caboose **5.95**

**152-237** U-Boats

**152-238** Dash 9-44CW

**152-251** F45

**152-253** FP45

**152-276** SD9

**152-277** Trainmaster SP

**152-278** Trainmaster Standard

**152-290** PA-1

**152-291** PB-1

**152-292** S-12

**152-2289** B Units (2 sets) **3.95**

**152-2381** Dash-9 For Low Number Board Cab

**152-2382** Dash-9 For Gull Wing Cab

## Atlas 4.95 ea

**152-301** GP30/GP40

**152-302** SD35

**152-344** SD24 High or Low Nose **4.95**

## Bowser Pennsylvania Cabooses

**152-255** N-5 Cars **4.95**

**152-256** N-5C Cars **5.95**

**152-345** Modernized N5 Cars **4.95**

**152-346** N8 Cars **4.95**

## Kato 4.95 ea

**152-307** SD40

**152-308** GP35 Phases 1a, b & c

**152-309** SD45

**152-317** SD40-2

## Walthers/PROTO 2000 4.95 ea

**152-248** Proto 2000 E7A

**152-249** Proto 2000 E7B

**152-250** F40PH

**152-254** Proto 2000 E8/9 (Early Tooling)

**152-300** Proto 2000 PA

**152-303** GP60 Standard Cab

**152-304** SD60M 2-Window Cab

**152-306** SD60M 3-Window Cab

**152-313** SD60 Standard Cab

**152-314** GP30

**152-315** GP7 Phase II Second Release

**152-316** GP9 Phase II

**152-318** Proto 2000 SD45

**152-348** PROTO 2000 GP38-2

## High Tech Details

**152-319** GE Cabs (#5000-5008) **4.95**

## MDC/Roundhouse

**152-347** "Northeastern" Style 26' Two-Window Caboose **4.95**

## Rail Power Products 4.95 ea

**152-240** SD45

**152-241** SD60

**152-242** CF7 w/Topeka Cab

**152-244** SD60M

**152-243** Dash 8-40CW All Cabs & Dash 9

**152-245** GP35

**152-246** CF7 w/Round Cab

**152-247** SD7/9

**152-252** Dash 8-40B

**152-257** SD90MAC

**152-264** SD38/40

**152-265** SD60M 3 Piece Windshield

**152-266** GP60

**152-267** GP60M

**152-268** SD45-2

**152-269** B23-7

**152-274** C30-7

**152-275** C32-8

**152-336** GP40X

# STRUCTURE PARTS

## ATSF (Santa Fe) -Style Structure Parts

**152-337** Stand Alone Bay Window **11.95**

**152-338** Brackets **8.95**

**152-339** Windows and Doors **21.95**

**152-280** Santa Fe - Rio Grande Style Chimney pkg(3) **4.95**

**152-283** Santa Fe Style Shingles **20.95**

## Chimneys 4.95 ea

**152-279** Smoke Jacks

**152-281** Single Farber Style pkg(3)

**152-282** Double Farber Style pkg(2)

## Gas Pumps

**152-334** 1950s Era pkg(2) **4.95**

## Grain Spouts

**152-333** Flexible Style pkg(4) **4.95**

## Loading Docks

**152-327** "L" Shaped & Straight pkg(2) **11.95**

**152-331** Freight Platform **8.95** Measures 9-1/4 x 1-3/8".

## Screen Doors & Windows 4.95 ea

**152-310** Atlantic Coast Line Depot

**152-311** Post Office

**152-312** Dill's Market

## Shingles

**152-284** Hex Shaped **12.95**

**152-285** Tabbed **16.95**

**152-286** Rolled Roofing **8.95**

**152-335** Shake **16.95**

## Stairs

**152-332** Stair Set pkg(2) **7.95**

# MISCELLANEOUS

**152-106** Stationary Boiler Kit **34.95**

**152-107** Stationary Steam Engine Kit **36.95**

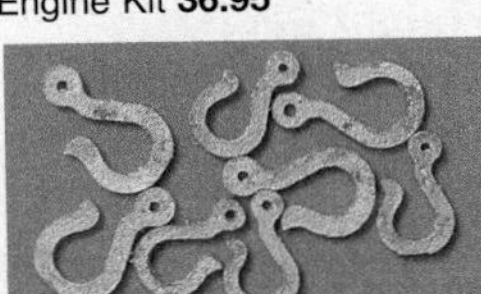

**152-402** Hooks pkg(6) **4.95**

**152-404** Fire Hydrants pkg(6) **4.95**

See What's New and Exciting at **www.walthers.com**

## BUSCH

IMPORTED FROM GERMANY BY WALTHERS

# INTERIOR DETAILS

## Office Set

**189-5402 23.99**
Perfect for adding realism to building interiors, this modern office furniture set looks great in any structure. Includes four desks with computer workstations complete with mouse and keyboard details. Two monitors are illuminated by white LEDs. Set also includes four office chairs and is ready for hookup to a 14-16V DC or AC power supply (sold separately).

# DETAIL PARTS

## AEI System

Now appearing on locos and cars, Automatic Equipment Identification (AEI) computerized system keeps track of prototype equipment.

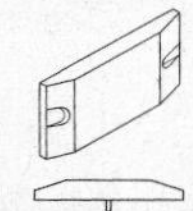

**116-29460** Tags pkg(28) **3.25**
Prototypically correct, tags feature small mounting pins for easy installation on painted models without damaging the finish.
**116-29461** Reader Antennas & RF Module **TBA**

## Brass Diesel Steps 3.75 ea (Unless Noted)

Give your diesel fleet a new level of detail with these photo-etched steps, which provide scale thickness and see-through realism. Can be installed directly on your model, or used to replace molded steps. Available for many popular models.

### For Athearn Shells

**116-29236** SD40-2
**116-29237** GP60, 50, 40, 38
**116-29249** C44-9W
**116-29252** UB/UC
**116-29254** SW7
**116-29255** SW1500
**116-29256** F45/FP45
**116-29262** SD70/75 3-Step

**Limited Quantity Available**
**116-29261** SD70/75 4-Step

### For Railpower Shells

**116-29230** SD45
**116-29231** SD60
**116-29232** 8-40CW
**116-29233** B23-7
**116-29234** SD60M
**116-29235** GP35
**116-29244** GP60B, M
**116-29245** C30-7
**116-29246** C32-8/8-40B
**116-29247** SD45-2
**116-29248** 9-44CW
**116-29250** SD40/38
**116-29257** SD90MAC **4.95**

### For Assorted Shells

**116-29239** Front Range GP7/9

### Kato Shells

**116-29238** SD40/45
**116-29260** C44-9W

## Chain

Includes 12" of chain.

### Brass 3.50 ea

**116-29216** 40 Links Per Inch
**116-29217** 27 Links Per Inch
**116-29218** 15 Links Per Inch
**116-29270** 13 Links Per Inch
**116-29271** 6 Links Per Inch

### Black 3.95 ea

**116-29219** 40 Links Per Inch
**116-29220** 27 Links Per Inch
**116-29221** 15 Links Per Inch
**116-29272** 13 Links Per Inch
**116-29273** 6 Links Per Inch

### Silver 3.95 ea

**116-29222** 40 Links Per Inch
**116-29223** 27 Links Per Inch
**116-29224** 15 Links Per Inch
**116-29274** 13 Links Per Inch
**116-29275** 6 Links Per Inch

## E Unit Parts

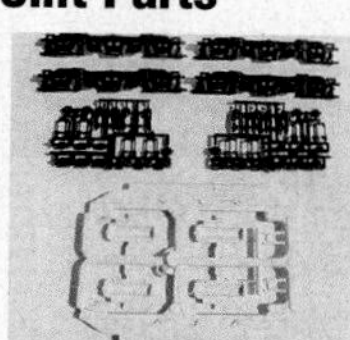

**116-29300** Sideframe Set **8.95**
Set of four sideframes with separate hangers, brake cylinders, and different journal box covers. Fits Athearn SD45, U, C, F45 and FP45 three-axle trucks.
**116-29301** Fuel Tank Skirt/Air Tank Set **3.25**

## Electric Generator Set

**116-29462 3.50**
Portable or stationary generator and fuel tank.
**NEW 116-29463** Modern Freight Car Levers **3.50**
**NEW 116-26702** Intermodal Parts Sprue **3.50**

## Freight Car Parts

**116-29400** Tank Car Ends pkg(6) **3.50**
Includes two each: "recessed" (ACF insulated), "hard edge" (GATX/Trinity Insulated) and "soft edge" (GATX/Trinity Insulated). Fits Model Die Casting 50' tank car.

## Grab Irons

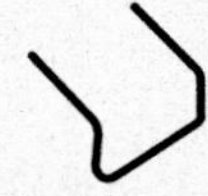

**116-29100** pkg(50) **4.75**
Fine scale, formed brass wire is unplated for better paint adhesion. Use on locos and cars.

## Windshield Wipers

Molded in nonbreakable Delrin®.
**116-29200** Long & Short pkg(8) **3.75**
**116-29201** Short Only pkg(8) **3.25**

## Stirrups pkg(25) 3.50 ea

Formed brass steps.

116-29000

116-29001

116-29002

**116-29000** Style "A"
**116-29001** Style "B"
**116-29002** Style "C"

## Sun Shades Set 3.25 ea

Replace fragile plastic shades with durable brass etchings. Great for models which are handled often. Shades are adjustable and include mounting instructions.

116-29210

116-29211

116-29212

**116-29210** Hood Unit Diesels pkg(6)
**116-29211** E&F Unit pkg(6)
**116-29212** Comfort Cab pkg(4)

## Weights

Motor Mount Cradle Weights for locos are listed in the Lighting-Electrical-Motors section.

## Athearn 85' Flat Car

**116-13202** Flat Car w/End Weights **14.95**
Improve the looks and operation of Athearn 85' Flat Cars with this custom weight set. Parts fit center sill and ends, lowering the car to a more prototypical height. Lower center of gravity and additional weight improve tracking, so the car can be operated easily without a load. Can be used on cushioned or noncushioned cars and adds more realistic detail to the end of the car. Includes complete Athearn kit, end weight castings and instructions.

See What's New and Exciting at
**www.walthers.com**

## Weight Sets 8.75 ea

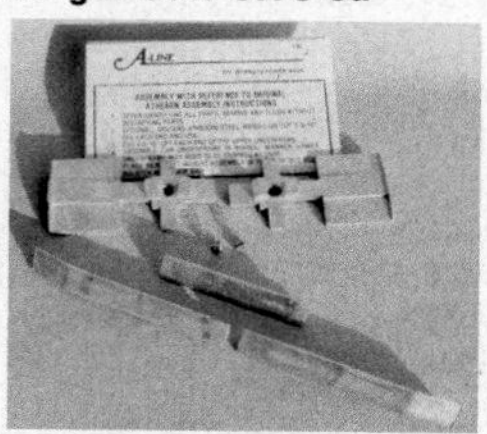

**116-13200** 85' Flat Car End Weight Kit
**116-13201** Center Sill Kit
Fits Athearn 85' and Custom Rail and Accurail 89' flat cars, plus Walthers Auto Rack.

## Flat Weights 5.95 ea

An easy way to add extra weight to locos and cars. Lead is precut, with double-sided backing tape for easy installation. Thickness dimension includes tape.
**116-13000** 1/2 x 1/2 x 3/16" 12.7 x 12.7 x 4.7mm 3oz 84g pkg(2)
**116-13001** 1/2 x 3/4 x 5/32" 12.7 x 19 x 3.9mm 3oz 84g pkg(2)
**116-13002** 1/2 x 3/4 x 1/4" 12.7 x 19 x 6.3mm 6oz 168g

## Pourable Lead

**116-13015** 6oz (168g) **4.95**
An easy way to add weight in tight spaces, tiny lead balls are .080" or about 5/64" diameter. Easily poured into any area and set with diluted white glue.

## Moldable Lead

**116-13010** Moldable Lead Weight 1oz **9.95**
Mold with fingers, can be glued with most adhesives, will not harden over time.

## Lead Sheets

All sheets are 4-1/2" long and 2-3/4" wide.
**116-13016** 4oz, 1/32" Thick **3.50**
**116-13018** 6oz, 1/16" Thick **3.95**
**116-13020** 9oz, 3/32" Thick **4.95**

## Scale Label Set

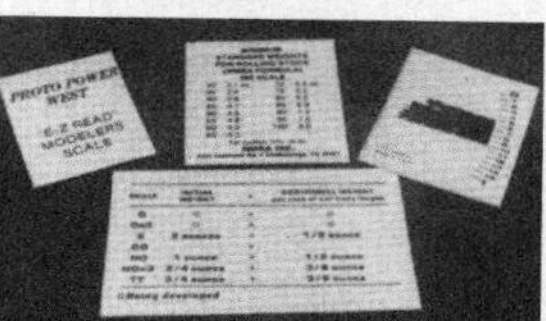

**116-13111 3.25**
Improve the performance of your freight car fleet by making sure every car meets NMRA weight standards. Self-adhesive label converts a 16oz postal scale (sold separately) to an E-Z read modeler's weighting scale. Use with A-Line "weigh-it yourself" lead weights.

## 12" Diameter Roof Ve

**231-241 2.95**

## 18" Diameter Roof Ven 2.95 ea

White metal castings.

231-240

231-242

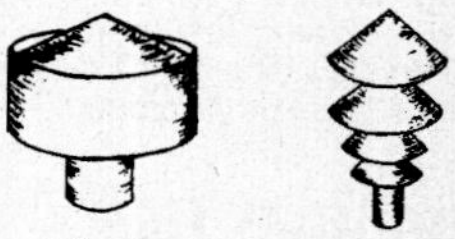

**231-240** Round pkg(5)
**231-242** Stacked Cones pkg(

## 18" Diameter Wind Vane Vents pkg(3) 2.95 ea

White metal castings.

231-243

231-244

**231-243** Mouth Down Wind
**231-244** Mouth Up Wind

## Plywood Sheets

**231-1010** 1/2 x 1" pkg(12) **2.9**
Real wood cut to a scale 4 x 8 sheet, great for lumber yards, freight car or pickup bed loads, boarded-up windows or scale models of layouts!

## Slat Vent Kits 9.95 ea

These larger slatted vents can be used on engine sheds, industrial buildings or any structure that needs realistic roof detail.

**231-17** Small
9/16 x 1-1/8" 1.4 x 2.8cm
Makes up to five vents.

**231-19** Large
1 x 2" 2.5 x 5cm
Makes up to three vents.

Item listed below is available by Special Order (see Legend Page).
**231-18** Medium
3/4 x 1-1/2" 1.9 x 3.8cm
Makes up to four vents.

...prove the looks of any ...del with this selection of ...stic, brass and white metal ...rts. All items are unpainted.

## ...ITBITS PARTS

### ...aboose Parts

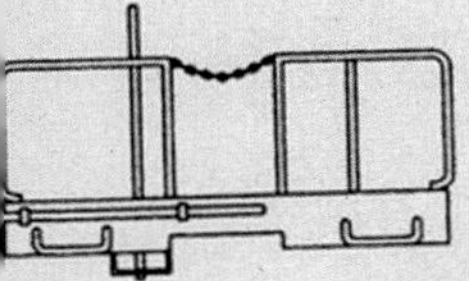

...8-6 End Beam w/Railing - ...hite Metal **2.45**

...8-60 Steps w/Round ...orners pkg(4) **2.25**

...8-61 Awnings - White Metal ...25

### ...mokejacks pkg(2) ....25 ea

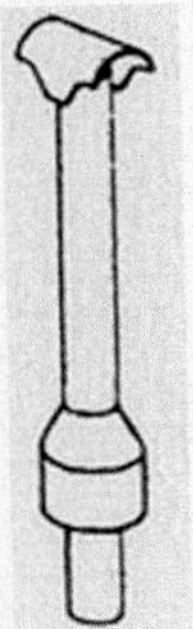

### Cupola 2.95 ea

...718-64 Tall – Old Style

...718-70 Short – Modern Style

### Ends 1 Pair 2.95 ea

**718-65** Wood Sheathed w/Windows

**718-66** Steel w/Windows

**718-67** Wood Sheathed – No Windows

### Windows pkg(4) 2.25 ea

**718-68** 2-Light

**718-69** 1-Light

### Freight Car Parts

**718-78** AB Brake System - White Metal **2.25**

**718-1102** Pennsylvania H-25 Hopper Ends - 1 Pair **2.95**

### Passenger Car Parts

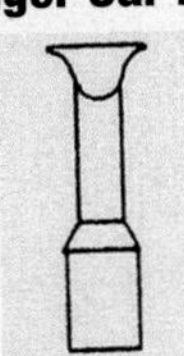

**718-7** Smokestack pkg(2) **2.25**

**718-10** Steam Traps **2.25**

**718-14** Diaphragms - 2 Pair w/Springs **3.95**

**718-41** 27 x 108" Water Tanks **2.95**

**718-42** Holding Tanks **2.95**

**718-43** Air Conditioner Box **2.95**

**718-44** Regulator **2.95**

**718-45** Trip Valve **2.95**

**718-46** Air Compressor **2.95**

**718-47** Double Air Tank **2.95**

**718-49** PRR Roof Ducts **2.25**

**718-50** Coach Doors **2.25**

**718-93** RPO Exterior Window Bar pkg(4) **4.95**

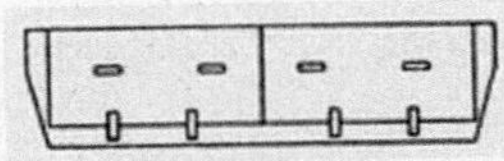

**718-370** Tool Box **2.25**

**718-371** Retaining Valve **2.25**

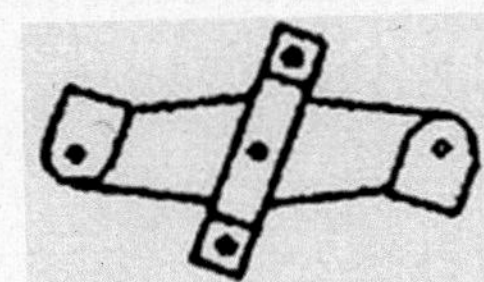

**718-372** Brake Lever **2.25**

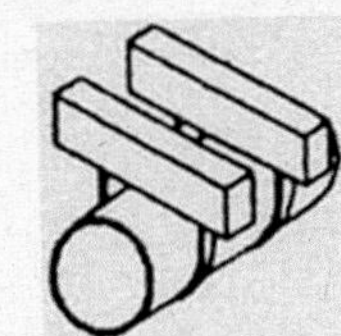

**718-373** Air Tank **2.25**

**718-374** Generator **2.25**

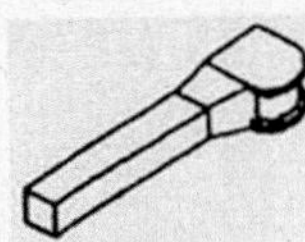

**718-375** Truss Rod Tie-Downs pkg(4) **2.45**

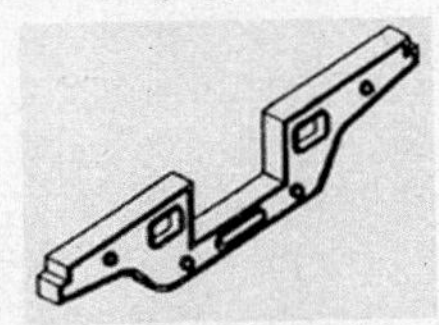

**718-376** Wood Cross Bearers **2.45**

**718-377** Queen Post Assembly **2.45**

### Air Brake System

**718-12** Type UC Plastic 2 Sets **6.95**

### Air Conditioner

**718-73** Air Conditioner Unit **2.25**

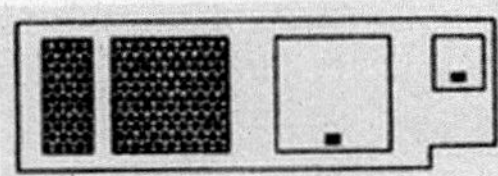

**718-378** York **3.45**

### Battery Box

**718-18** With Generator & Bracket - Plastic **2.95**

**718-19** Notch-Cornered w/Generator & Bracket **2.95**

**718-75** Battery Box **3.45**

**718-77** Utility Box **3.45**

**718-80** Pullman **3.45**

**718-83** Pullman **3.45**

**718-94** Erie **3.45**

### Car Sides 1 Pair 5.95 ea

**718-21A** Coach

**718-21B** Combine

**718-21C** RDG Double-Door Baggage Car

**718-21D** RDG Modern Baggage Car

**718-21E** CNJ Baggage Car

**718-21F** WM Baggage Car

### Doors - 6' Baggage 4.95 ea

**718-89** Brass

**718-96** Plastic

### Dress-Up Kit

**718-32** Railway Post Office **4.95**
Includes two each external window bars, internal window bars and smash plates.

### Ends

#### Coach

**718-22A** Rounded Roofline **5.95**

**718-22G** Rounded Roofline w/Windows **5.95**

**718-22H** Flat Roofline w/Windows **5.95**

#### Baggage Car

**718-22B** Flat Roofline Type 1 **5.95**

**718-22C** Flat Roofline Type 2 **2.95**

**718-22D** Angled Roofline **5.95**

**718-22E** Rounded Roofline **2.95**

**718-22F** PRR-Style **2.95**

**718-201** Rounded Roofline w/End Door **3.95**

### Heavyweight Bulkhead Kits 3.95 ea

**718-23A** Coaches, Diners, Smokers & Pullmans; 2 Bulkheads & Strip Styrene

**718-24A** Heavyweight Combines; 3 Bulkheads & Strip Styrene

### Pullman Ice Bunker

**718-81** Single **3.45**

**718-82** Double **3.95**

### Roofs

**718-25** 70' Arch Roof w/Lavatory Vents **4.95**

**718-27** 70' Clerestory Roof w/Lavatory Vents **5.95**

**718-40** PRR Arch Roof 11" Center Piece w/2 End Caps **4.95**

**718-102** 11" Roof For Heavyweight Rebuilds **3.95**

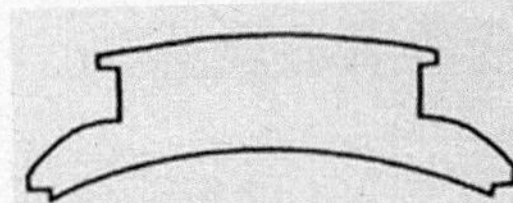

**718-130** 11" Wood Clerestory Roof w/Plastic End Caps **9.95**

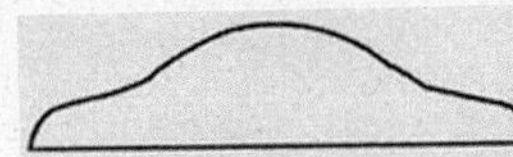

**718-131** Wood Stillwell Roof w/Resin End Caps **9.95**

**718-132** Wood DL&W Arch Roof w/Resin End Caps **9.95**

### Steps

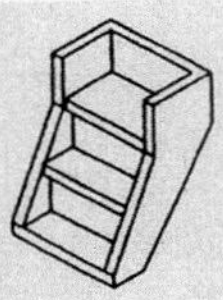

**718-8** 3-Step Type pkg(4) **2.95**

**718-33** 4-Step Type pkg(4) **2.95**

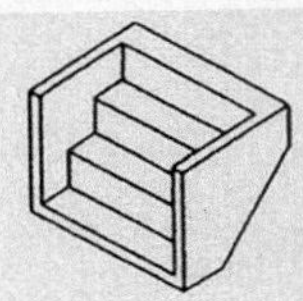

**718-72** For Troop Sleeper **2.25**

**718-86** Baggage Steps - 1 Scale Foot Wide pkg(8) **3.95**

**718-87** Baggage Steps (4) 30", (4) 12" **3.95**

### Underframe

**718-30B** Fishbelly Style - Plastic **3.95**

### Vents

**718-28** Long Garland Roof Vents **3.95**

**718-34** Gold Vents pkg(12) **3.95**

**718-35** Lavatory Vent **2.45**

**718-36** Diner Vent **2.45**

**718-37** Box Vent **2.45**

**718-38** Ward Vents **3.95**

**718-39** Osgood-Bradley Vents **6.95**

**718-16** Utility Roof Vents **2.25**

**718-138** Ward Vents For Stillwell Roofs **3.95**

**718-254** Pullman Garland - Double **2.25**

**718-256** Pullman Garland - Single **2.25**

### Windows 2.25 ea

Printed on clear acetate.

**718-101** White On Clear

**718-103** White On Clear

### Locomotive Parts

**718-62** Back-Up Light on Bracket **2.25**
Designed for Bachmann 2-8-0 (sold separately) adaptable to other models.

**718-31** Marker Lights For ALCO RS-3 pkg(4) **2.25**

## BRANCHLINE TRAINS

BLUEPRINT SERIES

### BLUEPRINT SERIES CAR KIT PARTS

Great for kitbashing or modifying Blueprint Series cars or customizing your own rolling stock. Parts are injection-molded plastic.

#### Box Car Parts

**Box Car Ends 4.98 ea**
Includes grab irons and ladders.

**181-100001** Early Dreadnaught
**181-100002** Late Improved Dreadnaught
**181-100003** Dartnot
**181-100004** 4/4 Dreadnaught

**Box Car Roofs 2.98 ea**

**181-100005** 50' Diagonal Panel
**181-100006** 50' Overhanging Diagonal Panel
**181-140001** 40' Box Car Diagonal Panel
**181-140002** 40' Box Car Straight Panel
**181-200001** 50' Modern "X-Panel"

**Box Car Doors 2.98 ea (Unless Noted)**

**181-100010** 8' Superior 7-Panel pkg(2)
**181-100011** 8' Superior 6-Panel pkg(2)
**181-100012** 8' Youngstown pkg(2)
**181-100013** 9' Youngstown pkg(2)
**181-100014** 7' & 8' Double Youngstown **4.98**
**181-140004** 6' Youngstown pkg(2)
**181-140005** 7' Superior pkg(2)
**181-140006** 7' Youngstown pkg(2)

**Box Car Detail Sets 2.98 ea (Unless Noted)**

**181-100007** 50' Despatch Ends & Roof Kit **4.98**
Includes 2 ends, 50' roof, end ladders and grab irons.
**181-100008** 50' Apex Roofwalk
**181-100015** Box Car End Details
Includes ladders, grabs, handbrake, air hose and cut levers.
**181-100016** Box Car Side Details
Includes ladders, grab irons, stirrup steps and tack boards.
**181-100017** 50' Underframe & Brake Gear **4.98**
**181-200002** 50' Modern Box Car Details
**181-200003** 50' Modern Box Car Brake Detail **4.98**

**Reefer Details 2.98 ea (Unless Noted)**

**181-120001** Roofwalk
**181-120002** Reefer Detail Parts
Includes side and end grab irons, ladders and details.
**181-120004** 40' Wood Reefer Underframe Kit **4.98**

#### HO Passenger Car Details

**2.98 ea (Unless Noted)**

**Body Cores**

**181-151002** HO Coach Body Core
**181-151113** Pullman Body Core

**Car Sides**

**181-151001** 80' Single Window Coach Sides
**181-151101** Pullman 8-1-2 Plan 3979
**181-151102** Pullman 10-1-2 Plan 3585
**181-151103** Pullman 12-1 Plan 3410
**181-151104** Pullman 10-1-1 Plan 3973
**181-151105** Pullman 14-Section Plan 3958
**181-151106** Pullman 6-3 Plan 3523a
**181-151110** Pullman 10-1-1 Plan 3973

**Car Roofs**

**181-151011** Coach Roof W/Vents **3.98**
**181-151107** Pullman 8-1-2 Plan 3979
**181-151108** Pullman 10-1-2 Plan 3585
**181-151109** Pullman 12-1 Plan 3410
**181-151111** Pullman 14-Section Plan 3958
**181-151112** Pullman 6-3 Plan 3523a

**Miscellaneous**

**181-151003** Center Sill W/Brake Gear **3.98**
**181-151004** Battery Boxes, Air Tanks & Steam Traps
**181-151005** Operating Diaphragms
**181-151006** Passenger Car End Details
Includes safety chains, steam piping and signal lines.
**181-151007** Passenger Car Steps
**181-151008** Vestibule Interior Walls
**181-151010** Coach Interior **3.98**
**181-151114** Pullman Center Sill W/Brake Gear **3.98**
**181-151115** Pullman Battery Boxes & Air Tanks
**181-151116** Pullman Ice & Mechanical A/C Parts
**181-151117** Pullman Steam Ejector A/C Parts

## BRAWA

LIEBE ZUM DETAIL

IMPORTED FROM GERMANY BY WALTHERS
Metal details for layout scenes.

### STREET DETAILS

**186-5438** Telephone Station w/Lighting pkg(2) **21.99**

**186-5439** Telephone Box FH32 w/Lighting **24.99**

**186-5440** Police Emergency Phone **16.99**
Green, approximately 1" 2.54cm tall, illuminated.

186-5441

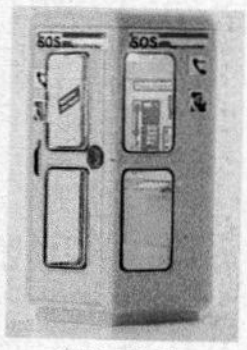

186-5442

**186-5441** Illuminated Phone Booth **11.99**
**186-5442** Phone Shanty **15.99**
**186-5443** English Phone Booth w/Clock **28.99**

**186-5444** Pay Phone Booth **20.99**

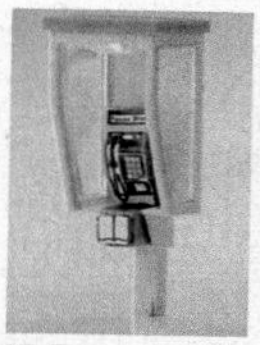

**186-5445** Freestanding Pay Phone **13.99**
**186-5446** Freestanding Tall Pay Phone **14.99**

**186-5447** FH 32 Era III/IV **24.99**

186-5448

186-5449

**186-5448** FH 32 Era II **24.99**
**186-5449** Swisscom **17.99**

### TRACKSIDE DETAILS

**186-2652** Distance Posts pkg(10) **7.99**
Prototypes are spaced 100 meters apart.

**186-2653** Switch Heater **13.99**
Includes two propane tanks, 3-3/4" 9.3cm wide.

**186-2654** Lineside Phone Box **6.99**
1 x 3/4" 2.5 x 1.8cm.

Get the Scoop!
Get the Skinny!
Get the Score!
Check Out Walthers Web site at
**www.walthers.com**

## CMA

Make your models look th
best with these plastic par
For a complete listing of C
products, visit Walthers W
site at www.walthers.com.

**Crates**

**363-1020** pkg(8) **4.95**

**Ladders**

**363-1010** For Freight Cars pkg(16) **4.95**

**Phosphor Bronze Wi 2.50 ea**
Make handrails, grab irons, plumbing and more.

**363-1100** .008" pkg(10)
**363-1101** .010" pkg(12)
**363-1102** .015" pkg(12)
**363-1103** .020" pkg(12)
**363-1104** .025" pkg(12)
**363-1105** .032".pkg(12)
**363-1106** .0125" pkg(12)

**Roofwalks**

**363-1016** 40' Steel pkg(3) **5.**
Make any 40' box car, stock car or reefer more realistic w these parts. One-piece roofwalk and separate corne walkways have a very thin cross section and see-throug tread.

## CLASSIC MINIATURES

Cast metal details.

Visit Walthers Web site at www.walthers.com for a complete listing of Classic Miniatures products.

**Chimney & Smoke Jac 3.00 ea**

**225-20003** Brick Chimney pkg(2)
**225-20008** Smokejack pkg(4)

**Staircase**

**225-20002** Ornamental Iron Staircase **7.00**
0.10" thick. Includes stripwooc for stairs and scribed wood porch.

**Stove Pipe**

**225-20009** Elbow Stove Pipe pkg(3) **3.00**

# CANNON & COMPANY DIESEL COMPONENTS

ake your motive power look like the real thing with these jection molded parts. Each is carefully engineered to match ajor structural components of second and third generation EMD comotives. Parts are molded in light gray styrene. Easily added most plastic locos and a great starting point for scratchbuilt or itbashing projects. All include instructions for assembly and stallation. All parts are for EMD locomotives.

## ir Filter Hatch

**91-1901** AAF Angled Paper lter **2.95**
orrect for post-1976 P38-2s and SD38-2s.

## ir Reservoirs

**91-2155** Standard pkg(2) **.95**
hese reservoirs are used on ll EMD switchers, GPs and Ds starting with the first 40 eries units to the current D70/75s.

## nticlimbers 2.95 ea Unless Noted)

hange or upgrade the look of ny EMD, from the first GP35s the latest SD90.

191-2101 191-2102

**191-2101** Small pkg(4)
ncludes two different styles.

**191-2102** Full Width pkg(2)
Used on early SD units.

**191-2103** Standard Dash 2 Type pkg(2)

**191-2104** Tunnel Motor Style pkg(2)
Used on SD40T-2 and SD45T-2 Rear, includes two styles.

**191-2105** 50 Series, Late Dash 2 and GP15-1 pkg(2)

**191-2106** SD60, SD60M & SD50 pkg(2)
Used on front and rear.

**191-2107** SD70, Late GP60 pkg(2)
Used on front and rear of SD70 and on front of GP60.

**191-2108** SD80/90 Front & Rear w/Ditch Lights pkg(2) **3.50**
Includes one set of forward ditch lights.

## Blower Housings pkg(2) 3.50

Blower housings are a distinguishing feature of modern EMD power.

191-1601 191-1602 191-1603

**191-1601** Angled
Used on some GP/SD40-2s, GP/SD50s, all GP/SD60s and the SD70MAC.

**191-1602** 35 & 40
Used on all GP/SD35s, most GP/SD38s, GP/50, GP40s and SD45s.

**191-1603** Late-40
Used on 1971 built GP/SD38 & 39, GP/SD40s and SD45s.

**191-1604** Dash 2
Used on the majority of Dash 2 GPs and SDs, plus all early GP/SD50s.

## Brake Chain Tensioner

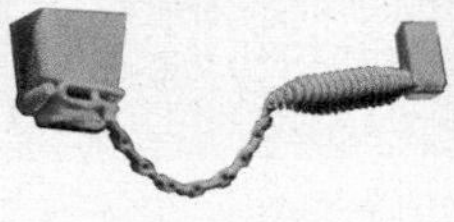

**191-2152** For Dash 2 & 50/60 Series SD Units pkg(2) **2.95**

## Cab Sub Base & Optional Doors

Kits replace the entire structure under the cab and nose. Includes enough parts to build two different sub bases.

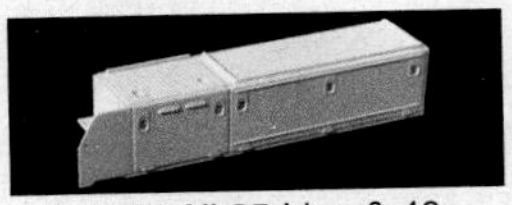

**191-1201** All 35 Line & 40 Series Units 2 Pair **6.95**

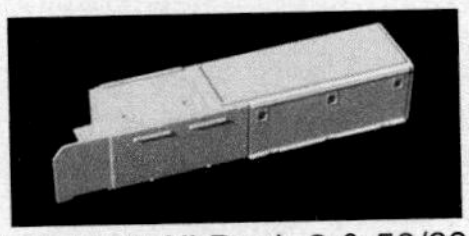

**191-1202** All Dash 2 & 50/60 Series Units 2 Pair **6.95**

**191-1203** SP "Split" Equipment Doors pkg(6) **2.95**

**191-1204** CR "Split" Battery Box Doors, Chessie "Mailslot" Battery Box Doors pkg(8) **2.95**

## Cast Brakewheels

**191-1108** 22" pkg(6) **3.95**
Used on almost all EMD units and all GEs up to the Dash 7.

## Dynamic Brakes

191-1801 191-1803

**191-1801** Hatch For SD50s to Mid SD60s **2.95**

**191-1802** Hatch For EMD SD60, 70 & 75 **2.95**

**191-1803** Intake Grilles pkg(2) **3.50**
For SD50s through SD75s.

## Extended Range Doors 4.50 ea

191-1804 191-1805 191-1806

**191-1804** For GP35 pkg(9)

**191-1805** For GP40 pkg(9)

**191-1806** For 40 Series SDs pkg(16)

## Electrical Cabinet Air Filter Box pkg(2) 2.95 ea

191-1902 191-1903 191-1904

**191-1902** For 40 Series

**191-1903** For Early To Mid Dash 2s

**191-1904** Built-In Style For Mid Dash 2s & 50/60 Series

## Fuel Tank Detail Set

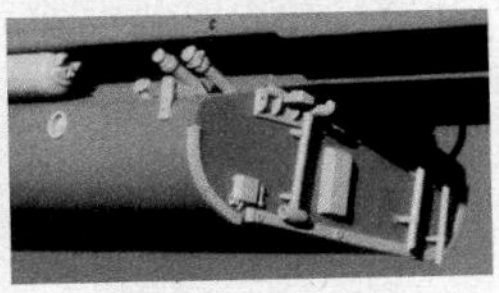

**191-2156 4.95**
This 32 part set incorporates every possible detail found on contemporary EMD fuel tanks including: hangers, gauges, breathers, drains and more.

## Hood Unit Doors

These newly revised doors are interchangeable with the previous series, except that they are completely solid. Also, please note new size.

### Engine Compartment Doors pkg(8) 2.50 ea

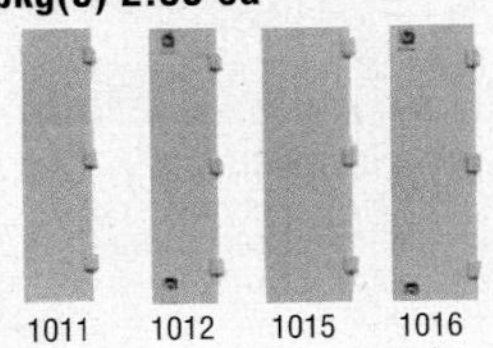

1011 1012 1015 1016

**18 x 78"**

**191-1011** Plain

**191-1012** Latched

**22 x 78"**

**191-1015** Plain

**191-1016** Latched

### Generator/Alternator Access pkg(4) 2.50 ea

Includes access doors and plates.

**191-1018** 35/40 Series

**191-1019** Dash 2, 50/60/70 Series

### Radiator Compartment Doors pkg(8) 2.50 ea

Measure a scale 22 x 65", unless noted.

**191-1013** Plain

**191-1014** Latched

**191-1017** 16 x 17 x 65"
Includes both Plain and Latched types.

**191-1020** Plain & Latched pkg(8) **2.50**
18 x 65"

## Inertial Filter Hatches pkg(2) 2.95 ea

One of the more prominent features on the roof, inertial filter hatches or "dust bins" feature deeply molded, ultra-fine exhaust grilles, and a raised mounting surface that "floats" the hatch just off the top of the long hood.

**191-1351** Early 35 Line Units

**191-1352** GP/SD38

191-1353 191-1354

**191-1353** Late 35 Line Units
Used on GP/SD39, GP/SD40, SD45 and SD38-2, SD40-2, SD45-2.

**191-1354** GP38-2, GP15-1, GP15T

**191-1355** GP40-2 & Phase I GP39-2

**191-1356** Phase II GP39-2

**191-1357** GP49 & GP50

**191-1358** GP59, GP60, GP60B, GP60M

**191-1359** SD50, SD60M

**191-1360** SD70, SD70M

## Inertial Filter Screens

These screens all feature correct depth and contour as well as hex head bolts on the extra-thin mounting flange.

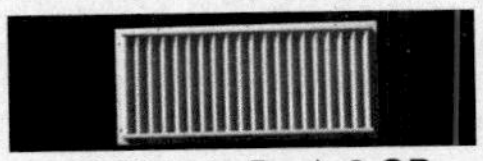

**191-1301** Late Dash 2 GPs pkg(4) **2.50**
Correct for late GP38-2s, GP39-2s, GP40-2s and SD38-2s.

**191-1302** 35 Line, GP pkg(4) **2.95**
Correct for GP35 and SD35 and some SD39s.

**191-1303** pkg(4) **2.50**
Correct for GP38, GP39, GP40 and some SD39s. Also used on early GP38-2, GP39-2, GP40-2, GP15-1 and SD38-2s.

**191-1304** pkg(4) **2.50**
Correct for SD38, SD40, SD45 and early SD40-2 and SD45-2.

**191-1305** Post-1984 EMD SD40-2 pkg(4) **2.50**

**191-1306** Inertial Filter Screens **2.50**
Set includes long and short for GP49, GP50, GP59 and GP60.

**191-1307** SD50 to SD90 pkg(4) **2.50**
Used on SD50, SD60, SD60M, SD70, SD75, SD80 and SD90.

## Long Hood Ends pkg(2) 3.50 ea

Four different components essential to upgrade any scale width EMD long hood to an exact prototype match.

**191-SE1** Dash 2 Hood End without Class Lights
Used on EMD SD70, 75, late Dash 2 and BL20-2.

191-1151 191-1153

**191-1151** 35 Series
Correct hood end for GP/SD28s and 35s.

**191-1152** 40 Series
Standard hood end for GP/SD38s, 39s and 40s.

**191-1153** Dash 2
Fully equipped hood end with numberboards and class lights, for Dash 2s, plus 50, 60 and 70 Series.

**191-1154** Blank Dash 2
Blank hood end for later Dash 2, 50, 60 and 70 Series locos.

# CANNON & COMPANY
DIESEL COMPONENTS

## Pilot Lift Tabs

**191-2051** EMD 40 Series Through SD90 pkg(24) **2.50**

## Radiator Grilles & Screens

The early radiator grilles feature all of the visible layers of detail right back to the shutters. The later style screens accurately represent the depth and rounded corrugations of the prototype.

**191-1401** Radiator Screens Pkg(4) **2.95**
Used on late GP38-2, GP39-2 and SD45-2.

**191-1402** 35 Line Radiator Grilles pkg(4) **3.50**
Used on all 35 Line units: GP28, GP35, SD28 and SD35.

**191-1403** Radiator Screens pkg(4) **3.50**
Used on late GP40-2s and SD40-2s.

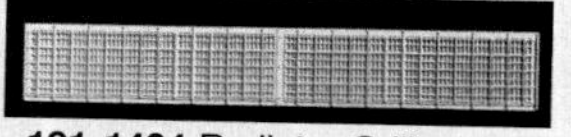

**191-1404** Radiator Grilles pkg(4) **3.95**
Correct for all GP40s and SD40s, also early GP40-2s and SD40-2s.

**191-1405** Radiator Grilles pkg(4) **3.95**
Precise wire mesh grilles for GP/SD38/39 and Phase I GP39-2, plus early GP38-2.

**191-1406** GP50/60 Radiator Screens pkg(2) **3.95**
Used on GP49, GP50, GP59 and all versions of GP60.

**191-1407** SD50-75 Radiator Screens pkg(2) **3.95**
Used on SD50, SD60, SD60M, SD70 and SD75.

**191-1408** SD80/90 Radiator Screens pkg(2) **3.95**
Used on SD80 and SD90.

**191-1409** Farr Radiator Grille pkg(2) **2.95**
Unique grilles for most Southern Pacific SD39s.

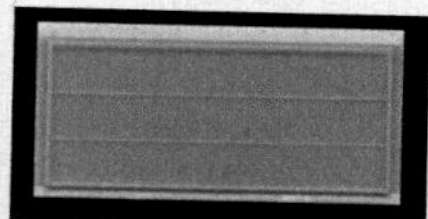

**191-1410** SD45 Farr Radiator Grilles pkg(6) **3.95**
Unique grills for many SP SD45s.

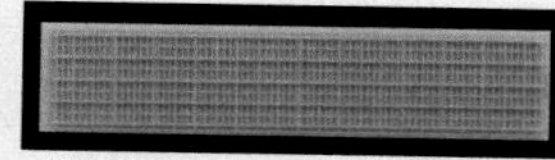

**191-1411** EMD SD45-2 Wire Grilles pkg(4) **3.95**

## Roof Stock

**191-1751** Blank pkg(2) **3.95**
Features exact scale edge radius and a highly detailed sand filler. It is long enough to build the radiator compartment of any unit up to and including the SD45-2.

## Safety Tread & Step Kits 4.50 ea (Unless Noted)

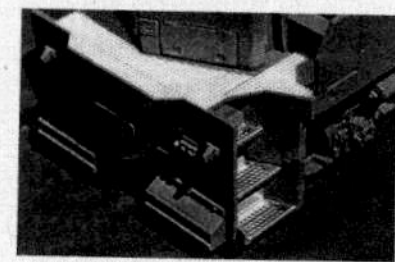

**191-2001** For Athearn GP38-2 & GP40-2s **16.50**
Features a near scale diamond grid pattern on ultra thin brass, exact scale hole layout in the steps and a perfect drop-in fit.

**191-2002** Safety Step & Tread Kit For Athearn SW1000 & SW1500 **12.50**

191-2003

191-2004

**191-2003** Step Set For All Kato SDs

**191-2004** Step Set For All Kato GP35s

**191-2005** Safety Tread & Step Kit For Athearn SD40-2 **18.50**

**191-2006** Step Set For Proto 2000 SD60

**191-2007** Step Set For Athearn SD70 (3 Step)

**191-2008** Step Set For Athearn SD70/75 (4 Step)

**191-2009** Step Set for Proto 2000 GP60

**191-2010** Safety Tread & Step Set for Walthers GP15-1 **16.50**
Features extra front platform piece for 81" nose, hood side step and left walkway strips for both versions of this model.

**191-2011** Step Set for Athearn SD50

191-2012

191-2013

**191-2012** Step Set for Proto 2000 SD45

**191-2013** Step Set for Athearn SD70MAC

**191-2014** Step Set for Proto 2000 SD50

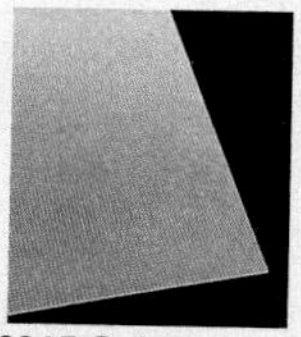

**191-2015** Safety Tread Stock **16.50**
Full sheet of tread material, 1.42 x 5.7".

**191-2016** Walkway Safety Tread **16.50**
Five tread strips, .245 x 5.46".

**191-2017** Anticlimber Safety Tread pkg(6) **4.95**
Fits our AC-2102 full-width anticlimber.

**191-2018** Anticlimber Safety Tread pkg(6) **4.95**
Fits our AC-2103 standard anticlimber.

**191-2019** Anticlimber Safety Tread pkg(6) **4.95**
Fits our AC-2105 50 series anticlimber.

**191-2020** Anticlimber Safety Tread pkg(6) **4.95**
Fits our AC-2106 60 series anticlimber.

**191-2021** Anticlimber Safety Tread pkg(6) **4.95**
Fits our AC-2107 and 2108 70 to 90 series anticlimber.

**191-2022** Step Set for Proto 2000 GP7, 9, 18 & 20
Includes four extra steps for battery boxes or unusual prototypes.



Kits contain all deck tread and steps for Athearn SD40T-2 models indicated.

**NEW 191-2030** 81" Nose **TBA**

**NEW 191-2031** 88" Nose **TBA**

These safety tread nose only kits are supplemental to #s 191-2005, 2030 and 2031, each sold separately, and contain only the short hood tread for the Athearn SD40T-2 and SD40-2 models indicated.

**NEW 191-2032** 116" Nose **TBA**

**NEW 191-2033** 123" Nose **TBA**

**NEW 191-2034** Safety Tread Nose Only For Athearn SD40-2 81" Nose **TBA**
This kit is supplemental to #191-2005 and has only the short hood tread for the 81" nose.

## Side Step Sets 4.50 ea (Unless Noted)

**191-2023** For Athearn SD 45T-2

**NEW 191-2024** For Athearn SD 45-2

**NEW 191-2025** For Athearn MP15AC

**191-2026** For PROTO 2000 GP30

**NEW 191-2028** For Athearn Genesis F45 & FP45 **4.95**

**NEW 191-2029** Steps Only For Athearn SD40T-2 **4.95**

**NEW 191-2035** Steps Only For Athearn SD40-2 **4.95**

## SD Jacking Pads pkg(4) 2.95 ea

191-2153

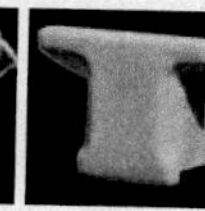

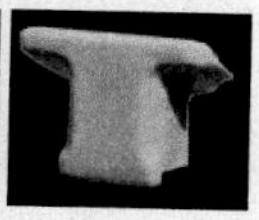

191-2154

**191-2153** For All 40 Series SDs & Dash 2 SDs Built Before January 1974

**191-2154** For All Dash 2 SDs Built Between January 1974 & Late 1977

## Short Hood Accessories

191-1102

191-1107

**191-1102** EMD Low Nose Toilet Hatch pkg(4) **2.50**
A post-1981 addition to most 88" low noses (use with #1104) used on both GP and SD units.

**191-1107** 88" Optional Left Side pkg(2) **2.95**
Recessed brake wheel side for post-1990 units with 88" nose, use with #1104 (sold separately).

## Short Hood Kits & Accessories 6.95 ea

Five different conversion ki replicate the variety of shor hoods used by EMD from 1 to the present. Each kit includes at least 40 parts to cover the many differences brake gear, class lights, ver and other appliances.

191-1101

191-1103

**191-1101** High Nose
Used on most units from the GP/SD35 through the GP50 Includes clear numberboard material.

**191-1103** 81"
Introduced in 1963, used on hood units, from early 35 lin through early Dash 2s.

191-1104

191-1105

**191-1104** 88"
Introduced in 1977, this is th standard nose for all post-19 Dash 2s through the GP60s and SD70s.

**191-1105** 116"
The first of the "snoots," usec on early SP SD40T-2 "tunnel motors" and UP SD40-2s.

**191-1106** 123"
The final version of the "snoo used on ATSF and Kansas C Southern SD40-2s, plus SP and SSW SD40T-2s.

## Spartan Cab Sides, 4-Window pkg(2) 2.95 ea

**191-1506** For 40 Series

**191-1507** For Dash 2s

## SP Jacking Plates

**191-2151** pkg(12) **2.50**
Late 70s to early 80s.

## Step Guard

**191-1605** For SD80 & SD90 **2.95**

ANNON
COMPANY
ESEL COMPONENTS

## inwall EMD Cab Kits Accessories

esigned to fit EMD comotive models from rious manufacturers. Cab s feature "thinwall" nstruction for a highly alistic appearance. Doors d windows (with flush fitting lass," included in all kits) are parate and can be modeled en or closed.

### ood Units 7.95 ea

**91-1501** Dash 2, 50/60/70 eries
ncludes optional front wall with ." shaped window used by ome roads. Now includes ser-cut cab windows.

**91-1502** "35" / 40 Series
low includes laser-cut cab windows.

### witcher Cabs 8.50 ea

**91-1503** Early Switcher
rched window style used on W1s through SW7s built rom 1939 to 1950.

**191-1504** Late Switcher
Squared window style used on SW7-SW1200s built from 1950-1966.

### Cab Details

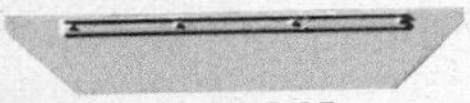

**191-1551** pkg(8) **2.95**
Traditional styled sunshades with reinforcing bracket and razor-sharp edges. Exact fit for brackets in Cannon cab kits and carefully molded to be flexible.

**191-1552** Padlocks & Wiper Motors pkg(17) **2.50**

**191-1553** Super Cab Sunshades pkg(4) **2.95**

### Step Lights

**191-2052** pkg(6) **2.95**

### Window Sets

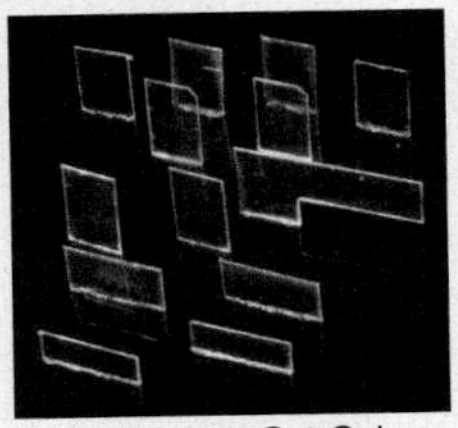

**191-1505** Laser-Cut Cab Windows **3.50**
Precision laser-cut window sets for #1501 and 1502 cab kits.

## Thinwall EMD Fans

The primary characteristic of nearly all EMD hood units is the roof top fans. Now you can upgrade most models from the GP30 to the end of the Dash 2 series with these components, which feature ultra-thin top and mounting flanges, completely detailed hubs, motor supports and motor housing. The nickel-silver grilles employ two-layer or three-layer etching to replicate the prototype assemblies. Application data is for as-built units.

### 36" Radiator Fans

**191-1706** pkg(2) **9.50**
Center radiator fans for all GP35s, SD35s and SDP35s. Also used as dynamic fan on SD38s. Features new three-level grille etching.

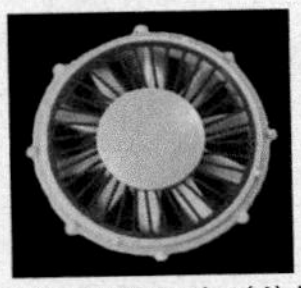

**NEW 191-1707** pkg(4) **TBA**
36-inch cap top radiator fan for first generation EMD diesels. Used on GP/SD7, GP/SD9, GP20, SD18 and SD24.

### 48" Radiator Fans pkg(3) 10.50 ea

191-1701

191-1702

**191-1701** Correct for all GP30s & Early GP/SD35s

**191-1702** Used on all Late GP/SD35 & Early GP/SD38, GP/SD40s

**191-1703** 9-Blade Version for all GP/SD39s & Early SD45s

**191-1704** Late GP/SD38, GP/SD40 & Pre-1980 GP/SD38-2s & GP/SD40-2s

**191-1705** Correct for Late GP/SD39s, SD45s & Pre-1980 GP39-2s & SD45-2s

### 48" Dynamic Brake Fans pkg(2) 6.95 ea (Unless Noted)

**191-1851** Early Style for all GP30s & Early GP/SD35s

**191-1852** For all Late GP/SD35s & Early GP/SD38, 39, 40 & SD45s

**191-1853** Final Design for Late GP/SD38, 39, 40, SD45 & all Dash 2 Units

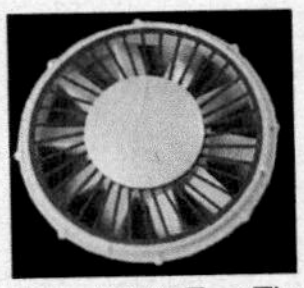

**NEW 191-1854** For First Generation EMD Diesels **TBA**
Used on GP7 and GP9.

### Turbo Hatches pkg(2) 3.95 ea

Correct exhaust assemblies for any turbocharged unit from the first GP/SD35s to the last Dash 2s before silencers were mandated. Components feature see-through stacks with .008" bars, plus correct angles and dimensions.

191-1951

191-1952

**191-1951** GP/SD35

**191-1952** 40 Series & Dash 2

BLMA MODELS

## NEW PRODUCTS

### Locomotive Parts

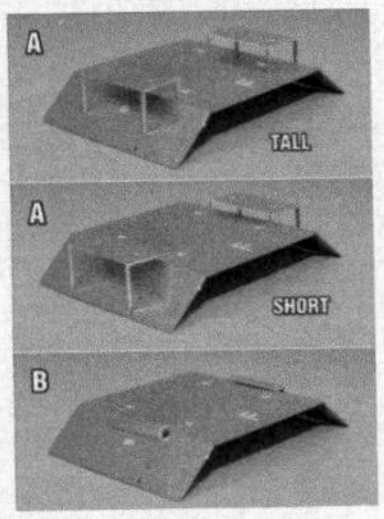


**NEW 176-4550** Remote Controlled Antenna Stands **8.95**
Etched brass detail set includes four of the most common styles.

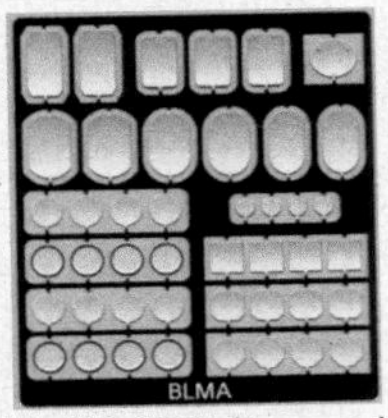


**NEW 176-4551** Removed Headlight Covers **5.50**
Many railroads changed their headlight/class light configuration over time and patched the holes with metal scraps. This detail set includes several common styles so you can easily model these removed lights on your favorite diesels.

**NEW 176-4552** Modern RV Style Air Conditioner pkg(4) **4.75**
Upgrade your modern locos with these RV style air conditioners found on UP, CN, IC, Florida Tri-Rail and more.

### Grab Iron Drill Template

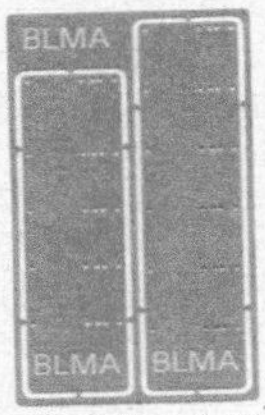


**NEW 176-4500** **4.00**
This set of templates will help even the most experienced modeler align and drill precise holes for grab iron installation on any locomotive. Jigs are spaced at 15, 18, 20 & 24". Simply tape in place, align and drill.

### Grab Irons

Made of .008" stainless steel wire, these grab irons feature prototypical dimensions including the correct wire diameter.

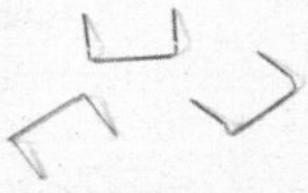

**NEW 176-4510** 18" Drop pkg(20) **5.75**

**NEW 176-4511** 18" Straight pkg(60) **15.50**

**NEW 176-4512** 18" Straight pkg(20) **5.75**

CAL-SCALE

From the golden age of steam to the latest diesels, modeling your favorite equipment is easy with these brass and plastic parts.

## NEW PRODUCTS

### Super Detailing Parts

**NEW 190-522** Coupler Lift Bars for EMD GP & SD Units 1 Pair **2.90**

**NEW 190-523** Curved Roof Grabs for EMD GP & SD Diesels pkg(8) **2.90**

**NEW 190-526** Tongue for Bowser RoadRailer pkg(2) **4.95**

**NEW 190-524** Detail Kit for Athearn EMD GP38-2, GP40-2, SD40-2 Diesels **14.00**

**NEW 190-525** Detail Kit for Athearn EMD SW1500, SW1000 Diesels **14.00**

**NEW 190-527** Detail Kit for Atlas Trainman RS-32/36 Diesels **14.80**

**NEW 190-528** Detail Kit for Atlas Trainman GP38-2 **14.00**

## STEAM DETAILS

### Air Brakes

**190-313** "ABD" Plastic pkg(2) **4.05**
Three-piece, for modern freight cars.

### Air Conditioning Receptacle

**190-355** pkg(2) **3.60**

### Air Hoses

**190-276** Freight Car & Caboose, Plastic pkg(20) **2.60**
Standard design, enough for 10 cars.

**190-277** Standard Type-Brass pkg(4) **2.95**
Use on locomotives, tenders and cars.

**190-319** Steam Freight Locos pkg(2) **2.45**

### Air Pumps

**190-240** Westinghouse Cross Compound **4.40**

**190-334** Side Mounting **6.80**
Dual pumps mounted side by side, with full piping. Used on right side of most locos. This is a different configuration than smokebox mounted pumps (#190-349).

### Cross Compound-Piped 6.00 ea

Pumps include basic air piping, which can be bent for custom installations, or expanded with wire and fittings, sold separately.

**190-346** With Remote Strainer

**190-347** Standard Strainer

**190-349** Front Mounting
Used on front of smoke boxes, most locos had two.

### Single Phase w/Bracket 5.20 ea

Older style with single cylinder, used on early steam locos.

**190-256** 9-1/2"

**190-257** 11"

### Alternator

**190-365** Passenger Car **3.05**
Prototype converts DC to AC for car lighting systems.

### Ash Pans

**190-248** Drop-Door Type pkg(2) **4.40**
Typically used on engines with small fire boxes built between 1900 and late 1930s.

**190-249** Commonwealth Cast Type pkg(2) **5.70**
Used on larger, modern engines but also applied to older types. Castings can be cut to fit any length fire box.

**190-479** Pennsylvania Type pkg(2) **4.35**

### Backhead Details

**190-372** Gauges, Engineer's & Fireman's Side **4.05**

**190-373** Reverse Quadrant For Power Reverse **4.85**

**190-374** Small Quadrant pkg(2) **3.95**
Use for injectors, small power reverse, etc.

### Battery Receptacles

**190-354** pkg(2) **3.60**

### Bells

**190-281** Standard Rope Pull **3.85**

**190-285** Air Ringer **3.85**

**190-299** Angle Bracket Boiler Front Mounting **4.60**

**190-317** Modern Steam Loco **3.85**

**190-328** With Top Bar **4.05**

**190-329** Rigid Old Ball Top **3.05**

### Blow-Off Cocks

**190-308** Blow-Off Cocks (2) & Inspection Plugs (6) **4.40**

### Brake Cylinders

**190-219** Engines pkg(2) **4.35**

**190-220** Westinghouse "PC" High Speed System (3 pieces) **7.40**
Used on older engine tenders and passenger cars. Includes cylinder with levers and triple valve, reducing valve and auxiliary reservoir.

**190-221** Tender **3.45**

### Brake Shoes 12.10 ea

Each set includes insulated bushing.

**190-444** Fits 57 to 64"

**190-445** Fits 64 to 80"

**190-446** Fits Bowser M1, M1A, Northern & USRA Mountain

**190-447** Fits Bowser G-5

### Brake Wheels

**190-289** Brass, 6-Spoke pkg(6) **4.40**

**190-351** Plastic pkg(6) **3.40**

### Cab Details

**190-381** Roof Hatch **2.90**

**190-385** Deck Plate w/Hinges **5.50**

### Cab Walkways pkg(2) 3.25 ea

**190-379** 25/32" 19.8mm

**190-380** 1-1/16" 26.9mm

### Coal Pusher

**190-255** Standard **5.50**

### Damper

**190-269** Damper Control **2.45**

### Detail Kits

Sets include all handrails, grab irons, lift rings, windshield wipers and more.

**190-519** EMD FT & F A Unit Diesels **12.50**

**190-520** EMD FT & F B Unit Diesels **12.50**

**190-521** Alco C-628 or C-630 **14.80**

**190-2001** Modern Pennsy Freight Engines **12.08**
Modernize Bowser engines with this kit and #236 Smoke Box front. Includes modern headlight, Pyle dual generator, bracket for generator, modern Pennsy marker lights, Keystone number plate and chin platform.

**190-2021** Detail Kit Roundhouse Harriman Locomotives **57.44**

**190-2022** Steam Loco Super Detail Kit **57.44**
PRR L-2, fits Athearn Genesis 2-8-2 Mikado.

### Domes

#### Auxiliary

Each includes dome base, valves and whistle.

**190-227** Exposed Set **5.10**

**190-228** Exposed w/Fittings **4.40**

#### 1860-70 Vintage

Each includes sand and steam domes.

**190-338** Round Steam Tapered Sand Domes **4.75**

**190-342** Fluted Sand, Tapered Steam Domes **9.50**

### Eccentric Crank

**190-384** pkg(2) **5.50**

### Feedwater Heater Kits

#### Elesco

**190-2003** Feedwater Heater Kit (8 Pieces) **12.08**
Build with exposed or covered head, castings for both are included.

**190-343** Feedwater Pipe Set **6.00**
Includes one each hot and cold water pipes.

#### Worthington

**190-270** Worthington Type SA Feedwater Heater (3 Pieces) **9.50**

### Generators 3.05 ea

**190-211** Turbo

**190-212** Sunbeam

**190-213** Loco Light

**190-214** Buda Ross

**190-215** Pyle-GE

**190-234** Pyle, Dual Voltage

**190-335** With Muffler

**190-348** Passenger Car

**190-362** Large, Dual Voltage

#### Spicer Shaft Driven Types

**190-352** Type GL, 20kw **6.90**

**190-353** Type GL, 25kw **6.90**

**190-357** Type G, 35kw **7.40**

### Headlights

**190-204** Lima Arc **3.05**

**190-206** Standard, w/Wing Board & Visor **3.05**

**190-207** Plain **3.05**

**190-208** Northern Pacific Style **3.05**

**190-263** Mars Light - Twin Type **3.40**
Used on steam and diesels, includes bracket for mounting on steam loco smokebox.

**190-282** GN Style **3.05**

**190-304** Switcher **4.10**
Used at front and rear on small locos and as back-up light on bigger tenders.

**190-305** Large Baldwin Oil Lamp (1890s) **4.60**

#### Pennsylvania Styles 3.05 ea

**190-235** Modern

**190-477** Flat Back

#### Pyle 3.05 ea

**190-201** With Visor

**190-205** With Wing Board

**190-230** Twin Sealed Bean

#### Pyle - Flat Sided 3.05 ea

**190-327** Standard

**190-331** With Visor

#### Santa Fe Styles

**190-203** Large, Old **3.05**

**190-209** With Bracket **3.40**

**190-210** Standard **3.05**

#### Sunbeam 3.05 ea

**190-202** Standard

**190-229** With Visor

### Headlight Brackets

**190-241** Standard w/Numberboard **3.05**

**190-246** High Mounting w/Grab Irons **4.40**
Fits all Cal-Scale headlights.

**190-478** Pennsy Type **2.45**
Use with headlights #235 or 477, sold separately.

#### Center-Mounting 3.05 ea

**190-258** UP

**190-279** CNW

### Heaters

**190-225** Locomotive Oil Hea **4.40**

### Injectors

**190-262** Non-Lifting Nathan Type "4000" **3.40**

**190-264** Non-Lifting Sellers Type **3.40**

**190-288** Lifting, Large Monitc pkg(2) **6.80**

**190-337** Check Valve & Injector Set **6.70**

**190-341** Check Valve & Injector (3 Pieces) **7.15**

### Locomotive Air Brakes 3.85 ea

**190-272** Double Kit

**190-273** Single Phase
Three-piece set, use with engines equipped with single phase air pump.

### Markers pkg(2) 3.05 ea (Unless Noted)

#### For Caboose

**190-325** Caboose, Less Jewels **3.30**

**190-463** Pennsylvania Style

**190-464** PRR, Penn Central & CR

**190-465** CR

#### For Locomotives

**190-280** Modern

**190-312** "Standard Era" Including USRA

**190-375** A&W Style
Used on some early engines, passenger cars and cabooses.

#### For Passenger Cars

**190-490** PRR Type 2 Pair

## iscellaneous

**0-226** Locomotive Radiator **40**

**0-239** Over-Fire Jet Set :g(16) **8.30**

**0-271** Mechanical ıbricators w/Brackets pkg(4) **60**

**0-286** Sanders pkg(2) **4.00**

**0-326** Wood Burning Stack 'Spark Arrestor Screen **9.50**

**0-382** Window Shade pkg(2) **25**

**0-383** Three-Way Junction ox pkg(2) **2.90**

**90-452** PRR Modern "Dog ouse" **9.45**
ıstalled on tender deck of ome larger PRR steam locos, oused a seat for the head rakeman.

**90-493** PRR Tender Water coop Controls (3 Piece Set) **.05**

**90-2004** Water Scoop Kit **9.49**
complete with scoop, control nd other details.

## ufflers

**90-222** Exhaust w/Valve **3.45**

**90-223** Exhaust, Wilson **3.05**

## umber Boards

**90-260** 4 Character pkg(2) **.80**

**90-389** Oval pkg(2) **2.80**

## Number Plates 2.45 ea

**190-238** PRR pkg(3)

**190-244** B&O Capitol Dome pkg(2)

**190-245** Plain pkg(3)

## Passenger Air, Signal, Steam Lines

**190-274** Loco & Tender-Brass **5.65**
Set of five hoses and brackets for equipping a single engine and tender.

**190-320** Bracketed Air & Signal Lines pkg(2) **2.45**
Parts for two engines.

**190-2002** Double Pump Set **9.48**
Includes two air pumps, plus distributing valve and equalizing reservoir.

Info, Images, Inspiration! Get It All at
**www.walthers.com**

## Pilots 8.30 ea (Unless Noted)

**190-261** Commonwealth Drop Coupler
Used on 4-8-4s, Big Boys and Challengers.

**190-296** Commonwealth w/Swing Coupler pkg(5 Pieces)

**190-298** General Steel Castings w/Coupler

**190-315** Standard Boiler Tube

**190-318** Boiler Tube w/Coupler, Hoses & Sheet Metal Guard

**190-336** Wood, 5' 6", CP

**190-340** Wood, 4' 6", UP **8.40**

**190-344** Commonwealth Cast Late Version w/Couplers

**190-387** PRR **7.80**

**190-388** PRR-Slatted w/Stops **7.80**

## Piping

### Brackets pkg(6) 2.55 ea

Cored for .020 wire, sold separately.

**190-480** Four Hole

**190-481** Three Hole

**190-482** Two Hole

### Clamps

**190-483** Clamp for .020 Wire pkg(10) **2.85**

### Unions 4.05 ea

**190-484** Hexagonal pkg(16)
Includes six medium and two large unions.

**190-485** Square & Round pkg(16)
Includes eight square and eight round unions.

## Power Reverse 4.50 ea (Unless Noted)

**190-216** Type "C"

**190-217** Type "T"

**190-218** Type "P" **3.60**

**190-237** Pennsylvania-Modern **2.45**

**190-297** Articulated Locos **4.40**

**190-303** Early 1900s **4.40**

**190-330** Ragonnet B **4.40**

**190-332** Ragonnet B1 **4.40**

**190-360** Standard Reverse Gear (Rear)
Typically used on small engines. **4.40**

**190-363** Large Reverse Gear Rear Facing **4.40**

## Shields

Available separately or in kits containing pump mounting brackets, radiator casting and equalizing reservoir.

**190-259** Air Pump Shield **6.80**
Used on modern locomotives.

### Large 7' 9"

**190-266** Shield Only **5.65**

**190-2005** Kit **9.49**
Used on UP Challengers, Big Boys and other large, modern locomotives.

### Small 7' 3"

**190-267** Shield Only **5.65**

**190-2006** Kit **9.49**
Used on conventional sized locomotives.

## Smoke Box Fronts

**190-236** PRR Modern 7' 6" w/Number Plate **5.20**
Used on K-5s and M-1s.

**190-242** Harriman Type 86" Diameter w/Number Plate **5.45**

**190-243** USRA Type, 81" Diameter w/Number Plate **5.45**

**190-278** CNW w/Bracket **5.10**

## Steam Loco Cab Brake Stands 4.40 ea

**190-366** Single Valve, Older or Smaller Engines

**190-367** Standard Era - All Engines (2 Valve)

**190-368** Modern Medium & Large Engines

## Steps

**190-377** Boiler pkg(2) **2.45**

**190-475** Pennsy Cabin Car (Caboose) pkg(4) **4.85**

**190-495** PRR Tender Steps **5.70**

## Stoker Engines

**190-224** Standard Two Cylinder **5.60**

**190-254** Single Cylinder Duplex Type **3.85**

## Tender Brake Set

**190-306** Westinghouse "U" Set **9.20**
Standard equipment on most tenders built from 1920-1950.

## Tender Hatches

**190-231** Large **5.10**

**190-232** Rectangular Base **3.85**

**190-233** Rounded Base **3.85**

## Tool Box

**190-295** Loco Tool Box **3.60**

**190-364** Tool Box, Tender **4.85**

## Throttles

**190-268** Front End w/Rods & Guides **3.85**

**190-369** Horizontal-Early Engines **3.60**

**190-370** Front End, Medium & Large #1 **4.40**

**190-371** Front End, Medium & Large #2 **4.40**

**190-376** Dome, Mounts On Side of Steam Dome **3.05**

## Train Control

**190-252** Train Control Box w/Bracket, Union 3-Speed **6.45**

**190-390** Trailing Truck Bearing Plates pkg(2) **3.05**

## Valves

**190-247** Pop-Valves, Large pkg(6 Pieces) **2.45**

### Check Valves

**190-251** Nathan Double Top Feed **3.05**

**190-253** With Stop Valve pkg(2) **3.40**

**190-265** Vertical pkg(2) **3.40**

### Globe Valves

**190-314** Valves & Drain Cocks pkg(13) **5.65**

**190-361** 2 & 3" Valves pkg(4) **4.40**

### Starter Valves

**190-293** Large, Left Hand **3.85**

**190-294** Small, Right & Left Hand pkg(2) **4.40**

## Vapor Traps

**190-350** For Heavyweight Passenger Cars pkg(2) **3.60**

**190-358** For Streamline Cars pkg(2) **4.40**

## Water Pump

**190-287** Steam Water Pump & Hose Reel **6.80**
Fairbanks-Morse design.

**190-333** Low Water Alarm **4.05**

## Whistles & Accessories

**190-250** Large Modern Type **2.45**

**190-307** Saturated Steam w/Pipe **4.40**

**190-339** Assorted Whistles pkg(3) **4.75**

**190-378** Whistle Shield **2.80**

# DIESEL DETAILS

## Antenna Supports

Accurate models of the induction phone (an early form of radio) antennas and brackets used on Pennsylvania cabooses and locos.

### Diesel Sets 11.50 ea (Unless Noted)

Brass parts, plus complete instructions with photos.

**190-401** RS-3

**190-402** F-Unit

**190-403** Alco PA

**190-404** F-M Trainmaster

**190-405** Baldwin S-12

**190-406** GP30 **12.50**

**190-407** RS-1

**190-408** GP7/9

**190-409** Baldwin Sharks

**190-410** U-25B

**190-411** RS-11

**190-412** E Unit **12.50**

**190-438** FP7 **12.10**

**190-459** FA **10.95**

**190-466** RS12 **12.10**

**190-498** F-M C-Liner **12.60**

**190-499** PRR -Erie Built **12.60**

**190-500** F-M "Baby Trainmaster" **13.75**

### Cabooses

**190-455** N5 Stand & Receiver-Brass **12.95**

**190-474** Brackets & Receiver-Plastic **4.85**

### Receivers

**190-391** Transmitter - Loco & Caboose pkg(2) **3.95**

**190-392** Antenna Stand Only pkg(2) **4.40**

**190-457** GP7/9 **2.45**

**190-458** F-M Trainmaster **2.45**

## Air Horns-Nathan

**190-316** 5-Chime **3.60**

**190-400** 3-Chime w/Mounting Brackets **5.20**

**190-420** 3-Chime P3 **6.00**

**190-421** 5-Chime P5 **8.30**

**190-422** KS-1 pkg(2) **3.05**

**190-423** KS-2 pkg(2) **3.05**

**190-424** 2-Chime K2 **6.00**

**190-425** 3-Chime K3 **6.00**

**190-426** 4-Chime K4 **6.00**

**190-427** 5-Chime K5 **8.30**

**190-428** 3-Chime M3 **7.15**

**190-429** 5-Chime M5 **8.30**

## Alco FA Parts

**190-460** Water Cooled Turbo Exhaust Stack **2.45**

**190-461** Dynamic Brake-Plastic **2.45**

**190-462** Dynamic Brake-Brass **6.25**

## Bells

**190-322** Hood Unit - Bracketed **3.30**

**190-430** Underframe Mounted pkg(2) **3.60**

**190-435** Road Switcher Style w/Bracket EL **4.35**

## Coupler Lift Bar

**190-476** Lift Bar w/Stanchions pkg(2) **4.55**
Typical of lift bars used on many diesels.

## Fuel System

**190-431** Fillers pkg(3) **3.05**

**190-432** Filters pkg(2) **4.60**

## Grab Irons 2.90 ea

All grab irons are preformed of .012" diameter wire

**190-506** Type 1 pkg(12)
**190-507** Straight #1 pkg(20)
**190-508** Straight #2 pkg(20)
**190-509** Drop Style pkg(20)
**190-515** Pilot Grab Bar pkg(12)
**190-516** Alco "Century Series" Body Corner Grabs

### For EMD FT & F Unit Diesels pkg(12) 2.90 ea

**190-502** Side Door
**190-503** Cab Door
**190-504** Side Grabs
**190-505** Roof Window

## Headlights

**190-417** Mars Light for F3A **2.45**

## GE 44 Tonner pkg(2) 3.05 ea

**190-413** Modern

**190-414** Visor

## Pyle National pkg(2) 3.20 ea

**190-395** Dual Sealed Beam

**190-396** Single Beam

## Lift Rings

**190-501** .012" Wire pkg(20) **2.90**

## MU Stands pkg(2) 3.20 ea

**190-393** With Nonworking Light & Battery Connector

**190-394** With Battery Connector

## Numberboards

**190-397** 3-Character pkg(2) **3.40**

**190-398** 5-Character pkg(2) **3.75**

**190-416** Early F Unit w/Marker pkg(2) **3.05**

**190-443** PRR E & F Unit pkg(2) **3.05**

## Pilots - F Units

**190-441** Doors Only **3.05**

**190-442** Passenger Pilot w/Coupler Cover **12.95**
Complete assembly for Athearn F and Cary E units.

## Spark Arrestor pkg(2) 3.10 ea

**190-439** Half-Round Top

**190-440** Flat Top

## Steps

**190-399** Step pkg(2) **2.80**

**190-434** Stanchion Style - End Platform EL **7.15**

**190-448** E, F & BL2 pkg(6) **4.35**

**190-449** For FP45 & F45 (4 large & 1 small) pkg(5) **4.35**

**190-450** For PA, PBs & FAs pkg(4) **4.35**

## Miscellaneous Details

**190-415** Nose Lift Rings EMD F & E pkg(2) **2.45**

**190-418** Ladder for Baldwin Shark **3.60**

**190-419** Windshield Wipers pkg(4) **4.35**

**190-433** RS Marker Lights EL pkg(4) **4.85**

**190-436** Dynamic Brake Access Panel **2.45**

**190-437** Sunshade w/Mounting Lugs **4.85**

**190-451** Water Tank FP7 **7.15**

**190-456** Modern Pilot Plow **7.20**

**190-488** Receiver Box for PRR RS Locos **3.05**

**190-489** Slack Adjuster for PRR RS Locos 2 Pair **3.05**

**190-497** Lift Rings For F-M C-Liner Diesels **3.75**

## "U" Bolts pkg(20) .012" Wire

## 2.90 ea

**190-512** Small

**190-513** Large

**190-514** Coupler Lift Bar .012" Wire pkg(4)

## Windshield Wipers 2 Pair 2.90 ea

**190-517** Single Arm Style

**190-518** Dual Arm Style

# CAR PARTS

## Freight Details

**190-283** AB Brake System, Plastic (black) **3.40**

**190-491** Styrene Roofwalks (2 35' Walks & 4 Laterals) **5.70**
Just .020" thick with see-through surface.

**190-492** Hoses - Air & Signal pkg(16) **2.60**
Includes eight of each hose type.

**190-494** Brake Levers - Plastic 4 Pair **2.50**

## Freight Car Parts 2.90 ea

**190-510** Roof Corner Grabs pkg(12)

**190-511** Ladder Grabs pkg(12)

**190-512** Coupler Lift Bar pkg(4) .012" Wire

## Passenger Details

**190-309** Tailgate-Brass pkg(2) **4.40**

**190-321** End Railing Set Wood Cars **17.20**

**190-345** Mail Catcher for Railway Post Office pkg(2) **5.55**

**190-486** Passenger Car Tail Gate **2.25**

**190-487** Brake Wheel, Plastic pkg(6) **2.45**

## Brake Sets

**190-359** Westinghouse HSC (6 Pieces) **8.30**
Used on streamline cars.

## Steps

**190-356** Passenger Car - Standard Era pkg(4) **8.30**

**190-386** Passenger/Baggage Car pkg(4) **7.50**

*Campbell Scale Models*

Use these parts to detail modern, Old West or Victorian-era buildings. Windows, doors and trim are molded in white plastic unless noted.

## Barrels

Made from turned hardwood, with raised trim and bands.

**200-249** Red pkg(12) **6.61**

**200-250** Plain pkg(12) **5.98**

## Chain

**200-256** Black **6.61**
12" length, 36 links per inch. Dealers MUST order in multiples of 6.

## Corrugated Aluminum 7.71 ea

Easy way to model corrugated walls or roofing. Each sheet is 7-1/2" long by .002" thick. Dimension listed is scale width.

**200-804** 4' pkg(10)

**200-805** 6' pkg(9)

**200-801** 8' pkg(9)

**200-802** 10' pkg(7)

**200-803** 12' pkg(6)

## Doors 4.49 ea

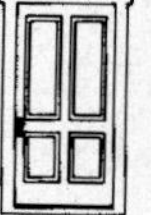
200-912

200-913

200-914

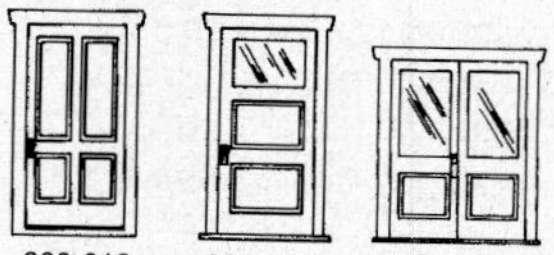

**200-912** pkg(3)

**200-913** pkg(3)

**200-914** pkg(2)

200-915

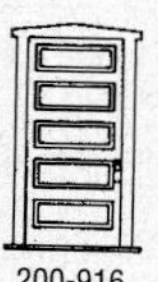
200-916

200-917

**200-915** pkg(3)

**200-916** pkg(3)

**200-917** pkg(2)

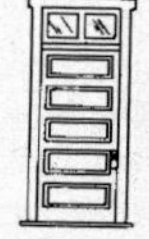
200-918

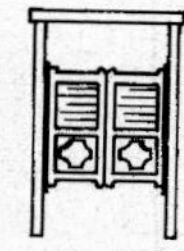
200-919

**200-918** pkg(2)

**200-919** pkg(2)

**200-941** Victorian Door/Vent pkg(2)

## Oil Drums pkg(12) 6.61 ea (Unless Noted)

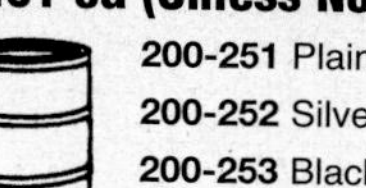

**200-251** Plain **5.98**

**200-252** Silver

**200-253** Black

**200-254** Red

## Profile Shingles

**200-800** 100' Roll **11.39**
Modeling realistic shingled roofs is easy with profile shingles. Made of paper with a natural wood color, one edge is notched to resemble individual shingles while the other is solid. The back is coated with water-soluble glue. Simply cut to length, moisten and apply in overlapping strips. Enough material to cover approximately 9 x 12".

## Skylights 4.49 ea

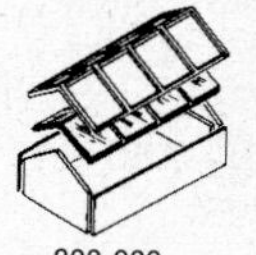
200-909

200-910

**200-909** pkg(2)

**200-910** Corrugated pkg(4)

## Structural Details 4.49 ea

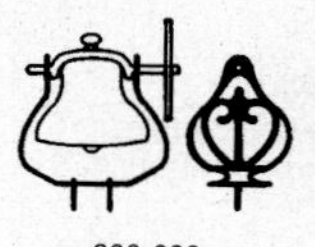
200-920 200-927

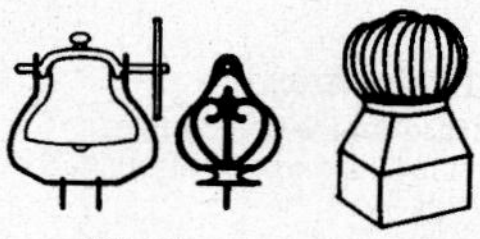

**200-920** Bell & Bracket

**200-927** Cyclone Vent pkg(3)

200-921 200-922

**200-921** Corbels pkg(28)

**200-922** Porch Railing pkg(4)

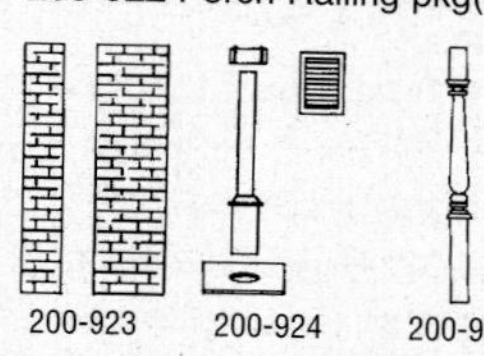
200-923 200-924 200-926

**200-923** Chimneys pkg(2)

**200-924** Two Smoke Jacks & Four Attic Vents

**200-926** Turned Post pkg(5)

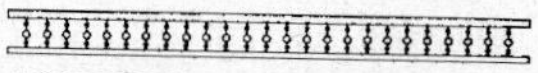

**200-932** Spool Trim pkg(4)

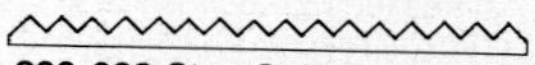

**200-933** Step Stringer pkg(4)

## Windows 4.49 ea

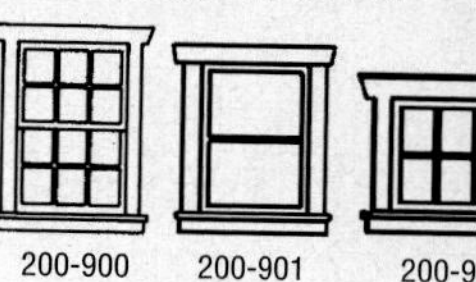
200-900 200-901 200-9

**200-900** pkg(4)

**200-901** pkg(5)

**200-902** pkg(5)

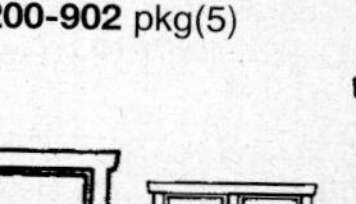

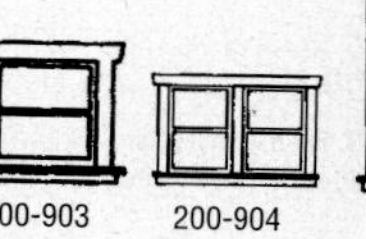
200-903 200-904 200-9

**200-903** pkg(6)

**200-904** pkg(3)

**200-905** pkg(4)

200-906 200-907

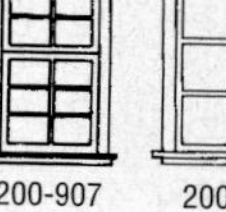
200-90

**200-906** pkg(4)

**200-907** pkg(4)

**200-908** pkg(3)

200-911 200-929 200-93

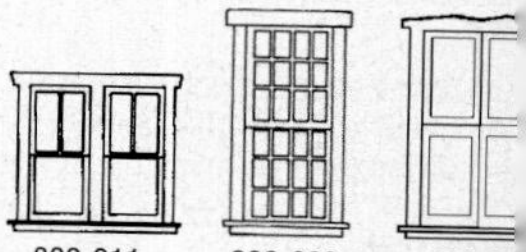

**200-911** pkg(3)

**200-929** pkg(2)

**200-937** pkg(3)

**200-936** pkg(3)

**200-939** Large Victorian pkg(

**200-940** Small Victorian pkg(

## Miscellaneous

**200-255** Brass Light Shades pkg(6) **5.98**
Dealers MUST order in multiples of 6.

**200-925** Nuts & Bolts pkg(60) **4.49**
One-piece plastic, molded in gunmetal gray, but easily painted to match your project.

**200-930** Park Benches pkg(4) **4.89**
Plastic sides with plastic slats.

**200-931** Flagpole & 48 Star Flag **4.49**
Plastic pole, printed paper flag and basic assembly instructions.

**200-934** Smoke Stack pkg(2) **4.49**
Molded in black plastic.

**200-935** Hinges, Large pkg(8) **4.49**
Molded in black plastic.

## ıstom Finishing

ıd a new dimension to your odels with this line of brass ıd pewter detail parts for cos and passenger cars. ach is finely detailed and ady for installation. Most ems include basic mounting structions and can be tached using ACC or solder.

or a complete listing of ustom Finishing parts, visit /althers Web site at ww.walthers.com.

### ntennae 4.95 ea Unless Noted)

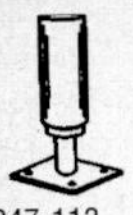
247-113

247-201

**47-113** Firecracker pkg(2)

**47-201** Sinclair pkg(2) **3.95**

**47-208** Motor

**47-229** Pickup Shoe
'or mounting on truck side 'ames.

### Bells 4.95 ea

#### ligh-Hood Mount

247-109

247-110

**247-109** Boston & Maine Type

**247-110** MEC 1

247-111

247-138

**247-111** MEC Type 2

**247-138** Dual Lever

247-246

247-250

**247-246** Hood

**247-250** EMD SW

### Brake Details

**247-147** Hand Brake Chain Guide pkg(6) **5.95**

### Diesel Details

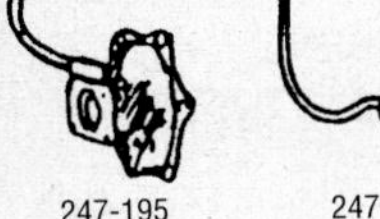
247-195 247-196

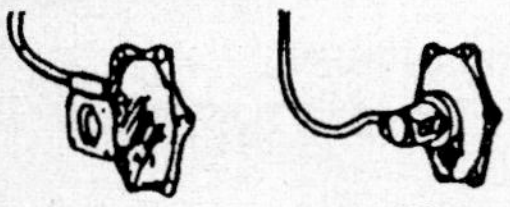

**247-195** Wheel Slip Modulator pkg(4) **4.95**

**247-196** Speed Recorder pkg(4) **4.95**

**247-205** RS-2/3 Curved Grab Irons pkg(10) **3.95**

### Headlights/Lighting

**247-112** Pyle Dual Beam Ground Light w/Bracket pkg(2) **4.95**

### Horns

#### EMD

**247-215** Single Chime pkg(2) **5.95**

### Lineside Details

247-171

247-194

**247-171** Buda Wheel Stops pkg(2) **6.95**

**247-194** Durable Bumper Model D **7.95**

**247-327** Industrial-Size Acetylene Cutting Torch w/Cart (Pewter & Brass Wire Kit) **10.95**

### MU Hoses

**247-257** 3-Hose **7.95**

**247-258** Diesel **7.95**
With bracket; two left, two right.

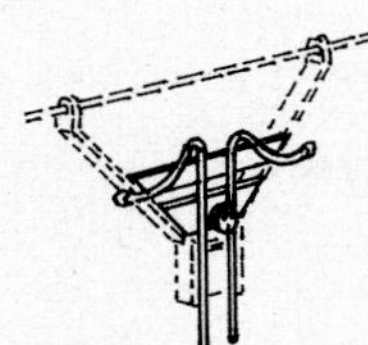

**247-347** End Platform Railing Mounting for MU Hoses. For ALCO RS-2 Diesels 1 Pair **4.95**

### Stacks (Intake/Exhaust)

247-214

247-247

**247-214** EMD Steam Generator pkg(2) **5.95**

**247-247** Extended Height Exhaust Stack GP, SD Pair **4.95**

### 14" Steam Generator Intake

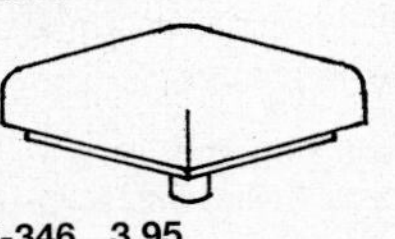

**247-346 3.95**

## CVMW
## CENTRAL VALLEY MODEL WORKS

### Large Double-Stop Doors

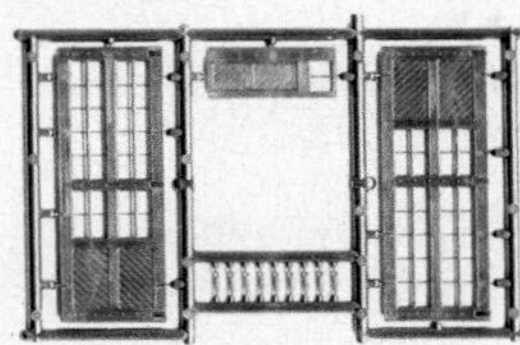

**210-1605** pkg(3) **5.98**
Each package includes three pairs (six in all) large shop doors with working hinges. These doors are the correct size for engine houses and locomotive shop buildings.

### Switch Stands

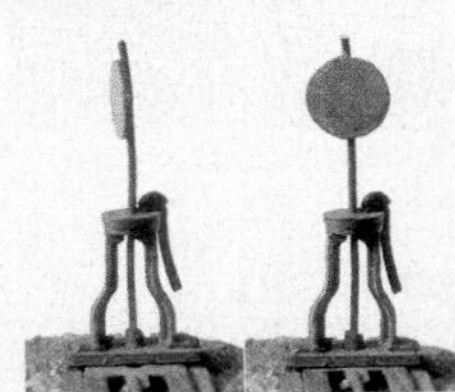

**210-1604** pkg(6) **5.98**
Includes six switch stand kits with optional target styles.

### 40' Freight Car Roof

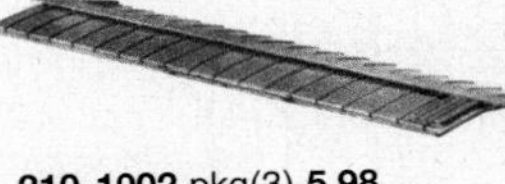

**210-1002** pkg(3) **5.98**
Each package includes three roofs with separate see-through running board details.

### 40' Underframe Kit

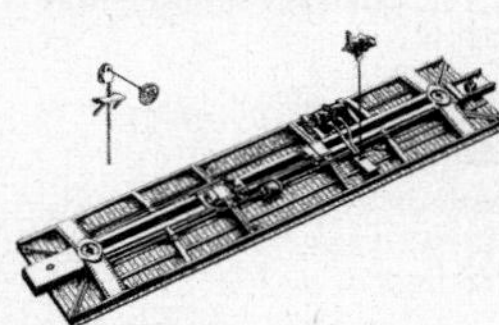

**210-1000** pkg(3) **5.98**
Each package includes three steel underframes with separate wood floor, Ajax brake wheel, detailed triple valve and air pressure reservoir.

## DEPOTS BY JOHN

### Air Conditioner

**87-109** Window Air Conditioner Kit pkg(2) **3.50**
Easy-to-build kit with pre-cut block, metal grill and foil covering.

### Chimneys 2.95 ea

87-126

**87-124** 36' Tall w/Caps

**87-125** 18" Square w/Caps pkg(2)

**87-126** Victorian pkg(2)

### Eave Brackets

**87-138** Large w/Acute Angle pkg(8) **2.49**

### Steps

**87-129** Concrete pkg(2) **2.49**

**87-140** Concrete Dock pkg(2) **2.95**

### Windows

**87-139** Glass Block 2-1/2 x 4" (Clear) **2.99**

Latest New Product News Daily! Visit Walthers Web site at

**www.walthers.com**

## EASTERN CAR WORKS

Plase visit Walthers web site at www.walthers.com for a complete listing of all available items.

### Caboose Detail Set

**117-9111** Superdetails for Athearn & MDC Cars **10.00**
Fits center cupola models.

### Caboose Window Sets 3.00 ea

**117-9108** Bowser N5c

**117-9113** Bowser N5

### Covered Hopper Parts

**117-9100** M&K Ballast Doors **3.00**

**117-9105** Detail Set **4.00**

### Floats & Fittings

**117-9118** Marine Car Float & GMA Barge Fittings **10.00**
Includes one each of #s 9119, 9120, 1921 and 9122.

**117-9120** Kleets & Chocks **3.00**

### Passenger Car Details 3.00 ea (Unless Noted)

**117-9101** Pennsylvania Ice Air Conditioner

**117-9102** Car Roof Vents

**117-9115** Car Stirrup **4.00**

### Passenger Car Underbody Details

**117-9103** PRR/ Pullman **5.00**

### Roof for Covered Gondola

**117-9116** 52' 6" Mid-Height **8.00**
Fits Walthers, E&C Shops, Roundhouse, Life-Like and Con-Cor cars.

Turn any model into a detailed replica with this line of injection-molded plastic, brass and cast metal parts. Many items include basic assembly and installation instructions.

Items listed in blue ink may not be available at all times (see Legend Page).

# DIESEL DETAILS

## Air Horns

### Nathan pkg(2) 1.75 ea

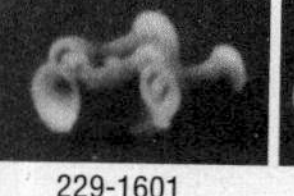

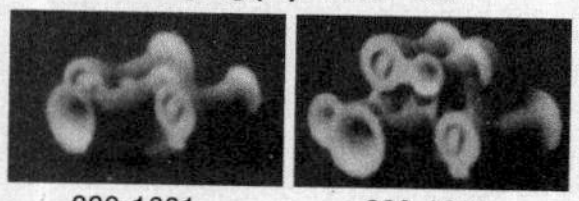

229-1601 229-1602

**229-1601** 3-Chime M3

**229-1602** 5-Chime M5

**229-1603** P3/P5

### Leslie

**229-1608** Tyfon A200 pkg(4) **2.00**

## Air Filters

Cast metal.

**229-2706** Horst Paducah **8.75**

## Air Grilles

### EMD-Early

Etched stainless steel.

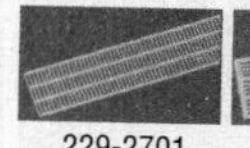

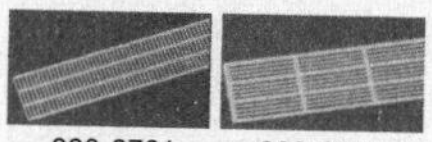

229-2701 229-2704

**229-2701** "Farr" F&E Units pkg(2) **9.00**

**229-2704** F7A pkg(2) **6.00**

229-2705 229-2711

**229-2705** F7B pkg(2) **6.00**

**229-2711** "Chicken Wire" - Early F Units pkg(2) **8.50**

**229-2727** Proto 2000 SW9/1200 **5.00**

### EMD-Late

**229-2012** 48" Flat Top Grille pkg(2) **3.00**
Photo-etched metal.

### ALCO

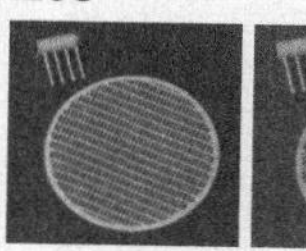

229-2702 229-2703

**229-2702** 64" Diameter pkg(2) **4.00**

**229-2703** 57" Diameter pkg(2) **3.00**
Sets include photo-etched round grille and plastic bolts.

### EMC FT, Stewart

**229-2728** Fan & Dynamic Brake Grilles **3.50**

### Fairbanks-Morse

**229-2712** Exhaust, Vent & Intake pkg(4) **2.50**

## Air Reservoirs 2.25 ea

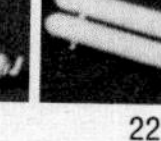

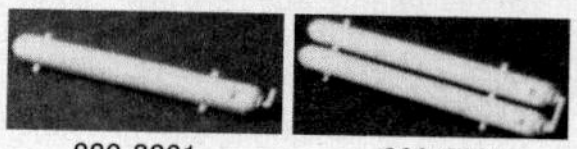

229-3201 229-3202

**229-3201** Single 15" Diameter Top or Side Mount pkg(2)

**229-3202** Double 12" Diameter Top Mount pkg(2)

**229-3203** 15" GP35/40 Side Mount pkg(4)

## Air Vents

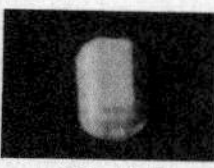

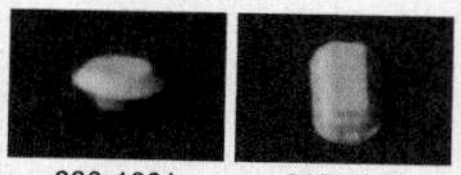

229-1901 229-1902

**229-1901** Round pkg(12) **1.00**
Mounted on cab roof or low nose.

**229-1902** Flat - Roof or Side Mount pkg(8) **1.00**

229-1903 229-1904

**229-1903** Flat - Roof Mount pkg(4) **1.50**

**229-1904** Dynamic Brake pkg(2) **1.50**
Mounted on roof of hood units.

**229-1905** EMD Body Louvers **3.95**

## Air Hoses

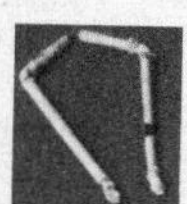

**229-1508** MU pkg(16) **2.50**

## Bells pkg(2) 1.25 ea (Unless Noted)

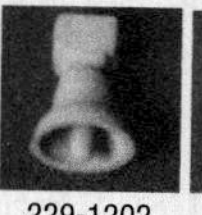

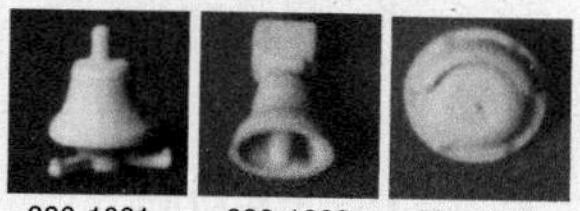

229-1201 229-1202 229-1204

**229-1201** EMD Cab Mount **1.50**

**229-1202** Underframe Mount

**229-1204** Western

## Brake Cylinders

**229-2801** Diesel Trucks pkg(8) **3.00**

## Cabs-North American Safety Design

**229-3604** Canadian Type **10.95**

## Cab Details

### Air Conditioners 1.50 ea

229-2308 229-2309

**229-2308** "Prime"

**229-2309** "Vapor"

### Armrests 1.25 ea

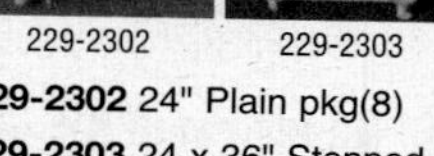

229-2302 229-2303

**229-2302** 24" Plain pkg(8)

**229-2303** 24 x 36" Stepped pkg(4)

### Air Deflectors "Prime" Type pkg(4) 1.25 ea

Molded in clear plastic, with raised frame, which can be painted for added realism.

229-2310 229-2311 229-2312

**229-2310** Deflector/Mirror - UP Type

**229-2311** Angled

**229-2312** Straight

### Wind Deflector Set

**229-2304** pkg(3) **2.50**
Includes three styles of scale thickness deflectors, made of photo-etched brass. Eyebolts are included so deflectors can be open or closed.

### Windows

**229-2301** All Weather pkg(2) **3.00**
Double type for GP, SD units.

**229-2551** Clear Plastic Window Material pkg(5) **1.25**

**229-3306** EMD pkg(4) **1.25**

## Chain

**229-2210** Safety Chain (black) 12" Long-40 Links Per Inch **2.75**

## Classification Lights 1.25 ea

**229-1017** Early EMD pkg(6)
Used on GP7, GP9, GP18, GP20 and SD24.

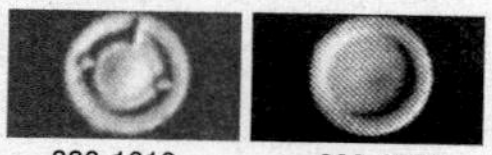

229-1019 229-1020

**229-1019** Late EMD pkg(8)
Used from GP30 on, can be illuminated from inside.

**229-1020** Blank Knock-Out pkg(8)
Used On EMD Dash 2s.

## Cooling Fans

### Flat Top pkg(4) 2.75 ea

229-2001 229-2004

**229-2001** 34"

**229-2003** Dynamic Brake 48" Flat Top pkg

**229-2004** 48"

### Q Type

**229-2006** 48" pkg(3) **7.00**

## Coupler Lift Bars

Parts match equipment on front and rear of most hood units. Bars are preformed wire and fit plastic or brass brackets.

### AAR Type 1

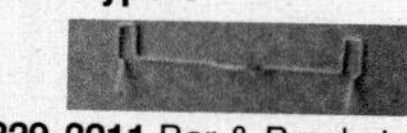

**229-2211** Bar & Brackets pkg(2) **2.50**

**229-2212** Bar Only pkg(10) **5.50**

### Brackets Only

**229-2213** Plastic pkg(16) **3.00**

**229-102213** Brass pkg(8) **2.75**

### Miscellaneous

**229-2204** Bar w/Bracket pkg(2) **2.00**

**229-2205** Bar Only pkg(10) **2.75**

## Diesel Truck Journals pkg(8) 2.25 ea

229-2805

**229-2804** Hyatt Roller Beari

**229-2805** EMD Blomberg Square Type

**229-2806** EMD Blomberg Slope Style

## Drop Steps

### EMD pkg(2) ea 1.50

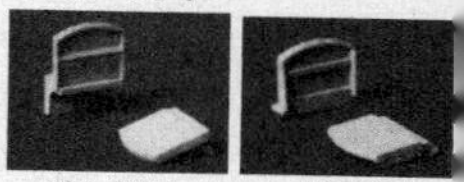

229-1401 229-1402

**229-1401** Early GP, SD, SW

**229-1402** Late GP, SD

**229-1404** Dash 2 Series

### General Electric

**229-1403** U Series pkg(2) 1.

### ALCO pkg(2) 3.00 ea

229-1405 229-1406

**229-1405** Short-RS/RSDs

**229-1406** Long-Century

**229-1408** Long-RSD

## Exhaust Stacks

### EMD pkg(2) 1.25 ea

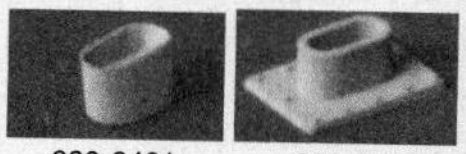

229-2401 229-2402

**229-2401** F3, F7, F9, BL2

**229-2402** Non-Turbo

## Eye Bolts pkg(24)

**229-2206** Formed Wire **3.25**

**229-2222** Long Shank **3.75**

## Flashers pkg(2) 1.50 ea

Nonoperating units feature base and appropriately colored globe.

229-2901 229-2902 229-2903

**229-2901** Western Cullen

**229-2902** Stratolite

**229-2903** Xenon Strobe

## Footboards

**229-2208** Metal pkg(2) **3.25**

## Fuel Tank Parts 1.00 ea

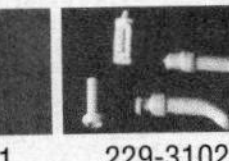
229-3101 229-3102

**229-3101** EMD Flush-Mount Fuel Gauge pkg(6)

**229-3102** Fitting Set pkg(8) Includes filler necks, plus sight gauge and flush mount gauge.

## Grab Irons

Scale size, made of formed wire and precut (unless noted).

### Drop Type

229-2201 229-2202

**229-2201** With Nut/Bolt/ Washer Castings pkg(18) **2.25**

**229-2202** Grab Irons Only pkg(24) **2.50**

### Straight Type pkg(12) 2.00 ea

**229-2224** 11"

**229-2225** 14"

**229-6605** 36"

**229-6210** With Nut/Bolt/ Washer Castings 17"

**229-6423** 22" Straight

**229-6425** 22" Drop

**229-6426** 19-1/2" Straight

**229-6427** 19-1/2" Drop

### Locomotives

**229-2215** 28" Ladder Grabs for E & F Units **2.00**

### Pilot

**229-2216** Curved, Anti-Climber pkg(12) **2.00**

**229-2220** Pilot Grab Bar - SW/GP, 8'-4" pkg(6) **1.25**

### Fan pkg(3) 1.50 ea

Mounted on roof of hood units in front of the last radiator fan.

**229-2217** Circular, GP30-GP/SD60

**229-2218** Angular Dash 2

### Roof

**229-2221** Cab Roof Grab Bar pkg(6) **1.25**

## Headlights

### Oscillating Pyle

**229-1001** Plastic pkg(2) **1.00**

### Oscillating Mars 1.00 ea

229-1005 229-1008

**229-1005** Plastic pkg(2)

**229-1008** Dual Plastic pkg(2)

### Oscillating Dual Pyle Gyralight pkg(2) 1.00 ea

229-1002 229-1009

**229-1002** Plastic

**229-1009** Recessed

### Dual Pyle

229-1003 229-1004

**229-1003** EMD-Late Plastic pkg(2) **1.00**

**229-101003** EMD-Late Brass **1.35**

**229-1004** Early Plastic pkg(2) **1.00**

**229-101024** Brass w/Vertical Shield **1.35**

### Pyle - Large "Mountain" Type For WP, CN, CP

**229-1010** Plastic pkg(2) **1.25**

**229-101010** Brass **1.50**

### Pyle - Dual w/Visors pkg(2) 1.00 ea

**229-1023** Horizontal

**229-1024** Vertical

### Pyle Conversion Plate

**229-1012** For 14-1/2" Headlight pkg(2) **1.00** Modifies older single beam units into dual sealed beam lights, used on many first generation units.

### EMD Switchers pkg(2)

229-1011 229-1015

**229-1011** Dual Pyle w/Numberboards & Sealed Beams **3.00**

**229-1015** Original (Large, Single Beam) NW/SW Series **1.50**

### Dual Mars pkg(2) 1.00 ea

229-1006 229-1007

**229-1006** Standard

**229-1007** Oscillating Dual Recessed

### Back-Up Light

**229-1014** Canadian Type pkg(2) **1.00**

### Ditch Lights

**229-1013** Canadian Type pkg(2) **1.00**

**229-1022** With Stand pkg(4) **1.25**

**229-1026** MU Stand-SP High Type 1 set **1.25**

**229-1029** BN Style Strobe Flashers pkg(4) **1.25**

### Southern Pacific Types pkg(2)

**229-1025** High Type w/MU Stand **1.25**

**229-1027** Low Type **1.00**

## Ladders

### Locomotive

**229-2207** SD 7/9 Kit **3.50**

## Lenses pkg(12) 1.25 ea

### Clear Classification Lights

**229-1708** 4-1/2" (.052") Diameter

**229-1709** 7" (.080") Diameter

### Headlight Lenses

**229-1710** 12" (.138") Diameter

**229-1711** 14-1/2" (.167") Diameter

## Lift Rings

229-1102 229-1103 229-1104

**229-1101** Plastic pkg(36) **1.50**

**229-101101** Brass pkg(24) **2.25**

**229-1102** EMD F&E Unit Nose pkg(6) **1.25**

**229-1103** Flat - Mounts on Pilot Beam pkg(8) **1.25**

**229-1104** Tabs - Roof and Side Hood Mount pkg(16) **1.50**

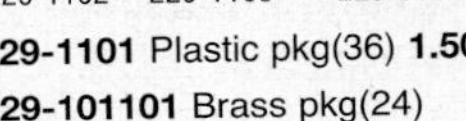
229-1105 229-1106 229-1107

**229-1105** Switcher Side Mount pkg(4) **1.50**

**229-1106** Alco FA/PA Century Type pkg(12) **1.25**

**229-1107** Alco S/RS Type pkg(12) **1.25**

**229-1108** GE w/Hinges pkg(12) **1.50**

## Miscellaneous

**229-2307** SD7-35 Circular Access Cover pkg(6) **1.00**

**229-2809** Truck Air Line EMD Blomberg "B" pkg(4) **1.50**

## MU Stands pkg(2) 1.25 ea

### Early GP

229-1501 229-1502

**229-1501** Low

**229-1502** High

### Intermediate GP/SD

229-1503 229-1504

**229-1503** Single

**229-1504** Double

### Late GP/SD

229-1505 229-1506

**229-1505** Single

**229-1506** Double

## MU Receptacles 1.25 ea (Unless Neted)

**229-1507** Receptacles & Blank Covers pkg(2) Three different types of receptacles and two styles of covers.

**229-101507** Brass pkg(30) **2.25**

**229-1509** Modern Receptacles

**229-1510** Head-End Power Receptacle Set

## Numberboards

### ALCO pkg(4) 3.00 ea

Plastic boards and brackets, with photo-etched brass fronts for large or five-digit style numberboards.

229-2602 229-2603

**229-2602** Curved Back

**229-2603** Angled Back

### Miscellaneous

**229-2601** Stencils (Photo-Etched Brass) pkg(2) **3.00**

**229-2604** Numberboard & Headlight WP/UP GP35/40 **3.50**

## Radiators

### EMD Switchers pkg(2) 3.50 ea

Kits include photo-etched screen and plastic frame to model large radiators on the front of EMD switchers. Includes instructions.

**229-2709** SW Units

**229-2710** NW Units

### Fairbanks-Morse

**229-2713** Photo-Etched Fan Screen **3.00**



## Radio Antennas

229-1801 229-1802 229-1803

### Can Type

Used by ATSF and UP.

**229-1801** Plastic pkg(6) **1.00**

### Whip Type

Used by ATSF and UP.

**229-1802** Plastic pkg(3) **1.25**

### Sinclair

**229-1803** Plastic pkg(4) **1.50**

**229-101803** Brass pkg(4) **2.50**

**229-1806** Small **2.00**

### Motorola Firecracker

**229-1805** pkg(6) **1.25**

**229-101805** Brass pkg(3) **2.00**

## Sand Fillers

### EMD Locos

**229-3001** Late-GP35 pkg(6) **1.25**

**229-3002** Early-GP7/9 pkg(4) **1.00**

### EMD Cab Units pkg(4)

**229-3003** Early **1.00**

## Shock Absorber/ Snuber pkg(4) 1.75 ea

229-2803

**229-2802** EMD Style

**229-2803** GE Style

## Short Nose Conversions

**229-3605** CP Rail 102" **6.95**

## Signal Boxes pkg(2) 1.50 ea

229-2305 229-2306

**229-2305** 3 Strap-Early

**229-2306** 2 Strap-Late

## Spark Arrestors

### MILW Types pkg(2) 3.25 ea

Cast metal.

**229-2105** SW Switchers

**229-2106** F Units

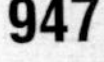

### Miscellaneous

229-2101 229-2102 229-2103

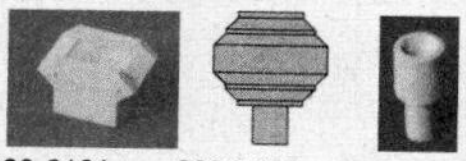

**229-2101** Super Flared Switcher Type pkg(2) **1.25**

**229-2102** Round Type pkg(2) **1.25**

**229-2103** Round Wire Screen Type pkg(2) **2.50**
Used on EMD Switchers, cast metal.

229-2104 229-4001

**229-2104** ATSF Type Cast Metal pkg(2) **2.50**

**229-4001** Steam Locos **2.00**

### Speed Recorders pkg(4) 1.75 ea

**229-2807** Flange Type

**229-2808** GE Type

### Sunshades

#### Plastic

229-1301 229-1302

**229-1301** GP/SD Units pkg(6) **1.50**

**229-1302** F&E Units pkg(4) **1.25**

**229-1303** EMD Wide Cabs pkg(4) **1.50**

#### Brass

**229-101302** F&E Units pkg(4) **1.75**

### Window Sets

Individual clear plastic windows replace solid window casting in locos.

**229-3303** Athearn F7A **1.75**

**229-3304** Athearn F7B **1.00**

### Winterization Hatches 2.00 ea

229-2013 229-2014

**229-2013** GP9 & GP18

**229-2014** GP/SD60

## MINIATURE TOOLS

**229-7101** Hand Tool Set **4.00**
Photo-etched, 35 pieces.

**229-7102** Screw Jack pkg(2) **1.35**

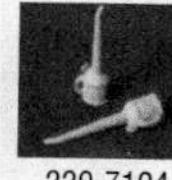
229-7103 229-7104

**229-7103** Rerail Frog pkg(2) **2.25**

**229-7104** Oil Can pkg(2) **1.35**

229-7106 229-7107

**229-7106** Lathe **3.50**

**229-7107** Drill Press **2.50**

## FREIGHT CAR PARTS

### Air Hoses

**229-6206** Freight Car pkg(6) **2.00**

### Box Car Parts

229-6211 229-6213

**229-6211** Brake Platform pkg(4) **2.75**

**229-6213** Handles, Hatches & Tack Boards (14 Pieces) **2.25**

### Door Parts

**229-6216** Hennesy Door Opener pkg(2) **2.00**

### Superior Panel Doors pkg(2)

**229-6311** 10 x 9'-3", 6-Panel **3.85**

### Brake Details

#### Brake Gear Sets

229-6238 229-6401

**229-6227** AB Brake Set **5.75**

**229-6238** Hand Brake & Valve pkg(2) **1.50**

**229-6247** ABDXL Brake Set **4.75**

**229-6401** Equipco pkg(2) **1.25**

**229-6402** Miner pkg(2) **1.25**

**229-6403** Ukeco pkg(2) **1.25**

### Car Ends & Parts

**229-6239** Cushion Draft Gear pkg(4) **TBA**

### Dreadnaught Ends pkg(4) 1.75 ea

#### 40s & 50s AAR Box Car

**229-6235** 4/5 Type

**229-6430** Car-End Walkover w/Handrail Set

### Caboose Parts

**229-6502** End Platform & Stops pkg(2) Etched Metal **4.00**

229-6503 229-6504

**229-6503** Curved Grab Irons-Ends & Sides pkg(12) **2.75**

**229-6504** "L" Shaped Grab Irons- Ends pkg(12) **2.75**

### Radio Antennas pkg(3)

229-1804 229-6501

**229-1804** Wagon Wheel **3.25**
Photo-etched brass with plastic antenna casting.

**229-6501** Dish Type **2.50**

### Coupler Lift Bars

#### Freight Car

**229-6215** Standard Type pkg(10) **2.50**
Formed wire cut lever and eyebolt for mounting on end of car.

**229-6240** Modern pkg(6) **2.25**

### Covered Hopper Parts

229-6212 229-6218

**229-6212** Square Hatch pkg(8) **2.75**

**229-6218** Round Hatch pkg(8) **2.00**

**229-6229** Discharge Gate pkg(4) **2.00**

**229-6429** Roping/Lift Tab for ACF Cars pkg(8) **1.50**

### Gondola Parts

**229-6214** Roping Ring Flat, Gondola or Hopper, Wire Formed pkg(12) **1.50**

**229-6221** Dreadnaught Ends pkg(2) **2.50**

### Grab Irons

**229-6205** Running Board Corner pkg(12) **2.25**

**229-6209** Bracket Type, 22" pkg(8) **2.00**
Molded in Delrin® plastic.

**229-6217** 18" Curved for Tank Car pkg(12) **2.00**

### Ladders

**229-6207** Long pkg(10) **2.85**

**229-6208** Short (Modern) pkg(8) **2.00**

### Ladder Sets 2.25 ea

**229-6241** 8-Rung

**229-6242** 7-Rung

### Running Boards

Includes pre-formed corner grab irons.

#### Metal 7.50 ea

Photo-etched metal.

**229-6203** 40' Cars

**229-6204** 50' Cars

### Stirrups

#### Offset Bottom Mount pkg(8) 1.65 ea

229-6411 229-6412 229-6413

**229-6411** Angled 18 x 12-1/2"

**229-6412** Stepped 17 x 14"

**229-6413** Double 18-1/2 x 12"

#### Straight Bottom Mount pkg(8) 1.65 ea

229-6414 229-6417

**229-6414** 16 x 11-1/2"

**229-6417** 8-1/2 x 13"

#### Side Mount pkg(8) 1.65 ea

229-6415 229-6416

**229-6415** Slant, 13-1/2 x 13"

**229-6416** Straight, 9 x 12"

#### Miscellaneous 1.75 ea (Unless Noted)

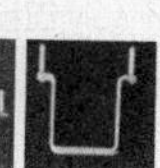
229-6418 229-6420

**229-6418** Mechanical Reefer pkg(7)

**229-6420** Thrall Type pkg(8)

**229-6428** ACF Centerflow Hoppers pkg(8)

### Tank Car Parts

**229-6219** Dome for Athearn 40' Tank Cars **3.50**

**229-6237** Tank Car Placards pkg(8) **1.25**



## PASSENGER CA DETAILS

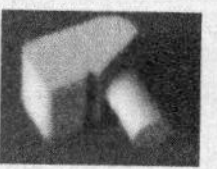

**229-6604** Roof Vent-Harrima Type pkg(16) **1.75**

**229-6609** Head-End Power Receptacle Set **1.25**

**229-6642** Modern Coupler L Bar pkg(4) **2.50**

### Grab Irons pkg(12) 1.75 ea

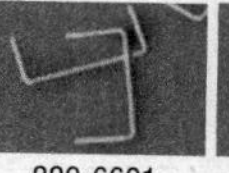
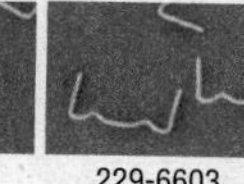
229-6601 229-6603

**229-6601** Vestibule

**229-6602** Roof

**229-6603** Roof Ladder

### Car Steps pkg(6) 1.75 ea

**229-6607** Material Handling Car

**229-6608** Stirrup for Baggage Car

## STRUCTURE DETAILS

### Nut/Bolt/Washer Castings 2.00 ea

Simulates 3/4" bolt with 2" washer.

**229-2203** Plastic pkg(48)

**229-102203** Brass pkg(18)

**229-7202** Footing Piers, Concrete pkg(12)

## HARDWARE

### Wire

#### Brass

**229-2513** 1/16" Diameter pkg(6) **3.00**

#### Flat Brass pkg(6) 3.00 ea

**229-2522** .015 x .018"

**229-2524** .015 x .030"

**229-2526** .015 x .024"

**229-2528** .015 x .042"

**229-2530** .015 x .060"

#### Stainless Steel 2.50 ea

Measurement indicates diameter.

**229-3503** .010" pkg(5)

**229-3504** .012" pkg(10)

**229-3505** .015" pkg(10)

**229-3506** .019" pkg(10)

**ound Brass 3.00 ea**
ieal for modeling all types of pe, railings etc., brass wire is asily bent to fit your pplications. Size is outside iameter in HO Scale inches, ollowed by actual dimensions. = Size; OD = Outside iameter; WS = Wire Size.

**29-2501** S = 1/4", OD = .5400", WS = .006" pkg(5)

**29-2502** S = 3/8", OD = .6750", WS = .008" pkg(5)

**29-2503** S = 1/2", OD = .8400", WS = .010" pkg(5)

**29-2504** S = 3/4", OD = .2150", WS = .012" pkg(10)

**29-2505** S = 1", OD = .6600", WS = .015" pkg(10)

**29-2506** S = 1-1/4", OD = .9900", WS = .019" pkg(10)

**29-2507** S = 1-1/2", OD = .3750", WS = .022" pkg(10)

**229-2508** S = 2", OD = .8750", WS = .028" pkg(10)

**229-2509** S = 2-1/2", OD = .5000", WS = .033" pkg(10)

**229-2510** S = 3", OD = 4.0000", WS = .040" pkg(6)

**229-2511** S = 3-1/2", OD = 4.0000", WS = .046" pkg(6)

**229-2512** S = 4", OD = 4.5000", WS = .052" pkg(6)

**Steel Hex Nuts pkg(6)**
**229-2557** 2/56 **1.50**

**Steel Washers pkg(6)**
**229-2558** 2/56 **1.50**

**Steel Panhead Screws 1.50 ea**

**2/56 pkg(6)**
**229-2552** 1/8"
**229-2553** 3/16"
**229-2554** 1/4"
**229-2555** 1/2"
**229-2556** 3/8"

Durango Press

Parts are metal castings unless noted.

## NEW PRODUCTS

### Detail Parts

**2.95 ea (Unless Noted)**

**NEW 254-48** Mine Hand Pick pkg(3)

**NEW 254-71** Heavy-Duty Winch Kit **6.95**

**NEW 254-96** "Jerry Can" Gas Cans pkg(5)

**NEW 254-132** Freight Door Style #1 pkg(2)

**NEW 254-133** Freight Door Style #2 (Flat) pkg(2)

**NEW 254-134** Freight Door Style #3 (Single) pkg(2)

### Caboose Parts

254-16

254-24

**254-16** Windows, Doors & Steps **10.95**

**254-24** Steps pkg(8) **3.50**

### Chain-36LPI

**254-121** Brass (12") **2.50**

### Chimneys

254-18

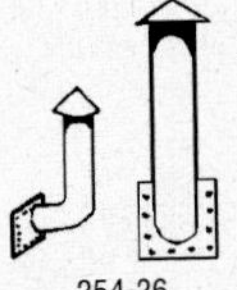
254-26

**254-18** Victorian Chimney **2.50**

**254-26** Smoke Jacks pkg(3) **3.25**

### Coal Buckets

**254-76** With Handle pkg(2) **3.95**
Used at small coaling facilities, can be used as small buckets in O Scale.

### Garbage Cans

**254-80** Half-Full Garbage Cans pkg(5) **3.25**

**254-95** Covered Garbage Cans pkg(6) **3.95**

### Headlight

**254-45** Rio Grande, Early Box Type pkg(2) **4.95**

### Interior Details

**254-108** Stove **2.25**

**254-122** Box of Bottles pkg(4) **2.50**

**254-123** Cafe Chairs pkg(8) **2.50**

### Kegs 2.95 ea

**254-77** Small Aluminum pkg(5)

**254-78** Large Aluminum pkg(5)

### Miniature Tools

**254-64** Small Hand Tool Boxes pkg(4) **2.95**

**254-104** Ladder, Plastic pkg(2) **2.50**

**254-106** Rerailer Shoes pkg(4) **1.95**

**254-107** Large Tool Boxes pkg(2) **1.95**

**254-109** Lanterns pkg(4) **2.95**

**254-110** Shovels pkg(4) **2.50**

**254-111** Brooms pkg(4) **2.50**

### Plastic Doors pkg(4)

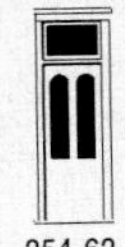
254-62

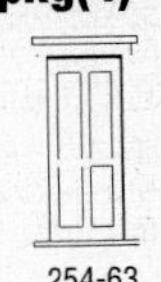
254-63

**254-62** With Transom **1.95**

**254-63** Four Panel **2.50**

### Plastic Windows Double-Hung 1.95 ea

254-60

254-61

**254-60** Tall pkg(4)

**254-61** Double pkg(2)

### Screws

**254-127** Wood Truck (1/4") pkg(12) **1.95**

### Tires

**254-93** Auto pkg(12) **5.50**

### Water Tank

**254-124** Round Rooftop **6.95**

### Wooden Barrels

**254-15** Large pkg(4) **2.50**

**254-23** Small pkg(10) **3.50**

### Miscellaneous

254-25

254-81

**254-25** Rural Mailbox pkg(5) **2.95**

**254-34** Bridge Shoes pkg(4) **2.25**

**254-46** hooks, Block & Tackle **2.25**

**254-65** Car Battery pkg(4) **2.95**

**254-69** Freight Dock/Door Bumper pkg(4) **2.95**

**254-75** Electrical Box pkg(3) **2.50**

**254-79** Coal Box 2 pc **3.25**

**254-81** 8-Gallon Gas Can pkg(4) **2.95**

254-82 254-83

**284-82** Upright Air Compressor pkg(2) **2.95**

**254-83** Manhole Covers pkg(5) **2.95**

254-84 254-85

**254-84** Acetylene Tanks **3.25**

**254-85** Fire Extinguishers pkg(5) **2.95**

**254-86** Pallets pkg(8) **2.95**

**254-87** Sewer Grates pkg(5) **2.95**

**254-92** Large Truck Tires pkg(6) **2.95**

254-94

254-128

**254-94** Assorted Gears pkg(8) **5.50**

**254-103** Band Fasteners/Turnbuckles Plastic 3 Sizes pkg(26) **1.95**

**254-128** Speeder Wheels pkg(4) **2.50**

## Information STATION

### Modeling Mortar

Are you finding that your brick buildings look kind of boring? There's an easy way to add function, realism and detail to any brick structures. By creating the appearance of mortar in each level of brickwork, you've got a building that's brought to life!

Brick buildings are constructing by stacking brick one on top of the other in rows. Between each stack is a layer of mortar, which acts as an adhesive that holds the bricks together. But most kits simulate the brickwork, and leave the layer of mortar invisible. This, however, can be modified with a few creative ideas.

What you want to do is apply a thin wash of either white or gray paint, allowing it to flow down between the bricks. Then wipe it away from the surface before it dries. This gives the paint a chance to settle in the ridges between the bricks, thus simulating the appearance of mortar between layers of brick. There are also some commercial mortars available to simplify the job. Whatever you choose, it's likely that your houses, industries and churches will look more realistic after the mortar is used!

# DETAILS WEST

These detail parts are white metal castings or styrene parts. Illustrations are not to scale.

## NEW PRODUCTS

### Diesel Detail Parts

**Mirrors**
**NEW 235-353** Rear View **2.95**

**Wind Deflector**
**NEW 235-354 2.50**

**Adaptor Plates**
**NEW 235-355 3.95**
For mounting Athearn Blomberg sideframes on Atlas trucks, sold separately.

**NEW 235-356 8.25**
For Atlas trucks, sold separately, includes Blomberg sideframes.

### Freight Car Details

**Scale Cushion Draft Gears**
For 50 and 60' Freight Cars.

**NEW 235-1025** "20" Style w/Cut Bars **4.25**

**NEW 235-1026** "Wide Mouth" Style w/Cut Bars 1 set **4.25**

For Cabooses

**NEW 235-1027** With Cut Bars & Brackets **4.50**

## DIESEL DETAIL PARTS

### Air Conditioners

**235-158** Vapor Type **1.00**
Mounted atop cab of 2nd generation hood units. Styrene.

### Air Cooling Coils

**235-159** Prime Type **1.25**
Roof mount with adapter for GE hood unit. Styrene.

**235-260** Dayton/Phoenix Type **2.00**
For GE Dash 9, white metal.

**235-318** Rooftop **2.50**
GN, SP&S, & some eastern roads.

### Air Filters

**Early Types 1.00 ea**

235-139

235-154

**235-139** 2nd Generation EMD & GE Units pkg(2)

**235-154** 1st & Early 2nd Generation Hood Units

**GE Type**
Used on CNW and UP Dash 8, 9 and AC4400CW locos.

**235-248** Filter Set w/Mount & Pipes **2.25**

**Prime Type 1.25 ea**

235-198

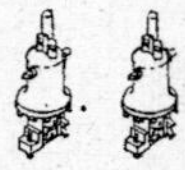

235-199

**235-198** Prime Type 1

**235-199** Prime Type 2
Used on second generation EMD hood units.

**Salem Type**

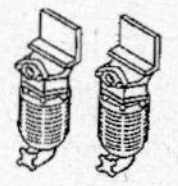

235-225

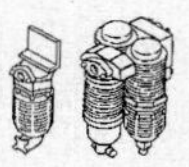

235-226

**235-225** Small pkg(2) **1.50**

**235-226** Set pkg(2) **1.75**

**235-237** Air Dryer Filter w/Pipes & Mounts **4.75**

### Air Horns

**235-131** Hancock Type 4700 pkg(2) **1.00**
Used by PC, MILW, L&N, SCL and others, also used on industrial switchers.

235-173

235-174

**235-173** Flat Type Single-Chime pkg(2) **3.95**
For 1st generation diesels, brass.

**235-174** Wabco Type E, Single-Chime pkg(2) **3.95**
For 1st generation diesels.

**235-347** Shrouded Three Chime (pewter) **2.95**
CB&Q, GN.

**Leslie**
**235-190** RSL-3L-R **3.99**

**235-191** RS-ST-RF, 5-Chime Horn **4.25**

**235-326** S-3L Nonspiked Caps BN, GN, Katy & many eastern roads. **3.75**

**235-327** S5T-RR 3 Bells Facing Forward, 2 Facing Back For CSX, NS, MKT, N&W, UP & Others. **3.75**

**235-351** 5 Chime, 4 Forward, 1 Reverse (brass) **4.25**
GM&O, UP, others.

**Nathan 3.75 ea (Unless Noted)**

235-175

235-186

235-187

**235-175** P3, Three-Chime
For all types of 1st and 2nd generation units, brass.

**235-186** M3, brass.

**235-187** M5, brass.

**235-250** K5HR24
CNW, SP, CSX, NS and Canadian roads, brass.

**235-251** K5 Low Profile w/Reverse #3 & 4 Bells
CSX, DRGW, NS and others, brass.

**235-252** K5 Low Profile w/All Bells Forward
Amtrak, CSX, NS, Metro, brass.

**235-253** K3 w/Reverse #4 Bell
ATSF, BNSF, CN, CP, SP and others, brass.

**235-254** K3 w/All Bells Forward
CP, CN and others, brass.

**235-346** P-3 Large Right Bell Configuration (pewter) **2.95**
NP, others.

### Air Horn Stand

**235-329** Tall **1.25**

### Air Hose pkg(2) 1.25 ea

**235-267** Locomotive Type w/Bracket

**235-268** Locomotive Type w/Extension & Angle Cock

**235-302** Drop Elbow Style

### Air Tanks

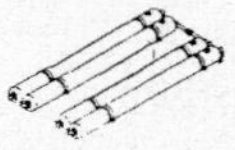

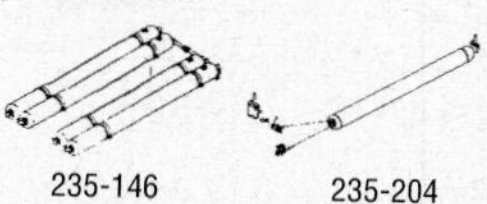

235-146

235-204

**235-146** Geeps-Roof Mount **2.50**
Used on EMD GP7 through GP20s and CNW GP35s.

**235-204** EMD Hood Units-Underframe **2.05**

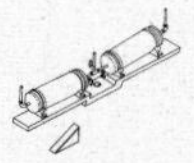

235-261

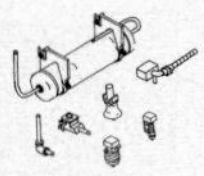

235-263

**235-261** Bottom-Mount for Post 1995 GE Dash 9 AC4400CW **5.25**
Kit includes tanks with brackets, cast metal.

**235-263** 4- & 6-Axle GE Diesels **5.25**
Kit includes tanks with brackets, pipes, air filter, moisture ejector and bell, cast metal.

### Air Tank Details

**235-242** Pipes & Moisture Ejectors-Set **1.95**

**235-259** GE Dash 8, 9 & AC4400CW Pipe & Bracket Details **2.95**
Used on right side underframe, white metal and brass.

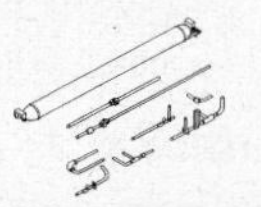

**235-304** With Pipes **4.25**
For early to late era EMD hood units.

### Antennas

235-157

235-214

**235-157** "Firecracker" Type pkg(5) **2.25**
Brass, used on all types of locos and cabooses.

**235-214** Sinclair w/Ground Plane **1.50**
Used by SP, ATSF and others.

235-274

235-275

**235-274** Sinclair (Long Type) pkg(2) **1.00**

**235-275** Sinclair (Short Type) pkg(4) **1.25**

235-276

235-277

**235-276** "Can" Type pkg(2) **1.00**

**235-277** "Wide Cone" Type pkg(2) **1.00**

235-278

235-279

**235-278** "Cone" Type pkg(2) **1.00**

**235-279** "Tear Drop" Type pkg(2) **1.00**

**235-280** "Lollipop" Type pkg **1.00**

**235-322** "Nail" Type pkg(2) **1.25**
All roads.

### Antenna Mounting Stands pkg(2) 1.75 ea (Unless Noted)

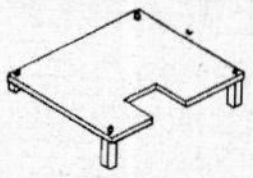

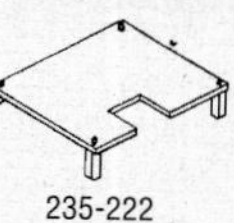

235-222

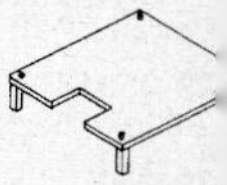

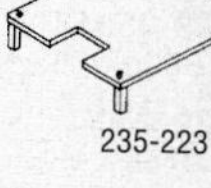

235-223

**235-222** Style 1

**235-223** Style 2

**235-352** Multi-type Configuration Set (brass etched) **5.25**

### Automatic Train Contr 1.25 ea

235-170

235-184

**235-170** Control Box
For hood units of PRR (later PC, CR) ATSF, UP and others

**235-184** Automatic Train Stop
Used by Santa Fe, Amtrak.

### Bells pkg(2) 1.25 ea (Unless Noted)

235-127

235-128

**235-127** Frame Mount
For all types of units.

**235-128** Fabricated Type
Standard equipment for EMD switchers, post 1952.

235-129

235-134

**235-129** Hood-Side Mount
GE and other hood units.

**235-134** Roof Mount
GE hood units.

235-135

235-151

**235-135** Front Mount **1.50**
N&W and SOU hood units

**235-151** Curved Base-Fabricated Type
For Alco-built switchers.

# ETAILS WEST

235-152 235-176

**35-152** Gong Type **1.00**
or nose of CNW and Detroit, oledo & Ironton units, also nstalled on some Bangor and roostook, BN and MP power.

**35-176** Hood-Side Mount

235-238 235-292

**35-238** End of Fuel Tank lount

**35-292** Roof Top **1.75**
or SP units.

## Electronic Bells pkg(2) 3.15 ea

**235-336** Electronic, Small Round Type
For MILW, SOO & others.

**235-337** Electronic, Dual Large Speaker Type
For MILW, BN, SOO & others.

## Bearing Cap

**235-244** Axle Bearing Caps pkg(4) **1.25**

## Brake Vent Valve

**235-245** Brake Vent Regulator Valve pkg(2) **1.25**

## Cab & Body Vents pkg(12) 1.00 ea

**235-121** Round Styrene
Used on hood units and cabooses.

**235-122** Square
Used on cabs of 2nd generation EMD and GE units.

## Coupler Cut Lever, F Unit Front

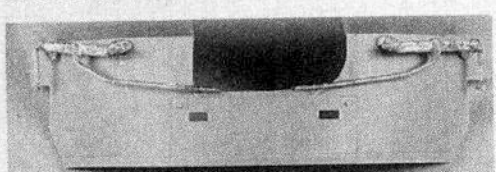

**235-316** For All Roads **2.75**

**235-317** For SP **1.95**

## Coupler Knuckle Brackets

235-196 235-210

**235-196** Spare Knuckle/ Bracket pkg(2) **1.00**

**235-210** Knuckle Holder GP50/60 **1.75**
Many roads install these brackets on locos, so crews have spare knuckles handy for occasional repairs.

## Diesel Parts

235-118 235-119

**235-118** Steam Generator Set (3 pieces) **1.50**

**235-119** Rerail Frog Set **1.50**
Includes two "butterfly" rerailers, right and left hanging brackets and basic instructions.

235-172 235-188

**235-172** Loco & Cab Step Lights pkg(8) **1.25**
For virtually all diesels and many roads' cabooses.

**235-188** Diesel Sun Visor, Styrene pkg(4) **1.00**

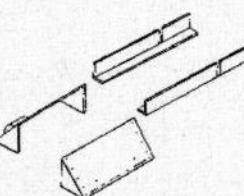

**235-194** Awning/Smoke Deflector **1.50**

**235-195** Coupler Buffer Plate pkg(2) **1.50**
Fills empty space below couplers on most plastic hood units, includes installation instructions.

**235-324** Sun Visor for Cab Interior pkg(2) **1.50**

**235-325** Rooftop Pipe pkg(2) **1.25**
For F-Units, "Gooseneck"

## Ditch Lights

235-228 235-229

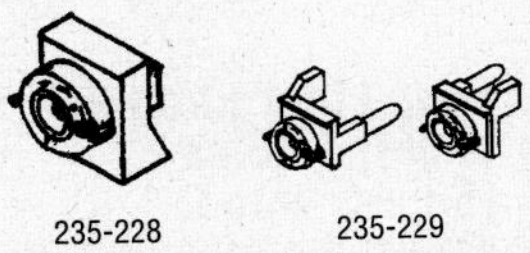

**235-228** EMD Style (Pilot Top Mount) **2.95**

**235-229** GE Style w/Lenses (Pilot End Mount) **2.95**
Working accessory, includes lamp housings and lenses.

**235-243** With Platforms & Lenses **3.50**

**235-301** Late Style w/Lenses **3.15**

## End-Of-Train Device

**235-227** End-of-Train Device w/Red Bulb **1.95**
One-piece metal casting, simulates devices used to protect modern freight trains.

## Flag Holder Brackets

**235-323** All F-Units pkg(4) **1.50**

## Fuel Fillers pkg(4)

235-149 235-166 235-167

**235-149** GE Hood Units **1.25**

**235-166** EMD Road Units **1.00**

**235-167** EMD Switcher Type **1.00**

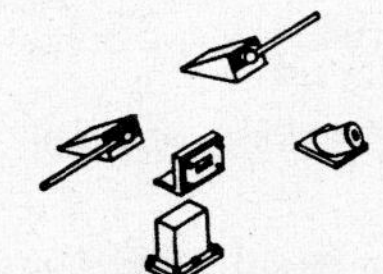

**235-258** GE Dash 8, 9 & AC4400CW Fillers & Gauges **2.95**

**235-348** "Y" Neck Type pkg(2) **1.50**

## Fuel Shut-Off

**235-247** Emergency Fuel Shut-Off Box pkg(2) **1.25**

## Fuel Tank Brackets

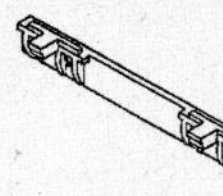

235-197 235-240

**235-197** End Bracket pkg(2) **1.50**

**235-240** GE Style Brackets pkg(4) **1.75**

## Fuel Tank Details

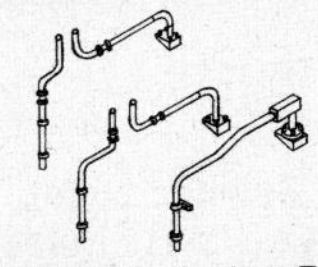

**235-305** Drain & Vent Pipes for EMD pkg(5) **2.50**

**235-349** Vent Pipe, Dual Pipe Type pkg(2) **1.50**
SP, others.

## Fuel Tank Extension w/Fuel Fillers, Gauge & Side Skirting

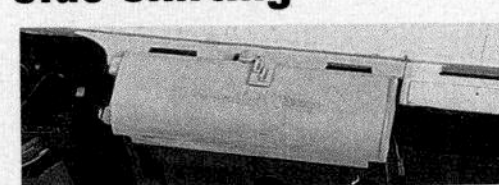

**235-315** **4.95**
For SP, WP & others.

## Fuel Tank Mounts

**235-111** Breather Pipe **1.00**
For SD7/9, 18, 24 and 26.

## GPS Dome

**235-320** Small Round, UP **1.95**

**235-321** Small Square, Angled Top w/Conduit **1.50**

## Handbrakes

235-179 235-132 235-177

**235-179** EMD/GE Wheel Only pkg(2) **1.00**

**235-132** Ratchet Handbrake **1.00**
Standard on most EMD and other hood units.

**235-177** Locomotive Type - Wheel w/Gear Box **1.50**

**235-246** Handbrake Chain Pulley Beam pkg(2) **1.50**

**235-1016** Handbrake & Pulley Mount **1.50**

## Headlight Sets - Southern Pacific

To make diesels more visible, SP applied additional warning lights to virtually all types of diesels. Sets are complete with mounting brackets, lights and basic instructions.

### Mars Lights, Pre-1958 Hood Units

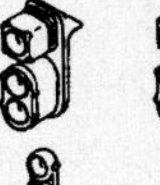
235-100 235-101

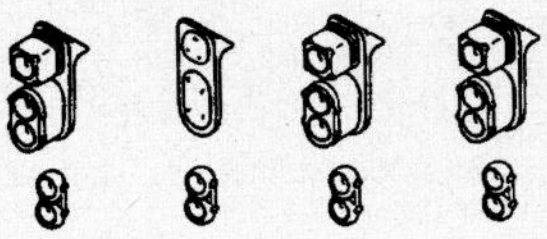

**235-100** Single End (6 pieces) **2.25**

**235-101** Double End (8 pieces) **2.75**

New Arrivals Updated Every Day! Visit Walthers Web site at **www.walthers.com**

### Mars Lights, SD7/9

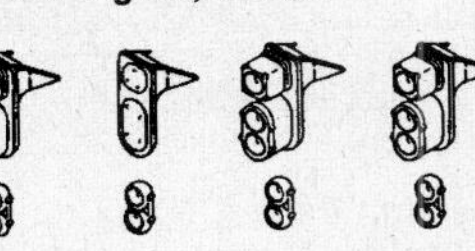
235-104 235-105

**235-104** Single End (6 pieces) **2.25**

**235-105** Double End (8 pieces) **2.75**

### Pyle Lights, Post 1958 Hood Units

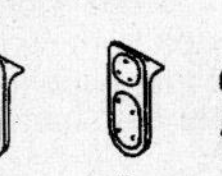

235-102 235-103

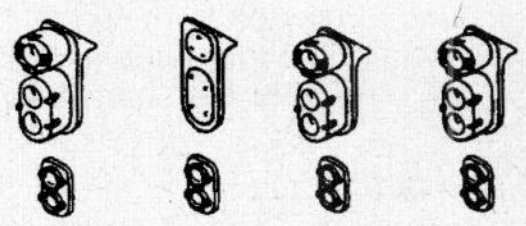

**235-102** Single End (6 pieces) **2.25**

**235-103** Double End (8 pieces) **2.75**

## Loco Detail Sets

### Amtrak Loco Super Detail Kit

**235-271** AMD-103 (P-40, P-42) **22.95**
Kit includes sander brackets, underframe bell, screen guard, toilet drain, K5LA horn, HEP cables, air dryers with mounts, battery box brackets, Sinclair radio antenna and many pipe assortments. Parts are white metal and brass.

### Athearn/Genesis Detail Sets

**235-296** SD70 ATSF & BNSF **14.95**

**235-297** SD75I BNSF **22.95**

**235-298** SD70I/75I CN **24.95**

**235-299** SD70M UP **19.95**

**235-300** Auxiliary Set for #s 296, 297, 298 & 299 **6.95**

### EMD Detail Sets

**235-331** EMD GP60 Diesels (47 Pieces) **23.50**
For ATSF, BNSF.

**235-332** EMD GP60 Diesels (47 Pieces) **24.50**
SP, Cotton Belt, DRGW.

**235-333** EMD GP60 Diesels NS (44 Pieces) **22.75**

**235-339** Southern Pacific SD45T-2 **20.95**

**235-340** EMD SD70MAC **19.50**

# DETAILS WEST

## F Unit Parts 5.50 ea (Unless Noted)

235-208

235-209

**235-208** A Unit, For Athearn, Stewart & other F units. Includes front step, walkway platform, coupler draft gear, draft gear detail and rear door.

**235-209** B Unit For Athearn, Stewart & other F units. Includes door, coupler draft gear and backup light for each end.

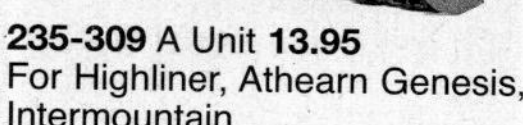

**235-309** A Unit **13.95**
For Highliner, Athearn Genesis, Intermountain.

**235-310** B Unit **12.95**
For Highliner, Athearn Genesis, Intermountain.

## GE Detail Sets

Complete sets of parts to detail your Dash 9-44CW or AC4400CW to match specific prototypes.

**235-230** SP, CSX, NS, CP **15.95**

**235-231** CNW, UP **13.95**

**235-232** ATSF, BNSF **14.95**

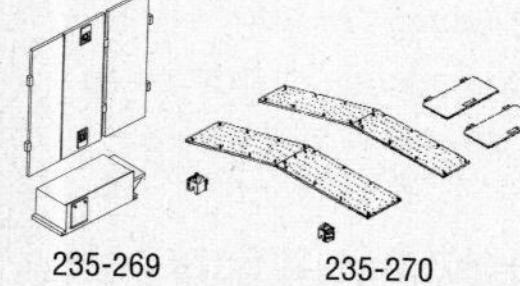
235-269 235-270

**235-269** Brass Etched Access Doors & Capacitor Starter Box **3.95**
White metal and bronze. For post 1995 GE AC4400CW.

**235-270** Bronze Etched Walkway Detail Set **5.95**
White metal and bronze. For GE Dash 9-44CW or AC4400CW. Includes rear radiator walkway plates, walkway access hatches and lifting lugs.

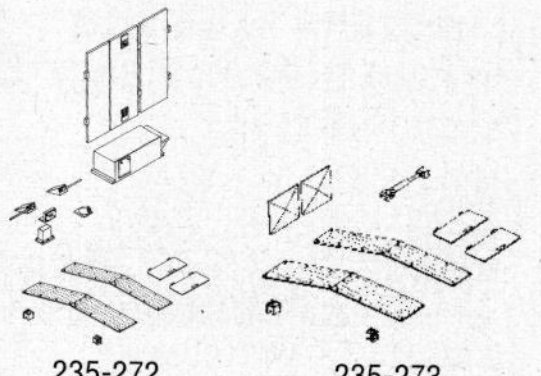
235-272 235-273

**235-272** Locomotive Detail Set **12.50**
White metal, brass and bronze. Set includes brass access doors, capacitor starter box, etched bronze walkway plates, lifting lugs and fuel filler.

**235-273** Bronze Etched Detail Kit **8.50**
White metal and bronze. Set includes radiator plates, access hatches, lifting lugs, four "x" panels and anti-hunting dampers for BNSF and NS GE Dash 9-44CWs.

## Proto 2000 GP30 Detail Sets

**235-281** DRGW **14.95**

**235-282** BN/GN **16.95**

**235-283** SP/SSW **14.75**

## Southern Pacific

**235-339** SD 45T-2 **20.95**

## MU Cables 2.15 ea (Unless Noted)

235-218

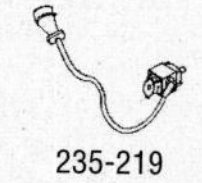
235-219

**235-218** Double Plugs pkg(4)

**235-219** Receptacle, Plug pkg(2)

**235-220** Receptacle w/Two Plugs pkg(2)

**235-221** Dummy Receptacle pkg(2)

**235-236** Double-Ended Receptacle & Two Receptacle pkg(2)

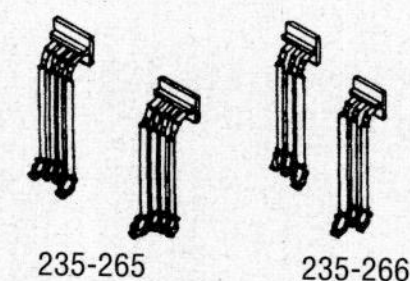
235-265 235-266

**235-265** Locomotive 4 Cluster Set pkg(4) **3.75**

**235-266** Locomotive 3 Cluster Set pkg(4) **3.50**

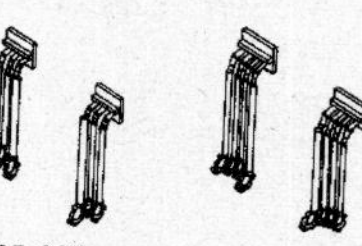
235-294 235-295

**235-294** 3 Cluster Set, Pre 1980 Locos pkg(4) **3.50**

**235-295** 4 Cluster Set, Pre 1980 Locos pkg(4) **3.75**

**235-452** With Two Types of Stands **2.95**

## Number Boards pkg(2)

### Auxiliary-For Switchers

235-136

235-156

**235-136** EMD **1.00**

**235-156** Alco **1.25**

### For Road Units

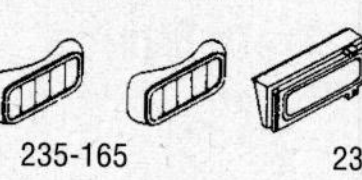
235-165 235-249

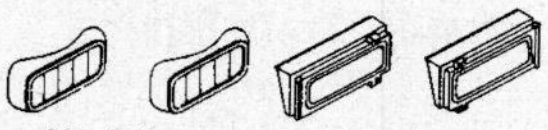

**235-165** F Unit **1.00**
Correctly scaled and designed for Athearn F7A, also used on some E units.

**235-249** GE Dash 7/8/9, AC4400CW **1.35**

## Pilots

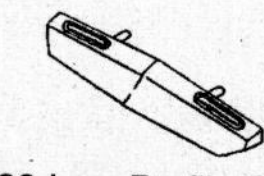

**235-130** Low Profile Snowplow **1.95**
Replaces footboards on 2nd generation EMD and GE hood units.

235-192

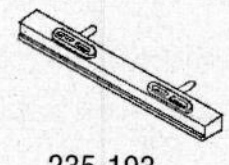
235-193

**235-192** Beam w/Footboards pkg(2) **1.50**

**235-193** Beam Only pkg(2) **1.25**

## Pyle Headlights

### Gyralight pkg(2) 1.00 ea

235-115

235-116

235-148

**235-115** Single

**235-116** Twin - Early

**235-148** Twin - Flush Mount

**235-291** Twin "Cab" Type
For SP, CB&Q and others.

## Mars Lights pkg(2) 1.00 ea

235-112

235-113

**235-112** Signal

**235-113** Twin Signal

## Nose Mounted Lights 1.00 ea (Unless Noted)

**235-133** Barrel Type pkg(2) **2.00**
For GP7/9s of Western Pacific and CN.

**235-137** Mars

**235-138** Pyle
Integral with nose, used on some EMD 2nd generation hood units, one-piece casting with mounting instructions, locos require modification.

235-162

235-200

**235-162** E & F Unit Back-Up Light, pkg(2)
Single sealed beam.

**235-200** Nose Headlight/Warning Light **1.25**
Used by SP and some other roads, mounted on low nose.

**235-290** Mars, Twin Signal DRGW & others.

## Twin Sealed Beam pkg(2) 1.00 ea

235-114

235-117

**235-114** Early

**235-117** Late

## Rerail Frog w/Brackets

**235-293** (4 pieces) **1.75**
For DRGW, UP & others.

## Rotary Beacons

White metal base with styrene lens.

235-106

235-126

**235-106** Roof Mount **1.25**

**235-126** "Western-Cullen" **1.25**
Type D-312 used by UP, BN, ATSF and others.

**235-306** Pyle National w/Cored Lens **2.25**
Includes cap and base.

## Sander Brackets

**235-330** 4 Axle & 6 Axle Trucks **2.75**
ABS styrene.

## Sand Filler Hatches pkg(4) 1.25 ea (Unless Noted)

**235-201** EMD GP7 through GP20

**235-202** Alco

**235-203** GE

**235-241** GE Dash 8, 9 & AC Series-Set **1.75**
Rear housing and filler hatches for newer GE power.

## Snow Plows 1.95 ea (Unless Noted)

Metal castings duplicate various styles of pilot plows installed on many diesels.

235-110

235-120 235-14

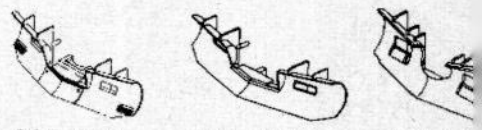

**235-110** With Footboards
For 2nd generation hood un of SP, UP and Western Paci

**235-120** Early Hood Units
1st and some 2nd generatio hood units of Spokane, Portland & Seattle (BN), IC, SP, CN including Alco Centuries.

**235-140** Western Style
Used on 2nd generation hoo units of SP, UP and WP.

235-150

235-155

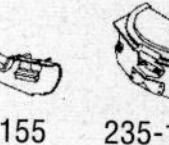
235-160

**235-150** Weed Cutter
For hood units of ATSF, Conr and others.

**235-155** Standard
Most common type, used by ATSF, BN, CNW and WP.

**235-160** F & E Unit Type **2.5**
Used by Amtrak, GN (BN), S and WP.

235-180 235-185 235-205

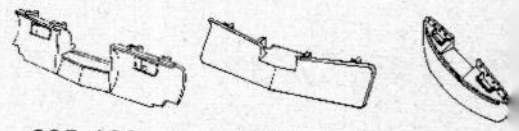

**235-180** Flat

**235-185** Low Profile, NP

**235-205** Convex
Used on Chessie System EM hood units.

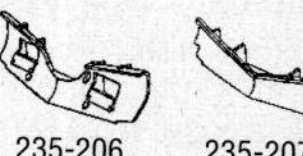
235-206 235-207

**235-206** 2nd Generation Hoo Units

**235-207** Low Profile
ATSF & other roads.

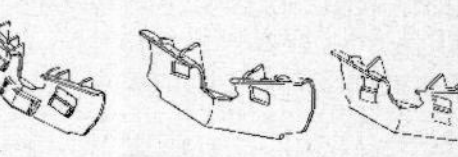
235-217 235-233 235-234

**235-217** EMD Passenger Hood Unit Plow

**235-233** SP, CP Type

**235-234** CNW & UP Type

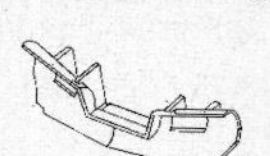

**235-235** Santa Fe Type

**235-255** Open MU Doors ATSF & BN

**235-256** CSX, NS

**235-257** Canadian Roads BCR & CN

## DETAILS WEST

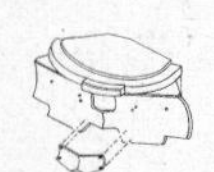

**35-264** Alco PA Pilot (SP) **.50**

235-286

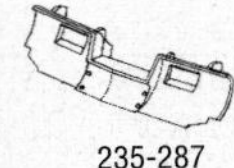
235-287

**35-286** DRGW

**35-287** BN, GN, Others

**35-303** No MU Doors

**35-313** w/Cast Coupler Cut ever **3.75**
or SP, WP & other roads.

**35-314** w/Cast Coupler Cut ever **3.75**
or GN, NP & other roads.

### Spark Arrestors pkg(2) 1.50 ea

**235-319** Half-Rounded Top
For F-Units and early Geeps.

**"Super"**
Used on nonturbocharged units.

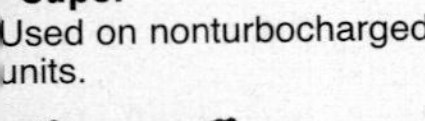

235-123

235-124

235-125

**235-123** Lifting Type

**235-124** Nonlifting Type
For EMD units of DRGW, MP, CNW, GM&O and SOO.

**235-125** Harco Centrifugal Type pkg(2)
For nonturbocharged EMDs from UP, BN, BAR and ARR.

### SP Barrel Type Headlights 1.25 ea

235-108

235-109

**235-108** Bolted Face

**235-109** Hinged Face
For first generation GP and SD units.

### Speed Recorders

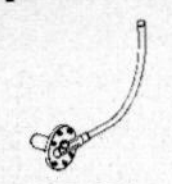
235-284

235-285

**235-284** With Cable Line pkg(2) **1.95**
For early to late era locos.

**235-285** pkg(2) **1.95**
For late era locos

### Traction Motor Cable Sets

**235-224** Traction Motor Cable Set **1.95**

**235-239** Traction Motor Cable Set **3.25**

### Truck Journal pkg(4) 1.25 ea

235-288

235-289

**235-288** Square Type

**235-289** Slope Type

### Vent & Electrical Cabinet Sets 1.00 ea

235-107

235-161

**235-107** Late 2nd Generation

**235-161** EMD Dash-2
Cast metal, includes vent for top of hood and electrical cabinet filter.

### Wheel Slip Modulation Device

**235-350** All Roads pkg(4) **2.95**

### Winterization Hatches

Used on locos of roads operating in colder areas. Hatches redirect radiator heat back into the hood to keep electrical equipment warm and dry. Styrene parts.

**Early EMD 1.00 ea**

235-163

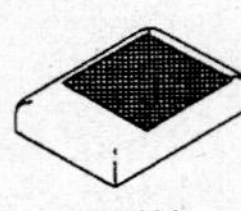
235-164

**235-163** F Units
Used on both A and B units.

**235-164** GP/SD Units
For EMD GP7/9, GP20 and SD7/9.

**48" - Later EMD 1.50 ea**

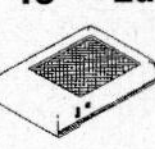
235-211

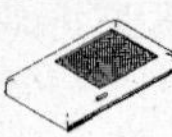
235-212

235-213

**235-211** GP50

**235-212** SD45, F45, GP18

**235-213** Square, SD45, F45



### Miscellaneous

235-307

235-308

**235-307** Steerable Truck Sideframe **8.95**
For GE Phase I.

**235-308** Air Dryer Filter, Cylinder/Box Style pkg(2) **1.95**
For late-era model GE and EMD locos.

## FREIGHT CAR DETAILS

### Brake Gear Sets 1.85 ea

Complete exterior and underbody details for box cars, adaptable to other cars. Styrene.

**235-1020** Modern 1960-Present.
Includes slack adjuster vertical "Hook & Eye" lever detail.

**235-1021** Early 1940-1975
Includes Ajax brakewheel.

### Coupler Pockets

Freight cars shown in photos are not included.

**Cushion**

**235-1009** Caboose & Freight Cars **2.50**

**235-1010** Most 60' Cars **2.50**

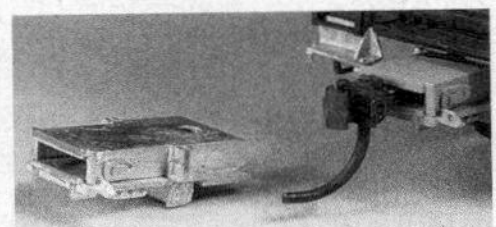

**235-1023** "20 Inch," For 50' & 60' Freight Cars **2.75**

**235-1024** Long Cushion Type, For 60' to 86' Freight Cars **2.75**

**Non-Cushion**

**235-1022** For Early to Late Era 40' & 50' Freight Cars **2.50**

### Doors

**8' Doors**

**235-181** With Guides & Tack Boards pkg(2) **1.75**

### Hitches 3.45 ea (Unless Noted)

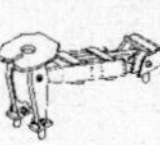
235-1004

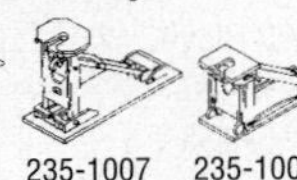
235-1007 235-1008

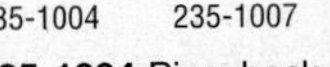

**235-1004** Piggyback Hitch **6.95**

**235-1007** Pullman-Standard Rigid

**235-1008** ACF Model 6-2 Cushioned Fixed Hitch

235-1011

235-1012

235-1013

**235-1011** Trailer Train TT-2 Rigid Fixed Hitch pkg(2)

**235-1012** Pullman-Standard Cushioned Fixed Hitch pkg(2)

**235-1013** ACF Model 5 Rigid-Wrench Operated Retractable Hitch pkg(2)

**235-1014** Spine Car Hitch pkg(5) **7.95**

### Intermodal Details

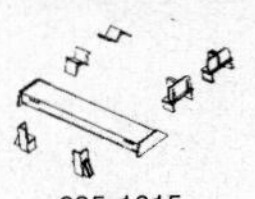
235-1015

235-1017

**235-1015** Flat Car Restraint Curbs **5.95**
Includes container end fixed restraint curbs and fold down restraint curbs, fits 60' and 89' flat cars.

**235-1017** Bridge Plates for Piggyback Flats pkg(2) **1.75**

**235-1018** Spine Car Detail Kit **15.95**

### Ladders pkg(4) 1.25 ea

235-1005 235-1006

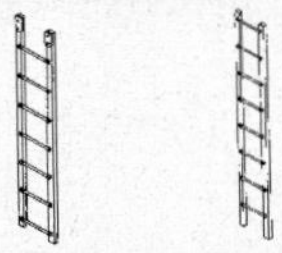

**235-1006** 7-Rung Ladder w/Brackets pkg

**235-1005** 8-Rung ladder

### Log Bunks

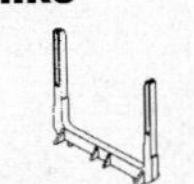

**235-171** Pacific Car & Foundry Type pkg(4) **2.50**
Converts 40' and 50' flat cars into log carriers, used by BN, MILW and UP.

### Underframes 2.25 ea

Styrene parts can be used with many freight car kits, include under-car cushioning details.

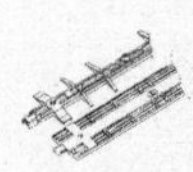
235-182

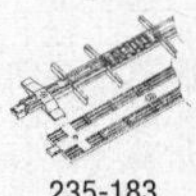
235-183

**235-182** 50' Hydra-Cushion w/Brake Set

**235-183** 50' "Evans 20" Cushion w/Brake Set

## TRACKSIDE DETAILS

### Battery Vaults pkg(2)

Prototypes house storage batteries to power trackside signals, crossing protection and other electrical gear.

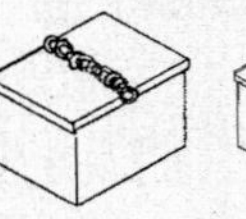
235-909 235-910

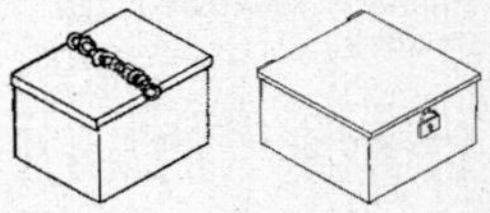

**235-909** Small **1.25**

**235-910** Medium **1.50**

**235-911** Large **1.75**

### Crossing Flasher

**235-913** Crossing Signal w/LEDs **19.95**
Includes crossbuck, pole, base and LEDs.

### Detectors

To prevent derailments, the prototypes of this equipment monitor passing trains for overheated wheel bearings (#900) or anything dragging beneath a car (#905). Nonworking kits include castings to build a typical installation and instructions.

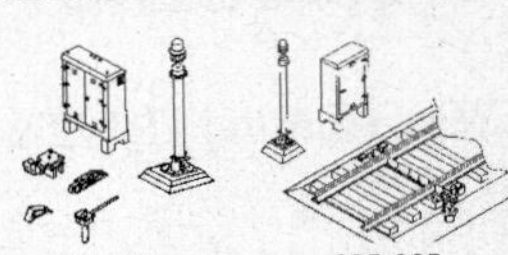
235-900 235-905

**235-900** Hot Box **7.95**

**235-905** Dragging Equipment **4.95**

### Electric Relay Cabinets

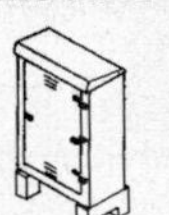
235-901

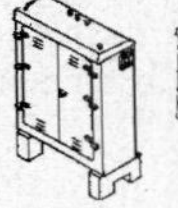
235-902

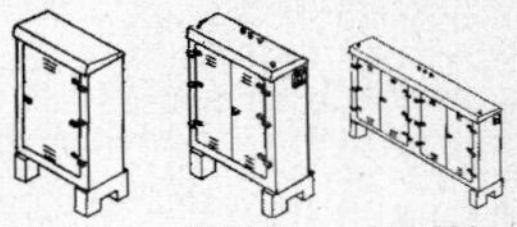

235-904

**235-901** 1-Door **1.98**

**235-902** 2-Door **2.10**

**235-904** 4-Door **2.20**
Prototypes house controls for crossing gates, flashers, signals, etc.

### Instrument Sheds

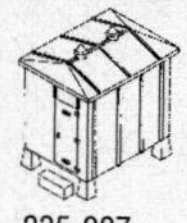
235-907

235-908

**235-907** 6 x 8' **4.25**

**235-908** 5 x 7' **3.25**

### Jack & Stands

**235-450** Air Jack & Car Stands pkg(2) **2.25**
Used in shops to lift and support freight cars being repaired.

## TRACK DETAILS

### Light Poles

**235-455** w/Light Heads pkg(2) **4.25**
Nonworking. For yards, industrial, engine facility, etc.

### Phone Box

**235-912** Telephone Box w/Wood Post **1.50**

### Lubricator

**235-906** Flange Lubricator Set **2.95**
Installed on curves to reduce wheel and flange wear, prototype automatically applies grease to passing wheel flanges before car or loco enters a curve.

### Men Working Sign/Blue Flag

**235-451** Men At Work Sign **1.95**
Collapsible sign with bracket, mounts between tracks, includes decal sign. Prototype protects repair or inspection crews working on equipment.

### Railbars

#### 6 & 4 Bolt

**ABS Plastic pkg(36) 2.50 ea**

**235-931** Code 83

**235-933** Code 70

**Brass pkg(12) 3.75 ea**

**235-932** Code 83

**235-934** Code 70

#### 4 Bolt

**235-935** Code 55 Pewter pkg(24) **2.50**

### Rail Details

#### Rail Joint Bars pkg(12) 2.75 ea

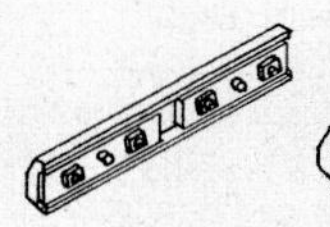
235-921 235-922

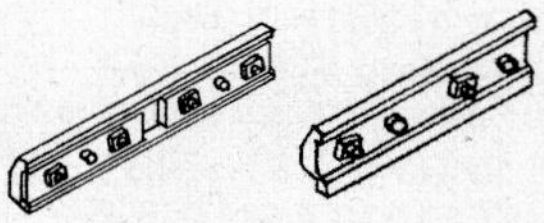

**235-921** 3-Bolt Fish Plate, Code 83, 70

**235-922** 2-Bolt Fish Plate, Code 70

#### Turnout Rail Braces pkg(12) 2.95 ea

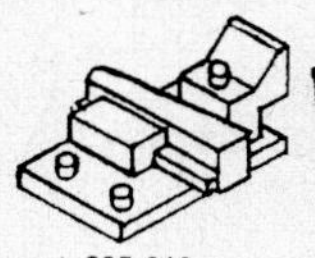
235-919

235-920

**235-919** Adjustable

**235-920** Rigid

### Switch Controls

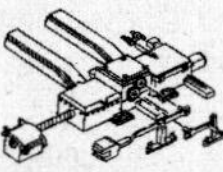

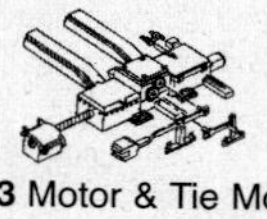

**235-903** Motor & Tie Mount **1.75**
Simulates electric motors used on prototype turnouts controlled by a dispatcher.

### Switch Stands

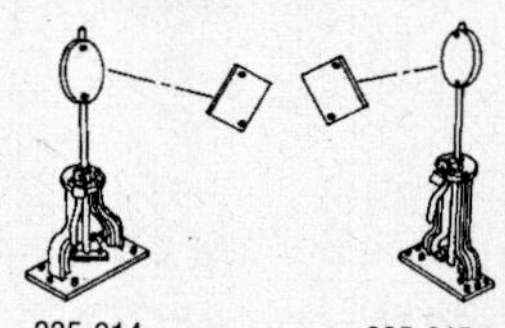
235-914 235-915

**235-914** Style 1 pkg(2) **2.95**

**235-915** Style 2 pkg(2) **2.95**

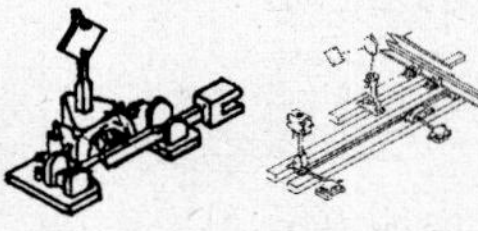
235-916 235-917

**235-916** Ground Throw Switch 2 Sets **2.75**

**235-917** With Interlock **3.75**

### Turnout Parts

#### Frog Sets 8.95 ea (Unless Noted)

Manganese insert type with plastic railbars and pewter guard rails.

**Code 83**

**235-926** #8

**235-927** #9

**Code 70**

**235-928** #9

**235-929** #8

**235-937** #7

#### Frog & Points Code 55 15.75 ea

**235-930** #8

Manganese insert type with plastic railbars and pewter guard rails.

**235-936** #7

White bronze with pewter guard rails and railbars

### Miscellaneous

**235-453** Air Stand w/Hose For Engine & Freight Car Shops **2.25**

**235-454** Yard Speakers - For Yards, Engine Facilities, Etc. pkg(2) **1.95**

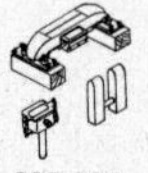
235-923

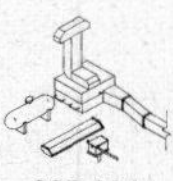
235-924

**235-923** Automatic Train Stop (ATS) Inductor **2.50**
For mainline track.

**235-924** Switch Heater **4.50**
With blower, propane tank and heater duct.

**235-925** Spur & Yard Track Derail **3.95**
With two style posts, decals & switch stand

## VEHICLE DETAILS

### Hy-Rail Wheels

**235-918** For Trident Vehicles Set **6.95**
Converts Chevy Pickup, Suburban or Blazer to railroad inspection/repair vehicle. Includes front and rear hy-rail wheels, toolbox and welding tanks.

## CATALOG

**235-1** Catalog **No Charge**

For Up-To-Date Information and News Bookmark Walthers Web site at
**www.walthers.com**

Detail parts are pewter castings. Visit Walthers web site at www.walthers.com for a complete listing of available parts from Evergreen Hill.

### Cans & Drums 2.75 ea

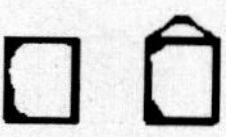
261-609

261-613

**261-609** Lube Cans Set pkg(6)

**261-613** 2-1/2 Gallon Gas Can pkg(4)

261-618

261-659

261-661

**261-618** 25-Gallon Drum pkg(5)

**261-659** Milk Can pkg(6)

**261-661** Garbage Can pkg(4)

### American Hoist & Derrick Equipment

**261-505** Stationary Boiler **14.95**

**261-506** Two Spool Hoist **29.95**

### Interior Details 2.75 ea (Unless Noted)

261-626

261-637

261-638

**261-626** Work Bench **2.50**

**261-637** Toilet pkg(2)

**261-638** Sink & Towel Dispenser

261-639

261-640

261-641

**261-639** Wall Telephone pkg(3)

**261-640** Radio pkg(3)

**261-641** Chair pkg(2)

**261-642** Stove & Pipe

**261-660** Lamp Shade pkg(6

### Miniature Tools 2.75 ea (Unless Noted)

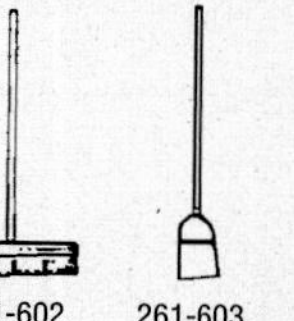
261-602 261-603 261-604

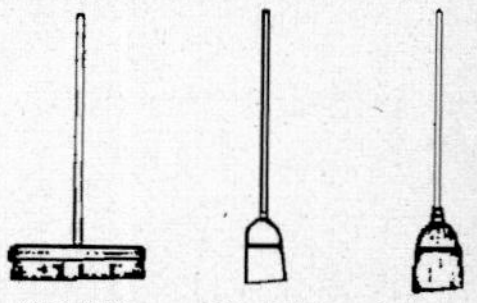

**261-602** Push Broom pkg(4)

**261-603** Street Broom pkg(4

**261-604** Shovel pkg(4)

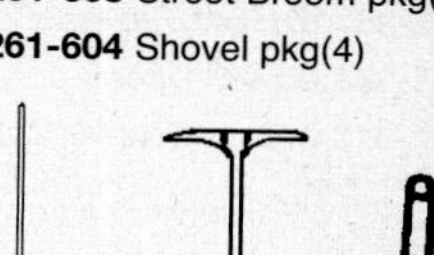

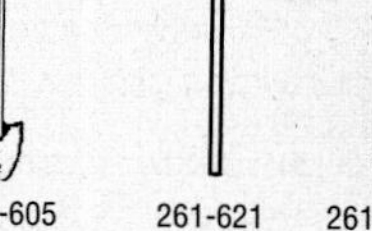
261-605 261-621 261-650

**261-605** Spade pkg(4)

**261-621** Picks pkg(6)

**261-650** Fire Extinguisher pkg(5)

### Power Meter

**261-606** Power Head/Box 2.2

### Roller Bearings pkg(4) 2.75 ea

**261-632** Small

**261-633** Large

### Shingles

These genuine cedar shingles are .015" thick. Two sheets pe package, each with cap shingles and starter strips.

**16"**

**261-301** Self-Adhesive **9.95**

**261-303** Non-Adhesive **9.79**

**24"**

**261-305** Self-Adhesive **9.49**

**261-307** Non-Adhesive **9.29**

### Welding Tanks pkg(5) 2.75 ea

261-622 261-624

**261-622** Oxygen Bottle

**261-624** Acetylene Bottle

# GCLaser

## NEW PRODUCTS

### Roof-Top Antenna

**NEW 292-1267** pkg(4) **6.99**

### Adirondack Chairs

**NEW 292-12731** pkg(4) **9.99**

### Plywood Crates pkg(2) 8.99 ea (Unless Noted)

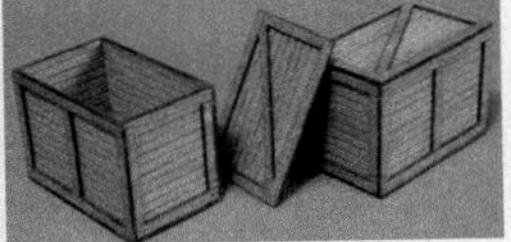

**NEW 292-91001** 13/16 x 1/2 x 5/8"

**NEW 292-91002** 1-1/16 x 13/16 x 5/8"

**NEW 292-91003** 1-1/16 x 13/16 x 1/2"

**NEW 292-91004** 1-1/16 x 13/16 x 1/4"

**NEW 292-91005** 1-15/16 x 13/16 x 1/2" **15.99**

**NEW 292-91006** Double Lid 1-1/16 x 13/16 x 1/4"

**NEW 292-91007** 13/16 x 1/2 x 5/8"

**NEW 292-91008** 1-1/16 x 13/16 x 5/8"

**NEW 292-91009** 1-1/16 x 13/16 x 1/2"

**NEW 292-910010** 1-1/16 x 13/16 x 1/4"

**NEW 292-910011** 1-15/16 x 13/16 x 1/2" **15.99**

**NEW 292-910012** Double Lid 1-1/16 x 13/16 x 1/4"

## Detail Kits

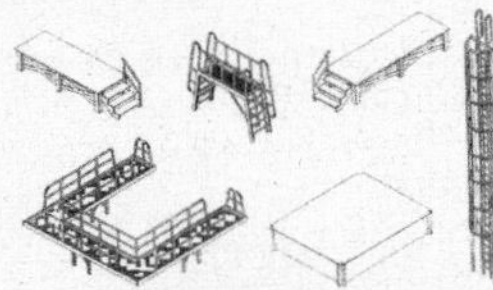

**292-1310041** Detail Kit for McGraw Oil #933-2913 (sold separately) **24.99**
Features berm and tank walkover, windows, doors and decks.

**292-1256** Berm Walkover **9.99**
Measures: 1-1/2 x 3/8 x 1-1/4"

## Feed Troughs

**292-1241** pkg(4) **9.99**
Measures: 1-1/4 x 9/32 x 7/16"

## Lumber Loads

### 2 x 12" 14.99 ea

**292-113311** One Each 8 & 20'

**292-113312** One Each 10 & 18'

**292-113313** One Each 12 & 16'

**292-113314** Two 14' Loads

### 3 x 12" 12.99 ea

**292-113315** One Each 8 & 20'

**292-113316** One Each 10 & 18'

**292-113317** One Each 12 & 16'

**292-113318** Two 14' Loads

### 2 x 6" 16.99 ea

**292-113319** One Each 8 & 20'

**292-113320** One Each 10 & 18'

**292-113321** One Each 12 & 16'

**292-113322** Two 14' Loads

## Pergolas & Trellises

**292-1234** Pergola Set w/Two Trellises **19.99**
One each large and small pergola, one arbor and two trellises.

**292-12341** Small Pergola w/Two Trellises **9.99**

**292-12342** Large Pergola w/Two Trellises **12.99**

**292-12343** Arbor w/Two Trellises **9.99**

## Tool Set

**292-1154** Miniature Tool Set **3.99**
Includes 10 shovels, four saws, two picks & 14 hammers.

## Truck Bodies

Create a custom replica with these kits, designed to fit Classic Metalworks Mini-Metals International flatbed trucks (sold separately.) Kits feature laser-cut and detailed parts, plus instructions with isometric drawings.

**292-12231** Stake Bed **9.99**

**292-12232** Cattle Bed **10.99**

**292-12233** Grain Bed **11.99**

## Truck Body Kits

### Fit Classic Metal Works R-190 (sold separately)

**292-12235** Materials **12.99**

**292-12236** Flat Bed **7.99**

### Fit Athearn Ford "C" Trucks (sold separately)

**292-12237** Stake Bed **11.99**

**292-12238** Cattle **12.99**

**292-12239** Flatbed **10.99**

**NEW 292-122317** Cable Reel Hauler **15.99**
Fits R-190 or White dual axle only. Includes 2 cable reels.

### For Sylvan Trucks (sold separately)

**Maple Leaf V-002**

**NEW 292-12381** Stake Bed **13.99**

**NEW 292-12386** Flatbed **10.99**

**Super Power V-021**

**NEW 292-12387** Stake Bed **15.99**

**NEW 292-123812** Flatbed **12.99**

**COE V-006**

**NEW 292-123813** Stake Bed **15.99**

**NEW 292-123818** Flatbed **12.99**

**White 4000 V-020**

**NEW 292-123819** Stake Bed **15.99**

**NEW 292-123824** Flatbed **12.99**

**GMC 600 V-022**

**NEW 292-123825** Stake Bed **15.99**

**NEW 292-123830** Flatbed **12.99**

### For Classic Metal Works Trucks (sold separately)

**292-12361** Cold Storage Platform **9.99**

**292-12362** Dry Transfer Platform **9.99**

**292-12363** Bulk Ice Platform **9.99**

### Trailer Office

**292-122316** **10.99**
2-7/8 x 2-1/8 x 2-3/16"
Features etched base and includes doors, windows and meter socket. Fits Athearn Ford "C" Box (sold separately).

## Rooftop Details

Once you've gotten everything set up on your layout (roads laid, track set up, cars placed, buildings built), make sure you take a look at your little city from a bird's-eye view. You might have forgotten one importan detail. Have your rooftops been forgotten? Don't forget that many structures place details atop their roofs. Modelers have a bevy of choices to choose from when detailing their rooftops

Think about the type of roof you want each building to feature. Most feature a shingle style, but don't forge you can vary the color of the shingles. Also think about adding some sun damage to the shingles. Fading the colors on some of the shingles will make the roof seem more realistic. You could also place a team of workers atop a roof to show a building in a state of repair. In addition, you could show a few exposed trusses to show the project in progress!

Keep ventilation sources in mind when installing factories and businesses on your layout. Large industrial-style chimneys are needed atop most hard-working factories. You could also install an access door, dust collectors, smokestacks, air handles or neon signs to create more visual interest,

For your houses, think what sits atop your home. Chimneys for fireplaces, air conditioning units, television antennas, satellite pools and even swimming pools atop skyscrapers could be the perfect touch!

## GCLaser

### Cable Reels

**292-1119** Empty pkg(3) **12.99**
Kit Includes laser-cut pieces to build three complete reels with laser-etched end boards. Includes complete instructions with isometric drawings.

### 5/8 x 1-1/16" Diameter 3-Packs 12.99 ea

292-11191

292-11192

**292-11191** Loaded
**292-11192** Covered

### Ladders

**292-11101 14.99**
Kit includes 75 laser-cut pieces and builds four 20' ladders, four 10' ladders; three 8' step ladders, three 6' step ladders, four 4' step ladders and four sawhorses.

### Pallets

**292-11102** pkg(36) **15.99**
Includes 108 laser-cut pieces, enough to build 36 wood pallets with notched forklift supports.

### Tables & Chairs

**292-11103 13.99**
Kit includes 73 laser-cut pieces and builds three round tables with interlocking supports, two rectangular tables with bracing, two picnic tables with bracing, four benches with supports, four back rest benches with supports and four chairs with supports.

## FRENCHMAN RIVER MODEL WORKS

## NEW PRODUCTS

### Boat Parts

Transform your marine models with thesde detailed parts, which can be adaptred to all sorts of vessels. Parts are lead-free Britania (pewter) castings unless noted.

### Anchor

**NEW 267-1071** 65" pkg(3) **6.00**

### Bridge Hooks

**NEW 267-1141** pkg(2) **2.50**

### Car Float Track Bumper

**NEW 267-1201** Cast Resin pkg(3) **7.00**

### Cleats

**NEW 267-1121** Large 54" Long pkg(10) **11.50**

**NEW 267-1131** Small 45" Long pkg(10) **10.00**

### Companion Way

**NEW 267-1161** Cast Resin pkg(2) **3.00**

### Deck Storage Box

**NEW 267-1151** Cast Resin pkg(2) **3.00**

### Firewood Stack

**NEW 267-1181** Cast Resin pkg(2) **2.25**

### 4-Blade Propeller

**NEW 267-1021** Small pkg(5) **5.75**

**NEW 267-1031** Large pkg(5) **7.25**

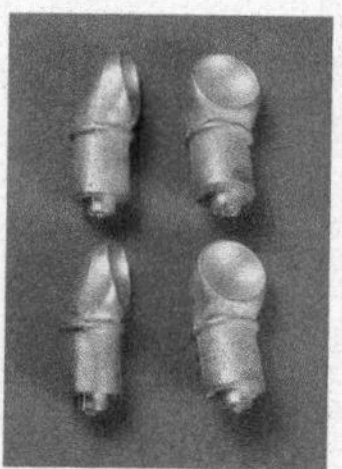

### Funnels

**NEW 267-1051** Short; 49" Tall pkg(4) **3.00**

**NEW 267-1061** Tall; 68" Tall pkg(4) **4.00**

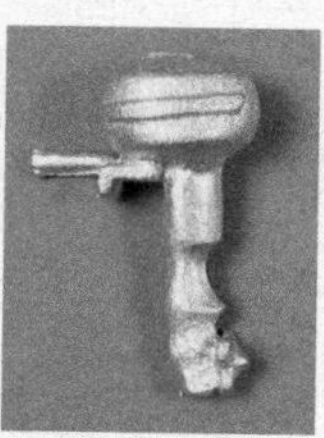

### Outboard Motor

**NEW 267-1091 4.75**

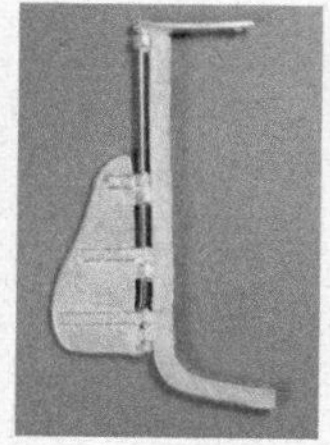

### Rudder

**NEW 267-1041** Scale 36 x 21" pkg(5) **5.75**

**NEW 267-1101** Scale 16'6" **14.75**

### Ship's Wheel & Oars

**NEW 267-1011** Laser-Cut Wood **2.00**

### Smoke Stack

**NEW 267-1171** Cast Resin pkg(2) **3.00**

### Steam Boiler

**NEW 267-1191** Cast Resin **3.00**

### Tire Bumpers/Fenders

**NEW 267-1111** pkg(10) **5.75**

### Winch

**NEW 267-1081** 2-Piece Set **7.00**
52 x 49" base and 70" long winch drum.

# GRANDT LINE

Parts for HO and HOn3 equipment are highly detailed, made of injection-molded styrene plastic unless noted.

## NEW PRODUCT

### Feed Sacks

**NEW 300-5304** pkg(20) **3.00**

## STRUCTURAL DETAILS

### Brackets & Corbels

**300-5074** Double-S Corbels 38" pkg(12) **3.00**

300-5151 300-5178

**300-5151** 14 x 17-1/2" Bracket pkg(20) **2.50**

**300-5178** Porch Bracket pkg(24) **2.50**

300-5171 300-5172

**300-5171** Victorian Corbels pkg(28) **3.00**

**300-5172** Eave Bracket & Louvered Vent pkg(4) **3.00**

**300-5275** pkg(12) **3.00**

### Building Details 3.00 ea

300-5218 300-5219

**300-5218** Corrugated Metal Roofing (2 Sheets)

**300-5219** Date Plaques/ Numbers (2 Sets)

**300-5279** Corrugated Iron Sheet 3.5 x 1.825" pkg(2)

### Chimneys & Vents

**300-5057** Chimney pkg(3) **3.00**

300-5084 300-5107 300-5297

**300-5084** Engine House Stack Set pkg(3) **3.95** Includes two 18" and one 9" stacks.

**300-5107** Louvered Victorian Attic Vents pkg(4) **3.00**

**300-5297** Chimney for Winters Mansion #225-38908 (sold separately) **3.00** 1/2 x 5/16 x 3/4" 1.3 x 0.8 x 2cm

### Cornices

300-5076 300-5020

**300-5076** 6 x 6 x 20" pkg(120) **4.75**

**300-5020** "Wells Fargo" Office-Brick Set pkg(4) **3.00**

### Depot Details

#### Rio Grande Southern - "Ophir"

300-5025 300-5026

**300-5025** Eaves pkg(6) **3.00**

**300-5026** Gables pkg(4) **3.00**

300-5197 300-5198

**300-5197** 36 x 84" Doors pkg(4) **3.00**

**300-5198** Freight Doors pkg(3) **3.95**

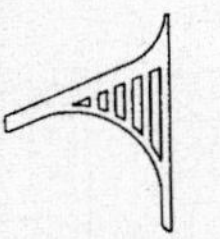

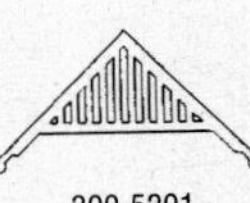

300-5200 300-5201

**300-5200** Eave Trim pkg(4) **2.50**

**300-5201** Gable Trim pkg(4) **2.50**

300-5202 300-5027

**300-5202** Roof Cresting Trim **3.95**

**300-5027** Station Roof Trim (7 Pieces) **4.00**

**300-5263** Residence Door w/Arched Window Set **2.50**

#### Rio Grande Southern Depot Windows 3.00 ea

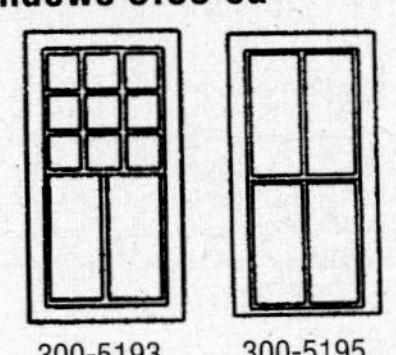

300-5193 300-5195

**300-5193** 36 x 76" pkg(8)

**300-5195** 4-Pane 36 x 82" pkg(4)

**300-5194** 9-Pane 32 x 53", 58 x 53" Each

**300-5196** Single/Double 24 x 82", 72 x 82" pkg(4)

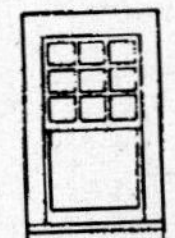

**300-5199** 10-Pane, 24 x 44", 51-1/2 x 51"

**300-5203** Double, 36 x 82" pkg(4)

#### Durango & DRGW Stations

300-5013 300-5014

**300-5013** Doors pkg(2) **2.50**

**300-5014** Windows 36 x 87" pkg(8) **4.25**

**300-5015** Wainscot pkg(5) **3.25**

**300-5016** Windows 36 x 44" pkg(8) **3.00**

300-5042 300-5058

**300-5042** Doors w/Oval Window pkg(2) **2.50**

**300-5058** Door w/Frame & Transom pkg(3) **3.00**

**300-5080** Baggage Room Door pkg(3) **3.00**

### Door Grab Bag Assortment

**300-5243** **18.95**

### Doors

300-5021 300-5022

**300-5021** Five Panel w/Frame pkg(3) **2.50**

**300-5022** "Assay Office" Double, 5-3/4' pkg(2) **2.50**

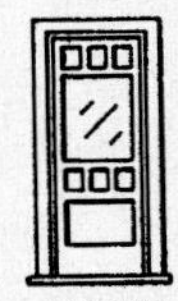

300-5028 300-5072

**300-5028** 30" w/Window & Separate Frame pkg(3) **2.50**

**300-5072** 4-Light w/Transom pkg(4) **3.00**

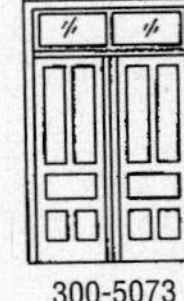

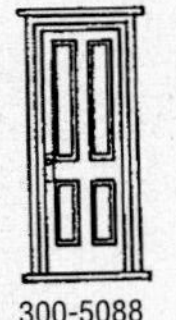

300-5073 300-5088

**300-5073** Double pkg(2) **2.50**

**300-5088** Station 4-Panel, 2'6" x 7'6" pkg(3) **3.00**

300-5102 300-5109

**300-5102** Engine House w/Hinges pkg(4) **3.95**

**300-5109** Double w/Transom Round & Rectangular Panes pkg(3) **3.00**

**300-5115** Victorian Store Front **2.50**

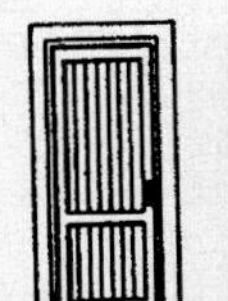

**300-5131** 2-Panel w/Frame (Tongue & Groove) pkg(3) **2.50**

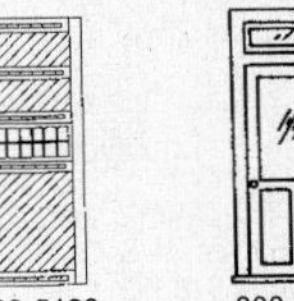

300-5133 300-5134

**300-5133** Roundhouse w/Windows & Doors **3.95** Fits 14-1/2' x 19' opening.

**300-5134** 36" w/Window and Transom pkg(3) **2.50**

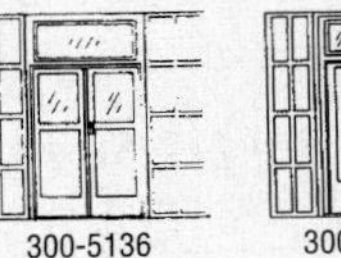

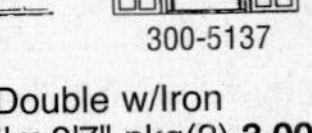

300-5136 300-5137

**300-5136** Double w/Iron Shutters, 5' x 9'7" pkg(2) **3.00**

**300-5137** Single w/Iron Shutters, 4'2" x 9'7" pkg(2) **3.00**

300-5139 300-5149

**300-5139** Factory Front w/Transom pkg(2) **2.50** For masonry buildings, measures a scale 39 x 92".

**300-5149** Double w/Transom & 2 Side Lights pkg(2) **2.50**

## GRANDT LINE

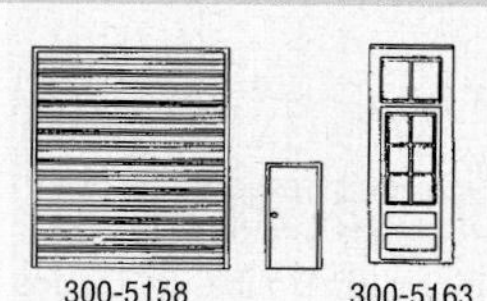

300-5158 300-5163

**300-5158** Warehouse, Roll-Up & 36" Personnel (2 Sets) **3.00** 12'6" x 14'3"

**300-5163** 33" w/Window & Transom pkg(3) **3.00**

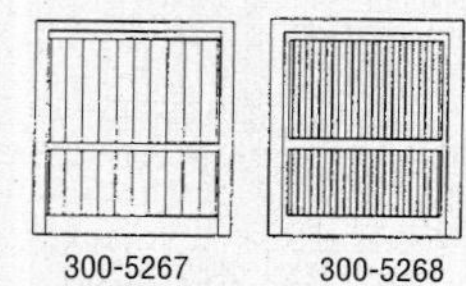

300-5267 300-5268

**300-5267** Warehouse .9 x 1.05" pkg(2) **3.00**

**300-5268** Warehouse .8 x 1" pkg(2) **3.00**

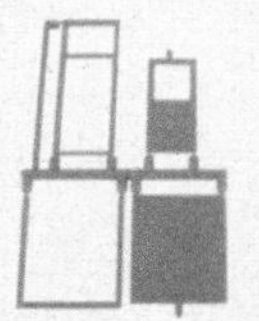

**NEW 300-5301** Paneled Door Set w/Transom & Crossbraced Door pkg(2) **3.00**

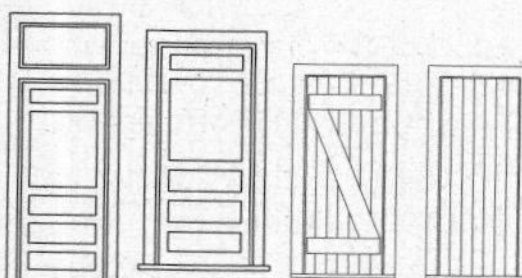

300-5291 300-5292 300-5293

### Doors pkg(2) 2.50 ea

**300-5291** With Frame, Window & Transom 34" x 6'-10"

**300-5292** With Frame & Window 34" x 6'-10"

**300-5293** Z-Braced Plank Door & Frame Scale 30 x 66"

### Fence

**300-5119** Victorian Picket Fence Set **3.00**

### Lattice Work

**300-5064** Band Stand pkg(8) **3.50**
Can be adapted to Campbell Bandstand.

### Louvered Shutters pkg(16) 3.00 ea

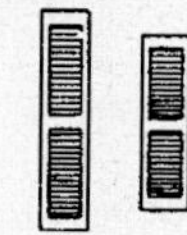

**300-5173** 18 x 56"

**300-5174** 18 x 68"

**300-5175** 18 x 87"

### Porch Railings 3.00 ea (Unless Noted)

300-5017 300-5019

**300-5017** "Wells Fargo" Balcony pkg(3)

**300-5019** "Gay Nineties" pkg(4)

300-5034 300-5035

**300-5034** Ornamental w/Roof Bracket (4 Pieces)

**300-5035** Turned Spindle pkg(3)

**300-5065** "Masonic Hall" Balcony, Brackets (2 Pieces) **3.25**

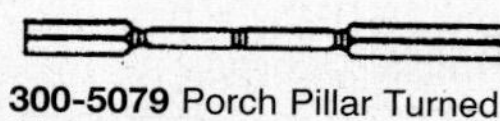

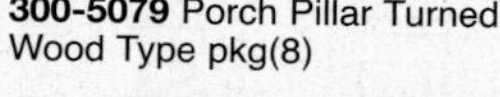

**300-5079** Porch Pillar Turned Wood Type pkg(8)

**300-5083** 35" High, 1" Bars on 6" Centers pkg(6) **3.95**
Approximately 100 scale feet.

### Railings

**300-5294** Decorative Iron Railing 4 Sets **3.00**

**300-5295** Iron Bar Railing pkg(4) **3.00**

**300-5296** Iron Bar Railing Set **3.00**

Small 1-5/16 x 7/16" 3.3 x 1.1cm

Large 1-5/8 x 7/16" 4.1 x 1.1cm



### Roofs

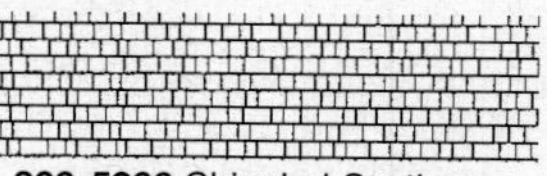

**300-5266** Shingled Sections pkg(4) **5.25**
Two sections 3.58 x 1.65", one section 2.4 x 1.475", one section 1.3 x 1.5".

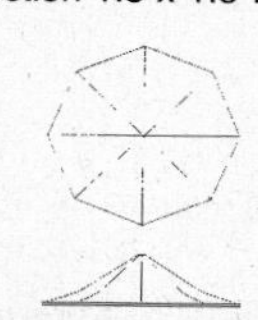

**300-5269** Octagonal Bandstand **3.95**

### Shingles

**300-5216** Scalloped pkg(2) **3.00**

### Staircases

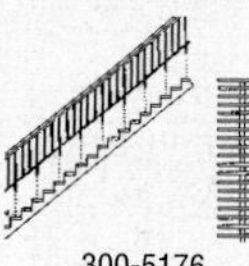

300-5176 300-5177

**300-5176** Modern Cast Iron **3.00**

**300-5177** Open Wood **3.95**

### Station Details

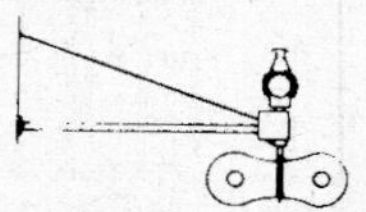

**300-5089** Rotary Order Board **3.00**
Used by many Colorado narrow gauge lines.

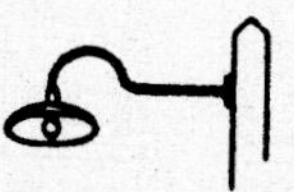

**300-5062** Lamp Reflectors & Bulbs pkg(18) **3.00**
Nonworking, molded in clear plastic. Simulates outdoor lighting used on all types of railroad, commercial and industrial buildings.

### Stoves

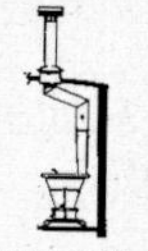

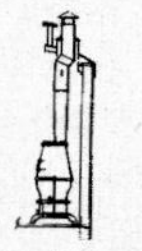

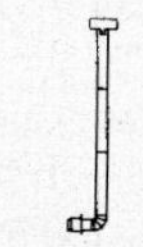

300-5007 300-5008 300-5023

**300-5007** DRGW Caboose Car w/Stack **3.00**

**300-5008** DRGW Passenger Car w/Stack **2.50**

**300-5023** Stovepipe w/Elbow Bonnet, Thimble **2.50**

### Trim

**300-5018** Spool for Upper Porch (4 Pieces) **3.00**

**300-5075** Corbel Double S 26" **3.00**

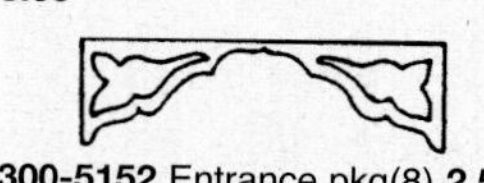

**300-5152** Entrance pkg(8) **2.50**

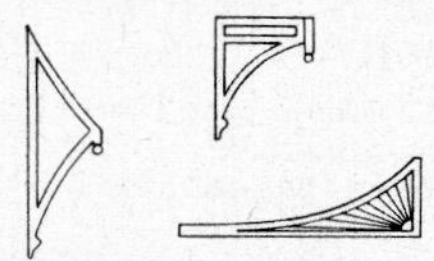

**300-5162** Queen Anne Trim **3.00**

**300-5211** Architectural Details-Dentils pkg(3) **2.50**

300-5227 300-5228

**300-5227** Gable pkg(4) **2.50**

**300-5228** Newel Post pkg(8) **2.50**

**300-5229** Spool Bracket pkg(8) **2.50**

**300-5246** Widow's Walk Iron Railing (4 Pieces) **3.95**

**300-5258** Gable Trim Assortment pkg(8) **3.00**

### Trim Grab Bag

**300-5244 19.95**
Assorted trim pieces, ideal for scratchbuilding, kitbashing or superdetailing.

### Windows 3.00 ea (Unless Noted)

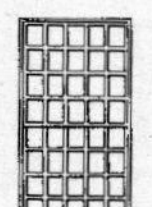

300-5009 300-5010 300-5029

**300-5009** Double Hung 36 x 56" pkg(8)

**300-5010** Roundhouse 60 x 120" pkg(6)

**300-5029** 27 x 64" Double Hung pkg(8)

300-5011 300-5030

**300-5011** 30" Silverton Static Attic pkg(4)

**300-5030** Double Hung 27 x 48" pkg(8)

300-5031 300-5032

**300-5031** Double Hung 36 x 64" pkg(8)

**300-5032** Double Hung 36 x 52" pkg(8)

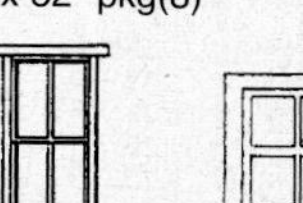

300-5060 300-5081

**300-5060** Station 30 x 69" pkg(8)

**300-5081** Horizontal Sliding 5 x 33" pkg(8)

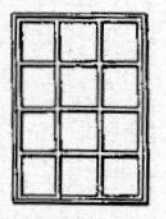

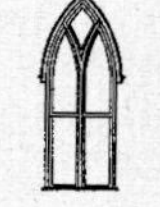

300-5077 300-5087 300-5092

**300-5077** Double-Hung Masonry 72 x 102" pkg(4)

**300-5087** Gothic Church 48 x 90" pkg(4)

**300-5092** Round Top 60 x 150" pkg(4)

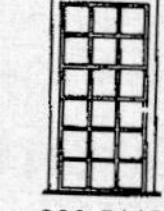

300-5097 300-5112

**300-5097** Engine House 18-Pane, 42 x 91" pkg(8)

**300-5112** Attic

**300-5116** Victorian, 4 Single, 2 Double (2 Sets)

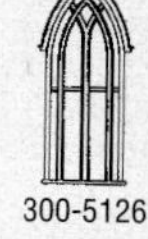

300-5117 300-5126

**300-5117** Double Hung 36 x 64", 4-Pane pkg(8)

**300-5126** Gothic Church & Residence pkg(4)

## GRANDT LINE

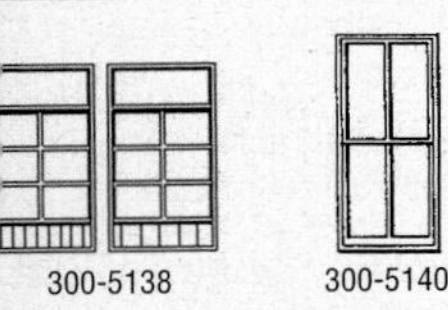

300-5138 300-5140

**300-5138** Store Window, 65 x 115" pkg(4)

**300-5140** Double Hung 4-Pane Factory 42 x 91" pkg(4)

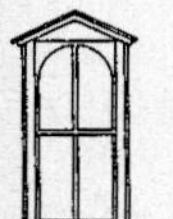

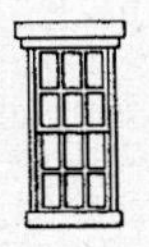

300-5150 300-5154

**300-5150** Peak Cap 41 x 90" pkg(8)

**300-5154** Mason 30 x 65" pkg(8)

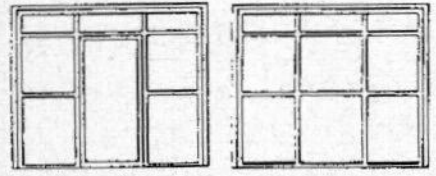

**300-5157** Window & Door Set 115 x 97" (2 Sets)

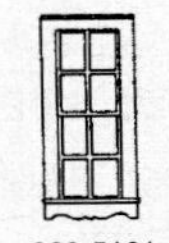

300-5160 300-5161

**300-5160** Queen Anne pkg(3)

**300-5161** Queen Anne Single pkg(3)

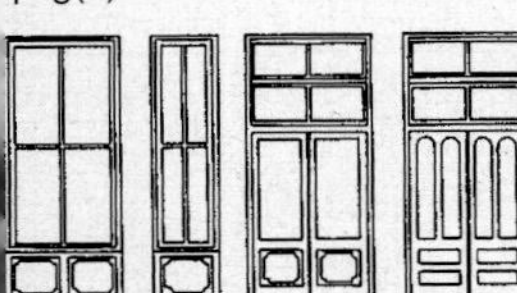

**300-5165** Storefront Set **3.95**

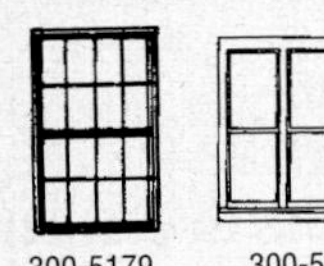

300-5179 300-5204

**300-5179** Double Hung, 42 x 72" pkg(6)

**300-5204** 6-Pane Double Hung, Triple 100 x 92" pkg(3)

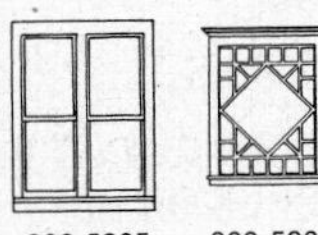

300-5205 300-5206

**300-5205** 4-Pane Double Hung, Double 65 x 92" pkg(3)

**300-5206** Diamond Patterned pkg(2) **2.50**

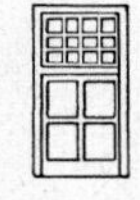

300-5208 300-5209

**300-5208** Double Hung 85 x 48" pkg(4)

**300-5209** Double Hung 34 x 67" pkg(7)

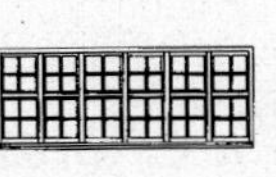

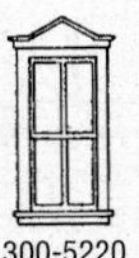

300-5210 300-5220

**300-5210** 48-Pane Double Hung 186 x 70" pkg(2)

**300-5220** Double Pointed 33 x 88" pkg(8)

300-5212 300-5215

**300-5212** Double Round-Top pkg(4)

**300-5215** Double 4-Pane 30 x 62" pkg(8)

300-5221 300-5222

**300-5221** 8-Pane Double 63 x 69" pkg(4)

**300-5222** 16-Pane Double 59 x 64" pkg(4)

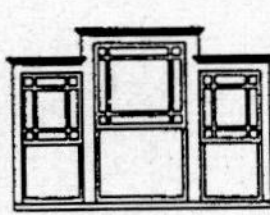

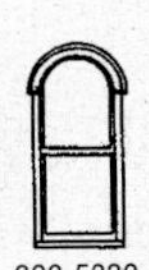

300-5223 300-5230

**300-5223** Dormer/Gable pkg(4)

**300-5230** Round Top 2' x 6' pkg(8)

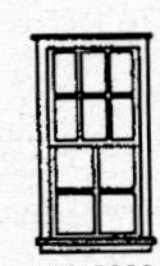

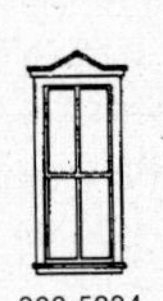

300-5233 300-5234

**300-5233** Double Hung 32 x 70" pkg(8)

**300-5234** Pointed Top 30 x 86" pkg(8)

300-5239 300-5240

**300-5239** Single Sash 28 x 26" pkg(4)

**300-5240** Round, Masonry 65" Diameter pkg(2) **2.50**

300-5241 300-5242

**300-5241** Shed or Attic pkg(8)

**300-5242** Horizontal pkg(8)

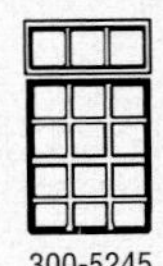

300-5245 300-5247

**300-5245** Window/Transom Set pkg(4)

**300-5247** Double Hung 11-Pane pkg(8)

300-5248 300-5249

**300-5248** Attic Peaked Single Pane pkg(8)

**300-5249** Victorian Attic pkg(8)

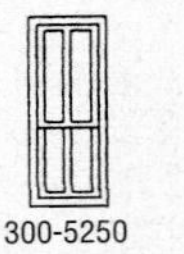

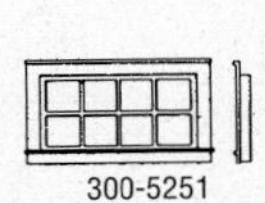

300-5250 300-5251

**300-5250** Double-Hung 4-Pane pkg(8)

**300-5251** Horizontal pkg(8)

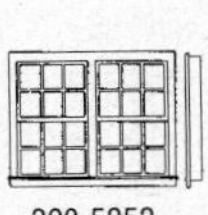

300-5252 300-5254

**300-5252** Double pkg(8)

**300-5254** Gothic pkg(8)

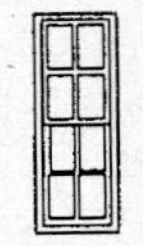

300-5255 300-5256

**300-5255** 8-Pane Double-Hung pkg(8)

**300-5256** 20-Pane Arched pkg(8)

**300-5259** Peaked Top Window/Door Set pkg(2)

**300-5261** Windows 4-Pane pkg(8)

**300-5262** Half Round 13-Pane pkg(6)

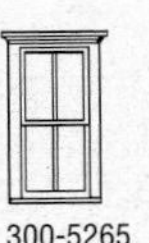

300-5264 300-5265

**300-5264** 4-Pane Single, 8-Pane Double pkg(2)

**300-5265** 4-Pane pkg(8)

**300-5273** Double-Hung 2-Pane pkg(8) **3.00**

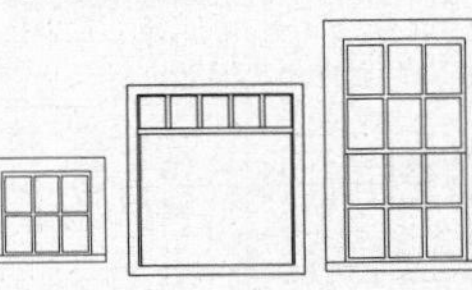

300-5280 300-5281 300-5282

**300-5280** Single Sash 6-Light 30 x 28" pkg(6)

**300-5281** Commerical 5-Light 63 x 75" pkg(4)

**300-5282** Double-Hung 6 Over 6 30 x 56" pkg(6)

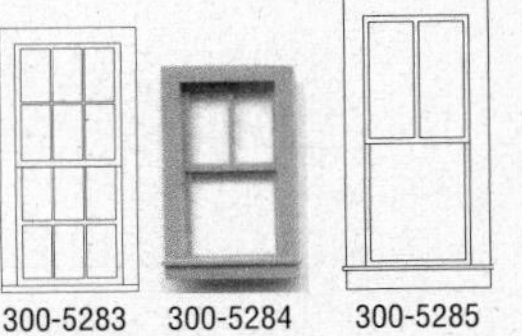

300-5283 300-5284 300-5285

**300-5283** Double-Hung 6 Over 6 38 x 86" pkg(4)

**300-5284** Double-Hung 2 Over 1 28" x 48" pkg(9)

**300-5285** Double-Hung 2 Over 1 28 x 64" pkg(9)

300-5286 300-5287

**300-5286** Double-Hung 2 Over 1 42 x 62" pkg(6)

**300-5287** For Pool Hall 3-1 Light Scale 56 x 82" pkg(4)

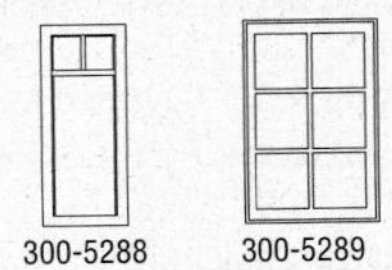

300-5288 300-5289

**300-5288** 3-Pane 2 Over 1 27 x 78" pkg(6)

**300-5289** 6-Light Masonry Scale 42 x 72" pkg(6)

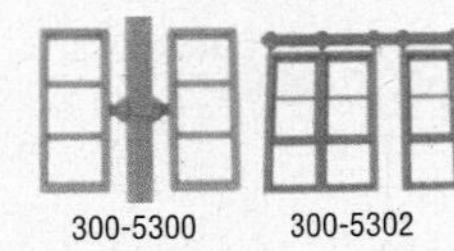

300-5300 300-5302

**NEW 300-5300** Horizontal 3-Pane pkg(8)

**NEW 300-5302** Double Hung 3-Pane 30 x 88 & 64 x 88" 4 sets

300-5303 300-5305

**NEW 300-5303** Horizontal 3-Pane

**NEW 300-5305** 4-Pane Attic pkg(8) 27 x 30"

### Masonry Windows 3.00 ea

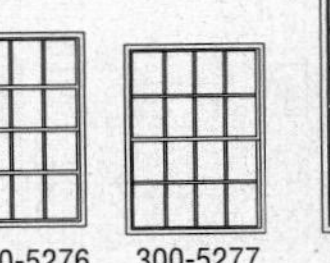

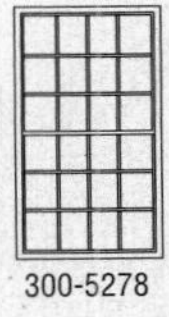

300-5276 300-5277 300-5278

**300-5276** 35 x 68" 6 Over 6 pkg(8)

**300-5277** 48 x 68" 8 Over 8 pkg(8)

**300-5278** 48 x 86.5" 12 Over 12 pkg(8)

**NEW 300-5299** 38 x 55" pkg(8)

### Window Grab Bag

**300-5192 19.95**
An assortment of windows for kitbashing, scratchbuilding, etc.

## HARDWARE

### Hinges

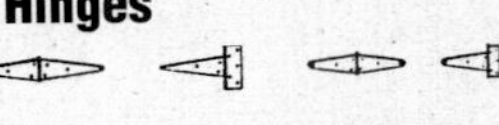

**300-5095** Assortment (2 Sets) **2.50**

**300-5168** Reefer Door Hinge pkg(48) **3.00**

**NEW 300-5298** Strap Hinge pkg(48) **3.00**

### Lift Rings

**300-5085** Plastic Assortment pkg(108) **3.00**

### Nut-Bolt-Washer 3.00 ea

Illustrations enlarged to show detail.

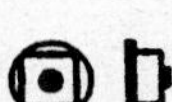

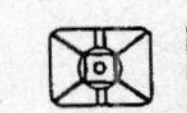

300-5101 300-5113

**300-5101** 7/8" Nut, 3-3/16" Steel Washer pkg(175)

**300-5113** 2-1/2" Nut w/Rectangular Washers pkg(100)

## GRANDT LINE

**300-5123** 2-1/2" Nut, 6-1/2" Washer pkg(100)

**300-5135** 2-1/2" Hex Nut, No Washer pkg(100)

**300-5156** 2-1/2" Nut-Bolt Washer Cored, .020" pkg(80)

**300-5045** 1" Square Nut pkg(175)

**300-5046** 1-3/4" Square Nut pkg(175)

**300-5066** 1-1/4" Nut, 3" Malleable Iron Washer pkg(175)

**300-5093** 2-1/2" Nut, 5" Malleable Washer pkg(100)

**300-5094** 2-1/2" Nut w/Carter Brothers Elliptical Washer pkg(100)

**300-5096** 2-1/2" Nut, 6" Square Washer pkg(100)

**300-5098** 2-1/4" Nut-Bolt, 4-1/2" Washer pkg(100)

**300-5099** 3" Nut, 4-1/2" Washer pkg(100)

**300-5100** 1-3/4" Nut-Bolt, 2-1/2" Washer pkg(175)

**300-5270** Star pkg(100)

### Sheaves 3.00 ea

**300-5091** Minehead Frame - 60" Diameter Plastic (2 Sets)

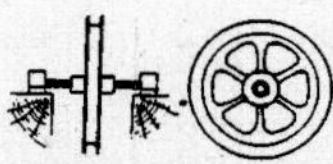

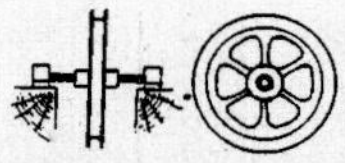

**300-5122** 43" Diameter Cable Sheave w/Bearings pkg(2)

### Turnbuckles

**300-5039** Plastic pkg(24) **3.00**
DRGW prototypes are full-scale and cored for .015 wire.

## FREIGHT CAR DETAILS

### Brake Gear Sets

#### Westinghouse Narrow Gauge Type K

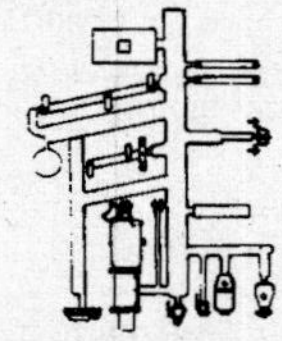

**300-5040** Plastic **2.50**

**300-5224** Colorado & Southern NY Type **2.50**
Used on Colorado & Southern cars with truss rod underframes, also used on Florence & Cripple Creek box cars.

**300-5232** Westinghouse AB **4.75**
Complete set with reservoirs, valve, rods, bell levers, chain and more.

### Brake Wheels pkg(4) 3.00 ea

**300-5037** DRGW 16" Spoke Plastic

**300-5067** 15" Lovested Plastic

**300-5225** Colorado & Southern Brake Wheel

### Brake Rods

**300-5184** With Clevis pkg(6) **3.00**

**300-5189** With Chain pkg(2) **2.50**

### Reefer Door Latch Kits pkg(4) 3.00 ea

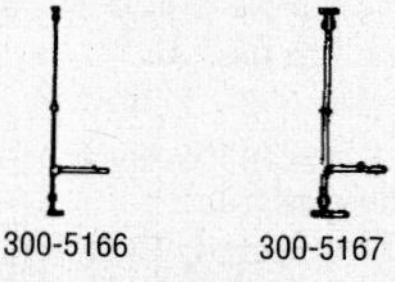


**300-5166** Narrow Gauge

**300-5167** Standard Gauge

### Caboose Details

#### Rio Grande/Rio Grande Southern

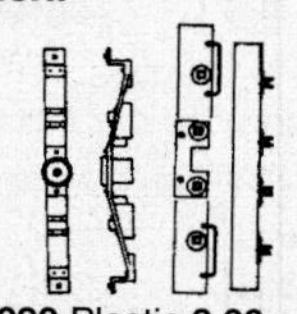

**300-5090** Plastic **3.00**
Short Rio Grande/Rio Grande Southern caboose end detail, bolsters and needlebeams.

#### Colorado & Southern

**300-5128** Needlebeam & Queenpost Subassembly for High-Side Gondola pkg(4) **3.00**

**300-5236** Pedestals & Journal Box Lids pkg(4) **3.25**

**300-5237** Steps **2.50**

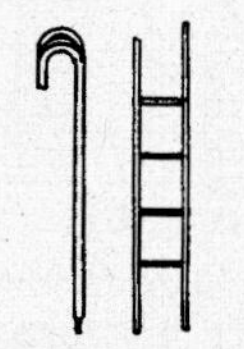

**300-5238** Ladders pkg(2) **3.95**

### Freight Car Doors

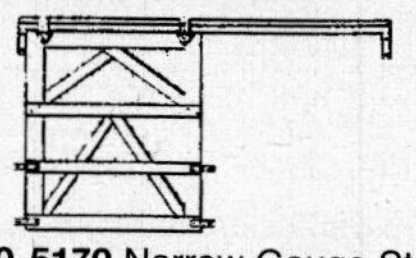

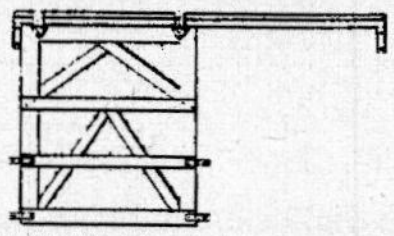

**300-5170** Narrow Gauge Stock Car pkg(2) **2.50**

**300-5207** Standard Box Car w/Camel Hardware pkg(2) **3.00**

### Flat Car Details

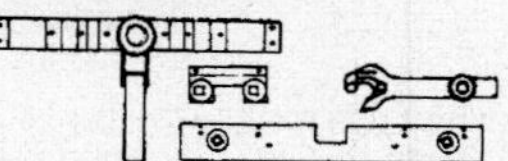

**300-5183** Plastic-2 Complete Sets **2.50**
Includes bolster, end beam, striker plate and coupler used on DRGW 6000 series narrow gauge flat cars.

### Gondola Parts

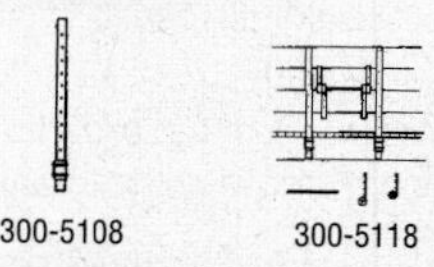


**300-5108** Stake & Stake Pockets for 12" Boards pkg(40) **3.50**

**300-5118** Hinge Set for Side Dump Gondola (2 Sets) **2.50**

**300-5125** Standard Gauge Bolster pkg(4) **2.50**
Based on modified cast steel bolsters on high-side gondolas.

### Grab Iron Bending Fixture

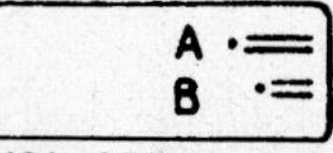

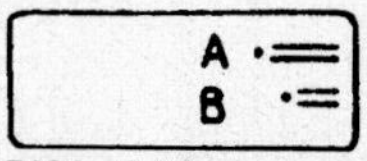

**300-5191** **2.50**
Make scale 17 and 20" straight grab irons for your equipment in minutes with this handy tool. Just insert a length of .008" wire (sold separately), bend with gentle finger pressure and trim.

### Hardware Kits

Sets include the steel parts found on the prototypes.

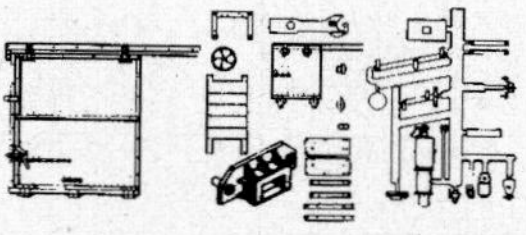

**300-5001** DRGW Box Car **5.00**

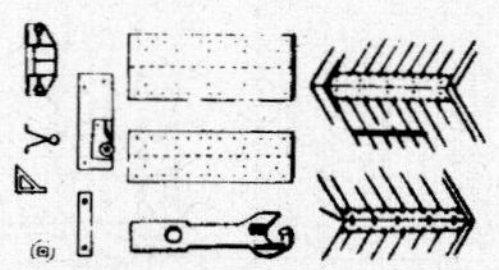

**300-5002** DRGW High Side Gondola **4.50**

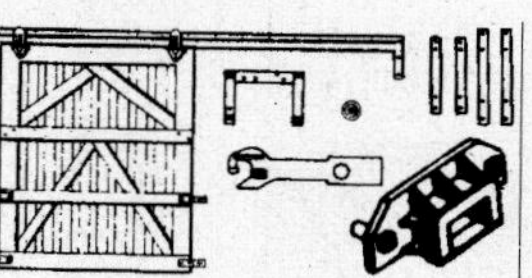

**300-5004** DRGW Stock Car **4.50**

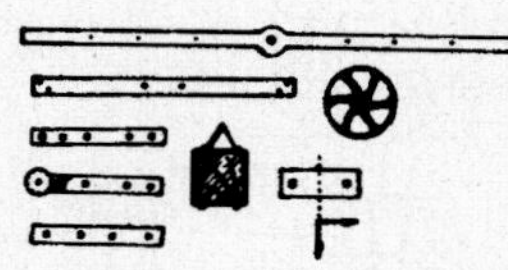

**300-5103** Russell Log Car **2.50**

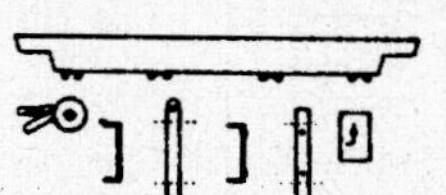

**300-5105** Westside Lumber Co. Flat Car **2.50**

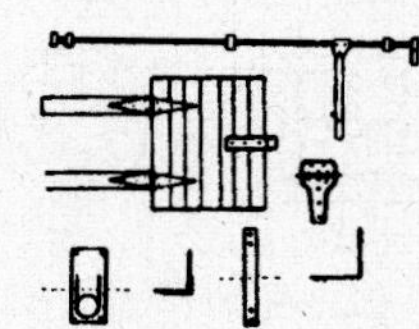

**300-5106** Standard Gauge Reefer **3.25**

### Log Bunks

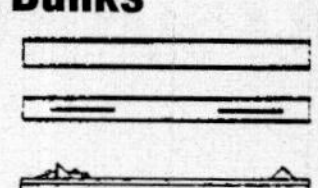

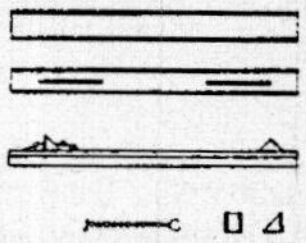

**300-5104** Pacific Car & Foundry Type pkg(2) **2.50**

### Narrow Gauge Freight Car Details

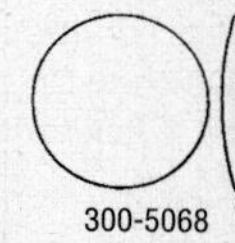


**300-5056** DRGW Box Car Er Roof Walks pkg(4) **3.00**

**300-5068** UTLX Tank Car Ends, 77" pkg(2) **2.50**

**300-5124** Ladders pkg(20) **2.50**

**300-5169** Box Car Corner Plates pkg(4) **3.00**

**300-5185** Uncoupling Levers pkg(2) **3.00**

### Queenposts 3.00 ea

#### With Beam pkg(4)

Plastic.

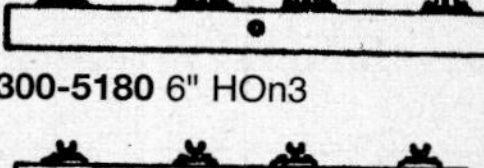

**300-5180** 6" HOn3

**300-5181** 3"

#### Plain pkg(24)

**300-5050** 6"

**300-5052** 3"

#### Queenposts Only pkg(24)

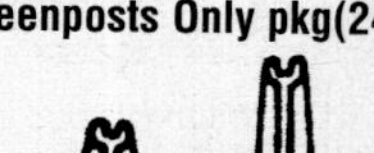

**300-5051** 5"

**300-5053** 10"

### Stake Pockets U Bolt pkg(24) 3.00 ea

Plastic.

**300-5012** Single

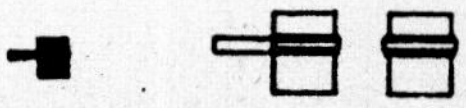

**300-5036** DRGW Double

## GRANDT LINE

### Stirrup Steps 3.00 ea

Used on box cars, flat cars, stock cars and high-side gondolas.

**300-5129** Brown Delrin pkg(24)

300-5130 300-5190

**300-5130** Black Delrin pkg(24)

**300-5190** DRGW pkg(20)

## PASSENGER CAR DETAILS

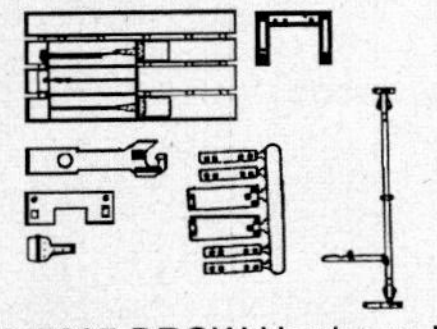

**300-5005** DRGW Hardware Kit **4.50**

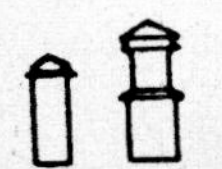

**300-5043** Roof Detail **3.00**
Plastic vents, smokejacks and more.

### Doors pkg(4) 3.00 ea

300-5063 300-5070

**300-5063** Caboose

**300-5070** Straight Top Coach End

300-5071 300-5078

**300-5071** Combine Baggage

**300-5078** Arch Top Coach End

**300-5274** Freight Door

### Windows

300-5059 300-5069

**300-5059** Outfit (Work) Car pkg(8) **3.00**

**300-5069** Narrow for DRGW Coach pkg(30) **3.75**

## MISCELLANEOUS

### Baggage Wagon Kit

**300-5033** Plastic **3.25**

### Cribbing Sections

**300-5260** 1 x 4" pkg(6) **6.50**

### Drums & Barrels

300-5041 300-5217

**300-5041** 55-Gallon Steel Drum w/Fire Lid pkg(12) **3.00**

**300-5217** Wooden Barrels pkg(12) **3.50**

### Fairmont Push Car Kits 3.00 ea

**300-5164** HO

**300-5024** HOn3-Plastic

### Wagon Wheels

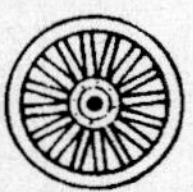

**300-5143** Circus Wagon pkg(8) **3.50**
Includes 36" front and 48" diameter rear wheels, adaptable to other types of heavy wagons.

### Water Tank Parts

**300-5038** Hoop Fasteners pkg(99) **4.50**

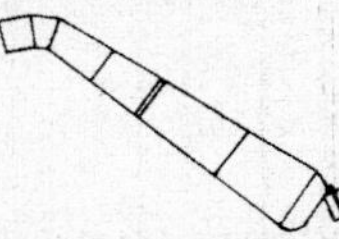

**300-5054** Spout Set **3.00**

## CATALOG

**300-9993** Grandt Line Catalog - Small Scale Miniatures **6.95**

**300-9991** Grandt Line Catalog HO & N **5.50**

## Great West Models, Inc.

Details are all high-quality resin, plastic or white metal castings.

## NEW PRODUCTS

### Stacked Cargo

**NEW 24-4139** Feed Sacks w/Pallet **2.50**

**NEW 24-4140** Seed Sacks w/Pallet **2.50**

**NEW 24-4141** Medium Boxes w/Pallet **2.50**

**NEW 24-4142** Large Boxes w/Pallet **2.50**

### Air Conditioning Units

**24-4107** Assorted Ductwork **8.50**

**24-4108** Large **3.95**

**24-4109** Medium **2.95**

**24-4110** Small **2.20**

### Evaporative Coolers

**24-4111** Large **2.75**

**24-4112** Small **2.25**

### Garage Doors pkg(2) 1.25 ea

**24-4101** Double Car

**24-4102** Single Car

### Gas Station Details

**24-316** Fuel Island **9.98**
Includes island, two fuel pumps, 55-gallon trash drum and signs.

**24-4126** Mechanics Tool Chest & Base **3.75**

**24-4127** 1960s-1980s Single Handle Gas Pumps w/Signs pkg(2) **5.50**

**24-4128** Modern Gas Island w/Metal Edge **2.30**

**24-4129** Old Style Gas Island **2.20**

**24-4130** Fuel Island Protector Posts pkg(4) **2.20**

**24-4131** Tire Rack **3.10**

**24-4132** Tires #1 pkg(7) **2.80**

**24-4133** 1960s-1980s Car Lift **3.95**

**24-4134** Wall-Mounted Air Pumps pkg(2) **2.20**

**24-4138** 1940-1950s Gas Pump pkg(2) **5.50**

For Daily Product Information Click

**www.walthers.com**

### Old Style Gas Station Details 22.98 ea

Includes island, two pumps, oil can racks, two oil bunkers, five tires, two 55-gallon drums, one car lift, one tire pump and signs.

**24-3131** Lesters & Phillips

**24-3132** Lesters & Shell

**24-3133** Lesters & Mobil

**24-3134** Lesters & Sinclair

### Sacks pkg(6) 2.75 ea

**24-4136** Feed Sack

**24-4137** Seed Sack

### Vents

**24-4113** J Vent **2.20**

**24-4114** Assorted pkg(5) **1.75**

**24-4117** Large Industrial **2.60**

**24-4118** Small Industrial **2.20**

**24-4119** Large Motorized Exhaust **2.30**

**24-4120** Small Motorized Exhaust **2.30**

**24-4121** Large Old Style **2.30**

**24-4122** Small Old Style **2.20**

**24-4123** Large Wall Or Roof Exhaust **2.20**

**24-4124** Small Wall Or Roof Exhaust **2.10**

**24-4125** Large Assorted pkg(4) **2.50**

### Miscellaneous Building Details

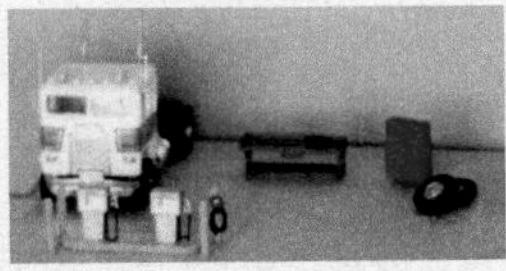

**24-315** Tractor/Trailer Details **24.98**
Tool chest and base, work-bench, two fuel pumps and island, grinder, air pump and hose, 12 building protectors, four-way wrench, two tires, two wheels and signs.

**24-314** Assorted Warehouse Details **6.98**
Includes pallet jack, pallets, feed bags, seed bags and signs.

**24-4103** Stair & Railing **1.50**

**24-4104** Office Entries pkg(2) **1.25**

**24-4105** Industrial Square Windows pkg(4) **1.25**

**24-4106** Assorted Downspouts & Scuppers pkg(4) **2.25**

**24-4115** Industrial Electric Meter **2.75**

**24-4116** Dock Bumpers pkg(6) **1.25**

**24-4135** Insulated Dock Door Surrounds pkg(2) **3.50**

## HERPA

### Box Car Parts

**326-3015 3.95**
Includes four ladders, brake wheels and roof walk for Canadian NSC 40' Box Cars.

## KIBRI

IMPORTED FROM GERMANY BY WALTHERS

Plastic parts molded in colors.

## VENTS

**405-8609** Exhaust Vents pkg(2) **13.99**

# DETAIL PARTS

## SP Locomotive Details

**331-5014** EMD Cab Front **4.95**
Features patched "L" window and extended-vision window front.

**331-6029** G.R.I.P. Radiator Doors for SD45T-2 Pair **2.95**

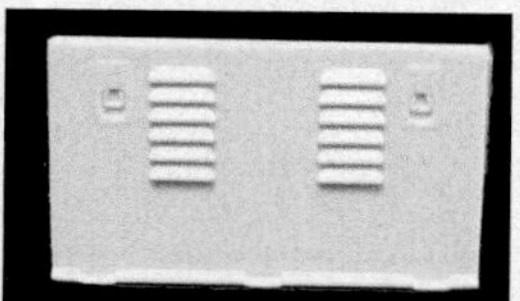

**331-6030** G.R.I.P. Battery Box Door Set for Various Units **2.95**

## GE Locomotive Details

**331-6028** Louvered Doors for "EUC" Box on XR Series U Boats **2.95**

**331-6032** Plain Doors for "EUC" Box on XR Series U Boats **2.95**

## Locomotive Detail

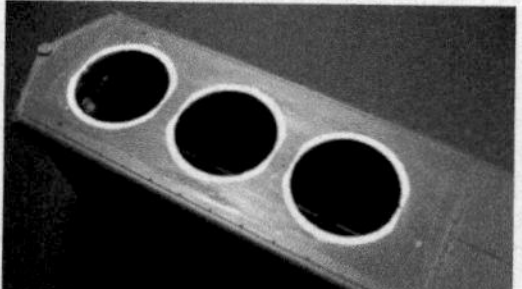

**331-6031** Radiator Fan Shroud Inserts for Proto 2000 SD45s **2.95**
For use with Cannon & Co. fans.(Sold Sepaeately)

## Box Car Door Conversion

**331-4000** Landis Doors Pair **3.95**
As used on Evergreen Leasing, SP and SSW cars. Fits Athearn Genesis PC&F box cars.

## GE Diesel Cabs 6.95 ea (Unless Noted)

Carefully engineered for prototype accuracy and ease of construction, each thinwall kit is designed for use on locos with scale width hoods. Each cab features separate windows and doors of the correct size, which can be positioned open or closed. Separate door handles are provided for extra realism. The roof contour matches the real thing.

### Pre 1972

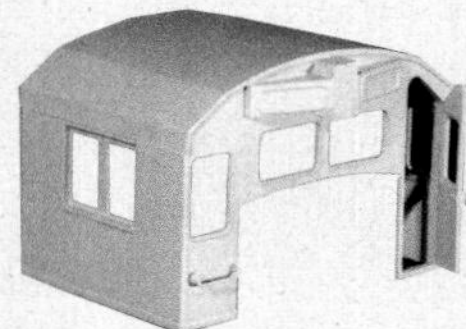

**331-5000** 2-Window

**331-5001** 4-Window

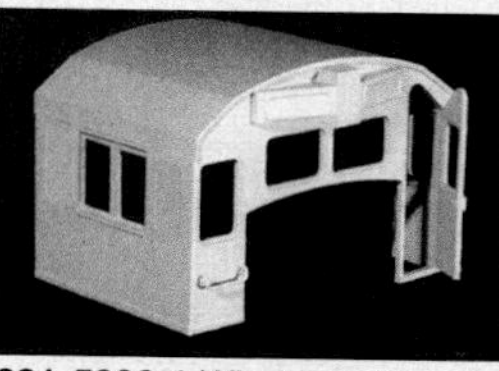

**331-5002** 4-Window w/Small Windows Plated Over



### Post 1972

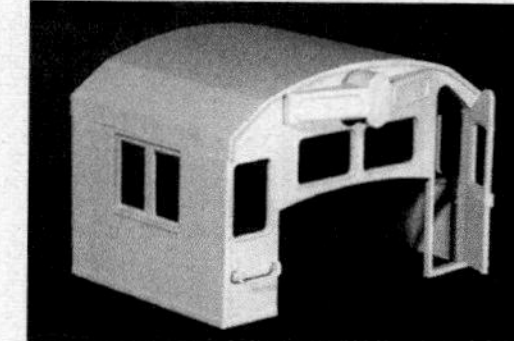

**331-5003** 2-Window

**331-5004** 4-Window

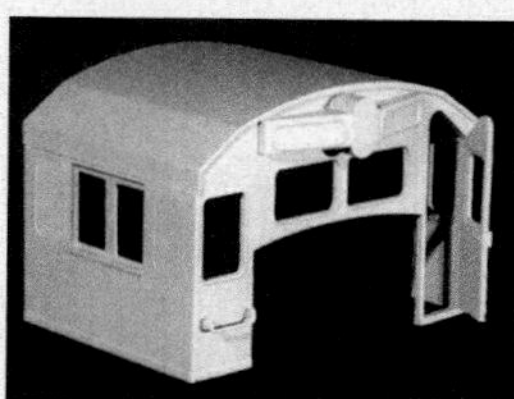

**331-5005** 4-Window w/Small Windows Plated Over

### High Hood

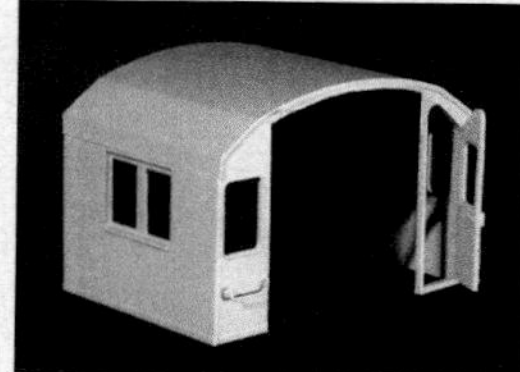

**331-5006** 2-Window Cab

**331-5007** 4-Window Cab

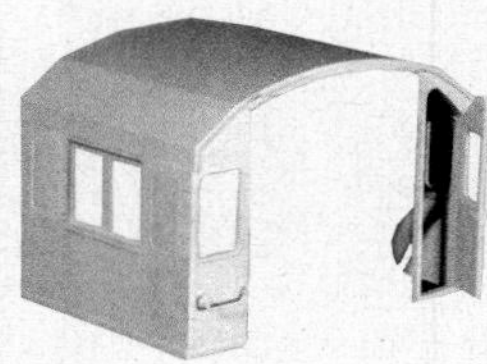

**331-5008** 4-Window Cab w/Small Windows Plated Over

### SP Cab Kit

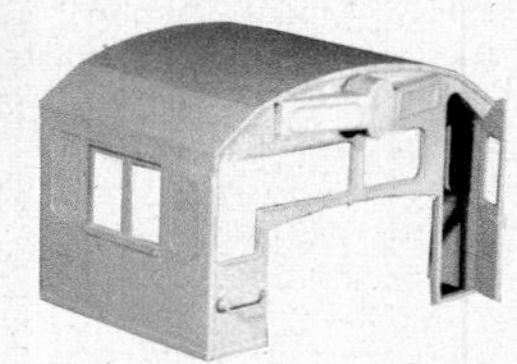

**331-5009** "L" Window **7.50**

B Unit Conversion Kits For Proto 2000 GP9 Diesels UP/PRR 331-5011

### U-25 Series

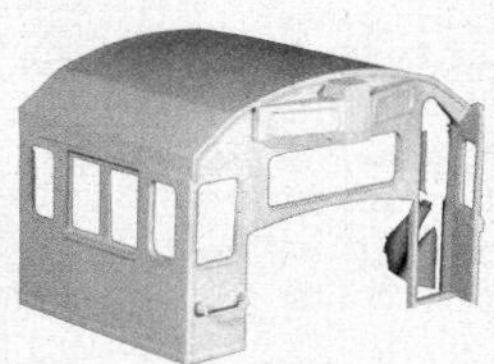

**331-5010** Single-Pane Front Window

## GE Exhaust Stack 2.95 ea

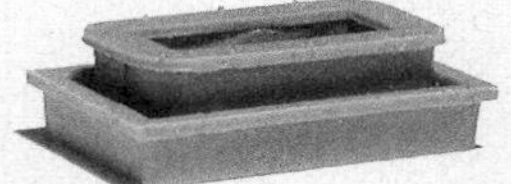

**331-6000** U-Boats Through Dash-7

**331-6001** Dash-7 Through Dash-8

**331-6002** Dash-8 Through Dash-9

## B Unit Conversion Kits

**331-5011** For Proto 2000 GP9 Diesels UP/PRR **6.95**

## Waste Fluid Containment Tank EMD 2.95 ea

**331-6008** Square

**331-6009** Angled Corners

**331-6010** UP Style

## Antenna Domes 2.95 ea

**331-6003** Round

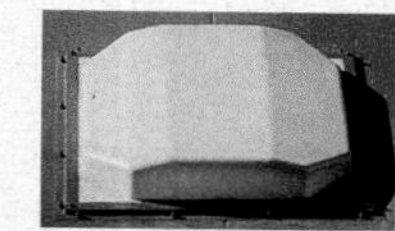

**331-6007** Octagon

**331-6027** Small BNSF, UP, NS, CSX and others

## Intake Grilles 2.95 ea

**331-6005** C-30-7 Rear

**331-6006** C-36-7 Dynamic

## Ice Breaker Bars

**331-6016** SP, Tall **2.95**
For F units.

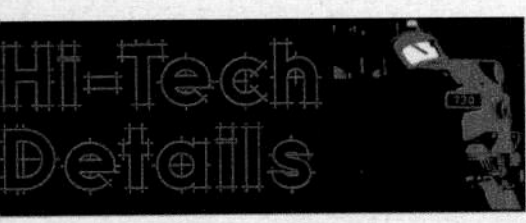


## Cab Window Shades

**331-6017** For SOU & NS Diesels **2.95**

## Battery Box & Air Tank Kit

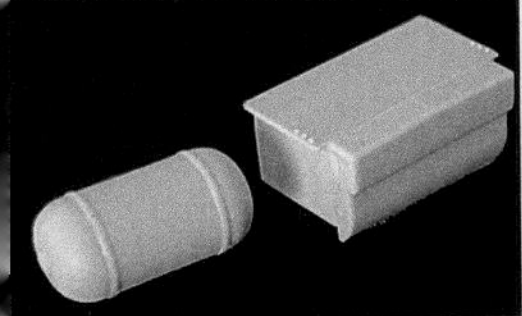

**331-6026** F Unit **9.95**

## Fuel Gauge

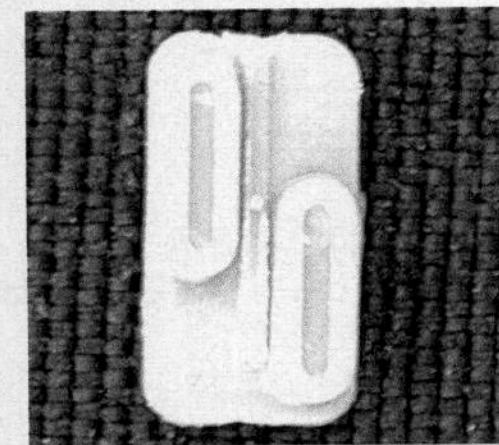

**331-6023** Large E & F Unit 1 Pair **2.95**

## Fuel Tank

**331-6024** F Unit – 1500 Gallon **6.95**

## Fuel Tank Brackets

**331-6025** E & F Units 3 Pieces **2.95**

## Inertia Grill

**331-6022** ATSF F Unit **2.95**

## Lift Lugs - E & F Units 2 Pair 2.95 ea

### EMD

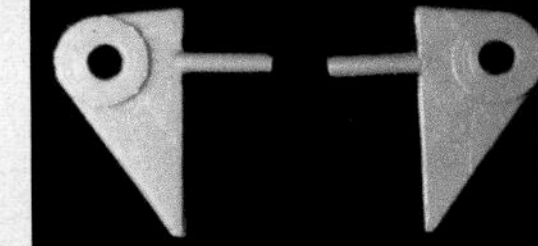

**331-6018** Front

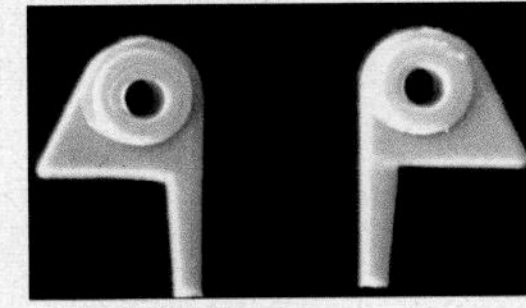

**331-6019** Rear

### ATSF

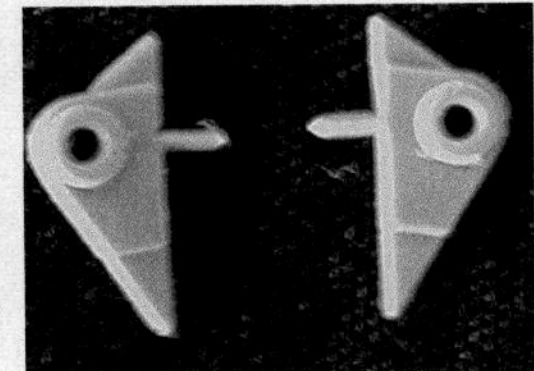

**331-6020** Front

**331-6021** Rear

**NEW 331-6033** Lift Lugs Pilotbeam Mount **2.95**

## GE High Nose Kit

**331-5012 6.95**

## GE Anticlimber

**331-6004** C-30-7 **2.95**

Designed, Manufactured & Assembled entirely in the U.S.A.

# FREIGHT CAR DETAILS

## Brake Pads

380-441

380-442

**380-441** For Use On All Kadee® Trucks (Except #s 513, 518, 555 & 558) pkg(4) **1.90**

**380-442** For Use On Kadee Trucks #s 513, 518, 555 & 558) pkg(4) **1.90**

## Brake Wheels

### Metal

**380-440** 18" Metal pkg(6) **1.65**

### Plastic pkg(8) 2.65 ea

#### Ajax

**380-2020** Box Car Red
**380-2030** Red Oxide
**380-2040** Black

#### Equipco

**380-2021** Box Car Red
**380-2031** Red Oxide
**380-2041** Black

#### Miner

**380-2022** Box Car Red
**380-2032** Red Oxide
**380-2042** Black

#### Universal

**380-2023** Box Car Red
**380-2033** Red Oxide
**380-2043** Black

#### Champion

**380-2024** Box Car Red
**380-2034** Red Oxide
**380-2044** Black

#### Modern

**380-2025** Box Car Red
**380-2035** Red Oxide
**380-2045** Black

## Doors 2 Pair 3.50 ea

Detailed, plastic sliding doors for 40' and 50' Kadee PS-1 or other manufacturers' box cars.

### Camel-Youngstown

**380-2200** 6' High Tackboard (Red Oxide)

**380-2201** 6' High Tackboard (Box Car Red)
**380-2202** 6' Low Tackboard (Red Oxide)
**380-2203** 6' Low Tackboard (Box Car Red)
**380-2215** 8' High Tackboard (Red Oxide)
**380-2216** 8' High Tackboard (Box Car Red)
**380-2220** 8' Low Tackboard (Red Oxide)
**380-2221** 8' Low Tackboard (Box Car Red)
**380-2234** 7' High Tackboard (Red Oxide)
**380-2235** 7' High Tackboard (Box Car Red)
**380-2236** 7' Low Tackboard (Red Oxide)
**380-2237** 7' Low Tackboard (Box Car Red)

### Superior

**380-2205** 6' 5-Panel High Tackboard (Red Oxide)
**380-2206** 6' 5-Panel High Tackboard (Box Car Red)

**380-2207** 6' 5-Panel Low Tackboard (Red Oxide)
**380-2208** 6' 5-Panel Low Tackboard (Box Car Red)
**380-2210** 6' 7-Panel High Tackboard (Red Oxide)
**380-2211** 6' 7-Panel High Tackboard (Box Car Red)
**380-2230** 8' 6-PanelLow Tackboard (Red Oxide)
**380-2231** 8' 6-Panel low Tackboard (Box Car Red)
**380-2238** 7' 5-Panel High Tackboard (Red Oxide)

**380-2239** 7' 5-Panel High Tackboard (Box Car Red)
**380-2240** 7' 5-Panel Low Tackboard (Red Oxide)
**380-2241** 7' 5-Panel Low Tackboard (Box Car Red)

### Pullman-Standard

**380-2225** 8' 5-Panel Low Tackboard (Red Oxide)
**380-2226** 8' 5-Panel Low Tackboard (Box Car Red)

## Running Boards

"Look at the Detail"

### Apex 1 Pair 4.35

Highly detailed, see-through plastic running boards for 40' and 50' Kadee PS-1 or other manufacturers' box cars.

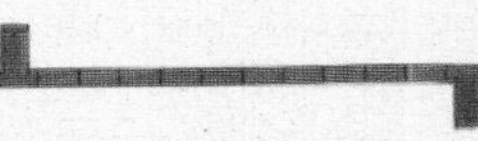

**380-2000** 40' Red Oxide
**380-2001** 40' Box Car Red
**380-2002** 40' Black
**380-2003** 40' Galvanized Metal
**380-2010** 50' Red Oxide
**380-2011** 50' Box Car Red
**380-2012** 50' Black
**380-2013** 50' Galvanized Metal

## Ladders 1 Set 3.00 ea

Near-to-scale seven-rung ladders for 40' and 50' Kadee PS-1 or other manufacturers' box cars. Set includes side and end ladders.

**380-2101** Oxide Red
**380-2102** Box Car Red
**380-2103** Black

## Parts

380-438

380-439

**380-438** Air Hose & Angle Cock w/Mounting Bracket pkg(20) **1.65**

**380-439** Nut-Bolt-Washer Detail pkg(36) **1.65**

Decorated white metal castings.

## NEW PRODUCTS

### Gas Station Curb Signs

#### pkg(3) 4.49 (Unless Noted)

Use these layout-ready signs along the sidewalks in front of your gas stations. Figures not included.

**NEW 361-462** Texaco
**NEW 361-463** Mobil
**NEW 361-464** Shell
**NEW 361-465** Flying A
**NEW 361-466** Sinclair
**NEW 361-467** Phillips 66
**NEW 361-468** Oilzum pkg(4)
**NEW 361-469** Conoco

**NEW 361-472** Quaker State pkg(4)

**NEW 361-473** Pennzoil
**NEW 361-474** Kendall
**NEW 361-475** Sunoco

### Port-a-Potty Set

**NEW 361-499** **7.99**

## CRATES

### Assorted Crates pkg(4) 4.49 ea

A variety of food product crates with colorful labels, including: Irish Beauty, Smoky Jim's Sweet Potatoes, Washington Apples, Jo Jo Melons, Greenspot, American Maid Pears, Red Crown and Big Chief Tomatoes.

#### Large

**361-323** Brown
**361-423** Gray
**361-523** Green

#### Small

**361-324** Brown
**361-424** Gray
**361-524** Green

### Auto Parts Crates pkg(4) 4.49 ea

**361-823** Brown
**361-824** Gray
**361-825** Green

### Deluxe Crates pkg(5) 4.98 (Unless Noted)

**361-714** Tan

**361-715** Terra Cotta

**361-716** White w/Weathering **5.49**

**361-717** Square/Mixed Colors

### Custom REA Crates

**361-723** pkg(5) **4.98**

## BARRELS

Prepainted barrels with product labels. Great detail for railroad shop, gas stations and bulk oil dealers, refineries, farms and almost any industry.

### Gas Station pkg(5) 4.49 ea

Labels from Blau, Deep Rock, Texaco, Pennzoil, Veedol, Sunoco and Sinclair.

**361-312** Green

**361-313** Red

**361-812** Orange

**361-813** White

### Industrial pkg(5) 4.49 ea

Labels from FMC, Dow, Monsanto, RP, J&L Steel, Glidden, BPS and IC.

**361-412** Silver
**361-413** Yellow

### Feed & Seed Fertilizer pkg(5) 4.49 ea

**361-512** Blue w/Yellow Tops

**361-513** Black

**361-912** Paint & Chemical (gray, red top) pkg(5)

### Food & Flour

**361-712** Custom Barrels Wood (brown) **4.49**
Includes labels from Karo, Gold Medal, Pasier Pickles, Swan Flour and Fleischmanns Yeast.

### Oil Barrels pkg(5) 4.79

Add realism to your service station and oil dealer scenes with these layout-ready barrels.

**361-558** Sunoco (blue, yellow)

**361-559** DX (red, cream)

**361-562** Texaco (red, green)

**361-563** Mobil (red, black)

**361-564** Shell (yellow, red)

**361-565** Flying A (flat red, black)

**361-566** Sinclair (green, flat white)

**361-567** Phillips 66 (orange, black)

**361-568** Gilmore (Mustard, red)

**361-569** Conoco (Ivory, green)

### Custom Fencing

**361-305** Assorted Custom 6" Board Fence **4.49**

**361-818** 3-Rail Metal (silver) pkg(2) **5.99**

### Flour Sacks

**361-713** Mixed pkg(3) **4.49**

### Gas Pumps

Prepainted and decorated with the logo of the company shown.

#### Custom pkg(2) 5.98 ea

**361-814** Texaco
**361-815** Mobil
**361-816** Sinclair
**361-817** Phillips 66
**361-828** Richfield
**361-829** Skelly

#### Deluxe Custom pkg(2) 6.99 ea

**361-514** Texaco
**361-515** Mobil

**361-516** Sinclair

**361-517** Phillips 66
**361-518** Shell
**361-572** Gilmore
**361-573** Conoco
**361-588** Sunoco
**361-589** Flying "A"

### Highway Cones

**361-897** 1950s Yellow w/Black Top pkg(5) **3.49**

**361-898** pkg(5) **2.98**

**361-899** pkg(10) **4.98**

### Ice Blocks

**361-205** pkg(25) **2.89**

### Ladders

**361-554** 8' Step (brown) **1.79**
**361-555** 10' Lean-To Ladders (unfinished) pkg(4) **1.79**

### Oil Highboys pkg(2) 4.49 ea

Prepainted and decorated with the logo of the company shown.

**361-914** Texaco
**361-915** Mobil
**361-916** Sinclair
**361-917** Phillips 66
**361-918** Shell

## Oil Racks

**361-826** Mixed Brands pkg(3) **4.98**

## Picket Fences

Measure 11" total.(unless noted)

**361-705** Clean (white) pkg(2) **3.98**

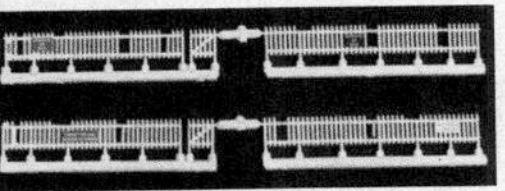

**361-805** Weathered w/Signs pkg(2) **5.49**

## Propane Tanks

### Small 4.49 ea

**361-724** Silver

**361-725** White

**361-726** Light Blue

**361-730** Mustard Yellow

### Large 5.49 ea

**361-727** Silver

**361-728** White

**361-729** Light Blue

**361-731** Mustard Yellow

## Soda Cases

**361-827** Mixed Brands pkg(3) **4.49**

## Soda Machines

**361-732** Upright Soda Machine/Case **5.99**
Mixed brands available.

### Chest Type 5.99 ea

**361-733** 7-Up

**361-734** Pepsi

**361-735** RC

## Tire Displays

**361-316** Painted & Labeled pkg(3) **4.98**

## Detail Sets - Unfinished

### Marine & Nautical Details

**361-457** Unpainted **10.95**
Includes three outboard motors, three life rings, three life preservers, four mushroom anchors, three fuel cans, one dolly and four oars.

### Deluxe Gas Station Interior

**361-510** Unpainted **14.95**
Unfinished cast-metal details to complete the look of your filling station interior. Features 18 pieces including floor jacks, tool chests, tires, broom, air compressor and more.

### Stacks of Stuff

**361-500** Junk Piles pkg(11) **16.95**

### Unfinished

**361-501** Stovepipes & Chimneys pkg(10) **9.98**

**361-502** Mainline **11.95**
With relay and phone boxes.

**361-503** Roof Vent & Stack **9.98**

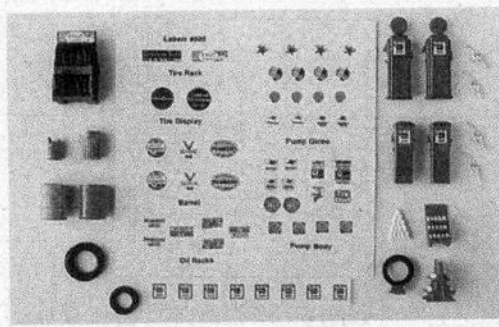

**361-504** Old-Time Gas Station Pre-1940s **9.98**

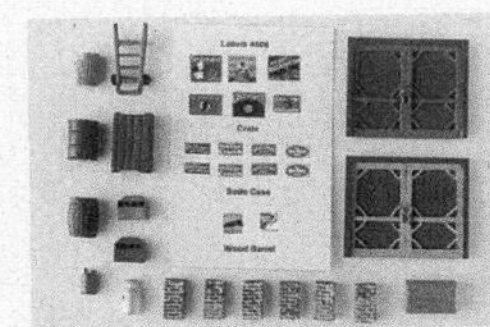

**361-505** Post-1940s Gas Station **11.95**

**361-506** Loading Dock **9.98**

**361-507** Deluxe Roof Stacks & Vents **9.98**

**361-508** Feed & Seed Elevator **10.95**

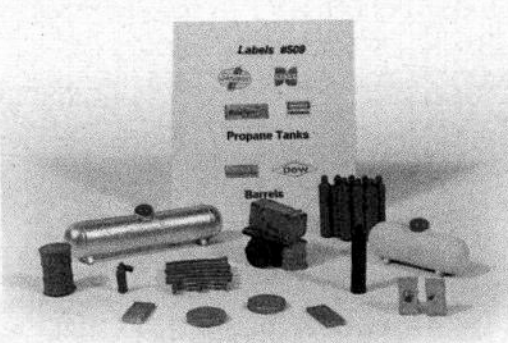


**361-509** Commercial & Industrial **11.95**

**361-511** Crates, Kegs & Barrels pkg(30) **15.95**



# Keystone Locomotive Works

Parts are metal pressure castings; kits include brass rod and wire as required.

Visit www.walthers.com for a complete listing of Keystone Locomotive Works Products.

## Boilers

**395-20** Vertical, Small **2.25**

**395-101** Horizontal, Portable **15.95**

## Engines

**395-31** Donkey Engine C&D **12.95**

**395-32** Boiler w/Small Mill Engine **11.95**

**395-1106** Large Horizontal Engine Only **14.95**

## Junk

**395-2** Engine House **3.95**
Includes various steam parts.

**395-12** Set of 8 Drivers and Axles **5.95**

**395-14** Logging **3.95**
Includes 70- and 90-Ton Shay parts.

**395-15** Diesel Engine House **5.95**

## Miniature Tools

**395-1** Logging Tool Set **3.95**

## Sawmill Details

**395-19** Cheese Blocks pkg(4) **1.25**

**395-34** Sumner 6' Band Saw **12.95**

**395-35** Shotgun Carriage w/Ways & Track **10.95**

**395-36** Edger Kit **10.95**

**395-37** Live Rolls **10.95**

**395-38** Cut-off Saw **10.95**

**395-39** Logging Mill Transfer Table **10.95**

**395-102** Working Jill Poke Unloader Kit **9.95**

## Windshield Wipers 1.98 ea

**395-3401** Metal pkg(4).

# METAL MINIATURES

Parts are lead alloy castings. Illustrations are not to scale.

Please visit Walthers Web site at www.walthers.com for a complete listing of all available items.

## Diesel Snow Plows 4.00 ea

**340-50** GP/SD Series Locos
Fits Athearn locos, adaptable to Tyco and PFM.

### 1960s-1970s Diesels

Used on many EMD GP and SD, and GE U28-U33 units. Fits Athearn, Life-Like and Bachmann as well as Alco and imported brass locos.

**340-56** Notched Corner

**340-59** Large Coupler Opening

**340-61** EJ&E, LIRR "Weedcutter" Style

## Fork Lift

**340-32** Clark Fork Lift pkg(2) **4.00**

## Trackside Details

**340-100** Track Siding Bumper Post **4.00**
Bolted tie crib and earth works, for all types of shortline or industrial trackage.

Detailed, injection-molded styrene plastic, unless noted.

### Bridge Parts

#### Plate Girders

**255-80180** 85' Girder pkg(4) **8.30**

**255-80166** 50' Girder pkg(4) **5.70**

**255-80167** 30' Girder pkg(4) **5.20**

#### Bridge Shoes

Made from white metal.

**255-80034** pkg(4) **4.85**

**255-80035** Assorted pkg(16) **9.15**

### Doors 2.95 ea

255-80161

**255-80062** Transom pkg(4)

**255-80063** Four Panel pkg(4)

**255-80065** Baggage pkg(3)

**255-80160** Warehouse Overhead pkg(3)

**255-80161** Office Front pkg(8)

**255-80162** Warehouse Personnel pkg(4)

**255-80165** Store Front pkg(4)

### Windows 2.95 ea

255-80061 255-80064

**255-80061** Double 66 x 104" pkg(2)

**255-80064** Eight Pane 28 x 64" pkg(8)

255-80067 255-80068

**255-80067** Eight Pane 25 x 50" pkg(8)

**255-80068** Two Pane 28 x 64" pkg(8)

### Building Details

**255-80066** Board Walks pkg(2) **2.95**

**255-80105** Pallets pkg(12) **2.95**

**255-80163** Gutters & Downspouts pkg(6) **2.95**

**255-80164** Electric Meter Box & Mast pkg(2) **2.95**

**255-80173** Ore Gate **3.20**

## TAURUS PRODUCTS/ TROUT CREEK ENGINEERING

Visit Walthers web site at www.walthers.com for a complete listing of parts available from Taurus Products/Trout Creek Engineering.

### Ladders

**707-2002** 5-Rung Caboose pkg(2) **7.00**

**707-2005** Freight Car, Long pkg(4) **5.00**
Measures .010" thick. Includes instructions to adapt to cars using five-, six- or seven-rung ladders.

**707-2006** Freight Car, Short pkg(8) **5.00**
Measures .010" thick.

**707-2012** 4-Rung Caboose Ladder **7.00**

### Railings

**707-2004** Platform Railings for Observation Cars Kit **6.00**
Includes brake stanchion and handle.

## moloco

## CABOOSE KITS

### Tool Box & End Gate Kit

**504-1151 5.95**
Upgrade your cabooses easily with the addition of this toolbox, battery box and end gates. This kit replicates GN caboose details, later owned by BN, BNSF, Montana Rail Link and others.

### End Step & Platform Kit

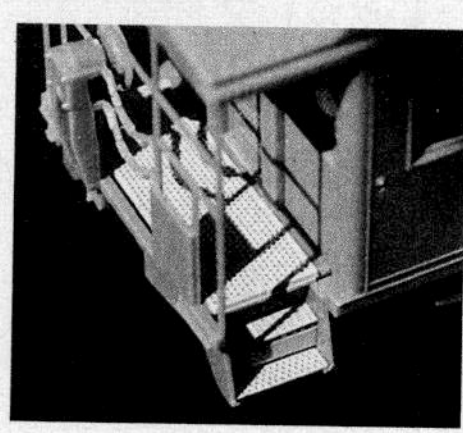

2-Step Version Shown

3-Step Version Shown

**504-1201 9.95**
Includes four step grid patterns, six platforms in four grid patterns for two- and three-step versions, three step risers (including CB&Q, Colorado & Southern and Forth Worth & Denver tall version) and DRGW coupler platform extension.

## CUPOLA KITS

**504-1501 6.95**
For Atlas or Athearn HO Scale models, sold separately. Includes correct Stanray roof contours and details, flush mounting laser-cut windows, body filler sections for easy conversion, separate movable side windows, ultra-thin roof overhang and optional roofwalk brackets. Suitable for BN, B&M, GN, N&W, NS, Trona and Montana Rail Link.

Daily New Arrival Updates! Visit Walthers Web site at **www.walthers.com**

**504-1502** With Centered Side Windows **7.95**
This style of cupola was seen on railroads from 1961-1964, as well as similar versions between 1961-1976. Suitable for BN, GN, NP, Montana Rail Link, Maine Central, Chicago Central & Pacific, Illinois Central Gulf, and Gulf, Mobile & Ohio.

## FREIGHT CAR PARTS

**504-801** Stanray Overhanging Diagonal-Panel Roof **5.00**
Fits all 50-foot box car models. Features thin edges and scale details.

**504-802** Roofwalk Support Brackets **2.95**
These roofwalk brackets. They'll add an extra touch of prototypical realism to cars that have had roofwalks removed.

# M.V. PRODUCTS
REALISTIC LIGHT LENSES FOR MODELS

## HEADLIGHT & MARKER LENSES

Add realistic headlights to your favorite models with this unique lens system. Each comes fully assembled, with a parabolic metal mirror mounted behind a solid lens made of hybrid epoxy. This design picks up and reflects all available light for a highly realistic appearance. The lens is heat-resistant, and may be modified for installation over existing light sources, such as bulbs or light pipes. Adaptable to any scale, in addition to clear, many sizes are produced in red, green, amber, blue and black (IR) colors. These can be used to detail trains, autos, trucks, fire trucks, military vehicles, police and emergency vehicles, or aircraft models.

Lighting the Lens – Make a starter hole with a pointed tool in the center of the metal backing. Select a drill size representative of a scale bulb and drill a hole approximately halfway into the lens. During power-on operation, the whole lens will glow, with a bright center that looks like a scale bulb.

HO Scale sizes are shown for individual lenses, along with actual diameter in inches and drill number needed for mounting.

### Engine Sets

Designed for brass steam engines, include lenses for headlight(s) and tender back-up lamp. Some include a red lamp where required.

**516-1** One Clear & One Red pkg(2) **1.85**
PFM ATSF 4-6-4, 4-8-4, 2-10-4.
**516-2** Clear 18" pkg(2) **1.95**
PFM ATSF #1337 4-6-2, B2 & B3 Shays with balloon stacks, Michigan 3-Cylinder Shay, Custom Brass NP A & A1 4-8-4.
**516-3** Clear pkg(2) **1.95**
Balboa/Hallmark ATSF 9000 series 0-6-0.
**516-4** Two Clear & One Red pkg(3) **2.45**
Sunset ATSF 0-8-0 & 2-8-0, Custom Brass/Balboa/Key ATSF 2-6-2.
**516-5** Clear pkg(2) **1.95**
Hallmark ATSF 2-8-0 #2507.
**516-6** Clear pkg(2) **1.45**
Tenshodo GN, M2, N3, R2, P2 and Q1, Westside NYC J1e 4-6-4, PFM MoPac 4-8-4.
**516-7** Clear pkg(2) **1.45**
Tenshodo GN, S1, S2 and O8. Van Hobbies CN N-5d 2-8-0, CP T-1a, and H.1a.b 4-6-4.
**516-8** Clear pkg(3) **2.85**
Westside/Balboa/Max Gray SP GS4.
**516-9** Two Clear & One Red pkg(3) **2.85**
PFM CNW 4-6-2 E2a. Westside/Max Gray UP FEF2 & FEF3.
**516-10** Clear pkg(2) **1.85**
PFM SOU F1 & PS4, WP 4-8-2.
**516-12** Clear pkg(2) **1.85**
Athearn Alco PA.
**516-13** Clear pkg(2) **1.95**
PFM Pacific Coast Shay & NP S4 4-6-0. NWSL E2a 4-6-2.
**516-14** Clear pkg(2) **1.95**
PFM Frisco 2-10-0, Westside SP B1. Alco Models SP C15 2-8-0.
**516-15** Clear pkg(2) **1.85**
PFM Western Pacific 2-8-2, DRGW L131, C&O K4, UP FEF1, MILW F6a.
**516-16** Clear pkg(2) **1.45**
PFM DRGW & Western Pacific 4-6-0, MP 4-6-2 & 4-8-4. Westside NYC J3a, J3b & J1e. Van Hobbies CN #6060.

### Individual Lenses

#### 4" HO, 3-1/2" 1/72 & 7" N pkg(4) 2.20 ea (Unless Noted)

1/72 aircraft, vehicle and train lights. Measures .046", Drill #56. HO marker and class lights.
**516-700** Clear
**516-701** Red
**516-703** Blue (formation lights)
**516-704** Green
**516-705** Amber
**516-702** Red, Green & Amber Recognition Lights set(3) **1.65**

#### 4-1/2" pkg(4) 2.20 ea (Unless Noted)

Measures .052", Drill #55. Class lights for most EMD hood units and GE U-Boats. Fits Detail Associates headlights 1017, 1018, 1019 and 1020 each sold separately. Drop-in mount for marker light castings from Cal-Scale, Precision Scale and most HO brass steam engines.
**516-300** Clear
**516-301** Red
**516-302** Green
**516-303** Amber
**516-304** Blue
**516-500** Red, Green & Amber set(3) **1.65**

#### 5-1/2" pkg(4) 2.20 ea (Unless Noted)

Measures .063", Drill #52. Class lights for Athearn, AHM and most brass U-Boats, headlights for Athearn RDC and various Alco Models. Also fits Cal-Scale, Precision Scale and most brass steam loco marker light castings.
**516-22** Clear
**516-220** Red
**516-221** Green
**516-222** Amber
**516-223** Blue
**516-501** Red, Green & Amber set(3) **1.65**

#### 6-1/8" pkg(4) 2.20 ea

Measures .070", Drill #50.
**516-600** Clear
**516-601** Red
**516-602** Green
**516-603** Amber

#### 6-1/2"

Measures .073", Drill #49.
**516-18** Six Clear & One Red pkg(7) **3.50**
Athearn U-Boats, Details West headlight 102 and 1012.
**516-26** Clear pkg(4) **2.20**
Details West headlight 117 and 138, Detail Associates headlight 1003.
**516-103** Eight Clear & Two Red pkg(10) **5.00**
Details West headlight 103.

#### 6-3/4"

Measures .078", Drill #47.
**516-19** Six Clear & One Red pkg(7) **3.60**
Athearn EMDs, Atlas GP40, AHM U25C, Gem SDP40F, AHM, Model Power, Trains and PMI EMD FP45. Details West headlights 100 and 104.
**516-23** Four Clear & One Red pkg(5) **2.50**
Athearn F45, FP45, SD9. Alco Models Century Series, SD40, GP40, C643. Details West headlights 101 and 105 - use two sets.
**516-24** Red pkg(2) **1.10**
Details West headlights 112, 113, 115 and 116. Detail Associates headlights 1001, 1002, 1005, 1007, 1008 and 1009. Utah Pacific 70, 71 and 84.
**516-25** Clear pkg(4) **2.20**
Athearn SD9. Details West headlights 113, 114, 116 and 137. Detail Associates headlights 1002-1004, 1006-1009 and 1011.

#### 7"

Measures .082", Drill #45.
**516-28** One Clear, One Red pkg(2) **1.10**
Cal-Scale #263 Mars light, PFM Burlington 05 with Mars light.
**516-280** Clear pkg(4) **2.20**
Sealed beam headlights for EMD hood units, GE U-Boat & electrics - all manufacturers.
**516-281** Red pkg(4) **2.20**

#### 7-1/2" pkg(4) 2.20 ea (Unless Noted)

Measures .086", Drill. #44
**516-20** Clear
**516-27** Clear - Tender pkg(2) **1.10**
**516-200** Red
**516-201** Green
**516-202** Amber
**516-203** Blue
**516-502** One Red, One Green & One Amber set(3) **1.65**

#### 8-1/2" pkg(2) 1.10 ea

Measures .096", Drill #44.
**516-409** Clear
**516-410** Red
**516-411** Green
**516-412** Amber

#### 9" pkg(2) 1.10 ea

Measures .101", Drill #38.
**516-29** Clear
Headlights for SS Ltd. old trucks and 1/43 Scale (measures 4.46") vehicles.
**516-30** Red
**516-31** Amber
**516-32** Blue

#### 9-1/2" pkg(2) 1.75 ea

Measures .110", Drill #35.
**516-109** Clear
**516-110** Red

### Train, 1/35 & 1/43 Vehicle & 1/32 Aircraft Lights .90 ea (Unless Noted)

#### 10" HO

Measures .116", Drill #32. HO headlights. 3.7" lights for 1/35 Scale military vehicles with large bezels.
**516-116** Clear
**516-117** Red (for signal lamps)
**516-118** Black (for infra-red)

#### 11" HO

Measures .128", Drill #30. HO headlights. 4.46" headlights for 1/35 Scale military vehicles with small bezels. 5/7" headlight in 1/43 Scale.
**516-128** Clear
**516-129** Red (for signal lamps)
**516-130** Amber (for fog lamps)
**516-131** Blue (for signal lamps)
**516-132** Black (for infra-red)
**516-17** Clear pkg(2) **1.75**
Athearn SW7, Alco/Westside GE 44-Ton Diesel.
**516-800** Red, Green & Amber set(3) **2.50**
Approximately 11" HO. Measures .125", drill 1/8". Used for 1/32 Scale aircraft recognition lights.

#### 12"

Measures .136", Drill #29.
**516-21** Clear for Athearn Baldwin S12 pkg(2) **1.75**
**516-136** Clear
**516-137** Red
**516-138** Amber
**516-139** Blue

#### 13" .90 ea

Measures .149", Drill #25.
**516-149** Clear
**516-150** Red

#### 14" .90 ea

Measures .159", Drill #21.
**516-159** Clear
**516-160** Red

#### 14-1/2" 1.00 ea

Measures .166", Drill #19. Use for vehicle lights in 1/35 Scale (measures 5.7") or 1/43 Scale (measures 7").
**516-166** Clear
**516-167** Red
**516-168** Amber
**516-169** Blue

#### 15" 1.00 ea

Measures .173", Drill #17.
**516-173** Clear
**516-174** Red

#### 15-1/2" 1.00 ea

Measures .180", Drill #15.
**516-180** Clear
**516-181** Red
**516-182** Amber
**516-183** Blue

#### 16"

**516-185** Clear **1.00**
Measures .185", Drill #13.

#### 17"

**516-193** Clear **1.00**
Measures .193", Drill #10.

#### 17-1/2" 1.00 ea

Measures .199", Drill #8. Use with 7" lamps on 1/35 Scale vehicles.
**516-197** Amber
**516-198** Red
**516-199** Clear

#### Athearn F7A Set(2) 1.95 ea

Scale 17-1/2" fits nose and front door headlights.
**516-11** Clear
**516-111** One Clear & One Red
Can be used to fashion a lamp with a red emergency stop signal.

#### 18"

**516-204** Clear **1.00**
Measures .204", Drill #6.

#### 18-1/2" 1.00 ea

Measures .209", Drill #4. Ideal for marker lights (measures 4-1/2") in G Scale.
**516-209** Clear
**516-210** Red
**516-211** Green
**516-212** Amber

#### 19" 1.00 ea

Measures .221", Drill #2. Use for 7" lamps in 1/32 Scale.
**516-216** Red
**516-217** Amber
**516-218** Clear

#### 20" 1.00 ea

Measures .228", Drill #1. Use for 5.7" lamps in 1/24 - 1/25 Scale vehicles.
**516-228** Clear
**516-229** Red
**516-230** Amber
**516-231** Blue

#### 21-1/2"

**516-401** Clear **2.00**
Measures/Drill 15/64".

#### 22"

**516-248** Clear **1.05**
Measures .248", Drill 1/4".

#### 23"

**516-402** Clear **2.00**
Measures/Drill 17/64".

#### 24-1/2" 2.00 ea

Measures/Drill 9/32". Use for 7" lamps on 1/24 - 1/25 Scale vehicles.
**516-403** Clear
**516-414** Red
**516-415** Amber

#### 26"

**516-404** Clear **2.00**
Measures/Drill 19/64".

### Catalog

**516-1001 1.50**
A comprehensive list of MV Products lenses, with sizes and applications for over a thousand models.

## New England Rail Service, Inc.

Model Pullman-built heavyweight cars with these highly detailed parts. Parts are designed especially for the Rivarossi 12-1 Sleeper (sold separately), and are plastic unless noted.

For more photos and information, see the complete listing at www.walthers.com.

### PASSENGER CAR PARTS

#### Air Conditioning Parts

**529-250** Air Conditioning Duct **7.50**
Universal kit can be applied to almost any Pullman car. Duct can be cut to any length. Includes four different end pieces.

**529-253** Pullman Sump Tank 1 Pair **4.95**
For use with ice-activated air condition kits. Cast resin.

**529-255** Air Conditioner Compressor Box pkg(2) **4.95**

**529-256** Holdover Coil Box for Mechanical Air Conditioner pkg(2) **4.95**

#### Conversion Kits

These kits include replacement side windows and details

**529-300** Coach **5.95**
**529-301** Combination Car **4.95**
**529-310** Plan 3584 10-2 Sleeper **5.95**
**529-312** Plan 2410 12-1 Sleeper **5.95**
**529-313** Plan 2412 16 Section Sleeper **7.95**
**529-316** Plan 4046B 12-2 Sleeper **5.95**
**529-317** Plan 4090 8-1-3 Sleeper **4.95**
**529-318** Plan 4084 6-6 Sleeper **9.95**
**529-319** Plan 2585 10-1-2 Sleeper **9.95**
**529-320** Plan 4158 12 Room, 2 Single Bedroom, 3 Double Bedroom Sleeper **4.95**
**529-330** Plan 2416 28 Chair, 1 Drawing Room Parlor Car **4.95**

#### Ice Bunkers pkg(2) 4.95 ea

Used with ice activated air conditioning systems.

**529-251** 6' Single
**529-252** Double

#### Miscellaneous

**529-210** Interior Vestibule Wall pkg(8) **5.95**
Separates the vestibule area from the interior.

**529-211** 5' 6" Baggage Doors w/Frames pkg(8) **5.95**
Pullman designed, used on many combination and/or club cars.

**529-212** Diner Kitchen Windows & Food Service Doors **3.95**
Includes four of the most common paired window styles, two each of two other styles and two each 24" and 28" food service doors.

**529-230** 145-Gallon Pressurized Water Tank pkg(2) **4.95**
Used on all Pullman cars; parts for two complete tanks.

**529-231** 8-Cell Battery Box pkg(2) **4.95**
Models feature floor drains and screened vent ports. Parts for two complete boxes included.

### FREIGHT CAR PARTS

#### 1-1/2 Door Box Car Conversion Kit

**529-1000 5.95**
Used for automobiles and similar large loads. Kit includes doors, hardware and details to modify an Accurail 4000 or 4200 series box car (sold separately).

## NEAL'S N GAUGING TRAINS

### MESH

#### 20.95 ea (Unless Noted)

Made of stainless steel, mesh measures 2-1/2 x 3-3/4" 6.2 x 9.3cm.

#### Square

**530-313** .2mm Spacing
**530-314** .3mm Spacing
**530-315** .5mm Spacing

#### Diamond

**530-316** .20mm Spacing
**530-317** .35mm Spacing
**530-318** .50mm Spacing

#### Hexagonal

**530-319** .5mm Spacing **18.95**

#### Octagonal

**530-320** .25mm Spacing **18.95**

### WINDOW GRAPHICS

#### 12.98 ea (Unless Noted)

**530-201** The Boom-Boom Room Fits Design Preservation Models 243-101

**530-202** Curtis's Critters Fits Design Preservation Models 243-102

**530-203** David's Drugstore Fits Design Preservation Models 243-108

**530-204** Dan's Diner Fits Design Preservation Models 243-116

**NEW 530-204** Softee Furnishings Fits Design Preservation Models 243-117 **14.98**

### NEW PRODUCTS

#### Making-A-Scene™ Series

**NEW 716-20049** Trash Cans w/Lids pkg(8) **10.95**

**NEW 716-20050** Garage Rubbish Set **12.95**
Junk Chassis & 3 Different Junk Clusters

**NEW 716-20051** Chemical Dump Set **14.95**
Drum Cluster, Spills & 8 Single Drums

**NEW 716-20052** Freight Cluster Set #1 **14.95**
3 Different Clusters & Scale

**NEW 716-20053** Freight Cluster Set #2 **14.95**
3 Different Clusters & Scale

### MAKING A SCENE DETAILS

**716-20031** Freight Assortment **13.95**
Three barrels, with one stack of 15 and 3 standing sacks.

**716-20042** Milk Cans pkg(10) **11.95**

**716-20043** Old-Time Conical Milk Cans pkg(10) **11.95**

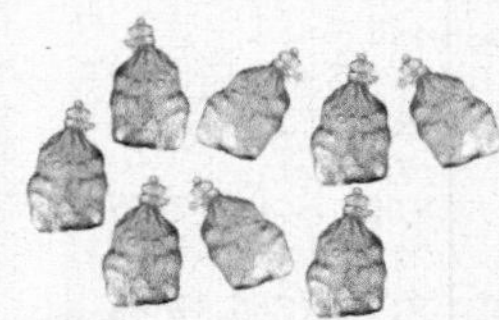

**716-20044** Onion Sacks pkg(8) **11.95**

**716-20045** Potato Sacks pkg(10) **11.95**

**716-20046** Motor Bikes pkg(3) **10.95**

### WOODEN BARRELS

**716-20030** pkg(6) **10.95**

### FREIGHT ASSORTMENT

**716-20031 11.95**
Includes three barrels, one stack of 15 sacks and three individual sacks

### CLOSED SACK ASSORTMENT

**716-20029 11.95**
Includes one stack of 15 sacks and three individual sacks

See What's New and Exciting at
**www.walthers.com**

## Nu-Line Structures

Manufacturer of Fine Scale Products

Nu-Line Structures, Inc. produces a line of fine scale detail parts designed for use with locomotives or their line c modern structures (see the Structures section of this Reference Book for a look at the kits available).

### LOCOMOTIVE DETAILS

#### Tunnel Motor Rear Grilles

**533-87007** pkg(4) **6.25**
Package contains enough grilles to detail two locomotives.

### STRUCTURE DETAILS

#### Doors

#### Cargo Doors

**533-87001** Truck 8 x 10' pkg(6) **4.25**

**533-87002** Rail 10 x 10' pkg(3 **3.25**

#### Access Doors

**533-87003** Building 12 x 15' pkg(2) **1.75**

**533-87004** Rail Building 19 x 20' pkg(2) **2.75**
Doors allow a train to enter directly into a structure.

#### Fencing

**533-160501** 4' Tall x 7' Wide 24" total length **10.50**

#### Gates

**533-160101** Steel 4 x 12.5' pkg(4) **4.95**

#### Ramp

**533-87005 3.25**
Will rise up from zero to four feet.

#### Sidewalks

**533-87006** pkg(2) **1.75**
Includes two sizes: scale 6 x 38' and 3 x 40'

#### Skylights

**533-87008** Low Profile pkg(10) **6.75**

#### Walls

**533-160201** 3, 5 & 6' Tall **7.95**

# PRECISION SCALE CO

HO/HOn3 Passenger/Freight Car Parts Catalog 585-9739

## Air Conditioning Systems

**585-31003** Passenger Car Air Conditioner Compressor (Frigidaire) **4.50**

**585-33212** Pullman Car Reservoir **2.50**

**585-33214** Pullman Car Mechanical Speed Control **3.50**

**585-33233** Pullman Car Mechanical Standby Switch Box **3.25**

## Air Horns

**585-39044** Alco pkg(2) **2.50**

**585-39083** Alco pkg(2) **2.50**

**585-39084** 3-Chime w/Ring Mount **2.75**

**585-39085** 3-Chime w/Bracket **2.75**

## Air Hoses

**585-3150** With Angle Cock & Glad Hand pkg(6) **3.00**

**585-3152** With Glad Hand, Less Angle Cock pkg(6) **3.00**

**585-3307** HOn3 Short w/Angle Cock & Glad Hand pkg(8) **3.00**

**585-3281** Dual w/Bracket for Pilot **2.25**

## Air Pumps

**585-3092** 8-1/2" Westinghouse Cross Compound **3.25**

**585-3188** 9-1/2" Single Phase Westinghouse **3.50**

## Books

### Styrene Fabrication

**585-9784 6.00**
Fully illustrated handbook by Al Armitage explains simple techniques of building with styrene. Loose leaf form, 8-1/2 x 11".

### Plan Books By Al Armitage

**585-9785** Railroad Structures **3.75**

**585-9786** Western Buildings Vol. 1 **3.75**

**585-9787** Western Buildings Vol. 2 **3.75**

**585-9788** Western Buildings Vol. 3 **3.75**

**585-9789** JS Cain Residence Bodie, California **5.00**

**585-9790** Sacramento Building **3.75**

**585-9791** Brick Dwellings Eureka, Nevada **3.75**

**585-9792** Churches **3.50**

**585-9793** Donkey Engines **4.50**

**585-9794** Logging Cars **3.50**

**585-9795** Heisler Locomotive **5.75**

**585-9796** Shay Locomotive **5.75**

**585-9797** Climax Standard **6.50**

**585-9798** #14 Heavy Motor Trucks (HO/O) **6.25**

**585-9799** #15 Wagons (HO/O) **6.50**

## Booster Engines

**585-3296** Franklin Type Plumbing Connections 1 Pair **3.00**

## Chain & Chain Hooks

**585-3304** Inboard pkg(6) **2.50**

**585-3305** Outboard pkg(6) **2.50**

**585-32042** Inboard, Plastic pkg(10) **2.00**

**585-32043** Outboard, Plastic pkg(10) **2.00**

## Diaphragms

**585-33309** Working 1 Pair **8.00**

HO/HOn3 Steam Locomotive Parts Catalog 585-9740

HO/HOn3 Diesel Locomotives Parts Catalog 585-9741

## Catalogs

Within the pages of these three HO/HOn3 catalogs, a modeler will find everything needed to outfit a freight car, passenger car or locomotive the way it should be done. Easy to use, each catalog is organized alphabetically by the more common terms used by modelers. Full of valuable information like critical dimensions and correct scale sizes, these catalogs give readers exactly what they need. Throughout these fully illustrated catalogs you will find many "Super Detailing Kits" which will enable you to detail existing wood, plastic and brass models. Each catalog includes a complete listing of Precision Scale detail parts for its respective category. Note: Color of catalog covers shown is not actual color of catalogs.

**585-9739** Passenger/Freight Car **10.00**
132 pages.

**585-9740** Steam Locomotive **18.00**
Third edition, over 200 pages.

**585-9741** Diesel Locomotive **7.00**
54 pages.

## Gear Boxes & Accessories

**585-31214** HOn3 C-16 Gear Cover **2.25**

**585-48324** 13:1 Nylon Gear **2.00**

## Passenger Car Interiors pkg(8) 5.75 ea

Parts constructed from plastic.

### Tavern/Lounge Car

Includes two settees and six semi-circular tables.

**585-33318** Brown

**585-333181** Gray

**585-333182** Blue

### Dining Car

Includes two settees, four chairs and two square tables.

**585-33319** Brown

**585-333191** Gray

**585-333192** Blue

## HOn3 Freight Car Kits

These Craft Train Kits consist of unpainted brass, plastic and wood parts.

**585-10608** 30' Wood Reefer DRGW **28.00**

**585-10640** 40' Wood Reefer DRGW **26.75**

**585-10650** Tank Car UTLX **28.75**

## Seats

### Cab Seats 2.75 ea (Unless Noted)

**585-3413** Modified pkg(2)

**585-39091** Engineer

**585-39092** Diesel, Auxiliary

### Passenger Cars (40 Double, 12 Single) 4.50 ea

**585-33312** Brown

**585-333121** Gray

**585-333122** Light Blue

### Lightweight & Heavyweight Passenger Cars

Includes arm rests.

**Single pkg(6) 4.50 ea**

**585-33315** Brown

**585-333151** Gray

**585-333152** Blue

**Double pkg(6) 5.25 ea**

**585-33316** Brown

**585-333161** Gray

**585-333162** Blue

Triple pkg(6) 6.00 ea

**585-33314** Brown

**585-333141** Gray

**585-333142** Blue

## Short Caboose Kits

### Single Cupola w/Square Ends

**585-10670** With Angle Corner Steps, DRGW w/Decals for #0500 & #0573 **27.50**

**585-106701** With Angle Corner Steps, Brass End Railings & Trucks, DRGW #0500 & #0573 **28.50**

**585-10674** With Square Corner Steps, DRGW w/Decals for #0577 & #0578 **27.50**

**585-106741** With Square Corner Steps, Brass End Railings & Trucks, DRGW #0577 & #0578 **28.50**

### Double Cupola w/Round Ends

**585-10672** With Angle Corner Steps, DRGW w/Decals for #0575 **27.50**

**585-106721** With Angle Corner Steps, Brass End Railings & Trucks, DRGW #0575 **28.50**

**585-10676** With Square Corner Steps, No Awning, DRGW w/Decals for #0580 **27.50**

**585-106761** With Square Corner Steps, Brass End Railings & Trucks, No Awning, DRGW #0580 **28.50**

### DRGW Long Caboose

**NEW 585-106821 31.50**

## Springs

### Journals pkg(8) 3.00 ea

**585-44** Undersize

**585-8054** Oversize

### Drivers pkg(12)

**585-381** Small **2.75**

**585-382** Large **3.50**

## Tables

### pkg(12) 4.00 ea

Six each of plastic round and corner triangular styles.

**585-33313** Brown

**585-333131** Gray

**585-333132** Blue

### Assorted Dining Car Interior pkg(24) 6.00 ea

Plastic.

**585-33317** Brown

**585-333171** Gray

585-333172 Blue

## Track pkg(6) 27.50 ea (Unless Noted)

Allows long wheelbase locos to negotiate sharper curves. All rail is nickel silver, scale 9' ties and 36" track length.

### Curved Flex

**585-4926** Elevated, Code 100

**585-4928** Elevated, Code 83

**585-4930** Elevated, Code 70

**585-4932** Main Line, Code 83

### Straight Track

**585-4925** Code 100

**585-4927** Code 83

**585-4929** Code 70

**585-4931** Code 83 HO/HOn3 **30.50**

# PLANO

Made of photo-etched metal for near-scale thickness and see-through surfaces on grilles, platforms and walkways. For a complete list of parts and current availability, see walthers.com

## NEW PRODUCTS

### Diesel Loco Parts

**Fan Hatch for Cannon Thin Wall Fans (Brass) 3.50 ea**

NEW **565-11852** For SD40-2, GP/SD40

NEW **565-11862** For GP30/35

NEW **565-11872** For GP/SD38, GP/SD39

NEW **565-11882** For GP38-2

### Freight Car Parts

**Covered Hopper Walkway - Apex Pattern**

NEW **565-11036** Atlas Trainman® ACF 3560 Covered Hopper **8.50**

## DIESEL LOCO PARTS

### Bell

**565-18421** Gong Bell Nose Insert Plates w/Cutout template pkg(3) **3.50**
For CNW and DT&I Units

### Body Louvers

**565-461** For EMD GP7/GP9 pkg(12) **2.25**

### Brackets

**Rotary Beacon Bracket 2.25 ea**

**565-182** Cab Corner pkg(3)

**565-183** Cab Center, Low pkg(2)

**565-462** No Hole; for Cab Corner Mounting pkg(3)

**Radio Antenna**

**565-184** Small - Cab Center pkg(3) **2.25**

### 48" Fan Grilles

**565-467** " Flat Top pkg(2) **3.00**

**565-468** Dynamic Brake w/Lift Rings - Fits Kato Models **3.50**

### Fan Hatches

**565-180** SD45 **4.00**

**565-186** SD40-2 **3.50**

**565-187** GP38 **3.50**

**565-188** GP38-2 **3.00**

### Intake Grills for PROTO 2000™ EMD SD45 7.25ea

**565-11805** Early

**565-11806** Late

### Lift Rings

**565-120** pkg(60) **2.25**

### Safety Tread

**565-208** Diamond **10.50**

### Santa Fe GP30u

**Filter Shrouds w/Smoke Deflectors 6.25 ea**

**565-14801** Phase I Cab

**565-14802** Phase II Cab

**Smoke Deflectors**

**565-14803** **2.75**
Fits PROTO 2000 GP30.

### SP SD45 "Elephant Ears" Air Intake Shrouds 8.50 ea

**565-14851** EMD-Built Round Top Style

**565-14852** SP-Built Angled Top Style

### Step Guards

**565-189** EMD Blower Housing-Angled Slots pkg(4) **1.00**
Photo-etched brass, fits many EMD hood units.

### Winterization Hatch Screens

**565-476** For PROTO 2000 GP7/9 and SD7/9 w/36" Fans pkg(4) **3.25**

**565-477** For PROTO 2000 EMD SD60 Stainless Steel pkg(2) **4.00**

## FREIGHT CAR PARTS

### Autorack Anti-Vandal Bars Sets 7.25 ea

**565-13371** For Walthers Bi-level Cars

**565-13372** For Walthers Tri-level Cars

### Brake Platforms

**565-130** Open, Round pkg(2) **1.25**

**565-131** Slotted pkg(2) **1.50**

**565-132** Diamond pkg(2) **1.25**

**565-13112** Apex Slotted Pattern pkg(12) **5.75**

### Container Car Details

**565-137** End Load Guides pkg(20) **1.75**

**565-171** For A-Line Husky Stack **3.00**

### Coupler Cut Lever Bars w/Hangers - Adjustable Style

**565-12002** pkg(3) **3.25**

**565-12003** pkg(6) **5.50**

**565-12004** pkg(12) **8.75**

### Coupler Platforms

**Partial Width 1.95 ea**

**565-127** Round

**565-128** Slotted

**565-129** Open Diamond

**Full Width 2.75 ea**

**565-133** Round

**565-134** Slotted Pattern

**Apex Slotted**

**565-1284** pkg(4) **6.00**

### Slotted Walkway Material 10.50 ea

Large, photo-etched sheets feature a slotted pattern. Each measures 1-7.8 x 8-1/2".

**565-201** Stainless Steel

**565-202** Brass

**Morton Round Pattern**

**565-203** Stainless Steel

**565-204** Brass

### Walkway Kits

Photo-etched metal for scale thickness and see-through tread in round, slotted and diamond patterns, as used on prototype cars.

**Walthers**

**Plastic Pellet Covered Hoppers**

**565-115** **8.25**

**Cement Hoppers**

**565-86** 2-Bay **5.75**

**Pullman-Standard PS2CD Covered Hoppers 8.50 ea**

**565-87** Morton, Round

**565-88** Apex, Slotted

**50' Airslide Covered Hoppers**

**565-95** Single-Bay Apex, Slotted **3.75**

**565-98** Double-Bay Apex, Slotted **4.50**

**565-99** Double-Bay Morton, Round **4.50**

**Pressure Differential (PD) Covered Hoppers**

**565-114** Morton, Round **7.25**

**Coil Cars**

**565-123** Apex, Slotted Full-Length **5.50**

**Front Runner Platforms**

**565-126** 2 Sets **3.00**

**48' Thrall Well Cars**

**565-153** Stand-Alone Single, Round **4.25**

**565-154** Five-Car Set **8.75**

**Spine Cars**

**565-158** Walkways **2.25**

**Funnel-Flow Tank Cars**

**565-301** Platform Walkway **5.25**

**NSC 53' Well Cars**

**565-13232** Three-Unit Set **15.00**

**565-13233** Three-Unit Set w/IBC Boxes **16.75**

**65' LPG/Anhydrous Ammonia Tank Cars**

**565-302** Center Handrail **7.75**

**565-303** Outside Handrail **6.75**

**565-304** Inside Handrail **6.75**

**20' Tank Container**

**565-316** Walkways **2.00**

**48' Thrall Double Stack Container Car**

**565-1533** 3 Sets **9.75**

**Husky Stack**

**565-125** General Purpose **5.25**

**ACF**

**70-Ton 2-Bay Hoppers**

**565-91** For Bowser & Kato **3.50**

**A-Line**

**Double Stack**

**565-148** 40' Gunderson Five-Unit Set **2.00**
Walkways with lift rings.

**Husky Stack**

**565-151** Walkway & Detail Parts **7.75**

**Atlas**

**565-96** ACF Cylindrical Hopper Walkway w/Risers **9.50**

**565-307** 33,000-Gallon Tank Car **6.25**

**565-10891** Apex for Retooled PS-2 2-Bay **3.50**

**565-11063** US Gypsum for ACF Pressure-Aide **9.25**

**Extended Vision Caboose**

**565-453** Apex **6.50**

**565-454** End Platforms & Steps **2.75**

**565-456** Apex Pattern, Right Hand Version **6.50**

**Con-Cor**

**3-Bay Covered Hoppers**

**565-92** Apex, Slotted **4.50**

**Intermountain**

**Pullman Standard Covered Hoppers (Morton, Round) 9.00 ea**

**565-82** Trinity Style

**565-83** PS4750

**Canadian Cylindrical Hoppers 8.25 ea**

**565-97** Morton

**565-100** Grain Cars

**4600 Cubic Feet Hopper 8.50 ea**

**565-11041** Morton - For Atlas or Intermountain

**565-11091** Morton

**565-11092** Apex

**565-11093** Early US Gypsum

**565-11094** Late US Gypsum

**McKean Centerflow Covered Hoppers**

**565-102** 2-Bay Apex Pattern **7.50**

**565-105** 3-Bay Apex Pattern **8.25**

## PASSENGER CAR PARTS

### Blinds

**565-300** Venetian Blinds, 3 Sizes, Stainless Steel **8.50**

## TRUCK & TRAILER DETAIL

### Fenders

**565-372** Chrome Quarter Fenders pkg(2) **2.25**

### Mudflaps

**565-352** Chrome Tipped Flap pkg(2) **2.25**

Fits Herpa and Promotex trucks, adaptable to others.

### Placard Frames

**565-310** Tank Cars **1.75**

**565-311** Truck/Trailer-Flush Mount **1.50**

### Racks For Trident Chevy Pickups

**565-378** Pipe Rack, 8' Box **3.25**

**565-379** Louvered Headache Rack **2.00**

### Radiator Grilles

**565-387** Square & Horizontal pkg(2) **2.50**
For Ford L9000 Tractor; Fits Walthers & Atlas models, sold separately.

### Running Boards For Trident Chevys

**565-382** Blazer **2.50**

**565-383** Suburban **3.00**

**565-384** Van **3.00**

### Mirror Sets 2.00 ea (Unless Noted)

**565-354** Ford Aeromax Set #1

**565-355** Ford Aeromax Set #2

**565-357** International Set #1

**565-374** International Set #2

**565-358** Mack CH13 Set #1 **2.50**

**565-373** Mack CH13 Set #2

**565-359** "Lollipop" Style pkg(8)

**565-360** Front Corner Bumper Post pkg(8)

**565-375** KW T600 Set for Herpa **2.25**

**565-376** UPS/Mack Truck Mirrors/Details for Herpa **3.24**

**565-377** UPS Box Delivery Van Mirror/Detail Set for Walthers & N.J. International

**565-386** Photo-Etched Wide Vision Mirrors w/Mounting Brackets - Fits Trident Chevy Trucks/Vans pkg(2) **2.50**

**565-13542** Mirror Set & Wipers For Athearn Ford C Cab **3.00**

*Division of* **Rix Products**

Parts are molded in plastic.

# CAR DETAILS

### Dome Car Window

**541-1** Dome Insert **4.25**
See-through green plastic dome fits Oriental Limited "California Zephyr" car, or any brass model of a Budd prototype dome car.

### Glazing pkg(4) 2.25 ea

Each measures 1 x 3" 2.5 x 7.5cm.

**541-1002** Green Tint

### Panel Hopper Conversion

**541-4000 2.75**
"Blisters" were applied on the side panels of some older cars to increase carrying capacity. Complete set fits Athearn 34' ribbed side hoppers.

### Passenger Car Seats pkg(36) 5.25 ea

For lightweight and streamlined cars.

**541-4100** Brown

**541-4101** Gray

**541-4102** Red

**541-4103** Blue

**541-4104** Green

# STRUCTURAL DETAILS

### Building Detail Set

**541-3001** Gutters, Downspouts, Chimney & Electric Meter **3.25**

### Doors 2.25 ea (Unless Noted)

**541-1100** Roll-Up Freight pkg(2)

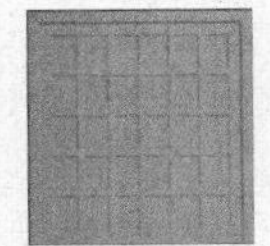

**541-1101** 30-Panel Wood pkg(2)

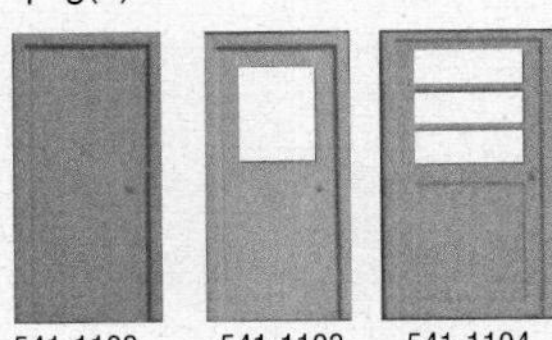

541-1102 541-1103 541-1104

**541-1102** Solid pkg(3)

**541-1103** Door w/Large Window pkg(3)

**541-1104** Door w/3-Panel Window pkg(3)

**541-1105** Window/Door Combo pkg(2)

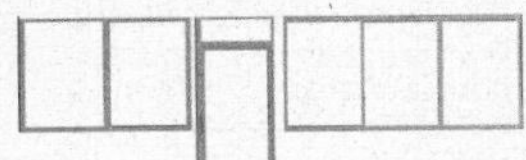

**541-1106** Store Front & Window

**541-1110** Two Car Garage, 16 x 7' pkg(2)

541-1108 541-1109

**541-1108** Engine House Door/Frame pkg(2) **2.50**

**541-1109** Roll-Up Loading, 9-1/2 x 12' pkg(2)

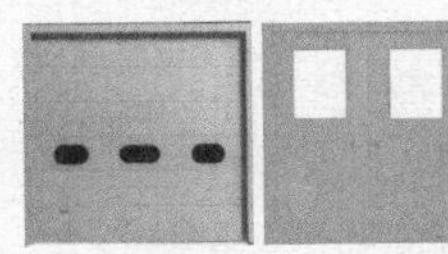

541-1107 541-1111

**541-1107** 12 x 12' Freight pkg(2)

**541-1111** Double Personnel pkg(2)

**541-1112** Fire Station Door w/Separate Frame (Open) pkg(2)

541-1113 541-1115

**541-1113** Roll-Up Freight Door, 9-1/2 x 10' pkg(2)

**541-1115** Window & Center Door Combo pkg(2)

**541-1200** Personnel Doors pkg(6) **3.00**

**541-1201** Windows Assorted pkg(6) **3.00**

**541-1202** Freight Doors Assorted pkg(6) **4.25**

**541-1203** Doors & Windows Assorted pkg(6) **4.25**

### Downspouts

**541-1116** Large Overhang pkg(4) **2.00**

**541-3101** Small Overhang pkg(6) **2.25**

### Guardrail

Kits include plastic molded parts and illustrated instructions.

**541-3** Guard **1.90**

**541-12** Highway Guardrail pkg(3) **3.25**

**541-13** Highway Guardrail pkg(6) **5.25**

### Machine Shop Doors/Windows

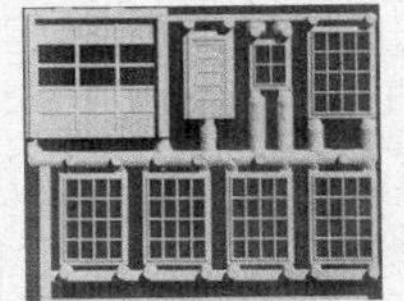

**541-3000** Doors & Windows pkg(8) **3.25**

**541-3002** Windows pkg(4) **2.25**

### Parking Barrier

**541-1016** Concrete pkg(12) **2.25**

### Stair Parts 2.25 ea

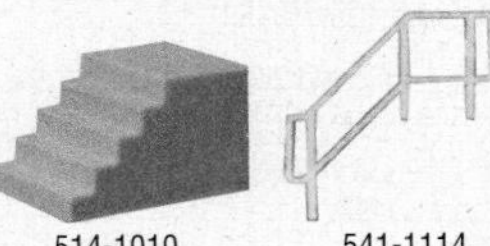

514-1010 541-1114

**541-1010** Concrete Staircase pkg(3)

**541-1114** Staircase Handrails pkg(2)

### Ventilators

541-1009

541-3102

**541-1009** Louvered pkg(3) **2.00**

**541-3102** Roof Ridge pkg(4) **2.75**

### Windows 2.25 ea

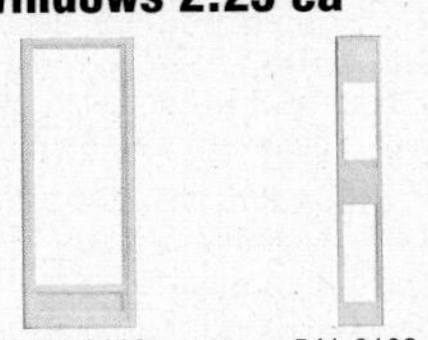

541-2100 541-2102

**541-2100** One-Story pkg(3)

**541-2102** Two-Story (Metal Buildings) pkg(2)

**541-2101** Vertical Pane Slide Window pkg(3)

541-2103

541-2104

**541-2103** Four-Pane pkg(3)

**541-2104** Eight-Pane pkg(2)



## RED CABOOSE

Items listed in blue ink may not be available at all times (see Legend Page).

# NEW PRODUCTS

### Freight Car Parts

### Cushion Coil Car

### Assembled Hoods pkg(2)

**13.95 ea**

**NEW 629-320004** Steel Pro

**NEW 629-320005** Spring Hill

**NEW 629-320006** Undecorated

# FREIGHT CAR PARTS

### Box Car

**629-800001** 40' Roof & Walkway **2.75**

**629-800004** Ladder/Detail Sprue **2.00**

**629-800005** 6' Doors (2 Youngstown, 2 Superior) **2.00**

**629-800006** Grab Irons **1.85**

**629-800007** AAR Laser-Cut Wood Roofwalk **2.95**

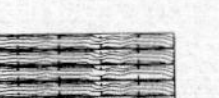

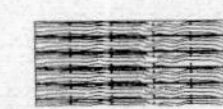

**629-800008** 10' Wooden Laser-Cut Interior & Roofwalk **9.95**
With peel and stick backing.

### Flat Car

**629-220001** 42' Laser-Cut Wood Flat Car Deck **3.95**
With peel and stick backing.

### X-29

**629-700001** Underframe **4.00**

**629-700002** Door/Detail **5.00**

**629-700003** Roof & Roofwalk **2.75**

### Reefer

**629-400010** K Brakes & Air Hoses **1.85**

**629-400011** Wood Ice Hatch/ Platform **2.75**

**629-400012** Reefer Detail Kit **3.50**

### Tank Car

**629-300002** Frame **2.75**

**629-300008** Frame Grab Irons **1.85**

## Railflyer Model Prototypes Inc.

### NEW PRODUCTS

Create exacting replicas of today's US- and Canadian-built diesels with these photo-etched and plastic conversion parts. Each is carefully researched for accuracy and can be adapted to a wide range of models. NOTE: To prevent damage in shipment, all photo-etched sets are secured to cardstock with double-sided tape. As many parts are small and may have sharp edges, these items should be kept away from children and pets.

### DIESEL DETAILS

#### Batten Strips

**NEW 631-1206** For EMD/GMD **7.49**

#### Spartan Cab Kits 46.49 ea

**NEW 631-4001** EMD w/81" Nose

**NEW 631-4002** EMD w/88" Nose

**NEW 631-4003** EMD w/High Nose

**NEW 631-4010** GMD w/81" Nose

**NEW 631-4011** GMD w/88" Nose

**NEW 631-4012** GMD w/102" Nose

#### Cab Steps 10.49 ea

Includes enough parts to do three locos.

**NEW 631-1048** GMDD

**NEW 631-1087** EMD

#### Coupler Plates 9.49 ea

Plastic parts.

**EMD**

**NEW 631-1061** For Type E Knuckle; GP/SD

**NEW 631-1062** For Type F Knuckle

**NEW 631-1063** Late Version; SD50 Series-on

**GE**

**NEW 631-1064** Early Production for Type E or F Knuckle

**NEW 631-1065** Late Production for E or F Type Knuckle

#### EMD/GMD Air Reservoirs

**NEW 631-1200** Standard Production **TBA**

**NEW 631-1201** GP Unit Split Style **TBA**

**NEW 631-1202** SD Unit Split Style **TBA**

**NEW 631-1203** SD Unit Split Style **TBA**

#### EMD/GMD Pilots 12.49 ea

Near-scale parts feature pilot holes for appliances such as handrails and coupler lift bars; can be used with Coupler Plates, available separately.

**NEW 631-900** Algoma Central, Ontario Northland Units w/4-Steps

**NEW 631-901** British Columbia Railway SD40-2 w/3-Steps

**NEW 631-902** CN GP38-2 & SD40 w/3-Steps

**NEW 631-903** CN GP38-2, GP40-2 & SD40-2 w/4 Steps

**NEW 631-904** Devco Units (SCR, NBSR & Louisville & Indiana Railway) w/4-Steps

**NEW 631-905** CP SD40 w/Non-recessed 3-Steps

**NEW 631-906** CP Early GP38AC, GP38-2 w/3-Steps

**NEW 631-907** CP Late GP38-2 w/3-Steps

**NEW 631-908** CP Early SD40-2 w/3-Steps

**NEW 631-909** CP Late SD40-2 w/Notched Top Corners; 3-Steps

#### EOT/Knuckle Holder

**NEW 631-1013** CN-Style **10.49**

#### Jack Pads pkg(8) 7.49 ea

Plastic parts.

**NEW 631-1066** All GP Units

**NEW 631-1067** Late SD40-2 through SD60

**NEW 631-1068** Late Production; SD70 Series-on

**NEW 631-1070** GE Dash-7 to Dash-9

#### Lift Tabs

**NEW 631-1069** EMD/GMD **7.49**

Parts for two locos with straight and one with angled brackets. Ridge and mounting tab ensure correct placement of these plastic parts.

#### Long Hood Lift Tabs

**NEW 631-1015** pkg(60) **10.49**
Fabricated steel lift tabs, used by CNR/UPR and others.

#### Pillow Blocks

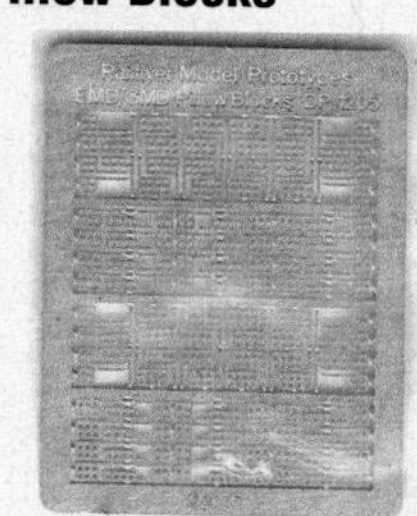

**NEW 631-1205** EMD/GMD **7.49**

#### EMD/GMDD Scale Profile Fuel Tanks 19.49 ea

Add an exact scale contoured and profiled fuel tank to your model. Can be used with walkway/frame modules (sold separately) or another existing locomotive product to upgrade non-scale components. Fuel tank is made from high quality, injection molded polystyrene and includes photo-etched end and top plates to give an exact rendering of the prototype. A contoured fit weight is also included. The top plate can be chosen to match specific fuel filler locations. If used with the walkway/frame modules, the fuel tank is properly aligned by a male/female connection and is slung a scale 1-1/2" from the bottom edge of the frame.

**NEW 631-4060** US 5000-Gallon - End Fill

**NEW 631-4061** US 5000-Gallon - Two End Fill

**NEW 631-4064** US 4400-Gallon - End Fill

**NEW 631-4065** US 4400-Gallon - Two End Fill

**NEW 631-4067** US 4000-Gallon - End Fill

**NEW 631-4068** US 4000-Gallon - Two End Fill

**NEW 631-4069** US 4000-Gallon - Center Fill

**NEW 631-4070** US 3600-Gallon - End Fill

**NEW 631-4074** US 3200-Gallon - End Fill

**NEW 631-4077** US 3000-Gallon - End Fill

**NEW 631-4080** US 2600-Gallon - End Fill

**NEW 631-4082** US 2600-Gallon - Center Fill

**NEW 631-4086** US 1700-Gallon - End Fill

#### Rear Pilot - No Foot Boards

**NEW 631-1089** For Converted EMD/GMD Locos **8.49**

#### Tread Plate

**Just Because Tread Plate**

Scale width matches tread plate on modern EMD/GMDD diesels.

**NEW 631-950** Walkways **9.49**

**NEW 631-951** Pilot Ends **9.49**

**NEW 631-952** Sheet **12.49**
Larger sheet can be cut to fit your models or patterns for custom applications.

**For Units with Spartan Cab 24.49 ea**

**NEW 631-1021** GMDD GP Units

**NEW 631-1022** GMD Early SD Units

**NEW 631-1023** GMD Dash-2 SD Units

#### Walkway Light Enclosures

**NEW 631-1207** **7.49**

#### Walkway Modules 32.49 ea

For EMD/GMDD second generation locos. Gives an accurate wheelbase, width, and coupler area detail. The system is designed to work with other locomotive building systems to offer a completely new and accurate model from the rails up. The walkway / frame modules allow you to choose detail components of your choice to match any specific locomotive class. Includes; walkway/frame, photo-etched side sills and bolster / jack pad mounts, coupler pocket cover, truck bolster insert, integral weights, and walkway duct. Constructed of high quality injection molded polystyrene, ABS plastic and photo-etch metal. Use with Next-Gen Steps, Treadplate and Pilots, each sold separately.

**GP38-2/GP39-2/GP40-2/GP50**

**NEW 631-4030** GP C4:E4 Side Sill Option

**NEW 631-4031** GP C4:E4/5 Side Sill Option

**NEW 631-4032** GP C4/5:E4/5 Side Sill Option

**NEW 631-4033** GP C4:E4/5 B Side Sill Option

**NEW 631-4034** GP C4:E4/5 P1 Side Sill Option

**NEW 631-4035** GP C4:E4/5 P2 Side Sill Option

**NEW 631-4036** GP C4:E4/5 B P2 Side Sill Option

**NEW 631-4037** GP Late Side Sill Option

**SD38-2/SD40-2/SD45-2/SD50**

**NEW 631-4040** SD C5:E5 Side Sill Option

**NEW 631-4041** SD C5:E5 DFCO Side Sill Option

**NEW 631-4042** SD C5/6:E5/6 DFCO Side Sill Option

**NEW 631-4043** SD C5/6:E6 Side Sill Option

**NEW 631-4044** SD Late Side Sill Option

### Wide Cab Diesel Parts

#### Anti-Climber

**NEW 631-1012** CN Locos **10.49**

#### Cab Kit

**NEW 631-4013** GMD **46.49**

#### Electrical Boxes 10.49 ea

**NEW 631-1014** CN GP38-2W & GP40-2W

**NEW 631-1016** CN SD Units; Early GP38-2W

#### Tread Plate 24.49 Each

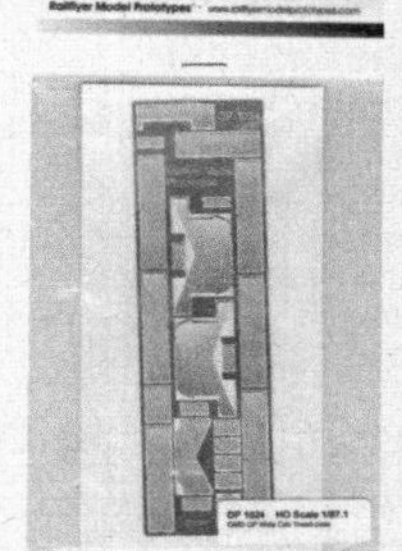

**NEW 631-1024** GP Units

**NEW 631-1025** SD Units

### EMD Diesel Parts

#### Raised Walkways

**NEW 631-1100** CN, Ontario Northland SD70I & SD75I **24.49**

**631-1101** EMD SD90 Series **TBA**

#### EMD US-Built Diesel Steps 18.99 ea

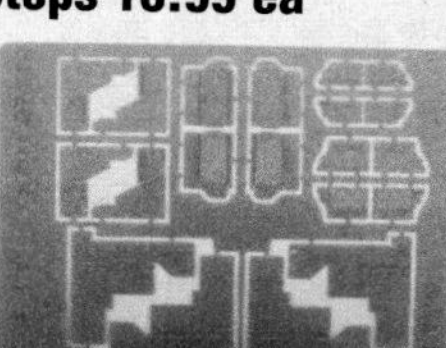

**NEW 631-1082** Late GP38-2 w/Low Middle Step; CNW, UP, CFW&E, NREX Units

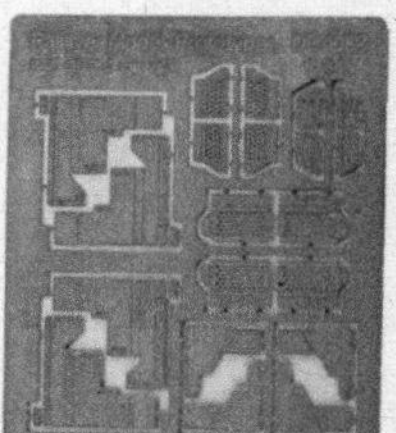

**NEW 631-1083** Late GP38-2 w/High Middle Steps, CP, Soo Units

**NEW 631-1085** CN, IC GP38-2 Platform Steps

## ailflyer Model Prototypes

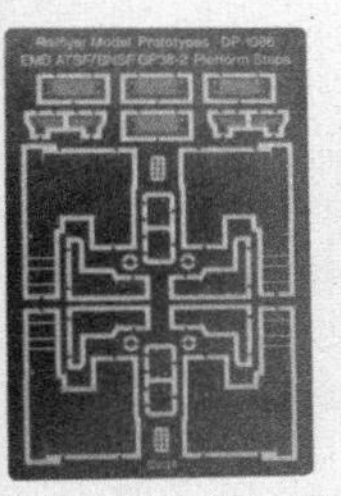

**NEW 631-1086** ATSF, BNSF GP38/39-2 Platform Steps

**NEW 631-1088** DT&I, Long Island Railroad GP38/39-2

## GMD Diesel Parts

### Canadian Style Steps & Stepwells

#### 4-Step Version 17.49 ea

**NEW 631-1001** Early; Units Built Before 1976

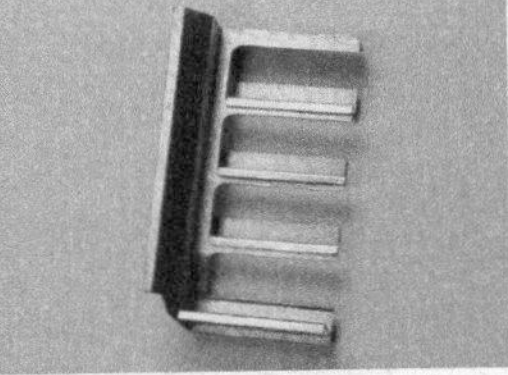

**NEW 631-1011** Late; Units Built After 1975

#### 3-Step Version 17.49 ea

**NEW 631-1031** GP38AC, GP40 & Early GP38-2

**NEW 631-1032** Mid-Production GP38-2

**NEW 631-1033** Late Production GP38-2

**NEW 631-1034** CN GP35 & GP40

**NEW 631-1035** CN Late GP40

**NEW 631-1041** Early SD40-2

**NEW 631-1042** Early/Mid-Production SD40-2

**NEW 631-1043** Mid-Production SD40-2

**NEW 631-1044** Mid/Late Production SD40-2

**NEW 631-1045** Late SD40-2

**NEW 631-1046** BCR SD40-2 #751-782 (Most Units)

**NEW 631-1071** CN Late SD40 & Alsthom Rebuilds

**NEW 631-1072** CN Early SD40

**NEW 631-1073** Retired CN SD40 & Alsthom Rebuilds

**NEW 631-1074** CP SD40

### Snow Shields

#### GP Units 10.49 ea

**NEW 631-1053** With Wide Cab

### Numberboard-Mounted Bell 12.99 ea (Unless Noted)

Kits consist of plastic and etched-metal parts.

**NEW 631-1057** Single Marker/Class Light

**NEW 631-1058** Two Marker/Class Light

**NEW 631-1059** Three Marker/Class Light

**NEW 631-1060** CN w/Rain Guards **8.49**

### Traction Motor Duct 8.49 ea

**NEW 631-1049** NBSR "Joey Door"

**NEW 631-1050** Canadian Style, No Reinforcement Strips (Plastic)

**NEW 631-1051** Short for CN Wide Cab GP38-2W (Plastic)

## Trackside Details

### Crossbucks 8.49 ea

**NEW 631-800** Modern Canadian Style pkg(12)

**NEW 631-801** Modern US Style

## Next-Gen by Railflyer Model Prototypes

Detail parts and accessories designed to increase the accuracy of your models and add to your enjoyment of model building with well thought out assembly and high quality materials. Injection molded parts are made with slide molds where applicable. Photo-etched metal components employ three-layer etching where additional detail is required.

### EMD Steps 16.49 ea

Designed to work with walkway/frame modules (sold separately) for a drop fit with no cutting or milling. Extensively researched and tested with 3D CAD modeling to ensure fit before final tooling.

**NEW 631-6014** GP Dash 2 Standard Production

**NEW 631-6015** SD Dash 2 Standard Production

**NEW 631-6016** GP Late Production - LMS

**NEW 631-6017** GP Late Production - HMS

**NEW 631-6018** GP Wide Platform Steps

**NEW 631-6019** GP35

**NEW 631-6020** GP38/40

**NEW 631-6021** GP38-2/GP39-2 Platform Steps

**NEW 631-6022** BN/BNSD/CN/IC SD40-2

**NEW 631-6023** UP SD38-2/SD40-2

**NEW 631-6024** CPR/SOO SD40-2

**NEW 631-6025** KCS SD40-2

### GMDD Steps 16.49 ea

Designed to work with walkway/frame modules (sold separately) for a drop fit with no cutting or milling. Next-Gen steps are redesigned for added strength and easier construction.

#### 4-Step

**NEW 631-6001** Early GP

**NEW 631-6002** Early SD

**NEW 631-6003** Late GP

**NEW 631-6004** Late SD

#### 3-Step

**NEW 631-6005** Early GP38AC, GP38-2 & Others

**NEW 631-6006** Mid GP

**NEW 631-6007** Late GP

**NEW 631-6008** Initial Production SD

**NEW 631-6009** Early Production SD

**NEW 631-6010** Mid-Production SD

**NEW 631-6011** Late Production SD

**NEW 631-6012** Final Production SD

**NEW 631-6013** BCR SD40-2

## PREISER

IMPORTED FROM GERMANY BY WALTHERS

## INTERIOR DETAILS

**590-17184** Office Equipment **37.99**

**590-17185** Workshop Equipment **33.99**

For Up-To-Date Information and News Bookmark Walthers Web site at

**www.walthers.com**

## SMOKEY VALLEY RAILROAD PRODUCTS

Please visit Walthers Web site at www.walthers.com for a complete listing of all available items.

## LOCOMOTIVE DETAILS

### B Unit Accessories

**676-72** GE High Short Hood/Dash 7 **7.45**

**676-73** GE Utility Cabs/B30-73 **7.45**

### Dynamic Brake Hatch

**676-88** EMD Late GPs **9.45**
For EMD GP60 Phase II. Fits Athearn GP50/60.

### EMD Fans w/Rotating Blades

#### 48" Original

**676-139** Single **3.45**

**676-140** Set of Three **8.95**
For GP50, GP60 and GP60M dynamic brakes. Also used on F45, FP45, SDP40F, SD40-2, SD40T-2 and other GP and SD units.

#### 48" Q Fans

**676-143** Set of Three **8.95**
For later GP and SD units.

#### 52"

**676-141** Single **3.45**
For SD50, SD60, SD60M, SD70 and other units.

### Grilles

**676-138** GP9 **3.45**
Designed to backdate the Proto 2000 GP18 to a GP9. Can be adapted to other engines where a see-through GP9 grille is desired.

### Handrail Kits 16.95 ea (Unless Noted)

Make any diesel more realistic. Includes .015" wire, brass handrail stanchion castings (cored for .015" wire) and bending templates.

**676-14** GE U Boat-Bachmann U36B, Athearn B Units

**676-19** T&D SD40-2, SD40T-2 & Athearn SD40-2

**676-23** Cary & Athearn SW1500/SW1000.

**676-30** Athearn GP38-2/40-2

**676-31** Atlas-Stewart RS-3

**676-41** Con-Cor MP15

**676-42** Athearn SD45 & SDP40

**676-45** Atlas RS-11 & RSD-12 **16.95**

**676-82** Atlas GP7 **17.95**

**676-87** Railpower CF7

**676-200** Dash 8-40CW **17.95**

**676-211** GP60M

**676-212** GP60B

**676-214** GP35

**676-216** GE AC4400 CW **17.95**

**676-252** SD90MAC **17.95**

### Handrail Stanchions

#### Brass

Castings cored for .015" wire, sold separately.

**676-100** EMD 1st Generation **13.95**
GP/SD7 and Early GP9.

**676-101** Old GP/SD9 pkg(28) **12.95**
Fits GP9, GP18 and GP20; SD9, SD18 and SD24.

**676-103** Modern GP pkg(28) **12.95**
Also fits SD second generation diesels.

**676-104** Modern SD pkg(37) **12.95**

**676-108** Alco Road Switchers - Old pkg(22) **8.95**

**676-110** GE U Boats pkg(30) **12.95**

**676-118** GE Dash 8/9 CW **13.95**

**676-135** SD60 pkg(59) **13.95**

#### Plastic 6.45 ea

**676-205** EMD 2nd Generation pkg(28)

**676-206** GP9, GP18, GP20, GP50, GP18, GP20, GP24

### Handrail Tees

**676-102** Plastic pkg(8) **4.45**

## STEWART PRODUCTS

### Cast Metal Details 3.10 ea

**683-804** Fire Extinguishers pkg(10)

**683-820** Open Wood Barrels pkg(10)

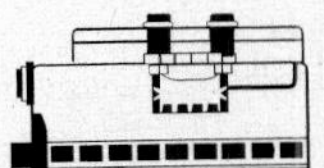

**683-821** Diesel Engine

**683-823** Semi-Trailer Hoses pkg(6)

Customize any kit or scratchbuilt marine model with this line of highly detailed parts, made of polyurethane resin or metal. See the complete line of Seaport Model Works boat kits in the Vehicles section.

# BOAT PARTS

## Bitts pkg(4) 3.95 ea (Unless Noted)

663-P35HO 663-P36HO

**663-P35HO** Double - 1/4" Tall
**663-P36HO** Single - 3/8" Tall
**NEW 663-P79HO** Double Bitt pkg(2) **3.50**

## Bollards pkg(4) 2.95 ea

663-P13HO 663-P19HO

**663-P13HO** Double - 5/32" Tall
**663-P19HO** Bollard Crossbar - 9/32" pkg(3)

**663-P48HO** With Crossbar - 7/32" Tall

## Capstans pkg(2) 3.00 ea

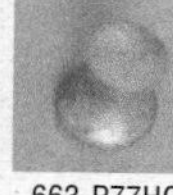

663-P37HO 663-P77HO

**663-P37HO** Powered - 3/8" Tall
**663-P77HO** Unpowered - 7/32" Tall

## Cleats

663-P15HO 663-P30HO

**663-P15HO** 9/32 x 3/32" pkg(8) **3.50**
**663-P30HO** 3/8 x 1/8" pkg(8) **3.95**

## Companions pkg(4) 3.95 ea

663-M39HO 663-M52HO

**663-M39HO** Measures 1/2 x 1/2 x 9/16"
**663-M52HO** Measures 17/32 x 15/32 x 7/16"

## Fittings

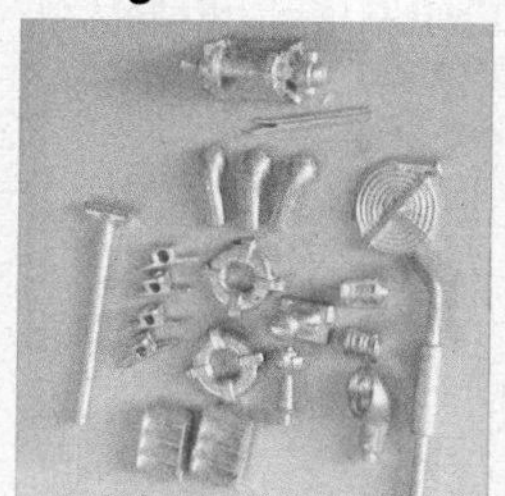

**663-SA12HO** Sardine Carrier - Set of 20 Metal Parts **16.95**

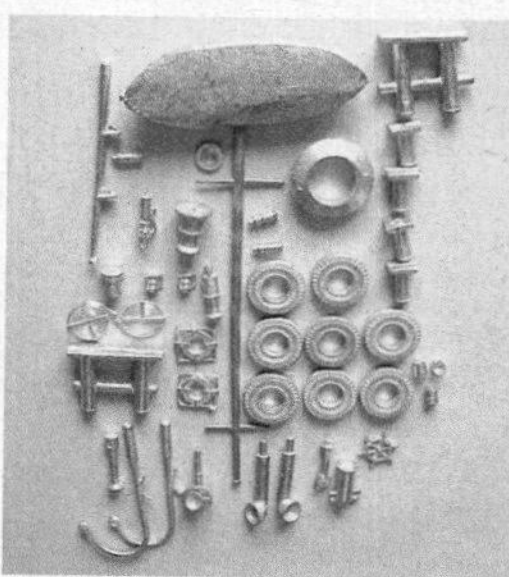

**663-SA19HO** Tugboat - Set of 46 Metal Parts **36.95**

## Hatches

663-M38HO 663-M40HO

**663-M38HO** Cargo Hatch w/Cover - 1-1/8 x 1" pkg(4) **5.95**
**663-M40HO** Deck Hatch pkg(5) **3.95**

663-M41HO 663-M49HO

**663-M41HO** Companion/Hatchway pkg(4) **3.95**
**663-M49HO** Deck Hatch w/Cover -3/4 x 11/16" pkg(4) **4.95**
**663-M51HO** Deck Hatch pkg(4) **3.95**

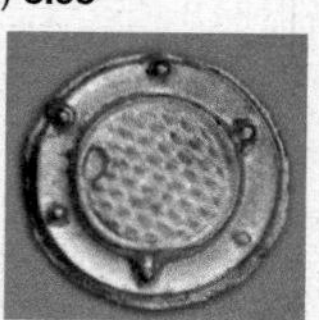

**663-P56HO** Manhole Cover/Car Float Hatch -7/16" Diameter pkg(6) **4.95**

## Life Rings

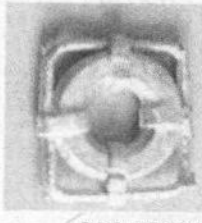

663-P25HO 663-P41HO

**663-P25HO** With Rope - 3/8" Diameter pkg(4) **3.95**
**663-P41HO** Plain - 5/16" Diameter pkg(4) **2.95**

## Pilot House Details

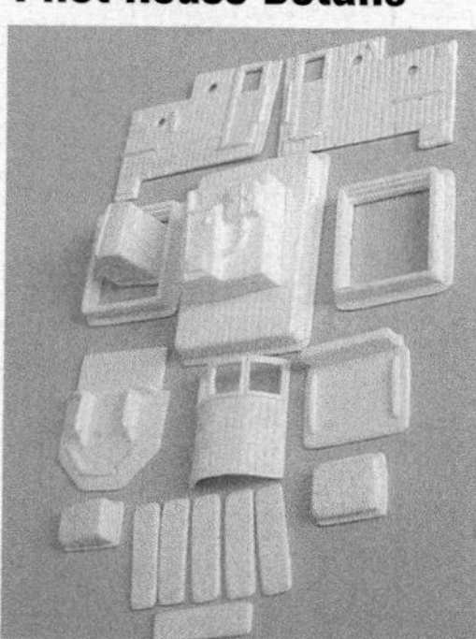

**663-SA3HO** Pilot House Cabin & Deck Furniture For Sardine Carrier **15.00**
Includes Pilot House (SA18HO), plus four hatches and one companion.

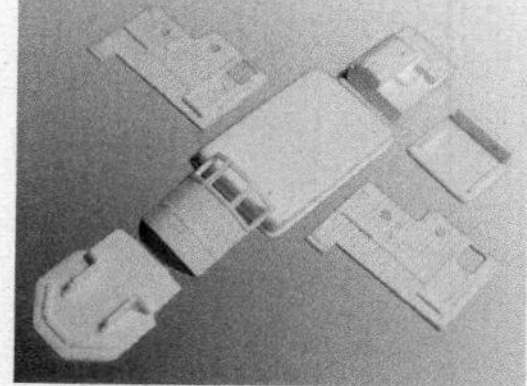

**663-SA18HO** Pilot House - Set of 7 Resin Parts **8.95**

**663-P22HO** Interior Fitting Set **4.75**
Includes compass, speed telegraph, wheel mount and wheel.

## Searchlights

663-P27HO 663-P43HO

**663-P27HO** 9/16" Tall pkg(2) **3.00**
**663-P43HO** 9/32" Tall pkg(3) **2.95**

## Ship's Wheel

**663-P80HO** 3/8" Diameter **3.50**

## Smokestacks pkg(4) 3.00 ea

663-P38HO 663-P39HO

**663-P38HO** Galley - 1/2" Tall
**663-P39HO** 7/16" Tall

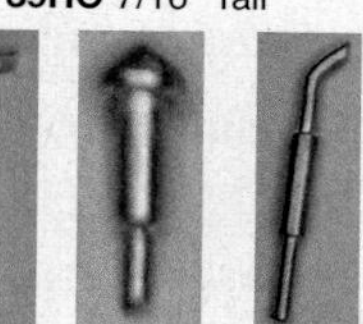

663-P46HO 663-P50HO 663-P51HO

**663-P46HO** "Tee"-Shaped - 1-1/2" Tall
**663-P50HO** Galley - Straight - 1/4" Tall
**663-P51HO** Curved Top - 1-1/16"

## Tug Boat Bitts

Each measures 5/8" tall.

663-P71HO 663-P73HO

**663-P71HO** Forward **3.50**
**663-P73HO** Aft **3.50**

## Steps

**663-P70HO** 3/8 x 5/8" **3.50**

## Ventilators & Accessories

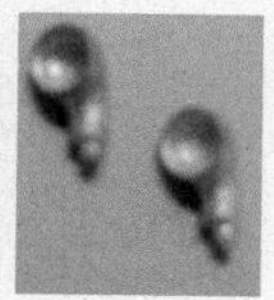

663-P24HO 663-P32HO

**663-P24HO** Ventilator Long Cowl Type - 3/4" Tall pkg(3) **3.50**
**663-P32HO** Ventilator Stubby Cowl Type - 11/32" Tall pkg(4) **3.00**

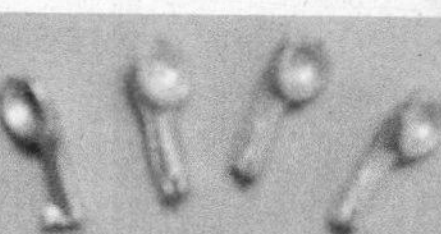

**663-P47HO** Cowls - 3/8" Tall pkg(4) **2.95**

## Miscellaneous

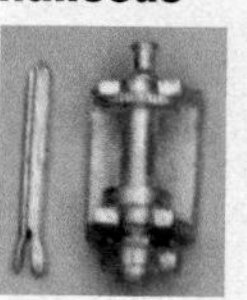

**663-P17HO** Single Drum Winch (3-Piece Set) **3.75**
Measures 5/8" long x 7/32" ta

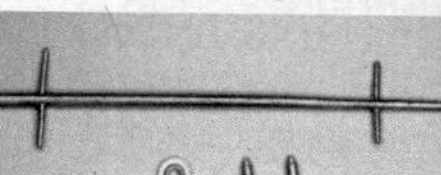

**663-P18HO** Main Mast - 3-1/2" Tall **3.50**
Includes mast, spreaders, lights and base.

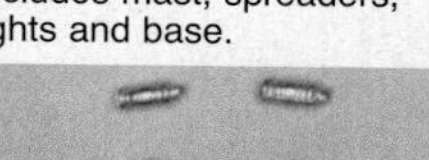

**663-P23HO** Cabin Top Mast w/Lights 1-13/16" Tall **2.95**

**663-P26HO** Fire Hose Coil - 3/8" Diameter pkg(3) **2.95**

**663-P28HO** Cabin Top Running Light - 5/32" Tall pkg(4) **2.95**
**663-P31HO** Buckets - 1/8" Tall pkg(4) **3.00**

**663-P52HO** 3 Steps pkg(4) **3.00**
Measures 7/32" wide x 5/16" high.

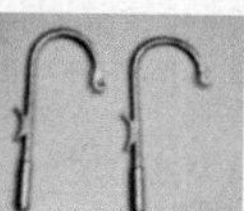
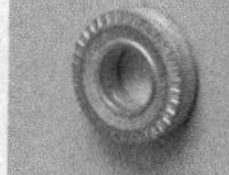

663-P33HO 663-P34HO

**663-P33HO** Davits 1-3/8" Tall 1 Pair **2.95**
**663-P34HO** Old Tires - 1/2" Diameter pkg(6) **3.75**
Use as "fenders" to protect the sides of a hull.

**663-P74HO** Tug Whistle -1/2" Tall pkg(2) **3.00**

# CARFLOAT ACCESSORIES

All parts listed below fit Walthers Carfloat #933-3152, sold separately.

**663-P64HO** Rail Fasteners for Carfloat/Ferry Deck - Each 3" Long pkg(16) **7.95**

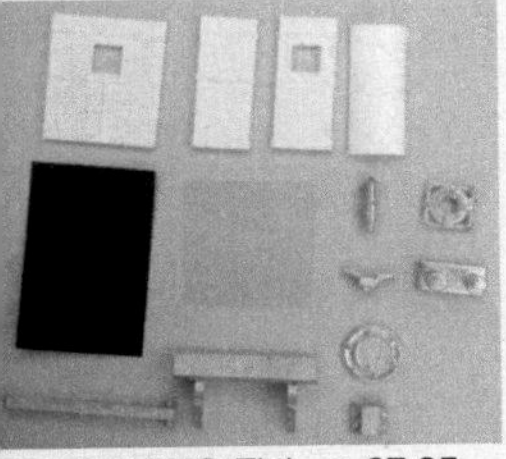

**663-SA10HO** Fittings **27.95**
Set of 54 parts includes three carstops, eight manholes, 8 cleats, eight double bitts, 20-piece toggle bar assembly, one life ring, and one smokejack in cast metal, plus a five-piece resin cabin assembly.

**663-SA13HO** Transfer Building Framework 28 Pieces; Extends to 22" **22.95**
Includes seven building frames, 15 large platform supports, one medium and one small 2-step stairways and two life preservers. All parts are cast metal.
**663-SA14HO** Transfer Building Framework Kit; 9" Building Extension **8.95**

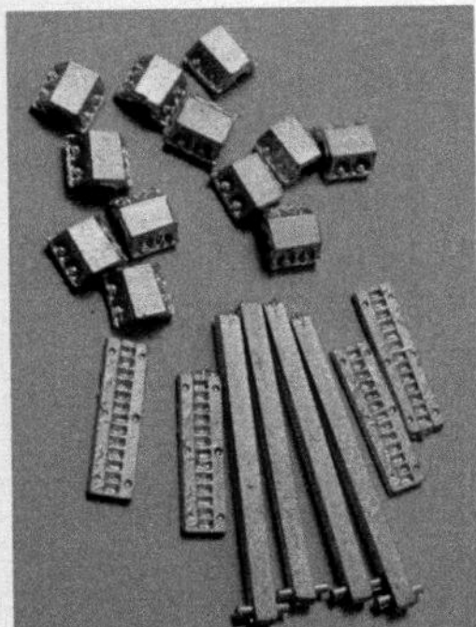

**663-SA15HO** Toggle Bar Assembly **10.95**
Set includes 20 metal castings: 12 toggle pockets, four toggle bars and four racks.

DIVISION OF CIRCUITRON
Easy-to-build white metal kits (unless noted) include detailed parts and assembly instructions.

## Electric Motors

**652-3512** Industrial Electric Motors **5.95**

## Fence Hardware

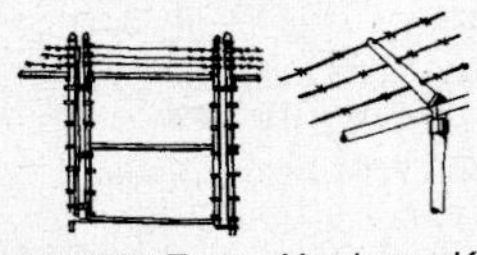

**652-3504** Fence Hardware Kit **8.95**
Great detail around any factory, business, parking lot, locomotive on display in the city park, or anywhere you need a realistic security fence. Includes cast metal posts, gate, latch and flat wire. Posts are 12 scale feet tall, can be cut. Also makes a nice smaller fence in O or S Scale. For the finishing touch, add Micro-Mesh fence material (sold separately) and barbed wire.

## Flat Wire

**652-1504** Nickel Silver (5') **2.95**
Measures .010 x .030", can be used to model load restraint banding.

## LP TANK

**652-3505** LP Gas Tank pkg(2) **5.95**
Industrial-sized propane tanks are common throughout rural areas. Includes styrene parts for two tanks.

## Micro-Mesh

Lightweight, non-woven, raised diamond pattern mesh. Measures just .005" thick; 3 x 6" 7.5 x 15cm.

**652-3500** Aluminum **4.95**

**652-3501** Brass **5.95**

## Pallets

**652-5002** Wooden Pallet pkg(12) **2.95**
4' square, molded in brown styrene.

# S&S HOBBY PRODUCTS

## ATSF Radio Antennas

**643-310** pkg(2) **8.99**
Adds realistic detail to E units, F units, PAs, GP7s and many other engines and cabooses. Kit includes etched stainless steel platforms and legs, brass rod and Detail Associates can-type antennas.

## Photo-Etched Diesel Grille Kits

**643-306** For Athearn SD40T-2 **4.99**

**643-307** For Athearn AMD103 **5.99**

**643-308** For Walthers F40PH **6.99**

## E-Z Safety Tread

**643-311** pkg(2) **6.99**
Super thin polypropylene realistic raised tread. Easy to trim, paint and glue to any engine or model. Each package comes with two 3-1/2 x 5-3/4" sheets.

# SELLEY Finishing Touches

Detail parts are unpainted metal castings.

## Boat

**675-673** Rowboat **2.30**

## Brake Parts 2.00 ea

**675-50** Brake Cylinder

## Cans, Cases, Buckets, Barrels & Drums pkg(12) 3.30 ea (Unless Noted)

**675-151** Oil Drums

**675-152** Flour Barrels

**675-153** Packing Cases

**675-154** Milk Cans

**675-298** Buckets pkg(3) **2.30**

**675-299** Beer Kegs

## Carts, Trailers & Trucks

**675-142** Hand Truck **2.30**

**675-143** Baggage Cart **4.00**

**675-144** 4-Wheel Baggage Truck **4.00**

**675-145** 2-Wheel Baggage Truck **2.60**

**675-148** Industrial Trailer pkg(2) **2.30**

**675-149** Stake Trailer **2.60**

## Feedwater Heater

**675-379** Elesco Type w/Bracket **2.00**

## Fire Hose

**675-595** On Rack **2.00**

## Gas Pumps w/Man 3.60 ea

**675-175** Shell

**675-176** ESSO

**675-177** Texaco

## Interiors

**675-166** Pump & Tub **2.30**

**675-419** Country Store Set **8.60**
Includes figures, scale, pot belly stove, pail and shovel, dolly, two chairs, barrel, hatchet and assorted cases.

**675-646** Stove, Hod & Shovel **2.60**

## Luggage

**675-150** pkg(12) **4.00**

**675-656** Trunks (Assortment) pkg(6) **3.30**



## Mailboxes 2.60 ea (Unless Noted)

**675-173** Letter Boxes pkg(4)

**675-174** Package Mailboxes pkg(3)

**675-235** Rural Mailboxes pkg(4)

**675-641** Mail Crane **3.30**

## Miniature Tools

**675-140** Tools (Set of 5) **2.60**

**675-141** Scales pkg(2) **2.30**

**675-290** Mower & Roller **2.60**

**675-605** Step Ladder **2.60**

**675-659** Compressor Kit **3.50**

**675-1391** Wheelbarrows pkg(2) **2.40**

## MOW Car Kits

**675-283** Hand Car **6.60**

**675-608** Go Devil **13.20**

## Passenger Car Weights 3.00 ea

Flat, cast metal weights for improved rolling performance.

**675-703** 1/2oz Athearn pkg(4)

**675-704** 1/2oz pkg(4)

**675-705** 3/4oz pkg(3)

**675-706** 1-1/4oz pkg(2)

**675-707** 1oz pkg(2)

## Street Details

**675-113** Parking Meters pkg(12) **3.00**

**675-172** Fire Alarm Boxes pkg(4) **2.60**

**675-180** Fire Hydrants pkg(12) **3.30**

**675-184** Trash Boxes pkg(2) **2.30**

**675-230** Barricades pkg(2) **3.00**

## Transformers

**675-257** Large **7.20**

**675-510** Giant **8.60**

**675-637** Line Pole Type pkg(6) **3.30**

## Vending Machines

**675-679** pkg(3) **3.90**
Includes ice, soft drink and newspaper machines.

## CATALOG

**650-9999** HO #10 Catalog **4.00**
Add more realism to your layout with the complete line of structures, cast metal parts and details. The complete selection is illustrated in this catalog, and all items are available from Walthers by special order.

## CAST METAL DETAILS

All castings are unpainted white metal.

### Air Conditioners

**650-2467** Window pkg(7) **2.95**

**650-2473** 20-Ton Roof **4.35**

### Barrels, Baskets, Cans & Kegs

**650-2017** Barrel w/Top (separate) pkg(4) **2.89**

**650-2162** Reed Basket pkg(3) **2.49**

**650-2164** Bushel Basket pkg(3) **2.49**

**650-2277** Milk Can pkg(6) **2.69**

**650-2314** Trash Can pkg(3) **2.89**

**650-2403** Garbage Can 30-Gallon pkg(3) **2.89**

**650-2406** Cream Cans pkg(6) **2.49**

**650-2421** Open Garbage Can 30-Gallon pkg(4) **2.89**

**650-2429** Open Garbage Can 20-Gallon pkg(4) **2.89**

**650-2430** Garbage Can 20-Gallon pkg(4) **2.89**

**650-2555** Small Wood Beer Keg pkg(4) **2.69**

### Brackets

650-2019

650-2021

**650-2019** Double pkg(6) **3.49**

**650-2021** Finial Small pkg(12) **2.89**

650-2022

650-2023

**650-2022** Porch "Fan" pkg(6) **3.19**

**650-2023** Eave Small pkg(10) **3.19**

650-2024

650-2026

**650-2024** Eave Medium pkg(10) **3.39**

**650-2026** Porch pkg(3) **2.89**

650-2027

650-2060

**650-2027** Sign pkg(3) **2.89**

**650-2060** Eave Ornate pkg(6) **3.49**

650-2107

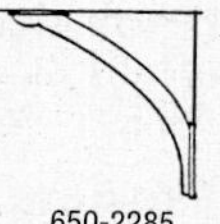
650-2285

**650-2107** Roof Overhang Eave pkg(6) **3.49**

**650-2285** Eave-Large pkg(10) **3.69**

**650-2289** Ornate Eave-Large pkg(10) **3.19**

**650-2290** Ornate Eave-Small pkg(10) **2.99**

**650-2527** Eave pkg(3) **2.89**

**650-2548** Wooden Eave pkg(3) **2.89**

**650-2556** Gable End pkg(4) **2.89**

### Chimneys

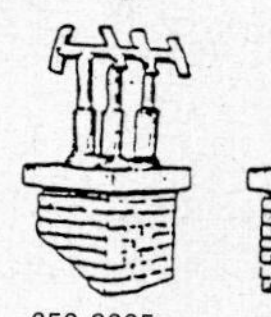
650-2005

650-2006

**650-2005** Tenement Chimney Porch Roof 3-Vent **3.19**

**650-2006** Tenement Chimney Floor Roof 3-Vent **3.19**

650-2007

650-2008

**650-2007** Tenement Chimney Porch Roof 4-Vent **3.39**

**650-2008** Tenement Chimney Flat Roof 4-Vent **3.39**

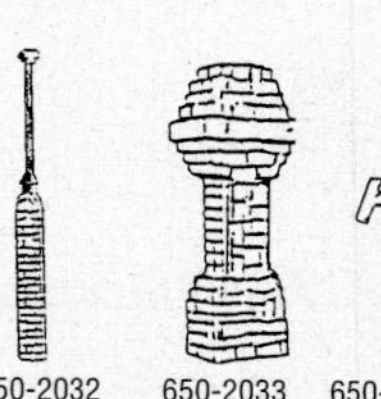
650-2032 650-2033 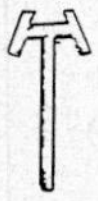 650-2066

**650-2032** Emporium Chimney **3.19**

**650-2033** Tall Brick Chimney pkg(2) **3.19**

**650-2065** Smokejack Pitch Roof w/Cap pkg(4) **3.19**

**650-2066** Tall 2-Vent Jack pkg(4) **3.39**

**650-2166** Short Smokejack-Pitched pkg(4) **2.99**

**650-2167** Tall Smokejack-Pitched pkg(4) **2.99**

650-2178 650-2284 650-2329

**650-2178** Stackable Brick Chimney pkg(2) **2.69**

**650-2284** Short Brick Chimney pkg(2) **2.49**

**650-2329** Two-Vent Brick Chimney **2.99**

**650-2358** Short Chimney pkg(2) **2.69**

**650-2428** Chimney 7' w/Tapered Flue **2.99**

**650-2441** Smokejack w/Taper-Straight pkg(2) **3.19**

**650-2443** Smokejack w/Taper "T" pkg(2) **3.19**

**650-2452** Cone Top Smoke-jack w/Taper pkg(2) **3.19**

**650-2487** Tenement Chimney pkg(2) **2.49**

**650-2499** Brick Chimney Flat pkg(2) **2.49**

**650-2503** Brick Chimney Stone pkg(2) **2.49**

**650-2505** Tall Chimney Stone Cap pkg(2) **3.19**

**650-2515** Tenement Chimney 2-Vent **2.99**

**650-2517** Tall Brick Chimney pkg(2) **3.19**

**650-2518** Short Brick Chimney pkg(2) **2.49**

**650-2519** Round Smokestack pkg(2) **3.19**

**650-2532** T-Style Smokejack pkg(4) **3.39**

**650-2536** Tall Round Smokejack **3.19**

**650-2542** Brick Chimney Stone pkg(2) **2.49**

**650-2544** Large Stone Chimney pkg(2) **3.19**

**650-2546** Short Brick Chimney Concrete pkg(2) **2.49**

**650-2550** Short Chimney w/Flue pkg(2) **2.49**

**650-2551** Tall Chimney w/Flue pkg(2) **3.19**

**650-2553** Brick Chimney w/Taper pkg(2) **2.49**

### City Street Details

**650-2011** City Tree Planters w/Post Small pkg(2) **3.39**

650-2012

650-2036

650-2037

**650-2012** City Tree Planters w/Post Large pkg(2) **3.39**

**650-2036** Industrial Lamp Large pkg(10) **2.69**

**650-2037** Industrial Lamp Small pkg(10) **2.49**

650-2039

650-2040

**650-2039** Porch Lamp pkg(2) **2.69**

**650-2040** Back Door Lamp pkg(2) **2.69**

**650-2058** City Canopy pkg(2) **2.89**

**650-2318** Electric Street Lamp-Single Light (Nonworking) **3.39**

650-2319

650-2336

**650-2319** Gas Street Lamp-Single Light (Nonworking) **3.39**

**650-2320** Park Bench pkg(2) **2.99**

**650-2333** Manhole Cover pkg(6) **2.49**

**650-2334** Sewer Grating pkg(3) **2.49**

**650-2335** Police Call Box-Wall Mount pkg(3) **2.49**

**650-2336** Fire Call Box on Post pkg(3) **2.69**

**650-2337** Water Hydrant pkg(4) **3.19**

**650-2345** Electric Street Lamp-Double Light (Nonworking) **4.49**

**650-2393** Telephone Pole Crossarms pkg(12) **2.99**

**650-2427** Drinking Fountain pkg(3) **2.49**

**650-2486** Street Lamp J Top **3.89**

**650-2491** Fire Plug #2 pkg(4) **2.49**

**650-2493** Cast Iron Bench pkg(2) **2.99**

**650-2516** Barber Pole pkg(2) **2.99**

**650-2525** Two Arm Utility Pole pkg(2) **4.19**

**650-2534** Four Arm Utility Pole pkg(2) **4.89**

**650-2549** Metal Lamp pkg(1? **2.69**

### Construction Equipment

**650-9124** Jensen Oil Pump **27.95**

**650-9125** Jennings Lumber Co. Log Skidder **34.95**

**650-9126** V&T Jib Crane **34.9?**

### Cornices

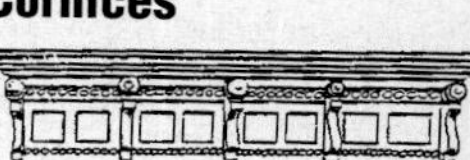

**650-2173** Ornate Storefront **4.29**

**650-2181** Ornate #3 pkg(2) **3.39**

**650-2346** Ornate #4 **4.19**

**650-2347** Ornate #5 **3.79**

**650-2432** Ornate #6 **4.19**

### Crates

650-2151

650-2152

**650-2151** 24 x 18 x 24" pkg(3) **3.19**

**650-2152** 42 x 30 x 18" pkg(3) **3.19**

650-2153

650-2154

**650-2153** 36 x 30 x 36" pkg(2) **3.19**

**650-2154** 30 x 36 x 66" pkg(2) **3.19**

650-2155

650-2156

**650-2155** 54 x 54 x 54" pkg(2) **3.49**

**650-2156** Stacked 2-High Empty pkg(4) **2.49**

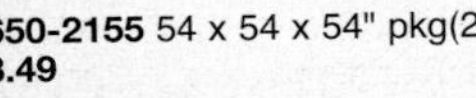

650-2157

650-2158

**650-2157** Stacked 3-High Empty pkg(4) **2.69**

**650-2158** Stacked 4-High Empty pkg(4) **2.89**

650-2159

650-21560

**650-2159** Stacked 2-High Filled pkg(4) **2.49**

**650-2160** Stacked 3-High Filled pkg(4) **2.69**

**650-2161** Stacked 4-High Filled pkg(4) **2.89**

**650-2278** Stack of Filled-5 High pkg(4) **2.99**

**650-2279** Single-Filled pkg(4) **2.49**

**650-2280** Single-Empty pkg(4) **2.49**

**650-2310** Stack of Crates-Empty 5 High pkg(4) **2.99**

**650-2385** Filled (3)-Flat pkg(4) **2.69**

**650-2386** Empty (3)-Flat pkg(4) **2.69**

## Depot Details

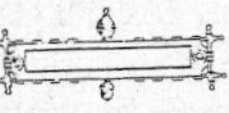

**650-2096** Station Signboard pkg(2) **4.29**

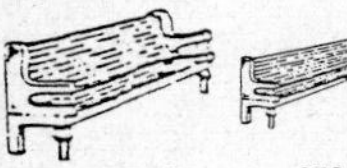
650-2148

650-2149

**650-2148** Station Bench (Interior/Exterior) Straight pkg(2) **3.69**

**650-2149** Station Bench (Interior/Exterior) Corner In pkg(2) **3.69**

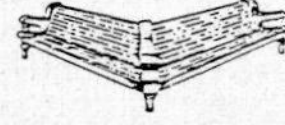

**650-2150** Station Bench (Interior/Exterior) Corner Out pkg(2) **3.69**

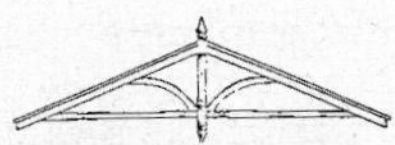

**650-2176** Passenger Station Platform Truss pkg(2) **4.49**

**650-2182** Telegraph Sounder pkg(3) **2.69**

**650-2275** Train Order Signal pkg(2) **2.89**

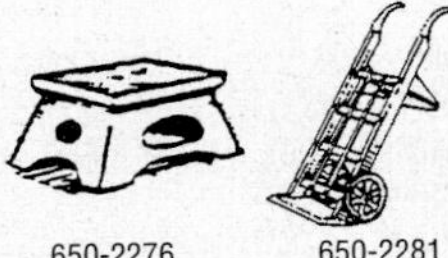
650-2276 650-2281

**650-2276** Passenger Assist Steps pkg(4) **2.89**

**650-2281** Two Wheel Dolly pkg(2) **3.39**

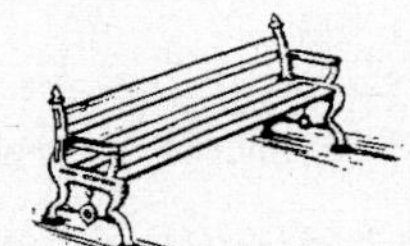

**650-2282** Cast Iron Bench w/Wood Slates pkg(2) **2.99**

**650-2283** Baggage Barrow **4.49**

**650-2369** Train Order Signal **7.99**

**650-2370** Station Platform Lamps pkg(3) **4.99**

**650-2387** Ornate Sign Panel pkg(2) **3.79**

**650-2390** Bay Ticket Window **3.69**

**650-2501** Large Wooden Pallets pkg(6) **3.89**

**650-2540** Telegraph Pole pkg(2) **4.19**

## Doors

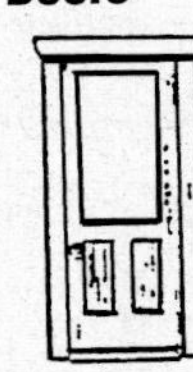
650-2061

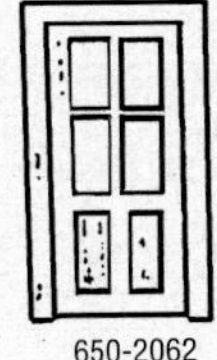
650-2062

**650-2061** 2-Panel 1-Lite pkg(2) **2.69**

**650-2062** 2-Panel, 4-Lite Steel Frame pkg(2) **2.69**

**650-2085** Door Hinges pkg(12) **2.69**

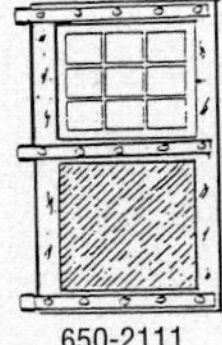
650-2111

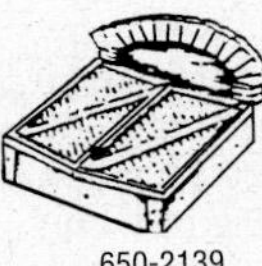
650-2139

**650-2111** English House Door w/Hinge pkg(2) **4.19**

**650-2139** Cellar Door, Brick, Set **3.39**

**650-2165** Commercial-Recessed **3.39**

650-2199

650-2200

**650-2199** Narrow 4-Panel 6-Lite pkg(2) **2.69**

**650-2200** Narrow 2-Panel 1 Lite pkg(2) **2.69**

**650-2256** Virginia City pkg(2) **3.19**

**650-2258** Colonial Arch pkg(2) **3.19**

**650-2260** 4-Panel w/Transom pkg(2) **3.19**

650-2262 650-2264

**650-2262** Colonial Ornate pkg(2) **3.19**

**650-2264** 2-Panel, 4-Lite pkg(2) **2.69**

**650-2265** Saloon pkg(2) **2.89**

**650-2268** 6-Panel pkg(2) **2.69**

**650-2269** 4-Panel pkg(2) **2.69**

**650-2327** Ornate to Match Windows #650-2326 pkg(2) **3.19**

**650-2351** Curved Arch Door pkg(2) **3.19**

**650-2360** Store Front **2.99**

**650-2363** Freight w/Transom **2.99**

**650-2365** Freight Without Transom pkg(2) **2.99**

**650-2366** Steel Fire pkg(2) **3.69**

**650-2367** Wood Frame, 1-Lite, 2-Panel pkg(2) **2.69**

**650-2368** Victorian 2-Lite pkg(2) **3.19**

**650-2435** Wood Brace, Factory **2.99**

**650-2482** 2-Lite Door w/Transom pkg(2) **2.69**

**650-2524** Two Panel Wood Door pkg(2) **2.69**

## Drums

**650-2328** 55-Gallon Oil pkg(6) **2.89**

**650-2349** Stack 55-Gallon **2.99**

**650-2417** 15-Gallon pkg(8) **2.89**

**650-2418** 30-Gallon pkg(7) **2.89**

**650-2419** #2 55-Gallon pkg(6) **2.89**

**650-2449** 55-Gallon w/Trash pkg(5) **2.89**

**650-2462** Open/Used 55-Gallon pkg(7) **3.65**

**650-2463** Open/New 55-Gallon pkg(7) **3.65**

**650-2488** 55-Gallon Oil #3 pkg(6) **2.89**

**650-2514** 55-Gallon Oil #4 pkg(6) **2.89**

## Emergency Vehicle

**650-9119** Gould 1890 Fire Engine **21.95**

## Farm Details

**650-7209** Farm Machinery **39.95**

**650-7269** Farm Yard Details **9.95**

**650-9139** Drag Disc **6.95**

**650-9140** Harrow (Drag Rack) **6.95**

**650-9141** Foot Treadle Grinding Wheel **5.95**

**650-9142** Plow **6.95**

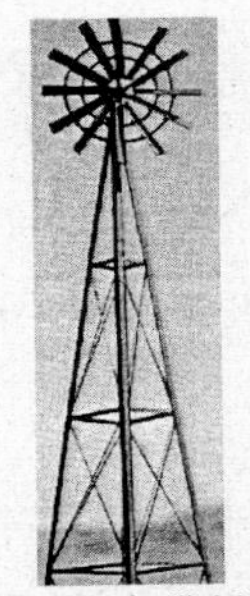

**650-9143** Windmill **14.95**

## Fences

650-2030

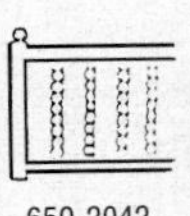
650-2042

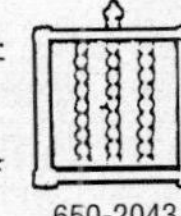
650-2043

**650-2030** Ornate Gate pkg(3) **2.69**

**650-2042** Ornate Section pkg(3) **2.49**

**650-2043** Gate for Ornate Fence Section #650-2042 pkg(2) **2.49**

**650-4127** Corrugated Iron Fence w/Gates Scale 200' (Metal) Kit **14.95**

**650-4128** Chain Link w/Gates Scale 200' (Brass) Kit **26.15**

## Finials

**650-2287** Large pkg(8) **2.49**

**650-2288** Small pkg(8) **2.49**

**650-2395** Extra Large Ball pkg(4) **2.69**

**650-2433** Ball Large pkg(6) **2.89**

## Freight Car Loads

Resin castings.

**650-8050** Banded Lumber pkg(4) **11.95**

**650-8051** Covered Machine pkg(3) **12.95**

## Gas Station Details

650-2015

650-2016

**650-2015** Engine Block 4 Cycle w/Exhaust & Transmission **2.69**

**650-2016** Engine Block 4 Cycle w/Exhaust, Transmission & Mounts **2.69**

**650-2067** Gas Station Hoist Platform **2.69**

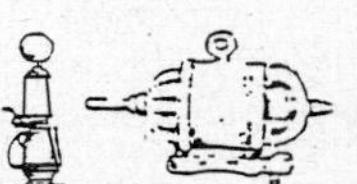
650-2068 650-2098 650-2174

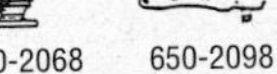

**650-2068** Ornate 1929 Gas Pump **4.19**

**650-2098** Electric Motor Large pkg(2) **2.89**

**650-2174** Oil Can Rack pkg(2) **2.49**

# SUPER DETAILING PARTS

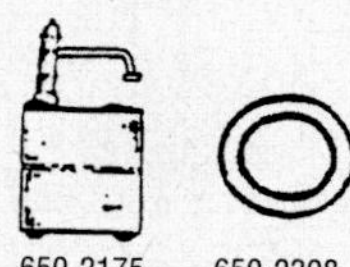
650-2175 650-2308

**650-2175** Oil Highboy (Bulk Oil) pkg(3) **3.49**

**650-2308** Tires pkg(10) **2.69**

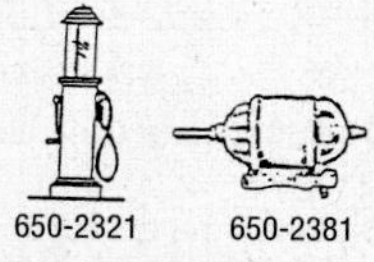
650-2321 650-2381

**650-2321** 1929 Gas Pump **4.19**

**650-2381** Small Electric Motor pkg(4) **2.69**

**650-2394** Gas Pump Island **2.49**

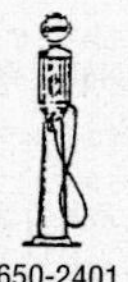
650-2401

650-2402

**650-2401** 1930s Gas Pump **4.19**

**650-2402** Round Gas Can pkg(4) **2.69**

**650-2407** Auto Tires #2 pkg(10) **2.69**

**650-2408** Auto Tires #3 pkg(10) **2.69**

**650-2409** Auto Tires #4 pkg(10) **2.69**

**650-2453** 1950s Electric Gas Pump pkg(2) **2.69**

**650-2454** Junk Barrel w/Trash Pile pkg(3) **2.89**

**650-2476** Auto Engines Kit pkg(3) **7.45**

**650-2496** Auto Tire Stand pkg(2) **2.49**

**650-2520** Gas Station Hoist Kit **2.69**

**650-2521** Auto Tire Pump w/Stand pkg(4) **2.69**

**650-8028** Auto Junk Piles **15.95**

## Gears

**650-2184** Small Gears pkg(6) **2.49**

**650-2185** Large Gears & Sheave pkg(3) **2.49**

**650-2377** Set of Gears pkg(12) **4.49**

## Interior Detail Sets

Complete sets of parts.

**650-7200** Commercial Office Interior **43.95**

**650-7201** Grocery Store Interior **49.95**

**650-7202** Passenger Depot, Exterior/Interior **36.95**

**650-7203** General Store, Exterior/Interior **51.95**

**650-7204** Roundhouse Interior **51.95**

**650-7205** Furniture Factory **29.95**

**650-7206** Hardware Store Interior & Exterior **26.96**

**650-7207** Pool Hall **49.95**

**650-7208** Barber Shop **41.95**

**650-7212** Service Station **26.95**

**650-7213** Wischer's Washers **26.96**

**650-7214** Martha's Country Market **16.97**

**650-7215** Dixie's Diner **9.95**

**650-7217** Living Room w/Walls **16.95**

**650-7218** Country Kitchen w/Walls **21.95**

**650-7219** Master Bedroom w/Walls **13.95**

**650-7220** Guest Bedroom w/Walls **13.95**

**650-7221** Dining Room w/Walls **13.95**

**650-7222** Study w/Walls **19.95**

**650-7223** Family Room w/Walls **19.95**

**650-7224** Full Bath w/Walls **13.95**

**650-7226** Machine Shop **44.95**

**650-7227** Street Details **13.95**

**650-7228** San Francisco Office Building Millwork (For Kit #1113) **16.95**

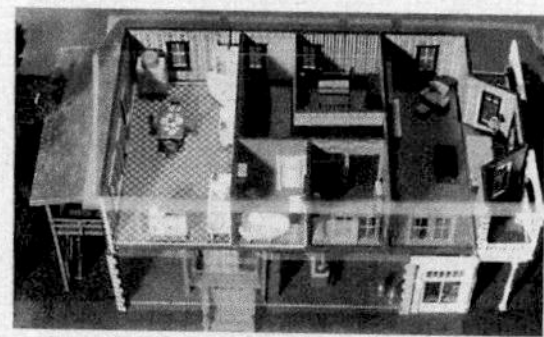

**650-7229** The Store Interior (For Kit #1118) **86.95**



## Loco Details

**650-2189** Gauge Cluster pkg(2) **2.49**

**650-2222** Loco Cab Seat pkg(2) **2.99**

**650-2223** Johnson Bar pkg(2) **2.99**

**650-2224** Coal Rake pkg(3) **2.69**

**650-7230** Loco Detail Set #1 **5.95**

**650-7231** Loco Detail Set #2 **5.95**

## Logs & Stumps

All except #650-2539 are resin castings.

**650-2539** Tree Stump Small & Large pkg(2) **4.19**

**650-8007** Small Stumps pkg(20) **11.95**

**650-8008** Large Stumps pkg(16) **11.95**

**650-8020** Large Floating Logs pkg(9) **5.95**

**650-8021** Small Floating Logs pkg(18) **11.95**

## Master Touch Details

**650-7233** Industrial Roof-Top Set **21.95**

**650-7234** Commercial Roof-Top Set **21.95**

**650-7235** For Bachmann Sears Home **26.95**
Set of interior furnishings and additional exterior details, designed especially for the "Sears Catalog House" kit.

## Miniature Tools

650-2048

650-2049

**650-2048** Dynamite Plunger pkg(3) **2.69**

**650-2049** Dynamite Keg pkg(4) **2.69**

**650-2089** Steel Ladder pkg(4) **2.89**

**650-2090** Fire Extinguisher No. 2 pkg(6) **3.19**

**650-2101** Nuts/Bolts/ Washers-15° pkg(12) **2.69**

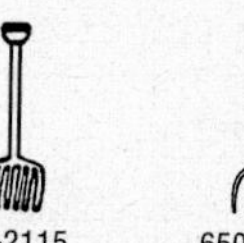
650-2115 650-2116

**650-2115** Manure Fork pkg(3) **2.69**

**650-2116** Pitch Fork pkg(3) **2.69**

**650-2117** Hoe pkg(3) **2.69**

**650-2118** Post Hole Digger pkg(3) **2.89**

**650-2119** Scythe w/Blade pkg(3) **2.89**

650-2123

650-2146

**650-2123** Hand Axe pkg(3) **2.49**

**650-2146** Fire Axe pkg(3) **2.49**

**650-2147** Anvil pkg(2) **2.49**

**650-2168** Small Winch pkg(2) **4.19**

**650-2201** Push Broom pkg(3) **2.69**

**650-2202** Tamp Bar pkg(3) **2.69**

**650-2203** Spike Maul pkg(3) **2.69**

**650-2204** Pry Bar pkg(3) **2.69**

650-2205

650-2206

**650-2205** Spud Wrench pkg(4) **2.49**

**650-2206** Monkey Wrench pkg(3) **2.69**

**650-2207** Screw Jack pkg(3) **3.39**

**650-2208** Track Jack pkg(3) **3.39**

**650-2209** Vice-Jaws Closed pkg(2) **2.89**

**650-2210** Bench Grinder pkg(3) **2.69**

**650-2211** C-Clamp-Large pkg(3) **2.49**

**650-2212** 5-Gallon Can pkg(3) **2.49**

**650-2213** Oil Can-Large pkg **2.49**

**650-2214** Oil Can-Small pkg **2.49**

**650-2215** Pail w/Handle Up pkg(3) **2.69**

**650-2216** Pail w/Handle Dow pkg(3) **2.69**

**650-2217** Canteen pkg(3) **2.6**

**650-2218** Water Bag pkg(3) **2.49**

**650-2219** Water Keg pkg(3) **2.89**

**650-2220** Tin Dipper pkg(6) **2.89**

**650-2221** Grease Pot pkg(3) **2.49**

**650-2233** Scoop pkg(6) **2.89**

**650-2234** Push Cart pkg(2) **3.19**

**650-2238** Scoop Shovel pkg( **2.69**

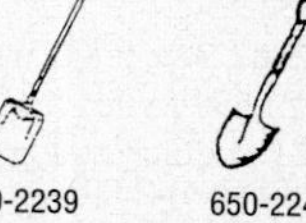
650-2239 650-2240

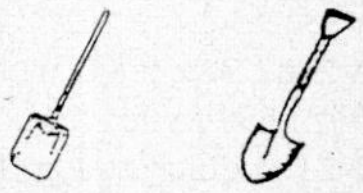

**650-2239** Long Handle Shove pkg(3) **2.69**

**650-2240** Spade Shovel pkg( **2.69**

**650-2298** Lanterns pkg(6) **3.1**

**650-2299** Acetylene Bottle w/Valve pkg(3) **2.69**

**650-2300** Oxygen Bottle w/Valve pkg(3) **2.69**

**650-2301** Tiny Tools-Set A **3.39**

**650-2302** Tiny Tools-Set B **3.39**

**650-2303** Tool Box pkg(3) **2.69**

**650-2304** Lug Wrench pkg(4) **2.69**

**650-2305** Oil Bottle-Small pkg(12) **2.69**

**650-2306** Tire Pump pkg(4) **2.69**

**650-2307** Air Compressor **2.69**

**650-2311** Welding Cart **2.99**

**650-2312** Welding Hose & Nozzle **2.49**

**650-2313** Straight Broom pkg(3) **2.49**

**650-2322** Work Cart **3.69**

**650-2324** Fire Extinguisher #1 pkg(6) **3.19**

**650-2379** Cross Cut Saw & Ax pkg(2) **2.69**

**650-2391** Arc Welder Kit **3.39**

**650-2410** Air Compressor, Large **2.89**

**650-2412** Small Welding Cart & Tanks pkg(3) **2.49**

**650-2415** Acetylene Tanks #2 pkg(4) **2.49**

**650-2416** Oxygen Tanks #2 pkg(4) **2.49**

**650-2468** Portable "A" Frame Hoist **6.15**

**650-2470** Work Tables (3 types) **6.15**

**650-2471** 6' Wooden Stepladder pkg(2) **2.95**

**650-2504** Wooden Ladder pkg(4) **2.89**

**650-2507** Long Spade Shovel pkg(3) **2.69**

**650-2508** Long Scoop Shovel pkg(3) **2.69**

**650-2509** Straight Broom No. 2 pkg(3) **2.69**

**650-2535** Step Stool pkg(4) **2.89**

**650-7211** Blacksmith's Tools & Equipment **8.95**

## Pallets

**650-2455** Wood Pallets (3 Each Small & Large) pkg(6) **3.39**

**650-2466** Hydraulic Pallet Jack pkg(2) **2.95**

## Passenger Car Parts 2.89 ea

**650-2106** Old-Time Water Cooler pkg(3)

**650-2317** Heater pkg(2)

## Piers

**650-2099** Concrete Pier Single pkg(6) **3.39**

**650-2100** Concrete Pier Double pkg(4) **3.79**

**650-2197** Concrete Triple pkg(2) **3.39**

**650-2447** Concrete Pier - Rectangular pkg(2) **2.89**

## Pipes

650-2044

650-2045

**650-2044** 8" w/Flange, Straight pkg(4) **2.49**

**650-2045** 8" w/Flange, 90° pkg(3) **2.49**

**650-2190** 6" Expansion Union pkg(3) **2.49**

**650-2193** With Gas Line Valve pkg(3) **2.49**

**650-2194** Pipe Section w/Inlet Valve pkg(3) **2.49**

## Pulleys

**650-2378** Set #1 pkg(4) **2.99**

**650-2389** Set #2 pkg(4) **2.99**

## Rails & Posts

650-2028 650-2029

**650-2028** Ornate Rail w/Post Small pkg(3) **2.69**

**650-2029** Ornate Rail w/Post Large pkg(3) **2.89**

**650-2133** Post w/Carved Top 11' pkg(4) **2.99**

**650-2134** Post w/Carved Top 10' pkg(4) **2.99**

**650-2135** Post w/Carved Top & Bottom pkg(4) **2.99**

**650-2170** Ornate Half-Round Column pkg(4) **2.99**

**650-2136** Fluted Post 1/2 Round 13'6" pkg(4) **2.99**

**650-2137** Fluted Post Round 13'6" pkg(4) **3.39**

**650-2138** Fluted Post Square 12' pkg(4) **3.19**

**650-2291** Balcony Railing pkg(2) **3.39**

**650-2292** Railing w/Post pkg(3) **2.89**

**650-2295** Post-Small pkg(4) **3.19**

**650-2296** Post-Large pkg(4) **3.39**

**650-2343** Stoop Railing pkg(2) **2.49**

**650-2481** Post w/Finial Top pkg(4) **3.19**

**650-2483** Post w/Double Corbel pkg(4) **3.19**

**650-2484** Post w/Flatback pkg(4) **3.19**

## Sacks

650-2031

650-2126

**650-2031** Stack of 6 pkg(3) **2.49**

**650-2126** Pile of 4 pkg(3) **2.49**

650-2127

650-2128

**650-2127** Stack of 18 **2.49**

**650-2128** 3 Leaning pkg(3) **2.49**

**650-2229** Grain pkg(6) **3.19**

**650-2230** Flour pkg(6) **3.19**

**650-2231** Open Feed pkg(6) **3.19**

**650-2232** Leaning pkg(6) **3.19**

**650-2338** Stack of 3 pkg(3) **2.69**

**650-2350** Stack of 36 **3.79**

## Signs

**650-2371** Large Boot (Old-Time Store Sign) pkg(2) **2.49**

**650-2372** Large Dentures (Old-Time Store Sign) pkg(2) **2.49**

**650-2373** Large Tooth (Old-Time Store Sign) pkg(2) **2.49**

**650-2374** Drug Store pkg(2) **3.79**

**650-2422** Coke Button pkg(6) **2.69**

## Stairs & Steps

**650-2041** Stair Stringer 6 Riser pkg(8) **2.49**

**650-2144** Ornate Stair Stringer 14-Riser pkg(4) **3.19**

**650-2359** Exterior Staircase **4.19**

**650-2538** Wooden Steps pkg(4) **2.99**

**650-2552** Long Wooden Stairs pkg(3) **3.39**

## Stoves

**650-2251** Pot Belly Stove #1 pkg(2) **3.39**

**650-2316** Pot Belly Stove #2 pkg(2) **2.99**

**650-2339** Pot Belly Stove #3 pkg(2) **2.89**

**650-2480** Pot Belly Stove #4 pkg(2) **3.39**

**650-2531** Pot Belly Stove w/Pipe pkg(2) **3.39**

## Telephones

**650-2245** Wall Phone pkg(3) **2.69**

**650-2246** Extension Phone pkg(3) **2.69**

**650-2247** Candlestick Phone pkg(3) **2.69**

## Trackside Details

650-2052

650-2053

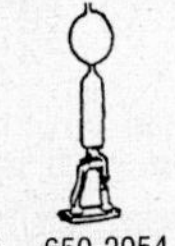
650-2054

**650-2052** Switch Stand Harp (Dummy) **3.19**

**650-2053** Switch Stand w/Cast Base (Dummy) **3.19**

**650-2054** Switch Stand w/Frame Base (Dummy) **3.19**

650-2103

650-2120

**650-2103** Water Tank Spout w/Counterweights **4.49**

**650-2120** Water Pump pkg(2) **3.39**

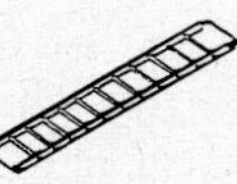
650-2124

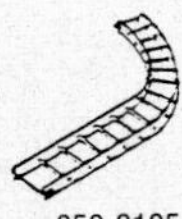
650-2125

**650-2124** Freight Roller Straight Section pkg(3) **3.19**

**650-2125** Freight Roller 90° Curve Section pkg(2) **2.89**

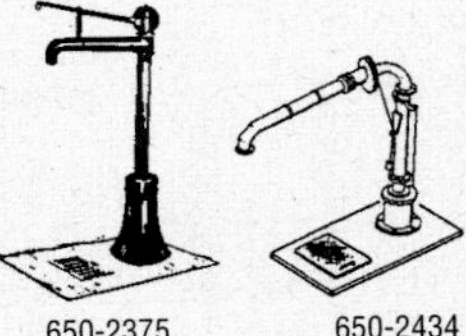
650-2375 650-2434

**650-2375** Water Column **5.99**

**650-2426** Water Tank Spout Kit **4.49**

**650-2434** DRGW Water Column **4.99**

**650-2460** Water Tank Spout w/Counterweights #2 **3.39**

**650-2497** Crossing Gate Kit-2 Gates **5.99**

## Trim

650-2013 650-2014

**650-2013** Box Style Roof pkg(4) **2.99**

**650-2014** Ridge DRGW Style pkg(4) **3.19**

**650-2056** Spanish Tile Ridge pkg(4) **3.19**

**650-2169** Curved Eave pkg(4) **3.19**

**650-2180** Store Corner pkg(4) **2.99**

**650-2293** Diamond Roof pkg(4) **3.19**

**650-2294** Low Relief Roof pkg(4) **2.99**

Item listed below is available by Special Order (see Legend Page).

**650-2537** Gable End pkg(4) **2.99**

## Valves

650-2046

650-2105

**650-2046** 8" Gate w/Wheel pkg(2) **2.69**

**650-2105** 3-Way pkg(3) **2.49**

**650-2195** Check pkg(3) **2.49**

**650-2196** Quick Close pkg(3) **3.39**

## Vents

650-2047

650-2108

**650-2047** Tank pkg(5) **2.49**

**650-2084** Foundation pkg(10) **2.69**

**650-2108** Roof w/Fin pkg(2) **4.19**

**650-2273** Round Gable Vent pkg(3) **2.69**

**650-2330** Roof pkg(3) **2.89**

**650-2382** Turbine Vent-Flat Roof **3.39**

**650-2383** Turbine Vent-Slope Roof pkg(2) **3.39**

**650-2423** Globe 24" pkg(4) **2.89**

**650-2450** Mushroom Roof pkg(6) **2.69**

**650-2489** Large Flat Roof pkg(2) **2.89**

**650-2498** Round Industrial Roof pkg(3) **2.89**

**650-2500** Round Roof pkg(3) **2.69**

**650-2502** Large Round Roof **2.69**

**650-2512** Roof & Wind Vane pkg(2) **2.69**

**650-2529** Roof for Peak pkg(2) **2.49**

**650-2543** 24" Globe Roof pkg(3) **2.99**

**650-2554** Roof Pitch Roof pkg(2) **3.19**

## Wheels

**650-2237** Wagon Wheel-Large pkg(4) **3.19**

**650-2309** Wagon Wheels-Small pkg(4) **2.89**

## Windows

650-2063 650-2069

**650-2063** Emporium Front pkg(2) **3.19**

**650-2069** Brick Cellar 2-Lite pkg(4) **3.19**

650-2070

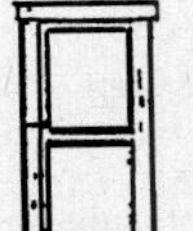
650-2071

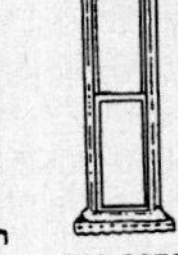
650-2072

**650-2070** Elliptical pkg(4) **2.69**

**650-2071** Double-Hung pkg(3) **2.89**

**650-2072** Ornate Narrow 2-Lite pkg(3) **2.99**

650-2073

650-2074

650-2075

**650-2073** Tall Narrow 12-Lite pkg(3) **3.19**

**650-2074** Double-Double-Hung 4-Lite pkg(2) **2.89**

**650-2075** Ornate Double-Hung 2-Lite pkg(3) **3.19**

SCALE STRUCTURES LIMITED

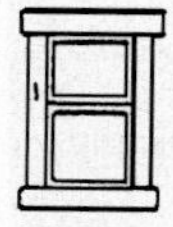
650-2076

650-2077

**650-2076** Short Double-Hung pkg(3) **2.89**

**650-2077** Steel Sash 9-Lite Double pkg(2) **2.89**

650-2078

650-2079

**650-2078** Steel Sash 9-Lite pkg(3) **2.89**

**650-2079** Steel Sash 3-Lite Basement pkg(5) **3.19**

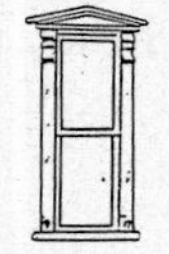
650-2080

650-2081

**650-2080** Tall Virginia City 2-Lite pkg(3) **3.19**

**650-2081** Double-Double-Hung 2-Lite Ornate pkg(2) **2.99**

650-2082

650-2092

**650-2082** Steel Sash 1-Lite Basement pkg(5) **3.19**

**650-2083** Steel Sash 18-Lite pkg(3) **3.19**

**650-2092** Wood Window Casement Detail pkg(2) **2.69**

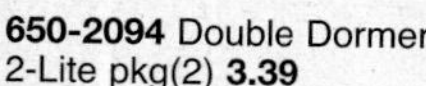
650-2094

650-2095

**650-2094** Double Dormer 2-Lite pkg(2) **3.39**

**650-2095** Tall Ornate 2-Lite pkg(3) **3.39**

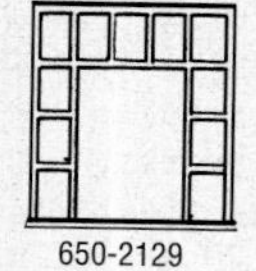
650-2129

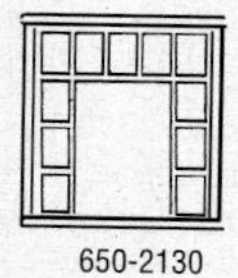
650-2130

**650-2129** Factory 9-Lite Without Frame pkg(3) **3.39**

**650-2130** Factory 9-Lite w/Frame pkg(3) **3.49**

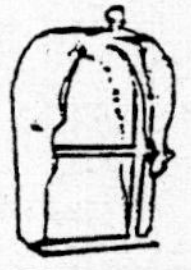
650-2140

650-2141

**650-2140** Mansard 2-Lite Small pkg(3) **2.69**

**650-2141** Mansard 2-Lite Tall pkg(3) **3.79**

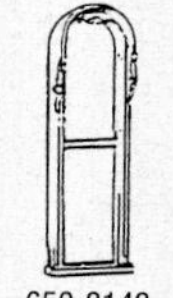
650-2142

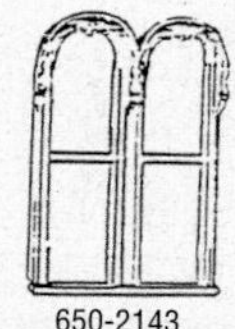
650-2143

**650-2142** Victorian Round Top 2-Lite Tall pkg(2) **3.79**

**650-2143** Victorian Double Top 2-Lite Tall pkg(2) **3.19**

650-2179

650-2261

**650-2179** Ornate Bay **3.39**

**650-2257** Virginia City pkg(3) **3.19**

**650-2259** Colonial Arch pkg(3) **3.19**

**650-2261** Double-Hung 3-Lite pkg(3) **2.89**

650-2263

650-2266

**650-2263** Colonial Ornate pkg(3) **3.19**

**650-2266** Double-Double-Hung 3-Lite pkg(2) **2.89**

650-2267

650-2272

**650-2267** Tall 4-Lite pkg(3) **2.99**

**650-2272** Round Gable pkg(3) **2.69**

650-2325

650-2326

**650-2325** Tall City Double-Hung 8-Lite pkg(3) **3.19**

**650-2326** Ornate Double-Double-Hung 3-Lite pkg(2) **2.89**

650-2352

650-2353

**650-2352** Curved Arch Double 2-Lite **2.99**

**650-2353** Curved Arch Tall 3-Lite pkg(3) **3.79**

**650-2354** Curved Arch Short 3-Lite pkg(3) **3.39**

650-2355

650-2356

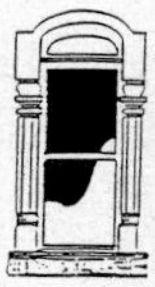

**650-2355** Cast Concrete 2-Lite-Single pkg(3) **3.69**

**650-2356** Cast Concrete 2-Lite-Double **2.99**

**650-2357** Cast Concrete 2-Lite-Triple **3.39**

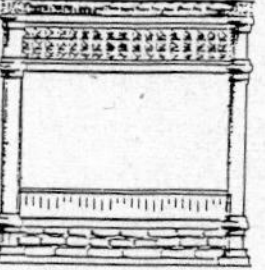
650-2361

650-2437

**650-2361** Store Front 1-Lite **3.49**

**650-2437** Double-Hung 4-Pane pkg(3) **2.69**

**650-2442** Double-Hung 8-Pane pkg(2) **3.19**

**650-2526** Wood 2-Lite pkg(3) **2.89**

**650-2533** Two-Story Bay **4.29**

Window listed below is available by Special Order (see Legend Page).
**650-2523** Wood 2-Lite pkg(3) **2.89**

## Miscellaneous

**650-2010** Porch Lattice Curved pkg(4) **3.19**

**650-2018** Small Power Head w/Meter pkg(3) **2.49**

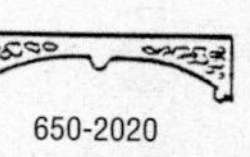
650-2020

650-2035

**650-2020** Porch Header Ornate pkg(4) **3.19**

**650-2034** City Apartment Mailbox Cluster pkg(4) **2.69**

**650-2035** McClellan Saddle pkg(2) **2.69**

**650-2038** Spitoon Number 4 pkg(4) **2.69**

**650-2050** Bed Roll pkg(3) **2.49**

**650-2051** Bridle pkg(3) **3.39**

**650-2055** Spanish Tile Roof Peak pkg(5) **2.69**

**650-2057** Octagon Gusset Plate pkg(12) **2.49**

**650-2059** Ornate Building Cap #1 **3.79**

**650-2091** Front Stoop, Round pkg(2) **3.19**

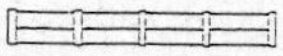

**650-2093** Wall Cap Strip Narrow pkg(4) **3.39**

**650-2104** Strap Turnbuckles pkg(10) **2.89**

**650-2112** Wall Capstrip Wide pkg(4) **3.49**

**650-2113** Shingle Bolt pkg(10) **3.19**

650-2114

650-2121

**650-2114** Cyclone w/Support Bracket **4.49**

**650-2121** Horse Collar pkg(3) **2.89**

**650-2122** Water Tub **2.99**

**650-2163** Lug Box pkg(3) **2.49**

**650-2171** Electric Main Switch-Small pkg(3) **2.49**

**650-2177** Drawer Cluster **2.49**

**650-2183** Pillow Blocks pkg(8) **2.89**

**650-2188** Valve Cluster pkg(3) **2.69**

**650-2191** Tee Section 8" pkg(3) **2.69**

**650-2192** Electric Insulators pkg(12) **2.69**

**650-2198** Bridge Girder Section pkg(2) **4.49**

**650-2225** Western Saddle pkg(2) **2.99**

**650-2226** Pack Rack pkg(2) **2.49**

**650-2227** Colt .45 w/Holster pkg(3) **2.69**

**650-2228** Rifle pkg(3) **2.69**

**650-2234** Push Cart pkg(2) **3.19**

**650-2235** Scale-Large pkg(2) **2.99**

**650-2236** Cowboy Hat pkg(6) **2.99**

**650-2241** Desk #1 **2.99**

**650-2242** Desk Top for #650-2241 **2.69**

**650-2243** Swivel Chair Without Arms pkg(2) **2.69**

**650-2244** Steel Safe-Large pkg(2) **2.69**

**650-2248** Typewriter pkg(2) **2.69**

**650-2249** Books pkg(4) **2.69**

**650-2250** Desk Lamp #1 pkg(2) **2.69**

**650-2252** Coal Hod pkg(3) **2.69**

**650-2253** Coal Scoop pkg(3) **2.49**

**650-2254** Cuspidor #1 pkg(4 **2.69**

**650-2255** Wall Clock w/Print Sheet **2.49**

**650-2274** Trunk pkg(2) **2.49**

**650-2297** Lamps (7 Kinds) pkg(7) **3.39**

**650-2315** Water Cooler w/Faucet pkg(3) **2.69**

**650-2322** Work Cart **3.69**

**650-2323** Ice Wagon **3.69**

**650-2331** Industrial Power Head-Large pkg(3) **2.49**

**650-2332** Industrial Power Head-Small pkg(3) **2.49**

**650-2340** Flower Pot pkg(12) **2.49**

**650-2341** Lattice, Style #1 pkg(4) **3.19**

**650-2342** Stoop w/Worn Mat **2.99**

**650-2344** Skylight-Small pkg(2) **3.19**

**650-2348** Ornate Gable End Panel **3.39**

**650-2376** Gas Meter w/Valve-Medium pkg(2) **3.19**

**650-2380** Single Water Fauce pkg(10) **3.19**

**650-2384** Coal Bin pkg(2) **2.4**

**650-2388** Factory Whistle pkg(4) **2.69**

**650-2396** Residential Power Head pkg(6) **2.89**

**650-2397** Residential Gas Regulator pkg(6) **2.89**

**650-2398** Pulley Trolley & Hook pkg(3) **3.19**

**650-2399** Wall-Mounted Fire Plug pkg(6) **2.69**

**650-2400** Power Control Pane pkg(4) **2.69**

**650-2404** Open Top Coke Machine pkg(2) **3.19**

**650-2405** Upright Coke Machine pkg(2) **3.19**

**650-2411** Fuel Oil Tank 200-Gallon **4.49**

**650-2413** Exterior Plumbing-4 Pieces, 2 Types **2.49**

**650-2414** Electrical Meter Box pkg(6) **2.69**

**650-2420** Oil Bunker #2 pkg(4) **3.19**

**650-2424** Oil Can Rack #2 pkg(2) **2.49**

**650-2425** Hand Water Pump #2 pkg(3) **2.69**

**650-2431** Portable Scale pkg(2) **2.99**

**650-2440** Hydraulic Pump Jack pkg(3) **2.89**

**650-2445** Ornate Ceiling Panels pkg(2) **3.39**

**650-2456** Shaded Lamp w/Wire Loop pkg(5) **2.89**

**650-2461** Rubbish Bin **2.95**

**650-2464** Clark Forklift (1947 Model) **6.15**

SCALE STRUCTURES LIMITED

**650-2465** 4 x 8' Diamond Plate Sheets pkg(7) **3.65**

**650-2468** Portable "A" Frame Hoist **6.15**

**650-2469** Wood Barrel Racks w/6 Barrels **6.15**

**650-2470** Work Tables (3 Types) **6.15**

**650-2471** 6' Wooden Stepladder pkg(2) **2.95**

**650-2472** Squirrel Cage Exhaust Blower **4.35**

**650-2474** Wooden Reels (Small, Medium, Large) pkg(9) **4.35**

**650-2475** Roof Water Tower **7.45**

**650-2477** Roll-Off Trash Body Kit **8.95**

**650-2478** Skipper's Dog House pkg(2) **2.95**

**650-2479** Safety Cones pkg(8) **2.95**

**650-2485** Drain Scuppers pkg(8) **2.49**

**650-2490** Roof Top Cyclone #2 **3.79**

**650-2492** Corner Mailbox #2 pkg(3) **2.69**

**650-2494** Small Ornate Eagle pkg(3) **2.69**

**650-2495** Bell w/Bracket pkg(3) **3.19**

**650-2510** Building Corner Stone pkg(2) **2.69**

**650-2511** Wooden Ramp pkg(3) **2.69**

**650-2513** Swivel Chair w/Arms pkg(2) **2.69**

**650-2530** Platform Roof Support pkg(3) **4.29**

**650-2541** Warehouse Work Station pkg(2) **2.99**

**650-2547** Industrial Electric Insulator pkg(8) **2.99**

**650-2557** Short Wooden Counter pkg(2) **2.99**

**650-4100** Facing Brick-Brown pkg(3) **3.69**

**650-4124** Rubble Stone-Brown pkg(3) **3.69**

**650-4125** Facing Stone-Brown pkg(3) **3.69**

**650-5161** Cash Register & Paper Roll **2.89**

**650-7232** Fire Hose Stand Kit **7.95**

Items listed below are available by Special Order (see Legend Page).

**650-2522** Deck Braces pkg(4) **3.49**

**650-2528** Steel Stantions pkg(6) **2.99**

**650-2545** Ornate Metal Column pkg(4) **3.39**

Sunrise Enterprises

Turn a plain model into a detailed replica with this line of metal castings.

## LOCOMOTIVE DETAILS

### Antennas

**NEW 695-133002** Model 221 Sinclair 21" pkg(6) **5.75**

**695-133003** 21" Model 221 Sinclair pkg(6) **5.75**

**NEW 695-133004** Ground Plane w/Sinclair & Whip Base **TBA**

**NEW 695-133011** SP/St. Louis Southwestern Caboose Radio w/3' Ground Plane **TBA**

**NEW 695-133012** EMD, Alco PA Wagon Wheel w/Stand & Whip **TBA**

**695-133015** Whip Antenna Base w/Bolts pkg(12) **5.50**

**NEW 695-133016** UHF Radio For Engines pkg(6) **5.50**

### Lift Rings

**NEW 695-133000** 2-3/4" pkg(36) **5.25**

**NEW 695-133005** ATSF E & F Unit Diesel Nose & Rear **6.00**

**NEW 695-133006** Most Roads E & F Unit Diesel Nose & Rear pkg(6) **6.00**

**NEW 695-133007** Geep Pilot NP/BN pkg(6) **6.00**

**Flat Bottom Pkg(36) 6.00 Ea**

**695-133008** 3-1/2 x 7/8"

**695-133009** 5-1/2 x 7/8"

**695-133010** 8-1/2 x 7/8"

### Knuckle Buster Latches pkg(48) 6.50 ea

**695-133017** Late Style

**695-133020** Early Style

### Hinges 6.50 ea

**695-133018** Dual Wing Long pkg(48)

**695-133019** One Short Left Hinge & One Long Right Hinge

### Sets

**NEW 695-133013** SP Commuter GP9 Wagon Wheel Antenna & Steam Generator Set **TBA**

**NEW 695-133014** ATSF Caboose "High Ball" Wig-Way Cupola Signal Set **14.95**



### Station Signs ATSF Split Poles pkg(2) 3.75 ea

**695-14135** 6'

**695-14136** 8'

**695-14137** 10'

### Miscellaneous

**NEW 695-14124** Electric Relay Box Twin **6.15**

**NEW 695-14125** Electric Relay Box Single **7.45**

**NEW 695-14131** ATSF Warning Boards w/ Decals **2.95**

## SHEEPSCOT

Bring a new level of realism to your modeling with this line of details.

### Photo-Etched Details

Unassembled brass.

**668-75001** Fire Escape - Five Flights **10.00**
Includes parts for five flights of stairs, with landings and railings.

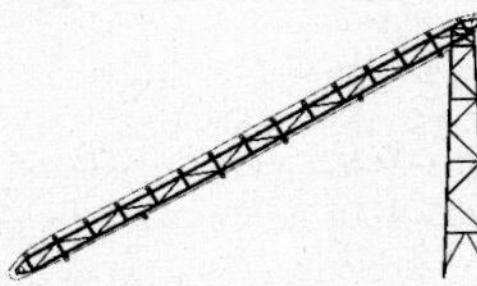

**668-75002** Conveyor 60' **10.00**
Includes 15 top and six return rollers.

**668-75004** Crane Boom **10.00**
35' long, with two 20' inserts, can be used to build a 75' boom.

**668-75012** 100-Ton Crane Boom **20.00**
100' long, includes 60' basic boom and two 20' inserts.

**668-75014** Tug Boat Railings **10.00**
Designed for Walthers Railroad Tug Boat Kit #933-3153, sold separately.

## SMALLTOWN U.S.A.

Molded plastic detail parts.

### Doors pkg(2) 2.25 ea

699-4 699-5

**699-4** Overhead, 10 x 12'

**699-5** Hinged Freight, 10 x 9'

UTAH PACIFIC MODEL RAILROAD PRODUCTS

Parts are lost wax brass castings unless noted.

### Air Horn

**755-60** Five Chime for GE U-Boats, etc. **2.80**

### Antenna Masts

**755-91** Brass pkg(25) **7.35**

**755-92** Plastic pkg(25) **3.65**

### Arm Rests pkg(2) 2.95 ea

**755-79** Two Brackets

**755-80** Three Brackets

### Bells

755-81

755-98

**755-81** Diesel pkg(2) **2.25**

**755-98** Brass w/Bracket pkg(2) **3.20**

### Brake Parts

**755-68** Brake Wheel **2.80**

**755-82** Brake Cylinder Assembly **2.25**

### Caboose Stacks 2.95 ea

**755-73** 27" Tall

**755-74** 54" Tall

### Dynamic Brake Kit

**755-78** 7.35

### Exhaust Stack

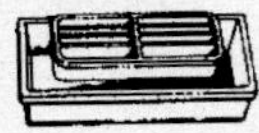

**755-69** GE Type **3.50**

### Grab Irons

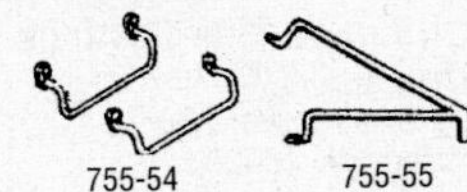

755-54 755-55

**755-54** Drop, Brass pkg(12) **8.45**

**755-55** Corner, Brass pkg(2) **2.80**

### Handrail Stanchions

**755-87** GE Type pkg(32) **11.60**
Cast in Beryllium copper.

### Hapco Spark Arrestors

**755-75** Stack Only **2.95**

**755-76** Two Stacks & Two Bases **6.95**

### Lift Rings

**755-62** GE Type pkg(10) **2.80**

### Marker Lights

**755-63** Adlake Caboose pkg(2) **5.25**

### Mirrors

**755-77** Cab Mirror w/Brackets pkg(2) **2.95**

### Pyle Gyralites

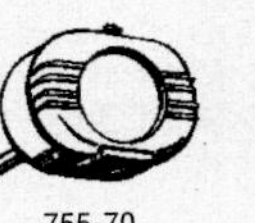

755-70

755-71

**755-70** Single **2.25**

**755-71** Single w/Bracket **2.65**

755-84

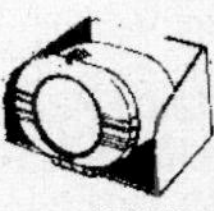

755-85

**755-84** Single w/Headlight - Nose Mount **2.95**

**755-85** Single - Nose Mount **2.25**

### Snow Plow

**755-99** Pilot Plow **7.35**

### Snow Shield

**755-83** pkg(2) **6.95**
Used on UP and Amtrak E units.

### Speed Recorders

755-61

755-65

**755-61** Early GE pkg(2) **2.10**
Early GE axle generator loco overspeed control.

**755-65** Axle Wheel Slip pkg(5) **2.80**
Chicago Pneumatic, axle-mounted speed recorder drive unit.

### Sun Visors

**755-93** Diesel Cab Visors pkg(4) **2.95**
Photo-etched in .005" brass.

### Tank Car Details

**755-53** Dome & Vent **2.80**

### Traction Motor

**755-67** GE 752 Style **4.05**
Early traction motor, less gear case.

### Vents

**755-72** Roof Vents **2.25**
For cabooses, passenger cars, structures, etc.

### Windshield Wipers

**755-94** Beryllium Copper pkg(4) **3.65**

**755-97** Plastic pkg(4) **2.25**

# TICHY TRAIN GROUP

Precision injection-molded impact-grade styrene parts. Measurements shown are to scale. Visit Walthers Web site at www.walthers.com for a complete listing of Tichy Train Group parts.

## NEW PRODUCT

### Lamp Posts

**NEW 293-8155** Early Style pkg(8) **4.00**

### Brake Parts 2.50 ea (Unless Noted)

**293-3003** Brake Wheel, Bracket & Staff pkg(4) **1.50** For 1895-1920 era flats and gondolas. Cored for .018 and .020 wire.

**293-3005** KC West Brake

**293-3013** AB Brake Set

**293-3034** Split K Brake System

### Chimneys

**293-8123** Brick Chimney w/2 Course Top Corbel (Red-Brown w/Open Core) pkg(3) **3.00**

**NEW 293-8156** Chimney Cap pkg(8) **3.00**

### Coal Chute

**293-8003 3.00**

### Doors 3.00 ea (Unless Noted)

**293-8009** Wooden Structure pkg(3) **1.50**

**293-8049** 4 Panel 36 x 80" pkg(6)

**293-8108** 4 Panel Utility 36 x 60" (Fits .5 x .7" Opening) pkg(6)

**293-8111** Double w/2 Lite Transom 72 x 115" (Fits .875 x 1.36" Opening) pkg(3)

**293-8112** 1 Lite Masonry w/3 Lite Transom & Steel Shutters 50 x 115" (Fits .57 x 1.3" Opening) pkg(3)

**293-8116** 1 Lite Residential w/Transom & Separate Frame 36 x 80" (Fits .47 x 1.175" Opening) 3 Sets

**293-8117** Storefront Set w/2 Different Door Styles 2 Sets

**293-8118** 4 Lite Factory w/3 Lite Transom & Separate Masonry Frame 39 x 92" (Fits .5 x 1.35" Opening) 3 Sets

**293-8119** Framed w/Transom & Frame 3 Sets

**293-8121** Double w/Sidelights & Transom, Separate Frame 89-1/2 x 130" (Fits 1.075 x 1.53" Opening) pkg(3)

**293-8124** 5 Pane Double 54 x 80" (Fits .66 x .975" Opening) pkg(4)

**293-8125** Freight w/5 Lite Transom 72 x 108" (Fits .95 x 1.29" Opening) pkg(4)

**293-8130** 1 Lite Residential w/3 Lite Transom 36 x 96" (Fits .45 x 1.15" Opening) pkg(6)

**293-8132** 6 Lite w/2 Lite Transom 33 x 110" (Fits .42 x 1.31" Opening) pkg(4)

**293-8140** Double w/Transom & Iron Shutters 65 x 115" (Fits .76 x 1.32" Opening) pkg(3)

**293-8150** Single 6-Light, 3-Panel 33 x 80" (Fits .415 x .965" Opening) pkg(4)

**293-8151** Double 6-Light, 3-Panel 66 x 80" (Fits .79 x .95" Opening) pkg(3)

### Eyebolts

**293-3037** pkg(80) **3.00**

### Fire Escape Platform

**293-8060** With Railing, Vertical Ladder & See-Through Grate pkg(2) **3.00**

### Grab Irons 3.00 ea

Preformed wire.

**293-3015** 18" Drop pkg(100)

**293-3021** 18" Straight pkg(100)

**293-3028** Roof Corner pkg(100)

**293-3053** 24" Straight pkg(50)

**293-3054** Curved Caboose pkg(25)

**293-3057** 24" Drop pkg(50)

### Hardware

#### Nut-Bolt-Washer Castings 2.50 ea

**293-8016** 1-3/4" Nut w/2-1/2" Washer pkg(2000)

**293-8082** 3" Square Nut, Bolt, 6" Square Washer pkg(96)

**293-8142** 1" Bolt, 2" Nut, 3-1/2" Washer pkg(200)

**293-8143** 3" Bolt, 5" Nut, 12" Square Washer pkg(48)

**293-8144** 2" Bolt, 3" Nut, 5" Washer pkg(96)

#### Star Washers 2.50 ea

**293-8145** 8" pkg(96)

**293-8146** 12" pkg(48)

#### Scale Rivet Heads 2.50 ea

**293-8017** .020" pkg(200)

**293-8018** .025" pkg(200)

**293-8019** .030" pkg(200)

**293-8020** .035" pkg(200)

**293-8075** .04" Diameter pkg(96)

**293-8076** .05" Diameter pkg(96)

**293-8077** .06" Diameter pkg(96)

**293-8078** .07" Diameter pkg(96)

**293-8079** .08" Diameter pkg(96)

### Jib Crane

**293-8007 5.95**

### Ladders

**293-3033** Freight Car **293-3066** Box Car pkg(8) **2.00**

**293-8002** Safety Cage Ladder/Staircase **3.00**

### Pipe Railings

**293-8013** pkg(4) **1.50**

### Platforms

**293-3023** Reefer Wood Ice pkg(4) **2.50**

**293-8001** Open Grate **3.00**

### Porch Details 3.00 ea

**293-8101** Double S Corbell pkg(32)

**293-8109** Round Spindle Porch Railing pkg(3)

**293-8110** Lattice Trim pkg(6)

**293-8122** Lattice Panel pkg(3) 1 x 1-1/2"

**293-8129** Double "S" Corbel w/Top Detailing pkg(28)

**293-8147** Rafter Tails w/Decorative French Curve, 88 pieces 3/8" long, 22 pieces 7/8" long

**293-8148** Decorative Wrought Iron Railing 1.8" long pkg(4)

**293-8152** Square Trim Pieces for 8" (.93") Porch Columns pkg(42)

### Roofing Shingles

**293-8135** Slate, 36 Square Inches **14.95**

### Roofwalk

**293-3029** 40' Wood **2.00**

### Stake Pockets

**293-3006** pkg(32) **1.50**

### Stovepipe

**293-8141** w/Rain Cap & Flashing pkg(4) **3.00**

### Turnbuckles

**293-8021** pkg(24) **2.50**

### Water Column

**293-8006 4.95**

### Windows 3.00 ea

**293-8024** 6/6 Double Hung pkg(12)

**293-8028** 4/4 Double Hung 27 x 62" pkg(12)

**293-8029** 4/4 Double Hung 25 x 48" pkg(12)

**293-8036** Double Hung Masonry 20/20 pkg(8)

**293-8046** 9 Pane Masonry 52 x 34" pkg(12)

**293-8052** 6/6 Double-Hung Masonry 72 x 102" pkg(12)

**293-8054** 9/9 Double Hung 44" x 90" (Fits .54 x 1.07" Opening) pkg(12)

**293-8055** 9/9 Double Hung Arch Top 44 x 90" (Fits .54 x 1.07" Opening) pkg(12)

**293-8062** 2/2 Double Hung 24 x 56" (Fits .33 x .71" Opening pkg(12)

**293-8067** Work Car Horizontal Windows 24 x 24" pkg(12)

**293-8068** Work Car Windows w/Sash Vertical 18 x 28" pkg(12)

**293-8069** 4/4 Double Hung w/Open Lower Sashes (Matches #293-8028) 27" Wide x 62" High pkg(12)

**293-8072** 2/2 Double Hung Arch Top 30" Wide x 60" High pkg(10)

**293-8074** 2 Panel Small Horizontal 36" Wide x 9" High pkg(12)

**293-8086** 8/8 Double Hung Masonry 38" Wide x 68" High pkg(12)

**293-8087** Masonry 20 Pane Industrial w/Tilting Center 7" Wide x 9.5" High pkg(3)

**293-8088** 4/4 Double Hung w/Separate Adjustable Sash 34 x 88" (Fits .44 x .98") pkg(12)

**293-8090** 6 Pane w/Tilt Out Top Sash 34 x 64" (Fits .44 x .78") pkg(12)

**293-8100** 27 Pane Industrial, Enginehouse 44 x 104" pkg(8)

**293-8102** Single Sash (Same Size as #8061) 136 x 82" (Fits .50 x 1.0" Opening) pkg(12)

**293-8103** Double Hung Double Unit (Matches 8025) 64 x 62" (Fits .75 x .75" Opening) pkg(6)

**293-8104** Double Hung Triple Unit (Matches 8025) 98 x 62" (Fits .75 x 1.14" Opening) pkg(3)

**293-8105** 2/2 Double Hung 40 x 47" (Fits .36 x .58" Opening) pkg(12)

**293-8106** 2/2 Double Hung Double Unit (Matches #8105) 64 x 74" (Fits .75 x .58" Opening) pkg(6)

**293-8107** 2 Pane Masonry 35 x 35" (Fits .4 x .4" Openir pkg(12)

**293-8113** Round Top 1/1 24 72" (Fits .34 x .825 Opening) pkg(12)

**293-8114** Round Top Double Unit 1/1 52 x 72" (Fits .64 x .87" Opening) pkg(6)

**293-8115** 2/2 Masonry pkg(8

**293-8120** 6 Lite Store w/Top Transom & Lower Wood Pan 65 x 115 (Fits .75 x 1.325" Opening) pkg(6)

**293-8126** 4/4 Double Hung Double Unit (Matches #8030) 64 x 80" (Fits .81 x .99" Opening) pkg(6)

**293-8127** 4/4 Double Hung Triple Unit (Matches #8030) 98 x 80" (Fits 1.225 x .99" Opening) pkg(3)

**293-8128** 13 Pane Half Roun Masonry (Use Over #8036, 8133) 60 x 30" (Fits .675 x .3 Opening) pkg(8)

**293-8131** 4/4 Double Hung Double Unit 27 x 64" (Fits .36 x .78" Opening) pkg(12)

**293-8133** 25 Pane Masonry Industrial/Roundhouse w/Separate Tilt Out 60 x 104" (.68 x 1.19") pkg(8)

**293-8136** 12/12 Double Hung w/Mantle 31 x 62" (Fits .4 x .75" Opening) pkg(12)

**293-8137** 4/4 Double Hung 8( x 62" (Fits .955 x.76" Opening pkg(6)

**293-8138** 2/2 Double Hung Storefront 76 x 82" (Fits .925 .98" Opening) pkg(6)

**293-8139** Double Casement 30 x 40" (Fits .39 x .5" Opening) pkg(12)

**293-8149** Round Attic 30" Diameter (Fits .415" Opening) pkg(6)

**NEW 293-8153** 6/6 Double Hung pkg(12)

**NEW 293-8154** 12-Pane Masonry pkg(12)

Photo by Pelle Søeberg

Building a current-era layout presents unique challenges, especially when going from mountains to desert. Where real landscapes appear larger than life, it takes restraint to model these wide-open spaces on an HO layout. In *Mountain To Desert: Building the HO Scale Daneville & Donner River*, Pelle Søeberg, a frequent contributor to *Model Railroader* magazine, explains the techniques that conquered his American West railroad. Painting a backdrop is an effective way to cover a lot of territory, but Pelle believes that it shouldn't be the main attraction on a layout. For this reason, Pelle doesn't have clouds on his backdrop since, as in nature, they attract too much attention. He painted the distant mountains in light blue and green shades, using photos of the Feather River area as reference. He dabbed on hundreds of pine trees to create a forested effect, not trying to make each tree realistic. After adding Woodland Scenics pine trees, brush and other scenery, the backdrop blended in beautifully.

Pelle's book is just one of many great resources you'll discover as you explore this section. Get new ideas, research your favorite railroad, choose fun software or find the perfect railroad print or collectible. A great collection of books, videos, DVDs, CDs, collectibles, software and more is all just a page turn away.

## LIFE-LIKE®

Div. of Wm. K. Walthers, Inc.

### Books

**Basics For Beginners 13th Edition**

**433-8003 1.00**
Useful tips on detailing, building and landscaping your layout

## BUSCH

IMPORTED FROM GERMANY BY WALTHERS

### NEW PRODUCTS

**2007 Catalogs**

Discover the entire exciting line of Busch models with these catalogs. Full-color photos of the entire selection of electronic accessories, scenery, signals, vehicles and much more.

**NEW 189-49996** 2007 Vehicle Catalog **1.99**

**NEW 189-999903** 2007 New Products Flyer **No Charge**

**NEW 189-999897** 2007 Catalog **9.99**

**189-999895** 2006 Catalog w/CD ROM **4.99**

### BOOKS

**Blueprints For Ten True-Track® Layouts**

**150-15 3.25**
Great for beginners who want to use popular Atlas True-Track for their layout. Includes track plans for 10 fun layouts complete with diagrams and lists of which track components are needed for each. For a complete listing of True-Track roadbed style track, see the Track & Accessories section of the Reference Book. 44 pages.

**Beginner's Guide To HO Model Railroading**

**150-9 5.50**
Perfect for the novice, this book contains 12 layouts built with either Atlas Code 100 or Code 83 track. Includes Atlas Master DCC wiring instructions; large, clear layout diagrams; and complete construction and wiring instructions.

**HO Layouts For Every Space**

**150-11 6.50**
Contains 11 challenging layouts for unusual spaces, large and small. Each plan has complete instructions on benchwork, tracklaying, wiring, scenery and more.Includes Code 83 & 100 track products required listings.Intermediate to advanced skill levels.

**The Complete Atlas Wiring Book**

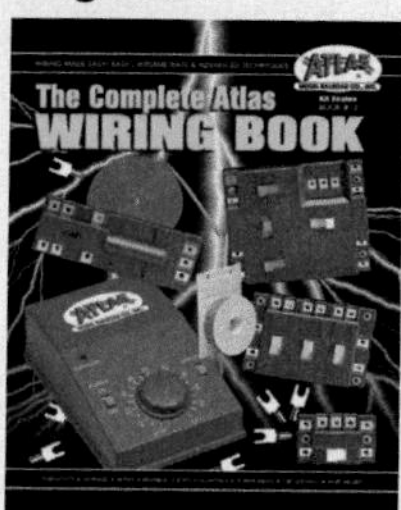


**150-12 6.50**
Learn how to install and use Atlas' quality components on any layout. Starts beginners with the basics of wiring, and takes advanced modelers through some complex wiring situations. Complemented by more than 100 diagrams and complete glossary. For all scales and skill levels.

**Seven Step-By-Step HO Railroads**

**150-13 6.50**
This book will show you, step-by-step, how to build the layout of your choice. Includes tips on benchwork, track laying, wiring and scenery. All skill levels. Includes plans using Code 83 or Code 100 track.

**King-Size Plan Book**

**150-14 10.95**
Contains six layout plans that are large and relatively complex. Four out of the six plans fold out to 11 x 17", and each plan is in a 2" to-the-foot scale format. Includes complete building instructions, including detailed diagrams for a few cookie-cutter layout plans. Intermediate to advanced skill levels.

### BOOKS

**Air Brushing**

**Hobby & Craft Guide To Air-Brushing**

**165-500 7.90**
Preparation for painting, mixing paint, cleaning and maintenance. 32 pages, 8-1/2 x 11".

**Step By Step Modelers Guide to Air-Brushing**
**165-505 11.65**
Covers painting models, figures and dioramas. Techniques from shadowing to properly mixing paint. 32 pages, 8-1/2 x 11".

**Introduction to Airbrushes, Accessories & Airbrushing Mediums**
**165-222001 22.00**

Items listed below are available by Special Order (see Legend Page).

**The Fundamentals of Airbrush Technique: Basic Exercises**
**165-222002** Volume I **22.00**

**Intermediate Airbrush Technique: Working In Color**
**165-222003** Volume II **22.00**

### VIDEO

**Aging and Weathering Models (and Stuff) With an Airbrush**

**165-11 22.00**
With a few basic colors and a little ingenuity you'll learn the techniques necessary to weather your own models for a truly realistic look. 60 minutes.

## BRASS CAR SIDES

### DVDs

Classic scenes of passenger and freight trains in the Midwest, West and Canada from 1964 to 1991. Color, digitally transferred to DVD, with informative narration by photographer Dennis C. Henr

**Indiana and Early Railroad Memories 1964-72/ Minnesota Railroad Memories 1964-1971**
**173-412 34.75**

Thirteen chapters by railroad location. CB&Q, Chicago, C&EI, CSS&SB, GN/BN, Lafayette, IN, PC/NYC, N&W/WAB/NKP, Monon, NP, MILW, Northfield, MN, CRIP, MN&S, P&E/NYC, St. Paul, Early Amtrak. 107 minutes.

**U.S. Trains in the 1970s**
**173-413 TBA**

Trackside, dome and cab ride aboard MILW, BN, Amtrak, DRGW, UP, ICG, Rock Island, CNW, MNS, CSS&SB and 4449 in Northern Illinois, Colorado, Iowa, Wisconsin, Minnesota, Indiana, Wyoming and the West. Grouped by region or road.

**Great Canadian Passenger Trains**
**173-414 TBA**

CP and CN out west in 1972, Ontario in 1974, and VIA in the west in 1978 and 1991. VIA-E&N Victoria-Nanaimo RDC from cab, BCR "Royal Hudson."

## BACHMANN

### NEW PRODUCT

**Catalog**

**2007 Bachmann Catalog**

**NEW 160-99907 10.00**
This full-color, catalog shows the top-of-the-line products included in the Bachmann and Spectrum® lines.

## N-COR

# USIC CDS

### eat American Train assics 19.99 ea

usic for your railroad room or lfanning trip! CDs feature iginal performances on iitar, banjo, fiddle and more.

23-990221 Volume 1: 16 All me Favorite Songs elections include: Orange lossom Special, Wabash annonball, Chattanooga hoo Choo, Nine Pound ammer, Wreck of the Old 97, ohn Henry, City of New Drleans, Moving On, Choo Choo Cha Boogie, Waiting for Train, Freight Train Boogie, ilendale Train, Freight Train, ake the A Train, Night Train to Memphis and Life's Railway to Heaven.

223-990222 Volume 2: Coal, Water & Steel
Selections include: Coal Water & Steel, The Night they Drove Old Dixie Down, Casey Jones, Engine 143, Folsom Prison Blues, Good Morning Railroad Man, I've Been Working on the Railroad, King of the Road, New River Train, In the Pines, The Rock Island Line, 900 Miles, Way Out there and Train 45.

Daily New Arrival Updates! Visit Walthers Web site at

**www.walthers.com**

## C M SHOPS, INC.

# MUGS

Full-color, baked enamel ceramic mugs. Dishwasher safe.

12-9095

12-8012

### Railroad Heralds 5.95 ea

**12-9001** EL
**12-9002** CNJ
**12-9004** Lehigh & Hudson River
**12-9005** B&O
**12-9006** Family Lines
**12-9007** BN
**12-9008** Illinois Central Gulf
**12-9009** Lehigh & New England
**12-9010** CNW (Employee Owned)
**12-9011** PRR (Keystone)
**12-9012** PC
**12-9013** RDG
**12-9014** Erie
**12-9015** Lackawanna Railroad
**12-9016** ATSF
**12-9017** Rio Grande
**12-9018** Chessie
**12-9020** CNW
**12-9021** The Rock
**12-9023** LV
**12-9024** SOU
**12-9026** Erie Western
**12-9027** CB&Q
**12-9028** WP
**12-9031** WM
**12-9032** Seaboard Air Line
**12-9033** Providence & Worchester
**12-9034** Richmond, Fredericksburg & Potomac
**12-9035** MP
**12-9036** Boston & Maine
**12-9037** SP
**12-9038** New York, Susquehanna & Western
**12-9039** Frisco
**12-9040** NP
**12-9041** Pennsylvania - Reading Seashore Lines
**12-9042** New York, Ontario & Western
**12-9043** Kansas City Southern
**12-9044** Ann Arbor
**12-9045** MKT
**12-9046** C&O
**12-9047** Maine Central
**12-9048** Detroit, Toledo & Ironton
**12-9049** CR
**12-9050** N&W
**12-9051** SOO
**12-9052** Rock Island
**12-9053** Green Bay & Western
**12-9054** Rutland
**12-9055** Raritan River
**12-9056** Wabash
**12-9057** Vermont Railway
**12-9058** Gulf, Mobile & Ohio
**12-9059** IC
**12-9060** Long Island-Dashing Dan
**12-9061** Bangor & Aroostook
**12-9062** Duluth, Missabe & Iron Range
**12-9063** NKP
**12-9064** L&N
**12-9065** SOO-Modern
**12-9067** SSW-Blue Streak
**12-9068** Clinchfield
**12-9069** NH (McGinnis)
**12-9070** Pittsburgh & Lake Erie
**12-9072** Florida East Coast
**12-9073** New York, Susquehanna & Western - Susie Q
**12-9074** Chicago Great Western
**12-9075** Chattahoochee Industrial
**12-9076** Spokane, Portland & Seattle
**12-9077** Minneapolis, Northfield & Southern
**12-9078** Atlantic Coast Line
**12-9079** CV-Old
**12-9080** Grand Trunk Western
**12-9081** CP-Old
**12-9082** Delaware Otsego
**12-9083** Seaboard
**12-9084** Model Railroader 50th Anniversary
**12-9085** Morristown & Erie
**12-9086** Chicago & Illinois Midland
**12-9087** Texas & Pacific
**12-9088** NMRA 50th Anniversary
**12-9089** Appalachicola Northern
**12-9090** Central of Georgia
**12-9091** Seaboard Coast Line
**12-9092** MON
**12-9093** Bessemer & Lake Erie
**12-9094** Amtrak®
**12-9095** Colorado Midland
**12-9096** NS
**12-9097** Alaska
**12-9098** Virginian
**12-9099** Texas-Mexican Railway
**12-9100** NJ Transit
**12-9101** Mexican National Railways
**12-9102** CNW System
**12-9103** C&O Kitten
**12-9104** Boston & Maine (McGinnis)
**12-9105** CP Rail
**12-9106** Erie Centennial
**12-9107** GN (Big Sky Blue)
**12-9109** Montana Rail Link
**12-9110** WC
**12-9111** UP "Overland"
**12-9112** Trona
**12-9113** Toronto, Hamilton & Buffalo
**12-9114** Reading Anthracite
**12-9115** British Columbia
**12-9116** Belt Railway of Chicago
**12-9117** Bangor & Aroostook (shield)
**12-9118** Monongahela
**12-9119** Connecticut Central
**12-9120** Ashley, Drew & Northern
**12-9121** BNSF
**12-9122** Chicago & Eastern Illinois
**12-9123** Housatonic
**12-9124** Detroit, Toledo & Ironton - Compass Herald
**12-9125** CSX
**12-9126** Rio Grande Thru the Rockies

### F Units 5.95 ea

**12-8001** Ontario & Western
**12-8002** LV
**12-8003** GN
**12-8004** DRGW
**12-8005** CNW
**12-8006** Gulf, Mobile & Ohio
**12-8007** SP
**12-8008** L&N
**12-8009** CN
**12-8010** EL
**12-8011** ATSF
**12-8012** NYC
**12-8013** PRR
**12-8014** Wabash
**12-8016** PRR (Passenger)
**12-8017** Southern
**12-8018** ATSF
**12-8019** Erie
**12-8020** Clinchfield
**12-8021** Burlington Route
**12-8022** NP
**12-8023** Frisco
**12-8024** WP
**12-8025** CP
**12-8026** B&O

## DPA-LTA ENTERPRISES

# NEW PRODUCT

### Books

#### Official Locomotive Rosters & News

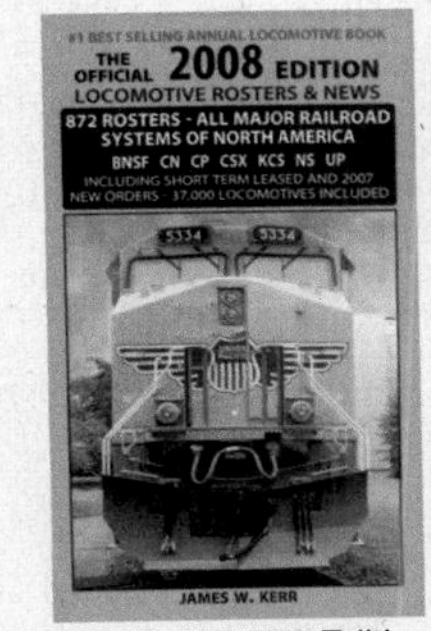


**NEW 237-17** 2008 Edition **29.95**
870 current listings (in alphabetical order) of all North American railroads, listing all their locomotives, plus all new orders for 2008, as well as rented locomotives seen on the trains.This book is used by the railroad industry as a valuable operations tool.

#### Illustrated Modern Freight Cars of North America

**237-102 19.95**
A great modeler's reference, this book includes 220 large builder's photos of all kinds of cars. Perfect bound, softcover, 120 pages.

## BRAWA

IMPORTED FROM GERMANY BY WALTHERS

### Catalog

**NEW 186-1071** 2007 **13.99**
Pages of full-color photos of locos, scenery, signals and all other items. English text.

# Carstens PUBLICATIONS, INC.

An assortment of railroad publications from plan books to electrical handbooks. Books are softcover unless noted.

## NEW PRODUCT

### Book

**On30 Annual**
Captures the best of On30 modeling featuring three stunning layouts plus hands-on locomotive, rolling stock and structure articles. Includes construction plans and product features. 84 pages.

**NEW 205-10** 2007 Edition **14.95**

**NEW 205-11** 2008 Edition **TBA**

## BOOKS

### Railroads

**The Pennsylvania - The Eastern Lines**

**205-1 30.95**
All-color photo book showing diesel era and electric operations from Long Island to Harrisburg. Written by Steve Stewart with photography by Dave Augsburger.

**Seaboard Coastline**
**205-46 20.95**
Beginning with the merger of SAL and ACL, covers Florida operations until the CSX era. Rare photos showing shop yard, freight and passenger scenes.

**Passenger Cars 32.95 ea (Unless Noted)**

**205-3** Volume 1
Covers pioneer and wooden cars, as well as heavyweight steel cars. 104 pages show many B&W photos and historical sketches.

**205-4** Volume 2
Focuses on streamline passenger cars, including baggage, RPO, dome cars, diner, lounge cars and more.

**NEW 205-5** Volume 3
All about solariums, sleepers and inspection cars.

**NEW 205-6** Passenger Cars Combo **75.00**
Volumes 1, 2 and 3 combined in one package.

**B&O Thunder In The Alleghenies**

**205-97 14.95**
Discover how the B&O was driven to run rail through this treacherous stretch of mountain range. 70 pages.

**The V&O Story**

**205-47 19.95**
Examines the philosophy concepts and history behind W. Allen McClelland's mythical Virginia & Ohio super layout. Photos (some color), 100 pages, 8-1/2 x 11".

**Lehigh & New England**

**205-81 13.95**
Covers the road's turbulent history as a bridge road and major coal hauler. Photos, 80 pages.

**Locomotive Terminals & Railroad Structures**

**205-98 18.95**
Learn historical, structural and design information on a variety of buildings, from roundhouses and water tanks, to signal towers, ash handlers and more. Full of B&W photos. 120 pages.

**NC&STL Dixie Line**

**205-87** Hardcover **27.95**
Enjoy this look at the Nashville, Chattanooga & St. Louis Railway. Many pictures of the road's steam and diesel operations complement an informative history. 98 pages.

**Connecticut Company's Sreetcars**

Depicts operations in Hartford, New Haven, Norwich, New London, Derby, Waterbury, Bridgeport and more. Over 150 photos and illustrations.

**205-83** Hardcover **26.95**

Item listed below is available by Special Order (see Legend Page).
**205-82** Softcover **21.95**

**The Railroad That Came Out At Night**

**205-65 12.95**
Covers railroading in and around Boston as it was from the time South Station was built through the present.

**Extra South**

**205-53 21.95**
Nostalgic look at southern steam railroading. Reprint of 1964 edition with expanded text and photos. 144 pages, 8-1/2 x 11".

**Rails Beyond The Rutland**

**205-54 12.95**
Contemporary operations of the Vermont Railway, Green Mountain Railroad and Clarendon & Pittsford. Pictures of rail action in Vermont's green mountains and a remembrance of Rutland steam power.

**UPRR: The Overland Route**

**205-60 12.95**
Big power and long trains of this great American carrier in the last great days of steam. 11 x 8".

See What's New and Exciting at
**www.walthers.com**

**Cumberland & Pennsylvania**

**205-63 10.95**
Western Maryland acquired famous old C&P. Photos of steam power and unusual g electrics operating in the Alleghenies. 11 x 8".

**Baltimore & Ohio Heritag 1945-1955**

**205-52 7.95**
From 2-8-8-4s and 2-10-2s t 4-4-2s on the old Buffalo & Susquehanna. 48 pages, 11 x 8-1/2".

**Grand Trunk Heritage**

**205-66 11.95**
Covers Grand Trunk steam in Maine, New Hampshire and Quebec. 64 pages.

**Susquehanna: NYS&W**

**205-80 16.95**
From Erie steam and railcars through RS-1s to GP18s. 98 pages, 11 x 8-1/2".

### Modeling

**Traction Planbook (2nd Edition)**



**205-16 9.95**
Packed with specially drawn traction plans. Photos, 98 pages, 8 x 11".

## Carstens
PUBLICATIONS, INC.

### odeling The Wild West

05-62 15.95
earn how to build such period ieces as a wooden trestle, oaling station, water tower, epot, windmill, stock yard, vater mill, grain mill, firehouse nd gold mine. 8 pages full of &W photos.

### peration Handbook For Aodel Railroaders

205-74 12.95
Provides in-depth information of methods and procedures of prototype railroads for transporting freight and passengers, and ways to duplicate prototype activities on model railroads.

### Electrical Handbook For Model Railroads Volume 2, 4th Edition

205-89 14.95
The latest edition of Paul Mallery's advanced electronic handbook. Walkaround, digital control, relays, transistor throttles, track circuits, interlocking signals, cab and command control, TV interference, lighting, trouble-shooting and more. 100 pages.

### Electrical Handbook for Model Railroads Volume 1

205-92 9.95
Basic model railroad electrical information for beginner and advanced modeler. Packed with diagrams and photos. A must for trouble-free operation. 68 pages.

### 150 Years Of Train Models

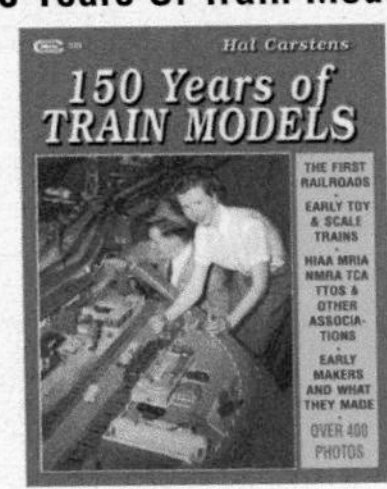


205-95 30.95
A complete history of model railroading from 1846 to the present. Covers a large number of scales, over 150 pages, over 400 photos and illustrations.

### Complete Layout Plans (3rd Edition)

205-96 8.95
A track book for beginners and others who prefer sectional track, whether in N, HO, TT, S or O Scale. Nearly 150 designs, 186-piece track-planning kit, 36 pages, 8 x 11".

### Bridge & Trestle Handbook

205-99 22.95
Details bridge and trestle engineering, construction elements and various types.

### Miscellaneous

### The Circus Moves By Rail

205-84 39.95
A giant collection of rare photos, posters and illustrations that documents the history of the railroad circus. 400 pages.

### Talking To The World From Pan Am's Clippers

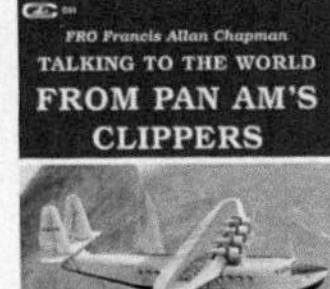

205-91 21.95
Francis Allan Chapman describes his worldwide flying adventures aboard Pan American Airways Clippers. 128 pages.

### Lionel Standard Gauge Era

205-13 4.00
Locos and car types made by Lionel in Standard Gauge 1906-1941. 34 pages, 8-1/2 x 11".

### The Life And Times Of A Locomotive Engineer

205-94 19.95
Account of 40 years on the SP Railroad. 312 pages.

Item listed below is available by Special Order (see Legend Page).

### Toy Trains Of Yesteryear

205-67 5.00
52 pages, 8-1/4 x 11".

## Country Trains

Items are printed in full color except as noted.

Please visit Walthers Web site at www.walthers.com for a complete listing of all available items.

### Bumper Stickers .89 ea
Silkscreen printed, red and black. 10 x 2" unless noted.

**203-21** I Love Trains
**203-24** My Wife Says If I Buy One More Train She'll Leave Me. Gee, I'll Miss Her. (4 x 8")
**203-29** No Smoking Unless You Are a Locomotive
**203-39** Railroaders Love To Couple Up (2 x 12") .

### Logos 1.98 ea
8 x 8" decal stickers.

**203-304** BN
**203-306** Chessie
**203-307** CNW
**203-309** DRGW
**203-322** Texas & Pacific
**203-341** ATSF
**203-342** SP
**203-343** UP
**203-345** Amtrak®
**203-347** PRR
**203-349** MILW
**203-351** D&H
**203-364** NP
**203-365** NS
**203-366** NYC
**203-369** Rock Island
**203-374** UP "Overland"

### Roadname Signs 2.49 ea
12 x 12" unless noted. All signs are heavy cardboard.

**203-877** D&H (10 x 12")
**203-878** SSW (11 x 11")
**203-884** LV
**203-888** CNW
**203-893** Burlington Route (10 x 11")
**203-895** CP
**203-897** Rock Island (11-1/4 x 8")
**203-899** MILW (12-1/2 x 8-1/2")
**203-901** Boston & Maine
**203-908** N&W
**203-909** Maine Central
**203-913** Georgia Railroad
**203-926** Railway Express Agency
**203-929** NKP
**203-930** MKT (10 x 11")
**203-941** Chessie System
**203-946** CSX (9 x 12")
**203-953** NYC Oval
**203-954** NYC Lines (5 x 12")
**203-955** NH (8 x 12")
**203-956** Erie
**203-957** NS "Horse" (8 x 12")
**203-960** Penn Central (5 x 12")
**203-961** B&O
**203-963** Wabash
**203-964** Virginia & Truckee
**203-965** L&N
**203-970** MP Lines (18 x 12")
**203-971** NP (10 x 11")
**203-972** SOO
**203-973** Western Pacific (12-1/8 x 12-1/8")
**203-974** Amtrak (12-1/2 x 7")
**203-975** ATSF (11-3/4 x 11-3/4")
**203-976** GN (11-3/4 x 11-3/4")
**203-977** BNSF Circle Herald
**203-978** SP (12-1/8 x 12-1/8")
**203-979** SP Daylight (12 x 6")
**203-981** PRR (12-1/8 x 12-1/8")
**203-984** CR Quality (4-1/2 x 12")
**203-988** DRGW (9 x 12")
**203-991** BN (12 x 8-3/4")
**203-992** UP
**203-996** SOU

### Wall Signs 2.95 ea (Unless Noted)
Printed in prototypical colors on heavy cardboard. 12 x 12" unless otherwise noted.

**203-872** It's Not My Job to Run the Train
**203-875** To the Trains
**203-914** Caution Model Railroaders At Play
**203-915** No Parking On Railroad Tracks Except When Train Is Coming (12 x 18")
**203-916** Railroad Crossing (round)
**203-918** Railroad Crossing (23 x 23")
**203-919** Stop, Look & Listen (6 x 12")
**203-969** No Smoking Unless You Are A (Locomotive) (4 x 12") .98

## DESIGN PRESERVATION MODELS®

### Structure Catalog

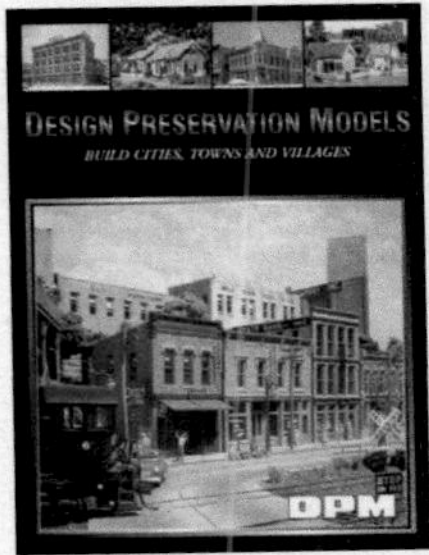


243-13 1.95
A complete listing of all HO, N and O Scale kits, shown in full color.

## RAILROAD SIGNS

**16.59 ea**

Colorful, authentic graphics on porcelain/enamel base. Sized 8 x 8", 8 x 12" and 9" round (unless noted). Graphics identical to magnets shown at left.

234-101

234-102

**234-101** NYC Pay Toilet 3-1/2 x 12"
**234-102** ATSF "The Chief"

234-103

234-104

**234-103** BN
**234-104** Railway Express Agency

234-105

234-106

**234-105** Wells Fargo & Co. Express
**234-106** Maine Central

234-108

234-109

**234-108** Boston & Maine
**234-109** Finck's Overalls

234-110

234-200

**234-110** Telephone
**234-200** ATSF

234-200

234-202

**234-201** Western Pacific
**234-202** NKP

**234-203** Erie
**234-204** UP "The Overland Route"

234-205

THE MILWAUKEE ROAD

234-206

**234-205** Chessie 12 x 8"
**234-206** MILW

234-207

234-208

**234-207** SP
**234-208** GN RY

234-209

234-210

**234-209** NP
**234-210** ROCK 12 x 8"

234-211

234-212

**234-211** Seaboard Railroad
**234-212** CNW

234-213

234-214

**234-213** IC
**234-214** PRR

234-215

234-216

**234-215** MKT
**234-216** Atlantic Coast Line

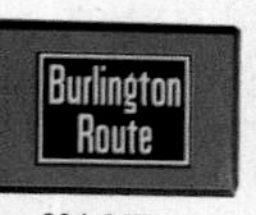


234-217

234-219

**234-217** Burlington Route
**234-219** American Flyer

234-220

234-221

**234-220** B&O
**234-221** DRGW

234-222

234-224

**234-222** Southern
**234-224** MP Eagle

234-225

234-226

**234-225** MON
**234-226** N&W

234-228

234-229

**234-228** NYC
**234-229** Wabash

234-230

234-231

**234-230** RDG
**234-231** SOO

234-232

234-233

**234-232** Railroad Crossing
**234-233** White Pass & Yukon Route

234-234

234-235

**234-234** L&N
**234-235** Frisco

234-236

234-237

**234-236** Durango & Silverton
**234-237** NH

234-239

234-240

**234-239** NS
**234-240** CR

234-241

234-242

**234-241** CNJ
**234-242** To the Trains

234-243

234-244

**234-243** Kansas City Southern
**234-244** D&H

234-245

234-246

**234-245** San Francisco Cable Car Crossing
**234-246** WC

234-247

234-249

**234-247** My Job 8 x 10"
**234-249** BNSF

234-250

234-251

**234-250** Lackawanna
**234-251** CSX

234-252

234-253

**234-252** Canadian Pacific
**234-253** CN

234-254

234-255

**234-254** Mopac (Buzzsaw)
**234-255** Cotton Belt

**NEW 234-256** C&O

## RAILROAD MAGNETS 2.98 ea

Authentic graphics and durable construction. Sized approximately 2 x 2", 2 x 3" and 2-1/4" round.

**234-2** American Flyer Trains
**234-4** Atlantic Coast Line
**234-5** Boston & Maine
**234-6** B&O
**234-7** BN
**234-8** Burlington Route
**234-9** C&O
**234-10** Chessie System
**234-11** CNW
**234-12** Cotton Belt
**234-13** Durango & Silverton
**234-14** Erie

**234-15** Florida East Coast
**234-16** Frisco
**234-17** GN
**234-18** IC
**234-19** L&N
**234-20** MKT
**234-21** Maine Central
**234-22** MILW
**234-23** MON
**234-24** MP Eagle
**234-25** N&W
**234-26** NYC
**234-27** NH
**234-28** NKP
**234-29** NP
**234-30** Pacific Electric
**234-31** PRR
**234-32** RDG
**234-33** DRGW
**234-34** ROCK
**234-35** ATSF
**234-36** ATSF Chief
**234-37** Seaboard Railroad
**234-38** SOO
**234-39** SP
**234-40** Southern
**234-41** UP

**234-42** Virginia & Truckee
**234-43** Wabash
**234-44** Western Pacific
**234-45** White Pass & Yukon Route
**234-46** Railway Express Agency
**234-47** Wells Fargo & Co. Express
**234-48** Railroad Crossing
**234-49** Finck's Overalls
**234-50** AT&T

**234-51** I Love Trains
**234-52** Public Telephone
**234-64** WC
**234-65** BNSF
**234-66** Lackawanna
**234-67** Cable Car Crossing
**234-68** CR
**234-69** NS
**234-70** Kansas City Southern
**234-72** CSX
**234-73** Canadian Pacific
**234-74** CN
**234-75** Mopac (Buzzsaw)
**234-77** D&H
**234-78** CNJ

234-80

234-81

**NEW 234-80** We Can Do It
**NEW 234-81** I Want You

## DOVER PUBLICATIONS

Visit Walthers web site at www.walthers.com for a complete listing of Dover Publications releases.

## NEW PRODUCTS

### Coloring Books

**NEW 241-460665** All Aboard! Trains Activity Kit - Stickers, Crosswords & More **16.95**

**NEW 241-486451747** All Aboard! Trains Activity & Coloring Book **2.95**

**NEW 241-486440095** Famous Trains **3.95**

### CD-ROM Clip Art & Fonts

Use these to print your own billboards, posters, decals and more. Includes CD and book.

**NEW 241-486996840** World War I & II Posters **19.95**

**NEW 241-486998274** Vintage Advertising Illustrations in Color **19.95**

**NEW 241-486999858** 24 Circus Display Fonts **16.95**

## BOOKS

**241-5312** Iron Horses: American Locomotives 1829-1900 **19.95**

**241-8249** The Golden Age Of The Steam Locomotive **21.95**

**241-412474** Illustrated Encyclopedia Of World Railway Locomotives **34.95**

**241-3786** Railroad Engines Around The World Coloring Book **3.95**

**241-23293** Antique Locomotive Coloring Book **3.95**

## FALLER

IMPORTED FROM GERMANY BY WALTHERS

### Catalog

**272-190886 15.99**
Latest edition, with complete listing of structures, auto system cars and accessories, scenery material, lighting and more in HO, N, TT and Z scales. English, French and German text.

## FINE SCALE MINIATURES

### The Fabulous Franklin & South Manchester Railroad

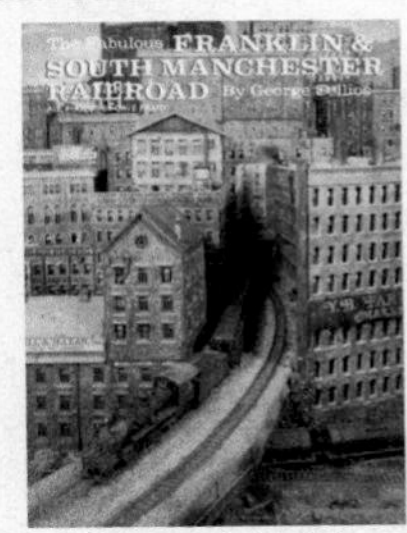


**275-1** Volume 1 **19.95**
A visual treat, from the towering 20-story buildings, down to the tiniest details, such as weeds growing in sidewalk cracks. Softcover, 82 color photos, 80 pages, 8-1/2 x 11".

## GOLDEN WEST BOOKS

Please visit Walthers Web site at www.walthers.com for a complete listing of all available items.

### Union Pacific in Southern California

**NEW 290-95** 1890-1990 **49.95**

### Electric Railways Around San Francisco 24.95 ea

**290-1** Volume 1
**290-2** Volume 2

### The Streamline Era

**290-5 65.95**

### Pacific Electric Railway

**290-10** Volume 4 The Western Division **39.95**

### The Southern Pacific in Los Angeles 1873-1996

**290-7 69.95**

### Union Pacific in Southern California

**290-11 49.95**

### Railroad Photography Western States

**290-12 36.95**

### The Budd Diesel Rail Car

**290-84 57.95**

### Santa Fe RR Getaway 59.95 ea

**290-955** Volume 1
**290-956** Volume 2

### Donner Pass

**290-959 57.95**

Get Your Daily Dose of Product News at
**www.walthers.com**

## NEW PRODUCTS

### Books

### Norfolk & Western: Steam's Last Stand

**NEW 65-475 59.95**
8-1/2 x 11" Landscape Format.

### Stock Car Cyclopedia Volume 1

**NEW 65-476 29.95**
This book features photos and scale drawings, making it an excellent reference for modelers. 100 Pages, Softcover, 8-1/2 x 11" Landscape Format.

## PROTOTYPE RAILROADING

### The South Park Line

**65-399 89.95**
By Mallory Hope Ferrell. 368 pages, 8-1/2 x 11" Format.

### The Allegheny Lima's Finest

**65-448 44.95**
The story of the 2-6-6-6 steam locos built for C&O and the Virginian. 260 pages, Hardcover, 8-1/2 x 11" Format.

### Green Bay & Western The First 111 Years

**65-449 47.95**
350 pages, Hardcover, 8-1/2 x 11" Format.

### NS 1995 Review

**65-450 36.95**
16 full-color pages, 144 pages, Softcover, 8-1/2 x 11" Format.

### Diesel Data Series

In-depth look at the design, development and operational history of various diesel engines.

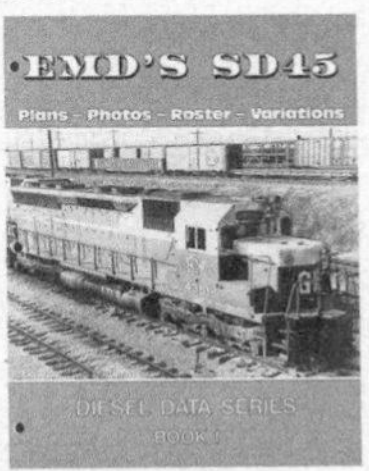


**65-451** EMD SD45 **5.95**
**65-452** ALCO FA-2 **5.95**
**65-453** EMD BL2 **5.95**
**65-454** EMD SD24 **5.95**
**65-455** EMD GP15 **12.95**
**65-460** EMD GP49 **17.95**

### SP Oregon Division

**65-456 59.95**
128 Pages, Hardcover, 12 x 9" Format.

### NP Classic Steam Era

**65-457 59.95**
A complete look at NP steam power. 320 pages, Hardcover, 8-1/2 x 11" Format.

### The Milwaukee Electrics

**65-458 49.95**
304 pages, Hardcover, 11 x 8-1/2" Format.

### Locomotive Cyclopedia

Covers engines from the 0-6-0 and 4-4-0 up to the 2-6-6-6 and 2-8-8-4. 11 x 14" Hardcover. Landscape format with scale drawings
**65-459** Volume I **59.95**

**65-470** Volume II **69.95**
271 pages

### Burlington Northern Northwest Passage

**65-461 59.95**
128 Pages, Hardcover.

### Pere Marquette Revenue Freight Cars

**65-463 34.95**
55 car diagrams 14 lettering diagrams, 200 builder's and in-service photos are provided. 180 pages, Hardcover, 8-1/2 x 11" Format.

### Pennsy Diesels 1924 - 1968

**65-464 55.95**
Hardcover, 8-1/2 x 11" Format.

### The Northern Pacific

**65-465 74.95**
176 pages, Hardcover, 11 x 9" Format, 264 color photos, nine detailed full-color maps.

### Dixie Lines – The L& N Railroad

**65-467 64.95**
160 pages, 12 x 9" Format, 213 color photos, color maps.

### The Virginia & Truckee – The Bonanza Road

**65-468 49.95**
144 pages with 16 full-color pages, Hardcover, 8-1/2 x 11" Format.

### Lima The History

**65-469 59.95**
This 8-1/2 x 11" hardcover book has over 350 pages and more than 550 illustrations.

### The Omaha Road

**65-471 59.95**
The history of the Chicago, St. Paul, Minneapolis & Omaha.

### Slow Trains Down South

**65-472** Volume I Daily 'Cept Sunday **59.95**
Shortlines and logging railroads of the northeastern portion of the "Bible Belt." By Mallory Hope Ferrell

**65-474** Volume II **59.95**
Small steam powered lines of the deep south including Arkansas and Eastern Texas just before abandonement and dieselization.

## EVERGREEN SCALE MODELS

### Books

#### Styrene Modeling

**269-14 14.95**
The first complete and informative text on styrene modeling. Some of the top authors in modeling use projects called "Case Studies In Styrene" to describe their tips and techniques for building and finishing styrene models. Along with easy-to-follow text, there are 174 color and 106 B&W photos. 88 pages, 8-1/2 x 11".

# GIL REID

All prints are packed in a sturdy cardboard tube to protect against dirt and moisture. The larger prints are priced as shown under the color image.

## RAILROAD PRINTS

**PRR-The Intruder-Banks Tower**

70-43 50.00

**The Thrill of a Fast Train-CNW, Morrison, IL**

70-44 42.00

**Chris Burger At The Throttle**

70-36 50.00

**How Not To Fire An M-1**

70-39 50.00

**Apex of the Atlantics**

70-41 35.00

**The 400 At Eau Claire**

70-1020 50.00

**The Cannonball - Milwaukee Road**

70-1016 42.00

**Bad Night On The East End**

70-37 42.00

**Omaha Union Station**

70-1017 42.00

**Oiling 'Round**

70-25 42.00

**The Old Reliable**

70-42 38.00

**Railroad Ghosts**

70-1015 42.00

**Railroad Bull**

70-38 50.00

**Pennsylvania Standard**

70-1019 50.00

**Back Home Again**

70-40 38.00

**SOO Action at Duplainville**

70-34 42.00
17-1/2 x 11-1/2" image on 22 x 16" heavy stock.

**NYC's Great Hudson**

70-1014 42.00
The J-1d, NYC's Hudson 5298, is ready, waiting for the next call for mainline service.

**PRR-Hand Off at Harrisburg**

70-26 42.00

**NYC-Headquarters is Watching**

70-24 42.00

**NYC 79 mph**

70-1018 50.00

## Great Trains Of America

Prints priced at $30.00 are printed on 22 x 16" stock. Interurban prints are on 12 x 15" stock.

**Ten-Wheeler Tradition**

70-27 30.00
CNW engine at Butler Yard.

**The Competitors**

70-32 30.00
A CNW "H" on a bridge, while a MILW S2 goes underneath.

**Union Pacific Flagship**

70-7 30.00
UP Overland Limited drives through the snow at night.

**MILW-Roaring Through Rondout**

70-8 30.00
Hiawatha sweeps north at 100 mph.

**PRR T1 5536: 120 mph Plus?**

70-35 42.00

**Juice Vs. Steam**

70-21 30.00
An interurban from Chicago, South Shore & Bend races o of Chicago.

**PRR-Pennsy's Finest**

70-11 30.00
K4 5425 is smoking it up (fireman's side).

**MILW-Happy Hiawatha Holiday**

70-31 30.00
Engine 1 leaves Milwaukee in 1935.

**NYC-Centuries Pass at Night**

70-13 30.00
J3a passes Valley series observation car.

**NKP-Berkshire at Midnight**

70-14 30.00
S-2 765s crew ready for a fast run.

# IL REID

RR-No. 65 The American

0-4 30.00
tays on time despite driving now.

Vabash, IC, Chicago & lton

0-6 30.00
hose Night Trains at St. Louis Union Station.

PRR-Still on the Payroll 1935

70-30 30.00

PRR-Pennsy Perfection

70-18 30.00

Seaboard Air Line-A Name Like a Cocktail

70-10 30.00
The Orange Blossom Special at speed.

NYC/PRR-Race of the Century

70-2 30.00

CUT-Queen City Quietude

70-3 30.00
Five locos at Cincinnati Union Terminal.

IC-6.6 Miles from Destiny

70-19 30.00
It's Casey Jones on No. 1 tonight!

SP-Gray plus Orange and Red

70-12 30.00
Lark headed by Daylight 4-8-4.

Chicago North Shore & Milwaukee 763 with Diner Passes 757

70-20 30.00

Cincinnati & Lake Erie-Red Devil Fast as a Plane

70-22 30.00

New York Central & Hudson River 999

70-28 30.00
The day before 112.5 mph and the Empire State Express.

# HEIMBURGER HOUSE PUBLISHING

## BOOKS

### Prototype Rail

**Narrow Gauge Country 1870-1970**
30-115 by Mallory Hope Ferrell 59.95

**Norfolk & Western Coal Car Equipment**
30-28 6.95

**The Pioneer Zephyr**
30-111 18.95

**Glover Steam Locomotives: The South's Last Steam Builder**
30-55 41.95

**Mason Steam Locomotives**
30-108 53.95

**The Milwaukee Road: 1928-1985**
30-99 59.95

**Uintah Railway: The Gilsonite Route - Revised**
30-43 44.95

**Rayonier**
30-90 Revised Edition 42.95

**Gilpin Gold Tram**
30-29 39.95

**North Shore/South Shore**
30-93 42.95

**Fiddletown & Copperopolis**
30-12 14.95

**Nevada County Narrow Gauge**
30-911581464 41.95

**The Search For Steam**
30-37 45.95

**Desert Railroading**
30-102 46.95

**America's Rail Pictorial**
30-88 44.95

**Monon Route**
30-58 49.95

**Wabash**
30-9 43.95

**Wabash Standard Plans & References**
30-30 22.95

**Train Country**
30-47 28.95

**The Maine Two-Footers**
30-911581472 44.95

**The American Streamliner: Post-War Years**
30-104 46.95

**Trains Of America**
30-19 45.95

**The Last Of Steam**
30-38 42.95

**Illinois Central: Main Line of Mid-America**
30-46 43.95

**West Side Pictorial**
30-103 53.95

**Colorful East Broad Top**
30-31 26.95

**Rio Grande Steam Locomotives: Standard Gauge**
30-42 43.95

**Chicago & North Western - Milwaukee Road Pictorial**
30-36 32.95

**The American Streamliner (Pre-War Years)**
30-56 44.95

### John Norwood

**Rio Grande Narrow Gauge**
30-7 45.95

**Rio Grande Memories**
30-25 42.95

**John Norwood's Railroads**
30-39 44.95

**Classic Vintage Crawlers and Dozers Vol. I**
30-107 54.95

### Robert W. Richardson

**Rio Grande: Chasing The Narrow Gauge**
30-105 Volume 1 55.95
30-112 Volume 2 55.95
30-109 Chasing Trains 62.95

### Modeling

**Sn3 Modeling**
30-6 14.95

**A.C. Gilbert's Famous American Flyer Trains**
30-911581480 43.95

**The Man Who Lives In Paradise**
30-22 26.95
The autobiography of A.C. Gilbert.



# INTERNATIONAL HOBBY CORP.

## BOOKS

All books are hardcover.

**Steam Locomotive 3-D Pop-Up Book**

348-51795 2.98
A pop-up guide to the history and use of steam engines. Seven intricate dimensional spreads show famous steam locomotives, and the accompanying text is full of facts.

**Stations**

348-52100 3.98
The fictional journey we each take along the tracks of memory, where time and place intersect the lost world of home.

# KROMER CAP CO.

**Railroad Cap**

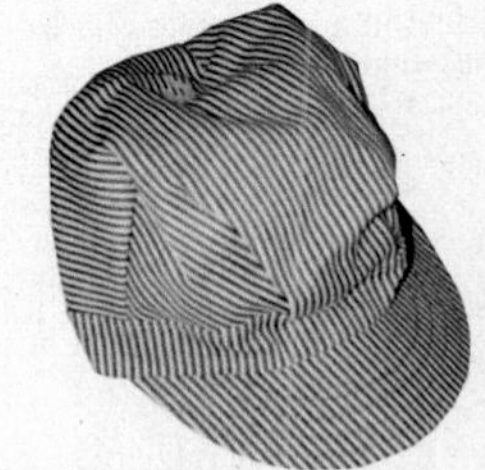

407-775 Adjustable Cap 9.99
Blue-and-white striped cotton cap. Fully washable. Pleated one-piece top.

# GREEN FROG PRODUCTIONS

## NEW PRODUCTS

### Prototype Railroading

**Tracks of the Old Pennsylvania Railroad**

NS conquers the Allegheny mountains with hard working locomotives and helpers from Spruce Creek westward to the scenic Conemaugh Gorge. Enjoy mountain railroading amid blazing fall colors in this video shot by professional photographer Rich Scheid. About 90 minutes with Dolby Digital 5.1 Surround.

**NEW 302-20109** DVD **29.95**

**In Search of Narrow Gauge Mikados**

Tim Lab spent five years finding and photographing classic narrow gauge 2-8-2s including the 464, 473, 476, 478, 480, 481, 484, 487, 488, 489 and 497. All were beautifully filmed performing their daily duties, many in locations you've never seen before, including the Huckleberry Railroad in Michigan and the "off limits" areas of the Durango roundhouse and yards as well! Approx. 81 minutes.

**NEW 302-31687** DVD **24.95**

**The 60s: Passenger, Steam & Electrics**

A fascinating look at 1960s vintage action in and around Chicago including equipment and operations on the Wabash, Rock Island, IC, ATSF, B&O, PRR, and C&O, plus the last days of steam on the CNW and GTW. Approx. 78 minutes.

**NEW 302-31688** DVD **24.95**

**Oakley Narrow Gauge**

This two CD set starts out with amazing footage from 1995 of Rio Grande's narrow gauge #463, a class K-27, showing her stuff working an authentic D&RGW freight through the mountains and prairies of the Rockies. This one includes many, many run-bys in remote locations, mostly only accessible by train! The second disk stars Rio Grande Derrick OP, along with authentic maintenance of way cars and caboose, all pulled by #463. This is the ONLY time this train has ever appeared in this configuration, and follows its run from Chama to Antonito and return... including beautiful scenes throughout the line...both tunnels, Toltec Gorge, water stops, and much, much more. Each disc is about 60 minutes long.

**NEW 302-31689** Two DVD Set **29.95**

**Rocky Mountain Steam Trains**

Green Frog's professional Hi-Definition cameras capture two of the most scenic railroads in the United States... the Cumbres and Toltec, and the Durango & Silverton. From Chama, New Mexico, to Silverton, Colorado, you'll see great coverage of these tourist Railroads, as well as spectacular scenery and mountains in all their glory.

**NEW 302-31690** Standard TV (4x3) Format **29.95**
Complete program formatted for current standard TVs and DVD players. One hour and 44 minutes.

**NEW 302-31691** Wide Screen High-Definition **29.95**
Complete program in 1080i high-definition for amazing clarity and picture quality, with Dolby Digital 5.1 surround sound audio. PLEASE NOTE: Requires HD DVD format player; will not operate on regular or Blu Ray DVD players. Two disk set, approx. 80 minutes total.

### Model Railroading

**Building the Denver & Rio Grande Western Narrow Gauge**

Watch as the famed narrow gauge line comes to life in HOn3 in this series of DVDs. Each volume covers several phases of construction, with plenty of great how-to tips and ideas that can be used to build any layout.

**NEW 302-20104** Volume I **29.95**
The project layout begins with the Durango yard. You'll see how the basement room was finished, and the scenic backdrop was painted. Next it's on to building benchwork, laying dual gauge track, adding some structures and scenery, and building and wiring the yard control panel. 60 minutes.

**NEW 302-20107** Volume II **24.95**
This program covers building of the complete Garden Flower Mill. The scenery along the river at Durango gets finished with great looking Cottonwood trees, rocks and shrubs. The yard area gets additional details and scenery, while the town gets a concrete street and the station tracks are ballasted. 60 minutes.

**The Appalachian Coal Industry Modeling the Prototype**

Here's a complete look at this fascinating industry, which has inspired modelers for years. Examine the history of the coal industry in Appalachia, then see how coal moves from mines to end-users. You'll see all phases of the operation, from the inside of a mine, preparation plants, storage facilities, loaders, a rotary dumper, coking operations to steel mills and of course, plenty of trains. And there are excellent examples of model railroads based on the industry too! To help you get started with your model coal facilities, a demonstration on building a conveyer belt system is featured. Approx. 61 minutes.

**NEW 302-31679** DVD **24.95**

For Up-To-Date Information and News Bookmark Walthers Web site at

**www.walthers.com**

**Painting Backdrops**

Greg Gray, a professional ar with over 30 backdrops to hi credit and over 30 years of experience in teaching and giving clinics at model railroa conventions, shows how to change blank walls into far reaching vistas. You'll learn how to sketch in a rough outline, fill-in with preliminary washes, and add in detail. Learn how to select brushes and paints, prepare the surface, and even install a curved corner, then paint tre sky, clouds, bushes, and buildings that appear three-dimensional. Approx. 81 minutes.

**NEW 302-31680** DVD **24.95**

**Railfanning the Santa Fe**

Gary Hoover's layout showcases his favorite locations from Illinois to the Pacific with scenes that railfar would have to travel for days cover. But we cover them all i this video adventure, includin Castle Gate, Utah, the desert of the southwest, the mountains of Colorado, a Pacific coast scene with a working lighthouse, and more As an added bonus, Gary demonstrates how he modele ocean waves and offers tips o building a prototype scene for photography. Approx. 54 minutes.

**NEW 302-31681** DVD **24.95**

### Styrene The Ideas, Tips & Techniques of Dean Freytag

Learn how to work with plastic from the master himself, Dean Freytag. This exclusive in-depth video presents Dean's many ideas on creating interesting and unique models, and shows how to apply these tips and techniques to your own projects. Dean covers adhesives, materials and parts, construction basics, tools, kitbashing, scratchbuilding and finishing in this 61 minute DVD.

**NEW 302-31682** DVD **24.95**

# VIDEOS & DVDS

## Prototype Railroading

### CN North America Volume 4

Rich Scheid's camera follows CN's North American operations from Niagara Falls, NY across the border to Canada, then up to Toronto. Cross Ontario to Windsor and climb aboard a freight train for a cab ride through the Detroit River tunnels under the international border to Detroit, MI. Features fantastic shots of the Niagara rapids, Niagara River Gorge, downtown Toronto, the world-famous CN tower and CN's Macmillan Yard. Visits many North American CN depots and crosses the rolling farmland of Southern Ontario. 90 minutes.

**302-20089** DVD **29.95**

### Emery Gulash Collection

**5 Disc DVD Set 59.95 ea**

Some of Emery Gulash most popular videos are now available in 5-pack DVD sets.

**302-20087** First Generation Diesels and Classic Steam Over five hours of classic steam and first-generation diesels from the 50s, 60s and 70s. Includes The Nickel Plate, California Zephyr, Pennsylvania Railroad, The Wabash Railroad and Western Maryland (End of an Era).

**302-20097** Narrow Gauge Collection Almost six hours of narrow gauge from the 50s, 60s and 70s. Includes Top Frog Volume 1, The East Broad Top, Rotary on the Rio Grande, The Chama Turn and the three episode set Switchin' Along the Rio Grande, Twilight of the Rio Grande and Worktrain to Silverton.

### Feather River Volume 2: Tracks of the Old Western Pacific

Travel along with professional photographer Rich Scheid as he captures great footage of the Feather River canyon along the old Western Pacific between Portola and Oroville in Northern California. Visit the Portola Railroad Museum before going through Clio to view trains from many angles on the longest trestle along the route. From there, head west to Williams Loop and the Keddie Wye trestle for more great camera angles. Then it's on through the canyon for spectacular views of trains hugging granite cliffs as they roll above the roaring white water rapids of the Feather River. Your tour ends at the canyon's west end with lots of UP and BSNF trains. Approximately 85 minutes.

**302-20083** DVD **29.95**

### Illinois Hot Spots

More action-packed video from the camera of Steve Neff. Contemporary action from 1989-1990 is captured at Galesburg, Tuscola, Effingham, Benton, East Dubuque, Centralia and East Clinton. You'll see operations on the UP, ATSF, BN, CR and NW in one of America's favorite train-watching areas. 1 hour.

**302-31666** DVD **24.95**

### Marion: The Train Watching Capitol of Ohio

With 30 scheduled trains per day running through town, Marion is a railfan's delight. Follow Steve Neff's camera as he captures the incredible action on Conrail, CSX and Norfolk Southern in Marion. 57 minutes.

**302-31665** DVD **24.95**

### The Monongahela Railway

The Monongahela, a major coal hauling railroad in Pennsylvania and West Virginia is organized into two operating divisions. Catch the action on the Western Division Branches including West Brownsville, Ten Mile, Waynesburg, Miracle Run and the Manor Branch including Bailey Mine. Unit trains from Detroit Edison, Somerset Railway, Wisconsin Electric and others are shown. See motive power from the Pittsburgh and Lake Erie, CNW, CSX, Detroit Edison and Conrail as well as the Monon's own Super 7s. 59 minutes.

**302-31664** DVD **24.95**

### The New Georgia Railroad: Steam at its Best Ala The 1950s

During 1986, the state of Georgia leased loco number 750, a sparkling, high-wheeled 4-6-0 Pacific type from the Atlanta Chapter of the Railroad Historical Society. Originally built for the Florida East Coast Railroad, this loco was eventually sold to the Savannah and Atlanta railroad where it remained in service until retired. The Atlanta chapter of the NRHS obtained it in the 60s and refurbished it for runs by the state of Georgia. The 50s train makes its way around an 18 mile loop 4 times a day each day it runs. Speeds up to 60 MPH are attained. Includes scenes with a beautifully restored E-8 painted in the colors of the New Georgia Railroad. Approx. 28 minutes.

**302-31667** DVD **24.95**

## Narrow Gauge

### The Cumbres & Toltec In '73

In the fall of 1973, the Cumbres & Toltec was a very different railroad than today. Double headers were the norm, and no passenger cars existed. Covered in this video is Mike #483, now out of service. Mike 487 also helps out sporting its snowplow for these runs. This is a fall color bonanza, shot in September when the aspen are at their peak by noted photographer Jerry Carson. Approx. 37 minutes.

**302-31668** DVD **24.95**

### The Shasta Route: Tracks of the Old Southern Pacific

The action begins in Klamath Falls, Oregon and follows the Cascade line south into California along the base of Mt. Shasta and then through towns at its base all the way south to Redding. 83 minutes.

**302-20067** DVD **29.95**

### Tracks of the Old C&O and the Ohio Central Steam Specials

The action starts at the Kentucky-Ohio border and follows the old C&O North-South mainline (now CSX) up through Columbus, Ohio. Then it's off to eastern Ohio on the Ohio Central to chase a steam special headed by ex-GTW 4-8-4 #6325 back to Columbus, Ohio. CSX action then continues north from Columbus up the old C&O mainline to just south of Fostoria, Ohio. 87 Minutes.

**302-20060** DVD **29.95**

### I've Been Working on the Railroad
This action video tells it all by comparing trackwork done by the railroads in the 1950s and earlier with the heavily automated way it is done today. First we see work being done in the days of steam. We fast forward to the mid-1990s, where wood ties are being replaced with concrete ties. 45 minutes.

**302-20065** DVD **29.95**

### BNSF Spokane To Portland
**302-20028** DVD **29.95**

### BNSF, Cajon Pass, Canyon Diablo & Flagstaff
Travel through spectacular Cajon Pass, Canyon Diablo, and Flagstaff on this whirlwind railroad video adventure through the far West. Approx. 58 minutes.

**NEW 302-31684** DVD **24.95**

### BNSF: The Front Range. Crawford Hill, The Plains
An exciting journey along the Front Range of the Rocky Mountains and across the vast expanse of the Great Plains, showcasing spectacular railroad action on BNSF and UP amid beautiful western scenery.

**NEW 302-31685** DVD **19.98**

### BNSF: Tracks Of The Goat
Volume 1: Over Marias Pass and Thru Glacier Park. Volume 2 travels through the Cascade Mountains of Washington, down Steven's Pass, and ends up visiting Tacoma and Vancouver.

**302-20034** DVD Volume 1 **29.95**

**302-20029** DVD Volume 2 **29.95**

### BNSF: Tracks Of The Old Santa Fe
Follow the old Santa Fe line from Cajon Pass Summit through Victorville and on to Barstow, California. Then on to Needles, California and Topock where the BNSF crosses the Colorado River. Also features Kingman Canyon, Kingman, Walapai, Hackberry, Valentine, Seligman and Williams, Arizona. Approximately 60 minutes.

**Volume 1**
**302-20003** DVD **29.95**

**Volume 2**
Travel from Arizona to New Mexico, enjoying the ride aboard ATSF Warbonnets and BNSF Pumpkins.
**302-20036** DVD **29.95**

**Volume 3**

**NEW 302-20102** DVD **29.95**

### Cass & Mower Logging Trains
**302-20030** DVD **29.95**

### Classic Steam Of The 20s Through The 40s
**302-31606** DVD **24.95**

### CN North America - Volume I
Join photographer Rich Scheid as he visits CN operations in Southern Ontario and CN's South Eastern subsidiary, Grand Trunk, on the Mt. Clemens Subdivision.
**302-20100** DVD **24.95**

### CN North America - Volume II
See operations in Southern Michigan on the old Grand Trunk Western's Flint and Holly Subdivisions. Visit Battle Creek, Bellevue, Charlotte, and Potterville, Durand, Flint, Lapeer, Emmet, Imlay City and Port Huron, Fenton and Waterford and finally Pontiac, Michigan. Approximately 60 minutes.
**302-20007** DVD **29.95**

### CN North America - Volume 3
Action on CN's former GTW Holly and Shoreline Subdivisions. Includes Royal Oak, Detroit, Delray Tower, Milwaukee Jct and a cab ride on a Detroit Edison coal train. Flat Rock Yard to Toledo's Lang Yard are also covered. 96 minutes.

**302-20056** DVD **29.95**

### Conrail Middle Division
From Altoona to Harrisburg, visit the "longest stone arch bridge in the world" at Rockville, PA, the famous Horseshoe Curve and more. 60 minutes.
**302-20091** DVD **29.95**

### Conrail Pittsburgh To Crestline
Go through over 20 locations, including Conway Yard, where over 4000 cars a day are classified. 60 minutes.
**302-20092** DVD **29.95**

### Conrail - The West Slope
Tremendous action between Gallitzin, PA, and Johnstown, PA. 60 minutes.

**NEW 302-20090** DVD **29.95**

### Conrail Winter
**302-20094** DVD **29.95**

### Conrail's Big-4
Visit places such as Terre Haute, Greencastle and Avon, Indiana, as well as Effingham and East St. Louis, Illinois and more. Highlights include IC, UP, BN, NS and CSX. 60 minutes.
**302-20093** DVD **29.95**

### The East Broad Top
Includes coverage from the early 1950s through the 1970s. 120 minutes.

**302-31624** DVD **34.95**

### Feather River Canyon Spectacular
Visit the spectacular Shasta Route under the snow-covered Mt. Shasta, the fabulous Feather River Canyon and treacherous Donner Pass where two steam locomotives, the UP's 844 on the point and its Challenger behind, pull 22 passenger cars. 55 minutes.
**302-20095** DVD **29.95**

### Florida East Coast
Videographer Rob McCormack of Canrail Video captures the line from Jacksonville to Miami... including some beautiful night shots, as well as daytime action galore. Approx. 74 minutes.
**NEW 302-20101** DVD **29.95**

### Illinois Central
37 years of the Illinois Central from steam to diesel. Disc 1 covers the last of steam from original 16mm footage by Jerry Carson. Disc 2 shows contemporary action on the "Mainline of Mid America." Also included is a slide show of IC images never before on DVD. 140 minutes.

**302-20059** DVD **39.95**

### The Last Steam Operated Sawmill
The state of Oregon is home to the very last steam operated sawmill in the U.S. Enjoy a grand tour; following the logs from delivery, to the mill pond, to debarking, sawing, edging, sorting and finished goods. Approximately 30 minutes.
**302-31631** DVD **19.95**

### NASA Railroad
An in-depth look at a truly different railroad that moves rocket motors, rocket fuel an a wide range of items with a fleet of special cars. Color, 6 minutes.
**302-20064** DVD **29.95**

### Norfolk Southern
**Volume I: Atlanta to Chatanooga**

**302-20071** DVD **29.95**

**Volume II: The Kentucky Divisior**
Covers the action between Debutts Yard in Chattanooga the crew change point at Oakdale.

**302-20072** DVD **29.95**

**Volume III: Deeper Into the Rathole**
Venture into Norfolk Southern's throbbing Rathole line from Oakdale, TN to Somerset, KY. Watch as trains highball through spectacular deep cuts dug in the early 1960s. Enjoy vintage steam scenes on the K&T. Take a cab ride in the Big South Fork train, pulled by an Alco S-1 equipped with a steam whistle! You'll also visit a partially reconstructed coal mine. 55 minutes.

**302-20073** DVD **29.95**

**Limited Quantity Available**
**302-53177** VHS **29.95**

**Volume IV: Tracks of the Old N&W**
Visit the coal mountains of West Virginia, beginning in Blue Field, West Virginia and working north through Mayberry, Switch Back, Elkhorn, Kyle, Northfork, Keystone, Kimball, Superior, Welch and Roderfield. Approximately 56 minutes.

**302-20070** DVD **29.95**

**Volume V: Tracks of the Old N&W Part 2**
**302-20016** DVD **29.95**

**Northern Pacific**
**302-31610** DVD **24.95**

**Rails Chicago**
Switching and mainline running in the "Windy City." Revised. 56 minutes.
**302-31673** DVD **24.95**

**Rails New York Metro**
Follow photographer Richard Kugel as he documents action around New York City in the months prior to the Conrail split and the weeks that followed.
**302-31669** DVD **24.95**

**The Rio Grande Southern/ Denver & Rio Grande Western**
Visit the Black Canyon at Gunnison, now under a lake, as well as Lizard Head Pass, Durango, Cerro Summit and many more.
**302-31645** DVD **24.95**

**Rock Island Railroad**
Follow the history of the Rock Island with photography captured from 1958 to 1970.
**302-31603** DVD **24.95**

**South Shore Line**
A look at the South Shore in 1975-78.
**302-31635** DVD **24.95**

**The St. Louis Sojourn**
Visit St. Louis Station and other locations in and around St. Louis. 60 minutes.
**302-31629** DVD **24.95**

**Steam Giants Across America**
Witness the exciting action of massive articulated steam locomotives. Featuring Stereo Hi-Fi sound. 60 minutes.
**302-31608** DVD **24.95**

**Steam In The 50s**
Three volumes cover steam's final years. Volume I: MP, NP, Pennsy, IC, B&O and more; 60 minutes. Volume II: UP, DM&IR, CNW and more; 35 minutes. Volume III: NP, Klickitat Lumber, N&W and more. 60 min.
**302-31618** DVD Volume I **24.95**
**302-31619** DVD Volume II **24.95**
**302-31620** DVD Volume III **24.95**

**Steam Shortlines Of The South**
A fantastic tape of 15 different steam operated railroads in the South, shot in the 1950s and 60s.
**302-31675** DVD **24.95**

**Suwanee Steam Special**
Features #1218 in the Florida sun. 60 minutes.
**302-31628** DVD **24.95**

**Three Decades Of Excursion**
See and hear number 4501 as she pulls three decades of steam excursions. Color, 90 minutes.
**302-31621** DVD **24.95**

**Top Frog Volume 4**
1950s to 1970s passenger train action from NYC, PRR, EL, MON, MP, CB&Q, Gulf, Mobile & Ohio, B&O, IC, C&O, MILW, Penn Central and Grand Trunk. 60 minutes.
**302-31614** DVD **24.95**

**Top Frog 5 Early Diesels**
Footage from ATSF, UP, EL, DRGW, MILW, NYC, Gulf, Mobile & Ohio, SOO, B&O, PRR, NKP and ROCK. 60 minutes.
**302-31615** DVD **24.95**

**Top Frog Volume 6**
Covers the DRGW action of the 50s and 60s on the now abandoned line between Durango and Chama. 30 minutes.
**302-31616** DVD **24.95**

**Top Frog Volume 7**
50s, 60s and 70s equipment and trains are featured in this 45 minute video. Highlights include passenger, freight and many first generation diesels of CB&Q.
**302-31617** DVD **24.95**

**Train Mountain Museum**
Located in Southern Oregon near Chiloquin, Train Mountain has over 200 acres of operation, including storage and maintenance facilities.
**302-31640** DVD **24.95**

**Train Mountain Museum 2000**
Explore this incredible, live steam operation that now has over 75,000 feet (over ten miles!) of track making it the largest 7-1/2" gauge road in the world. This railroad can handle 300 trains!
**302-31641** DVD **24.95**

**Twilight Of Steam**
A fantastic collection of steam from the 1960s and 70s. 60 minutes.
**302-31605** DVD **24.95**

**Union Pacific Super Railroad**

**Volume I: Western Illinois to Cheyenne, Wyoming**
Lots of action, multiple train meets and more. 60 minutes.

**302-20075** DVD **29.95**

**Volume II: Cheyenne to Ogden**
Visit the mines in the Powder River Basin, follow the UP to Sherman Hill, by way of the Hermosa tunnels and much more! Stereo Hi-Fi sound and 90 minute running time.

**302-20076** DVD **29.95**

**Volume III: Butte to Pocatello**

**302-20077** DVD **24.95**

**Volume IV: The Oregon Short Line**

**302-20078** DVD **29.95**

**Volume V: The LaGrande Subdivision**

**302-20079** DVD **24.95**

**Volume VI: The Lordsburg Sub, the Scenic Southwest**

**302-20080** DVD **29.95**

**Union Pacific Tracks Of The Old Mopac**
**302-20017** DVD Volume I **29.95**
**302-20018** DVD Volume II **29.95**

**Western Maryland - End Of An Era**
Original color films chronicling the final years of the Western Maryland.
**302-31637** DVD **24.95**

**The Circus & The Railroad**
In the "good ol' days" most circuses traveled by railroad. You'll get to see how it was done first hand as you view how equipment and animals were loaded and unloaded, a circus parade and Wisconsin's Circus World Museum. 30 minutes.
**302-31663** DVD **24.95**



**Gateway To The Pacific: BNSF & UP**
Travel along the Columbia River Gorge with BNSF on the north side and follow the UP along the south side. You'll also visit places like Stampede Pass, Stevens Pass and more. 60 minutes.

**NEW 302-31686** DVD **24.95**

**Rails New Orleans**
**302-31674** DVD **24.95**

**Top Frog 3 The Best Of Passenger Trains**
Great photography, action and color. 60 minutes.
**302-31613** DVD **24.95**

**The Golden Twilight of Postwar Steam**

**Part 1: The Pennsy's West End and its Neighbors**
Features an incredible array of steamers from the Pennsy including J-1, T-1, K-4, M-1A, H Class 0-8-0, H-6, H-10 locos. Early diesels include F units and Baldwin Centipedes. Also featured are vintage neighboring Chicago and St Louis railroads. From original color and black-and-white footage by Gene Miller. 54 minutes.

**302-20058** DVD **34.95**

GREEN FROG PRODUCTIONS

**Part 2: Rails in the Heartland**
Features Chicago and Eastern Illinois Railway and L&N action in and around Evansville, Indiana just after WWII From original color and black-and-white footage by Gene Miller. 46 minutes.

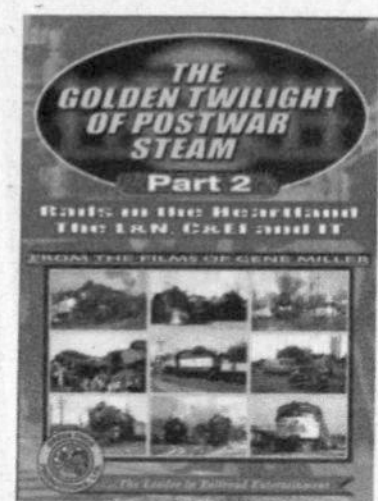

**302-20066** DVD **34.95**

**Part 3: Cajon to Horseshoe**
Classic film taken by Gene Miller during the 40s and 50s when steam power was disappearing and the first generation diesels appeared. Travel with Gene as he captures train action in the metro Chicago and St. Louis areas west to the UP, Santa Fe and SP, then heads back to the B&O in Kentucky and wraps it up on PRR's legendary Horseshoe Curve.

**302-20088** DVD **34.95**

### 70s & 80s Steam Celebration
**302-20027** DVD **29.95**

### Atlanta Railroads-Their History & Their Story
A documentary covering the history from the very first train to today's operations. 60 minutes.

**302-31632** DVD **24.95**

### The California Zephyr
Filmed in 1965 aboard and trackside the California Zephyr. 60 minutes.

**302-31623** DVD **24.95**

### Chicago Odyssey
Volume I: Action in and around Chicago in the 1950s and 1960s. Volume II: 1960s and 1970s. 2-1/2 hours.

**302-20012** DVD Volume I, 2-Disc Set **39.95**

**302-20013** DVD Volume II, 2-Disc Set **39.95**

### Erie Lackawanna
Begins in early 1962 after the merger of the Erie and Delaware, Lackawanna & Western and continues to the formation of Conrail in 1976.

**302-31627** DVD **39.95**

### New York Central Odyssey
**Volume I**
Two-disc set features action of first-generation diesels. 150 minutes.

**302-20014** DVD Volume I, 2-Disc Set **39.95**

**Volume II**
Summer 1963. Transition to the Cigar Band Herald, action on Toledo Division and merger into Penn Central. 2 hours, 40 minutes. 2-Disc set.

**302-20015** DVD Volume II, 2-Disc set **39.95**

### The Nickel Plate
Steam and First Generation diesels in the 50s and 60s as well as the Akron, Canton & Youngstown. 45 minutes.

**302-31601** DVD **24.95**

### Northeast Vintage Diesels
**302-31633** DVD **24.95**

### Pacific Northwest Kaleidoscope
Full color, 16mm footage in the 1930s through early 1970s. Lots of Milwaukee Road action. 60 minutes.

**302-31604** DVD **24.95**

### Passenger Trains Of The 60s
Three episodes on one DVD! See the last few years of pre-Amtrak® passenger action in New England, Memphis, Atlanta and Birmingham. Railroads include the NH, L&N, IC, SOU, SAL, ACL and more. 2 hours, 13 minutes.

**302-20063** DVD **29.95**

### The Penn Central
**Volume I**
Scenes before the PRR and NYC merger around Valparaiso, Indiana and Wayne, Michigan. Post merger scenes include Detroit and St. Louis. Tape two: later operations in Michigan, Ohio, Windsor, Canada and Buffalo, New York. Two tapes, color, narration, Stereo Hi-Fi sound and 180 minute running time.

**302-31609** DVD Volume I, 2-Disc Set **39.95**

**Volume II**
Visit Chicago, Ohio and Michigan, including Detroit, Ann Arbor, Ypsilanti, Niles, Toledo, Jackson and Carleton. 60 minutes.

**302-31634** DVD Volume II **24.95**

**Volume III**
Original footage from Emery Gulash taken in 1971-72 including early Amtrak action in Chicago and Detroit, TurboTrain demonstrations, Chessie specials and a wide range of daily PC operations in Ohio and Michigan.

**NEW 302-20103** DVD Volume III **34.95**

### Pennsylvania Railroad
From 1952 until the merger with the NYC, covers the end of steam and classic First Generation diesels.

**302-31607** DVD **24.95**

### Rails in Transition Odyssey
Noted rail photographer Jerry Carson captured a time of major change for the railroad industry. See plenty of 60s and 70s action in this two-disc set including vintage MP, N&W, GM&O, PRR, Frisco, CNW, C&O, B&O, South Shore, MKT, ATSF and more. 1hour, 44 minutes.

**302-20062** DVD **39.95**

### Rio Grande Odyssey
From the early 60s until the 80s, see First Generation Geeps, narrow gauge steam and great freight and passenger train action. 2-1/2 hours.

**302-20019** DVD 2-Disc Set **39.95**

Latest New Product News Daily! Visit Walthers Web site at **www.walthers.com**

### The RoadRailers
First introduced by C&O as far back as 1955, this unique method of freight operation still exists today. 30 minutes.

**302-31622** DVD **24.95**

### Santa Fe Odyssey
**Volume I**
From 1952 until 1980, rail photographer Emery Gulash shot the Santa Fe from Chicago to the west. See the Santa Fe FT freight units, the PA passenger power, and a variety of switchers and road trains. The "Warbonnet" paint scheme and the change to the Santa Fe blue scheme is also covered in this chronology. 2 hours, 10 minutes.

**302-20002** DVD Volume I w/Bonus Features **39.95**

**Volume II**
Santa Fe revitalizes its diesel fleet in the 1970s. 120 minutes.

**302-20032** DVD Volume II **39.95**

**Volume III**
Santa Fe from the 1950s to the 1980s. 105 minutes.

**302-20033** DVD Volume III **39.95**

### Top Frog 2 - Best Of Steam
Steam scenes from the 50s along with fan trip runs in the 60s and 70s. 1 hour.

**302-31611** DVD **24.95**

### Wabash Railroad
From 1954 until the merger with the N&W. First Generation diesels and plenty of passenger trains. 60 minutes.

**302-31602** DVD **24.95**

### Traction N' Trolleys
Great film from the 30s, 40s and some from the 50s and 60s. Shows how it used to be when traction and trolleys were an integral part of our economy. 60 minutes.

**302-31671** DVD **24.95**

### All Aboard TV Series
11 hours of railroad excitement, as 26 separate episodes of All Aboard are combined into one five-disc set, showcasing the many aspects of the North American railroad scene.

**302-20057** 5-Disc Set **99.95**

### Amtrak's California Zephy Discovering The Great American West
Chicago to the West Coast, aboard and off train. Visit wit crews, stop at the Golden Spike Monument and visit the California State Railroad Museum. 48 minutes.

**302-31625** DVD **24.95**

### CSX Volume I: Atlanta To Chattanooga
Fast paced action meets, branch line operations and yard activity. 60 minutes.

**302-20039** DVD **29.95**

### CSX Volume 2: Chattanooga To Nashville
Spectacular scenery including Cowan tunnel, Cumberland Mountain and Nickajack Lake.

**302-20041** DVD **29.95**

**CSX Volume 3: Nashville To Louisville**
See two ex-L&N branch lines, CF-7s and the Kentucky Railroad Museum. Civil War history, fast paced CSX action, including Radner Yard.

**302-20042** DVD **29.95**

**CSX Volume 4: Louisville To Cincinnati**
Travel the line from yard to yard and see fantastic bridges, tunnels and fast paced action.

**302-20043** DVD **29.95**

**CSX Volume 5: Evansville To Chicago**
Covers fast paced action at the Ohio River bridge, night action at Evansville yard, Vincennes, Indiana, Terra Haute and more.

**302-20044** DVD **29.95**

**CSX Volume 6: Pittsburgh to Willard, Ohio**
Follow over 200 miles of track through beautiful fall scenery. 60 minutes.

**302-20045** DVD **29.95**

**CSX Volume 7: Jacksonville To Plant City, Florida**

**302-20046** DVD **29.95**

**CSX Volume 8: Baltimore Service Lane**

**302-20047** DVD **29.95**

**CSX Volume 9: VHS Willard to Deshler, Ohio**
You'll see the addition of a new main, an expansion addition to the yard at Willard and contractors installing new track and new signaling systems. Visit a hobo stew party, meet locals of Deshler and learn about the important history of this town to the B&O.

**302-20048** DVD **29.95**

**CSX Volume 10: VHS Augusta to Spartanburg**
Travel along CSX's hilly regions between Augusta, GA, and Spartanburg, SC. Includes heavy freight action with helpers at the rear, a cab ride in a new wide cab AC engine, visits to the yards on both ends of the line and more.

**302-20049** DVD **29.95**

**CSX Volume 11: Greenwood To Atlanta (Abbeville Subdivision)**
Includes spectacular coverage of the long bridge over the Hartwell Reservoir, train meets, a crew change at Abbeville, fast runbys, as well as archival footage from the 80s.

**302-20050** DVD **29.95**

**CSX Volume 12: Pennsylvania & Western Maryland Fall Spectacular**
View Amtrak, freights with helper service, yard action, track crews keeping the railroad running and Ohio River crossings throughout Pennsylvania and Maryland. Approximately 60 minutes.

**302-20051** DVD **29.95**

**CSX Volume 13: The Big Sandy Sub: A Story About Eastern Kentucky Coal**
See coal being loaded, visit the coal mines of Shelby, Kentucky, ride a set of pushers from Shelby over the Pine Mountains to Virginia, and then ride the head end back through Elkhorn City and on to Shelby. Approximately 70 minutes.

**302-20052** DVD **29.95**

**CSX Volume 14: Selkirk (Albany), NY: The Capital District & The Hudson/ Mohawk Valleys**
Explore the CSX lines including the River Line, the Hudson Line and the Boston Line, as well as the Chicago Line and witness a non-stop parade of trains. In addition to CSX, we will also enjoy trains of Conrail, Amtrak, MBTA, Metro- North, New England Central, Canadian National and Canadian Pacific. Approximately 58 minutes.

**302-20053** DVD **29.95**

**CSX Volume 15: Clinchfield Autumn**
Spectacular. Go deep into the valleys of Kentucky, Virginia and Tennessee along CSX's former Clinchfield Kingsport line. Enjoy mountain railroading in the Blue Ridge Mountains. Approximately 60 minutes.

**302-20008** DVD **29.95**

**Empire Builder**
Volume I is a documentary about the Amtrak train from Chicago. Includes interviews with crew members. Volume II is a railfan-oriented tape with aerial shots, in-cab scenes, run-bys and train action.

**302-31636** DVD Volume I **34.95**

**From Coal To Kilowatts - The Coal Trains Of Detroit Edison**
The most comprehensive coal train tape ever produced. From the mines to dumping at the power plant. 90 minutes.

**302-31661** DVD **24.95**

**Maintenance Of Way Yesterday & Today**
Hear from the experts how railroads manage this impressive operation and see how it's done. 45 minutes.
**302-20065** DVD **29.95**

**Railroading Through The Winter Of '93**
Great coverage of the blizzard of 1993 in the Northeast corner of the U.S. and in Southeast Canada. You'll see CN, CP, Amtrak, CSX, Grand Trunk and more. 60 minutes.

**302-31670** DVD **24.95**

**Steel Rails - Private Varnish**
Action inside and out of the best private cars in North America. 60 minutes.

**NEW 302-31683** DVD **34.95**

**The Toledo, Peoria & Western**
**302-31630** DVD **24.95**

**Union Pacific Odyssey**
Volume I: History of the UP. 120 minutes. Volume II: More First Generation diesels, "City" trains, new Second Generation diesels, more turbines, DD 35s and Centennials. 120 minutes, Color.

**302-20020** DVD Volume I, 2-Disc Set **39.95**

**302-20021** DVD Volume II, 2-Disc Set **39.95**

Modern Day Railroading Videos listed below are available by Special Order (see Legend Page).

**Magnolia Cut-Off Of The CSX**
Sweeping curves, tunnels, trestles and fall foliage serve as a back drop for GP40s, GP50s and rare U30Cs.

**302-20040** DVD **29.95**

**The Way West**
Modern action from the Mississippi to the Feather River Canyon. 60 minutes.

**302-20061** DVD 2-Disc set **39.95**

## Narrow Gauge

**50s Memories Of The Rio Grande Narrow Gauge**
Travel through the Black Canyon with Bumble Bee #268 before moving on to Marshall Pass to catch the scrap train. Then witness some limestone operations at Monarch Pass prior to seeing one of the Rio Grande Mikes switching industries in Farmington, and much more.

**302-31643** DVD **24.95**

**Best Of Narrow Gauge**
Rio Grande narrow-gauge action assembled from previously released footage by Emery Gulash. 62 minutes.

**302-31612** DVD **24.95**

**The Chama Turn**
Action and operations over Cumbres.

**302-31644** DVD **24.95**

**Colorado - Steam Mecca**
Coverage of all Colorado major steam railroads. Digital stereo sound.

**302-20004** DVD **29.95**

**DRGW And The Bumblebee—#268**
Incredible 1950s narrow gauge action shot around Gunnison, Alamosa, the Farmington branch, the Monarch branch and between Durango and Chama. 45 minutes.

**302-31626** DVD **24.95**

**Narrow Gauge Combo**
Includes three short films; "Switchin' Along The Rio Grande," "Twilight Of The Rio Grande" and "Worktrain to Silverton." Approximately one hour, 20 minutes.

**302-31638** DVD **29.95**

**Rotary On The Rio Grande Narrow Gauge**
Follow the Cumbres & Toltec in 1975 and 1976 as it opened its line using the former Rio Grande rotary snow plow OM.

**302-31639** DVD **24.95**

### Ghost Train From the Past
Follow the Rio Grande Southern in 1997 through such locations as Lower Gallagher, Keystone Hill, Bridge 45A and Brown/Meadow Creek.

**302-20005** DVD **29.95**

## Kids' Tapes & DVDs

### Trains, Trains, Trains! For Kids 2 To 92
K.C. Frog takes you on a tour of old and new trains, talks about steam and diesel engines and how they work, and takes you on a cab ride through the mountains.

**302-31662** DVD **24.95**

### Trains, Trains, Trains for Kids 2
Join K.C. Frog and his pal "Buddy" on an educational and hilarious trip on Amtrak's California Zephyr. K.C. Frog lives with a beautiful model railroad, and his pal Buddy visits him in this episode, and K.C. tells Buddy all about his exciting trip on Amtrak.

**302-20010** DVD **24.95**

### Everything Trains for Kids
Five DVD set includes five modeling programs: Trains, Trains, Trains Volumes 1 and 2, Live Steam in Florida 2002, I've Been Working on the Railroad, The Circus and the Railroads. 195 minutes (almost 4 hours!).

**302-20069** DVD **49.95**

## Model Railroading

### 4 Narrow Gauge Layouts
Visit four beautiful finished layouts of well-known modelers Paul Scoles, Dave Woodrell, Jim Noonan and Bill Busacca.

**302-31642** DVD **24.95**

### Building a Model Railroad Series
Disc 1: Designing, Benchwork and Laying Track; Disc 2: Wiring for Command Control, Building Structures and Rolling Stock; Disc 3: Scenery, Adding Realism and Operating.

**302-20037** 3-DVD Set **79.95**

### Building The Rio Grande Southern
This "Modeling the Prototype Series" covers the building of a Rio Grande Southern-based layout in several stages. Offers plenty of tips and techniques on building structures, benchwork and trackwork as well as detailing and painting techniques. Most volumes are 60 to 70 minutes long.

**Volume I**
Building Durango of the 1930s. Covers benchwork, tracklaying, locomotive facility and more.

**302-20022** DVD **29.95**

**Volume II**
Building Durango part two. Covers how-to add fascia board, lay down ballast in the yard, create access hatches, and build detailed scenery.

**302-20023** DVD **29.95**

**Volume III**
Building Dolores part one.

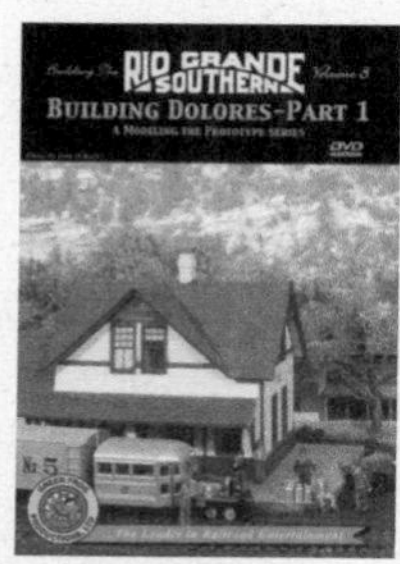


**302-20024** DVD **29.95**

**Volume IV**
Building Dolores part two. Covers the final portions of building the town of Dolores, including the river that flows through town.

**302-20025** DVD **29.95**

**Volume V**
Building the New Mexico Lumber Company part one.

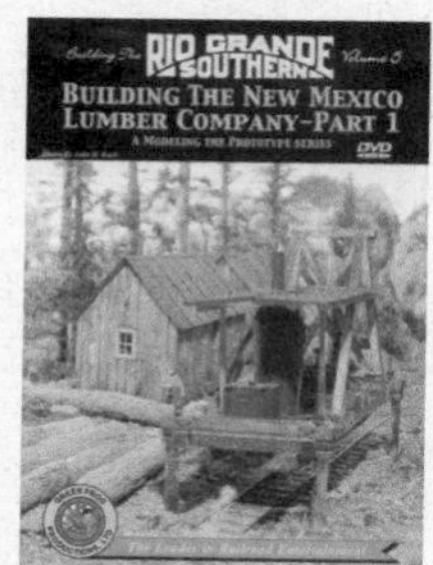


**302-20011** DVD **29.95**

**Volume VI**
Building the New Mexico Lumber Company part two.

**302-20026** DVD **29.95**

**Volume VII**
Building the New Mexico Lumber Company part three. Covers installation of a photo mural backdrop in the logging area, basic construction techniques used for a huge sawmill, construction of slash burner and engine house, and town scenery.

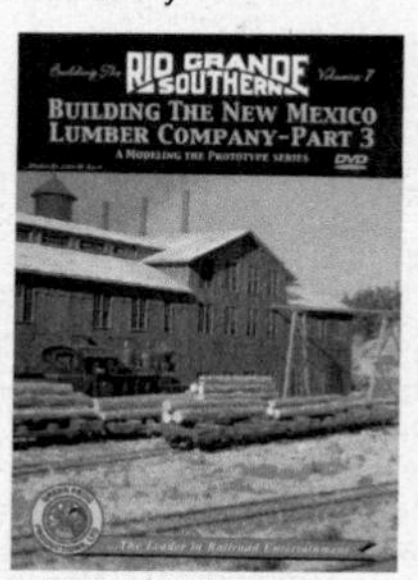


**302-20031** DVD **29.95**

**Volume VIII**
Back to Durango. Build a flour mill, set up stock pens, add a return loop around the roundhouse and create a storage yard.

**302-20035** DVD **29.95**

See What's Available at

**www.walthers.com**

**Volume IX**
Dolores to Rico. Build a rock wall, construct a long tunnel, add backdrops, learn scenery painting technqiues, add a sampling mill and an ore bin complex.

**302-20038** DVD **29.95**

**Limited Quantity Available**
**302-53220** VHS **29.95**

### Building Structures
Covers a variety of techniques including preparing pieces before assembly, painting, scratchbuilding, decaling, dry transfers, mortar and bricks and weathering.

**Limited Quantity Available**
**302-70006** VHS **19.95**

## Expanding Your Model Railroad

### 29.95 ea (Unless Noted)
This series of how-to videos gives you plenty of ideas about expanding your current layout and how to do it. The three volumes cover benchwork, roadbed and trackwork, tying new layout sections into your existing railroad plus upgrading topics like installing DCC with sound, photo mural backdrops and operation. An added bonus includes a layout plan you can print on your PC.

**Volume 1**
**302-20074** DVD

**Volume 2**
**302-20084** DVD

**Limited Quantity Available**
**302-53230** VHS

**Volume 3**
**302-20085** DVD

**Limited Quantity Available**
**305-53231** VHS

**Three Disc Set**
**302-20086** DVD **49.95**

### Installing & Blending Photo Mural Backdrops
302-20054 DVD 29.95

### Live Steam in Florida 2002
Join the Green Frog cameras in fast paced live steam action on the following railroads: Bob Zuckerman's Lockhart & Lakewood Forest has almost 1000 feet of track on his property, and the layout provides great action as the tracks roam around his home. Larry Smith's Manatee Central Railroad includes tunnels, long runs, passing sidings, a lake and more. Ridge Live Steamers: Richard Dobler's 2,600-foot mainline through an old Orange Grove in Central Florida. Long bridges, fast track, a steaming bay, as well as great operation featuring long trains. Largo Central Railroad is a club layout featuring 1.2 miles of main line track in beautifully landscaped Largo Central Park. Great steaming bays, a large yard, junctions, stations, and passing sidings are featured. 55 Minutes.

302-20009 DVD 24.95

### Modeling & Beyond
Five DVD set includes five modeling programs: Photo Mural Backdrops, Scratch Building Structures, The Rio Grande Southern (Modeling the Prototype), Steam Operated Sawmill and 4 Narrow-Gauge Layouts. 276 minutes (over 5 hours!).

302-20068 DVD 49.95

### The Rio Grande Southern
On3 layout. Learn about the RGS and how you can model it, buildings, scenery, etc.

302-31646 DVD 19.95

### Scratch Building Structures
302-20055 DVD 29.95

### Logging Railroads/ Modeling The Prototype
Shows how the trees were cut and loaded, then unloaded at the saw mill. 60 minutes.

302-31672 DVD 24.95

## AUDIO CDS
### 14.95 ea
Test your sound system and your ears with these digitally recorded, edited and mastered CDs. Sit back and enjoy a listening experience that makes you feel like you are on vacation.

302-60005 Steam Soliloquy

302-60006 Sounds of #1218

302-60007 Sounds of CSX 10 Soundtrack (No Narration)

302-60008 Sounds of CSX 11 Soundtrack (No Narration)

302-60009 Norfolk Southern-2 Soundtrack (No Narration)

302-60010 The GP9s

302-60011 Steam/Diesel Sounds of 50s New Georgia

302-60012 Steam/Diesel Sounds of the 80s

302-60013 1st Generation Diesels

302-60014 Sounds of the East Broad Top

302-60015 Sounds of the Silverton

302-60016 Rails New York Metro

302-60017 Remembering Steam - Volume I Trackside

302-60018 Remembering Steam - Volume II Train

**krause publications**

## NEW PRODUCTS
### Books

### Standard Catalog Series
Handy reference books feature plenty of photos, a rarity scale, condition criteria, typical prices and more to help determine the worth of used toy trains.

### Lionel® Train Sets 1945-1969

NEW 213-515 29.99

### American Flyer Trains

NEW 213-812 32.99

### Collector's Guide Series
These books are loaded with color photos of the trains along with typical selling prices based on condition.

213-724

213-725

213-945

### Classic O-Gauge Trains
NEW 213-724 19.99

### Prewar Lionel Trains 1900-1942
NEW 213-725 19.99

### Postwar Lionel Trains 1945-1969
NEW 213-945 19.99

## BOOKS
### Warman's Lionel Train Field Guide 1945-1969

213-2999 12.99

A great reference for collectors. Offers tips on identifying specific pieces and determining values.

### O'Brien's Collecting Toy Trains

213-7690 Sixth Edition 29.99

Covers pre- and post-war Lionel as well as American Flyer, Buddy L, Marx, Ives, Kusan and AMT.

### Standard Catalog of Lionel Trains

213-8909 213-8910

213-8909 1945-1969 Revised 2nd Edition 39.99

213-8910 1900-1942 29.99

**Limited Quantity Available**

### Railway Photography
213-7 19.99

Full of inspiration and how-tos, this tribute to railroading contains images from well-known contemporary photographers. Covers history, equipment, film, planning photo journeys, working with light, photo storage and presentation, publishing and more.

### Classic Railroad Advertising
213-1201 19.99

Collection spans from 1917 through the present. Hardcover, 224 pages, 212 color photos, 8-1/4 x 10-7/8".

### Railway Masterpieces
213-1209 19.99

This pictorial captures some of the most impressive, significant and interesting elements of railroading from today and yesterday. Hardcover, 160 pages, 100 color and 100+ B&W photos, 10-7/8 x 8-1/4".

## Information STATION

### Interesting Dates in Railroad History

May 8, 1837 – The first American 4-4-0 steam locomotive is completed in Philadelphia, Pennsylvania.

June 15, 1842 – Newspapers report the development of refrigerated cars cooled by ice.

May 10, 1869 – The Golden Spike is driven at Promontory Point, Utah, commemorating the completion of the first US Transcontinental Railroad.

April 14, 1872 – The YMCA organizes to house train crews.

September 16, 1875 – The first Fast Mail train departs New York's Grand Central Station.

September 5, 1876 – Southern Pacific officials drive a golden spike at Lang Station (Santa Clarita), linking northern and southern California.

June 28, 1895 – The first electric train service in the US begins on the seven-mile Nantasket Branch of the New Haven Railroad.

August 29, 1916 – The United States Railway Adminsitration is formed to operate U.S. railroads during World War One.

May 12, 1936 – The first run of the legendary Super Chief departs Chicago.

March 11, 1966 – The last factory-built rotary snow plow is retired and sold for scrap.

October 30, 1970 – President Nixon signs the Railpax Bill into law, which leads the way for the development of the Amtrak®.

December, 2005 – Mainline steam on China's JiTong Railway ends. Two locos brought to U.S. in summer 2006 for resale.

## NEW PRODUCTS

Model Railroader BOOKS

### Booklets

#### Get Started in N Scale

**NEW 400-12414 7.95**
N Scale is perfect for small spaces and this guide shows you how to create a complete layout to fit tight areas. Booklet explains the advantages of N Scale and offers a variety of ideas on getting started. Softcover, 8-1/4 x 10-3/4", 16 pages, 45 color photos.

### Books

#### Planning Scenery for Your Model Railroad

**NEW 400-12410 21.95**
Explains how to use natural landscapes as the basis to create more realistic scenery. Projects incorporate natural effects like rock strata, water forms, field crops and space-saving industries. Softcover, 8-1/4 x 10-3/4", 96 pages, 175 color photos, 25 b&w photos, 10 illustrations.

#### Mountain to Desert: Building the HO Scale Danville and Donner River

**NEW 400-12416 19.95**
Pelle Soeborg teaches you innovative techniques for your layout. Topics include constructing basic terrain, ballasting track, choosing scenery materials, painting backdrops, scratchbuilding modern businesses, installing a truss bridge, weathering and more. Softcover, 8-1/4 x 10-3/4", 96 pages, 200 color photos, 15 illustrations.

#### The DCC Guide

**NEW 400-12417 19.95**
Learn how to take advantage of all the realistic sound and smoother switching and running features in today's models. This comprehensive all-new guide helps you get the most out of digital command control (DCC). Diagrams and photos illustrate wiring, installation and setting decoders and throttle equipment. Includes an overview of available products to aid in selecting the right system for your needs. Softcover, 8-1/4 x 10-3/4", 80 pages, 80 color photos, 55 illustrations.

#### Building a Model Railroad Step by Step

**NEW 400-12418 21.95**
Follow the construction of Model Railroader Senior Editor David Popp's N Scale layout. More that 30 projects take you through the complete process from start to finish. Step-by-step photos and illustrations make it easy to apply the techniques to your layout. Softcover, 8-1/4 x 10-3/4", 112 pages, 260 color photos, 20 illustrations.

#### Detailing Freight Cars

**NEW 400-12420 18.95**
Use the tips in this comprehensive guide and your freight cars will look and run just like the real thing. Features include upgraded details, wheels, couplers and loads. Ideal for intermediate modelers who want to improve their equipment. Softcover, 8-1/4 x 10-3/4", 88 pages, 100 color and 50 b&w photos, 5 illustrations.

#### Detailing Diesel Locomotives

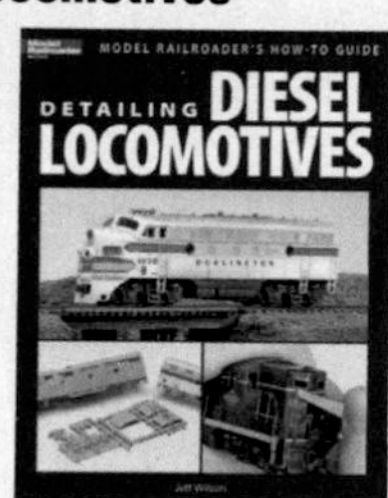

**NEW 400-12421 19.95**
Improve the look of your diesel locomotives. This illustrated volume guides you through the finer points of adding realism to your motive power. Softcover, 8-1/4 x 10-3/4", 88 pages, 175 color and 25 b&w photos, 2 illustrations.

FineScale Modeler BOOKS

#### Classic Combat Aircraft

**NEW 400-12431 Vol. 2 18.95**
Learn to build, modify, detail and paint these legendary WWII warbirds. Eighteen illustrated projects include the P-51 Mustang, P-47 Thunderbolt, B-17 Flying Fortress as well as Axis aircraft like the Bf 109 and Stuka. Introduction by Paul Boyer. Softcover, 96 pages, 300 color photos, 8-1/4 x 10-3/4".

Garden RAILWAYS BOOKS

### Booklet

#### Get Started in Garden Railroading

**NEW 400-12415 7.95**
Combine two great hobbies - gardening and model railroading. Explains how you can turn your backyard into beautiful natural setting complete with a working large-scale model train. Softcover, 8-1/4 x 10-3/4", 16 pages, 45 color photos, 5 illustrations.



### Book

#### How to Design and Build Your Garden Railroad

**NEW 400-12406 21.95**
Plan, design and install a garden railway in your own backyard. Master garden railroader Jack Verducci shows you how to landscape with natural materials, create water features and add drama with structures, bridges and trestles. Softcover, 8-1/4 x 10-3/4", 96 pages, 190 color photos, 25 illustrations.

### Book

#### Tourist Trains Guidebook

**NEW 400-1207 18.95**
A must-have for railfans, this completely new guide lists hundreds of tourist train sites and train-related attractions in North America. Features information on when to go, how to get there and tips on what to do when you arrive. Includes a laminated discount card good for hundreds of dollars of savings on admission fees. Softcover, 5-1/4 x 8", 320 pages, 150 b&w photos.

## Calendars

### The Art of Model Railroading 2008

**NEW** 400-68151 12.95
Large, full-color photographs capture the detailed, lifelike scenes created by some very talented model railroaders. Features layouts by Pelle Soeborg, Rob Enrico and Bernard Kempinski. 13 x 10-1/2".

### Railroads at Work 2008

**NEW** 400-68152 12.95
Colorful, contemporary images show trains at work moving people and freight across scenic regions of North America. Features BNSF, CR, UP, Utah Railway, CN, Durango & Silverton, CSX, CNW and more. 13 x 10-1/2".

Model Railroader BOOKS

### DCC Projects & Applications

400-12407 17.95
This book takes the reader through a series of DCC projects, including setting up a DCC layout, decoder installation, lighting effects, sound effects, layout wiring projects, advanced decoder programming and tips and ideas for advanced DCC projects. Also includes a list of important considerations for choosing a DCC system. More technical than DCC Made Easy but still comprehensible to the average modeler. Softcover, 8-1/4 x 10-3/4", 96 pages, 150 color photos, 30 illustrations.

### The Model Railroader's Guide to Junctions

400-12408 18.95
Get the scoop on railroad junctions —where tracks meet and cross. Photos show how junctions work and the details that surround them. Softcover, 8-1/4 x 10-3/4", 88 pages, 150 color photos, 20 illustrations.

### The Model Railroader's Guide to Industries Along the Tracks 2

400-12409 19.95
Provides insights, photos, and guidelines for modeling several rail-served industries. Includes overviews of creameries and milk traffic, the paper industry, breweries, iron ore mining and transloading, coal customers, freight houses and less-than-carload traffic. Softcover, 8-1/4 x 10-3/4", 88 pages, 120 color photos, 70 b&w photos, 12 illustrations.

### Basic Wiring For Model Railroaders - 2nd Edition

400-12412 19.95
Revised, full-color second edition provides simple instructions for beginning hobbyists. Includes instructions for block wiring, turnout wiring, loop track wiring and other principles essential to building a layout. Softcover, 80 Pages, 8-1/4 x 10-3/4". 225 color photos, 25 illustrations.

### The Model Railroader's Guide to Passenger Equipment & Operations

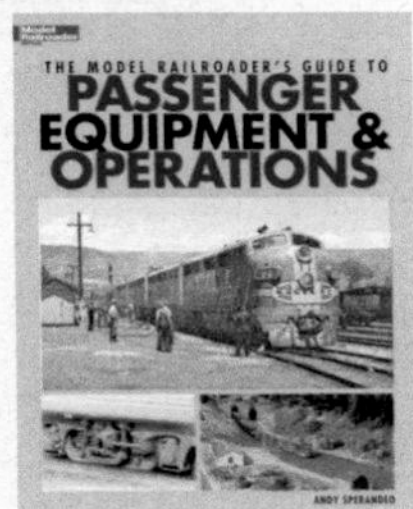

400-12244 19.95
Helps modelers integrate realistic passenger trains and operations into any layout. Learn about passenger train history, types, equipment and terminals. Softcover, 8-1/4 x 10-3/4", 96 pages, 130 color photos, 70 b&w photos, 20 illustrations.

### The Model Railroader's Guide to Coal Railroading

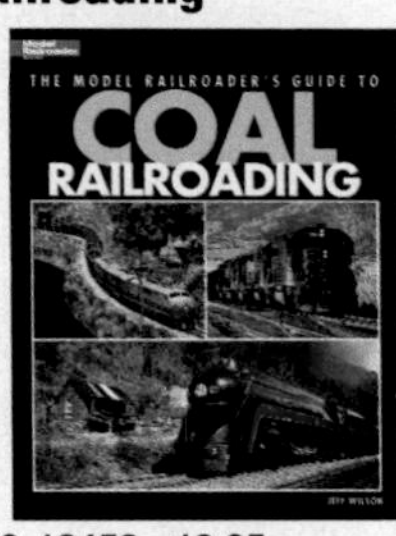

400-12453 19.95
Handy reference for modeling a coal-hauling prototype-based or freelance railroad. Includes information on modeling coal trains, company towns, and coal customers, plus operating tips. Softcover, 8-1/4 x 10-3/4", 96 pages, 130 color photos, 70 b&w photos, 20 illustrations.

### Steam Locomotive Projects and Ideas

400-12221 18.95
Learn to detail, kitbash, paint and maintain a steam locomotive of any scale. Includes information about the history of steam motive power and components of the prototype. Compiled from the pager of Model Railroader, with additional new material from John Pryke. Softcover, 80 pages, 100 color and 50 B&W photos, 40 illustrations, 8-1/4 x 10-3/4".

### The Model Railroader's Guide to Freight Cars

400-12450 19.95
Get a brief history of each type of North American freight car, then learn how car designs have changed since WWI. Includes detailed information for modeling realistic rolling stock in any scale. Softcover, 96 pages, 75 color and 110 B&W photos, 6 illustrations, 8-1/2 x 10-3/4".

### Realistic Model Railroad Operation

400-12231 19.95
Covers the history, practice, terminology and benefits of operating realistically. Guides the reader through the steps leading to realistic operation, and includes pictorial examples of working model railroads and operating sessions. Softcover, 96 pages, 125 color and 25 B&W photos, 40 illustrations, 8-1/4 x 10-3/4".

### Trackside Scenes You Can Model

400-12234 18.95
Historic photographs capture intriguing prototype railroad settings from all over the U.S. The author details how you can realistically model each prototype scene on your own layout. Each chapter features a description of the scene including trackage, structures, and operating environment, and a suggested track plan. Softcover, 80 pages, 80 color and 20 B&W photos, 25 illustrations, 8-1/4 x 10-3/4".

## Basic Model Railroad Benchwork: The Complete Photo Guide

**400-12241 18.95**
A concise, illustrated teaching method takes the mystery out of model railroad benchwork. Covers the materials, tools and basic skills required to make sturdy benchwork for any size or scale layout. Softcover, 96 pages, 300 B&W photos, 25 illustrations, 8-1/4 x 10-3/4".

## DCC Made Easy

**400-12242 14.95**
Explains DCC methods and techniques in a straightforward way. Covers the history of Command Control, dissects the components of a DCC system, and addresses the full range of commercially available systems. Softcover, 48 pages, 100 color photos, 10 illustrations, 8-1/4 x 10-3/4".

## The New Scenery Tips & Techniques

**400-12243 19.95**
Compiled from the pages of *Model Railroader,* this completely revised edition includes intriguing ideas on how to create realistic ground cover, trees, bushes, rocks, water and more, for your model railroad. Softcover, 104 pages, 225 color and 25 B&W photos, 8-1/4 x 10-3/4".

## HO Scale Model Railroading

**400-12246 19.95**
Starting with benchwork and ending with realistic scenery, this guide provides insight into the fundamentals of model railroading. Features many up-to-date techniques, and references many significant new products. Softcover, 96 pages, 200 color photos, 8-1/4 x 10-3/4".

## Basic Painting & Weathering for Model Railroaders

**400-12247 19.95**
Presents step-by-step techniques to finish, paint, decal and weather railroad models. Introduces the tools, products, and techniques while guiding hobbyists through several basic projects. Softcover, 80 pages, 250 color photos, 8-1/4 x 10-3/4".

## The Model Railroader's Guide To Freight Yards

**400-12248 18.95**
Learn the basic techniques and facilities needed for building a freight yard on a layout of any size, scale or era! A great book for skilled beginners or intermediate-level modelers. Softcover, 80 pages, 180 color and B&W photos, 8-1/4 x 10-3/4".

## Realistic Model Railroad Design

**400-12250 19.95**
Learn creative and do-able options for building your next model railroad. From choosing a theme to selecting a scale to bringing in creative design, it's all covered! Softcover, 96 pages, 150 color and B&W photos, 20 illustrations, 8-1/4 x 10-3/4".

## Basic Trackwork For Model Railroaders

**400-12254 19.95**
Using a step-by-step photographic approach, this book offers proven, easy-to-follow techniques for the installing of sturdy trackwork, including fitting the roadbed, laying sectional or flexible track, and finishing the track with lineside details. Also covers installing turnouts, cleaning and maintaining trackwork, and other special techniques suitable for a layout of any size or scale.

## The Model Railroader's Guide To Industries Along The Tracks

**400-12256 19.95**
Learn how to add great industries like mining, refining and agriculture to your layout. Detailed descriptions and illustrations make expanding these operations easier than ever. Softcover, 80 pages, 180 color and B&W photos, 8-1/4 x 10-3/4".

## Basic Scenery For Model Railroaders

**400-12233 19.95**
Covers simple techniques for making realistic scenery (including ground cover, trees, water, rocks, roads and trackside details) for any size or scale layout. Includes color photos and diagrams that demonstrate basic steps to adding prototypical scenery to a model railroad. Softcover, 96 pages, 200 color photos, 8-1/4 x 10-3/4".

## The Model Railroader's Guide To Locomotive Servicing Terminals

**400-12228 18.95**
Includes tips and techniques for modeling trackage, structures and terminal details appropriate for the steam or diesel era. Softcover, 80 pages, 125 color and 50 B&W photos, 8-1/4 x 10-3/4".

## Basic Model Railroad Track Plans

**400-12237 16.95**
Includes simple, ideal layout designs for beginning model railroaders. Features plans for a variety of HO and N Scale starter layouts. Also includes general construction techniques that are useful in building any layout. Softcover, 64 pages, 15 color and B&W photos, 60 illustrations, 8-1/4 x 10-3/4".

## A Realistic HO Layout For Beginners

**400-12141 18.95**
Shows how to build a realistic HO layout with all the details. 96 pages, 120 B&W and 60 color photos, 8-1/4 x 10-7/8".

## Building City Scenery For Your Model Railroad

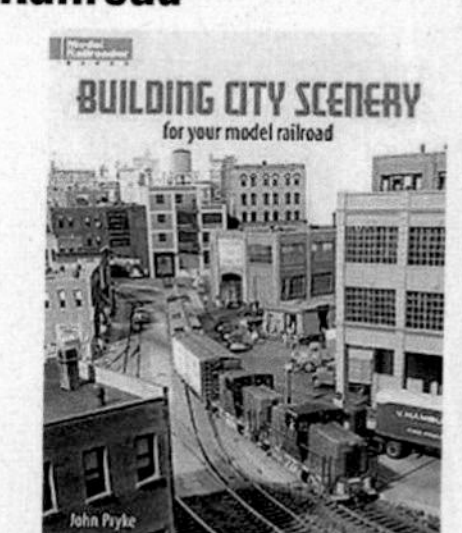


**400-12204 19.95**
Learn how to model realistic city structures and objects. Softcover, 96 pages, 120 color and 40 B&W photos, 25 illustrations, 8-1/4 x 10-3/4".

## How To Build Realistic Model Railroad Scenery

**400-12216 24.95**
Featuring today's newest products and equipment, this third-edition guide will attract modelers with contemporary images. Includes new chapters on Western, desert and urban settings. Ideal for any modeler planning a layout. Softcover, 144 pages, 300 color and 150 B&W photos, 20 illustrations, 8-1/4 x 10-3/4".

## How To Build and Detail Model Railroad Scenes

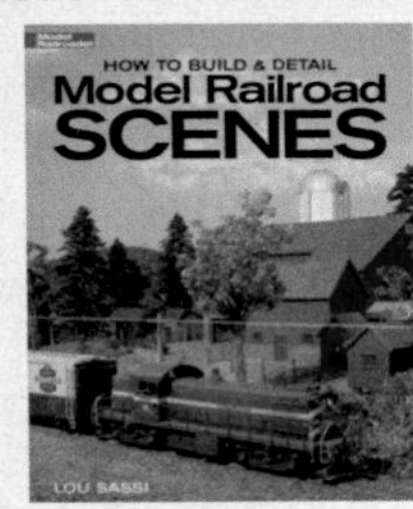


**400-12249 21.95**
This practical, photo-driven guide covers the principles and techniques of designing and constructing detailed, realistic model railroad scenes. The various projects include structure, scenery, and detailing techniques for both urban and rural settings. It's the essential information modelers need to make a good layout look great. Softcover, 88 pages, 230 color photos, 20 illustrations, 8-1/4 x 10-3/4".

## Project Railroads You Can Build

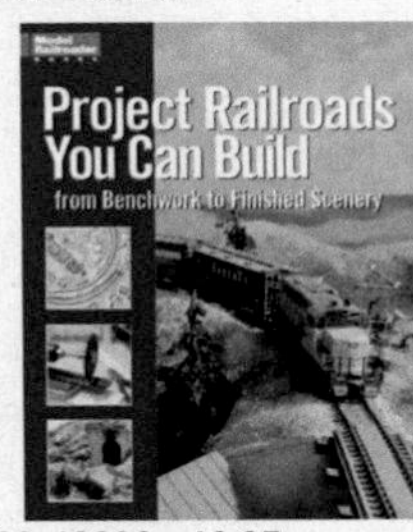


**400-12236 16.95**
Includes easy-to-follow instructions for constructing moderately-sized N or HO Scale model railroads from benchwork through finished scenery. Ideal for novice model railroaders or experienced hobbyists interested in exploring other scales. Softcover, 80 pages, 180 B&W photos, 8-1/4 x 10-3/4".

## Scenery For Your Model Railroad

**400-12194 18.95**
Teaches you everything you need to know about scenery from ground cover and rockwork, to trees, water, and more. Includes photos of models and prototype scenes for inspiration. Softcover, 8-1/4 x 10-3/4".

## Basic Wiring For Model Railroaders

**400-12212 18.95**
Teaches basic electrical connections for a two-rail DC-powered layout of any size or complexity. Basic layout wiring techniques are presented simply, with numerous photos, illustrations and diagrams. Softcover, 8-1/4 x 10-3/4".

## Trackwork & Lineside Detail For Your Model Railroad

**400-12235 19.95**
An introduction to the basics of tracklaying and lineside detailing. Includes tips, techniques and ideas for working with track and the details immediately alongside it. Softcover, 96 pages, 150 color photos, 50 Illustrations, 8-1/4 x 10-3/4".

## Basic Structure Modeling for Model Railroaders

**400-12258 19.95**
Learn the reasons for including structures on your layout, then select and build your own! Photo-driven projects demonstrate the tools, materials, and techniques used for modeling plastic and wood structures. Includes tips for realistic finishing, painting, weathering, sign making, interior detailing and more. A great resource for beginner model railroaders. Softcover, 88 pages, 225 color photos, 1 illustration, 8-1/2 x 10-3/4".

## Track Planning for Realistic Operations

**400-12148** 3rd Edition **21.95**
Must-have for track planning. Includes design tips and techniques. 144 pages, 45 B&W and 120 illustrations, 8-1/4 x 10-3/4".

## Basic Model Railroading: Getting Started In The Hobby

**400-12197 17.95**
Packed with simple tips and techniques, detailed photos, diagrams and drawings. Basics of tracklaying, wiring, maintaining locomotives, scenery, painting, weathering and more. 80 pages, 150 color photos, 8-1/4 x 10-3/4".

## HO Railroad From Start To Finish

**400-12121 17.95**
Beginner's book on the construction of the HO Scale Cripple Creek Central. Covers everything from benchwork to rolling stock, avoids power tools and messy materials. 100 photos, 8-1/4 x 10 x 3/4".

## Realistic Model Railroad Building Blocks

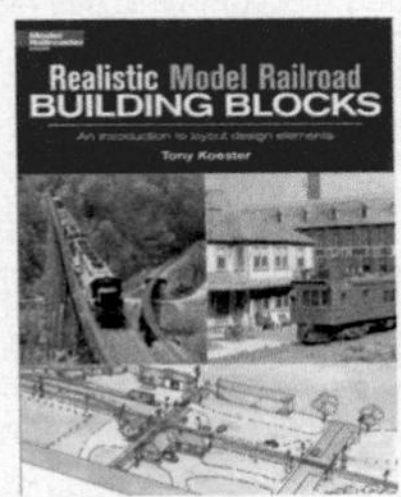


**400-12405 19.95**
Offers techniques for incorporating layout design elements into a larger layout. Perfect for intermediate and advanced modelers. Softcover, 96 pages, 125 color and 10 B&W photos, 75 illustrations, 8-1/4 x 10-3/4".

Info, Images, Inspiration! Get It All at
**www.walthers.com**

## Easy Model Railroad Wiring

**400-12207** 2nd Edition **21.95**
Provides easy and reliable layout wiring techniques that every level of modeler needs to know. Each chapter includes photos, illustrations and detailed schematics. Softcover, 128 pages, 80 B&W photos, 160 illustrations, 8-1/4 x 10-3/4".

## The Model Railroader's Guide to Bridges, Trestles & Tunnels

**400-12452 19.95**
Each chapter shows prototype examples and ways to model, paint, weather and install different types of bridges, trestles and tunnels. Ideal for intermediate and advanced hobbyists. Softcover, 88 pages, 75 color and 100 B&W photos, 15 illustrations, 8-1/4 x 10-3/4".

## Model Railroad Bridges And Trestles

**400-12101 21.95**
Includes 12 construction plans, prototype photos and over 20 sets of scale drawings. 152 pages, 8-1/2 x 11".

### How To Build Model Railroad Benchwork

**400-12175** 2nd Edition **16.95**
New tools, materials and techniques that make benchwork construction easy. 80 pages, 115 B&W photos and 120 illustrations.

### Maintaining & Repairing Your Scale Model Trains

**400-12210 17.95**
With simple, instructional information, this book covers the basic techniques needed to maintain and repair DC-powered scale model locos, rolling stock and layouts. 80 pages, 150 B&W photos, 8-1/4 x 10-3/4".

### Model Railroader Cyclopedia Vol. 1: Steam Locomotives

**400-1001 49.95**
Tells what all the piping, springs and pumps are for. 272 pages, 127 HO Scale drawings, 700 photos, 14 x 11".

### 48 Top-Notch Track Plans

**400-12132 18.95**
You'll find a layout to fit any space limit or scale preference including HO (HOn2-1/2 and HOn3), O, S, N and Z Scales. 120 pages, 100 color and 220 B&W photos, 8-1/4 x 10-3/4".

### 101 Track Plans For Model Railroaders

**400-12012 14.95**
Easy-to-use plans in every size, shape and scale — from tiny card-table layouts to giant garage-size railroads. Demonstrates how to design a railroad to fit any space and shows how to convert plans to N, HO, S, and O Scales. 8-1/4 x 11-1/4", 72 pages.

### Easy Model Railroading Booklets 7.95 ea

Aimed at beginners, this new booklet series will educate new hobbyists about the basics of model railroading. Each booklet covers one important aspect of the hobby in enough detail to get readers started so that they can move on to more detailed work as their skills progress. Adapted from the pages of Model Railroader's "Back to Basics" columns and Model Trains Step-by-Step. Softcover, 16 pages, all color photos and illustrations, 8-1/4 x 10-3/4".

### Tables for your Trains

**400-12401**

### Tips on Track

**400-12402**

### Wiring Basics

**400-12403**

### Simple Scenery

**400-12404**

### Basic Buildings

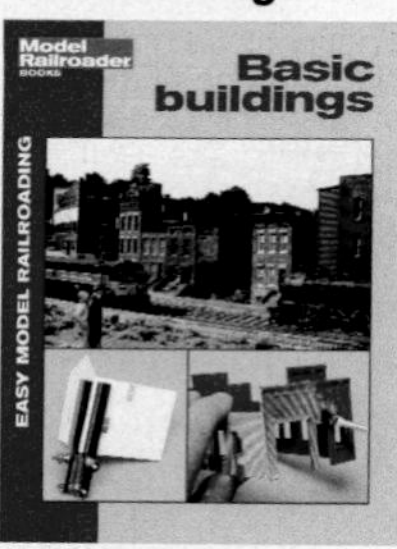


**400-12413 7.95**
Learn the basic skills to build realistic models! Step-by-step photos and instructions cover the basic building methods, kitbashing unique structures, and finishing with paint, signs and details. Perfect for beginners. Softcover, 8-1/4 x 10-3/4", 16 pages, 45 color photos.

Get Daily Info, Photos and News at

**www.walthers.com**

**Model Railroader VIDEO**

### Building Your First Model Railroad

**400-10002** VHS **12.95**
**400-10003** DVD **12.95**
Teaches you everything you need to know to build a model railroad layout. Narrated by Michael Gross, actor and model railroad enthusiast.

### Scenery & Airbrushing Made Easy

**400-15060 DVD 29.95**
Covers everything you need to build layout scenery, as well as use an airbrush to apply scenery paint. Covers tools, applications and special techniques. 120 minutes; stereo sound; color.

**FineScale Modeler BOOKS**

### Airbrushing Basics

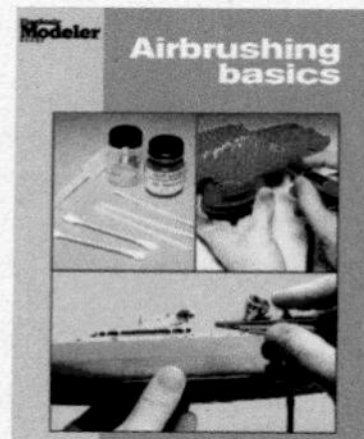


**400-12430 7.95**
Learn airbrushing tips and techniques from the experts! This booklet provides a clear guide on getting the most out of your airbrush, including proper cleaning and maintenance techniques. Softcover, 8-1/4 x 10-3/4", 16 pages, 45 color photos, 5 illustrations.

### Modeler's Guide to Realistic Painting & Finishing

**400-12257 16.95**
Perfect for the beginning plastic modeler who wants to learn more advanced techniques, this photo-driven guide includes an introduction to airbrushing and sections on brush painting, dry-brushing, applying washes and pastel chalk weathering. Softcover, 8-1/4 x 10-3/4", 80 pages, 200 color photos, 10 illustrations.

### The Basics of Scale Modeling

**400-12251 16.95**
Beginning scale modelers are full of questions: What tools do I need? What glue works best? How do I put a model together? How are decals applied? Modelers will find the answers to these questions and more compiled in this book. Softcover, 80 pages, 230 color photos, 10 illustrations, 8-1/2 x 10-3/4".

### Easy Scale Modeling

**400-12259 7.95**
Simple techniques, detailed photos and easy-to-follow diagrams get new modelers started. Offers basic information on assembling, painting, finishing and displaying scale models. Softcover, 16 pages, 64 color photos, 8-1/2 x 10-3/4".

## Figures

### How To Paint Realistic Military Figures

**400-12240 21.95**
Covers military figures and horses from medieval times to Desert Storm. Softcover, 96 pages, 120 color and 75 B&W photos, 8-1/4 x 10-3/4".

## Armor

### How To Build Armor Dioramas

**400-12239 22.95**
Learn the steps to building detailed armored vehicles. Then gets tips on the best ways to display your new models. Also includes great tips on figure modeling, kit assembly and finishing details. Softcover, 112 pages, 300 color photos, 8-1/4 x 10-3/4".

### Modeling Classic Combat Aircraft

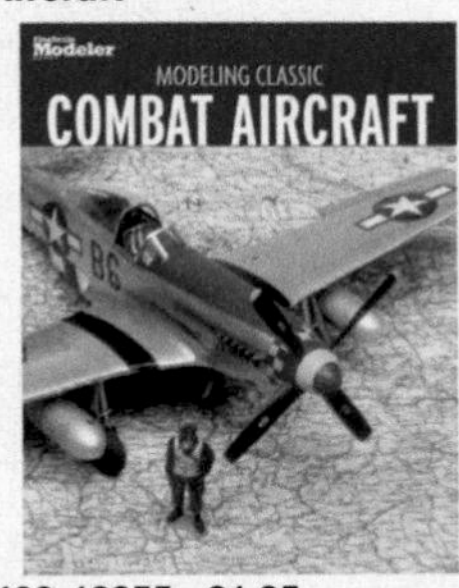


**400-12255 21.95**
Learn to build, paint and finish military aircraft models from WWII to today. Over 15 projects are featured, including the P-51 Mustang, F-18 Sabre, the A-7D Corsair, the B-17 Flying Fortress, and more. Compiled from the pages of FineScale Modeler magazine and edited by Mark Thompson. Softcover, 96 pages, 300 color photos, 8-1/4 x 10-3/4".

### How To Model World War II German Armor

**400-12232 22.95**
Offers techniques for creating most types of German armored vehicles. Covers weathering, special battle effects, airbrushing camouflage and German armor paint schemes, working with flexible track, working with resin, creating accessories, using photo-etched brass, creating figures and dioramas, and more. Softcover, 104 pages, 230 color photos, 8-1/4 x 10-3/4".

### How To Use An Airbrush

**400-12173 21.95**
Learn how to achieve special airbrushing effects on a variety of plastic models. Eleven projects teach the basics of realistic finishes, camouflage, weathering and other special effects for scale plastic modeling. Softcover, 96 pages, 196 color photos, 8-1/4 x 10-3/4".

### Basics Of Ship Modeling

**400-12220 19.95**
Step-by-step photos guide you from basic assembly techniques to painting and weathering, detailing, masking and displaying your model ships. Softcover, 112 pages, 25 color and 400 B&W photos, 8-1/4 x 10-3/4".

### Building And Displaying Scale Model Aircraft With Paul Boyer

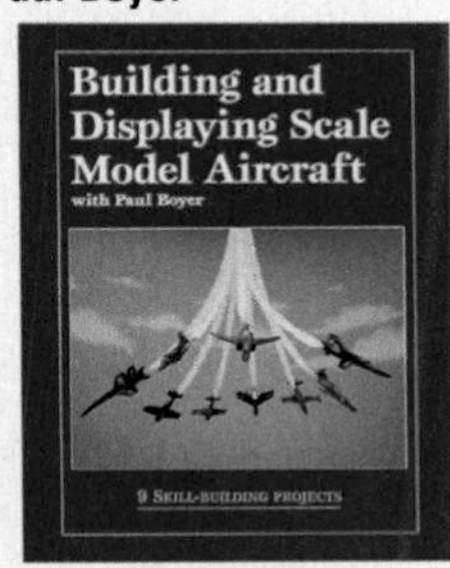


**400-12151 12.95**
Teaches basic aircraft modeling preparation and assembly techniques. Includes suggestions for painting and decaling with special attention to creative displays and mounting tips for finished projects. 88 pages, 50 color and 110 B&W photos, 8-1/4 x 10-3/4".

### How To Build Dioramas

**400-12136** 2nd Edition **24.95**
With this newly updated book, making realistic dioramas has never been easier. Includes new projects and photos, along with tips on weathering, painting, detailing and more. Softcover, 144 pages, 290+ photos, 41 illustrations, 8-1/4 x 10-3/4".

Trains BOOKS

## Books

### Guide To North American Railroad Hot Spots

**400-1097 24.95**
This guide takes you to 100 of the busiest, most interesting train-watching sites across the U.S. and Canada. Each spread includes a color photo and authoritative text about the site written by train-watching experts. Softcover, 208 pages, 200 color photos, 8-1/2 x 5-1/2".

### American Shortline Railway Guide

**400-1073** 5th Edition **24.95**
A ready reference for nearly 600 shortline and regional railroads in the United States and Canada. 320 pages, 100 B&W photos, 8-1/4 x 5-1/2".

### Guide To North American Steam Locomotives

**400-1051 29.95**
The development of steam locomotives on all North American railroads since 1900. 400 pages, 400+ B&W photos, 8-1/4 x 5-1/2".

## KIBRI

IMPORTED FROM GERMANY BY WALTHERS

## CATALOG

**405-99902** 2006-2007 **19.99**
A full-color guide to Kibri's complete line of HO scale vehicles and structures plus scenery and N Scale too.

## Information STATION

### Mining Terms

Adit - Horizontal tunnel for the earth's surface.

Brow - A low place in the roof of a mine, giving insufficient headroom.

Bullion Furnace - The final furnace in which refined gold is melted.

Cage - The platform used to lower/raise men and material in a vertical shaft.

Contact - The place or surface where two different kinds of rocks meet.

Cornish Pump - Used for pumping water out of the mines to prevent flooding

Conveyor - An apparatus for moving material from one point to another in a continuous fashion.

Fall - A mass of roof rock or coal which has fallen in any part of a mine.

Gallows - A vertical shaft's head frame, usually open.

Head Frame - An above-ground structure at a mine shaft used a support so that cages and skips can be raised above the surface for unloading.

Hoist - A drum on which hoisting rope is wound in the engine house, as the cage or skip is raised in the hoisting shaft.

Intake - The passage through which fresh air is drawn or forced into a mine or to a section of a mine.

Mining District - An area in which minerals have been located.

Shaft - An opening used for ventilation or drainage and/or for hoisting of personnel or materials.

Water Hole - A miner's slang for a bar or tavern.

Signature Series, signed and numbered except where indicated.

Items listed below are available by Special Order (see Legend Page).

## LARGE-FORMAT COLOR PRINTS

**413-47300** The Winter San Juan Express - Limited Edition **75.00**
A dramatic full-color rendering. 22 x 30", numbered, signed and dated.

**413-2479** SP "2479" **60.00**
18 x 22" print of engine No. 2479 at San Jose, California, in the 1930s. Image size 17 x 24". Limited edition of 300 prints.

**413-9039** UP "9039" On Archer Hill **45.00**
This special "unpublished" print by Mike Kotowski is of a run of 500. 18 x 14-1/4".

## MOUNTED FULL-COLOR PRINTS

**24.95 ea**
13 x 16" mount, 8 x 11" image.

### Streamliners

413-1380

**413-100** MILW "100"
**413-118** RDG "118"
**413-652** SP "652"
**413-1026** Frisco "1026"
**413-1380** Southern "1380"
**413-1400** NH "1400"
**413-2102** LV "2102"
**413-2906** UP "2906"
**413-3768** PRR "3768"
**413-4001** CNW "4001"
**413-5304** B&O "5304"
**413-5450** NYC J3A "5450"

### Mighty Mallets

413-1981

**413-7** "Skookum" Deep River
**413-200** Out of the Moffat Tunnel
**413-208** WP, M-80 Class Mallets
**413-800** Virginian 800 Class
**413-1218** Class "A" Number 1218
**413-1399** ATSF Passenger Mallet
**413-1601** Allegheny Barrels Toward Sunlight
**413-1981** GN "1981" 2-6-8-0
**413-2601** Erie L-1 Class Mallet
**413-3705** DRGW Challenger
**413-4015** UP Big Boy
**413-4294** Cab Forward

### Mountain Classics

**413-179** WP "179" FEC 414, MT44
**413-1460** Saluda Mountain "1460"
**413-1522** Frisco "1522" at Fork Valley
**413-1607** DRGW "1607" M-75 Heavyweight
**413-2523** GN "2523" Fast Tracking
**413-3001** NYC Mohawk "3001"
**413-4117** Hercules "4117" B&M
**413-4352** San Joaquin SP "4352"
**413-5594** F3 Class "5994" B&O
**413-6755** PRR "6755"
**413-7002** Pony Express "7002" UP
**413-60603** Bullet Nose Betty "6060"

### California Classics

413-9205

**413-9201** Pacific Coast "105" at Santa Maria
**413-9202** ATSF "3450" at Fresno
**413-9203** SP "2921" at Capitola Trestle
**413-9204** SP "2479" at San Jose
**413-9205** SP "2412" at Milbrae
**413-9206** Napa Valley Line "60"
**413-9207** SP "4100" at Niles Tower
**413-9208** SP "4402" at Salinas
**413-9209** Modesto & Empire Traction "100"
**413-9210** WP "94" & SP "3025" at Altamont Pass
**413-9211** Stockton Terminal & Eastern "1"
**413-9212** ATSF "3940" at Pinole

### Last High Steppers

413-700

**413-700** Wabash Cannonball
**413-1801** Dixie Flyers
**413-2584** The First High Stepping GN
**413-2925** All the Way w/ATSF
**413-3000** An Ageless High Stepper, SP
**413-3460** The Tallest High Stepper, ATSF
**413-5200** The Hudson
**413-5302** B&O
**413-8000** The Race of the Iron Thoroughbreds
**413-8444** The Last of the High Steppers
**413-44492** A Reprieve from the Past

### The Last Steamers

413-199004

**413-199001** NYC's Niagra "5500"
**413-199002** NKP
**413-199003** SP "4294"
**413-199004** RDG G3 "219"
**413-199005** West Point
**413-199006** ATSF
**413-199007** N&W's Last Y-6 "2200"
**413-199008** NP's Last Challenger "5149"
**413-199009** C&O "1309"
**413-199010** Rutland
**413-199011** PRR
**413-199012** Big Boy

### Narrow Gauge West

413-198603

**413-198601** White Pass & Yukon at Dead Horse Gulch
**413-198602** Pacific Coast Ry "106"
**413-198603** WSL Shay "9" Tuolomne
**413-198604** Lake Tahoe's Railroad
**413-198605** The Suntan Route
**413-198606** Rio Grande Southern at Trout Lake
**413-198607** Uintah Ry, Morro Castle
**413-198608** Morenci Southern
**413-198609** Sumpter Valley, Baker
**413-198610** DRGW at Chama
**413-198611** SP Narrow Gauge from Keeler
**413-198612** Nevada County Narrow Gauge Bear River Bridge

### Contemporary Steam

413-9213

**413-9213** Spokane, Portland & Seattle "700"
**413-9214** Sierra Railroad "3" & "34"
**413-9215** Cotton Belt "819"
**413-9216** NKP "765" vs Pere Marquette "1225"
**413-9217** Nevada Northern "40"
**413-9218** SP "2472"
**413-9219** Cumbres & Toltec "488"
**413-9220** Atlantic & West Poin "290"
**413-9221** ATSF "3751"
**413-9222** N&W "611"
**413-9223** UP "3985"
**413-9224** Blue Mountain & Reading "2102"

## UNMOUNTED FULL-COLOR PRINTS

**24.95 ea**
11-3/4 x 14" print, 8-1/2 x 11-1/2" image (unless noted)

413-2860

**413-808** UP "808" Kansas 11 x 14" print, 6-3/4 x 10" image
**413-836** UP "838"
**413-2860** UP "2860"
**413-5011** SP "5011"

## DUO-TONE PRINTS

### Iron Horse Vignettes

**15.95 ea**
Duo-tone color process prints, (printed in brown and black) representing both narrow and standard gauge and the 4-4-0 to the 2-8-8-4 locomotives. Printed on 15 x 20" six-point cover stock.
Included with each print is a description of each loco, a short informative statement on its wheel arrangement, and its disposition. Unsigned and unnumbered.

**413-2** Wildcat RR "2" 2-6-2
**413-4** Clover Valley "4" 2-6-6-2T
**413-29** Virginia & Truckee "29" 2-8-0
**413-94** WP "94" 4-6-0
**413-488** DRGW "488" 2-8-2
**413-610** Texas & Pacific "610" 2-10-4
**413-765** NKP "765" 2-8-4
**413-2839** Southern "Royal Hudson" "2839" 4-6-4
**413-3025** SP "3025"
**413-3811** SP "3811"
**413-6060** CN "6060"

MBI Publishing Company

## NEW PRODUCTS

### GE Evolution Locomotives

**NEW 503-139934 36.95**
Sean Graham-White. A new generation of locomotives for a changing world: greener, cleaner and just as powerful. This book introduces readers to General Electric's Evolution Series, the company's latest achievement. Today's most up-to-date railfans will want to read about the development, testing, production, and use of the locomotive that, in its first year of production, has already been ordered by every Class 1 railroad in North America. Hardcover, 8-1/4 x 10-5/8", 144 pages, 160 color photos.

### Regional Railroads of the Midwest

**NEW 503-140304 36.95**
Steve Glischinski. They may not be the biggest or the best known, but regional carriers are the heart of the American rail system - and of the Midwest. Highly respected rail writer and photographer Glischinksi draws on his own knowledge and archive, as well as the photography of several colleagues, to offer an authoritative, lavishly illustrated account of the histories, motive power and operations of twelve of the Midwest's most vital current carriers, including a system map of every road covered. Paperback, 8-1/4 x 10-5/8", 160 pages,150 color photos.

Daily New Arrival Updates! Visit Walthers Web site at
**www.walthers.com**

### North American Railroad Bridges

**NEW 503-142999 36.95**
Brian Solomon. This photographic history pays tribute to the railroad bridge from the quaint wooden trestle to the graceful arched viaduct. Accompanying Solomon's account are images depicting railroads large and small hauling traffic over bridges across the continent. Hardcover, 8-1/4 x 10-5/8", 160 pages, 100 color and 50 b/w photos.

### Intermodal Railroading

**NEW 503-143000 36.95**
Brian Solomon. Richly illustrated history chronicles one of the most revolutionary developments in freight railroading during the twentieth century: intermodal shipping. Begins with attempts at "piggybacking" in the 1930s, and moves on to the period from World War II through the 1960s. Hardcover, 8-1/4 x 10-5/8", 192 pages, 150 color and 50 b/w photos.

### VIA Rail

**NEW 503-143021 36.95**
Chris Greenlaw. Go VIA Rail and see Canada. Archival and modern photography, route maps and print ads help detail the history of VIA Rail's motive power and passenger cars, as well such passenger trains as The Canadian and The Atlantic. Hardcover, 8-1/4 x 10-5/8", 160 pages. 100 color and 50 b/w photos.

### Southern Railway

**NEW 503-143022 36.95**
Tom Murray. This illustrated account of the venerable Southern is both the story of the railroad's 88-year tenure as the transporation force in the region and a fascinating chapter of Southern history. Murray explores this complex history right up to its 1982 merger with Norfolk & Western to form Norfolk Southern. Book includes system maps, period ads and timetables. Hardcover, 8-1/4 x 10-5/8", 160 pages, 100 color and 50 b/w photos.

### Long Island Rail Road Railroad Color History

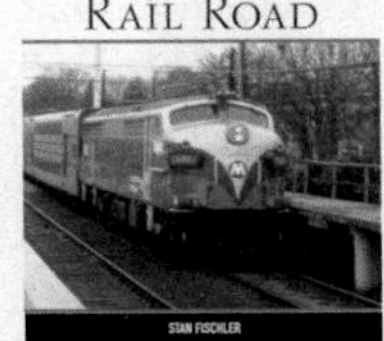


**NEW 503-143360 36.95**
Stan Fischler. Chartered in 1834, the Long Island Rail Road is still running today and is the oldest American railway operating under its original name. It is also the busiest commuter railroad on the continent. This illustrated history features archival and modern photography, route maps, print ads and timetables Includes such colorful tales as Mile-a-Minute Murphy and the Great Bicycle-Long Island Rail Road Race. Hardcover, 8-1/4 x 10-5/8", 160 pages, 100 color and 50 b/w photos.

### Burlington Route Streamlined Observation Cars

**NEW 503-143423** Burlington Signature Cars **22.95**
Jonathan Boyle, Sr. Chronicles the life of Burlington's premier cars of the streamlined era, the obervation cars that brought up the rear of the great trains and carried their names - the "signature" cars of the fleet. Paperback, 8-1/2 x 11", 80 pages.

### Southern Railway Steam Trains

**NEW 503-144016** Vol 2: Freight **32.95**
Curt Tillotson Jr.Portrays Southern Railway's freight trains from the 1930s to the end of steam featuring many superb B&W photos with extended captions. Tillotson captures the essence of the Southern's remarkable stable of older, yet well-maintained and superbly-operated, steam locomotives. Hardcover, 8-1/2 x 11". 112 pages, 112 b/w photos.

### The Railway Dictionary, Worldwide Railway Facts and Terminology

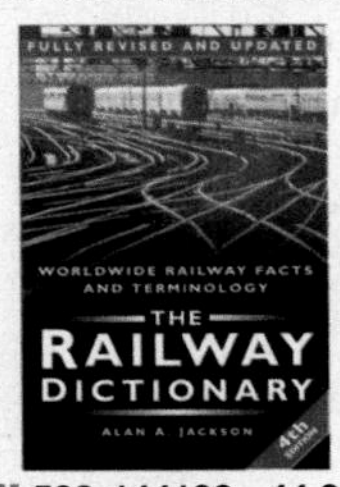


**NEW 503-144100 44.95**
Alan Jackson. International in scope and covering all aspects of railway terminology, past and present, this fourth edition includes among much else proper names of trains, companies and manufacturers, and clarifies a profusion of abbreviations. Hardcover, 6-1/4 x 9-3/8", 416 pages, 45 b/w photos.

### Railroads Across North America

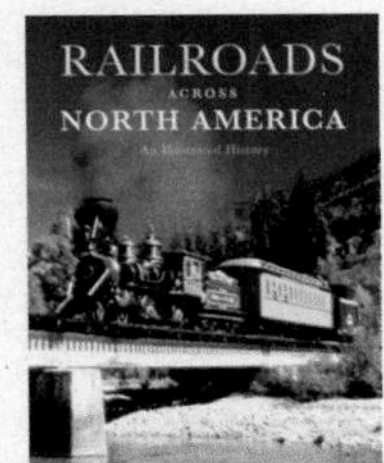


**NEW 503-144187** An Illustrated History **29.95**
Claude Wiatrowski. From the might of the major rail companies and their empires to the romance of rail travel, this book celebrates the glory and grandeur of American railroading. Features vintage photographs, modern images, maps, timetables, tickets, brochures and more. Hardcover, 9 x 12", 256 pages, 350 color and 150 b/w photos, 25 diagrams.

### New York Central Railroad

**NEW 503-144344 36.95**
Brian Solomon and Mike Schafer. For decades the New York Central reigned as one of America's most important railroads. This illustrated history covers the NYC through its 1968 merger with PRR and the eventual merger of Pennsylvania Central's successor Conrail into Norfolk Southern and CSX. Features archival photographs, route maps, period ads and timetables. Hardcover, 8-1/4 x 10-5/8", 160 pages, 100 color and 50 b/w photos.

### Southern Pacific Railroad

**NEW 503-144347 36.95**
Brian Solomon. More than just a railroad, the Southern Pacific was an empire. From austere western roots, the "Espee" grew into a railroad of some 17,000 route miles.This illustrated history tells the tale of SP's development from 1861 through its 1996 acquisition by the Union Pacific through archival photographs, route maps, period ads and timetables. Hardcover, 8-1/4 x 10-5/8", 160 pages, 100 color and 50 b/w photos.

### The West Point Route

**NEW 503-145061** The Atlanta & West Point Railroad & Western RR of Alabama **43.95**
Robert Hanson. The West Point Route had full-blown passenger and freight operations. This book gives a detailed, cogent, and well-documented history of this well-known but little understood operation. Hardcover, 8-3/4 x 11-1/4", 191 pages.

MBI Publishing Company

### Northern Pacific Railway Photo Archive

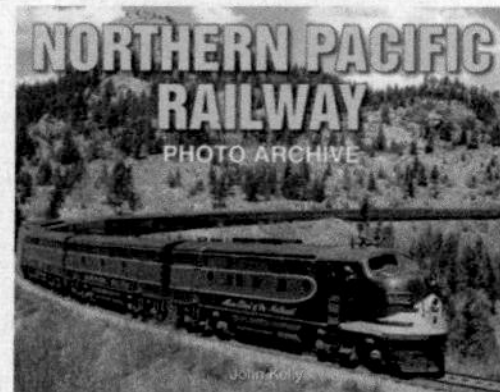


**NEW 503-145348 29.95**
John Kelly. All aboard the streamlined Vista-Dome North Coast Limited. Covering the 30s through the 60s, this book's outstanding vintage photography highlights the North Coast Limited, Vista-Dome passenger trains, NPs team and diesel locomotives, and freight cars, maintenance-of-way and cabooses. Paperback, 10-1/4 x 8-1/2", 128 pages, 122 b/w photos.

### Chicagoland Commuter Railroads

**NEW 503-145352** Metra & Northern Indiana Commuter Transportation District **32.95**
Patrick Dorin. Commuter or suburban rail passenger train services have been an important part of the Chicago Metro area for well over 100 years. This book reviews Chicago area commuter before the development of the RTA, Metra and NICTD. Paperback, 8-1/2 x 11", 128 pages, 40 color and 160 b/w photos.

### Tugboats of the Great Lakes

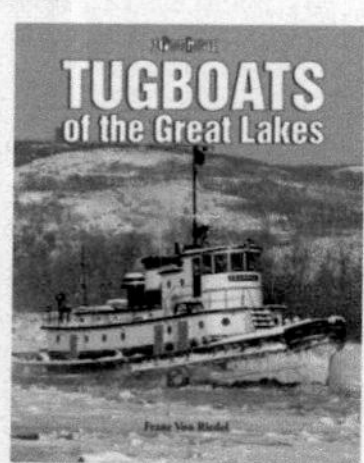


**NEW 503-145354** A Photo Gallery **34.95**
Franz Von Riedel. From the early days of commercial navigation on the Great Lakes, tugboats were needed to guide the ships in and out of ports. This book takes an in-depth look into Great Lakes ice-breaking, ship-assistance and towing. Paperback, 8-1/2 x 11", 160 pages, 120 color and 200 b/w photos.

### The Atlantic & Danville RR Company

**NEW 503-145912** The Railroad of Southside Virginia 2nd Ed. **29.95**
William E. Griffin, Jr. Here is the complete history of the railroad built to transport cotton from the farms of Southside Virginia to the port of Norfolk. Out of print since 1987, the book has been updated to cover the history of the railroad since the creation of the Norfolk Southern Corporation and provides a new color section. Hardcover, 8-3/4 x 11-1/4", 108 pages, 32 color and 193 b/w photos.

### Interurban Trains to Chicago

**NEW 503-145948 29.95**
John Kelly. Follows Samuel Insull's Great Chicago Systems, three superb interurban routes powered by electric traction that carried passengers from the north, west and southwest into downtown Chicago. Vintage photographs, timetables and poster advertising are featured. Paperback, 8-1/2 x 10-1/4", 128 pages.

### Great Lakes Ore Docks and Ore Cars

**NEW 503-145951 29.95**
Patrick Dorin. All of the iron ore throughout the Lake Superior Iron Ore District was carried by rail to ports on Lakes Superior, Michigan and Huron. This book lists all of the ore docks on The Great Lakes, as well as their operational life span right up to the present time. Includes the types of ore docks, photos, a roster of ore cars from the 1940s to the present and ore car schematics and pertinent data. Hardcover, 8-1/2 x 11", 128 pages.

### Santa Fe Passenger Trains in California

**NEW 503-146104** From the 1940s Thru Amtrak and More **29.95**
Patrick Dorin. The latest in Dorin's series on Santa Fe passenger trains tells the story of the line's trains in California in the period from the first streamliner up to Amtrak. Ideal for passenger buffs, Santa Fe fans and modelers. Hardcover, 8-3/4 x 11-1/4", 90 pages.

## MBI RAILROAD COLOR HISTORIES®

### New Haven Railroad

**503-135464 36.95**
Author Peter Lynch, a former New Haven employee, guides us through the history of the New Haven. Also includes a wide variety of New Haven motive power from multiple builders including: steam, 44-tonners, EP-2s, EP-3s, EP-4s, EF-4s, FL-9s, FAs, PAs, DL-109s, C-Liners, RDCs, H-16-44s U25Bs and much more in rare archival imagery. Hardcover, 8-1/4 x 10-5/8", 160 pages, 100 color and 50 B&W images.

### Rio Grande Railroad

**503-135758 36.95**
Features Rio Grande motive power including: steam, 44-tonners, FTs and later F units, PAs, H-15-44s, H-10-44s, Kraus-Maffei and all later EMD units. Also covers passenger trains such as Vista-domed California Zephyr and the Royal Gorge.

### Penn Central Railroad

**503-137234 36.95**
Peter Lynch. Penn Central was the result of the merger of the New York Central and Pennsylvania railroads and is the subject of this fine history. Former PC employee Lynch offers a colorful collection of images from the archives of numerous photographers. Covers rolling stock, motive power, operations and facilities along the 20,000 mile right of way. Hardcover, 8-1/4 x 10-5/8", 160 pages, 200 color photos.

### The Milwaukee Road

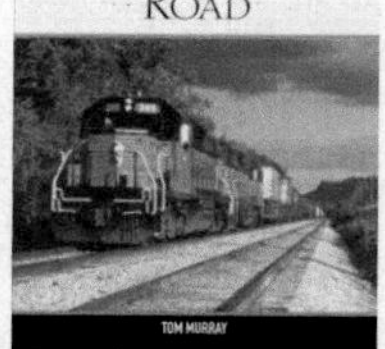


**503-137377 36.95**
Murray. Words and pictures carry readers across the vast tracts of land and time traversed by the Chicago, Milwaukee, St. Paul & Pacific—better known as the Milwaukee Road. Ranging from the railroad's late-19th century beginnings to its purchase by onetime rival Soo Line in 1985, this book also looks at the road's Hiawatha passenger trains, its "Little Joe" electrics and its Milwaukee, Wisconsin shops. Hardcover, 8-1/4 x 10-5/8", 160 pages, 150 color photos.

### Amtrak

**503-137466 36.95**
Brian Solomon. This pictorial history traces the 30-plus-year history of Amtrak from 1971 to 1991. Modern and period color photos illustrate motive power, including the high-speed Acela Express; rolling stock and equipment, much of it inherited from predecessor roads; famous long-distance trains past and present; short-haul corridors. Hardcover, 8-1/4 x 10-5/8", 160 pages, 150 color photos.

### Canadian National Railway

**503-137469 36.95**
Tom Murray. The 80 year history of the Canadian National Railway –"The World's Best Railroad." Covers equipment, operations, and features great archival and modern photos, timetables, advertisements, and a clear explanation of CNR's role in the settling of Canada. Hardcover, 8-1/4 x 10-5/8", 160 pages, 100 color and 50 B&W photos.

### Canadian Pacific Railway

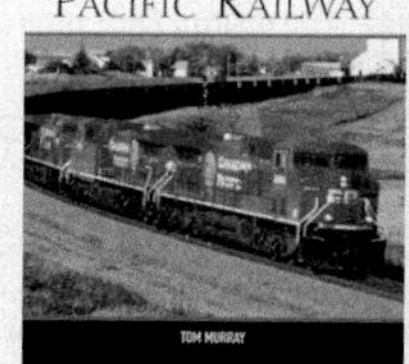


**503-139856 36.95**
Murray. CPR's story unfolds in spectacular sweep and gritty detail, from incorporation to multinational presence. This richly illustrated volume depicts locomotives, rolling stock, employees, the operations and the diverse terrain CPR traversed that made it "The World's Greatest Travel System." Hardcover, 8-1/4 x 10-5/8", 160 pages, 100 color and 50 B/W photos

### Chessie System

**503-139937 34.95**
Ori. In 1972 three great railroads joined forces as the Chessie System. This book traces the railroad's origins from the B&O and C&O in the early 1960s to the inclusion of the WM a decade later, and examines the Chessie System itself, from its major facilities, diesel fleet and intermodal operation to the technological advances that distinguished its reign. Hardcover, 8-1/4 x 10-5/8", 160 pages, 100 color and 50 B/W photos.

MBI Publishing Company

### Conrail

**503-137222 36.95**
Timothy Doherty & Brian Solomon. The 25 year history of Conrail is chronicled in this colorful book. Covers motive power, rolling stock, yards, terminals, its most interesting routes as well as operations. Interviews with former Conrail employees round out this fine history. Hardcover, 8-1/4 x 10-5/8", 144 pages, 100 color and 50 B&W photos.

### Duluth, Missabe & Iron Range Railroad

**503-138617 36.95**
John Leopard. Tucked away in scenic Northern Minnesota, the DMIR hauled taconite pellets and ore from the region's iron mines to the huge ore docks of Lake Superior. This illustrated history traces the road's origins in the Duluth & Iron Range and the Duluth, Missabe & Northern railroads and focuses on the period from their merger under U.S. Steel, covering its legendary steam power, to today and the current ownership by Canadian National.

### CSX

**503-139313 34.95**
Brian Solomon. Formed in 1980 as a holding company for the Chessie and Seaboard Systems, CSX merged them into CSX Transportation in 1986. This book explains how CSX and Norfolk Southern divided up the operations of their rival Conrail. Covers CSX diesel-electric powered freight operations in the East and Midwest as well as CSX hardware, facilities, and operations from 1980 to today.

### Illinois Central Railroad

**503-139848 36.95**
Murray. One of America's greatest railroads, the Illinois Central ran some of the nation's most famous passenger trains, as well as a freight service renowned for its quality. Drawing on archival records and interviews, this comprehensive and beautifully illustrated history of the "Main Line of Mid-America" looks at motive power and rolling stock, passenger service, freight operations, and the IC's most interesting routes. Hardcover, 8-1/4 x 10-5/8", 160 pages, 100 color and 50 B/W photos.

### Pennsylvania Railroad

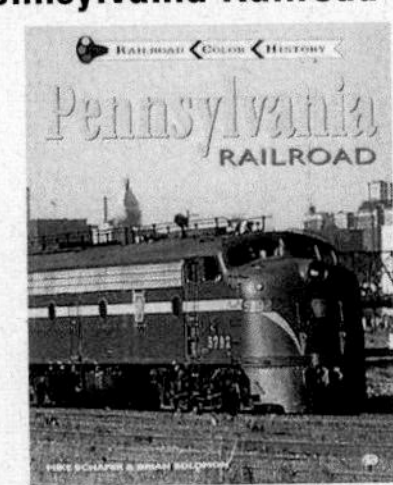


**503-124439 24.95**
Filled with archival and color photos of locomotives, trains and events of the PRR from the 1950s and 60s, and includes coverage of the Broadway Limited and Pennsylvania Limited passenger trains.

### Santa Fe Railway

**503-125094 24.95**
A classic tribute to the Atchison, Topeka and Sante Fe Railway that became the premier transportation company in the U.S. This book also includes information on the famous Super Chief, El Capitan and The Chief luxury passenger trains.

### Southern Pacific Railroad

**503-128918 24.95**
A colorful look at the great American railroad - the Southern Pacific. The SP was one of the most important railroads in the US. In its heyday, SP operating revenues were overshadowed only by the NYC and PRR. SP is famous for participating in the building of the transcontinental railroad, its fleet of Daylight streamlined passenger trains, and its 200 "Cab-Forward" steam locomotives. Softcover, 8-1/4 x 10-3/4", 128 pages, 40 B&W illustrations, 80 color.

### Baltimore & Ohio Railroad

**503-129825 24.95**
Takes you on a colorful journey through the hard-working history of the B&O Railroad, famous for its great passenger trains, including the Capital Limited and the National Limited, innovative technology, and aesthetic equipment. Softcover, 8-1/4 x 10-3/4", 128 pages, 40 B&W illustrations, 80 color images.

See What's New and Exciting at
**www.walthers.com**

### Union Pacific Railroad

**503-130130 24.95**
Since its beginnings in the 1860s, the UP has become one of the largest railroads in North America. Famous for its "Big Boy" steam locomotives and M10000 streamlined passenger train.

## GREAT PASSENGER TRAINS SERIES

### 20th Century Limited

**503-135743 34.95**
Zimmermann. Authoritative history from 1902 to its demise in 1967. Examines the train and its steam, electric and diesel motive power; its swank passenger cars and services and tells the complete story from the days of opulent wooden cars to the cutbacks leading to the formation of Amtrak.

### Burlington Zephyrs

**503-137237 36.95**
Karl Zimmerman. 2004 marked the 70th anniversary of the original Zephyr. This authoritative, illustrated history examines the trains, motive power, streamline designs, rolling stock including the Vista-Dome, and stations. Also features period advertising, route maps, timetables, and more. Hardcover, 8-1/2 x 11", 128 pages, 50 color and 75 B&W photos.

### Great Northern Empire Builder

**503-139310 36.95**
Bill Yenne. This illustrated history covers the Empire Builder through its 1970 demise. Included here are the trains, their various forms of motive power and rolling stock, and their services. A wealth of black and white archival images and period color photography depict the Empire Builder along its scenic route plus related facilities, advertising and more. Hardcover, 8-1/2 x 11", 160 pages, 90 color and 90 black-and-white images.

### The Milwaukee Road's Hiawathas

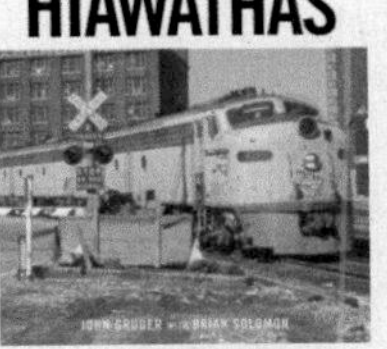


**503-139853 34.95**
Gruber. The Hiawathas became known as the "Fastest Trains in America," clocking over 100 miles per hour on daily runs. This authoritative history of Milwaukee Road passenger service is illustrated with evocative color photography detailing the renowned steam and diesel locomotives and their distinctive rolling stock. Includes design drawings, car interiors, route maps and period ads. Hardcover, 8-1/4 x 10-5/8", 160 pages, 120 color and 60 B/W photos.

MBI Publishing Company

### Santa Fe Chiefs

**503-139315 36.95**
Bill Yenne. This illustrated history of the Santa Fe's flagship passenger trains carries readers back to an era of luxury travel on America's rails—when movie stars and moguls booked rooms on the Super Chief for the 40-hour trip from Chicago to Los Angeles. Tells the story of America's most celebrated passenger train from its first run in 1936 to its takeover by Amtrak in 1971. Hardcover, 8-1/2 x 10-5/8", 160 pages, 90 color and 90 black-and-white images.

### Southern Pacific Passenger Trains

**503-139312 34.95**
Brian Solomon. Well into the 1950s, the SP operated an extensive fleet of popular, colorful passenger trains that became the preferred mode of travel for the West Coast's nouveau riche and everyday travelers alike. This history covers their motive power, rolling stock and the SP's services. Archival photographs depict the trains on their routes systemwide from Portland to Los Angeles, Texas and New Orleans. Hardcover, 8-1/2 x 11", 160 pages, 90 color and 90 black-and-white photos.

### New Haven Passenger Trains

**503-139921 34.95**
Lynch. This illustrated history revisits the days when trains like the Merchants Limited, Yankee Clipper, Cranberry, and Quaker carried tourists and commuters to the great cities of the East Coast. Plenty of photographs and authoritative text chronicle trains and routes—detailing motive power, rolling stock, advertising, stations and services that made the New Haven a passenger giant. Hardcover, 8-1/2 x 11", 160 pages, 180 photos.

### Pennsylvania Railroad's Broadway Limited

**503-139416 34.95**
Welsh. This authoritative, illustrated history tells the story of Pennsylvania Railroad's Broadway Limited. An institution in New York-to-Chicago rail travel from 1902 to 1955. Text and pictures introduce readers to the posh cars and powerful engines, the luxuries and amenities on board, the stations, terminals and timetables-everything that made the train the pride of the Pennsylvania. Hardcover, 8-1/4 x 10-5/8", 160 pages, 90 color and 90 B/W photos.

## RAILROAD BOOKS

### Lionel: America's Favorite Toy Trains

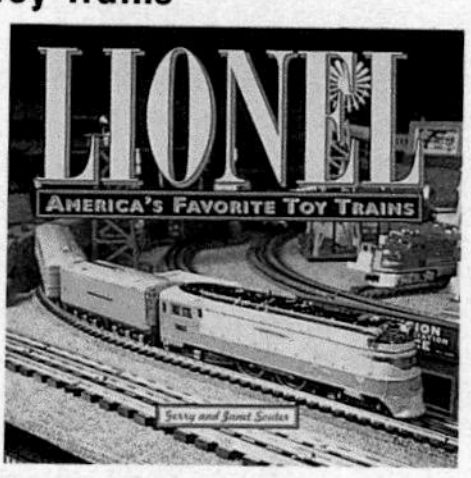


**503-137319 19.95**
Souter. This colorful volume illustrates the history of Lionel electric toy trains. Learn of Lionel's greatest years in the 1950s and 1960s and its resurgence in the 1990s—just in time for the company's 100th anniversary celebration in 2000. Paperback, 10 x 10", 156 pages, 150 color and 50 black-and-white photos.

### The Lionel FasTrack Book

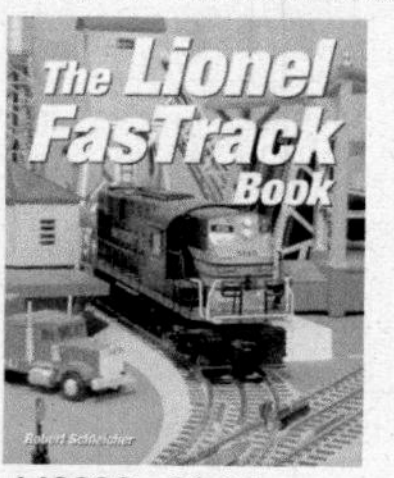


**503-140296 29.95**
Schleicher. This book presents the first complete guide to the FasTrack system. Amply illustrated with color photos and 36 track diagrams, it instructs readers on every aspect of the system, from assembling and disassembling, to designing unique layouts, or planning layouts for smaller areas. Paperback, 8-1/4 x 10-5/8", 160 pages, 150 color photos and 36 diagrams.

### The Big Book of Lionel

**503-138620** The Complete Guide to Owning and Running America's Favorite Toy Trains **29.95**
Robert Schleicher. A one-stop, hands-on guide for those who buy Lionel trains with the intention of actually running them. Paperback, 8-1/4 x 10-5/8", 256 pages, 200 color and 150 B&W photos, 20 maps.

### Classic Toy Trains

**Limited Quantity Available**

**503-135109 19.95**
Souter. Rediscover the beloved collectible toy trains of Carlisle & Finch, American Flyer, Ives, Hafner and Lionel displayed here in this nostalgic and colorful volume. Paperback, 8-1/4 x 10-3/4", 256 pages, 250 color and 150 B/W photos.

### Big Book Of Model Railroad Track Plans

**503-135813 34.95**
Schleicher. This book features 81 model track plan options. Project descriptions include technical advice and prototype photos that will inspire any modeler. Projects feature obstacles that might be encountered during construction and helpful tips for getting it right the first time. Includes line art diagrams layout routes, dimensions, and photographs of the finished layout. Softcover, 8-1/4 x 11-5/8", 256 pages, 75 color and 75 B&W images.

### North American Railyards

**503-136276 36.95**
Michael Rhodes. This comprehensive, illustrated guide is the definitive reference to more than 70 major railyards across the U.S. and Canada. Schematic track plans identify every track and its purpose – essential for train watchers and modelers. Covers intermodal, hump and traditional classification yards. Hardcover, 8-1/4 x 10-5/8", 240 pages, 100 color and 100 B&W photos, track plans.



### Travel by Pullman: A Century of Service

**503-138625 34.95**
Joe Welsch & Bill Howes. During the 1910s and 1920s Pullman carried more than 35 million passengers annually in 9,000+ sleeping and parlor cars. Text examines Pullman's entire operation from the equipment and car shops to the roles of the porter, cleaners, cooks, barbers, shoe-shiners and more. Historic photos of car interiors plus ads, and sales literature. Hardcover, 10 x 10", 160 pages, 100 color and 100 B&W photos.

### Burlington Northern Santa Fe Railway

**503-139304 50.00**
Brian Solomon. Here is the detailed and fascinating history of how two legendary railroads—the Santa Fe and the Burlington Northern—merged in 1995 to create one of America's new rail icons, the Burlington Northern Santa Fe (BNSF). Hardcover, 10-1/2 x 12", 288 pages, 200 color and 50 black-and-white images, 10 diagrams.

### Atlas of North American Railroads

**503-139926 36.95**
Bill Yenne. Classic system maps produced by North American railroads, collected for the first time in a single volume, offer a sweeping view of the industry's remarkable reach in the period of its greatest power. Each railroad's routes unfold in multi-page spreads featuring a capsule history, vital specs such as track mileage and years of operation, and period photographs, all detailing their mid-twentieth-century might. Hardcover 8-1/4 x 10-5/8", 176 pages, 25 color and 25 black-and-white photos, 150 diagrams.

MBI Publishing Company

## Railroad Signaling

**503-136335 36.95**
Solomon. Complete and illustrated guide to railroad signaling in the U.S. simplifies and presents the bewildering array of mechanisms, procedures and rules that have evolved since the 1830s to promote safety, on America's railways. Provides photos of equipment and explanations of how this equipment is used. Hardcover, 8-1/4 x 10-5/8", 128 pages, 250 color photos.

## EMD Locomotives

**503-140308 40.00**
Solomon. This overview of the great locomotive maker provides a comprehensive account of EMD's history, from the 1920s railcars to the mid-century F units, workhorse GP and SD locomotives, and Dash series; including the company's race with its chief competitor, General Electric, to reach 6,000 horsepower. Hardcover, 10 x 10", 176 pages, 125 color and 75 B/W photos.

## GE Locomotives

**503-135762 36.95**
This book covers a broad cross-section of GE's locomotive history, from first electric S motors to today's colossal 6,000 HP diesel-electrics. Includes Pennsy's E44s, Amtrak's E60s and Milwaukee Road's "Little Joes"

## Images Of Western Railroading

**503-136414 34.95**
Schmollinger. From dizzying mountain passes to green pine valleys and arid desert canyons, the regions spanning the Rocky Mountains to the Pacific Coast have always presented the railroad with a geography that challenges the equipment. But what's a hinderance to the railroad is a scenic delight for fans. Hardcover, 10 x 10", 168 pages, 200 color photos.

## The American Freight Train

**503-131562 34.95**
Boyd. Includes a large selection of archival color photos depicting rolling stock and the steam and diesel engines that pulled them. Hardcover, 10 x 10", 156 pages, 150 color and 50 B&W images.

## The American Passenger Train

**503-133363 34.95**
Schafer & Welsh. This photographic history rambles though two centuries of passenger trains, presenting a wealth of modern and period color photographs. Hardcover, 10 x 10", 168 pages, 150 color and 50 B&W photos.

## The American Railroad: Working for the Nation

**503-140568 24.95**
This nostalgic, authoritative history of U.S. railroads is richly illustrated and covers everything from a road's beginning to the heyday of the 1940s and 50s, up to the present. Rail buffs will appreciate the detail and focus on railroading's five most fascinating components-locomotives, freight trains, passenger trains, depots and workforce. Softcover 10 x 10", 160 pages, 163 color and 40 B/W photos.

## American Steam Locomotive

**503-126474 29.95**
Solomon. The mighty trains that once ruled the tracks are shown against scenic mountains, plains and small towns. Hardcover, 10 x 10", 160 pages, 150 color and 50 B&W images.

## Classic American Railroad Terminals

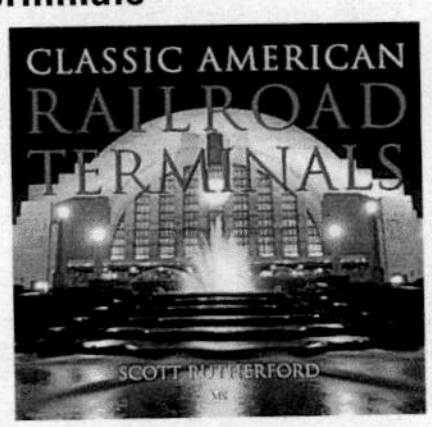


**503-131565 34.95**
Rutherford. Archival and modern photography tells the stories behind the design, the architecture, and the use of terminals. Hardcover, 10 x 10", 156 pages, 150 color and 50 B&W photos.

## Classic American Railroads

**503-123457 34.95**
Schafer. America's famous railroads—Santa Fe; the Milwaukee; NYC; Pennsy; UP; Denver & Rio Grande; GN; and more. Hardcover, 10 x 10", 160 pages, 50 color and 150 B&W images.

## The Great Book of Trains

**503-133796 24.98**
Hollingsworth. This book provides lavishly illustrated and technically detailed descriptions of more than 300 of the world's most famous locomotives. The text is complemented by dozens of historical photographs and 160 beautifully drawn full-color sideviews. Hardcover, 8-1/2 x 11", 416 pages, 600 color and 177 B/W photos.

## More Classic American Railroads

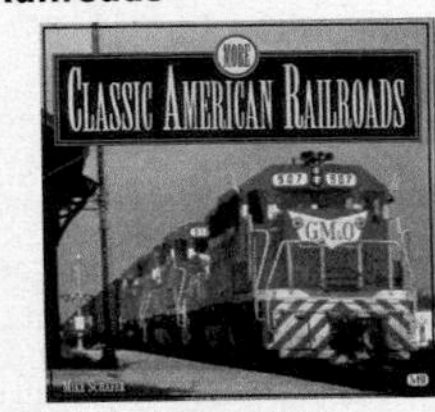


**503-130133 39.95**
Schafer. Features railroads like the D&H; EL; Gulf, Mobile & Ohio; LV; NYC, Chicago & St. Louis; MP; SOU; Wabash; and others. Hardcover, 10 x 10", 160 pages, 150 color and 50 B&W images.

## Railway Maintenance Equipment

**503-133371 24.95**
Solomon. Find the true identity of the equipment used to build and maintain railbeds and lines including tie pullers, rail grinders and more. Detailed photos show the machines and tools in action. This is a handy reference guide for fans of full-size railways or modelers. Softcover, 8-1/4 x 11", 128 pages, 40 images, 80 color illustrations.

## Rail Power

**503-143024 14.95**
Barry. This concise volume traces the transformation and evolution of steam, electric and diesel locomotives from the early 19th century right up to the present. Detailed descriptions identify the more than 100 locomotive types pictured and explain their roles in the history of American motive power. Paperback, 6-1/2 x 8-1/4", 192 pages, 200 color and 50 B/W photos.

## Streamliners: A History Of A Railroad Icon

**503-135136 19.95**
Streamliners centers on various aspects of the trains such as their development, rolling stock, motive power, interior design and operations. Photographs zero in on the lounges, dining-car china, sleeping-car cabins, and so forth. A softcover reprint of Classic American Streamliners. 10 x 10", 160 pages, 150 color and 80 B&W images.

## MBI Publishing Company

### Steam Trains: A Photographic Gallery

**503-139906 34.95**
Bell. Few images speak as clearly of a time and a place as a dramatic black-and-white photograph of an American steam locomotive. All the new photographs in this beautiful book meticulously recreate with stunning images that original monochromatic style, capturing the bygone age of steam rail against the settings of its heyday. Hardcover, 10 x 10", 192 pages, 120 B/W photos.

### Working on the Railroad

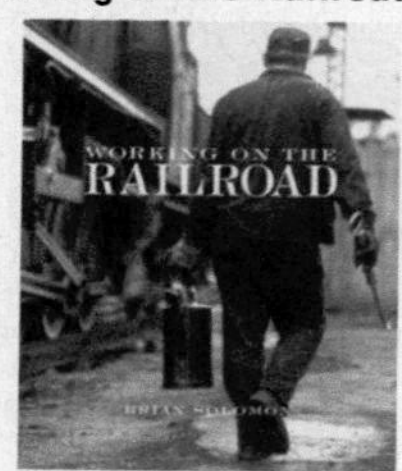


**503-139628 34.95**
This richly illustrated volume takes us behind the scenes to show what goes into keeping a railroad running. Includes anecdotes from railroad workers as well as the historical evolution of railway vocations and descriptions of how each job has changed over time. Hardcover, 8-1/4 x 10-5/8", 160 pages, 150 color and 75 B/W photos.

## TLC RAILROAD BOOKS

### North American Steam Locomotive Builders and Their Insignia

**503-144648 43.95**
Davies. This book gives a fascinating look into the successes and failures of the locomotive builders, then on the cutting edge of technology. Philadelphia, Schenectady and Lima, Ohio are here with a host of other locations from New England to San Francisco. The Canadian builders are included. Hardcover, 8-3/4 x 11-1/4", 266 pages, 300 B/W photos.

### Seaboard Coast Line & Family Lines Railroad 1967-1986 — A CSX Predecessor

**503-140323 34.95**
This book brings together great SCL photos and text to form a cohesive history of this important system that combined two of the greatest Southeastern railroads (SAL and ACL) and set the stage for the 1986 merger with Chessie System that resulted in today's CSX. Hardbound, 160 pages, over 200 black & white and color illustrations.

### Santa Fe's Super Chief and El Capitan 1936-1971

**503-140418 28.95**
Patrick C. Dorin tells the history of these two great Santa Fe streamliners. Includes descriptions of cars, service, timetables, diagrams and photos. Hardbound, 100 pages, over 100 illustrations.

### Baltimore & Ohio Steam Locomotives

**503-137125** The Last 30 Years 1928-1958 **29.95**
Dixon. Primarily a photo album of late B&O steam – most previously unpublished. Hardcover, 8-1/2 x 11", 128 pages, 200 color photos.

### Chesapeake & Ohio's Pere Marquette

**503-136297** America's First Post-War Streamliner **21.95**
Dixon. Pere Marquette Railway story told in great detail from original documents and with great photos, many from C&O official files. Softcover, 8-1/2 x 11", 80 pages, 130 color and B&W photos.

### Chicago & North Western Freight Trains & Equipment

**503-136298 29.95**
Dorin. An overview of the line's freight trains and cars over the years, with emphasis from the 1930s to modern times. There are great illustrations showing steam and diesel locomotives, cars of all types, and information about how the trains were operated. Hardcover, 128 pages, 8-1/2 x 11", 200 color and B&W photos.

### Clinchfield Railroad In The Coal Fields

**503-135944 32.95**
Covers the history of the railroad and its towns, operations, structures and equipment with maps, B&W and color photos and first-hand stories. Included are the accounts of riding and working some of the actual jobs on the railroad written in railroad lingo. Hardcover, 144 pages, 8-1/2 x 11", 220 color and B&W photos.

### Milwaukee Road Passenger Service

**503-138599** From the Hiawatha to Amtrak **29.95**
Dorin. An excellent overview starting with the original Hiawatha pulled by 4-4-2s and later 4-6-2 F7 steam locos until the last train before Amtrak. Hardcover, 8-1/2 x 11", 144 pages, 200 B&W photos.

### Michigan-Ontario Iron Ore Railroads

**503-134778 25.95**
Dorin. Covers the Lake Superior & Ishpeming, Chicago & North Western/Union Pacific, Milwaukee Road, Soo Line, DSS&A, Canadian Pacific, Canadian National, Escanaba & Lake Superior, Wisconsin Central and Algoma Central. Hardcover, 112 pages, 8-1/2 x 11", 175 B&W photos.

### Minnesota-Ontario Iron Ore Railroads

**503-134777 25.95**
Dorin. Covers the Duluth, Missabe & Iron Range, BN, Soo Line, Canadian National, North Shore Mining and LTV operations. Hardcover, 8-1/2 x 11", 112 pages, 175 B&W photos.

### Missouri Pacific Passenger Trains

**503-134779** The Postwar Years **28.95**
Dorin. This volume overviews the first streamlined trains and ends with the arrival of Amtrak in May 1971. Hardcover, 8-1/2 x 11", 128 pages, 175 B&W and color images.

### Nashville, Chattanooga & St. Louis

**503-134782** A History Of The Dixie Line **39.95**
Schult. This is a complete history of the Nashville, Chatanooga & St. Louis Railroad from its beginnings in the 1840s through the Civil War, to its end. Hardcover, 8-1/2 x 11", 280 pages, 200 B&W photos.

For Up-To-Date Information and News Bookmark Walthers Web site at

**www.walthers.com**

MBI Publishing Company

## New Haven Railroad

**503-135931**Dining On The Shore Line Route **24.95**
Frattasio. Along with the cars themselves, the spotlight shines on the people behind this New England railroad's highly regarded dining and grill car services. China patterns are illustrated, with an appetizing selection of authentic railroad recipes. Softcover, 8-1/2 x 11", 112 pages, 200 B&W photos.

## Passenger Trains Of Northern New England 1935-1966

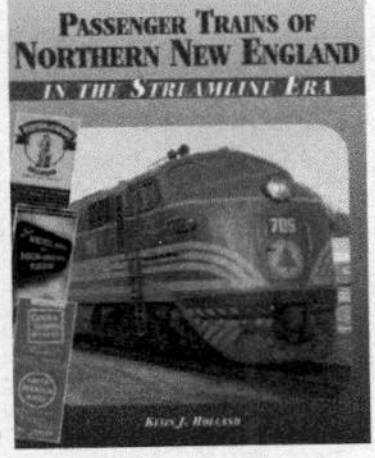

**503-134781 29.95**
Holland. Passenger trains are chronicled in this examination of their role in the vanguard of streamlining in the mid-1930s through the 1960s. Over 200 B&W and color illustrations. Hardcover, 144 pages, 8-1/2 x 11", 200 B&W photos.

## Pennsylvania Railroad Passenger Train Consists And Cars

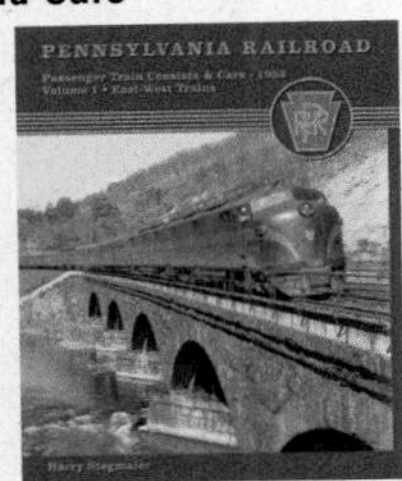

**503-135928** Vol.1 East-West Trains **39.95**
Stegmaier. The author uses a 1952 PRR official consist book and traces the background of the service, the type of cars used, their regular and special assignments, and shows the exact makeup of all Pennsy's important East-West passenger trains in this transition year. Hardcover, 8-1/2 x 11", 112 pages, 150 color and 30 B&W photos.

## Santa Fe Passenger Trains in the Streamlined Era

**503-138611 32.95**
Dorin. Extensive text depicts ATSF's superb passenger trains from the 1940s through 1971. Exterior and interior photos, train roster, locos, rolling stock, timetables and more. Hardcover, 8-1/2 x 11", 144 pages, 150 B&W photos.

## Santa Fe Streamlined Observation Cars

**503-138612 20.95**
Boyle. Interior and exterior photos, floor plans and PR photos. A must for modelers of ATSF's named trains such as the "Super Chief." Paperback, 8-1/2 x 11", 80 pages, 50 color and 150 B&W photos.

## Southern Railway Steam Trains

**503-138609** Volume 1: Passenger **29.95**
Tillotson. 150 superb photos of steam passenger trains throughout the Southern system. Features information on mountain lines and operations. Hardcover, 8-1/2 x 11", 112 pages, 200 B&W photos,

## Southern Railway Diesel Locomotives And Trains 1960-1982

**503-135930 29.95**
Tillotson. A look at each and every class from beginning to end. Fully illustrated both with roster photos and action pictures. Hardcover, 8-1/2 x 11", 112 pages, 30 color and 162 B&W images.

## Tennessee Central Railroad

**503-136299** The Nashville Route **30.95**
Downey.The trains, equipment, and operations, with excellent B&W and color photos, maps and illustrations. It fell on bad days after WWII and eventually its trackage was taken over after 1968 and operated by Southern, Louisville & Nashville, and Illinois Central. Hardcover, 144 pages, 8-1/2 x 11", 200 color and B&W illustration.

## Way of the Zephyrs: The Postwar Years

**503-140484 34.95**
Doughty. Traces the postwar Zephyr fleet from the birth of the modern dome car in 1945 through the Burlington Northern merger in 1970. Covers such streamlined passenger train icons as California Zephyr, Denver Zephyr. Hardcover, 8-1/2 x 11", 128 pages, 29 color and 175 B/W photos.

## West Virginia's Last Logging Railroad: The Meadow River Lumber Company

**503-135929 19.95**
Bagdon.The complete story from 1912 to its end in 1971, when the last log train arrived in Rainelle, West Virginia, just before the mill was closed. In 1958 the first diesels came to supplant the Shays, Heisler and Climax that had powered the trains up until that time. Some of Meadow River's equipment went to the Cass Scenic Railroad. Softcover, 80 pages, 8-1/2 x 11", 130 B&W illustrations.

## West Virginia Central & Pittsburg Railway

**503-136300** A Western Maryland Predecessor **32.95**
Clarke. A must for those interested in West Virginia, mountain railroading, and coal and lumber development. Hardcover, 8-1/2 x 11", 160 pages, 200 B&W photos.

## Wheeling And Lake Erie

**503-135927** Volume 2: Ohio Coal Hauler **29.95**
Corns. This 500-mile Ohio coal hauler had lumbering 2-6-6-2's, fast 2-8-4s, home built 0-6-0s and 0-8-0s. Cars, locomotives, stations, terminals, shops, facilities, iron ore piers on Lake Erie. From 1870s through merger with Nickle Plate in 1949. Hardcover, 128 pages, 11 x 8-1/2", 360 B&W illustrations.

## Appalachian Coal Hauler

**503-134774** The Innerstate Railroad's Mine Runs And Coal Trains **29.95**
Wolfe. This latest volume deals with the coal mines, tipples, and switching operations, including coal trains and mine runs. The photos, drawings and track plans give wonderful background to modelers. Hardcover, 160 pages, 8-1/2 x 11", 175 B&W photos.

## B&O Caboose: Photos And Diagrams Volume 1

**503-127318 26.95**
Each class of caboose features a dimensioned drawing and photographs showing the car in actual service. Hardcover, 11 x 8-1/2", 124 pages, 110 B&W illustrations.

## Chesapeake & Ohio Passenger Cars In Color

**503-130616 32.95**
Outstanding color history documents C&O passenger cars and trains from 1945 to the emergence of Amtrak® in 1971.

## Chesapeake & Ohio Steam in Color As Modeled

**503-143504 39.95**

## Chesapeake & Ohio Super Power Steam Locomotives

**503-143505 32.95**

## Chespeake & Ohio West Virginia 1940-1960

**503-143506 19.95**

## Chessie: The Railroad Kitten

**503-124122 11.95**
A wonderfully nostalgic tribute to the lovable kitten. Softcover, 8-1/2 x 11", 64 pages, 70 B&W illustrations, 12 color.

## Chicago & North Western Passenger Cars

**503-133437 19.95**
Dorin. This illustrated volume provides complete data about cars used for passenger service operations from 1945 to 1995. Softcover, 8-1/2 x 11", 64 pages, 100 B&W images.

## New Haven Railroad's Streamline Passenger Fleet 1934–1953

**503-130611 28.95**
Engaging history explains how New Haven managed to order streamline passenger fleets in the midst of both the Great Depression and WWII.

## The New Haven Railroad In The Steam Era

**503-127311 33.95**
Color photographs illustrate the history of the New Haven Railroad's passenger operations in the era of the streamlined train beginning in 1934.

## New York Central's Lightweight Passenger Cars, Trains & Travel

**503-124625 28.95**
This volume spans the period from the inauguration of the Mercury in 1936 to the end of the NYC with merger into the Penn Central in 1967. Hardcover, 8-1/2 x 11", 160 pages, 200+ B&W and color illustrations.

## Nickel Plate Road Diesel Locomotives

**503-127319 26.95**
The complete story of Nickel Plate Road's dieselization traces the history of all diesel locomotives before and after the N&W merger.

## Richmond, Fredericksburg & Potomac Passenger Service: 1935–1975

**503-130614 26.95**
The story of the 113-mile railroad that linked Northeast railways to Southern operations via the nation's capital.

## Steam's Camelot

**503-130615 38.95**
Southern/Norfolk Southern Excursions in Color. Color photos of bygone behemoths and a fascinating text detail nostalgic PR steam operations.

MBI Publishing Company

**Steam Locomotive Coaling Stations And Diesels**
**503-135660 19.95**
Dixon. This book reproduces material originally contained in articles appearing in Railway Age and other trade magazines of the era, and combines this material with many photos of various types of coaling stations and fueling facilities. Softcover, 80 pages, 8-1/2 x 11".

**Western Pacific Locomotives & Cars**
**503-127313 24.95**
This photographic chronicle illustrates the steam and diesel locomotives, passenger, freight and work cars used in the post-1930 period. Hardcover, 8-1/2 x 11", 112 pages, 190 B&W illustrations.

## MOTORBOOKS ENTHUSIAST COLOR SERIES®

These books offer a range of fact-filled and photo-packed titles that give complete coverage of your favorite subjects... at a great price! Each is softcover, 8-1/4 x 9", 96 pages, 80 color photos.

**Caboose**

**503-124445 15.95**

**Electric Locomotives**

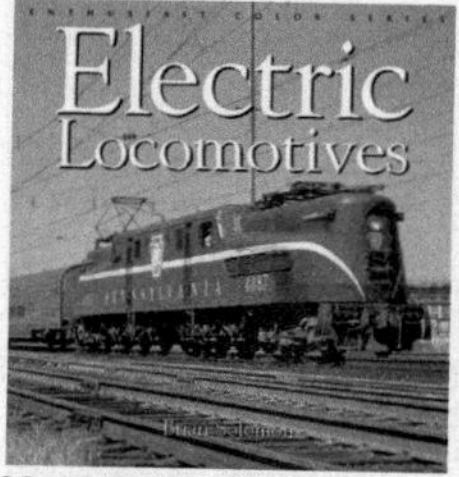


**503-136258 15.98**

**Freight Train Cars**

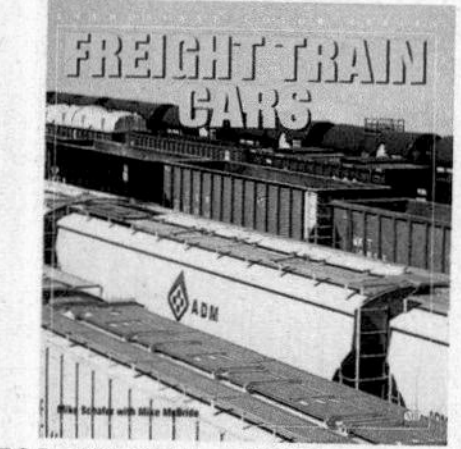


**503-128956 14.95**

**Modern Diesel Locomotives**

**503-123265 14.95**

**Modern Lionel Trains**

**503-136431 14.95**

**Modern Toy Trains**

**503-135129 14.95**

**Santa Fe Railway**

**503-135808 15.95**

**Super Steam Locomotives**

**503-130120 15.95**

**Subways Of The World**

**503-129992 14.95**

**Vintage Diesel Locomotives**

**503-126374 14.95**

## PHOTO ARCHIVES BY ICONOGRAFIX

**CNW Passenger Trains of the 400 Fleet Photo Archive**

**503-143198 29.95**
Kelly. The "400 Fleet" brought people from Wisconsin, Upper Michigan and southern Minnesota into Chicago. Coverage includes the Twin Cities 400, Minnesota 400, Peninsula 400, Flambeau 400, Kate Shelley 400 and commuter streamliners. Paperback, 10-1/4 x 8-1/2", 128 pages, 121 B/W photos.

**Classic Streamliners Photo Archive**

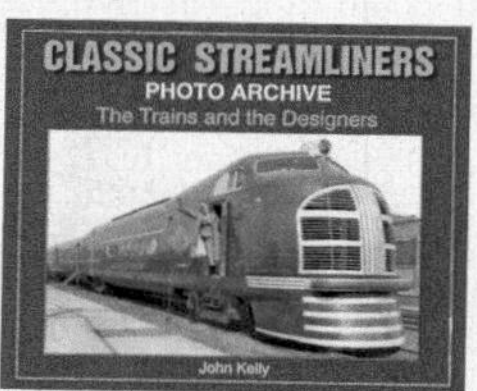


**503-137517** The Trains and the Designers **29.95**
John Kelly. Covers the streamliners designed by Raymond Lowey for the PRR, Henry Dreyfuss for the NYC, Otto Kuhler for the MILW and B&O, and the Electro Motive styling team. Paperback 10-1/4 x 8-1/2", 128 pages, 121 B&W photos.

**Locomotives of the Upper Midwest Photo Archive**

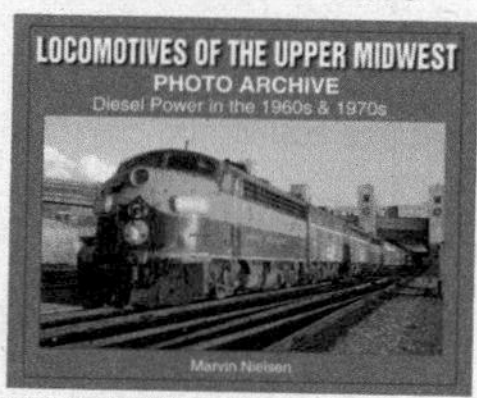


**503-137475** Diesel Power in the 1960s & 1970s **29.95**
Nielsen. Covers the locomotives used by SOO C&NW, BN, MILW, WCI, GB&W and others. Paperback 10-1/4 x 8-1/2", 128 pages, 121 B&W photos,

**Steam Locomotives of the B&O Railroad Photo Archive**

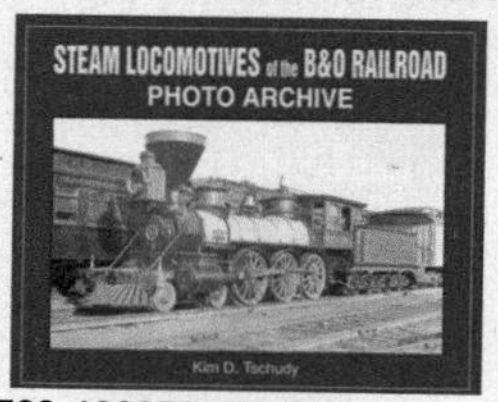


**503-136379 29.95**
Kim Tshudy. This book takes a look at the Steam locos of America's oldest railroad from the Civil War through the end of steam. Paperback 10-1/4 x 8-1/2", 128 pages, 121 B&W photos,

**Marion Mining & Dredging Machines**
**503-135915 29.95**

**Illinois Central Railroad 1875-1970**
**503-134604 29.95**

**Great Northern Railway Ore Docks Of Lake Superior**
**503-135242 29.95**

**Circus & Carnival Tractors 1930-2001**
**503-135239 29.95**

**Marion Construction Equipment 1883-1975**
**503-134599 29.95**

**Chicago, St Paul, Minneapolis & Omaha 1880-1940**
**503-124384 29.95**

**Great Northern Railway 1945-1970, Vol. 2**
**503-126127 29.95**

**Milwaukee Road 1850-1960**
**503-123566 29.95**

**Milwaukee Road Depots 1856-1954**
**503-131748 29.95**

**Show Trains Of The 20th Century**
**503-130665 29.95**

**Soo Line 1975-1992**
**503-124385 29.95**

**Trains Of The Circus 1872–1956**
**503-130085 29.95**

**Trains of the Twin Ports Duluth-Superior In The 1950s**
**503-129095 29.95**

**Trains Of The Upper Midwest: Steam & Diesel in the 1950s/1960s**
**503-131684 29.95**

## DVDs

These high-quality DVDs capture railroading in the United States at its finest.

**Santa Fe Vintage West**

**NEW 503-146234** DVD **29.50**
Early film from the 50s through the 80s with synchronized, accurate sound. See more action from pre-merger 1993 with the last of the new Warbonnets. Many F-units on mail, freight and passenger trains. Lots of older Alco and early EMD and GE power. The Tehachapis, Cajon Pass, Eastbay and Stockton. The Needles sub brings stunning desert action. 94 minutes.

**Scarlet & Gray Memories**

**NEW 503-146233** DVD **29.50**
Join us for a look back at the SP in the 1990s and in earlier views of the 1970s. See the SP power taken away by the 1996 UP-SP merger. More action and views from the San Fernando Valley, Cajon Pass and Beaumont Hill bring you a SP that you can fondly remember. These are the missing views that define the SP to every fan who misses the railroad. Lots of fun and lots of older SP power. The Bakersfield Yard scenes are compared from 1993 and back in 1971. Don't miss this video! 100 minutes.

MBI Publishing Company

### Diesel Power Of The Santa Fe

**503-136538** DVD **28.50**
Vintage film of freight and passenger. Rare Pasadena Sub., Franklin Canyon, Stockton, Cajon, Tehachapi, Mojave to Barstow, Illinois and much more. See PA, F-units, GP9 and more. 91 minutes.

### Diesel Power On The Southern Pacific

**503-136405** DVD **29.50**
Trace SP's conversion to diesel from WWII's steam powered troop and freight trains to the end in the 50s. See F-units, Geeps, SDs, ALCOs, FM, Baldwin and finally the rise of GE. Rare Burbank and Santa Paula branch action. Mainlines from Shasta down to Sunset lines with old Taylor Yard. Kaiser ore, LAUPT, old "West-line" and much more. 103 minutes.

### Donner Pass Thunder

**503-136902** DVD **28.50**
Features views from 1959 to the end. See freight and passenger trains in blizzards and sunshine with steep grades and beautiful scenery. See snow fighting equipment and the snow-shed history. 90 minutes.

### Electric Rails Around The Bay

**503-136551** DVD **34.50**
Sacramento Northern, SP-IER and Peninsular Railway history and action in B&W and beautiful color film. See early passenger, ferry and the freight of the SN in the Oakland Hills. Fifty years of great electric filming. 61 minutes.

### Electric Rails of Utah

**503-140422** DVD **29.50**
See electrics from the 20s to the 50s in and around Salt Lake, Utah. Covers the Bamberger, Salt Lake & Utah, Saltair Line, Utah Idaho central and more. Also includes the Kennecott electrics at Bingham Canyon open-pit copper mine and KCC operations in Nevada.

### Empire Of The North

**503-135373** DVD **29.50**
See GN, NP, CB&Q and the SP&S from the fifties into the seventies with late steam and diesel power. 91 minutes.

### Extreme SP

**503-136536** DVD **28.50**
Action from early 90s to the end. Heavy Shasta action and Donner Pass with floods, snow storms and blue skies. Lots of old power and great coverage of rotaries, flangers, snow-cats and spreaders. 112 minutes.

### Key System Empire

**503-135949** DVD **28.50**
See the Key System from its early days with ferryboats to the Bay Bridge era. Visit all the lines and cross the bay by ferry and bridge-rails to San Francisco. Streetcars, Bridge-articulated units and many surprises, plus cameo appearances of early Muni and IER make this a great story. 61 minutes.

### Milwaukee Road Scrapbook

**503-140423** DVD **29.50**
Features all the Milwaukee Road favorites including Bi-Polars, Quills, Little Joes and Boxcabs on passenger and freight trains. Also looks at the lineside scene along the Milwaukee including structires, wrecks, snow and MOW. Includes NP, GN and Butte, Anaconda & Pacific electrics and more.

### SP by the Bay

**503-140424** DVD **29.50**
Revised and rereleased on DVD, see commuter action on the San Francisco Peninsula. Features the last of steam plus FM Trainmasters, GP9 and EMD and Alco freight and local power.

### SP Scrapbook

**503-136540** DVD **26.50**
Visit numerous locations from 1985 to 1997. Elvas tower, Stockton Jct. tower and lots of older SP power such as Geeps and SD9s. Beet trains, Oil-cans, manifest freights and intermodals. 90 minutes.

### SP Vintage West

**503-137625** DVD **29.50**
This look at the SP between 1950 and 1978 features SP favorites like Cab-Forwards and F Units on Donner Pass. Bay Area action includes a run on the San Jaoquin Daylight to Tracy and Lathrop, commuter trains, the City of San Francisco and diesel and steam on northern California routes form Donner to Tehachapi.

### SP When The Empire Was Intact

**503-140421** DVD **28.50**
Action on Shasta and Donner Pass lines from 1965 to 1979 and coverage of the Siskiyou and NWP lines. 103 minutes.

### Tennessee Pass

**503-140174** DVD **26.50**
Helpers, foreign power, 10,000-ton trains and more battled three percent grades on this stretch of rugged mountain railroad back when it was a busy stretch of line. Covers Pueblo to Dotsero including pacing shots and two-camera views, plus maps, graphics and more.

### Union Pacific Vintage West

**503-144115** DVD **28.50**
Follow UP from the 50s and the end of steam to diesel takeover. See geeps, E and F-units and the rise of second generation power. Color film with history, graphics, maps and narration. 98 minutes.

### WP Vintage West

**503-135561** DVD **29.50**
Remembers the WP from the late steam era into the 80s. We bring the WP and Sacramento Northern to the screen with freight and passenger trains plus interchange with other roads. Follow the Zephyr story from 1934 to 1970 with extra coverage of the Rio Grande and CB&Q. 90 minutes.

## NEW PRODUCTS

### Books 59.95 ea

#### Color Series

**Burlington Northern in Color**
**NEW 484-1289** Vol 1: The Urge to Merge

**NEW 484-1298** Vol 2: A Cascade of Color

**Canadian Pacific Facilities In Color**
**NEW 484-1276** Volume 1

**Chicago, North Shore & Milwaukee in Color**
**NEW 484-1282** Vol 2: Point of No Return

**Duluth, Winnipeg & Pacific in Color**
**NEW 484-1273**

**Erie Railroad Facilities In Color**

**NEW 484-1178** Vol 1: New Jersey

**NEW 484-1278** Vol 2: New York State

**NEW 484-1286** Vol 3: PA, OH, IN & IL

**Great Northern In Color**
**NEW 484-1179** Vol 1: Lines West

**Lackawanna Railroad Facilities In Color**
**NEW 484-1294** Vol 1: Hoboken to Dover

**Lehigh Valley in Color**
**NEW 484-1287** Vol 4

**Norfolk & Western Steam in Color**
**NEW 484-1295 59.95**

**Spokane, Portland & Seattle In Color**
**NEW 484-1293** Diesels of the Northwest's Own Railway

**Terminal Railroad Association of St. Louis in Color**
**NEW 484-1292**

**Toledo, Peoria & Western in Color**
**NEW 484-1277**

**Wabash in Color**
**NEW 484-1290** Vol 2

#### Color Guides

**Canadian Railways Color Guide to Freight & Passenger Equipment**

**NEW 484-1285** Vol 1

**Wabash/Nickel Plate/DT&I Color Guide to Freight and Passenger Equipment**
**NEW 484-1300**

#### Trackside Series Books

**Trackside Around Louisville (West)**
**NEW 484-1180** 1947-58

**Rock Island Trackside**

**NEW 484-1272** 1960-1980

**Erie Lackawanna Trackside**
**NEW 484-1274**

**Trackside Around West Virginia**
**NEW 484-1275** 1963-1968

**Trackside Grand Trunk-New England Lines**
**NEW 484-1279**

**Trackside Around the Big Apple**
**NEW 484-1280** 1964-73

**Trackside in Search of Southern New England Steam**
**NEW 484-1283**

**Trackside Around Youngstown**
**NEW 484-1284** 1962-1982

**Trackside In The Northeast**
**NEW 484-1288** 1946-1959

**Trackside Around Montreal**
**NEW 484-1296** 1955-1979

**Trackside In The Mid-Atlantic States**
**NEW 484-1297** 1946-1959

**Trackside With "Mr Alco" George W. Hockady**
**NEW 484-1301**

#### Atchison, Topeka & Santa Fe

**Santa Fe In Color 1940-1971 49.95 ea**
**484-30** Volume 1: Chicago to KC

**484-130** Volume 2: KC to Albuquerque

**484-224** Volume 3: Albuquerque to L.A.

**484-232** Volume 4: Texas and the El Capitan

**Color Guide To Freight And Passenger Equipment**
**484-958 49.95**

**Santa Fe All The Way**
**484-1011** Volume 1 **49.95**

**Santa Fe Facilities in Color 59.95 ea**
**484-1141** Volume 1

**484-1163** Volume 2

**Santa Fe Trackside**
**484-1021 54.95**

#### Atlantic Coast Line

**Color Guide To Freight And Passenger Equipment**
**484-1034 54.95**

#### Baltimore & Ohio

**B&O Steam In Color**
**484-1050 54.95**

**Color Guide To Freight And Passenger Equipment**
**484-969 49.95**

**Trackside with Willis McCaleb**
**484-1005 49.95**

**Trackside Along The B&O 1957-1958**
**484-1033 54.95**

**484-1097** Baltimore & Ohio In Color Volume 1 **59.95**

#### Bangor & Aroostook

**Bangor & Aroostook in Color**
**484-1133 59.95**

#### Boston & Maine

**B&M In Color**
**484-991** Volume 1 **49.95**

**NEW 484-1299** Vol 2 **59.95**

**Trackside With Arthur E. Mitchell**
**484-1025 54.95**

#### Buffalo, Rochester & Pittsburgh Railway

**Buffalo, Rochester & Pittsburgh Railway in Color**
**484-1114** Volume 1: New York **59.95**

**NEW 484-1291** Vol 2: Pennsylvania-Middle Division **59.95**

#### Burlington Northern

**Color Guide To Freight And Passenger Equipment**
**484-1068 59.95**

#### Canadian National

**Color Guide To Freight And Passenger Equipment**
**484-1035** Volume 1 **54.95**

**484-1054** Volume 2 **54.95**

**Canadian National Steam in Color**
**484-1145** Volume 1: Ontario & East **59.95**

**484-1159** Volume 2: Ontario & West **59.95**

#### Canadian Pacific

**Color Guide To Freight And Passenger Equipment**
**484-947 49.95**

**Canadian Pacific In Color**
**484-1092** Volume 1: Eastern Lines **59.95**

**Canadian Pacific Steam in Color 59.95 ea**
**484-1162** Vol. 1

**484-1172** Vol. 2: Montreal & West

#### Central RR Of New Jersey

**CNJ In Color**
**484-19** Volume 2 **49.95**

**484-1091** Volume 3 **59.95**

**CNJ Steam In Color**
**484-1048 54.95**

**CNJ/Lehigh Valley Color Guide To Freight And Passenger Equipment**
**484-954 49.95**

#### Central Vermont

**CV In Color**
**484-1044 54.95**

#### Chesapeake & Ohio

**Color Guide To Freight And Passenger Equipment**
**484-944 49.95**

**Chesapeake & Ohio In Color 59.95 ea**
**484-1083** Volume 1

**484-1101** Volume 2

**484-1130** Volume 3

#### Chessie System

**484-1094** Color Guide To Freight Equipment **59.95**

#### Chicago, Burlington & Quincy

**CB&Q In Color**
**484-229** Volume 1 **49.95**

**484-959** Volume 2 **49.95**

**484-1031** Volume 3 **54.95**

**484-1084** Volume 4 **59.95**

**Color Guide To Freight And Passenger Equipment**
**484-953 49.95**

#### Chicago & Eastern Illinois

**C&EI In Color**
**484-1051 54.95**

See What's Available at
**www.walthers.com**

#### Chicago Great Western

**Chicago Great Western In Color**
**484-987 49.95**

**Color Guide To Freight And Passenger Equipment**

**484-1009 49.95**

#### Chicago, Milwaukee, St. Paul & Pacific/ Milwaukee Road

**Milwaukee Road In Color 49.95 ea (Unless Noted)**
**484-962** Volume 1: The East End

**484-970** Volume 2: The Milwaukee Area

**484-971** Volume 3: Wisconsin & Michigan

**484-972** Volume 4: Iowa, Missouri, Minnesota & the Dakotas **54.95**

**Color Guide To Freight And Passenger Equipment**
**484-974** Volume 1 **49.95**

**484-1036** Volume 2 **54.95**

**Under Milwaukee Wires**
**484-985 49.95**

#### Chicago, North Shore & Milwaukee Railway in Color

**484-1166** Vol. 1 **59.95**

#### Chicago & North Western

**CNW In Color**
**484-997** Volume 1: 1941-53 **49.95**

**484-1029** Volume 2: 1954-58 **54.95**

**484-1142** Volume 3: 1959-1964 **59.95**

**CNW Official Color Photography**
**484-1020 54.95**

#### Chicago, Rock Island & Pacific

**Rock Island In Color 49.95 ea**

**484-234** Volume 1: 1948-64

**484-951** Volume 2: 1965-80

**Color Guide To Freight and Passenger Equipment**
**484-981 49.95**

**Chicago, South Shore & South Bend in Color**
**484-1137** Volume 1: 60 Years of the South Shore **59.95**

## Clinchfield

**Clinchfield in Color**
**484-1113 59.95**

## Conrail

**Color Guide To Freight Equipment**
**484-1042 54.95**

## Delaware & Hudson

**D&H Steam In Color**
**484-1053 54.95**

**484-1124** Volume 3: D&H in the Diesel Years **59.95**

## Delaware, Lackawanna & Western

**Lackawanna Railroad Trackside**
**484-1017 54.95**

**Erie/DL&W Color Guide To Freight And Passenger Equipment**
**484-1059 54.95**

**Lackawanna Railroad In Color 59.95 ea**
**484-1098** Volume 2

**484-1138** Volume 3: The Transition Years

**Erie Lackawanna Through Passenger Service**
**484-1168** Vol. 1: 1960-1965 **59.95**

**Erie Lackawanna in Color**
**484-1173** Vol. 6 **59.95**

## Denver & Rio Grande Western

**DRGW In Color**
**484-114** Volume 1: Colorado **45.00**

**Rio Grande Narrow Gauge in Color**
**484-1153** Vol. 1 1947-1959 **59.95**

**484-946** Volume 2: Utah **49.95**

**484-1061** Volume 3 **59.95**

**Color Guide To Freight And Passenger Equipment**
**484-982** Volume 1 **49.95**

**Rio Grande Trackside**
**484-1019 54.95**

## Detroit, Toledo & Ironton

**DT&I In Color**
**484-1057 54.95**

## Duluth, Missabe & Iron Range

**Duluth, Missabe & Iron Range In Color**
**484-1088 59.95**

## Erie Lackawanna

**Erie Lackawanna in Color**
**484-1120** Volume 5: Merger and Memories **59.95**

## Grand Trunk Western 59.95 ea

**Grand Trunk Western In Color**
**484-1106** Volume 1: Steam & Green 1941-61

**484-1118** Volume 2: Visual Redesign

## Great Northern

**GN Steam & Electric In Color**
**484-1016 54.95**

**Color Guide To Freight And Passenger Equipment**
**484-952 49.95**

## Illinois Central

**IC In Color**
**484-975 49.95**

**IC/GM&O Color Guide To Freight And Passenger Equipment**
**484-1073 59.95**

## Illinois Terminal

**Illinois Terminal In Color**
**484-1003** Volume 1 **49.95**

**484-1058** Volume 2 **54.95**

## Kansas City Southern

**Kansas City Southern In Color**
**484-1102 59.95**

## Lehigh & Hudson River In Color

**484-1064 59.95**

## Locomotive & Car Builders

**Pullman-Standard Color Guide To Freight Equipment**
**484-955 49.95**

**Fairbanks-Morse In Color**
**484-978 49.95**

**Alco Official Color Photographs**
**484-1008 49.95**

**Passenger Alcos In Color**
**484-1043 54.95**

**Baldwin Diesels In Color 59.95 ea**
**484-1070** Volume 1: A-G

**484-1079** Volume 2: H-P

**484-1085** Volume 3: Q-Z

**Refrigerator Car Color Guide**

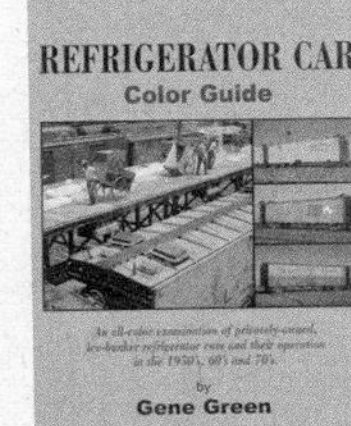


**484-1156 59.95**

## Louisville & Nashville

**Color Guide To Freight And Passenger Equipment**
**484-1046** Volume 1 **54.95**

**484-1132** Volume 2 **59.95**

**Louisville & Nashville In Color Volume 1**
**484-1111 59.95**

## Maine Central

**Maine Central In Color**
**484-1007** Volume 1 **49.95**

**484-1028** Volume 2 **54.95**

## Minneapolis & St. Louis

**M&St.L In Color**
**484-984 49.95**

## Missouri-Kansas-Texas

**MKT In Color**
**484-225 49.95**

## Missouri Pacific 59.95 ea

**484-1115** Color Guide to Freight and Passenger Equipment **59.95**

**Missouri Pacific in Color**
**484-1129** Volume 1: The Era of the Eagles

**484-1150** Volume 2: Screamin' Eagles

## Monon

**Monon In Color**
**484-1089 59.95**

## National Railways Of Mexico

**NdeM In Color**
**484-1047 54.95**

## New Haven

**NH Trackside**
**484-1010 49.95**

**Trackside Along The New Haven**
**484-1086 59.95**

**New Haven In Color 59.95 ea**
**484-1107** Volume 1: The Battle For Profits 1945-61

**484-1126** Volume 2: The Struggle for Survival

**484-1149** Volume 3: 1961-1968

## New York Central

**New York Central Lightning Stripes**
**484-67** Volume 1 **45.00**

**484-165** Volume 2 **49.95**

**NYC Color Guide To Freight And Passenger Equipment**
**484-228 49.95**

**484-1151** Volume 2 **59.95**

**New York Central Trackside w/Eugene Van Dusen**
**484-950 49.95**

**Michigan Central Trackside w/Emery Gulash**
**484-1055 54.95**

NYC In Color
**484-1066** Volume 1 **59.95**

**484-1082** Volume 2 **59.95**

**NYC Facilities In Color**
**484-1087 59.95**

**Trackside along New York Central's Western Division 1949-55**
**484-1099 59.95**

## New York, Ontario & Western

**NYO&W In Color**
**484-990 49.95**

**New York, Susquehanna & Western In Color**
**484-1072 59.95**

## Norfolk & Western

**N&W In Color**
**484-988** Volume 1 **49.95**

**Color Guide To Freight And Passenger Equipment**
**484-1039 54.95**

## Northern Pacific

**Color Guide To Freight And Passenger Equipment**
**484-963 49.95**

**Northern Pacific In Color**
**484-1074** Volume I:1949-1959 **59.95**

## Pacific Electric

**Pacific Electric In Color**
**484-999** Volume I **49.95**

**484-1024** Volume II **54.95**

## Penn Central

**Color Guide To Freight And Passenger Equipment**
**484-948 49.95**

## Pennsylvania Railroad

**Color Guide To Freight And Passenger Equipment**
**484-968** Volume 2 **49.95**

**484-1071** Volume 3 **59.95**

**Pennsy, Standard Railroad Of The World**
**484-1018** Volume 1 **54.95**

**Trackside Under Pennsy Wires**
**484-1045 54.95**

**Trackside On The PRR North Of Washington, DC**
**484-1052 54.95**

**Central Pennsylvania**
**484-1127 59.95**

**Pennsy Steam Years**
**484-1060** Volume 3 **54.95**

**New York Harbor Railroads In Color**
**484-1049** Volume 1 **54.95**

**484-1082** Volume 2 **59.95**

**Pennsy Electric Years**
**484-1069** Volume 2 **59.95**

**484-1158** Volume 3 **59.95**

## Pittsburgh & Lake Erie In Color

**484-1076** Volume 1: 1976-1992 **59.95**

**484-1136** Volume 2: 1956-1976

## Reading

**Reading Company In Color**
**484-1078** Volume 2 **59.95**

## Richmond, Fredericksburg & Potomac

**Richmond, Fredericksburg & Potomac In Color**
**484-1093 59.95**

## Rutland

**Rutland In Color**
**484-1103 59.95**

## St. Louis-San Francisco

**Frisco In Color**
**484-961 49.95**

## Seaboard Air Line

**Color Guide To Freight And Passenger Equipment**
**484-1004 49.95**

## Soo Line

**Soo Line In Color**
**484-993 49.95**

## Southern Railway

**Southern Railway In Color**
**484-1013** Volume 2 **49.95**

**Color Guide To Freight And Passenger Equipment**
**484-977 49.95**

**Southern Railway Through Passenger Service in Color**
**484-1161 59.95**

## Southern Pacific

**Southern Pacific In Color**
**484-1096** Volume 3: Classic Scarlet **59.95**

**484-1109** Volume 4: The Tunnel Motor Era **59.95**

**484-1121** Volume 5: Merger and Memories **59.95**

**Color Guide To Freight And Passenger Equipment**
**484-1015** Volume 1 **49.95**

**484-1148** Volume 2 **59.95**

**484-1169** Volume 3 **59.95**

**Official Color Photography**
**484-1038 54.95**

## Spokane, Portland & Seattle

**Color Guide To Freight And Passenger Equipment**
**484-945 49.95**

## Traction 59.99 ea (Unless Noted)

**Baltimore - Washington Trolleys In Color**
**NEW 484-1181**

**Ohio Valley Trolleys in Color**
**NEW 484-1281**

**Pennsylvania Trolleys In Color**

**484-1022** Volume III: The Pittsburgh Region **54.95**

**484-1108** Volume IV

**Street Car Scenes Of The 1950s In Color**
484-1032 54.95

**New Jersey Trolleys In Color**
484-1077

**New York City Trolleys In Color**
484-1080

**California Trolleys In Color**
484-1081 Volume 1: San Diego & Los Angeles

**Boston Trolleys in Color**
484-1117 Volume 1: The North Side

484-1128 Volume 2: The South Side

**Great Lakes Trolleys in Color**
484-1119

**Canadian Trolleys in Color**
484-1177 Vol. 1: Eastern Canada

### Union Pacific

**UP Steam In Color**
484-957 49.95

**UP Trackside**
484-1006 49.95

**Union Pacific Official Photography**
484-254 Volume I 49.95

484-1023 Volume II 54.95

**Color Guide To Freight And Passenger Equipment**
484-262 Volume 1 49.95

484-986 Volume 2 49.95

**Union Pacific Diesels In Color Volume 1: 1934-59**

484-1105 59.95

### Union Railroad

**URR In Color**
484-1056 54.95

484-1140 Virginian Railway in Color 59.95

### Wabash

**Wabash Trackside With Emery Gulash 1954-74**
484-1112 59.95

### Western Maryland

**Trackside with George M. Leilich**
484-1075 59.95

### Western Pacific

**Trackside w/Bob Larson**
484-1027 54.95

**Color Guide To Freight and Passenger Equipment**
484-1063 59.95

**Western Pacific in Color**
484-1171 59.95

### Regional Interest 59.95 ea (Unless Noted)

**Southern States Trolleys in Color**
484-1134

**Northern New England Color Guide To Freight And Passenger Equipment**
484-233 49.95

**East Of The Hudson: 1941-1953 w/Bill McChesney**
484-949 49.95

**Chicago 1957-1965**
484-1026 54.95

**Scranton, PA 1952-1976**
484-1030 54.95

**Philadelphia 1945-1969**
484-1037 54.95

**St. Louis 1952-59 w/Jim Ozment**
484-1040 54.95

**Boston 1942-62 w/Lawson Hill**
484-1041 54.95

**Buffalo 1953-1976**
484-1062

**New York City 1953-1968**
484-1065

**Allentown, PA 1947-68**
484-1067

**Sayre-Towanda-Waverly Pa. With Lloyd Hall**
484-1095

**Frisco/Katy Color Guide To Freight Equipment**
484-1100

**Pennsylvania Shortlines In Color**
484-1104 Volume 1

484-1147 Volume 2

### Trackside Series 59.95 ea

**Trackside Around Ontario 1955-60**
484-1110

**Trackside Around Massachusetts 1950-1970**
484-1116

**Trackside Around the Niagara Peninsula 1953-1976**
484-1122

**Trackside Around Illinois 1960-1973**

484-1123

**Trackside Around Atlanta 1955-1975**
484-1125

**Trackside Detroit Downriver 1946-1976**
484-1135 With Emery Gulash

**Trackside Along the Boston & Maine 1945-1975**
484-1139

**Trackside Around Granger Country 1952-1955**
484-1131

**Trackside Around Cleveland 1965-1979**
484-1143

**Trackside with EMD Field Representative Casey Cavanaugh 1960-1962**
484-1144

**Trackside Along the Erie-Lackawanna New Jersey Commuter Zone**
484-1146

**Trackside in Louisville (East) 1948-1958**
484-1152

**Trackside in Appalachia**
484-1176 w/Gene Huddleston

**Trackside Around British Columbia**
484-1167 w/Matt Herson

**Trackside Around Charlottesville, VA**
484-1170 1967-1984

**Trackside Around Duluth**
484-1154 1957-1960

**Trackside Around Kansas**
484-1175 1950-1975 w/Lloyd Stagner

**Trackside Around New Jersey**
484-1164 1968-1983 w/Robert Yanosey

**Trackside: Milwaukee Road East**
484-1157

**Trackside: Milwaukee Road West**
484-1165 w/Jim Boyd

**Trackside In Search Of Northern New England Steam**
484-1174 w/John Morrison

**Trackside Reading Anthracite Country**
484-1160

## MICROSCALE®

## RAILROAD SIGNS

### 10.95 ea (Unless Noted)

Colorful metal signs are great for decorating train rooms, dens and studies. High-quality and lightweight, these metal signs are die-cut to retain the shape of the original railroad logos. They're also embossed, giving them a slight 3-D effect. Signs are printed in vivid, authentic and durable colors, measure approximately eight inches in height and have pre-drilled holes for mounting.

**460-10001** PRR
**460-10002** UP
**460-10003** ATSF
**460-10004** GN
**460-10005** SP
**460-10006** NYC
**460-10008** Western Pacific
**460-10010** CP
**460-10011** CNW
**460-10013** NP
**460-10017** Rock Island
**460-10020** B&O
**460-10022** DRGW
**460-10023** CB&Q
**460-10028** Frisco
**460-10029** MKT
**460-10031** Microscale Logo (blue, black, white)
**460-10032** Pacific Electric
**460-10034** N&W
**460-10200** Railroad Crossing (24" Crossbuck) **34.95**
**460-10201** Railroad Crossing Advance Warning (round; yellow & black) **29.95**
18" heavy duty aluminum sign
**460-10501** SP Daylight **14.95**
19-1/2" long
**460-10502** ATSF Indian Head **14.95**
17-1/2" long

**Limited Quantity Available**
**460-10007** NH
**460-10009** SOU
**460-10012** Atlantic Coast Line
**460-10014** Kansas City Southern
**460-10015** IC
**460-10016** Florida East Coast
**460-10018** RDG
**460-10019** Seaboard Air Line
**460-10021** Erie
**460-10024** LV
**460-10025** Boston & Maine
**460-10026** CR
**460-10027** BN
**460-10030** Penn Central
**460-10033** Northwestern Pacific

## DIECUT 4" VINYL STICKERS

### 2.50 ea

**460-20001** Pennsy Keystone
**460-20002** UP
**460-20004** GN
**460-20005** SP
**460-20009** SOU
**460-20010** CN

## NOCH

IMPORTED FROM GERMANY BY WALTHERS

## NEW PRODUCT

### Books

**English Landscaping Guidebook**
**NEW 528-71543 24.99**

## CATALOGS

**528-71070** 2007 Noch Catalog **12.99**

**NEW 528-71080** 2008 Noch Catalog **TBA**

### CD-Rom

**528-71071** 2007 Noch Catalog **14.99**

**NEW 528-71081** 2008 Noch Catalog **TBA**

## NORTHWEST SHORT LINE

### Catalog

**NWSL Full-Line Catalog**
53-1 9.00

### Books

**Logging To The Salt Chuck-100 Years Of Simpson Timber Co. Railroad Logging**

**53-5069** Hardcover **45.95**

**Logging Railroads In Skagit Co.**
**53-5089** Hardcover **59.95**
The history of logging railroads in Skagit County, Washington. Excellent photographic coverage with over 400 photos.

**The Pacific Northwest Railroads Of McGee & Nixon -1940s & 50s**
**53-5099** Hardcover **59.95**
Classic photos from NPRY employees and official photographers Warren McGee and Ron Nixon. From steam to shiny new diesels. 300 photos, 38 in color.

**Northern Pacific Railway Of McGee & Nixon - 1930s Thru 50s**

**53-5109** Hardcover **49.95**
Steam to diesel. 300 photos, many full page.

## Oso Publishing Company

### BOOKS

**Logging Railroads of Weyerhaeuser's Vail-McDonald Operation**

**537-1931064059 49.95**
Covers the fascinating history of northwest railroad logging starting with steam and evolving to diesel as only Weyerhaeuser could do it. Authors Frank Telewski and Scott Barrett capture the story making this a must for any logging enthusiast, model railroader or forest historian. 371 photos, 10 drawings and 65 maps.

**The MODOC: Southern Pacific's Back Door to Oregon**

**537-1931064091 49.95**
Noted authors Tom Dill and Jack Bowden give a historical look at SP's shortcut from the Overland line to Oregon: the Modoc Line. Great for SP modelers and fans as it covers an often overlooked, but spectacular area of the railroad. Hardbound, 352 pages.

**Railroad Logging in the Klamath Country**

**537-1931064113 49.95**
During the first half of the 20th century more than two dozen rail lines were pushed into the forests of Klamath, Deschutes, Lake and Jackson Counties. Includes over 140 photos and a concise history of every lumber company in the region that operated a railroad plus a roster of its locomotives and one or more maps of its rail lines.

**Narrow Gauge Railway Scene**
**537-920698417 24.95**
A collection of over 400 photographs taken by various photographers of a variety of different railroad lines.

**Vista-Dome North Coast Limited**

**537-1931064067 74.95**
Bill Keubler's carefully researched work on the Northern Pacific's luxurious named train.

**Discovering Washington's Historic Mines,**
**537-964752123** Volume 1
**24.95**
Covers the discovery of gold in the West Central Cascade Mountains and the subsequent boom of towns like Silverton and Monte Cristo. Softbound, 230 pages.

**537-1931064040** Volume 2
**34.95**
Covers mining in the East Central Cascade Mountains and Wenatchee Mountains. Softbound, 400 pages, maps, photos, index.

**537-1931064156** Volume 3: The North Cascade Mountains
**39.95**
Covers the search for minerals and the colorful history of the people who searched for treasure. Includes photographs, mine locations and drawings.

## PLASTRUCT

### Books

**The Cyclopedia of Industrial Modeling**

**570-115 32.00**
A step-by-step book with color pictures featuring numerous industrial modeling projects by one of the leading scratch model builders, Dean Freytag. Each accurate model is accompanied by a detailed bill of materials and highlights the creative ways to use styrene for structural shapes. 90 pages.

### Catalogs

**Universal Model Parts Catalog**

**570-7** Volume 8 **5.00**



## RAPIDO TRAINS

### NEW PRODUCT

### Book

**TurboTrain: A Journey**

**NEW 606-102008 24.95**
Jason Shron. This is the first book ever to tell the story of the TurboTrain through history, anecdotes and photographs, the majority of which have never been published before. It has been 40 years since the TurboTrain first rocketed to its record-breaking speeds and touched the hearts of a new generation of railfans. Part train, part jet aircraft, the TurboTrain was the latest in ground transport innovation. But the Turbo's promise of a new era of passenger travel sadly went unfulfilled. A gas turbine powered train introduced at a time of unprecedented hostility towards passenger train travel and unprecedented high fuel prices had little chance. Despite its obstacles, the TurboTrain was a success with the travelling public and, by the time the last trains were retired in 1982, Turbo was running at 97 percent efficiency. This made it one of the most reliable passenger trains in North America.

Pentrex produces DVDs of exciting prototype railroading. For a complete listing of Pentrex DVD and VHS video productions visit walthers.com.

## NEW PRODUCTS

### DVDs

### Prototype Railroads 29.95 ea (Unless Noted)

**Conrail Hot Spots**

**NEW 561-2612** East 2 Hours

**NEW 561-2615** West 2 Hours

**Great American Circus & Show Trains**

**NEW 561-2613** 1 Hour 45 Minutes

**Into the Allegheny Range**

**NEW 561-2616** Volume 1 Hancock, WV to Cumberland, MD. 3 Hours.

**Montana Rail Link**

**NEW 561-2617** 1 Hour 10 Minutes

**Steam Over Tennessee Pass**

**NEW 561-2618** 1 Hour 30 Minutes

**The Alaska Railroad**

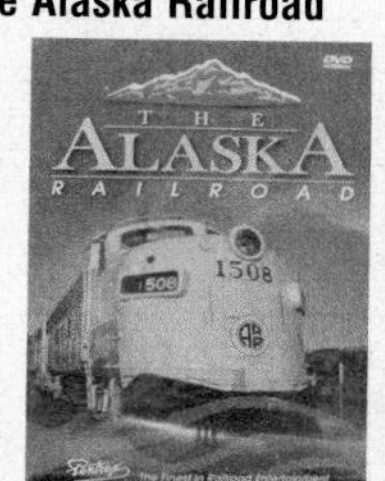


**NEW 561-2619** 1 Hour 30 Minutes

**The Ultimate Tehachapi**

**NEW 561-2620** 2-Disc Set 8 Hours

**Union Pacific Feather River Route**

**NEW 561-2621** 1 Hour

**BC Rail Collection**

**NEW 561-2622** 3 Hours 24 Minutes
Collection of five shows.

**The Heritage Collection**

**NEW 561-2623** 1 Hour 35 Minutes
Five separate shows covering American railroads of the 40s and 50s.

**Empire Builders to Milwaukee**

**NEW 561-2624** 50 Minutes

**Mexico's Pacifico Railroad**

**NEW 561-2625** 2 Hours

**Cumbres & Toltec Scenic Freight Train**

**NEW 561-2700** 1 Hour

**Raton Pass-King Coal-The Chief-BALJ**

**NEW 561-2701** 1 Hour 30 Minutes

**Sunrise/Sunset- A Day at Gibbon Junction**
**NEW 561-2702** 1 Hour 13 Minutes

**Santa Fe's Mojave Mainline**
**NEW 561-2703** 1 Hour 15 Minutes

**Sacramento Steam '99**
**NEW 561-2704** 3 Hours 30 Minutes

**Pentrex Previews**

**NEW 561-2705** Volume 2 2 Hours 15 Minutes

**Early Amtrak Across Wisconsin**
**NEW 561-2706** 1 Hour

## DVDs

From contemporary operations to the classic trains of yesteryear, you'll find a wide range of railroad action in these top-quality railroad DVDs. Each is in full-color with sound (unless noted). All titles are videos unless noted.

**1522 Galloping Through Texas**
**561-2032** DVD **29.95**
70 minutes.

**Above The Rails**
**561-2207** DVD **29.95**
Combines two classic Pentrex videos – "Above Southern California Rails" and "Above 3751 Over Cajon" into an exciting two-hour DVD.

**Collection**
Contains four classic AAR films covering the years 1952, 1956, 1966 and 1967. 76 minutes.
**561-2206** DVD Combo Volume 1 & 2 **29.95**

**Amtrak's Northeast Corridor Combo**

**561-2523** DVD **29.95**
A 1992 look at Amtrak's. Two Hours, 40 Minutes. Two Hours

**Amtrak Surfline Combo**
**561-2524** DVD **29.95**

**American Railroad Beaumont Hill Combo**
**561-2518** DVD **29.95**
SP's high-speed crossing of the daunting San Gorgonio Pass. Two Hours, 30 Minutes.

**The Best of 1989**
**561-2601** DVD **29.95**
Highlights the special railroading events of 1989. Two Hours.

**The Best Of The Midwest 29.95 ea**

**561-2516** Volume 1 DVD **29.95**
67 Minutes.

**561-9843** Volume I Video
Visit Missouri, Nebraska, Iowa, South Dakota and Minnesota.

**561-2519** Volume 2 DVD **29.95**
Visit South Dakota, Iowa, Wisconsin, Illinois, Minnesota and Nebraska to see the best in Midwestern railroading. 97 minutes.

**561-2520** Volume 3 DVD **29.95**
Mainlines and regionals in Kansas, Missouri, Iowa, Minnesota and Wisconsin. 81 minutes.

### Big Boy Combos

**561-2502** Part 1 DVD **29.95**
Last of the Giants and Cheyenne Shops. One hour, 23 minutes.

**561-2503** Part 2 DVD **29.95**
Last of the Giants Volume 3 – Sherman Hill and Big Boys on TV on one disc. Two hours, 20 minutes.

### B&O Odyssey, Volume 1
Ohio and Pennsylvania from 1954 to 1964 60 minutes.

**561-2015** Volume 1 DVD **29.95**

### B&O Odyssey, Volume 2
1965 through 1968. 60 minutes.

**561-2202** Volume 2 DVD **29.95**

### Cajon Pass – Tehachapi Loop
**561-2500** DVD **29.95**
Two hours, 10 minutes.

### Cajon II Combo

**561-2522** DVD **29.95**
Two Hours, 30 Minutes.

### Christmas Trains
**561-2525** DVD **29.95**
68 Minutes.

### China Steam Spectacular
**561-2406** DVD **29.95**
Two hours, 28 minutes.

### Classic St. Louis Railroading/Santa Fe Vintage Diesels
**561-2303** DVD **29.95**
Filmed during the 1960s and 1970s. 98 minutes.

### Columbia River Gorge Volume 1
Spectacular vistas and nonstop railroading along BNSF's Fallbridge Subdivision. Two Hours

**561-2607** DVD **29.95**

### CSX Mountain Sub: Up, Over, Around & Through
**561-2034** DVD **29.95**
96 minutes.

### Daylight 4449 Combo
**561-2410** DVD **29.95**

### Daylight Freedom Special 29.95 ea
The Daylight 4449 in the Columbia River Gorge and the Deschutes River Canyon. 85 minutes.

**561-2210** DVD

### Denver and Rio Grande
**561-2417** DVD **29.95**

### Donner Combo
**561-2314** DVD **29.98**
Includes "Battle for Donner Pass" and "Across Donner Summit." Three hours, 17 minutes.

### Durango & Silverton Narrow Gauge Railroad
**561-2506** DVD **29.95**

### Extreme Steam Volume 2: 12 Steam Locos
**561-2603** DVD **29.95**

### Fallen Flag Series
**561-2214** DVD **29.95**
Visit the railroads of Chicago and the Twin Cities in this collector's edition DVD. Two hours, 16 minutes.

### Final Run Over Cajon Pass
**516-2412** DVD **29.95**

### Goin' To Kansas City
Travel aboard the BNSF to discover a 225-mile rural route through southeastern Kansas. 95 minutes.

**561-2008** DVD **29.95**

### Grand Canyon Railway

**561-2517** DVD **29.95**
Ride the daily Williams Flyer excursion train. 60 Minutes.

### Great Northern Railways Combo
**561-2512** Volumes 1, 2 & 3 **29.95**
Two Hours, 15 Minutes.

### The Green Bay Route

**561-2605** DVD **29.95**
72 Minutes.

### Historic Hot Spots Combo
**561-2313** DVD **29.95**
Includes "Railfanning Southern California in the 1950s" and "Santa Fe's Pasadena Subdivision."

### Horseshoe Curve & Sand Patch Grade Combo
**561-2600** DVD **29.95**
Late 80s, early 90s action. Two Hours, 15 Minutes.

### King Coal Combo
**561-2307** DVD **29.95**
Includes "King Coal Powder River Rails/Mines" and "Powder River Basin Coal Trains."

### Last Run of a Cab Forward Over Donner Pass
**561-2409** DVD **29.95**

### Pacific Electric, Los Angeles Streetcars Combo

**561-2515** DVD **29.95**
65 Minutes.

### Pentrex DVD Previews
**561-2504** DVD **19.95**
Sampling of 43 different programs. Two hours, 30 minutes.

### Pittsburgh Mainlines
**561-2407** DVD **29.95**

### Runnin' The Highline: BNSF's Gateway Subdivision
**561-2511** DVD **29.95**
Travel the former Western Pacific highline aboard a BNSF freight train. 107 minutes.

### Santa Fe Into LA
**561-2416** DVD **29.95**



### Santa Fe 3751: Route of the Chiefs
Los Angeles to Chicago and back.

**561-2508** DVD **29.95**
90 Minutes.

### Santa Fe's Arizona Mainline
**561-2610** DVD **29.95**
80 Minutes.

### Santa Fe Combo

**561-2602** Across the Heartland & Countdown to Merger DVD **29.95**
Two Hours, 49 Minutes.

### Santa Fe New Mexico Mainline Combo
**561-2521** Clovis & Gallup Subdivisions DVD **29.95**

### Southern California Rails
**561-2404** DVD **29.95**

### Southern Pacific Classic Collectors Series
**561-2505** DVD **29.95**
Three SP steam programs originally produced by Video Rails on one disc. 90 minutes.

### Southern Pacific Film Archives
**561-2301** DVD **29.95**
Includes "Daylights, Cab Forwards & Early Diesels" and "Flangers, Spreaders and Rotary Snow Plows."

### Special Trains
**561-2310** DVD **29.95**
60 minutes.

### Steam Across America
**561-2408** Volume 1 DVD **29.95**

**561-2609** Volume 1 combo **19.95**

### Steam Across The Pacific Northwest
Engine #4449 travels former BN trackage.

**561-2013** DVD **29.95**
115 minutes.

### Steam Photo Freights & Passenger Extras
**561-2030** DVD **29.95**
96 minutes.

### Steam To The Grand Canyon
**561-2212** DVD **29.95**
120 minutes.

### Steam To Spokane
**561-2025** DVD **29.95**
63 minutes.

### Street Running
A collective look at 20 locations around the country where railroads continue to run trains down the middle of main streets. 104 minutes.

**561-2418** DVD **29.95**

### Those Incredible Alcos 29.95 ea
**561-2419** Volume 1 DVD

**561-2420** Volume 2 DVD

**561-2501** Volume 3 DVD

### Today's Chicago Railroads
**561-2611** DVD **29.95**
Two Hours.

### Today's Northwestern Pacific
**561-2606** DVD **29.95**
110 Minutes.

### Train Meets – Double The Action 29.95 ea
**561-2219** DVD Volume 1

**561-2573** DVD Volume 2
48 minutes.

### Train Wrecks, Crashes, Disasters
**561-2507** DVD **29.95**

### Union Pacific Big Boy Collection
**561-2036** DVD **39.95**

### Union Pacific Classic Collectors' Series Combo
**561-2510** DVD **29.95**
90 Minutes.

### Union Pacific Streamliner Collection
**561-2312** DVD **39.95**
100 minutes.

### Union Pacific's Mighty Turbines

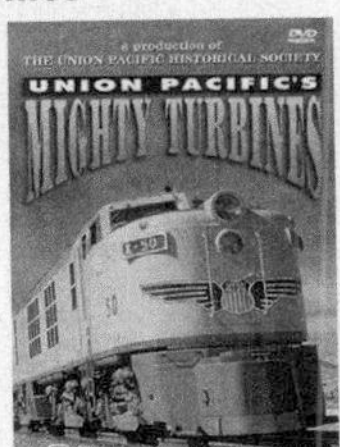


**561-2514** DVD **29.95**
46 Minutes.

### Virginia & Ohio: Afton Division Finale
**561-2028** DVD **29.95**

### Workin' On The Railroad
**561-2414** DVD **29.95**

RAILROAD AVENUE ENTERPRISES

### Railroad Stations Of New England

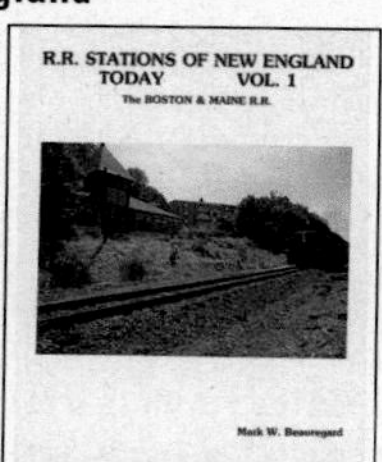

**615-5** Volume 1 **4.00**
At the turn of the century, stations were radiant, better kept than many private homes. They were the yardstick by which the public measured and valued individual railroads. 190 B&W photos, 72 pages, 8-1/2 x 11".

### Lehigh Valley Passenger Cars

**615-6 7.00**
Features blueprints redrawn from original LV shop prints. Follows the changes particular cars went through over the years. 64 pages, B&W photos and illustrations.

### 26 Miles To Jersey City

**615-7 8.95**
Pictorial documents the conditions of stations existing in New Jersey during the early 1970s and early 80s. Focuses on CNJ stations. 62 pages, B&W photos.

### The Morristown & Erie Railway

**615-9 8.95**
Features 48 pages of B&W photography depicting the railroad after its 1982 reorganization which brought it out of bankruptcy.

### A Colorful Look At The Chicago & North Western

**615-19 19.95**
Looks at the line from the mid 60s to the UP merger. Includes 80 color photos showcasing a wide range of diesels across the system. 48 pages, full color.

### The Hard Coal Carriers

**615-14** Volume 1: First Generation Geeps **19.95**
Covers the CNJ, Lackawanna, Erie, EL, LV and RDG. 130 photos, 80 pages.

**615-16** Volume 2: Camelback Twilight **19.95**
Covers the CNJ, Lackawanna, Erie, Erie Lackawanna, LV and RDG with complete roster information and detail data. 11 color and 119 B&W photos, 80 pages.

### Conrail's SD40 & SD40-2

**615-17 19.95**
Complete roster and specifications. 66 color photos.

### Anthracite Country Color

**615-20 19.95**
Pennsylvania's central coal region during the 1950s. Includes 64 photos from the RDG, CNJ, Pennsy and LV operating in Schuylkill and Carbon County. Lots of steam and early diesels from a by-gone era. 48 pages, full color.

### Diamondbugs

**615-21 14.95**
Over 80 black and white photos illustrate the evolution of the gas-electrics on the Erie. Also included are diagrams and charts giving a comprehensive look at these cars. 64 pages.

### Colorful Memories Of Reading's Shamokin Division

**615-22 19.95**
Covers the Reading Co. during the steam-to-diesel transition era with 48 pages of full color.

### Memories Of Eastern Pennsylvania Railroading

**615-23 24.95**
Contains photos from the 1950s and 1960s of PRR, LV, CNJ, RDG, EL, Erie and Delaware, Lackawanna & Western. Full color, 64 pages.

### Dutch Country Trolleys

**615-24 15.95**
Covers the Conestoga Traction Company and the Hershey Transit Company. 64 pages.

### Third Avenue Railway: A Cityscape Of Manhattan & The Bronx

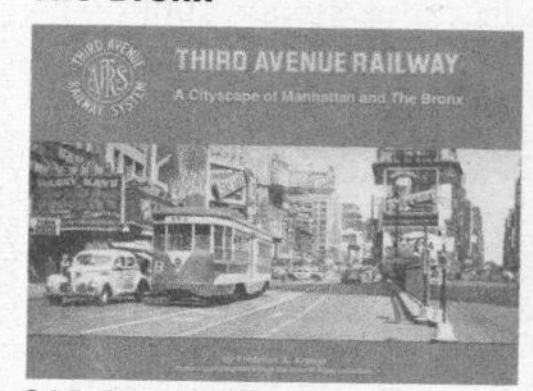

**615-25 18.95**
Pictorial review of the Third Avenue Railway during the 1940s. Full of nostalgic B&W photos of Manhattan and the Bronx street scenes. 80 pages.

### Unifying The Subways

**615-26 17.95**
Covers New York City Subway System from its unification through the Transit Authority's control. 72 pages, B&W photos. Written by Frederick A. Kramer.

### A Colorful Look At The Erie Lackawanna

**615-27 24.95**
A full-color photo essay by an employee of the EL; Rich Pennisi. 64 pages, 8-1/2 x 11"

### BQT: The Brooklyn & Queens Transit

**615-28 19.95**
Historic review through 1960 featuring numerous, nostalgic B&W photos. 80 pages.

### A Colorful Look At Selected Pennsylvania Shortlines

**615-29 19.95**
Take a look at the work of Carl Connelly as he traveled across the state in pursuit of his hobby during the 1960s and 70s. 48 pages, 90 color photos.

### Operation CUT...The First 30 Years (Cleveland Union Terminal)

**615-30 18.95**
Depicts rail operations, both railroad and transit, that ran out of the Cleveland Union Terminal from 1930 to 1960. 72 pages, B&W photography.

RailDriver®

# DESKTOP TRAIN CAB CONTROLLER FOR PERSONAL COMPUTER

**560-120** RailDriver Desktop Cab Controller **169.95**
Ever want to sit behind the controls of a real locomotive? The RailDriver Desktop Train Cab Controller lets you run train simulation games on your personal computer with prototypical reverser, throttle and brake levers. Compatible with most popular train simulation programs made by Microsoft®, TrainMaster, Auran and Kuju. Features an internal subwoofer to add the vibration of the engine to the levers. 28 programmable buttons and navigation controls let you park the keyboard and mouse and run your train from the RailDriver. Control stand measures 13-1/2 x 7 x 4" 34 x 18 x 10cm about 1/3 the size of the real thing. Requires USB computer connection.

# TRAILER HITCH COVER

Item listed below is available by Special Order (see Legend Page).

**560-270** Knuckle Coupler Decorative Hitch Cover (rusty dark brown) **39.95**
Now it's easy to pretend you're driving a train. This solid cast aluminum hitch cover looks like a knuckle coupler. Fits either 1-1/4 or 2" receiver. Use for decorative purposes only.

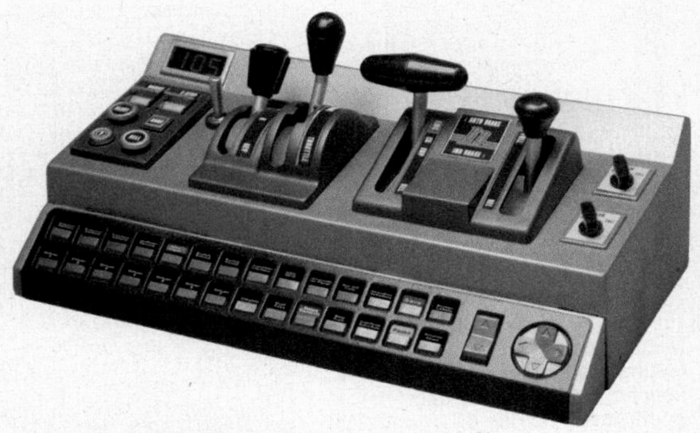

Desktop Train Cab Controller for Personal computer 560-120

# SOFTWARE

RailDriver reference software brings you hard-to-find books on easy-to-use CD-ROMs. Each book has been scanned, so they are easily navigated like a Web site. While optimized for Microsoft Internet Explorer, the CDs can also be read on other systems including Macintosh.

## Cyclopedias 29.95 ea

Railway cyclopedias were used by railroaders for maintenance and modifications. Because the information was supplied by the railroads or their suppliers, everything is accurate, making this information a must for modelers wanting to recreate railroading as it was in the steam era. Also included on each CD is the RailDriver Scale Print Utility (PC only) that makes it easy to enlarge or reduce the drawings and photos to any size.

**560-90** 1922 Locomotive Cyclopedia

**560-91** 1922 Car Builders Cyclopedia

**560-92** 1921 Maintenance of Way Cyclopedia

**560-93** 1911 Electric Railroad (Traction) Cyclopedia

**560-269** 1906 Locomotive Dictionary First Edition **29.95**

## Train Simulator Expansion Packs

These CD-ROM sets add new routes, features and tools to the Microsoft Train Simulator.

**560-135** Cambrian Route **29.99**

560-137 560-138

**560-137** Black Forest Route **29.99**

**560-138** Glacier Express **35.99**

560-146 560-147

**560-146** Severn Valley Route **34.95**

**560-147** American Classics **22.95**

## RK PUBLISHING

# DVDs

## Dome Car Magic

**611-20059** A History of Dome Cars **19.95**
From Burlington's 1945 Silver Dome to present-day full-length domes operating in Canada and Alaska, this program chronicles the history of those glamorous sightseeing dome cars. Includes archival footage of the Empire Builder, Super Chief, California Zephyr and more. Produced by award-winner Richard Luckin and Narrated by Michael Gross. 26 minutes.

## Super Chief: Speed, Style, Service

**611-20029 24.95**
Tells the story of Santa Fe's legendary Super Chief as told through interviews and vintage footage. Long regarded as an icon of America's southwest, this silver speedster was THE way for movie stars and VIPs to travel between Chicago and Los Angeles. Hosted by Michael Gross. 56 minutes.

## Silver Thread Through The West: The California Zephyr

**611-20039 24.95**
Touted as "America's most talked-about train" the California Zephyr took travelers from Chicago to Oakland/San Francisco in style. It was the flagship of the CB&Q, DRGW and Western Pacific and was known for the spectacular scenery of the Rockies as seen through its domes. 56 minutes.

## Daylight: The Most Beautiful Train In The World

**611-20049 24.95**
Flagship of the SP, these colorful speedsters were the preferred way for travelers to get from Los Angeles to San Francisco. Hosted by Michael Gross. 56 minutes.

## S&S HOBBY PRODUCTS

## My Train Coloring Book

**643-700 4.49**
Fun for kids of all ages. Twenty pages of the many faces of North America's Railroads.

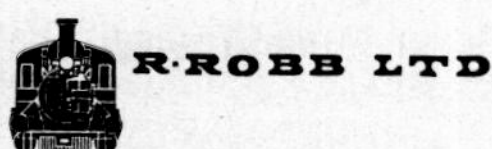


## BOOKS

### Narrow Gauge Pictorials

Colorado narrow gauge equipment from various roads, is featured in these softcover books. Each has a horizontal format and more than 100 B&W photos.

**DRGW Refrigerator, Stock and Tank Cars**

622-4 Volume IV **30.00**

**DRGW Cabooses**

622-5 Volume V **28.00**

**Motive Power of the C&S**

622-6 Volume VI **35.00**

**DRGW Number Work Equipment**

622-10 Volume X **35.00**

**Locomotives of the DRGW**

622-11 Volume XI **33.00**
Includes roster, folios and photographs of all modern narrow gauge steam locos.

**Pino Grande**

622-201 Softcover **35.00**
Reprint of Howell North Publication.

**The Grand Mountains**

622-301 **35.00**
Features 4-8-2 Mountain class M-67, M-69, M-75 and M-78 locomotives.

**The Mudhens**

622-302 **30.00**
Photographic history of the D&RGW K-27 2-8-2 Mikado Type Locomotive.

**Rio Grande Narrow Gauge - the Final Years, Alamosa To Chama**

622-304 **28.00**
This photographic journey chronicles the final three years (1965-1968) of freight and passenger operations over the Rio Grande's line between Alamosa, Colorado and Chama, New Mexico.

Computerize everything from operations to equipment maintenance records with this new line of software, designed especially for model railroading. Pentium-based system (recommended Pentium 3 or higher), 128 MB RAM, 20 MB HD, SVGA.

## NEW PRODUCTS

### Computer Software

**Fort Knox Model Railroading Appraising System™**

**NEW** 702-FNAS **29.95**
Now you can easily determine how much your collection is worth. This advanced appraising software analyzes the purchase price, current value and estimated appreciation then forecasts what it may be worth at any given time in the future. The fully customizable program maintains your entire collection in an easy to manage, easy to view system. Records vital information like purchase date, purchase price, manufacturer, condition and much more. Allows you to include an image with each item listed and print inventory reports and forecasts. Compatible with MS Windows XP and Vista.

**Service Tracker™**

**NEW** 702-STPRO
Professional Edition **29.95**
Maintenance, service and testing are key functions to keeping your equipment in good running order. This advanced software lets you keep track of service schedules and reminds you about inspections, maintenance and test runs for each piece of equipment. User-friendly system includes inventory control, advanced reporting, image storage and more. Compatible with MS Windows XP and Vista.

**Train Trek Layout Simulation**

702-TTLS05 For Marklin Digital Systems **84.95**
Plan your railroad and simulate the action on-screen before running it in real life. This user-friendly, yet comprehensive program makes it easy to assemble a complete layout including locomotives, cars, turnouts, sensors and scenery. Designed to maximize Marklin digital systems, it supports all train types and scales. Work out the bugs of experimental routes with Track Editor, create an endless number of customized routes with Time Table and finish it all off with Scenery Editor. Program features digital ID, manual and automatic control and advanced graphics that won't clog your system's memory. Instruction manual included. Ideal for beginners and experts alike. Compatible with MS Windows XP and Vista.

702-14132 Ultimate Data Professional RR Edition + Service Tracker **49.95**
This customizable database will help you keep track of any collection of any size. Up to 11 images of each item can be added, and a handy Total Value category helps you keep track of costs for insurance purposes. The program also includes ServiceTracker™ so you can keep accurate records of repairs and regularly scheduled maintenance. Compatible with MS Windows 98, XP and Vista.

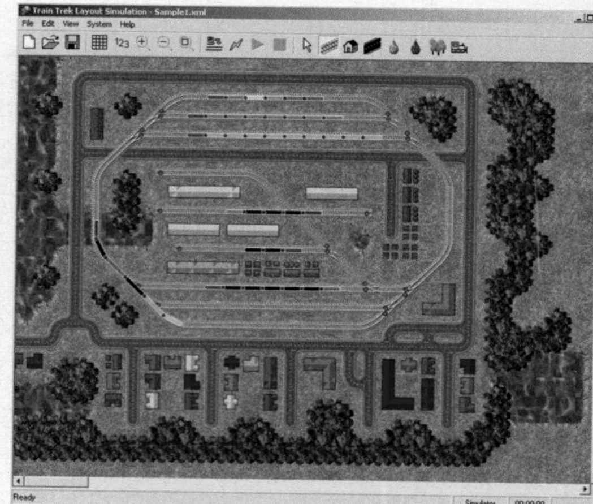

702-TTLS05

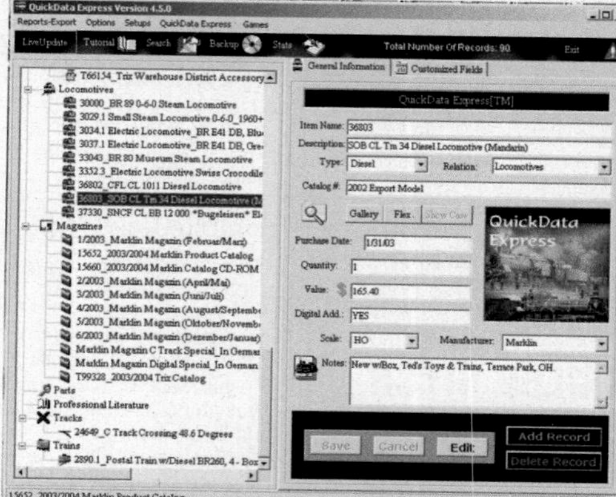

702-14142

702-14142 Quick Data Express **19.95**
Keep track of your collection easily. Provides eight different categories (Locos, Trains, Cars, Track, Accessories, Professional Literature and Magazines) and icons for one-click retrieval. You can also store digital images of items, and customize fields as needed. Database can easily be exported to MS Excel, MS Word, Text, HTML, Lotus and other formats. Compatible with MS Windows 98, XP and Vista.

Daily New Product Announcements! Visit Walthers Web site at **www.walthers.com**

**All Aboard Data Express™**

702-15172 **29.95**
Build a customized, personalized database for your collection with this software designed especially for model railroaders. Now, you can create an unlimited number of categories, subcategories and item listings with as many images of each item as you wish — capacity is limited only by the size of your hard drive!

Compatible with MS Windows XP (Home and Professional Edition) and Vista, the system also includes import and export features that work directly with Microsoft Excel and text format. And it's built with the latest encryption security.

The system also comes with the Model Railroad Toolbox that includes digital and analog clocks, system hardware analyzer, calculator, hobby shop address book, sticky notes reminder and more.

# NEW PRODUCTS

## Books

### World Famous Horseshoe Curve

**NEW 52-40 9.95**
Offers readers an overview of the history of this landmark from its construction through its 150th anniversary in 2004. Published in cooperation with the Railroader's Memorial Museum in Altoona, PA.

### Hawaiian Railway Album WWII Photos

**Volume 3: Plantation Railways on Oahu**

**NEW 52-41 23.95**
Continuing the popular series, this volume is packed with 105 images of the seven railways on Oahu. Also includes rosters and two full-page maps from the 40s. 72 Pages, softbound.

### Hawaiian Railway Album WWII Photos Volume 4

**NEW 52-45 TBA**

### New York Central Steam Power West of Buffalo

**NEW 52-42** Volume 1 **21.95**

### PRR Lines West Volume 2: Pittsburgh and Northeast Ohio 1960-1999

**NEW 52-43 TBA**

### Railroading in Downtown Chicago

**NEW 52-44** Volume 2 **TBA**

# BOOKS

## Prototype Railroading

### ALCO Reference #1

**52-15 29.95**
200 black-and-white photos show the locomotives built at the ALCO plant in Schenectady, New York.

### Altoona Action

**52-18 44.95**
Railroading around Horseshoe Curve! Color and black-and-white photos show PRR, Penn Central and CR in the area between the mid-1960s and the mid-1990s.

### Anthracite Classics

**52-23 19.95**
This all-color book covers steam and diesel engines from PRR, RDG, LV and CNJ from the early 1950s to the mid-1960s. 48 pages.

### Delaware & Hudson: Thunder & Lightning Stripes

**52-21 19.95**
All-color look at the D&H, famous for its Alcos and brilliant paint schemes. 48 pages.

### Canadian Steam in the Prairies, Towns and Cities

**52-33 16.95**
Features beautiful black-and-white steam photography, mainly from the 1930s and 1940s, with many surprises—great for modelers of that era! 40 pages, 60 photos, softbound.

### Railroaders in the Lehigh River Valley

**52-34 24.95**
This beautiful book features brilliant photography that gives readers a first-hand look at railroading in this region. It's packed with plenty of images of Alcos, GE's and cabooses.

### Hawaiian Railway Album WWII Photos

**Volume 2: Along the Main Lines of the Oahu Railway & Land Co. and The Hawaii Consolidated Railway**

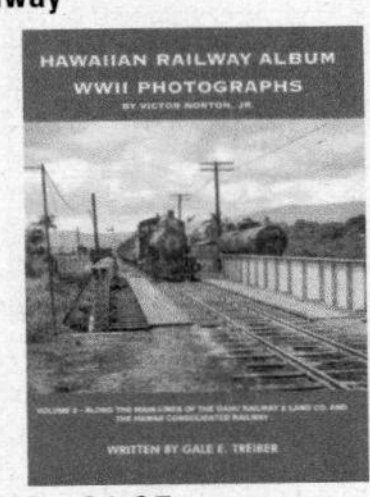


**52-35 21.95**
This book features plenty of freight and passenger equipment, structure and trackside photos. Includes 13 maps, plus schedules, rosters and more.

### Illinois Central: North of the Ohio River

**52-2 59.95**
All-color hardcover book covering the IC in depth, with maps, freight schedules and nearly 200 photos of trains, towers and structures. 136 pages.

### Chessie System: Cumberland Action

**52-16 39.95**
All-color book covering the B&O, WM and Chessie in the Allegheny Mountains. Includes roster, track charts. 112 pages.

### Freight Equipment of the New York Central, Volume 1: Box Cars, Stock Cars & Reefers

**52-24 13.95**
Covers from turn-of-the-century wood cars to the modern steel cars of the 1950s and 1960s. 48 pages.

### CF7 Locomotives: From Cleburne to Everywhere

**52-12 24.99**
Details their conversion from ATSF F-Units. Includes complete roster and dispositions for entire fleet. Hundreds of photos and diagrams. 112 pages.

### Wellsboro's Own Railroad

**52-31 11.95**
An all-encompassing history of the railroad from its humble beginnings in 1859 through its different incarnations. 40 pages.

### New England 1930s Steam Action - Worcester

**52-17 11.95**
Discover the impact of steam power in Massachusetts during the 1930s, from railroads like Boston & Albany, NH, Boston & Maine and Maine Central. 48 pages.

### New England Classics, Volume 1

**52-22 19.95**
An all-color tribute to Boston & Maine, Central Vermont, Maine Central, Bangor & Aroostook and more. 48 pages.

### Passenger Cars of New England 13.95 ea

Featuring wooden coaches, milk cars and more. 48 pages.

**52-28** Volume 1: Boston & Maine

**52-29** Volume 2: Bangor & Aroostook/Maine Central

**52-30** Volume 3: Central Vermont/Rutland

### New York Central Power Along the Hudson 18.95 ea

Packed with plenty of black-and-white photos taken before WWII by noted photographer Ed May, these volumes capture the essence of NYC steam, electric and diesel railroading along the mighty Hudson.

**52-36** Volume 1: Harmon

**52-37** Volume 2: Oscawana to Albany

### New York Central Steam on the Harlem and Putnam Divisions

**52-39 19.95**
NYC steam photography from 1917 thru 1952 from the collection of Ed May, with commentary by Richard Stoving. Most of the images are pre-WWII.

### PRR Lines West, Volume 1: Pittsburgh to St. Louis 1960-1999

**52-19 59.95**
Features over 190 color photos of stations, towers and trains from the latter half of the 20th century. Hardcover 136 pages.

### Railroading in Downtown Chicago

**52-38 18.95**
Vintage photography featuring Chicago freight and passenger action by Robert P. Olmsted. Includes Monon, PRR, C&NW, EL, CB&Q, C&EI, NYC, B&O, C&O and more!

## Coloring Books

### The Alphabet Train Coloring Book

**52-26 5.00**
Ages 2 through 8.

### Railroads in 50 States Coloring Book

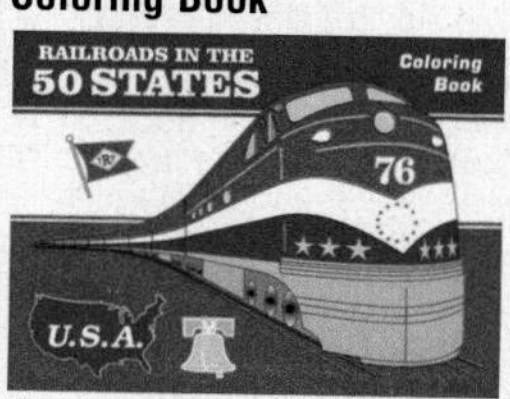


**52-25 5.00**
Also teaches state capitals, mottos, nicknames and symbols. Ages 6 through 12.

### Railroad Learning & Activity Book

**52-27 5.95**
Features fun activities like word games, connect-the-dots, and matching exercises. Ages 2 through 8.

Info, Images, Inspiration! Get It All at
**www.walthers.com**

## Sandia Software

### DVD

### Denver & Rio Grande Multimedia Adventure Kit

**645-11 99.95**
The largest collection of Rio Grande information ever assembled into one product. This multimedia product covers D&RG, D&RGW, RGW, RGS, and Moffat lines. Narrow and standard gauge (emphasis on the narrow gauge circle) from 1871 to present. Over 200 town descriptions with history, USGS maps, yard drawings. Over 3000 images of rolling stock, bridges, buildings, towns, mines, etc. Includes interactive software browser that is fully searchable by keyword, index, or contents. CAD drawings of buildings, bridges, etc. you can view and print to any scale. Hours of high quality MPEG2 video, slide shows, walk throughs, sounds, clip art, track profiles. Complete ebooks: 1922 DRG USGS summary, 1930s travel book, 1925 employee magazines, 1930s rule book, 1950s MOW standard drawings, locomotive catalog, time tables, equipment rosters and more. A must for any modeler or fan of the Rio Grande. System requires a PC running Windows 98 or higher, 1078 x 768 monitor, MPEG2 capability (for videos), DVD player and mouse.

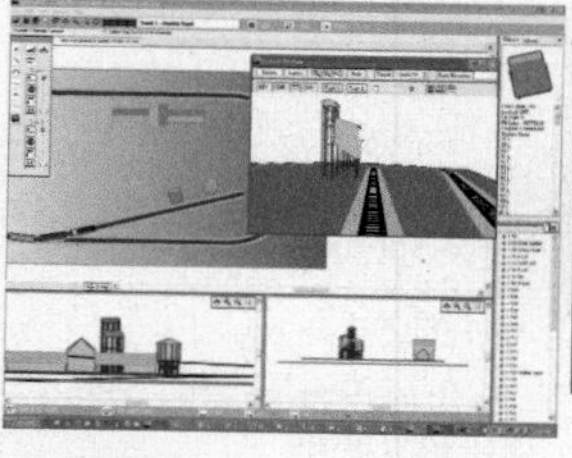

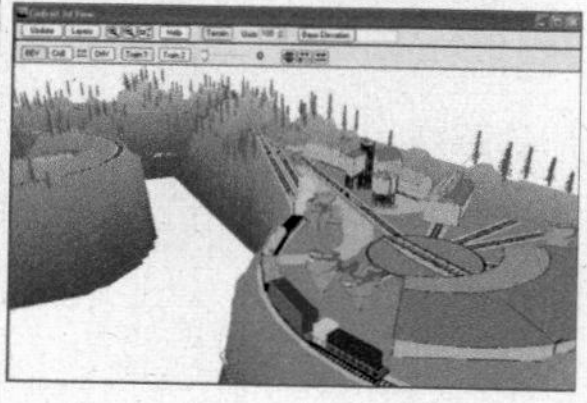

### Cadrail

**NEW 645-3** Version 9 **99.95**
Version 9 is updated to make use of Microsoft's .net framework making Cadrail more powerful than ever and fully compatible with Windows Vista operating system. Version 9 still supports all other systems running Windows 98 or higher. Easy-to-use flexible CAD tools allow you to design complex shapes, snap track sections together, add turnouts, create complex combinations of yard ladders, sidings and crossovers, add your walls and benchwork to the drawing and more. Version 9 features better 3-D drawing support, new 3-D views and improved graphics. You can open multiple drawings and copy and paste between them. Operate the train in real time with a 3-D cab view, overhead view or birdseye view. Improved drawing tools allow you to edit freehand, create 3-D shapes and rotate in three directions. Also features better defined figures, improved printing and more. Allows you to make printouts to any scale, in any unit of measurement and in any device supported by Windows. Software comes with printed manual, interactive computerized help file and extensive libraries with thousands of shapes you can use for layouts, buildings, bridges, scenery, track and more. Requires VGA, mouse, CD-ROM.

## VOLLMER

IMPORTED FROM GERMANY BY WALTHERS

## NEW PRODUCT

### CATALOG

**NEW 770-2007** 2007 **12.99**
Separate sections for G, HO, N & Z Scale, with measurements for all buildings. Full-color, 8-1/4 x 11-3/4".

## WHISTLES UNLIMITED

### Wood Train Whistles

**753-30** Mini **4.00**

**753-20** Junior **4.50**

**753-10** Regular **4.95**

Weekend Chief publishes and distributes a wide range of prototype railroading books, with a special focus on operations in the eastern United States. Each book is loaded with photos, making them an ideal reference for the modeler or historian.

## NEW PRODUCTS

### Books

#### Railroad Books

**Diesel Demonstrators**

**NEW 779-110** 69.95
Exciting book showcases the various demonstrators developed by Alco, Fairbanks-Morse, GM Electro Motive Division, General Electric, Lima Hamilton and Baldwin. Covers switchers, road units, experimental units and more. Features lots of great color images including a special photo section of locos at work in freight train service.

**Erie Lackawanna Diesel Locomotives**

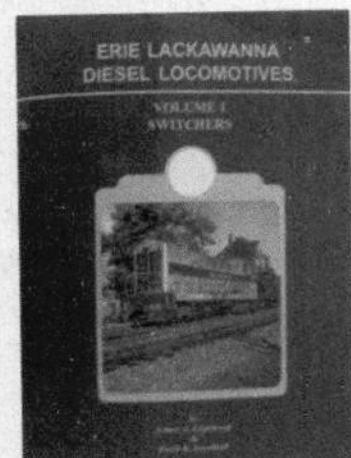


**NEW 779-150** Volume 1: Switchers 20.00

**South Shore Line Electric Locomotives & Interurban Cars**

**NEW 779-155** 20.00

**Pennsylvania Dining Cars**

**NEW 779-156** 20.00

#### Four Ways West Publications

**Miss Katy in the Lone Star State**

**NEW 779-145** 59.95

**Burlington Route Passenger Trains**

**NEW 779-146** Volume 1 59.95

**Wisconsin Central Heritage**

**NEW 779-153** Volume 1 59.95

#### Train Tech Series by Specialty Press

**Southern Pacific Daylight Steam Locomotives**

**NEW 779-151** 24.95

## BOOKS

### Railroad Books

**Mainline Steam Revival**
**779-4** 39.95
Learn how the steam locomotive restoration craze has brought many engines out of retirement. 208 pages, over 300 photos.

**Railway Milk Cars 15.00 ea (Unless Noted)**
Widely varied and dressed in colorful schemes, these refrigerated cars carried milk between rural dairies and brokers and processors in key cities. Each volume is packed with photos.

**779-27** Volume 1

**779-28** Volume 2

**779-29** Volume 3

**779-73** Volume 4 20.00

**Creameries of Upstate New York at the Turn of the Century**
**779-30** 18.00
A look at the businesses once served by railroads using milk cars. Plenty of black and white photos. Makes a great reference for modeling the railway milk industry.

**Equipment of the Boston & Maine 15.00 ea**
Each photo roster book is packed with black and white images.

**779-31** Volume 1: Diesel Switchers & Road Switchers

**779-32** Volume 2: Diesel Cab Units

**779-33** Volume 3: Gas/Diesel Railcars, Talgo and Electric Locos

**Equipment of the Delaware & Hudson 15.00 ea**
Photo roster books are packed with black and white images. Softbound.

**779-34** Volume 1: Passenger Cars

**779-35** Volume 2: Steam Locomotives

**NYC Electric Locomotives and MU Cars**
**779-36** 15.00

**New Haven Railroad 15.00 ea (Unless Noted)**
Each softbound book is packed with black and white photos.

**779-37** The Electrified Zone

**779-38** The Boston Division 13.95

**779-41** Passenger Cars

**779-42** The Old Colony Division

**779-53** Electrics and MUs

**Rolling Stock of New England 15.00 ea**
An excellent reference for any modeler, each softbound volume features plenty of B&W roster and action views.

**779-39** Volume 1: New Haven RR Work Equipment

**779-40** Volume 2: New Haven RR Freight Equipment

**Boston, Revere Beach & Lynn Railroad**
**779-43** 18.00

**Railroad Cities 15.00 ea (Unless Noted)**
Each volume is a nostalgic photographic overview of a major railroad city.

**779-44** Providence, Rhode Island

**779-45** Concord, New Hampshire

**779-46** Springfield, Massachusetts 13.95

**779-54** Conneaut, Ohio

**Passenger Equipment of the PRR 15.00 ea (Unless Noted)**
**779-47** Volume 2: Sleepers

**779-49** Volume 3: Parlor Cars

**779-50** Volume 1: Coaches 13.95

**The Reading in the Conrail Era**
**779-48** Volume 2: 1976-1998 49.95

**Virginian Railroad Equipment**
**779-51** Volume 2: Diesels and Electric Locomotives 18.00

**Rails Across Boston 18.00 ea**
A look at Beantown's railroading heyday through black and white photos.

**779-55** Volume 1: South and West

**779-56** Volume 2: North

**Boston & Maine 79.95 ea**
A glimpse of the B&M in the transition era.

**779-57** Volume 1: City and Shore

**779-58** Volume 2: Forest, River and Mountain

**Boston & Albany**

**779-59** Volume 2 49.95
Tells the story of the NYC's lines in New England.

**Green Mountain Rails**
**779-60** 64.95
Showcases Vermont's colorful railroads.

**Pennsylvania Railroad Electric Locomotives & MUs**
**779-63** 18.00

**Atlantic Coast Line Freight Cars**
**779-64** 18.00

**Portrait of the Pennsylvania Railroad**

**779-61** 49.95
Transition-era action captured on film by noted photographer Philip R. Hastings. Hardbound.

**New Haven Diesel Locomotives**
**779-66** Volume 1: Switchers & Road Switchers 18.00

**NEW 779-152** Volume 2: DL 109s, FAs and Demonstrators 20.00

**NEW 779-154** Volume 3: PAs, C-Liners & FL9s **20.00**

### Central Vermont Diesels
**779-70 18.00**

### Steel Rails & Silver Wings: The Story of the PRR & TAT Airline

**779-71 34.95**

### Pennsylvania Railroad Mail & Baggage Cars

**779-72 18.00**

### Rails Across New Haven

**779-74 20.00**
Passenger and freight terminals from the early 1900s to the 1930s.

### Brooklyn's Waterfront Railways
**779-109 24.95**
Brooklyn steam, diesel and electrics in color and black & white. Maps and brochures. Softcover, 64 pages.

### Diesels To Park Avenue: The FL-9 Story
**779-111 44.00**
Chronicles the use of the FL9 for forty years, despite questions surrounding its real ability to operate on both diesel and third rail. 116 pages.

### The New Haven Railroad Old Colony Division
**779-138** Volume 2 **20.00**
Early steam to early diesel locomotives along the routes out of Boston.

### Railroad Cities Jersey City, NJ
**779-139 20.00**
Early steam to early diesel around Jersey City.

### New York Connecting Railroad
**779-140 35.95**

### B&O Switchers
**779-142 20.00**

### Victorian Railroad Stations Of Long Island
**779-1004 39.95**

## Four Ways West Publications

### Windy City to the Twin Cities
**779-78** BurlingtonRoute/BN/BNSF **59.95**

### BNSF Motive Power Annual

**779-79** 1998-1999 **49.95**

**779-80** 1997 **49.95**

**779-81** 1996 **44.95**

**779-82** 1994 **44.95**

### Burlington Route Color Pictorial 49.95 ea
CB&Q motor cars, steam and diesel locos. Complete with locomotive rosters.

**779-83** Volume 1

**779-84** Volume 2

### Chesapeake & Ohio Color Pictorial
**779-86** Volume 2 **59.95**

### Colorado & Southern - Southern Division Color Pictorial
**779-87 49.95**
C&S steam and first-generation diesels south of Denver to the Texas border.

### Dragon Steel
**779-88 49.95**
An ALCO action album.

### EMD's Classic Cowl Units
**779-89 59.95**
All about these classic units from Santa Fe's FP45s to Amtrak SDP40Fs, EMD test units and commuter F40Cs. Lots of color photos.

### Great Northern Color Pictorial
**779-90** Volume 2 **49.95**

**779-91** Volume 3 **49.95**

**779-93** Volume 6 **64.95**

**779-94** Volume 7 **64.95**

### Great Northern Equipment in Color 49.95 ea
**779-95** Volume 1: Box & Stock Cars

**779-96** Volume 3: Western Fruit Express, Cabooses & Maintenance Equipment

### Green Bay & Western Color Pictorial

**779-97 59.95**

### Illinois Central Color Pictorial
**779-98** Volume 1 **59.95**
Passenger operations during the diesel era featuring 235 color photos.

**NEW 779-143** Volume 2 **59.95**

### Kansas City Southern Color Pictorial
**779-99 49.95**

### Milwaukee Road Locomotives

**779-144** Volume One **59.95**
In depth coverage of MILW motive power. First of series covers passenger and freight cab and booster units from FTs to E9s. Hundreds of vintage black and white and color photos, complete rosters and more.

### New Haven Color Pictorial
**779-100** Volume 1: The West End **54.95**

**779-101** Volume 2: Central Connecticut & Rhode Island **59.95**

**NEW 779-148** Volume 3: The East End **59.95**

### New England's Colorful Railroads

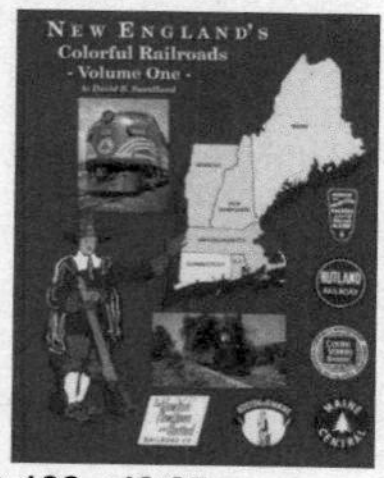

**779-102 49.95**
Railroad's glory years from the 1940s to the 1970s.

### New York Central Color Pictorial
**779-103** Volume 1: Chicago to Boston **49.95**

**779-104** Volume 2: St. Louis to New York City **59.95**

**779-105** Volume 3: Peoria, IL to Brewster, NY **59.95**

### Northern Pacific Color Pictorial
**779-106** Volume 1 **49.95**

**779-107** Volume 3 **49.95**

**779-108** Volume 4 **59.95**

### Pennsylvania Railroad Color Pictorial
**779-137** Volume 1: Altoona to York City **49.95**

**779-112** Volume 2: St. Louis to NewYork City **49.95**

**779-113** Volume 3: Chicago to Camden, NJ **59.95**

**779-114** Volume 4: Louisville to Washington, D.C. **59.95**

**NEW 779-147** Volume 5: Chicago to Phillipsburg, New Jersey **59.95**

### Pool Power West

**779-115 49.95**

### Railroads of the Pine Tree State 49.95 ea
Maine's colorful railroads featuring the Boston & Maine, Grand Trunk, Bangor & Aroostook, CP and shortlines including Belfast and Moosehead Lake.

**779-116** Volume 1

**779-117** Volume 2

### Rio Grande Color Pictorial
**779-118** Volume 1 **59.95**

### Rock Island Color Pictorial 1960-1969
**779-119** Volume 2: 1959-1969 **49.95**

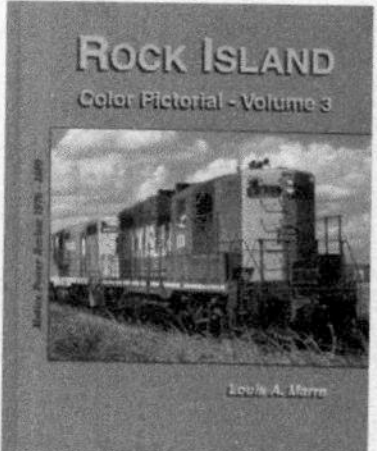

**779-120** Volume 3: The Final Decade **54.95**

### Down South on the Rock Island 1940-1969
**779-121 59.95**
Steam and early-day diesels on freight and passenger trains along RI's southern system.

### Santa Fe in the Lone Star State 1940-1969
**779-122 49.95**

### Southern Pacific Passenger Trains
**779-123** Volume 2: Day Trains of the Coast Line **74.95**

### Southern Pacific in Transition
**779-124 49.95**
One last look after SP merged with DRGW but before the SP/UP merger.

### Southern Pacific's Historic Overland Route 1950s-1960s
**779-125 49.95**
Scenes from the 1950s and 60s of the western portion from Oakland to Ogden, Utah.

### Southern Pacific's San Joaquin Valley Line 1950s-1960s
**779-126 59.95**

### Southern Pacific's Scenic Coast Line Color Pictorial

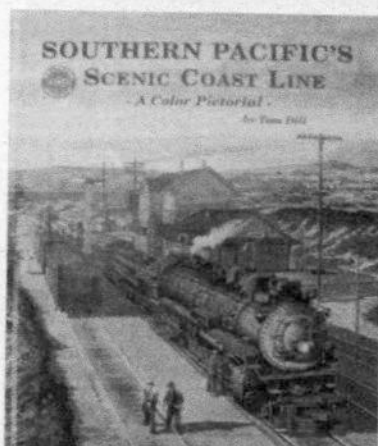

**779-127 59.95**

**Southern Pacific's Texas & New Orleans Color Pictorial**
**779-128** 59.95

**Union Pacific Motive Power Annual 49.95 ea**
**779-129** 1997
**779-130** 1998/1999

**Western Pacific Color Pictorial**
**779-131** Volume 1 **49.95**
**779-132** Volume 2 **59.95**

**Life on the Feather River Route**

**779-133** 59.95

**ALCO FAs**
**779-134** 59.95
Comprehensive history of Alco-GE and MILW-FA series locos.

**Northern Pacific Color Pictorial**

**779-135** Volume 5: Passenger Operations 1951-71 **65.00**
**779-136** Volume 6: Freight Operations 1930s Through BN Merger **64.95**

**Traintech Series by Specialty Press 24.95 ea**

**779-76** Burlington Zephyrs
**779-77** EMD F-Unit Locomotives
**779-141** EMD Early Road Switchers: GP7-GP20 Locomotives

**Build a Display For Collectible Houses Video 19.98 ea**

Create the magic through this step-by-step, detailed video that teaches you how to build a 31 x 44" 77.5 x 110cm display for your collectible houses. This enchanted scenery display can be shown year round and modified to fit any table, buffet, TV, dresser, fireplace opening or mantel. You'll learn how to: build a base including different levels using lightweight foam components, install street and house lights into the base and out of sight, learn how to make rocks, hillsides, roads, bushes, trees, streams and a waterfall and complete your masterpiece, landscaping it with Turf and Snow. A pamphlet listing all of the products needed is included, and the one hour video also provides various tips, techniques, ideas and instructions for each product.

785-1055

785-1056

**785-1055** DVD
**785-1056** VHS

**Model Scenery Made Easy Video 24.98 ea**

785-973

785-993

**785-973** DVD
**785-993** VHS

A comprehensive, detailed account of scenery modeling. Provides helpful information for modelers of any skill level, and shows how to do scenery the easy way. Approximately 60 minutes.



**SubTerrain: A How-To Video 24.98 ea**

785-1400

785-1401

**785-1400** DVD
**785-1401** VHS

A step-by-step video that shows you how to build a model railroad layout with the revolutionary SubTerrain Layout System. Approximately 60 minutes.

**The Clinic® Video 24.98 ea**

785-970

785-990

**785-970** DVD
**785-990** VHS

Learn by watching the professionals demostrate landscaping and terrain modeling techiques. In this video, you'll see just how easy it is. 1 hour and 15 minutes.

**SubTerrain Manual**

**785-1402 7.98**
An illustrated how-to manual that teaches you how to create the ideal base for scenery and landscaping from start to finish.

**The Scenery Manual**

**785-1207 10.98**
An illustrated start-to-finish guide, with new spiral binding, teaches terrain construction and landscaping. It is full of basics for beginners and secrets of skilled scenery modelers.

WB VIDEO PRODUCTIONS

For a complete listing of WB titles, visit www.walthers.com.

## NEW PRODUCTS

### DVDs

**Challenger 82**
**NEW 798-2DVD** 39.95

**Diesels on the Union Pacific**
**NEW 798-13DVD** 39.95
Two-disc special.

**Excursion to the 30s**
**NEW 798-3DVD** 29.95

**Rio Grande Narrow Gauge**
**NEW 798-6DVD** 29.95

**The Rio Grande Today**
**NEW 798-22DVD** 39.95

**Silver Rails and Golden Memories**
**NEW 798-26DVD** 39.95

**The Sugar Cane Train**
**NEW 798-18DVD** 9.95
15 minutes.

**Tehachapi Part 1: The Santa Fe & Part 2: The Southern Pacific**
**NEW 798-20DVD** 39.95
Two-disc special.

## DVDS

**Abo Canyon & the BNSF**
**798-43DVD** 24.95

**Allegheny Rails 39.95 ea**
**798-24DVD** Volume I B&O Steam
**798-25DVD** Volume II WM in the 50s

**America On Rails 29.95 ea**
**798-30DVD** Volume I
**798-36DVD** Volume II
**798-37DVD** Volume III

**Assault On Snow**
**798-27DVD** 39.95

**Blue Ridge Steam**
**798-35DVD** 39.95

**BNSF: A Time Of Change 24.95 ea**
**798-44DVD** Volume I
**798-45DVD** Volume II
**798-46DVD** Volume III

**BNSF's Land of Enchantment**
**798-48DVD** 24.95

**Kindig's Diesels**
**798-29DVD** 29.95

**Last Steamers of the Colorado & Southern**
**798-19DVD** 39.95

**The Milwaukee's Mighty Electrics**
**798-28DVD** 39.95

**Santa Fe's New Mexico Main: The Belen Cutoff**
**798-39DVD** 39.95

**Santa Fe's Raton Route**
**798-42DVD** 39.95

**Santa Fe's Seligman Sub**
**798-33DVD** 39.95

**Steam Over Sherman**
**798-11DVD** 39.95

**Union Pacific's Last Steam Giants**
**798-38DVD** 24.95

**Union Pacific Superpower**

**798-47DVD** 24.95

# RAILROAD BOOKS

Each volume is packed with photos that will provide endless ideas for modeling projects.

## NEW PRODUCT

### Locomotive Directory

#### Norfolk Southeren

**NEW 95-99 24.95**
Compact and convenient guides provides a unit-by-unit listing (accurate through January 1, 2007), and dozens of photos. Handy 6 x 9" 15 x 22.5cm format fits easily in pocket or camera bag for railfan excursions.

#### Alcos

**95-56** Volume 1: Century Series Four-Axle Units **35.00**

**95-97** Alco's High-Hood Switchers **29.95**
Between 1932 and 1940, Alco built 176 HH switchers ranging from 600 to 1,000 horsepower. Many Class I railroads stepped up to try out these early models, and even in the 21st Century a handful still serve as industrial switchers. Includes photos and drawings. 120 pages, softbound.

#### Conrail

The Final Years

**95-66 48.00**
Hardcover, 200 pages, 500 photos.

#### CSX

**95-92** CSX 2004-2005 Locomotive Directory **24.95**

#### Norfolk Southeren

**Limited Quantity Available**

**95-95** NS **24.95**

#### PRR Series

This softcover series examines specific models and provides a comprehensive collection of photos.

#### Volume 1: Alco RS Series

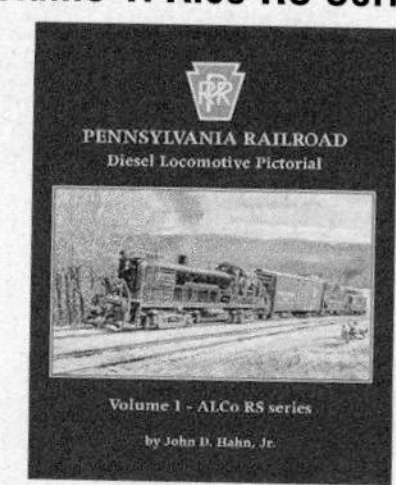


**95-61 16.95**

#### Volume 3: EMD Second Generation Road Switchers

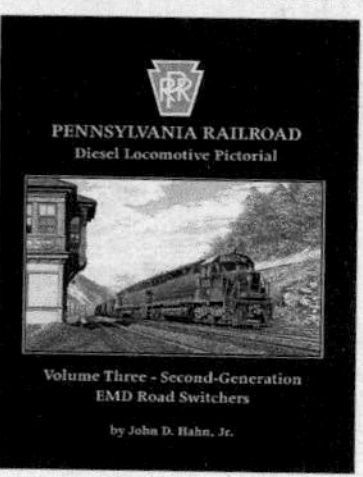


**95-63 16.95**
GP30s to pre-merger SD45s. 80 pages, over 150 photos.

#### Volume 5: Fairbanks-Morse Locomotives

**95-83 17.95**
72 pages, over 130 B&W photographs.

#### Volume 6: EMD And Alco Freight Cab Units

**95-86 24.95**
Softcover, 120 pages, 295 photos.

#### Volume 7: EMD E Units And Alco PAs

**95-87 24.95**
Softcover, 120 pages, 250+ photos.

#### Volume 8: EMD GP7s & GP9s

**95-55 24.95**

#### Volume 9: Alco & GE Switchers

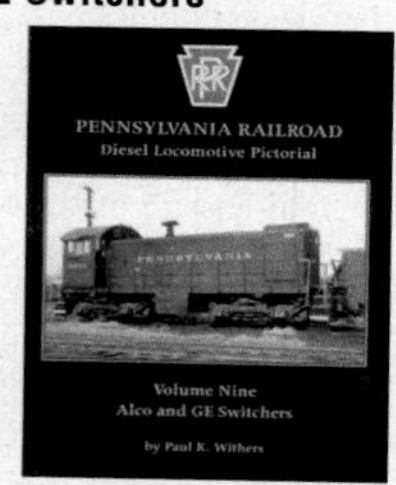


**95-93 19.95**

#### Pennsy Electric Pictorial

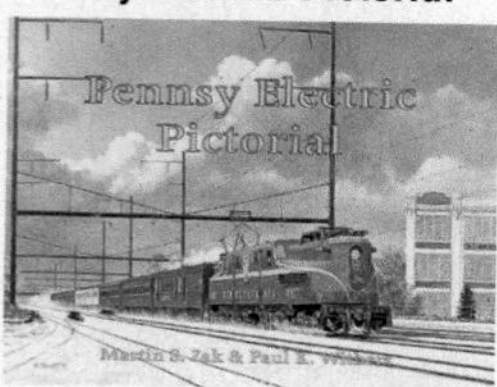


**95-78 39.95**
Hardcover, over 300 B&W photographs.

Get Daily Info, Photos and News at

**www.walthers.com**

#### UP

Switchers & Slugs

**95-65 24.95**
Softcover, 116 pages (24 in color) with over 275 B&W photos.

#### Union Pacific's Sherman Hill In The Diesel Era

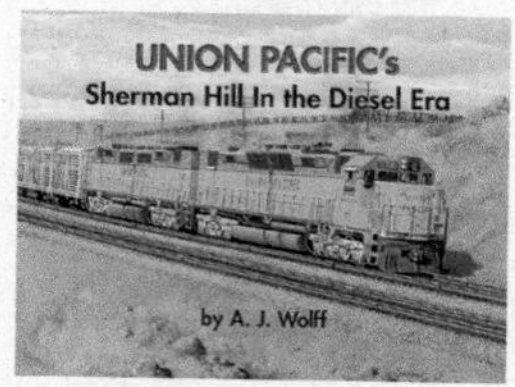


**95-75 48.00**
Over 500 photos, 224 pages.

#### Diesels Of The Union Pacific 1934-82: The Classic Era

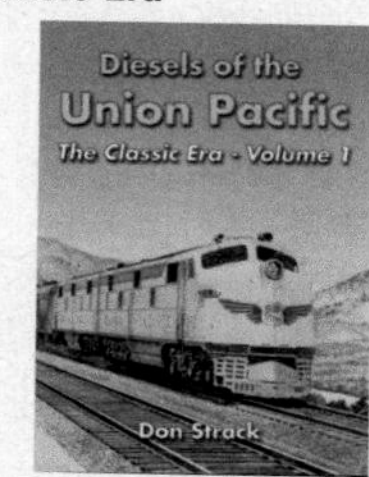


**95-79** Volume 1 **45.00**
Over 500 photos, hardcover, 224 pages.

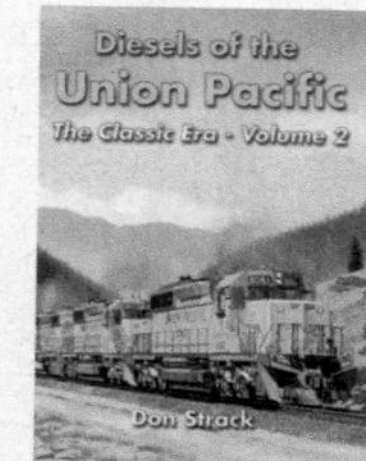


**95-84** Volume 2 **50.00**

#### Union Pacific's Turbine Era

**95-82 55.00**
Color and B&W photographs, 224 pages.

#### Union Pacific Locomotive Directory

**95-89** 2003/2004 **24.95**

**95-98** UP 2005/2006 **TBA**

### Miscellaneous

#### Rockville Bridge: Rails Across the Susquehanna

**95-58 29.95**
A historical look at the century old Rockville Bridge, the world longest stone arch and concrete railroad bridge. Softcover, 112 pages, 200+ photos.

#### Diesels Of The Southern Railway 1939-1982

**95-68 65.00**
Hardcover, 384 pages with more than 1,000 photos.

#### The GP20 & SD24 EMD's Turbocharged Duo

**95-70 29.95**
112 pages, over 200 color and B&W photos.

#### Kansas City Southern In The Deramus Era

**95-73 48.00**
Hardcover, 224 pages featuring maps, rosters and over 500 photos.

#### The Contemporary Diesel Spotter's Guide

**95-76 24.95**
Use distinguishing features (parts locations, truck type, etc.) to pick out a diesel locomotive. Full of color and B&W photographs.

### Fairbanks-Morse Erie-Builts & H20-44S

**95-77 24.95**

### EMDs SW8: America's Medium-Horsepower Switcher Choice

**95-88 19.95**
Softcover, 72 pages (4 color pages), 250 photos (20 color photos).

### EMD's SW1500

**95-96 35.00**
Introduced at the zenith of switcher production in the 60s and 70s, these versatile 645-powered switchers were ideal for yard, local and road service. Owned by over 20 major railroads, plus shortlines and industries, the SW1500 was EMD's most popular post-60s switcher. Includes photos and drawings. 120 pages, softbound.

### Fairbanks-Morse H15-44/H16-44

**95-90 29.95**

### Diesels Of The CNW

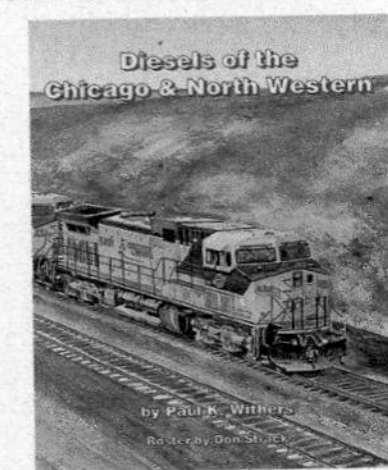


**95-900 59.95**
Hardcover, 320 pages (32 in full-color) and 400+ photos.

### Revolutionary Diesel EMC's FT

**95-1000 24.95**
Softcover second edition with 132 pages, 250+ color and B&W photos.

### Train Master-the Most Useful Locomotive Ever Built

**95-250 29.95**

## JOIN THE NATIONAL MODEL RAILROAD ASSOCIATION

You may know that the NMRA developed interchange standards for model railroad products. Maybe you've been to a club open house, or heard about regional and national conventions. But there are many other benefits for members.

Whether you invest in a brass loco, a bag of detail parts or a complete kit, you expect to get your money's worth of fun and relaxation from your purchase. A one-year membership is just $45.00, far less than most craft train kits, a brass model or a hardcover book. And the return on your investment, in the form of new friends, knowledge and modeling skills, is priceless.

In today's fast-changing world, the NMRA can help you keep up with your favorite hobby. The monthly "Scale Rails" provides the latest news, along with how-to articles and much more. The Kalmbach Memorial Library, located near the National Headquarters in Chattanooga, Tennessee, houses thousands of articles, books and other reference materials on model and prototype railroading. And, the NMRA is also publishing prototype reference books, in addition to the Data Sheets covering recommended practices.

Whether on a local, regional or national level, you'll be able to meet fellow modelers.

We think you'll agree that it makes good sense to belong to an organization that's doing so much for so many people—and doing it all for fun! Use the application blank below (or make a photocopy) and join today.

Phil Walther

## NEW PRODUCTS

### The History, Making and Modeling of Steel

**NEW 98-20 65.95**
Required reading for steel modelers, this limited edition is a reprint of Walthers classic how-to book originally published in the mid-90s. It's loaded with information and photos and features a brand new forward by steel modeling authority, Dean Freytag.

## MEMBERSHIP APPLICATION

NMRA, INC. • 4121 CROMWELL RD. • CHATTANOOGA, TN 37421-2119
Telephone (423) 892-2846 • Fax (423) 899-4869

- ❏ **Regular**, One Year ................. $45.00
- ❏ **Regular**, Five Year ................. $215.00
- ❏ **Sustaining**, One Year ............. $90.00
- ❏ **Student**, One Year ................. $30.00 (Under 25 Years)
- ❏ **Affiliate**, One Year (No Scale Rails) .... $23.00
- ❏ **Family Member**, One Year ............. $9.00 (Available to Spouse or Minor Child of Member)
- ❏ **Life Membership**, Apply to Headquarters Office with date of birth for a quotation.

enclose . . . ❏ Check ❏ Money Order ❏ Charge

Occupation ____________ Date of Birth ____________
Scale & Gauge ____________ NMRA # (renewals only) ____________
Special Interests (include prototype) ____________
(U.S. FUNDS ONLY) ❏ NEW ❏ RENEWAL

Name ____________
Street ____________
City ____________
State ____________
Telephone ____________

JW/Revised 3/95

Charge to:
❏ American Express
❏ VISA ❏ Master Card ❏ Discover
Expiration Date ____________
CARD NUMBER

Recommended by **WALTHERS**

Signature ____________

2008
HO
Model Railroad
Reference Book